June 22–27, 2013
New York, New York, USA

Association for Computing Machinery

Advancing Computing as a Science & Profession

SIGMOD'13

VOL 1 of 2

International Conference on

Management of Data

Sponsored by:

ACM SIGMOD

Supported by:

SAP, ORACLE, Goldman Sachs, Microsoft, Facebook, Google, IBM Research, Linked in, VMware, EMC^2, AT&T, CISCO, kx, NEC, TURN, Yahoo!, NSF, Morgan & Claypool Publishers, Cambridge University Press, ELSEVIER, and Morgan Kaufmann

Association for
Computing Machinery

Advancing Computing as a Science & Profession

The Association for Computing Machinery
2 Penn Plaza, Suite 701
New York, New York 10121-0701

ISBN: 978-1-4503-2155-6 (Digital)

ISBN: 978-1-4503-2613-1 (Print)

Additional copies may be ordered prepaid from:

ACM Order Department
PO Box 30777
New York, NY 10087-0777, USA

Phone: 1-800-342-6626 (USA and Canada)
+1-212-626-0500 (Global)
Fax: +1-212-944-1318
E-mail: acmhelp@acm.org
Hours of Operation: 8:30 am – 4:30 pm ET

Printed in the USA

Table of Contents

Research Session 5: Schema Matching and Spatial Databases I

Research Session 6: Graph Connectivity

Research Session 7: Crowdsourcing

Research Session 8: Social Media

Research Session 9: Systems, Performance I

Research Session 10: Graph Management

Research Session 11: Text Databases

Research Session 12: Systems, Performance II

Research Session 13: Information Extraction

Research Session 14: Query Processing and Optimization

Research Session 15: Cloud Computing

Research Session 16: Data Cleaning

Research Session 17: Complex Event Processing

Research Session 18: Systems, Performance III

Research Session 23: Data Mining

Research Session 24: Road Networks and Trajectories

Research Session 25: Security

Research Session 26: Indexing

Keynote Addresses

Panel

Tutorials

Demo Session 1: Data Intensive Applications

Demo Session 2: Data Analysis and Mining; Privacy; Security

Demo Session 3: Database Optimization; Performance

Demo Session 4: Graphs and Networks; Potpourris

Industry Session 1: Big Data I

Industry Session 2: Enterprise Data Management

Industry Session 3: Big Data II and Web

Industry Session 4: Systems and New Hardware Trends

Industry Session 5: Big Data III and More

Undergraduate Research

New Researcher Symposium

SIGMOD 2013 Conference Organization

General Chairs: Kenneth Ross (Columbia University)
Divesh Srivastava (AT&T Research)

Program Chair: Dimitris Papadias (HKUST)

Proceedings Chair: Stavros Papadopoulos (HKUST)

Tutorial Chair: Yufei Tao (CUHK Hong Kong)

Keynote and Panel Chair: Mike Stonebraker (MIT)

Industrial Program Chair: Nick Koudas (University of Toronto)

Demonstration Chair: Cyrus Shahabi (USC)

Workshop Chair: Christian S. Jensen (Aarhus University)

Undergraduate Research Program Chairs: Xiaokui Xiao (NTU Singapore)
Alexandra Meliou (UMASS Amherst)

Finance Chair: Graham Cormode (AT&T Research)

Finance Vice Chair: Flip Korn (AT&T Research)

Publicity/Social Media Chair: Amelie Marian (Rutgers University)

Sponsorship Chairs: Divyakant Agrawal (University of California at Santa Barbara)
Dennis Shasha (New York University)

Exhibit Chair: Mustafa Canim (IBM)

Local Arrangements Chairs: Cong Yu (Google)
Wendy Hui Wang (Stevens Institute of Technology)

Registration Chair: John Cieslewicz (Google)

Demonstration and Workshop Local Arrangements Chairs: Bishwaranjan Bhattacharjee (IBM)
Tasos Kementsietsidis (IBM)

Web/Information Chair: Hila Becker (Google)

Program Committee Group Leaders:

Walid Aref (Purdue)
Amr El Abbadi (UCSB)
Christos Faloutsos (CMU)
Phillip B. Gibbons (Intel Research)
Jayant Haritsa (Indian Institute of Science)
Ihab Ilyas (Qatar Computing Research Institute)
Sam Madden (MIT)
Tamer Oszu (University of Waterloo)
Thomas Seidl (Aachen University)
Vasilis Vassalos (AUEB)
K.Y Whang (KAIST)
Marianne Winslett (UIUC and ADSC)
Jun Yang (Duke)

Program Committee:

Ashraf Aboulnaga (University of Waterloo)
Gustavo Alonso (ETH)
Sihem Amer-Yahia (CNRS LIG)
Lyublena Antova (EMC and Greenplum)
Subi Arumugam (University of Florida)
Ira Assent (Aarhus University)
Ilaria Bartolini (University of Bologna)
Philip Bernstein (Microsoft Research)
Christian Boehm (LMU Munich)
Francesco Bonchi (Yahoo! Labs)
Peter Boncz (CWI)
Angela Bonifati (Lille 1 University)
Bogdan Cautis (Telecom ParisTech)
Chee Yong Chan (National University of Singapore)
Kevin Chang (UIUC)
Shimin Chen (HP Labs)
Lei Chen (HKUST)
James Cheng (CUHK)
Reynold Cheng (HKU)
Junghoo Cho (UCLA)
Tyson Condie (Microsoft Research)
Graham Cormode (AT&T Research)
Bin Cui (Peking University)
Carlo Curino (Yahoo! Research)
Sudipto Das (Microsoft Research)
Gautam Das (UTA and QCRI)
Khuzaima Daudjee (University of Waterloo)
Antonios Deligiannakis (Technical University of Crete)
Daniel Deutch (Ben Gurion University)
Alin Deutsch (UCSD)
Jens Dittrich (Saarland University)

Program Committee (continued):

Cecilia Procopiuc (AT&T Research)
Lin Qiao (LinkedIn)
Krithi Ramamritham (IIT Bombay)
Louiqa Raschid (UM College Park)
Christopher Re (University of Wisconsin Madison)
Matthias Renz (LMU)
Benjamin Rubinstein (Microsoft Research)
Elke Rundensteiner (WPI)
Dimitris Sacharidis (IMIS Athena Research)
Simonas Saltenis (Aalborg University)
Anish Das Sarma (Google Research)
Pierre Senellart (Telecom ParisTech and HKU)
Yasin Silva (Arizona State University)
Ambuj Singh (UCSB)
Yannis Sismanis (IBM Research)
Julia Stoyanovich (Drexel University)
Jimeng Sun (IBM Research)
Nesime Tatbul (ETH)
Evimaria Terzi (Boston University)
Hanghang Tong (IBM Research)
Nikos Triandopoulos (Boston University)
Kostas Tzoumas (TU Berlin)
Leong Hou U (University of Macau)
Haixun Wang (Microsoft Asia)
Steven Whang (Stanford)
Raymond Chi-Wing Wong (HKUST)
Xiaokui Xiao (Nanyang Technological University)
Jierui Xie (Oracle)
Lin Xuemin (UNSW)
Xifeng Yan (UCSB)
Yin Yang (ADSC)
Man Lung Yiu (Hong Kong Polytechnic University)
Jeffrey Xu Yu (CUHK)
Ting Yu (NCSU)
Zhenjie Zhang (ADSC)
Rui Zhang (University of Melbourne)

Demonstration Program Committee:

Enrique Alfonseca (Google)
Mohamed Ali (Microsoft)
Klaus Berberich (Max-Planck Institute)
Michael Cafarella (University of Michigan)
Ugur Demiryurek (USC)
Ada Fu (Chinease University of Hong Kong)
Wolfgang Gatterbauer (Carnegie Mellon University)
Thomas Heinis (EPFL)
Bijit Hore (UCI)
Ling Hu (Google)
Yan Huang (University of North Texas)
Shengyue Ji (Google)
Dmitri V. Kalashnikov (UCI)
Kyoungsook Kim (NICT)
Sang-goo Lee (Seoul National University)
Nikos Mamoulis (University of Hong Kong)
Atsuyuki Morishima (Tsukuba University)
Mario Nascimento (University of Alberta)
Athanasios Papaioannou (EPFL)
Jorge Quiane-Ruiz (Saarland University)
Mirek Riedewald (Northeastern University)
Junho Shim (Sookmyung Women's University)
Kyuseok Shim (Seoul National University)
Houtan Shirani-Mehr (USC)
Michal Shmueli-Scheuer (IBM)
Jaideep Vaidya (Rutgers University)
Arjen De Vries (CWI)
Xiaochun Yang (Northeastern University)
Demetris Zeinalipour (University of Cyprus)
Xiaofang Zhou (U. of Queensland)
Roger Zimmermann (National University of Singapore)

Industrial Program Committee:

Albert Angel (Google)
Anish Das Sarma (Google)
Marios Hadjieleftheriou (AT&T Labs Research)
Panos Ipeirotis (NYU)
Chaitanya Mishra (Facebook)
Berthold Reinwald (IBM Research, Almaden)
Jingren Zhou (Microsoft)
Calisto Zuzarte (IBM)

Travel Award Selection Committee:

Anastasia Ailamaki (EPFL)
Anthony Tung (NUS)
Dan Suciu (University of Washington)
Gustavo Alonso (ETH Zurich)
HV Jagadish (University of Michigan)
Joseph Hellerstein (University of California, Berkeley)
Laks Lakshmanan (University of British Columbia)
Michael Benedikt (University of Oxford)
Michael Franklin (University of California, Berkeley)
Nick Koudas (University of Toronto)
Timos Sellis (RMIT University)
Vagelis Hristidis (University of California, Riverside)

Additional Reviewers:

Alexander Alexandrov
Antoine Amarilli
Yael Amsterdamer
Panayiotis Andreou
Nikos Armenatzoglou
Anastasios Arvanitis
Cigdem Aslay
Daniel Barowy
Senjuti Basu Roy
George Beskales
Nikos Bikakis
Christoph Boden
Matthias Boehm
Petko Bogdanov
Kenneth Bøgh
Panagiotis Bouros
Douglas Burdick
Jesus Camacho-Rodriguez
Lei Cao
Lijun Chang
Georgios Chatzimilioudis
Aamir Cheema
Ling Chen
Shiwen Cheng
Euijin Choo
Byung-Gon Chun
Costantinos Costa
Xuan-Hong Dang
Mahashweta Das
Nazli Dereli
Cristian Diaconu
David Eisenstat
Mohammed El Seidy
Abdallah Elguindy
Amr ElHelw
Sameh Elnikety
Dora Erdos
Alexandre Evfimievski
Stephan Ewen
Antonino Freno
Yiming Gao
Giorgos Giannopoulos
Nikos Giatrakos
Behzad Golshan
Xi Gong
Francesco Gullo
Manish Gupta
Minh Hoang
Katja Hose
Haibo Hu
Weishu Hu
Silu Huang
Fabian Hueske
Patricia Iglesias
Elena Ikonomovska
Minhao Jiang
Alekh Jindal
Zachary Jorgensen
Abhijith Kashyap
Asterios Katsifodimos
Georgios Kellaris
Fabian Keller
James Kelley
Arijit Khan
Yannis Klonatos
David Konopnicki
Andreas Konstantinidis
Arun Kumar
Yongchul Kwon
Theodoros Lappas
Georgios Larkou
Julien Leblay
Jeong-Hoon Lee
Ki-Hoon Lee
Chuan Lei
Marcus Leich
Vincent Leroy
Justin Levandoski
Yuhong Li
John Liagouris
Bailong Liao
Xika Lin
Cheng Long
Arlei Lopes da Silva
Hua Lu
Daniel Lupei
Matteo Magnani
Manuel Mayr
Natwar Modani
Bongki Moon

Additional Reviewers (continued):

Michael Mortensen
Abdullah Mueen
Abhishek Mukherji
Jaeseok Myung
Hoang-Vu Nguyen
Milos Nikolic
Andres Noetzli
Olga Ohrimenko
Adam O'Neill
Christopher Oßner
Erdem Ozdemir
Endre Palatinus
Nana Pan
Dimitrios Papadopoulos
Odysseas Papapetrou
Panos Parchas
Sungchan Park
Youngki Park
Marco Patella
Peng Peng
Shangfu Peng
Mathias Peters
Olga Poppe
Vijayan Prabhakaran
Miao Qiao
Lu Qin
Venkatesh Raghavan
Vijayshankar Raman
Sriram Rao
Stefan Richter
Alexandra Roatis
Haggai Roitman
Natali Ruchansky
Eduardo Ruiz
Matthias Sax
Hassan Sayyadi
Joerg Schad
Sebastian Schelter
Tom Schreiber
Stefan Schuh
Rusty Sears
Russell Sears
Prithviraj Sen
Zechao Shang
Shuo Shang
Dafna Sheinwald
Yanyan Shen
Entong Shen
Vishwakarma Singh
Emil Stefanov
Yuzhou Sun
Ameet Talwalkar
Tian Tan
Lu-An Tang
Jiao Tao
Shirish Tatikonda
Saravanan Thirumuruganathan
Christian Thomsen
Quoc-Trung Tran
Honglei Tu
Alexander Ulrich
Minhas Umar
Thanasis Vergoulis
Aleksandar Vitorovic
Jia Wang
Yilei Wang
Di Wang
Chi Wang
Jingjing Wang
Wei Wei
Medhabi Wei
Jeroen Weijers
Markus Weimer
Tim Weninger
Matthew Wiley
Huanhuan Wu
Yinghui Wu
Shanchan Wu
Ming-Chuan Wu
Yanyan Xu
Hui Yan
Shengqi Yang
Jongheum Yeom
Stamatis Zampetakis
Bohan Zhan
Ying Zhang
Wenjie Zhang
Yuanyuan Zhu
Zhou Zhuojie
Bo Zong
Haitao Zou

SIGMOD 2013 Sponsor & Supporters

ACM Sponsor:

ACM SIGMOD

Diamond Supporter:

SAP®

Platinum Supporters:

ORACLE®

Goldman Sachs

Microsoft®

Gold Supporters:

facebook

Google™

IBM Research

LinkedIn®

vmware®

EMC²

Silver Supporters:

at&t

CISCO

KX

NEC

TURN

YAHOO!®

Student Travel:

NSF

Platinum Publisher:

MORGAN & CLAYPOOL PUBLISHERS

Silver Publishers:

CAMBRIDGE UNIVERSITY PRESS

ELSEVIER

MK MORGAN KAUFMANN

Cumulon: Optimizing Statistical Data Analysis in the Cloud*

Botong Huang
Duke University
bhuang@cs.duke.edu

Shivnath Babu
Duke University
shivnath@cs.duke.edu

Jun Yang
Duke University
junyang@cs.duke.edu

ABSTRACT

We present Cumulon, a system designed to help users rapidly develop and intelligently deploy matrix-based big-data analysis programs in the cloud. Cumulon features a flexible execution model and new operators especially suited for such workloads. We show how to implement Cumulon on top of Hadoop/HDFS while avoiding limitations of MapReduce, and demonstrate Cumulon's performance advantages over existing Hadoop-based systems for statistical data analysis. To support intelligent deployment in the cloud according to time/budget constraints, Cumulon goes beyond database-style optimization to make choices automatically on not only physical operators and their parameters, but also hardware provisioning and configuration settings. We apply a suite of benchmarking, simulation, modeling, and search techniques to support effective cost-based optimization over this rich space of deployment plans.

Categories and Subject Descriptors

H.2.8 [**Database Management**]: Database Applications—*Statistical databases*

Keywords

statistical computing; cloud; data parallelism; linear algebra

1 Introduction

"Big data" are growing in volume and diversity at an explosive rate. Data analysis has become increasingly sophisticated and statistical. In many situations, simple database reporting queries are no longer sufficient for deriving insights from high-dimensional and noisy datasets. There are also more people interested in analyzing data than ever before. They are not limited to HPC (High-Performance Computing) centers or big Internet companies; instead, they range from statisticians to biologists, social scientists, and journalists, many of whom have little computing expertise (or access thereto).

The rise of the cloud in recent years presents an interesting opportunity for big-data analytics. There are many successful private clouds (e.g., used by large Internet companies), public cloud service providers (e.g., Amazon's Elastic Compute Cloud, or EC2), as well as software for the cloud (e.g., Apache Hadoop). Users can "rent" a variety of computing options instantaneously from the cloud, pay only for their use according to clear price tags (e.g., Table 1), and avoid hardware acquisition and maintenance costs. Users also benefit from simpler programming models (the most prominent example being MapReduce [7], which Hadoop implements) and a wealth of tools, some of which have started to target machine learning and statistical computing—Apache Mahout, Greenplum/MADlib [5, 10], HAMA [19], RHIPE [9], Ricardo [6], Haloop [3], SystemML [8], ScalOps [1], just to name a few.

Machine type	CPU cores	Memory (GB)	Cost ($/hour)
m1.small	1	1.7	0.065
c1.median	2	1.7	0.165
m1.large	2	7.5	0.260
c1.xlarge	8	7.0	0.660
m1.xlarge	4	15.0	0.520

Table 1: A sample of machine types available from Amazon EC2.

Despite these advantages, it remains frustratingly difficult for most users to use the cloud for any non-trivial statistical analysis of big data—especially when the analysis is novel or ad hoc, and there is no existing program or library already highly tuned for the problem, platform, and budget at hand. First, ***developing*** efficient statistical analysis programs require a great deal of expertise and effort. Popular cloud programming platforms, such as Hadoop, require users to code and think in low-level, platform-specific ways, and, in many cases, resort to extensive manual tuning to achieve acceptable performance. Second, ***deploying*** such programs in the cloud is hard. Users are faced with a maddening array of choices, ranging from hardware provisioning (e.g., type and number of machines to request on Amazon EC2), configuration (e.g., number of map and reduce slots in Hadoop), to implementation alternatives and execution parameters. Some of these choices, as we shall demonstrate through experiments later in this paper, can be critical to meeting deadlines and staying within budget. However, current systems offer little help to users in making such choices.

Our Contributions In this paper we present Cumulon, an end-to-end solution that simplifies both the development and deployment of matrix-based statistical computing programs in the cloud.

When ***developing*** such programs, users of Cumulon will be able to think and code in a natural way using the familiar language of linear algebra. A lot of statistical data analysis (or computationally expensive components thereof) can be succinctly written in the matrix notation and with basic operations such as multiply, add, transpose, etc. Here are two examples that we will revisit later:

- Singular value decomposition (SVD) of a matrix has extensive applications in statistical analysis. In the randomized algorithm

*This work is supported by NSF grants 0916027, 0917062, 0964560, and a 2010 HP Labs Innovation Research Award.

Algorithm 1: Simplified pseudocode for PLSI. Here, $\circ$ denotes element-wise multiply and $\circ\!/$ denotes element-wise divide.

Data: $\mathbf{O}$: $m \times n$ sparse word-document matrix, where m is the vocabulary size and n is the number of documents;
k: number of latent topics (much less than m and n).
Result: $\mathbf{B}$: $n \times k$ dense document-topic matrix;
$\mathbf{C}$: $m \times k$ dense word-topic matrix;
$\mathbf{E}$: $k \times k$ diagonal matrix representing topic frequencies.

initialize $\mathbf{B}, \mathbf{C}, \mathbf{E}$;
repeat
  $\mathbf{F} \leftarrow \mathbf{O} \circ\!/ (\mathbf{C} \times \mathbf{E} \times \mathbf{B}^\mathsf{T})$;
  $\mathbf{E}' \leftarrow \mathbf{E} \circ (\mathbf{C}^\mathsf{T} \times \mathbf{F} \times \mathbf{B})$;
  $\mathbf{C}' \leftarrow (\mathbf{C} \times (\mathbf{I} \circ\!/ \mathbf{E}')) \circ (\mathbf{F} \times \mathbf{B} \times \mathbf{E})$;
  $\mathbf{B}' \leftarrow (\mathbf{B} \times (\mathbf{I} \circ\!/ \mathbf{E}')) \circ (\mathbf{F}^\mathsf{T} \times \mathbf{C} \times \mathbf{E})$;
  $\mathbf{B}, \mathbf{C}, \mathbf{E} \leftarrow \mathbf{B}', \mathbf{C}', \mathbf{E}'$;
until *termination condition*;

of [18] for computing an approximate SVD, the first (and most expensive) step involves a series of matrix multiplies. Specifically, given an $m \times n$ input matrix $\mathbf{A}$, this step uses an $l \times m$ randomly generated matrix $\mathbf{G}$ whose entries are i.i.d. Gaussian random variables of zero mean and unit variance, and computes $\mathbf{G} \times (\mathbf{A} \times \mathbf{A}^\mathsf{T})^k \times \mathbf{A}$. Typically, l is much smaller than m and n, and k is small (say 5). We refer to this step as RSVD-1.

- A popular method in information retrieval and text mining is *Probabilistic Latent Semantic Indexing* (*PLSI*) [13]. The algorithm can be conveniently written in the matrix notation with just a few lines, as shown in Algorithm 1.

Cumulon allows users to rapidly develop in this R-like language, without having to learn MapReduce or SQL, or to worry about how to map data and computation onto specific hardware and platforms.

When ***deploying*** statistical data analysis programs in a cloud, users of Cumulon will be presented with best "deployment plans" meeting their requirements, along with information that is actually useful in making decisions—in terms of completion time and monetary cost. For instance, given a target completion time, Cumulon can suggest the best plan on Amazon EC2 that minimizes the expected monetary cost. This plan encodes choices of not only implementation alternatives and execution parameters, but also cluster provisioning and configuration settings. For example, Figure 1 shows, for various Amazon EC2 machine types under different time constraints, the cost of best deployment plans for RSVD-1, the critical step of the randomized SVD algorithm discussed earlier. Figures like this one show a clear tradeoff between completion time and cost, as well as relative cost-effectiveness of various machine types for the given program, making it easier for users to make informed decisions. Cumulon generates this figure automatically by building cost models and performing cost-based optimization in the space of possible deployment plans. In general, across different machine types and as time constraint varies, the optimal cluster size, configuration, and execution parameters vary; choosing them by hand would have been tedious and difficult.

We make a number of technical contributions in this paper:

1) We show that MapReduce is a poor fit for matrix-based analysis. We adopt a simplified parallel execution model that is more efficient, flexible, and easier for automatic optimization. Instead of building completely new storage and execution engines, we show how to implement Cumulon on top of HDFS and Hadoop, in a way that departs significantly from the MapReduce model. This novel strategy offers large savings over more "traditional" uses of Hadoop for matrix operations, such as SystemML [8].

2) Thanks to Cumulon's focus on matrix-based data analysis, we can model programs not as black boxes, but as plans consisting of a set of commonly used physical operators. Cumulon's simple yet

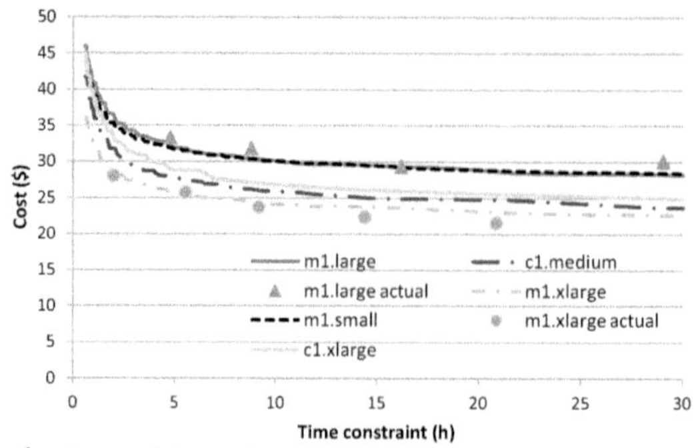

Figure 1: Costs of the optimal deployment plans for RSVD-1 (with l = 2k, m = 200k, n = 200k, k = 5) using different machine types under different time constraints. Curves are predicted; costs of actual runs for sample data points are shown for comparison.

flexible execution model enables us to develop a specialized set of operators with predictable computation and network I/O patterns. We also introduce new operators. For example, "masked matrix multiply" captures an efficient execution strategy involving interacting sparse and dense matrix operations, which has previously only been possible with manual low-level coding.

3) Building on our understanding of Cumulon's physical operators, we show how to obtain good cost estimates for matrix-based programs in a cloud by benchmarking, simulation, and modeling. Various sources of performance uncertainty in the cloud makes cost estimation particularly challenging. We show how to cope with the variance among the speeds of individual tasks (threads of parallel execution) and account for the behavior of the task scheduler when predicting overall completion time.

4) We demonstrate the benefit of considering a bigger deployment plan space that encodes the choices of not only physical operators and their execution parameters, but also hardware provisioning and configuration settings. Experiments show that, without jointly optimizing these choices, one can get far inferior plans. While Cumulon currently assumes homogeneous clusters, it considers deployment plans that switches clusters dynamically between steps; we give examples where such plans make sense.

5) We devise efficient strategies for searching through this much bigger plan space, by exploiting the properties and common characteristics of our programs for pruning and prioritization. Cumulon can optimize fairly complex programs (such as PLSI, which involves 16 operators) in a reasonable time (under one minute for PLSI) on a desktop with moderate hardware.

6) Hadoop-based Cumulon inherits important features of Hadoop such as failure handling, and is able to leverage the vibrant Hadoop ecosystem. While targeting matrix operations, Cumulon can support programs that also contain traditional, non-matrix Hadoop jobs. For example, we will demonstrate a complete text analytics program consisting of both downloading and preprocessing of documents (to build input matrices) and matrix-based PLSI (Algorithm 1). At the same time, Cumulon is not tied to Hadoop; because of its generic execution model, Cumulon can be extended to multiple storage/execution engines in the future.

2 System Overview and Road Map

We begin with an overview of how Cumulon turns a program into an optimized form ready for deployment in the cloud.

Logical Plan and Rewrites Cumulon first converts the program into a *logical plan*, which consists of *logical operators* corresponding to standard matrix operations, e.g., matrix transpose, add, multiply, element-wise multiply, power, etc. Then, Cumulon conducts a series of rule-based *logical plan rewrites* to obtain "generally bet-

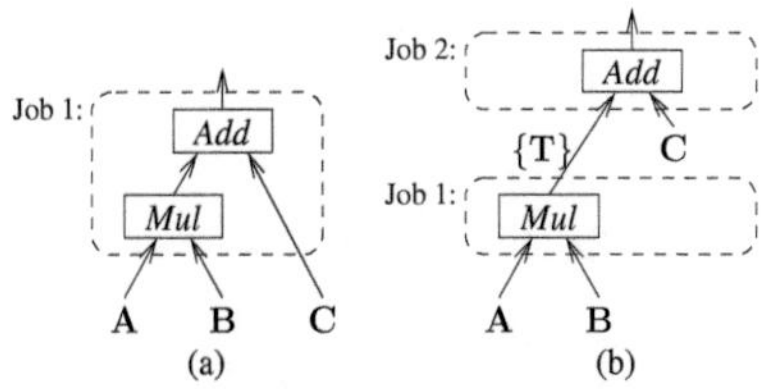

Figure 2: Two physical plan templates for $\mathbf{A} \times \mathbf{B} + \mathbf{C}$. In (b), the output from *Mul*, $\{\mathbf{T}\}$, is a list of matrices whose sum is $\mathbf{A} \times \mathbf{B}$.

ter" logical plans. Such rewrites consider input data characteristics (e.g., matrix sizes and sparsity) and apply linear algebra equivalences to reduce computation or I/O, or increase parallelism.

For example, consider again the expression $\mathbf{G} \times (\mathbf{A} \times \mathbf{A}^\top)^k \times \mathbf{A}$ in RSVD-1 from Section 1. The original logical plan raises $\mathbf{A} \times \mathbf{A}^\top$ to the k-th power, which repeatedly multiplies large $m \times m$ matrices. However, a better approach (when l and k are small) would be to use associativity of matrix multiply to rewrite the logical plan as:

$$\underbrace{((\cdots((\mathbf{G} \times \mathbf{A}) \times \mathbf{A}^\top) \times \cdots \times \mathbf{A}) \times \mathbf{A}^\top)}_{2k \text{ multiplies}} \times \mathbf{A},$$

which involves repeatedly multiplying a matrix with only l rows by another matrix, which is much cheaper.

Physical Operators and Plan Templates For each logical plan, Cumulon translates it into one or more *physical plan templates*, each representing a parallel execution strategy for the program. A physical plan template represents a workflow of *jobs*, where each job is in turn a DAG (directed acyclic graph) of *physical operators*. We will provide more details on these concepts in Section 3. For now, think of a job as a unit of work that is executed in a data-parallel fashion, where each thread of execution, or *task*, runs an instance of the physical operator DAG in a pipelined fashion over a different input split. The translation procedure attempts to group operators into as few jobs as possible, but if doing so causes one job to contain multiple resource-hungry physical operators, alternatives will be generated. Also note that one logical operator may be translated into one or more physical operators, and sometimes one physical operator may implement multiple logical operators.[1]

For example, Figure 2 shows two possible physical plan templates for $\mathbf{A} \times \mathbf{B} + \mathbf{C}$. The first one (a) has one job while the second one (b) has two. The reason why two jobs might be preferable will become apparent when we discuss in Section 3 how Cumulon implements matrix multiply in detail. Roughly speaking, the physical operator *Mul* only multiples submatrices from $\mathbf{A}$ and $\mathbf{B}$. In general, to complete $\mathbf{A} \times \mathbf{B}$, these results need to be further grouped and aggregated; in Figure 2b, *Add* performs this aggregation (as well as addition with $\mathbf{C}$) in a separate job. On the other hand, Figure 2a applies in the special case where submatrices multiplied by *Mul* include complete rows from $\mathbf{A}$ and complete columns from $\mathbf{B}$; no further aggregation is needed and *Add* can perform addition with $\mathbf{C}$ in the same job as *Mul*.

Deployment Plan Note that a physical plan template does not completely specify how to execute the program in the cloud. A complete specification, which we call a *deployment plan*, is a tuple $\langle \mathcal{L}, \mathcal{O}, \mathcal{P}, \mathcal{Q} \rangle$, where:

- $\mathcal{L}$ is a physical plan template.
- $\mathcal{O}$ represents parameters settings for all physical operators in $\mathcal{L}$. For example, for the *Mul* operator in Figure 2b, we need to specify the sizes of the submatrices multiplied in each task.
- $\mathcal{P}$ represents hardware provisioning settings, e.g., what machine type and how many machines to reserve on Amazon EC2. In general, such settings may change during the course of execution; for example, when a program shifts from an I/O-intensive stage to a computation-intensive stage, we may want to switch to fewer machines with more powerful CPUs.
- $\mathcal{Q}$ represents configuration settings. For example, for a Hadoop-based implementation of Cumulon, we need to specify the number of map/reduce "slots" per machine. In general, these setting can also change during the course of execution.

Given a physical plan template $\mathcal{L}$ and user requirements (e.g., minimizing monetary cost while capping completion time), Cumulon performs cost-based optimization to find a deployment plan based on $\mathcal{L}$ that satisfies the user requirements. Cumulon then carries out the deployment plan in the cloud. Cumulon will monitor the execution, and alert the user if it detects deviation from the assumptions made or guarantees offered by the optimization.

3 Storage and Execution

As MapReduce has been the prevalent model for data-parallel programming in the cloud, a natural question is whether we can build our support for matrix-based data analysis on this model. Before presenting our approach for Cumulon in Section 3.2, we first show, in Section 3.1, why MapReduce is a poor fit for this type of programs. In Section 3.2, after describing Cumulon's storage and execution models, we sample a couple of interesting physical operators designed for matrices, and show how to implement Cumulon conveniently on top of Hadoop (without adhering to MapReduce).

3.1 Why not MapReduce

A MapReduce job consists of a *map* phase followed by a *reduce* phase. The map phase partitions the input (modeled as key-value pairs) disjointly across multiple map tasks for parallel processing. For the reduce phase, the intermediate output data from the map tasks are grouped by their keys and *shuffled* over the network to be processed by multiple reduce tasks. Each group of intermediate output is processed by the same reduce task to produce final output.

Implementing efficient matrix-based computation within the confines of MapReduce is awkward. In general, in a parallel matrix operation, each task may request specific subsets of input data items. Assignment of input to map tasks in MapReduce can be controlled to some extent by representing input in different ways (such that all data needed by a task is packed as one key-value pair), or with custom input splitting supported by some implementations of MapReduce (e.g., Hadoop). However, such control is still limited in supporting the general data access patterns of matrix operations.

In particular, map tasks in MapReduce are supposed to receive *disjoint* partitions of input, but for many matrix operations, one input data item may be needed by multiple tasks. A workaround in MapReduce is for mappers to read in the input items, replicate them—one copy for each reduce task that needs it, and then shuffle them to reduce tasks. The map phase thus does nothing but to make extra copies of data, which could have been avoided completely if map tasks are allowed to receive overlapping subsets of input.

Next, we illustrate the limitation of MapReduce using a concrete example of matrix multiply, and discuss the inefficiency in existing MapReduce-based implementations.

Example: Matrix Multiply Consider multiplying two big matrices $\mathbf{A}$ (of size $m \times l$) and $\mathbf{B}$ (of size $l \times n$). Let $\mathbf{C}$ denote the result (of size $m \times n$). On a high level, virtually all efficient parallel matrix multiply algorithms work by dividing input into submatrices: $\mathbf{A}$ into $f_m \times f_l$ submatrices, each with size ${}^{m}/_{f_m} \times {}^{l}/_{f_l}$, and

[1] We will not discuss logical plan rewrites and translation into physical plan templates further: because of space constraints, they are not the focus of this paper. Their solutions are orthogonal from and should readily work with the techniques in this paper.

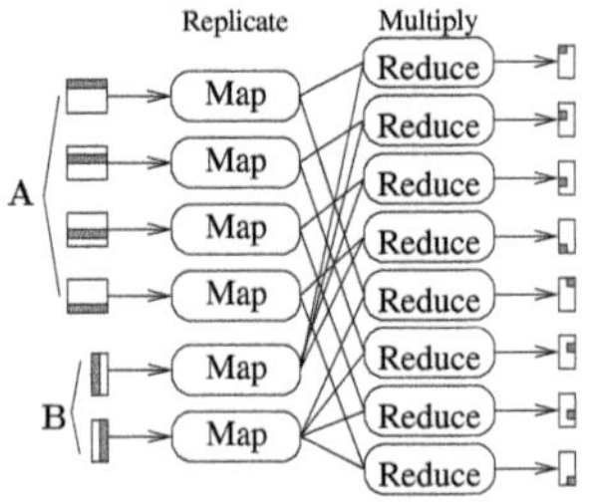

Figure 3: MapReduce job for $\mathbf{A} \times \mathbf{B}$ using SystemML's RMM; $f_l = 1$ is required.

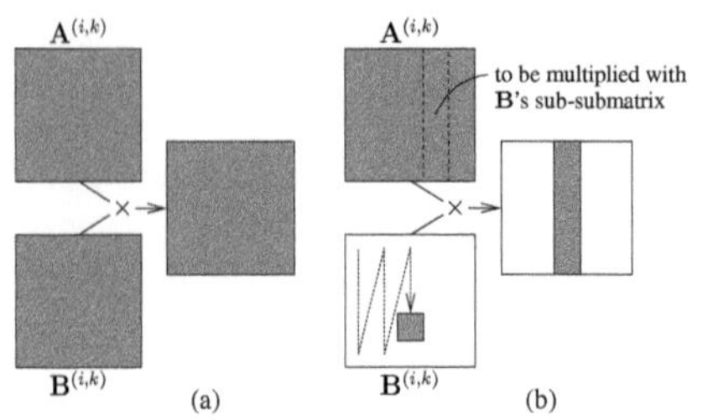

Figure 4: Options for multiplying submatrices within a task. Shaded portions are kept in memory.

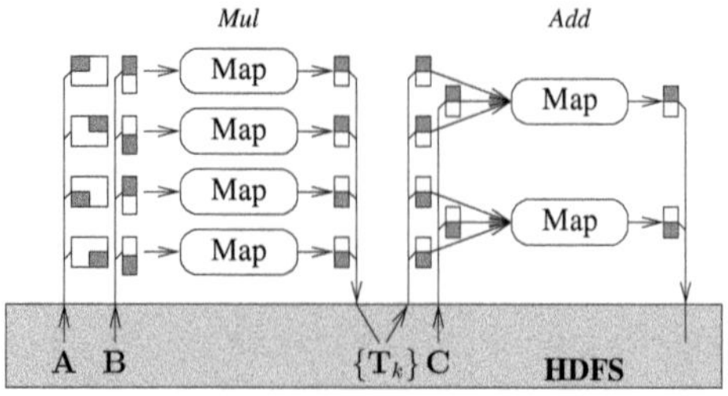

Figure 5: Cumulon's map-only Hadoop jobs for $\mathbf{A} \times \mathbf{B} + \mathbf{C}$ using the physical plan template of Figure 2b.

$\mathbf{B}$ into $f_l \times f_n$ submatrices, each with size $^l/_{f_l} \times {}^n/_{f_n}$. We call f_m, f_l, and f_n *split factors*. The output will consist of $f_m \times f_n$ submatrices. Let $\mathbf{M}^{(i,j)}$ denote the submatrix of $\mathbf{M}$ at position (i, j). The output submatrix at position (i, j) is then computed as $\mathbf{C}^{(i,j)} = \sum_{k=1}^{f_l} \mathbf{A}^{(i,k)} \times \mathbf{B}^{(k,j)}$. Computation typically proceeds in two steps: first, pairs of submatrices from $\mathbf{A}$ and $\mathbf{B}$ are multiplied in parallel; second, the results of the multiplies are grouped (by the output submatrix position they contribute to) and summed. Note that if $f_l = 1$, the second step is not needed.

Indeed, matrix multiply is an example where one input submatrix may be needed by multiple tasks in the first step (unless $f_m = f_n = 1$, a special case that we will discuss later). If we adhere to MapReduce, we have to use the map phase to replicate the input submatrices and shuffle them to the reduce phase to be multiplied. Next, if $f_l \neq 1$, we need a second MapReduce job to perform the required summation, adding even more overhead. SystemML [8] takes this approach (called *RMM* there), but to avoid the second MapReduce job, it requires $f_l = 1$ (see Figure 3 for illustration).

However, SystemML's RMM turns out to be suboptimal on many accounts. First, the map phase performs no useful computation; input replication and shuffling are just expensive workarounds to allow reduce tasks to access data they need. Second, $f_l = 1$ severely limits the choice of execution strategies: it basically amounts to multiplying rows of $\mathbf{A}$ with columns of $\mathbf{B}$. It is well known in the literature on out-of-core linear algebra [21] that such an aspect ratio is suboptimal for matrix multiply (assuming sufficiently large m, l, and n). The number of element multiplications per task in this case is only linear in the number of input elements per task; in contrast, using square submatrices of size $k \times k$, for example, would yield k^3 multiplications per $2k^2$ input elements. Since the total number of element multiplications across all tasks is fixed ($m \times l \times n$), strategies that require fewer input elements for the same number of multiplications have lower I/O. We will experimentally confirm the suboptimality of SystemML's RMM strategy in Section 6.1.

In the other special case of $f_m = f_n = 1$, we basically multiply columns of $\mathbf{A}$ with rows of $\mathbf{B}$: each submatrix multiply generates a matrix of the same size as the final output $\mathbf{C}$, and these matrices simply need to be added to produce $\mathbf{C}$. Note that in this case the submatrix multiply tasks work on disjoint input data, though each task needs to draw a specific pair of submatrices from $\mathbf{A}$ and $\mathbf{B}$. If we relax the MapReduce model to allow custom input splitting, it would be possible to use a map phase to perform all submatrix multiplies, and a reduce phase to perform the final add. However, under a "pure" MapReduce model, we would need one full MapReduce job for the submatrix multiplies and another one for the add: the map phase in both jobs serves the sole purpose of routing appropriate data to reduce tasks, which still incurs considerable overhead. This two-job strategy for $f_m = f_n = 1$ is called *CPMM* in SystemML [8]. RMM and CPMM together are the two matrix multiply strategies supported by SystemML.

HAMA [19] supports arbitrary split factors for matrix multiply. It assumes that input has already been preprocessed for a MapReduce job such that each map task receives the two submatrices to be multiplied as one input data item. The result submatrices are then shuffled to reduce tasks to be added. Thus, HAMA carries out all computation in a matrix multiply in a single MapReduce job. However, the preprocessing step would still take another MapReduce job to replicate the input submatrices.

3.2 The Cumulon Approach

Having seen how the pure MapReduce model is not suitable for matrix operations, we now turn to a simpler but more flexible model.

Storage Since Cumulon targets matrix-based computation, it provides an abstraction for distributed storage of matrices. Matrices are stored and accessed by *tiles*. A tile is a submatrix of fixed (but configurable) dimension. Cumulon's execution model guarantees that, at any given time, a tile has either multiple concurrent readers, or one single writer.

Tile size is chosen to be large enough to amortize the overhead of storage and access, and to enable effective compression. However, they should not be so big that they limit execution options (e.g., split factors in matrix multiply). See Section 6 for the default setting in experiments. Within a tile, elements are stored in column-major order. Both sparse and dense formats are supported: the sparse format enumerates indices and values of non-zero elements, while the dense format simply stores all values.

Jobs and Tasks A Cumulon program executes as a workflow of *jobs*. A job reads a number of input matrices and writes a number of output matrices; input and output matrices must be disjoint. Dependencies among jobs are implied by dependent accesses to the same matrices. Dependent jobs execute in serial order. Each job executes as multiple independent *tasks* that do not communicate with each other. All tasks within the job run identical code, but read different (possibly overlapping) parts of the input matrices (*input splits*), and write disjoint parts of output matrices (*output splits*). Hence, this execution model can be seen as a restricted variant of the *Bulk Synchronous Parallel* model [22] where data are only communicated through the global, distributed storage in the unit of tiles.

It is worth noting that tiles do not correspond to input/output splits. A task may work on input/output splits that each consist of multiple tiles. Also, unlike MapReduce, input splits do not need to be disjoint across tasks, and a task can read its input split and write its output split anytime during its execution.

Slots and Waves Available hardware is configured into a number of *slots*, each of which can be used to execute one task at a time. A *scheduler* assigns tasks to slots. If a job consists of more tasks than slots, it may take multiple *waves* to finish. Each wave consists of a number of concurrently executing tasks no more than the number of slots. There may not be a clear boundary between waves, as a slot can be assigned another task in the same job immediately after the current task completes. However, as stated earlier, dependent jobs do not start until the current job is completely done.

Physical Plan Templates and Operators As defined in Section 2, a *deployment plan* completely specifies how to execute a Cumulon program. The *physical plan template* component ($\mathcal{L}$) of the deployment plan specifies a workflow of jobs, where each job is a DAG of *physical operators*. Each physical operator has a list of parameters, whose settings (by the $\mathcal{O}$ component in the deployment plan) control their execution behavior. During job execution, each task executes an instance of the DAG. Similar to database query execution, the physical operators execute in a pipelined fashion through an iterator-based interface. To reduce the overhead of element-wise data passing, the unit of data passing among iterators is a tile (when appropriate). Physical operators can read and write tiles in the input and output splits (respectively) assigned to their tasks.

Example Recall the two physical plan templates for $\mathbf{A} \times \mathbf{B} + \mathbf{C}$ in Figure 2. Here we fill in more details. The *Mul* physical operator has split factors f_m, f_l, and f_n as its parameters (they are not the only ones; more discussion will follow shortly): set by $\mathcal{O}$, they control the dimensions of two submatrices being multiplied. *Mul* reads these submatrices directly from distributed storage.

The physical plan template in Figure 2a works for $f_l = 1$, where *Mul* produces a submatrix of $\mathbf{A} \times \mathbf{B}$ directly (no summation is required), and passes this submatrix to *Add* in the same job (one tile at a time) to be added to the corresponding submatrix of $\mathbf{C}$.

The physical plan template in Figure 2b works in the general case of $f_l > 1$ and requires two jobs. The first job multiplies submatrices from $\mathbf{A}$ and $\mathbf{B}$, and writes f_l intermediate matrices, where the k-th intermediate matrix $\mathbf{T}_k$ consists of submatrics $\mathbf{T}_k^{(i,j)} = \mathbf{A}^{(i,k)} \times \mathbf{B}^{(k,j)}$; each instance of *Mul* is responsible for one submatrix in one of the intermediate matrices. The second job computes $(\sum_{k=1}^{f_l} \mathbf{T}_k) + \mathbf{C}$; each instance of *Add* reads corresponding tiles from $\mathbf{T}_1, \ldots, \mathbf{T}_k, \mathbf{C}$, adds them, and writes an output tile.

A Closer Look at *Mul* So far, our discussion of *Mul* has remained at a high level; next, we discuss how two input submatrices $\mathbf{A}^{(i,k)}$ and $\mathbf{B}^{(k,j)}$ are actually multiplied. There are many options, with different performance tradeoffs. We begin with two options illustrated in Figure 4. **1)** The most straightforward option is to read two submatrices entirely into memory and multiply them using a highly tuned BLAS library. This option has good CPU utilization but also high memory requirement. The amount of memory available to each slot limits the size of the submatrices that can be multiplied without thrashing. **2)** Another option, aimed at reducing memory requirement, is to read one submatrix in memory and stream in the other one in a specific order tile by tile. Say $\mathbf{A}^{(i,k)}$ is read and buffered in memory. Conceptually, each column of output tiles is produced by multiplying $\mathbf{A}^{(i,k)}$ with each column of tiles in $\mathbf{B}^{(k,j)}$. To this end, we reserve memory for a column of output tiles, and stream in tiles of $\mathbf{B}^{(k,j)}$ in column-major order. The p-th tile in the current column of $\mathbf{B}^{(k,j)}$ would be multiplied with the p-th column of tiles in $\mathbf{A}^{(i,k)}$ and accumulated into the column of output tiles. While this option has a lower memory requirement, its multiplications are performed in a more piecemeal fashion, so it tends to result in lower CPU utilization than the first option.

There actually exist a range of options between the two above. Besides the split factors f_m, f_l, f_n, which control the dimensions of submatrices to be multiplied, *Mul* also includes parameters that further specify the input submatrix to buffer in memory and the *granularity of streaming* the other submatrix as "sub-submatrices." These parameters provide a smooth tradeoff between CPU utilization and memory requirement. The first option above is the case where $\mathbf{B}^{(k,j)}$ has just one sub-submatrix; the second option is where the sub-submatrices are tiles. Further details are omitted.

MaskMul Besides improving standard physical operators (e.g., making *Mul* more flexible and allowing *Add* to take multiple inputs), we have also found the need to introduce new operators in order to capture efficient execution strategies for complex expressions. *MaskMul* is one such example.

To motivate, consider Line 3 of PLSI (Algorithm 1), where a large, but very sparse, matrix $\mathbf{O}$ is element-wise divided by the equally large result of a chain of dense matrix multiplies. With standard matrix operators, we will be forced to fully evaluate the expensive dense matrix multiplies. A well-known trick in hand-coded PLSI implementations is to exploit the sparsity in $\mathbf{O}$ to avoid full dense matrix multiplies: if a particular element of $\mathbf{O}$ is 0, there is no need to compute the corresponding element in the result of multiplies, because element-wise divide would have returned 0 anyway.

Therefore, we introduce a new physical operator, *MaskMul* (for *masked* matrix multiply). In addition to input matrices $\mathbf{A}$ and $\mathbf{B}$ to be multiplied, *MaskMul* receives a "mask" in the form of a sparse matrix $\mathbf{M}$ to be element-wise multiplied or divided by $\mathbf{A} \times \mathbf{B}$. Execution of *MaskMul* is driven by the non-zero elements in $\mathbf{M}$. Conceptually, we multiply row i of $\mathbf{A}$ with column j of $\mathbf{B}$ only if $m_{i,j} \neq 0$. Details are omitted because of space constraints.[2]

As we will see in Section 6.1, *MaskMul* can improve performance dramatically. In particular, it speeds up Line 3 of PLSI (Algorithm 1) by more than an order of magnitude (Figure 11).

Need for Automatic Optimization From the discussion of physical operators, it is clear that we want automatic optimization of matrix-based data analysis programs. Even for simple programs with the most basic matrix operations, there are many choices to be made. For example, for Figure 2, should we choose two jobs, or one job with potentially suboptimal split factors? For matrix multiply, what are the best choices of split factors and streaming granularity? Depending on sparsity, should we use *Mul* or *MaskMul*? Some of these choices are related to each other, and to hardware provisioning and configuration settings that affect number of tasks (and split size per task), memory, CPU utilization, relative costs of CPU and I/O, etc. Making these choices manually may be infeasible, error-prone, or simply not cost-effective.

Implementation in Hadoop Our discussion so far only assumes generic storage and execution platforms. While this generality is by design—as we want Cumulon to be able to work with a variety of alternative platforms in the future—our current implementation of Cumulon is based on Hadoop and HDFS, which allows us to readily leverage its features, flexibility, and ecosystem of tools and users. We now describe this implementation, highlighting how it departs from the traditional MapReduce-based usage of Hadoop.

We use HDFS for distributed matrix storage. A matrix is stored using one or more data files in HDFS. Tiles of a matrix written by the same task go into the same data file. For each matrix, we also store metadata (including information such as dimension and sparsity) and index (which maps the position of a tile to a data file and the offset and length therein) in HDFS. Additional details are omitted because of space constraints.

Each Cumulon job is implemented as a *map-only* Hadoop job. Cumulon slots correspond to Hadoop map slots (we do not have reduce slots because we never use the reduce phase). Unlike MapRe-

[2] Although the optimization enabled by *MaskMul* is reminiscent of "pushing selections down through a join" in databases, it cannot be achieved in our context using just rewrite rules involving standard matrix operators. The reason is that the mask cannot be pushed below the multiply to its input matrices—unless the mask has rows or columns consisting entirely of zeros, every element of the input matrices will be needed by some non-zero element of the mask. Thus, we need the new operator *MaskMul* to handle this non-standard filtering of computation.

duce, a map task does not receive input as key-value pairs; instead, it simply gets specifications of the input splits it is responsible for, and reads directly from HDFS as needed. In-memory dense matrix multiplies call a (multi-threaded) JBLAS library. Each map task also writes all its output to HDFS; there is no shuffling.

For example, Figure 5 illustrates how Cumulon implements the physical plan template in Figure 2b with Hadoop and HDFS. Contrasting with SystemML's use of Hadoop in Figure 3, we see that Cumulon is simpler, more flexible (e.g., by supporting any choice of split factors), and has less overhead (by avoiding map tasks that do nothing but route and replicate data). These advantages will be confirmed by experiments in Section 6. Section 6.1 will also compare with another possible implementation of Cumulon on Hadoop that use reduce tasks (to get fewer jobs); we will see that the map-only approach described here works better.

4 Cost-Based Optimization

Overview We now turn to cost-based optimization of deployment plans for matrix-based data analysis in the cloud. Given a physical plan template $\mathcal{L}$—recall from Section 2 that Cumulon obtains possible $\mathcal{L}$'s from the original logical plan through rewrites and translation—we would like to find a deployment plan for $\mathcal{L}$ that is optimal in terms of completion time and total (monetary) cost. Recall that a deployment plan for $\mathcal{L}$ is a tuple $\langle \mathcal{L}, \mathcal{O}, \mathcal{P}, \mathcal{Q} \rangle$, where $\mathcal{O}$ represents the physical operator parameter settings, $\mathcal{P}$ represents the hardware provisioning settings, and $\mathcal{Q}$ represents the configuration settings. Let $\mathfrak{T}(\cdot)$ and $\mathfrak{C}(\cdot)$ denote the completion time and cost of a deployment plan, respectively. In this paper, we focus on:

$$\textbf{minimize}_{\mathcal{O},\mathcal{P},\mathcal{Q}}\ \mathfrak{C}(\langle \mathcal{L}, \mathcal{O}, \mathcal{P}, \mathcal{Q} \rangle)\ \textbf{s.t.}\ \mathfrak{T}(\langle \mathcal{L}, \mathcal{O}, \mathcal{P}, \mathcal{Q} \rangle) \le T_{\max};$$

i.e., minimizing cost given a completion time constraint ($T_{\max}$). Other problem formulations may also be appropriate (e.g., minimizing time given a cost budget, or finding all Pareto-optimal plans); techniques in this section can be extended to these formulations.

We currently make two simplifying assumptions. First, while we support intra-job parallelism (i.e., we execute each job using parallel tasks), we do not consider inter-job parallelism (i.e., two jobs cannot execute at the same time even if they are not dependent on each other). Second, at any point during the execution of a job, the cluster is homogeneous (i.e., consisting of identical machines). What partially compensates for these limitations is our support for dynamic cluster switching between jobs. Thus, the cluster can be heterogeneous across jobs and over time.

Hadoop and Amazon EC2 Currently, Cumulon is implemented on top of Hadoop and targets deployment on Amazon EC2. Under this setting, we can spell out the components $\mathcal{P}$ and $\mathcal{Q}$ of a deployment plan. $\mathcal{P}$ specifies, for each job, the type and number (N) of machines to reserve on EC2; a change in either type or number of machines across adjacent jobs implies cluster switching. $\mathcal{Q}$ specifies the Hadoop/HDFS configuration settings for each job. From our experience, the most relevant setting with a significant impact on plan performance is the number of map slots (S) per machine; we will therefore focus on this setting. Appropriate values for other settings can either be derived using S (such as memory available for each task) or chosen in ways independent from particular plans (such as HDFS block size).

For EC2, the monetary cost of a cluster is calculated by multiplying the hourly per-machine rate for the cluster type, the number of machines in the cluster, and the number of hours (rounded up to the nearest integer) that the cluster is in use. In this paper, we simplify the cost function by assuming no rounding up, as we estimate expected costs anyway. It is straightforward to extend our techniques to work with rounding and other billing schemes.

Next, we discuss how to estimate the completion time and cost of a deployment plan (Section 4.1), and how to search the space of feasible plans for the optimal one (Section 4.2). Although much of the discussion will be specific to Hadoop and EC2, our technique should be applicable to other scenarios as well.

4.1 Time and Cost Estimation

On EC2, the total completion time and cost of a deployment plan come from the following sources: **1)** running Hadoop jobs; **2)** cluster initialization; **3)** cluster switching; **4)** data ingress/egress. (1) is the most significant source and will be the emphasis of this section. Time and cost for (2), (3), and (4) are relatively easier to estimate. (2) and (3) depend on the size and type of the clusters involved. (3) and (4) depend the amount of data transferred. For (3), the matrices that need to be copied to the new cluster can be obtained via live variable analysis. For (4), the cost depends on the method used for data ingress/egress. Currently we assume that all input/output data of a program reside on Amazon EBS, but other methods and cost functions can be plugged in. For (2), (3), and (4), we will not go into additional details because of space constraints.

Since the cost of running a Hadoop job on EC2 can be readily calculated from the completion time, we will focus on estimating the expected completion time of a job in this section. Our overall approach is to build a model for job completion time using data collected from benchmarking and simulation. Since the number of possible settings of $\mathcal{L}$, $\mathcal{O}$, $\mathcal{P}$, and $\mathcal{Q}$ is huge, we cannot afford a single high-dimensional model; instead, we decompose it into components and build each component separately. In the remainder of subsection, we first discuss how to estimate completion time of individual tasks (Section 4.1.1) by modeling computation and network I/O separately, and then how to estimate job completion time from task completion time (Section 4.1.2).

Several challenges differentiate cost estimation in Cumulon from non-cloud, database settings. First, cardinality estimation, key in databases, is a not an issue in our setting because the dimensions of matrices (even intermediate ones) are easy to derive at compile time. Instead, the closest analogy in our setting is estimation of matrix sparsity, which affects the cost of sparse matrix operations. Second, in matrix-based computation, CPU accounts for a significant fraction of the total running time, so unlike the database setting, we cannot count only I/O (in our case, network I/O). Third, performance uncertainty that arises from parallel execution in the cloud makes estimation especially challenging. For example, we need to model how variance among individual task completion times affects the overall job completion time (even if we care only about its average). Finally, we note that accurate cost modeling of arbitrary statistical computing workloads is extremely difficult, because it entails predicting data- and analysis-dependent convergence properties. Techniques in this section aim at predicting "per-iteration" time and cost instead of the number of iterations; Section 5 discusses how Cumulon handles this challenge pragmatically.

4.1.1 Estimating Task Completion Time

We estimate the running time of a task as the sum of three components: computation, network I/O (from/to the distributed matrix store), and task initialization. The simplicity of this approach stems from the simplicity of the Cumulon execution model, which gives map tasks direct control of their I/O and eliminates the reduce phase and shuffling. Task initialization is a fixed overhead given a slot and is easy to estimate; we focus on computation and network I/O next.

Estimating Computation Time of a Task Recall that a task consists of a DAG of physical operators. We build a model of computation time for each operator and compose (add) them into a model for the task. A possible approach is to analytically derive a FLOP

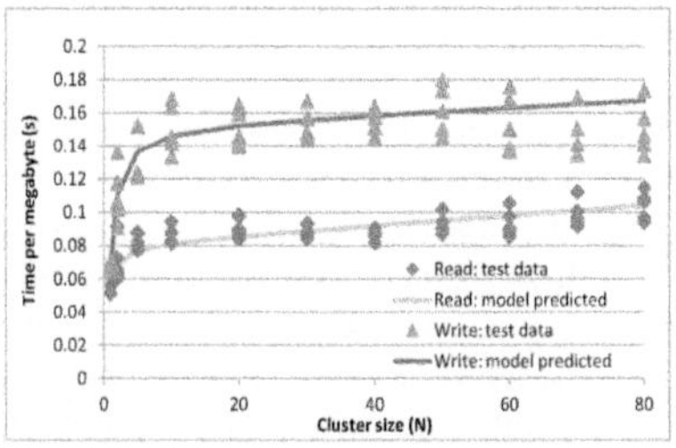

Figure 6: Estimated vs. actual times per unit I/O for machine type c1.medium with $S = 2$. The program measured here multiplies two dense matrices.

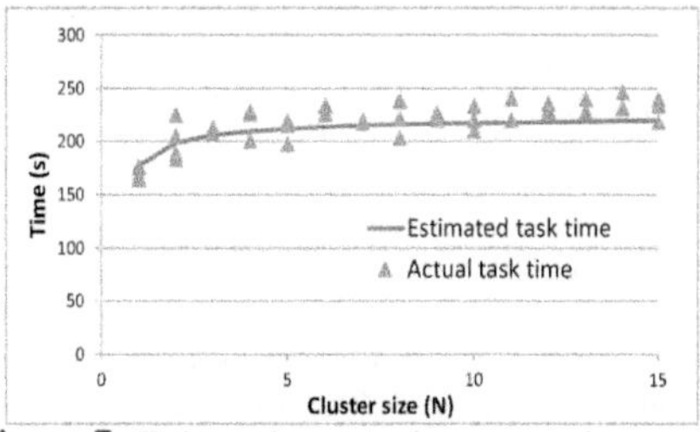

Figure 7: Estimated vs. actual average task completion times for machine type c1.medium with $S = 2$. The program here multiplies two 6k × 6k dense matrices.

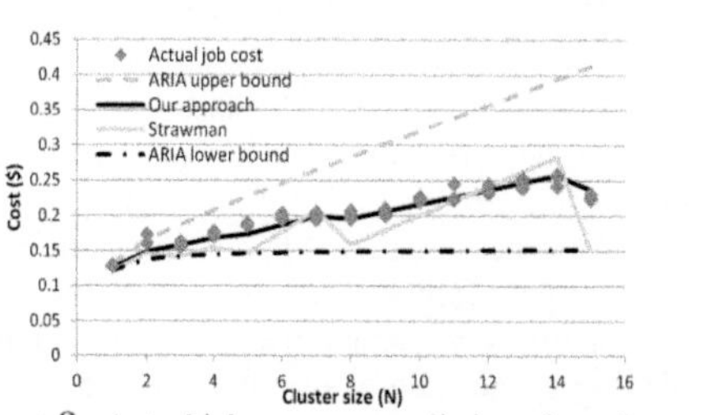

Figure 8: Actual job costs vs. predictions from the strawman approach, ours, as well as ARIA upper/lower bounds. The job multiplies two dense matrices of sizes 12k×18k and 18k × 30k. Machine type is c1.medium; $q = 30$; $S = 2$.

(floating-point operations) count model for each operator, but we have found that FLOP counts alone do not lead to an accurate estimate of computation time. For example, a JBLAS implementation of matrix multiply is easily orders-of-magnitude faster than hand-coded loops, despite the same FLOP counts; a sparse matrix multiply is much slower than a dense one with the same FLOP count. Therefore, we build a model for each operator by benchmarking.

In general, the model inputs include machine type, number of slots per machine, operator parameter settings, input split size, and input sparsity. There is no need to consider the number of machines in the cluster because computation is local. For some operators, the model can be pared down further. For example, for dense matrix *Mul*, we only need to benchmark for combinations of machine type, number of slots, and dimensions of sub-submatrices it chooses to multiply-accumulate each time using JBLAS. Then, the computation time of the whole *Mul* operator can be computed by multiplying the estimated time per JBLAS call by the number of such calls, which can be easily and analytically derived from the input split size, split factors, and granularity of streaming (recall Section 3.2).

Instead of benchmarking every possible setting of model inputs, we sample the space of feasible settings. For example, for *Mul*, machine type and number of slots limit the amount of memory available to each slot, and in turn bounds the sizes of sub-submatrices, which we additionally constrain to be integral multiples of tile sizes. The number of slots is also naturally limited on a given machine type; it makes no sense to allot a large number of slots on a machine with few cores because matrix computation is CPU-intensive. We repeat the benchmark for each setting multiple times; beside the mean, the sample variance will also be useful later (Section 4.1.2). Estimates for unseen settings are obtained using interpolation from neighboring benchmarked settings.

Though this approach is simple, we have found it very effective so far, both for highly predictable dense matrix operators, and for sparse matrix operators where the distribution of non-zero entries is random enough with respect to how input is split—this case happens, for example, to our PLSI program because when it generates **O**, it orders documents and words randomly (by their hashes). Future work is needed to better model the impact of skew in sparsity; new models can be readily incorporated into Cumulon.

Estimating Network I/O Time per Task Modeling of network I/O time is quite different from modeling computation. First, the average I/O speed depends on the size of the cluster (see Figure 6 for an example). Second, the total I/O volume is a reasonable predictor for I/O time (unlike FLOP count for computation time). Therefore, we estimate the total I/O volume per task, model time per unit I/O, and multiply them to obtain the I/O time estimate.

The total I/O volume per task is the sum of the I/O volume for each of its operators, which can be analytically derived from input split size, input sparsity, and relevant operator parameters settings.

To model the time per unit I/O, or inverse speed v^{-1}, we note that it depends on the machine type, number of slots per machine (S), and number of machines (N). Reads and writes need to be modeled differently. Because of space constraints, we focus on reads here. In our setting, some reads may be local because some HDFS blocks (or replicas thereof) may happen to reside on machines reading them. For each machine type and S, we benchmark local and remote reads. Let $v^{-1}_{\text{r.local}}$ denote the inverse speed (seconds per MB transferred) of local reads, and let $v^{-1}_{\text{r.remote}}$ denote the inverse speed of remote reads. Given a machine type and S, we estimate $v^{-1}_{\text{r.local}}$ as a constant and $v^{-1}_{\text{r.remote}}$ an affine function of N from the benchmark results. (It turns out that a larger N slows down $v^{-1}_{\text{r.remote}}$, but the effect is small.) We then estimate the inverse read speed v^{-1}_{r} as $\frac{1}{N}(\gamma v^{-1}_{\text{r.local}} + (N-\gamma)v^{-1}_{\text{r.remote}})$, where γ is the HDFS replication factor. Intuitively, γ/N is the probability that a read is local. Again, just like for computation time, we also derive a variance estimate for v^{-1} from sample variances obtained from benchmarking.

Figure 6 compares our model predictions with actual times per unit of data read/written by a dense matrix multiply program. A total of 108 actual measurements are plotted (60 of which are from multiplying two 6k × 6k matrices, and 48 are from multiplying a 4k × 8k matrix with an 8k × 8k one). The read/write models are each trained using 22 data points (disjoint from the 108 above) obtained by benchmarking the multiplication of 6k×6k matrices. The figure shows that our models are quite effective, with coefficients of determination 0.92 (for reads) and 0.91 (for writes).

Putting It Together To estimate the expected completion time of a task, we add our estimates for the three components: computation, I/O, and task initialization. Figure 7 shows our estimate to be fairly consistent with the actual average task completion time for dense matrix multiply, over a wide range of cluster sizes. In this figure, each of the 40 data points plotted represents the measured average task completion for a test run (not used for training models). To obtain the variance in task completion time (which will be needed in Section 4.1.2 for estimating expected job completion time), we assume that the three component times are uncorrelated, and simply add their variances. The variance for the I/O time component is derived by scaling the standard deviation (root of variance) in v^{-1} (in seconds per MB) by the I/O volume (in MB).

4.1.2 Estimating Job Completion Time

Before presenting our approach to estimating job completion time, we start by discussing a strawman approach and a previous approach by *ARIA* [23]. Let q denote the number of tasks in a job (which can be derived from the input split size and total input size), and let μ denote the mean task completion time. Note that the total number of slots available for executing these tasks is NS.

Strawman With the strawman approach, we simply compute the number of waves as $\lceil q/NS \rceil$, and multiply it by μ to get the expected job completion time. If this approach works, we should see, as depicted by the plot for strawman in Figure 8, lots of jaggedness in the completion times (and hence costs) of a given job when N varies. Here, since each task remains the same, its completion time changes little with N. As N increases, $\lceil q/_{NS} \rceil$ does not decrease smoothly; it decreases only at specific "breakpoints" of N. Thus, by this model, job completion time dips only at these points and remains flat otherwise; cost dips at the same points but goes up (because we get charged by N) otherwise. However, the actual job completion time/cost behavior, also shown in Figure 8, is smoother.

This discrepancy can be explained by the variance in task completion times and the behavior of the task scheduler. Suppose that the last wave has just a few remaining tasks. If every task takes exactly μ time, the job completion time will indeed be μ times the number of waves. However, because the variance in task completions, some slots will finish earlier, and the scheduler will assign the remaining tasks to them; thus, the last wave may complete under μ. Overall, the variance in task completion times actually make the job completion time behavior smoother over N.

ARIA ARIA [23] characterizes task completion times by the observed average, minimum, and maximum among past runs of the same exact task. From these quantities, ARIA analytically derives an lower bound and an upper bound for job completion time. Figure 8 shows how these bounds translate to bounds on job cost (here ARIA is given 100 observations). ARIA estimates the expected job time/cost to be the average of the lower/upper bounds. From Figure 8, we see that the bounds are quite loose; although their average matches the general trend in actual job costs, it is too smooth and fails to capture the variations—its root-mean-square error (relative to actual average job costs) is 0.0189 (compared with 0.0078 for our approach). Also, ARIA's analytical bounds do not consider different custom scheduler behaviors, which are possible in Hadoop.

Our Approach To account for the effect of variance (denoted σ^2) in task completion times, Cumulon models job completion time as a function of q, NS, and μ as well as σ^2. Specifically, the function has form $\mu(\lceil q/_{NS} \rceil + (\frac{q \bmod NS}{NS} - \alpha(\frac{\sigma}{\mu})) \cdot \beta(\frac{\sigma}{\mu}))$. Intuitively, the number of waves is adjusted by a fraction that accounts for σ^2 and the scheduler behavior. We take a simulation-based approach to support custom scheduler behavior. Given q, NS, and σ/μ, we draw task completion times from a truncated Gaussian with $(1, (\sigma/\mu)^2)$, and simulate the scheduler to obtain the expected job time. Using simulation results, we fit $\alpha(\frac{\sigma}{\mu})$ and $\beta(\frac{\sigma}{\mu})$ as low-degree polynomials. As Figure 8 shows, this approach models the job costs best, capturing both general trends and local variations.

To summarize, starting with models for components of the individual task completion times, we have shown, step by step, how to accurately estimate expected costs of jobs. Capturing the variance in task completion times is crucial in our approach. In this paper we have focused on predicting expected job costs; further quantifying the error variance would be a natural next step.

4.2 Search Strategy

Having seen how to estimate expected completion time and cost of a deployment plan, we now discuss how to solve the optimization problem posed at the beginning of this section:

$$\textbf{minimize}_{\mathcal{O},\mathcal{P},\mathcal{Q}}\ \mathfrak{C}(\langle \mathcal{L}, \mathcal{O}, \mathcal{P}, \mathcal{Q} \rangle)\ \textbf{s.t.}\ \mathfrak{T}(\langle \mathcal{L}, \mathcal{O}, \mathcal{P}, \mathcal{Q} \rangle) \leq T_{\max}.$$

As Section 6.2 will demonstrate with experiments, it is necessary to jointly consider operator parameter settings as well as hardware provisioning and configuration settings. The main challenge addressed in this section is how to cope with the large search space.

Establishing the Range of Cluster Sizes The number of machines (N) is a parameter in $\mathcal{P}$ with a potentially large range. We can narrow down this range by making two observations. For a given job running on a cluster with a particular machine type: **1)** as we decrease N, the job's best possible expected completion time cannot decrease; **2)** we can find a function $\check{c}(N)$ that lower-bounds the expected cost of the job on a cluster of size N, such that $\check{c}(N)$ is non-decreasing in N. Both observations are intuitive. (1) states that a job cannot run slower with more resources. While not always true for extremely large values of N (where the overhead of distribution could make a job run slower), the observation will likely hold in the range of N we actually consider in practice (unless we are given unreasonably tight $T_{\max}$). As for (2), while cost may not always increase with N, the general trend is increasing (as exemplified by Figure 8) as the overhead of parallelization kicks in. Our model of job time in Section 4.1.2 allows us to derive $\check{c}(N+1)$ after searching the deployment plans for a cluster of size N (details omitted because of space constraints).

Given an upper bound on completion time, (1) naturally leads to a lower bound $\check{N}$ on N for meeting the completion time constraint. Using a procedure $\mathsf{opt}_{\mathcal{O},\mathcal{Q}}$ (see Algorithm 2 for pseudocode) that finds the optimal deployment plan given $\mathcal{L}$ and $\mathcal{P}$, Cumulon finds lower bound $\check{N}$ efficiently by performing an exponential search in N, using $O(\log \check{N})$ calls to $\mathsf{opt}_{\mathcal{O},\mathcal{Q}}$.

Given an upper bound on cost, (2) naturally leads to an upper bound on N required for beating the given cost. Starting from the lower bound on N found earlier, we can examine each successive N, which involves calling $\mathsf{opt}_{\mathcal{O},\mathcal{Q}}$ with this N, until $\check{c}(N+1)$ (obtained as a by-product of the $\mathsf{opt}_{\mathcal{O},\mathcal{Q}}$ call) exceeds the given cost.

Searching for Plans Without Cluster Switching We are now ready to describe the algorithm $\mathsf{opt}_{\mathcal{O},\mathcal{P},\mathcal{Q}}$ (Algorithm 2) for finding the optimal deployment plan for $\mathcal{L}$ without cluster switching. The idea is simple. For each machine type, we establish the range of relevant cluster sizes as described earlier—the time constraint is given; the cost constraint is given by the best plan found so far, because any plan with a higher cost need not be considered.

The innermost loop of $\mathsf{opt}_{\mathcal{O},\mathcal{P},\mathcal{Q}}$ calls $\mathsf{opt}_{\mathcal{O},\mathcal{Q}}$. Since $\mathsf{opt}_{\mathcal{O},\mathcal{Q}}$ is given a cluster of fixed type and size, $\mathsf{opt}_{\mathcal{O},\mathcal{Q}}$ can optimize each job $j \in \mathcal{L}$ independently. Currently, we use a straightforward method to find the optimal $\mathcal{O}$ and $\mathcal{Q}$ for each j. We loop through possible values of S (which are naturally capped by a small multiple of the number of cores per machine, because our programs are CPU-intensive), and, for each S, sample the space of feasible operator parameter settings such that the total memory required by j's operators does not exceed a slot's available memory. As mentioned earlier, we also extend this method to compute a cost lower bound for a cluster of the same type and size $N+1$ (details omitted). Finally, $\mathsf{opt}_{\mathcal{O},\mathcal{Q}}$ returns the optimal $\mathcal{O}$ and $\mathcal{Q}$ for $\mathcal{L}$, which consists of the optimal settings for each job in $\mathcal{L}$. Although simple, this method is fast enough in practice, because each job tends not to have many operators (see Section 6.2 for some optimization time numbers). The modular design of Cumulon's optimization algorithm allows more sophisticated methods to be plugged in if needed.

Searching for Plans with Cluster Switching Cluster switching blows up the already big search space by another factor exponential in the number of jobs in the program. Therefore, we have to resort to heuristics. We conjecture that the for real programs, there likely exist near-optimal deployment plans that do not switch clusters many times. One reason is that switching incurs considerable overhead. Another reason is that real programs often contain a few steps whose costs are dominating; it might make sense to switch clusters for these steps, but additional switching between other steps will unlikely result in significant overall improvement.

Operating under this assumption, we search the plan space by first considering plans with no switches (using $\mathsf{opt}_{\mathcal{O},\mathcal{P},\mathcal{Q}}$ described above), and then those with one more switch in each successive iteration. This prioritization allows the search to be terminated when optimization runs out of time, and ensures that the most promising plans are considered first.

Very briefly, the algorithm for searching for the optimal plan with

Algorithm 2: Optimizing deployment plan with no cluster switching.

```
opt_{O,Q}(L, P): L: physical plan template;
                 P: type and number of machines in the cluster.
returns: deployment plan with lowest cost for given L and P;
  if two return values are expected, the second lower-bounds the cost
  on larger clusters of the same type (details omitted).
O, Q ← ∅, ∅;
foreach job j ∈ L do
    C_best, S_best, O_best = ∞, ⊥, ⊥;
    foreach reasonable slot number per machine S do
        foreach feasible setting O of j's operator parameters do
            if C(⟨j, O, P, (S)⟩) < C_best then
                C_best, S_best, O_best = C(⟨j, O, P, (S)⟩), S, O;
    O ← O ∪ {(j, O_best)}; Q ← Q ∪ {(j, S_best)};
return ⟨L, O, P, Q⟩;
```

```
opt_{O,P,Q}(L, T_max): L: physical plan template;
                       T_max: maximum completion time.
returns: lowest-cost deployment plan for L that runs under T_max.
C_max, D_best ← ∞, ⊥;
foreach machine type m do
    N ← min{N | C(opt_{O,Q}(L, (m, N))) ≤ T_max} by exponential
    search;
    repeat
        D, č ← opt_{O,Q}(L, (m, N));
        if C(D) < C_max then C_max, D_best ← C(D), D;
        ;
    until č ≥ C_max;
return D_best;
```

x switches works by partitioning jobs in $\mathcal{L}$ into $x+1$ groups, where cluster switching takes place on partition boundaries. Once a plan is chosen for a partition, its time and cost update the time/cost budgets available to remaining partitions, which restrict the search for their plans. Details are omitted because of space constraints.

5 Other Issues

Iterative Programs For simplicity of presentation, we have not yet discussed loops. Cumulon supports a loop construct in the workflow of jobs. It is intended for iterative programs (not for writing low-level, C-style loops that implements matrix multiply, for example). As mentioned in Section 4.1, cost estimation for iterative programs is very difficult, because convergence depends on factors ranging from input characteristics (e.g., condition numbers of matrices) to starting conditions (e.g., warm vs. cold).

Cumulon takes a pragmatic approach in this regard. We focus on predicting the per-iteration time and cost of an iterative program. For short loop bodies (such as PLSI), we first unroll it to enable more optimization opportunities. The user can either reason with this per-iteration "rate" produced by Cumulon, or specify the desired number of iterations to get the overall cost. In practice, this limitation is not severe, because users often start with trial runs until they understand the convergence properties on full datasets. An interesting direction of future work is to look for cases where we can do more, e.g., when factors affecting convergence are understood and can be efficiently computed without running the program.

Coping with Performance Variance In Section 4.1.2, we have shown how to deal with variance in task completion time, which can result from transient behaviors or self-interference among tasks, and affect our prediction of expected job completion time. But this step is only a beginning. Performance uncertainty can arise for many reasons. It can stem from our optimizer's incomplete or inaccurate knowledge of the input properties: e.g., whether and where non-zero entries are clustered in a sparse matrix. In a cloud setting, for a (virtual) machine of given type, a cloud provider may assign an AMD instead of an Intel CPU, which affects the performance of linear algebra libraries. Depending on where the provisioned machines are located in the provider's data center, the network characteristics may vary. Performance can also be impacted by other virtual machines running on the same physical machine, and by other workloads sharing the same physical network.

While Cumulon is far from sophisticated in tackling performance variance from such sources, it offers a practical guard against wrong decision with its runtime monitoring support. When a deployment plan is executing, Cumulon monitors its performance and alerts the user as soon as it detects potentially significant deviations from the optimizer's time and cost predictions, e.g., when the first iteration takes much longer than expected. Upon receiving an alert, the user may decide to cancel the deployment to avoid sinking more money. As future work, we plan to investigate the possibility of dynamic reoptimization using data collected during ongoing execution.

6 Experiments

Our experiments are conducted on Amazon EC2. We consider the EC2 machine types listed in Table 1, and use the published rates (but without rounding up usage hours). The HDFS block size is 32MB; Cumulon's tiles have the same size by default (equivalent of a 2048×2048 dense double matrix). HDFS replication factor is set to 3 or the cluster size (N), whichever is smaller. These configuration settings do impact performance and reliability, but unlike the number of slots per machine (S), their choices are far less dependent on particular Cumulon programs. We have found these settings to work well for all workloads we tested, and therefore we do not include them in $\mathcal{Q}$ for plan optimization.

We use a variety of programs to evaluate Cumulon. 1) ***Matrix multiplies*** with varying dimensions and sparsity allow us to experiment with different input characteristics. 2) ***RSVD-1***, introduced in Section 1, is the dominating step in a randomized SVD algorithm. 3) ***GNMF-1***, also used by SystemML [8] for evaluation, is an expensive step in one iteration of the popular Gaussian Non-Negative Matrix Factorization algorithm. 4) ***PLSI-1*** is Line 3 in Algorithm 1, an expensive step in a PLSI iteration. 5) ***PLSI-full*** is a Hadoop program consisting of a non-Cumulon part, which downloads and preprocesses documents into the word-document matrix **O**, followed by a Cumulon part, which performs PLSI on **O**.

6.1 Execution Engine and Physical Operators

We now demonstrate the advantages of the executions strategies enabled by Cumulon's flexible model and physical operators as well as their efficient implementation on top of Hadoop/HDFS. Here, we focus on showing how, given a cluster, our approach achieves faster running time (and hence lower cost).

Comparison with SystemML First, we compare Cumulon with SystemML using a number of matrix multiply programs with varying sizes, shape, and sparsity. Their running times on the same cluster, broken down by jobs and phases, are shown in Figure 9. For SystemML, the number of map slots and that of reduce slots are always 2, and we choose the faster one of their RMM and CPMM strategies for each program. For Cumulon, we use the deployment plans picked by Cumulon; the number of (map) slots is also always 2. Table 2 shows the input dimensions and the split factors ended up being used by SystemML and Cumulon.

For Cumulon, we omit streaming granularity settings (Section 3.2) here and in subsequent discussion; in most cases choosing this granularity to be a tile works best, as CPU under-utilization can be compensated with a large enough S.

From Figure 9, we see that Cumulon is significantly faster than SystemML (and hence proportionally cheaper in terms of mone-

	$\mathbf{A}$ $(m \times l)$	$\mathbf{B}$ $(l \times n)$	SystemML	Cumulon
	if sparse, sparsity shown in parentheses		split factors f_m, f_l, f_n	
1	24k × 24k	24k × 24k	8, 1, 8	4, 4, 4
2	1 × 100k	100k × 100k	1, 1, 50	1, 10, 10
3	100 × 100k	100k × 100k	1, 1, 50	1, 10, 10
4	160k × 100	100 × 160k	8, 1, 8	8, 1, 8
5	100 × 20000k	20000k × 100	1, 80, 1	1, 80, 1
6	200k × 200k (0.1)	200k × 1000	100, 1, 1	10, 10, 1
7	1000k × 1000k (0.01)	1000k × 1	100, 1, 1	10, 10, 1

Table 2: Choices of split factors by SystemML and Cumulon for $\mathbf{A} \times \mathbf{B}$.

tary cost), for all but one program (#4). For #4, the two inputs are small and shaped like column and row vectors, where SystemML's RMM strategy happens to use the same (optimal) split factors as Cumulon; thus the two have comparable performance.

Two factors attribute to Cumulon's advantage: 1) Cumulon's map tasks do more useful work than SystemML's; 2) SystemML's choices of split factors are severely limited. We examine these factors in isolation later when discussing Figures 10 and 12.

More Complex Workflows and Advantage of *MaskMul* Figure 11 compares SystemML and Cumulon on two workflows, GNMF-1 and PLSI-1, on the same cluster. For PLSI-1, $m = 3375104$, $n = 131151$, $k = 100$. GNMF-1 computes $\mathbf{H} \circ (\mathbf{H}^\mathsf{T} \times \mathbf{V}) \circ\!/ (\mathbf{W}^\mathsf{T} \times \mathbf{W} \times \mathbf{H})$, where $\mathbf{H}$ is $k \times m$, $\mathbf{V}$ is $n \times m$, and $\mathbf{W}$ is $n \times k$ as in PLSI-1. There are two map slots per machine, and for SystemML, also two reduce slots. SystemML uses 5 full MapReduce jobs for GNMF-1, and 1 for PLSI-1; in contrast, Cumulon uses 4 and 1 *map-only* jobs, respectively. From Figure 11, we see that advantages of Cumulon carry over to more complex workflows.

Figure 11 further compares two plans for PLSI-1 in Cumulon: one that does not use the *MaskMul* operator (recall Section 3.2) and one that uses it. We see that performance improvement enabled by *MaskMul* is dramatic (more than an order of magnitude), further widening the lead over SystemML.[3]

Comparison with Other Hadoop-Based Implementations Going beyond SystemML, we examine more broadly how to implement matrix multiply with general split factors on top of Hadoop. We compare three options. 1) Cumulon: Two map-only jobs, where the first multiplies and the second adds. 2) ***Pure MapReduce***: Two map-reduce jobs, where the map tasks in the first job simply replicate and shuffle input to reduce tasks to be multiplied, like in SystemML. Unlike SystemML, however, flexible choices of split factors are allowed, so the second job may be required for adding. (This option enables us to study the impact of different uses of map tasks in isolation from the effect of different split factors.) 3) ***Cumulon+reduce***: One full map-reduce job, where the map tasks read directly from HDFS to multiply, like Cumulon; however, the results are shuffled to reduce tasks to be added.

Figure 10 compares the running times of these options in the same cluster, as well as settings of split factors and number of slots (optimized for respective options). First, we see that pure MapReduce incurs a significant amount of pure overhead in its map tasks; in contrast, other options' map tasks perform all multiplications. Second, the map-only approach of Cumulon allows it to focus all resources on map tasks, without the overhead and interference caused by having to shuffle to reduce tasks. For example, because of resource contention, Cumulon+reduce is forced to allocate 3 map slots for multiplication (vs. 4 for Cumulon) and use bigger split factors (which lead to more I/O). Also, general sorting-based shuffling supported by Hadoop is an overkill for routing data to matrix operators, who know exactly which tiles they need. Thus, in spite of the fact that writes to HDFS are slower than to local disks (for shuffling), Cumulon's approach of passing data through HDFS between map-only jobs is the better option.

6.2 Deployment Plan Space and Optimization

We begin with experiments that reveal the complexity of the search space and motivate the need for jointly optimizing settings of operator parameters ($\mathcal{O}$), hardware provisioning ($\mathcal{P}$), and configuration ($\mathcal{Q}$). These experiments also exercise the Cumulon optimizer. Then, we see examples of how Cumulon helps users make deployment decisions and works with a program with non-matrix Hadoop components. We also explore plans with cluster switching.

Impact of Operator Parameter and Configuration Settings We show that even if we are given a fixed cluster, different $\mathcal{O}$ and $\mathcal{Q}$ settings can have a big impact on performance. Figure 12 compares a number of deployment plans for a dense matrix multiply on the same cluster, while the number of slots per machine (S) varies. For each S setting, we consider the plan with the optimal $\mathcal{O}$ (split factors) for this S, as well as a plan with same split factors as SystemML's RMM (which requires $f_l = 1$). However, this latter plan is implemented in Cumulon and does not carry the overhead of SystemML's pure MapReduce implementation. (Thus, this plan helps reveal the impact of SystemML's suboptimal split factor choices in isolation from the overhead of its restricted use of map tasks.)

From Figure 12 we make two observations. First, poor choices of $\mathcal{O}$ and $\mathcal{P}$ lead to poor performance; e.g., the second plan for $S = 1$ is nearly three times more expensive than the optimal plan with $S = 6$. Second, the choices of $\mathcal{O}$ and $\mathcal{P}$ are interrelated. As S increases, memory available to each slot decreases, which obviously limits the input split size. However, the effect of S on the optimal split factors is more intricate than simply scaling them proportionally to make splits fit in memory, as we can see from Figure 12.

Also note that the optimal S setting in general is not the number of cores per machine (8 in this case). One of the reasons is that JBLAS, which we use for submatrix multiply, is multi-threaded, so even a smaller S can fully utilize the CPU; overcommitting hurts performance. In this case, automatic cost-based optimization works much more reliably than general rules of thumb.

Impact of Machine Type Next, we see how machine types influence optimality of deployment plans. Figure 13 explores various plans for dense matrix multiply on a 20-machine cluster of four types. There are four "base" plans, each optimized for one type. As the legend shows, they have rather different $\mathcal{O}$ and $\mathcal{Q}$ settings.

Figure 13 also shows what happens if one simply "retools" a plan optimized for one machine type for another. In particular, if the target machine type does not have enough memory run this plan, we lower the plan's S setting so that it can run without thrashing. This retooling is not always feasible; e.g., Plan 4, optimized for m1.xlarge, cannot be retooled for m1.small and c1.medium. In general, retooled plans are suboptimal, and in some cases (e.g., Plan 1 retooled for c1.xlarge) can incur twice as much cost as the optimal.[4]

Impact of Cluster Size Even if we fix the machine type, optimal settings for $\mathcal{O}$ and $\mathcal{Q}$ will change as we vary the cluster size N. In Figure 14, we consider RSVD-1 on increasing large clusters of c1.xlarge machines. First, we find Plan 1 as the best for $N = 1$, and Plan 2 as the best for $N = 250$. Their $\mathcal{O}$ and $\mathcal{Q}$ settings are shown in the legend. We retool the plans for different cluster sizes in a straightforward way: they simply run with their $\mathcal{O}$ and $\mathcal{Q}$ settings, so work done by each task remains the same, and varying N translates

[3]In more detail, *MaskMul* is applied to the second multiply (between $\mathbf{C} \times \mathbf{E}$ and $\mathbf{B}^\mathsf{T}$) under $\circ\!/$. This second multiply is where the bulk of the computation is—recall that $\mathbf{C}$ is $m \times k$, $\mathbf{E}$ is $k \times k$, $\mathbf{B}^\mathsf{T}$ is $k \times n$, and $m, n \gg k$.

[4]Figure 13 shows monetary cost, not time. As a side note on how to interpret such figures, having the lowest cost (Plan 2 and c1.medium in this case) may not imply the best deployment plan in the presence of tighter completion time constraints. Here, Plans 3 and 4 actually complete quicker, but are costlier because the rates of their machine types are higher.

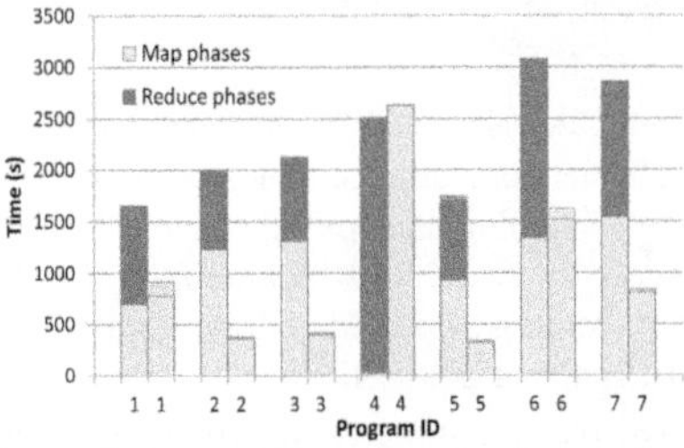

Figure 9: SystemML vs. Cumulon for matrix multiply programs (see table in text), on 10 m1.large machines. For each program, the left bar shows SystemML and the right bar shows Cumulon.

Time ‖ slots ↘	Cumulon	pure MapReduce	Cumulon +reduce
1st map	1980s ‖ 4	1885s ‖ 2	2465s ‖ 3
1st reduce	n/a	2759s ‖ 4	924s ‖ 2
2nd map	510s ‖ 4	d/c†	n/a
2nd reduce	n/a	d/c†	n/a
split factors	6, 6, 6	6, 6, 6	8, 8, 8

Figure 10: Options for multiplying two dense 48k × 48k matrices using flexible split factors, on 10 c1.xlarge machines. († Implementation-dependent; irrelevant here as pure MapReduce's first job alone is already more costly than other options.)

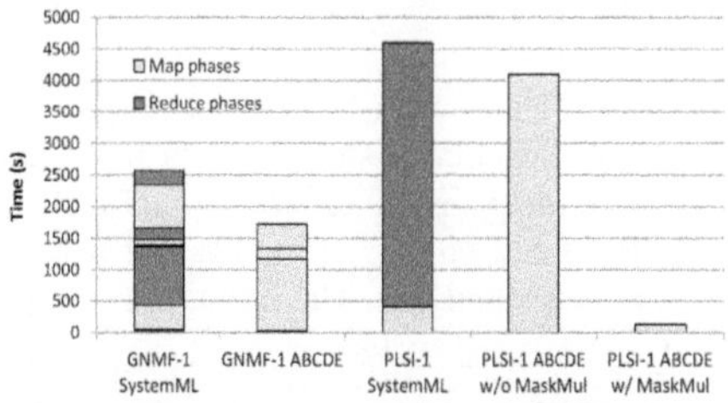

Figure 11: SystemML vs. Cumulon for GNMF-1 and PLSI-1, on 10 m1.large machines (some jobs/phases are short and thus may be difficult to discern from the figure).

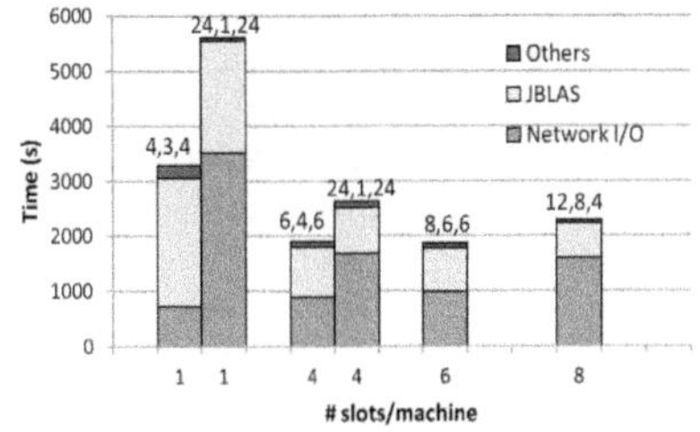

Figure 12: Effect of operator parameter and configuration settings (split factors and number of slots per machine) on running time of multiplying two 48k × 48k dense matrices. The cluster has 10 c1.xlarge machines. The split factors for *Mul* are shown on top of the respective bars.

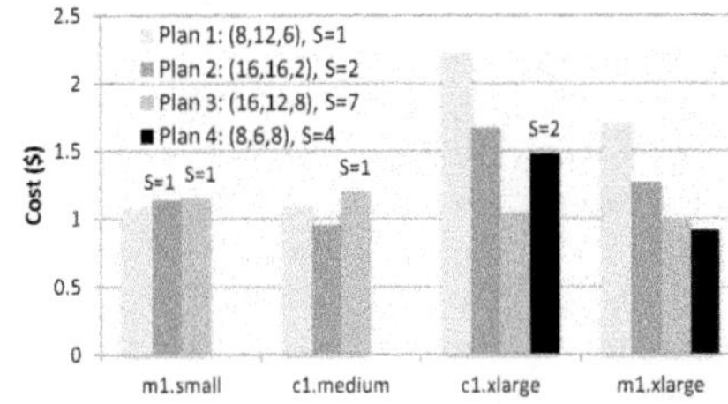

Figure 13: Effect of machine type on the cost of multiplying two 96k × 96k dense matrices. $N = 20$. The legend shows, for each base plan, its settings of the three split factors and the number (S) of slots per machine. Adjustment to S (if needed) is shown on top of the respective bar.

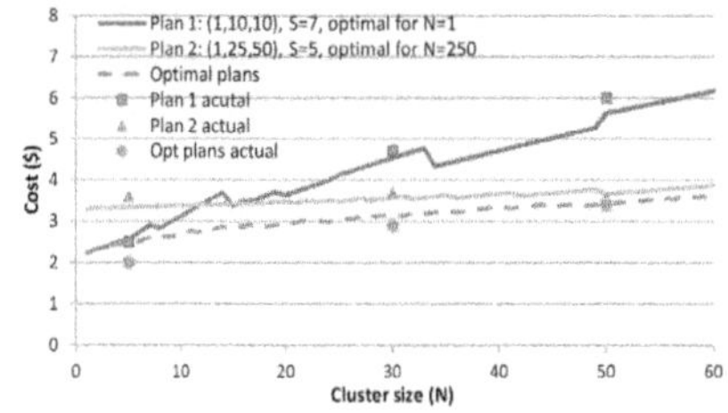

Figure 14: Effect of cluster size on the cost of RSVD-1 (with $l = 2\text{k}, m = 200\text{k}, n = 200\text{k}, k = 5$) on c1.xlarge machines. Cost curves are predicted; costs of actual runs for sample data points are shown for comparison.

to varying number of waves. The predicted costs of running these plans retooled from Plans 1 and 2 are plotted in Figure 14. For comparison, the figure also plots the predicted cost of the optimal plan found by our optimizer for every N.

As we can see from the figure, sticking to the same $\mathbb{O}$ and $\mathbb{Q}$ settings when N changes is suboptimal. Intuitively, Plan 1 performs more work per task and requires overall fewer tasks, but when N grows, many slots may idle in the last wave, leading to waste. On the other hand, Plan 2 has a lot of tasks, which are an overkill and carry more overhead and I/O when N is small. The optimal settings of $\mathbb{O}$ and $\mathbb{Q}$ change with N, and result in lower costs than Plans 1 and 2 (except for the two N's they are optimized for).

Since the cost curves in this figure are predicted by Cumulon, we also conduct a number of actual runs and plot their costs for comparison. These costs are consistent with our predictions.

Putting It Together We now show how Cumulon can help users make intelligent deployment decisions by generating Figure 1 seen earlier in Section 1. The figure visually presents the tradeoff between completion time and monetary cost[5] across different machine types, and enables users to ask "what-if" questions with different deadline and budget scenarios. Each data point of a cost curve is obtained by invoking the Cumulon optimizer to find the lowest-cost deployment plan for RSVD-1 that completes within the given time for the given machine type. This plan specifies not only parameter settings for its physical operators but also the cluster size and the number of slots per cluster. On a desktop machine with moderate hardware, it took under a minute to generate the whole figure (excluding the costs of actual runs for sample data points). This optimization overhead is well worth the benefit provided by Figure 1—one actual run can easily take hours to complete.

To see that Cumulon's cost estimation is effective, we also conducted actual runs for some data points; the results are largely in line with the predictions. Additional evaluation of cost estimation can be found in Figure 14 and figures in Section 4.1.

Cluster Switching and PLSI-Full Finding a simple program that warrants cluster switching turned out to be difficult. Cluster switching did not bring significant benefit to matrix multiplies, RSVD-1, GNMF-1, or PLSI-1, or complete versions of the last three algorithms. For example, in complete RSVD, while cluster switching at the end of RSVD-1 may seem obvious, it actually makes little difference because so little work remains after this dominating RSVD-1 step. Hence, our experience confirms our conjecture in Section 4.2 and justifies our approach of prioritizing the search for plans with few or no switches.

Nonetheless, to test our optimizer's support for cluster switching, we constructed a synthetic program with two dense matrix multiplies: the first one is between two 60k × 60k matrices; the second one is between 400k × 100 and 100 × 400k. Even for this program, one c1.medium cluster turns out to work well. Things become more interesting if we assume that c1.medium is no longer available. Among the remaining four machine types, c1.xlarge is most suited for the first multiply, while m1.small is best for the second. Our optimizer is able to find that the optimal plan involves a switch from c1.xlarge to m1.small when $T_{\max} \geq 1.4$ hours. Under tighter completion time constraints, however, the cost of switching itself makes it unattractive. We omit the details.

Finally, we consider PLSI-full, which includes both non-matrix and matrix parts. The second part runs Algorithm 1 (3 iterations) and is handled by Cumulon. The first part consists of hand-optimized Hadoop jobs that download a document collection as separate bz2 files (about 13GB total), decompress them, and extract a sample of text documents (3.5GB) form the collection to prepare a 9460k × 1095k (with sparsity of 2×10^{-5}) word-document matrix for the second part. Since Cumulon is built on top of Hadoop, it is easy to execute these two parts as a series of Hadoop jobs. While Cumulon optimizes the second part, we have to manually tune the first.

It turns out that while the first part of PLSI-full prefers a large number of small machines, the second part prefers fewer but larger

[5]Cost of data ingress/ogress depends on the setup, and is not shown here. Assuming Amazon EBS for stable storage, this cost would be no more than $2 (same for all deployment plans in Figure 1).

machines. Thus, we select two candidate clusters: C_1, with 20 c1.medium machines, and C_2, with 6 m1.xlarge machines. We consider three plans: 1) run the entire PLSI-full on C_1; 2) run the entire PLSI-full on C_2; 3) run the first part on C_1, switch to C_2, and run the second part. The results are summarized below.

	Time (s)				Cost ($)			
Plan	Preprocess	Switch	PLSI	Total	Preprocess	Switch	PLSI	Total
C_1	10757.5	0	13830	24587.5	9.90	0	12.72	22.62
C_2	14480.5	0	11712	26192.5	12.51	0	10.12	22.63
$C_1 \rightarrow C_2$	10757.5	670	11712	23139.5	9.90	0.58	10.12	20.59

Here, cluster switching reduces the cost from $22.62 to $20.59.

7 Related Work

A number of recent projects supporting statistical computing on big data subject scientists and statisticians to new, and in most cases, lower-level, programming abstractions. RHIPE [9], Ricardo [6], and Analytics' R/Hadoop enable R code to invoke Hadoop and vice versa, but programmers are responsible for parallelization and tuning. Apache Mahout and MADlib [5, 10] offer libraries of statistical analysis routines (for Hadoop and a parallel database system, respectively). Historically, library-based approaches have been either limited by hard-coded assumptions tied to particular data representations and execution environments, or ridden with knobs that are difficult to tune for new deployment settings.

Automatic, cost-based optimization is a staple of database systems. Indeed, MADlib leverages a database optimizer to alleviate tuning burden, but database optimizers are often inadequate for matrix-based workloads. Database-style optimization has also been applied to general MapReduce systems, e.g., by Starfish [11]. However, such work faces difficult challenges in modeling arbitrary map and reduce functions. Because Cumulon focuses on matrix-based programs, we are able to take a white-box approach specialized for such workloads. SystemML [8] takes an approach similar to ours, but as we have seen earlier, Cumulon avoids some significant overheads that SystemML incurs with its MapReduce-based implementation. Furthermore, SystemML only considers optimization of execution, while Cumulon also jointly considers hardware provisioning and configuration settings.

Automatic resource provisioning has been studied recently for general MapReduce systems [14, 23, 25, 12]. In contrast to the black-box workloads that these systems face, we focus on declaratively specified statistical workloads, which lead us to a different challenges and opportunities as we have shown in this paper.

On a high level, we share the goal of making big-data analytics easier with many recent systems. For example, projects such as SciDB [2] are rebuilding entire systems from the ground up for specific workload types. Targeting graph mining, PEGASUS [15] implements *generalized iterated matrix-vector multiply* efficiently on Hadoop. RIOT [24] and RevoScaleR focus on making statistical computing workloads in R I/O-efficient; pR [16] automatically parallelizes function calls and loops in R. Pig [17], Hive [20], and SciHadoop [4] are examples of higher-level languages and execution plan generators for MapReduce systems. Our work goes beyond these systems by addressing important usability issues of automatic hardware provisioning and configuration.

8 Conclusion and Future Work

We have presented Cumulon, a system that simplifies both the development and deployment of matrix-based data analysis programs in the cloud. We have shown how pure MapReduce is a poor fit for such workloads, and demonstrated how Cumulon's flexible execution model, new operators, and unconventional implementation on top of Hadoop/HDFS together provide significant performance improvements over existing Hadoop-based systems for statistical data analysis. We have motivated the need for automatic and joint optimization of not only physical operators and their parameter settings, but also hardware provisioning and configuration settings in the cloud. We have shown how a suite of benchmarking, simulation, modeling, and search techniques provide effective cost-based optimization over this vast space of possibilities.

We have already pointed out a number of directions for future work throughout this paper, such as more sophisticated handling of performance variance, exposing variance in cost estimation to users, and dynamic reoptimization. We also plan to consider the HPC offerings by Amazon EC2 and intelligently choose between HPC- and Hadoop/HDFS-based implementations. While we currently focus on addressing an individual user's need, it will be nice to extend Cumulon to optimize, schedule, and provision for workloads of multiple users programs in a shared cluster setting. Going a step further, it would be interesting to see, from a cloud provider's perspective, how a better understanding of matrix-based workloads can help in deciding what machine types to offer to support such workloads, and how to price these machine types sensibly.

References

[1] V. R. Borkar, Y. Bu, M. J. Carey, J. Rosen, N. Polyzotis, T. Condie, M. Weimer, and R. Ramakrishnan. Declarative systems for large-scale machine learning. *IEEE Data Engineering Bulletin*, 35(2):24–32, 2012.

[2] P. G. Brown. Overview of SciDB: Large scale array storage, processing and analysis. *SIGMOD 2010*.

[3] Y. Bu, B. Howe, M. Balazinska, and M. D. Ernst. HaLoop: Efficient iterative data processing on large clusters. *PVLDB*, 3(1):285–296, 2010.

[4] J. B. Buck, N. Watkins, J. LeFevre, K. Ioannidou, C. Maltzahn, N. Polyzotis, and S. A. Brandt. SciHadoop: Array-based query processing in Hadoop. *Supercomputing 2011*.

[5] J. Cohen, B. Dolan, M. Dunlap, J. M. Hellerstein, and C. Welton. MAD skills: New analysis practices for big data. *VLDB 2009*.

[6] S. Das, Y. Sismanis, K. S. Beyer, R. Gemulla2, P. J. Haas, and J. McPherson. Ricardo: Integrating R and Hadoop. *SIGMOD 2010*.

[7] J. Dean and S. Ghemawat. MapReduce: Simplified data processing on large clusters. *OSDI 2004*.

[8] A. Ghoting, R. Krishnamurthy, E. Pednault, B. Reinwald, V. Sindhwani, S. Tatikonda, Y. Tian, and S. Vaithyanathan. SystemML: Declarative machine learning on MapReduce. *ICDE 2011*.

[9] S. Guha. *Computing Environment for the Statistical Analysis of Large and Complex Data.* PhD thesis, Purdue University, 2010.

[10] J. M. Hellerstein, C. Re, F. Schoppmann, Z. D. Wang, E. Fratkin, A. Gorajek, K. S. Ng, C. Welton, X. Feng, K. Li, and A. Kumar. The MADlib analytics library or MAD skills, the SQL. *PVLDB*, 5(12):1700–1711, 2012.

[11] H. Herodotou and S. Babu. Profiling, what-if analysis, and cost-based optimization of MapReduce programs. *PVLDB Endowment*, 4(11):1111–1122, 2011.

[12] H. Herodotou, F. Dong, and S. Babu. No one (cluster) size fits all: Automatic cluster sizing for data-intensive analytics. *SoCC 2011*.

[13] T. Hofmann. Probabilistic latent semantic indexing. *SIGIR 1999*.

[14] K. Kambatla, A. Pathak, and H. Pucha. Towards optimizing hadoop provisioning for the cloud. *HotCloud 2009*.

[15] U. Kang, C. E. Tsourakakis, and C. Faloutsos. PEGASUS: A peta-scale graph mining system. *ICDM 2009*.

[16] J. Li, X. Ma, S. B. Yoginath, G. Kora, and N. F. Samatova. Transparent runtime parallelization of the R scripting language. *J. Parallel & Distributed Computing*, 71(2):157–168, 2011.

[17] C. Olston, B. Reed, U. Srivastava, R. Kumar, and A. Tomkins. Pig latin: A not-so-foreign language for data processing. *SIGMOD 2008*.

[18] V. Rokhlin, A. Szlam, and M. Tygert. A randomized algorithm for principal component analysis. *SIAM J. Matrix Analysis & Applications*, 31(3), 2009.

[19] S. Seo, E. J. Yoon, J.-H. Kim, S. Jin, J.-S. Kim, and S. Maeng. HAMA: An efficient matrix computation with the MapReduce framework. *CloudCom 2010*.

[20] A. Thusoo, J. S. Sarma, N. Jain, Z. Shao, P. Chakka, S. Anthony, H. Liu, P. Wyckoff, and R. Murthy. Hive - a warehousing solution over a map-reduce framework. *PVLDB*, 2(2):1626–1629, 2009.

[21] S. Toledo. A survey of out-of-core algorithms in numerical linear algebra. In *DIMACS Series In Discrete Mathematics And Theoretical Computer Science: External Memory Algorithms*, pages 161–179. 1999.

[22] L. G. Valiant. A bridging model for parallel computation. *CACM*, 33(8), 1990.

[23] A. Verma, L. Cherkasova, and R. H. Campbell. ARIA: automatic resource inference and allocation for mapreduce environments. *ICAC 2011*.

[24] Y. Zhang, H. Herodotou, and J. Yang. RIOT: I/O-efficient numerical computing without SQL. *CIDR 2009*.

[25] Z. Zhang, L. Cherkasova, A. Verma, and B. T. Loo. Meeting service level objectives of Pig programs. In *2012 Intl. Workshop on Cloud Computing Platforms*.

Shark: SQL and Rich Analytics at Scale

Reynold S. Xin, Josh Rosen, Matei Zaharia,
Michael J. Franklin, Scott Shenker, Ion Stoica

AMPLab, EECS, UC Berkeley
{rxin, joshrosen, matei, franklin, shenker, istoica}@cs.berkeley.edu

ABSTRACT

Shark is a new data analysis system that marries query processing with complex analytics on large clusters. It leverages a novel distributed memory abstraction to provide a unified engine that can run SQL queries and sophisticated analytics functions (*e.g.*, iterative machine learning) at scale, and efficiently recovers from failures mid-query. This allows Shark to run SQL queries up to 100× faster than Apache Hive, and machine learning programs more than 100× faster than Hadoop. Unlike previous systems, Shark shows that it is possible to achieve these speedups while retaining a MapReduce-like execution engine, and the fine-grained fault tolerance properties that such engine provides. It extends such an engine in several ways, including column-oriented in-memory storage and dynamic mid-query replanning, to effectively execute SQL. The result is a system that matches the speedups reported for MPP analytic databases over MapReduce, while offering fault tolerance properties and complex analytics capabilities that they lack.

Categories and Subject Descriptors

H.2 [**Database Management**]: Systems

Keywords

Databases; Data Warehouse; Machine Learning; Spark; Shark; Hadoop

1 Introduction

Modern data analysis faces a confluence of growing challenges. First, data volumes are expanding dramatically, creating the need to scale out across clusters of hundreds of commodity machines. Second, such high scale increases the incidence of faults and stragglers (slow tasks), complicating parallel database design. Third, the *complexity* of data analysis has also grown: modern data analysis employs sophisticated statistical methods, such as machine learning algorithms, that go well beyond the roll-up and drill-down capabilities of traditional enterprise data warehouse systems. Finally, despite these increases in scale and complexity, users still expect to be able to query data at interactive speeds.

To tackle the "big data" problem, two major lines of systems have recently been explored. The first, consisting of MapReduce [17] and various generalizations [22, 13], offers a fine-grained fault tolerance model suitable for large clusters, where tasks on failed or slow nodes can be deterministically re-executed on other nodes. MapReduce is also fairly general: it has been shown to be able to express many statistical and learning algorithms [15]. It also easily supports unstructured data and "schema-on-read." However, MapReduce engines lack many of the features that make databases efficient, and thus exhibit high latencies of tens of seconds to hours. Even systems that have significantly optimized MapReduce for SQL queries, such as Google's Tenzing [13], or that combine it with a traditional database on each node, such as HadoopDB [4], report a minimum latency of 10 seconds. As such, MapReduce approaches have largely been dismissed for interactive-speed queries [31], and even Google is developing new engines for such workloads [29].

Instead, most MPP analytic databases (*e.g.*, Vertica, Greenplum, Teradata) and several of the new low-latency engines proposed for MapReduce environments (*e.g.*, Google Dremel [29], Cloudera Impala [1]) employ a coarser-grained recovery model, where an entire query has to be resubmitted if a machine fails.[1] This works well for short queries where a retry is inexpensive, but faces significant challenges for long queries as clusters scale up [4]. In addition, these systems often lack the rich analytics functions that are easy to implement in MapReduce, such as machine learning and graph algorithms. Furthermore, while it may be possible to implement some of these functions using UDFs, these algorithms are often expensive, exacerbating the need for fault and straggler recovery for long queries. Thus, most organizations tend to use other systems alongside MPP databases to perform complex analytics.

To provide an effective environment for big data analysis, we believe that processing systems will need to support *both* SQL and complex analytics efficiently, and to provide fine-grained fault recovery across both types of operations. This paper describes a new system that meets these goals, called Shark. Shark is open source and compatible with Apache Hive, and has already been used at web companies to speed up queries by 40–100×.

Shark builds on a recently-proposed distributed shared memory abstraction called Resilient Distributed Datasets (RDDs) [39] to perform most computations in memory while offering fine-grained fault tolerance. In-memory computing is increasingly important in large-scale analytics for two reasons. First, many complex analytics functions, such as machine learning and graph algorithms, are iterative, scanning the data multiple times; thus, the fastest systems deployed for these applications are in-memory [28, 27, 39]. Second, even traditional SQL warehouse workloads exhibit strong temporal and spatial locality, because more-recent fact table data

[1]Dremel provides fault tolerance within a query, but Dremel is limited to aggregation trees instead of the more complex communication patterns in joins.

SIGMOD'13, June 22–27, 2013, New York, New York, USA.

and small dimension tables are read disproportionately often. A study of Facebook's Hive warehouse and Microsoft's Bing analytics cluster showed that over 95% of queries in both systems could be served out of memory using just 64 GB/node as a cache, even though each system manages more than 100 PB of total data [6].

The main benefit of RDDs is an efficient mechanism for fault recovery. Traditional main-memory databases support fine-grained updates to tables and replicate writes across the network for fault tolerance, which is expensive on large commodity clusters. In contrast, RDDs restrict the programming interface to *coarse-grained* deterministic operators that affect multiple data items at once, such as *map*, *group-by* and *join*, and recover from failures by tracking the *lineage* of each dataset and recomputing lost data. This approach works well for data-parallel relational queries, and has also been shown to support machine learning and graph computation [39]. Thus, when a node fails, Shark can recover mid-query by rerunning the deterministic operations used to build lost data partitions on other nodes, similar to MapReduce. Indeed, it typically recovers within seconds by parallelizing this work across the cluster.

To run SQL efficiently, however, we also had to extend the RDD execution model, bringing in several concepts from traditional analytical databases and some new ones. We started with an existing implementation of RDDs called Spark [39], and added several features. First, to store and process relational data efficiently, we implemented in-memory columnar storage and columnar compression. This reduced both the data size and the processing time by as much as 5× over naïvely storing the data in a Spark program in its original format. Second, to optimize SQL queries based on the data characteristics even in the presence of analytics functions and UDFs, we extended Spark with *Partial DAG Execution (PDE)*: Shark can reoptimize a running query after running the first few stages of its task DAG, choosing better join strategies or the right degree of parallelism based on observed statistics. Third, we leverage other properties of the Spark engine not present in traditional MapReduce systems, such as control over data partitioning.

Our implementation of Shark is compatible with Apache Hive [34], supporting all of Hive's SQL dialect and UDFs and allowing execution over unmodified Hive data warehouses. It augments SQL with complex analytics functions written in Spark, using Spark's Java, Scala or Python APIs. These functions can be combined with SQL in a single execution plan, providing in-memory data sharing and fast recovery across both types of processing.

Experiments show that using RDDs and the optimizations above, Shark can answer SQL queries up to 100× faster than Hive, runs iterative machine learning algorithms more than 100× faster than Hadoop, and can recover from failures mid-query within seconds. Shark's speed is comparable to that of MPP databases in benchmarks like Pavlo et al.'s comparison with MapReduce [31], but it offers fine-grained recovery and complex analytics features that these systems lack.

More fundamentally, our work shows that MapReduce-like execution models can be applied effectively to SQL, and offer a promising way to combine relational and complex analytics. In addition, we explore why current SQL engines implemented on top of MapReduce runtimes, such as Hive, are slow. We show how a combination of enhancements in Shark (*e.g.,* PDE), and engine properties that have not been optimized in MapReduce, such as the overhead of launching tasks, eliminate many of the bottlenecks in traditional MapReduce systems.

2 System Overview

As described in the previous section, Shark is a data analysis system that supports both SQL query processing and machine learning functions. Shark is compatible with Apache Hive, enabling users to run Hive queries much faster without any changes to either the queries or the data.

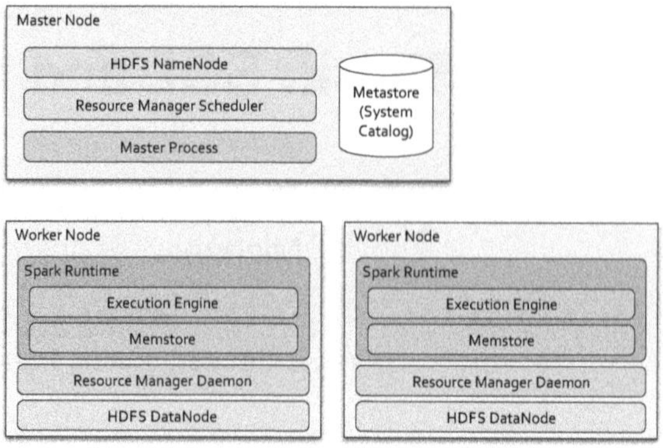

Figure 1: Shark Architecture

Thanks to its Hive compatibility, Shark can query data in any system that supports the Hadoop storage API, including HDFS and Amazon S3. It also supports a wide range of data formats such as text, binary sequence files, JSON, and XML. It inherits Hive's schema-on-read capability and nested data types [34].

In addition, users can choose to load high-value data into Shark's memory store for fast analytics, as illustrated below:

```
CREATE TABLE latest_logs
  TBLPROPERTIES ("shark.cache"=true)
AS SELECT * FROM logs WHERE date > now()-3600;
```

Figure 1 shows the architecture of a Shark cluster, consisting of a single master node and a number of worker nodes, with the warehouse metadata stored in an external transactional database. It is built on top of Spark, a modern MapReduce-like cluster computing engine. When a query is submitted to the master, Shark compiles the query into operator tree represented as RDDs, as we shall discuss in Section 2.4. These RDDs are then translated by Spark into a graph of tasks to execute on the worker nodes.

Cluster resources can optionally be allocated by a resource manager (*e.g.,* Hadoop YARN [2] or Apache Mesos [21]) that provides resource sharing and isolation between different computing frameworks, allowing Shark to coexist with engines like Hadoop.

In the remainder of this section, we cover the basics of Spark and the RDD programming model, and then we describe how Shark query plans are generated and executed.

2.1 Spark

Spark is the MapReduce-like cluster computing engine used by Shark. Spark has several features that differentiate it from traditional MapReduce engines [39]:

1. Like Dryad [22] and Hyracks [10], it supports general computation DAGs, not just the two-stage MapReduce topology.
2. It provides an in-memory storage abstraction called Resilient Distributed Datasets (RDDs) that lets applications keep data in memory across queries, and automatically reconstructs any data lost during failures [39].
3. The engine is optimized for low latency. It can efficiently manage tasks as short as 100 milliseconds on clusters of thousands of cores, while engines like Hadoop incur a latency of 5–10 seconds to launch each task.

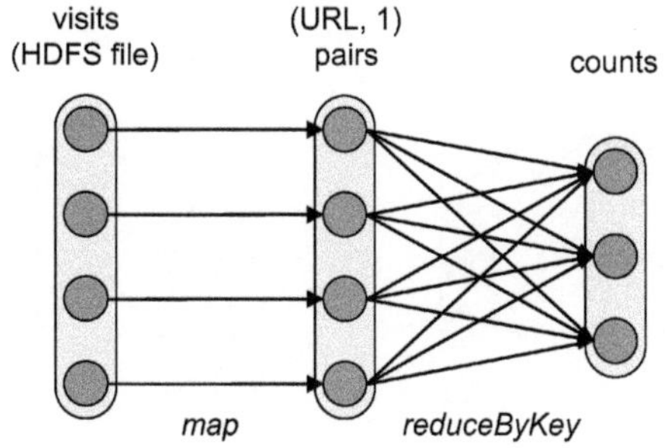

Figure 2: Lineage graph for the RDDs in our Spark example. Oblongs represent RDDs, while circles show partitions within a dataset. Lineage is tracked at the granularity of partitions.

RDDs are unique to Spark, and were essential to enabling mid-query fault tolerance. However, the other differences are important engineering elements that contribute to Shark's performance.

In addition to these features, we have also modified the Spark engine for Shark to support *partial DAG execution,* that is, modification of the query plan DAG after only some of the stages have finished, based on statistics collected from these stages. Similar to [25], we use this technique to optimize join algorithms and other aspects of the execution mid-query, as we shall discuss in Section 3.1.

2.2 Resilient Distributed Datasets (RDDs)

Spark's main abstraction is *resilient distributed datasets* (RDDs), which are immutable, partitioned collections that can be created through various data-parallel *operators* (*e.g., map, group-by, hash-join*). Each RDD is either a collection stored in an external storage system, such as a file in HDFS, or a derived dataset created by applying operators to other RDDs. For example, given an RDD of (visitID, URL) pairs for visits to a website, we might compute an RDD of (URL, count) pairs by applying a *map* operator to turn each event into an (URL, 1) pair, and then a *reduce* to add the counts by URL.

In Spark's native API, RDD operations are invoked through a functional interface similar to DryadLINQ [24] in Scala, Java or Python. For example, the Scala code for the query above is:

```
val visits = spark.hadoopFile("hdfs://...")
val counts = visits.map(v => (v.url, 1))
                   .reduceByKey((a, b) => a + b)
```

RDDs can contain arbitrary data types as elements (since Spark runs on the JVM, these elements are Java objects), and are automatically partitioned across the cluster, but they are immutable once created, and they can only be created through Spark's deterministic parallel operators. These two restrictions, however, enable highly efficient fault recovery. In particular, instead of replicating each RDD across nodes for fault-tolerance, Spark remembers the *lineage* of the RDD (the graph of operators used to build it), and recovers lost partitions by *recomputing* them from base data [39].[2] For example, Figure 2 shows the lineage graph for the RDDs computed above. If Spark loses one of the partitions in the (URL, 1) RDD, for example, it can recompute it by rerunning the *map* on just the corresponding partition of the input file.

The RDD model offers several key benefits in our large-scale in-memory computing setting. First, RDDs can be written at the speed of DRAM instead of the speed of the network, because there is no need to replicate each byte written to another machine for fault-tolerance. DRAM in a modern server is over 10× faster than even a 10-Gigabit network. Second, Spark can keep just one copy of each RDD partition in memory, saving precious memory over a replicated system, since it can always recover lost data using lineage. Third, when a node fails, its lost RDD partitions can be rebuilt *in parallel* across the other nodes, allowing speedy recovery.[3] Fourth, even if a node is just slow (a "straggler"), we can recompute necessary partitions on other nodes because RDDs are immutable so there are no consistency concerns with having two copies of a partition. These benefits make RDDs attractive as the foundation for our relational processing in Shark.

2.3 Fault Tolerance Guarantees

To summarize the benefits of RDDs, Shark provides the following fault tolerance properties, which have been difficult to support in traditional MPP database designs:

1. Shark can tolerate the loss of *any set of worker nodes.* The execution engine will re-execute any lost tasks and recompute any lost RDD partitions using lineage.[4] This is true even within a query: Spark will rerun any failed tasks, or lost dependencies of new tasks, without aborting the query.
2. Recovery is parallelized across the cluster. If a failed node contained 100 RDD partitions, these can be rebuilt in parallel on 100 different nodes, quickly recovering the lost data.
3. The deterministic nature of RDDs also enables straggler mitigation: if a task is slow, the system can launch a speculative "backup copy" of it on another node, as in MapReduce [17].
4. Recovery works even for queries that *combine* SQL and machine learning UDFs (Section 4), as these operations all compile into a single RDD lineage graph.

2.4 Executing SQL over RDDs

Shark runs SQL queries over Spark using a three-step process similar to traditional RDBMSs: query parsing, logical plan generation, and physical plan generation.

Given a query, Shark uses the Hive query compiler to parse the query and generate an abstract syntax tree. The tree is then turned into a logical plan and basic logical optimization, such as predicate pushdown, is applied. Up to this point, Shark and Hive share an identical approach. Hive would then convert the operator into a physical plan consisting of multiple MapReduce stages. In the case of Shark, its optimizer applies additional rule-based optimizations, such as pushing `LIMIT` down to individual partitions, and creates a physical plan consisting of transformations on RDDs rather than MapReduce jobs. We use a variety of operators already present in Spark, such as *map* and *reduce*, as well as new operators we implemented for Shark, such as broadcast joins. Spark's master then executes this graph using standard MapReduce scheduling techniques, such as placing tasks close to their input data, rerunning lost tasks, and performing straggler mitigation [39].

While this basic approach makes it possible to run SQL over Spark, doing it *efficiently* is challenging. The prevalence of UDFs and complex analytic functions in Shark's workload makes it difficult to determine an optimal query plan at compile time, especially for new data that has not undergone ETL. In addition, even with

[2] We assume that external files for RDDs representing data do not change, or that we can take a snapshot of a file when we create an RDD from it.

[3] To provide fault tolerance across "shuffle" operations like a parallel reduce, the execution engine also saves the "map" side of the shuffle in memory on the source nodes, spilling to disk if necessary.

[4] Support for master recovery could also be added by reliabliy logging the RDD lineage graph and the submitted jobs, because this state is small, but we have not implemented this yet.

such a plan, naïvely executing it over Spark (or other MapReduce runtimes) can be inefficient. In the next section, we discuss several extensions we made to Spark to efficiently store relational data and run SQL, starting with a mechanism that allows for *dynamic*, statistics-driven re-optimization at run-time.

3 Engine Extensions

In this section, we describe our modifications to the Spark engine to enable efficient execution of SQL queries.

3.1 Partial DAG Execution (PDE)

Systems like Shark and Hive are frequently used to query fresh data that has not undergone a data loading process. This precludes the use of static query optimization techniques that rely on accurate a priori data statistics, such as statistics maintained by indices. The lack of statistics for fresh data, combined with the prevalent use of UDFs, requires dynamic approaches to query optimization.

To support dynamic query optimization in a distributed setting, we extended Spark to support *partial DAG execution* (PDE), a technique that allows dynamic alteration of query plans based on data statistics collected at run-time.

We currently apply partial DAG execution at blocking "shuffle" operator boundaries where data is exchanged and repartitioned, since these are typically the most expensive operations in Shark. By default, Spark materializes the output of each map task in memory before a shuffle, spilling it to disk as necessary. Later, reduce tasks fetch this output.

PDE modifies this mechanism in two ways. First, it gathers customizable statistics at global and per-partition granularities while materializing map outputs. Second, it allows the DAG to be altered based on these statistics, either by choosing different operators or altering their parameters (such as their degrees of parallelism).

These statistics are customizable using a simple, pluggable accumulator API. Some example statistics include:

1. Partition sizes and record counts, which can be used to detect skew.
2. Lists of "heavy hitters," *i.e.,* items that occur frequently in the dataset.
3. Approximate histograms, which can be used to estimate partitions' data distributions.

These statistics are sent by each worker to the master, where they are aggregated and presented to the optimizer. For efficiency, we use lossy compression to record the statistics, limiting their size to 1–2 KB per task. For instance, we encode partition sizes (in bytes) with logarithmic encoding, which can represent sizes of up to 32 GB using only one byte with at most 10% error. The master can then use these statistics to perform various run-time optimizations, as we shall discuss next.

Partial DAG execution complements existing adaptive query optimization techniques that typically run in a single-node system [7, 25, 36], as we can use existing techniques to dynamically optimize the local plan *within* each node, and use PDE to optimize the global structure of the plan at stage boundaries. This fine-grained statistics collection, and the optimizations that it enables, differentiates PDE from graph rewriting features in previous systems, such as DryadLINQ [24].

3.1.1 Join Optimization

Partial DAG execution can be used to perform several run-time optimizations for join queries.

Figure 3 illustrates two communication patterns for MapReduce-style joins. In *shuffle join*, both join tables are hash-partitioned by

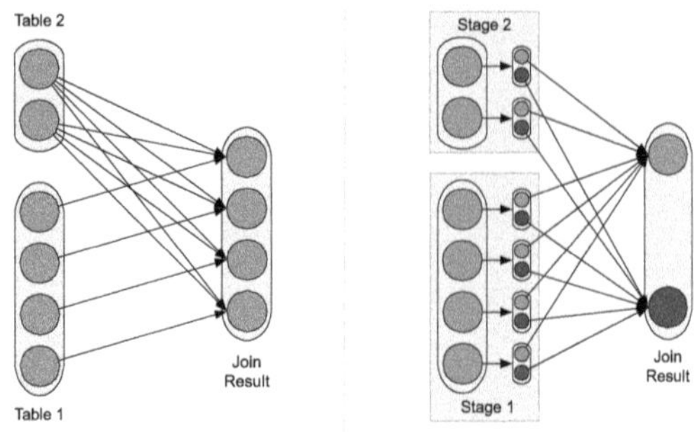

Figure 3: Data flows for map join and shuffle join. Map join broadcasts the small table to all large table partitions, while shuffle join repartitions and shuffles both tables.

the join key. Each reducer joins corresponding partitions using a local join algorithm, which is chosen by each reducer based on run-time statistics. If one of a reducer's input partitions is small, then it constructs a hash table over the small partition and probes it using the large partition. If both partitions are large, then a symmetric hash join is performed by constructing hash tables over both inputs.

In *map join*, also known as *broadcast join*, a small input table is broadcast to all nodes, where it is joined with each partition of a large table. This approach can result in significant cost savings by avoiding an expensive repartitioning and shuffling phase.

Map join is only worthwhile if some join inputs are small, so Shark uses partial DAG execution to select the join strategy at run-time based on its inputs' exact sizes. By using sizes of the join inputs gathered at run-time, this approach works well even with input tables that have no prior statistics, such as intermediate results.

Run-time statistics also inform the join tasks' scheduling policies. If the optimizer has a prior belief that a particular join input will be small, it will schedule that task before other join inputs and decide to perform a map-join if it observes that the task's output is small. This allows the query engine to avoid performing the pre-shuffle partitioning of a large table once the optimizer has decided to perform a map-join.

3.1.2 Skew-handling and Degree of Parallelism

Partial DAG execution can also be used to determine operators' degrees of parallelism and to mitigate skew.

The degree of parallelism for reduce tasks can have a large performance impact: launching too few reducers may overload reducers' network connections and exhaust their memories, while launching too many may prolong the job due to task scheduling overhead. Hive's performance is especially sensitive to the number of reduce tasks [8], due to Hadoop's large scheduling overhead.

Using partial DAG execution, Shark can use individual partitions' sizes to determine the number of reducers at run-time by coalescing many small, fine-grained partitions into fewer coarse partitions that are used by reduce tasks. To mitigate skew, fine-grained partitions are assigned to coalesced partitions using a greedy bin-packing heuristic that attempts to equalize coalesced partitions' sizes [19]. This offers performance benefits, especially when good bin-packings exist.

Somewhat surprisingly, we discovered that Shark can obtain similar performance improvement simply by running a larger number of reduce tasks. We attribute this to Spark's low scheduling and task-launching overhead.

3.2 Columnar Memory Store

In-memory computation is essential to low-latency query answering, given that memory's throughput is orders of magnitude higher than that of disks. Naïvely using Spark's memory store, however, can lead to undesirable performance. For this reason, Shark implements a columnar memory store on top of Spark's native memory store.

In-memory data representation affects both space footprint and read throughput. A naïve approach is to simply cache the on-disk data in its native format, performing on-demand deserialization in the query processor. This deserialization becomes a major bottleneck: in our studies, we saw that modern commodity CPUs can deserialize at a rate of only 200MB per second per core.

The approach taken by Spark's default memory store is to store data partitions as collections of JVM objects. This avoids deserialization, since the query processor can directly use these objects, but leads to significant storage space overheads. Common JVM implementations add 12 to 16 bytes of overhead per object. For example, storing 270 MB of TPC-H lineitem table as JVM objects uses approximately 971 MB of memory, while a serialized representation requires only 289 MB, nearly three times less space. A more serious implication, however, is the effect on garbage collection (GC). With a 200 B record size, a 32 GB heap can contain 160 million objects. The JVM garbage collection time correlates linearly with the number of objects in the heap, so it could take minutes to perform a full GC on a large heap. These unpredictable, expensive garbage collections cause large variability in response times.

Shark stores all columns of primitive types as JVM primitive arrays. Complex data types supported by Hive, such as `map` and `array`, are serialized and concatenated into a single byte array. Each column creates only one JVM object, leading to fast GCs and a compact data representation. The space footprint of columnar data can be further reduced by cheap compression techniques at virtually no CPU cost. Similar to columnar database systems, *e.g.*, C-store [32], Shark implements CPU-efficient compression schemes such as dictionary encoding, run-length encoding, and bit packing.

Columnar data representation also leads to better cache behavior, especially for for analytical queries that frequently compute aggregations on certain columns.

3.3 Distributed Data Loading

In addition to query execution, Shark also uses Spark's execution engine for distributed data loading. During loading, a table is split into small partitions, each of which is loaded by a Spark task. The loading tasks use the data schema to extract individual fields from rows, marshal a partition of data into its columnar representation, and store those columns in memory.

Each data loading task tracks metadata to decide whether each column in a partition should be compressed. For example, the loading task will compress a column using dictionary encoding if its number of distinct values is below a threshold. This allows each task to choose the best compression scheme for each partition, rather than conforming to a global compression scheme that might not be optimal for local partitions. These local decisions do not require coordination among data loading tasks, allowing the load phase to achieve a maximum degree of parallelism, at the small cost of requiring each partition to maintain its own compression metadata. It is important to clarify that an RDD's lineage does not need to contain the compression scheme and metadata for each partition. The compression scheme and metadata are simply byproducts of the RDD computation, and can be deterministically recomputed along with the in-memory data in the case of failures.

As a result, Shark can load data into memory at the aggregated throughput of the CPUs processing incoming data.

Pavlo et al.[31] showed that Hadoop was able to perform data loading at 5 to 10 times the throughput of MPP databases. Tested using the same dataset used in [31], Shark provides the same throughput as Hadoop in loading data into HDFS. Shark is 5 times faster than Hadoop when loading data into its memory store.

3.4 Data Co-partitioning

In some warehouse workloads, two tables are frequently joined together. For example, the TPC-H benchmark frequently joins the lineitem and order tables. A technique commonly used by MPP databases is to co-partition the two tables based on their join key in the data loading process. In distributed file systems like HDFS, the storage system is schema-agnostic, which prevents data co-partitioning. Shark allows co-partitioning two tables on a common key for faster joins in subsequent queries. This can be accomplished with the `DISTRIBUTE BY` clause:

```
CREATE TABLE l_mem TBLPROPERTIES ("shark.cache"=true)
AS SELECT * FROM lineitem DISTRIBUTE BY L_ORDERKEY;

CREATE TABLE o_mem TBLPROPERTIES (
  "shark.cache"=true, "copartition"="l_mem")
AS SELECT * FROM order DISTRIBUTE BY O_ORDERKEY;
```

When joining two co-partitioned tables, Shark's optimizer constructs a DAG that avoids the expensive shuffle and instead uses map tasks to perform the join.

3.5 Partition Statistics and Map Pruning

Typically, data is stored using some logical clustering on one or more columns. For example, entries in a website's traffic log data might be grouped by users' physical locations, because logs are first stored in data centers that have the best geographical proximity to users. Within each data center, logs are append-only and are stored in roughly chronological order. As a less obvious case, a news site's logs might contain `news_id` and `timestamp` columns that are strongly correlated. For analytical queries, it is typical to apply filter predicates or aggregations over such columns. For example, a daily warehouse report might describe how different visitor segments interact with the website; this type of query naturally applies a predicate on timestamps and performs aggregations that are grouped by geographical location. This pattern is even more frequent for interactive data analysis, during which drill-down operations are frequently performed.

Map pruning is the process of pruning data partitions based on their natural clustering columns. Since Shark's memory store splits data into small partitions, each block contains only one or few logical groups on such columns, and Shark can avoid scanning certain blocks of data if their values fall out of the query's filter range.

To take advantage of these natural clusterings of columns, Shark's memory store on each worker piggybacks the data loading process to collect statistics. The information collected for each partition includes the range of each column and the distinct values if the number of distinct values is small (*i.e.*, enum columns). The collected statistics are sent back to the master program and kept in memory for pruning partitions during query execution.

When a query is issued, Shark evaluates the query's predicates against all partition statistics; partitions that do not satisfy the predicate are pruned and Shark does not launch tasks to scan them.

We collected a sample of queries from the Hive warehouse of a video analytics company, and out of the 3833 queries we obtained, at least 3277 of them contained predicates that Shark can use for map pruning. Section 6 provides more details on this workload.

4 Machine Learning Support

A key design goal of Shark is to provide a single system capable of efficient SQL query processing and sophisticated machine learning. Following the principle of pushing computation to data, Shark

```
def logRegress(points: RDD[Point]): Vector {
  var w = Vector(D, _ => 2 * rand.nextDouble - 1)
  for (i <- 1 to ITERATIONS) {
    val gradient = points.map { p =>
      val denom = 1 + exp(-p.y * (w dot p.x))
      (1 / denom - 1) * p.y * p.x
    }.reduce(_ + _)
    w -= gradient
  }
  w
}

val users = sql2rdd("SELECT * FROM user u
   JOIN comment c ON c.uid=u.uid")

val features = users.mapRows { row =>
  new Vector(extractFeature1(row.getInt("age")),
             extractFeature2(row.getStr("country")),
             ...)}
val trainedVector = logRegress(features.cache())
```

Listing 1: Logistic Regression Example

supports machine learning as a first-class citizen. This is enabled by the design decision to choose Spark as the execution engine and RDD as the main data structure for operators. In this section, we explain Shark's language and execution engine integration for SQL and machine learning.

Other research projects [16, 18] have demonstrated that it is possible to express certain machine learning algorithms in SQL and avoid moving data out of the database. The implementation of those projects, however, involves a combination of SQL, UDFs, and driver programs written in other languages. The systems become obscure and difficult to maintain; in addition, they may sacrifice performance by performing expensive parallel numerical computations on traditional database engines that were not designed for such workloads. Contrast this with the approach taken by Shark, which offers in-database analytics that push computation to data, but does so using a runtime that is optimized for such workloads and a programming model that is designed to express machine learning algorithms.

4.1 Language Integration

In addition to executing a SQL query and returning its results, Shark also allows queries to return the RDD representing the query plan. Callers to Shark can then invoke distributed computation over the query result using the returned RDD.

As an example of this integration, Listing 1 illustrates a data analysis pipeline that performs logistic regression over a user database. Logistic regression, a common classification algorithm, searches for a hyperplane w that best separates two sets of points (e.g. spammers and non-spammers). The algorithm applies gradient descent optimization by starting with a randomized w vector and iteratively updating it by moving along gradients towards an optimum value.

The program begins by using `sql2rdd` to issue a SQL query to retreive user information as a `TableRDD`. It then performs feature extraction on the query rows and runs logistic regression over the extracted feature matrix. Each iteration of `logRegress` applies a function of w to all data points to produce a set of gradients, which are summed to produce a net gradient that is used to update w.

The highlighted `map`, `mapRows`, and `reduce` functions are automatically parallelized by Shark to execute across a cluster, and the master program simply collects the output of the `reduce` function to update w.

Note that this distributed logistic regression implementation in Shark looks remarkably similar to a program implemented for a single node in the Scala language. The user can conveniently mix the best parts of both SQL and MapReduce-style programming.

Currently, Shark provides native support for Scala, Java and Python. We have modified the Scala shell to enable interactive execution of both SQL and distributed machine learning algorithms. Because Shark is built on top of the JVM, it would be relatively straightforward to support other JVM languages, such as Clojure or JRuby.

We have implemented a number of basic machine learning algorithms, including linear regression, logistic regression, and k-means clustering. In most cases, the user only needs to supply a `mapRows` function to perform feature extraction and can invoke the provided algorithms.

The above example demonstrates how machine learning computations can be performed on query results. Using RDDs as the main data structure for query operators also enables one to use SQL to query the results of machine learning computations in a single execution plan.

4.2 Execution Engine Integration

In addition to language integration, another key benefit of using RDDs as the data structure for operators is the execution engine integration. This common abstraction allows machine learning computations and SQL queries to share workers and cached data without the overhead of data movement.

Because SQL query processing is implemented using RDDs, lineage is kept for the whole pipeline, which enables end-to-end fault tolerance for the entire workflow. If failures occur during the machine learning stage, partitions on faulty nodes will automatically be recomputed based on their lineage.

5 Implementation

While implementing Shark, we discovered that a number of engineering details had significant performance impacts. Overall, to improve the query processing speed, one should minimize the tail latency of tasks and the CPU cost of processing each row.

Memory-based Shuffle: Both Spark and Hadoop write map output files to disk, hoping that they will remain in the OS buffer cache when reduce tasks fetch them. In practice, we have found that the extra system calls and file system journaling adds significant overhead. In addition, the inability to control when buffer caches are flushed leads to variability in shuffle tasks. A query's response time is determined by the last task to finish, and thus the increasing variability leads to long-tail latency, which significantly hurts shuffle performance. We modified the shuffle phase to materialize map outputs in memory, with the option to spill them to disk.

Temporary Object Creation: It is easy to write a program that creates many temporary objects, which can burden the JVM's garbage collector. For a parallel job, a slow GC at one task may slow the entire job. Shark operators and RDD transformations are written in a way that minimizes temporary object creations.

Bytecode Compilation of Expression Evaluators: In its current implementation, Shark sends the expression evaluators generated by the Hive parser as part of the tasks to be executed on each row. By profiling Shark, we discovered that for certain queries, when data is served out of the memory store the majority of the CPU cycles are wasted in interpreting these evaluators. We are working on a compiler to transform these expression evaluators into JVM bytecode, which can further increase the execution engine's throughput.

Specialized Data Structures: Using specialized data structures is an optimization that we have yet to exploit. For example, Java's hash table is built for generic objects. When the hash key is a primitive type, the use of specialized data structures can lead to more compact data representations, and thus better cache behavior.

6 Experiments

We evaluated Shark using four datasets:

1. Pavlo et al. Benchmark: 2.1 TB of data reproducing Pavlo et al.'s comparison of MapReduce vs. analytical DBMSs [31].
2. TPC-H Dataset: 100 GB and 1 TB datasets generated by the DBGEN program [35].
3. Real Hive Warehouse: 1.7 TB of sampled Hive warehouse data from an early industrial user of Shark.
4. Machine Learning Dataset: 100 GB synthetic dataset to measure the performance of machine learning algorithms.

Overall, our results show that Shark can perform more than 100× faster than Hive and Hadoop, even though we have yet to implement some of the performance optimizations mentioned in the previous section. In particular, Shark provides comparable performance gains to those reported for MPP databases in Pavlo et al.'s comparison [31]. In some cases where data fits in memory, Shark exceeds the performance reported for MPP databases.

We emphasize that we are *not* claiming that Shark is fundamentally faster than MPP databases; there is no reason why MPP engines could not implement the same processing optimizations as Shark. Indeed, our implementation has several disadvantages relative to commercial engines, such as running on the JVM. Instead, we aim to show that it is possible to achieve comparable performance while retaining a MapReduce-like engine, and the fine-grained fault recovery features that such engines provide. In addition, Shark can leverage this engine to perform machine learning functions on the same data, which we believe will be essential for future analytics workloads.

6.1 Methodology and Cluster Setup

Unless otherwise specified, experiments were conducted on Amazon EC2 using 100 `m2.4xlarge` nodes. Each node had 8 virtual cores, 68 GB of memory, and 1.6 TB of local storage.

The cluster was running 64-bit Linux 3.2.28, Apache Hadoop 0.20.205, and Apache Hive 0.9. For Hadoop MapReduce, the number of map tasks and the number of reduce tasks per node were set to 8, matching the number of cores. For Hive, we enabled JVM reuse between tasks and avoided merging small output files, which would take an extra step after each query to perform the merge.

We executed each query six times, discarded the first run, and report the average of the remaining five runs. We discard the first run in order to allow the JVM's just-in-time compiler to optimize common code paths. We believe that this more closely mirrors real-world deployments where the JVM will be reused by many queries.

6.2 Pavlo et al. Benchmarks

Pavlo et al. compared Hadoop versus MPP databases and showed that Hadoop excelled at data ingress, but performed unfavorably in query execution [31]. We reused the dataset and queries from their benchmarks to compare Shark against Hive.

The benchmark used two tables: a 1 GB/node *rankings* table, and a 20 GB/node *uservisits* table. For our 100-node cluster, we recreated a 100 GB *rankings* table containing 1.8 billion rows and a 2 TB *uservisits* table containing 15.5 billion rows. We ran the four queries in their experiments comparing Shark with Hive and report the results in Figures 4 and 5. In this subsection, we hand-tuned Hive's number of reduce tasks to produce optimal results for Hive. Despite this tuning, Shark outperformed Hive in all cases by a wide margin.

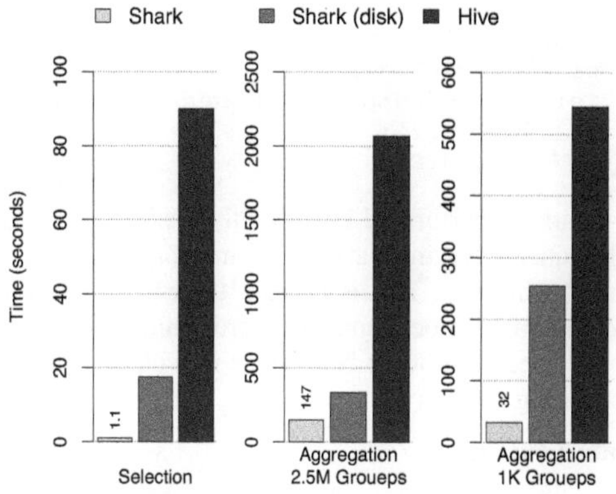

Figure 4: Selection and aggregation query runtimes (seconds) from Pavlo et al. benchmark

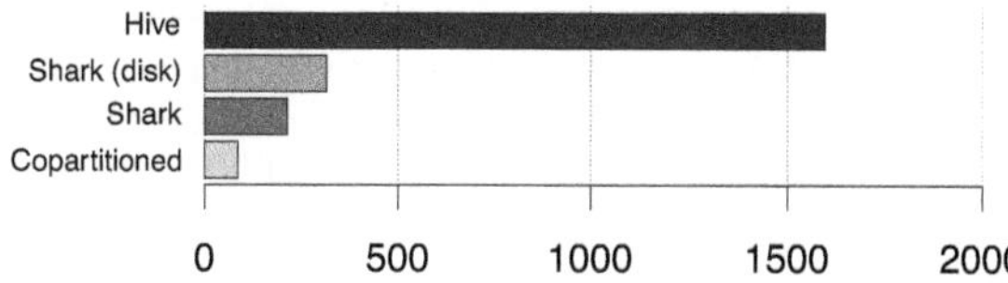

Figure 5: Join query runtime (seconds) from Pavlo benchmark

6.2.1 Selection Query

The first query was a simple selection on the *rankings* table:

```
SELECT pageURL, pageRank
FROM rankings WHERE pageRank > X;
```

In [31], Vertica outperformed Hadoop by a factor of 10 because a clustered index was created for Vertica. Even without a clustered index, Shark was able to execute this query 80× faster than Hive for in-memory data, and 5× on data read from HDFS.

6.2.2 Aggregation Queries

The Pavlo et al. benchmark ran two aggregation queries:

```
SELECT sourceIP, SUM(adRevenue)
FROM uservisits GROUP BY sourceIP;

SELECT SUBSTR(sourceIP, 1, 7), SUM(adRevenue)
FROM uservisits GROUP BY SUBSTR(sourceIP, 1, 7);
```

In our dataset, the first query had two million groups and the second had approximately one thousand groups. Shark and Hive both applied task-local aggregations and shuffled the data to parallelize the final merge aggregation. Again, Shark outperformed Hive by a wide margin. The benchmarked MPP databases perform local aggregations on each node, and then send all aggregates to a single query coordinator for the final merging; this performed very well when the number of groups was small, but performed worse with large number of groups. The MPP databases' chosen plan is similar to choosing a single reduce task for Shark and Hive.

6.2.3 Join Query

The final query from Pavlo et al. involved joining the 2 TB *uservisits* table with the 100 GB *rankings* table.

```
SELECT INTO Temp sourceIP, AVG(pageRank),
SUM(adRevenue) as totalRevenue
FROM rankings AS R, uservisits AS UV
WHERE R.pageURL = UV.destURL
AND UV.visitDate BETWEEN Date('2000-01-15')
AND Date('2000-01-22')
GROUP BY UV.sourceIP;
```

Again, Shark outperformed Hive in all cases. Figure 5 shows that for this query, serving data out of memory did not provide much benefit over disk. This is because the cost of the join step dominated the query processing. Co-partitioning the two tables, however, provided significant benefits as it avoided shuffling 2.1 TB of data during the join step.

6.2.4 Data Loading

Hadoop was shown by [31] to excel at data loading, as its data loading throughput was five to ten times higher than that of MPP databases. As explained in Section 2, Shark can be used to query data in HDFS directly, which means its data ingress rate is at least as fast as Hadoop's.

After generating the 2 TB *uservisits* table, we measured the time to load it into HDFS and compared that with the time to load it into Shark's memory store. We found the rate of data ingress was 5× higher in Shark's memory store than that of HDFS.

6.3 Micro-Benchmarks

To understand the factors affecting Shark's performance, we conducted a sequence of micro-benchmarks. We generated 100 GB and 1 TB of data using the DBGEN program provided by TPC-H [35]. We chose this dataset because it contains tables and columns of varying cardinality and can be used to create a myriad of micro-benchmarks for testing individual operators.

While performing experiments, we found that Hive and Hadoop MapReduce were very sensitive to the number of reducers set for a job. Hive's optimizer automatically sets the number of reducers based on the estimated data size. However, we found that Hive's optimizer frequently made the wrong decision, leading to incredibly long query execution times. We hand-tuned the number of reducers for Hive based on characteristics of the queries and through trial and error. We report Hive performance numbers for both optimizer-determined and hand-tuned numbers of reducers. Shark, on the other hand, was much less sensitive to the number of reducers and required minimal tuning.

6.3.1 Aggregation Performance

We tested the performance of aggregations by running group-by queries on the TPC-H *lineitem* table. For the 100 GB dataset, *lineitem* table contained 600 million rows. For the 1 TB dataset, it contained 6 billion rows.

The queries were of the form:

```
SELECT [GROUP_BY_COLUMN], COUNT(*) FROM lineitem
GROUP BY [GROUP_BY_COLUMN]
```

We chose to run one query with no group-by column (*i.e.*, a simple count), and three queries with group-by aggregations: SHIPMODE (7 groups), RECEIPTDATE (2500 groups), and SHIPMODE (150 million groups in 100 GB, and 537 million groups in 1 TB).

For both Shark and Hive, aggregations were first performed on each partition, and then the intermediate aggregated results were partitioned and sent to reduce tasks to produce the final aggregation. As the number of groups becomes larger, more data needs to be shuffled across the network.

Figure 6 compares the performance of Shark and Hive, measuring Shark's performance on both in-memory data and data loaded from HDFS. As can be seen in the figure, Shark was 80× faster than hand-tuned Hive for queries with small numbers of groups, and 20× faster for queries with large numbers of groups, where the shuffle phase domniated the total execution cost.

We were somewhat surprised by the performance gain observed for on-disk data in Shark. After all, both Shark and Hive had to read data from HDFS and deserialize it for query processing. This difference, however, can be explained by Shark's very low task launching overhead, optimized shuffle operator, and other factors; see Section 7 for more details.

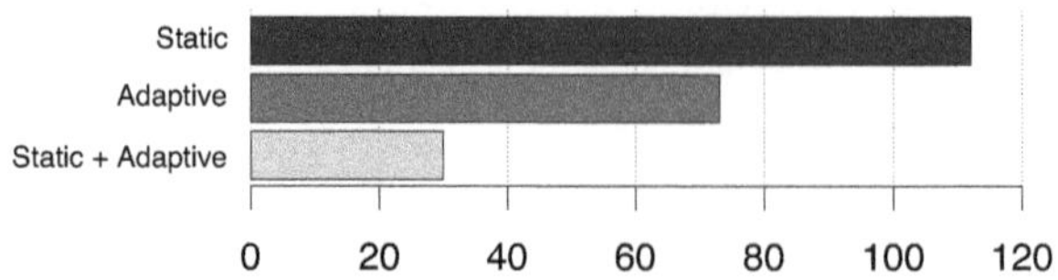

Figure 7: Join strategies chosen by optimizers (seconds)

6.3.2 Join Selection at Run-time

In this experiment, we tested how partial DAG execution can improve query performance through run-time re-optimization of query plans. The query joined the *lineitem* and *supplier* tables from the 1 TB TPC-H dataset, using a UDF to select suppliers of interest based on their addresses. In this specific instance, the UDF selected 1000 out of 10 million suppliers. Figure 7 summarizes these results.

```
SELECT * from lineitem l join supplier s
ON l.L_SUPPKEY = s.S_SUPPKEY
WHERE SOME_UDF(s.S_ADDRESS)
```

Lacking good selectivity estimation on the UDF, a static optimizer would choose to perform a shuffle join on these two tables because the initial sizes of both tables are large. Leveraging partial DAG execution, after running the pre-shuffle map stages for both tables, Shark's dynamic optimizer realized that the filtered *supplier* table was small. It decided to perform a map-join, replicating the filtered *supplier* table to all nodes and performing the join using only map tasks on *lineitem*.

To further improve the execution, the optimizer can analyze the logical plan and infer that the probability of *supplier* table being small is much higher than that of *lineitem* (since *supplier* is smaller initially, and there is a filter predicate on *supplier*). The optimizer chose to pre-shuffle only the *supplier* table, and avoided launching two waves of tasks on *lineitem*. This combination of static query analysis and partial DAG execution led to a 3× performance improvement over a naïve, statically chosen plan.

6.3.3 Fault Tolerance

To measure Shark's performance in the presence of node failures, we simulated failures and measured query performance before, during, and after failure recovery. Figure 8 summarizes fives runs of our failure recovery experiment, which was performed on a 50-node `m2.4xlarge` EC2 cluster.

We used a group-by query on the 100 GB *lineitem* table to measure query performance in the presence of faults. After loading the *lineitem* data into Shark's memory store, we killed a worker machine and re-ran the query. Shark gracefully recovered from this failure and parallelized the reconstruction of lost partitions on the other 49 nodes. This recovery had a small performance impact, but it was significantly cheaper than the cost of re-loading the entire dataset and re-executing the query (14 vs 34 secs).

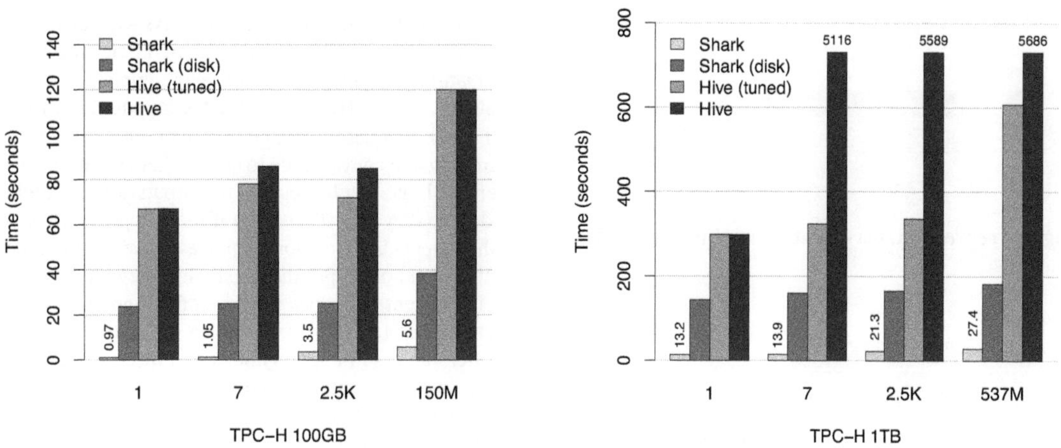

Figure 6: Aggregation queries on *lineitem* table. X-axis indicates the number of groups for each aggregation query.

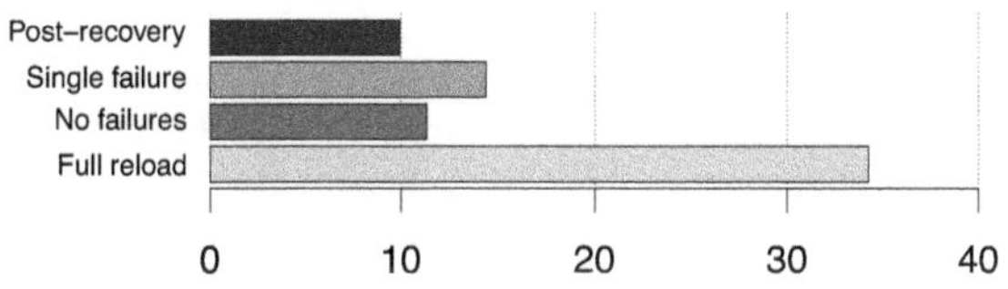

Figure 8: Query time with failures (seconds)

After this recovery, subsequent queries operated against the recovered dataset, albeit with fewer machines. In Figure 8, the post-recovery performance was marginally better than the pre-failure performance; we believe that this was a side-effect of the JVM's JIT compiler, as more of the scheduler's code might have become compiled by the time the post-recovery queries were run.

6.4 Real Hive Warehouse Queries

An early industrial user provided us with a sample of their Hive warehouse data and two years of query traces from their Hive system. A leading video analytics company for content providers and publishers, the user built most of their analytics stack based on Hadoop. The sample we obtained contained 30 days of video session data, occupying 1.7 TB of disk space when decompressed. It consists of a single fact table containing 103 columns, with heavy use of complex data types such as `array` and `struct`. The sampled query log contains 3833 analytical queries, sorted in order of frequency. We filtered out queries that invoked proprietary UDFs and picked four frequent queries that are prototypical of other queries in the complete trace. These queries compute aggregate video quality metrics over different audience segments:

1. Query 1 computes summary statistics in 12 dimensions for users of a specific customer on a specific day.
2. Query 2 counts the number of sessions and distinct customer/-client combination grouped by countries with filter predicates on eight columns.
3. Query 3 counts the number of sessions and distinct users for all but 2 countries.
4. Query 4 computes summary statistics in 7 dimensions grouping by a column, and showing the top groups sorted in descending order.

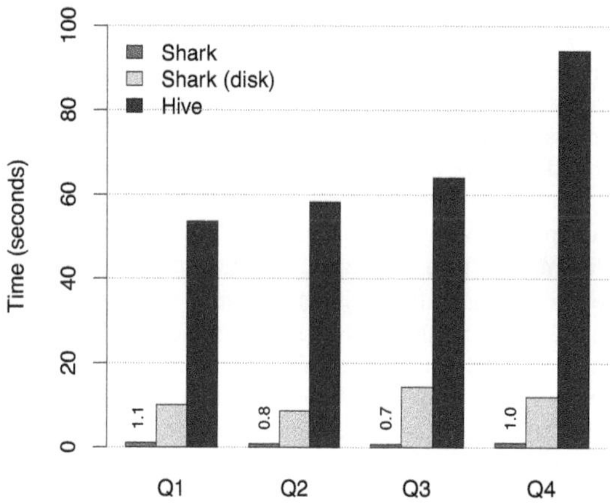

Figure 9: Real Hive warehouse workloads

Figure 9 compares the performance of Shark and Hive on these queries. The result is very promising as Shark was able to process these real life queries in sub-second latency in all but one cases, whereas it took Hive 50 to 100 times longer to execute them.

A closer look into these queries suggests that this data exhibits the natural clustering properties mentioned in Section 3.5. The map pruning technique, on average, reduced the amount of data scanned by a factor of 30.

6.5 Machine Learning

A key motivator of using SQL in a MapReduce environment is the ability to perform sophisticated machine learning on big data. We implemented two iterative machine learning algorithms, logistic regression and k-means, to compare the performance of Shark versus running the same workflow in Hive and Hadoop.

The dataset was synthetically generated and contained 1 billion rows and 10 columns, occupying 100 GB of space. Thus, the feature matrix contained 1 billion points, each with 10 dimensions. These machine learning experiments were performed on a 100-node `m1.xlarge` EC2 cluster.

Data was initially stored in relational form in Shark's memory store and HDFS. The workflow consisted of three steps: (1) selecting the data of interest from the warehouse using SQL, (2) extracting features, and (3) applying iterative algorithms. In step 3, both algorithms were run for 10 iterations.

Figures 10 and 11 show the time to execute a single iteration

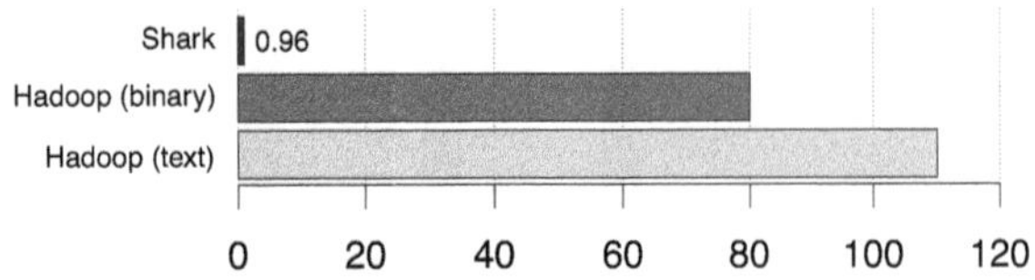

Figure 10: Logistic regression, per-iteration runtime (seconds)

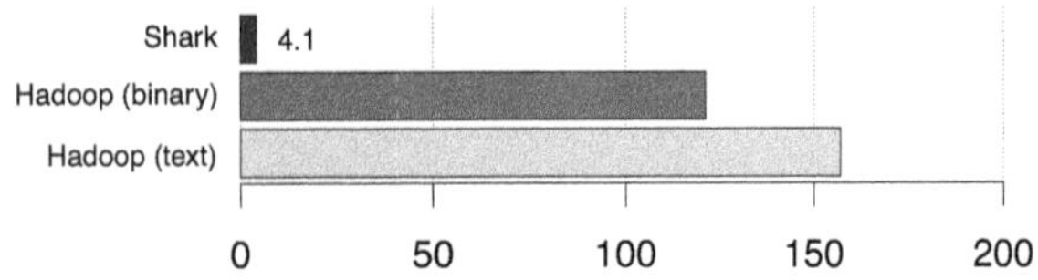

Figure 11: K-means clustering, per-iteration runtime (seconds)

of logistic regression and k-means, respectively. We implemented two versions of the algorithms for Hadoop, one storing input data as text in HDFS and the other using a serialized binary format. The binary representation was more compact and had lower CPU cost in record deserialization, leading to improved performance. Our results show that Shark is 100× faster than Hive and Hadoop for logistic regression and 30× faster for k-means. K-means experienced less speedup because it was computationally more expensive than logistic regression, thus making the workflow more CPU-bound.

In the case of Shark, if data initially resided in its memory store, step 1 and 2 were executed in roughly the same time it took to run one iteration of the machine learning algorithm. If data was not loaded into the memory store, the first iteration took 40 seconds for both algorithms. Subsequent iterations, however, reported numbers consistent with Figures 10 and 11. In the case of Hive and Hadoop, every iteration took the reported time because data was loaded from HDFS for every iteration.

7 Discussion

Shark shows that it is possible to run fast relational queries in a fault-tolerant manner using the fine-grained deterministic task model introduced by MapReduce. This design offers an effective way to scale query processing to ever-larger workloads, and to combine it with rich analytics. In this section, we consider two questions: first, why were previous MapReduce-based systems, such as Hive, slow, and what gave Shark its advantages? Second, are there other benefits to the fine-grained task model? We argue that fine-grained tasks also help with multitenancy and elasticity, as has been demonstrated in MapReduce systems.

7.1 Why are Previous MapReduce-Based Systems Slow?

Conventional wisdom is that MapReduce is slower than MPP databases for several reasons: expensive data materialization for fault tolerance, inferior data layout (*e.g.,* lack of indices), and costlier execution strategies [31, 33]. Our exploration of Hive confirms these reasons, but also shows that a combination of conceptually simple "engineering" changes to the engine (*e.g.,* in-memory storage) and more involved architectural changes (*e.g.,* partial DAG execution) can alleviate them. We also find that a somewhat surprising variable not considered in detail in MapReduce systems, the task scheduling overhead, actually has a dramatic effect on performance, and greatly improves load balancing if minimized.

Intermediate Outputs: MapReduce-based query engines, such as Hive, materialize intermediate data to disk in two situations. First, *within* a MapReduce job, the map tasks save their output in case a reduce task fails [17]. Second, many queries need to be compiled into *multiple* MapReduce steps, and engines rely on replicated file systems, such as HDFS, to store the output of each step.

For the first case, we note that map outputs were stored on disk primarily as a convenience to ensure there is sufficient space to hold them in large batch jobs. Map outputs are *not* replicated across nodes, so they will still be lost if the mapper node fails [17]. Thus, if the outputs fit in memory, it makes sense to store them in memory initially, and only spill them to disk if they are large. Shark's shuffle implementation does this by default, and sees far faster shuffle performance (and no seeks) when the outputs fit in RAM. This is often the case in aggregations and filtering queries that return a much smaller output than their input.[5] Another hardware trend that may improve performance, even for large shuffles, is SSDs, which would allow fast random access to a larger space than memory.

For the second case, engines that extend the MapReduce execution model to general task DAGs can run multi-stage jobs without materializing any outputs to HDFS. Many such engines have been proposed, including Dryad, Tenzing and Spark [22, 13, 39].

Data Format and Layout: While the naïve pure schema-on-read approach to MapReduce incurs considerable processing costs, many systems use more efficient storage formats within the MapReduce model to speed up queries. Hive itself supports "table partitions" (a basic index-like system where it knows that certain key ranges are contained in certain files, so it can avoid scanning a whole table), as well as column-oriented representation of on-disk data [34]. We go further in Shark by using fast in-memory columnar representations within Spark. Shark does this without modifying the Spark runtime by simply representing a block of tuples as a single Spark record (one Java object from Spark's perspective), and choosing its own representation for the tuples within this object.

Another feature of Spark that helps Shark, but was not present in previous MapReduce runtimes, is control over the data partitioning across nodes (Section 3.4). This lets us co-partition tables.

Finally, one capability of RDDs that we do not yet exploit is random reads. While RDDs only support coarse-grained operations for their *writes*, *read* operations on them can be fine-grained, accessing just one record [39]. This would allow RDDs to be used as indices. Tenzing can use such remote-lookup reads for joins [13].

Execution Strategies: Hive spends considerable time on sorting the data before each shuffle and writing the outputs of each MapReduce stage to HDFS, both limitations of the rigid, one-pass MapReduce model in Hadoop. More general runtime engines, such as Spark, alleviate some of these problems. For instance, Spark supports hash-based distributed aggregation and general task DAGs.

To truly optimize the execution of relational queries, however, we found it necessary to select execution plans based on data statistics. This becomes difficult in the presence of UDFs and complex analytics functions, which we seek to support as first-class citizens in Shark. To address this problem, we proposed partial DAG execution (PDE), which allows our modified version of Spark to *change* the downstream portion of an execution graph once each stage completes based on data statistics. PDE goes beyond the runtime graph rewriting features in previous systems, such as DryadLINQ [24], by collecting fine-grained statistics about ranges of keys and by allowing switches to a completely different join strategy, such as broadcast join, instead of just selecting the number of reduce tasks.

[5] Systems like Hadoop also benefit from the OS buffer cache in serving map outputs, but we found that the extra system calls and file system journalling from writing map outputs to files still adds overhead (Section 5).

Task Scheduling Cost: Perhaps the most surprising engine property that affected Shark, however, was a purely "engineering" concern: the overhead of launching tasks. Traditional MapReduce systems, such as Hadoop, were designed for multi-hour batch jobs consisting of tasks that were several minutes long. They launched each task in a separate OS process, and in some cases had a high latency to even submit a task. For instance, Hadoop uses periodic "heartbeats" from each worker every 3 seconds to assign tasks, and sees overall task startup delays of 5–10 seconds. This was sufficient for batch workloads, but clearly falls short for ad-hoc queries.

Spark avoids this problem by using a fast event-driven RPC library to launch tasks and by reusing its worker processes. It can launch thousands of tasks per second with only about 5 ms of overhead per task, making task lengths of 50–100 ms and MapReduce jobs of 500 ms viable. What surprised us is how much this affected query performance, even in large (multi-minute) queries.

Sub-second tasks allow the engine to balance work across nodes extremely well, even when some nodes incur unpredictable delays (*e.g.,* network delays or JVM garbage collection). They also help dramatically with skew. Consider, for example, a system that needs to run a hash aggregation on 100 cores. If the system launches 100 reduce tasks, the key range for each task needs to be carefully chosen, as any imbalance will slow down the entire job. If it could split the work among 1000 tasks, then the slowest task can be as much as 10× slower than the average without affecting the job response time much! After implementing skew-aware partition selection in PDE, we were somewhat disappointed that it did not help compared to just having a higher number of reduce tasks in most workloads, because Spark could comfortably support thousands of such tasks. However, this property makes the engine highly robust to unexpected skew.

In this way, Spark stands in contrast to Hadoop/Hive, where using the wrong number of tasks was sometimes 10× slower than an optimal plan, and there has been considerable work to automatically choose the number of reduce tasks [26, 19]. Figure 12 shows how job execution times vary as the number of reduce tasks launched by Hadoop and Spark in a simple aggregation query on a 100-node cluster. Since a Spark job can launch thousands of reduce tasks without incurring much overhead, partition data skew can be mitigated by always launching many tasks.

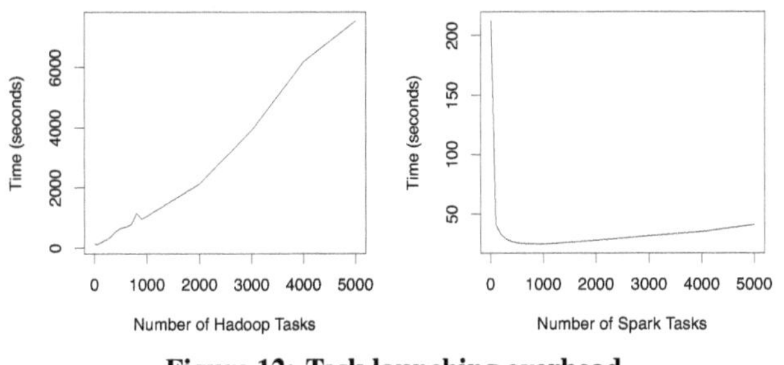

Figure 12: Task launching overhead

More fundamentally, there are few reasons why sub-second tasks should not be feasible even at higher scales than we have explored, such as tens of thousands of nodes. Systems like Dremel [29] routinely run sub-second, multi-thousand-node jobs. Indeed, even if a single master cannot keep up with the scheduling decisions, the scheduling could be delegated across "lieutenant" masters for subsets of the cluster. Fine-grained tasks also offer many advantages over coarser-grained execution graphs beyond load balancing, such as faster recovery (by spreading out lost tasks across more nodes) and query elasticity [30]; we discuss some of these next.

7.2 Other Benefits of the Fine-Grained Task Model

While this paper has focused primarily on the fault tolerance benefits of fine-grained deterministic tasks, the model also provides other attractive properties. We wish to point out two benefits that have been explored in MapReduce-based systems.

Elasticity: In traditional MPP databases, a distributed query plan is selected once, and the system needs to run at that level of parallelism for the whole duration of the query. In a fine-grained task system, however, nodes can appear or go away during a query, and pending work will automatically be spread onto them. This enables the database engine to naturally be elastic. If an administrator wishes to remove nodes from the engine (*e.g.,* in a virtualized corporate data center), the engine can simply treat those as failed, or (better yet) proactively replicate their data to other nodes if given a few minutes' warning. Similarly, a database engine running on a cloud could scale *up* by requesting new VMs if a query is expensive. Amazon's Elastic MapReduce [3] already supports resizing clusters at runtime.

Multitenancy: The same elasticity, mentioned above, enables dynamic resource sharing between users. In some traditional MPP databases, if an important query arrives while another large query is using most of the cluster, there are few options beyond canceling the earlier query. In systems based on fine-grained tasks, one can simply wait a few seconds for the current tasks from the first query to finish, and start giving the nodes tasks from the second query. For instance, Facebook and Microsoft have developed fair schedulers for Hadoop and Dryad that allow large historical queries, compute-intensive machine learning jobs, and short ad-hoc queries to safely coexist [38, 23].

8 Related Work

To the best of our knowledge, Shark is the only low-latency system that can efficiently combine SQL and machine learning workloads, while supporting fine-grained fault recovery.

We categorize large-scale data analytics systems into three classes. First, systems like ASTERIX [9], Tenzing [13], SCOPE [12], Cheetah [14], and Hive [34] compile declarative queries into MapReduce-style jobs. Although some of them modify the execution engine they are built on, it is hard for these systems to achieve interactive query response times for reasons discussed in Section 7.

Second, several projects aim to provide low-latency engines using architectures resembling shared-nothing parallel databases. Such projects include PowerDrill [20] and Impala [1]. These systems do not support fine-grained fault tolerance. In case of mid-query faults, the entire query needs to be re-executed. Google's Dremel [29] does rerun lost tasks, but it only supports an aggregation tree topology for query execution, and not the more complex shuffle DAGs required for large joins or distributed machine learning.

A third class of systems take a hybrid approach by combining a MapReduce-like engine with relational databases. HadoopDB [4] connects multiple single-node database systems using Hadoop as the communication layer. Queries can be parallelized using Hadoop MapReduce, but within each MapReduce task, data processing is pushed into the relational database system. Osprey [37] is a middleware layer that adds fault-tolerance properties to parallel databases. It does so by breaking a SQL query into multiple small queries and sending them to parallel databases for execution. Shark presents a much simpler single-system architecture that supports all of the properties of this third class of systems, as well as statistical learning capabilities that HadoopDB and Osprey lack.

The partial DAG execution (PDE) technique introduced by Shark resembles adaptive query optimization techniques proposed in [7,

36, 25]. It is, however, unclear how these single-node techniques would work in a distributed setting and scale out to hundreds of nodes. In fact, PDE actually complements some of these techniques, as Shark can use PDE to optimize how data gets shuffled *across* nodes, and use the traditional single-node techniques *within* a local task. DryadLINQ [24] optimizes its number of reduce tasks at run-time based on map output sizes, but does not collect richer statistics, such as histograms, or make broader execution plan changes, such as changing join algorithms, like PDE can. RoPE [5] proposes using historical query information to optimize query plans, but relies on repeatedly executed queries. PDE works on queries that are executing for the first time.

Finally, Shark builds on the distributed approaches for machine learning developed in systems like Graphlab [27], Haloop [11], and Spark [39]. However, Shark is unique in offering these capabilities in a SQL engine, allowing users to select data of interest using SQL and immediately run learning algorithms on it without time-consuming export to another system. Compared to Spark, Shark also provides far more efficient in-memory representation of relational data, and mid-query optimization using PDE.

9 Conclusion

We have presented Shark, a new data warehouse system that combines fast relational queries and complex analytics in a single, fault-tolerant runtime. Shark significantly enhances a MapReduce-like runtime to efficiently run SQL, by using existing database techniques (e.g., column-oriented storage) and a novel *partial DAG execution (PDE)* technique that leverages fine-grained data statistics to dynamically reoptimize queries at run-time. This design enables Shark to approach the speedups reported for MPP databases over MapReduce, while providing support for machine learning algorithms, as well as mid-query fault tolerance across both SQL queries and machine learning computations. Overall, the system can be up to 100× faster than Hive for SQL, and more than 100× faster than Hadoop for machine learning. More fundamentally, this research represents an important step towards a unified architecture for efficiently combining complex analytics and relational query processing.

We have open sourced Shark at `shark.cs.berkeley.edu`. The latest stable release implements most of the techniques discussed in this paper, and more advanced features such as PDE and data copartitioning will be incorporated soon. We have also worked with two Internet companies as early users. They report speedups of 40–100× on real queries, consistent with our results.

10 Acknowledgments

We thank Cliff Engle, Harvey Feng, Shivaram Venkataraman, Ram Sriharsha, Tim Tully, Denny Britz, Antonio Lupher, Patrick Wendell, Paul Ruan, Jason Dai, Shane Huang, and other colleagues in the AMPLab for their work on Shark. We also thank Andy Pavlo and his colleagues for making their benchmark dataset and queries available. This research is supported in part by NSF CISE Expeditions award CCF-1139158 and DARPA XData Award FA8750-12-2-0331, and gifts from Amazon Web Services, Google, SAP, Blue Goji, Cisco, Clearstory Data, Cloudera, Ericsson, Facebook, General Electric, Hortonworks, Huawei, Intel, Microsoft, NetApp, Oracle, Quanta, Samsung, Splunk, VMware and Yahoo!, and by a Google PhD Fellowship.

11 References

[1] https://github.com/cloudera/impala.

[2] http://hadoop.apache.org/.

[3] http://aws.amazon.com/elasticmapreduce/.

[4] A. Abouzeid et al. Hadoopdb: an architectural hybrid of mapreduce and dbms technologies for analytical workloads. *VLDB*, 2009.

[5] S. Agarwal et al. Re-optimizing data-parallel computing. In *NSDI'12*.

[6] G. Ananthanarayanan et al. Pacman: Coordinated memory caching for parallel jobs. In *NSDI*, 2012.

[7] R. Avnur and J. M. Hellerstein. Eddies: continuously adaptive query processing. In *SIGMOD*, 2000.

[8] S. Babu. Towards automatic optimization of mapreduce programs. In *SoCC'10*.

[9] A. Behm et al. Asterix: towards a scalable, semistructured data platform for evolving-world models. *Distributed and Parallel Databases*, 29(3):185–216, 2011.

[10] V. Borkar et al. Hyracks: A flexible and extensible foundation for data-intensive computing. In *ICDE'11*.

[11] Y. Bu et al. HaLoop: efficient iterative data processing on large clusters. *Proc. VLDB Endow.*, 2010.

[12] R. Chaiken et al. Scope: easy and efficient parallel processing of massive data sets. *VLDB*, 2008.

[13] B. Chattopadhyay, , et al. Tenzing a sql implementation on the mapreduce framework. *PVLDB*, 4(12):1318–1327, 2011.

[14] S. Chen. Cheetah: a high performance, custom data warehouse on top of mapreduce. *VLDB*, 2010.

[15] C. Chu et al. Map-reduce for machine learning on multicore. *Advances in neural information processing systems*, 19:281, 2007.

[16] J. Cohen, B. Dolan, M. Dunlap, J. Hellerstein, and C. Welton. Mad skills: new analysis practices for big data. *VLDB*, 2009.

[17] J. Dean and S. Ghemawat. MapReduce: Simplified data processing on large clusters. In *OSDI*, 2004.

[18] X. Feng et al. Towards a unified architecture for in-rdbms analytics. In *SIGMOD*, 2012.

[19] B. Guffler et al. Handling data skew in mapreduce. In *CLOSER'11*.

[20] A. Hall et al. Processing a trillion cells per mouse click. *VLDB*.

[21] B. Hindman et al. Mesos: A platform for fine-grained resource sharing in the data center. In *NSDI'11*.

[22] M. Isard et al. Dryad: distributed data-parallel programs from sequential building blocks. *SIGOPS*, 2007.

[23] M. Isard et al. Quincy: Fair scheduling for distributed computing clusters. In *SOSP '09*, 2009.

[24] M. Isard and Y. Yu. Distributed data-parallel computing using a high-level programming language. In *SIGMOD*, 2009.

[25] N. Kabra and D. J. DeWitt. Efficient mid-query re-optimization of sub-optimal query execution plans. In *SIGMOD*, 1998.

[26] Y. Kwon et al. Skewtune: mitigating skew in mapreduce applications. In *SIGMOD '12*, 2012.

[27] Y. Low et al. Distributed graphlab: a framework for machine learning and data mining in the cloud. *VLDB*, 2012.

[28] G. Malewicz et al. Pregel: a system for large-scale graph processing. In *SIGMOD*, 2010.

[29] S. Melnik et al. Dremel: interactive analysis of web-scale datasets. *Proc. VLDB Endow.*, 3:330–339, Sept 2010.

[30] K. Ousterhout et al. The case for tiny tasks in compute clusters. In *HotOS'13*.

[31] A. Pavlo et al. A comparison of approaches to large-scale data analysis. In *SIGMOD*, 2009.

[32] M. Stonebraker et al. C-store: a column-oriented dbms. In *VLDB'05*.

[33] M. Stonebraker et al. Mapreduce and parallel dbmss: friends or foes? *Commun. ACM*.

[34] A. Thusoo et al. Hive-a petabyte scale data warehouse using hadoop. In *ICDE*, 2010.

[35] Transaction Processing Performance Council. *TPC BENCHMARK H*.

[36] T. Urhan, M. J. Franklin, and L. Amsaleg. Cost-based query scrambling for initial delays. In *SIGMOD*, 1998.

[37] C. Yang et al. Osprey: Implementing mapreduce-style fault tolerance in a shared-nothing distributed database. In *ICDE*, 2010.

[38] M. Zaharia et al. Delay scheduling: A simple technique for achieving locality and fairness in cluster scheduling. In *EuroSys 10*, 2010.

[39] M. Zaharia et al. Resilient distributed datasets: a fault-tolerant abstraction for in-memory cluster computing. NSDI, 2012.

Parallel Analytics as a Service

Petrie Wong Zhian He Eric Lo
Department of Computing
The Hong Kong Polytechnic University
{cskfwong, cszahe, ericlo}@comp.polyu.edu.hk

ABSTRACT

Recently, massively parallel processing relational database systems (MPPDBs) have gained much momentum in the big data analytic market. With the advent of hosted cloud computing, we envision that the offering of MPPDB-as-a-Service (MPPDBaaS) will become attractive for companies having analytical tasks on only hundreds gigabytes to some ten terabytes of data because they can enjoy high-end parallel analytics at a cheap cost. This paper presents *Thrifty*, a prototype implementation of MPPDB-as-a-service. The major research issue is how to achieve a lower total cost of ownership by consolidating thousands of MPPDB tenants on to a shared hardware infrastructure, with a performance SLA that guarantees the tenants can obtain the query results as if they are executing their queries on dedicated machines. Thrifty achieves the goal by using a *tenant-driven design* that includes (1) a *cluster design* that carefully arranges the nodes in the cluster into groups and creates an MPPDB for each group of nodes, (2) a *tenant placement* that assigns each tenant to several MPPDBs (for high availability service through replication), and (3) a *query routing* algorithm that routes a tenant's query to the proper MPPDB at run-time. Experiments show that in a MPPDBaaS with 5000 tenants, where each tenant requests 2 to 32 nodes MPPDB to query against 200GB to 3.2TB of data, Thrifty can serve all the tenants with a 99.9% performance SLA guarantee and a high availability replication factor of 3, using only 18.7% of the nodes requested by the tenants.

Categories and Subject Descriptors

H.2.4 [**Systems**]: [Parallel databases; Query processing]

Keywords

cloud databases, consolidation, database-as-a-service, multi-tenant databases, parallel databases

1. INTRODUCTION

Recently, massively parallel processing relational database systems (MPPDBs) like Vertica, Microsoft SQL Server Parallel Database Warehouse, and Greenplum have gained much momentum in the big data analytic market. These MPPDBs feature SQL interface, fast data loading, easy scale-out, fast recovery, and short analytical query processing time. With the advent of hosted cloud computing, we envision that the offering of **MPPDB-as-a-Service (MPPDBaaS)** will become attractive for companies having analytical tasks on hundreds gigabytes to some ten terabytes of data. From the viewpoint of tenants who rent the service, they can enjoy parallel analytics on their "big" data, but the hardware cost, the operation cost (e.g., administration), and especially the software license (which costs about USD 15K per core or USD 50K per TB of data for a commercial MPPDB we know) they pay for a share of the service are likely to be much lower than running everything themselves. From the viewpoint of the service providers, they can achieve a lower total cost of ownership by consolidating the tenants on to a shared hardware infrastructure, so that the service can be run using far fewer machine nodes than the sum of the number of the machine nodes requested by the tenants. When sharing resources among tenants, it is challenging to ensure the service level agreements (SLA) for the tenants are met after consolidation. Ideally, a tenant that rents a 4-node MPPDB should have the feeling that the queries are really executed by a MPPDB that runs on four dedicated machine nodes. Therefore, a service provider that offers MPPDB-as-a-service should regard the *query latency before consolidation* as the performance SLA.

One approach to offer database-as-a-service (DaaS) is based on the use of virtual machines (VM) [24]. The VM approach offers hard isolation among tenants and thus performance isolation among tenants could be easily achieved. However, the VM approach incurs significant redundancy on the resources (e.g., multiple copies of the OS and DBMS, etc.) [8, 7]. Therefore, the recent trend for DaaS is to use the *shared-process multi-tenancy* [13] model (i.e., sharing the same database process among tenants). Relational Cloud [8, 7] and SQL Azure [4] are using this model so that a much higher consolidation effectiveness could be obtained. But so far they focus on tenants with *transactional workloads*.

Let us see some interesting results when applying the shared-process multi-tenancy model to host tenants with *parallel analytical workloads*. Figures 1a and b show the query performance of TPC-H Q1 on a commercial MPPDB. We use this MPPDB to host multiple tenants using the same database process (the detailed experimental setup is given in Section 7). Each tenant holds a TPC-H scale factor 100 dataset. In Figure 1a, the line 1T shows the speedup of Q1 in a single-tenant setting. We can see that Q1 scales out linearly with the number of nodes.

Transactional (OLTP) workloads generally touch a small amount of data per transaction. So, OLTP-database-as-a-service using the shared-process model could still support a large number of concurrent query executions after consolidation [8, 7]. In contrast, analytical workloads are I/O-intensive, so concurrent query executions on the same database instance *easily increase the query latency*

SIGMOD'13, June 22–27, 2013, New York, New York, USA.

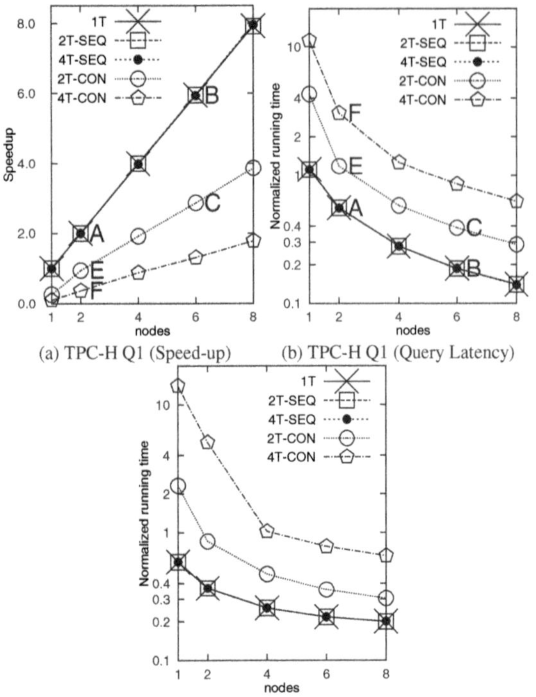

(a) TPC-H Q1 (Speed-up) (b) TPC-H Q1 (Query Latency)

(c) TPC-H Q19 (Query Latency)

Figure 1: Query performance in a commercial MPPDB with multi-tenants. xT-SEQ means there are x tenants submitting queries sequentially xT-CON means there are x active tenants submitting queries concurrently.

and violate the SLA. In Figure 1a, the lines 2T-CON and 4T-CON show the speedup of Q1 (with respect to 1-node) when there are respectively two tenants and four tenants sharing the same database instance, and the tenants submit Q1 together. We can see that Q1's performance are 2× (in 2-tenant setting) and 4× slower (in 4-tenant setting). That is, once the tenants submit queries together, none of their SLAs could be met. This is a challenge of using the shared-process multi-tenancy model to serve analytical workloads.

Yet, Figure 1a reveals a consolidation opportunity. In the figure, the line 2T-SEQ shows the speedup of Q1 (with respect to 1-node) in a 2-tenant setting where one tenant first submits an instance of Q1, and after that finishes, another tenant then submits another instance of Q1; and the average query latency of Q1 is calculated. Not surprisingly, as shared-process multi-tenancy incurs little overhead [8], when two Q1 instances are executed one after the other on a MPPDB with multiple tenants, their individual query latency is close to that when running a single Q1 instance on a MPPDB with a single tenant. This observation also holds at a higher degree of multi-tenancy with four tenants (see the line 4T-SEQ in Figure 1a). The above shows that even for analytical workloads, if the consolidated tenants are not active together, it is possible that the tenants' individual SLA could still be met.

The second consolidation opportunity can be observed by looking at Figure 1b, which shows the query latency of Q1. First, assume there are four tenants, each rents a 2-node MPPDB to process a TPC-H scale factor 100 dataset. The service provider basically requires a total of $4 \times 2 = 8$ separate nodes to host them. The SLA of TPC-H Q1 for each tenant is then A seconds, as illustrated in Figure 1b. What if the service provider uses a 6-node MPPDB to host all four tenants (i.e., every tenant partitions their data on to those six nodes)? Let us assume that only one out of the four tenant is *active* (e.g., submit a Q1 instance) and the rest of them are *inactive*, i.e., not submitting any query. That active tenant then can obtain the result of Q1 in B seconds — the SLA is met. When two out of the four tenants are active together and they concurrently submit an instance of Q1 to the 6-node MPPDB, each tenant can obtain the result of Q1 in C seconds — their SLAs are also met. The above shows that it is a consolidation opportunity that is more specific to parallel analytic workload.

This paper presents the design, implementation, and experimental evaluation of *Thrifty*, a system that offers MPPDB-as-a-service. Thrifty employs shared-process multi-tenancy and exploits opportunities mentioned above to consolidate tenants on to a shared cluster. Low active tenant ratios are commonly found in real multi-tenancy environments. For example, in IBM's database-as-a-service, the active tenant ratio is only 10% [20]. Such a low active tenant ratio gives Thrifty many opportunities to meet the SLAs after consolidation. Nevertheless, there are still some challenges left. First, consider a production cluster of 6000 nodes, a total of 4000 tenants, and each tenant requests a 2-node MPPDB. In this case, shall Thrifty put all 4000 tenants onto a 6000-node MPPDB instance? Second, the above discussion has not yet covered the issue of *high availability*, which is important for database-as-a-service. Third, Thrifty has to avoid SLA violations like some cases above where many tenants become active together. Fourth, notice that TPC-H Q1 is a *linear scale-out* query under our experimental setting. Thrifty also has to consider other cases such as concurrent execution of *non-linear scale-out queries*. Figure 1c shows the performance of TPC-H Q19 in the same experimental environment. TPC-H Q19 does not scale out linearly in our setting. For those queries, the second consolidation opportunity mentioned above cannot be easily applied.

In a nutshell, Thrifty aims to offer MPPDBaaS using few machines with the following requirements:

R1) Supporting thousands of tenants and machine nodes.
R2) Offering high availability services.
R3) Offering query-latency based performance SLA guarantees.
R4) Each tenant requests a multi-node MPPDB that serves multiple users; some user queries may linear scale-out but some may not.
R5) Tenants' query templates may be known or unknown beforehand. For report generating applications, the query templates could be found in the applications' stored procedures. For interactive analysis, however, a data analyst may craft and submit an ad-hoc query at any time.

R1 and R2 are two general cloud computing requirements. R3 is a DaaS requirement specific to analytical workloads.[1] R4 is specific to MPPDBaaS and R5 is necessary if we want to offer a real MPPDBaaS. These requirements together make the design and implementation of Thrifty very challenging. For example, sharing the database process among tenants (to enjoy higher consolidation ratio) makes R3 challenging because there is no more hard isolation. While performance prediction techniques for concurrent analytical workload [9, 1, 21, 16, 2] may help there on the surface, these techniques require the knowledge of the query sets as input, which contradicts with R5 above.

This paper makes three principal contributions for this problem:

1. Tenant-Driven Design (TDD) (Section 3) — the core framework to implement MPPDB-as-a-Service. TDD includes three parts: (a) [Cluster Design] arrange the machine nodes in the cluster into *groups* and create an MPPDB for each group of

[1]DaaS supporting OLTP workloads defines their SLA based on the throughput before-and-after consolidation [7].

nodes, (b) [Tenant Placement] assign each tenant to several MPPDBs (for replication), and (c) [Query Routing] route a tenant's query to a MPPDB containing that tenant's data at runtime. We can show that the use of TDD can tackle requirements R2 to R5 in a row. Furthermore, based on TDD, we can show that solving R1 could be treated as solving a *new variant of vector bin packing optimization problem.* We then present heuristics solutions that solve that problem effectively (Section 4).

2. Thrifty — a prototype implementation of MPPDB-as-a-service based on TDD. The architecture design of Thrifty (Section 2) as well as system issues like elastic scaling (Section 5) and system tuning (Section 6) are presented.
3. An experimental testbed to evaluate the consolidation effectiveness and the performance guarantees of any MPPDBaaS. Experiments show that in a MPPDBaaS with 5000 tenants, where each tenant requests 2 to 32 nodes MPPDB to query against 200GB to 3.2TB of data, Thrifty can serve all the tenants with a 99.9% performance SLA guarantee and a high availability replication factor of 3, using only 18.7% of the nodes requested by the tenants (Section 7).

After presenting the above, we discuss related work in Section 8 and conclude this work and outline some future work in Section 9.

2. SYSTEM OVERVIEW

Thrifty adopts a pricing model that charges a tenant based on the number of requested nodes (the degree of parallelism) and its active usage. It begins with a set of independent MPPDB tenants running parallel analytical workloads, where each tenant runs a MPPDB on a disjoint set of machine nodes. Figure 2 shows the architecture of Thrifty. The components of Thrifty are:

(a) *Tenant Activity Monitor*: The Tenant Activity Monitor automatically collects the query logs of the deployed MPPDBs, derives the tenant activities, and summarizes the query characteristics of individual tenants. For example, it continuously monitors the active tenant ratio of all tenants in the past 30 days. These information is passed to the *Deployment Advisor* for further processing, and is available to the system administrator for advanced system tuning.

(b) *Deployment Advisor*: The Deployment Advisor takes as inputs the tenant activity statistics, the individual tenant information (e.g., number of nodes requested), a replication factor R (specified by a system administrator for high availability), and a performance SLA guarantee P (also specified by the system administrator which ensures that, after consolidation, the tenants can still meet their SLA for a P%, e.g., 99.9%, of time). It returns as output a *deployment plan*. The deployment plan consists of two parts: *cluster design* and *tenant placement*. The cluster design details how the machine nodes in the cluster are arranged into groups. Each group of nodes then runs a single MPPDB instance. The tenant placement specifies which MPPDB instances a tenant should be deployed on; and a tenant is deployed on R MPPDB instances. At run-time, the Deployment Advisor may fine-tune the deployment plan according to the live-updated tenant activities supplied by the Tenant Activity Monitor. Currently, Thrifty assumes all nodes in the cluster are identical in configurations (e.g., CPU, RAM).

(c) *Deployment Master*: The Deployment Master follows the deployment plan devised by the Deployment Advisor to start the MPPDB instances and deploy the tenants onto them. It also switches off/hibernates nodes that are not listed in the deployment plan. The deployment is supposed to be static for days. A (re)-consolidation process is expected to be executed periodically, because it is expected that there are new tenants register with and existing tenants de-register with the service.

(d) *Query Router*: The Query Router accepts queries from tenants and routes the queries to the proper MPPDB instance according to the tenant placement.

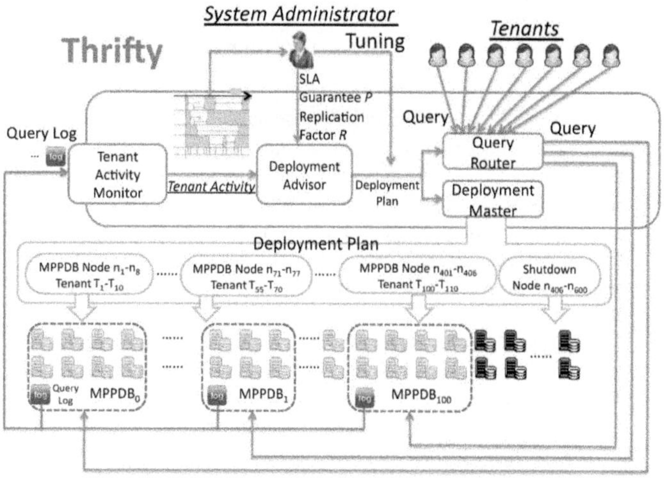

Figure 2: The architecture of the Thrifty system.

The crux of Thrifty is to devise a good deployment plan to serve thousands of tenants using fewer machine nodes. Thrifty targets on tenants with temporal skew [19] analytical workloads, e.g, tenants from different time zones and mostly submit queries within a certain period (e.g., 9am to 5pm) but not in a 24×7 fashion. That type of temporal skew workload is not uncommon in today's data analytical market [5]. The target tenants are supposed to have up to only some tens terabytes of data but hope to enjoy the parallel speedup offered by the expensive MPPDB products. These are what enable consolidation. Tenants that are always active and/or with more than terabytes of data could be detected by Thrifty and they will be excluded from consolidation.[2]

3. TENANT-DRIVEN DESIGN (TDD)

The principle of Tenant-Driven Design (TDD) is to exploit the low active tenant ratio found in real multi-tenant cloud environments to design a deployment plan that let each active tenant exclusively use an MPPDB that just fits (or, over-fits) its parallelism requirement. By using TDD, we can show that requirements R2 to R5 (Section 1) are all tackled in a row.

The whole Tenant-Driven Design consists of three parts: (1) Cluster Design (Section 3.1), (2) Tenant Placement (Section 3.2), and (3) Query Routing (Section 3.3).

3.1 Cluster Design

The cluster design of TDD is to divide a set of machine nodes into A groups (we will discuss how to set the value of A later). Then, each group of nodes form a separate MPPDB. Let T be the number of tenants, n_i be the number of nodes requested by tenant T_i, and N be the total number of nodes requested by all T tenants

[2]Those tenants offer little room for consolidation, and they are served by dedicated nodes under another service plan.

Tenant	T_1	T_2	T_3	T_4	T_5	T_6	T_7	T_8	T_9	T_{10}
n_i	6	6	5	5	5	4	4	3	2	2

(a) Tenant Characteristics (42 nodes requested)

Group	G_0	G_1	G_2
MPPDB	MPPDB_0	MPPDB_1	MPPDB_2
Parallelism	6-node	6-node	6-node

(b) Cluster Design (18 nodes)

MPPDB	MPPDB_0	MPPDB_1	MPPDB_2
Hosting	$T_1 - T_{10}$	$T_1 - T_{10}$	$T_1 - T_{10}$

(c) Tenant Placement

Figure 3: A Toy Example

(i.e., $N = \sum_1^T n_i$). Without loss of generality, we assume $n_i \le n_j$ if $i > j$. Then, our tenant-driven design assigns n_1 nodes to groups $G_1, G_2, ..., G_{A-1}$. Group G_0 is a special group. Our tenant-driven design assigns a variable of U nodes to G_0, where $n_1 \le U \le (N - (A-1)n_1)$. We call the MPPDB created from group G_0 as the "tuning MPPDB", which is used for system tuning. We will discuss more about the choice of U in Section 6 and now we assume $U = n_1$.

As a toy example, assume that there are $T = 10$ tenants and the number of nodes requested by each tenant is listed in Figure 3a. In this toy example, the service provider requires a total of $N = 42$ nodes to host these tenants before consolidation. So, assume that $A = 3$, there are three groups and TDD results in a 18-node cluster design as listed in Figure 3b.

3.2 Tenant Placement

The tenant placement of TDD is very simple. Specifically, each MPPDB is assigned to host all tenants. Figure 3c illustrates the tenant placement for the example. From the above discussion, we observe the Property 1.

PROPERTY 1. *The tenant-driven design enforces a replication factor of A for each tenant.*

Replication is a standard way to ensure high availability and load balancing. Usually, the replication factor is around two to four.

3.3 Query Routing

Algorithm 1 presents the query routing algorithm based on our tenant-driven design. The idea is to "route an active tenant" (compare with the concept of "route a query") to an MPPDB and let that MPPDB exclusively process all that tenant's (concurrent) queries until that tenant becomes inactive. Here, we use a strong notion of *inactive* — as long as a tenant does not have any queries being executed by any MPPDB, that tenant is inactive at that moment.

Algorithm 1: TDD Query Routing Algorithm

```
   Input: Tenant T_i, Query Q
1  if T_i has queries running on MPPDB_x then
2      route Q to MPPDB_x;
3  else
4      if MPPDB_0 currently is free then
5          route Q to MPPDB_0;
6      else
7          if there is any free MPPDB then
8              route Q to a free MPPDB_j;
9          else
10             route Q to MPPDB_0 for concurrent processing;
```

We explain the query routing by walking through an example of tenant activities listed in Figure 4. In the example, the maximum

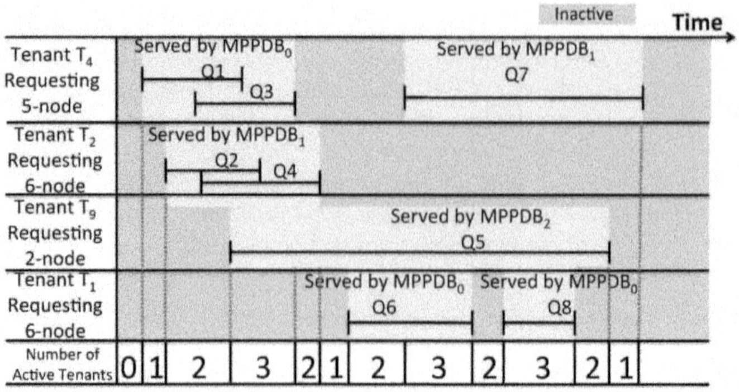

Figure 4: Tenant Activities and Query Routing

number of concurrent active tenant is three. In the beginning, tenant T_4 becomes active and submits a query Q_1. As all MPPDBs in the cluster are initially free (not serving any queries), Q_1 gets routed to MPPDB_0 (Line 5). Next, tenant T_2 becomes active and submits a query Q_2. As MPPDB_0 is currently busy (serving T_4's Q_1), Q_2 is routed to MPPDB_1, which is free (Line 8). Next, tenant T_4 has a query Q_3 submitted while Q_1 is still running on MPPDB_0. So, Q_3 is also routed to MPPDB_0 (Line 2). Continuing the example, Q_4 is the next query arriving to the system. As Q_4 is submitted by T_2 and MPPDB_1 is still serving a query of tenant T_2, Q_4 is routed to MPPDB_1 as well (Line 2). Tenant T_9 becomes active next and submits a query Q_5. In this case, Q_5 is routed to MPPDB_2, which is free (Line 8). Next, tenant T_1 becomes active and submits query Q_6, since T_4 has just finished Q_1 and Q_3, Q_6 is routed to MPPDB_0 (Line 5). Q_7 is the next query submitted by tenant T_4 after Q_1 and Q_3. Since Q_1 and Q_3 have already finished, Q_7 of T_4 is not necessary be routed to MPPDB_0. It is thus routed to MPPDB_1 because MPPDB_0 is busy serving tenant T_1. Q_8 of tenant T_1 is the last query in our example. Although Q_8 is submitted almost right after Q_6 (e.g., with a short "think-time" during a user's interactive analysis session), tenant T_1 is still regarded as inactive for a short while. Therefore, it is not necessary for Q_8 to follow Q_6 to go to MPPDB_0. In this example, however, it is still routed to MPPDB_0 because all other MPPDBs are busy.

3.4 SLA Guarantee and Load Balancing

GUARANTEE 1. *No matter a tenant's queries are* linear-scale-out, non-linear-scale-out, *submitted* sequentially and possibly in an ad-hoc manner *(interactive analysis), or* submitted in a batch for concurrent execution (report generation) at any multi-programming-level (MPL). *Tenant-Driven Design ensures the SLAs of a maximum of A active tenants are met.*

Although simple, TDD can obtain a strong performance SLA guarantee under a general and practical MPPDB-as-a-service setting. In essence, TDD has tackled requirements R2 to R5 in a row. In the example above, all tenants's SLA are met because their queries are *served by dedicated MPPDBs with exact (e.g., Q_2, Q_4, Q_6, Q_8) or higher degree of parallelism (e.g., Q_1, Q_3, Q_5, Q_7).*

TDD achieves load balancing among tenants implicitly. That is because TDD uses a strong notion of inactive and it applies replication on the tenant data, therefore the tenants can be quickly served by an available MPPDB. We remark that load balancing *within* a tenant is not TDD's but the tenant's own issue. The pricing model of Thrifty is to charge a tenant based on the number of nodes it requested. Therefore, if a tenant rents only a 2-node MPPDB instance to serve many concurrent users (e.g., MPL=100), the possibly slow down of the tenant's performance due to the high load is brought by the tenant's own node-choice — TDD is just offering what the tenant should get.

Node failure is handled directly by the MPPDB. All MPPDB products we know can still stay online even with (some) node failure. Thrifty will replace a failed node by starting a new node upon receiving node failure notification from the underlying MPPDB. Node failure, or having more than A active tenants at run-time may cause performance delay and thus SLA violations. We will address this in the next two sections.

4. SERVING THOUSANDS OF TENANTS

With the use of TDD, Thrifty is able to handle a general type of MPPDBaaS tenants (R4 and R5) while offering high availability services (R2) with performance SLA guarantees (R3). However, the discussion so far has only considered a small number of tenants and the total cluster size (i.e., the total number of nodes involved) is small. If there are a lot of tenants, say $T = 5000$, and if the (average) active tenant ratio is 10%, the average number of active tenants at a certain point may reach 500 and the maximum number of active tenants could be even larger. According to Guarantee 1, in order to ensure all that 500+ active tenants can meet their SLAs together, we need to set $A > 500$. That would enforce each tenant's data get replicated more than 500 times, according to Property 1. We approach this issue (R1) by grouping the tenants into *tenant-groups* so that there are only some tens tenants in each tenant-group.

There are two considerations when grouping the tenants. First, we want to group the tenants in a way that can minimize the total number of nodes used after consolidation. Second, we want to ensure the active tenant ratio in each tenant-group is low enough to meet the replication factor R. For example, if we put 30 tenants that are always active together into the same tenant-group, we still need to set $A = 30$ for that tenant-group in order to meet all tenant's SLA.

Finding an optimal tenant-group formation that can address the two considerations above, unfortunately, is $\mathcal{NP}$-hard. To explain, consider a simple scenario that $R = 3$ and six tenants, whose activities are divided into sequences of d fix-width time epochs like in Figure 5. Based on that representation, finding the optimal tenant-group formation is equivalent to a **Largest Item Vector Bin Packing Problem with Fuzzy Capacity** (LIVBPwFC), which is a new variant of the classic vector bin packing problem. Specifically, a tenant (item) T_i is charactered by a tuple $(\vec{A_i}, n_i)$, where n_i denotes the number of nodes requested by T_i, and $\vec{A_i} = \langle a_1, a_2, \cdots, a_d \rangle$ depicts the activity of T_i: $a_k = 1$ if T_i is active in the k-th epoch or $a_k = 0$ otherwise. For example, in Figure 5, there are 10 epochs. Tenant T_1's activity $\vec{A_1}$ is represented as $\langle 1, 1, 1, 1, 1, 1, 0, 0, 0, 0 \rangle$, meaning that it was active from t_1 to t_6 and inactive from t_7 to t_{10}. Each tenant group (bin) TG_j is charactered by a tuple $(\vec{B_j}, P)$, where $\vec{B_j}$ is a d-dimensional vector $\vec{B_j} = \langle R, R, \cdots, R \rangle$. $\vec{B_j}$ and P together characterize the *fuzzy capacity constraint* of a bin such that it is not full as long as the set of items S that are packed in this bin have more than or equal to P% of epochs having less than R active tenants. In other words, a set S of tenants (items) fits into a TG_j (bin) if $COUNT^{\leq R}(\sum_{T_i \in S} \vec{A_i})/d \geq P\%$, where $COUNT^{\leq R}(\vec{V_i})$ is a function that counts the number of dimensions in a vector $\vec{V_i}$ whose values are less than or equal to R. For example, consider $S = \{T_1, T_4, T_5, T_6\}$ in Figure 5. $\sum_{T_i \in S} \vec{A_i}$ results in a vector $\langle 2, 2, 2, 2, 4, 3, 2, 1, 2, 1 \rangle$ and $COUNT^{\leq R}(\sum_{T_i \in S} \vec{A_i})$ returns 9 if $R = 3$.

Concerning the optimization goal, recall that for T tenants, our tenant-driven design uses at least $A \cdot n_1$ nodes. That is, the total number of nodes used is dominated by the largest tenant that requests the most number of nodes. For the example in Figure 3, T_1 is the largest tenant and it requests six nodes, so a total of $A \cdot n_1 = 3 * 6 = 18$ nodes is required. Therefore, the optimization goal is to minimize the total of number of nodes requested by the *largest item* (tenant) in each created bin.

The classic vector bin packing problem is a special case of our LIVBPwFC problem in which only $\vec{A_i}$ and $\vec{B_j}$ are considered (i.e., n_i are ignored and $P = 100\%$). The classic vector bin packing problem is $\mathcal{NP}$-hard and recent work [18] states that First-Fit-Decreasing (FFD) is a practical heuristic to get approximate solutions. FFD suggests to sort all items according to a scalar value and inserts the items into a bin according to that order. An item is inserted into a new bin if the current bin is full. In order to get a single scalar value for a d-dimensional item, one heuristic is to take the product of the dimension values. However, FFD was not especially designed for our LIVBPwFC problem and it did not take into account the fuzzy capacity constraint and the largest item. Another direction is to phrase the problem as a mixed integer non-linear optimization problem (MINLP). Appendix A details such a formulation. However, the formulation contains non-linear constraints and many local minima. Therefore, only general-purpose global optimization algorithms/solvers (e.g., DIRECT [14]) could be used. Unfortunately, these general-purpose global optimization algorithms/solvers run extremely slow for more than 20 variables.

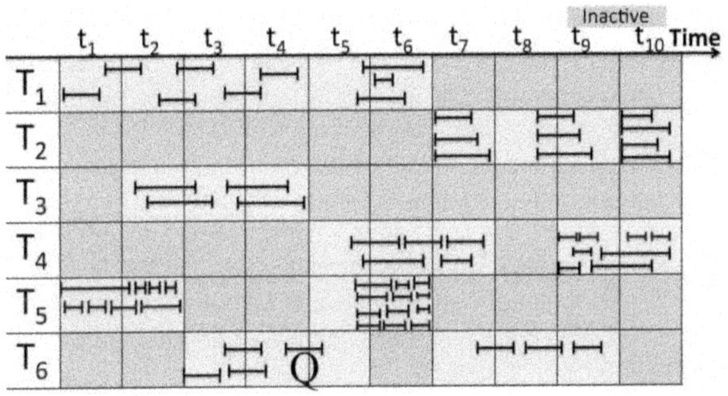

Figure 5: Tenant Activities with Fixed-Width Time Epochs

As recent work [18] suggests using heuristics to solve vector bin packing style problems is more practical, we have developed our own heuristic algorithm that exploits properties of TDD. The algorithm works by solving the two considerations separately. Specifically, we first look at *what kind of grouping can generate a cluster design that can save more nodes?* Recall that the total number of nodes used by a cluster design is dictated by the largest tenant that requests the most number of nodes. In Figure 3, T_1 is the largest tenant and it requests six nodes, so that cluster design saves $42 - 3 * 6 = 24$ nodes. If we group ten tenants of equal size, each requests six nodes, the resulting cluster design would still be the same, but that could save a total of $6 \times 10 - 18 = 42$ nodes. Therefore, our first intuition is that *we should put tenants of the*

Figure 6: Example Tenant Distribution

Num. of Tenants	900	800	700	600	500	400	300	200	100
Parallelism	2	3	4	5	6	7	8	9	10

$TG_1 = \{T_3\}$	1-active	2-active
+ T_1?	30% → 30%	0% → 30%
+ T_2?	30% → 70%	0% → 0% *
+ T_4?	30% → 80%	0% → 0%
+ T_5?	30% → 50%	0% → 10%
+ T_6?	30% → 50%	0% → 20%

(a) T_2 is chosen

$TG_1 = \{T_3, T_2\}$	1-active	2-active	3-active
+ T_1?	70% → 70%	0% → 30%	0% → 0%
+ T_4?	70% → 60%	0% → 30%	0% → 0%
+ T_5?	70% → 90%	0% → 10%	0% → 0% *
+ T_6?	70% → 30%	0% → 50%	0% → 0%

(b) T_5 is chosen

$TG_1 = \{T_3, T_2, T_5\}$	1-active	2-active	3-active
+ T_1?	90% → 40%	10% → 50%	0% → 10%
+ T_4?	90% → 40%	10% → 60%	0% → 0% *
+ T_6?	90% → 30%	10% → 70%	0% → 0%

(c) T_4 is chosen

$TG_1 = \{T_2 - T_5\}$	1-active	2-active	3-active	4-active
+ T_1?	40% → 10% †	60% → 60%	0% → 30%	0% → 0%
+ T_6?	40% → 10%	60% → 60%	0% → 30%	0% → 0% *

†: Explanation: With T_2–T_5 only, epochs t_1, t_3, t_4, and t_8 have 1 active tenant (40%). With T_1 added, epoch t_8 has 1 active tenant (10%).

(d) All ties; T_6 is chosen

$TG_1 = \{T_2 - T_6\}$	1-active	2-active	3-active	4-active
+ T_1?	10% → 0%	60% → 30%	30% → 60%	0% → 10%

TTP (for $R \leq 3$) before adding T_1: 10% + 60% + 30% = 100%
TTP (for $R \leq 3$) if T_1 is added: 0% + 30% + 60% = 90%

(e)

Figure 7: Second Step of Tenant-Grouping (* means that tenant is chosen in that iteration)

same size (i.e., requesting the same number of nodes) into the same tenant-group.

Next, we look at the second consideration, i.e., *how to ensure a low active tenant ratio within each tenant-group?* A natural intuition is that *we should analyze the tenants' activities, and put a tenant into a tenant-group that (a) minimizes the increase in the maximum number of active tenants of that tenant-group and (b) ensures that fuzzy capacity constraint of each resulting tenant-group is not violated.*

Based on the intuitions above, we have developed a two-step tenant grouping heuristic algorithm. In the first step, we put all tenants with homogenous node-size into the same tenant-group (we call those *initial-groups*). Consider the tenant distribution in Figure 6, there would be nine initial-groups (e.g., all 300 tenants that request 8-node MPPDBs are in the same initial-group).

In the second step, we further split the tenant in each initial group into tenant-groups. Specifically, for all tenants in the same initial group, we first insert the least active tenant into a tenant-group. Next, we pick the tenant T_{best} that minimizes the increase in time percentage (measured in terms of the number of time epochs) of the maximum number of active tenants. Take the tenant activities in Figure 5 as an example. Assume tenant T_3 is put as the first member of the first tenant-group TG_1. So, when putting T_1 into TG_1, the total time percentage that has two active tenants, is increased from 0% to 30% (i.e., there are three epochs, t_2, t_3, t_4, out of ten, have two active tenants). If putting T_2 into TG_1, the total time percentage of having two active tenants does not increase. Figure 7a shows the potential time percentage changes of different numbers of active tenants when adding a tenant into the tenant-group TG_1 (with T_3 there). In the example, both T_2 and T_4 can keep the maximum number of active tenant to be one if any one of them is added to TG_1. So, we break the tie by examining the increase of the total time percentage time of having one active tenants — T_2 is then chosen and added to TG_1. Figure 7b shows the potential time percentage changes of different number of active tenants if adding either T_1, T_4, T_5, or T_6 to the tenant-group TG_1, which now contains T_3 and T_2. T_5 is chosen because it incurs the least increase in the total time percentage of the maximum number of active tenants. The process continues by adding T_4 (Figure 7c) and T_6 to TG_1 (Figure 7d), one-by-one. Note that after TG_1 has five tenants T_2, T_3, T_4, T_5, and T_6, the maximum number of active tenants is only three (see Figure 5).

Let TTP be total time percentage that the number of active tenants is smaller than or equal to R in a tenant-group, and recall that P be a performance SLA guarantee that is specified by the system administrator, who wants to ensure that for a P% of time the tenants can meet their SLA. So, the adding of a tenant to a tenant-group stops only when that would result in $TTP < P$. In our example, assume the system administrator specifies $R = 3$ and she wants to ensure that for a 99.9% of time the tenants can meet their SLA. From Figure 7e, we can see that if T_1 is added into the tenant-group, the total time percentage that the number of active tenants is smaller than or equal to $R = 3$ will drop from 100% to 90%. That in contrast means there is 10% of time that there would be more than three active tenants. So, if $A = 3$, Thrifty may violate those tenants' SLA guarantee at those epochs. Therefore, T_1 would not add to tenant-group TG_1 and the tenant-grouping process starts a new iteration by creating a new tenant-group TG_2. The two-step tenant grouping algorithm is summarized in Algorithm 2. The first step takes $\mathcal{O}(T)$ time to form initial groups. For each initial group of size g_i, it searches from the g_i tenants the tenant T_{best} with the least increase in TTP and add it to a tenant group TG_j. The process repeats for the remaining $g_i - 1$ tenants, $g_i - 2$ tenants, so on and so forth and thus it requires $\mathcal{O}(g_i^2)$ searches for each initial group. Nevertheless, the algorithm running time is not a major issue because tenant-grouping is an offline process, triggered only occasionally, the number of tenants involved is usually in the order of thousands, and most importantly our experiments show that it yields deployment plans that save more than 3.6% to 11.1% nodes than standard heuristic. After tenant grouping, the resulting tenant-groups follow the tenant-driven design to generate the cluster design and tenant placement, using $A = R$.

Algorithm 2: 2-Step Tenant Grouping Algorithm

```
Input: Tenants 𝒯, Replication Factor R, SLA Guarantee P%
   // First Step
1  Put tenants requesting the same number of nodes into the same initial
   groups
   // Second Step
2  for each initial groups do
3      i = 1;
4      Create tenant group TG_i;
5      Identify the tenant T_best ∈ 𝒯 that will minimize the increase of
       time percentage of the maximum number of active tenants in
       TG_i;
6      if adding T_best to TG_i, and TG_i's TTP is still ≥ P% then
7          Remove T_best from 𝒯 and add T_best to TG_i;
8          Goto Line 5;        ▷Try to add another tenant into this group
9      else
10         i++;
11         Goto Line 4;        ▷ Create another tenant-group
```

The epoch size has an influence on the grouping quality. For example, Query Q of T_6 in Figure 5 actually only spans a very small portion of epoch t_5. If the epoch size is halved, T_6 can be

Tenant / Data Size	Node Starting & MPPDB Initialization	Bulk Loading
2-node / 200GB	462s	10172s
4-node / 400GB	850s	20302s
6-node / 600GB	1248s	30121s
8-node / 800GB	1504s	40853s
10-node / 1TB	1779s	50446s

Table 1: Starting and Bulk Loading a MPPDB

added to the tenant group TG_1 as well. Empirically, we found that epoch sizes of 10 seconds to 30 seconds could achieve the best consolidation effectiveness.

Before we go to the next section, we remark that our two-step tenant-grouping method relies on the assumption that "the tenant history repeats itself", which has been proven in realistic DaaS environments [8, 20]. So, when the TTP of a tenant-group at $R = 3$ is 99.9%, we have a high confidence that the number of active tenants is less than or equal to three at run-time. Of course, it is still possible that the number of active tenants exceeds three at run-time (e.g., 0.08% of time having four active tenants and 0.04% of time having five active tenants, which results in a 0.12% of time having more than three active tenants). Thrifty uses a reactive approach that elastically adds more nodes for that tenant group to handle those situations (will discuss this in the next section). This approach is pragmatic and makes good use of the elastic nature of cloud computing.

5. LIGHTWEIGHT ELASTIC SCALING

At run-time, tenants' activities may deviate from the history. Consider a tenant-group having a TTP of 99.95% during tenant-grouping. At run-time, some tenants in that group may become more active than what the past tenant activities have indicated, and that will result in a lower run-time TTP (RT-TTP). When the RT-TTP drops to, say 98%, that implies there is 2% of time the tenants are not exclusively served by dedicated MPPDBs and some of their queries may not meet the SLA. Thrifty handles this issue using a standard elastic scaling approach as in other cloud systems. The Tenant Activity Monitor monitors the RT-TTP of each tenant-group using a time window (e.g., 24-hour). When it detects the RT-TTP of a tenant-group of the past 24 hours has just dropped below the performance SLA guarantee P, Thrifty will call the Deployment Advisor to take action.

One possible action is to elastically scale up A by one, i.e., adding one more MPPDB. In MPPDBaaS, however, scaling up A is not as simple and efficient as scaling resources (e.g., RAM) in VM-based cloud environment. Specifically, it takes hours to start a new MPPDB and bulk load all tenants' data before it is ready to use. Table 1 shows the time of starting up a MPPDB and bulk loading tenant data into a MPPDB in our environment. We see that the data loading time dominates the times of starting the machines and creating the MPPDB instances, although it has already achieved a reasonable loading rate (about 1.2GB/min). Take starting a 10-node MPPDB that contains 1TB of tenant data as an example. After detecting the RT-TTP of a tenant-group of the past 24 hours has dropped below the, say, 99.9% performance SLA guarantee threshold, Thrifty needs about 14.5 hours (50446s+1779s) to prepare the new MPPDB. Assume that the RT-TTP of the tenant group is consistently 98% during those 14.5 hours, that would result in about 17.4 minutes (14.5 hours $\times$ 2%) having concurrent query processing at $MPPDB_0$. Consider a reasonable time frame of, say, one month, Thrifty has about 43 minutes (1 month $\times$ 0.1%) of "grace period" for not meeting the SLA guarantee of a tenant group.[3] So, that grace period is barely enough to tolerate the scaling of A twice. Therefore, we look for a more lightweight approach to implement the elastic scale-up operation such that we can tolerate more scale-up operations or possibly other performance-influencing operations (e.g., node failure) in the grace period.

Our lightweight approach is to identify the "over-active" tenant(s) in that tenant group and add a new MPPDB to serve only those tenant(s), instead of adding a MPPDB that serves *the whole tenant-group*. We see from Table 1 the data loading time scales linearly with the data size. As the data size of a tenant in a tenant-group must always be less than the data size of *all* tenants in that group, the elastic scale-up operation that starts a new MPPDB and loads data for only the over-active tenants would be more efficient. Specifically, on detecting the RT-TTP of a tenant-group of the past 24 hours has dropped below P, Thrifty will run an over-active-tenant-identification algorithm to identify the tenant(s) that are more active than the history indicated, and create a new MPPDB to serve them. The over-active-tenant-identification algorithm is similar to the tenant-grouping algorithm presented in Algorithm 2, with the only change that takes only the tenants of a particular tenant-group as inputs. It is expected some tenant(s) cannot join the same tenant group anymore, and they are identified as over-active and their data are bulk loaded[4] to a new MPPDB. When the new MPPDB is ready, the Deployment Advisor will notify the Query Router to route queries from the over-active tenant(s) to the new MPPDB.

For any tenant-group that has ever gone through the above elastic scaling process, Thrifty will add tenants in those tenant-groups to a re-consolidation list. Those tenants, together with new tenants, over-active tenants, and tenants in tenant-groups with de-registered tenants, will get re-consolidated in the next (re)-consolidation cycle. Finally, tenants with regular bursts in tenant activity (e.g., there are usually bursts near the end of a fiscal year) could be identified by Thrifty's regular activity monitoring and they would be excluded from consolidation before the bursts arrive.

We regard our approach as a reactive approach to maintain the SLA performance guarantee. A pessimistic approach is to use $A + 1$ MPPDBs upfront to serve a tenant group, which is not cost-effective. A proactive approach is to predict at run-time whether the RT-TTP will soon drop below P and proactively trigger lightweight elastic scaling if so. That approach, however, is subjected to prediction error and spikes (e.g, sharp drop of RT-TTP followed by sharp rise) in tenant activities.

6. MANUAL TUNING

The elastic scaling operation of Thrifty automatically adds a MPPDB to serve the over-active tenants when the RT-TTP of a tenant-group of the past 24 hours stays below the SLA performance guarantee P. That MPPDB will be there until the next re-consolidation cycle (to minimize the overhead of scaling up and down). A system administrator may override this action. Consider a performance SLA guarantee of 99.9%, and a tenant-group of tenants served by three 10-node MPPDBs ($A = R = 3$). If there is a minor increase of active tenant ratio of that group, resulting in a RT-TTP of, say, 99.8%, in the past 24 hours, and if a system administrator realizes from the Tenant Activity Monitor that the RT-TTP of

[3]That 43 minutes is only an optimistic estimate because some tenants should have already consumed some of that grace period before Thrifty takes action.

[4]For MPPDB products that support parallel data loading, we would enable that option.

that group is not continuously dropping but stays flat, she may think that Thrifty's elastic scaling that starts a new 10-node MPPDB for the over-active tenants is overkilling (because there is only 99.9%−99.8%=0.1% of tiny time percentage of possibly SLA violations).

In situations like this, the system administrator may instead use the parameter U to manually tune the performance SLA guarantee of that tenant-group. Recall that the tenant-driven design reserves a parameter U to control the number of nodes used by the $MPPDB_O$ (Section 3). In our example above, the system administrator may override Thrifty's elastic scaling but increase U from 10 to, say, 12. Recall that the query routing algorithm of Thrifty routes a query to $MPPDB_O$ if all MPPDBs are busy (Algorithm 1 Line 10). Whenever the 0.2% of time the fourth (or the fifth...) active tenant submits a query, that is routed to $MPPDB_O$ for concurrent processing. So, it is possible that the 99.9% SLAs can be met *empirically* by having a higher degree of parallelism and more computation power (U+2) in $MPPDB_O$ (like Point C in Figure 1b).

7. EVALUATION

Multi-tenancy is an important topic in cloud database research. However, due to privacy, tenant logs are seldom available to the public. In view of this, we begin by describing a methodology to create close-to-realistic multi-tenant DaaS tenant logs. Next, we study the consolidation effectiveness of Thrifty based on those generated tenants. Finally, we evaluate the lightweight elastic scaling feature of Thrifty.

7.1 Generation of Tenant Logs

The objective of this section is to describe a methodology to generate close-to-realistic MPPDBaaS tenant activity logs . The resulting logs are useful to validate the consolidation effectiveness of the two-step tenant grouping algorithm.

To imitate the realistic scenarios, the log generation process has two steps: (1) Real Query Log Collection and (2) Multi-Tenant Log Composition. In the first step, we imitate the activity of different kinds of tenants, submit queries to MPPDBs, and collect the corresponding real query logs from the MPPDBs. In the second step, we compose activity logs of a large number of tenants from those real query logs.

Step 1: Real Query Log Collection We use TPC-H and TPC-DS data and queries in this step. We use a commercial MPPDB product to create five MPPDB instances: 2-node, 4-node, 8-node, 16-node, 32-node. We assume a tenant has more data if it requests more nodes. A tenant may either hold TPC-H data or TPC-DS data (with equal probability). So, the 2-node, 4-node, 8-node, 16-node, and 32-node MPPDB instances respectively hold 200GB, 400GB, 800GB, 1.6TB and 3.2TB of TPC-H/TPC-DS data (each node gets a 100GB data partition).

We then imitate a tenant and submit queries to each MPPDB by following the procedure below: Each tenant has at most S autonomous users, where S is a random integer between 1 and 5. Each user follows a probability distribution P to carry out the following: (a) either submit a random TPC-H/DS query to a MPPDB, or (b) submit a batch of M random TPC-H/DS queries to a MPPDB, where M is a random integer between 1 and 10. The user will not take any action until the single query (for (a)) or the query batch (for (b)) is complete. A batch of queries is complete only when all its submitted queries have finished. After the completion of a query/query batch, a user will pause for W seconds before the next event takes place, where W is a random integer from 3 to 600. We have repeated the above procedure 100 times. Each time the above procedure is carried out for 3 hours, on the 2-node, 4-node, 8-node, 16-node, and 32-node MPPDBs, using a uniform distribution as P. The query logs of the above executions are collected. Each query log collected is essentially a 3-hour real query log of an artificial tenant, which requests, say, a 16-node MPPDB with a maximum of 4 active users.

Step 2: Multi-Tenant Log Composition There are two inputs in this step: (i) the total number of tenants T; and (ii) the skewness of the tenant size distribution. The skewness of the tenant size is chosen by sampling from the CDF of a Zipf distribution with a parameter $0 < \theta < 1$, where a smaller θ tends to uniform whereas a larger θ tends to skew. The default θ is 0.8.[5] An example input in this step looks like Figure 6, where $T = 5400$ but the tenant can only request 2/4/8/16/32-node MPPDB instances because we have only prepared those in Step (1).

Given the tenant characteristics, the next step is to generate the tenant activity log of each tenant. We illustrate this by giving an example of generating a one-day activity log of a tenant that requests a 4-node MPPDB instance. In the beginning, the tenant first gets a random time offset O from the following:

Offset O	$+0$	$+3$	$+5$	$+8$	$+16$	$+17$	$+19$
Example	Seattle	New York	Sao Paulo	London	Beijing	Japan	Sydney

Next, the tenant randomly picks a 4-node 3-hour query log from the logs prepared in Step 1, and copies that into its activity log but with the time offset O added. That offset is used to imitate the start of the office hour of that tenant in a particular time zone. After that, the tenant randomly picks another 4-node 3-hour query log from the logs prepared in Step 1, and copies into its activity log but with the time offset $O + 3 + 2$ added. That offset is used to imitate the start of the afternoon office hour after three hours of morning office hour plus two hours of lunch. Finally, the tenant randomly picks yet another 3-hour query log, and copies into its activity log but with the time offset $O + 3 + 2 + 9$ added. That offset is used to imitate some report generation activities scheduled 6 hours after the office hour and some queries posed by users in remote offices (in different time zones).

We generate 30-day query activities for each tenant. In each week, each tenant is active for five (week)days and then inactive two days (for the weekend). Within the 30 days, each tenant is inactive in two weekdays to imitate two days of public holiday. That two days are randomly chosen, but they are the same for the tenants in the same time zone.

7.2 Experimental Setting

All the experiments are done on Amazon EC2 Extra Large Instance (15 GB memory and 8 EC2 Compute Units) running a commercial MPPDB on Linux. We follow the physical design suggested by the accompanied tuning advisor of the MPPDB to do the partitioning and create the indexes. The MPPDB product we used supports parallel loading, so we enable that option. Thrifty is implemented using Python and we use $U = n_1$.

7.3 Consolidation Effectiveness under Different Tenant Characteristics

This first set of simulation experiments is to evaluate the consolidation effectiveness of our two-step tenant-grouping algorithm under different tenant characteristics. The consolidation effectiveness is measured as the percentage of nodes saved. For example,

[5]According to [11], the database sizes (measured in terms of amount of data) of different companies follow a skew distribution. Among the parallel database user community, a company tends to determine the number of nodes based on the data size. So, the tenant size also follows a skew distribution.

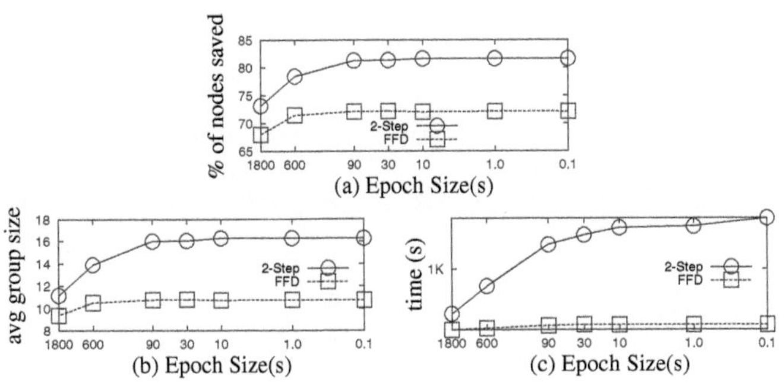

Figure 8: Varying Epoch Size E

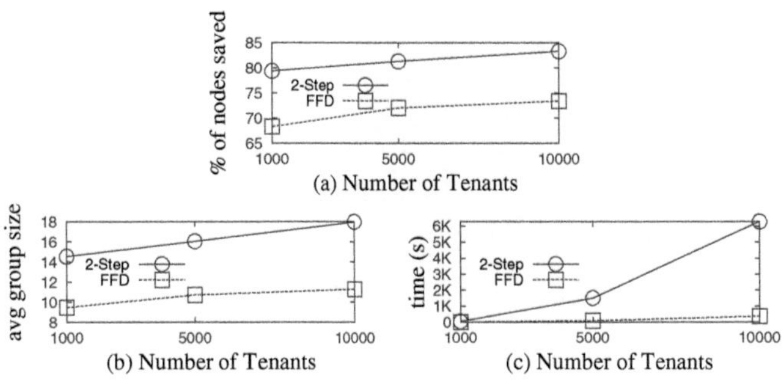

Figure 9: Varying Number of Tenants T

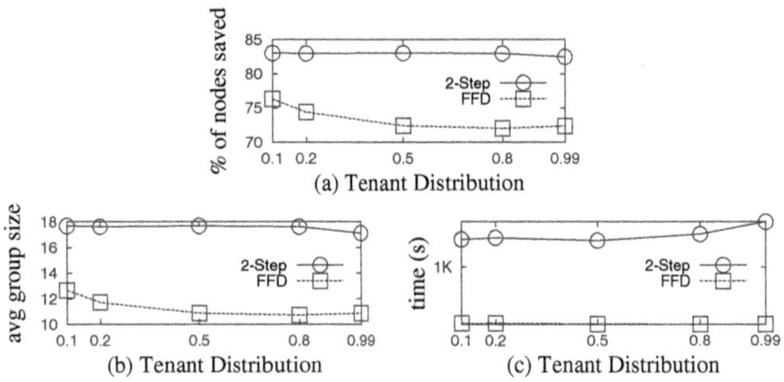

Figure 10: Varying Tenant Distribution θ

a 80% consolidation effectiveness means that if the tenants all together request 10000 machine nodes, Thrifty can serve all of them using 2000 nodes only, meaning 8000 machine nodes are saved.

Table 2 shows the parameters we varied in this part of experiments. The default values are in bold face. The generated logs according to these parameters have average active tenant ratios range from 8.9% to 12%, which is close to the real 10% in DaaS [20]. The active tenant ratio under the default parameter value is 11.9%. We have implemented an optimal tenant-grouping solution based on solving the MINLP formulation (Appendix A) using DIRECT [14] but it has taken about 12 days to compute the optimal solution for only 20 tenants. Therefore, we only compare with the FFD heuristic. In our experiments, our 2-step heuristic algorithm always generates better deployment plans by saving 3.6% to 11.1% more nodes than FFD.

Parameter	Ranges
Epoch Size (E)	0.1s, 1s, **10s**, 30s, 90s, 600s, 1800s
Number of Tenants (T)	1000, **5000**, 10000
Tenant Distribution (θ)	0.1, 0.2, 0.5 **0.8**, 0.99
Replication Factor (R)	1, 2, **3**, 4
Performance SLA (P)	95%, 99% **99.9%**, 99.99%

Table 2: Evaluation Parameters

Varying Epoch Size Recall from Section 4 that the consolidation effectiveness of Thrifty is influenced by the choice of epoch size E in the tenant-grouping algorithm. This experiment is to evaluate the influence of that parameter and let us choose a suitable one for the rest of the experiments. Figure 8a shows the consolidation effectiveness of Thrifty under different choices of E. When the epoch size is large, 1800s, the consolidation effectiveness of FFD and our 2-step heuristic are about 68.0% and 73.1%, respectively. The consolidation effectiveness increases with the use of smaller epoch size. For our 2-step heuristic, the consolidation effectiveness is high up to 81.5% when a 10s epoch size is used, where smaller epoch size does not yield further improvement. Figure 8c shows the execution time of running FFD and our 2-step heuristic algorithms. FFD is efficient because it just spends $\mathcal{O}(T \log T)$ time to sort the tenants. Although slower, our 2-step heuristic algorithm consistently generates deployment plans that save 5.1% to 9.4% more nodes than FFD over all epoch sizes and it finishes in 30 minutes even with the finest 0.1s epoch size is used. So, we adopt 10s as the default epoch size. Figure 8b shows the average size of the resulting tenant-groups. Tenant-groups formed by our 2-step heuristic algorithm can pack more tenants than FFD.

Varying Number of Tenants Figure 9a shows that Thrifty's consolidation effectiveness is not significantly influenced by the number of tenants. When the number of tenants increases from 1000 to 10000, consolidation effectiveness of our 2-step heuristic is increased from 79.3% to 83.3% The minor increase is brought by giving more choices to the algorithm to pick when inserting a tenant into a tenant-group. Figure 9b supports the observation by showing that the average tenant-group size also slightly increases with the number of tenants. Figure 9c shows that the execution time of our 2-step heuristics algorithm. Overall, our 2-step heuristic spends about two hours to find a deployment plan that saves 83.3% of nodes for 10000 tenants. In contrast, although the FFD heuristic spends only about 6 minutes, it finds a deployment plan that can only save 73.4% of nodes for 10000 tenants.

Varying Tenant Distribution Figure 10a shows that the consolidation effectiveness of our 2-step heuristic is not influenced by the tenant distribution as significant as FFD does. Figure 10b supports the observation. Figure 10c shows that the tenant distribution has a small influence on running time of the 2-step heuristic, because the second step of our heuristic scans the list of tenants once per insertion of a tenant into a tenant-group and thus an initial group with more tenants takes more time to finish the grouping.

Varying Replication Factor This experiment is to evaluate the consolidation effectiveness under different replication factors R. As one of the considerations of our two-step tenant-group algorithm is to ensure that the maximum number of active tenants in the resulting tenant-group does not exceed R for $P\%$ of time, a higher replication factor would put more tenants into a tenant-group. Figure 11b shows that the average tenant-group size of 2-step heuristic is increased from 4.7 to 22.2 , when R is increased from 1 to 4. Figure 11a shows that 2-step's consolidation effectiveness is increased from 78.8% to 82.0% accordingly. The increase of consolidation effectiveness is not as significant as the increase of the average tenant-group size because when R is 4, more machines are used, and that waters down the number of machines saved. Figure 11c shows that the running time of our 2-step heuristic increases with

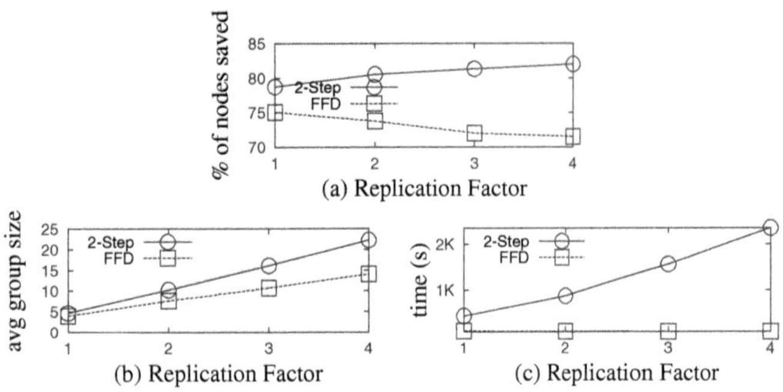

(a) Replication Factor
(b) Replication Factor
(c) Replication Factor

Figure 11: Varying Replication Factor R

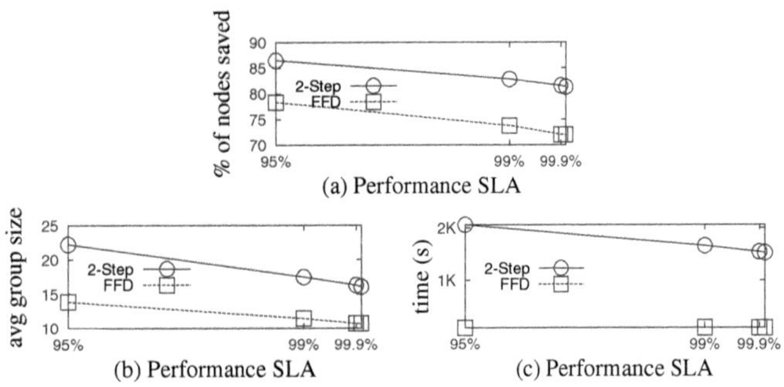

(a) Performance SLA
(b) Performance SLA
(c) Performance SLA

Figure 12: Varying Performance SLA P

R because more tenants can be tried when inserting a tenant into a tenant-group.

Varying Performance SLA guarantee This experiment is to evaluate the consolidation effectiveness under different performance SLA guarantees. Figure 12a shows that the consolidation effectiveness of our 2-step heuristic can be as high as 86.5% if only a 95% performance guarantee is required, and it drops back to 81.6% and 81.3%, respectively, when more stringent performance SLA guarantees, 99.9% and 99.99%, are required. The experimental results show that 99.9% is stringent enough such that an even more stringent performance SLA guarantee of 99.99% does not reduce the consolidation effectiveness further. When the performance guarantee is not so stringent (95%), Figure 12b shows that both heuristics can pack more tenants into the same tenant group, and Figure 12c shows that our 2-step heuristics has a higher running time than FFD because more tenants can be tried to be inserted into a tenant-group.

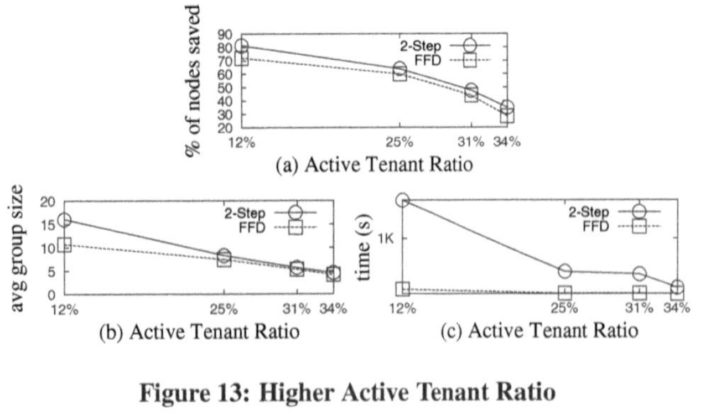

(a) Active Tenant Ratio
(b) Active Tenant Ratio
(c) Active Tenant Ratio

Figure 13: Higher Active Tenant Ratio

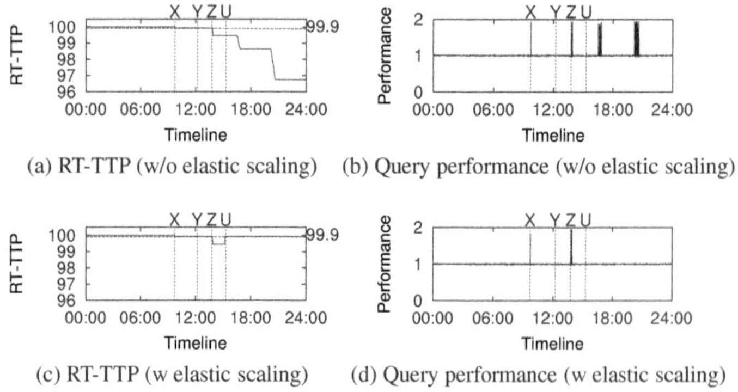

(a) RT-TTP (w/o elastic scaling) (b) Query performance (w/o elastic scaling)
(c) RT-TTP (w elastic scaling) (d) Query performance (w elastic scaling)

Figure 14: Lightweight Elastic Scaling in a Tenant Group

7.4 Consolidation Effectiveness under Higher Active Tenant Ratio

This second set of experiments is mainly used to get a feeling of the consolidation effectiveness under some unusual scenarios where the active tenant ratio is much higher than 10%. We generate tenant logs that with higher active tenant ratios by using the default parameter values listed in Table 2 but with the following modifications in Step 2 (Multi-Tenant Log Composition) of the log generation process:

	Modification Made & Meaning	Resulting Active Tenant Ratio
	-	11.9%
(1)	Tenants get either +0 or +3 offsets only (imitating tenants are all from North America)	25.1%
(2)	Tenants of (1) but with no lunch hour	30.7%
(3)	All tenants get the same +0 offset (imitating tenants are all from the west coast) and with no lunch hour	34.4%

Figure 13a shows the consolidation effectiveness of our 2-step heuristic algorithm drops from 81.3% to 34.8% when the active tenant ratio increases from 11.9% to 34.4%. That makes sense because when the history shows that many tenants have been very active, the tenant-grouping algorithm cannot put many tenants into the same tenant group. When the active tenant ratio is high up to 34.4%, Figure 13b shows that a tenant-group can contain only five tenants on average. In this experiment, $R = 3$, so it means Thrifty has to use three MPPDBs to serve five tenants and thus only nodes requested by two tenants could be saved, resulting in a 34.8% consolidation effectiveness.

Generally the active tenant ratio in a realistic DaaS has active tenant ratio as low as 10% [20]. For tenants that have high active tenant ratio, as mentioned, Thrifty could detect them easily and exclude them from consolidation. Even when the active tenant ratio is high up to 30.7% and 34.4%, respectively, our 2-step heuristic can still save 47.6% and 34.8% of the requested nodes, and not to forget that includes three replicas for each tenant as a high availability service.

7.5 Lightweight Elastic Scaling

In this section, we aim to take a look at how Thrifty's lightweight elastic scaling takes action in practice. We choose to present some real production information about a tenant-group generated from the previous tenant-grouping experiment that uses the default values (Table 2). That tenant-group consists of 14 tenants that request 4-node MPPDBs ($R = 3$; deploy on EC2 clusters). Figure 14a shows an excerpt of run-time tenant-activities of that tenant-group with Thrifty's elastic scaling disabled. In the beginning of the excerpt, the RT-TTP of that tenant-group is 100%, meaning there were at most three active tenants in the past 24 hours. At time X, the RT-TTP of that tenant-group slightly dropped to 99.92%. We checked the query log and found that there was once a fourth tenant active and $MPPDB_0$ had concurrently processed two queries for a very short duration. Figure 14b shows the corresponding excerpt of the performance of queries in Thrifty. The performance is normalized, so 1.0 means a query has finished execution as quick as it should be when measured in an isolated environment. A performance, say, 1.2 means a query has finished execution 1.2 time slower than it should be when measured in an isolated environment. At time X where there were two queries concurrently processed by $MPPDB_0$, that two queries respectively obtained 50% and 80% query latency delay. However, that was the first such event in the past 24 hours and the duration of that event was short. Thus no elastic scaling took place — this showcases how Thrifty's reactive scaling approach can deal with some one-off spikes.

In order to study the effect of Thrifty's elastic scaling, we manually took over a tenant at time Y and continuously submitted queries to the system on behalf of that tenant. Figure 14c shows the run-time tenant-activities of that tenant-group with Thrifty's elastic scaling enabled. From time Y to time Z, only two tenants were active concurrently and thus nothing happened even though we were submitting queries continuously as being the third tenant. At time Z, three other tenants became concurrently active and this time the tenant-group had accumulated more than 0.1% of time more than three active tenants in the past 24 hours. Therefore, Thrifty carried out elastic scaling. Thrifty took about 2 seconds to identify the over-active tenant and it spent about 5000 seconds to load the data of the over-active tenant. At time U, the new MPPDB was ready. Since then, Thrifty routed all our queries to the new MPPDB and the tenant-group excluded all the activities of the removed tenant. Therefore, the RT-TTP of that tenant group returned back to 99.9% and above. Figure 14d shows the corresponding excerpt of the performance of queries in Thrifty with elastic scaling enabled. As multiple queries were concurrently processed by $MPPDB_0$ at time Z, they exhibited performance delay. However, after scaling up, Thrifty had been able to deal with the subsequent over-active scenarios. In contrast, Figure 14b shows the expected scenarios where some subsequent queries cannot meet the performance SLA as we kept on submitting queries to the system while the elastic scaling option was disabled. These together showcases how Thrifty's elastic scaling approach can deal with over-active tenants that deviate from the history.

8. RELATED WORK

To the best of our knowledge, this is the first paper to discuss MPPDB-as-a-service and provide a real implementation to support the stringent query-latency SLA for parallel analytical workloads.[6]

DaaS There are several approaches to provide database-as-a-service [13]: (1) The VM approach, (2) the Shared Table Approach, and (3) the Shared Process Approach.

(1) The VM approach is to pack each individual tenant's database instance into a virtual machine (VM) and multiple VMs on a single physical machine [24]. The VM approach achieves hard isolation. Therefore, the performance SLA of individual tenants could be easily maintained. However, this approach incurs significant redundancy among the tenants (e.g., multiple copies of the OS and DBMS) and thus [7] states that it is not cost-effective for DaaS.

(2) The Shared Table approach is to share a single database instance and *the same set of tables among all tenants*. This approach requires the tenants' schemas are mostly identical or similar, which is common in software-as-a-service (e.g., Salesforce.com) with database as the backend. The Shared Table approach can largely reduce the redundancy and thus thousands of small (data size) and mostly inactive tenants can be packed onto a single server [3, 22, 12]. This approach is orthogonal to our work, as our tenants are autonomous and tenants' schemas are typically different.

(3) The Shared Process approach is to share a single database instance among the tenants but each tenant can own its private set of tables. This approach achieves a much higher consolidation effectiveness than the VM approach and and it supports autonomous tenants with arbitrary schemas. MIT's Relational Cloud [8] is based on this approach. It includes a consolidation engine, Kairos [7], to consolidate many *centralized OLTP databases* on to a shared hardware infrastructure. The SLA of consolidating OLTP workloads in Kairos is the database throughput before-and-after consolidation.

Thrifty uses the Shared Process approach in order to attain a higher consolidation effectiveness. Different from Relational Cloud [8], our tenants (a) request multiple-node MPPDBs and (b) issue analytical workloads. The former requires a skillful cluster design that arranges the nodes in the cluster into groups of MPPDBs and a corresponding tenant placement scheme that assign a tenant to R different MPPDBs. That is not an issue in Relational Cloud for which tenants hosts only a single centralized database. The latter makes the consolidation concerns and methodology of Thrifty different from Relational Cloud: as mentioned, OLTP workloads generally touch a small amount of data per transaction. So the same database instance could still support a large number of concurrent query executions from different tenants after consolidation. Therefore, the consolidation concerns of Relational Cloud are (i) how to estimate the resource (e.g., CPU, RAM) of each OLTP-workload and (ii) how to compute the aggregated resource consumptions of multiple workloads. In contrast, analytical workloads are mostly I/O intensive, so any concurrent query execution on the same database instance would easily increase the query latency and cause SLA violation (see Points E and F in Figure 1). Therefore, our consolidation concern is how to avoid concurrent query execution when consolidating the tenants.

Parallel Databases In parallel databases, performance speedup is brought by partitioning the data across multiple machine nodes to maximize intra-query parallelism. Recent research related to parallel database mostly focuses on finding a good data partitioning strategy to minimize the overhead of shipping data across multiple nodes [17, 6]. Temporal access skew was also used by a recent NewSQL system to aid the data partitioning design [19]. In this paper we leverage temporal access skew, i.e., low active tenant ratio, to aid our cluster design to deal with the SLA guarantee problem caused by concurrent executions of analytical queries in a shared database process.

Optimization problems in cloud computing VM-based tenant placement is a hot topic in cloud computing [10, 15]. Yet, to the best our knowledge, these works have not considered any MPPDBaaS-specific requirements like query-latency performance SLA (R3) or requesting multiple nodes by a single tenant (R4). In this paper, after using TDD, we get a Largest Item Vector Bin Packing Problem with Fuzzy Capacity (LIVBPwFC), which a variant of the classic vector bin packing (VBP) problem. The VBP problem has been used to model many forms of VM placement problem recently [15]: a VM is represented by a *vector of resource demands* $\langle r_1, r_2, \ldots, r_d \rangle$ (each r_i denotes the demand of a particular resource, say, RAM) and a machine is represented by a *vector of resource capacity* $\langle c_1, c_2, \ldots, c_d \rangle$ (each c_i denotes the capacity of

[6]During the paper review process, Amazon has announced Redshift, which is a MPPDBaaS. Its underlying technology however is not publicly available.

a particular resource, say, RAM, of a node). As LIVBPwFC is new and more general than VBP, we devise new heuristics for that.

Elastic resource scaling in cloud computing Finally, substantial research in cloud computing has looked at the problem of elastic resource scaling (e.g., [23]). Thrifty follows those reactive approaches with the unique challenges that the scaling of MPPDB is a heavyweight operation, comparing with the elastic scaling of hardware resources like the memory allocated to a virtual machine.

9. FUTURE WORK AND CONCLUSION

In this paper, we present Thrifty, a prototype that offers massively parallel processing relational database system as a service (MPPDBaaS). The technologies associated with Thrifty include the cluster design that details the arrangement of thousands of machines nodes to form MPPDBs of different degree of parallelism, the tenant-placement that details the tenant-to-MPPDB assignment, the query routing algorithm that routes tenant queries to a proper MPPDB for processing, the implementation of elastic scaling, and the system tuning methodologies. Experimental results show that Thrifty can save around 73.1% to 86.5% of nodes in a wide range of usual settings.

Thrifty is currently a research prototype and there are a lot of interesting future work. First, Thrifty currently assumes the machine nodes in the cluster are homogeneous, extending Thrifty to deal with a cluster of heterogeneous machines is thus an important yet challenging task. Second, data privacy is an important issue in DaaS. Fortunately, privacy-aware query processing techniques have no significant difference between centralized databases and parallel databases. We plan to incorporate techniques like adjustable security (e.g., [7]) into Thrifty. Third, currently Thrifty targets a very general setting where some tenants may submit ad-hoc queries. Our plan is to separate the tenants in Thrifty into two classes in the future, where tenants that would not submit ad-hoc queries (e.g., those only run reporting generation applications and agree to let us extract their query templates) are treated as a special class (they will get another service plan). For tenants in that class, we will host them using a specialized tenant-driven divergent design that uses $U > n_1$ nodes for MPPDB_0 *upfront* and use different partition schemes for different MPPDBs [6] in order to deal with the non-linear scale-out problem. That would be a special case of our tenant-driven design. Although only applicable to a restricted type of tenants, that design would incur fewer elastic scalings and with a higher consolidation effectiveness. The crux of that specialized design is to identify the minimum value of U that can afford different degrees of concurrent query processing on MPPDB_0 without performance SLA violations, which requires extending concurrent workload performance prediction techniques to parallel databases.

Acknowledgement We thank Ben Kao, Andrew Lamb, and the anonymous reviewers for their valuable comments. This work is partly supported by the Research Grants Council of Hong Kong (GRF PolyU 525009 and 521012).

10. REFERENCES

[1] M. Ahmad, S. Duan, A. Aboulnaga, and S. Babu. Predicting completion times of batch query workloads using interaction-aware models and simulation. In *EDBT*, pages 449–460, 2011.

[2] M. Akdere, U. Ćetintemel, M. Riondato, E. Upfal, and S. Zdonik. Learning-based query performance modeling and prediction. In *ICDE*, pages 390 – 401, 2012.

[3] S. Aulbach, T. Grust, D. Jacobs, A. Kemper, and J. Rittinger. Multi-tenant databases for software as a service: schema-mapping techniques. In *SIGMOD*, pages 1195–1206, 2008.

[4] P. A. Bernstein, I. Cseri, N. Dani, N. Ellis, A. Kalhan, G. Kakivaya, D. B. Lomet, R. Manne, L. Novik, and T. Talius. Adapting Microsoft SQL server for cloud computing. In *ICDE*, pages 1255–1263, 2011.

[5] Y. Chen, S. Alspaugh, and R. H. Katz. Interactive analytical processing in big data systems: A cross-industry study of mapreduce workloads. *PVLDB*, 5(12):1802–1813, 2012.

[6] M. P. Consens, K. Ioannidou, J. LeFevre, and N. Polyzotis. Divergent physical design tuning for replicated databases. In *SIGMOD*, pages 49–60, 2012.

[7] C. Curino, E. P. C. Jones, S. Madden, and H. Balakrishnan. Workload-aware database monitoring and consolidation. In *SIGMOD*, pages 313–324, 2011.

[8] C. Curino, E. P. C. Jones, R. A. Popa, N. Malviya, E. Wu, S. Madden, H. Balakrishnan, and N. Zeldovich. Relational cloud: a database service for the cloud. In *CIDR*, pages 235–240, 2011.

[9] J. Duggan, U. Ćetintemel, O. Papaemmanouil, and E. Upfal. Performance prediction for concurrent database workloads. In *SIGMOD*, pages 337–348, 2011.

[10] D. Gmach, J. Rolia, L. Cherkasova, G. Belrose, T. Turicchi, and A. Kemper. An integrated approach to resource pool management: Policies, efficiency and quality metrics. In *DSN*, pages 326 –335, 2008.

[11] J. Gray, P. Sundaresan, S. Englert, K. Baclawski, and P. J. Weinberger. Quickly generating billion-record synthetic databases. In *SIGMOD*, pages 243–252, 1994.

[12] M. Hui, D. Jiang, G. Li, and Y. Zhou. Supporting database applications as a service. In *ICDE*, pages 832 –843, 2009.

[13] D. Jacobs and S. Aulbach. Ruminations on multi-tenant databases. In *BTW Proceedings*, pages 514–521, 2007.

[14] D. R. Jones. Direct global optimization algorithm. *Encyclopedia of Optimization*, pages 725–735, 2009.

[15] S. Lee, R. Panigrahy, V. Prabhakaran, V. Ramasubramanian, K. Talwar, L. Uyeda, and U. Wieder. Validating heuristics for virtual machines consolidation. In *Microsoft Research Technical Report*, 2011.

[16] G. Luo, J. F. Naughton, and P. S. Yu. Multi-query SQL progress indicators. In *EDBT*, pages 921–941. Springer, 2006.

[17] R. V. Nehme and N. Bruno. Automated partitioning design in parallel database systems. In *SIGMOD*, pages 1137–1148, 2011.

[18] R. Panigrahy, K. Talwar, L. Uyeda, and U. Wieder. Heuristics for vector bin packing. In *Microsoft Research Technical Report*, 2011.

[19] A. Pavlo, C. Curino, and S. Zdonik. Skew-aware automatic database partitioning in shared-nothing, parallel OLTP systems. In *SIGMOD*, pages 61–72, 2012.

[20] B. Reinwald. Multitenancy. *University of Washington and Microsoft Research Summer Institute*, 2010.

[21] J. Schaffner, B. Eckart, D. Jacobs, C. Schwarz, H. Plattner, and A. Zeier. Predicting in-memory database performance for automating cluster management tasks. In *ICDE*, pages 1264 –1275, 2011.

[22] O. Schiller, B. Schiller, A. Brodt, and B. Mitschang. Native support of multi-tenancy in RDBMS for software as a service. In *EDBT*, pages 117–128, 2011.

[23] Z. Shen, S. Subbiah, X. Gu, and J. Wilkes. Cloudscale: elastic resource scaling for multi-tenant cloud systems. In *SOCC*, pages 5:1–5:14, 2011.

[24] A. A. Soror, U. F. Minhas, A. Aboulnaga, K. Salem, P. Kokosielis, and S. Kamath. Automatic virtual machine configuration for database workloads. *ACM TODS*, 35(1), 2010.

APPENDIX

A. FORMULATION OF THE LIVBPWFC

$$\text{Minimize} \quad \sum_{j=1}^{\lceil \frac{T}{R} \rceil} \max_i (R * n_i * x_{ij}) \quad (1)$$

$$\text{Subject to} \quad \sum_{k=1}^{d} H[R - \sum_{i=1}^{T} \vec{A}_i[k] * x_{ij}] \geq P\% * d, \forall j \quad (2)$$

$$\sum_{j=1}^{\lceil \frac{T}{R} \rceil} x_{ij} = 1, \forall i \quad (3)$$

$$x_{ij} \in \{0, 1\}, \forall i, \forall j \quad (4)$$

where $i \in [1, \cdots, T], j \in [1, \cdots, \lceil \frac{T}{R} \rceil]$ and $H[n]$ is the discretization format of the *Heaviside step function*:

$$H[n] = \begin{cases} 0, & \text{if } n < 0, \\ 1, & \text{otherwise.} \end{cases}$$

Variable $x_{ij} = 1$ if tenant T_i is packed to tenant-group TG_j or $x_{ij} = 0$ otherwise.

Objective function: There are T tenants. Each tenant-group has R replicas and can support R concurrently active tenants. So, there are at most $\lceil \frac{T}{R} \rceil$ tenant-groups. Each tenant-group TG_j requires $R * n_i$ machines, where i is the largest tenant that requests the most nodes in that tenant-group.

MESSIAH: Missing Element-Conscious SLCA Nodes Search in XML Data

Ba Quan Truong[§] Sourav S Bhowmick[§] Curtis Dyreson[†] Aixin Sun[§]
[§]School of Computer Engineering, Nanyang Technological University, Singapore
[†]Department of Computer Science, Utah State University, USA
bqtruong|assourav|axsun@ntu.edu.sg, curtis.dyreson@usu.edu

ABSTRACT

Keyword search for smallest lowest common ancestors (SLCAs) in XML data has been widely accepted as a meaningful way to identify matching nodes where their subtrees contain an input set of keywords. Although SLCA and its variants (*e.g.,*MLCA) perform admirably in identifying matching nodes, surprisingly, they perform poorly for searches on *irregular schemas* that have *missing elements*, that is, (sub)elements that are optional, or appear in some instances of an element type but not all (*e.g.,* a <population> subelement in a <city> element might be optional, appearing when the population is known and absent when the population is unknown). In this paper, we generalize the SLCA search paradigm to support queries involving missing elements. Specifically, we propose a novel property called *optionality resilience* that specifies the desired behaviors of an XML keyword search (XKS) approach for queries involving missing elements. We present two variants of a novel algorithm called MESSIAH (**M**issing **E**lement-con**S**ciou**S** h**I**gh-quality **SLCA** searc**H**), which are optionality resilient to irregular documents. MESSIAH *logically* transforms an XML document to a *minimal full document* where all missing elements are represented as empty elements, *i.e.,* the irregular schema is made "regular", and then employs efficient strategies to identify *partial* and *complete full* SLCA nodes (SLCA nodes in the full document) from it. Specifically, it generates the same SLCA nodes as any state-of-the-art approach when the query does not involve missing elements but avoids irrelevant results when missing elements are involved. Our experimental study demonstrates the ability of MESSIAH to produce superior quality search results.

Categories and Subject Descriptors

H.2.4 [**Database Management**]: Systems - Query processing

General Terms

Algorithms, Experimentation, Performance

Keywords

XML keyword search, missing elements, optionality resilience, full SLCA

Dataset	Number of Labels	Missing Label Ratio
Mondial	70	64.3%
SIGMOD	12	0%
DBLP	41	68.3%
Uniprot	94	72.3%
PDB	267	1.12%
Interpro	68	41.1%
Shakespeare	22	40.9%

Figure 1: Missing label ratio on different datasets.

1. INTRODUCTION

Keyword search on XML data (XKS) has gained popularity as it relieves users from learning complex XML query languages (*e.g.,* XPath, XQuery) and from having to know the structure of underlying data. However, the lack of expressivity and inherent ambiguity bring in two key challenges in performing XKS [9]. First, we need to automatically connect the nodes that match the search keywords in an intuitive, meaningful way. Second, we should effectively identify the desired return information. Specifically, the first challenge involves finding some nodes (*e.g.,* SLCA nodes) whose subtrees contain all matching nodes [2,8,17] while the second challenge focuses on filtering nodes within these subtrees to produce relevant and coherent results [1,4,7,9,10]. In this paper, we focus on the first challenge.

The *smallest lowest common ancestor* (SLCA) [17] is arguably the most popular technique for locating highly-related data nodes and has become the foundation for many recent XKS approaches [1, 4, 7, 9, 10]. A keyword search using the SLCA semantics returns nodes in the XML tree that satisfy the following two conditions: (a) the subtrees rooted at the nodes contain all the keywords, and (b) the nodes do not have any proper descendant that satisfies condition (a). The set of returned data nodes is referred to as the SLCAs of the keyword search query. For example, the only SLCA node satisfying the query Q_1 (Provo area) on the XML document D_2 in Figure 2(a) is the node with ID 0.4.3 (for brevity, in the sequel we will use n_{id} to denote a node with ID id). Figure 3(a)(i) shows the SLCA node $n_{0.4.3}$ (shaded) along with its matches to all Q_1's keywords.

1.1 A Problem with SLCA

Nested, tagged elements are the building blocks of XML. Each tagged element has a sequence of zero or more attribute/value pairs, and a sequence of zero or more subelements. An implication of this "relaxed" structure of XML data is that a subelement may appear in one nested substructure of an XML document but not in another "similar" substructure. For example, consider the XML document D_1 in Figure 2(a). Notice that although the area element ap-

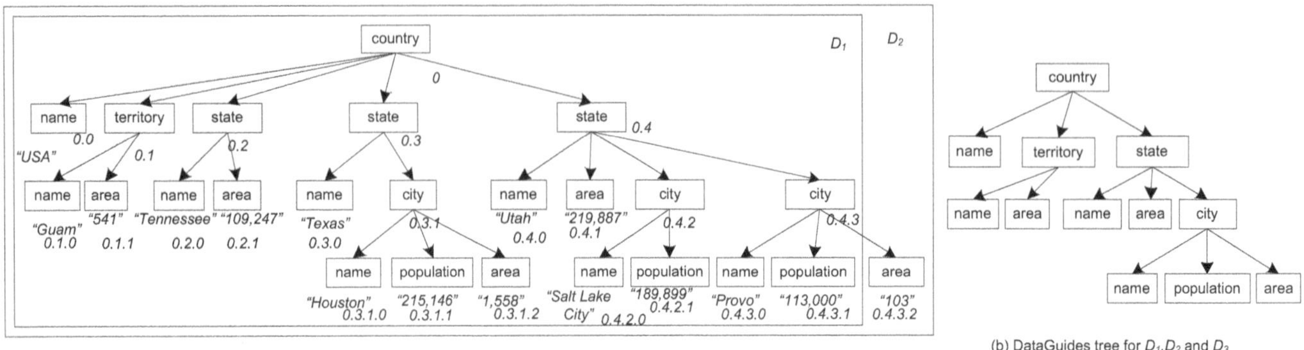

(a) Sample Documents

(b) DataGuides tree for D_1, D_2 and D_3

Figure 2: Sample XML documents D_1 and D_2 (D_2 contains all the nodes of D_1 and an additional `area` element (rightmost node)) and their DataGuide.

pears in the first `city` substructure, it is missing in the last two substructures.

There can be many reasons for such missing elements. For instance, a specific entity may not have an element (as an attribute) as it is meaningless in this context (*e.g.*, the `spouse` attribute of a `person` entity who is single is meaningless). Elements may also be missing due to incompleteness of data or human error. Whatever may be the semantics of a missing (or optional) element in a specific context, we refer to this scenario collectively as the *missing element*[1] phenomenon and the label of the missing element (*e.g.*, `area`) a *missing label.* Note that "missing element" covers the "missing attribute" scenario as well. Furthermore, the missing element could contain subelements that are also missing, *i.e.*, it could be a missing subtree in a data model instance. Note that in XML documents it is not mandatory to explicitly mark such missing data using *empty elements* (*i.e.*, `<tag></tag>` or `<tag/>`) or *empty attributes* (*i.e.*, `tag=""`)).

Is the missing element phenomenon prevalent in real XML documents? Interestingly, our initial investigation with several popular real-world XML datasets reveal that it is indeed so. Figure 1 shows a glimpse of this phenomenon. The third column shows the *missing label ratio*, which is the ratio between the number of missing labels and the number of unique labels in a specific dataset. Notice that in all but one of the datasets more than 40% of the labels are missing labels. Hence, it is highly possible for users' queries to involve missing elements. However, it is unrealistic to expect the users to be aware of elements which may be missing. Hence, it is imperative for the underlying XKS engine to handle this phenomenon appropriately.

Surprisingly, SLCA-based XML keyword search (XKS) techniques perform poorly in the presence of the missing element phenomenon. Specifically, the quality of SLCA nodes is adversely affected when a keyword query contains a missing label. For instance, for Q_1 on D_1, $n_{0.4}$ is selected as the SLCA node by [14, 17] as shown in Figure 3(a)(ii). However, $n_{0.4.1}$ is not a relevant match as it is not `Provo`'s area and does not conform to the user's search intention in Q_1. That is, selecting $n_{0.4}$ as an SLCA node would produce a result subtree containing irrelevant data.

At first glance, an advocate of classical SLCA computation techniques may argue that the selection of $n_{0.4}$ as an SLCA node may be considered relevant and meaningful if we accept that it gives an "approximation" of the desired result. However, we argue that such approximation is often irrelevant to the search intention. To illustrate this point further, let us consider the query Q_M (`York latitude`) on the *Mondial* dataset. One of the cities containing the keyword `York` but without latitude information is `York` city in the UK. For this result, SLCA-based approaches [14, 17] will return the `country` node of the UK which contains *all* cities in the UK. Observe that this result has two core drawbacks. First, it is too broad. There are nearly 100 cities of the UK in the dataset and it is unrealistic to expect users to explore all of them to find desired results. Second, it does not provide a precise or direct answer to the query and user's search intention. Since Q_M is specifically about `York`'s latitude information, retrieving "approximate" results containing many irrelevant data without answering the question directly may annoy users. Note that the core reason for such poor performance is that most XKS techniques consider matches "close" to each other as relevant but when the most relevant matches (*e.g.*, $n_{0.4.3.2}$ or `York`'s latitude) are missing, even the closest one may be irrelevant.

It may also seem that approaches built on top of SLCA nodes that effectively identify the desired return information (*e.g.*, [1, 4, 7, 9, 10]) can address the above limitation. Although these efforts certainly improve the result quality, when querying in the presence of missing elements, they make the same assumptions as SLCA-based techniques and cannot improve the poor input from [14, 17] significantly. In fact, for Q_1 on D_1, these techniques produce the same result as [14, 17].

1.2 Challenges

A straightforward approach to address the aforementioned limitation is to first modify the XML document by adding *empty* elements (`<tag/>`) to *represent missing* elements and then adopt an existing technique (*e.g.*, [17]) to find SLCA nodes. We refer to such a modified XML document as a *full document.* The intuition being that if there is no missing element in the full document, the aforementioned problem does not occur. For example, document D_3 in Figure 3(b) is a full document of D_1 in which all missing elements are represented by empty elements (depicted by a dotted box). For instance, the `area` node for `Provo`, which is missing in D_1, is now shown in D_3 using an empty `area` element. Clearly, an existing SLCA-based XKS can now find high quality SLCA nodes in the full document. For instance, Figure 3(a)(iii) shows the SLCA node $n_{0.4.3}$ (and all of its matches) for Q_1 on D_3. Notice that the irrelevant `area` node $n_{0.4.1}$ is no longer considered a match. The node $n_{0.4.3.2}$ is depicted in a dotted box to indicate that it is not originally in D_1.

Unfortunately, the aforementioned naïve solution to identify high quality SLCA nodes demands modification of the XML document which is usually undesirable in real-world applications. Firstly, an XML document may be accessed by multiple, heterogeneous appli-

[1] We adopt the "missing element" term from [13] where it refers to elements that are declared optional in the DTD.

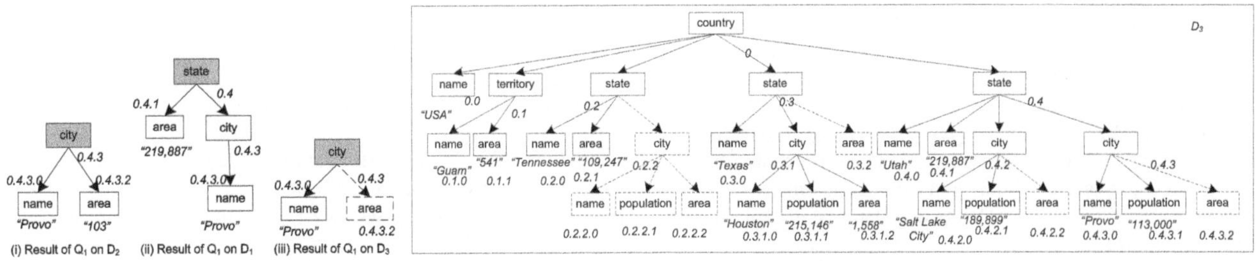

(a) Results of Q_1 (Provo area)

(b) Full document

Figure 3: Results of a keyword query and an example of full document.

cations such that altering it may have undesirable effect on some of these applications. Secondly, creating a copy of the existing document and adding empty elements to it will necessitate strict consistency checks, which is usually expensive to maintain especially for frequently updated documents. Thirdly, a full document version is not as space efficient as the original document, potentially affecting XML query performance. Fourthly, as mentioned earlier, an element may be missing in a document for various reasons. For instance, it may be meaningless for certain entities. Hence, explicitly adding it into these entities compromises data semantics. Lastly, often write permission of an XML document on the Web may not be available due to technical or legal reasons, making the aforementioned approach impractical. Furthermore, a direct consequence of such modification is the necessity of automatically pruning SLCA nodes in the full document which are empty elements. Otherwise, it may confuse end-users as they will not be able to locate some SLCA nodes when they browse the original XML document.

1.3 Contributions

Given a query Q on document D, how can we identify high-quality SLCA nodes in D that are also SLCAs in the full document version of D without physically creating the latter? In this paper, we address this core challenge. To the best of our knowledge, this is the first work that systematically addresses the SLCA computation problem germinated from the missing element phenomenon in XML data. More specifically, we make the following contributions.

- In Section 3, we propose a novel property called *optionality resilience* that specifies the desired behaviors of an XKS approach for queries with missing elements. We analyze the optionality resilience of existing XKS approaches to systematically identify their limitations in handling the missing element phenomenon.
- In Section 4, we introduce the notion of *full* SLCA (FSLCA) that satisfies the optionality resilience property. *Full* SLCAs are SLCAs in the original document as well as in the full document version of it. Specifically, the set of FSLCA nodes is identical to SLCA nodes when the query does not contain missing elements but avoids irrelevant results when missing elements are involved. Hence, identifying FSLCA nodes in a document enables us to produce high-quality SLCA nodes even when the query involves missing elements.

  We introduce two variants of FSLCA nodes, namely *partial* and *complete* FSLCA, to give users flexibility in viewing results containing missing elements. *Complete* FSLCA does not return result nodes containing missing elements ($n_{0.4.3}$ in D_1 for Q_1). Alternatively, *partial* FSLCA returns result nodes with missing elements (*e.g.,* Figure 3(a)(iii)). In this representation the user is explicitly informed that the desired data is missing.
- In Section 5, we propose two variants of a novel algorithm called MESSIAH (**M**issing **E**lement-con**S**ciou**S** h**I**gh-quality **SLCA** searc**H**), that efficiently identifies sets of complete and partial FSLCA nodes for a given keyword query (possibly containing missing labels) on document D. An important feature of MESSIAH is that it *does not physically* add missing elements to D. Particularly, a full document is *logically* created with the sole goal of facilitating the generation of superior quality FSLCA nodes. Furthermore, MESSIAH can be integrated seamlessly with state-of-the-art techniques for retrieving relevant information (Step 2 of XKS) [1, 7, 9–11], potentially inheriting the strengths of these approaches.
- In Section 6, extensive experiments with real datasets are conducted to validate our solution's effectiveness, superiority, efficiency, and scalability. Specifically, we show that the quality of results generated by MESSIAH is identical to state-of-the-art SLCA computation techniques when the query does not contain missing labels. However, when the query contains missing labels then MESSIAH consistently generates superior quality results compared to these state-of-the-art techniques. Importantly, such superior result quality is achieved *without* any significant performance overhead of the proposed algorithms.

2. PRELIMINARIES

We model an XML document D as an ordered and node-labeled tree. Each node $n \in D$ is assigned two functions $\mathbb{L}(n)$ and $\mathbb{F}(n)$ returning n's label (*i.e.,* tag) and text value, respectively. A node n is called an **empty node (element)** when $\mathbb{F}(n)$ returns empty string. We use notation $n_1 \prec n_2$ to denote n_2 is a descendant of n_1. Each node $n \in D$ is assigned an identifier (ID), denoted as $id(n)$, satisfying the following condition: $\forall n_1, n_2 \in D$, $id(n_1) < id(n_2)$ iff n_1 precedes n_2 in document order. Note that the preorder attribute in containment encoding scheme [18] or Dewey number in Dewey encoding scheme [15] can be used as identifiers of nodes. Consistent with several existing XKS techniques, we also use Dewey numbers as node identifiers which enable fast LCA computation. The IDs of nodes in Figures 2(a) and 3(b) are their Dewey numbers in the corresponding documents.

Similar to [1, 7], we use prefix paths to indicate the **type** of a node. Two nodes are considered of the *same* type when they share the *same* prefix path. Using path as type enables us to use *DataGuide* [3] as type structure. A DataGuide $\mathbb{S}$ is a prefix tree representing all unique paths in D *i.e.,* each unique path p in D is represented in $\mathbb{S}$ by a node (referred to as *schema node*) whose root-to-node path is p. Hence, each schema node in $\mathbb{S}$ also corresponds to a type and the hierarchical relationship among schema nodes represents type relations. Specifically, a type t_2 is called a *child (descendant) type* of another type t_1 if t_2's corresponding schema node is a child (descendant) of t_1's schema node in $\mathbb{S}$. We shall use $t_1 \prec_{\mathbb{S}} t_2$ to denote t_2 is a *descendant type* of t_1. Notice the subscript $\mathbb{S}$ is added to indicate type relation on $\mathbb{S}$. For instance, Figure 2(b) depicts the DataGuide of document D_1 in which $t_{state} \prec_{\mathbb{S}} t_{city}$. We also denote $N_D(t)$ as the set of all nodes of type t. For example, $N_{D_1}(t_{state}) = \{n_{0.2}, n_{0.3}, n_{0.4}\}$. Note that it is not mandatory for an XML document to be accompanied by its DataGuide as it can be easily extracted from a "schemaless" document in linear time [3]. In fact, DataGuides have been exploited in research related to XKS [1,7,9].

Given a query $Q(w_1, \ldots, w_k)$, if a keyword w_i is contained in either $\mathbb{L}(n)$ or $\mathbb{F}(n)$ then the node n is called a **label match** or a **value match** to w_i, respectively. The sets of all label and value matches to w_i in D are denoted as $L_D(w_i)$ and $V_D(w_i)$, respectively. The set of all **matches** to w_i in D, $M_D(w_i)$, is equal to $L_D(w_i) \cup V_D(w_i)$. Notably, if a node is a label match to w_i then all nodes of the same type are also label matches to w_i. We call this type a **type match** to w_i whose set is denoted as $T_D(w_i)$. When the context is clear, we denote $V_D(w_i)$, $L_D(w_i)$, $M_D(w_i)$, $T_D(w_i)$ as V_i, L_i, M_i, T_i, respectively. For example, in D_1 (Figure 2(a)), $V_{D_1}(\texttt{city}) = \{n_{0.4.2.0}\}$, $L_{D_1}(\texttt{city}) = \{n_{0.3.1}, n_{0.4.2}, n_{0.4.3}\}$, $T_{D_1}(\texttt{city}) = \{t_{city}\}$.

Given a query $Q(w_1, \ldots, w_k)$, the XKS process can be broadly divided into two steps: (a) locating result nodes and (b) retrieving result matches [9]. The first step corresponds to selecting a set of **result nodes** $R(Q, D)$ from document D satisfying Q. For each result node $r \in R(Q, D)$, the second step retrieves a set of matches $S_D(r) \subseteq (M_D(w_1) \cap \cdots \cap M_D(w_k) \cap desc_D(r))$ where $desc_D(r)$ is the descendant set of r in D. In this paper, we focus on the first step.

As mentioned in Section 1, one of the most popular approaches to represent results nodes is SLCA [17]. Formally, for a query $Q(w_1 \ldots w_k)$ on a document D, let $lca(m_1, \ldots, m_k)$ be the LCA of k matches $m_1, \ldots, m_k$ and $LCA(Q, D) = \{lca(m_1, \ldots, m_k) | m_i \in M_k \forall i \in [1, k]\}$. Then, SLCA returns the result nodes $R(Q, D) = SLCA(Q, D) = \{n \in LCA(Q, D) | \nexists n' \in LCA(Q, D), n \prec n'\}$. Since each type corresponds to a schema node in $\mathbb{S}$, we extend the LCA and SLCA concepts to types as well. For instance, $lca_{\mathbb{S}}(t_{state/name}, t_{state/city}) = t_{state}$.

3. OPTIONALITY RESILIENCE

Optionality resilience describes the desired behaviors of an XKS system when handling the missing element phenomenon. Specifically, it captures how the query result changes when an optional node is missing from the document. In this section, we first identify two types of optionality resilience, namely *result resilience* and *match resilience*, corresponding to the two steps of XKS. Next, we analyze existing XKS approaches in terms of these two properties.

3.1 Result Resilience

In an XKS query, the relevance of a result depends on the search intention as well as result matches. Since users are rarely aware of the missing element phenomenon, missing nodes should not change the search intention (*i.e.,* an XKS system should not return new results that are irrelevant to the search intention). More specifically, a missing element may make an existing result irrelevant but should not add a new result. For example, consider the documents D_1 and D_2 where $n_{0.4.3.2}$ is the only node missing in D_1 but appears in D_2. Consider now the query Q_2 `(city, area)` on D_1 and D_2. The search intention is probably to find the areas of all cities. Hence, the results should include all `city` subtrees in the document with an `area` child (*e.g.,* $n_{0.3.1}$ and $n_{0.4.3}$ on D_2). However, when the `area` of $n_{0.4.3}$ is missing as in D_1, the corresponding `area` subtree becomes irrelevant. Consequently, introducing new result $n_{0.4}$ related to `state` for Q_2 on D_1 is likely to be irrelevant. Similarly, absence of the `area` of *Provo* ($n_{0.4.3.2}$) should not make `areas` of other `cities` such as *Salt Lake City* (*e.g.,* $n_{0.4.2}$) more relevant to *Provo* than *Salt Lake City*.

DEFINITION 1. ***[Result Resilience]*** *Let Q be an XKS query on two documents D and D' where $D' = D \backslash \{n\}$ and n is a label match to Q. Then, an XKS system is called result-resilient if $R(Q, D') \subseteq R(Q, D)$.*

3.2 Match Resilience

In an XKS query, label keywords reflect the desired data in the final result tree [1,9]. Reconsider the query Q_2 on D_1 and D_2. The node $n_{0.3.1}$ is a common result of Q_2 in both these documents. The *match resilience* property asserts that the match set of $n_{0.3.1}$ should remain the same in D_1 and D_2 as $n_{0.4.3.2}$ is not a descendant of $n_{0.3.1}$. On the other hand, consider the query Q_3 `(Utah, city, population, area)`. The common result of this query is the subtree rooted at $n_{0.4}$. Then, the match resilience property also asserts that the result tree of $n_{0.4}$ should be (non-strictly) smaller in D_1 than in D_2 as the missing node $n_{0.4.3.2}$ in D_1 is a descendant of this subtree in D_2.

DEFINITION 2. ***[Match Resilience]*** *Consider a label query $Q(w_1, \ldots, w_n)$ and two documents D, D' where $D' = D \backslash \{n\}$ and n is a label match to Q. An XKS system is match-resilient if for each result $r \in R(Q, D) \cap R(Q, D')$ any one of the following holds: (a) $S_{D'}(r) = S_D(r)$ if $n \notin S_D(r)$; (b) $S_{D'}(r) \subseteq S_D(r)$ if $n \in S_D(r)$.*

3.3 Optionality Resilience Analysis of Existing Approaches

Smallest Lowest Common Ancestor (SLCA). The SLCA approach introduced in [17] has been arguably the most popular technique to locate the result nodes and has become the backbone of various other approaches such as XSeek [9], XReal [1], XBridge [7], MaxMatch [10], etc. However, SLCA violates result resilience which explains its inability to handle missing elements as highlighted in Section 1. For example, consider the query Q_1 `(Provo, area)` on D_2. The SLCA approach returns the node $n_{0.4.3}$ but it returns $n_{0.4}$ on $D_1 = D_2 \backslash \{n_{0.4.3.2}\}$.

Meaningful Related Lowest Common Ancestor (MLCA). The MLCA-based technique [8] returns each result tree as a group of matches, called *pattern match*, containing exactly one match for each keyword. Two nodes n_1 and n_2 that match keywords w_1 and w_2, respectively, are *meaningfully related* if there does not exist n_1' and n_2' that match w_1 and w_2 such that the LCA of n_1 and n_2 is an ancestor of the LCA of n_1' and n_2'. When a set of nodes are pair-wise meaningfully related, their LCA is called an MLCA. Each returned pattern match contains an MLCA node and its corresponding pair-wise related matches.

MLCA does not satisfy result resilience. Consider the query Q_4 `(USA, Tennessee, Utah, area)` to find the areas of both *Tennessee* and *Utah*. The results on D_1 is empty since no matter which `area` node is chosen in the pattern match, it is not related to at least one value match. Specifically, node $n_{0.4.1}$ is not related to $n_{0.2.0}$ and node $n_{0.2.1}$ is not related to node $n_{0.4.0}$. Meanwhile, if $n_{0.4.1}$ is removed from the document, MLCA returns a pattern match in which $n_{0.0}$, $n_{0.2.0}$, $n_{0.4.0}$ and $n_{0.2.1}$ are matches for `USA`, `Tennessee`, `Utah` and `area`, respectively.

XSEarch. In XSEarch [2], two nodes n_1 and n_2 are considered *related* if the path between them consists of no same-label nodes except n_1 and n_2 themselves. For example, in D_1 (Figure 2(a)), nodes $n_{0.4.3.0}$ and $n_{0.4.1}$ are considered related. A pattern match is considered related if all of its matches are related to each other. XSEarch considers two semantics, namely, *all-pair* and *star*. *All-pair* semantics requires all pairs of matches to be related. *Star*-semantics only requires at least one match which is related to all other matches.

XSEarch also violates result resilience. For Q_1, XSEarch returns same results as SLCA on D_1 and D_2. Notice that $n_{0.4.3.0}$ is considered related to both $n_{0.4.3.2}$ and $n_{0.4.1}$.

Structural Consistency. In [6], the authors propose a new constraint for the SLCA list called *structural consistency*. A list of SLCA nodes are *structural consistent* when there are no ancestor-descendant relationships among them not only in instance-level (as in the original definition of SLCA) but also in schema-level. However, structural consistency is not sufficient to ensure result resilience when missing elements are involved. In fact, [6] returns same results as SLCA for Q_1 on D_1 and D_2 since there is only one SLCA node in both cases.

XSeek. A sub-task in retrieving result nodes is to deduce the result type. XSeek is a result type deduction technique built on top of SLCA [17]. Specifically, it attempts to locate entity nodes using a heuristic that entity nodes usually have same-label siblings. Then, for each SLCA node n_a, XSeek's result node is the lowest entity node n_e such that $n_e \preceq n_a$. However, XSeek still violates result resilience. For example, for Q_1, it produces identical results to SLCA on D_1 and D_2 since both $n_{0.4}$ and $n_{0.4.3}$ are entity nodes.

XReal and XBridge. XReal [1] and XBridge [7] are also result type detection techniques but based on *match statistics*. In a nutshell, XReal computes the *confidence* of a type T to be the result type by counting the number of T-typed nodes containing the matches for each query keyword but penalizes types that are too close to the root node. On the other hand, XBridge computes the result type confidence by aggregating the confidence for all results of that type. The confidence of each result is computed based on its match frequency and distribution in the query answer. Notably, the confidence value from both XReal and XBridge is zero when the result type has no results with at least one match for each keyword (*i.e.*, non-zero match frequency). Consequently, both these approaches fail to satisfy result resilience. For example, for Q_1 on D_2, the returned result type is `city` since the only result with non-zero match frequency for all keywords is of that type. On D_1, however, the returned result type is `state`. Since the result types are different, their results fail to satisfy result resilience.

AllMatch. *PathReturn* and *SubtreeReturn* are two typical techniques for the second step of XKS [4,9,10]. *PathReturn* returns all descendant matches of each result node and the paths connecting them while *SubtreeReturn* returns the full subtrees rooted at each result node. Since *PathReturn* and *SubtreeReturn* return the same set of matches (*i.e.*, all descendant matches) for each result node, in this paper, we refer to them as AllMatch. The result trees from AllMatch satisfy match resilience. For each result node r, all descendant matches are returned. On the other hand, when a node is removed from the document, r will not get any new descendants. Thus, no new descendant matches of r are introduced.

MaxMatch and Relaxed Tightest Fragment (RTF). While *PathReturn* and *SubtreeReturn* do not violate result resilience, they suffer from low recall and precision [9]. MaxMatch [10] and RTF [4] are introduced to address this problem. MaxMatch filters irrelevant matches under an SLCA node by returning only *contributors*. For each node n, its *contribution* is defined as the set of query keywords whose matches are descendant of n. A node is a *contributor* if its contribution is not subsumed by any of its siblings. RTF extends this notion of contributor to the so-called *valid contributor*, which is a node whose contribution is not subsumed by any of its *same-label* siblings.

MaxMatch [10] also incorporates four desirable properties of XKS by comparing XKS results when the document or query changes. However, these properties do not guarantee desirable behavior when missing elements are involved in the query. Specifically, both MaxMatch and RTF violate match resilience. For instance, consider Q_5 (`Utah, city, population, area`) whose intention is probably to find the population and area of all cities of *Utah*. The only result node from [1,9,17] on both D_1 and D_2 is $n_{0.4}$. For $n_{0.4}$, on D_2, both MaxMatch and RTF select $n_{0.4.3.1}$ as relevant match. Notice that $n_{0.4.2.1}$, the `population` of *Salt Lake City*, is not selected since it only has `population` but not `area` whereas *Provo* city has both these elements. On the other hand, on D_1 the matches for both *Salt Lake City* and *Provo* are returned as *Provo*'s area information is missing.

4. FULL SLCA (FSLCA)

Recall from Section 1, if an XML document is *full* then all missing elements are specified by empty elements. Consequently, SLCA nodes identified during keyword search on a *full* XML document will be able to satisfy optionality resilience property as there are no missing elements. Among these identified SLCA nodes, we refer to the nodes that exist in the original document as *full* SLCA (FSLCA) nodes. For example, reconsider the query Q_1 on D_1. The only SLCA node matching the query is $n_{0.4}$ which is undesirable. Document D_3 (Figure 3(b)) displays the full version of D_1. If we now compute the SLCA nodes on D_3 for Q_1, it would produce $n_{0.4.3}$ since its descendant node $n_{0.4.3.0}$ matches to `Provo` and node $n_{0.4.3.2}$ matches to `area`. Since $n_{0.4.3}$ also exists in D_1, it is an FSLCA of Q_1. We now formally introduce the concepts of *full* XML document and FSLCA.

4.1 Full XML Document

DEFINITION 3. ***[Full Node]*** *Given a document D, a node $n \in D$ with type t is full, denoted as $FullNode(n)$, if for each child type t_c of t, n has at least one child node with type t_c.*

For example, in D_1, $n_{0.3.1}$ is a full node since type `city` has three child types, namely `name`, `population` and `area`, and $n_{0.3.1}$ has corresponding child nodes $n_{0.3.1.0}$, $n_{0.3.1.1}$ and $n_{0.3.1.2}$, respectively.

DEFINITION 4. ***[Full Document]*** *An XML document D is considered full, denoted as $F(D)$, iff all of its nodes are full. That is, $\forall n \in D$, $FullNode(n) =$ `true`.*

For example, D_3 in Figure 3(b) is a full document. Noticeably, a document D can be transformed to a full document $F(D)$ by adding empty elements as children to nodes that are not full in D. For instance, D_1 can be transformed to D_3 by adding empty elements (in dotted rectangles). Observe that there are infinite numbers of full documents $F(D)$ of D. For example, adding any numbers of `area` nodes as siblings of $n_{0.4.3.2}$ would create another full document of D_1. In practice, we only consider the *minimal* full document of D.

DEFINITION 5. ***[Minimal Full Document]*** *Given an XML document D, a full document $F(D)$ is minimal, denoted as $F_{min}(D)$ iff the following conditions are true: (a) $\forall n \in D$, $n \in F_{min}(D)$; (b) for each $n' \in F_{min}(D)$, n' is either in D or removing it would make $F_{min}(D)$ no longer a full document; and (c) all nodes in $F_{min}(D) \backslash D$ are empty nodes.*

For example, D_3 in Figure 3(b) is a minimal full document of D_1. In the sequel, for brevity, we shall use $F(D)$ or F instead of $F_{min}(D)$ when the context is clear. Clearly, given a document D, the DataGuides of D and $F(D)$ are identical.

4.2 FSLCA Definition

Since a full document may contain empty nodes that do not exist in the original document, each FSLCA node belongs to one of the following two categories:

- *Category 1*: Both the FSLCA node *and* its matches are in the original document D. For example, consider the query Q_2(`area`, `city`) on D_1. Then the FSLCA node $n_{0.3.1}$ belongs to this category as its subtree includes matches for both `city` and `area`.
- *Category 2*: The FSLCA node is in D but its matches *are not* in D. For example, for Q_2 on D_1, FSLCA nodes $n_{0.4.2}$ and $n_{0.4.3}$ belong to this category as both do not have any `area` element as descendant.

In this paper, we refer to the result sets consisting of only Category 1 FSLCA nodes as *complete* FSLCA nodes while the results sets consisting of both the aforementioned categories are called *partial* FSLCA nodes. Formally,

DEFINITION 6. ***[Partial & Complete*** **FSLCA*]*** *Given a query Q on a document D,*

- *the set of partial* FSLCA *nodes of Q on D, denoted as $PFSLCA(Q,D)$ is defined as, $PFSLCA(Q,D) = SLCA(Q,F(D)) \cap D$.*
- *the set of complete* FSLCA *nodes of Q on D, denoted as $CFSLCA(Q,D)$ is defined as, $CFSLCA(Q,D) = PFSLCA(Q,D) \cap SLCA(Q,D)$.*

Remark. The complete and partial FSLCAs are designed to allow two different strategies of returning result nodes containing missing elements. The most obvious approach is to ignore result nodes containing missing elements, which is realized by complete FSLCA. For example, consider the query Q_2 (`city`, `area`) on D_1. Here, $CFSLCA(Q_2, D_1) = \{n_{0.3.1}\}$ as $n_{0.4.2}$ and $n_{0.4.3}$ do not have `area` element as descendant. Alternatively, partial FSLCA does not eliminate such results nodes and returns them explicitly indicating the missing elements. For example, $PFSLCA(Q_2, D_1) = \{n_{0.3.1}, n_{0.4.2}, n_{0.4.3}\}$ and the `area` elements in $n_{0.4.2}$ and $n_{0.4.3}$ are represented as empty nodes (an empty node is represented as a box with a dashed line border).

4.3 Proofs for Optionality Resilience

THEOREM 1. *Both partial and complete* FSLCA *nodes satisfy result resilience.*

PROOF. For any pairs of document D and $D' = D \backslash \{n\}$ where $n \in D$, we have $F(D) = F(D')$. Therefore, $SLCA(Q, F(D)) = SLCA(Q, F(D'))$ for any query Q. Since $D' \subset D$, $PFSLCA(Q, D') \subseteq PFSLCA(Q, D)$.

For all result nodes $r \in CFSLCA(Q, D')$, r has descendant matches to all keywords in D'. Meanwhile, since $D \subseteq F(D) = F(D')$, there are no results in $SLCA(Q, D)$ that is a descendant of r. Thus, $r \in SLCA(Q, D)$. But $r \in SLCA(Q, F(D')) = SLCA(Q, F(D))$. Therefore, $r \in CFSLCA(Q, D)$. □

The following lemmas prove that existing XKS approaches built on top of FSLCA nodes instead of SLCA nodes satisfy the optionality resilience property.

LEMMA 1. *The results of XSeek on top of either partial or complete* FSLCA *nodes satisfy result resilience.*

PROOF. Let n_0 be a node in document D. Let $xseek(n_0)$ be a function returning the lowest ancestor entity node of n_0 as described in Section 3.3. Since $PFSLCA(Q, D') \subseteq PFSLCA(Q, D)$ and $CFSLCA(Q, D') \subseteq CFSLCA(Q, D)$, their images through function $xseek()$ maintain inclusion relation $\subseteq$. □

LEMMA 2. *If matches to empty elements are considered, the results of MaxMatch and* RTF *on top of either partial or complete* FSLCA *nodes satisfy match resilience.*

PROOF. Let Q be a query on two documents such that $D' = D \backslash \{n\}$, $n \in D$ and n is a label match of Q. Let r be a result node and r_0 be a node within the result tree rooted at r. If n is not a descendant of r_0, its contribution is unchanged in D and D'. If n is a descendant of r_0, r_0 would have at least one label match with same label with n in $F(D)$ and $F(D')$. Therefore, the contribution of r_0 is unchanged for both MaxMatch and RTF. □

5. FSLCA COMPUTATION

In this section, we present two variants of the MESSIAH algorithm, namely P-MESSIAH and C-MESSIAH, to compute partial and complete FSLCA nodes, respectively. These algorithms can retrieve FSLCA nodes without the need of physically generating full documents. Also, it is not necessary for the XML document to be accompanied by its schema or DTD as a DataGuide tree can be easily generated from a "schemaless" XML document [3]. Note that such DataGuide tree has also been used in several prior work related to XKS [1,7,9]. We first summarize the principle behind existing SLCA computation approach which serves as a foundation for the FSLCA computation problem.

5.1 Principles for SLCA Computation

The core idea behind all existing SLCA computation techniques can be summarized by the following lemmas (see [17] for full proofs).

LEMMA 3. *Given a node $n \in D$ and a query keyword w, the level of the* SLCA *between n and matches of w on D, denoted as $slcaLvl(n, D, w)$, is equal to $max(lvl(lca(n, lm(n, M_D(w)))),$ $lvl(lca(n, rm(n, M_D(w)))))$ where $lvl()$ returns the level of a node and $lm(n, M_D(w))$ and $rm(n, M_D(w))$ return the last node before n and the first node after n in $M_D(w)$, respectively.*

LEMMA 4. *Given a node $n \in D$ and keywords $w_1, \ldots, w_k$, the level of the* SLCA *between n and matches of $w_1, \ldots, w_k$ on D, denoted as $slcaLvl(n, D, w_1, \ldots, w_k)$, is equal to $min(slcaLvl(n, D, w_1), \ldots, slcaLvl(n, D, w_k))$.*

Lemma 3 focuses on a special case of SLCA computation where there are only two sets in which one set is a single element n. It reduces the SLCA into the LCA of n to either $lm()$ or $rm()$. Lemma 4 extends this results to multiple sets. The final SLCA computation is then achieved by computing $slcaLvl(n, D, w_1, \ldots, w_k)$ for all nodes n of a set M as candidates and then pruning those SLCA candidates with at least one descendant candidate. The difference between [17] and [14] lies on how to get M. [17] chooses $M = M_D(w_1)$ in which w_1 is the keyword with smallest match set whereas [14] reduces M further by exploiting several optimizations. Meanwhile, [19] considers all ancestor-or-self of $M_D(w_1)$ as M but uses equality comparison instead of $lm()$ and $rm()$.

Both [17] and [14] exploit a non-indexed and an indexed approach to support $lm()$ and $rm()$. The indexed approach uses random access to retrieve $lm()$ and $rm()$ from a B-tree, which is suitable when M is small. When M is large, non-indexed approach using sequential scan is more suitable. For all cases, the time complexity is $O(dk|M|log(|M_{max}|)$ where d is the document depth and M_{max} is the largest match set.

5.2 Key Strategies behind MESSIAH

The key idea of FSLCA computation using MESSIAH is based on the following two observations. First, SLCA or FSLCA computation only requires *checking* whether a node has descendant matches but not *retrieving* the matches directly. Note that existing approaches compute SLCA by retrieving the matches first (*i.e.*, $lm()$, $rm()$) and then computing SLCA from them. However, this approach cannot be used in MESSIAH as some matches are "virtual" (missing elements) and cannot be retrieved. Second, since a full document does not have missing nodes, we can infer the subtree structure of a node by analyzing its type only. For instance, in a full document, we can infer that each `state` has some `city` as child and each `city` has `name`, `population` and `area` as children. These two observations are materialized in the following theorem.

THEOREM 2. *In a minimal full document F, given a node n with type t, n has a descendant label match n' to a keyword w iff there exists a type match t' to w such that $t \preceq_{\mathbb{S}} t'$.*

PROOF. It follows from the definition of minimal full document (Definition 5). □

COROLLARY 1. *Let F be the minimal full document of D. Given node $n \in D$ and a query keyword w, $slcaLvl(n, F, w) = max(lvl(lca(n, lm(n, M_D(w)))), lvl(lca(n, rm(n, M_D(w)))), slcaLvl(t, \mathbb{S}, w))$ where t is the type of n and $slcaLvl(t, \mathbb{S}, w)$ is the level of the SLCA between t and all type matches of w in $\mathbb{S}$.*

COROLLARY 2. *Given a node $n \in D$, minimal full document F, and keywords $w_1, \ldots, w_k$, $slcaLvl(n, F, w_1, \ldots, w_k) = min(slcaLvl(n, F, w_1), \ldots, slcaLvl(n, F, w_k))$.*

Corollary 1 and 2 are useful generalization of Lemma 3 and 4, respectively. Observe that the left-hand-sides of the equations in these corollaries leverage F while the matches are retrieved from D (*i.e.*, $M_D(w)$). Importantly, as DataGuides for most practical datasets are small [1], $slcaLvl(t, \mathbb{S}, w)$ can be computed efficiently (can even be pre-computed).

5.3 Partial FSLCA Computation

Partial FSLCA computation needs to address a novel challenge compared to existing SLCA computation techniques. Observe that Lemma 3-4 and Corollary 1-2 assume that each SLCA/FSLCA node has a match n in D (called *anchor node* in [14]). However, some partial FSLCA nodes may not have any match in D. To address this challenge, we split the partial FSLCA computation problem into two cases, namely FSLCA node with at least one value match and FSLCA node with only label match, and address each them in turn.

Case 1: FSLCA with at least one descendant value match. Corollary 1 and 2 can be applied for Case 1 since all value matches are in D (converting D to F is not necessary). However, since the value matches can be matches of any keywords, the set of anchor nodes is $V_1 \cup \cdots \cup V_k$ instead of M_1 as used in SLCA computation.

Case 2: FSLCA with at least one label match to each keyword. When a partial FSLCA node n_a has at least one descendant label match n_ℓ to each keyword, it may not have any match in the original document D. Consequently, locating anchor nodes is challenging. We propose a technique to retrieve the candidate node n_a *without* using anchors.

Based on Theorem 2, n_a has a descendant label match to keyword w if and only if its type t_a has a descendant type match to w.

Algorithm 1: The P-MESSIAH Algorithm.

Input: A query Q with k keywords $w_1 \ldots w_k$
Input: The list of value matches V_i and type matches T_i for each w_i in document D whose Dataguide is $\mathbb{S}$
Output: The list of FSLCA nodes of Q on D

1 $Result = \emptyset$;
2 $T = SLCA_{\mathbb{S}}(T_1, \ldots, T_k)$;
3 $Cand_2 \leftarrow$ **merge**($\{N_D(t)|t \in T\}$);
4 $Anchor_1 \leftarrow$ **merge**($V_1, \ldots, V_k$);
5 $c'_1 \leftarrow root$;
6 $c_2 \leftarrow Cand_2$.**next**();
7 **while** *there are more nodes in* $Anchor_1$ **do**
8     $a_1 \leftarrow Anchor_1$.**next**();
9     $t_1 \leftarrow$ the type of a_1;
10   **for** $i = 1 \rightarrow k$ **do**
11   **if** $a_1 \notin V_i$ **then**
12             $\ell_i = max(lvl(lca(a_1, Anchor_1.\mathbf{peekLast}(i))), lvl(lca(a_1, Anchor_1.\mathbf{peekNext}(i))), slcaLvl(t_1, \mathbb{S}, w_i))$;
13     $\ell = min_{1 \leq i \leq k}(\ell_i)$;
14     $c_1 = ancestor(a_1, \ell)$;
15   **if** $id(c'_1) <= id(c_1)$ **then**
16   **if** $c'_1 \not\preceq c_1$ *and* $c'_1 \not\preceq c_2$ **then**
17             $Result = Result \cup \{c'_1\}$;
18   **while** c_2 *is not null and* $id(c_2) < id(c_1)$ **do**
19   **if** $c_2 \not\preceq c_1$ **then**
20                 $Result = Result \cup \{c_2\}$;
21             $c_2 \leftarrow Cand_2$.**next**();
22         $c'_1 \leftarrow c_1$;
23 **if** c_2 *is null or* $c'_1 \not\preceq c_2$ **then**
24     $Result = Result \cup \{c'_1\}$;
25 **while** c_2 *is not null* **do**
26     $Result = Result \cup \{c_2\}$;
27     $c_2 \leftarrow Cand_2$.**next**();
28 **return** $Result$

Therefore, t_a must have at least one descendant type match to each keyword. In other words, t_a is an SLCA of the type matches of all keywords w (*i.e.*, given a query $Q(w_1, \ldots, w_k)$ on D, $t_a \in SLCA_{\mathbb{S}}(T_D(w_1), \ldots, T_D(w_k))$). Thus, to retrieve n_a, we can find all t_a and then retrieve all corresponding n_a in D. Notice that this strategy does not require any anchors. Furthermore, it is extremely efficient since label matches are not retrieved and the number of possible values of t_a is small.

The P-MESSIAH Algorithm. Algorithm 1 outlines the procedure of P-MESSIAH which realizes our above discussion on partial FSLCA nodes computation. Observe that the inputs are value matches and type matches for Q which can be retrieved directly from D. Lines 2-3 correspond to our technique for Case 2. All candidate nodes generated for this case (*i.e.*, having at least one descendant label match for each keyword) are stored in $Cand_2$. The $Anchor_1$ stores all value matches for Q which shall serve as anchor matches. The **merge()** function in Lines 3 and 4 merges the input sets into a single sorted set of nodes and returns them in stream format. Note that if all of the input sets are sorted stream, the **merge()** function can be implemented efficiently without sorting and consumes minimal memory. Both $Anchor_1$ and $Cand_2$ are required to be sorted for pruning which we shall discuss later. The symbols a_1 and c_2 denote the current cursor node of streams $Anchor_1$ and $Cand_2$, respectively. They are assumed to be null when there are no more nodes in the stream.

Lines 7-14 materialize Case 1. The loop in Lines 7-22 is executed for each anchor node a_1 in $Anchor_1$. Lines 10-14 use Corollary 1 and 2 to ensure that the candidate node c_1 of a_1 has descendant matches to all keywords. Notably, instead of using $lm()$ and $rm()$ functions, we use **peekLast**(i) and **peekNext**(i) which return the last and next node, respectively, in the i-th input stream (*i.e.*, V_i) in $Anchor_1$. Although the latter functions return same results as $lm(a_1, V_i)$ and $rm(a_1, V_i)$, respectively, **peekLast**(i) and **peekNext**(i) are more efficient since they can be easily supported in streams by storing the last retrieved node and looking ahead the next retrieved node of each input stream. Specifically, they take $O(1)$ time compared to $O(log(V_i))$ time of $lm(a_1, V_i)$ and $rm(a_1, V_i)$.

Lines 15-22 check whether the new candidate nodes can be partial FSLCA nodes. Since the candidates come from two cases, they need to check against each other. Lines 15-17 check c'_1 against Case-1 candidate c_1 and Case-2 candidate c_2. Lines 18-21 check all following Case-2 candidates against Case-1 candidate c_1. Notice that Case-2 candidates do not require checking against each other since they cannot have $\prec$ relation. Lines 23-27 are similar to Lines 16-22 to evaluate the last c'_1.

Time Complexity. Let T be the result returned in Line 2 and d be the document depth. Then the time complexity of Algorithm 1 is $O(dk \sum_{1 \le i \le k} |V_k| + dlog(k) \sum_{t \in T} |N_D(t)|)$. These two terms correspond to Case 1 and 2, respectively. In particular, Case 1 produces $O(\sum_{1 \le i \le k} |V_k|)$ candidate nodes, each takes $O(dk)$ time (due to Line 12). Case 2 produces $O(\sum_{t \in T} |N_D(t)|)$ candidates, each takes $O(d \log(k))$ time (due to the **merge** function in Line 3).

Remark 1. Since the complexity of ILE algorithm [17] is $O(kd|M_1|log(|M_k|)$, it may seem that our complexity is worse. However, notice that the result size between two cases are not equal. In practice, as demonstrated in Section 6, P-MESSIAH outperforms ILE. First, the ILE algorithm uses $lm()$ and $rm()$ functions with random access while our algorithm exploits stream extensively without random access. Second, for most keywords w, $L(w) \gg V(w)$. Hence, $\sum_{1 \le i \le k} |V_k|$ is potentially much smaller than $|M_1|log(|M_k|)$. Third, the $dlog(k) \sum_{t \in T} |N_D(t)|$ term only appears when $T(w_i) \neq \varnothing \forall i$.

Remark 2. P-MESSIAH follows an "eager" strategy *i.e.*, FSLCA nodes are returned in document-order and the first output node can be returned even before all of input nodes are read. This property is highly desirable in practice since it greatly reduces query response time (*i.e.*, the time the users need to wait to view the first result).

EXAMPLE 1. Consider Q_2(city, area) on D_1. We have $V_{D_1}(\texttt{city}) = \{n_{0.4.2.0}\}$, $T_{D_1}(\texttt{city}) = \{t_{city}\}$, $V_{D_1}(\texttt{area}) = \varnothing$, $T_{D_1}(\texttt{area}) = \{t_{territory/area}, t_{state/area}, t_{city/area}\}$. Using the DataGuide in Figure 2(b), Line 2 returns t_{city}. Thus, $Cand_2 = \{n_{0.3.1}, n_{0.4.2}, n_{0.4.3}\}$. Meanwhile, $Anchor_1 = \{n_{0.4.2.0}\}$ so that the first and only value for a_1 is $n_{0.4.2.0}$. For this a_1, $\ell = 3$ and $c_1 = n_{0.4.2}$. The condition in Line 15 is satisfied but not the one in Line 16. As $c_2 = n_{0.3.1}$ precedes $c_1 = n_{0.4.2}$, the while-loop in Lines 18-21 proceeds to check Line 19 condition and adds $n_{0.3.1}$ as the first result. Next, $c_1 = n_{0.4.2}$ is assigned to c'_1. At Line 23, the condition fails since both c'_1 and c_2 refer to the same node $n_{0.4.2}$ so that c'_1 is not added to the results. Finally, Lines 25-26 add the two remaining nodes in $Cand_2$, $n_{0.4.2}$ and $n_{0.4.3}$, as results. The final results is $\{n_{0.3.1}, n_{0.4.2}, n_{0.4.3}\}$. ∎

5.4 Complete FSLCA Computation

The C-MESSIAH algorithm is outlined in Algorithm 2. Similar to [17], each node a in M_1 (assumedly the smallest match set) is processed one-by-one[2] (Lines 4-5) and the computed candidate c is pruned based on document order and $\prec$ relation (Lines 12-13). Since our purpose is to get the SLCA nodes of Q in F and not D, Corollary 1 and 2 are used instead of Lemma 3 and 4 (Lines 8-11). The filtering is accomplished using the $isSLCA$ flag which indicates whether the current node stored in c' is $SLCA(Q, D)$ and is set at Line 16. Notice that $min_{2 \le i \le k}(\ell'_i)$ is equal to $slcaLvl(a, D, w_2, \ldots, w_k)$ (Lemma 4). When this value is larger than ℓ, it means the candidate c is an SLCA node for Q on D.

Algorithm 2: The C-MESSIAH Algorithm.

Input: A query Q with k keywords $w_1 \ldots w_k$
Input: The matches M_i in document D whose Dataguide is $\mathbb{S}$
Output: The list of complete FSLCA nodes of Q on D

1 $Result = \emptyset$;
2 $c' \leftarrow root$;
3 $isSLCA \leftarrow \texttt{false}$;
4 **while** *there are more nodes in* M_1 **do**
5     $a \leftarrow M_1$.**next**();
6     $t \leftarrow$ the type of a_1;
7   **for** $i = 2 \rightarrow k$ **do**
8         $\ell'_i = \max(lvl(lca(a_1, lm(a_1, M_i))), lvl(lca(n, rm(a_1, M_i))))$;
9         $\ell_i = \max(\ell'_i, slcaLvl(t, \mathbb{S}, w))$;
10     $\ell = min_{2 \le i \le k}(\ell_i)$;
11     $c = ancestor(a_1, \ell)$;
12   **if** $id(c') <= id(c)$ **then**
13   **if** $c' \npreceq c$ *and* $isSLCA = \texttt{true}$ **then**
14             $Result = Result \cup \{c'\}$;
15         $c' \leftarrow c$;
16         $isSLCA \leftarrow (\ell = min_{2 \le i \le k}(\ell'_i))$;
17 **if** $isSLCA = \texttt{true}$ **then**
18     $Result = Result \cup \{c'\}$;
19 **return** $Result$

Time Complexity. Assume that $slcaLvl(t, \mathbb{S}, w)$ in Line 9 can be computed in $O(1)$ since $\mathbb{S}$ is usually much smaller than D. Then the time complexity of Algorithm 2 is $O(dk|M_1| \log(|M_{max}|))$ where d is the document depth, M_1 and M_{max} are the smallest and largest match sets.

EXAMPLE 2. Consider Q_2(city, area) on D_1. $M_{D_1}(\texttt{city}) = \{n_{0.3.1}, n_{0.4.2}, n_{0.4.2.0}, n_{0.4.3}\}$ and $M_{D_1}(\texttt{area}) = \{n_{0.1.1}, n_{0.2.1}, n_{0.3.1.2}, n_{0.4.1}\}$. Since the match sets have equal size, we can use either one as M_1. Lets choose $M_{D_1}(\texttt{city})$. For $n_{0.3.1}$, the nodes returned by lm and rm functions are $n_{0.2.1}$ and $n_{0.3.1.2}$, respectively, whose LCA levels with $n_{0.3.1}$ are 1 and 3, respectively (Lines 7-8). Thus, ℓ'_i in Line 8 is 3. Since the type t of $n_{0.3.1}$ is city, $slcaLvl(t, \mathbb{S}, \texttt{area})$ is 3 and $\ell_i = 3$. In Line 11, $c = n_{0.3.1}$ which is assigned to the empty c' with $isSLCA$ set to true. Similarly, for the next node $n_{0.4.2}$, we get candidate $c = n_{0.4.2}$ with $\ell'_i = 2$ and $\ell_i = 3$. Since $n_{0.3.1} \not\prec n_{0.4.2}$, $n_{0.3.1}$ is returned as the first result node. $n_{0.4.2}$ is then assigned to c' but with $isSLCA$ set to false. For the next node $n_{0.4.2.0}$, $c = c_{0.4.2.0}$ and $isSLCA$ is set to false. Lastly, for $n_{0.4.3}$, the candidate node $c = n_{0.4.3}$ but $isSLCA$ is still false. Therefore, it is also not added to the results. Hence, $n_{0.3.1}$ is the only result node.

5.5 Heuristics-based Algorithm Selection

Recall that C-MESSIAH ignores result nodes containing missing elements (returns complete FSLCA) whereas P-MESSIAH does not

[2] More optimized technique such as [14] can also be applied. However, it is orthogonal to the problem.

eliminate such results nodes and returns them explicitly indicating the missing elements as empty nodes (returns partial FSLCA). That is, P-MESSIAH returns all complete FSLCA nodes of C-MESSIAH as well as additional results containing missing elements. Given a query Q, how can we automatically deduce which variant of MESSIAH needs to be executed? In this section, we present a heuristics-based selection strategy to answer this question. Specifically, our heuristic is based on the statistics of underlying XML data and not on their semantics.

Intuitively, the selection choice is influenced by the usefulness of the additional results generated by P-MESSIAH. We advocate that it depends on the number of complete FSLCAs as well as the number of results (denoted by N) desired by a user. In the context of keyword search, N is typically small. So if an XKS system returns more than N complete FSLCA results, then a user may not be interested in the results with missing elements. Consequently, C-MESSIAH is relatively more appropriate for this case. On the other hand, if there are fewer than N complete FSLCA results, then displaying additional results with missing elements using P-MESSIAH will be potentially useful.

The challenge here is to estimate the number of complete FSLCAs *apriori*. We address it by adopting a lightweight version of the *XSketch*-index [12]. In short, an *XSketch*-index is a directed acyclic graph synopsis G where each *synopsis node* g represents a set of data nodes with same labels and each edge (g_p, g_c) signifies the parent-child relationship between the data nodes of g_p and g_c. Each internal (resp. leaf) synopsis node stores the structural (resp. value) distribution of the child labels (resp. value tokens) among its data nodes. For example, a synopsis node g_{city} representing all `city` elements in D_1 will have the structural distribution of 100% for `name` and `population` but 33% for `area` since all `city` elements have `name` and `population` but only one out of three has `area`. Similarly, for the $g_{city/area}$ synopsis node representing all `city/area` elements in D_1, the value distributions of `Houston`, `Salt`, `Lake`, `City`, and `Provo` are all 33%.

We use a *lightweight* version of *XSketch*-index where the synopsis graph G is represented using the DataGuide tree $\mathbb{S}$. Specifically, each synopsis node corresponds to exactly one schema node in $\mathbb{S}$. Note that G can be built while computing $\mathbb{S}$ and stored with it. It is worth mentioning that although a more detailed *XSketch*-index would provide a better estimation, it takes more space. A detailed discussion on the space-accuracy trade-off is provided in [12]. As we shall see later, such lightweight version is sufficient to select the correct variant of MESSIAH with high accuracy.

To illustrate the estimation process, let us reconsider Q_1 and Q_2 on D_1. For Q_1 `(Provo area)`, from the *XSketch*-index, all `cities` have `name` but only 33% of `name` have value `Provo`. Meanwhile, only 33 % of `cities` have `area`. Assuming independent distribution between the two, 11% of `cities` have both `Provo` and `area`. Since there are 3 `city` elements in D_1, the estimated result size is $3 \times 0.11 = 0.33$. Similarly, for Q_2 `(city area)`, 33% of `city` elements have `area` which leads to the estimated result size of 1. Let $N = 1$. Since $0.33 < 1$, P-MESSIAH is used for Q_1 but C-MESSIAH is used for Q_2. This estimation reflects the intuition that Q_1 is more likely to have no relevant results in the document so results with missing elements are desirable.

6. EXPERIMENTAL STUDY

We conducted experiments to compare performance of MESSIAH against state-of-the-art SLCA computation approaches, namely, SE and ILE [17]; and IMS and IIMS [14]. For complete FSLCA, we also provide two implementations, non-indexed (denoted by NC-MESSIAH) and indexed (denoted by IC-MESSIAH), corresponding

Id	Queries	Num. of Complete FSLCA	Num. of Partial FSLCA	Num. of SLCA
QM1	London	4	4	4
QM2	California Arizona	1	1	1
QM3	country Muslim	98	98	98
QM4	country name Laos	1	1	1
QM5	Fresno longitude	0	1	1
QM6	York latitude	1	5	3
QM7	city longitude latitude	801	3111	801
QM8	river Lualaba area length	0	4	1
QP1	Kringle	38	38	38
QP2	Kringle Domain	8	8	8
QP3	journal Nature	1572	1572	1572
QP4	publication 2002 Science	281	281	281
QP5	Filaggrin parent_list	0	1	1
QP6	publication journal year	40292	41950	40292
QP7	Desmoglein interpro Pemphigus class_list	2	4	2
QP8	Peptidase S1A prothrombin Patthy sec_list	1	3	1
QD1	XML	7913	7913	7913
QD2	Torsten Grust	46	46	46
QD3	Aradhye title	16	16	16
QD4	XML Keyword Search inproceedings	50	50	50
QD5	inproceedings cite	6374	872535	6374
QD6	Aradhye inproceedings cite	0	11	1
QD7	volume XML book	7	13	7
QD8	XQuery XIME proceedings cite	0	4	1
QS1	Hamlet	469	469	469
QS2	Juliet speech	173	173	173
QS3	to be or not to be speaker	659	659	659
QS4	wherefore art thou Romeo Act	3	3	3
QS5	King Lear Tragedy prologue	0	1	1
QS6	play title subtitle	1	125	1
QS7	Othello Act IV epilogue	0	2	1
QS8	Troilus Cressida Act VI prologue epilogue	0	1	1

Figure 4: Query set.

to two methods to realize $lm()$ and $rm()$ functions as in [14, 17]. Notice that partial FSLCA does not use $lm()$ and $rm()$, so we only provide one implementation (P-MESSIAH). All techniques are implemented using Java 1.7 on top of Berkeley DB 4.0.103. The experiments were performed on an Intel Xeon X5570 machine with 4GB memory. Since the techniques to select relevant return nodes within the SLCA subtrees (*e.g.*, [1, 9, 10]) are orthogonal to MESSIAH, we do not compare them.

6.1 Experimental Setup

Dataset. The experiments are performed on four XML datasets, Mondial (1.72MB), INTERPRO (69MB), DBLP (740MB) and SHAKESPEARE (9.1MB). Mondial is a data-centric XML dataset with many short texts while SHAKESPEARE is a text-centric XML document consisting of mostly long texts. INTERPRO and DBLP are datasets with both short and long text. Note that these data sources are also used for empirical study in prior works [1, 9, 10, 17].

Queryset. The set of queries studied for each dataset is reported in Figure 4. The queries for Mondial, INTERPRO, DBLP, and SHAKESPEARE are denoted as QM1-QM8, QP1-QP8, QD1-QD8, and QS1-QS8, respectively. They are selected as follow. We employ ten unpaid volunteers who have knowledge of XML but are not involved in this project. Since our focus is on queries involving missing elements, for each volunteer, we ask them to generate four queries without missing labels and four with missing labels for each dataset. The missing labels for each dataset are provided beforehand. For each dataset, with 80 sample queries, we keep 8 queries with diversity in numbers of keywords, keyword selectivity and whether the keyword matches to a label or a value for experiments. The first four queries do not contain missing elements whereas the last four queries do. Thus, the result size of each of the first four queries is identical for all benchmark approaches. Ob-

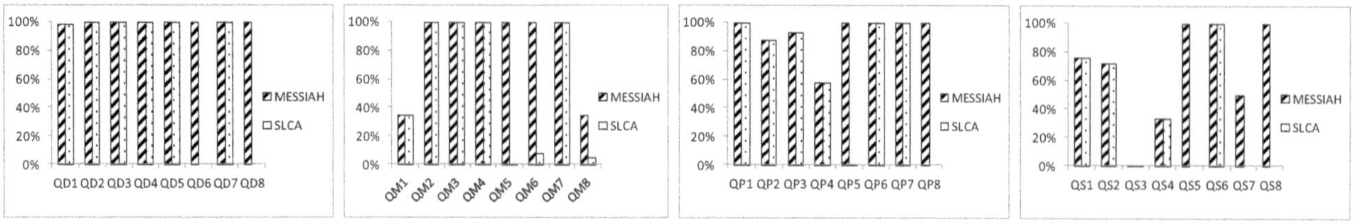

(a) DBLP (b) Mondial (c) INTERPRO (d) SHAKESPEARE

Figure 5: Precision.

serve that the result sizes of complete FSLCA, partial FSLCA and SLCA may not be identical in the last four queries. Note that the first four queries are used to compare the performance of MESSIAH with state-of-the-art techniques when missing labels are not in users' queries.

Indexes used. To support efficiently evaluation of Algorithm 1, we exploit the following two indexes. (a) *Inverted List:* Our inverted list maps each keyword w to a sorted set of value matches to w and a set of type matches to w. They are used to find the input set for Algorithm 1. Notice that while the value match is sorted, a sorted index such as B+-tree is not required for P-MESSIAH since we do not employ random access at all. Instead, a hash index can be used which allows faster sequential traversal. The node order is maintained when the index is built while parsing the document. (b) *Type Index:* It maps each type t to a sorted $N_D(t)$. It is invoked in Line 3 of Algorithm 1. Similar to the inverted list, the order of $N_D(t)$ is not required to be maintained by a B+-tree but by inserting them in correct order.

6.2 Results

Search quality. In this experiment, we compare the quality of results returned by SLCA and FSLCA approaches. Since all SLCA approaches return the same results, we only use the results returned by [17] as representative results. Since the difference between partial and complete FSLCA approaches are some explicitly marked missing data results which do not contribute to precision or recall, we use complete FSLCA (C-MESSIAH) as representative for FSLCA.

For each query, we ask each volunteer to specify the search intention. We then provide document schema and ask them to convert their intention to XQuery/XPath query. The results of these queries are considered as correct results. The volunteers can discuss among themselves but unanimity is not required.

To measure the search quality, we use *precision* and *recall*, defined as follow:

$$precision = \frac{|Rel \cap Ret|}{|Ret|}, recall = \frac{|Rel \cap Ret|}{|Rel|}$$

where Rel is the set of nodes retrieved by an XML query (as described above) and Ret is the set of result type matches returned by SLCA/FSLCA. For instance, for QM6, the XPath query agreed by all of our volunteers is `//city[contains(name,'York')]/latitude`. The set of `latitude` nodes retrieved by this query is denoted as Rel. Ret is the set of all `latitude` matches returned by FSLCA(resp. SLCA)-based techniques.

Since the focus of our paper is on queries with missing labels, some of our experimental queries actually do not have relevant results (QD6, QD8, QM5, QM8, QP5, QP8, QS5, QS7 and QS8). For these queries, recall is not available since the sets of relevant nodes, Rel, are empty. Hence, for precision measurement, if the approach returns empty results, we consider the precision in this case (0/0) is 100%. On the other hand, if non-empty results are returned, the precision is considered 0%.

The recall of both SLCA and FSLCA are consistently high. Specifically, except for the no-relevant-result queries (QD6, QD8, QM5, QM8, QP5, QP8, QS5, QS7 and QS8) whose recall is unavailable, the recall of both SLCA and FSLCA are 100% for all other queries. *It shows that our approach matches* SLCA*'s ability to produce high recall [9, 10].*

Figure 5 reports the precision of MESSIAH in comparison with SLCA-based techniques. It is clear that our approach has higher or equal precision than SLCA-based approaches for all queries, especially queries with missing elements (*i.e.,* queries with subscripts 5 to 8). In particular, for queries QD6, QD8, QM5, QM8, QP5, QP8, QS5, QS7 and QS8, SLCA approaches have zero precision. There are no relevant results for these queries. For complete FSLCA approach, no results are returned. On the other hand, SLCA returns lots of irrelevant result matches. For instance, consider QD6. The intention of this query is to find the citations in all of `Aradhye`'s papers. Notice that DBLP only stores the citation information for only few publications [5] and do not have any data on `Aradhye`'s citations. For this query, complete FSLCA returns empty results. Meanwhile, existing SLCA techniques' only result is the root node containing many irrelevant `cite` nodes.

A similar problem also arises for QM6. Note that there are five cities in the world with name containing `York` but only one (*i.e.,* `New York`) contains `latitude` data in the Mondial dataset. For this query, complete FSLCA approach returns a single `city` node corresponding to `New York`. Meanwhile, partial FSLCA will return all 5 cities with `York`. Except for `New York`, the remaining cities' subtrees do not include any `latitude` data. Hence, these partial FSLCAs explicitly indicate that their `latitude` data are missing. On the other hand, for SLCA, besides the `latitude` of `New York city`, the `latitudes` of cities belonging to the same province or same country as `York` are returned instead.

While FSLCA consistently outperforms SLCA-based approaches, for some queries, both suffer poor precision. For instance, considering QM1, most of our volunteers expect the result to be the city of `London, UK`. However, there are other cities containing `London` such as `East London` in South Africa which are unexpectedly returned by both FSLCA and SLCA. Consider another example QP4 whose intention is probably to find proteins published in `Science` in 2002. However, a protein can be involved in multiple publications. Hence if a protein has one publication in `Science` but not in 2002 and another publication in 2002 but not in `Science`, then this protein is still returned as a result. All volunteers agree that both `Science` and 2002 should be associated with the same publication. Nevertheless, we note that *these problems lie on the semantics of* SLCA *itself which is orthogonal to this work.*

We also notice that both FSLCA and SLCA have low precision on text-centric documents (*e.g.,* SHAKESPEARE) compared to data-centric documents (*e.g.,* DBLP, Mondial). The reason is that all SLCA approaches match each keyword individually while, for long-text-attributes, collective matching is expected. For example, consider QS3. Its intention is probably to find the speaker of the line

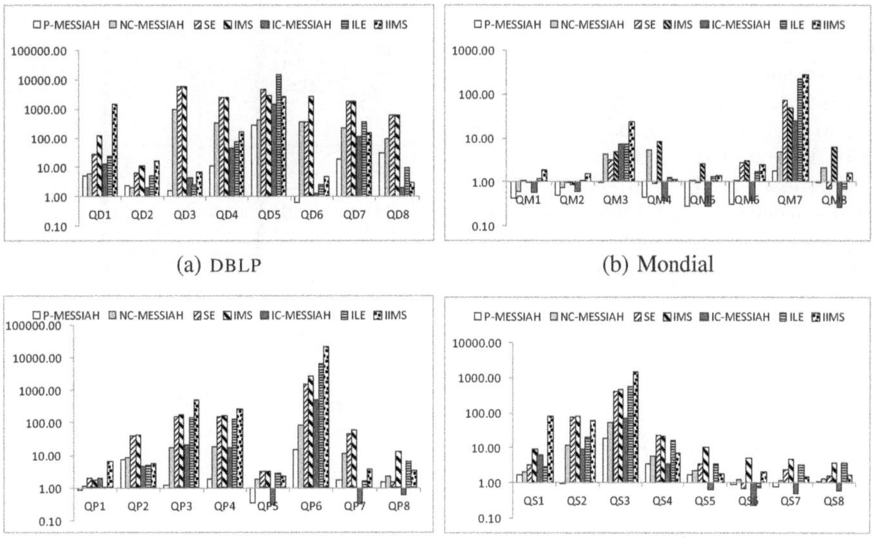

(a) DBLP (b) Mondial

(c) INTERPRO (d) SHAKESPEARE

Figure 6: Execution times (in msec). Note that y-axis is in log scale.

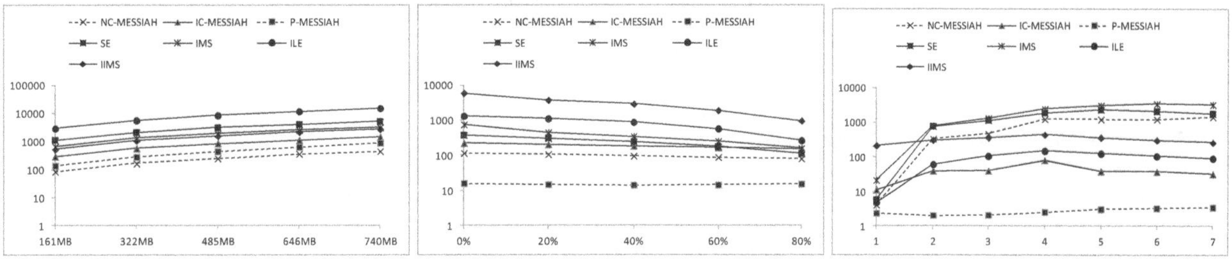

(a) Scalability (b) Percentage of missing elements (c) Number of keywords

Figure 7: Execution times (in msec).

to be or not to be. Thus, the keywords to be or not to be are expected to be matched collectively to a single node in that order. However, FSLCA and all SLCA-based approaches process those keywords individually so that a result can have different matches for to, be, not, etc. Nevertheless, this problem can be solved by ranking [1, 16] or collective matching as used in IR.

Execution times. In this set of experiments, we study the execution times of MESSIAH against state-of-the-art algorithms to compute SLCA nodes. Notice that we only measure the time to retrieve the SLCA/FSLCA nodes without retrieving the matches. The results are reported in Figure 6 (MESSIAH is shown in solid colors).

Clearly, P-MESSIAH *is faster than most of the* SLCA*-based approaches for majority of the queries*. It is an order of magnitude faster than the *fastest* SLCA-based approaches for several queries (*e.g.,* QD4, QM7, QP3, QP4, QS3). Notice that these queries have a lot of label keywords (*e.g.,* publication, inproceedings). In an XML document, these keywords typically have a huge number of matches, significantly deteriorating performance of SLCA algorithms while P-MESSIAH is independent of the number of label matches (see Section 5.3). Also, C-MESSIAH is consistently fast for all queries with only one query exceeding 100*ms*.

On the other hand, the execution times of C-MESSIAH (both indexed and non-indexed) are generally worse than P-MESSIAH even when its result size is smaller. It is because, unlike P-MESSIAH, C-MESSIAH requires retrieval of label matches. As discussed in [17], the indexed implementations (IC-MESSIAH, ILE, IIMS) are generally faster and perform well when there are selective keywords in the query (*i.e.,* QM6, QP5, etc.) while the non-indexed implementations are generally slower but perform well when all keywords have high frequency (*e.g.,* QD5). However, notice that C-MESSIAH is still faster than its corresponding counterparts in [14] and [17].

Note that larger result size of P-MESSIAH compared to SLCA-based approaches does not mean slower subtree retrieval cost for the former. Since MESSIAH is conscious of the missing element phenomenon, results of P-MESSIAH are usually specific descendants of SLCA's results. Thus, the size of each result subtree returned by P-MESSIAH is smaller than that of SLCA-based approaches. For instance, consider QD6. The result size of SLCA is 1 but its only result subtree is, in fact, the whole XML tree!

Scalability. In this experiment, we vary the data size of DBLP dataset by trimming it to 161MB, 322MB, 485MB and 646MB. The performance of QD5 is then measured on these datasets. Note that QD5 is chosen because it involves missing elements and has a large result size, ensuring significantly different result size when the data size varies. The results are shown in Figure 7(a). Expectedly, the execution time increases when the data size increases for all approaches. More importantly, *our approaches are significantly faster than all* SLCA *approaches across all datasets*. Also notice that, in this case, NC-MESSIAH is faster than P-MESSIAH. It is because cite is a relatively rare label in DBLP [5] so that there are much fewer complete FSLCA nodes than partial FSLCA nodes.

Number of missing elements. In this experiment, we vary the number of nodes which are missing in the document and study its effect on the execution times of the benchmark approaches. The query used for this experiment is interpro name on the IN-

TERPRO dataset. Notice that each `interpro` node in INTERPRO has exactly one leaf child with label `name`. We remove $K\%$ of these `name` nodes and measure the performance on the modified document with missing nodes. Here, we vary K from 0 to 80 where $K = 0\%$ refers to the original document. The results are reported in Figure 7(b). We can make two key observations. Firstly, for existing SLCA algorithms and C-MESSIAH algorithms, more missing elements tend to reduce the execution time. It is expected since more missing elements means fewer SLCA (complete FSLCA) `interpro` nodes to be returned. Secondly, the execution time of P-MESSIAH does not change significantly when the number of missing nodes varies. Recall that the time complexity of Algorithm 1 is independent of the number of label matches. Observe that removing the `name` node for query `interpro name` only affects the number of label matches to `name`.

Number of keywords. Next, we study the effect of number of keywords in a query on the execution time. We use the query `XML title inproceedings author Torsten Grust 2007` (on DBLP) containing seven keywords for this purpose. We first start with the query `XML` and then incrementally add more keywords from left to right. In each step, the execution time is measured and reported in Figure 7(c). The results show that the performances of all approaches except P-MESSIAH vary with different number of keywords. On the other hand, the execution time of P-MESSIAH is faster than these approaches and generally do not vary significantly with the number of keywords. Observe that when the number of keywords increases, a query has more input nodes but the result size also decreases. For SLCA-based approaches the effect of the input nodes dominates since output size is generally not as large as input size. However, for P-MESSIAH, for each keyword, we only retrieve the value matches and type matches and not the label matches. Hence, the input size is typically much smaller resulting in significant performance gain. Also notice that, when the number of keywords increase, the query becomes more selective so that indexed algorithms tend to be faster than non-indexed algorithms. Figure 7(c) also clearly shows that our C-MESSIAH algorithms are faster than the corresponding SLCA counterparts.

Heuristics for algorithm selection. Lastly, we study the accuracy of our proposed heuristic in choosing C-MESSIAH or P-MESSIAH appropriately. As C-MESSIAH and P-MESSIAH share identical result set for all queries with subscripts 1 to 4, we only consider sample queries with subscripts 5 to 8. We set $N = 20$ (desired number of results). Figure 8 shows the results of our study. Clearly, our approach estimates the number of complete FSLCA nodes with reasonable accuracy (see Figure 4) and more importantly uses it to make accurate choice. Specifically, for all queries where C-MESSIAH would return empty results (*e.g.*, QD5, QP5, QD6) or very few results (*e.g.*, QP7, QS6), P-MESSIAH is suitably chosen to effectively inform a user existence of missing elements in desired result sets. On the other hand, for queries with reasonably large results size (*e.g.*, QM7, QP6, QD5), C-MESSIAH is employed as discussed in Section 5.5.

Id	Estimated Num. of Complete FSLCA	Id	Estimated Num. of Complete FSLCA	Id	Estimated Num. of Complete FSLCA	Id	Estimated Num. of Complete FSLCA
QM5	0.221	QP5	0.865	QD5	6373.971	QS5	0.000
QM6	1.104	QP6	40292	QD6	0.029	QS6	0.070
QM7	228.017	QP7	0.000	QD7	11.691	QS7	0.047
QM8	2.882	QP8	0.000	QD8	0.000	QS8	0.000

Figure 8: Heuristic-based algorithm selection (underline means C-MESSIAH is selected, otherwise P-MESSIAH).

7. CONCLUSIONS

The quest for high quality keyword search in XML data has become more pressing because many users favor the simplicity and familiarity of search queries to formulating a syntactically correct query using a complex XML query language. State-of-the-art XML keyword search techniques adopt smallest lowest common ancestors (SLCAs) and its variants as a meaningful way to identify matching nodes in XML data. However, SLCA-based approaches perform poorly for queries involving missing elements as they are not optionality resilient. In this paper, we present two variants of a novel algorithm called MESSIAH which identify optionality-resilient FSLCA nodes instead of SLCA nodes to address this limitation. MESSIAH exploits the notion of a full document and the small size of its DataGuide to efficiently identify superior quality FSLCA nodes. A compelling benefit of MESSIAH is that it can be integrated seamlessly with state-of-the-art techniques for relevant return nodes selection, potentially improving the strengths of these approaches. Our empirical study demonstrated that MESSIAH not only produces superior quality results but also is significantly faster than state-of-the-art SLCA computation techniques.

8. REFERENCES

[1] Z. Bao, J. Lu, T. W. Ling, and B. Chen. Towards an effective xml keyword search. *IEEE TKDE*, 22(8):1077–1092, 2010.

[2] S. Cohen, J. Mamou, Y. Kanza, and Y. Sagiv. Xsearch: A semantic search engine for xml. In *VLDB*, pages 45–56, 2003.

[3] R. Goldman and J. Widom. Dataguides: Enabling query formulation and optimization in semistructured databases. In *VLDB*, 1997.

[4] L. Kong, R. Gilleron, and A. Lemay. Retrieving meaningful relaxed tightest fragments for xml keyword search. In *EDBT*, 2009.

[5] M. Lay. Dblp - some lessons learned. In *VLDB*, 2009.

[6] K.-H. Lee, K.-Y. Whang, W.-S. Han, and M.-S. K. 0002. Structural consistency: enabling xml keyword search to eliminate spurious results consistently. *VLDB J.*, 19(4):503–529, 2010.

[7] J. Li, C. Liu, R. Zhou, and W. Wang. Suggestion of promising result types for xml keyword search. In *EDBT*, pages 561–572, 2010.

[8] Y. Li, C. Yu, and H. V. Jagadish. Schema-free xquery. In *VLDB*, pages 72–83, 2004.

[9] Z. Liu and Y. Chen. Identifying meaningful return information for xml keyword search. In *SIGMOD*, pages 329–340, 2007.

[10] Z. Liu and Y. Chen. Reasoning and identifying relevant matches for xml keyword search. *PVLDB*, 1(1):921–932, 2008.

[11] Z. Liu and Y. Chen. Return specification inference and result clustering for keyword search on xml. *ACM TODS*, 35(2), 2010.

[12] N. Polyzotis, M. Garofalakis, and Y. Ioannidis. Selectivity estimation for xml twigs. In *ICDE*, pages 264–275. IEEE, 2004.

[13] A. Schmidt, F. Waas, M. L. Kersten, M. J. Carey, I. Manolescu, and R. Busse. Xmark: A benchmark for xml data management. In *VLDB*, pages 974–985, 2002.

[14] C. Sun, C.-Y. Chan, and A. K. Goenka. Multiway slca-based keyword search in xml data. In *WWW*, 2007.

[15] I. Tatarinov, S. Viglas, K. S. Beyer, J. Shanmugasundaram, E. J. Shekita, and C. Zhang. Storing and querying ordered xml using a relational database system. In *SIGMOD*, pages 204–215, 2002.

[16] A. Termehchy and M. Winslett. Effective, design-independent xml keyword search. In *CIKM*, pages 107–116, 2009.

[17] Y. Xu and Y. Papakonstantinou. Efficient keyword search for smallest lcas in xml databases. In *SIGMOD*, pages 537–538, 2005.

[18] C. Zhang, J. F. Naughton, D. J. DeWitt, Q. Luo, and G. M. Lohman. On supporting containment queries in relational database management systems. In *SIGMOD*, pages 425–436, 2001.

[19] J. Zhou, Z. Bao, W. Wang, T. W. Ling, Z. Chen, X. Lin, and J. Guo. Fast slca and elca computation for xml keyword queries based on set intersection. In *ICDE*, pages 905–916, 2012.

Indexing for Subtree Similarity-Search using Edit Distance

Sara Cohen
Dept. of Computer Science and Engineering
Hebrew University of Jerusalem
Jerusalem, Israel
sara@cs.huji.ac.il

ABSTRACT

Given a tree Q and a large set of trees $\mathcal{T} = \{T_1, \ldots, T_n\}$, the *subtree similarity-search problem* is that of finding the subtrees of trees among $\mathcal{T}$ that are most similar to Q, using the tree edit distance metric. Determining similarity using tree edit distance has been proven useful in a variety of application areas. While subtree similarity-search has been studied in the past, solutions required traversal of all of $\mathcal{T}$, which poses a severe bottleneck in processing time, as $\mathcal{T}$ grows larger. This paper proposes the first index structure for subtree similarity-search, provided that the unit cost function is used. Extensive experimentation and comparison to previous work shows the huge improvement gained when using the proposed index structure and processing algorithm.

Categories and Subject Descriptors

H.3.1 [**Information Storage and Retrieval**]: Content Analysis and Indexing—*Indexing methods*

Keywords

Edit distance; Indexing

1. INTRODUCTION

In many applications, data is naturally modeled as a labeled ordered tree. Such trees may be compared to determine their similarity. One of the most common methods of comparing trees is by using tree edit distance, i.e., similarity is measured by the number of edit operations required to "transform" one tree into the other. Some examples of application areas where this approach has been taken include comparison of RNA secondary structures [6, 12], discovering and comparing shape classes [13, 22], natural language processing [14], character recognition [18], quantifying neuronal morphology [11], cerebral vascular tree matching [21], information extraction [17], document similarity [15], and similarity joining and querying of XML documents [1, 2, 8].

SIGMOD'13, June 22–27, 2013, New York, New York, USA.

It is well known [20, 23] that the edit distance between two ordered trees can be computed in polynomial time, using dynamic programming. Due to the importance of the tree edit distance metric in a variety of applications, further optimizing the computation of tree edit distance has been a topic of extensive research, e.g., [4, 5, 7, 16], among many others. Thus, a huge body of work has focused on efficiently comparing two trees to determine their similarity with respect to the edit distance metric. However, there has been very little work on the following problem: Given a user tree and a large database of trees, quickly identify the trees in the database (or subtrees thereof) that are most similar to that of the user. We call this the *subtree similarity-search problem.*[1] Clearly the ability to efficiently find trees that are similar to the user's input is an important task, in light of the many applications of tree edit distance discussed above.

Since *(1)* the number of subtrees of trees to be considered is polynomial (there is one subtree for each node of each tree in the database) and *(2)* edit distance can be computed in polynomial time, it follows that the subtree similarity-search problem is solvable in polynomial time. This is achieved by simply computing the edit distance from the user provided tree, for each subtree in the database (using any one of the many efficient algorithms for tree edit distance), and then returning the best results. However, in practice, this strategy is highly non-feasible with a huge running time. Recently, [1, 2] presented a the first non-trivial solution to the subtree similarity-search problem that makes an effort to decrease the number of edit-distance computations needed, while also using bounded memory. Unfortunately, their solution requires traversal of all the entire database, which is a severe bottleneck, as the database grows bigger.

Our main contribution is a new approach to the subtree similarity-search problem (for the unit cost function), that significantly reduces processing time. In particular, we introduce a novel index structure that takes advantage of both general structural regularities in the trees, as well as selectivity of uncommon data items. We then devise a Dewey stack-based algorithm [9] that can take advantage of the index structure to quickly identify subtrees in the result. Finally, we perform extensive evaluation to demonstrate the excellent performance of our index and algorithm, as well as its superiority over the state-of-the-art.

[1] In [1, 2] this is called the *approximate subtree matching problem.*

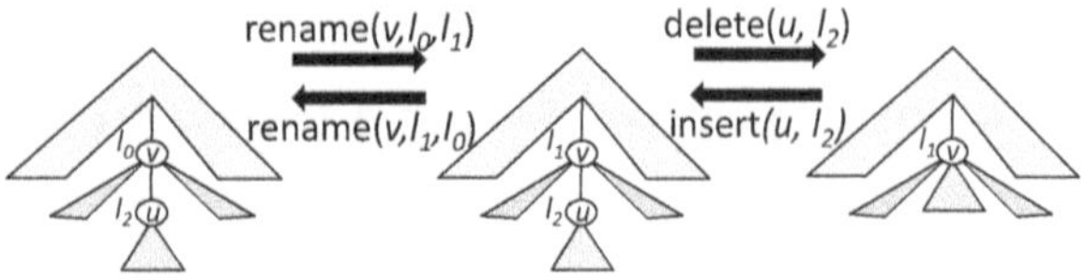

Figure 1: Edit operations rename, insert and delete.

2. FORMAL FRAMEWORK

2.1 Trees and Forests

We use Σ to denote an infinite alphabet of labels. Our trees are directed and ordered, and have labels drawn from Σ. If $T = (V, E)$ is a tree, we use $r(T)$ to denote the root of T, $l(v) \in \Sigma$ to denote the label of node $v \in V$, and $<$ to denote the complete ordering of nodes, as defined by a pre-order traversal of T.

We will sometimes use $\mathcal{V}(T)$ and $\mathcal{L}(T)$ to denote the nodes and the labels associated with nodes, respectively, of T. Given a node v, we denote by T_v the *subtree* rooted at v. We denote by $SubTrees(T)$ the set of all subtrees of T, i.e.,

$$SubTrees(T) = \{T_v \mid v \in V(T)\}.$$

Note that $T \in SubTrees(T)$. If $\mathcal{T}$ is a set of trees, then we define $SubTrees(\mathcal{T})$ as $\bigcup_{T \in \mathcal{T}} SubTrees(T)$.

For the purpose of computing edit distance, we also need the notion of a forest. A *forest* F is simply a sequence $T_1, \ldots, T_n$ of rooted, directed, labeled, ordered trees. The complete ordering $<$ of the nodes is defined by a pre-order traversal of the trees in the order given (i.e., $T_1, T_2, \ldots$).

2.2 Tree Edit Distance

We recall the standard definition of edit operations and edit distance on trees and forests [4]. There are three allowed *edit operations*. First, one may *delete* a node v, labeled l_1, written $del(v, l_1)$, in which case the children of v are promoted to be children of the parent of v, while retaining their relative order. If v is a root of a tree in a forest, then the children of v form roots of new trees within the forest. Second, one may *insert* a node u, labeled l_2, written $ins(u, l_2)$, into a tree. When inserting u as a child of some node v, a continuous subsequence of the children of v can be demoted to be children of u. Finally, one may *rename* a node w, written $rename(w, l_1, l_2)$, by changing the label of w from l_1 to l_2. The three edit distance operations are depicted in Figure 1.

Each edit operation is associated with a cost. Let $\epsilon \notin \Sigma$ denote the *null label* and let Σ_ϵ be $\Sigma \cup \{\epsilon\}$. Formally, a *cost function* c associates every pair l_1, l_2 from $\Sigma_\epsilon \times \Sigma_\epsilon$ with a cost $c(l_1, l_2)$, where

- $c(l, \epsilon)$ is the cost of deleting a node labeled l;
- $c(\epsilon, l)$ is the cost of inserting a node labeled l;
- $c(l_1, l_2)$ is the cost of renaming a node labeled l_1 to l_2.

Cost functions must be a distance metric, i.e., for any $l_1, l_2, l_3 \in \Sigma_\epsilon$ the following conditions are satisfied:

1. $c(l_1, l_2) \geq 0$, $c(l_1, l_1) = 0$;
2. $c(l_1, l_2) = c(l_2, l_1)$;
3. $c(l_1, l_3) \leq c(l_1, l_2) + c(l_2, l_3)$.

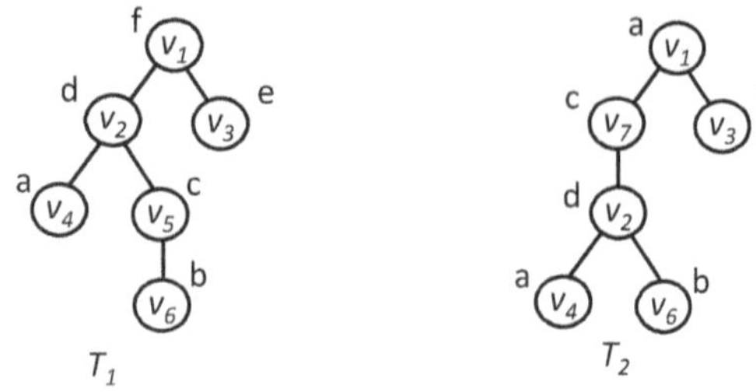

Figure 2: The edit distance between these trees is 3, when using the unit cost function.

One special cost function of interest is the *unit* cost function, which assigns the cost of one to every editing operation, i.e., $c(l_1, l_2) = 1$ when $l_1 \neq l_2$. *In this paper, we will consider only the unit cost function.* In Section 5.1 we briefly discuss the problem of adapting our algorithm to other cost functions.

Given trees T_1 and T_2, or more generally, forests F_1 and F_2, there is always a series of operations (actually many different series of operations) that transform F_1 to F_2. The edit distance between F_1 and F_2, denoted $ed(F_1, F_2)$ is simply the sum of costs of the cheapest series of operations transforming F_1 to F_2. Since c is a metric, for all forests it holds that $ed(F_1, F_2) = ed(F_2, F_1)$.

EXAMPLE 2.1. *Figure 2 demonstrates the notion of edit distance. The two trees in this figure have an edit distance of three (using the unit cost function), as demonstrated by the series of operations*

$$rename(v_1, f, a), ins(v_7, c), del(v_5, c),$$

which transform the first tree into the second, by first renaming the root, then inserting a node labeled c as a child of the root, and finally, deleting node v_5. Note the use of the same node identifiers in both trees to make the correspondence apparent.

2.3 Problem of Interest

Given a (small) tree Q and a corpus of (large) trees $\mathcal{T} = T_1, \ldots, T_n$, our goal is to find the subtrees of trees in $\mathcal{T}$ that are most similar to Q. We will usually refer to Q as the *query*. Our problem gets two parameters: a similarity bound m, and a quantity bound k. Intuitively, we will be returning trees whose similarity to Q is bound by m, and, among these, we will return the best k trees.

Given a set of trees $\mathcal{T}$, a query Q and a non-negative number m, we use $Bound_m(Q, \mathcal{T})$, to denote all subtrees of trees in $\mathcal{T}$ within an edit distance of m from Q, i.e., the set

$$\{S \mid S \in SubTrees(\mathcal{T}) \text{ and } ed(Q, S) \leq m\}.$$

We now formally define the problem of interest.

PROBLEM 1 (SUBTREE SIMILARITY-SEARCH). *Let Q be a query and $\mathcal{T}$ be a set of trees. Let m be a non-negative number and k be a positive integer. The* m-bounded top-k subtree similarity-search problem *(or simply the subtree similarity-search problem for short) is to return a set of trees $Top_{m,k}(Q, \mathcal{T})$ which satisfies the following two conditions:*

- *Size is k (if possible):*

$$|Top_{m,k}(Q, \mathcal{T})| = \min\{|Bound_m(Q, \mathcal{T})|, k\};$$

- *Contains best subtrees: For every pair of trees $S_1, S_2 \in SubTrees(\mathcal{T})$, if*
  - $S_1 \in Top_{m,k}(Q, \mathcal{T})$ and
  - $S_2 \notin Top_{m,k}(Q, \mathcal{T})$,

  then $ed(Q, S_1) \leq ed(Q, S_2)$.

Choosing a high value for m essentially turns this problem into a regular (non-bounded) top-k search problem. On the other hand, choosing a high value for k turns this problem into that of finding all results (and not just the best results) within the bound of m. (We note that [2] has proven that there is an easily computable upper bound on the maximum possible edit distance among the k best answers, which is dependent only on the size of Q and on k, and is independent of the size of the tree $\mathcal{T}$. Thus, larger values of m need not be considered.)

The edit distance between two trees was shown to be computable in polynomial time, provided that the trees are ordered [4,20]. Since every tree T has a linear number of subtrees, the subtree similarity-search problem can be solved in polynomial time in a straightforward fashion: For each tree $T \in \mathcal{T}$ and for each subtree $S \in SubTrees(T)$, compute $ed(Q, S)$ and then return a set of subtrees satisfying the required criteria.

Notwithstanding the theoretical polynomial bound on computing tree edit distance, since $SubTrees(\mathcal{T})$ will typically be very large, simply computing edit distance for every subtree of $\mathcal{T}$ is not practically feasible. Instead, our focus in this paper is on index structures and algorithms that can significantly speed up the processing time by efficiently identifying a small subset of subtrees of $\mathcal{T}$ that must be examined.

3. NAIVE ALGORITHM

We present a rather naive algorithm for the problem of subtree similarity-search, using a basic index structure. This algorithm serves as a building block for the more intricate algorithm presented later. It also highlights the difficulties that are encountered when trying to solve the subtree similarity-search problem using index structures.

The very basic skeleton of this (as well as the subsequent) algorithm consists of two stages.

- *Identify Candidates:* Find subtrees S of $SubTrees(\mathcal{T})$ likely to be within edit distance m of Q. Such subtrees are called *candidates.*
- *Compute Edit Distance:* For each candidate S, compute $ed(Q, S)$ and check whether this value is within the bound of m. Finally, return the top-k among all subtrees S that were considered.

To boost performance (as will be apparent later), these two stages are actually performed in an interleaved fashion—immediately after a candidate S is identified, we compute the edit distance of S from Q.

Compared to most of our algorithm (which does linear time computations on posting lists), computing edit distance is a relatively expensive operation (as it is polynomial in the size of Q and S). Therefore, it is critical to minimize the number of tree edit distance computations that are necessary, i.e., the number of candidates identified. Our indices are used for this purpose, and are described next. We note that the index structure for the algorithm of Section 4 is somewhat different and is described later in Section 4.1.

3.1 Indices

Given a corpus $\mathcal{T}$ containing possibly many trees, we assume that each tree $T \in \mathcal{T}$ is associated with an integer identifier $doc(T)$. Each node v in a tree is associated with a node identifier $id(v)$ using the Dewey encodings [9]. We review Dewey encodings briefly. For the root node r of a tree T, we define $id(r) = doc(T)$. For the remainder of the nodes, the identifiers are defined inductively. Let w be the k-th child of the node v. Then, $id(w) = id(v).k$, i.e., it is simply the concatenation of the identifier of v, with the index of w among the children of v. Dewey encodings are useful, as they allow the relationship among nodes to be quickly determined, e.g., w is a descendant of v if and only if $id(v)$ is a prefix of $id(w)$.

We will use $\bar{d}$ and $\bar{e}$ to abstractly denote Dewey encodings (node identifiers), and ϵ to denote the empty Dewey encoding (i.e., a series of numbers of length zero). When convenient, we will often avoid differentiating between a node and its identifier. For example, we will say "the subtree of $\bar{d}$," and write $T_{\bar{d}}$, when referring to the subtree T_v where $id(v) = \bar{d}$.

For the naive algorithm, we use two types of indices: label indices and node indices, described next.

- **Label Index:** For every label l in a tree of $\mathcal{T}$, we store the list of identifiers $id(v)$ of nodes v such that v is labeled l. The nodes are stored, sorted according to a pre-ordering of the nodes (i.e., the relation $<$). We will use $\mathcal{I}_l$ to refer to the list of nodes associated with label l, and call $\mathcal{I}_l$ the *posting list* for l. We use *Dict* to denote the dictionary, i.e., the set of all label indices. In our implementation, the dictionary is a BTree of (label, posting-list) pairs, thus allowing logarithmic access to posting lists, given a label.
- **Node Index:** For each node v, we store its identifier $id(v)$, along with the following information about T_v:
  - number of nodes in T_v, denoted $size(T_v)$;
  - depth of T_v, i.e., the number of nodes on the longest root to leaf path of T_v, denoted $depth(T_v)$;
  - label $l(v)$ of v;

  We will use $NodeInd$ to denote the index containing all node information. Again, this index is implemented as a BTree, to allow easy access to the information about each individual node. The BTrees stores the node information sorted by node identifiers, according to a pre-ordering.

Note that the node identifiers are sorted by a pre-ordering. This is particularly important for $NodeInd$, as it ensures that subtrees can be recreated by a continuous reading of $NodeInd$. This is important as our algorithms must recreate subtrees S before applying a standard edit distance computation algorithm to compute $ed(Q, S)$. *We emphasize that at no point in our computation do we need to directly access the original trees; rather all accesses are to the index.*

3.2 Algorithm

We use a Dewey-Stack-style algorithm [9] to find candidate subtrees. The algorithm *NaiveSearch* appears in Figure 3. This algorithm gets as input a user query Q, a set of trees $\mathcal{T}$, a non-negative bound m, and a positive integer

Algorithm *NaiveSearch*$(Q, \mathcal{T}, m, k)$

1. $\mathcal{PL} \leftarrow$new List
2. **for** $l \in \mathcal{L}(Q)$
3. **do** Add $\mathcal{I}_l$ to $\mathcal{PL}$
4. $\mathcal{S} \leftarrow$ new Stack
5. *Results* $\leftarrow$new BoundedPriorityQueue(k)
6. **while** not $\mathcal{PL}.isEmpty()$
7. **do** $(\bar{d}, l) \leftarrow \mathcal{PL}.next()$
8. $L \leftarrow \{\!\{\}\!\}$
9. **while** not $\mathcal{S}.isEmpty()$ and $\mathcal{S}.top().id$ is not a prefix of $\bar{d}$
10. **do** $(\bar{d}_{prev}, L_{prev}) \leftarrow \mathcal{S}.pop()$
11. $L \leftarrow L \uplus L_{prev}$
12. $m \leftarrow FilterAndAdd(Q, L, \bar{d}_{prev}, m, Results)$
13. $\bar{d}_{top} \leftarrow \epsilon$
14. **if** not $\mathcal{S}.isEmpty()$
15. **then** $(\bar{d}_{prev}, L_{prev}) \leftarrow \mathcal{S}.pop$
16. $\mathcal{S}.push(\bar{d}_{prev}, L \uplus L_{prev})$
17. $\bar{d}_{top} \leftarrow \bar{d}_{prev}$
18. **for each** $\bar{e}$ such that $\bar{d}_{top} \sqsubset \bar{e} \sqsubset \bar{d}$, in order
19. **do** $\mathcal{S}.push(\bar{e}, \{\!\{\}\!\})$
20. $\mathcal{S}.push(\bar{d}, \{\!\{l\}\!\})$
21. $L \leftarrow \{\!\{\}\!\}$
22. Perform the loop of Lines 9-12, until $\mathcal{S}$ is empty
23. **return** *Results*

Algorithm *FilterAndAdd*$(Q, L, \bar{d}, m, Results)$

1. $i \leftarrow |\mathcal{L}(Q) \cap L|$
2. $labelDiff \leftarrow \max\{(size(Q) - i), (size(T_{\bar{d}}) - i)\}$
3. $depthDiff \leftarrow$ absValue$(depth(Q) - depth(T_{\bar{d}}))$
4. **if** $labelDiff \leq m$ and $depthDiff \leq m$
5. **then** $c \leftarrow ed(Q, T_{\bar{d}})$
6. **if** $c < m$ or ($c = m$ and $Results.size < k$)
7. **then** $Results.boundedEnqueue(c, \bar{d})$
8. **if** $Results.size = k$
9. **then return** $Results.getTopScore()$
10. **else return** m

Figure 3: A naive algorithm for solving the subtree similarity-search problem.

k. Intuitively, the naive algorithm searches for subtrees of $\mathcal{T}$ that have at least one label in common with Q. For each such subtree S, the algorithm finds all common labels with Q. Then, using a simple computation, a lower bound on the edit distance of Q and S is computed. If this lower-bound is less than m, the actual edit distance is computed. Depending on the result of the computation, the tree S can be added to the set of results. We note that m may also be updated during the process, to derive a tighter upper bound.

We now examine the algorithm in more detail.

Data Structures. *NaiveSearch* uses the following data structures:

- A list $\mathcal{PL}$ of posting lists: The structure $\mathcal{PL}$ contains a set of posting lists (one for each label in Q). Although not explicitly written in the algorithm, for each posting list $\mathcal{I}_l$ added to $\mathcal{PL}$, the system initializes a pointer that points at the first Dewey identifier in the posting list of l. Using these pointers, $\mathcal{PL}$ supports two operations:
  - *next*: When this operation is called, a search is performed among all pointers to posting lists in $\mathcal{PL}$. A posting list $\mathcal{I}_l$ is found which has a pointer that points to the smallest Dewey id $\bar{d}$ (according to a pre-ordering) among all pointers to lists in $\mathcal{PL}$. The pair $(\bar{d}, l)$ is returned, and the pointer to $\mathcal{I}_l$ is incremented.
  - *isEmpty*: Returns true when all pointers to posting lists have reached the end of their lists (and are, therefore, pointing to a null value).
- A stack $\mathcal{S}$: The stack $\mathcal{S}$ contains pairs of the form $(\bar{d}, L)$ where $\bar{d}$ is a Dewey identifier and L is a *multiset* of labels.[2] This multiset L is used to store labels that appear in the subtree of $\bar{d}$, and are common with Q. Note that a multiset, denoted $\{\!\{\cdot\}\!\}$, and not a set, is used, as the same label may appear multiple times within a single subtree. The operations *top, pop, push,* and *isEmpty* are supported, with their usual meaning.
- A bounded priority queue of results *Results*: A bounded priority queue is similar to a priority queue, except it has a predefined size bound k. The elements inserted into *Results* are pairs $(c, \bar{d})$, such that $c = ed(Q, T_{\bar{d}})$. The queue is ordered so that the elements with the greatest value for c are at the top. Since *Results* is a k-bounded priority queue, it will always contain at most k elements. To this end, the queue supports the operation *boundedEnqueue*, which inserts a new element, and then, if the queue contains more than k elements, removes the top element (i.e., that with the greatest edit distance from Q). Note that *Results* also supports *size*, which returns the number of elements currently in the queue and *getTopScore*, which returns the score (i.e., the edit distance) for the topmost element in the queue.

Execution. In Lines 1 to 5, the data structures are initialized, including adding all posting lists corresponding to labels in Q to the structure $\mathcal{PL}$. In Lines 6 to 20, we loop until all Dewey identifiers in all posting lists of $\mathcal{PL}$ have been considered (i.e., until $\mathcal{PL}$ is empty). During each iteration of the list, we find the first pair identifier $\bar{d}$, among all those that have not yet been considered.

In Line 8, we initialize L to contain an empty multiset of labels. Note that all subsequent operations on L are multiset operations, e.g., $\uplus$ is the multiset union operation. Next, in Line 9, we examine the stack $\mathcal{S}$, and check whether its topmost element is a prefix of $\bar{d}$ (in which case it is an ancestor of $\bar{d}$). While it is not a prefix (Lines 9–12), we pop entries $(\bar{d}_{prev}, L_{prev})$. For such entries we have already discovered all labels in common with their subtrees and Q. In particular if S contains $(\bar{d}_{prev}, L_{prev})$, then $T_{\bar{d}_{prev}}$ contains all labels in L_{prev}, as well as all labels in the multisets L' that are above this stack entry (as entries above $\bar{d}_{prev}$ correspond to its descendants). Line 11 updates the multiset of labels in the tree rooted at $\bar{d}_{prev}$ as we iterate over the stack.

Since we have determined all labels of Q that are in common with $T_{\bar{d}_{prev}}$, we can determine whether $T_{\bar{d}_{prev}}$ may possibly be within the edit distance bound of m. For this purpose, in Line 12, the algorithm *FilterAndAdd* is called. Using L (and the depth of $T_{\bar{d}_{prev}}$), we can compute a lower bound on $ed(Q, T_{\bar{d}_{prev}})$ (Lines 1–3 of *FilterAndAdd*). The correctness of this lower bound is stated in Proposition 3.2. If the

[2]Since $\mathcal{S}$ is a stack containing Dewey identifiers, this style of algorithm is referred to as a Dewey stack algorithm [9].

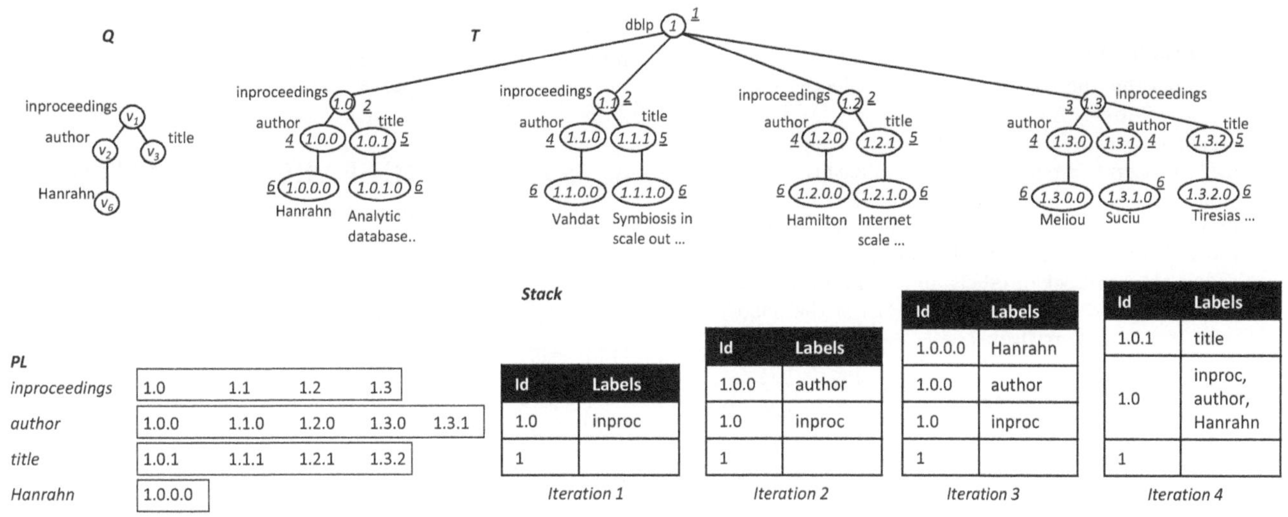

Figure 4: Query Q, excerpt from DBLP Tree T and data structures while running *NaiveSearch*.

lower bound is at most m, we compute the edit distance, and if this value is within the bound of m, the Dewey identifier (along with value of the edit distance) is added to *Results* (Lines 4–7 of *FilterAndAdd*). Actually, the Dewey identifier will be added if *Results* has not yet reached its bounded size of k, or if the new score is strictly lower than m. Note that in Lines 8–10 of *FilterAndAdd*, we return (and thereby, update) m so that it is equal to the cost of the top-most element in *Results*, once we have found k Dewey identifiers within the bound. This can effectively lower m, and hence, help to filter out additional results.

Back in *NaiveSearch*, at this point, either $\mathcal{S}$ is empty, or its topmost entry is a prefix of $\bar{d}$. If $\mathcal{S}$ is indeed not empty, the multiset L is added to the label multiset of the topmost entry (Lines 14–17). This reflects the fact that all labels in L are in the tree rooted at the Dewey encoding of the top of the stack. Note that $\mathcal{S}$ always satisfies the invariant that each entry in the stack is a descendant of each entry appearing above it (i.e., inserted before it) of the stack.

In Lines 18–19, all Dewey identifiers $\bar{e}$ that are descendants of the top-most identifier in the stack $\bar{d}_{top}$, and are predecessors of $\bar{d}$ are added to the stack. (Note that if $\mathcal{S}$ is empty, $\bar{d}_{top}$ is initialized to ϵ, the empty Dewey identifier, and all predecessors of $\bar{d}$ will be added.) This ensures that we will eventually pop each predecessor (as it contains a label from Q in its subtree). In Line 20, we add $\bar{d}$, along with the multiset of labels $\{\!\{l\}\!\}$, since $\bar{d}$ contains l in its subtree (as indicated by the posting list entry of Line 7).

Finally, if $\mathcal{S}$ is not empty when the loop of Line 6 terminates, we continue popping entries, and checking whether they may be within the edit distance bound (Line 22). At this point, we have examined all subtrees that contain at least one label in common with Q, and we return *Results*, which contains the k best such subtrees (Line 23).

EXAMPLE 3.1. *Consider the query Q and tree T of Figure 4. (For now, ignore the underlined numbers appearing next to the nodes.) Suppose that we choose $k = 1$ and $m = 2$. Note that this tree has document identifier 1, and hence, the root is identified by the Dewey encoding 1. When running NaiveSearch, for this query and tree, the set of posting lists of interest $\mathcal{PL}$ (those containing labels from Q) are depicted at the lower left-side of the figure.*

The first pair to be returned by Line 7 of the main loop is $(1.0, \mathit{inproceedings})$. *Since $\mathcal{S}$ is empty, the loop of Line 9 is not entered. Similarly, the condition of Line 14 does not hold. Hence, we add all encodings between $\bar{d}_{top} = \epsilon$ and 1.0 to the stack, deriving the first stack depicted in the lower right-side of the Figure.*

The next pair returned by Line 7 is $(1.0.0, \mathit{author})$. *Since* 1.0 *is a prefix (i.e., ancestor) of* 1.0.0, *nothing is popped in the loop of Line 9. Lines 15-16 have no effect (since L is the empty multiset), and Line 17 initializes $\bar{d}_{top}$ to* 1.0. *Hence, in the loop of Line 18, only* 1.0.0 *is added, yielding the second stack depicted in the Figure. Similarly, the pair* $(1.0.0.0, \mathit{Hanrahn})$ *is returned next by Line 7. Once again, the top of the stack* 1.0.0 *is a prefix of* 1.0.0.0, *causing similar execution, and yielding the third stack depicted.*

The fourth pair to be returned by Line 7 is $(1.0.1, \mathit{title})$. *Entries* 1.0.0.0 *and* 1.0.0 *are popped from the stack, as they are not prefixes of* 1.0.1. *While popping, we first call FilterAndAdd for* 1.0.0.0 *with* $\{\!\{\mathit{Hanrahn}\}\!\}$. *We compute the values labelDiff* $= \max\{4-1, 1-1\} = 3$ *and depthDiff* $= \text{absValue}(3-1) = 2$. *Since one of these values is larger than m, no edit distance computation is performed. Next, we call FilterAndAdd for* 1.0.0 *with* $\{\!\{\mathit{author}, \mathit{Hanrahn}\}\!\}$. *In this case, labelDiff* $= \max\{4-2, 2-2\} = 2$ *and depthDiff* $= \text{absValue}(3-2) = 1$. *Since both values are less than m, we compute the edit distance* $ed(Q, T_{1.0.0}) = 2$, *and* $(2, 1.0.0)$ *is added to Results. In this case, the value of m need not be updated. After considering both popped values, we update the set of labels of* 1.0, *and add* 1.0.1 *with* $\{\!\{\mathit{title}\}\!\}$ *to the stack.*

Execution proceeds in a similar fashion. Note that after popping 1.0 *during the execution, we will discover that* $ed(Q, T_{1.0}) = 1$, *and* $(1, 1.0)$ *will replace the previous value entry in our 1-bounded priority queue (k was chosen as 1).*

In addition, m will be updated to 1 to reflect the fact that any tree with greater edit distance cannot be part of the result (as there are k answers already found with a lower edit distance).

3.3 Discussion

We now consider the correctness and efficiency of the algorithm *NaiveSearch*. As will be clear from the discussion below, in some cases, *NaiveSearch* may miss results, and, in general, *NaiveSearch* is not particularly efficient.

Correctness. We first state that our filtering condition of *FilterAndAdd* is correct. In the following proposition, recall that $\mathcal{L}(T)$ is the multiset of labels appearing in T, $size(T)$ is the number of nodes in T and $depth(T)$ is the length of the longest root to leaf path in T.

PROPOSITION 3.2. *Let Q be a query and S be a subtree. Let i be the size of the bag intersection of $\mathcal{L}(S)$ and $\mathcal{L}(Q)$. Then,*

$$ed(Q, S) \geq (size(Q) - i)$$
$$ed(Q, S) \geq (size(S) - i)$$
$$ed(Q, S) \geq \text{absValue}(depth(Q) - depth(S))$$

The proof of Proposition 3.2 is straightforward. Translating Q to S requires, at the minimum, achieving the same multiset of labels, and the same depth. As we consider the unit cost function, each edit operation has a cost of 1, and hence, the size of differences in label multisets, as well as the size of differences in depth, are a lower bound on the edit distance.

NaiveSearch only examines subtrees that have at least one label in common with Q. If m is larger than the number of nodes in Q, then there may be subtrees satisfying the requirements that have no label in common with Q. Such subtrees with never be examined, and hence, will not be returned. However, for the more natural case that m is less than $size(Q)$, all answers must have at least one label in common with Q, and *NaiveSearch* is correct. Note that Proposition 3.3 follows from Proposition 3.2, and an easy analysis of the algorithm. This analysis is omitted, as it is similar to showing the correctness of the Dewey-stack algorithm for keyword search in [9].

PROPOSITION 3.3. *If $m < size(Q)$ then NaiveSearch returns $Top_{m,k}(Q, \mathcal{T})$.*

Efficiency. Obviously, *NaiveSearch* runs in polynomial time, as it examines each node at most once and performs at most a linear number of edit distance computations. However, unfortunately *NaiveSearch* is quite inefficient! The main problem is that it must traverse the entire posting lists of all labels appearing in the query. If the labels in the query are very common, then the posting lists can collectively be about as large as the original trees. To make things worse, the stack S will eventually contain not only nodes labeled by a query label, but also all ancestors of such nodes. Hence, again, we are likely to traverse a significant portion of the tree.

In a nutshell, while the goal of indexing is to avoid a scan of the entire trees in the corpus, accessing posting lists that contain most document identifiers of nodes in the corpus (and then also accessing their ancestors) does not provide performance gains. This is demonstrated intuitively next.

EXAMPLE 3.4. *Consider, again, the example from Figure 4. A total of 14 out of the 23 nodes in T appear in the posting lists $\mathcal{PL}$. Including all ancestors of such nodes, yields 15 nodes that are inserted into the stack throughout the execution. Given sufficiently large values of k and m, we may require close to 15 edit distance computations. For example, given $k = 4$ and $m = 3$, it is not difficult to see that NaiveSearch would perform 13 edit distance computations.*

4. STRUCTURE SEARCH ALGORITHM

In this section we introduce the *StructureSearch* algorithm that allows structural commonalities to be leveraged, in order to avoid the scan of large posting lists, and to significantly reduce the number of edit distance computations required. We start by demonstrating the intuition behind our approach.

EXAMPLE 4.1. *Consider the query Q and tree T appearing in Figure 4. The tree T has 23 nodes, and hence, defines 23 subtrees, all of which may be in $Top_{m,k}(Q, T)$, for large enough values of m and k. Hence, given sufficiently large m and k, one might assume that 23 edit distance computations are necessary to return all 23 subtrees within $Top_{m,k}(Q, T)$. However, careful observation of T reveals much regularity, that can be leveraged to reduce the number of edit distance operations required. As we show later in our experimentation, such regularity is common in real tree datasets (and is much more pronounced in large trees).*

To demonstrate how edit distance computations may be avoided, consider subtrees $T_{1.1}$ and $T_{1.2}$. It is not difficult to see that $ed(Q, T_{1.1}) = ed(Q, T_{1.2})$ must hold, and therefore, one of these edit distance computations can be avoided. This is true since, with respect to the labels in Q, trees $T_{1.1}$ and $T_{1.2}$ are identical. To be more precise, replacing every label of $T_{1.1}$ and $T_{1.2}$ that does not also appear in Q, with some new unused label δ would yield trees $T^{\delta}_{1.1}$ and $T^{\delta}_{1.2}$ that are identical. Since our cost function uses a unit cost for operations, the precise labels appearing in a subtree are irrelevant to the cost, for labels not appearing in Q. On the other hand, we would not expect $ed(Q, T_{1.1})$ to be equal to $ed(Q, T_{1.0})$, as the latter has an additional label (Hanrahn) in common with Q. Similarly, We would also not expect $ed(Q, T_{1.1})$ to be equal to $ed(Q, T_{1.3})$, as it has a different structure.

Example 4.1 shows how edit distance computations can be avoided by leveraging similarities among subtree structures. However, in practice, computations can be avoided only if these similarities can be recognized *efficiently at runtime*. This requires some sort of auxiliary indexing information, to avoid subtree scans during query processing. However, such indexing is not completely straightforward, as determining that two subtrees will have the same edit distance from Q, is a query dependent operation, as it takes into consideration the labels of Q.

We formalize the above idea. Let L be a set of labels and T be a tree. Let δ be a new, unused label. We use $T^{L,\delta}$ to denote the result of replacing every label l in T, such that $l \notin L$, with δ. Thus, $T^{L,\delta}$ will contain only the labels in $L \cup \{\delta\}$. We define L-equivalence of trees, as follows. Let S and T be trees. We say that S and T are L-equivalent, written $S \equiv_L T$, if $S^{L,\delta}$ is *identical* to $T^{L,\delta}$.

EXAMPLE 4.2. *Consider the tree T of Figure 4. Define the sets of labels $L_1 = \{inproceedings, author, title\}$, $L_2 =$*

$\mathcal{L}(Q)$ *and* $L_3 = \emptyset$. *Then,* $T_{1.0} \equiv_{L_1} T_{1.1}$, $T_{1.0} \not\equiv_{L_2} T_{1.1}$, $T_{1.1} \equiv_{L_2} T_{1.2}$, *and* $T_{1.0.0} \equiv_{L_3} T_{1.0.1}$, *are just a few of the equivalences that can be observed.*

The following easy proposition states that L-equivalence is useful for avoiding edit distance computations, and it holds since the unit cost function is used.

PROPOSITION 4.3. *The following properties hold:*

- *If* $S_1 \equiv_{\mathcal{L}(Q)} S_2$, *then* $ed(Q, S_1) = ed(Q, S_2)$.

While it would be useful to have an index that immediately identifies whether two subtrees are equivalent with respect to the labels of a given query Q, we cannot take into consideration, during the indexing phase, every possible set of labels. Instead, while indexing, we identify a set of labels in the input, denoted $\mathcal{L}_c$. Typically, we will choose $\mathcal{L}_c$ to be the set containing the most common labels appearing in the input.[3] Structural similarities among subtrees will be identified, with respect to the set $\mathcal{L}_c$.

To be precise, each node v in $\mathcal{T}$ will be associated with a *structural identifier*, denoted *struct*(v). These identifiers precisely divide the subtrees of $\mathcal{T}$ into equivalence classes, with respect to $\mathcal{L}_c$, i.e.,

$$struct(v) = struct(u) \iff T_v \equiv_{\mathcal{L}_c} T_u\,.$$

Given a structural identifier s, we will use $[s]$ to denote the set of trees that have the structural identifier s. We will use $T_{[s]}$ to denote the tree derived by taking any tree in $[s]$, and replacing all its labels that are not from $\mathcal{L}_c$ with δ. Thus, $T_{[s]}$ is, in a sense, an abstraction of all trees in $[s]$.

We use *structSet*($\mathcal{T}$) to denote the set of all structural identifiers of nodes in $\mathcal{T}$. Note that the size of *structSet*($\mathcal{T}$) is the number of distinct subtrees in $\mathcal{T}$, with respect to the labels in $\mathcal{L}_c$ (and is also a measure of the regularity of $\mathcal{T}$ with respect to $\mathcal{L}_c$).

4.1 Indices

We now describe the indices used for *StructureSearch*. Let $\mathcal{L}$ be all labels appearing among $\mathcal{T}$, $\mathcal{L}_c$ be a subset of $\mathcal{L}$ and $\mathcal{L}_u$ be $\mathcal{L} \backslash \mathcal{L}_c$, i.e., the remainder of the labels. (The subscript u is a reminder that $\mathcal{L}_u$ usually contains uncommon labels.) In the following, we use $\mathcal{L}_c(T)$ (resp. $\mathcal{L}_u(T)$) to denote the multiset containing all labels from T that belong to $\mathcal{L}_c$ (resp. $\mathcal{L}_u$).

- **$\mathcal{L}_u$-Label Index:** As in the label index of Section 3.1, for each label $l \in \mathcal{L}_u$, we store the list of identifiers of nodes v, such that v is labeled l. We use the same notation $\mathcal{I}_l$ and *Dict* to refer to this dictionary of posting lists.
- **Structure Index:** For each identifier s in *structSet*($\mathcal{T}$), we store
  - $|\mathcal{L}_c(T_{[s]})|$, i.e., the number of nodes in $T_{[s]}$ labeled with labels from $\mathcal{L}_c$,
  - $size(T_{[s]}) - |\mathcal{L}_c(T_{[s]})|$, i.e., the number of nodes in $T_{[s]}$ labeled with δ,
  - the depth of $T_{[s]}$ and
  - a sorted list of Dewey identifiers of all roots of trees in $[s]$.
- **$\mathcal{L}_c$-Label Index:** For each label $l \in \mathcal{L}_c$, we store the list of structural identifiers s for which $l \in \mathcal{L}(T_{[s]})$, along with the number of times that l appears in $T_{[s]}$.[4]
- **Node Index:** In addition to the information specified in Section 3.1 (size, depth and label), we also store the structural identifier *struct*(v) for each node v.

[3]For now, it use useful to think of $\mathcal{L}_c$ as comprising the set of labels of internal nodes, as these are usually very common in a tree. Further discussion of how $\mathcal{L}_c$ is chosen will be given in Section 5.

L_c-Label Index

label	*(structure id, multiplicity)*
dblp	(1,1)
inproceedings	(1, 4), (2,1), (3,1)
author	(1, 5), (2, 1), (3,2), (4,1)
title	(1, 4), (2, 1), (3,1), (5,1)

Structure Index

structure id	*nodes labeled L_c*	*other nodes*	*depth*	*Dewey identifiers*
1	14	9	4	1
2	3	2	3	1.0, 1.1, 1.2
3	4	3	3	1.3
4	1	1	2	1.0.0, 1.1.0, 1.2.0, 1.3.0, 1.3.1
5	1	1	2	1.0.1, 1.1.1, 1.2.1, 1.3.2
6	0	1	1	1.0.0.0, 1.0.1.0, 1.1.0.0, 1.1.1.0, 1.2.0.0, 1.2.1.0, 1.3.0.0, 1.3.1.0, 1.3.2.0

Figure 5: $\mathcal{L}_c$-label index and structure index for excerpt from DBLP Tree T.

EXAMPLE 4.4. *Figure 5 depicts the structure index and the* $\mathcal{L}_c$*-label index for the tree* T *of Figure 4, when choosing* $\mathcal{L}_c = \{dblp, inproceedings, author, title\}$. *Note that the structural identifier of each node in* T*, appears next to the node, and is underlined.*

4.2 Algorithm

We now describe the algorithm *StructureSearch*. To simplify, we start by describing a slight variation of this algorithm that will only return trees that contain at least one label in common with Q (as does *NaiveSearch*). In Section 4.4, we explain how to further extend this algorithm, to also return trees containing no labels in common with Q.

Our algorithm has three major components:

- **Gathering Information:** In this first component, we gather information about structure ids s such that $T_{[s]}$ has at least one label from $\mathcal{L}_c$ in common with Q.

[4]Complete label information is stored for each structural identifier s. It is possible to save space by leveraging the nesting of the trees. However, in practice, the size of this index was reasonable, and hence, this optimization was not employed.

Algorithm *GatherInformation*$(Q, \mathcal{T})$

$\mathcal{PL} \leftarrow$new List
for $l \in \mathcal{L}_c(Q)$
  do Add $\mathcal{I}_l$ to $\mathcal{PL}$
$\mathcal{H} \leftarrow$new Hashtable
$s_{prev} \leftarrow \perp$
$L \leftarrow \{\!\{\}\!\}$
while (not $\mathcal{PL}.isEmpty()$)
  do $((s, n), l) \leftarrow \mathcal{PL}.next()$
    if $s \neq s_{prev}$ and $s_{prev} \neq \perp$
      then $\mathcal{H}.put(s_{prev}, |\mathcal{L}_c(Q) \cap L|)$
    $L \leftarrow \{\!\{\}\!\}$
    Add n occurrences of l to L
    $s_{prev} \leftarrow s$
if $s_{prev} \neq \perp$ **then** $\mathcal{H}.put(s_{prev}, |\mathcal{L}_c(Q) \cap L|)$
return $\mathcal{H}$

Figure 6: A structure-based algorithm for solving the subtree similarity-search problem.

- **Finding $\mathcal{L}_u$ Answers:** In the second component we find the top-k answers (within the edit bound of m) among all those that have *at least one label from $\mathcal{L}_u$ in common with Q.*
- **Finding $\mathcal{L}_c$ Answers:** In the third component, we find additional answers that have labels from $\mathcal{L}_c$ in common with Q (but have no labels from $\mathcal{L}_u(Q)$). These are added to the answers found in the previous component, in order to find the top-k answers sharing a label in common with Q.

Each of these components in discussed in detail next.

4.2.1 Gathering Information

In the algorithm *GatherInformation*, we find all structural identifiers s, such that trees in $[s]$ contain at least one label in $\mathcal{L}_c$ that is also in Q. The algorithm returns a hash table containing, for each such s, the size of the multiset intersection of $\mathcal{L}_c(T_{[s]}) \cap \mathcal{L}_c(Q)$. These values will be used to compute a bound to filter our candidates in the next two components. Observe that *GatherInformation* is a simple loop over the $\mathcal{L}_c$-label index for entries corresponding to labels from $\mathcal{L}_u(Q)$. Note also that, as described above, the entry for label l contain pairs (s, n) such that $T_{[s]}$ contains n occurrences of label l.

Algorithm *GatherInformation* appears in Figure 6. As in *NaiveSearch*, this algorithm also uses a data structure $\mathcal{PL}$, which supports finding the next entry among the posting lists from the $\mathcal{L}_c$-label Index. Thus, it returns the next pair (s, n), along with the corresponding label, as ordered by the structural identifiers s. The algorithm continually adds to the set L, while the same structural identifier is seen. When a new identifier is seen, complete information has been derived about the previous, and thus, the multiset-intersection size can be added to the hashtable.

Example 4.5. *The result of GatherInformation for the query and tree of Figure 4 (with $\mathcal{L}_c = \{dblp, inproceedings, author, title\}$), appears in the left-hand side of Figure 7.*

4.2.2 Finding $\mathcal{L}_u$ Answers

The goal of $\mathcal{L}_u$-*FindAnswers* is to find the top-k subtrees, among all those that share a label in common with $\mathcal{L}_u(Q)$.

Structure Id	Intersection Size
1	3
2	3
3	3
4	1
5	1

Hashtable
Algorithm: GatherInformation

Id	Labels
1.0.0.0	Hanrahn
1.0.0	
1.0	
1	

Stack
Algorithm: L_c-FindAnswers

Figure 7: Data structures for algorithms.

Since $\mathcal{L}_u$ will typically be chosen as the most uncommon labels from $\mathcal{T}$, there are relatively few subtrees that will be considered at this point.

Observe that the posting lists for $\mathcal{L}_u$ are identical in form to the posting lists for $\mathcal{L}$ from the previous section. Therefore, we actually use the algorithm *NaiveSearch* to implement $\mathcal{L}_u$-*FindAnswers*, with two significant changes:

1. In Line 2, we iterate only over the labels in $\mathcal{L}_u(Q)$, instead of over all labels of Q.
2. Our implementation of *FilterAndAdd* is slightly different. To compute the variable *labelDiff*, we first find the structural identifier s of $\bar{d}$, using the node index. We then look up s in the hashtable $\mathcal{H}$ returned by *GatherInformation*, to find the number of labels from $\mathcal{L}_c(Q)$ that are in common with $T_{\bar{d}}$. (Note that if s is not in $\mathcal{H}$, then there are no such labels in common.) Given the information in the structural index, we know the number of nodes with labels from $\mathcal{L}_c$, and the number of nodes with labels from $\mathcal{L}_u$, among $T_{\bar{d}}$. The Dewey stack algorithm has computed the number of labels from $\mathcal{L}_u(Q)$ that are in common with $T_{\bar{d}}$. Therefore, we can easily compute the minimum number of label changes needed to change Q into $T_{\bar{d}}$, and this value is assigned to *labelDiff*.

The remainder of the algorithm remains the same.

Example 4.6. *The query Q of Figure 4 contains one label in $\mathcal{L}_u$, namely Hanrahn. There is a single node containing this label in the tree T. The right-hand size of Figure 7 depicts the stack, when running the adaptation of NaiveSearch to $\mathcal{L}_u$-FindAnswers. After the single Dewey identifier 1.0.0.0 is added, all entries will be popped and we will consider (using FilterAndAdd) the subtrees $T_{1.0.0.0}, T_{1.0.0}, T_{1.0}, T_1$ as possible answers to the search problem. Note that these are precisely all subtrees of T that contain a label from $\mathcal{L}_u$ that also appears in Q.*

4.2.3 Finding $\mathcal{L}_c$ Answers

At the end of $\mathcal{L}_u$-*FindAnswers*, we have identified the top-k answers (with an edit distance bounded by m) among all those subtrees of $\mathcal{T}$ that share at least one label from $\mathcal{L}_u$ with Q. However, in two cases we must also consider candidates which have no labels from $\mathcal{L}_u$.

- **Case 1:** First, it is possible that $\mathcal{L}_u$-*FindAnswers* did not return enough answers, i.e., there were fewer than k subtrees containing a label from $\mathcal{L}_u$ that were within the edit distance bound of m. If $m \geq |\mathcal{L}_u(Q)|$, then there may be additional answers that have no label from $\mathcal{L}_u(Q)$ that should be returned.

- **Case 2:** Second, even if $\mathcal{L}_u$-*FindAnswers* returns k results, it is possible that there are superior answers, which do not contain any label from $\mathcal{L}_u(Q)$. This is possible if $|\mathcal{L}_u(Q)|$ is less than the edit distance of the worst answer returned thus far.

The pseudo-code of the algorithm $\mathcal{L}_c$-*FindAnswers* is omitted due to space limitations. However, this algorithm is easy to understand—it simply iterates over the hash table $\mathcal{H}$ returned by *GatherInformation*. For each structure identifier s in the hashtable, a bound is computed on the edit distance between $T_{[s]}$ and Q. This is possible, since we have stored the size of $|\mathcal{L}_c(Q) \cap \mathcal{L}_c(T_{[s]})|$ in the hashtable, and we know that $|\mathcal{L}_u(Q) \cap \mathcal{L}_u(T_{[s]})| = \{\!\!\{\}\!\!\}$ (since $T_{[s]}$ contains no labels from $\mathcal{L}_u$.) If this bound is less than m then we compute the edit distance between $T_{[s]}$ and Q.[5] If the edit distance is below m, we add trees with structural identifier s, that do not yet appear in *Results*. Note that at this point we may add many new trees (e.g., if *Results* has less than k answers), but a single edit distance computation for each structural identifier is all that is needed.

EXAMPLE 4.7. *When examining structural identifier 2, $\mathcal{L}_c$-FindAnswers would compute a lower bound of two for the edit distance, as the hashtable indicates that (1) $T_{[s]}$ has 3 labels from $\mathcal{L}_c$ in common with Q, which are precisely all labels from $\mathcal{L}_c$ in both Q and in $T_{[s]}$ and (2) $T_{[s]}$ has a two nodes labeled δ. If $2 < m$, an edit distance computation would be performed, yielding the edit distance of two (as the bound and actual edit distance coincide). Both $T_{1.1}$ and $T_{1.2}$ would be added to the result at this point.*

4.3 Discussion

We use *StructureSearch* to refer to the algorithm that performs the three components discussed above.[6] Proposition 3.3 holds for *StructureSearch*, i.e., the algorithm correctly returns all answers if the edit distance bound is at most the size of Q. Again, *StructureSearch* will miss answers that do not contain labels in common with Q. This will be remedied in Section 4.4.

In practice, it turns out that *StructureSearch* is quite efficient (Section 5). To understand intuitively why this is so, recall that $\mathcal{L}_c$ is chosen to be the set of common labels in $\mathcal{T}$, while $\mathcal{L}_u$ is chosen to be the set of uncommon labels. With respect to the common labels, there are relatively few subtrees that are structurally different one from another, i.e., *structSet*($\mathcal{T}$) contains few structural identifiers. Hence, the first component of *StructureSearch* will iterate over relatively small posting lists of structural identifiers. Similarity, the third component of *StructureSearch* will iterate over the relatively small hashtable returned by *GatherInformation*, and it performs at most one edit distance computation for each entry of $\mathcal{H}$.

The second component of *StructureSearch* iterates over the posting lists corresponding to labels in $\mathcal{L}_u(Q)$. Since these labels are uncommon, the posting lists are quite short, and again, relatively few edit distance computations are required. We will demonstrate in our experimentation later on that good choices of $\mathcal{L}_c$ and $\mathcal{L}_u$ are critical to achieving an efficient implementation.

4.4 Answers Without Labels from Q

To efficiently find answers that do not have any labels in common with Q, we need an additional index structure. We associate each node v with a *pure structural identifier* $pure(v)$ such that

$$pure(v) = pure(u) \iff T_v \equiv_\emptyset T_u\,.$$

In other words, $pure(v)$ would coincide with $struct(v)$ if $\mathcal{L}_c$ was chosen to be $\emptyset$. Since pure structural identifiers completely ignore labels, there are typically very few different pure structural identifiers, even for a large $\mathcal{T}$.

In addition to the indices discussed above, we also store a *pure structural index*. This index contains, for each pure structural identifier p, the size of $T_{[p]}$, as well as the list of all nodes structural identifiers s, such that the trees in $[s]$ have the pure structural identifier p. We organize this index sorted by the size of $T_{[p]}$.

Now, finding results with no labels in common with Q is quite simple. For a given bound m, we search the pure structural index for all pure structural identifiers p such that $size(T_{[p]})$ is at most m (since every label must be replaced). For each such pure structural identifier p, we make a *single* edit distance computation to determine the value of $ed(Q, T_{[p]})$. If this value is within our bound of m, then all new subtrees with pure structural identifier p can be added to the result.

After incorporating this change to *StructureSearch*, one can show correctness of the algorithm:

PROPOSITION 4.8. *StructureSearch returns $Top_{m,k}(Q, \mathcal{T})$.*

5. EXPERIMENTATION

We experimentally evaluate our algorithms, and show that *StructureSearch* significantly outperforms the state-of-the-art solution. We consider both real and synthetic datasets, and study scalability as a function of the data size, query size, or number of answers desired. All experimentation was run on a 32-bit Windows 7 laptop with a 2.53GHz processor, 4GB internal memory, running Java 1.6 with only 1GB internal memory. Within our *StructureSearch* algorithm, we used the dynamic algorithm from [23] to compute actual edit distance values. We used the Berkeley DB to store all index structures. We do not provide experimentation for *NaiveSearch* as it is clearly inferior to *StructureSearch*. (See also the related discussion on choosing $\mathcal{L}_c$, below.)

The runtime of our algorithm is compared with the state-of-the-art—algorithm *TASM-postorder* from [1, 2]. The authors of this work kindly provided us with their source code. All queries used in the experimentation are chosen randomly from the subtrees of the datasets. In addition, each point appearing in our graphs actually reflects the result of running four experiments (using randomly chosen queries of the same size), and returning the average of the runtimes.[7] All times are measured in seconds.

[5] Recall that m may not be smaller than the value given by the user, as it is updated by is updated by *NaiveSearch*, i.e., by $\mathcal{L}_u$-*FindAnswers*.

[6] Actually, we will soon extend *StructureSearch* to also return trees containing no labels in common with Q.

[7] The only exceptions to this rule is for some of the larger experiments with *TASM-postorder*, where we ran only two experiments per point, due to the lengthy runtime of this algorithm.

Name Name	Size (MB)	Nodes (millions)	Structures (thousands)
XMark100	114	3.6	116
XMark200	230	7.2	166
XMark400	465	14.5	228
XMark900	932	28.9	265
XMark1800	1866	57.8	289
DBLP	319	17.6	11
SProt	112	9.4	163

Table 1: Dataset statistics.

Recall that the subtree similarly search problem gets two parameters: k, the number of answers to be returned, and m, the maximum edit distance from any answer to the query. When not otherwise stated, we choose $k = 5$, and we choose m as the number of nodes in the query. We note that in all cases the number of answers returned is equal to the number k of answers requested.

Datasets. Most of our experiments use the XMark benchmark [19], as it can create datasets of varying sizes. We also considered two non-synthetic datasets: a DBLP dataset[8] (bibliographic information) and a SwissProt dataset[9] (annotated protein sequences). Some statistics about the size of the datasets appear in Table 1. All numbers are rounded for readability.

The third column of Table 1 contains the total number of nodes in each dataset, while the fourth column contains the number of different structures, with respect to the set of labels $\mathcal{L}_c$ chosen. We discuss our choice of $\mathcal{L}_c$ later. However, observe that the number of different structures is always significantly smaller than the number of nodes (which is equal to the number of subtrees in the dataset). Note that even when the size of the XMark benchmark is doubled, the number of distinct structures only grows moderately. Note also that the non-synthetic datasets also have a relatively small number of distinct structures, e.g., DBLP has only about 11 thousand distinct structures, while it has close to 18 million subtrees. This dataset regularity is important, as it significantly speeds up the processing of our algorithms.

Choosing $\mathcal{L}_c$. Throughout this paper, we have used the term *label* to refer to the textual value associated with each tree node. Using this single notion is convenient, as it hides implementation details of XML documents, that are of no importance to the algorithm definition. When considering the problem of effectively choosing the set $\mathcal{L}_c$, it is useful to note that the labels of an XML tree are of three distinct types, namely *(1)* element names, *(2)* attribute names and *(3)* textual data.

As explained earlier, for our algorithm to work well, $\mathcal{L}_c$ should contain the most common labels in the datasets. For this reason, $\mathcal{L}_c$ will always contain all element and attribute names. It turns out that there are also textual data values that are extremely common within the datasets. Hence, we considered also adding some of the textual data values to the set $\mathcal{L}_c$. In Figure 8a we depict the runtime for varying sets of $\mathcal{L}_c$, over the XMark100 dataset, for queries of varying sizes. The sets $\mathcal{L}_c$ were chosen by including element names, attribute names, and the n most common textual data values (where n ranges from 0 to 10000).

Observe that even including a small number (i.e., 10) of the most common textual data values already significantly improves the runtime of the queries. Further expanding of $\mathcal{L}_c$ can eventually degrade the runtime (e.g., query of size 64, with 10000 most common textual data values) as the number of distinct structures with respect to $\mathcal{L}_c$ can grow significantly. Note that this experiment also gives an indication of the fact that *NaiveSearch* would perform quite poorly, as *NaiveSearch* is similar to *StructureSearch* when $\mathcal{L}_c$ is chosen as the emptyset (not even including any element or attribute names).

The performance for $n = 1000$ and $n = 10000$ is quite similar. In the remainder of the experiments we have built all indices for all datasets by taking $\mathcal{L}_c$ to include element names, attribute names and the 1000 most common textual data values. It is possible that choosing a different number of values to include, for each dataset, would yield superior results. However, we leave the problem of choosing optimal values for future work.

Varying Query Size. In Figure 8b we show the results of running queries of varying sizes (from 4 to 64 nodes) on the datasets XMark100, XMark400 and XMark1800. We use SS and TASM to denote the *StructureSearch* and *TASM-postorder* algorithms, respectively. The time (measured in seconds) is displayed using a log-scale axis, in order to make the runtimes clearer, despite their wide ranges. Note that for each query size, the first three bars display results for *StructureSearch*, while the final three display results for *TASM-postorder*.

Observe that the runtime of *StructureSearch* is quite reasonable, even when considering large queries of size 64, and large datasets such as XMark1800. In particular, *StructureSearch* runs significantly better than *TASM-postorder*, achieving between 4x and 59x speedup. This huge improvement in time follows from three distinct advantages of *StructureSearch*:

- *StructureSearch* does not traverse the input document.
- *StructureSearch* significantly reduces the number of necessary edit distance computations, by leveraging structural similarities.
- When running queries one after another, *StructureSearch* can take advantage of common indices that were already read from disk by a previous query. This "caching effect" reduces disk read time, when multiple queries are evaluated. *TASM-postorder*, on the other hand, traverses the document in order, and hence, little of it is likely to be left in memory during the next query execution (particularly for large documents).

Varying Document Size. Figure 8c depicts the results of running queries of sizes 4, 8 and 64 over datasets of varying sizes. As before, the runtime is displayed using a log-scale axis, and the first (resp. last) three bars represent *StructureSearch* (resp. *TASM-postorder*). As before, *StructureSearch* has a reasonable runtime with gradual increases in runtime as the document size doubles. The relative speedup with respect to *TASM-postorder* is between 5x and 63x.

[8]http://dblp.uni-trier.de/xml
[9]http://www.expasy.ch/sprot

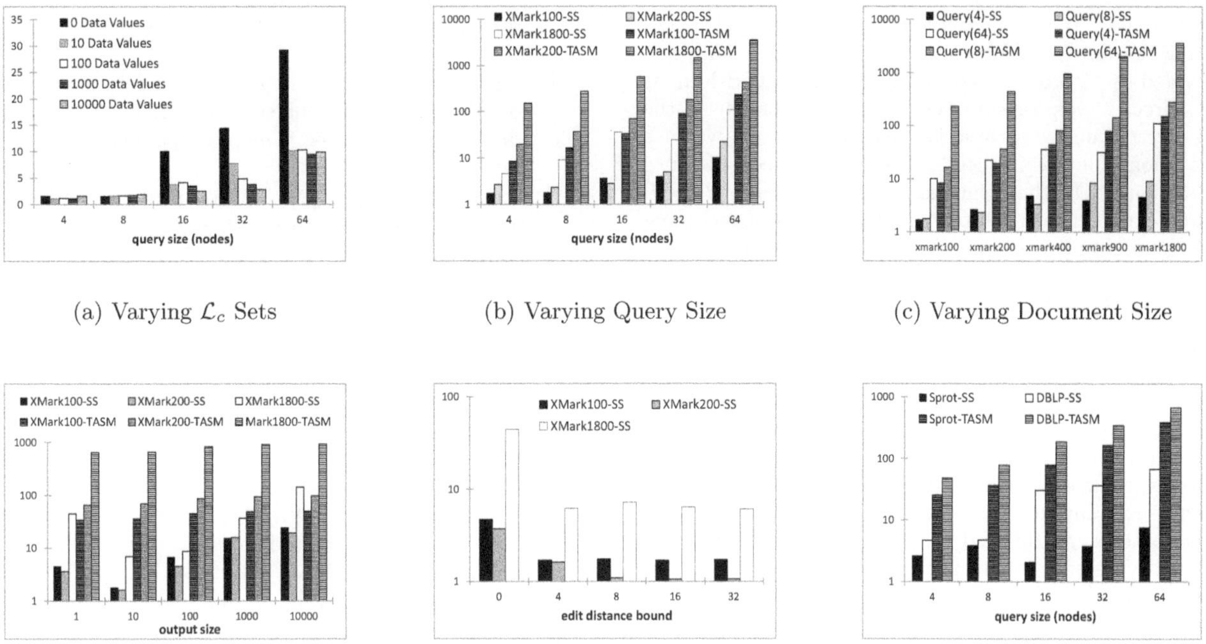

(a) Varying $\mathcal{L}_c$ Sets (b) Varying Query Size (c) Varying Document Size

(d) Varying Number of Results (e) Varying Edit Bound (f) Non-synthetic Datasets

Figure 8: Execution times for varying $\mathcal{L}_c$ sets, query sizes, document sizes, number of results and edit distance bounds.

Varying Results Size. Figure 8d shows the runtime for queries of size 16, over datasets XMark100, XMark200 and XMark1800 for varying values of k. Observe that the runtime for *TASM-postorder* does not increase significantly as the number of results generated grows. This is not the case with *StructureSearch* whose runtime grows as a function of the number of desired results. Regardless, *StructureSearch* still outperforms *TASM-postorder* even for large number of results.

We note that the graph contains an anomaly with regards to the runtime of *StructureSearch* which seems to decrease at first (as the number of results increases), and only later to increase. It seems that this is due to the caching effect observed earlier. Subsequent runs of the same queries (with only a change in the number of results), access the same indices, and hence, these may already be on disk from before, thereby avoiding additional disk accesses. While effort was made to avoid such caching effects on the experiments, in this case we did not succeed in overcoming the natural caching mechanism. In any case, it is clear by simply adding the runtime of the case where $k = 1$ to the runtime of the other cases that even if all accesses to the indices were disk accesses, the runtime would still be reasonable.

Varying Edit Distance Bound. Figure 8e shows the runtime for queries of size 16, over the datasets XMark100, XMark200 and XMark1800 for varying values of m. This figure contains results only for *StructureSearch*, as the algorithm *TASM-postorder* does not get a bound m on edit distance as part of its input. Once again, the experiment involved running the same queries multiple times (with different values of m), and hence, the decreasing runtime is most likely attributable to the caching effect mentioned earlier. In any case, it seems that increasing m will not not significantly increase runtime, as a major runtime component is the accesses to indices on disk. The size of m does not (significantly) effect the number of indices that must be read.

Non-synthetic Datasets. We now consider non-synthetic datasets: DBLP and SProt. Figure 8f shows the runtime of *StructureSearch* and *TASM-postorder* for queries of varying sizes over these datasets. Once again, *StructureSearch* performs well, outperforming *TASM-postorder* by a speedup of 6x to 50x. Thus, *StructureSearch* has excellent performance on both synthetic and real datasets.

5.1 Discussion

In the experiments above we have clearly shown the reasonable runtime of *StructureSearch*, it scalability with respect to various parameters (such as query and document size), and its superiority over the state-of-the-art.

Our indices have a linear number of entries, with respect to the data size.[10] In practice, however, the indices were a bit large, requiring an average of 1GB of memory per 100MB of the input document. No efforts were made to compress the indices, and we leave that for future work. We note, however, that the key reason for the large index size seems to be the extensive use of Dewey identifiers. This issue can easily be remedied, either by giving running identifiers to nodes, and storing only a single running identifier to Dewey iden-

[10]An exception is the $\mathcal{L}_c$-label index that can be quadratic in the size of the data. As noted in Footnote 4, it is actually possible to use only linear space for this index, and in practice it was quite small.

tifier translation index, or by using one of the recently proposed methods for compressing Dewey identifiers, e.g., [10].

A final issue is that *StructureSearch* was developed specifically for the unit cost function. The fact that a unit cost is provided is leveraged extensively by the algorithm, as *(1)* we directly look for subtrees containing labels from the query, and *(2)* unit cost functions easily define equivalence classes among subtrees, which are used to avoid edit distance computations. On the other hand, the algorithm *TASM-postorder* can deal with arbitrary cost functions. Leveraging indices for non-unit cost functions is an open problem.

6. CONCLUSION

In this paper we presented new index structures and a new algorithm for efficiently solving the subtree similarity-search problem, for the tree edit distance metric, when a unit cost function is provided. Our algorithm takes advantage both of structural similarities, and of selectiveness of uncommon data items, to achieve significant speedup.

Careful examination of the general framework indicates that same ideas can be used to find the top-k subtrees, for additional types of distance metrics. To understand why, observe that the idea of dividing trees into equivalence classes according to their structure, and utilizing these classes to reduce the number of computations of the metric, is indifferent to the precise metric chosen. Thus, it is possible to utilize the same basic algorithm (and avoid iterating over the entire database) for other metrics. The efficiency of this process will be dependent on two factors: *(1)* the ability to provide effective lower bounds on similarity of a given tree structure to the user query, via carefully chosen indices and *(2)* the actual time that it takes to compute the metric, when the estimated metric bound is within the user's threshold. The first item will determine how effectively the algorithm weeds out early on subtrees that will not be in the result, while the second item determines how efficiently the metric will be computed for subtrees not eliminated early on.

In the future we intend to test our framework for other metrics, such as the recently proposed *pq*-gram distance [3]. Additional problems for future work, include compressing the indices, and adapting the algorithm (or developing a new index structure and algorithm) for non-unit cost functions.

7. ACKNOWLEDGMENTS

Sara Cohen was partially supported by the Israel Science Foundation (Grant 143/09) and the Ministry of Science and Technology (Grant 3-8710). Sara Cohen is grateful to Omer Balash for implementing a different version of this system.

8. REFERENCES

[1] N. Augsten, D. Barbosa, M. Böhlen, and T. Palpanas. TASM: top-k approximate subtree matching. In *ICDE*, 2010.

[2] N. Augsten, D. Barbosa, M. H. Böhlen, and T. Palpanas. Efficient top-k approximate subtree matching in small memory. *IEEE Trans. Knowl. Data Eng.*, 23(8):1123–1137, 2011.

[3] N. Augsten, M. H. Böhlen, and J. Gamper. The *pq*-gram distance between ordered labeled trees. *ACM Trans. Database Syst.*, 35(1), 2010.

[4] P. Bille. A survey on tree edit distance and related problems. *Theor. Comput. Sci*, 337, 2005.

[5] E. D. Demaine, S. Mozes, B. Rossman, and O. Weimann. An optimal decomposition algorithm for tree edit distance. *ACM Trans. on Algorithms*, 6(1), 2009.

[6] S. Dulucq and L. Tichit. RNA secondary structure comparison: exact analysis of the Zhang-Shasha tree edit algorithm. *Theor. Comput. Sci*, 306(1-3):471–484, 2003.

[7] S. Dulucq and H. Touzet. Analysis of tree edit distance algorithms. In *CPM*, 2003.

[8] M. Garofalakis and A. Kumar. Correlating xml data streams using tree-edit distance embeddings. In *PODS*, 2003.

[9] L. Guo, F. Shao, C. Botev, and J. Shanmugasundaram. Xrank: Ranked keyword search over xml documents. In *SIGMOD*, 2003.

[10] T. Härder, M. P. Haustein, C. Mathis, and M. Wagner. Node labeling schemes for dynamic xml documents reconsidered. *Data Knowl. Eng.*, 60(1):126–149, 2007.

[11] H. Heumann and G. Wittum. The tree-edit-distance, a measure for quantifying neuronal morphology. *Neuroinformatics*, 7:179–190, 2009.

[12] I. Hofacker, W. Fontana, P. Stadler, L. Bonhoeffer, M. Tacker, and P. Schuster. Fast folding and comparison of RNA secondary structures. *Chemical Monthly*, 125:167–188, 1994.

[13] P. Klein, S. Tirthapura, D. Sharvit, and B. Kimia. A tree-edit-distance algorithm for comparing simple, closed shapes. In *SODA*, 2000.

[14] M. Kouylekov and B. Magnini. Combining lexical resources with tree edit distance for recognizing textual entailment. In *MLCW*, 2005.

[15] P. Lakkaraju, S. Gauch, and M. Speretta. Document similarity based on concept tree distance. In *HT*, 2008.

[16] M. Pawlik and N. Augsten. Rted: A robust algorithm for the tree edit distance. *PVLDB*, 5(4):334–345, 2011.

[17] D. C. Reis, P. B. Golgher, A. S. Silva, and A. F. Laender. Automatic web news extraction using tree edit distance. In *WWW*, 2004.

[18] J. R. Rico-Juan and L. Micó. Comparison of AESA and LAESA search algorithms using string and tree-edit-distances. *Pattern Recognition Letters*, 24(9-10):1417–1426, 2003.

[19] A. Schmidt, F. Waas, M. L. Kersten, M. J. Carey, I. Manolescu, and R. Busse. Xmark: A benchmark for xml data management. In *VLDB*, 2002.

[20] K.-C. Tai. The tree-to-tree correction problem. *J. ACM*, 26(3):422–433, July 1979.

[21] W. Tang and A. C. Chung. Cerebral vascular tree matching of 3D-RA data based on tree edit distance. In *Medical Imaging and Augmented Reality*, volume 4091, pages 116–123. 2006.

[22] A. Torsello, A. Robles-Kelly, and E. R. Hancock. Discovering shape classes using tree edit-distance and pairwise clustering. *International Journal of Computer Vision*, 72, 2007.

[23] K. Zhang and D. Shasha. Simple fast algorithms for the editing distance between trees and related problems. *SIAM Journal of Computing*, 18, 1989.

Discovering XSD Keys from XML Data

Marcelo Arenas
PUC Chile &
University of Oxford
marenas@ing.puc.cl

Jonny Daenen
Hasselt University &
Trans. University of Limburg
jonny.daenen@uhasselt.be

Frank Neven
Hasselt University &
Trans. University of Limburg
frank.neven@uhasselt.be

Martin Ugarte
PUC Chile
mgugarte@uc.cl

Jan Van den Bussche
Hasselt University &
Trans. University of Limburg
jan.vandenbussche@uhasselt.be

Stijn Vansummeren
Université Libre de Bruxelles
(ULB)
stijn.vansummeren@ulb.ac.be

ABSTRACT

A great deal of research into the learning of schemas from XML data has been conducted in recent years to enable the automatic discovery of XML Schemas from XML documents when no schema, or only a low-quality one is available. Unfortunately, and in strong contrast to, for instance, the relational model, the automatic discovery of even the simplest of XML constraints, namely XML keys, has been left largely unexplored in this context. A major obstacle here is the unavailability of a theory on reasoning about XML keys in the presence of XML schemas, which is needed to validate the quality of candidate keys. The present paper embarks on a fundamental study of such a theory and classifies the complexity of several crucial properties concerning XML keys in the presence of an XSD, like, for instance, testing for consistency, boundedness, satisfiability, universality, and equivalence. Of independent interest, novel results are obtained related to cardinality estimation of XPath result sets. A mining algorithm is then developed within the framework of levelwise search. The algorithm leverages known discovery algorithms for functional dependencies in the relational model, but incorporates the above mentioned properties to assess and refine the quality of derived keys. An experimental study on an extensive body of real world XML data evaluating the effectiveness of the proposed algorithm is provided.

Categories and Subject Descriptors

H.2.8 [**Information Systems**]: Database Management—*Database Applications, Data Mining*

Keywords

XML key mining

1. INTRODUCTION

The automatic discovery of constraints from data is a fundamental problem in the scientific database literature, especially in the context of the relational model in the form of key, foreign key, and functional dependency discovery (e.g., [22]). Although the absence of DTDs and XML Schema Definitions (XSDs) for XML data occurring in the wild has driven a multitude of research on learning of XML schemas [6, 7, 8, 9, 10, 18], the automatic inference of constraints has been left largely unexplored (we refer to Section 2 for a discussion on related work). In this paper, we address the problem of *XML key mining* whose core formulation asks to find all XML keys valid in a given XML document. We use a formalization of XSD keys (defined in Section 3) consistent with the definition of XML keys by W3C [31]. We develop a key mining algorithm within the framework of levelwise search that additionally leverages discovery algorithms for functional dependencies in the relational model. Our algorithm iteratively refines keys based on a number of quality requirements; a significant portion of the paper is devoted to a study of the complexity of testing these requirements.

EXAMPLE 1.1. *Consider the key,*

$$\phi := (\underbrace{(order, q_{\texttt{order}})}_{context\ c},\ \underbrace{\texttt{.//book}}_{target\ path\ \tau},\ \underbrace{(\texttt{.//title},\ \texttt{.//year})}_{key\ paths\ p_1,\ p_2,\ \ldots}).$$

Here, the pair $(order, q_{\texttt{order}})$ is a context *consisting of the label 'order' and the state or type $q_{\texttt{order}}$[1], which identifies the context-nodes for which ϕ is to be evaluated. Further,* `.//book` *is an XPath-expression, called* target path*, selecting within every context node a set of target nodes. The key constraint now states that every target node must be uniquely identified by the record determined by the key paths* `.//title` *and* `.//year`*, which are XPath-expressions as well. In other words, no two target nodes should have both the same title and the same year. A schematic representation of the semantics of a key is given in Figure 2. So, over the XML document t displayed in Figure 1, the key ϕ gives rise to the table $R_{\phi,t}$:*

$(order, q_{\texttt{order}})$	`.//book`	`.//title`	`.//year`
$(o_1,$	$b_1,$	'Movie analysis',	2012)
$(o_1,$	$b_2,$	'Programming intro',	2012)
$(o_2,$	$b_3,$	'Programming intro',	2012)

In Figure 1, the names of the order and book nodes from left to right are o_1, o_2, and b_1, b_2, b_3, respectively, and every order node has type $q_{\texttt{order}}$. Then, ϕ holds in t if the functional dependency

$$(order, q_{\texttt{order}}), \texttt{.//title}, \texttt{.//year} \ \rightarrow\ \texttt{.//book}$$

holds in $R_{\phi,t}$. That is, within the same context node, 'title' and 'year' uniquely determine the 'book' element.

[1]Types are defined in the accompanying schema which is not given here but discussed in Section 3.

SIGMOD'13, June 22–27, 2013, New York, New York, USA.

As a necessary condition for a key to be valid on a tree t, the XML key specification ([31, Section 3.11.4]) requires every key path to always select precisely one node carrying a data-value.[2] The key is then said to *qualify* on t. As an example,

$$\phi' := ((\text{bookshop}, q_{\texttt{bookshop}}), \quad \texttt{.//order}, \quad (\texttt{.//address})),$$

qualifies for the particular tree given in Figure 1 (assuming every node labeled 'bookshop' has type $q_{\texttt{bookshop}}$) since every target node o_1 and o_2 has precisely one address node. But, the accompanying XSD might allow XML documents *without* or with *multiple* addresses, for which ϕ' would not qualify. So, qualifying for the given document does not necessarily entail qualifying for every document in the schema. We say that a key is *consistent* w.r.t. an XSD if the key qualifies on every document satisfying the XSD. As a quality criterion for keys, we want our mining algorithm to only consider consistent keys. We, therefore, start by studying the complexity of deciding consistency and obtain the pleasantly surprising result that consistency can be tested in polynomial time for keys disallowing disjunction on the topmost level. We show that consistency for general keys is CONP-hard and even PSPACE-hard for keys with regular expressions (which are not allowed in W3C keys).

In addition to consistency, we want to enforce a number of additional quality requirements on keys. In particular, we want to disregard keys that can only select an a priori bounded number of target nodes independent of the size of the input document. Since the main purpose of a key is to ensure uniqueness within a collections of nodes, it does not make sense to consider bounded keys for which the size of this collection is fixed in advance and can not grow with the size of the document. Similarly, we want to ignore so-called universal keys that hold in every document. We obtain that testing for bounded and universal keys is tractable.

A final theoretical theme of this paper is that of reasoning about keys. On the negative side, and in strong contrast to reasoning about relational keys [3, 29] or XML keys without an accompanying schema [14, 15], we show that testing satisfiability, equivalence, and implication between keys is EXPTIME-hard. As an aside, we show that a milder form of equivalence, namely, that of target path equivalence, i.e., determining that two target paths always select the same set of target nodes over documents satisfying the schema, is tractable. The latter can be used as an instrument to reduce the number of candidate target paths.

After laying the above theoretical groundwork, we turn to the theme of mining. Example 1.1 indicates how XML key mining can leverage algorithms for the discovery of functional dependencies (FDs) over a relational database. Indeed, once a context c and a target path τ are determined, any FD of the form $c, p_1, \ldots, p_n \rightarrow \tau$ that holds in the relational encoding $R_{(c,\tau,\overline{P}),t}$ entails the key $(c, \tau, (p_1, \ldots, p_n))$ in t where $\overline{P}$ is a sequence consisting of all possible consistent key paths. Of course, it remains to investigate how to efficiently explore the search space of candidate contexts c, target paths τ, and consistent key paths p. To this end, we embrace the framework of levelwise search (as, e.g., described by Manilla and Toivonen [24]) to enumerate target and key paths. The components of this framework consist of a search space U, a Boolean search predicate q, and a specialization relation $\preceq$ that is a partial order on U and monotone w.r.t. q. In particular, the partial order arranges objects from most general to most specific and when q holds for an object then q should also hold for all generalizations of that object. The solution then consists of all objects $u \in U$ for which $q(u)$ holds, enumerated according to the specialization relation while avoiding testing objects for which q can not hold anymore given already obtained information.

We define a target path miner within the above framework as follows: the search predicate holds for a target path when the number of selected target nodes exceeds a predetermined threshold value; and, the partial order $\preceq$ is determined by containment among target paths. To streamline computation, we utilize a syntactic one-step specialization relation $\prec_1$ that we prove to be optimal w.r.t. the considered partial order. Furthermore, the search predicate can be solely evaluated on a much smaller prefix tree representation of the input document and, therefore, does not need access to the original document. In addition, we define a one-key path miner which searches for all consistent single key paths p (w.r.t the already determined context and target path). Specifically, the search predicate holds for a key path p when p selects *at most one* key node (w.r.t. the given context and target path). Even though consistency requires the selection of exactly one key node, this mismatch can be solved by confining the search space to all key paths that appear as paths from target nodes in the prefix tree. Even though the search predicate can not always be computed on the much smaller prefix tree without access to the original document, we provide sufficient conditions for when this is the case. The partial order is defined as the set inclusion relation defined on key paths for which the one-step specialization relation is the inverse of $\prec_1$. Once all consistent one-key paths are determined, as explained above, a functional dependency miner can be used to determine the corresponding XML key (e.g., [11, 21, 23]).

Contributions. We make the following contributions:
(*i*) We characterize the complexity of the consistency problem for XML keys w.r.t. an XSD for different classes of target and key paths (Theorem 4.4). As a basic building block, and of independent interest, we study the complexity of cardinality estimation of those XPath-fragments in the presence of a schema (an overview is given in Table 1). In addition, we characterize the complexity of boundedness, satisfiability, universality, and implication of XML keys (Theorem 4.5) as well as equivalence of target paths (Theorem 4.6).

(*ii*) We develop a novel key mining algorithm leveraging on algorithms for the discovery of relational functional dependencies and on the framework of levelwise search by employing an optimal one-step specialization relation for which the search relation can be computed, if not completely, then at least partly on a prefix tree representation of the document. (Section 5)

(*iii*) We experimentally assess the effectiveness of the proposed algorithm on an extensive body of real world XML data.

Outline. In Section 2, we discuss related work. In Section 3, we introduce the necessary definitions. In Section 4, we investigate the complexity of decision problems concerning keys in the presence of XSDs. In Section 5, we discuss the XML key mining algorithm. In Section 6, we experimentally validate our algorithm. We conclude in Section 7.

2. RELATED WORK

XML Keys. One of the first definitions of keys for XML was introduced by Buneman et al. [14, 15]. These keys are of the form $(Q, (Q', P))$ where Q is the context-path, Q' is the target path and P is a set of key paths. Although the W3C definition of keys was largely inspired by this work, there are some important differences. First, Buneman et al.'s keys allow more expressive target and key

[2]Actually, the specification is a bit more general in allowing the use of attributes. For ease of presentation, we disregard attributes and let leaf nodes carry data values. We note that all the results in the paper can be easily extended to include attributes.

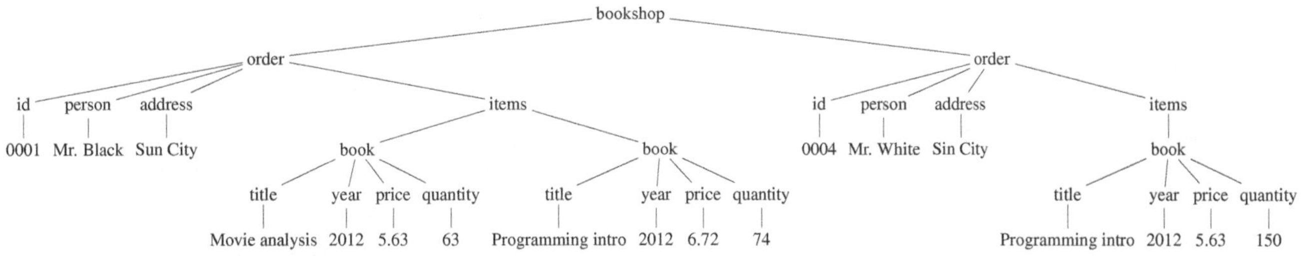

Figure 1: An example XML tree (order and book nodes are named o_1, o_2 and b_1, b_2, b_3 from left to right).

paths by allowing several occurrences of the descendant operator. Context paths, however are less expressive since W3C keys allow the context to be defined by an arbitrary DFA, while Buneman et al.'s keys limit themselves to path expressions. Furthermore, Buneman et al.'s key paths are allowed to select several nodes whereas W3C keys paths are restricted to select precisely one node. We stress that in this paper we follow the W3C-specification for the definition of keys. As is the case for the relational model, much is known about the complexity of key inference for Buneman et al.'s keys [14, 15, 20]. Unfortunately, these results do not carry over to W3C keys as the latter are defined w.r.t. an XML Schema but the former are not.

Decision problems in the presence of a schema. A number of consistency problems of XML keys w.r.t. a DTD have been considered by Fan and Libkin [17]. They have shown, for instance, that key implication in the presence of a DTD is decidable in polynomial time. The keys that they consider, however, are much simpler than the W3C keys considered in the present paper. Basically, a key in their setting is determined by an element name and a number of attributes. Their model is subsumed by ours since each such key can be defined by an XML key and every DTD can be represented by an XSD. We point out that [17] contains many more results on the interplay between keys, foreign keys, inclusion dependencies and DTDs. Arenas et al. [4] discuss satisfiability[3] of XML keys w.r.t. a DTD. The result most relevant to the present paper is NP-hardness of satisfiability w.r.t. a non-recursive DTD and for keys with only one key path. We show that the problem becomes hard for EXPTIME in the presence of XSDs.

XML constraint mining. The automatic discovery of Buneman et al.'s keys from XML data has previously been considered by a number of researchers. Grahne and Zhu [19] considered mining of approximate keys and proposed an Apriori style algorithm which uses the inference rules of [15] for optimization. Necaský and Mlýnková [28] ignore the XML data but present an approach to infer keys and foreign keys from element/element joins in XQuery logs. Fajt et al [16] consider the inference of keys and foreign keys building further on algorithms for the relational model. The above algorithms can not be used for W3C keys since they do not take the presence of XSDs into account and keys are not required to be consistent. Yu and Jagadish [32] consider discovery of functional dependencies (FDs) for XML. Similar to Buneman et al.'s keys, the considered FDs have paths that can select multiple data elements, and contexts are defined w.r.t. a selector expression as opposed to w.r.t. a DFA. For these reasons, W3C keys can not be encoded as a special case of FDs. Barbosa and Mendelzon [5] proposed algorithms to find ID and IDREFs attributes in XML documents. They show that the natural decision problem associated to this discovery problem is NP-complete, and present a heuristic algorithm. Abiteboul et al. [2] consider probabilistic generators for XML collections in the presence of integrity constraints but do not consider mining of such constraints.

[3]We note that satisfiability is called consistency in [4].

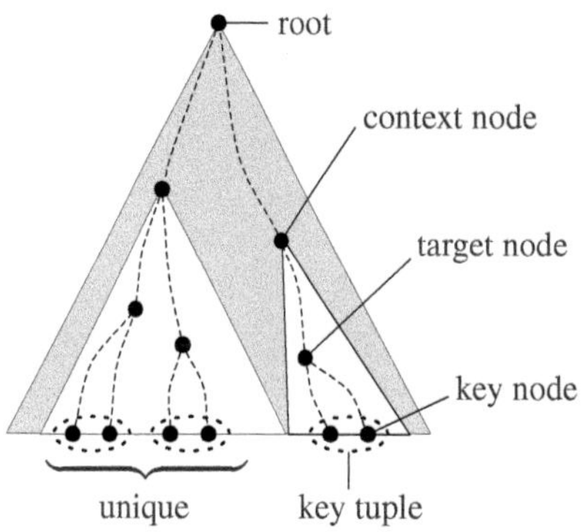

Figure 2: Schematic representation of a key.

3. DEFINITIONS

In this section we introduce the required definitions concerning trees, XSDs, and XML keys, and formally define the XML key mining problem. The correspondence between our definition of XML keys and the W3C definition is discussed in Section 3.3.

For a finite set R, we denote by $|R|$ the cardinality of R.

3.1 Trees and XML

As is standard, we represent XML documents by means of labeled trees. Formally, for a set S, an *S-tree* is a pair (t, lab_t) where t is a finite tree and lab_t maps each node of t to an element in S. To reduce notation, we identify each tree simply by t and leave lab_t implied. We assume the reader to be familiar with standard common terminology on trees like *child*, *parent*, *root*, *leaf*, and so on. For a node v, we denote by $\text{anc-string}_t(v)$ the string formed by the labels on the unique path from t's root to (and including) v, called the *ancestor string* of v. By $\text{child-string}_t(v)$, we denote the string obtained by concatenating the labels of the children of v. If v is a leaf then $\text{child-string}_t(v)$ is the empty string, denoted by ε. Here, we assume that trees are sibling-ordered. We fix a finite set of element names Σ and an infinite set $\mathbf{Data}$ of data elements. An *XML-tree* is a $(\Sigma \cup \mathbf{Data})$-tree where non-leaf nodes are labeled with Σ and leaf nodes are labeled with elements from $(\Sigma \cup \mathbf{Data})$. As the XSD specification does not allow mixed content models for fields in keys [31], we ignore 'mixed' content models altogether to simplify presentation, and assume that when a node is labeled with a $\mathbf{Data}$-element it is the only child of its parent. We then

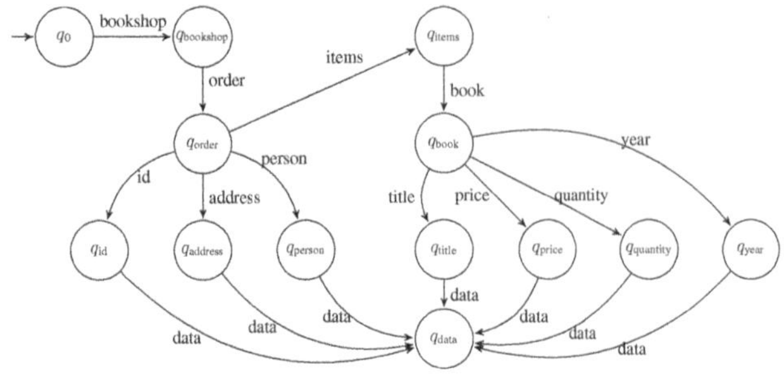

Figure 3: The type automaton of X_{bookshop}.

denote by $\text{value}_t(v)$ the **Data**-label of v's unique child when it exists; otherwise we define $\text{value}_t(v) = \perp$ with $\perp$ a special symbol not in **Data**. When $\text{value}_t(v) \in \textbf{Data}$, we also say that v is a **Data**-node.

EXAMPLE 3.1. *Figure 1 displays an XML-tree t. In this tree,* $\text{anc-string}_t(b_1) =$ `bookshop order items book`, *and also* $\text{child-string}_t(b_1) =$ `title year price quantity`. *Furthermore, every node labeled* `id`, `person`, `address`, `title`. `year`, `price`, *or* `quantity` *is a* **Data**-*node, while, for instance,* b_1 *is not.*

3.2 XSDs

XML keys are defined within the scope of an XSD. We make use of the DFA-based characterization of XSDs introduced by Martens et al. [25]. An *XSD* is a pair $X = (A, \lambda)$ where $A = (\text{Types}, \Sigma \cup \{\texttt{data}\}, \delta, q_0)$ is a Deterministic Finite Automaton (or DFA for short) without final states (called the type-automaton) and λ is a mapping from Types to deterministic[4] regular expressions over the alphabet $\Sigma \cup \{\texttt{data}\}$. Here, Types is the set of states; `data` is a special symbol, not in Σ, which will serve as a placeholder for **Data**-elements; $\delta : \text{Types} \times \Sigma \cup \{\texttt{data}\} \to \text{Types}$ is the (partial) transition function; and $q_0 \in \text{Types}$ is the initial state. Additionally, the labels of transitions leaving q should be precisely the symbols in $\lambda(q)$. That is, for every $q \in \text{Types}$, $Out(q) = Symb(\lambda(q))$, where $Out(q) = \{\sigma \in \Sigma \mid \delta(q, \sigma) \text{ is defined}\}$ and $Symb(r)$ consists of all Σ-symbols in regular expression r.

A *context* $c = (\sigma, q)$ is a pair in $\Sigma \times \text{Types}$. By $\text{CNodes}_t(c)$, we denote all nodes v of t for which $\text{lab}_t(v) = \sigma$ and A halts in state q when started in q_0 on the string $\text{anc-string}_t(v)$. Let $\mathcal{L}(r)$ denote the language defined by the regular expression r. We say that the tree t *adheres to* X, if for every context $c = (\sigma, q)$ and every v in $\text{CNodes}_t(c)$ one of the following holds.

- $\text{value}_t(v) \in \textbf{Data}$ and $\texttt{data} \in \mathcal{L}(\lambda(q))$; or
- $\text{value}_t(v) = \perp$ and $\text{child-string}_t(v) \in \mathcal{L}(\lambda(q))$.

Intuitively, A determines the vertical context of a node v by the state q it reaches in processing $\text{anc-string}_t(v)$. When v is a **Data**-node, the content model specified by q, that is $\lambda(q)$, should contain the placeholder `data`. Otherwise, when v is not a **Data**-node, $\text{child-string}_t(v)$ should satisfy the content-model $\lambda(q)$. We stress that this DFA-based characterization of XSDs corresponds precisely to the more traditional abstraction in terms of single-type grammars [26, 27]. We let $\mathcal{L}(X)$ denote the set of all trees adhering to XSD X.

[4] Also referred to as 1-unambiguous regular expressions [13].

EXAMPLE 3.2. *Let* $X_{bookshop} = (A, \lambda)$ *be the XSD where A is given in Figure 3 and* λ *is defined as follows.*

$$q_0 \mapsto \texttt{bookshop}$$
$$q_{bookshop} \mapsto \texttt{order}^+$$
$$q_{order} \mapsto \texttt{id person address items}^+$$
$$q_{items} \mapsto \texttt{book}^+$$
$$q_{book} \mapsto \texttt{title year? price quantity}$$

For all other types q, $\lambda(q) = \texttt{data}$.

Then tree t in Figure 1 adheres to $X_{bookshop}$. *Moreover,* $b_1 \in \text{CNodes}_t(book, q_{book})$ *and* $\text{child-string}_t(b_1) \in \mathcal{L}(\lambda(q_{book}))$.

3.3 XML keys

A *selector expression* is a restricted XPath-expression of one of the three forms '.' (the dot symbol) or $./l_1/l_2/\dots/l_k$ (starting with the child axis) or $.//l_1/l_2/\dots/l_k$ (starting with the descendant axis), where $k \geq 1$, and $l_1, \dots, l_k$ are element names or the wildcard symbol '*'. A string $w = w_1 \cdots w_k$, where each w_i is an element name, is said to *match* $./l_1/l_2/\dots/l_k$ when $w_i = l_i$ or $l_i = *$ for each i. For selector expressions starting with the descendant axis, we say that w matches $.//l_1/l_2/\dots/l_k$ if a suffix of w matches $./l_1/l_2/\dots/l_k$. For a tree t, a node v of t, and a selector expression τ, the set $\tau(t, v)$ is defined as follows. If $\tau =$ '.', then $\tau(t, v) = \{v\}$. Otherwise τ is of the form either $./l_1/l_2/\dots/l_k$ or $.//l_1/l_2/\dots/l_k$, and $\tau(t, v)$ contains all nodes v' such that v' is a descendant of v and the path of labels from v (but excluding the label of v) to (and including) v' matches τ. A *disjunction of selector expressions* is of the form $\tau = \tau_1 \mid \cdots \mid \tau_m$ where each τ_i is a selector expression. In this case, $\tau(t, v)$ is defined as the union of all $\tau_i(t, v)$. When v is the root of the document, we simply write $\tau(t)$ for $\tau(t, v)$. We denote by $\mathcal{SE}$ and $\mathcal{DSE}$ the class of selector expressions and disjunctions of selector expressions, respectively.

DEFINITION 3.3. *An* XML key, *defined w.r.t. an XSD X, is a tuple* $\phi = (c, \tau, P)$, *where* (i) *c is a context in X;* (ii) $\tau \in \mathcal{DSE}$ *is called the* target path, *and* (iii), *P is an ordered sequence of expressions in* $\mathcal{DSE}$ *called* key paths.

To emphasize that ϕ is defined w.r.t. X, we sometimes write a key simply as a pair (ϕ, X).

We stress that the definition of XML keys given above, corresponds to the definition of keys in XML Schema [31]. In particular, the context is given implicitly by declaring a key inside an element and an element has a label and a certain type. Target paths are called *selector paths* [31, Section 3.11.6.2] and key paths are called *fields*. They obey the same grammar as used here with the difference that we do not make use of attributes but require key paths to select data nodes.

The semantics of an XML key is as follows. The context c defines a set of context nodes which divides the document into separate (but not necessarily disjoint) parts. Specifically, each node in $\text{CNodes}_t(c) = \{v_1, \dots, v_n\}$ can be considered as the root of a separate tree. For each of those trees, i.e., for each $i \in \{1, \dots, n\}$, every node in $\tau(t, v_i)$ should uniquely define a record. Such a record is determined by the key paths in $P = (p_1, \dots, p_k)$. That is, each v in $\tau(t, v_i)$ defines the record $[\text{value}_t(u_1), \dots, \text{value}_t(u_k)]$, denoted by $\text{record}_P(t, v)$, where $p_j(t, v) = \{u_j\}$ for all $j \in \{1, \dots, k\}$. We graphically illustrate the above in Figure 2.

Note that $p_j(t, v)$ might select more than one node or might select a node u for which $\text{value}_t(u)$ is undefined; both are disallowed by the XML Schema specification:

DEFINITION 3.4. *A key* $\phi = (c, \tau, P)$ qualifies *in a document* t *if for every* $v \in \text{CNodes}_t(c)$*, every* $u \in \tau(t, v)$ *and every* $p \in P$*,* $p(t, u)$ *is a singleton containing a* $\mathbf{Data}$*-node.*

Finally, following the W3C specification, we define satisfaction of an XML key w.r.t. a document:

DEFINITION 3.5. *An XML tree* t satisfies *a key* $\phi = (c, \tau, P)$ *or a key is* valid *w.r.t.* t*, denoted by* $t \models \phi$*, iff* (i) ϕ *qualifies in* t*; and,* (ii) *for every node* v *in* $\text{CNodes}_t(c)$*,* $\text{record}_P(t, u) \neq \text{record}_P(t, u')$*, for every two different nodes* u *and* u' *in* $\tau(t, v)$*.*

Notice that, there can be two causes for a key to be invalid: (*i*) the key does not qualify in the document and actually is ill-defined w.r.t. the document; or (*ii*) the data values in the document invalidate the key. The first cause can be seen as structural invalidation, while the second cause is semantical and more informative.

In this paper, we are interested in inferring keys that *always* qualify to a document satisfying the schema. We call such keys consistent. In Section 4, we show that consistency can be decided efficiently for target and key paths in $\mathcal{SE}$, and is intractable otherwise.

DEFINITION 3.6. *A key is consistent w.r.t. a schema if the key qualifies in every document adhering to the schema.*

EXAMPLE 3.7. *Consider the key* ϕ *from Example 1.1. Then* ϕ *is valid w.r.t. the tree in Figure 1 but* ϕ *is not consistent w.r.t.* X_{bookshop}*. Indeed,* X_{bookshop} *defines the 'year'-element of a 'book'-element to be optional.*

3.4 XML key mining

Given an XML document t adhering to a given XSD, we want to derive all supported XML keys ϕ that are valid w.r.t. t.[5] We define the support of a key as the quantity measuring the number of nodes captured by the key. Define $\text{TNodes}_t(\phi)$ as the set of target nodes selected by $\phi = (c, \tau, P)$ on t. That is,

$$\text{TNodes}_t(\phi) = \bigcup_{v \in \text{CNodes}_t(c)} \tau(t, v).$$

Then, following Grahne and Zhu [19], we define the *support* of ϕ on t to be the total number of selected target nodes: $\text{supp}(\phi, t) = |\,\text{TNodes}_t(\phi)|$. Since this support only depends on the context c and the target path τ of ϕ, we also write $\text{supp}(c, \tau, t)$ for $\text{supp}(\phi, t)$.

We are now ready to define the problem central to this paper.

DEFINITION 3.8. **(XML key mining problem)** *Given an XSD* X*; an XML document* t *adhering to* X*; and a minimum support threshold* N*, the* XML key mining problem *consists of finding all keys* ϕ *consistent with* X *such that* $t \models \phi$ *and* $\text{supp}(\phi, t) > N$*.*

The above is only the core definition of the XML key mining problem. We will discuss some quality requirements in the next section.

4. BASIC DECISION PROBLEMS

A basic problem in data mining is the abundance of found patterns. In this section, we address a number of fundamental decision problems relevant to identifying low quality keys which can then be removed from the output of the key mining algorithm. Specifically, we consider testing for consistency and show that the problem becomes tractable when top-level disjunction is disallowed. We also study universality and boundedness, and show that they are tractable. Finally, we show that testing for satisfiability and implication of keys is EXPTIME-hard, even when disallowing disjunction, which complicates the inference of minimal keys.

[5]W.l.o.g. and to simplify presentation, we restrict attention to a single document as multiple XML-documents can always be combined into one by introducing a common root.

$\mathcal{P}$	$\forall_{\text{tree}}^{>k,\mathcal{P}}$	$\forall_{\text{tree}}^{<k,\mathcal{P}}$	$\forall_{\text{tree}}^{=k,\mathcal{P}}$
$\mathcal{RE}$	EXPTIME-complete	in PTIME	in EXPTIME PSPACE-hard ($k \geq 1$)
$\mathcal{DSE}$	EXPTIME-complete	in PTIME	in EXPTIME CONP-hard ($k \geq 1$)
$\mathcal{SE}$	EXPTIME-complete	in PTIME	in PTIME
$\mathcal{SE}^*$	in EXPTIME	in PTIME	in PTIME
$\mathcal{SE}^{//}$	in PTIME	in PTIME	in PTIME

Table 1: Complexity of $\forall_{\text{tree}}^{\bullet k,\mathcal{P}}$**.**

4.1 Consistency

As detailed in Section 3.3, the W3C specification requires keys to be consistent. We therefore define CONSISTENCY as the problem to decide whether ϕ is consistent w.r.t. X, given a key ϕ and an XSD X. In this section, we show that CONSISTENCY is in fact solvable in PTIME when patterns in keys are restricted to $\mathcal{SE}$. The proof of this result is the most technical result of the paper. Actually, the PTIME result is also surprising since a minor variation of consistency is known to be EXPTIME-hard, as we explain next.

Consistency requires that on every document adhering to X, every key path should select precisely *one* data node for every target node. This is related to deciding whether an XPath selector expression selects *at least* and *at most* a given number of nodes, on every document satisfying a given XSD. Indeed, define $\forall_{\text{tree}}^{\bullet k}$ with $k \in \mathbb{N}$ and $\bullet \in \{<, =, >\}$ to be the problem of deciding, given an XSD X and a selector expression p, whether it holds that $|p(t)| \bullet k$, for every $t \in \mathcal{L}(X)$. We show in Lemma 4.3 that CONSISTENCY can be easily reduced to $\forall_{\text{tree}}^{=1}$. Although Bjorklund, Martens, and Schwentick [12] showed that $\forall_{\text{tree}}^{>k}$ is EXPTIME-complete, we obtain below that $\forall_{\text{tree}}^{=1}$ can in fact be solved in polynomial time through an intricate translation to the equivalence test for unambiguous tree automata [30].

4.1.1 *Cardinality of XPath result sets*

Because of its relevance to cardinality estimation of XPath result sets, we investigate in more detail the complexity of $\forall_{\text{tree}}^{\bullet k,\mathcal{P}}$ and it restriction to strings, denoted by $\forall_{\text{string}}^{\bullet k,\mathcal{P}}$, relative to the XPath-fragment $\mathcal{P}$.

To obtain a more complete picture, we also consider the class of all regular expressions, denoted by $\mathcal{RE}$. For a regular expression r and a tree t, $r(t)$ then selects all nodes whose ancestor string[6] matches r. Furthermore, denote by $\mathcal{SE}$ the set of all selector expressions and by $\mathcal{SE}^{//}$ and $\mathcal{SE}^*$, the set of all selector expressions *without* descendant and wildcard, respectively. For a class of patterns $\mathcal{P} \in \{\mathcal{RE}, \mathcal{DSE}, \mathcal{SE}, \mathcal{SE}^{//}, \mathcal{SE}^*\}$, we denote by $\forall_{\text{tree}}^{\bullet k,\mathcal{P}}$ the problem $\forall_{\text{tree}}^{\bullet k}$ where expressions are restricted to the class $\mathcal{P}$.

THEOREM 4.1. *The complexity of the problem* $\forall_{\text{tree}}^{\bullet k,\mathcal{P}}$ *is as stated in Table 1.*

Notice that the problem $\forall_{\text{tree}}^{=k,\mathcal{RE}}$ is PSPACE-hard for every value $k \geq 1$, while $\forall_{\text{tree}}^{=k,\mathcal{DSE}}$ is CONP-hard for every value $k \geq 1$. On

[6]Defined in Section 3.2 as the string formed by the labels on the path from the root to the considered node.

the other hand, $\forall_{\text{tree}}^{=0,\mathcal{RE}} = \forall_{\text{tree}}^{<1,\mathcal{RE}}$ and $\forall_{\text{tree}}^{=0,\mathcal{DSE}} = \forall_{\text{tree}}^{<1,\mathcal{DSE}}$ and, thus, these two problems can be solved in polynomial time given the results in the second column of Table 1. Below we provide a sketch of the proof that $\forall_{\text{tree}}^{=1,\mathcal{SE}}$ can be solved in polynomial time, which is a key problem in our study of consistency.

PROOF SKETCH OF $\forall_{\text{tree}}^{=1,\mathcal{SE}} \in$ PTIME. In this proof, we need an encoding of XML trees as binary trees. More precisely, for an XML tree t, denote by fcns(t) a binary tree such that for every node v of t: (1) v is a node in fcns(t); (2) the left child of v in fcns(t) is the first child of v in t (if v is a leaf in t, then a node with label # is placed as the left child of v in fcns(t)); and (3) the right child of v in fcns(t) is the next sibling of v in t (if such a sibling does not exist in t, then a node with label # is placed as the right child of v in fcns(t)). Moreover, in this proof we also make use of tree automata which operate in a top-down fashion over binary trees, which are called binary tree automata (BTA). Given a BTA A, we denote by $\mathcal{L}(A)$ the set of trees accepted by A, and we say that A is unambiguous if for every $t \in \mathcal{L}(A)$, there is only one accepting run of A on t, but there could many non-accepting ones.

In order to show that $\forall_{\text{tree}}^{=1,\mathcal{SE}} \in$ PTIME, we first need the following results: (1) given an XSD X, one can construct in polynomial time a deterministic BTA A_X such that for every tree t: fcns$(t) \in \mathcal{L}(A_X)$ if and only if $t \in \mathcal{L}(X)$; (2) given a selector expression p, one can construct in polynomial time a non-deterministic BTA B_p such that for every XML tree t: fcns$(t) \in \mathcal{L}(B_p)$ if and only if $|p(t)| > 0$; and (3) there is a deterministic BTA $A_\#$ such that $t' \in \mathcal{L}(A_\#)$ if and only if $t' =$ fcns(t) for some XML tree t. With these ingredients, the polynomial time algorithm for $\forall_{\text{tree}}^{=1,\mathcal{SE}}$ works as follows.

Let X be an XSD and p a selector expression. In order to test whether $(X,p) \in \forall_{\text{tree}}^{=1,\mathcal{SE}}$, we first verify whether $(X,p) \in \forall_{\text{tree}}^{<2,\mathcal{SE}}$, which can be done in polynomial time (see Table 1). If this is not the case, then we know that $(X,p) \notin \forall_{\text{tree}}^{=1,\mathcal{SE}}$, so the algorithm returns *false*. Otherwise, the algorithm continues by computing deterministic BTAs A_X, $A_\#$ and non-deterministic BTA B_p. Then to check whether $(X,p) \in \forall_{\text{tree}}^{=1,\mathcal{SE}}$, the algorithm needs to verify whether $\mathcal{L}(A_X \times A_\#) \subseteq \mathcal{L}(B_p)$, where $A_X \times A_\#$ is the usual product of BTAs that accepts $\mathcal{L}(A_X) \cap \mathcal{L}(A_\#)$ and can be computed in polynomial time. The key observations to make here are: (1) testing whether $\mathcal{L}(A_X \times A_\#) \subseteq \mathcal{L}(B_p)$ is equivalent to verifying whether $\mathcal{L}(A_X \times A_\#) \subseteq \mathcal{L}(A_X \times B_p)$; (2) containment for BTAs is an intractable problem, but it becomes tractable for unambiguous BTAs [30]; (3) $A_X \times A_\#$ is an unambiguous BTA as it is deterministic; and (4) although $A_X \times B_p$ is non-deterministic, by using the fact that $(X,p) \in \forall_{\text{tree}}^{<2,\mathcal{SE}}$, it is possible to prove that $A_X \times B_p$ is an unambiguous BTA. Therefore, we can test in polynomial time whether $\mathcal{L}(A_X \times A_\#) \subseteq \mathcal{L}(A_X \times B_p)$ and, thus, we can test in polynomial time whether $(X,p) \in \forall_{\text{tree}}^{=1,\mathcal{SE}}$. □

Finally, we consider the corresponding problem for strings as well. We denote by $\forall_{\text{string}}^{\bullet k,\mathcal{P}}$ the problem to decide whether, given a DFA A and a pattern $p \in \mathcal{P}$, $|p(s)| \bullet k$ for every $s \in \mathcal{L}(A)$. Here, as every string can be viewed as a unary tree, $p(s)$ simply denotes the nodes selected by p when evaluated from the root.

THEOREM 4.2. *The complexity of the problem* $\forall_{\text{string}}^{\bullet k,\mathcal{P}}$ *is as for* $\forall_{\text{tree}}^{\bullet k,\mathcal{P}}$ *with the exception that:*

1. $\forall_{\text{string}}^{>k,\mathcal{RE}}$, $\forall_{\text{string}}^{>k,\mathcal{DSE}}$, $\forall_{\text{string}}^{>k,\mathcal{SE}}$ *are* PSPACE*-complete and* $\forall_{\text{string}}^{>k,\mathcal{SE}^*}$ *is in* PTIME*;*
2. $\forall_{\text{string}}^{=k,\mathcal{RE}}$ *is* PSPACE*-complete for every* $k \geq 1$*; and*
3. $\forall_{\text{string}}^{=k,\mathcal{DSE}}$ *is* CONP*-complete for every* $k \geq 1$.

The results in Theorem 4.2 are important for our investigation not only because they can be used to obtain lower bounds for the complexity of the problems $\forall_{\text{tree}}^{\bullet k,\mathcal{P}}$, but also because the extension of some of the techniques developed to prove them played a key role in pinpointing the complexity of some of the problems $\forall_{\text{tree}}^{\bullet k,\mathcal{P}}$, most notably in the case of $\forall_{\text{tree}}^{=k,\mathcal{SE}}$.

4.1.2 Main result on consistency

For a class of patterns $\mathcal{P}$, we denote by CONSISTENCY($\mathcal{P}$) the problem CONSISTENCY restricted to keys using expressions in $\mathcal{P}$. We introduce the following definition. Let $k \in \mathbb{N}$, $\bullet \in \{<,=,>\}$, and $\mathcal{R},\mathcal{S}$ be two pattern languages. We denote by $\forall_{\text{key}}^{\bullet k,\mathcal{R},\mathcal{S}}$ the problem to decide whether for a given XSD X and a key $\phi = (c,\tau,(p))$ with $\tau \in \mathcal{R}$ and $p \in \mathcal{S}$, it holds that $|p(t,u)| \bullet k$ for every $t \in \mathcal{L}(X)$, every node v in CNodes$_t(c)$, and for every node u in $\tau(t,v)$.

Let *root* stand for the class containing only the selector expressions '.', that is, the expression which selects the root. The following lemma now allows to transfer upper and lower bounds from the previous section:

LEMMA 4.3. *Let* $k \in \mathbb{N}$*, let* $\bullet \in \{<,>,=\}$*, and let* $\mathcal{P} \in \{\mathcal{RE},\mathcal{DSE},\mathcal{SE},\mathcal{SE}^{//},\mathcal{SE}^*\}$*. Then*

1. $\forall_{\text{key}}^{\bullet k,\mathcal{RE},\mathcal{P}}$ *is polynomial time reducible to* $\forall_{\text{tree}}^{\bullet k,\mathcal{P}}$*; and,*
2. $\forall_{\text{tree}}^{\bullet k,\mathcal{P}}$ *is polynomial time reducible to* $\forall_{\text{key}}^{\bullet k,root,\mathcal{P}}$.

The main result of this section immediately follows from Theorem 4.1 and Lemma 4.3:

THEOREM 4.4. *1.* CONSISTENCY($\mathcal{SE}$) *is in* PTIME*;*

2. CONSISTENCY($\mathcal{DSE}$) *is* CONP*-hard and in* EXPTIME*;*
3. CONSISTENCY($\mathcal{RE}$) *is* PSPACE*-hard and in* EXPTIME*;*

4.2 Determining the quality of keys

We investigate a number of additional criteria to determine the quality of keys. Since the number of keys mined from a given document can be quite large, we are interested in identifying irrelevant keys that can be disregarded from the output of any key mining algorithm. Examples are keys that hold in any document, that only address a bounded number of target nodes, and keys that are implied by keys that have already been found.

Thereto, let X be an XSD, ϕ a key and Ψ be a set of keys such that every key in $\Psi \cup \{\phi\}$ is consistent w.r.t. X. Then,

- UNIVERSALITY is the problem to decide whether $t \models \phi$ for every tree in $t \in \mathcal{L}(X)$;
- BOUNDEDNESS is the problem to decide whether there is an $N \in \mathbb{N}$, such that for every tree $t \in \mathcal{L}(X)$,

$$|\,\text{TNodes}_t(\phi)| \leq N.$$

- KEY IMPLICATION, denoted by $\Psi \sqsubseteq \phi$, is the problem to decide whether for all trees $t \in \mathcal{L}(X)$ such that $\bigwedge_{\psi\in\Psi} t \models \psi$ it holds that $t \models \phi$.
- SATISFIABILITY is the problem to decide whether there is a tree $t \in \mathcal{L}(X)$ with $t \models \phi$;

Intuitively, a bounded key can only select a bounded number of target nodes independent of the size of the input document. Since the main purpose of a key is to ensure uniqueness of nodes within a collection of nodes, bounded keys are not very interesting.

We next show that identifying universal and bounded keys is algorithmically feasible, while determining implication (and even satisfiability) of keys is intractable. Therefore, determining a smallest set of keys (aka, a cover) is practically infeasible. Note that, while the EXPTIME-completeness of SATISFIABILITY is discouraging, it does not pose a problem for key mining algorithms in practice. Indeed, by Definition 3.8 a key mining algorithm will, on input (X, t) with $t \in \mathcal{L}(X)$ only return keys ϕ with $t \models \phi$ (which can efficiently be checked). As such, the keys ϕ it returns are necessarily satisfiable.

Similar to the previous section, we parametrize the problems above by a class $\mathcal{P}$ of expressions, to restrict attention to input keys that only use expressions in $\mathcal{P}$.

THEOREM 4.5. *1.* UNIVERSALITY($\mathcal{DSE}$) *is in* PTIME.

2. BOUNDEDNESS($\mathcal{DSE}$) *is in* PTIME.

3. KEY IMPLICATION($\mathcal{SE}$) *is* EXPTIME*-hard.*

4. SATISFIABILITY($\mathcal{SE}$) *is* EXPTIME*-complete.*

Next, we consider *target path containment* and *equivalence*. Given an XSD X, a context c, and two selector expressions τ and τ', TARGET PATH CONTAINMENT is the problem to decide whether for every tree $t \in \mathcal{L}(X)$ and every node $v \in \text{CNodes}_t(c)$, $\tau(t, v) \subseteq \tau'(t, v)$. We denote the latter condition by $\tau \subseteq_{X,c} \tau'$. By TARGET PATH EQUIVALENCE we denote the corresponding equivalence problem.

THEOREM 4.6. TARGET PATH CONTAINMENT *and* TARGET PATH EQUIVALENCE *are in* PTIME.

TARGET PATH EQUIVALENCE is a particularly relevant problem for key mining since it allows to identify, within the mined set of keys, the semantically equivalent but distinct keys (c, τ, P) and (c, τ', P) with τ target path equivalent to τ'. In this sense, target path equivalence is a sufficient condition for key implication, but which can be solved efficiently.

5. XML KEY MINING ALGORITHM

In this section, we provide an algorithm for solving the XML key mining problem. Recall from Definition 3.8 that the input to this algorithm is an XSD X, an XML tree t and a minimum support threshold N, and that it should output keys that are consistent with X, are satisfied by t, and whose support exceeds N[7]. For the remainder, let $X = (A_X, \lambda_X)$ with the type-automaton $A_X = (\text{Types}, \Sigma \cup \{\texttt{data}\}, \delta, q_0)$.

The overall structure of the XML key mining algorithm is outlined in Algorithm 1.

Algorithm 1 XML Key Mining Algorithm

for all $c \in \text{ContextMiner}_{t,X}$ **do**
  for all $\tau \in \text{TargetPathMiner}_{t,X}(c)$ **do**
    $S = \text{OneKeyPathMiner}_{t,X}(c, \tau)$
    $\mathcal{P} = \text{MinimalKeyPathSetMiner}_{t,X}(c, \tau, S)$
    for each $P \in \mathcal{P}$ return (c, τ, P)

Basically the algorithm consists of four components:

- $\text{ContextMiner}_{t,X}$ returns a list of possible contexts based on t and X;
- $\text{TargetPathMiner}_{t,X}(c)$ returns a list of unique target paths with minimal support in t given a context c;

[7] If no XSD is available, one can be derived, e.g., using algorithms from [9].

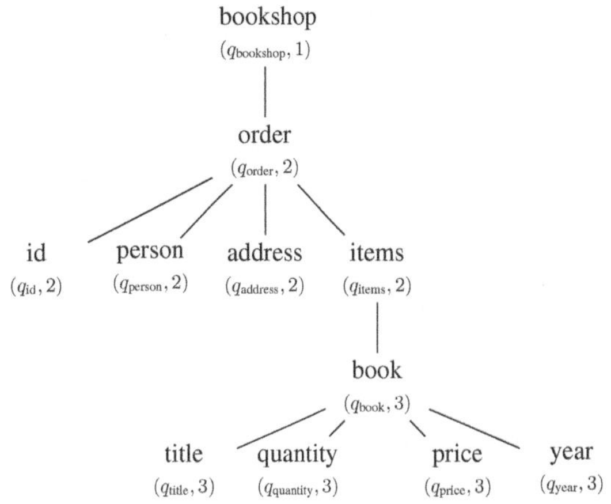

Figure 4: Prefix tree for the XML tree in Figure 1.

- $\text{OneKeyPathMiner}_{t,X}(c, \tau)$ returns a maximal set S of unique key paths for which $(c, \tau, \{p\})$ is consistent for every $p \in S$; and,
- $\text{MinimalKeyPathSetMiner}_{t,X}(c, \tau, S)$ returns a set $\mathcal{P}$ of minimal subsets P of S for which $t \models (c, \tau, P)$.

$\text{TargetPathMiner}_{t,X}(c)$ and $\text{OneKeyPathMiner}_{t,X}(c, \tau)$ are different instantiations of levelwise search [24], while the function $\text{MinimalKeyPathSetMiner}_{t,X}(c, \tau, S)$ leverages on discovery algorithms for functional dependencies in the relational model. In the remainder, we explain each function in detail. We will only consider target and key paths up to a given length k_{max} which can be at most the maximum depth of the document. Since the presence of top-level disjunction renders testing for consistency intractable (cf. Theorem 4.4), we focus on a key mining algorithm that disregards the union operator.

5.1 Prefix Tree and Context Miner

We first define a basic data structure that is used to speed-up various parts of the mining algorithm. Denote by $\text{PT}(t)$ the prefix tree obtained from t by collapsing all nodes with the same ancestor string. Recall that the ancestor string of a node is the string obtained by concatenating all labels on the unique path from the root to (and including) that node. Let h be the function mapping each node in t to its corresponding node in $\text{PT}(t)$. Then, we label every node m in $\text{PT}(t)$ with the number of nodes in t mapped to m, i.e., $|h^{-1}(m)|$ together with the state assigned to m by the type-automaton A_X. For example, the prefix tree for the XML tree in Figure 1 is shown in Figure 4. Note that $\text{PT}(t)$ does not contain data nodes. The prefix tree can be computed in time linear in the size of t (see, e.g., [19]).

We next discuss the context miner. Clearly, the set of all contexts $c = (\sigma, q)$ with $\sigma \in \Sigma$ and $q \in \text{Types}$, can be directly inferred from the given XSD. But, since only contexts that are actually realized in t can give rise to a non-zero support, the context miner enumerates all unique contexts c occurring in $\text{PT}(t)$ through a depth-first traversal.

5.2 Target Path Miner

Next, we describe the target path miner which finds all target paths exceeding the support threshold for a given context c. The algorithm follows the framework of *levelwise search* described by Mannila and Toivonen [24]. In brief, the algorithm is of a generate-and-test style that starts from the most general target path, .//*

Algorithm 2 Basic algorithm for levelwise search [24]

$C_0 :=$ set of most general elements of U;
$i := 0$;
while $C_i \neq \emptyset$ **do**
  $F_i := \{\tau \in C_i \mid q(\tau)\}$;
  $C_{i+1} := \{\tau \in U \mid \forall \tau' \in U : \tau' \prec \tau \Rightarrow \tau' \in \bigcup_{j\leq i} F_j\} \setminus \bigcup_{j\leq i} C_j$;
  $i := i + 1$;
Return(F_i);

Algorithm 3 TargetPathMiner$_{t,X}(c)$

$C_0 :=$ set of minimal elements of U;
$i := 0$;
while $C_i \neq \emptyset$ **do**
  $F_i := \{x \in C_i \mid q(x)\}$;
  $G_{i+1} := \{x \in U \mid \exists y \in F_i : y \prec_1 x\}$;
  $C_{i+1} := \{x \in G_{i+1} \mid \forall y : y \prec_1 x \Rightarrow y \in \bigcup_{j\leq i} F_j\}$;
  $i := i + 1$;
Return(F_i);

in our case, and generates increasingly more specific paths while avoiding paths that cannot be interesting given the information obtained in earlier iterations.

The components of any levelwise search algorithm consist of a set U called the *search space*; a predicate q on U called the *search predicate*; and a partial order $\preceq$ on U called the *specialization relation*. The goal is to find all elements of U that satisfy the search predicate. Obviously, U in our case is the set of selector expressions up to length k_{max}. A standard approach is to use a support threshold for the search predicate. Accordingly, we define the search predicate as $q(\tau) := \text{supp}(c, \tau, t) > N$, for the given input threshold N. That is, τ is deemed interesting when its support exceeds N.

For levelwise search to work correctly, q should be *monotone* (actually, monotonically decreasing) with respect to $\preceq$, meaning that if $\tau' \preceq \tau$ and $q(\tau)$ holds, then $q(\tau')$ holds as well. The intuition of $\tau' \preceq \tau$ is that τ is more specific than τ', or in other words, that τ' is more general than τ. For our purposes, it would be ideal to use the semantic containment relation $\tau \subseteq_{X,c} \tau'$ in context c (as defined in Section 4.2). Although this containment relation is shown to be tractable (Theorem 4.6), through a translation to the inclusion test of unambiguous string automata, it is not well-suited to be used within the framework of levelwise search which requires fast testing of specialization due to the large number of such tests. In strong contrast, as we show below, the containment of selector expressions that disregards the presence of a schema, has a syntactic counterpart which can be implemented efficiently. Therefore, we define $\tau' \preceq \tau$ if and only if for every XML tree t, the set $\tau(t)$ is a subset of $\tau'(t)$. With respect to this definition it is obvious that q is monotone. Notice also that $\tau \subseteq \tau'$ implies $\tau \subseteq_{X,c} \tau'$.

Now, levelwise search computes sets F_i iteratively as shown in Algorithm 2. Here, $\prec$ is the strict version of $\preceq$, so $\tau' \prec \tau$ if $\tau' \preceq \tau$ and $\tau' \neq \tau$. Each step computing C_{i+1} is called *candidate generation*; those candidates that satisfy q then end up in the corresponding set F_{i+1} (the letter F is a shorthand for "frequent", referring to the support threshold). It can formally be shown that the union of all sets F_i indeed equals the set of all elements of U satisfying q [24]. Moreover, the algorithm is terminated as soon C_i is empty, because then all later sets F_j and C_j with $j \geq i$ will be empty as well.

The above abstract framework, however, leaves a number of questions to be answered: (i) *How can we efficiently evaluate the search predicate $q(\tau)$?*; and, (ii) *How can we efficiently generate candidate sets C_{i+1}?*. We will next answer these questions in detail.

Search predicate. The search predicate $\text{supp}(c, \tau, t)$ can be entirely evaluated on the prefix tree $\text{PT}(t)$ and does not need access to the original document t. A single XPath-expression can be used to aggregate the counts of all nodes matching τ below nodes in context c.[8] Indeed, for $c = (\sigma, q)$, the support can be obtained from $\text{PT}(t)$ using the following XPath expression:

$$\text{sum}(//\sigma[\text{@state} = id_q]/\tau/\,\text{@matches}),$$

where id_q is the internally used id of the state q. The attributes `@state` and `@matches` contain respectively the state id assigned to the node in the prefix tree and the number of nodes with the same ancestor path in t.

Specialization relation and candidate generation. Since our chosen specialization relation is purely semantic, we need an equivalent algorithmic definition to show that containment can be effectively decided. Thereto, we define a "one-step specialization relation" as follows: $\tau' \prec_1 \tau$ if τ is obtained from τ' by one of the following operations: (a) if τ' starts with the descendant axis, replace it by the child axis; (b) if τ' starts with the descendant axis, insert a wildcard step right after it; or, (c) replacing a wildcard with an element name.

We establish that $\tau' \preceq \tau$ if and only if τ' can be transformed into τ by a sequence of $\prec_1$-steps, or, more formally:

PROPOSITION 5.1. *The relation $\preceq$ equals the reflexive and transitive closure of the relation $\prec_1$.*

Note that the definition of $\prec_1$ makes it impossible that $\tau' \prec_1 \tau'' \prec_1 \tau$ while at the same time $\tau' \prec_1 \tau$. Hence, Proposition 5.1 implies that $\prec_1$ as defined above really is the "successor" relation of $\preceq$. More formally, $\tau' \prec_1 \tau$ holds precisely if and only $\tau' \prec \tau$ and there exists no intermediate τ'' such that $\tau' \prec \tau'' \prec \tau$. Moreover, $\prec_1$ is very efficient to compute. Thus armed, we can perform candidate generation in a effective manner as given in Algorithm 3. Here, candidate generation is split up in two steps, which in practice can be interleaved. The set G_{i+1} takes all successors of the current set F_i; the set C_{i+1} then prunes away those elements that have a predecessor that does not satisfy q. It can be shown formally that the sets F_i computed in this concrete manner are exactly the same as those prescribed by the levelwise algorithm:

THEOREM 5.2. *Algorithms 2 and 3 are equivalent.*

Duplicate elimination. Often, a nuisance in mining logical formulas such as selector expressions is duplicate elimination: different expressions may be logically equivalent. Fortunately, in our setting, it follows from Proposition 5.1 that only identical selector expressions can be equivalent.

Regardless, it can happen that two derived, and therefore, inequivalent, target paths τ and τ' select precisely the same set of target nodes on the given document t. As these paths are equivalent from the perspective of t, it holds that $t \models (c, \tau, P)$ iff

[8]Recall that in the prefix tree every node contains its corresponding context and count.

$t \models (c, \tau', P)$ for all sets P. Therefore, w.r.t generation of key paths P, it does not makes sense to consider all of these equivalent path separately. Rather we should choose among them one canonical path. One possibility, e.g., is to opt for the most specific path according to $\prec_1$ minimizing the length and number of wildcards. Notice that equivalence of target paths on t can be tested on the prefix tree $\mathrm{PT}(t)$ without access to the original document.

Boundedness elimination. The quality of the mining result can be improved using the results of Section 4.2. Indeed, target paths that are bounded but that have still passed the support threshold N, which may happen with low values of N, may be eliminated at this stage.

5.3 One-Key Path Miner

Our task here is to find all key paths p for which $(c, \tau, (p))$ is consistent on the given document: that is, for every $v \in \mathrm{CNodes}_t(c)$ and every $u \in \tau(t, v)$, it holds that $p(t, u)$ is a singleton containing a $\mathbf{Data}$-node. Afterwards, only those key paths p are retained for which $(c, \tau, (p))$ is consistent w.r.t. X. The reason for this two-step approach is to reduce the number of costly consistency tests. Although testing for consistency w.r.t. a schema is in polynomial time (cf., Theorem 4.4), it can be slow for large schemas and is ill-suited to be used directly as a search predicate. Therefore, we test for document consistency in a first step and make use of the fact that inconsistency on t implies inconsistency on X. That is, key paths which are not consistent on t and which are therefore pruned in the first step, can never be consistent w.r.t. X.

It turns out that again a levelwise search may be used, utilizing the converse of the specialization relation $\preceq$ for target-path mining. So, define $p' \preceq^{\text{key}} p$ iff $p \preceq p'$. That is, $p' \preceq^{\text{key}} p$ iff $p' \subseteq p$. The search predicate $q_\tau^{\text{key}}(p)$ is now defined to hold if p selects *at most* one node in t for each of the target nodes selected by τ in context c. This q_τ^{key} is indeed monotonically decreasing w.r.t. the converse of containment among selector expressions: $p' \preceq^{\text{key}} p \equiv p' \subseteq p$ and $q_\tau^{\text{key}}(p)$ together imply $q_\tau^{\text{key}}(p')$. We note that consistency requires the selection of exactly one, rather than at most one, node. However, this mismatch can be solved by confining the search space U_{key} to all selector expressions up to length k_{max} that from a target node select a leaf node in the prefix tree: these expressions select at least one node by virtue of their being present in the prefix tree. The "most general" elements from which the levelwise search is started are then the paths in the prefix tree from target nodes to leafs. Obviously, U_{key} can be computed directly from $\mathrm{PT}(t)$.

It remains to discuss how to compute q_τ^{key} efficiently. Unfortunately, q_τ^{key} can not always be computed solely on $\mathrm{PT}(t)$. Indeed, consider the documents $t_1 = a(b(d), b(d))$ and $t_2 = a(b(d, d), b)$, where each d-node is a $\mathbf{Data}$-node. Then, $\mathrm{PT}(t_1) = \mathrm{PT}(t_2)$ yet ϕ is consistent on t_1 but inconsistent on t_2 for $\phi = (c_{\text{root}}, ./a/b, (./d))$ with c_{root} the root context.

We next present a sufficient condition for inconsistency which can be tested on the prefix tree. Thereto, consider $\phi = (c, \tau, (p))$ and let $t' = \mathrm{PT}(t)$. For a node m in t', we denote by $\#_{t'}(m)$ the number assigned to m in t', that is, $|h^{-1}(m)|$ for h as defined in Section 5.1. Define the following conditions: (C1) There exists a $v \in \mathrm{CNodes}_{t'}(c)$ and a $u \in \tau(t', v)$ such that $\#_{t'}(u) < \sum_{w \in p(t', u)} \#_{t'}(w)$; and, (C2) There exists a $v \in \mathrm{CNodes}_{t'}(c)$, a $u \in \tau(t', v)$, a $w \in p(t', u)$, and a node m on the path from u to w such that $\#_{t'}(m) < \#_{t'}(w)$.

Here, (C1) says that the number of target nodes u is strictly smaller than the number of nodes selected by p, and (C2) says that there is a leaf node selected by p and an ancestor with a smaller number of corresponding nodes in t. Both conditions imply that there are at least two nodes selected by p which belong to the same target node in t and which contradict consistency.

Formally, we have that:

PROPOSITION 5.3. *Given $\phi = (c, \tau, (p))$ and a document t. If condition C1 or C2 holds on $\mathrm{PT}(t)$, then ϕ is inconsistent on t.*

So, only when the tests for the above two conditions fail, we evaluate p on t to determine the value of $q_\tau^{\text{key}}(p)$.

Finally, define $\prec_1^{\text{key}}$ as the inverse of $\prec_1$, that is, $p' \prec_1^{\text{key}} p$ iff $p \prec_1 p'$. Then, the first step of $\mathrm{OneKeyPathMiner}_{t,X}(c, \tau)$ is the same algorithm as depicted in Algorithm 3 with U, q, and $\prec_1$, replaced by U_{key}, q_τ^{key}, and $\prec_1^{\text{key}}$, respectively. The second step in $\mathrm{OneKeyPathMiner}_{t,X}(c, \tau)$ retains from all of the returned key paths p, those for which $(c, \tau, (p))$ is consistent w.r.t. X employing the algorithm of Theorem 4.4. A duplicate elimination step similar to the one of the previous section is performed as well.

5.4 Minimal Key Path Set Miner

At this point, we have computed the maximal set S for which every $p \in S$, $(c, \tau, \{p\})$ is consistent w.r.t. X. Next, we are looking for minimal and meaningful sets $P \subseteq S$ such that $t \models (c, \tau, P)$, that is, such that (c, τ, P) is a key for t.

We capitalize on existing relational techniques for mining functional dependencies (e.g., [11, 21, 23]). To this end, we define a relation $R_{S,t}$ with the following schema

$$(CID, TID, p_1, p_2, \ldots, p_{|S|}),$$

where CID and TID are columns for the selected context nodes and target nodes, respectively, and every p_i corresponds to the unique $\mathbf{Data}$-value selected by the corresponding key path p_i. Then, $(v, u, \bar{o}) \in R_{S,t}$ if and only if $v \in \mathrm{CNodes}_t(c)$, $u \in \tau(t, v)$ and $\mathrm{record}_S(t, u) = \bar{o}$. Now, it follows that $t \models (c, \tau, P)$ iff

$$CID, p_1, p_2, \ldots, p_n \rightarrow TID.$$

is a functional dependency in $R_{S,t}$ for $P = (p_1, \ldots, p_n)$. We can now plug in any existing functional dependency discovery algorithm.

6. EXPERIMENTS

For our experiments, we use a corpus of 90 high quality XML documents and associated XSDs obtained from [1]. The input can therefore be seen as 90 pairs consisting each of a unique XML-document and a unique XSD. The maximal and average number of elements occurring in documents is 91K and 5K, respectively, while the maximal and average number of elements occurring in XSDs is 532 and 52, respectively. All experiments are w.r.t. to this corpus and were run on a 3GHz Mac Pro with 2GB of RAM. In all experiments, we set k_{max} to 4 for target paths and to 2 for key paths, unless explicitly mentioned otherwise.

Prefix tree. As different parts of the algorithm can avoid access to the input document t by operating directly on $\mathrm{PT}(t)$, it is instrumental to investigate the compression rate of $\mathrm{PT}(t)$ over t. Figure 5 plots the number of nodes in documents versus the number of nodes in the corresponding prefix trees. Note that the scale is logarithmic. In essence, every document is compressed to a prefix tree with at most 200 nodes even for large documents containing ten or even hundred thousand of nodes.

Contexts. A key $\phi = (c, \tau, P)$ consists of three interdependent components: target paths need only to be considered w.r.t. a context, and key paths need only to be considered w.r.t. a context and a target path. To avoid an explosion of the size of the search space

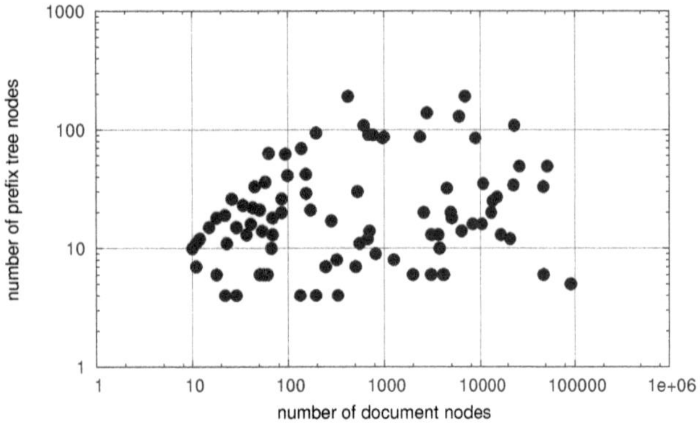

Figure 5: Number of documents versus number of nodes in prefix trees.

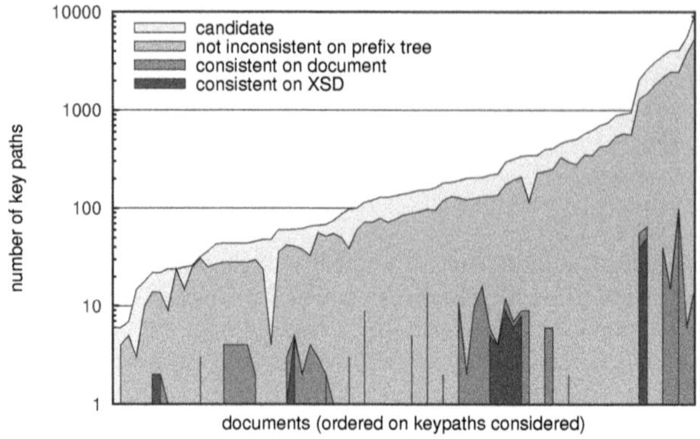

Figure 7: Behavior of one-key path miner.

it is paramount to reduce the number of considered contexts, target paths and key paths. We next assess the effectiveness of the algorithm in this respect.

We start with the number of contexts considered by the algorithm. An analysis comparing the number of contexts allowed by XSDs with the number of contexts actually used in the XML documents, shows that for 40% of the documents all allowable contexts materialize in the corresponding XML documents, i.e., there is no improvement as no allowable context can be omitted. Nevertheless, it appears that this mostly happens for smaller XSDs. Indeed, the total sum of allowable contexts over all 90 documents is 4639 while the total sum of contexts found in actual documents is 2217 which indicates that over the complete data set 52% of all possible contexts do *not* have to be considered. Keeping in mind that every context that can be removed in this step, eliminates a call to the target path *and* key path miner underlines the effectiveness of context search driven by the XML data at hand.

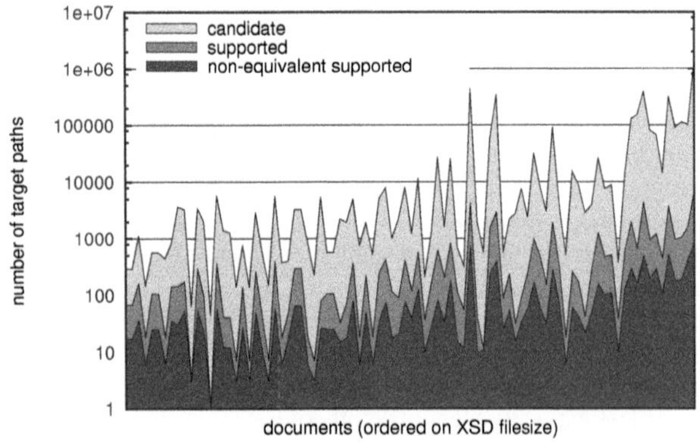

Figure 6: Behavior of the target path miner.

Target paths. Next, we discuss the behavior of the target path miner when the support threshold N equals 10. The results are illustrated in Figure 6 (cases with $k_{max} = 5$ and/or lower support threshold were also tested but are similar and therefore not shown). For presentation purposes, the X-axis enumerates all document-XSD pairs increasingly ordered by the size of the XSD. The figure then shows per pair, the number of candidate, supported, and non-equivalent derived target paths. Its purpose is to provide a visual inspection on the considered quantities on a per document basis. By candidate target paths we mean those that occurred in a candidate set C_i during the execution of Algorithm 3. Non-equivalent target paths are those which remain after duplicate elimination (as explained in Section 5.2). The number of possible target paths to consider (that is, the cardinality of the search space U times the number of allowable contexts) is not shown as the target path miner only considers a small fraction of those, to be precise, only 3% on average. Furthermore, on average, only 7% of all candidate target paths turn out to be supported and of all supported paths only 27% remain after duplicate elimination. To get a feeling for the magnitude of the reduction in target paths (TPs) provided by the algorithm, we give the following table of absolute numbers which are summed up over the whole data set of document-XSD pairs:

possible TPs	2.4×10^{11}
candidate TPs	6.7×10^{6}
supported TPs	8.4×10^{4}
unique TPs	1.3×10^{4}

One-key paths. Figure 7 provides a visual interpretation of the reduction in number of key paths by the consecutive steps of the one-key path miner as described in Section 5.3. Again, for presentation purposes, the X-axis enumerates all document-XSD pairs increasingly ordered by the number of resulting candidate key paths. Specifically, the figure plots on a per document basis the following numbers: candidate key paths, paths for which the inconsistency test fails on the prefix tree, paths which are consistent on the document, and paths which are consistent w.r.t. the XSD. We first discuss the average improvement on a per document basis. Specifically, on average 29% of candidate paths are inconsistent over the prefix tree. This means that for 61% of the remaining key paths consistency needs to be tested on the document. On average, only 6% of key paths are consistent w.r.t. the document and of these 68% turn out to be consistent w.r.t. the XSD. Absolute numbers summed up over the whole data set of document-XSD pairs, give the following picture for key paths (KPs):

candidate KPs	48144
inconsistent KPs on prefix tree	29190
consistent KPs on document	484
consistent KPs on XSD	288

It is interesting to observe that on the considered sample of real-world documents, consistency on the document does not always imply consistency w.r.t. the associated XSD. Specifically, the above table shows that overall only roughly 60% of KP which are consistent on documents are consistent on the XSD as well.

Keys. Next, we discuss the keys returned by our algorithm. We use the hypergraph transversal algorithm to mine relational functional dependencies as, for instance, described in [22], but any such algorithm can be readily plugged in. We consider keys with target path length at most 4 and key path length at most 2. In the following, we refer to testing consistency of a key w.r.t. its XSD, that is, by applying the algorithm of Theorem 4.4, as the schema consistency test. Table 2 and Table 3 then gather some statistics of discovered keys without and with the schema consistency test. First of all, it can be observed that not every document contains a key with the required support: only 30% and 16% of all documents using support 10 and 100, respectively (Table 2). The latter might seem strange at first sight, but note that not all XML documents are in fact databases and that the requirement for a key to qualify (cf., Definition 3.4) is a severe one. Indeed, even lowering the support threshold to a value of two (experiment not shown here) only provides a key for 60% of the documents, but of course a key with support two is not very relevant. We note that the average supports for discovered keys in this section is 404 and 612 for support thresholds equal to 10 and 100, respectively, while the maximum support encountered is 2011, indicating that the discovered keys indeed cover a large number of elements.

The figures in the two tables nicely illustrate the effectiveness of schema consistency as a quality measure. Indeed, without schema consistency Table 2 shows that 107 and 54 keys are derived for support threshold 10 and 100, respectively. Interestingly, in both cases, there is a document with a rather large number of keys: 23 to be specific. But, after the schema consistency test each of these keys is removed as they all contain a key path which select elements of which the schema says they are optional. Of course, one could debate about whether the schema is actually always correct or may be too liberal. One could always opt to offer keys which do not pass schema consistency to the user. However, after an inspection of the derived keys from our corpus, it becomes apparent that in many cases keys rejected by the schema are probably not keys at all. As an illustrative example, consider the three derived keys (all with support 340, and where `root` refers to the root context):

```
(root,/Products,{/ID})
(root,/Products,{/Other_Information,
                                  /Catalogue-Name})
(root,/Products,{/Type, /Other_Information})
```

where after the schema consistency test only the first key remains. In this case, it should be clear that the second and third keys are not accurate but a glitch in the data. Therefore, one could say that the reduction from 107 to 43 and from 54 to 16 keys in Tables 2 and 3 actually improves the quality at the expense of lowering the quantity which in our opinion can be seen as a good thing as most data mining problem suffer from an explosion in derived patterns.

Quality. It remains to discuss the quality of the keys. When the provided schema is accurate, the schema consistency test, as discussed above, provides a quality criterion in its own. A second quality criterion can be the high support of derived keys: as mentioned above the found support of derived keys is on average 404 and 612 for support thresholds equal to 10 and 100, respectively, while the maximum support encountered is 2011. Furthermore, when inspecting found keys it appeared that in many cases keys select elements whose name contains 'ID'.

We finish with a discussion on implication of keys. Usually, in key discovery, the goal is to find a minimal set of keys, called cover,

	sup = 10	sup = 100
derived keys	107	54
docs with keys	27	15
average nr. of keys per doc	4	3.6
max nr. of keys per doc	23	23
average nr. of key paths	1.3	1.3
max key nr. of key paths	2	2

Table 2: Statistics of mined keys *without* the requirement to be consistent w.r.t. the associated XSD.

	sup = 10	sup = 100
derived keys	43	16
docs with keys	19	10
average nr. of keys per doc	2.2	1.6
max nr. of keys per doc	9	4
average nr. of key paths	1.3	1.2
max key nr. of key paths	2	2

Table 3: Statistics of mined keys *with* the requirement to be consistent w.r.t. the associated XSD.

from which all other keys can be derived. For instance, to this end Grahne and Zhu [19] make use of the inference algorithms for XML keys investigated and shown to be polynomially computable by Buneman et al. [15]. Unfortunately, Theorem 4.5 shows that key implication in the presence of a schema is EXPTIME-hard. Still, there is opportunity to detect duplicate keys. For instance, the next pair of discovered keys turn out to be equivalent (both with support 90):

```
((State: 188,Symbol: ConstraintID),/*,{/*})
((State: 167,Symbol: PureOrMixtureData),
          /Constraint/ConstraintID/*,{/*})
```

as `ConstraintID` can only occur under a `Constraint`-element. We can therefore consider the keys to be equivalent as they select precisely the same set of target nodes.

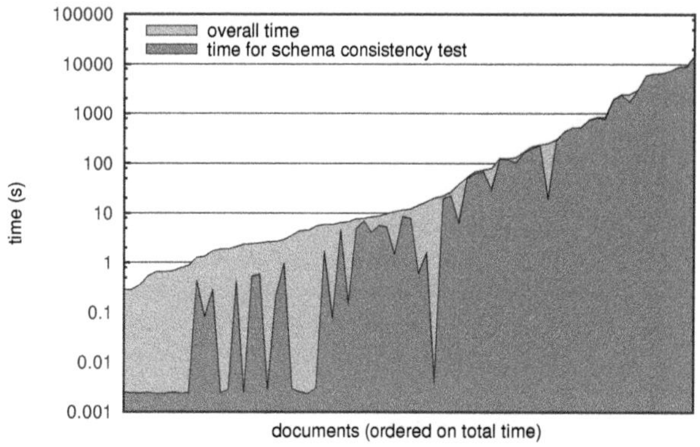

Figure 8: Proportion of the running time consumed by the schema consistency check.

Running time. We next discuss the runing time of the algorithm. Of course, the previous sections have already illustrated how the different mining steps succeed in reducing the number of considered contexts, target paths and key paths and every such reduction

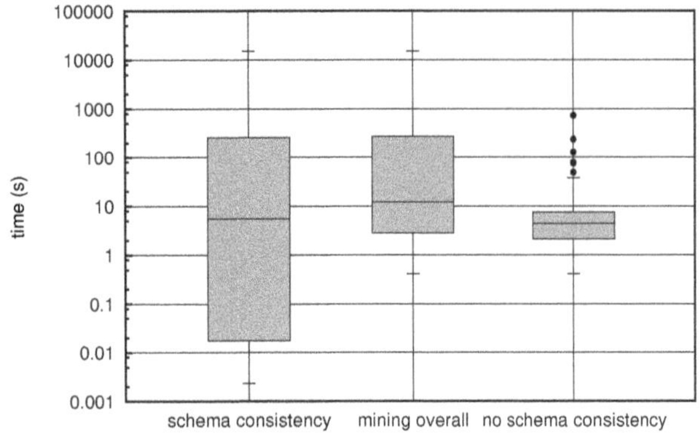

Figure 9: Boxplots indicating average run times.

induces a gain in speed. Figure 9 gives insight in the overall running time. Here, a large fraction of the time is taken up by the schema consistency test. Furthermore, Figure 8 gives an indication of the proportion of time taken by the schema consistency test w.r.t. the overall running time. For presentation purposes, the X-axis enumerates all document-XSD pairs increasingly ordered by the time required for the schema consistency test. Note that the figure does not imply an exponential growth of the running time. In fact, as the X-axis does not corresponds to a quantity, no inference can be made about the asymptotic growth of the running time.

We want to stress that key discovery is not a time critical task and that the algorithm only has to be run once for an XML-document and XSD. Nevertheless, the above figures also show that the most room for improvement lies within a speed up of the schema consistency test and less in other components of the algorithm.

7. DISCUSSION

In this paper, we initiated a fundamental study of properties of W3C XML keys in the presence of a schema and introduced an effective novel key mining algorithm leveraging on the formalism of levelwise search and on algorithms for the discovery of functional dependencies in the relational model.

A number of interesting issues remain open and require further investigation. The most direct one is to close the gaps between some of the obtained lower and upper bounds. It would be interesting to investigate tractable subcases especially w.r.t. key implication. An observed bottleneck of the proposed approach is to check consistency of a derived key w.r.t. the associated schema, even though the number of keys which have to be tested is greatly reduced by testing for inconsistency on the XML document, it should be investigated how schema consistency can be accelerated. This would require advances in string and tree automata theory. Another approach would be to try to find fast heuristic algorithms or to study the problem for subclasses of XSDs.

8. ACKNOWLEDGEMENTS

We used the infrastructure of the VSC - Flemish Supercomputer Center, funded by the Hercules foundation and the Flemish Government. We acknowledge financial support of the Fondecyt Grant #1131049, FP7-ICT-233599 and ERC grant agreement DIADEM, no. 246858.

9. REFERENCES

[1] University of Amsterdam XML web collection. `http://data.politicalmashup.nl/sgrijzen/xmlweb/`.

[2] S. Abiteboul, Y. Amsterdamer, D. Deutch, T. Milo, and P. Senellart. Finding optimal probabilistic generators for XML collections. In *ICDT*, pages 127–139, 2012.

[3] S. Abiteboul, R. Hull, and V. Vianu. *Foundations of Databases*. Addison-Wesley, 1995.

[4] M. Arenas, W. Fan, and L. Libkin. What's hard about XML schema constraints? In *DEXA*, pages 269–278, 2002.

[5] D. Barbosa and A. O. Mendelzon. Finding id attributes in XML documents. In *XSym*, pages 180–194, 2003.

[6] G. J. Bex, W. Gelade, W. Martens, and F. Neven. Simplifying XML schema: effortless handling of nondeterministic regular expressions. In *SIGMOD*, pages 731–744, 2009.

[7] G. J. Bex, W. Gelade, F. Neven, and S. Vansummeren. Learning deterministic regular expressions for the inference of schemas from XML data. *TWEB*, 4(4), 2010.

[8] G. J. Bex, F. Neven, T. Schwentick, and S. Vansummeren. Inference of concise regular expressions and DTDs. *ACM TODS*, 35(2), 2010.

[9] G. J. Bex, F. Neven, and S. Vansummeren. Inferring XML schema definitions from XML data. In *VLDB*, pages 998–1009, 2007.

[10] G. J. Bex, F. Neven, and S. Vansummeren. Schemascope: a system for inferring and cleaning XML schemas. In *SIGMOD*, pages 1259–1262, 2008.

[11] D. Bitton, J. Millman, and S. Torgersen. A feasibility and performance study of dependency inference. In *ICDE*, pages 635–641, 1989.

[12] H. Björklund, W. Martens, and T. Schwentick. Validity of tree pattern queries with respect to schema information. 2012.

[13] A. Brüggemann-Klein and D. Wood. One-unambiguous regular languages. *Inf. Comput.*, 140(2):229–253, 1998.

[14] P. Buneman, S. B. Davidson, W. Fan, C. S. Hara, and W. C. Tan. Keys for XML. *Computer Networks*, 39(5):473–487, 2002.

[15] P. Buneman, S. B. Davidson, W. Fan, C. S. Hara, and W. C. Tan. Reasoning about keys for XML. *Inf. Syst.*, 28(8):1037–1063, 2003.

[16] S. Fajt, I. Mlynkova, and M. Necasky. On mining XML integrity constraints. In *ICDIM*, pages 23–29, 2011.

[17] W. Fan and L. Libkin. On XML integrity constraints in the presence of DTDs. *J. ACM*, 49(3):368–406, 2002.

[18] M. N. Garofalakis, A. Gionis, R. Rastogi, S. Seshadri, and K. Shim. XTRACT: Learning document type descriptors from XML document collections. *Data Min. Knowl. Discov.*, 7(1):23–56, 2003.

[19] G. Grahne and J. Zhu. Discovering approximate keys in XML data. *CIKM*, page 453-460, 2002.

[20] S. Hartmann and S. Link. Efficient reasoning about a robust XML key fragment. *ACM TODS*, 34(2), 2009.

[21] H. Mannila and K.-J. Raiha. Practical algorithms for finding prime attributes and testing normal forms. In *PODS*, 1989.

[22] H. Mannila and K.-J. Räihä. *The design of relational databases*. Addison- Wesley, 1991.

[23] H. Mannila and K.-J. Räihä. Algorithms for inferring functional dependencies from relations. *Data Knowl. Eng.*, 12(1):83–99, 1994.

[24] H. Mannila and H. Toivonen. Levelwise search and borders of theories in knowledge discovery. *Data Min. Knowl. Discov.*, 1(3):241–258, 1997.

[25] W. Martens, F. Neven, and T. Schwentick. Simple off the shelf abstractions for XML schema. *SIGMOD Record*, 36(3):15–22, 2007.

[26] W. Martens, F. Neven, T. Schwentick, and G. J. Bex. Expressiveness and complexity of XML schema. *ACM TODS*, 31(3):770–813, 2006.

[27] M. Murata, D. Lee, M. Mani, and K. Kawaguchi. Taxonomy of XML schema languages using formal language theory. *ACM Trans. Internet Techn.*, 5(4):660–704, 2005.

[28] M. Necaský and I. Mlýnková. Discovering XML keys and foreign keys in queries. In *SAC*, pages 632–638. ACM, 2009.

[29] R. Ramakrishnan and J. Gehrke. *Database management systems (3. ed.)*. McGraw-Hill, 2003.

[30] H. Seidl. Deciding equivalence of finite tree automata. *SIAM J. Comput.*, 19(3):424–437, 1990.

[31] W3C. XML schema part 1: Structures, 2nd edition.

[32] C. Yu and H. V. Jagadish. XML schema refinement through redundancy detection and normalization. *VLDB J.*, 17(2):203–223, 2008.

A Scalable Lock Manager for Multicores

Hyungsoo Jung
NICTA
Sydney, Australia
hyungsoo.jung@gmail.com

Hyuck Han*
Samsung Electronics
Hwasung, South Korea
hyuck.han@samsung.com

Alan D. Fekete
University of Sydney
Sydney, Australia
alan.fekete@sydney.edu.au

Gernot Heiser
NICTA and UNSW
Sydney, Australia
gernot@nicta.com.au

Heon Y. Yeom
Seoul National University
Seoul, South Korea
yeom@snu.ac.kr

ABSTRACT

Modern implementations of DBMS software are intended to take advantage of high core counts that are becoming common in high-end servers. However, we have observed that several database platforms, including MySQL, Shore-MT, and a commercial system, exhibit throughput collapse as load increases, even for a workload with little or no logical contention for locks. Our analysis of MySQL identifies latch contention within the lock manager as the bottleneck responsible for this collapse.

We design a lock manager with reduced latching, implement it in MySQL, and show that it avoids the collapse and generally improves performance. Our efficient implementation of a lock manager is enabled by a staged allocation and de-allocation of locks. Locks are pre-allocated in bulk, so that the lock manager only has to perform simple list-manipulation operations during the acquire and release phases of a transaction. De-allocation of the lock data-structures is also performed in bulk, which enables the use of fast implementations of lock acquisition and release, as well as concurrent deadlock checking.

Categories and Subject Descriptors

H.2.4 [**Database Management**]: Systems—*concurrency, transaction processing*; D.1.3 [**Programming Techniques**]: Concurrent Programming

General Terms

Algorithms, Design, Performance

Keywords

Multicores, scalable lock manager, concurrent programming

*Affiliation: Memory Solutions Lab, Memory Division, Samsung Semiconductor.

SIGMOD'13, June 22–27, 2013, New York, New York, USA.

1. INTRODUCTION

Present high-end computing platforms, as they are frequently used for database servers, now feature dozens of processor cores, and will soon exceed 100 cores. It is therefore important that database transaction processing can utilise such a large number of cores efficiently.

This is not trivial, as higher core counts result in increased contention for shared data structures in the DBMS internals. A few years ago, studies [11, 17] showed that many open-source and commercial database engines exhibit limited multi-core scalability, and even performance collapse, due to bottlenecks in their lock, log or transaction manager. This has triggered significant research activity [3, 5, 12, 14–17, 19] aimed at reducing lock or latch contention.

Yet, significant scalability problems still exist for serializable transactions, surprisingly even under read-only workloads, where the locks never conflict with one another (though of course they must still be taken, since the system must work properly if updates are submitted). This is illustrated in Figure 1, which shows throughput of a serializable, read-only workload on MySQL under varying load using 4, 8 or 16 cores of the same 32-core platform. (Detailed specification of the setup is given in Section 5.)

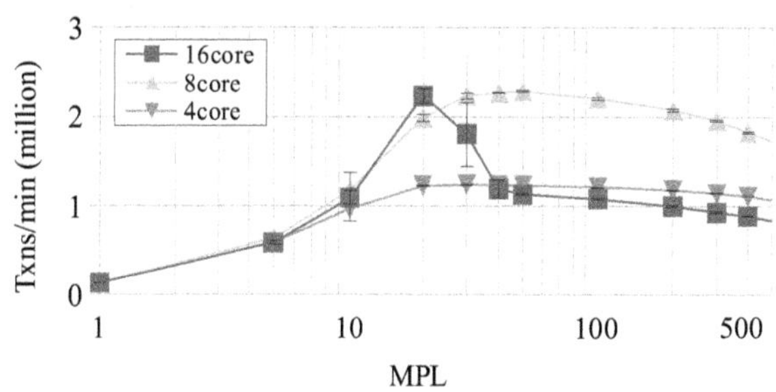

Figure 1: MySQL throughput under varying multiprogramming level (MPL) on 4 (green), 8 (yellow) and 16 cores (red).

The figure clearly shows that on 4 cores the database behaves as expected, with 8 cores throughput degrades at high load to about 75 % of peak throughput. On 16 cores, high-load performance collapses to about 1/3 of peak, and well below what the 4-core configuration can handle. The peak throughput of 16 cores is also below that of 8.

Our analysis of this undesirable effect shows that it is caused by latch contention in the lock manager. Each time a transaction acquires or releases a lock, it grabs the mutex protecting the global table of locks. Even though the mutex is only held briefly, *cache-line bouncing* [18] makes acquiring or releasing it expensive under high contention [4].

We propose a solution to this problem, based on a (mostly) latch-free implementation of the lock manager. The design is enabled by the observation that the lock acquisition and release operations can be split into two: the allocation (and initialisation) and de-allocation of the lock data structure, and the manipulation of this data structure. The latter can be implemented latch-free, and thus contention-free. We perform allocation and de-allocation of locks in bulk, thus amortising any remaining latching overhead over a large number of locks. Furthermore, de-allocation becomes a garbage-collection exercise which can be performed asynchronously to transaction processing. We refer to this approach as *staged lock acquisition and release*.

This paper makes the following contributions:

- We identify scalability issues leading to performance collapse under high workloads when running on a platform featuring dozens of cores. We show that this collapse occurs on multiple open-source (MySQL, Shore-MT) as well as on a commercial database engine (Section 5.2).
- We propose a design for the lock manager in which much less latching is needed, and we describe its implementation in MySQL (Section 3).
- A key idea that enables our design is bulk allocation and de-allocation of locks, asynchronous to transaction processing (Section 4);
- we evaluate our implementation, demonstrating that staged lock handling avoids the throughput collapse and also leads to improved peak throughput (Section 5.2).

2. BACKGROUND AND RELATED WORK

This paper is related to an extensive literature on managing concurrency, both in database systems and more general programs. Here we point to a few essential concepts needed for understanding our contribution.

2.1 The Lock Manager

Database management platforms are expected to provide the application programmers with an abstraction of ACID transactions, freeing the programmer from worrying about anomalies that might arise from concurrency or failure. This enables independent development of multiple database clients. Authoritative coverage on the field of transaction management, and its subfield of concurrency control can be found in the textbooks by Bernstein *et al.* [2] and Weikum and Vossen [20]. The internal design of a DBMS is described by Hellerstein *et al.* [9]. The usual approach is for the lower, storage-focused parts of the DBMS to contain a component called a lock manager. Code that fetches or updates a record obtains an appropriate lock in the lock manager; this lock is then held until the transaction completes ("strict two phase locking"). Locks are taken in various modes, such as shared mode for a read, or exclusive mode for a write; other modes are important for preventing phantoms and allowing locking on different granularities of item (such as records, pages and tables). The lock manager arbitrates access by putting a transaction, which attempts to acquire an incompatible lock, into a wait state, and wakes it up when the lock becomes available. Design principles for a lock manager are presented by Gray and Reuter [8].

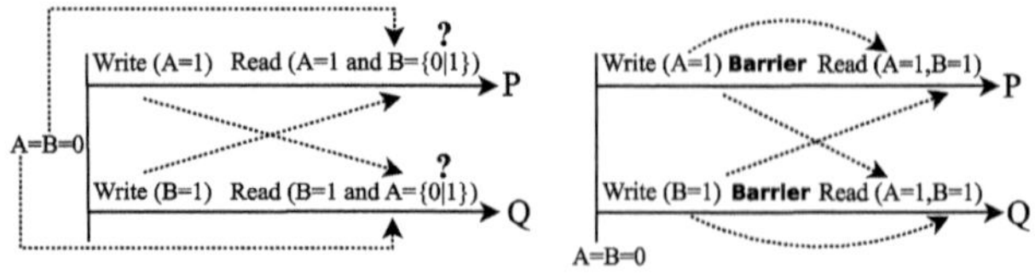

(a) Non-serialisable execution (b) Safe with barriers

Figure 2: Unsafe vs. safe RAW execution.

While the lock manager prevents logical interference between concurrent transactions, there is also a need to prevent interference between DBMS threads as they manipulate the shared physical structures within the DBMS, including within the lock manager. This is typical of the problems of concurrent programming, and is traditionally addressed by what the DB community calls latches (or mutexes) that surround any DBMS internal code that deals with shared data structures. The distinctions between locks and latches are clarified by Graefe [6]. Early open-source DBMS code used a coarse-grained latch on the whole of the kernel internals, but more recent releases (e.g., the InnoDB system we used as the baseline for our evaluation) have moved to a more sophisticated design with separate latches for different parts of the kernel, such as the lock manager, the buffer pool, etc.

Recent research has addressed some bottlenecks in transaction processing on multi-core platforms [11,17], proposing some radical changes to the system architecture or access structures [7, 12, 14, 15, 19]. In contrast, we here consider a localized change to the lock manager, without requiring other parts of the platform to be recoded.

2.2 Synchronising Multithread Programs

Concurrent programs are notoriously hard to code correctly. The simplest approach relies on an ability to make a segment of code execute without interleaving, allowing repeated use of a variable, as in the synchronisation pattern called *atomic write after read* (AWAR) where a thread or process atomically reads and then writes a shared variable. The atomicity of AWAR is typically achieved through latches (such as spin locks) using atomic machine instructions, such as Compare-and-Swap or Test-and-Set. On multiprocessor architectures with a snoop-based cache coherence protocol, this can lead to expensive *cache invalidation storms*.

An alternative coding style is *read after write* (RAW) where a process writes to some shared variable A, followed by the process reading a different shared variable B, without process writing to B in between [1]. Use of the RAW pattern must ensure that concurrent processes only see a compatible (linearizable or sequentially consistent) state of shared variable. The problem is illustrated in Figure 2(a), where concurrent processes P and Q access shared variables A and B according to the RAW pattern. Executing unconstrained, the data race could result in P seeing the value of $B = 0$ **and** Q seeing the value $A = 0$, which violates serialisability. Figure 2(b) shows how correctness can be enforced though the introduction of *memory barriers*, making the data race benign.

While memory barriers can be expensive, the advantage of the RAW pattern over AWAR is that the hardware overhead is paid at most once per thread. This is in contrast to cache lines potentially bouncing repeatedly between processes in AWAR. Hence the RAW pattern tends to scale better with increasing number of cores and processes.

The textbook by Herlihy and Shavit [10] provides extensive coverage on multiprocessor programming, for a wide range of interesting data structures.

3. LOCKING WITH LESS LATCHING

We now describe the approach we take to make the lock manager (mostly) latch-free. As explained earlier, the core idea is to separate the allocation and de-allocation of the lock data structures from lock acquisition and release, and perform the allocation and de-allocation in bulk and asynchronous to transaction processing.

In this section we describe the algorithms for lock acquisition and release, while the bulk allocation and de-allocation of the lock hash table is presented in Section 4.

The LHS of Figure 3 shows high-level pseudo-code of the implementation of the lock acquisition (top) and release (bottom) operations in MySQL; other database engines use a similar approach. Most of the acquisition and all of the release are protected by a mutex on the lock data structure. This ensures the consistency of the lock table and correct synchronisation of transactions.

3.1 Lock Acquisition

The fundamental observation which allows us to reduce latching is that some of the data races in the code are benign: when obtaining a slot in the hash table, it does not matter which slot goes to a particular transaction, as long as all transactions obtain different slots.

Looking at the acquire code in the LHS column of Figure 3, we can see that the transaction first creates a lock on the data item and inserts it into its list of held locks.[1] It then checks whether other transactions hold incompatible locks on the same data, in which case it marks the new lock as being in waiting state, followed by checking for deadlocks. The complete sequence is protected by a latch on the hash table.

The second part makes the transaction wait until all preceding incompatible locks are released, as required for the usual database locking protocols. It does this by calling the operating system to suspend the process, until the holder of the incompatible lock signals its release. This code is protected by the transaction latch.[2]

Re-writing this operation in the RAW pattern allows us to eliminate the hash-table latch, as shown on the RHS of Figure 3. Inserting the lock into the hash table is now performed by a latch-free implementation of the insertion function (**S1**), discussed below. Each occurrence of writ-

Traditional Lock Manager | **Our Lock Manager**

Lock Acquire in Growing Phase

Traditional Lock Manager:

```
mutex_enter(lock_table->mutex);
n_lock = lock_create();
n_lock->state = ACTIVE;
lock_insert(n_lock);
for all locks (lock) in hash_bucket
  if (lock is incompatible with n_ lock)
    n_lock->state = WAIT;
    if (deadlock_check() ==TRUE)
        abort Tx;
      break;
  else
      continue;
  end if
end for
mutex_exit(lock_table->mutex);
if (n_lock->state==WAIT)
  mutex_enter(Tx->mutex);
  Tx->state = WAIT;
  os_cond_wait(Tx->mutex);
  mutex_exit(Tx->mutex);
end if
```

Our Lock Manager:

```
A1:  n_lock = lock_create();
A2:  n_lock->state = ACTIVE;                        S1
A3:  atomic_lock_insert(n_lock);
A4:  for all locks (lock) in hash_bucket
A5:    if (lock is incompatible with n_lock)
A6:      n_lock->state = WAIT;                      S2
A7:      atomic_synchronize();
A8:      if (lock->state==OBSOLETE)
A9:        n_lock->state=ACTIVE;                    S3
A10:       atomic_synchronize();
A11:       continue;
A12:     if (new_deadlock()==TRUE)
A13:       abort Tx;
A14:     break;
A15:   end if
A16: end for
A17: if (n_lock->state == WAIT)
A18:   mutex_enter(Tx->mutex);                      S4
A19:   atomic_synchronize();
A20:   if ( n_lock has to wait )
A21:     Tx->state = WAIT;
A22:     os_cond_wait(Tx->mutex);
A23:   else
A24:     n_lock->state = ACTIVE;                    S5
A25:     atomic_synchronize();
A26:   end if
A27:   mutex_exit(Tx->mutex);
A28: end if
```

Lock Release in Shrinking Phase

Traditional Lock Manager:

```
mutex_enter(lock_table->mutex);
for all locks (lock1) in Tx
  lock_release(lock1);
  for all locks (lock2) following lock1
    if ( lock2 doesn't have to wait )
      lock_grant( lock2 );
      lock2->state=ACTIVE;
    end if
  end for
end for
mutex_exit(lock_table->mutex);
```

Our Lock Manager:

```
R1:  for all locks (lock1) in Tx
R2:    lock1->state = OBSOLETE;                     S6
R3:    atomic_synchronize();
R4:    for all locks (lock2) that follow lock1
R5:      mutex_enter(lock2->Tx->mutex);
R6:      if ( lock2->Tx->state==WAIT &&
R7:           lock2 does not have to wait )
R8:        lock2->Tx->state=ACTIVE;
R9:        lock2->state=ACTIVE;                     S7
R10:       atomic_synchronize();
R11:       os_cond_signal(lock2->Tx);
R12:     end if
R13:     mutex_exit(lock2->Tx->mutex);
R14:   end for
R15: end for
```

Figure 3: Implementation of lock acquisition and release in MySQL. The left column shows the existing lock manager code, while the right column shows our reduced-latch implementation. S1, . . . , S7 represent *RAW synchronisation points*.

ing a shared variable followed by reading a different one (**S2**, **S3**) is protected by a barrier (represented by the `atomic_synchronize()` function), in line with the safe RAW pattern of Figure 2(b) . The new lock state `OBSOLETE` is a result of the staged de-allocation, and indicates that the lock is no longer in use. The deadlock-checking function (line **A12**) must be replaced by a race-tolerant implementation `new_deadlock()`.

Operation of `atomic_lock_insert()` is shown in Figure 4. The function inserts a new lock into the hash table by using `atomic_fetch_and_store()` on the tail pointer of the hash chain, returning the old tail pointer. The old tail is then made to point to the new lock. The function `next_pointer_update()` implements a *compare-and-swap-*

[1]Since InnoDB uses a small bitmap in a lock to represent other record locks of the same transaction in the same page, and the use of the bitmap can only be decided by seeing all locks in the hash list, `lock_create()` occurs while the hash table mutex is held.

[2]In InnoDB, when a MySQL thread is suspended, it should release the mutex it holds, and after being woken up, the thread must regain the mutex and do the post-processing.

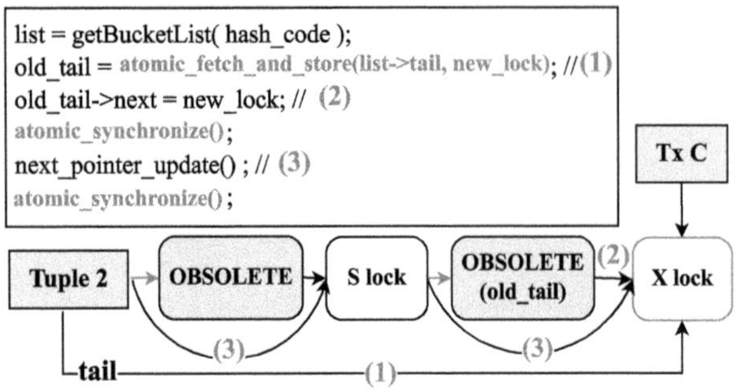

Figure 4: Operation of `atomic_lock_insert()` on a lock hash chain.

based concurrent update [10] of the next pointers of all active locks in the list. Barriers are again used to ensure safe RAW execution. Since the next pointer update follows the atomic update of the tail pointer, we have to guarantee that other concurrent transactions accessing this list see a consistent view of this list.

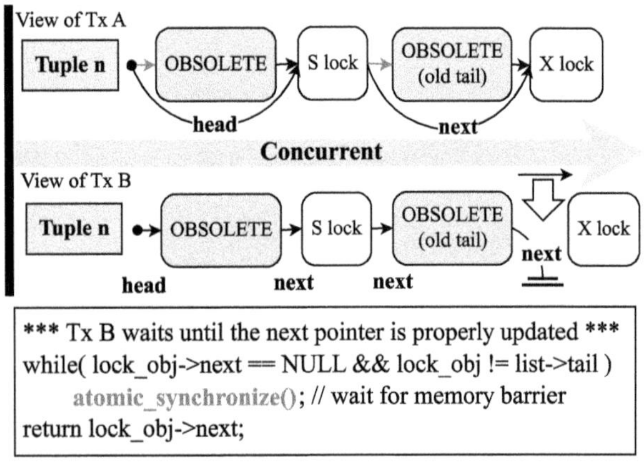

Figure 5: Pseudo-code of latch-free list iteration.

The traversal of the lock list (line **A4** of Figure 3) must preserve the invariant that all locks inserted before the present one are examined. The implementation of the iterator is explained in Figure 5. The original iterator in LHS of Figure 3 simply traverses the list by using the next pointer of a lock until the end of the list. Our iterator is augmented with the `while` loop, and this ensures that any locks previously inserted into the list become visible by waiting until the next pointer of a lock points to a newly inserted lock. As shown in Figure 4, since the next pointer update is done after the atomic update of a tail pointer, concurrent list traversal should see either the new lock or the old tail. This is why we need the while loop.

The second part of the acquire function retains the transaction latch, which is fine, as this latch is not contented by multiple processes. Barriers must again be inserted to ensure safe RAW execution.

3.2 Lock Release

The release code is shown in the bottom part of Figure 3. Our implementation again removes the lock-table latch, and inserts barriers according to the RAW pattern. Note that, rather than de-allocating the lock, its status is set to `OBSOLETE`, so that *no dangling pointers are generated.* The actual de-allocation is performed asynchronously and in bulk.

Importantly, the release code must examine locks which were allocated after the present lock, to detect any sleeping transactions trying to acquire an incompatible lock on the same data. These are signaled via a system call which wakes up the sleeping process.

3.3 Deadlock Detection

The deadlock checking function is to find any cycle in the wait-for graph by traversing a lock hash table. The traditional approach does this traversal while holding the lock-table latch. We avoid this by keeping any released lock and transaction data structures until they are guaranteed to be no longer required, thus avoiding dangling-pointer dereferences in the deadlock checker. By making any other data structures required for deadlock detection transaction-local, we enable a latch-free implementation.

When a deadlock is detected in the traditional, latch-based implementation, the lock manager can use a number of different policies for selecting a victim transaction to abort. For example, it can choose the transaction which (1) holds the smallest number of (write) locks, (2) generates the fewest log records, or (3) actually causes the deadlock (joining lock).

In our latch-free implementation, safety prevents a thread from changing the transaction state while other threads may access the state. Hence, the thread must abort its own transaction when detecting a deadlock, i.e., we can only implement the above policy (3).

3.4 Correctness

The main correctness concern is that concurrent acquisition and release operations operate correctly, and that deadlock detection is correct.

Figure 6(a) illustrates the scenario where a transaction Tx A executes `COMMIT` and is about to release lock1. Concurrently, transaction Tx B tries to insert an exclusive lock (lock2) into the same lock hash list (and is sent to sleep). We must guarantee that the commit of Tx A will wake up Tx B.

Figure 6(b) shows possible schedules resulting from the interleaving of the two transactions. The critical point is the change of the state of the lock by Tx A (**S6**), we must ensure that Tx B will be woken, no matter how the execution of **S6** is interleaved with its own execution. Depending on where **S6** occurs during Tx B's execution, we have five different interesting cases, as indicated in Figure 6(b).

The correctness argument is summarised in Figure 6(c). In the first three schedules, (1)–(3), **S6** happens before Tx B examines the state of `lock1`, and the barriers ensure that Tx B sees the correct lock state. For schedule (4), Tx B may or may not see the updated lock state. If it does, (4)(ii) then this is the same as schedules (1)–(3), and thus executes correctly. Else the checking routine **R6-7** of Tx A, which follows Tx B's wait execution due to Tx B's transaction mutex, correctly captures Tx B's "WAIT" state and wakes up Tx B correctly. In schedule (5), Tx B cannot detect `S6` and waits until Tx A correctly finds Tx B's state, as in schedule (4)(i).

To reason about the correctness of concurrent deadlock checking, suppose we have multiple transactions, all executing **S2**, changing their lock state to `WAIT`. Assuming that

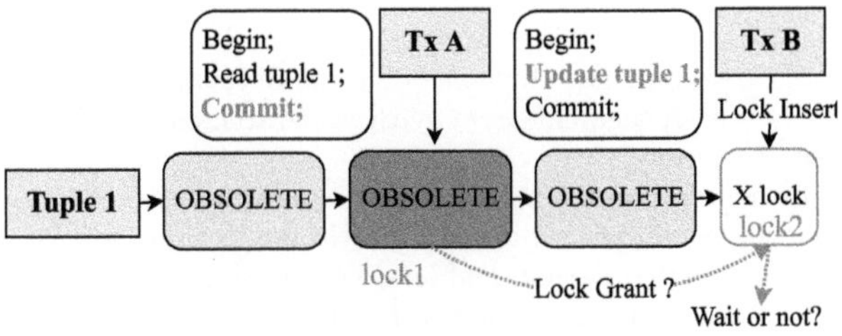

(a) Illustration

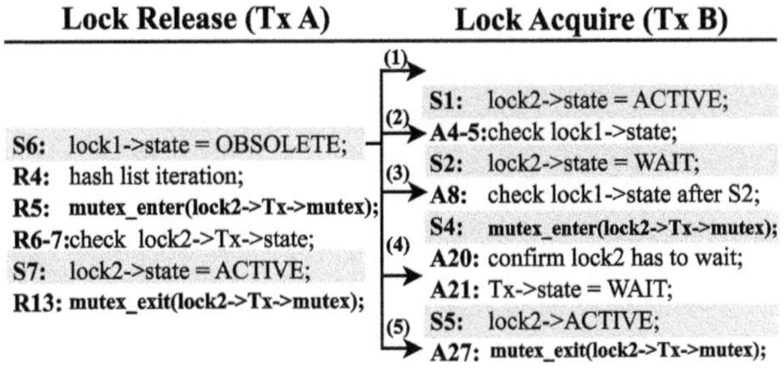

(b) All possible schedules

Schedule	Result
(1) S6 < S1 .. S7 (2) S1 < S6 < S2 .. S7 (3) S1 < S2 < S6 < S4 .. S7	(A4-5), (A8), and (A20) correctly detect lock1's OBSOLETE state. (correct)
(4) S1 .. S4 < S6 < S5 .. S7 implies (A27 < R5)	(i) If (A21) excutes, then (R4) detects; and (R6-7) and (S7) wake up Tx B. (correct) (ii) If (A20) detects lock1's OBSOLETE, then it is the same as schedule (3). (correct)
(5) S1 .. S5 < S6 < S7 implies (A27 < R5)	(R6-7) detects Tx B's WAIT, and (S7) correctly wakes up Tx B. (correct)

(c) Correctness

Figure 6: Concurrent execution of `Lock Acquire` and `Lock Release`.

these transactions create a real deadlock, then all interleaving schedules of concurrent deadlock checking must guarantee that at least one of the checks must see the `WAIT` state of all other locks. This is ensured by the RAW pattern. Note that, unlike the traditional approach, latch-free deadlock checking may abort more than one transaction, if multiple deadlock checking invocations find the same deadlock simultaneously. This is correctness-neutral (but may result in performance degradation).

4. LOCK MANAGEMENT

The RAW-style algorithms for acquisition and release of locks described in the previous section can only work because we do not de-allocate a lock as soon as it has been released—this is the essential idea of staged lock release. It means that we can tolerate dangling references to a released lock, as long as its obsolete status is visible to any transaction still holding such a reference.

4.1 Safe Lock De-allocation

Locks must be de-allocated eventually, else we would be creating a memory leak. Given that de-allocation is delayed, the time when it happens is flexible, as long as we ensure that no dangling references are left, and that de-allocation happens eventually—a classical garbage-collection problem.

The timing flexibility means that we can reduce overheads by cleaning up locks in bulk. The same is true for allocation: by pre-allocating locks, we can also reduce overheads through bulk operations.

When is it safe to de-allocate a lock? As each lock belongs to a unique transaction which created it, and transactions do not pass to other transactions references to locks, a sufficient condition is the following: *A lock L can be safely de-allocated if the oldest transaction in the system has started after L's transaction terminated.*

For bulk de-allocation of a group of locks, this means that we need to keep track of the highest transaction commit ID for the group, and check that this ID is less than the oldest active transaction ID in the transaction table. A simple way to achieve this is to record the highest commit ID, T_M, for each group whenever one of the group's transaction terminates, and maintain the ID, $T_{\min}$ of the oldest still active transaction. The group can then be cleaned up when (i) all of its transactions have terminated and (ii) $T_M < T_{\min}$ for the group.

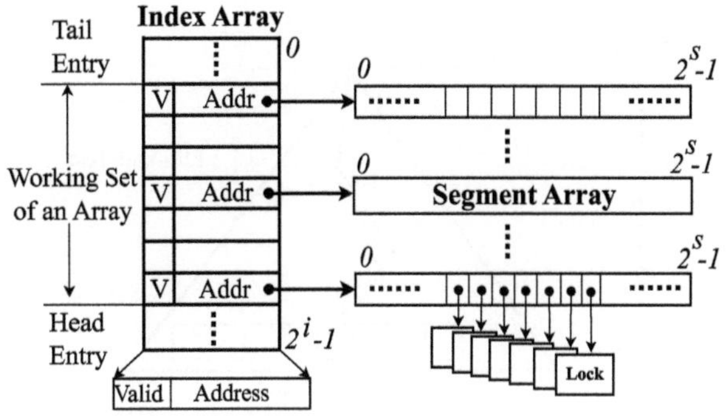

Figure 7: Lock index data structure.

4.2 Lock Pool Implementation

To support bulk allocation and de-allocation of locks, we use a data structure which can grow and shrink on demand and naturally groups locks of similar age, and allows us to locate locks quickly. Specifically, we use a page-table-like index structure to locate a lock from its ID, as shown in Figure 7.

The data structure consists of a top-level *index array* of 2^i entries. Each entry has a valid flag and a pointer to a second-level *segment array* of size 2^s, and both fields are packed into a single 8-byte word together. A segment array contains pointers to lock objects, as well as other meta data, such as an index number that is assigned to a lock when it is allocated to a transaction. The index array has two associated pointers, the *head entry* and the *tail entry*. Index-array entries between the head and the tail may point to segment arrays (if their valid flag is set), entries outside do not point to segment arrays (irrespective of the valid flag). The array is accessed in a circular fashion, meaning that if head<tail then the potentially valid entries are the ones ≤head as well as those ≥tail. A third pointer (not shown) points to the highest (newest) used segment, all segments between that pointer and the head are unused.

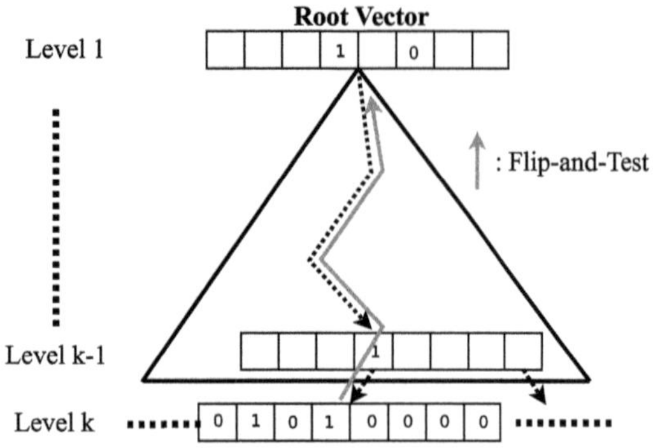

(a) Byte-vector forest

```
/* C-like pseudo-code for Flip-and-Test with a byte-vector of level k.
 * BVector      : char *          /* a bytevector array */
 * index        : int             /* index for s-array */
 * BVector_size : int             /* the size of byte vector */
 */
int j   =  k-1;
int i   =  BVector_size - (0x8 << (3*j));
int pos =  index;
for(  ;  i>= 0;  i -= (0x8 << (3*(- - j)))) {
    BVector[i+pos] = 0x0 ;
    __sync_synchronize() ;        /* memory barrier */
    if( * (long *) ( BVector + i + (pos&0xFFFFFFF8 ) ) != 0 )
        return;
    pos>>=3;                      /*position for a next level vector*/
}
```

(b) Latch-free pseudo code for Flip-and-Test

Figure 8: Hierarchical free-list maintenance.

4.3 Pre-allocation of Locks

A background pre-allocator will allocate additional segment arrays if the number of unused segments falls below a low-water mark (i.e. the highest used segment is close to the head). This is done by finding an index-array entry whose valid flag is FALSE, starting from the tail pointer. This array is then moved to the head, its valid flag set to TRUE, and the head and possibly tail pointers are incremented (modulo array size). If no invalid segment is found, a new one must be allocated and initialised. As long as lock consumption does not outrun the pre-allocator, pre-allocation and lock consumption never overlaps, avoiding contention. However, a dangerous race condition in this producer-consumer loop occurs if `lock_create()` finds no free locks. We use the CAS instruction to make `lock_create()` (consumer) wait until the pre-allocator (producer) creates (or recycles) and initializes a new free segment array.

4.4 Lazy De-allocation of Locks

Bulk cleanup of locks happens at the granularity of segment arrays, once the whole array is invalidated (and the safety condition is satisfied). Simple approaches to detecting the invalidated state of the whole segment array would be (1) scanning the entire segment array frequently, or (2) keeping a single reference counter, which should be atomically incremented/decremented by concurrent transactions. The first approach needs a dedicated scanning process (not efficient), and the second one has a shortcoming of serializing atomic instructions on a single shared variable, which we aim to avoid. For efficient detection of invalid arrays, we associate each segment array with a hierarchical free list, as shown in Figure 8.

The list uses hierarchical byte-vector compression. At the leaf level, each byte represents a valid flag for an individual lock. Each byte of a non-leaf level compresses 8 bytes of the level below, and maintains the invariant that if the byte is zero, all the lower-order bytes mapped by it are zero as well. The top-level byte is the valid flag for the whole segment array.

The free list is updated latch-free (using hierarchical byte flipping implemented in the RAW pattern) whenever the state of a lock is changed to "OBSOLETE" (**R2** in Figure 3). The transaction first clears the valid flag of the lock, and invokes a memory barrier. Then it reads the complete 8-byte word containing the valid flag just cleared. If the word is zero, the transaction clears the next byte up the hierarchy. This is repeated until either a non-zero word is found, or the top-level valid flag is cleared (red line in Figure 8(a)). Flags are encoded as bytes (rather than bits) as the x86 architecture supports atomic updates of bytes but not of individual bits. Figure 8(b) is the C-like pseudo-code for the implementation of latch-free Flip-and-Test. This pseudo code depends on the assumption that, before executing Flip-and-Test, `next_pointer_update()` is performed to correctly adjust pointer values (Figure 4). This ensures that transactions started after the release of a lock can never see the obsolete lock.

Once the top-level valid flag is cleared, the complete segment array and the locks it references can be cleaned up (recycled) *as soon as the safety condition holds.* As indicated in Section 4.1, we do this by keeping for each segment track of the highest commit ID, T_M, whenever a lock is freed. The nontrivial part is to keep a system-wide oldest active transaction ID, $T_{\min}$. This bookkeeping can be done rather easily by using an existing global transaction table (or list) in database systems. For example, MySQL maintains a global shared transaction list, and it adds a newly started transaction to the end of the list, while removal can happen anywhere. This global list meets two important invariants; (1) the youngest live transaction is placed at the end of the list and (2) the oldest live transaction is always at the beginning of the list. The ID of the first transaction in the list is the one that we look for. By comparing that oldest live transaction ID with T_M for a given segment array, we can decide whether or not the segment array can be safely recycled.

4.5 Lock Manager Architecture

The resulting lock manager architecture is shown in Figure 9. The traditional hash-based lock manager architecture [8], prevalent in contemporary database engines, is augmented by the lock index data structure.

A new lock is obtained by using an atomic `fetch_and_add` on a shared pointer into the segment array; something like a *sloppy counter* [3], could be used should this atomic increment turn into a bottleneck. Once a transaction has obtained a unique lock ID, it can access the lock data structure directly. Locks released by committed transactions are not safe to be cleaned, since some old active transactions can still hold the references to these locks. Advancing the head

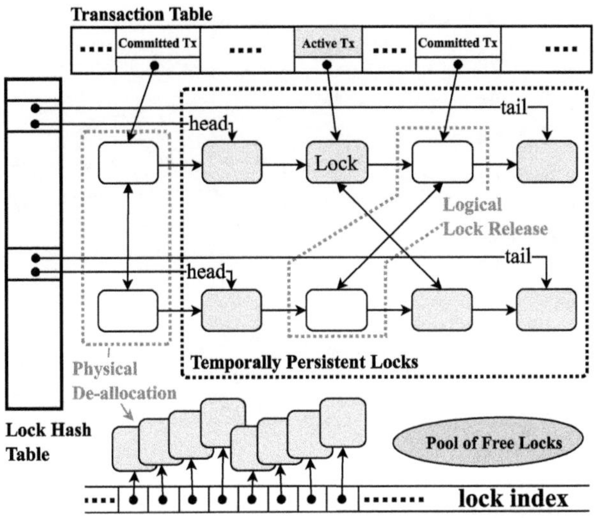

Figure 9: High-level view of the lock manager data structures.

pointer of a lock list eventually makes obsolete locks ready for clean-up, and we then physically de-allocate those locks.

MySQL recycles TRANSACTION objects. We therefore have locks point not at the TRANSACTION object of its owner, but a small shadow transaction data structure, which is also indexed by transaction ID. These shadow objects can be cleaned up safely when the segment array is cleaned, as the safety criterion on locks ensures that the transactions are no longer active.

5. EVALUATION

We measured multicore scalability on two open-source and one commercial database: MySQL-5.6.10-GA with InnoDB storage engine-1.2.10, Shore-MT-6.0 (the official Wisconsin branch), and a commercial DBMS X.[3] We also measured an implementation of our design (Section 3 and Section 4) for a reduced-latching lock manager using staged allocation and de-allocation; this was coded as modifications to the InnoDB storage engine as back-end for the same MySQL code, and we refer to it below as "Our System."

5.1 Evaluation Setup

5.1.1 System Setup

All databases are running on a 32-core Dell PowerEdge server whose hardware characteristics are listed in Table 1. The operating system is Linux 3.1.5, which incorporates the scalability improvement patch by Boyd-Wickizer *et al.* [3].

We run MySQL with the default configuration, except for the following parameters:

`max-connections`	1000
`innodb_buffer_pool_size`	20 GiB
`innodb_log_file_size`	256 MiB
`innodb_log_buffer_size`	16 MiB
`innodb_flush_method`	fsync
`innodb_flush_log_at_trx_commit`	2

The last setting (2) means the log flushing policy of "writing at commit, flushing once per second." Shore-MT is also configured with 20 GiB of buffer pool (`sm_bufpoolsize`), 256 MiB of log file (`sm_logsize`), and 16 MiB of log buffer (`sm_logbufsize`). All transactions in Shore-MT experiments are committed enabling the "`lazy`" option to enable the lazy log-flushing policy. Shore-MT provides the "group commit" function that enables multiple transactions to commit together with a single log record, and this leads to modification of the benchmark program. Thus, we do not use the "group commit" function in all Shore-MT experiments. DBMS X is configured with similar parameters: the same size of buffer pool, log file, and log buffer, and the group commit policy.

[3]The commercial system's license prohibits us from identifying it.

Component	Specification
Processors	8-Core Intel Xeon CPU E7-8837
Processor Sockets	4 Sockets
Hardware Threads	32 (No HyperThreading Support)
Clock Speed	2.66 GHz
L1 D-Cache	32 KiB (per core)
L1 I-Cache	32 KiB (per core)
L2 Cache	256 KiB (per core)
L3 Cache	24 MiB (per socket)
Memory	128 GiB DDR3 1066 MHz
Network	Ethernet 1 Gbps

Table 1: Dell PowerEdge R810 hardware specifications.

We use the isolation level `SERIALIZABLE` in all databases, and in addition we have run MySQL with `REPEATABLE READ` (RR) isolation for comparison. For Shore-MT, we use key-value locking for the B-tree index and the record-level locking iterator in accessing data records.

All experiments have a single database instance running on the server. A varying number of clients is emulated on a separate client computer (also multi-core, 128 GiB of RAM, running Linux 3.0.0). To expose performance bottlenecks in the lock manager, we configure all databases to have plenty of buffer pool space (i.e., 20 GiB). We store all data to *tmpfs*, an in-memory file system, to avoid disk bottlenecks.

Client and server machines are connected with a 1 Gbps Ethernet network. The benchmark client runs the OpenJDK 64-Bit Server Java VM (build 19.0-b09, mixed mode) with the MySQL connector JDBC driver version 5.1.1. The only exception is that in the Shore-MT experiments, all clients are running on the server machine and directly call API functions of Shore-MT to access data, eliminating communication overhead. This is the setup used by Johnson *et al.* [11], which we retain to make our results comparable to theirs. This gives Shore-MT a potential performance advantage over the other systems, but the purpose of our evaluation is to examine scalability, not to compare performance across databases.

5.1.2 Microbenchmark

Our microbenchmark schema uses three tables called `txbench-{1, 2, 3}` with two non-null integer and ten variable sized character columns (`b_value-{1, 2, ..., 10}`); one of the integer columns (`b_int_key`) is a primary key. Each table is populated with 100 k randomly chosen items.

We use two types of queries: query transactions (read-only) and update-after-read transactions (read-update). A transaction reads S data items, either $S = 10$ or $S = 100$.

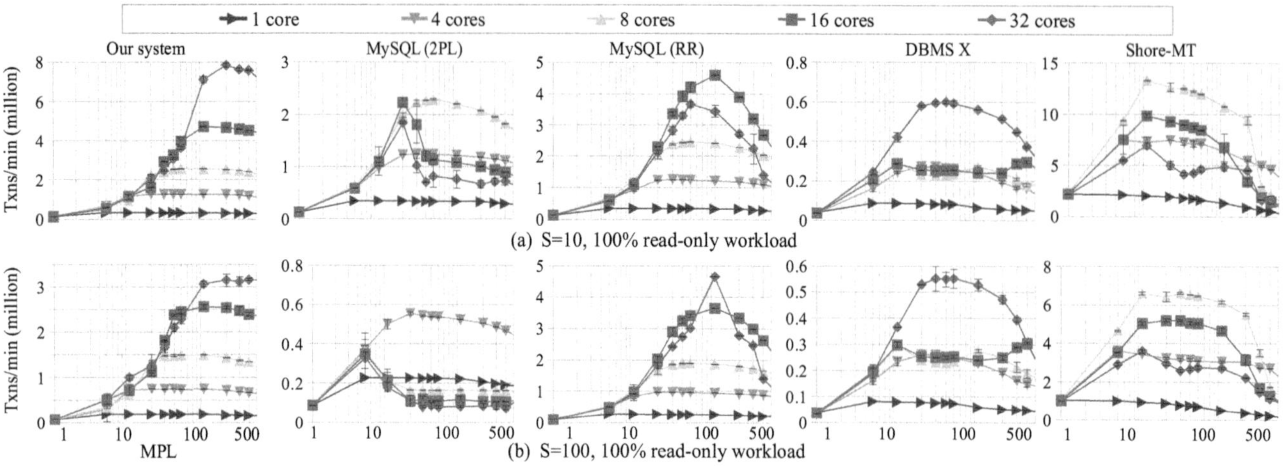

Figure 10: Throughput as a function of load (MPL) for varying number of cores.

To create *rw*-conflicts, we configure the read-update transactions to use the following access rules: a transaction reading data items from `txbench-i` updates rows from `txbench-j`, where `j=i + 1 mod 3`.

The read-only transaction consists of a single Select-From-Where query:

```
SELECT sum(b_int_value)*rand_number FROM txbench-i
 WHERE b_int_key > :id and b_int_key <= :id+S
```

This means that the DBMS scans S rows in the table and aggregates their integer column. This keeps the size of the result small (a single integer), to minimise network traffic.

The read-update transaction first reads S rows from `txbench-i` and updates $0.2 \times S$ rows from `txbench -((i+1)%3)`. The reading part of this transaction uses the same range query as the read-only transaction, and the update part consists of just a single SQL statement (again to minimize network cost):

```
UPDATE txbench-((i+1)%3) SET b_value-k = rand_str
 WHERE b_int_key = :id1
       OR b_int_key = :id2
```

Note that the read-update transactions are not serializable in `REPEATABLE READ` isolation due to cyclic dependency among these transactions. Our measurements are done with a limited implementation, to read and write records (but not to insert or delete).

We vary the multiprogramming level (MPL) from 1 to 500, with all clients trying to execute transactions as fast as possible without think time. Each experiment was repeated five times, with each run consisting of one minute ramp-up period and one minute measurement period. All plotted points in the figures of Section 5 are the average of these five test runs.

5.1.3 *System configuration and profiling*

To profile various system activities, we used OProfile, a system-wide, statistical, continuous profiler for Linux systems. We also used Intel VTune to verify function call traces. We use profiling to break total execution time into four categories: Idle for the idle state, Kernel for Linux kernel functions, Database for non-mutex related database functions, and Mutex for all mutex related functions in the DBMS. For DBMS X we cannot break down the time spent inside the database, so we use DBMS X for the total time spent inside the database code (corresponding to the sum of Database and Mutex).

To evaluate the impact of various CPU configurations, we use the CPU hotplug feature of modern processors. The hotplug function can make CPUs (or cores) available or unavailable to the Linux kernel. For a given number of cores, we use the minimum number of sockets (i.e., 1 socket for ≤ 8 cores and 2 sockets for $9 \cdots 16$ cores). This minimises cache coherence costs and thus represents a best case for latch-based approaches.

5.2 Experimental Results

5.2.1 *Performance under load*

We evaluate the scalability of the various database systems with respect to the number of cores utilized, and to the workload. A partial result was shown in Figure 1, which motivated our reduced-latch approach to lock management. Our purpose here is to confirm that the collapse is not an artefact of a poor implementation of one system, but rather applies to a diversity of platforms, and also to show that our design eliminates the collapse.

Figure 10 shows the complete results for read-only transactions. The leftmost graphs (Our system) show MySQL with the implementation of our reduced-latch, staged lock manager, while the other graphs show unmodified existing systems. Note that the scales on the y-axis differ, as attempting to display all graphs on the same scale would make the results of the less-performing systems unreadable. In any case, our purpose is not to compare performance across platforms (except between MySQL and Our System), but to show which systems experience performance collapse, at high (but not logically contending) load and on many cores.

We can see that even with 4 cores, all the vanilla configurations show a throughput peak, with performance degrading when load increases further.

At 16 cores (2 sockets) the performance degradation turns into an outright collapse for both open-source systems. Interestingly, DBMS X roughly maintains peak performance, but its peak is about an order of magnitude less than that

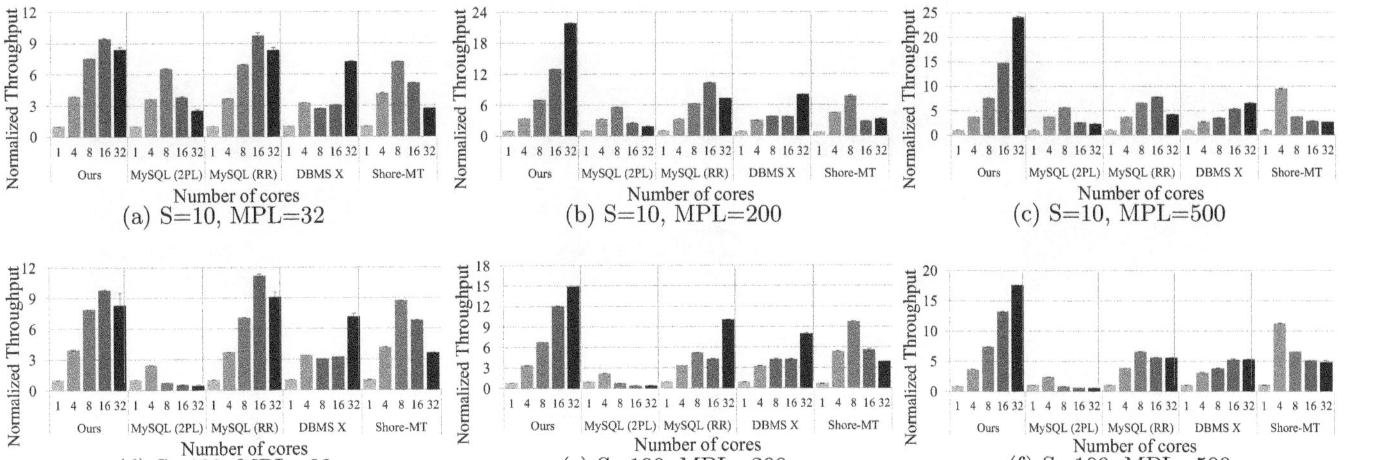

(a) S=10, MPL=32 (b) S=10, MPL=200 (c) S=10, MPL=500

(d) S=100, MPL=32 (e) S=100, MPL=200 (f) S=100, MPL=500

Figure 11: Read-only throughput normalised to single-core performance.

of the open-source systems, and throughput remains below that of the open-source systems even at the highest loads we applied.

At 32 cores (4 sockets), the performance collapse can be observed for all vanilla configurations, including DBMS X. For MySQL, even the peak performance is degraded below that of configurations with fewer cores. The best scalability is exhibited by MySQL in the RR configuration with the larger (S=100) transactions.

In contrast, our system never shows a performance collapse, at worst there is a small degradation from the peak at increasing load. Furthermore, adding cores increases the peak throughput in all cases. The throughput of our systems is also always at least as high as that of the vanilla MySQL(2PL) system it is based on. For the smaller transactions it even matches or exceeds the performance of the RR configuration. The reason why our system outperforms MySQL(RR) is because MySQL(RR) uses the transaction-system mutex whenever it opens a consistent read-view, when a transaction begins or commits. As MPL grows, the mutex duration also increases and incurs high contention among transactions. This leads to the unexpected performance behavior under high load of smaller transactions.

5.2.2 *Core scalability*

For a more detailed analysis of the scalability of the different core configurations with increasing core count, we zoom in on three "interesting" values of MPL: 32, 200 and 500.

We choose MPL 32 as a good proxy for peak throughput of the vanilla databases, as all of them, except MySQL(RR), peaked in the vicinity of that load. Furthermore, 32 is the maximum core count, so in the full hardware configuration there would be one transaction per core, representing something of an ideal case. MPL 200 is interesting as our system is at or near peak performance there. MPL 500 is the most extreme load we ran, and the one which triggered the most serious performance collapses.

The results are shown in Figure 11. MPL 32, subfigures (a) and (d), is fairly benign, all systems exhibit at worst a small degradation of throughput with increasing core count (although MySQL(2PL) with S=100 degrades starting with as few as 8 cores).

At MPL 200, MySQL shows a significant degradation, and Shore-MT performance plateaus for small transactions (b), while the system degrades for the large transactions (e). DBMS X shows a somewhat strange behaviour, with flat performance at intermediate core counts but roughly doubling from 16 to 32 cores. Our system is well behaved, scaling well with small transactions and saturating but not degrading for the large transactions.

At the highest load, our system scales almost perfectly with the small transactions until 16 cores and then saturates, with the large transactions the saturation starts earlier. DBMS X scales similar to or system for large transactions, but much worse for small ones. Shore-MT scales to 4 cores but then saturates (but remember that this system shows performance degradation under high load even on a single core). MySQL shows performance degradation with increasing core numbers.

5.2.3 *Where does the time go?*

Profiling allows us to peek inside the systems, as shown in Figure 12. The leftmost column stands out for its virtual absence of the (yellow) mutex times, thanks to latch-free implementation of lock management. This is in stark contrast to the second column, showing the MySQL system ours was derived from, which has in excess of 50 % of time spent spinning on mutexes. The lowest fraction of spinning is in the 8-core configuration with small transactions. As Figure 10 shows, this is the configuration where MySQL performs best. It is obvious that the performance degradation of MySQL results from high mutex contention.

Surprisingly, at 32 cores the overloaded MySQL system actually has significant idle time! MySQL implements all mutexes using the atomic Test-and-Set instruction, with an additional random backoff mechanism. After a failed attempt to acquire a mutex it busy-waits. After the predefined (but configurable) number of failures, the mutex routine puts the calling thread to sleep until the mutex is released. This explains the idle time at times of high mutex contention.

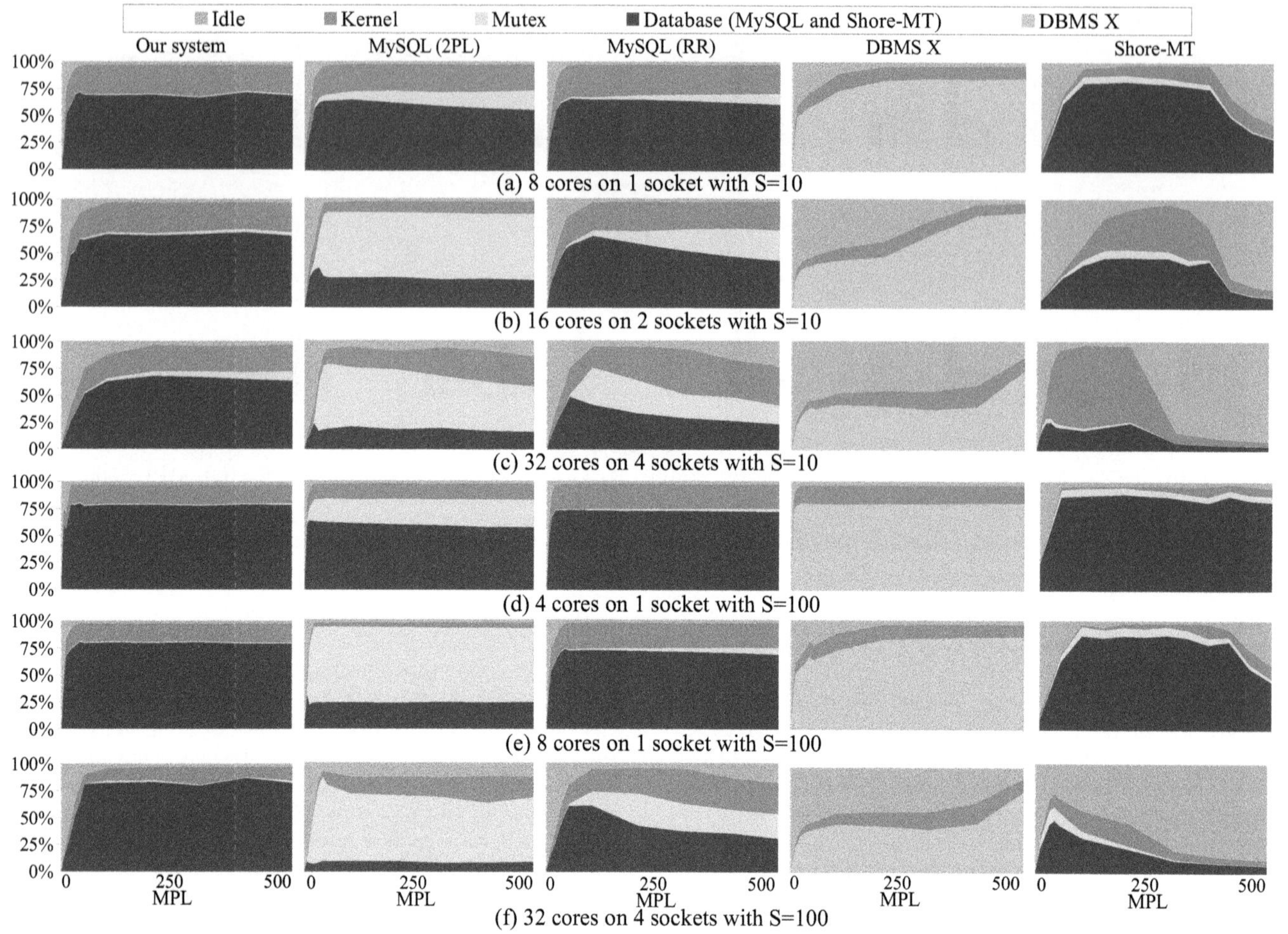

Figure 12: Breakdown of profiled results of our system, MySQL (2PL), MySQL (RR), DBMS X, and Shore-MT (from left to right) with different core/socket configurations (from top to bottom) and 100% read-only workloads.

Also noticeable is that for small transactions, MySQL(RR) also shows significant mutex overhead (as well as idle time), despite the lower isolation level. The explanation is that in RR isolation, when a read view is to be opened, MySQL uses the transaction-system mutex to find a serialisable point. Consequently, for the larger transaction size the relative mutex overhead is much reduced.

DBMS X, where we could not break down the in-database time due to lack of access to internals, also exhibits a large amount of idle time in overload situations.

Shore-MT does not show much mutex time, but large amounts of OS time. At early stages of MPL, Shore-MT spends most time in the operating system. At very high load, the system is mostly idle. Further analysis can explain these two phenomena. Shore-MT uses the `pthread_mutex_lock/unlock` routines as default latch functions, and those pthread functions are based on the `futex` system call. If the latch is uncontended, `futex` can acquire the latch with simply calling `atomic_swap` and memory barrier functions and return the locked latch without context switch. This explains why Shore-MT spends most of time in Kernel, especially in the kernel function `cpu_relax()`, which keeps invoking a memory barrier until it gets to hold a mutex. However, if latch contention is detected during the futex call, the calling process or thread sleeps until the latch is released. This explains the huge idle time in high load conditions. If Shore-MT is configured to use MCS locks [13] instead of pthread mutex functions, the throughput at MPL 500 on 32 cores drops dramatically to about 5,000 tpm, with >95% of time spent in the idle state.

5.2.4 Read-update workload

Our previous experiments included no updates, so that there was no logical contention at all between locks, in order to focus attention on the contention between latches. However, all OLTP workloads do include some updates, which are the reason even read-only queries need to set locks at all. Figure 13 shows a direct comparison of our system with MySQL(2PL). Figure 13(a) repeats the throughput data for read-only workloads (32-core lines of the two leftmost graphs in the bottom row of Figure 10). Figure 13(b) shows the same configuration, except that we now use a read-update workload with 20 % update transactions. Update transactions acquire locks which are incompatible with those of both read-only and update transactions, and this leads to blocking and deadlocks. Figure 13(c) shows the abort rates for the workload with 20% update transactions; these aborts in-

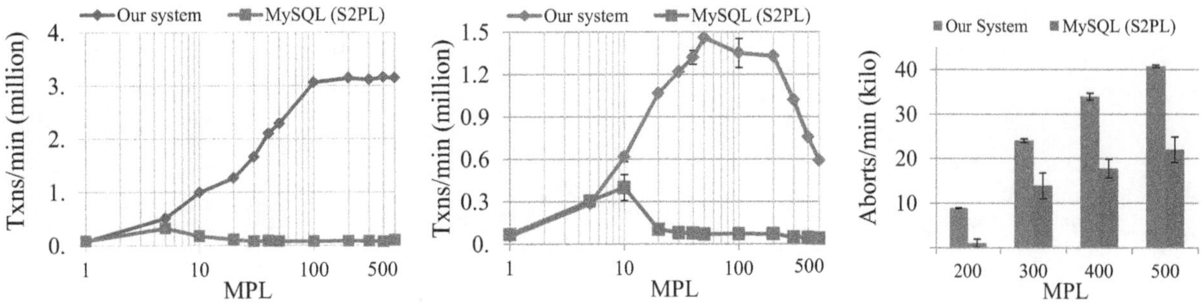

(a) Throughput, R/O workload (b) Throughput, with 20% updates (c) Aborts, with 20% updates

Figure 13: Our system vs. MySQL(2PL) on 32 cores, S=100.

crease dramatically at high loads, with up to 46 % of MySQL transactions aborted at top load. Our system has similar overall abort rates, but due to the higher throughput, the fraction of aborts is much lower; at worst about 6.7 % of transactions are aborted with our system. This shows the benefit of concurrent deadlock checking. Our system shows performance degradation in high workload due to lock conflicts, not because of latch contention.

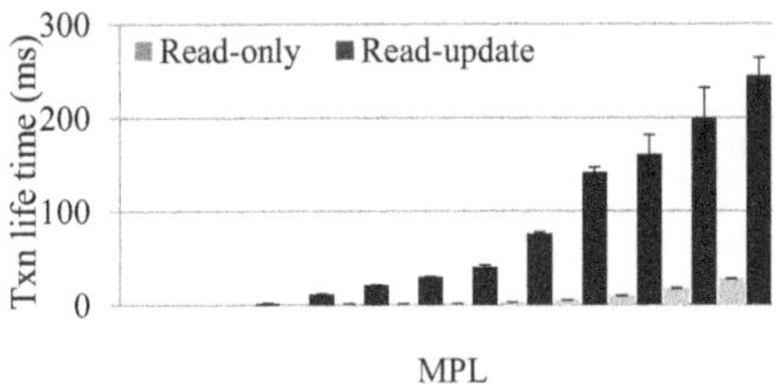

(a) Our system

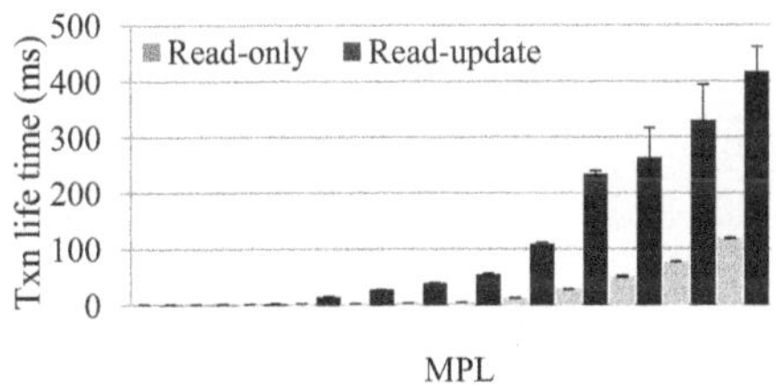

(b) MySQL(2PL)

Figure 14: Transaction lifetimes for configuration of Figure 13(b).

An examination of transaction lifetimes, shown in Figure 14, provides additional insight. The duration of read-only as well as update transactions increases dramatically with load in MySQL, indicating long periods of spinning on mutexes. In contrast, in our system the durations of R/O transactions do not show unexpected increase by load, and even the duration of update transactions increases only moderately with load, as one would expect in an ideal system.

5.2.5 *Lock hash chain*

A potential bottleneck of our staged lock management is the lock hash list, which needs to be scanned during lock acquisition (lines **A4. . . A15** of Figure 3). In our implementation, this list is potentially much longer than in vanilla MySQL, as it may contain many obsolete locks. We therefore devised a benchmark which stresses this part of the code, by increasing contention for data items.

Our *hotspot* benchmark is a variant of our standard $S = 10$ benchmark with 20 % update transactions. In this case we restrict transactions to access only 5 % of all table rows, thus increasing logical contention twentyfold. Figure 15(b) shows the results for throughput and Figure 15(c) shows abort rates. The standard $S = 10$, R/O benchmark throughput is shown in Figure 15(a) for comparison. We can see from Figure 15 that the hotspot load degrades throughput of our system moderately again due to lock conflicts, the degradation is actually more pronounced in MySQL(2PL). Under the read-only workload (Figure 15(a)), the throughput of our system hits the peak of 8 million tpm (at MPL 200) and decreases to 6.8 million tpm (at MPL 500), while that of MySQL(2PL) reaches the peak of 1.8 million tpm (at MPL 20) and collapses to 0.7 million tpm (at MPL 500). With the read-update workload (Figure 15(b)), the throughput of our system has the peak of 6.1 million (at MPL 200, 75 % of that of the R/O workload) and then decreases to 3.3 million tpm (at MPL 500, again 48 % of R/O). In contrast, MySQL(2PL) achieves a peak of 1.6 million tpm (at MPL 20, 90 % of R/O) and collapses to 0.2 million tpm (at MPL 500, 30 % of R/O). This is also reflected in the abort rates, which for our system are a tiny 0.19 %, while MySQL(2PL) suffers 44 % aborted transactions. In other words, there is no indication that the increased length of our hash chains is becoming a bottleneck.

6. CONCLUSION

We have found that contemporary database systems are not yet ready for the multicore age. Our evaluation has demonstrated a collapse of transaction throughput under high load, even read-only load, for all the database systems we analysed. In the case of the open-source systems, MySQL and Shore-MT, we could identify latch contention in the lock manager as the bottleneck. While we could not perform the same in-depth analysis on the commercial DMBS X, its observable behaviour is similar enough to the open-source systems to suspect that the cause is similar.

We proposed to address this problem by an improved implementation of the lock manager, which adopts the RAW pattern and barrier synchronization to greatly reduce the use of latches. We have described the design for such a lock manager which is based on staged lock management, where locks are pre-allocated and lazily de-allocated in bulk,

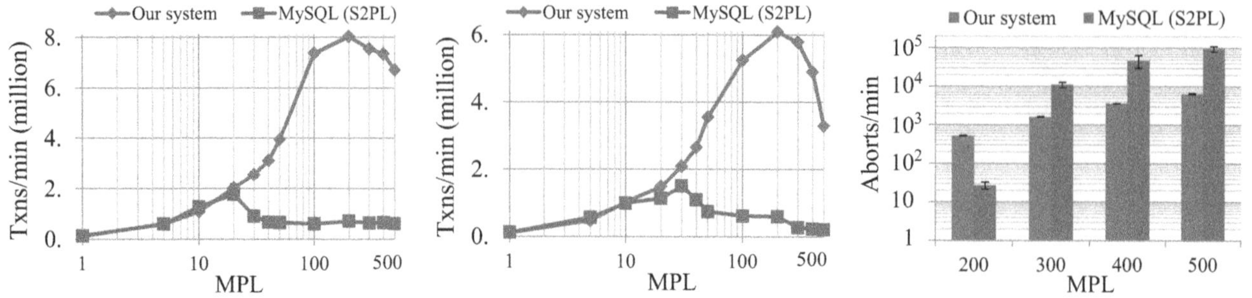

(a) Throughput, R/O workload (b) Throughput, 20% updates, hotspot (c) Abort rate, 20% updates, hotspot

Figure 15: Exploring hotspot behaviour, 32 cores, S=10.

and deadlock checking can be done concurrently. We coded this design as a variant of the backend storage of MySQL. Our experiments show that this approach (i) eliminates the performance collapse by essentially eliminating latch contention, and (ii) always achieves at least the same performance as the baseline system.

The potential weak point of our staged approach is the longer hash chains, resulting from obsolete locks which have not yet been cleaned up. Our attempts to stress this part of the system by forcing a high rate of contention on individual data items did not indicate that this causes any performance problems. We conclude that the staged, reduced-latch approach to lock management looks promising.

7. ACKNOWLEDGMENTS

We would like to thank Michael Cahill for providing valuable comments on the initial draft, and SeongJae Park for helping in many places. We would like to thank the anonymous SIGMOD reviewers for insightful comments which helped to improve the paper.

8. REFERENCES

[1] H. Attiya, R. Guerraroui, D. Hendler, P. Kuznetsov, M. Michael, and M. Vechev. Laws of Order: Expensive Synchronization in Concurrent Algorithms Cannot be Eliminated. In *POPL*, pages 487–498, 2011.

[2] P. A. Bernstein, V. Hadzilacos, and N. Goodman. *Concurrency Control and Recovery in Database Systems.* Addison-Wesley, 1987.

[3] S. Boyd-Wickizer, A. T. Clements, Y. Mao, A. Pesterev, M. F. Kaashoek, R. Morris, and N. Zeldovich. An Analysis of Linux Scalability to Many Cores. In *OSDI*, pages 1–8, 2010.

[4] S. Boyd-Wickizer, M. F. Kaashoek, R. Morris, and N. Zeldovich. Non-scalable Locks are Dangerous. In *Proceedings of the Linux Symposium*, Ottawa, Canada, July 2012.

[5] A. T. Clements, F. Kaashoek, and N. Zeldovich. Scalable Address Spaces Using RCU Balanced Trees. In *ASPLOS*, pages 199–210, 2012.

[6] G. Graefe. A Survey of B-tree Locking Techniques. *ACM Trans. Database Syst.*, 35(3):16:1–16:26, July 2010.

[7] G. Graefe, H. Kimura, and H. Kuno. Foster B-trees. *ACM Trans. Database Syst.*, 37(3):17:1–17:29, Sept. 2012.

[8] J. Gray and A. Reuter. *Transaction Processing: Concepts and Techniques.* Morgan Kaufmann, 1993.

[9] J. M. Hellerstein, M. Stonebraker, and J. Hamilton. *Architecture of a Database System.* Now Publishers Inc., Hanover, MA, USA, 2007.

[10] M. Herlihy and N. Shavit. *The Art of Multiprocessor Programming.* Morgan Kaufmann, 2008.

[11] R. Johnson, I. Pandis, N. Hardavellas, A. Ailamaki, and B. Falsafi. Shore-MT: a Scalable Storage Manager for the Multicore Era. In *EDBT*, pages 24–35. ACM, 2009.

[12] R. Johnson, I. Pandis, R. Stoica, M. Athanassoulis, and A. Ailamaki. Scalability of Write-ahead Logging on Multicore and Multisocket Hardware. *The VLDB Journal*, 21(2):239–263, 2012.

[13] J. M. Mellor-Crummey and M. L. Scott. Algorithms for Scalable Synchronization on Shared-Memory Multiprocessors. *ACM Trans. Computer Systems*, 9(1):21–65, 1991.

[14] I. Pandis, R. Johnson, N. Hardavellas, and A. Ailamaki. Data-oriented Transaction Execution. *PVLDB*, 3(1-2):928–939, 2010.

[15] I. Pandis, P. Tözün, R. Johnson, and A. Ailamaki. PLP: Page Latch-free Shared-everything OLTP. *Proc. VLDB Endow.*, 4(10):610–621, 2011.

[16] A. Pesterev, J. Strauss, N. Zeldovich, and R. T. Morris. Improving Network Connection Locality on Multicore Systems. In *EuroSys*, pages 337–350, 2012.

[17] T.-I. Salomie, I. E. Subasu, J. Giceva, and G. Alonso. Database Engines on Multicores, Why Parallelize When You Can Distribute? In *EuroSys*, pages 17–30, 2011.

[18] C. Schimmel. *UNIX Systems for Modern Architectures: Symmetric Multiprocessing and Caching for Kernel Programmers.* Addison-Wesley Professional, 1994.

[19] J. Sewall, J. Chhugani, C. Kim, and P. Dubey. PALM: Parallel Architecture-Friendly Latch-Free Modification to B+Trees on Many-Core Processors. In *PVLDB*, pages 795–806, 2011.

[20] G. Weikum and G. Vossen. *Transactional Information Systems: Theory, Algorithms, and the Practice of Concurrency Control and Recovery.* Morgan Kaufmann, 2001.

Controlled Lock Violation

Goetz Graefe, Mark Lillibridge, Harumi Kuno, Joseph Tucek, Alistair Veitch
Hewlett-Packard Laboratories

ABSTRACT

In databases with a large buffer pool, a transaction may run in less time than it takes to log the transaction's commit record on stable storage. Such cases motivate a technique called early lock release: immediately after appending its commit record to the log buffer in memory, a transaction may release its locks. Thus, it cuts overall lock duration to a fraction and reduces lock contention accordingly.

Early lock release also has its problems. The initial mention of early lock release was incomplete, the first detailed description and implementation was incorrect with respect to read-only transactions, and the most recent design initially had errors and still does not cover unusual lock modes such as 'increment' locks. Thus, we set out to achieve the same goals as early lock release but with a different, simpler, and more robust approach.

The resulting technique, controlled lock violation, requires no new theory, applies to any lock mode, promises less implementation effort and slightly less run-time effort, and also optimizes distributed transactions, e.g., in systems that rely on multiple replicas for high availability and high reliability. In essence, controlled lock violation retains locks until the transaction is durable but permits other transactions to violate its locks while flushing its commit log record to stable storage.

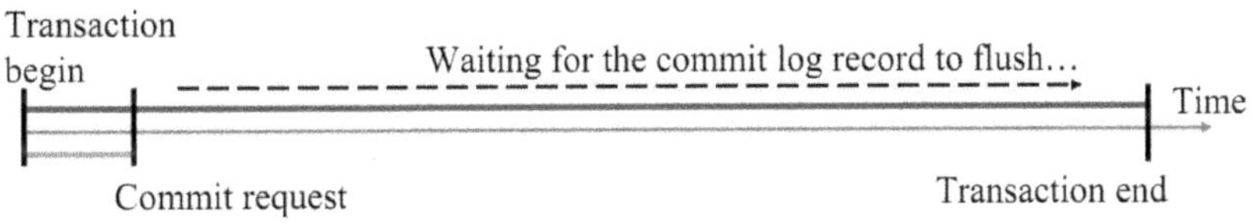

Figure 1. Lock retention times in traditional and optimized commit sequences.

Categories and Subject Descriptors

H.2.4 [**Database Management**]: Systems – *transaction processing: concurrency.*

Keywords

Transaction processing, DBMS, locking, concurrency.

1 INTRODUCTION

A simple database transaction takes 20,000 to 100,000 instructions [1], depending on the transaction logic, on index structures, on the quality of the implementation, and on compiler optimizations. For example, assuming 40,000 instructions per transaction, 1 instruction per CPU cycle on average, a 4 GHz CPU clock, and no buffer faults, a modern processor core can execute the transaction logic in about 0.01 ms. Committing such a transaction, however, may take much longer. If "stable storage" for the recovery log is a pair of traditional disk drives, the time to commit might approach 10 ms. If stable storage for the recovery log is provided by flash storage, commit time might be faster by two orders of magnitude, i.e., 0.1 ms, but it is still an order of magnitude longer than transaction execution.

If a transaction acquires locks right at its start, e.g., key value locks in a B-tree index, and holds them until transaction commit is complete, it retains the locks for about 0.01 ms while the transaction logic proceeds and for another 0.1 ms (or even 10 ms) during commit processing, i.e., after the transaction logic is complete. Given these relationships, it is not surprising that researchers have sought to reduce lock contention during commit processing. Retaining locks for only 0.01 ms, not 0.11 ms (or even 10.01 ms), should appreciably reduce lock contention, in particular for "hot spot" locks such as appending index entries to an index on transaction time or on an attribute with high correlation to transaction time, e.g., order number or invoice number.

Figure 1 illustrates the relationship between transaction execution time and commit duration. The diagram shows a factor of 10. In the traditional sequence of actions during commit processing, each transaction holds its locks for the entire time shown by the blue line above the time line. In a transaction with early lock release, lock retention is as short as the green line below the time line. The same performance improvement is achieved by a new technique, controlled lock violation, even in its simple form.

Multiple prior research efforts have described early lock release, which lets a transaction release its locks immediately after space for a commit record is allocated in the log buffer in memory. In other words, the locks are released before the commit record is flushed to stable storage and thus before the transaction becomes durable. Soisalon-Soininen and Ylönen [2] proved this technique correct, i.e., recoverable, but their proof does not address concurrency control and transaction isolation. Johnson et al. [3] and Kimura et al. [4] measured dramatic improvements in lock contention and in transaction throughput. Unfortunately, early lock release can also produce wrong results, including incorrect updates, because an implementation may fail to respect commit dependencies among participating transactions, as illustrated in **Figure 2**. In essence, one transaction must not publish or persist another transaction's update until the update is durable.

Recent work [4] describes a new variant of early lock release that avoids these wrong results yet preserves performance and scalability. The principal idea is to remove the locks from the lock manager early but to retain "tags" to convey commit dependencies among transactions. In some cases, commit dependencies are respected that do not exist, i.e., the technique is too conservative. As importantly, the tags do not fully optimize distributed transactions, e.g., in modern database systems that maintain multiple replicas for high availability and high reliability. Nonetheless, lacking other correct implementations, we take this as the prototypical representative of early lock release.

Controlled lock violation is a new and superior alternative to early lock release. It eschews early lock release and the need for tags. Instead, each transaction retains its locks until its commit process is complete. With respect to concurrency, controlled lock violation matches early lock release as it permits subsequent transactions to violate or ignore lock conflicts, but only in very controlled situations. More specifically, a subsequent transaction may acquire a lock that violates an existing lock if the transaction holding the lock is already in its commit process, i.e., if it has allocated a commit record in the log buffer. Thus, controlled lock violation enables concurrency in all situations in which early lock release (corrected with tags) enables concurrency.

Moreover, controlled lock violation can improve the concurrency not only of centralized, single-site transactions but also of distributed transactions. Thus, controlled lock violation can increase concurrency during commit processing in modern system designs that rely on replicas. The same issue – multiple separate recovery logs and two-phase commit – equally applies to many partitioned databases. For example, in a large database partitioned such that individual partitions (and their individual recovery logs) can easily move in order to achieve elastic scaling, transactions over multiple partitions require two-phase commit even when all affected partitions currently reside on the same server. In contrast to early lock release, controlled lock violation optimizes commit processing and lock conflicts in all those settings.

The contributions of our new technique are these:

1. In a single-site setting, controlled lock violation achieves the same transaction processing performance as early lock release, but without new theory, with fewer special cases, and without new data structures.
2. Controlled lock violation covers a broader set of lock modes than early lock release and all granularities of locking, including multi-granularity locking and key-range locking.
3. By retaining the original locks during commit activities, subsequent conflicting transactions can analyze the conflict more precisely than is possible in early lock release.
4. In a distributed setting, controlled lock violation optimizes both phases of two-phase commit. Thus, the conflicts of participant transactions can be reduced tremendously compared to two-phase commit execution. (Early lock release can optimize only the final phase of two-phase commit.)
5. For "canned transactions" coded as stored procedures, static code analysis can enable controlled lock violation even before a transaction's commit request.

The following section reviews related prior work, in particular on early lock release and two-phase commit. Section 3 introduces controlled lock violation and contrasts it to early lock release. Section 4 extends controlled lock violation to two-phase commit and Section 5 applies it to canned transactions. Section 6 compares the performance of controlled lock violation with that of early lock release in those cases when early lock release applies. Section 7 compares controlled lock violation with further related techniques, e.g., speculative execution. The final section contains our summary and conclusions.

2 RELATED PRIOR WORK

DeWitt et al. described early lock release back in 1984, albeit without an implementation [5]. Ailamaki and her research group have described a highly optimized implementation as well as the resulting speed-up in transaction processing [6]. Kimura et al. describe an oversight in the earlier designs as well as a technique to avoid over-eager commit of read-only transactions [4]. These efforts are discussed below, followed by a summary of other but unrelated cases of early lock release as well as some background information on distributed two-phase commit.

We assume concurrent and serializable transactions implemented by commonly used techniques, including write-ahead logging, log sequence numbers, record-level locking, logical "undo" by logged compensating updates rather than rigid physical "undo," an in-memory buffer pool for data and recovery log plus persistent block-access storage such as traditional disks, durability by forcing commit records to the recovery log on "stable storage," two-phase commit in distributed transactions, etc. The intention behind these assumptions is broad applicability of the work.

2.1 Main memory databases

An early paper [5] on implementation techniques for main memory database systems described early lock release as follows (original emphasis):

"A scheme that amortizes the log I/O across several transactions is based on the notion of a pre-committed transaction. When a transaction is ready to complete, the transaction management system places its commit record in the log buffer. The transaction releases all locks *without waiting for the commit record to be written to disk*. The transaction is delayed from committing until its commit record actually appears on disk. The 'user' is not notified that the transactions has committed until this event has occurred.

By releasing its locks before it commits, other transactions can read the pre-committed transaction's dirty data. Call these *dependent transactions*. Reading uncommitted data in this way does not lead to an inconsistent state as long as the pre-committed transaction actually commits *before* its dependent transactions. A pre-committed transaction does not commit only if the system crashes, never because of a user or system induced abort. As long as records are sequentially added to the log, and the pages of the log buffer are written to disk in sequence, a pre-committed transaction will have its commit record on disk before dependent transactions."

In this design, locks are released early, without distinction by lock mode, e.g., shared or exclusive. It is well known that read locks can be released early, e.g., during the pre-commit phase of distributed transactions with two-phase commit. Write locks, on the other hand, require longer retention in traditional transaction processing. Similarly, this design does not distinguish between read-only and read-write transactions among the dependent transactions. It turns out that the next design repeats this erroneous omission. (**Figure 2** shows an example error scenario.)

2.2 Early lock release in Shore-MT

Researchers at CMU and EPFL implemented early lock release as part of tuning Shore-MT [6], specifically to remove logging from the critical path of transaction processing by avoiding all lock contention while a transaction becomes durable.

Johnson et al. demonstrate "speedup due to ELR [early lock release] when running the TPC-B benchmark and varying I/O latency and skew in data accesses" while logging on different forms of stable storage, including logging to a slow traditional disk (10 ms for a write to stable storage) and logging to flash (write in 0.1 ms) [3]. Running TPC-B (which produces many lock conflicts) against a traditional logging device, their work shows that early lock release can speed up system throughput 30-fold; for a fast logging device, system throughput improves 3-fold.

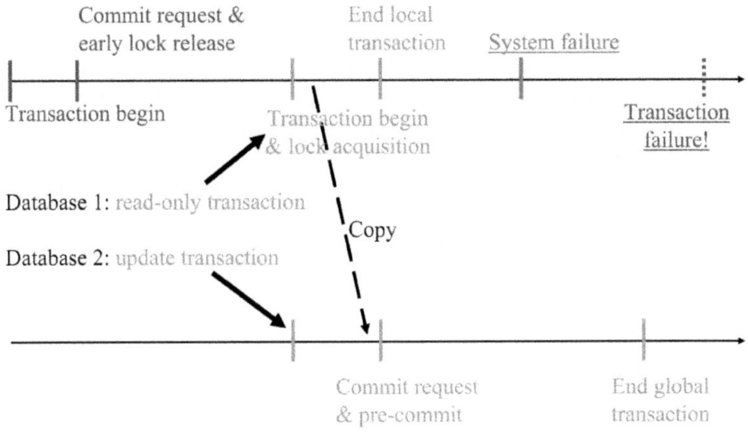

Figure 2. Bad database contents due to early lock release.

While the speed-ups are impressive, early lock release as originally described and implemented in Shore-MT can produce wrong results and even wrong database contents [4]. For example, consider a transaction T_0 acquiring an exclusive lock to update a database record, then releasing the lock after formatting a commit record in the log buffer, whereupon transaction T_1 acquires a lock on the same database record. If both transactions T_0 and T_1 are update transactions, then the sequencing of commit records enforces the commit dependency between them. What happens, however, if the dependent transaction T_1 does not require a commit record because it is a read-only transaction? In this case, it may read and report a value written by transaction T_0 before the commit of transaction T_1 is complete. Transaction T_1 may terminate successfully and thus commit to the user a value that may never exist in the database if the commit record of transaction T_0 is never saved on stable storage, e.g., due to a system crash.

For an example resulting in bad database contents, consider a transaction T_0 that updates a record in the database D_0 from old value 10 to new value 11 and then begins its commit activities. After T_0 has formatted its commit record in the log buffer and released its locks, transaction T_1 reads the value 11, copies it into another database D_1, and then performs its own commit. This commit is a two-phase commit between databases D_0 and D_1. Assume that database D_1 provides commit coordination and logs global commit records. Since transaction T_1 is a read-only transaction in database D_0, the pre-commit phase is sufficient there, the second commit phase is not required, and no log record is written in database D_0 for transaction T_1. Moreover, assume that stable storage for database D_1 is fast (e.g., flash storage) whereas stable storage for database D_0 is slower (e.g., a traditional disk). In this case, it is quite possible that transaction T_1 commits, including saving its final global commit record on stable storage, before transaction T_0 can do the same and become durable. If database D_0 crashes in the meantime, database D_0 rolls the data record back to value 10, whereas database D_1 contains value 11. Clearly, this result of "copying" from database D_0 to database D_1 is not acceptable transactional behavior.

Figure 2 illustrates this example. There are two parallel timelines for the two databases. One transaction (blue) in Database 1 reaches its commit point but never achieves durability due to a system failure (red); thus, this transaction and all its updates are rolled back during system recovery. The distributed transaction (green) attempts a two-phase commit prior to the system failure; the local read-only sub-transaction in Database 1 immediately responds and does not participate in the second commit phase. The coordinator may commit the global transaction even after one of the participating sites fails, because the local sub-transaction on Database 1 terminated successfully. At the end, the value copied from Database 1 to Database 2 will remain in Database 2 but be rolled back in Database 1, such that Database 2 is no longer a faithful copy of Database 1.

2.3 *Early lock release in Foster B-trees*

As part of an effort to prototype and evaluate a new B-tree variant, early lock release was also implemented in the context of prototyping Foster B-trees [7], although design and implementation of the locking subsystem are orthogonal to its usage in any specific data structure. This is the first implementation of early lock release to avoid the danger of wrong results and wrong database contents. The technique employed relies on tags in the lock manager's hash table [4]. When an update transaction releases a lock as part of early lock release, it leaves a tag containing the log sequence number of its commit record. Any subsequent transaction acquiring a lock on the same object must not commit until the appropriate log page has been written to stable storage.

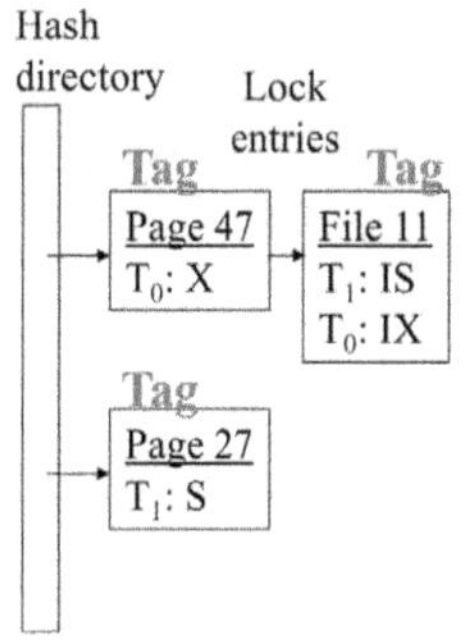

Figure 3. Hash table with tags.

Figure 3 illustrates where tags are attached in the lock manager's hash table. The tag contains a high water mark, i.e., a log sequence number. Any transaction acquiring any lock on the same object cannot commit until this log record is on stable storage.

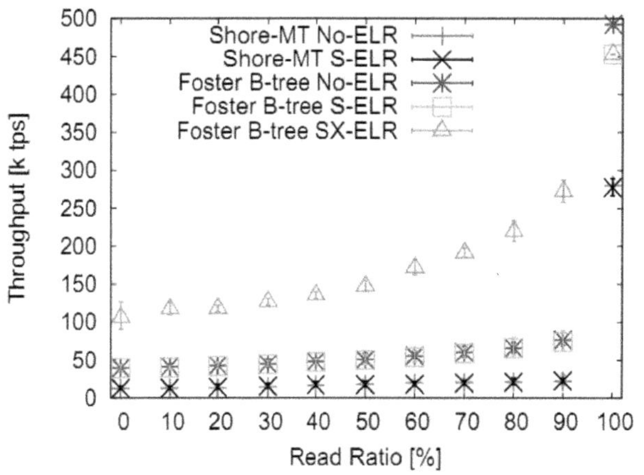

Figure 4. Performance effects of early lock release, © VLDB Endowment.

Figure 4, copied from [4], shows performance improvements due to early lock release in Shore-MT [6], including the version with Foster B-trees [7] instead of the original Shore-MT indexes. The relative performance of Foster B-trees and the original Shore-MT B-tree implementation is not relevant here as it is partially due to differences in representation and compression of records in pages. A comparison of fully implemented early lock release (purple triangles) with the same code minus early lock release (blue stars) demonstrates performance advantages across almost the entire range from an insert-only workload (read ratio 0%) to read-only queries (read ratio 100%). The performance advantage reverses for a read-only workload "because ELR checks the transaction's lock requests twice at commit time" [4]. This experiment logs on flash storage; the effects are similar or stronger with the recovery log on traditional disks.

The performance of early lock release in **Figure 4** is also indicative of the performance of controlled lock violation. This is because they are equivalent in their effect, at least in single-site cases (they are not in the context of two-phase commit). After all, one transaction releasing its locks is effectively the same as other transactions ignoring those same locks (in the same cases).

Unfortunately, after the introduction of tags had "repaired" early lock release, it needed yet another repair. Early lock release for intention locks requires tags just like absolute locks (i.e., non-intention locks), but they require a different kind of tag. For example, two transactions may both acquire intention locks on the same index but may touch different index entries. Thus, tags for intention locks should introduce commit dependencies only in conflicts with absolute locks but not with intention locks [4].

Of course, one wonders how many additional kinds of tags might be required. For example, Microsoft SQL Server uses multiple special locks such as 'insert' locks, 'bulk insertion' locks, 'schema stability' and 'schema modify' locks, etc. In other words, what seems needed is either a theory for deriving appropriate tags from lock modes (as in [8]) or a mechanism (including an appropriate theory and policy) that avoids tags altogether.

One may also wonder how early lock release may optimize distributed transactions with two-phase commit. It turns out, unfortunately, that the optimizations of early lock release apply to the final commit phase only but not to the pre-commit phase. In other words, a participant transaction may release its read-only locks during the pre-commit phase (as is well known) but it must retain its update locks until the local participant transaction has appended its final commit record to the log buffer. Lock retention time is reduced only by the time to write the final commit record to stable storage but not by the time for writing the pre-commit record during the initial phase or for communication and coordination during a two-phase commit. This is discussed further in Section 4.

2.4 Other cases of early lock release

In addition to the instances outlined above, other instances of early lock release have been mentioned in the literature or are used in real systems.

First, when a transaction employs "save points," e.g., between individual SQL statements, and if a transaction rolls back to an earlier save point, then it may release the locks it acquired after that save point. For example, if a transaction's first statement touched only index I_1 and the second statement touched index I_2, but the second statement failed and the transaction rolls back to the save point between the two statements, then all locks on index I_2 may be released during this partial rollback.

Second, when a transaction must abort, it may release all its read-only locks immediately. Only the write locks are required to protect the rollback actions. As the rollback logic proceeds, it may release locks as it completes the rollback ("undo", compensation) actions, i.e., in reverse order of lock acquisition.

Third, when the global coordinator in a two-phase commit requests that local participant transactions prepare for transaction commit, read-only participants may terminate immediately [9]. This includes releasing all their locks; obviously, those are all read-only locks. In addition, a read-only participant has no need to participate in the second phase of the two-phase commit. This is perhaps the most well known example of early lock release.

Fourth, read-write participants in a two-phase commit may release their read-only locks immediately upon receiving the request to prepare for a transaction commit. In other words, early lock release in two-phase commit is not dependent on the overall behavior of the local participant but on the nature of the locks – a transaction may release its read-only locks immediately after the commit request.

Fifth, even in the absence of distribution and two-phase commit, a transaction may release its read-only locks as soon as it has allocated space for a commit record in the log buffer. This technique requires that each transaction scans its set of locks twice, once to find (and release) its read-only locks and once again (at the very end) to release the remaining locks. Early lock release requires only one such scan, which releases all locks and inserts tags into the lock manager's hash table. These tags will be cleared out by subsequent transactions finding tags that expired. Controlled lock violation requires only the final scan after all commit activities; it may, however, use an earlier scan over all its locks in order to identify all transactions already waiting for those locks and able to resume with controlled lock violation.

	IS	*IX*	*S*	*X*	*SIX*
IS	ok	ok	ok		ok
IX	ok	ok			
S	ok		ok		
X					
SIX	ok				

Figure 5. Compatibility of hierarchical locks.

Sixth, existing locks may be modified in their lock modes in order to strip out the read-only aspects. For example, an SIX lock [10] may be reduced to a lock in IX mode. (An SIX lock combines a shared S lock and an intent-exclusive IX lock on the same object – the compatibility matrix for intention locks is shown in **Figure 5**.) Locks may also be reduced in their coverage or granularity of locking. For example, an exclusive X lock on an entire index may be reduced to an IX lock on the index combined with appropriate X locks on individual pages or index entries. Note that lock de-escalation can proceed without checking for lock conflicts and cannot create a deadlock. Thus, the X lock on the index is not released but instead it is much reduced in its strength or coverage.

Finally, key range locking raises special cases for the last two points. Some key range locks guarantee the absence of possible future database contents, specifically locks on the open interval between two existing key values in an ordered index such as a B-tree. Such locks are required to prevent phantoms and to ensure true serializability [11]. As special forms of read-only locks, they can be released prior to the transaction's commit activities. Other key range locks combine read-only and update parts, with only the update aspect required during commit activities. For example, a XS lock ("key exclusive, gap shared") [12] can be reduced to an XN lock ("key exclusive, gap free") as part of releasing all read-only locks. **Figure 6** shows a B-tree node with a few key values as well as some of these lock modes and their scope.

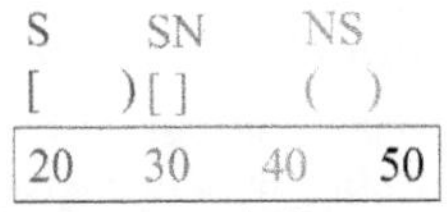

Figure 6. Lock scopes in key range locking.

2.5 *Distributed commit*

The traditional standard for committing a transaction over multiple nodes (or multiple recovery logs) has been two-phase commit, with all locks retained until all commit activities are complete. Thomson et al. [13] observe that "The problem with holding locks during the agreement protocol is that two-phase commit requires multiple network round-trips between all participating machines, and therefore the time required to run the protocol can often be considerably greater than the time required to execute all local transaction logic. If a few popularly-accessed records are frequently involved in distributed transactions, the resulting extra time that locks are held on these records can have an extremely deleterious effect on overall transactional throughput." Therefore, their design sequences transactions deterministically in order to "eliminate distributed commit protocols, the largest scalability impediment of modern distributed systems." In contrast, controlled lock violation reduces the "contention footprint" [13] of two-phase commit by judiciously violating locks held by committing transactions.

Kraska et al. [14] similarly aim to reduce lock conflicts by reducing commit communication. They "describe a new optimistic commit protocol for the wide-area network. In contrast to pessimistic commit protocols such as two-phase commit, the protocol does not require a prepare phase and commits updates in a single message round-trip across data centers if no conflicts are detected" [14]. An essential part of this protocol seems to be that each request for work includes a request to prepare for commit, quite comparable to the first phase of a traditional two-phase commit. In either case, a local transaction guarantees that it will abide by a subsequent global decision to commit or abort.

With this guarantee in place, a single message carrying the global decision can achieve the final commit, comparable to the second phase of a traditional two-phase commit. As each work request includes a request for commit preparation, each work step with local database updates requires a prepared-to-commit log record in each local recovery log. Moreover, a prepared local transaction is protected, i.e., it cannot be terminated, e.g., if it becomes part of a deadlock. Note that a local participant may subsequently receive additional work requests for the same transaction. If the additional work request includes database updates, it invalidates the prior commit preparation and requires a new one, including another suitable log record written to stable storage.

Kraska et al. measured round-trip response times between various regions on Amazon's EC2 cluster over a number of days [14]. Even communication links with response times around 0.1-0.2 seconds most of the time can spike to about 1 second and even to about 4 minutes. Note that these are message delays, not failures. If such delays affect communication during two-phase commit, and if transactions retain locks during commit coordination, spikes in communication latency likely produce spikes in lock contention.

Kraska et al. [14] propose to address the problem by imposing the cost to prepare a two-phase commit on every remote invocation within every transaction, whether or not network latency is currently spiking. In contrast, controlled lock violation addresses the problem by permitting subsequent transactions to violate locks and proceed while earlier transactions run their commit activities.

3 CONTROLLED LOCK VIOLATION

While early lock release removes locks from the lock manager before writing the commit record to stable storage, controlled lock violation retains the locks until transaction end. In order to match the concurrency and performance of early lock release, however, controlled lock violation permits new transactions to acquire conflicting locks in a controlled way. Specifically, in the simplest form of controlled lock violation, lock acquisition is permitted if the transaction holding the lock has appended its commit record to the log buffer. The advanced forms of controlled lock violation have more relaxed rules, e.g., for two-phase commit (Section 4) or for canned transactions (Section 5).

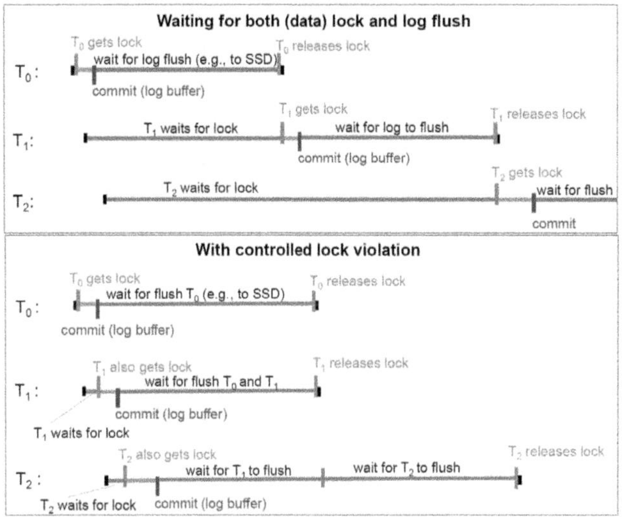

Figure 7. Sequences of three transactions (T_0, T_1, and T_2) without (top) and with (bottom) controlled lock violation.

Figure 7 illustrates a sequence of three transactions that all require a lock on the same database object. The green horizontal lines represent the time needed to execute transaction logic; the red horizontal lines represent time spent waiting for locks or for log records to flush to stable storage. The top diagram shows subsequent transactions acquiring the contested lock only after each preceding transaction has finished all its commit activities. The bottom diagram shows how subsequent transactions may acquire the contested lock and run the transaction logic immediately after the preceding transaction has started its commit activities, specifically after adding its commit log record to the in-memory log buffer. Note that in the lower figure, the commit log records of transactions T_0 and T_1 happen to go to stable storage in the same I/O operation. Obviously, controlled lock violation enable transactions to follow each other in faster succession. The "price" for this performance gain is that multiple transactions require rollback during recovery in case of a system failure; recall that a transaction with a commit log record in the log buffer can fail only if the entire system crashes.

3.1 *Principles*

It is well known that if a transaction T_1 reads an update by a preceding yet uncommitted transaction T_0, also known as a dirty read, then T_1 incurs a commit dependency on T_0. In other words, in a serializable transaction execution schedule, transaction T_1 may commit only after transaction T_0 commits. More generally, if a transaction T_1 ignores or violates a concurrency control conflict, e.g., conflicting locks, with another transaction T_0, a commit dependency results.

The only exception is a read-only lock held by the earlier transaction. In this case, a commit dependency is not required. On the other hand, a read-only lock acquired in conflict with an earlier lock causes a commit dependency. In fact, this is the case overlooked in early designs for early lock release.

Of course, should transaction T_0 subsequently read or update a data item after transaction T_1 has updated it, then a circular dependency results. In such cases, serializability becomes impossible and transaction T_1 must abort.

One can consider a rollback of transaction T_0 as such a case: modern recovery techniques essentially "update back" the changes of failed transactions rather than reverse byte for byte. Logical transaction compensation is required whenever the granularity of locking, e.g., key value locking, lets multiple concurrent transactions modify the same physical data structure, e.g., a B-tree node. If transaction T_0 fails and rolls back after transaction T_1 has updated a data item already updated by transaction T_0, then the "update back" action completes a circular dependency that can be resolved only by aborting transaction T_1. Thus, thinking of rollback as "updating back" nicely explains the commit dependency mentioned above.

3.2 *Approach*

In a traditional database system without early lock release, imagine a transaction T_0 holding a lock and another transaction T_1 requesting a conflicting lock. In this case, T_1 might wait for T_0's commit (and the implied lock release) or T_1 might abort T_0 (and thus force immediate lock release). For a decision between these alternatives, it compares the priorities of T_0 and T_1. It also checks the state of T_0. If T_0 has already added a commit record to the log buffer, or if T_0 is part of a distributed transaction in pre-commit state, or if T_0 is already aborting and rolling back, then T_0 is protected and T_1 cannot force T_0 to abort. Importantly, before transaction T_1 decides on a course of action, it must acquire information about transaction T_0 and its transactional state.

Controlled lock violation aims to achieve the performance advantages of early lock release (corrected with tags) but without releasing locks until all commit activities are complete. In controlled lock violation, transaction T_0 retains all its locks until its commit record indeed is on stable storage. However, if transaction T_1 comes along and looks at transaction T_0 (in order to decide its course of action, e.g., whether to abort T_0), and if T_0 already has a commit record in the log buffer (even if not yet on stable storage), then T_1 may proceed in spite of any locks T_0 still holds. Specifically, transaction T_1 may acquire its desired lock in spite of the conflict but it must take a commit dependency on T_0. Transaction T_0 retains its locks, so the lock manager may grant and hold conflicting locks in this case.

Actually, the commit dependency is required only if the lock held by transaction T_0 is an update lock, e.g., an exclusive lock, 'intent exclusive' lock, 'increment' lock, etc. In other words, violation of anything but a read-only lock creates a commit dependency. A write lock acquired in conflict with an earlier lock must be registered as a commit dependency, even if two update transactions and their commit records usually ensure a correct commit ordering. This is necessary because the write lock might be used only for reading: if the entire transaction remains a read-only transaction without any log records, then no commit record is required and the error case may occur unless the commit dependency is explicitly enforced.

3.3 *Implementation techniques*

In the above examples, the crucial task missing from transaction T_0's commit is writing the commit record to stable storage; the other tasks are acknowledgement of the commit to the user (or application) and releasing locks and other resources such as threads and memory. As soon as the log write is complete and thus the transaction durable, the commit dependency is resolved.

Thus, the commit dependency is really equivalent to a high water mark in the recovery log. When the recovery log has been written to stable storage up to and including this high water mark, transaction T_1 is free to commit. In other words, when transaction T_1 acquires a lock that conflicts with a non-read-only lock held by transaction T_0, which is permitted because transaction T_0 has already written its commit record to the log buffer, then the LSN (log sequence number) of T_0's commit record is registered as the high water mark governing the commit of T_1. Transaction T_1 cannot commit until the recovery log has been written to stable storage up to and including this log record.

If transaction T_1 is an update transaction, then it will eventually append its own commit record to the log buffer and the log on stable storage. In this case, the sequencing of commit records in the recovery log will ensure correct enforcement of the commit dependency. In other words, the commit dependency is almost meaningless and enforced as a matter of course.

If, on the other hand, transaction T_1 is a read-only transaction without any log records and thus without a commit record, and if transaction T_1 has incurred a commit dependency by violating a lock of a committing transaction T_0, then T_1 must wait until the commit record of T_0 is saved on stable storage. This is precisely what the high water mark enforces. Thus, this technique delays a committing read-only transaction only if a lock violation has indeed occurred and only as much as absolutely necessary.

If transaction execution is faster than writing a commit record to stable storage, perhaps even orders of magnitude faster, then transactions may form long chains of commit dependencies. In the extreme example of 0.01 ms execution time and 10 ms commit time, a chain of 1,000 transactions seems possible. If only one of those transactions were to abort, all subsequent ones must abort, too. In other words, this seems to be a bad case of "abort amplification" or "cascading abort."

One must recognize, however, that a traditional transaction processing system would have let none of the subsequent transactions acquire conflicting locks; thus, transactions aborted in this design would never even have started or made progress past the conflicting lock request. More importantly, all transactions whose locks may be violated have reached their commit point and have appended a commit record to the log buffer; thus, practically the only cause for a transaction failure is a system failure, in which all subsequent transactions would fail even without the chain of commit dependencies.

3.4 *Comparison with early lock release*

Controlled lock violation is similar to early lock release, at least in some aspects. First, a transaction T_1 can proceed as soon as an earlier, conflicting transaction T_0 has added its commit record to the log buffer in memory (or at least allocated space and an address for it). Second, most read-only transactions can commit instantly, except those that encounter a lock conflict and incur a commit dependency. (In this exception case, controlled lock violation is "slower" than early lock release because controlled lock violation behaves correctly whereas early lock release does not – see **Figure 2** and the corresponding discussion).

Controlled lock violation is also quite different from early lock release. First, transaction T_0 retains its locks in controlled lock violation as long as in traditional lock release, so it does not release any locks early. Second, locks can be violated while transaction T_0 commits, but only after T_0 has added its commit record to the log buffer. Third, hardly any new mechanism is required – for example, neither the allocation nor the clean up of tags are required. Fourth, if there is no conflict between committing and active transactions, controlled lock violation does not impose any restrictions or overheads, whereas early lock release forces committing transactions to install tags in the lock manager's hash table just in case a subsequent transaction might create a lock conflict. Finally, and perhaps most importantly, controlled lock violation requires very little if any new theory – violation of lock conflicts and resulting commit dependencies are already part of the traditional theory of concurrency control and recovery.

3.5 *Combined locks*

Retaining the original locks during commit activities is more precise than early lock release. This is because controlled lock violation preserves all lock information during commit activities whereas early lock release reduces that information to a tag. The detailed information about locks is particularly useful in cases with combined lock modes such as SIX (see **Figure 5**).

A conflict involving a combined lock mode does not always induce a commit dependency, because a combined lock may include read-only and update parts. Thus, controlled lock violation is more precise than early lock release, because early lock release reduces the conflict analysis to tags whereas controlled lock violation retains the precise lock. Early lock release would introduce commit dependencies in all of the following examples.

Consider, for example, transaction T_0 holding a combination lock, e.g., an SIX lock on a file (to read the entire file and update selected pages). A commit dependency is required only if a lock acquired by a later transaction conflicts with the update part. For example, if transaction T_1 requests an IS lock (in preparation of locking individual pages in S mode), there is no conflict at all because lock modes SIX and IS are compatible. (There is no conflict over this lock for the entire file; there may be a conflict if T_0 and T_1 attempt to lock the same page.) Further, if transaction T_2 acquires an IX lock on the file (in preparation of acquiring X locks on individual pages), which conflicts only with the read-only S part of the SIX lock of transaction T_0, no commit dependency is required. On the other hand, if another transaction T_3 acquires an S lock on the file, which conflicts with the IX part of the SIX lock of transaction T_0, then T_3 incurs a commit dependency on T_0. (In this particular case, transaction T_3 also incurs a commit dependency on T_2 due to the conflict between IX and S locks.)

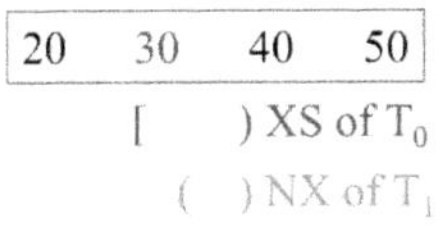

Figure 8. Conflicts and dependencies in key range locking.

Another example is key range locking in B-tree indexes. Consider the specific case illustrated in **Figure 8**. Transaction T_0 has locked key value 30 in XS mode ("key exclusive, gap shared") [12] and is in its commit phase with the commit record in the log buffer. If transaction T_1 acquires a violating NX lock ("key free, gap exclusive" – N stands for no lock), should that imply a commit dependency? The correct answer is 'no'. If transaction T_2 acquires a violating SN lock ("key shared, gap free"), should that imply a commit dependency? The correct answer is 'yes'. With early lock release and a tag in the lock manager's hash table, it is impossible to derive these correct answers. Controlled lock violation makes the correct decision easy: As the NX lock of transaction T_1 conflicts only with the read-only part of the XS lock held by transaction T_0, no commit dependency is required. On the other hand, since the SN lock of transaction T_2 conflicts with the update part of the XS lock held by transaction T_0, T_2 incurs a commit dependency on T_0. (Locks of modes SN and NX do not conflict; therefore, T_2 does not incur a commit dependency on T_1.)

3.6 *Weak transaction isolation levels*

Many databases and their applications run with a transaction isolation level weaker than serializability, e.g., "read committed." This isolation level permits releasing read-only locks immediately after use, e.g., when a scan advances to the next record. Write locks, on the other hand, are retained until the transaction ends.

If a transaction finds a desired data item locked, it waits. Only the "dirty read" transaction isolation level ignores existing locks (and consequently provides no meaningful transaction isolation). With controlled lock violation, this wait may not be required – a subsequent transaction may violate locks held by a transaction already in its commit activities. If a read-only lock of transaction T_1 violates a write lock of an earlier transaction T_0, it incurs a commit dependency. This is true even if the transaction T_1 releases this read-only lock soon thereafter, i.e., long before it attempts to commit.

A special case is an earlier transaction T_0 that deletes a record. Most implementations employ ghost records, also known as invalid records or pseudo-deleted records. These records still exist in the data structure but are marked as logically deleted. Their value is that a locked data item remains in the data structure until the transaction commits, thus avoiding special cases in the concurrency control code and simplifying rollback code. Any scan or query must ignore ghost records. If a transaction T_1 finds a locked ghost record, and if the lock-holding transaction T_0 is in its commit activities, then T_1 may violate the lock but it incurs a commit dependency. Transaction T_1 may commit only if transaction T_0 indeed commits the ghost record. If transaction T_0 fails and rolls back, transaction T_1 erroneously ignored a valid record and it therefore must abort as well.

3.7 *Summary*

In summary, controlled lock violation matches early lock release in the principal goal: when and where early lock release applies, controlled lock violation permits the same concurrency. However, controlled lock violation is simpler, e.g., with respect to data structures, yet it is more general, e.g., with respect to lock modes, and more accurate, e.g., with respect to combined locks and key range locking.

Early lock release and controlled lock violation can complement each other, for example in the following way. Once a transaction has determined its commit LSN, it may release its read-only locks. All remaining locks remain active but subsequent lock requests may violate them.

The early lock release part of this hybrid design can also weaken combined locks by removing the read-only component, e.g., from SIX to IX in hierarchical locking or from XS to XN in key-range locking. Moreover, it may notify waiting threads and transactions of released or weakened locks. Weakening SIX to IX locks seems particularly valuable in systems that let threads retain intention lock (e.g., IX) from one transaction to another, a technique known as speculative lock inheritance [15]. Incidentally, both early lock release and controlled lock violation can treat a U (upgrade [8]) lock as if it were an S lock.

Hybrid models are readily possible because in some sense, controlled lock violation differs from early lock release only in the information they retain: while tags in corrected early lock release retain a synopsis of the released lock, controlled lock violation retains the entire lock with all its detailed information. Retaining all lock information permits precision and functionality impossible with early lock release, unless each retained tag effectively replicates the released lock.

4 DISTRIBUTED TRANSACTIONS

As mentioned earlier, early lock release applies only to the final commit phase of two-phase commit, not to the pre-commit phase. In other words, early lock release cuts the lock retention time by the time for writing the final commit record but not by the time for communication during the two-phase commit and for writing the pre-commit record to stable storage.

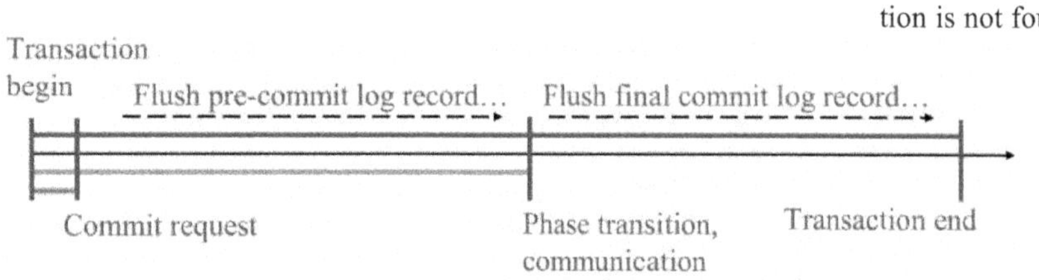

Figure 9. Lock retention times in two-phase commit.

Figure 9 illustrates a distributed transaction and its two commit phases. The execution time is short but each commit phase requires communication and at least one write to stable storage. Traditional lock release retains locks until all commit activities are complete, shown by a blue line above the time line. Early lock release retains locks throughout the first phase of a two-phase commit, shown by a green line below the time line. In contrast, controlled lock violation enforces locks only during transaction execution, shown by a short red line at the bottom left.

Using the times for transaction execution and for flushing commit records to stable storage from the introduction, and assuming for simplicity negligible communication times, execution takes 0.01 ms and each commit phase takes 10 ms (logging on a pair of traditional disks) or 0.1 ms (logging on flash memory). Traditional commit processing holds all locks for 20.01 ms (log on disks) or 0.21 ms (log on flash); early lock release holds all locks for 10.01 ms or 0.11 ms; and controlled lock violation enforces locks for only 0.01 ms (independent of the log device). In other words, with the log on a pair of traditional disks, effective lock retention times are 2,000 times shorter than with traditional commit processing and 1,000 times shorter than with early lock release; with the log on flash memory, effective lock retention times are 20 or 10 times shorter, respectively.

Specifically, imagine an update transaction T_1 that is a local participant in a distributed transaction coordinated by remote transaction T_0, and another transaction T_2 that requests a lock conflicting with a lock held by T_1. With early lock release, T_2 must wait until T_1 has added its final commit record to the log buffer. With controlled lock violation, once the local transaction T_1 has received the request for the first commit phase, T_2 may acquire a conflicting lock. Of course, T_2 incurs a commit dependency on T_1 and thus on T_0. If those fail, T_2 must roll back as well.

4.1 Implementation of commit dependencies

Implementation of commit dependencies in distributed settings are somewhat complex. Fortunately, the commit dependencies required here are always within a single site (node). Thus, fairly simple mechanisms suffice.

A recent detailed description of such mechanisms was published, for example, by Larson et al. [16]. They call their design a "register-and-report approach" in which "T1 registers its dependency with T2 and T2 informs T1 when it has committed or aborted." Essential to the implementation is a counter (similar to a reference counter) and a set data structure capturing dependent transactions. They explain further:

"To take a commit dependency on a transaction T2, T1 increments its CommitDepCounter and adds its transaction ID to T2's CommitDepSet. When T2 has committed, it locates each transaction in its CommitDepSet and decrements their CommitDepCounter. If T2 aborted, it tells the dependent transactions to also abort by setting their AbortNow flags. If a dependent transaction is not found, this means that it has already aborted. Note that a transaction with commit dependencies may not have to wait at all - the dependencies may have been resolved before it is ready to commit. Commit dependencies consolidate all waits into a single wait and postpone the wait to just before commit." [16]

4.2 Performance effects

Perhaps a concrete example is best to illustrate the advantages of eliminating lock conflicts during both phases of a two-phase commit. If the transaction logic runs 0.01 ms (e.g., 40,000 instruction cycles on a core running at 4 GHz) and each commit phase runs 0.1 ms (to force a commit record to flash storage), then early lock release improves the contention footprint by almost a factor of 2 (0.21 ms ÷ 0.11 ms) whereas controlled lock violation improves the time with lock conflicts by more than a factor of 20 (0.21 ms ÷ 0.01 ms). If stable storage is realized with traditional disks, and if the time to force a log record to stable storage is 10 ms, then the factor for early lock release remains at about 2 (20.01 ms ÷ 10.01 ms) whereas the factor is about 2,000 (20.01 ms ÷ 0.01 ms) for controlled lock violation.

If locks can be violated immediately after a distributed transaction begins its commit sequence, lock contention during the two-phase commit sequence may cease to be a concern for performance and scalability. In other words, the major concern about or argument against two-phase commit loses weight and credibility. By removing lock conflicts during communication and coordination of two-phase commit, controlled lock violation may substantially contribute to increased use of two-phase commit with distributed transactions and thus to the consistency and reliability of distributed systems.

4.3 Summary

Both early lock release and controlled lock violation reduce the effective lock retention times during two-phase commit. Neither improves the elapsed time, communication time, or logging effort during commit processing. However, since early lock release pertains only to the final phase of the two-phase commit, its improvement of effective lock retention times is very small in comparison to that of controlled lock violation.

5 CANNED TRANSACTIONS

In some cases, controlled lock violation may be advantageous even before the user (or application) requests a transaction commit for the transaction holding the lock. In general, such lock violation is a bad idea. For example, if transaction T_0 needs and acquires a lock, transaction T_1 violates this lock, and then T_0 performs another action that requires the same lock again, then transaction T_0 needs to violate the lock held by T_1 and transactions T_0 and T_1 have mutual, i.e., circular, commit dependencies on each other. Only aborting transaction T_1 can resolve this situation.

If, however, it is certain that transaction T_0 will not require again a specific lock that it holds, then another transaction T_1 may violate this lock. For example, a "canned" transaction T_0 may run a stored procedure, that stored procedure may consist of multiple statements, and each statement may touch its own set of tables, i.e., disjoint from the tables in other statements. All of these are not unreasonable assumptions as many stored procedures satisfy them. When they apply, then another transaction T_1 may violate any lock from an earlier statement. The precise condition is that locks may be violated if neither the current nor any future statement might need them.

```
Begin transaction
Update accounts set balance += …
Update accounts set balance −= …
Insert activities values (…)
Commit transaction
```

Figure 10. A canned transaction.

Figure 10 shows source code for a very simple stored procedure. It moves money from one account to another and then inserts a record of it in a table of activities. After the first two statements, the table of accounts will not be touched again, except perhaps to roll back the updates in case of a transaction failure, e.g., due to a deadlock. Thus, while the third statement is still executing, a later transaction may violate the locks on the accounts table still held by an active transaction. Even in this simple example, controlled lock violation during one of three statements reduces the time with lock conflicts for the accounts table by one third (not including lock retention after the commit request). In other words, in addition to eliminating lock contention while a commit record is written to stable storage, controlled lock violation can reduce lock contention even further.

Note that controlled lock violation of read-only locks does not incur a commit dependency. In other words, controlled lock violation of a read-only lock has no negative effect at all. Thus, for tables touched only by a single statement of a stored procedure, controlled lock violation gives the semantics and consistency of full serializability but with the contention footprint and with the lock conflicts of "read committed" transaction isolation.

The tables involved in each statement can easily be extracted from the source code of the stored procedure. If disambiguation of table names requires a binding based on the user invoking the stored procedure, such static analysis might not be possible, in particular if tables and views may have multiple names or aliases. Cases requiring user-specific name resolution are discouraged in practice, because these cases also prevent precompilation, cached query execution plans, and compile-time query optimization. Therefore, static analysis is usually possible. It might focus on tables and materialized views (i.e., objects of the logical database design) or on indexes and partitions (i.e., objects of the physical database design). In the former case, it is sufficient to analyze the request syntax; in the latter case, query execution plans must also be considered.

Gawlick and Kinkade [17] wrote: "Consider, for example, an ultra-hot spot: a counter updated by every transaction. To achieve a high transaction rate, we want a transaction to be able to access the counter without waiting for any other transaction. We also want to guarantee the integrity of the counter, consistency with other parts of the data base, etc." Their solution introduced a new "change" verb to the language, i.e., a restriction to increment and decrement operations instead of general read and write operations. Note that an 'increment' lock is perfectly compatible with serializable transactions but it does not imply a read lock, i.e., it does not bestow the right to expect repeatable reads.

Wolfson [18] described a static analysis of stored procedures and an algorithm to identify points when explicit early lock release may be permitted without the danger of deadlocks. The analysis algorithm is, unfortunately, NP-complete and needs to run whenever the text of a stored procedure is altered. Moreover, the work is limited to single-site deployments and to shared and exclusive locks.

The present design offers an alternative to both prior approaches: a transaction may acquire a traditional write (exclusive) lock on the counter, increment its value, and then hold the lock until all commit activities are complete. Because such a transaction touches the counter only once, subsequent transactions may violate this lock immediately after the increment operation. In other words, controlled lock violation can offer practically the same concurrency but without the need for 'increment' locks.

In summary, controlled lock violation can happen even before the commit request in some cases that may be expected common in practice. It might for many applications combine the advantages of "read committed" and serializable transaction isolation levels. In many cases, it also enables traditional exclusive locks with the concurrency of special 'increment' locks.

6 PERFORMANCE EVALUATION

We implemented and measured controlled lock violation in the context of Shore-MT [6], an experimental database system.

6.1 Implementation

We implemented controlled lock violation in Shore-MT by adding a binary flag to each transaction descriptor that indicates whether other transactions may violate the transaction's locks. Lock acquisition ignores conflicts with locks held by transactions with this flag set when determining if locks can be granted. The flag starts unset and is set at the same point early lock release would release locks, namely once the commit record has been allocated in the log buffer.

We also modified the lock acquisition code so that when a transaction violates another transaction's lock, the acquiring transaction advances its high-water mark to equal or exceed the holding transaction's commit LSN. A transaction's high water mark (part of the preexisting implementation of early lock release) is the highest LSN that must be flushed to stable storage before a read-only transaction is allowed to commit and return data to a client. The preexisting code to implement this delay takes less than 60 lines of C++ including comments and debugging code but not tests. Such delays affect only read-only transactions.

The present implementation omits many possible optimizations. For example, it maintains a transaction's high-water mark even when a lock acquisition violates a read-only lock and it fails to wake up waiting transactions when lock violation becomes possible. (We expect to have this remedied very soon.) We also have not yet implemented controlled lock violation in the context of two-phase commit or of canned transactions.

6.2 *Results*

In the following, we report the performance of controlled lock violation versus two variants of early lock release (releasing S locks only and releasing both S and X locks) for the industry standard TPC-B benchmark, which models simple database transactions. To cover a range of logging delays, we logged to a RAM disk but added an extra delay ranging from 0.1 ms to 10 ms to simulate a range of stable storage devices. The database data itself was stored on disk and our experimental machine is a 4-socket Intel Xeon X7542 machine running at 2.7 GHz with 24 cores.

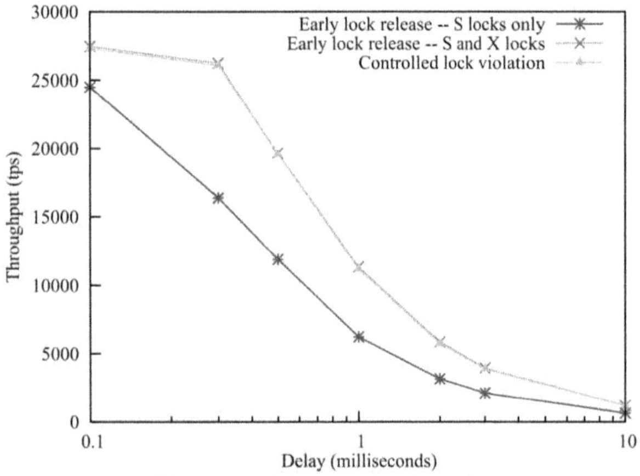

Figure 11. 24 cores, 24 threads.

Figure 11 and **Figure 12** show the transaction throughput (transactions per second) for competing commit processing techniques as the extra delay is varied. **Figure 11** is for 24 threads (one per core) while **Figure 12** is for 48 threads (two per core). Extra threads can perform useful work when other threads are blocked, waiting for locks or, more likely in the case of controlled lock violation, for their commit record to be flushed to stable storage.

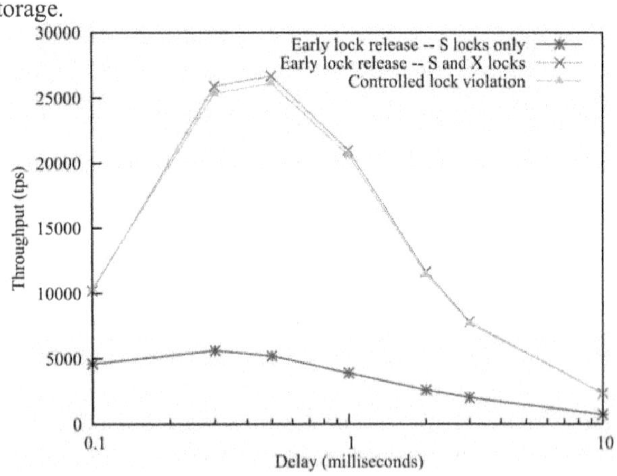

Figure 12. 24 cores, 48 threads.

Note that the relatively low performance for 48 cores at small delay is expected, since the threads block only for a very short time and hence the additional threads merely add overhead (e.g., due to true contention, context switching overhead, etc.).

As can be seen, both controlled lock violation and early lock release for S and X locks outperform the traditional approach of releasing read-only locks early by large factors for sizable delays: up to 5× at 1 ms commit delay and 2× at 10 ms commit delay. The improvement is smaller at small delays: up to 2.2× at 0.1 ms commit delay and 4.5× at 0.3 ms commit delay. The performance of controlled lock violation and early lock release for S and X locks are not significantly different; a T-test fails to reject the null hypothesis at p=0.05. However, as our implementation of controlled lock violation is missing several possible optimizations (see Section 6.1) it may be possible for controlled lock violation to exceed the performance of early lock release.

Since controlled lock violation sometimes delays read-only transactions, we also experimented with a variant of TPC-B with 70% of the transactions made read-only by omitting their writes. The results, shown in **Figure 13** for 48 threads, again show sizable improvements for controlled lock violation.

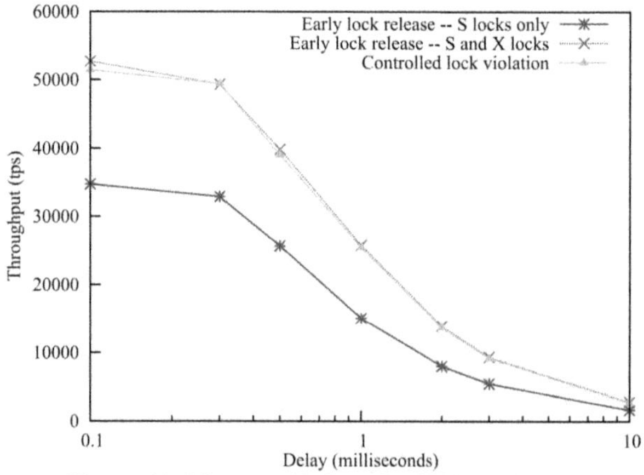

Figure 13. 24 cores, 48 threads, 70% read-only.

7 DISCUSSION

Both early lock release and controlled lock violation are specific forms of speculative execution. The speculation risk, however, is very small, as both techniques require that the earlier transaction reaches its commit point and formats a commit record in the log buffer before speculative execution begins. Nonetheless, with all other things equal, a system should schedule (process) a transaction without commit dependency ahead of one with, or one with fewer commit dependencies ahead of one with more. In other words, a transaction with commit dependencies should progress only if there no is work pending that is less speculative, or when the processing resources would remain idle except for speculative work. This is particularly true in the advanced forms of controlled lock violation discussed in later sections.

Outside the research area of database management, Nightingale et al. [19] investigated scenarios similar to ours. The issue was the same – guaranteeing durability yet hiding the latency until information had been written to disk. Their context was a file system and its "sync" operations. Their solution acknowledges the write operation immediately and lets the invoking process continue while preventing the process from communication. In other words, speculative execution of the process enabled further local progress but in the unlikely case that the sync operation failed, the process can be rolled back and the speculative execution is wasted. Thus, by relying on inexpensive checkpoints and speculative execution, their system achieved performance similar to asynchronous writes to disks but the semantics of synchronous writes.

Early lock release and controlled lock violation similarly rely on speculative execution with an extremely low risk of failure and of wasted work.

Both early lock release and controlled lock violation also seem related to optimistic concurrency control, in the sense that new transactions may proceed ignoring existing transactions and their concurrency footprint. Both techniques, however, are forms of pessimistic concurrency control, i.e., locking. Both techniques employ traditional locking techniques for synchronization atomicity or concurrency control – only during the phase that ensures durability of transaction, i.e., flushing the commit record to stable storage, are locks released or violated.

This reliance on pessimistic concurrency control is very deliberate. Carey's extensive simulation studies (e.g., [20] and multiple subsequent studies) point out that the mechanism of concurrency control matters little in systems with few conflicts. In systems with many conflicts, avoiding wasted work by early detection of conflicts is the most important determinant of performance (other than a fine granularity of locking). Controlled lock violation wastes work (due to "cascading aborts" or "abort amplification") only if a transaction fails after reaching its commit point.

In a single-site or single-log system, a transaction starts cascading aborts only if a system failure (crash) occurs in the time between adding a commit record to the log buffer and completing the write to stable storage, i.e., the time required for a single write operation. Moreover, in a traditional system that retains locks until a transaction is durable, the transactions failed due to cascading abort would not have started. In other words, controlled lock violation is pessimistic with respect to synchronization atomicity but it is optimistic with respect to durability once a transaction has started its commit activities. The risk and extent of wasted work are miniscule compared to the performance advantage of early lock release and controlled lock violation.

In a system with multiple logs and thus with two-phase commit, frequent failures during the first commit phase would suggest delaying controlled lock violation to the second phase. If, however, most transactions that start their commit activities also finish them successfully, the risk of cascading aborts is low. Similar considerations apply to controlled lock violation prior to the commit point of canned transactions – if failures are frequent, controlled lock violation should be restricted to the commit phase.

Early lock release and controlled lock violation avoid multi-version concurrency control and its complexities by delaying any conflicting transaction until the lock-holding transaction has finished its updates. Thus, there is no need for multiple versions of the same record. However, should a rollback be required, e.g., because a distributed transaction fails in the second phase of its two-phase commit, it is possible that multiple transactions need to roll back, which could take a single record back in time through multiple states. Nonetheless, at any one time, there is only a single version of each record in the database.

8 SUMMARY AND CONCLUSIONS

In summary, the simple form of controlled lock violation is comparable to early lock release. Early lock release can boost the performance of transaction processing by a small factor or even an order of magnitude as shown in **Figure 4**. In those cases in which early lock release applies, controlled lock violation enables the same amount of additional concurrency compared to traditional commit processing. However, there are multiple reasons to prefer controlled lock violation over early lock release.

First, controlled lock violation is simpler and more robust because it has fewer special cases. It applies to all lock types – any lock may be violated and violation of any but a read-only lock induces a commit dependency. Even after multiple rounds of correction and improvement, early lock release still does not cover 'increment' locks. The same is true for more specialized locks that are used in real database systems, e.g., 'bulk insertion' or 'schema stability' or 'schema modify' locks in SQL Server, as well as the various special designs for key range locking and their lock modes. Controlled lock violation is a simple, consistent solution for all of these lock types, easy enough for implementation, quality assurance, and maintenance by most software engineers working on data management code.

Second, controlled lock violation is more precise than early lock release with tags. For key range locking, a precise separation of concurrency and conflict is required, in particular for hot spots known in many databases and their indexes. Controlled lock violation carries that precision to the commit dependency, whereas early lock release may introduce a commit dependency where none is required.

Third, controlled lock violation works well with two-phase commit. With early lock release, a transaction can avoid lock conflicts if an earlier transaction is in the final phase of the two-phase commit. With controlled lock violation, a transaction can avoid lock conflicts during both phases, i.e., already during the initial phase. Thus, the opportunity for lock conflicts during two-phase commit is much smaller with controlled lock violation than with early lock release. It could be argued that this reduction in lock conflicts takes most of the performance costs out of two-phase commit. For example, it might enable immediate (as opposed to eventually consistent) maintenance of all copies in a system relying on replicas for high reliability and high availability. These effects and their implications require further research.

Fourth, controlled lock violation applies even before the user (or application) requests a commit. In a "canned" transaction with a fixed sequence of statements, locks can be violated prior to the commit request if neither the current nor any future statement might need the locks, and this can be based on static analysis of the stored procedure and its source code.

In conclusion, we believe that controlled lock violation matches the promise of early lock release but it is simpler, more accurate, and more general. In other words, we believe it is superior in multiple dimensions.

ACKNOWLEDGEMENTS

Hideaki Kimura implemented the tag-based design for early lock release with read-only transactions. Eric Anderson pointed out the possible relationship between controlled lock violation and optimistic concurrency control. Haris Volos helped with the performance evaluation. Martin Scholl alerted us to the recent work on MDCC. Gary Smith suggested some concerns regarding dispatching waiting transactions and transaction isolation levels weaker than serializability. Barb Peters suggested some improvements in style and grammar.

We thank all developers and researchers of the Shore-MT team at EPFL, CMU and UW-Madison for making the Shore-MT code-base available. We especially thank Anastassia Ailamaki and her students for their thoughtful work on early lock release.

REFERENCES

[1] Anon et al.: A measure of transaction processing power. Datamation, 1 April 1985. Also: http://research.microsoft.com/~gray/papers/AMeasureOfTransactionProcessingPower.doc; retrieved 11/10/2012.

[2] Eljas Soisalon-Soininen, Tatu Ylönen: Partial strictness in two-phase locking. ICDT 1995: 139-147.

[3] Ryan Johnson, Ippokratis Pandis, Radu Stoica, Manos Athanassoulis, Anastasia Ailamaki: Aether: a scalable approach to logging. PVLDB 3(1): 681-692 (2010).

[4] Hideaki Kimura, Goetz Graefe, Harumi Kuno: Efficient locking for databases on modern hardware. ADMS workshop, Istanbul August 2012.

[5] David J. DeWitt, Randy H. Katz, Frank Olken, Leonard D. Shapiro, Michael Stonebraker, David A. Wood: Implementation techniques for main memory database systems. ACM SIGMOD 1984: 1-8.

[6] Ryan Johnson, Ippokratis Pandis, Nikos Hardavellas, Anastasia Ailamaki, Babak Falsafi: Shore-MT: a scalable storage manager for the multicore era. EDBT 2009: 24-35.

[7] Goetz Graefe, Hideaki Kimura, Harumi Kuno: Foster B-trees. ACM TODS 37(3) (2012).

[8] Henry F. Korth: Locking primitives in a database system. JACM 30(1): 55-79 (1983).

[9] Irving L. Traiger, Jim Gray, Cesare A. Galtieri, Bruce G. Lindsay: Transactions and consistency in distributed database systems. ACM TODS 7(3): 323-342 (1982).

[10] Jim Gray, Raymond A. Lorie, Gianfranco R. Putzolu, Irving L. Traiger: Granularity of locks in a large shared data base. VLDB 1975: 428-451.

[11] Jim Gray, Raymond A. Lorie, Gianfranco R. Putzolu, Irving L. Traiger: Granularity of locks and degrees of consistency in a shared data base. IFIP Working Conf. on Modeling in Data Base Management Systems 1976: 365-394.

[12] Goetz Graefe: A survey of B-tree locking techniques. ACM TODS 35(3) (2010).

[13] Alexander Thomson, Thaddeus Diamond, Shu-Chun Weng, Kun Ren, Philip Shao, Daniel J. Abadi: Calvin: fast distributed transactions for partitioned database systems. ACM SIGMOD 2012: 1-12.

[14] Tim Kraska, Gene Pang, Michael J. Franklin, Samuel Madden: MDCC: multi-data center consistency. Submitted for publication, available at http://mdcc.cs.berkeley.edu.

[15] Ryan Johnson, Ippokratis Pandis, Anastasia Ailamaki: Improving OLTP scalability using speculative lock inheritance. PVLDB 2(1): 479-489 (2009)

[16] Per-Åke Larson, Spyros Blanas, Cristian Diaconu, Craig Freedman, Jignesh M. Patel, Mike Zwilling: High-performance concurrency control mechanisms for main-memory databases. PVLDB 5(4): 298-309 (2011).

[17] Dieter Gawlick, David Kinkade: Varieties of concurrency control in IMS/VS Fast Path. IEEE Database Eng. Bull. 8(2): 3-10 (1985).

[18] Ouri Wolfson: An algorithm for early unlocking of entities in database transactions. J. Algorithms 7(1): 146-156 (1986).

[19] Edmund B. Nightingale, Kaushik Veeraraghavan, Peter M. Chen, Jason Flinn: Rethink the sync. ACM TOCS 26(3): (2008).

[20] Michael J. Carey, Michael Stonebraker: The performance of concurrency control algorithms for database management systems. VLDB 1984: 107-118.

X-FTL: Transactional FTL for SQLite Databases

Woon-Hak Kang[†] Sang-Won Lee[†] Bongki Moon[‡]

Gi-Hwan Oh[†] Changwoo Min[†]

[†]College of Info. and Comm. Engr.
Sungkyunkwan University
Suwon, 440-746, Korea
{woonagi319,swlee,wurikiji,multics69}@skku.edu

[‡]School of Computer Science and Engineering
Seoul National University
Seoul, 151-744, Korea
bkmoon@snu.ac.kr

ABSTRACT

In the era of smartphones and mobile computing, many popular applications such as Facebook, twitter, Gmail, and even Angry birds game manage their data using SQLite. This is mainly due to the development productivity and solid transactional support. For transactional atomicity, however, SQLite relies on less sophisticated but costlier page-oriented journaling mechanisms. Hence, this is often cited as the main cause of tardy responses in mobile applications.

Flash memory does not allow data to be updated in place, and the copy-on-write strategy is adopted by most flash storage devices. In this paper, we propose *X-FTL*, a transactional flash translation layer(FTL) for SQLite databases. By offloading the burden of guaranteeing the transactional atomicity from a host system to flash storage and by taking advantage of the copy-on-write strategy used in modern FTLs, *X-FTL* drastically improves the transactional throughput almost for free without resorting to costly journaling schemes. We have implemented *X-FTL* on an SSD development board called OpenSSD, and modified SQLite and `ext4` file system minimally to make them compatible with the extended abstractions provided by *X-FTL*. We demonstrate the effectiveness of *X-FTL* using real and synthetic SQLite workloads for smartphone applications, TPC-C benchmark for OLTP databases, and FIO benchmark for file systems.

Categories and Subject Descriptors

H.2.4 [**DATABASE MANAGEMENT**]: Systems—*Transaction procesing*

General Terms

Design, Performance, Reliability

Keywords

SQLite, Transactional Atomicity, Flash Storage Devices, Flash Translation Layer, Copy-On-Write

SIGMOD'13, June 22–27, 2013, New York, New York, USA.

1. INTRODUCTION

An update action in a database system may involve multiple pages, and each of the pages in turn usually involves multiple disk sectors. A sector write is done by a slow mechanical process and can be interrupted by a power failure. If a failure occurs in the middle of a sector write, the sector might be only partially updated. A sector write is thus considered non-atomic by most contemporary database systems [4, 16].

Atomic propagation of one or more pages updated by a transaction can be implemented by shadow pages or physical logging. However, the cost will be considerable during normal processing. Most commercial database systems adopt a solution based on physiological logging, which is more I/O efficient in handling updates and more flexible in the locking granularity. On the other hand, *SQLite*, developed as an embedded database system, faces additional challenge to limit the scale of its code base. Hence SQLite relies on costlier but less sophisticated mechanisms similar to shadow paging.

In order to support transactional atomicity, SQLite processes a page update by copying the original content to a separate *rollback* file or appending the new content to a separate *write-ahead log*. This is often cited as the main cause of tardy responses in smartphone applications [11, 12]. According to a recent survey [12], such popular applications as Facebook, Gmail, twitter, web browsers, and even Angry birds game manage their data using SQLite on smartphone platforms like Android, and approximately 70% of all write requests are for SQLite databases and related files. Considering the increasing popularity of smart mobile platforms, improving the I/O efficiency of SQLite is a practical and critical problem that should be addressed immediately.

Most contemporary mobile devices, if not all, use flash memory as storage media to store data persistently. Since flash memory does not allow any page to be overwritten in place, a page update is commonly carried out by leaving the existing page intact and writing the new content into a clean page at another location [9, 13]. This strategy is called *copy-on-write (CoW)*. Whether it is intended or not, the net effect of copy-on-write operations by a flash memory drive remarkably resembles what the shadow paging mechanism achieves [15]. This provides an excellent opportunity for supporting atomic update propagation almost for free.

In this paper, we present *X-FTL* that (1) realizes low-cost atomic update for individual pages, (2) provides the awareness of database semantics in page updates to support the atomicity of transactions, and (3) exposes an extended abstraction (and APIs) to not only SQLite but also other upper layer applications such as a journaling file system.

The key contributions of this work are summarized as follows.

- *X-FTL* provides an extended abstraction at the storage device level and guarantees the atomicity of transactions and the durability of committed changes almost at no cost. SQLite and journaling file systems can build on *X-FTL* to minimize the overhead of transactional support and metadata journaling.

- When running on top of *X-FTL*, a journaling file system may turn journaling off and can still achieve the same level of consistency provided by full journaling. This indicates that a lightweight transactional file system can be developed without taking extra burden for duplicate data and metadata writes and synchronous write ordering [10, 23, 24].

- We have implemented *X-FTL* on an open SSD development hardware platform called *OpenSSD* by enhancing its FTL code with the *X-FTL* features presented in this paper. We have demonstrated SQLite and `ext4` file system can take advantage of *X-FTL* with only minimal changes in their code.

The rest of the paper is organized as follows. Section 2 describes the transactional support and I/O efficiency of SQLite and presents the motivation of our work. Section 3 reviews the existing techniques for atomic updates and journaling file systems and flash translation layer (FTL) approaches. In Section 4, we present the design principles and the architecture of *X-FTL* and discuss its advantage for SQLite databases. Section 5 presents the implementation details of the *X-FTL* architecture. In Section 6, we evaluate the performance impact of *X-FTL* on SQLite databases as well as file systems. Lastly, Section 7 summarizes the contributions of this paper.

2. MOTIVATION

2.1 Transactional Support in SQLite

For its portability on a wide spectrum of platforms, SQLite makes a few assumptions on the underlying hardware and operating system. While some of them are optimistic, some are pessimistic. One of the critical and pessimistic assumptions is that a disk sector write is not atomic [4]. If a failure occurs in the middle of a sector write, it might be that part of the sector is modified, while the rest is left unmodified.

In order to support the atomicity of transaction execution without the atomicity of a sector write, SQLite operates usually in either *rollback* mode [4] or *write-ahead log* mode [6]. If a transaction updates a page in *rollback* mode, the original content of the page is copied to the rollback journal before updating it in the database, so that the change can always be undone if the transaction aborts. The opposite is done in *write-ahead log* mode. If a transaction updates a page in *write-ahead log* mode, the original content is preserved in the database and the modified page is appended to a separate log, so that any committed change can always be redone by copying it from the log. The change is then

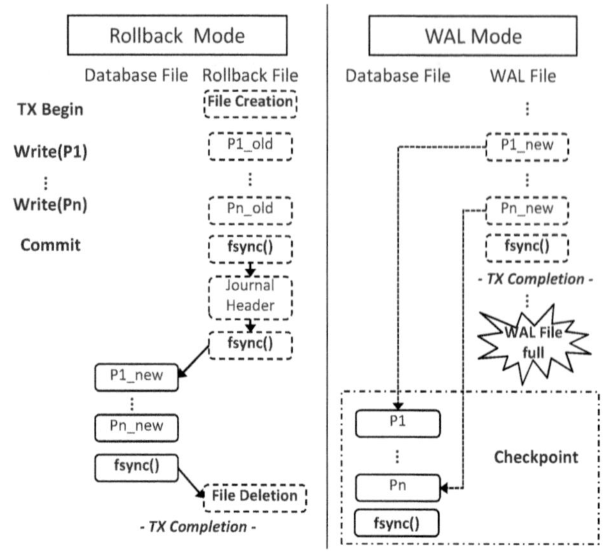

Figure 1: SQLite Journal Modes

later propagated to the database by periodical checkpointing. The delayed propagation in *write-ahead log* mode allows a transaction to maintain its own *snapshot* of the database and enable readers to run fast without being blocked by a writer.

Other notable features of SQLite are summarized below for the background information [4]. SQLite is a software library that implements a serverless transactional SQL database engine. It manages tables and indexes in a single database file on an underlying file system such as `ext4`. SQLite adopts *force* and *steal* policies for buffer management. When a transaction commits, all the pages updated by the transaction are force-written to a stable storage using the `fsync` command. When the buffer runs out of free pages, even uncommitted updates can be written to a stable storage.

2.2 I/O Efficiency of SQLite

The pessimistic side of SQLite further assumes that, for a file that grows in size, the file size is updated before the file content. This requires SQLite to do extra work to ensure that the metadata and content of a file are written to persistent media in particular order, so that a failure between the two events does not cause inconsistency in the database. One popular approach to imposing write ordering is to execute a sync operation as a barrier between a pair of ordered write operations [22].[1] This may be the reason why SQLite is criticized for excessive use of the sync file system call [11].

SQLite assumes that a file deletion is atomic. This assumption is essential for SQLite to maintain consistency in the database, because the presence of a *hot* rollback journal in *rollback* mode, for example, indicates that a transaction was committing when a failure occurred. This assumption cannot be made without support for atomic update of file metadata, which SQLite again assumes is guaranteed by the metadata journaling of an underlying file system.

[1]Most SCSI or SATA drives support the force unit access (FAU) command to bypass the internal cache for reading and writing.

The I/O behaviors of SQLite, as depicted in Figure 1, depend on which mode it runs in. If SQLite runs in *rollback* mode, a journal file is created and deleted whenever a new transaction begins and ends. This increases I/O activities significantly for updating metadata. If SQLite runs in *write-ahead log* mode, a log file is reused and shared by many transactions until the log file is cleared by a checkpointing operation. Thus, the overhead of updating metadata is much lower when SQLite run in *write-ahead log* mode. Another aspect of I/O behaviors is how frequently files are synced. SQLite invokes `fsync` system calls more often when it runs in *rollback* mode than in *write-ahead log* mode. Since the header page of a journal file requires being synced separately from data pages, SQLite needs to invoke at least one more `fsync` call for each committing transaction.

2.3 Problem Statement

SQLite relies heavily on the use of *rollback* journal files and *write-ahead log* as well as frequent file sync operations for transactional atomicity and durability. The I/O inefficiency of this strategy is the main cause of tardy responses of applications running on SQLite. Our goal is to achieve I/O efficient, database-aware transactional support at the flash based storage level so that SQLite and similar applications can simplify their logics for transaction support and hence run faster. We have developed a new flash translation layer (FTL) called *X-FTL*. With *X-FTL*, SQLite and other upper layer applications such as a file system can achieve transactional atomicity and durability as well as metadata journaling with minimum overhead and redundancy.

3. RELATED WORK

By taking advantage of the *copy-on-write* mechanism of flash storage, *X-FTL* can efficiently guarantee that all the pages updated by a transaction are successfully propagated or no pages are written at all upon a failure. In this regard, three types of existing work are closely related to *X-FTL*: shadow paging technique [15], journaling file systems [7, 19, 21, 25], and a few FTL techniques for atomic write of file system journal data [17, 18, 20]. Now, let us briefly explain each work and compare it with *X-FTL*.

3.1 Shadow Paging Technique

In the shadow paging approach [15], when a transaction updates pages, a new version of each page is created, instead of overwriting the existing one. The reason for preserving the old copy (called *shadow page*) is to make page updates atomic by replacing a long page write process with a short pointer manipulation. Hence, the database system needs to keep two page tables: one for new versions and the other for old copies. In fact, each mode of *rollback* and *write-ahead log* in SQLite can be regarded as a variant of this shadow paging technique.

In this respect, our *X-FTL* is conceptually no less than offloading the shadow paging overhead from the database engine to the flash storage layer. This simple offloading opens up new opportunities for implementing the transactional atomicity inside flash storage much more efficiently because most contemporary FTLs rely on *copy-on-write* for update operations. That is, by extending an existing FTL which does not overwrite an old copy, atomic update of pages can be achieved at the flash storage level at no additional cost.

Besides, with *X-FTL*, unlike the traditional shadow paging technique, SQLite-like applications are relieved from the burden of managing two separate page tables and reclaiming the space occupied by old copies.

3.2 Journaling File Systems

Modern file systems take a journaling approach to guarantee the consistency of both metadata and data [10, 19, 21]. The consistency provided by the journaling file systems is aimed at updating a fixed set of pages atomically, which is not semantically sufficient to support more general database transactions. Recently, a few flash-aware journaling file systems such as JFFS [25] and YAFFS [7] have been developed. These file systems, when writing data or metadata to storage upon explicit sync calls by users or upon periodic flush, do not overwrite the original copies. Instead, the new copies are saved in a separate journal area until they are propagated to their original location by checkpointing. This way they achieve data consistency at the expense of increased IOs required for journaling.

In contrast, *X-FTL* provides at least the same level of consistency as provided by modern journaling file systems and can boost transaction performance significantly without resorting to redundant journal files.

3.3 FTL Approaches

Recently, mainly from the storage and file system communities, a few interesting suggestions have been made to support atomic updates on flash-based storage devices [17, 18, 20]. Like journaling file systems described above, those FTL approaches focus more on updating a fixed set of pages atomically.

The *atomic write FTL* by Park *et al.* [18], among the first studies for supporting atomic write in flash storage, exploits the out-of-place update characteristics of flash storage. In particular, this work deals with supporting atomic write of multiple pages specified in a *single* write call like $\texttt{write}(p_1, .., p_n)$. Each write call leaves a commit record after writing all the data pages so that they can be rolled back together if necessary. This approach was recently applied to FusionIO flash SSDs, which helped MySQL achieve atomicity of multiple page writes [17].

Prabhakaran *et al.* proposed a transactional FTL called *txFlash* to support atomic writes for file system journaling [20]. In addition to supporting atomicity of mult-page writes, TxFlash provides isolation among multiple atomic write calls by ensuring that no conflicting writes are issued. It relies on a new commit protocol called Simple Cyclic Commit (SCC) to eliminate the need of a separate commit record for each write, which would impose a write ordering and additional latency.

The common limitation of these approaches is that the atomicity of a multi-page write can be supported only on a per-call basis or only when the whole set of pages are flushed from the buffer pool at once. This requirement clearly contradicts the steal policy of buffer management SQLite and most database systems adopt for performance reasons. Unlike these FTL approaches, *X-FTL* allows for any data page to be written at any time and still supports atomicity of any group of pages belonging to a transaction. Consequently, we can realize flexible and efficient support for general transaction semantics with *X-FTL*, which can also be used to provide atomic writes required in a journaling file system.

3.4 Different Media

It has been recently reported that SQLite database is one of the main performance bottlenecks in smartphone applications [11, 12]. However, no solution has been proposed yet to address the performance problem of SQLite, except for a few suggestions that DRAM or PRAM be utilized as storage for shorter latency and higher bandwidth instead of flash-based storage [11]. The *X-FTL* solution we propose assumes only flash storage which is more common, more economical and has strong market ground. In this respect, *X-FTL* is, as far as we know, the first flash-based approach to tackling SQLite performance concerns.

4. ARCHITECTURE OF X-FTL

In the previous sections, we have reviewed how SQLite and a journaling file system achieve atomic page updates on a storage device that does not support it natively, and identified heavy redundancy in page writes (required by SQLite in the *rollback* or *write-ahead log* mode and by a file system for data and metadata journaling) as the main cause of long latency in update operations. In this section, we present a new method called *X-FTL* that supports atomic page updates at the flash based storage level, so that upper layers such as SQLite and a file system can be freed from the burden of heavy redundancy of duplicate page writes. The design principles and the abstractions of *X-FTL* will be presented.

4.1 Design Principles

In order to have a flash based storage layer provide a transactional support, we have designed a new flash translation layer called *X-FTL*. The design objectives of *X-FTL* are threefold. First, *X-FTL* takes advantage of the copy-on-write mechanism adopted by most flash-based storage devices [9], so that it can achieve transactional atomicity and durability at low cost with no more redundant writes than required by the copy-on-write operations themselves. This is especially important for SQLite that adopts the *force* policy for buffer management at commit time of a transaction. Second, *X-FTL* aims at providing atomic propagation of page updates for individual pages separately or as a group without being limited to SQLite or any specific domain of applications. So the abstractions of *X-FTL* must introduce minimal changes to the standards such as SATA, and the changes must not disrupt existing applications. Third, SQLite and other upper layer applications should be able to use *X-FTL* services without considerable changes in their code. In particular, required changes, if any, must be limited to the use of extended abstractions provided by *X-FTL*.

This approach is novel in that it attempts to turn the weakness of flash memory (*i.e.*, being unable to update in place) into a strong point (*i.e.*, inherently atomic propagation of changes). Unlike the existing FTLs with support for atomic write [17, 18, 20], *X-FTL* supports atomicity of transactions without contradicting the steal policy of database buffer management at no redundant writes. This enables low-cost transactional support as well as minimal write amplification, which extends the life span of a flash storage device.

4.2 X-FTL Architecture and Abstractions

In the core of *X-FTL* is the *transactional logical-to-physical page mapping table* (or *X-L2P* in short) as shown in Figure 2. The *X-L2P* table is used in combination with a traditional page mapping table (or *L2P* in short) maintained by most FTLs. The *L2P* and *X-L2P* tables appear in the left and right sides of Figure 2, respectively. In order to provide transactional support at the storage level, we add to it more information such as the transaction id of an updater, the physical address of a page copied into a new location, and the status of the updater transaction. This will allow us to have full control over which pages can be reclaimed for garbage collection. Specifically, an old page invalidated by a transaction will not be garbage-collected as long as the updater transaction remain active, because the old page may have to be used to rollback the changes in case the transaction gets aborted. If the updater transaction commits successfully, the information on the old page can be released from the *X-L2P* table so that it can be reclaimed for garbage collection.

Obviously the additional information on transactions must be passed from transactions themselves to the flash-based storage, but it cannot be done through the standard storage interface such as SATA. We have extended the SATA interface so that the transaction id can be passed to the storage device by `read` and `write` commands. Besides, two new commands, `commit` and `abort`, have been added to the SATA interface so that the change in the status of a transaction can also be passed. The extensions we have made to the SATA interface are summarized below.

write(tid t, page p) The write command of SATA is augmented with an id of a transaction t that writes a logical page p. This command writes the content of p into a clean page in flash memory and add a new entry $(t, p, paddr, active)$ into the *X-L2P* table, where *paddr* is the physical address of the page the content of p is written into.

read(tid t, page p) The read command of SATA is also augmented with an id of a transaction t that reads a logical page p. This command reads the copy of p from the database snapshot of transaction t. Depending on whether t is the transaction that updated p most recently or not, a different version of p may be returned.

commit(tid t) This is a new command added to the SATA interface. When a commit command is given by a transaction t, the physical addresses of new content written by t become permanent and the old addresses are released so that the old page can be reclaimed for garbage collection.

abort(tid t) This is a new command added to the SATA interface. When an abort command is given by a transaction t, the physical addresses of new content written by t are abandoned and those pages can be reclaimed for garbage collection.

Note that the SATA command set is not always available for SQLite and other applications that access files through a file system. Instead of invoking the SATA commands directly from SQLite, we have extended the `ioctl` and `fsync` system calls so that the additional information about transactions can be passed to the storage device through the file system.

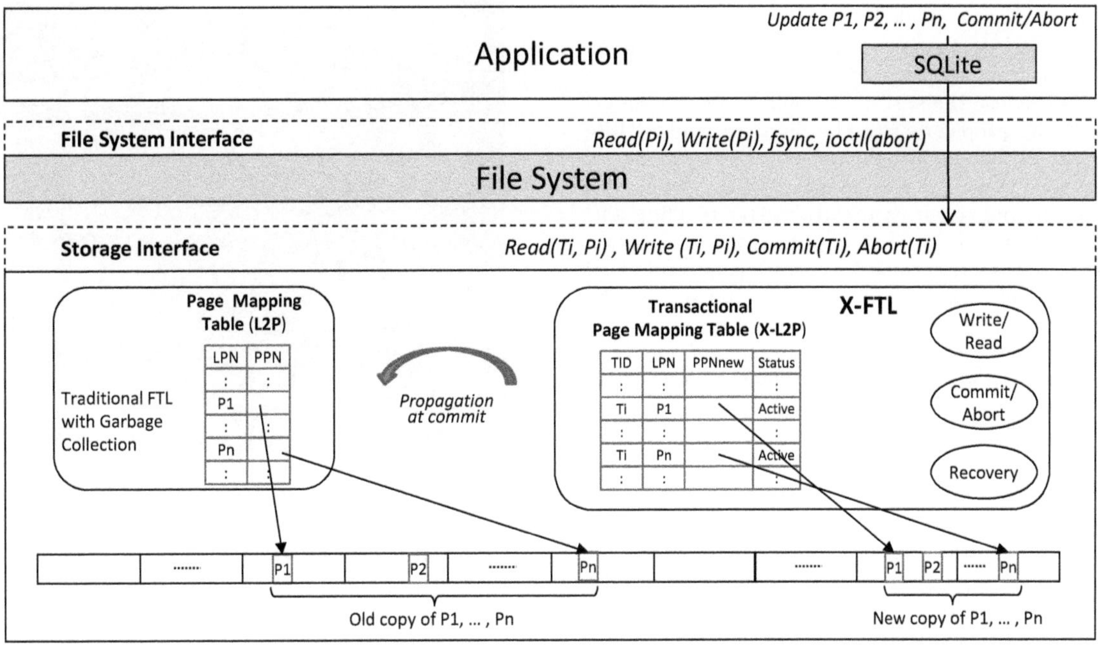

Figure 2: *X-FTL* Architecture: an FTL for Transactional Atomicity

4.3 X-FTL Advantages for SQLite

When SQLite runs in *rollback* mode, it creates a journal file for every transaction when it begins so its changes can be rolled back if necessary, and deletes the journal file when the transaction ends. The amount of overhead incurred by frequent file creations and deletions is non-trivial. Whenever a page is about to be updated by a transaction, the old content of the page is synchronously copied into a journal file. When a transaction commits, `fsync` system calls must be invoked for both the log and database files to guarantee the durability of the transaction. This makes SQLite execute the costly `fsync` system call excessively.

When SQLite runs in *write-ahead log* mode, for a page that is about to be updated by a transaction, the new content of the page is written to the log file. So, reading a certain page may require accessing both the log file and the database file to find the correct version of the page. This process can be facilitated by an in-memory index but reading the two files may still be unavoidable and the overhead is not trivial when it happens.

With *X-FTL* that supports atomic page updates at the storage device level, the runtime overhead of SQLite can be reduced dramatically. First, SQLite does not have to write a page (physically) more than once for each logical page write. Second, a single invocation of `fsync` call will be enough for each committing transaction because all the updates are made directly to the database file. Consequently, the I/O efficiency and the transaction throughput of SQLite can improve significantly for any workload with non-trivial update activities.

The current version (3.7.10) of SQLite supports the atomicity of a transaction that updates multiple database files but it is awkward or incomplete [4, 6]. When a transaction updates two or more database files in *rollback* mode, a master journal file, in addition to regular journal files, should be created to guarantee the atomic propagation of the entire set of updates made against the database files [4]. With *X-FTL*, in contrast, SQLite keeps trace of the multi-file updates in the *X-L2P* table under the same transaction id and supports the atomicity of the transaction without additional effort.

5. IMPLEMENTATIONS

This section presents the implementation details of the *X-FTL* architecture depicted in Section 4. The dominant portion of the *X-FTL* implementation is made into the firmware of the OpenSSD development board by cross-compiling the source code written in C. As an intermediary between *X-FTL* and SQLite, the file system accepts the information of active transactions through the `fsync` and `ioctl` system calls and passes it to *X-FTL* via the extended SATA command set. To carry this out, additional changes are also made in the system calls and the SATA interface. As will be described below, the changes made in SQLite is minimal.

We have chosen the `ext4` as the underlying file system, as it is the most common file system in Android platforms and any improvement in performance by *X-FTL* would have direct impact on many real-world mobile applications running on `ext4`.

5.1 Changes made in SQLite

The original SQLite runs in either *rollback* or *write-ahead log* mode to achieve atomic propagation of updated pages. However, if SQLite runs on *X-FTL*, it does not have to run in either mode. Instead, it can simply turn them off, because *X-FTL* supports transactional atomicity and durability at the storage level. When running in *off* mode, SQLite applies changes directly to database pages and the metadata of the database file. Recall that, even in *off* mode, the database buffer is still managed by the steal and force policies.

The force policy can be enforced by simply force-writing all the pages updated by a committing transaction to the database using `fsync` system call of an underlying file system. For an aborting transaction, however, the process of rolling back the changes made by the transaction is not defined [4] when SQLite runs in *off* mode. Consequently, an aborting transaction may leave a database in an inconsistent state. This is because the steal policy allows an uncommitted change to be propagated to the database and SQLite does not undo the uncommitted change in the *off* mode.

Unfortunately, there is no counterpart of the `fsync` system call that can undo changes already written to a file. The only way to address this problem is to pass the information of an aborting transaction to *X-FTL*, so that uncommitted changes can be rolled back inside a flash-based storage device. This is done by modifying SQLite such that it invokes a new system call for an aborting transaction, and this is the only change we have made to SQLite. The new system call is implemented in the file system by adding a new request type '*abort*' to the `ioctl` system call.

5.2 Changes made in File System

A file system plays a messenger role in passing the transactional context of database accesses from SQLite to *X-FTL*. For example, when a page is updated by a transaction, its id needs to be passed to *X-FTL* along with the content of the page so that *X-FTL* can keep track of the pages that are updated by the transaction. When the transaction requests a read or write operation, it is translated into `read(t,p)` or `write(t,p)`, where `t` and `p` are the id of the transaction and the logical address of a page, respectively. As will be described in Section 5.3, `read(t,p)` and `write(t,p)` are new commands added to the standard SATA command set. Note that transaction ids are managed by the file system instead of SQLite. This implementation decision is made because SQLite does not run as a stand-alone server but instead is linked to an application as a library, and thus it is difficult for applications to manage transaction ids globally.

Similarly, a commit or abort command is passed from a transaction to *X-FTL* via the file system. When a transaction t is about to commit, the file system is notified of that via an `fsync` system call invoked for the transaction so that all updated pages are force-written to the database. The `fsync` system call is translated to one or more `write(t,p)` commands for all updated pages. This is then followed by a `commit(t)` command passed to *X-FTL* via the extended SATA interface. We have added a new `commit(t)` command to the SATA command set by extending the parameter set of `trim` command.

When a transaction t is about to abort, the file system is notified of that via an `ioctl` system call given for the transaction. Since SQLite adopts the steal policy for buffer management, some of the pages updated by the transaction may have already been propagated to the database, while the rest may still be cached in the file system buffer. Undoing the cached changes is done simply by dropping them from the file system buffer. To rollback the changes written to the database, an `abort(t)` command is issued to *X-FTL*. Similarly to the `commit(t)` command, the `abort(t)` command is implemented by extending the parameter set of `trim` command.[2] The detailed implementation of `commit(t)` and `abort(t)` commands is described in the next section.

[2]An eMMC flash memory card, commonly used in smartphones, allows to add application-specific commands to the storage interface [5]. With an eMMC card, the commit and abort commands could be added without modifying the trim command.

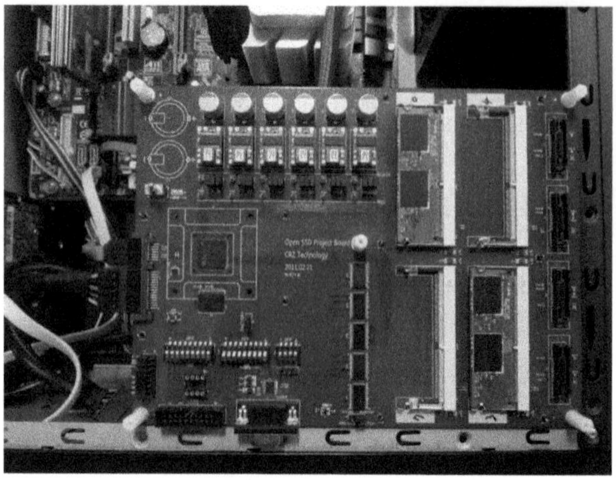

Figure 3: OpenSSD connected to host system

5.3 Changes made in FTL

In order to prototype *X-FTL*, we have implemented *X-FTL* on the OpenSSD platform. OpenSSD is an SSD development platform that is made publicly available by the OpenSSD Project to promote research and education on the recent flash-based solid state drive technology [3]. The OpenSSD platform is based on the *Barefoot* controller, which is an early commercial product by Indilinx. Thus it has the same performance characteristics as a commercial SSD equipped with the Barefoot controller. OpenSSD adopts a page mapping scheme for flash memory management like most contemporary SSD products and eMMC flash memory cards. The OpenSSD board is connected to a host system through the SATA interface as shown in Figure 3.

The *X-L2P* table is maintained persistently in the flash memory of the OpenSSD development board. The most recent changes are cached in DRAM until they are committed. As shown in Figure 2, the *X-L2P* table stores an entry (t, la_p, pa_a, s) for each page p updated by an active transaction t, where la_p is the logical address of p, pa_p is the (new) physical address of p, and s is the status of transaction t. The physical address pa_p is determined by the FTL when the new content of p is written to a free page in flash memory. The value of s can be *active*, *committed* or *aborted*. Note that a new entry for page p is added to the *X-L2P* table only when p is updated for the first time. If the same page p is updated again, the existing entry is just updated with a new physical address.

Each entry in the *X-L2P* table serves dual purposes. First, it keeps track of the latest version of a page while maintaining the older but committed copy intact so that a correct version of the page can be read by concurrent transactions. Specifically, when a `read(t,p)` command is given, if t matches the transaction id of an entry of p in the *X-L2P* table, then the copy of p whose physical address in the entry is returned. Otherwise, the older committed copy is found in the *L2P* table and returned to the reader. Second, the entry of p in the *X-L2P* table prevents the latest uncommitted copy of p from being garbage-collected. When a flash memory block is picked up for garbage collection, the pages in the block are considered valid and copied into a new block if their physical addresses are found in the *X-L2P* table. That is, a page is considered invalid only when it is not found in either the *L2P* table or the *X-L2P* table.

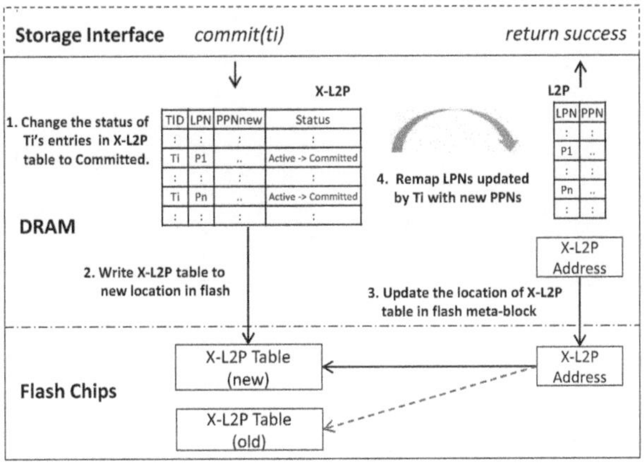

Figure 4: Commit procedure in X-FTL

When a `commit(t)` command is received (via a `trim` command), all the pages updated by t must have been written to flash memory persistently and their physical addresses must have been saved in the *X-L2P* table. Thus, the only remaining steps are to change the status field of each entry from *active* to *committed*, and flush all the entries created by t persistently to flash memory. From this moment on, transaction t is considered committed, and the *X-L2P* table entries with a *committed* status become available for reuse by other transactions. Besides, the *L2P* table is updated so that its entries point to the committed physical copies of the pages updated by t. Note that the propagation of committed changes from the *X-L2P* table to the *L2P* table is idempotent and it is the original FTL that is responsible for backing the *L2P* table up persistently in flash memory and getting prepared for crash recovery.

The *X-L2P* table can be configured to have any number of entries, but it is very small in the current implementation – either 500 entries (8KB) or 1000 entries (16KB).[3] This is because the minimum required number of entries is a few tens due to the relatively small number of concurrent transactions running for SQLite databases and each *X-L2P* entry is only 16 bytes long. Thus, when a transaction commits, the entire *X-L2P* table is written to flash memory in copy-on-write fashion. The physical location of the *X-L2P* table is kept track of by a meta-data block in flash memory reserved by an FTL. We assume that updating the physical location in the meta-data block is done atomically. The commit procedure of *X-FTL* is summarized in Figure 4.

Processing an `abort(t)` command is much simpler and done in two steps. First, for all t's entries in the *X-L2P* table, the status fields are changed from *active* to *aborted*. Second, all the corresponding pages in flash memory are invalidated.

5.4 Recovery

For the recovery of a database, we consider two types of common failures. The first type of a failure occurs when SQLite is terminated abnormally but without failing the entire system. The other type occurs when the entire system fails, for example, by a power outage.

In the first case, since the file system and *X-FTL* are still functioning normally, the system kernel can detect the file opened by a killed process. Then, using the abort logic described in Sections 5.2 and 5.3, the file system drops all the dirty pages of the file from the file system cache, and *X-FTL* rolls back all the uncommitted updates that are already written to the database file.

In the second case, on a system reboot, both the *L2P* and *X-L2P* tables are loaded from the flash memory to determine the status of transactions killed by a system crash. All the *X-FTL* table entries with a *committed* status are reflected to the *L2P* table. This operation is idempotent and the only step required to ensure durability of all recently committed transactions. Propagation of committed changes (*i.e.*, updated pages) must have been done already to the database for all committed transactions by the commit logic described in Section 5.3. For an incomplete transaction at the time of a crash, all the uncommitted changes are undone by the same abort logic described above.

6. PERFORMANCE EVALUATION

In this section, we present the performance evaluation carried out to analyze the impact of *X-FTL* on SQLite as well as a file system. To understand the impact on SQLite, we picked three different database workloads. We then ran SQLite in *rollback* and *write-ahead log* modes on top of the (unchanged) `ext4` file system with the OpenSSD board running the original FTL. We also ran the modified SQLite on top of the `ext4` file system with the changed system calls with the OpenSSD board running *X-FTL*. We included a file system benchmark to evaluate the impact of *X-FTL* on the performance of the `ext4` file system.

6.1 Experimental Setup

The OpenSSD development platform is equipped with Samsung K9LCG08U1M flash memory chips. These flash memory chips are of MLC NAND type with 8KB pages and 128 pages per block. The OpenSSD has a Barefoot controller with 87.5MHz ARM processor, and the controller contains 96KB SRAM to store the firmware and 64MB Mobile SDRAM to store metadata such as mapping tables. The version of SATA interface is 2.0 that supports 3 Gbps.

The host machine is a Linux system with 3.5.2 kernel running on Intel core i7-860 2.8GHz processor and 2GB DRAM. We used the `ext4` file system in *ordered* mode for metadata journaling when SQLite ran in *rollback* or *write-ahead log* mode. When SQLite ran on *X-FTL*, the file system journaling was turned off but the changes we added to the file system (described in Section 5.2) were enabled.

The version of SQLite used in this paper was 3.7.10, which supports both *rollback* and *write-ahead log* modes. The page size was set to 8KB to match the page size of the flash memory chips installed on the OpenSSD board.

6.2 Workloads

We used three database workloads and a file system benchmark. The database workloads are a synthetic workload, a set of traces from and a popular benchmark for Android smartphones, and the TPC-C benchmark. The Flexible I/O (FIO) was used as a file system benchmark.

[3]Most eMMC flash memory cards are equipped with 512KB SRAM, 128KB of which is used for maintaining the L2P mapping table. We believe it is not so impractical to store an *X-L2P* table of 8KB $\sim$ 16KB in the SRAM of an eMMC card.

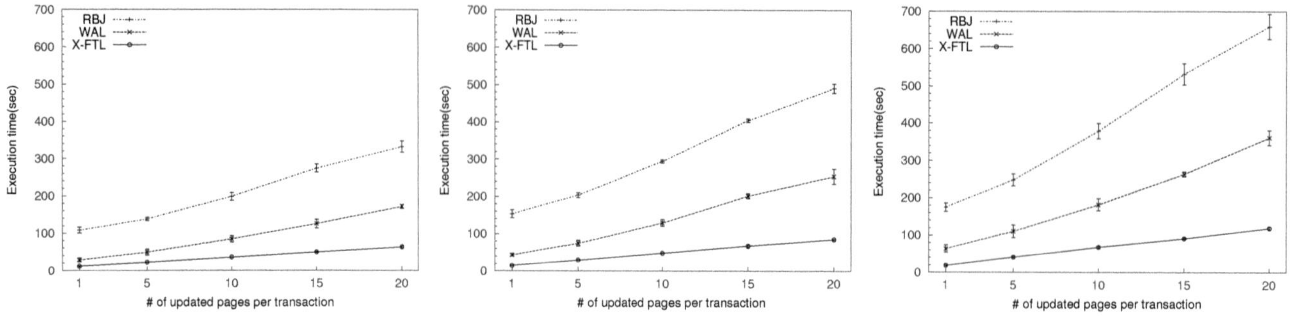

(a) GC validity 30% (b) GC validity 50% (c) GC validity 70%

Figure 5: SQLite Performance (x1,000 Synthetic Transactions)

Mode	Host-side					FTL-side			
	SQLite DB	SQLite Journal	File System	Total Counts	fsync calls	Write	Read	GC	Erase
RBJ	6,230	7,222	15,987	29,439	2,999	243,639	9,792	756	2,044
WAL	3,523	5,754	3,646	12,923	1,013	92,979	3,472	409	897
X-FTL	5,211	0	994	6,205	994	33,239	2,011	115	243

Table 1: I/O Count (# of updated pages per transaction = 5, GC validity = 50%)

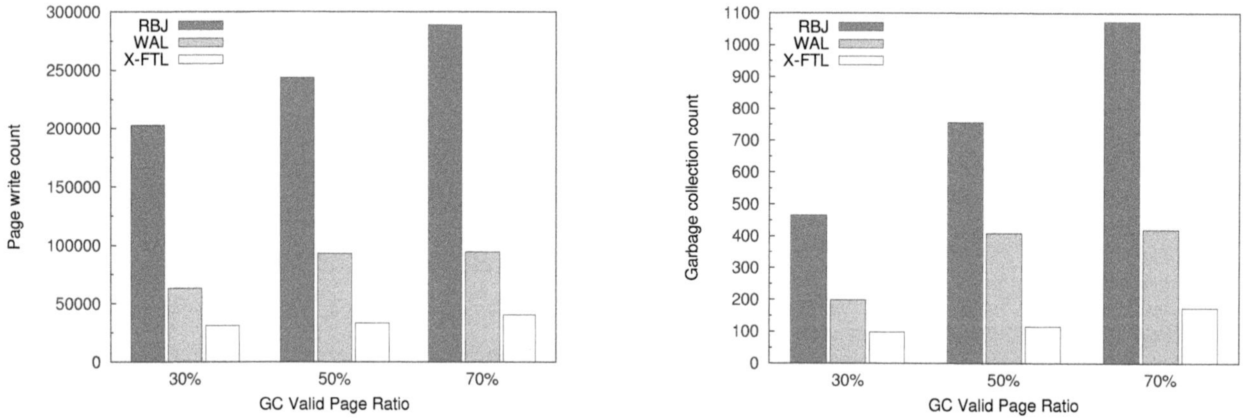

(a) Write count (b) Garbage collection count

Figure 6: I/O Activities inside OpenSSD (# of updated pages per transaction = 5)

Synthetic This workload consists of a `partsupply` table created by the `dbgen` tool of the TPC-H benchmark. This table contains 60,000 tuples of 220 bytes each. Each transaction reads a fixed number of tuples using random `partkey` values, updates the `supplycost` field of each tuple, and commits.

Android Smartphone This workload consists of traces obtained by running four popular applications on an Android 4.1.2 Jelly Bean SDK, namely, RL Benchmark [2], Gmail, Facebook, and a web browser. RL Benchmark is a popular benchmark used for performance evaluation of SQLite on Android platforms. We modified the source code of SQLite to capture all the transactions and their SQL statements.

TPC-C The DBT2 tool was used for TPC-C benchmarking with 10 warehouses [1, 14]. Two separate workloads, mix and read-intensive, were created by adjusting the ratio of five transaction types. Since the locking granularity of SQLite is a database file, the number of database connections was set to one in order to avoid frequently aborting update transactions.

File System Benchmark The Flexible I/O (FIO) benchmark is commonly used to test the performance of file and storage systems [8]. It spawns a number of threads or processes doing a particular type of I/O operations as specified by the user parameters. This benchmark was added to evaluate the effects of *X-FTL* on the random write performance of a file system.

6.3 Run-Time Performance

This section demonstrates the effectiveness of *X-FTL* by comparing the performance of SQLite with and without *X-FTL*. Similarly, the performance of `ext4` was tested with and without *X-FTL* for file system benchmark. We use the `RBJ`, `WAL` and `X-FTL` symbols to denote the execution of SQLite

	RLBenchmark	Gmail	Facebook	WebBrowser
# of database files	1	2	11	6
# of tables	3	31	72	26
# of queries	82,234	15,533	4,924	7,929
# of select queries	5,200	3,540	1,687	1,954
# of join queries	0	1,381	28	1,351
# of insert queries	51,002	7,288	2,403	1,261
# of update queries	26,000	889	430	1,813
# of delete queries	2	2,357	117	1,373
Average updated pages per transaction	3.31	4.93	2.29	2.95
# of DDL/SQLite commands	30	78	259	177

Table 2: Analysis of Android Smartphone Traces

in *rollback* mode, *write-ahead log* mode and with *X-FTL* enabled, respectively. Each performance measurement presented in this section was an average of five runs or more. The standard deviation is also presented as an error bar whenever it was large enough to be visible in the graph.

6.3.1 Synthetic workload

In the synthetic workload, we varied the number of updates requested by a transaction from one to 20, and 1,000 transactions were executed for each fixed number of updates. To evaluate the effect of garbage collections by FTL, we controlled aging of the OpenSSD flash memory chips such that the ratio of valid pages carried over by garbage collection was approximately 30%, 50% or 70%.

Figure 5 shows the elapsed times of SQLite when it ran in *rollback* or *write-ahead log* mode on the original FTL of the OpenSSD and when it ran in *off* mode on *X-FTL* under various configurations. As is shown clearly in Figure 5(b), *X-FTL* helped SQLite process transactions much faster than *write-ahead log* and *rollback* modes by 3.5 and 11.7 times. The standard deviation of elapsed times was 6.04% on average.

The considerable gain in performance was direct reflection of reductions in the number of write operations and `fsync` system calls. Recall that, with the force policy, SQLite force-writes all the updated pages when a transaction commits. Table 1 compares *rollback* and *write-ahead log* modes with *X-FTL* with respect to the number of writes and `fsync` calls. In the case of *rollback*, in particular, both numbers were very high. This is because SQLite had to create and delete a journal file for each transaction and consequently had to use `fsync` call very frequently. In *write-ahead log* mode, SQLite wrote twice as many pages as running it with *X-FTL*, because it had to write pages to both log and database files.

Table 1 drills down the I/O activities further for the case when the number of pages updated per transaction was five. In the 'Host-side' columns, we counted the number of page writes requested by SQLite and the number of metadata page writes requested by the file system separately as well as the total number of `fsync` calls. In the 'FTL-side' columns, we counted the number of pages written and read (including those copied-back internally in the flash memory chips) as well as the frequencies of garbage collection and block erase operations. Garbage collection is always done for an individual flash memory block. The block erase count includes the data blocks garbage collected and the metadata blocks erased by FTL. Figure 6 visualizes two key measurements from the 'FTL-side' column in Table 1 in bar charts: (a) the number of pages written and (b) the frequencies of garbage collection. Figures 5 and 6 show that the trend in elapsed times among the three modes is consistent with the trend in the I/O activities.

In *rollback* mode, each transaction writes 5 data pages and one header page to the journal file. This incurs two `fsync` calls, one for data pages and the other for a head page. When it commits, the transaction writes 5 data pages and one header page to the database file, which is followed by a single `fsync` call.

Similarly, in *write-ahead log* mode, each transaction writes 5 data pages and one header page to the log file. Then the transaction invokes a single `fsync` call before it commits. The propagation of the changes to the database file, however, is not done until a checkpointing operation is triggered. Since SQLite carries out checkpointing every 1,000 page writes by default, a total of five checkpointing operations were done for 1,000 transactions. The number of page writes requested for the database file was less than 5,000, because pages updated more than once are flushed to the storage only once by a checkpointing operation.

When SQLite ran with *X-FTL*, the total number of page writes requested by SQLite and the file system was about a half of that for *write-ahead log* mode, because SQLite did not have to write anything to the log file.

6.3.2 Android Smartphone Workload

The four Android smartphone traces, whose characteristics are summarized in Table 2, were replayed with SQLite on the OpenSSD board. SQLite ran in *rollback* mode, *write-ahead log* mode or *off* mode with *X-FTL*. In Figure 7, we measured the elapsed time taken by SQLite to process each workload completely. Since the performance gap between the *rollback* and *write-ahead log* modes was similar to that

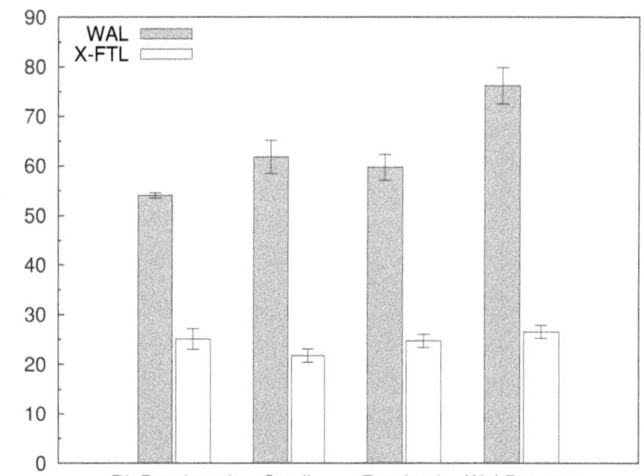

Figure 7: Smartphone Workload Performance

observed in the synthetic workload, we did not include the elapsed time of *rollback* mode for the clarity of presentation. Across all the four traces, SQLite performed 2.4 to 3.0 times faster when it ran with *X-FTL* than when it ran in *write-ahead log* mode. These results match the elapsed times and the trend of I/O activities observed in the synthetic workloads (shown in Figure 5(b) and Figure 6). The standard deviation of elapsed times was 5.02% on average.

To provide better insight into the observations, the characteristics of the traces are described below with respect to database query processing.

RL Benchmark is a write-intensive workload that consists of 13 different types of SQL statements performed on a single table with three attributes. The workload includes roughly 50,000 insertions, 5,000 selections, 25,000 updates, an index creation, and a table drop.

Gmail trace includes common operations such as saving new messages in the inbox, reading from and searching for keywords in the inbox. The Gmail application relies on SQLite to capture and store everything related to messages such as senders, receivers, label names and mail bodies in the *mailstore* database file. This trace includes a large number of insert statements. The read-write ratio was about 3 to 7 with more writes than reads.

Facebook trace was obtained from a Facebook application that reads news feed, sends messages and uploads photo files. A total of 11 files were created by the Facebook application, but `fb.db` was accessed most frequently by many SQL statements. Similarly to Gmail, this trace includes a large number of insert statements, because Facebook uses SQLite to store most of the information on the screen in a database. In addition, Facebook stores many small thumbnail images in the SQLite database as blobs. This makes the number of updates per transaction tend to be high. The read-write ratio was about 3 to 7 like the Gmail trace.

Browser trace was obtained while the Android web browser read online newspapers, surfed several portal sites and online shopping sites, and SNS sites. The web browser uses SQLite to manage the browsing history, bookmarks, the titles and thumbnails of fetched web pages. Since the URLs of all visited web pages are stored, the history table receives many update statements. In addition, cookie data are frequently inserted and deleted when web pages are accessed. Thus, the cookie table also received a large number of update statements. Among the six files the browser creates, `browser2.db` was the dominant target of most SQL statements as the main database file. Another interesting thing about this trace is that it includes quite a large number of join queries. The read-write ratio was about 4 to 6.

6.3.3 TPC-C Benchmark

By adjusting the relative frequencies of the five types of transactions, we created four separate workloads: write-intensive, read-intensive, selection-only, and join-only. Table 3 shows the configuration of each workload. The TPC-C benchmark results measured in transactions processed per minute (tpmC) are summarized in Table 4.

Transaction Types	Delivery	Order Status	Payment	Stock Level	New Order
Write-intensive	4%	4%	43%	4%	45%
Read-intensive	0%	50%	0%	45%	5%
Selection-only	0%	100%	0%	0%	0%
Join-only	0%	0%	0%	100%	0%

Table 3: TPC-C Workloads

(measured in tpmC)	Write intensive	Read intensive	Selection only	Join only
WAL	251	3,942	281,856	35,662
X-FTL	582	9,925	277,586	35,888

Table 4: TPC-C Performance

In the write-intensive workload, each transaction updates two pages on average. The performance gap between *X-FTL* and *write-ahead log* mode was not as wide as what was observed in the synthetic workload, which is purely update only, but the gain in the transaction throughput was still considerable. SQLite with *X-FTL* achieved about 130 percent higher transaction throughput than SQLite in *write-ahead log* mode.

In the read-intensive workload, the results were somewhat surprising. The performance gap was even higher in the read-intensive workload. With *X-FTL*, SQLite achieved about 152 percent improvement in transaction throughput than running in *write-ahead log* mode. This was due to the additional overhead incurred for SQLite to retrieve the most recent version of a page requested by each read. When it ran in *write-ahead log* mode, for each page to read, SQLite had to access the *write-ahead log* to find the most recent version. If it is not found in the *write-ahead log*, then it needs to be read from the database file. This is a well known problem common in the database systems that maintain multiple versions of a data page. This also clearly demonstrates the advantage of *X-FTL*, which allows SQLite to run in *off* mode without the burden of maintaining and accessing a log file.

In the selection-only or join-only workload, the performance of SQLite in *write-ahead log* mode and with *X-FTL* was comparable. This is obviously because, with no pages updated, SQLite did not have to read from or write into the log file. Since SQLite uses the nested-loop join algorithm, it does not create any temporary file for intermediate result.

6.3.4 File System Benchmark

As is described in Section 4, *X-FTL* supports atomic update propagation not only for SQLite but also for other applications such as a file system. We used the FIO benchmark (version 2.0.10) to evaluate the effects of *X-FTL* on the random write performance of a file system.

In this experiment, the average write IOPS was measured while a single thread updated data pages in a 4GB file randomly for 600 seconds. The size of a page was 8KB. An `fsync` system call was invoked every 1, 5, 10, 15, or 20 page writes to mimic the different sizes of transactions in the synthetic workload. In each test case, the `ext4` file system ran in *ordered* journaling mode (for metadata only), in *full* journaling mode (for both data and metadata), or in *off* mode with *X-FTL* enabled. Their throughput measured in IOPS is shown in Figure 8.

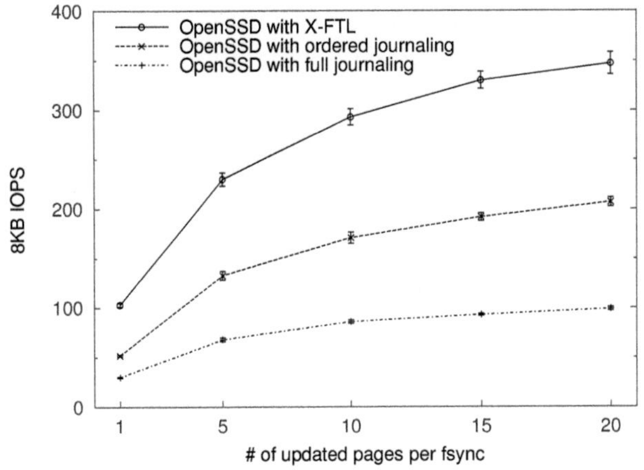

Figure 8: FIO Benchmark with a Single Thread

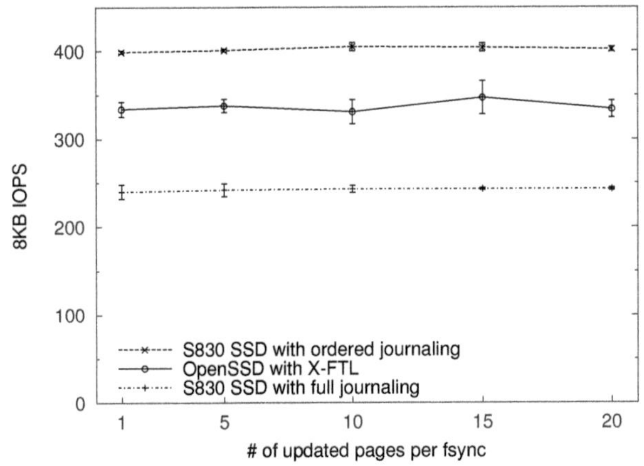

Figure 9: FIO Benchmark: *X-FTL* vs. S830 SSD (with 16 Concurrent Threads)

The IO throughput increased steadily in all the three cases as the `fsync` interval increased, obviously because less frequent `fsync` calls lowered the overhead of force-write operations. More importantly, the `ext4` file system with *X-FTL* achieved the highest IO throughput consistently across all `fsync` intervals by about 67 to 99% and 240 to 254% over the ordered and full journaling, respectively. The standard deviation was 2.34% on average. The full journaling guarantees the atomicity of page writes at the expense of writing each data page twice. The ordered journaling writes a data page only once but does not guarantee the atomicity of page writes. Besides, it requires two write barriers to guarantee the write order of data pages and metadata [22]. On a flash based storage device including OpenSSD, a write barrier command stores the mapping table as well as data pages persistently in flash memory chips. On the other hand, *X-FTL* invokes a commit command once as part of a `fsync` system call, which plays the same role as a write barrier. Therefore, the cost of an additional write of mapping table to flash memory contributed to the gap in IOPS between *X-FTL* and the *ordered* journaling.

To put the results from the OpenSSD development board in perspective, we repeated the same file system benchmark with an MLC based SSD, Samsung S830 (128GB), with 16 concurrent threads. Figure 9 shows the I/O throughput of S830 in ordered and full journaling modes as well as the I/O throughput of OpenSSD with *X-FTL*. In comparison with the results shown in Figure 8, the I/O throughput of OpenSSD was less than 25% and higher than 35% that of S830 in ordered and full journaling modes, respectively. This should not be surprising given that the controller of OpenSSD is at least one generation older than that of S830. The standard deviation was 2.00% on average in this experiment.

In summary, *X-FTL* achieves the level of consistency that can be achieved by a file system operating in full journaling mode at the cost even lower than that of ordered journaling mode.

6.4 Recovery Performance

In order to evaluate recovery performance, the OpenSSD board was turned off while SQLite was executing the synthetic workloads presented in Section 6.3.1. This test was repeated in *rollback*, *write-ahead log*, and *X-FTL* modes to examine the impact of the three execution modes on the recovery time of SQLite. We measured the time taken to restart the SQLite database in each mode.

mode	*Rollback*	*Write-ahead log*	*X-FTL*
(msec)	20.1	153.0	3.5

Table 5: SQLite Restart Time

Table 5 presents the average recovery times of three modes. For each mode, we took the average of restart times measured from five separate runs. The restart time given in Table 5 includes the time taken by SQLite to recover the database in each mode. Note that it does not include the common time taken by the OpenSSD to recover its FTL data structures (for example, the *L2P* table) and the time taken by the file system to remount the OpenSSD device. We observed the time taken by each step using a debugging tool attached to the OpenSSD.

In the case of *rollback* mode, the recovery time includes the time taken to carry out two steps. The first is to copy the old versions of pages updated by active transactions from the *rollback* journal file, if exists, to the original database file. The second is to delete the *rollback* file for undo purpose. The number of pages to be copied in this experiment was approximately ten.

In the case of *write-ahead log* mode, the recovery time includes the time taken to copy the latest copies of pages updated by committed transactions from a *write-ahead log* file to the original database file. Because the *write-ahead log* file is sized to one thousand pages by default, the recovery time in *write-ahead log* mode (153.0 milliseconds) was much longer than that in *rollback* mode (20.1 milliseconds).

Since only one SQLite database was updated in the experiment, the recovery times observed in *rollback* and *write-ahead log* modes represent the time to recover the database when accessed for the first time after the crash. If multiple databases were running at failure time, each database needs to be recovered individually.

In the case of *X-FTL* mode, the recovery steps include loading the *X-L2P* table and reflecting the *X-L2P* table entries with a *committed* status to the *L2P* table. All these steps took only about 3.5 milliseconds. The restart time of *X-FTL* was much shorter, because it did not involve copying any data page from the database or log file.

7. CONCLUSION

Considering the increasing popularity of SQLite in smartphone applications, improving the I/O efficiency of SQLite is a practical and critical problem that need be addressed immediately. This paper proposes a novel transactional FTL called *X-FTL*, which can efficiently support atomic propagation of multiple pages updated by transactional applications (*e.g.*, SQLite databases and file systems) to a flash memory storage device. The existing solutions such as running SQLite in *rollback* or *write-ahead log* mode and relying on the full journaling of `ext4` file system are essentially equivalent in that they are based on data journaling and managing the journal data is done by a host system.

X-FTL can relieve the host system of the burden of guaranteeing the transactional atomicity. *X-FTL* offloads the responsibility to the flash storage layer. By taking advantage of a copy-on-write mechanism adopted by existing FTLs, *X-FTL* implements all-or-nothing propagation of multiple pages without resorting to the costly journaling schemes. Therefore, *X-FTL* halves the amount of data to be written to the storage, and doubles the transactional performance and the life span of flash storage.

We have implemented *X-FTL* on an SSD development platform called OpenSSD by enhancing its FTL code with the *X-FTL* features. We have modified SQLite and *ext4* file system to take advantage of *X-FTL* with only minimal changes in their code. Using a comprehensive set of synthetic and real workloads for SQLite databases and file systems, we have demonstrated that *X-FTL* achieves a significant improvement in transaction performance.

8. ACKNOWLEDGMENTS

This research was supported in part by National Research Foundation of Korea(NRF) (2012R1A1A2A10044300, No.2010-0026511, No.2012-0006423), the IT R&D program of MKE/KEIT [10041244, SmartTV 2.0 Software Platform], and the IT/SW creative research program of MKE/NIPA (A-2012- H0505-12-1013). This work was also supported by Research Resettlement Fund for the new faculty of SNU.

9. REFERENCES

[1] OSDL Database Test 2(DBT-2). `http://osdldbt.sourceforge.net`.

[2] RL Benchmark:SQLite. `http://redlicense.com/`.

[3] OpenSSD Project. `http://goo.gl/JOTs5`, 2011.

[4] Atomic Commit In SQLite. `http://www.sqlite.org/atomiccommit.html`, 2012.

[5] Embedded Multi-Media Card (eMMC), Electrical Standard (4.5.1). `http://www.jedec.org`, Jun 2012.

[6] Write-Ahead Logging. `http://www.sqlite.org/wal.html`, 2012.

[7] YAFFS: A NAND-Flash Filesystem. `http://www.yaffs.net/`, 2012.

[8] J. Axboe. FIO (Flexible IO Tester). `http://git.kernel.dk/?p=fio.git;a=summary`.

[9] A. Ban. Flash file system, Apr 1995. US Patent 5,404,485.

[10] V. Chidambaram, T. Sharma, A. C. Arpaci-Dusseau, and R. H. Arpaci-Dusseau. Consistency Without Ordering. In *Proceedings of USENIX conference on File and Storage Technologies (FAST '12)*, pages 101–116, 2012.

[11] H. Kim, N. Agrawal, and C. Ungureanu. Revisiting storage for smartphones. In *Proceedings of USENIX conference on File and Storage Technologies (FAST'12)*, 2012.

[12] K. Lee and Y. Won. Smart Layers and Dumb Result: IO Characterization of an Android-Based Smartphone. In *Proceedings of ACM EMSOFT*, pages 23–32, 2012.

[13] S.-W. Lee, D.-J. Park, T.-S. Chung, D.-H. Lee, S. Park, and H.-J. Song. A Log Buffer-based Flash Translation Layer using Fully-associative Sector Translation. *ACM Transactions on Embedded Computing Systems*, 6(3):18, 2007.

[14] S. T. Leutenegger and D. Dias. A Modeling Study of the TPC-C Benchmark. In *Proceedings of ACM SIGMOD*, pages 22–31, 1993.

[15] R. A. Lorie. Physical Integrity in a Large Segmented Database. *ACM Transactions on Database Systems*, 2(1):91–104, Mar 1977.

[16] C. Mohan. Disk Read-Write Optimizations and Data Integrity in Transaction Systems Using Write-Ahead Logging. In *Proceedings of ICDE*, pages 324–331, 1995.

[17] X. Ouyang, D. W. Nellans, R. Wipfel, D. Flynn, and D. K. Panda. Beyond Block I/O: Rethinking Traditional Storage Primitives. In *Proceedings of International Conference on High-Performance Computer Architecture (HPCA '11)*, pages 301–311, 2011.

[18] S. Park, J. H. Yu, and S. Y. Ohm. Atomic Write FTL for Robust Flash File System. In *Proceedings of the Ninth International Symposium on Consumer Electronics (ISCE 2005)*, pages 155 – 160, Jun 2005.

[19] V. Prabhakaran, A. C. Arpaci-Dusseau, and R. H. Arpaci-Dusseau. Analysis and Evolution of Journaling File Systems. In *Proceedings of USENIX Annual Technical Conference*, pages 105–120, 2005.

[20] V. Prabhakaran, T. L. Rodeheffer, and L. Zhou. Transactional Flash. In *Proceedings of Symposium on Operating Systems Design and Implementation (OSDI)*, pages 147–160, 2008.

[21] M. Rosenblum and J. K. Ousterhout. The Design and Implementation of a Log-Structured File System. *ACM Transactions on Computer Systems*, 10(1):26–52, Feb 1992.

[22] M. Steigerwald. Working with Write Barriers and Journaling File Systems. Imposing Order. *Linux Journal*, May 2007.

[23] A. Sweeney, D. Doucette, W. Hu, C. Anderson, M. Nishimoto, and G. Peck. Scalability in the XFS File System. In *Proceedings of USENIX Annual Technical Conference*, pages 1–14, 1996.

[24] S. C. Tweedie. Journaling the Linux ext2fs File System. In *Proceedings of Annual Linux Expo (LinuxExpo '98)*, 1998.

[25] D. Woodhouse. JFFS: The Journaling Flash File System. In *Proceedings of the Ottawa Linux Symposium*, 2001.

Optimal Splitters for Temporal and Multi-version Databases

Wangchao Le[1] Feifei Li[1] Yufei Tao[2,3] Robert Christensen[1]
[1]University of Utah [2]Chinese University of Hong Kong [3]Korea Advanced Institute of Science and Technology
{lew, lifeifei}@cs.utah.edu taoyf@cse.cuhk.edu.hk robertc@eng.utah.edu

ABSTRACT

Temporal and multi-version databases are ideal candidates for a distributed store, which offers large storage space, and parallel and distributed processing power from a cluster of (commodity) machines. A key challenge is to achieve a good load balancing algorithm for storage and processing of these data, which is done by partitioning the database. We introduce the concept of *optimal splitters* for temporal and multi-version databases, which induce a partition of the input data set, and guarantee that the size of the maximum bucket be minimized among all possible configurations, given a budget for the desired number of buckets. We design efficient methods for memory- and disk-resident data respectively, and show that they significantly outperform competing baseline methods both theoretically and empirically on large real data sets.

Categories and Subject Descriptors

H.2.4 [**Information Systems**]: Database Management – *Systems*

Keywords

Optimal splitters, temporal data, multi-version databases

1. INTRODUCTION

Increasingly, user applications request the storage and processing of historical values in a database, to support various auditing, provenance, mining, and querying operations for better decision making. Given the fast development in distributed and parallel processing frameworks, applications can now afford collecting, storing, and processing large amounts of multi-versioned or temporal values from a long-running history. Naturally, it leads to the development of multi-version databases and temporal databases. In these databases, an object o is associated with multiple disjoint temporal intervals in the form $[s, e]$, each of which is associated with the valid value(s) of o during the period of $[s, e]$.

Consider two specific examples as shown in Figure 1. Figure 1(a) shows a multi-version database [6, 17], and Figure 1(b) shows a temporal database, where each object is represented by a piecewise linear function. A multi-version database keeps all the historical values of an object. A new interval with a new value is created whenever an update or an insertion to an object has occurred. An existing interval with a (now) old value terminates when an item has been deleted or updated.

On the other hand, for large temporal or time-series data, we can represent the value of a temporal object as an arbitrary function $f : \mathbb{R} \rightarrow \mathbb{R}$ (time to value). In general, for arbitrary temporal data, f can be expensive to describe and process. In practice, applications often approximate f using a piecewise linear function g [3, 7, 13]. The problem of approximating an arbitrary function f by a piecewise linear function g has been extensively studied (see [3, 7, 13, 19] and references therein). Other functions can be used for approximation as well, such as a piece-wise polynomial function, for better approximation quality. The key observations are: 1) more intervals lead to better approximation quality, but also are more expensive to represent; 2) adaptive methods, by allocating more intervals to regions of high volatility and less to smoother regions, are better than non-adaptive methods with a fixed segmentation interval.

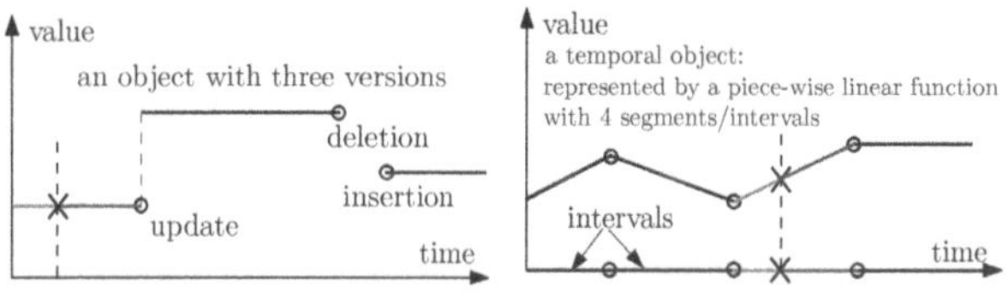

(a) Multi-version database. (b) Temporal database.

Figure 1: Databases with Intervals.

How to approximate f with g is beyond the scope of this paper, and we assume that the data has already been converted to a set of intervals, where each interval is associated with a mapping function (piece-wise linear, or piece-wise polynomial) by *any* segmentation method. In particular, we require *neither* them having the same number of intervals *nor* them having the aligned starting/ending time instances for intervals from different objects. Thus it is possible that the data is collected from a variety of sources after each applying different preprocessing modules.

Lastly, large interval data may also be produced by any time-based or range-based partitioning of an object, such as a log file or a spatial object, from a big data set.

That said, we observe that in the aforementioned applications users often have to deal with big interval data. Meanwhile, storing and processing big data in a cluster of (commodity) machines, to tap the power of parallel and distributed computation, is becoming increasingly important. Therefore, storing and processing the large number of intervals in a distributed store is a paramount concern, in enabling the above applications to leverage the storage space and the computation power from a cluster.

Since most analytical tasks and user queries concerning interval data in a multi-version or temporal database are time-based, e.g.,

SIGMOD'13, June 22–27, 2013, New York, New York, USA.

find the object ids with valid values in $[50, 100]$ at time-instance t, the general intuition is to partition the input data set into a set of buckets based on their time-stamps. Intervals from one bucket are then stored in one node and processed by one core from a cluster of (commodity) machines. By doing so, user queries or transactions concerning a time instance or a time range can be answered in selected node(s) and core(s) independently without incurring excessive communication, which also dramatically improves the spatial and temporal locality of caching in query processing.

A challenge is to achieve load-balancing in this process, i.e., no single node and core should be responsible for storing and processing too many intervals. In particular, *given the number of buckets to create, the size of the maximum bucket should be minimized.* This is similar to the concept of *optimal splitters* in databases with points [21] or array data sets [14, 18]. However, the particular nature of interval data sets introduces significant new challenges.

Specifically, a partitioning boundary (known as a splitter) may split an interval into two intervals. As a result, buckets on both sides of a splitter need to contain an interval that intersects with a splitter; see examples in Figure 1 where the dashed line with a cross represents a splitter. Furthermore, intervals from different objects may overlap with each other, which complicates the problem of finding the optimal splitters. Finally, a good storage scheme should also be capable to handle ad-hoc updates gracefully. In contrast, in a point or array data set, any element from the original data set will only lead to one element in one of the buckets; and elements do not overlap with each other.

Our contributions. Given n objects with a total of N intervals from all objects, and a user-defined budget k for the number of buckets to create, a baseline solution is a dynamic programming formulation with a cost of $O(kN^2)$. However, this solution is clearly not scalable for large data sets. Our goal is to design I/O and computation efficient algorithms that work well regardless if data fits in main memory or not. A design principle we have followed is to leverage on existing indexing structures whenever possible (so these methods can be easily adopted in practice). Specifically, we make the following contributions:

- We formulate the problem of finding optimal splitters for large interval data in Section 2.
- We present a baseline method using a dynamic programming formulation in Section 3.
- We design efficient methods for memory-resident data in Section 4. Our best method finds optimal splitters of a data set for any budget values k in only $O(N \log N)$ cost.
- We investigate external memory methods for large disk-based data in Section 5. Our best method finds optimal splitters of a data set for any budget value k in only $O(\frac{N}{B} \log_{M/B} \frac{N}{B})$ IOs, where B is the block size and M is the memory size.
- We extend our methods to work for the queryable version of the optimal splitters problem in Section 6, where k is the query parameter. We also discuss how to make our methods dynamic to handle ad-hoc updates in Section 6.
- We examine the efficiency of the proposed methods with extensive experiments in Section 7, where large real data sets with hundreds of millions of intervals were tested.

We survey related work in Section 8, and conclude in Section 9.

2. PROBLEM FORMULATION

Let the database D be a set of objects. Each object has an *interval attribute* (e.g., time) whose universe U is the real domain representable in a computer. An object's interval attribute contains a sequence of non-overlapping intervals, as demonstrated in Figure 1. Given an interval $[s, e]$, we refer to both s and e as its *endpoints*, and s (e) as its *starting (ending) value.* Although the intervals from one object are disjoint, the intervals of different objects may overlap. Let N be the total number of intervals from *all* objects in D. Denote by I the set of these N intervals.

The objective is to partition I into smaller sets so that they can be stored and processed in a distributed and parallel fashion. A *size-k partition P over I*, denoted as $P(I, k)$, is defined as follows:

1. P contains m *splitters*, where $0 \le m \le k$. Each splitter is a vertical line that is orthogonal to the interval dimension at a *distinct* value $\ell \in U$. We will use ℓ to denote the splitter itself when there is no confusion. Let the splitters in P be $\ell_1, \dots, \ell_m$ in ascending order, and for convenience, also define $\ell_0 = -\infty$, $\ell_{m+1} = \infty$. These splitters induce $m+1$ buckets $\{b_1, \dots, b_{m+1}\}$ over I, where b_i $(1 \le i \le m+1)$ represents the interval $[\ell_{i-1}, \ell_i]$.
2. If $s \ne e$, an interval $[s, e]$ of I is assigned to a bucket b_i $(1 \le i \le m+1)$, if $[s, e]$ has an intersection of *non-zero length* with the interval of b_i. That is, the intersection cannot be a point (which has a zero length).

   If $s = e$, $[s, e]$ degenerates into a point, in which case we assign $[s, e]$ to the bucket whose interval contains it. In the special case where $s = \ell_i$ for some $i \in [1, m]$ (i.e., the point lies at a splitter), we follow the convention that $[s, e]$ is assigned to b_{i+1}.
3. We will regard b_i as a set, consisting of the intervals assigned to it. The size of bucket b_i, denoted as $|b_i|$, gives the number of such intervals.

Define the *cost of a partition P* with buckets $b_1, \dots, b_{m+1}$ as the size of its maximum bucket:

$$c(P) = \max\{|b_1|, \dots, |b_{m+1}|\}. \tag{1}$$

Since the goal is to partition I for storage and processing in distributed and parallel frameworks, a paramount concern is to achieve load-balancing, towards which a common objective is to minimize the maximum load on any node, so that there is no single bottleneck in the system. The same principle has been used for finding optimal splitters in partitioning points [21] and array datasets [14, 18]. That said, an optimal partition for I is formally defined as follows.

Definition 1 An optimal partition of size k for I is a partition $P^*(I, k)$ with the smallest cost, *i.e.*,

$$P^*(I, k) = \underset{P \in \mathcal{P}(I,k)}{\operatorname{argmin}}\ c(P) \tag{2}$$

where $\mathcal{P}(I, k)$ is the set of all the size-k partitions over I.

$P^*(I, k)$ is thus referred to as an *optimal partition.* If multiple partitions have the same optimal cost, $P^*(I, k)$ may represent any one of them. In what follows, when the context is clear, we use P^* and P to represent $P^*(I, k)$ and $P(I, k)$, respectively.

Note that it is an equivalent definition if one defines $P(I, k)$ in step 2 such that, bucket b_i gets assigned only the *intersection* of $[s, e]$ with b_i – namely, only a *portion* of $[s, e]$ is assigned to b_i, instead of the entire $[s, e]$. This, however, does not change the number of intervals stored at b_i, which therefore gives rise to the same partitioning problem. Keeping $[s, e]$ entirely in b_i permits conceptually cleaner and simpler discussion (because it removes the need of remembering to take intersection). Hence, we will stick to this problem definition in presenting our solutions.

Consider the example from Figure 2, where I contains 9 intervals from 3 objects. When $k = 2$, the optimal splitters are $\{\ell_1, \ell_2\}$,

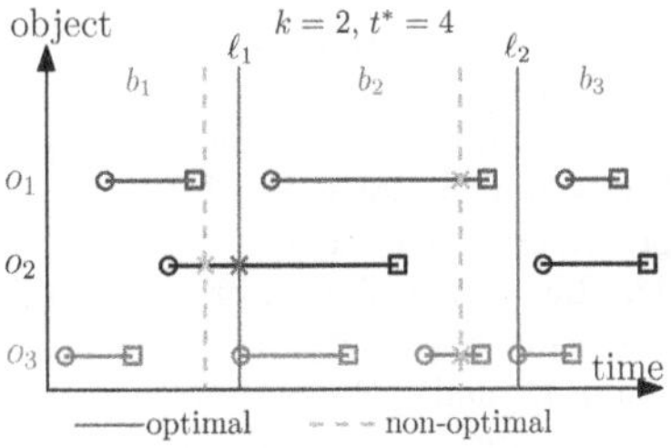

Figure 2: An example.

which yields 3 buckets b_1, b_2, b_3 with 3, 4, and 3 intervals respectively; hence, $c(P^*) = 4$. An alternative partition of 2 splitters is also shown in Figure 2 with dashed lines. It induces 3 buckets with 3, 4, and 5 intervals, so its cost 5 is worse than the aforementioned optimal partition. Note that we use t^* to represent $c(P^*)$.

Depending on whether k is given apriori or not, there are two versions of the optimal splitters problem. In the first case, k is fixed and given at the same time with the input set I. This fits the scenario where the number of nodes/cores in a cluster available for processing I is already known. In the second case, a user is not certain yet how many nodes/cores should be deployed. Thus, he/she wants to explore the cost of the optimal partition for different budget values of k. In this case, k is unknown, and we are allowed to pre-process I in order to quickly find the optimal splitters for any subsequent queries over I with different k values. Formally:

Problem 1 *The static interval splitters problem is to find P^* and $c(P^*)$ for an interval set I and a fixed budget value k.*

Problem 2 *The queryable interval splitters problem is to find P^* and $c(P^*)$ over an interval set I, for any value k that is supplied at the query time as a query parameter.*

Clearly, any solution to the queryable version can be applied to settle the static version, and vice versa (by treating I and k as a new problem instance each time a different k is supplied). However, such brute-force adaptation is unlikely to be efficient in either case. To understand why, first note that, in Problem 2, the key is to pre-process I into a suitable structure so that all subsequent queries can be answered fast (the pre-processing cost is *not* a part of a query's overhead). In Problem 1, however, such preprocessing cost must be counted in an algorithm's overall running time, and can be unworthy because we only need to concentrate on a single k, thus potentially avoiding much of the computation in the preprocessing aforementioned (which must target all values of k).

We investigate the static problem in Sections 3, 4, and 5, and the queryable problem in Section 6. In the queryable problem, handling updates in I becomes an important issue, and presents additional challenges, which are also tackled in Section 6.

3. A BASELINE METHOD

Let us denote the N intervals in I as $[s_1, e_1], \ldots, [s_N, e_N]$. Suppose, without loss of generality, that $s_1 \leq \ldots \leq s_N$. Let $S(I) = \{s_1, \ldots, s_N\}$, *i.e.*, the set of starting values of the intervals in I. When I is clear from the context, we simply write $S(I)$ as S.

Where to place splitters? For any splitter ℓ, denote by $\ell(1)$ the splitter that is placed at the smallest starting value in S that is larger than or equal to ℓ. If no such starting value exists, $\ell(1)$ is undefined. Note that if ℓ itself is a starting value, $\ell(1) = \ell$.

It turns out that, to minimize the cost of a partition over I, it suffices to place splitters only at the values in S. This is formally stated in the next two lemmas:

Lemma 1 *Consider any partition P with distinct splitters $\ell_1, \ldots, \ell_m$ in ascending order, such that $\ell_m(1)$ is undefined. Let P' be a partition with splitters $\ell_1, \ldots, \ell_{m-1}$. Then, it always holds that $c(P') = c(P)$.*

PROOF. Let b_m and b_{m+1} be the last two buckets in P (which are separated by ℓ_m), and b'_m be the last bucket of P' (which is to the right of ℓ_m). When $\ell_m(1)$ is undefined, there are no new intervals starting to the right of ℓ_m. Hence, it is not hard to show that $b_{m+1} \subseteq b_m = b'_m$. This proves the lemma because all the other buckets in P exist directly in P'. □

If s_{max} is the largest starting value in S, the above lemma suggests that we can drop all those splitters greater than s_{max} without affecting the cost of the partition. Hence, it does not pay off to have such splitters.

Lemma 2 *Consider any partition P with distinct splitters $\ell_1, \ldots, \ell_m$ in ascending order, such that $\ell_m(1)$ exists. Let ℓ_i be the largest splitter that does not belong to S (i.e., $\ell_j \in S$ for all $j < i \leq m$). Define P' as a partition with splitters*

- *$\ell_1, \ldots, \ell_{i-1}, \ell_i(1), \ell_{i+1}, \ldots \ell_m$, if $\ell_i(1) \neq \ell_{i+1}$;*
- *$\ell_1, \ldots, \ell_{i-1}, \ell_{i+1}, \ldots \ell_m$, otherwise.*

Then, it always holds that $c(P') \leq c(P)$.

PROOF. We consider only the first bullet because the case of the second bullet is analogous. Let b_i (b_{i+1}) be the bucket in P that is on the left (right) of ℓ_i. Similarly, let b'_i (b'_{i+1}) be the bucket in P' that is on the left (right) of $\ell_i(1)$. We will show that $b'_i \subseteq b_i$ and $b'_{i+1} \subseteq b_{i+1}$, whose correctness implies $c(P') \leq c(P)$, because all the other buckets in P still exist in P', and vice versa.

We prove only $b'_i \subseteq b_i$ because a similar argument validates $b'_{i+1} \subseteq b_{i+1}$. Given an interval $[s, e]$ assigned to b'_i, we will show that it must have been assigned to b_i, too. Note that, by definition of $\ell_i(1)$, *no starting value can exist in* $[\ell_i, \ell_i(1))$. This means that $s < \ell_i$ because s would not be assigned to b'_i if $s = \ell_i(1)$.

If $s = e$, then s must fall in $[\ell_{i-1}, \ell_i)$, which means that s is also assigned to b_i. On the other hand, if $s \neq e$, a part of $[s, e]$ needs to intersect (ℓ_{i-1}, ℓ_i) so that $[s, e]$ can have intersection of non-zero length with b'_i. This means that $[s, e]$ also has non-zero-length intersection with b_i, and therefore, is assigned to b_i. □

This shows that if a partition has a splitter that is not in S, we can always "snap" the splitter to a value in S, without increasing the cost of the partition (may decrease the cost of the partition).

Dynamic programming. Given a splitter ℓ, we define $I^-(\ell)$, $I^+(\ell)$, and $I^o(\ell)$ as the subset of intervals in I whose starting values are less than, greater than, and equal to ℓ, respectively:

$$\begin{aligned} I^-(\ell) &= \{[s_i, e_i] \in I \mid s_i < \ell\} \\ I^+(\ell) &= \{[s_i, e_i] \in I \mid s_i > \ell\} \\ I^o(\ell) &= \{[s_i, e_i] \in I \mid s_i = \ell\}. \end{aligned}$$

An interval $[s, e]$ is said to *strongly cover* a splitter ℓ if $s < \ell < e$ (note that both inequalities are strict). Let $I^\times(\ell)$ be the subset of intervals from I that strongly cover ℓ:

$$I^\times(\ell) = \{[s_i, e_i] \in I \mid s_i < \ell < e_i\}.$$

The following fact paves the way to a dynamic programming algorithm solving Problem 1:

Lemma 3 *If $k = 0$, $c(P^*(I, k)) = |I|$. For $k \geq 1$, $c(P^*(I, k)) =$*

$$\min\left\{|I|,\ \min_{\ell \in S}\{\max\{c(P^*(I^-(\ell), k-1)), \lambda\}\}\right\}. \quad (3)$$

where $\lambda = |I^o(\ell)| + |I^+(\ell)| + |I^\times(\ell)|$.

PROOF. The case of $k = 0$ is obvious, so we concentrate on $k \geq 1$. A partition of size-k over I is allowed to use m splitters, where m ranges from 0 to k. If $m = 0$, then apparently the partition has cost $|I|$. The rest of the proof considers $m \geq 1$.

Lemmas 1 and 2 indicate that it suffices to consider partitions where all splitters fall in S. Let us fix a starting value $x \in S$. Consider an arbitrary partition $P(I, k)$ *whose last splitter ℓ is at position x*. Let $m \in [1, k]$ be the number of splitters in $P(I, k)$. Let $P(I^-(x), k-1)$ represent the partition over $I^-(x)$ with the first $m-1$ splitters of $P(I, k)$. Denote by $b'_1, ..., b'_m$ the buckets of $P(I^-(x), k-1)$ in ascending order.

Let $b_1, ..., b_{m+1}$ be the buckets of $P(I, k)$ in ascending order. As $P(I, k)$ shares the first $m-1$ splitters with $P(I^-(x), k-1)$, we know $b_i = b'_i$ for $1 \leq i \leq m-1$. Next, we will prove:

- Fact 1: $b_m = b'_m$
- Fact 2: $|b_m + 1| = |I^o(x)| + |I^+(x)| + |I^\times(x)|$.

These facts indicate:

$$\begin{aligned} c(P(I,k)) &= \max\{|b_1|, ..., |b_{m+1}|\} \\ &= \max\{|b'_1|, ..., |b'_m|, |b_{m+1}|\} \\ &= \max\{c(P(I^-(x), k-1)), |b_{m+1}|\} \\ &\geq \max\{c(P^*(I^-(x), k-1)), |b_{m+1}|\} \end{aligned}$$

where the equality can be achieved by using an optimal partition $P^*(I^-(x), k-1)$ to replace $P(I^-(x), k-1)$. Then, the lemma follows by minimizing $c(P(I, k))$ over all possible x.

Proof of Fact 1. We will prove only $b_m \subseteq b'_m$ because a similar argument proves $b'_m \subseteq b_m$. Let $[x', x]$ be the interval of b_m. Accordingly, the interval of b'_m is $[x', \infty)$. Consider an interval $[s, e]$ of I that is assigned to b_m. If $s = e$, then it must hold that $x' \leq s < x$ (note that $s \neq x$; otherwise, $[s, e]$ is assigned to b_{m+1}), which means that $[s, e] \in I^-(x)$, and hence, $[s, e]$ is assigned to b'_m. On the other hand, if $s \neq e$, then $[s, e]$ has a non-zero-length intersection with $[x', x]$, implying that $[s, e]$ intersects (x', x). Hence, $s < x$, and $[s, e]$ has a non-zero-length intersection with $[x', \infty)$. This proves that $[s, e]$ is also assigned to b'_m.

Proof of Fact 2. By definition, an interval $[s, e]$ in I is assigned to b_{m+1} in three disjoint scenarios: 1) $s > x$, 2) strongly covers x, and 3) $s = x$. The numbers of intervals in these scenarios are given precisely by $I^+(x)$, $I^\times(x)$, and $I^o(x)$, respectively. □

We are now ready to clarify our dynamic programming algorithm, which aims to fill in an N by k matrix, as shown in Figure 3. Cell $[i, j]$ (at the i-th row, j-th column) records the optimal cost for a sub-problem $c(P^*(I(i), j))$, where $I(i)$ denotes the set of intervals in I with ids 1, ..., i (we index intervals in I in ascending order of their starting values, break ties first by ascending order of their ending values, and then arbitrarily). Thus, Cell $[i, j]$ represents the optimal cost of partitioning $I(i)$ using up to j splitters.

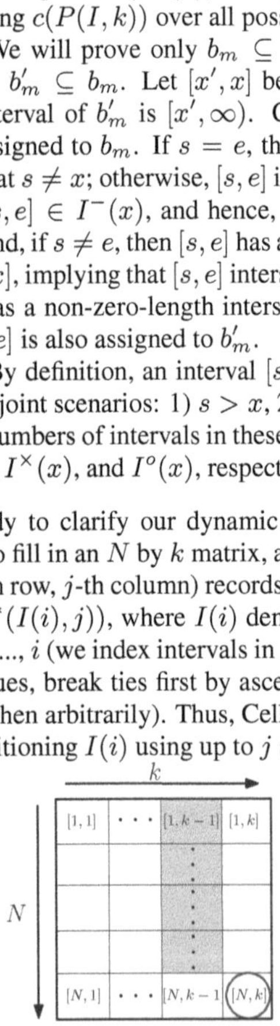

Figure 3: The DP method.

Specifically, we fill the matrix starting from the top-left corner to the bottom-right corner. To fill the cost in Cell $[i, j]$, according to Lemma 3, the last splitter in a partition $P(I(i), j)$ may be placed at any value in $\{s_1, ..., s_i\}$. Hence, one needs to check $i-1$ cells from the $(j-1)$-th column, i.e., from $[1, j-1]$ to $[i-1, j-1]$. For instance, in Figure 3, to find the value for the cell $[N, k]$, we need to check $N-1$ cells from the previous column (the gray cells). We refer to this approach as the *DP* method.

The above algorithm can be slightly extended in the straightforward manner to remember also the partitions found, so that the DP method outputs both P^* and $c(P^*)$.

Cost analysis. Sorting I by starting values takes $O(N \log N)$ time. Next, we focus on the cost of DP. Given a splitter ℓ_j, using ideas to be explained in Section 4, we can determine λ in $O(1)$ time with the help of a structure that can be built in $O(N \log N)$ time. Hence, to fill in Cell $[i, j]$, it requires to check $i-1$ cells in the preceding column plus $O(1)$ cost for obtaining λ. Completing an entire column thus incurs $O(\sum_{i=1}^{N} i) = O(N^2)$ time. As k columns need to be filled, the overall running time is $O(kN^2)$.

4. INTERNAL MEMORY METHODS

The DP method clearly does not scale well with the database size N due to its quadratic complexity. In this section, we develop a more efficient algorithm for Problem 1, assuming that the database can fit in memory.

The decision version of our problem is what we call the *cost-t splitters problem*: determine whether there is a size-k partition P with $c(P) \leq t$, where t is a positive integer given as an input parameter. If such P exists, t is *feasible*, or otherwise, *infeasible*. If t is feasible, we define $\bar{t}$ as an arbitrary value in $[1, t]$ such that there is a size-k partition P with $c(P) = \bar{t}$, i.e,

$$\bar{t} = \text{an arbitrary } x \in [1, t] \text{ s.t. } \exists P \in \mathcal{P}(k, I), c(P) = x. \quad (4)$$

When t is infeasible, define $\bar{t} = 0$. An algorithm solving the cost-t splitters problem is required to output $\bar{t}$, and if $\bar{t} > 0$ (i.e., t is feasible), also a P with $c(P) = \bar{t}$. The following observation follows immediately the above definitions:

Lemma 4 *If t is infeasible, then any $t' < t$ is also infeasible.*

A trivial upper bound of t is N. Hence, the above lemma suggests that we can solve Problem 1 by carrying out binary search to determine the smallest feasible t in $[1, N]$. This requires solving $O(\log N)$ instances of the cost-t splitters problem. In the sequel, we will show that each instance can be settled in $O(k)$ time, using a structure constructable in $O(N \log N)$ time. This gives an algorithm for Problem 1 with $O(N \log N + k \log N) = O(N \log N)$ overall running time.

As before, we denote the intervals in I as $[s_1, e_1], ..., [s_N, e_N]$ sorted in non-descending order of their starting values; break ties by non-descending order of their ending values first, and then arbitrarily. Interval $[s_i, e_i]$ is said to have *id* i. We consider that I is given in an array where the i-th element is $[s_i, e_i]$ for $1 \leq i \leq N$.

Stabbing-count array. As will be clear shortly, the key to attacking the cost-t splitters problem is to construct a *stabbing-count array A*. For each $i \in [1, N]$, define $\sigma[i]$ as the number of intervals in I strongly covering the value s_i, i.e.,

$$\sigma[i] = |I^\times(s_i)|. \quad (5)$$

Furthermore, define $\delta[i]$ as the number of intervals in I with starting values equal to s_i but with ids less than i. Formally, if $I^o_<(s_i) = \{[s_j, e_j] \in I \mid s_j = s_i \wedge j < i\}$, then

$$\delta[i] = |I^o_<(s_i)|. \quad (6)$$

A stabbing-count array A is simply an array of size N where $A[i] = (\sigma[i], \delta[i])$, $1 \leq i \leq N$. Figure 4 shows an example

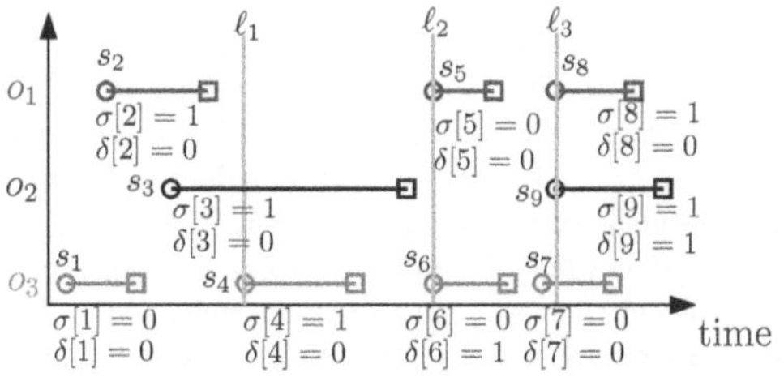

Figure 4: Stabbing-count array.

where I has $N = 9$ intervals, and the values of $\sigma[i]$, $\delta[i]$ have been shown under the interval with id i. For instance, $\sigma[4] = 1$ because there is one interval $[s_3, e_3]$ strongly covering s_4, whereas $\delta[6] = 1$ because one interval $[s_5, e_5]$ has the same starting value as $[s_6, e_6]$, and yet, has a smaller id than $[s_6, e_6]$.

Lemma 5 *The stabbing count array can be built in $O(N \log N)$ time.*

PROOF. This is done with a sweeping technique. First, use $O(N \log N)$ time to sort in ascending order the $2N$ endpoints (starting and ending values) of the N intervals in I, breaking ties as follows:

- A starting value is always put before an ending value;
- If both endpoints are starting values, the one belonging to an interval with a smaller id is put earlier (similarly, if both endpoints are ending values).

Denote by E the sorted list. For each endpoint $x \in E$, we associate it with the id i of the interval where x belongs, and if x is an ending value, also with the starting value s_i of that interval.

Next, we scan E once by its ordering. In this process, an interval $[s, e]$ is *alive* if s has been scanned, but e has not. At any moment, we keep track of 1) s_{last}: the last starting value scanned, 2) the number c of alive intervals, and 3) the number c_δ of alive intervals whose starting values equal s_{last}. As we will see, all this information can be updated in constant time per endpoint in E, and allows us to generate an entry of stabbing count array A in constant time after a starting value is scanned.

Specifically, at the beginning of the scan, $c = c_\delta = 0$ and $s_{last} = -\infty$. Let x be the next endpoint to be scanned, and i the id of the interval to which x belongs. We proceed as follows:

- Case 1: x is an ending value e_i. Decrease c by 1. Furthermore, if $s_i = s_{last}$, also decrease c_δ by 1.
- Case 2: x is a starting value. Increase c by 1. Furthermore, if $x = s_{last}$, increase c_δ by 1; otherwise, set s_{last} to x, and reset c_δ to 1. We also generate an entry $(\sigma[i], \delta[i])$ of A, where $\sigma[i] = c - c_\delta$, and $\delta[i] = c_\delta - 1$.

The scan clearly takes $O(N)$ time, thus completing the proof. □

Cost-t splitters in memory. Given the stab-counting array A, we now describe an algorithm, called *t-jump*, for solving the cost-t splitters problem in $O(k)$ time. If t is feasible, our algorithm outputs $\bar{t}$ and a partition P with splitters $\ell_1, ..., \ell_m$, where m is some integer between 0 and k, such that $c(P) = \bar{t} \le t$. Each ℓ_j ($1 \le j \le m$) is a starting value of a certain interval in I. We denote by $p(j)$ the id of that interval, namely, $\ell_j = s_{p(j)}$.

Algorithm 1 illustrates the details of t-jump. At a high level, the main idea is to place the splitters in ascending order, and particularly, in such a way that the next splitter is pushed as far away from the preceding one as possible, aiming to let the new bucket have size exactly t (hence, the name t-jump). However, as we will see, due to the overlapping among intervals, the aim is not always achievable. When it is not, we need to settle for a bucket with a smaller size, by moving the next splitter backwards, but just enough to make the new bucket's size drop below t.

Algorithm 1: t-jump (I, k, t)

1 **if** $t \ge N$ **then**
2   **return** $\bar{t} = N$, and an empty splitter set;
3 $p(1) = t + 1 - \delta[t+1]$; $|b_1| = t - \delta[t+1]$;
4 **if** $|b_1| = 0$ **then**
5   **return** $\bar{t} = 0$;
6 $\bar{t} = |b_1|$;
7 **for** $j = 2, \ldots, k$ **do**
8     $x_j = p(j-1) + t - \sigma[p(j-1)]$;
9   **if** $x_j > N$ **then**
10         $|b_j| = N - p(j-1) + 1 + \sigma[p(j-1)]$;
        $\bar{t} = \max(\bar{t}, |b_j|)$;
11   **return** $\bar{t}$, and splitters $s_{p(1)}, ..., s_{p(j-1)}$;
12     $p(j) = x_j - \delta[x_j]$;
13   **if** $p(j) = p(j-1)$ **then**
14   **return** $\bar{t} = 0$;
15   /* $p(j) < p(j-1)$ cannot happen */
16     $|b_j| = t - \delta[x_j]$; $\bar{t} = \max(\bar{t}, |b_j|)$;
17 $|b_{k+1}| = N - p(k) + 1 + \sigma[p(k)]$;
18 **if** $|b_{k+1}| > t$ **then**
19   **return** $\bar{t} = 0$;
20 $\bar{t} = \max(\bar{t}, |b_{k+1}|)$;
21 **return** $\bar{t}$, and splitters $s_{p(1)}, ..., s_{p(k)}$.

Now, let us walk through the algorithm. In the outset, Lines 1-2 deal with the trivial case where $t \ge N$ (such t is always feasible, even if no splitter is used). Lines 3-6 place the first splitter ℓ_1 at the *largest starting value that guarantees* $|b_1| \le t$. The rationale of these lines is from the next lemma:

Lemma 6 *We have:*

- *For $\ell_1 = s_{p(1)}$ where $p(1)$ is set as in Line 3, $|b_1| = t - \delta[t+1] \le t$. On the other hand, if $\ell_1 > s_{p(1)}$, $|b_1| > t$.*
- *If $|b_1|$ as set in Line 3 equals 0, t is infeasible.*

PROOF. To prove the first sentence in the first bullet, note that b_1 does not include the interval with id $p(1)$. The bucket includes exactly the intervals with ids 1, ..., $p(1) - 1$, namely, $t - \delta[t+1]$ of them. To prove the second sentence, if $\ell_1 > s_{p(1)}$, b_1 includes at least the first $t + 1$ intervals, and hence, $|b_1| > t$.

Now we show that the second bullet is also true. In fact, since $t = \delta[t+1]$, the intervals with ids 1, ..., $t+1$ all have the same starting values. These intervals will be assigned to an identical bucket in any partition. This bucket must have a size at least $t + 1$. □

Hence, if $|b_1| = 0$, the algorithm terminates at Line 5, indicating that t is infeasible. Otherwise (*i.e.*, $|b_1| > 0$), we know that the cost of the current partition is $\bar{t} = |b_1|$ (Line 6).

For every $j \in [2, k]$, Lines 8-16 determine splitter ℓ_j, assuming $\ell_1, ..., \ell_{j-1}$ are already available. These lines set ℓ_j to *largest starting value that guarantees* $|b_j| \le t$, based on the next lemma:

Lemma 7 *We have:*

- *For $\ell_j = s_{p(j)}$ where $p(j)$ is set as in Line 12, $|b_j| = t - \delta[x_j] \le t$. On the other hand, if $\ell_j > s_{p(j)}$, $|b_j| > t$.*
- *If $p(j) = p(j-1)$ at Line 13, t is infeasible.*

PROOF. Regardless of the position of ℓ_j, b_j *must* contain $\sigma[p(j-1)]$ intervals, i.e., those in $I^{\times}(s_{p(j-1)})$ because they strongly cover $s_{p(j-1)}$, and hence, have non-zero-length intersection with b_j. If ℓ_j is placed at $s_{p(j)}$, then besides the intervals of $I^{\times}(s_{p(j-1)})$, b_j also includes those intervals with ids $p(j-1)$, ..., $p(j)-1$. By definition of the stabbing count array, $|I^{\times}(s_{p(j-1)})| = \sigma[p(j-1)]$. Hence, b_j contains in total $|I^{\times}(s_{p(j-1)})|+p(j)-p(j-1) = t-\delta[x_j]$ intervals. This proves the first sentence of the first bullet.

If $\ell_j > s_{p(j)}$, then besides $I^{\times}(s_{p(j-1)})$, b_j also includes at least the intervals with ids $p(j-1)$, ..., x_j (due to line 12 and the definition of the stabbing count array for $\delta[i]$, $s_{p[j]} = s_{x[j]}$). In this case, $|b_j|$ is at least $x_j - p(j-1) + 1 + |I^{\times}(s_{p(j-1)})| = t+1$. This proves the second sentence of the first bullet.

Next, we show that the second bullet is also true. Notice that $p(j) = p(j-1)$ implies $\delta[x_j] = t - \sigma[p(j-1)]$. By the way x_j is calculated, there are exactly $t - \sigma[p(j-1)] - 1$ starting values between $s_{p(j-1)}$ and s_{x_j}. Hence, since $\delta[x_j] > t - \sigma[p(j-1)] - 1$, we know that the interval with id $p(j-1)$ is counted by $\delta[x_j]$ (i.e., the interval belongs to $I^{\circ}_{<}(x_j)$). This means that $s_{p(j-1)} = s_{x_j}$.

Now we have found $\sigma[p(j-1)]$ intervals of I strongly covering $s_{p(j-1)}$, in addition to $\delta(x_j)+1$ intervals whose starting values are $s_{p(j-1)}$ (the $+1$ is due to the interval with id x_j). These $\sigma[p(j-1)] + \delta(x_j) + 1 = t+1$ intervals will always be assigned to an identical bucket in any partition. Therefore, no partition can have cost at most t. □

Hence, Lines 13-15 declare t infeasible if $p(j) = p(j-1)$. Otherwise, Line 16 correctly sets $|b_j|$, and updates the current partition cost $\bar{t}$ if necessary.

Now let us focus on Lines 9-11. They handle the scenario where *less than* k splitters are needed to obtain a partition of cost at most t. Specifically, the final partition has only $j-1$ splitters. Line 10 determines the size of the last bucket, and adjusts the partition cost $\bar{t}$ accordingly. The algorithm terminates at Line 11 by returning the results.

At Line 17, we have obtained all the k splitters, and hence, the last bucket b_{k+1} has been automatically determined. The line computes its size, while Lines 18-20 check its feasibility (a negative answer leads to termination at Line 19), and update the partition cost if needed. Finally, Line 21 returns the k splitters already found, as well as the cost $\bar{t}$ of the partition.

We illustrate the algorithm with the example in Figure 4, setting $t = k = 3$. To find the first splitter ℓ_1, we compute $p(1) = 4$, and hence, place ℓ_1 at s_4. To look for the second splitter ℓ_2, Line 8 calculates $x_2 = p(1) + t - \sigma[p(1)] = 4 + 3 - 1 = 6$. However, as $\delta[6] = 1 > 0$, we move $p(2)$ back to $x_2 - \delta[x_2] = 6 - 1 = 5$. For the third splitter ℓ_3, we derive $p(3) = p(2) + t - \sigma[p(2)] = 5 + 3 - 0 = 8$. Finally, the algorithm checks the size of the last bucket, which is $N - p(3) + 1 + \sigma[p(3)] = 9 - 8 + 1 + 1 = 3$, namely, still within the target cost t. Hence, t-jump outputs $\bar{t} = 3$, and splitters $\ell_1 = s_4, \ell_2 = s_5$, and $\ell_3 = s_8$.

Lemma 8 *If t-jump does not return $\bar{t} = 0$, then the splitters output constitute a partition with cost $\bar{t} \le t$. Otherwise (i.e., $\bar{t} = 0$), then t must be infeasible.*

PROOF. The first sentence is easy to show, given that the sizes of all buckets have been explicitly given in Algorithm 1. Next, we focus on the case where $\bar{t} = 0$. The algorithm may return $\bar{t} = 0$ at three places: Lines 5, 14, and 19. Lemmas 6 and 7 have already shown that termination at Lines 5 and 14 is correct. It thus remains to show that Line 19 termination is also correct.

Assume, for the purpose of contradiction, that j-jump reports $\bar{t} = 0$ at Line 19, but there exists a size-k partition P' over I such that $c(P') \le t$. Suppose that P' has splitters $\ell'_1, \dots, \ell'_m$ in ascending order for some $m \le k$, which define $m+1$ buckets $b'_1, \dots, b'_{m+1}$ again in ascending order. By Lemmas 1 and 2, we can consider that ℓ'_1, ..., ℓ'_m are all starting values in S.

We will establish the following statement: *for each $j \in [1, m]$, t-jump always places the jth smallest splitter ℓ_j in such a way that $\ell_j \ge \ell'_j$* – referred to as the *key statement* henceforth. This statement will complete the proof of Lemma 8. To see this, notice that it indicates $\ell_k \ge \ell_m \ge \ell'_m$, which in turn means $|b_{k+1}| \le |b'_{m+1}|$. However, as Line 19 tells us $|b_{k+1}| > t$, it thus must hold that $|b'_{m+1}| > t$, thus contradicting the fact that $c(P') \le t$.

We now prove the key statement by induction. As the base step, $\ell_1 = s_{p(1)} \ge \ell'_j$ because if not, then by Lemma 6 $|b'_1|$ must be strictly greater than t, violating $c(P') \le t$.

Now assuming that the key statement is correct for $j = z$, next we show that it is also correct for $j = z+1$. In fact, if $\ell_{z+1} = s_{p(z+1)} < \ell'_{z+1}$, then by Lemma 7 a bucket with interval $[\ell_z, \ell'_{z+1}]$ will have a size greater than t. However, since $\ell_z \ge \ell'_z$, we know that the interval $[l'_z, l'_{z+1}]$ of bucket b'_z contains $[\ell_z, \ell'_{z+1}]$, and therefore, $|b'_{z+1}|$ must also be greater than t, contradicting $c(P') \le t$. This completes the proof of the key statement. □

Algorithm t-jump in Algorithm 1 clearly runs in linear time to the number of splitters, i.e., $O(k)$ time. Putting everything in this section together, we have arrived at the first main result of the paper.

Theorem 1 *The static interval splitters problem can be solved in $O(N \log N)$ time in internal memory.*

5. EXTERNAL MEMORY METHODS

This section discusses how to solve the static interval splitters problem I/O-efficiently when the input set I of intervals does not fit in memory. Our analysis will be carried out in the standard *external memory* model of computation [2]. In this model, a computer has M words of memory, and a disk has been formatted into *blocks* (a.k.a. pages) of size B words. An I/O operation either reads a block from the disk to memory, or conversely, writes a block in memory to the disk. The objective of an algorithm is to minimize the number of I/Os. We assume $M \ge 3B$, i.e., the memory is large enough to store at least 3 blocks of data.

Initially, the input set I is stored in a disk-resident array that occupies $O(N/B)$ blocks. When the algorithm finishes, we should have output the $m \le k$ splitters of the final partition to a file of $O(k/B)$ blocks in the disk. Define:

$$SORT(N) = (N/B)\log_{M/B}(N/B).$$

It is well-known that sorting a file of N elements entails $O(SORT(N))$ I/Os by the textbook external sort algorithm. The rest of the section serves as the proof for the theorem below:

Theorem 2 *The static interval splitters problem can be solved using $O(SORT(N))$ I/Os in external memory.*

As before, denote the intervals in I as $[s_1, e_1]$, $[s_2, e_2]$, ..., $[s_N, e_N]$ in ascending order of s_i (break ties by ascending order of their ending values first, and then arbitrarily), $1 \le i \le N$, where $[s_i, e_i]$ is said to have id i. Henceforth, we consider that I is stored as a disk-resident array where the i-th element is $[s_i, e_i]$. This can be fulfilled by simply sorting the original input I, whose cost is within the budget of Theorem 2.

Adapting the main-memory algorithm. The previous section has settled the static interval splitters problem in $O(N \log N)$ time when the input I fits in memory. Recall that our algorithm has two steps: it first creates the stabbing count array A in $O(N \log N)$

time, and then solves $O(\log N)$ instances of the cost-t splitters problem, spending $O(k)$ time on each instance.

In external memory, a straightforward adaptation gives an algorithm that performs $O(SORT(N) + \min(k, \frac{N}{B}) \log N)$ I/Os. Recall from Section 4 that the computation of the stabbing count array A requires only sorting $2N$ values followed by a single scan of the sorted list. Hence, the first step can be easily implemented in $O(SORT(N))$ I/Os in external memory. The second step, on the other hand, trivially runs in $O(\min(k, \frac{N}{B}) \log N)$ I/Os, by simply treating the disk as virtual memory.

This algorithm is adequate when k is not very large. The term $\min(k, \frac{N}{B}) \log N$ is asymptotically dominated by $O(SORT(N))$ when $k = O(\frac{N}{B \log_2(M/B)})$ (note that the base of the logarithm is 2). However, the solution falls short for our purpose of claiming a clean bound $O(SORT(N))$ for the entire range of $k \in [1, N]$ (as is needed for proving Theorem 2).

In practice, this straightforward solution can be expensive when k is large, which may happen in a cluster. Note that k could be the total number of cores in a cluster, when each core is responsible for processing one bucket in a partition. So it is not uncommon to have k in a few thousand, or even tens of thousands in a cluster.

Next, we provide an alternative algorithm in the external memory that performs $O(SORT(N))$ I/Os.

Cost-t splitter in external memory. The *cost-t splitters problem* (defined in Section 4) determines whether there is a size-k partition P with cost $c(P) \leq t$; moreover, if P exists, an algorithm also needs to output such a partition (any P with $c(P) \leq t$ is fine). Assuming that the stabbing-count array A has been stored as a file of $O(N/B)$ blocks, next we explain how to solve this problem with $O(N/B)$ I/Os.

The algorithm implements the idea of our main-memory solution by scanning the arrays A and I synchronously once. Following the notations in Section 4, let $\ell_1, \ldots, \ell_m$ be the splitters of P (where $1 \leq m \leq k$), and $p(i)$ an interval id such that $\ell_i = s_{p(i)}$, $1 \leq i \leq m$. We start by setting $p(1)$ as in Line 3 of Algorithm 1, fetching the $p(1)$-th interval of I, and writing it to an output file. Iteratively, having obtained $p(i)$, for $1 \leq i \leq m-1$, we forward the scan of A to $A[p(i)]$, and compute $p(i+1)$ according to Lines 8-16 in Algorithm 1. Then, we forward the scan of I to retrieve the $p(i+1)$-th interval of I, and append it to the output file. Recall that the main-memory algorithm would declare the absence of a feasible P under several situations. In external memory, when any such situation occurs, we also terminate with the absence declaration, and destroy the output file.

The total cost is $O(N/B)$ I/Os because we never read the same block of I or A twice. The algorithm only requires keeping $O(1)$ information in memory. In particular, among $p(1), \ldots, p(i)$ (suppose $p(i+1)$ is not available yet), only $p(i)$ needs to be remembered. We will refer to $p(i)$ as the *front-line value* of the algorithm. By definition, once $p(i+1)$ is obtained, it becomes the new front-line value, thus allowing us to discard $p(i)$ from memory.

Cost-t testing. Let us consider an easier variant of the cost-t splitters problem called *cost-t testing*, which is identical to the former problem except that it does not require an algorithm to output a partition in any case (i.e., even if P exists). An algorithm outputs only a boolean answer: yes (that is, P exists), or no.

Clearly, the cost-t testing problem can also be solved in $O(N/B)$ I/Os. For this purpose, we slightly modify our algorithm for cost-t splitter: (i) eliminate the entire part of the algorithm dealing with the output file (which is unnecessary for cost-t testing), and (ii) if the algorithm declares the absence of a feasible P, we return no for cost-t testing; otherwise, i.e., the algorithm terminates without such a declaration, we return yes.

What do we gain from such a modification, compared to using the cost-t splitter algorithm to perform cost-t testing directly? The answer is the avoidance of writing $O(k/B)$ blocks. Recall that the cost-t splitter algorithm would produce during its execution an output file whose length can reach k. Doing away with the output file turns out to be crucial in attacking a concurrent extension of cost-t testing, as discussed next, which is the key to proving Theorem 2.

Concurrent testing. The goal of this problem is to solve multiple instances of the cost-t testing problem simultaneously. Specifically, given h integers satisfying $1 \leq t_1 < t_2 < \ldots < t_h \leq N$, the *concurrent testing problem* settles h instances of cost-t testing for $t = t_1, \ldots, t_h$, respectively. Following the result in Lemma 4, cost-t testing obeys the monotonicity that if cost-t testing returns yes (or no), then cost-t' with any $t' > t$ (or $t' < t$, respectively) will also return yes (no). Therefore, the output of concurrent testing can be a single value τ, equal to the smallest t_j ($1 \leq j \leq h$) such that t_j-testing returns yes. Note that τ does not need to always exist: the algorithm returns nothing if t_h-testing returns negatively (in which case, the t_j-testings of all $j \in [1, h-1]$ must also return no).

Assuming $h \leq cM$ where $0 < c < 1$ is to be decided later, we can perform concurrent testing in $O(N/B)$ I/Os. We concurrently execute h cost-t testings, each of which sets t to a distinct t_j, $1 \leq j \leq h$. The concurrency is made possible by several observations on the cost-t testing algorithm we developed earlier:

1. Regardless of t, the algorithm scans I and A only *forwardly*, i.e., it never reads any block that has already been passed.
2. The next block to be read from I (A) is uniquely determined by its front-line value $p(i)$. In particular, if $p(i)$ is larger, then the block lies further down in the array I (A).
3. As one execution of the algorithm requires only $c' = O(1)$ words of memory, by setting
$$c = \frac{1}{c'}\left(1 - \frac{2B}{M}\right) \tag{7}$$
we ensure that h concurrent threads of the algorithm demand at most $cM \cdot c' = M - 2B$ words of memory. This will always leave us with two available memory blocks, which we deploy as the input buffers for reading I and A, respectively. Note that since $M \geq 3B$, we have $c \geq 1/(3c')$, indicating that $cM = \Omega(M)$.

In memory, the algorithm uses a min-heap H to manage the front-line values of the h threads of cost-t testing. At each step, it de-heaps the smallest value p from H. Suppose without loss of generality that p comes from the thread of cost-t_j testing, for some $j \in [1, h]$. We execute this thread until having obtained its new front-line value, which is then en-heaped in H. This continues until all threads have terminated, at which point we determine the output τ as explained before. A trivial improvement is to stop testing t_j's for $t_j > t_i$ if the testing on t_i returns that t_i is feasible. The fact that it performs only $O(N/B)$ I/Os follows directly from the preceding observations about each thread of cost-t testing.

Solving the static interval splitters problem. Our I/O efficient algorithm for the static interval splitters problem has three steps:

1. Construct the stabbing count array A.
2. Obtain the minimum t^* such that cost-t^* testing returns yes.

3. Solve the cost-t^* splitters problem to retrieve the splitters of an optimal partition P^*.

We refer to this algorithm as the *concurrent t-jump* method, or in short *ct-jump*. The correctness of the algorithm is obvious, noticing that Step 2 guarantees t^* to be the cost of an optimal partition.

We explained previously how to do Step 1 in $O(SORT(N))$ I/Os and Step 3 in $O(N/B)$ I/Os. Next, we will show that Step 2 requires only $O((N/B)\log_M N)$ I/Os. This will establish Theorem 2 because, for $N \geq M$, it holds that[1]

$$\frac{\log N}{\log M} \leq \frac{\log N - \log B}{\log M - \log B}$$

Note that the left hand side is $\log_M N$ whereas the right hand side is $\log_{M/B}(N/B)$.

The rest of the section will concentrate on Step 2. It is easy to see that t^* falls in the range $[1, N]$. We will gradually shrink this *permissible range* until eventually it contains only a single value, i.e., t^*. We achieve the purpose by launching multiple rounds of concurrent testing such that, after each round, the permissible range will be shrunk to $O(1/M)$ of the original length. An example for performing concurrent testings to shrink the permissible range is shown in Figure 5.

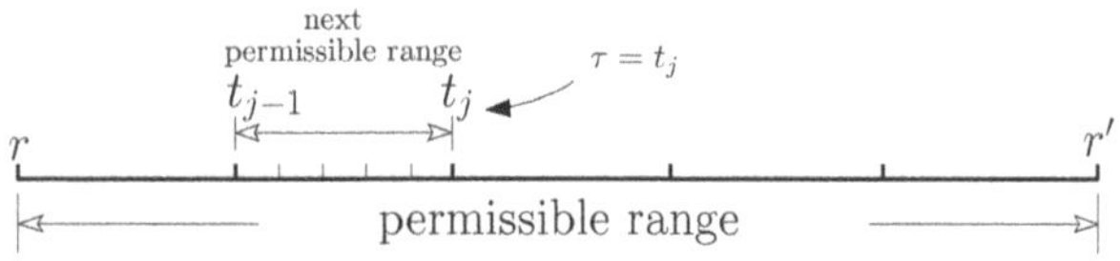

Figure 5: Concurrent testing on permissible ranges.

Specifically, suppose that the permissible range is currently $[r, r']$ such that $r' - r \geq cM$, where c is the constant given in (7). We choose $h = cM$ integers $t_1, ..., t_h$ to divide $[r, r']$ as evenly as possible, namely: $t_j = r + \lceil j(r' - r)/(h+1) \rceil$, for $j = 1, ..., h$. Then, we carry out concurrent testing with $t_1, ..., t_h$. Let τ be the output of the concurrent testing. Then, the permissible range can be shortened to:

- $[t_h + 1, r']$ if τ does not exist (*i.e.*, the concurrent testing returned nothing).
- $[r, t_1]$ if $\tau = t_1$.
- $[t_{j-1} + 1, t_j]$ if $\tau = t_j$ for some $j > 1$.

It is easy to verify that the length of the new permissible range is at most $2/(cM) = O(1/M)$ that of the old one.

Finally, when the permissible range $[r, r']$ has length at most cM, we acquire the final t^* by one more concurrent testing with $h = r' - r + 1$ values $t_1, ..., t_h$, each of which is set to a distinct integer in $[r, r']$. The value of t^* equals the output τ of this concurrent testing.

It is clear that we perform $O(\log_M N)$ rounds of concurrent testing in total. As each round takes linear I/Os, we thus have obtained an algorithm that implements Step 2 in $O((N/B)\log_M N)$ I/Os. In other words, the algorithm *concurrent t-jump* has IO cost $O(SORT(N))$. This completes the proof of Theorem 2.

6. QUERYABLE INTERVAL SPLITTERS AND UPDATES

In this section, we tackle the challenges in solving the queryable interval splitters problem (*i.e.*, Problem 2).

Queryable interval splitters. Our solutions for the static interval splitters problem also lead to efficient solutions to the queryable interval splitters problem.

In internal memory, we can use the t-jump algorithm for answering any queries with different k values. In a preprocessing step, we build the stabbing count array A (which occupies $O(N)$ space) in $O(N \log N)$ time. For subsequent queries, each query with a different k value takes $O(k \log N)$ time to answer, by solving $\log N$ cost-t splitters problems and each taking $O(k)$ time.

In external memory, the preprocessing cost of the *t-jump method* is $O(SORT(N))$ I/Os to build and maintain the disk-based stabbing count array A. The size of the index (which is just A) is $O(N/B)$, and the query cost is $O(\min\{k, N/B\} \log N)$ I/Os.

The preprocessing step of the *concurrent t-jump method* is the same. Hence, it also takes $O(SORT(N))$ I/Os, and its index also uses $O(N/B)$ space. Each query takes $O((N/B)\log_M N)$ I/Os.

Updates. In the queryable problem, another interesting challenge is to handle dynamic updates in the interval set I. Unfortunately, in this case, update costs in both the *t-jump* and *concurrent t-jump* methods are expensive. The indexing structure in both methods is the stabbing-count array A. To handle arbitrary updates, in the worst case, all elements in A need to be updated. Hence, the update cost is $O(N)$ time in internal memory, and $O(N/B)$ I/Os in external memory. This is too expensive for large data sets.

This limitation motivates us to explore update-efficient indexing structures and query methods for the queryable interval splitters problem. We again leverage the idea of solving $O(\log N)$ instances of the cost-t splitters problems (the decision version of our problem), in order to answer an optimal splitter query with any k value. The challenge boils down to designing an update-friendly indexing structure for answering a cost-t splitters query efficiently.

Observe that the key step in our algorithm for solving a cost-t splitters query in Section 4 is to figure out which starting value to use for placing the next splitter, which is given by Lines 8 and 12 in Algorithm 1. The critical part is to find out:

1) the number of intervals in I that strongly cover a starting value s, which is where a splitter has been placed at, i.e., $|I^\times(s)|$.
2) the number of intervals in I that share the same starting values as an interval $[s_i, e_i]$ ($1 \leq i \leq N$), but with smaller ids less than i, i.e., $|I^o_<(s_i)|$.

Hence, to solve a cost-t splitters problem instance, we just need to use an update-friendly index that answers any stabbing count query efficiently, i.e., an index that finds $|I^\times(s)|$ and $|I^o_<(s)|$ for any point s efficiently. This can be done efficiently using a *segment B-tree* [23]. In internal memory, this structure occupies $O(N)$ space, can be built in $O(N \log N)$ time, answers a stabbing count query in $O(\log N)$ time, and supports an insertion/deletion in $O(\log N)$ time. In external memory, the space, construction, query, and update costs are $O(N/B)$, $O((N/B)\log_{M/B}(N/B))$, $O(\log_B N)$ and $O(\log_B N)$, respectively.

Finally, answering a cost-t splitters query requires answering k different stabbing count queries; and answering a queryable interval splitters problem then takes $O(\log N)$ cost-t splitters problem instances. Hence, the overall query cost of this approach is $O(k \log^2 N)$ time in internal memory, and $O(k \log_B N \cdot \log N)$ I/Os in external memory. We denote this method as the *stabbing-count-tree* method, or just *sc-tree*.

7. EXPERIMENTS

We implemented all methods in C++. The external memory methods were implemented using the TPIE-library [4]. All exper-

[1] Let x, y, z be positive values such that $x \geq y > z$, then $\frac{x}{y} \leq \frac{x-z}{y-z}$.

iments were performed on a Linux machine with an Intel Core i7-2600 3.4GHz CPU, a 4GB memory and a 1TB hard drive.

Datasets. We used several large real datasets. The first one *Temp* is from the MesoWest project. It contains temperature measurements from Jan 1997 to Oct 2011 from 26,383 distinct stations across the United States. There are almost 2.6 billion total readings from all stations with an average of 98,425 readings per station. For our experiments, we view each year of readings from a distinct station as *a distinct object*. Each new reading in an object is viewed as an update and creates *a new version of that object*. This leads to a multi-version database and every version of an object defines an interval in the database. *Temp* has 145,628 objects with an average of 17,833 versions per object. So *Temp* has approximately 2.6 billion intervals in total.

The second real dataset, *Meme*, was obtained from the Memetracker project. It tracks popular quotes and phrases which appear from various sources on the Internet. Each record has the URL of the website containing the memes, the time Memetracker observed the memes, and a list of the observed memes. We view each website as an object. Each record reports a new list of memes from a website, and it is treated as an update to the object representing that website, which creates a new version that is alive until the next update (a record containing the same website). *Meme* has almost 1.5 million distinct websites and an average of 67 records per website. Each version of an object in *Meme* also defines an interval, and we have approximately 100 million intervals in total.

We have also obtained the popular time series datasets [12] from the UCR Time Series website. In particular, we used three of the largest datasets from this collection; but they are all much smaller than *Temp* and *Meme* as described above. All real datasets are summarized in Table 1, with their number of intervals.

Temp	Meme	CMU	Mallat	NHL
2.6×10^9	1.0×10^8	1.57×10^5	2.39×10^6	1.41×10^6

Table 1: Number of intervals in real datasets tested.

Setup. We primarily used *Meme* in internal memory and *Temp* in external memory. In order to test the scalability, we randomly selected subsets from *Meme* and *Temp* to produce data with different number of intervals. Unless otherwise specified, the default values for important parameters in our experiments are summarized in Table 2. The page size is set to 4096 bytes by default. The default fill factor in the *sc-tree* is 0.7. In each experiment, we varied the value of one parameter of interest, while setting other parameters in their default values. Since the UCR time series datasets are all relatively small in size compared to *Meme* and *Temp*, we only used them for evaluating the internal memory methods.

	Internal	External
Dataset	a subset of *Meme*	a subset of *Temp*
Size	~ 21 MB	~ 4.1 GB
N	~ 1 million	~ 200 million
k	40	5000
h	not applicable	5

Table 2: Default datasets and default values of key parameters.

7.1 Results from internal memory methods

In this case, we focus on the results from the *static interval splitters* problem.

Figure 6 studies the effect of k and N. Clearly, the *DP* method is linear to k as shown in Figure 6(a) and quadratic to N as shown in Figure 6(b). DP is 4-5 orders of magnitude more expensive than our t-jump method. On the other hand, even though the second step in t-jump is to solve $O(\log N)$ instances of cost-t splitters problem and each instance takes $O(k)$ time, the dominant cost for

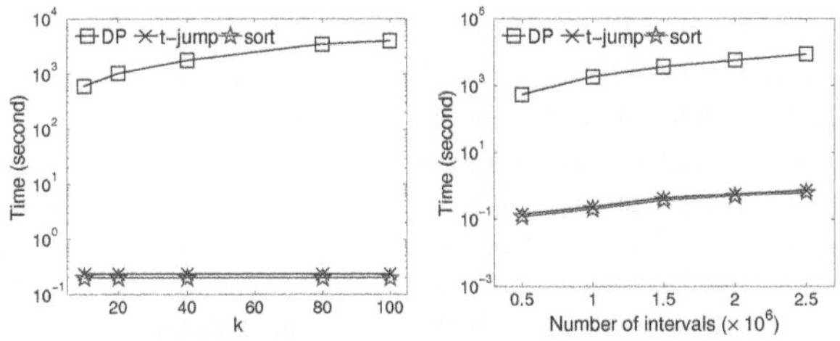

(a) Vary k. (b) Vary N.

Figure 6: Running time of internal memory methods.

t-jump is the sorting operation in its step, which is to construct the stabbing count array. Hence, its overall cost is $O(N \log N)$. As a result, its running time is almost not affected by k as seen in 6(a), but (roughly) linearly affected by N as seen in 6(b). In conclusion, t-jump is extremely efficient for finding optimal splitters, and it is highly scalable (as cheap as main memory sorting methods). It takes only about 1 second to find optimal splitters for size-40 partitions over 2.5 million intervals, when they are not sorted. Note that t-jump will be even more efficient and scalable if data is already sorted; in that case, its cost reduces to only $O(k \log N)$.

In Figure 7, we report the experimental results on the datasets from the UCR time series collection. The trend is similar to our observations from the *Meme* dataset. Our best solution t-jump consistently performs 3-4 orders of magnitudes faster than the DP approach in all three datasets. The dominant cost for t-jump is from sorting the input data, which is clearly shown in Figure 7.

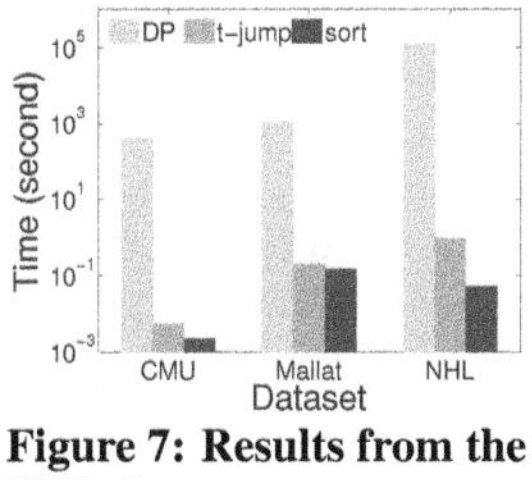

Figure 7: Results from the UCR datasets.

7.2 Results from external memory methods

We first present the results for the *static interval splitters* problem, then analyze the results for the *queryable interval splitters* problem. In both problems, we need to study the effect of h from the second step in our concurrent t-jump method. Hence, we first evaluate the impact of h as shown in Figure 8.

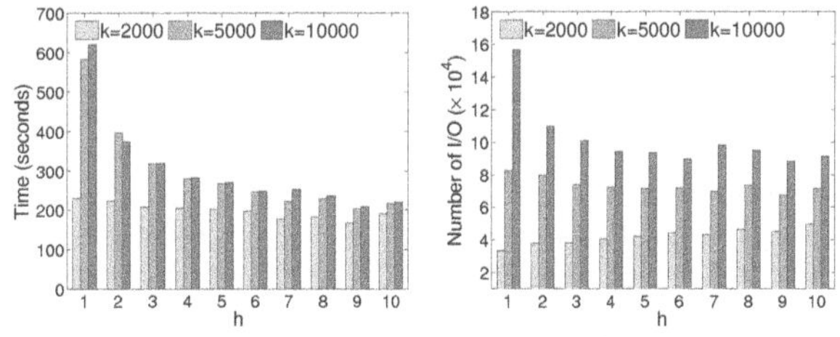

(a) Time. (b) IO.

Figure 8: Effect of h in the second step of ct-jump.

To isolate the impact of h, we show only running time from the second step of the ct-jump method, i.e., we assume that the stabbing count array has already been constructed and do not include its construction cost in Figure 8. We vary h between 1 to 10, and repeat the same experiment for $k = 2,000$, $k = 5,000$ and $k = 10,000$. What is interesting to observe from Figure 8(a) is that the running time initially deceases sharply and then slightly increases (very slowly), when we increase h. The same trend (albeit being less obvious and consistent) can also be observed for the number of IOs in Figure 8(b). This is because that the initial increment in h helps quickly reduce the permissible range, but subsequent increases in h lead to little gain (in shrinking the permissible range), but require more unnecessary testings. These results show that a small h value is sufficient for ct-jump to produce consistently good performance for a wide-range of k values. Hence, we set $h = 5$ as the default value for the rest of the experiments.

Results for static interval splitters. Recall that in this case, the overall cost includes the cost for building either the stabbing count array or the stabbing count tree, and the cost for finding the optimal splitters with the help of such a data structure. Also recall that the cost in this case, in terms of IOs, for ct-jump, t-jump, and sc-tree is $O(SORT(N))$, $O(SORT(N) + k \log N)$, and $O(SORT(N) + k \log_B N \log N)$ respectively.

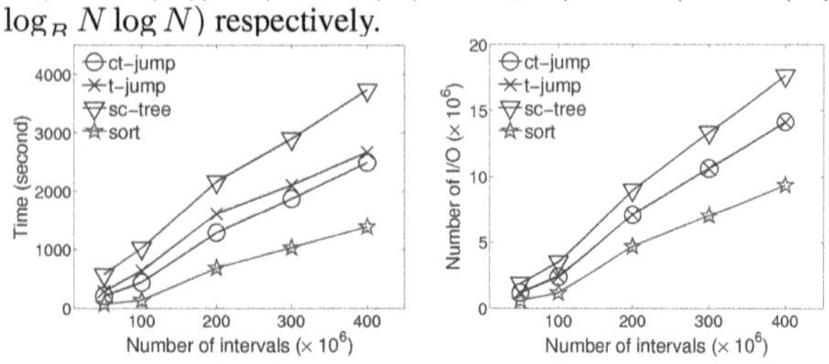

(a) Running time. (b) Total IO.

Figure 9: Static splitters, vary N.

Figure 9 studies the scalability of different methods by varying N from 50 million to 400 million. Not surprisingly, all methods have an almost linear dependence to N in terms of both running time and IOs. But obviously ct-jump achieves the best overall running time in Figure 9(a), and both ct-jump and t-jump have clearly outperformed the sc-tree method. The ct-jump method also has better IOs than t-jump, but the difference is not clearly visible in Figure 9(b), because that the dominant IO cost for both methods is the external sort. Both methods have fewer IOs than sc-tree, especially for larger data. Overall, ct-jump is the best method that is almost as efficient and scalable as external sorting. With $N = 400$ million intervals, ct-jump achieves a 30% speedup over the *sc-tree* method and a 10% speedup over the t-jump method.

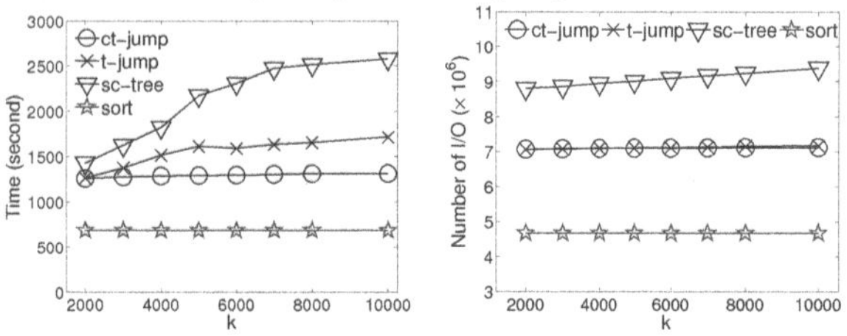

(a) Running time. (b) Total IO.

Figure 10: Static splitters, vary k.

We also investigated the impact of k by varying k from $2,000$ to $10,000$. As k becomes larger, both the running time and the number of IOs increase in all methods, especially for the sc-tree method as shown in Figure 10. A larger k value increases the cost of solving a cost-t splitters problem, which is the essential step for all methods. However, the benefit of concurrent testing in ct-jump is clearly reflected in Figure 10(a) for larger k values. Its cost is still very much just the sorting cost, which is consistent with our theoretical analysis. In contrast, the t-jump method displays a clear increase in running time over larger k values. The ct-jump method is more than 2 times faster than sc-tree, and about 20-30% faster than the t-jump method, as we increase k.

In conclusion, ct-jump is the best method for the static interval splitters problem in external memory.

Results for queryable interval splitters. We first study the preprocessing cost to construct the indices for different external memory methods, which is to construct either the stabbing count array in ct-jump and t-jump, or the stabbing count tree in sc-tree. Figure 11 compares the size of the indices in different methods when we increase N from 50 million to 400 million. Both stabbing count array and stabbing count tree are linear to N, however, a stabbing count tree does require much more space, almost by a factor 2 when N becomes 400 million. The stabbing count array in both ct-jump and t-jump is the same in size as the size of all intervals. This means that it will be much smaller than the size of the database, which contains other values than just an interval for each record.

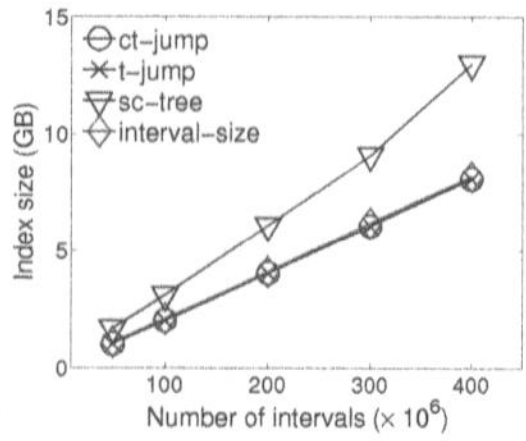

Figure 11: Index size.

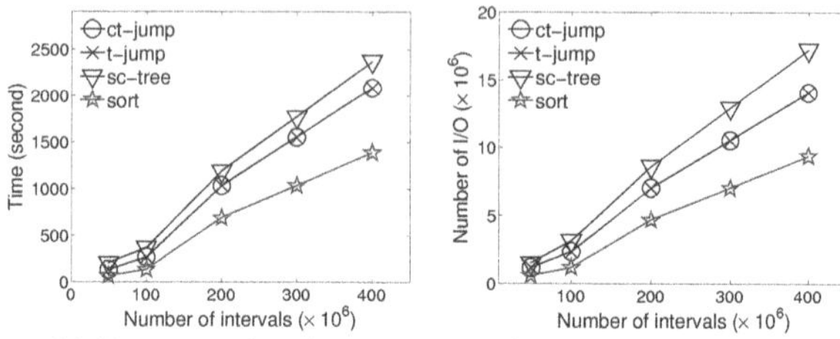

(a) Preprocessing time. (b) Preprocessing IO.

Figure 12: Preprocessing cost.

In terms of the construction cost of indices in these methods, Figure 12 shows that building a stabbing count array is slightly cheaper than building a stabbing count tree. But both are dominated by the external sorting cost, and obviously the ct-jump and the t-jump methods share the same preprocessing cost. All three methods have an almost linear construction cost to N.

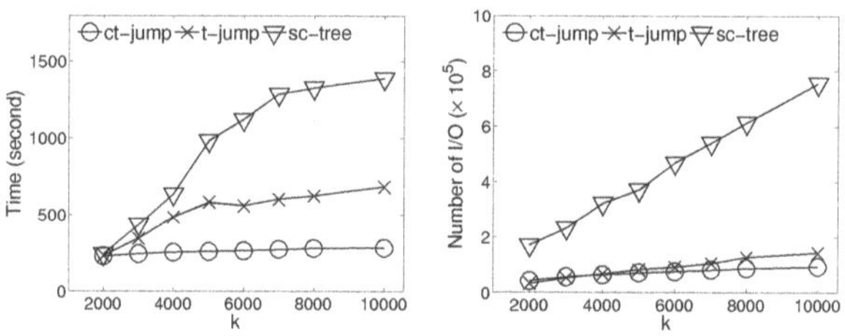

(a) Query time. (b) Query IO.

Figure 13: Queryable splitters, vary k.

We next study the query cost. Figure 13 investigates the impact of k when it changes from $2,000$ to $10,000$. The query time for all three methods increase, as shown in Figure 13(a), but the cost of ct-jump increases at the slowest rate. Specifically, we observe that ct-jump answers a query 3-4 times faster than sc-tree, and about 1-2 times faster than t-jump. A similar trend can be observed in the IO cost, as shown in Figure 13(b). However, in this case, the IO difference between ct-jump and t-jump appears to be much smaller, compared to their difference in query time.

So one may wonder why the query time of ct-jump is much better than t-jump, when the difference in terms of the number of IOs is not so significant. This is explained by the (much) better caching behavior in ct-jump. Recall that ct-jump performs concurrent testing of several cost-t testing instances. As a result, it makes very small leaps while scanning through the stabbing count array, compared to the big leaps made by t-jump over the stabbing count array. These small leaps result in much better hit rates in buffer and cache, leading to much better running time.

Next, we examine the scalability of our query methods when we increase the size of the data from 50 million to 400 million. Figure 14(a) reports the query cost in terms of number of IOs. Not surprisingly, larger N values only increase the query IOs by a small amount. In contrast to the linear dependence on k, the query cost of ct-jump and t-jump only depends on N by a $O(\log N)$ factor, and

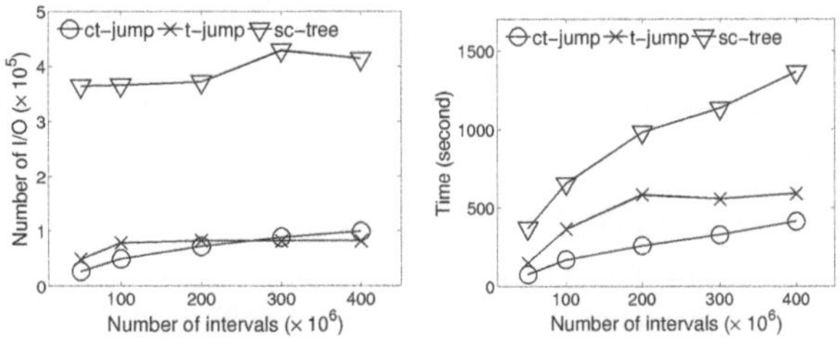

(a) Query IO. (b) Query time.

Figure 14: Queryable splitters, vary N.

the query cost of sc-tree only depends on N by a $O(\log_B N \log N)$ factor. On the other hand, the increases in running time for all three methods are more significant when N increases, as shown in Figure 14(b). This is because that as N becomes larger, for a fixed k value, the distance between two consecutive splitters also becomes larger. Since all three methods essentially make k jumps over the data to solve a cost-t splitters problem instance, a larger jump in distance leads to poorer caching performance, which explains the more notable increase in query time than that in query IO when N increases. Nevertheless, ct-jump outperforms sc-tree by about 60% and t-jump by about 30% in time on average.

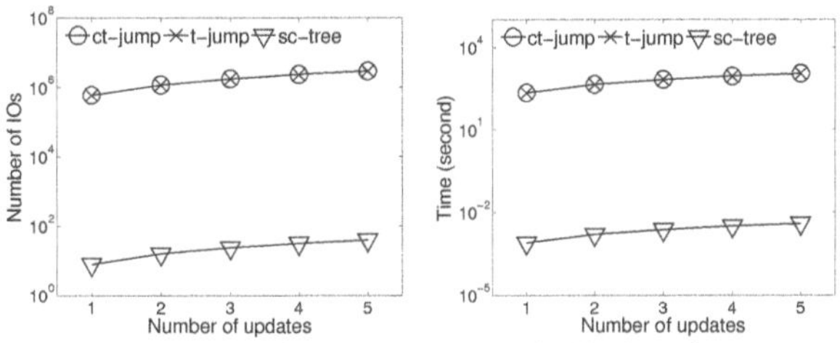

(a) Update IO. (b) Update time.

Figure 15: The update cost for queryable splitters.

Lastly, updates to the data may happen for the queryable splitters problem. When dealing with updates is important, as we have analyzed earlier in Section 6, sc-tree becomes a much more attractive method than ct-jump and t-jump. The fundamental reason is that a stabbing count tree is a dynamic indexing structure with an update cost of $O(\log_B N)$ IOs, while a stabbing count array is not with an update cost of $O(N/B)$ IOs. Of course, the update-friendly property in a stabbing count tree comes with the price of having more expensive query cost, as we have already shown.

That said, we generate a number of updates by randomly issuing a few insertions/deletions on the initial set of intervals. We report the average cost in IOs and time from 10 updates, as shown in Figure 15(a) and Figure 15(b). Clearly, the *sc-tree* method is much more efficient in handling updates than *t-jump* and *ct-jump*.

In summary, for the queryable splitter problem in external memory, when data is static (which is often the case for big data), the *ct-jump* method is the most efficient method. When dealing with dynamic updates is important, *sc-tree* works the best. Nevertheless, all three methods have excellent efficiency and scalability on big data, and the key idea behind all three methods is our observation on solving $O(\log N)$ cost-t problem (or testing) instances.

7.3 Optimal Point Splitters

A special case of our problem is when *all intervals degenerate to just points*, where *each interval* starts and ends at one same time instance.

Our solution can gracefully handle such special case, i.e., to find the optimal splitters for a point set. The state-of-the-art method for finding the optimal splitters in a point set runs in $O(k \log^2 N)$ time [21], assuming the set of input points has already been sorted. We dub this approach the p-split method. The details of this study will be surveyed in Section 8. In contrast, t-jump runs in only $O(k \log N)$ time, saving a $O(\log N)$ factor compared to the state-of-the-art on a point dataset. Note that the investigation from [21] focuses only on the RAM model, i.e., p-split is an internal memory method. Therefore, in this experiment, we compare p-split against our internal memory method t-jump by using all the internal memory datasets. In particular, we represent each interval only by its starting value and report the running time for finding the optimal point splitters. The results are shown in Figure 16. Not surprisingly, t-jump performs 3-4 times faster than the state-of-the-art method p-split across all datasets.

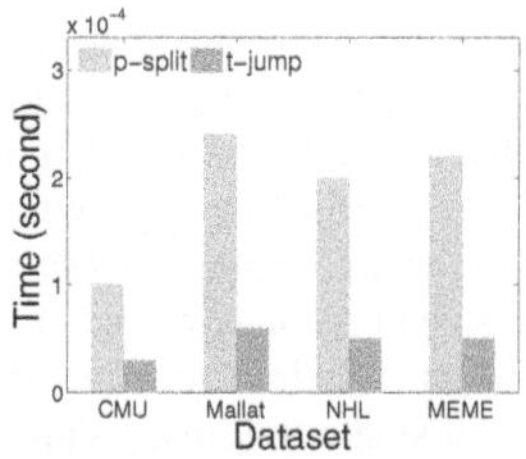

Figure 16: Comparison with p-split [21] to find optimal point splitters.

7.4 Final Remark

It is also interesting to point out our algorithms, t-jump, ct-jump, and sc-tree also produce very balanced buckets while minimizing the size of the maximum bucket. This is due to the fact that they all use our algorithm for solving the cost-t splitters (or cost-t testing) problem as a basic building block. And the way we solve the cost-t splitters (or cost-t testing) problem is to attempt to produce each bucket with a size t. When this is not possible, our algorithm finds a bucket with a size that is as close as possible to t, before producing the next bucket. In other words, in the optimal partition P^* that our algorithms find with the maximum bucket size being equal to t^*, the size of each bucket in P^* is in fact very close to t^*.

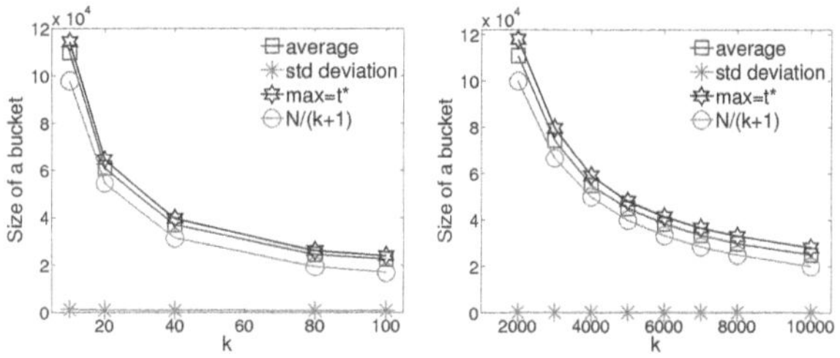

(a) Meme Data. (b) Temp Data.

Figure 17: Balanced partitions produced by our algorithms.

Figure 17 verifies this claim over both real data sets, when we vary k and show the average and the standard deviation for the sizes of all buckets in the optimal partition P^* produced by our algorithms, along with $t^* = c(P^*)$, the size of the maximum bucket in P^*. In all cases, the average bucket size is very close to t^*, and the standard deviation is very small (hundred to a thousand, compared to tens of or hundred thousand for the average bucket size). Furthermore, note that the average size of a bucket is not necessarily $\frac{N}{k+1}$ in our problem, since an interval may span over multiple buckets. In fact, it is always $\geq \frac{N}{k+1}$ and varies for different partitions depending on the data set I, the budget k, and the partitioning algorithm used. Nevertheless, all three of our methods, t-jump, ct-jump, and sc-tree, produce the same P^* for a given k and I.

8. RELATED WORK

To the best of our knowledge, this is the first work that investigates the problem of finding optimal splitters for large interval data.

Ross and Cieslewicz studied the problem of finding optimal splitters for a set of one dimensional points [21]. In their problem, a partition consists a set of disjoint buckets over the point dataset. The buckets are produced by k splitters. However, a set of k splitters will produce $(2k + 1)$ buckets instead of just $(k + 1)$ buckets:

they count all points that have values equal to a splitter as a separate bucket, so k splitters form k distinct buckets by themselves (which we refer to as the *splitter buckets*), plus the other $(k+1)$ buckets formed by any two neighboring splitters (which we refer to as the *non-splitter buckets*). Their goal, however, is to minimize the size of the maximum bucket from only the $(k+1)$ non-splitter buckets. Their motivation was to disregard buckets that contain only a single (but many duplicates) value. This finds applications in incremental sorting, distributed and parallel processing (of some applications), etc., as they argued in [21]. They have proposed a $O(k \log^2 N)$ method for memory-resident point sets. Clearly, their problem is fundamentally different from the interval splitters problem. Interestingly, it is possible to extend our stabbing-count array based methods, namely, *t-jump* and *concurrent t-jump*, to solve this problem in internal and external memory respectively. In that case, our solution leads to a $O(k \log N)$ method, which improves the results in [21] by a $O(\log N)$ factor for the point splitters problem.

On the other hand, the array partitioning problem is as follows. The input is an one-dimension array E of N non-negative numbers, and a *weight function* w that maps a contiguous segment of A to a non-negative integer. The k-partition of E is a division of E into $(k+1)$ contiguous segments, that is, setting dividers $\ell_0 = 0 < \ell_1 < \cdots < \ell_k < \ell_{k+1} = N$. Here, the ith segment is $E[\ell_{i-1}+1 \cdots \ell_i]$. The MAX norm of a partition over E is $\max_{i=1}^{k+1} w(E[\ell_{i-1}+1 \cdots \ell_i]$. The goal is to find a partition of size k that minimizes the MAX norm of any size-k partitions over E. Typical weight function includes addition and Hamming weight function [14, 18] among others. This problem can also be extended to 2-dimensional arrays, where a partition consists of a number of disjoint but complete-covering 2-dimensional blocks over the 2-dimensional array E. Khanna et al. studied this problem and gave an $O(N \log N)$ algorithm for memory resident arrays in 1d for arbitrary k. This problem is NP-hard in 2d and they gave approximation methods instead. More efficient and effective approximations were then given in [18]. This problem is related but certainly very different from our work. An interesting open problem is the interval array partitioning problem, which is defined similarly as the array partitioning problem, except that each element in the array is an interval of values (e.g., those from an uncertain object).

Our study may find interesting applications in parallel interval scheduling problems [9], where each job has a specified interval within which it needs to be executed. Each machine has a *busy interval* which contains all the intervals corresponding to the jobs it processes. Given the parallelism parameter $g \geq 1$, which is the maximal number of jobs that can be processed simultaneously by a single machine. The goal is to assign the jobs to machines such that the total busy time of the machines is minimized. This problem is known to be NP-hard for $g \geq 2$. Nevertheless, it is an intriguing future work to explore if our techniques can help design efficient approximate solutions for such problems.

Lastly, the DP method follows the general intuition of bucketization that finds application in optimal histogram constructions, e.g., the DP method for constructing a V-optimal histogram [11,20]. The construction of the stabbing count array is somewhat related to the prefix sum array that finds applications in data warehouses and histogram constructions, e.g., [10, 15]. Our study is also generally related with the management of interval and temporal data [1,5,8,16,16,22].

9. CONCLUSION

Temporal and multi-version databases often generate massive amounts of data. Therefore, it becomes increasingly important to store and process these data in a distributed and parallel fashion. This paper makes an important contribution in solving the optimal splitters problem, which is essential in enabling efficient distributed and parallel processing of such data. An interesting open problem is to extend our study to higher dimensions.

10. ACKNOWLEDGMENT

Wangchao Le, Feifei Li, and Robert Christensen were supported in part by NSF Grants IIS-0916488, IIS-1053979 and an REU supplement. Yufei Tao was supported in part by (i) projects GRF 4166/10, 4165/11, and 4164/12 from HKRGC, and (ii) the WCU (World Class University) program under the National Research Foundation of Korea, and funded by the Ministry of Education, Science and Technology of Korea (Project No: R31-30007).

11. REFERENCES

[1] P. K. Agarwal, L. Arge, and K. Yi. An optimal dynamic interval stabbing-max data structure. In *SODA*, pages 803–812, 2005.

[2] A. Aggarwal and J. S. Vitter. The input/output complexity of sorting and related problems. *CACM*, 31(9):1116–1127, 1988.

[3] A. Anagnostopoulos, M. Vlachos, M. Hadjieleftheriou, E. Keogh, and P. S. Yu. Global distance-based segmentation of trajectories. In *KDD*, 2006.

[4] L. Arge, O. Procopiuc, and J. S. Vitter. Implementing I/O-efficient data structures using TPIE. In *ESA*, 2002.

[5] L. Arge and J. S. Vitter. Optimal external memory interval management. *SIAM Journal on Computing*, 32(6):1488–1508, 2003.

[6] B. Becker, S. Gschwind, T. Ohler, B. Seeger, and P. Widmayer. An asymptotically optimal multiversion b-tree. *VLDBJ*, 5(4):264–275, 1996.

[7] Q. Chen, L. Chen, X. Lian, Y. Liu, and J. X. Yu. Indexable PLA for efficient similarity search. In *VLDB*, 2007.

[8] J. Chomicki, D. Toman, and M. H. Böhlen. Querying ATSQL databases with temporal logic. *ACM TODS*, 26(2):145–178, 2001.

[9] M. Flammini, G. Monaco, L. Moscardelli, H. Shachnai, M. Shalom, T. Tamir, and S. Zaks. Minimizing total busy time in parallel scheduling with application to optical networks. In *IPDPS*, 2009.

[10] C.-T. Ho, R. Agrawal, N. Megiddo, and R. Srikant. Range queries in OLAP data cubes. In *SIGMOD*, pages 73–88, 1997.

[11] H. V. Jagadish, N. Koudas, S. Muthukrishnan, V. Poosala, K. C. Sevcik, and T. Suel. Optimal histograms with quality guarantees. In *VLDB*, 1998.

[12] E. Keogh and et. al. The UCR time series classification/clustering homepage. www.cs.ucr.edu/~eamonn/time_series_data.

[13] E. J. Keogh, S. Chu, D. Hart, and M. J. Pazzani. An online algorithm for segmenting time series. In *ICDM*, 2001.

[14] S. Khanna, S. Muthukrishnan, and S. Skiena. Efficient array partitioning. In *ICALP*, pages 616–626, 1997.

[15] N. Koudas, S. Muthukrishnan, and D. Srivastava. Optimal histograms for hierarchical range queries. In *PODS*, pages 196–204, 2000.

[16] H.-P. Kriegel, M. Pötke, and T. Seidl. Managing intervals efficiently in object-relational databases. In *VLDB*, 2000.

[17] D. Lomet, M. Hong, R. Nehme, and R. Zhang. Transaction time indexing with version compression. *PVLDB*, 1(1):870–881, 2008.

[18] S. Muthukrishnan and T. Suel. Approximation algorithms for array partitioning problems. *J. Algorithms*, 54(1):85–104, 2005.

[19] T. Palpanas, M. Vlachos, E. Keogh, D. Gunopulos, and W. Truppel. Online amnesic approximation of streaming time series. In *ICDE*, 2004.

[20] V. Poosala, Y. E. Ioannidis, P. J. Haas, and E. J. Shekita. Improved histograms for selectivity estimation of range predicates. In *SIGMOD*, 1996.

[21] K. A. Ross and J. Cieslewicz. Optimal splitters for database partitioning with size bounds. In *ICDT*, pages 98–110, 2009.

[22] Y. Tao and D. Papadias. MV3R-Tree: A spatio-temporal access method for timestamp and interval queries. In *VLDB*, 2001.

[23] J. Yang and J. Widom. Incremental computation and maintenance of temporal aggregates. *The VLDB Journal*, 12(3):262–283, 2003.

Building an Efficient RDF Store Over a Relational Database

Mihaela A. Bornea [1], Julian Dolby [2], Anastasios Kementsietsidis [3]
Kavitha Srinivas [4], Patrick Dantressangle [5], Octavian Udrea [6], Bishwaranjan Bhattacharjee [7]
IBM Research
{[1]mbornea, [2]dolby, [3]akement, [4]ksrinivs, [6]oudrea, [7]bhatta}@us.ibm.com, [5]dantress@uk.ibm.com

ABSTRACT

Efficient storage and querying of RDF data is of increasing importance, due to the increased popularity and widespread acceptance of RDF on the web and in the enterprise. In this paper, we describe a novel storage and query mechanism for RDF which works on top of existing relational representations. Reliance on relational representations of RDF means that one can take advantage of 35+ years of research on efficient storage and querying, industrial-strength transaction support, locking, security, etc. However, there are significant challenges in storing RDF in relational, which include data sparsity and schema variability. We describe novel mechanisms to shred RDF into relational, and novel query translation techniques to maximize the advantages of this shredded representation. We show that these mechanisms result in consistently good performance across multiple RDF benchmarks, even when compared with current state-of-the-art stores. This work provides the basis for RDF support in DB2 v.10.1.

Categories and Subject Descriptors

H.2 [**Database Management**]: Systems

Keywords

RDF; Efficient Storage; SPARQL; Query optimization

1. INTRODUCTION

While the Resource Description Framework (RDF) [14] format is gaining widespread acceptance (*e.g.,* Best Buy [3], New York Times [18]), efficient management of RDF data is still an open problem. In this paper, we focus on two aspects of efficiency, namely, storage and query evaluation. Proposals for storage of RDF data can be classified into two categories, namely, *Native* stores (*e.g.,* Jena TDB [23], RDF-3X [13], 4store [1]) which use customized binary RDF data representations, and *Relationally-backed* stores (*e.g.,* Jena SDB [23], C-store [2]) which shred RDF data to appropriate relational tables. While there is evidence that going native pays in terms of efficiency, we cannot completely disregard relationally-backed stores. For one thing, relational stores come with 35+ years of research on efficient storage and querying. More importantly, relational-backed stores offer important features that are mostly lacking from native stores, namely, scalability, industrial-strength transaction support, compression, security, to name a few. However, there are important challenges in using a relational database as an RDF store, the most important of which stem from the inherent mismatch between the relational and RDF models. Dynamic RDF schemas and data sparsity are typical characteristics of RDF data which are not commonly associated with relational databases. So, it is not a coincidence that existing approaches that store RDF data over relational stores [2,21,23] cannot handle this dynamicity without altering their schemas. More importantly, existing approaches cannot scale to large RDF stores and cannot handle efficiently many complex queries. Our first contribution is an innovative relational storage representation for RDF data that is both flexible (it does not require schema changes to handle dynamic RDF schemas), and scalable (it handles efficiently the most complex queries).

Efficient querying is our next contribution, with the query language of choice in RDF currently being SPARQL [16]. Although there is a large body of work in query optimization (both in SPARQL [8,11,13,17,19] and beyond), there are still important challenges in terms of (a) SPARQL query optimization, and (b) translation of SPARQL to equivalent SQL queries. Typical approaches perform bottom-up SPARQL query optimization, *i.e.,* individual triples [17] or conjunctive SPARQL patterns [13] are independently optimized, and then the optimizer orders and merges these individual plans into one global plan. These approaches are similar to typical relational optimizers which rely on statistics to assign costs to query plans (in contrast to approaches [19] where statistics are ignored). While these approaches are adequate for simple SPARQL queries, they are not as effective for more complicated, but still common, SPARQL queries, as we illustrate in this paper. Such queries often have deep, nested sub-queries whose inter-relationships are lost when optimizations are limited by the scope of single triple or individual conjunctive patterns. To address such limitations, we introduce a hybrid two-step approach to query optimization. As a first step, we construct a specialized structure, called a data flow, that captures the inherent inter-relationships due to the sharing of common variables or constants of different query components. These inter-relationships often span the boundaries of simple conjuncts (or disjuncts) and are often across the different levels of nesting of a query, *i.e.,* they are not visible to existing bottom-up optimizers. As a second step, we use the data flow and cost estimates to decide both the order with which to optimize the different query components, and the plans we are to consider.

While our hybrid optimizer searches for optimal plans, this search must be qualified by the fact that our SPARQL queries must be converted to SQL. That is, our plans should be such that when they

SIGMOD'13, June 22–27, 2013, New York, New York, USA.

are implemented in SQL, they are (a) amenable to optimizations by the relational query engine; and (b) can be efficiently evaluated in the underlying relational store. So in our setting, SPARQL acts as a declarative query language that is optimized, while SQL becomes a procedural implementation language for our plans. This dependence on SQL essentially transforms our problem from a purely query optimization problem into a combined query optimization and translation problem. The translation part is particularly complex since there are many equivalent SQL queries that implement the same SPARQL query plan. Consistently finding the right SQL query is one of the key challenges and contributions of our work.

Note that both the hybrid optimization and the efficient SPARQL-to-SQL translation are contributions that are not specific to our work, and both techniques are generalizable and can be applied in any SPARQL query evaluation system. So our hybrid optimizer can be used for SPARQL query optimization, independent of the selected RDF storage (with or without a relational back-end); our efficient translation of SPARQL to SQL can be generalized and used for any relational storage configuration of RDF (not just the one we introduce here). The combined effects of these two independent contributions drive the performance of our system.

The effectiveness of both our optimizer and our relational back-end are illustrated through detailed experiments. There has been lots of discussion [6, 9] as to what is a representative RDF dataset (and associated query workload) for performance evaluation. Different papers have used different datasets with no clear way to correlate results across works. To provide a thorough picture of the current state-of-the-art, and illustrate the novelty of our techniques, we provide as our last contribution an experimental study that contrasts the performance of *five* systems (including ours) against *four* different (real and benchmark) data sets. Our work provides the basis for RDF support in DB2 v.10.1.

2. RDF OVER RELATIONAL

There have been many attempts to shred RDF data into the relational model. One approach involves a single *triple-store* relation with three columns, for the subject, predicate and object. Then, each RDF triple becomes a single tuple, which for a popular dataset like DBpedia results in a relation with 333M tuples (one per RDF triple). Figure 1(a) shows a sample of DBpedia data, used as our running example. The triple-store can deal with dynamic schemas since triples can be inserted without a priori knowledge of RDF data types. However, efficient querying requires specialized techniques [13]. A second alternative is a *type-oriented* approach [23] where one relation is created for each RDF data type. So, for our data in Figure 1(a), we create one relation for people (*e.g.,* to store Charles Flint triples) and another for companies (*e.g.,* to store Google triples). Dynamic schemas require schema changes as new RDF types are encountered, and the number of relations can quickly get out of hand if one considers that DBpedia includes 150K types. Finally, a third alternative [2, 21] considers a *predicate-oriented* approach centered around column-stores where a binary subject-object relation is created for each predicate. So, in our example, we create one relation for the *born*, one for the *died* predicate etc. Similar to the type-oriented approach, dynamic schemas are problematic as new predicates result in new relations, and in a dataset like DBpedia these can number in the thousands. In what follows, we introduce a fourth *entity-oriented* alternative which avoids both the skinny relation of the first approach, and the schema changes (and thousands of relations) required by the latter two.

2.1 The DB2RDF schema

The triple-store offers flexibility in the tuple dimension since new triples irrespectively of type or predicate are added to the relation. The intuition behind our entity-oriented approach is to carry this flexibility in the column dimension. Specifically, the lesson learned from the latter two alternatives is that there is value in storing objects of the same predicate in the same column. So, we introduce a mechanism in which we treat the columns of a relation as flexible storage locations that are not pre-assigned to any predicate, but predicates are assigned to them *dynamically*, during insertion. The assignment ensures that a predicate is always assigned to the same column or more generally the same set of columns.

We describe the basic components of DB2RDF schema in Figure 1. The *Direct Primary Hash (DPH)* (shown in Figure 1(b) and populated with the data from Figure 1(a)) is the main relation in the schema. Briefly, DPH is a wide relation in which each tuple stores a subject s in the *entry* column, with all its associated predicates and objects stored in the $pred_i$ and val_i columns $0 \leq i \leq k$, respectively. If subject s has more than k predicates, *i.e.,* $|pred(s)| > k$, then $((|pred(s)|/k) + 1)$ tuples are used for s, *i.e.,* the first tuple stores the first k predicates for s, and s *spills* (indicated by the *spill* column) into a second tuple and the process continues until all the predicates for s are stored. For example, all triples for Charles Flint in Figure 1(a) are stored in the first DPH tuple, while the second DPH tuple stores all Larry Page triples. Assuming more than k predicates for Android, the third DPH tuple stores the first k predicates while extra predicates, like graphics, spill into the fourth DPH tuple.

Multi-valued predicates require special treatment since their multi-values (objects) cannot fit into a single val_i column. Therefore, we introduce a second relation, called the *Direct Secondary Hash (DS)*. When storing a multi-valued predicate in DPH, a new unique identifier is assigned as the value of the predicate. Then, the identifier is stored in the DS relation and is associated with each of predicate values. To illustrate, in Figures 1(b) and (c), the industry for Google is associated with lid:1 in DPH, while lid:1 is associated in the DS relation with object values Software and Internet.

Note that although a predicate is always assigned to the same column (for any subject having this predicate), the same column stores multiple predicates. So, we assign the founder predicate to column $pred_3$ for both the Charles Flint and the Larry Page subjects, but the same column is also assigned to predicates like kernel and graphics. Having all the instances of a predicate in the same column provides us with all the advantages of traditional relational representations (*i.e.,* each column stores data of the same type) which are also present in the type-oriented and predicate-oriented representations. Storing different predicates in the same column leads to significant space savings since otherwise we would require as many columns as predicates in the data set. In this manner, we use a relatively small number of physical columns to store datasets with a much larger number of predicates. This is also consistent with the fact that although a dataset might have a large number of predicates, not all subjects instantiate all predicates. So, in our sample dataset, the predicate born is only associated with subjects corresponding to humans, like Larry Page, while the founded predicate is associated only with companies. Of course, a key question is how exactly we do this assignment of predicates to columns and how we decide this value k. We answer this question in Section 2.2 and also provide evidence that this idea actually works in practice.

From an RDF graph perspective, the DPH and DS relations essentially encode the outgoing edges of an entity (the predicates *from* a subject). For efficient access, it is advantageous to also encode the incoming edges of an entity (the predicates *to* an object). To this end, we provide two additional relations, called the *Reverse*

(Charles Flint, born, 1850)
(Charles Flint, died, 1934)
(Charles Flint, founder, IBM)
(Larry Page, born, 1973)
(Larry Page, founder, Google)
(Larry Page, board, Google)
(Larry Page, home, Palo Alto)
(Android, developer, Google)
(Android, version, 4.1)
(Android, kernel, Linux)
(Android, preceded, 4.0)
...
(Android, graphics, OpenGL)
(Google, industry, Software)
(Google, industry, Internet)
(Google, employees, 54,604)
(Google, HQ, Mountain View)
(IBM, industry, Software)
(IBM, industry, Hardware)
(IBM, industry, Services)
(IBM, employees, 433,362)
(IBM, HQ, Armonk)

(a) Sample DBpedia data

entry	*spill*	$pred_1$	val_1	$pred_2$	val_2	$pred_3$	val_3	...	$pred_k$	val_k
Charles Flint	0	died	1934	born	1850	founder	IBM	...	*null*	*null*
Larry Page	0	board	Google	born	1973	founder	Google	...	home	Palo Alto
Android	1	developer	Google	version	4.1	kernel	Linux	...	preceded	4.0
Android	1	*null*	*null*	*null*	*null*	graphics	OpenGL	...	*null*	*null*
Google	0	industry	lid:1	employees	54,604	*null*	*null*	...	HQ	Mtn View
IBM	0	industry	lid:2	employees	433,362	*null*	*null*	...	HQ	Armonk

(b) Direct Primary Hash (DPH)

l_id	*elm*
lid:1	Software
lid:1	Internet
lid:2	Software
lid:2	Hardware
lid:2	Services

(c) Direct Secondary Hash (DS)

entry	*spill*	$pred_1$	val_1	...	$pred_{k'}$	$val_{k'}$
1850	0	born	Charles Flint	...	*null*	*null*
1973	0	born	Larry Page	...	*null*	*null*
1934	0	*null*	*null*	...	died	Charles Flint
IBM	0	*null*	*null*	...	founder	Charles Flint
			...			
Software	0	industry	lid:3	...	*null*	*null*
Hardware	0	industry	lid:4	...	*null*	*null*

(d) Reverse Primary Hash (RPH)

l_id	*elm*
lid:3	IBM
lid:3	Google
lid:4	IBM
lid:4	Google

(e) Reverse Secondary Hash (RS)

Figure 1: Sample DBpedia RDF data and the corresponding DB2RDF schema

Predicate Set	Freq.
SV_1 SV_2 SV_3 SV_4 MV_1 MV_2 MV_3 MV_4	.01
SV_1 SV_2 SV_3 MV_1 MV_2 MV_3	.24
SV_1 SV_3 SV_4 MV_1 MV_3 MV_4	.25
SV_2 SV_3 SV_4 MV_2 MV_3 MV_4	.25
SV_1 SV_2 SV_4 MV_1 MV_2 MV_4	.24
SV_5 SV_6 SV_7 SV_8	.01

Table 1: Micro-Bench Characteristics

Query	Star query predicate set	Results
Q1	SV_1 SV_2 SV_3 SV_4	938
Q2	MV_2 MV_2 MV_3 MV_4	10313
Q3	SV_1 MV_1 MV_2 MV_3 MV_4	10313
Q4	SV_1 SV_2 MV_1 MV_2 MV_3 MV_4	10313
Q5	SV_1 SV_2 SV_3 MV_1 MV_2 MV_3 MV_4	10313
Q6	SV_1 SV_2 SV_3 SV_4 MV_1 MV_2 MV_3 MV_4	10313
Q7	SV_5	2500
Q8	SV_5 SV_6	2500
Q9	SV_5 SV_6 SV_7	2500
Q10	SV_5 SV_6 SV_7 SV_8	2500

Table 2: Micro-Bench Queries

```
SELECT ?s WHERE { ?s SV1 ?o1 . ?s SV2 ?o2 . ?s SV3 ?o3 . ?s SV4 ?o4 }
```

(a) SPARQL for Q1

```
SELECT  T.entry FROM DPH AS T
WHERE   T.PRED0='SV1' AND T.PRED1='SV2' AND T.PRED2='SV3' AND T.PRED3='SV4'
```

(b) Entity-oriented SQL

```
SELECT  T1.SUBJ FROM TRIPLE AS T1, TRIPLE AS T2, TRIPLE AS T3, TRIPLE AS T4
WHERE   T1.PRED='SV1' AND T2.PRED='SV2' AND T3.PRED='SV3' AND T4.PRED='SV4' AND
        T1.SUBJ = T2.SUBJ AND T2.SUBJ = T3.SUBJ AND T3.SUBJ = T4.SUBJ
```

(c) Triple-store SQL

```
SELECT  SV1.ENTRY FROM COL_SV1 AS SV1, COL_SV2 AS SV2, COL_SV3 AS SV3, COL_SV4 AS SV4
WHERE   SV1.ENTRY = SV2.ENTRY AND SV2.ENTRY = SV3.ENTRY AND SV3.ENTRY = SV4.ENTRY
```

(d) Predicate-oriented SQL

Figure 2: SPARQL and SQL queries for Q1

Primary Hash (RPH) and the *Reverse Secondary Hash (RS)*, with samples shown in Figures 1(d) and (e).

Advantages of DB2RDF *Layout.*

An advantage of the DB2RDF schema is the elimination of joins in star queries (i.e., queries that ask for multiple predicates for the same subject or object). Star queries are quite common in SPARQL workloads, and complex SPARQL queries frequently contain subgraphs that are stars. Star queries can involve purely single valued predicates, purely multi-valued predicates, or a mix of both. While for single valued predicates the DB2RDF layout reduces star query processing to a single row lookup in the DPH relation, processing of multi-valued or mixed stars requires additional joins with DS relation. It is unclear how these additional joins impact the performance of DB2RDF when compared to the other types of storage.

To this end, we designed a micro benchmark that contrasts query processing in DB2RDF with the triple-store and predicate-oriented approaches[1]. The benchmark has 1M RDF triples with the characteristics defined in Table 1. Each table row represents a predicate set along with its relative frequency distribution in the data. So, subjects with the predicate set $\{SV_1, SV_2, SV_3, SV_4, MV_1, MV_2, MV_3, MV_4\}$ (first table row) constituted 1% of the 1 million dataset. The predicates SV_1 to SV_8 were all single valued, whereas MV_1 to MV_4 were multi-valued. The predicate sets are such that a single valued star query for SV_1, SV_2, SV_3 and SV_4 is highly selective *but only when all four predicates are involved in the query.* The predicates by themselves are not selective. Similarly, a multi-valued star query for MV_1, MV_2, MV_3 and MV_4 is selective, but only if it involves all four predicates. We also consider a set of selective single valued predicates (SV_5 to SV_8) to separately examine the effects of changing the size of a highly selective single valued star on query processing, while keeping the result set size constant.

[1]We omitted the type-oriented approach because for this micro-benchmark it is similar to the entity-oriented approach.

Table 2 shows the predicate sets used to construct star queries. Figure 2(a) shows the SPARQL star query corresponding to the predicate set for Q1 in Table 2. For each constructed SPARQL query, we generated three SQL queries, one for each of the DB2RDF, triple-store, and predicate-oriented approaches (see Figure 2 for the SQL queries corresponding to Q1). In all three cases, we only index subjects, since the queries only join subjects. Q1 examines single valued star query processing. As shown in Figure 3, for Q1 DB2RDF was 12X faster than the triple-store, and 3X faster than the predicate-oriented store (78, 940, and 237 ms respectively). Q2 data shows that this result extends to multi-valued predicates, because of the selectivity gain. DB2RDF outperformed the triple-store by 9X and the predicate-oriented store by 4X (124, 1109 and 426 ms respectively). Q3-Q6 show that the result extends to mixed stars of single and multi-valued predicates, with query times significantly worsening with increased number of conjuncts in the query for the triple-store (1287-1850 ms), while times in the predicate-oriented store show noticeable increases (514-614 ms). In contrast, DB2RDF query times are stable (131-139 ms). Q7-Q10 show a similar trend in the single valued star query case, when any one of the predicates in the star is selective (66-73 ms for DB2RDF, 203-249 for triple-store, and 2-6 ms in the predicate-oriented store). When each predicate involved in the star was highly selective, the predicate-oriented store outperformed DB2RDF. However,

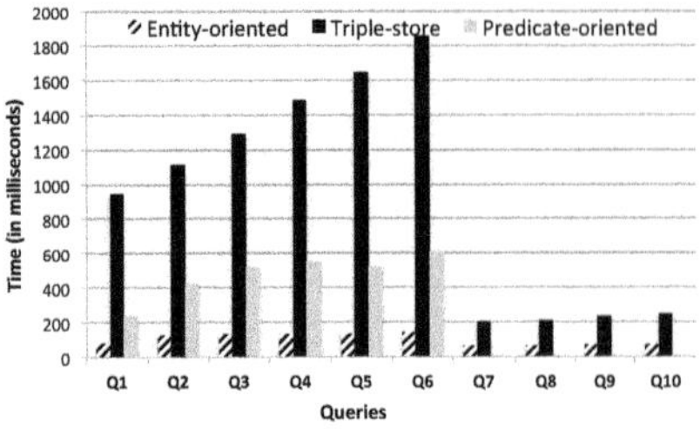

Figure 3: Schema micro-bench results

DB2RDF is more stable across different conditions (all 10 queries), whereas the performance of the predicate-oriented store depends on predicate selectivities and fluctuates significantly. Overall, these results suggest that DB2RDF has significant benefits for processing generic star queries. Beyond star queries, in Section 4 we show that for a wide set of datasets and queries, DB2RDF is significantly better when compared to existing alternatives.

2.2 Predicate-to-Column assignment

The key to entity-oriented storage is to fit (ideally) all the predicates for a given entity on a single row, while handling the inherent variability of different entities. Because the maximum number of columns in a relational table is fixed, the goal is to dynamically assign each predicate of a given dataset to a column such that:
1. the total columns used across all subjects is minimized.
2. for a subject, mapping two different predicates into the same column (assignment conflict) is minimized to reduce *spills*, since spills cause self-joins, which in turn degrades performance[2].

At an abstract level, a predicate mapping is simply a function that takes an arbitrary predicate p and returns a column number.

Definition 2.1 (Predicate Mapping). A *Predicate Mapping* is a function URI $\rightarrow \mathfrak{N}$ the domain of which is URIs of predicates and the range of which is natural numbers between 0 and an implementation-specified maximum m. Since these mappings are assigning predicates to columns in a relational store, m is typically chosen to be the largest containable on a single database row.

A single predicate mapping function is not guaranteed to minimize spills in predicate insertion, i.e., the mapping of two different predicates of the same entity into the same column. Hence, we introduce predicate mapping compositions to minimize conflicts.

Definition 2.2 (Predicate Mapping Composition). A *Predicate Mapping Composition*, written $f_{m,1} \oplus f_{m,2} \oplus \ldots \oplus f_{m,n}$, defines a new predicate mapping that combines the column numbers from multiple predicate mapping functions $f_1, \ldots f_n$:

$$f_{m,1} \oplus f_{m,2} \oplus \ldots \oplus f_{m,n}(p) \equiv \{v_1, \ldots, v_n \,|f_{m,i}(p) = v_i\}$$

A single predicate mapping function assigns a predicate in exactly one column; so data retrieval is more efficient. However, there are greater possibilities for conflicts, which would force self-joins to gather data across spill rows for the same entity. When predicate composition is used, then the implementation must select a column number in the sequence for predicate insertion and must potentially check all those columns when attempting to read data. This can negatively affect data retrieval, but could reduce conflicts in the data, and eliminate self-joins across multiple spill rows.

We describe two varieties of predicate mapping functions, depending upon whether, or not, a sample of the dataset is available (e.g., due to an initial bulk load, or in the process of data reorganization). If no such sample is available, we use a hash function based on the string value of any URI; when such a sample is available, we exploit the structure of the data sample using graph coloring.

[2]The triple store illustrates this point clearly since it can be thought of as a *degenerate* case of DB2RDF that uses a single $pred_i$, val_i column pair and where naive evaluation of queries always requires self-joins.

Hashing.

A straightforward implementation of Definition 2.1 is a hash function h_m computed on the string value of a URI and restricted to a range from 0 to m. To minimize spills, we compose n independent hashing functions to provide the column numbers

$$h_m^n \equiv h_{m1} \oplus h_{m2} \oplus \ldots \oplus h_{mn}$$

To illustrate how composed hashing works, consider the Android triples in Figure 1(a) and the two hash functions in Table 3. Further assume these triples are inserted one-by-one, in order, into the database. The first triple (Android, developer, Google) creates a new tuple for subject Android and predicate developer is inserted into $pred_1$, since h_1 puts it there and the column is currently empty. The next triple, (Android, version, 4.1), inserts in the same tuple predicate version in $pred_2$. The third triple, (Android, kernel, Linux), is mapped to $pred_1$ by h_1, but the column is full, so it is inserted into $pred_3$ by h_2. (Android, preceded, 4.0) is inserted into $pred_k$ by h_1. Finally, (Android, graphics, OpenGL) is mapped to column $pred_3$ by h_1 and $pred_2$ by h_2; however, both of these locations are full. Thus, a spill tuple is created which results in the layout shown in Figure 1(b).

predicate	h_1	h_2
developer	1	3
version	2	1
kernel	1	3
preceeded	k	1
graphics	3	2

Table 3: Hashes

Graph Coloring.

When a substantial dataset is available (say, from bulk loading), we exploit the structure of the data to minimize the number of total columns and the number of columns for any given predicate. Specifically, our goal is to ensure that we can overload columns with predicates that do not co-occur together, and assign predicates that do co-occur together to different columns. We do that by creating an interference graph from co-occurring predicates, and use graph coloring to map predicates to columns.

Definition 2.3 (Graph Coloring Problem). A graph coloring problem is defined by an *interference graph* $G =< V, E >$ and a set of *colors* C. Each edge $e \in E$ denotes a pair of nodes in V that must be given different colors. A *coloring* is a mapping that assigns each vertex $v \in V$ to a color different from the color of any adjacent node; note that a coloring may not exist if there are too few colors. More formally,

$$M(G, C) = \left\{ \langle v, c \rangle \;\middle|\; \begin{array}{l} v \in V \wedge \\ c \in C \wedge \\ (\langle v_i, c_i \rangle \in M \wedge \langle v, v_i \rangle \in E \rightarrow c \neq c_i) \end{array} \right\}$$

Minimal coloring would be ideal for predicate mapping, but to be useful the coloring must have no more colors than the maximum number of columns. Since computing a truly minimal coloring is NP-hard in general, we use the Floyd-Warshall greedy algorithm to approximate a minimal coloring.

To apply graph coloring to predicate mapping, we formulate an interference graph consisting of edges linking every pair of predicates that both appear in any subject. That is, we create $G_D =< V_D, E_D >$ for an RDF dataset D where

$$V_D = \{p \,|< \mathtt{s}, \mathtt{p}, \mathtt{o} >\in \mathtt{D}|\}$$
$$E_D = \{< p_i, p_j > |< \mathtt{s}, \mathtt{p_i}, \mathtt{o} > \in \mathtt{D} \wedge < \mathtt{s}, \mathtt{p_j}, \mathtt{o} > \in \mathtt{D}|\}$$

If a coloring $M(G_D, C)$ such that $|C| \leq m$ exists, then it provides a mapping of each predicate to precisely one database column. We use c_m^D to be a predicate mapping defined by coloring

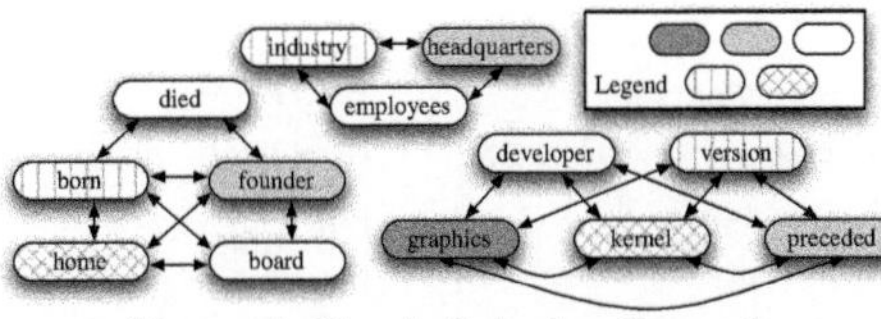

Figure 4: Graph Coloring Example

of dataset D with m or fewer colors. All of our datasets (see Section 4 for details on them) except DBpedia could be colored to fit on a database row. When a coloring does not exist, as in DBpedia, this means there is no way to put all the predicates into the columns such that every entity can be placed on one row and each predicate for the entity be given exactly one column. In this case, we can color a subset of predicates (e.g., based on query workload and the most frequently occurring predicates), and compose a predicate mapping function based on this coloring and hash functions.

We define more formally what we mean by coloring for a subset. Specifically, we define a subset P of the predicates in dataset D, and we write $D \otimes P$ to be all triples in D that have a predicate from P. If we choose P such that the remaining data is colorable with $m-1$ colors, then we define a mapping function

$$\hat{c}_m^{D \otimes P} \equiv \begin{cases} c_{m-1}^{D \otimes P} & p \in P \\ m & p \notin P \end{cases}$$

This coloring function can be composed with another function to handle the predicates not in P, for instance $\hat{c}_m^{D \otimes P} \oplus h_m$. With this predicate mapping composition, we were able to fit most of the data for a given entity on a single row, and reduce spills, while ensuring that the number of columns usage was minimized. Note that this same compositional approach can be used to handle dynamicity in data. If a new predicate p gets added after coloring, the second hash function is used to specify the column assignment for p.

Figure 4 shows how coloring works for the data in Figure 1(a). Predicates died, born, and founder have interference edges because they co-occur for entity Charles Flint. Similarly, founder, born, home and board co-occur for Larry Page and are hence connected. Notice further that the coloring algorithm will color board and died the same color even though both are predicates for the same type of entity (e.g., Person) because they never co-occur together (in the data). Overall, for the 13 predicates, we only need 5 colors.

2.3 Graph Coloring in practice

We evaluated the effectiveness of coloring using four RDF datasets (see Section 4 for details). Our datasets were chosen so that they covered a wide range of skews and distributions [6]. So, for example, while the average out-degree in DBpedia is 14, in LUBM and SP2B it's 6. The average in-degree in DBpedia is 5, in SP2B 2 and in LUBM 8. Beyond averages, out-degrees and in-degrees in DBpedia follow a power-law distribution [6] and therefore some subjects have significantly more predicates than others.

The results of graph coloring for all datasets are shown in Table 4. For the first three datasets, coloring covered 100% of the dataset, and reduced from 30% to as much as 85% the number of columns required in the DPH and RPH relations. So, while the LUBM dataset has 18 predicates, we only require 10 columns in the DPH and 3 in the RPH relations. In the one case where coloring could not cover all the data, it could still handle 94% of the dataset in DPH with 75 columns, and 99% of the dataset in RPH with 51 columns, when we focused on the frequent predicates and the query workload. To put this in perspective, a one-to-one mapping from predicates to columns would require 53,796 columns for DBpedia (instead of 75 and 51, respectively).

We now discuss spills and nulls. Ideally, we want to eliminate spills since they affect query evaluation. Indeed, by coloring in full

Dataset	Triples	Total Predicates	DPH Columns	Percent. Covered	RPH Columns	Percent. Covered
SP2Bench	100M	78	54	100%	53	100%
PRBench	60M	51	35	100%	9	100%
LUBM	100M	18	10	100%	3	100%
DBpedia	333M	53,976	75	94%	51	99%

Table 4: Graph Coloring Results

the first three datasets, we have *no spills* in the DPH and RPH relations. So, storing 100M triples from LUBM in DB2RDF results in 15,619,640 tuples in DPH (one per subject) and 11,612,725 tuples in RPH (one per object). Similarly, storing 100M triples of SP2B in DB2RDF results in 17,823,525 in DPH and 47,504,066 tuples in RPH, without any spills. In DBpedia, storing 333M triples results in DPH and RPH relations with 23,967,748 and 78,697,637 tuples, respectively, with only 808,196 spills in the former (3.37% of the DPH) and 35,924 spills in the latter (0.04% of RPH). Of course, our coloring considered the full dataset before loading so it is interesting to investigate how successful coloring is (in terms of spills) if only a subset of the dataset is considered. Indeed, we tried coloring only 10% of the dataset, using random sampling of records. We used the resulted coloring from the sample to load the full dataset and counted any spills along the way. For LUBM, by only coloring 10% of the records, we were still able to load the whole dataset without any spills. For SP2B, loading the full dataset resulted in a negligible number of spills, namely, 139 spills (out of 17,823,525 entries) in DPH, and 666 (out of 47,504,066 entries) in RPH. More importantly, for DPpedia we only had 222,423 additional spills in DPH (a 0.9% increase in DPH) and 216,648 additional spills in RPH (a 0.3% increase). So clearly, our coloring algorithm performs equally well for bulk and for incremental settings.

In any dataset, each subject does not instantiate all predicates, and therefore even in the compressed (due to coloring) DPH and RPH relations not all subjects populate all columns. Indeed, our statistics show that for LUBM, in the DPH relation 64.67% of its predicate columns contain NULLs, while this number is 94.77% for the RPH relation. For DBpedia, the corresponding numbers are 93% and 97.6%. It is interesting to see how a high percentage of NULLs affects storage and querying. In terms of storage, existing commercial (*e.g.,* IBM DB2) and open-source (*e.g.,* Postgres) database systems can accommodate large numbers of NULLs with small costs in storage, by using *value compression*. Indeed, this claim is also verified by the following experiment. We created a 1M triples dataset in which each triple in the dataset had the same 5 predicates and loaded this dataset in our DB2RDF schema using IBM DB2 as our relational back-end. The resulting DPH relation has 5 predicate columns and no NULL values (as expected) and its size on disk was approximately 10.1MB. We altered the DPH relation and introduced (i) 5 additional null-populated predicate/value columns, (ii) 45 null-populated columns, or (iii) 95 null-populated columns. The storage requirements for these relations changed to 10.4MB, 10.65MB and 11.4MB respectively. So, increasing by 20-fold the size of the original relation with NULLs only required 10% of extra space.

We also evaluated queries across all these relations. The impact of NULLs is more noticeable here. We considered both fast queries with small result sets, and longer running queries with large result sets. The 20-fold increase in NULLs resulted in differences in evaluation times that ranged from as low as 10% to as much as a two-fold increase on the fastest queries. So, while the presence of NULLs has small impact in storage, it can noticeably affect query performance, at least for very fast queries. This illustrates the value of our coloring techniques. By reducing both the number of columns with nulls, and the number of nulls in existing columns, we improve query evaluation and minimize space requirements.

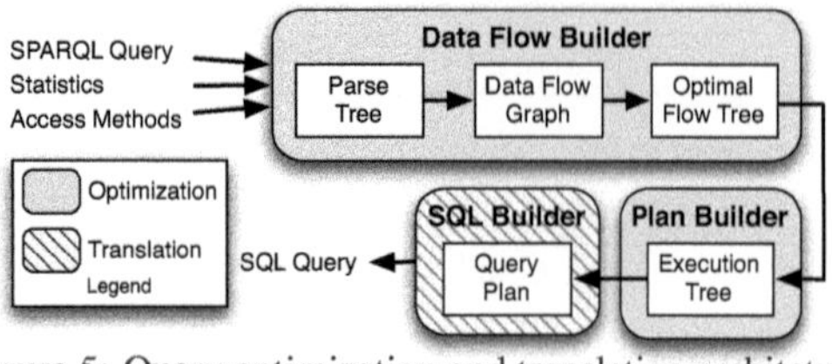

Figure 5: Query optimization and translation architeture

3. QUERYING RDF

Relational systems have a long history of query optimization, so one might suppose that a naive translation from SPARQL to SQL would be sufficient, since the relational optimizer can optimize the SQL query once the translation has occurred. However, as we show empirically here and in Section 4, huge performance gains can occur when SPARQL and the SPARQL to SQL translation are independently optimized. In what follows, we first present a novel hybrid SPARQL query optimization technique, which is generic and independent of our choice of representing RDF data (in relational schema, or otherwise). In fact these techniques can be applied directly to query optimization for native RDF stores. Then, we introduce query translation techniques tuned to our schema representation. Figure 5 shows the steps of the optimization and translation process, as well as the key structures constructed at each step.

3.1 The SPARQL Optimizer

There are three inputs to our optimization:

1. The query $\mathcal{Q}$: The SPARQL query conforms to the SPARQL 1.0 standard. Therefore, each query $\mathcal{Q}$ is composed of a set of hierarchically nested graph patterns $\mathcal{P}$, with each graph pattern $P \in \mathcal{P}$ being, in its most simple form, a set of triple patterns.

2. The statistics $\mathcal{S}$ **over the underlying RDF dataset**: The types and precision with which statistics are defined is left to specific implementations. Examples of collected statistics include the total number of triples, average number of triples per subject, average number of triples per object, and the top-k URIs or literals in terms of number of triples they appear in, etc.

3. The access methods $\mathcal{M}$: Access methods provide alternative ways to evaluate a triple pattern t for some pattern $P \in \mathcal{P}$. The methods are system-specific, and dependent on existing indexes. For example, for a system like DB2RDF with only subject and object indexes (no predicate indexes), the methods would be *access-by-subject* (acs), by *access-by-object* (aco) or a *full scan* (sc).

Figure 6 shows a sample input where query $\mathcal{Q}$ retrieves the people that founded or are board members of companies in the software industry. For each such company, the query retrieves the products that were developed by it, its revenue, and optionally its number of employees. The statistics $\mathcal{S}$ contain the top-k constants like *IBM* or *industry* with counts of their frequency in the base triples. Three different access methods are assumed in $\mathcal{M}$, one that performs a data scan (sc), one that retrieves all the triples given a subject (acs), and one that retrieves all the triples given an object (aco).

The optimizer consists of two modules, namely, the *Data Flow Builder* DFB, and the *Query Plan Builder* QPB.

• **Data Flow Builder** (DFB): Query triple patterns typically share variables, and hence the evaluation of one is often dependent on that of another. For example, in Figure 6(a) triple pattern t_1 shares variable $?x$ with both triples patterns t_2 and t_3. In DFB, we use sideways information passing to construct an optimal flow tree, that considers cheaper patterns (in terms of estimated variable bindings) first before feeding these bindings to more expensive patterns.

• **Query Plan Builder** (QPB): While the DFB considers information passing irrespectively of the query structure (*i.e.,*, the nesting of patterns and pattern operators), the QPB module incorporates this structure to build an execution tree (a storage-independent query plan). Our query translation (Section 3.2) uses this execution tree to produce a storage specific query plan.

```
SELECT *
WHERE { ?x home "Palo Alto" (t1)
        { ?x founder ?y (t2) UNION
          ?x member ?y (t3) }
        { ?y industry "Software" (t4)
          ?z developer ?y (t5)
          ?y revenue ?n (t6) }
        OPTIONAL {
            ?y employees ?m (t7) } }
```

(a) Sample query $\mathcal{Q}$

value	count
IBM	7
industry	6
Google	5
Software	2
Avg triples per subject	5
Avg triples per object	1
Total triples	26

(b) top-k stats in $\mathcal{S}$

$\mathcal{M} = \{sc, acs, aco\}$

(c) Access methods $\mathcal{M}$

Figure 6: Sample input for query optimization/translation

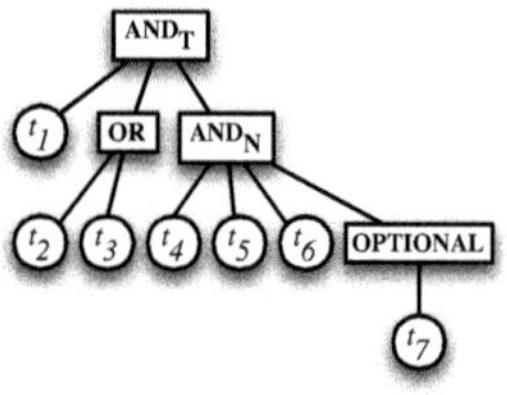

Figure 7: Query parse tree

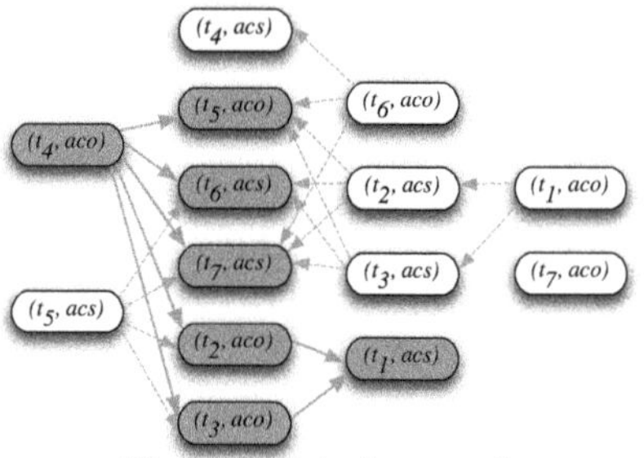

Figure 8: Data flow graph

3.1.1 *The Data Flow Builder*

The DFB starts by building a parse tree for the input query. The tree for the query in Figure 6(a) is shown in Figure 7. Then it uses sideways information passing to compute the data flow graph which represents the dependences amongst the executions of each triple pattern. A node in this graph is a pair of a triple pattern and an access method; an edge denotes one triple producing a shared variable that another triple requires. Using this graph, DFB computes the optimal flow tree (the blue nodes in Figure 7) which determines an optimal way (in terms of minimizing costs) to traverse all the triple patterns in the query. In what follows, we describe in detail how all these computations are performed.

Computing cost.

Definition 3.1 (Triple Method Cost)**.** Given a triple t, an access method m and statistics $\mathcal{S}$, function $\mathsf{TMC}(t, m, \mathcal{S}) :\rightarrow c, c \in \mathbb{R}_{\leq 0}$ assigns a cost c to evaluating t using m wrt statistics $\mathcal{S}$.

The cost estimation clearly depends on the statistics $\mathcal{S}$. In our example, $\mathsf{TMC}(t_4, aco, \mathcal{S}) = 2$ because the exact lookup cost using the object Software is known. For a scan method, $\mathsf{TMC}(t_4, sc, \mathcal{S}) = 26$, *i.e.,* the total number of triples in the dataset. Finally, $\mathsf{TMC}(t_4, acs, \mathcal{S}) = 5$, *i.e.,* the average number of triples per subject, assuming subject is bound by a prior triple access.

Building the Data Flow Graph.

The data flow graph models how using the current set of bindings for variables can be used to access other triples. In modeling this flow, we need to respect the semantics of AND, OR and OPTIONAL patterns. We first introduce a set of helper functions that are used to define the graph. We use $\uparrow$ to refer to parents in the query tree structure: for a triple or a pattern, it is the immediately enclosing pattern. We use $*$ to denote transitive closure.

Definition 3.2 (Produced Variables). $\mathcal{P}(t, m) :\rightarrow \mathcal{V}_{prod}$ maps a triple and an access method pair to a set of variables that are bound after the lookup, where t is a triple, m is an access method, and $\mathcal{V}_{prod}$ is the set of variables.

In our example, for the pair $(t4, aco)$, $\mathcal{P}(t_4, aco) :\rightarrow y$, because the lookup uses *Software* as an object, and the only variable that gets bound as a result of the lookup is y.

Definition 3.3 (Required Variables). $\mathcal{R}(t, m) :\rightarrow \mathcal{V}_{req}$ maps a triple and an access method pair to a set of variables that are required to be bound for the lookup, where t is a triple, m is an access method, and $\mathcal{V}_{req}$ is the set of variables.

Back to the example, $\mathcal{R}(t_5, aco) :\rightarrow y$. That is, if one uses the *aco* access method to evaluate t_5, then variable y must be bound by some prior triple lookup.

Definition 3.4 (Least Common Ancestor). $\mathsf{LCA}(p, p')$ is the first common ancestor of patterns p and p'. More formally, it is defined as follows:

$$\mathsf{LCA}(p, p') = x \iff \\ x \in \uparrow^*(p) \wedge x \in \uparrow^*(p') \wedge \nexists y. y \in \uparrow^*(p) \wedge y \in \uparrow^*(p') \wedge x \in \uparrow^*(y)$$

As an example, in the Figure 7, the least common ancestor of AND_N and OR is AND_T.

Definition 3.5 (Ancestors To LCA). $\uparrow\uparrow (p, p')$ refers to the set of $\uparrow^*$ built from traversing from p to the $\mathsf{LCA}(p, p')$:

$$\uparrow\uparrow (p, p') \equiv \{x \,|\, x \in \uparrow^*(p) \wedge \neg x \in \uparrow^*(\mathsf{LCA}(p, p'))\}$$

For instance, for the query shown in Figure 7, $\uparrow\uparrow (t_1, \mathsf{LCA}(t_1, t_2)) = \{\mathsf{AND}_T, \mathsf{OR}\}$

Definition 3.6 (OR Connected Patterns). $\cup$ denotes that two triples are related in an OR pattern, i.e. their least common ancestor is an OR pattern: $\cup(t, t') \equiv \mathsf{LCA}(t, t')$ is OR.

In the example, t_2 and t_3 are $\cup$.

Definition 3.7 ($\mathsf{OPTIONAL}$ Connected Pattern). $\mathsf{OPTIONAL}$ Connected Patterns $\hat{\cap}$ denotes if one triple is optional with respect to another, i.e. there is an OPTIONAL pattern guarding t' with respect to t:

$$\hat{\cap}(t, t') \equiv \exists p : p \in \uparrow\uparrow(t', t) \wedge p \text{ is } \mathsf{OPTIONAL}$$

In the example, t_6 and t_7 are $\hat{\cap}$, because t_7 is guarded by an $\mathsf{OPTIONAL}$ in relation to t_6.

Definition 3.8 (Data Flow Graph). The *Data Flow Graph* is a graph of $G =< V, E >$, where $V = (\mathcal{T} \times \mathcal{M}) \cup \mathsf{root}$, where root is a special node we add to the graph. A directed edge $(t, m) \rightarrow (t', m')$ exists in V when the following conditions hold:

$$\mathcal{P}(t, m) \supset \mathcal{R}(t', m') \wedge \neg\,(\cup(t, t') \vee \hat{\cap}(t', t))$$

In addition, a directed edge from root exists to a node (t, m) if $\mathcal{R}(t, m) = \emptyset$.

In the example , a directed edge $\mathsf{root} \rightarrow (t_4, aco)$ exists in the data flow graph (in Figure 8 we show the whole graph but for simplicity in the figure we omit the root node), because t_4 can be accessed by an object with a constant, and it has no required variables. Further, $(t_4, aco) \rightarrow (t_2, aco)$ is part of the data flow graph, because (t_2, aco) has a required variable y that is produced by (t_4, aco). In turn, (t_2, aco) has an edge to (t_1, acs), because (t_1, acs) has a required variable x which is produced by (t_2, aco).

The *Data Flow Graph* $\mathcal{G}$ is weighted, and the weights for each edge between two nodes is determined by a function:

$$\mathsf{W}((t, m), (t', m')), \mathcal{S}) :\rightarrow w$$

The w is derived from the costs of the two nodes, i.e., $\mathsf{TMC}(t, m, \mathcal{S})$, and $\mathsf{TMC}(t', m', \mathcal{S})$. A simple implementation of this function, for example could apply the cost of the target node to the edge. In the example, for instance, w for the edge $\mathsf{root} \rightarrow (t_4, aco)$ is 2, whereas the edge $\mathsf{root} \rightarrow (t_4, asc)$ is 5.

Computing The Optimal Flow Tree.

Given a weighted data flow graph $\mathcal{G}$, we now study the problem of computing the optimal (in terms of minimizing the cost) order for accessing *all* the triples in query $\mathcal{Q}$.

Theorem 3.1. *Given a dataflow graph $\mathcal{G}$ for a query $\mathcal{Q}$, finding the minimal weighted tree that covers all the triples in $\mathcal{Q}$ is NP-hard.*

The proof is by reduction from the TSP problem and is omitted here due to lack of space. In spite of this negative result, one might think that the input query $\mathcal{Q}$ is unlikely to contain a large number of triples, so an exhaustive search is indeed possible. However, even in our limited benchmarks, we found this solution to be impractical (e.g., one of our queries in the tool integration benchmark had 500 triples, spread across 100 OR patterns). We therefore introduce a greedy algorithm to solve the problem: Let T denote the *execution tree* we are trying to compute. Let τ refer to the set of triples corresponding to nodes already in the tree:

$$\tau \equiv \{t_i \,|\, \exists m_i \;(t_i, m_i) \in \mathcal{T}\}$$

We want to add a node that adds a new triple to the tree while adding the cheapest possible edge; formally, we want to choose a node (t', m') such that

$$\begin{array}{l}
(t', m') \in V \wedge \textit{ \# node to add} \\
t' \notin \tau \wedge \textit{ \# node adds new triple} \\
\exists (t, m) : \\
\left(\begin{array}{l}
(t, m) \in \mathcal{T} \wedge \textit{ \# node currently in tree} \\
(t, m) \rightarrow (t', m') \wedge \textit{ \# valid edge to new node} \\
\textit{\# no similar pair of nodes such that...} \\
\nexists (t'', m''), (t''', m''') : \\
\left(\begin{array}{l}
(t'', m'') \in \mathcal{T} \wedge \\
t''' \notin \tau \wedge \\
(t'', m'') \rightarrow (t''', m''') \wedge \\
\textit{\# ...adding } (t''', m''') \textit{ is cheaper} \\
\mathsf{W}((t'', m''), (t''', m''')) < \mathsf{W}((t, m), (t', m'))
\end{array}\right)
\end{array}\right)
\end{array}$$

On the first iteration, $\mathcal{T}_0 = \mathsf{root}$, and $\tau_0 = \emptyset$. $\mathcal{T}_{i+1}$ is computed by applying the step defined above, and the triple of the chosen node is added to τ_{i+1}. In our example, $\mathsf{root} \rightarrow (t_4, aco)$ is the cheapest edge, so $\mathcal{T}_1 = (t_4, aco)$, and $\tau_0 = t_4$. We then add (t_2, aco) to $\mathcal{T}_2$, and so on. We stop when we get to $\mathcal{T}_n$, where n is the number of triples in $\mathcal{Q}$. Figure 8 shows the computed tree (marked blue nodes) while Figure 9 shows the algorithm, where function $triple(j)$ returns the triple associated with a node in $\mathcal{G}$.

3.1.2 *The Query Plan Builder*

Both the data flow graph and the optimal flow tree largely ignore the query structure (the organization of triples into patterns) and the operators between the (triple) patterns. Yet, they provide useful information as to how to construct an actual plan for the input query, the focus of this section and output of the QPB module.

In more detail, Figure 10 shows the main algorithm $\mathsf{ExecTree}$ of the module. The algorithm is recursive and takes as input the optimal flow tree F computed by DFB, and (the parse tree of) a pattern P, which initially is the main pattern that includes the whole query

```
Input: The weighted data flow graph G
Output: An optimal flow tree T
τ ← ∅;
T ← root;
E ← SortEdgesByCost(G);
while |T| < |Q| do
  for each edge e_ij ∈ E do
    if i ∈ T ∧ j ∉ T ∧ triple(j) ∉ τ then
      T ← T ∪ j;
      τ ← τ ∪ triple(j);
      T ← e_ij;
```

Figure 9: The algorithm for computing the optimal flow tree

```
   Input: The optimal flow tree F of query Q, a pattern P in Q
   Output: An execution tree T for P, a set L of execution sub-trees
1  T ← ∅; L ← ∅;
2  switch the type of pattern P do
3    case P is a SIMPLE pattern
4      for each triple pattern t_i ∈ P do
5        T_i ← GetTree(t_i, F); L_i ← ∅;
6        if isLeaf(T_i, F) then L ← L ∪ T_i;
7        else (T, L) ← AndTree(F, T, L, T_i, L_i)
8    case P is an AND pattern
9      for each sub-pattern P_i ∈ P do
10       (T_i, L_i) ← ExecTree(F, P_i);
11       (T, L) ← AndTree(F, T, L, T_i, L_i);
12   case P is an OR pattern
13     for each sub-pattern P_i ∈ P do
14       (T_i, L_i) ← ExecTree(F, P_i);
15       (T, L) ← OrTree(F, T, L T_i, L_i);
16   case P is an OPTIONAL pattern
17     (T', L') ← ExecTree(F, P);
18     (T, L) ← OptTree(F, T, L T', L');
19   case P is a nested pattern
20     (T, L) ← ExecTree(F, P);
21 return (T, L)
```

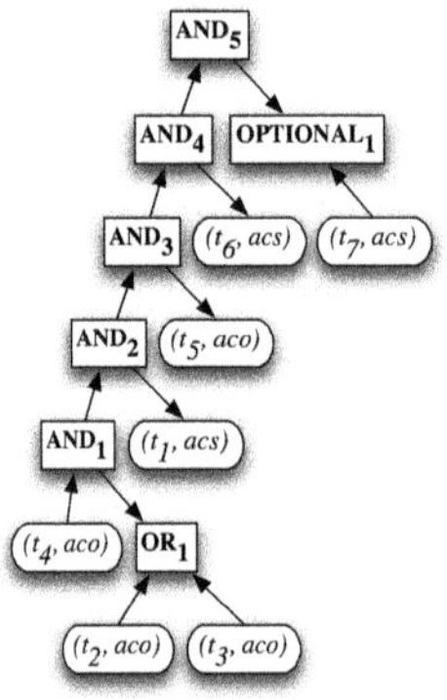

Figure 10: The ExecTree Algorithm and resulting execution tree

$\mathcal{Q}$. So in our running example, for the query in Figure 6(a), the algorithm takes as input the parse tree in Figure 7 and the optimal flow tree in Figure 8. The algorithm returns a schema-independent plan T, called the *execution tree* for the input query pattern P. The set of returned execution sub-trees $\mathcal{L}$ is guaranteed to be empty when the recursion terminates, but contains important information that the algorithm passes from one level of recursion to the previous one(s), while the algorithm runs (more on this later).

There are four main types of patterns in SPARQL, namely, *SIMPLE*, AND, UNION (a.k.a OR), and OPTIONAL patterns, and the algorithm handles each one independently, as we illustrate through our running example. Initially, both the execution tree T and the set $\mathcal{L}$ are empty (line 1). Since the top-level node in Figure 7 is an AND node, the algorithm considers each sub-pattern of the top-level node and calls itself recursively (lines 8-10) with each of the sub-patterns as argument. The first sub-pattern recursively considered is a *SIMPLE* one consisting of the single triple pattern t_1. By consulting the flow tree F, the algorithm determines the optimal execution tree for t_1 which consists of just the node (t_1, acs) (line 5). By further consulting the flow (line 6) the algorithm determines that node (t_1, acs) is a leaf node in the optimal flow and therefore it's evaluation depends on the evaluation of other flow nodes. Therefore, the algorithm adds tree (t_1, acs) to the local *late fusing* set $\mathcal{L}$ of execution trees. Set $\mathcal{L}$ contains execution sub-trees that should not be merged yet with the execution tree T but should be considered later in the process. Intuitively, late fusing plays two main roles: (a) it uses the flow as a guide to identify the proper point in time to fuse the execution tree T with execution sub-trees that are already computed by the recursion; and (b) it aims to optimize query evaluation by minimizing the size of intermediate results computed by the execution tree, and therefore it only fuses sub-trees at the latest possible place, when either the corresponding sub-tree variables are needed by the later stages of the evaluation, or when the operators and structure of the query enforce the fuse. The first recursion terminates by returning $(T_1, \mathcal{L}_1) = (\emptyset, \{L_1 = (t_1, acs)\})$. The second sub-pattern in Figure 7 is an OR and is therefore handled in lines 12-15. The resulting execution sub-tree contains three nodes, an OR node as root (from line 15) and nodes (t_2, aco) and (t_3, aco) as leaves (recursion in line 14). This sub-tree is also added to local set $\mathcal{L}$ and the second recursion terminates by returning $(T_2, \mathcal{L}_2) = (\emptyset, \{L_2 = \{\text{OR}, (t_2, aco), (t_3, aco)\}\})$. Finally, the last sub-pattern in Figure 7 is an AND pattern again, which causes further recursive calls in lines 8-11. In the recursive call that processes triple t_4 (lines 5-7), the execution tree node (t_4, aco) is the root node in the flow and therefore it is merged to the main execution tree T. Since T is empty, it becomes the root of the tree T. The three sub-trees that include nodes (t_5, aco), (t_6, acs), and $OPT = \{(\text{OPTIONAL}), (t_7, aco)\}$ are all becoming part of set $\mathcal{L}$. Therefore, the third recursion terminates by returning $(T_3, \mathcal{L}_3) = ((t_4, aco), \{L_3 = \{(t_5, aco)\}, L_4 = \{(t_6, acs)\}, L_5 = \{(\text{OPTIONAL}), (t_7, aco)\}\}$. Notice that after each recursion ends (line 10), the algorithm considers (line 11) the returned execution T_i and late-fuse $\mathcal{L}_i$ trees and uses function AndTree to build a new local execution T and set $\mathcal{L}$ of late-fusing trees (by also consulting the flow and following the late-fusing guidelines on postponing tree fusion unless it is necessary for the algorithm to progress). So, after the end of the first recursion and the first call to function AndTree, $(T, \mathcal{L}) = (T_1, \mathcal{L}_1)$, *i.e.*, the trees returned from the first recursion. After the end of the second recursion, and the second call to AndTree, $(T, \mathcal{L}) = (\emptyset, \mathcal{L}_1 \cup \mathcal{L}_2)$. Finally, after the end of the third recursion, $(T, \mathcal{L}) = ((t_4, aco), \mathcal{L}_1 \cup \mathcal{L}_2 \cup \mathcal{L}_3)$. The last call to AndTree builds the tree to the right of Figure 10 in the following manner. Starting from node (t_4, aco), it consults the flow and picks from the set $\mathcal{L}$ the sub-tree L_2 and connects this to node (t_4, aco) by adding a new AND node as the root of the tree. Sub-trees L_3 , L_4 and L_5 can be added at this stage to T but they are not considered as they violate the principles of late-fusing (their respective variables are not used by any other triple, as is also obvious by the optimal flow). On the other hand, there is still a dependency between the latest tree T and L_1 since the selectivity of t_1 can be used to reduce the intermediate size of the query results (especially the bindings to variable $?y$). Therefore, a new AND is introduced and the existing T is extended with L_1. The process iterates in this fashion until the whole tree in Figure 10 is generated.

Note that by using the optimal flow tree as a guide, we are able to *weave* the evaluation of different patterns, while our structured-based processing guarantees that the associativity of operations in the query is respected. So, our optimizer can generate plans like the one in Figure 10 where only a portion of a pattern is initially evaluated (*e.g.*, node (t_4, aco)) while the evaluation of other constructs in the pattern (*e.g.*, node (t_5, aco)) can be postponed until it no longer can be avoided. At the same time, this de-coupling from query structure allow us to safely push the evaluation of patterns early in the plan (*e.g.*, node (t_1, acs)) when doing so improves selectivity and reduces the size of intermediate results.

3.2 The SPARQL to SQL Translator

The translator takes as input the execution tree generated from the QPB module and performs two operations: first, it transforms the execution tree into an equivalent query plan that exploits the entity-oriented storage of DB2RDF; second, it uses the query plan to create the SQL query which is executed by the database.

3.2.1 *Building the Query Plan*

The execution tree provides an access method and an execution order for each triple but assumes that each triple node is evaluated

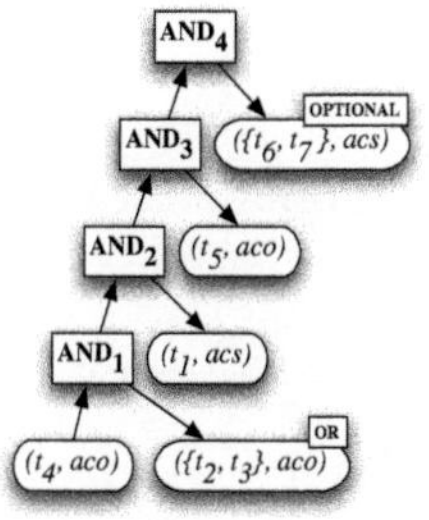

Figure 11: The query plan tree

```
SELECT ...
FROM  1:| DPH | AS T
WHERE 2:| T.ENTITY = ... | AND
      3:| T.PREDn1 = ... AND T.PREDn2 = ... |

   4:| LEFT OUTER JOIN DS AS S0
     | ON T.VALn1 = S0.lid
```

Figure 12: SQL code template

independently of the other nodes. However, one of the advantages of the entity-oriented storage is that a single access to, say, the DPH relation might retrieve a row that can be used to evaluate multiple triple patterns (star-queries). To this end, starting from the execution tree the translator builds a query plan where triples with the same subject (or the same object) are *merged* in the same plan node. A merged plan node indicates to the SQL builder that the containing triples form a star-query and must be executed with a single SQL select. Merging of nodes is always advantageous with one exception: when the star query involves entities with spills. The presence of such entities would require self-joins of the DPH (RPH) relations in the resulting SQL statement. Self-joins are expensive and therefore we use the following strategy to avoid them: When we *know* that star-queries involve entities with spills, we choose to *cascade* the evaluation of the star-query by issuing multiple SQL statements, each evaluating a subset of the star-query while at the same time filtering entities from the subsets of the star-query that have been previously evaluated. The multiple SQL statements are such that no SQL statement accesses predicates stored into different spill rows. Of course, the question remains on how we determine whether spills affect a star query. In our system this is straightforward. With only a tiny fraction of predicates involved in spills (due to coloring – see Section 2.3), our optimizer consults an in-memory structure of predicates involved in spills to determine during merging whether any of the star-query predicates participate in spills.

During the merging process we need to respect both the *structural* and *semantic* constraints. The structural constraints are imposed by the entity-oriented representation of data. To satisfy the structural constraints, candidate nodes for merging need to refer to the same entity, have the same access method and do not involve spills. As an example, in Figure 8 nodes t_2 and t_3 refer to the same entity (due to variable $?x$) and the same access method *aco*, as do nodes t_6 and t_7, due to the variable $?y$ and the method *acs*.

Semantic constraints for merging are imposed by the control structure of the SPARQL query (*i.e.,* the AND, UNION, OPTIONAL patterns). This restricts the merging of triples to constructs for which we can provide the equivalent SQL statements to access the relational tables. Triples in conjunctive and disjunctive patterns can be safely merged because the equivalent SQL semantics are well understood. Therefore, with a single access we can check whether the row includes the non-optional predicates in the conjunction. Similarly, it is possible to check the existence of any of the predicates mentioned in the disjunction. More formally, to satisfy the semantic constraints of SPARQL, candidate nodes for merging need to be ANDMergeable, ORMergeable or OPTMergeable.

Definition 3.9 (AND Mergeable Nodes)**.** Two nodes are ANDMergeable iff their least common ancestor and all intermediate ancestors are AND nodes:

$$\text{ANDMergeable}(t,t') \iff$$
$$\forall x : x \in (\uparrow\uparrow(t,\text{LCA}(t,t')) \cup \uparrow\uparrow(t',\text{LCA}(t,t'))) \implies x \text{ is AND}$$

Definition 3.10 (OR Mergeable Nodes)**.** Two nodes are ORMergeable iff their least common ancestor and all intermediate ancestors are OR nodes:

$$\text{ORMergeable}(t,t') \iff$$
$$\forall x : x \in (\uparrow\uparrow(t,\text{LCA}(t,t')) \cup \uparrow\uparrow(t',\text{LCA}(t,t'))) \implies x \text{ is OR}$$

Going back to the execution tree in Figure 10, notice that ORMergeable (t_2, t_3) is true, but ORMergeable (t_2, t_5) is false.

Definition 3.11 (OPTIONAL Mergeable Nodes)**.** Two nodes are OPTMergeable iff their least common ancestor and all intermediate ancestors are AND nodes, except the parent of the higher order triple in the execution plan which is OPTIONAL:

$$\text{OPTMergeable}(t,t') \iff$$
$$\forall x : x \in (\uparrow\uparrow(t,\text{LCA}(t,t')) \cup \uparrow\uparrow(t',\text{LCA}(t,t')))$$
$$\implies x \text{ is AND} \vee \{x \text{ is OPTIONAL} \wedge x \text{ is parent of } t'\}$$

As an example, in Figure 10 OPTMergeable (t_6, t_7) is true.

Given the input execution tree, we identify pairs of nodes that satisfy *both* the structural and semantic constraints introduced, and we merge them. Due to lack of space, we omit here the full details of the node merging algorithm and illustrate the output of the algorithm for our running example. So, given as input the execution tree in Figure 10, the resulting query plan tree is shown in Figure 11. Notice that in the resulting query plan there are two node merges, one due to the application of the ORMergeable definition, and one by the application of the OPTMergeable definition. Note that each merged node is annotated with the corresponding semantics under which the merge was applied. As a counter-example, consider node (t_5, aco) which is compatible structurally with the new node $(\{t_2, t_3\}, aco)$ since they both refer to the same entity through variable $?y$, and have the same access method *aco*. However, these two nodes are not merged since they violate the semantic constraints (*i.e.,* they do not satisfy the definitions above since their merge would mix a conjunctive with a disjunctive pattern). Even for our simple running example, the two identified node merges result in significant savings in terms of query evaluation. Intuitively, one can think of these two merges as eliminating two extra join operations during the translation of the query plan to an actual SQL query over the DB2RDF schema, the focus of our next section.

3.2.2 The SQL *Generation*

SQL generation is the final step of query translation. The query plan tree plays an important role in this process, and each node in the query plan tree, be it a triple, merge or control node, contains the necessary information to guide the SQL generation. For the generation, the SQL builder performs a post order traversal of the query plan tree and produces the equivalent SQL query for each node. The whole process is assisted by the use of SQL code templates.

In more detail, the base case of SQL translation considers a node that corresponds to a single triple or a merge. Figure 12 shows the template used to generate SQL code for such a node. The code in box 1 sets the target of the query to the DPH or RPH tables, according to the access method in the triple node. The code in box 2 restricts the entities being queried. As an example, when the subject is a constant and the access method is *acs*, the *entry* is connected to the constant subject values. When the subject is variable and the method is *acs*, then *entry* is connected with a previously-bound variable from a prior SELECT sub-query. The same reasoning applies for the *entry* component for an object when the access method is *aco*. Box 3 illustrates how one or more predicates are selected. That is, when the plan node corresponds to a merge, multiple $pred_i$ components are connected through conjunctive or disjunctive SQL operators. Finally, box 4 shows how we do outer join with the secondary table for multi-valued predicates.

```
WITH QT4RPH AS
 SELECT T.val1 AS val1 FROM RPH AS T WHERE T.entry='Software' AND T.pred1 ='industry',
QT4DS AS
 SELECT COALESCE (S.elm, T.val1 ) AS y
 FROM   QT4RPH AS T LEFT OUTER JOIN DS AS S ON T.val1 =S.l_id
QT23RPH AS
 SELECT QT4DS.y,
        CASE T.predm ='founder' THEN valm ELSE null END AS valm,
        CASE T.pred0 ='member' THEN val0 ELSE null END AS val0
 FROM   RPH AS T, QT4DS
 WHERE  T.entry =QT4DS.y AND (T.predm ='founder' OR T.pred0 ='member'),
QT23 AS
 SELECT LT.val0 AS x, T.y FROM QT23RPH as T, TABLE (T.valm, T.val0) as LT(val0)
 WHERE  LT.val0 IS NOT NULL
QT1DPH AS
 SELECT T.entry AS x, QT23.y FROM DPH AS T, QT23
 WHERE  T.entry =QT23.x AND T.predk ='home' AND T.val1 ='Palo Alto',
QT5RPH AS
 SELECT T.entry AS y, QT1DPH.x FROM RPH AS T, QT1DPH
 WHERE  T.entry =QT1DPH.y AND T.pred1 ='developer',
QT67DPH AS
 SELECT T.entry AS y, QT5RPH.x, CASE T.predk ='employees' THEN valk ELSE null END as z
 FROM   DPH AS T, QT5RPH WHERE T.entry =QT5RPH.y AND T.predm ='revenue'
SELECT x, y, z FROM QT67DPH
```

Figure 13: Generated SQL for SPARQL Query in Figure 6

The operator nodes in the query plan are used to guide the connection of instantiated templates like the one in Figure 12. We have already seen how AND nodes are implemented through the variable binding across triples as in box 2. For OR nodes we use the SQL UNION operator to connect its components' previously defined SELECT statements. For OPTIONAL we use LEFT OUTER JOIN between the SQL template for the main pattern and the SQL template for the OPTIONAL pattern. Figure 13 shows the final SQL for our running example where the SQL templates described above are instantiated according to the query plan tree in Figure 11.

In Figure 13, several Common Table Expressions (CTEs) are used for each plan node. t_4 is evaluated first and accesses RPH using the Software constant. Since industry is a multivalued predicate, the RS table is also accessed. The remaining predicates in this example are single valued and the access to the secondary table is avoided. The ORMergeable node t_{23} is evaluated next using the RPH table where the object is bound to the values of y produced by the first triple. The WHERE clause enforces the semantic that at least one of the predicates is present. The CTE projects the values corresponding to the present predicates and null values for those that are missing. The next CTE just flips these values, creating a new result record for each present predicate. The plan continues with triple t_5 and is completed with node the OPTMergeable node t_{67}. Here no constraint is imposed for the optional predicate making its presence optional on the record. In case the predicate is present, the corresponding value is projected, otherwise null. In this example, each predicate is assigned to a single column. When predicates are assigned to multiple columns, the position of the value is determined with CASE statements as seen in the SQL sample.

3.3 Advantages of the SPARQL Optimizer

To examine the effectiveness of our query optimization, we conducted experiments using both our 1M triple microbenchmark of Section 2.1 (which offers more control) and queries from the datasets used in our main experimental section (Section 4). As an example, for our microbenchmark we considered two constant values O_1 and O_2 with relative frequency in the data of .75 and .01, respectively. Then, we issued the simple query shown in Figure 14(a) that allowed data flows in either direction; i.e., evaluation could start on t_1 with an *aco* using O_1, then use the bindings for $?s$ to access t_2 with an *acs*, or start instead on t_2 with an *aco* using O_2 and use bindings for $?s$ to access t_1. The latter case is of course better. Figure 14(b) shows the SQL generated by our SPARQL optimizer while Figure 14(c) shows an equivalent SQL query corresponding to the only alternative but sub-optimal flow. The former query took 13 ms to evaluate, whereas the latter took 5X longer, that is 65 ms, suggesting that our optimization is in fact effective even in this simple query. Using real and benchmark queries from datasets resulted in even more striking differences in evaluation times. For example, when optimized by our SPARQL optimizer query, PQ1 from PRBench (Section 4) was evaluated in 4ms, while the translated SQL corresponding to a sub-optimal flow required 22.66 seconds!

```
SELECT ?s WHERE { ?s SV1 O1 (t1) . ?s SV2 O2 (t2) }
```

(a) SPARQL Query

```
SELECT T.ENTRY, D.ENTRY FROM RS AS R, DPH AS D
WHERE   R.ENTRY='O2' AND R.PROP='SV2' AND D.ENTRY=T.ENTRY AND D.VAL0='O1' AND D.PROP0='SV1'
```

(b) Optimized SQL

```
SELECT T.ENTRY, D.ENTRY FROM RS AS R, DPH AS D
WHERE R.ENTRY='O1' AND R.PROP='SV1' AND D.ENTRY=T.ENTRY AND D.VAL0='O2' AND D.PROP0='SV2'
```

(c) Alternative SQL

Figure 14: Query Translation

4. EXPERIMENTS

We compared the performance of DB2RDF, using IBM DB2 as our relational back-end, to that of Virtuoso 6.1.5 OpenSource Edition, Apache Jena 2.7.3 (TDB), OpenRDF Sesame 2.6.8, and RDF-3X 0.3.5. DB2RDF, Virtuoso and RDF-3X were run in a client server mode on the same machine and all other systems were run in process mode. For both Jena and Virtuoso, we enabled all recommended optimizations. Jena had the BGP optimizer enabled. For Virtuoso we built all recommended indexes. For DB2RDF, we only added indexes on the entry columns of the DPH and RPH relations (no indexes on the $pred_i$ and val_i columns).

We conducted experiments with 4 different benchmarks: LUBM [7], SP2Bench [15], DBpedia [12], and a private benchmark PRBench that was offered to us by an external partner organization. For the LUBM and SP2Bench benchmarks, we scaled them up to 100 million triples each and used their associated published query workloads. The DBpedia 3.7 benchmark [5] has 333 million triples. The private benchmark included data from a tool integration application, and it contained 60 million triples about various software artifacts generated by different tools (e.g., bug reports, requirements, etc). For all systems, we evaluated queries in a warm cache scenario. For each dataset, benchmark queries were randomly mixed to create a run, and each run was issued 8 times to the 5 stores. We discarded the first run and reported the average result for each query over 7 consecutive runs. For each query, we measured its running time excluding the time taken to stream back the results to the API, in order to minimize variations caused by the various APIs available. As shown in Figure 15, the evaluated queries were classified into four categories. Queries that failed to parse SPARQL correctly, we reported as *unsupported*. The remainder supported queries were further classified as either *complete*, *timeout*, or *error*. We counted the results from each system and when a system provided the correct number of answers we classified the query as completed. If the system returned the wrong number of results, we classified this as an error. Finally, we used a timeout of 10 minutes to trap queries that do not terminate within a reasonable amount of time. In the figure, we also report the average time taken (in seconds) to evaluate complete and timeout queries. For queries that timeout, their running time was set to 10 minutes. For obvious reasons, we do not count the time of queries that return the wrong number of results.

This is the most comprehensive evaluation of RDF systems. Unlike previous works, this is the first study that evaluates 5 systems using a total of *78 queries*, over a total of *600 million triples*. Our experiments were conducted on 5 identical virtual machines (one per system), each equivalent to a 4-core, 2.6GHz Intel Xeon system with 32GB of memory running 64-bit Linux. Each system was not memory limited, meaning it could consume all of its 32G. None of the systems came close to this memory limit in any experiment.

4.1 The datasets

• **LUBM:** The LUBM benchmark requires OWL DL inference, which is not supported across all tested systems. Without inference, most benchmark queries return empty result sets. To address this issue, we expanded the existing queries and created a set of *equivalent* queries that implement inference and do not require this feature from the evaluated system. As an example, if the LUBM ontology stated that $GraduateStudent \sqsubseteq Student$, and the query asks for *?x rdf:type Student*, the query was expanded into *?x rdf:type Student UNION ?x rdf:type Graduate Student*. We performed this set of expansions and issued the same expanded query to all systems. From the 14 original queries in the benchmark, only 12 (denoted as LQ1 to LQ10, LQ13 and LQ14) are included here because 2 queries involved ontological axioms that cannot be expanded.

• **SP2Bench:** SP2Bench is an extract of DBLP data with corresponding SPARQL queries (denoted as SQ1 to SQ17). We used this benchmark as is, with no modifications. Prior reports on this benchmark were conducted with at most 5 million triples (even in the paper where the benchmark was introduced). We scaled to 100 million triples, and noticed that some queries (by design) had rather large result sets. SQ4 in particular created a cross product of the entire dataset, which meant that *all* systems timeout on this query.

• **DBpedia:** The DBpedia SPARQL benchmark is a set of query templates derived from actual query logs against the public DBpedia SPARQL endpoint [12]. We used these templates with the DBpedia 3.7 dataset, and obtained 20 queries (denoted as DQ1 to DQ20) that had non-empty result sets. Since templates were derived for an earlier DBpedia version, not all result in non-empty queries.

• **PRBench:** The private benchmark reflects data from a tool integration scenario where specific information about the same software artifacts are generated by different tools, and RDF data provides an integrated view on these artifacts across tools. This is a quad dataset where triples are organized into over 1 million 'graphs'. As we explain, this caused problems for some systems which do not support quads (e.g., RDF-3X, Sesame). We had 29 SPARQL queries (denoted as PQ1 to PQ29), with some being fairly complex queries (e.g., a SPARQL union of 100 conjunctive queries).

4.2 Experimental results

Main Result 1. Figure 15 shows that DB2RDF is the only system that evaluates correctly and efficiently 77 out of the 78 tested queries. As mentioned, SQ4 was the only query in which our system did timeout (as did all the other systems). If we exclude SQ4, it is clear from Figure 15 that each of the remaining systems had queries returning incorrect number of results, or queries that timeout without returning any results. We do not emphasize the advantage of DB2RDF in terms of SPARQL support, since this is mostly a function of system maturity and continued development.

Main Result 2. Given Figure 15, it is hard to make direct system comparisons. Still, when the DB2RDF system is compared with systems that can evaluate approximately the same queries (*i.e.,* Virtuoso and Jena), then DB2RDF is in the worst case slightly faster, and in the best case, as much as an order of magnitude faster than the other two systems. So, for LUBM, DB2RDF is significantly faster than Virtuoso (2X) and Jena (4X). For SP2Bench, DB2RDF is on average times about 50% faster than Virtuoso, although Virtuoso has a better geometric mean (not shown due to space constraints), which reflects Virtuoso being much better on short running queries. For DBpedia, DB2RDF and Virtuoso have comparable performance, and for PRBench, DB2RDF is about 5.5X better than Jena. Jena is actually the only system that supports the same queries as DB2RDF, and across all datasets DB2RDF is in the worst case 60%, and in the best case as much as two orders of magnitude faster. A comparison between DB2RDF and RDF-3X is also possible, but only in the LUBM dataset where both systems support a similar number of queries. The two systems are fairly close in performance and out-perform the remaining three systems. When compared between themselves across 11 queries (RDF-3X did not run one query), DB2RDF is faster than RDF-3X in 3 queries, namely in LQ8, LQ13 and LQ14 (246ms, 14ms and 4.6secs versus 573ms, 36ms and 9.5secs, respectively), while RDF-3X has clearly an advantage in 3 other queries, namely in LQ2, LQ6, LQ10 (722ms, 12secs and 1.57secs versus 20secs, 33secs and 3.42secs, respectively). For the remaining 5 queries, the two systems have almost identical performance with RDF-3X being faster than DB2RDF by approximately 3ms for each query.

Dataset	System	Supported			Unsupported	Mean
		Complete	Timeout	Error		(secs)
LUBM (100M triples) (12 queries)	Jena	12	-	-	-	35.1
	Sesame	4	-	8	-	164.7
	Virtuoso	12	-	-	-	16.8
	RDF-3X	11	-	-	1	2.8
	DB2RDF	12	-	-	-	8.3
SP2Bench (100M triples) (17 queries)	Jena	11	6	-	-	253
	Sesame	8	8	1	-	330
	Virtuoso	16	1	-	-	211
	RDF-3X	6	2	2	7	152
	DB2RDF	16	1	-	-	108
DBpedia (333M triples) (20 queries)	Jena	18	1	1	-	33
	Virtuoso	20	-	-	-	0.25
	DB2RDF	20	-	-	-	0.25
PRBench (60M triples) (29 queries)	Jena	29	-	-	-	5.7
	Virtuoso	25	-	-	4	3.9
	DB2RDF	29	-	-	-	1.0

Figure 15: Summary results for all systems and datasets

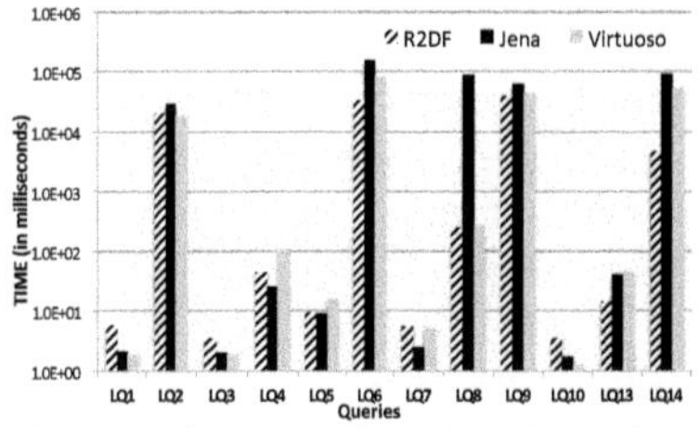

Figure 16: LUBM benchmark results

Detailed results: For a more detailed per-query comparison, we turn to Figure 16 which illustrates the running times for DB2RDF, Virtuoso and Jena for all 12 LUBM queries (reported times are in milliseconds and the scale is logarithmic). Notice that DB2RDF outperforms the other systems in the long-running and complicated queries (*e.g.,* LQ6, LQ8, LQ9, LQ13, LQ14). So, DB2RDF takes approximately 33secs to evaluate LQ6, while Virtuoso requires 83.2secs and Jena 150secs. Similarly, DB2RDF takes 40secs to evaluate LQ9, whereas Virtuoso requires 46 and Jena 60secs. Most notably, in LQ14 DB2RDF requires 4.6secs while Virtuoso requires 53secs and Jena 94.1secs. For the sub-second queries, DB2RDF is slightly slower than the other systems, but the difference is *negligible* at this scale. So, for LQ1, DB2RDF requires 5ms, while Virtuoso requires 1.8ms and Jena 2.1ms. Similarly, for LQ3 DB2RDF requires 3.4ms while Virtuoso takes 1.8ms and Jena 2.0ms.

The situation is similar in the PRBench case. Figure 17 shows the evaluation time of 4 long-running queries. Consistently, DB2RDF outperforms all other systems. For example, for PQ10 DB2RDF takes 3ms, while Jena requires 27 seconds and Virtuoso requires 39 seconds! For each of the other three queries, DB2RDF takes approx 4.8secs while Jena requires a minimum of 32 and Vir-

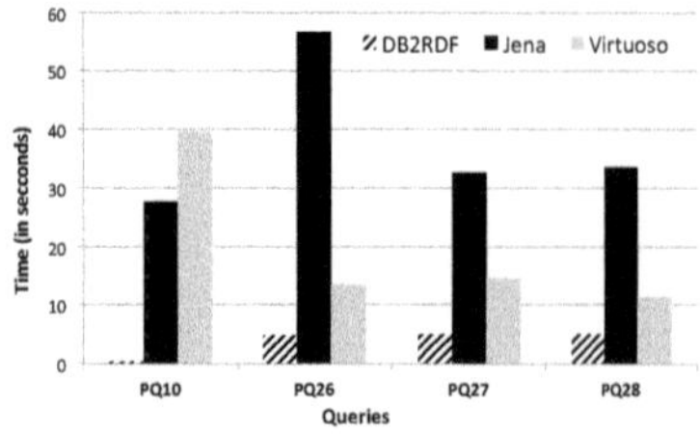

Figure 17: PRBench sample of long-running queries

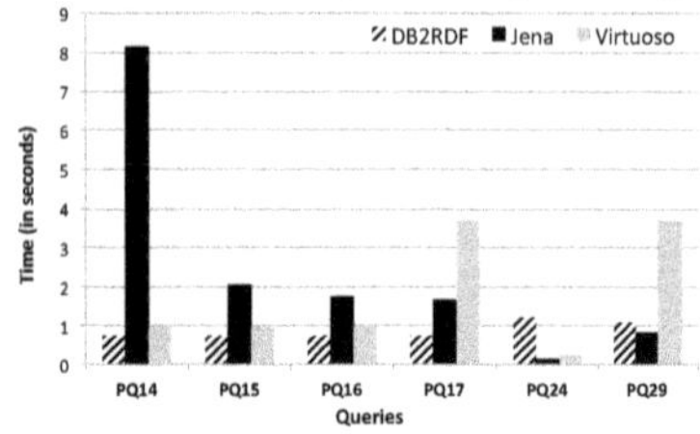

Figure 18: PRBench sample of medium-running queries

tuoso a minimum of 11secs. Figure 18 shows that the situation is similar for medium-running queries where DB2RDF consistently outperforms the competition.

5. RELATED WORK

Abadi et al. [2] propose a predicate-oriented storage for efficient RDF management which uses column stores technology and avoids many of the self-join operations in the final SQL. A recently proposed index structure for RDF called GRIN [20] uses a grouping technique to determine a small subset of the RDF database that contains the answers to a query and can be used independently of the underlying RDF representation. Stocker et al. [17] and Hartig and Heese [8] propose techniques for algebraic re-writing of SPARQL queries to help the query engine devise a better query plan (we already commented about the limitations of these and the following technique in previous sections). Madulo et al. [11] describe a technique to estimate the selectivity of a triple pattern by gathering frequency statistics of the subject, predicate and object and then assuming probabilistic independence between their distributions.

Chen et al. [4] improve the performance of relational-based XML engines. As in our work, the authors store XML documents in a single wide and sparse table. Unlike our work, the management of null values is shifted to the relational engine, and spills are not handled, *i.e.,* it is not clear the work handles the case when an XML element is too large to fit in a record.

Weiss et al. [22] propose an *in-memory* store based on six extended indexes for RDF triples. While the authors argue the benefits of of this approach for query processing, there are important scalability concerns: memory requirements scale linearly with data size and for 6M triples (the largest dataset evaluated) the system requires 8GB of memory. Accordingly, for, say, the 100M LUBM dataset they would require approximately 120GB of memory. Our disk-based store scales without such requirements.

Huang et al. [10] focus on storage and query execution for clustered RDF databases with datasets distributed using graph partitioning algorithms and queries split into chunks that can be executed in parallel. Our work focuses on a centralized setting.

6. CONCLUSIONS

In this paper, we introduced a novel representation and querying mechanism for RDF data on top of relational databases. We introduced DB2RDF, an innovative relational schema that deals with RDF sparsity and schema variability. We showed that DB2RDF has additional benefits during query processing including the reduction of join operations for star queries. We also introduced an innovative SPARQL query optimization technique and novel SPARQL-to-SQL translation techniques, and we showed that these outperform existing RDF stores on standard datasets and query workloads.

For future work, we are preparing a study on insertion, bulk load and update performance and we are planning to extend our system to support the SPARQL 1.1 standard (including property paths). We are also planning to support inferencing, a topic we briefly discussed during the presentation of the LUBM benchmark.

7. REFERENCES

[1] 4store - scalable RDF storage. `http://4store.org/`http://4store.org/.

[2] D. J. Abadi, A. Marcus, S. R. Madden, and K. Hollenbach. Scalable semantic web data management using vertical partitioning. In *VLDB*, pages 411–422, 2007.

[3] Best Buy jump starts data web marketing. `http://www.chiefmartec.com/2009/12/best-buy-jump-starts-data-web-marketing.html`.

[4] L. J. Chen, P. A. Bernstein, P. Carlin, D. Filipovic, M. Rys, N. Shamgunov, J. F. Terwilliger, M. Todic, S. Tomasevic, and D. Tomic. Mapping XML to a Wide Sparse Table. In *ICDE*, pages 630–641, 2012.

[5] DBpedia dataset. http://dbpedia.org.

[6] S. Duan, A. Kementsietsidis, K. Srinivas, and O. Udrea. Apples and oranges: a comparison of RDF benchmarks and real RDF datasets. In *SIGMOD*, 2011.

[7] Y. Guo, Z. Pan, and J. Heflin. LUBM: A benchmark for OWL knowledge base systems. *Journal of Web Semantics*, 3(2–3):158–182, 2005.

[8] O. Hartig and R. Heese. The SPARQL Query Graph Model for Query Optimization. pages 564–578. 2007.

[9] O. Hassanzadeh, A. Kementsietsidis, and Y. Velegrakis. Data management issues on the semantic web. In *ICDE*, pages 1204–1206, 2012.

[10] J. Huang, D. J. Abadi, and K. Ren. Scalable SPARQL Querying of Large RDF Graphs. *PVLDB*, 4(11):1123–1134, 2011.

[11] A. Maduko, K. Anyanwu, A. Sheth, and P. Schliekelman. Estimating the cardinality of rdf graph patterns. In *WWW*, pages 1233–1234, 2007.

[12] M. Morsey, J. Lehmann, S. Auer, and A.-C. Ngonga Ngomo. DBpedia SPARQL Benchmark – Performance Assessment with Real Queries on Real Data. In *ISWC 2011*, 2011.

[13] T. Neumann and G. Weikum. The RDF-3X engine for scalable management of RDF data. *The VLDB Journal*, 19(1):91–113, Feb. 2010.

[14] Resource Description Framework (RDF). `http://www.w3.org/RDF/`.

[15] M. Schmidt, T. Hornung, G. Lausen, and C. Pinkel. SP2Bench: A SPARQL Performance Benchmark. *CoRR*, abs/0806.4627, 2008.

[16] SPARQL Query Language for RDF. `http://www.w3.org/TR/rdf-sparql-query/`.

[17] M. Stocker, A. Seaborne, A. Bernstein, C. Kiefer, and D. Reynolds. SPARQL basic graph pattern optimization using selectivity estimation. In *WWW*, pages 595–604, 2008.

[18] The New York Times Linked Open Data. `http://data.nytimes.com/`.

[19] P. Tsialiamanis, L. Sidirourgos, I. Fundulaki, V. Christophides, and P. Boncz. Heuristics-based query optimisation for SPARQL. In *EDBT*, pages 324–335, 2012.

[20] O. Udrea, A. Pugliese, and V. S. Subrahmanian. GRIN: A Graph-based RDF Index. In *AAAI*, pages 1465–1470, 2007.

[21] Virtuoso Open-Source Edition. http://virtuoso.openlinksw.com/wiki/main/main/.

[22] C. Weiss, P. Karras, and A. Bernstein. Hexastore: sextuple indexing for semantic web data management. *PVLDB*, 1(1):1008–1019, 2008.

[23] K. Wilkinson, C. Sayers, H. A. Kuno, and D. Reynolds. Efficient RDF Storage and Retrieval in Jena2. In *Semantic Web and Databases Workshop*, pages 131–150, 2003.

Automatic Synthesis of Out-of-Core Algorithms

Yannis Klonatos Andres Nötzli Andrej Spielmann Christoph Koch Viktor Kuncak
School of Computer and Communications Sciences, EPFL
{yannis.klonatos, andres.notzli, andrej.spielmann, christoph.koch, viktor.kuncak}@epfl.ch

ABSTRACT

We present a system for the automatic synthesis of efficient algorithms specialized for a particular memory hierarchy and a set of storage devices. The developer provides two independent inputs: 1) an algorithm that ignores memory hierarchy and external storage aspects; and 2) a description of the target memory hierarchy, including its topology and parameters. Our system is able to automatically synthesize memory-hierarchy and storage-device-aware algorithms out of those specifications, for tasks such as joins and sorting. The framework is extensible and allows developers to quickly synthesize custom out-of-core algorithms as new storage technologies become available.

Categories and Subject Descriptors

I.2.2 [**Artificial Intelligence**]: Automatic Programming—*Program synthesis*; D.4.2 [**Operating Systems**]: Storage Management—*Storage hierarchies*; H.2.4 [**Database Management**]: Systems—*Query processing*

Keywords

Out-of-core algorithms, synthesis, memory hierarchies

1. INTRODUCTION

The design of performance-critical software systems must depend on the hardware on which these systems run. This is particularly true for data-intensive computations. The research literature describes numerous out-of-core algorithms designed and optimized for a variety of hardware and storage device configurations [23, 13, 9, 25, 5, 21, 27, 16, 18]. These are case studies of how understanding memory hierarchies and data locality can drive algorithm design.

To this day, no methodology exists for creating such algorithms. We must rely on significant creative talent to serve our need for such algorithms, which remain publishable as original research contributions.

The introduction of a new storage or memory technology requires the development of new versions of most out-of-core algorithms. This leads to an arms race between the developers of hardware on one hand and of software systems and out-of-core algorithms on the other. Each new development in hardware calls for numerous research contributions on the software side, to update a multitude of algorithms and systems. Given the rapid rate of hardware innovation and the increasing popularity of hardware specialization, the ultimate consequence is a modest software crisis.

To address this challenge, we propose the use of software synthesis to automatically generate specialized out-of-core algorithms. The input is a naive memory hierarchy oblivious algorithm and a description of the target hardware setup and memory hierarchy. We encode fundamental principles of out-of-core algorithm design, many of which aim at the maximization of data locality, as transformation rules. The application of such a rule to the algorithm results in an equivalent algorithm which *may* have better performance on real hardware. By applying transformation rules, we create a navigable search space of equivalent algorithms. To be able to choose an optimal algorithm, we develop a cost estimation procedure based on the given hardware description.

The next example illustrates our approach:

EXAMPLE 1. The simplest way to implement a join algorithm on relations R and S is with two nested for-loops:

for $(x \leftarrow \mathsf{R})$ for $(y \leftarrow \mathsf{S})$ if joinCond(x,y) then $[\langle x,y\rangle]$ else []

This program is an intuitive description of the programmer's intention. Let us assume a scenario where the input is stored on a hard disk and the output is not written anywhere (e.g., it is consumed by the CPU). Then, ignoring any buffering of the hard disk and the operating system, this program transfers every tuple of R and S from the hard disk separately. The efficiency of the algorithm can be improved significantly if we reduce the number of disk seeks by accessing the relations in larger contiguous blocks. Also, the semantics of the program does not change if the loops are reordered so that the outer relation is the smaller, but this further reduces the amount of seeking. By expressing such knowledge as transformation rules, we can automatically transform the above program into one that implements these two optimizations:

$(\lambda\langle \mathsf{R},\mathsf{S}\rangle.$for $(xBlock\ [k_1] \leftarrow \mathsf{R})$
  for $(yBlock\ [k_2] \leftarrow \mathsf{S})$ for $(x \leftarrow$ xBlock)
    for $(y \leftarrow yBlock)$ if joinCond(x,y) then $[\langle x,y\rangle]$ else [])
(if length(R) $\leq$ length(S) then $\langle$R, S$\rangle$ else $\langle$S, R$\rangle$)

When the block-size k1 of *xBlock* is maximized, this is the canonical Block Nested Loops Join. □

In the above example, we used the following transformation rule that turns a loop into a buffered scan with block-based transfers of block size k:

for ($x \leftarrow$ S) $e \Rightarrow$
for ($xBlock$ [k] $\leftarrow$ S) for ($x \leftarrow xBlock$) e

This rule says that the left-hand side program is equivalent to the right-hand side and suggests that, subject to the targeted memory hierarchy, the latter is likely to be more efficient than the former. Indeed, the latter program requires less seeking on the hard disk.

To realize our vision of out-of-core algorithm synthesis, we have addressed the following challenges:

Design of a new language. We have designed a domain-specific language (DSL) called OCAL (Out-of-Core Algorithm Language), described in Section 3. The primary design goals of OCAL are (i) to be expressive enough for a variety of out-of-core algorithms, (ii) to be succinct enough to keep typical algorithms short and the search space for program synthesis manageable, and (iii) to keep syntax and semantics of the language simple to facilitate analysis and program transformation. In order to make it reasonably easy to cost programs and apply transformations, we should avoid constructs such as unrestricted recursion, mutable values, and side effects. As a consequence, we avoid imperative and low-level languages such as C for program representation during synthesis.

OCAL is defined as Monad Calculus on lists [8, 26] with a fold expression. It satisfies the above three design desiderata. (i) It is expressive, extending the power of nested relational algebra by the ability to process collections sequentially and exploiting order, which is central to capturing the essence of most out-of-core algorithms. (ii) Named OCAL function definitions can be used to keep OCAL programs short; these definitions are treated like language extensions in our synthesis system. (iii) OCAL is a simple purely functional language without side-effects in which recursion is confined to fold (and flatMap). Transformations in OCAL can be applied locally due to its functional and algebraic qualities. Finally, since full recursion is excluded and for-comprehensions (functional for-loops as in, say, XQuery and Scala) are straightforward to define in OCAL, even users only familiar with imperative languages can read most OCAL programs without great difficulty. It is relatively easy to map OCAL programs to imperative (C) code.

Cost Estimation and Cost Minimization. We need a systematic cost estimation framework to reason about the efficiency of OCAL programs. This requires an easily computable cost measure for evaluating the performance of each program that we explore. This measure, presented in Section 5, is a function of the algorithm, the memory hierarchy and statistics about the input. One contribution of this paper is the demonstration that in this domain it is possible to efficiently and automatically perform such estimation, and that the estimates are predictive enough to differentiate more efficient from less efficient algorithms on a given memory hierarchy.

There are two orthogonal aspects of cost estimation: structural program transformations and parameter selection. For the former, we use a breadth-first search strategy to explore the space of structurally different programs, and we use constants derived from the given memory hierarchy to build a cost function. To perform the latter, each program is also parameterized with values such as sizes of blocks and buffers. In Example 1, k is one such parameter. We use our cost estimation rules to characterize the running time estimate as a (possibly non-linear) function of those parameters. We have also implemented the non-linear optimization solver described in [19] to tune the values of parameters so as to minimize the cost estimate. We have found this strategy to be computationally feasible and to yield efficient programs for various memory hierarchies.

Development of a program synthesizer. Based on the language, rewrite rules, and costing framework, we have implemented OCAS, the Out-of-Core Algorithm Synthesizer. The input to OCAS consists of two orthogonal items: (1) a naive memory-oblivious algorithm given in OCAL; and (2) the structure and parameters of a memory hierarchy and storage devices. From this input, OCAS automatically derives efficient algorithms that have the same functional behavior as the initial specification algorithm, but whose performance is tuned to the given memory hierarchy. To do so, it uses a library of transformation rules, which we discuss in Section 6. OCAS then generates C code out of the optimized algorithm, using an OCAL-to-C code generator. Our approach also necessitates a technique, presented in Section 4, for describing memory hierarchies, such that device properties can be expressed sufficiently abstractly.

Because OCAS operates automatically, it is possible to deploy it even in environments where the system configuration changes dynamically, such as cloud infrastructures. OCAS can be used at installation time to adapt a piece of data management software to a computer, or at deployment time via just-in-time-compilation to make best use of fresh information on the availability of system resources.

Most importantly, the design of OCAS provides the so far missing methodology for designing efficient out-of-core algorithms, and even automatizes algorithm creation. Developers may need to make use of the extensibility of OCAS to adapt to unforeseen developments, but there is no need to "reinvent the wheel"; The basic machinery of OCAS will remain unchanged.

Providing an extensible architecture. Extensibility is an important property of the design of OCAS. Developers should be able to easily adapt OCAS as new hardware platforms become available and new algorithms are proposed. The library of program transformation rules of OCAS can be extended to implement new ways of using data locality considerations to create better algorithms. Furthermore, we can create named definitions in OCAL that can subsequently be used like new language operations. For each such definition, we can extend OCAS by matching code generator and cost function plugins to allow the synthesizer to make use of a particularly efficient implementation of that new language feature. Thus, definitions (in conjunction with code generator and cost function extensions) do *not* increase the expressiveness of the language but the efficiency of the algorithms created.

We conclude with an experimental evaluation of our system. We use OCAS to derive C code for algorithms such as Block Nested Loops Join, GRACE Hash Join and the External Merge-Sort in their canonical textbook forms starting from a naive specifications of joins and sorting. We also present examples of algorithms specialized for memory hierarchies that are not yet found in textbooks, such as a join

$$\frac{}{x : \mathsf{Type}(x)} \quad \frac{}{c : \mathsf{Type}(c)} \quad \frac{}{p : \mathsf{IType}(p) \rightarrow \mathsf{OType}(p)} \quad \frac{e : \tau}{\lambda x.e : \mathsf{Type}(x) \rightarrow \tau} \quad \frac{e_1 : \tau_2 \rightarrow \tau_1 \quad e_2 : \tau_2}{e_1 e_2 : \tau_1} \quad \frac{e_1 : \tau_1 \ldots\ e_n : \tau_n}{\langle e_1, \ldots, e_n \rangle : \langle \tau_1, \ldots, \tau_n \rangle}$$

$$\frac{e : \langle \tau_1, \ldots, \tau_n \rangle \quad i : \mathsf{Int}}{e.i : \tau_i} \quad \frac{e : \tau}{[e] : [\tau]} \quad \frac{e : \tau_1 \rightarrow [\tau_2]}{\mathsf{flatMap}(e) : [\tau_1] \rightarrow [\tau_2]} \quad \frac{c : \mathsf{Bool},\ e_1 : \tau,\ e_2 : \tau}{\mathsf{if}\ c\ \mathsf{then}\ e_1\ \mathsf{else}\ e_2 : \tau} \quad \frac{c : \tau_2,\ f : \langle \tau_2, \tau_1 \rangle \rightarrow \tau_2}{\mathsf{foldL}(c, f) : [\tau_1] \rightarrow \tau_2}$$

Figure 1: The type system of OCAL.

algorithm for flash drives. We present these case studies and their evaluation in Section 7.

2. RELATED WORK

There is very little work on automating out-of-core algorithm design. In contrast, a great amount of work has been done on manually developing specialized out-of-core algorithms for various tasks and memory hierarchies. In our work, we often refer to canonical algorithms for certain database management tasks. Their descriptions can be found in the standard text books like [23]. More recently, effort has been expended on designing algorithms for flash memory [21, 18, 5], the intricate memory hierarchies of graphics cards [9, 13, 25, 27], and multi-level memory hierarchies [16]. These papers demonstrate that the state of the art in developing out-of-core algorithms is to manually carry out ad-hoc effort; one cannot yet rely on automation or a clear design methodology.

The idea of automatic program transformation is present in [17]. However, this work does not take into account the characteristics of the architecture as OCAS does. This makes the approach limited as new architectures become available. Furthermore, the authors focus only on for-loops while OCAS proposes the use of a new language that (i) supports a wider set of constructs and (ii) is extensible to allow for easy addition of new definitions. Synthesis appears in domains other than data management as well. For instance, hardware-specific synthesis of linear transforms and other mathematical functions is the aim of SPIRAL [22].

In the Sequoia project [24], a general-purpose C-like language is presented that has *explicit* knowledge of the topology of the machine, and allows writing programs that efficiently utilize the hierarchy and the available parallelism. The Sequoia system does not perform software synthesis, so the programmers must specify the out-of-core algorithms themselves. However, it still handles other aspects of out-of-core algorithms like our tool, such as parameter selection.

OCAS performs algebraic manipulations to obtain more efficient equivalent programs; this idea can also be found in work on functional programming [20, 7]. Recursion schemas like folding [12] also play an important role in our work, especially for our sorting algorithms.

For static analysis of the running costs of functional programs, we draw inspiration from [15, 14, 10, 11]. COSTA [4] is a general-purpose cost estimation system for Java bytecode. This makes it applicable to languages more powerful than the one described in this paper. However, for the same reason, COSTA often fails to deduce bounds as tight as those of our system when working with a restricted custom-designed language. In particular, for the Merge-Sort algorithm that we use in one of our examples, we could not bring COSTA to estimate the asymptotically correct cost bound of $O(n \log n)$.

3. THE OUT-OF-CORE DSL

In this section we present OCAL (Out-of-Core Algorithm Language) which OCAS uses to represent data processing algorithms. The design of OCAL provides enough expressive power to describe commonly used algorithms ranging from traditional relational algebra operators, such as selection, projection and joins, to additional aspects of data processing such as sorting. At the same time, OCAL also allows easy application of transformation rules and costing as it will be discussed in more detail in Section 5 and Section 6.

The base language. OCAL extends Monad Calculus on lists [8, 26] with a fold expression. Consequently, the proposed language is more expressive than nested relational calculus. Starting from a totally ordered set D of atomic values that includes integers, booleans and strings, values are built inductively from D using list and tuple construction as formalized by the following grammar:

$$\tau ::= \mathsf{D} \mid \langle \tau, \ldots, \tau \rangle \mid [\tau]$$

The typing rules of the language are presented in Figure 1 where $e, e_1, \ldots, e_n$ range over expressions, x over variables, c over primitive constants and $\tau, \tau_1, \ldots, \tau_n$ over types. Each value x is assigned a $\mathsf{Type}(x)$ and, similarly, constants c have a type $\mathsf{Type}(c)$. Functions in OCAL are of type $\tau_1 \rightarrow \tau_2$ where τ_1 and τ_2 are value types. As an example, the type of a join operator for two binary relations on D is:

$$\langle [\langle \mathsf{D}, \mathsf{D} \rangle], [\langle \mathsf{D}, \mathsf{D} \rangle] \rangle \rightarrow [\langle \mathsf{D}, \mathsf{D}, \mathsf{D}, \mathsf{D} \rangle]$$

In the same figure, p ranges over primitive functions including boolean connectives ($\wedge$, $\vee$, $\neg$); equality of values of various types and comparison of basic data types D ($==$, $\leq$, $\geq$); a list union operator $\sqcup$, and further functions on tuples of values of D that only require a constant amount of memory (e.g., arithmetic operations). IType and OType are the input and output types of p, respectively.

The addition of a fold expression to Monad Calculus adds the ability to express sequential computation, which is essential for data processing algorithms including sorting. Folding from the left – $\mathsf{foldL}(c,f)$ – encodes a restrictive recursion pattern, an iterative application of the binary function f to elements of an input list. When using an infix operator $\oplus$, foldL is defined as follows:

$$\mathsf{foldL}(c,\oplus)([v_1,v_2,\ldots,v_n]) = (\cdots((c \oplus v_1) \oplus v_2) \oplus \cdots \oplus v_n)$$

Extensibility. Developers also have the ability to provide additional *definitions*, expressed in terms of the base language. Figure 2 presents schemes of definitions, where we use symbol _ as a placeholder for an unused function argument. We make the following observations regarding these definitions.

The head and tail constructs are used to extract elements from a list. They are undefined when the list is empty.

The functional for loop returns a value of a list type, which is the concatenation of list-typed values computed by its body at each iteration. This is similar to the for loop in XQuery and to flatMap/ext in other languages [3, 8]. The parameter k concerns blocking and is explained in detail in Section 6. Whenever omitted, its value is assumed to be 1.

The treeFold construct generates a tree-shaped bracketing for the applications of a function f which takes k arguments. For example, for a ternary f we have:

$$\text{treeFold}[3](c,f)([v_1,v_2,\ldots,v_6]) = f(f(v_1,v_2,v_3),f(v_4,v_5,v_6),c)$$

This construct is used to represent divide and conquer strategies, as found in e.g. Merge-Sort. It uses a queue to store the initial elements and the intermediate results.

The unfoldR function iterates over a tuple of n lists simultaneously. In every iteration the n-ary function f is applied, which computes part of the output and removes at most one element from the beginning of each list. The computation terminates when all lists are empty. The result of each iteration is appended to the intermediate result from the previous iteration starting with an empty list. We can use unfoldR to express the merging of two sorted lists as unfoldR(mrg) and the zipping of n lists as unfoldR(z).

The partition function groups a set of tuples by their first elements.

For a given fixed k, the $\text{funcPow}[k](f)$ definition scheme yields a nonrecursive definition to obtain a 2^k-ary function using multiple applications of a binary function f.

$$\begin{array}{l} \text{head} : [\tau] \rightarrow \tau \\ \quad := \lambda l.\text{foldL}(\langle \text{true}, 0\rangle, \lambda\langle a, x\rangle.\text{if } a.1 \text{ then } \langle \text{false}, x\rangle \text{ else } a)(l).2 \end{array}$$

$$\begin{array}{l} \text{tail} : [\tau] \rightarrow \tau \\ \quad := \lambda l.\text{foldL}(\langle \text{true}, []\rangle, \lambda\langle a, x\rangle. \\ \qquad \text{if } a.1 \text{ then } \langle \text{false}, []\rangle \text{ else } \langle \text{false}, a.2 \sqcup [x]\rangle)(l).2 \end{array}$$

$$\begin{array}{l} \text{length} : [\tau] \rightarrow \text{Int} \\ \quad := \text{foldL}(0, \lambda\langle sum, \_\rangle.sum + 1) \end{array}$$

$$\begin{array}{l} \text{avg} : [\text{D}] \rightarrow \text{D} \\ \quad := (\lambda x.(x.1/x.2))(\text{foldL}(\langle 0, 0\rangle, \lambda\langle a, x\rangle.\langle a.1 + x, a.2 + 1\rangle)) \end{array}$$

$$\begin{array}{l} \text{for } (x\ [k] \leftarrow \text{R})\ e : [\tau_1] \rightarrow [\tau_2] \\ \quad := \text{foldL}(\langle [], []\rangle, \lambda\langle a, x\rangle.\text{if length}(a.1) - 1 == \text{k then} \\ \qquad \langle [], a.2 \sqcup f(a.1 \sqcup x)\rangle \text{ else } \langle a.1 \sqcup x, a.2\rangle) \end{array}$$

$$\begin{array}{l} \text{treeFold}[k](c, f) : [\tau_1] \rightarrow [\tau_2] \\ \quad := \lambda seed.\text{foldL}(\langle [], seed\rangle, \lambda\langle a, \_\rangle. \\ \quad\ \text{if length}(a.2) == 1 \wedge a.1 == [] \text{ then } a \\ \quad\ \text{else if length}(a.1) == k \text{ then } \langle [], a.2 \sqcup f(a.1)\rangle \\ \quad\ \text{else if tail}(a.2)\ != []\text{ then } \langle a.1 \sqcup \text{head}(a.2), \text{tail}(a.2)\rangle \\ \quad\ \text{else } \langle a.1 \sqcup \text{head}(a.2), [c]\rangle)(seed \sqcup seed) \end{array}$$

$$\begin{array}{l} \text{unfoldR}(f) : \langle [\tau_1], \ldots, [\tau_n]\rangle \rightarrow [\tau_r] \\ \quad := \lambda seed.(\text{foldL}(\langle [], seed\rangle, \lambda\langle a, \_\rangle. \\ \quad\ \text{if } a.2 == \langle [], \ldots, []\rangle \text{ then } \langle a.1, \langle [], \ldots, []\rangle\rangle \\ \quad\ \text{else } \langle a.1 \sqcup f(a.2).1, f(a.2).2\rangle))(seed.1 \sqcup \ldots \sqcup seed.n) \end{array}$$

$$\begin{array}{l} \text{mrg} : \langle [\tau], [\tau]\rangle \rightarrow \langle [\tau], \langle [\tau], [\tau]\rangle\rangle \\ \quad := \lambda\langle l_1, l_2\rangle. \\ \quad\ \text{if length}(l_1) == 0 \wedge \text{length}(l_2) == 0 \text{ then } \langle [], \langle [], []\rangle\rangle \\ \quad\ \ \text{else if length}(l_1) == 0 \text{ then } \langle [\text{head}(l_2)], \langle [], \text{tail}(l_2)\rangle\rangle \\ \quad\ \ \text{else if length}(l_2) == 0 \text{ then } \langle [\text{head}(l_1)], \langle \text{tail}(l_1), []\rangle\rangle \\ \quad\ \ \text{else if head}(l_1) < \text{head}(l_2) \text{ then } \langle [\text{head}(l_1)], \langle \text{tail}(l_1), l_2\rangle\rangle \\ \quad\ \ \text{else } \langle [head(l_2)], \langle l_1, tail(l_2)\rangle\rangle \end{array}$$

$$\begin{array}{l} \text{z} : \langle [\tau_1], \ldots, [\tau_n]\rangle \rightarrow \langle [\langle \tau_1, \ldots, \tau_n\rangle], \langle [\tau_1], \ldots, [\tau_n]\rangle\rangle \\ \quad := \lambda\langle l_1, \ldots, l_n\rangle. \\ \qquad \langle [\langle \text{head}(l_1), \ldots, \text{head}(l_n)\rangle], \langle \text{tail}(l_1), \ldots, \text{tail}(l_n)\rangle\rangle \end{array}$$

$$\begin{array}{l} \text{partition} : [\langle \tau_1, \ldots, \tau_n\rangle] \rightarrow [\tau_1, [\langle \tau_2, \ldots, \tau_n\rangle]] \\ \quad := \text{foldL}([], \lambda\langle ps, x\rangle. \\ \quad\ (\lambda nps.\text{if } nps.1 \text{ then } nps \text{ else } ps \sqcup \langle x.1, [x.2]\rangle)(\\ \qquad \text{foldL}(\langle \text{false}, []\rangle, \lambda\langle nps, xs\rangle.\text{if } xs.1 == x.1 \\ \qquad\ \text{then } \langle \text{true}, nps \sqcup [xs \sqcup [x.2]]\rangle \text{ else } \langle \text{false}, nps \sqcup [xs]\rangle)(ps))) \end{array}$$

$$\begin{array}{l} \text{funcPow}[1](f) : \langle \tau_1, \tau_2\rangle \rightarrow \tau_3 \\ \quad := f \\ \text{funcPow}[k+1](f) : \langle \tau_1, \ldots, \tau_{2^k}\rangle \rightarrow \tau_r \\ \quad := \lambda\langle a.1, \ldots, a.2^{k+1}\rangle. \\ \quad\ f(\text{funcPow}[k](f)(a.1, \ldots, a.(2^k)), \\ \qquad \text{funcPow}[k](f)(a.(2^k + 1), \ldots, a.2^{k+1})) \end{array}$$

Figure 2: Examples of definitions

Generating C code from OCAL. As we mentioned earlier, OCAS generates C code out of programs written in OCAL by translating each expression to an appropriate sequence of C statements. C is the target language since it is widely used in database systems development. By default, OCAS expands definitions and generates code for each individual expression of the base language. In order to increase efficiency, developers can overwrite the default code generators for expressions and definitions using generator plugins. OCAS contains efficient generator plugins for all definitions in Figure 2. For instance, our partition definition as shown in Figure 2 has $O(n^2)$ complexity, even though there exists a linear implementation with the same semantics. By providing a code generator plugin for this construct, the linear implementation can be used. Similarly, the definitions of the head and length functions have linear time complexity, even though there exist suitable implementations for constant time execution. Finally, because the inner function of unfoldR can only access the head of the lists and the output is produced sequentially, we can transfer *blocks* of elements at once, as we present in Section 6.

4. MEMORY AND STORAGE MODEL

Automated transformations in OCAS are driven by a model of the memory hierarchy. For this purpose, the developer must specify a tree-shaped hierarchy where every node represents a hardware component able to store data and an edge represents the ability to transfer data between two nodes. In Example 1, the hierarchy consists of a main memory node at the root with a single child node representing a hard disk.

Every node is attributed a set of properties that provide information about its characteristics. This is merely an abstract description of each node's characteristics, since precise modeling of the architectural and physical attributes of nodes is beyond the scope of this work. Examples of such properties are presented in Figure 3.

Our model makes three assumptions. First, events between distinct hierarchy levels do not interfere with each other (we assume DMA transfers). Second, there exists a single processing unit which executes all computation and can only access data that is stored at the root node of the tree. Third, we assume synchronous I/O and that the hardware properties, such as the throughput and seek time of hard disks, remain constant.

For a program, the location of the input data, as well as the output node, must both be specified. If the output node is not set, we assume that the output is consumed by the CPU. Each data value resides in a node. In order to perform computation on those values, they must be transferred to the root node. Thus, for a given program, OCAS has to

Size. The size of the device. This property must be set for all nodes.

Pagesize. The data at this node must be accessed by pages of this size. If it is possible to address every byte individually then pagesize = 1.

Maximum length of a write sequence (maxSeqW). The maximum amount of data that it is possible to write in a sequence, using a single I/O request. For flash drives this is equal to the erase block size.

Maximum length of a read sequence (maxSeqR). The maximum amount of data that it is possible to read in a sequence, using a single I/O request.

Edge properties: Weights of InitCom[m1 → m2] and UnitTr[m1 → m2] cost events.

Figure 3: Examples of properties of the hierarchy

infer transfers for the set of values that have to be accessible by the processing unit throughout the execution of the program. In Example 1, values x and y have to be transferred to RAM before performing the join.

Moving a data value v from one hierarchy level to another induces *costs*. We leave the specifics of cost computation of OCAL expressions for Section 5, but we note here that the final cost depends on the paths used for data transfers. The act of transferring data concerns not only the input and the output but intermediate results as well.

In order to model the cost of moving data along an edge in the memory hierarchy, each edge has two cost metrics associated with it. Using different costs for different edges enables more accurate cost estimation. First, we consider the cost of initiating a transfer between the two hierarchy nodes (InitCom event). If either of the nodes is a hard disk, this corresponds to a seek in our model. Similarly, in order to transfer data to a flash drive, a block has to be erased before data can be written. The second metric is the cost of transferring a unit of data between the two hierarchy levels (UnitTr event). If the developer chooses to ignore certain cost events, he can set their value to zero. This allows our system to, for example, ignore the cost of InitCom for RAM when considering I/O intensive workloads. Both costs can be collected either from the device specifications or using standard tools like e.g. Seeker [2] for hard disk seeks. We follow this approach in our evaluation.

Because we model memory hierarchies as trees whose leaves are storage devices and whose root is the fastest level of the hierarchy, we cannot model, say, general parallel computation. We are currently working on a way of modeling hardware deeply with the goal of ultimately being able to automatically infer program transformation rules and cost functions from the hardware description.

5. AUTOMATED COST ESTIMATION

Sufficiently accurate cost estimation of programs is essential because it is used by OCAS to compare programs in terms of efficiency. In the domain of out-of-core algorithms we are mainly interested in costs introduced by moving data around in the memory hierarchy. Thus, we currently neglect the actual computation cost of a program in our system. Instead, we opt for modeling only the two aspects of data transfers that we introduced in Section 4: initiating the transfer and actually transferring the requested data.

This section provides a stepwise description of the communication cost computation. First, we describe *how* to compute the result size of each OCAL expression. This is needed since the input typically represents structured data, and thus we need to estimate not only the total size, but also the sizes of nested components that may be separately used in subcomputations. Then, we describe *when* data transfers are introduced in our cost model. Finally, we analyze how the cost estimator separately computes two aspects of data transfers in order to provide the final cost formula and we discuss the extensibility of the costing.

Note that the costing of a program in OCAS does not require to actually run the program. This is important, since actual execution may be very costly. This aspect enables our methodology to be used to compare a large number of programs efficiently, which is essential when exploring variations of a program by applying transformations. We discuss transformation rules in greater detail in Section 6 and in this section we focus on how to cost one single program.

Figure 4 provides a guiding example for this section. It shows the different steps carried out by the cost estimation engine for every expression of a block nested loop join that reads two relations R and S from HDD into RAM, joins them there and finally writes the result back to HDD.

5.1 Estimating the result size of expressions

Given that OCAL programs are compositions of expressions, and that each expression may increase the amount of output, we must estimate the result size of every expression in OCAL. To do that, we introduce the notion of *annotated types*, which annotate lists types with cardinalities. The corresponding grammar is:

$$\alpha ::= [\alpha]^x \mid \langle \alpha_1, \ldots, \alpha_n \rangle \mid c$$

An annotated type α is either a list of form $[\alpha]^x$ where x is the cardinality, a tuple of annotated types or a constant size c. This notation allows us to represent the size of values while retaining their structure. It is worth mentioning that the length of a list is not restricted to integer constants but can be described by an arithmetic expression containing variables. As an example of an annotated type, $\langle [[1]^y]^x, [\langle 1, 1\rangle]^z \rangle$ represents a tuple composed of a list of lists and a list of tuples. By using variables we can express the result size as a function of the input sizes and other parameters without having to recompute the cost of a program every time the size of its inputs or other parameters change.

By using annotated types, the result size of expressions can be then estimated as shown in Figure 5. In what follows, we sometimes write $x \cdot [b]^y$ to denote $[b]^{x \cdot y}$. The recursive function R defines the result size as an annotated type for an expression in a context Γ, which is a set that maps symbols to annotated types. This context is extended every time new symbols are referenced. In order to turn the estimate of a result size into a single arithmetic expression, we define the function size which turns an annotated type to an integer-valued arithmetic expression representing the size of the annotated type in bytes. In addition, we define card and elem to extract information about lists. Since function definitions do not produce any results until they are applied to a value, in our costing we assume that all of them are matched with corresponding function applications. The cost of the flatMap construct is the same as that of for with k set to 1.

Observe that we perform *worst-case* analysis of the result size of each expression. For instance, for nested lists, we take the maximum of the lengths of the inner lists. This design choice may lead to overestimation of result sizes, e.g. in the

Expression	Context	Result size	UnitTr $m_{\mathsf{HDD}} \rightarrow m_{\mathsf{RAM}}$	UnitTr $m_{\mathsf{RAM}} \rightarrow m_{\mathsf{HDD}}$	InitCom $m_{\mathsf{HDD}} \rightarrow m_{\mathsf{RAM}}$	InitCom $m_{\mathsf{RAM}} \rightarrow m_{\mathsf{HDD}}$
$\mathsf{for}\ (xB\ [k_1] \leftarrow \mathsf{R})$	$\Gamma_1 = \mathsf{R} \mapsto [1]^x, \mathsf{S} \mapsto [1]^y$	$[\langle 1,1\rangle]^{x \cdot y}$	$x + \frac{x}{k_1}y$	$2xy$	$x/k_1 + \frac{xy}{k_1 k_2}$	$2xy/k_o$
$\mathsf{for}\ (yB\ [k_2] \leftarrow \mathsf{S})$	$\Gamma_2 = \Gamma_1 \cup xB \mapsto [1]^{k_1}$	$[\langle 1,1\rangle]^{k_1 \cdot y}$	y	$2k_1 y$	y/k_2	$2k_1 y/k_o$
$\mathsf{for}\ (x \leftarrow \mathrm{xB})$	$\Gamma_3 = \Gamma_2 \cup yB \mapsto [1]^{k_2}$	$[\langle 1,1\rangle]^{k_1 \cdot k_2}$	0	$2k_1 k_2$	0	$2k_1 k_2/k_o$
$\mathsf{for}\ (y \leftarrow yB)$	$\Gamma_4 = \Gamma_3 \cup x \mapsto 1$	$[\langle 1,1\rangle]^{k_2}$	0	$2k_2$	0	$2k_2/k_o$
$\mathsf{if\ joinCond}(x,y)$	$\Gamma_5 = \Gamma_4 \cup y \mapsto 1$	$[\langle 1,1\rangle]^{1}$	0	0	0	0
$\mathsf{then}\ [\langle x, y\rangle]$	Γ_5	$[\langle 1,1\rangle]^{1}$	0	0	0	0
$\mathsf{else}\ []$	Γ_5	0	0	0	0	0

Figure 4: Costing of an example of two unary relations R and S of type [Int]. The hierarchy has two nodes, an HDD and a RAM (root node), and we assume that the size of Int is 1.

$$\mathsf{card}([\alpha]^x) := x \qquad \mathsf{elem}([\alpha]^x) := \alpha \qquad \mathsf{size}([\alpha]^x) := x \cdot \mathsf{size}(\alpha) \qquad \mathsf{size}(\langle \alpha_1, \ldots, \alpha_n\rangle) := \mathsf{size}(\alpha_1) + \ldots + \mathsf{size}(\alpha_n)$$

$$\mathsf{size}(c) := c \qquad \mathsf{R}(\Gamma, x) := \Gamma(x) \qquad \mathsf{R}(\Gamma, [e]) := [\mathsf{R}(\Gamma, e)]^1 \qquad \mathsf{R}(\Gamma, \mathsf{if}\ c\ \mathsf{then}\ e_1\ \mathsf{else}\ e_2) := \mathsf{max}(\mathsf{R}(\Gamma, e_1), \mathsf{R}(\Gamma, e_2))$$

$$\mathsf{R}(\Gamma, c) := \mathsf{sizeof}(c) \qquad \mathsf{R}(\Gamma, e.i) := \mathsf{R}(\Gamma, e).i \qquad \mathsf{R}(\Gamma, e_1 \sqcup e_2) := \mathsf{R}(\Gamma, e_1) + \mathsf{R}(\Gamma, e_2) \qquad \mathsf{R}(\Gamma, \langle e_1, \ldots, e_n\rangle) := \langle \mathsf{R}(\Gamma, e_1), \ldots, \mathsf{R}(\Gamma, e_n)\rangle$$

$$\mathsf{R}(\Gamma, \mathsf{for}(x\ [k] \leftarrow e_1)\ e_2) := \frac{\mathsf{card}(\mathsf{R}(\Gamma, e_1))}{k} \cdot \mathsf{R}(\Gamma \cup \{x \mapsto [\mathsf{R}(\Gamma, \mathsf{elem}(e_1))]^k\}, e_2)) \qquad \mathsf{R}(\Gamma, (\lambda x.e_1)(e_2)) := \mathsf{R}(\Gamma \cup \{x \mapsto \mathsf{R}(\Gamma, e_2)\}, e_1)$$

$$\mathsf{R}(\Gamma, \mathsf{foldL}(c, \lambda\langle a, x\rangle.e_1)(e_2)) := \mathsf{R}(\Gamma, c) + \mathsf{card}(\mathsf{R}(\Gamma, e_2))\Big(\mathsf{R}(\Gamma \cup \{a \mapsto \mathsf{R}(\Gamma, c), x \mapsto \mathsf{R}(\Gamma, \mathsf{elem}(e_2))\}, e_1) - \mathsf{R}(\Gamma, c)\Big)$$

Figure 5: Data size estimation rules for every expression of OCAL.

case of if-then-else, the branch that gives the largest result may not be the one that will actually be taken during execution. However, as we show in our evaluation, even with this overestimation, OCAS can still differentiate more efficient programs from less efficient ones, with respect to the given memory hierarchy. Finally, we also allow the programmer to annotate any expression with a custom result size estimate. This may be needed since the static rules that OCAS uses for data size estimation may not capture specific algorithm semantics. A fold which produces a very small output in its last iteration, but very large outputs in all others is one example where these annotations allow programmers to explicitly express the intention of their algorithm.

5.2 Determining data transfer occurrences

OCAS models data transfers implicitly: whenever the execution context is extended with a new value, we account for an appropriate amount of transfers for this value. After modeling the transfer, this value is then considered to be in its new location. Furthermore, as soon as a value is not in the context anymore, it does not consume space for the hierarchy level it belonged to. By implicitly modeling data transfers, we enable separation between a program and its execution environment (memory hierarchy). This alleviates the need for programmers to annotate where intermediate values are stored throughout the execution of a program.

We use the following notation and semantics for data transfers. First, values are transferred from a hierarchy node m_s, where they originally reside, to a memory node m_d. In order to simplify costing of a program, we assume that data transfers happen only between adjacent memory nodes (m_s is directly connected to m_d in the tree). Furthermore, if m_d is the root node, then an expression will be executed to process the fetched data, thus producing an output written at a node m_o, which has to be a child of m_d, possibly different from m_s (because otherwise no transfers are needed).

Finally, data transfers between adjacent hierarchy levels are constrained by the physical size of the participating nodes. Given that modeling replacement algorithms at each level of the memory hierarchy is a very complicated task, we choose a simpler solution. We use dedicated space for input (b_{in}) and output (b_{out}) buffers at each level, per value, so that their combined size does not exceed the size of the specific level. These buffers determine the amount of transfers necessary to process each value and will be utilized by the transformation rules presented in Section 6. Furthermore, when the output buffer is filled, it is completely evicted to the output memory level. Choosing good values for input and output buffer sizes is a critical aspect of designing high performance out-of-core algorithms. It is also a non-trivial task for developers, since choosing locally optimal solutions at each node may not give a globally optimal solution for the whole hierarchy. Thus, the automation that our system provides in that respect is very helpful to developers.

5.3 Estimating cost events

The core of cost computation concerns estimating the cost of InitCom and UnitTr transfer events occurring between adjacent nodes. OCAS estimates these events independently. Figure 6 shows how our system counts the amount of data transferred for various kinds of functions. For function definitions (along with their applications), the size of the argument determines how many bytes are transferred from m_s to m_d. The size of the result tells how many bytes are written out. In addition, as flatMap executes its inner function for every element, we have to multiply the number of the elements caused by this function by the length of the list. For foldL the situation is very similar but we also have to take into account that c has to be transferred to m_d as well.[1] Every expression other than function application basically just aggregates the number of events of its subexpressions. Calculating the amount of InitCom events is similar to computing the amount of data transferred. The total cost is then found if we add up the two separate costs, which gives a sin-

[1]The presented cost function is simplified and adapted to our examples. The general cost function is more complicated because OCAL is able to express algorithms with super-exponential running time.

Expression e	Cost of InitCom events $\mathsf{C}(\Gamma, e)$	Cost of UnitTr events $\mathsf{T}(\Gamma, e)$
$(\lambda x.e_1)(e_2)$	$\mathsf{C}(\Gamma \cup \{x \mapsto \mathsf{R}(\Gamma, \mathsf{elem}(e_2))\}, e_1) + \mathsf{C}(\Gamma, e_2)$ $+\mathsf{size}(\mathsf{R}(\Gamma, e_2))\ \mathsf{InitCom}[m_s \to m_d]$ $+\mathsf{size}(\mathsf{R}(\Gamma, e))\ \mathsf{InitCom}[m_d \to m_o]$	$\mathsf{T}(\Gamma \cup \{x \mapsto \mathsf{R}(\Gamma, \mathsf{elem}(e_2))\}, e_1) + \mathsf{T}(\Gamma, e_2)$ $+\mathsf{size}(\mathsf{R}(\Gamma, e_2))\ \mathsf{UnitTr}[m_s \to m_d]$ $+\mathsf{size}(\mathsf{R}(\Gamma, e))\ \mathsf{UnitTr}[m_d \to m_o]$
$(\mathsf{for}(x\ [\mathrm{k}] \leftarrow e_2)\ e_1)$	$\frac{\mathsf{card}(\mathsf{R}(\Gamma, e_2))}{k} \mathsf{C}(\Gamma \cup \{x \mapsto [\mathsf{R}(\Gamma, \mathsf{elem}(e_2))]^k\}, e_1)$ $+\mathsf{C}(\Gamma, e_2) + \frac{\mathsf{size}(\mathsf{R}(\Gamma, e_2))}{k} \mathsf{InitCom}[m_s \to m_d]$ $+\frac{\mathsf{size}(\mathsf{R}(\Gamma, e))}{b_{out}}\ \mathsf{InitCom}[m_d \to m_o]$	$\frac{\mathsf{card}(\mathsf{R}(\Gamma, e_2))}{k} \mathsf{T}(\Gamma \cup \{x \mapsto [\mathsf{R}(\Gamma, \mathsf{elem}(e_2))]^k\}, e_1)$ $+\mathsf{T}(\Gamma, e_2) + \mathsf{size}(\mathsf{R}(\Gamma, e_2))\ \mathsf{UnitTr}[m_s \to m_d]$ $+\mathsf{size}(\mathsf{R}(\Gamma, e))\ \mathsf{UnitTr}[m_d \to m_o]$
$(\mathsf{foldL}(c, \lambda\langle a, x\rangle.e_1))(e_2)$	$\sum_{i=0}^{\mathsf{card}(\mathsf{R}(\Gamma, e_2))-1} \mathsf{C}\Big(\Gamma \cup \{a \mapsto i \cdot (\mathsf{R}(\Gamma \cup$ $\{a \mapsto \mathsf{R}(\Gamma, c), x \mapsto \mathsf{R}(\Gamma, \mathsf{elem}(e_2))\}, e_1) - \mathsf{R}(\Gamma, c)),$ $x \mapsto \mathsf{R}(\Gamma, \mathsf{elem}(e_2))\}, e_1\Big) + \mathsf{C}(\Gamma, e_2)$ $+(\mathsf{size}(\mathsf{R}(\Gamma, c)) + \mathsf{size}(\mathsf{R}(\Gamma, e_2)))\ \mathsf{InitCom}[m_s \to m_d]$ $+\mathsf{size}(\mathsf{R}(\Gamma, e))\ \mathsf{InitCom}[m_d \to m_o]$	$\sum_{i=0}^{\mathsf{card}(\mathsf{R}(\Gamma, e_2))-1} \mathsf{T}\Big(\Gamma \cup \{a \mapsto i \cdot (\mathsf{R}(\Gamma \cup$ $\{a \mapsto \mathsf{R}(\Gamma, c), x \mapsto \mathsf{R}(\Gamma, \mathsf{elem}(e_2))\}, e_1) - \mathsf{R}(\Gamma, c)),$ $x \mapsto \mathsf{R}(\Gamma, \mathsf{elem}(e_2))\}, e_1\Big)$ $+\mathsf{T}(\Gamma, e_2) + (\mathsf{size}(\mathsf{R}(\Gamma, c))$ $+\mathsf{size}(\mathsf{R}(\Gamma, e_2)))\ \mathsf{UnitTr}[m_s \to m_d]$ $+\mathsf{size}(\mathsf{R}(\Gamma, e))\ \mathsf{UnitTr}[m_d \to m_o]$

Figure 6: Rules for computing the cost of InitCom and UnitTr events.

gle expression depicting the cost of a program as a function of various parameters like block and input sizes.

We end this section with two remarks. First, our system also allows the developer to define custom costs for definitions by extending the mechanisms for counting events and estimating result sizes with special cases. This feature allows to specify tighter bounds for special cases using the developer's expertise. If the developer does not specify a cost formula for his definitions, OCAS extends each definition and costs its inner expressions in order to get a cost estimation metric. Second, observe that when the target memory hierarchy changes, the costing formulas are changed accordingly, based on the above analysis. This may make a different set of transformation rules applicable and may, as a result, generate a different program as output. In the next section, we discuss the transformation rules in more detail, and show how they can generate a better program based on the cost formulas we presented here.

6. TRANSFORMATION RULES

In the previous section we discussed how to estimate the cost of a program based on the amount of data transfers it performs. In this section, we discuss the set of rules that transform a given program to another one with equivalent functionality that may have better performance with respect to a given memory hierarchy. Since it is rarely possible to determine analytically whether the application of a rule results in a performance improvement, we opt for cost-based optimization rather than using a deterministic recipe for obtaining efficient programs. OCAS exhaustively searches the space of equivalent programs, estimates the cost of each and then selects one with the best performance. For example, consider the following sequence of equivalent join algorithms between relations R and S of type list of tuples:

```
for (x ← R) for (y ← S) if joinCond(x,y) then [⟨x,y⟩] else []
⇓ [rule apply−block applied twice, for R and S respectively]
for (xBlock [k1] ← R) for (x ← xBlock) for (yBlock [k2] ← S)
  for (y ← yBlock) if joinCond(x,y) then [⟨x,y⟩] else []
⇓[rules swap−iter and seq−ac]
for (xBlock [k1] ← R) for[HDD⇝RAM] (yBlock [k2]← S)
  for (x ← xBlock) for (y ← yBlock)
    if joinCond(x,y) then [⟨x,y⟩] else []
⇓[rule order−inputs]
(λ⟨R, S⟩.for (xBlock [k1] ← R) for[HDD⇝RAM] (yBlock [k2]←S)
  for (x ← xBlock) for (y ← yBlock)
    if joinCond(x,y) then [⟨x,y⟩] else [])
(if length(R) ≤ length(S) then ⟨R, S⟩ else ⟨S, R⟩)
```

The first program is a naive implementation of a Nested Loops Join algorithm that issues a disk read every time it accesses a tuple from either of the two relations. The final program is a Block Nested Loops Join that uses the smaller relation in the outer loop. Both programs discard the output. Every step in the derivation is annotated with a transformation rule presented in Subsection 6.2.

6.1 From Principles to Transformation Rules

We have identified three main principles that drive the transformations performed by our system:

Data locality and block-based transfers. One heuristic that OCAS uses is to fetch the largest possible block of data to the processing unit *at once*. The justification is that, unless the input contains data that is never looked at by the algorithm, every data element has to be eventually fetched. Thus, if fetching is performed in larger chunks, then the number of InitCom events, which represent disk seeking and the costly erasure on flash drives, decreases. The transformation rule that applies this optimization is called apply−block.

The order in which individual data elements are accessed can also be changed by rules swap−iter and order−inputs. This is a class of optimizations whose effectiveness depends on the interaction of several levels of the memory hierarchy, rather than the properties of each individual level. Therefore, there does not exist a generally valid characterization of the cases when these optimizations are effective, other than suggesting that the performance after the application of the rule should improve.

Sequential versus random access. Some devices perform significantly better if data on them is accessed sequentially rather than in random order. A notable example are hard disks, but also writing sequentially to flash drives is more efficient because an erased block can be filled before another one has to be erased somewhere else. Pre-fetching data by blocks into a level that does not have a performance penalty for random access can improve performance in programs where random access is confined to happen within blocks. Blocking is introduced through the apply−block rule.

Minimizing the number of passes through the input. Some programs require accessing every element of the input several times to compute the result. There are abundant examples of this behavior in data management systems: join algorithms may have to consider all pairs of members from two relations, comparison-based sorting algorithms have a theoretical bound of at least $\log n$ accesses to each input element, etc. OCAS uses two techniques based on this principle: Partitioning data by hash, represented by the rule hash−part; and Divide-And-Conquer, represented by the rule inc−branching. Both rules have the effect that the individual input elements need to be accessed fewer times, in fact only two times in the case of hash−part, but in a more random order. Therefore there is a trade off between the total amount of data transferred and the amount of seeking that this rule introduces.

In addition to the previous ideas, another class of optimization rules target improving the asymptotic computational complexity of the algorithm, such as the fldL−to−trfld rule. However, we do not make this kind of rules a priority of this paper, because they are rather independent of the usage of the memory hierarchy and they form a broad enough research topic on their own. Application of functional-style transformations to improve the asymptotic complexity of programs has been studied in e.g. [7] and [6], although not in the context of *automatic* synthesis of programs.

6.2 List of Transformation Rules

We write our rules as $e_1 \Rightarrow e_2$ where e_1 and e_2 are OCAL expressions. This means that whenever a part of a program matches e_1 then this part is equivalent to and can be replaced by e_2, leading to a new program. Most rules come with additional conditions on e_1 that determine when the rule can be applied. These conditions pose a challenge: some are undecidable in the general case or deciding them is too computation-intensive. In such cases, we implement a conservative estimation procedure that returns no false positives by deciding a stronger but simpler condition. This approach may lead our tool to fail to notice opportunities when a rule could be correctly applied but it never allows it to apply a rule in a non-valid context. We now describe the motivation of each rule, the conditions under which it can be applied and some examples of usage.

We show in the experimental section that this set of rules already covers a rich collection of programs. There are other principles that OCAS does not yet deal with. However, our tool can be easily extended by such principles in the form of new transformation rules that follow the same pattern as the ones presented in this section.

Increasing the Block Size (apply−block). The fold and flatMap constructs, as specified in Section 3, iterate over the elements of a list one by one, as they appear, in a sequential fashion. However, OCAS provides the for construct which allows iterating over blocks of elements, instead of one by one. Using the blocked for in place of the more granular counterpart is the aim of the following transformation rule:

for (x [1] $\leftarrow$ R) [1] $e \Rightarrow$
  for ($xBlock$ [k_1] $\leftarrow$ R) for ($x \leftarrow xBlock$) [k_2] e

This rule can be applied both when fetching data towards the processing unit as well as to the data that is written as a result of evaluating expression e. To use it, we introduce the new annotation [k_2] (in the place shown) for buffering the output. In general, apply−block increases the amount of data read or written in a single I/O request, from the default single element to blocks of size k_1 and k_2, respectively. The value of k_2 is limited by the space and the maxSeqW property of the node where the elements are being written to, and k_1 by the maxSeqR property of the source node. The actual values of k_1 and k_2 are determined by the non-linear optimizer that we have implemented based on [19]. In short, for a single loop, a good heuristic is that both k_1 and k_2 should be as big as possible, subject to the aforementioned restrictions. However, if several nested loops over different ranges compete for space at the same node, this trivial heuristic does not work and we use the optimization solver to determine the block sizes.

If R is originally stored at node m_0, is fetched at m_1 and the output is written to node m_2, this rule reduces the number of InitCom[$m_0 \to m_1$] cost events k_1-fold, and the number of InitCom[$m_1 \to m_2$] events k_2-fold, as long as $m_0 \neq m_2$. If some of these nodes are hard disks, this rule decreases the number of disk seeks. In general, our system aims to replace every list-iterative construct with block size 1 with as many levels of nested equivalent constructs with larger block size as there are levels in the memory hierarchy. We note that we also use an analogous rule to introduce bigger blocks to our implementation of unfoldR.

Swapping The Order Of Iterative Constructs (swap−iter). Given two for or two flatMap constructs that iterate over two different lists, we can then change the order in which these two constructs are applied, as follows:

for (x_1 [k_{11}] $\leftarrow$ $range_1$) [k_{12}] for (x_2 [k_{21}] $\leftarrow$ $range_2$) [k_{22}] e $\Rightarrow$
  for (x_2 [k_{21}]$\leftarrow$ $range_2$) [k_{22}] for (x_1 [k_{11}]$\leftarrow$ $range_1$) [k_{12}] e

This rule can be applied provided that the value of $range_2$ does not depend on x_1. We also have an analogous rule for loops with a condition:

for (x_1 [k_{11}] $\leftarrow$ $range_1$) [k_{12}]
 if c then for (x_2 [k_{21}] $\leftarrow$ $range_2$) [k_{22}] e_1 else e_2
$\Downarrow$
for (x_2 [k_{21}] $\leftarrow$ $range_2$) [k_{22}]
 for (x_1 [k_{11}] $\leftarrow$ $range_1$) [k_{12}] if c then e_1 else e_2

Ordering Input Lists by Length (order−inputs)

$f \Rightarrow \lambda\langle x_1, x_2\rangle.$
  f(if length(x_1) $\leq$ length(x_2) then $\langle x_1, x_2\rangle$ else $\langle x_2, x_1\rangle$)
$f \Rightarrow \lambda\langle x_1, x_2\rangle.$
  f(if length(x_1) $\leq$ length(x_2) then $\langle x_2, x_1\rangle$ else $\langle x_1, x_2\rangle$)

The target of this rule are applications where the input is a tuple of lists whose order does not matter for the calculated result but may matter for efficiency. For instance, a Block Nested Loops join is more efficient if the outer relation is the smaller. These two rules can be applied if f is of type $\langle[\tau_1], [\tau_1]\rangle \to \tau_2$. It is easy to generalize this rule for functions whose input is a tuple of type $\langle[\tau_1], \ldots, [\tau_1]\rangle \to \tau_2$.

Hash Partitioning of Input (hash−part). The following procedure can sometimes improve the performance of an algorithm. Given a tuple of lists, we distribute the elements of each of the lists into subsets, each containing elements that hash into a particular range. We thus obtain a tuple of lists of lists, where each list of lists represents the set of hash partitions of one of the original lists. These are then zipped together to form a value L of type list of tuples of lists, that has length s and contains all the tuples of corresponding partitions. The original algorithm is then mapped over the tuples. OCAS provides an efficient implementation of the partition definition, which is executed in linear time. The following transformation rule captures this idea:

$$f \Rightarrow \lambda\langle x_1, \ldots, x_k\rangle.(\mathsf{flatMap}(f)\ (\mathsf{zip}(\langle \mathsf{partition}(x_1), \ldots, \mathsf{partition}(x_k)\rangle)))$$

This rule works for any s when f is a function that iterates over a tuple of lists, for example a join. Most importantly, f must be such that when one takes the union of results of f applied to the s partitions, one gets the same result as applying f to the original input lists. This means that we do not care about the order in which the function processes the input elements.

If f is a program that accesses every element of its input more than once, applying this rule has the effect that all of the data is read only twice: once during the partitioning phase and once when applying f to the partitions, provided they are small enough to fit in the node into which f reads the data to from their original location. This is ensured by choosing s to be large enough. This rules is needed for synthesizing hash joins.

Increasing the Branching of treeFold (inc−branching).

$\mathsf{treeFold}[2^k](c, \mathsf{funcPow}[k](f)) \Rightarrow$
$\quad \mathsf{treeFold}[2^{k+1}](c, \mathsf{funcPow}[k+1](f))$

The condition for this rule to work is that f has to be associative. When this rule is applied, the number of applications of the function inside the treeFold decreases but the function becomes more complicated as it accepts more arguments. More precisely, we get approximately $\frac{n}{2^k-1}$ applications of funcPow[k](f) instead of approximately n applications of f, where n is the length of the input list. Also, when initially converting treeFold[2] into treeFold[4], the use of this rule is usually preceded by a use of an auxiliary rule $f \Rightarrow \mathsf{funcPow}[1](f)$ which applies to any f.

In Section 7, we provide the example of deriving 2^k-way External Merge-Sort. There, the sorting algorithm operates on a list of lists, which necessitates the usage of the unfold definition. In this particular case, it is more efficient to actually execute the above transformation rule as follows:

$\mathsf{treeFold}[2^k](c, \mathsf{unfoldR}(\mathsf{funcPow}[k](f))) \Rightarrow$
$\quad \mathsf{treeFold}[2^{k+1}](c, \mathsf{unfoldR}(\mathsf{funcPow}[k+1](f)))$

A detailed explanation is omitted due to space constraints.

Change of Folding Pattern (fldL−to−trfld).

$\mathsf{foldL}(c, f) \Rightarrow \mathsf{treeFold}[2](c, f)$

This rule works whenever f is associative and c is an identity element for f. The treeFold[2] pattern applies f the same number of times as foldL. However, if the size of the result of f and its computational complexity grow at least linearly with the size of its input, then treeFold[2] achieves better performance by balancing f's input sizes more equally.

Adding a Sequentiality Annotation (seq−ac). To enhance the precision of the cost estimation, we allow an expression to be annotated with a token $[m_1 \rightsquigarrow m_2]$. This

Hard disk: size = 1T	pagesize = 4K
Flash drive: size = 512G	maxSeqW = 256K
Cache: size = 3M	pagesize = 512B
InitCom[HDD ↦ RAM] = 15ms	InitCom[RAM ↦ HDD] = 15ms
InitCom[RAM ↦ SSD] = 1.7ms	InitCom[RAM ↦ Cache] = 0.1ms
UnitTr[HDD ↦ RAM] = 1s/30M	UnitTr[RAM ↦ HDD] = 1s/30M
UnitTr[SSD ↦ RAM] = 1s/120M	UnitTr[RAM ↦ SSD] = 1s/120M

Figure 7: Node properties and associated cost units

notifies the costing engine that for this expression, all data transfers from m_1 to m_2 happen sequentially. This annotation serves only as an indicator for the costing engine and it does not change the semantics and implementation of the program. It can be applied when no other part of the program causes any communication to m_2. A syntactic check provides a sufficient condition.

For example, a for-loop that reads a page of the hard disk to the main memory in every iteration and does not otherwise touch the hard disk is allowed to have this annotation. In this case, instead of counting one such event for every iteration (which is the result of ordinary cost inference), the new InitCom cost is given by: $\max\left(1, \frac{\mathsf{totaltransfers}}{\min(m_1.\mathsf{maxSeqR}, m_2.\mathsf{maxSeqW})}\right)$. Another natural interpretation of this cost function optimization is writing multiple blocks of data to a flash drive after a block, usually much larger, has been erased.

7. EXPERIMENTAL EVALUATION

In this section we present our experimental platform and evaluate our approach with respect to the following points:

1. The quality of synthesized algorithms. We evaluate this aspect in two ways. First, we manually inspect the generated C code obtained from OCAS and check whether the code matches our expectations. Particularly for disk-based joins and sorting, we check whether we obtain exactly the standard textbook algorithms. Then, we evaluate the performance of the synthesized algorithms by running the generated C code on actual data on a hardware configuration that matches our memory hierarchy description.

2. The accuracy of the predictions compared to the actual execution times of the algorithms. We examine two aspects of this issue, the imprecision of the estimations caused by the fact that the cost formulas do not currently consider CPU costs, and the degree of overestimation caused by the fact that OCAS performs worst-case analysis.

3. The execution time of the synthesizer, given that the search space grows as longer chains of transformation rules are evaluated on larger programs.

7.1 Experimental Platform

Our platform[2] is a Mac OS X machine with an i7-2620M processor, standard 1TB Western Digital hard disk drives and one 500GB Apple SSD TS512C. Input and RAM buffer sizes are reported in bytes, and are specifically chosen for each experiment. The properties of our devices and the cost of unit events are listed in Figure 7. Costs not included are assumed to be zero. OCAS is implemented in Scala, so we use a Java Virtual Machine with 256MB of heap space. The C programs generated by OCAS are compiled using GCC

[2]This is for all experiments other than measuring cache misses.

Program	Spec. [s]	Opt. [s]	Act. [s]	Relation size		Total buffer size	Search space	Steps	OCAS Runtime [s]
				R	S				
BNL - No writeout	4×10^9	411	545	1G	32M	8M	9287	6	17
BNL with cache - No writeout	4×10^9	445	533	1G	32M	8M	54202	7	370
(GRACE) hash join - No writeout	4×10^9	356	491	1G	32M	8M	28471	7	78.5
BNL writing to HDD	1016144	5058	4704	32K	256M	20K	2566	6	8.2
BNL wr. to other HDD	1016144	1689	2176	32K	256M	20K	7443	6	14.4
BNL writing to flash	561179	307	455	32K	256M	20K	7443	6	12.7
External sorting	1×10^9	157	272	1G	-	260K	130	10	2.9
Set Union	251931	396	499	2G	2G	48K	21	3	0.07
Multiset Union (sorted list)	251931	396	479	2G	2G	48K	21	3	0.06
Multiset Union (value-multiplicity)	251931	396	487	2G	2G	48K	21	3	0.07
Multiset Diff. (sorted list)	126033	266	137	2G	2G	48K	21	3	0.07
Multiset Diff. (value-multiplicity)	126033	266	153	2G	2G	48K	21	3	0.07
Column Store Read 5 cols.	125965	197	196	4G	-	5M	7	3	0.01
Column Store Read 10 cols.	251931	395	382	8G	-	10M	7	3	0.01
Duplicate Removal from a Sorted List	503862	546	882	16G	-	16K	7	3	0.16
Aggregation	125965	136	168	4G	-	32K	7	3	0.25

Table 1: Cost estimates for the naive specification algorithm (Spec) and the synthesized algorithm (Opt), actual running times of the generated C programs for the synthesized algorithms (Act), data sizes, and statistics on synthesis (search space size and depth, and synthesizer running time).

4.2. In what follows, the running time refers to the *actual execution time* of the generated programs.

7.2 Inspection and Performance Evaluation

The aim of this work is to automatically generate algorithms tuned for a particular memory hierarchy. To that end, we do not claim the optimality of the generated algorithms. We have instead manually verified that the generated algorithms are the same as those in textbooks [23]. Table 1 presents results for all of our experiments and it also contains the cost of the naive algorithm the user provides, which assumes one I/O (and one seek) per tuple processed.

Next, we analyze variations of the running BNL Join example and we explain in detail how OCAS automatically derives an External Merge-Sort of $n \cdot \log n$ complexity from a naive specification of an insertion sort of n^2 complexity. The purpose of these examples is to show that OCAS generates optimized algorithms and adapts its cost formulas and generated algorithms when the memory hierarchy changes.

Block Nested Loops (BNL) and Hash Join. All join examples start with the same naive join algorithm of Example 1. We create different algorithms from different memory hierarchy descriptions and parameterizations. Results for the BNL Join with no write-out are shown in the first line of Table 1. This corresponds to the example used so far in the paper.

When a memory hierarchy that consists of a hard disk and the main memory is extended with one level of CPU cache, OCAS generates a version of Block Nested Loops join with additional for loops that make use of the available cache.

The reader can verify that by applying this transformation, which corresponds to loop tiling, the program becomes more cache-friendly. As a result, there is a small performance improvement, as shown in Table 1. We make two observations. First, the underestimation of OCAS is smaller in this experiment, because a previously ignored part of the memory hierarchy is modeled in the cost formulas. Second, using the tool *perf* [1] we measured the number of data cache misses. This number is reduced by 98.2%, compared to the previous example (the non-cache conscious BNL join). However, the execution time does not reflect this significant improvement, since this experiment is I/O bound.[3]

Furthermore, by applying the partitioning rule from Section 6, OCAS is capable of transforming the Block Nested Loops Join into a variant of the GRACE hash join. Our experiments show that, as expected, the hash join performs better than the BNL join.

Next, we turn our attention to three examples where the output of the join is written to a device and not discarded.

When the output is written back to the same hard disk that stores the input, sequential reading from the hard disk is no longer possible, because the write operations interfere with the reads. Table 1 shows that the cost formula successfully depicts the considerably increased running time, even though the size of the input relations is significantly smaller compared to the original BNL join with no write-out.

If the memory hierarchy changes so that another hard disk HDD2 stores the output, reading and writing do not interfere with each other, so both can be executed sequentially. By doing so, even though the amount of data transfers remains the same, hard disk seeking is significantly reduced, as indicated by our cost formulas. As a result, Table 1 shows that both the estimated and the actual execution times are reduced by more than 50%. Note that we use the join condition "true" (thus we compute a relational product between the two relations) in the BNL join examples which write their output to a drive. Thus, write cost dominates read cost, which explains why the BNL join writing to a different disk is much slower than the BNL join discarding its output.

Finally, we consider an example with the same memory hierarchy as above, but a flash drive used in place of the second hard disk. In this case, OCAS generates the same program as before. However, both the estimated and the actual execution times are reduced due to the significantly better sequential write speed of SSDs. This is true, even though the factor of the InitCom events changes to depict their different meaning on flash. They do not correspond to seeks, but rather to an erasure occurring before each sequence of write operations, the length of which is given by the maxSeqW property of the flash drive. OCAS estimates better execution time for the example with flash and, thus, it accurately captures this trade-off between sequential writ-

[3]We have acquired the cache miss ratio of this experiment on a Linux server with an Intel Xeon E5-2620 CPU. The relative speedup between the Block Nested Loops join and the cache example remains the same.

ing and erase operations. The actual execution time of this experiment presents a similar behavior.

External Merge Sort. This example uses the fact that folding merge over a list of singleton lists of integers yields a sorting algorithm, and, thus, demonstrates how our rules for changing the folding patterns can bring us from Insertion Sort to a version of the External Merge-Sort. As a starting point, Insertion Sort can be represented as:

$$\mathsf{foldL}([], \mathsf{unfoldR}(\mathsf{mrg}))(\mathsf{R})$$

where mrg is the supporting function presented in Section 3 and the input is a list R of length x of singleton lists of integers. In this naive version, the elements are transferred one by one from HDD to RAM and back. The cost is:

$$\sum_{j=0}^{x-1}(\mathsf{InitCom}[\mathsf{HDD} \mapsto \mathsf{RAM}] + (j+1)(\mathsf{UnitTr}[\mathsf{HDD} \mapsto \mathsf{RAM}]$$
$$+ \mathsf{UnitTr}[\mathsf{RAM} \mapsto \mathsf{HDD}] + \mathsf{InitCom}[\mathsf{RAM} \mapsto \mathsf{HDD}]))$$

Our system includes a basic engine for simplifying arithmetic expressions, capable of finding closed forms of some sums, which automatically simplifies the above formula to:

$$x\ \mathsf{InitCom}[\mathsf{HDD} \mapsto \mathsf{RAM}] + \frac{x(x+1)}{2}(\mathsf{UnitTr}[\mathsf{HDD} \mapsto \mathsf{RAM}]$$
$$+ \mathsf{UnitTr}[\mathsf{RAM} \mapsto \mathsf{HDD}] + \mathsf{InitCom}[\mathsf{RAM} \mapsto \mathsf{HDD}])$$

By applying rule fldL−to−trfld, rule inc−branching and finally rule apply−block, we obtain 4-way External Merge-Sort. If we then apply rule inc−branching k − 1 more times, we get to 2^{k}-way External Merge-Sort, whose code is:

$$\mathsf{treeFold}[2^k]([], \mathsf{unfoldR}(\mathsf{funcPow}[k](\mathsf{mrg})))$$

The cost of running this program is, after simplification:

$$\left\lceil \frac{\lceil \log x \rceil x}{\mathsf{k}} \right\rceil (\mathsf{UnitTr}[\mathsf{RAM} \mapsto \mathsf{HDD}] + \mathsf{UnitTr}[\mathsf{HDD} \mapsto \mathsf{RAM}]$$
$$+ \frac{1}{b_{in}}\mathsf{InitCom}[\mathsf{HDD} \mapsto \mathsf{RAM}] + \frac{1}{b_{out}}\mathsf{InitCom}[\mathsf{RAM} \mapsto \mathsf{HDD}])$$

Our non-linear optimization solver determines that this cost is minimal when the all the input blocks and the output block are as large as possible, which means $b_{out} = b_{in} = \frac{m_s.\mathsf{size}}{2^k+1}$, and hence the number of units transferred decreases with k and is proportional to $1/k$, while the amount of seeking *increases* with k and is proportional to $2^k/k$. Choosing the right k is again accomplished using the optimization solver and depends on the ratio between the seek-time and reading speed of the hard disk.

To sum up, the output algorithm of OCAS is always better than the specification algorithm provided by the user, and is adapted to the given memory hierarchy.

Manual inspection of the generated C programs shows that OCAS produces exactly the standard textbook (disk-based) BNL and hash join and external sorting algorithms.

7.3 Accuracy of Cost Formulas

General Overview In Table 1, we present the actual execution times of the generated C code for the optimized algorithms. As we can see, the estimates of OCAS are in general not far from the actual execution time, and in some cases our tool underestimates. This is because, as we explain below, the cost formulas are very simple and they do not

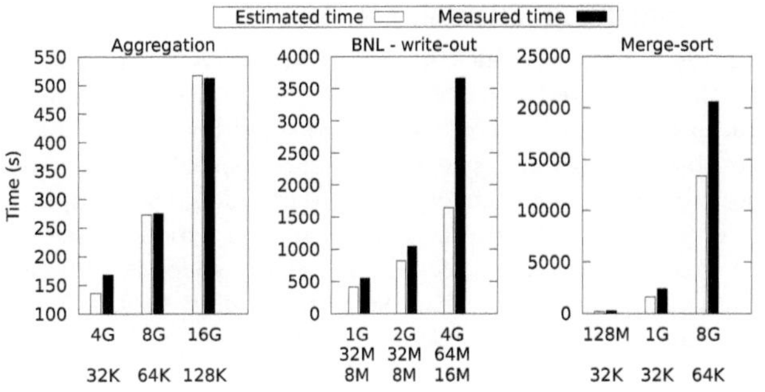

Figure 8: Estimated and actual running times for varying input and buffer sizes. The x-axis label shows the size of the first input relation, the second input relation (if applicable) and buffer size.

completely represent the actual execution properties, especially for CPU dominated workloads. The important point to notice is that, when comparing equivalent algorithms like we did above in the case of BNL join with writing to different devices, the predictions follow the same trend as the actual execution times. Next, we examine two different aspects of accuracy in more detail: the effects of not modeling computation cost and of performing worst-case analysis.

Impact of Computation Costs. OCAS does not currently model computation costs. This can cause our system to underestimate, as shown in Table 1. Moreover, underestimation should grow the more CPU intensive a task is. To examine this hypothesis, we run a set of experiments with a variety of different algorithms, input and buffer sizes. The results for these experiments, presented in Figure 8, confirm the initial assumption: For tasks that are not CPU-intensive, such as aggregation, the estimations are very accurate. However, for tasks like joins or sorting, which consume a significant amount of CPU cycles, underestimation grows with the input size. This raises the need of a more precise modeling of the CPU. However, we leave this for future work.

Impact of Worst-Case Analysis. The worst case analysis that OCAS performs can lead to significant overestimation of the output size, resulting in overestimation of the number of write operations. This is important, since this amount proportionally affects the reported estimations. To better understand this behavior, we present three examples in Table 1: one that calculates the union of sets represented as a sorted list of unique values, another that returns the union of multisets represented as a list of value-multiplicity pairs, and finally one that calculates their difference. For the union examples, the estimated output is equal to $\mathsf{length}(L_1)+\mathsf{length}(L_2)$ and for difference it is $\mathsf{length}(L_1)$. The latter follows because in the worst case there is no element that is the same amongst the two relations. The results of Table 1 show that there is overestimation due to predicting more write operations than those actually happening for the difference example. The union algorithm, however, is estimated correctly in both examples.

The join operator has a similar behavior due to selectivity: the higher the selectivity, the closer the estimation is to the actual running time. As Table 1 shows, with the selectivity of 100%, which corresponds to a relational product, the predictions become very accurate.

7.4 Running Time of OCAS

Table 1 presents the time required for OCAS to generate the optimized algorithms. As we can see, our tool is practical, since its execution time is small for all examples. We observe that the size of the search space depends on the number of steps needed for the derivation, the complexity of the input program, and the memory model used in the experiment. As expected, the search space is growing roughly exponentially with the number of transformation steps and the execution time is linked to the size of the search space. However, it is not dependent on the input size because OCAS uses cost-based optimization, which does not need to execute the programs in order to estimate their cost.

8. CONCLUSIONS

In this paper we describe OCAS, a code synthesizer that, given a memory hierarchy oblivious algorithm, automatically generates an efficient out-of-core version by exploiting characteristics of the provided memory hierarchy. OCAS applies transformation rules to a program, and exhaustively searches the space of generated equivalent programs to locate the one with the best performance metric. This metric is an estimation of the data transfers occurring at execution time. Our preliminary results show that OCAS adapts the generated algorithms to changes in the memory hierarchy and that it produces optimized versions of algorithms quickly. Its estimations are accurate when I/O cost dominates CPU cost. Otherwise, the underestimation increases proportionally with the CPU costs. This does not affect the correctness of the approach, as OCAS is able to always differentiate between more efficient and less efficient algorithms. Finally, OCAS efficiently performs estimation of parameters like buffer sizes, a task which is non-trivial for developers.

Acknowledgments

This work was supported by ERC grants 279804 and 306484.

9. REFERENCES

[1] perf: Linux profiling with performance counters. https://perf.wiki.kernel.org/index.php/Main_Page.

[2] Seeker: a utility to measure disk performance. http://www.linuxinsight.com/how_fast_is_your_disk.html.

[3] Xquery 1.0: An xml query language. http://www.w3.org/TR/xquery/.

[4] E. Albert, P. Arenas, S. Genaim, and G. Puebla. Closed-form upper bounds in static cost analysis. *J. Automated Reasoning*, 46(2):161–203, 2011.

[5] P. Andreou, O. Spanos, D. Zeinalipour-Yazti, G. Samaras, and P. K. Chrysanthis. FSort: External sorting on flash-based sensor devices. In *Data Management for Sensor Networks*, 2009.

[6] L. Augusteijn. Sorting morphisms. In *3rd Int'l Summer School on Advanced Functional Programming, volume 1608 of LNCS*, 1998.

[7] R. S. Bird. Algebraic identities for program calculation. *The Computer Journal*, 32(2):122–126, April 1989.

[8] V. Breazu-Tannen, P. Buneman, and L. Wong. Naturally embedded query languages. In *Proceedings of 4th International Conference on Database Theory (ICDT)*, pages 140–154. Springer-Verlag, 1992.

[9] D. Cederman and P. Tsigas. A practical quicksort algorithm for graphics processors. In *Proc. 16th European Symp. Algorithms*, 2008.

[10] W. Chin and S. Khoo. Calculating sized types. *Journal of Higher-Order and Symbolic Computation*, 14(2-3), September 2001.

[11] N. A. Danielsson. Lightweight semiformal time complexity analysis for purely functional data structures. In *Proc. POPL*, January 2008.

[12] J. Gibbons. Origami programming. In J. Gibbons and O. de Moor, editors, *The Fun of Programming*, page chapter 3. Palgrave, 2003.

[13] N. K. Govindaraju, R. Kumar, and D. Manochas. GPUTeraSort: High performance graphics coprocessor sorting for large database management. In *Proc. SIGMOD*, 2006.

[14] M. Hoffmann and S. Jost. Static prediction of heap space usage for first-order functional programs. In *Proc. POPL*, 2003.

[15] S. Jost, K. Hammond, H. Loidl, and M. Hoffmann. Static determination of quantitative resource usage for higher-order programs. In *Proc. POPL*, 2010.

[16] C. Kim, J. Chhugani, N. Satish, E. Sedlar, A. D. Nguyen, T. Kaldewey, V. W. Lee, S. A. Brandt, and P. Dubey. Fast: fast architecture sensitive tree search on modern CPUs and GPUs. In *Proc. SIGMOD*, 2010.

[17] S. Krishnan, S. Krishnamoorthy, G. Baumgartner, C.-C. Lam, and J. Ramanujam. Efficient synthesis of out-of-core algorithms using a nonlinear optimization solver. In *IPDPS*, page 34, 2004.

[18] Y. Liu, Z. He, Y. P. Chen, and T. Nguyen. External sorting on flash memory via natural page run generation. *The Computer Journal*, 2011.

[19] G. Liuzzi, S. Lucidi, and M. Sciandrone. Sequential penalty derivative-free methods for nonlinear constrained optimization. *SIAM Journal on Optimization*, 20(5):2614–2635, 2010.

[20] E. Meijer, M. Fokkinga, and R. Patterson. Programming with bananas, lenses, envelopes and barbed wire. In *FPCA*, 1991.

[21] H. Park and K. Shim. Fast: Flash-aware external sorting for mobile database systems. *J. Systems and Software*, 82(8):1298–1312, 2009.

[22] M. Püschel, F. Franchetti, and Y. Voronenko. *Encyclopedia of Parallel Computing*, chapter Spiral. Springer, 2011.

[23] R. Ramakrishnan and J. Gehrke. *Database Management Systems, 3rd ed.* McGraw-Hill, 2002.

[24] M. Ren, M. Houston, J.-Y. Park, W. Dally, and A. Aiken. A tuning framework for software-managed memory hierarchies. In *Proc. PACT*, October 2008.

[25] E. Sintorn and U. Assarsson. Fast parallel gpu-sorting using a hybrid algorithm. *J. Parallel and Distributed Computing*, 68(10):1381–1388, October 2008.

[26] V. Tannen and R. Subrahmanyam. Logical and computational aspects of programming with sets/bags/lists. In *Proc. ICALP*, pages 60–75, 1991.

[27] X. Ye, D. Fan, W. Lin, N. Yuan, and P. Ienne. High performance comparison-based sorting algorithm on many-core GPUs. In *Proc. IPDPS*, 2010.

InfoGather+: Semantic Matching and Annotation of Numeric and Time-Varying Attributes in Web Tables

Meihui Zhang*
National University of Singapore
mhzhang@comp.nus.edu.sg

Kaushik Chakrabarti
Microsoft Research
kaushik@microsoft.com

ABSTRACT

Users often need to gather information about "entities" of interest. Recent efforts try to automate this task by leveraging the vast corpus of HTML tables; this is referred to as "entity augmentation". The accuracy of entity augmentation critically depends on semantic relationships between web tables as well as semantic labels of those tables. Current techniques work well for string-valued and static attributes but perform poorly for numeric and time-varying attributes.

In this paper, we first build a semantic graph that (i) labels columns with unit, scale and timestamp information and (ii) computes semantic matches between columns even when the same numeric attribute is expressed in different units or scales. Second, we develop a novel entity augmentation API suited for numeric and time-varying attributes that leverages the semantic graph. Building the graph is challenging as such label information is often missing from the column headers. Our key insight is to leverage the wealth of tables on the web and infer label information from semantically matching columns of other web tables; this complements "local" extraction from column headers. However, this creates an interdependence between labels and semantic matches; we address this challenge by representing the task as a probabilistic graphical model that jointly discovers labels and semantic matches over all columns. Our experiments on real-life datasets show that (i) our semantic graph contains higher quality labels and semantic matches and (ii) entity augmentation based on the above graph has significantly higher precision and recall compared with the state-of-the-art.

Categories and Subject Descriptors

H.3.5 [**Information Storage and Retrieval**]: Online Information Services, Web-based services

Keywords

Web Table, Semantic Matching

*Work done while visiting Microsoft Research.

SIGMOD'13, June 22–27, 2013, New York, New York, USA.

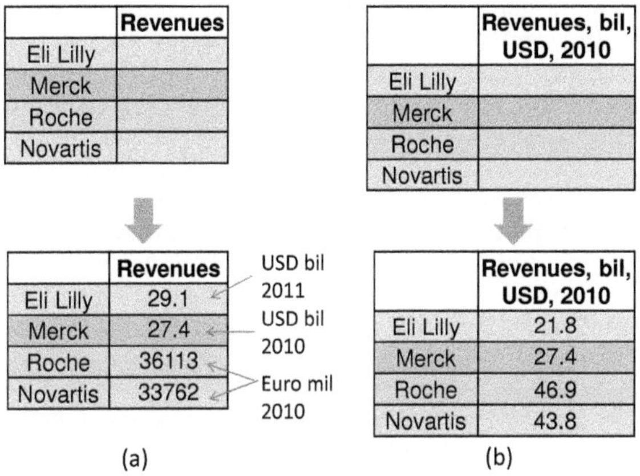

Figure 1: (a) Existing entity augmentation approach (b) Proposed entity augmentation operation for numeric and time-varying attributes

1. INTRODUCTION

Users often need to gather information about "entities" of interest [5, 21, 16]. For example, an analyst in an enterprise might want to gather revenue and market capitalization information of its customers in a particular sector (say, pharmaceutical sector) to predict its sales for that sector. Or a student might want to gather to information about colleges, such as their tuition fees, number of enrolled students, acceptance rates and average SAT scores, in order to choose the college to go to.

Such information gathering tasks are extremely labor-intensive today. The Web contains a vast corpus of HTML tables. In this paper, we focus on relational HTML tables where each row corresponds to an entity and each column corresponds to an attribute [5, 21]. In many cases, they contain the information sought by these tasks [5, 21, 19, 14, 12]. The desired information is typically scattered among various tables. To automate information gathering, researchers have recently proposed the *"entity augmentation"* operation (EA) [5, 21, 14](referred to as EXTEND in [5]). Given the names of a set of entities and a few keywords describing the name of an attribute, the entity augmentation operation leverages the vast corpus of HTML tables to automatically "fill in" the values of the specified entities on the specified attribute. Figure 1(a) shows an example of an EA query where the entities are 4 pharmaceutical companies and the keyword is 'revenues'.

To support EA, we first find tables that "match" with the query table, i.e., contains some of the entities and an attribute whose name matches the keywords. We then consolidate the matching tables to fill in the desired values.

For high precision and recall, it is critical that the matching tables are *semantically consistent.* Matching the attribute names with the keywords using IR techniques does not ensure this. For example, the query shown in Figure 1(a) might match with tables containing 2010 revenues as well as those containing 2011 revenues, those containing revenues in billions of USD as well as those containing revenues in millions of Euros (because they all contain the keyword 'revenues'). Consolidating values from such different tables without understanding the semantic relationships between them leads to erroneous augmentation.

Baseline Approach: The baseline approach to compute semantically consistent matches is to build a *semantic matching graph over web tables* [21]. Suppose each web table is a binary relation with the first column corresponding to the entity name and the second to an attribute of the entity (referred to as entity-attribute binary (EAB) relations). Each web table is a node in the graph. There is an edge between two nodes iff (i) the first columns of the two web tables contain the same type of entities and (ii) the second columns refer to the same attribute of those entities. The edges are computed using schema matching techniques [21].

The accuracy of entity augmentation critically depends on the accuracy of the semantic graph. While the baseline technique works well for string-valued and static attributes, it is inadequate for *numeric* and *time-varying* attributes.

EXAMPLE 1. *Consider the 5 web tables shown in Figure 2. The baseline technique identifies the 3 edges shown using solid, black lines (referred to as simple(S) edges as they capture simple, 1:1 mappings): between T_2 and T_3, T_1 and T_4 and T_4 and T_5. Consider the query table Q in Figure 1(a). The baseline technique matches with all 5 tables. The result of entity augmentation is shown in Figure 1(a). For Eli Lilly, T_4 and T_5 provides the value* 29.1 *while T_1 provides* 21.8*; hence, it selects* 29.1 *(based on aggregate score). For Merck, T_1 provides* 27.4*, T_5 provides* 45.9 *and T_2 provides* 21091*; say, it selects* 27.4 *based on matching score. For Roche and Novartis, T_3 provides the values* 36113 *and* 33762 *respectively. The result is undesirable: the value for Eli Lilly is in USD billion and from 2011, the one for Merck is also in USD billion but from 2010 and the ones for Roche and Novartis are in Euro million and from 2010.*

Why does the baseline approach produce semantically inconsistent results? First, we observe that *a large fraction attributes in web tables are numeric* and the same semantic attribute occurs in a *wide variety of units and scales across different web tables.* For example, in Figure 2, T_1 has 2010 revenue in billions of USD while T_2 and T_3 have it in millions of Euros. The baseline approach has no knowledge of unit and scale; without this knowledge, it is impossible to produce semantically consistent results. Second, many numeric attributes are time-varying in nature: different tables, possibly created at different times, contain values of the same attribute at different points of time. For example, T_1 has the revenue information for 2010 while T_4 and T_5 have the same information for 2011. The baseline approach has no knowledge of time; without this, it is again impossible to produce semantically consistent results. Finally, the baseline approach fails to detect relationships where the same semantic attribute is expressed in different units or scales. For example, it fails to detect that T_1, T_2 and T_3 contain the same semantic attribute (2010 revenue) and the values can be converted from one to another. Without this knowledge, it is impossible convert the values in the matching tables into the desired scale and unit.

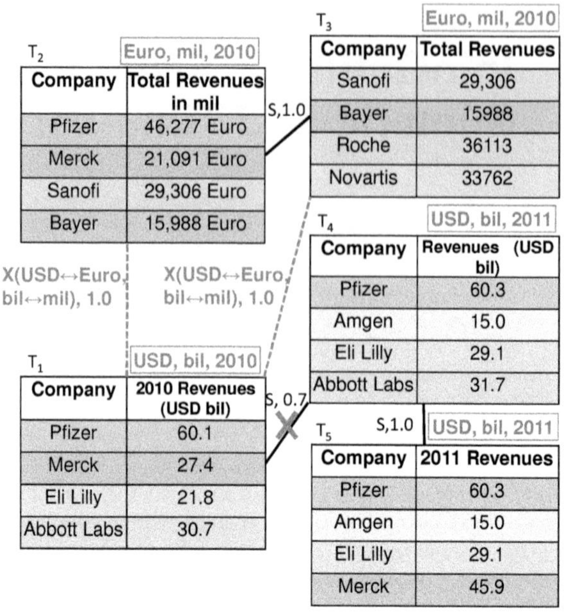

Figure 2: Example of Semantic Graph over Web Tables

Main insights and contributions: In this paper, we build a semantic graph over web tables suited for numeric and time-varying attributes. It consists of:

(i) *Semantic labels*: Annotates each attribute column with unit, scale and timestamp (referred to as *"semantic labels"*). In this paper, we focus on year as the timestamp.[1] The semantic labels are shown in red inside boxes in Figure 2).

(ii) *Semantic matches*: Computes semantic matches between columns representing the same semantic attribute, even if they are expressed in different units and scales. For example, in addition to the S edges, the graph should contain edges between T_1 and T_2 and between T_1 and T_3 (shown using dashed, red lines) in Figure 2. We refer to these as X edges (X referring to transformations/conversions). We assume a set of pre-defined *conversion rules.* An X edge between a pair of tables T and T' is associated with a set of conversion rules which together convert the values between $T.B$ and $T'.B$. For example, the X edge between T_1 and T_3 is associated with two conversion rules: $Euro = 1.3 \times USD$ and $bil = 1000 \times mil$.

There are several technical challenges in building such a graph. First, identifying the semantic labels as well as the X edges is hard as the unit and scale information is often missing in the column headers or values [19, 14]. For example, table T_3 does not specify that the information is in millions of Euros. *Our key insight is to leverage the wealth of tables on the web: even if the column header does not contain the label information, the semantically matching columns of other web tables might contain the label information (in their column headers). We can "propagate" those labels to this table.* For example, T_3 semantically matches with T_2; assuming we can extract T_2's labels *mil* and *Euro* "locally" from its column header and column values, we can propagate them to T_3. Although this shows propagation over an S edge, such propagation can occur even over X edges. However, this creates an interdependence between labels and semantic matches: we need semantic matches to compute the labels and we need the labels to compute the matches. We address this challenge by *representing the task as a*

[1]Our approach can handle other granularities of timestamp like quarter, month, day, etc. We focus on year for simplicity of explanation.

probabilistic graphical model (Markov random field) that simultaneously discovers labels and semantic matches over all columns. Second, making such inferences can lead to inconsistencies. For example, the same table might be assigned both *Euro* and *USD* as labels. We address this challenge by defining hard constraints to control such inconsistent labels and integrating them into the inference algorithm. Finally, schema matching techniques can compute spurious matches. For example, the values of an attribute (say, revenues) may not change significantly from one year to another; this can lead to spurious matches. In Figure 2, the revenues of Pfizer and Abbott Labs did not change significantly from 2010 to 2011; this leads to a spurious semantic match between T_1 and T_4. This leads to semantically inconsistent results as shown in Example 2. Our main insight is to leverage the discovered labels to eliminate such spurious edges. For example, we can infer that the edge between T_1 and T_4 is spurious based on the discovered labels 2010 and 2011 respectively (hence marked with a red cross). We encode this knowledge as hard constraints into our graphical model.

We have built the INFOGATHER+ system based on the above insights. Our contributions can be summarized as follows:

- We propose a novel technique based on probabilistic graphical models to discover the semantic labels of columns and semantic matches between columns over all web tables collectively instead of individually. Our model elegantly combines diverse signals such as "local" extraction of labels from the column headers and values, semantic matches computed using traditional schema matching techniques and label propagation. We develop efficient algorithms to solve the joint discovery task.
- We present a novel entity augmentation API suited for numeric and time-varying attributes. Specifically, we allow users to specify unit, scale and time information to unambiguously specify the augmentation task. An example of the API and the desired output (based on the graph shown in Figure 2) is shown in Figure 1(b). We develop novel query processing algorithms for the new entity augmentation operation.
- We perform extensive experiments on three real-life datasets of web tables. Our experiments show that the graph produced by our graphical model has significantly higher quality in terms of semantic labels and semantic matches compared with the baseline approach. Furthermore, entity augmentation based on the above graph has significantly higher precision and recall compared with the baseline approach.

The rest of the paper is organized as follows. We formulate the semantic graph building problem in Section 2. Section 3 describes the system architecture. We present our model and inference algorithms in Section 4. We describe the entity augmentation API and query processing algorithm in Section 5. Experiments, related work and conclusions appear in Section 6, 7 and 8.

2. PROBLEM DEFINITION

2.1 Data Model

We assume that each web table is an entity-attribute binary (EAB) relation, i.e., a web table $T \in \mathcal{T}$ is of the form $T(K, B)$ where K denotes the entity name attribute and B is an attribute of the entity. Figure 2 shows five web tables (T_1,T_2,T_3,T_4,T_5) satisfying the EAB property. We assume that each web table T has (i) a column header H_T of the attribute column $T.B$ (e.g., H_{T_1} for table T_1 in Figure 2 is

Rule Id	LHS	Conversion Factor (θ)	RHS
r1	euro	1.3	usd
r2	bil	1000	mil
r3	usd	6.2	cny
r4	mil	1000	k
r5	usd	80.2	jpy
r6	mts	3.28	ft
r7	ft	12	inches
r8	inches	2.54	cms

(a)

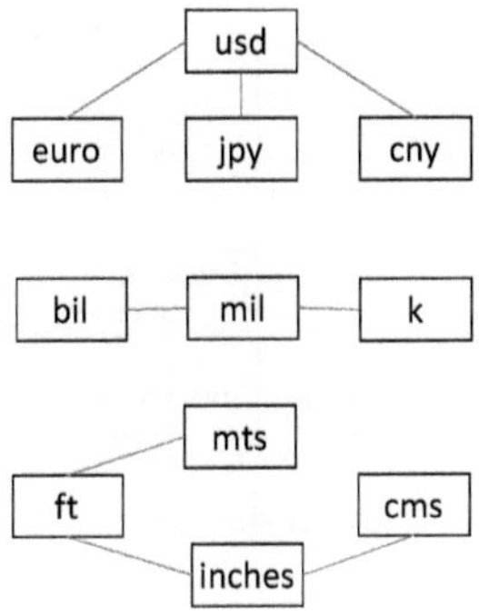

(b)

Figure 3: (a)Conversion rules (b) Mutex groups

"2010 Revenues (USD bil)"). H_T can be empty if the table has no column headers. (ii) context information C_T including header rows that describes the table (that spans across all the columns), caption of the table, text surrounding the table and the url and title of the web page from which it was extracted. In our system, we distinguish between the different context fields. For simplicity, we ignore these distinctions in this paper.

In practice, not all web tables are EAB relations. Most such tables have a "subject column"; this column contains the names of the entities. All other columns are attributes of these entities [19]. Furthermore, there are effective heuristics to detect the subject column [19]. We can therefore split the $n-$ary table into $(n-1)$ EAB relations: the subject column with each of the other $(n-1)$ columns.

2.2 Conversion Rules

We assume that the set of conversion rules are known upfront. They are specified by the system administrator (or domain experts) using a simple, rule specification language. Each rule has 3 components: a left-hand side (LHS), a conversion factor (θ) and a right-hand side (RHS). The LHS and RHS are strings describing units and scales. For example, for the rule $Euro = 1.3 \times USD$, the LHS is *Euro*, θ is 1.3 and the RHS is USD. Figure 3(a) shows more examples of rules.

The same unit and scale can be referred to in several ways. For example, USD is also referred to as \$ and *US Dollar*; *mil* is also referred to as *mln*, *million* and *millions*. We assume there is a canonical string for every unit and scale; the rules are specified using the canonical strings. Furthermore, we assume that all the synonyms are known so that their occurrences can be detected in column headers and column values.

For simplicity, we assume if a rule $a = \theta \times b$ is present, the reverse rule $b = \frac{1}{\theta} \times a$ is also present in the rule database (not shown in Figure 3(a) to avoid clutter). Finally, our system can handle ranges as the conversion factor in order to capture fluctuating conversion factors. For example, one might specify the conversion factor between Euro and USD to be anywhere between 1.2 and 1.3. For simplicity, we focus on a single number as the conversion factor. Note that the rules can change with time: the system administrator can insert new rules, delete existing rules or modify the LHS, conversion factor or RHS of existing rules.

2.3 Problem Statement

Given the corpus of web tables and a set of conversion rules, the goal is to build a semantic graph G over web tables that enables us to perform accurate entity augmentation. Each web table $T \in \mathcal{T}$ is a node in G. The ideal semantic

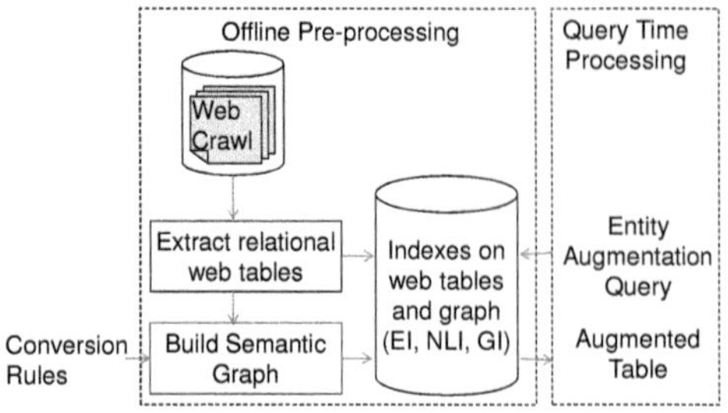

Figure 4: InfoGather+ system architecture

graph G should contain:
(i) **S edges**: between two nodes $T(K, B)$ and $T(K', B')$ iff $T.K$ and $T.K'$ refer to the same type of entities and $T.B$ and $T.B'$ refer to the same attribute of those entities, expressed in the same unit and scale and reflect information of the same points of time (i.e., same year).
(ii) **X edges**: between two nodes $T(K, B)$ and $T(K', B')$ iff $T.K$ and $T.K'$ refer to the same type of entities and $T.B$ and $T.B'$ refer to the same attribute of those entities (at the same points of time) but expressed in different units and scales. Each X edge is associated with a set of conversion rules which converts the values from $T.B$ to $T'.B'$. Since the reverse rule is present for each forward rule, for every X edge from T to T', there is an X edge with an equivalent set of rules from T' to T. Hence, we ignore the directionality of X edges in the discussions except when necessary.
(iii) **Semantic labels**: for unit, scale and year at each node. We distinguish between the unit and scale labels (*SU labels* in short) and *year labels* as a node can be assigned multiple SU labels but only one year label.

3. SYSTEM ARCHITECTURE

Figure 4 shows the architecture of the InfoGather+ system. It has two components: offline preprocessing and query time processing.
Offline preprocessing: There are 3 main steps in this component:
• *Extract HTML tables* from the web crawl and distinguish the relational tables from other types of tables, such as layout tables and attribute-value tables. Our approach is similar to the one in [7]; we do not discuss this further as it is not the focus of this paper.
• *Build the semantic graph.* This is the focus of the paper and is discussed in detail in Section 4.
• *Build indexes on the web tables and the graph* for efficient query time processing. We build 3 indexes: (i) An inverted index on entities (EI). Given a query table Q, EI(Q) returns the set of web tables (along with scores) that contains at least one of the query entities. (ii) An inverted index on column names and semantic labels (NLI): Given a query table Q, NLI(Q) returns the set of tables (along with scores) whose column headers contain the query keywords and/or the set whose semantic labels match with the query labels. (iii) An index on graph edges (GI): Given a web table T, $GI(T)$ returns the set of tables that are connected to T in the semantic graph along with a score indicating the strength of the matching relationship.

Our offline processing needs to scale to hundred of millions of tables. Steps 1 and 3 are easily parallelizable (e.g., using the MapReduce framework). We discuss scalable implementation of Step 2 in Section 4.
Query time processing: We focus on entity augmentation queries in this paper. We can support other classes of queries like augmentation by example [21], attribute discovery [21] and search by column keywords [14] using this architecture. There are two main steps:
• *Identify matching tables and edges*: along with their scores for the query. We leverage the EI, NLI and GI indexes for this purpose.
• *Fill-in values*: For each query entity, we then collect the corresponding values in these matching tables along with the scores, convert to the desired unit and scale, aggregate the scores for each value and select the one with the highest aggregate score.

4. SEMANTIC GRAPH CONSTRUCTION

One option is to follow a *"staged" approach*: start with the semantic graph proposed in the baseline approach [21] (which contains only S edges), then add semantic labels and finally add X edges as follows:
• *Semantic labels*: Let $\mathcal{L}$ denote the set of scale and unit descriptor strings that appear in the LHSs and RHSs of the conversion rules. Formally,

$$\mathcal{L} = \bigcup_{r \in \mathcal{R}} r.LHS \cup \bigcup_{r \in \mathcal{R}} r.RHS$$

where $\mathcal{R}$ denotes the set of conversion rules and $r.LHS$ ($r.RHS$) the scale or unit descriptor constituting LHS (RHS) of rule r. We assume that we know the synonyms for each scale or unit descriptor $l \in \mathcal{L}$. We annotate a web table T with a label $l \in \mathcal{L}$ if either l or one of its synonyms occur in either the column header H_T of $T.B$ or column values of $T.B$. For example, we annotate T_1 in Figure 2 with $\{USD, bil\}$ and T_2 with $\{Euro, mil\}$.

Let $\mathcal{Y}$ denote the set of year strings; we use all year strings from "1900" to "2050". We annotate a web table T with $y \in \mathcal{Y}$ if the y occurs in either in the column header H_T of $T.B$ or in the context C_T of T. For example, we annotate T_1 in Figure 2 with 2010. We refer to this approach as *"local extractions"* as the labels are extracted locally from this table.
• *X edges*: After we have added the semantic annotations as described above, we add an X edge between T and T' associated with the set $R \subseteq \mathcal{R}$ of conversion rules iff (i) the set L_T of labels of T contains LHS of each rule $r \in R$, i.e., $\bigcup_{r \in R} r.LHS \subseteq L_T$ (ii) the set L'_T of labels of T' contains RHS of each rule $r \in R$, i.e., $\bigcup_{r \in R} r.RHS \subseteq L'_T$ and (iii) the values of the common entities in the two tables can be converted from one to the other by multiplying with the product of the conversion factors, i.e., $Sim_X(T, T', R) > \delta$ where $Sim_X(T, T', R)$ denotes the fraction of common entities that can be converted using the product of the conversion factors and δ is a threshold. Formally,

$$Sim_X(T, T, R) = \frac{|(t, t') \in T \times T' \text{ s.t. } t.A = t'.A \wedge \frac{t'.B}{t.B} \sim \Pi_{r \in R} r.\theta|}{|(t, t') \in T \times T' \text{ s.t. } t.A = t'.A|}$$

For example, we add an X edge between T_1 and T_2 corresponding to conversion rules $R = \{USD = 0.77 \times Euro, bil = 1000 \times mil\}$ because (i) T_1 has labels $\{USD, bil\}$ (ii) T_2 has labels $\{Euro, mil\}$ and (iii) the values of the common entities (i.e., Pfizer and Merck) satisfy the product of the conversion factors, i.e., $\frac{46277}{60.1} \sim (0.77 \times 1000)$ for Pfizer and $\frac{21091}{27.4} \sim (0.77 \times 1000)$ for Merck. So, $Sim_X(T_1, T_2, R) = 1.0$. Note that we allow slight variations in values while checking the convertibilities.

This approach suffers from two problems:
• *Low precision*: Text in the context fields as well as column

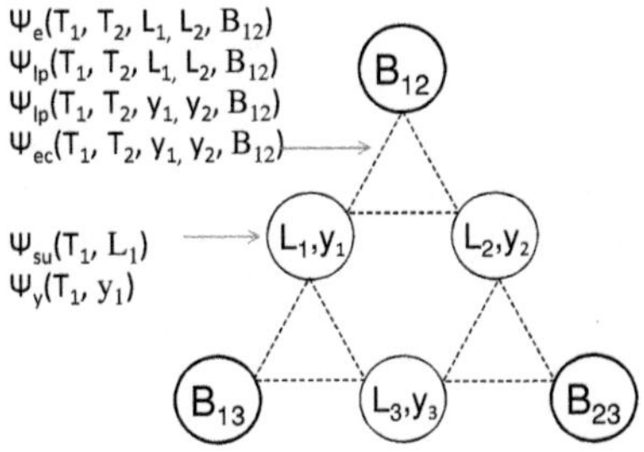

Figure 5: Graphical model for matching and annotating 3 tables T_1, T_2 and T_3

headers can be noisy and ambiguous. Annotations based on only local extraction might lead to incorrect labels.

- *Low coverage*: Often, unit, scale and year information is missing in the column headers, values and context. For example, T_3 does not contain this information. So, the staged approach fails to annotate T_3 with the unit, scale and year information; consequently, it fails to detect the two X edges (corresponding to conversion rules R_1 and R_2 listed in Figure 3) between T_1 and T_3. This is exacerbated by the fact that many tables do not have column headers and/or context information.

Our main insight is that we can improve the precision and coverage if we compute the labels not just using local extractions but also using labels of semantically matching columns. This creates an interdependence between labels and semantic matches: we need semantic matches to compute the labels and we need the labels to compute the matches. We propose a global approach that *collectively computes all the labels and matches and combines the diverse signals.* We present an elegant problem formulation based on probabilistic graph models (Markov random field). We first provide a brief overview of graphical models and then present our formulation.

4.1 Probabilistic Graphical Models

We use undirected graphical models in this paper, referred to as Markov networks or Markov random fields. A graphical model represents the joint distribution over a set of random variables $\mathcal{X} = \{X_1, \cdots, X_n\}$ where each X_i can take values from the space of labels [11]. The model represents each element of $\mathcal{X}$ as a node in a graph G and captures the dependencies between them with a set of cliques of G.

We identify the cliques and define a potential function $\psi(C, X_C) \to \mathbb{R}$ for each clique. $\psi(C, X_C)$ captures the compatibility of the labels X_C assigned to the variable subset C. We use two kinds of potentials: node potentials $\psi(i, X_i)$ defined on the label X_i of a single node i and edge potentials $\psi(i, j, X_i, X_j)$ defined over edge (i, j) in G and labels (X_i, X_j) assigned to the two nodes it connects. The overall probability distribution is the normalized product of all of the potentials. In logarithmic representation,

$$P(X_1, \cdots, X_n) \propto \exp(\sum_i \psi(i, X_i) + \sum_i \sum_j \psi(i, j, X_i, X_j))$$

The inference problem is to find $\arg\max_{\mathcal{X}} P(X_1, \cdots, X_n)$, the most likely joint assignment of labels to variables.

We describe how we model semantic annotation and matching task as a graphical model by defining the random variables, node and edge potentials, the overall objective and finally the inference algorithm.

4.2 Variables

For every table T, we associate two random variables: L_T to denote the set of SU labels and y_T to denote the year label. There can be multiple SU labels assigned to T; hence, L_T can take a value from the set $\mathcal{P}(\mathcal{L})$ where $\mathcal{P}(\mathcal{S})$ denotes the powerset of any set $\mathcal{S}$. Recall $\mathcal{L}$ denotes the set of scale and unit descriptor strings that appear in the LHSs and RHSs of the conversion rules. On the other hand, there can be at most one year label assigned to T; hence, y_T can take a value from the set $\mathcal{Y} \cup \{NA\}$ (NA denotes no year). For every pair of tables T, T', we associate a random variable $B_{TT'}$ denoting the semantic match between T and T'. There can be either an X edge (represented by a set of one or more conversion rules) or an S edge or no edge at all; hence $B_{TT'}$ can take a value from the set $\{\mathcal{P}(\mathcal{R})-\{\phi\}\}\cup\{S, NA\}$. Recall $\mathcal{R}$ denotes the set of conversion rules.

4.3 Node and Edge Potentials

We define node and clique potentials to combine diverse signals like local extraction of labels from the column headers and values, semantic matches computed using traditional schema matching techniques and label propagation.

4.3.1 Local extraction of SU labels

One important signal in assigning SU labels is the local extraction technique described in the staged approach, i.e., we assign an SU label $l \in \mathcal{L}$ to web table T iff either l or one of its synonyms occur in either the column header H_T of $T.B$ or column values of $T.B$. We define two features for this purpose. We define a binary feature function $f_H(T, l)$ which is set to 1 if H_T contains either the label l or a synonym of l, and 0 otherwise. For column values, we extract the strings that precede and follow the numeric values in column $T.B$. Let $PFStrings(T)$ denote the set of strings that *consistently* precede or follow the values across the entire column (e.g., in more than 80% of the rows). For example, in Figure 2, $PFStrings(T_2) = \{Euro\}$. We define a binary feature function $f_V(T, l)$ which is set to 1 if there exists a $s \in PFStrings(T)$ such that s either contains l or a synonym of l, and 0 otherwise. A set L_T of labels is a good assignment if either $f_H(T, l)$ or $f_V(T, l)$ is 1 for all or most labels in it. We define the node potential $\psi_{su}(T, L_T)$ as follows:

$$\psi_{su}(T, L_T) = \frac{\sum_{l \in L_T} \max(f_H(T, l), f_V(T, l))}{|L_T|}$$

SU labeling, especially with label propagation, can lead to inconsistencies. For example, the same table might be assigned both *Euro* and *USD* as labels. We define hard constraints to control such inconsistent labels and integrate them into our node potential $\psi_{su}(T, L_T)$. We define a set of mutually exclusive groups (referred to as "mutex groups") such that any table can be assigned at most one label from a mutex group. Two strings l and l' are in the same mutex group if l is connected to l' via a chain of one or more conversion rules $l = \theta_1 \times p_1$, $p_1 = \theta_2 \times p_2$, $\cdots$, $p_{n-1} = \theta_n \times l'$. Suppose the system has the 8 conversion rules shown in Figure 3(a). The mutex groups for the 8 rules are shown in Figure 3(b). The mutex groups can be computed simply as follows. Construct a graph with each label $l \in \mathcal{L}$ as a node. Insert an edge between two nodes if there is a rule with the two strings as its LHS and RHS. Compute all the connected components of the graph. Each connected component corresponds to a mutex group. Let $Mutex(l, l')$ denote a binary variable which is true if there exists a mutex group containing both l and l' and false otherwise. We modify $\psi_{su}(T, L_T)$ to disallow inconsistent labeling by taking large negative values for inconsistent labels. The final node potential $\psi_{su}(T, L_T)$ is:

$$\begin{aligned}\psi_{su}(T, L_T) &= -\infty \text{ if } l, l' \in L_T \text{ s.t. } Mutex(l, l') \text{ is true} \\ &= \frac{\sum_{l \in L_T} \max(f_H(T,l), f_V(T,l))}{|L_T|} \text{ otherwise}\end{aligned}$$

4.3.2 S and X edge computation

We discuss computing semantic matches between pairs of tables. The schema matching technique proposed for web tables in [21] is an important signal to determine S edges, i.e., there is likely to be an S edge between two web tables T and T' if the common entities in the two tables have equal values on the second column. Define tuple similarity $Sim_S(T, T')$ as the fraction of common entities that have approximately equal values:

$$Sim_S(T, T') = \frac{|(t, t') \in T \times T' \text{ s.t. } t.A = t'.A \wedge t.B \sim t'.B|}{|(t, t') \in T \times T' \text{ s.t. } t.A = t'.A|}$$

Note that we allow slight variations in values while checking the equalities. S is a good assignment for $B_{TT'}$ if $Sim_S(T, T')$ is above a certain threshold, say δ.

For X edges, we follow the computation technique described in the staged approach, i.e., there is likely to be an X edge associated with a set $R \in \mathcal{R}$ of conversion rules between T and T' if (i) T's labels contain the LHSs of R (ii) T''s labels contains the RHSs of R and (iii) the values of the common entities can be converted using the product of the conversion factors. Recall $Sim_X(T, T', R)$ denotes the fraction of common entities that can be converted using the product of the conversion factors. An X edge associated with set of rules R is a good assignment if (i) and (ii) are true and $Sim_X(T, T', R)$ is above a certain threshold, say δ. We define the final clique potential $\psi_e(T, T', L_T, L'_T, B_{TT'})$ as follows:

$$\begin{aligned}&\psi_e(T, T', L_T, L'_T, B_{TT'}) \\ =\ & Sim_S(T, T') \text{ if } Sim_S(T, T') > \delta \ \wedge\ B_{TT'} = S \\ =\ & Sim_X(T, T', R) \text{ if } Sim_X(T, T', R) > \delta \ \wedge\ B_{TT'} = R \\ & \wedge \bigcup_{r \in R} r.LHS \subseteq L_T \ \wedge\ \bigcup_{r \in R} r.RHS \subseteq L'_T \\ =\ & 0 \text{ otherwise}\end{aligned}$$

4.3.3 Local Extraction of year labels

Just like SU labels, local extraction is an important clue in assigning year labels, i.e., we assign a year label $y \in \mathcal{Y}$ to T if the y occurs either in the column header H_T of T_B or in the context C_T of T. As in the previous case, we define two binary feature functions: (i) $f_H(T, y)$, which is set to 1 if H_T contains y and to 0 otherwise and (ii) $f_C(T, y)$ which is set to 1 if C_T contains y and to 0 otherwise. y_T is a good assignment if either $f_H(T, y_T)$ or $f_C(T, y_T)$ is 1. We define the node potential $\psi_y(T, y_T)$ as follows:

$$\psi_y(T, y_T) = \max(f_H(T, y_T), f_C(T, y_T))$$

4.3.4 SU and year label propagation

If there is an S edge between T and T', by definition, we can propagate all the labels $l \in L_T$ of T to T' and vice-versa. For example, in figure 2, we propagate the labels (mil and $Euro$) from T2 to T3. L_T and L'_T are good assignments to two tables T and T' connected by an S edge if all or most of their elements are the same, i.e., the set similarity (e.g., Jaccard Similarity) is high.

If there is an X edge (associated with a set R of rules) from T to T', we can propagate all labels $l \in (L_T - \bigcup_{r \in R} r.LHS)$ from T to T' and all labels $l \in (L'_T - \bigcup_{r \in R} r.RHS)$ from T' to T.[2] The insight here is that T and T' are semantically identical except in the scales and units present in the rules connecting them; so, all the other labels of T apply to T' and vice-versa. For example, consider two tables T and T': T has labels $L_T = \{mil, USD\}$ and there is an X edge associated with the rule $USD = 0.77 \times Euro$ from T to T'. We can propagate the label $\{mil, USD\} - \{USD\} = \{mil\}$ from T to T'. L_T and L'_T are good assignments to two tables T and T' connected by an X edge associated with the set R of rules if all or most of the elements in $L_T - \bigcup_{r \in R} r.LHS$ and $L'_T - \bigcup_{r \in R} r.RHS$ are the same, i.e., the set similarity (e.g., Jaccard Similarity) between those two sets is high. We define the edge potential $\psi_{lp}(T, T', L_T, L'_T, B_{TT'})$ as follows:

$$\begin{aligned}&\psi_{lp}(T, T', L_T, L'_T, B_{TT'}) \\ =\ & JaccSim(L_T, L'_T) \text{ if } B_{TT'} = S \\ =\ & JaccSim(L_T - \bigcup_{r \in R} r.LHS, L'_T - \bigcup_{r \in R} r.RHS) \text{ if } B_{TT'} = R \\ =\ & 0 \text{ otherwise}\end{aligned}$$

We can propagate the year label from T to T' if there is either a S edge or X edge between them. y_T and y'_T are good assignments to two tables T and T' connected by an S or X edge if $y_T = y'_T \neq NA$. We define the edge potential $\psi_{lp}(T, T', y_T, y'_T, B_{TT'})$ as follows:

$$\begin{aligned}\psi_{lp}(T, T', y_T, y'_T, B_{TT'}) &= 1 \text{ if } y_T = y'_T \wedge y_T \neq NA \\ &= 0 \text{ otherwise}\end{aligned}$$

4.3.5 Spurious edge elimination

Schema matching techniques can introduce spurious edges. One significant source of errors is time-varying attributes: if the values of an attribute (say, revenues) did not change significantly from one year to another, it can lead to a spurious match. In Figure 2, the revenues of Pfizer and Abbott Labs did not change significantly from 2010 to 2011; this leads to a spurious semantic match between T_1 and T_4. We disallow such spurious matches by taking large negative values when the year labels are not identical. We define the clique potential $\psi_{ec}(T, T', y_T, y'_T, B_{TT'})$ as follows:

$$\begin{aligned}\psi_{ec}(T, T', y_T, y'_T, B_{TT'}) &= -\infty \text{ if } y_T \neq y'_T \wedge y_T \neq NA \\ &\quad \wedge y'_T \neq NA \wedge B_{TT'} \neq NA \\ &= 0 \text{ otherwise}\end{aligned}$$

4.4 Overall Objective

The goal is to find the assignment to the variables L_T, y_T and $B_{TT'}$ such that the following objective is maximized:

$$\begin{aligned}&\sum_T \psi_{su}(T, L_T) + \sum_T \psi_y(T, y_T) \text{ (local extraction)} \\ &+ \sum_{T,T' \in \mathcal{T}} \psi_e(T, T', L_T, L'_T, B_{TT'}) \text{ (S and X edges)} \\ &+ \sum_{T,T' \in \mathcal{T}} \psi_{lp}(T, T', L_T, L'_T, B_{TT'}) \text{ (SU label propagation)} \\ &+ \sum_{T,T' \in \mathcal{T}} \psi_{lp}(T, T', y_T, y'_T, B_{TT'}) \text{ (year label propagation)} \\ &+ \sum_{T,T' \in \mathcal{T}} \psi_{ec}(T, T', y_T, y'_T, B_{TT'}) \text{ (edge constraint)} \qquad (1)\end{aligned}$$

[2] We consider the directionality here. However, considering the reverse direction (from T' to T) yields the same result.

4.5 Inference Algorithm

4.5.1 *Independent Inference*

We first show how to find the optimal node and edge ing to maximize the above objective in the case of no propagation. This optimization can be solved in polyn time because the optimization for each objective comp can be solved completely based on local information. T similar to the *staged approach* described before. The p code is shown in Algorithm 1. The local extraction of scale and year is first performed based on feature fun defined above. Once the node labels have been detern we compute the S and X edges using the similarity fu and the computation technique described above. The labels can then be obtained accordingly. Finally, we c the edge label to NA for those having different years o sides to satisfy the edge constraint ψ_{ec}.

Algorithm 1: Independent Inference

```
foreach table T ∈ 𝒯 do
    Initialization: L_T = {}, y_T = NA
    // local extraction of unit and scale
    foreach label l ∈ ℒ do
        if max(f_H(T, l), f_V(T, l)) = 1 then
            L_T.add(l);
    // local extraction of year
    foreach year y ∈ 𝒴 do
        if max(f_H(T, y), f_C(T, y)) = 1 then
            y_T = y;
// S and X edge computation
foreach table pair T, T' do
    B_TT' = arg max ψ_e(T, T', L_T, L'_T, B_TT');
// Spurious edge elimination
foreach table pair T, T' do
    if ψ_ec(T, T', y_T, y'_T, B_TT') = −∞ then
        B_TT' = NA;
return L_T, y_T, B_TT';
```

4.5.2 *Hardness of Collective Inference*

We next show that finding the labels that maximize the final objective function with label propagation is NP-Hard, even for a simple case where we only have one variable y_T. In this simple case, our objective is turned to

$$\max_{\mathbf{y}} \quad \sum_{T\in\mathcal{T}} \psi_y(T, y_T) + \sum_{T,T'\in\mathcal{T}} \psi_{ec}(T, T', y_T, y'_T) + \sum_{T,T'\in\mathcal{T}} \psi_{lp}(T, T', y_T, y'_T) \quad (2)$$

THEOREM 1. *Finding the optimal labeling for objective (2) is NP-Hard.*

PROOF. We prove it by reduction from metric labeling problem [10]. Metric labeling is defined over a weighted undirected graph $G = (V, E)$ and a label set L, where the weight (nonnegative) $w(v, v')$ indicates the strength of the relationship between node v and v'. We are given: (1) a nonnegative cost function $c(v, l)$ for assigning label l to the node v; (2) a distance $d(l, l')$ between label l and l'. The objective is to find a labeling function $f : V \to L$ such that the following total cost is minimized:

$$\mathcal{C}(f) = \sum_{v\in V} c(v, f(v)) + \sum_{(v,v')\in E} w(v, v') \cdot d(f(v), f(v'))$$

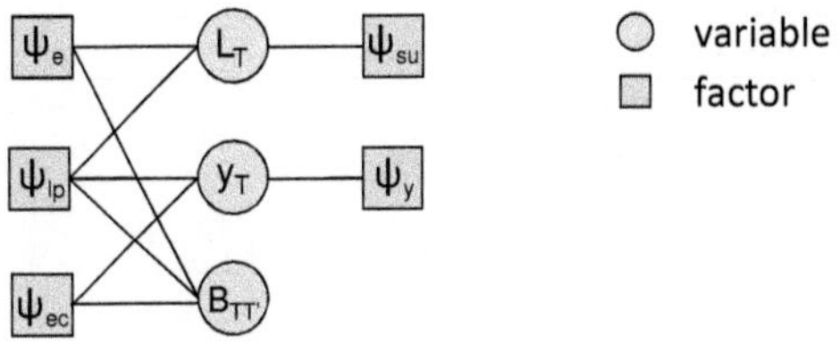

Figure 6: Factor graph.

To reduce the metric labeling to our problem, we let each node $v \in V$ corresponds to one $T \in \mathcal{T}$. The variable y_T can only take labels from set L and can not be NA. Then we define node potential ψ_y and edge potential ψ_{ec}, ψ_{lp} as follows:

$$\begin{aligned} \psi_y(v, l) &= -c(v, l) \\ \psi_{ec}(v, v', l, l') &= -w(v, v') \cdot d(l, l') \\ \psi_{lp}(v, v', l, l') &= 0 \end{aligned}$$

Since the the cost c and distance d are both nonnegative, maximizing $\psi_y(v, l)$ is equivalent to minimizing the cost for assigning l to v. Similarly, maximizing $\psi_{ec}(v, v', l, l')$ is e-quivalent to minimizing the cost for assigning l and l' to a pair of nodes. We let ψ_{lp} be zero so that it does not affect the final labeling. Hence, the objective function (2) is consistent with the total cost in metric labeling. If a labeling function f can be found in polynomial time to maximize the objective (2), it can also minimize the total cost $\mathcal{C}$ in metric labeling problem. □

4.5.3 *Approximation Algorithm*

We develop an approximation algorithm to resolve the collective inference by adapting the techniques proposed in probabilistic graphical model, specifically, the belief propagation algorithm [11]. Belief propagation algorithm operates on a factor graph which contains variable nodes and factor n-odes, and proceeds by passing "belief" via messages between variable nodes and factor nodes. In our problem, there are three variables and five factors. We show the factor graph in Figure 6. There is an edge between a variable x and a factor ψ iff x appears in ψ.

The algorithm starts with initializing the node potential ψ_{su} and ψ_y for each table T by doing the local extraction of scale, unit and year labels. The collective inference is then processed by iteratively passing messages between neighboring nodes. At each iteration, we schedule the message passing process in three steps. The first step is centered on edge potential ψ_e. The messages are sent from the scale/unit label L_T to ψ_e, then to the edge label $B_{TT'}$ and then sent back. This step tries to create more edges between tables based on current belief on node labeling and, at the same time, tries to select labels that are beneficial for edge creation. At the second step, the focus is on the edge potential ψ_{lp} for label propagation. The messages are passed from L_T, y_T and $B_{TT'}$ to ψ_{lp}; ψ_{lp} then sends back messages according to the set of labels that produce the highest potential. The final step deals with the constraint ψ_{ec} for eliminating spurious edges. The passing schedule for this step is similar to Step 1 except that the messages are sent between year label y_T, edge label $B_{TT'}$ and ψ_{ec}. The algorithm stops when the message values converge or the number of iteration reaches the max limit. The final values of variables are derived from the messages. The details of the algorithm is presented in Algorithm 2.

Algorithm 2: Collective Inference

foreach *table* $T \in \mathcal{T}$ **do**
  Compute $\psi_{su}(T, L_T), \psi_y(T, y_T)$;
Initialization: $M = 0$
while *Iteration* $\leq$ *max_iteration* **do**
  foreach *table pair* T, T' **do**
    `// Step 1`
    $M(L_T \to \psi_e) = \psi_{su}(T, L_T) + \sum_{T'} M(\psi_{lp} \to L_T)$;
    $M(L_{T'} \to \psi_e) = \psi_{su}(T, L_{T'}) + \sum_{T''} M(\psi_{lp} \to L_{T'})$;
    $M(\psi_e \to B_{TT'}) = \max_{L_T, L_{T'}} [\psi_e + M(L_T \to \psi_e) + M(L_{T'} \to \psi_e)]$;
    $M(B_{TT'} \to \psi_e) = M(\psi_{lp} \to B_{TT'}) + M(\psi_{ec} \to B_{TT'})$;
    $M(\psi_e \to L_T) = \max_{L_{T'}, B_{TT'}} [\psi_e + M(L_{T'} \to \psi_e) + M(B_{TT'} \to \psi_e)]$;
    $M(\psi_e \to L_{T'}) = \max_{L_T, B_{TT'}} [\psi_e + M(L_T \to \psi_e) + M(B_{TT'} \to \psi_e)]$;
    `// Step 2`
    $M(L_T \to \psi_{lp}) = \psi_{su}(T, L_T) + \sum_{T'} M(\psi_e \to L_T)$;
    $M(L_{T'} \to \psi_{lp}) = \psi_{su}(T, L_{T'}) + \sum_{T''} M(\psi_e \to L_{T'})$;
    $M(y_T \to \psi_{lp}) = \psi_y(T, y_T) + \sum_{T'} M(\psi_{ec} \to y_T)$;
    $M(y_{T'} \to \psi_{lp}) = \psi_y(T, y_{T'}) + \sum_{T''} M(\psi_{ec} \to y_{T'})$;
    $M(B_{TT'} \to \psi_{lp}) = M(\psi_e \to B_{TT'}) + M(\psi_{ec} \to B_{TT'})$;
    $M(\psi_{lp} \to B_{TT'}) = \max_{L_T, L_{T'}, y_T, y_{T'}} [\psi_{lp} + M(L_T \to \psi_{lp}) + M(L_{T'} \to \psi_{lp}) + M(y_T \to \psi_{lp}) + M(y_{T'} \to \psi_{lp})]$;
    $M(\psi_{lp} \to L_T) = \max_{L_{T'}, y_T, y_{T'}, B_{TT'}} [\psi_{lp} + M(L_{T'} \to \psi_{lp}) + M(y_T \to \psi_{lp}) + M(y_{T'} \to \psi_{lp}) + M(B_{TT'} \to \psi_{lp})]$;
    $M(\psi_{lp} \to L_{T'}) = \max_{L_T, y_T, y_{T'}, B_{TT'}} [\psi_{lp} + M(L_T \to \psi_{lp}) + M(y_T \to \psi_{lp}) + M(y_{T'} \to \psi_{lp}) + M(B_{TT'} \to \psi_{lp})]$;
    $M(\psi_{lp} \to y_T) = \max_{y_{T'}, L_T, L_{T'}, B_{TT'}} [\psi_{lp} + M(y_{T'} \to \psi_{lp}) + M(L_T \to \psi_{lp}) + M(L_{T'} \to \psi_{lp}) + M(B_{TT'} \to \psi_{lp})]$;
    $M(\psi_{lp} \to y_{T'}) = \max_{y_T, L_T, L_{T'}, B_{TT'}} [\psi_{lp} + M(y_T \to \psi_{lp}) + M(L_T \to \psi_{lp}) + M(L_{T'} \to \psi_{lp}) + M(B_{TT'} \to \psi_{lp})]$;
    `// Step 3`
    $M(y_T \to \psi_{ec}) = \psi_y(T, y_T) + \sum_{T'} M(\psi_{lp} \to y_T)$;
    $M(y_{T'} \to \psi_{ec}) = \psi_y(T, y_{T'}) + \sum_{T''} M(\psi_{lp} \to y_{T'})$;
    $M(\psi_{ec} \to B_{TT'}) = \max_{y_T, y_{T'}} [\psi_{ec} + M(y_T \to \psi_{ec}) + M(y_{T'} \to \psi_{ec})]$;
    $M(B_{TT'} \to \psi_{ec}) = M(\psi_{lp} \to B_{TT'}) + M(\psi_e \to B_{TT'})$;
    $M(\psi_{ec} \to y_T) = \max_{y_{T'}, B_{TT'}} [\psi_{ec} + M(y_{T'} \to \psi_{ec}) + M(B_{TT'} \to \psi_{ec})]$;
    $M(\psi_{ec} \to y_{T'}) = \max_{y_T, B_{TT'}} [\psi_{ec} + M(y_T \to \psi_{ec}) + M(B_{TT'} \to \psi_{ec})]$;
  if *converged* **then**
    break;
return $\mathbf{L_T}$, $\mathbf{y_T}$, $\mathbf{B_{TT'}}$;

4.5.4 *Scalable Implementation of Collective Inference*

There are hundreds of millions of tables on the web; to build the semantic graph over all web tables, the belief propagation algorithm need to scale to factor graphs containing billions of nodes. Many large scale graph processing tasks can be expressed as a sequence of iterations, in each of which a vertex can receive messages sent in the previous iteration, send messages to other vertices, and modify its own state and that of its outgoing edges or mutate graph topology. Hence, several systems have been developed for above computation model over very large-scale graphs (e.g., Pregel [13], Trinity [17]). Since the belief propagation algorithm follows the same computational model, we can leverage those technologies for scalable implementation of collective inference.

5. QUERY PROCESSING

We focus on entity augmentation queries in this section. Our system can support other types of web table search queries [21, 14]. We first define the query interface of our system.

5.1 Query Interface

DEFINITION 1 (QUERY INTERFACE). *An entity augmentation query $Q = \langle A, E, SU, Y \rangle$ consists of four components:*
A: keywords describing attribute name.
E: the set of entities of interest.
SU: unit and scale (optional).
Y: timestamp (optional).

The proposed API significantly extends the previously proposed entity augmentation API which takes only attribute name and entity set as input [21]. We extend the query language with *SU* and *Y* to unambiguously specify the augmentation task. Furthermore, it better leverages the semantic graph we build in this paper.

5.2 Query Time Processing

We briefly introduced the two main steps for EA queries in Section 3. We also described the indexes built for efficient query time processing. We now present the processing in detail. The pseudo code is shown in Algorithm 3.

Step 1: Identify matching tables. Given the query Q, we first leverage the EI index to identify the set of tables that contains at least one of the entities in $Q.E$. Among these tables, we use the NLI index to identify the subset of tables that satisfy the following conditions: (1) The column header matches with the attribute name keywords in $Q.A$; (2) The year label matches with the query label in $Q.Y$ (if any); (3) The unit and scale labels match with each of the query labels in $Q.SU$. A unit/scale label is considered a match if it occurs in the same mutex group as $Q.SU$. This is because they are convertible from one to another; we can convert values from the units they are available in to the desired query unit. Finally, for each qualified table, we search for its semantically matching tables using GI index. The qualified tables together with their matching tables become our sources for filling in values at next step.

Step 2: Fill-in values. For each table identified at Step 1, we collect the values provided in the table for each of

Algorithm 3: Query Processing

// Step 1: Identify matching tables
$\mathcal{S} = EI(Q)$;
$\mathcal{S} = \mathcal{S} \cap NLI(Q)$;
$\mathcal{S} = \mathcal{S} \cup \bigcup_{T \in \mathcal{S}} GI(T)$;
// Step 2: Fill-in values
foreach *table* $T \in \mathcal{S}$ **do**
  foreach *tuple* $t \in T$ **do**
    if $t.e \in Q.E$ **then**
      v = Convert($t.v$, L_T, $Q.SU$);
      Aggregate($t.e$, v);
AugmentEntity($Q.E$);

the query entities. We compare the table's semantic labels (unit and scale) with the query labels. If they do not agree, we convert the values to the desired unit and scale. The converted values are then aggregated. Finally, we augment the query entities with the values with the highest aggregate score.

EXAMPLE 2. *Consider the web tables shown in Figure 2. Suppose the collective inference approach has discovered the semantic labels and edges shown in Figure 2. Consider the EA query in Figure 1(b). The query processing algorithm will identify T_1, T_2 and T_3 as matching tables because (1) their column headers contain "revenues" (2) their year labels match with '2010' and (3) they contain unit/scale labels that are in the same mutex group as USD (USD, Euro and Euro respectively). For Eli Lilly, T_1 provides* 21.8 *which is already in USD bil. For Merck, T_1 provides* 27.4 *and T_2 provides* 21091*; the latter is converted to USD bil which also results in* 27.4*. For Roche and Novartis, T_3 provides the values* 36113 *and* 33762 *respectively; they are converted to USD bil resulting in* 46.9 *and* 43.8 *respectively. This produces the desirable, semantically consistent results (all from 2010 and all in USD bil) shown in Figure 1(b).*

6. EXPERIMENTS

We present an experimental evaluation of the techniques proposed in the paper. The goals of the experimental study are:
• To evaluate the quality of the semantic labels (unit, scale and year) and semantic matches discovered by our collective inference approach
• To evaluate the impact of the discovered labels and matches on entity augmentation (EA) queries and to compare with the baseline approach
• To evaluate the efficiency of processing EA queries specified using the proposed query interface

6.1 Experimental Setup

Datasets: We conducted experiments on three real-life datasets of web tables: Company, Country and City, which are extracted from a recent snapshot of Microsoft Bing search engine. Table 1 shows the detailed statistics of the datasets including the number of web tables, the total number of numeric attributes across all the tables and the average number of numeric attributes per table.

EA Queries and golden truth: We conducted experiments for the following EA queries:
• *Company revenue and profit:* We compiled the golden truth by extracting the Forbes Global 2000 list of year 2011

Table 1: Datasets statistics

Domain	Tables	Numeric Attrs	Average
Company	39,223	80,149	2.04
City	81,977	140,459	1.71
Country	159,730	344,509	2.16

from [2]. We chose various subsets of those companies as the entities. We considered multiple EA queries with "revenue" and "profit" as attribute keywords, in various units and scales and from year 2011.
• *Country area:* We compiled the golden truth by extracting the list of 249 countries along with their total area from a Wikipedia page [3]. We chose various subsets of those countries as entities. We considered multiple EA queries with "area" as attribute keyword and in different units.
• *Country taxrate:* We compiled the golden truth by extracting the list of corporate income tax rates of 34 OECD member countries from Tax Foundation [4]. We chose various subsets of those countries as entities. We considered multiple EA queries with "tax rate" as attribute keywords and from different years.
• *City population:* We compiled the golden truth by extracting the list top 600 largest cities in 2011 from the City Mayors site [1]. We chose various subsets of those cities as entities. We considered multiple EA queries with "population" as attribute keyword, in various scales and from year 2011.

Conversion rules: The set of conversion rules are shown in Table 2. We list only the ones relevant to the EA queries reported in the paper. We omit the conversion factors and only show the units/scales involved in the rules. For example, for the city population EA query, the relevant rules are those for converting between four scale labels, i.e. billion, million, thousand and NA. We also have a database containing synonyms of unit and scale descriptors.

Table 2: Conversion rules

Query Attribute	Conversion tokens
Company revenue/profit	euro usd
	billion million thousand NA
City population	billion million thousand NA
Country area	sq.meter sq.feet sq.km sq.mile

Our algorithms are implemented in C# and the experiments were performed on a Windows server with a Quad-Core AMD Opteron 2.3 GHz CPU and 128GB RAM.

6.2 Evaluating Quality of Semantic Graph

We evaluate the graph quality in terms of the quality of the semantic labels (unit, scale and year) and semantic matches. In this set of experiments, we report the results on Company dataset.

6.2.1 Node Label Quality

We manually selected a random set of 1000 EAB tables whose attributes are related to company revenue. We compare the labels on these tables discovered by our collective inference approach (CI in short) with the ones discovered by the independent inference approach (II in short). Table 3 shows the quality results of the node labels. Recall that II computes labels based on local extractions only and X edges based on those labels. For SU labels (scale and unit), *CI discovers more labels* compared with II (labels for 35% more nodes) and *with high precision* ($\sim$ 97%). II annotates 510 out of 1000 tables; CI annotate 180 more tables (due to label propagation).

We first analyze the new tables annotated by CI approach. We randomly sampled 100 (out of 180) tables and manually checked the labels. We found 97 tables are labeled correctly and completely and 3 tables (all in <million, usd>) are partially correct. We further analyze those 3 partially correct tables. CI annotates two of them with million only and one with usd only. By manually checking the original web page, we found that the first two tables contain revenue values of year 1955. Since the majority of web tables contain recent information and those values are very different from the ones of recent years, they are not connected to the majority of tables in the semantic graph. Hence, CI fails to propagate the correct unit to those two tables. The other error occurs on the table which contains information about Revenue per Employee instead of total revenue.

We now evaluate the labels discovered by both II and CI. We observe 428 out of 510 labels are identical. CI annotates 81 of those 510 tables with additional labels (e.g., usd → <usd, million>). Interestingly, CI even made a correction to one of the tables[3]. The table header specifies million, whereas the values are in fact in billion.

For year labels, *CI labels 4X more nodes* compared with II and *with a precision of* ∼ 89%. II annotates only 129 out of 1000 tables while CI annotates 527 tables (due to label propagation). Again, we take a random sample of 100 tables and manually check the year annotation. The accuracy is 89%. From a careful analysis of the data, the mistakes made on the 11% tables can be mostly attributed to the similar values between different years. For example, we notice there are two tables, one of year 2006 and one 2011. However, there are 6 out of 8 entities in the 2006 table having values very close to 2011 revenue values. Similar to the SU label, our approach can also make correction to year labels. While analyzing the annotation results, we encounter a 2011 revenue table[4] that happens to have "2010 revenue" in the header – our approach correctly assigned the label 2011 to it.

Table 3: Node label quality

SU	II	510	same:	428
			diff:	1
	CI	690	more:	81 (100%)
			new :	180 (∼97%)
Year	II	129	same:	127
			diff:	2
	CI	527	more:	–
			new :	398 (∼89%)

6.2.2 Edge Quality

We study the quality of the semantic matches (i.e., edges) produced by our techniques. We evaluate it on the Company dataset as well. We consider the edges between the 1000 revenue tables. Table 4 shows the edge quality results. Recall that our approach creates new X edges and eliminates spurious edges (between tables that contain information from different years). In the table, we show the number of X edges created and the spurious edges eliminated by II and CI approaches. For X edge creation, II creates 205 edges while CI creates 405. For spurious edge elimination, II removes only 4 edges while CI eliminates 336 edges (out of 1935 S edges). Both are due to label propagation: more labels lead to more X edge creation and more spurious edge elimination. To evaluate the accuracy of the edges we created and eliminated, we randomly took 100 sample edges from each of the set and performed another round of manual checking. The accuracy results are included in the Table 4 as well. The accuracy of CI is 83% and 79% for created and eliminated edges respectively. By analyzing the data, we found that the mistakes are again caused by the same (or similar) values shared by tables from different years.

Table 4: Edge quality

	X Edge		Elimination	
	II	CI	II	CI
Number	205	405	4	336
Accuracy	∼90%	∼83%	100%	∼79%

6.3 Evaluating Entity Augmentation Quality

We implemented four different approaches (2 baseline approaches and 2 variations of our approach):

- *S:* This is a baseline approach which treats unit/scale and year specified in the query as normal keywords in attribute name. It considers a table relevant to query Q only if the table header contains all of the keywords in $Q.A$, $Q.SU$ and $Q.Y$. The edges between tables are simple S edges.
- *S-Syn:* This is similar to S approach except that we leverage synonyms of attribute names. We mine the attribute synonyms using the approach proposed in [21]. For attribute name, a table T is considered a match to Q if the union of the synonyms of T's attribute covers all the keywords in $Q.A$, $Q.SU$ and $Q.Y$.
- *Independent Inference(II):* This approach computes SU and year labels based on local extraction and X edges based on those labels. It also eliminates spurious edges based on those local labels. It uses the query processing algorithm proposed in Section 5.
- *Collective Inference(CI):* This is our proposed approach based on the collective inference algorithm. It also uses the query processing algorithm proposed in Section 5.

In this section, we report the EA quality for the above approaches. We use two metrics to measure EA quality: coverage and precision.

$coverage = \frac{\#entities\_augmented}{\#entities\_in\_query}$

$precision = \frac{\#entities\_correctly\_augmented}{\#entities\_augmented}$

We first present the results for two simple scenarios where the query specifies only SU (no year) and only Y (no SU) (Country-area and Country-tax rate respectively). We then present the results for the scenario where both SU and Y are specified in the query.

6.3.1 SU-only Scenario

Figure 7 shows the coverage and precision results of augmenting country area in square km. The x-axis represents different entity sets: the top-k countries in descending order of the country area for various values of k. We did this to study the sensitivity of the approaches to head and tail entities [5] All the four approaches achieve high coverage; the coverage decreases as we encounter more tail entities. However, S and S-Syn approaches have poor precision: the highest is 0.22 on 250 countries. In contrast, II and CI achieve consistently high precision across all entity sets: an average

[3]http://www.americanet.de/html/wirtschaft__grosste_firmen.html

[4]http://waste360.com/corporate-sustainability-50/2011

[5] This assumes that the countries with larger area are head countries and the ones with smaller area are tail. There is a correlation between area and query popularity but this, in general, is not true; hence, the sensitivity aspect of this study is not conclusive.

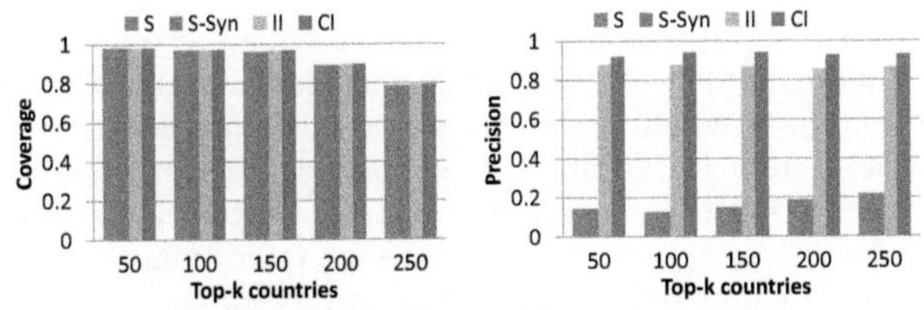

Figure 7: Country area: square km

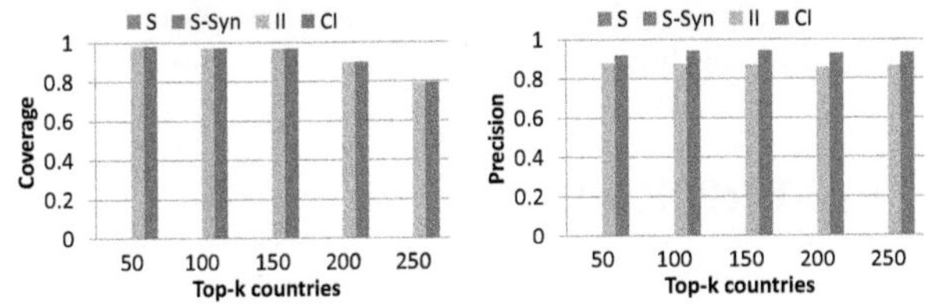

Figure 8: Country area: sqft

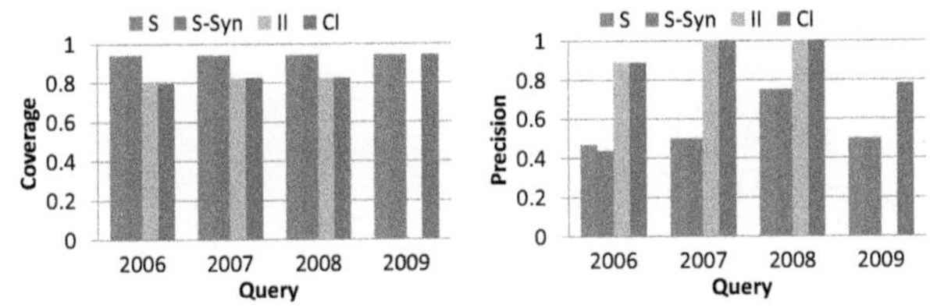

Figure 9: Country taxrate

precision of 0.87 for II approach and 0.93 for CI. This confirms that adding X edges and semantic labels significantly impacts the quality of EA queries. The improvement is more significant in CI where we create more X edges and labels via label propagation.

Figure 8 shows the results of augmenting country area using a different unit: sqft. The drawback of baseline approaches is more obvious in this query. The baseline approaches fail to augment even a single entity. This is because country area is not available in the desired unit; hence, *S* and *S-Syn* finds zero relevant tables. On the other hand, our approaches achieve high coverage and precision as we can convert the values from the units they are available in to the desired unit.

6.3.2 Year-only Scenario

Figure 9 shows the results of augmenting country tax rate for year 2006-2009. The baseline approaches reach high coverage for all years. However, the average precision is only 0.55 and 0.54 for *S* and *S-Syn* respectively. This is due to spurious edges between tables that contain information from different years; hence, the results contain values from years different from the query year. II and CI improves the average precision to 0.72 and 0.92 respectively by eliminating spurious edges. Note that II returns zero result for year 2009. This is because II fails to hit the tables that contain the query answer without propagating the years. Overall, CI significantly outperforms II and the baselines as it does a better job in propagating the labels and eliminating spurious edges (as shown in Table 4).

6.3.3 SU+Year Scenario

We compare the approaches for the scenario where the query specifies both unit/scale and year. We present results for four entity augmentation queries on Company and City datasets. For this set of experiments, we omit the *S* approach in the figures, because *S* either returns zero results or similar results as *S-Syn*.

Figure 10 compares the 3 approaches for the company-revenue query in <million, \$> for year 2011. The baseline

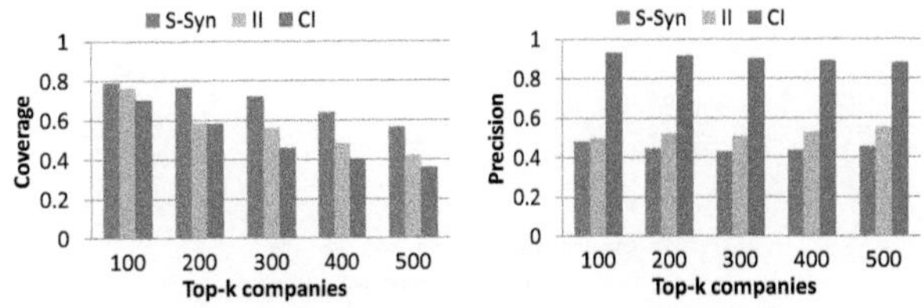

Figure 10: Company revenue: million \$

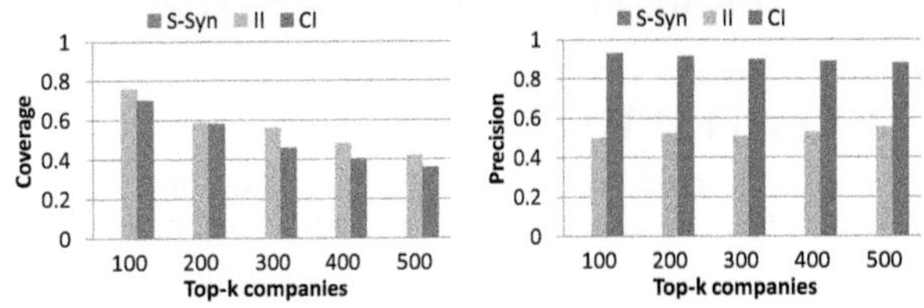

Figure 11: Company revenue: billion \$

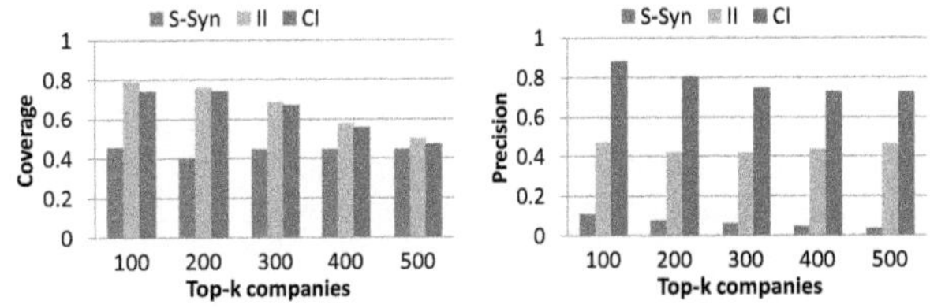

Figure 12: Company profit: million \$

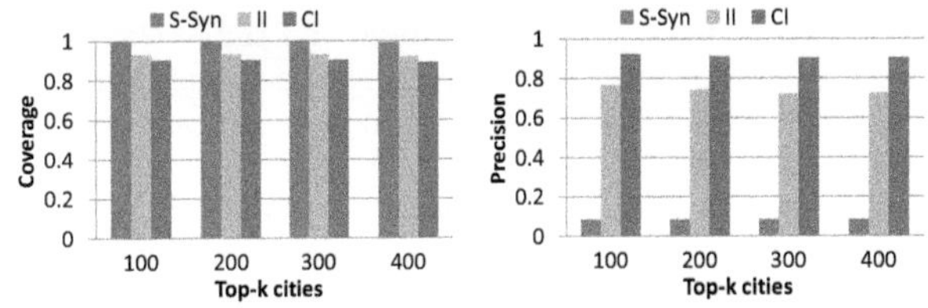

Figure 13: City population: million

approach has good coverage but suffers from poor precision (~ 0.4). II does not improve the precision significantly but CI improves the precision to 0.9. This indicates that the higher quality labels and edges produced by CI significantly improves the quality of EA queries.

Figure 11 shows the results for the company-revenue query in <billion, \$> for year 2011. Similar to augmenting country area in sqft, the baseline approach returns zero results, whereas CI is not affected by changing of query scale from million to billion. This is due to the unavailability of information in <billion, \$> and our ability to convert the values from the units they are available into <billion, \$>.

Figure 12 plots the results of the company-profit query in <million, \$> for year 2011. CI consistently outperforms both II and the baseline approach. Figure 13 shows the results for the city-population in million for year 2011. Again, CI significantly outperforms both II and the baseline approach on precision and achieves high coverage as well. The average coverage and precision are 0.9 and 0.9 respectively.

6.4 EA Query Efficiency

We evaluate the efficiency of processing EA queries using the CI approach. Figure 14 shows the query response time as we increase the number of entities from 50 to 400. The response time is within 1 second and increases sub-linearly with the number of entities, making our approach usable in interactive applications.

In summary, our experiments show that our collective inference approach produces higher quality semantic matches and semantic labels which significantly improves the quality of entity augmentation queries.

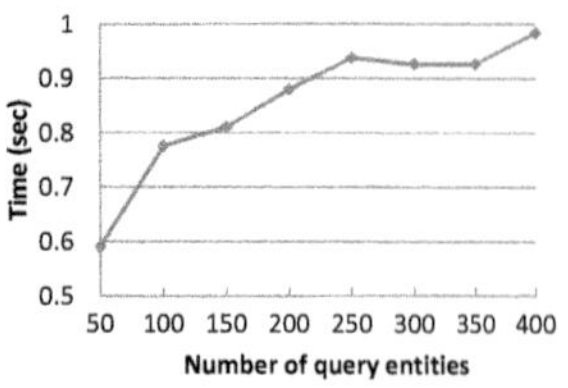

Figure 14: Query response time

7. RELATED WORK

Our work is most related to works on annotating web tables [12, 19] and semantic matching between web tables [21]. Given a catalog (e.g., YAGO), Limaye et. al. annotates columns in web tables with those catalog types, pairs of columns with those catalog relationships and table cells with those catalog entities [12]. In contrast, Venetis et. al. leverages a database of classes, instances and relationships extracted automatically from the web to perform such annotations. Our annotations are fundamentally different from those annotations: we annotate columns with unit, scale and year information. To the best of our knowledge, such annotations have not been studied before in the context of web tables. Our work significantly extends the semantic matching in InfoGather [21]. InfoGather focuses only on S edges which is inadequate for numeric and time-varying attributes. InfoGather+ discovers X edges and semantic labels in addition to S edges; as a result, it performs significantly better compared with InfoGather.

Search over web tables has received significant research attention recently [6, 5, 21, 14]. Cafarella et. al. proposes a simple keyword search that returns a ranked list of web tables [5]. More recent works propose to consolidate matching tables to synthesize the desired table for the user. One example is the entity augmentation operation proposed in [5, 21]. Another example is the user specifying sets of keywords she wishes to see in the answer table (e.g., "Pain killer|Side effects"); the system consolidates a single answer table for such queries [14]. Our work on semantic graph is orthogonal to these works; it is critical for all consolidation-based approaches. Secondly, we significantly extend the entity augmentation API for numeric and time-varying attributes.

Our work on semantic graph is related to the vast body of work on schema matching [15, 9]. Traditional schema matching works find semantic matches between two database schemas. Most works focus on one-to-one mappings; the works that deal with complex matches rely only on "local" extraction [8] (i.e., looks for labels in the column headers and values). In this paper, we argue that this is inadequate for web tables as such information is often missing from column headers. We leverage the fact that there are millions of tables on the web; even if the local header does not contain the information, some semantically matching table will contain it. Furthermore, we annotate tables with semantic labels which is not considered in schema matching works.

Recently, researchers have started studying ways to assign a timestamp (or time span) to facts in a knowledgebase (like YAGO or Freebase) [20, 18]. In this paper, we study year annotation in conjunction with scale and unit annotation and semantic matches in the context of web tables.

8. CONCLUSION

In this paper, we present the InfoGather+ system to answer entity augmentation queries accurately for numeric and time-varying attributes. We build a semantic graph that (i) labels columns with unit, scale and year information and (ii) computes semantic matches between columns even when the same numeric attribute is expressed in different units or scales. Our experiments demonstrate that by leveraging the semantic graph, we can answer such queries much more accurately compared with the state-of-the-art.

Our work can be extended in multiple directions. In this paper, we focused on leveraging the semantic graph for entity augmentation; how to leverage it for other modes of web table search is an item of future work.

9. REFERENCES

[1] City Mayors. http://www.citymayors.com/statistics/largest-cities-mayors-1.html.

[2] Forbes Global 2000. http://www.forbes.com/lists/2012/18/global2000_2011.html.

[3] List of countries by area. http://en.wikipedia.org/wiki/List_of_countries_and_dependencies_by_area.

[4] Tax Foundation. http://taxfoundation.org/article/oecd-corporate-income-tax-rates-1981-2012.

[5] M. J. Cafarella, A. Y. Halevy, and N. Khoussainova. Data integration for the relational web. *PVLDB*, 2(1):1090–1101, 2009.

[6] M. J. Cafarella, A. Y. Halevy, D. Z. Wang, E. Wu, and Y. Zhang. Webtables: exploring the power of tables on the web. *PVLDB*, 1(1):538–549, 2008.

[7] M. J. Cafarella, A. Y. Halevy, Y. Zhang, D. Z. Wang, and E. Wu. Uncovering the relational web. *WebDB*, 2008.

[8] R. Dhamankar, Y. Lee, A. Doan, A. Halevy, and P. Domingos. iMAP: discovering complex semantic matches between database schemas. *SIGMOD*, pages 383–394, 2004.

[9] A. Doan and A. Y. Halevy. Semantic integration research in the database community: A brief survey. *AI Magazine*, 26:83–94, 2005.

[10] J. Kleinberg and E. Tardos. Approximation algorithms for classification problems with pairwise relationships: metric labeling and markov random fields. *J. ACM*, 49(5):616–639, Sept. 2002.

[11] D. Koller and N. Friedman. *Probabilistic Graphical Models: Principles and Techniques.* MIT Press, 2009.

[12] G. Limaye, S. Sarawagi, and S. Chakrabarti. Annotating and searching web tables using entities, types and relationships. *PVLDB*, 3(1):1338–1347, 2010.

[13] G. Malewicz, M. H. Austern, A. J. C. Bik, J. C. Dehnert, I. Horn, N. Leiser, and G. Czajkowski. Pregel: a system for large-scale graph processing. *SIGMOD*, pages 135–146, 2010.

[14] R. Pimplikar and S. Sarawagi. Answering table queries on the web using column keywords. *PVLDB*, 5(10):908–919, 2012.

[15] E. Rahm and P. A. Bernstein. A survey of approaches to automatic schema matching. *VLDB J.*, 10(4):334–350, 2001.

[16] A. D. Sarma, L. Fang, N. Gupta, A. Y. Halevy, H. Lee, F. Wu, R. Xin, and C. Yu. Finding related tables. *SIGMOD*, pages 817–828, 2012.

[17] B. Shao, H. Wang, and Y. Li. The trinity graph engine.

[18] P. P. Talukdar, D. Wijaya, and T. Mitchell. Coupled temporal scoping of relational facts. *WSDM*, pages 73–82, 2012.

[19] P. Venetis, A. Y. Halevy, J. Madhavan, M. Pasca, W. Shen, F. Wu, G. Miao, and C. Wu. Recovering semantics of tables on the web. *PVLDB*, 4(9):528–538, 2011.

[20] Y. Wang, B. Yang, L. Qu, M. Spaniol, and G. Weikum. Harvesting facts from textual web sources by constrained label propagation. *CIKM*, pages 837–846, 2011.

[21] M. Yakout, K. Ganjam, K. Chakrabarti, and S. Chaudhuri. Infogather: entity augmentation and attribute discovery by holistic matching with web tables. *SIGMOD*, pages 97–108, 2012.

Value Invention in Data Exchange

Patricia C. Arocena
University of Toronto
prg@cs.toronto.edu

Boris Glavic
Illinois Institute of Technology
bglavic@iit.edu

Renée J. Miller
University of Toronto
miller@cs.toronto.edu

ABSTRACT

The creation of values to represent incomplete information, often referred to as *value invention*, is central in data exchange. Within schema mappings, Skolem functions have long been used for value invention as they permit a precise representation of missing information. Recent work on a powerful mapping language called *second-order tuple generating dependencies* (SO tgds), has drawn attention to the fact that the use of arbitrary Skolem functions can have negative computational and programmatic properties in data exchange. In this paper, we present two techniques for understanding when the Skolem functions needed to represent the correct semantics of incomplete information are computationally well-behaved. Specifically, we consider when the Skolem functions in second-order (SO) mappings have a first-order (FO) semantics and are therefore programmatically and computationally more desirable for use in practice. Our first technique, *linearization*, significantly extends the Nash, Bernstein and Melnik *unskolemization* algorithm, by understanding when the sets of arguments of the Skolem functions in a mapping are related by set inclusion. We show that such a linear relationship leads to mappings that have FO semantics and are expressible in popular mapping languages including source-to-target tgds and nested tgds. Our second technique uses source semantics, specifically functional dependencies (including keys), to transform SO mappings into equivalent FO mappings. We show that our algorithms are applicable to a strictly larger class of mappings than previous approaches, but more importantly we present an extensive experimental evaluation that quantifies this difference (about 78% improvement) over an extensive schema mapping benchmark and illustrates the applicability of our results on real mappings.

Categories and Subject Descriptors

H.2.5 [**Heterogeneous Databases**]: Data Translation

Keywords

Data Exchange, Schema Mappings, Value Invention, Unskolemization

SIGMOD'13, June 22–27, 2013, New York, New York, USA.

1. INTRODUCTION

Schema mappings are constraints that model the relationship between schemas and have been used extensively in data exchange and integration. In data exchange, schema mappings are used as a logical specification of how to map data from a source to a target schema. In data integration, mappings are used to specify how target queries can be translated into source queries. For decades, Skolem functions have played an important role in schema mappings [18]. Skolem functions can be used to model object identifier (OID) invention or *value invention* [18], and more generally to provide a precise model of how missing values are correlated to known source values [27, 29], and to other missing values [1]. The representational power of functions in mappings was recognized by Fagin et al. [12], with their presentation of a class of existential second-order (SO) formulas with arbitrary function symbols, called *second-order tuple-generating dependencies* (SO tgds). SO tgds are the right choice for modeling many data exchange and integration problems, such as mapping composition [12] and correlation of mappings [1]. Some, but not all, SO tgds are equivalent to *first-order (FO)* mappings (that is, mappings expressible in FO logic) [12]. While having the right expressive power, SO tgds do have some drawbacks. Model checking, determining whether a pair of instances satisfies a mapping, is intractable for SO tgds, while polynomial in data complexity for FO mappings [12]. Model checking is important for supporting updates, peer data-exchange [15], and data coordination [20]. Furthermore, SO tgds are not closed under target homomorphisms [31], a property that has undesirable consequences in practice. If a data exchange solution (for an SO tgd) is modified by a homomorphism that preserves constants and only modifies `NULLs` (for example by filling in missing information), then the result may no longer be a valid solution.

As a result, most systems, including Clio [29], Orchestra [17], ++Spicy [24], and OpenII [30], use FO mapping languages based on the popular language of *source-to-target (s-t)* tgds (also known as Global-and-Local-As-View or *GLAV* for short [21]), and the more general *nested* tgds (*nested GLAV*) [14]. Fuxman et al. [14] argued that nested GLAV, which permits nesting of mappings, instead of correlation of mappings via Skolem functions (as in SO tgds), are a less powerful, but more user-friendly programming concept. Both GLAV and nested GLAV mappings are closed under target homomorphisms [31]. Translations of these FO mapping languages into efficient transformation code (in, e.g.,

Source Schema
WorksOn (Department, Project, BudgetId)
Audit (BudgetId, Auditor)
City (Department, City)

Target Schema
Project (PId, BudgetId)
Dept (Department, Year, Project, NumEmp)
Location (Department, DepId, City, State)
Budget (Project, Leader, Size)

Figure 1: Example Schema

SQL, XQuery, or XSLT) are well-known, [14, 24] and others, but the same is not true for arbitrary SO tgds.

Fortunately, many (though of course not all) SO tgds are equivalent to (nested) GLAV mappings. However, testing if an SO tgd is equivalent to a (nested) GLAV mapping is undecidable, so it is not possible to have a complete characterization of all SO tgds that are rewritable (this follows from the result of Feinerer et al. [13]). Nash et al. [26] were the first to present a polynomial-time sufficient condition for when an SO tgd is equivalent to a GLAV mapping and to motivate why finding such rewritings can be important in practice. They provided a transformation algorithm to map SO tgds produced by mapping composition to an equivalent GLAV mapping, which can be of exponential size. We generalize their work to understand when the potentially correlated functions in an arbitrary SO tgd are well-behaved. We provide a more general condition that is able to transform more SO tgds to GLAV. We also consider transformations to the more expressive language of nested GLAV. The size of a nested GLAV mapping produced by these transformations is linear in the size of the input SO tgd.[1] We call SO tgds that can be transformed by our techniques *linearizable*. Finally, we consider source semantics, specifically functional dependencies (FDs). We show that in the presence of FDs (including keys), a larger set of SO tgds can be transformed to equivalent nested GLAV mappings.

1.1 Nesting and Linearization

The language of SO tgds is the right language for model management operators [9] like composition [12] and MapMerge [1], and has found important application in other operators including mapping inversion [6]. To motivate our work, we consider through examples, when such mappings can be simplified and expressed as a set of equivalent FO mappings (either GLAV or nested GLAV). Consider the source and target schemas of Figure 1. Primary key attributes are underlined.

EXAMPLE 1.1. *Suppose we wish to map the source information* `WorksOn.BudgetId` *to the* `Project` *relation in the target. The project id* (`PId`) *of the target is not present in the source, so a mapping must* invent *this value using an existential or Skolem function. One mapping (θ_1) that expresses the semantics that the target attribute* `PId` *should depend on the source values* `Department` *(d) and* `Project` *(p), is shown in Figure 2. This mapping is an SO tgd as it contains an existentially quantified function. Intuitively, this function models that any tuples with the same* `Department` *and* `Project` *values must necessarily share the same* `PId` *value. It is well known that this mapping is equivalent to the FO mapping Ω_1 (a nested GLAV mapping which permits interleaving of universal and existential quantifiers [14]). The position of the existential variable in Ω_1 (nested after d and p) expresses the same semantics as the existential function in θ_1. Fagin et al. [12] proved that this mapping is not equivalent to* **any** *GLAV mapping. As a result, the only known algorithm for simplifying SO tgds [26] would fail as it only considers transformation into GLAV mappings, not nested GLAV.*

In our work, we present a sufficient condition for simplifying SO tgds into nested GLAV mappings that would produce Ω_1. Intuitively, our condition characterizes when Skolem functions are well-behaved in that they do not interact with other Skolem functions in a way that would prohibit a simple FO substitution of a Skolem function with an appropriately nested existential. Of course, in the above example there is a single Skolem function so the replacement of the Skolem function by an existential only requires examination of its arguments. When there are multiple Skolem functions, we must understand how their arguments interact.

EXAMPLE 1.2. *Consider the second mapping in Figure 2 adapted from Libkin and Sirangelo [22], which maps the* `WorksOn` *relation to a target* `Dept` *relation. This example illustrates a mapping in which the arguments to the Skolem functions have been* customized *to precisely model the application semantics. In the SO tgd θ_2, the two Skolem functions f and g are used to generate values for the* `Year` *and* `NumEmp` *attributes. The target attribute* `Year` *depends on the department and, thus, d* (`Department`)*, is the only argument for Skolem function f. The Skolem function g has two arguments, because the number of employees* (`NumEmp`) *depends on the* `Department` *and* `Project`*. Again, this SO tgd is not equivalent to any GLAV mapping [22]. Our algorithm succeeds by placing the (FO) existentials in the correct scope, and would produce Ω_2, an equivalent nested GLAV mapping.*

Notice that to produce an equivalent nested mapping, the Skolem functions in the SO tgd (and corresponding existentials) must be placed in a **linear** order. This example adapts an existing SO quantifier elimination method, often called *linearization* to the case of SO tgds. We are not the first to make use of this technique for data exchange. Pichler and Skritek [28] proposed a fragment of SO tgds named SO^{ord} for which the complexity of model checking, both data and combined complexity, can be reduced to that of FO formulas. In their reduction, the authors impose conditions that rely on the existence of a total ordering of the Skolem functions (based on set containment of their argument sets). Our rewriting techniques will generalize this by using a novel partitioning strategy that allows us to apply linearization over sets of clauses in a complex SO tgd. When these clauses can be partitioned into sets (which we call blocks) with pairwise disjoint sets of (linearizable) Skolem functions, our condition is more general. Furthermore, unlike Pichler and Skritek [28], we present a constructive (and efficient) algorithm for translating this more general set of SO tgds into nested GLAV mappings.

1.2 (Un)Skolemization Revisited

Our examples illustrate that we will be replacing Skolem functions with existentials, a process known under various

[1]This does not contradict the result from Nash et al. [26] stating that GLAV rewritings can be exponential in size, because we are rewriting into nested GLAV mappings which are more expressive.

Ex. 1: Key Invention
$\theta_1 = \exists f\,(\forall d \forall p \forall b\; W(d,p,b) \rightarrow P(f(d,p),b))$
$\Omega_1 = \forall d \forall p\, \exists v_f\, \forall b\; W(d,p,b) \rightarrow P(v_f,b)$

Ex. 2: Skolems with Overlapping Arguments
$\theta_2 = \exists f \exists g\,(\forall d \forall p \forall b\; W(d,p,b) \rightarrow D(d,f(d),p,g(d,p)))$
$\Omega_2 = \forall d\, \exists v_f\, \forall p\, \exists v_g\, \forall b\; W(d,p,b) \rightarrow D(d,v_f,p,v_g)$

Ex. 3.A: Skolems with Disjoint Arguments
$\theta_3 = \exists f \exists g\,(\forall d \forall c\; C(d,c) \rightarrow L(d,f(d),c,g(c)))$
Ex. 3.B: FD on City: Department $\rightarrow$ City
$\theta_3' = \exists f \exists g\,(\forall d \forall c\; C(d,c) \rightarrow L(d,f(d,c),c,g(c)))$
$\Omega_3 = \forall c\, \exists v_g\, \forall d\, \exists v_f\; C(d,c) \rightarrow L(d,v_f,c,v_g)$

Ex. 4: Arguments from Distinct Source Relations
$\theta_4 = \exists f \exists g\,(\forall d \forall p \forall b \forall a\; W(d,p,b) \wedge A(b,a) \rightarrow B(p,f(d,p,b),g(b,a)))$
$\Omega_4 = \forall b \forall a\, \exists v_g\, \forall d \forall p\, \exists v_f\; W(d,p,b) \wedge A(b,a) \rightarrow B(p,v_f,v_g)$
WorksOn FD: Department, Project $\rightarrow$ BudgetId
Audit FD: BudgetId $\rightarrow$ Auditor

Figure 2: SO tgds and First-order Translations

names such as *unskolemization*, *reversed Skolemization*, and *deskolemization* [16, 26]. Important to our solutions will be determining the right placement of the existentials (nested within universal quantifiers) based on the arguments of the Skolem functions and also whether such a placement is possible. As our examples make clear, the existential quantifier must be placed after any universal quantifiers representing its arguments (and not after universals on which it does not depend). To understand this, it is helpful to consider both unskolemization and its complement Skolemization. Indeed, in the integration literature, Skolemization is often used as a process for transforming FO formulas into a normal form that *eliminates* existential quantifiers by replacing them with functions. The reverse process (unskolemization) is always possible for Skolemized FO formulas, but not for SO tgds because SO tgds can have arbitrary arguments in the Skolem functions. Our work considers sufficient conditions for when this is possible. So while our algorithms can be considered unskolemization algorithms, it is important to recognize that our goal is not to get rid of Skolem functions, but rather to understand when the Skolem functions in a mapping are well-behaved (and have a computationally desirable FO semantics). If a complex SO tgd can be shown to be equivalent to a (nested) GLAV mapping then we guarantee that the Skolem functions can be untwisted to produce a well-behaved nested mapping, and therefore efficient transformation code.

EXAMPLE 1.3. (PART A) *Consider the mapping θ_3 in Figure 2 that maps the source relation* `City` *to the target relation* `Location`. *The target relation has two attributes,* `DepId` *and* `State`, *which depend respectively on the* `Department` *and* `City` *attributes from the source. This SO tgd is* **not** *equivalent to Ω_3 or to any nested GLAV mapping [12]. Thus, for example, if the source and target evolve independently of each other it may be computationally hard to check whether the modified instances fulfill the mapping, because this is model checking which is NP-complete for SO tgds (and in P for nested GLAV mappings).*

1.3 Source Constraints

Often the source contains constraints, most commonly keys or FDs. We can use these constraints to simplify SO mappings that otherwise would not be equivalent to any nested mapping (like θ_3).

EXAMPLE 1.3.(PART B) *Suppose each* `Department` *in the source has a single* `City` *(modeled by the FD* `Department` $\rightarrow$ `City`*). If this is the case, then we will show that θ_3 is equivalent to θ_3' (Figure 2) where the Skolem f has arguments d and c (both* `Department` *and* `City`*). This enables us to use our linearization criteria to show that θ_3 with this FD, is equivalent to the nested mapping Ω_3.*

Source constraints are a powerful tool for simplifying mappings, but we can do even better by considering implied dependencies. If we consider a source expression as a view, the set of FDs implied by the view can be computed [19]. The next example illustrates how to use such inferred constraints to simplify SO tgds.

EXAMPLE 1.4. *Consider the SO tgd θ_4 which maps a join of* `WorksOn` *and* `Audit` *to the target relation* `Budget` *(adapted from Alexe et al. [1]). Suppose we have source keys* (`Department, Project`) *for* `WorksOn` *and* `BudgetId` *for* `Audit`. *These keys alone cannot be used to augment the arguments of Skolem functions f or g (since both already contain the keys). However, if we compute the implied dependencies on the source join, we will see that $d, p \rightarrow b, a$ (over the exchanged data). Hence, we can augment the arguments of f to include all four variables and easily see that θ_4 with these keys is equivalent to Ω_4 which linearizes g before f.*

1.4 Summary of Contributions

The main contributions of this work are the following.

- We prove a sufficient condition for an SO tgd to be equivalent to a nested tgd. This condition is broader than the condition used in previous work by Nash et al. [26], and we experimentally compare this difference.
- We develop an algorithm (called `Linearize`) for rewriting SO tgds satisfying our condition into nested GLAV mappings. Our algorithm is more general in that it produces nested GLAV mappings, uses linearization of Skolem arguments, and includes a new partitioning scheme for complex, multi-clause SO tgds.
- We introduce an equivalence preserving transformation of SO tgds exploiting the existence of FDs in the source schema. Our transformation computes attribute closures for the source expression considered as a view, and uses these to augment the arguments of Skolem functions.
- We present an algorithm `LinearizeFDs` that extends our linearization technique with source FDs, and show that this combination presents many more opportunities for rewriting. Specifically, many SO tgds that cannot be rewritten, can be written in the presence of source keys or FDs. We compare this against Marnette et al.'s re-Skolemization strategy [23], originally proposed to compute compact solutions.
- We use STBenchmark 2.0 [7] to produce SO tgds and mapping scenarios with source keys or FDs. We use this extended system to generate a large set of mapping scenarios that include schemas produced by composition, evolu-

tion, or manual customization of Skolem functions. We also present real-life mapping scenarios. Our evaluation shows that (1) our partitioning and linearization techniques permit the rewriting of significantly more SO tgds than previous techniques (approximately 78% more), (2) by using source keys (that is, normalized source schemas where the only FDs are keys) we can rewrite over twice as many SO tgds as without any keys.

The remainder of the paper is organized as follows. We introduce some formal definitions and background in Section 2. Section 3 presents our new partitioning and linearization conditions followed by our rewriting algorithm `Linearize` in Section 4. Building on these results, Section 5 demonstrates how to use FDs to provide more opportunities for rewriting and presents our `LinearizeFDs` algorithm. We empirically evaluate our techniques in Section 6, discuss additional related work in Section 7, and conclude in Section 8.

2. PRELIMINARIES

Schemas and Instances. A *schema* is a non-empty finite set $\mathbf{R}$ of relation symbols where each $R_i \in \mathbf{R}$ has a fixed arity. We define the notion of *instance* I over a schema $\mathbf{R}$ in the normal way for relational schemas, that is, as the union of relation instances over R_i, where $R_i \in \mathbf{R}$. Let $\mathbf{S} = (S_1, \ldots, S_n)$ and $\mathbf{T} = (T_1, \ldots, T_m)$ be two disjoint schemas. We follow the convention of referring to $\mathbf{S}$ as the *source* schema and to $\mathbf{T}$ as the *target* schema. The notation $(\mathbf{S}, \mathbf{T})$ denotes the schema $(S_1, \ldots, S_n, T_1, \ldots, T_m)$. When necessary, we extend this nomenclature to instances by adding the prefix *source* and *target*, respectively.

Satisfaction, Quantifier Scope, and Substitution. We use the standard notion of satisfaction of a formula in FO logic. If K is an instance and φ is a formula, we write $K \models \varphi$ to denote that K satisfies φ. The same notion is applied over a set of formulas Σ. The scope of an occurrence of a quantifier $Q \in \{\forall, \exists\}$ in a formula is the subformula controlled by the quantifier. For example, given $\forall x \exists y \psi(x, y)$, the scope of quantifier $\forall x$ is the subformula $\exists y \phi(x, y)$, where x appears as a free variable, and the scope of $\exists y$ is the subformula $\phi(x, y)$, where both x and y are free. Let ϕ be a formula. We use $\phi[t \leftarrow t']$ to denote the formula that is derived from ϕ by replacing all occurrences of term t with term t'.

Schema Mappings. A *schema mapping* is a triple $\mathcal{M} = (\mathbf{S}, \mathbf{T}, \Sigma)$, where $\mathbf{S}$ and $\mathbf{T}$ are schemas with no relation symbols in common and Σ is a set of logical formulas over $(\mathbf{S}, \mathbf{T})$ [11]. An *instance of* $\mathcal{M}$ is an instance $\langle I, J \rangle$ over $(\mathbf{S}, \mathbf{T})$ that satisfies every formula in Σ. If $\langle I, J \rangle \models \mathcal{M}$, then we call J a *solution of* I *under* $\mathcal{M}$.

First-Order Tgds. A *source-to-target tuple-generating dependency* (s-t tgd) [11] is a formula of the form $\forall \mathbf{z}, \mathbf{x}(\phi(\mathbf{z}, \mathbf{x}) \rightarrow \exists \mathbf{y} \psi(\mathbf{x}, \mathbf{y}))$, where $\mathbf{z}$, $\mathbf{x}$, and $\mathbf{y}$ are disjoint vectors of variables; $\phi(\mathbf{z}, \mathbf{x})$ is a conjunction of atomic formulas over the source schema $\mathbf{S}$; and $\psi(\mathbf{x}, \mathbf{y})$ is a conjunction of atomic formulas over the target schema $\mathbf{T}$. All variables of $\mathbf{z} \cup \mathbf{x}$ are used in ϕ and all variables of $\mathbf{x} \cup \mathbf{y}$ are used in ψ. We adopt the term **GLAV mappings** [21] for sets of s-t tgds. A *nested tgd* [14] is an FO sentence of the form $Q(\mathbf{x}, \mathbf{y})((\phi_1(\mathbf{x}) \rightarrow \psi_1(\mathbf{x}, \mathbf{y})) \wedge \ldots \wedge (\phi_n(\mathbf{x}) \rightarrow \psi_n(\mathbf{x}, \mathbf{y})))$ where (1) $Q(\mathbf{x}, \mathbf{y})$ is a sequence of quantifiers - universal quantifiers for $\mathbf{x}$ and existential quantifiers for $\mathbf{y}$; (2) each $\phi_i(\mathbf{x}, \mathbf{y})$ is a conjunction of atomic formulas over the source schema $\mathbf{S}$; (3) each $\psi_i(\mathbf{x}, \mathbf{y})$ is a conjunction of atomic formulas over the target schema $\mathbf{T}$; and (4) each variable from $\mathbf{x}$ appears in some formula ψ_i and each variable from $\mathbf{y}$ appears in some formula ψ_j. Nested tgds, also known as **nested GLAV mappings**, are a proper extension of GLAV mappings that allows alternation of $\forall$ and $\exists$ quantifiers [31].

Second-Order Tgds. A *second-order tuple-generating dependency* (SO tgd) [12] is an existential second-order formula of the form $\exists \mathbf{f}((\forall \mathbf{x_1}(\phi_1 \rightarrow \psi_1)) \wedge \cdots \wedge (\forall \mathbf{x_n}(\phi_n \rightarrow \psi_n)))$ where (1) each member of $\mathbf{f}$ is a function symbol; (2) each ϕ_i is a conjunction of (a) atomic formulas over the source schema $\mathbf{S}$ and (b) equalities of the form $t = t'$ where t and t' are terms based on $\mathbf{x_i}$ and $\mathbf{f}$; (3) each ψ_i is a conjunction of atomic formulas over the target schema $\mathbf{T}$; and (4) each variable in $\mathbf{x_i}$ appears in some atom of ϕ_i. Even though SO tgds may allow equalities between or with Skolem terms in general settings, such equalities do not play a role for data exchange and can be eliminated [32]. Arenas et al. [5] have generalized previous results from Nash et al. [26] to prove that every SO tgd is equivalent to another SO tgd with no nested Skolem functions (e.g., $f(g(a), b)$). Thus, in what follows, we assume SO tgds without equalities between or with Skolem terms and no nesting of Skolem terms.

Clausal Normal Form. Any SO tgd can be transformed into an equivalent SO tgd in *clausal normal form*. Let $\exists \mathbf{f} \, \forall \mathbf{x_1} \ldots \forall \mathbf{x_n} (\chi_1 \wedge \cdots \wedge \chi_n)$ be an SO tgd θ, where each implication clause χ_i is a quantifier-free formula (i.e., θ is in prenex normal form). Let $N = \{C_1, \ldots, C_n\}$ be a set of clauses where $C_i = \chi_i$ for $1 \leq i \leq n$. We refer to N as the clausal normal form of θ where the variables in N are implicitly universally quantified, and the clauses are related by conjunction [16]. Unless otherwise stated, we assume SO tgds in clausal normal form.

Skolemization. Let α be an FO formula. The SO *Skolemization* of α is an SO formula that results from replacing existential quantifiers with Skolem functions, based on the equivalence $\forall \mathbf{x} \exists y \, \delta(\mathbf{x}, y) \equiv \exists f \forall \mathbf{x} \, \delta(\mathbf{x}, y)[y \leftarrow f(\mathbf{x})]$ [10]. Informally, this transformation removes $\exists y$ from α, introduces a new existentially quantified *Skolem function* f of *arity* k, where k is the number of universally quantified variables in $\mathbf{x}$, and replaces y wherever it appears in the scope of $\exists y$ with the Skolem term $f(\mathbf{x})$. The *argument sequence* of a Skolem function $f(x_1, x_2, \ldots, x_k)$, denoted as $arg(f)$, is the sequence of variables $x_1, x_2, \ldots, x_k$ on which f depends. We use the term *argument set* (and abuse the notation $arg(f)$) to refer to the set of variables in the argument sequence.

3. SUFFICIENT REWRITING CONDITION

We now present the first contribution of the paper, a *new* sufficient condition for rewriting SO tgds into nested GLAV mappings. This condition relies on the notions of *consistency* and *linearity*, which we adapt from SO quantifier elimination methods [16]. We first present the intuition, then prove the correctness of our condition. Importantly, we turn this condition into a practical rewrite algorithm in Section 4.

3.1 Intuition of Unskolemization

Our approach for rewriting SO tgds relies heavily on unskolemization. Consider an SO tgd θ in prenex form [10]

$$\exists \mathbf{f} \, \forall \mathbf{x_1} \ldots \forall \mathbf{x_n} (\chi_1 \wedge \cdots \wedge \chi_n) \tag{1}$$

The aim of unskolemization is to eliminate the $\exists \mathbf{f}$ quantifiers from θ and produce an equivalent set (Ω in our examples) of FO formulas, in our case a nested GLAV mapping, without Skolem functions. This involves systematically introducing

FO existential quantifiers in place of Skolem functions. To do this, we resort to the same logical equivalence transformation [10] used to Skolemize FO formulas, i.e.,

$$\forall \mathbf{x} \exists y\, \delta(\mathbf{x}, y) \equiv \exists f \forall \mathbf{x}\, \delta(\mathbf{x}, y)[y \leftarrow f(\mathbf{x})] \qquad (2)$$

For unskolemization, we aim to apply Eq. (2) from right-to-left. For instance, reversing the original Skolemization of an FO formula involves repeated applications of this single-step equivalence over each Skolem function symbol. Notice that when doing this, we implicitly obey an equation's predetermined order of universal and existential quantifiers (some of which may have been introduced by previous applications of the equivalence). That is, for $f(\mathbf{x})$, we must add $\exists y$ immediately after all universal quantifiers binding $\mathbf{x}$.

EXAMPLE 3.1. *Consider a single clause SO tgd:*

$$\exists f \exists g\, (\forall x_1 \forall x_2 (R(x_1, x_2) \rightarrow S(f(x_1), g(x_1, x_2), x_2)))$$

To transform this SO tgd into an equivalent nested GLAV mapping, we apply Eq. (2) twice. First, we replace g with an existential variable v_g that is introduced right after the quantification of x_1 and x_2, the arguments of g. The resulting SO formula θ' is $\exists f (\forall x_1 \forall x_2 \exists v_g\, (R(x_1, x_2) \rightarrow S(f(x_1), v_g, x_2)))$. We can now apply Eq. (2) again to remove the function f. An existential variable v_f representing f can be introduced right after the quantifier for x_1 (the argument of f). The resulting equivalent nested GLAV mapping is:

$$\forall x_1 \exists v_f \forall x_2 \exists v_g (R(x_1, x_2) \rightarrow S(v_f, v_g, x_2))$$

In this example, the first application of Eq. (2) (to remove g) did not hinder us from applying the equation a second time to remove the function f. However, when reversing the Skolemization of an arbitrary SO tgd, this may not always be the case, i.e., a rewriting step may result in a formula that can not be further unskolemized using this equation. This is not surprising, because there are SO tgds that are not equivalent to any FO formula. The conditions over SO tgds we introduce next make use of a careful ordering of unskolemization steps to ensure that this type of rewriting is indeed possible, i.e., they are *sufficient*.

3.2 Consistency

The first condition we consider is *consistency*. Consistency models whether all occurrences of a Skolem function symbol in a formula use exactly the same arguments.

DEFINITION 3.2. **[Consistency]** *A Skolem function f is consistent with respect to an SO tgd θ if 1) any two occurrences of f in θ have the same argument sequence, and 2) for any occurrence of f, each argument position is filled with a universally quantified source variable and no variables are repeated. An SO tgd θ is consistent when all its Skolem functions are consistent.*

By requiring each argument position to be filled with a universally quantified source variable, our definition disallows nesting of Skolem functions. At first sight, this may appear restrictive, but recall from Section 2 that any SO tgd is equivalent to an SO tgd without nesting of functions.

EXAMPLE 3.3. *Consider the following set of clauses:*

$$C_1 : S(x_1, x_2) \rightarrow T_1(x_1, f(x_1), g(x_1, x_2)) \wedge T_2(g(x_2, x_1))$$
$$C_2 : R(x_3, x_4) \rightarrow W(x_3, x_4, h(x_3, x_3))$$

The function f is consistent, g is not (because the two occurrences of g do not share the same argument sequence), and h is not (it contains a repeated variable).

Lack of consistency is problematic when we try to unskolemize a formula because it may prevent us from choosing the same existential variable $\exists v_f$ to replace all occurrences of a given Skolem function f. Unification can often be applied to achieve consistency [16] but this is orthogonal to our discussion. Importantly, consistency has also been used by Nash et al. [26] (though using a different condition).

3.3 Maximal Partition

Consistency on its own does not guarantee rewritability. The linearity condition we motivated in Section 1 (based on conditions used in SO logic [16]) with consistency is still not sufficient for SO tgds. To apply linearity and consistency, we must first consider how the multiple clauses of an SO tgd are related. We present a new partitioning strategy for SO tgds (in which all clauses using a Skolem function f must be grouped together) that we use to guide rewriting.

DEFINITION 3.4. **[Maximal Partition]** *Let θ be an SO tgd and $\Pi = \{\pi_1, \ldots, \pi_b\}$ a partition of the clauses of θ into sets of disjoint clauses called blocks. A partitioning Π is called a* maximal partition *of θ if (1) every two distinct blocks π_i and π_j are pairwise disjoint with respect to Skolem functions and (2) there exists no partition Π' of θ satisfying (1) that has more elements than Π.*

Note that every SO tgd θ has a unique maximal partition. For example, the maximal partition of an SO tgd with clauses $C_1 : R(x_1) \rightarrow S(f(x_1), g(x_1))$, $C_2 : T(x_1) \rightarrow U(g(x_1))$, and $C_3 : V(x_3) \rightarrow W(h(x_3))$ is $\{C_1, C_2\}, \{C_3\}$. This method of splitting an SO tgd into a conjunction of SO tgds based on the blocks in its maximal partition is equivalence preserving, because we split the input using the rules of quantifier distribution and SO tgds are closed under conjunction [12]. Thus, each block can be unskolemized separately and it is sufficient to check the linearity condition introduced next for each block individually. This is a less strict condition than requiring it to hold for the complete SO tgd as used in Pichler and Shritek [28].

3.4 Linearity

Linearity requires the Skolem functions of each block in the maximal partition Π of an SO tgd θ to form a linear order according to the set inclusion of their arguments.

DEFINITION 3.5. **[Linearity]** *Let θ be an SO tgd and Π its maximal partition. A block π in Π is linear if for all distinct Skolem functions f and g occurring in π (with arity n and m, respectively) their argument sets can be linearly ordered by set inclusion. Assuming $n \leq m$, we have that the set of arguments of f is a subset of the set of arguments of g, i.e., $arg(f) \subseteq arg(g)$. We say an SO tgd θ is linear if all blocks π in Π are linear.*

EXAMPLE 3.6. *Consider an SO tgd with a single block that contains Skolem terms $f(x_1, x_2)$, $g(x_1)$ and $h(x_3)$. While the argument sets of Skolem functions f and g can be linearly ordered by set inclusion (that is, $arg(g) \subseteq arg(f)$), notice that there is no set inclusion relationship between f and h, and between g and h. This block of clauses is not linear. However, if Skolem h would have been in a different block than f and g, then the SO tgd would be linear.*

3.5 Sufficient Condition

Linearity on top of consistency guarantees that we can produce an FO rewriting, where all the quantifier dependencies implied by Skolem function arguments can be morphed into a single linear quantifier prefix (as required to generate nested GLAV). It guarantees that when more than one existential variable needs to be introduced to replace the Skolem functions, Eq. 2 can be repeatedly applied, i.e., the result of each application of this equation is structured as required for the next application. More precisely, the equation should be applied to each Skolem function symbol in order of decreasing arity. For example, the SO tgd from Ex. 3.1 is linear ($f(x_1) < g(x_1, x_2)$) and, as has been shown in that example, can be transformed successfully into nested GLAV by replacing *first* Skolem function g and *then* f.

THEOREM 3.7. *Let θ be an SO tgd without equalities between or with Skolem terms. If θ is both consistent and linear, then θ can be successfully rewritten as a logically equivalent nested GLAV mapping.*

4. LINEARIZATION ALGORITHM

We now present a polynomial-time algorithm, called `Linearize`, that rewrites an SO tgd using our new sufficient condition from Section 3, and the right-to-left direction of the equivalence shown in Eq. (2). Algorithm 1 takes as input an SO tgd θ in clausal normal form. It attempts to rewrite the input by applying a number of transformation steps.

Check Consistency. Compute the maximal partition and test consistency. If any Skolem function is inconsistent, report that the rewriting failed.

Check Linearity. Recall from Example 3.6 that linearity can be checked on each block π of the maximal partition separately. We sort the list O_π of Skolem functions of block π according to set inclusion of their arguments using procedure `SortArgIncl`. If two Skolem functions are incomparable according to argument set inclusion, we report that the rewriting failed.

Rewrite into Nested GLAV. If the linearity condition is satisfied, rewrite each block of clauses π as a single nested tgd, yielding a nested GLAV mapping Ω. The algorithm creates a total order over the universally quantified variables based on the sorted order O_π of Skolem functions. Proceeding from lowest to highest function in sort order, for each Skolem term f, we add $\forall x$ to the mapping (for all $x \in arg(f)$ that are not already in the mapping due to an earlier Skolem term, notice that the ordering among these does not matter), then we add an existential variable for f, $\exists v_f$ (directly after the quantifiers for variables from the arguments of f). Once we have processed all variables used as arguments for any Skolem, we add an universal quantification $\forall x'$ for each remaining variable x'.

THEOREM 4.1. *Let θ be an SO tgd without equalities between or with Skolem terms, then `Linearize`$(\theta) \equiv \theta$.*

To illustrate Algorithm 1 consider our example SO tgds.

EXAMPLE 4.2. *Consider θ_1 from Figure 2. This SO tgd is trivially consistent and linear, because it consists of only a single clause and the only Skolem function f is just used once. Procedure `SortArgIncl` would create the following order over the quantified variables: $d = p < b$ (b is last because it is not used in any function). The resulting quantifier prefix is $\forall d \forall p \exists v_f \forall b$. Now consider θ_2 with two Skolem terms f and g which will be ordered $f < g$ and, thus, θ_2 is linear. Ordering the variables results in the quantifier prefix $\forall d \exists v_f \forall p \exists v_g \forall b$. Since SO tgds θ_3 and θ_4 are not linear, they can not be rewritten using Algorithm 1.*

Algorithm 1 `Linearize` (θ)

Input : A SO tgd θ without Skolem equalities.
Output : If successful, a nested GLAV mapping Ω; otherwise, θ.

$\mathbf{f} \leftarrow$ the set of Skolem functions in θ
$\Pi \leftarrow$ the maximal partition of θ
{Check Consistency}
for each $f \in \mathbf{f}$ **do**
  $\pi_f \leftarrow$ block that contains f
  $arg(f) \leftarrow (t_1, \ldots, t_a)$ for a term $f(t_1, \ldots, t_a)$ in π_f
  for each term $f(t'_1, \ldots, t'_a)$ in π_f **do**
    $arg(f)' \leftarrow (t'_1, \ldots, t'_a)$
    if $\exists i, j : t'_i = t'_j$ **or** $arg(f) \neq arg(f)'$ **then**
      return θ {Not consistent}
{Check Linearity}
for each π in Π **do**
  $O_\pi \leftarrow$ list of Skolem terms in π
  if not SORTARGINCL(O_π) **then**
    return θ {Not linear}
{Unskolemize}
$\Omega \leftarrow \emptyset$ {nested GLAV}
for each π in Π **do**
  $\Omega \leftarrow \Omega \cup$ REDUCETONESTED(π, O_π)
return Ω

5. LINEARIZATION USING FDS

The `Linearize` algorithm fails if two Skolem terms in a block have unrelated (by set containment) argument sets. However, in many cases there is a hidden connection between these arguments based on constraints that hold on the source schema. In this section, we present the main contribution of this paper, an algorithm for rewriting SO tgds in the presence of source keys or FDs. We use these constraints to augment Skolem terms with additional arguments, thus increasing the chance of rewriting. We first prove that this type of augmentation preserves equivalence. Then we introduce our extended rewriting algorithm and prove its correctness. Moreover, we show that augmentation of Skolem arguments never transforms a linearizable SO tgd (or more precisely one on which our Algorithm `Linearize` would succeed) into an SO tgd that is not linearizable by our algorithm, i.e., using the source constraints can never hurt our ability to find a rewriting.

5.1 Equivalence Preserving Augmentation of Skolem Terms based on Source FDs

Consider a consistent SO tgd θ and a set Σ_S of source FDs over **S**. Each FD fd is of the form $fd : X \rightarrow Y$ where X, Y and U are vectors of attributes; $X, Y \subseteq U$ and U is the set of all attributes over a given source relation. The intuition of using FDs to augment Skolem terms is that if a Skolem term $f(\mathbf{x})$ contains variables corresponding to the left-hand-side of a source FD fd, then adding variables corresponding to the right-hand-side of fd to the list of arguments of f, is an *equivalence preserving transformation.* Adding additional arguments to Skolem terms can help us rewrite SO tgds into nested GLAV mappings, as we show next.

EXAMPLE 5.1. *Recall θ_3 from Example 1.3 over source relation* `City` *and target relation* `Location`, *with disjoint Skolem terms f and g. This SO tgd is consistent but not linear. Assume that* `Department` $\to$ `City` *holds over relation* `City`. *If we apply this FD over Skolem term f, then by adding variable c to f we can rewrite θ_3 as an equivalent formula*

$$\exists f \exists g\, (\, \forall d \forall c\; C(d,c) \to L(d, f(d,c), c, g(c))\,)$$

This equivalent consistent and linear SO tgd can be rewritten into a nested GLAV mapping using Algorithm 1.

Intuitively, the type of augmentation exemplified above can be applied to all occurrences of a Skolem term $f(\mathbf{x})$ only if the base FDs in Σ_S imply an FD $fd : \mathbf{x} \to \mathbf{y}$ over the variables in *each* clause that references f. When this condition is fulfilled, we can safely replace $f(\mathbf{x})$ with $f(\mathbf{x}, \mathbf{y})$ in all clauses containing f. Let C be a clause of an SO tgd. We use Σ_C, called the *clausal FDs* for C, to denote the set of FDs that are implied by Σ_S over the variables of the left-hand-side of the clause (the source expression). Of course it is well known how to compute Σ_C for FDs over conjunctive expressions [19]. Next, we show that augmentation based on implied source FDs preserves equivalence.

THEOREM 5.2. *Let θ be a consistent SO tgd, Σ_S a set of source FDs, and $f(\mathbf{x})$ a Skolem term used in θ. Moreover, let π_f be the set of clauses of θ that mention f, and let $\mathbf{x}' \to \mathbf{y}$ with $\mathbf{x}' \subseteq \mathbf{x}$ be an implied clausal FD that holds for all clauses in π_f. Then the following equivalence holds:*

$$\theta[f(\mathbf{x}) \leftarrow f(\mathbf{x}, \mathbf{y})] \cup \Sigma_S \equiv \theta \cup \Sigma_S$$

There may be cases where applying FDs will not help us achieve a successful rewriting of SO tgds. However, as we show in the experimental evaluation, in practice this approach is very effective. This is because the arguments of Skolem functions are usually not chosen randomly, but rather in a principled way to encapsulate certain desired grouping or correlation semantics [1, 22, 23, 29].

5.2 Algorithm and Correctness Proof

We now introduce a polynomial time algorithm for rewriting SO tgds in the presence of source FDs. Algorithm 2, called `LinearizeFDs` (θ, Σ_S), takes as input a consistent SO tgd θ in clausal normal form and a set Σ_S of source FDs. The algorithm consists of two main steps, augmenting Skolem terms based on implied FDs and applying our rewriting algorithm to the result of this equivalent transformation.

As before, we generate the maximal partition of θ (Line 2). Lines 3 and 4 compute the clausal FDs Σ_C (procedure `InferFDs`) that hold over the variables of a clause. Afterwards (Lines 5 to 8), for each Skolem function f, we retrieve the block π_f that contains f and compute Σ_f, the set of FDs that holds over all clauses in π_f. Recall from Theorem 5.2 that a Skolem function can be augmented based on FDs that hold over all clauses using f. The clauses in block π_f are clearly a superset of these clauses. Thus, by intersecting the sets of FDs from the clauses in π_f, we know that each FD in Σ_f can be used to augment the arguments of f. Method `VariableClosure` is used to replace the arguments $arg(f)$ of f with their attribute closure according to Σ_f. This step is equivalent to a repeated application of our equivalence preserving transformation and thus, generates an SO tgd that is equivalent to the input SO tgd. Last, we run the rewriting algorithm over the resulting SO tgd θ^{aug} (Line 9).

Algorithm 2 `LinearizeFDs` (θ, Σ_S)

Input : A consistent SO tgd θ without Skolem equalities
A set Σ_S of FDs over source schema **S**
Output : If successful, a nested GLAV mapping Ω; otherwise, θ.

```
1: θ^aug ← θ
2: Π ← maximal partition of θ^aug
   {Compute FDs for each Clause}
3: for each clause C in θ^aug do
4:     Σ_C ← InferFDs(C, Σ_S)
   {Augment Skolem Terms}
5: for each Skolem f in θ do
6:     π_f ← block that contains f
7:     Σ_f ← ⋂_{C∈π_f} Σ_C {FDs valid for all Clauses in π_f}
8:     arg(f) ← VariableClosure(arg(f), Σ_f)
   {Run Linearization Algorithm}
9: return Linearize(θ^aug)
```

EXAMPLE 5.3. *Consider the SO tgd θ_4 from Figure 2 which joins relations* `WorksOn` *and* `Audit` *on the attribute* `BudgetId`. *The source FDs,* `Department, Project` $\to$ `BudgetId` *and* `BudgetId` $\to$ `Auditor`, *together with the reuse of variable b (the join) imply the FD $d, p \to b, a$ over the source expression. This (implied) dependency enables us to augment f with variable a to produce the rewriting*

$$W(d,p,b) \wedge A(b,a) \to B(p, f(d,p,b,a), g(b,a)),$$

where as before we assume existential quantification over Skolems and universal quantification over source variables. This equivalent augmented SO tgd is now linear.

Proving the correctness of Algorithm 2 amounts to showing that the transformed SO tgd θ^{aug} is equivalent to the input θ, under the assumption that the source FDs Σ_S hold.

THEOREM 5.4. *Let θ be a consistent SO tgd without equalities between or with Skolem terms and let Σ_S be a set of source FDs, then*

$$\textit{LinearizeFDs}(\theta, \Sigma_S) \cup \Sigma_S \equiv \theta \cup \Sigma_S.$$

According to Theorem 5.4, the rewritten SO tgd θ^{aug} produced by `LinearizeFDs` is equivalent to the input. However, does this algorithm also preserve the sufficient condition?

THEOREM 5.5. *Let θ be a consistent SO tgd, Σ_s a set of source FDs, and θ^{aug} be the equivalent SO tgd derived by algorithm* **`LinearizeFDs`**. *If θ can be rewritten by* **`Linearize`** *so can θ^{aug}. The opposite direction does not hold in general.*

5.3 Discussion

The algorithm presented in this section divides the task of rewriting in two steps: (1) apply an equivalence preserving re-Skolemization strategy, and (2) check the linearity condition on the result. In the first step, we could use any re-Skolemization strategy as long as it preserves equivalence. Of course, the first re-Skolemization strategy that comes to mind is that of Marnette et al. [23], which has been applied in the context of efficiently computing compact data exchange solutions under target constraints using SQL queries. This sound but not complete strategy uses source FDs to minimize the arguments of Skolem functions in a GLAV mapping, and uses target FDs to choose the most general Skolemization among competing ones.[2] We can take the first part

[2]Like ours, the intuition behind this technique is that of injectively creating and equating labelled `NULLs`.

Name	Description	Example	Skolems
ADD	Copy a relation and add new attributes	$R(a,b) \rightarrow S(a,b,f(a,b))$	Variable
ADL	Copy a relation, add and delete attributes in tandem	$R(a,b) \rightarrow S(a,f(a))$	Variable
CP	Copy a relation	$R(a,b) \rightarrow S(a,b)$	-
DL	Copy a relation and delete attributes	$R(a,b) \rightarrow S(a)$	-
HP	Horizontally partition a relation into multiple relations	$R(a,b) \wedge a = c_1 \rightarrow S_1(b)$ $R(a,b) \wedge a = c_2 \rightarrow S_2(b)$	-
ME	Inverse of vertical partitioning (merge)	$R(a,b) \wedge S(b,c) \rightarrow T(a,b,c)$	-
MA	Inverse of vertical partitioning + adding attributes	$R(a,b) \wedge S(b,c) \rightarrow T(a,b,c,f(a,b,c))$	Variable
OF	Object fusion, e.g., inverse of horizontal partitioning	$R(\underline{a},b) \rightarrow T(a,b,f(a))$ $S(\underline{a},c) \rightarrow T(a,g(a),c)$ $R(\underline{a},b) \wedge S(\underline{a},c) \rightarrow T(a,b,c)$	Fixed
SJ	Copy relation (S) and create a relationship table (T) through a self-join	$R(\underline{a},b,c) \rightarrow S(a,c)$ $R(\underline{a},b,c) \wedge R(\underline{b},d,e) \rightarrow T(a,b)$	-
SU	Copy a relation and create a surrogate key	$R(a,b) \rightarrow S(\underline{f(a,b)},b,g(b))$	Fixed / Variable
VH	Vertical partitioning into a HAS-A relationship	$R(a,b) \rightarrow S(\underline{f(a)},a) \wedge T(\underline{g(a,b)},b,f(a))$	Fixed
VI	Vertical partitioning into an IS-A relationship	$R(\underline{a},b,c) \rightarrow S(\underline{a},b) \wedge T(\underline{a},c)$	-
VNM	Vertical partitioning into an N-to-M relationship	$R(a,b) \rightarrow S_1(\underline{f(a)},a) \wedge M(\underline{f(a)},\underline{g(b)}) \wedge S_2(\underline{g(b)},b)$	Fixed
VP	Vertical partitioning	$R(a,b) \rightarrow S_1(\underline{f(a,b)},a) \wedge S_2(\underline{f(a,b)},b)$	Variable

Figure 3: Mapping Primitives

of this strategy and use it to replace the argument set $arg(f)$ of a Skolem function f with a minimal subset $min(args(f))$ such that both share the same closure according to the implied source FDs. We call this new strategy `LinearizeMin`. We ask, then, what are the implications of minimizing instead of maximizing the argument sets?

EXAMPLE 5.6. *Recall again Ex. 4 from Figure 2 with Skolem functions $f(d,p,b)$ and $g(b,a)$. If we minimize these, we obtain $f(d,p)$ and $g(b)$, respectively. The resulting formula is not linear, in contrast to the re-Skolemized formula we would obtain using `LinearizeFDs`. Now, consider a linear variation of this same example where $f(d,p,b)$ is replaced by $f(d,p,b,a)$ and $g(b,a)$ stays the same. Applying minimization, the re-Skolemizations for Skolems f and g are $f(d,p)$ and $g(b)$ which again are not linear.*

This example demonstrates that our approach of maximizing argument sets can solve cases for which minimization fails and, even more important, the example also shows that minimization may turn a linear SO tgd into a non-linear one. The following theorem proves that our approach is strictly better than minimization for the purpose of translating SO tgds into (nested) GLAV mappings.[3]

THEOREM 5.7. *Let θ be a consistent SO tgd and Σ_s a set of source FDs. Let θ^{Min} be the result of minimizing the argument sets of each Skolem f in θ. Furthermore, let θ^{aug} be the equivalent SO tgd derived by algorithm `LinearizeFDs`. If θ^{min} can be rewritten by `Linearize` so can θ^{aug}.*

6. EXPERIMENTS

To evaluate our techniques, we used STBenchmark 2.0 [7], a benchmark for generating SO tgds that extends the well-known STBenchmark [2], a GLAV mapping benchmark. The main motivation of our evaluation is to put into practice our rewriting algorithms for SO tgds, and to compare against the state-of-the-art using an implementation of Nash et al.'s [26] sufficient condition. This sufficient condition, which we call `NBM` after the authors, requires consistency and that every universally quantified source variable that appears in the target expression (right-hand-side expression) of an SO tgd also appears as an argument in every consistent Skolem function. We also compare against the minimization strategy [23] discussed in Section 5.3 (`LinearizeMin`), which minimizes the argument sets of Skolem functions using implied FDs before checking our linearity condition. Using STBenchmark 2.0, we generate a large number of SO tgds, and we measure the success of rewriting into nested GLAV (referred to as *success rate*) independently for each technique, i.e., `NBM`, `Linearize`, `LinearizeFDs`, and `LinearizeMin`. We start by describing the features of STBenchmark 2.0 that we use, and then describe our experimental study.

6.1 Mapping Generator

STBenchmark 2.0 [7] is able to randomly generate a broad range of SO tgds by combining basic mapping primitives into complex mappings. The mapping generator takes as input a set of configuration parameters and returns as output a schema mapping $\mathcal{M} = (\mathbf{S}, \mathbf{T}, \Sigma)$. The benchmark supports different variants of vertical partitioning primitives, some of which offer specialized support for generating mappings with (possibly repeated) Skolem functions, including functions with both overlapping and disjoint arguments. This permits the modeling of complex correlations, including Skolem functions that cannot be unskolemized and rewritten into GLAV. In Figure 3, we outline the benchmark mapping primitives used in our study. For each primitive, we offer a brief description and an example mapping, in which we underline those attributes which are part of primary keys, when these are essential for understanding the semantics of the transformation. Moreover, we indicate whether each primitive generates no Skolem terms (–), or some Skolem terms, using fixed or variable Skolemization strategies (*Fixed* and *Variable*, respectively). Note that the original STBenchmark [2] only uses Skolem functions in surrogate key (SU) and vertical partitioning (VP) scenarios, and only a single function in each. Hence, the original STBenchmark scenarios could always be unskolemized (i.e., they were nested GLAV), whereas STBenchmark 2.0 generates SO tgds. Note that the example mappings in the figure represent the simplest version of each primitive. The generated mappings may be much more involved and diverse. For instance, a vertical partitioning may split a relation into more than two

[3] This is not surprising because the minimization strategy was not designed with unskolemization in mind.

Parameter	Min	Max
Number of Primitives (per type)	0	10
Number of Relations Per Schema	1	100+
Number of Attributes Per Relation	2	15
Number of Key Attributes	1	3
Join Path Length	2	4
Join Type	Star	Chain
Primary Key FDs	No	Yes
Source FDs	0%	50%
Skolem Noise	0%	50%
Source Reuse	0%	50%

Figure 4: Some Configuration Parameters

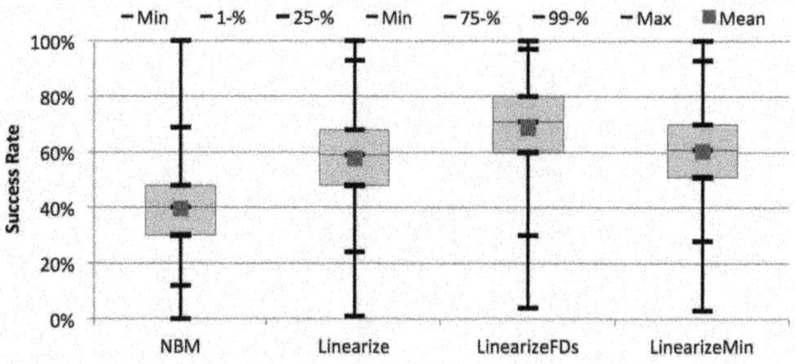

Figure 5: 12,500,000 Random Schema Mappings

fragments (depending on how the configuration parameters are set). For primitives that support variable Skolemizations, we use three different strategies (i.e., *Key*, *All*, and *Random* chosen through a parameter called *Skolem Mode*).

We made use of STBenchmark 2.0's ability to support the generation of primary keys, and random multi-attribute and partial FDs over the source. Configuration parameters, *Primary Key FDs* and *Source FDs*, are used to turn these features on and off as desired. We also made extensive use of the benchmark's ability to reuse schema elements across primitives. For example, two instances of a *CP* primitive may copy from the same source relation. This is of importance for generating correlations among mappings and in a sense, more realistic cases of Skolem terms across clauses used in the complex SO tgds we wish to consider.

Composition of schema mappings, like schema evolution, can lead to complex interactions between Skolem terms (specifically the arguments of the Skolem functions). In addition to Skolem terms introduced in the benchmark's primitives, we introduce additional Skolem terms by randomly choosing source attributes to be replaced (in the target) with Skolem functions (using the benchmark's configuration parameter *Skolem Noise* [7]). For instance, assume the Skolem term $f(a)$ was assigned to attribute b of relation $S(a,b)$. We would transform the SO tgd $S(x_1,x_2) \rightarrow T(x_1,x_2)$ into $S(x_1,x_2) \rightarrow T(x_1,f(x_1))$.

6.2 Random Scenarios

To analyze the effectiveness of the four rewriting techniques (NBM, Linearize, LinearizeFDs and LinearizeMin), we randomly generated a broad and large number of schema mappings using STBenchmark 2.0 [7]. Figure 4 outlines some of the most important configuration parameters involved in this experimental run and their valid ranges. For example, we randomly selected the number of instances for each mapping primitive (from 0 to 10, following a uniform distribution). The size of the source and target schema was determined not only by the number of requested attributes per relation (plus/minus deviations), but also by the type of requested primitives and some other additional parameters, such as the length of join paths. We consider variable types of joins (i.e., star and chain), key sizes, percentages of source FDs, Skolem noise, and source reuse.

To understand the stability of our experiments over these random configurations, we initially repeated each experiment up to 1,000 times. For all four techniques, we found that the values were already stable at 100 repetitions per configuration (less than 1% difference for each percentile of the distribution, with most percentiles being identical). For all experiments, the reported data values are averaged across 250 runs. This guarantees stable results for the whole breadth of schema mappings that can be generated with STBenchmark 2.0 (using these parameter ranges). Figure 5 plots the distribution of the success rate (i.e., minimum, 1-percentile, 25-percentile, median, 75-percentile, 99-percentile, maximum) for the four techniques, over a total of 12,500,000 schema mappings. By *success rate*, we mean the fraction of SO tgds from a schema mapping that were successfully rewritten, e.g., for a schema mapping with 10 SO tgds, 30% would indicate that 3 SO tgds were successfully rewritten. For a few mappings, all methods performed very well or very bad. Given the random nature of the generated schema mappings, this was an expected outcome. Recall that even the types of primitives used in the mappings were chosen randomly. Figure 5 shows that `NBM` is already able to rewrite 40% of the scenarios, `Linearize` can rewrite almost 50% more achieving a 58% success rate while `LinearizeFDs` achieves an average 71% success rate. The success rate of `LinearizeMin` is only slightly higher than `Linearize`. We will thus only consider the latter technique over real-life scenarios on Section 6.6. These results suggest that significant gains are possible by exploiting our more general rewriting techniques and the presence of source FDs.

6.3 Mapping Primitives

Next we ran experiments using only one primitive at a time to understand how the techniques deal with different types of real world scenarios. Figures 6 and 7 present the average success rate (over 250 runs) for each primitive with 0% and 50% Skolem noise, respectively. In both cases, we use 50% of source FDs. In the case of 0% Skolem noise, we found that all methods perform very well, i.e., we achieve 100% success rate for many primitives. This can be attributed to the fact that 6 of the 14 mapping primitives do not generate any Skolem terms (see Figure 3, e.g., CP and DEL). `Linearize` and `LinearizeFDs` perform better for the "harder" primitives. In particular, `LinearizeFDs` is the only technique that can successfully deal with vertical partitioning into N-to-M relationships (VPN). This success is due to the presence of source FDs which can be exploited to linearize Skolem terms with disjoint argument sets. As revealed by Figure 7, the importance of applying FDs is very noticeable in the case of 50% Skolem noise (i.e., high prevalence of Skolem functions with random arguments). For many primitives, `LinearizeFDs` succeeds in over 80% of the cases, `Linearize` in about 40%, and `NBM` in about 20%. However, some primitives result in Skolem terms that are more difficult to rewrite than others. Notably, merge primitives (i.e., MA and ME, which encode denormalization or the reversal of vertical partitioning) may use long sequences of joins in

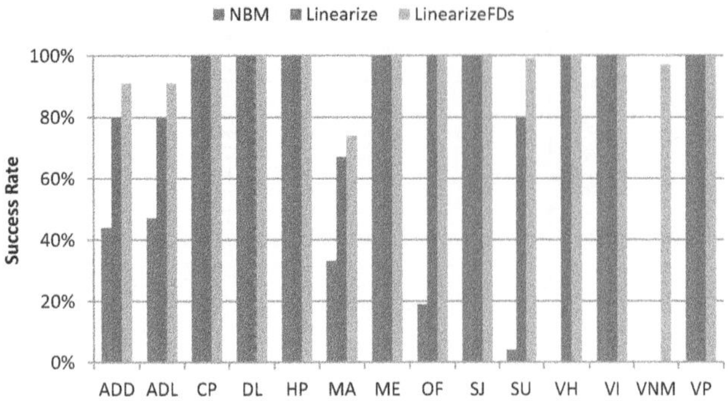

Figure 6: Per Primitive with 0% Skolem Noise

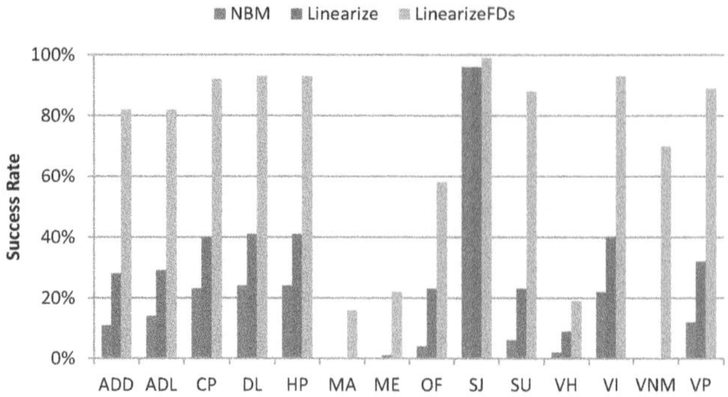

Figure 7: Per Primitive with 50% Skolem Noise

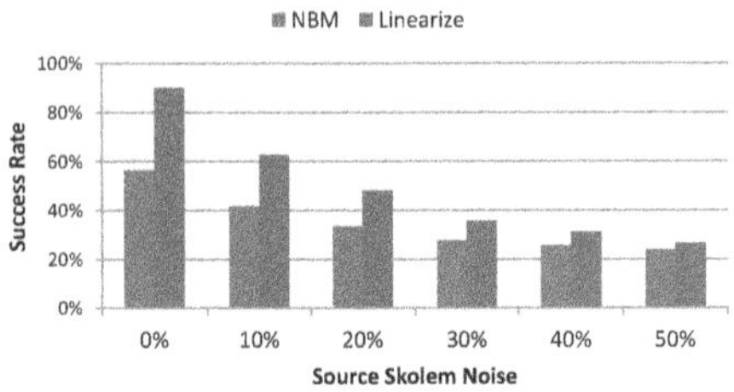

Figure 8: Increasing Skolem Noise

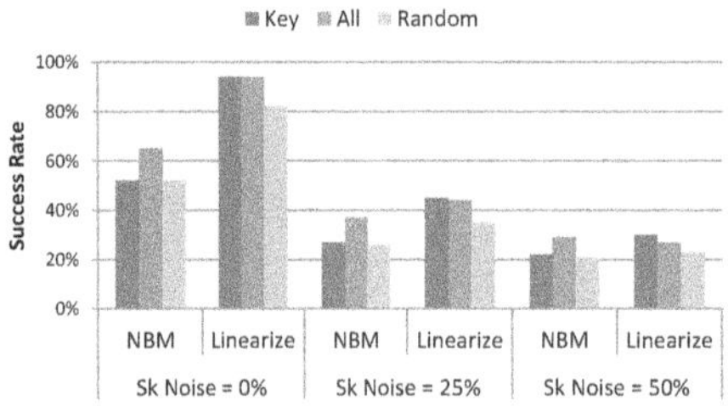

Figure 9: Skolem Mode vs. Noise

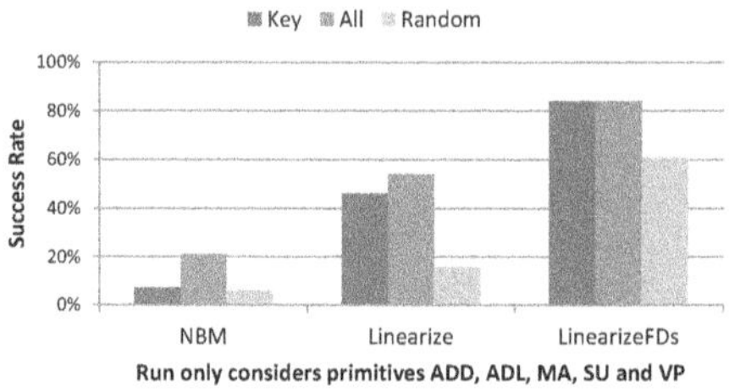

Figure 10: Varying Skolem Modes

a single SO tgd. The longer the join sequence, the higher the chance that randomly introduced Skolem terms are not rewritable, not even using FDs. We also found that, in general, `NBM` achieves lower success rates for higher percentages of Skolem noise and, in particular, for most vertical partitioning primitives. This finding aligns with the results reported by Bernstein et al. [8] who also point out the difficulty of rewriting these types of primitives.[4]

6.4 Amount and Type of Skolem Terms

We now investigate how the amount and types of Skolem terms influence success rate. Recall that in STBenchmark 2.0 [7], the configuration parameter *Skolem Noise* simulates that the mapping scenario is the result of composition or correlation operations. The SO tgd mapping generator supports three strategies for choosing the arguments of Skolem functions. *Key* uses the key attributes of a source expression as arguments for a given Skolem function; *All* uses all attributes of a source expression; and *Random* randomly selects a number of attributes. Figure 8 shows the average success rates over all Skolem modes for techniques `NBM` and `Linearize`, with Skolem noise varying from 0% to 50%. FDs were deactivated for this experiment. In general, we observe that the performance of both techniques decreases as we increase the amount of Skolem noise. This was expected, because intuitively the more Skolem noise is present, the higher the chance that an SO tgd contains Skolems that can not be rewritten. `Linearize` succeeds in over 80% percent of the cases for 0% Skolem noise and only in 27% of the cases for 50% Skolem noise. Note that 50% of Skolem noise causes an unrealistically large number of Skolem terms that are unlikely to appear in practical schema mappings. Nonetheless, we included these measurements to understand how the techniques behave under extreme conditions.

[4]Note that their experiments measure the success of composition rather than the success rate of rewriting [8].

Figure 9 shows the breakdown for each of the three Skolem modes (i.e., Key, All and Random). As can be seen, `NBM` achieves the best success rate if all attributes of a relation (*All*) are used as Skolem arguments, and exhibits similar behavior for *Random* and *Key* Skolem arguments. This behavior stems from the fact that *NBM*'s sufficient condition explicitly requires all exchanged source variables to appear as arguments to every Skolem term, a condition that is easily met under mode *All*. In contrast, `Linearize` works similarly well for both modes *Key* and *All*.

Not all primitives generate Skolem terms and for some primitives the Skolem arguments are predetermined by the semantics of the mapping transformation (i.e., Fixed vs. Variable Skolemization, as outlined in the last column of Figure 3). In the next experiment, we consider only those primitives that support variable Skolemization strategies (i.e., AD, ADL, MA, SU, and VP). Using a fixed Skolem noise percentage of 25%, we compare the success rate of the three techniques for the different Skolem strategies. We show the results of this experiment in Figure 10. Notice that `NBM` performs poorly, in particular for random Skolem terms (about 3% success rate). The success rates for `Linearize` and `LinearizeFDs` are better in general, but are also significantly lower for *Random* (about 20%).

6.5 Impact of Primary Keys and FDs

As part of our experimental plan, we also studied the effect of key and functional dependencies in rewriting SO tgds. We varied three main configuration parameters: *Skolem Mode* (i.e., Key, All and Random), Percentage of *Source FDs* (i.e., 0%, 25%, and 50%), and *Primary Key FDs*. Each separate run considered all mapping primitives, variable type of joins, and primary keys between 1 and 3 attributes. Source Skolem noise was fixed to 50%. We generated mappings with and without primary key FDs, and also with various degrees of additional source FDs. The results are depicted in Figure 11. We include `Linearize` as a baseline (the best we can do

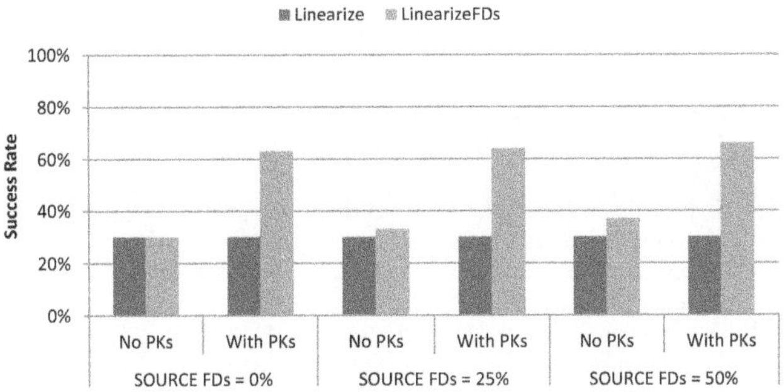

Figure 11: Impact of Primary Keys

Amalgam

Scenario	NBM	Linearize	LinearizeFDs	LinearizeMin
$S_1 \to S_2$	0	3	8	3
$S_1 \to S_3$	1	8	8	8
Total (16 SO tgds)	**6%**	**68%**	**100%**	**68%**

Bio

Scenario	NBM	Linearize	LinearizeFDs	LinearizeMin
GUS $\to$ BioSQL	0	4	7	4
Total (8 SO tgds)	**0%**	**50%**	**87%**	**50%**

3SDB

Scenario	NBM	Linearize	LinearizeFDs	LinearizeMin
$S_1 \to S_2$	4	6	10	9
$S_2 \to S_3$	7	9	9	9
$S_1 \to S_3$	2	4	11	4
Total (30 SO tgds)	**43%**	**63%**	**100%**	**73%**

Figure 12: Real-world Mappings

without using FDs). As we increase the percentage of source FDs, there is a slight increase (5% for 25% FDs and 10% for 50% FDs) in the success rate of **LinearizeFDs**. This experiment shows that primary keys act as a catalyst for rewriting, yielding at least a 75% increased success rate. This finding confirms our hypothesis about the advantages of considering FDs for rewriting.

6.6 Real-World Mappings

Last, we applied our techniques over three real-life mapping scenarios. The first scenario, *Amalgam* [25], consists of schemas describing scientific bibliographies. The second and third scenarios, *Bio* [3] and *3SDB* [4], are from the biological domain. We created SO mappings by relying on the semantics of the schemas and documented data transformations. We compared all rewriting techniques including **LinearizeMin**. Figure 12 reports the number of SO tgds that were successfully rewritten by each technique.

Amalgam. This scenario comprises two mappings between schemas S_1 and S_2, and between S_1 and S_3. Schemas S_1, S_2, and S_3 consists of 15, 27, and 5 relations, respectively. Each mapping is specified by 8 SO tgds, and all Skolem functions include keys. **LinearizeFDs** succeeds on all SO tgds, followed by **Linearize** and **LinearizeMin** with a success rate of 68%. NBM only succeeds for one SO tgd as the remaining ones require a more expressive mapping language.

Bio. We use a mapping between fragments of the Genomics Unified Schema *GUS* and the generic relational Biological Schema *BioSQL*.[5] The source schema *GUS* consists of 7 relations, and the target schema *BioSQL* consists of 6 relations. The schema mapping is specified by 8 SO tgds. **LinearizeFDs** succeeds on rewriting all but one SO tgd due to the presence of disjoint Skolem argument sets, thus outperforming the other techniques by at least 74%. NBM did not succeed on any of the tgds.

3SDB. This scenario consists of three mappings representing the evolution of three versions (S_1, S_2, and S_3) of a biological sample database schema used for gene expression analysis [4]. All rewriting techniques perform reasonably well, in particular with respect to the second mapping which consists mostly of full tgds with fewer Skolem functions. The third mapping from S_1 to S_3 models the composition of the evolution mappings and exhibits complex Skolem argument sets, resulting in a lower success rate for all techniques except **LinearizeFDs**. Notice that while **LinearizeMin** accomplishes similar performance as **LinearizeFDs** for the simpler evolution mappings, it only succeeds in rewriting up to 36% of the tgds in the composed mapping.

[5]From www.gusdb.org and www.biosql.org, respectively.

6.7 Discussion

In summary, our technique **LinearizeFDs** consistently outperforms both **Linearize** and NBM by a large margin over both synthetic and real-world mappings (e.g., over 95% success rate in the latter). The performance of **LinearizeFDs** is largely improved by the existence of primary keys in the source. Using implied FDs to *augment* Skolem terms appears to be more beneficial than using FDs to minimize Skolem terms [23] before checking our linearity condition (i.e., **LinearizeMin**). Since primary keys are available in most schemas or can be added without much effort, we expect our method to perform very well in practice.

7. RELATED WORK

The *NBM* algorithm [26] was used as part of a mapping composition framework presented by Bernstein et al. [8]. This work presented a composition algorithm based on view unfolding and a comprehensive experimental study in the context of schema evolution (whereas our work and evaluation considers general SO tgds). In Bernstein et al., source key dependencies were used to minimize the argument sets of Skolem functions (for example, a Skolem function $f(x, y)$ could be minimized to $f(x)$ if $x \to y$). We have found that such minimization can sometimes hide a linearization opportunity and instead use an algorithm that augments function arguments using FDs. Importantly, Bernstein et al. [8] suggest as future work that it may be possible to exploit key dependencies "in a more direct way". We have confirmed their conjecture and also shown how to leverage more general source FDs along with dependencies implied by a mapping.

A number of techniques, logical and otherwise, have been proposed for reducing the argument sets of Skolem functions in SO tgds. Using SO Skolemization [10], Fagin et al. [12] show that every s-t tgd is equivalent to an SO tgd without equalities. It is often possible to apply a prior step to this transformation that leads to Skolem terms with fewer arguments. Practically, this means obtaining SO tgds with Skolem terms depending *only* on the universal variables that are effectively being exchanged, instead of using all universal variables as dictated by the standard Skolemization strategy [10]. Yu and Popa [32] exploit this optimization, among others, in their mapping composition algorithm and use it to simplify SO tgds by replacing every equality between two Skolem terms with an equality of their arguments. This simplification guarantees chase equivalence. In the context of exchanging data in open and closed worlds, Libkin and Sirangelo [22] discuss the use of *custom* Skolemization strategies to encapsulate the semantics of 1-to-1 and 1-to-n relationships over target attributes. Our approach of using FDs to modify the arguments sets of Skolem functions may be seen as proposing yet another Skolemization strategy, albeit one that has the property of generating more opportunities for the successful unskolemization of the resulting SO tgd.

8. CONCLUSIONS

We introduced two approaches for transforming SO tgds into equivalent nested GLAV mappings. Our approach assumes we are given an (arbitrary) SO tgd (without Skolem equalities) and provides sufficient conditions for when the rich Skolem functions in SO tgds are well-behaved and have an FO semantics. We experimentally showed that these conditions are able to handle a very large number of real schema mappings. Going forward, we would like to incorporate our insights on both linearization and using FDs directly into mapping operators including composition and MapMerge. This could lead to more concise Skolemizations and in general a better understanding of how to determine the arguments of newly introduced Skolem functions within mappings. This follows a trend of using FDs to simplify data exchange [23], but holds the promise of being able to use FDs and more general Skolem management techniques directly within a host of model management operators.

Acknowledgments. We thank the anonymous referees for their valuable suggestions. Special thanks to Sheila McIlraith for relevant discussions, and to Bodgan Alexe and Yuan An for providing us with real-life schemas and mappings. Arocena was supported by the NSERC Business Intelligence Network.

9. REFERENCES

[1] B. Alexe, M. A. Hernández, L. Popa, and W. C. Tan. MapMerge: Correlating Independent Schema Mappings. *VLDB J.*, 21(2):191–211, 2012.

[2] B. Alexe, W. C. Tan, and Y. Velegrakis. STBenchmark: Towards a Benchmark for Mapping Systems. *PVLDB*, 1(1):230–244, 2008.

[3] B. Alexe, B. ten Cate, P. Kolaitis, and W. Tan. Designing and refining schema mappings via data examples. In *SIGMOD*, pages 133–144, 2011.

[4] Y. An, A. Borgida, R. J. Miller, and J. Mylopoulos. A Semantic Approach to Discovering Schema Mapping Expressions. In *ICDE*, pages 206–215, 2007.

[5] M. Arenas, R. Fagin, and A. Nash. Composition with Target Constraints. *Logical Methods in Comput. Sci.*, 7(3), 2011.

[6] M. Arenas, J. Pérez, J. Reutter, and C. Riveros. Inverting Schema Mappings: Bridging the Gap between Theory and Practice. *PVLDB*, 2(1):1018–1029, 2009.

[7] P. C. Arocena, M. D'Angelo, B. Glavic, and R. J. Miller. STBenchmark 2.0. Technical report, University of Toronto, 2013. `http://dblab.cs.toronto.edu/project/STBench2.0.`

[8] P. A. Bernstein, T. J. Green, S. Melnik, and A. Nash. Implementing Mapping Composition. *VLDB J.*, 17(2):333–353, 2008.

[9] P. A. Bernstein, A. Y. Halevy, and R. A. Pottinger. A Vision for Management of Complex Models. *SIGMOD Record*, 29(4):55–63, Dec. 2000.

[10] H. B. Enderton. *A Mathematical Introduction to Logic*. Harcout Academic Press, 2nd. Edition, 2001.

[11] R. Fagin, P. Kolaitis, R. J. Miller, and L. Popa. Data Exchange: Semantics and Query Answering. *Theor. Comput. Sci.*, 336(1):89–124, 2005.

[12] R. Fagin, P. Kolaitis, L. Popa, and W. C. Tan. Composing Schema Mappings: Second-Order Dependencies to the Rescue. *TODS*, 30(4):994–1055, 2005.

[13] I. Feinerer, R. Pichler, E. Sallinger, and V. Savenkov. On the Undecidability of the Equivalence of Second-Order Tuple Generating Dependencies. In *AMW*, 2011.

[14] A. Fuxman, M. A. Hernández, H. Ho, R. J. Miller, P. Papotti, and L. Popa. Nested Mappings: Schema Mapping Reloaded. In *VLDB*, pages 67–78, 2006.

[15] A. Fuxman, P. Kolaitis, R. J. Miller, and W. C. Tan. Peer Data Exchange. *TODS*, 31(4):1454–1498, 2006.

[16] D. Gabbay, R. Schmidt, and A. Szalas. *Second Order Quantifier Elimination: Foundations, Computational Aspects and Applications*. College Publications, 2008.

[17] T. J. Green, G. Karvounarakis, N. E. Taylor, O. Biton, Z. G. Ives, and V. Tannen. ORCHESTRA: Facilitating Collaborative Data Sharing. In *SIGMOD*, pages 1131–1133, 2007.

[18] R. Hull and M. Yoshikawa. ILOG: Declarative Creation and Manipulation of Object Identifiers. In *VLDB*, pages 455–468, 1990.

[19] A. Klug and R. Price. Determining View Dependencies Using Tableaux. *TODS*, 7(3):361–380, 1982.

[20] M. K. Lawrence, R. A. Pottinger, and S. Staub-French. Data Coordination: Supporting Contingent Updates. *PVLDB*, 4(11):831–842, 2011.

[21] M. Lenzerini. Data Integration: a Theoretical Perspective. In *PODS*, pages 233–246, 2002.

[22] L. Libkin and C. Sirangelo. Data Exchange and Schema Mappings in Open and Closed Worlds. *J. Comput. Syst. Sci.*, 77(3):542–571, 2011.

[23] B. Marnette, G. Mecca, and P. Papotti. Scalable Data Exchange with Functional Dependencies. *PVLDB*, 3(1):105–116, 2010.

[24] B. Marnette, G. Mecca, P. Papotti, S. Raunich, and D. Santoro. ++Spicy: an OpenSource Tool for Second-Generation Schema Mapping and Data Exchange. *PVLDB*, 4(12):1438–1441, 2011.

[25] R. J. Miller, D. Fisla, M. Huang, D. Kymlicka, F. Ku, and V. Lee. The Amalgam Schema and Data Integration Test Suite. `www.cs.toronto.edu/~miller/amalgam`, 2001.

[26] A. Nash, P. A. Bernstein, and S. Melnik. Composition of Mappings Given by Embedded Dependencies. *TODS*, 32(1):4, 2007.

[27] Y. Papakonstantinou, S. Abiteboul, and H. Garcia-Molina. Object Fusion in Mediator Systems. In *VLDB*, pages 413–424, 1996.

[28] R. Pichler and S. Skritek. The Complexity of Evaluating Tuple Generating Dependencies. In *ICDT*, pages 244–255, 2011.

[29] L. Popa, Y. Velegrakis, R. J. Miller, M. A. Hernández, and R. Fagin. Translating Web Data. In *VLDB*, pages 598–609, 2002.

[30] L. Seligman, P. Mork, A. Y. Halevy, K. P. Smith, M. J. Carey, K. Chen, C. Wolf, J. Madhavan, A. Kannan, and D. Burdick. OpenII: an Open Source Information Integration Toolkit. In *SIGMOD*, pages 1057–1060, 2010.

[31] B. ten Cate and P. Kolaitis. Structural Characterizations of Schema-Mapping Languages. In *ICDT*, pages 63–72, 2009.

[32] C. Yu and L. Popa. Semantic Adaptation of Schema Mappings when Schemas Evolve. *VDLB*, pages 1006–1017, 2005.

Indexing Methods for Moving Object Databases: Games and Other Applications*

Hanan Samet[§] Jagan Sankaranarayanan[‡†] Michael Auerbach[§]
[§]University of Maryland, College Park, MD [‡]NEC Labs America, Cupertino, CA
hjs@cs.umd.edu, jagan@nec-labs.com, mikea@umd.edu

ABSTRACT

Moving object databases arise in numerous applications such as traffic monitoring, crowd tracking, and games. They all require keeping track of objects that move and thus the database of objects must be constantly updated. The cover fieldtree (more commonly known as the loose quadtree and the loose octree, depending on the dimension of the underlying space) is designed to overcome the drawback of spatial data structures that associate objects with their minimum enclosing quadtree (octree) cells which is that the size of these cells depends more on the position of the objects and less on their size. In fact, the size of these cells may be as large as the entire space from which the objects are drawn. The loose quadtree (octree) overcomes this drawback by expanding the size of the space that is spanned by each quadtree (octree) cell c of width w by a cell expansion factor p ($p > 0$) so that the expanded cell is of width $(1+p) \cdot w$ and an object is associated with its minimum enclosing expanded quadtree (octree) cell. It is shown that for an object o with minimum bounding hypercube box b of radius r (i.e., half the length of a side of the hypercube), the maximum possible width w of the minimum enclosing expanded quadtree cell c is just a function of r and p, and is independent of the position of o. Normalizing w via division by $2r$ enables calculating the range of possible expanded quadtree cell sizes as a function of p. For $p \geq 0.5$ the range consists of just two values and usually just one value for $p \geq 1$. This makes updating very simple and fast as for $p \geq 0.5$, there are at most two possible new cells associated with the moved object and thus the update can be done in $O(1)$ time. Experiments with random data showed that the update time to support motion in such an environment is minimized when p is infinitesimally less than 1, with as much as a one order of magnitude increase in the number of updates that can be handled vis-a-vis the $p = 0$ case in a given unit of time. Similar results for updates were obtained for an N-body simulation where improved query performance and scalability were also observed. Finally, in order amplify the paper, a video titled "Crates and Barrels" was produced which is an N-body simulation of 14,000 objects. The video as well as a JAVA applet that illustrates the behavior of the loose quadtree are both available from `http://www.cs.umd.edu/~hjs/loosequad/`.

*This work was supported in part by the National Science Foundation under grants CCF-05-15241, IIS-0713501, IIS-10-18475, IIS-12-19023, Microsoft Research, Google, NVIDIA, the E.T.S. Walton Visitor Award of the Science Foundation of Ireland, and the National Center for Geocomputation at the National University of Ireland at Maynooth.

†Work done while the author was at the University of Maryland.

SIGMOD'13, June 22–27, 2013, New York, New York, USA.

Categories and Subject Descriptors

E.1 [**Data**]: Data Structures

General Terms

Algorithm, Performance

Keywords

game databases, moving objects, spatial data structures, cover fieldtree, loose quadtree, loose octree, spatial indexing, spatial databases, game programming

1. INTRODUCTION

One of the motivations for the development of geographic information systems (GIS) is to keep track of objects (e.g., QUILT [38, 41], and the SAND Browser [11, 36]) for both location-based and feature-based queries [4]. Similar needs arise in game applications (e.g., [9,16]), where the difference is that the objects are not usually static. Instead, they are constantly moving and thus the database of objects must be constantly updated. An attractive method of representing spatial objects to support the tracking process uses an object hierarchy where minimum bounding hypercube boxes (e.g., an R-tree [15,37]) are used to speed up the process of detecting if objects are present or overlap other objects. One of the drawbacks of such a representation is that the hierarchies of different sets of objects are not in registration thereby making set operations between the two sets such as unions and intersections more complex.

A solution is to use a hierarchy of congruent cells while still not decomposing the objects. In this case, the hierarchy is based on a regular decomposition of the underlying space such as a region quadtree (e.g., [37]) and then associates each object with its minimum enclosing quadtree cell. Methods that employ this technique include the MX-CIF quadtree [1, 24, 45], multilayer grid file [44], R-file [19], filter tree [40] (used for spatial join algorithms [18,20,21]), and SQ-histogram [3] (used for selectivity estimation in processing spatial queries) where the primary difference lies in the nature of the access structure that is used. For example, Figure 1a is the cell decomposition induced by the MX-CIF quadtree for a collection of rectangle objects, while Figure 1b is its tree representation. Notice that more than one object is associated with some of the nodes in the tree which means that the objects have the same minimum enclosing quadtree cell (e.g., the root and its NE child, where the children are referred to as NW, NE, SW, and SE denoting the Northwest, Northeast, Southwest, and Southeast quadrants, respectively, of corresponding cells).

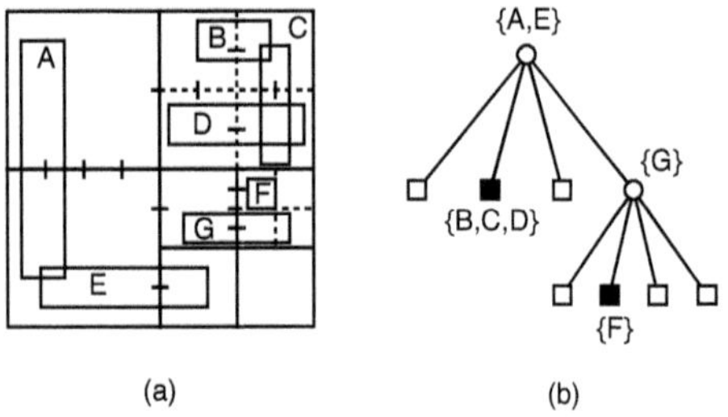

Figure 1: (a) Cell decomposition induced by the MX-CIF quadtree for a collection of rectangle objects and (b) its tree representation (from [37]).

The drawback of these methods is that the size of these minimum enclosing quadtree cells depends on the position of the centroids of the objects and is independent of the size of the objects, subject to a minimum which is the size of the object. In fact, it may be as large as the entire space from which the objects are drawn. This has bad ramifications for applications where the objects move including games, traffic monitoring, and streaming. In particular, if the objects are moved even slightly, then they usually need to be reinserted in the structure.

The cover fieldtree [12,13] and the more commonly known loose quadtree (octree) [47] are designed to overcome this independence of the size of the minimum enclosing quadtree cell and the size of the object (see also the expanded MX-CIF quadtree [2], multiple shifted quadtree methods [7,26,27], and the partition fieldtree [12, 13]). This is done by expanding the size of the space that is spanned by each quadtree cell c of width w by a cell expansion factor p ($p > 0$) so that the expanded cell is of width $(1+p)\cdot w$ and an object is associated with its minimum enclosing expanded quadtree (octree) cell. The notion of an expanded quadtree cell can also be seen in the quadtree medial axis transform [34, 35]. For example, letting $p = 1$, Figure 2 is the loose quadtree corresponding to the collection of objects in Figure 1(a) and its MX-CIF quadtree in Figure 1(b). In this example, there are only two differences between the loose and MX-CIF quadtrees:

1. Rectangle object E is associated with the SW child of the root of the loose quadtree instead of with the root of the MX-CIF quadtree.

2. Rectangle object B is associated with the NW child of the NE child of the root of the loose quadtree instead of with the NE child of the root of the MX-CIF quadtree.

To further understand the loose quadtree and its behavior, see the publicly available web site at `http://www.cs.umd.edu/~hjs/loosequad/`. The web site also contains a video titled "Crates and Barrels" that shows an N-body simulation containing 14,000 objects. The video illustrates the improvement in in performance when using a loose quadtree over an MX-CIF quadtree.

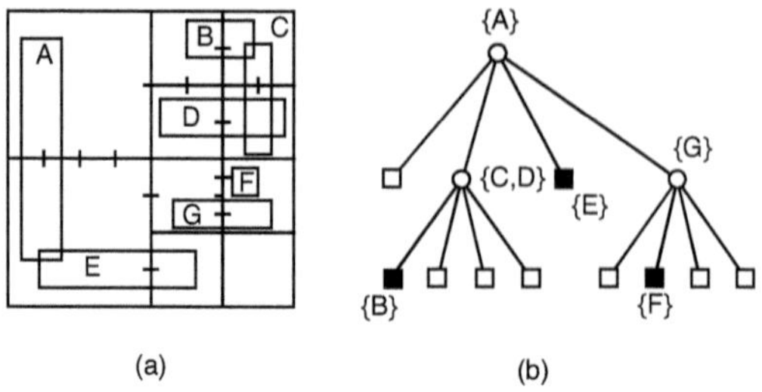

Figure 2: (a) Cell decomposition induced by the loose quadtree for a collection of rectangle objects identical to those in Figure 1, and (b) its tree representation (from [37]).

Ulrich [47] has shown that given a loose quadtree cell c of width w and cell expansion factor p, the radius r of the minimum bounding hypercube box b of the smallest object o that could possibly be associated with c must be greater than $pw/4$.

Our contribution is the realization that the real utility of the loose quadtree is best evaluated in terms of the inverse of the above relation as we are interested in minimizing the maximum possible width w of c given an object o with minimum bounding hypercube box b of radius r (i.e., half the length of a side of the hypercube) denoted by MBHR(o,b,r). This is because reducing w is the real motivation and goal for the development of the loose quadtree as an alternative to the MX-CIF quadtree for which w can be as large as the width of the underlying space. We achieve our goal in Section 3 by examining the range of the relative widths of c and b as this provides a way of taking into account the constraints imposed by the fact that the range of values of w is limited to powers of 2. In particular, the novelty of our work lies in our showing this range to be just a function of p, and hence independent of the position of o. Moreover, we prove that for $p \geq 0.5$, the relative widths of c and b take on at most two values, and usually just one value for $p \geq 1$. This makes updating the index very simple when objects are moving as there are at most two possible new cells associated with a moved object, instead of $\log_2$ of the width of the space in which the objects are embedded (which can be as large as 16 assuming a $2^{16} \times 2^{16}$ embedding space as used by us). In other words, we have shown how to update in $O(1)$ time for $p \geq 0.5$ which is of great importance as there is no longer a need to perform a search for the appropriate quadtree cell.

The rest of this paper is organized as follows. Section 2 discusses related work in the context of the moving object databases literature. Section 3 shows how to achieve position independence for the width of the minimum enclosing quadtree cell c by examining the range of the relative widths of c and the minimum bounding hypercube box b of object o, denoted by MBH(o,b), and also how to take into account the constraints imposed by the fact that the range of values of the width of c is limited to powers of 2. Section 4 presents a cell insertion algorithm for the loose quadtree. Section 5 discusses the ramifications of the results of Section 3. Section 6 contains an experimental evaluation of the loose quadtree with respect to the extent that it needs to be updated on account of object motion for different values of p and object size distribution, Section 7 shows the results of using the Loose Quadtree in an N-body simulation which is typical of the type of functionality needed in modern video games and hence is conducted in a main memory environment unlike the experiments in Section 6 which used secondary storage. Concluding remarks are drawn in Section 8.

2. RELATED WORK

As pointed out in [43], updates to spatial indices, such as those that occur due to motions of the objects, require a coarse tree-level locking instead of object-level as entire sub-trees may have to locked to facilitate deletion of an object from its prior position and reinsertion into its newer position. Several approaches [22, 29, 33, 46, 49] have been proposed which we broadly classify based on the strategy that they use to minimize the updates to the spatial index. If the movement of the data is *predictive*, or in other words, the future position of the object is known for a short future time period, then the structure can be optimized to answer queries for a short period without having to rebuild the structure. This is the strategy adopted by the TPR-tree [33], its variant the TPR*-tree [46].

[22, 49] resort to space-filling curves and B-trees in lieu of a more traditional spatial index, such as an R*-tree [6] in order to take advantage of the B-tree's ability to handle high rates of updates. Similarly, [25, 31] transform the position of a moving object using a Hough transformation into a dual space, such that updates are only required when the velocity of the object changes resulting in overall fewer updates. A method for indexing trajectories of moving objects is given in [32], while a method to index objects moving on a road network that takes advantage of the restricted motions of these objects along the road network within prescribed speed limits is given in [29]. To make spatial indices more update efficient, [42, 43] propose a general method to take advantage of the many cores in modern computer architectures even as queries are applied to the spatial data structure.

Our work is unique in the sense that we deal with objects that have extents (i.e., geometries), while most of the work in this area deals with point objects. While the geometry of the moving objects may not be important in vehicular or people tracking applications, it is not so for games and physics-based applications. Note that we cannot assume that the position of the object and its trajectory can be reasonably estimated. A typical game scenario consists of several dynamic objects which move in response to other dynamic or static objects in the scene, making long term prediction of their movement quite difficult. Moreover, rendering the scene requires that the spatial data structures be queried tens of times per second in order to ascertain which objects are visible in the scene, how they are interacting, and even how light interacts with them in order to produce the desired interactivity that users expect from games. A B-tree could be used to speed up updates in lieu of a spatial index such as an R*-tree or a quadtree. In this paper we use two experimental setups: one involving a loose quadtree indexed by a B-tree where the blocks of the quadtree are represented by their location codes, and another using a pointer-based quadtree structure. Finally, in contrast to methods that increase the throughput of a spatial index by harnessing the work of multiple threads updating the spatial index (e.g., [42, 43]), our method avoids as many updates to the spatial index as possible. Our method and multi-threaded update intensive methods are not mutually exclusive in the sense that one does not preclude the application of the other.

3. CALCULATION OF THE MAXIMUM LOOSE QUADTREE CELL WIDTH

A key principle to observe is that in the loose quadtree, the smallest expanded quadtree cell c of width w that contains the object o has the property that the centroid of o (actually of MBHR(o,b,r)) is contained in the non-expanded portion of c. Thus insertion proceeds by finding the smallest quadtree cell c that contains the centroid of b, and whose expanded cell also contains o. The traditional way of finding c is to recursively search the quadtree starting at the root and descend to the appropriate child based on the value of the centroid. In fact, it turns out that there is even an easier way of determining c, which involves little search (i.e., few descents in the quadtree). In particular, we show below that the width w of c must lie within a relatively small range of values, thereby greatly restricting the number of possible cells that must be tested for the inclusion of o.

Recall that one of the key drawbacks of data structures such as the MX-CIF quadtree that associate an object o with the minimum sized quadtree cell c of width w that encloses object o's MBHR(o,b,r) is that w is a function of the position of o, and to a lesser extent, a function of r in the sense that only its minimum is a function of r. In contrast, in the loose quadtree, as we show in the rest of this section, the dependence of w on the position of o is reduced significantly. In particular, we demonstrate that w lies within a range of values that only depend on the radius r of o's MBH(o,b) and the value of the cell expansion factor p. In fact, normalizing w via division by $2r$ leads to Theorem 3.1, given below, which enables the calculation of a range of expanded quadtree cell sizes whose lower and upper bounds only depend on p. As we will see, restricting of the cell sizes to be powers of 2 (i.e., $1, 2, 4, \ldots 2^n$) makes these bounds quite tight, with the range taking on at most two values for $p \approx 1$, which turns out to be the primary p value of interest. Thus the size of the containing quadtree cell is almost the size of the object or the size of the next larger quadtree cell.

THEOREM 3.1. *The ratio $w/2r$ of the widths of the expanded minimum enclosing quadtree cell c and MBH(o,b) obeys*

$$\frac{1}{1+p} \leq \frac{w}{2r} < \frac{2}{p}.$$

PROOF. We first derive a lower bound on the range of the ratios. From the definition of the cell expansion factor p, we know that given an object o with MBHR(o,b,r) the smallest quadtree cell c of width w with which o can be associated so that o's centroid lies in the non-expanded portion of c arises when the centroids of b and c coincide, and moreover the cell c' resulting from the expansion of c (i.e., having width $(1+p)w$) is just large enough to contain b of width $2r$ (see Figure 3(a)). This leads to the following inequality:

$$(1+p)w \geq 2r \qquad (1)$$

and can be rewritten as

$$\frac{w}{2r} \geq \frac{1}{1+p}. \qquad (2)$$

We can use similar reasoning to obtain an upper bound on the range of the ratios, and in the process use a similar construction to that of Ulrich [47] except that for a given cell expansion factor p, Ulrich assumed the existence of a quadtree cell c of width w and was seeking the radius r of the minimum bounding hypercube box b of the smallest object o that could possibly be associated with the expanded cell c, while we are assuming that for a given cell expansion factor p, we are given an object o with minimum bounding hypercube box b of radius r and are seeking the width w of the largest cell c with whose expanded cell b would be associated. We make use of our observation that the centroid of the object o with MBHR(o,b,r) is always required to be contained in the non-expanded portion of the associated quadtree cell.

An alternative way of casting our goal is that we want to find the width of the smallest object o that can have a minimum enclosing expanded quadtree cell c of width w. Doing this enables us to calculate an upper bound on the range of $w/2r$. Given our requirement that the centroid of the object is always in the non-expanded portion of the minimum enclosing expanded quadtree cell c, we find that one of c's corners is coincident with the centroid of o, and that the radius r of b is not too large so that b is too large for the expanded region of c (i.e., an attainable upper bound on r of $pw/2$ as shown in Figure 3(b)), and just large enough so that b does not fit in the expanded region of one of the subcells of c of width $w/2$

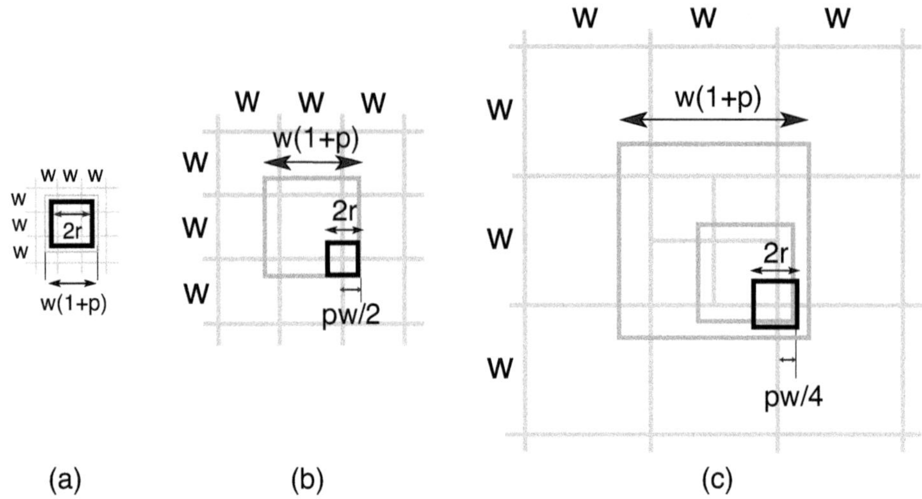

Figure 3: Assuming cell expansion factor p and an examples showing the (a) smallest ratio of the width w of the quadtree cell c associated with b and the width of b which is attained when the centroids of o and c coincide, and the (b) lower and (c) upper bounds on the largest ratio attained when the centroid of o coincides with one of the corners of c. Note that (c) is drawn at a different scale than (b).

(i.e., an unattainable lower lower bound on r of $pw/4$ as shown in Figure 3(c)). Equivalently, for this particular configuration, we say that $pw/4 = 2^{k-1} = r - \delta' < r \leq 2^k = pw/2$ for some value of k and $\delta' > 0$. Simplifying the notation by letting $\delta' = \delta w/4$, we have $pw/4 = 2^{k-1} = r - \delta w/4 < r \leq 2^k = pw/2$ for some $\delta > 0$. Since the width w of c is the same for all values of r in this range, we point out that c's width relative to that of b is maximized when r takes on the value:

$$r = pw/4 + \delta w/4, \delta > 0. \tag{3}$$

which can be rewritten as:

$$w/2r = \frac{w}{\frac{pw}{2} + \delta\frac{w}{2}}, \delta > 0, \tag{4}$$

$$w/2r = \frac{2}{p+\delta} < \frac{2}{p}, \tag{5}$$

$$w/2r < \frac{2}{p}. \tag{6}$$

Combining relations 2 and 6 yields the range:

$$\frac{1}{1+p} \leq \frac{w}{2r} < \frac{2}{p}. \tag{7}$$

□

We interpret Theorem 3.1 as follows. Without loss of generality, we assume that the quadtree cell corresponding to the root of the loose quadtree has length 2^g, where g is an integer. This enables us to avoid dealing with negative values of k, which is somewhat counter intuitive, as would be the case were we to continue with the unit hypercube assumption. In this case, all cells c in the loose quadtree have width $w = 2^k$, such that $k \leq g$ is an integer. Now, for any given value x, let us define a function $M(x)$ which determines a k such that $2^{k-1} < x \leq 2^k$, and returns the value 2^k. In other words,

$$M(x) = 2^k, \text{ s.t. } 2^{k-1} < x \leq 2^k. \tag{8}$$

Moreover, we also have that

$$1 \leq \frac{M(x)}{x} < 2. \tag{9}$$

The rationale behind the function $M(x)$ is that it *quantizes* x to the next higher power of 2 unless it is already a power of 2. To explain the utility of $M(x)$ from a geometric point of view, consider an input object R with a minimum bounding hypercube box of radius r. We have that $M(r)$ is the radius of the smallest quadtree cell (i.e., half the width) that can potentially contain R. We now derive the minimum and maximum possible ratios of $w/2r$ in terms of $M(.)$. Our motivation is to be able to identify a set of quadtree cells (typically a few) in the loose quadtree that can potentially contain R. From relation 7, we are given that $w/2r$ is greater than or equal to $1/(p+1)$, but is less than $2/p$. The number of levels of the loose quadtree spanned by the range $[1/(p+1), 2/p)$ is upper-bounded by the number of integers of the form 2^k, where k is an integer, that is contained in the range $[1/(p+1), 2/p)$. That is, we have just shown that the number of levels spanned by the range in relation 7 cannot exceed V, which is given by Lemma 3.1 below.

LEMMA 3.1. *The number of levels in the loose quadtree at which the expanded minimum quadtree cell of the object could possibly lie is upper bounded by V, where*

$$V = \log_2(M(2/p)) - \log_2(M(1/(p+1))). \tag{10}$$

Now, let us make some observations on the possible ranges of relative cell widths on the basis of relations 7 and 10. First, for the degenerate case of the MX-CIF quadtree, in which case no expansion takes place (i.e., $p = 0$), we have an unbounded upper bound on the range of values and a lower bound of 1. As p increases towards 1, the range of values decreases. For example, for $p = 1/4$, we have a range of relative cell widths $[4/5, 8)$. This means that the relative cell widths of the set of possible quadtree cells containing a given input rectangle R with a minimum bounding hypercube box of radius r lie between $[M(4/5) = 1, M(8) = 8) = \{1, 2, 4\}$. In other words, the quadtree cells containing R in the loose quadtree can be of radius $M(r)$, $2M(r)$, and $4M(r)$ (i.e., half the width). In fact, these radii hold for all values of p such that $1/4 \leq p < 1/2$.

For $p = 1/2$, there are just two possible relative cell widths corresponding to $[M(2/3) = 1, M(4) = 4) = \{1, 2\}$. In other words, the associated quadtree cells of R can be either the quadtree cell of radius $M(r)$ or of radius $2M(r)$. These radii hold for all values of p such that $1/2 \leq p < 1$. For $p = 1$, there are also just two possible relative cell widths corresponding to $[M(1/2) = 1/2, M(2) = 2) = \{1/2, 1\}$. In other words, the associated quadtree cells of R can be either the quadtree cell of radius $M(r)$, or can be of radius half of $M(r)$. These radii hold for all values of p such that $1 \le p < 2$. As p increases beyond 1, the number of possible ratios of relative cell widths oscillates between one and two. In particular, for $\lfloor p \rfloor = 2^k - 1$, where $k \ge 1$ is an integer, the ratio $w/2r$ takes on two values $[M(1/2^k) = 2^{-k}, M(2/(2^k - 1)) = 2^{2-k})$, while for all other values of p (i.e., $2^k \le p < 2^{k+1} - 1$, where $k \ge 1$ is an integer), $w/2r$ takes on just one value $M(1/2^k) = 2^{-k}$.

4. INSERTION IN A LOOSE QUADTREE

In this section we show how Theorem 3.1 and Lemma 3.1 can be used to derive a simple $O(1)$ time object insertion algorithm for the loose quadtree. We first give an example of the algorithm using $p = 1/4$. From Theorem 3.1, we have that the quadtree cells containing a given input rectangle object o with a minimum bounding hypercube box of radius r can be associated with one of three possible cells of radius $M(r)$, $2M(r)$, and $4M(r)$. The insertion algorithm proceeds as follows. We first find a cell b of radius $M(r)$, such that it contains the centroid of o. This can be done in $O(1)$ time by noting that $M(r) = 2^{\lceil \log_2 r \rceil}$. At this point, we have that either b, the parent of b (say b') of radius $2M(r)$, or the parent of b' (say b") of radius $4M(r)$ contains o and we insert o in the smallest one whose expanded region contains o.

The actual insertion algorithm is given by procedure LOOSEQUADTREEINSERT below. It uses Lemma 3.1 to determine the number of quadtree cells and their corresponding sizes that are to be checked in the loop in lines 8–22 to determine the minimum-sized quadtree cell that is to contain the object to be inserted. The algorithm does not assume that the loose quadtree is represented as a tree structure with out degree 4 (8 for a loose octree in three dimensions). Instead, it assumes the use of a pointerless quadtree representation (e.g., [14,37]) that just keeps track of the leaf nodes (i.e., cells) of the loose quadtree which are represented using, for example, a number, termed a *locational code* (referred to as the Morton Representation [28] in Section 6), that uniquely identifies each leaf node. This number can be formed by concatenating the size of the cell, say i for a cell of width 2^i, with a number j resulting from interleaving the binary representations of the coordinate values of a predefined corner such as the lower-left corner assuming that the origin of the underlying space is at the lower-left corner (e.g., (a, b) in two dimensions) so that i is at the right of j. The collection of these numbers can be represented using any access structure including binary search trees, balanced binary search trees, B-trees, etc. although our implementation in the experimental setup in Section 6 uses a B-tree. Thus the role of LOOSEQUADTREEINSERT is simply to create records for the loose quadtree which consist of the locational code and a reference to the object so that we can differentiate between objects that are associated with the same leaf node (i.e., cell) of the loose quadtree. In this case, the cell is replicated in the access structure.

1 **pointer loose_quadtree_block procedure** LOOSEQUADTREEINSERT(P, O)

2 /* Given a loose quadtree with expansion factor p, create and return a loose quadtree record for object o which contains the object and its locational code. Object o is represented by a record of type *object* having the fields XCENT, YCENT, and MBBRADIUS corresponding to the x and y coordinate values of o's centroid, and the radius of o's minimum bounding hypercube box. The function $M(r)$ returns the integer 2^k such that $2^{k-1} < r \le 2^k$. The locational code is obtained by applying bit interleaving to the binary representations of x_{low} and y_{low}, the x and y coordinate values of the lower-left corner of the loose quadtree cell b of width w which contains o and concatenating it to the depth of b (i.e., $\log_2(w)$) and its value is a pointer to object o. If several objects are associated with the same cell of the loose quadtree, then the cell is replicated. These replicated loose quadtree cells are differentiated by virtue of the objects that are associated with them. The actual loose quadtree record for the cell including its locational code is constructed by procedure FORMBLOCK (not given here). Note the use of "$\div$" to denote integer division, "/" to denote real division, and $\uparrow$ to denote exponentiation. */

3 **value real** p
4 **value object** o
5 **real** r
6 **integer** i, w, x_{low}, y_{low}
7 $r \leftarrow$ MBBRADIUS(o)
8 **for** $i \leftarrow \log_2(M(1/(p+1)))$ **step** 1
9   **until** $\log_2(M(2/p)) - 1$ **do**
10   /* Calculate width of smallest possible cell b containing o */
11   $w \leftarrow (2 \uparrow (i+1)) * M(r)$
12   /* Determine b's lower-left corner (x_{low}, y_{low}) */
13   $x_{low} \leftarrow$ (XCENT(o) $\div w) * w$
14   $y_{low} \leftarrow$ (YCENT(o) $\div w) * w$
15   /* Determine if b's expanded region contains o */
16   **if** $x_{low} - p * w/2 \le$ XCENT(o) $- r$ **and**
17   XCENT(o) $+ r \le x_{low} + (1 + p/2) * w$ **and**
18     $y_{low} - p * w/2 \le$ YCENT(o) $- r$ **and**
19   YCENT(o) $+ r \le y_{low} + (1 + p/2) * w$
20   **then exit_for_loop**
21   **endif**
22 **enddo**
23 **return**(FORMBLOCK(x_{low}, y_{low}, w, o))

5. DISCUSSION

The calculations of the possible containing quadtree cell widths for $p = 1/4$, $p = 1/2$, and $p = 1$ lead to the observation that as p takes larger values (even for p as small as $1/4$), the loose quadtree treats the input objects as if they are points and it is their centroid that determines their associated quadtree cell, while their size and the value of the cell expansion factor determine the size of their associated quadtree cell. Actually, the above statement must be tempered a bit. In particular, although it implies that the position of object o is not a factor in the determination of the width w of the expanded quadtree cell c with which o's MBH(o,b) is associated, this is not quite true as the existence of a range of values for the ratio $w/2r$ of the widths of c and b is a direct result of the variation in the position of o along with that of the value of p. However, as we showed above, for values of $p \ge 1/2$, the values of the ratio of the widths of c and b take on at most two values which differ by one where, in the case of $p \ge 1$, the only reason for the two possible ratio values is the fact that at times p takes on a value which is one less than a power of 2.

At this point, it is appropriate to ask what value p should one use. The answer must bear in mind that as p gets large, the radii (i.e., half the width) of the associated expanded quadtree cells get larger and thus they overlap adjacent quadtree cells of half the radius for $p = 1$ and of equal radius for $p = 2$, and even greater radii as p increases further. On the other hand, as p approaches 0, the radii of the quadtree cells associated with object o are increasingly dependent on the position of the centroid of object o and can get disproportionately large independent of the radius of o's minimum bounding hypercube box. The cardinality of the set of possible values of these radii is minimized at 1 when $p \ge 2$ with the exception of $p = 2^k - 1$ for integer values of k in which case the cardinality of the set is 2 corresponding to radius values 2^i and 2^{i+1} for some integer i. Clearly, there is no point in letting p get larger than 2 in which case the radius of the associated quadtree cell is pre-determined and depends solely on the value of the radius of o's minimum bounding hypercube box.

Thus we remain with the range $1/2 \leq p < 2$ for which the cardinality of the set of possible values of the radii of the quadtree cells is 2 corresponding to radius values 2^i and 2^{i+1} for some integer i. Our rationale for choosing p in this range is that the expanded quadtree cells are not so large as is the case for $p = 2$ and hence the extent of the overlap with adjacent quadtree cells is reduced, while the burden of having two possible radii for the quadtree cells is not great. Of course, procedure LOOSEQUADTREEINSERT in Section 4 is not as simple for $p = 1$ as it is for $p = 2$, in which case there is no need for the loop in lines 8–22. Nevertheless, for $p = 1$, the loop in lines 8–22 need only be executed twice, which is still quite simple. Ulrich [47] lets $p = 1$, while results of our experiments described in Section 6 make a case for choosing p to be infinitesimally smaller than 1. It is important to observe that all of the results that we have described hold for loose quadtrees of arbitrary dimension (e.g., three dimensions such as the loose octree) as they are all formulated in terms of the radii of the quadtree cells.

Algorithms that make use of the loose quadtree are simplified by our observation that the centroid of object o (actually of o's MBHR(o,b,r) is always contained in the non-expanded portion of the quadtree cell c with which o is associated. However, there are scenarios where users may wish to violate this property. For example, for certain values of r and p, r may be sufficiently small so that both the centroid of o lies in the expanded portion of c and o still fits in the expanded cell c. This situation is desirable when users want to move o as much as possible without having to associate it with another quadtree cell just because o's centroid is no longer in the non-expanded region of c. Interestingly, this modification does not change the ranges of relative cell widths as the example in Figure 3(c) still corresponds to the largest value of the ratio. The difference is that now the motion of the object so that the centroid of o is also in the expanded portion of c does not result in the association of o with another cell as long as o lies entirely in the expanded portion of c. Of course, this complicates subsequent searches (as well as delete operations), as now instead of just looking for a cell whose non-expanded portion contains the centroid of o, we must examine all possible cells whose expanded cells can contain o. Notice that in essence, we have transformed the search problem from one involving points (i.e., centroids of the objects) to one involving regions (i.e., the minimum bounding hypercube boxes of the objects).

6. EXPERIMENTAL EVALUATION

Experiments were run on a Linux (2.6.18) quad 1.86 GHz Xeon server with four gigabyte of RAM. The algorithms were implemented using GNU C++. The experiments studied the behavior of loose quadtrees in an environment where the objects are in motion. Our experimental setup consisted of a large collection of rectangle objects. For most, but not all, of our experiments, we used random rectangle data obtained by generating their centroid and extents at random, which is equivalent to the method used by Ulrich [47]. Each object (i.e, rectangle) in the collection is associated with its minimum enclosing quadtree cell (actually minimum enclosing expanded quadtree cell), which is represented by its bit-interleaved Morton representation [28]. The Morton representation is indexed using a B-tree index, which is referred to as a *linear* quadtree [14, 37].

In our setup, we use a non-spatial index (e.g., array, B-tree, Hash) to index the input objects by their identifier and a spatial index (i.e., loose quadtree in our case represented as a linear quadtree) to index the current positions of the objects. As an object's position changes, we first update its current position using the non-spatial index. This operation is fairly quick as updating the position of the object requires no modification to the non-spatial index itself. Next, we must update the spatial index which poses a real computational bottleneck as even small changes in the position of the object result in an update to the index. We remedy this problem to a limited extent by representing an object by the quadtree cell with which it is associated (not necessarily containing it as the loose quadtree permits objects to be associated with smaller cells). This means that the index does not store the exact geometry of the object. However, given that we know that the ratio of the sizes of the object's minimum enclosing expanded quadtree cell and of the object is bounded by a small value which is a function of p, we are in some sense implicitly recording the geometry of the object in the index. Moreover, the Morton representation that is stored in the B-tree contains a reference to the actual object, which is stored in an array and also indexed by the non-spatial index in order to facilitate quick updates, when necessary.

In this respect, the loose quadtree is distinguished from all other spatial indices, such as an R-tree, that explicitly store the positions of objects (i.e., rectangles). This means that when the position of an object changes, in the case of an R-tree and related spatial indices, we would have to always update the indices as they depend on the minimum bounding hypercube boxes of the objects which have changed, while in the case of the loose quadtrees, we only need to update the index if if the object is associated with a different quadtree cell. This property of the loose quadtree makes it attractive for serving as a spatial index for moving object applications. In contrast, as we pointed out, updates in spatial indices such as the R-tree, as well as other related spatiotemporal indices, will often require a complete rebuild step when the position of the object changes, which is quite complicated. Nevertheless, for the sake of completeness, we provide a comparison of comparison of loose quadtree with a suitable implementation of a R-tree in Section 7.

We ran a number of experiments to test the sensitivity of the loose quadtree to the motion of the objects that it stores. We used a collection of one million randomly generated rectangles in a two-dimensional space, which were stored in a B-tree based loose quadtree index. Our implementation of the B-tree is single threaded with a node size of 8 kb that can store up to 64 objects per node. Furthermore, we cache 10% of the nodes in an in-memory cache. The non-spatial index is an in-memory array indexed by the object identifier. For this set of experiments we chose a disk-based data structure such as a B-tree to index the objects instead of an in-memory spatial data structure. The B-tree is better than the pointer-based quadtree in the sense that it provides access to each quadtree cell (node) in the tree using its locational code in constant time (i.e., time proportional to the height of the B-tree, which we view as a constant) whereas in the pointer-based quadtree our access time is proportional to the base 2 logarithm of the width (i.e., maximum depth) of the underlying embedding space.

We let the expansion factor p vary between 0 and 5. Recall that for the case $p = 0$, the loose quadtree corresponds to an MX-CIF quadtree. We first built an index for all the objects in a loose quadtree for a given p. Next, we translated the objects in order to mimic a moving object application. If the translations resulted in an object being associated with a different quadtree cell, then we updated the index, which involves deleting an entry from the B-tree index and adding a new entry corresponding to the minimum expanded quadtree cell containing the object after the translation. We tabulated the number of objects for which the index needed to be updated. We controlled the motion of the objects using a value s, denoting the maximum translation of the object across a single dimension. For example, suppose that s is 5%, then all of the rectangles are translated across each of the dimensions by a value that is at most 5% of its side length across each of the dimensions.

In order to provide a better understanding of the effect of motion on the loose quadtree index, we distinguish between two types of motion, namely *uniform* and *fixed* translations. In the case of a uniform translation, the motion is controlled by a random variable, which is bounded by s. In other words, all the objects are subjected to different translations, where the translation across any dimension is less than s. In the case of a fixed translation, all of the objects are translated by a fixed value (i.e., s) across each of the dimensions, which basically represents the worst case scenario (in terms of the maximum amount of motion) of any moving object application.

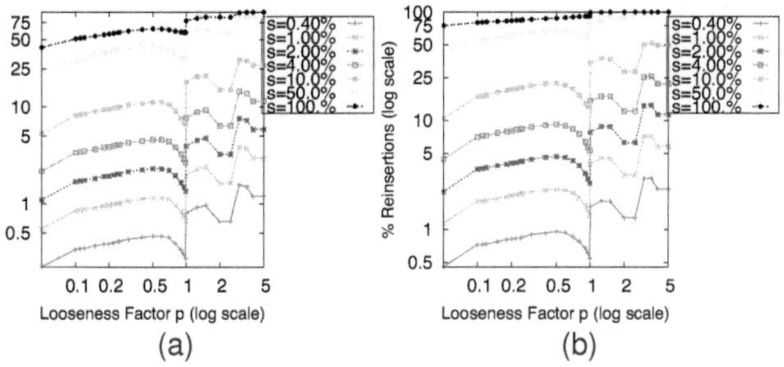

Figure 4: Reinsertion rates for two-dimensional rectangle input for varying values of p and s with $\delta = 10$, for a) uniform and b) fixed translations.

Finally, we also varied the sizes of the input rectangle objects by using the value δ, which denotes the ratio of the largest side length of a rectangle object in the data set to the smallest side length of a rectangle object in the data set. It should be clear that a large value of δ means a large range of rectangle object sizes, while a small value of δ means that the rectangle objects are more or less of the same size. All of the experiments whose results we present varied one or more of these variables to showcase the utility of loose quadtrees for moving object applications. Note that this is a far more extensive experimental evaluation than the one conducted by Ulrich [47] who only studied the loose quadtree's behavior for culling operations and only compared the $p = 0$ and $p = 1$ cases.

Our first experiment considered the case of one million two-dimensional rectangle objects for values of p ranging between 0 and 5, and values of s ranging between 0.40% and 100%. The value of δ was kept constant at 10. Figure 4 shows the percentage of objects that required reinsertion as a function of p, while the different curves in the plot show the behavior of the loose quadtree index for different values of s. As expected, the percentage of objects that require reinsertion increases as s increases. From the figure, we observe that this percentage increases with p with a precipitous drop at $p = 0.999$ where the results are comparable to $p = 0$. Figure 5 provides a more vivid illustration of the comparability of the results for $p = 0.999$ with those for $p = 0$ by showing the result of normalizing the reinsertion rates for the different values of p and s vis-a-vis those for $p = 0.999$. Here we see that the reinsertion rate for $p = 0.999$ is superior to the other values of p for all reasonable values of s (i.e., less than s <50%). It is interesting to note that for all values of s, for small values of p, this percentage increases with p with a local maximum at around $p = 0.5$, at which time it has a precipitous drop at $p = 0.999$ where the results are comparable to $p = 0$, and then increases sharply for $p = 1$, and continues to increase, but at a lesser rate, as p continues to increase (i.e., p >1). This phenomenon is explained in greater detail below.

The percentage of objects requiring reinsertion is relatively low at $p = 0$ since the range of the values of the side lengths of the minimum enclosing quadtree cells is large as is also the value of the maximum side length. This means that objects often have a large area in which to move without requiring reinsertion. As p in-

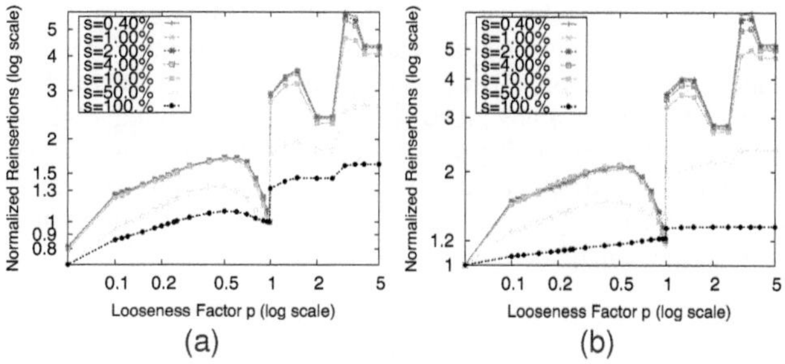

Figure 5: Reinsertions for two-dimensional rectangle input for varying values of p and s with $\delta = 10$, normalized with the reinsertion rate for $p = 0.999$ for a) uniform and b) fixed translations.

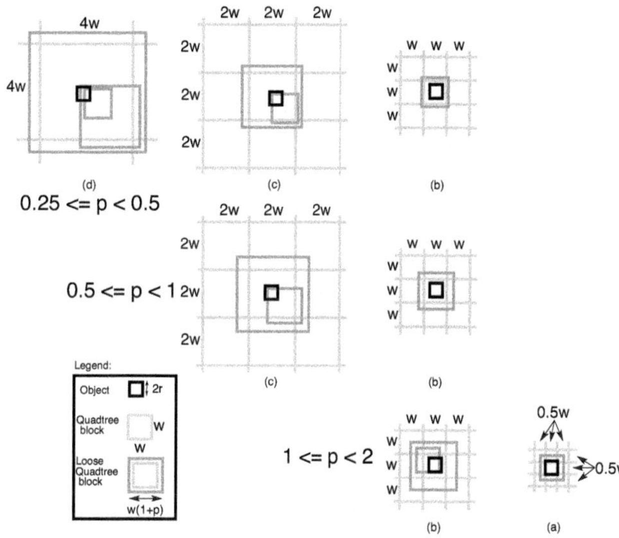

Figure 6: Illustration of the variation of the relative sizes of the minimum enclosing expanded quadtree cells and of the minimum bounding hypercube boxes of the objects with respect to different ranges of values of p: (first row) 0.25≤p<0.5, (second row) 0.5≤p<1, and (third row) 1≤p<2.

creases, we observe that the range of values of the side lengths of the minimum enclosing expanded quadtree cells become increasingly smaller, which means that the area in which the objects can move without requiring reinsertion gets smaller. Figure 6 illustrates this observation using an example object with minimum bounding hypercube box of radius r. In particular, we can see that for values of p in the range $[0.25, 0.5)$, the side length of the minimum enclosing expanded quadtree cell is either 2, 4, or 8 times the radius of the minimum bounding hypercube box of the object (first row of Figure 6) ; while for values of p in the ranges $[0.5, 1)$, the side length of the minimum enclosing expanded quadtree cell is either 2 or 4 times the radius of the minimum bounding hypercube box of the object (second row of Figure 6); and for values of p in the ranges $[1, 2)$ the side length of the minimum enclosing expanded quadtree cell is either 1 or 2 times the radius of the minimum bounding hypercube box of the object (third row of Figure 6). Notice that the percentage of objects requiring reinsertion starts to decrease at $p = 0.5$ with a minimum at $p = 0.999$. This is because at $p = 0.5$ there are only two choices for the size of the minimum enclosing expanded quadtree cell, having eliminated the cell with side length 8 times the radius of the minimum bounding hypercube box of the object. Moreover, the number of objects associated with the eliminated cell are relatively small. On the other hand, at $p = 1$, there are again only two choices for the minimum enclosing expanded quadtree cell, but now a large such cell is replaced by one with a quarter of its area thereby greatly limiting the ability of the objects to move without requiring reinsertion. The pattern of increasing percentages requiring reinsertion continues unabated for $p > 1$ as we have increasingly smaller replacement cells with saw-tooth like behavior in the neighborhood of $p = 2^k$.

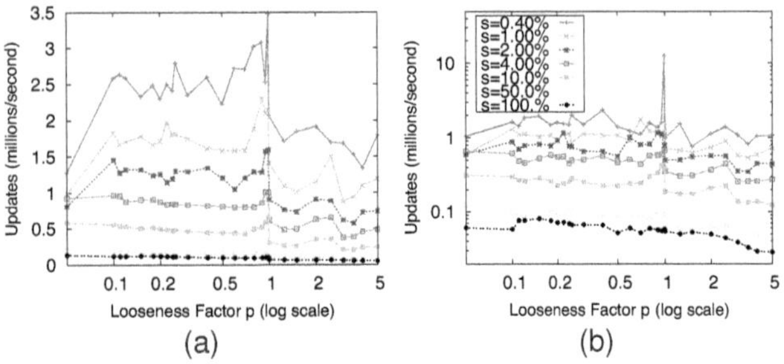

Figure 7: Update rates for two-dimensional rectangle objects for varying values of p and s with $\delta = 10$, for a) uniform and b) fixed translations.

For some data structures, the update process can be sped up by batching the updates using bulk loading methods (e.g., [5, 48, 10, 17]). For example, Dittrich et al. [10] assume that updates can come at fast rates so it may not be good to handle one update at a time. Instead, they use "snapshots", which are basically large static data structures and an update pool, which is a fast data structure stored in the main memory. In this case, updates are collected in the update pool, and once enough of them have been accumulated, they are applied en mass to the snapshot structure to create a new snapshot structure; hence a variant of bulk updates which are cheaper than single updates. In our method, all insertions and deletions are always performed in O(1) time, and thus there is no need for pooling the updates.

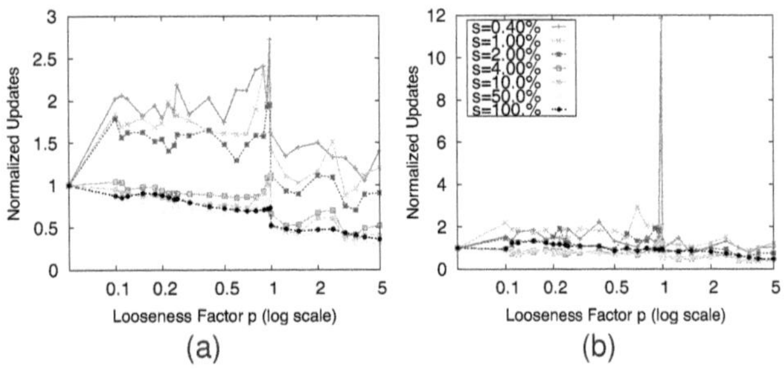

Figure 8: Update rates for two-dimensional rectangle objects for varying values of p and s with $\delta = 10$, normalized with the reinsertion rate for $p = 0$ for a) uniform and b) fixed translations.

The second set of experiments used the above environment and measured the number of updates in millions/second that can be supported by the loose quadtree data structure since this correlates with updating the spatial index with the new positions of the objects. Recall that an update in a loose quadtree involves deleting an entry from the B-tree index and inserting another entry. The key advantage of the loose quadtree structure is that small motions of objects, most likely, do not require any changes to the index, and if they do, then they are less complex as p becomes increasingly larger than 0 since the range of possible minimum enclosing expanded quadtree cells is much smaller. Figure 7 shows the number of updates in millions/second that a loose quadtree index can support under both the uniform and fixed translation cases. We see that this number decreases as s increases with performance generally peaking at $p = 0.999$, although this is most noticeable for s <50%. We also observe that the number of updates per second for a given value of s does not vary greatly across different value of p with the exception of relatively small values of s (0.40% and 1.0%), for which performance peaks noticeably at $p = 0.999$, especially with respect to $p = 0$. Figure 8 provides a more vivid illustration of this improvement by showing the result of normalizing the number of updates per second for the different values of p and s vis-a-vis those for $p = 0$, where for a fixed translation s =0.40% we see a one order of magnitude improvement. Again, these results are primarily due to the dramatically reduced cost of insertion since the new minimum enclosing expanded quadtree cell can be determined in at most 2 look up operations for $p = 0.999$ versus a significantly higher number for $p = 0$. This figure shows that the improved throughput is observed for most values of p for $s \leq 50\%$.

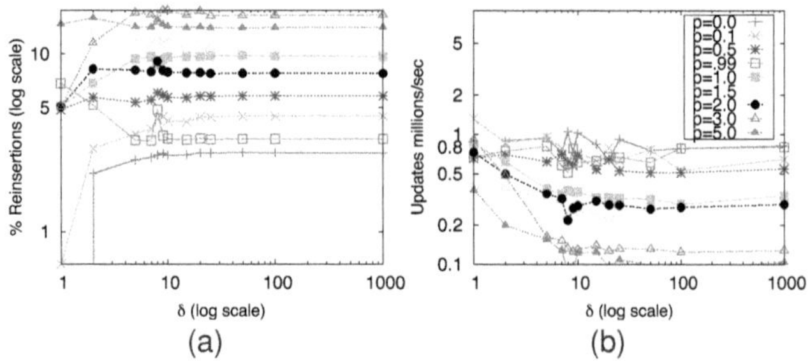

Figure 9: a) Reinsertion and b) update rates in millions/second for two-dimensional rectangle input for varying values of δ and p keeping s=5% with uniform translations.

The third set of experiments examined the effect of varying δ on the performance of the loose quadtree data structure. Recall that δ bounds the ratio of the length of the largest side of a rectangle object in the input data set to the length of the smallest side of a rectangle object in the input data set. In other words, if δ is small, then all the objects in the input are of the same size. If δ is large, then the objects are of different sizes. Figure 9 measures the reinsertion and update rates in millions/second for varying values of δ and p, keeping s fixed at 5% with uniform translations. We can see that both the reinsertion and update rates are relatively independent of δ, which means that the loose quadtree data structure is suitable for handling data sets containing objects of varying sizes.

Finally, we compared the efficacy of loose quadtrees on a real world data set. We used a 2D rectangle data set generated from taking a TIGER road data set of Los Angeles County, CA and then fitting a bounding box around the line segments forming the edges in the road network. This resulted in a data set containing 267K 2D rectangles with a good mix of rectangles of different sizes. We subjected the input rectangles to both uniform and fixed translations as in prior experiments described in Figures 4 and 7. As before, we report both the percentage of the objects that had to be reinserted due to the translation, and the time that it took to perform the reinsertion (i.e., to update the data structure) which we report in terms of the number of updates per second. Figure 10a and 10c shows the percentage of updates (i.e., reinsertions) needed for uniform and fixed translations, and once again it is easy to see that, for $p = 0.999$, very few updates to the data structure are needed. Figure 10b and 10d shows the number of updates per second for uniform and fixed translations, and again it is not surprising that, for $p = 0.999$, the number of updates that can be done per second sky rockets due to the savings in the reinsertion cost.

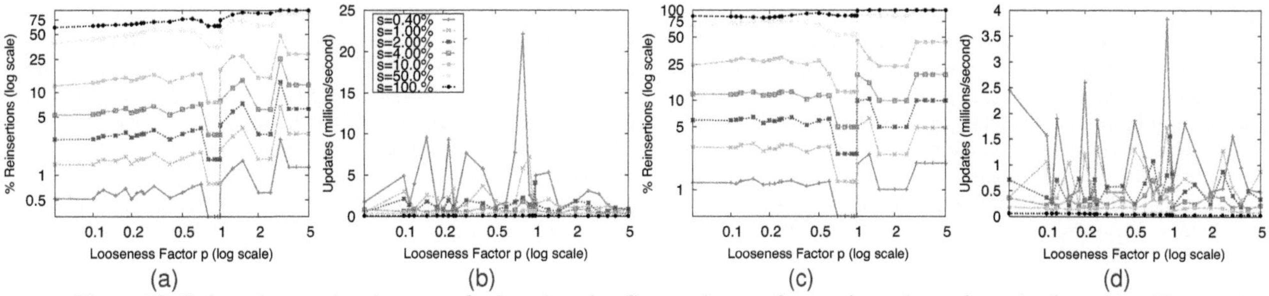

Figure 10: Reinsertions and update rates for Los Angeles County data set for varying values of p and s for a–b) uniform and c–d) fixed translations

7. N-BODY SIMULATION

We also ran a set of experiments designed to replicate common conditions for object dimension, object placement, object movement, and object frequency based on modern video games. The data structure was tested using an N-body simulation [30] which consists of insertion, deletion, update, range, and collision detection queries on the data structure that stores them. We record how much time is needed to fixed number of frames, as well as operation statistics for different numbers of objects and values of p. During each frame, objects are allowed to move, to receive force from external sources to simulate player interaction, and to collide with each other. Every object is processed in a physics engine and the objects are stored using a loose quadtree (with values of the expansion factor p ranging from 0 to 1.0). The physics engine works by processing every object in the simulation every frame. If an object is moving, then the engine performs a range query on the area occupied by the object's bounding hypercube box to return a list of hit objects. Each hit object is then entered into a physics equation and the object's velocities and positions (i.e., trajectories) are updated. At any given time, about 50% of the objects are moving over our entire 1 kilometer squared game universe.

These experiments were run on a Windows 7 enterprise quad core 2.6GHz I7 workstation with eight gigabytes of 1600MHz DDR3 RAM and an Nvidia GT650m discrete GPU. The simulation and related code were compiled using Microsoft Visual Studio 2010's integrated 32 bit compiler. The experiments compared the MX-CIF quadtree ($p = 0$) with variants of the loose quadtree for a few values of p. A pointer-based quadtree implementation was used here in order to simplify the algorithms as the main focus was on evaluating the efficacy of the loose quadtree data structure for the moving object applications such as, but not limited to, video games. In addition, the pointer-based environment enables all execution to occur in main memory which is the environment used in video games.

The rest of this section is organized as follows. Section 7.1 provides more details on the update (i.e., insertion) costs in comparison to the total cost of the N-body simulation. Section 7.2 examines the costs of the different queries involved in the N-body simulation as well as the scalability of the loose quadtree. In order to provide an additional reference point on our performance measures, Section 7.3 reports on a limited comparison with an R-tree data structure in terms of insertion costs and times for a window query as part of the N-body simulation. Extensive modifications were needed to make the R-tree work in this setting due to its inherently poor insertion behavior as outlined in the prologue of this section.

7.1 Insertion and N-Body Simulation Costs

The N-body simulation consists of two-dimensional objects that interact with one another. Each object exerts a force on all the other objects in the scene and consequently each object moves due to the resulting force that is applied on it. In such a simulation, computing the force interaction between the objects is the single most time-consuming operation. Periodically, a large radial force is exerted on the system. These explosions are designed to simulate common game play cases where movement of many objects occurs in only a subset of the game universe. However, since all the objects move by varying amounts, updating the spatial data structure used to index the objects can be a significant bottleneck. We use this setup to test the update performance of the MX-CIF quadtree and three variants of the loose quadtree having p values of 0.5, 0.999 and 1.0.

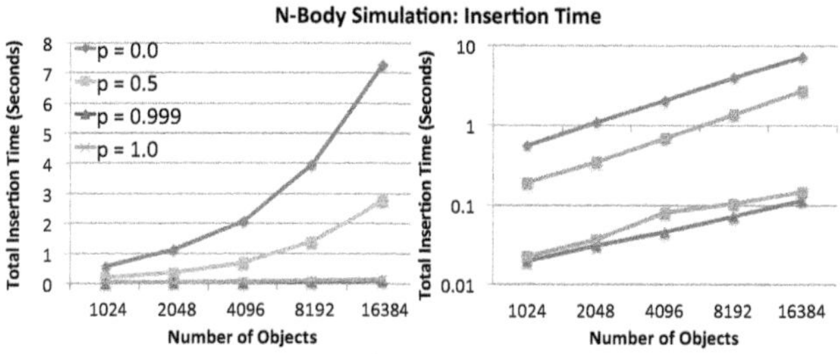

Figure 11: CPU execution time for insertions in the N-body simulation using a normal scale (left) and a log scale (right).

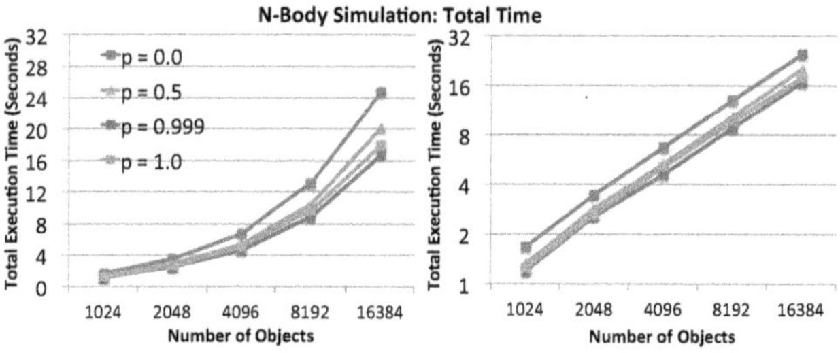

Figure 12: CPU execution time for insertions in the N-body simulation using a normal scale (left) and a log scale (right).

The total execution time is recorded which corresponds to the number of seconds required to perform the simulation for a fixed number of time steps. We record the total time in seconds spent performing insertion operations into the loose quadtree during execution of the N-body simulation. We also record the total number of insertion operations needed (i.e., the number of objects that need to be reinserted after a motion). Figure 11 shows amount of time spent doing insertion using both a normal scale (left of Figure 11) and a log scale (right of Figure 11), while Figure 12 shows the total amount of time spent in the N-body simulation using both a normal scale (left of Figure 12) and a log scale (right of Figure 12). Note the similar behavior for the four variants with $p = 0.999$ performing the best. In fact, there is a one half order of magnitude difference in the insertion and total N-body simulation execution times between $p = 0$ and $p = 0.999$. It is interesting to note that the difference between the total execution times of the N-body simulation with the use of $p = 0.999$ versus with the use of $p = 0$ is accounted for by the savings in the insertion costs (approximately 7 seconds). Figure 13 shows the relatively large reduction in the number of objects that need reinsertion when using $p = 0.999$ vis-a-vis $p = 0$. It is also interesting to note that all of the log plots show a linear relationship which means that all of the statistics that we collected obey a power law of $y = ax^b$ where a and b are constants with b varying between 1.60 and 1.75. It is clear from this data that the loose quadtree outperforms the MX-CIF quadtree ($p = 0$), and that the value of $p = 0.999$ leads to better performance than $p = 1$. In fact, we see almost two orders of magnitude less insertions for $p = 0.999$ vis-a-vis $p = 0$. In the case of $p = 1.0$ and $p = 0.999$ we see reductions as high as 30% in both the total number of insertions (Figure 13) and time spent in insertions (Figure 11), and as high as 10% in the total execution time of the N-body simulation, which is less as expected since we are looking at the total execution time which involves more operations than insertions, but is still very good.

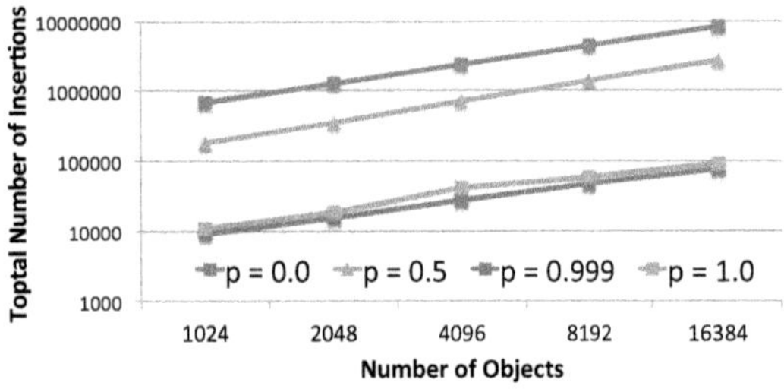

Figure 13: Number of insertions in the N-body simulation using a log scale.

7.2 Query Performance and Scalability

We now examine the performance of the loose quadtree for the queries that form the key geometric operations in an N-body simulation. Our motivation is to show that the good update performance of the loose quadtree (i.e., minimization of reinsertions upon object motion) does not come at the expense of query performance, and that it scales. In order to do this, our first set of experiments measured the time taken to perform a number of different queries as well as recorded the number of blocks and objects in the loose quadtree that are visited by each query. Our second set of experiments examines the performance of the loose quadtree on simulations with varying sizes of objects. In particular, we show that the loose quadtrees can scale to handle really large simulations way beyond the limitations of the MX-CIF quadtree (i.e., a loose quadtree with $p = 0$).

In order to test the query performance of the data structures, we use a different environment than the one in Section 7.1. In particular, we recreate a game environment to simulate a complex 3D scene. In this scenario, the objects do not exert force on one another but move due to gravity. Hence, the bottleneck in this environment is not computing the inter-object forces but rather capturing the interactions between the objects as they collide with one another. Capturing these interactions between the objects requires knowledge of which objects are in close proximity to which other objects in the scene. All objects in the environment are updated dynamically using a physics simulation solver. Furthermore, we also render the scene which requires the application of geometrical operations such as ray tracing, view frustum culling and window queries on the spatial data structures.

We note that the time taken to compute each time step in the simulation is roughly broken down as follows: About 70% of the time is spent on updating the data structure, 20% of the time is spent on performing geometric operations such as frustum culling, ray tracing, window and nearest neighbor search, while the remaining 10% of the time is spent on rendering the scene. Note that rendering is GPU assisted, so that the 10% time only corresponds to the time needed to transfer the objects to the GPU, which makes it relatively independent of the complexity of the scene. Moreover, the time taken to render the scene is also common to all the data structures that we examine in this section.

Below, we examine the time needed to execute a number of queries as part of an N-body simulation with 14,000 dynamic objects. Figure 14a shows the average times in nanoseconds needed to perform each of the queries, while Figure 14b shows the average number of blocks and objects visited while processing the queries. RAY corresponds to ray tracing which is used to find the objects that intersect a single ray (i.e., line) in the scene. FRUS refers to the frustum culling operation which identifies all the objects that are inside the scene being rendered. Geometrically speaking, this operation captures the intersection of a hyperplane with the objects in the simulation. NN refers to a nearest neighbor search that given an object o, find another object that is closest to o. In an N-body simulation, NN is used for collision detection purposes. Finally, WIN-L and WIN-S capture window (region) query operations that obtain a list of objects overlapping with a window query, where WIN-L is a large window search that covers most of the blocks in the data structure, while WIN-S applies a smaller window that only intersects a few blocks.

Figure 14a shows that $p = 0.999$ performs better than $p = 0$ for all query cases. The figure also indicates the percentage improvement resulting from use of $p = 0.999$ over the MX-CIF quadtree ($p = 0$). In particular, the loose quadtree yields an improvement of up to 43% over the MX-CIF quadtree for these common spatial queries. Furthermore, $p = 0.999$ performs better than $p = 1$ for all cases, although the difference is often too small to be discernible in the figure. It is interesting to note from Figure 14b that $p = 0.999$ and 1 both visited more blocks than $p = 0$. This is not surprising as the MX-CIF quadtree is sensitive to the position and size of the objects which results in its association of many objects with the larger-sized blocks in the quadtree thereby ultimately using fewer blocks. On the other hand, the loose quadtree, whether at $p = 0.999$ or $p = 1$, is not sensitive to the position of the objects so it distributes the objects more evenly using up more blocks. However, as can be seen in Figure 14b, the MX-CIF quadtree examines way too many objects resulting in wasted work. On the other hand, the loose quadtree for our values of p (i.e., 0.999 and 1). only examines blocks that have the potential to contain relevant objects but it needs to look at more of them. Even though these two forces negate each other, they still result in the loose quadtree outperforming the MX-CIF quadtree for our values of p.

Notwithstanding the query performance of the loose quadtree, it is important to note that the act of updating objects constitutes the majority of the time of an N-body simulation, which is where the loose quadtree really excels. Figure 15 shows the update cost incurred per frame due to the moving objects in the scene as well as the time needed in milliseconds to render a frame using the loose quadtree with $p = 0.999$ and MX-CIF quadtree for varying sizes of the simulation. The performance of $p = 1$ is slightly worse than $p = 0.999$ but better than the MX-CIF quadtree and is not shown in the Figure. From the figure we see that the loose quadtree can render frames 2–5 times faster than the MX-CIF quadtree. In particular, even at 100,000 objects, the loose quadtree could still sustain about 5 frames per second (210 milliseconds per frame) in contrast to the MX-CIF quadtree which at this size could not even render one frame per second (to be precise it took 1.4 seconds per frame). To put the size of the problem in a proper perspective, we note that current commercial games available in the market as of 2012 typically do not involve more 15,000 thousand moving objects [8]. In

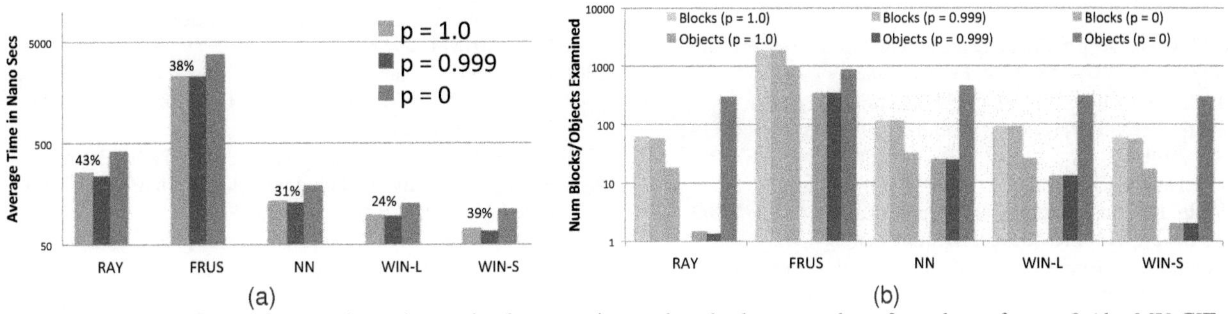

Figure 14: (a) Query times, using a log scale, for operations using the loose quadtree for values of $p = 0$ (the MX-CIF quadtree), $p = 0.999$, and $p = 1$ where $p = 0.999$ performs best as indicated with the percent improvement over the MX-CIF quadtree. (b) The average number of blocks and objects visited by the query

this sense, we have shown that using loose quadtree makes it possible to scale significantly these simulations vis-a-vis the state of the art. Furthermore, from Figure 15 we see that the time spent needed to update the underlying data structure using an MX-CIF quadtree is at least 3 times more expensive when compared with the time needed when using a loose quadtree with $p \approx 1$.

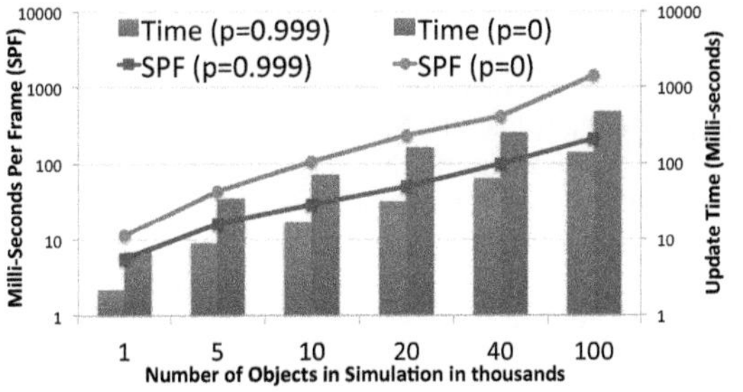

Figure 15: Figure shows the milliseconds to render a frame and the time in milliseconds spent per frame to update the data structure for varying sizes of the simulations

7.3 R-tree

We have justified the use of the loose quadtree which permits p to vary by comparing it with the MX-CIF quadtree which is a loose quadtree with $p = 0$. In order to provide an additional reference point we also present a limited comparison with the R-tree data structure, described in Section 1, which is an object hierarchy that makes use of minimum bounding hypercube boxes somewhat in the same spirit as the MX-CIF quadtree except that the hierarchies of different sets of objects are not in registration. We used the Hilbert R-tree [23] in our comparison as it is easy to construct. However, as expected, we found that updating the position of the objects in the R-tree for each individual object was prohibitively expensive, taking several orders of magnitude time more than the loose quadtree to perform the reinsertions upon execution of an update after a motion thereby making it practically unusable. Therefore, in order to improve the R-tree's performance, we batched up all the objects that required reinsertion and then reinserted them as a single batch rather than one at a time. This approach was found to be faster than rebuilding the structure from scratch. For the simulation with 14,000 objects, the update time for the R-tree structure was 106.99 milliseconds per frame of the simulation. In comparison, the update time for $p = 0.999$ was 22.11 milliseconds, while for the MX-CIF quadtree (i.e., $p = 0$), it was 82.26 milliseconds. So, our modified R-tree structure was still 25% worse than the MX-CIF quadtree but significantly worse (i.e., 5 times worse) than the loose quadtree with $p = 0.999$.

Next, we compared the query performance of the R-tree for the two window queries, WIN-L and WIN-S. Using the R-tree, the average time to execute them was 167 nanoseconds for WIN-L and 142 nanoseconds for WIN-S. In contrast, the query times of WIN-L and WIN-S were 128 and 113 nanoseconds, respectively, for the MX-CIF quadtree and 98 and 73 nanoseconds, respectively, for $p = 0.999$. These results show that the loose quadtree is superior even when compared against an appropriately modified R-tree variant resulting in the loose quadtree being almost twice as fast.

8. CONCLUDING REMARKS

We have shown how to determine for a loose quadtree the maximum possible width w of the minimum enclosing expanded quadtree cell c for an object o with MBHR(o,b,r) and cell expansion factor p. We have also shown that w is independent of the position of o. This property enables determining the cell with which o is associated and can be used, for example, in an algorithm to build a loose quadtree in an environment that deploys a pointerless quadtree. In particular, this independence means that the algorithm requires little or no search and could be used, for example, to populate a spatial database with the latest wave of multiprocessors such as those that make use of GPUs (e.g., [27]). It could also be used in point cloud applications (e.g., [39]). Our experiments (including the N-body simulation which did not rely on a pointerless quadtree) have demonstrated that letting p take on a value infinitesimally smaller than 1 leads to the best results in minimizing the need to update the index when objects are moving thereby increasing the size of the collection (i.e., database) of objects that can be supported. This is in contrast to the conventional use of $p = 1$ [47].

9. REFERENCES

[1] D. J. Abel and J. L. Smith. A data structure and algorithm based on a linear key for a rectangle retrieval problem. *CVGIP*, 24(1):1–13, Oct. 1983.

[2] D. J. Abel and J. L. Smith. A data structure and query algorithm for a database of areal entities. *Australian Computer Journal*, 16(4):147–154, Nov. 1984.

[3] A. Aboulnaga and J. F. Naughton. Accurate estimation of the cost of spatial selections. In *ICDE*, pp. 123–134, San Diego, CA, Feb. 2000.

[4] W. G. Aref and H. Samet. Efficient processing of window queries in the pyramid data structure. In *PODS*, pp. 265–272, Nashville, TN, Apr. 1990.

[5] L. Arge, K. H. Hinrichs, J. Vahrenhold, and J. S. Vitter. Efficient bulk operations on dynamic R-trees. In *ALENEX*, LNCS 1619, pp. 328–348, Baltimore, MD, Jan. 1999.

[6] N. Beckmann, H.-P. Kriegel, R. Schneider, and B. Seeger. The R*-tree: an efficient and robust access method for points

and rectangles. In *SIGMOD*, pp. 322–331, Atlantic City, NJ, June 1990.

[7] T. M. Chan. Approximate nearest neighbor queries revisited. In *SCG*, pp. 352–358, Nice, France, June 1997.

[8] D. Collin. Culling the battlefield data oriented design in practice. *Game Developers Conference*, San Francisco, CA, Feb. 2011.

[9] A. J. Demers, J. Gehrke, C. Koch, B. Sowell, and W. M. White. Database research in computer games. In *SIGMOD*, pp. 1011–1014, Providence, RI, June 2009.

[10] J. Dittrich, L. Blunschi, and M. A. Vaz Salles. Indexing moving objects using short-lived throwaway indexes. *SSTD*, LNCS 5644, pp. 189–207, Aalborg, Denmark, July 2009.

[11] C. Esperança and H. Samet. Experience with SAND/Tcl: a scripting tool for spatial databases. *JVLC*, 13(2):229–255, Apr. 2002.

[12] A. U. Frank. Problems of realizing LIS: storage methods for space related data: the fieldtree. TR 71, ETH, Zurich, Switzerland, June 1983.

[13] A. U. Frank and R. Barrera. The Fieldtree: a data structure for geographic information systems. In *SSD*, LNCS 409, pp. 29–44, Santa Barbara, CA, July 1989.

[14] I. Gargantini. An effective way to represent quadtrees. *CACM*, 25(12):905–910, Dec. 1982.

[15] A. Guttman. R-trees: a dynamic index structure for spatial searching. In *SIGMOD*, pp. 47–57, Boston, June 1984.

[16] E. Haines. Loose octrees for dynamic raytracing. The ray tracing news, Aug. 2001.

[17] G. R. Hjaltason and H. Samet. Speeding up construction of PMR quadtree-based spatial indexes. *VLDBJ*, 11(2): 109–137, Oct. 2002.

[18] E. G. Hoel and H. Samet. Benchmarking spatial join operations with spatial output. In *VLDB*, pp. 606–618, Zurich, Switzerland, Sept. 1995.

[19] A. Hutflesz, H.-W. Six, and P. Widmayer. The R-file: an efficient access structure for proximity queries. In *ICDE*, pp. 372–379, Los Angeles, Feb. 1990.

[20] E. Jacox and H. Samet. Spatial join techniques. *TODS*, 32(1):7, Mar. 2007.

[21] E. Jacox and H. Samet. Metric space similarity joins. *TODS*, 33(2):7, June 2008.

[22] C. S. Jensen, D. Lin, and B. C. Ooi. Query and update efficient B^+-tree based indexing of moving objects. In *VLDB*, pp. 768–779, Toronto, Canada, Sept. 2004.

[23] I. Kamel and C. Faloutsos. Hilbert R-tree: an improved R-tree using fractals. In *VLDB*, pp. 500–509, Santiago, Chile, Sept. 1994.

[24] G. Kedem. The quad-CIF tree: a data structure for hierarchical on-line algorithms. In *DAC*, pp. 352–357, Las Vegas, NV, June 1982.

[25] G. Kollios, D. Papadopoulos, D. Gunopulos, and V. J. Tsotras. Indexing mobile objects using dual transformations. *VLDBJ*, 14(2):238–256, Apr. 2005.

[26] S. Liao, M. A. Lopez, and S. T. Leutenegger. High dimensional similarity search with space filling curves. In *ICDE*, pp. 615–622, Heidelberg, Germany, Apr. 2001.

[27] M. D. Lieberman, J. Sankaranarayanan, and H. Samet. A fast similarity join algorithm using graphics processing units. In *ICDE*, pp. 1111–1120, Cancun, Mexico, Apr. 2008.

[28] G. M. Morton. A computer oriented geodetic data base and a new technique in file sequencing. TR, IBM Ltd., Ottawa, Canada, 1966.

[29] T. Nguyen, Z. He, R. Zhang, and P. Ward. Boosting moving object indexing through velocity partitioning. *VLDB*, 5(9):860–871, 2012.

[30] L. Nyland, M. Harris, and J. Prins. Fast n-body simulation with CUDA. In *GPU Gems 3*, pp. 677–695. Addison-Wesley, Upper Saddle River, NJ, 2007.

[31] J. M. Patel, Y. Chen, and V. P. Chakka. STRIPES: an efficient index for predicted trajectories. In *SIGMOD*, pp. 635–646, Paris, France, June 2004.

[32] D. Pfoser and C. S. Jensen. Trajectory indexing using movement constraints. *GeoInformatica*, 9(2):93–115, 2005.

[33] S. Šaltenis, C. S. Jensen, S. T. Leutenegger, and M. A. López. Indexing the positions of continuously moving objects. In *SIGMOD*, pp. 331–342, Dallas, TX, May 2000.

[34] H. Samet. A quadtree medial axis transform. *CACM*, 26(9):680–693, Sept. 1983.

[35] H. Samet. Reconstruction of quadtrees from quadtree medial axis transforms. *CVGIP*, 29(3):311–328, Mar. 1985.

[36] H. Samet. Depth-first k-nearest neighbor finding using the MaxNearestDist estimator. In *IAPR*, pp. 486–491, Mantova, Italy, Sept. 2003.

[37] H. Samet. *Foundations of Multidimensional and Metric Data Structures*. Morgan-Kaufmann, San Francisco, 2006.

[38] H. Samet, A. Rosenfeld, C. A. Shaffer, and R. E. Webber. A geographic information system using quadtrees. *PR*, 17(6):647–656, November/December 1984.

[39] J. Sankaranarayanan, H. Samet, and A. Varshney. A fast all nearest neighbor algorithm for applications involving large point-clouds. *C&G*, 31(2):157–174, Apr. 2007.

[40] K. Sevcik and N. Koudas. Filter trees for managing spatial data over a range of size granularities. In *VLDB*, pp. 16–27, Mumbai (Bombay), India, Sept. 1996.

[41] C. A. Shaffer, H. Samet, and R. C. Nelson. QUILT: a geographic information system based on quadtrees. *IJGIS*, 4(2):103–131, April–June 1990.

[42] D. Šidlauskas, K. A. Ross, C. S. Jensen, and S. Šaltenis. Thread-level parallel indexing of update intensive moving-object workloads. In *Adv. in STD*, LNCS 6849, pp. 186–204. 2011.

[43] D. Šidlauskas, S. Šaltenis, and C. S. Jensen. Parallel main memory indexing for moving-object query and update workloads. In *SIGMOD*, pp. 37–48, Scottsdale, AZ, June 2012.

[44] H.-W. Six and P. Widmayer. Spatial searching in geometric databases. In *ICDE*, pp. 496–503, Los Angeles, Feb. 1988.

[45] E. Tanin, A. Harwood, and H. Samet. A distributed quadtree index for peer-to-peer settings. In *ICDE*, pp. 254–255, Tokyo, Japan, Apr. 2005.

[46] Y. Tao, D. Papadias, and J. Sun. The TPR*-tree: an optimized spatio-temporal access method for predictive queries. In *VLDB*, pp. 790–801, Berlin, Germany, Sept. 2003.

[47] T. Ulrich. Loose octrees. In *Game Programming Gems*, pp. 444–453. Charles River Media, Rockland, MA, 2000.

[48] J. van den Bercken, B. Seeger, and P. Widmayer. A generic approach to bulk loading multidimensional index structures. In *VLDB*, pp. 406–415, Athens, Greece, Aug. 1997.

[49] M. L. Yiu, Y. Tao, and N. Mamoulis. The B^{dual}-tree: indexing moving objects by space filling curves in the dual space. *VLDBJ*, 17(3):379–400, Sept. 2008.

I/O Efficient: Computing SCCs in Massive Graphs

Zhiwei Zhang†, Jeffrey Xu Yu†, Lu Qin†, Lijun Chang‡, Xuemin Lin‡

†The Chinese University of Hong Kong, China, {zwzhang,yu,lqin}@se.cuhk.edu.hk

‡The University of New South Wales, Australia, {ljchang,lxue}@cse.unsw.edu.au

ABSTRACT

A strongly connected component (SCC) is a maximal subgraph of a directed graph G in which every pair of nodes are reachable from each other in the SCC. With such a property, a general directed graph can be represented by a directed acyclic graph (*DAG*) by contracting an SCC of G to a node in *DAG*. In many real applications that need graph pattern matching, topological sorting, or reachability query processing, the best way to deal with a general directed graph is to deal with its *DAG* representation. Therefore, finding all SCCs in a directed graph G is a critical operation. The existing in-memory algorithms based on depth first search (*DFS*) can find all SCCs in linear time w.r.t. the size of a graph. However, when a graph cannot resident entirely in the main memory, the existing external or semi-external algorithms to find all SCCs have limitation to achieve high I/O efficiency. In this paper, we study new I/O efficient semi-external algorithms to find all SCCs for a massive directed graph G that cannot reside in main memory entirely. To overcome the deficiency of the existing *DFS* based semi-external algorithm that heavily relies on a total order, we explore a weak order based on which we investigate new algorithms. We propose a new two phase algorithm, namely, tree construction and tree search. In the tree construction phase, a spanning tree of G can be constructed in bounded sequential scans of G. In the tree search phase, it needs to sequentially scan the graph once to find all SCCs. In addition, we propose a new single phase algorithm, which combines the tree construction and tree search phases into a single phase, with three new optimization techniques. They are early acceptance, early rejection, and batch processing. By the single phase algorithm with the new optimization techniques, we can significantly reduce the number of I/Os and CPU cost. We conduct extensive experimental studies using 4 real datasets including a massive real dataset, and several synthetic datasets to confirm the I/O efficiency of our approaches.

Categories and Subject Descriptors

G.2.2 [**Graph Theory**]: Graph algorithms

Keywords

graph algorithm; I/O efficient; SCC computing

1. INTRODUCTION

Finding all Strongly Connected Components (SCCs) is an important operation for directed graphs. Here, an SCC is a maximal subgraph S for a given directed graph G, such that for every pair of nodes u and v in S, there is a directed path from u to v in S and there is also a directed path from v to u in S. Many real applications that deal with a directed graph need to find all SCCs first.

Topological Sort: Topological sort is widely used in many applications especially in planning and scheduling. In a topological sort, nodes in a directed graph are ranked according to a partial order specified by the edges. If there are cycles in the graph, all nodes in a cycle are considered as equal rank and merged into one. This is done by finding all SCCs in the graph. In [13], Hellings et al. propose an algorithm for external bisimulation on graphs where all nodes are assumed to be in the reverse topological order and stored on disk. This needs to find all SCCs in a preprocessing step.

Reachability Query Processing: Reachability query is a widely studied query to ask whether a node u can reach another node v through a directed path in a directed graph. There are many applications in social networks, biological networks, software analysis, and semantic web. Because two nodes in an SCC are reachable from each other, in the literature, almost all algorithms to process reachability queries over a general directed graph G first convert G into a directed acyclic graph (*DAG*) by contracting an SCC into a node, which needs to find all SCCs in a prepossessing step. As an example, for handling reachability queries over a massive directed graph, the GRAIL index [22] needs to be built on *DAG*. The key point is that it must compute all SCCs before constructing an index for a general directed graph.

Graph Pattern Matching: Pattern matching in *XML* data and graph data has been widely studied. Computing SCCs is an optimization technique to compress a large graph for processing pattern matching queries [12].

In the literature, many efficient in-memory algorithms for finding all SCCs have been studied. The Kosaraju-Sharir algorithm [3] can find all SCCs for a directed graph in linear time w.r.t. the size of the graph, by depth first searching the graph twice in memory. However, due to the fact that the sizes of many real graphs are increasing rapidly, a graph cannot reside entirely in the main memory. As an example, there are more than 901 million active nodes and more than 125 billion edges.[1] As a small part of the entire web, WEBSPAM-UK2007[2] contains 105,896,555 pages in 114,529 hosts in the .UK domain in May 2007. This graph contains nearly 4 billion edges.

---

[1]http://newsroom.fb.com/

[2]http://barcelona.research.yahoo.net/webspam/datasets/uk2007/

For handling a large directed graph $G(V, E)$, a naive way to externalize the in-memory *DFS* based algorithm requires $O(|E|)$ I/Os. Chiang et al [8] propose an algorithm with I/O complexity $O(|V| + \frac{|V|}{M} \cdot scan(|E|) + sort(|E|))$. Later, Kumar and Schwabe [14] and Buchsbaum et al. [7] improve the I/O complexity to $O((|V| + \frac{|E|}{B}) \log_2 \frac{|V|}{B} + sort(|E|))$ by maintaining the list of edges that should not be traversed using tournament trees [14] and buffered repository trees [7], respectively. Here, B is the disk block size. Despite their theoretical guarantees, these algorithms are considered impractical for general directed graphs that encountered in real applications. Cosgaya-Lozano et al. [10] study a heuristic external algorithm to compute all SCCs for a directed algorithm based on contraction used by Chiang et al [8] which is for undirected graphs. But, for directed graphs, the algorithm may end up an infinite loop and cannot compute all SCCs. Sibeyn et al. [20] study a semi-external algorithm, which constructs two Depth First Search (*DFS*) trees on the directed graph, based on the Kosaraju-Sharir algorithm, to find all SCCs. But, the algorithm generates a large number of I/Os, and is hard to be optimized.

In this paper, we propose a new I/O efficient semi-external algorithm to compute all SCCs for a directed graph G. The main contributions of this work are summarized below. First, we observe that the total order used in Kosaraju-Sharir algorithm [3] to handle an in-memory graph is too strong for an I/O efficient algorithm to handle a graph on disk. We propose a weaker order which is based on the depth of a node in a graph. By the weaker order, we can significantly reduce the number of I/Os. Second, we analyze the main costs incurring in the algorithm by Sibeyn et al. [20], and propose new techniques to reduce such costs using a single tree. Third, based on the weak order, we propose a new two phase algorithm. In the first phase it constructs a tree, and in the second phase it searches the tree constructed to find all SCCs. In the tree construction phase, it needs $\mathsf{depth}(G) \cdot |E|/B$ I/Os in the worst case, where $\mathsf{depth}(G)$ is the longest simple path in G, and B is the disk block size. In the tree search phase, it only needs to use $|E|/B$ I/Os. As a comparison, the algorithm in [20] finds all SCCs by two *DFS* over a graph G. One *DFS* needs $\mathsf{depth}(G) \cdot |E|/B$ I/Os. Fourth, we further propose a new single phase algorithm, which combines the tree construction and tree search phases into one phase. We propose new optimization techniques, namely, early acceptance, early rejection, and batch processing. By early acceptance, we contract a partial SCC into a node in an early stage while constructing a tree. By early rejection, we remove nodes that will not participate in any SCCs while constructing the tree in an early stage. In addition, we use batch processing techniques to reduce the CPU cost. By the single phase algorithm, we can significantly reduce the number of I/Os and CPU cost. Finally, we conduct extensive experimental studies using 4 real datasets including a massive real dataset, and several synthetic datasets to confirm the I/O efficiency of our approach.

The remainder of this paper is organized as follows. In Section 3, we discuss the preliminaries and give the problem statement for computing SCCs. In Section 4, we discuss two existing solutions. In Section 5, we outline our approaches. We discuss a new two phase single tree approach with a tree construction phase and a tree search phase in Section 6 and a new single phase single tree approach with new optimization techniques in Section 7. In Section 2, we discuss the related work. We report our experimental results in Section 8 and conclude the paper in Section 9.

2. RELATED WORK

Finding strongly connected components of a directed graph G is a primitive operation in directed graph exploration, which has been studied for both internal memory model and external memory model. In the internal memory model, where the whole graph resides in main memory, strongly connected components of a directed graph can be computed in $O(n + m)$ where $n = |V(G)|$ and $m = |E(G)|$ based on Depth-First Search (*DFS*) [9].

The difference between accessing an element in main memory and fetching an element on disk is captured by the external memory model (or the I/O model) [2], which counts disk accesses incurred by an algorithm using the following parameters: M is the memory size and B is the block size. In the I/O model [2], scanning n elements requires $scan(n) = \Theta(\frac{n}{B})$ I/Os, and sorting n elements requires $sort(n) = \Theta(\frac{n}{B} \cdot \log_{\frac{M}{B}} \frac{n}{B})$ I/Os.

A naive way to externalize the internal *DFS* algorithm requires $O(|E|)$ I/Os. Chiang et al [8] propose an algorithm with I/O complexity $O(|V| + \frac{|V|}{M} \cdot scan(|E|) + sort(|E|))$. Later, Kumar and Schwabe [14] and Buchsbaum et al. [7] improve the I/O complexity to $O((|V| + \frac{|E|}{B}) \log_2 \frac{|V|}{B} + sort(|E|))$ by maintaining the list of edges that should not be traversed using tournament trees [14] and buffered repository trees [7], respectively. Despite their theoretical guarantees, these algorithms are considered impractical for general directed graphs that encountered in real applications. As an example, for the WEBSPAM-UK2007 graph with 105,895,555 nodes used in our experiment, the algorithm by Buchsbaum et al. [7], needs about 1,566,000,000 I/Os for a certain *DFS*, and our algorithm uses about 4,000,000 I/Os to find all SCCs in the large graph.

Two approaches are proposed recently targeting at designing efficient algorithms with good performance in real applications [20, 10]. Sibeyn et al. [20] propose an implementation of semi-external *DFS*, i.e., assuming that the main memory can hold the node set but not the edge set of the graph. Cosgaya-Lozano and Zeh [10] present a contraction-based algorithm which does not follow the line of *DFS*-based algorithms. Their algorithm identifies and contracts SCCs repeatedly until the graph fits in memory, then an internal memory algorithm is run to find the final SCCs.

Other than the problem of finding SCCs or *DFS* tree on external directed graphs, several problems in the external memory model are studied in the literature. Dementiev et al. [11] provide an implementation of an external memory minimum spanning tree algorithm based on the ideas of [19], which performs extremely well in practice, even though theoretically inferior to the algorithms of [1, 8]. Ajwani et al. [4, 6] propose implementations of external undirected breadth-first search algorithm with the idea from [15]. Ulrich Meyer et al. [17, 18, 16] design and implement practical I/O-efficient single source shortest paths algorithm on general undirected sparse graphs. Surveys about designing I/O efficient algorithms for massive graphs can be found at [21, 5].

3. PROBLEM DEFINITION

We model a directed graph as $G(V, E)$, where $V(G)$ represents the set of nodes and $E(G)$ represents the set of directed edges in G, and denote the number of nodes and the number of edges of graph G by n and m, i.e., $n = |V(G)|$ and $m = |E(G)|$. For simplicity, we also use V and E to denote $V(G)$ and $E(G)$ of G respectively, when it is obvious. Given a graph G, a path $p = (v_1, v_2, \cdots, v_k)$ is a sequence of k nodes in V such that, for each $v_i (1 \leq i < k)$, $(v_i, v_{i+1}) \in E$. A node v_i can reach a node v_j in G, denoted $v_i \to v_j$, iff there exists a path from v_i to v_j in G. The length of a path p, denoted as $\mathsf{len}(p)$, is the number of edges in p. A simple path is a path $(v_1, v_2, \cdots, v_k)$ with k distinct nodes. A longest simple path p is a simple path in G with the largest $\mathsf{len}(p)$. We use $\mathsf{depth}(G)$ to denote the length of the longest simple path in G. A cycle is a path where a same node appears more than once, and a

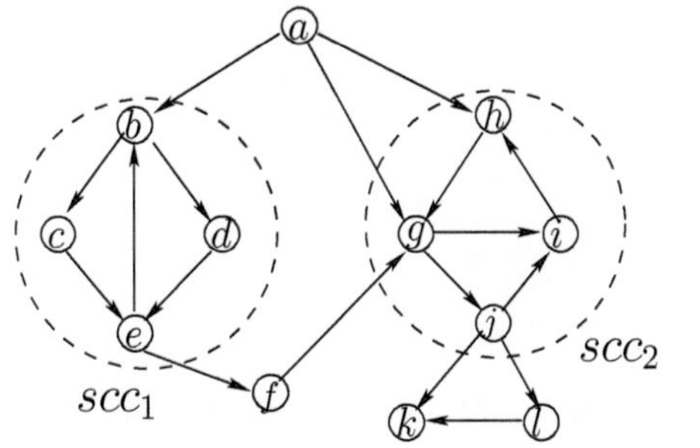

Figure 1: A Graph G with 2 SCCs

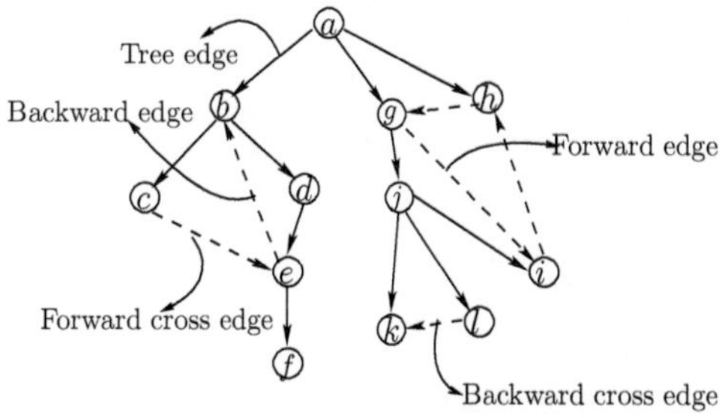

Figure 2: A *DFS* Tree T with Different Edge Types

simple cycle is a path $(v_1, v_2, \cdots, v_{k-1}, v_k)$ where the first $k-1$ nodes are distinct but $v_k = v_1$.

Given a directed graph G, node v_i is strongly connected to node v_j, denoted as $v_i \leftrightarrow v_j$, iff $v_i \rightarrow v_j$ and $v_j \rightarrow v_i$ in G. Here, $\leftrightarrow$ is an equivalence relation, which is reflexive, symmetric, and transitive. We use $v_i \not\leftrightarrow v_j$ to denote that node v_i is not strongly connected to node v_j. A strongly connected component (SCC) of G is the maximal set of nodes V_c ($\subseteq V$) such that, for every pair of nodes v_i and v_j in V_c, $v_i \leftrightarrow v_j$, and for every pair of nodes v_i and v_k $v_i \in V_c$ and $v_k \notin V_c$, $v_i \not\leftrightarrow v_k$. Fig. 1 shows a graph G with 12 nodes and 18 edges. There are 2 SCCs, SCC_1 and SCC_2.

Finding SCCs in a directed graph G can be done with a spanning tree of G. A spanning tree $T(V, E)$ of $G(V, E)$ is a connected directed tree that consists of all nodes ($V(T) = V(G)$) for a connected graph G. For a directed graph G that has several connected components, a spanning tree can be constructed with a virtual node v_0 which links to every spanning tree constructed for a connected component in G. The depth of a node v in a directed tree T is denoted by $\mathsf{depth}(v, T)$, where $\mathsf{depth}(v_0, T) = 0$.

Problem Statement: compute all SCCs for a large directed graph $G(V, E)$ with limited memory M. Here $c|V| \leq M \ll \|G\|$ where c is a small constant number for example $c = 2$, $|V|$ is the number of nodes, and $\|G\|$ is the space for the entire graph G.

4. EXISTING SOLUTIONS

In the literature, there are an external algorithm and a semi-external algorithm to find all SCCs of a directed graph G. The external algorithm is based on contraction [10], and the semi-external algorithm is based on depth first search (*DFS*) [20].

Contraction Based EM-SCC: Cosgaya-Lozano et al. [10] provide a heuristic algorithm, called EM-SCC, to compute all SCCs for a large directed graph, by taking the idea of the contraction-based algorithm for undirected graphs by Chiang et al. in [8]. Given limited memory M, EM-SCC compresses a graph iteratively by contraction until a graph can fit in M, In brief, it processes G in iterations, $G = G_0, G_1, G_2, \cdots, G_f$. In the i-th iteration, EM-SCC contracts some partial SCCs into a node and compresses G_i to be a smaller G_{i+1} for next iteration. The last G_f must fit in M. In the i-th iteration ($i < f$), G_i cannot fit in M. EM-SCC partitions G_i into smaller partitions, $G_{i_1}, G_{i_2}, \cdots$ where G_{i_j} can fit in M. EM-SCC computes SCCs using an in-memory algorithm for G_{i_j}, and compresses G_i by contracting an SCC in G_{i_j} into a node, which maintains the connectivity between nodes in the SCC with other nodes in G.

Unlike the case for undirected graphs where Chiang et al. [8] ensure an undirected graph G can fit into main memory in a log number of iterations, EM-SCC has its limitation to use the same idea for directed graphs. EM-SCC cannot stop in a finite number of iterations in the following cases to compute all SCCs. (Case-1) An SCC of G_i appears across a number of partitions, and the partitions cannot be further compressed by contraction. (Case-2) G_i is a directed acyclic graph, but cannot fit in M. When G contains a large SCC or a large number of small/mid sized SCCs, the probability of Case-1 to happen is high. When G is a *DAG*-liked graph, the probability of Case-2 to happen is high. Due to its problem of finding all SCCs in a finite number of iterations, we will mainly discuss our approach with the semi-external algorithm based on depth first search.

Depth First Search Based DFS-SCC: Sibeyn et al. [20] propose a semi-external algorithm, which finds all SCCs by depth first searching G twice. With a depth first search of G, it constructs a *DFS* tree T which is a spanning tree of G. Given a spanning tree T, every edge (u, v) in G is categorized into tree-edge and non-tree-edge. A tree-edge (u, v) is an edge in T. There are 4 types of non-tree-edges: (1) forward-edge: u is an ancestor of v in T, (2) backward-edge: u is a descendant of v in T, (3) forward-cross-edge: u and v do not have ancestor/descendant relationship and u appears before v by the preorder of T for G, and (4) backward-cross-edge: u and v do not have ancestor/descendant relationship and u appears after v by the preorder of T for G. A spanning tree is a *DFS* tree if and only if there is no forward-cross-edges in the graph. In order to find such tree, the idea is to reduce the number of forward-cross-edges until none can be found. Fig. 2 shows such a tree T rooted at a with solid edges for the graph G in Fig. 1. Given T, (a, b) is a tree-edge because $(a, b) \in E(T)$, (e, b) is a backward-edge because b is an ancestor of e in T, (g, i) is a forward-edge because g is an ancestor of i in T, (c, e) is a forward-cross-edge, because c appears before e by the preorder of T, and (l, k) is a backward-cross-edge because l appears after k by the preorder of T.

The semi-external depth first search algorithm is shown in Algorithm 1, denoted as DFS-Tree(G) [20]. Algorithm 1 constructs a *DFS* tree. Among the 4 types of non-tree-edges, backward-edge, forward-edge, and backward-cross-edge are excluded by the ancestor/descendant relationship and preorder. Algorithm 1 repeatedly reconstructs a *DFS* tree by reducing the number of forward-cross-edges (lines 8-10) in every iteration (lines 7-12). In an iteration, Algorithm 1 accesses all edges in $E(G)$ on disk in sequential order, and attempts to reduce the number of forward-cross-edges as many as possible. The iteration stops when there are no forward-cross-edges ($updated$ = false), and the number of iterations is $\mathsf{depth}(G)$ in the worst case. There are theoretical approaches in the literature to reduce the I/O complexity but are impractical [8, 14, 7], as discussed in the related work.

The DFS-SCC algorithm (Algorithm 2) finds all SCCs by depth first searching G twice, or in other words, by calling Algorithm 1 twice. The first time is to obtain a decreasing postorder of nodes over the *DFS* tree obtained by DFS-Tree(G) (lines 1-2). It then constructs a graph $\overline{G}$ by reversing every edge in G (line 3). Because $V(\overline{G}) = V(G)$, with the same decreasing postorder, it calls DFS-Tree($\overline{G}$) again to obtain a new *DFS* tree T_S (line 4). Here, all nodes in a subtree rooted at a child of the virtual node v_0 of T_S

Algorithm 1 DFS-Tree(G)

for all nodes $v \in V(G)$ in the order as specified **do**
  add edge (v_0, v) in T where v_0 is a virtual node;
construct an initial *DFS* tree T and assign all nodes in $V(T)$ with preorder;
$updated \leftarrow$ true;
while $updated =$ true **do**
  $updated \leftarrow$ false;
  for all edges $(u, v) \in E(G)$ **do**
    if (u, v) is a forward-cross-edge **then**
      $w \leftarrow$ the parent of v in T;
      delete the edge (w, v) from T and add the edge (u, v) in T;
      $updated \leftarrow$ true;
  reassign all nodes in $V(T)$ with preorder by *DFS* of T if $updated =$ true;
return T;

Algorithm 2 DFS-SCC(G)

$T \leftarrow$ DFS-Tree(G);
sort $V(G)$ in decreasing postorder by traversing T;
construct a graph $\overline{G}$ from G by reversing every edge in G, where $V(\overline{G}) = V(G)$ (with the same postorder);
$T_S \leftarrow$ DFS-Tree($\overline{G}$);
output that all nodes in a subtree of the virtual node v_0 of T_S forms an SCC;

are in the same SCC. The main idea of Algorithm 2 is to develop a semi-external algorithm based on the Kosaraju-Sharir algorithm which finds all SCCs in main memory [3].

Consider G in Fig. 1. The first *DFS* traverses G in $abcefgjklihd$, and its decreasing postorder is $abdcefgjihlk$. With the decreasing postorder, in the second *DFS*, the root v_0 of the *DFS* tree computed has 6 subtrees representing 6 SCCs $\{a\}$, $\{b, c, d, e\}$, $\{f\}$, $\{g, h, i, j\}$, $\{k\}$, and $\{l\}$.

There are 3 main costs in DFS-SCC. (Cost-1) DFS-SCC needs to traverse G twice using *DFS* to compute all SCCs. In each *DFS*, it needs the number of $\mathsf{depth}(G) \cdot |E(V)|/B$ I/Os in the worst case where B is the block size. In the literature, there are no efficient external *DFS* algorithms due to a large number of random I/O accesses produced in the in-memory algorithm designed for *DFS*. (Cost-2) Even though there are partial SCCs which can be possibly contracted to save space while *DFS*, or in other words, while constructing a *DFS* tree, it cannot be done. We explain the reasons. As implied by the Kosaraju-Sharir algorithm [3], DFS-SCC uses a total order of nodes (decreasing postorder), computed in the first *DFS*, in the second *DFS*. Therefore, the nodes cannot be contracted in the first *DFS*. In the second *DFS*, we can possibly contract some partial SCCs into a node, but we have to maintain which node belongs to which SCC while reading edges $E(G)$ sequentially from disk to construct the second *DFS* tree. In other words, we cannot save space for free. All SCCs have to be identified at the same time when the entire second *DFS* tree is constructed. (Cost-3) In *DFS* (Algorithm 1), to reduce the number of forward-cross-edges, when forward-cross-edge, (u, v), is found, it needs to reshape the tree by updating the preorder of nodes in all subtrees rooted on the path from u to the root of the *DFS* tree constructed. Fig. 3 shows an example. Suppose a node, u, in subtree B to node g is a forward-cross-edge. The edge (a, g) will be deleted, and the edge (u, g) will be added. Also, the preorder of all nodes in the subtrees rooted at nodes, e, f, and g must be redone. Such process can be done in main memory but consumes high CPU cost.

In this paper, we propose a new algorithm in order to reduce the large CPU/IO cost produced by the DFS-SCC algorithm.

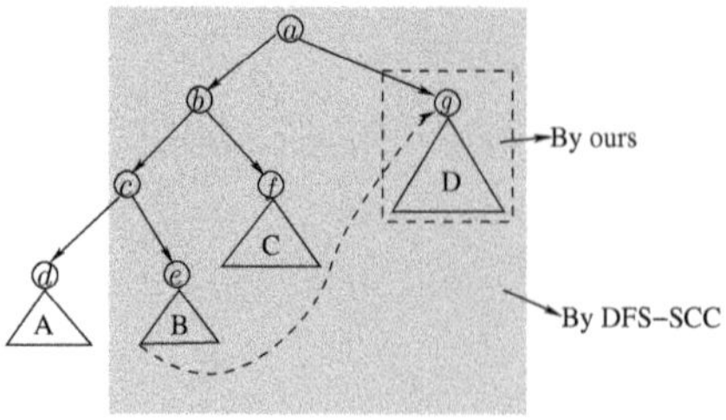

Figure 3: CPU Cost for Updating an Edge

5. THE NEW APPROACHES

In this section, we outline our new approaches to compute all SCCs for a directed graph G. Our key observation is that the Kosaraju-Sharir algorithm [3] is very efficient based on the total order over $V(G)$ when G can be held in main memory entirely, because all memory accesses can be done in constant time. In designing I/O efficient algorithms, such a total order is too strong in the sense that it cannot be used to reduce the number of I/Os and/or save space, and there is no obvious relationship between the total order and SCCs per se.

Instead of the decreasing postorder used in DFS-SCC, in this paper, we use a rather weak order. The idea behind the weak order is as follows. For an SCC, there must exist at least one cycle. While constructing a spanning tree T for G, a cycle (a part of SCC) will appear as to contain at least one edge (u, v) that links to a higher level node in T. A necessary condition can be specified as $\mathsf{depth}(u) > \mathsf{depth}(v)$ in T, or in other words, node u at a level, $\mathsf{depth}(u)$, links to a node v at a higher level, $\mathsf{depth}(v)$. There are two cases when $\mathsf{depth}(u) > \mathsf{depth}(v)$ holds. First, v is an ancestor of u in T. In such a case, (u, v) is a backward-edge and the cycle can be identified by combining tree-edges on the path from v to u plus the edge (u, v). Second, v is not an ancestor of u on T. In this paper, we call such an edge an up-edge. For the second case, we can locally reshape T in a similar way as done in Algorithm 1 when dealing with forward-cross-edges. In brief, let w be the parent of v for an up-edge (u, v), we delete (w, v) from T and add (u, v) in T. By doing so, we reduce an up-edge.

To reduce Cost-1 in the DFS-SCC algorithm, we create a BR-Tree, to compute all SCCs. Our algorithm can compute all SCCs efficiently by traversing the BR-Tree constructed only once. To reduce Cost-2, we propose new optimization techniques namely, early acceptance and early rejection. By early acceptance, we contract a partial SCC into a node in an early stage while constructing BR-Tree. By early rejection, we identify necessary conditions to remove nodes that will not participate in any SCCs while constructing BR-Tree. It is worth noting that such optimizations can not be easily introduced into the DFS-SCC algorithm as discussed before. To show the effectiveness of our approach, consider a tree T in Fig. 4. The 3 nodes e, f, and g can be contracted into a node e' by early acceptance, and node a as well as all nodes on the subtrees C and D can be removed by early rejection if the conditions are met. A large number of nodes/edges can be removed in every iteration in our algorithm. To reduce Cost-3, we show that when an up-edge (u, v) is found while constructing a BR-Tree, we only need to update the depths of nodes on the subtree rooted at node u. Reconsider Fig. 3, when eliminating an up-edge, (u, g) where u is in B, in the DFS-SCC algorithm, the order of all nodes under subtrees denoted by B, C and D need to be updated. We only need to update the nodes in the subtree D.

In the following we discuss our approach step-by-step based on a spanning tree called BR-Tree for G. A BR-Tree T can be constructed in any traversal order with which all non-tree edges in G

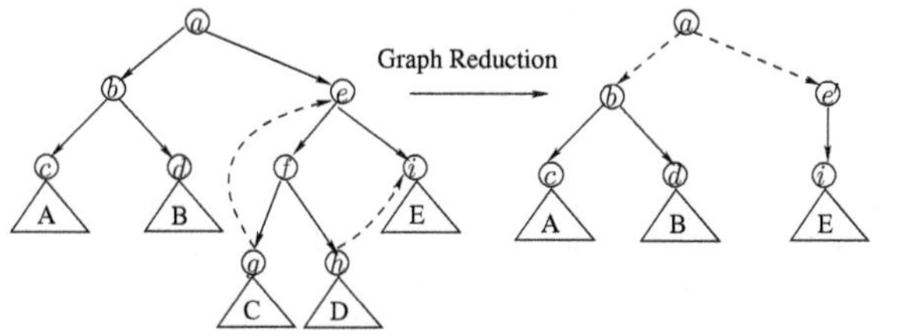

Figure 4: Early Acceptance and Early Rejection

are either backward-edge, up-edge, or down-edge. An edge (u, v) is a backward-edge if v is an ancestor of u. An edge (u, v) is an up-edge w.r.t. T iff $\mathsf{depth}(u, T) \geq \mathsf{depth}(v, T)$. An edge (u, v) is a down-edge w.r.t. T iff u is not an ancestor of v, v is not an ancestor of u in T, and $\mathsf{depth}(u, T) < \mathsf{depth}(v, T)$. The size of BR-Tree is $2|V(G)|$, because a node only needs to maintain its parent node in T.

Single Tree: We discuss a single BR-Tree T to compute all SCCs with a naive approach as follows.

construct a BR-Tree T; no-up-edge $\leftarrow$ true;
while no-up-edge = true **do**
  compute partial SCCs by contracting nodes in T with sequential scanning $E(G)$;
  if there is a new up-edge found in T **then** construct a BR-Tree T **else** no-up-edge $\leftarrow$ false;

Here, we can construct a BR-Tree T in a similar manner as shown in Algorithm 1 using the notion of up-edge[3] instead with I/O complexity $\mathsf{depth}(G) \cdot |E(G)|/B$ where B is a block size. Assume N up-edges are found in the while loop statement while contracting nodes, it needs to reconstruct BR-Tree T N times. Due to the high I/O complexity, this naive single tree approach is infeasible.

A Two Phase Construct and Search Approach: To significantly reduce the I/O complexity with a single tree for computing all SCCs, we give a new two phase approach, named 2P-SCC (Algorithm 3). In the first phase we construct a tree, and in the second phase we compute all SCCs by searching the tree constructed. The I/O complexity for the first construction phase is $\mathsf{depth}(G) \cdot |E(G)|/B$, and the I/O for the second search phase is only one scan of $E(G)$. We show that we can do the one scan of $E(G)$ in the second phase using a special spanning tree, BR$^+$-Tree, where a node u maintains its parent node in T plus one of its ancestors v by a backward-edge (u, v) in G. Here the size of BR$^+$-Tree is $3|V(G)|$. We will discuss the two phase approach using the special spanning BR$^+$-Tree, and then we show that we can do the same using BR-Tree instead of BR$^+$-Tree.

The one sequential scan of $E(G)$ is achieved based on a refined "up-edge". We give its new definition we use in this work which is based on two functions: $\mathsf{drank}(u, T)$ and $\mathsf{dlink}(u, T)$.

$$\mathsf{drank}(u, T) = \min\{\mathsf{depth}(v, T) | v \in \mathsf{Rset}(u, G, T)\}$$
$$\mathsf{dlink}(u, T) = \operatorname{argmin}_v \{\mathsf{depth}(v, T) | v \in \mathsf{Rset}(u, G, T)\}$$

Here, $\mathsf{Rset}(u, G, T)$ denotes the set of nodes including u and nodes that v can reach by a BR$^+$-Tree T of G. The function $\mathsf{drank}(u, T)$ gives the minimum depth of v that u can reach in BR$^+$-Tree T, and $\mathsf{dlink}(u, T)$ specifies the unique node v that is with $\mathsf{drank}(u, T)$. Given BR$^+$-Tree T of G, we redefine an up-edge below.

Definition 5.1: (Up-Edge) Given a BR$^+$-Tree T of graph G, an edge $e = (u, v) \in E(G)$ is an up-edge w.r.t. T iff the following two conditions are satisfied: (1) u is not an ancestor of v and v is not an ancestor of u in T, and (2) $\mathsf{drank}(u, T) \geq \mathsf{drank}(v, T)$. □

[3]The up-edge will be used instead forward-cross-edge in the condition (line 8, Algorithm 1).

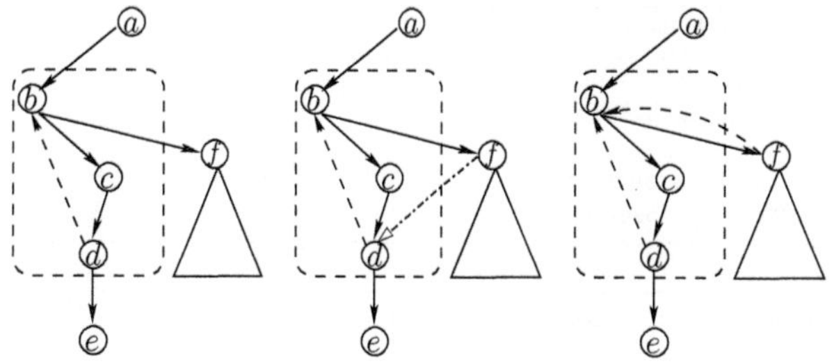

(a) (b) (c)

Figure 5: The Refined up-edge

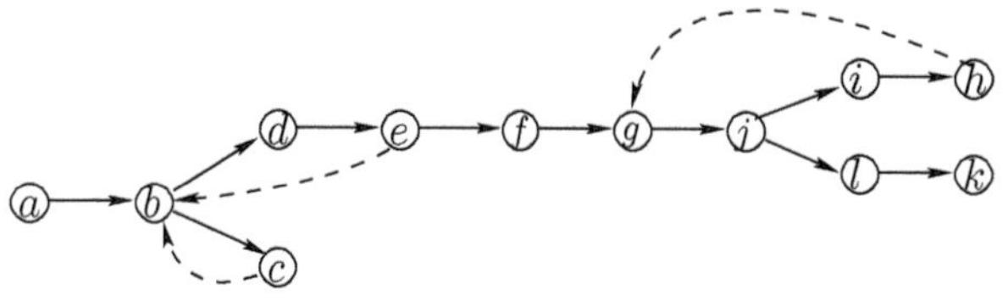

Figure 6: A BR-Tree T of G in Fig. 1

We explain the new up-edge using an example. Fig. 5(a) shows a BR$^+$-Tree T. The spanning tree part is shown by the solid edges and the additional backward-edges are shown by dotted edges. By the initial definition of up-edge, the edge (f, d) is not an up-edge over the spanning tree. By the new definition of up-edge, (f, d) becomes an up-edge (Fig. 5(b)). We handle this up-edge of (f, d) by indicating that f is in a cycle in G. This is done by deleting (f, d) from T, but adding a backward-edge of (f, b) to BR$^+$-Tree. As a result, all SCCs of G induce a connected subtree of BR$^+$-Tree T of G in the tree search phase by a single sequential scan of $E(G)$. As an example, Fig. 6 shows a BR$^+$-Tree T for G in Fig. 1. There are no up-edges in T. The SCC with nodes $\{b, c, d, e\}$ induces a subtree rooted at b in T. The SCC with nodes $\{g, h, i, j\}$ induces a subtree rooted at g in T. We will discuss the two-phase approach in Section 6.

A Single Phase Approach: To further improve the I/O efficiency with a single tree for computing all SCCs, we propose a new single phase approach, named 1P-SCC (Algorithm 6). 1P-SCC uses a single BR-Tree T with $2|V(G)|$ space instead of BR$^+$-Tree, which is achieved by two optimization techniques, early acceptance and early rejection. On the other hand, the two optimization techniques can further reduce the space to keep $V(G)$ in iterations. The space reduced can be used as a buffer to reduce the I/O cost for reading $E(G)$. We will discuss it in Section 7.

6. TWO PHASE SINGLE TREE

In this section, we discuss the two phases of the 2P-SCC algorithm (Algorithm 3), namely, Tree-Construction (Algorithm 4) and Tree-Search (Algorithm 5).

6.1 Tree Construction

We show an algorithm for tree construction, and the algorithm is named Tree-Construction as shown in Algorithm 4. Our Algorithm 4 shares similarity with Algorithm 1 but is with several main differences. Like Algorithm 1, Algorithm 4 traverses G and constructs a tree by reshaping the tree iteratively. Unlike Algorithm 1, Algorithm 4 does not request to use *DFS* to construct a spanning tree. The algorithm is to construct a tree by eliminating up-edges, lines 7-12, which can reduce CPU cost as indicated in Fig. 3. The elimination of an up-edge is done in one of two ways. One is explained in Fig. 5. The other is to reshape the tree with a pushdown operation.

Algorithm 3 2P-SCC(G)

Input: A directed graph G.
Output: All the SCCs in G.

```
T ← Tree-Construction(G);
return Tree-Search(G, T);
```

Algorithm 4 Tree-Construction(G)

Input: A directed graph G.
Output: A spanning tree T of G.

```
1: T ← a spanning tree of G;
2: update-drank(G, T);
3: updated ← true;
4: while updated = true do
5:     updated ← false;
6:     for all edge (u, v) ∈ E(G) in sequential order on disk do
7:         if (u, v) is an up-edge then
8:             if dlink(T, v) is an ancestor of u then
9:                 delete the edge (u, v) from T;
10:                add the edge (u, dlink(T, v)) in T;
11:            else
12:                T ← T⇓(u, v);
13:                updated ← true;
14:    update-drank(G, T);
15: return T;
```

The operation pushdown (⇓): Given a spanning tree T of G, for an up-edge $(u, v) \in E(G)$ w.r.t. T, pushdown operation $T\Downarrow(u, v)$ modifies T to be T' as follows. Let $T' = T$. (1) Cut the subtree T_v rooted at v from T'. (2) Paste the subtree T_v as a new subtree of u in T'. (3) Update depth(v) for every node in T_v w.r.t. T'.

Since u and v do not have ancestor/descendant relationship by the definition of up-edge, the operation ⇓ will result in another spanning tree T' of G, but reduce an up-edge. The cost of changing node depth (the step (3) in pushdown) is done locally. On the other hand, when *DFS* tree reshapes, Algorithm 1 needs to change the preorder globally. Algorithm 4 is more efficient than Algorithm 1, as indicated in Fig. 3.

In Algorithm 4, the while loop statement (lines 4-14) repeats by sequentially scanning $E(G)$ until no up-edges are found. In Algorithm 4, the procedure update-drank(G, T) updates the drank of all nodes in T in one scan of all edges of $E(G)$, where for each node $v \in V(T)$ we keep a backward-edge (v, u) with the smallest depth(u, T) if there is any. The procedure of update-drank does not incur additional I/Os because it can be done at the same time when accessing $E(V)$ (line 6).

Algorithm 4 needs at most $3 \times n \times b$ bytes of memory, where $n = |V(G)|$ and b is the number of bytes to store a node in G.

Lemma 6.1: *Algorithm 4 stops in at most* depth(G) *iterations.* □

Example 6.1: We show how to build a BR$^+$-Tree T for G (Fig. 1). An initial spanning tree T is shown in Fig. 7(1). First, for the up-edge (f, g), we cut the edge (a, g) and add a new edge (f, g). The result is shown in Fig. 7(2). For the up-edge (i, h), we cut the edge (a, h) and add a new edge (i, h). The result is shown in Fig. 7(3). Then, we find the up-edge (l, k), we cut the edge (i, k) and add another edge (l, k). For the up-edge (c, e), because dlink$(e, T) = b$ is an ancestor of c, thus we cut the edge (c, e) and add an edge (c, b). The final BR$^+$-Tree is shown in Fig. 7(4) without up-edges. □

6.2 Tree Search

Given a directed graph G, one way to compute all SCCs of G is to contract all nodes in an SCC into a node. We take this idea

Algorithm 5 Tree-Search(G, T)

Input: A directed graph G, and a BR$^+$-Tree T.
Output: All SCCs of G.

```
for all edge (u, v) ∈ E(G) in sequential order on disk do
    if (u, v) is a backward edge and has not been merged then
        p ← the path on T from v to u;
        contract all nodes in p into one node;
for all node u ∈ V(T) do
    output all nodes v represents as an SCC;
```

using a BR$^+$-Tree T constructed by sequential scan of $E(G)$ once. First, recall that a BR$^+$-Tree T is a spanning tree where a node u maintains its parent node in T plus one of its ancestors v by a backward-edge (u, v) in G. And there are no up-edges in G w.r.t T by Definition 5.1. We reemphasize that by definition an edge $(u, v) \in E(G)$ is an up-edge iff drank$(u, T) \geq$ drank(v, T) and there is no ancestor/descendant relationship between u and v in T. It is important to note that drank(u, T) gives the minimum depth of v that u can reach in BR$^+$-Tree T. Second, a partial SCC is represented by a cycle in BR$^+$-Tree which is a path with tree-edges from u to v plus a backward-edge from v to u. We denote it as $p = (v_1, v_2, \cdots, v_{k-1}, v_k)$ where $u = v_1 = v_k$ and $v = v_{k-1}$. All nodes on the path p belong to an SCC, and can be contracted into a node u with drank(v, T), due to the backward-edge (v, u). Importantly, there will not be any new up-edges when contracting such a path into a node in G w.r.t. the T contracted. We show it in two cases after all nodes in p are contracted in u. In the first case, let (v_i, w) be an edge from a node v_i on the path p to a node that does not appear in the path p. The edge (v_i, w) cannot be a new up-edge by definition. In the second case, let (w, v_i) be an edge from a node that does not appear in the path p to a node v_i on the path p. The edge (w, v_i) cannot be a new up-edge by definition. In addition, all other non-up-edges in G w.r.t. T cannot be up-edges because they are not affected by the contraction of nodes in p. This ensures that one scan of $E(G)$ can compute all SCCs.

We give the tree search algorithm in Algorithm 5. While scanning all edges in $E(G)$, if an edge is a non-tree edge w.r.t. BR$^+$-Tree, the edge can be either a backward-edge or a down-edge. A backward-edge will lead to contract more nodes into a node which may represent a partial SCC already. The contraction will not introduce new up-edges as discussed above, and it only needs one sequential scan of $E(G)$.

Example 6.2: We show how Algorithm 5 works using an example. Suppose we have constructed the BR$^+$-Tree as shown in Fig. 8(1). There are three backward edges, (c, b), (e, b) and (h, g). First, we contract nodes using the backward-edge (c, b), and obtain a partial SCC bc as shown in Fig. 8(2). Second, we contract nodes using the backward-edge (e, b). The nodes on the path (bc, d, e) are contacted into an SCC $bcde$ as shown in Fig. 8(3). Finally, we can contract nodes using the backward-edge (h, g) in a similar way. The 6 SCCs are represented by the 6 nodes in the tree in Fig. 8(4). □

7. SINGLE PHASE SINGLE TREE

The two-phase approach (Algorithm 4) uses a BR$^+$-Tree which consumes $3|V(G)|$ space, and requires at most depth(G) sequential scans of $E(G)$ in the construction phase and 1 sequential scan of $E(G)$ in the tree search phase. In this section, we discuss a single phase approach. We can reduce the space from $3|V(G)|$ to $2|V(G)|$ using BR-Tree based on the notion of BR$^+$-Tree. We can significantly reduce the number of sequential I/Os by further

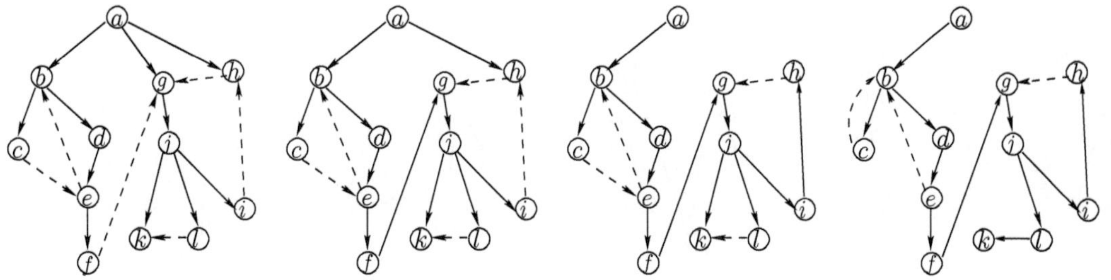

Tree T (1) — $T \leftarrow T \Downarrow (f,g)$ (2) — $T \leftarrow T \Downarrow (i,h)$ (3) — $T \leftarrow T \Downarrow (l,k)$ (4)

Figure 7: Tree Construction Example for G in Fig. 1

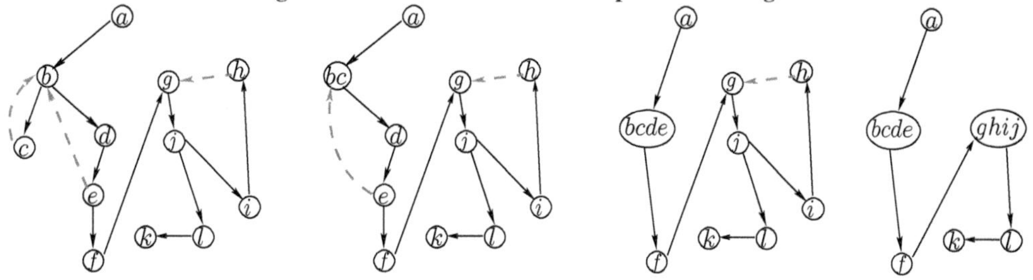

(1) — merge using (c,b) (2) — merge using (e,b) (3) — merge using (h,g) (4)

Figure 8: Tree Search Example of T in Fig. 7

Algorithm 6 1P-SCC(G)

Input: A directed graph G.
Output: All the SCCs in G.

```
1:  G' ← G; T ← a spanning tree of G'; updated ← true;
2:  while updated = true do
3:      updated ← false;
4:      for all edge (u, v) ∈ E(G') in sequential order on disk do
5:          if (u, v) is a backward edge then
6:              p ← the path on T from v to u;
7:              contract all nodes in p into a node;
8:              updated ← true;
9:          if (u, v) is an up-edge then
10:             T ← T ⇓ (u, v);
11:             updated ← true;
12:     early-acceptance(G', T) if the size of a large SCC is ≥ τ;
13:     early-rejection(G', T); {early-rejection and early-acceptance
        can be done together.}
14: for all node u ∈ V(G') do
15:     output all nodes that contract to a single u as an SCC;
```

reducing graph G to be processed in every iteration. The graph reduction is achieved by our optimization techniques, namely, early acceptance, early rejection, and batch edge reduction. Early acceptance is to contract cycles as soon as a backward-edge is found in an iteration. Early rejection is to remove those nodes that will not be used to form any new SCCs. Batch edge reduction is to process as many edges as possible together to reduce CPU cost by making full use of the main memory.

7.1 Early Acceptance

By early acceptance, we mean to contract cycles while constructing a BR-Tree. In this sense, all backward edges are eliminated while constructing a BR-Tree, therefore there is no need to maintain the backward-edges in the first tree construction phase for the later contraction in the second tree search phase. Because the contraction is done in tree construction, $\mathsf{drank}(u,T)$ can be easily computed as $\mathsf{drank}(u,T) = \mathsf{depth}(u,T)$.

The single phase algorithm is shown in Algorithm 6, which combines Tree-Construction and Tree-Search into one phase. Like Tree-Construction, it processes iteratively. In an iteration, for an up-edge (u,v), it conducts in a similar way as it is done in Tree-Construction (lines 11-13). The single phase algorithm needs to reshape the tree using pushdown ($\Downarrow$), but does not need to replace an up-edge to a backward-edge as done in Tree-Construction, because the same is replaced by the contraction. For a backward-edge (u,v), we find the tree path from v to u in T, and contract all nodes in the path (lines 7-10) as done in Tree-Search. The single phase algorithm stops when no up-edges and no backward-edges are found. For such a BR-Tree, a node in T represents an SCC in G.

The early-acceptance (line 12) reduces a graph G' into a smaller graph G' to be used in the next iteration if the algorithm finds that there are large SCCs whose size is greater than a given threshold τ. It is done as follows. Let T be the current spanning tree for G'. (1) For a node u in T, which represents a set of nodes V_u contracted, we exclude all induced edges in V_u from G', and use u to represent all nodes in V_u. (2) For all edges (v_i, v_j) where $v_i \in V_u$ and $v_j \notin V_u$, the edge (v_i, v_j) is replaced with (u, v_j). (3) For all edges (v_i, v_j) where $v_j \in V_u$ and $v_i \notin V_u$, the edge (v_i, v_j) is replaced with (v_i, u). As we will show later, a significant number of nodes and edges will be eliminated and a smaller graph will be used in the following iterations.

Example 7.1: We show an example of early acceptance. Suppose initially we construct a spanning tree T as shown in Fig. 9(1). We find that edge (e,b) is a backward edge. At this time, instead of eliminating up-edges, we merge nodes using edge (e,b). We merge nodes in the tree path (b,d,e) and create a new partial SCC node bde. The result is shown in Fig. 9(2). We find the up-edge (f,g), and thus we cut the edge (a,g) from T and add a new edge (f,g). The result after eliminating up-edge (f,g) is shown in Fig. 9 (3). Similarly, we eliminate up-edge (i,h) by cutting edge (a,h) and adding edge (i,h), and we eliminate up-edge (l,k) by cutting edge (j,k) and adding edge (l,k), and we get another tree as shown in Fig. 9 (4). We find the backward edge (h,g) and we merge nodes

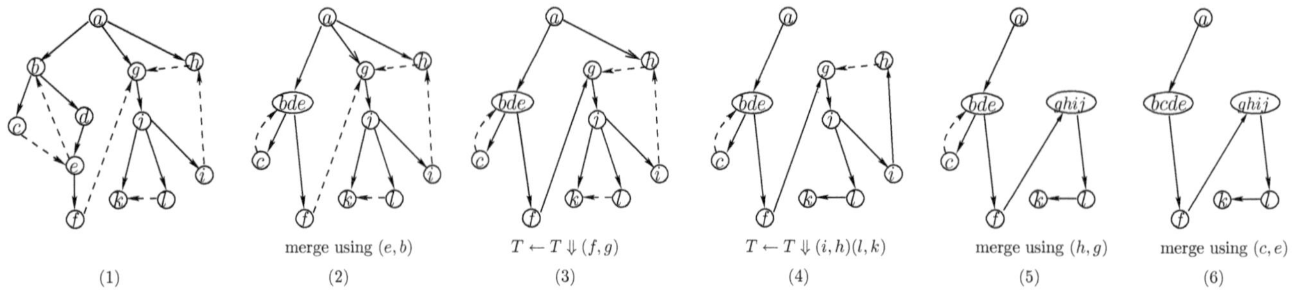

Figure 9: Early Acceptance Example for G in Fig. 1

Algorithm 7 early-rejection(G, T)

1: **for all** node u in G **do**
2:   **if** drank(u) < drank$_{min}$ **or** drank(u) > drank$_{max}$ **then**
3:     **output** the nodes u represents as an SCC;
4:     remove u from T;

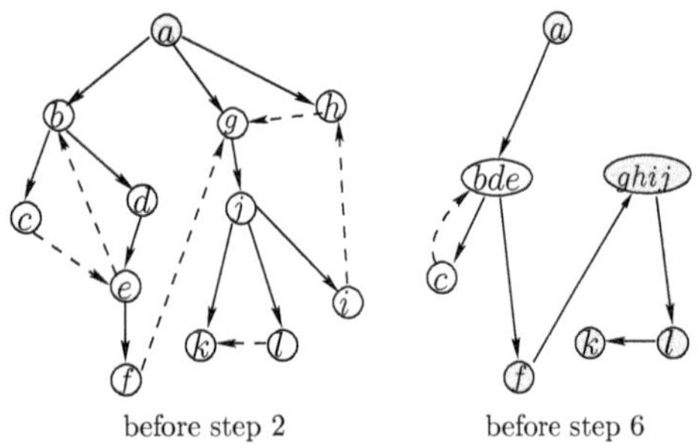

Figure 10: Early Rejection Example

in the path from g to h on T. We created an SCC node $ghij$, which is shown in Fig. 9 (5). Finally, we find backward edge (c, e), merge nodes in the path from e to c on T, and end up with the graph as shown in Fig. 9(6) with 2 SCCs, $bcde$ and $ghij$. □

We will discuss early-rejection (line 13) which removes the nodes that will not be involved in a new SCC, in the next subsection. Note that both early-acceptance and early-rejection can be done at the same time to reduce cost.

7.2 Early Rejection

We discuss how to remove those nodes that will not be involved in a new SCC in an early stage by early-rejection(G, T). The condition is specified by a min drank (drank$_{min}$) and a max drank (drank$_{max}$) for the graph G, w.r.t. its spanning tree T.

$$\text{drank}_{min} = \min\{\text{drank}(v), \text{ for all}(u, v) \text{ with drank}(u) \geq \text{drank}(v)\}$$
$$\text{drank}_{max} = \max\{\text{drank}(u), \text{ for all}(u, v) \text{ with drank}(u) \geq \text{drank}(v)\}$$

Given a spanning tree T of a graph G, for an edge (u, v), drank$(u) \geq$ drank(v) suggests that u and v are possibly in an SCC. drank$_{min}$ and drank$_{max}$ specify the upper and lower bound, respectively, over all such edges in a graph G. Here, drank$_{min}$ suggests that any node u with drank(u) ($<$ drank$_{min}$) cannot be in a larger SCC than what SCC u may be involved in already, and drank$_{max}$ suggests that any node u with drank(u) ($>$ drank$_{max}$) cannot be in a larger SCC than what SCC u may be involved in already. The condition holds because in the single phase approach, nodes are contracted during construction and drank(u) = depth(u).

The early-rejection algorithm is shown in Algorithm 7. When the condition is held on a node u, all the nodes, represented by u as an SCC in T for G, are output, and u will be removed from T. As a result, all the edges connected to/from u can be excluded in the further iteration.

Algorithm 8 1PB-SCC(G)

Input: A directed graph G.
Output: All the SCCs in G.

1: $G' \leftarrow G$; $T \leftarrow$ a spanning tree of G'; $updated \leftarrow$ true;
2: **while** $updated =$ true **do**
3:   $updated \leftarrow$ false;
4:   divide $E(G')$ into batches $B = \{B_1, B_2, \cdots\}$ where $B_i \in B$ can fit in main memory;
5:   **for all** $B_i \in B$ **do**
6:     $G" \leftarrow T \cup B_i$;
7:     compute all SCCs in $G"$ using an in-memory algorithm, and construct a *DAG* by contracting nodes in an SCC into one node;
8:     let topological order for all nodes in $|V(G")|$ be $\{v_1, v_2, \cdots, v_{|V(G")|}\}$;
9:     **for** $j = 1$ **to** $|V(G")|$ by the topological order **do**
10:       **for all** $(v_i, v_j) \in E(G")$ **do**
11:         **if** drank$(v_i) \geq$ drank(v_j) **then**
12:           $T \leftarrow T \Downarrow (v_i, v_j)$; $update \leftarrow$ true;
13:   early-acceptance(G', T) if the size of a large SCC is $\geq \tau$;
14:   early-rejection(G', T); {early-rejection and early-acceptance can be done together.}
15: **for all** node $u \in V(G')$ **do**
16:   **output** all nodes that contract to a single u as an SCC;

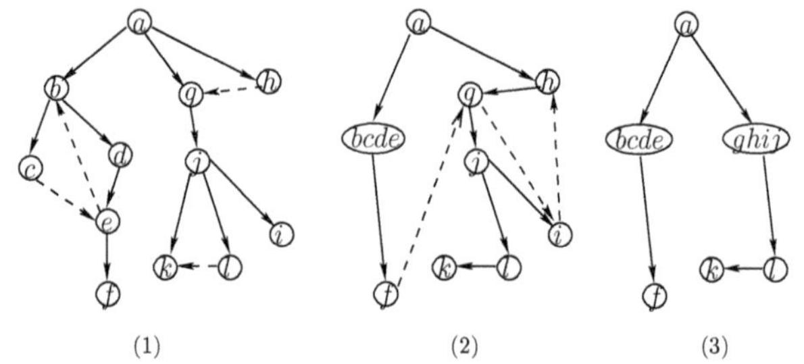

Figure 11: 1PB-SCC Construction Example for G in Fig. 1

Example 7.2: We show an example on early rejection. Consider the spanning tree T shown in Fig. 9(1) for G in Fig. 1. Here, drank$_{min}$ = 1 and drank$_{max}$ = 4. Node a can be early rejected because drank$(a) = 0$. We can remove a from T. And the edges (a, b), (a, g), (a, h) do not need to be considered in the following iterations. The result after the early rejection is shown in Fig. 10 (before step 2). Consider the spanning tree T shown in Fig. 9(5). Here, drank$_{min}$ = drank$_{max}$ = 1. All nodes, f, k, l, and $ghij$ can be removed from the graph, as shown in Fig. 10 (before step 6). All related edges can be removed in further processing. □

7.3 Batch Edge Reduction

In the 1P-SCC algorithm (Algorithm 6), CPU cost is rather high. We explain it below. For an edge (u, v) (line 4), in order to determine whether (u, v) is a backward-edge/up-edge, by Definition 5.1, it needs to check whether there is an ancestor/descendant relationship between u and v over the spanning tree T. Assume that we use $O(|V(G')|)$ memory to maintain a spanning tree T for G'. T

is possibly updated frequently, because it will be updated when an up-edge is found. When T is updated, the existing techniques for ancestor/descendant relationship detection in constant time cannot be used. To find whether v is an ancestor of u, it needs to check whether v is on the path from u towards the root of T in main memory. Such CPU cost depends on the average length of a path, or in other words, the average depth in T. In Algorithm 6, when BR-Tree is reshaped by pushdown ($\Downarrow$) for an up-edge (u, v), the depth of all nodes under the subtree rooted at v increase by at least one. When more $\Downarrow$ operations are conducted on T, the average depth of nodes in T will be larger. Therefore, the CPU cost to check ancestor/descendant relationship increases. We discuss how to reduce the cost of computing ancestor/descendant relationships as well as the cost to maintain depth of nodes when finding up-edges on T below.

Our algorithm is shown in Algorithm 8 which enhances Algorithm 6 by batch processing to reduce CPU cost. Given memory M_B which is available to edges in main memory. First, we read all edges we can read from disk into main memory as a batch, and denote it as B_i (line 5). Second, we construct a graph G" in memory by the current T plus the edges in B_i, use an in-memory algorithm to compute all SCCs (Kosaraju-Sharir algorithm [3]), and construct a *DAG* of G" (lines 7-8). By the *DAG* of G", all SCCs are eliminated and therefore no backward edges exist in the *DAG*. The CPU cost for computing ancestor/descendant relationships for edges in G" are shared in the process of constructing *DAG*. Third, we construct a new BR-Tree T for the *DAG*, which is also for G" in memory (lines 9-12). In order to reduce the CPU cost for maintaining the depth of nodes when eliminating up-edges, we sort all nodes in G" in topological order which can be done in constructing *DAG* without extra cost. We process nodes in the topological order, and we can guarantee that all incoming nodes of v in G" have been processed. The depth of v in the new T can be simply computed as $\mathsf{drank}(v) = \max_{(u,v)\in E(G")}\{\mathsf{drank}(u) + 1\}$ using dynamic programming. In such a way, when eliminating (u, v) using $\Downarrow$ (line 12), we do not update the drank of all nodes in the subtree rooted at v, but only update the $\mathsf{drank}(v)$ by setting $\mathsf{drank}(v) \leftarrow \mathsf{drank}(u) + 1$. Fourth, like Algorithm 6, we conduct early-acceptance and early-rejection (line 13-14), and output all SCCs (lines 15-16).

CPU Cost Saving: Consider G' to be processed, where $m = |E(G')|$ and $n = |V(G')|$. By the 1P-SCC algorithm (lines 4-11), all nodes are in memory. Assume all m edges are processed one by one, and there are m' up-edges. Suppose the average cost for updating the drank values of nodes in a subtree is C_T and the average cost for up-edges checking is C_V. The CPU cost for the 1P-SCC algorithm is $C_{\text{1P-SCC}} = O(m' \cdot C_T + m \cdot C_V)$. It is important to note that C_T is to update all nodes in a subtree and C_V is to check a path from a node towards the root. Both are costly. On the other hand, by the 1PB-SCC algorithm, there are β batches to process (lines 4-12). The graph G' with n nodes and $n-1+\frac{m}{\beta}$ edges are constructed in each batch, where $n-1$ is the number of edges in the spanning tree in main memory, and $\frac{m}{\beta}$ is the number of edges can be loaded into main memory in a batch. In one batch, finding all SCCs using the Kosaraju-Sharir algorithm [3] in such a graph G' in memory will cost $O(2n - 1 + \frac{m}{\beta}) = O(\frac{m}{\beta} + n)$ time, where n is the number of nodes, and $n - 1 + \frac{m}{\beta}$ is the number of edges. And there are β batches, the total becomes $O(m + \beta n)$. When β is small, where a large number of edges can be processed in a batch, the 1PB-SCC algorithm is efficient. When $\beta = \frac{m}{n}$, which means n edges are processed in each batch, the CPU cost for the 1PB-SCC algorithm is $C_{\text{1PB-SCC}} = O(m)$ which is obviously better than the CPU cost for the 1P-SCC algorithm $C_{\text{1P-SCC}} = O(m' \cdot C_T + m \cdot C_V)$.

Example 7.3: We show an example of finding SCCs of the graph shown in Fig. 1 using Algorithm 8. The procedure is shown in Fig. 11. Suppose the initial BR-Tree is shown as the solid edges in Fig. 11(1). The G' is shown in Fig. 11(1) by adding four more edges (dotted lines) into memory. After finding SCCs in G', nodes b, c, d, and e are merged into one node $bcde$ and after topological sorting and performing dynamic programming by finding the longest paths on G', the new BR-Tree T is shown as the solid edges in Fig. 11(2). We then form a new G' as shown in Fig. 11(2) by adding three more edges (dotted lines) into memory. After finding SCCs and topological sorting on G', we find a new SCC $ghij$ by merging nodes g, h, i and j, and the final BR-Tree is shown in Fig. 11(3). □

7.4 I/O Efficiency

It is worth noting that the total number of I/O accesses depends on the number of iterations, where in an iteration it needs to access batches of edges of $E(G)$ for G sequentially. Reducing the effective number of iterations becomes a key point. Assume we can find all strongly connected components in L iterations, and assume on average P nodes are merged/rejected in the i-th iteration. These P nodes and Q edges between any pair of these P nodes will be eliminated in the following j-th iteration for $i < j \leq L$. The saving in the i-th iteration is $(P + 2Q)(L - i)b/B$, where b is the number of bytes to store a node, and B is the block size. In total, the number of I/Os we can save is

$$\sum\nolimits_{i=1}^{L}(P + 2Q)(L - i)b/B = (P + 2Q)\frac{(L-1)L}{2B}b$$

In addition, more space saved, the better to make batch edge reduction more effective, because $P/2$ more edges can be loaded in the next (i+1)-th iteration when P nodes are eliminated on average in i-th iteration. In the total L iterations,

$$\sum\nolimits_{i=1}^{L}(P/2)(i-1) = P(L-1)L/4$$

more edges can be loaded in main memory. Our techniques significantly reduce the number of iterations and therefore the I/O accesses.

We show how effective our single phase algorithm is using a large real dataset as an example. WEBSPAM-UK2007 consists 105,896,555 web-pages in 114,529 hosts in the .UK domain. The graph contains 105,895,908 nodes and 3,738,733,568 edges with the average degree 35 per node. There exist 193,670 SCCs including 84,498,517 nodes. The biggest strongly connected component contains 68,582,555 nodes and the second biggest one contains 235,228 nodes. The smallest strongly connected component contains 2 nodes. Our 1PB-SCC algorithm with early acceptance and early rejection occurs 21 iterations to find all SCC. Without early acceptance and early rejection, we need more than 50 iterations. After the last iteration, the graph to be processed only consists of 35,769,598 edges. More than 99% of edges are pruned in the first 20 iterations. Table 1 shows information for the first 5 iterations. In the first 5 iterations, 29.5M nodes and 646M edges have been pruned. Among all the nodes pruned in the first 5 iterations, 9,757,730 nodes are pruned by early rejection and 22,591,413 nodes are pruned by early acceptance. Early acceptance outperforms early rejection because 80% nodes belong to an SCC and only 20% nodes do not belong to any strongly connected component. In the first iteration, by reducing 7.6M nodes, we can load additional 3.8M edges into the memory to process in a batch in the following iter-

Iteration	1	2	3	4	5
# of Nodes Reduced	7.6M	6.8M	5.4M	5.3M	4.4M
# of Edges Reduced	113M	145M	109M	142M	137M
% of Nodes Reduced	8.61%	7.66%	5.86%	5.98%	4.77%
% of Edges Reduced	3.02%	3.87%	2.93%	3.79%	3.66%

Table 1: Nodes and Edges Reduced in the First 5 Iterations

ations, and the more space we saved by pruning nodes, the more I/Os we can reduce.

8. PERFORMANCE STUDIES

In this section, we show our experimental results by comparing our algorithms with the external contraction based algorithm EM-SCC [10] and the semi-external *DFS* based algorithm DFS-SCC (Algorithm 2). Our algorithms are all based on BR-Tree: the basic 2P-SCC algorithm (Algorithm 3), the 1P-SCC algorithm which is with both early-acceptance and early-rejection, and 1PB-SCC (Algorithm 8) which is 1P-SCC plus batch processing. In 1P-SCC and 1PB-SCC, the parameter τ for early-acceptance is 0.5% of $|V(G)|$. That is, when an SCC is greater than 0.5% of $|V(G)|$, the algorithm will do early-acceptance the graph. The early rejection is processed in every 5 iterations. All the algorithms are implemented using Visual C++ 2005 and tested on a PC with Intel Core2 Quard 2.66GHz CPU and 3.43GB memory running Windows XP. The disk block size is 64KB. The default memory size M is the memory to hold $3|V(G)|$ plus one disk block, that is $M = 4 \times (3|V(G)|) + 64K$ where 4 is the number of bytes to keep a node. We set the max time cost to be 5 hours. If a test does not stop in the time limit, we will denote it using INF. In our experiments, we do not show the result of EM-SCC since it is much slower than all other algorithms and cannot stop in most cases.

Datasets: In our experiments, we use 4 large real datasets including a massive dataset, and several synthetic datasets.

The 4 real large datasets are: cit-patent, go-uniprot, citeseerx, and WEBSPAM-UK2007. The cit-patent[4] includes all citations in patents granted in the US between 1975 and 1999. The cit-patents contains 3,774,768 nodes and 16,518,947 edges, with average degree 4.37 per node. Go-uniprot includes the gene ontology and annotations from the UniProt dataset[5]. The graph of go-uniprot contains 6,967,956 nodes and 34,770,235 edges, with average degree 4.99 per node. The citeseerx is the complete citation graph as of March 2010[6]. The graph of citeseerx contains 6,540,399 nodes and 15,011,259 edges, with average degree 2.3 per node. Among the datasets, go-uniprot and cit-patents are dense graphs and citeseerx is a sparse graph. Because these real graphs always contain small SCCs, we add random edges to make it contain more and larger SCCs. For every graph, we add 10% more edges. WEBSPAM-UK2007[7] consists of 105,896,555 webpages in 114,529 hosts in the .UK domain. The graph contains 105,895,908 nodes and 3,738,733,568 edges, with the average degree 35 per node.

We also generate 3 different kinds of synthetic graph datasets, in order to test the scalability in all situations. All the graphs contain nodes from 30M to 70M with average degree varying from 3 to 7. A synthetic graph is generated as follows. We construct a graph G by randomly selecting all nodes in SCCs first. Then we add edges among the nodes in an SCC until all nodes form an SCC. Finally, additional random nodes and edges are added to the graph. For the Massive-SCC case, a graph contains at least a massive SCC with 200,000 to 600,000 nodes. For the Large-SCC case, a graph contains at least a large SCC with 4,000 to 12,000 nodes. For the Small-SCC case, the largest SCC in a graph is less than 100 nodes. The parameters and their default values are shown in Table 2.

[4]snap.stanford.edu/data

[5]www.uniprot.org

[6]citeseerx.ist.psu.edu

[7]barcelona.research.yahoo.net/webspam/datasets/uk2007/links/

Parameter	Range	Default
Size of $\|V\|$	30M,40M,50M,60M,70M	30M
Average Degree D	3,4,5,6,7	5
Size of Massive-SCC	200K,300K,400K,500K,600K	400K
Size of Large-SCC	4K,6K,8K,10K,12K	8K
Size of Small-SCC	20,30,40,50,60	40
Number of Massive-SCCs	1	1
Number of Large-SCCs	30,40,50,60,70	50
Number of Small-SCCs	6K,8K,10K,12K,14K	10K

Table 2: Range and Default Value for Parameters

Name	1PB-SCC	1P-SCC	2P-SCC	DFS-SCC
cit-patents (T)	24s	22s	701s	840s
go-uniprot (T)	22s	21s	301s	856s
citeseerx (T)	10s	8s	517s	669s
cit-patents (I/O)	16,031	13,331	133,467	667,530
go-uniprot (I/O)	26,034	47,947	471,540	619,969
citeseerx (I/O)	15,472	13,482	104,611	392,659

Table 3: Real Large Datasets (T: time, I/O: # of I/Os)

Exp-1 (Performance on Real Large Datasets): Table 3 shows the results for the 3 real large datasets: cit-patents, go-uniprot, and citeseerx. 1P-SCC runs fastest and DFS-SCC is the slowest. 1PB-SCC has similar performance with 1P-SCC. The processing time for 1PB-SCC is slightly larger than 1P-SCC in all the three datasets. This is because in all the three datasets, the number of nodes that are involved in at least one SCC is small. As a result, even if many edges are processed together in a batch by 1PB-SCC, the number of up-edges in each batch is small, and thus 1PB-SCC has to spend more time on topological sort all the other edges. Such cost makes 1PB-SCC slower than 1P-SCC. For the number of I/Os, 1PB-SCC consumes more I/Os than 1P-SCC in the cit-patents and citeseerx datasets, but less I/Os than 1P-SCC in the go-uniprot dataset. This is because the average size of SCCs in the go-uniprot dataset is smaller than the other two datasets. In such a situation, the probability for an SCC to be merged in a certain batch is high. As a result, although the CPU cost cannot be reduced, the number of iterations for 1PB-SCC is smaller than 1P-SCC in the go-uniprot dataset. Thus the I/O cost for 1PB-SCC is small.

Exp-2 (Performance on the Massive WEBSPAM-UK2007): We test the massive WEBSPAM-UK2007 which contains 105,895,908 nodes and 3,738,733,568 edges. To store all edges on disk, we need at least 30GB. In our testing, the default memory size is set as $M = 1.18G$. We conduct two testings. The first is to test by varying the size of its graph. We extract a subgraph of WEBSPAM-UK2007 G which is an induced subgraph over a subset of nodes selected in G, ranging from 20% to 100%. The second is to test by varying the internal memory from 1GB to 3GB. The results are shown in Fig. 12 and Fig. 13 respectively.

Fig. 12(a) shows the time cost of algorithms when varying the graph size, and Fig. 12(b) shows the corresponding I/O cost. 1PB-SCC can find all SCCs for any sizes of the graph. 1P-SCC can find all SCCs when the size of graph is below 60% of the original graph. 1PB-SCC performs well to handle a massive SCC which contains more than 60 million nodes by our optimization techniques. Fig. 13 shows the effectiveness of our algorithms when there is additional memory space available. Even with a large main memory, DFS-SCC, 2P-SCC, and 1P-SCC cannot compute all SCCs. 1PB-SCC can make full use of the additional memory with additional batch processing.

Exp-3 (Vary Node Size $|V|$ in Synthetic Data): We vary the num-

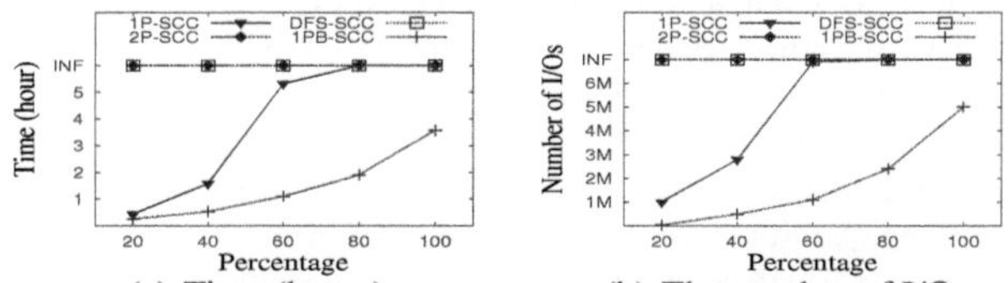

(a) Time (hours) (b) The number of I/Os

Figure 12: WEBSPAM-UK2007: Varying Node Size

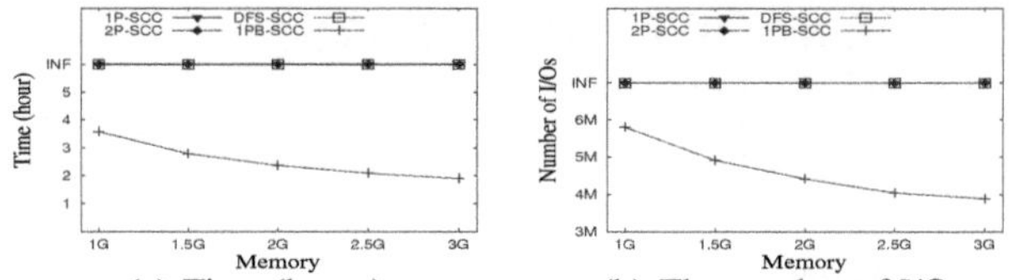

(a) Time (hours) (b) The number of I/Os

Figure 13: WEBSPAM-UK2007: Vary Memory

ber of nodes $|V(G)|$ in the graph G from 30,000,000 to 70,000,000 and we have three sets of graphs. Fig. 14(a) and Fig. 14(b) show the processing time and number of I/Os for Massive-SCC graphs. Fig. 14(c) and Fig. 14(d) show the performance for Large-SCC graphs, Fig. 14(e) and Fig. 14(f) show the performance for Small-SCC graphs. The average degree for each graph is 5. When the graph size increases, the processing time and the number of I/Os for all tests increase. For Massive-SCC, DFS-SCC increases sharply, and costs much more time and I/O. 2P-SCC cannot stop within the time limit if the size of graph is more than 40M. This is because when the graph size increases, the depth and the width of BR-Tree will also increase and the cost to calculate the dlink of edges increases very fast. The cost of 1P-SCC is much smaller. This is because the graph size decreases significantly by early-acceptance and early-rejection. 1PB-SCC performs best. This is because when the memory can hold a large number of edges, in addition to early-rejection and early-acceptance, 1PB-SCC can build the desired BR-Tree without checking each edge one by one. The topological sort reduces the cost significantly, especially when the size of an SCC is large. Although 1PB-SCC has smallest time cost, the gap of I/O between 1PB-SCC and 1P-SCC is very small, because 1PB-SCC aims to reduce the CPU cost of checking up-edges other than the I/O cost. The results for Large-SCC and Small-SCC are shown in Fig. 14(c), Fig. 14(d), Fig. 14(e), and Fig. 14(f). They share the similarity with Massive-SCC.

Exp-4 (Vary Average Degree in Synthetic Data): We vary the average degree D of nodes in a graph from 3 to 7. We also test on three sets of graphs with Massive-SCC, Large-SCC, and Small-SCC respectively. In each test, the default number of SCCs and the default average size are used. When the average degree of graph increases, the processing time and I/O cost increase for all algorithms. Among all algorithms, 1PB-SCC performs best for both time cost and I/O cost. The increasing rate is very slow. This is because that even higher degree means larger search space and more I/Os, it also indicates that more edges will stay in one SCC. 1PB-SCC takes advantage of this by merging SCCs according to the partial graph in the internal memory. The results are shown in Fig. 15.

Because the gap between DFS-SCC/2P-SCC and the others is big, we omit DFS-SCC and 2P-SCC in Fig. 15. DFS-SCC and 2P-SCC can only handle with degree 3 and 4. The DFS-SCC and 2P-SCC increase sharply, because when the average degree increases, the total number of edges that need to be checked increases, and more edges will introduce more search space and more iterations that needed to find out the *DFS* tree or BR-Tree. When

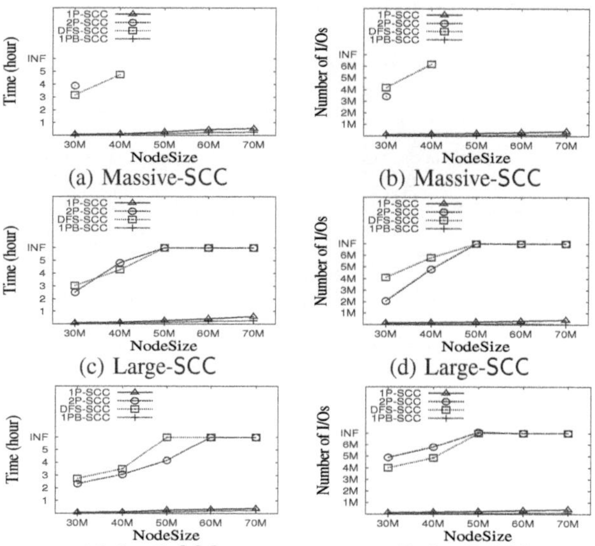

(a) Massive-SCC (b) Massive-SCC

(c) Large-SCC (d) Large-SCC

(e) Small-SCC (f) Small-SCC

Figure 14: Synthetic Data: Vary Node Size

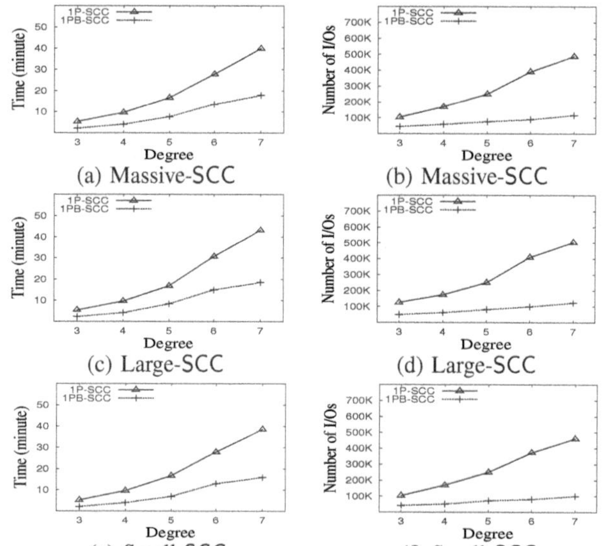

(a) Massive-SCC (b) Massive-SCC

(c) Large-SCC (d) Large-SCC

(e) Small-SCC (f) Small-SCC

Figure 15: Synthetic Data: Vary Degree

the size of SCC is small, 2P-SCC outperforms DFS-SCC, because each SCC contains a small number of nodes. These nodes are easy to be put together when searching BR-Tree. When the size of SCC becomes very large, 2P-SCC does perform well. But, when the size of SCC is large but not enough, DFS-SCC may outperform 2P-SCC. Consider degree 4. In Massive-SCC, DFS-SCC and 2P-SCC take 4.45 and 4.18 hours. In Large-SCC, DFS-SCC and 2P-SCC take 3.56 and 4.18 hours. In Small-SCC, DFS-SCC and 2P-SCC take 3.05 and 2.81 hours.

Exp-5 (Vary SCC Size in Synthetic Data): We vary the size of each SCC in each set of the graphs. For Massive-SCC graphs, we vary the size of SCC from 200,000 to 600,000. The results are shown in Fig. 16(a) and Fig. 16(b). Only 1P-SCC and 1PB-SCC can find all SCCs within the time limit. All the other algorithms cannot. 1PB-SCC performs best. The results for Large-SCCs are shown in Fig. 16(c) and Fig. 16(d). The results for Small-SCC are shown in Fig. 16(e) and Fig. 16(f). 2P-SCC cannot compute all SCCs for Massive-SCC and Large-SCC cases. For Small-SCC, 2P-

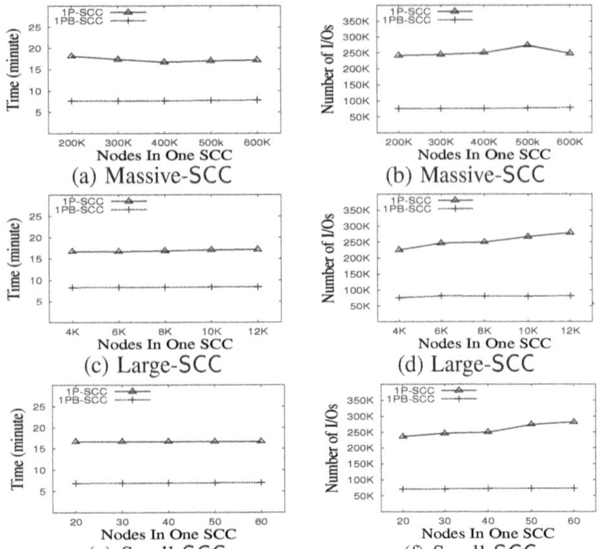

(a) Massive-SCC (b) Massive-SCC

(c) Large-SCC (d) Large-SCC

(e) Small-SCC (f) Small-SCC

Figure 16: Synthetic Data: Vary SCC Size

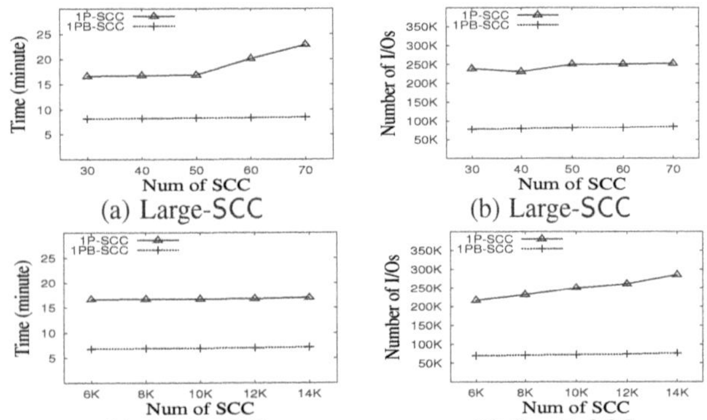

(a) Large-SCC (b) Large-SCC

(c) Small-SCC (d) Small-SCC

Figure 17: Synthetic Data: Vary the Number of SCCs

SCC takes 3.51, 4.07, and 4.17 hours when the numbers of SCCs in an SCC are, 20, 30, and 40, respectively. DFS-SCC cannot process any cases.

Exp-6 (Vary the Number of SCCs in Synthetic Data): We also test different number of SCCs for Large-SCC and Small-SCC, because we only create one SCC for Massive-SCC. The results are shown in Fig. 17. For Large-SCC, we vary the number of SCCs from 30 to 70 and each SCC contains 8,000 nodes. For Small-SCC, we vary the number of SCCs from 6K to 14K. For all tests, both 1PB-SCC and 1P-SCC can find all SCCs, and 1PB-SCC outperforms 1P-SCC. 2P-SCC cannot handle Large-SCC graphs, and takes hours for Small-SCC graphs. DFS-SCC cannot process any cases.

9. CONCLUSIONS

In this paper, we study new I/O efficient semi-external algorithms to find all SCCs for a large directed graph. We propose a new two phase algorithm with a tree construction followed by a tree search to find all SCCs. The two phase algorithm uses a bounded number of sequential scans of the graph. In order to further improve its I/O efficiency and reduce CPU cost, we propose a new single phase algorithm which combines the two phases into one phase. The three new optimization techniques we proposed along with the single phase algorithm are early acceptance, early rejection, and batch processing. By early acceptance, we contract a partial SCC into a node in an early stage while constructing a tree. By early rejection, we remove nodes that will not participate in any SCCs while constructing the tree in an early stage. The two techniques reduce the number of I/Os by reducing the graph to deal with as a smaller graph in iterations. In addition, we use batch processing technique to reduce the CPU cost. Our extensive performance studies confirm that we can significantly reduce the number of I/Os and CPU cost, and compute all SCCs that cannot be done by others in limited time.

10. ACKNOWLEDGEMENTS

The work was partially supported by grant of the Research Grants Council of the Hong Kong SAR, China No. 418512 and the fifth author was partially supported by NSFC61232006, NSFC61021004, ARCDP110102937 and ARCDP120104168.

11. REFERENCES

[1] J. Abello, A. L. Buchsbaum, and J. Westbrook. A functional approach to external graph algorithms. *Algorithmica*, 32(3), 2002.

[2] A. Aggarwal and J. S. Vitter. The input/output complexity of sorting and related problems. *Commun. ACM*, 31(9), 1988.

[3] A. V. Aho, J. E. Hopcroft, and J. D. Ullman. *Data Structures and Algorithms*. Addison-Wesley, 1983.

[4] D. Ajwani, R. Dementiev, and U. Meyer. A computational study of external-memory bfs algorithms. In *Proc. of SODA'06*, 2006.

[5] D. Ajwani and U. Meyer. *Algorithmics of Large and Complex Networks*, chapter 1: Design and Engineering of External Memory Traversal Algorithms for General Graphs. Springer, 2009.

[6] D. Ajwani, U. Meyer, and V. Osipov. Improved external memory bfs implementation. In *Proc. of ALENEX'07*, 2007.

[7] A. L. Buchsbaum, M. H. Goldwasser, S. Venkatasubramanian, and J. Westbrook. On external memory graph traversal. In *Proc. of SODA'00*, 2000.

[8] Y.-J. Chiang, M. T. Goodrich, E. F. Grove, R. Tamassia, D. E. Vengroff, and J. S. Vitter. External-memory graph algorithms. In *Proc. of SODA'95*, 1995.

[9] T. H. Cormen, C. Stein, R. L. Rivest, and C. E. Leiserson. *Introduction to Algorithms*. McGraw-Hill, 2001.

[10] A. Cosgaya-Lozano and N. Zeh. A heuristic strong connectivity algorithm for large graphs. In *Proc. of SEA'09*, 2009.

[11] R. Dementiev, P. Sanders, D. Schultes, and J. F. Sibeyn. Engineering an external memory minimum spanning tree algorithm. In *IFIP TCS*, 2004.

[12] W. Fan, J. Li, S. Ma, H. Wang, and Y. Wu. Graph homomorphism revisited for graph matching. *PVLDB*, 3(1), 2010.

[13] J. Hellings, G. H. Fletcher, and H. Haverkort. Efficient external-memory bisimulation on dags. In *Proc. of SIGMOD'12*, 2012.

[14] V. Kumar and E. J. Schwabe. Improved algorithms and data structures for solving graph problems in external memory. In *Proc of SPDP'96*, 1996.

[15] K. Mehlhorn and U. Meyer. External-memory breadth-first search with sublinear i/o. In *Proc. of ESA'02*, 2002.

[16] U. Meyer and V. Osipov. Design and implementation of a practical i/o-efficient shortest paths algorithm. In *Proc. of ALENEX'09*, 2009.

[17] U. Meyer and N. Zeh. I/O-efficient undirected shortest paths. In *Proc. of ESA'03*, 2003.

[18] U. Meyer and N. Zeh. I/O-efficient undirected shortest paths with unbounded edge lengths. In *Proc. of ESA'06*, 2006.

[19] J. F. Sibeyn. External connected components. In *Proc. of SWAT'04*, 2004.

[20] J. F. Sibeyn, J. Abello, and U. Meyer. Heuristics for semi-external depth first search on directed graphs. In *Proc. of SPAA'02*, 2002.

[21] J. S. Vitter. External memory algorithms and data structures. *ACM Comput. Surv.*, 33(2), 2001.

[22] H. Yildirim, V. Chaoji, and M. J. Zaki. Grail: Scalable reachability index for large graphs. *PVLDB*, 3(1), 2010.

TF-Label: a Topological-Folding Labeling Scheme for Reachability Querying in a Large Graph

James Cheng, Silu Huang, Huanhuan Wu, Ada Wai-Chee Fu
Department of Computer Science and Engineering
The Chinese University of Hong Kong
{jcheng, slhuang, hhwu, adafu}@cse.cuhk.edu.hk

ABSTRACT

Reachability querying is a basic graph operation with numerous important applications in databases, network analysis, computational biology, software engineering, etc. Although many indexes have been proposed to answer reachability queries, most of them are only efficient for handling relatively small graphs. We propose TF-label, an efficient and scalable labeling scheme for processing reachability queries. TF-label is constructed based on a novel topological folding (TF) that recursively folds an input graph into half so as to reduce the label size, thus improving query efficiency. We show that TF-label is efficient to construct and propose efficient algorithms and optimization schemes. Our experiments verify that TF-label is significantly more scalable and efficient than the state-of-the-art methods in both index construction and query processing.

Categories and Subject Descriptors

E.1 [**DATA**]: DATA STRUCTURES—*Graphs and networks*

General Terms

Algorithms, Performance

Keywords

Graph reachability, graph indexing, graph querying

1. INTRODUCTION

A **reachability query** asks whether there exists a path from one vertex to another vertex in a directed graph. Reachability querying is one of the fundamental operations in directed graphs. It has a wide range of applications such as processing recursive queries in data and knowledge base management, querying associations and logical reasoning in Web and Semantic Web graphs, pattern matching in graphs and XML documents, analyzing the biological function of genes, checking connections in geographic navigation systems, social network analysis, ontology querying, program analysis, and many more.

Reachability querying has been extensively studied in the past [1, 2, 3, 4, 5, 6, 10, 11, 12, 14, 17, 18, 19, 20, 21, 23, 24, 25, 26, 28]. In recent years, there is a shift of interest to handle large graphs. The more recent works [6, 18, 19, 25, 28] have highlighted the applications of reachability querying in large graphs such as Web graphs, Semantic Web and RDF graphs, social networks, large XML databases, etc., and more efforts have been given to the development of scalable methods for answering reachability queries.

As pointed out in [18], most existing methods can only handle relatively small graphs with tens to hundreds of thousands vertices and edges. For processing larger graphs, these methods are either too costly in indexing or in query processing (more discussion in Section 9), thus limiting their application to real world graphs.

For graphs with millions of vertices and edges, only a few methods can process them with reasonably good efficiency [19, 25, 28]. For larger graphs with tens of millions of vertices and edges, the only known method that attains reasonable indexing and querying efficiency is the recently proposed *backbone* structure [18]. A reachability query, where a vertex s can reach another vertex t, can be answered by (1) first finding all backbone vertices B_s that can be reached from s and all backbone vertices B_t that can reach t, and then (2) check whether any vertex in B_s can reach any vertex in B_t. Any existing method can be applied to the backbone graph to process Step (2), and querying is generally faster since the backbone can be significantly smaller than the original graph.

Although the backbone is used as a general framework (called *SCARAB* [18]) to further improve the scalability of a reachability index (including ours), an efficient and scalable method itself is still most crucial for query performance for the two main reasons (both verified in our experiments). First, SCARAB itself may not be scalable to large graphs. Second, the backbone of a large graph may still be too large for existing methods.

We propose an efficient and scalable labeling scheme, which can process large graphs that cannot be handled by SCARAB and other existing methods. Given the labels of s and t, i.e., a set of vertices that are reachable from s and can reach t respectively, we can answer whether s can reach t efficiently by simply intersecting their labels (as in [14]). We give the main idea of our method as follows.

We propose a novel data structure, called **topological folding (TF)**, based on which we develop our labeling scheme, **TF-label**. Given a directed graph, we can convert it into a directed acyclic graph (DAG) by condensing each strongly connected component (SCC) in the graph into a super node. Reachability queries can be answered on the DAG since all vertices are reachable from each other within an SCC. We define a *topological structure* $\mathcal{T}$ for the DAG. TF is intuitively a structure obtained by folding $\mathcal{T}$ into half each time, which essentially implies a great reduction in the label size as labeling is processed in $O(\lg \ell)$ levels instead of a total of ℓ levels in $\mathcal{T}$. Then, we apply a labeling technique, inspired by the

SIGMOD'13, June 22–27, 2013, New York, New York, USA.

work of [16], on the TF structure to construct labels for answering reachability queries.

We summarize the main contribution of our work as follows.

- We propose an efficient and scalable TF-based labeling scheme for reachability query processing.
- We propose optimization techniques such as special handling of high-degree vertices to further improve the scalability.
- We propose efficient algorithms for constructing the TF structure and then the labels from the TF, as well as the optimization techniques.
- Our experiments on a wide spectrum of real and synthetic datasets verify that TF-label achieves competitive indexing performance and significantly better query performance than the state-of-the-art methods [18, 19, 25, 28]. In many cases, TF-label is an order to several orders of magnitude faster in query processing. We also show that TF-label is more scalable and has stable performance with the change in various graph properties.

The rest of the paper is organized as follows. We first give some basic notations and problem definition in Section 2. Then, through Sections 3 to 7 we present the details of TF and TF-label with their design and algorithms. We evaluate the performance of TF-label in Section 8. Finally, we discuss related work in Section 9 and conclude the paper in Section 10.

2. NOTATIONS/PROBLEM DEFINITION

Given a directed graph $\mathcal{G}$, a **reachability query** asks whether there is a path from a vertex u to another vertex v in $\mathcal{G}$. We assume $u \neq v$ as it is trivial to process $u = v$. Formally, a *directed edge*, or simply an *edge* (since all edges are directed in this paper), from u to v is denoted by (u, v). A *path* P from v_1 to v_p in $\mathcal{G}$ is defined by $P = \langle v_1, \ldots, v_p \rangle$ such that (v_i, v_{i+1}) is an edge in $\mathcal{G}$ for $1 \leq i < p$. We use $u \rightarrow v$ to indicate that u can reach v (or v is reachable from u), and $u \nrightarrow v$ to indicate that u cannot reach v.

Given any two vertices u and v in a *strongly connected component (SCC)* of $\mathcal{G}$, u can always reach v. With this observation, existing methods first compute a compressed graph, $G = (V_G, E_G)$, of $\mathcal{G}$ as follows: the set of vertices V_G of G is the set of SCCs of $\mathcal{G}$, and a directed edge is created in G from one SCC C_1 to another SCC C_2 if there exists a directed edge (v_1, v_2) in $\mathcal{G}$, where v_1 is a vertex in C_1 and v_2 is a vertex in C_2. Then, a reachability query is answered by checking whether there is a path from C_u to C_v in G, where $C_u, C_v \in V_G$, u is a vertex in C_u and v is a vertex in C_v.

The compressed graph G created above is in fact a *directed acyclic graph (DAG)*. Thus, for simplicity, we call G the DAG of $\mathcal{G}$ in this paper. Since the SCCs of $\mathcal{G}$ can be computed efficiently [15], we follow the convention of existing methods and assume that the input to our algorithm is the DAG of the input directed graph.

Given a DAG, $G = (V_G, E_G)$, we define the set of *in-neighbors* (*out-neighbors*) of a vertex $v \in V_G$ as $nb_{in}(v, G) = \{u : (u, v) \in E_G\}$ ($nb_{out}(v, G) = \{u : (v, u) \in E_G\}$), and the *in-degree* (*out-degree*) of v as $deg_{in}(v, G) = |nb_{in}(v, G)|$ ($deg_{out}(v, G) = |nb_{out}(v, G)|$).

Problem definition. We study the following problem: given a DAG $G = (V_G, E_G)$, compute a set of vertex labels (also called an index) for processing reachability queries, i.e., given $s, t \in V_G$, the query whether s can reach t can be efficiently answered using the labels of s and t.

3. TOPOLOGICAL FOLDING

Through Sections 3 to 6, we present our main indexing scheme, called **TF-label**, which is designed based on a novel **topological folding** scheme of the DAG of a directed graph. We first present the concept of topological folding in this section.

3.1 Basic Topological Folding

Given a DAG $G = (V_G, E_G)$, we start by assigning each vertex in G a topological level number as follows.

DEFINITION 1 (TOPOLOGICAL LEVEL NUMBER). *Given a DAG $G = (V_G, E_G)$, the **topological level number** of a vertex $v \in V_G$, denoted by $\ell(v, G)$, is defined as follows:*

- *If $nb_{in}(v, G) = \emptyset$: $\ell(v, G) = 1$;*
- *Else: $\ell(v, G) = \max\{(\ell(u, G) + 1) : u \in nb_{in}(v, G)\}$.*

*The **topological level number** of G, denoted by $\ell(G)$, is given by $\ell(G) = \max\{\ell(v, G) : v \in V_G\}$.*

Since G is a DAG, it is easy to see that every vertex $v \in V_G$ has *exactly one* topological level number, which can be derived from a topological ordering of the DAG.

Given the topological level number, we now define the *topological levels* of a DAG and state an important property that will be used in the definition of topological folding later on.

DEFINITION 2 (TOPOLOGICAL LEVELS). *A DAG $G = (V_G, E_G)$ consists of t* topological levels *of vertices, denoted by $\{L_1(G), \ldots, L_t(G)\}$, where $t = \ell(G)$, and $L_i(G) = \{v : v \in V_G, \ell(v, G) = i\}$ for $1 \leq i \leq t$.*

LEMMA 1. *Each topological level $L_i(G)$ of a DAG G, for $1 \leq i \leq \ell(G)$, is an* independent set *of G.*

PROOF. $L_i(G)$ is an independent set of G if $\forall u, v \in L_i(G)$, $(u, v) \notin E_G$ and $(v, u) \notin E_G$. Suppose to the contrary if $(u, v) \in E_G$ or $(v, u) \in E_G$, then we have either $\ell(u, G) < \ell(v, G)$ or $\ell(v, G) < \ell(u, G)$, contradicting the fact that $u, v \in L_i(G)$, i.e., $\ell(u, G) = \ell(v, G) = i$. □

To clearly illustrate the concepts, for now let us assume that the DAG G only has edges going from vertices in $L_i(G)$ to vertices in $L_{i+1}(G)$, and there is no edge going from any vertex in $L_i(G)$ to a vertex in $L_j(G)$ where $j > i + 1$ (we will handle such edges in Section 3.2). We call such a DAG a ***k*-partite DAG**, where $k = \ell(G)$. Figure 1(a) shows an example of a k-partite DAG where $k = 6$.

We define a *topological folding scheme* that recursively folds up G by taking away half of the levels, as follows.

DEFINITION 3 (TOPOLOGICAL FOLDING (TF)). *Given a $\ell(G)$-partite DAG $G = (V_G, E_G)$, the **topological folding (TF)** of G is a set of DAGs, $\mathbb{G} = \{G_1, G_2, \ldots, G_f\}$, where each $G_i = (V_{G_i}, E_{G_i})$ is defined as follows:*

- *$V_{G_1} = V_G$ and for $2 \leq i \leq f$, $V_{G_i} = \bigcup_{1 \leq j \leq \lfloor \ell(G_{i-1})/2 \rfloor} L_{2j}(G_{i-1})$;*
- *For $1 \leq i \leq f$, E_{G_i} is a set of edges with which G_i is a $\ell(G_i)$-partite DAG and $\forall u, v \in V_{G_i}$, $u \rightarrow v$ in G_i if and only if $u \rightarrow v$ in G.*

*The **topological folding number**, or **TF number**, of G, denoted by $tf(G)$, is given by $tf(G) = f = |\mathbb{G}| = \lfloor \log_2 \ell(G) \rfloor + 1$.*

Intuitively, TF folds each G_i into half (i.e., taking away half of the levels together with their vertices) to obtain G_{i-1}, starting from $G_1 = G$ to G_f which has only one level and cannot be folded any more. Hence, we have the name "topological folding".

To correctly process reachability queries, it is necessary for the edge sets E_{G_i} to maintain the reachability of the vertices. To efficiently process reachability queries, we also want each E_{G_i} to be as small as possible. The following lemma leads to a simple and efficient method to construct E_{G_i}.

LEMMA 2. *Let $G = (V_G, E_G)$ be a $\ell(G)$-partite DAG and $\mathbb{G} = \{G_1, G_2, \ldots, G_{tf(G)}\}$ be a topological folding of G. For $2 \le i \le tf(G)$, $V_{G_{i-1}} \backslash V_{G_i}$ is an* independent set *of G_{i-1}.*

PROOF. According to Lemma 1, each $L_j(G_{i-1})$ for $1 \le j \le \ell(G_{i-1})$ is an independent set of G_{i-1}. According to the definition of $\mathbb{G}$, $V_{G_1} = V_G$ and for $2 \le i \le tf(G)$, $V_{G_{i-1}} \backslash V_{G_i}$ are the vertices at all the odd levels of G_{i-1}. Since each G_{i-1} is a $\ell(G_{i-1})$-partite DAG, the union of the vertices at all the odd levels of G_{i-1} is clearly an independent set of G_{i-1}. □

We construct the edge sets E_{G_i} as follows.

- $E_{G_1} = E_G$;
- For $2 \le i \le tf(G)$, E_{G_i} is constructed from G_{i-1} as follows: for each $v \in L_j(G_{i-1})$, where j is odd, create a new edge in E_{G_i} from each in-neighbor (if any in G_{i-1}) of v to each out-neighbor (if any in G_{i-1}) of v.

LEMMA 3. *The edge sets E_{G_i} constructed above give a valid topological folding $\mathbb{G}$ of a $\ell(G)$-partite DAG $G = (V_G, E_G)$.*

PROOF. First, each G_i is a $\ell(G_i)$-partite DAG since each edge in E_{G_i} only goes from $L_j(G_i)$ to $L_{j+1}(G_i)$, for $1 \le j \le \ell(G_i)$. Second, reachability from each vertex to another is maintained because each $u_{in} \in L_{j-1}(G_{i-1})$ is connected to each $u_{out} \in L_{j+1}(G_{i-1})$ by an edge in E_{G_i} if the edges (u_{in}, v) and (v, u_{out}) exist in G_{i-1}, where $v \in L_j(G_{i-1})$ and j is odd. □

Note that the correctness of the proof of Lemma 3 also depends on the validity of Lemma 2, because if any edge (u, v), where $u, v \in V_{G_{i-1}} \backslash V_{G_i}$, exists in G_{i-1}, then the reachability established in the proof of Lemma 3 will not be valid.

The following example illustrates the idea of topological folding.

EXAMPLE 1. *Figure 1 shows the topological folding of a 6-partite DAG G ($\ell(G) = 6$). G_2 is constructed from G_1 by adding edges $(c, f), (d, f)$, and (f, h), and then removing all vertices in the odd levels of G_1. Next, odd level vertices of G_2 are removed to form G_3.*

3.2 Dealing with Cross-Level Edges

In Section 3.1 we introduced the basic concepts and structure of topological folding of a DAG and some of its essential properties. However, the DAG G of a real world directed graph is rarely $\ell(G)$-partite. On the contrary, there can be many **cross-level edges** in G, i.e., there can be edges from vertices in $L_i(G)$ to vertices in $L_j(G)$, where $1 \le i < i+1 < j \le \ell(G)$, as shown in Figure 2.

To deal with these cross-level edges in the DAG, we observe that each DAG G_i in a topological folding $\mathbb{G}$ need not be $\ell(G_i)$-partite, but only need the following essential properties to be maintained in each G_i: **(1)** *the set of vertices to be removed from G_i is an independent set of G_{i-1} for $2 \le i \le tf(G)$*; and **(2)** *$\forall u, v \in (V_{G_i} \cap V_G)$, $u \to v$ in G_i if and only if $u \to v$ in G.*

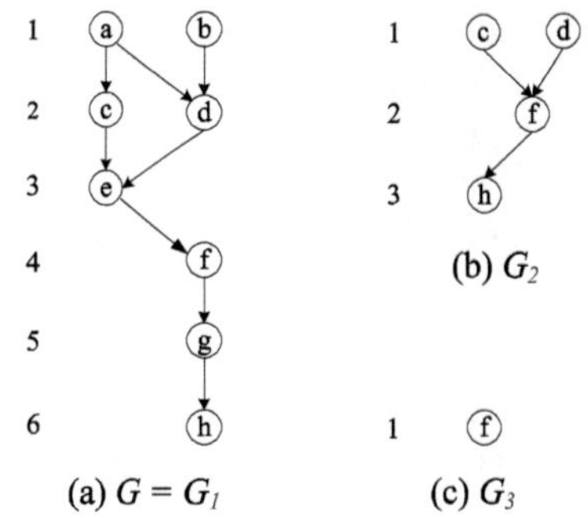

Figure 1: Topological folding

To construct each G_i that satisfies the above two properties, we devise a transformation scheme for G_{i-1}, for $2 \le i \le tf(G)$, with which we construct the corresponding **transformed topological folding** as follows:

Procedure 1. TRANSFORMED TF CONSTRUCTION:

1. $G_1 = G$, and set $i = 1$;
2. Initialize $G_i^* = G_i$, then do the following three steps in order:
   - 2.1. For $1 \le j \le \ell(G_i^*)$ and j is odd, for each $v \in L_j(G_i^*)$: Let $U = (L_k(G_i^*) \cap nb_{out}(v, G_i^*))$, where $k > j+1$. If $U \ne \emptyset$, then add a **dummy vertex** w to $L_{j+1}(G_i^*)$, add a new edge set $\{(w, u_{out}) : u_{out} \in U\}$ and a new edge (v, w) to $E_{G_i^*}$, and remove the edge set $\{(v, u_{out}) : u_{out} \in U\}$ from $E_{G_i^*}$.
   - 2.2. For $1 \le j \le \ell(G_i^*)$ and j is odd, for each $v \in L_j(G_i^*)$: Let $U = (L_k(G_i^*) \cap nb_{in}(v, G_i^*))$, where $k < j-1$ and k is even. If $U \ne \emptyset$, then add a **dummy vertex** w to $L_{j-1}(G_i^*)$, add a new edge set $\{(u_{in}, w) : u_{in} \in U\}$ and a new edge (w, v) to $E_{G_i^*}$, and remove the edge set $\{(u_{in}, v) : u_{in} \in U\}$ from $E_{G_i^*}$.
   - 2.3. For $1 \le j \le \ell(G_i^*)$ and j is odd, for each $v \in L_j(G_i^*)$: add a new edge set $\{(u_{in}, u_{out}) : u_{in} \in (L_{j-1}(G_i^*) \cap nb_{in}(v, G_i^*)), u_{out} \in (L_{j+1}(G_i^*) \cap nb_{out}(v, G_i^*))\}$ to $E_{G_i^*}$.
3. If $\ell(G_i^*) > 1$, initialize $G_{i+1} = G_i^*$, and remove all vertices at odd levels of G_{i+1} together with all edges incident to them; then, set $i = i+1$ and go to Step 2. Otherwise, return the **transformed topological folding** $\mathbb{G}^* = \{G_1^*, \ldots, G_{tf(G)}^*\}$ and quit.

Note that Step 2.2 ignores all Level-k in-neighbors of v if k is odd, because for this case a dummy vertex must have been created at an even level in Step 2.1, and is thus also handled in Step 2.2.

Also note that we do not increase the number of levels in any G_i or G_i^*, and hence $tf(G)$ is still defined in the same way as in Definition 3. We also define the *TF number* of a vertex as follows.

DEFINITION 4 (TOPOLOGICAL FOLDING NUMBER). *Let $G = (V_G, E_G)$ be a DAG, $\mathbb{G}^* = \{G_1^*, \ldots, G_{tf(G)}^*\}$ be the transformed topological folding of G, and let V^* be the set of dummy vertices created in $\mathbb{G}^*$. The* TF number *of a vertex $v \in (V_G \cup V^*)$, denoted by $tf(v)$, is given by $tf(v) = \max\{i : v \in V_{G_i^*}\}$.*

The TF number *of G is given by $tf(G) = |\mathbb{G}^*| = \lfloor \log_2 \ell(G) \rfloor + 1$. Also note that $tf(G) = \max\{tf(v) : v \in V_G\}$.*

We illustrate the concept using the following example.

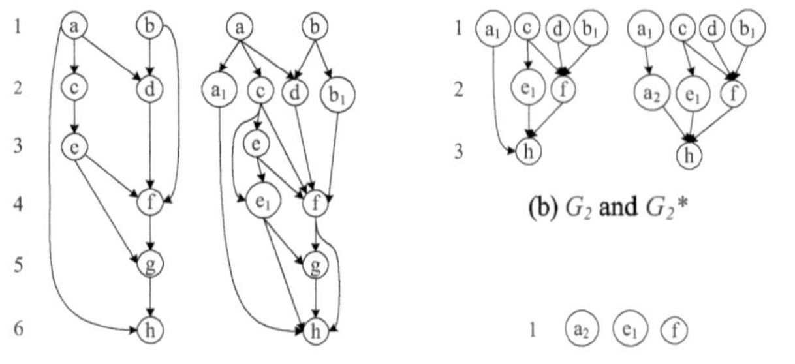

(a) G=G_1 and G_1*

(b) G_2 and G_2*

(c) $G_3 = G_3$*

Figure 2: Transformed topological folding

EXAMPLE 2. *Figure 2 shows the transformed topological folding of a DAG. The DAG G in Figure 2(a) contains a number of cross-level edges: $(a, h), (b, f), (d, f), (e, g)$. By Procedure 1, we first transform $G = G_1$ to G_1^*. At level 1, Step 2.1 is executed, we add dummy vertex a_1 for a, and add edges (a, a_1) and (a_1, h), then edge (a, h) is removed; similarly, we add b_1, (b, b_1) and (b_1, f), and remove (b, f). Next consider level 3, e_1 is added for e, and we add $(e, e_1), (e_1, g)$, and remove (e, g). At Step 2.3, we add (c, e_1) and (c, f). Finally for level 5, at Step 2.3, we add (e_1, h) and (f, h). Thus, we have constructed G_1^*, i.e., the figure on the right in Figure 2(a). Note that in G_1^*, the vertices at all the odd levels are independent of each other. At Step 3 these vertices are removed, and we obtain G_2, as shown in Figure 2(b). Repeating the process, we obtain G_2^* and G_3, while G_3^* is simply the same as G_3.*

By Definition 4, $tf(v) = 1$ for $v \in \{a, b, e, g\}$ since their last occurrence is in G_1^*. Similarly, $tf(v) = 2$ for $v \in \{a_1, c, d, b_1, h\}$, $tf(v) = 3$ for $v \in \{a_2, e_1, f\}$, and $tf(G) = 3$.

One concern in the process of Procedure 1 is that many dummy vertices and edges may be created. We will handle these cases in Sections 5 and 6. In fact, G_i^* (or G_i) is also not useful for reachability processing and hence deleted after the labeling process.

The following lemma are important in establishing the correctness of our method for reachability query answering in Section 4.1.

LEMMA 4. *Let $\mathbb{G}^* = \{G_1^*, \ldots, G_{tf(G)}^*\}$ be the transformed topological folding of a DAG $G = (V_G, E_G)$. Let G_i be the graph from which G_i^* is transformed. Then,* **(1)** *$V_{G_{i-1}^*} \backslash V_{G_i}$ is an independent set of G_{i-1}^* for $2 \leq i \leq tf(G)$; and* **(2)** *$\forall u, v \in (V_{G_i} \cap V_{G_i^*})$, where $1 \leq i \leq tf(G)$, $u \rightarrow v$ in G_i^* if and only if $u \rightarrow v$ in G_i; and* **(3)** *$\forall u, v \in (V_{G_i^*} \cap V_{G_j^*})$, where $j = i - 1$ and $1 < i \leq tf(G)$, $u \rightarrow v$ in G_i^* if and only if $u \rightarrow v$ in G_j^*.*

PROOF. We first prove **(1)**. According to Procedure 1, we obtain G_i by removing the odd levels of G_{i-1}^*, i.e., $V_{G_{i-1}}^* \backslash V_{G_i}$. Since there is no edge from a vertex to another vertex at the same level in G_{i-1}^*, each level of G_{i-1}^* is an independent set of G_{i-1}^*. For any edge that goes from u at an odd level to v at another odd level, the edge is removed from G_{i-1}^* and a dummy vertex is created to preserve the connection from u to v. Thus, for any $u, v \in V_{G_{i-1}}^* \backslash V_{G_i}$, (u, v) does not exist in G_{i-1}^*.

Next we prove **(2)**. From G_i to G_i^*, Procedure 1 either converts a cross-level edge to a path with a middle dummy vertex or adds an edge from an in-neighbor to an out-neighbor of an odd-level vertex in G_i. Thus, in both cases, **(2)** is true.

Lastly, we prove **(3)**. According to Procedure 1, all the cross-level edges in G_j are removed from G_j^* and hence a vertex w at L_k of G_j^*, where $1 \leq k \leq \ell(G_j^*)$ and k is odd, has only in-neighbors at L_{k-1} (if any) and out-neighbors at L_{k+1} (if any). Since Procedure 1 creates an edge from every in-neighbor of w to every out-neighbor of w, we have $u \rightarrow v$ in G_i if and only if $u \rightarrow v$ in G_j^* for any $u, v \in (V_{G_i} \cap V_{G_j^*})$, which together with **(2)** implies **(3)**. □

Note that by a recursive analysis on **(3)** of Lemma 4, we can actually prove a stronger lemma that shows $u \rightarrow v$ in G_i^* if and only if $u \rightarrow v$ in G_j^*, for all $u, v \in (V_{G_i^*} \cap V_{G_j^*})$, where $1 \leq j < i \leq tf(G)$ (instead of $j = i - 1$ as in **(3)** of Lemma 4).

4. LABELING AND QUERY ANSWERING

In this section, we present our TF-based labeling scheme and discuss reachability query answering using the labels.

4.1 The Labeling Scheme

The label of a vertex is defined as follows.

DEFINITION 5 (VERTEX LABEL). *Let $G = (V_G, E_G)$ be a DAG, $\mathbb{G}^* = \{G_1^*, \ldots, G_{tf(G)}^*\}$ be the transformed topological folding of G, and let V^* be the set of dummy vertices created in $\mathbb{G}^*$. The* ***in-label*** *and* ***out-label*** *of a vertex $v \in (V_G \cup V^*)$, denoted by $label_{in}(v)$ and $label_{out}(v)$, are defined as follows:*

- *$label_{in}(v)$: (1) $v \in label_{in}(v)$, and (2) for any $u \in label_{in}(v)$, $nb_{in}(u, G_{tf(u)}^*) \subset label_{in}(v)$.*
- *$label_{out}(v)$: (1) $v \in label_{out}(v)$, and (2) for any $u \in label_{out}(v)$, $nb_{out}(u, G_{tf(u)}^*) \subset label_{out}(v)$.*

Intuitively, we add to $label_{in}(v)$ and $label_{out}(v)$ recursively the in-neighbors and out-neighbors in the folding graph G_i^* of each vertex u currently in $label_{in}(v)$ and $label_{out}(v)$, where $i = tf(u)$.

The following property between a vertex and its in-neighbors/out-neighbors shows that, in constructing the labels for a vertex, we only go for reachable vertices with higher TF number and ignore all other reachable vertices. This is a crucial design principle of our labeling scheme that leads to *a significant reduction on the label size (compared with transitive closure), since each vertex has $O(\ell(G))$ levels of reachable vertices, but only $O(\lg \ell(G))$ levels of reachable vertices with higher TF number.*

LEMMA 5. *If $w \in nb_{in}(u, G_{tf(u)}^*)$ or $w \in nb_{out}(u, G_{tf(u)}^*)$, then $tf(w) > tf(u)$.*

PROOF. Since w is in $G_{tf(u)}^*$, we have $tf(w) \geq tf(u)$. However, $tf(w) = tf(u)$ implies that both w and u are in an independent set of $G_{tf(u)}^*$, which contradicts the fact that the edge (u, w) or (w, u) exists in $G_{tf(u)}^*$. Thus, $tf(w) \neq tf(u)$ and $tf(w) > tf(u)$. □

We use the following example to illustrate the labeling scheme.

EXAMPLE 3. *Consider the labeling for vertex a. Initially, a is added to $label_{in}(a)$ and $label_{out}(a)$. Since $tf(a) = 1$ and $nb_{in}(a, G_1^*) = \emptyset$, we finalize $label_{in}(a) = \{a\}$. Next, since $nb_{out}(a, G_1^*) = \{a_1, c, d\}$, $\{a_1, c, d\}$ are added to $label_{out}(a)$. Since a_1 has an out-neighbor a_2 in $G_{tf(a_1)}^* = G_2^*$, we add a_2 to $label_{out}(a)$. We also add $\{e_1, f\}$ to $label_{out}(a)$ for $nb_{out}(c, G_2^*) = \{e_1, f\}$ and $nb_{out}(d, G_2^*) = \{f\}$. The vertices $\{a_2, e_1, f\}$ have TF number of 3 but they have no out-neighbor in G_3^*, and hence the labeling for a is completed. The labels for all vertices are shown in Table 1.*

4.2 Reachability Querying using Labels

We now discuss how we use the vertex labels to process reachability queries. Given two vertices s and t in G, we ask whether s can reach t, the query answer is given by the following equation.

vertex	$label_{out}$	$label_{in}$
a	{a, a_1, c, d, e_1, f}	{a}
b	{b, b_1, d, f}	{b}
e	{e, e_1, f}	{c, e}
g	{g, h}	{e_1, f, g}
a_1	{a_1, a_2}	{a_1}
c	{c, e_1, f}	{c}
d	{d, f}	{d}
b_1	{b_1, f}	{b_1}
h	{h}	{a_2, e_1, f, h}
a_2	{a_2}	{a_2}
e_1	{e_1}	{e_1}
f	{f}	{f}

Table 1: Labeling for the example in Figure 2

$$s \to t = \begin{cases} \texttt{true}, & \text{if } label_{out}(s) \cap label_{in}(t) \neq \emptyset; \\ \texttt{false}, & \text{if } label_{out}(s) \cap label_{in}(t) = \emptyset. \end{cases} \quad (1)$$

We give an example of reachability query processing as follows.

EXAMPLE 4. *Consider the example in Figure 2, the labeling is shown in Table 1. Suppose the query is to ask whether c can reach h: since $label_{out}(c) \cap label_{in}(h) = \{e_1, f\}$, the answer is* `true`. *Now consider whether a can reach b: since $label_{out}(a) \cap label_{in}(b) = \emptyset$, the answer is* `false`.

Lemmas 6-9 and Theorem 1 establish the correctness of reachability query answering by Equation (1). The lemmas themselves also reveal important properties and the design of the TF structure, and hence how TF labeling works for reachability query answering.

LEMMA 6. *Given a path $P = \langle u_1, \ldots, u_\alpha \rangle$ in any graph in $\mathbb{G}^*$, there exists a sequence of vertices $S = \langle u_1 = v_1, \ldots, v_\beta = u_\alpha \rangle$ such that for $1 \leq i < \beta$:* **(1)** *the edge (v_i, v_{i+1}) is in G^*_j where $j = \min(tf(v_i), tf(v_{i+1}))$; and* **(2)** *the sequence S is maximal, i.e., no sub-sequence can be inserted between any v_i and v_{i+1} such that the resultant sequence also satisfies* **(1)**.

PROOF. The path P implies that there exists a sequence $S = \langle u_1, S_1, u_2, S_2, \ldots, u_{\alpha-1}, S_{\alpha-1}, u_\alpha \rangle$, where each S_i for $1 \leq i < \alpha$ is constructed (according to Procedure 1) as follows.

If $\ell(u_i, G^*_j) = \ell(u_{i+1}, G^*_j) + 1$, where $j = \min(tf(u_i), tf(u_{i+1}))$, then either u_i or u_{i+1} will be removed in G_{j+1} and hence S_i must be an empty set. In this case, we have (u_i, u_{i+1}) in G^*_j.

Otherwise, (u_i, u_{i+1}) is a cross-level edge in G_j, where $j = \min(tf(u_i), tf(u_{i+1}))$, then S_i is a sequence of dummy vertices. Assume $j = tf(u_i)$ (the case $j = tf(u_{i+1})$ can be processed similarly). To preserve the reachability from u_i to u_{i+1} in G_j, at least one dummy vertex w must be created in G^*_j together with the edges (u_i, w) and (w, u_{i+1}). Thus, we have the edge (u_i, w) in G^*_j. If (w, u_{i+1}) is still a cross-level edge in $G_{j'}$, where $j' = \min(tf(w), tf(u_{i+1}))$, then another dummy vertex is to be created in $G^*_{j'}$ to preserve the reachability from w to u_{i+1} in G^*_j. A recursive expansion in this way gives the sub-sequence $S'_i = \langle u_i = w_1, w_2, \ldots, w_{\gamma-1}, w_\gamma = u_{i+1} \rangle$, where $S_i = \langle w_2, \ldots, w_{\gamma-1} \rangle$, and for $1 \leq k < \gamma$, (w_k, w_{k+1}) in G^*_j and $j = \min(tf(w_k), tf(w_{k+1}))$. S'_i is ensured to be maximal if the above recursive expansion is executed until no more sub-sequence can be generated.

By relabeling the vertices, we obtain $S = \langle u_1 = v_1, \ldots, v_\beta = u_\alpha \rangle$ such that S satisfies both **(1)** and **(2)**. □

Lemma 6 is used to show that a sequence of vertices S with a special property (as specified in the lemma) exists for a path P in any graph in $\mathbb{G}^*$. The existence of such a sequence is essential in proving the correctness of Lemma 9 and hence Theorem 1.

LEMMA 7. *Given a sequence of vertices $S = \langle s = v_1, \ldots, v_\beta = t \rangle$, where for $1 \leq i < \beta$, the edge (v_i, v_{i+1}) is in G^*_j where $j = \min(tf(v_i), tf(v_{i+1}))$: if s and t are both in some graph $G^*_\phi \in \mathbb{G}^*$, then $s \to t$ in G^*_ϕ.*

PROOF. First, each edge (v_i, v_{i+1}) in G^*_j implies $v_i \to v_{i+1}$ in G^*_j. We can derive the reachability from v_1 to v_β in G^*_ϕ as follows.

Consider the vertex $v_i \in S$ where $tf(v_i) < \phi$ and $tf(v_i) \leq tf(v)$ for all $v \in S \backslash \{v_i\}$. If v_i exists in S, then according to Procedure 1, v_{i-1} must be connected to v_{i+1} in $G^*_{tf(v_i)}$ in order to preserve the the reachability from v_{i-1} to v_{i+1} via v_i. Thus, removing v_i from S we still have $v_{i-1} \to v_{i+1}$ in G^*_j, where $j = \min(tf(v_{i-1}), tf(v_{i+1}))$. We repeat the above process with $S = S \backslash \{v_i\}$ until we have $tf(v) \geq \phi$ for all remaining vertices v in S, and let $S' = \langle s = v_1, \ldots, v_{\beta'} = t \rangle$ be the new sequence obtained at the end of this process. We continue with S' as follows.

Consider the vertex $v_i \in S'$ that is not in G^*_ϕ and $tf(v_i) \geq tf(v)$ for all $v \in S' \backslash \{v_i\}$. If v_i exists in S', then we have $v_{i-1} \to v_i$ in $G^*_{tf(v_{i-1})}$ and $v_i \to v_{i+1}$ in $G^*_{tf(v_{i+1})}$. Since v_i is not in G^*_ϕ and $tf(v_i) > \phi$, v_i is a dummy vertex and v_i preserves the reachability from v_{i-1} to v_{i+1} in G^*_j, where $j = \min(tf(v_{i-1}), tf(v_{i+1}))$. Thus, removing v_i from S' we still have $v_{i-1} \to v_{i+1}$ in G^*_j. We repeat the above process with $S' = S' \backslash \{v_i\}$ until all the remaining vertices are in G^*_ϕ. Let $S'' = \langle s = v_1, \ldots, v_{\beta''} = t \rangle$ be the new sequence obtained at the end of this process.

Note that both s and t are still in S'' since s and t are in G^*_ϕ. According to the derivation process, we have $v_i \to v_{i+1}$ in G^*_ϕ for $1 \leq i \leq \beta''$, from which we have $s = v_1 \to \cdots \to v_{\beta''} = t$. Thus, $s \to t$ in G^*_ϕ. □

Lemma 7 reveals an important reachability relation between vertices in a sequence as defined in Lemma 6. This reachability relation is also crucial in the proofs of Lemmas 8 and 9.

LEMMA 8. *Given two vertices $s, t \in V_G$, if there exists a vertex $x \in label_{out}(s) \cap label_{in}(t)$, then $s \to t$ in G.*

PROOF. Let us first assume that $x \neq s$ and $x \neq t$. Then, according to Definition 5, if $x \in label_{out}(s)$, there exists a vertex $u \in label_{out}(s)$ such that $x \in nb_{out}(u, G^*_{tf(u)})$. Moreover, $u \in label_{out}(s)$ in turn implies that there exists $u' \in label_{out}(s)$ such that $u \in nb_{out}(u', G^*_{tf(u')})$. Thus, we obtain a sequence $S_{out} = \langle s = u_1, \ldots, u_\alpha = x \rangle$, where for $1 \leq i < \alpha$ the edge (u_i, u_{i+1}) is in $G^*_{tf(u_i)}$. Similarly, we obtain another sequence $S_{in} = \langle x = v_\beta, \ldots, v_1 = t \rangle$, where for $1 \leq i < \beta$ the edge (v_{i+1}, v_i) is in $G^*_{tf(v_i)}$. According to Lemma 5, $tf(u_i) < tf(u_{i+1})$ for $1 \leq i < \alpha$ and $tf(v_i) < tf(v_{i+1})$ for $1 \leq i < \beta$. Thus, according to Lemma 7, the sequence $S = \langle s = u_1, \ldots, u_\alpha = x = v_\beta, \ldots, v_1 = t \rangle$ implies that $s \to t$ in G^*_1, and hence $s \to t$ in $G = G_1$ by Lemma 4. If $x = t$, then $t \in label_{out}(s)$ gives the sequence $S = \langle s = u_1, \ldots, u_\alpha = x = t \rangle$, which implies that $s \to t$ in G. And similarly for $x = s$. □

The following lemma proves the reverse statement of Lemma 8.

LEMMA 9. *Given two vertices $s, t \in V_G$, if $s \to t$ in G, then there exists a vertex $x \in label_{out}(s) \cap label_{in}(t)$.*

PROOF. We show that if $s \to t$ in G, then there exists a sequence of vertices $S = \langle s, \ldots, t \rangle$ such that there is a vertex x in S, where $x \in label_{out}(s)$ and $x \in label_{in}(t)$.

First, $s \to t$ in G implies that there is a path $P = \langle s = \ldots, t \rangle$ in G^*_1 (by Procedure 1 and Lemma 4). According to Lemma

6, there exists a sequence $S = \langle s = w_1, \ldots, w_\gamma = t\rangle$ such that for $1 \le i < \gamma$, the edge (w_i, w_{i+1}) is in G_j^* where $j = \min(tf(w_i), tf(w_{i+1}))$, and S is maximal.

Next, we show that there exists a unique vertex x in S such that $tf(x) > tf(w)$ for all $w \in S\backslash\{x\}$. It is trivially true that there exists x such that $tf(x) \ge tf(w)$ for all $w \in S\backslash\{x\}$. To remove the '=' sign, suppose to the contrary that there exists another vertex x' such that $tf(x') = tf(x) = j$, which implies that x and x' are both in G_j^*. Assume, without loss of generality, that x appears before x' in S. Then, $tf(x') = tf(x) = j$ implies that x and x' are both in an independent set of G_j^* according to Lemma 4. The independence between x and x' implies that either (1) $x \not\twoheadrightarrow x'$ or (2) x reaches x' via some other vertex x'' in G_j^* such that $tf(x'') > tf(x)$. For (1), it is a contradiction since $x \rightarrow x'$ in G_j^* according to Lemma 7. For (2), we have the path $P' = \langle x, \ldots, x'', \ldots, x'\rangle$ in G_j^* and by Lemma 6 we can obtain another sequence $S' = \langle x, \ldots, x'', \ldots, x'\rangle$ from P', which contradicts to the fact that S is maximal.

We complete the proof by showing that the unique vertex x, where $tf(x) > tf(w)$ for all $w \in S\backslash\{x\}$, is in both $label_{out}(s)$ and $label_{in}(t)$. Let $S = \langle s = u_1, \ldots, u_\alpha = x = v_\beta, \ldots, v_1 = t\rangle$. We first consider the sub-sequence $\langle s = u_1, \ldots, u_\alpha = x\rangle$. If $s = u_1 = u_\alpha = x$, then $x \in label_{out}(s)$ by Definition 5. If $\alpha > 1$, for each u_i, we find the first u_j, where $1 \le i < j \le \alpha$, such that $tf(u_i) < tf(u_j)$. Such a u_j must exist since there is at least one vertex u_α where $tf(u_i) < tf(u_\alpha)$. Moreover, $u_i \rightarrow u_j$ in $G_{tf(u_i)}^*$ according to Lemma 7. Thus, (u_i, u_j) is an edge in $G_{tf(u_i)}^*$ because otherwise, u_i reaches u_j in $G_{tf(u_i)}^*$ via some other vertex u_k, which contradicts to the fact that S is maximal.

Thus, we obtain a sequence $\langle s = u_1', \ldots, u_{\alpha'}' = x\rangle$, where $tf(u_i') < tf(u_{i+1}')$ and (u_i', u_{i+1}') is an edge in $G_{tf(u_i')}^*$ for $1 \le i < \alpha'$. According to Definition 5, $s = u_1' \in label_{out}(s)$, $u_2' \in label_{out}(s)$ since $u_1' \in label_{out}(s)$ and $u_2' \in nb_{out}(G_{tf(u_1')}^*)$, …, $u_{i+1}' \in label_{out}(s)$ since $u_i' \in label_{out}(s)$ and $u_{i+1}' \in nb_{out}(G_{tf(u_i')}^*)$, …, $x = u_{\alpha'}' \in label_{out}(s)$ since $u_{\alpha'-1}' \in label_{out}(s)$ and $u_\alpha' \in nb_{out}(G_{tf(u_{\alpha'-1}')}^*)$. Finally, a similar analysis shows that $x \in label_{in}(t)$. □

We note that the sequence S in the proof of Lemma 9 may not be unique, but we only need to show the existence of one such sequence for the proof.

The following theorem proves the correctness of reachability query answering by vertex labels.

THEOREM 1. *Given a reachability query whether a vertex $s \in V_G$ can reach another vertex $t \in V_G$, the answer given by Equation 1 is correct.*

PROOF. The proof follows directly from Lemmas 8 and 9. □

5. REMOVING DUMMY VERTICES

The vertex labels constructed in Section 4 contain dummy vertices, which may take up a lot of space and incur extra processing in query answering. In this section, we propose a new label with all dummy vertices removed.

According to Procedure 1, a dummy vertex w is created only as either an out-neighbor of u or an in-neighbor of v for a cross-level edge (u, v). If w is created as an out-neighbor of u (or an in-neighbor of v), then u (or v) is called the **in-source vertex** (or **out-source vertex**) of w, denoted by $src(w) = u$ (or $src(w) = v$). If $src(w) = v$ is a vertex in G, i.e., v is not a dummy vertex, then v is called the **root vertex** of w, denoted by $rt(w)$. In general, we have $rt(w) = src(src(\cdots src(w) \cdots))$.

With the definition of in-source/out-source vertices and root vertices, we define a new vertex label as follows.

DEFINITION 6 (VERTEX LABEL WITHOUT DUMMIES). *Let $f(u)$ be a function such that $f(u) = rt(u)$ if u is a dummy vertex, and $f(u) = u$ otherwise. The new labels of a vertex $v \in V_G$, denoted by $label2_{in}(v)$ and $label2_{out}(v)$, are defined as follows:*

- *$label2_{in}(v) = \{f(u) : u \in label_{in}(v)\}$.*
- *$label2_{out}(v) = \{f(u) : u \in label_{out}(v)\}$.*

Intuitively, $label2_{in}(v)$ is obtained by replacing every dummy vertex u in $label_{in}(v)$ with $rt(u)$, and similarly for $label2_{out}(v)$.

For all $v \in V_G$, $|label2_{in}(v)| \le |label_{in}(v)|$ and $|label2_{out}(v)| \le |label_{out}(v)|$, since there can be multiple dummy vertices with the same root vertex and/or the root vertex may already exist in the set. Thus, compared with *label*, *label2* reduces index storage space and improves querying efficiency.

The following lemma and theorem prove the correctness of query answering using *label2*.

LEMMA 10. *Given $s, t \in V_G$, **(1)** if $x \in label_{out}(s)$ and $rt(x) \notin label_{out}(s)$, then $s \rightarrow rt(x)$ in G; and **(2)** if $x \in label_{in}(t)$ and $rt(x) \notin label_{in}(t)$, then $rt(x) \rightarrow t$ in G.*

PROOF. We first prove **(1)**. From the proof of Lemma 8, $x \in label_{out}(s)$ implies a sequence $S = \langle s = u_1, \ldots, u_\alpha = x\rangle$, where for $1 \le i < \alpha$ the edge (u_i, u_{i+1}) is in $G_{tf(u_i)}^*$. Since x is a dummy vertex, according to Procedure 1 there exists another sequence $S_2 = \langle rt(x) = v_1, \ldots, v_{\beta-1} = src(x), v_\beta = x\rangle$, where for $1 \le i < \beta$: either the edge (v_i, v_{i+1}) is in $G_{tf(v_i)}^*$ if $rt(x)$ is an in-source vertex, or (v_{i+1}, v_i) is in $G_{tf(v_i)}^*$ if $rt(x)$ is an out-source vertex.

If $rt(x)$ is an in-source vertex, then we construct the proof as follows. Let $y = x$. Start from $i = \alpha - 1$ to $i = 2$, we re-assign $y = u_i$ if $u_i = src(y)$ (note that $i \ne 1$ since $s = u_1 = rt(x)$ contradicts $rt(x) \notin label_{out}(s)$). Let $\langle s = u_1, \ldots, u_{\alpha'} = y\rangle$ be the sub-sequence such that $u_{\alpha'-1} \ne src(y)$. According to Procedure 1, $u_{\alpha'-1}$ is an in-neighbor of $rt(x)$ so that $u_{\alpha'-1}$ is also connected to v_2 in $G_{tf(rt(x))}^*$ to preserve the reachability from $u_{\alpha'-1}$ to $rt(x)$'s cross-level out-neighbors (now via v_2). Note that v_2 may not be in $label_{out}(s)$, i.e., S, because v_2 may not be an out-neighbor of $u_{\alpha'-1}$ in $G_{tf(u_{\alpha'-1})}^*$, i.e., $tf(v_2) < tf(u_{\alpha'-1})$. Thus, we have the sequence $\langle s = u_1, \ldots, u_{\alpha'-1}, rt(x)\rangle$, where $(u_{\alpha'-1}, rt(x))$ in $G_{tf(rt(x))}^*$, from which we have $s \rightarrow rt(x)$ in G by Lemma 7.

If $rt(x)$ is an out-source vertex, then we have $\langle s = u_1, \ldots, u_\alpha = x = v_\beta, v_{\beta-1} = src(x), \ldots, v_1 = rt(x)\rangle$. Again, by Lemma 7 we have $s \rightarrow rt(x)$ in G.

Similarly we can prove **(2)**. □

THEOREM 2. *Given a reachability query whether a vertex $s \in V_G$ can reach another vertex $t \in V_G$, the answer given by Equation 1 with "label" replaced by "label2" is correct.*

PROOF. Let $X = label_{out}(s) \cap label_{in}(t)$ and $X2 = label2_{out}(s) \cap label2_{in}(t)$. We show that **(1)** if $X \ne \emptyset$, then $X2 \ne \emptyset$, and **(2)** if $X = \emptyset$, then $X2 = \emptyset$.

We first prove **(1)**. If $X \ne \emptyset$, then either (i) $\exists x \in X$, x is not a dummy vertex, or (ii) $\forall x \in X$, x is a dummy vertex. For (i), x is also in $X2$ according to Definition 6 and hence $X2 \ne \emptyset$. For (ii), $rt(x)$ is in $X2$ and hence $X2 \ne \emptyset$.

We now prove **(2)**. Suppose to the contrary that $X2 \ne \emptyset$, which must be caused by the replacement of some dummy vertex x by $rt(x)$, i.e., $rt(x) \in X2$ for some dummy vertex x. We have the following possible cases:

vertex	$label2_{out}$	$label2_{in}$
a	{a, c, d, e, f}	{a}
b	{b, d, f}	{b}
e	{e, f}	{c, e}
g	{g, h}	{e,f,g}
c	{c, e, f}	{c}
d	{d, f}	{d}
h	{h}	{a,e,f,h}
f	{f}	{f}

Table 2: Removing dummy vertices from the labels in Table 1

(i) If $x \in label_{out}(s)$ and $rt(x) \notin label_{out}(s)$: then we have $rt(x) \in label2_{out}(s)$ as a replacement of x. Thus, by Lemma 10, we have $s \rightarrow rt(x)$ in G.

Otherwise, $rt(x)$ is originally in $label_{out}(s)$ since $rt(x) \in X2$. Thus, we have $rt(x) = s$, or $s \rightarrow rt(x)$ in G by Lemma 8 since $rt(x) \in label_{out}(s)$ and $rt(x) \in label_{in}(rt(x))$.

(ii) If $x \in label_{in}(t)$ and $rt(x) \notin label_{in}(t)$: then similarly as (i) we have $rt(x) \rightarrow t$ in G by Lemma 10.

Otherwise, similarly as (i) we have either $rt(x) = t$, or $rt(x) \rightarrow t$ in G.

For every combination of the cases in (i) and (ii) above, we have $s \rightarrow t$ in G, which implies $X \neq \emptyset$ by Lemma 9 and thus a contradiction. Therefore, we have our result that $X = \emptyset$ implies $X2 = \emptyset$.

Given **(1)** and **(2)**, the correctness of the theorem follows directly from Theorem 1. □

The following example illustrates the concept of *label2*.

EXAMPLE 5. *Table 2 shows the labeling of the same graph in Example 3 with dummy vertices removed. In Table 1, we have* $label_{out}(b) = \{b, b_1, d, f\}$, *but* $label2_{out}(b) = \{b, d, f\}$ *in Table 2 since* $rt(b_1) = b$ *already exists in* $label_{out}(b)$. *For* $label_{out}(c) = \{c, e_1, f\}$ *in Table 1, we replace dummy vertex* e_1 *with* $rt(e_1) = e$ *and obtain* $label2_{out}(c) = \{c, e, f\}$ *in 2. Similarly, we obtain label2 for all other vertices in G.*

6. HANDLING HIGH-DEGREE VERTICES

In the construction of G^*_{i+1} from G^*_i, or G^*_i from G_i, many new edges may be created to connect the in-neighbors of a vertex v to v's out-neighbors. Although such connections are necessary to preserve reachability after v is removed, the construction is costly in the presence of high-degree vertices since the number of edges created is given by $(deg_{in}(v, G_i) * deg_{out}(v, G_i))$. The following example illustrates the problem caused by high-degree vertices.

EXAMPLE 6. *Consider the example in Figure 3(a), f is a high-degree vertex with* $deg_{in}(f, G_1) * deg_{out}(f, G_1) = 3*5 = 15$. *By Procedure 1, f is removed at the first iteration and we need to add many edges in order to maintain reachability in* G_2 *as shown in Figure 3(b). In the DAG of many real graphs, often we have a few vertices with very high degree (these vertices normally correspond to giant SCCs in the original directed graph). For example, in the p2p dataset, we have a vertex v with* $deg_{in}(v, G_1) = 43562$ *and* $deg_{out}(v, G_1) = 366$. *Such high-degree vertices will take up a lot of space in the intermediate graphs and hence incur a significant amount of extra processing in the overall labeling process.*

Here we propose a method to address this problem. For simplicity, in the subsequent discussion we focus on handling high-degree

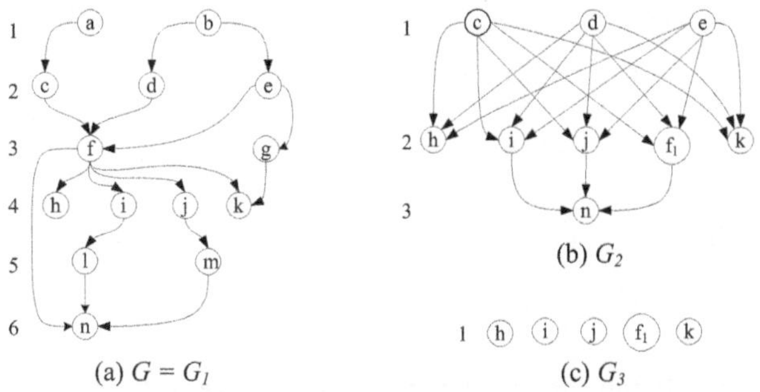

Figure 3: Problem caused by high-degree vertices

vertices in $G_1 = G$, but we remark that the method applies to other G_i in the same way.

Given a vertex $v \in V_G$, we define the set of vertices that are reachable from v as $reach_{out}(v, G) = \{u : v \rightarrow u\}$, and the set of vertices that can reach v as $reach_{in}(v, G) = \{u : u \rightarrow v\}$. Let H be the set of top-k high-degree vertices defined as follows: $\forall h \in H$ and $v \in V_G \backslash H$, $(deg_{in}(h, G) * deg_{out}(h, G)) \geq (deg_{in}(v, G) * deg_{out}(v, G))$. We may set k as the h-index value of a graph [8, 9].

We propose a new vertex label of a vertex $v \in V_G$, denoted by $label3_{in}(v)$ and $label3_{out}(v)$, which have *dummy vertices removed* as in Section 5 and *high-degree vertices handled* as follows:

1. For each $h \in H$, $label3_{in}(h) = \{h\}$ and $label3_{out}(h) = \{h\}$.
2. For each $v \in V_G \backslash H$, initialize $label3_{in}(v) = \{h : h \in H, v \in reach_{out}(h, G)\}$ and $label3_{out}(v) = \{h : h \in H, v \in reach_{in}(h, G)\}$.
3. Remove all vertices in H, together with all edges incident to them, from G. Let G' be the remaining graph.
4. For each $v \in V_{G'}$ (i.e., $v \in V_G \backslash H$), construct $label2_{in}(v)$ and $label2_{out}(v)$ from G' as discussed in Sections 3-5.
5. For each $v \in V_G \backslash H$, $label3_{in}(v) = label2_{in}(v) \cup label3_{in}(v)$ and $label3_{out}(v) = label2_{out}(v) \cup label3_{out}(v)$.

The following theorem proves the correctness of reachability query answering using *label3* obtained from the above steps.

THEOREM 3. *Given a reachability query whether a vertex* $s \in V_G$ *can reach another vertex* $t \in V_G$, *the answer given by Equation 1 with "label" replaced by "label3" is correct.*

PROOF. First, we show that if $s \rightarrow t$ in G, i.e., there exists a path $P = \langle s, \ldots, t \rangle$ in G, then the answer returned is `true`.

1. If P contains no vertex in H, then P must be in the remaining graph G'. Thus, query answering using "*label2*", which is constructed from G' and contained in "*label3*", returns `true` as proved in Theorem 2.
2. If P contains at least one vertex $h \in H$, then we must have $h \in label3_{out}(s)$ and $h \in label3_{in}(t)$. Thus, the answer returned is `true`.

Next, we show that if $s \nrightarrow t$ in G, then the answer returned is `false`. Suppose to the contrary that the answer is `true`, i.e., $\exists x \in (label3_{out}(s) \cap label3_{in}(t))$.

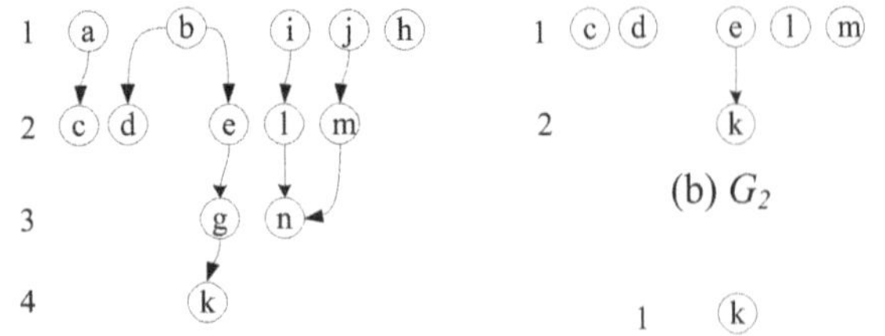

(a) $G = G_1$ (b) G_2 (c) G_3

Figure 4: Topological folding with high-degree vertex removed

	$label3_{out}$	$label3_{in}$
a	{a,c,f}	{a}
b	{b,d,e,f,k}	{b}
c	{c,f}	{c}
d	{d,f}	{d}
e	{e,f,k}	{e}
f	{f}	{f}
g	{g,k}	{e,g}
h	{h}	{f,h}
i	{i,l}	{f,i}
j	{j,m}	{f,j}
k	{k}	{f,k}
l	{l}	{f,l}
m	{m}	{f,m}
n	{n}	{f,l,m,n}

(a)

	$label2_{out}$	$label2_{in}$
a	{a,c,f,h,i,j,k}	{a}
b	{b,d,e,f,h,i,j,k}	{b}
c	{c,f,h,i,j,k}	{c}
d	{d,f,h,i,j,k}	{d}
e	{e,f,h,i,j,k}	{e}
f	{f,h,i,j,k}	{c,d,e,f}
g	{g, k}	{e,g}
h	{h}	{h}
i	{i}	{i}
j	{j}	{j}
k	{k}	{k}
l	{l,n}	{i,l}
m	{m,n}	{j,m}
n	{n}	{f,i,j,n}

(b)

Table 3: Labeling for G in Figure3(a): (a) $label3$; (b) $label2$

1. If $x \in H$, then we have $s \in reach_{in}(x, G)$ and $t \in reach_{out}(x, G)$, assuming that $x \neq s$ and $x \neq t$. Thus, we have $s \to x$ and $x \to t$ in G, which implies $s \to t$ in G. Now if $x = s$ or $x = t$, then $t \in reach_{out}(x = s, G)$ or $s \in reach_{in}(x = t, G)$, which again implies $s \to t$ in G. In each case, the result contradicts to the fact that $s \not\to t$ in G.

2. If $x \notin H$, then $x \in label2_{out}(s)$ and $x \in label2_{in}(t)$, which implies $s \to t$ in G' by Theorem 2. Since G' is a subgraph of G, we have $s \to t$ in G, which is a contradiction.

□

The following example further illustrates the idea.

EXAMPLE 7. *Consider the example in Figure 3. We first obtain* $reach_{in}(f, G) = \{a, b, c, d, e\}$ *and* $reach_{out}(f, G) = \{h, i, j, k, l, m, n\}$. *Then, we initialize label3 for the vertices:* $label3_{out}(v) = \{f\}$ *for each* $v \in \{a, b, c, d, e\}$, *and* $label3_{in}(v) = \{f\}$ *for each* $v \in \{h, i, j, k, l, m, n\}$. *Then, we remove f and all edges incident to f, which gives the graph as shown in Figure 4(a). Next we construct the TF and then label2 from the DAG in Figure 4(a). Finally, we merge label2 and label3 to obtain the final label3 as shown in Table 3(a).*

Compared with label2 computed for the graph in Figure 3(a), which is shown in Table 3(b), label3 is considerably smaller. The example also reveals that after removing the high-degree vertices, the graph becomes much easier to handle.

7. ALGORITHM AND COMPLEXITY

In this section, we discuss the algorithmic and complexity issues of our proposed method. Our method consists of two main phases, namely, the pre-processing or indexing phase and the query processing phase. Query processing is just an intersection of two sets which terminates as soon as the first common element is found and thus the complexity is bounded by the label size. The pre-processing phase includes computing the DAG from an input directed graph, topological sorting of the resulting DAG, construction of the transformed TF structure, and the label construction. The steps before labeling are either simple or have been presented in sufficient details. We therefore focus our discussion on the labeling algorithm here.

Algorithm 1: Labeling($\mathbb{G}^* = \{G_1^*, \ldots, G_{tf(G)}^*\}$)

1 Let $V_{G_i} = \emptyset$, where $i = tf(G) + 1$;
2 **for** $i = 1, ..., tf(G)$ **do**
3   **foreach** $v \in (V_{G_i^*} \backslash V_{G_{i+1}})$ **do**
4     $label_{in}(v) \leftarrow \{v\} \cup \{u : (u, v) \in G_i^*\}$;
5     $label_{out}(v) \leftarrow \{v\} \cup \{u : (v, u) \in G_i^*\}$;
6 **for** $i = tf(G), ..., 1$ **do**
7   **foreach** $v \in (V_{G_i^*} \backslash V_{G_{i+1}})$ **do**
8   **foreach** $u \in label_{in}(v)$ **do**
9       $label_{in}(v) \leftarrow label_{in}(v) \cup label_{in}(u)$;
10   **foreach** $u \in label_{out}(v)$ **do**
11       $label_{out}(v) \leftarrow label_{out}(v) \cup label_{out}(u)$;
12 **return** $label_{in}(v)$ and $label_{out}(v)$ for all vertices v;

We propose an efficient top-down algorithm to construct the vertex labels defined in Definition 5. As shown in Algorithm 1, Lines 1-5 initializes $label_{in}(v)$ and $label_{out}(v)$ for each vertex v to contain the in-neighbors and out-neighbors of v in $G_{tf(v)}^*$. Note that for each $v \in (V_{G_i^*} \backslash V_{G_{i+1}})$, $tf(v) = i$ since v no longer exists in G_{i+1}. Line 1 is introduced so that $(V_{G_i^*} \backslash V_{G_{i+1}}) = V_{G_i^*}$ when $i = tf(G)$ in Lines 3 and 7, since $G_{tf(G)+1}$ does not really exist.

Lines 6-11 performs a top-down operation starting at the highest level of the TF structure. At each level i, for each vertex $v \in (V_{G_i^*} \backslash V_{G_{i+1}})$, we simply include the in-label (out-label) of v's in-neighbors (out-neighbors) in $label_{in}(v)$ ($label_{out}(v)$).

The correctness of Algorithm 1 follows from Definition 5 and Lemma 5. While the algorithm does not remove dummy vertices, we discuss how it can be handled with little additional overhead, as inspired by the following lemma.

LEMMA 11. *For any vertex* $v \in V_G$ *and any* $G_i^* \in \mathbb{G}^*$, *at most two dummy vertices will be created in* G_i^* *whose root vertex is* v.

PROOF. According to Procedure 1, initially we may create one dummy vertex u_{out} as an out-neighbor of v and/or another dummy vertex u_{in} as an in-neighbor of v. And u_{out} and u_{in} must be created in $G_{tf(v)}^*$. At most one dummy vertex (let it be w_{out}) will be created as an out-neighbor of u_{out} since all incoming edges of u_{out} are not cross-level edges by construction. And w_{out} must be created in G_j^*, where $j = tf(u_{out})$. Similarly, at most one dummy vertex will be created as an out-neighbor of w_{out}, and so on. A similar analysis applies to u_{in} and thus in any $G_i^* \in \mathbb{G}^*$, we have at most two dummy vertices created whose root vertex is v. □

If v is the root vertex of any dummy vertex and v is the in-source vertex, then Lemma 11 implies the existence of a unique sequence $S_{out} = \langle v = u_1, \ldots, u_\alpha \rangle$, where u_{j-1} is the in-source vertex of u_j for $1 < j \leq \alpha$; thus, we can use only two labels, $label_{in}(u_j)$ and $label_{out}(u_j)$, to keep the labels for all dummy vertices u_j at each level $i = tf(u_j)$ in Lines 6-11 of Algorithm 1. Similarly, the same strategy applies to another unique sequence if v is the root vertex of a set of dummy vertex and v is the out-source vertex.

Thus, in the top-down labeling process, in total we maintain at most four labels for each vertex $v \in V_G$ for all dummy vertices created with v as their root vertex.

Next we analyze the complexity of the pre-processing phase. Computing the DAG takes linear time in the size of the input directed graph. Given the DAG $G = (V_G, E_G)$, topological sorting takes $O(|V_G| + |E_G|)$ time. Then, we apply Procedure 1 to construct the TF structure, which takes $O(\lg \ell(G))$ iterations of Steps 2 and 3. At the i-th iteration, we need $O(\sum_{v \in V_{G_i^*}} (deg_{in}(v, G_i^*) * deg_{out}(v, G_i^*)))$ time for the construction. From Lemma 11, $|V_{G_i^*}| \leq 2|V_{G_i}|$ and the degree of a dummy vertex w is bounded by that of $src(w)$. The total time complexity is given by $C1 = O(\sum_{1 \leq i \leq \lg \ell(G)} \sum_{v \in V_{G_i}} (deg_{in}(v, G_i) * deg_{out}(v, G_i)))$. The complexity of Algorithm 1, together with dummy vertex handling, is bounded by $C2 = O(\sum_{1 \leq i \leq \lg \ell(G)} \sum_{v \in (V_{G_i^*} \setminus V_{G_{i+1}})} (\sum_{u \in nb_{in}(v, G_i^*)} label_{in}(u) + \sum_{u \in nb_{out}(v, G_i^*)} label_{out}(u)))$. Both $C1$ and $C2$ depend on the characteristics of the input DAG, especially the vertex degree. Both $C1$ and $C2$ can be significantly reduced by removing the set of high-degree vertices H, which takes $O(|H|(|V_{G_i}| + |E_{G_i}|))$ time to remove H and add $h \in H$ to the labels of other vertices as discussed in Section 6.

8. EXPERIMENTAL EVALUATION

We implemented our method, **TF-label**, in C++ (source code available in authors' webpage). We compare TF-label with the following state-of-the-art methods for processing reachability queries: **PathTree** [19], **GRAIL** [28], **PWAH8** [25], **ScaPathTree** and **ScaGRAIL**. ScaPathTree and ScaGRAIL are the application of PathTree and GRAIL in the **SCARAB** framework [18], i.e., first computing the backbone of the input DAG and then applying PathTree or GRAIL for reachability querying (more details in Section 1). Though in theory any existing method can be applied in SCARAB, we were not able to do so for PWAH8 and TF-label due to unfamiliarity with their system. ScaPathTree and ScaGRAIL were provided by the authors of [18].

All source codes of the methods we compare with are the latest version provided by their authors, and all were implemented in C++ and compiled using the same gcc compiler as TF-label. We ran all experiments on a computer with an Intel 3.3 GHz CPU, 16GB RAM, and running Ubuntu 11.04 Linux OS.

8.1 Performance on Real Datasets

We first evaluate the performance of our method on real-world datasets from a wide spectrum of domains. As shown below, the first set of 7 datasets are from 3 different domains, while the second set of 5 datasets are from 5 different domains. We want to examine the differences in the spectrum of datasets that our method can handle versus those of existing methods.

Real datasets. We used the following 7 large real datasets that are used in [18, 28] for scalability test: `citeseer`, `citeseerx` and `cit-patent` (`patent`) are citation networks, in which non-leaf vertices have an average out-degree of 10 to 30; `go-uniprot` is the joint graph of Gene Ontologyterm and the annotations from the UniProt database (*www.uniprot.org*), which is the universal protein resource; `uniprot22m`, `uniprot100m` and `uniprot150m` are the subsets of the complete RFG graph of UniProt.

We also used 5 real datasets from Stanford Large Network Dataset Collection. We selected one large directed graph from each of the following categories: `email-EuAll` (`email`) from communication networks, `soc-LiveJournal1` (`LJ`) from social networks, `p2p-Gnutella31` (`p2p`) from Internet peer-to-peer networks, `web-Google` (`web`) from Web graphs, and `wiki-talk` (`wiki`) from Wikipedia networks. In addition, `cit-patent` from citation networks is already included in the first 7 graphs. Detailed descriptions of the datasets can be found in (*snap.stanford.edu/data*).

Table 4: Real datasets (K = 10^3)

Dataset	$\lvert V_\mathcal{G}\rvert$	$\lvert E_\mathcal{G}\rvert$	$\lvert V_G\rvert$	$\lvert E_G\rvert$	$\ell(G)$	d_{avg}
`citeseer`	–	–	694K	312K	13	0.45
`citeseerx`	–	–	6540K	15011K	59	2.30
`go-uniprot`	–	–	6968K	34770K	21	4.99
`patent`	–	–	3775K	16519K	32	4.38
`uniprot22m`	–	–	1595K	1595K	4	1.00
`uniprot100m`	–	–	16087K	16087K	9	1.00
`uniprot150m`	–	–	25038K	25038K	10	1.00
`email`	265K	420K	231K	223K	7	0.97
`LJ`	4848K	68994K	971K	1024K	24	1.05
`p2p`	63K	148K	48K	55K	14	1.14
`web`	876K	5105K	372K	518K	34	1.39
`wiki`	2394K	5021K	2282K	2312K	8	1.01

Table 4 lists the number of vertices and edges in the original directed graph, $\mathcal{G}$, as well as in the DAG G of $\mathcal{G}$, respectively. We do not show $|V_\mathcal{G}|$ and $|E_\mathcal{G}|$ for the datasets obtained from [28] since the authors did not provide these numbers. Note that existing methods for reachability querying assume that the input is a DAG. We also show the topological level number of G, $\ell(G)$, as well as the average degree of the vertices (denoted by d_{avg}) in G.

Indexing Performance. We first report indexing performance results, but remark that (online) query performance should be the more important performance indicator, provided that (offline) indexing performance is reasonable. We report the index construction time (total elapsed time in seconds) in Table 5. The shortest time for each dataset is highlighted in **bold**.

Table 5: Index construction time (in sec)

	TF-label	PathTree	ScaPathTree	GRAIL	ScaGRAIL	PWAH8
`citeseer`	**0.73**	26.76	1.60	0.79	0.98	0.76
`citeseerx`	63.60	–	–	**7.80**	15.43	8597.02
`go-uniprot`	47.49	–	724.67	**13.95**	16.60	52.46
`patent`	162.44	–	–	**7.24**	36.23	1380.76
`uniprot22m`	2.27	–	10.26	2.10	**2.09**	**2.09**
`uniprot100m`	40.29	–	1301.71	27.25	28.94	**24.10**
`uniprot150m`	55.48	–	4107.77	43.86	48.22	**41.07**
`email`	**0.10**	–	0.61	0.26	0.26	166.98
`LJ`	**0.55**	–	31.93	1.08	1.17	–
`p2p`	**0.03**	2.16	0.13	0.04	0.04	1.40
`web`	**0.40**	–	11.12	0.41	0.62	1559.91
`wiki`	**0.96**	–	–	2.54	2.35	–

For the datasets from [28], GRAIL has the best performance and the performance of ScaGRAIL is close to that of GRAIL. The indexing time of TF-label is comparable to that of PWAH8 for most datasets. For `citeseerx` and `patent`, TF-label is 135 and 8.5 times faster than PWAH8. Compared with ScaPathTree, our method is from a few times to 74 times faster. ScaPathTree was not able to obtain the results for `citeseerx` and `patent`, while PathTree can only run on `citeseer`.

For the datasets from the Stanford Collection, TF-label is the best for indexing all the datasets. TF-label is about twice faster than GRAIL and ScaGRAIL on average, and up to orders of magnitude faster than PWAH8, PathTree and ScaPathTree. We note that we did not specifically pick these datasets, but rather simply selected one large graph from each category of directed graphs (we did leave out two categories because the DAGs of these graphs are too small, for which most existing methods will be efficient enough). Therefore, the result shows that our method is able to perform well for graphs from various domains.

Table 6 reports the index size (in MB). For the 3 uniprot datasets, TF-label is from about 3 to 10 times smaller than all other methods. For citeseer, TF-label is only worse than PathTree, but much better than the other methods. But for citeseerx, patent and go-uniprot, TF-label is much larger. However, for the second set of 5 datasets, TF-label is much smaller in all cases except p2p for which it is larger than PathTree.

Table 6: Index or label size (in MB)

	TF-label	PathTree	ScaPathTree	GRAIL	ScaGRAIL	PWAH8
citeseer	2	**1**	28	11	28	7
citeseerx	1524	–	–	**100**	285	149
go-uniprot	431	–	403	**106**	387	244
patent	4732	–	–	**58**	206	5334
uniprot22m	**6**	–	68	24	67	19
uniprot100m	**77**	–	685	246	673	209
uniprot150m	**132**	–	1071	382	1049	349
email	**0.9**	–	10	4	10	2
LJ	**4**	–	41	15	41	–
p2p	0.2	**0.1**	2	0.7	2	0.2
web	**3**	–	16	6	16	4
wiki	**9**	–	–	35	95	–

Overall, the results of indexing time and index size show that our method is very competitive in indexing performance, especially for the datasets from the Stanford Collection. In fact, only GRAIL and ScaGRAIL are able to beat TF-label for indexing a few datasets. However, next we will show that GRAIL and ScaGRAIL are significantly slower in query processing than TF-label for all datasets.

Query Performance. We randomly generate 1 million queries for each dataset and Table 7 reports the total time taken to run the queries (the shortest time for each dataset is highlighted in **bold**).

Table 7: Total query processing time (in milli-sec)

	TF-label	PathTree	ScaPathTree	GRAIL	ScaGRAIL	PWAH8
citeseer	**6**	98	85	174	63	112
citeseerx	**160**	–	–	18861	684	187
go-uniprot	**48**	–	142	365	109	449
patent	**419**	–	–	6726	1240	14593
uniprot22m	**34**	–	115	259	97	210
uniprot100m	**79**	–	198	407	155	275
uniprot150m	**95**	–	862	433	183	294
email	**14**	–	124	6715	93	146
LJ	**51**	–	207	3741919	999	–
p2p	12	22	36	9192	24	**11**
web	**49**	–	196	436682	1548	142
wiki	**39**	–	–	457529	139	–

The result clearly shows that TF-label outperforms all other methods in all cases except for p2p, for which TF-label is comparable with PWAH8. ScaGRAIL can run on all datasets, but is from about 2 to 32 times slower than TF-label. ScaPathTree and PWAH8 are also significantly slower than TF-label, and they cannot scale to run on a number of datasets. GRAIL is up to orders of magnitude slower than TF-label and PathTree cannot scale for processing most of the datasets.

Another important feature of TF-label is that it has stable good-performance for all datasets, unlike the other methods which are slow for processing some datasets. For example, ScaGRAIL is particularly slow in processing web, for which ScaPathTree and PWAH8 perform reasonably well. Similarly, ScaPathTree is slow in processing uniprot150m and PWAH8 is slow in processing patent. Such a stable performance from TF-label is important for handling datasets from various application domains.

We also emphasize that TF-label can be further applied in the SCARAB framework, as do ScaGRAIL and ScaPathTree, to improve the performance. Thus, our result is impressive since TF-label even significantly outperforms the existing methods applied in SCARAB. In the next experiment, we show that TF-label scales well where all existing methods, including SCARAB, cannot scale, for both indexing and querying.

8.2 Scalability and Effects of Various Graph Properties

We use synthetic datasets to control the different properties of the DAG graph and hence assess their effects on the performance of our method, for both efficiency and scalability.

Synthetic datasets. We consider three important properties of the DAG graph: (1) *the number of vertices* (V_G), (2) *the average vertex degree* (d_{avg}), and (3) *the number of topological levels* ($\ell(G)$). We generate three categories of datasets as follows (let $M = 10^6$):

(C1) Fix $d_{avg} = 3$ and $\ell(G) = 7$, then: set $V_G = 5M$, $10M$, $20M$, $40M$ and $80M$, respectively.

(C2) Fix $V_G = 1M$ and $\ell(G) = 7$, then: set $d_{avg} = 10, 20, 30,$ 40 and 50, respectively.

(C3) Fix $V_G = 1M$ and $d_{avg} = 3$, then: set $\ell(G) = 3, 7, 15, 31$ and 63, respectively.

For the generation of a DAG G with $|V_G|$ vertices, $|\ell(G)|$ levels, and average degree d_{avg}, we first create $|V_G|$ vertices and distribute them to the $|\ell(G)|$ levels. Then, for each vertex v at each level i, where $1 < i < |\ell(G)|$, we add one edge from a vertex selected randomly at level $i-1$ to v, and add edges from v to $(d_{avg} - 1)$ randomly selected vertices at level $j > i$ in G. To test query performance, we randomly generate 1 million queries for each dataset.

Effect of number of vertices. Figure 5 reports the performance results of processing the (C1) datasets, where we vary the number of vertices $|V_G|$ from $5M$ to $80M$ ($M = 10^6$).

For index construction, TF-label is significantly faster than all other methods except GRAIL. Compared with GRAIL, TF-label is slower when $|V_G| \leq 20M$, but is 3 times faster when $|V_G| \geq 40M$. When $|V_G| = 80M$, all other methods failed (we terminated GRAIL after it took two orders of magnitude longer time than ours). PWAH8 could only handle $5M$ vertices, while PathTree failed even with $5M$ vertices (thus not shown in Figure 5). Moreover, ScaPathTree and ScaGRAIL also cannot scale well, since SCARAB failed to construct the backbone for such large datasets.

The index size of TF-label is about twice that of GRAIL, and is 1.5 to 3 times smaller than that of the other methods (for the datasets they can handle).

For query processing, TF-label is again significantly faster than all the other methods. Moreover, we also see that GRAIL is the slowest and is over an order of magnitude slower than TF-label. When $|V_G| = 40M$, GRAIL is 6400 times slower than TF-label.

Overall, TF-label is shown to be much more scalable than the existing methods with the increase in the number of vertices, i.e., also in the graph size. The results also show that the indexing performance of TF-label scales linearly with the increase in the graph size, but remains reasonably stable in query performance. The reason that query time does not increases much when the graph size increases is because the average label size remains stable, which can be observed as the index size increases only linearly.

Effect of average vertex degree. Figure 6 reports the performance results of processing the (C2) datasets, where we vary the average vertex degree from 10 to 50.

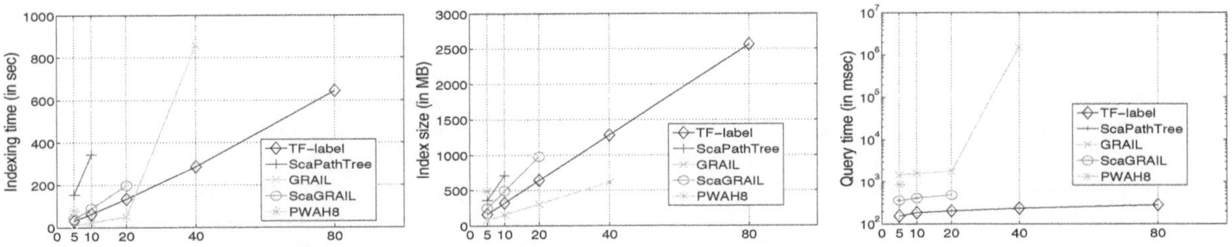

Figure 5: Performance on varying number of vertices: from $5M$ to $80M$ ($M = 10^6$)

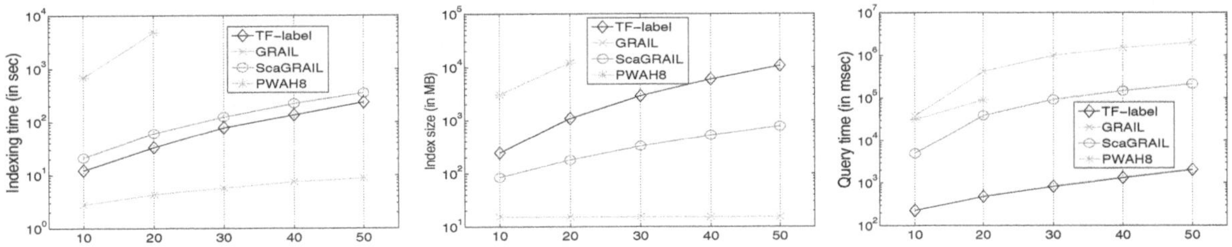

Figure 6: Performance on varying average degree: from 10 to 50

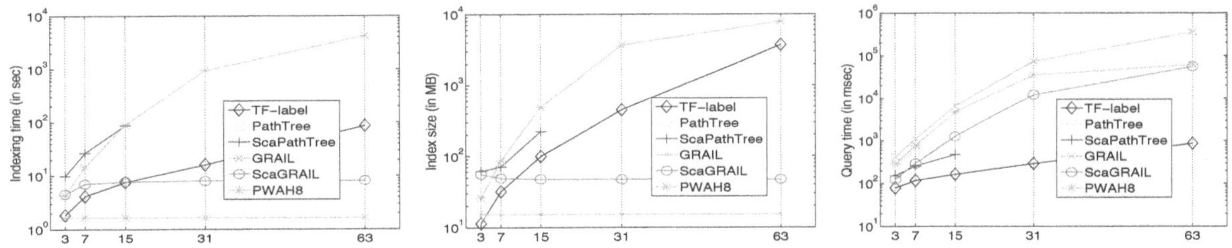

Figure 7: Performance on varying topological level number: from $(2^2 - 1)$ to $(2^6 - 1)$

The results show that both PathTree and ScaPathTree cannot scale to process datasets with average degree of even 10 (thus not shown in Figure 6). PWAH8 can only process datasets with average degree up to 20, and is up to two orders of magnitude worse than TF-label in both indexing and query performance.

TF-label is about twice faster than ScaGRAIL but is significantly slower than GRAIL in indexing, while the index size of TF-label is also much larger. However, for the more critical online query performance, both ScaGRAIL and GRAIL are too slow. ScaGRAIL is about two orders of magnitude slower and GRAIL is three orders of magnitude slower than TF-label in query processing for most of the cases.

As an index without reasonable query performance is not really useful, we can conclude that TF-label is the only method shown to be scalable with the increase in average vertex degree. TF-label scales linearly when average degree increases.

Effect of number of topological levels. Figure 7 reports the performance results of processing the (C3) datasets, where we vary the number of topological levels from $(2^2 - 1)$ to $(2^6 - 1)$ (which means that $tf(G)$ ranges from 2 to 6).

For index construction, TF-label is from a few times to 60 times faster than PathTree, ScaPathTree, and PWAH8. TF-label is faster than ScaGRAIL for the level number up to 15, but is slower than both ScaGRAIL and GRAIL in other cases. But in these cases ScaGRAIL and GRAIL are too slow in query processing. The index size also shows a similar trend.

For query processing, TF-label significantly outperforms all the other methods in all cases. Especially when the level number increases to 15 or more, TF-label is an order to two orders of magnitude faster than the other methods.

The results also show that TF-label scales roughly linearly when the level number increases, while the other methods scale poorly especially for query processing.

9. RELATED WORK

A reachability query can be answered in $O(|V_G| + |E_G|)$ time by a BFS or DFS in the input graph G, or in $O(1)$ time by precomputing the transitive closure [23] in $O(|V_G||E_G|)$ time. Existing methods all strive to attain high online query efficiency with a low offline index construction cost.

The full transitive closure is often too large and hence various labeling or compression schemes have been processed to reduce the label size [1, 5, 6, 17, 19, 25, 26]. Although these methods achieve reasonable query efficiency, most of them have a high indexing cost and are not efficient enough for processing large graphs.

There is another category of methods that construct vertex labels by traversing the graph only [4, 24, 28], and hence have a relatively low index construction cost. While these methods can efficiently answer a subset of queries that are supported by the labels, in general a much larger subset of queries are not covered by the index and are very costly to process as it requires graph traversal.

There are also a number of methods [2, 3, 10, 11, 12, 20, 21] that can be considered as improvements over the 2-hop labels [14], which constructs $label_{in}(v)$ and $label_{out}(v)$ for each vertex v and queries are answered as in Equation (1). Unlike our method, these methods are all very costly to construct and cannot scale to large graphs.

A backbone structure was proposed as a general framework [18] on which existing methods such as [19] can be applied to handle larger graphs. However, Section 8 shows that the performance of our method is significantly better than the state-of-the-art methods [19, 28] applied in the backbone framework. We are also aware of a recent work [22] that trades off query performance for reduced index size and indexing cost.

Due to space limit, we cannot discuss every method in greater details. More detailed discussions on the above existing methods can be found in [6, 18, 28, 29].

This work is inspired by the work [16], where a hierarchical structure is proposed for processing shortest path distance queries. However, the application of the topological structure and the design of topological folding are unique. In particular, our TF structure has at most $\lg \ell(G)$ levels, which is small for real graphs, while the hierarchical structure in [16] can have many levels.

10. CONCLUSIONS

We introduced a novel and highly effective indexing scheme, TF-label, for reachability querying in large graphs. Based on an extensive set of experimental studies, we showed that TF-label has a very stable high performance in query processing, which is typically an order of magnitude faster than the best previous methods [18, 19, 25, 28], while TF-label also enjoys competitive indexing performance. To our knowledge TF-label is the only truly scalable method since known scalable methods suffer from slow query response time for graphs with large sizes, large average degrees or large number of topological levels, while TF-label stays efficient. The ability to handle a wide range of different graph properties also demonstrates the suitability of TF-label for processing graphs from various application domains.

A useful extension of the current work is to develop I/O-efficient algorithms to index graphs that cannot fit in main memory. Methods developed in [7, 13, 27] may be applied to achieve this task.

11. REFERENCES

[1] R. Agrawal, A. Borgida, and H. V. Jagadish. Efficient management of transitive relationships in large data and knowledge bases. In *SIGMOD Conference*, pages 253–262, 1989.

[2] R. Bramandia, B. Choi, and W. K. Ng. On incremental maintenance of 2-hop labeling of graphs. In *WWW*, pages 845–854, 2008.

[3] J. Cai and C. K. Poon. Path-hop: efficiently indexing large graphs for reachability queries. In *CIKM*, pages 119–128, 2010.

[4] L. Chen, A. Gupta, and M. E. Kurul. Stack-based algorithms for pattern matching on DAGs. In *VLDB*, pages 493–504, 2005.

[5] Y. Chen and Y. Chen. An efficient algorithm for answering graph reachability queries. In *ICDE*, pages 893–902, 2008.

[6] Y. Chen and Y. Chen. Decomposing DAGs into spanning trees: A new way to compress transitive closures. In *ICDE*, pages 1007–1018, 2011.

[7] J. Cheng, Y. Ke, S. Chu, and C. Cheng. Efficient processing of distance queries in large graphs: a vertex cover approach. In *SIGMOD Conference*, pages 457–468, 2012.

[8] J. Cheng, Y. Ke, A. W.-C. Fu, J. X. Yu, and L. Zhu. Finding maximal cliques in massive networks by h*-graph. In *SIGMOD Conference*, pages 447–458, 2010.

[9] J. Cheng, Y. Ke, A. W.-C. Fu, J. X. Yu, and L. Zhu. Finding maximal cliques in massive networks. *ACM Trans. Database Syst.*, 36(4):21, 2011.

[10] J. Cheng, Z. Shang, H. Cheng, H. Wang, and J. X. Yu. K-reach: Who is in your small world. *PVLDB*, 5(11):1292–1303, 2012.

[11] J. Cheng, J. X. Yu, X. Lin, H. Wang, and P. S. Yu. Fast computation of reachability labeling for large graphs. In *EDBT*, pages 961–979, 2006.

[12] J. Cheng, J. X. Yu, X. Lin, H. Wang, and P. S. Yu. Fast computing reachability labelings for large graphs with high compression rate. In *EDBT*, pages 193–204, 2008.

[13] S. Chu and J. Cheng. Triangle listing in massive networks. *TKDD*, 6(4):17, 2012.

[14] E. Cohen, E. Halperin, H. Kaplan, and U. Zwick. Reachability and distance queries via 2-hop labels. In *SODA*, pages 937–946, 2002.

[15] T. Cormen, C. Leiserson, R. Rivest, and C. Stein. *Introduction to algorithms*. MIT press, 2001.

[16] A. W.-C. Fu, H. Wu, J. Cheng, and R. C.-W. Wong. Is-label: an independent-set based labeling scheme for point-to-point distance querying. *PVLDB*.

[17] H. V. Jagadish. A compression technique to materialize transitive closure. *ACM Trans. Database Syst.*, 15(4):558–598, 1990.

[18] R. Jin, N. Ruan, S. Dey, and J. X. Yu. Scarab: scaling reachability computation on large graphs. In *SIGMOD Conference*, pages 169–180, 2012.

[19] R. Jin, N. Ruan, Y. Xiang, and H. Wang. Path-tree: An efficient reachability indexing scheme for large directed graphs. *ACM Trans. Database Syst.*, 36(1):7, 2011.

[20] R. Jin, Y. Xiang, N. Ruan, and D. Fuhry. 3-hop: a high-compression indexing scheme for reachability query. In *SIGMOD Conference*, pages 813–826, 2009.

[21] R. Schenkel, A. Theobald, and G. Weikum. Hopi: An efficient connection index for complex xml document collections. In *EDBT*, pages 237–255, 2004.

[22] S. Seufert, A. Anand, S. J. Bedathur, and G. Weikum. Ferrari: Flexible and efficient reachability range assignment for graph indexing. In *ICDE*, 2012.

[23] K. Simon. An improved algorithm for transitive closure on acyclic digraphs. *Theor. Comput. Sci.*, 58(1-3):325–346, 1988.

[24] S. Trißl and U. Leser. Fast and practical indexing and querying of very large graphs. In *SIGMOD Conference*, pages 845–856, 2007.

[25] S. J. van Schaik and O. de Moor. A memory efficient reachability data structure through bit vector compression. In *SIGMOD Conference*, pages 913–924, 2011.

[26] H. Wang, H. He, J. Yang, P. S. Yu, and J. X. Yu. Dual labeling: Answering graph reachability queries in constant time. In *ICDE*, page 75, 2006.

[27] J. Wang and J. Cheng. Truss decomposition in massive networks. *PVLDB*, 5(9):812–823, 2012.

[28] H. Yildirim, V. Chaoji, and M. J. Zaki. Grail: Scalable reachability index for large graphs. *PVLDB*, 3(1):276–284, 2010.

[29] J. X. Yu and J. Cheng. Graph reachability queries: A survey. In *Managing and Mining Graph Data*, pages 181–215. 2010.

Efficiently Computing k-Edge Connected Components via Graph Decomposition

Lijun Chang[†£], Jeffrey Xu Yu[‡], Lu Qin[‡], Xuemin Lin[†£], Chengfei Liu[§], Weifa Liang[¶]

[†]East China Normal University, China
[£]University of New South Wales, Australia, {ljchang,lxue}@cse.unsw.edu.au
[‡]The Chinese University of Hong Kong, China, {yu,lqin}@se.cuhk.edu.hk
[§]Swinburne University of Technology, Australia, cliu@swin.edu.au
[¶]Australian National University, Australia, wliang@cs.anu.edu.au

ABSTRACT

Efficiently computing k-edge connected components in a large graph, $G = (V, E)$, where V is the vertex set and E is the edge set, is a long standing research problem. It is not only fundamental in graph analysis but also crucial in graph search optimization algorithms. Consider existing techniques for computing k-edge connected components are quite time consuming and are unlikely to be scalable for large scale graphs, in this paper we firstly propose a novel graph decomposition paradigm to iteratively decompose a graph G for computing its k-edge connected components such that the number of drilling-down iterations h is bounded by the "depth" of the k-edge connected components nested together to form G, where h usually is a small integer in practice. Secondly, we devise a novel, efficient threshold-based graph decomposition algorithm, with time complexity $O(l \times |E|)$, to decompose a graph G at each iteration, where l usually is a small integer with $l \ll |V|$. As a result, our algorithm for computing k-edge connected components significantly improves the time complexity of an existing state-of-the-art technique from $O(|V|^2|E| + |V|^3 \log |V|)$ to $O(h \times l \times |E|)$. Finally, we conduct extensive performance studies on large real and synthetic graphs. The performance studies demonstrate that our techniques significantly outperform the state-of-the-art solution by several orders of magnitude.

Categories and Subject Descriptors

H.2.8 [**Database Applications**]: Data mining; G.2.2 [**Graph Theory**]: Graph algorithms

Keywords

k-edge connected components; graph decomposition; minimum cut

1. INTRODUCTION

In many real applications, various data and their relationships can be modeled as a graph $G = (V, E)$, where vertices in V represent the entities of interest and edges in E represent the relationships between the entities. With the proliferation of graph data based applications, such as social networks, information networks, web search, bi-chemistry, biology, and road networks, significant research effort has been made towards many fundamental problems in managing and analyzing graph data. Given a graph $G = (V, E)$, the problem of computing k-edge connected components of G is to find a collection of maximal induced subgraphs $\{G_i\}$ of G such that each G_i is k-edge connected, i.e., the resulting graph is still connected after the removal of any $(k-1)$ edges from G_i [3, 20]. Fig. 1 shows an example; the graph in Fig. 1 is 2-edge connected, and it has four 3-edge connected components highlighted by the dotted circles, respectively.

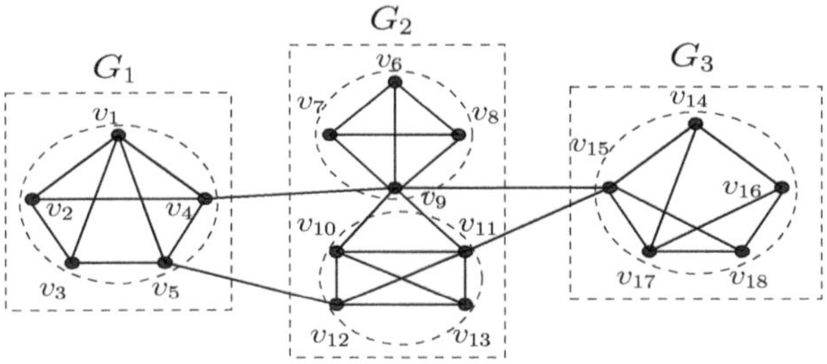

Figure 1: 3-edge connected components

Computing k-edge connected components has many real applications. For example, in social networks, computing k-edge connected components can identify the closely related entities to provide useful information for social behavior mining [1]. In a web-link based graph, a highly connected graph may be a group of web pages with a high commonality, which is useful for identifying the similarities among web pages. In computational biology, a highly connected subgraph is likely to be a functional cluster of genes for biologists to conduct the study of gene microarrays. Computing k-edge connected components also potentially contributes to many other technology developments such as graph visualization, robust detection of communication networks, community detection in a social network (e.g., Facebook), graph sparsification, etc, [7, 16, 19, 20]. Motivated by these, the problem of computing k-edge connected components has been studied very recently in [17, 20].

Clearly, if a graph G is not k-edge connected, there must be a set C of edges, namely a cut, such that the number $|C|$ of edges in C is smaller than k (i.e., $|C| < k$) and the removal of the edges in C cuts the graph G into two disconnected subgraphs G_1 and G_2. Based on this observation, the authors in [17, 20] develop a cut-based technique to iteratively cut a non k-edge connected graph into two disconnected subgraphs by applying the *global min-cut* algorithm in [14] (to be defined in the next section) till all remaining connected subgraphs are k-edge connected or no edge is remaining in the graph. For example, considering the graph in Fig. 1 and a given $k = 3$, suppose that a cut $\{(v_4, v_9), (v_5, v_{12})\}$ is first discovered. The cut-based technique in [17, 20] cuts the graph into G_1 and $(G_2 \cup G_3)$ where G_1 is induced by vertices $v_1, v_2, \ldots, v_5$, and $(G_2 \cup G_3)$ is induced by $v_6, \ldots, v_{18}$. In the next iteration, the cut-based technique is executed against subgraphs G_1 and $(G_2 \cup G_3)$, respectively. Since the time complexity of the technique in [14] is $O(|V||E| + |V|^2 \log |V|)$, the cut-based technique runs in $O(|V||E| + |V|^2 \log |V|)$ time to find one cut. Consequently, the cut-based technique in [17, 20] runs in time $O(|V|^2(|E| + |V| \log |V|))$ to compute k-edge connected components of G. The authors in [20] also develop a set of novel techniques to reduce the running time of the proposed algorithm in practice. Nevertheless, due to its high order time complexity and the nature of the framework (cut-based), the techniques and the framework are not scalable to efficiently process large scale graphs; this is also confirmed by our empirical studies in Section 5. Motivated by this, in this paper we study the problem of efficiently computing k-edge connected components.

Our Approach. Our technique is based on a graph decomposition paradigm. We here use the graph G in Fig. 1 as an illustrative example, which consists of three subgraphs G_1, G_2, and G_3, as depicted by dotted rectangles, such that G_1 is connected to the other part of G by two edges, and G_3 is also connected to the other part of G by two edges. Assuming that $k = 3$, we can decompose the graph into three disconnected subgraphs G_1, G_2, and G_3 instead of separating G_1 from G.

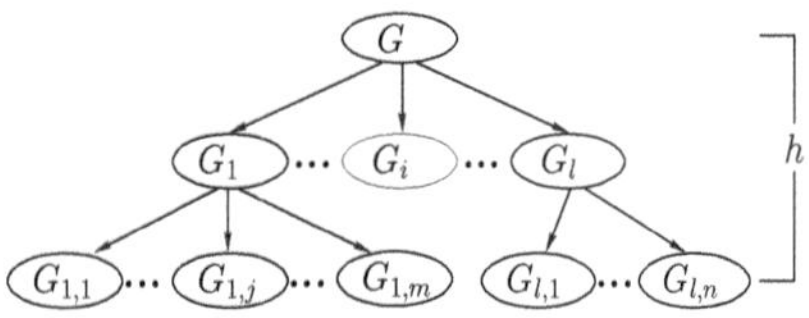

Figure 2: Graph decomposition tree

Generally, a non k-edge connected ($k > 1$) graph G can be represented by a decomposition tree as depicted in Fig. 2 such that each k-edge connected component of G is represented by a leaf node, and each intermediate node of the tree is a connected subgraph of G that is not k-edge connected. Moreover, the sibling nodes (subgraphs) in the tree have the property that each of them is connected to the remaining part of the parent graph by less than k edges except one sibling subgraph. For example, in Fig. 2, $G_1, G_2, ..., G_l$ are the sibling graphs with the parent graph G, and there are at least $(l - 1)$ graphs among $G_1, G_2, ..., G_l$ each of which (say G_i) is connected to the remaining part of G (i.e., $G - G_i$) by less than k edges. Our graph decomposition paradigm guarantees to decompose an intermediate graph G by detecting and removing all inter edges cross its children subgraphs.

To efficiently compute k-edge connected components of a graph using the graph decomposition paradigm, we develop a novel, efficient algorithm to decompose graph G for a given k, which runs in time $O(l|E|)$ and has the following property that 1) if G is not k-edge connected, it will remove all the edges cross its children subgraphs (in the decomposition tree), and 2) each k-edge connected component will not be broken into several parts. Iteratively running graph decomposition algorithm (till all remaining connected subgraphs are k-edge connected) gives a solution to the problem of computing k-edge connected components; this gives the overall time complexity $O(h \times l|E|)$ instead of $O(|V|^2(|E| + |V| \log |V|))$, where h is the height of the decomposition tree (see Fig. 2) and $l \ll |V|$.

Contributions. Our primary contributions are summarized as follows.

- We propose an effective graph decomposition paradigm to efficiently compute k-edge connected components.
- We develop a novel graph decomposition technique to efficiently decompose a non k-edge connected graph in $O(l \times |E|)$ time, where l usually is a small integer with $l \ll |V|$. Consequently, our technique for computing k-edge connected components runs in $O(h \times l \times |E|)$ instead of $O(|V|^2(|E| + |V| \log |V|))$ time of the state-of-the-art technique in [20], where h is the height of the decomposition tree and is practically a small integer.
- We conduct both theoretical and empirical studies on large real and synthetic graphs. Extensive performance studies demonstrate that the proposed algorithm significantly outperforms the state-of-the-art algorithm by several orders of magnitude.

Organization. The rest of the paper is organized as follows. A brief overview of related work is given below. Section 2 provides the necessary background information, including the problem definition, the global min-cut algorithm in [14], and an existing algorithm for testing edge connectivity [11]. Section 3 presents the graph decomposition paradigm, while Section 4 presents the graph decomposition technique. The experimental results are reported in Section 5. Finally, a conclusion is given in Section 6.

Related Work. Efficiently computing subgraphs, based on some designated densities, has recently drawn a great deal of attentions from both database and algorithm communities. The designated densities can be classified into two categories, 1) local density, and 2) connectivity density.

1. Local Density. Efficient techniques for computing all maximal *cliques* and *quasi-cliques* of a graph are presented in [6, 4] and [18], respectively. The authors in [16] investigate the problem of efficiently enumerating another kind of dense induced subgraphs, namely DN-subgraphs, where a DN-subgraph has the property that for each pair of adjacent vertices, u and v, they share at least λ common neighbors. Problems of efficiently computing other dense subgraphs, including k-core [5], triangle k-core motifs [19], etc., have also been recently investigated. An extension of k-core, i.e., finding dense subgraphs g of each graph G such that the h-hop neighborhood of a vertex in g has at least k vertices whose attributes satisfy a certain constraint, is also studied in [9]. Nevertheless, due to inherently different problem natures, these existing techniques are inapplicable to computing k-edge connected components.

2. Connectivity Density. The authors in [17] investigate the problem of efficiently computing frequent closed k-edge connected subgraphs from a set of data graphs with the focus on k-edge connectivity and the number of occurrence of subgraphs. The edge connectivity of a graph is the minimum number of edges whose removal disconnects the graph. Note that a frequent closed subgraph is not necessarily an induced subgraph. The only existing technique to tackle the scalability of computing k-edge connected components is reported in [20]. The technique is based on iteratively cutting a graph with lower (than k) connectivity into two parts, and the authors in [20] also develop a set of novel pruning rules to reduce the running time in practice. Similar (to that in [20]) framework is also used to compute SkyGraph in [13]. Here, the problem of computing SkyGraph outputs a subset $\mathcal{S}$ of induced subgraphs of G with the properties: 1) for each induced subgraph $g \notin \mathcal{S}$, there must be a subgraph g' in $\mathcal{S}$ such that both the connectivity of g' and the number of vertices of g' are no smaller than those of g with at least one of these two strictly larger; and 2) none of two subgraphs in S has such property regarding each other. As pointed out earlier, due to the high order time complexity and the nature of the framework (cut-based), the techniques and the framework in [20] are not scalable enough to efficiently process large scale graphs.

The problem of efficiently computing every maximal subset V_i of vertices of G, such that each pair of vertices in V_i is k-edge connected in G, has been studied in [8, 12, 10, 15]. Note that in such a maximal vertex subset V_i of G, each pair of vertices that are k-edge connected in G is not necessarily k-edge connected in the induced subgraph by V_i; in fact, the induced subgraph may be disconnected. Therefore, computing all such maximal vertex subsets is inherently different from computing the k-edge connected components of G. Note that, although [10] also uses the term "k-edge connected component", the meaning is different as discussed above.

2. BACKGROUND INFORMATION

In this paper, we focus on an *undirected graph* $G = (V, E)$, where V is the set of vertices and E is the set of edges. We denote the number of vertices and the number of edges by $|V|$ and $|E|$, respectively.

Given a vertex subset $V_s \subseteq V$, the *induced* subgraph $G[V_s]$ by the vertices in V_s is a subgraph of G with V_s as its vertex set such that the edge set of $G[V_s]$ consists of only the edges in G with both endpoints in V_s. That is, $G[V_s] = (V_s, \{(u, v) \in E \mid u, v \in V_s\})$.

2.1 Problem Statement

Definition 2.1: A graph G is *k-edge connected* if the remaining graph is still connected after the removal of any $(k-1)$ edges from G. □

For example, the graph G in Fig. 3 is 2-edge connected, while the two subgraphs G_1 and G_3 in Fig. 3 are 3-edge connected.

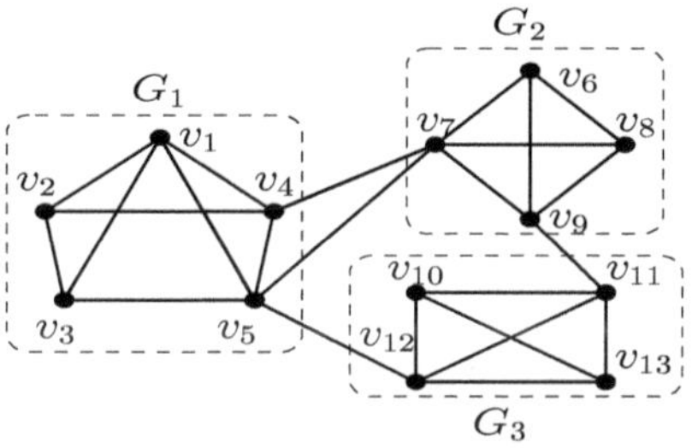

Figure 3: A graph and its 3-edge connected components

Definition 2.2: Given a graph G, a subgraph g of G is a *k-edge connected component* if 1) g is k-edge connected, and 2) any supergraph of g in G is not k-edge connected. □

Problem Statement: Given a graph G and an integer k, we study the problem of efficiently computing k-edge connected components of G.

Properties of k-edge connected components:

- A k-edge connected component is an *induced* subgraph;
- A k-edge connected component is *maximal*; that is, by adding any vertex or a set of vertices into a k-edge connected component, the resulting induced subgraph will not be k-edge connected;
- All k-edge connected components of a graph are *disjoint*.

2.2 Cut-based Framework, Global Min-Cut, and Connectivity Test

Definition 2.3: Given a graph $G = (V, E)$, a *cut* $C = (S, T)$ is a partition of V into two non-empty, disjoint subsets, $S \cup T = V$ and $S \cap T = \emptyset$. □

We also denote a cut by the set of edges whose endpoints are in different subsets, i.e., $\{(u, v) \in E \mid u \in S, v \in T\}$. The value of a cut is the number of edges in the cut, i.e., $w(C) = w(S, T) = |\{(u, v) \in E \mid u \in S, v \in T\}|$.

Definition 2.4: A cut $C = (S, T)$ is called an *s–t cut* if s and t are in different partitions, and it is a *minimum s–t cut* if its value is no larger than the value of any other s–t cuts. □

Let $\lambda(s, t; G)$ denote the value of a minimum s–t cut in G. The *connectivity* between s and t in G is defined as $\lambda(s, t; G)$. Two vertices s and t are called k-edge connected in G if and only if $\lambda(s, t; G) \geq k$. In the following, we simply denote k-edge connected as *k-connected*.

Definition 2.5: The *global min-cut* of a graph G is the cut of G that has the smallest value among all cuts of G. □

Let $\lambda(G)$ denote the value of the global min-cut of G, or equivalently, $\lambda(G) = \min_{s,t \in G, s \neq t} \lambda(s, t; G)$. A graph G is k-connected if and only if $\lambda(G) \geq k$. For example, $C_1 = \{(v_4, v_7), (v_5, v_7), (v_5, v_{12})\}$ and $C_2 = \{(v_5, v_{12}), (v_9, v_{11})\}$ are cuts of the graph in Fig. 3. C_1 is a minimum v_1–v_8 cut and C_2 is a global min-cut.

Cut-based framework: For computing k-edge connected components of a graph G, an existing solution [20] uses a cut-based framework by iteratively computing a small cut of each connected subgraph by running a variant of the global min-cut algorithm, and removing all edges in cuts with values less than k. The connected subgraphs in the final graph are k-edge connected components of G. The pseudocode is shown below.

```
Procedure: find k-edge connected components (G, k)
Find a small cut, C, of G;
if the value of C is less than k then
    Remove all edges of C from G;
    Find k-edge connected components of each connected subgraph of
    G;
else
    Output G as a k-edge connected component;
```

Computing a global min-cut: We introduce an approach to finding global min-cut of graphs [14]. The general idea is finding minimum s–t cuts for $(|V| - 1)$ pairs of vertices, and reporting the one with the smallest value as a global min-cut. Instead of computing maximum flows, the authors in [14] propose a procedure called the *maximum adjacency search* or *maximum cardinality search*, denoted by Mas, to find a minimum s–t cut. Given a graph as input, Mas returns the minimum cut for a pair of vertices s and t. The efficiency of this approach is due to the fact that s and t are determined by Mas rather than its input. Whenever a minimum s–t cut is found by Mas, s and t are merged into a super-vertex, and the resulting graph is given as an input to Mas for another iteration. The global min-cut is found after $(n - 1)$ iterations.

The procedure Mas computes an order of all vertices in G, denoted by a list L. Let t be the last vertex in L and s be the vertex prior to t in L. Then it has the property that the adjacent edges of t in G is the minimum s–t cut. The list L is constructed as follows. It is initialized as a singleton list containing an arbitrary vertex from V. As long as there are vertices not included in L, the vertex u, which is the one most tightly connected to L, i.e., $u = \arg\max_{v \in V \setminus L} w(L, v)$, where $w(L, v)$ denotes the number of edges between v and the vertices in L, is added to the tail of L.

Theorem 2.1: *[14] Let s and t be the two vertices (in the order) most recently added to L, then $(L \setminus \{t\}, \{t\})$ is a minimum s–t cut. The time complexity of* Mas *is $O(|E| + |V| \log |V|)$ if the Fibonacci heap is used for finding the most tightly connected vertex.* □

As a consequence of Theorem 2.1, the time complexity of finding a global min-cut of G is $O(|V||E| + |V|^2 \log |V|)$ [14]. In [20], the authors propose that, in order to compute k-edge connected components, as long as the value of the minimum cut found by Mas in an iteration is smaller than k, the procedure for finding a small cut will terminate. Note that the time complexity of Mas is $\Omega(|E|)$, i.e., it is lower bounded by $|E|$. Therefore, if a graph is k-connected, the running time of [20] is $\Omega(|V||E|)$ which limits the algorithm to be only applicable to small graphs.

Testing edge connectivity: The problem of testing whether a graph is k-edge connected is also studied in the literature. For unweighted simple graphs, the best previous known algorithm runs in time $O(|V||E|)$ which is based on dominating set and maximum flow techniques [11], denote by TestConnect. If the minimum degree of a graph G is less than k, then G is not k-edge connected. Otherwise, the algorithm maintains three disjoint vertex subsets S, T, U of V, where T consists of all vertices adjacent to but not in S, and U consists of all remaining vertices. S is initialized to contain an arbitrary vertex. Whenever U is non-empty, it picks a vertex v from U and computes the minimum cut C between v and S. If the value of C is less than k, then G is not k-edge connected, otherwise, v is added to S, and T and U are updated accordingly. Finally if U is empty, then G is k-edge connected. For more details, please refer to [11]. Note that, TestConnect terminates when a cut of value less than k is found or U is empty, and with a slight modification it can be used in the cut-based framework to replace the procedure of finding global min-cut. However, existing works for computing k-edge connected components of a graph are unaware of this algorithm. We also evaluate the performance of using TestConnect in our empirical studies (see Section 5).

3. COMPUTING K-EDGE CONNECTED COMPONENTS

Before presenting techniques to compute k-edge connected components, we claim that the set of k-edge connected components of a graph is unique.

Lemma 3.1: *Given a graph G, all its k-edge connected components are unique.* □

Proof Sketch: We prove it by contradiction. Assume that there are two different sets of k-edge connected components. Then there must exist two k-edge connected components from each one of the two sets, g_1 and g_2, that are non-disjoint and also non-identical. Otherwise, the two sets of k-edge connected components are the same. Therefore, $(g_1 \cup g_2)$ is also k-connected (since there is no cut of value less than k that can disconnect $(g_1 \cup g_2)$), which contradicts that both g_1 and g_2 are k-edge connected components which should be maximal. □

3.1 Graph Decomposition-based Framework

Given a graph G and an integer k, our graph decomposition-based framework for computing k-edge connected components is iteratively decomposing a non k-connected subgraph into several (possibly more than two) connected subgraphs by removing edges in all cuts of G with values less than k. More specifically, initially, we have one connected graph which is G, and whenever there are connected subgraphs that are not k-connected, we try to decompose them into sets of smaller subgraphs. The algorithm terminates when all connected subgraphs are k-connected. The pseudocode of our framework is shown in Alg. 1, where Decompose denotes an algorithm to decompose a graph which will be discussed shortly.

The connected subgraphs (including the intermediate subgraphs and the final k-edge connected components) can be organized into a tree structure as depicted in Fig. 2, called *decomposition tree*, where each ellipse represents a connected subgraph. The root represents the input graph G, and the children of a connected subgraph represent the set of connected subgraphs obtained by decomposing that subgraph (using Decompose). Therefore, all k-edge connected components of G are represented by leaf nodes of the tree. Decomposition tree is further characterized in Section 3.3. Alg. 1 generates all k-edge connected components by conducting a Breadth-First Search traversal on the decomposition tree.

Algorithm 1 Computing k-edge connected components

Input: A graph $G = (V, E)$ and an integer k.
Output: k-edge connected components of G.

Initialize a queue Q_g consisting of a single graph G;
for each subgraph g **in** Q_g **do**
  $\phi_k(g) \leftarrow$ Decompose(g, k);
  if $\phi_k(g)$ consists of only one subgraph **then**
    Output $\phi_k(g)$ as one of the k-edge connected components;
  else
    Push all subgraphs of $\phi_k(g)$ into Q_g;

We define a *partition graph PG* and two operators, the *merge operator* $\rho_{u,v}(PG)$ and the *split operator* $\gamma_{S,T}(PG)$, on it in the following.

Partition Graph: A partition graph $PG = (G, D)$ of a graph $G = (V, E)$ is obtained from G by augmenting each vertex $u \in V$ with a set of elements from domain D, such that $\cup_{u \in V} D(u) = D$ and $D(u) \cap D(v) = \emptyset, \forall u \neq v$, where $D(u)$ denotes the set of elements associated with vertex $u \in V$. That is, sets of elements associated with the vertices in V form a partition of D.

An ordinary graph $G = (V, E)$ is a special partition graph with $D = V$, where $D(u) = \{u\}, \forall u \in V$. Therefore, the input to our algorithm is a partition graph $PG = (G = (V, E), D(= V))$ where $D(u) = \{u\}, \forall u \in V$.

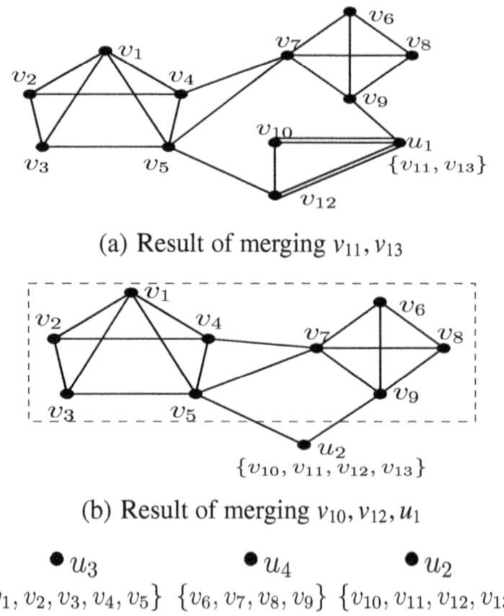

(c) Final partition graph

Figure 4: Partition graphs

Merge Operator: A merge operator $\rho_{u,v}(PG)$ merges two vertices u and v of PG into a single super-vertex, denote the new super-vertex by v_{uv}. More specifically, the operator adds v_{uv} to PG with $D(v_{uv}) = D(u) \cup D(v)$, and adds parallel edges (v_{uv}, x) to PG for each $x \in V \backslash \{u, v\}$, where the number of parallel edges is equal to the total number of parallel edges (u, x) and (v, x), and then removes vertices u and v and their associated edges from PG. Note that, after the merge, edge (u, v) is removed if it is in PG, and other edges are retained.

For example, Fig. 4(a) shows the result of the merge operator $\rho_{v_{11},v_{13}}(PG)$ where PG is the partition graph implied by Fig. 3. There are two parallel edges between v_{10} and u_1. Edge (v_{11}, v_{13}) is removed in the resulting partition graph.

Split Operator: A split operator $\gamma_{S,T}(PG)$ removes all edges of cut C from PG, where $C = (S, T)$ is a cut of PG.

Given an arbitrary partition graph $PG = (G = (V, E), D)$, the resulting graph obtained by performing either the merge operator or the split operator is still a partition graph. To simplify the presentation, in the rest of the paper, we use $\rho_{s,t}(PG)$ and $\gamma_{S,T}(PG)$ to denote the resulting partition graphs after applying the corresponding operators, respectively.

Graph Decomposition: The general idea of our graph decomposition algorithm, Decompose, is iteratively applying merge and split operators on the partition graph $PG = (G = (V, E), D(= V))$ to finally obtain a special partition graph $PG_r = (G_r = (V_r, E_r), D(= V))$ with $E_r = \emptyset$, such that each $D(u), u \in V_r$, induces a connected subgraph of G. Let $\phi_k(PG_r)$ denote the set of connected subgraphs represented by PG_r, i.e. $\phi_k(PG_r) = \{G[D(u)] \mid u \in V_r\}$. Decompose returns $\phi_k(PG_r)$ as the decomposed graph. For example, for the graph in Fig. 3, if we decompose it for $k = 3$, the final special partition graph will be in the form of Fig. 4(c), from which we can see that $\phi_3(G) = \{G_1, G_2, G_3\}$. The pseudocode of Decompose is shown in Alg. 2. Given an input graph G and an integer k. The algorithm first constructs the corresponding partition graph PG (Line 1). Then, it proceeds iteratively to update the partition graph until its edge set is empty (Lines 3-8), through the split operator (Line 5) and the merge operator (Line 7). To choose which operator to be applied depends on the value of the cut found by MinCut (Line 3) which computes the minimum cut for a pair of vertices.

Algorithm 2 Decompose(G, k)

```
1: Construct the corresponding partition graph PG of G, PG_0 ← ((G_0 ←
   G), (D ← V)), i ← 0;
2: while The edge set of PG_i is non-empty do
3:     (s, t, S, T) ← MinCut(PG_i, k);
4:     if w(S, T) < k then
5:         PG_{i+1} ← γ_{S,T}(PG_i);
6:     else
7:         PG_{i+1} ← ρ_{s,t}(PG_i);
8:     i ← i + 1;
9: return φ_k(PG_i);
```

Example 3.1: Consider the graph in Fig. 3 and $k = 3$. Assume the first iteration of computing minimum cut is computed between vertices v_{11} and v_{13}. As the value of the cut is 3, v_{11} and v_{13} are merged and the resulting partition graph is shown in Fig. 4(a). Fig. 4(b) shows the partition graph after merging v_{10}, v_{12}, u_1. The next pair of vertices, whose minimum cut is computed, is v_9 and u_2, then edges in the cut $C = \{(v_5, u_2), (v_9, u_2)\}$ are removed since the cut consists of only two edges. The resulting partition graph is the union of the subgraph shown in the dotted rectangle in Fig. 4(b) and the isolated vertex u_2. After applying a few more merge operators and split operators, we will get the special partition graph shown in Fig. 4(c) from which we can get the 3-edge connected components. □

3.2 Algorithm Correctness

In this section, our goal is to prove the correctness of the framework (Alg. 1) provided that MinCut in Alg. 2 correctly returns the minimum cut for a pair of vertices.

Lemma 3.2: *Given a partition graph PG, after applying a total number of $(|V| - 1)$ of merge operators and split operators,* Decompose *will produce a partition graph with no edges.* □

Proof Sketch: We prove it by induction. (Base Case) for $|V| = 1$, the claim is trivially true. (General Case) for $|V| > 1$, we consider two cases based on the type of the first operator applied. If the first operator is a merge operator, then the resulting partition graph has $|V'| = |V| - 1$ vertices which requires $(|V'| - 1)$ iterations of merge operators and split operators to remove all the edges. Therefore, the claim is true. If the first operator is a split operator, assuming that the split operator divides the partition graph into two disconnected subgraphs with $|V_1|$ and $|V_2|$ vertices each. Then all edges can be removed in $1 + (|V_1| - 1) + (|V_2| - 1)$ operations. Therefore, the claim is true. □

Atomicity property: Here, we prove the atomicity of Decompose, i.e., each of the connected subgraphs returned by Decompose will contain either all vertices of a k-edge connected component or none of its vertices.

Proof Sketch: To prove the claim, we prove that all edges in a k-edge connected component $g = (V_g, E_g)$ will not be removed during the execution of Decompose. As the algorithm removes only edges in cuts with values less than k, it is equivalent to prove that any edge of g will not be included in any cut with value less than k.

We prove it by contradiction. Assume that some of the edges of g are included in cuts with values less than k, and let (u, v) be the first such edge included in a cut C; that is, cuts are considered in the order of being found by iterations of MinCut. Let V_1 and V_2 denote the vertices of the two disconnected subgraphs that contain u and v respectively after removing all edges in C. Then $C \cap E_g$ is a cut of g which cuts V_g into $V_1 \cap V_g$ and $V_2 \cap V_g$. This means that there is a cut $C \cap E_g$ of g with value less than k, which contradicts that g is a k-edge connected component. □

Cutability property: To prove the cutability of Decompose, we prove that if a graph is not k-connected, then Decompose will decompose it into at least two disconnected subgraphs.

Proof Sketch: Given a non k-connected graph G, there must exist cuts of value less than k that can cut G into at least two disconnected subgraphs. The rest is to prove that Decompose can find at least one such cut eventually during the decomposition process.

We prove it by contradiction. Assume that Decompose are not able to find any cut of value less than k during the decomposition process. Consider such a cut C of value less than k. For any edge $(u, v) \in C$, u and v are not going to be merged since they are not k-connected. Therefore, all the edges in C are retained after merge operators, which contradicts that there is no edge remaining in the final partition graph obtained by Decompose (Lemma 3.2). □

Having shown the atomicity property and the cutability property of Decompose, we are now ready to show the correctness of the graph decomposition-based technique for computing k-edge connected components (Alg. 1) of a graph.

Theorem 3.1: *Alg. 1 correctly computes all k-edge connected components of a graph, provided that* MinCut *in Alg. 2 returns the minimum cut for a pair of vertices.* □

Proof Sketch: From the atomicity property, we know that a k-edge connected component will never be further decomposed into multiple subgraphs during the decomposition process (atomicity property). As long as a graph is not k-connected, Decompose will decompose it into at least two disconnected subgraphs (cutability property). Therefore, the input graph will be decomposed into a set of k-edge connected components by Alg. 1 eventually. □

3.3 Complexity

Time complexity of Alg. 1: Let h denote the height of the decomposition tree as illustrated in Fig. 2 and defined in Section 3.1, and $T_{\mathsf{Dec}}(G)$ denote the time complexity of decomposing a graph G using Decompose, which will be discussed in the next section. Then, the time complexity of Alg. 1 is $O(h \times T_{\mathsf{Dec}}(G))$.

Characterization of the decomposition tree: A decomposition tree of G, as depicted in Fig. 2, is a representation of the iterative process that decomposes non k-connected subgraphs of G into smaller subgraphs. Each k-edge connected component of G is represented by a leaf node, and each intermediate node is a connected subgraph of G that is not k-connected itself. The sibling nodes (subgraphs), e.g., $G_{1,1}, \ldots, G_{1,m}$, represent the result of decomposing its parent graph, G_1.

In a simple way, the sibling subgraphs have the property that each of them is connected to the remaining part of its parent graph by less than k edges except one sibling subgraph. For example, consider the graph in Fig. 1 and $k = 3$, G_1, G_2, G_3 form the sibling subgraphs for the parent graph G. Both G_1 and G_3 are connected to the remaining part of G by 2 edges, while G_2 is connected to the remaining part of G by 4 edges. Now, consider another graph in Fig. 3 and $k = 3$, $(G_1 \cup G_2), G_3$ form the sibling subgraphs, because both G_1 and G_2 are connected to the remaining part of the parent graph by 3 edges. More rigorously, the sibling subgraphs have the property that each of them is connected to any vertex in the remaining part of the parent graph by less than k edge-disjoint paths. Given a graph $G = (V, E)$, we define a partition of V based on the connectivity between pairs of vertices, denote by $\mathcal{V}_p = \{V_1, \cdots, V_m\}$, such that each pair of vertices in the same partition is k-connected in G, and otherwise not k-connected. Then, the vertex set of each subgraph obtained by Decompose(G, k) is contained in exactly one of the partitions of $\mathcal{V}_p$. As a result, a non k-connected graph G will be decomposed into at least $m \geq 2$ disconnected subgraphs. For example, if we attach a four-vertex clique G_4 to be adjacent to v_{16} in Fig. 1 by two edges, then Decompose can decompose the graph into four subgraphs G_1, G_2, G_3, and G_4, in one iteration.

By iteratively constructing children subgraphs for each non k-connected subgraph in the above way as defining the sibling subgraphs, the decomposition tree can be constructed. Each level of the tree can be computed from the union of their parent graphs by a single iteration of Decompose. The height h of the decomposition tree reflects the "depth" of the k-edge connected components nested together to form G. After each iteration of Decompose, the "depth" of nestedness is reduced by one. For example, in Fig. 1, the "depth" is two. After the first iteration of Decompose with $k = 3$, there are three disconnected subgraphs G_1, G_2, and G_3, where G_2 consists of two k-edge connected components nested together and can now be decomposed in the next iteration.

Potentially a smaller h: Intuitively, given a non k-connected graph G, the more the number of disconnected subgraphs returned by Decompose, the shorter the height h of the decomposition tree. The minimum number of disconnected subgraphs that will be returned by Decompose is guaranteed by the number of sibling subgraphs as discussed above. Usually, we will get more disconnected subgraphs. For example, consider the graph in Fig. 3, there are only two sibling subgraphs $(G_1 \cup G_2)$ and G_3 as discussed above. However, in practice, if G_3 is split from G before any merge of a pair of vertices where one is from G_1 and the other is from G_2, then G_1 and G_2 will also be split by a following split operator in the same iteration of Decompose. Therefore, three disconnected subgraphs will be returned by Decompose, and we get $h = 1$. This phenomenon is observed in our experimental studies. For example, each of the Amazon and web-Google dataset has almost 1,000 10-edge connected components, however, h is only 3. We also observe that, in our testing, the small value of h is quite steady across different sizes of graphs and different numbers of k-edge connected components in a graph.

4. GRAPH DECOMPOSITION

In this section, we first discuss a baseline algorithm for graph decomposition, and then propose a simple yet efficient data structure to replace the Fibonacci heap as required by the baseline algorithm. Finally, we propose several optimization techniques to further improve the performance of our decomposition approach based on the threshold k of computing k-edge connected components.

4.1 Baseline algorithm

The baseline algorithm for graph decomposition is by calling the procedure of maximum adjacency search (Mas in Section 2.2) to compute the minimum cut between a pair of vertices, i.e., replace MinCut in Alg. 2 by Mas, denoted by BaseLine. Recall that, Mas computes a linear order L for the vertices of G, and let s and t be the two vertices that are most recently added to L, and t be the last one, then the adjacent edges of t is a minimum s–t cut.

Iterations	List L
1	$v_1, v_2, v_3, v_4, v_5, v_7, v_6, v_8, v_9, v_{11}, v_{12}, v_{10}, v_{13}$
2	$v_1, v_2, v_3, v_4, v_5, v_7, v_6, v_8, v_9, v_{11}, v_{12}, \{v_{10}, v_{13}\}$
3	$v_1, v_2, v_3, v_4, v_5, v_7, v_6, v_8, v_9, v_{11}, \{v_{10}, v_{12}, v_{13}\}$
4	$v_1, v_2, v_3, v_4, v_5, v_7, v_6, v_8, v_9, \{v_{10}, v_{11}, v_{12}, v_{13}\}$
5	$v_1, v_2, v_3, v_4, v_5, v_7, v_6, v_8, v_9$
6	$v_1, v_2, v_3, v_4, v_5, v_7, \{v_8, v_9\}, v_6$
7	$v_1, v_2, v_3, v_4, v_5, v_7, \{v_6, v_8, v_9\}$
8	$v_1, v_2, v_3, v_4, v_5, \{v_6, v_7, v_8, v_9\}$
9	v_1, v_2, v_3, v_4, v_5
10	$v_1, \{v_4, v_5\}, v_2, v_3$
11	$v_1, \{v_2, v_3\}, \{v_4, v_5\}$
12	$v_1, \{v_2, v_3, v_4, v_5\}$

Table 1: Execution of BaseLine

Example 4.1: Consider the graph in Fig. 3 and $k = 3$. The first iteration of Mas will produce the order $L = (v_1, v_2, v_3, v_4, v_5, v_7, v_6, v_8, v_9, v_{11}, v_{12}, v_{10}, v_{13})$. Then $s = v_{10}$ and $t = v_{13}$, and it can be verified that $\{(v_{10}, v_{13}), (v_{11}, v_{13}), (v_{12}, v_{13})\}$ is a minimum v_{10}–v_{13} cut.

The lists L obtained from all 12 iterations of Mas during the running of BaseLine are shown in Table 1, where super-vertices are denoted by their associated elements. We omit those isolated vertices. For the first three iterations, we apply the merge operator since the value of cut found is no less than 3, and the resulting partition graph after the first three iterations is shown in Fig. 4(b). After the fourth iteration, we find a cut with value 2, then the split operator is applied. The graph is decomposed into three disconnected subgraphs after 12 iterations. □

Time complexity of BaseLine: Since the time complexity of Mas is $O(|E| + |V| \log |V|)$ (Theorem 2.1), and BaseLine will invoke at most $(|V| - 1)$ iterations of Mas (Lemma 3.2), the time complexity of BaseLine thus is $O(|V||E| + |V|^2 \log |V|)$.

4.2 A Simple Efficient Data Structure

The term $|V| \log |V|$ in the time complexity of BaseLine is due to finding the most tightly connected vertex in Mas using the Fibonacci heap, which assumes that the *update-key* operation and the *extract-max* operation takes $O(1)$ and $O(\log |V|)$ time, respectively. Note that extract-max and update-key are the only two operations of Fibonacci heap needed in Mas, assuming that *insert* and *remove* are special cases of the update-key operation. However, the Fibonacci heap is complicated and does not guarantee good performance in practice for a reasonable size graph. Motivated by this, we propose a simple yet efficient data structure to accelerate BaseLine as follows.

Data Structure: Let *key*(v) denote the key of vertex v during the execution of Mas, i.e., $key(v) = w(L, v)$ which is the number of edges between v and vertices in L. Let $\bar{c}$ denote the maximum value among all minimum cuts for different pairs of vertices. We have $key(v) \leq \bar{c}, \forall v \in V$, and $\bar{c} \leq |E|$. We propose to use doubly linked lists coupled with a head table to accommodate the *extract-max* and *update-key* operations.

For the doubly linked lists, we use an array of size $3|V|$ to store the data; that is, for each vertex $u \in V$, $key(u)$ stores the key, $pre(u)$ and $next(u)$ store the predecessor and successor vertices in the doubly linked list, respectively. Each doubly linked list links all the vertices with identical keys. In the head table H, $H(x)$ stores the first vertex in the doubly linked list whose key value equals to x. For example, in Fig. 5, assume that vertices v_i and v_j have the same key value x, and v_i is the first vertex in this doubly linked list, then $H(x) = v_i$, $pre(v_j) = v_i$, and $next(v_i) = v_j$. Since the maximum key value can be potentially be $\bar{c}$, the size of head table H is $\bar{c}$ in worst case. We discuss in the next subsection how to lower the size of H.

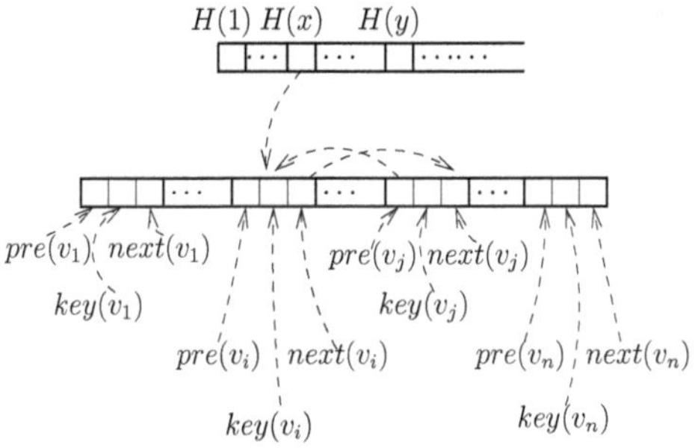

Figure 5: Data Structure

In addition to the two arrays, we also record a value *po*, which is the potential of the current maximum key value for all vertices in the data structure, and is initialized as 0. The value of *po* is updated after only the update-key operation.

Extract-max: To extract the next vertex with the largest key value, we first decrease *po* until $H(po) \neq nil$, and then report the first vertex pointed by $H(po)$ and remove it from that doubly linked list, as shown below.

Extract-max(u):

while $H(po) = nil$ **do**
  $po \leftarrow po - 1$;
$u \leftarrow H(po)$, and remove u from $H(po)$;

Update-key: To update the key of vertex v from x to y, we first remove v from the doubly linked list represented by $H(x)$, and then insert v to the doubly linked list $H(y)$. We also update $po \leftarrow y$ if $y > po$.

Update-key(v):

remove v from the doubly linked list $H(key(v))$;
update $key(v)$ and insert v into $H(key(v))$;
$po \leftarrow key(v)$ if $key(v) > po$;

Example 4.2: Consider Fig. 5, assume that $H(x)$ denotes a doubly linked list containing vertices v_i and v_j, i.e., $key(v_i) = key(v_j) = x$, and v_i is the first vertex in the doubly linked list. Assume *po* is now set as y and the largest key value with non-empty doubly linked list is x. To extract the vertex with maximum key value, we first decrease *po* to x which takes $O(y - x)$ time, and then report and remove v_i which takes $O(1)$ time. □

Time Complexity: The worst time complexity of the update-key operation is $O(1)$ as ensured by the properties of doubly linked lists. In the following, we discuss the time complexity of the extract-max operation which is nontrivial.

Lemma 4.1: *The worst time complexity of extract-max is* $O(\bar{c})$*, which can be as large as* $|E|$. □

Proof Sketch: For extract-max, we need to decrease *po* until $H(po) \neq nil$. As *po* can be potentially as large as $\bar{c}$ and the only non-empty doubly linked list could be $H(1)$, therefore, in worst case, extract-max takes $O(\bar{c})$ time. □

Although the worst time complexity of one extract-max is bounded by $|E|$, we show that the total running time of $|V|$ extract-max operations is still bounded by $|E|$ through the following theorem.

Theorem 4.1: *Given a graph* $G = (V, E)$*,* Mas *can find a minimum cut for an arbitrary vertex pair s and t in time* $O(|E|)$ *using our data structure, denoted by* Mas-Linear. □

Proof Sketch: The correctness of Mas-Linear directly follows from the correctness of extract-max and update-key using our data structure and the correctness of Mas.

Let $In(i)$ and $De(i)$ denote the increase value and decrease value of *po* when finding the most tightly connected vertex for the i-th time in Mas, i.e., to compute the i-th vertex of L, respectively. Then, the time complexity is bounded by $O(|E|+\sum_{j=1}^{|V|} De(j))$, where $O(|E|)$ is the total time of update-key operations and $\sum_{j=1}^{|V|} De(j)$ is the total time of extract-max operations. We have the property that $\sum_{j=1}^{|V|} In(j) \leq |E|$ since the update-key operation is executed once for each edge in the graph and the value of *po* is increased by the amount of at most one after each update-key operation. Then, $\sum_{j=1}^{|V|} De(j) \leq \sum_{j=1}^{|V|} In(j) \leq |E|$. Therefore, the total time complexity of Mas-Linear follows. □

4.3 Optimization

In the following, we propose three optimization techniques to further improve the performance of Decompose based on the threshold k of computing k-edge connected components.

Early merge based on k-connectivity. From Line 7 of Alg. 2, we can see that the only requirement for applying the merge operator is that the connectivity between s and t should be no less than k. Therefore, we can merge more than one pair of vertices during one iteration of Mas, as long as each pair of vertices is guaranteed to be k-connected in the input graph, based on the following lemmas. Recall that, after finding a minimum cut, Alg. 2 merges only one pair of vertices if applicable.

Consider the list L obtained by Mas on graph G. For any $v \in L$, let L_v denote the list of vertices added to L prior to v (excluding v), and p_v denote the last vertex in L_v. We call $w(L_v, v)$ as the key value of v, $\forall v \in V$. Then, we have the following property.

Lemma 4.2: *Given a graph G, for any vertex* $v \in L$*, if* $w(L_v, v) \geq k$*, then* p_v *and* v *are k-connected in G.* □

Proof Sketch: Consider the subgraph of G induced by the vertex set $L_v \cup \{v\}$, i.e., $G[L_v \cup \{v\}]$, applying Mas on it will produce exactly the same list $L_v \cup \{v\}$. This is because that, considering the two executions of Mas on G and $G[L_v \cup \{v\}]$ respectively and assuming that the same initial vertex (i.e., the first vertex in L_v) is chosen, then, for any vertex $u \in L_v \cup \{v\}$, its key value will be the same for both executions. Therefore, provided that $w(L_v, v) \geq k$, p_v and v are k-connected in $G[L_v \cup \{v\}]$ (Theorem 2.1), which implies that p_v and v are k-connected in G. □

Following Lemma 4.2, we can merge more than one pair of vertices after obtaining the list L. However, this will result in one additional scan on L of size $|V|$. Therefore, we propose to merge pairs of vertices on-the-fly following the lemma below.

Lemma 4.3: *During the execution of* Mas, *whenever there is a vertex v with key value no less than k, we then apply the merge operator on u and v where u is the vertex last added to the current list L, and continue this execution.* □

Proof Sketch: Let L denote the list obtained by Mas, and L_1 denote the list obtained by merging all pairs of vertices of L satisfying Lemma 4.2. Note that, in L_1, it merges only pairs of consecutive vertices in L. Since L_1 is obtained by getting L first, the set of merge operators will not affect the correctness of the algorithm as guaranteed by Lemma 4.2. Let L_2 denote the list obtained by this lemma. We prove that L_2 is exactly the same as L_1.

Note that, we consider each super-vertex , after merging pairs of vertices, in L_1 and L_2 as a set of vertices, and call it an item of L_1 and L_2. Let $L_{1,i}$ and $L_{2,i}$ denote the i-th item of L_1 and L_2, respectively. We prove that $L_1 = L_2$ by induction. For $i = 1$, if $L_{1,1}$ consists of only one vertex u, which means that $w(u, v) < k, \forall v \neq u$, then $L_{1,1} = L_{2,1}$. Otherwise, for any vertex v other than the initial vertex u in $L_{1,1}$, we have $w(L_v, v) \geq k$, then v will be included in $L_{2,1}$; for any vertex $v \notin L_{1,1}$, we have $w(L_v, v) < k$, then v will not be included in $L_{2,1}$. Therefore $L_{1,1} = L_{2,1}$. For $i > 1$, the first vertex in $L_{1,i}$ and $L_{2,i}$ is identical as guaranteed by the selection of vertex with maximum key value. Similarly to the proof for the case $i = 1$, we have $L_{1,i} = L_{2,i}$. Therefore, $L_1 = L_2$. □

Following Lemma 4.3, consider the graph in Fig. 3 with $k = 3$, when L is initialized as $\{v_1\}$, the list L obtained after the first execution of Mas is $(v_1, v_2, v_3, \{v_4, v_5\}, v_7, v_6, \{v_8, v_9\}, v_{11}, v_{12}, \{v_{10}, v_{13}\})$, in which three pairs of vertices are merged in one iteration.

List sharing after applying split operators. Consider Alg. 2, if a minimum cut of value less than k is found by Mas, after applying the split operator, a minimum cut of the resulting graph can be determined from the same list L, without actually running Mas on the resulting graph. Therefore, the list L can be shared across different executions of Mas after applying split operators.

Lemma 4.4: *Given a graph G, if the value of a minimum s–t cut* (S, T) *returned by* Mas *is less than k, then, in the resulting graph after applying the split operator, i.e.,* $\gamma_{S,T}(G)$, $(S \setminus \{s\}, \{s\})$ *is a minimum r–s cut, where r is the vertex added to L prior to s.* □

Proof Sketch: Note that, in the cut (S, T), T consists of only a single vertex t. After the split operator which removes all adjacent edges of t from G, we obtain $\gamma_{S,T}(G)$. The list L' obtained by applying Mas on $\gamma_{S,T}(G)$ will be exactly the same as S. Therefore, $(S \setminus \{s\}, \{s\})$ is a minimum r–s cut in $\gamma_{S,T}(G)$. □

Consider the execution example shown in Table 1, the minimum cut obtained at iteration 4 has value 2 which is less than $k = 3$. Therefore, we can get the list L of iteration 5 without running Mas again. Note that, this optimization can be applied iteratively until a merge operator is applied.

Efficient vertex reduction by degree. In a k-edge connected component, each vertex will have degree at least k. Therefore, we can remove all vertices with degrees less than k from the input graph. Efficient algorithm to recursively remove all vertices with degree less than k is studied in [2], which runs in $O(|V| + |E|)$ time. The general idea is that, it maintains a queue Q of vertices which is initialized to contain all vertices with degree less than k in the current graph G. It iteratively removes the vertices in Q from G. After the removal of vertices, the degrees of some vertices not in Q will change from at least k to below k, and then those vertices are added to Q and the process of removing vertices from G continues until no new vertex is added to Q. We use this efficient vertex reduction method based on degree k in our optimization. For more details, please refer to [2]. Without this optimization, to remove vertices with degrees less than k would require scanning the graph multiple times.

4.4 Algorithm with Optimization

The overall algorithm by incorporating the optimization techniques is shown in Alg. 3, denoted by Decompose-LMS, where the **L**inear data structure, early **M**erge, and list **S**haring optimization techniques are used. In procedure Mas-LMS, the vertices in queue Q are recursively merged with u (Lines 13-20), and the split operator is recursively applied if the minimum cut implied by the current list L has value less than k (Lines 21-23).

Algorithm 3 Decompose-LMS (G, k)

Input: A graph $G = (V, E)$ and an integer k.
Output: Subgraphs of G if $\lambda(G) < k$, and G otherwise.

1: Construct the corresponding partition graph PG of G, $PG_0 \leftarrow (G_0(\leftarrow G), D(\leftarrow V))$, $i \leftarrow 0$;
2: **while** The edge set of PG_i is non-empty **do**
3:   $PG_{i+1} \leftarrow$ Mas-LMS (PG_i, k);
4:   $i \leftarrow i + 1$;
5: **return** $\phi_k(PG_i)$;

6: **procedure** Mas-LMS (G, k)
7: $L \leftarrow$ {an arbitrary vertex u of V};
8: Initialize our data structure;
9: **while** $L \neq V$ **do**
10:   $u \leftarrow$ extract-max;
11:   Add u to L and remove u from the data structure;
12:   Initialize a queue Q with u;
13:   **while** $Q \neq \emptyset$ **do**
14:     $v \leftarrow Q.pop()$;
15:     **for each** $(v, s) \in E$ **with** $s \notin L$ **do**
16:       **if** the key of s increases to pass k **then**
17:         Add s to Q, remove s from the data structure;
18:       **else**
19:         Update-key for s;
20:     Merge u and v if $u \neq v$;
21: **while** $|L| > 1$ **and** the value of the cut implied by the last two vertices in L is less than k **do**
22:   Split the cut;
23:   Remove the last vertex from L;

In Decompose-LMS where the optimization of early merge based on k-connectivity is applied, whenever the key of a vertex v is increased to pass k, v is removed from our data structure. Therefore, the maximum key value in our data structure is bounded by k, which means that we need only k entries for our head table which is discussed in Section 4.2.

Theorem 4.2: *Given a graph* $G = (V, E)$, Decompose-LMS *correctly decomposes it into at least two disconnected subgraphs if* $\lambda(G) < k$ *and returns G otherwise. The time complexity is* $O(l \times |E|)$, *where* l $(\leq |V|)$ *is the number of iterations of* Mas-LMS, *i.e., the value of i at Line 5 of Alg. 3.* □

Proof Sketch: The correctness of Decompose-LMS directly follows from the correctness of Mas, and Lemmas 4.2, 4.3, and 4.4. For the time complexity, since Mas-LMS takes $O(|E|)$ time and there are totally l iterations of Mas-LMS, the time complexity of Decompose-LMS follows. □

Bound on the value of l**:** Now, we characterize the value of l in two situations based on whether G is k-connected or not.

Given a non k-connected graph $G = (V, E)$, let $\mathcal{G}_k = \{g_1 = (V_1, E_1), \cdots, g_m = (V_m, E_m)\}$ be the set of k-edge connected components of G. Then, $l \leq \max_{j=1}^{m} |V_j|$. The reason is that, for any two k-edge connected components of G, g_i and g_j, Decompose-

LMS either splits the two subgraphs or merges them into a single subgraph. If g_i and g_j are split into two subgraphs by Decompose-LMS, then the number of vertices of g_i and g_j is each reduced by at least one after one iteration of Mas-LMS. The reason is that, let u_i and u_j be the last node of g_i and g_j on L respectively, then the keys of u_i and u_j are at least k, therefore, u_i and u_j are merged with other vertices. Otherwise, vertices of g_i and g_j are merged into super-vertices. Let sg_i^a and sg_j^a denote the subgraph induced by vertices (or super-vertices) of g_i and g_j after a iterations of Mas-LMS, respectively. Note that super-vertices in sg_i^a and sg_j^a can overlap. Then the number of vertices in sg_i^{a+1} (sg_j^{a+1}) is strictly less than sg_i^a (sg_j^a), since both sg_i^a and sg_j^a are k-connected. Therefore, after each iteration of Mas-LMS, the number of vertices in each of g_i will be reduced by at least one, and $l \leq \max_{j=1}^{m} |V_j|$.

Given a k-connected graph G, each vertex of G will have a degree at least k and Decompose-LMS will merge all vertices in G into a single super-vertex. In Decompose-LMS, an iteration of Mas-LMS computes an order L of vertices in G and merges each such vertex having $w(L_v, v) \geq k$ with its predecessor vertex in L (refer to early merge optimization). Let $k(L)$ denote the number of vertices having $w(L_v, v) \geq k$ in L. Then, after each iteration of Mas-LMS which computes an order L, the number of vertices is reduced by $k(L)$. Recall that $w(L_v, v)$ is the number of edges between v and vertices prior to v in L. Implicitly, for a pair of vertices u and v that have more than $k-1$ parallel edges between them, Mas-LMS ensures to merge the two vertices into a super-vertex. Given a random order L and a vertex v with degree no less than $2k$, the probability that v will be merged with other vertices is at least $\frac{1}{2}$. Let V_{2k} denote the subset of vertices in G whose degrees are no less than $2k$. The expected number of vertices that will be reduced after one iteration of Mas-LMS is at least $\frac{|V_{2k}|}{2}$. After merging vertices into super-vertices, degrees of super-vertices are tend to become larger. Therefore, the number of vertices reduces rapidly after each iteration of Mas-LMS. For a special graph that every vertex has degree no less than $2k$, the number of iterations l is expected to be bounded by $\log |V|$. The same phenomenon also applies to each k-edge connected component of G if G is not k-connected.

In our empirical studies, the sizes of the largest k-edge connected components of as-Skitter and SSCA-20 dataset are over 0.3 million and 1 million, while the value of l is 9 and 8, respectively. Of all the real and synthetic graphs we tested, the values of l are no more than 21 regardless of the sizes of graphs and the sizes and/or numbers of k-edge connected components of a graph. Therefore, algorithm Decompose-LMS is able to process large graphs. Note that our optimization techniques are inapplicable to those connectivity testing algorithms (such as TestConnect [11] as discussed in Section 2.2) which are based on maximum flow techniques, since flows computed for different pairs of vertices are unrelated.

Example 4.3: Given the graph in Fig. 3 and $k = 3$. The list L obtained for each iteration of Mas-LMS is shown in Table 2, where super-vertices are denoted by their associated elements. Decompose-LMS computes a graph decomposition for $k = 3$ in four iterations. Therefore, Decompose-LMS is much faster than BaseLine (Section 4.1), which takes 12 iterations as shown in Table 1. □

Iterations	List L
1	$v_1, v_2, v_3, \{v_4, v_5\}, v_7, v_6, \{v_8, v_9\}, v_{11}, v_{12}, \{v_{10}, v_{13}\}$
2	$v_1, \{v_4, v_5\}, \{v_2, v_3\}, v_7, \{v_6, v_8, v_9\}, v_{11}, \{v_{10}, v_{12}, v_{13}\}$
3	$v_1, \{v_2, v_3, v_4, v_5\}, \{v_6, v_7, v_8, v_9\}, \{v_{10}, v_{11}, v_{12}, v_{13}\}$
4	$\{v_1, v_2, v_3, v_4, v_5\}$

Table 2: Execution of Decompose-LMS

Remarks on the range of the value of h: Our algorithm Decompose-LMS will decompose a graph G into a set of subgraphs sg_i, each of which possibly contains several k-edge connected components. Assume that two different k-edge connected components g_i and g_j have equal probabilities to be split and to be merged. Then, the decomposition tree (see Section 3) tends to be a balanced tree on average, and h is expected to be bounded by $\log |V|$. In our empirical studies, the largest h is 5 across graphs whose vertex numbers vary from 4 thousand to 2 million.

5. EXPERIMENTS

We conduct extensive performance studies to evaluate the efficiency of our framework (proposed in Section 3) and our graph decomposition algorithm based on several optimization techniques (studied in Section 4) for the computation of k-edge connected components in graphs. The following algorithms are implemented:

- CutB-GMC: The cut-based framework plugged in a variant of finding **G**lobal **M**in-**C**ut algorithm as discussed in Section 2.2. We also incorporate the optimization techniques and pruning rules proposed in [20] into CutB-GMC.
- CutB-TC: The cut-based framework plugged in the **T**esting **C**onnectivity algorithm (TestConnect) which can find a minimum cut with value less than k by a slight modification, as discussed in Section 2.2.[1]
- DecB-LMSD: Our graph decomposition-based framework (Section 3) plugged in our graph decomposition algorithm with all the optimization techniques proposed in Section 4, i.e., the framework in Alg. 1 plus the decomposition algorithm in Alg. 3.
- DecB: Our graph decomposition-based framework plugged in the baseline algorithm BaseLine for graph decomposition.
- CutB-LMD: The cut-based framework plugged in a modification of our decomposition algorithm to cut a graph into only two disconnected subgraphs. All the optimization techniques proposed in Section 4 are applied except the list sharing optimization which is inapplicable.

All algorithms are implemented in C++ and compiled with GNU GCC with the -O3 optimization. All experiments are conducted on a PC with an Intel(R) Core(TM) i5-2400 CPU (3.10GHz) and 4GB memory running Ubuntu 12.04. We evaluate the performance of all algorithms on both real and synthetic graphs as follows.

Real Graphs: We evaluate the algorithms on eight real graphs, Arxiv General Relativity collaboration network (ca-GrQc), Arxiv Condensed Matter collaboration network (ca-CondMat), email network from a EU research institution (email-EuAll), who-trusts-whom network of Epinions.com (soc-Epinions1), Amazon product co-purchasing network (amazon0601), web graph from Google (web-Google), Wikipedia talk (communication) network (wiki-Talk), and Internet topology graph (as-Skitter). All the graphs are downloaded from the Stanford SNAP library[2], and detailed descriptions about these graphs can also be found there. Sizes of these graphs are shown in Table 3.

Synthetic Graphs: We evaluate the algorithms on three kinds of synthetic graphs, all of which are generated by the graph generator GTGraph[3]. The three kinds of synthetic graphs are as follows.

- Random graphs: Random graphs with $a \times 1000$ vertices and $b \times 1000$ edges are denoted by *Random-a-b*, where a and b are integers and the $b \times 1000$ edges are added by randomly choosing a pair of vertices for each edge.

[1]Note that, TestConnect was not studied in previous works for computing k-edge connected components.
[2]`http://snap.stanford.edu/data/`
[3]`http://www.cse.psu.edu/~madduri/software/GTgraph/`

ID	Dataset	#Vertices	#Edges
D1	ca-GrQc	5,242	14,484
D2	ca-CondMat	23,133	93,439
D3	email-EuAll	265,214	364,481
D4	soc-Epinions1	75,879	405,740
D5	wiki-Talk	2,394,385	4,659,565
D6	amazon0601	403,394	2,443,408
D7	web-Google	875,713	4,322,051
D8	as-Skitter	1,696,415	11,095,298

Table 3: Sizes of real graphs

- PowerLaw graphs: Similar to Random-a-b, *PowerLaw-a-b* denote a PowerLaw graph with $a \times 1000$ vertices and $b \times 1000$ edges. The degree distributions of PowerLaw graphs conform with the power-law distribution.
- SSCA graphs: *SSCA-a* denote a SSCA graph with 2^a vertices. A SSCA graph contains a collection of randomly sized cliques, and then inter-clique edges are added randomly.

We generated two random graphs, Random-20-120, and Random-20-140, two power-law graphs, PowerLaw-20-120, and PowerLaw-20-140, and five SSCA graphs, SSCA-12, SSCA-14, SSCA-16, SSCA-18, and SSCA-20. The sizes of the five SSCA graphs are shown in Table 4.

Dataset	#Vertices	#Edges
SSCA-12	4,096	24,584
SSCA-14	16,384	143,744
SSCA-16	65,536	896,759
SSCA-18	262,144	5,640,272
SSCA-20	1,048,576	35,318,325

Table 4: Sizes of SSCA graphs

For all these testings, we vary k for the connectivity requirement of k-edge connected components. Each experiment is run three times, and the average CPU time is reported here.

5.1 Decomposition-based Against Cut-based

In this test, we evaluate the effectiveness of our proposed graph decomposition-based framework against the cut-based framework studied in [20]. CutB-GMC, CutB-TC, CutB-LMD are cut-based algorithms while DecB-LMSD is a graph decomposition-based algorithm.

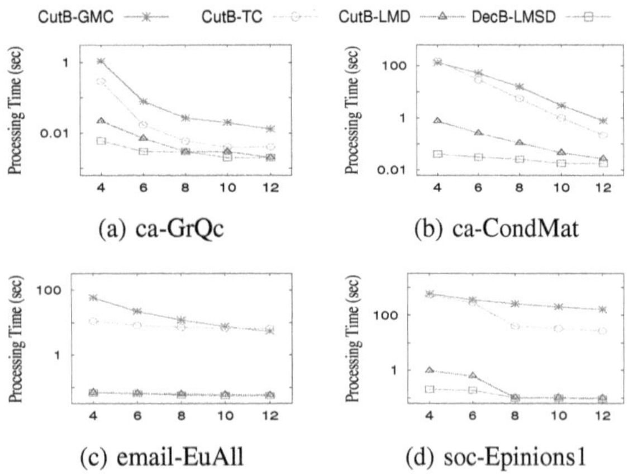

Figure 6: Against cut-based algorithms (Varying k)

Results on Real Graphs: We evaluate CutB-GMC, CutB-TC, CutB-LMD, and DecB-LMSD on four of the real graphs, since the other four real graphs are too large for the slow algorithms to finish in reasonable time. The processing time are shown in Fig. 6. A similar trend found in all figures of Fig. 6 is that the processing times of all four algorithms tend towards smaller when k increases. When k becomes larger, the resulting graph after removing all vertices with degrees less than k becomes smaller, therefore all algorithms run faster.[4] CutB-TC runs slightly faster than CutB-GMC on all four graphs which conforms with their time complexity differences as discussed in Section 2.2, i.e., $O(|V||E|)$ for testing connectivity versus $O(|V||E| + |V|^2 \log |V|)$ for finding global min-cut. DecB-LMSD outperforms both CutB-GMC and CutB-TC by several orders of magnitude. Although CutB-LMD runs much faster than CutB-GMC due to our optimization techniques, it is still much slower than DecB-LMSD. In Fig. 6(c), the processing times of CutB-LMD and DecB-LMSD are almost the same. The reason is that, after removing all vertices with degree less than k, the remaining graph consists of a single k-edge connected component, i.e., $h = 1$, then the performance between the cut-based algorithm and the graph decomposition-based algorithm becomes marginal on this graph.

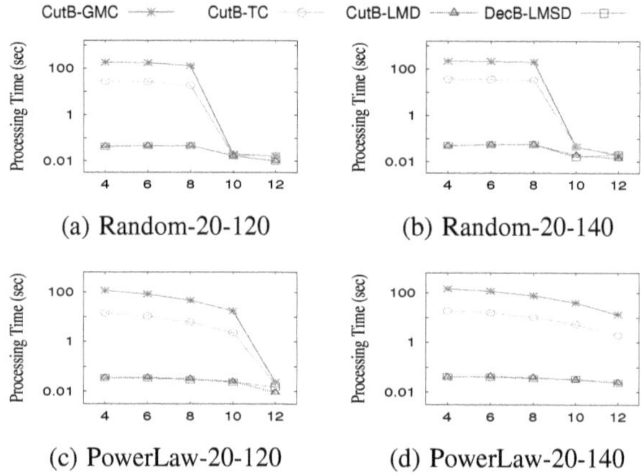

Figure 7: Against cut-based algorithms (Varing k)

Results on Random and PowerLaw Graphs: The processing times of CutB-GMC, CutB-TC, CutB-LMD, DecB-LMSD on random graphs and power-law graphs are plotted in Fig. 7. Similar to that shown in Fig. 6, DecB-LMSD outperforms both CutB-GMC and CutB-TC by more than three orders of magnitude. As shown in all figures of Fig. 7 except Fig. 7(d), when k is larger than a certain value (e.g., $k \geq 10$ in Fig. 7(a)), the processing times of all four algorithms are almost the same, due to that there is no subgraph that is k-connected, i.e., the graph is empty after removing all vertices with degree less than k. The ratio between the processing time of CutB-TC and that of CutB-GMC is almost the same for all graphs with different k values. The process times of DecB-LMSD and CutB-LMD are the same on all graphs, since the random graphs and power-law graphs tend to either have no subgraph with connectivity at least k or have only one giant subgraph with connectivity at least k. By comparing Fig. 7(a) and Fig. 7(c), Fig. 7(b) and Fig. 7(d). We can infer that power-law graphs tend to have larger connectivity compared with random graphs.

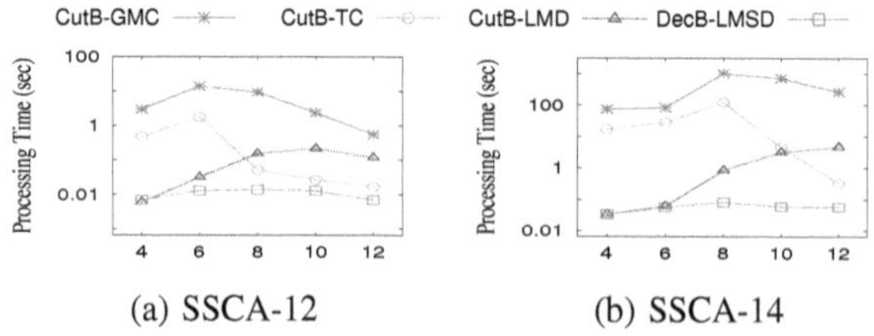

Figure 8: Against cut-based algorithms (Varying k)

[4]Note that, the technique of removing all vertices with degrees less than k is applied on all of the tested algorithms, while our optimization of efficient vertex reduction by degree is an efficient approach to realize this reduction.

Results on SSCA Graphs: Fig. 8 shows the evaluation results of the four algorithms on two SSCA graphs. As a SSCA graph contains a set of randomly sized cliques, the processing times shown in Fig. 8 have different patterns as compared with that shown in Fig. 7. In Fig. 8(a), the processing time of CutB-GMC increases when k increases from 4 to 6 as opposite to that in Fig. 6 and Fig. 7. This is because that, when k increases from 4 to 6, the size of each k-edge connected component decreases, however, the number of k-edge connected components increases as a result of the large number of cliques contained. DecB-LMSD still outperforms CutB-GMC by several orders of magnitude. However, CutB-TC also performs well for larger k, because the size of k-edge connected components becomes very small for larger k and TestConnect tends to find more balanced cut than Mas. Intuitively, TestConnect divides a non k-connected subgraph by the minimum cut between a pair of random vertices whose minimum cut values are less than k, while finding global minimum cut using Mas removes all the adjacent edges of a subgraph after contracting all vertices in it into a single super-vertex. Therefore, CutB-TC can reduce the size of each connected subgraph very quickly, while CutB-GMC divides a graph into one large and one small subgraph each time. As shown in Fig. 8, unlike those shown in Fig. 6 and Fig. 7, CutB-LMD performs much worse than DecB-LMSD, due to the larger number of k-edge connected components contained in SSCA graphs than the small real graphs, random graphs, and power-law graphs. Therefore, CutB-LMD needs to compute a global minimum cut for a lot of large subgraphs of the input graph.

Dataset	Number of components	Max size of components	h	l
ca-GrQc	10	80	2	5
ca-CondMat	14	2,020	2	7
email-EuAll	1	2,762	1	2
soc-Epinions1	1	9,337	1	3
wiki-Talk	1	47,081	1	3
amazon0601	979	8,855	3	21
web-Google	1,031	171,398	3	11
as-Skitter	9	325,486	2	9
SSCA-12	166	94	3	7
SSCA-14	359	346	5	15
SSCA-16	79	59,387	3	11
SSCA-18	30	254,996	3	9
SSCA-20	22	1,037,606	2	8

Table 5: Value of h and l of DecB-LMSD (k = 10)

The value of h and l: We test the value of h and l which contributes to the time complexity $O(h \times l \times |E|)$ of our DecB-LMSD algorithm. The values of h and l by applying DecB-LMSD on the eight real graphs and the five SSCA graphs with $k = 10$ are shown in Table 5, in which we also list out the number of k-edge connected components and the maximum size of k-edge connected components (in terms of number of vertices in it) of those graphs with $k = 10$. Among the real graphs, amazon0601 and web-Google have the largest number of k-edge connected components, and they also have large size of k-edge connected components. SSCA graphs either have a lot of small k-edge connected components (for large k) or have just a few large k-edge connected components (for small k), but not both. Despite the large number of k-edge connected components and/or the large size of k-edge connected components, both h and l in our DecB-LMSD computation are of small values. Combining this fact with our $O(h \times l \times |E|)$ time complexity, DecB-LMSD can finish in a few seconds even on large graphs.

Scalability Testing: We test the scalability of CutB-GMC, CutB-TC, CutB-LMD, and DecB-LMSD. We generate four Random graphs, Random-a-10a, and four PowerLaw graphs, PowerLaw-a-10a, with

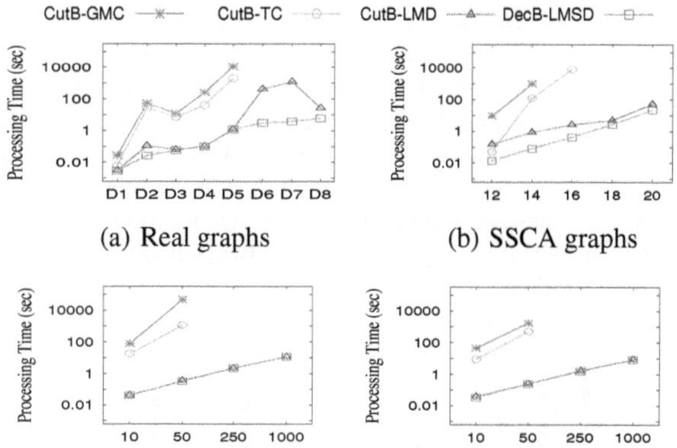

(a) Real graphs (b) SSCA graphs

(c) Random graphs (d) PowerLaw graphs

Figure 9: Scalability test (Varying graphs, k = 8)

$a = 10, 50, 250, 1000$, respectively. The testing results with $k = 8$ are shown in Fig. 9. The x-axis denotes the different graphs. The corresponding graphs in Fig. 9(b) can be inferred from the label of the x-axis with "SSCA-" omitted, e.g., 12 means the SSCA-12 graph. The exact name of the corresponding graphs in Fig. 9(a) can be found from Table 3. The x-axis of Fig. 9(c) and Fig. 9(d) denote the number of vertices ($\times 10^3$). Some of the results are not plotted in Fig. 9, because the corresponding algorithms fail to terminate in five hours on the corresponding configurations. CutB-GMC and CutB-TC are not scalable to large graphs. The performance of CutB-LMD depends on the number of k-edge connected components. For example, among the eight real graphs, D5 (amazon0601) and D6 (web-Google) have large number of k-edge connected components, then CutB-LMD performs much worse than DecB-LMSD. DecB-LMSD scales almost linearly with respect to the size of input graphs as shown in Fig. 9(b), where the sizes of the five SSCA graphs increase exponentially. From Fig. 9(c) and Fig. 9(d), we see that the processing times of CutB-LMD and DecB-LMSD are almost the same, because there is only one large k-edge connected component in each of these graphs.

5.2 Evaluating Optimization Techniques

In this subsection, we evaluate the effectiveness of the proposed optimization techniques in Section 4. Note that, we also consider the data structure proposed in Section 4.2 as an optimization. Therefore, there are four optimization techniques: **L**inear data structure, early **M**erge, list **S**haring, and efficient vertex reduction by **D**egree. Let the four letters (**L**, **M**, **S**, **D**) denote the corresponding optimization applied in an algorithm, respectively. We evaluated a series of algorithms, DecB-M, DecB-LM, DecB-MSD, DecB-LMS, DecB-LMD, DecB-L, DecB-LSD. For example, DecB-LMS is an algorithm by applying the first three optimization techniques.

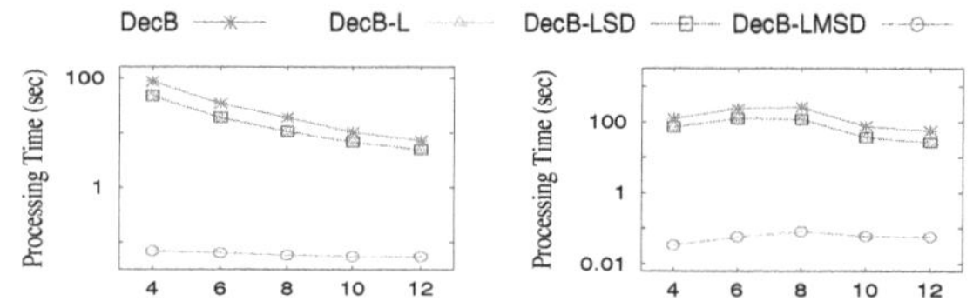

(a) email-EuAll (b) SSCA-14

Figure 10: Testing early merge optimization(Varying k)

Testing the early merge optimization: We evaluate the effectiveness of the early merge optimization by comparing DecB-LMSD with other algorithms without this optimization, such as DecB, DecB-L, DecB-LSD. The results of running these algorithms on email-EuAll graph and SSCA-14 graph are reported in Fig. 10. DecB-L and DecB-LSD run slightly faster than the baseline algorithm DecB, however, both of them run much slower than DecB-LMSD by several orders of magnitude. The effectiveness of early merge optimization is due to the fact that a lot of vertex-pairs are merged in one iteration. Therefore, the number of vertices reduces rapidly after each iteration of Mas-LMS in Alg. 3 as discussed in Section 4.4, which results in a very small l. Without this optimization, for a k-connected graph $G(V, E)$, the running time would be $\Omega(|V||E|)$. In the following testings, we always include the early merge optimization.

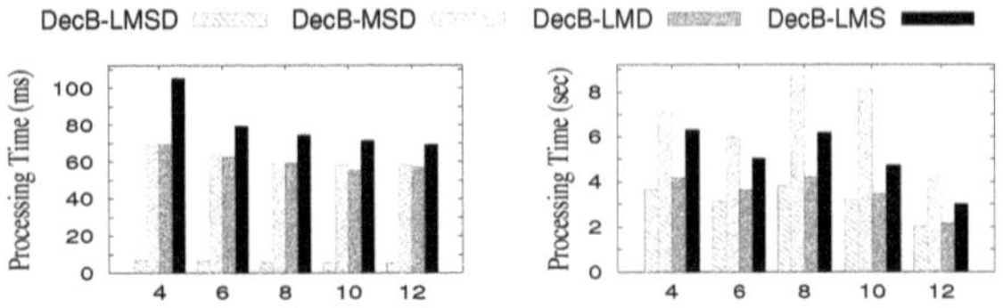

(a) email-EuAll (b) web-Google

Figure 11: Testing L, S, D optimization techniques (Varying k)

Testing L, S, D optimization techniques: We test the effectiveness of the three optimizations, linear data structure, list sharing, and efficient vertex reduction by degree, by not considering the corresponding optimization in an algorithm while applying all other optimization techniques. The testing results are shown in Fig. 11. On the email-EuAll graph, leaving out any optimization will increase the processing time as shown in Fig. 11(a), while on the web-Google graph leaving out the list sharing optimization does not affect the performance of DecB-LMSD as shown in Fig. 11(b).

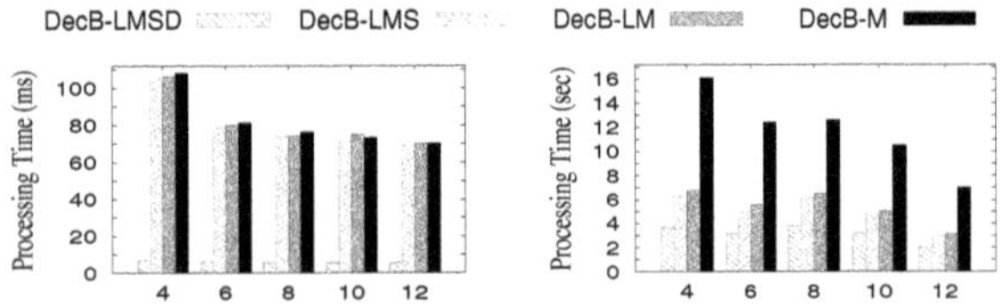

(a) email-EuAll (b) web-Google

Figure 12: Adding optimization incrementally(Varying k)

Adding optimization techniques incrementally: We test the effect of adding one optimization at a time incrementally, starting from the DecB-M algorithm. The optimization techniques are added in the following order, linear data structure, list sharing, and vertex reduction by degree, where the final algorithm is DecB-LMSD. In Fig. 12(a) we see that, the performance does not improve until all optimization techniques are added. However, in Fig. 12(b), we can see performance improvement after adding each of the three optimization techniques.

From the above evaluations, we conclude that the early merge optimization improves the performance substantially, while the other optimization techniques also improve the performance of algorithms after applying the early merge optimization.

6. CONCLUSION

In this paper, we have proposed a novel graph decomposition paradigm to iteratively decompose a graph G for computing its k-edge connected components with a very small decomposition depth h. To compute k-edge connected components efficiently based on this decomposition paradigm, we devised an efficient threshold-based graph decomposition algorithm with time complexity $O(l \times |E|)$ with a small integer l (usually $l \ll |V|$). As a result, we have improved the time complexity of an existing state-of-the-art solution of computing k-edge connected components of a graph from $O(|V|^2|E| + |V|^3 \log |V|)$ to $O(h \times l \times |E|)$, where l and h are usually bounded by a small constant in all the real and synthetic graphs we tested. As their relationships and the average case behavior of $h \times l$ are very challenging to deal with, we will put this issue in our future work. We finally conducted experiments to evaluate the performance of the proposed algorithm, and the experimental results demonstrate that our techniques outperform the existing one by several orders of magnitude.

Acknowledgements: The work was started when the first author was at CUHK, and partially done when the first and the fourth authors were at East China Normal University. The second author was partially supported by grants of the Research Grants Council of the Hong Kong SAR, China, No.418512. The fourth author was partially supported by NSFC61232006, NSFC61021004, ARC DP110102937, ARC DP120104168. The second, the fifth and the sixth authors were partially supported by ARC DP120102627.

7. REFERENCES

[1] R. Agrawal, S. Rajagopalan, R. Srikant, and Y. Xu. Mining newsgroups using networks arising from social behavior. In *Proc. of WWW'03*, 2003.

[2] V. Batagelj and M. Zaversnik. An o(m) algorithm for cores decomposition of networks. *CoRR*, cs.DS/0310049, 2003.

[3] A. A. Benczúr and D. R. Karger. Randomized approximation schemes for cuts and flows in capacitated graphs. *CoRR*, cs.DS/0207078, 2002.

[4] L. Chang, J. X. Yu, and L. Qin. Fast maximal cliques enumeration in sparse graphs. *Algorithmica*, 66(1), 2013.

[5] J. Cheng, Y. Ke, S. Chu, and M. T. Özsu. Efficient core decomposition in massive networks. In *Proc. of ICDE'11*, 2011.

[6] J. Cheng, Y. Ke, A. W.-C. Fu, J. X. Yu, and L. Zhu. Finding maximal cliques in massive networks by h*-graph. In *Proc. of SIGMOD'10*, 2010.

[7] W. S. Fung, R. Hariharan, N. J. A. Harvey, and D. Panigrahi. A general framework for graph sparsification. In *Proc. of STOC'11*, 2011.

[8] Z. Galil and G. F. Italiano. Reducing edge connectivity to vertex connectivity. *SIGACT News*, 22(1), Mar. 1991.

[9] S. Günnemann, B. Boden, and T. Seidl. Finding density-based subspace clusters in graphs with feature vectors. *Data Min. Knowl. Discov.*, 25(2), 2012.

[10] N. Hiroshi and W. Toshimasa. Computing k-edge-connected components of a multigraph (special section on discrete mathematics and its applications). *IEICE transactions on fundamentals of electronics, communications and computer sciences*, 76(4), 1993-04-25.

[11] D. W. Matula. Determining edge connectivity in 0(nm). In *Proc. of FOCS'87*, 1987.

[12] H. Nagamochi and T. Ibaraki. A linear time algorithm for computing 3-edge-connected components in a multigraph. *Japan Journal of Industrial and Applied Mathematics*, 9, 1992.

[13] A. N. Papadopoulos, A. Lyritsis, and Y. Manolopoulos. Skygraph: an algorithm for important subgraph discovery in relational graphs. *Data Min. Knowl. Discov.*, 17(1), Aug. 2008.

[14] M. Stoer and F. Wagner. A simple min-cut algorithm. *J. ACM*, 44(4), 1997.

[15] Y. H. Tsin. Yet another optimal algorithm for 3-edge-connectivity. *J. of Discrete Algorithms*, 7(1), 2009.

[16] N. Wang, J. Zhang, K.-L. Tan, and A. K. H. Tung. On triangulation-based dense neighborhood graph discovery. *Proc. VLDB Endow.*, 4(2), Nov. 2010.

[17] X. Yan, X. J. Zhou, and J. Han. Mining closed relational graphs with connectivity constraints. In *Proc. of KDD'05*, 2005.

[18] Z. Zeng, J. Wang, L. Zhou, and G. Karypis. Out-of-core coherent closed quasi-clique mining from large dense graph databases. *ACM Trans. Database Syst.*, 32(2), June 2007.

[19] Y. Zhang and S. Parthasarathy. Extracting analyzing and visualizing triangle k-core motifs within networks. In *Proc. of ICDE'12*, 2012.

[20] R. Zhou, C. Liu, J. X. Yu, W. Liang, B. Chen, and J. Li. Finding maximal k-edge-connected subgraphs from a large graph. In *Proc. of EDBT'12*, 2012.

An Online Cost Sensitive Decision-Making Method in Crowdsourcing Systems

Jinyang Gao†, Xuan Liu†, Beng Chin Ooi†, Haixun Wang§, Gang Chen‡

†School of Computing, National University of Singapore, Singapore

§Microsoft Research Asia, Beijing, P.R. China

‡College of Computer Science, Zhejiang University, Hangzhou, P.R. China

†{jinyang.gao, liuxuan, ooibc}@comp.nus.edu.sg, §haixunw@microsoft.com, ‡cg@zju.edu.cn

ABSTRACT

Crowdsourcing has created a variety of opportunities for many challenging problems by leveraging human intelligence. For example, applications such as image tagging, natural language processing, and semantic-based information retrieval can exploit crowd-based human computation to supplement existing computational algorithms. Naturally, human workers in crowdsourcing solve problems based on their knowledge, experience, and perception. It is therefore not clear which problems can be better solved by crowdsourcing than solving solely using traditional machine-based methods. Therefore, a cost sensitive quantitative analysis method is needed.

In this paper, we design and implement a cost sensitive method for crowdsourcing. We online estimate the profit of the crowdsourcing job so that those questions with no future profit from crowdsourcing can be terminated. Two models are proposed to estimate the profit of crowdsourcing job, namely the linear value model and the generalized non-linear model. Using these models, the expected profit of obtaining new answers for a specific question is computed based on the answers already received. A question is terminated in real time if the marginal expected profit of obtaining more answers is not positive. We extends the method to publish a batch of questions in a HIT. We evaluate the effectiveness of our proposed method using two real world jobs on AMT. The experimental results show that our proposed method outperforms all the state-of-art methods.

Categories and Subject Descriptors

H.3.m [**Information Storage and Retrieval**]: Miscellaneous

Keywords

Crowdsourcing, Decision-making

1. INTRODUCTION

Crowdsourcing has attracted a great deal of interest as a platform for leveraging crowd-based human computation and intelligence. It is to some extent inspired by the vast amount of collaboration in Web 2.0 communities, where users share not only information, but also their knowledge and intelligence. Platforms such as, for example, the Amazon Mechanical Turk (AMT) [1], facilitate the refinement of data and reduction of noise by passing complex jobs to human workers. These complex jobs include image tagging, semantic-based information retrieval, and natural language processing, which are hard for computers, but relatively easy for human workers. Instead of designing sophisticated algorithms or spending a lot of money to consult experts, many of these jobs can be solved by human workers on a crowdsourcing platform at a much lower cost. Some successful crowdsourcing applications that appear recently include CrowdDB [4], CrowdSearch [19], and HumanGS [14].

Despite the success of crowdsourcing systems, employing crowdsourcing effectively remains challenging for three reasons. First, for most crowdsourcing jobs, we need to obtain multiple answers to guarantee their quality. Thus, we have to decide when to stop obtaining new results provided by human workers. Most existing work uses the accuracy or the cost as the optimization objective. These turn out to be too rigid in practice. However, the trade-off is not trivial. Typically crowdsourcing jobs may have different level of difficulty (e.g. homework of kids vs. research problems), risks (e.g. Flickr image tagging vs. cancer diagnosing), and profits (e.g. survey for personal interest vs. design for investment model). Therefore, it is important to have an online economic model that considers all these factors of crowdsourcing jobs.

Second, none of the current research focuses on whether a problem is suitable for crowdsourcing or not. Intuitively, crowdsourcing based techniques are more fitting for problems that require semantic processing. For example, sentiment analysis, image tagging, and information retrieval are good problems for crowdsourcing while large scale numerical analytics are better handled by machines.

Finally, the estimation of crowdsourcing quality is still primitive. Low quality answers may sharply reduce the quality of crowdsourcing, and introduce noises. To resolve the quality issue, several methods have been proposed, such as Crowdscreen [12] and CDAS [9]. Both proposals only consider the accuracy of the answers provided by the workers, without taking into account the difficulty of the tasks. However, it is very challenging to predict the difficulty of the tasks, and a robust algorithm that can handle problems of varied levels of difficulty and answers of varied levels of quality is needed.

In this paper, we propose a novel online cost sensitive decision-making model to address the above three challenges. Our contributions include:

SIGMOD'13, June 22–27, 2013, New York, New York, USA.

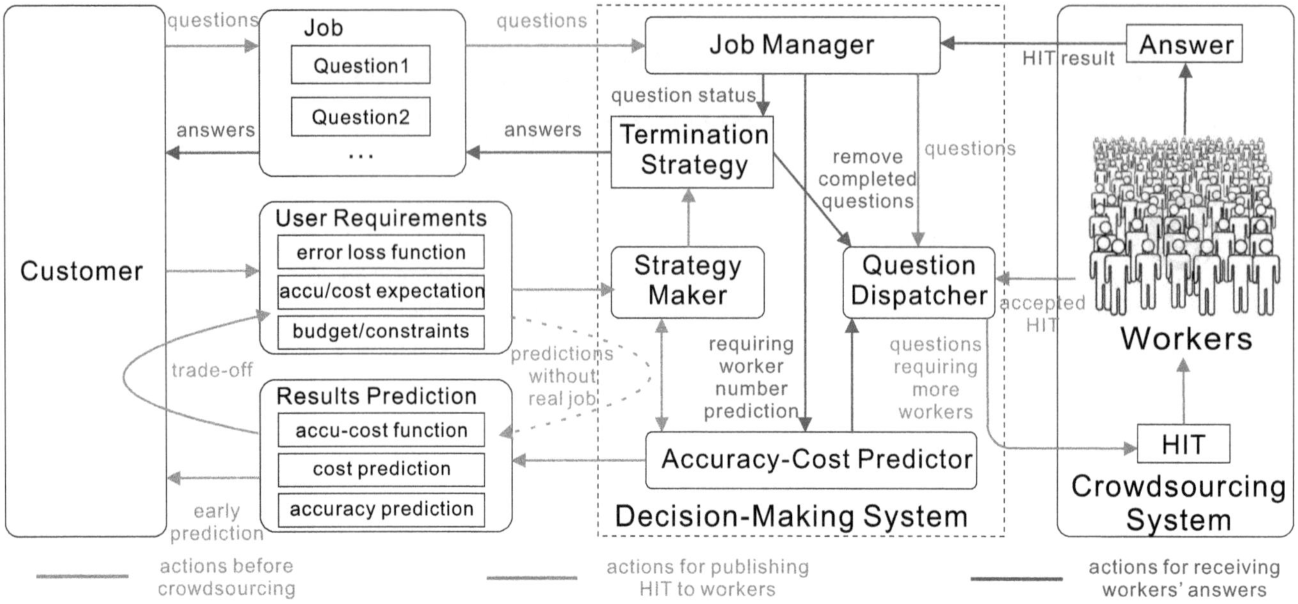

Figure 1: The Architecture of Cost Sensitive Decision Making System

- We propose an online, cost sensitive decision-making model to analyze and decide whether to stop the question in its current status, given the value of the question, the risk of getting incorrect answers, and the cost of workers in the crowdsourcing system. To the best of our knowledge, our model is the first that provides an online quantitative profit analysis of crowdsourcing jobs. We further extend our algorithm to support online cost sensitive decision-making with constraints, such as limited budgets etc.
- An application or task may contain questions of diverse difficulty levels. We propose a model for measuring the difficulty of a question and We design and implement a robust algorithm that handles such questions.
- We propose a novel algorithm called Accuracy-Cost to perform the marginal analysis of the accuracy and the cost in crowdsourcing. The algorithm calculates the incremental profit when the number of workers is increased.
- We conduct extensive experimental studies on two real datasets obtained from the answers of workers in AMT to evaluate the effectiveness of our proposed method. The results show that our method obtains precise results while keeping the cost low. We also develop an automatic question dispatching method that assigns multiple questions in a HIT while each question can be terminated at any time.

The rest of this paper is organized as follows. Section 2 gives an overview of our method. Section 3 explains the preliminaries. Section 4 presents our proposed linear model to get real time decisions and analyse the profit. Section 5 extends our linear model to the non-linear model, which demonstrates the relationship between cost and accuracy and gives our model widespread applicability. Section 6 discusses the experimental studies. Section 7 reviews the related works. Finally, we conclude in Section 8.

2. OVERVIEW

In this section, we give an overview of our cost sensitive decision-making method for crowdsourcing.

Figure 1 shows the architecture of our proposed method. The core part is the decision-making system (the dashed box), which consists of five components, namely the job manager, the question dispatcher, the accuracy-cost predictor, the strategy maker, and the termination strategy manager. The job manager passes the questions from the crowdsourcing customer to the question dispatcher. It keeps collecting the answers of the workers and reporting the updated question status to the termination strategy manager. After receiving the questions, the question dispatcher allocates these questions to several workers using a question dispatching algorithm (will be discussed in Subsection 5.2). The termination strategy manager determines whether we should stop getting more answers for a question and return the results to the customer based on the status of the question. These termination strategies are generated by the strategy maker according to user's requirements, namely the error loss function, the accuracy/cost expectation, the budget, or other constraints. The strategy maker employs a linear model we propose in Section 4. Note that the generated strategies are stored in the termination strategy manger so that our decision-making system is able to decide if we should terminate a question in real-time. The accuracy-cost predictor provides two major functionalities. First, it predicts the results as well as the accuracy/cost ratio. Second, it generates the termination strategies using a generalized non-linear model together with the strategy maker. The details of the non-linear model is discussed in Section 5.

In summary, our proposed decision-making system automatically dispatches questions to the workers. It terminates the questions and returns the answers in real-time according to the generated termination strategies. This decision-making system also provides an early prediction of the results before running a real crowdsourcing job in order to help the customer set proper user requirements. In the following sections, we present the idea and the method of implementing this decision making system.

3. PRELIMINARIES

Before describing our method in Section 4 and 5, we discuss the required prior knowledge to understand the problem.

For the sake of brevity, in our model we assume the questions are two-choice problems. We can think of the two choices as binary values 0 and 1. However, we can easily extend our method to problems that have more than two choices.

Question status: We model the status of a question by a pair (m, l) that represents the numbers of the two different answers received from the workers. Since the values 0 and 1 are just two symbols to represent both choices, the 0s and 1s in the answers can be exchanged. As a result, the following two cases: (1) m 0s and l 1s; (2) m 1s and l 0s can be viewed as identical to represent the agreement of the workers on the two choices. Without loss of generality, in the remainder of this paper, we use (m, l) $(m \geqslant l)$ to represent the above two cases.

Intuitively, the question status indicates the difficulty of the question. When m is far larger than l, most of the workers agree on one choice. It could be that this question is easy. On the other hand, when m is close to l, it is likely that the question is too difficult so that the workers are just making guesses.

Question run: A question run r is a sequence of question statuses as we get answers from workers for this question, i.e.,

$$r = \{(m_0, l_0), (m_1, l_1), \cdots, (m_n, l_n)\}$$

where $(m_0, l_0) = (0, 0)$ is the initial status. Every non-initial status (m_i, l_i) has exactly one more answer than its previous status (m_{i-1}, l_{i-1}), i.e., $(m_i, l_i) = (m_{i-1}, l_{i-1}+1)$ or $(m_{i-1}+1, l_{i-1})$. In the above question run r, the question is terminated at question status (m_n, l_n), after which it will not accept more answers. For example, $\{(0, 0), (1, 0), (2, 0), (2, 1)\}$ is a valid question run that stops after getting three answers but $\{(0, 0), (1, 0), (2, 1), (2, 0)\}$ is not a valid question run.

Accuracy of question answer: We use A_Q to denote the accuracy of an answer to question Q, i.e. the probability that a worker provides the correct answer. Most of existing works considering the accuracy of answers assume that the accuracy is a fixed value that can be computed from sampled answers, e.g. [9][12]. The major drawback of these models is that they do not take the difficulty of questions into consideration. Using these models, for a single worker, his answers to different questions would have the same quality. However, this observation contradicts the intuition that the answers of a hard question might be poor.

In our paper, instead of modelling the accuracy as a single fixed value and employing sampling based methods to estimate this value, we represent the accuracy as a probability distribution. The probability distribution provides the ability of modelling answer quality based on the observed question status. We model the accuracy A_Q as a random variable and we estimate the value of A_Q by the observation of the question status (m, l). Specifically, we assume that A_Q obeys the Beta distribution:

ASSUMPTION 1. *Given a question Q, the probability density function of A_Q is:*

$$f(A_Q = \mu) = \mu^{a-1}(1-\mu)^{b-1}/Beta(a, b)$$

We thus have $E[A_Q] = a/(a+b)$. a and b are parameters of the Beta distribution, representing the prior prediction of the random variable. The Beta distribution is actually a two-dimensional Dirichlet distribution [1]. We can replace the Beta distribution by the more general Dirichlet distribution for multiple choice questions.

If the prior distribution is $B(\mu|1, 1)$, i.e., the uniform distribution, then the estimation of A_Q is only determined by the observation of the question status. In other words, our method is a generalized form of both the traditional fixed accuracy model and the uniform distribution. It takes both the prior knowledge and the question status observation into consideration to adapt the estimated distribution of the difficulty of problems. Ideally the estimated distribution performs best when it is the same as the empirical distribution of problem difficulty. However, the empirical distribution is always difficult to obtain. Moreover, it is not feasible to compute Bayesian inference based on the empirical distribution. The Beta distribution is used to simplify the computation, as it is the conjugate prior distribution of Binomial and Bernoulli distribution. While on the other hand, Beta distribution with proper parameters fits the accuracy distribution well.

We have observed that our model is robust since using different prior prediction parameters a, b almost does not change the results. This is because our model is based on a probability distribution and it can be adaptively adjusted to be applied on questions with diversified difficulties. Moreover, we observed that the empirical distribution of A_Q in several real question sets, including the tweet sentiment analysis questions and common sense questions used in our experiments, is similar to the $B(\mu|6, 2)$ distribution. On the other hand, our experiments also show that when distribution changes, this estimation still works well. In Section 4, we explain the reason that the probability distribution based accuracy model outperforms the fixed value based accuracy models. In the experiment section, we use empirical data to support the above two observations.

Accuracy of question result: We use A_R to represent the accuracy of the result based on a majority voting on the current question status (m, l). We always choose the answer represented by the majority m. As a result, A_R is the probability that the majorities m choose the correct answer. We define $\langle x, y \rangle$ as the status having x correct answers and y incorrect answers. As the status (m, l) represents either m correct answers or m incorrect answers, $(m, l) = \langle m, l \rangle \cup \langle l, m \rangle$. By Bayesian analysis, the conditional probability, A_R given A_Q and observation (m, l) is:

$$A_R = \frac{Pr(\langle m, l \rangle)}{Pr(\langle m, l \rangle) + Pr(\langle l, m \rangle)} = \frac{{A_Q}^{m-l}}{{A_Q}^{m-l} + (1 - A_Q)^{m-l}}$$

Note that A_R is also a random variable as A_Q is a random variable.

The notations used in the following sections of this paper are listed in Table 1.

4. LINEAR DECISION-MAKING

In this section, we introduce a linear model for online decision making. We first estimate the accuracy of the answers according to the question status and prior distribution. Based on the estimation of the answer accuracy, we obtain the marginal income and the profit of each status. This enables us to make decisions at each status according to the economic profit. In this paper, we employ a dynamic programming algorithm to calculate the profit and generate the strategy for each question status. We prove that the time complexity of our strategy generating algorithm is $O(n^2)$ (n is the maximum possible number of answers for a single question, i.e. the search space), which is a significant improvement compared with existing methods such as CrowdScreen's $O(n^4)$ linear programming. In this section, we also discuss the techniques of extending our method to solve a more complex problem, namely linear model with constraints of accuracy and cost.

4.1 Linear model

For a question Q, the linear model has three variables: the question value V_Q, the error loss L_Q, and the question cost per worker

[1]http://en.wikipedia.org/wiki/Dirichlet_distribution

Table 1: Notations

Q	a question in a crowdsourcing job
V_Q	the value of a crowdsourcing question Q
L_Q	the loss of getting a wrong answer for Q
C_Q	the cost of assigning a question to a worker
(m, l)	the status of the crowdsourcing question Q
A_R	the probability that the voting result of Q is correct
A_Q	the probability that a worker provides the correct answer to the question Q
$MI(m, l)$	the marginal income of the question accuracy A_R in status (m, l)
$P(m, l)$	the expected economic profit of the question in status (m, l)
$P_S(m, l)$	the expected economic profit of stopping the question in status (m, l)
$P_C(m, l)$	the expected economic profit of continuing the question in status (m, l)
$\mathrm{B}(\mu\|a, b)$	PDF of Beta distribution
$\Gamma(n)$	Gamma function
$Beta(a, b)$	Beta function

C_Q. As discussed in Section 2, these values are preset by the crowdsourcing customer. V_Q is the value of this question given an answer (not necessarily a correct one). The error loss L_Q is the penalty of obtaining a wrong answer for Q. C_Q represents the cost of hiring a worker for Q. According to the definition of V_Q, L_Q and C_Q, we propose the following linear model:

DEFINITION 4.1 (PROFIT OF A QUESTION). *Suppose a question Q ends after it receives k answers, and the result is ans. The profit P of Q is:*

(1) ans is correct: $P = V_Q - kC_Q$.

(2) ans is incorrect: $P = V_Q - L_Q - kC_Q$.

However, in practice we do not know whether the answer ans is correct or not. Thus, we compute the expected value $E[P]$ of the profit to estimate the average profit of question Q. The expected profit is computed by:

$$\begin{aligned} E[P] &= (V_Q - kC_Q)E[A_R] + (V_Q - L_Q - kC_Q)(1 - E[A_R]) \\ &= L_Q E[A_R] + V_Q - L_Q - kC_Q \end{aligned}$$

where A_R is the probability that ans is correct. Note that A_R is a random variable, we thus use the expected $E[P]$ with respect to all possible worlds of A_R.

We use two functions, namely the value function $f^V(E[A_R])$ and the cost function $f^C(E[A_R])$, to describe the expected profit function $E[P](E[A_R])$. $f^V(E[A_R])$ is the expected gain from the job, while $f^C(E[A_R])$ is the cost of crowdsourcing. In this model, obviously $f^V(E[A_R])$ (i.e. $L_Q E[A_R] + V_Q - L_Q$) is a linear function of accuracy $E[A_R]$. It is remarkable that the expected profit function is not a linear function for $E[A_R]$, since larger $E[A_R]$ requires more answers (larger number of k). We will discuss the non-linear $f^V(E[A_R])$ in next section for some special needs in multi-question situation.

In Subsection 4.2, we describe the method to estimate $E[A_R]$ based on the prior distribution $\mathrm{B}(\mu|a, b)$ of the difficulty A_Q and the observations on the final status (m, l) of Q.

We formally define the decision-making problem based on the linear model.

PROBLEM DEFINITION 1. *Given V_Q, L_Q and C_Q of a question Q, find the decision-making algorithm to maximize $E[P]$ among all possible runs of Q on any answer sequence provided by the workers.*

We next show the method of deriving $E[A_Q]$, $E[A_R]$ etc. in Subsection 4.2 and we discuss the algorithm of finding the question run that maximizes $E[P]$ in Subsection 4.3.

4.2 Accuracy Estimation

Suppose the observation of the final status is (m, l), we can derive the $E[A_Q]$ based on the prior distribution $\mathrm{B}(\mu|a, b)$ using Bayesian Analysis. The posterior result is our estimation of $E[A_Q]$.

THEOREM 4.1.

$$E[A_Q] = \frac{\Gamma(a+m+1)\Gamma(b+l) + \Gamma(a+l+1)\Gamma(b+m)}{(a+b+m+l)(\Gamma(a+m)\Gamma(b+l) + \Gamma(a+l)\Gamma(b+m))}$$

where $\Gamma(n)$ is the Gamma function such that $\Gamma(n) = (n-1)!$ for any positive integer n.

PROOF. We prove the theorem using Bayesian Theorem. The conditional probability density function of the observation $O = (m, l)$ given the condition $A_Q = x$ ($x \sim \mathrm{B}(\mu|a, b)$) is

$$f_O(m, l|A_Q = x) = \binom{m+l}{m}(x^m(1-x)^l + x^l(1-x)^m)$$

Note that the probability density function contains two cases: (1) m correct answers, l incorrect answers and (2) m incorrect answers, l correct answers. Using Bayesian Theorem, we have:

$$\begin{aligned} f_{A_Q}(A_Q = x|m, l) &= \frac{f_O(m, l|A_Q = x) f_{A_Q}(A_Q = x)}{f_O(m, l)} \\ &= \frac{(x^m(1-x)^l + x^l(1-x)^m)x^{a-1}(1-x)^{b-1}}{\int_0^1 (x^m(1-x)^l + x^l(1-x)^m)x^{a-1}(1-x)^{b-1}dx} \\ &= \frac{x^{a+m-1}(1-x)^{b+l-1} + x^{a+l-1}(1-x)^{b+m-1}}{\int_0^1 x^{a+m-1}(1-x)^{b+l-1} + x^{a+l-1}(1-x)^{b+m-1}dx} \end{aligned}$$

Therefore, the expected value of A_Q is:

$$\begin{aligned} E[A_Q] &= \int_0^1 x f_{A_Q}(A_Q = x|m, l)dx \\ &= \int_0^1 \frac{x^{a+m}(1-x)^{b+l-1} + x^{a+l}(1-x)^{b+m-1}}{\int_0^1 (x^{a+m-1}(1-x)^{b+l-1} + x^{a+l-1}(1-x)^{b+m-1})dx} dx \\ &= \frac{\int_0^1 x^{a+m}(1-x)^{b+l-1}dx + \int_0^1 x^{a+l}(1-x)^{b+m-1}dx}{\int_0^1 (x^{a+m-1}(1-x)^{b+l-1}dx + \int_0^1 x^{a+l-1}(1-x)^{b+m-1})dx} \\ &= \frac{Beta(a+m+1, b+l) + Beta(a+l+1, b+m)}{Beta(a+m, b+l) + Beta(a+l, b+m)} \\ &= \frac{\Gamma(a+m+1)\Gamma(b+l) + \Gamma(a+l+1)\Gamma(b+m)}{(a+b+m+l)(\Gamma(a+m)\Gamma(b+l) + \Gamma(a+l)\Gamma(b+m))} \end{aligned}$$

□

Theorem 4.1 gives the average accuracy of the answers. Based on this theorem, we can further derive the expectation of the accuracy of the results A_R using Bayesian Analysis. We have the following theorem:

THEOREM 4.2. *Given observations on the final status (m, l) of a question, the expected accuracy of the results $E[A_R]$ is:*

$$E[A_R] = \frac{\Gamma(a+m)\Gamma(b+l)}{\Gamma(a+m)\Gamma(b+l) + \Gamma(a+l)\Gamma(b+m)}$$

Table 2: Trends of A_Q and A_R

	Prior Distribution \ Question Status	(1,0)	(3,3)	(4,0)	(8,2)	(100,100)	(101,100)	(110, 100)
A_Q	Fixed accuracy 0.75	0.75	0.75	0.75	0.75	0.75	0.75	0.75
	$B(\mu\|6,2)$	0.75	0.643	0.821	0.762	0.51	0.51	0.513
	Fixed accuracy 0.80	0.8	0.8	0.8	0.8	0.8	0.8	0.8
	$B(\mu\|8,2)$	0.8	0.687	0.853	0.79	0.514	0.514	0.52
A_R	Fixed accuracy 0.75	0.75	0.5	0.988	0.999	0.5	0.75	1
	$B(\mu\|6,2)$	0.75	0.5	0.962	0.953	0.5	0.51	0.591
	Fixed accuracy 0.80	0.8	0.5	0.996	1	0.5	0.8	1
	$B(\mu\|8,2)$	0.8	0.5	0.985	0.983	0.5	0.514	0.634

PROOF. Note that A_R is a function of A_Q. Thus, the expected value of A_R is:

$$
\begin{aligned}
E[A_R] &= \int_0^1 A_R f_{A_Q}(A_Q = x|m,l)dx \\
&= \int_0^1 \frac{x^m(1-x)^l}{x^m(1-x)^l + x^l(1-x)^m} \\
&\quad \times \frac{x^{a+m-1}(1-x)^{b+l-1} + x^{a+l-1}(1-x)^{b+m-1}}{\int_0^1 x^{a+m-1}(1-x)^{b+l-1} + x^{a+l-1}(1-x)^{b+m-1}dx}dx \\
&= \frac{\int_0^1 x^{a+m-1}(1-x)^{b+l-1}dx}{\int_0^1 x^{a+m-1}(1-x)^{b+l-1} + x^{a+l-1}(1-x)^{b+m-1}dx} \\
&= \frac{Beta(a+m,b+l)}{Beta(a+m,b+l)+Beta(a+l,b+m)} \\
&= \frac{\Gamma(a+m)\Gamma(b+l)}{\Gamma(a+m)\Gamma(b+l)+\Gamma(a+l)\Gamma(b+m)}
\end{aligned}
$$

□

Theorem 4.1 and 4.2 show that the expected values of A_Q and A_R only depend on the status (m,l) and the prior parameters a, b.

To illustrate Theorem 4.1 and 4.2, we show several examples of trends of A_Q and A_R on different question status given specified prior distribution of difficulty of questions in Table 2. We compare the two Beta distributions $B(\mu|6,2)$ and $B(\mu|8,2)$ with two fixed value based models with accuracy 0.75 and 0.8, which are the expected values of the two Beta distributions respectively. We obtain the following facts from Table 2: in status $(3,3)$, the predicted value of A_Q of the $B(\mu|8,2)$ distribution model (0.687) is smaller than that of fixed value model (0.75); in status $(4,0)$, the predicted value of A_Q of the $B(\mu|6,2)$ distribution model (0.821) is larger than that of fixed value model (0.8). These two facts show that the Beta distribution model provides a better prediction than the fixed value based models, since the predicted values of A_Q according to the fixed value based models are always the same no matter what the current question status is.

Moreover, the predicted values of different distribution models converge while the number of answers goes up. Therefore, the choice of prior parameters in the distribution model is not important, because the distribution model can adaptively adjust the predicted values according to the observation of question status Consider the status $(8,2)$, the two fixed value models (0.75 and 0.8) provide very aggressive predictions on A_R, i.e. 0.999 and 1 respectively. However, in practice, 8 of 10 workers agree may not always guarantee the correctness of the results.

When the status is (100, 100), we intuitively believe A_Q is likely to be close to 0.5 rather than 0.75 or 0.8. Based on the status $(100,100)$, we consider the case of accepting one more answer, i.e. question status $(101,100)$. Obviously A_R should still be close to 0.5 as the votes of both choices are very close. However, the two fixed value based models provide the prediction of A_R as 0.75 and 0.8 respectively, which are the same as the predicted values in question status $(1,0)$. This example shows that the Beta distribution model outperforms the fixed value based models by considering the question status.

According to Theorem 4.1 and 4.2, we can predict the possible future answers based on $E[A_Q]$, $E[A_R]$ and the current status (m,l). We define two transitive probabilities:

(1) $Pr(+1|m,l)$: probability from status (m,l) to $(m+1,l)$.

(2) $Pr(-1|m,l)$: probability from status (m,l) to $(m,l+1)$.

Intuitively $Pr(+1|m,l)$ and $Pr(-1|m,l)$ represent the probability that the next answer is the same value as the value voted by m and l answers respectively. Obviously $Pr(+1|m,l) + Pr(-1|m,l) = 1$. We have the following theorem:

THEOREM 4.3.

$$
\begin{aligned}
&E[Pr(+1|m,l)] \\
= &\frac{\Gamma(a+m+1)\Gamma(b+l)+\Gamma(b+m+1)\Gamma(a+l)}{(a+b+m+l)(\Gamma(a+m)\Gamma(b+l)+\Gamma(a+l)\Gamma(b+m))}
\end{aligned}
$$

The proof is analogous to Theorem 4.1. Based on these above theorems, we can quantitatively derive the decision-making strategies.

4.3 Decision Making

We consider the marginal income of accuracy at each status (m,l). Then we derive the profit according to the marginal income of accuracy. We define the marginal income of accuracy at status (m,l) as the expected increase of the $E[A_R]$ after obtaining a new answer. We denote the marginal income of accuracy at status (m,l) as $MI(m,l)$.

DEFINITION 4.2.

$$MI(m,l) \quad = \quad E'[A_R|m,l] - E[A_R|m,l]$$

where $E'[A_R|m,l]$ is the expected accuracy of the results after getting one more answer, i.e. $E'[A_R|m,l] =$

if m>l: $E[E[A_R|m+1,l]Pr(+1|m,l) + E[A_R|m,l+1]Pr(-1|m,l)]$, *i.e.* $E[A_R|m+1,l]E[Pr(+1|m,l)] + E[A_R|m,l+1]E[Pr(-1|m,l)]$

if m=l: $E[E[A_R|m+1,l]Pr(+1|m,l) + E[A_R|l+1,m]Pr(-1|m,l)]$, *i.e.* $E[A_R|m+1,l]E[Pr(+1|m,l)] + E[A_R|l+1,m]E[Pr(-1|m,l)]$

By simplifying the equations in Definition 4.2, we have the following theorem:

THEOREM 4.4. *The marginal income of accuracy $MI(m,l)$ satisfies:*

(1) $MI(m,l) = 0$ *when* $m > l$.

(2) $MI(m,m) = \dfrac{a-b}{2(a+b+2m)}$.

Algorithm 1: Generate Linear Strategy Algorithm

```
Input: Parameter a, b of prior distribution, Error Loss L_Q, question
       cost C_Q
Output: Strategy S for each status (m, l)
M ← ⌈1/2 (L_Q(a−b)/(6C_Q) − (a + b))⌉;
S.M ← M;
for i from M to 0 do
    S.(M, i) ← stopping;
    S.P_S(M, i) ← V_Q − (1 − E[A_R|M, i])L_Q − (M + i)C_Q;
    S.P(M, i) ← S.P_S(M, i);
for i from M − 1 to 0 do
    for j from i to 0 do
        S.P_S(i, j) ← V_Q − (1 − E[A_R|i, j])L_Q − (i + j)C_Q;
        S.P_C(i, j) ← E[Pr(+1|i, j)]S.P(i + 1, j) +
            E[Pr(−1|i, j)]S.P(i, j + 1) − C_Q;
        S.P(i, j) ← max{S.P_S(i, j), S.P_C(i, j)};
        if S.P_S(i, j) >= S.P_C(i, j) then
            S.(i, j) ← stopping;
        else
            S.(i, j) ← continuing;
return S
```

PROOF. We prove the theorem by calculating $MI(m,l)$. When $m > l$, getting an extra answer cannot change the result of the majority voting. Therefore, the marginal income of accuracy is 0. As a result, $MI(m,l) = 0$ when $m > l$.

When $m = l$,

$$\begin{aligned} & MI(m,m) = E[A_R|(m+1,m)] - E[A_R|(m,m)] \\ = & \frac{\Gamma(a+m+1)\Gamma(b+m)}{\Gamma(a+m+1)\Gamma(b+m)+\Gamma(a+m)\Gamma(b+m+1)} \\ & - \frac{\Gamma(a+m)\Gamma(b+m)}{\Gamma(a+m)\Gamma(b+m)+\Gamma(a+m)\Gamma(b+m)} \\ = & \frac{(a+m)\Gamma(a+m)\Gamma(b+m)}{((a+m)+(b+m))\Gamma(a+m)\Gamma(b+m)} - \frac{1}{2} \\ = & \frac{a+m}{a+b+2m} - \frac{1}{2} \\ = & \frac{a-b}{2(a+b+2m)} \end{aligned}$$

□

Note that $a > b$ is guaranteed by the prior distribution. Therefore, $MI(m,m)$ decreases while m increases.

Based on the marginal income of the accuracy, we can further derive the profit $P(m,l)$ of a question in status (m,l). The profit is defined as the maximum economic profit at status (m,l) given the linear model in Subsection 4.1. We introduce two more profit functions before formally defining $P(m,l)$, namely the profit $P_S(m,l)$ of stopping the question at status (m,l) and the profit $P_C(m,l)$ of continuing the question at status (m,l). Since a question has only two choices (stopping and continuing) at any status, we therefore formally define the profit at status (m,l) as:

DEFINITION 4.3.

$$P(m,l) = \max\{P_S(m,l), P_C(m,l)\}$$

Intuitively, we should stop the question when $P_S(m,l) >= P_C(m,l)$ because we cannot benefit from this question any more by waiting for more answers.

Now we consider the two profit functions $P_S(m,l)$ and $P_C(m,l)$. Given the accuracy $E[A_R]$, we know that the result is incorrect with probability $1 - E[A_R]$. Therefore, according to the linear model, the profit $P_S(m,l)$ satisfies:

$$P_S(m,l) = V_Q - (1 - E[A_R])L_Q - (m+l)C_Q$$

When we continue a question, we will pay one more C_Q and get a new answer from a new worker. Meanwhile, the status is also changed to a new status. It is easy to find that the next status is $(m+1,l)$ with probability $Pr(+1|m,l)$ and $(m,l+1)$ with probability $Pr(-1|m,l)$. Thus, the profit $P_C(m,l)$ is recursively defined as following:

$$\begin{aligned} P_C(m,l) &= E[Pr(+1|m,l)]P(m+1,l) \\ &\quad + E[Pr(-1|m,l)]P(m,l+1) - C_Q \end{aligned}$$

Given the recursive definition, it is difficult to calculate them directly. Now we discuss the condition to guarantee the strategy of one status (m,l) stopping, i.e.

$$P_S(m,l) \geqslant P_C(m,l)$$

m that satisfies $MI(m,m)L_Q < C_Q$ is obvious a lower bound, as we will not get a positive profit in each future step. Moreover, we have found a looser lower bound of m. We have the following theorem:

THEOREM 4.5 (TERMINATION THEOREM). *A sufficient condition of $P_S(m,l) \geqslant P_C(m,l)$ is*

$$m \geqslant \frac{1}{2}\left(\frac{L_Q(a-b)}{6C_Q} - (a+b)\right)$$

and $l < m$.

PROOF. We define $P'(m,l) = P(m,l) - P_S(m,l)$. Based on this definition, we can rewrite the Definition 4.3 by

$$\begin{aligned} P'(m,l) &= \max\{0, MI(m,l)L_Q + E[Pr(+1|m,l)]P'(m+1,l) \\ &+ E[Pr(-1|m,l)]P'(m,l+1) - C_Q\} \end{aligned}$$

We have the observations $P'(m,l) \geqslant P'(m,l-1)$ and $P'(m,l) \geqslant P'(m+1,l)$ for all $m > l$. For a large enough number m, we have $MI(m,m) < C_Q/L_Q$ since $\lim_{m\to+\infty} MI(m,m) = 0$. Based on $MI(m,m)L_Q < C_Q$, there exist some m such that $P'(m+1,m) = 0$. We can prove the following Lemma:

LEMMA 4.1. *$P'(m,m-1) = 0$ if $P'(m+1,m) = 0$ and $m \geqslant \frac{1}{2}(\frac{L_Q(a-b)}{6C_Q} - (a+b))$*

Based on Lemma 4.1, we therefore state that $P'(m,m) = 0$ when $m \geqslant \frac{1}{2}(\frac{L_Q(a-b)}{6C_Q} - (a+b))$. □

PROOF OF LEMMA 4.1. *We prove the lemma by contradiction. If $P'(m,m-1) > 0$, we have the following inequality: $MI(m,m-1)L_Q + E[P(+1|m,m-1)]P'(m+1,m-1) + E[P(-1|m,m-1)]P'(m,m) - C_Q > 0$ where $MI(m,m-1) = 0$. Meanwhile, we have*

$$P'(m+1,m-1) <= P'(m+1,m)$$

As a result, $P'(m+1,m-1) = 0$. Obviously, $E[P(-1|m,m-1)] < 1/2$. Therefore, we have $P'(m,m) > 2C_Q$.

Note that

$$P'(m,m) = MI(m,m)L_Q + P'(m+1,m) - C_Q$$

According to the fact that $P'(m+1,m) = 0$, we have

$$P'(m,m) = MI(m,m)L_Q - C_Q$$

Therefore,

$$MI(m,m)L_Q - C_Q > 2C_Q$$

Algorithm 2: Generate Linear Strategy Algorithm with Constraints

Input: Parameter a, b of prior distribution, Error Loss L_Q, question cost C_Q, Budget constraint θ
Output: Strategy $\mathcal{S}$ for each status (m, l)

1 $M \leftarrow \lceil \frac{1}{2}(\frac{L_Q(a-b)}{6C_Q} - (a+b)) \rceil$;
2 $\mathcal{S}.M \leftarrow M$;
3 **for** *i from M to 0* **do**
4 $\quad \mathcal{S}.(M, i) \leftarrow stopping$;
5 $\quad \mathcal{S}.P_S(M, i) \leftarrow V_Q - (1 - E[A_R|M, i])L_Q - (M + i)C_Q$;
6 $\quad \mathcal{S}.P(M, i) \leftarrow \mathcal{S}.P_S(M, i)$;
7 **for** *i from* $M - 1$ *to 0* **do**
8 $\quad$ **for** *j from i to 0* **do**
9 $\quad\quad$ **if** $(i + j + 1)C_Q > \theta$ **then**
10 $\quad\quad\quad \mathcal{S}.P_S(i, j) \leftarrow V_Q - (1 - E[A_R|i, j])L_Q - (i + j)C_Q$;
11 $\quad\quad\quad \mathcal{S}.P(i, j) \leftarrow \mathcal{S}.P_S(i, j)$;
12 $\quad\quad\quad \mathcal{S}.(i, j) \leftarrow stopping$;
13 $\quad\quad$ **else**
14 $\quad\quad\quad \mathcal{S}.P_S(i, j) \leftarrow V_Q - (1 - E[A_R|i, j])L_Q - (i + j)C_Q$;
15 $\quad\quad\quad \mathcal{S}.P_C(i, j) \leftarrow E[Pr(+1|i, j)]\mathcal{S}.P(i + 1, j) + E[Pr(-1|i, j)]\mathcal{S}.P(i, j + 1) - C_Q$;
16 $\quad\quad\quad \mathcal{S}.P(i, j) \leftarrow \max\{\mathcal{S}.P_S(i, j), \mathcal{S}.P_C(i, j)\}$;
17 $\quad\quad\quad$ **if** $\mathcal{S}.P_S(i, j) >= \mathcal{S}.P_C(i, j)$ **then**
18 $\quad\quad\quad\quad \mathcal{S}.(i, j) \leftarrow stopping$;
19 $\quad\quad\quad$ **else**
20 $\quad\quad\quad\quad \mathcal{S}.(i, j) \leftarrow continuing$;
21 **return** $\mathcal{S}$

Moreover, $MI(m, m) = (a - b)/(2(a + b + 2m))$. *As a result, we have* $m < \frac{1}{2}(\frac{L_Q(a-b)}{6C_Q} - (a + b))$ *, which contradicts with* $m \geqslant \frac{1}{2}(\frac{L_Q(a-b)}{6C_Q} - (a + b))$. □

We have designed the linear model based algorithm (Algorithm 1) to generate the strategy deciding whether the question should stop at each status (m, l). The search space bound M is the upper-bound of m in all possible *continuing* status (m, l) in Theorem 4.5:

$$M = \lceil \frac{1}{2}(\frac{L_Q(a - b)}{6C_Q} - (a + b)) \rceil \quad (1)$$

We apply dynamic programming to iteratively compute the decision of the generated strategy $\mathcal{S}$ from the upper-bound back to 0. For each status (m, l), we compute $P_S(m, l)$ and $P_C(m, l)$ based on $P(m + 1, l)$ and $P(m, l + 1)$. In strategy $\mathcal{S}$, the decision is made for each status (m, l) by comparing $P_S(m, l)$ and $P_C(m, l)$. As a result, the question run that maximizes $P(m, l)$ is found by stopping the question at the first status (m^*, l^*) such that $P_S(m^*, l^*) \geqslant P_C(m^*, l^*)$. Algorithm 1 can be applied to find the question run that maximize $P(m, l)$ for all input 0-1 sequences. Obviously, the time complexity of Algorithm 1 is $O(M^2)$ where M is computed in Equation 1. Note that Algorithm pre-computes all possible decisions offline and it only takes $O(M)$ time to make decisions online by querying $\mathcal{S}.(m, l)$ in $O(1)$ time for each status (m, l).

4.4 Model with Constraints

In this subsection, we discuss the decision-making problem with constraints on the accuracy and cost of the result of the question. Suppose the constraints are represented by $cost \leqslant Budget$. We solve this problem by simply adapting Algorithm 1. We mark the status (m, l) as stopping when $(m + l + 1)C_Q > Budget$. This adapted algorithm is outlined in Algorithm 2. We can extend algorithm 2 to support other constraints such as accuracy etc.

Algorithm 3: Accuracy-Cost Algorithm

Input: Parameter a, b of prior distribution, question cost C_Q
Output: List of tuples of accuracy, cost and error loss $\{\langle accu, cost, L_Q \rangle\}$

result $\leftarrow \emptyset$;
$L_Q \leftarrow 1000C_Q$;
while $L_Q > 0$ **do**
$\quad \mathcal{S} \leftarrow$ GenerateLinearStrategy(a, b, L_Q, C_Q);
$\quad$ accu $\leftarrow$ ComputeAccuracy($\mathcal{S}$);
$\quad$ cost $\leftarrow$ ComputeCost($\mathcal{S}$);
$\quad$ result $\leftarrow$ result $\cup \langle$accu[0][0], cost[0][0], $L_Q\rangle$;
$\quad max \leftarrow 0$;
$\quad$ **foreach** *Non-stop status* (m, l) *in* $\mathcal{S}.status$ **do**
$\quad\quad c \leftarrow$ cost$[m][l]$;
$\quad\quad l_Q \leftarrow cL_Q/(P_C(m, l) - P_S(m, l) + c)$;
$\quad\quad$ **if** $l_Q > max$ **then** $max \leftarrow l_Q$;
$\quad L_Q \leftarrow max$;
return result;

In Algorithm 2, the upper bound of search space M is computed in line 1. Line 3-6 pre-computes the strategy for status (M, i). All statuses (M, i) are set to be *stopping*. Line 7-20 the strategy of each status (i, j) is computed. When status (i, j) does not satisfy the constraints, it is set to be *stopping* in line 10-12. Otherwise, $P_S(i, j)$ and $P_C(i, j)$ are computed respectively in line 14-15. The decision of status (i, j) is decided by comparing $P_S(i, j)$ with $P_C(i, j)$ in line 17-20. The computed strategy $\mathcal{S}$ is returned as the result of Algorithm 2 (line 21).

5. NON-LINEAR DECISION-MAKING

In this section, we discuss a non-linear model based approach to predict the relationship between the accuracy and the cost of the question without prior knowing L_Q. We have presented the decision making algorithm in Section 4 for a single question, where the job value is a linear function of the accuracy. However, considering the case of making decisions on a batch of questions, the value function might be more complicated than a linear function. For example, we list three non-linear functions in Figure 2, representing the cases that we have constraints on the quality of the data and we use the information entropy to measure the informativeness of the data. Therefore, the value functions are not linear. Moreover, the non-linear model based method is also driven by situations where the customers are not able to estimate the error loss function L_Q of some problems. The method we have discussed in Section 4 cannot be simply applied to make decisions for the question in the above situations. Since the quality of data can be well estimated by the accuracy when the number of questions is large enough, we propose Algorithm 3 to find the relationship between accuracy and cost (shown in the bottom of Figure 2) in Subsection 5.1. Algorithm 3 calculates the difference between the value function and the cost function as the profit function (as illustrated on the right hand side of Figure 2). Thus, the maximum point of the profit function (star point in Figure 2) is the trade-off point to maximize the profit. We extend our method to solve the problem of decision making for multiple questions in Subsection 5.2.

5.1 Accuracy-Cost Relationship

To obtain the cost function of accuracy, we propose the non-linear model based algorithm (Algorithm 3) by iteratively applying Algorithm 1. According to the Algorithm 1, we know that given fixed $a, b, L_Q/C_Q$, we have a determined strategy to find the question run that maximizes the profit.

The basic idea of this non-linear model based algorithm is to:

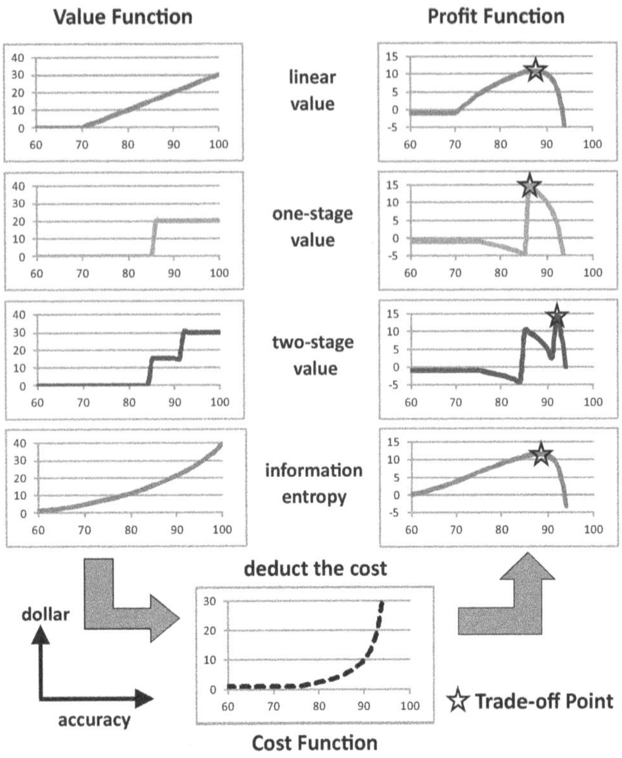

Figure 2: Examples of non-linear decision making

Step 1. initialize L_Q to be a sufficiently large value (i.e. $1000C_Q$) and compute the accuracy and cost based on L_Q.

Step 2. iteratively adjust the value of L_Q by reducing L_Q such that the decision of only one status (m, l) changes from *continuing* to *stopping*.

Step 3. compute accuracy and cost and go back to Step 2.

This method is to enumerate the accuracy and cost pairs by gradually reducing the value of L_Q. We show the detailed method in Algorithm 3. In Algorithm 3, we record the expected accuracy and cost for each status (m, l) using the strategy generated from L_Q. Algorithm 3 iteratively reduces L_Q by selecting the maximum l_Q that can change exactly one *continuing* status to *stopping*. l_Q is computed in line 11. The correctness is guaranteed by the following lemma:

LEMMA 5.1. *Given a continuing status (m, l), we reduce L_Q to be $cost[m][l]L_Q/(P_C(m, l) - P_S(m, l) + cost[m][l])$. If the stopping/continuing status of all status (m', l') other than (m, l) are not changing, we have $P_C(m, l) = P_S(m, l)$.*

PROOF OF LEMMA 5.1. *By the definition of the two profits, i.e. $P_S(m, l)$ and $P_C(m, l)$:*

$$\begin{aligned} P_S(m,l) &= V_Q - L_Q + E[A_R|m,l]L_Q - (m+l)C_Q \\ P_C(m,l) &= V_Q - L_Q + accu[m][l]L_Q - (m+l)C_Q \\ &\quad -cost[m][l] \end{aligned}$$

We therefore have

$$P_S(m,l) - P_C(m,l) = L_Q \Delta accu - cost[m][l]$$

where $\Delta accu = accu[m][l] - E[A_R|m,l]$. We assume that $l_Q \Delta accu - cost[m][l] = 0$. Thus,

$$l_Q = \frac{cost[m][l]}{\Delta accu} = \frac{cost[m][l]L_Q}{P_C(m,l) - P_S(m,l) + cost[m][l]} \quad \square$$

Algorithm 4: Compute Accuracy

Input: Strategy $\mathcal{S}$
Output: Expected accuracy accu of the problem in every status (m, l) using Strategy $\mathcal{S}$

```
M ← S.M;
for i from M to 0 do
    for j from i to 0 do
        if (i, j) is stopped then
            accu[i][j] ← E[A_R|i, j];
        else
            accu[i][j] ←
              Pr(+1|i, j)accu[i+1][j] + Pr(−1|i, j)accu[i][j−1];
return accu
```

Algorithm 5: Compute Cost

Input: Strategy $\mathcal{S}$
Output: Expected accuracy cost of the problem in every status (m, l) using Strategy $\mathcal{S}$

```
M ← S.M;
for i from M to 0 do
    for j from i to 0 do
        if (i, j) is stopped then
            cost[i][j] ← (i + j)C_Q;
        else
            cost[i][j] ← Pr(+1|i, j)cost[i + 1][j] +
              Pr(−1|i, j)cost[i][j − 1] + C_Q;
return cost
```

The strategy is generated according to the newly updated L_Q. We employ dynamic programming method to compute the accuracy and cost in Algorithm 4 and 5. These two algorithms compute the accuracy and cost respectively for each status (m, l) from (M, M) (*stopping*) back to $(0, 0)$.

We formally define the non-linear value function problem as:

PROBLEM DEFINITION 2. *Given the functions of the value of question quality $f^V(accu)$ and cost $f^C(accu)$ with respect to the accuracy of the result, find the strategy to maximize $f^P(accu) = f^V(accu) - f^C(accu)$ on each possible question run.*

Algorithm 3 provides the accuracy-cost relationship $f^C(accu)$, which makes it possible to find a trade-off point when user requirements $f^V(accu)$ is clear. Moreover, this can be used to give customer the accuracy and cost predictions early and help the user to choose suitable requirements like $f^V(accu)$ or special point of $\langle accu, cost, L_Q \rangle$.

The solution of those non-linear $f^V(accu)$ requirements can be done as follows:

1. Compute $result = \{\langle accu, cost, L_Q \rangle\}$ by calling Algorithm 3.

2. Find $\max_{accu \in result}\{f^V(accu) - f^C(accu)\}$ by computing the difference between the non-linear value and cost for each *accu* in the *result*. Generate the strategy using the corresponding L_Q of *accu* as parameter of Algorithm 2.

Notice that in general case the $f^P(accu)$ is not convex (e.g. the profit function for stage value). As a result, we have to calculate every point for computing $f^P(accu)$.

This method can also be applied to solve the problem with constraints on the expectation of accuracy or cost. We only need to modify the non-linear functions $f^V(accu)$ to present the constraints (e.g.stage value function gives a strict constraint of accuracy).

Algorithm 6: Question Dispatching Algorithm

Dispatcher:
Initialize min-heap $heap$ to be empty;
foreach *non-stop question* Q_i **do**
    $C_i \leftarrow cost[0][0]$;
    $P_i \leftarrow 0$;
    $E_i \leftarrow C_i - P_i$;
    if *heap.size()<k* **then**
        $heap.push(Q_i)$;
while *not all questions are stopped and a new worker comes* **do**
    foreach *question* Q_i *in heap* **do**
        Assign Q_i to the HIT; $P_i \leftarrow P_i + 1$;
        $E_i \leftarrow C_i - P_i$;
    foreach *non-stop question* Q_i *in heap* **do**
        Maintain $heap$ using E_i;

Updater:
while *any question* Q_i *gets into a stopping status* $(Q_i.m, Q_i.l)$ **do**
    Mark Q_i as a stopped question.
while *any question* Q_i *gets a new answer to the status* $(Q_i.m, Q_i.l)$ **do**
    $P_i \leftarrow P_i - 1$;
    $C_i \leftarrow cost[Q_i.m][Q_i.l]$;
    $E_i \leftarrow C_i - P_i$;
    Maintain $heap$ using E_i;

5.2 Decision-Making for Multiple Questions

We discuss the question dispatching algorithm (Algorithm 6) in this subsection. This algorithm aims to build a question dispatcher that assigns HITs containing a batch of questions to the workers. Batching questions in a HIT is an effective approach to reduce the average cost of each question. However, our proposed algorithm only generates strategies for a single question. Questions may be included multiple times in different HITs and their decisions are made in real-time. The numbers of required workers are different among the questions. Therefore, we need to design an algorithm to dynamicly batch non-stopped questions in a HIT. The question dispatching algorithm is designed in order to reduce the rate of already stopped questions in the HITs.

The key idea of our question dispatching algorithm is to manage all the questions to be finished at almost the same time. We store all the unfinished questions in a question pool and maintain the number of questions included in the HITs. Attributed to the fact that the randomness of receiving order of the answers, it is difficult to design a deterministic method to find the best assignment of questions. Instead, we maintain the expected number of asking questions from current status such that these numbers are synchronously decreased. As a result, we put questions with the largest expected number of asking questions into a HIT.

We outline the function of dispatcher and updater in Algorithm 6. For the question, the number of expected asking questions C_i at status $(Q_i.m, Q_i.l)$ is retrieved from $cost[Q_i.m][Q_i.l]$ computed by Algorithm 5. Meanwhile, there are some HITs on the worker's hand. We record the number of HITs that are posted but have not yet received answers of each question Q_i as P_i. We use $E_i = C_i - P_i$ as the estimation of expected asking questions. When a HIT is posted or its answer is received, the expectations of effected questions are updated and the questions with the largest expected numbers are maintained with a min heap.

6. EXPERIMENTAL STUDIES

This section will discuss the experiment results of our methods. To evaluate the performance of our proposed methods, we have conducted extensive experiments on two real-world datasets on the AMT. Besides, various robustness tests and theoretical results are studied using synthetic datasets. We show that our proposed method: (1) works better than any other existing method in terms of both the accuracy and the cost; (2) is robust to handle questions with diversified difficulty distribution and unexpected data quality; (3) is scalable when the maximum number of workers is increased; (4) works well on various kinds of crowdsourcing questions.

6.1 Experiment Setup

We use the following two datasets for our performance studies, namely tweet sentiment analysis (*TSA*) dataset and common sense question (*CSQ*) dataset. Humans are good at comprehension and perform well on problems requiring background knowledge. These two datasets focus on the two main advantages of crowdsourcing respectively.

TSA dataset: A real-world tweets dataset containing 400 comments of 20 movies is crawled from Twitter. We generate a sentiment analysis question (positive, negative) for each of the comments as a candidate crowdsourcing task. We assign each of the 400 questions to up to 50 workers using the question dispatching algorithm (Algorithm 6). We repeat the question dispatching algorithm 10 times to get 10 different question runs for each question. In total, we get 200,000 answers from the workers as the *TSA* dataset.

CSQ dataset: We crawl 400 common sense problems from the Internet as the candidate crowdsourcing tasks. We also assign each of the 400 questions to up to 50 workers by repeatedly using Algorithm 6 10 times. In total, we also get 200,000 answers from the workers as the *CSQ* dataset.

Figure 3 compares the distribution of the difficulty of the questions with $B(\mu|6,2)$ distribution. The average accuracy of results A_R is tested on more than 200 answers. This figure indicates that $B(\mu|6,2)$ distribution can be well used to model the distribution of the difficulty of the Tweet sentiment analysis questions. Moreover, the results also show that about 6.8% of questions have an average A_R smaller than 0.5, which fits the prediction well. The predicted value of the proportion is 6.25% based on $B(\mu|6,2)$ distribution. The accuracy of these questions become even worse when more workers answer them. As a result, the overall accuracy of results on all questions can only achieve 93%-94% rather than very close to 100%. We also observe that the questions in both datasets are a bit more difficult than the expectation based on the prior $B(\mu|6,2)$ distribution.

To compare the performance of proposed algorithm with other existing algorithms, we implement four algorithms, i.e. Accuracy-Cost (Algorithm 3), Crowdscreen [12], Majority Voting and Naive Majority Voting Algorithm. In the majority voting algorithm, when the number of providers of a value is more than a half of the maximum number of workers, the online majority voting algorithm outputs this value and stops, whereas in the offline naive majority voting algorithm, all the values from all workers are collected and output the majority results.

6.2 Problem-Crowdsourcing Fitness

In this subsection we give the analysis on whether a job is appropriate for crowdsourcing or not. We use C_Q as the unit. The results in Figure 4 show that the lower bound of V_Q to get benefit from crowdsourcing job in various L_Q. The loss and cost $V_Q - P(0,0)$ means the total cost of solving a question by crowdsourcing (notice that $P(0,0)$ contains V_Q in it, this measure only contains the error loss expectation and questions cost and is irrelevant to V_Q).

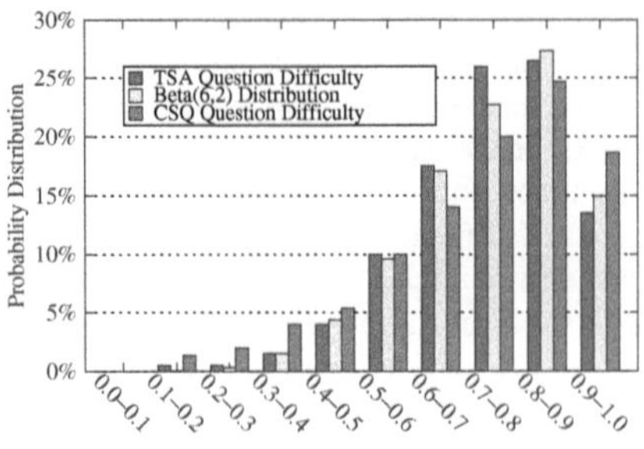

Figure 3: **Distribution of the difficulty of problems vs. B(μ|6, 2) distribution**

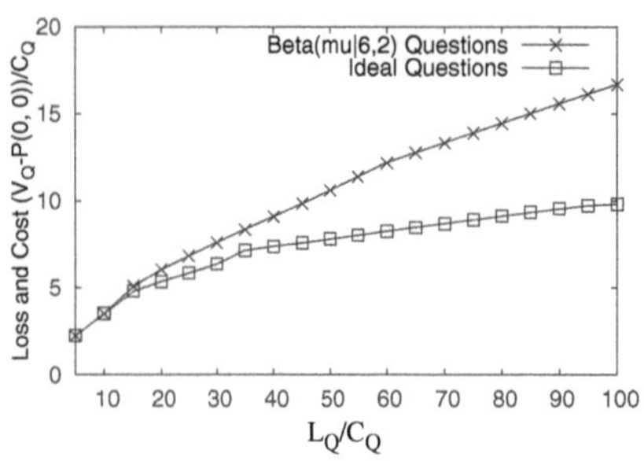

Figure 4: **Lower bound of V_Q**

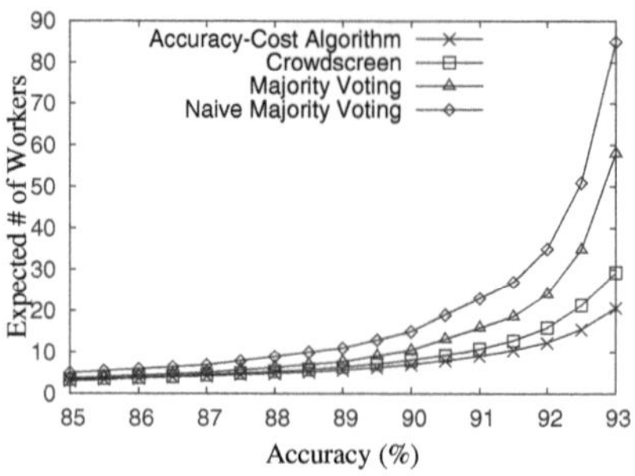

Figure 5: **Expected number of workers given required accuracy**

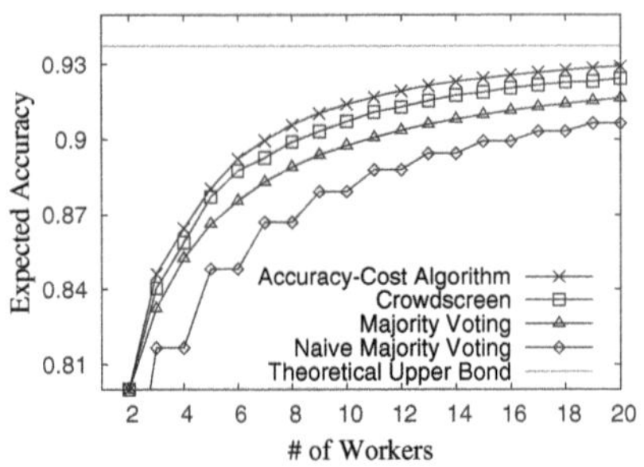

Figure 6: **Expected accuracy given the number of workers**

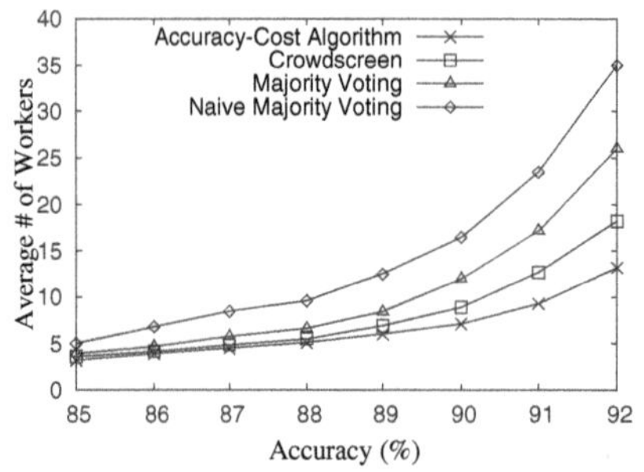

Figure 7: **Empirical number of workers given required accuracy on TSA dataset**

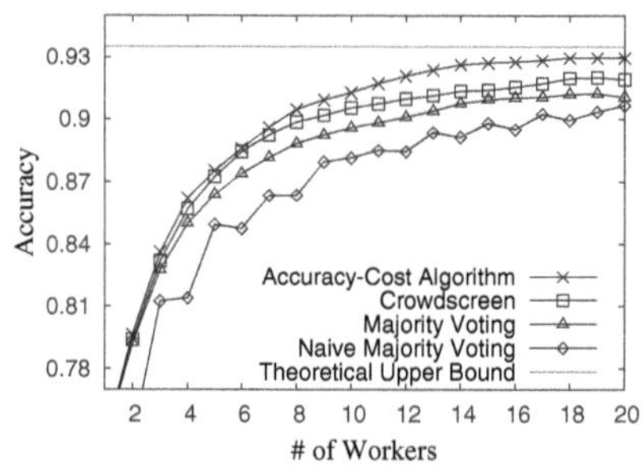

Figure 8: **Empirical accuracy given the number of workers on TSA dataset**

For those jobs where L_Q is too high or V_Q is not enough, crowdsourcing is not a cost-effective way. We compare the loss and cost on two set of questions, namely the questions obeying $B(\mu|6, 2)$ distribution and the questions having the ideal same $A_Q = 0.75$.

6.3 Performance of Accuracy-Cost Algorithm

We test the performance of our Accuracy-Cost Algorithm by investigating the accuracy-cost relationship on both datasets *TSA* and *CSQ*. The results of the number of workers given required accuracy and the accuracy given the number of workers are showed here. We compare the four algorithms, namely Accuracy-Cost, CrowdScreen, Majority Voting and Naive Majority Voting. All four algorithms make the trade-off according to their strategy.

Figure 5 and Figure 6 present the theoretical predictions of the number of workers given a required accuracy and the accuracy given the number of workers respectively based on the $B(\mu|6, 2)$ distribution model.

Experimental results on the *TSA* dataset: Figure 7 shows the empirical number of workers hired in the crowdsourcing system. In Figure 7, the results show that our Accuracy-Cost Algorithm needs the smallest number of workers and Naive Majority Voting needs the largest number. Meanwhile, comparing Figure 7 with Figure 5, the empirical results validate the theoretical predictions. Figure 8 shows the empirical accuracy of the crowdsourcing tasks on the *TSA* dataset. The results in Figure 8 show that our Accuracy-Cost Algorithm has the highest accuracy while Naive Majority Voting has the lowest. The empirical results also fit the theoretical predictions well by comparing Figure 8 with Figure 6. Our Accuracy-Cost Algorithm outperforms other algorithms because our Accuracy-Cost Algorithm computes the maximum accuracy for each possible cost and the smallest cost for each possible accuracy (in Algorithm 3).

Experimental results on the *CSQ* dataset: Figure 9 shows the empirical number of workers hired in the crowdsourcing system. We observe similar trends in Figure 9, i.e. the number of workers of Accuracy-Cost Algorithm is the smallest. The empirical results in Figure 9 also fit the theoretical prediction of the results in Figure 5 well. Figure 10 shows the empirical accuracy of the crowdsourcing tasks on the *CSQ* dataset. The results in Figure 10 are similar to the results in Figure 6.

The experimental results on these two datasets show that our method can be applied on various crowdsourcing questions and yield good accuracy while requiring the least number of workers.

6.4 Robustness

We study the robustness of our algorithm by varying the distribution of question difficulty. We vary variance and expectation of the difficulty distribution of questions such that the distribution is different from our prior $B(\mu|6, 2)$ distribution. The robustness of obtaining satisfied results on unexpected hard questions (or low quality users) is another key requirement, since low data quality without expectation is usually unacceptable.

Figure 11 demonstrates the empirical accuracy of our Accuracy-Cost Algorithm, CrowdScreen and Majority Voting working on unexpected low quality answers with an average 65% accuracy. Note that these four algorithms expect the difficulty of questions to be 75% based on the prior $B(\mu|6, 2)$ distribution. Figure 11 shows that our algorithm still produces results with accuracy very close to the accuracy required by the customer while the other two algorithms fail to obtain results with high accuracy. This phenomenon is due to the fact that our algorithm models the probability of a worker providing an answer as a random variable. This property provides the ability to detect the decrease of accuracy and guarantee high quality results by asking more questions automatically. We can see that

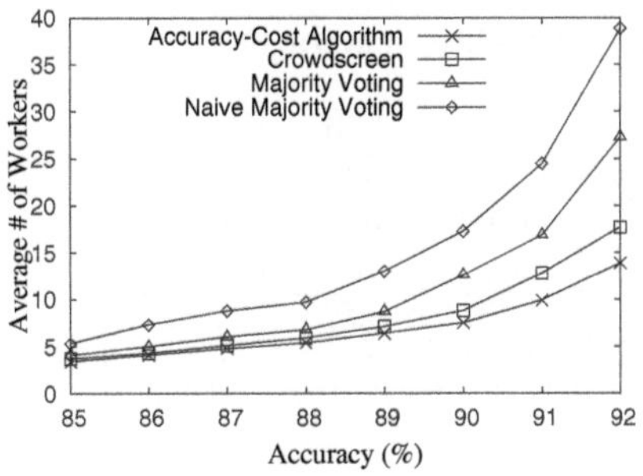

Figure 9: Empirical number of workers given required accuracy on CSQ dataset

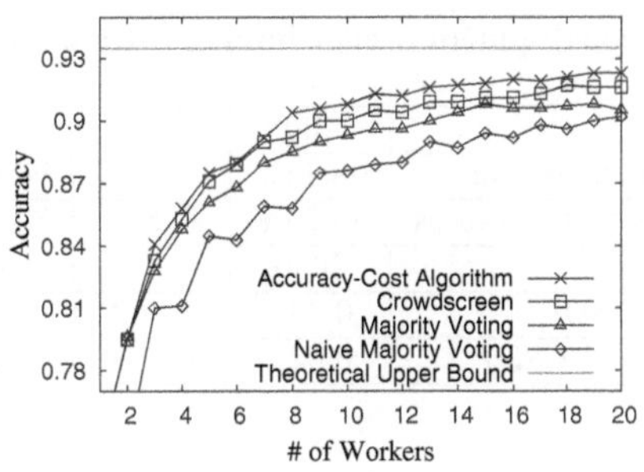

Figure 10: Empirical accuracy given the number of workers on CSQ dataset

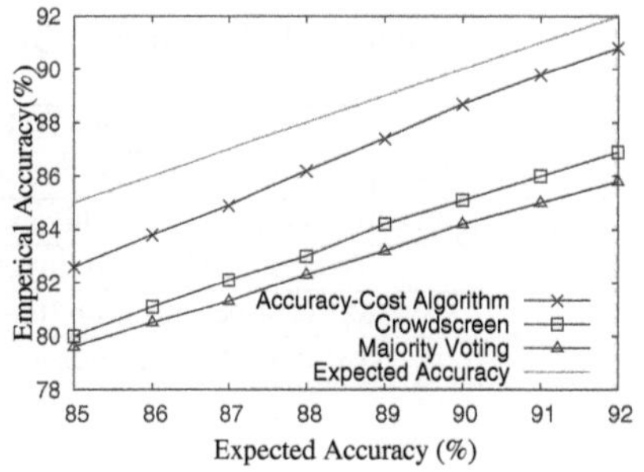

Figure 11: Accuracy of the algorithms on hard questions

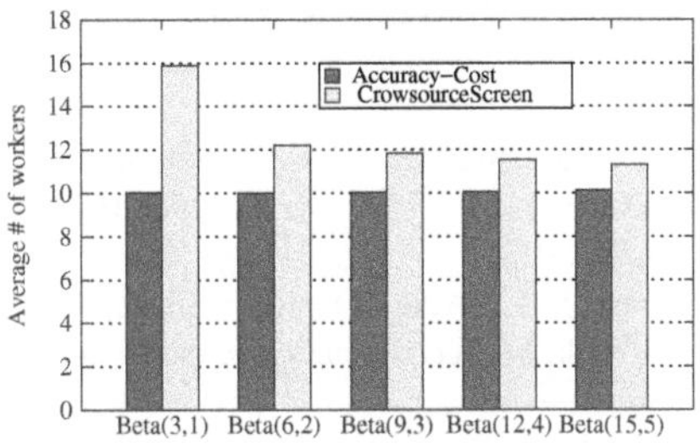

Figure 12: Vary the variance of difficulty of questions

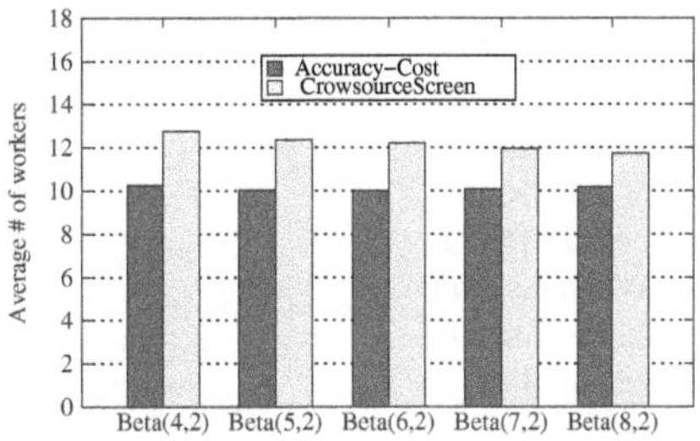

Figure 13: Vary the expectation of difficulty of questions

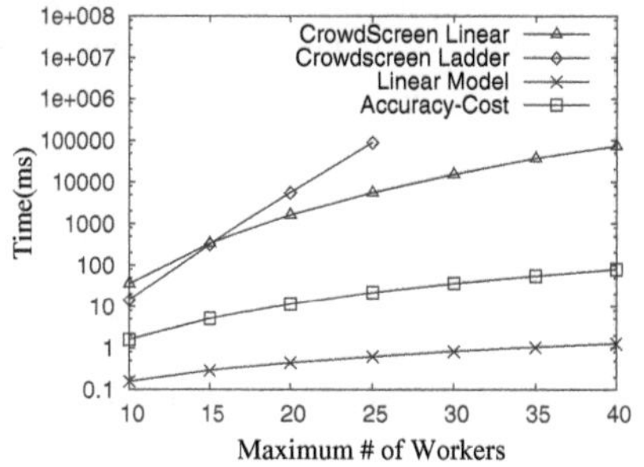

Figure 14: Strategy Generating Time

with the growth of the number of workers(i.e. the increase of accuracy requirement), our method obtains more answers and produces more precise estimation, which results in stronger resistance.

Figure 12 and Figure 13 show the performance when we vary the difficulty distribution of questions. In both experiments algorithm with $B(\mu|6,2)$ distribution and CrowdScreen algorithm are compared to the algorithm using the exact prior distribution (our algorithm outputs the best strategy when data exactly match the prior distribution). In our experiments, we use the accuracy that the exact prior distribution algorithm using 10 workers can achieve as the accuracy requirements. We report the number of needed workers to achieve the accuracy requirements for both algorithms. Figure 12 reports the results of varying the variance of the distribution and Figure 13 reports the results of varying the expectation of the distribution. The results in these two figures indicate that our Accuracy-Cost algorithm needs almost the same number (less than 2% increment) of workers as the exact prior distribution algorithm when we vary the difficulty distribution of the questions, while Crowdscreen algorithm needs more workers when the variance of the distribution is increased.

Instead of using a fixed value, this random variable based probability model is more robust.This implies that our algorithm can by applied to solve unexpected hard questions or working on data sources with unpredictable quality in real crowdsourcing applications.

6.5 Scalability and Question Dispatching

In this subsection, we discuss the scalability of our algorithm when the number of workers and the number of questions increases.

We first report the results on the running time of our algorithms with respect to the number of workers in Figure 14. We compare both our linear and non-linear algorithms with the CrowdScreen's linear and ladder algorithms. Note that the time reported is the offline strategy generating time. The results show that our algorithms are scalable when the number of workers is increased. The linear strategy generating algorithm takes 1.29 milliseconds and non-linear algorithm takes 80.06 milliseconds when there are 40 workers. The results also show that the two CrowdScreen algorithms need to take a lot more time to generate the strategy.

We report the performance of the question dispatching algorithm in Table 3. In this experiment, the maximum number of questions in a HIT is varied from 400 to 10. The measurements contain the average percentage of valid questions in each HIT, average finishing time, average cost per question and average cost per effective question. The valid question refers to the not yet stopped questions in the HIT. We compare the average percentage of valid questions of our question dispatching algorithm to that of randomly assigning questions. The results show that our question dispatching algorithm assigns up to 10.9% and on average 4.53% more valid questions in each HIT than randomly assigning algorithm.

7. RELATED WORK

Crowdsourcing has been widely used to solve challenging problems by human intelligence in comprehensive areas. In crowdsourcing systems, complex and difficult problems are partitioned to simple tasks. These tasks are assigned to several workers. The crowdsourcing system collects and integrates the answers from the workers as the results of the crowdsourcing jobs. Kitter et al. [8] studied the user behaviour in micro-task markets to show that user performs different behaviours.

Recently, crowdsourcing has been adopted and applied in several research areas such as database researches, machine learning and information retrieval. CrowdDB [3, 4], Qurk [10, 11] and TurkDB [13] designed three databases that are incorporated with crowdsourcing systems. These three databases allow queries to be partially answered through the AMT system. Selke et al. [16] expanded database schemas with additional attributes through querying the crowdsourcing systems. CrowdER [17] applied crowd-

Table 3: Performance of Question dispatching algorithm (2 USD per hour per worker on average)

# of questions in a HIT	400	200	100	50	20	10
Effective questions rate using question dispatcher	48.20%	88.40%	94.60%	98.40%	99.50%	99.80%
Effective questions rate by randomly assigning questions	48.20%	77.50%	87.30%	93.60%	96.70%	98.40%
Average HIT finish time (s)	2850	1472	765	393	189	113
Average cost per question (0.01 USD)	0.396	0.409	0.425	0.437	0.526	0.627
Average cost per effective question (0.01 USD)	0.822	0.463	**0.449**	**0.444**	0.529	0.628

sourcing to find the matching entities. In [9], we proposed a quality sensitive answering model for our system CDAS to manage the crowdsourcing tasks. In [15], Raykar et al. discussed the method of applying crowdsourcing in supervised learning without absolute golden standard. In [5], Guo et al. proposed a method to find the maximum element in a crowdsourcing database. Alonso et al. [2] developed a crowdsourcing based relevance evaluation method for information retrieval while Kazai et al. [7] proposed a crowdsourcing based book search evaluation method. Ipeirotis et al. [6] designed an approach to rank the workers by quality. Welinder et al. [18] proposed a crowdsourcing based online algorithm to find the ground truth. Crowdsourcing techniques has also been applied on other database based applications, such as graph search [14].

CrowdScreen [12] was designed to improve the accuracy and reduce the cost of binary choice problems in crowdsourcing systems by using a probabilistic method. Our work is different in that (1) we consider the three factors that affect the profit of the crowdsourcing job, namely the value of the questions, the risk of obtaining an incorrect answer and the cost of assigning questions to workers; we consider both linear and non-linear model of the accuracy-cost relationship; (2) we model the accuracy of an answer to a question as a random variable instead of a fixed value; (3) we have optimized the algorithms to build more scalable and robust algorithms.

8. CONCLUSION

Crowdsourcing has attracted a great deal of interest in solving challenging problems by integrating human intelligence with algorithms. However, the system cannot be applied with unreliable data quality. Moreover, it is even harder to decide whether a problem is suitable to be solved by crowdsourcing. In this paper, we propose an online cost sensitive decision making method with novel data quality estimation. To show the effectiveness and efficiency of our method, we conduct extensive experiments over two real datasets on the Amazon Mechanical Turk. The experimental results show that our proposed method achieves a better accuracy-cost performance than all the existing methods. Moreover, our method is both scalable and robust such that it outputs reliable answers with diversified crowdsourcing data quality.

9. ACKNOWLEDGEMENT

The work of this paper was in part supported by a Faculty Award from Microsoft Research Asia and Singapore NRF grant R-252-000-511-281.

10. REFERENCES

[1] http://www.mturk.com.

[2] O. Alonso, D. Rose, and B. Stewart. Crowdsourcing for relevance evaluation. In *SIGIR Forum*, volume 42, pages 9–15. ACM, 2008.

[3] A. Feng, M. Franklin, D. Kossmann, T. Kraska, S. Madden, S. Ramesh, A. Wang, and R. Xin. Crowddb: Query processing with the vldb crowd. *VLDB*, 4(12), 2011.

[4] M. Franklin, D. Kossmann, T. Kraska, S. Ramesh, and R. Xin. Crowddb: answering queries with crowdsourcing. In *SIGMOD*, pages 61–72, 2011.

[5] S. Guo, A. Parameswaran, and H. Garcia-Molina. So who won?: dynamic max discovery with the crowd. *SIGMOD*, pages 385–396. ACM, 2012.

[6] P. Ipeirotis, F. Provost, and J. Wang. Quality management on amazon mechanical turk. *SIGKDD workshop*, pages 64–67. ACM, 2010.

[7] G. Kazai, J. Kamps, M. Koolen, and N. Milic-Frayling. Crowdsourcing for book search evaluation: impact of hit design on comparative system ranking. *SIGIR*, 2011.

[8] A. Kittur, E. Chi, and B. Suh. Crowdsourcing user studies with mechanical turk. *SIGCHI*, pages 453–456. ACM, 2008.

[9] X. Liu, M. Lu, B. Ooi, Y. Shen, S. Wu, and M. Zhang. Cdas: a crowdsourcing data analytics system. *VLDB*, 5(10):1040–1051, 2012.

[10] A. Marcus, E. Wu, D. Karger, S. Madden, and R. Miller. Crowdsourced databases: Query processing with people. CIDR, 2011.

[11] A. Marcus, E. Wu, D. Karger, S. Madden, and R. Miller Demonstration of Qurk: a query processor for humanoperators. *SIGMOD*, pages 1315–1318. ACM, 2011.

[12] A. Parameswaran, H. Garcia-Molina, H. Park, N. Polyzotis, A. Ramesh, and J. Widom. Crowdscreen: Algorithms for filtering data with humans. *SIGMOD*, pages 361–372. ACM, 2012.

[13] A. Parameswaran and N. Polyzotis. Answering queries using humans, algorithms and databases. CIDR, 2011.

[14] A. Parameswaran, A. Sarma, H. Garcia-Molina, N. Polyzotis, and J. Widom. Human-assisted graph search: it's okay to ask questions. *VLDB*, 4(5):267–278, 2011.

[15] V. Raykar, S. Yu, L. Zhao, G. Valadez, C. Florin, L. Bogoni, and L. Moy. Learning from crowds. *JMLR*, 11:1297–1322, 2010.

[16] J. Selke, C. Lofi, and W. Balke. Pushing the boundaries of crowd-enabled databases with query-driven schema expansion. *VLDB*, 5(6):538–549, 2012.

[17] J. Wang, T. Kraska, M. Franklin, and J. Feng. Crowder: crowdsourcing entity resolution. *VLDB*, 5(11):1483–1494, 2012.

[18] P. Welinder and P. Perona. Online crowdsourcing: rating annotators and obtaining cost-effective labels. *CVPR workshop*, pages 25–32. IEEE, 2010.

[19] T. Yan, V. Kumar, and D. Ganesan. Crowdsearch: exploiting crowds for accurate real-time image search on mobile phones. *MobiSys*, pages 77–90, 2010.

Leveraging Transitive Relations for Crowdsourced Joins

Jiannan Wang[#], Guoliang Li[#], Tim Kraska[†], Michael J. Franklin[‡], Jianhua Feng[#]
[#]Department of Computer Science, Tsinghua University, [†]Brown University, [‡]AMPLab, UC Berkeley
wjn08@mails.tsinghua.edu.cn, ligl@tsinghua.edu.cn, tim_kraska@brown.edu
franklin@cs.berkeley.edu, fengjh@tsinghua.edu.cn

ABSTRACT

The development of crowdsourced query processing systems has recently attracted a significant attention in the database community. A variety of crowdsourced queries have been investigated. In this paper, we focus on the crowdsourced join query which aims to utilize humans to find all pairs of matching objects from two collections. As a human-only solution is expensive, we adopt a hybrid human-machine approach which first uses machines to generate a candidate set of matching pairs, and then asks humans to label the pairs in the candidate set as either matching or non-matching. Given the candidate pairs, existing approaches will publish all pairs for verification to a crowdsourcing platform. However, they neglect the fact that the pairs satisfy transitive relations. As an example, if o_1 matches with o_2, and o_2 matches with o_3, then we can deduce that o_1 matches with o_3 without needing to crowdsource (o_1, o_3). To this end, we study how to leverage transitive relations for crowdsourced joins. We propose a hybrid transitive-relations and crowdsourcing labeling framework which aims to crowdsource the minimum number of pairs to label all the candidate pairs. We prove the optimal labeling order and devise a parallel labeling algorithm to efficiently crowdsource the pairs following the order. We evaluate our approaches in both simulated environment and a real crowdsourcing platform. Experimental results show that our approaches with transitive relations can save much more money and time than existing methods, with a little loss in the result quality.

Categories and Subject Descriptors: H.2.4 [Database Management]: Systems—*Query processing*;

Keywords: Crowdsourcing, Join Operator, Transitive Relations, Entity Resolution

1. INTRODUCTION

The development of crowdsourced query processing systems has recently attracted a significant attention in the database community [4,14,16]. A variety of crowdsourced queries have been investigated, such as crowdsourced MAX query [6,22], crowdsourced SELECT query [19,21], and crowdsourced JOIN query [3,14,24,25]. In this paper, we focus on the crowdsourced join query for entity resolution which aims to identify all pairs of *matching* objects between two collections of objects, where humans are utilized to decide whether a pair of objects is matching, i.e. referring to the same real-world entity. The crowdsourced join query can help to solve many real problems that are hard for computers. For example, given two collections of product records from two online retailers, there may be different records that refer to the same product, e.g. "iPad 2nd Gen" and "iPad Two". In order to integrate them, we can perform a crowdsourced join query to find all pairs of matching products.

A human-only implementation of crowdsourced joins is to ask humans to label every pair of objects from the two collections as either matching or non-matching [14]. Since the human-only solution is wasteful, prior works [3,24,25] showed how to build hybrid human-machine approaches. In our paper, we adopt a hybrid approach which first uses machines to generate a candidate set of matching pairs, and only then asks humans to label the pairs in the candidate set. Given the candidate pairs, existing hybrid solutions will publish all of them to a crowdsourcing platform, e.g., Amazon Mechanical Turk (AMT). However, existing hybrid solutions neglect the fact that the pairs satisfy transitive relations. By applying transitive relations, we can deduce some pairs' labels without asking humans to label them, thus reducing the number of crowdsourced pairs. For example, if o_1 and o_2 are matching, and o_2 and o_3 are matching, we do not need to crowdsource the label for (o_1, o_3) since they can be deduced as matching based on transitive relations.

Based on this idea, in our paper, we study the problem of combining transitive relations and crowdsourcing to label the candidate pairs generated by machines. We formulate this problem, and propose a hybrid labeling framework which aims to crowdsource the minimum number of pairs for labeling all the candidate pairs. We find that the labeling order, i.e. which pairs should be labeled first, has a significant effect on the total number of crowdsourced pairs. We prove that labeling first all matching pairs, and then the other non-matching pairs leads to the optimal labeling order. However, the optimal order requires to know the real matching pairs upfront which cannot be achieved in reality. Therefore, we propose a heuristic labeling order which labels the pairs in the decreasing order of the likelihood that they are a matching pair. The likelihood could be given by some machine-learning methods [24]. We prove the order can lead to the minimum *expected* number of crowdsourced pairs. In

SIGMOD'13, June 22–27, 2013, New York, New York, USA.

order to label the pairs in this order, one simple way is to label them from the first pair to the last pair one by one. However, this method prohibits workers from doing tasks in parallel and leads to a long completion time. To address this problem, we devise a parallel labeling algorithm which can identify the pairs that must need to be crowdsourced, and ask crowd workers to label them in parallel. To summarize, we make the following contributions in the paper:

- We formulate the problem of utilizing transitive relations to label the candidate pairs in crowdsourcing, and propose a hybrid transitive-relations and crowdsourcing labeling framework to address this problem.
- We find the labeling order has a significant effect on the number of crowdsourced pairs, and respectively propose an optimal labeling order and an expected optimal labeling order.
- We devise a parallel labeling algorithm to reduce the labeling time, and propose two optimization techniques to further enhance the performance.
- We present our evaluations using both simulation and AMT. The experimental results show that our approaches with transitive relations can save much more money and time than existing methods, with a little loss in the result quality.

Organization. We formulate our problem in Section 2 and propose a hybrid labeling framework in Section 3. Section 4 proves the optimal and expected optimal labeling orders. We devise a parallel labeling algorithm and two optimization techniques in Section 5. Experimental study is presented in Section 6. We cover related work in Section 7, and present our conclusion and future work in Section 8.

2. PROBLEM FORMULATION

In this section, we first introduce crowdsourcing (Section 2.1) and then define transitive relations (Section 2.2). Finally, we formulate our problem of utilizing transitive relations to label a set of pairs in crowdsourcing (Section 2.3).

2.1 Crowdsourcing

There are many crowdsourcing platforms, such as AMT and MobileWorks, which provide APIs for easily calling large numbers of workers to complete micro-tasks (called Human Intelligent Tasks (HITs)). To label whether two objects in a pair are identical through crowdsourcing, we create an HIT for the pair, and publish it to a crowdsourcing platform. Figure 1 shows an example HIT for a pair ("iPad 2", "iPad two"). In the HIT, the workers are required to submit "YES" if they think "iPad 2" and "iPad two" are the same or submit "NO" if they think "iPad 2" and "iPad two" are different. After the workers have completed the HIT, we obtain the crowdsourced label of the pair.

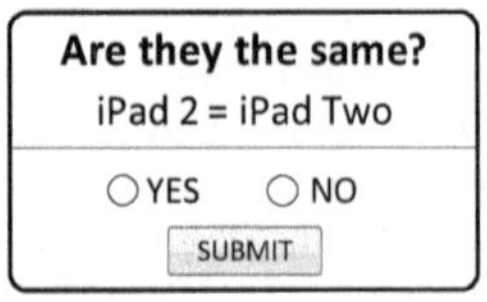

Figure 1: An example HIT for an object pair.

Assumption: Of course, workers might return wrong results and ambiguities in the question might exist. Techniques to address this problem were, for example, proposed in [2,7,13,23]. However, this problem can be treated as an orthogonal issue, as shown by [18,25], and we assume only correct answers for the remainder of the paper.

2.2 Transitive Relations

In this section, we discuss how to utilize transitive relations to deduce the label of a pair. We use the following notations. Let $p = (o, o')$ denote an object pair. The label of $p = (o, o')$ could be either "matching" or "non-matching", which respectively means that o and o' refer to the same real-world entity, and o and o' refer to different real-world entities. If o and o' are matching (non-matching), they are denoted by $o = o'$ $(o \neq o')$.

There are two types of transitive relations.

Positive Transitive Relation: Given three objects, o_1, o_2 and o_3, if $o_1 = o_2$, and $o_2 = o_3$, then we have $o_1 = o_3$. For example, consider the three objects "iPad 2nd Gen", "iPad Two" and "iPad 2". As "iPad 2nd Gen" and "iPad Two" are matching, and "iPad Two" and "iPad 2" are matching, then "iPad 2nd Gen" and "iPad 2" can be deduced as a matching pair based on positive transitive relation.

Negative Transitive Relation: Given three objects, o_1, o_2 and o_3, if $o_1 = o_2$, and $o_2 \neq o_3$, then we have $o_1 \neq o_3$. For example, consider the three objects "iPad Two", "iPad 2" and "iPad 3". As "iPad Two" and "iPad 2" are matching, and "iPad 2" and "iPad 3" are non-matching, then "iPad Two" and "iPad 3" can be deduced as a non-matching pair based on negative transitive relation.

By applying positive and negative transitive relations to n objects, we have the following lemma.

LEMMA 1. *Given a set of objects, $o_1, o_2, \cdots, o_n$, (1) if $o_i = o_{i+1}$ $(1 \leq i < n)$, then we have $o_1 = o_n$; (2) if $o_i = o_{i+1}$ $(1 \leq i < n, i \neq k)$, and $o_k \neq o_{k+1}$, then we have $o_1 \neq o_n$.*

Given a set of labeled pairs, to check if a new pair (o, o') can be deduced from them, we build a graph for the labeled pairs for ease of presentation. In the graph, each vertex represents an object, and each edge denotes a labeled pair. (For simplicity, an object and a pair of objects are respectively mentioned interchangeably with its corresponding vertex and edge in later text.) From Lemma 1, we can easily deduce the following conditions:

1. If there exists a path from o to o' which only consists of matching pairs, then (o, o') can be deduced as a matching pair;
2. If there exists a path from o to o' which contains a single non-matching pair, then (o, o') can be deduced as a non-matching pair;
3. If any path from o to o' contains more than one non-matching pair, (o, o') cannot be deduced.

EXAMPLE 1. *Consider seven labeled pairs: three matching pairs $(o_1, o_2), (o_3, o_4), (o_4, o_5)$ and four non-matching pairs $(o_1, o_6), (o_2, o_3), (o_3, o_7), (o_5, o_6)$. To check whether the unlabeled pairs $(o_3, o_5), (o_5, o_7), (o_1, o_7)$ can be deduced from them, we first build a graph as shown in Figure 2.*

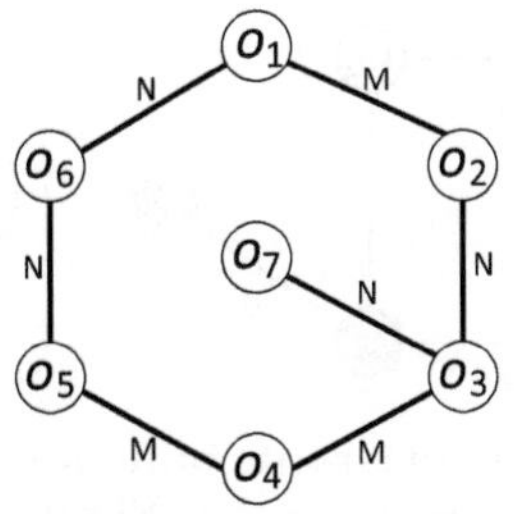

Figure 2: Graph illustrating Example 1 ("M" denotes "matching", and "N" denotes "non-matching").

For the unlabeled pair (o_3, o_5), there is a path $o_3 \rightarrow o_4 \rightarrow o_5$ from o_3 to o_5 which only consists of matching pairs, i.e. $o_3 = o_4$, $o_4 = o_5$, thus (o_3, o_5) can be deduced as a matching pair.

For the unlabeled pair (o_5, o_7), there is a path $o_5 \rightarrow o_4 \rightarrow o_3 \rightarrow o_7$ from o_5 to o_7 which contains a single non-matching pair, i.e. $o_5 = o_4$, $o_4 = o_3$, $o_3 \neq o_7$, thus (o_5, o_7) can be deduced as a non-matching pair.

For the unlabeled pair (o_1, o_7), there are two paths $o_1 \rightarrow o_2 \rightarrow o_3 \rightarrow o_7$ and $o_1 \rightarrow o_6 \rightarrow o_5 \rightarrow o_4 \rightarrow o_3 \rightarrow o_7$ from o_1 to o_7. As both of them contain more than one non-matching pair, (o_1, o_7) cannot be deduced.

2.3 Problem Description

To process crowdsourced joins, we first use machine-based techniques to generate a candidate set of matching pairs. This has already been studied by previous work [24]. The goal of our work is to study how to label the candidate pairs. Since in our setting, some pairs will be labeled by crowd workers, and others will be deduced using transitive relations. We call the former as *crowdsourced (labeled) pairs*, and the latter as *deduced (labeled) pairs*. Typically, on a crowdsourcing platform, we need to pay for crowdsourced pairs, thus there is a financial incentive to minimize the number of crowdsourced pairs. Based on this idea, we define our problem as below.

DEFINITION 1. *Given a set of pairs that need to be labeled, our goal is to crowdsource the minimum number of pairs such that for the other pairs, their labels can be deduced from the crowdsourced pairs based on transitive relations.*

EXAMPLE 2. *Figure 3 shows eight pairs, i.e., $p_1, p_2 \cdots, p_8$, generated by machine-based methods for labeling (Please ignore the Likelihood column for now). We build a graph for these pairs, where the vertices with the same grey level represent the matching objects. One possible way to label them is to crowdsource seven pairs $p_1, p_2, p_3, p_5, p_6, p_7, p_8$. For the other pair p_4, as shown in the graph, it can be deduced from p_1 and p_2 based on transitive relations. A better way to label them only needs to crowdsource six pairs $p_1, p_2, p_3, p_5, p_7, p_8$. For the other pairs, as shown in the graph, p_4 can be deduced from p_1 and p_2, and p_6 can be deduced from p_5 and p_8. It is not possible to further reduce the amount of crowdsourced pairs. Thus, six is the optimal amount.*

3. LABELING FRAMEWORK

We propose a hybrid transitive-relations and crowdsourcing labeling framework in this section. Our framework takes as input a set of unlabeled pairs generated by machine-based techniques, and identifies these pairs' labels either through crowdsourcing or by using transitive relations. As shown in Figure 4, our framework mainly consists of two components, `Sorting` and `Labeling`. Their details will be described in Sections 3.1 and 3.2, respectively.

ID	Object
o_1	iPhone 2nd Gen
o_2	iPhone Two
o_3	iPhone 2
o_4	iPad Two
o_5	iPad 2
o_6	iPad 3rd Gen

(a) A set of objects

ID	Object Pairs	Likelihood
p_1	(o_2, o_3)	0.85
p_2	(o_1, o_2)	0.75
p_3	(o_1, o_6)	0.72
p_4	(o_1, o_3)	0.65
p_5	(o_4, o_5)	0.55
p_6	(o_4, o_6)	0.48
p_7	(o_2, o_4)	0.45
p_8	(o_5, o_6)	0.42

(b) A set of object pairs

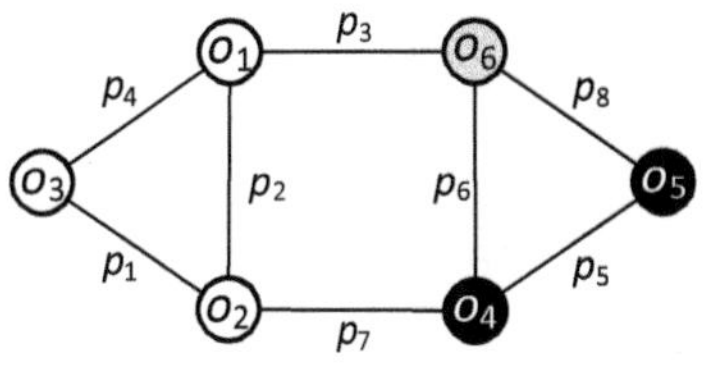

(c) A graph built for the set of object pairs

Figure 3: A running example.

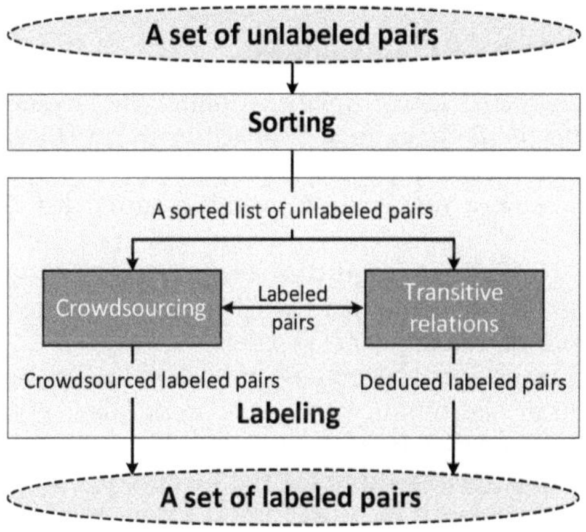

Figure 4: Hybrid transitive-relations and crowdsourcing labeling framework.

3.1 Sorting Component

Given a set of unlabeled pairs, we have an interesting finding that the labeling order of the pairs will affect the number of crowdsourced pairs. A labeling order can be taken as a sorted list of pairs, denoted by $\omega = \langle p_1, p_2, \cdots, p_n \rangle$, where p_i $(2 \leq i \leq n)$ will be labeled after $p_1, p_2, \cdots, p_{i-1}$. For example, suppose we need to label three pairs, (o_1, o_2), (o_2, o_3), (o_1, o_3), where $o_1 = o_2$ and $o_2 \neq o_3$ and $o_1 \neq o_3$. If the labeling order is $\omega = \langle (o_1, o_2), (o_2, o_3), (o_1, o_3) \rangle$, after labeling the first two pairs through crowdsourcing, we obtain $o_1 = o_2$ and $o_2 \neq o_3$. For the third pair, we can deduce $o_1 \neq o_3$ from $o_1 = o_2$ and $o_2 \neq o_3$ based on transitive relations, thus ω requires crowdsourcing *two* pairs. However, if we use a dif-

```
Algorithm 1: DEDUCELABEL(p, L)
   Input: p = (o, o') : an object pair; L: a set of labeled pairs
   Output: ℓ: the deduced label
1  begin
2      Build a CLUSTERGRAPH for L;
3      Let cluster(o) and cluster(o') denote the cluster of
       objects o and o' respectively;
4      if cluster(o) = cluster(o') then
5          ℓ = "matching";
6      else
7          if there is an edge between cluster(o) and cluster(o')
           then
8              ℓ = "non-matching";
9          else
10             ℓ = "undeduced";
11     return ℓ;
12 end
```

Figure 5: DeduceLabel algorithm.

ferent labeling order $\omega' = \langle (o_2, o_3), (o_1, o_3), (o_1, o_2) \rangle$, after labeling the first two pairs through crowdsourcing, we obtain $o_2 \neq o_3$ and $o_1 \neq o_3$. We are unable to deduce $o_1 = o_2$ from $o_2 \neq o_3$ and $o_1 \neq o_3$ based on transitive relations, thus ω' requires crowdsourcing *three* pairs which is more than that required by ω.

Based on this observation, in our framework, the sorting component attempts to identify the optimal labeling order to minimize the number of crowdsourced pairs. Thus, it takes as input a set of unlabeled pairs and outputs a sorted list of unlabeled pairs. The details of identifying the optimal labeling order will be presented in Section 4.

3.2 Labeling Component

Given a sorted list of unlabeled pairs, the labeling component labels the pairs in the sorted order. In this section, we present a very simple, one-pair-at-a-time, labeling algorithm to achieve this goal. Consider a sorted list of pairs $\omega = \langle p_1, p_2, \cdots, p_n \rangle$. The algorithm will start with labeling from the first pair, and then label each pair one by one. When labeling the i-th pair p_i, if its label cannot be deduced from the already labeled pairs (i.e., $\{p_1, p_2, \cdots, p_{i-1}\}$) based on transitive relations, we publish p_i to a crowdsourcing platform and obtain its crowdsourced label; otherwise, we deduce its label from $p_1, p_2, \cdots, p_{i-1}$, and output the deduced label. After obtaining the label of p_i, we begin to process the next pair p_{i+1}, and use the same method to get its label. The algorithm stops until all the pairs are labeled.

Next, we discuss how to check whether an unlabeled pair $p = (o, o')$ can be deduced from a set of labeled pairs based on transitive relations. As mentioned in Section 2.2, we can build a graph for the labeled pairs, and check the graph whether there is a path from o to o' which contains no more than one non-matching pair. If there exists such a path, p can be deduced from the labeled pairs; otherwise, p cannot be deduced. One naive solution to do this checking is enumerating every path from o to o', and counting the number of non-matching pairs in each path. However, the number of enumerated paths may increase exponentially with the number of vertices in the graph, thus we propose an efficient graph-clustering-based method to solve this problem.

When enumerating each path, we find that only non-matching pairs in the path can affect the checking result. In other words, the matching pairs have no effect on the

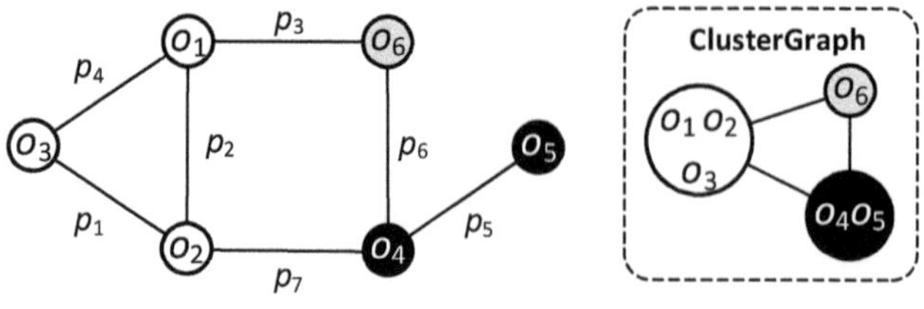

Figure 6: A ClusterGraph built for the first seven labeled pairs $\{p_1, p_2, \cdots, p_7\}$ in Figure 3.

checking result. This observation inspires us to merge the matching objects into the same cluster, and then, for each pair of non-matching objects, we add an edge between their corresponding clusters. We call the new graph a CLUSTERGRAPH. By using the CLUSTERGRAPH, we can efficiently check whether an unlabeled pair $p = (o, o')$ can be deduced from the already labeled pairs. Figure 5 shows the pseudo-code of the algorithm. Given a set of labeled pairs $\mathcal{L}$, we first build a CLUSTERGRAPH for $\mathcal{L}$ using Union-Find algorithm [20] (Line 2). Then for the unlabeled pair $p = (o, o')$,

(1) If o and o' are in the same cluster, then there is a path from o to o' which only consists of matching pairs. Thus, p can be deduced as a matching pair (Lines 4-5);

(2) If o and o' are in two different clusters,

(2.1) If there is an edge between the two clusters, there exists a path from o to o' with a single non-matching pair. Thus, p can be deduced as a non-matching pair (Lines 7-8);

(2.2) If there is no edge between the two clusters, there does not exist a path from o to o' with no more than one non-matching pair. Thus, p cannot be deduced (Lines 9-10).

EXAMPLE 3. *Suppose we have already labeled seven pairs $\{p_1, p_2, \cdots, p_7\}$ in Figure 6. To check whether $p_8 = (o_5, o_6)$ can be deduced from them, we first build a* CLUSTERGRAPH *as follows. Since o_1, o_2, o_3 are matching, we merge them into one cluster. As o_4 and o_5 are matching, we merge them into another cluster. Since o_6 does not match with any other object, we take itself as one cluster. There are three non-matching pairs, i.e., $p_3 = (o_1, o_6)$, $p_6 = (o_4, o_6)$ and $p_7 = (o_2, o_4)$. We respectively add three non-matching edges between* cluster(o_1) *and* cluster(o_6), cluster(o_4) *and* cluster(o_6), cluster(o_2) *and* cluster(o_4).

Consider the unlabeled pair $p_8 = (o_5, o_6)$. In the CLUSTERGRAPH, *since o_5 and o_6 are in different clusters, and* cluster(o_5) *and* cluster(o_6) *have an edge, then there must exist a path from o_5 to o_6 which contains a single non-matching pair (e.g., $o_5 \to o_4 \to o_6$), thus $p_8 = (o_5, o_6)$ can be deduced as a non-matching pair from $\{p_1, p_2, \cdots, p_7\}$.*

The labeling algorithm needs to enumerate each pair one by one and it can only publish a single pair to the crowdsourcing platform. Hence, every time there is only one available HIT in the crowdsourcing platform. This constraint makes the workers unable to do HIT simultaneously and results in long latency. Notice that batching strategies [14,24], which place multiple pairs into a single HIT, have been proved useful in reducing the money cost. However, the simple approach is unable to support the batching techniques since only one pair is allowed to publish every time, and thus results in more money cost. To overcome these drawbacks, we propose a parallel labeling algorithm in Section 5, which can crowdsource multiple pairs every time without increasing the total number of crowdsourced pairs.

4. SORTING

As observed in Section 3.1, different labeling orders result in different numbers of crowdsourced pairs. In this section, we explore the optimal labeling order to minimize the number of crowdsourced pairs. We begin with the formulation of this problem and discuss how to find the optimal labeling order in Section 4.1. However, the optimal order cannot be achieved in reality. Thus, in Section 4.2, we propose a heuristic labeling order, called expected optimal labeling order, which can be proved to minimize the expected number of crowdsourced pairs.

4.1 Optimal Labeling Order

Given a labeling order $\omega = \langle p_1, p_2, \cdots, p_n \rangle$, let $\mathcal{C}(\omega)$ denote the number of crowdsourced pairs required by ω. Our goal is to identify the optimal labeling order which results in the minimum number of crowdsourced pairs. The formal definition of this problem is as follows.

DEFINITION 2 (OPTIMAL LABELING ORDER). *Given a set of object pairs, the problem of identifying the optimal labeling order is to get a sorted list of pairs, ω_{op}, such that the number of crowdsourced pairs is minimal using the order, i.e. $\mathcal{C}(\omega_{op}) \leq \mathcal{C}(\omega)$ holds for any other order ω.*

For example, assume three object pairs, $p_1 = (o_1, o_2)$, $p_2 = (o_2, o_3)$, $p_3 = (o_1, o_3)$, where p_1 is a matching pair, and p_2, p_3 are two non-matching pairs. We can label them in six different labeling orders, $\omega_1 = \langle p_1, p_2, p_3 \rangle$, $\omega_2 = \langle p_1, p_3, p_2 \rangle$, $\omega_3 = \langle p_2, p_3, p_1 \rangle$, $\omega_4 = \langle p_2, p_1, p_3 \rangle$, $\omega_5 = \langle p_3, p_1, p_2 \rangle$, and $\omega_6 = \langle p_3, p_2, p_1 \rangle$. The numbers of crowdsourced pairs of the six orders are respectively $\mathcal{C}(\omega_1) = 2$, $\mathcal{C}(\omega_2) = 2$, $\mathcal{C}(\omega_3) = 3$, $\mathcal{C}(\omega_4) = 2$, $\mathcal{C}(\omega_5) = 2$, and $\mathcal{C}(\omega_6) = 3$. As ω_1, ω_2, ω_4, ω_5 lead to the minimum number of crowdsourced pairs, any one of them can be seen as the optimal labeling order.

Notice that any labeling order can be changed to another labeling order by swapping adjacent pairs. We first study how swapping two adjacent pairs affects the number of crowdsourced pairs. We have an observation that it is always *better* to first label a matching pair and then a non-matching pair, i.e., it will lead to fewer or equal number of crowdsourced pairs. Recall $\omega_3 = \langle p_2, p_3, p_1 \rangle$ and $\omega_4 = \langle p_2, p_1, p_3 \rangle$ in the above example. ω_3 labels a non-matching pair p_3 before a matching pair p_1 while ω_4 swaps the positions of p_1 and p_3, and labels a matching pair p_1 before a non-matching pair p_3. As $\mathcal{C}(\omega_3) = 3$ and $\mathcal{C}(\omega_4) = 2$, the example shows that ω_4, which first labels a matching pair, needs to crowdsource fewer pairs than ω_3. Lemma 2 formulates this idea.

LEMMA 2. *Consider two labeling orders,*

$$\omega = \langle p_1, \cdots, p_{i-1}, \boldsymbol{p_i}, \boldsymbol{p_{i+1}}, p_{i+2}, \cdots p_n \rangle,$$

$$\omega' = \langle p_1, \cdots, p_{i-1}, \boldsymbol{p_{i+1}}, \boldsymbol{p_i}, p_{i+2}, \cdots p_n \rangle,$$

where ω' is obtained by swapping p_i and p_{i+1} in ω. If p_i is a non-matching pair, and p_{i+1} is a matching pair, then we have $\mathcal{C}(\omega') \leq \mathcal{C}(\omega)$.

PROOF. For a pair p_j, if $j \notin \{i, i+1\}$, it is easy to see that $\{p_1, p_2, \cdots, p_{j-1}\}$ in ω is the same as that in ω'. Therefore, if p_j is a crowdsourced pair in ω, it must be a crowdsourced pair in ω', and vice versa. Hence, we only need to check whether p_i, p_{i+1} are crowdsourced pairs in ω and ω'.

There are four possible cases for p_i, p_{i+1} in ω: deduced and crowdsourced pairs, crowdsourced and crowdsourced pairs, deduced and deduced pairs, or crowdsourced and deduced pairs. We prove that in any case, $\{p_i, p_{i+1}\}$ in ω' would contain fewer or equal number of crowdsourced pairs than $\{p_i, p_{i+1}\}$ in ω, thus $\mathcal{C}(\omega') \leq \mathcal{C}(\omega)$ holds.

Case 1: *p_i is deduced and p_{i+1} is crowdsourced.* As p_i in ω can be deduced from $\{p_1, p_2, \cdots, p_{i-1}\}$, in the graph built for them, there is a path from one object of p_i to the other with no more than one non-matching pairs. Such path still exists in the graph built for more pairs $\{p_1, p_2, \cdots, p_{i-1}, p_{i+1}\}$, thus p_i in ω' is also a deduced pair. Similarly, as p_{i+1} in ω cannot be deduced from $\{p_1, p_2, \cdots, p_i\}$, it cannot be deduced from fewer pairs $\{p_1, p_2, \cdots, p_{i-1}\}$, thus p_{i+1} in ω' is also a crowdsourced pair. Therefore, $\mathcal{C}(\omega') \leq \mathcal{C}(\omega)$ holds in Case 1.

Case 2: *p_i is crowdsourced and p_{i+1} is crowdsourced.* In the worst case, both p_i and p_{i+1} in ω' still need to be crowdsourced, so $\mathcal{C}(\omega') \leq \mathcal{C}(\omega)$ holds in Case 2.

Case 3: *p_i is deduced and p_{i+1} is deduced.* As p_i in ω can be deduced from $\{p_1, p_2, \cdots, p_{i-1}\}$, it can also be deduced from more pairs $\{p_1, p_2, \cdots, p_{i-1}, p_{i+1}\}$, thus p_i in ω' is also a deduced pair. As p_{i+1} in ω can be deduced from $\{p_1, p_2, \cdots, p_i\}$, it is easy to derive that p_{i+1} can also be deduced from the *crowdsourced* pairs in $\{p_1, p_2, \cdots, p_i\}$. Since p_i is not a *crowdsourced* pair based on the given condition, p_{i+1} can be deduced from the *crowdsourced* pairs in $\{p_1, p_2, \cdots, p_{i-1}\}$, thus p_{i+1} in ω' is a deduced pair. As p_i and p_{i+1} in ω' are both deduced pairs, $\mathcal{C}(\omega') \leq \mathcal{C}(\omega)$ holds in Case 3.

Case 4: *p_i is crowdsourced and p_{i+1} is deduced.* As the matching pair p_{i+1} in ω can be deduced from $\{p_1, p_2, \cdots, p_i\}$, in the graph built for $\{p_1, p_2, \cdots, p_i\}$, there exists a path from one object of p_{i+1} to the other which only consists of matching pairs. As p_i is a non-matching pair, after removing p_i from the graph, the path still exists in the graph built for $\{p_1, p_2, \cdots, p_{i-1}\}$, thus p_{i+1} can be deduced from $\{p_1, p_2, \cdots, p_{i-1}\}$. Hence, p_{i+1} in ω' is also a deduced pair. In the worst case, p_i in ω' still need to be crowdsourced, so $\mathcal{C}(\omega') \leq \mathcal{C}(\omega)$ holds in Case 4. □

For a given labeling order, by using the above method to swap adjacent object pairs, we can put all the matching pairs prior to the non-matching pairs. As it is better to label a matching pair first and then a non-matching pair, the new order will require fewer or equal number of crowdsourced pairs than the original labeling order.

Next we prove that swapping adjacent matching pairs or non-matching pairs will not change the number of crowdsourced pairs.

LEMMA 3. *Consider two labeling orders,*

$$\omega = \langle p_1, \cdots, p_{i-1}, \boldsymbol{p_i}, \boldsymbol{p_{i+1}}, p_{i+2}, \cdots p_n \rangle,$$

$$\omega' = \langle p_1, \cdots, p_{i-1}, \boldsymbol{p_{i+1}}, \boldsymbol{p_i}, p_{i+2}, \cdots p_n \rangle,$$

where ω' is obtained by swapping p_i and p_{i+1} in ω. If p_i and p_{i+1} are both matching pairs or both non-matching pairs, then we have $\mathcal{C}(\omega') = \mathcal{C}(\omega)$.

PROOF. Since swapping p_i and p_{i+1} will not affect the other pairs except p_i and p_{i+1} (see the proof in Lemma 2), we only need to prove that $\{p_i, p_{i+1}\}$ in ω' requires the same number of crowdsourced pairs as $\{p_i, p_{i+1}\}$ in ω, thus $\mathcal{C}(\omega') = \mathcal{C}(\omega)$ holds. We still consider the four cases.

Case 1: *p_i is deduced and p_{i+1} is crowdsourced.* As in the proof of Case 1 in Lemma 2, we have p_i in ω' is also a deduced pair, and p_{i+1} in ω' is also a crowdsourced pair. Therefore, $\mathcal{C}(\omega') = \mathcal{C}(\omega)$ holds in Case 1.

Case 2: *p_i is crowdsourced and p_{i+1} is crowdsourced.* As p_{i+1} in ω cannot be deduced from $\{p_1, p_2, \cdots, p_i\}$, it cannot be deduced from fewer pairs $\{p_1, p_2, \cdots, p_{i-1}\}$, thus p_{i+1} in ω' is also a crowdsourced pair.

Next, we prove by contradiction p_i in ω' is also a crowdsourced pair. Assume p_i in ω' is not a crowdsourced pair. Then p_i can be deduced from $\{p_1, p_2, \cdots, p_{i-1}, p_{i+1}\}$. In the graph built for $\{p_1, p_2, \cdots, p_{i-1}, p_{i+1}\}$, there exists a path from one object of p_i to the other which contains no more than one non-matching pair. And since p_i in ω is crowdsourced, p_i cannot be deduced from $\{p_1, p_2, \cdots, p_{i-1}\}$, thus p_{i+1} must be in the path. By removing p_{i+1} from the path and adding p_i to the path, we obtain a new path from one object of p_{i+1} to the other. Since p_{i+1} is removed and p_i is added, the path must be in the graph built for $\{p_1, p_2, \cdots, p_i\}$. As p_i, p_{i+1} are either both matching pairs or both non-matching pairs, the path contains no more than one non-matching pair. Therefore, p_{i+1} can be deduced from $\{p_1, p_2, \cdots, p_i\}$ which contradicts p_{i+1} in ω is a crowdsourced pair. Hence, the assumption does not hold, and p_i in ω' is a crowdsourced pair. Since p_i, p_{i+1} in ω' are both crowdsourced pairs, $\mathcal{C}(\omega') = \mathcal{C}(\omega)$ holds in Case 2.

Case 3: *p_i is deduced and p_{i+1} is deduced.* As in the proof of Case 3 in Lemma 2, we have p_i in ω' is also a deduced pair, and p_{i+1} in ω' is also a deduced pair. Therefore, $\mathcal{C}(\omega') = \mathcal{C}(\omega)$ holds in Case 3.

Case 4: *p_i is crowdsourced and p_{i+1} is deduced.* As p_{i+1} in ω can be deduced from $\{p_1, p_2, \cdots, p_i\}$, in the graph built for $\{p_1, p_2, \cdots, p_i\}$, there exist some paths from one object of p_{i+1} to the other which contains no more than one non-matching pair. There are three cases about these paths:

(a) If none of these paths contains p_i, that is, p_i and p_{i+1} will not affect each other, then p_i in ω' is also a crowdsourced pair and p_{i+1} in ω' is also a deduced pair. Therefore, $\mathcal{C}(\omega') = \mathcal{C}(\omega)$ holds in Case 4(a).

(b) If some of these paths contain p_i but others do not, then we can infer that in the graph built for $\{p_1, p_2, \cdots, p_{i-1}\}$, there exists a path from one object of p_i to the other with no more than one non-matching pair, thus p_i can be deduced from $\{p_1, p_2, \cdots, p_{i-1}\}$ which contradicts p_i in ω is a crowdsourced pair. Hence, Case 4(b) is impossible.

(c) If all of the paths contain p_i, after removing p_i from these paths, in the graph built for $\{p_1, p_2, \cdots, p_{i-1}\}$, there will be no path from one object of p_{i+1} to the other which contains no more than one non-matching pair, thus p_{i+1} cannot be deduced from $\{p_1, p_2, \cdots, p_{i-1}\}$. That is, p_{i+1} in ω' is a crowdsourced pair. Next we prove that p_i in ω' is a deduced pair. Consider one of these paths that contain p_i. After removing p_i from the path and adding p_{i+1} to the path, we obtain a new path from one object of p_i to the other. Since p_i is removed and p_{i+1} is added, the path must be in the graph built for $\{p_1, p_2, \cdots, p_{i-1}, p_{i+1}\}$. As p_i, p_{i+1} are either both matching pairs or both non-matching pairs, the path contains no more than one non-matching pair. Therefore, p_i can be deduced from $\{p_1, p_2, \cdots, p_{i-1}, p_{i+1}\}$, thus it is a deduced pair in ω'. As p_i in ω' is a deduced pair, and p_{i+1} in ω' is a crowdsourced pair, $\mathcal{C}(\omega') = \mathcal{C}(\omega)$ holds in Case 4(c). □

For two different labeling orders, if they both first label all the matching pairs and then label the other non-matching pairs, we can change one labeling order to the other by swapping adjacent matching pairs and adjacent non-matching pairs. Based on Lemma 3, the two labeling orders require the same number of crowdsourced pairs. Therefore, any labeling order, which puts all the matching pairs to the front of the other non-matching pairs, is the optimal.

THEOREM 1. *Given a set of object pairs, the optimal labeling order is to first label all the matching pairs, and then label the other non-matching pairs.*

For example, consider the pairs in Figure 3. $\omega_{op} = \langle p_1, p_2, p_4, p_5, p_3, p_6, p_7, p_8 \rangle$ is the optimal labeling order since all the matching pairs, i.e., p_1, p_2, p_4, p_5, are labeled before the other non-matching pairs, i.e., p_3, p_6, p_7, p_8.

Now we have proved that the optimal labeling order is to first label all the matching pairs, and then label the other non-matching pairs. However, when identifying the labeling order, we have no idea about whether a pair is matching or non-matching, therefore, the optimal labeling order cannot be achieved in reality. To address this problem, we propose an expected optimal labeling order in the next section.

4.2 Expected Optimal Labeling Order

In this section, we aim to identify a labeling order that requires as few crowdsourced pairs as possible. Recall the optimal labeling order which first labels the matching pairs and then labels the non-matching pairs. Although we do not know the real matching pairs upfront, machine-based methods can be applied to compute for each pair the likelihood that they are matching. For example, the likelihood can be the similarity computed by a given similarity function [24]. In the previous section, we have proved that it is better to label a matching pair before a non-matching pair (Lemma 2). Based on this idea, we pose a conjecture that it is better to label the object pairs in the decreasing order of the likelihood that they are matching.

To formulate the conjecture, consider a labeling order $\omega = \langle p_1, p_2, \cdots, p_n \rangle$. Suppose each pair in ω is assigned with a probability that they are matching. Then the number of crowdsourced pairs required by ω becomes a random variable. Its expected value is computed as the sum of the probability that p_i is a crowdsourced pair ($1 \le i \le n$), i.e.,

$$\mathrm{E}\big[\mathcal{C}(\omega)\big] = \sum_{i=1}^{n} \mathbb{P}(p_i = \mathsf{crowdsourced}).$$

To compute $\mathbb{P}(p_i = \mathsf{crowdsourced})$, we enumerate the possible labels of $\{p_1, p_2, \cdots, p_{i-1}\}$, and for each possibility, since the labels of $\{p_1, p_2, \cdots, p_{i-1}\}$ are known, we can derive whether p_i is a crowdsourced pair or not. Hence, $\mathbb{P}(p_i = \mathsf{crowdsourced})$ is the sum of the probability of each possibility that p_i is a crowdsourced pair.

We aim to identify a labeling order that can minimize the expected number of crowdsourced pairs since the order is expected to require the number of crowdsourced pairs. We call such an order an *expected optimal labeling order*. The following definition formulates this problem.

DEFINITION 3 (EXPECTED OPTIMAL LABELING ORDER). *Given a set of object pairs, and each object pair is assigned with a probability that they are matching, the problem of* *identifying the expected optimal labeling order ω_{eop} is to compute a sorted list of pairs such that the expected number of crowdsourced pairs is minimal using the order, i.e. $\mathrm{E}[\mathcal{C}(\omega_{eop})] \le \mathrm{E}[\mathcal{C}(\omega)]$ holds for any other order ω.*

EXAMPLE 4. *Consider three pairs, $p_1 = (o_1, o_2)$, $p_2 = (o_2, o_3)$ and $p_3 = (o_1, o_3)$. Suppose the probabilities that p_1, p_2 and p_3 are matching pairs are respectively 0.9, 0.5 and 0.1. There are six different labeling orders, $\omega_1 = \langle p_1, p_2, p_3\rangle$, $\omega_2 = \langle p_1, p_3, p_2\rangle$, $\omega_3 = \langle p_2, p_3, p_1\rangle$, $\omega_4 = \langle p_2, p_1, p_3\rangle$, $\omega_5 = \langle p_3, p_1, p_2\rangle$, and $\omega_6 = \langle p_3, p_2, p_1\rangle$. We first compute the excepted number of crowdsourced pairs for $\omega_1 = \langle p_1, p_2, p_3\rangle$. For the first pair p_1, as there is no labeled pairs, it must be crowdsourced, thus $\mathbb{P}(p_1 = \mathsf{crowdsourced}) = 1$. For the second pair p_2, as $p_2 = (o_2, o_3)$ cannot be deduced from $p_1 = (o_1, o_2)$, it must need crowdsourcing, thus $\mathbb{P}(p_2 = \mathsf{crowdsourced}) = 1$. For the third pair, $p_3 = (o_1, o_3)$ can be deduced from $p_1 = (o_1, o_2)$ and $p_2 = (o_2, o_3)$ only when either p_1 or p_2 is a matching pair. Hence, the probability that p_3 is a crowdsourced pair is equal to the probability that both p_1 and p_2 are non-matching pairs, i.e. $(1-0.9)\cdot(1-0.5) = 0.05$. By adding up the probabilities that p_1, p_2, p_3 are crowdsourced pairs, we have $\mathrm{E}[\mathcal{C}(\omega_1)] = 1 + 1 + 0.05 = 2.05$. Similarly, we can compute $\mathrm{E}[\mathcal{C}(\omega_2)] = 2.09$, $\mathrm{E}[\mathcal{C}(\omega_3)] = 2.45$, $\mathrm{E}[\mathcal{C}(\omega_4)] = 2.05$, $\mathrm{E}[\mathcal{C}(\omega_5)] = 2.09$, and $\mathrm{E}[\mathcal{C}(\omega_6)] = 2.45$. As ω_1 and ω_4 require the minimum expected number of crowdsourced pairs, either one of them can be taken as the optimal expected labeling order.*

Similar to Lemmas 2 and 3, we can prove that, for two adjacent pairs p_i and p_{i+1}, (1) if the probability that p_i is a matching pair is less than that for p_{i+1}, swapping them will lead to a less or equal expected number of crowdsourced pairs; (2) if the probability that p_i is a matching pair is the same as that for p_{i+1}, swapping them will not affect the expected number of crowdsourced pairs. Therefore, the expected optimal labeling order is to label the pairs in the decreasing order of the probability that they are a matching pair (as formalized in Theorem 2). Due to space constrains, we omit the proof.

THEOREM 2. *Given a set of object pairs, the expected optimal labeling order is to label the pairs in the decreasing order of the probability that they are a matching pair.*

Consider the unlabeled pairs $p_1, p_2, \cdots, p_8$ in Figure 3. To identify their expected optimal labeling order, we first use a machine-based method to compute a likelihood for each pair that it is a matching pair. The higher the likelihood, the larger the probability. Therefore, based on Theorem 2, the expected optimal labeling order is to check the pairs in the decreasing order of the likelihood, i.e., $\omega_{eop} = \langle p_1, p_2, p_3, p_4, p_5, p_6, p_7, p_8\rangle$.

In this section, we have proved the correctness of our conjecture from a theoretical perspective. In Section 6.2, we also evaluate the expected optimal labeling order on real-world datasets, and experimental results show the expected optimal labeling order has good performance in practice.

5. PARALLEL LABELING

After identifying the expected optimal labeling order, our labeling framework will label the unlabeled pairs in this order. In Section 3.2, we present a simple approach to achieve this goal. However, the approach only allows to publish a single pair to the crowdsourcing platform, which is unable to label the pairs simultaneously and results in long latency. To alleviate this problem, we propose a parallel labeling algorithm in Section 5.1, which can crowdsource multiple pairs every time without increasing the total number of required crowdsourced pairs. To further improve the parallelism, we present two optimization techniques in Section 5.2.

```
Algorithm 2: ParallelLabeling(ω)
   Input: ω = ⟨p1, p2, ··· , pn⟩ : a sorted list of unlabeled pairs
   Output: L = {(pi, ℓ) | 1 ≤ i ≤ n}: a set of labeled pairs
 1 begin
 2     L = {};
 3     while there is an unlabeled pair in ω do
 4         P = ParallelCrowdsourcedPairs(ω);
 5         L ∪= CrowdsourceLabels(P);
 6         for each unlabeled pair p ∈ ω do
 7             if DeducedLabel(p, L) then
 8                 Add (p, ℓ) into L;
 9     return L;
10 end
```

Figure 7: Parallel labeling algorithm.

5.1 Parallel Labeling Algorithm

We first use an example to show our basic idea. Consider the labeling order $\omega = \langle (o_1, o_2), (o_2, o_3), (o_3, o_4)\rangle$. The simple labeling approach will first crowdsource the first pair (o_1, o_2), and cannot crowdsource the second pair until the first pair is labeled. However, for the second pair (o_2, o_3), we observe that no matter which label the first pair gets, we must need to crowdsource it since the second pair (o_2, o_3) cannot be deduced from the first pair (o_1, o_2). For the third pair (o_3, o_4), we have a similar observation that no matter which labels the first two pairs get, we must crowdsource it since the third pair (o_3, o_4) cannot be deduced from the first two pairs (o_1, o_2) and (o_2, o_3). Therefore, all the pairs in ω can be crowdsourced together instead of individually. Based on this idea, we propose a parallel labeling algorithm as shown in Figure 7.

Algorithm Overview: Our parallel labeling algorithm employs an iterative strategy. In each iteration, the algorithm first identifies a set of pairs that can be crowdsourced in parallel (Line 4). Then the algorithm publishes the pairs simultaneously to the crowdsourcing platform, and obtains their crowdsourced labels (Line 5). After that, the algorithm utilizes the already labeled pairs to deduce subsequent unlabeled pairs (Lines 6-8). The algorithm repeats the iterative process until all the pairs are labeled.

A big challenge in the algorithm is to identify a set of pairs that can be crowdsourced in parallel. We know that a pair $p_i = (o, o')$ needs to be crowdsourced if and only if p_i cannot be deduced from $\{p_1, p_2, \cdots, p_{i-1}\}$.

In the case that $\{p_1, p_2, \cdots, p_{i-1}\}$ are labeled, we need to check the graph built for $\{p_1, p_2, \cdots, p_{i-1}\}$. If every path from o to o' contains more than one non-matching pair, then p_i cannot be deduced from $\{p_1, p_2, \cdots, p_{i-1}\}$. However, some pairs in $\{p_1, p_2, \cdots, p_{i-1}\}$ may have not been labeled. In this case, we have no idea about the exact number of non-matching pairs in some paths. In order to see if every path must contain more than one non-matching pair, we compute the minimum number of non-matching pairs in

```
Algorithm 3: PARALLELCROWDSOURCEDPAIRS(ω, L)
   Input: ω = ⟨p_1, p_2, ··· , p_n⟩ : a sorted list of unlabeled pairs
          L: a set of labeled pairs
   Output: P: a set of pairs that can be crowdsourced in parallel
1  begin
2      P = {};
3      Initialize an empty CLUSTERGRAPH;
4      for i = 1 to n do
5          if (p_i, ℓ) ∈ L then
6              Insert (p_i, ℓ) into CLUSTERGRAPH;
7          else
8              p_i = (o, o');
9              if cluster(o) ≠ cluster(o') and there is no edge
               between cluster(o) and cluster(o') then
10                 Add p_i into P;
11             Insert (p_i, "matching") into CLUSTERGRAPH;
12     return P;
13 end
```

Figure 8: ParallelCrowdsourcedPairs algorithm.

each path by supposing all the unlabeled pairs are matching pairs. If the minimum number of non-matching pairs in each path is larger than one, then whatever the unlabeled pairs in $\{p_1, p_2, \cdots, p_{i-1}\}$ are labeled, the number of non-matching pairs in each path must be larger than one, thus p_i cannot be deduced from $\{p_1, p_2, \cdots, p_{i-1}\}$, and needs to be crowdsourced.

Based on this idea, given a sorted list of object pairs, $\omega = \langle p_1, p_2, \cdots, p_n \rangle$, where some pairs have not been labeled, to identify which pairs can be crowdsourced in parallel, we first suppose all the unlabeled pairs are matching pairs, and then for each pair p_i $(1 \le i \le n)$, we output p_i as a crowdsourced pair if it cannot be deduced from $\{p_1, p_2, \cdots, p_{i-1}\}$. As discussed in Section 3.2, CLUSTERGRAPH can be utilized to efficiently decide whether p_i cannot be deduced from $\{p_1, p_2, \cdots, p_{i-1}\}$. Note that to make a decision for each p_i $(1 \le i \le n)$, we do not need to build the CLUSTERGRAPH from scratch since the CLUSTERGRAPH can be easily obtained by inserting p_{i-1} into the CLUSTERGRAPH built for $\{p_1, p_2, \cdots, p_{i-2}\}$.

Figure 8 shows the algorithm for identifying the pairs that can be crowdsourced in parallel in each iteration. The algorithm first initializes an empty CLUSTERGRAPH, and then checks each pair p_i $(1 \le i \le n)$. If p_i has already been labeled, it does not need to be crowdsourced any more, thus we update the CLUSTERGRAPH by inserting p_i, and go to the next pair p_{i+1} (Lines 5-6); otherwise, we check whether p_i can be deduced from $\{p_1, p_2, \cdots, p_{i-1}\}$. In the CLUSTERGRAPH, if $\mathsf{cluster}(o) \neq \mathsf{cluster}(o')$ and there is no edge between $\mathsf{cluster}(o)$ and $\mathsf{cluster}(o')$, p_i cannot be deduced, and thus needs to be crowdsourced (Lines 9-10). In this case, since p_i is unlabeled, we suppose it is a matching pair, and insert p_i into the CLUSTERGRAPH, and go to the next pair p_{i+1} (Line 11). After checking all the pairs, we return the obtained crowdsourced pairs.

EXAMPLE 5. *Consider the running example in Figure 3. Given the labeling order $\langle p_1, p_2, \cdots, p_8 \rangle$, Figure 9 shows how to use the parallel labeling algorithm to label the pairs (The solid edges represent labeled pairs and the dotted edges represent unlabeled pairs.).*

In the first iteration, since all the given pairs are unlabeled, we first suppose $\{p_1, p_2, \cdots, p_8\}$ are matching pairs, and then identify five pairs (i.e., p_1, p_2, p_3, p_5, p_6) that can be crowdsourced in parallel (the bold solid edges in Figure 9(a)). For example, p_5 is identified since it cannot be deduced from $\{p_1, p_2, p_3, p_4\}$ while p_7 is not identified since it can be deduced from $\{p_1, p_2, p_3, p_4, p_5, p_6\}$ (Note that they are supposed as matching pairs). We are able to publish $\{p_1$, p_2, p_3, p_5, $p_6\}$ simultaneously to the crowdsourcing platform. After obtaining their labels, based on transitive relations, we can deduce p_4 from p_1 and p_2, and deduce p_8 from p_5 and p_6 (the bold solid edges in Figure 9(b)). Since there still exists an unlabeled pair (i.e. p_7), we repeat the iteration process.

In the second iteration, since only p_7 is unlabeled, we first suppose p_7 is a matching pair, and then identify one pair (i.e., p_7) for crowdsourcing (the bold-solid edges in Figure 9(c)). We publish p_7 to the crowdsourcing platform. After it is labeled, we find all the pairs have been labeled, thus the algorithm is terminated, and the labeled pairs are returned.

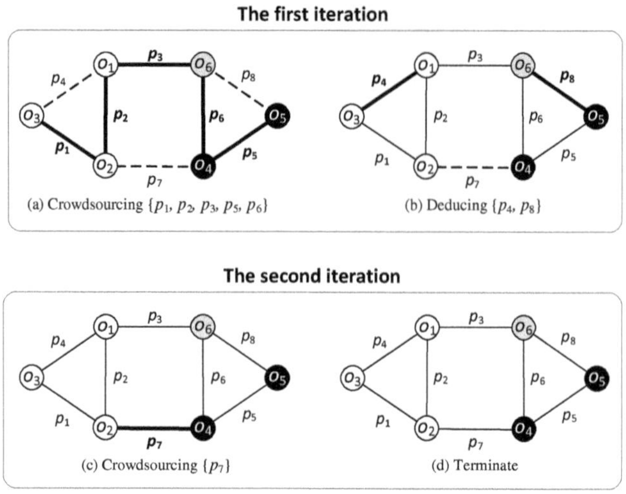

Figure 9: An illustration of parallel labeling algorithm.

5.2 Optimization Techniques

In this section, we propose two optimization techniques, instant decision and non-matching first, to further enhance our parallel labeling algorithm.

Instant Decision: Recall our parallel labeling algorithm. The algorithm will first publish some pairs to the crowdsourcing platform, and after all the published pairs have been labeled, decide which pairs can be crowdsourced next. Notice that we do not need to wait until all the published pairs have been labeled to decide the next-round crowdsourced pairs. Instead when some of the published pairs are labeled, we can utilize them instantly to crowdsource the remaining pairs. For example, in Figure 9, we first publish $\{p_1$, p_2, p_3, p_5, $p_6\}$ together to the crowdsourcing platform. If p_3 and p_6 are labeled, we can deduce that $p_7 = (o_2, o_4)$ must be a crowdsourced pair, and can be published instantly instead of waiting for the other pairs. This is because, in the graph built for $\{p_1, p_2, p_3, p_4, p_5, p_6\}$, there are two paths from o_2 to o_4, i.e., $o_2 \to o_1 \to o_6 \to o_4$ and $o_2 \to o_3 \to o_1 \to o_6 \to o_4$. Both paths contain at least two non-matching pairs (i.e., p_3 and p_6), thus p_7 cannot be deduced from $\{p_1$, p_2, p_3, p_4, p_5, $p_6\}$ based on transitive relations.

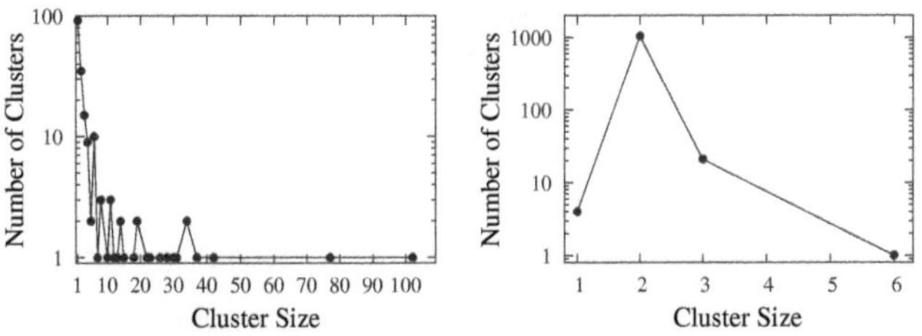

(a) Paper (b) Product

Figure 10: Cluster-size distribution.

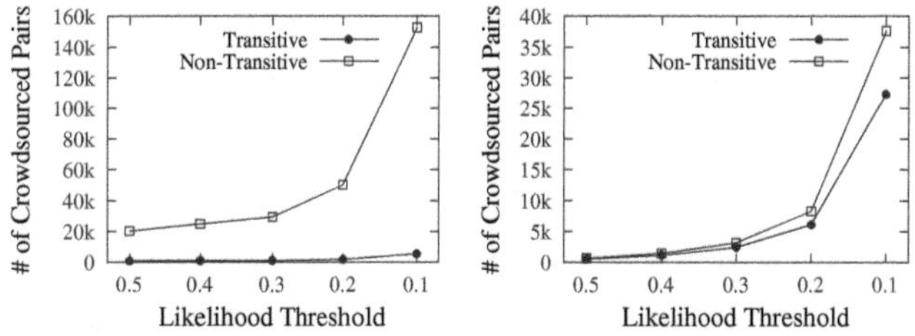

(a) Paper (b) Product

Figure 11: Effectiveness of transitive relations.

Based on this idea, we propose an optimization technique, called *instant decision*, which will make an instant decision on which pairs can be published next whenever a single published pair (instead of all the published pairs) is labeled. Achieving this goal requires a minor change to the algorithm in Figure 8 by excluding the already published pairs from $\mathcal{P}$ in Line 12. By applying the optimization technique to our parallel labeling algorithm, we are able to increase the number of the available pairs in the crowdsourcing platform to enhance the effect of parallelism.

Non-matching First: If we utilize the instant-decision optimization technique, when a published pair is labeled, we need to decide which pairs can be crowdsourced next. We find if the labeled pair is a matching pair, that will not lead to publishing any other pair. This is because when deciding which pairs can be crowdsourced in Figure 8, we have assumed that all the unlabeled pairs are matching pairs. Hence, knowing an unlabeled pair is a matching pair will have no effect on the algorithm. Based on this idea, we propose an optimization technique, called *non-matching first*. Consider the published pairs in the crowdsourcing platform. If we could ask the crowd workers to label the potentially non-matching pairs first, i.e., label the published pairs in the increasing order of the probability that they are a matching pair, that would increase the number of the available pairs in the crowdsourcing platform so as to enhance the effect of parallelism. It is worth noting that this order is for the published pairs in the parallel labeling algorithm, which is different from the order for labeling all pairs in Section 4.

6. EXPERIMENT

In this section, we evaluate our method. The goals of the experiments are to (1) examine the effectiveness of transitive relations in reducing the number of crowdsourced pairs, (2) compare the number of crowdsourced pairs required by different labeling orders, (3) validate the advantage of our parallel labeling algorithm over the non-parallel labeling algorithm, and (4) illustrate the performance of our method in a real crowdsourcing platform.

We used two public real-world datasets to evaluate our approaches which were widely adopted by prior works. (a) Paper (a.k.a Cora)[1] is a dataset of research publications. Each object in the dataset is a record with five attributes, *Author*, *Title*, *Venue*, *Date* and *Pages*. There are 997 distinct records, leading to $\frac{997*996}{2} = 496,506$ pairs. (b) Product (a.k.a Abt-Buy)[2] is a product dataset containing information on 1081 products from *abt.com* and 1092 products from *buy.com*. Each object is a product record with two attributes, *name* and *price*. The dataset contains a total of $1081 * 1092 = 1,180,452$ pairs.

[1] http://www.cs.umass.edu/~mccallum/data/cora-refs.tar.gz

[2] http://dbs.uni-leipzig.de/file/Abt-Buy.zip

We see that compared to PRODUCT PAPER has far larger clusters and should thus benefit more from using transitive relations.

We chose Paper and Product datasets in the experiment due to their different characteristics in the number of matching objects. To visualize the difference, we clustered the true matching objects in each dataset, and plotted the cluster-size distribution in Figure 10. We see that compared to Product, Paper has far larger clusters and should thus benefit more from using transitive relations. For example, there is a cluster consisting of 102 matching objects on the Paper dataset. For such a large cluster, using transitive relations can reduce the number of crowdsourced pairs from $\frac{102*101}{2} = 5151$ to 101. However, for smaller clusters, e.g. cluster size = 3, using transitive relations can only reduce the number of crowdsourced pairs from $\frac{3*2}{2} = 3$ to 2.

It was found that most of the pairs in the datasets look very dissimilar, and can easily be weeded out by algorithmic methods [24]. We followed this method to compute for each pair a likelihood that they are matching, and only asked the crowd workers to label the most likely matching pairs, i.e. those pairs whose likelihood is above a specified threshold.

6.1 Effectiveness of Transitive Relations

In this section, we evaluate the effectiveness of transitive relations on the Paper and Product datasets. If the labeling method did not apply transitive relations, denoted by Non-Transitive, all of the pairs need to be crowdsourced. On the contrary, if the labeling method utilized transitive relations, denoted by Transitive, many pairs can be deduced based on transitive relations, and only the remaining pairs need to be crowdsourced. We varied the likelihood threshold from 0.5 to 0.1 on both the Paper and Product datasets, and respectively used Non-Transitive and Transitive to label the pairs whose likelihood is above the threshold. Figure 11 compares the number of crowdsourced pairs required by Non-Transitive and Transitive (with the optimal labeling order). On the Paper dataset, we can see Transitive reduced the number of crowdsourced pairs by 95%. For example, when the likelihood threshold was 0.3, Transitive only needed to crowdsource 1065 pairs while Non-Transitive had to crowdsource 29,281 pairs. On the Product dataset, even if there are not so many matching objects in the dataset (Figure 10), Transitive can still save about 20% crowdsourced pairs compared to Non-Transitive. For example, when the threshold is 0.2, 6134 pairs needed to be crowdsourced by Transitive while Non-Transitive required to crowdsource 8315 pairs.

6.2 Evaluating Different Labeling Orders

Having shown the benefits of transitive relations in reducing the crowdsourced pairs, we now turn to examining how different labeling orders affect the effectiveness of transitive relations. We compare the number of crowdsourced

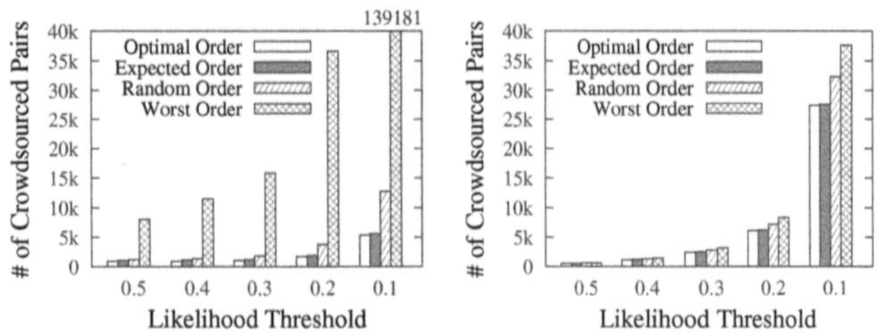

(a) Paper (b) Product

Figure 12: The number of crowdsourced pairs required by different labeling orders.

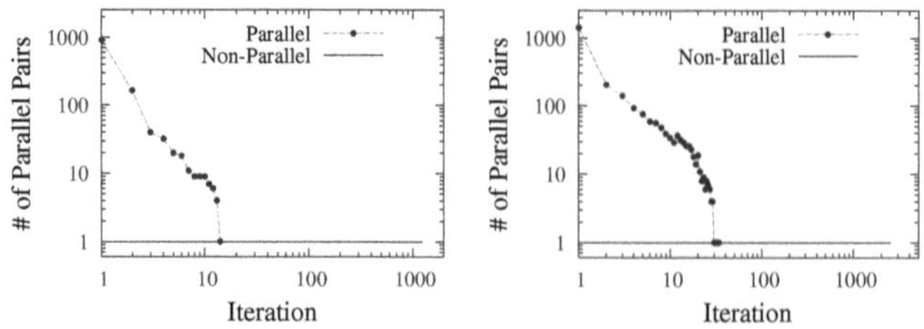

(a) Paper (b) Product

Figure 13: Parallel v.s. non-parallel labeling algorithm (likelihood threshold = 0.3).

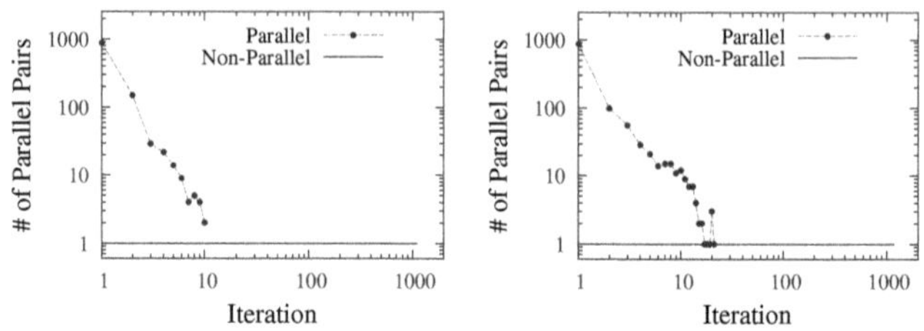

(a) Paper (b) Product

Figure 14: Parallel v.s. non-parallel labeling algorithm (likelihood threshold = 0.4).

pairs required by different labeling orders in Figure 12. Optimal Order, Expect Order, Random Order, and Worst Order respectively denote the labeling orders which label first all matching pairs then the other non-matching pairs, label the pairs in the decreasing order of likelihood, label the pairs randomly, and label first all non-matching pairs then the other matching pairs. By comparing Worst Order with Optimal Order, we can see the selection of labeling orders has a significant effect on the number of required crowdsourced pairs. For example, on the Paper dataset, if labeling the pairs whose likelihood is above 0.1 in the worst order, we needed to crowdsource 139,181 pairs, which was about 26 times more than the crowdsourced pairs required by the optimal order. By comparing Expect Order and Random Order with Optimal Order, we can see that the expected optimal order needed to crowdsource a few more pairs than the optimal order but the random order involved much more crowdsourced pairs, which validated that the expected optimal order has a very good performance in practice. Unless otherwise stated, we will use the expected optimal order to label the pairs in later experiments.

6.3 Evaluating Parallel Labeling Algorithm

In this section, we evaluate our parallel labeling algorithm as well as the corresponding optimization techniques.

We first compare the parallel labeling algorithm (referred to as Parallel) with the non-parallel labeling algorithm (referred to as Non-Parallel). We respectively used Parallel and Non-Parallel to label the pairs whose likelihood was above 0.3. Figure 13 illustrates their number of parallel pairs in each iteration. Compared to Non-Parallel, Parallel significantly reduced the total number of iterations. For example, on the Paper dataset, there were a total of 1237 crowdsourced pairs. For this, Non-Parallel required 1237 iterations, i.e., in each iteration only a single pair could be crowdsourced. But Parallel reduced the number of iterations to 14, where in each iteration, 908, 163, 40, 32, 20, 18, 11, 9, 9, 9, 7, 6, 4, and 1 pair(s) respectively have been crowdsourced in parallel. We also evaluated Parallel for other likelihood thresholds, and found that a better performance can be achieved for higher likelihood thresholds. For example, Figure 14 shows the result for a threshold of 0.4. Comparing to the result in Figure 13 (threshold=0.3), Parallel involved fewer iterations on both datasets. This is because for a larger threshold, there were fewer number of pairs whose likelihood was above the threshold. Thus the graph built for the pairs became more sparse, and allowed to crowdsource more pairs per iteration.

Next we evaluate optimization techniques for parallel labeling algorithm. In Figure 15, Parallel, Parallel(ID), and Parallel(ID+NF) respectively denote the parallel algorithm without any optimization technique, the parallel algorithm with the instant-decision optimization technique, and the parallel algorithm with both instant-decision and non-matching-first optimization techniques. (Note that the parallel algorithm with only the non-matching-first optimization technique is the same as Parallel.) At the beginning, all of the three algorithms published a set of pairs to the crowdsourcing platform, and then waited for the crowd workers to label them. Parallel and Parallel(ID) were supposed to label the pairs randomly while Parallel(ID+NF) was supposed to first label the most unlikely matching pairs. When a pair was labeled, Parallel would not publish any new pairs until all the pairs in the crowdsourcing platform had been labeled, whereas both Parallel(ID) and Parallel(ID+NF) would instantly decide which pair to publish next. Figure 15 illustrates that the number of available pairs in the crowdsourcing platform changed with the increasing number of pairs labeled by the crowd. Unlike Parallel, Parallel(ID) and Parallel(ID+NF) ensured that at any time, there were sufficient pairs available in the crowdsourcing platform, which kept the crowd doing our work continuously. For example, on the Product dataset, after 1420 pairs were crowdsourced, Parallel only had one available pair in the crowdsourcing platform while Parallel(ID) and Parallel(ID+NF) respectively had 219 pairs and 281 pairs in the crowdsourcing platform. In addition, we can also see from the figure that Parallel(ID+NF) lead to more available pairs than Parallel(ID), which validated the effectiveness of the non-matching-first optimization technique.

6.4 Evaluating our approaches in a real crowdsourcing platform

Finally we evaluate our approaches with AMT. We paid workers 2 cents for completing each HIT. In order to reduce the cost, we adopted a batching strategy [14,24] by placing 20 pairs into one HIT. To control the result quality, each HIT was replicated into three assignments. That is, each pair would be labeled by three different workers. The final decision for each pair was made by majority vote.

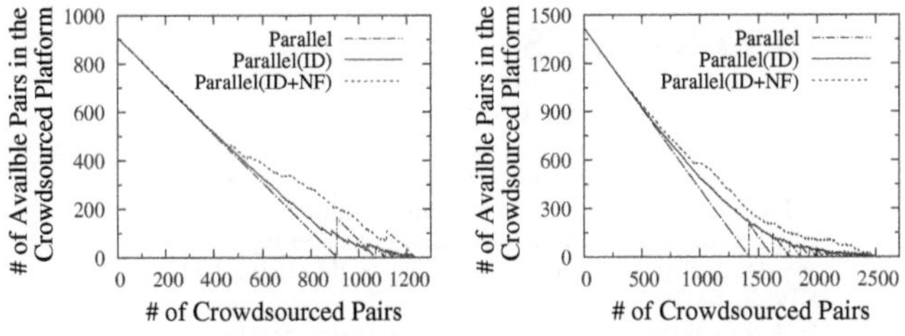

(a) Paper (b) Product

Figure 15: Optimization techniques for the parallel labeling algorithm (likelihood threshold = 0.3).

We first compare Parallel(ID) with Non-Parallel in AMT using a threshold of 0.3. (We were unable to evaluate Parallel(ID+NF) in AMT since the current AMT can only randomly assign HITs to workers.) As we only focused on the difference between their completion time, we simulated that the crowd in AMT always gave us correct labels. In this way, the two algorithms would crowdsource the same number of pairs, thus requiring the same amount of money. As discussed in Section 3.2, the batching strategy is not applicable to Non-Parallel. To make a fair comparison, Non-Parallel used the same HITs as Parallel(ID), but published a single one per iteration. Table 1 compares their completion time. We can see Parallel(ID) significantly improved the labeling performance over Non-Parallel. For example, on the Paper dataset, if we used Non-Parallel to publish 68 HITs in a non-parallel way, we had to wait for 78 hours. However, if we published them in parallel, the waiting time reduced by almost one order of magnitude.

Table 1: Comparing Parallel(ID) with Non-Parallel in AMT (likelihood threshold = 0.3).

Dataset	# of HITs	Non-Parallel	Parallel(ID)
Paper	68	78 hours	8 hours
Product	144	97 hours	14 hours

In order to evaluate the effectiveness of transitive relations with AMT, we respectively used Transitive and Non-Transitive to label the pairs whose likelihood was above 0.3, where Transitive adopted Parallel(ID) to label the pairs in the expected optimal labeling order, and Non-Transitive simply published all the pairs simultaneously to the crowdsourcing platform. We compared Transitive with Non-Transitive in terms of completion time, number of HITs, and result quality. Table 2 shows the respective results on the Paper and Product datasets. We employed *Precision*, *Recall*, and *F-measure* to evaluate the result quality. Let tp denote the number of correctly labeled matching pairs, fp the number of wrongly labeled matching pairs, and fn the number of falsely labeled non-matching pairs. Precision and recall are respectively defined as $\frac{\text{tp}}{\text{tp+fp}}$ and $\frac{\text{tp}}{\text{tp+fn}}$. F-measure is defined as the harmonic mean of precision and recall, i.e. $\frac{2\cdot\text{precison}\cdot\text{recall}}{\text{precison+recall}}$.

We used qualification tests to improve the result quality. A qualification test consisted of three specified pairs. Only the workers who correctly labeled the pairs were allowed to do our HITs. In Table 2(a), to label 29,281 pairs on Paper dataset, Non-Transitive published $\frac{29281}{20} = 1465$ HITs, and waited for 755 hours until all the HITs were completed, whereas Transitive can reduce the HITs by 96.5% and the time by 95.8% with about 5% loss in the result quality. This experimental result indicates that for the dataset with a lot of matching objects, Transitive can save a large amount of cost and time with a little loss in result quality. The reason for the loss of quality is that some pairs' labels were falsely deduced from incorrectly labeled pairs based on transitive relations.

Table 2: Comparing Transitive with Non-Transitive in AMT (likelihood threshold = 0.3)

(a) Paper

	# of HITs	Time	Quality		
			Precision	Recall	F-measure
Non-Transitive	1465	755 hours	68.82%	95.03%	79.83%
Transitive	52	32 hours	62.96%	90.47%	74.25%

(b) Product

	# of HITs	Time	Quality		
			Precision	Recall	F-measure
Non-Transitive	158	22 hours	95.69%	68.94%	80.14%
Transitive	144	30 hours	94.70%	68.82%	79.71%

Next we turn to the experimental result on Product dataset. In Table 2(b), 3154 pairs needed to be labeled, and Non-Transitive published $\frac{3154}{20} = 158$ HITs, and waited for 22 hours until all the HITs were completed. Since there are not so many matching objects in the dataset, Transitive can only save about 10% of the HITs. Due to the iterative process of publishing HITs, Transitive lead to a little longer completion time. But in terms of quality, Transitive was almost the same as Non-Transitive. This experimental result indicates that for the dataset with not so many matching objects, transitive relations can help to save some money with almost no loss in result quality but may lead to longer completion time.

7. RELATED WORK

Recently, several projects on crowd-enabled query processing system [4,14,16] and hybrid crowd-machine data integration system [9] were proposed in the database community. To implement such systems, there are many studies in processing a variety of crowdsourced queries [3,6,14,17,18, 21,22,24,25]. As one of the most important queries, crowdsourced joins have been widely investigated in [3,14,24,25]. Marcus et al. [14] proposed a human-only technique with some batching and feature filtering optimizations for crowdsourced joins. Wang et al. [24] developed a hybrid human-machine workflow which first utilized machine-based techniques to weed out a large number of obvious non-matching pairs, and only asked the crowd workers to label the remaining pairs. Demartini et al. [3] also employed a hybrid human-machine technique, and in addition, they developed a probabilistic framework for deriving the final join result. Whang et al. [25] proposed a budget-based method for crowdsourced joins which assumed there was not enough money to label all the pairs, and explored how to make a good use of limited money to label a certain number of pairs. When using the crowd workers to label a set of pairs, the prior works neglected the fact that transitive relations hold among the pairs. Therefore, our work complements them by leveraging transitive relations to reduce the number of crowdsourced pairs. In a recent technical report, Gruenheid et al. [5] also explored how to leverage transitive relations for crowdsourced joins, but they mainly studied how to decide whether two objects refer to the same entity when crowd workers give inconsistent answers, which has a different focus than our work.

Some real applications such as entity resolution [1,15,26] also seek to benefit from transitive relations. Essentially, these works first label pairs using some sophisticated algorithms, and then utilize transitive relations to obtain the final result. They mainly focused on how to resolve the conflicts introduced by transitive relations rather than reduce the precious human effort. In a pay-as-you-go data integration system, Jeffrey et al. [8] studied the problem of minimizing the human work to achieve the best data-integration quality. But their approach aimed to identify the most uncertain pairs for verification, without considering the benefits of transitive relations.

There are also some studies on parallel crowdsourcing. Little et al. [11] compared iterative crowdsourcing model with parallel crowdsourcing model in a variety of problem domains, and provided some advice about the selection of models. TurKit [12] is a toolkit based on the crash-and-rerun programming model which makes it easier to write parallel crowdsourcing algorithms. CrowdForge [10] is a map-reduce style framework which partitions a complex task into subtasks that can be done in parallel. These tools can help us to easily implement the parallel labeling algorithm in a real crowdsourcing platform.

8. CONCLUSION AND FUTURE WORK

We studied the problem of leveraging transitive relations for crowdsourced joins (e.g., for entity resolution), to minimize the number of crowdsourced pair verifications. Our approach consists of two components: (1) The sorting component takes the pre-matched pairs from a machine-based method and determines the best order for verification. We found that the labeling order has a significant effect on the number of crowdsourced pairs. We proved that the optimal labeling order, which minimizes the number of crowdsourced pairs, has to first label all the matching pairs, and then label the other non-matching pairs. As this is impossible to achieve (we do not know the real matching pairs upfront), we proved that the expected optimal labeling order is to label the pairs in the decreasing order of the probability that they are a matching pair. (2) For the labeling component, we found that a simple labeling method lead to longer latency and increased cost. We devised a novel parallel labeling algorithm to overcome these drawbacks. We have evaluated our approaches, both using simulation and with AMT, and showed, that transitive relations can lead to significant cost savings with no or little loss in result quality.

Various future directions exist for this work including to detect non-transitive relations, automate money/time/quality trade-offs for joins, explore other kinds of relations (e.g. one-to-one relationship) or extend to non-equality joins (i.e., general theta-joins). In this work, we showed that transitive relations can lead to significant cost savings in crowdsourced joins for entity resolution.

Acknowledgements. This work was partly supported by the National Natural Science Foundation of China under Grant No. 61003004 and 61272090, National Grand Fundamental Research 973 Program of China under Grant No. 2011CB302206, and a project of Tsinghua University under Grant No. 20111081073, and the "NExT Research Center" funded by MDA, Singapore, under Grant No. WBS:R-252-300-001-490, and NSF CISE Expeditions award CCF-1139158 and DARPA XData Award FA8750-12-2-0331, and gifts from Amazon Web Services, Google, SAP, Blue Goji, Cisco, Clearstory Data, Cloudera, Ericsson, Facebook, General Electric, Hortonworks, Huawei, Intel, Microsoft, NetApp, Oracle, Quanta, Samsung, Splunk, VMware and Yahoo!.

9. REFERENCES

[1] N. Bansal, A. Blum, and S. Chawla. Correlation clustering. *Machine Learning*, 56(1-3):89–113, 2004.

[2] O. Dekel and O. Shamir. Vox populi: Collecting high-quality labels from a crowd. In *COLT*, 2009.

[3] G. Demartini, D. E. Difallah, and P. Cudré-Mauroux. ZenCrowd: leveraging probabilistic reasoning and crowdsourcing techniques for large-scale entity linking. In *WWW*, pages 469–478, 2012.

[4] M. J. Franklin, D. Kossmann, T. Kraska, S. Ramesh, and R. Xin. CrowdDB: answering queries with crowdsourcing. In *SIGMOD*, pages 61–72, 2011.

[5] A. Gruenheid, D. Kossmann, S. Ramesh, and F. Widmer. Crowdsourcing entity resolution: When is A=B? Technical report, ETH Zürich.

[6] S. Guo, A. G. Parameswaran, and H. Garcia-Molina. So who won?: dynamic max discovery with the crowd. In *SIGMOD Conference*, pages 385–396, 2012.

[7] P. G. Ipeirotis, F. Provost, and J. Wang. Quality management on amazon mechanical turk. In *Proceedings of the ACM SIGKDD Workshop on Human Computation*, pages 64–67, 2010.

[8] S. R. Jeffery, M. J. Franklin, and A. Y. Halevy. Pay-as-you-go user feedback for dataspace systems. In *SIGMOD Conference*, pages 847–860, 2008.

[9] S. R. Jeffery, L. Sun, M. DeLand, N. Pendar, R. Barber, and A. Galdi. Arnold: Declarative crowd-machine data integration. CIDR, 2013.

[10] A. Kittur, B. Smus, S. Khamkar, and R. E. Kraut. CrowdForge: crowdsourcing complex work. In *UIST*, pages 43–52, 2011.

[11] G. Little, L. B. Chilton, M. Goldman, and R. C. Miller. Exploring iterative and parallel human computation processes. In *Proceedings of the ACM SIGKDD workshop on human computation*, pages 68–76. ACM, 2010.

[12] G. Little, L. B. Chilton, M. Goldman, and R. C. Miller. TurKit: human computation algorithms on mechanical turk. In *UIST*, pages 57–66, 2010.

[13] X. Liu, M. Lu, B. C. Ooi, Y. Shen, S. Wu, and M. Zhang. CDAS: A crowdsourcing data analytics system. *PVLDB*, 5(10):1040–1051, 2012.

[14] A. Marcus, E. Wu, D. R. Karger, S. Madden, and R. C. Miller. Human-powered sorts and joins. *PVLDB*, 5(1):13–24, 2011.

[15] A. E. Monge and C. Elkan. An efficient domain-independent algorithm for detecting approximately duplicate database records. In *DMKD*, pages 23–29, 1997.

[16] A. Parameswaran, H. Park, H. Garcia-Molina, N. Polyzotis, and J. Widom. Deco: Declarative crowdsourcing. Technical report, Stanford University. http://ilpubs.stanford.edu:8090/1015/.

[17] A. G. Parameswaran, H. Garcia-Molina, H. Park, N. Polyzotis, A. Ramesh, and J. Widom. CrowdScreen: algorithms for filtering data with humans. In *SIGMOD Conference*, pages 361–372, 2012.

[18] A. G. Parameswaran, A. D. Sarma, H. Garcia-Molina, N. Polyzotis, and J. Widom. Human-assisted graph search: it's okay to ask questions. *PVLDB*, 4(5):267–278, 2011.

[19] A. D. Sarma, A. Parameswaran, H. Garcia-Molina, and A. Halevy. Finding with the crowd. Technical report, Stanford University.

[20] R. E. Tarjan. Efficiency of a good but not linear set union algorithm. *J. ACM*, 22(2):215–225, 1975.

[21] B. Trushkowsky, T. Kraska, M. J. Franklin, and P. Sarkar. Crowdsourced enumeration queries. In *ICDE*, pages 673–684, 2013.

[22] P. Venetis, H. Garcia-Molina, K. Huang, and N. Polyzotis. Max algorithms in crowdsourcing environments. In *WWW*, pages 989–998, 2012.

[23] P. Wais, S. Lingamneni, D. Cook, J. Fennell, B. Goldenberg, D. Lubarov, D. Marin, and H. Simons. Towards building a high-quality workforce with mechanical turk. *Proceedings of Computational Social Science and the Wisdom of Crowds (NIPS)*, pages 1–5, 2010.

[24] J. Wang, T. Kraska, M. J. Franklin, and J. Feng. CrowdER: Crowdsourcing entity resolution. *PVLDB*, 5(11):1483–1494, 2012.

[25] S. E. Whang, P. Lofgren, and H. Garcia-Molina. Question selection for crowd entity resolution. Technical report, Stanford University.

[26] S. E. Whang, D. Menestrina, G. Koutrika, M. Theobald, and H. Garcia-Molina. Entity resolution with iterative blocking. In *SIGMOD Conference*, pages 219–232, 2009.

Crowd Mining

Yael Amsterdamer
Tel Aviv University
Tel Aviv, Israel
yaelamst@post.tau.ac.il

Yael Grossman
Tel Aviv University
Tel Aviv, Israel
yaelgros@post.tau.ac.il

Tova Milo
Tel Aviv University
Tel Aviv, Israel
milo@cs.tau.ac.il

Pierre Senellart
Télécom ParisTech & The University of Hong Kong
Paris, France & Hong Kong
pierre.senellart@telecom-paristech.fr

ABSTRACT

Harnessing a crowd of Web users for data collection has recently become a wide-spread phenomenon. A key challenge is that the human knowledge forms an open world and it is thus difficult to know what kind of information we should be looking for. Classic databases have addressed this problem by data mining techniques that identify interesting data patterns. These techniques, however, are not suitable for the crowd. This is mainly due to properties of the human memory, such as the tendency to remember simple trends and summaries rather than exact details.

Following these observations, we develop here for the first time the foundations of crowd mining. We first define the formal settings. Based on these, we design a framework of generic components, used for choosing the best questions to ask the crowd and mining significant patterns from the answers. We suggest general implementations for these components, and test the resulting algorithm's performance on benchmarks that we designed for this purpose. Our algorithm consistently outperforms alternative baseline algorithms.

Categories and Subject Descriptors

H.2.8 [**Database Applications**]: Data mining

Keywords

crowd mining, crowdsourcing, association rule learning

1. INTRODUCTION

Problem. Social scientists, micro-economists, journalists, marketers, public health specialists, and politicians alike routinely analyze people's behaviors to find new trends, understand and document behaviors, and possibly put forward adequate policies in response. Discovering statistically significant patterns in the crowd's habits is however a challenging task, and traditional tools (interviews, polls, surveys) to collect data from individuals about their daily life are costly to implement, and moreover, it is often hard to know which are the best questions to ask. This is in part due to the fact that human knowledge forms an *open world* [13]; it is often the case that one wants to use the crowd to find out what is *interesting and significant* about a particular topic, without full knowledge about what the topic consists of.

In traditional settings where one has access to a database of all relevant information, the problem of finding significant, as-yet-unknown patterns has been addressed via *data mining*. In particular, *association rules* [1], which capture when one set of data items indicates the presence (or values) of another set, were shown to be useful in identifying significant patterns. The typical application is shopping baskets: a store can, by analyzing purchase records, mine rules about which items are bought together. In this traditional setting, the significant rules are assumed to be initially unknown, and data mining algorithms dynamically construct database queries to identify them, relying on indicators such as *support* and *confidence*.

However, association rule mining is based on the assumption that *transactions* (e.g., sets of items bought together in the shopping basket application) are available. When dealing with the crowd's behavior, it is often impossible to have access to these transactions, i.e., to ask individuals for extensive descriptions of their past activities.

As a motivating example, consider a health researcher, Alice, who is interested in discovering and testing new drugs by analyzing the practices of folk medicine (also known as traditional medicine, i.e., medicinal practice that is neither documented in writing nor tested out under a scientific protocol). Alice is interested in discovering association rules such as "Garlic and oregano leaves can be used to treat a sore throat" or "Chamomile tea drinkers tend to experience sleepiness" together with their support and confidence. Alice can interview folk healers, but it is unrealistic for her to ask them for an exhaustive list of all cases they treated over the years. A database of transactions, each corresponding to the symptoms and treatments of a particular illness case, simply cannot be constructed. As another example, consider a social scientist analyzing life habits of people, in terms of activities (watching TV, jogging, reading, etc.) correlated with their contexts (time of the day, weather, presence of friends, etc.). Here too it is impossible to obtain a comprehensive database of transactions, representing all the "events" (mornings, evenings...) with their context and all the activities performed in them, for a large community. Or

SIGMOD'13, June 22–27, 2013, New York, New York, USA.

consider a public health researcher studying a population's eating habits to understand how best to fight an obesity epidemics (in which case transactions correspond to types of food eaten or cooked together); an ergonomics consultant who surveys work habits in a company to detect positive or negative patterns in work organization that should be encouraged or corrected (transactions correspond to events in the day-to-day work life, e.g., a particular meeting with the communication means used for it). In all these cases, we deal with an open world (no pre-existing list of relevant activities, foodstuff, or work environment factors) and it is impossible to obtain an exhaustive database of all transactions.

Crowd-based data sourcing is a new and powerful data procurement paradigm that engages Web users to collectively contribute data [12]. Information is often gathered by posing *questions* to users, which they may answer for some small payment, for social or moral reasons, or in the context of a game [17, 25]. Even though people cannot recall all of their transactions, social studies show that they can often provide simple summaries, and even more complicated ones when asked targeted questions [5]. Summaries can be viewed as *rules that apply to individuals*, or personal rules. As an example, a folk healer may be able to tell Alice, when asked which symptoms he usually encounters (an *open question*), that he deals with nausea cases almost every week. He can also answer perhaps more complex but targeted questions (named *closed questions*), such as "When a patient has both headaches and fever, how often do you use a willow tree bark infusion to treat him?" The answer might be something like "A few times a year, that is, perhaps for a half of all such patients." Mining the crowd thus differs from traditional data mining in two fundamental ways: on the one hand, one cannot have access to the transactions in extension, but on the other hand, summaries allow obtaining, with one request, information that encapsulates many transactions.

The problem we address is thus: *How to exploit the unique capabilities of the crowd to mine data from the crowd?*

Note that even when transactions are partly available, we can use the crowd to gather complementary information: a store might have easy access to its consumers' shopping baskets and use classic mining approaches on them, but it does not know what its consumers buy outside of its stores and cannot grasp the subjective consumer experience; for this, stores and marketing agencies use consumer panels and surveys. However, these may be time-consuming, expensive and inaccurate, and we would like to use crowdsourcing for a more efficient alternative.

If people are aware of the rules that apply to them, why mine these rules? First and most importantly, our goal is to identify trends in the entire population. Each person is only familiar with her own habits, which form partial information about the general trends. Mining many users allows us to piece together the complete picture. Second, it is hard for people to list even their personal rules – only prominent rules may be recalled in this manner [5]. Our mining process asks users concrete, well-defined questions, which help digging deeper into their memory.

Contributions. To tackle the crowd mining problem, we present in this article the following contributions:

1. We define a model for the average behavior of the crowd. We model the types of questions a user may be asked (open and closed), and the data we retrieve as a result. This relies on per-user notions if pattern significance. The formal model allows defining the ultimate goal of crowd mining: finding the association rules that are *overall* significant. This highlights the required changes in the data mining paradigm to make it suitable for the crowd. (Section 2)
2. We present an effective crowd-mining framework. The generic components of this framework can be used for iteratively choosing the best crowd questions, processing the answers, and upon demand, deciding which rules are the significant ones. Some framework components are "black boxes" which allow plugging in different implementations for different applications. (Section 3)
3. Since computing the exact overall significance of a rule would require posing questions to all the users, it is infeasible for large crowds. As an important component of our framework, we perform a probabilistic modeling of the crowd and their behavior, and develop a formulation for well-founded probabilistic estimates of the significance of a rule, the potential error in this estimation, and the impact of asking a given question on this significance and uncertainty. (Section 4)
4. We also propose a specific implementation of the remaining components of the framework, based on adaptations of classic mining algorithms [2], and general techniques from sequential sampling [24]. The unique settings of crowd mining prevent us from using existing data mining algorithms as-is. The main reason is that at each point we may have only discovered a subset of the items domain and, for the rules composed of the items discovered so far, estimations are always inaccurate to some degree. Our solution also serves as an illustration of how to adapt classic association rule mining algorithms to the crowd. (Section 5)
5. Finally, we propose benchmark datasets that enable systematic evaluation of crowd-mining algorithms performance. We show, by means of an extensive experimental evaluation on an implementation of our algorithm, that it consistently outperforms alternative baseline algorithms, and identifies significant rules with greater accuracy, while asking fewer questions. The results also demonstrate the viability of our crowd-mining framework, even with simple implementations of some of the black boxes. (Section 6)

We discuss related work in Section 7 and conclude with possible extensions in Section 8.

2. PRELIMINARIES

We are interested in asking users about personal rules, and inferring about overall important rules and general trends. For that, we start with basic definitions of association rules and their quality measurements per individual. We claim that these simple definitions, based on classic association rule theory [1], can capture the summarized manner in which people tend to record certain types of information. This also guides us in the types of questions we ask the crowd and the interpretation we give to their answers.

Let $\mathcal{U}$ be a set of human users, and let $\mathcal{I} = \{i_1, i_2, i_3, \dots\}$ be a non-empty finite set of unique items. Define a *transaction* t as a subset of $\mathcal{I}$. Each user u is associated with a *personal database* D_u, which is a bag (multiset) of transactions. $|D_u|$ denotes the number of transactions in D_u.

Let $A, B \subseteq \mathcal{I}$, $A \cap B = \emptyset$. Then $A \rightarrow B$ is an *association rule*, which may be used to signify that in a personal database D_u, $A \subseteq t$ implies $B \subseteq t$, for any $t \in D_u$. From this point we sometimes use the notation $a, b \rightarrow c, d$ instead of $\{a, b\} \rightarrow \{c, d\}$, for brevity.

When mining folk medicine, for instance, items may represent symptoms, treatments and medicine ingredients. An association rule might be flu→garlic, signifying that when a user has the flu, she takes garlic.

In data mining, rules are considered interesting when they occur frequently in the data. We recall the standard definitions of support and confidence, which are used here as indicators for rule significance *per user*.

DEFINITION 2.1 (USER CONFIDENCE AND SUPPORT). *Given a user u with database D_u and a rule $A \rightarrow B$, let the* user support *of $A \rightarrow B$ in the transactions of u be defined as:*

$$supp_u(A \rightarrow B) := \frac{|\{t \in D_u \mid A, B \subseteq items(t)\}|}{|D_u|}$$

and similarly, define the user confidence *of $A \rightarrow B$ as:*

$$conf_u(A \rightarrow B) := \frac{|\{t \in D_u \mid A, B \subseteq items(t)\}|}{|\{t \in D_u \mid A \subseteq items(t)\}|}$$

Questions and answers. Data mining techniques generally rely on processing transactions for association rule learning. While we model the knowledge of every user from the crowd as an underlying personal database of transactions, this database is *completely virtual*, and not available to us for mining directly. For instance, a transaction in folk medicine may represent a particular case of the flu with all the symptoms and treatments used. People usually do not remember many such elaborate details, and instead tend to remember summaries, which can be viewed as rules.

Consequently, we give a definition for the method of accessing personal databases based on association rules (rather than transactions) and their user support and confidence. For a given rule, users can tell us the significance of the rule in their personal databases. Moreover, users can spontaneously recall rules. Thus, the two following types of questions to users are considered.

- **Closed questions.** Questions modeled as $A \xrightarrow{?} B$. We interpret the answer of a user u as the support and confidence of the rule $A \rightarrow B$ w.r.t. D_u, i.e., the pair $\langle supp_u(A \rightarrow B), conf_{D_u}(A \rightarrow B)\rangle$.
- **Open questions.** Questions modeled as $? \xrightarrow{?} ?$. The answer of a user u is interpreted as some A, B, along with the confidence and support of $A \rightarrow B$ in D_u.

We show in the sequel how these types of questions can be used for mining interesting rules from the crowd.

In order to be presented to users, questions must be phrased in natural language. For instance, consider the closed question flu$\xrightarrow{?}$garlic. One way of displaying it is by two natural language questions, corresponding to the support of "flu" and the confidence of flu$\xrightarrow{?}$garlic, respectively: "How often do you usually have the flu?" and "When you have the flu, how often do you take garlic?" An open question may be formed as "Tell us about an illness, the way you treat it and how often this occurs." Users may then enter their answer in natural language, e.g., "When I have the flu I take garlic about 80% of the time. This usually happens twice a year." In such a case, NLP tools must be used for interpreting the answer. Alternatively, users may also be given multiple options to choose from (e.g., "always", "often", "sometimes", "rarely"); or fill in the frequency by providing a number of occurrences and the time period from closed lists.

The way in which people answer the questions in practice reveals another challenge: people mostly give only *rough estimations* for the support and confidence of rules. For instance, when the exact support is 0.879 they may give an approximate answer ("about 90% of the time"), a range ("80–100% of the time") or even be slightly off the correct answer ("90–100% of the time") [5]. In our definitions we assume that both user support and confidence are provided to us as a single, perhaps approximate, number.[1] One way of modeling the error in user answers might be, e.g., assuming some error range per user. As we explain next, our choice of overall quality measures for rules allows us to ignore individual user errors and still obtain good estimations.

Note that support and confidence of *different* association rules may be dependent. For instance, the support of $A \cup B \rightarrow C$ is bounded by the support of $A \rightarrow C$. We consider these dependencies in asking about rules for which we have no samples (see Section 5), but not in our approximations (for computation simplicity). This means that we gather information on each rule separately from the crowd. Note that this does not affect the algorithm correctness, but gathering information on several rules at once could be a further optimization (see extensions in Section 8).

Overall Rule Significance. We are interested in inferring general trends, i.e., rules that have overall significance in a group of users. For that, we first need to choose how to *aggregate* user answers into an overall quality measure per rule. Since our focus in this work is on users rather than transactions, we define significant rules as rules with high *average* user support and confidence.[2] Formally:

DEFINITION 2.2 (SIGNIFICANT RULES). *Let $\mathcal{U}$ be a group of users. We say that a rule $r = A \rightarrow B$ is* significant *in $\mathcal{U}$ if it satisfies $\text{avg}_{u \in \mathcal{U}}\, supp_u(r) \geqslant \Theta_s$ and $\text{avg}_{u \in \mathcal{U}}\, conf_u(r) \geqslant \Theta_c$, where $0 \leqslant \Theta_s, \Theta_c \leqslant 1$ are predetermined threshold values.*

Note that in order to obtain the true average support and confidence one must ask every user in $\mathcal{U}$ about r. In practice this is impossible, since the number of relevant users and rules may be huge. Thus, we resort to sample-based empirical estimations. As described in Section 4, the choice of average as the aggregation function allows us to employ rigorous statistical tools for such estimations.

Another advantage of choosing avg here is for handling the error in individual user answers. In many case studies, it was shown that on average, individual user errors "cancel" each other out such that the average of the answers is very close to the truth. This phenomenon forms the foundations for the theory of the *wisdom of the crowd* [22]. It is particularly relevant in situations when user answers are independent, and indeed, as the answers we seek are personal, there is a good reason to assume such independence.

The choice of thresholds for the average support and confidence in Definition 2.2 is taken from classic data mining. We note that the solution we present can be adapted to support other functions on the average support and confidence, e.g., a threshold on their sum or product.

[1] Answers that describe the frequency of habits may be interpreted w.r.t. a fixed time period. For instance, "x times a week" may be interpreted as $\frac{x}{7}$.

[2] Other possible aggregates are discussed in Section 8.

Choice of users. Different works in the area of crowdsourcing focus either on the choice of questions, the choice of users to ask, or both [19, 8, 4]. While the ability to choose the questions to ask the users always exists, the ability to choose users is inherently limited. This is due to the fact that particular users may not always be available, or willing to answer more than a few questions. We therefore make the *least restrictive assumption*, namely that the users who answer our questions are chosen randomly each time. As we show next, this assumption is actually useful in our settings, since it allows treating user answers as random samples.

3. FRAMEWORK

Having identified the general settings in which our crowd mining algorithm works, we turn to design the general structure of a novel crowd-mining framework. This framework is composed of theoretical components that are used as *black-boxes*. Depending on prior knowledge, particular estimations about the data distribution, a different choice of the target function, etc. – different *implementations* of the black-boxes may be preferred. This observation is not unique to crowd mining, and also applies to different data mining algorithms, machine learning algorithms, etc.

The framework structure we suggest is designed to facilitate a crowd-mining algorithm. A few unique properties of crowd mining (as opposed to classic data mining) guide the course of this algorithm, as follows.

1. **Using the crowd wisely.** The most costly resource in our settings, both in latency and possibly monetary cost, are the crowd questions. Thus, we aim to minimize the number of questions by maximizing the knowledge gain per question.
2. **Data access model.** As defined in Section 2, a user answer gives us information only w.r.t. a particular rule. Thus, the algorithm is directed by the choice of rules to ask about.
3. **Estimated quality.** As it is impossible to ask all users each question, our algorithm relies on estimations for rule significance, as well as for the effect of a question on our confidence.

Based on these characteristics, our algorithm is an *interactive* one, and works in iterations. At each iteration, we use the knowledge gained so far to decide which question to ask next. The question should be chosen so as to maximize knowledge gain. This is the most challenging part of the algorithm, and the main role of the component framework. Once the user answer is obtained, the framework components can be used to update our estimations for the significance of different rules. In addition, at each point of the algorithm, we can rely on these estimations for computing and returning the set of significant rules.

Remark. For simplicity, we assume that the algorithm only selects *one question at a time*. We briefly discuss the selection of the best bulk of K next questions, which may be then posed to the crowd in parallel, in Section 8.

Our framework components are organized in a *hierarchy*. Each black-box implementation in this hierarchy may use lower-tier black-boxes. If the implementation of this black-box is replaced, the lower-level black-boxes may not be required anymore. An overview of the hierarchy of our framework components is given in the diagram in Figure 1. The boxes with light background are boxes for which the implementation is straightforward, using the boxes of the level below. The black-box components are colored black.

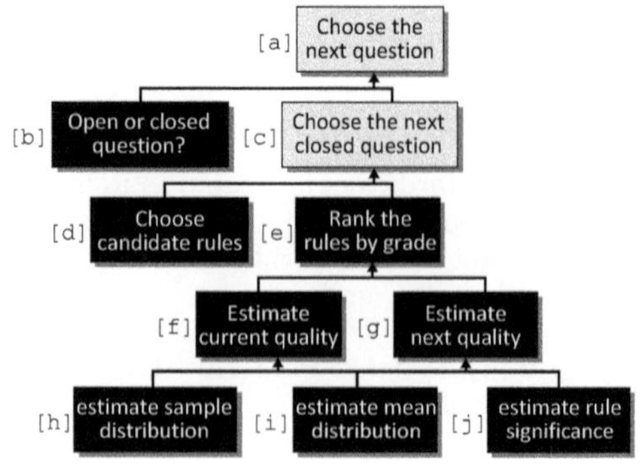

Figure 1: Framework Component Hierarchy

Data: Set of users $\mathcal{U}$, a budget N
Result: S: a set of association rules
Initialize *Enabled* `[d]`;
for *every* $i \in \{1, \ldots, N\}$ *OR until stopped* **do**
  $u \leftarrow$ a random user;
  if *Ask open question?* `[b]` **then**
    $q \leftarrow$ an open question;
    $(r', s, c) \leftarrow$ the answer of u for q;
  else
    $r' \leftarrow \arg\max_{r \in Enabled} grade(r)$ `[e]`;
    $q \leftarrow$ a closed question about r';
    $(s, c) \leftarrow$ the answer of u for q;
  Update *Enabled* `[d]`;
  Add (s, c) to the samples of r';
$S \leftarrow \emptyset$;
for *every* $r \in$ *Enabled* **do**
  if *r is significant* `[j]` **then**
    Add r to S;
return S;

Algorithm 1: Crowd-mining association rules

Algorithm 1 gives a high-level description of a crowd-mining algorithm using the framework components. The use of a particular component is indicated by marking the relevant lines with the component letter. Some of the components are called implicitly, such as in the call to the *grade* function `[e]`, which involves components `[f-j]`, or the choice of the next question `[a]` which appears decomposed and spans over the **if-then-else** part inside the loop.

The course of the algorithm. Given a budget of N questions to pose to the crowd, the algorithm completes at most N iterations. It may be stopped at any point, e.g., if too much time has elapsed or if we have obtained satisfactory accuracy. At each iteration we first choose a random user u, according to our assumption from Section 2. Then, we use the framework components to decide which question to ask.

Note that, as in many other learning problems, we have a tradeoff between obtaining (possibly) new information by asking open questions, and refining the accuracy of our estimations by asking closed questions. In particular, items of the domain, which are initially unknown, can only be discovered by open questions, thus expanding the set of rules which we can compose and evaluate. On the other hand, the fact that we can cleverly select where to refine our knowledge (by asking closed questions) gives us the advantage over random sampling (asking only open questions). Thus, the first black-box component used in the algorithm is responsible for choosing between closed and open questions (box [b]), while aiming to balance the tradeoff. Its particular implementation may depend on assumptions about answers to open questions (according to which distribution they are selected), and on the need in exploration (e.g., how much of the item domain has been discovered).

If the chosen type is *open*, an open question is posed to the user u, who returns a rule r' with its support and confidence (according to Section 2).

The case of a *closed* question is the more algorithmically challenging one. When selecting the next closed question to ask, we do not want to consider all the possible rules that can be composed of the known data items. This is because 1) there is a huge amount of rules, and 2) most of them are not interesting. Instead, we can focus on a small subset of more interesting rules, called *enabled* rules (box [d]). The choice of which rules to enable can be inspired by the rule exploration order of existing data mining algorithms (See Section 5). However, it must also take into account unique features of the crowd mining scenario, such as the fact that no full information about a rule is ever collected.

Now, among the enabled rules, we ask about the rule with the highest *grade* (box [e]). The grade is computed in an elaborate way so as to reflect the effect of asking a question on r'. We would like to choose the rule that, if this were the final iteration, would maximize our *overall output quality*. After selecting a rule r', we ask the user u about it and record his answer (user support and confidence).

At the end of Algorithm 1, the set of significant rules is computed and returned as the output. Component [j] is reused here for finding significant rules.

The lower tiers. We now turn to explain the lower level components in the hierarchy, which are used in the implementation of box [e]. See Section 4, where we describe the non-trivial implementation for these components, which is a key contribution of this paper.

The second-lowest-level components in Figure 1 refer to estimation of the current quality of the algorithm output (box [f]), and the "next" quality, namely the quality after asking one more question on a particular rule r' (box [g]). The difference between those measures, i.e., the effect of the answer about r' on the quality, may be used for rule ranking.

To estimate the quality before and after asking about r', we must first estimate the overall support and confidence of each rule (recall Definition 2.2). For generality, instead of computing just one estimation, we compute a *distribution* that reflects the probability for different values of the means, given the collected knowledge (box [i]). Next, we decide whether r' is significant (box [j]). The decision method should minimize the probability of making an error. Finally, the estimation of the next quality depends on the next user answer about r' (box [h]). We can use the samples (user answers) and any standard fitting method for estimating the distribution of the next user answer.

4. ERROR ESTIMATION, RULE RANKING

In order to rank closed questions (box [e]), we need to predict the expected effect of each answer on the overall output quality. We suggest, as a possible quality measure, the *expected total number of errors* (to be formally defined in the sequel). We show that this simple option proves to be a useful and practical one.

Table 1: Running Example for rule $\hat{r}$

	current	next (expected)
Sample mean	$\mu = (0.5125, 0.5125)$	μ
Sample covariance	$\Sigma = 10^{-2} \cdot \begin{pmatrix} 1.72 & 0.39 \\ 0.39 & 1.72 \end{pmatrix}$	Σ
$f_{\hat{r}}$ covariance	$\frac{\Sigma}{4}$	$\frac{\Sigma}{5}$
$P_{\text{err}}(\hat{r})$	0.367	0.332

We next describe in detail a key contribution of this paper, namely, suggested implementations for components [e-j], which work together to minimize the expected output error. For generality, our choices are based on the assumption of *zero prior knowledge*, and some of them include parameters that may be tweaked experimentally. This way, and as we show in our experiments (See Section 6), we construct a general-purpose crowd-mining algorithm. The implementations are explained in a bottom-up fashion, with the letter of the relevant component next to each section title.

Estimating the mean [i]. According to Section 2, we are interested in approximating the average support and confidence. When we ask a closed question about a particular rule r, we in fact choose a user randomly (uniformly) out of a huge number of users, and obtain his user support and confidence for r. This may be modeled as *sampling from an unknown distribution* $\tilde{g}_r$, the distribution of the user answers. Each sample is a 2D vector, where the first dimension is the support and the second is the confidence. According to the central limit theorem, the sample mean, denoted f_r, approaches a normal distribution. We thus approximate the distribution of the sample mean f_r by the bivariate normal distribution with mean vector $\tilde{\mu}$ and covariance matrix $\frac{1}{N}\tilde{\Sigma}$, where $\tilde{\mu}$ is the (unknown) mean of $\tilde{g}_r$, $\tilde{\Sigma}$ is the (unknown) covariance of $\tilde{g}_r$ and N is the sample size. I.e., $f_r \sim \mathrm{N}(\tilde{\mu}, \frac{1}{N}\tilde{\Sigma})$.

Both $\tilde{\mu}$ and $\tilde{\Sigma}$ are unknown but, using the samples for rule r, we can approximate $\tilde{\mu}$ as the *sample average* μ and $\tilde{\Sigma}$ as the *sample covariance* Σ. Now the sample mean distribution f_r may be approximated as a normal distribution with mean μ and covariance $\frac{1}{N}\Sigma$. I.e., $f_r \sim \mathrm{N}(\mu, \frac{1}{N}\Sigma)$.

EXAMPLE 4.1. *Assume that for a particular rule $\hat{r} = A \rightarrow B$, we have obtained so far the answers of 4 users:*

	User support	*User confidence*
User 1	0.4	0.4
User 2	0.4	0.6
User 3	0.6	0.4
User 4	0.65	0.65

The sample mean and covariance are shown in Table 1, under the column "current". The rest of the table is not necessary at this point, but will be useful as we continue with this example throughout the section. The obtained estimated Gaussian distribution of the mean $f_{\hat{r}}$ is depicted in Fig. 2(a). The dark circle is the mean, the light circles are the actual samples, and the background is darker according to where the probability mass lies.

This estimation of the mean is based on the fact that, other than samples, we have no information about the mean. If we had some prior estimation for the mean distribution, this method could be extended to take it into account.

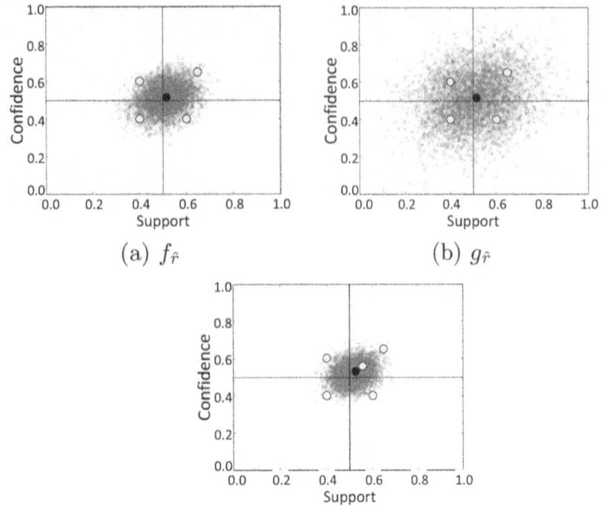

(a) $f_{\hat{r}}$ (b) $g_{\hat{r}}$

(c) $f'_{\hat{r}}$ when the next sample is $(0.55, 0.55)$

Figure 2: Distribution figures for rule $\hat{r}$ (x-axis is confidence, y-axis is support)

Estimating the sample distribution `[h]`. In order to choose the best next question, we need to estimate what the next answer might be for each rule. Recall that $\tilde{g}_r$ is an unknown distribution. We already know that the sample mean μ and sample covariance Σ are unbiased estimators for its mean $\tilde{\mu}$ and covariance $\tilde{\Sigma}$, respectively. Here, we choose to roughly approximate $\tilde{g}_r$ by $g_r \sim \mathrm{N}(\mu, \Sigma)$. Note that g_r cannot be precisely normal, since the support and confidence values are taken from the range $[0, 1]$. Thus, for a sample (s, c) we use the PDF $g_r((s, c) \mid s, c \in [0, 1])$ (truncated Gaussian). The notation $\mid s, c$ is omitted for brevity.

A normal distribution is a simple and general choice for describing the distribution of real-life data. However, other distributions may make good choices as well. For instance, it may be the case that user either have frequent or rare headaches. This produces two groups of samples, one with high values, and another with low ones. Such a situation may be better described by a bimodal distribution rather than a normal one.

EXAMPLE 4.2. *Consider again the samples from Ex. 4.1. The distribution of $g_{\hat{r}}$, computed using μ and Σ as mean and covariance, is depicted in Fig. 2(b). Compare to Fig. 2(a) to see the difference in variance w.r.t. $f_{\hat{r}}$.*

Estimating rule significance `[j]`. At any point of the algorithm, based on the current best estimations for the overall confidence and support, we would like to decide for every rule r whether it is significant or not. Note that the probability of the mean being above both thresholds is the *unbiased estimator* for whether the mean is above both thresholds, since for a binary random variable, the probability for 1 is also the expectation. In addition, note that as the number of samples N grows, the covariance approaches the 0 matrix; this happens since the sample covariance Σ approaches the constant, real covariance $\tilde{\Sigma}$, and we divide it by N to estimate the covariance of the mean.

Thus, to decide on rule significance, we check whether, according to f_r, the probability for the mean to be above both thresholds is greater than 0.5. This is done by testing whether $\int_{\Theta_s}^{\infty}\int_{\Theta_c}^{\infty} f_r(s,c)\, \mathrm{d}c\,\mathrm{d}s > 0.5$ (numerical integration of bivariate normal distributions is well-studied and fast algorithms exist to reach a very high precision [14]).

EXAMPLE 4.3. *Let us return to our running example. Assume that $\Theta_s = \Theta_c = 0.5$. The probability that the mean is above both thresholds, computed using the formula above, is* 0.367. *This means that there is a greater probability for the overall support and confidence of $\hat{r}$ to be below one of the thresholds, and thus our algorithm decides that it is not a significant rule.*

Example 4.3 provides another important observation: although the sample mean $\mu = (0.5125, 0.5125)$ is above both thresholds, the probability of being below one of the thresholds is greater than 0.5. Thus, using the mean itself to decide whether a rule is significant may be misleading.

Estimating current quality `[f]`. We suggest, as an output quality measure, the *total number of errors*. Recall that the ground truth in our case is unknown, rendering exact computation impossible; instead, we compute the *expected* number of errors, according to the probability of giving an erroneous answer on each rule. Let X_i be a random variable whose value is 1 if our algorithm makes an error in classifying rule r_i. Denote the error probability for rule r_i by $P_{\mathrm{err}}(r)$, and the domain of all possible rules by $\mathcal{R}$. The expected total number of errors is given by the formula

$$\mathbb{E}\left[\sum_{r_i \in \mathcal{R}} X_i\right] = \sum_{r_i \in \mathcal{R}} \mathbb{E}\left[X_i\right] = \sum_{r_i \in \mathcal{R}} P_{\mathrm{err}}(r_i) \qquad (1)$$

Let us now develop the formula for $P_{\mathrm{err}}(r)$. In the case that our algorithm decides that a rule r is significant, the error probability is the probability for r not to be significant, i.e., $P_{\mathrm{err}}(r) = 1 - \int_{\Theta_c}^{\infty}\int_{\Theta_s}^{\infty} f_r(s,c)\, \mathrm{d}c\,\mathrm{d}s$. In the case when the algorithm decides r is not significant, the complement of this formula to 1 is used. Note that if the decision method described above is used, $P_{\mathrm{err}}(r)$ is the probability of being on the side of the thresholds with the smaller distribution mass. In particular, it is guaranteed to be 0.5 or less.

EXAMPLE 4.4. *Returning to our running example, we can now easily compute the error probability. The algorithm decides that $\hat{r}$ is not significant, the error probability is the probability of being above both thresholds –* 0.367. *This also appears in Table 1.*

The computation explained above works only for rules that have at least two samples (this is necessary for f_r to be well-defined). In order to handle rules without any user samples, we allot each rule an initial set of samples by a new user $u^* \notin \mathcal{U}$. These samples can be chosen such that the initial error probability is maximal (0.5) and the covariance is large, to reflect the fact that we have no information about this rule, yet. This also means that the next user answer is likely to reduce the error probability and covariance, i.e., our estimation becomes more accurate, as we would expect when knowledge is gained. As we obtain more user samples, the effect of these initial samples becomes negligible.

Estimating next quality `[g]`. We next want to estimate the effect of the next question on the total number of errors. First, we need to know how an additional sample may affect the error probability of rule r. Recall that we have estimated the sample distribution as g_r. Given one more sample from g_r in addition to the collected user samples, we are able to compute a new sample mean μ', a new sample covariance Σ', and based on these two – a new distribution of the mean f'_r. Since every sample may result in a different f'_r, we aim at finding the *expected* error $\mathbb{E}\left[P'_{\text{err}}(r)\right]$, over all possible next samples. We split the computation into two cases, depending on the probability of $\tilde{\mu}$ to be above both thresholds given the new average μ'. Formally, let s and c be the support and confidence of the next sample, drawn from g_r, and f'_r the new sample mean distribution based on them. Denote by $\varphi(s,c)$ the area of the next sample values for which r is estimated to be significant. Then,

$$\mathbb{E}\left[P'_{\text{err}}(r)\right] = \iint\limits_{\varphi(s,c)} g_r(s,c)\cdot\left[1-\int_{\Theta_c}^{\infty}\int_{\Theta_s}^{\infty} f'_r(s',c')\,\mathrm{d}c'\mathrm{d}s'\right]\mathrm{d}c\,\mathrm{d}s$$
$$+\iint\limits_{\neg\varphi(s,c)} g_r(s,c)\cdot\left[\int_{\Theta_c}^{\infty}\int_{\Theta_s}^{\infty} f'_r(s',c')\,\mathrm{d}c'\mathrm{d}s'\right]\mathrm{d}c\,\mathrm{d}s$$

The first summand refers to the error probability if the rule is significant after the next sample. In the outer integral we integrate over all relevant values of the next sample, and in the inner integral we compute the error probability as the chance of the mean not being above both thresholds. We compute the average of such error probabilities, weighted according to the probability of the particular next sample. Similarly, the second summand refers to the error probability if the rule is *not* significant after the next sample.

This integral cannot be computed directly, and thus we use a numerical Monte Carlo method to estimate its value [18]. This is done by repeatedly sampling s, c from g_r. For each such sample, we add it as the ith sample to the $i-1$ samples obtained from the users. From this set of i samples we compute a new sample mean and sample covariance, to find the new distribution f'_r. Now we can compute the error probability of f'_r in the exact same manner as we did with f_r above. Finally, after taking enough samples, we can average the error probabilities computed for each sample and obtain the estimator for $\mathbb{E}\left[P'_{\text{err}}(r)\right]$.

This estimator can then be plugged into formula 1 to compute the expected next total number of errors. We are now in fact computing the expectation of the expected total number of errors $\mathbb{E}\left[\mathbb{E}\left[\sum_{r_i\in\mathcal{R}} X_i\right]\right] = \sum_{r_i\in\mathcal{R}}\mathbb{E}\left[\mathbb{E}\left[X_i\right]\right]$. Note that we only ask on r, and since we treat the rules as independent, the answer only impacts r's error probability. Thus, if $r_i = r$, then $\mathbb{E}\left[\mathbb{E}\left[X_i\right]\right] = \mathbb{E}\left[P'_{\text{err}}(r)\right]$, and $\mathbb{E}\left[\mathbb{E}\left[X_i\right]\right] = P_{\text{err}}(r_i)$ otherwise.

EXAMPLE 4.5. *Returning to our running example, we examine the effect of an additional sample on the mean distribution. Assume that the fifth sample is* $(0.55, 0.55)$. *The new sample mean and covariance would be*

$$\mu' = (0.52, 0.52), \quad \Sigma' = 10^{-3}\cdot\begin{pmatrix} 2.64 & 0.65 \\ 0.65 & 2.64 \end{pmatrix}$$

Fig. 2(c) depicts the new distribution $f'_{\hat{r}}$, where notably the covariance decreases w.r.t. $f_{\hat{r}}$ (Fig. 2(a)). The expected next error, 0.332 *is lower than the current one,* 0.367.

Final ranking of the rules [e]. Given the estimations discussed thus far, we want to rank the association rules. The grade used for ranking a rule r should reflect the *expected effect* of an answer about r, on some global output quality measure, in our case the total number of errors. The chosen closed question is about the highest-ranked rule.

We explained in the previous two sections how to estimate the current error probability for a rule r and the expected error probability after one more question. Based on these two values, we can compute the expected error probability decrease resulting from one question on r, as $grade(r) = \mathbb{E}\left[P_{\text{err}}(r) - P'_{\text{err}}(r)\right] = P_{\text{err}}(r) - \mathbb{E}\left[P'_{\text{err}}(r)\right]$. This error decrease also reflects the effect on the total number of errors, since the only summand in formula 1 that changes when we ask about r is $P_{\text{err}}(r)$, which is replaced with the expected value of $P'_{\text{err}}(r)$.

The total number of errors has practical advantages as the quality measure. Given the current and next error probabilities for every rule, the effect on this measure is easy to compute. Consider an alternative quality measure for the output. In search algorithms such as ours, two types of quality measures are typically noted: *precision*, or the ratio of relevant results within the output, and *recall*, or the ratio of output data within the relevant data. Since there is typically a tradeoff between the two, it is common for algorithms to optimize a measure that balances between them. The standard such measure is the F-measure, defined as $2\cdot\frac{\text{precision}\cdot\text{recall}}{\text{precision}+\text{recall}}$.[3] One may choose the question to ask based on the answer's expected effect on the F-measure. We found this approach less practical, since precision and recall can only be estimated very roughly, when the ground truth is unknown. Moreover, due to computation complexity, significant numerical errors may be encountered. In tests, while the general trends were similar, using the former approach provided higher-quality results, also w.r.t. the F-measure. See Section 6.

5. OTHER COMPONENTS

We next describe implementations for the two remaining black-boxes that are independent of ranking.

Choosing the enabled rules [d]. The following challenge is classic in association rule learning. Making computations (e.g., error estimations) for the entire domain of rules is infeasible, since it is huge. We would like to consider only a relatively small subset of rules, that are more likely to be significant than others, at each point of the algorithm. We refer to these rules as *enabled*. A closed question may only be asked on an enabled rule.

Classic data mining algorithms rely on different strategies for choosing the order in which rules are considered. Denote by *k-rule* a rule $A \to B$ such that $|A \cup B| = k$. Apriori and following works consider first only 1-rules, then only 2-rules, etc [2]. This relies on the fact that according to the definition of support, if a $k+1$-rule has a high support, all its k-sub-rules (made of subsets of its items) also have high support values. Other data mining algorithms may "jump" from k to $k+k'$, where $k' > 1$ [3]. While these jumps lead to rules that are less likely to be significant, if they turn out to be significant, we gain information not only on the considered rule but also on all of its sub-rules .

The unique settings of crowd mining prevents us from using existing strategies as-is. First, at any point we never gain "enough" information about significant k-rules. The reason is the approximate nature of our algorithm, which

[3]In our experiments in Section 6, we use the F-measure to test the performance of our algorithm.

always involves some degree of uncertainty. Thus, "exhaustive" approaches such as Apriori cannot be used. Second, the ability of people to remember large rules is limited, which calls to a focus on smaller rules. Last, we treat the rules as independent in our estimations. This renders jumps rather useless, as they increase the risk of wasting a question, without the benefit of gaining more information. How to utilize rule dependencies in our settings is left for future work.

We suggest the following variation for the order of considered rules, designed for our settings as described above. Note that unlike Apriori, the set of enabled rules at each point contains rules of different sizes.

1. We enable smaller rules first, starting from all 1-rules (using discovered items).
2. In Apriori, a $k+1$-rule is considered only if *all* its k-sub-rules have a high support. In crowd mining, rather than waiting for all significant k-rules to be known, we enable a $k+1$-rule as soon as *two* of its k-sub-rules are enabled, and have a high support. We need at least two rules in order to "cover" the $k+1$ items.
3. No jumps are taken.

This strategy is rather simple, but performs well for our settings, see Section 6. More sophisticated strategies will be considered in future work.

Deciding open vs closed questions [b]. So far, we have only focused on asking closed questions. However, as explained in Section 3, open questions are also a vital part of crowdsourcing. One reason is that open questions allow discovering new items from $\mathcal{I}$. Another pragmatic reason is that people tend to spontaneously recall only prominent rules – with very low or very high support and confidence (for instance, "When I have a stomach ache, I *almost always* drink tea"). Thus, an answer to an open question may improve our recall, by discovering an unknown significant rule.

On the other hand, open questions are closer to random samples, since the rule in the answer is unknown. As we show in Experiment 4 in Section 6, asking only open questions results in low precision and does not measure up to algorithms with closed questions. This is true even when we assume that the user answers always regard significant rules.

The decision between open and closed questions relates to the general, well-studied, problem of *exploration vs. exploitation* in sequential sampling [24]. The tradeoff is between gaining more information (in our case, finding where uncertainty exists), and utilizing existing information (in our case, reducing the uncertainty). To optimally balance the two, one must make specific assumptions on the answer distribution. Since we do not make such assumptions, we experiment with two general strategies of the exploration-exploitation paradigm, which provide approximate solutions [24].

One possible strategy, called the *ε-greedy strategy* is choosing a constant proportion of the questions to be open. This can be done by *flipping a weighted coin* with probability $1-\varepsilon$ at each iteration. This option is the simplest one, and balances the number of closed and open questions. A more sophisticated strategy, called the *ε-decreasing strategy*, relies on the fact that as we gain more information, less exploration is required. The weight for choosing an open question is initially high, and gradually decreases as more knowledge is collected. In Section 6 we compare the performance of the two strategies and show that the simple approach performs just as well as the more sophisticated one. This is also in accordance with the empirical studies in [24].

6. EXPERIMENTS

We introduce *CrowdMiner*, a system for mining association rules from the crowd. The *CrowdMiner* system is implemented in Python using an SQLite database. External libraries used were StatsModels[4], containing an implementation of multivariate Gaussian integration through MC sampling [14], and the Orange data mining library [9]. Experiments were executed on a Lenovo ThinkPad with 8GB of RAM and a 2.80 GHz Intel Core i7 processor, running Windows 7 x64. All results are averaged over 5 executions per algorithm for accuracy.

6.1 Benchmark Datasets

Since the concept of mining rules from the crowd is a new one, no benchmark datasets currently exist in the form of rules assigned to users. We propose 3 benchmark datasets upon which we run our experiments. The benchmarks are constructed in the following way.

To simulate the real world, we begin with a transaction dataset. Each user is assigned a set of transactions, which are then translated into personal association rules using the standard Apriori algorithm. Each user u now has a set of rules R_u which represent the user's "world", and their respective confidence and support values; these values are stored in what we refer to as the *real-world database.* They may then be queried as part of the crowd-mining process.

Recall that Apriori itself uses thresholds in order to decide which rules to generate. We therefore supply the Apriori algorithm with support and confidence thresholds, *lower than the thresholds used to determine rule significance.* We refer to these thresholds as the *Apriori thresholds.* The support threshold for each user was set to $\frac{2}{\#transactions}$, to ensure that each rule is supported by at least two different transactions. The confidence threshold may vary per dataset, but was generally set to 0.1 to ensure a database of manageable size.

Given the users' individual rule sets, we simulate the answers to questions as follows. When a user u is asked a closed question about some rule $r \in R_u$, she returns the support and confidence $supp_u(r)$, $conf_u(r)$. If u is asked about a rule $r \notin R_u$, she returns "don't-know", a default value having low support and confidence. A user u who is asked an open question returns one of her k-best rules, sorted first by support and then by confidence (k was usually set to 50). This is because support is generally the dominant factor when deciding whether a rule is significant or not.

The support and confidence thresholds are determined based on the data distribution so as to ensure an adequate number of significant rules. If the threshold is set too low, the difference between a significant and a non-significant rule may be negligible; if the threshold is set too high, we may not obtain enough significant rules.

Synthetic Dataset. This dataset contains transactions that were generated using the IBM Quest Data Generator [2]. We have generated three types of transactions, such that the items in the transactions of each type were selected from a domain of a different size: 200K transactions over a domain of 20 items, 100K transactions over 100 items and 50K transactions over 500 items. By combining the 3 types, we

[4]http://statsmodels.sourceforge.net/

ensured the existence of rules with low, medium and high support and confidence. This transaction set was then uniformly assigned to a set of 1,000 users. The resulting dataset is sparse, but well distributed: some rules are common to almost all the users, but most of the rules are known to only a few. We experimented with different subsets of these users, of sizes between 100 and 1,000 (over the same transaction distribution). Since the results did not change significantly, we present the results for the entire set of 1,000 users.

Retail Dataset. The retail dataset was constructed from a list of transactions representing purchases at a retail store [6]. This real-world dataset is available online, and used for benchmarking in many data mining applications. The dataset reflects the transactions of approximately 3,000 users. Since the data was anonymized, transactions were uniformly assigned to a set of users.

Wikipedia Dataset. The third dataset was extracted from Wikipedia and contains a list of real Wikipedia users and the categories they edited (each transaction is an edit session, with the categories of edited articles). We chose Simple English Wikipedia[5] because of its smaller scale, making the extraction of contributors for every article more manageable. However, the obtained database was overly specific and noisy, containing multiple categories representing the same concept (such as "movie" and "film"), and required cleaning. To do this, we made use of YAGO [21], a massive semantic taxonomy constructed from Wikipedia. First, we mapped Simple English Wikipedia articles to YAGO entities. We then used the YAGO taxonomy to "climb up" the category hierarchy, selecting for each category in each article the relevant high-level categories. This provided cleaner data with a greater degree of similarity between users, enabling meaningful rule mining. This database contains roughly 600 users, all of whom have at least one association rule.

6.2 Experimental results

Algorithms. We compare three different algorithms, each of which selects the queries in a different way:

- *Random* is a naïve algorithm that asks at each point about a random rule in the known database.
- *Greedy* is a simple algorithm that asks about the rule with the *fewest samples* at each point.
- *CrowdMiner* uses all the techniques detailed in Sections 4 and 5. At each point, it selects the question that maximizes our grade function.

The output of each algorithm is a list of its significant rules: rules which satisfy the threshold with probability > 0.5. Each experiment below compares the performance of these algorithms over time, given different scenarios.

Metrics. We evaluate our experiments using two metrics. *Errors* represents the absolute number of errors made by each algorithm: it is calculated as the sum of false-positives and false-negatives. *F-measure* is the harmonic mean of precision and recall, used to characterize the results more accurately. Naturally, we also measured precision and recall for all the experiments; some of the graphs are not shown for lack of space. All metrics were re-measured after every iteration of the algorithm. Combining all results provided us with a progression chart, showing how the F-measure / number of errors progressed over time in the execution of the algorithm. Every test used 2,000 crowd questions.

We now present the results of our empirical evaluation.

Experiment 1: Zero-Knowledge Mining. This experiment tests the performance of the 3 algorithms over a dataset for which they have no prior information: i.e., they begin with an empty sample database, and fill it by querying the real-world database. This experiment allows us to examine how accurately the algorithms mine association rules while simultaneously constructing a database.

Figure 3 shows the results for this experiment over the three benchmark datasets, for both F-measure and error metrics. Note that the error and F-measure graphs behave in a symmetric fashion (when the F-measure is high, the error number is low), and therefore in future experiments we show only the F-measure. During the execution of the algorithms, open questions and newly enabled rules increase the number of rules in the database, while closed questions improve the knowledge about existing rules. As the experiments show, the noted improvement is derived primarily from recall obtained from the enabling of larger rules: our algorithm is able to extract the largest number of significant rules. The precision differences are somewhat smaller. An example of precision–recall breakdown is shown in Figure 3(g) and 3(h) respectively. The Wikipedia dataset (Figure 3(f)) exhibits lower F-measure levels for all algorithms, since this data is highly distributed and there are many rules that apply only to small groups or even single users. Even so, *CrowdMiner* outperforms the other two algorithms.

Experiment 2: Mining Over Known Item-Domains. In contrast to the previous scenario, we now examine a scenario in which the domain of items is given in advance. This simulates a case where, for example, there exists a large catalog listing all the items available for purchase in Chicago, while no information exists about consumer habits. The execution of the algorithms thus starts with a database where all the items in the domain exist as 1-rules, having initial "don't know" values.

Figure 4 shows the results for this experiment over the three benchmarks. These results are very similar to the zero-knowledge experiment, but it appears that in the first few crowd questions, the greedy algorithm benefits from the additional information provided by the catalog. Since initially all the 1-rules are in the same state, asking about the rule with the least samples is pretty much the best that can be done, and the precision of the greedy algorithm is relatively high. However, it is soon overtaken by *CrowdMiner*, which discovers more rules by enabling larger rules with a high potential for being significant.

Experiment 3: Refinement for a Given Set of Rules. In this experiment, we are interested in isolating and examining the performance of the *closed question functionality* in *CrowdMiner* vs. the two competitor algorithms. All the algorithms are given an initial, randomly selected set of 400 rules. They then ask a series of closed questions only. For lack of space, we only show results for the synthetic dataset.

Figure 4 shows the results for this experiment in two metrics: (i) F-measure and (ii) errors. Since there are no open questions and no enabling of larger rules, the scope of the recall is limited.This means that the change in the F-measure graph is mainly caused by the change in precision.

[5]`http://simple.wikipedia.org/`

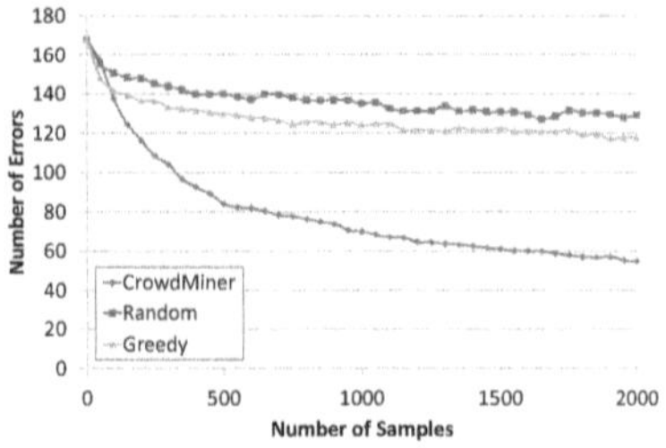

(a) Synthetic: Errors

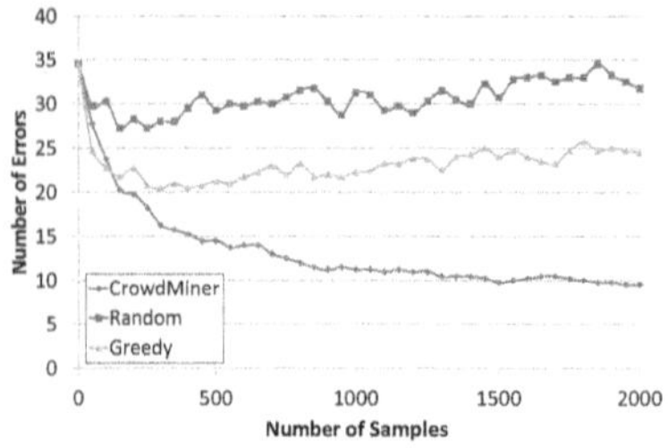

(b) Retail: Errors

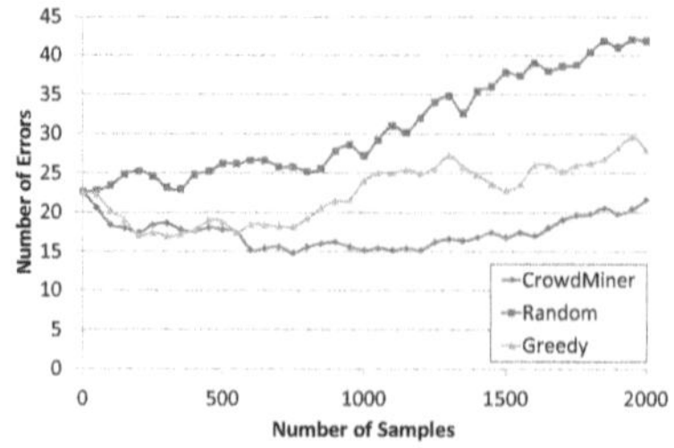

(c) Wikipedia: Errors

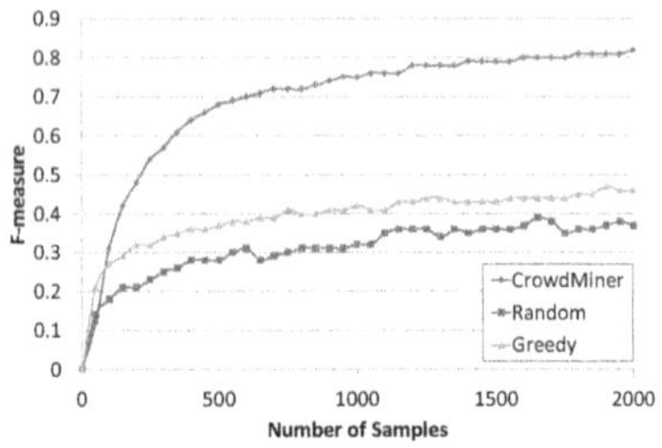

(d) Synthetic: F-measure

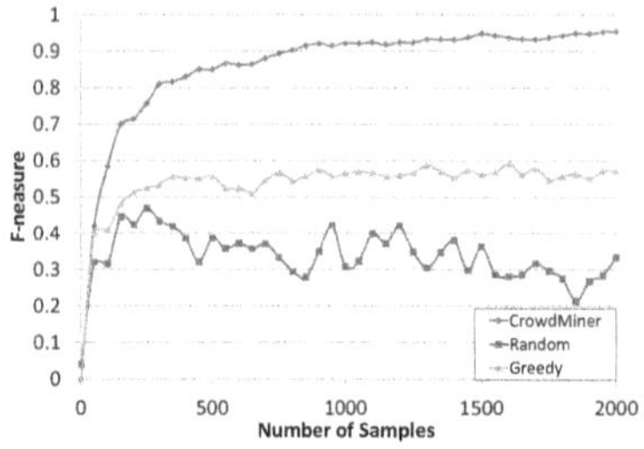

(e) Retail: F-measure

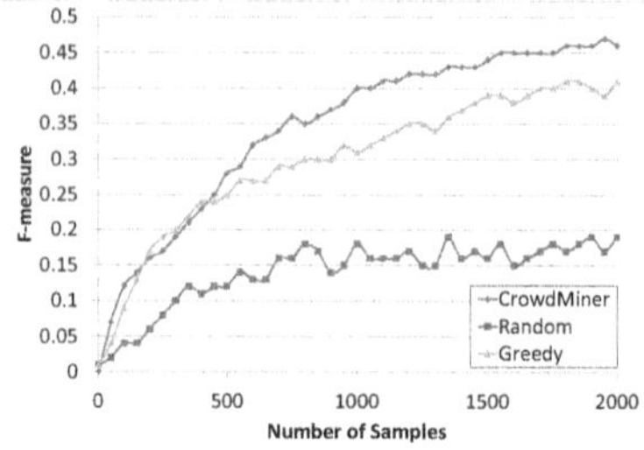

(f) Wikipedia: F-measure

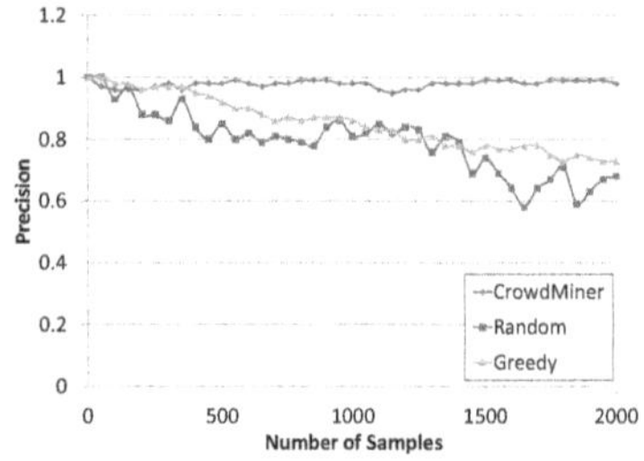

(g) Retail: Precision

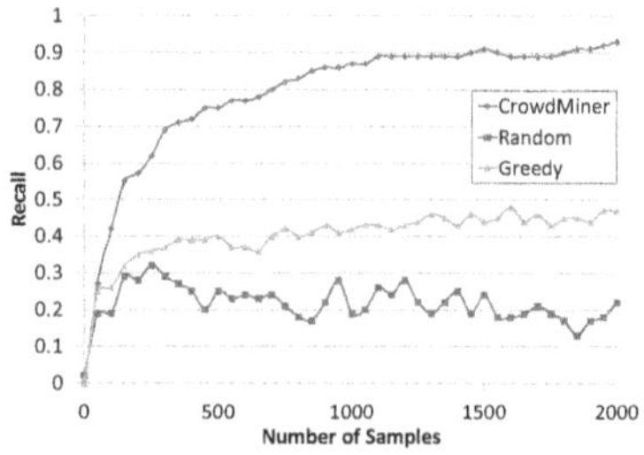

(h) Retail: Recall

Figure 3: Zero-knowledge rule mining

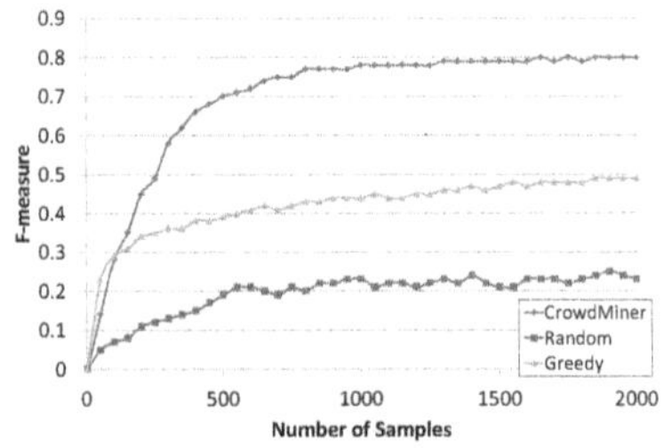

(a) Synthetic: F-measure

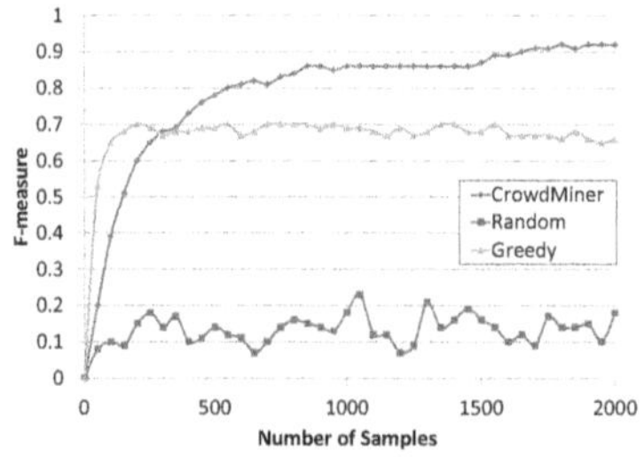

(b) Retail: F-measure

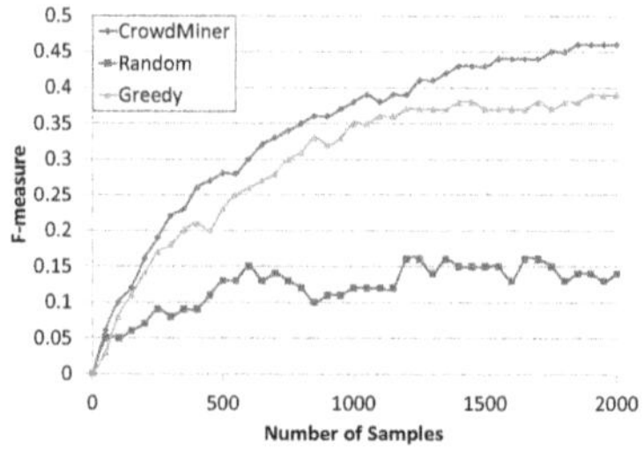

(c) Wikipedia: F-measure

Figure 4: Rule mining for known items

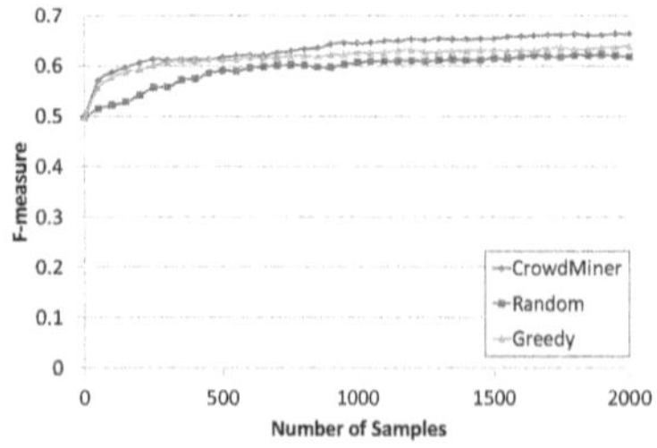

(a) Synthetic: F-measure

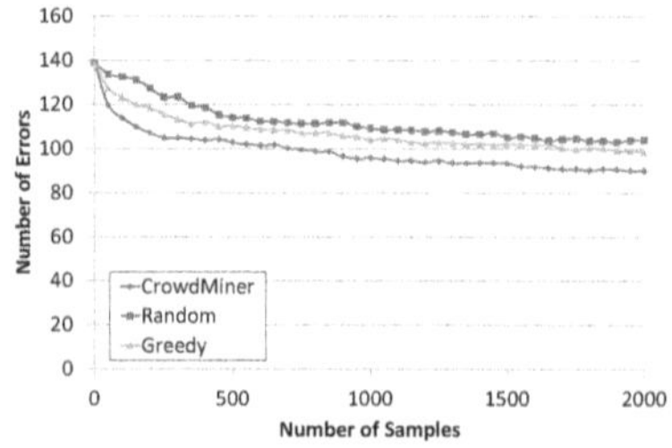

(b) Synthetic: Errors

Figure 5: Rule mining over initial sample

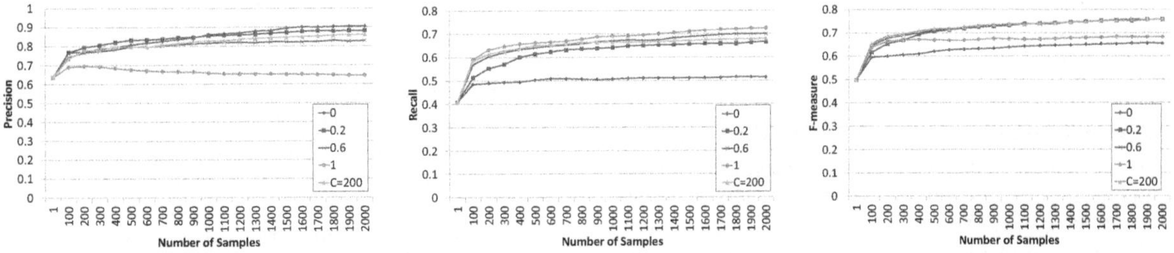

(a) Precision (b) Recall (c) F-measure

Figure 6: Determining the coin flip value

The advantage of *CrowdMiner* here is statistically significant, and is preserved across additional experiments that were run using different initial sample sizes.

Experiment 4: Choosing Open or Closed Questions. As described in Section 5, we study two strategies of deciding between open and closed questions, and their effect on the performance of *CrowdMiner*. Both strategies rely on flipping a weighted coin, where the weight represents the probability of asking an open question.

The first strategy, ε-*greedy*, assigns the coin a constant weight which we range from 0 (ask only closed questions) to 1 (ask only open questions). In effect, a coin flip of 0 cannot introduce any new information into the system, while a coin flip of 1 is equivalent to sampling rules at random from users. The second strategy, ε-*decreasing* reduces the coin flip weight as a function of time: $weight(t) = \frac{C}{C+t}$. This function was run for different values of C. The first 4 values in the legends of Figure 6 represent the results for particular ε-greedy coin flip values. The last represents the best results for ε-decreasing, which were obtained for $C = 200$.

We use an initial database as in Experiment 3.

Figure 6(a) shows the precision of the results, for different weights of the coin flip. The highest precision of ε-greedy is achieved when the weight is 0, and *CrowdMiner* asks only closed questions. This makes sense, since asking closed questions leads to higher confidence within the set of known rules, and in particular within the rules estimated to be significant. In general, the higher the weight is, the lower the precision is. Figure 6(b) shows the recall of the results. Note that the highest recall is achieved when the weight is 1 (*CrowdMiner* asks only open questions), and the lowest when the weight is 0. However, note that there is a significant gap between the recall for a weight of 0 (no new information is introduced into the system) and the recall for a weight of 0.2 (a small amount of new information is introduced into the system). We also observe that a varying coin flip value does not yield better results than a fixed value. The best results, for $C = 200$, were similar to those of a fixed weight of 0.6.

We set the default weight of the coin flip to a fixed value of 0.1 for all the other experiments. This is done in order to reduce randomness in the execution of *CrowdMiner*, while still allowing enough exploration of rules and items.

7. RELATED WORK

Data procurement is one of the most important and challenging aspects of crowdsourcing [12]. Some recent works (e.g., [11, 13, 16, 19]) suggest the construction of database platforms where some components of the database (e.g., values, query parts) are crowdsourced. In such platforms, the choice of crowd questions by the query plan has to take into account various aspects such as the monetary cost, latency, accuracy, etc. For the same reasons, in the current work we attempt to maximize the accuracy of the output while asking a minimal number of crowd questions. The works of [4, 10] deal with deciding which user should be asked what questions, with the particular goal of minimizing uncertainty. However, the settings for crowd mining are more complicated: we do not know in advance what knowledge we are looking for, and in particular, which questions may be asked, or what the answers might be (for open questions).

To support the collection of open-world data, several platforms (e.g., Wikipedia) allow users to decide what data to contribute. Such platforms may collect an unbounded amount of valuable data, solely depending on contributor efforts. In contrast, our algorithm poses targeted questions, which help users recall information they may have not provided spontaneously. The knowledge gain maximization at each question leads, in particular, to user effort minimization.

Our motivation for turning to the crowd is similar to that of surveys. In surveys, the set of questions is usually small, and is *chosen in advance*, typically by experts (e.g., [7]). However, in an open world, it may be hard to know what to ask in advance. We deal with this difficulty by dynamically constructing questions based on collected knowledge.

This work has strong connections with *association rule learning*. As we noted, some principles of our algorithm are inspired by the Apriori algorithm [2]. A particularly relevant line of works [23, 27] considers cases when accessing the entire database is impossible, and learning must be done based on *data samples*. While they sample transactions, such information is not available in our settings at all. One could sample rules, which corresponds to asking only open questions. However, this allows much less control over the collected information. Our experiments (where the flip coin weight is 1, see Sec. 6) show that this approach performs worse than ours, and in particular leads to a low precision.

The goal in *active learning* [15], another related research field, is incrementally choosing data items that should be labeled by an expert, in a manner that maximizes the knowledge gain. Some works in this field are focused on scenarios with human experts, whose labels may be erroneous [8, 20, 26]. They address this problem by trying to identify preferred experts, or to filter the noise (error rate) in the answers. In contrast, we try to learn about the distribution of user answers, and there are no "wrong" answers. An interesting research direction would be utilizing techniques from these works for identifying, e.g., "representative" users, whose personal rules tend to reflect the population average. Giving more weight to these users may improve our algorithm's learning curve, but is non-trivial as explained in Section 8.

The well-studied multi-armed bandit [24] problem is: given a set of slot-machines, which should be played at each step to maximize reward? In Sections 5 and 6.2 we examine strategies for balancing exploration and exploitation, developed for this kind of problems.

8. CONCLUSION AND EXTENSIONS

This work studies, for the first time, mining association rules from the crowd, in common scenarios where transactions are not available. We have defined a formal model for crowd mining, and identified the differences from the classic data mining paradigm; presented the generic components of an effective crowd-mining framework; suggested an implementation for these components, including error probability estimation where the ground truth is unknown; and conducted an experimental study with the prototype system *CrowdMiner*, proving that our algorithm outperforms baseline competitor algorithms for different data benchmarks. In particular, it outperforms an algorithm which relies solely on rule sampling (via open questions). In our experiments we also show the importance of cleverly choosing closed questions, and gradually enabling larger rules.

We note that our algorithm, as presented in the paper, can be extended in a natural manner from choosing a single question to choosing the *best bulk of next K questions*, by means of dynamic programming. Such an extension may improve the latency of the algorithm, since it allows posing the K questions in parallel. Details about the required adjustments to the error estimations and the algorithm are omitted because of lack of space.

One possible optimization for our algorithm is by taking into account the *dependencies* between rules when interpreting user answers. In this manner, more knowledge may be extracted and utilized from each answer.

We have chosen the aggregation function to be the *average*, which gives all the users equal weights. For some applications, however, one may want to give more weight to users who are trusted, or have more underlying transactions (e.g., users that practice folk medicine more often). Extending our results to this case is not trivial, since when the distribution of weights is not known in advance, it is hard to predict the effect of a user answer. We leave this for future research.

Finally, our framework consists of many black-boxes. We presented one promising implementation for them, but it is interesting to study other implementations, which use prior knowledge on the data distribution, the users, etc.

Acknowledgments. This work has been partially funded by the European Research Council under the FP7, ERC grants Webdam, agreement 226513, and MoDaS, agreement 291071, and by the Israel Ministry of Science.

9. REFERENCES

[1] R. Agrawal, T. Imieliński, and A. Swami. Mining association rules between sets of items in large databases. *SIGMOD Record*, 22(2), 1993.

[2] R. Agrawal and R. Srikant. Fast algorithms for mining association rules. In *VLDB*, 1994.

[3] R. J. Bayardo Jr. Efficiently mining long patterns from databases. *SIGMOD Record*, 27(2), 1998.

[4] R. Boim, O. Greenshpan, T. Milo, S. Novgorodov, N. Polyzotis, and W. Tan. Asking the right questions in crowd data sourcing. In *ICDE*, 2012.

[5] N. Bradburn, L. Rips, and S. Shevell. Answering autobiographical questions: The impact of memory and inference on surveys. *Science*, 236(4798), 1987.

[6] T. Brijs, G. Swinnen, K. Vanhoof, and G. Wets. Using association rules for product assortment decisions: A case study. In *KDD*, 1999.

[7] J. M. Converse and S. Presser. *Survey questions: Handcrafting the standardized questionnaire.* Number 63 in Quantitative Applications in Social Sciences. Sage Publications Inc., 1986.

[8] O. Dekel and O. Shamir. Vox populi: Collecting high-quality labels from a crowd. In *COLT*, 2009.

[9] J. Demšar, B. Zupan, G. Leban, and T. Curk. Orange: From experimental machine learning to interactive data mining. *PKDD*, 2004.

[10] D. Deutch, O. Greenshpan, B. Kostenko, and T. Milo. Declarative platform for data sourcing games. In *WWW*, 2012.

[11] A. Doan, M. Franklin, D. Kossmann, and T. Kraska. Crowdsourcing applications and platforms: A data management perspective. *PVLDB*, 4(12), 2011.

[12] A. Doan, R. Ramakrishnan, and A. Y. Halevy. Crowdsourcing systems on the World-Wide Web. *Commun. ACM*, 54(4), 2011.

[13] M. Franklin, D. Kossmann, T. Kraska, S. Ramesh, and R. Xin. CrowdDB: answering queries with crowdsourcing. In *SIGMOD*, 2011.

[14] A. Genz. Numerical computation of rectangular bivariate and trivariate normal and t probabilities. *Statistics and Computing*, 14, 2004.

[15] M. Lindenbaum, S. Markovitch, and D. Rusakov. Selective sampling for nearest neighbor classifiers. *Machine Learning*, 54(2), 2004.

[16] A. Marcus, E. Wu, D. Karger, S. Madden, and R. Miller. Crowdsourced databases: Query processing with people. In *CIDR*, 2011.

[17] Amazon's Mechanical Turk. `https://www.mturk.com`.

[18] M. Newman and G. Barkema. *Monte Carlo methods in statistical physics.* Oxford University Press, 1999.

[19] A. G. Parameswaran and N. Polyzotis. Answering queries using humans, algorithms and databases. In *CIDR*, 2011.

[20] V. Sheng, F. Provost, and P. Ipeirotis. Get another label? Improving data quality and data mining using multiple, noisy labelers. In *SIGKDD*, 2008.

[21] F. M. Suchanek, G. Kasneci, and G. Weikum. Yago: A core of semantic knowledge. In *WWW*, 2007.

[22] J. Surowiecki. The wisdom of crowds: Why the many are smarter than the few and how collective wisdom shapes business. *Economies, Societies and Nations*, 2004.

[23] H. Toivonen. Sampling large databases for association rules. In *VLDB*, 1996.

[24] J. Vermorel and M. Mohri. Multi-armed bandit algorithms and empirical evaluation. *ECML*, 2005.

[25] L. von Ahn and L. Dabbish. Designing games with a purpose. *Commun. ACM*, 51(8), 2008.

[26] Y. Yan, R. Rosales, G. Fung, and J. Dy. Active learning from crowds. In *ICML*, 2011.

[27] M. Zaki, S. Parthasarathy, W. Li, and M. Ogihara. Evaluation of sampling for data mining of association rules. In *RIDE*, 1997.

Efficient Sentiment Correlation for Large-scale Demographics

Mikalai Tsytsarau
University of Trento, via Sommarive 14, Trento, Italy
tsytsarau@disi.unitn.eu

Sihem Amer-Yahia
CNRS, LIG, France
Sihem.Amer-Yahia@imag.fr

Themis Palpanas
University of Trento, via Sommarive 14, Trento, Italy
themis@disi.unitn.eu

ABSTRACT

Analyzing sentiments of demographic groups is becoming important for the Social Web, where millions of users provide opinions on a wide variety of content. While several approaches exist for mining sentiments from product reviews or micro-blogs, little attention has been devoted to aggregating and comparing extracted sentiments for different demographic groups over time, such as 'Students in Italy' or 'Teenagers in Europe'. This problem demands efficient and scalable methods for sentiment aggregation and correlation, which account for the evolution of sentiment values, sentiment bias, and other factors associated with the special characteristics of web data. We propose a scalable approach for sentiment indexing and aggregation that works on multiple time granularities and uses incrementally updateable data structures for online operation. Furthermore, we describe efficient methods for computing meaningful sentiment correlations, which exploit pruning based on demographics and use top-k correlations compression techniques. We present an extensive experimental evaluation with both synthetic and real datasets, demonstrating the effectiveness of our pruning techniques and the efficiency of our solution.

Categories and Subject Descriptors

H.2.8 [**Database Applications**]: Data mining — *correlations*

Keywords

sentiment analysis; sentiment demographics; correlation;

1. INTRODUCTION

Today, sentiment analysis has become a platform that provides valuable information on people's opinions regarding different topics, and is widely used by businesses [5] and social study institutions [17]. Sentiment extraction and aggregation has been applied in various domains, from *movie reviews* to product *reputation management*. While multiple efforts focused on developing machine learning and statistical methods for characterizing sentiment within large bodies of text or for brief opinions and tweets [11, 14], not much attention has been devoted to aggregating sentiment along users' demographics [15]. Studies along this direction have traditionally focused on an off-line analysis and aggregation of polling data for pre-determined demographic groups. However, it is difficult to organize polling on a large scale and conduct it regularly enough to analyze trends and correlations over time.

Nevertheless, the need to provide fine-grained analytics of social data is growing. Readily available users' demographics along with opinion data constitute a gold mine for extracting insights on what a particular user group thinks and how their opinion evolves over time and compares to opinions of others.

Some recent studies have already made a step along this direction. For instance, "A Demographic Analysis of Online Sentiment during Hurricane Irene" [6] revealed dynamic (temporal) sentiment differences between Southern USA and New England, and at the same time a constant (inherent) difference in the sentiments expressed by males and females, referred to as *sentiment bias*. Indeed, different demographic groups may have different points of reference when they express their sentiments for different topics. For example, while youngsters tend to prefer relatively cheap restaurants and are comfortable with a certain level of noise, pensioners generally prefer quieter and moderately priced restaurants. In addition, sentiments of demographic groups may evolve differently over time. For example, "French farmers" and "German farmers" had initially positive sentiments for the topic "organic farming", but later disagreed when the French government introduced additional taxes for organic goods superseding laws set by the European union and in disfavor of French farmers. In the above example, if the two groups have equal average sentiments for a specific topic during some time period, it will be hard to say if they really have the same attitude towards the events in that period, or if their equal sentiments are merely the result of an instantaneous convergence of otherwise diverse sentiments.

Our examples suggest the need for sophisticated methods that can compare and correlate sentiments of demographic groups over time regardless of their inherent biases. One important aspect in the design of appropriate methods is the definition of sentiment correlation as a function of aggregated sentiment over a time period. We explore Pearson's correlation using several variations of the average sentiment. Second, it is important to use efficient correlation methods, which allow online updates. Here again, we evaluate several ways of constructing a time interval of sentiment correlations and show that correlations remain meaningful and robust to noise when time intervals are assembled from smaller ones, which allows to apply efficient top-k and windowed correlation methods.

There are two computational challenges when implementing our methods: 1) finding demographic groups requires the exploration of all possible combinations of values for demographics attributes; 2) in order to find correlations between pairs of demographic groups, one potentially needs to explore all sub-intervals of the input time interval. We show that both challenges render traditional database

SIGMOD'13, June 22–27, 2013, New York, New York, USA.

approaches inefficient, and describe algorithms that exploit the *lattice structure induced by demographics attributes* in order to prune the search space. Our algorithms also make use of *hierarchical time aggregation* to achieve efficient and scalable indexing and retrieval of aggregated sentiments. The contributions of this work can be summarized as follows:

- We formalize a novel large-scale sentiment analytics problem, focusing on the efficient aggregation of sentiment and computation of high and significant sentiment correlations between maximal demographic groups within dynamically determined time intervals.
- Specific to demographics sentiments, we describe efficient correlation pruning methods based on the demographics lattice. Furthermore, we introduce two novel methods for correlation compression, which allow for the efficient implementation of our algorithms.
- We conduct an extensive set of experiments to validate our problem, and evaluate the performance of our solution. We use synthetic datasets, which contain large-scale artificial correlations with added noise, and the MovieLens real dataset, which comes with rich user demographics. The experiments demonstrate that correlated demographic groups can be identified very efficiently with the help of our specialized indexing storage and effective pruning. Finally, our evaluation provides interesting insights on correlations among real demographic groups in MovieLens.

This paper is organized as follows. Section 2 defines our framework and the problem we tackle, while Section 3 develops the properties of correlation with respect to our problem. Section 4 describes our algorithms for correlated groups and correlation compression. Our user study and performance experiments are reported in Section 5. Section 6 provides a summary of the related work. We conclude in Section 7.

2. FORMALISM

We are given a database $\mathscr{X}$ of records $x = (u,t,s,p)$ where $u \in \mathscr{U}$ denotes a user expressing sentiment $s \in$ [-1,1] on a topic $t \in \mathscr{T}$ in a time period p characterized with a start and end timestamps.

In our definitions we assume that sentiments are extracted for a given topic. For example, the record $x_1 = (u_1, Politics, 0.8, p_1)$ means that user u_1 expressed a positive sentiment (i.e., +0.8) for "Politics" during time period p_1. Such information can be extracted from the tweets of user u_1 during that time period. The record $x_2 = (u_2, Drama, \text{-}0.5, p_2)$ expresses a negative sentiment for "Drama" movies by user u_2 during time period p_2. This information can be computed from movie rating datasets such as MovieLens.

2.1 Definitions

We assume that each user $u \in \mathscr{U}$ is associated with a collection of values for a set of demographics attributes $\{a_i\}$. For example, *25* for attribute a_1 : `age`, *Student* for a_2 : `occupation`, and *Italy* for a_3 : `location`. Each attribute a_i is associated with a demographics hierarchy $\mathscr{D}_i$ whose nodes hierarchically partition the set of values for that attribute. Correspondingly, each demographics hierarchy node contains all users from $\mathscr{U}$ whose attribute values are covered by that node. The top left part of Figure 1 shows an example demographics hierarchy associated with attribute `location`. The top node covers users from all available geographic locations (corresponding to $\mathscr{U}$), and the descendant nodes partition those users into non-intersecting subsets according to their geographic locations.

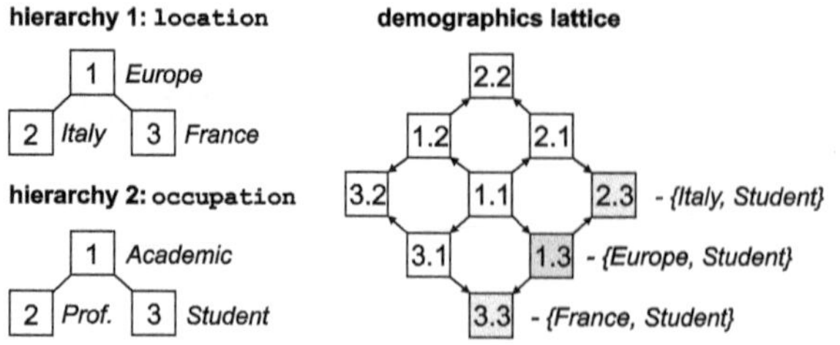

Figure 1: Two demographics hierarchies forming a lattice.

Definition 1. (Demographics Criteria) $\boldsymbol{d} = \{a_1 = d_1, \cdots, a_k = d_k\}$ is a set of predicates over demographics attributes a_i, where each predicate requires attribute's values to be contained in a node from a demographics hierarchy.

For example, $\boldsymbol{d} = \{\texttt{age} : Young, \texttt{location} : Italy, \texttt{occupation} : Student\}$ refers to a combination of predicates on user attributes `age`, `location` and `occupation`. To simplify our notation, we will use $\boldsymbol{d} = \{Young, Italy, Student\}$ to refer to the same set of predicates. Values in demographics criteria correspond to hierarchy nodes and are therefore a fixed set, which can be enumerated. We note that user attributes with continuous values (for example, `age`) can be transformed to categorical values in order to induce a hierarchy.

Definition 2. (Demographics Generality) Demographics criteria $\boldsymbol{d}$ is more (less) general than $\boldsymbol{d}'$ if: $\forall\,(d_i, d'_i) : \quad d'_i \in d_i \quad (d_i \in d'_i)$. We denote these relationships as $\boldsymbol{d} \prec \boldsymbol{d}' \quad (\boldsymbol{d} \succ \boldsymbol{d}')$.

All demographics criteria and their generality relationships form a *demographics lattice L*, with a size equal to the product of the hierarchies' sizes. We show an example of such a lattice in the right part of Figure 1, where a nine-element demographics lattice is formed by all node combinations of two hierarchies, each containing three nodes (shown left). The links that go from one lattice node to another indicate generality relations. For example, such criteria as $\{Italy, Student\}$ and $\{France, Student\}$ are less general than $\{Europe, Student\}$, which is itself less general than $\{Europe, Academic\}$.

Definition 3. (Demographic Group) $\mathscr{U}^{\boldsymbol{d}}$, defined by demographics criteria $\boldsymbol{d}$, is a set of users $u \in \mathscr{U}$, who satisfy predicates in $\boldsymbol{d}$.

An example of demographic group is European students defined by the demographics criteria $\{Europe, Student\}$, shown in Figure 1, right. In this paper, we only consider groups of users, that can be defined using demographics criteria and use demographics criteria to denote demographic groups in all our equations.

Definition 4. (Group Sentiment) Given a demographics criteria $\boldsymbol{d}$, a topic t and a time period p, we define the group sentiment of $\mathscr{U}^{\boldsymbol{d}}$ as an aggregation of sentiments s_x over records $x = (u_x, t_x, s_x, p_x)$ where $u_x \in \mathscr{U}^{\boldsymbol{d}}$, $t_x = t$, s_x is the sentiment of u_x for t, and $p_x \in p$: $s(\boldsymbol{d}, p) = \frac{1}{|x|} \sum s_x \mid \{u_x \in \mathscr{U}^{\boldsymbol{d}}, p_x \in p\}$.

In the rest of the paper, we assume that sentiments are aggregated and analyzed with respect to the same topic t, and therefore we omit t where applicable.

The main scope of this paper is to analyze time-behavior of sentiment. Therefore, we need to consider a time series of sentiments, aggregated using fixed intervals to allow meaningful comparisons of individual points within, as well as across time series.

Definition 5. (Sentiment Time Series) is a sequence of values s_i computed by aggregating sentiments on a time interval p, using fixed sub-intervals p_i of the same length: $s_i = s(\boldsymbol{d}, p_i)$.

Our further analysis of sentiment dynamics is centered on sentiment time series for a given group, topic and time period. Before going into details about the right time granularity and a sentiment correlation function $\rho()$, we consider the relations between demographic groups, and discuss how they affect the formulation of our problem.

Definition 6. (Maximal Demographic Group) Given a sentiment time series similarity function $\rho()$, a threshold θ and a time period p, we call a demographic group $\mathcal{U}^{\boldsymbol{d}}$ maximal, if and only if: $\nexists\, \boldsymbol{d}' \prec \boldsymbol{d}$, *s.t.* $\rho(\boldsymbol{d}, \boldsymbol{d}', p) > \theta$.

Intuitively, the above definition says that a demographic group is maximal if there is no other, more general group, that for the time period of interest shares the same sentiment behavior with the given demographic group. We define maximal demographic groups with respect to their sentiment time series similarity, by analogy to the definition of maximal itemsets in frequent itemset mining.

Demographics relations may also be of a partial-overlap type, e.g., between {*Europe, Students*} and {*Italy, Academic*} (where *Europe* is a superset of *Italy*). However, we can argue that while for negative correlations all relationships between groups can be interesting, for positive correlations, generality and partial-overlap relations represent trivial cases of sentiment dependency. Sentiment correlations in this case can be caused by aggregating the same sentiments from the overlap for both groups. Therefore, we need to consider a disjoint type of relation.

Definition 7. (Demographics Disjointness) between two demographic criteria $\boldsymbol{d}$ and $\boldsymbol{d}'$ is strictly opposite to demographics generality: $\exists(d_i, d_i') : d_i \cap d_i' = \emptyset$. We denote these relationships as $\boldsymbol{d} \not\perp \boldsymbol{d}'$.

In other words, disjointness on any of the attributes makes the entire criteria also disjoint. Based on the above observations, for the rest of this paper we limit the scope of possible relations to those between non-overlapping groups and fully-overlapping groups only.

2.2 Problem Definition

In this paper we are interested in finding strong and significant positive and negative correlations among the sentiments time series of demographic groups. For the sake of simplicity, we will only work with positive thresholds, specifying the sign of the correlation if needed.

Problem Statement. (Correlated Sentiment) Given a period of time p and correlation ρ_{min}, find pairs of maximal disjoint demographic groups $\{\boldsymbol{d}, \boldsymbol{d}'\}$ and the longest time interval $p' \in p$ where their sentiments correlate: $|\rho(\boldsymbol{d}, \boldsymbol{d}', p')| > \rho_{min}$.

Note that we can further restrict the answer set to only contain demographic groups whose correlation is statistically significant. That is, we require that $|\rho(\boldsymbol{d}, \boldsymbol{d}', p')| > \rho_{min}$ at a significance level r_{min}. We discuss this issue in more detail in the following sections.

A proper solution to the above-formulated problem will allow identifying sentiment behavior at a much finer level of detail than currently possible, finding cases that are counter-intuitive and can only be observed by processing huge amounts of data. We further discuss some interesting examples of such findings in Section 5, where we report the results of applying the proposed approach to the analysis of movie opinions.

3. SENTIMENT CORRELATION

Similarity of sentiments between two demographic groups is measured using a correlation coefficient of their sentiment time series.

Definition 8. (Sentiment Correlation) Correlation ρ of two time series s and s' of length n (with averages $\bar{s}$ and $\bar{s}'$) is defined as the normalized inner product $(s \circ s')_1^n$ of local deviations from averages:

$$\rho = \frac{(s \circ s')_1^n}{n\sigma_s\sigma_{s'}} = \frac{\sum_{i=1}^{n}(s_i - \bar{s}) \cdot (s_i' - \bar{s}')}{\sqrt{\sum_{i=1}^{n}(s_i - \bar{s})^2 \cdot \sum_{i=1}^{n}(s_i' - \bar{s}')^2}}$$

Indices $_1^n$ in the inner product denote that it is computed using data points from 1 to n. Correlation ρ takes values in the interval [-1, 1], where a positive (resp., negative) sign indicates that sentiments are changing in the same (resp., opposite) way and the absolute value measures the strength of the correlation.

Sentiment average can be computed in different ways in order to reflect different dependencies between time series. In addition, the period of time during which correlation is computed may vary depending on on whether the whole period is considered at once or if it is processed into sub-intervals. In the next two sub-sections we discuss different sentiment average computation and interval processing. We use the examples in Figure 2.

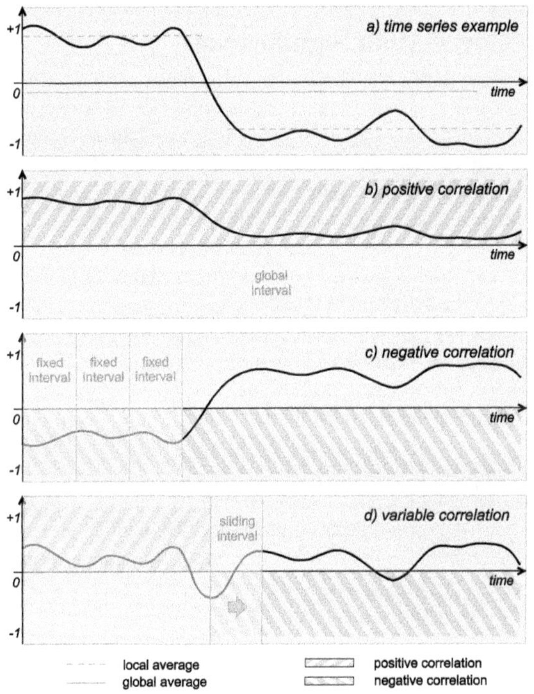

Figure 2: Examples of different correlation types.

3.1 Sentiment Averages

Global Average: This correlation detects co-variation of sentiments regardless of their sentiment bias. In Figure 2, a strong positive correlation between a and b is detected even though time series b is entirely positive.

Zero Average: When an average is substituted with a zero value, the correlation formula detects *polarity correlation* (e.g., between a and c in Figure 2). Polarity correlation indicates a much stricter dependency between sentiments: not only their local deviations, but also their signs (polarity) should be synchronized. As an additional benefit, it is easier to compute, as it does not need to compute average values of sentiments.

Local Average: If we compute correlation with local average (shown as dashed grey lines in time series a), we are able to detect correlation between local deviations. For example, the time series d has the same deviations of sentiment as the series a during the first period, and inverse deviations during the second period. These periods can be detected by computing correlation using sliding windows with the running average.

3.2 Time Intervals

Global Interval: We compute a single correlation value for the entire input time interval.

Fixed Interval: The input time interval is divided into fixed-length sub-intervals within which correlations are computed.

Sliding Interval: The input time interval is divided into variable-length sub-intervals in a way that maximizes correlations. This goal can be achieved by optimizing sizes of correlation intervals, or by using a greedy algorithm that identifies intervals on-the-fly.

We observe, that for very long time intervals, global average sentiment is likely to be close to zero, so global average and zero average effectively become the same. The same is true for local average, which becomes closer to the global one with increased interval sizes. We will use the above variations of the sentiment correlation in our algorithms, which we describe in the following sections.

3.3 Correlation Significance

When computing the correlation value between two time series, we also need a measure that expresses how confident we are that this value accurately captures reality (e.g., we can be more confident that the correlation value between two particular time series is true when these time series are long than when they are comprised of just a few data points). This measure is the correlation significance. Given the correlation coefficient ρ, computed from n samples, we consider two *Null Hypotheses* about the correlation, which have the following test statistics:

Hypothesis H1 ($\rho = 0$): the value $z = \rho\sqrt{(n-2)/(1-\rho^2)}$ is distributed as the *t-distribution* with $(n-2)$ degrees of freedom.

Hypothesis H2 ($\rho < \rho_{min}$): the value $z = (Z(\rho) - Z(\rho_{min}))\sqrt{n-3}$ is distributed as the *standard normal*, where $Z(\rho) = artanh(\rho)$.

Definition 9. (Correlation Significance) r is defined as the probability at which the considered null hypothesis is supported. For large n, the (one-tailed) significance of H1 and H2 is computed using the cumulative distribution function of the standard normal:

$$r = 1 - \Phi(z) = 1 - \frac{1}{\sqrt{2\pi}}\int_{-\infty}^{z} e^{-\frac{x^2}{2}}dx$$

While the first hypothesis is intended to verify if there exists any correlation between the two time series, the second hypothesis tests if they are correlated at least as high as ρ_{min}. For example, if $\rho = 0.9$, $\rho_{min} = 0.7$ and $n = 10$, we have that $r_{H1} \approx 0.0002$ and $r_{H2} \approx 0.06$. Relying on the significance threshold $r_{min} = 0.05$, H1 can be rejected as improbable, meaning that the two time series are indeed correlated. On the contrary, H2 cannot be rejected, signifying that ρ can be smaller than 0.7 and thus it is subject for pruning.

4. METHOD AND ALGORITHMS

In this section, we present our methods for storing sentiment time series for demographic groups and efficiently extracting correlations. We begin with the outline of our sentiment storage, followed by a description of our algorithms. Finally, we present smart pruning and compression techniques which take a full advantage of our storage and allow efficient problem solving.

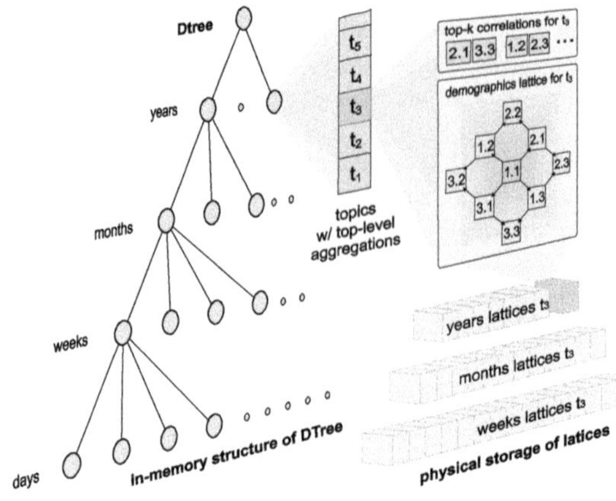

Figure 3: The DTree, a time-indexed sequential storage of aggregated demographics sentiments over multiple topics.

4.1 Data Storage and Management

Our problem requires ad-hoc navigation of time series at different aggregation granularities, and fast access to sentiments for demographic groups. Therefore, it makes sense to organize the data storage around a time-indexed and aggregating structure named *Demographics Tree (DTree)*, which at its nodes provides access to aggregated sentiment values via the demographics lattice. We demonstrate this structure in Figure 3 and describe below.

DTree is a hierarchically organized balanced tree, where each level in the hierarchy stores information relevant to years, month, weeks, and days. Each node in the tree corresponds to one of these intervals, and is connected to the parent and children nodes in the hierarchy, as well as to the adjacent nodes at the same level. Each DTree node stores statistical aggregations of sentiments for different topics for the specific time interval: *(count, sum, sum of squares)*$_t$, where topic $t \in \mathcal{T}$. These aggregations allow us to reconstruct sentiment mean, variance, volume and their derivatives, and they are also incrementally maintainable, allowing the easy update of the DTree as new data come in. In addition, DTree nodes store top-k correlations for the particular time interval and topic, in order to facilitate query answering. We provide more details on the construction of top-k correlations in Section 4.3. DTree nodes maintain physical aggregations only for the top-level demographic groups for each topic (e.g., only for group (1.1) in Figure 3). Detailed aggregations for all individual groups are accessible by following a pointer to a separate structure, the sequential file storage for lattices. This pointer indicates an offset in the file that contains the demographics lattice snapshot with the aggregations for all demographic groups for the particular topic and time interval. By traversing this sequential file storage structure, we can simultaneously reconstruct the sentiment time series for all demographic groups for a particular topic and time aggregation level.

Thanks to this layout, a time index with high-level aggregates and pointers remains compact and can be kept in main memory (Figure 3, left), while sentiment time series can be organized as a collection of individual files (Figure 3, right). The additional benefit of this organization is that it ensures fast sequential access for time series of sentiments, compared to relational databases [16].

We note that the number of sentiment values monotonically decreases as we navigate down the demographics lattice and down the DTree levels, so many of the demographics leaf nodes will contain zeroes at lower time granularities. This allows storing sentiment values in a more compact way, by storing only non-zero values (e.g., using run-length encoding methods [19]).

4.2 Overview of Algorithms

Our algorithm for extracting significant correlations is based on the DTree storage and is listed in Algorithm 1. Due to lack of space, we present our algorithm for the sliding time interval and conventional correlation formula (see Section 3). The other approaches, using fixed or global intervals, can be reduced from it by considering subsequent time intervals of constant sizes (fixed), or the entire time series (global).

The process of mining sentiment time series is performed in a top-down fashion, going from higher to lower granularities in a DTree and from root to leaf nodes in a demographics lattice. Our approach achieves hierarchical correlation management and pruning through remembering for every pair of groups which of the identified time intervals to `refine` or `exclude` at the next granularity level. Lines 13 and 16 of the algorithm only show the invocation of these functions, assuming that the corresponding time interval pruning takes an immediate effect on the next iteration.

In the second loop, we sequentially access the time series, while computing correlations between demographic groups in the third loop, where candidates are evaluated going from higher order nodes to their children. If a high correlation is detected for some candidate groups (line 12), then their positively correlated children are excluded, meaning that the corresponding lattice branches are not revisited in subsequent iterations of the loop. This pruning asserts the maximality of identified correlations and also reduces the candidate set.

The described algorithm employs the sliding interval approach, where correlation interval boundaries are determined in a greedy fashion: by comparing correlation coefficients between a forward (sliding) interval w_{next} of a fixed size, and an interval that runs from the previous boundary w_{prev}. We note, that while the sliding time interval w_{next} is updated for all demographics pairs as we scan the time series, the correlation time intervals w_{prev} are computed and maintained for each demographics pair individually, and their starting boundaries do not necessarily coincide (however, all their ending boundaries border with w_{next} while it slides). When global or fixed time interval approaches are used, it is possible to prune candidate demographic groups on-the-fly according to their estimated value of correlation, so that less and less computations are needed as we advance along the time series.

Finally, for all detected pairs of groups and correlation intervals, the algorithm can start the greedy generalization step, described in Algorithm 2. It iteratively supersedes groups with their maximal parents until they are disjoint and highly correlated.

Computing and storing correlation coefficients for all combinations of demographics nodes is only possible for small lattices, since it requires a quadratic space on the size of a lattice. But since we are interested in finding only high and significant correlations, it is possible to compute and store only such values, while still being able to answer queries with a good precision. In the following sections, we describe how correlation pruning and compression enable efficient implementation of our method.

Algorithm 1: Sliding algorithm for discovering sentiment correlations. Employs pruning using correlation estimates based on Lemma 1 and significance threshold based on Lemma 2.

```
Input : Time interval p, significance r_min, correlation ρ_min, lattice L,
        sliding interval size m
Output: demographic groups and correlation intervals
1  for granularity = max ... 1 do
2    for p_i = {p_1 ... p_n} ∈ p do
3      w_next = w_next + p_i − p_{i−m}; //push next, pop last
4      //w_prev are individual for each candidate
5      //candidates are ordered by height(d,d') top-down
6      for (d,d') ∈ L × L | d⊓̸d' do
7        w_prev = w_prev + p_{i−m}; //update previous interval
8        ρ_prev = correlation(d,d',w_prev);
9        ρ_next = correlation(d,d',w_next);
10       if |ρ_prev − ρ_next| > ρ_min then
11         //correlation interval is detected
12         if r(ρ_prev < ρ_min) < r_min then
13           refine (d,d',w_prev,granularity - 1);
14           //exclude all correlated children groups
15           for (d_1 ∈ d, d_2 ∈ d', ρ > ρ_min) do
16           exclude (d_1,d_2,w_prev,granularity);
17         end
18         w_prev = ∅;
19       end
20       //prune for the next granularity using Lemma 1
21       w_BW = p_{i−2..i};    ρ_BW(d,d',w_BW) = Lemma1(n);
22       if r(ρ_BW > ρ_min) < r_min then
23         exclude (d,d',w_BW,granularity - 1);
24       end
25     end
26   end
27 end
```

Algorithm 2: Group generalization algorithm

```
Input : Correlation ρ, time interval p, demographic groups d,d',
        maximality threshold θ
Output: Maximal demographic groups
//start from initial demographic groups complying to criteria
while d⊓̸d' & correlation(d,d',p) ≥ ρ do
  d = arg max {correlation(d,parent(d),p) > θ};
  d' = arg max {correlation(d',parent(d'),p) > θ};
end
return the last (d,d') complying to criteria;
```

4.3 Computing Correlations

In this section we describe an efficient way for computing correlations: first, by discarding insignificant results, and, second, by discarding correlations of children groups according to the maximality principle given in Definition 6. Furthermore, we propose efficient methods of storing precomputed correlation values for fixed time intervals. We note that the proposed hierarchical pruning and correlation compression methods are applied on top of correlation values, and can be used in combination with various correlation algorithms. Some existing correlation methods [21, 7] can also be applied to our case, but are otherwise orthogonal to the pruning and compression methods discussed in this paper.

4.3.1 *Pruning Correlations*

To find a pair of demographic groups with correlated sentiment, we have to evaluate all pairs of nodes in demographics lattice. However, we observe that correlation holds certain regularity properties on a demographics lattice and on time granularities, which are useful for pruning. We can apply pruning based on correlation estimates from the higher-granularity data (*vertical pruning*), and based on the observed part of the time series (*horizontal pruning*), as described below.

Vertical Pruning:

Given the DTree, we would like to be able to estimate correlations for a smaller time granularity based on the averages computed for a higher time granularity. This is possible using the Spruill and Gastwirth correlation estimation method [13], which relies on the Bartlett and Wald regression estimator.

LEMMA 1. *The estimate ρ_{BW} of correlation and its asymptotic standard deviation are computed using the following formula:*

$$\rho_{BW}(\boldsymbol{d},\boldsymbol{d}',p) = \frac{s'_{U3}-s'_{L3}}{s_{U3}-s_{L3}} \cdot \frac{\sigma(\boldsymbol{d},p)}{\sigma(\boldsymbol{d}',p)}, \quad \sigma(\rho_{BW}) = c\frac{1-\rho^2}{\sqrt{N}}$$

In the above equations, s_{U3} (s_{L3}) and s'_{U3} (s'_{L3}) are the averages of intermediate aggregates $s(\boldsymbol{d},p_i)$ and $s(\boldsymbol{d}',p_i)$ computed for $i \geq 2n/3$ ($i \leq n/3$), where n is the number of intermediate aggregates. The factor c is linearly depending on ρ and n and is estimated using the tabulation data given in [13]. We note that all standard deviations and intermediate aggregates used in this formula are directly accessible in the DTree at every granularity level.

Horizontal pruning:

If both the correlation threshold ρ_{min} and the time interval p of size n are known, then for every subinterval $p_1 \dots p_k$, $k < n$, with the corresponding inner product $(s \circ s')_1^k$, we can compute the upper bound of the correlation coefficient over p. We can then use this estimate to prune small correlations as more and more points of p are observed.

LEMMA 2. *If δ_s and $\delta_{s'}$ are the maximum sentiment deviations and the inner product of sentiment deviations $(s \circ s')_1^k$ at point k is less than $(n\rho_{min}\sigma_s\sigma_{s'} - (n\text{-}k)\delta_s\delta_{s'})$, then $\rho(s,s') < \rho_{min}$.*

PROOF.

$$\rho(s,s') = \frac{(s \circ s')_1^k + (s \circ s')_{k+1}^n}{n\sigma_s\sigma_{s'}} < \frac{(s \circ s')_1^k + (n\text{-}k)\delta_s\delta_{s'}}{n\sigma_s\sigma_{s'}} < \frac{n\rho_{min}\sigma_s\sigma_{s'}}{n\sigma_s\sigma_{s'}} = \rho_{min}$$

We note that estimating maximum deviations is only possible for bounded time series. This is true in our case, where sentiments are distributed between [-1,1]. Thus, we can set $\delta_s = |\bar{s}| + 1$, which occurs when a sentiment is the most distant from the mean value (deviating in the opposite direction).

As in the case of vertical pruning, the standard deviations and mean values of time series, used in the above estimation, are stored at a higher granularity level in the DTree and thus directly available.

4.3.2 Compressing Correlations

Although the pruning techniques help to efficiently compute top-k correlations, the number of these correlations can sometimes grow very large. There exists a tradeoff between the precision and recall of storing top-k correlations, which is defined by size k. Improving both characteristics is only possible for larger top-k sizes. In contrast, performance and scalability requirements demand top-k size to be small. This problem can be addressed by compressing top-k correlations, as described below.

We propose two algorithms of top-k compression: a greedy algorithm of triangulation correlation compression, TCC, and clustering correlation compression, CCC, based on density clustering. Nevertheless, other existing methods of clustering and graph compression can be adapted to compress top-k correlations.

Triangulation correlation compression TCC

Given correlation coefficients between two demographics nodes and a third one, we can estimate upper and lower limits for the correlation between them. Based on the correspondence between correlation coefficients and angles of vectors, representing local deviations of time series to their mean, we can apply the triangular inequality, which gives us the following lemma:

LEMMA 3. *If $\rho(\boldsymbol{d},\boldsymbol{d}') = \rho_1$, $\rho(\boldsymbol{d},\boldsymbol{d}'') = \rho_2$ and $\rho(\boldsymbol{d}',\boldsymbol{d}'') = \rho$ then*

$$\rho_1\rho_2 - \sqrt{(1-\rho_1^2)(1-\rho_2^2)} \leq \rho \leq \rho_1\rho_2 + \sqrt{(1-\rho_1^2)(1-\rho_2^2)}.$$

The detailed proof can be found in [3]. From the above inequality it follows that the transitivity of a positive and a negative correlation holds only if $\rho_1^2 + \rho_2^2 > 1$. This property requires absolute correlation values between two time series to be above 0.7 in order for the inequality to have any valuable prediction power. We note that this property is naturally achievable between nodes in a demographics lattice thanks to regularity and monotonicity of aggregated data. Therefore, Lemma 3 suits to our needs to compactly store correlations and recover missing values.

The simple greedy compression algorithm is listed in Algorithm 3. It removes elements from the top-k, which can be approximated using the triangulation principle. The compression process starts with a sorted list of correlations, which size is larger than k. Correlations are removed from the list one by one, being replaced with the next candidate in the list ($k+1$) until the removal of any correlation introduces an error, larger than the one gained by adding a candidate. TCC algorithm can be further optimized by removing several correlations at once, until their approximations do not depend on each other. Such an optimization leads to a considerable performance benefit, since the approximation errors are not recomputed at every modification of a top-k list. However, the algorithm may become less optimal in this case. For the lack of space, we evaluate only the basic version of TCC, leaving possible extensions of this method for a future work.

Algorithm 3: Triangulation correlation compression TCC. Removes correlations which can be approximated using Lemma 3.

```
Input : demographics lattice L, number k
Output: Top-k correlations
for (d,d') ∈ L × L do
  | add ρ(d,d') to topk;
end
sort topk descending by ρ;
while find (d,d',d'') ∈ topk s.t.
    err = min|ρ(d,d') - Lemma3(d,d',d'')| do
  | if err < |topk[k+1]| then
  |   | remove ρ(d,d') from topk;
  |   | add topk[k+1] to topk;
  |   | keep ρ(d,d'') and ρ(d',d'') in the topk;
  | else trim topk to the size k; break ;
end
```

Clustering correlation compression CCC

Correlation coefficient between time series of sentiment can be transformed to Euclidean Distance [21]. Relying on this distance metric, we can identify groups of time series, which are highly-correlated on the same fixed time interval. We propose to apply unsupervised clustering to find such groups and to compactly store only their average and pairwise correlations. Since the space needed to allocate pairwise correlations is quadratic on the number of lattice nodes, replacing the correlations of individual nodes with those of their clusters can yield a significant compression ratio.

Because of the transitivity property of high correlations (according to Lemma 3), any set of highly correlated nodes is going to be densely packed in the Euclidean space, with a good cluster separation. Therefore, we find density-based algorithms of clustering more suitable, as their complexity in our case becomes asymptotically proportional to the number of elements in a cluster. Our clustering method uses the density-based algorithm DBSCAN [4], although any other distance-based algorithm can be used as well.

The compression process, described in Algorithm 4, starts with grouping lattice nodes into clusters based on their pairwise correlations. Clustering is performed using the absolute correlation

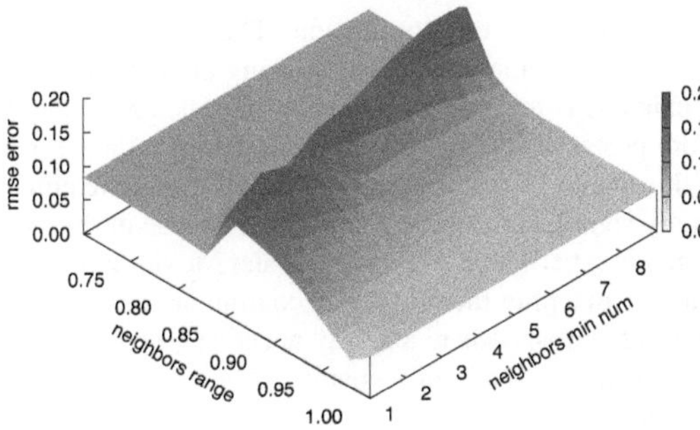

Figure 4: DBSCAN parameters space and optimization.

values, and the sign of each node's correlation with respect to its cluster is stored and later recovered. Unlike in euclidean spaces, where a cluster has a mean value or a centroid, in the correlation space there are only distances between nodes available. Therefore, we replace individual correlations between nodes with average correlations between their clusters: for different clusters the average is computed from pairwise correlations between their nodes, and for nodes in the same cluster the average is computed across all pairwise correlations within that cluster. Finally, correlations between outlier nodes and clusters or between outlier nodes are added to the output list which is trimmed to fit the top-k size.

Algorithm 4: Clustering correlation compression CCC. Replaces correlations with cluster averages.

Input : demographics lattice L, number k
Output: Top-k correlations

```
clusters = DBSCAN(L × L);
for i = 0; i < |clusters|; i++ do
    for j = i; j < |clusters|; j++ do
        ρ(i, j) = 0; //add cluster-cluster correlations
        for (d,d') ∈ clusters[i] × clusters[j] do
            ρ(i, j) += ρ(d,d');
        end
        ρ(i, j) = ρ(i, j)/|clusters[i] × clusters[j]|;
        add ρ(i, j) to topk;
    end
    for d ∉ clusters do
        ρ(i,d) = 0; //add outlier-cluster correlations
        for d' ∈ clusters[i] do
            ρ(i,d) += ρ(d,d');
        end
        ρ(i,d) = ρ(i,d)/|clusters[i]|;
        add ρ(i,d) to topk;
    end
end
for (d,d') ∈ L × L, d,d' ∉ clusters do
    add ρ(d,d') to topk; //add outlier-outlier correlations
end
while |topk| > k do
    remove the lowest;
end
```

To achieve a good clustering, the density parameter should be set to a correct value, which is not known a-priori. As a minimum density parameter, DBSCAN uses a combination of neighbors range (which we substitute for minimal correlation) and their minimum number. We note that a lower minimum correlation corresponds to a broader neighbors range, unlike in original DBSCAN implementation. Figure 4 demonstrates an example of our parameters space and their corresponding compression errors for a fixed top-k size. We observe that for a broader range (Figure 4, left valley), DBSCAN tends to aggregate all nodes into one cluster. The error in this case remains constant, since we approximate all correlations with a single value. When we increase the density parameter, the clustering error tends to grow due to outliers and since there are still not many clusters. Finally, for the optimum parameters, all the highly correlated nodes are clustered together and all the smaller correlations are represented by cluster distances, significantly reducing the compression error (Figure 4, right valley). Since it is not known which of the valleys contains the global optimum, we propose to broadly scan the space of possible DBSCAN parameters and then refine the optimum value using the gradient descent method. Nevertheless, DBSCAN is a one-pass method that relies on a precomputed distances index, and multiple clusterings used for optimization do not result in a significant performance degradation.

We note that top-k list can hold correlations not only between nodes, but also between clusters and between nodes and clusters. Depending on their presence in the top-k list and attribution to clusters, we retrieve correlation values in the way, described in Algorithm 5. It is also possible to apply a triangulation compression for clustering distances, creating a hybrid method that takes advantage of both TCC and CCC.

Algorithm 5: Top-k correlation retrieving method

Input: demographics pair $(d,d') \in L \times L$

```
//Determine a cluster id for each node (if clustered).
if clustered then d = cluster(d);   d' = cluster(d');
//If the value for a pair of ids is present, return it.
if topk(d,d') ≠ null then return topk(d,d');
//If the value is not present, estimate using Lemma 3.
ρ_low = −1;   ρ_high = +1;
for all (d,d',d'') do
    (ρ'_low, ρ'_high) = Lemma3(d,d',d'');
    if ρ_low < ρ'_low then ρ_low = ρ'_low;
    if ρ_high > ρ'_high then ρ_high = ρ'_high;
end
return (ρ_low + ρ_high)/2;
```

5. EXPERIMENTS

We ran experiments using both synthetic and real data. We first experiment with the synthetic data to evaluate the efficiency and performance of our algorithms, following it with the qualitative evaluation of correlations detected on a real dataset.

We implemented our algorithms in Java, and ran the experiments using Java JRE 1.7.0 on a machine with dual core 2.53 GHz CPU and 1.5 Gb of main memory.

5.1 Datasets

Synthetic Dataset

In order to accurately measure the precision of our system in identifying sentiment correlations, we conduct a series of experiments on synthetic data, containing time series of sentiments with artificially added positive and negative correlations, level biases and sentiment noise as demonstrated in Figure 5. We describe the layout of our dataset below.

Hierarchies. As a preliminary step, we generated a set of demographics hierarchies, for such attributes as age, gender, occupation, and location, containing 8, 3, 4 and 65 nodes respectively. Each node in every hierarchy was randomly assigned with a weight and a bias probability. Weights of nodes are distributed according to a *Zipf's* distribution, and normalized to add up to 1 at every level of a

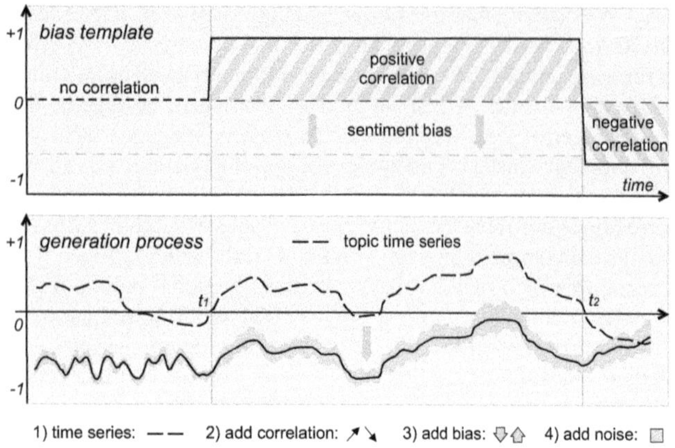

Figure 5: Generating biased sentiment time series.

hierarchy. Nodes from different hierarchies, when combined, form a lattice of 6240 demographic groups as shown in Figure 1. The sentiment volume of each demographic group was taken as a multiplication of weights of attribute nodes, and its bias as a weighted sum of their individual biases. That way, we achieve natural regularity in the demographics lattice, providing a natural distribution of sentiments, which is necessary for a proper evaluation of extracting maximal groups and pruning.

Topic Sentiment. The dataset itself contains time series of sentiments generated independently for multiple topics over a time span of 8 years. Each topic is represented by a unique *topic time series*, produced using a *random walk* method, which aggregates *uniformly* distributed sentiments, whose timestamps follow *Poisson* distribution. We vary the parameter of rate for timestamps to produce faster or slower changing time series for each topic. Since sentiments for the topic time series are sampled uniformly, its mean value is close to zero in a long run, meaning that it crosses the zero line a few times (for example, at points t_1 and t_2 in Figure 5). The original topic time series is stored for a randomly chosen demographic node, and we generate time series for other lattice nodes using individual *bias templates* for each of them. Bias templates contain sentiment bias levels and intervals of correlation with the topic time series (positive, negative or zero, randomly changed at "zero sentiment" points). The goal of our evaluation is then to correctly extract these correlation intervals between topic and biased time series, generated as described below.

Biased Sentiment. We produce a biased time series in a correspondence with the template, by copying (inverting) the topic time series in the case of positive (negative) correlation, or outputting randomized data otherwise (as seen in Figure 5, bottom). Following that, we add a certain positive or negative bias to the whole time series (shifting all the values) and the uniformly-distributed noise (for each value). Finally, we scale the time series to make sure that sentiments lay within the boundaries of [-1,1]. After generating a biased time series for the node, we insert raw sentiment data into the index in a proportion corresponding to node's volume. Then, we proportionally distribute these sentiments for all node's children (Figure 1), ensuring the maximality of that node.

MovieLens Dataset

MovieLens dataset[1] consists of 1 million ratings left by 6 thousand users on 4 thousand movies. It also comes with rich demographics attributes: age, gender, occupation, and location, which we directly imported to our application. These attributes result in a lattice of over 30 thousand nodes, making almost *half a billion* possible pairwise combinations. We extracted the geographical location from postal codes, however the number of ratings for many nodes in this hierarchy was exceedingly small. Since we aim at extracting only significant results, we disabled the use of the location attribute in this experiment. We used five-star MovieLens ratings as sentiments, by mapping them to [-1,1] continuous sentiment scale, where one star corresponds to a highly negative (-1) sentiment, and five stars correspond to a highly positive (+1) sentiment, and other ratings are distributed evenly.

Since comments for movies usually appear during a period of their showtime and then fade out, we propose using genres as topics, thus providing a stream of sentiments with rather constant rate, where new movies serve a role of events, leading to sentiment changes. The dataset has 18 genres, and most of movies belong to several genres at once, with their ratings contributing equally to all of them. This results in a certain regularity of sentiments across topics and demographic groups and challenges the detection of interesting correlations.

[1] http://www.grouplens.org/node/73

5.2 Evaluation Methodology

Efficiency evaluation is conducted on a synthetic dataset constructed as described in Section 5.1. It contains 10 topics with 400 biased time series for each of the topics, excluding children copies, while the much larger fraction of time series are generated randomly. We vary the level of noise added to time series in this dataset from 0.0 to 0.4 in absolute values, resulting in the same signal-to-noise ratios as sentiments are distributed on [-1,1]. We apply the scaling of time series after the noise was added.

We measure the average accuracy, precision and recall over all topics and all bias templates by measuring the correctness of correlation values over the extracted time intervals. For each of the time series, the extracted correlations are mapped to the binary scale [-1, 0, 1] according to a 0.5 threshold, and compared to binary values stored in the corresponding template.

We report additional measurements, such as precision and recall, to break down the observed performance for a more detailed analysis. Precision is computed as the percentage of the length of extracted high-correlation intervals, which are found in the template as such (this is relevant for either +1 or -1 correlations). Recall is computed as the percentage of the length of high correlation intervals from the template, which were extracted as high correlations. Accuracy is computed as the precision of extracting all kinds of intervals from the template, including zero-correlation intervals. Finally, the root mean squared error (RMSE) is computed by measuring the actual differences between extracted correlation values and those stored in templates. It is computed as a square root of the average of squared errors, where the average is computed by weighting errors according to their time interval lengths.

5.3 Efficiency Evaluation

We conduct the evaluation of efficiency to demonstrate the properties of the proposed correlation extraction methods, and their usefulness when applied on noisy data. We evaluate our methods against noise for time granularities of 1 day and 10 days to demonstrate the effects that sentiment aggregation and time interval coarseness have on the accuracy of correlation. The size of fixed and sliding windows in both cases was equal to 10 samples. The observed behavior is not specific to our implementation alone. Rather, it marks the best possible performance for computing correlations using various fixed or sliding interval methods at particular levels of aggregation and noise.

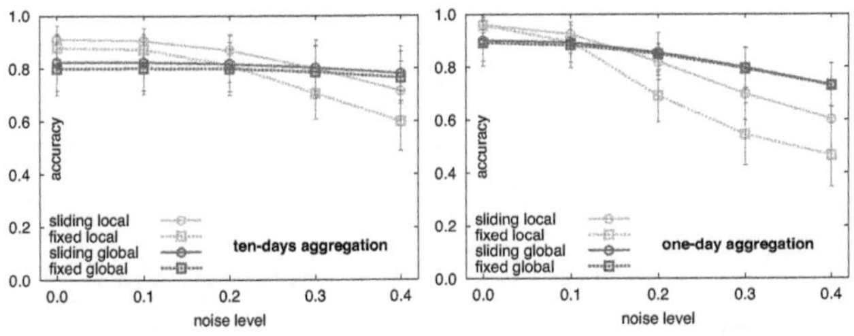

Figure 6: Accuracy of baseline correlations vs aggregation.

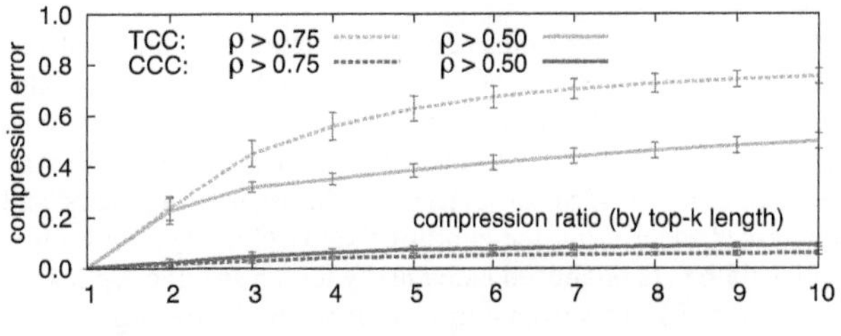

Figure 8: Compression error for top-k correlations.

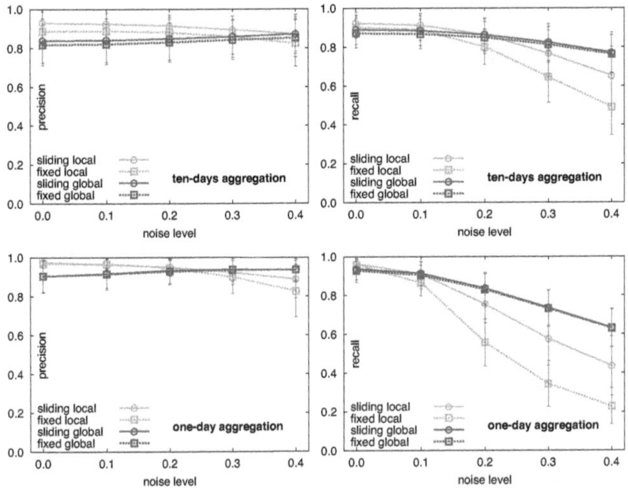

Figure 7: Precision and recall of baseline correlations.

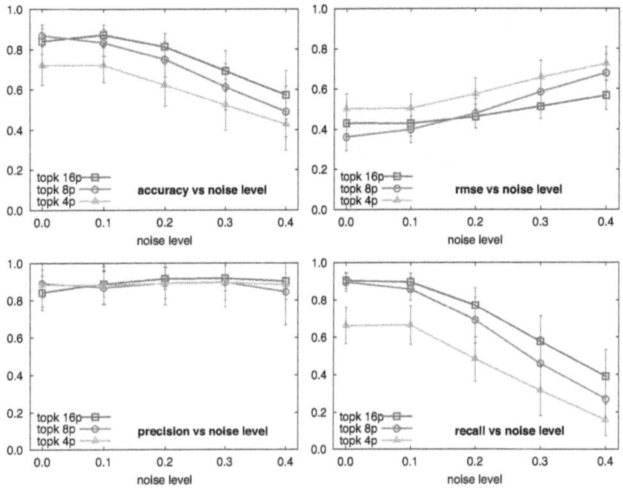

Figure 9: Accuracy of top-k correlations, 10 days aggregation.

5.3.1 Baseline Correlation Methods

The results achieved by baseline correlation methods are depicted in Figures 6 and 7, respectively. We observe that the best accuracy[2] is achieved in the case of local average methods, albeit, only at a proper aggregation granularity (in our case, ten days). Using same methods at granularities that are affected by noise results in a substantial performance drop, as can be seen in Figure 6, right. Very high levels of noise, usually present at low granularities, can lower or even reverse the actual correlation between the time series, affecting precision and recall. On the other hand, increased granularity may reduce precision because of the discretization errors when identifying correlation interval boundaries. This can be observed by comparing zero-noise accuracy values for one- and ten-days aggregations: the latter shows slightly lower accuracy solely by the coarseness of time intervals. Using global average (computed for the whole period and same for all windows) has proven to be more noise-resistant although it is not always as precise as local average, and cannot be applied in ad-hoc scenario, requiring pre-specified global time interval. From the discussion above it is evident that correlations must be analyzed using sliding or fixed windows and at varying aggregation granularities.

5.3.2 Top-K Correlation Method

We evaluate the individual performance of *TCC* and *CCC*, by measuring their average compression error and its variance while varying top-k sizes from 1 to 10 times of their initial length. To construct the top-k list, we computed correlations over disjoint pairs of demographic nodes for fixed time intervals (with local averages), taken from 17 different topics in MovieLens. Then, we filtered correlations according to the significance and minimum correlation criteria, obtaining the lists of (approximately) 12K high ($\rho > 0.50$) and 2K very high ($\rho > 0.75$) top-k correlations for an initial set of 140K disjoint pairs.

Compression error is computed as the root mean squared error (RMSE) between actual correlations and those retrieved according to Algorithm 5. We note that an optimal compression (with the smallest error) for CCC clustering method was sometimes achieved with a size, smaller than that required by the compression ratio parameter. In such cases the remaining space was filled with the highest non-clustered correlations.

In Figure 8 we present the results of our evaluation. We observe that TCC triangulation compression shows better performance when it is able to fit all the high correlations necessary for describing the rest of correlations, what happens in the case of large initial top-k list ($\rho > 0.50$). In the case when all correlations are high ($\rho > 0.75$) and there is a high compression ratio, there is a large portion of correlations which do not fit into the compressed top-k list and neither can be triangulated from the correlations present in the list. The error in this case is the highest. On the other hand, CCC clustering compression benefits from compressing higher correlations as soon as there is enough space in top-k to store an optimal number of clusters. In this case most of the high correlations appear within clusters and the amount of correlations which are not approximated by cluster-cluster distances becomes relatively small. Nevertheless, CCC can become inefficient due to the clustering information overhead if there are many distanced small clusters of 3 items. Since TCC method is able to approximate the third correlation using the remaining two, it can be a good companion in such cases. We recommend to use hybrid CCC+TCC method for compressing correlations as the most universally applicable, especially in the case of moderate compression ratios.

[2]The best achieved accuracy is not 100%, because some correlation intervals are smaller than the minimal correlation window.

We now look at the efficiency of correlation extraction of our top-k method using the same synthetic dataset, we used to evaluate the baseline methods. We calculated lists of high correlations ($\rho_{min} = 0.5$) for each of the fixed time intervals, containing 20-50K top-k values out of 15M (disjoint) and 40M (total) group pairs, and compressed them using the hybrid CCC+TCC method with clustering parameters optimized individually for the specific top-k size. We varied top-k sizes from 4 to 16 four-kilobyte disk pages (each page can hold up to 800 correlations or cluster distances). Figure 9 demonstrates that with the sufficient list of top-k correlations, computed for fixed-windows, it is possible to match the accuracy of conventional methods. A more detailed inspection shows that the drop in accuracy for smaller top-k sizes is caused mainly by a decreasing recall, due to the inability of top-k to fit all the high correlations, which our synthetic dataset is mainly composed of.

5.4 Scalability Evaluation

Performance of Indexing Sentiments

When new sentiments are being inserted into the DTree, they go through a number of levels in the tree index. First, the updates are aggregated in buckets, corresponding to the lowest time granularity. Second, the aggregated values are inserted in a single update, populating nodes of the index from top to bottom. For the DTree, updates are accumulated and inserted for each demographic group individually. Nevertheless, this method still improves the performance since disk pages are being accessed only once for each batch. During every update and at every granularity level, sentiment values are inserted into corresponding demographics lattices, for the specified group and *all of its parents*.

Demographic lattices can be stored on disk using different structures. The simplest of such structures is a *fixed array*, suitable for constant demographics lattices. It allows fast indexed access to the lattice values. The other is a *binary tree* of variable size and structure, which has reasonably fast $\log|L|$ access time and allows demographics lattices to be extended. However, this structure requires more space for storage and extra processing time.

We evaluate update performance for both structures by measuring index throughput versus main memory cache size. Smaller cache sizes require disk pages to be flushed more often, while larger cache sizes allow to have a smaller number of sequential updates. With the cache size of one page, the system becomes persistent, i.e. all changes are immediately stored on disk. Larger memory cache sizes demonstrate higher throughput, which is ultimately bounded by disk writing speed, as the processing time is sufficiently smaller than the input-output time. Another advantage of a larger cache is that in-memory updates are extremely fast if a cache has enough space. Nevertheless, the update rate drops back to nominal once the cache is full, and until it is flushed to disk, there is a risk of loosing the data in the case of memory or system fault. The results of our evaluation are presented in Figure 10. We observed that disk writes occur every time the DTree is updated up until when the cache size reaches the maximum number of parent nodes in the tree. In our experiment, the updating rate stayed constant until 4 pages. After that, when the cache is further increased, we see a linear improvement in performance, which is then asymptotically reaches the maximum value, bounded by the disk write speed. Binary tree (dynamic) storage features smaller update rate compared to the fixed array storage, since its disk pages occupy twice more space and since a binary tree is dynamically constructed.

Performance of Extracting Correlations

In Figure 11 we compare the time needed to extract correlation intervals using the same setup as in our accuracy evaluation.

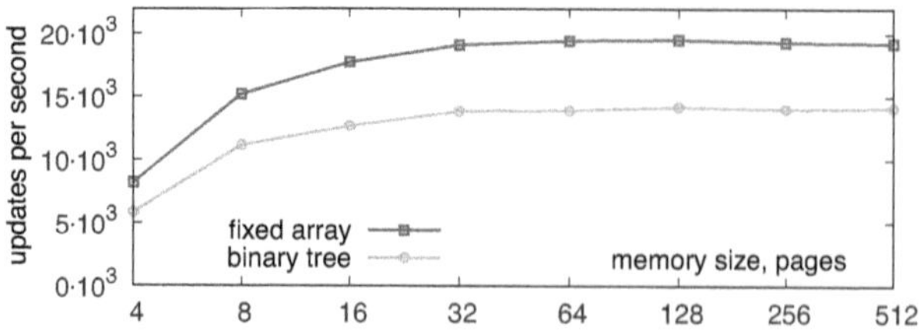

Figure 10: Performance of DTree versus memory cache size.

In the top chart, we report average times for the proposed methods using sliding and fixed time intervals (left), and the top-k technique (right). The time needed to compute correlations using sliding time intervals is approximately one third larger than the time taken by a fixed-interval method, since the prior needs to incrementally compute and compare correlations for two intervals: one is a fixed-length interval, sliding in front of the cursor, and another one is a dynamically expanding interval behind the cursor. The time of baseline methods remains fairly large since they compute correlations for a set proportional to $|L \times L|$.

In the bottom chart, we demonstrate the effect of hierarchical pruning for fixed-interval correlations and compare it to the grid-hashing correlation pruning used by StatStream [21]. We note that StatStream cannot be applied for sliding-interval correlations when sliding intervals among time series are of different lengths, as in our method. Moreover, the kind of time series approximation used in StatStream can not be used for bounded sentiments, where it results in numerous false positives at shorter interval lengths.

Both methods lead to significantly improved execution times in comparison to baseline methods, with hierarchical exhibiting better relative performance. The advantage of our method on highly correlated data is more pronounced with lower correlation thresholds, when maximality constraints allow earlier pruning. On the other hand, StatStream's performance benefits from better selectivity of higher thresholds and when time series are sparsely correlated, making it a good complementary approach.

Overall, we observe that the best performance is achieved by top-k correlations, which we report in both charts (with and without hierarchical pruning) for varying top-k sizes (16, 8 and 4 disk pages). It is evident, that top-k method is much faster even in the case of larger top-k sizes, where it matches the accuracy of direct methods. Furthermore, the top-k method demonstrates sub-linear scalability, sustaining almost the same performance even with exponentially increasing top-k sizes.

5.5 Usefulness Evaluation

To demonstrate the usefulness of our approach, we automatically identified the highest (i.e., exceeding 0.9) maximal significant correlations between disjoint demographic groups in the MovieLens dataset. We note that a naive solution to this problem will require computing and comparing almost half a billion of time series. In Figures 12-13 we represent positive and negative correlations organized using a graph-like structure. Correlations are visualized as edges between demographic groups, labeled according to topics (genres). For brevity, we visualize only a small fraction (up to 10) of high correlations identified for each topic. We note that due to this filtering, some of the correlation edges are not present in the graph. This does not necessarily mean that such correlations are below the specified threshold. Finally, we do not report correlations between some highly-overlapping (but still disjoint) demographic groups, such as between {*Under 18*} and {*K-12 student*} or {*56+*} and {*retired*}.

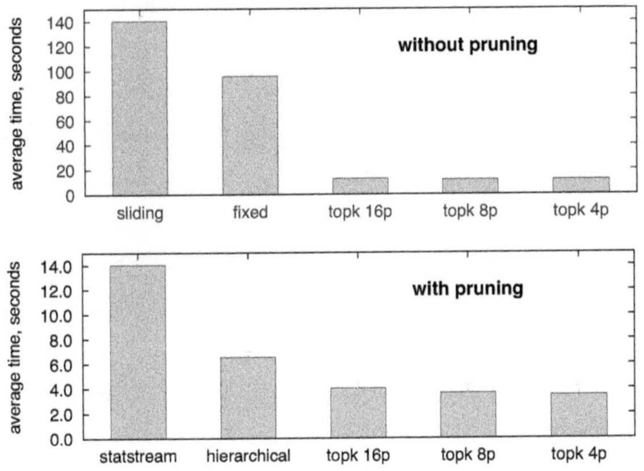

Figure 11: Comparison of correlation methods performance

We highlight nodes with the most unusual and interesting correlations, which took our particular attention, and provide their additional details in Table 1. For instance, in the top right corner of Figure 12 we observe a cluster of correlations on topic *animation* between the three very different groups: {*F, 56+*}, {*M,customer service*} and {*M,grad student*}. A more careful examination of this figure reveals that {*F, retired*} think of *thrillers* as {*M, 18-24, programmer*} - a short of a surprise, knowing that they have the same attitude to *romance* as {*M, K-12 student*}. Finally, {*academic*} and {*writer*} people have shown the most vibrant and unusual behavior in MovieLens dataset, producing many of the anti-correlations we observed in Figure 13.

Such results can be used to drive the work in a number of directions: in sociology, researchers may investigate why these unexpected correlations exist, and examine more carefully and in greater detail the interests of users; in marketing, knowledge of group sentiments, how they change over time and how they are related to other groups could help expand existing markets, by influencing similar target groups, gaining a better understanding of the fan base, and monitoring the reaction of opposing groups; in collaborative filtering, new systems may expand their range of recommendations on particular topics with results from correlated groups, resulting in an enhanced user experience.

6. RELATED WORK

The problem of identifying sentiment behavior in demographic groups has been traditionally addressed by polling. Polling requires long-term monitoring of a large sample of the population in order to allow for a meaningful comparison of sentiments among demographic groups. However, this process is rather expensive and error-prone [8, 6]. Therefore, many scientists look towards evaluating online sentiments, especially considering their existing correlation with actual opinions.

Online sentiments monitoring has been approached by scientists using a variety of data mining algorithms, from trend monitoring [18] to contradiction detection [11, 16], although these studies were not specifically accounting for relationships between demographic groups, their sentiment's correlation and hierarchical organization.

Recently, the work of Das et al. [2] introduced complex mining of sentiment data in the form of ratings, where the authors aimed at extracting meaningful demographic patterns. Our work differs in that we study the complementary problem of extracting groups with correlated sentiments over time, that is, groups that react similarly over time to external events. Then, this kind of analysis can also help provide a more meaningful interpretation for the biases observed in the sentiments expressed by the different groups.

Zhang et al. [20] introduced a sentiment aggregation and visualization system, which interactively displays sentiments based on the selected geographical location. The system represents a world map featuring a time evolution of sentiments expressed in news articles coming from different geographical regions. It automatically retrieves and displays sentiments around some particular time period for *ad-hoc* queries, aggregating them over different locations as the user navigates the map, or zooms in and out. However, it only targets small-scale data aggregation using a single demographics hierarchy. A work of Mandel et al. [6] is a step up in this direction, featuring sentiment aggregation over time for demographic groups formed by gender and location attributes. The authors analyzed Twitter messages for hurricane *Irene* and revealed sentiment differences among demographic groups. Their study suggested a necessity to account for classification errors (sentiment noise) and sentiment biases, thus forestalling our analysis, which addresses both of these problems.

Problems related to the identification of correlations among multiple time series have been studied by the data streams community, using a variety of techniques. These techniques focused on the efficient computation [21, 7], hidden variables [9], local correlations [10], pruning of candidate pairs [1], and lagged correlations [12]. Among them, StatStream [21] is the one that is closest to our work. StatStream computes correlations using sliding time intervals of specified sizes, composed of a number of sub-intervals of fixed length. It employs the *Discrete Fourier Transformation (DFT)* to compute correlations in an approximate and incremental manner. Our solution is different from the above works in a number of ways: (a) it analyzes time series using multiple aggregation granularities and detects correlations on ad-hoc time intervals; (b) it applies effective top down pruning both on time and demographics hierarchies; and (c) it uses correlation compression techniques to achieve efficiency and scalability.

7. CONCLUSIONS AND FUTURE WORK

In this work we approach the novel problems of characterizing sentiment evolution in a demographic group and identifying correlated groups, which address the large-scale sentiment aggregation. We design efficient algorithms for sentiment aggregation based on a careful indexing of time and demographics into hierarchies and demonstrate that our problems can be solved effectively on a large scale using clever pruning, top-k and compression methods.

Our approach allows observing sentiment behavior at a much finer level of detail than currently possible, helping to identify cases that are counter-intuitive and can only be observed by processing large amounts of data. Moreover, it enables an unprecedented scale-up of traditional social studies and raises new data analysis opportunities, useful for sociology and marketing researchers.

We outline some interesting problems and extensions of this paper, which we plan to work on. We consider only a disjoint type of relation, although it is possible to expand the notion of relations between groups to any arbitrary path in a demographics lattice, and use it as a filtering argument to our problems. Also we are investigating the case where disjoint groups appear to be the same sets of users due to a strict dependency among attributes. Filtering high correlations between such groups is possible when their sets of users are known and can be done as a preprocessing step. Alternatively, we can compare the volume of sentiments between these groups, which becomes possible since our DTree storage preserves this information.

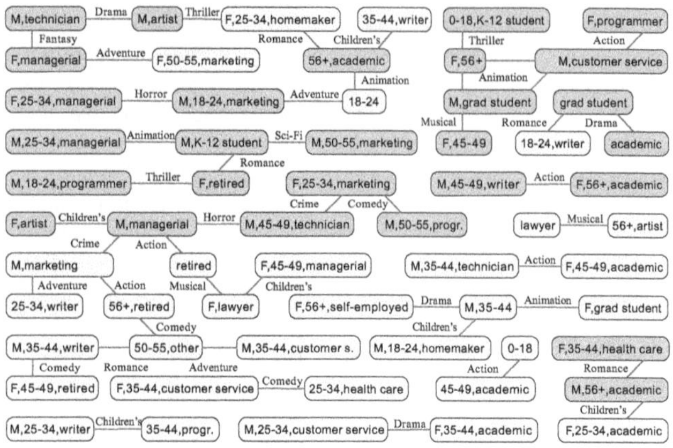

Figure 12: Positive sentiment correlations in MovieLens.

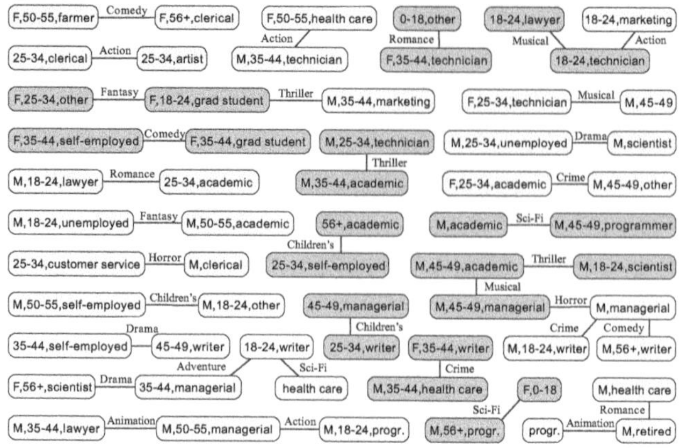

Figure 13: Negative sentiment correlations in MovieLens.

8. REFERENCES

[1] R. Cole, D. Shasha, and X. Zhao. Fast window correlations over uncooperative time series. In *KDD*, pages 743–749, 2005.

[2] M. Das, S. Amer-Yahia, G. Das, and C. Yu. Mri: Meaningful interpretations of collaborative ratings. In *VLDB*, 2011.

[3] N. S. Eric Langford and M. Owens. Is the property of being positively correlated transitive? *TAS*, 55(4):322–325, 2001.

[4] M. Ester, H.-P. Kriegel, J. Sander, and X. Xu. A density-based algorithm for discovering clusters in large spatial databases with noise. pages 226–231. AAAI Press, 1996.

[5] IBM. Social sentiment index. *IBM Smarter Analytics*, 2012.

[6] B. Mandel, A. Culotta, J. Boulahanis, D. Stark, B. Lewis, and J. Rodrigue. A demographic analysis of online sentiment during hurricane irene. In *LSM 2012*, pages 27–36, 2012.

[7] A. Mueen, S. Nath, and J. Liu. Fast approximate correlation for massive time-series data. In *SIGMOD*, pages 171–182, 2010.

[8] B. O'Connor, R. Balasubramanyan, B. R. Routledge, and N. A. Smith. From tweets to polls: Linking text sentiment to public opinion time series. In *ICWSM*, 2010.

[9] S. Papadimitriou, J. Sun, and C. Faloutsos. Streaming pattern discovery in multiple time-series. In *VLDB*, pages 697–708, 2005.

[10] S. Papadimitriou, J. Sun, and P. S. Yu. Local correlation tracking in time series. In *ICDM*, pages 456–465, 2006.

[11] A. M. Popescu and M. Pennacchiotti. Detecting controversial events from twitter. In *CIKM*, pages 1873–1876, 2010.

[12] Y. Sakurai, S. Papadimitriou, and C. Faloutsos. Braid: Stream mining through group lag correlations. In *SIGMOD*, pages 599–610, 2005.

[13] N. L. Spruill and J. L. Gastwirth. On the estimation of the correlation coefficient from grouped data. *JASA*, 77(379):614–620, Sept. 1982.

[14] M. Thelwall, K. Buckley, and G. Paltoglou. Sentiment in twitter events. *JASIST*, 62(2):406–418, 2011.

[15] M. Tsytsarau and T. Palpanas. Survey on mining subjective data on the web. *DAMI*, 24(3):478–514, 2012.

[16] M. Tsytsarau, T. Palpanas, and K. Denecke. Scalable detection of sentiment-based contradictions. In *DiversiWeb, WWW 2011*, 2011.

[17] A. Tumasjan, T. O. Sprenger, P. G. Sandner, and I. M. Welpe. Predicting elections with twitter: What 140 characters reveal about political sentiment. In *ICWSM*, 2010.

[18] I. Varlamis, V. Vassalos, and A. Palaios. Monitoring the evolution of interests in the blogosphere. In *ICDE Workshops*, 2008.

[19] F. Wang, N. Helian, and Y. J. Yip. Run-length encoding applied to grid space storing and indexing. In *ICWI*, pages 461–471, 2002.

[20] J. Zhang, Y. Kawai, T. Kumamoto, and K. Tanaka. A novel visualization method for distinction of web news sentiment. In *WISE*, 2009.

[21] Y. Zhu and D. Shasha. Statstream: statistical monitoring of thousands of data streams in real time. In *VLDB*, pages 358–369, 2002.

Topic	Group 1	Group 2	Begin	End	Correlation	Significance H1	Significance H2
Animation	{M,college/grad student}	{F,56+}	30.07.00	17.11.00	0.96	8.68E-07	9.02E-02
Animation	{M,K-12 student}	{M,25-34,executive/managerial}	07.11.00	07.03.01	0.94	2.67E-05	2.13E-01
Children's	{M,executive/managerial}	{F,artist}	30.07.00	07.11.00	0.94	2.03E-05	2.41E-01
Children's	{25-34,writer}	{45-49,executive/managerial}	08.10.00	15.02.01	-0.95	1.64E-05	1.28E-01
Children's	{25-34,self-employed}	{56+,academic/educator}	21.04.00	29.08.00	-0.93	4.28E-05	2.78E-01
Comedy	{F,25-34,sales/marketing}	{M,50-55,programmer}	17.11.00	13.09.01	0.97	4.11E-08	6.36E-04
Comedy	{customer service}	{45-49,artist}	18.10.00	26.01.01	0.96	3.25E-06	1.05E-01
Comedy	{F,35-44,self-employed}	{F,35-44,college/grad student}	07.12.00	16.04.01	-0.95	1.33E-05	1.28E-01
Fantasy	{M,technician/engineer}	{F,executive/managerial}	18.10.00	05.02.01	0.92	6.50E-05	3.71E-01
Fantasy	{F,18-24,college/grad student}	{F,25-34,other}	08.09.00	17.11.02	-0.92	6.80E-05	1.53E-01
Romance	{F,35-44,doctor/health care}	{M,56+,academic/educator}	17.12.00	02.11.01	0.98	4.23E-04	4.40E-06
Romance	{F,retired}	{M,K-12 student}	07.11.00	15.02.01	0.96	3.27E-06	1.05E-01
Romance	{M,artist}	{56+,academic/educator}	08.09.00	27.12.00	0.96	5.40E-06	9.02E-02
Romance	{F,35-44,technician/engineer}	{Under 18,other}	27.11.02	07.03.03	-0.96	3.69E-06	1.05E-01
Drama	{college/grad student}	{academic/educator}	18.09.00	27.12.00	0.96	4.34E-06	1.05E-01
Crime	{F,35-44,writer}	{M,35-44,doctor/health care}	05.02.01	29.08.02	-0.92	4.17E-03	1.95E-01
Action	{M,45-49,writer}	{F,56+,academic/educator}	30.07.00	26.01.01	0.96	3.55E-06	3.33E-02
Action	{F,programmer}	{M,customer service}	07.12.00	17.03.01	0.96	4.80E-06	1.05E-01
Thriller	{F,retired}	{M,18-24,programmer}	28.10.00	25.02.01	0.96	8.00E-06	7.76E-02
Thriller	{Under 18,K-12 student}	{F,56+}	17.11.00	25.02.01	0.95	9.07E-06	1.71E-01
Thriller	{M,25-34,technician/engineer}	{M,35-44,academic/educator}	17.11.00	27.03.01	-0.95	1.02E-05	1.28E-01
Thriller	{M,18-24,scientist}	{M,45-49,executive/managerial}	27.11.00	05.07.01	-0.95	3.75E-06	5.85E-02
Horror	{M,45-49,technician/engineer}	{M,executive/managerial}	17.11.00	07.03.01	0.96	3.48E-06	9.02E-02
Horror	{M,18-24,sales/marketing}	{F,25-34,executive/managerial}	21.04.00	07.03.03	0.96	3.28E-04	8.59E-07
Sci-Fi	{M,50-55,sales/marketing}	{M,K-12 student}	05.02.01	21.04.02	0.96	5.79E-06	1.21E-03
Sci-Fi	{M,45-49,programmer}	{M,academic/educator}	21.04.00	07.03.03	-0.98	3.07E-04	2.24E-01
Sci-Fi	{M,56+,programmer}	{F,Under 18}	16.01.01	11.01.02	-0.97	1.84E-04	1.94E-02

Table 1: Positive and negative sentiment correlations identified in MovieLens dataset.

EBM - An Entropy-Based Model to Infer Social Strength from Spatiotemporal Data

Huy Pham
Computer Science Dept.
Univ. of Southern California
huyvpham@usc.edu

Cyrus Shahabi
Computer Science Dept.
Univ. of Southern California
shahabi@usc.edu

Yan Liu
Computer Science Dept.
Univ. of Southern California
yanliu.cs@usc.edu

ABSTRACT

The ubiquity of mobile devices and the popularity of location-based-services have generated, for the first time, rich datasets of people's location information at a very high fidelity. These location datasets can be used to study people's behavior - for example, social studies have shown that people, who are seen together frequently at the same place and at the same time, are most probably socially related. In this paper, we are interested in inferring these social connections by analyzing people's location information, which is useful in a variety of application domains from sales and marketing to intelligence analysis. In particular, we propose an entropy-based model (EBM) that not only infers social connections but also estimates the strength of social connections by analyzing people's co-occurrences in space and time. We examine two independent ways: ***diversity*** and ***weighted frequency***, through which co-occurrences contribute to social strength. In addition, we take the characteristics of each location into consideration in order to compensate for cases where only limited location information is available. We conducted extensive sets of experiments with real-world datasets including both people's location data and their social connections, where we used the latter as the ground-truth to verify the results of applying our approach to the former. We show that our approach outperforms the competitors.

Categories and Subject Descriptors

H.2.8 [**Database Applications**]: Data mining, Spatial databases and GIS; H.3.3 [**Information Search and Retrieval**]: Retrieval models

Keywords

Social network; social strength; spatiotemporal; geospatial; spatial; data mining; social computing

1. INTRODUCTION

In the past, finding a person's location involved some detective work by following the person clandestinely. However, these days given all the online trails we leave behind, people's locations can be tracked at a very high resolution effortlessly. The location data can be inferred implicitly, for example from one's credit-card transactions or activities on mobile devices (through cell-phone towers, GPS, or WiFi hotspots). It can also be released explicitly, for example when someone distributes geo-tagged contents (e.g., tweets, uploads photos on Instagram, Flickr or Facebook), interacts with location-based-services online (e.g., Foursquare check-ins), or through a mobile app (e.g., Highlight, Glancee). Such a collection of people's locations over time (aka ***spatiotemporal*** data) is a rich source of information for studying various social behaviors. In particular, the one behavior we are interested in this paper is whether social relationships among people can be inferred from such a collection. The intuition is that if two people have been to the same places at the same time (aka ***co-occurrences***), there is a good chance that they are socially related. The ultimate goal is to derive the social-network of people and the social strength from their real-world location data as opposed to (or in addition to) their online activities.

The applications for such a physically inferred social network are plenty - it not only subsumes all the applications of online social networks such as marketing applications (e.g., target advertising, recommendation engines such as friendship suggestions), social studies (e.g., identifying influential people) and cultural studies (e.g., to examine the spreading patterns of new ideas, practices and rumors), but also has its own unique applications. For example, the network can be used to identify the new (or unknown) members of a criminal gang or a terrorist cell or it can be used in epidemiology to study the spread of diseases through human contacts.

However, the problem of inferring social connections from people's spatiotemporal data is particularly challenging for many reasons. First, it is not clear which attributes of co-occurrences should be measured to infer social connection. For example, if the number of co-occurrences of two people, called ***frequency***, is only considered, then one may arrive at a wrong conclusion about their social relationship. To illustrate, suppose two people study at the same library around the same time every day, which results in high frequencies, but they may not even know each other. This erroneous conclusion can be attributed to the fact that the library is a popular location and the observation that two people only co-occur at the library is not a strong indication of social connection. On the other hand, a few co-occurrences in a small private place are perhaps a better indication of friendship. Or alternatively, several co-occurrences at different popular places (e.g., coffeehouses, restaurants) may also be a better indication of friendships. Second, we are interested in inferring more information about social connections such as how close of a relationship two people have (aka ***social strength***). Third, there may be a lot of missing data, as people's location data may be sparse. Fourth, the spatiotemporal data is often extremely large, in the order of gigabytes, which could render

SIGMOD'13, June 22–27, 2013, New York, New York, USA.

the inference algorithms inefficient, taking too much time and/or resources to perform.

Our work is motivated by the following pioneering studies. First, Eagle et al. [9] showed there is a correlation between people's co-occurrences and their social connections by reporting on a study they conducted on a number of students and faculty members from a research institute. Following this observation, Crandall et al. [6] developed a probabilistic model to estimate the probability of two people being friends given their co-occurrences in space and time. Cranshaw et al. [7], on the other hand, introduced various features of co-occurrences and then utilized machine learning techniques to classify pairs of users as friends or not. Distinguished from these approaches is the work done by Li et al. [12], who represented each user's visit pattern as a trajectory, and friendship between two users is determined as the similarity between their trajectories. Lastly, in previous work [15], we studied this problem by introducing two properties, commitment and compatibility, that any social distance measure should follow to correctly infer social connections. While these studies showed the validity, importance and feasibility of inferring social connections from co-occurrences, they either made many simplifying assumptions (see Section 6) or failed to address some of the subtle questions about social connections. This paper is built on these studies by addressing the following questions: 1) inferring the strength of social connections from co-occurrences, 2) avoiding overestimation or underestimation of social connections by taking into account various features of co-occurrences and 3) focusing on the efficiency of the algorithms.

A naive approach to estimate the social strength is to simply count the number of unique locations two people co-occurred as their social strength. However, this measure would consider different locations equally important as it ignores the number of co-occurrences at each location. To address this problem, one could sum up the number of co-occurrences of two people across different locations as a measure of their social strength. The problem with this approach is that it may overestimate coincidences. For example, 10 random encounters at a crowded coffee shop (called coincidences) are considered 10 times more important than 1 interactive meeting at a private office.

To remedy for these shortcomings, we propose an Entropy-Based Model, named **EBM**, which successfully infers social strengths from spatiotemporal data with high accuracy. With EBM, we first use the Shannon entropy to measure the diversity of co-occurrences, which, for each pair of people, uses the number of their co-occurrences at each location to derive a relative co-occurrence measure, and use *only* diversity as social strength. This measure may give higher importance to outliers (i.e., local frequency), and thus may still overestimate the social strength due to coincidences. Hence, we generalize Shannon by using the Renyi entropy that can look at the global pattern of co-occurrences per user pair and has the flexibility of giving more or less weight to outliers by varying the order of diversity q. However, Renyi is still blind to the characteristic of a location (e.g., whether the location is a crowded public coffeehouse vs. a private office). Therefore, we incorporate weighted frequency, which utilizes location entropy to weigh each co-occurrence differently depending on the characteristics (crowdedness) of the location, thus it captures minor co-occurrences that can be a significant indication of a social connection. A summary list of our contributions is provided below.

- EBM quantifies the strength of each social connection by considering how diverse the distribution of the co-occurrences is in the context of locations (aka ***diversity***).
- EBM avoids overestimation by discounting coincidences, utilizing ***diversity's order*** - an important property of diversity.
- EBM compensates for the data sparseness by taking into account the local characteristics of locations (e.g., location popularity).
- We evaluated EBM using a large real-world dataset collected by a location-based social network called Gowalla. We 1) use **only** the Gowalla's location data to infer users' social connections, and 2) use the Gowalla's social-network as the **ground truth**.
- Our evaluation shows that EBM's predicted social strength is consistent with ground truth. 88% of social strengths are correctly predicted by our model.
- As for inferring friendships, by using the the diversity, we achieve a precision of 96.5%, but the recall was low due to the data sparseness. However, after incorporating location entropy into EBM, we improve the recall by a factor of 1.8.
- Our EBM's algorithm is parallelizable, thus can be implemented using the MapReduce framework in order to be efficient for massive data, which is critical in any online applications.
- Finally, we experimentally compared our model to the previous studies, including GEOSO [15], probabilistic model [6], the feature model [7] and the trajectory model [12], and the results show that EBM outperforms them in both efficiency and accuracy.

The rest of this paper is organized as follow: In Section 2, we formally define the problem and discuss the preliminaries necessary to construct the model. In Section 3 we explain the EBM model and how it answers the questions raised by the paper. Section 4 describes the optimization of the algorithm to deal with large datasets. We describe the experiment in Section 5, related work in Section 6, and make the conclusion of the paper in Section 7.

2. PROBLEM DEFINITION

In this section we will give the formal definition of the problem and introduce the notations and preliminaries that are used later to formulate the EBM model.

2.1 The Problem

As a user checks in at a location, the following information will typically be recorded and sent to the server: User's **ID** - u; User's **location** - l, which consists of latitude and longitude's values and a unique ID that represents a specific place such as a shopping center, a theater, a living house, etc; the **time** of the check-in - t. Therefore users' check-ins can be represented as a set of ***user-location-time*** triplets $< u, l, t >$, each of which states that User u visited location l at time t. We give the formal definitions of the problem as follow:

DEFINITION: ***Social strength*** is a quantitative measure that tells how socially close two people are.

DEFINITION: Given a set of users $U = (u_1, u_2, ..., u_M)$, a set of locations $L = (l_1, l_2 ..., l_N)$ and a set of check-ins in the forms of *user-location-time* triplets $< u, l, t >$, the problem is to infer the social strength for each pair of users.

Note: The only time-related input to the problem is the check-in's time. Another possible input that can greatly influence social strength is the amount of time two users stayed together at a place, often referred to as ***length of stay***. However, most location-based social networks nowadays, such as Facebook, Foursquare, Yelp, etc., *neither* record the length of stay *nor* provide such services. In fact, users check in at places, but never check out. Therefore, we design our model to capture such reality by limiting the input to only User IDs, locations and check-in times. Desirably, the length of stay can be a consideration in our future work once such information becomes readily available.

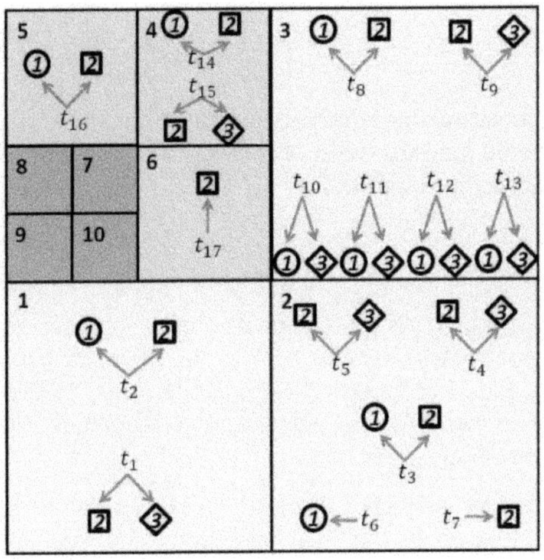

Figure 1: A quadtree storing areas of different levels of popularity, and the visits of Users $1, 2$ and 3

2.2 Preliminaries

2.2.1 Representation of Location

One popular way of storing visited locations is to use a grid to uniformly partition the space into disjoint cells of ***equal size*** [6, 15], where each cell represents only one ***place***, so that any two people, who check in within the same cell at the same time, are considered to have a ***co-occurrence***. However, a uniform grid is inflexible and inefficient due to the two following reasons: **1)** In a crowded area such as a downtown, a place, which represents the location of a co-occurrence, say a shopping center, is often much smaller compared to a place in a sparse mountainous region, say a national park. Hence, the method of partitioning the space into equal cells is not applicable here. **2)** Reducing the size of all the cells to fit small places in crowded areas would result in much waste of storage resources and look-up time in sparse areas, meanwhile, increasing the cells' size to fit to large places in sparse regions would result in misinterpreting the co-occurrences in crowded areas.

Therefore, to efficiently store spatial data, we use quadtree [17]. Fig. 1 shows a quadtree, where each quadrant, called ***cell***, has a unique ID, numbered from 1 to 10. Three users are shown as circles, diamonds and squares uniquely identified with user IDs 1, 2 and 3. The arrows show that a user checked in at the cell at time t_i. The darker, the denser the area. Geo-points inside a cell share the same cell ID, which is used along with time to determine co-occurrences. For example, looking at cell 1, we say Users 1 and 2 co-occurred at cell 1 at time t_2.

For simple presentation, we set the capacity of each cell of the quadtree to 1 so that each cell can cover a maximum of ***one*** place (in the experiment, the capacity is more than 1). The construction of the tree can be done by recursively dividing an area into four equal quadrants until each quadrant holds only one place.

2.2.2 Visit Vector

The visit history of a user is represented by a ***visit vector***, which shows the cell IDs and the check-in time. For example, the visit vector for User 1 in Fig. 1 is $V_1 = (< t_2 >, < t_3, t_6 >, ...)$, which states that User 1 visited cell 1 at time t_2; visited cell 2 at time t_3 and t_6, etc. The general format of the visit vector of User i is:

$$V_i = (< t_{1,1}, ..., t_{1,i_1} >, ..., < t_{M,1}, t_{M,2}, ..., t_{M,i_M} >) \quad (1)$$

where M is the number of leaves in the quadtree.

2.2.3 Co-occurrence Vector

If two users checked in at the same location within a time-interval τ, then we say that they have a co-occurrence. τ is an application-dependent parameter and can be set experimentally. Correspondingly, a ***co-occurrence vector*** between User i and User j represents all the co-occurrences of Users i and j is:

$$C_{ij} = (c_{ij,1}, c_{ij,2}, ..., c_{ij,M}) \quad (2)$$

where $c_{ij,l}$ is the number of co-occurrences between Users i and j at location l, which is referred to as ***local frequency***, which will be used throughout this paper.

For example, given the visit vectors of User 1 and User 2:

$V_1 = (< t_2 >, < t_3, t_6 >, < t_8, t_{10}, t_{11}, t_{12}, t_{13} >, < t_{14} >, < t_{16} >, 0, 0, 0, 0, 0)$

$V_2 = (< t_1, t_2 >, < t_3, t_4, t_5, t_7 >, < t_8, t_9 >, < t_{14}, t_{15} >, < t_{16} >, < t_{17} >, 0, 0, 0, 0)$

we see that the two users have one co-occurrence at location 1 at time t_2, one co-occurrence at location 2 at time t_3, etc, therefore the co-occurrence vector between User 1 and User 2 is:

$$C_{12} = (1, 1, 1, 1, 1, 0, 0, 0, 0, 0)$$

Usually, a user can only visit a limited number of locations, which makes the visit vector and the co-occurrence vector sparse (containing many zeroes). Therefore, we will introduce an alternative data structure and storage for optimization in Section 4. For now, we use this format to simplify the presentation.

3. THE EBM MODEL

The goal of this section is to devise a model, named ***Entropy-based Model*** (EBM), to quantify ***social strength*** between two users from their co-occurrence vectors. The overview diagram of EBM is shown in Fig. 2. In Section 3.1, we start by utilizing the diversity of the co-occurrence vectors as the main contributing factor to social strength. Consequently, we use the ***Shanon entropy*** to measure the diversity of co-occurrences (see Section 3.2), but we observe that this measure may overestimate the strength of social connections due to the impact of ***coincidences***, which are the case when people happen to co-occur by chance, but do not interact with each other, especially in crowded places such as downtown and shopping centers. Hence, we generalize Shanon entropy to the ***Renyi entropy*** (see Section 3.3), which gives us the flexibility of controlling how much coincidences can contribute to diversity via a parameter q, called the ***order of diversity***. Finally, to compensate for the problem of data sparseness, we incorporate ***weighted frequency***, which in turn uses ***location entropy***, into our model in Section 3.6 to increase the impact of co-occurrences at uncrowded places even at low frequencies to the strength of social connections. The resulting social strength is the ultimate measure that describes how close two people are based on the history of their spatiotemporal information.

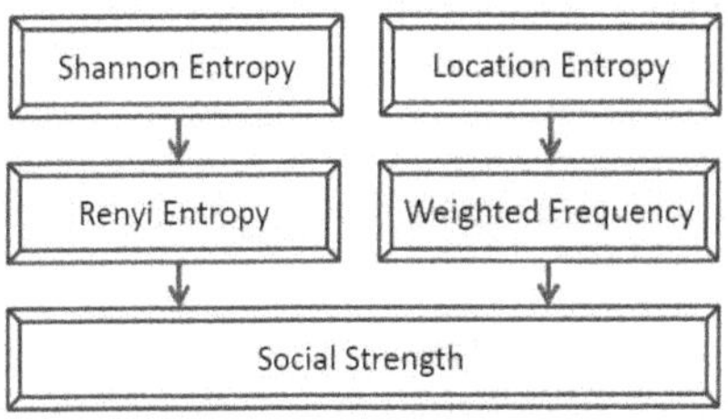

Figure 2: Diagram of EBM - Social strength is formulated via Renyi Entropy and Weighted Frequency

3.1 Diversity in Co-occurrences

The concept of diversity has long been used in Physics, Economics, Ecology, Information Theory, etc, as a quantitative measure to characterize the richness of a system [10, 11, 19]. Specifically, in Ecology, diversity is used to measure how diverse an ecosystem is; in the simplest case, it equals the number of different species in an ensemble. In Statistical Thermodynamics, diversity is the number of micro-states, in which a system can be [18].

Consider the co-occurrence vectors for each user pair in Fig. 1,

$$C_{12} = (1,1,1,1,1,0,0,0,0,0)$$
$$C_{23} = (1,2,1,1,0,0,0,0,0,0)$$
$$C_{13} = (0,0,4,0,0,0,0,0,0,0)$$

we see that User 1 and User 2 have 5 co-occurrences, so do User 2 and User 3. However, in the former case the co-occurrences are spread over 5 different locations, while in the latter case the co-occurrences happened in 4 different locations. Even simpler is the case of User 1 and User 3, for which all co-occurrences happened in one location - cell 3. We say that C_{12} is *more diverse* than C_{23}, and C_{23} is *more diverse* than C_{13}.

Intuitively, people, who are socially connected, tend to visit *various* places together [5, 6, 7, 9, 15]. This intuition is captured by our model as *how diverse* their co-occurrences are. Applying the general definition of diversity in [20], we formally define *diversity* in our model:

DEFINITION: Diversity is a measure that quantifies how many effective locations the co-occurrences between two people represent, given the mean proportional abundance of the actual locations.

3.2 Formulation of Diversity through Shannon Entropy

In this section, we use Shannon entropy, then we will extend EBM to a more generic one, called Renyi entropy, in Section 3.3.

First, we define the notations and quantities that will be used to construct EBM. $r_{i,j}^{l,t} =< i,j,l,t >$ is a co-occurrence of User i and User j at location l and at time t. $R_{ij}^{l} = \bigcup_t r_{i,j}^{l,t}$ is the set of co-occurrences of User i and User j, which happened at location l. R_{ij} is the set of all co-occurrences of User i and User j at all locations: $R_{ij} = \bigcup_l R_{i,j}^{l} = \bigcup_{l,t} r_{i,j}^{l,t}$

The probability that a randomly picked co-occurrence from the set R_{ij} happened at location l is:

$$P_{ij}^{l} = \frac{|R_{ij}^{l}|}{|R_{ij}|} \tag{3}$$

If we randomly pick a co-occurrence from the set R_{ij} and define its location as a random variable, then the uncertainty associated with this random variable is defined by the Shannon entropy for User i and User j as follow (the upper index S denotes *Shannon*):

$$H_{ij}^{S} = -\sum_{l} P_{ij}^{l} \log P_{ij}^{l} \tag{4}$$

Formulation of diversity: There exists a distinction between entropy and diversity, in which entropy often acts as the index of diversity. For illustration in the former research [11], Jost *et al* compared the *roles* of entropy and diversity as the radius and the volume of a sphere, respectively, where radius is used to calculate volume; and showed their relationship:

$$D = \exp(H) \tag{5}$$

where D is diversity, which indicates how diverse an ensemble is. Following this strategy, we construct the EBM model, where D shows how diverse the co-occurrences of two users are in terms of locations. The diversity of the co-occurrences of User i and User j, which is defined in Equation 5, becomes:

$$D_{ij} = \exp\left(H_{ij}^{S}\right) = \exp\left(-\sum_{l} P_{ij}^{l} \log P_{ij}^{l}\right) \tag{6}$$

Since we already defined the co-occurrence vector in Equation (2), we can rewrite the expression of diversity D_{ij} in terms of the co-occurrence vector as follow:

$$D_{ij} = \exp\left(-\sum_{l, c_{ij,l} \neq 0} \frac{c_{ij,l}}{f_{ij}} \log \frac{c_{ij,l}}{f_{ij}}\right) \tag{7}$$

where $f_{ij} = \sum_l c_{ij,l}$ is the total number of co-occurrences of User i and User j, named *frequency*. Note the difference between *frequency* f_{ij} and *local frequency* $c_{ij,l}$; the *frequency* of two users is the sum of all their *local frequencies*. From Equations (5), (6) and (7), we have observations:

- The higher the number of co-occurrence locations, the higher the uncertainty given by the Shannon entropy, and consequently the higher the diversity.
- If the number of co-occurrence locations is fixed, the diversity and the Shannon entropy reach their maximums when all the probabilities in Equations (5) and (6) are equal to each other.

To demonstrate the observations, let us consider the example of a group of three users in Fig. 1. The co-occurrence vectors, Shannon Entropy, Diversity value, the diverse information, the likelihood of coincidences and the probability of being friends for each pair of users are summarized in Table 1.

From Table 1, we see that C_{12} has the highest value of diversity due to the spread of co-occurrences over more locations, or in other words, C_{12} is the most diverse, followed by C_{23}, then followed by C_{13}, which is the least diverse as all the co-occurrences happened at only one place - cell 3. For C_{12}, the numbers of all co-occurrences are equal to each other (in the first five cells), which produces the maximum value of Shannon entropy, and consequently, the maximum value of diversity among the three co-occurrence vectors, together with the highest number of co-locations (i.e., 5), which makes it the most diverse, therefore, suggesting a high probability of User 1 and User 2 being friends. Furthermore, the value of diversity D_{12} coincides with the number of co-occurrence locations, which is the reason why diversity is often referred to as the ***effective number of states*** (in Statistical Mechanics [18]) or ***effective number of species*** (in Ecology [11]).

In addition, we see that the diversity of C_{23} (3.789) is less than the number of co-occurrence locations (i.e., 4), which is due to the fact that it has two co-occurrences at one place - cell 2 (*less diverse*), as compared to the case of C_{12}, where all co-occurrences are uniformly spread over five different cells (*more diverse*).

We also observe an interesting point where all four co-occurrences of User 1 and User 3 happened at a popular place - cell 3, which has been visited by all three users and has the highest number of co-occurrences in total. This fact implies the high likelihood of coincidences between User 1 and User 3, for example, they might just happen to be at a crowded public place (such as a shopping center or a library) at the same time. Therefore, even four co-occurrences in such a crowded place might still say very little about a possible social connection. We have the following observation:

Observation: A high number of co-occurrences at *only one place* might be an indicator of a friendship if the place is unpopular and uncrowded, but they might suggest the likelihood of coincidences in popular and crowded places. Shannon Entropy and its corresponding diversity, however, would treat multiple co-occurrences as coincidences independent of where took place. Also, Shannon Entropy does not allow us to adjust the impact of this type of co-occurrences on the diversity. Therefore, it is necessary to examine

Table 1: Example of Diversities

Co-occurrence Vector	Shannon Entropy	D_{ij} Value	Diversity	Likelihood of Coincidences	Prob. of a Friendship
$C_{12} = (1,1,1,1,1,0,0,0,0,0)$	1.609	5.000	High	Low	High
$C_{23} = (1,2,1,1,0,0,0,0,0,0)$	1.332	3.789	Medium	Medium	Medium
$C_{13} = (0,0,4,0,0,0,0,0,0,0)$	0.000	1.000	Low	High	Low

these issues to avoid any false predictions that coincidences might cause. We will address this in Sections 3.4 and 3.5.

3.3 Renyi Entropy-based Diversity

As we discussed in Section 3.2, even though the Shannon Entropy (and its corresponding diversity) can capture the likelihood of a social connection between two people, it cannot distinguish the cases when coincidences *might* or *might not* happen and does not allow us to adjust the impact of coincidences. Rennyi entropy and its corresponding diversity, on the other hand, will give us the utility to control how much coincidences can contribute to diversity. In fact, Shannon entropy is just a special case of Renyi entropy.

Consider the general case of entropy - Renyi entropy, given as:

$$H_{ij}^{R} = \left(-\log \sum_{l} \left(P_{ij}^{l}\right)^{q}\right) / (q-1) \tag{8}$$

where $q \geq 0$ is the order of diversity. The diversity given by Equation 5 becomes (The upper index R denotes *Renyi*):

$$D_{ij} = \exp(H_{ij}^{R}) = \exp\left[\left(-\log \sum_{l} \left(P_{ij}^{l}\right)^{q}\right) / (q-1)\right]$$

$$= \left[\exp\left(\log \sum_{l} \left(P_{ij}^{l}\right)^{q}\right)\right]^{1/(1-q)} = \left[\sum_{l} \left(P_{ij}^{l}\right)^{q}\right]^{1/(1-q)} \tag{9}$$

$$= \left[\sum_{l, c_{ij,l} \neq 0} \left(\frac{c_{ij,l}}{f_{ij}}\right)^{q}\right]^{1/(1-q)} \tag{10}$$

Equation (10) expresses the diversity in terms of a co-occurrence vector. The elegance of using the Renyi entropy in our problem lies inside the parameter q, called the ***order of diversity***, which indicates its ***sensitivity*** to the local frequency $c_{ij,l}$ [16]. Specifically:

- When $q > 1$ the Renyi entropy H_{ij}^{R}, and consequently the diversity D_{ij}, more favorably considers the high values of $c_{ij,l}$, which are the more popular events. In other words, the higher the local frequency $c_{ij,l}$, the more weight it gets from the diversity or the more impact the local frequency can make on diversity.
- When $q < 1$, in opposite, the diversity tends to give more weight to the local frequencies with low-values $c_{ij,l}$.
- When $q = 0$, the diversity is completely ***insensitive*** to $c_{ij,l}$ and gives the pure number of co-occurrence locations.
- Case $q = 1$: The Renyi entropy favors local frequencies $c_{ij,l}$ in opposite ways when $q < 1$ versus when $q > 1$, therefore $q = 1$ is the *pass-through* point where Renyi entropy and its diversity stop all of their biased favors and weight the local frequencies $c_{ij,l}$ by their *own* values, which is what Shannon entropy captures. This suggests a *meeting point* of the two entropies. Indeed, even though Equations (8), (9) and (10) are *undefined* at $q = 1$, their limits exist when $q \to 1$ (see the proof below) and become the Shannon entropy and the diversity defined in Section 3.2 .

Proof of Renyi Entropy's Limit: At $q = 1$ Equation (8) is undefined at its form $f(q)/g(q) = 0/0$, where $f(q) = -\log \sum_l \left(P_{ij}^{l}\right)^{q}$ and $g(q) = 1 - q$. Therefore, we use l'Hôpital's rule to find its limit, which is $\lim_{q \to 1} f(q)/g(q) = \lim_{q \to 1} f'(q)/g'(q)$. $f'(q) = \left(-1/\sum_l \left(P_{ij}^{l}\right)^{q}\right) \times \sum_l (P_{ij}^{l})^{q} \log P_{ij}^{l}$, and $g'(q) = -1$ (assuming natural logarithm for simplicity). Plug in the value $q = 1$ in the equation $f'(q)/g'(q)$, we get:
$\lim_{q \to 1} f(q)/g(q) = f'(q)/g'(q)|_{q=1} = \sum_l P_{ij}^{l} \log P_{ij}^{l}$. The last formula is nothing but Shannon entropy, thus the limit existence of Renyi entropy is proved. This also leads to the limit of diversity as $D = exp(H)$, and at $q = 1$ Equations (9) and (10) become Equations (6) and (7), respectively.

We see that the impact of the local frequency on the diversity is not always necessarily determined by just its own value $c_{ij,l}$, but also by the value of parameter q. This moves us one step closer to solving the problem of coincidences, which we are going to discuss in Section 3.4.

3.4 Coincidences

Coincidences occur when two people happen to be at the same places at the same time but never or rarely get a chance to see and communicate with each other, thus less possibility of being friends. This happens often in popular and crowded places where coincidences are frequent, such as cafeteria, public libraries, etc.

Consider the following example: assume there are 5 cells and consider two user pairs (*a*,*b*) and (*c*,*d*) with co-occurrence vectors: $C_{ab} = (10, 1, 0, 0, 9)$, $C_{cd} = (2, 3, 2, 2, 3)$, respectively. We also assume that cells 1 and 5 are *highly* crowded places, cell 2 is *medium*-crowded, while cell 3 and 4 are *non*-crowded, based on the number of visits. Intuitively, this example suggests that c and d are far more socially connected than a and b as the co-occurrences of a and b are likely coincidences; the co-occurrence at cell 2 would be the only one that is *medium*-significant for friendship of a and b, while c and d would have 7 of such or even more significant co-occurrences from cells 2, 3 and 4. First, obviously, using the total number of co-occurrences would give a wrong suggestion that (*a*,*b*) are socially closer to each other than (*c*,*d*). Second, using the number of co-occurrence locations (NL) for social strength would give us a relative value $NL_{ab}/NL_{cd} = 3/5$, which still indicates a recognizable level of connection of (*a*,*b*) compared to (*c*,*d*), but a *fair* measure would reasonably want that level to be low.

Now let's see how diversities of Shannon and Renyi entropies address the challenge in the example above. We set the value of q (order of diversity) to 0.5, less than 1, which, according to the discussion in Section 3.3, will limit the impact of coincidences. The relative value for Shannon entropy of two user pairs is $H_{ab}^{S}/H_{cd}^{S} = 0.86/1.59 = 0.54$, relative Shannon's diversity is $D_{ab}^{S}/D_{cd}^{S} = 2.35/4.90 = 0.48$, relative Renyi entropy is $H_{ab}^{R}/H_{cd}^{R} = 3.20/5.63 = 0.56$, relative Renyi's diversity is $D_{ab}^{R}/D_{cd}^{R} = 24.60/279.67 = 0.09$. First, the Renyi's diversity shows a relatively high level of social connection of $(c, d))$ compared to (a, b) ($D_{ab}^{R}/D_{cd}^{R} = 0.09$), which we would expect intuitively. Second, compared to Renyi's diversity, Shannon's diversity does *not* limit the impact of coincidences, consequently, the social strength of (*a*,*b*) is still high compared to that of (*c*,*d*) ($D_{ab}^{S}/D_{cd}^{S} = 0.48$). Third, using entropy (either Shannon or Renyi) instead of diversity as a metric of social strength still results in a relatively high level of connection of (*a*,*b*) compared to (c,d). Therefore, this example confirms our discussion in Section 3.2 that Entropy can only act as the index of diversity, but should not be used as a direct metric for social connection.

We see that coincidences often produce high local frequencies $c_{ij,l}$, which, if misjudged, can be overestimated. However, Renyi entropy and its diversity give us the ability to control the impact of coincidences on diversity through q, which is *sensitive* to the values of local frequencies. q is one of the optimization parameters and will be determined experimentally in Section 5.4.1.

Towards this end, we have focused on eliminating the impact of coincidences at crowded places. However, we have not yet answered the following two questions: **1)** What characterizes crowded and non-crowded places, or even further, the level of crowdedness? **2)** What can be used to determine the likelihood of coincidences in co-occurrences, even when local frequencies are low, and oppositely, the likelihood of non-coincidences when frequencies are low or high? We are going to answer these questions in Section 3.5 utilizing ***Location Entropy*** and ***Weighted Frequency***.

3.5 Location Entropy

Location entropy is a crucial part in **weighted frequency**. It was first introduced in [7] to describe the popularity of a location. Let l be a location, $V_{l,u} = \{< u, l, t >: \forall t\}$ be a set of check-ins at location l of User u and $V_l = \{< u, l, t >: \forall t, \forall u\}$ be a set of all check-ins at location l of all users. The probability that a randomly picked check-in from V_l belongs to User u is $P_{u,l} = |V_{l,u}|/|V_l|$. If we define this event as a random variable, then its uncertainty is given by the Shannon entropy as follow:

$$H_l = - \sum_{u, P_{u,l} \neq 0} P_{u,l} \log P_{u,l} \quad (11)$$

A high value of the location entropy indicates a popular place with many visitors and is *not* specific to anyone. On the other hand, a low value of the location entropy implies a private place with few visitors, such as houses, which are *specific* to a few people.

To help understand the meaning of location entropy, let's assume a simplified case, when N users have visited a location l and each user visited it exactly once. The location entropy then becomes:

$$H_l = - \sum_{u=1}^{N} \frac{1}{N} \log \frac{1}{N} = \log N \quad (12)$$

As we see in this simplified case, location entropy is the logarithm of the number of unique users, who have been at the place. We show the dependence of location entropy's value on the number of unique visitors for this simplified case in Fig 3(a). Fig 3(b) shows an example of location entropy for the case of three users from Fig 1, where the value of location entropy of each cell is underlined. Note that cell 7,8,9 and 10 have no visitors and they have a default value of 0 for location entropy (not shown in the figure). Fig. 3(b) tells us that location entropy is not really determined by the number of visits, but rather by the number of unique visitors. In addition, the location entropy is higher if the location is less specific to any user. Location entropy helps us answer two questions:

- Using location entropy, we can determine the places where coincidences are highly probable, even when the frequency of a user pair in such places is low. That is because location entropy for a place takes into account the visits of all others to that place.
- A low number of co-occurrences (low local frequency) at an uncrowded place can also be a significant indicator of social connections, ***even if*** the diversity is low. When the number of co-locations is low, the diversity will also be low, hence this type of co-occurrences cannot be captured by the diversity measure. Therefore, it is necessary to ensure that co-occurrences at highly private places are given more priority or weight.

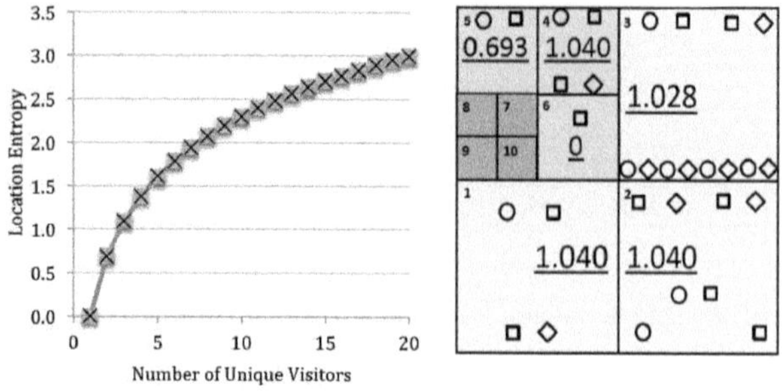

(a) Number of Unique Visitors vs. LE (b) Example of LE

Figure 3: Location Entropy (LE)

Using location entropy, we will introduce weighted frequency in Section 3.6 to capture this type of co-occurrences

3.6 Weighted Frequency

Co-occurrences in small uncrowded places, such as private houses, often results in more social interaction, as compared to those in crowded places. Therefore, the probability of friendships strongly depends on the locations of co-occurrences. Given the co-occurrence vector of Users i and j in Equation (2), we define the ***weighted frequency***, which tells us how important the co-occurrences at non-crowded places are to social strength, as follow:

$$F_{ij} = \sum_l c_{ij,l} \times \exp(-H_l) \quad (13)$$

It is interesting to note that $exp(-H_l)$ is the *inverse of diversity* of a location in terms of its visitors. This weighted frequency is inspired by ***tf-idf*** - a numerical statistic widely used in information retrieval and text mining [3] to measure the importance of a term/word t to a document in a corpus. ***tf*** is term frequency and often taken as the number of times the term appears in a document. ***idf*** is inverse document frequency, defined as $|D|/(|d \in D, t \in d| + 1)$ - the total number of documents $|D|$ divided by the number of documents that have t. In our problem, *location* is similar to *document* in ***tf-idf***, thus the number of co-occurrences at a location is similar to *term frequency* in a document. However, to weight co-occurrences, we use $exp(-H_l)$, not ***idf***, since location entropy provides insights into the intrinsic characteristics, i.e., the visiting patterns to a location. ***idf*** is not suitable here because by its definition, it says how important or how specific a user pair is to a location, but we want to answer a different question: how important a co-visit to that location is to a pair of user?

Another tempting approach, which is also inspired by ***tf-idf*** and in fact, used in [7], would be using $c_{ij,l}/\sum_l c_{ij,l}$ - the number of co-occurrences of a user pair at a location divided by the total number of co-occurrences by all user pairs at that location. To show the shortcoming of this approach, assume we have a private living house of a couple, who have made check-ins to produce 1000 co-occurrences. Another guest couple visited them once and made 1 co-occurrence. The $c_{ij,l}/\sum_l c_{ij,l}$ for the guest couple in this house is $1/(1000+1) = 1/1001$, which is very low and, therefore, would say nothing about the social connection of the guest couple, but as we know, such a co-occurrence, even just one, is a high indication of a social connection. Our ***weighted frequency***, however, looks at this case *differently*. Since the house is visited by few people, its location entropy is low (0.0079), which makes a high value of weight $exp(-H_l) = 0.9921$ (note that $0 < exp(-H_l) \leq 1$). Thus, this only co-occurrence makes a high impact on weighted frequency and is significant for the connection of the guest couple.

To continue the example in Section 3.4, we calculate weighted frequencies for the two couples (*a*,*b*) and (*c*,*d*). As we assumed earlier, cells 1 and 5 are crowded places. To compute location entropy, we also need the visit information of other users in each cell. To achieve that, assume there are additional 20 visitors at each of cells 1 and 5, and each of them visited the cell 10 times. For simplicity, also assume that each user *a*, *b*, *c* and *d* visited each cell as many times as they co-occurred with their partners. The weighted frequency for each pair is $F_{ab} = 1.10$ and $F_{cd} = 3.07$. Our analysis shows that F_{ab} is mostly impacted by cell 2, and F_{cd} is mostly impacted by cells 2, 3 and 4, which matches our expectation that only non-crowded places contribute to weighted frequencies.

Note: Diversity and weighted frequency answer two different question. Diversity *decreases* the impact of frequent coincidences while weighted frequency *increases* the impact of co-occurrences at less crowded places; the less crowded, the more impact.

Data sparseness: Weighted frequency plays an important role when it comes to data sparseness, i.e., when the availability of spatiotemporal data is very limited - only few co-occurrences for each couple, the Renyi's diversity can be very low. However, weighted frequency compensates for low diversity by further looking into location characteristics to capture the co-occurrences at non-crowded areas, which can be insignificant for diversity, but very significant for weighted frequency, and for friendship, consequently.

3.7 Social Strength

So far, we have formulated two independent ways, through which co-occurrences contribute to social strength: 1) **Diversity** (through Renyi entropy) - which measures how diverse the co-occurrences of two people are, and at the same time, can control and tell us how much coincidences can impact diversity, and 2) **Weighted frequency** - which favorably captures the local frequencies of co-occurrences at uncrowded places and can compensate for diversity in case of data sparseness. If we want to combine these two measure to produce an ultimate one for social strength, it is necessary to understand the *relative importance* of each component-measure to social strength. To illustrate, from the example discussed in Sections 3.4 and 3.6, we have ($D^R_{ab} = 24.60$, $F_{ab} = 1.10$), ($D^R_{cd} = 279.67$, $F_{cd} = 3.07$). We see that the two measures have different scales; as we decrease the order of diversity q, diversity will scale itself up to more clearly differentiate the impacts of coincidences and non-coincidences. As we see $D^R_{ab}/D^R_{cd} = 0.09$, but at the same time the diversity's scale goes up to 279.67 and weighted frequency remains at a low scale $F_{cd} = 3.07$. This challenge influences us in the way we combine the two measures together.

We now formulate the social strength, which ultimately tells how close two people are, by doing a linear regression over diversity D_{ij} and weighted frequency F_{ij}:

$$s_{ij} = \Phi(D_{ij}) + \Psi(F_{ij}) \tag{14}$$

where Φ and Ψ are two linear functions and s_{ij} is the ultimate strength measure we look for. Since D_{ij} focuses on the distribution of co-occurrences over different locations, while F_{ij} focuses on the intrinsic properties of locations, they are independent of each other, subsequently, Equation (14) takes us to a multiple regression problem over two independent variables D_{ij} and F_{ij}. For convenience of conducting the multiple regression, we rewrite Equation (14) in an explicit form through optimal parameters α, β and γ:

$$s_{ij} = \alpha.D_{ij} + \beta.F_{ij} + \gamma \tag{15}$$

where D_{ij} and F_{ij} are defined in Equations (10) and (13), respectively. Parameters α, β and γ [1] can be learned from dataset and/or provided by user. In Section 5.4.2 we show how these parameters can be learned from training data and applicable across networks.

Equation (15) is the final formula to determine social strength between two users given their co-occurrences in time and space.

4. OPTIMIZATION

To be efficient with massive datasets, we optimize the implementation by using k-d tree [1] for data structure and using MapReduce framework to parallelize the computation.

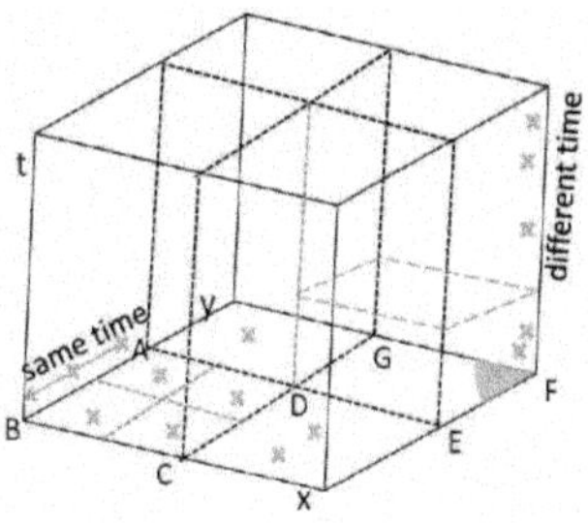

Figure 4: Data Structure

Data structure: We use k-d tree [1] with slight modifications to make it suitable for our problem. It is a 3-D tree shown in Fig. 4, with an (x, y) plane for representing locations, and a t-axis for time. The details of k-d tree's implementation can be found in literature [1]. Our focus here, however, is how to split the tree or sub-tree (named ***rectangular parallelepiped*** or **RP** for short) into smaller sub-trees when inserted data exceeds its capacity? To do that, we can either split the 1-D time interval into two equal halves or the 2-D spatial square of the **RP** into four equal quads. The former method is cheaper as it is a 1-D split. However, consider the case of quad $ABCD$ in Fig 4, spatial splitting is a better option as the spatial points are evenly spread out over the quad but all the temporal points shrink to one end of the time interval. In contrast, in the $DEFG$ quad, temporal splitting is a better option. To facilitate decision making, *one more time*, we use entropy. Assume we have N check-ins in an **RP**. Divide the **RP**'s spatial quad into $S = 4^n$ equal cells indexed from 1 to S, and the RP's time interval into $T = 2^m$ equal sub-intervals indexed from 1 to T (n and m are integers), then for the check-ins, the spatial Shannon entropy in the quad and the temporal Shannon entropy in the time interval are:

$$H_s = -\sum_i \frac{s_i}{N} \ln(\frac{s_i}{N}), \;\; H_t = -\sum_j \frac{t_j}{N} \ln(\frac{t_j}{N}) \tag{16}$$

where s_i and t_j are the numbers of check-ins in spatial cell i and time sub-interval j, respectively, and $1 \leq i \leq S$, $1 \leq j \leq T$. The more evenly spread-out the check-ins in the *quad* (or the time interval), the higher the entropy. These two quantities give us the clue of which dimension to split in an **RP** when it reaches capacity N. The empirical values for S and T is 16 ($n = 2$ and $m = 4$). In general, when the two entropies are roughly the same, time splitting is chosen to save storage cost.

Implementation with MapReduce: First, with k-d tree, the search for co-occurrences becomes efficient and standard as the time interval and the spatial quad can efficiently filter out all non-candidate points. The MapReduce implementation can be done in

[1]It is possible to keep only one parameter, say α, let $\beta = 1$ and skip γ. However, we keep all the three parameters just to follow the more traditional form of the multiple regression problem.

two phases. In the first phase, Maps build partial co-occurrence vectors in sub-trees, and Reduce combines them to make full co-occurrence vectors and compute diversities. In the second phase, Maps compute location entropy for each **RP**, while Reduce will use the entropy values to compute weighted frequencies.

5. PERFORMANCE EVALUATION

5.1 Dataset

The data used in the experiments was collected by Gowalla - a location-based social network, where users shared their locations through check-ins. The data was collected from February 2009 to October 2010 and consists of two different sets. The first set is spatiotemporal data, which has 6,442,890 check-ins from 196,591 users. Each check-in has format: <user ID, latitude, longitute, timestamp, location ID>. The second set is a social graph of friendships among users. It has 950,727 edges (or friendships).

Since Gowalla's spatial data are heavily concentrated in the US, we used only the spatiotemporal data within the US for the experiments. We divided the data into two subsets, **training** set and **evaluation** set. The **training** set contains $2,957,830$ check-ins in the West of USA (named L_{west}), and the social network of $102,320$ users who performed check-ins in the West (named S_{west}). The **evaluation** set contains $3,485,060$ check-ins in the East of USA (named L_{east}) and the corresponding social network of $95,725$ users (named S_{east}). Since some users performed check-ins in both the West and East parts, the two subsets S_{west} and S_{east} overlap. However, our analysis shows that the overlaps of users is just 0.74%, and of friendships is only 0.107%. Thus, the overlap is insignificant and cannot affect our evaluation.

5.2 Methodology

The two metrics we use to measure the accuracy of our techniques are precision and recall. Let TC be the set of true social connections reported by Gowalla's social network (i.e., **ground truth**) and RC be the set of user pairs that our model reported as socially connected. The **precision** and **recall** are defined as:

$$P = \frac{|TC \cap RC|}{|RC|}, \quad R = \frac{|TC \cap RC|}{|TC|} \tag{17}$$

where $\cap$ denotes the intersection operation.

5.3 Experiment Setup

We conducted our experiments on Amazon EC2 cluster with instances running on 64 bit Fedora 8 Linux Operating System with 15GB menory, 4 virtual cores and 4 disks with 1,690 GB storage. Our Map/Reduce algorithm is implemented using Hadoop version 0.22.0. To obtain consistent results, we used the same setup to perform all the experiments.

5.4 Results

5.4.1 *Order of Diversity*

In this set of experiments, we want to examine how the order of diversity q controls the impact of coincidences on diversity and find the optimal value for q. Towards this end, we use *only* diversity as social strength. To be completely unbiased, we do this experiment using only the training data L_{west} and S_{west}.

We perform this particular experiment through the following steps. **Step 1:** Vary the order of diversity q from 0 with a step of 0.1, then for each value of q, we calculate diversity D_{ij}^q based on Equation (10). **Step 2:** Since S_{west} only tells us if two users are friends or not, while our output D_{ij} gives us a numerical value (assumably strength), we need to somehow make the two comparable. To accomplish this, we define the threshold of diversity to be D^q so that: if $D_{ij}^q \geq D^q$ then User i and User j are considered to be friends by our model; otherwise they are not. Therefore, we vary threshold D^q from 0 with a step of $max(D_{ij})/1000$, take user pairs with diversity $D_{ij}^q \geq D^q$ (assuming they are friends) to compare with the real friendship information in S_{west} and calculate precision P and recall R. As a result of varying D^q, we get the dependence of precision and recall on q.

Figs. 5(a) and (b) show the results of how q impacts precision. The x-axis shows the order of diversity q and the y-axis shows the precision. To simplify the graph visualization, we split the graph into two, each shows three curves, each curve corresponds to one level of recall. In addition, we only show the results of q that ranges from 0 to 2.0 to keep a high level of details since further increasing q beyond 2.0 decreases the precision dramatically. We made the following **observations**:

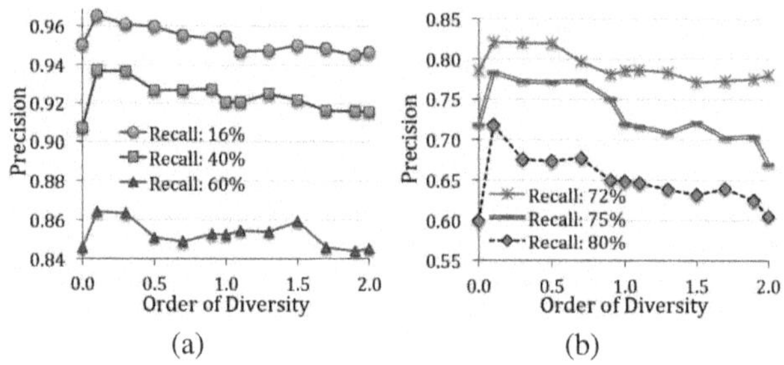

Figure 5: The impact of the order of diversity on precision.

- Our major observation is all the curves at 6 different recall's levels show the same behavior: they all peak at $q = 0.1$, which says $q = 0.1$ is the *optimal value* for limiting coincidences' impact. We believe this optimal value is a general phenomenon across networks for two reasons: first, all the networks nowadays share the same nature of check-ins as users share their locations with their friends; second, coincidences are general spatial phenomena and happen to all networks *without bias* to any particular network. To confirm this phenomenon, we repeated this experiment on another similar dataset from a different network - Brightkite, which consists of 58K users, 214K connections and 4.5M check-ins. The result showed a peak again at $q = 0.1$ with a very insignificant fluctuation (0.004), which can be considered as experimental uncertainty.
- The case $q = 0$ makes the diversity equal to the number of co-occurrence locations (a.k.a *richness*). Fig. 5 shows the fact that simply setting the diversity to the number of co-occurrence locations will produce ***low*** precision. This is because coincidences are completely ignored and all cases of co-occurrences are considered equally important.
- When q increases from 0.1 to 2.0, the diversity ***increasingly favors high*** local frequencies. Consequently it favors coincidences because coincidences often produce high local frequencies. Therefore coincidences now are out of control and have more impact on diversity, which causes false predictions, and consequently, causes the decrease in precision.
- Further decreasing q from 0.1 to 0 also results in the degradation of precision, because low values of q ($q < 0.1$) not only limits the impact of *coincidences* (*high* local frequencies), but also limits the impact of *non-coincidences* (*medium* local frequencies), which results in *excessive* controlling or *over*-limiting.

We will use the optimal value $q = 0.1$ for the rest of our experiments. Note that diversity mainly deals with precision since its role is to avoid coincidences. Therefore in Fig 5 we used precision to learn about the order of diversity. The low recall associated with diversity will be compensated by weighted frequency, which is what we are going to examine next.

5.4.2 Social Strength

Our goals in this set of experiments is 1) to compute the social strength by experimentally conducting multiple linear regression over diversity D_{ij} and weighted frequency F_{ij}; 2) to evaluate the social strength by relating it to friendship information from the ground truth S_{east}.

Linear Regression: In order to find the social strength in the evaluation dataset L_{east}, we first need to use the training set (L_{west} and S_{west}) to learn about the parameters α, β and γ in Equation (15) (See section 3.7). Thus, we need diversity D_{ij}, weighted frequency F_{ij} and strength $\hat{s}_{ij}$ (computed only based on social graph). We already have D_{ij} and F_{ij} computed from Equations (10) and (13). However, S_{west} is a social graph that only tells us if two users are friends or not, but not the strength. Fortunately, there exist different techniques to calculate social strength based *solely* on a social graph. We will use three techniques, which have been shown to have high performance [13], including **Jaccard's index**, **Adamic/Adar similarity** and **Katz score**.

Jaccard's index of Users i and j (J_{ij}) measures the probability that both i and j have a randomly selected person as a friend.

$$J_{ij} = |\Gamma(i) \cap \Gamma(j)| / |\Gamma(i) \cup \Gamma(j)| \tag{18}$$

where $\Gamma(i)$ and $\Gamma(j)$ are the sets of friends of i and j, respectively. Jaccard's index is inversely proportional to the total number of friends of i and j. Thus, the fewer friends that i and j have, the more *influential* their common friends are to Jaccard's index.

Adamic/Adar similarity (AA_{ij}) looks further at the popularity of each common friend of Users i and j and weights each of them differently. Consequently, a common friend, who is also a friend of *many* other people, has less impact on the similarity.

$$AA_{ij} = \sum_{k \in \Gamma(i) \cap \Gamma(j)} \frac{1}{\log \Gamma(k)} \tag{19}$$

Katz score K_{ij}: If we represent a social network as a undirected graph with users as nodes and edges as friendships between users, then the Katz score considers the ensemble of all paths between two nodes and sums over this ensemble:

$$K_{ij} = \sum_{l} \varepsilon^{l} \times |P_{ij,l}| \tag{20}$$

where $P_{ij,l}$ is the set of paths of length l from node i to node j, and ε is a small positive constant that defines the *attenuation* of Katz score as the length l grows. The optimal value of ε is shown in [13] to be of the order 10^{-3}.

Subsequently, $\hat{s}_{ij}$ can be any of the three measures above. Among the three, Katz score has the best performance, followed by Adamic/Adar similarity, and by Jaccard's index [13].

The optimal values of α, β and γ as the results of the *least-square method* in linear regression [2] are given as follow:

$$\alpha = \frac{(\sum F_{ij}^2)(\sum D_{ij}.\hat{s}_{ij}) - (\sum D_{ij}.F_{ij})(\sum F_{ij}.\hat{s}_{ij})}{(\sum D_{ij}^2)(\sum F_{ij}^2) - (\sum D_{ij}.F_{ij})^2} \tag{21}$$

$$\beta = \frac{(\sum D_{ij}^2)(\sum F_{ij}.\hat{s}_{ij}) - (\sum D_{ij}.F_{ij})(\sum D_{ij}.\hat{s}_{ij})}{(\sum D_{ij}^2)(\sum F_{ij}^2) - (\sum D_{ij}.F_{ij})^2} \tag{22}$$

$$\gamma = \overline{\hat{s}_{ij}} - \alpha.\overline{D_{ij}} - \beta.\overline{F_{ij}} \tag{23}$$

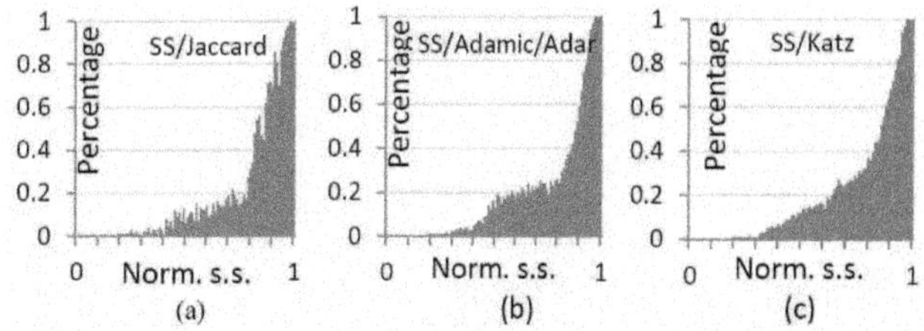

Figure 6: Percentage of real friendships vs. the social strength of buckets.

where $\overline{\hat{s}_{ij}}$, $\overline{D_{ij}}$, and $\overline{F_{ij}}$ are the corresponding mean values of $\hat{s}_{ij}$, D_{ij} and F_{ij}.

Applying each of the three techniques above to the social network S_{west} (i.e., the training data), we compute the social strength $\hat{s}_{ij}$. However, before computing parameters (α, β, γ), we first normalize diversity, weighted frequency and $\hat{s}_{ij}$ so that we can use the values of α and β to analyze the relative importance of each measure (diversity and weighted frequency) to social strength. The values of (α, β) for each of the Jaccard, Adamic/Adar and Katz methods are (0.441, 0.550), (0.476, 0.521), and (0.483, 0.520), respectively. As we see, the two measures are *comparable* in their importance to social strength in all three methods. Weighted frequency gets a slightly higher priority, which reveals a fact that many co-occurrences at uncrowded places have *low* frequencies. These are general phenomena because people check in more frequently at famous and popular places as those are more interesting to share with friends, while uncrowded places are less interesting to share, thus the check-in's frequencies there should be low. It is important and also interesting to note that this nature of check-ins is general to all networks since the main purpose of users' check-ins is to share their locations with friends, despite the fact that different networks might have different ways of encouraging users to perform check-ins. Therefore, consider two scenarios: first, if a partial social network is available explicitly for a spatiotemporal dataset, then it can be used to compute its own parameters (α, β, γ). Second, however, if no explicit social network is available, then the values of (α, β, γ) can be applied across networks without much sacrifice of precision due to the general phenomena discussed above.

Finally, applying these parameters to the evaluation dataset L_{east}, we compute the social strength s_{ij} for new user pairs based on their spatiotemporal data.

Social Strength and Friendship: Our goal now is to show the relationship of our *predicted social strength* with the *friendships*. We do this by *grouping* the user pairs with similar social strength together into subgroups called *buckets* and find the percentage of *real* friendships in each bucket. We perform this experiment through the following steps. **Step 1:** we divide the social strength axis into 100 intervals of equal length $\delta = 0.01$. **Step 2:** we group the user pairs with s_{ij} that belong to the same interval into a bucket. **Step 3:** we take the user pairs in each bucket and check with the social network (i.e., ground truth S_{east}) to find what percents of pairs in each bucket are truly friends as reported by Gowalla.

Fig 6 shows the results in forms of charts. The x-axis shows the middle value of normalized social strength of each bucket (or interval), while the y-axis shows the percentage of real friendships in each bucket as checked with the ground truth S_{east}. The three graphs in Fig 6(a)(b) and (c) correspond to three different cases of which technique is used in the linear regression of social strength in Section 5.4.2: (a) Jaccard's index is used; (b) Adamic/Adar similarity is used; (c) Katz score is used.

Observations: First, as observed in Fig. 6, our predicted social strength is consistent with the ground truth: user pairs with higher social strength have higher percentage of being friends than those user pairs with lower social strength. This also fits the *intuition* that user pairs with high social strength are more involved/interactive with each other, therefore they are more likely to be friends. Second, furthermore, as Katz score is a better metric than the other two [13], our predicted social strength also shows a better performance when Katz score is used in the regression. Fig. 6(c) shows a more consistent curve as the percentage is supposed to increase when the social strength of buckets increases. As Jaccard's index is the worst metric compared to Adamic/Adar similarity and Katz score, we see more fluctuations in 6(a) as the percentage goes up and down, while Fig 6(b) and Fig. 6(c) are smoother, which means more consistent with the ground truth.

5.4.3 Goodness of fit

Our goal in this experiment is to evaluate how well our *predicted* social strength from spatiotemporal data L_{east} fits the *observed* strength computed based only on social graph S_{east}? This is known as *goodness of fit*. This differs from the the previous experiments as in Section 5.4.2 we tested our social strength against friendship, but not observed strength. Hence, we use the **coefficient of determination** R^2 to measure the *variance* of our predicted social strength s_{ij} from $\hat{s}_{ij}$ computed *solely* based on ground truth S_{east} using each of the techniques above.

Coefficient of Determination measures how well the the predicted values fit the observed values. Let N be the number of user pairs, $\overline{\hat{s}_{ij}} = \sum \hat{s}_{ij}/N$ be the mean of the observed social strengths, $SS_{tol} = \sum_i (\hat{s}_{ij} - \overline{\hat{s}_{ij}})^2$ be the total sum of squares and $SS_{err} = \sum_i (\hat{s}_{ij} - s_{ij})^2$ be the sum of squares of residuals. The coefficient of determination is defined as:

$$R^2 = 1 - \frac{SS_{err}}{SS_{tol}} \tag{24}$$

R^2 is a statistic that shows the goodness of fit of the model. It ranges from 0 to 1.0; R^2 near 1.0 indicates that the regression results fit the real data well, while R^2 near 0 indicates the opposite.

Table 2: Coefficient of Determination

	Jaccard	Adamic/Adar	Katz
R^2	0.691	0.830	0.877

Table 2 shows the values of R^2 for each different technique used to compute $\hat{s}_{ij}$ in the evaluation's social network S_{east}. First, our model very well predicts the social strength. Particularly, if we use Katz score and assume its absolute reliability, then 87.7% of the social strengths in the East of USA are predictable by our model. Second, Katz and Adamic/Adar methods fit our linear regression better than the Jaccard's index. Logically, this also fits the evaluation in [13], which reported that Katz score is a better metric for social strength, followed by Adamic/Adar similarity, and followed by Jaccard's index. Third, the values of R^2 are high, which implies that linear regression is the right choice to integrate diversity and weighted frequency together.

5.4.4 Precision and Recall

We already showed that the precision of EBM is very high in Section 5.4.1, even just using diversity. Here, we would like to evaluate its recall. That is, what percentage of Gowalla's social connections can be predicted by ***just*** analyzing the check-in data? Note that this is a very tough challenge since the check-in data collected from Gowalla is very sparse (unlike more active social-networks such as Foursquare). For example, we analyzed the Gowalla users' co-occurrence vectors and found that out of $996,621$ user pairs who have co-occurred, only 4.3% of them co-occurred more than three times. 95% of pairs have few co-occurrences, which will inevitably limit the opportunity of exploring the social connections from this sparse spatiotemporal data. To alleviate this, we could have used other factors that can help us to infer social connections, such as common friends, common interests, etc. [4]. However, since the focus of this paper is on inferring social connections only from spatiotemporal data, we challenged EBM by limiting its knowledge to only the check-in data. Instead, to slightly level the field, we removed from our dataset those pairs of users who have zero or one co-occurrence and only included the pairs with more than one co-occurrence. This is a fair adjustment as it is almost impossible to infer friendship for those users with one or less co-occurrence (by any method that only relies on the check-in data).

To calculate precision and recall, we need to compare EBM's predictions with ground truth S_{east}. However, EBM gives us numerical strengths, while S_{east} only tells us if two users are friends or not. To work around this, we use the same technique as in Section 5.4.1 by defining a threshold s_0 for social strength and varying it to find precision and recall. Fig. 7(a) shows the results of the EBM's evaluation. The x-axis shows precision and the y-axis shows recall. The dotted line corresponds to the case when only diversity is used as social strength, while the other three are when both diversity and weighted frequency are integrated together to compute social strength, and correspond to three different techniques used in Section 5.4.2.

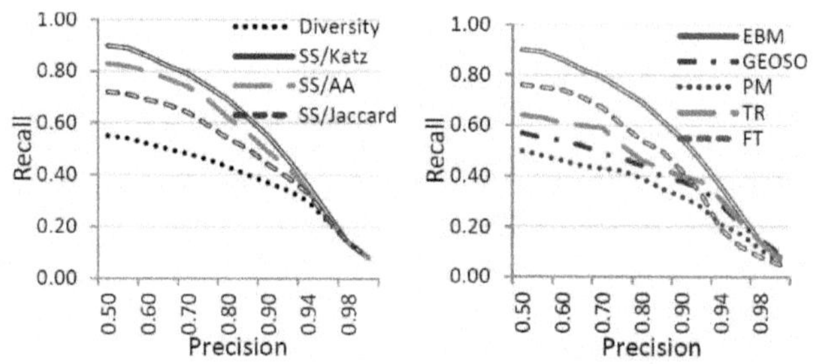

(a) EBM (b) EBM vs. other models

Figure 7: Precision vs. Recall

Observation 1: It is interesting to note that all the four curves practically meet together when recall is below 35% and start diverging as recall increases. This can be explained as follow: the low recall happens when we set high values for threshold s_0, thus only a *subset* of user pairs with *high* number of co-occurrences can pass through threshold s_0 and be considered. Therefore, handling coincidences is the only essential requirement for such subset. ***Diversity*** satisfies that requirement and it is used in all four cases, thus they all have the same performance level. However, when we reduce threshold s_0 is when user pairs with *fewer* co-occurrences can pass through the threshold and get considered. At this point, just handling coincidences is *not enough* and this is where ***weighted frequency*** comes into play to cope with data sparseness, as discussed in Section 3.6. Weighted frequency takes into account the location characteristics to predict social connections with very *low* number of co-occurrences. Such subtle co-occurrences cannot be captured by diversity, therefore its graph remains below the other three, which do use weighted frequency in addition to diversity.

Observation 2: As shown in Section 5.4.3 and in the related work [13], Katz score is a better metric for ground truth, followed by Adamic/Adar similarity and Jaccard index. Fig. 7(a) shows that our predicted social strength matches Katz score the best, which enhances the trustworthiness of our model.

Observation 3: Our model achieves both high precision and recall. Particularly, using Katz technique we can achieve (precision, recall) as high as (80%, 70%) or (70%, 82%). Moreover, considering the sparseness of the data where only 4.5% of co-occurred pairs have more than three co-occurrences, being able to get those high precision and recall is a major achievement.

5.4.5 *Comparison of EBM with other models*

Using the precision vs. recall graphs, we compare the performance of EBM with other four models, which have previously studied the problem, including probability model (PM) [6], GEOSO model [15], the model that utilizes various features (named FT for short) [7], trajectory model (TR) [12]. Fig. 7(b) shows the results.

Observations: *Precision*: EBM outperforms all other four models in precision. This is due to the EBM's ability of controlling the impact of coincidences, which is the real challenge to the other models since coincidences often produce very high local frequencies, which can easily misguide any method that wants to infer social connections from spatiotemporal data. The PM's precision remains the lowest; it assumes that each user can have *at most one* friend, which is almost never true; a possible fix would be removing that assumption, but that would severely interfere with its design and prevent it from formulating the probability of social connection. All PM, GEOSO and TR completely ignore location characteristics (aka *location entropy* in our work), thus there is no easy way for them to handle data sparseness, where *even* coincidences can have low frequencies, which is shown in our work as a difficult and challenging question. TR also does not clearly address coincidences at *high* frequencies. Finally, FT considers coincidences, however, it does not compute social strength but only answers if two people are friends or not. In addition, its ***tf-idf*** fails to capture co-occurrences at private places as shown in Section 3.6.

Recall: Since we challenged all five models with a *highly sparse* dataset, the result of recall truly shows how capable a model is of mining friendship's information. EBM achieves significantly higher recall compared to other models due to its knowledge of the locations (public or private, level of crowded-ness) and applies that knowledge to make *small* things (few co-occurrences) become *significant*. As discussed earlier, PM, GEOSO and TR have no knowledge about locations, thus cannot capture minor co-occurrences, consequently, have low recall. FT considers location characteristics to capture few co-occurrences in uncrowded locations, which explains its higher recall compared to GEOSO, PM and TR, but still lower than EBM's recall. The latter is because with EBM, *diversity* and *weighted frequency* can compensate for each other to avoid coincidences, and at the same time, handle sparse data.

Efficiency: We also parallelized the algorithms for GEOSO in [15], probability model (PM) in [6] and trajectory model in [12] to make the comparison. The feature model (FT) in [7] does not propose any data structure since the model was to target a relatively small proprietary data set, thus we do not examine its efficiency. Using the same setup, we run the experiments using different numbers of nodes (maps). Table 3 shows the number of seconds each model took to run in different setup: 100 nodes, 500 nodes and 1000 nodes. EBM outperforms the other three models. GEOSO and PM use a uniform grid to partition space into equal cells, thus results in high cost of storage as the number of cells grows enormously. TR has high cost in time due to its construction of trajectory (sequence) of user locations. Furthermore, EBM really takes advantages of parallelization as we see the rate, at which the running time decreases when we add more nodes to the computation.

Table 3: Efficiency of EBM and other models

	EBM	GEOSO	PM	TR
100 maps	159.12s	282.36s	203.25s	394.73s
500 maps	34.84s	92.46s	76.92s	129.32s
1000 maps	19.21s	39.22s	29.36s	64.291s

6. RELATED WORK

Given the experimental results are known now, we would like to elaborate on the related studies. Table 4 summarizes EBM and the previous studies with the same problem focus. The check-mark (✓) indicates that the question is addressed by the model, while the cross-mark (✗) indicates the opposite.

Table 4: Questions addressed by EBM and other models

	EBM	GEOSO	PM	FT	TR	BS
Coincidences	✓	✓	✗	✓	✗	✗
Location Characteristics	✓	✗	✗	✓	✗	✗
Data Sparseness	✓	✗	✗	✗	✗	✗
Social Strength	✓	✓	✓	✗	✓	✗

To examine the relationship between a friendship network and the human interactions, Eagle at al. [9] conducted their analysis on two different sets of data of the same group of users: one from mobile phone called "behavioral", another was reported by users called "self report" (shown as **BS** in Table 4). They examined the communications, locations and proximity of the users over an extended period of time, conducted a regression analysis over the data and finally compared the *behavioral* social network to *self-reported* relationships. Their results showed that the two are indeed related. In addition, communication was the most significant predictor of friendships, followed by number of common locations and proximity. However, this early study did not consider the impact of coincidences nor the importance of co-occurrence locations, which has been shown to be significant in our work.

Crandall et al. [6] used a probability model (**PM** in Table 4) to infer the probability of friendships given the co-occurrences in time and space and did the evaluation with a large dataset from Flickr. The first limit of this model is that it makes a simplifying assumption about the structure of the social network: each user can have only one friend, which is not the case in reality. Second, it does not consider the frequency of co-occurrences at each location; all the co-occurrences at one location only count as once. Finally, the impact of coincidences was not addressed, as well as the location characterics, known as location entropy in our work and in [7].

Cranshaw et al. [7] introduced various features such as specificity, location entropy, etc, in order to analyze the social connections (**FT** in Table 4). Their experiments showed that there exists a relationship between the mobility of patterns of a user and the number of the user's friends in the underlying social network. This is an in-depth study and provides much insight into the social network structure. However, they did not consider a subtle question of the social network: how close two people are (*aka* the social strength in our work)? In addition, they studied the location characteristics to avoid coincidences, but for each user pair, the local frequency was not clearly differentiated from location to location. Here, we show that the influences of local frequencies to social connections greatly vary from location to location. Furthermore, our weighted frequency also differs from TFIDF in their work in that we use the *inverse diversity* of a location ($exp(-H_l)$) to weight the local frequency, which considers the visiting patterns to a location and detects the significance of each single co-occurrence to social strength. Their TFIDF is more to show the specificity of a location to a user pair.

With a similar problem focus, Li et al. [12] also used the history of user locations to develop a similarity measure among users (**TR** in Table 4). They first represented each user as a trajectory in a hierarchical fashion, then used the similarity between the trajectories of two users as their social similarity. The model considers the movements of users in both micro and macro scales. This research is particularly promising for its scalability and its consideration of different level of movements. However, coincidences and location characteristics were not considered, which has been shown to be crucial in our work.

We previously proposed a geometrical model called GEOSO to infer the social connections based on co-occurrences in space and time (**GEOSO** in Table 4). We first defined the social distance geometrically and introduced two properties: *commitment* and *compatibility*, which must be considered by any distance measure. This approach is particularly interesting as the presence of the two properties help avoid coincidences. However, this approach suffers from complexity when working with massive data. In addition, all locations are considered equally important, therefore this is not an ideal approach to apply when it comes to data sparseness when the locations can be significant in predicting social connections.

In this work, we have addressed all the interesting, and at the same time, difficult challenges that the previous studies either ignored or suffered from. Our work does not make or simplify any assumptions and the experiment has proved the high accuracy of our model in predicting social connections with real-world data even when the data is sparse, as well as its efficiency when it comes to the problem of large-scale online processing.

7. CONCLUSIONS

In this paper, we studied the problem of inferring social connections from spatiotemporal data. Towards this end, we presented the EBM model to address some of the subtle questions about social connections, including how to infer the social strength of two people and how to avoid coincidences, which is a challenging problem due to its frequent nature. EBM also alleviated the problem of data sparseness by incorporating the location characteristics into the model when estimating the strength of social connections. Finally, our algorithm is efficient and parallelizable with Map-Reduce framework. Our experiments confirmed the high accuracy and efficiency of the EBM model and its superiority over competitors.

This work opens up new opportunities to answer some of the questions including: How do the social networks influence human physical behavior? How to use the social strengths inferred from spatiotemporal data to further study other aspects of a social network such as its durability and vulnerability? The issues of privacy are also likely to be raised such as how much of spatiotemporal data of a person is enough to maintain the social privacy of that person. These are some of the issues we would like to investigate as part of our future work.

7.1 Acknowledgments

This research has been funded in part by Award No. 2011-IJCX-K054 from National Institute of Justice, Office of Justice Programs, U.S. Department of Justice, as well as NSF grant IIS-1115153, the USC Integrated Media Systems Center (IMSC), and unrestricted cash gifts from Google, Northrop Grumman, and Microsoft. Any opinions, findings, and conclusions or recommendations expressed in this material are those of the author(s) and do not necessarily reflect the views of any of the sponsors such as the National Science Foundation or the Department of Justice.

8. REFERENCES

[1] J. Bentley. Multidimensional binary search trees used for associative searching. *Communications of the ACM*, 18(9):509–517, 1975.

[2] C. Bishop. *Pattern recognition and machine learning*, volume 4. springer New York, 2006.

[3] D. Blei, A. Ng, and M. Jordan. Latent dirichlet allocation. *the Journal of machine Learning research*, 3:993–1022, 2003.

[4] W. Bukowski, A. Newcomb, and W. Hartup. *The company they keep: Friendships in childhood and adolescence*. Cambridge University Press, 1998.

[5] E. Cho, S. A. Myers, and J. Leskovec. Friendship and mobility: user movement in location-based social networks. In *Proceedings of the 17th ACM SIGKDD*, KDD '11, pages 1082–1090, New York, NY, USA, 2011.

[6] D. J. Crandall, L. Backstrom, D. Cosley, S. Suri, D. Huttenlocher, and J. Kleinberg. Inferring social ties from geographic coincidences. *Proceedings of the National Academy of Sciences*, 107(52):22436–22441, 2010.

[7] J. Cranshaw, E. Toch, J. Hong, A. Kittur, and N. Sadeh. Bridging the gap between physical location and online social networks. In *Proceedings of the 12th ACM international conference on Ubiquitous computing*, Ubicomp '10, pages 119–128, New York, NY, USA, 2010. ACM.

[8] J. Dean and S. Ghemawat. Mapreduce: simplified data processing on large clusters. *Communications of the ACM*, 51(1):107–113, 2008.

[9] N. Eagle, A. S. Pentland, and D. Lazer. Inferring friendship network structure by using mobile phone data. *Proceedings of the NAS*, 106(36):15274–15278, 2009.

[10] M. O. Hill. Diversity and evenness: A unifying notation and its consequences. *Ecology*, 54:427–432, 1973.

[11] L. Jost. Entropy and diversity. *Oikos*, 113(2):363–375, 2006.

[12] Q. Li, Y. Zheng, X. Xie, Y. Chen, W. Liu, and W.-Y. Ma. Mining user similarity based on location history. In *Proceedings of the 16th ACM SIGSPATIAL*, GIS '08, pages 34:1–34:10, New York, NY, USA, 2008. ACM.

[13] D. Liben-Nowell and J. Kleinberg. The link-prediction problem for social networks. *Journal of the American society for IST*, 58(7):1019–1031, 2007.

[14] D. Papadias, Y. Tao, P. Kanis, and J. Zhang. Indexing spatio-temporal data warehouses. In *Proceedings. 18th International Conference on Data Engineering, 2002.*, pages 166–175. IEEE, 2002.

[15] H. Pham, L. Hu, and C. Shahabi. Towards integrating real-world spatiotemporal data with social networks. In *Proceedings of the 19th ACM SIGSPATIAL*, GIS '11, pages 453–457, New York, NY, USA, 2011. ACM.

[16] A. Renyi. On Measures of Entropy and Information. In *Berkeley Symposium Mathematics, Statistics, and Probability*, pages 547–561, 1960.

[17] H. Samet. The quadtree and related hierarchical data structures. *ACM Comput. Surv.*, 16(2):187–260, June 1984.

[18] D. V. Schroeder and H. Gould. An introduction to thermal physics. *Physics Today*, 53(8):44–45, 2000.

[19] H. Tuomisto. A consistent terminology for quantifying species diversity? yes, it does exist. *Oecologia*, 164:853–860, 2010. 10.1007/s00442-010-1812-0.

[20] H. Tuomisto. A diversity of beta diversities: straightening up a concept. *Ecography*, 33(1):2–22, 2010.

Online Search of Overlapping Communities

Wanyun Cui
Fudan University
wanyuncui1@gmail.com

Yanghua Xiao*
Fudan University
shawyh@fudan.edu.cn

Haixun Wang
Microsoft Research Asia
haixunw@microsoft.com

Yiqi Lu
Fudan University
luyiqi@gmail.com

Wei Wang
Fudan University
weiwang1@fudan.edu.cn

ABSTRACT

A great deal of research has been conducted on modeling and discovering communities in complex networks. In most real life networks, an object often participates in multiple overlapping communities. In view of this, recent research has focused on mining overlapping communities in complex networks. The algorithms essentially materialize a snapshot of the overlapping communities in the network. This approach has three drawbacks, however. First, the mining algorithm uses the same global criterion to decide whether a subgraph qualifies as a community. In other words, the criterion is fixed and predetermined. But in reality, communities for different vertices may have very different characteristics. Second, it is costly, time consuming, and often unnecessary to find communities for an entire network. Third, the approach does not support dynamically evolving networks. In this paper, we focus on online search of overlapping communities, that is, given a query vertex, we find meaningful overlapping communities the vertex belongs to in an online manner. In doing so, each search can use community criterion tailored for the vertex in the search. To support this approach, we introduce a novel model for overlapping communities, and we provide theoretical guidelines for tuning the model. We present several algorithms for online overlapping community search and we conduct comprehensive experiments to demonstrate the effectiveness of the model and the algorithms. We also suggest many potential applications of our model and algorithms.

Categories and Subject Descriptors

H.2.8 [**Database Management**]: Database Applications—*Data mining*

General Terms

Algorithms, Theory, Experimentation

Keywords

Community search; Social networks; Graph mining

*Correspondence author. This work was supported by the National NSFC (No. 61003001, 61170006, 61171132, 61033010); Specialized Research Fund for the Doctoral Program of Higher Education No. 20100071120032; NSF of Jiangsu Province (No. BK2010280).

SIGMOD'13, June 22–27, 2013, New York, New York, USA.

1. INTRODUCTION

Most complex networks in nature and human society contain *community structures* that serve as functional building blocks for the networks. Furthermore, communities often overlap with each other, that is, a vertex in a network may belong to more than one community.

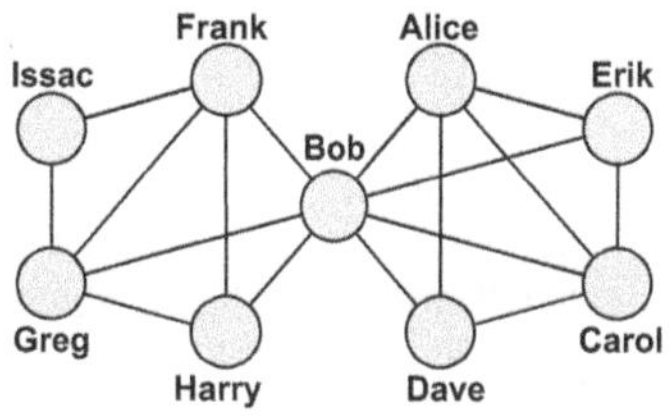

Figure 1: A toy social graph

1.1 Overlapping Communities

Overlapping community structures can be observed in many real networks, including social networks, biology networks, and sematic networks, and they are vital in revealing the internal structure of large networks [1]. The ubiquity of overlapping communities signifies the importance of finding overlapping communities in graphs.

Communities can be defined in many ways. In general, a community refers to a group of vertices that are densely connected to each other and sparsely connected to other vertices in the graph. The density of a community usually is measured by its average degree. In this paper, we use k-cliques [1] as the building blocks of a community. We will show the rational in Section 3. A k-clique is a complete graph of k vertices. Given a graph G, we can find all k-cliques in G. We say two k-cliques are adjacent if they share $k-1$ vertices in G. We can then create a k-clique graph for G. In the k-clique graph, each vertex is a k-clique and an edge between two vertices means the two k-cliques they represent are adjacent in G. A community is defined as a connected component, called a k-clique component, in the k-clique graph. Clearly, the larger the k value, the denser the communities. By tuning k, we obtain communities of different density. Next, we use a toy social network to illustrate overlapping communities.

EXAMPLE 1 (OVERLAPPING COMMUNITIES). *Consider the toy social graph shown in Figure 1. Suppose we need to find the communities containing Bob. When $k=3$, we get two overlapping communities: $abcde$[1] and $bfghi$ (for simplicity, we use the first character of a person's name to represent the person). When $k=4$, we find two communities: $abcde$ and $bfhg$. $bfhg$ is denser than*

[1] In the following text, we use 'abcde' to denote the clique consisting of vertex set $\{a, b, c, d, e\}$

bfhgi because Issac, who has fewer connections to the community, is excluded.

1.2 OCD vs OCS

There are two related problems: *overlapping community detection* (OCD), which finds overlapping communities in the entire network, and *overlapping community search* (OCS), which finds overlapping communities that a specific vertex belongs to.

The difference between OCD and OCS is clear. For a given graph, OCD takes k as input, and finds overlapping communities in the entire graph, using a batch process. As a result, all detected communities are of the density that is not less than the same threshold. On the other hand, OCS takes a vertex and a specific k as input, and finds overlapping communities containing the vertex, using an online process.

One common operation in community analysis is to retrieve the communities containing a vertex. To support online query answering by OCD, we need to detect and materialize all communities in an offline pre-computation stage and then index the communities. In contrast, with OCS, we just need to specify the vertex of interest in the query. Using OCD to support this common operation is less desirable for large graphs due to the following reasons.

- First, *it is costly and time consuming to find communities for the entire graph by OCD.* OCD in general is NP-hard, and many real life graphs are quite large, with millions or even billions of nodes. For example, the friendship network of Facebook [2] contains over 800 million nodes and 100 billion links. As a result, OCD is computationally prohibitive on real large graphs. In contrast, with OCS, we just need to find communities within the local neighborhoods of the vertex. In the experimental section, we will show that in most cases, our OCS solution only needs several milliseconds to find answers, independent of the entire graph size.

- Second, *OCD uses a global criterion for community detection for all vertices in a network.* The semantics of the discovered community in general heavily depends on the parameters. Example 1 has shown that for the same vertex, a different k leads to communities of different density and different semantics. Results on real networks (the details are presented in the experiment section) further show that under a given k, some vertices may have no corresponding valid communities. In other words, a fixed k is not appropriate for all vertices. OCD does not support using the most appropriate k for each individual vertex.

- Third, *it is difficult for OCD to support dynamically evolving graphs.* Graphs in real life are always evolving over time. OCD can only be used for offline analysis. Generally, we cannot afford to run OCD very frequently. As a result, a solution of OCD usually loses its freshness and effectiveness after a short period of time. In contrast, with OCS, we are free to issue queries for any vertex, which will not significantly hinder system performance.

In summary, OCD plus indexing suffers when the graph is dynamically evolving or users want to tune the density parameters for a better result. Because it is costly to rerun OCD and rebuild the index. Unfortunately, most real networks, such as Facebook friendship networks, are evolving and users in these networks usually expect to freely explore his or her neighborhood community. This motivates us to study online OCS.

1.3 Challenges

To understand the major challenges of OCS, we compare OCS with a related and well studied problem: *Community Search* (CS). Given a vertex (or a set of vertices), community search finds the community (instead of a set of overlapping communities) that contains the vertex [3]. In the following analysis, we show that CS and OCS are fundamentally different, and methods of CS cannot be directly applied to solve the OCS problem. The challenges of OCS are summarized as the follows:

- *Our first challenge lies in modeling the overlapping community search.* CS and OCS have different semantics. For OCS, each community has a "functioning model". For example, a person may be part of a "weekend hiking" community and a "software engineer community" at the same time. If we mix the two communities, then we incur a loss of semantics. Typical CS approaches cannot tell the difference. For example, one approach finds the subgraph that has the largest minimal degree as the community [3]. Clearly, if two subgraphs satisfy the criterion, then their union also satisfies the criterion. This shows that CS is not a good model for overlapping community. In comparison, OCS is more semantically aware in the sense that its goal is more about finding a functioning module that can better reveal the role of a vertex. Hence, we need to define the community more carefully and precisely to reflect this requirement. Specifically, we need to prescribe when two overlapping groups can be merged into a single community, and when they are two separate communities.

- *Our second challenge is that OCS is computationally harder than CS.* Intuitively, in OCS, all communities need to be enumerated. In some extreme cases, when there are an exponential number of valid communities, the enumeration is quite costly. Even if there is only a small number of valid communities, finding them among an exponential number of candidates is still a great challenge. In contrast, in most CS [3], for a given query vertex, there is at most one community to detect.

- *Our third challenge is to adopt approximate approaches so that we can scale to large graphs with millions of nodes.* Due to its computation intractability, it is difficult to scale up to million-node real life graphs. Finding the approximate results without compromising too much the quality of the solution (particularly the semantics of the community) is a challenge.

1.4 Contributions and Organization

In this paper, we propose a novel model for OCS, the theory based on the model, and the algorithms that solve OCS. More specifically, we make the following contributions:

- We introduce a model for OCS that satisfies not only the traditional community semantics, but also the semantics of overlapping. Furthermore, the two types of semantics are consistent in our model.

- We propose several algorithms to solve OCS. These algorithms produce meaningful results, and can handle million-node graphs.

- We offer the theoretical guidelines for parameter selection. The guidelines take into consideration the structural properties of real networks, and ensure the discovery of meaningful overlapping communities in real life complex networks.

- We conduct extensive experiments on real networks to justify our algorithms and theories. We also show many applications of OCS model and algorithms.

The rest of the paper is organized as follows. Section 2 discusses related work. Section 3 focuses on the model and the problem of overlapping community search. Section 4 describes a naive algorithm and an improved algorithm. We further propose a more efficient approximate algorithm. Experimental results in Section 5 show the performance and effectiveness of both the exact and the approximate algorithms. We show some potential applications for OCS model in Section 6. We conclude in Section 7.

2. RELATED WORK

Our work is closely related to work on several topics, including *overlapping community detection*, *dense subgraph discovery*, and *clique finding*.

Overlapping community detection. Palla et al. [1] first noticed that most real networks have overlapping community structures and proposed a percolation based method to detect overlapping communities in real networks. They also defined a community as a k-clique component. But they did not generalize it to allow relaxation. They developed a software called CFinder [4] based on the method to detect overlapping communities on biology networks. Their work was further extended with the EAGLE [5] algorithm that merges two cliques into one community if their Jaccard-similarity score is large enough. Gregory et al. [6] transformed the problem of overlapping community detection (OCD) on graph G into an equivalent non-overlapping community detection problem on another graph G', which is produced by duplicating certain vertices or edges in G. They used betweenness as the heuristic to select the vertex or edge to be duplicated. They further improved its performance by using local betweenness in a way that can be quickly computed to approximate the betweenness [7]. Ahn et al. [8] reinvented a community as a group of links instead of vertices so that they can always produce a hierarchical dendrogram on vertex-overlapped networks. Baumes et al. [9] proposed a greedy solution to grow overlapping communities. The algorithm first ranks all nodes according to some criterion, such as PageRank. Then, each node is added in turn into existing communities whose densities will increase after the acceptance of the new node as a member. Xu et al. [10] found that some vertices can not be classified into any communities. These vertices, called *hubs*, usually bridge different communities. So they proposed a linear algorithm, called SCAN, to find hubs and communities. Recently some efficient overlapping community detection algorithms were proposed, including SLPA [11], GCE [12] and OSLOM [13]. SLPA simulates the human communication behavior and realizes it into a speaker-listener label propagation algorithm. GCE identifies distinct cliques as seeds and expands these seeds by greedily optimizing a local fitness function. OSLOM finds overlapping communities by local optimization of a fitness function expressing the statistical significance of clusters with respect to random fluctuations.

Compared to OCD, OCS is a more light-weight problem model, and it is suitable for online query answering. By definition, OCD inherently implies intractable computation complexity. For example, CFinder needs to enumerate all k-cliques in a graph and then combine them in terms of overlap between cliques. Both clique enumeration and pairwise computation of clique similarity are costly. In contrast, in OCS, most resulting communities tend to occur around the local neighborhoods of the query vertex, allowing finding the answers by only exploring a part of the graph instead of processing the entire graph.

Dense subgraph discovery. In many graphs whose dense subgraphs have clear boundaries and can be separated from each other, communities are dense subgraphs. In this sense, our work is closely related to dense subgraph discovery. The problem of finding the densest subgraph is NP-hard, where the density of a graph $G(V, E)$ is usually measured by $\frac{2|E|}{|V|(|V|-1)}$. Doron et al. [14] gave an approximate algorithm for finding the dense k-vertex subgraphs of a given graph, with approximation ratio $O(n^{\delta})$ for some $\delta < \frac{1}{3}$. For practical use, Gibson et al. [15] used recursive shingling to find dense subgraphs on massive graphs. Their algorithms are scalable to web-scale graph with 50M hosts and 11B edges but without guarantees for the density of the result. To handle Internet-sized graph data in the form of stream, Bahman et al. [16] proposed a greedy solution for graph streams, which takes $O(log_{1+\epsilon}n)$ passes for any $\epsilon \geq 0$ yielding approximation factor of $2(1+\epsilon)$. Some other methods propose different definitions of dense subgraphs. For example, DN-graph is proposed in [17] and accompanied with a triangle-counting based solution. Although dense subgraph discovery is related to community discovery, they are essentially different from each other. A community is far beyond a dense subgraph. As a community, the density within the subgraph is expected to be significantly larger than the outside world of the subgraph. Furthermore, our problem is a typical search problem, in which a query vertex needs to be specified.

Clique finding. k-cliques underlie our community definition. There are already many k-clique related literatures. Most of them concern clique finding, i.e., finding a maximal clique or finding cliques with a size constraint. In general, the decision version of clique finding is NP-Complete [18]. Derényi [19] gave the threshold of edge-linking probability for the emergence of a giant k-clique component in an Erdos Renyi(ER) [20] random graph. To solve the problem practically, local search [21] is widely employed in many efficient solutions [22, 23, 24]. Along this direction, reactive local search (RLS) [22], dynamic local search (DLS) [23] and an improved DLS [24] have been proposed in turn. For disk-resident massive graphs, Cheng et al. [25] proposed an external-memory algorithm ExtMCE to reduce memory usage. They built a summary of small-sized graph, called H*-graph, to precisely encode the neighborhood information in the original graph. We only use k-clique to define community. In our problems, we not only need to find cliques around the query vertex, we also need to take care of clique adjacency. The second issue is not addressed in the clique-related work.

3. OVERLAPPING COMMUNITY

In the following, we first define the model as well as the problem (Section 3.1). Then, we justify the model by highlighting some of its important properties (Section 3.2). Finally, we discuss how to tune the parameters in the model to produce meaningful results (Section 3.3).

3.1 Model and Problem Definition

We start with the definition of OCS problem. Then, we generalize it into the (α, γ)-OCS problem.

3.1.1 OCS

Network communities are usually modeled by k-cliques [1]. Given an original network G, we derive a *k-clique graph* from G. In the k-clique graph, each node represents a k-clique in G, and an edge between two nodes means that the k-cliques the two nodes represent are adjacent in G, where adjacency is defined as follows:

DEFINITION 1 (CLIQUE ADJACENCY). *Two k-cliques are adjacent if they share $k-1$ vertices.*

We define OCS based on the concept of k-clique components.

DEFINITION 2 (k-CLIQUE COMPONENT). *Let C be a connected component in the k-clique graph. A k-clique component is the union of all k-cliques represented by nodes in C.*

Intuitively, given a vertex v_0, there may be multiple communities that contain v_0. All these communities naturally constitute the overlapping communities that contain v_0. Thus, the problem is finding all such communities.

PROBLEM 1 (OVERLAPPING COMMUNITY SEARCH (OCS)). *Given a graph $G(V, E)$, a query vertex v_0 and a positive integer k, we need to find all k-clique components containing v_0.*

EXAMPLE 2 (OCS). *Consider the graph shown in Figure 1. Assume we want to find overlapping communities that contain node b (i.e., $v_0 = b$). Let $k = 4$. We have three k-cliques containing b: $C_1 = abcd$, $C_2 = abce$ and $C_3 = bfhg$. The clique graph is*

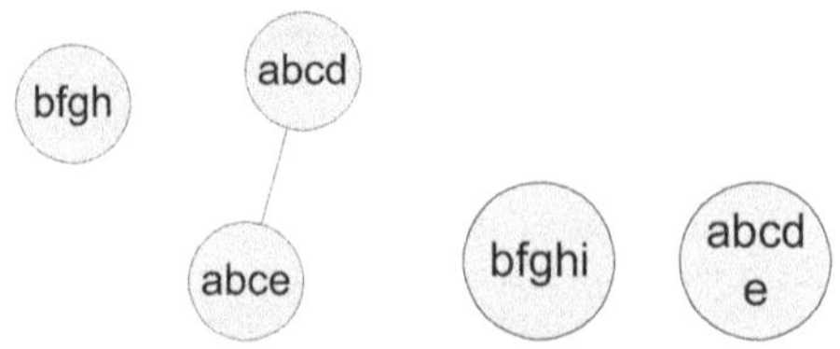

(a) The clique graph for $(3, 1)$-OCS (b) The clique graph for $(4, .8)$-OCS

Figure 2: Clique graphs are sensitive to the parameters of OCS.

shown in Figure 2(a). Hence, $C_1 \cup C_2$ and C_3 are returned as two overlapping communities containing the query vertex.

3.1.2 (α, γ)-OCS

The definition of overlapping community given above is too restrictive: First, every pair of nodes in each k-clique by definition must be connected. Second, two k-cliques are considered adjacent iff they share as many as $k-1$ nodes. In this section, we define a more general problem, (α, γ)-OCS, by relaxing the two constraints.

First, we relax the adjacency requirement. In (α, γ)-OCS, two k-cliques are considered adjacent if they share $\alpha \leq k-1$ vertices. This leads to the definition of α-adjacency.

DEFINITION 3 (α-ADJACENCY). *Two subgraphs G_1 and G_2 of graph $G(V, E)$ are α-adjacent if they share at least α vertices.*

Second, we relax the requirement of cliqueness. A k-clique is the densest graph among all k-node graphs. We generalize it to γ-quasi-clique by exposing parameter γ to tune the density of the subgraph.

DEFINITION 4 (γ-QUASI-k-CLIQUE [26]). *A γ-quasi-k-clique of graph G is a k-node subgraph of G with at least $\lfloor \gamma \frac{k(k-1)}{2} \rfloor$ edges (where $0 \leq \gamma \leq 1$).*

We now give a generalized version of overlapping community search: (α, γ)-OCS. Similar to the basic version, we also intend to find all overlapping communities containing a query vertex. But each community here is a γ-quasi-k-clique component and the clique adjacency is defined by α adjacency. Clearly, Problem 1 is simply $(k-1, 1)$-OCS.

PROBLEM 2 ((α, γ)-OCS). *For a graph G, a query vertex v_0 and a positive integer k, the (α, γ)-OCS problem finds all γ-quasi-k-clique components containing v_0.*

EXAMPLE 3 ((α, γ)-OCS). *To continue with the previous example, consider $(4, 0.8)$-OCS and $k = 5$ and $v_0 = b$. abcde and bghif are two resulting communities. This can be directly obtained from the clique graph shown in Figure 2(b).*

3.1.3 Complexity

We next analyze the complexity of overlapping community search. First, we show that $(k-1, 1)$-OCS is NP-hard. Given a query vertex v_0, the decision version of $(k-1, 1)$-OCS is to decide whether there are any k-cliques that contain v_0. When k is not a constant, this decision problem is NP-complete, which can be reduced from the k-clique problem (deciding whether a graph G has a k-clique). Then, as a more general problem, (α, γ)-OCS is also NP-hard.

3.2 The Rationale

Is the model proposed in Section 3.1 meaningful? In this section, we justify it from the following three aspects: community density, overlapping-awareness and consistency.

3.2.1 Community Density

To qualify as a community, a subgraph obviously needs to have *enough density*. In (α, γ)-OCS, the parameters α and γ together control the closeness among the members of a community. In this subsection, we establish a lower bound (Theorem 1) of the average degree for communities found by (α, γ)-OCS. Theorem 1 is based on Lemma 1. As an example of Theorem 1, the average degree of a community of $(k-1, 1)$-OCS is at least $k-1$.

LEMMA 1. *For a γ-quasi-k-clique, the number of edges incident to an arbitrary set of x vertices is at least $max\{0, \gamma\binom{k}{2} - \binom{k-x}{2}\}$.*

PROOF. The total number of edges of this clique is at least $\gamma\binom{k}{2}$. The subgraph induced by the rest $k-x$ vertices has at most $\binom{k-x}{2}$ edges, which are not incident to the selected vertices. Therefore, the lemma holds. □

THEOREM 1 (LOWER BOUND ON AVERAGE DEGREE). *The average degree of each community found by (α, γ)-OCS has a lower bound*

$$2\max\{0, \min\{f(1), f(\alpha), f(k)\}\}$$

where $f(x) = \frac{\gamma\binom{k}{2} - \binom{k-x}{2}}{x}$.

PROOF. First, we show that for $x \in \{1, 2, ..., \alpha, k\}$, it holds that $f(x) \geq \min\{f(1), f(\alpha), f(k)\}$. We have $f'(x) = -\frac{1}{2} + \frac{(1-\gamma)k(k-1)}{2x^2}$, which satisfies the following inequalities:

$$\begin{cases} f'(x) \geq 0, 0 < x \leq \sqrt{(1-\gamma)k(k-1)} \\ f'(x) < 0, x > \sqrt{(1-\gamma)k(k-1)} \end{cases}$$

Thus, $f(x)$ takes its minimum value at $x = 1$, $x = \alpha$ or $x = k$, which means $f(x) \geq \min\{f(1), f(\alpha), f(k)\}$.

Now, suppose C is a community found by (α, γ)-OCS, and C consists of t different cliques $C_1, C_2, ..., C_t$. Let $V_i = \bigcup_{1 \leq j \leq i} C_j$. Let $v_i = |V_i - V_{i-1}|$, we have $|C| = \sum_{1 \leq i \leq t} v_i$. Let e_i be the number of edges in $E[V_i] - E[V_{i-1}]$, where $E[V_i]$ is the edges induced by V_i. The average degree of C is $\frac{2|E(C)|}{|V(C)|}$, which equals $\frac{\sum_{1 \leq i \leq t} 2e_i}{|C|} = \frac{2}{|C|}\sum_{1 \leq i \leq t, v_i \neq 0} v_i \times \frac{e_i}{v_i}$. Using the minimal value of $\frac{e_i}{v_i}$ to replace each $\frac{e_i}{v_i}$, we get

$$\frac{2|E(C)|}{|V(C)|} \geq \frac{2\sum_{1 \leq i \leq t, v_i \neq 0} v_i}{|C|} \min_{1 \leq i \leq t, v_i \neq 0}\{\frac{e_i}{v_i}\} = 2 \min_{1 \leq i \leq t, v_i \neq 0}\{\frac{e_i}{v_i}\}$$

Due to the definition, $v_1 = k, \forall 2 \leq i \leq t, v_i \leq \alpha$. According to Lemma 1 and the fact that $f(x) \geq \min\{f(1), f(\alpha), f(k)\}$, we find that the average degree of a community found by (α, γ)-OCS has a lower bound $2\max\{0, \min\{f(1), f(\alpha), f(k)\}\}$. □

3.2.2 Overlapping Awareness

The model should be able to reveal the overlapping relationships of multiple communities. Note that this is not a trivial task. When two subgraphs overlap, it is hard to tell whether they are two components of a single community or two overlapping communities. In OCS, given two subgraphs H_1, H_2 that contain the query vertex, we have two choices: return $H_1 \cup H_2$ as a single community or return H_1, H_2 as two overlapping communities.

Previous models of communities were overlapping-unaware, and even overlapping-unfriendly. A widely adopted model [3] considers a subgraph whose minimal degree is larger than a given threshold as a valid community. Thus, the union of two communities is also a valid community. Hence, two communities can always be merged, even if they have very little overlap.

In (α, γ)-OCS, we use α to decide whether two components have enough overlapping to be considered and merged as a single community. Specifically, if two γ-quasi-k-cliques share fewer than α vertices and they are not reachable in any clique component, they are considered as two overlapping communities instead of a single community.

3.2.3 Consistency

Community search must be consistent, that is, if a community C is considered a community for a query vertex v_0, then if we use any other vertex in C as a query vertex, we should also obtain C as its community. We establish the consistency of (α, γ)-OCS in Theorem 2, which can be easily derived according to the fact that clique adjacency is an equivalence relationship.

THEOREM 2 (CONSISTENCY). *In (α, γ)-OCS, if C is a community that contains query vertex v_0, then for any other vertex $v \in C$ as the query vertex, C is also returned as its community.*

3.3 Parameter Selection

The model for overlapping community contains 3 parameters: k, α, γ. The selection of these parameters is crucial to producing meaningful results. In this section, we will give the theoretic guideline for selecting appropriate parameters.

3.3.1 Selection of γ and k

Parameter γ controls the density of the community. The selection of k and γ is related, in the sense that the larger the k, the more difficult it is to find communities with the high density. Hence, in order to generate meaningful results, γ should vary with k. Next, we will reveal the relationship between γ and k. We first give a simple relationship to avoid a trivial case. Then, we establish a more complicated relationship between them on ER random graphs.

A simple relationship. In general, as a meaningful community, the quasi clique needs to be connected. For k vertices, even when there are $\frac{k(k-1)}{2} - (k-1)$ edges among them, it is still possible that they are disconnected. It happens when the k-vertex graph consists of an isolated vertex and a $(k-1)$-vertex clique. To avoid the disconnected case, γ should be big enough. Hence, we need to ensure that:

$$\lfloor \gamma \frac{k(k-1)}{2} \rfloor > \frac{k(k-1)}{2} - k + 1,$$

By transformation, we have

$$\gamma \geq \frac{k-2}{k} + \frac{2}{k(k-1)} \tag{1}$$

Relationship on ER random graphs. Given a graph with N nodes and M edges, the density of the graph is given by $\frac{2M}{N(N-1)}$. Next, we use the ER random graph model [20] as an example to reveal the relationship between γ and k. The ER random graph is used to simulate real graphs, such as road networks. Consider an ER random graph $G \in \mathcal{G}(n, p)$ that has n vertices and each pair of vertices is linked with probability p, independent of other vertices and edges. Suppose we randomly pick k vertices from G. Let X be the random variable that represents the number of edges among the selected vertices. Then, the probability that $X = i$ is

$$Pr(X = i) = \binom{m}{i} p^i (1-p)^{m-i} \tag{2}$$

where $m = k(k-1)/2$. Let Y be the random variable that represents the density of the subgraph induced by the randomly selected k vertices. Clearly, we have $Y = X/m$. Then, the probability that k selected vertices have density γ is a function of k and γ, that is:

$$Pr(Y = \gamma) = \binom{\frac{k(k-1)}{2}}{\lfloor \frac{\gamma k(k-1)}{2} \rfloor} p^{\lfloor \frac{\gamma k(k-1)}{2} \rfloor} (1-p)^{\frac{k(k-1)}{2} - \lfloor \frac{\gamma k(k-1)}{2} \rfloor} \tag{3}$$

We give the simulation of $Pr(Y = \gamma)$ in Figure 3(a) for $p = 0.3$. We can clearly see that when γ is fixed, $Pr(Y = \gamma)$ in general is a decreasing function of k. This suggests that we can find communities for small k with high probability. We justify this in the experimental section by showing that for most real networks communities exist mostly for $4 \leq k \leq 10$.

When k is fixed, $Pr(Y = \gamma)$ reaches its maximum when γ is close to the average density. To show this more clearly, we give $Pr(Y = \gamma)$ as a function of γ for two fixed k in Figure 3(b). The simulation results imply that there are many subgraphs of average density in the networks. In general, a meaningful community should have a much larger density than the average density. Hence, we should select a large enough density to disfavor those trivial communities with average density.

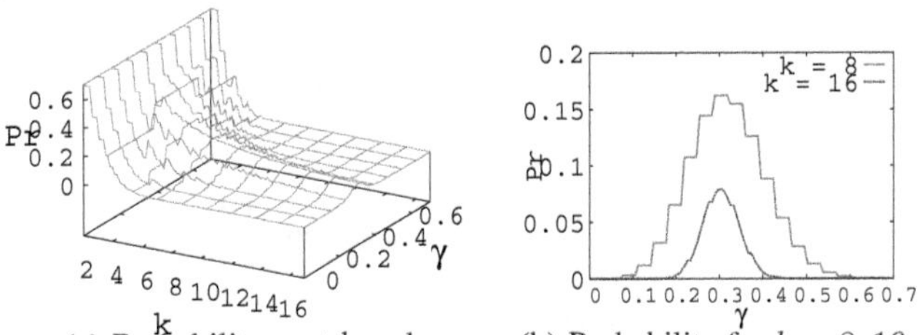

(a) Probability w.r.t k and γ (b) Probability for $k = 8, 16$

Figure 3: Simulation of density. This simulation shows the correlation between k and γ.

More formally, once k is given, we may use a confidence value such as $c = 0.05$ to construct an inequality $Pr(Y \geq \gamma) \leq c$ which is equivalent to

$$\sum_{i \leq j \leq m} \binom{m}{j} p^j (1-p)^{m-j} \leq c$$

, since $Pr(X \geq i) = Pr(Y \geq \gamma)$ when $i = \gamma m$. By solving above inequation, we find the appropriate i value and corresponding γ. By tuning c, we can control γ. A smaller c generally leads to a larger γ.

3.3.2 Selection of α

Parameter α, as we mentioned before, controls how strictly we consider two communities to be one community or components of the same community. Our major goal in selecting a meaningful α is to avoid two trivial cases.

The first trivial case occurs when the density of a γ-quasi-k-clique is contributed mainly by its α-size subset. As a result, any other $k - \alpha$ vertices outside of the clique combined with the subset will be a valid adjacent clique. This trivial case obviously leads to meaningless communities. To avoid this case, we need $\binom{\alpha}{2} < \gamma\binom{k}{2}$. By simple transformation, we have

$$\alpha \leq \lceil \sqrt{1/4 + k(k-1)\gamma} - 1/2 \rceil \tag{4}$$

The second trivial case occurs when two γ-quasi-k-cliques intersect at a α-size subset that is quite sparse. In real networks, if the common part of two subgraphs are too sparse, they can rarely be regarded as a single closely-connected community. If the common part of two subgraphs is too sparse, the two subgraphs can rarely be regarded as a single closely-connected community. This case happens if all edges are located among the rest $k - \alpha$ vertices. To avoid this, we set $\gamma\binom{k}{2} > \binom{k-\alpha}{2}$ so that the common part has at least one shared edge. By transformation, we have

$$\alpha \geq \lfloor k + 1/2 - \sqrt{\gamma k^2 - \gamma k + 1/4} \rfloor \tag{5}$$

Combining the two cases, given k and γ, we chose α to be an integer between the lower and upper bounds. As an example, when

$\gamma = 1$, we have $1 \leq \alpha \leq \lceil \sqrt{1/4 + k(k-1)} - 1/2 \rceil$. Furthermore, when $k = 4$, we have $1 \leq \alpha \leq 3$. Hence, usually we use $\alpha = 3$.

3.3.3 Practical selection of parameters

Based on the above analysis, we show that $\alpha = k - 1, \gamma = 1$ (or values close to 1) are typical settings of (α, γ)-OCS. By simple transformation of Eq. 1, we have

$$\gamma \geq 1 - \frac{2}{k}\frac{k-2}{k-1} = f(k)$$

. When $k > 3$, $f(k)$ converges to 1. It can be observed from the simulation of $f(k)$ in Figure 4. Hence, $\gamma = 1$ (or values close to 1) is a typical setting. Next, we show that $\alpha = k - 1$ is also a typical setting because *only* $\alpha = k - 1$ lies between the lower and upper bound of α for any k and $\frac{k-2}{k} + \frac{2}{k(k-1)} \leq \gamma \leq 1$ (shown in Theorem 3).

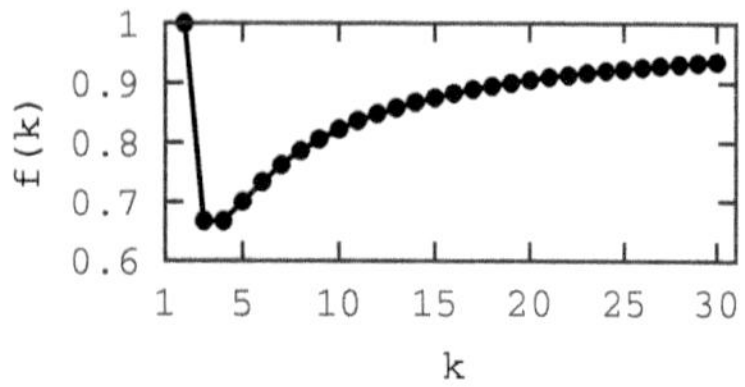

Figure 4: Simulation of $f(k)$.

THEOREM 3. *Let $\alpha = k - \Delta$ and Δ be a positive integer less than k. Only when $\Delta = 1$, α satisfies Eq. 4 and Eq. 5 for any $k \geq 2$ and $\frac{k-2}{k} + \frac{2}{k(k-1)} \leq \gamma \leq 1$.*

PROOF. First, consider $k = 2$. Since $0 < \alpha = k - \Delta < k$, we have $2 - \Delta > 0$. Hence, only $\Delta = 1$ satisfies this inequality. Next, for any k and $\frac{k-2}{k} + \frac{2}{k(k-1)} \leq \gamma \leq 1$, we have

$$\lceil \sqrt{1/4 + k(k-1)\gamma} - 1/2 \rceil \geq \lceil \sqrt{9/4 + (k-1)(k-2)} - 1/2 \rceil$$

, which is not less than $k - 1$; and

$$\lfloor k + 1/2 - \sqrt{\gamma k^2 - \gamma k + 1/4} \rfloor \leq \lfloor k + 1/2 - \sqrt{(k-1)(k-2) + 9/4} \rfloor$$

, which is not larger than $k - 1$. Thus only $\alpha = k - 1$, i.e., $\Delta = 1$, satisfies the constraints. □

4. ALGORITHMS

In this section, we will first propose two exact algorithms to solve OCS. The first is a straightforward solution. The second is a more efficient exact solution. To further improve the performance, we also propose a more efficient approximate algorithm.

4.1 Exact Algorithm

4.1.1 Naive Algorithm

We give a naive algorithm according to the definition of OCS. The direct solution for OCS consists of three major steps, which are shown in Algorithm 1. In the first step, we find the γ-quasi-k-clique that contains v_0. Then for each newly discovered vertex, we find all γ-quasi-k-cliques that contain the vertex. We repeat the above finding procedure until no new vertex can be discovered. In the second step, we calculate the clique adjacency for all cliques found in the first step. Finally, we return all clique components as the resulting communities.

4.1.2 New Algorithm Framework

The naive algorithm is not smart yet. As illustrated in Example 4, many cliques enumerated in the naive algorithm will not belong to a valid community. Hence, enumerating these invalid cliques

Algorithm 1 Naive OCS

Input: $G(V, E)$, v_0 α, γ, k;
Output: The overlapping communities containing v_0
//Stage 1. Find all the candidate cliques
$V_c \leftarrow \{v_0\}$
for all unvisited vertex $v \in V_C$ **do**
  $find\_clique(v)$; ▷ find *all* cliques that contain v
  Add all vertices of these cliques into V_C;
end for
//Stage 2. Calculate clique component
Calculate the adjacency matrix of candidate cliques;
//Stage 3. Return all clique components as communities

is wasteful. This can be avoided if we check the adjacency when a clique is enumerated. Following this idea, we proposed an improved algorithm, shown in Algorithm 2. The algorithm runs iteratively. In each iteration, we find an unvisited clique containing the query vertex by $next\_clique()$. If such a clique exists, we find the clique component that the clique belongs to by $expand()$.

EXAMPLE 4 (WASTEFUL ENUMERATION). *Consider (3, 1)-OCS with $k = 4$ and $v_0 = d$ on the graph shown in Figure 2(a), $\{a, b, c, d, e\}$ is the unique resulting community. By the naive algorithm, $bfgh$ will also be enumerated and participate in the succeeding computation, which is wasteful.*

Algorithm 2 Improved OCS

Input: $G(V, E)$, v_0 α, γ, k;
Output: The overlapping communities containing v_0
$\mathcal{R} \leftarrow \emptyset$;
while $C \leftarrow next\_clique(v_0), C \neq \emptyset$ **do**
  $\mathbf{C} \leftarrow expand(C)$; ▷ Find the clique component of C
  $\mathcal{R} \leftarrow \mathcal{R} \cup \{\mathbf{C}\}$;
end while
Return $\mathcal{R}$;

Note that for any two adjacent cliques, their clique components are identical. To avoid redundant enumeration, we record the visit status of each clique in both $next\_clique()$ and $expand()$, and only enumerate unvisited cliques. We illustrate this in Example 5. The new algorithm framework also allows us to further optimize it. We will present such optimizations in the following sections

EXAMPLE 5 (IMPROVED ALGORITHM). *Continue with the previous example but change v_0 to b. $next\_clique()$ may first return $bfgh$. By calling $expand()$ on this clique, we find the first community $\{b, f, g, h\}$. The next call of $next\_clique()$ may return abce. By calling $expand()$ on this clique, we find abcd. Thus, $\{a, b, c, d, e\}$ is the second community. Then, any further call of $next\_clique()$ will return nothing and the algorithm will terminate since all cliques have been visited either in $next\_clique()$ or $expand()$.*

4.1.3 Implementation of $next\_clique()$

$next\_clique(v_0)$ is responsible for enumerating each unvisited γ-quasi-k-clique containing vertex v_0. Finding all cliques is computationally hard. A naive solution needs to exhaustively enumerate all subsets with size k containing v_0, and check whether it is a valid clique. The solution costs $O(|V|^k k^2)$ time. Because there are $O(|V|^k)$ k-size subsets and checking whether the subset is a valid clique needs $O(k^2)$ time.

Clique enumeration is a well-known computationally hard problem. Even allowing approximation, clique finding is *hard to approximate*. Hence, brute-force enumeration seems to be inevitable to produce exact results. The major procedure is a depth-first search with backtracking. The procedure is shown in Algorithm 3. The search starts from $U = \{v_0\}$. Then, the procedure iteratively adds a new vertex into U until a new valid clique is found (line 5,6). The procedure will stop until all γ-quasi-k-cliques containing the query vertex are found.

The backtracking search can be improved from two aspects. First, we just need to select a new vertex from the neighbors of the current vertex (line 13). This is because as a valid parameter, γ needs to satisfy Eq. 1, which ensures the result is a connected subgraph. Second, we speedup the search by pruning the impossible enumeration (line 11). Let $|E(U)|$ be the number of edges in the subgraph induced by U. Thus the maximal number of edges that the resulting clique has is $|E(U)| + (k - |U|)|U| + \frac{(k-|U|)(k-|U|-1)}{2}$, which equals $|E(U)| + \frac{(k-|U|)(k+|U|-1)}{2}$. When the maximal number of edges is less than $\gamma\frac{k(k-1)}{2}$, that is

$$g(U) = |E(U)| + \frac{(k - |U|)(k + |U| - 1)}{2} < \gamma\frac{k(k-1)}{2} \quad (6)$$

, we can certainly prune the current U. The left side of the inequality is a function of U. We use $g(U)$ to denote it.

Algorithm 3 DFS procedure of $next\_clique(v_0)$

1: $U \leftarrow \{v_0\}$;
2: $DFS(U, v_0)$;
3: **procedure** DFS(U,u)
4:   **if** $|U| = k$ **then**
5:     **if** U is a γ-quasi-k-clique **And** U is unvisited **then**
6:       **Return** U;
7:     **else**
8:       **Return**;
9:     **end if**
10:   **end if**
11:   **if** $g(U) < \gamma\frac{k(k-1)}{2}$ **then Return;**
12:   **end if**
13:   **for all** $(u, v) \in E, v \notin U$ **do**
14:     $DFS(U \cup \{v\}, v)$;
15:   **end for**
16: **end procedure**

4.1.4 *Implementation of* $expand()$

Function $expand(C)$ is used for finding the clique component containing C. By any graph traverse on the clique graph, we can certainly find the connected component. But the traverse orders are influential on the performance. Here, we use DFS order.

The procedure of $expand(C)$ is shown in Algorithm 4. The major framework is a DFS traverse on the clique graph. In the algorithm, A is a global variable storing the currently found vertices in the clique component. The key operation in the traverse is *finding a subset* S_2 *from* C*'s neighborhoods to replace one of* C*'s subset* S_1 *so that the new combination* C' *is a valid clique.* To keep the size of the clique as k, we enforce $|S_1| = |S_2|$ (line 8). We can also use Eq. 6 to terminate the search that will not lead to a valid clique (line 6).

The function $Candidate(C - S_1)$ is used for finding a subset S_2 with the same size as $|S_1|$ from the *local neighborhoods* of $C - S_1$. Note that we do not need to enumerate S_2 from the entire V. Because under the constraint of Eq. 1, the induced graph of $(C-S_1) \cup S_2$ is always connected. Hence, in the worst case, we just need to explore the $|S_1|$*-hop-neighborhood of* $C - S_1$, which contains all vertices that are at most $|S_1|$ hops away from any vertex in $C-S_1$. When k is small, the exploration of $|S_1|$-hop-neighborhood is effective.

4.1.5 *Duplication detection*

In both $next\_clique()$ and $expand()$ functions, we may meet the same clique from different paths. For example, for the clique abc. We may meet it by $a - b - c$ or $a - c - b$. Hence, we need to tell whether a clique has ever been visited. For this purpose, we use a hash table to store visited cliques, allowing in constant time

Algorithm 4 $expand(C)$

Input: A γ-quasi-k-clique C;
Output: The clique component of C
1: $A \leftarrow C$;
2: $Expand\_clique(C)$;
3: **return** A;

4: **procedure** EXPAND_CLIQUE(C)
5:   **for all** $S_1 \subset C, |S_1| \leq k - \alpha$ **do**
6:     **if** $g(C - S_1) < \gamma\frac{k(k-1)}{2}$ **then** Continue
7:     **end if**
8:     **for all** $S_2 \in Candidate(C - S_1), |S_1| = |S_2|$ **do**
9:       $C' \leftarrow (C - S_1) \cup S_2$;
10:       **if** C' is unvisited **And** C' is a γ-quasi-k-clique **then**
11:         $A \leftarrow A \cup S_2$;
12:         $Expand\_Clique(C')$;
13:       **end if**
14:     **end for**
15:   **end for**
16: **end procedure**

to query a visited clique. We use the following hash function:

$$h(C) = (\sum_{v_i \in C} id(v_i) \times a^{id(v_i)}) \mod b \quad (7)$$

, where a, b are two large primes and $id(v_i)$ is the id of v_i. Hashing each k-size clique takes $O(k)$ time. By DFS, such complexity can be further reduced to $O(1)$. We only show this on $(k-1,1)$-OCS. In this case, two successively visited cliques have only two different vertices in the DFS traverse order. Thus, we can calculate the hash value in an incremental way. Suppose, $C_{i+1} = (C_i - \{v\}) \cup \{u\}$, we have

$$h(C_{i+1}) = (h(C_i) - id(v) \times a^{id(v)} + id(u) \times a^{id(u)}) \mod b \quad (8)$$

4.1.6 *Optimization on* $(k-1,1)$*-OCS*

In the exact solutions for the general OCS problem, we can only detect duplication after the enumeration of a clique. For a k-size clique, we may enumerate it $O((k-1)!)$ times. Next we show that on $(k-1,1)$-OCS, we can avoid such redundant enumerations. We only discuss it for $next\_clique(v_0)$. $Expand()$ can be optimized with the same technique. When we search for a γ-quasi ($\gamma < 1$) clique containing v_0, we need exhaustive enumerations to find a clique (line 13-15 in Algorithm 3). However, on $(k-1,1)$-OCS, we are searching for a standard clique (a complete subgraph). It is *order independent* to find such cliques. That is, for these cliques we can use any DFS order to enumerate the same clique. As a result, on $(k-1,1)$-OCS, we can pose an arbitrary linear order on V. Then, we search for a clique according to the linear order. That is only adding a vertex with a superior order into the partial solution. In this way, redundant enumerations of a k-clique can be avoided.

4.2 Approximate Algorithm

Next, we propose an efficient approximate algorithm for (α, γ)-OCS. The algorithm shares the same framework as Algorithm 2 with $next\_clique()$ and $expand()$ further approximated.

4.2.1 *Approximation in* $next\_clique()$

The $next\_clique()$ function may enumerate an exponential number of γ-quasi-k-cliques. To reduce the enumeration space, we only enumerate an unvisited clique which contains at least one new vertex that does not belong to any communities already found. This heuristic can be achieved by a slight change of the DFS procedure (Algorithm 3). Let $v_0, v_1, .., v_k$ be the vertex sequence (staring from the root v_0) in the DFS order. We require that the second vertex v_1 is a new vertex. In this way, we ensure that the new clique contains at least a new vertex. Note that we enforce that the vertex sequence contains a new vertex as early as possible and v_1 is the earliest vertex added into the sequence. Hence, v_1 is required to be a new vertex.

4.2.2 Approximation in $expand()$

We first study the traverse orders in $expand()$ function. We show in Example 6 that to meet all vertices in a community, the best case only requires a linear number cliques to be visited, while in the worst case, an exponential number of cliques may be visited.

EXAMPLE 6 (INFLUENCE OF TRAVERSE ORDERS). *Consider a complete graph with 100 vertices and $k = 4$. For $(k-1,1)$-OCS on any query vertex, the graph itself is the unique answer. To find the exact result, we need to visit $\binom{100}{4}$, approximately millions of k-cliques. Alternatively, if we always select a clique that is adjacent to previously visited cliques and contains at least one unvisited vertex, after visiting 97 cliques, all vertices in the result are met.*

The above example implies that we may find a community quite early before we exhaustively enumerate all γ-quasi-k-cliques in the community. Let C be a community of (α, γ)-OCS on graph G, in general we expect to find a shortest clique sequence $C_1, C_2, ...C_m$ such that each C_i is adjacent to at least one of its preceding cliques, and $\cup_{1\le i\le m} C_i = C$. However, in general, there exists an exponential number of possible sequences, it is hard to select the shortest sequence to visit.

Here, we will present a heuristic to find a short clique sequence. We still use DFS order. Consider $expand(C_1)$. Let C_i, C_{i+1} be two successively visited cliques; we always select C_{i+1} such that

$$C_{i+1} - \bigcup_{j\le i} C_j \neq \emptyset \tag{9}$$

. In other words, C_{i+1} is the clique containing at least one unvisited vertex. The traverse stops at C_m, to which no other unvisited cliques satisfying Eq. 9 are adjacent. In this way, the complete clique sequence $C_1, ...C_m$ is found. We return the union of them as the result of $expand(C_1)$. This heuristic can be implemented by simply adding a condition, $S_2 - A \neq \emptyset$, in line 10 of Algorithm 4.

4.2.3 Analysis

Consider a k-clique component C. Compared to the exact algorithm, which explores $O(\binom{|C|}{k})$ cliques, the approximate $expand()$ algorithm only explores exactly $O(|C|)$ cliques. Because the heuristic defined in Eq. 9 ensures finding a new vertex each time a clique is visited. $O(|C|)$ cliques will be visited and many wasteful enumerations are avoided. In this way, we reduce the exponential complexity to linear complexity. However, this heuristic may produce inexact results, which are illustrated in Example 7. We will show in the experimental section that this heuristic works quite well on real graphs, producing accurate results in most cases.

EXAMPLE 7 (BAD CASE). *Consider the $(2,1)$-OCS on the graph shown in Figure 1 with $k = 3$ and $v_0 = f$. The right community is $bfghi$. If cliques bfh, bgh were first visited, the search will stop since no new clique can be visited. As a result, i will be missed. If we first visit bfh and bfg, fgi is qualified to be visited and then we can find the right community.*

Due to the *NP-hardness to approximate* of clique finding, it is hard to give a theoretic guarantee of the approximation quality. However, we find that the approximate communities are *finer* than the exact ones. More formally, overlapping communities can be considered as a collection of subsets $P = \{C_1, C_2, ...C_k\}$. Then, for each community C_i in the approximate result, $\exists C'$ such that $C_i \subseteq C'$ and C' is an exact community of v_0. It clearly holds since the two approximations are equivalent to strengthen the constraint of a subgraph as a community. Since the community is finer, its size is smaller than or equal to the exact one. We have mentioned that the approximate algorithm only explores $O(|C|)$ cliques. Therefore, this property implies that the approximate algorithm is more efficient.

5. EXPERIMENTS

In this section, we present the experimental study and show the effectiveness and efficiency of our models and algorithms.

5.1 Experiment Setup

We ran all experiments on a PC with Intel Core2 at 2.13GHz, 4G memory running 64-bit Windows 7. We implemented all algorithms in C++. We compared the improved exact algorithm and the approximate algorithm. We also compared the OCS model and the OCD model. Except the study on the influence of parameters of γ and α, all results without explicit statement are obtained by $(k-1,1)$-OCS model.

We used four real networks to test our solution. The basic statistics of these networks are shown in Table 1. DBLP is a scientific collaboration network extracted from a recent snapshot of the D-BLP dataset [2]. Each vertex in the graph represents an author and each edge indicates a coauthoring relationship. Livejournal [3] is the friendship network of Livejournal, a social networking and blogging site. Google represents the web graph that was released in 2002 by Google. In the graph, nodes represent web pages and directed edges represent hyperlinks between them. We ignore the direction of the edges. WordNet is a semantic network in which each vertex represent a specific sense in language and each edge represents a certain semantic relationship between senses. WordNet has been widely used in a variety of real applications, such as word sense disambiguation, automatic text classification and automatic text summarization.

5.2 Case Study

We justify the model by two case studies: the scientific collaboration network and WordNet.

5.2.1 Scientific collaboration network

We run both the improved exact algorithm and the approximate algorithm on the scientific collaboration network extracted from D-BLP. The two algorithms produce almost the same results for most query vertices. Here, we use 'Jiawei Han' as the query vertex. Jiawei Han is a renowned computer scientist specializing in data mining and database. When $k = 6$, the exact result and the approximate result only differ in one community, where only two authors are missing in the approximate result. This justifies the effectiveness of the approximate algorithm. Hence, in the following evaluation, we will only use results produced by the approximate solution.

We show in Figure 5(a) part of the overlapping communities that Jiawei Han resides in. It only takes 18ms for the approximate solution to get the results, which justifies the efficiency of the approximate solution. Next, we focus on the effectiveness of the approach. We find that our overlapping community search model is meaningful in many aspects.

- First, it successfully unveils multiple research interests of an author. For example, in Jiawei Han's case, the community C_1 represents the topic of multimedia data mining and the community C_2 is about stream data mining. Each community has a clear boundary to be distinguished from others. We also can see that those authors with multiple research interests occur in different communities. For example, Jian Pei simultaneously occurs in C_2 and C_3, reflecting his research interest in both stream data mining and information network mining.
- Second, our model is flexible. By tuning parameter k, our model can discover communities with different closeness. For example, when $k = 9$, we discover more closely-connected communities of 'Jiawei Han' as shown in Figure 5(b). From

[2]Available at http://dblp.uni-trier.de/xml/

[3]This and Google are available at http://snap.stanford.edu/data.

Basic information				Performance of OCD and OCS				
Dataset	#Vertices	#Edges	average degree	LA	Amortized LA	OSLOM2	Amortized OSLOM2	OCS
WordNet	82670	133445	3.23	51s	0.61ms	1913s	23.1ms	0.15ms (k=3)
DBLP	560851	1816613	6.48	6183s	11ms	6993s	12.5ms	6.24ms (k=4)
Google	916427	4322051	9.43	22873s	25ms	84725s	92.5ms	31ms (k=6)
Livejournal	4847571	42851237	17.7	$>= 24h$	N/A	N/A	N/A	64ms (k=9)

Table 1: Datasets, performance of OCD and OCS

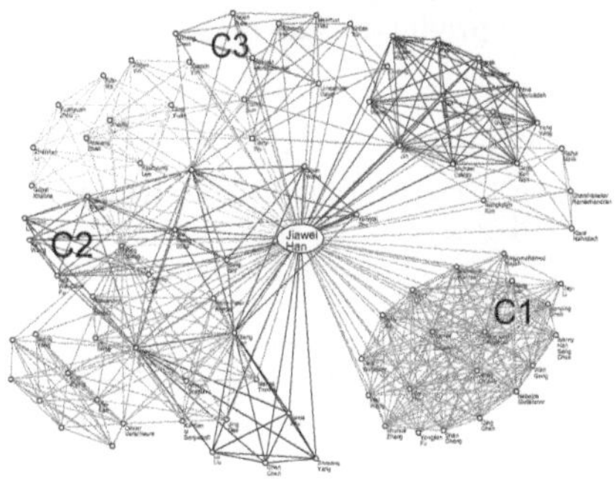

(a) $k = 6$

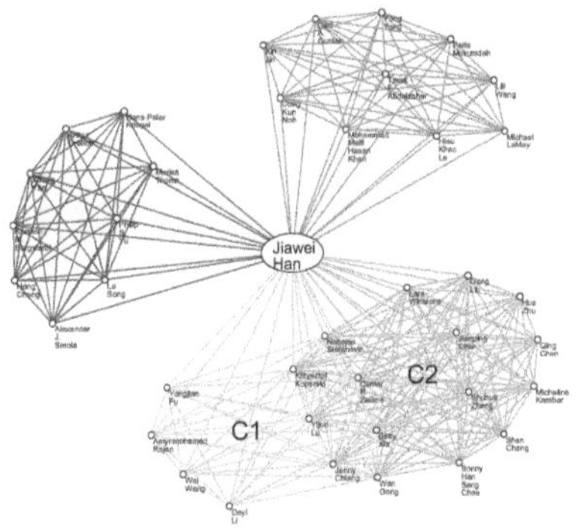

(b) k=9

Figure 5: Case study on DBLP. OCS can find communities representing different research topics. By tuning k, OCS can find communities with different closeness. This case study justifies the effectiveness of the OCS model.

the result, we can see that community C_1 of $k = 6$ is broken up into two more-closely connected overlapping communities C_1, C_2 of $k = 9$. The two communities respectively reflect Jiawei's more specific research interest. One is about multimedia data mining and the other is about association rule mining on large relational databases. When k becomes larger, many periphery members of communities who have relatively fewer collaborations with members in the community are excluded from the community. For example, we find that 59 authors in the result when $k = 6$ are excluded from the result when $k = 9$.

5.2.2 WordNet

In WordNet, we use the word *'vessel'* as the query vertex and we set $k = 3$. The result in Figure 6 shows that *'vessel'* occurs in multiple communities, and each community represents a certain sense of *'vessel'*. The community that contains *'bowl'*, *'dish'* corresponds to tablewares. The community consisting of *'barrel'* and *'tube'* represents the meaning of bucket. Another two communities represent the meaning of ships. The difference between these two communities is that the one consisting of *'ship'* and *'galley'* is generally used for describing ships with large tonnage and the other community are usually used for describing small boats. This example shows that our OCS model is helpful for finding different senses of a word, which is a fundamental task in natural language understanding.

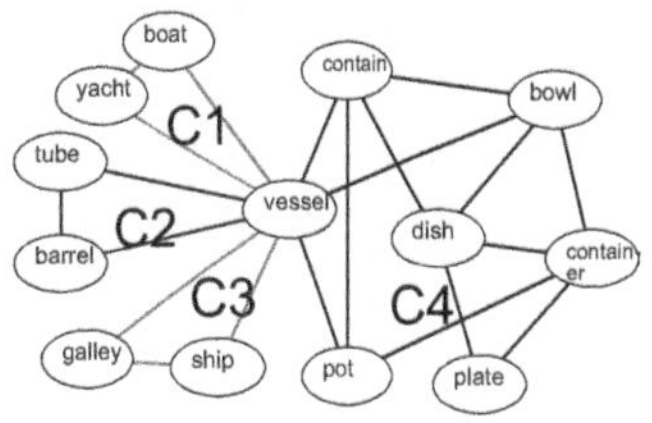

Figure 6: Case study on WordNet. OCS can find different senses of a word.

5.3 Performance

We first compare the performance of the exact algorithm and the approximate algorithm. Then, we compare the performance of OCS and OCD.

OCS: exact vs approximate methods. We tested the performance for both exact algorithms and approximate algorithms. For each k, we randomly selected 100 *valid query vertices* (with degree at least $k - 1$). We counted the average query answering time for these vertices under different k. Note that the exact solution has exponential enumeration cost. Hence, when the running time exceeds 60s, we terminated the exact algorithm and recorded the entire query response time as 60s. Clearly, this favors exact solutions. However, approximate solution still shows significant advantage over exact solutions as the following results indicate.

The results on three real networks are given in Figure 7. We can see that in general approximate algorithm is more than two orders of magnitudes faster than the exact one. Note that the performance priority of the approximation algorithm over the exact one is more striking than observed since we limit the running time of the exact algorithm to 60s. For Livejournal and Google, significant performance difference can be consistently observed over different k. When $k = 4$, most valid query vertices have non-trivial results and the approximate algorithm shows a much clearer advantage over the exact algorithm. On DBLP, an increase in speed by three orders of magnitudes is achieved for $k = 4$. For all the tested networks, the approximate solution's performance is quite stable compared to the exact solution, especially on DBLP. Even for the biggest two datasets, Livejournal and Google, both with approximately a million nodes and tens of millions edges, the approximation algorithm returns results within less than 100ms for almost all k. This sufficiently shows that the approximate solution can be used as online service for large real graphs.

OCS vs OCD. For comparisons, we also give the running time of the state-of-the-art OCD algorithmss LA [9] and OSLOM2 [13] in Table 1. We use the $-fast$ option to get the fastest results for OSLOM2. The time of OSLOM2 on Livejournal is not available. Because the program, which was downloaded from its official website, exited unexpectedly on Livejournal. We find that even on the smallest graph WordNet, two OCD algorithms still need 51s or 1913s, respectively. For a fair comparison, we also give the amortized running time of OCD, that is $\frac{\text{running time of OCD}}{|V|}$. Even con-

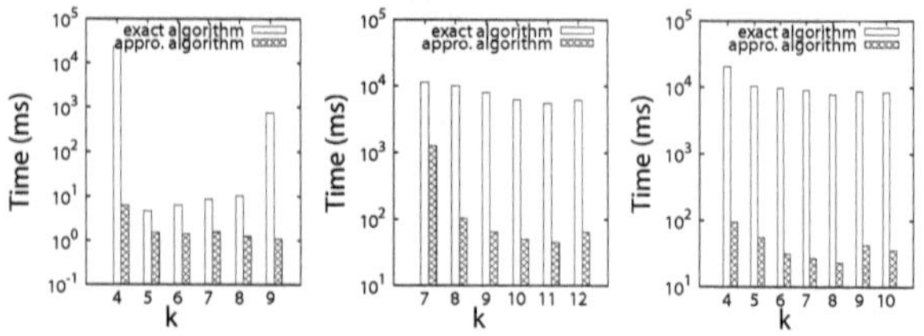

(a) DBLP (b) Livejournal (c) Google

Figure 7: Performance. The performance of the approximate solution is significantly better than that of the exact solution.

sidering the amortized running time, OCS is more efficient than OCD. From the comparison, we can clearly see that OCD is computationally prohibitive on large networks. In contrast, OCS is a lightweight solution to help us find overlapping communities.

5.4 Quality

In this subsection, we show the quality of the solution provided by the approximate algorithm. Overlapping communities express a certain equivalence relationship on V. Any two vertices in C_i are equivalent to each other under this equivalence relationship. Thus, we may use the overlapping ratio of the equivalence relationship to quantify the similarities between exact and inexact results. Let $P_1 = \{C_1, C_2, ...C_k\}$ be the approximate result, and let C'_i be one of the exact communities that contain C_i as a subset. Such C'_i certainly exists since P_1 is finer than the exact communities P_2. Then, we define the similarity between P_1 and P_2 as

$$sim(P_1, P_2) = \max_{1 \le i \le k} \sqrt{\frac{|C_i|(|C_i| - 1)}{|C'_i|(|C'_i| - 1)}} \tag{10}$$

. Clearly, we have $0 \le sim(P_1, P_2) \le 1$.

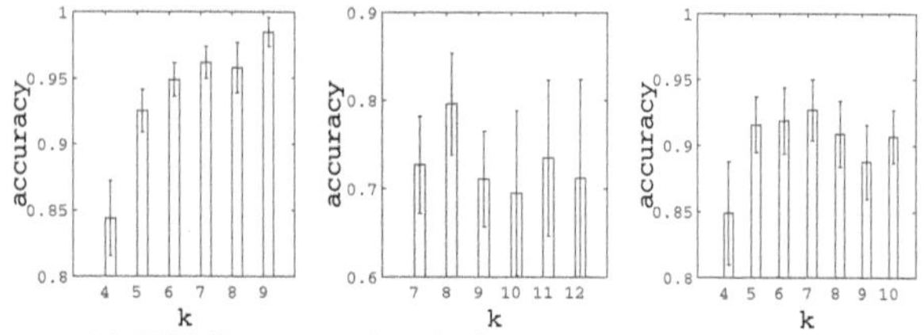

(a) DBLP (b) Livejournal (c) Google

Figure 8: Accuracy of approximate algorithm. Communities produced by approximate solutions are quite close to that produced by exact solutions.

We ran the approximate algorithm with 100 randomly selected valid query vertices on each network under different k. For each query vertex, we calculated the similarity value defined in Equation 10. We summarized the average and variance of the similarity value for 100 random query vertices. The results are shown in Figure 8. It is clear that for each tested network and each k, more than 70% accuracy can be achieved. In some special cases, for example, on DBLP and Google, almost 90% accuracy can be achieved.

We give the detailed accuracy results of DBLP in Table 2. In the table, for each k, 100 randomly selected valid vertices were queried. $\#has\ community$ denotes the number of vertices among them that have valid communities. $\#equivalent$ is the number of vertices for which the approximate algorithm produces the exact results. And $ratio = \frac{\#equivalent}{\#has\ community}$. We can see that for any k, more than 79% of query vertices have the exact results. When k increases, the accuracy increases. In many real applications where community has vague meanings, the accuracy of the community is not a strict requirement and our approximate algorithm is quite suitable for these applications.

k	4	5	6	7	8	9
$\#equivalent$	66	69	58	43	37	29
$\#has\ community$	84	83	65	49	40	30
ratio	79%	83%	89%	88%	93%	97%

Table 2: Accuracy on DBLP. For most query vertices, the approximate solution produces exact results.

5.5 Effectiveness

To show the effectiveness of the OCS model, we computed the proportion of valid query vertices that have communities. We ran the approximate algorithm on 100 randomly selected valid query vertices. For comparison, the proportions of valid query vertices are also given. The results are shown in Figure 9. From the figure, we can see that for each network, OCS model can discover meaningful communities for a significant number of vertices. On both DBLP and Google, when $k = 4$, more than 90% of valid query vertices have communities. For all the networks, the ratios of valid vertices and those with communities decrease as k increases. This can be naturally explained, since the constraint on the community is more restricted for a larger k.

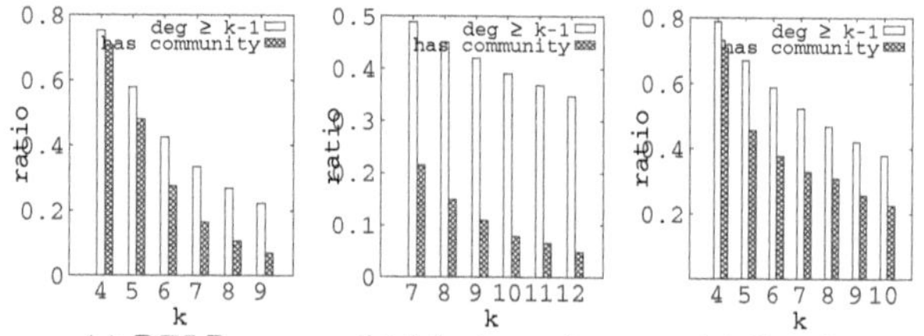

(a) DBLP (b) Livejournal (c) Google

Figure 9: Effectiveness of OCS. For most vertices, OCS model can find non-trivial results.

5.6 Influence of k

The value k is the most important parameter of OCS. In this subsection, we investigate the influence of k on the result of communities. We are interested in the number of communities as well as the size of communities.

We first give our analysis about the influence of k on community size and community number. In general, it is expected that the community size monotonically decreases with k. When k is small, the constraint for a group of vertices forming a community is weak. Consequently, it is easy to find large communities. When k grows, the community will become smaller. The influence of k on community number is a little bit more complicated. In general, there are two consequences caused by the growth of k:

- (1)The constraint on the closeness of a community becomes stronger. As a result, many communities found under a small k will not be a valid community any more. Consequently, the number of communities will reduce when k grows.
- (2)The condition for two communities to be merged into one single community becomes stronger. As a result, large communities will be broken up into small communities. Consequently, the number of communities will increase with k.

Hence, it is quite possible that there is a critical point on which two forces are balanced and maximal number of communities can be achieved. To verify this conjecture, we studied communities of 'Jiawei Han' in DBLP. We summarized the community number and community size of 'Jiawei Han' as the function of k.

Table 3: Performance on WordNet

k	3	4					
α	2	2	2	2	3	3	3
γ	1	0.8	0.9	1	0.8	0.9	1
Time (ms)	2298	36044	18022	6000	17882	17801	3395

The results are shown in Figure 10 and they verify our conjecture. From Figure 10(a), we can clearly see that the community size monotonically decreases with k. When $k = 5$ and larger, the community size is almost stable. These communities in general are core-coauthoring team members of 'Jiawei Han'. From Figure 10(b), we can clearly see that $k = 5$ is the critical point on which the maximal number of communities are found. Before this, larger communities are broken up into smaller communities when k increases. After this, valid communities quickly vanish due to the strong constraint on the closeness of a community.

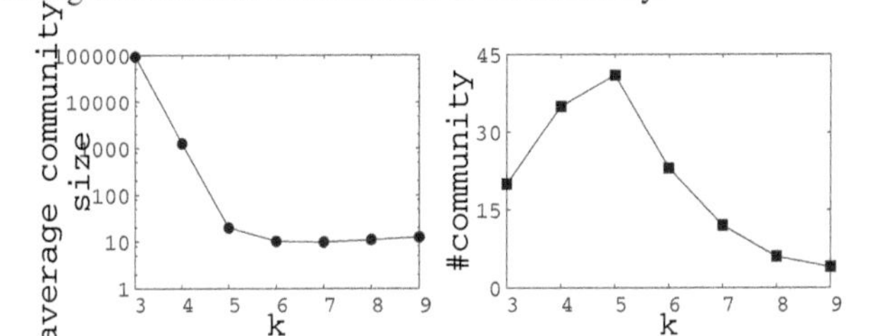

(a) Community size (b) Community number

Figure 10: Influence of k. Community size is monotonically decreasing with k.

5.7 Influence of α and γ

In this subsection, we study the influence of α and γ. We show our results on *WordNet*. Similar results were obtained on other networks. Since the graph is sparse, we only tested our approach on $k = 3$ and $k = 4$. According to Eq. 1, we have $\gamma \geq \frac{2}{3}$ for $k = 3, 4$. So we chose some representative γ satisfying these constraints. Note that for $k = 3$, only $\gamma = 1$ is meaningful. Hence, we only show the result for $\gamma = 1$ when $k = 3$. If $k = 4$, when $\frac{2}{3} \leq \gamma < \frac{5}{6}$, the quasi-4-clique has at least four edges; when $\frac{5}{6} \leq \gamma < 1$, the quasi-4-clique has at least five edges. We used $\gamma = 0.8$ and $\gamma = 0.9$ as two representative values of these two ranges, respectively. For each selected k and γ, we randomly selected 10 valid query vertices as v_0 and recorded their average running time in Table 3. When the query time of a vertex exceeds 60s, we considered it as 60s.

From the results, we found that, for the same k and α, generally a smaller γ costs more time. This is because a higher γ means a more strict constraint, which reduces the search space. For the same k and γ, the running time decreases with the growth of α. The reason is similar: a smaller α leads to a bigger search space.

6. APPLICATIONS

In this section, we propose two typical applications of OCS: *diversity based social network analysis* and *name disambiguation in social networks*. Our model and solution enable us to measure the diversity of social ties for a person, which is critical for the diversity based analysis in a quantitative manner. The OCS model and our solution also provide new insights to solve name disambiguation in social networks, which is well known as a hard problem. All the following studies are conducted on $(k-1, 1)$-OCS model.

6.1 Diversity-based Social Network Analysis

In social networks, an individual's social ties are diverse if he or she maintains connections to different communities or groups. Individuals with diverse social ties are more competitive than others [27, 28], because they serve as an intermediary with a position bridging different groups in a social network, and consequently own more opportunities than others in the network. Diversity leading to competition advantage has been widely acknowledged in real life, but has been rarely verified in a quantified manner. Computing overlapping communities is obviously a critical step to quantify the diversity of an individual. Due to the computational hardness of overlapping community detection, previous diversity measures use attributes to derive overlapping communities. For example, Shi et al. [29] uses the conferences at which an author has ever published a paper to obtain overlapping communities for DBLP scientific collaboration network.

Now, we can directly use our solution under the OCS model to calculate the diversity of an individual. Intuitively, the diversity of a person can be measured by the number of overlapping communities found by our approach. Next, we show some diversity related analysis on DBLP with diversity calculated by our OCS solution.

Diversity distribution. The first class of fundamental questions includes: *what is the distribution of diversity? Can we find people with really large diversity?* To answer these questions, we randomly select 1000 vertices and summarize the diversity distributions for $k = 3, 4, 5$. The results are shown in Figure 11. We find that most persons have diversity 1, indicating that they coauthor with authors in a local research community. These authors are mostly fresh hands in an area. However, there are some authors with large diversity. Some authors have diversity at about 20. These authors are mostly distinguished scientists in computer science. There are also some ambiguous names shared by more than one author. We will discuss this problem in the next application.

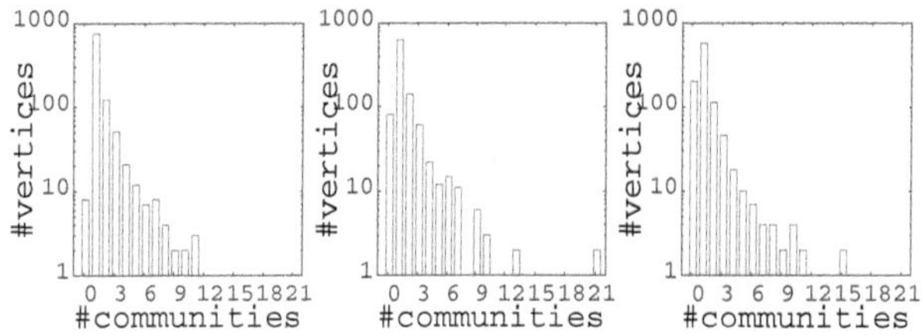

(a) $k = 3$ (b) $k = 4$ (c) $k = 5$

Figure 11: Distribution of diversity

Diversity leading to competitive advantage. Next, we verify the widely-established conjecture: *diversity of social ties leads to competitive advantage in a social network.* In a social network, a person's competitive power in general is positively correlated to his degree. Hence, to verify this conjecture, we summarize the correlation between degree and diversity. The result is shown in Figure 12. We find positive correlations between degree and diversity, which verifies the conjecture. This finding strongly suggests that diversity is one of the important driving forces for an author to become an academic star. This implication opens opportunity for some other interesting real applications, such as predicting rising stars.

6.2 Name Disambiguation

Name disambiguation is a typical problem in social network data management [30, 31]. For example, in DBLP there are at least 40 authors with the same name 'Wei Wang'. In general, name disambiguation is a challenging problem when person identity information is missing. The OCS model and its solution provide new insight to solve this problem. They are at least helpful in two aspects: First, they can be used to identify ambiguous names. Second, the overlapping communities themselves are candidate entities with the same name.

We ran our solution to $(k-1, 1)$-OCS with $k = 4$ on each vertex of DBLP. Table 4 presents the ambiguous names that have sig-

Ambiguous names			Renowned authors with large diversity		
Name	degree	# communities	Name	degree	# communities
Wei Li	589	113	Jennifer Widom	106	11
Xin Li	399	67	Alon Halevy	62	7
Ming Li	399	72	Hector Garcia-Molina	182	26
Li Zhang	486	95	David Dewitt	142	20
Ying Zhang	282	59	Michael Stonebraker	171	22
Hui Zhang	281	58	Jeffrey D. Ullman	97	11

Table 4: Ambiguous names, renowned authors in DBLP. Ambiguous names have a significantly large number of communities.

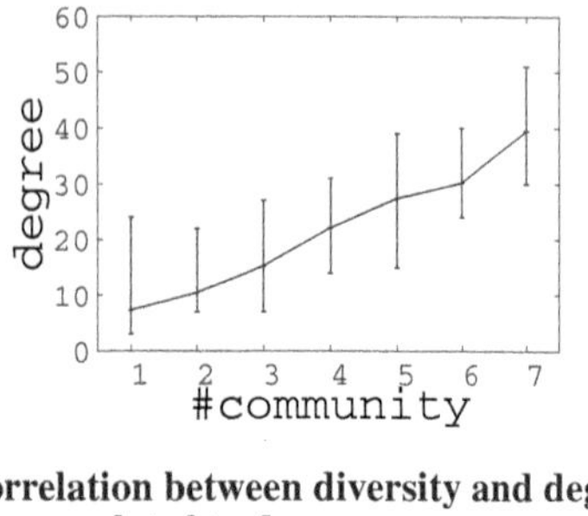

Figure 12: Correlation between diversity and degree (with $k = 4$). Diversity is correlated to degree.

nificant number of entities in DBLP. We found that most of these names have a large number of communities. Their community numbers in general can be considered as exceptions when compared to the community number distribution observed in Figure 11. For comparisons, we also give the community number of renowned scientists in the database community. It is clear that for a real person, even as famous scientists with many papers and abundant coauthoring relationships, their community numbers are smaller than the community number of ambiguous names. These facts strongly suggest that the large number of overlapping communities is a good indicator of ambiguous names referring to multiple entities. Besides name disambiguation in social networks, OCS is also helpful for sense disambiguation in semantic networks, as shown in the case study on WordNet.

7. CONCLUSION

Most real networks have overlapping community structures. In this paper we propose a novel overlappingness-aware community search problem: *overlapping community search*. Compared to overlapping community detection, our model is much lightweight and supports online query answering. We reveal the rationale behind the model and provide theoretical guidelines for tuning the model. We devise several exact algorithms and an efficient approximate algorithm to find meaningful overlapping communities. We conduct extensive experiments to show that both the exact algorithms and approximate algorithms are effective to discover meaningful overlapping communities in real networks, and the approximate solution is quite efficient, supporting online (within several ms) query answering on million-node graphs.

8. REFERENCES

[1] G. Palla, I. Derényi, I. Farkas, and T. Vicsek, "Uncovering the overlapping community structure of complex networks in nature and society." *Nature*, vol. 435, no. 7043, pp. 814–818, Jun. 2005.

[2] http://www.facebook.com/press/info.php?statistics.

[3] M. Sozio and A. Gionis, "The community-search problem and how to plan a successful cocktail party," in *KDD*, 2010.

[4] B. Adamcsek, G. Palla, I. J. Farkas, I. Derl̨enyi, and T. Vicsek, "Cfinder: locating cliques and overlapping modules in biological networks," *Bioinformatics*, vol. 22, no. 8, pp. 1021–1023, 2006.

[5] H. Shen, X. Cheng, K. Cai, and M.-B. Hu, "Detect overlapping and hierarchical community structure in networks," *Physica A*, vol. 388, no. 8, pp. 1706 – 1712, 2009.

[6] S. Gregory, "An algorithm to find overlapping community structure in networks," in *PKDD*, 2007.

[7] ——, "A fast algorithm to find overlapping communities in networks," in *Machine Learning and Knowledge Discovery in Databases*, ser. Lecture Notes in Computer Science, 2008, vol. 5211, pp. 408–423.

[8] Y.-Y. Ahn, J. P. Bagrow, and S. Lehmann, "Link communities reveal multiscale complexity in networks," *Nature*, vol. 466, pp. 761–764, Jun. 2010.

[9] J. Baumes, M. Goldberg, and M. Magdon-ismail, "Efficient identification of overlapping communities," in *ISI*, 2005, pp. 27–36.

[10] X. Xu, N. Yuruk, Z. Feng, and T. A. Schweiger, "Scan: a structural clustering algorithm for networks," in *KDD*, 2007.

[11] J. Xie, B. K. Szymanski, and X. Liu, "Slpa: Uncovering overlapping communities in social networks via a speaker-listener interaction dynamic process," in *ICDMW*, 2011.

[12] C. Lee, F. Reid, A. McDaid, and N. Hurley, "Detecting highly overlapping community structure by greedy clique expansion," *arXiv preprint arXiv:1002.1827*, 2010.

[13] A. Lancichinetti, F. Radicchi, J. J. Ramasco, and S. Fortunato, "Finding statistically significant communities in networks," *PloS one*, vol. 6, no. 4, p. e18961, 2011.

[14] D. Goldstein and M. Langberg, "The dense k subgraph problem," *CoRR*, vol. abs/0912.5327, 2009.

[15] D. Gibson, R. Kumar, and A. Tomkins, "Discovering large dense subgraphs in massive graphs," in *VLDB*, 2005.

[16] S. V. Bahman Bahmani, Ravi Kumar, "Densest Subgraph in Streaming and MapReduce," in *PVLDB*, 2012.

[17] N. Wang, J. Zhang, K.-L. Tan, and A. K. H. Tung, "On triangulation-based dense neighborhood graphs discovery," in *PVLDB*, 2010.

[18] R. M. Karp, "Reducibility Among Combinatorial Problems," in *Complexity of Computer Computations*, 1972, pp. 85–103.

[19] I. Derényi, G. Palla, and T. Vicsek, "Clique Percolation in Random Networks," *Physical Review Letters*, vol. 94, no. 16, pp. 160 202+, Apr. 2005.

[20] P. Erdos and A. Rényi, "On the evolution of random graphs," in *Publication of the Mathematical Institue of the Hungaria Academy of Sciences*, 1960, pp. 17–61.

[21] E. Aarts and J. K. Lenstra, Eds., *Local Search in Combinatorial Optimization*, 1997.

[22] R. Battiti and M. Protasi, "Reactive local search for the maximum clique problem," *Algorithmica*, vol. 29, no. 4, pp. 610–637, 2001.

[23] W. Pullan and H. H. Hoos, "Dynamic local search for the maximum clique problem," *J. Artif. Int. Res.*, vol. 25, pp. 159–185, February 2006.

[24] A. Grosso, M. Locatelli, and W. Pullan, "Simple ingredients leading to very efficient heuristics for the maximum clique problem," *Journal of Heuristics*, vol. 14, pp. 587–612, December 2008.

[25] J. Cheng, A. W.-c. Fu, and J. X. Yu, "Finding maximal cliques in massive networks by h*-graph," in *SIGMOD*, 2010.

[26] M. Brunato, H. Hoos, and R. Battiti, "On effectively finding maximal quasi-cliques in graphs," *Learning and Intelligent Optimization*, pp. 41–55, 2008.

[27] N. Eagle, M. Macy, and R. Claxton, "Network Diversity and Economic Development," *Science*, vol. 328, no. 5981, pp. 1029–1031, 2010.

[28] R. S. Burt, *Structural holes: The social structure of competition*. Harvard University Press, 1992.

[29] Q. Shi, B. Xu, X. Xu, Y. Xiao, W. Wang, and H. Wang, "Diversity of social ties in scientific collaboration networks," *Physica A*, vol. 390, no. 23?4, pp. 4627 – 4635, 2011.

[30] H. Han, H. Zha, and C. L. Giles, "Name disambiguation in author citations using a k-way spectral clustering method," in *ICDL*, 2005.

[31] H. Han, L. Giles, H. Zha, C. Li, and K. Tsioutsiouliklis, "Two supervised learning approaches for name disambiguation in author citations," in *JCDL*, 2004.

BitWeaving: Fast Scans for Main Memory Data Processing

Yinan Li
University of Wisconsin–Madison
yinan@cs.wisc.edu

Jignesh M. Patel
University of Wisconsin–Madison
jignesh@cs.wisc.edu

ABSTRACT

This paper focuses on running scans in a main memory data processing system at "bare metal" speed. Essentially, this means that the system must aim to process data at or near the speed of the processor (the fastest component in most system configurations). Scans are common in main memory data processing environments, and with the state-of-the-art techniques it still takes many cycles per input tuple to apply simple predicates on a single column of a table. In this paper, we propose a technique called BitWeaving that exploits the parallelism available at the bit level in modern processors. BitWeaving operates on multiple bits of data in a single cycle, processing bits from different columns in each cycle. Thus, bits from a batch of tuples are processed in each cycle, allowing BitWeaving to drop the cycles per column to below one in some case. BitWeaving comes in two flavors: BitWeaving/V which looks like a columnar organization but at the bit level, and BitWeaving/H which packs bits horizontally. In this paper we also develop the arithmetic framework that is needed to evaluate predicates using these BitWeaving organizations. Our experimental results show that both these methods produce significant performance benefits over the existing state-of-the-art methods, and in some cases produce over an order of magnitude in performance improvement.

Categories and Subject Descriptors

H.2.4 [**Information Systems**]: Database Management—*systems*

Keywords

Bit-parallel, intra-cycle parallelism, storage organization, indexing, analytics

1. INTRODUCTION

There is a resurgence of interest in main memory database management systems (DBMSs), due to the increasing demand for real-time analytics platforms. Continual drop in DRAM prices and increasing memory densities have made it economical to build and deploy "in memory" database solutions. Many systems have been developed to meet this growing requirement [2, 5–7, 9, 14, 21].

SIGMOD'13, June 22–27, 2013, New York, New York, USA.

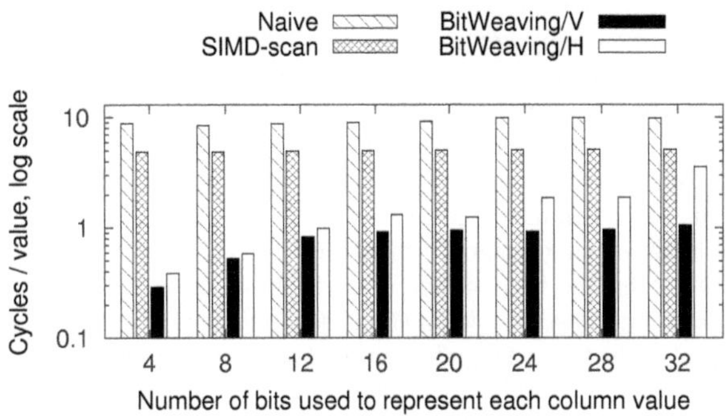

Figure 1: Performance Comparison

A key operation in a main memory DBMS is the full table scan primitive, since ad hoc business intelligence queries frequently use scans over tabular data as base operations. An important goal for a main memory data processing system is to run scans at the speed of the processing units, and exploit all the functionality that is available inside modern processors. For example, a recent proposal for a fast scan [18] packs (dictionary) compressed column values into four 32-bit slots in a 128-bit SIMD word. Unfortunately, this method has two main limitations. First, it does not fully utilize the width of a word. For example, if the compressed value of a particular attribute is encoded by 9 bits, then we must pad each 9-bit value to a 32-bit boundary (or what ever is the boundary for the SIMD instruction), wasting $32 - 9 = 23$ bits every 32 bits. The second limitation is that it imposes extra processing to align tightly packed values to the four 32-bit slots in a 128-bit SIMD word.

In this paper, we propose a set of techniques, which are collectively called BitWeaving, to aggressively exploit "intra-cycle" parallelism. The insight behind our intra-cycle parallelism paradigm is recognizing that in a single processor clock cycle there is "abundant parallelism" as the circuits in the processor core are simultaneously computing on multiple bits of information, even when working on simple ALU operations. We believe that thinking of how to fully exploit such intra-cycle parallelism is critical in making data processing software run at the speed of the "bare metal", which in this study means the speed of the processor core.

The BitWeaving methods that are proposed in this paper target intra-cycle parallelism for higher performance. BitWeaving does not rely on the hardware-implemented SIMD capability, and can be implemented with full-word instructions. (Though, it can also leverage SIMD capabilities if that is available.) BitWeaving comes in two flavors: BitWeaving/V and BitWeaving/H, corresponding to two underlying storage formats. Both methods produce as output a result bit vector, with one bit per input tuple that indicates if the input tuple matches the predicate on the column.

The first method, BitWeaving/V, uses a *bit-level* columnar data organization, packed into processor words. It then organizes the words into a layout that results in largely sequential memory address lookups when performing a scan. Predicate evaluation in the scan operation is converted to logical computation on these "words of bits" using the arithmetic framework proposed in this paper. In this organization, storage space is not wasted padding bits to fit boundaries that are set by the hardware. More importantly, in many cases, an early pruning technique allows the scan computation to be safely terminated, even before all the bits in the underlying data are examined. Thus, predicates can often be computed by only looking at some of most significant bits in each column. This scheme also naturally produces compact result bit vectors that can be used to evaluate the next stage of a complex predicate efficiently.

The second method, BitWeaving/H, uses a bit organization that is a dual of BitWeaving/V. Unlike the BitWeaving/V format, all the bits of a column value are stored together in BitWeaving/H, providing high performance when fetching the entire column value. Unlike previous horizontal bit packing methods, BitWeaving/H staggers the codes across processor words in a way that produces compact result bit vectors that are easily reusable when evaluating the next stage of a complex predicate.

Both BitWeaving methods can be used as a native storage organization technique in a column store database, or as an indexing method to index specific column(s) in row stores or column stores.

Figure 1 illustrates the performance of a scan operation on a single column, when varying the width of the column from 1 bit to 32 bits (Section 6 has more details about this experiment). This figure shows the SIMD-scan method proposed in [18], and a simple method (labeled Naive) that scans each column in a traditional scan loop and interprets each column value one by one. As can be seen in the figure, both BitWeaving/V and BitWeaving/H outperform the other methods across all the column widths. Both BitWeaving methods achieve higher speedups over other methods when the column representation has fewer number of bits, because this allows more column predicates to be computed in parallel (i.e. the intra-cycle parallelism per input column value is higher). For example, when each column is coded using 4 bits, the BitWeaving methods are **20X** faster than the SIMD-scan method. Even for columns that are wider than 12 bits, both BitWeaving methods are often more than **4X** faster than the SIMD-scan method. Note that as described in [18], real world data tends to use 8 to 16 bits to encode a column; BitWeaving is one order of magnitude faster than the SIMD-scan method within this range of code widths.

The contribution of this paper is the presentation of the BitWeaving methods that push our intra-cycle parallelism paradigm to its natural limit – i.e. to the bit level for each column. We also develop an arithmetic framework for predicate evaluation on BitWeaved data, and present results from an actual implementation.

The remainder of this paper is organized as follows: Section 2 contains background information. The BitWeaving methods and the related arithmetic framework is described in Sections 3 through 5. Section 6 contains our experimental results. Related work is covered in Section 7, and Section 8 contains our concluding remarks.

2. OVERVIEW

Main memory analytic DBMSs often store data in a compressed form [2, 4, 5, 10]. The techniques presented in this paper apply to commonly used column compression methods, including null suppression, prefix suppression, frame of reference, and order-preserving dictionary encoding [2,4,5,10]. Such a scheme compresses columns using a fixed-length order-preserving scheme, and converts the native column value to a *code*. In this paper, we use the term "code" to mean an encoded column value. The data for a column is represented using these codes, and these codes only use as many bits as are needed for the fixed-length encoding.

In these compression methods, all value types, including numeric and string types, are encoded as an unsigned integer code. For example, an order-preserving dictionary can map strings to unsigned integers [3, 10]. A scale scheme can convert floating point numbers to unsigned integers by multiplying by a certain factor [4]. These compression methods maintain an order-preserving one-to-one mapping between the column values to the codes. As a result, column scans can usually be directly evaluated on the codes.

For predicates involving arithmetic or similarity predicates (e.g. the `LIKE` predicates on strings), scans cannot be performed directly on the encoded codes. These codes have to be decoded, and then are evaluated in a conventional way.

2.1 Problem Statement

A *column-scalar scan* takes as input a list of n k-bit codes and a predicate with a basic comparison, e.g. $=, \neq, <, >, \leq, \geq,$ `BETWEEN`, on a single column. Constants in the predicate are also in the domain of the compressed codes. The column-scalar scan finds all matching codes that satisfy the predicate, and outputs an n-bit vector, called the *result bit vector*, to indicate the matching codes.

A *processor word* is a data block that can be processed as a unit by the processor. For ease of explanation, we initially assume that a processor word is an Arithmetic Logic Unit (ALU) word, i.e. a 64-bit word for modern CPUs, and in Appendix C of the extended version of this paper [12] we generalize our method for wider words (e.g. SIMD). The instructions that process the processor word as a unit of computation are called *full-word instructions*. Next, we define when a scan is a *bit-parallel method*.

DEFINITION 1. *If w is the width of a processor word, and k is the number of bits that are needed to encode a code in the column C, then a column-scalar scan on column C is a bit-parallel method if it runs in $O(\frac{nk}{w})$ full-word instructions to scan over n codes.*

A bit-parallel method needs to run in $O(\frac{nk}{w})$ instructions to make full use of the "parallelism" that is offered by the bits in the entire width of a processor word. Since processing nk bits with w-bit processor words requires at least $O(\frac{nk}{w})$ instructions, intuitively a method that matches the $O(\frac{nk}{w})$ bound has the potential to run at the speed of the underlying processor hardware.

2.2 Framework

The focus of this paper is on speeding up scan queries on columnar data in main memory data processing engines. Our framework targets the single-table predicates in the WHERE clause of SQL. More specifically, the framework allows conjunctions, disjunctions, or arbitrary boolean combinations of the following basic comparison operators: $=, \neq, <, >, \leq, \geq,$ `BETWEEN`.

For the methods proposed in this paper, we evaluate the complex predicate by first evaluating basic comparisons on each column, using a *column-scalar scan*. Each column-scalar scan produces a *result bit vector*, with one bit for each input column value that indicates if the corresponding column value was selected to be in the result. Conjunctions and disjunctions are implemented as logical AND and OR operations on these result bit vectors. Once the column-scalar scans are complete, the result bit vector is converted to a list of record numbers, which is then used to retrieve other columns of interest for this query. (See Appendix A in [12] for more details.) NULL values and three-valued boolean logic can be implemented in our framework using the techniques proposed in [13], and, in the interest of space, this discussion is omitted here.

We represent the predicates in the SQL WHERE clause as a binary predicate tree. A leaf node encapsulates a basic comparison operation on a single column. The internal nodes represent logical operation, e.g. AND, OR, NOT, on one or two nodes. To evaluate a predicate consisting of arbitrary boolean combinations of basic comparisons, we traverse the predicate tree in depth-first order, performing the column-scalar comparison on each leaf node, and merging result bit vectors at each internal node based on the logical operator that is represented by the internal node. Figure 8 illustrates an example predicate tree. In Section 3, we focus on single-column scans, and we discuss complex predicates in Section 4.3.

3. BIT-PARALLEL METHODS

In this section, we propose two bit-parallel methods that are designed to fully utilize the entire width of the processor words to reduce the number of instructions that are needed to process data. These two bit-parallel methods are called Horizontal Bit-Parallel (HBP) and Vertical Bit-Parallel (VBP) methods. Each method has a storage format and an associated method to perform a column-scalar scan on that storage method. In Section 4, we describe an early pruning technique to improve on the column-scalar scan for both HBP and VBP. Then, in Section 5 we describe the BitWeaving method, which combines the bit-parallel methods that are described below with the early pruning technique. BitWeaving comes in two flavors: BitWeaving/H and BitWeaving/V corresponding to the underlying bit-parallel method (i.e. HBP or VBP) that it builds on.

3.1 Overview of the two bit-parallel methods

As their names indicate, the two bit-parallel methods, HBP and VBP, organize the column codes horizontally and vertically, respectively. If we thought of a code as a tuple consisting of multiple fields (bits), HBP and VBP can be viewed as row-oriented storage and column-oriented storage *at the bit level*, respectively. Figure 2 demonstrates the basic idea behind HBP and VBP storage layouts.

Both HBP and VBP only require the following full-word operations, which are common in all modern CPU architectures (including at the SIMD register level in most architectures): logical and ($\wedge$), logical or ($\vee$), exclusive or ($\oplus$), binary addition ($+$), negation ($\neg$), and k-bit left or right shift ($\leftarrow_k$ or $\rightarrow_k$, respectively).

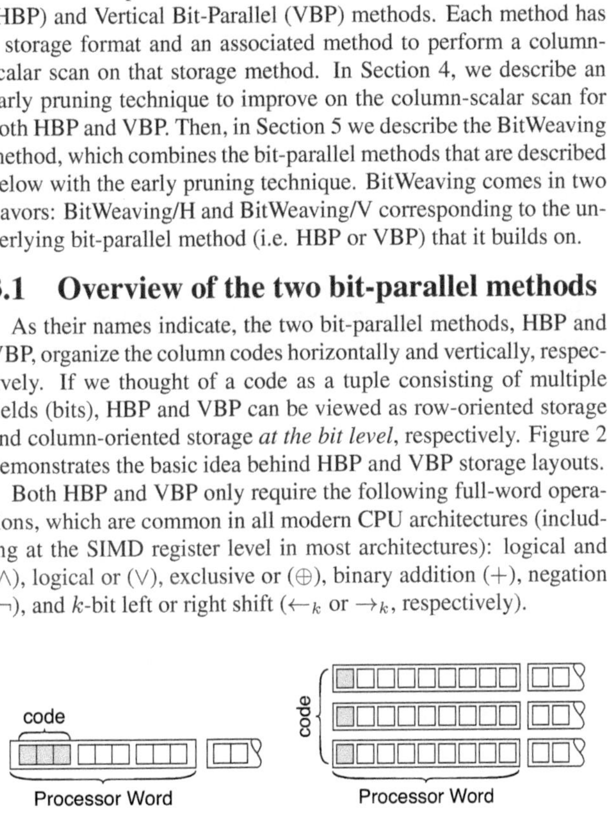

(a) Horizontal Bit-Parallel (b) Vertical Bit-Parallel

Figure 2: HBP and VBP layouts for a column with 3-bit codes. The shaded boxes represent the bits for the first column value.

Since the primary access pattern for scan operations is the sequential access pattern, both the CPU cost and the memory access cost are significant components that contribute to the overall execution time for that operation. Consequently, our methods are optimized for both the number of CPU instructions that are needed to process the data, as well as the number of CPU cache lines that are occupied by the underlying (HBP or VBP) data representations.

3.1.1 Running Example

To illustrate the techniques, we use the following example throughout this section. The data set has 10 tuples, and the column of interest contains the following codes: $\{1 = (001)_2, 5 = (101)_2, 6 = (110)_2, 1 = (001)_2, 6 = (110)_2, 4 = (100)_2, 0 = (000)_2, 7 = (111)_2, 4 = (100)_2, 3 = (011)_2\}$, denoted as $c1 - c10$ respectively. Each value can be encoded by 3 bits ($k = 3$). For ease of illustration, we assume 8-bit processor words (i.e. $w = 8$).

3.2 The Horizontal bit-parallel (HBP) method

The HBP method compactly packs codes into processor words, and implements the functionality of hardware-implemented SIMD instructions based on ordinary full-word instructions. The HBP method solves a general problem for hardware-implemented SIMD that the natural bit width of a column often does not match any of the bank widths of the SIMD processor, which leads to an under-utilization of the available bit-level parallelism.

We first present the storage layout of HBP in Section 3.2.1, and then describe the algorithm to perform a basic scan on a single column over the proposed storage layout in Section 3.2.2.

3.2.1 Storage layout

In the HBP method, each code is stored in a $(k + 1)$-bit section whose leftmost bit is used as a delimiter between adjacent codes (k denote the number of bits needed to encode a code). A method that does not require the extra delimiter bit is feasible, but is much more complicated than the method with delimiter bits, and also requires executing more instructions per code [11]. Thus, our HBP method uses this extra bit for storage.

HBP tightly packs and pads a group of $(k + 1)$-bit sections into a processor word. Let w denote the width of a processor word. Then, inside the processor word, $\lfloor \frac{w}{k+1} \rfloor$ sections are concatenated together and padded to the right with 0s up to the word boundary.

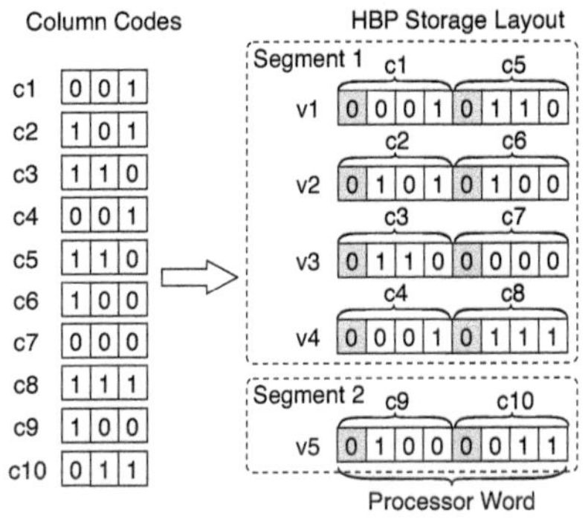

Figure 3: Example of the HBP storage layout ($k = 3, w = 8$). Delimiter bits are marked in gray.

In the HBP method, the codes are organized in a storage layout that simplifies the process of producing a result bit vector with one bit per input code (described below in Section 3.2.2). The column is divided into fixed-length *segments*, each of which contains $(k + 1) \cdot \lfloor \frac{w}{k+1} \rfloor$ codes. Each code represents $k + 1$ bits values, with k bits for the actual code and the leading bit set to the delimiter value of 0. Since a processor word fits $\lfloor \frac{w}{k+1} \rfloor$ codes, a segment occupies $k + 1$ contiguous processor words in memory space. Inside a segment, the layout of the $(k + 1) \cdot \lfloor \frac{w}{k+1} \rfloor$ codes, denoted as $c_1 \sim c_{(k+1)\cdot\lfloor \frac{w}{k+1} \rfloor}$, is shown below. We use v_i to denote the ith processor word in the segment.

$$
\begin{array}{llllll}
v_1: & c_1 & c_{k+2} & c_{2k+3} & \cdots & c_{k\cdot\lfloor \frac{w}{k+1} \rfloor+1} \\
v_2: & c_2 & c_{k+3} & c_{2k+4} & \cdots & c_{k\cdot\lfloor \frac{w}{k+1} \rfloor+2} \\
\vdots & \vdots & \vdots & \vdots & & \vdots \\
v_k: & c_k & c_{2k+1} & c_{3k+2} & \cdots & c_{(k+1)\cdot\lfloor \frac{w}{k+1} \rfloor-1} \\
v_{k+1}: & c_{k+1} & c_{2k+2} & c_{3k+3} & \cdots & c_{(k+1)\cdot\lfloor \frac{w}{k+1} \rfloor}
\end{array}
$$

	$v_1(c_1, c_5)$	$v_2(c_2, c_6)$	$v_3(c_3, c_7)$	$v_4(c_4, c_8)$	$v_5(c_9, c_{10})$
$X =$	$(0001\ 0110)_2$	$(0101\ 0100)_2$	$(0110\ 0000)_2$	$(0001\ 0111)_2$	$(0100\ 0011)_2$
$Y =$	$(0101\ 0101)_2$	$(0101\ 0101)_2$	$(0101\ 0101)_2$	$(0101\ 0101)_2$	$(0101\ 0101)_2$
$mask =$	$(0111\ 0111)_2$	$(0111\ 0111)_2$	$(0111\ 0111)_2$	$(0111\ 0111)_2$	$(0111\ 0111)_2$
$X \oplus mask =$	$(0110\ 0001)_2$	$(0010\ 0011)_2$	$(0001\ 0111)_2$	$(0110\ 0000)_2$	$(0011\ 0100)_2$
$Y + (X \oplus mask) =$	$(1011\ 0110)_2$	$(0111\ 1000)_2$	$(0110\ 1100)_2$	$(1011\ 0101)_2$	$(1001\ 1001)_2$
$Z = (Y + (X \oplus mask)) \wedge \neg mask =$	$(1000\ 0000)_2$	$(0000\ 1000)_2$	$(0000\ 1000)_2$	$(1000\ 0000)_2$	$(1000\ 1000)_2$

Figure 4: Evaluating a predicate $c < 5$ on the example column c

Figure 3 demonstrates the storage layout for the example column. Since each code in the example column is encoded by 3 bits ($k = 3$), we use $4 = 3 + 1$ bits to store each code and fit two codes into a 8-bit word ($w = 8$). As shown in the figure, the 10 values are divided into 2 segments. In segment 1, eight codes are packed into four 8-bit words. More specifically, word 1 contains code 1 and 5. Word 2 contains code 2 and 6. Word 3 contains code 3 and 7. Word 4 contains code 4 and 8. Segment 2 is only partially filled, and contains code 9 and code 10 that are packed into word 5.

3.2.2 *Column-scalar scans*

The HBP column-scalar scan compares each code with a constant C, and outputs a bit vector to indicate whether or not the corresponding code satisfies the comparison condition.

In HBP, $\lfloor \frac{w}{k+1} \rfloor$ codes are packed into a processor word. Thus, we first introduce a function $f_\circ(X, C)$ that performs simultaneous comparisons on $\lfloor \frac{w}{k+1} \rfloor$ packed codes in a processor word. The outcome of the function is a vector of $\lfloor \frac{w}{k+1} \rfloor$ results, each of which occupies a $(k+1)$-bit section. The delimiter (leftmost) bit of each section indicates the comparison results.

Formally, a function $f_\circ(X, C)$ takes as input a comparison operator $\circ$, a comparison constant C, and a processor word X that contains a vector of $\lfloor \frac{w}{k+1} \rfloor$ codes in the form $X = (x_1, x_2, \cdots, x_{\lfloor \frac{w}{k+1} \rfloor})$, and outputs a vector $Z = (z_1, z_2, \cdots, z_{\lfloor \frac{w}{k+1} \rfloor})$, where $z_i = 10^k$ if $x_i \circ C = \texttt{true}$, or $z_i = 0^{k+1}$ if $x_i \circ C = \texttt{false}$. Note that in the notation above for z_i, we use exponentiation to denote bit repetition, e.g. $1^4 0^2 = 111100$, $10^k = 1\underbrace{00 \cdots 00}_{k}$.

Since the codes are packed into processor words, the ALU instruction set can not be directly used to process these packed codes. In HBP, the functionality of vector processing is implemented using full-word instructions. Let Y denote a vector of $\lfloor \frac{w}{k+1} \rfloor$ instances of constant C, i.e. $Y = (y_1, y_2, \cdots, y_{\lfloor \frac{w}{k+1} \rfloor})$, where $y_i = C$. Then, the task is to calculate the vector Z in parallel, where each $(k+1)$-bit section in this vector, $z_i = x_i \circ y_i$; here, $\circ$ is one of comparison operators described as follows. Note that most of these functions are adapted from [11].

INEQUALITY ($\neq$). For the INEQUALITY, observe that $x_i \neq y_i$ iff $x_i \oplus y_i \neq 0^{k+1}$. Thus, we know that $x_i \neq y_i$ iff $(x_i \oplus y_i) + 01^k = 1{*}^k$ (we use $*$ to represent an arbitrary bit), which is true iff $((x_i \oplus y_i) + 01^k) \wedge 10^k = 10^k$. We know that $(x_i \oplus y_i) + 01^k$ is always less than 2^{k+1}, so overflow is impossible for each $(k+1)$-bit section. As a result, these computation can be done simultaneously on all x_i and y_i within a processor word. It is straightforward to see that $Z = ((X \oplus Y) + 01^k 01^k \cdots 01^k) \wedge 10^k 10^k \cdots 10^k$.

EQUALITY ($=$). EQUALITY operator is implemented by the complement of the INEQUALITY operator, i.e. $Z = \neg((X \oplus Y) + 01^k 01^k \cdots 01^k) \wedge 10^k 10^k \cdots 10^k$.

LESS THAN ($<$). Since both x_i and y_i are integers, we know that $x_i < y_i$ iff $x_i \leq y_i - 1$, which is true iff $2^k \leq y_i + 2^k - x_i - 1$. Observe that $2^k - x_i - 1$ is just the k-bit logical complement of x_i, which can be calculated as $x_i \oplus 01^k$. It is then easy to show that $(y_i + (x_i \oplus 01^k)) \wedge 10^k = 10^k$ iff $x_i < y_i$. We also know that $y_i + (x_i \oplus 01^k)$ is always less than 2^{k+1}, so overflow is impossible for each $(k+1)$-bit section. Thus, we have $Z = (Y + (X \oplus 01^k 01^k \cdots 01^k)) \wedge 10^k 10^k \cdots 10^k$ for the comparison operator $<$.

LESS THAN OR EQUAL TO ($\leq$). Since $x_i \leq y_i$ iff $x_i < y_i + 1$, we have $Z = (Y + (X \oplus 01^k) + 0^k 1) \wedge 10^k 10^k \cdots 10^k$ for the comparison operator $\leq$.

Then, GREATER THAN ($>$) and GREATER THAN OR EQUAL TO ($\geq$) can be implemented by swapping X and Y for LESS THAN ($<$) and LESS THAN OR EQUAL TO ($\leq$) operators, respectively.

Thus, the function $f_\circ(X, C)$ computes the predicates listed above on $\lfloor \frac{w}{k+1} \rfloor$ codes using 3–4 instructions.

Figure 4 illustrates an example when applying $f_<(v_i, 5)$ on the words $v_1 \sim v_5$ shown in Figure 3. The ith column in the figure demonstrates the steps when calculating $Z = f_<(v_i, 5)$ on the word v_i. The last row represents the results of the function. Each result word contains two comparison results. The value $(1000)_2$ indicates that the corresponding code is less than the constant 5, whereas the value $(0000)_2$ indicates that the corresponding code does not satisfy the comparison condition.

Algorithm 1 HBP column-scalar scan

Input: a comparison operator $\circ$
a comparison constant C
Output: BV_{out}: result bit vector

```
for each segment s in column c do
    m_s := 0
    for i := 1 ... k+1 do
        m_w := f_∘(s.v_i, C)
        m_s := m_s ∨ →_{i-1} (m_w)
    append m_s to BV_out
return BV_out;
```

Next, we present the HBP column-scalar scan algorithm based on the function $f_\circ(X, C)$. Algorithm 1 shows the pseudocode for the scan method. The basic idea behind this algorithm is to reorganize the comparison results in an appropriate order, matching the order of the original codes. As shown in the algorithm, for each segment in the column, we iterate over the $k+1$ words. In the inner loop over the $k+1$ words, we combine the results of $f_\circ(v_1, C) \sim f_\circ(v_{k+1}, C)$ together to obtain the result bit vector on segment s. This procedure is illustrated below:

$f_\circ(v_1, C)$:	$R(c_1)$	0	$\cdots$	0	0	$R(c_{k+2})$	$\cdots$
$\rightarrow_1 (f_\circ(v_2, C))$:	0	$R(c_2)$	$\cdots$	0	0	0	$\cdots$
$\vdots$	$\vdots$	$\vdots$		$\vdots$			
$\rightarrow_{k-1} (f_\circ(v_k, C))$:	0	0	$\cdots$	$R(c_k)$	0	0	$\cdots$
$\rightarrow_k (f_\circ(v_{k+1}, C))$:	0	0	$\cdots$	0	$R(c_{k+1})$	0	$\cdots$
$\sum_\vee$:	$R(c_1)$	$R(c_2)$	$\cdots$	$R(c_k)$	$R(c_{k+1})$	$R(c_{k+2})$	$\cdots$

In the tabular representation above, each column represents one bit in the outcome of $f_\circ(v_i, C)$. Let $R(c_i)$ denote the binary result of the comparison on $c_i \circ C$. Since $R(c_i)$ is always placed in

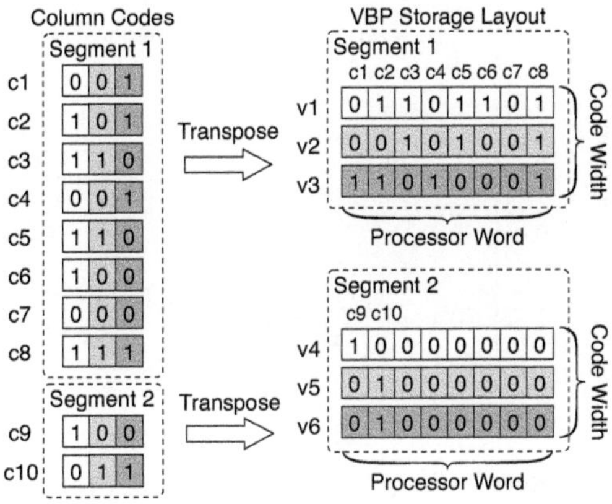

Figure 5: Example of the VBP storage layout. The middle bits of codes are marked in light gray, whereas the least significant bits are marked in dark gray.

the delimiter (leftmost) bit in a $(k+1)$-bit section, the output of $f_\circ(v_i, C)$ is in the form: $R(c_i)0^k R(c_{k+1+i})0^k \cdots$. By right shifting the output of $f_\circ(v_i, C)$, we move the result bits $R(c_i)$ to the appropriate bit positions. The OR ($\vee$) summation over the $k+1$ result words is then in the form of $R(c_1)R(c_2)R(c_3)\cdots$, representing the comparison results on the $\lfloor \frac{w}{k+1} \rfloor$ codes of segment s, in the desired result bit vector format.

For instance, to compute the result bit vector on segment 1 (v_1, v_2, v_3, and v_4) shown in Figure 3 and Figure 4, we perform $(1000\ 0000)_2 \vee \rightarrow_1 (0000\ 1000)_2 \vee \rightarrow_2 (0000\ 1000)_2 \vee \rightarrow_3 (1000\ 0000)_2 = (1001\ 0110)_2$. The result bit vector $(1001\ 0110)_2$ means that c_1, c_4, c_6, and c_7 satisfy the comparison condition.

Note that the steps above, which are carried out to produce a result bit vector with one bit per input code, are essential when using the result bit vector in a subsequent operation (e.g. the next step of a complex predicate evaluation in which the other attributes in the predicate have different code widths).

The HBP storage layout is designed to make it easy to assemble the result bit vector with one bit per input code. Taking Figure 3 as an example again, imagine that we lay out all the codes in sequence, i.e. put $c1$ and $c2$ in $v1$, put $c3$ and $c4$ in $v2$, and so forth. Now, the result words from the predicate evaluation function $f_\circ(v_i, C)$ on $v1, v2, \cdots$ are $f_\circ(v_1, C) = R(c_1)000R(c_2)000$, $f_\circ(v_2, C) = R(c_3)000R(c_4)000$, $\cdots$. Then, these result words must be converted to a bit vector of the form $R(c_1)R(c_2)R(c_3)R(c_4)\cdots$, by extracting all the delimiter bits $R(c_i)$ and omitting all other bits. Unfortunately, this conversion is relatively expensive compared to the computation of the function $f_\circ(v_i, C)$ (See Appendix B in [12] for more details). In contrast, the storage layout used by the HBP method does not need to execute this conversion to produce the result bit vector. In Section 6.1.1, we empirically compare the HBP method with a method that needs this conversion.

3.3 The Vertical bit-parallel (VBP) method

The Vertical Bit-Parallel (VBP) method is like a bit-level column store, with data being packed at word boundaries. VBP is inspired by the bit-sliced method [13], but as described below, is different in the way it organizes data around word boundaries.

3.3.1 Storage layout

In VBP, the column of codes is broken down to fixed-length segments, each of which contains w codes (w is the width of a processor word). The w k-bit codes in a segment are then transposed into k w-bit words, denoted as $v_1, v_2, \cdots, v_k$, such that the j-th bit in v_i equals to the i-th bit in the original code c_j.

Inside a segment, the k words, i.e. $v_1, v_2, \cdots, v_k$, are physically stored in a continuous memory space. The layout of the k words exactly matches the access pattern of column-scalar scans (presented below in Section 3.3.2), which leads to a sequential access pattern on these words, making it amenable for hardware prefetching.

Figure 5 illustrates the VBP storage layout for the running example shown in Section 3.1.1. The ten codes are broken into two segments with eight and two codes, respectively. The two segments are separately transposed into three 8-bit words. The word v_1 in segment 1 holds the most significant (leftmost) bits of the codes $c1 \sim c8$, the word v_2 holds the middle bits of the codes $c1 \sim c8$, and the word v_3 holds the least significant (rightmost) bits of the codes $c1 \sim c8$. In segment 2, only the leftmost two bits of the three words are used, and the remaining bits are filled with zeros.

3.3.2 Column-scalar scans

The VBP column-scalar scan evaluates a comparison condition over all the codes in a single column and outputs a bit vector, where each bit indicates whether or not the corresponding code satisfies the comparison condition.

The VBP column-scalar scan follows the natural way to compare two integers in the form of bit strings: we compare each pair of bits at the same position of the two bit strings, starting from the most significant bits to the least significant bits. The VBP method essentially performs this process on a vector of w codes in parallel, inside each segment.

Algorithm 2 VBP column-scalar comparison

Input: a predicate $C1 < c < C2$ on column c
Output: BV_{out}: result bit vector
1: **for** $i := 1 \dots k$ **do**
2:   **if** i-th bit in C1 is on **then**
3:     $C1_i := 1^w$
4:   **else**
5:     $C1_i := 0^w$
6: **for** $i := 1 \dots k$ **do**
7:   **if** i-th bit in C2 is on **then**
8:     $C2_i := 1^w$
9:   **else**
10:     $C2_i := 0^w$
11: **for** each segment s in column c **do**
12:   $m_{lt}, m_{gt} := 0$
13:   $m_{eq1}, m_{eq2} := 1^w$
14:   **for** $i := 1 \dots k$ **do**
15:     $m_{gt} := m_{gt} \vee (m_{eq1} \wedge \neg C1_i \wedge s.v_i)$
16:     $m_{lt} := m_{lt} \vee (m_{eq2} \wedge C2_i \wedge \neg s.v_i)$
17:     $m_{eq1} := m_{eq1} \wedge \neg(s.v_i \oplus C1_i)$
18:     $m_{eq2} := m_{eq2} \wedge \neg(s.v_i \oplus C2_i)$
19:   append $m_{gt} \wedge m_{lt}$ to BV_{out}
20: **return** BV_{out};

Algorithm 2 shows the pseudocode to evaluate the comparison predicate `BETWEEN` $C1$ `AND` $C2$.

At the beginning of the algorithm (Lines 1–5), we create a list of words $C1_1 \sim C1_k$ to represent w instances of $C1$ in the VBP storage format. If the i-th bit of $C1$ is 1, $C1_i$ is set to be all 1s, as all the i-th bits of the w instances of $C1$ are all 1s. Otherwise, $C1_i$ is set to be all 0s. Similarly, we create $C2_1 \sim C2_k$ to represent $C2$ in the VBP storage format (in Line 6–10).

In the next step, we iterate over all segments of the column, and simultaneously evaluate the range on all the w codes in each segment. The bit vector m_{gt} is used to indicate the codes such that they are greater than the constant $C1$, i.e. if the i-th bit of m_{gt} is on, then the i-th code in the segment is greater than the constant

$C1$. Likewise, m_{lt} is used to indicate the codes that are less than the constant $C2$. m_{eq1} and m_{eq2} are used to indicate the codes that are equivalent to the constant $C1$ and $C2$, respectively.

In the inner loop (Line 14–18), we compare the codes with the constants $C1$ and $C2$ from the most significant bits to the least significant bits, and update the bit vector m_{gt}, m_{lt}, m_{eq1}, and m_{eq2}, correspondingly. The k words in the segment s are denoted as $s.v_1 \sim s.v_k$. At the i-th bit position, for a code with the i-th bit on, the code must be greater than the constant $C1$ iff the i-th bit of $C1$ is off and all bits to the left of this position between the code and $C1$ are all equal ($m_{eq1} \wedge \neg C1_i \wedge s.v_i$). The corresponding bits in m_{gt} are then updated to be 1s (Line 15). Similarly, m_{lt} is updated if the i-th bit of a code is 0, the i-th bit of $C2$ is 1, and all the bits to the left of this position are all equal (Line 16). We also update m_{eq1} (m_{eq2}) for the codes that are different from the constant $C1(C2)$ at the i-th bit position (Line 17 & 18).

After the inner loop, we perform a logical AND between the bit vector m_{gt} and m_{lt} to obtain the result bit vector on the segment (Line 19). This bit vector is then appended to the result bit vector.

Algorithm 2 can be easily extended for other comparison conditions. For example, we can modify Line 19 to "append $m_{gt} \wedge m_{lt} \vee m_{eq1} \vee m_{eq2}$ to BV_{out}" to evaluate the condition $C1 \le c \le C2$. For certain comparison conditions, some steps can be eliminated. For instance, Line 15 and 17 can be skipped for a LESS THAN ($<$) comparison, as we do not need to evaluate m_{gt} and m_{eq1}.

4. EARLY PRUNING

The early pruning technique aims to avoid accesses on unnecessary data at the bit level. This technique is orthogonal to the two bit-parallel methods described in Section 3, and hence can be applied to both the HBP and the VBP methods. However, as the early pruning technique is more naturally described within the context of VBP, we first describe this technique as applied to VBP. Then, in Section 5.2 we discuss how to apply this technique to HBP.

4.1 Basic idea behind early pruning

It is often not necessary to access all the bits of a code to compute the final result. For instance, to compare the code $(110\underline{1}0101)_2$ to a constant $(110\underline{0}1010)_2$, we compare the pair of bits at the same position, starting from the most significant bit to the least significant bit, until we find two bits that are different. At the 4th position (underlined above), the two bits are different, and thus we know that the code is greater than the constant. We can now ignore the remaining bits.

	Constant	VBP words	m_{lt}
1st bit	0	01101101	00000000
2nd bit	1	00101001	10010010
3rd bit	1	11010001	-

Figure 6: Evaluating $c < 3$ with the early pruning technique

It is easy to apply the early pruning technique on VBP, which performs comparisons on a vector of w codes in parallel. Figure 6 illustrates the process of evaluating the eight codes in segment 1 of the example column c with a comparison condition $c < 3$. The constant 3 is represented in the binary form $(011)_2$ as shown in the second column in the figure. The first eight codes ($1 = (001)_2$, $5 = (101)_2$, $6 = (110)_2$, $1 = (001)_2$, $6 = (110)_2$, $4 = (100)_2$, $0 = (000)_2$, $7 = (111)_2$) of column c are stored in three 8-bit VBP words, as shown in the third column in the figure.

By comparing the first bit of the constant (0) with the first bits of the eight codes (01101101), we notice that no code is guaranteed to be less than the constant at this point. Thus, the bit vector m_{lt} is all 0s to reflect this situation. Next, we expand the comparison to the second bit between the constant and the codes. Now, we know that the 1st, 4th, and 7th codes are smaller than the constant because their first two bits are less than the first two bits of the constant (01). We also know that the 2nd, 3rd, 5th, 6th, and 8th codes are greater than the constant, as their first two bits are greater than the first two bits of the constant (01). At this point, all the codes have a definite answer w.r.t. this predicate, and we can terminate the VBP column-scalar scan on this segment. The bit vector m_{lt} is updated to be 10010010, and it is also the final result bit vector.

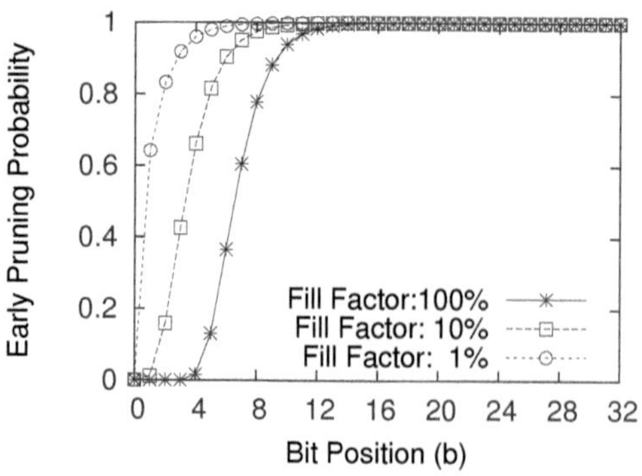

Figure 7: Early Pruning Probability $P(b)$

4.2 Estimating the early pruning probability

We first introduce the *fill factor* f of a segment, defined as the number of codes that are present over the maximum number of codes in the segment, i.e. the width of processor word w. For instance, the fill factor of the segment 1 in Figure 5 is $8/8 = 100\%$, whereas the fill factor of the segment 2 is $2/8 = 25\%$. According to this definition, a segment contains wf codes.

The early pruning probability $P(b)$ is defined as the probability that the wf codes in a segment are all different from the constant in the most significant b bits, i.e. it is the probability that we can terminate the computation at the bit position b.

We analyze the early pruning probability $P(b)$ on a segment containing wf k-bit codes. We assume that a code and the constant have the same value at a certain bit position with a probability of 1/2. Thus, the probability that all of the leading b bits between a code and the constant are identical is given by $(\frac{1}{2})^b$. Since a segment contains wf codes, the probability that these codes are all different from the constant in the leading b bits, i.e. the early pruning probability $P(b)$, is:

$$P(b) = (1 - (\frac{1}{2})^b)^{w \cdot f}$$

Figure 7 plots the early pruning probability $P(b)$ with a 64-bit processor word ($w = 64$) by varying the bit position b. We first look at the curve with a 100% fill factor. The early pruning probability increases as the bit position number increases. At the bit position 12, the early pruning probability is already very close to 100%, which indicates that in many cases we can terminate the scan after looking at the first 12 bits. If a code is a 32-bit integer, VBP with early pruning potentially only uses 12/32 of the memory bandwidth and the processing time that is needed by the base VBP method (without early pruning).

In Figure 7, at the lower fill factors, segments are often "cut-off" early. For example, for segments with fill factor 10%, we can prune the computation at bit position 8 in most (i.e. 97.5%) cases. This cut-off mechanism allows for efficient evaluation of conjunction/disjunction predicates in BitWeaving, as we will see next in Section 4.3.

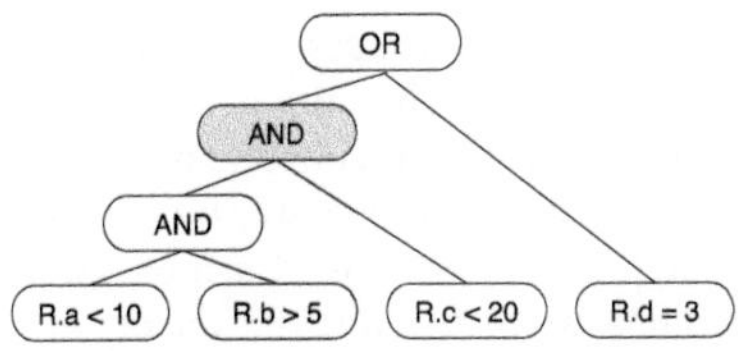

Figure 8: An example predicate tree for the expression `R.a < 10 AND R.b > 5 AND R.c < 20 OR R.d = 3`

4.3 Filter bit vectors on complex predicates

The early pruning technique can also be used when evaluating predicate clauses on multiple columns. Predicate evaluation on a single column can be pruned as outlined above in Section 4.1. But, early pruning can also be used when evaluating a series of predicate clauses with the result vector from the first clause being used to "initialize" the pruning bit vector for the second clause.

The result bit vector that is produced from a previous step is called the *filter bit vector* of the current column-scalar scan. This filter bit vector is used to filter out the tuples that do not match the predicate clauses that were examined in the previous steps, leading to a lower fill factor on the current column. Thus, the filter bit vector further reduces the computation on the current column-scalar scan (note that at the lower fill factors, predicate evaluation are often "cut-off" early, as shown in Figure 7).

As an example, consider the complex predicate: `R.a < 10 AND R.b > 5 AND R.c < 20 OR R.d = 3`. Figure 8 illustrates the predicate tree for this expression. First, we evaluate the predicate clause on column `R.a`, using early pruning. This evaluation produces a result bit vector. Next, we start evaluating the predicate clause on the column `R.b`, using early pruning. However, in this step we use the result bit vector produced from the previous step to seed the early pruning. Thus, tuples that did not match the predicate clause $R.a < 10$ become candidates for early pruning when evaluating the predicate clause on `R.b`, regardless of the value of their `b` column. As a result, the predicate evaluation on column `b` is often "cut-off" even earlier. Similarly, the result bit vector produced at the end of evaluating the AND node (the white AND node in the figure) is fed into the scan on column `R.c`. Finally, since the root node is an OR node, the complement of the result bit vector on the AND node (the gray one) is fed into the final scan on column `R.d`.

5. BIT WEAVING

In this section, we combine the techniques proposed above, and extend them, into the overall method called BitWeaving. BitWeaving comes in two flavors: BitWeaving/H and BitWeaving/V corresponding to the underlying bit-parallel storage format (i.e. HBP or VBP described in Section 3) that it builds on. As described below, BitWeaving/V also employs an adapted form of the early pruning technique described in Section 4.

We note that the BitWeaving methods can be used as a base storage organization format in column-oriented data stores, and/or as indices to speedup the scans over some attributes. For ease of presentation, below we assume that BitWeaving is used as a storage format. It is straightforward to employ the BitWeaving method as indices, and in Section 6.2 we empirically evaluate the performance of the BitWeaving methods when used in both these ways.

5.1 BitWeaving/V

BitWeaving/V is a method that applies the early pruning technique on VBP. BitWeaving/V has three key features: 1) The early pruning technique skips over pruned column data, thereby reducing the total number of bits that are accessed in a column-scalar scan operation; 2) The storage format is not a pure VBP format, but a *weaving* of the VBP format with horizontal packing into *bit groups* to further exploit the benefits of early pruning, by making access to the underlying bits more sequential (and hence more amenable for hardware prefetching); 3) It can be implemented with SIMD instructions allowing it to make full use of the entire width of the (wider) SIMD words in modern processors.

5.1.1 Storage layout

In this section, we describe how the VBP storage layout is adapted in BitWeaving/V to further exploit the benefits of the early pruning technique. In addition to the core VBP technique of vertical partitioning the codes at the bit level, in BitWeaving/V the codes are also partitioned in a horizontal fashion to provide better CPU cache performance when using the early pruning technique. This combination of vertical and horizontal partitioning is the reason why the proposed solution is called BitWeaving.

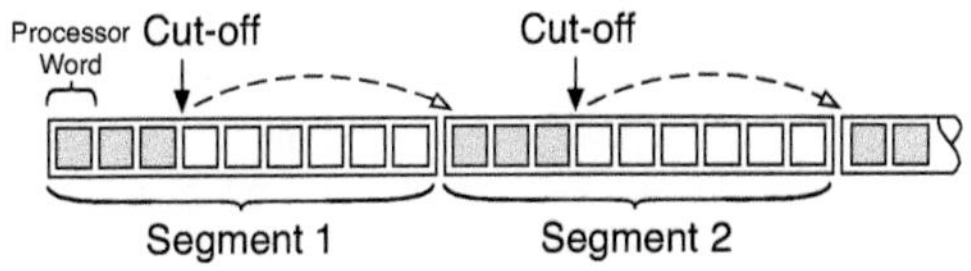

(a) VBP

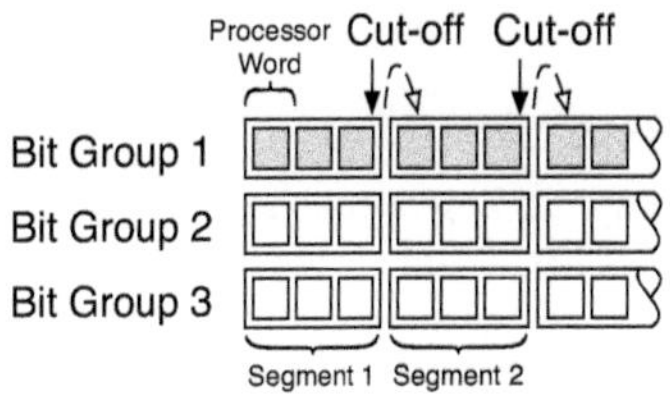

(b) BitWeaving/V

Figure 9: Early pruning on VBP and BitWeaving/V

The VBP storage format potentially wastes memory bandwidth if we apply the early pruning technique on the base VBP storage format. (See Section 3.3 for details.) Figure 9(a) illustrates a scan on a column stored in the VBP format. Suppose that with the early pruning technique (described in Section 4.1), the outcome of comparisons on all the codes in a segment is determined after accessing the first three words. Thus, the 4th to the 9th words in segment 1 can be skipped, and the processing can move to the next segment (as shown by the dashed arrow). Suppose that a CPU cache line contains 8 words. Thus, the six words that are skipped occupy the same CPU cache line as the first three words. Skipping over the content that has already been loaded into the CPU cache results in wasted memory bandwidth, which is often a critical resource in main memory data processing environments.

We solve this problem by dividing the k words in a segment into fixed sized *bit groups*. Let B denote the size of each bit group. The words in the same bit group are physically stored in continuous space. Figure 9(b) illustrates how the storage layout with the bit grouping reduces the amount of data that is loaded into the CPU cache. As shown in this figure, the nine words in each segment are divided into three bit groups, each containing three words per segment. Suppose that with the early pruning technique, the outcome of the comparisons on all the codes in a segment is determined after accessing the first three words. In this case, we only need to access the first three words of each segment, which are all laid out continuously and compactly in the first bit group. Consequently, the bit

Algorithm 3 BitWeaving/V column-scalar scan

Input: a predicate $C1 < c < C2$ on column c
BV_{in}: filter bit vector
Output: BV_{out}: result bit vector
1: initialize $C1$ and $C2$ (same as Lines 1-10 in Algorithm 2)
2: **for** each segment s in column c **do**
3: $m_{lt}, m_{gt} := 0$
4: $m_{eq1}, m_{eq2} := BV_{in}.s$ ◁
5: **for** $g := 1 \ldots \lfloor \frac{k}{B} \rfloor$ **do** □
6: **if** $m_{eq1} == 0$ **and** $m_{eq2} == 0$ **then** □
7: **break** □
8: **for** $i := gB + 1 \ldots \min(gB + B, k)$ **do** □
9: $m_{gt} := m_{gt} \vee (m_{eq1} \wedge \neg C1_i \wedge s.w_i)$
10: $m_{lt} := m_{lt} \vee (m_{eq2} \wedge C2_i \wedge \neg s.w_i)$
11: $m_{eq1} := m_{eq1} \wedge \neg(s.w_i \oplus C1_i)$
12: $m_{eq2} := m_{eq2} \wedge \neg(s.w_i \oplus C2_i)$
13: append $m_{gt} \wedge m_{lt}$ to BV_{out}
14: **return** BV_{out};

grouping technique uses memory bandwidth more judiciously, and results in a more sequential access pattern.

In the example above, if the early pruning triggers at two bits (instead of three bits), then we still save on memory accesses over a method that does not use bit groups. However, we will likely waste memory bandwidth bringing in data for the third bit. Picking an optimal bit group size is an interesting direction for future work. In Appendix D.2 of the full-length version of this paper [12], we empirically demonstrate the impact of the bit group size.

5.1.2 *Column-scalar scans*

We apply the early pruning technique on the VBP column-scalar scan, in two ways. First, when evaluating a comparison condition on a vector of codes, we skip over the least significant bits as soon as the outcome of the scan is fully determined. Second, a filter bit vector is fed into the scan to further speedup comparisons. This bit vector is used to filter out unmatched tuples even before the scan starts. This technique reduces the number of available codes in each segment, and thus speedups the scan (recall that early pruning technique often runs faster on segments with a lower fill factor as shown in Section 4.2).

The pseudocode for a VBP column-scalar scan with early pruning technique is shown in Algorithm 3. The algorithm is based on the VBP column-scalar scan shown in Algorithm 2. The modified lines are marked with ◁ and □ at the end of lines.

The first modification over the VBP scan method is to skip over the least significant bits once the outcome of the scan is fully determined (marked with □ at the end of lines). In the BitWeaving/V storage layout, k words representing a segment are divided into fixed-size bit groups. Each bit group contains B words in the segment. Predicate evaluation is also broken into a group of small loops to adapt to the design of bit groups. Before working on each bit group, we check the values of the bit masks m_{eq1} and m_{eq2}. If both bit masks are all 0s, then the leading bits between the codes and the constant are all different. Thus, the outcome of the scan on the segment is fully determined. As a result, we terminate the evaluation on this segment, and move to the next one.

We check the cut-off condition (in Line 6) in one of every B iterations of processing the k words of a segment. The purpose of this design is to reduce the cost of checking the condition as well as the cost of CPU branch mispredictions that this step triggers. If the cut-off probability at a bit position is neither close to 0% nor 100%, it is difficult for the CPU to predict the branch. Such branch misprediction can significantly slows down the overall execution. With the early pruning technique, checking the cut-off condition in one of every B iterations reduces the number of checks at the positions where the cut-off probability is in the middle range. We have observed that without this attention to branch prediction in the algorithm, the scans generally run slower by up to 40%.

The second modification is to feed a filter bit vector into the column-scalar comparisons. In a filter bit vector, the bits associated with the filtered codes are turned off. Filter bit vectors are typically the result bit vectors on other predicates in a complex WHERE clause (see Section 4.3 for more details).

To implement this feature, the bit masks m_{eq1} and m_{eq2} are initialized to the corresponding segment in the filter bit vector (marked with ◁ at the end of the line). During the evaluation on a segment, the bit masks m_{eq1} and m_{eq2} are updated by $m_{eq1} := m_{eq1} \wedge \neg(s.w_i \oplus C1_i)$ and $m_{eq2} := m_{eq2} \wedge \neg(s.w_i \oplus C2_i)$, respectively. Thus, the filtered codes remain 0s in m_{eq1} and m_{eq2} during the evaluation. Once the bits associated with the unfiltered codes are all updated to 0s, we terminate the comparisons on this segment following the early pruning technique. The filter bit vector potentially speedups the cut-off process.

5.2 BitWeaving/H

It is also feasible to apply early pruning technique on data stored in the HBP format. The key difference is that we store each bit group in the HBP storage layout (described in Section 3.2). For a column-scalar scan, we evaluate the comparison condition on bit groups starting from the one containing the most significant bits. In addition to the result bit vector on the input comparison condition, we also need to compute a bit vector for the inequality condition in order to detect if the outcome of the scan is fully determined. Once the outcome is fully determined, we skip the remaining bit groups (using early pruning).

However, the effect of early pruning technique on HBP is offset by the high overhead of computing the additional bit vector, and has an overall negative impact on performance (see Section 6.1.2). Therefore, the BitWeaving/H method is simply the HBP method.

5.3 BitWeaving/H and BitWeaving/V

In this section, we compare the two BitWeaving methods, in terms of performance, applicability, as well as ease of implementation. The summary of this comparison is shown in Table 1.

	BitWeaving/H	BitWeaving/V
Scan Complexity	$O(\lfloor \frac{n(k+1)}{w} \rfloor)$	$O(\frac{nk}{w})$
SIMD Implementation	Limited	Good
Early Pruning	No	Yes
Lookup Performance	Good	Poor

Table 1: Comparing BitWeaving/H and BitWeaving/V

Scan Complexity. BitWeaving/H uses $k + 1$ bits of processor word to store a k-bit code, while BitWeaving/V requires only k bits. As both methods simultaneously process multiple codes, the CPU cost of BitWeaving/H and BitWeaving/V are $O(\lfloor \frac{n(k+1)}{w} \rfloor)$ and $O(\frac{nk}{w})$, respectively; i.e., both are bit-parallel methods as per Definition 1. Both BitWeaving methods are generally competitive to other methods. However, in the extreme cases, BitWeaving/V could be close to 2X faster than BitWeaving/H due to the overhead of the delimiter bits (in BitWeaving/H). For instance, BitWeaving/H fits only one 32-bit code (with an addition delimiter bit) in a 64-bit process word, whereas BitWeaving/V fits two codes.

SIMD Implementation. The implementation of BitWeaving/H method relies on arithmetic and shift operations, which is generally not supported on an entire SIMD word today. Thus, BitWeaving/H

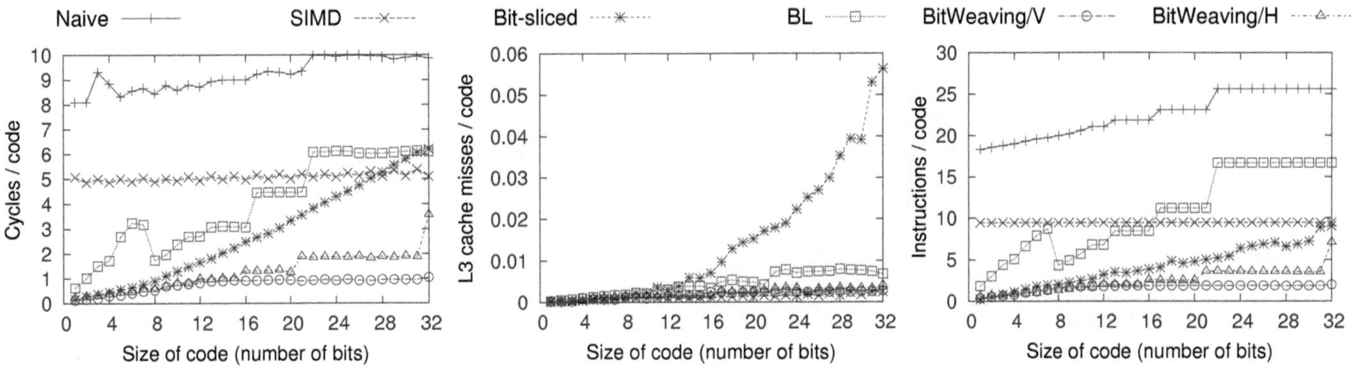

(a) Query Execution Time (b) Memory Performance (c) CPU Performance

Figure 10: Performance on query Q1.

has to pad codes to the width of banks in the SIMD registers, rather than the SIMD word width. This leads to underutilization of the full width of the SIMD registers. In contrast, BitWeaving/V method achieves the full parallelism that is offered by SIMD instructions. Appendix C in [12] describes how our methods can be extended to work with larger SIMD words.

Early Pruning. Applying early pruning technique on HBP requires extra processing that hurts the performance of HBP. As a result, BitWeaving/H does not employ the early pruning technique. In contrast, in BitWeaving/V, the early pruning technique works naturally with the underlying VBP-like format with no extra cost, and usually improves the scan performance.

Lookup Performance. With the BitWeaving/H layout, it is easy to fetch a code as all the bits of the code are stored contiguously. In contrast, for BitWeaving/V, all the bits of a code are spread across various bit groups, distributed over different words. Consequently, looking up a code potentially incurs many CPU cache misses, and can thus hurts performance.

To summarize, in general, both BitWeaving/H and BitWeaving/V are competitive methods. BitWeaving/V outperforms BitWeaving/H for scan performance whereas BitWeaving/H achieves better lookup performance. Empirical evaluation comparing these two methods is presented in the next section.

6. EVALUATION

We ran our experiments on a machine with dual 2.67GHz Intel Xeon 6-core CPUs, and 24GB of DDR3 main memory. Each processor has 12MB of L3 cache shared by all the cores on that processor. The processors support a 64-bit ALU instruction set as well as a 128-bit Intel SIMD instruction set. The operating system is Linux 2.6.9.

In the evaluation below, we compare BitWeaving to the SIMD-scan method proposed in [18], the Bit-sliced method [13], and a method based on Blink [8]. Collectively, these three methods represent the current state-of-the-art main memory scan methods.

To serve as a yardstick, we also include comparison with a naive method that simply extracts, loads, and then evaluates each code with the comparison condition in series, without exploiting any word-level parallelism. In the graphs below the tag *Naive* refers to this simple scan method.

Below, the tag *SIMD-scan* refers to the technique in [18] that uses SIMD instructions to align multiple tightly packed codes to SIMD banks in parallel, and then simultaneously processes multiple codes using SIMD instructions.

Below, the tag *Bit-sliced* refers to the traditional bit-sliced method proposed in [13]. This method was originally proposed to index tables with low number of distinct values; it shares similarities to the VBP method, but does not explore the storage layout and early pruning technique. Surprisingly, previous recent work on main memory scans have largely ignored the bit-sliced method.

In the graphs below, we use the tag *BL* (Blink-Like) to represent the method that adapts the Blink method [8] for column stores (since we focus on column stores for this evaluation). Thus, the tag *BL* refers to tightly (horizontally) packed columns with a simple linear layout, and without the extra bit that is used by HBP (see Section 3.2). The *BL* method differs from the BitWeaving/H method as it does not have the extra bit, and it lays out the codes in order (w.r.t. the discussion in the last paragraph in Section 3.2, the layout of the codes in *BL* is $c1$ and $c2$ in $v1$, $c3$ and $c4$ in $v2$, and so on in Figure 3).

Below, the tags BitWeaving/H (or BW/H) and BitWeaving/V (or BW/V) refer to the methods proposed in this paper. The size of the bit group is 4 for all experiments. The effect of the other bit group sizes on scan performance is shown in Appendix D.2 in [12].

We implemented each method in C++, and compiled the code using g++ 3.4.6 with optimization flags (O3).

In all the results below, we ran experiments using a single process with a single thread. We have also experimented using multiple threads working on independent data partitions. Since the results are similar to that of a single thread (all the methods parallelize well assuming that each thread works on a separate partition), in the interest of space, we omit these results.

6.1 Micro-Benchmark Evaluation

For this experiment, we created a table R with a single column and one billion uniformly distributed integer values in this column. The domain of the values are $[0, 2^d)$, where d is the width of the column that is varied in the experiments. The query (Q1), shown below, is used to evaluate a column-scalar scan with a simple LESS THAN predicate. The performance on other predicates is similar to that on the LESS THAN predicate. (See Appendix D.1 in [12] for more details.) The constants in the WHERE clause are used to control the selectivity. By default, the selectivity on each predicate is set to 10%, i.e. 10% of the input tuples match the predicate. Note, we also evaluate the impact of different selectivity (see Appendix D.3 in [12]), but by default use a value of 10%.

```
Q1:  SELECT COUNT(*) FROM R WHERE R.a < C1
```

6.1.1 *BitWeaving v/s the Other Methods*

In the evaluation below, we first compare BitWeaving to the

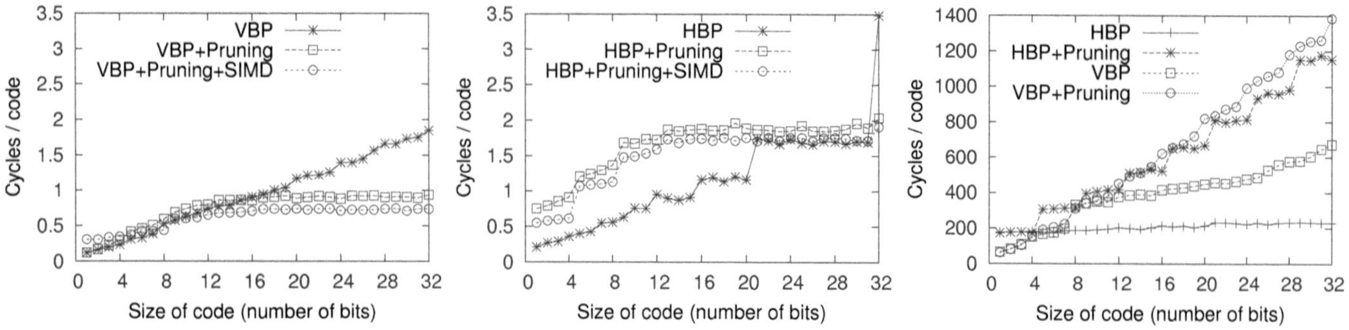

(a) VBP-related methods: Execution Time (b) HBP-related methods: Execution Time (c) Lookup Performance

Figure 11: Performance comparison between the HBP and the VBP related methods on Query Q1.

Naive, the SIMD-scan [18], the Bit-sliced [13], and the BL methods. Figure 10(a), Figure 10(b), and Figure 10(c) illustrate the number of cycles, cache misses, and CPU instructions for the six methods for Q1 respectively, when varying the width of the column code from 1 bit to 32 bits. The total number of cycles for the query is measured by using the RDTSC instruction. We divide this total number of cycles by the number of codes to compute the cycles per code, which is shown in Figure 10(a).

As can be observed in Figure 10(a), not surprisingly, the Naive method is the slowest. The Naive method shifts and applies a mask to extract and align each packed code to the processor word. Since each code is much smaller than a processor word (64-bit), it burns many more instructions than the other methods (see Figure 10(c)) on every word of data that is fetched from the underlying memory subsystem (with L1/L2/L3 caches buffering data fetched from main memory). Even when most of the data is served from the L1 cache, its CPU cost dominates the overall query execution time.

The SIMD-scan achieves 50%–75% performance improvement over the Naive method (see Figure 10(a)), but it is still worse compared to the other methods. Even though a SIMD instruction can process four 32-bit banks in parallel, the number of instructions drops by only 2.2-2.6X (over the Naive method), because it imposes extra instructions to align packed codes into the four banks before any computation can be run on that data. Furthermore, we observe that with SIMD instructions, the CPI (Cycles Per Instructions) increases from 0.37 to 0.56 (see Figure 10(c)), which means that a single SIMD instructions takes more cycles to executed than a ordinary ALU instruction. This effect further dampens the benefit of this SIMD implementation.

As can be seen in Figure 10(a), the Bit-sliced and the BL methods shows a near linear increase in run time as the code width increases. Surprisingly, both these methods are almost uniformly faster than the SIMD-scan method. However, the storage layout of the Bit-sliced method occupies many CPU cache lines for wider codes. As a result, as can be seen in Figure 10(b), the number of L3 cache misses quickly increases and hinders overall performance.

In this experiment, the BitWeaving methods *outperform all the other methods across all the code widths* (see Figure 10(a)). Unlike the Naive and the SIMD-scan methods, they do not need to move data to appropriate positions before the predicate evaluation computation. In addition, as shown in Figure 10(b) and 10(c), the BitWeaving methods are optimized for both cache misses and instructions due to their storage layouts and scan algorithms. Finally, with the early pruning technique, the execution time of BitWeaving/V (see Figure 10(a)) does not increase for codes that are wider than 12 bits. As can be seen in Figure 10(a), for codes wider than 12 bits, both BitWeaving methods are often more than 3X faster than the SIMD-scan, the Bit-sliced and the BL methods.

6.1.2 Individual BitWeaving Components

In this experiment, we compare the effect of the various techniques (VBP v/s HBP, early pruning, and SIMD optimizations) that have been proposed in this paper. Figure 11(a) and 11(b) plot the performance of these techniques for VBP and HBP for query Q1, respectively.

First, we compare the scan performance of the HBP and the VBP methods for query Q1. From the results shown in Figure 11(a) and 11(b), we observe that at certain points, VBP is up to 2X faster than HBP. For example, VBP is 2X faster than HBP for 32-bit codes, because HBP has to pad 32-bit code to a entire 64-bit word to fit both the code and the delimiter bit. In spite of this, HBP and VBP generally show a similar performance trend as the code width increases. This empirical results matches our analysis that both methods satisfy the cost-bound for bit-parallel methods.

Next, we examine the effects of the early pruning technique on both the VBP and the HBP methods. As can be seen in Figure 11(a), for wider codes, the early pruning technique quickly reduces the query execution time for VBP, and beyond 12 bits, the query execution time with early pruning is nearly constant. Essentially, as described in Section 4.2, for wider codes early pruning has a high chance of terminating after examining the first few bits.

In contrast, as can be seen in Figure 11(b), the effect of the early pruning technique on the HBP method is offset by the high overhead of computing the additional masks (see Section 5.2). Consequently, the HBP method (which is the same as BitWeaving/H, as discussed in Section 5.2) is uniformly faster than "HBP + Pruning".

Applying SIMD parallelism achieves marginal speedups for both the HBP and the VBP methods (see Figures 11(a) and 11(b)). Ideally, the implementation with a 128-bit SIMD word should be 2X faster than that with 64-bit ALU word. However, by measuring the number of instructions, we observed that the SIMD implementation reduces the number of instructions by 40%, but also increase the CPI by 1.5X. Consequently, the net effect is that the SIMD implementation is only 20% and 10% faster than the ALU implementation, for VBP and HBP respectively.

Next, we evaluate the performance of a lookup operation. A lookup operation is important to produce the attributes in the projection list after the predicates in the WHERE clause have been applied. In this experiment, we randomly pick 10 million positions in the column, and measure the average number of cycles that are needed to fetch (and assemble) a code at each position. The results for this experiment are shown in Figure 11(c).

As can be seen in Figure 11(c), amongst the four methods, the

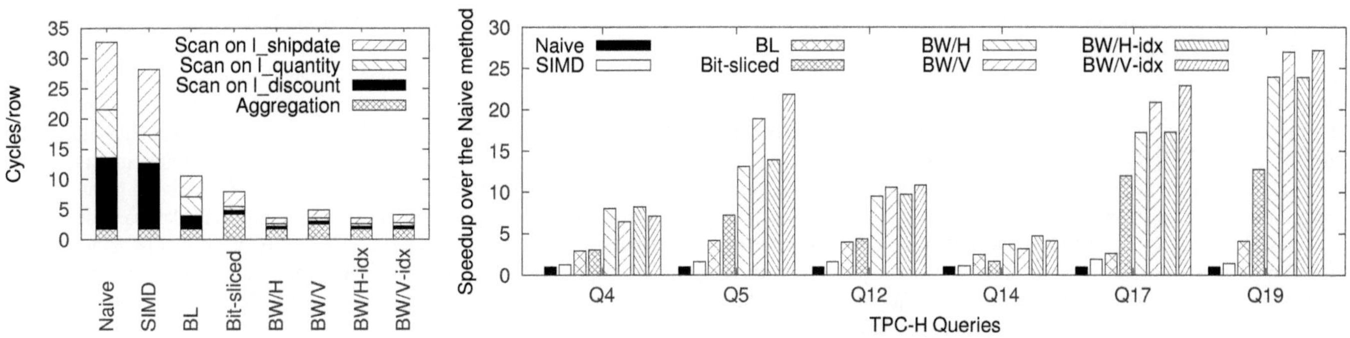

(a) Q6: Execution Time Breakdown

(b) Performance on TPC-H Queries with Materialized Join Inputs

Figure 12: Performance comparison with the TPC-H Queries (BW=BitWeaving).

lookup performance of the HBP method is the best, and its performance is stable across the code widths. The reason for this behavior is because all the bits of a code in the HBP method are located together. For the VBP method, all the bits of a code are stored in continuous space, and thus it is relatively fast to access all the bits and assemble the code. For the methods with the early pruning technique, the bits of a code are distributed into various bit groups. Assembling a code requires access to data across multiple bit groups at different locations, which incurs many CPU cache misses, and thus significantly hurts the lookup performance.

6.2 TPC-H Evaluation

In this experiment, we use seven queries from the TPC-H benchmark [17]. These experiments were run against a TPC-H dataset at scale factor 10. The total size of the database is approximately 10GB. First, we compare the performance of the various methods on the TPC-H scan query (Q6). This query is shown below:

```
SELECT sum(l_extendedprice * l_discount)
FROM lineitem
WHERE l_shipdate BETWEEN Date and Date + 1 year
 and l_discount BETWEEN Discount - 0.01
 and Discount + 0.01 and l_quantity < Quantity
```

As per the TPC-H specifications for the domain size for each of the columns/attributes in this query, the column `l_shipdate`, `l_discount`, `l_quantity`, `l_extendedprice` are encoded with 12 bits, 4 bits, 6 bits, and 24 bits, respectively. The selectivity of this query is approximately 2%.

Figure 12(a) shows the time breakdown for the scan and the aggregation operations for the BitWeaving and the other methods. Not surprisingly, the Naive method is the slowest. The SIMD-scan method only achieves about 20% performance improvement over the Naive method, mainly because the SIMD-scan method performs relatively poorly when evaluating the BETWEEN predicates (see Appendix D.1 in [12]). Evaluating a BETWEEN predicate is complicated/expensive with the SIMD-scan method since the results of the SIMD computations are always stored in the original input registers. Consequently, we have to make two copies for each attribute value, and compare each copy with the lower and upper bound constants in the BETWEEN predicate, respectively.

The BL method runs at a much higher speed compared to the Naive and the SIMD methods. However, compared to BitWeaving/H, the BL method uses more instructions to implement its functionality of parallel processing on packed data and the conversion process to produce the result bit vector, which hinders its scan performance.

Note that both the BitWeaving methods (BW/H and BW/V) outperform all existing methods. As the column `l_extendedprice` is fairly wide (24 bits), BitWeaving/V spends more cycles extracting the matching values from the aggregation columns. As a result, for this particular query, BitWeaving/H is faster than BitWeaving/V.

We also evaluated the effects of using the BitWeaving methods as indices. In this method, the entire WHERE clause is evaluated using the corresponding BitWeaving methods on the columns of interest for this WHERE clause. Then, using the method described in Appendix A in [12] , the columns involved in the aggregation (in the SELECT clause of the query) are fetched from the associated column store(s) for these attributes. These column stores use a Naive storage organization.

In Figure 12, these BitWeaving index-based methods are denoted as BW/H-idx and BW/V-idx. As can be seen in Figure 12(a), BW/H-idx and BW/H have similar performance. The key difference between these methods is whether the aggregation columns are accessed from either the BW/H format or from the Naive column store. However, since using BW/H always results in accessing one cache line per lookup, its performance is similar to the lookup with the Naive column store organization (i.e the BW/H-idx case). On the other hand, the BW/V-idx method is about 30% faster than the BW/V method. The reason for this behavior is that the vertical bit layout in BW/V results in looking up data across multiple cache lines for each aggregate column value, whereas the BW/V-idx method fetches these attribute values from the Naive column store, which requires accessing only one cache line for each aggregate column value.

Next, we selected six TPC-H join queries (Q4, Q5, Q12, Q14, Q17, Q19), and materialized the join component in these queries. Then, we ran scan operations on the pre-joined materialized tables. Here, we report the results of these scan operations on these materialized tables. The widths of the columns involved in the selection operations (i.e. the WHERE clause in the SQL query on the pre-joined materialized tables) ranges from 2 bits to 12 bits. All these queries, except for query Q19, contain a predicate clause that is a conjunction of one to four predicates. Query Q19 has a more complex predicate clause, which includes a disjunction of three predicate clauses, each of which is a conjunction of six predicates. These queries contain a variety of predicates, including $<, >, =, <>$, BETWEEN, and IN. Some queries also involve predicates that perform comparisons between two columns. The projection clauses of these six queries contain one to three columns with widths that vary from 3 to 24 bits.

Figure 12(b) plots the speedup of all the methods over the Naive method for the six TPC-H queries. For most queries, the BitWeaving methods are over one order of magnitude faster than the Naive method.

By comparing the performance of the BW/H and the BW/V methods, we observe that the answer to the question of which BitWeaving method has higher performance depends on many query characteristics. For Q4 and Q14, the BW/H method is slightly faster than the BW/V method, because the BW/H method performs better on the BETWEEN predicate on relative narrow columns (see Appendix D.1 in [12]). Query Q4 contains two predicate clauses, one of which is a BETWEEN predicate. In contrast, Query Q14 contains only one predicate clause, which is a BETWEEN predicate. For queries Q5, Q12, Q17, and Q19, the BW/V method outperforms the BW/H method as these four queries contain more than three predicate clauses. Although some of these queries also contain the BETWEEN predicate(s), the early pruning technique (of BW/V) speedups the scans with on BETWEEN predicates when performed at the end of a series of column-scalar scans. In general, we observe that the BW/V method has higher performance for queries with predicates that involve many columns, involve wider columns, and have highly selective predicates.

Using the BW/V method as an index improves the performance by about 15% for Q5 and Q17 (both queries contain wider columns in their projection lists), and has no significant gain for the other queries. In general, we observe that it is not very productive to use the BW/H method as an index, since it already has a low lookup cost as a base storage format. For the BW/V method, using it as an index improves the performance for some queries by avoiding the slow lookups that are associated with using the BW/V method as the base storage format.

We note that there are interesting issues here in terms of how to pick between BitWeaving/H vs. BitWeaving/V, and whether to use the BitWeaving methods as an index of for base storage. Building an accurate cost model that can guide these choices based on workload characteristics is an interesting direction for future work.

7. RELATED WORK

The techniques present in this paper are applicable to main-memory analytics DBMSs. In such DBMSs, data is often stored in compressed form. SAP HANA [5], IBM Blink [2,15], and HYRISE [10] use sorted dictionaries to encode values. Dynamic order-preserving dictionary was proposed to encode strings [3]. Other light-weight compression schemes can also be used for main-memory column-wise databases, such as [1,4,20].

SIMD instructions can be used to speed up database operations [19], and the SIMD-scan [18] method is the state-of-the-art scan method that uses SIMD. In this paper we compare BitWeaving with this scan method. We note that BitWeaving can also be used in processing environments that don't support SIMD instructions.

The BitWeaving/V methods shares similarity to the bit-sliced index [13], but the storage layout of a bit-sliced index is not optimized for memory access, as well as our proposed early pruning technique. A follow-up work presented the algorithms that perform arithmetic on bit-sliced indices [16]. Some techniques described in that paper are also applicable to our BitWeaving/V method.

The BitWeaving/H method relies on the capability to process packed data in parallel. This technique was first proposed by Lamport [11]. Recently, a similar technique [8] was used to evaluate complex predicates in IBM's Blink System [2].

8. CONCLUSIONS AND FUTURE WORK

With the increasing demand for main memory analytics data processing, there is an critical need for fast scan primitives. This paper proposes a method called BitWeaving that addresses this need by exploiting the parallelism available at the bit level in modern processors. The two flavors of BitWeaving are optimized for two common access patterns, and both methods match the complexity bound for bit-parallel scans. Our experimental studies show that the BitWeaving techniques are faster than the state-of-the-art scan methods, and in some cases by over an order of magnitude. For future work, we plan to explore methods to use BitWeaving effectively in other database operations, such as joins and aggregates. We also plan to study how to apply the BitWeaving technique within the context of broader automatic physical database design issues (e.g. replication, and forming column groups [8] automatically), multi-threaded scans, concurrent scans, other compression schemes, and considering the impact of BitWeaving on query optimization.

Acknowledgments

We would like to thank Jeffrey Naughton, Karu Sankaralingam, Craig Chasseur, Qiang Zeng, and the reviewers of this paper for their insightful feedback on an earlier draft of this paper. This work was supported in part by the National Science Foundation under grants IIS-1110948 and IIS-1250886, and a gift donation from Google.

9. REFERENCES

[1] D. J. Abadi, S. Madden, and M. Ferreira. Integrating compression and execution in column-oriented database systems. In *SIGMOD*, pages 671–682, 2006.

[2] R. Barber, P. Bendel, M. Czech, O. Draese, F. Ho, N. Hrle, S. Idreos, M.-S. Kim, O. Koeth, J.-G. Lee, T. T. Li, G. M. Lohman, K. Morfonios, R. Müller, K. Murthy, I. Pandis, L. Qiao, V. Raman, R. Sidle, K. Stolze, and S. Szabo. Business analytics in (a) Blink. *IEEE Data Eng. Bull.*, 35(1):9–14, 2012.

[3] C. Binnig, S. Hildenbrand, and F. Färber. Dictionary-based order-preserving string compression for main memory column stores. In *SIGMOD Conference*, pages 283–296, 2009.

[4] W. Fang, B. He, and Q. Luo. Database compression on graphics processors. *PVLDB*, 3(1):670–680, 2010.

[5] F. Färber, N. May, W. Lehner, P. Große, I. Müller, H. Rauhe, and J. Dees. The SAP HANA database – an architecture overview. *IEEE Data Eng. Bull.*, 35(1):28–33, 2012.

[6] M. Grund, J. Krüger, H. Plattner, A. Zeier, P. Cudré-Mauroux, and S. Madden. Hyrise - a main memory hybrid storage engine. *PVLDB*, 4(2):105–116, 2010.

[7] S. Idreos, F. Groffen, N. Nes, S. Manegold, K. S. Mullender, and M. L. Kersten. MonetDB: Two decades of research in column-oriented database architectures. *IEEE Data Eng. Bull.*, 35(1):40–45, 2012.

[8] R. Johnson, V. Raman, R. Sidle, and G. Swart. Row-wise parallel predicate evaluation. *PVLDB*, 1(1):622–634, 2008.

[9] A. Kemper, T. Neumann, F. Funke, V. Leis, and H. Mühe. Hyper: Adapting columnar main-memory data management for transactional and query processing. *IEEE Data Eng. Bull.*, 35(1):46–51, 2012.

[10] J. Krüger, C. Kim, M. Grund, N. Satish, D. Schwalb, J. Chhugani, H. Plattner, P. Dubey, and A. Zeier. Fast updates on read-optimized databases using multi-core CPUs. *PVLDB*, 5(1):61–72, 2011.

[11] L. Lamport. Multiple byte processing with full-word instructions. *Commun. ACM*, 18(8):471–475, 1975.

[12] Y. Li and J. M. Patel. BitWeaving: Fast scans for main memory data processing. http://research.cs.wisc.edu/quickstep/pubs/bitweaving-extended.pdf.

[13] P. E. O'Neil and D. Quass. Improved query performance with variant indexes. In *SIGMOD*, pages 38–49, 1997.

[14] *Oracle Exalytics In-Memory Machine: A Brief Introduction*, October 2011. Oracle White Paper.

[15] V. Raman, G. Swart, L. Qiao, F. Reiss, V. Dialani, D. Kossmann, I. Narang, and R. Sidle. Constant-time query processing. In *ICDE*, pages 60–69, 2008.

[16] D. Rinfret, P. E. O'Neil, and E. J. O'Neil. Bit-sliced index arithmetic. In *SIGMOD*, pages 47–57, 2001.

[17] Transaction Processing Performance Council. *TPC Benchmark H. Revision 2.14.3*. November 2011.

[18] T. Willhalm, N. Popovici, Y. Boshmaf, H. Plattner, A. Zeier, and J. Schaffner. SIMD-scan: Ultra fast in-memory table scan using on-chip vector processing units. *PVLDB*, 2(1):385–394, 2009.

[19] J. Zhou and K. A. Ross. Implementing database operations using SIMD instructions. In *SIGMOD*, pages 145–156, 2002.

[20] M. Zukowski, S. Héman, N. Nes, and P. A. Boncz. Super-scalar RAM-CPU cache compression. In *ICDE*, page 59, 2006.

[21] M. Zukowski, M. van de Wiel, and P. A. Boncz. Vectorwise: A vectorized analytical DBMS. In *ICDE*, pages 1349–1350, 2012.

Performance and Resource Modeling in Highly-Concurrent OLTP Workloads

Barzan Mozafari* Carlo Curino† Alekh Jindal* Samuel Madden*

*CSAIL MIT
{barzan,alekh,madden}@csail.mit.edu

†Microsoft
ccurino@microsoft.com

ABSTRACT

Database administrators of Online Transaction Processing (OLTP) systems constantly face difficult questions. For example, "*What is the maximum throughput I can sustain with my current hardware?*", "*How much disk I/O will my system perform if the requests per second double?*", or "*What will happen if the ratio of transactions in my system changes?*". Resource prediction and performance analysis are both vital and difficult in this setting. Here the challenge is due to high degrees of concurrency, competition for resources, and complex interactions between transactions, all of which non-linearly impact performance.

Although difficult, such analysis is a key component in enabling database administrators to understand which queries are eating up the resources, and how their system would scale under load. In this paper, we introduce our framework, called DBSeer, that addresses this problem by employing statistical models that provide resource and performance analysis and prediction for highly concurrent OLTP workloads. Our models are built on a small amount of training data from standard log information collected during normal system operation. These models are capable of accurately measuring several performance metrics, including resource consumption on a per-transaction-type basis, resource bottlenecks, and throughput at different load levels. We have validated these models on MySQL/Linux with numerous experiments on standard benchmarks (TPC-C) and real workloads (Wikipedia), observing high accuracy (within a few percent error) when predicting all of the above metrics.

Categories and Subject Descriptors

H.2.4 [**Systems**]: Relational databases

Keywords

OLTP, Performance Predictions, Multi-tenancy

1. INTRODUCTION

Operating a large database management system (DBMS) or a multi-tenant "database-as-a-service" [16] is a challenging and stressful task for database administrators (DBA), especially as the DBMS starts experiencing heavy concurrent load. Although some databases provide tools for measuring the run-time of an individual query, many performance problems are a result of *interactions* between concurrent queries, which existing systems are not capable of modeling. Many transactions that run fine in isolation become much slower when run together, as they interact in complex ways and contend for shared resources. Load that is added over time may cause resources that were previously abundant to become constrained, and query performance to plummet. Applications may generate unpredictable, time-varying load that puts strain on different resources (e.g., RAM, disk, or CPU) at different times. To handle all these scenarios, we need a way to *attribute* system load, on a per-resource basis to different queries, transactions, or applications. This attribution enables a number of useful applications, including:

- **Diagnosis / Performance Inspection:** Why is a given query running slow (in the presence of concurrency)? Which transaction groups are causing the spike of lock wait times in the DBMS?
- **Run-time Performance Isolation:** In a database supporting multiple applications, which application/transaction is using more than its allocated share of resources? At what rate should transactions of a given application be admitted/ dropped in order to avoid any SLA (service-level agreement) violations?
- **Billing:** What is the actual contribution of each workload to the overall resource consumption?

A second challenge for DBAs is to understand how database resource consumption and performance vary as load on the system changes, e.g., when partitioning the database, or when a sudden increase in popularity of a website imposes unexpected load on the back-end database To address the second challenge, we need *what-if analysis* tools to allow DBAs to answer two other classes of questions:

- **Performance Prediction:** What will the performance (e.g. latency or throughput) of a given query or application be if the rate of 'new order' transactions doubles?
- **Provisioning:** Which resource (e.g., disk, CPU, RAM) will bottleneck first if the load on the system increases? What is the hardware required to deliver a desired throughput?

To address these challenges, we introduce our approach, called DBSeer, for statistical *performance modeling and prediction.* Our techniques involve collecting a limited set of low-overhead statistics from the DBMS and the operating system, measured during normal system operation. We then use these statistics to build offline models for the given DBMS and the workload(s) running on it. These models allow us to perform attribution and what-if analysis by assessing the resource (e.g., CPU, disk, RAM, cache, DB locks) requirements of individual queries or applications and estimating how those requirements change as the database grows in size, as queries in the workloads change, or as allocated resources vary.

In DBSeer, we develop two classes of models and compare their performance. First, we develop *black-box models,* that make minimal assumptions about the nature of the underlying system, and train statistical regression models to predict future performance based on past performance statistics. Second, we develop *white-box models* that take the major components of the underlying database system into account, to enable more accurate predictions. Specifically, we develop white-box models for disk I/O, lock contention, and memory utilization of MySQL. Although these models are focused on MySQL, we believe that even solving performance prediction in the context of this one system represents an important step forward, as MySQL alone is used by millions of users. Moreover, in Section 8.5, we report preliminary (but promising) results in applying our models to another DBMS (PostgreSQL).

As we show in our experiments, the trade-off between these two classes of models is that black-box models are more general but are also less effective in making predictions outside of the range of inputs on which they were trained. Unfortunately, many interesting questions (including many what-if scenarios) require such "out of range" predictions, e.g., predicting performance when dramatic and heretofore unseen changes happen in the workload. This is why developing white-box models is also necessary: they are less general than black-box models (as they make assumptions about the nature of the database) but they provide higher extrapolation power.

Our approach in DBSeer[1] is specifically designed for highly concurrent OLTP (*transaction processing*) applications . These applications run lightweight transactions that read or write a few records at a time. We focus on this class of problems because OLTP settings are most frustrating for DBAs, due to their high levels of concurrency and the complex interactions between transactions (i.e., competition for different resources such as locks, cache, I/O). Such competitions can lead to non-linear effects, where a small change in load can trigger a large change in performance. Though some prior work has addressed performance prediction in the case of OLAP (a.k.a. *analytical*) databases [12, 3, 8], this problem has not been well studied in OLTP. Thus, a key contribution of our work is to develop non-linear models that capture highly concurrent locking and logging operations of OLTP workloads.

In summary, we make several contributions towards modeling transactional workload, including:

- **Resource Models:** we have developed white and black-box models for predicting different resources, including CPU, RAM, network, disk I/O, and lock contention. Our primary contribution here is a set of novel white-box models for predicting disk I/O and lock contention.
- **Extracting transaction types:** we have developed highly accurate clustering techniques to automatically extract and summarize "classes of similar transactions" from a query log that allow us to accurately group similar transactions. We show that this clustering is able, for example, to identify the 5 transaction classes in TPC-C, and the major query types in Wikipedia.
- **Evaluation:** we evaluate our models on a real database system, both using the well-known TPC-C benchmark and the real-life traces of Wikipedia, showing that we can predict the maximum throughput within 0-25% error. Additionally, we show that white-box models can avoid over-provisioning by at least 9× and predict disk I/O from 4× to 100× more accurately than simple black-box models when predicting resource utilization over a wide range of transaction rates.

2. SOLUTION OVERVIEW

In this paper, we focus on the problem of *resource prediction*. Given a set of transaction types (we describe our method for deriving these below) running at a certain rate (transactions per second, or TPS), with a certain mixture (fraction of each transaction type in the overall workload), the goal is to predict the CPU usage, disk I/O, minimum amount of RAM, network consumption, and time spent in lock contention. Such models are important for understanding how close a DBMS is to saturation and which resource will saturate first, as well as for diagnosis/investigation of performance problems (e.g., attributing utilization of particular resources to particular transactions).

2.1 DBSeer Overview

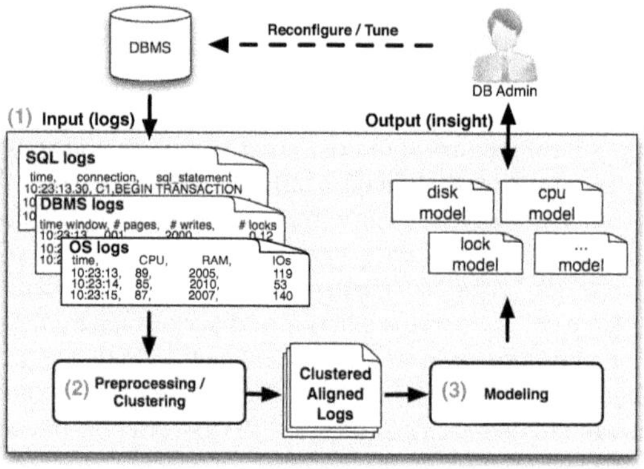

Figure 1: Workflow in DBSeer.

DBSeer consists of the following steps, shown in Figure 1:

1. **Collecting Logs.** We observe a DBMS during normal operation, i.e., running without modification in its production state. We collect standard SQL query logs, as well as various DBMS and OS statistics (over periods of hours or days).

2. **Preprocessing / Clustering.** We align (by time) and join the various logs, and extract a set of transaction types to categorize the types/classes of transactions that the system runs. We automatically cluster the transactions based on their SQL statements and the different tables that they have accessed. We also construct a concise profile of each transaction type, summarizing its access pattern to different tables in the database. These summaries are used in our lock contention model. Logging and clustering are described in more detail in Section 3. Note that the transaction types only differ based on features relevant for performance and resource consumption. This allows us to bound the number of classes we consider, while significantly improving the accuracy of our models. This also allows users to query the system with what-if scenarios that include changing the mixture of transactions (ratios of each transaction type in the workload).

3. **Modeling.** We build white- and black-box models to predict the resource utilization (CPU, RAM, disk I/O, Locks, etc.) of the system for different mixes and rates of transaction types. Our models can accurately answer attribution and what-if questions (e.g., for provisioning, diagnosis, etc) for any given mix of transactions or target transaction rate. This is shown in the figure as the Output/Insight arrow. Even for white-box models we relied on general knowledge of the functional component within the DBMS, without the need to modify nor access the source code of the system. A DB administrator (DBA) uses our system by providing as input a set of transaction logs (we use [1] to collect logs), and querying the resulting models to test a series of hypotheses. The DBA or automated tools running on his/her behalf can leverage our models to reconfigure or tune the DBMS, or perform other operational actions (migration, provisioning, etc.). Details of our models for different resources are presented in Section 4–6. Finally, we combine all these models in Section 7

[1]Source code for DBSeer is available at `http://dbseer.org`.

to accurately predict the maximum throughput that the system can deliver for a given mixture and rate.

All of our models accept a mixture $(f_1, \cdots . f_J)$ and a target TPS T, where f_i represents the fraction of the total transactions run from type i and J is the total number of types. The models are built from a small selection of training data collected over a narrow range of TPS and a specific mixture (such as the conditions of a system running in production), but can predict the expected resource utilization over a wide range of TPS and mixtures. We validate this experimentally in Section 8, showing that we can observe the system at a fixed mixture, and answer what-if and attribution questions about *never-seen-before* mixtures and rates.

3. PREPROCESSING

In this section, we describe our approach to logging (Sec. 3.1), transaction clustering (Sec. 3.2), and estimating page access distribution (Sec. 3.3). These are used as input to the prediction models described in the rest of the paper.

3.1 Gathering the Log and Statistics

We collected a number of aggregate statistics about the system. These statistics are collected passively, without affecting performance of the system or varying the rate or mix of transactions that are run, using standard operating system and database logging features. Specifically, we collected (i) resource consumption statistics from the OS (Linux, in our case), (ii) load statistics (e.g., number of dirty pages, number of logical reads, etc.) from the DBMS (MySQL, in our case), and (iii) a query log, containing start-time, duration, and the SQL for each statement run by the system. Practically this consists of running dstat (`http://dag.wieers.com/home-made/dstat/`), a python-based tool to collect OS and MySQL statistics on the server, and leveraging MySQL's query logging functionalities. Also, note that most production environments routinely monitor most of these statistics for administration and auditing purposes, and refer to this as telemetry.

The result of this logging is a number of features which we use in our models. These include:

1. The SQL statements and transactions executed by the system (that will be clustered using our clustering mechanism).
2. The run-time (latency) of each transaction.
3. Aggregate OS stats, including per-core CPU usage, number of I/O reads and writes, number of outstanding asynchronous I/Os, total network packets and bytes transferred, number of page faults, number of context switches, CPU and I/O usage.
4. Global status variables from MySQL including the number of `SELECT`, `UPDATE`, `DELETE`, and `INSERT` commands executed, number of flushed and dirty pages, and the total lock wait-time.

As we are focused on non-intrusive logging, we do not collect any statistics that significantly slow down performance, such as fine-grained locking information.

3.2 Transaction Clustering

We first use the logs to group transactions into a set of types or classes. The main goal of this step is to cluster transactions into classes that exhibit a similar access pattern, i.e. they access the same tables in the same order and perform similar operations on each table. (Note that different parts of a table might be accessed with different probabilities by each class of transactions.) Extracting transaction types allows us to model different mixtures of transactions in the workload, where the workload at any point in time is represented by the total number of transactions per second as well as the fraction of each transaction type in the mixture.

Extracting Transaction Summaries: Our clustering begins by parsing the query logs and extracting a *transaction summary* from each (successfully) committed transaction, defined as:

$$[t_0(mode_1, table_1, n_1, t_1), \cdots, (mode_k, table_k, n_k, t_k)] \quad (1)$$

where k is the number of tables accessed by the transaction (e.g., if it accesses table a, then table b and then again table a, we have $k = 3$), t_0 is the time lag between the `BEGIN` and the first SQL statement, and for $1 \le i \le k$, $table_i$ is the i'th table being accessed by this transaction, $mode_i$ is either w when accessing $table_i$ requires an exclusive lock (e.g. `DELETE`, `UPDATE`, `INSERT` or `SELECT...FOR UPDATE`), and is r if the access requires a read-only/shared lock (e.g. general `SELECT`). We define n_i as the approximate number of rows accessed from $table_i$. Finally, for $1 \le i < k$, t_i is defined as -1 when both the i'th and the $(i+1)$'th table accesses are caused by the same SQL statement. Otherwise, t_i is the time lag between the completion of the SQL statement causing the i'th access and the time that the $(i+1)$'th statement was issued. t_k is defined as the time between the last SQL statement and the final `COMMIT`. All of this information can be obtained from the SQL logs except the number of rows read or written from each table, which we estimate using the query rewriting technique described in Section 3.3.

Learning Transaction Types: Given the transaction summaries, we use the extracted features and apply the DBSCAN [9] clustering algorithm to group individual transactions based on their accesses. Note that DBSCAN is an unsupervised method (so it does not require labeled examples of each transaction type), and does not make any a priori assumptions about the number of clusters (as does, for example, k-means). As we show in Section 8.3, this clustering performs very well. In fact, it gives 0% misclassification compared to a manual clustering of the transactions based on their semantics. The input data consists of one row per transaction. Each row contains a set of transaction features. The feature set consists of 2 attributes for each table in the database, one for the number of rows read from and one for the number of rows updated/inserted in each table (many of these features will be zero as most transactions do not access all the tables). These simple features proved sufficient for clustering TPC-C and Wikipedia (as well as several other workloads [1]).

The output of this clustering is a workload summary that lists the major transaction types (along with representative queries) and provides their frequencies in the base workload. We found that the extracted classes are easy to understand and manipulate by the users, since we provide representative examples and allow the user to assign a name/label to each transaction type (e.g., the New Order transaction of TPC-C). This is a powerful abstraction that enables users to specify the rate at which *each* type of transaction will be executed (i.e., mixture and overall rate) as input to the prediction models. This allows us to explore hypothetical scenarios and understand how performance would vary for different mixtures of transactions.

3.3 Estimating Access Distributions

Our second use of the logs is to infer a rough probability distribution over all the pages in the database by access (read or write) and by transaction type—this is used in our locking and I/O prediction models to estimate conflict and update probabilities. We do this by processing the raw MySQL logs to extract individual queries/updates, and then rewriting queries to extract the primary keys accessed in the tables (using rewriting techniques in [6]). We then run our rewritten queries against the database to obtain sets of primary keys read/written by each query/update (grouped by transaction type). This analysis is done offline, imposing no overhead on the operational database. In the case of MySQL/InnoDB, primary keys are always the clustered index of a table, therefore we can assume that tuples with contiguous primary keys are stored consecutively on disk and hence, we can infer which pages are accessed. Here, we assume that all accesses to large tables are done via indexes, rather than sequential scans, which is true of well-tuned transactional applications. However, if needed, we could also use the `EXPLAIN` command to determine the exact access method in the query plan and hence, the exact set of pages that a given transaction will access. We then further aggregate these accesses into probability distributions (per table and per transaction type) necessary for our predictions.

4. MODELING DISK I/O AND RAM

In this section, we present our white-box models for disk I/O and RAM provisioning. Our models in this section are based on MySQL. While some of MySQL features are shared among other traditional DBMSs (e.g., LRU-based caching or 2-phase locking), some of the other features are specific to MySQL (e.g., the buffer pool flushing policy). Our main goal in this paper is to demonstrate that it is possible to build accurate models for a given DBMS. In particular, we focus on MySQL due to its popularity (used by millions of users). However, In Section 8.5, we also report preliminary results on applying our models to another DBMS (PostgreSQL).

Disk and memory are important aspects of performance in a database system. In fact, in a transactional database, such as MySQL, disk I/Os and RAM utilization are closely related to one another. The three main causes for disk I/Os are:

1. **Log writes**, needed to guarantee transactionality.
2. **Dirty pages write backs**, needed to bound recovery time, and allow transactionally-consistent reclamation of log files (all pages dirtied by transactions logged in the current log file need to be flushed to disk before the log file can be recycled).
3. **I/Os due to cache misses**, needed to read pages from disk that were not cached in the buffer pool, and possibly trigger eviction of dirty pages (which need to be written back to disk first).

These operations heavily depend on the size of the buffer pool: a smaller buffer pool leads to more I/Os.

In Section 4.1, we provide a brief overview of the aforementioned factors. Then, in Section 4.2, we introduce our white-box model for disk writes, which accounts for both log-related writes as well as those related to log reclamation. Finally, in Section 4.3, we present our models for disk reads and page writes caused by cache misses/evictions.

4.1 Background on Disk I/O in a DBMS

Log writes, due to their nature, can be easily modeled with linear regression, as they are proportional to the rate of each transaction type in the load (our linear models are discussed in Section 6). Therefore, in the rest of this section we focus on writes that are due to dirty page write-backs, or "flushes". Flushing happens for two main reasons: 1) *capacity misses*, when a new page is brought into the buffer pool and there are no free buffers, forcing an existing record to be flushed and 2) *log-triggered data flushes*, when the redo log file(s) is full and needs to be *rotated* or *recycled*. We handle capacity misses together with reads in Section 4.3, while in this section we focus on *log-triggered data flushes*.

Log-triggered data flushes exist because the dirty pages corresponding to the recycled log records need to be flushed to disk before recycling the log file. In a typical implementation, multiple log files are used in a circular fashion. Before recycling an old log file, the DBMS guarantees that all buffer pool pages dirtied by transactions logged in that file have been flushed back to disk. This means that the DBMS may temporarily stop serving transactions to flush dirty pages (this is needed to guarantee transactionality). Since this can cause a performance-hiccup for database users, modern DBMSs try to avoid this visible disruption of performance/service. This is achieved by means of a combination of heuristics that strike a balance between avoiding stalls due to log recycling and amortizing multiple writes to a page in the buffer pool before writing it back to disk, thus limiting the I/O pressure. In MySQL, this process is referred to as *adaptive flushing* of the buffer pool pages. Modeling the net effect of all these complex heuristics is a challenging task, and is one of our main contributions in this paper which is described next.

4.2 Disk Write Model

While different DBMSs use different heuristics for maintaining the balance between eagerly writing pages or lazily flushing them at the log rotation time, in the following we provide a simple analysis based on *conservation of flow* that abstracts the internal details and complicated heuristics of a particular DBMS (MySQL in our case) while still providing a reasonable prediction of the overall I/O behavior. To achieve this goal, we leverage the probability of pages being dirtied and evicted, as follows.

Probability of a page being dirtied. Let D be the number of pages in the database. For any given mixture of transactions, say $\tilde{f} = (f_1, \cdots, f_l)$, we build a probability distribution[2] $\tilde{p}_{write}$ over all the pages in the database, where every transaction drawn from this mixture writes to the i'th page with probability $p_{write,i}$. In other words, $\sum_{i=1}^{D} p_{write,i} = 1$. Here, for simplicity, we assume that a transaction only accesses one page. (similar analysis can be done when each transaction accesses multiple pages).

Given $\tilde{p}_{write}$, we would like to estimate the expected number of *unique* dirty pages after executing n transactions, drawn at random according to their corresponding weight in the mixture $\tilde{f}$. Here, we assume that different transactions arrive independently of each other. Let us denote this value with T_n, which can be written as

$$T_n = \sum_{i=1}^{D} T_{n,i} \qquad (2)$$

where $T_{n,i}$ is the probability of the i'th page being written to, at least once (i.e. being dirtied), calculated as:

$$T_{n,i} = 1 - (1 - p_{write,i})^n \qquad (3)$$

where $(1 - p_{write,i})^n$ is the probability of the i'th page staying clean (i.e., never been written to) after n transactions.

Next, we need to model the log rotation process using these probabilities. Note that, at any point in time, every page falls into exactly one of these three categories : (C1) where a page is dirty and the first transaction that made it dirty is logged in the old log, (C2) where a page is dirty and its first dirtying transaction is logged in the current (new) log, and finally (C3) where a page is still clean (i.e. is identical to its copy on the disk). Let $P_{1,i}$, $P_{2,i}$, and $P_{3,i}$ represent the probability of the i'th page belonging to each of these categories, respectively. Clearly, $P_{1,i} + P_{2,i} + P_{3,i} = 1$ for $i = 1, \cdots, D$. Let $d_{1,t}$, $d_{2,t}$ and $d_{3,t}$ represent the number of pages in categories (C1), (C2) and (C3) at time t, respectively. Also, let L be the maximum capacity of each log file, i.e., each log file can log up to L transactions on average. Clearly, the log needs to be rotated (i.e., the old log has to be deleted) at least as often as every L transactions, i.e. when the new log is full. However, the log rotation can only happen at time t if $d_{1,t} = 0$, otherwise a system crash could lead to data loss in any of the pages in category (C1), i.e., a loss of durability. Moreover, if a log rotation happens at t, we will have $d_{2,t+1} = 0$, i.e. the new log will be empty at the beginning of time $t + 1$.

In the following, we show how $P_{1,i}$, $P_{2,i}$, and $P_{3,i}$ can be expressed

[2] We use the notation $\tilde{X}$ to denote finite probability distributions, where X_i denotes the probability of the i'th outcome.

in terms of $T_{n,i}$. First, however, we provide the intuition behind our analysis.

Abstracting the main idea behind MySQL's adaptive flushing. The main idea behind MySQL's I/O heuristics, such as adaptive flushing (`http://bit.ly/bRN04A`), is that the flush rate (flow of pages out) should roughly match the rate at which pages are dirtied, such that at the time a log rotation happens, there will be no dirty pages waiting to be flushed. Specifically, if the system is running n transactions per second adaptive flushing chooses a flush rate of $F_t(n)$, where:

$$F_t(n) = \frac{d_{1,t}}{\frac{l_t}{n}} = \frac{d_{1,t} \cdot n}{l_t} \quad (4)$$

Here, l_t denotes the current capacity of the new log ($0 < l_t \leq L$) at time t, and thus, the new log is expected to get full in $\frac{l_t}{n}$ seconds given the current rate, over which $d_{1,t}$ pages need to be flushed back to disk. Thus, adaptive flushing attempts to write $\frac{d_{1,t} \cdot n}{l_t}$ dirty pages back to disk during each unit of time. Note that in reality MySQL uses several other heuristics to decide when to flush a page, but in Section 8 we show that this simplified model is a good enough predictor of the average flush rate.

Estimating flush rate (Monte-Carlo baseline). Given this basic model of flushing, the goal of the rest of this section is to predict the expected flush rate $F(n)$ for a given TPS of n, where $F(n) = E[F_t(n)]$, without directly observing the $d_{1,t}$ and l_t values. One approach to estimate $F(n)$ is to simply perform a MC (Monte-Carlo) simulation by randomly initializing l_0 and $d_{1,0}$ (to account for bias caused by different starting states), then for each t, selecting $\binom{D}{d_{t,0}}$ pages (as dirty ones), then selecting $F_t(n)$ out of these $d_{1,t}$ pages to flush, and then repeating this process for many values of l_0 and $d_{1,0}$ until we converge to a value for $F(n)$. This MC simulation, however, has several drawbacks. First, it provides little insight into the contribution of different characteristics of the workload or different tuning parameters towards the overall flush-rate (e.g., there is no way to attribute flushes to a given transaction type). Secondly, the straightforward MC simulation is quite slow—for TPC-C, we found it to be 6 to 10 orders of magnitude slower than the solution that is proposed in the rest of this section. This is due to the large number of variables and the numerous possible initial configurations. For instance, the TPC-C workload with 32 warehouses has about 750,000 different pages, and thus, in order to accurately estimate $F(n)$, we need to repeat the simulation for a reasonable portion of all the 2^{750000} possible sets of dirty pages, as starting states!

Estimating flush rate (Iterative approach). Instead, we develop a simple iterative algorithm that converges much more quickly and provides very accurate predictions as well as insight into how different transactions contribute to the overall I/O. Before presenting the details of our algorithm, we first simplify equation (4). Assuming that there is no log rotation at t and $t+1$, in expectation we have:

$$d_{1,t+1} = d_{1,t} - F_t(n)$$

Thus, the number of outstanding dirty pages can only decrease, since the old log is no longer being appended to. We also have $l_{t+1} = l_t - n$, since n log records are written to the new log at each time step. Substituting these two values into equation (4) for $F_{t+1}(n)$ we get:

$$F_{t+1}(n) = \frac{(d_{1,t} - F_t(n)) \cdot n}{l_t - n} = \frac{(d_{1,t} - \frac{d_{1,t} \cdot n}{l_t}) \cdot n}{l_t - n} = \frac{d_{1,t} \cdot n}{l_t}$$

Thus, in the absence of log rotations, $F_{t+1}(n) = F_t(n)$. By induction:

$$F_t(n) = \frac{d_{1,t_0} \cdot n}{L} \quad (5)$$

where t_0 is the time step immediately after any log rotation (i.e. log was rotated at $t_0 - 1$) and t is any time before the next log rotation. In other words, $t_0 \leq t < t_0 + \frac{L}{n}$. This holds because $l_{t_0} = L$, i.e., the new log is empty right after a log rotation.

Equation (5) is more desirable for estimating the expected flush rate, i.e. $E[F_t(n)]$, since n and L are time-independent. Thus, we only need to estimate $E[d_{1,t}]$. Due to the linearity of expectation, we have:

$$E[d_{1,t}] = \sum_{j=1}^{D} P_{1,j} \quad (6)$$

$$\text{Similarly,} \quad E[d_{2,t}] = \sum_{j=1}^{D} P_{2,j} \quad (7)$$

$$\text{and} \quad E[d_{3,t}] = \sum_{j=1}^{D} P_{3,j} \quad (8)$$

This equation, gives us a direct formula for estimating the average disk I/O (or flush rate), if we can accurately estimate $P_{1,i}$, $P_{2,i}$, and $P_{3,i}$. However, these variables are inter-dependent, since as pages are dirtied and flushed to disk, the probabilities change. To handle this, we define three time-series $\{P_{1,j,t}\}$, $\{P_{2,j,t}\}$, and $\{P_{3,j,t}\}$, where $P_{i,j,t}$ is the probability of the j'th page belonging to category Ci (where $i = 1,2,3$) at time t (where $t = 0,1,2,\cdots$). The final step of our modeling is to find the relationship between $\{P_{1,j,t}\}$, $\{P_{2,j,t}\}$, and $\{P_{3,j,t}\}$. Here, we omit several derivations (which are presented in detail in our technical report [15]), and present the final result, showing that for $m \geq 1$:

$$P_{1,i,t+m} = P_{1,i,t}(1 - \frac{n}{L})^m$$

$$P_{2,i,t+m} = 1 - P_{1,i,t+m} - P_{3,i,t+m}$$

$$P_{3,i,t+m} = \begin{cases} P_{3,i,t} \cdot (1 - \frac{n}{L})^m + P_{1,i,t} \cdot \frac{n}{L} \cdot m \cdot \frac{(1-\frac{n}{L})^m}{1-\frac{n}{L}} & \text{if } T_{n,i} = \frac{n}{L}, \\ P_{3,i,t} \cdot (1 - T_{n,i})^m + P_{1,i,t} \cdot \frac{n}{L} \cdot \frac{(1-T_{n,i})^m - (1-\frac{n}{L})^m}{\frac{n}{L} - T_{n,i}} & \text{if } T_{n,i} \neq \frac{n}{L}. \end{cases}$$

Our algorithm uses these equations by iteratively incrementing t, until they converge, thus estimating the values of $P_{1,i}$, $P_{2,i}$, and $P_{3,i}$. Having these values, we can use equation (6) and eventually (5) to estimate the flush rate.

4.2.1 Algorithm

Figure 2 shows the pseudo code for estimating the flush rate. The main idea behind this algorithm is to use equations above (line 2.4 to 2.6), to estimate $F(n)$ (line 2.3), and repeat this process until our estimator for $F(n)$ (i.e., $avgF$ in Figure 2) converges, i.e. it does not change more than a small value ϵ. The main difference between the algorithm and the aforementioned equations is that here, for efficiency, we pre-calculate the common expressions that remain constant throughout the iterations (e.g., T, Tp, $cachedCoef$ and sum). In each iteration, the algorithm predicts the flush rate in two stages. First, the algorithm chooses $m = \lfloor L/n \rfloor - 1$ which is the longest time interval without a log rotation, in order to estimate all the variables right before the next log rotation using the values of those variables from the last log rotation (lines 2.4–2.6). The second step is to apply the log rotation (lines 2.7–2.9) step, which simply involves swapping the $P(1,i)$ pages dirtied in the previous iteration into the old log, and discarding the previous $P(2,i)$ old pages. To compute the actual pages flushed during each iteration (F), we compute $d1$ using $P1$ (line 2.2) and then compute F from $d1$ using adaptive flushing (line 2.3), equation (4), ensuring that this value never exceeds

Algorithm I/O-predictor($\tilde{f}, n$)

1: $avgF \leftarrow \text{inf}, iter \leftarrow 0, F \leftarrow 0,$
   $P_{1,i} \leftarrow 0, P_{2,i} \leftarrow 0, P_{3,i} \leftarrow 1.$
   $period = \lfloor \frac{L}{n} \rfloor$ %time period between subsequent log rotations
   $m = period - 1$ %longest interval without a log rotation
   For $i = 1, \cdots, D$:
      $T(i) = 1 - (1 - p_{write,i})^n$
      $Tp(i) = (1 - T(i))^m,$
      $cachedCoef(i) = (1 - n/L)^m,$
      If $T(i) = \frac{n}{L}$,
         $sum(i) = m * Tp(i)/(1 - T(i)),$
      Else,
         $sum(i) = \frac{(1-T(i))^m - (1-\frac{n}{L})^m}{\frac{n}{L} - T(i)};$
2: While $|avgF - F| > \epsilon$,
2.1: $avgF = (iter * avgF + F)/(iter + 1),$
2.2: $d1 = \sum_{i=1}^{D} P_{1,i},$
2.3: $F = min(\frac{d1}{period}, MaxFlushRate),$
   %For the time step right before the log rotation, we have:
2.4: $P(3,i) = P(3,i) * Tp(i) + (n/L) * P(1,i) * sum,$
2.5: $P(1,i) = P(1,i) * cachedCoef,$
2.6: $P(2,i) = 1 - P(1,i) - P(3,i),$
   %Now flush the rest of the old log and rotate the logs
2.7: $P(3,i) = P(3,i) + P(1,i),$
2.8: $P(1,i) = P(2,i),$
2.9: $P(2,i) = 0$
   Return $avgF$

Figure 2: Expected I/O (flush rate) prediction algorithm (without page clustering).

$MaxFlushRate$, the maximum number of physical pages that a particular machine can perform.

Optimization, clustering similar pages: One of the major sources of time and space complexity in the pseudo code of Figure 2 is the total number of pages, i.e. D. However, after careful examination, it is apparent that one can cluster the pages based on the $p_{write,i}$ values. Thus, in the optimized version of this algorithm, we first cluster the D into $K(D,\epsilon)$ partitions (non-overlapping clusters) such that the i'th and j'th pages fall within the same partition if and only if $|p_{write,i} - p_{write,j}| \leq \epsilon$, where ϵ is a small enough constant. This is equivalent to running a K-means clustering over the $p_{write,i}$ values for the smallest K whose inter-cluster distance is no larger than ϵ. Choosing a proper value for ϵ is fairly straightforward, as one can use the algorithm's equations to find the largest value of ϵ for which the final error of the algorithm is less than user's tolerance threshold (We omit the math due to lack of space. However, note that our algorithm still works even without using this optimization).

This simple optimization further reduces the space and time complexity. For instance in TPC-C with 32 warehouses, we have $D \approx 750,000$ but there are only 8 unique values in the $p_{write,i}$'s, i.e. $K_{TPC\text{-}C}(D,0) = 8$.

Once the pages are clustered based on their $p_{write,i}$ values, the algorithm in Figure 2 remains the same except:

1. The algorithm takes an extra input parameter, i.e. ϵ.
2. Before the first line, run the clustering algorithm with ϵ, find $K(D,\epsilon)$. Then, replace D with $K(D,\epsilon)$, and for $i = 1, \cdots, K(D,\epsilon)$ use the mean of the i'th cluster for $p_{write,i}$.
3. Replace line 2.2 in Figure 2 with a weighted sum, namely $d1 = \sum_{i=1}^{D} P_{1,i} \cdot K_i$ where K_i is the number of pages in the i'th cluster.

4.3 Disk Reads and RAM Provisioning

As noted above, RAM and disk I/O are tightly coupled, as more RAM can reduce the number of capacity misses in the buffer pool, reducing the number of page reads and dirty page writes. Simply creating a buffer pool that is as large as possible, however, doesn't guarantee any particular level of capacity-related misses, so some model is needed to predict the rate at which capacity misses will occur for a given buffer pool size, transaction mixture, and per-transaction-type TPS target. This will then allow us to predict the maximum TPS that can be sustained given the available RAM and disk bandwidth, and also the measure the contribution of any one transaction to the overall load of the system.

To do this we built a Monte-Carlo simulation of the buffer pool. To estimate the miss rate for a database with N pages of RAM, we allocate an N element list bp. Using the page access distributions for each transaction type (derived as described in Sec. 3.3), we derive a *combined access distribution* that represents the probability of each of the D pages in the database being touched by the input mixture. We then simulate accesses to these D pages of the database by randomly selecting pages according to this combined distribution. When a page is accessed, it is added to the head of bp if it is not already present, other wise it is moved to the head of the list. When a page is added a counter C_{read} of the number of misses is incremented. If the access is a write, a bit on the page is set to mark it as dirty. If bp already contains N elements, the last element (tail) of bp is removed, and if the dirty bit is set, a counter C_{write} of the number of flushes is incremented. This simulates the behavior of an LRU cache eviction policy. We can then compute the number of page reads and flushes per second by dividing C_{read} and C_{write} by the TPS.

We further refine our simulation model to use LRU2 (which is used by MySQL), where when a page is first accessed it is added to somewhere in the middle of the list, and then moved to the head on a subsequent access. This prevents sequential scan operations of large tables from evicting all of the pages in the buffer pool. In Section 8.4 we show that this simple approach is able to estimate the number of buffer pool misses for a given mixture and RAM size.

In summary, combining our cache and log rotation models, our I/O model predicts that if we are running n TPS for a time period t, we will read $C_{read} \cdot t \cdot n$ data pages and write back $C_{write} \cdot t \cdot n + F_t(n)$ data pages, in addition to any sequential log I/O.

5. LOCK CONTENTION MODEL

In this section we develop a model of two-phase locking (2PL) that, given a mixture of concurrent transaction, allows us to predict the expected delay that a transaction will incur. The non-linearity of lock-contention makes this a challenging problem.

Our model for lock waits is based on an adaptation of Thomasian's model of two-phase locking (2PL) [21] (there have been a number of other locking models, as described in Sec. 9, but Thomasian's appears to be the most realistic).

In order to make Thomasian's model work for real workloads, we made several extensions and modifications to it. We first provide a high-level description of Thomasian's approach and then briefly describe our own modifications to the original model.

5.1 A Summary of Thomasian's 2PL Analysis

Input parameters. Thomasian's model assumes that the incoming transactions belong to a fixed number of *transaction classes*, $C_1, \cdots, C_J$, and the database consists of a fixed number of non-overlapping *regions* (e.g., rows, tables, etc), $D_1, \cdots, D_I$. All transactions in a class have the same access pattern to the database, consisting of a probability of accessing different regions. Thomasian's model also assumes that all transactions of class C_j always access the same (fixed) number of locks, say K_j, and therefore consist of $K_j + 1$ steps: an initialization step followed by K_j steps each preceded by a lock request. The processing times of transaction steps are assumed to be exponentially distributed and the mean processing times for the n'th step of a transaction of C_j is denoted by $S_{j,n}$. Transactions in

C_j access objects in the i'th region in their n'th step with probability $g_{j,n,i}$, and hence $\sum_{i=1}^{I} g_{j,n,i} = 1$.

General Idea. Here we provide a high level overview of Thomasian's work; see [21] for details. The approach assumes a non-homogeneous model where different transaction classes have different access patterns to the database regions. The approximate analysis is based on mean values of parameters to derive expressions for the probability of lock conflict (usually leading to transaction blocking) and the mean blocking time. The latter requires estimating the distribution of the effective wait-trees encountered by blocked transactions and the mean waiting time associated with different blocking levels. This is done is an iterative manner, as follows.

Let $U_{j,n}$ be the mean delay incurred by transaction from C_j due to encountering a lock conflict at its n'th step. At each step, $U_{j,n}$ is estimated based on (i) the probability of a conflict per transaction type and per each database region, (ii) the mean number of in-flight transactions that access the same region, and (iii) their current mean latencies (i.e., sum of their $S_{j,n}$ and $U_{j,n}$ values). This is done by calculating the mean depth of the wait-tree for each conflict. Once $U_{j,n}$ values are updated, new estimates for (i), (ii) and (iii) are calculated, because an increase in $U_{j,n}$ values will increase the aforementioned parameters as well. This iterative process continues until the estimates converge. The final lock delay for transactions of class j is $\sum_{i\in 1...n} U_{j,i}$.

5.2 Our Extensions to the Original Model

Despite several advantages over other theoretical work on 2PL modeling, some of the assumptions in Thomasian's original proposal [21] limit its applicability to real-life workloads and database systems, which we have addressed. The main difference between his model and our approach is that rather than assuming a particular set of transaction classes and database regions and distribution of page accesses, we learn these values from our test data. Moreover, instead of assuming a fixed processing time, we update transaction times during the analysis.

1. To decide on the database regions, we use the access distribution derived from the log (see Sec 3.2) and the same ϵ-page-clustering technique as in Section 4.2.1 to define each region as a cluster of pages in the database where each page is equally likely to be accessed.

2. To estimate $g_{j,n,i}$ values, we average the numbers extracted in the summaries of transactions of the same type (See Sec 3.2).

3. Measuring $S_{j,n}$ values is not as easy as computing regions and g values. The $S_{j,n}$ mean values are not constant and change depending on the number of active in-flight transactions. We address this problem by performing a linear regression (LR) to estimate $S_{j,n,m}$ which is the value of $S_{j,n}$ with m outstanding transactions. Our regression model is built using the transaction latencies of different transaction classes recorded in our log files.

4. The model also assumes "infinite resources", such that once the $S_{j,n}$ values are provided in the input, they do not change based on the number of active transactions in the system, as if each transaction is executing on its virtual processor with a processing rate independent of the number of active transactions in the system. We dynamically re-adjust these values at each iteration of the algorithm as follows. Based on Little's law from queuing theory we know that the average number of in-flight transactions at any point in time is $M = R * T$ where R is the average latency of a transaction and T is the system's throughput. Since our goal is to estimate the expected value of the lock waits in a steady state, without loss of generality, we can assume that T remains constant. At each iteration of the algorithm our estimation of R and M are refined. Therefore, at each iteration, instead of the original $S_{j,n}$ values, we use the adjusted values $S_{j,n} * c/M$ where c is the number of physical cores on the target machine. Although this linear approximation is not entirely accurate, it reasonably compensates for the decoupling assumption of the original model, as validated in our experiments.

5. The original model assumes that all the locks are exclusive. This is not true as in most workloads a considerable portion of the locks are read-only (i.e., shared). We solve this problem by using a Theorem from [20] stating that a database region with cardinality D_i in which locks are requested uniformly, in exclusive-mode with probability b and inclusive-mode with probability $1 - b$, is approximately equivalent to a region with cardinality D_i' in which all the locks are uniformly requested in exclusive-mode, where

$$D_i' = \frac{D_i}{1 - (1 - b)^2}$$

Thus, we adjust the original region cardinalities to compensate for the lack of inclusive locks in Thomasian's analysis.

6. The original model assumes that the transactions in each class always request the same number of locks, i.e. K_j is fixed for C_j. This assumption is again un-realistic. For instance, the 'delivery' transaction in TPC-C can request anywhere from 10 to 140 locks. Therefore, in our implementation we first cluster the transactions into different types, and then further re-partition the transactions of the same type into several transaction classes based on the number of locks that they acquire. This requires that we re-adjust the original mixture, i.e., substitute the f_j's with new probabilities for each class. We obtain these probabilities using the normalized frequencies in the training data per each transaction type. We also ignore very rare transaction classes (i.e., when $f_j < \epsilon$).

The accuracy of this improved model is evaluated in Section 8.

6. BLACK-BOX MODELS

In Sections 4 and 5, we introduced our white-box models (for RAM, disk I/O and lock contention) which are somewhat specific to MySQL, but as we will show in our experiments, enable us to make accurate predictions, well outside of the range of our training data. In this section, we present several choices of black-box models using off-the-shelf machine learning techniques for regression, which make minimal assumptions about the underlying system, and hence, are less specific to MySQL. In Section 8, we study the accuracy trade-off of these two types of models under different scenarios. Below, we divide the resources into linear and non-linear and discuss our models separately.

Linear Resources: Out of the resources that play a major role in the performance of a database, the following ones tend to grow generally linearly with the counts of each transaction type: CPU, network utilization and the number of log writes.

For example, for CPU, if a given transaction requires a certain number of CPU cycles to finish, it is likely that its execution involves almost the same instructions, regardless of others transactions that are running concurrently. Thus, for a given mixture $(f_1, \cdots, f_J)$, and a given TPS T, the CPU usage can be approximated as:

$$CPU = a_0 + a_1 \cdot f_1 \cdot T + \cdots + a_J \cdot f_J \cdot T$$

where a_i coefficients can be learned from training data (e.g. by minimizing squared error). Network I/O can be modeled similarly, as the number of messages sent for a transaction does not depend significantly on the concurrent transactions with which it is executing. Finally, the number of log writes and the number of logical records updated per second are also linearly related to the number of transactions of each type that are executed per second. Hence, these metrics can be predicted accurately across a wide range of mixtures and TPSs given a modest amount of training data.

Non-linear Resources: We have experimented with many statistical regression models to predict the lock contention and disk I/O, including (but not limited to) all regression algorithms that come with Weka (`www.cs.waikato.ac.nz/ml/weka/`) library. However, in this paper, we only mention a few models that either yield better accuracy or represent major approaches to regression.

Polynomial fitting. By specifying the degree of a polynomial, one can use the training data to learn the coefficients of the polynomial that minimize the squared error of the fit. In particular, theoretically it has been shown that lock wait times, in a perfect 2PL scheme, asymptotically converge to a *quadratic* function of the multi-programming level [11]. Thus, a reasonable block-box model of lock wait times can be:

$$LockWaitTime = a_0 + \sum_i a_i \cdot f_i \cdot T + \sum_{i,j} a_{i,j} \cdot f_i \cdot f_j$$

where a_i and $a_{i,j}$ coefficients need to be learned.

Kernel Canonical Correlation Analysis (KCCA). KCCA [4] is a powerful kernel-based technique that considers a pair of multivariate datasets and finds dimensions along which the two datasets are maximally correlated, whereby kernel functions are used as metrics of similarity. In our context, transaction counts are the first dataset, while performance metrics (lock, or I/O) constitute the second. Since KCCA has been successfully used in performance prediction for analytical workloads [10], we wanted to see if it could also be applied to transactional workloads.

Decision Trees. Decision trees are a well-known technique for both clustering and regression. For regression, the target value of a given test data is predicted as the average target value of the corresponding leaf node in the tree. We used Matlab's implementation of decision tree regression with default parameters, specifically with leaf-merging, no pruning and minimum of 1 item for forming a leaf node (all for maximizing the extrapolation power).

Neural Networks. Feed forward neural networks are another important class of regression techniques, used to fit an input-output relationship. Again, we used Matlab's implementation (called *fitnet*) with 10 hidden layers and Levenberg-Marquardt back-propagation algorithm as the training procedure.

7. THROUGHPUT PREDICTION

Now that we have described our white- and black-box models for individual resources, we briefly describe how we predict the overall throughput of the system and identify the bottleneck resource. Each model produces an estimate of resource utilization at a given TPS rate. To determine maximum system throughput, we need to identify the TPS at which each model predicts the resource will be saturated (e.g., the point where the disk I/O model predicts the disk will be saturated). For disk and CPU, we determined per-resource saturation points using the methodology for measuring the maximum resource capacity of a machine described in Curino et al. [5]. For disk, the maximum number of page flushes we could generate on our test machine was about 600 pages per second; for CPU, the maximum CPU load we could generate was about 90%. We use these to predict TPS maximums T_{disk} and T_{cpu}, based on the maximum TPS at which our disk model predicts an I/O rate of 600 page flushes per second, or our CPU model predicts a 90% usage.

For lock contention, our model produces an estimate of the latency for each transaction class, at a specified TPS. Using Little's Law (which says that the number of in-flight transactions is equal to the arrival rate, or TPS, times the mean transaction latency), we can compute the number of in-flight transactions. Since almost all production databases or websites use admission control to limit the number of outstanding clients, the maximum TPS T_{lock} we can achieve (based on our lock contention model) is the one at which this client limit is reached. Alternatively, users can specify a maximum per-transaction latency L, which we can use to select a TPS that keeps the latency below L. To estimate the overall maximum throughput of the system, we compute $T = \min(T_{disk}, T_{cpu}, T_{lock})$. The bottleneck is the resource that dictates this minimum throughput.

8. EXPERIMENTS & EVALUATION

The goal of our experiments is to understand the accuracy of our previously presented white- and black-box models at predicting resource utilization across a range of TPS and mixtures on real workloads, and to look at the end-to-end performance of our models on several "what if" and "attribution" scenarios, including:

- Finding bottlenecks: we show that we can identify the maximum throughput and the bottleneck resource for a given workload, TPS, and mixture, and that our bottleneck estimates are accurate enough to allow low-overhead provisioning of a system.
- Attribution: we show that we can predict the contribution of a given transaction type to the overall resource consumption of a system, given a workload, TPS, and mixture.

Overall, our results are promising, showing that we can often achieve low errors on individual models – e.g., within 20% relative error for CPU, 20% error for Disk writes and 0.5GB for RAM – and that we can identify bottleneck resources accurately in almost all cases and predict maximum throughput with a mean error of under 25% across a range of benchmarks.

Experimental Setup. Our experimental testbed is composed of two identical Dell PowerEdge R710 servers (one to generate load and the other one dedicated to MySQL) interconnected via a single gigabit Ethernet switch. Each server has two quad core Intel Xeon E5530 2.4 GHz processors, 24GB of RAM, and 6 disks (2TB 7200 RPM SAS) configured as a single RAID 5 volume. We used MySQL 5.5.7 running on Ubuntu 10.10 with kernel 2.6.35.

Datasets. We produced several datasets with different mixtures and different TPS, using both TPC-C benchmark and real-life Wikipedia transactions, all replayed using [1]. For each of these data sets we divided the workload into transaction types using our transaction clustering technique (we measure the accuracy of this clustering versus manual labeling in Section 8.3) and collected transaction summaries and access distributions as described in Section 3. Our main dataset consists of runs of TPC-C and Wikipedia at the following TPSs: 100, 200, 300, 400, 500, 600, 700, 800, 900. To further challenge our system we generated workloads sweeping very different mixtures of transaction types. For instance, in TPC-C, we gradually increased the fraction of the 'New Order' transactions from 0% to 88%, while decreasing the fraction of 'Payment' transactions from 88% to 0%, while keeping 'Order Status', 'Delivery', and 'Stock Level' at their original rate, namely 4% each. This is because most of the updates come from the first two types, allowing for better evaluation of our performance models. For Wikipedia, as with TPC-C, we varied the mixture of the two most frequent transactions, while keeping the other three at a fixed frequency.

Training Time. Across all of our experiments (some containing 30,000 training samples), training time of our white-box models for RAM, disk I/O and lock contention were all below 15 minutes. The black-box models exhibited a wider range of training times (from seconds for linear regression and curve fitting) to a few minutes for others. KCCA did not easily scale to large datasets (over 100 samples) and hence, we first clustered the training samples into at most 100 clusters before invoking KCCA. Since all our models are meant to be trained offline, we believe that these times are reasonable.

8.1 Verifying Throughput Prediction

In this section, we show that by using our resource models we can accurately predict the saturation point of each resource, which in turn can be used to predict the bottleneck resource and the overall maximum throughput, as described in Sec 7.

We compared our combined models ("Our combined WB model"), which consist of our white-box models for lock and disk I/O plus linear regression (LR) for CPU to simple linear regression on the CPU vs transaction counts ("LR for CPU"), and a simple linear regression on the number of page flushes vs transaction counts ("LR for #PF"). We chose linear regression since it seems the most natural choice for DBA, e.g. when the load is twice, expect twice the resources. Also, linear regression has been proposed by the previous work [2] as a more effective model for predicting the disk I/O compared to other types of regression such as Gaussian processes. We also present results of decision tree regression for predicting the maximum throughput via projecting the disk's flush rate ("Dec. Tree for #PF"). We omit other black-box models, as they all performed very poorly at predicting maximum throughput.

To compute the actual maximum throughput (i.e., "ground truth"), we warmed the buffer pool and then gradually increased the offered TPS until the performance leveled off at some maximum rate. We randomly generated 20 mixtures of TPC-C with different ratios of transaction types. We ran these mixtures on MySQL at a low to moderate throughput and collected test data which we used to train both our models as well the two LR models and the decision tree regression model. We used each model to predict the maximum expected throughput, and compared to ground truth.

The results of our experiments are shown in Figure 3, showing the average relative errors of each model at estimating the maximum throughput on different subsets of the mixtures. Specifically, we grouped the 20 mixtures into three sets, one for I/O bound mixtures, one for lock-bound mixtures, and one for CPU-bound mixtures, and computed the average performance of each model on each subset (only a few of our mixtures were I/O bound, and approximately equal numbers were CPU and lock bound). Our model's average error ranges between 0-25%, with its worst error on lock-bound mixtures. Our I/O model produces error that is less than 1% on average (mostly because our models for sequential logging and log rotation are quite accurate, as we show later in this section). Note that the LR-based CPU model performs much better on CPU bound workloads, and that the LR-based page flush model does better on the I/O bound workloads, but in all cases our model does better. Decision tree regression performed poorly across different workloads. This is expected, as decision trees are not capable of much extrapolation beyond the range of their training data, which is a requirement for accurate estimation of maximum throughput.

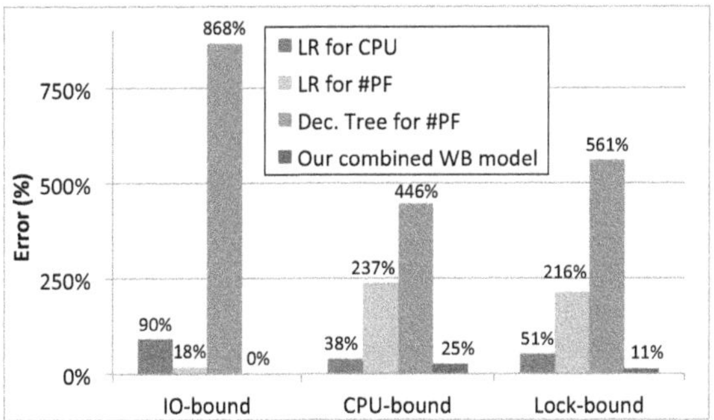

Figure 3: Max throughput prediction.

We also looked at the ability of our system to predict the bottleneck resource. On 19 out of 20 test data sets, we correctly predicted the true bottleneck. In the one case where we mispredicted, our model said the workload would be CPU bound, with a maximum throughput of 1578 TPS, while in reality the system was lock-bound and was able to run 1740 TPS (our locking model estimated the system would be able to run 1759 TPS). Hence, we underestimated the actual maximum TPS of the system by about 10%.

Although this is not a comprehensive study of system provisioning, the results of these experiments can also be used to look at our effectiveness at estimating whether a system is provisioned to handle a certain level of peak load. On these 20 data sets, our worst max throughput error is an overestimate of 44%, with mean error of 12%. In comparison, the worst case performance of the regression based models is 180% (49% mean) for the CPU model and 762% (200% mean) for the page flush model. Analyzing the detailed under and over-estimation of the maximum throughout by the other models, this results suggests that an administrator trying to estimate the resource requirements of a database system by linearly extrapolating CPU or I/O will over-provision the true resource needs of the system anywhere between 9× to two orders of magnitude more than if he used our models for provisioning. Similarly, he might under-provision the system between 8× to 10× using these models than if he used our combined models.

8.2 Attribution and Multi-tenancy Scenarios

In addition to estimating maximum throughput, our models allow us to answer questions about how much a given transaction type or tenant (e.g. in a database-as-a-service [16]) contributes to the overall load of a system. This is important for an administrator, e.g. to understand the impact on performance of migrating a database to a server. In this section, we present a few preliminary experiments showing the effectiveness of our models in two such scenarios.

In the first scenario, we consider two TPC-C workloads, $W1$ and $W2$, each running a single transaction together on a single machine. $W1$ runs the "new order" transaction at 275 TPS and $W2$ runs the "stock level" transaction at 225 TPS. Together, they result in 2.3 MB/sec of writes. Suppose the administrator wants to estimate how much the disk usage will be reduced if $W1$ is moved to another machine. We predict $W1$ alone will write 1.7 MB/sec, and in reality it writes 1.5 MB/sec, representing a 13.3% overestimation on our part. Note that a simple linear estimate would be unlikely to accurately answer such types of question, because as shown in Section 8.4 disk I/Os are highly nonlinear.

In the second scenario, we consider a full TPC-C workload running concurrently with a full Wikipedia workload, together on a single machine. This is meant to be representative of a multi-tenant database-as-a-service. We run Wikipedia at 200 TPS, and TPC-C at 100 TPS, each in isolation, and then predict the combined load when they are run together on the same machine. In this case, we are able to predict the CPU utilization of the combined workload to within 13% relative error (our pred = 4.6% CPU, actual = 4.0%), the disk write throughput to within 3% (our pred = 2.97 MB/s, actual = 3.01 MB/s), and the combined read throughput to within 97% (our pred = 330 KB/s, actual = 160 KB/sec). Although the relative error of our cache model is high (for reasons explained in Section 8.4 below), the absolute error is quite small; our later experiments show that our read model does quite well when the buffer pool is more heavily utilized.

These results show that our models are useful in several practical scenarios of great importance to database administrators. We now turn to detailed evaluations of our individual models.

8.3 Verifying Transaction Type Clustering

To test our transaction clustering, we ran our clustering algorithm described in Section 3.2 on a small log of SQL queries from Wikipedia and TPC-C. For TPC-C, we used the log of 7,361 transactions and for each we estimated the number of rows read and written (i.e., sum of rows updated, inserted or deleted) from each of the tables. Since the TPC-C benchmark has 9 tables, our dataset consisted of 18 numerical features. Applying Weka's (`www.cs.waikato.ac.nz/ml/weka/`) implementation of the DBSCAN clustering algorithm (with density parameters of $\epsilon = 0.9$ and minimum number of points 6) on this dataset, we obtained 5 clusters, precisely matching TPC-C transaction types.

For Wikipedia we used a log of 1,000 transactions and generated features corresponding to Wikipedia's 12 tables. We achieved the same accuracy using the same parameters to DBSCAN. The extracted clusters again matched the semantic notion of different transactions in Wikipedia workload, namely 'Add to Watch List' (type 1), 'Remove from Watch List' (type 2), 'Update Page' (type 3), 'Get Page Anonymous' (type 4), and finally 'Get Page Authenticated' (type 5). In both cases, we tried a range of parameters to DBSCAN and found that it was relatively insensitive to their values.

8.4 Verifying Resource Models

We now look at the performance of our individual resource models and their ability to predict resource utilization over a range of inputs. As with maximum throughput, we compared to two baselines: 1) linear regression and 2) linear regression with clustering.

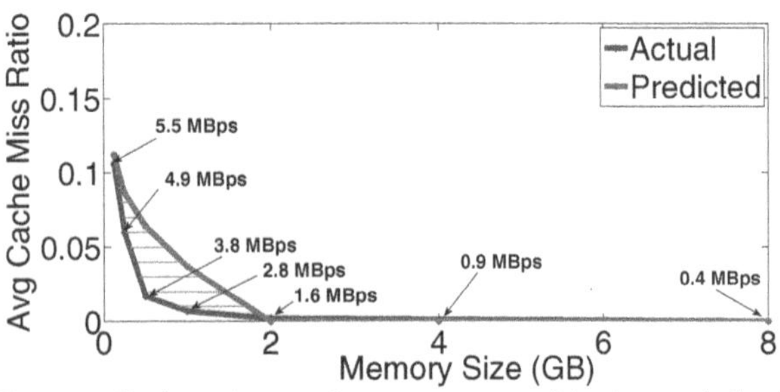

Figure 5: Cache-miss rate for memory provisioning and physical read prediction using the original TPC-C benchmark.

Disk Write Prediction. We used the datasets described at the beginning of Sec 8 to compare the accuracy of our model for predicting the data flush rate (described in Section 4.1). Figure 6 shows the results. Here, we used a limited range of training data from TPC-C where the average TPS was 900 and the fraction of 'New Order' transactions was less than 0.2 and predicted the number of page flushes on 9 different mixtures. These mixtures had an average TPS of 100 and varied the fraction of 'New Order' transactions roughly from 0% to 90% ('Payment' transactions were added to compensate, falling from roughly 90% to 0% of the load). In this experiment, the mean relative error of our white-box page flush model over the entire range was only 16%, while the errors for other black-box models ranged from 180% for LR without our transaction clustering to 3346% for decision tree regression. This dramatic difference confirms our theory that the mixture and TPS of training and test data are different (e.g. in what-if scenarios), our white-box models are significantly superior. LR-based methods are more accurate compared to others, due to their extrapolation capabilities, which methods like decision trees do not have.

We repeated similar experiments over many other ranges of data, both for TPC-C and Wikipedia. Due to lack of space, we have only summarized a few of them in Figure 4. In Figure 4, we use the notation '$D\ n_1 - n_2$' to denote the workload D (either TPC-C or Wikipedia), with a narrow range of different mixtures in the training set at the average TPS of n_1, and a complete range of different mixtures in the test data with an average TPS of n_2. In this figure, for each workload, we show different scenarios. In the left subfigure, the training TPS is close to the testing TPS (e.g., *wiki* 460 − 450 and *tpcc* 500 − 400): here the gap between the accuracy of our white-box model and that of the black-box models is considerably smaller (especially for LR with classification and decision trees), confirming our theory that we can rely on these black-model models when we have observed similar training data to the test range that we want to predict. In the right subfigure, the training TPS is either much lower than the test TPS or vise versa (e.g., *wiki* 100 − 900 and *wiki* 900−100). In these cases, the gap between our white and black box models widens dramatically: DBSeer out performs other methods by at least a factor of 4 in all cases, and up to 100× or more versus Neural Nets on Wikipedia. This gap is larger for Wikipedia mainly due to its higher degree of non-linearity in load (e.g. articles accessed/ edited almost follow a power law) compared to TPC-C. This experiment confirms our theory that white-box models can much more accurately model disk I/O when test data is far from training data.

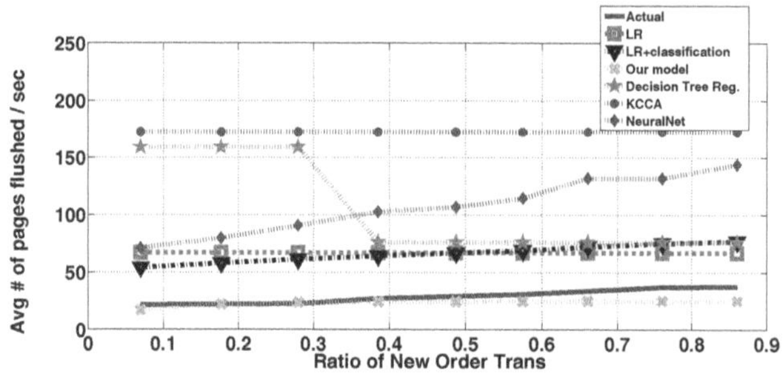

Figure 6: Predicting average page flush rate.

Disk Read/Memory Requirement Prediction. To validate our model of cache misses (which is used to relate buffer pool size to I/O), we used the original TPC-C mixture running at random TPS rates, and ran experiments for a wide range of buffer pool sizes. During each experiment, after the warm-up period of the database, we recorded the average cache-miss rate as well as the average number of physical reads per second and compared these actual numbers to the numbers predicted by our model. Figure 5 summarizes the result of this experiment, where we report the actual cache miss rate as well as that predicted by our model. As shown in this picture, our model slightly overestimates the cache miss rate. The error in memory provisioning for any cache miss rate (or equivalently, any number of physical reads) is the horizontal distance between the actual curve and our prediction curve, as illustrated with red horizontal lines in Figure 5. For instance, in order to ensure a cache miss rate of less or equal to 0.07, we need 224MB of buffer pool while our model's suggestion for the buffer pool size is 442MB, i.e. an over-provisioning. Our model follows the actual curve more closely at higher rates (i.e., above 0.06) and also at lower cache-miss rates (i.e., closer to zero) which is the ideal case where enough RAM could be allocated to dramatically reduce the amount of physical reads (and is where one would expect most OLTP databases to operate). Finally, the numbers with arrows show average disk reads in MB per second for each buffer pool size, showing a prediction of physical reads with less than 4.6MB average error.

Predicting CPU and other Linear Metrics. As mentioned in Section 6, CPU can be easily predicted using linear regression over the number of transactions from each type. We have validated the linearity of CPU across many different mixtures and TPS rates, both for TPC-C and Wikipedia. Here, due to space constraints, we only summarize a few experiments which are representative of the accuracy of linear regression for CPU prediction.

Fixed Mixtures. In Figure 7, we show the results of an experiments where we train on a Wikipedia workload of 1K articles, with a TPS

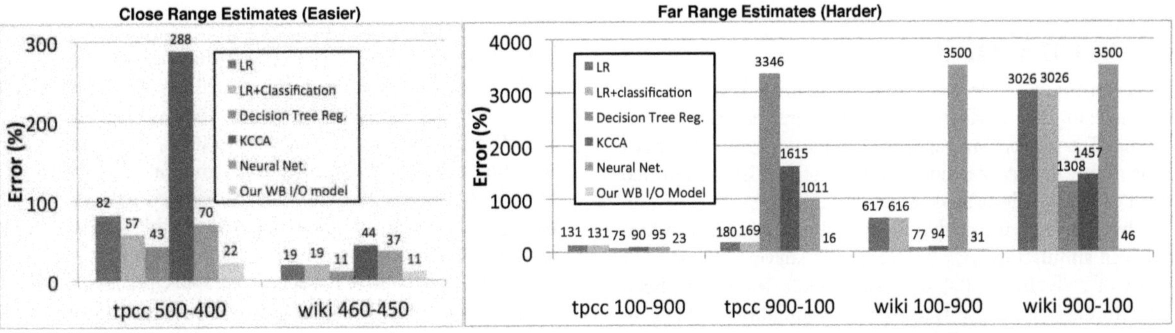

Figure 4: Disk write flush rate prediction for Wikipedia and TPC-C (percentage error) .

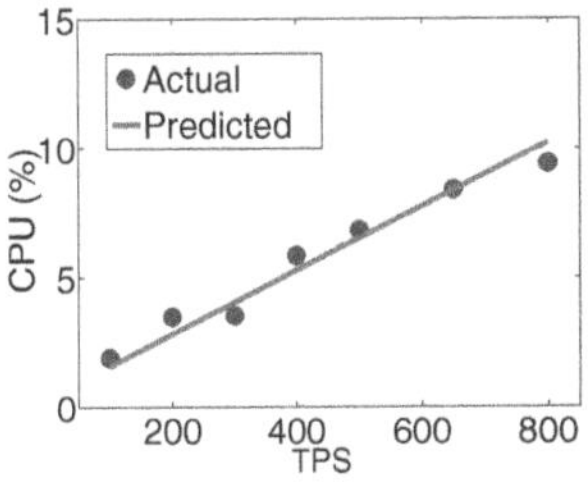

Figure 7: Predicting CPU, when varying the TPS for the Wikipedia database.

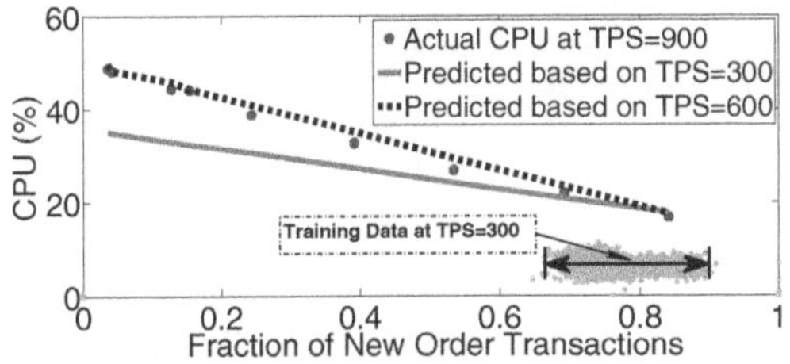

Figure 8: Predicting CPU, when varying both mixture and TPS.

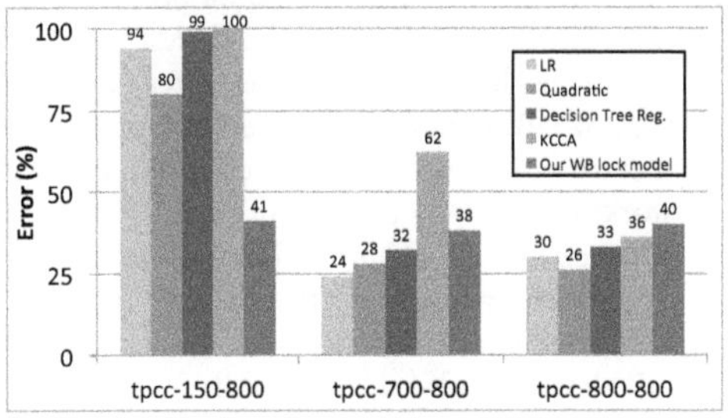

Figure 9: Predicting total lock wait times.

of 100 to 300, and then test it by predicting the CPU when increasing the TPS from 100 to 800. Our mean absolute error was 0.5 (in absolute CPU percentage) and mean relative error was 10.5%. A similar experiment for Wikipedia with 100K articles (training on a TPS between 100 to 300 and testing for CPU ranging between 400 to 800) leads to a mean absolute error of 1.5 and a mean relative error of 14.5%. For each TPS, we have shown the average CPU usage for more readability.

Varying both Mixture and TPS. In Figure 8, we report a set of experiments where we train on a very limited range of different mixtures at around TPS=300 (shown in green) and predict the average CPU usage through a much wider range of different mixtures and at a different TPS, namely at TPS=900. The mean absolute error (MAE) across these different mixtures is 6.3 and mean relative error (MRE) is 16.7%. In the same figure, we have also reported a similar set of experiments but using a training data at TPS=600. In this case, the error is lower (MAE=1.5 and MRE=5.8%). This is because the training data at 600 TPS is more similar to the test data at 900 TPS, compared to a training data of 300 TPS.

We have run similar experiments validating the linearity of network I/O for OLTP workloads, the number of logical reads and the amount of log I/O. Due to space limitations, we omit these results.

Verifying the Contention Model. The effectiveness of our lock contention model was demonstrated in Section 8.1 where we showed that it could predict the maximum throughput of lock-bound workloads, where the CPU and I/O were far from saturation However, we have also measured the accuracy of our lock model's prediction in isolation. We ran several experiments with TPC-C in which we increased the TPS by increasing the number of 'New Order' transactions (which typically cause a lot of contention due to their write-intensive nature). Figure 9 reports the error of our white-box model as well as a few other black-box models, where we use the same '$D\ n_1 - n_2$' notation as above. The same trend can be seen here where the accuracy of the white-box dominates black-box models as the ranges of training and testing data widen. Interestingly, when the training data is similar enough to the testing data, the LR and quadratic curves are more accurate than our white-box model. This is expected, as the white-box model makes a number of simplifying assumptions, and therefore only learns a few parameters from the data. This is why the accuracy of the white-box model does not improve, even when presented with more similar training data. The overall conclusion here is the same as before, however: when answering what-if questions or predicting performance regimes far from previously seen settings, use the white-box model. In other cases, quadratic fitting or LR seem are viable choices.

8.5 Generality to Other DBMSs

The focus of our paper is to show that, for a chosen DBMS, we can build very accurate models—hence our focus on MySQL. However, an interesting question is if and to what degree our MySQL-specific models apply to other DBMSs. In this section, we present some preliminary results on evaluating our models for predicting disk writes on another popular open-source DBMS: PostgreSQL. We apply the same models that we introduced in this paper (which target MySQL) to training and testing data collected from a PostgreSQL installation (on similar hardware). The white-box model of disk writes that we introduced in Section 4.2 was based on some general characteristics of traditional DBMSs as well as the specific flushing policy of MySQL. Thus, by using the same model for PostgreSQL we study the effect of different flushing policies in these two DBMSs on the accuracy of our predictions for disk writes in PostgreSQL.

We ran several experiments with the TPC-C workload, where we varied both the TPS range and the transaction mixtures. We collected similar combinations of training and testing data for PostgreSQL to those used for the MySQL experiment of Figure 6. In this experiment, our predictions for disk flush rate in Postures had an average relative error of 19.6%. Recall, from Section 8.4, that our error in predicting the same metric for MySQL in a similar setting (i.e., Figure 6) was 16%. Thus, the error of our flush rate predictions for Postures are comparable to that of our predictions for MySQL.

Although our experiments for PostgreSQL are not as comprehensive as those for MySQL, given that our models were originally designed for MySQL, even these preliminary results are quite promising, suggesting that with modest amount of additional modeling, accurate results might be achievable for other DBMSs as well.

9. RELATED WORK

Lock Contention. There have been numerous theoretical attempts at analyzing the performance of different variations of 2-phase locking. The pioneering paper by Thomasian [21] is the theoretical basis of our lock contention model which we have modified in a number of ways as described in Section 5.

Most of this literature uses either analytical modeling or random number-driven simulations [17] (see [22] for a survey). Because of the difficulty of collecting suitable measurements, there have been only a few studies which use trace-driven simulations. Also, to our knowledge no other work besides ours has implemented or evaluated an analytical model for predicting a real-world, deployed database system. Perhaps the closest to ours is an early work [19] where they have examined the degree to which three real workloads in IBM DB2 conformed to the assumptions commonly made in the literature, i.e. without predicting the contention degree of those workloads. In [7] the authors validated their model using an *abstraction* of TPC-C but on their own database *simulator*.

Performance and IO Prediction. There has been prior research on performance modeling for a database system, but mostly for OLAP workloads [12, 3, 8] and their optimal scheduling [14]. OLAP workloads are fundamentally different than OLTP. In OLAP, queries are mostly long-running and read-only with significantly lower degrees of concurrency. Therefore, the lock contention is typically not a problem in OLAP, e.g., the maximum concurrency level in [8] is 5, compared to thousands in an OLTP workload. Also, performance requirements in OLTP tend to be more stringent (e.g., a few milliseconds). Similarly, the authors in [10] only address scenarios with no concurrency, i.e. queries running one at a time. To the best of our knowledge, no prior work has tackled this problem for highly concurrent OLTP databases. The only exception is [2] where some preliminary results on CPU and IO prediction have been reported, where linear regression (LR) is shown to outperform Gaussian regression. The IO models presented in this paper improve on LR predictions by up to 71× in terms of accuracy. Moreover, lock contention, RAM, or other resources have not been addressed in [2].

Progress Indicators [13] also consider performance prediction but they need to continuously monitor the system to refine their previous estimates and thus, are more suitable to long-running queries. Finally, an early work has proposed models for buffer pool and bottleneck analysis [18], but they depend on many detailed specifications of the hardware and have been validated only in simulation.

In [16], we discussed our overall *vision* in the DBSeer project and enumerated important problems that arise in the context of a database-as-a-service and that require performance prediction, whereas in this paper we present our solution for performance prediction in a transactional database. In [5] we studied OLTP models for CPU, I/O, and RAM but in a very different setting, where the focus was consolidating existing workloads (without changing their rates or mixtures), rather than predicting the performance of each workload across variations in transaction rate and mixture. In the current paper, we do not consider consolidation but focus on more sophisticated resource models that relax several assumptions of our previous work: 1) we do not need to observe each workload in isolation, 2) our models in this paper are designed to make predictions even when the mixtures and rates that we predict for were never observed during the training/data collection phase.

10. CONCLUSION

In this paper, we presented a series of predictive models for resource utilization in OLTP databases as well as an experimental evaluation of those models on MySQL. For some resources, like CPU, Network, and log writes, we found that black-box models based on regression work quite well, yielding relative errors of just a few percent even when predicting resource utilization at very different rates or on different transaction mixtures than where they were trained. For other resources, e.g., RAM utilization, page flushes due to log recycling and buffer pool evictions, and database locks, white-box models that model the database are needed when making predictions about system performance over a wide range of transaction rates different than those observed at training. Our white-box models consist of a iterative model for log recycling, as well as a number of optimizations to an existing lock-contention model. Overall, our results evaluating these models are encouraging, yielding relative errors at predicting maximum throughput of a system ranging from 0–25% on a TPC-C like workload, with improvements of up to two orders of magnitude versus black box models in some cases.

Acknowledgments. This work was supported by the T-Party Project, a joint research program between MIT and Quanta Computer Inc., Taiwan, as well NSF grant IIS-1065219. We are grateful to Evan Jones, Y. C. Tay, Djellel E. Difallah, Purnamrita Sarkar and the anonymous reviewers for their comments.

11. REFERENCES

[1] OLTP Benchmark. `http://oltpbenchmark.com`.

[2] M. Ahmad and I. T. Bowman. Predicting system performance for multi-tenant database workloads. In *DBTest*. 2011.

[3] M. Ahmad, et al. Predicting completion times of batch query workloads using interaction-aware models and simulation. In *EDBT*. 2011.

[4] F. R. Bach and M. I. Jordan. Kernel Independent Component Analysis. *Journal of Machine Learning Research*, 3:1–48, 2002.

[5] C. Curino, et al. Workload-aware database monitoring and consolidation. In *SIGMOD*. 2011.

[6] C. Curino, et al. Update Rewriting and Integrity Constraint Maintenance in a Schema Evolution Support System: PRISM++. *PVLDB*, 2010.

[7] P. Di Sanzo, et al. Analytical modeling of lock-based concurrency control with arbitrary transaction data access patterns. In *ICPE*. 2010.

[8] J. Duggan, et al. Performance prediction for concurrent database workloads. In *SIGMOD*. 2011.

[9] M. Ester, et al. A Density-Based Algorithm for Discovering Clusters in Large Spatial Databases with Noise. In *KDD*. 1996.

[10] A. Ganapathi, et al. Predicting Multiple Metrics for Queries: Better Decisions Enabled by Machine Learning. In *ICDE*. 2009.

[11] J. Gray, et al. The dangers of replication and a solution. *SIGMOD Rec.*, 25(2), June 1996.

[12] C. Gupta, A. Mehta, and U. Dayal. PQR: Predicting Query Execution Times for Autonomous Workload Management. In *ICAC*. 2008.

[13] G. Luo, J. F. Naughton, and P. S. Yu. Multi-query SQL progress indicators. In *EDBT*. 2006.

[14] A. Mehta et al. BI batch manager: a system for managing batch workloads on enterprise data-warehouses. In *EDBT*. 2008.

[15] B. Mozafari, et al. DBSeer: Performance and Resource Modeling in Highly-Concurrent OLTP Workloads. Technical report, MIT, 2013.

[16] B. Mozafari, C. Curino, and S. Madden. Resource and performance prediction for building a next generation database cloud. *CIDR*, 2013.

[17] I. K. Ryu and A. Thomasian. Analysis of database performance with dynamic locking. *J. ACM*, 37, 1990.

[18] S. Salza and M. Renzetti. Performance Modeling of Paralled Database System. *Informatica (Slovenia)*, 22(2), 1998.

[19] V. Singhal and A. J. Smith. Analysis of locking behavior in three real database systems. *VLDBJ*, 6, 1997.

[20] Y. C. Tay, R. Suri, and N. Goodman. A Mean Value Performance Model for Locking in Databases: The Waiting Case. In *SIGMOD*. 1984.

[21] A. Thomasian. On a More Realistic Lock Contention Model and Its Analysis. In *ICDE*. 1994.

[22] P. S. Yu, D. M. Dias, and S. S. Lavenberg. On the analytical modeling of database concurrency control. *J. ACM*, 40, 1993.

ODYS: An Approach to Building a Massively-Parallel Search Engine Using a DB-IR Tightly-Integrated Parallel DBMS for Higher-Level Functionality

Kyu-Young Whang[†], Tae-Seob Yun[†], Yeon-Mi Yeo[†], Il-Yeol Song[‡], Hyuk-Yoon Kwon[†], In-Joong Kim[†]

[†]Department of Computer Science, Korea Advanced Institute of Science and Technology (KAIST)
Daejeon, Korea
{kywhang, tsyun, ymyeo, hykwon, ijkim}@mozart.kaist.ac.kr

[‡]College of Information Science and Technology, Drexel University
Philadelphia, USA
songiy@drexel.edu

ABSTRACT

Recently, parallel search engines have been implemented based on scalable distributed file systems such as Google File System. However, we claim that building a massively-parallel search engine using a parallel DBMS can be an attractive alternative since it supports a higher-level (i.e., SQL-level) interface than that of a distributed file system for easy and less error-prone application development while providing scalability. Regarding higher-level functionality, we can draw a parallel with the traditional O/S file system vs. DBMS. In this paper, we propose a new approach of building a massively-parallel search engine using a DB-IR tightly-integrated parallel DBMS. To estimate the performance, we propose a hybrid (i.e., analytic and experimental) performance model for the parallel search engine. We argue that the model can accurately estimate the performance of a massively-parallel (e.g., 300-node) search engine using the experimental results obtained from a small-scale (e.g., 5-node) one. We show that the estimation error between the model and the actual experiment is less than 2.13% by observing that the bulk of the query processing time is spent at the slave (vs. at the master and network) and by estimating the time spent at the slave based on actual measurement. Using our model, we demonstrate a commercial-level scalability and performance of our architecture. Our proposed system ODYS is capable of handling 1 billion queries per day (81 queries/sec) for 30 billion Web pages by using only 43,472 nodes with an average query response time of 194 ms. By using twice as many (86,944) nodes, ODYS can provide an average query response time of 148 ms. These results show that building a massively-parallel search engine using a parallel DBMS is a viable approach with advantages of supporting the high-level (i.e., DBMS-level), SQL-like programming interface.

Categories and Subject Descriptors

H.3.4 [**Information Storage and Retrieval**]: Systems and Software—*Performance evaluation (efficiency and effectiveness), Distributed systems*; C.4 [**Computer Systems Organization**]: Performance of Systems—*Measurement techniques, Modeling techniques*

Keywords

massively-parallel search engines, parallel DBMSs, DB-IR tight integration

1. INTRODUCTION

1.1 Motivation

A Web search engine is a representative large-scale system, which handles billions of queries per day for a petabyte-scale database of tens of billions of Web pages [9, 19]. Until now, commercial Web search engines have been implemented based on a scalable distributed file system such as Google File System (GFS) [12] or Hadoop Distributed File System (HDFS) [16]. These distributed file systems are suitable for large-scale data because they provide high scalability using a large number of commodity PCs. A storage system proposed for real-world scale data with better functionality is the key-value store. It stores data in the form of a key-value map, and thus, is appropriate for storing a large amount of sparse and structured data. Representative key-value stores are Bigtable [6], HBase [15], Cassandra [5], Azure [2], and Dynamo [11]. These systems are based on a large-scale distributed storage such as a distributed file system [6, 15] or a distributed hash table(DHT) [2, 5, 11].

However, both distributed file systems and key-value stores, the so-called "NoSQL" systems, have very simple and primitive functionality because they are low-level storage systems. In other words, they do not provide database functionality such as SQL, schemas, indexes, or query optimization. Therefore, to implement high-level functionality, developers need to build them using low-level primitive functions. Research for developing a framework for efficient parallel processing of large-scale data in large storage systems has been proposed. MapReduce [8] and Hadoop [14] are the examples of parallel processing frameworks. These frameworks are known to be suitable for performing extract-transform-load (ETL) tasks or complex data analysis. However, they are not suitable for query processing on large-scale data because they are designed for batch processing and scanning of the whole data [27]. Thus, commercial search engines use these frameworks primarily for data loading or indexing instead of user query processing.

High-level functionalities such as SQL, schemas, or indexes that are provided by the DBMS allow developers to implement queries that are used in search engines easily because they provide a higher expressive power than primitive functions in key-value stores, facilitating easy (and much less error-prone) application development and maintenance. In this sense, there have been many research efforts to support SQL even in the NoSQL systems. Fig. 1 shows the representative queries used in search engines that can be easily specified using the high-level functionality. Fig. 1 (a) shows a schema of a relation *pageInfo* that represents the information of Web pages. Fig. 1 (b) shows a SQL statement that represents a keyword query. The query finds the Web pages that contain the word "Obama" from the *pageInfo* relation. Fig. 1 (c) shows a SQL statement that represents a site-limited search. *Site-limited search* limits the scope of a user query to the set of Web pages collected from a specific site [29]. The query finds the Web pages that contain the word "Obama" from the site having *siteId* 6000. Fig. 1(d) shows one of its optimized versions. It requires an index-level join operation on *docId* with text predicates involving *contents* and *siteIdText* attributes (see Fig. 4(a) in Section 2).

Attribute Name	Attribute Type	Description
docId	integer	System defined identifier
pageId	integer	Page identifier
siteId	integer	Site identifier
siteIdText	text	Site identifier
title	text	Page title
URL	varchar	Page URL
content	text	Page content

(a) *pageInfo* relation.

```
SELECT p.pageId
FROM pageInfo p
WHERE MATCH(p.content, "Obama")>0;
```

(b) SQL statement for keyword search

```
SELECT p.pageId
FROM pageInfo p
WHERE MATCH(p.content, "Obama")>0
AND p.siteId = 6000;
```

(c) SQL statement for *site-limited search.*

```
SELECT p.pageId
FROM pageInfo p
WHERE MATCH(p.content, "Obama")>0 AND MATCH(p.siteIdText, "6000")>0;
```

(d) An optimized vertion of SQL statement for *site-limited search.*

Figure 1: An example of a schema and SQL statements.

These high-level functionalities allow us to easily develop advanced search engines with multiple search fields such as on-line discussion board systems as shown in Fig. 2 (a). The presented advanced search involves multiple fields as well as community-limited search capability. It requires complex index-level join operations among multiple fields, which require an implementation with high-level complexity. However, SQL allows us to implement those operations with a simple specification. Moreover, an index can be defined on any column by a simple declaration using SQL so that these complex index-level joins on multiple columns can be processed efficiently. Fig. 2 (b) shows a simple SQL statement for an advanced search that requires a four-way index-level join on *docId* with text predicates involving *title*, *content*, *communityIdText*, and *reg_date* attributes. Likewise, other search related applications can be easily developed by using SQL.

A parallel DBMS is a database system that provides both storage and parallel query processing capabilities. It could be considered an alternative to a large-scale search engine

(a) Advanced search with multiple fields.

```
SELECT p.pageId
FROM page p
WHERE MATCH(p.title, "database") > 0
AND MATCH(p.content, "index") > 0
AND MATCH(p.communityIdtext, "3") > 0
AND p.reg_date>="2001-01-01";
```

(b) An SQL statement for an advanced search using attribute embedding.

Figure 2: An example of advanced search.

because it has higher scalability and performance than traditional single node DBMSs and also has rich functionality such as SQL, schemas, indexes, or query optimization. Stonebreaker et al. [27] argue that parallel DBMSs are scalable enough to handle large-scale data and query loads. They claim that parallel DBMSs are linearly scalable and can easily service multiple users for database systems with multi-petabytes of data. However, parallel DBMSs have been considered as not having enough performance and scalability to be used as a large-scale search engine [1, 8], one outstanding reason being the lack of efficient information retrieval (IR) functionality.

To enable a DBMS to efficiently handle keyword search, tight integration of database (DB) and information retrieval (IR) functionalities has been proposed [28, 29]. The tight DB-IR integration implements IR functionality within the core of a DBMS, and thus, IR queries become efficient due to short access paths to the IR functionality. Two techniques for providing DB-IR integrated queries also have been proposed: 1) IR index join with posting skipping [28, 29] and 2) attribute embedding [29] to be explained in Section 2.

1.2 Our Contributions

In this paper, we make the following three contributions. First, we show that we can construct a commercial-level massively parallel search engine using a parallel DBMS, which to date has not been considered practical. Our proposed architecture, featuring a shared-nothing parallel DBMS, consists of masters and slaves. Our system, ODYS, following the proposed architecture achieves commercial-level scalability and efficiency by using Odysseus, which features DB-IR tight integration [28, 29], as its slaves. We have verified that each Odysseus is capable of indexing 100 million Web pages (loading and indexing in 9.5 days in a LINUX machine[1]), and thus, ODYS is capable of supporting a large volume of data with a small number of machines. Furthermore, the DB-IR tight integration enables the system to efficiently process a large number of queries arriving at a very fast rate. We show that ODYS can achieve a commercial-level performance especially for single-keyword searching, which is the most representative query.

Second, we propose an analytic and experimental performance model (simply, a *hybrid model*) that estimates the performance of the proposed architecture of the parallel DBMS, and then, validate the accuracy of the model. We argue that this model can accurately estimate the performance of a massively-parallel engine using the experimental results obtained from a small-scale one. For the master and network, we model each system component using the queuing model, and then, estimate the performance. For the slave, we propose an experimental method for accurately predicting the performance of a scaled-out (e.g., 300-node) system

[1]The machine is with a quad-core 2.5 GHz CPU, 4 Gbytes of main memory, and a RAID 5 disk having 13 disks (disk transfer rate: avg. 83.3 Mbytes/s) with a total of 13 Tbytes, a cache of 512 Mbytes, and 512 Mbytes/s bandwidth.

using a small-scale (e.g., 5-node) one. We note that the bulk (say, 92.28% ∼ 96.43%) of the query processing time is spent at the slave compared with the master and network. Our experimental method ensures high predictability of the slave side query processing time (which contributes most of the total processing time) since the estimation is directly derived from actual measurement. To verify the correctness of the model, we have built a ten-node parallel system of the proposed architecture and performed experiments with query loads compatible to those of a commercial search engine. The experimental results show that the estimation error between the model and the actual experiment is less than 2.13%. The proposed hybrid approach allows us to substantially reduce costs and efforts in building a large-scale system because we can accurately estimate its performance using a small number of machines without actually building it.

Last, by using the performance model, we demonstrate that the proposed architecture is capable of handling commercial-level data and query loads with a rather small number of machines. Our result shows that, with only 43,472 nodes, ODYS can handle 1 billion queries/day[2] for 30 billion Web pages with an average query response time of 194 ms. We also show that, by using twice as many (i.e., 86,944) nodes, ODYS can provide an average query response time of 148 ms. This clearly demonstrates the scalability and efficiency of the proposed architecture, and supports our argument that building a massively-parallel search engine using a parallel DBMS can be a viable alternative with advantages such as the high-level (i.e., DBMS-level) and SQL-like programming interface.

The rest of this paper is organized as follows. Section 2 introduces techniques of DB-IR integration as a preliminary. Section 3 proposes the architecture of ODYS, a massively parallel search engine using a DB-IR tightly integrated parallel DBMS. Section 4 proposes the performance model of ODYS. Section 5 presents the experimental results that validate the proposed performance model and demonstrate the scalability and performance of ODYS. Section 6 concludes the paper.

2. DB-IR INTEGRATION

In the database research field, integration of DBMS with IR features (simply, *DB-IR integration*) has been studied actively as the need of handling unstructured data as well as structured data is rapidly increasing. There are two approaches to DB-IR integration: loose coupling and tight coupling. The loose coupling method—used in many commercial systems—provides IR features as user defined types and functions outside of the DBMS engine (e.g., Oracle Cartridge and IBM Extender). This method is easy to implement because there is no need to modify the DBMS engine, but the performance of the system gets degraded because of long access paths to the IR feature. On the other hand, the tight coupling method [28, 29, 30] directly implements data types and operations for IR features as built-in types and functions of a DBMS engine (e.g., Odysseus [28, 29, 30] and MySQL [20]). The implementation of the method is difficult and complex because the DBMS engine should be modified but the performance is accelerated. Thus, the tight coupling method is appropriate for a large-scale system to efficiently handle a large amount of data and high query loads. The IR index of Odysseus [28][3] and MySQL are very close, but Odysseus has more sophisticated DB-IR algorithms for IR features as discussed below.

In a tightly integrated DB-IR system, an IR index is embedded into the system as shown in Fig. 3 (a). As in a typical DBMS, a B+-tree index can be constructed for an integer or formatted column. Similarly, an IR index is (automatically) constructed for a column having the text type. Fig. 3 (b) shows the structure of the IR index. The IR index consists of a B+-tree index for the keywords, where each keyword points to a *posting list*. The leaf node of the B+-tree has a structure similar to that of an inverted index. Each posting list for a keyword consists of the number of postings and the postings for the keyword. A *posting* has the document identifier (docId), and the location information where the keyword appears (i.e., docId, offsets). On the other hand, distinct from the inverted index, the IR index has a sub-index [28][3] for each posting list to search for a certain posting efficiently.

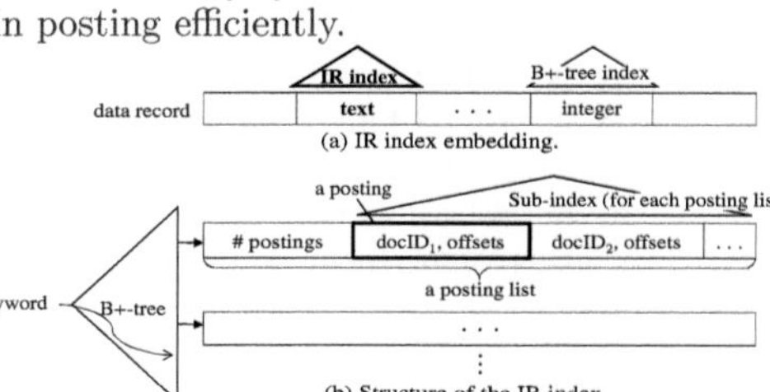

(a) IR index embedding.

(b) Structure of the IR index.

Figure 3: The IR index of the DB-IR tightly integrated DBMS.

In the DB-IR tightly integrated DBMS, two methods are used to improve the search performance: IR index join with posting skipping [28, 29] and attribute embedding [29]. *IR index join with posting skipping* is a technique for efficiently searching documents (e.g., Web pages) that have multiple co-occurring keywords. To search for documents having co-occurring keywords, the posting lists of the keywords should be joined. The posting skipping method identifies the part of the posting lists that need to be merged and skips the rest by using *sub-indexes* [28]. *Attribute embedding* is a technique for efficiently processing a DB-IR query that joins an attribute of a structured data type and an attribute of the text data type. For example, suppose that there are two attributes A and B having the text type and the integer type, respectively, and they are often accessed together. The attribute embedding method embeds the value of attribute B in each posting of attribute A. In this case, a DB-IR query that joins attributes A and B can be simply processed by one sequential scan of the posting list. In summary, it is the tightly integrated IR features, such as the embedded IR index with posting skipping, and attributed embedding, that makes ODYS a powerful search engine in the proposed parallel DBMS.

Example 1. Fig. 4 shows the processing of an IR query in a tightly integrated DB-IR system. Fig. 4 (a) shows an example of IR index join with posting skipping. When a site-limited query as in Fig. 1 (c) is given, *siteIdText* of type text is used instead of *siteId* of type integer as in Fig. 1 (d). Thus, the postings to be merged from each posting list are found efficiently using sub-indexes, as in the multiple keyword query processing. Fig. 4 (b) shows an example of attribute embedding. The values for *siteId* of type integer are embedded in the postings of *Content*. We can efficiently

[2]Nielsenwire [23] reports that Google handled 214 million queries/day in the U.S. in February 2010.

[3]Patented in the US in 2002; application filed in 1999.

process the queries involving both *siteId* and *Content* as in Fig. 1(c) by one sequential scan of the posting list. □

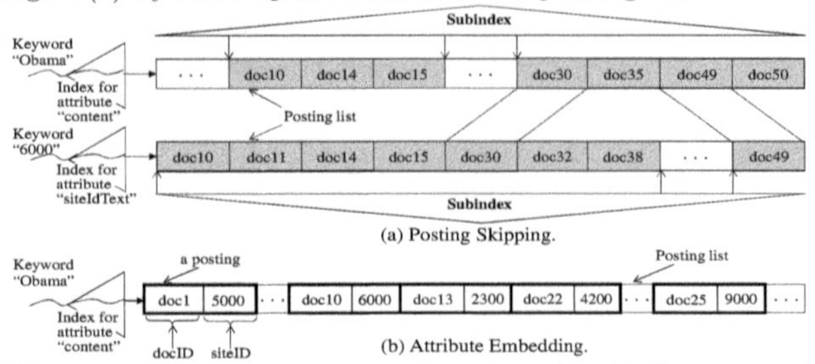

Figure 4: IR query processing in a tightly integrated DB-IR system [29].

3. ODYS MASSIVELY-PARALLEL SEARCH ENGINE

3.1 Architecture

Fig. 5 shows the architecture of ODYS. ODYS consists of masters[4] and slaves[5]. The masters share the slaves, and the slaves have a shared-nothing architecture. Each slave is Odysseus storing data in a disk array. The master and the slaves are connected by a gigabit network hub, and they communicate by using an asynchronous remote procedure call (RPC)[6].

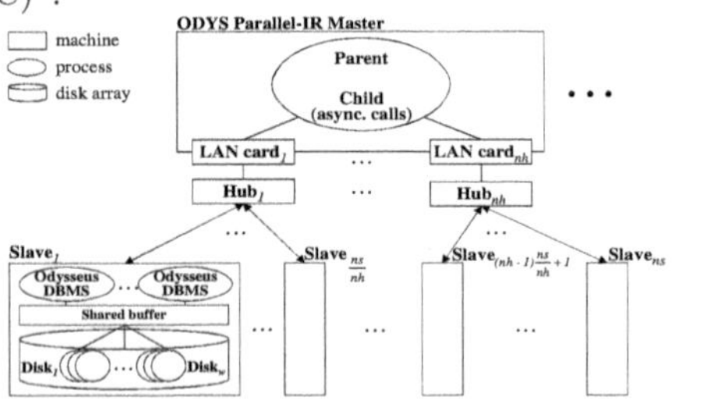

Figure 5: The architecture of ODYS.

The master stores metadata such as slaves' IP addresses, slaves' database paths (i.e., the location of the disk device storing each slave database), and schemas. The slaves store crawled Web pages and their IR indexes. There are two well-known methods for partitioning the index [9]: 1) *partitioning by documents* and 2) *partitioning by keywords*. For performance reasons, most commercial search engines including Google use the former method [9], which makes slaves work in parallel for processing the same query. Thus, we also employ the same method. That is, the entire set of Web pages is partitioned horizontally. Each slave stores a segment of the partitioned data and creates an IR index for each text-type attribute in the segment. To build a scalable shared-nothing parallel DBMS, we store tables into slaves in such a way to avoid a cross-node join. In search engines, typically there is one large-scale table, namely, the one for Web pages (say, 227 TBytes) and many small-scale tables (say, < 1 GBytes) such as tables for schema information, site information, and database statistics. We partition only the large-scale table into slaves and duplicate small-scale tables in every slave[7].

[4]The ODYS Parallel-IR Master consists of 58,000 lines of C and C++ code.

[5]The Odysseus (slave) consists of 450,000 lines of C and C++ code.

[6]We use socket-based RPC consisting of 17,000 lines of C, C++, and Python code developed by the authors.

[7]In this design, if two or more large-scale tables were used, join operations among those tables would not be allowed.

ODYS processes a user query as follows. When a user query arrives at a master, the master distributes the query to all slaves. Then, the master merges the results returned from the slaves and returns the final results to the user. The slaves process the query and return the results to the master. Each slave returns top-k results in the ranking order, and the master performs a merge operation for the results returned from the slaves to get the final top-k results. The slaves store each posting list of the IR index in the PageRank order (i.e., we are using query-independent ranking) to make top-k search efficient. Since the posting lists are stored in the PageRank order, the query processing performance is not much affected regardless how long the posting lists are or how big the database is. In this paper, we focus on the performance issues of the search engines and not on the effectiveness of ranking results. For performance reasons, we use query-independent ranking, which can be computed in advance, as many large-scale commercial search engines do, but any other ranking methods can be applied[8].

3.2 Updates and Fault Tolerance

In this paper, we focus on the performance issues of the search engine. Thus, we only briefly mention update and fault tolerance issues.

Updates and concurrency control: The search engines should handle a tremendous number of concurrent queries, which mostly consist of read-only transactions. Thus, in this paper, we focus on read-only transactions and the need for locking can be obviated[9]. Nevertheless, ODYS supports updates on a per-node basis with strong consistency [30]; thus, any transaction pertaining to individual nodes can be properly handled [29]. Update transactions can be processed on dedicated nodes and the nodes on service can be replaced with the updated nodes periodically.

Fault tolerance: Currently, fault tolerance features are being implemented in ODYS. We adopt an approach similar to the one proposed in Osprey [31]. In Osprey, Yang et al. [31] proposed a method implementing MapReduce-style fault tolerance functionality in a parallel DBMS. The proposed method maintains replicas and allocates small sized tasks dynamically to the nodes according to the loads of each node. As in Osprey, availability and reliability are achieved by maintaining multiple replicas of ODYS, and a middleware can be used for dynamically mapping masters and slaves of the multiple ODYS replicas. We call a replica of ODYS an *ODYS set*.

3.3 Other Parallel Processing Systems

In this section, we discuss the architectural relationships between ODYS and other recently developed parallel processing systems. We classify the existing DFS-based systems and parallel DBMSs into four types of layers as shown in Fig. 6[10]. In Fig. 6, the storage layer represents a distributed storage for large-scale data. The key-value store or a table layer represents a data storage storing data in

[8]Most commercial search engines use PageRank as a base ranking measure, and additionally, combines the query-dependent ranking (e.g., TF-IDF). However, since query-dependent ranking is only applied only to the top results that have been retrieved based on query-independent ranking [25], its processing cost is somewhat limited.

[9]Locking can be switched off in the search engine mode by selecting the consistency level 0.

[10]Modified and extended from the figure in p.4 of [4].

the form of key-value pairs or records in tables. The parallel execution layer represents a system for automatically parallelizing the given job. The language layer represents a high-level query interface.

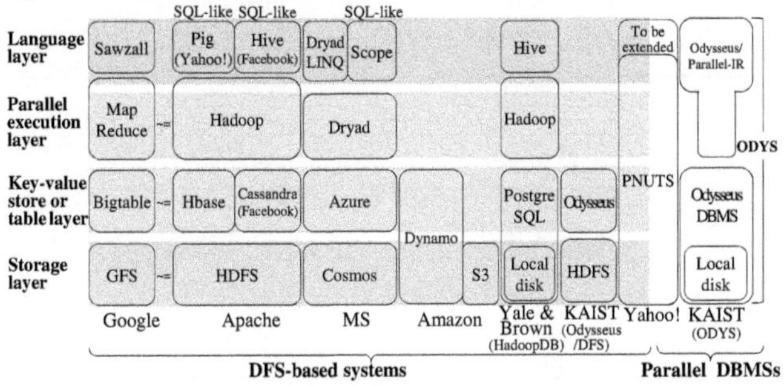

Figure 6: The map of ODYS and other parallel processing systems.

Most DFS-based systems that have been recently developed follow or modify Google's architecture. DFS-based systems developed by Apache and Microsoft (MS) have an architecture very close to Google's. On the other hand, Amazon's Dynamo and HadoopDB can be considered as variations of Google's architecture. Dynamo has a fully decentralized architecture and uses a relaxed consistency model called eventual consistency. HadoopDB has a hybrid architecture of the DFS-based system and the DBMSs; it is Hadoop on top of multiple single-node DBMSs. PNUTS is a highly scalable parallel DBMS that provides carefully chosen functionalities. It shares some design choices with the DFS-based system in that it provides simple functionalities, a relaxed consistency model, and flexible schema.

ODYS consists of two layers: Odysseus and Odysseus/ Parallel-IR. The Odysseus corresponds to the table layer. In ODYS, Odysseus DBMSs with local disks are used in parallel rather than key-value stores with a DFS system. The Odysseus/Parallel-IR is an integrated layer that combines the parallel execution layer and the language layer. Because ODYS uses a DBMS for the table layer, it can provide rich functionality for query processing by directly using most DBMS features including SQL.

There are several open source projects for search engines. Solr and Nutch are parallel search engines based on Apache Lucene [21], which is a search engine library for a single machine. They have a similar architecture consisting of masters and slaves where each slave is built on HDFS or a local file system. However, they do not support the high-level language layer such as SQL, but only support keyword queries. In addition, their performance and scalability are not enough to support commercial-level query loads. Moreira et al. [22] analyze performance and scalability of Nutch. The experimental results indicate that Nutch can process 33 queries/second (i.e., 2.8 million queries/day) for 480 GBytes dataset using 12 machines [22][11].

4. PERFORMANCE MODEL

In this section, we present a performance model of the proposed search engine architecture. Except for the specialized search engine companies, it is very difficult for a research center or an academic institute to build a real-world scale search engine because of limited resources including availability of hardware, space, and manpower. Therefore, an elaborate analytic or experimental model is needed to test and project the performance and scalability of a large-scale system without actually building it. For massively-parallel processing systems, analytic models using the queuing theory have been proposed to estimate the performance of the systems [17, 26]. However, those analytic models cannot be simply applied to our architecture because of the following reasons. First, the existing methods use simple parameters. In practice, however, to accurately estimate the performance of a large-scale system, all the specific parameters related to the performance of the system should be identified. Second, the existing methods assume that there is only one query type, while we consider multiple types of queries. Last, as the phenomenon that most significantly affects the performance, we show that the query response time is bounded by the maximum among slaves' query processing times, but no existing analytic method takes this into account. Therefore, we propose a performance model based on the queuing theory as well as intricate measurement schemes.

We claim that our performance model using a small-scale reference system (i.e., 5-node) can quite accurately predict the performance of a large-scale system (i.e., 300-node) due to the following reasons[12]. The performance model consists of two parts: 1) the master and network time and 2) the slave time. We show that the estimation error of the former is quite low, i.e., maximum 10.15% as shown in Fig. 11 in Section 5.2.2. Moreover, even if the estimation error of the master and network time were sizable, it could not affect the overall performance in a significant way since the overall performance largely depends on the performance of the slave time (e.g., 96.43% for 15.5 million queries/day) as shown in Fig. 14. We can be assured that the estimated performance of slaves is very close to the actual measurement since the estimation is directly derived from the measurement as presented in Section 4.2. Thus, our estimation of the total query response time is quite accurate (e.g., the estimation error is less than 2.13%) as shown in Fig. 11.

The assumptions related to query execution are as follows. We assume that every query is a top-k query where k is one of 10, 50 or 1000, and the set of input queries is a mix of single-keyword queries, multiple-keyword queries, and limited search queries as will be explained in Section 4.1.1. To evaluate a *lower-bound performance* of our system, we take two very conservative assumptions: 1) we run ODYS at "semi-cold start" and 2) we wait until "all" the slaves return the results. First, *semi-cold start* means that a query is executed in the circumstance where the internal nodes of the IR indexes (which normally fit in main memory) are resident in main memory while the leaf nodes (which normally are larger than available main memory), posting lists, and the data (i.e., crawled Web pages) are resident in disk. Typical commercial search engines process queries at *warm start* by storing the entire (or a large part of) indexes and data

[11]Moreira et al. [22] do not specify the ranking measure used. However, it must be that they used query-dependent ranking (e.g., TF-IDF) only since their results are significantly ($8 \sim 9$ times) worse than those of ten-node ODYS to be explained in Section 5.2.2. Thus, we do not directly compare their results with ours here.

[12]Cloud services (e.g., Amazon EC2, Microsoft Azure) cannot meet our requirements for constructing the precise performance model. We need to *exclusively* use and control physical machines (including CPUs and memory buses), network hubs, and disks to precisely reflect their effects to the performance model. However, cloud services cannot guarantee that environment.

in a massive-scale main memory [9]. This significantly helps reduce query response time. However, we do it at semi-cold start for the sake of evaluating a lower-bound performance[13]. To enforce semi-cold start, we use a buffer of only 12 MBytes sufficient for containing the internal nodes (occupying 11.5 MBytes) of the IR index for each slave[14]. Second, we wait until all the slaves return the results. This strategy guarantees the completeness of the results and projects the lower-bound performance. Performance can be improved by a deadline-driven technique, which waits for the results from slaves within limited time as in some commercial search engines, but then, we lose the completeness.

In the proposed performance model, each system component is modeled as a queue, and the query response time is estimated by summing up the expected sojourn time [7] of each queue. The following are the major considerations of the performance model. First, since each system component executes various types of tasks, the queue representing the component would receive various types of tasks that take different processing times. For example, a master CPU performs tasks of distributing the query to the slaves, merging the results returned from the slaves, etc. To simplify the problem, however, we regard the summation of all the types of tasks for a component as one request for the corresponding queue. Second, the service time is different depending on search condition types and the value of k of the top-k query. (The service time is the time for a request to be serviced in the queue, excluding the waiting time.) For instance, the time taken by a master CPU increases as the value of k gets larger because the merging cost increases. Therefore, we adopt the single-keyword top-10 query type—which has the shortest processing time—as the unit query, and transform(i.e., *normalize*) other query types in terms of the unit query. We explain this transformation in detail in Section 4.1. Finally, the times taken by slaves are bounded by the maximum value among all the sojourn times of slaves. In other words, we should calculate the expected maximum value of multiple sojourn times. However, this estimation is known to be very hard in the queuing theory [18]. Thus, we propose an estimation method for the slave maximum time through experiments, and it will be discussed in detail in Section 4.2.

4.1 Queuing Model

Among the ODYS system components, times taken by master CPUs, master memory bus, and network hubs are estimated by using a queuing model. Table 1 shows the notation used in the performance model.

4.1.1 Query Model

We consider nine types of queries. First, the queries are classified into three search condition types: single-keyword, multiple-keyword, and limited search queries. For each of the three search condition types, we further consider three types of top-k queries, where k = 10, 50, and 1,000. The performance of the master CPUs, master memory bus, and network hubs depend only on the k value while the performance of a slave depends on both the search condition type and the k value.

Table 1: The notation used in the performance model.

Symbols	Definitions
nm	the number of master nodes
ncm	the number of CPUs per master
ns	the number of slave nodes
nh	the number of network hubs
λ	the arrival rate of the ODYS
λ_C	the arrival rate of the system component C
λ'_C	the weighted arrival rate of the system component C
$w_C(k)$	the weight of the top-k query type in the system component C
$qmr(sct, k)$	the query mix ratio of top-k queries where sct is the search condition type
ST_C	the service time of the system component C
L_C	the average queue length of the system component C
X_C	the sojourn time of a customer in the queue of the system component C
r	the number of repetitions of a query set execution
np	the number of slaves in the small-sized system built
m_i	the master processing time for the ith slave
s_i	the query processing time of the ith slave
nt_i	the network transfer time of the ith slave's results

A *single-keyword query* is a query that has one keyword search condition. It is processed by finding the posting list that corresponds to the keyword from the IR index and by returning the first k results of the posting list. Single-keyword queries having the same k value can be processed within almost the same time regardless of the keyword because the top-k results have been stored according to a query-independent ranking calculated apriori.

A *multiple-keyword query* is a query that has two or more keyword search conditions. It is processed by finding the posting list for each keyword, performing a multi-way join for the posting lists, and returning the first k results of the joined results. A *limited search query* is a query having a keyword condition together with a site ID or a domain ID condition that limits the search scope. It is processed in the same way as a multiple-keyword query is. To process a limited search query using the multi-way join, site IDs or domain IDs are stored as text types and the IR indexes are created for them (see Example 1). Multiple-keyword or limited search queries take much longer processing time than single-keyword queries do because they require more disk accesses to find top-k results from the postings having the common docID's in multiple document lists.

As stated above, the query processing time varies depending on the search condition type and the k value of the top-k query. To simplify the queuing model, we normalize every query into one equivalent query type, i.e., the single-keyword top-10 query. For example, let us assume that a single-keyword top-10 query takes 2 ms while a multiple-keyword top-50 query takes 4 ms in some system component. Then, we regard a multiple-keyword top-50 query as two single-keyword top-10 queries for the component.

4.1.2 Arrival Rate (λ)

Suppose the query arrival rate is λ, and the requests are uniformly distributed to the components of the same type. Then, the arrival rate for a component is inversely proportional to the number of the components of the type, i.e., the number of queues. Table 2 shows the arrival rates for each component where nm, ncm, ns, and nh represent the

[13]We also performed experiments at warm start. It turns out that the total response time of our system at warm start is approximately 8.33% ~ 18.01% of that at semi-cold start for the single-keyword top-10 queries in Fig. 11(a).

[14]In our system, the size of the IR index excluding the posting lists is 1.34 Gbytes per slave, out of which leaf nodes occupy 1.33 Gbytes and the internal nodes 11.5 Mbytes for indexing 114 million Web pages.

numbers of masters, of CPUs per master, of slave nodes, and of network hubs, respectively. The queues for the master CPUs and the master memory bus process one request per user query while the queues for the network hubs process ns requests per user query because every slave processes the same query and returns the results through the network hubs.

Table 2: Arrival rates.

Component	A master CPU	A master memory bus	A network hub
Arrival rate	$\frac{\lambda}{ncm \cdot nm}$	$\frac{\lambda}{nm}$	$\frac{ns}{nh}\lambda$

4.1.3 *Weighted Arrival Rate (λ')*

In the query model, we normalize a query of an arbitrary type to an equivalent number of single-keyword top-10 queries. A *weighted arrival rate* of a component is the arrival rate of the normalized queries. For each component, we measure the processing time of each top-k query and calculate the relative weights of the processing time of top-50 and top-1000 queries compared with that of a single-keyword top-10 query as the unit. As an example, Fig. 7 (a) shows the average query processing time in the system component C of each top-k query type, and Fig. 7 (b) shows the weight $w_C(k)$ of each top-k query type in C. For the component C, the average processing time of a top-10 query is 25.01 ms, and its weight is considered to be 1.0. The weights of other top-k queries are calculated based on this value. The weighted arrival rate at the component C, λ_C', is obtained by calculating the sum of products of the weight and the query mix ratio of each query type. For example, consider an example of query mix ratio $qmr(sct, k)$ for top-k queries in Fig. 7 (c), where sct is a search condition type. Then, the weight of the arrival rate at the system component C for this query mix is calculated as 1.055.

search condition type \ k	Top-10	Top-50	Top-1000
All query types	25.010	25.519	36.467

(a) System component C time (ms).

search condition type \ k	Top-10	Top-50	Top-1000
All query types	1.0 query	1.02 queries	1.46 queries

(b) Weights of top-k types $w_C(k)$.

search condition type \ k	Top-10 (45%)	Top-50 (45%)	Top-1000 (10%)
Single keyword (98%)	44.1%	44.1%	9.8%
Multiple keyword (1%)	0.45%	0.45%	0.1%
Limited search (1%)	0.45%	0.45%	0.1%

(c) Query mix $qmr(sct, k)$.

$$\lambda'_C = \lambda_C \sum_{k \in top\text{-}k\ types} \left(w_C(k) \left(\sum_{sct \in search\ condition\ types} qmr(sct,k) \right) \right) = \lambda_C \times 1.055$$

Figure 7: An example of calculating a weighted arrival rate at the system component C.

The weighted arrival rate at each system component is as shown in Formulas (1) ~ (3). Here, we separate master CPUs from the master memory bus since we have multiple CPUs for each memory bus, and there is more contention in the memory bus than in a CPU. Since it is impossible to measure the weights of the master CPU and the master memory bus separately, we measure the master's total weight $w_{master}(k)$ for each top-k type and assume the same weight for both the master CPU and master memory bus.

4.1.4 *Parameters of the Performance Model*

To estimate a sojourn time at each component by using a queuing model, we measure the service time of each component. The service time at a component for each query type is obtained by measuring and averaging the processing times of all the queries of that type in a query set when executed alone. The master has two types of components: CPUs and the memory bus. Since the master CPU time and master memory access time cannot be measured independently, we first measure the total time taken by a master $ST_{master}(k, ns)$. Then, we obtain the service time of a master CPU $ST_{master\text{-}CPU}(k, ns)$ and that of the master memory bus $ST_{master\text{-}memory\text{-}bus}(k, ns)$ by dividing the total time by a given ratio, which will be discussed below. The total service time of a master $ST_{master}(k, ns)$ is obtained by Formula (4). In Formula (4), $T_{parent\text{-}proc}$ is the time spent by the parent process in the master for checking syntax of the query. $T_{child\text{-}proc}$ is the time spent by the child process for distributing the query to the slaves and storing the results received from the slaves into the result buffer. $T_{master\text{-}RPC}(k)$ is the time taken by the communication (RPC) module of the master; it varies according to k. $T_{child\text{-}proc}$ and $T_{master\text{-}RPC}(k)$ are multiplied by ns since they are repeated as many times as the number of slaves. $T_{merge}(k, ns)$ is the time for merging the results from the slaves to get the final top-k results. $T_{context\text{-}switch}(k, ns)$ is the time for the master processes to perform context switching. Formulas (5) and (6) show how to get the service times of a master CPU and a master memory bus. The service time of a master measured, $ST_{master}(k, ns)$, is divided according to the ratio of $\alpha : (1 - \alpha)$ to estimate the ratio of CPU time : memory access time ($0 \leq \alpha \leq 1$). The value of α is chosen in such a way that the estimated results fit the experimental results actually measured using the five-node reference system.

$$\lambda'_{master\text{-}CPU}(\lambda, nm, ncm) = \frac{\lambda}{ncm \cdot nm} \sum_{\substack{k \in top\text{-}k \\ types}} \left\{ w_{master}(k) \sum_{\substack{sct \in search \\ condition \\ types}} qmr(sct, k) \right\} \quad (1)$$

$$\lambda'_{master\text{-}memory\text{-}bus}(\lambda, nm) = \frac{\lambda}{nm} \sum_{\substack{k \in top\text{-}k \\ types}} \left\{ w_{master}(k) \sum_{\substack{sct \in search \\ condition \\ types}} qmr(sct, k) \right\} \quad (2)$$

$$\lambda'_{network}(\lambda, ns, nh) = \frac{ns}{nh}\lambda \sum_{\substack{k \in top\text{-}k \\ types}} \left\{ w_{network}(k) \sum_{\substack{sct \in search \\ condition \\ types}} qmr(sct, k) \right\} \quad (3)$$

$$ST_{master}(k, ns) = T_{parent\text{-}proc} + (T_{child\text{-}proc} + T_{master\text{-}RPC}(k)) * ns + T_{merge}(k, ns) + T_{context\text{-}switch}(k, ns) \quad (4)$$

$$ST_{master\text{-}CPU}(k, ns) = ST_{master}(k, ns) \times \alpha \quad (5)$$

$$ST_{master\text{-}memory\text{-}bus}(k, ns) = ST_{master}(k, ns) \times (1 - \alpha) \quad (6)$$

In Formula (4), $T_{parent\text{-}proc}$, $T_{child\text{-}proc}$, and $T_{master\text{-}RPC}(k)$ are measured using a small-sized (five-node) system since these values are independent of the number of slaves. On the other hand, since $T_{merge}(k, ns)$ and $T_{context\text{-}switch}(k, ns)$ depend on the number of slaves, we obtain them by using Formulas (7) and (8). To get the final top-k results, the results from the slaves are merged using a loser tree. In Formula (7), $t_{comparison}$ is the time spent by one comparison in the loser tree, and $\lceil \log_2 ns \rceil$, the height of the loser tree -1, is the number of comparisons for one result. t_{base} is the time spent for selecting a winner including the time to read streams and the time to copy the result to the result buffer but excluding the time for comparison. In Formula (8), $t_{per\text{-}context\text{-}switch}$ is the time spent by one context switch in the master. $ncs_{base}(k)$ is the initial number of context switches, and $ncs_{per\text{-}slave}(k)$ is the additional number of context switches per slave.

$$T_{merge}(k, ns) = k \times (\lceil \log_2 ns \rceil \times t_{comparison} + t_{base}) \quad (7)$$

$$T_{context\text{-}switch}(k, ns) = t_{per\text{-}context\text{-}switch} \times (ncs_{base}(k) + (ns \times ncs_{per\text{-}slave}(k))) \quad (8)$$

$ST_{network}(k)$, the service time of a network hub, is obtained by measuring the time taken by a network hub to transfer top-k results of a slave. Fig. 8 shows how to measure the service time of a network hub. For each top-k result, we measure the total time C of an RPC call. We then subtract M and S from C, where M is the CPU time taken by a master node, and S is the CPU time taken by a slave node. The CPU times are measured by using the time utility of LINUX. The CPU times M and S overlap the time O, which is the CPU time of the operating system to transfer data. However, the time is spent concurrently with the network transfer time, so we measure the time O and add it back. To measure the time O, we make a dummy RPC function by removing data transfer from the original RPC function, and measure the CPU time of the master node. The measured value corresponds to M−O, so we can obtain O from M and M−O. We assume that the CPU time of the operating system for network transfer at a slave is the same as that at the master. Therefore, we measure the service time of a network hub as (C−M−S)+2·O.

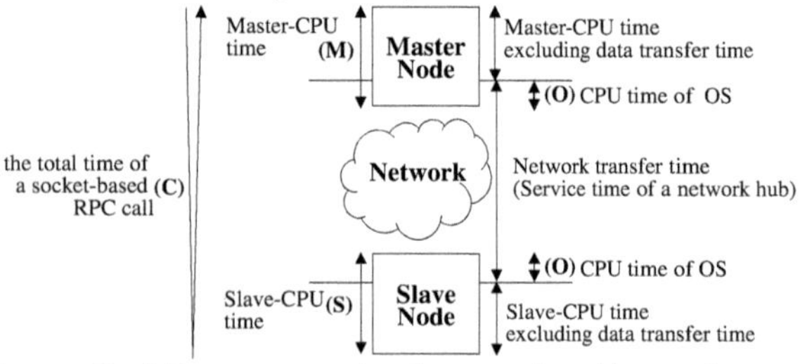

Figure 8: Measurement of a service time at a network hub.

4.1.5 *Average Queue Length and the Estimated Sojourn Time*

The average queue length of a component is the sum of the number of customers waiting in the queue and the number of customers being serviced. The sojourn time, i.e., the response time of a queue, is determined by the length of the queue. In this paper, every queue used in the performance model is an M/D/1 queue with a Poisson arrival process, a constant service time, and a single server. The average length of an M/D/1 queue is obtained by Formula (9). The average queue length for each component is obtained by Formulas (10) ∼ (12). To obtain the average queue length for the component C, we substitute λ in Formula (9) with the weighted arrival rate, and ST with the service time of top-10 query type for the component because the queries are normalized in terms of the single keyword top-10 query. We use a fixed value of ST, which is the average service time for the queue.

Meanwhile, the sojourn time X of a customer in a queue is the total time the customer spends inside the queue for waiting and for being served. The average sojourn time is obtained by Formula (13), where L is the average queue length and λ the arrival rate. Thus, the average sojourn time of single-keyword top-10 queries for each component is obtained by dividing the average length of the corresponding queue by the weighted arrival rate. The average sojourn times of queries having *other* top-k values are obtained by multiplying the weight for the top-k of the component.

$$L(\lambda, ST) = \frac{\lambda^2 E[ST^2]}{2(1 - \lambda E[ST])} + \lambda E[ST] \quad (9)$$

$$L_{master\text{-}CPU}(\lambda, nm, ncm, ns) = L(\lambda'_{master\text{-}CPU}(\lambda, nm, ncm), ST_{master\text{-}CPU}(k = 10, ns)) \quad (10)$$

$$L_{master\text{-}memory\text{-}bus}(\lambda, nm, ns) = L(\lambda'_{master\text{-}memory\text{-}bus}(\lambda, nm), ST_{master\text{-}memory\text{-}bus}(k = 10, ns)) \quad (11)$$

$$L_{network}(\lambda, ns, nh) = L(\lambda'_{network}(\lambda, ns, nh), ST_{network}(k = 10)) \quad (12)$$

$$E[X] = \frac{L}{\lambda} \quad (13)$$

$$E[X_{master\text{-}CPU}] = \frac{L_{master\text{-}CPU}(\lambda, nm, ncm, ns)}{\lambda'_{master\text{-}CPU}(\lambda, nm, ncm)} \times w_{master}(k) \quad (14)$$

$$E[X_{master\text{-}memory\text{-}bus}] = \frac{L_{master\text{-}memory\text{-}bus}(\lambda, nm, ns)}{\lambda'_{master\text{-}memory\text{-}bus}(\lambda, nm)} \times w_{master}(k) \quad (15)$$

$$E[X_{network}] = \frac{ns}{nh} \times \frac{L_{network}(\lambda, ns, nh)}{\lambda'_{network}(\lambda, ns, nh)} \times w_{network}(k) \quad (16)$$

For a network hub, ns/nh is additionally multiplied because ns/nh slaves are connected to one network hub.

4.2 Estimation of the Expected Slave Max Time

In ODYS, given a user query, all of the slaves process the query in parallel at semi-cold start. When a query is executed at semi-cold start, different slaves have much different processing times because the disk access time has a lot of variation. We note that, the total processing time is bounded by the maximum slave sojourn time (briefly, *slave max time*) since we must receive the results from all the slaves to answer the query. Here, we propose a method for estimating the slave max time based on measurement.

Fig. 9 shows the algorithm of the proposed estimation method for the slave max time. We call this algorithm the *partitioning-based estimation method* (simply, the *partitioning method*). The partitioning method estimates the slave max time of a large-sized (e.g., 300-node) target system by running a small-sized (e.g., 5-node) test system multiple times. Suppose r is the number of repetitions, np the number of slaves in the test system, and ns the number of slaves in the target system. In Step 1, the algorithm generates a sequence of $np \times r$ slave sojourn times for each query by running the test system r times. In Step 2, the algorithm partitions the sequence into segments of size ns, find the maximum value per segment, and average these values. Since the partitioning method provides the maximum value by measurement, the result must be very close to the actual measurement of the target system.

Algorithm ***Partitioning Method*** **for estimating the expected** ***Slave Max Time*****:**
Input: (1) Q: the query set,
(2) r: the number of repetitions of the query set execution
(3) np: the number of slaves of the prototype
(4) ns: the number of slaves of the target system
Output: The estimated slave max time for each query in Q
Algorithm:
Step1. Generate a sequence of slave sojourn times for each query:
1.1 Execute Q for r times at semi-cold start by using the np-node prototype and measure the slave sojourn times.
1.2 For the ith query in Q, make a sequence of the slave sojourn times as $< t_{i,1,1}, t_{i,1,2}, \ldots, t_{i,1,m}, t_{i,2,1}, \ldots, t_{i,2,m}, \ldots, t_{i,r,1}, \ldots, t_{i,r,np} >$, where $t_{i,p,q}$ is the slave sojourn time for the ith query in the pth repetition at the qth slave.
Step2. Estimate the average slave max time for ns slaves:
For each sequence obtained in Step1,
2.1 Partition the sequence into segments of size ns.
2.2 Find the maximum value per segment and average those values.

Figure 9: The algorithm for estimating the expected slave max time by using the partitioning method.

4.3 Estimation of the Average Total Query Response Time

Fig. 10 shows an overview of the estimation method for computing the average total query response time. In Fig. 10, m_i is the master processing time for a slave (i.e., for sending the query and receiving results from a slave), s_i, the query processing time of the ith slave, and nt_i, the network transfer time of the ith slave's result. Suppose that for all i, m_i, s_i, and nt_i have the same value m, s, and nt, respectively. Then, there are two cases for estimating the response time of a query. If m is less than or equal to nt, the total query response time is obtained as $(m_1+s_1+ns\times nt) = (m+s+ns\times nt) \approx (ns\times nt+s)$. Or, if m is greater than nt, the total query response time is obtained as $(ns \times m + s_{ns} + nt_{ns}) = (ns \times m + s + nt) \approx (ns \times m + s)$. (One m or one nt is negligible.) In other words, the total query response time is obtained by adding the bigger of the network hub's total sojourn time ($ns \times nt$) and the master's total sojourn time ($ns \times m$) to the slave sojourn time (s). Here, for s, we use the slave max time as discussed in Section 4.2. Formula (17) shows how to get the estimated value of the average total query response time.

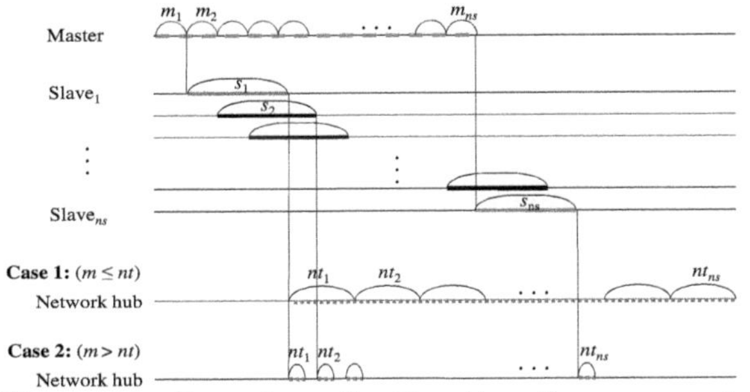

Figure 10: Overview of estimating the average total query response time.

5. PERFORMANCE EVALUATION

5.1 Experimental Data and Environment

We have built a ten-node parallel search engine according to the architecture shown in Fig. 5. Here, we have used one master, one 1-Gbps hub, and ten slaves each running 100 Odysseus processes with a shared buffer of 12 Mbytes. We have used one machine for the master, a Linux machine with a quad-core 3.06 GHz CPU[15] and 6 Gbytes of main memory. We have used two replicated five-node clusters: Cluster 1 and Cluster 2. Cluster 1 consists of four Linux machines each with two dual-core 3 GHz CPU, 4Gbytes of main memory, and a RAID 5 disk array. Each disk array has 13 disks (disk transfer rate: average 59.5 Mbytes/s) with a total of $0.9 \sim 3.9$ Tbytes disk space, a cache of $0.5 \sim 1$ Gbytes, and 200 Mbytes/s bandwidth. The remaining one is a Linux machine with a quad-core 2.5 GHz CPU, 4 Gbytes of main memory, and a RAID 5 disk array. The disk array has 13 disks (disk transfer rate: average 83.3 Mbytes/s) with a total of 13 Tbytes, a cache of 512 Mbytes, and 512 Mbytes/s bandwidth. Cluster 2 consists of five Linux machines each with a quad-core 2.4 GHz CPU, 8 Gbytes of main memory, and an internal RAID 5 disk array. The disk array has 10 disks (disk transfer rate: average 81.2 Mbytes/s) with a total of 5 Tbytes, a cache of 256 Mbytes, and 768 Mbytes/s bandwidth. In general, Cluster 2 is a bit faster than Cluster 1. The master and the slaves are connected by a 1-Gbps network hub.

We perform experiments using 114 million Web pages crawled. For each Web page, if its size is larger than 16 Kbytes, we extract and store important part of a fixed size (front 8 KBytes + rear 8 KBytes) to uniformly control the experiments. We build two replicated 5-node clusters (228 million Web pages total). For each cluster, we evenly partition the set of 114 million Web pages into five segments and allocate each segment to a slave. Thus, each slave stores and indexes 22.8 million Web pages[16]. We perform experiments using two query sets. One consists of only single-keyword top-10 queries, and the other consists of a mixed type of queries with different k (in top-k) values. We call the query sets SINGLE-10-ONLY and QUERY-MIX, respectively. For QUERY-MIX, we use the query mix ratio in Fig. 7 (c). Each query set includes 10,000 queries in which the keywords, site IDs, and domain IDs are all unique. Queries are generated at a Poisson arrival rate and issued by a separate machine.

We perform the following experiments. First, we measure the estimation error of the performance model by comparing its projected output with the results measured as the arrival rate and number of nodes are varied. We use the *estimation error* as defined in Formula (18). Second, we estimate the slave max time using the partitioning method using the five-node reference system (Cluster 1 only). Last, we project the performance of ODYS for real-world scale data and query loads by using the performance model. The value of α used in the performance model is 0.25. All the experimental results are measured at semi-cold start. To measure the time at semi-cold start, we first empty the DBMS buffers and disk array caches of all the slaves, and then, run 10,000 queries that are completely independent of the experimental queries (i.e., no keywords, site IDs, or domain IDs overlapping with those of the experimental queries) to load the internal nodes of the IR index into the DBMS buffer.

5.2 Experimental Results

5.2.1 Measurement of Parameters

We measure the parameters of the queuing model using the five-node system. The values are measured as described in Section 4.1.4. Table 3 shows the parameters measured.

5.2.2 Accuracy of the Performance Model

We vary the query loads from 5 to 24 million queries/day for the two query sets: SINGLE-10-ONLY and QUERY-MIX. Fig. 11 shows the average total query response time and the average processing time of the master and network for each query load. In Fig. 11[17], TOTAL-EXP-10 repre-

[15]State of the art CPUs use several features (e.g., EIST, Turbo Boost, C-State) for power saving. These features can cause a significant variance in the service time. To minimize this variance, we turn-off all these features.

[16]One ODYS slave is capable of indexing 100 million Web pages. But, we used 22.8 million/slave since we had only 114 million crawled. Nevertheless, this does not affect the query performance significantly since the postings are sorted according to the PageRank order, and only up to 1000 postings are retrieved for a single-keyword top-k query. For a multiple-keyword or limited search query, a larger number of postings are accessed, but a sufficient number of postings are available from 22.8 million Web pages.

[17]To avoid clutter, Fig. 11 shows only the results of the 10-node system. Others show similar trends.

$$
\begin{aligned}
& t_{parallel\text{-}n\text{-}node}(sct, k, \lambda, nm, ncm, ns, nh) \\
&= max\Big(\Big(E[X_{master\text{-}CPU}] + E[X_{master\text{-}memory\text{-}bus}]\Big), E[X_{network}]\Big) + t_{slave\text{-}max\text{-}time}(sct, k, \lambda, ns) \\
&= max\Big(\Big(\frac{L_{master\text{-}CPU}(\lambda, nm, ncm, ns)}{\lambda'_{master\text{-}CPU}(\lambda, nm, ncm)} \times w_{master}(k) + \frac{L_{master\text{-}memory\text{-}bus}(\lambda, nm, ns)}{\lambda'_{master\text{-}memory\text{-}bus}(\lambda, nm)} \times w_{master}(k)\Big), \\
& \frac{ns}{nh} \times \frac{L_{network}(\lambda, ns, nh)}{\lambda'_{network}(\lambda, ns, nh)} \times w_{network}(k)\Big) + t_{slave\text{-}max\text{-}time}(sct, k, \lambda, ns) \qquad (17)
\end{aligned}
$$

$$
\textit{estimation error} = \frac{\left| \textit{estimated average time of a query} - \textit{measured average time of a query} \right|}{\textit{measured average time of a query}} \qquad (18)
$$

Table 3: Parameters of the queuing model measured.

Parameters	Values
$T_{parent\text{-}proc}$	1.516 ms
$T_{child\text{-}proc}$	0.0081 ms
$T_{master\text{-}RPC}(k)$	0.01 ms, $k = 10$ 0.011 ms, $k = 50$ 0.031 ms, $k = 1000$
$t_{comparison}$	0.191 μs
t_{base}	0.28 μs
$t_{per\text{-}context\text{-}switch}$	2.105 μs
$ncs_{base}(k)$	56.490, $k = 10, 50$ 97.728, $k = 1000$
$ncs_{per\text{-}slave}(k)$	1.917, $k = 10, 50$ 3.316, $k = 1000$
$ST_{network}(k)$	0.129 ms, $k = 10$ 0.222 ms, $k = 50$ 0.318 ms, $k = 1000$

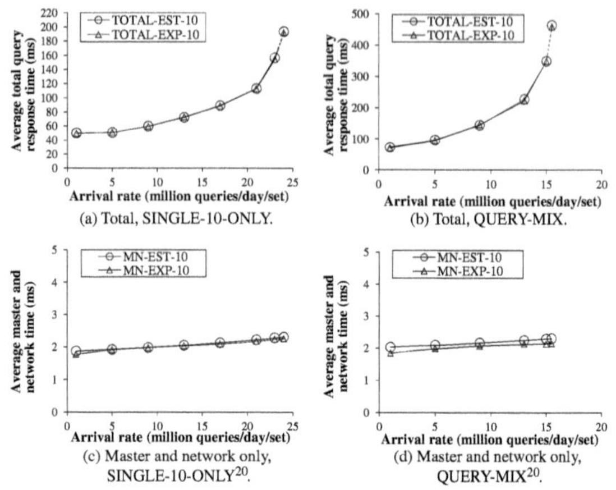

Figure 11: The estimated and experimental results of the ten-node system (ns=10) as the query arrival rate is varied. EST-10 represents estimated results for the 10-node system; EXP-10 experimental results.

sents the experimental results of the total query response time measured using the ten-node system as the query arrival rate is varied; TOTAL-EST-10 the estimated results from the hybrid performance model. That is, the slave max time is estimated from the measurement of the five-node reference system using the algorithm in Fig. 9 in Section 4.2; the master and network time is estimated from the queuing model; TOTAL-EST-10 is a sum of these two. MN-EXP-10 represents the experimental results of the master and network time; MN-EST-10 the estimated results. The results show that the maximum estimation error of the total query response time is 1.77% for SINGLE-10-ONLY, and 2.13% for QUERY-MIX. The maximum estimation error of the master and network time (i.e., the part modeled by the queuing model) is 6.29% for SINGLE-10-ONLY and 10.15% for QUERY-MIX[18]. For the same query load, the result of SINGLE-10-ONLY and QUERY-MIX shows a big difference. The reason is that the response time of the multiple-keyword and limited search queries are much longer than those of the single-keyword queries as discussed in Section 4.1.1[19]. In Fig. 11, dotted lines represent the regions where measurements become unstable since the number of input queries becomes close to the maximum possible throughput. The result in Fig. 11 (a) shows that the ten-node ODYS can stably process 266 queries/sec (23 million queries/day) with an average response time of 154 ms on a 1.52 TBytes dataset.

Fig. 12[21] shows the average total query response time and the average master and network time as the number of nodes is varied from 1 to 10 for two query sets: SINGLE-10-ONLY and QUERY-MIX. Here, EST-x represents the estimated results for x million queries/day/set; EXP-x the experimental results. In Figs. 12(a) and (b), due to variations of performance in individual machines, for 1- or 3-node configurations, the results vary depending on which machines we use in the experiment and do not average out. Thus, we represent the result as a range (i.e., from min using the fastest machine(s) to max using the slowest machine(s)). The results show that the maximum estimation error of the total query response time is 2.13%, and that of the master and network time is 10.15% when the number of nodes ≥ 5.

5.2.3 Estimation of the Slave Max Time

We analyze the effect of the number of slaves on the performance of ODYS. We estimate the slave max times for QUERY-MIX while increasing the segment size of the partitioning method for each query load. We measure 300 slave sojourn times for each query by running the query set 60 times using the five-node reference system. Fig. 13 shows the expected slave max time for each segment size. The results show that the expected slave max time increases up

[18]For sensitivity analysis, we have tested a different query mix having 20% of top-1000 queries obtaining a similar result where the maximum estimation error was 8.64%. We have not conducted sensitivity analysis on search condition types since the master and network time does not depend on search condition types, but only on the top-k value.

[19]It can be optimized by constructing separate ODYS sets dedicated to limited search queries. For the IR indexes of these ODYS sets, we can order the postings of each posting list by the domain ID, and then, by ranking the sets of the postings that have the same domain ID's independently of one another, significantly reducing the search over the posting list. However, these additional optimizations are beyond the scope of this paper and will be left as a further study.

[20]For Figures 11 (c) and (d), the master and network time is measured by subtracting the slave max time from the total query response time.

[21]To avoid clutter, Figs. 12(a) and (b) show the results only for three representative arrival rates; Figs. 12(c) and (d) only for one.

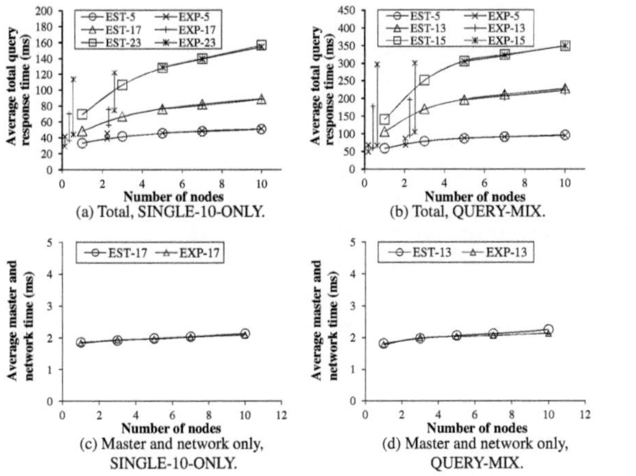

Figure 12: The estimated and experimental result as the number of nodes is varied. EST-x represents the estimated results for x million queries/day/set; EXP-x the experimental results.

to 1.5 ~ 2 times of the minimum value as the segment size increases, i.e., as the number of slaves increases. Interestingly, the slave max time gradually converges to a value less than twice the minimum instead of increasing indefinitely. Detailed analysis of this phenomenon is beyond the scope of this paper. We leave it as a further study.

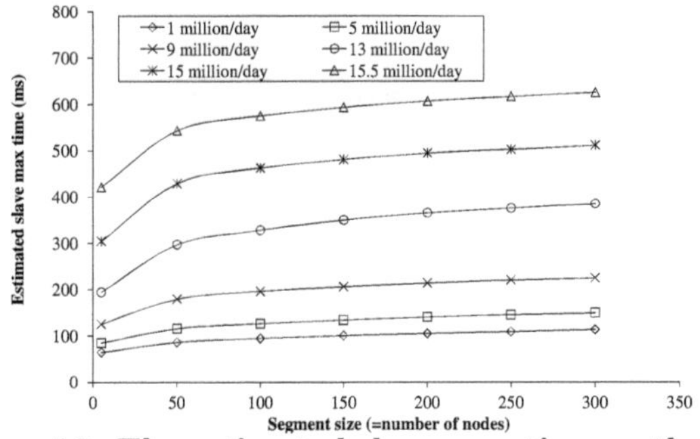

Figure 13: The estimated slave max time as the segment size is varied (QUERY-MIX, r=60, ns=5).

5.2.4 *Performance Projection of a Real-World-Scale (300-Node) ODYS*

By using the performance model, we estimate the average response time of ODYS for 30 billion[22] Web pages, which is considered real-world scale data [19]. Fig. 14 shows the estimated performance of a 300-node system for the query set QUERY-MIX. In the estimation, one ODYS set consists of 4 masters, 300 slaves, and 11 Gbit network hubs. Each master has a Quad-Core 3.06 GHz CPU, each slave has one 3 GHz CPU, 4 Gbytes of main memory, and 13 × 300 Gbytes SATA hard disks. Here, we select the number of masters (4) and network hubs (11) to make the queue lengths of master memory and network hubs similar to each other to avoid bottlenecks. In Fig. 14, TOTAL-EST-300 represents the estimated total response time of queries, and SLAVE-MAX-EST-300 represents the slave max time estimated using the partitioning method. SLAVE-MAX-EST-300 is identical to the results of the segment size 300 in Fig. 13.

[22]Google (as well as other commercial search engines such as MS Bing and Yahoo!) indexes approximately 25 billion Web pages. This is roughly indicated by the result of querying with frequently occurring keywords such as "a," "the," or "www."

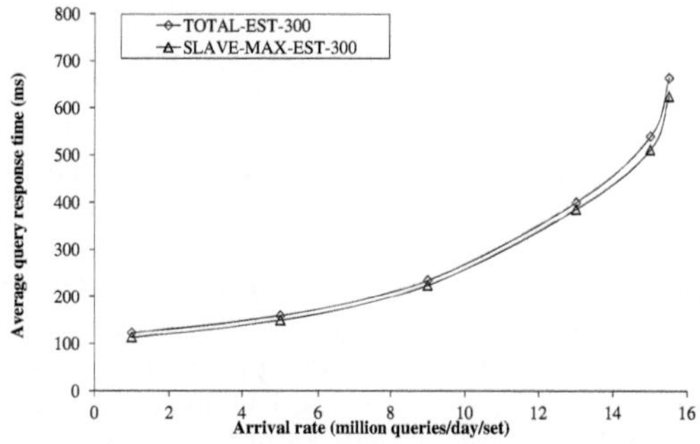

Figure 14: The projected average response time of ODYS for real-world scale service (ns=300). TOTAL-EST-300 is the average estimated total query response time; SLAVE-MAX-EST-300 the average estimated slave max time.

As we observed in Fig. 14, if an ODYS set were to take a higher query load, the total number of nodes required to handle the load could be reduced, but the performance would be degraded. Therefore, the trade-off between the number of nodes and the performance exists in providing reasonable performance with a minimal number of nodes. For example, suppose we run 7 million queries/day (81 queries /sec) per ODYS set, then ODYS can handle Google-scale service using 143 sets of 304 nodes (4 masters and 300 slaves), a total of 43,472 nodes, for 1 billion queries/day. In this case, the average query response time is only 194 ms. In contrast, if we ran 3.5 million queries/day (40.5 queries/sec), ODYS would need 286 sets with a total of 86,944 nodes with an average query response time of 148 ms[23]. The experiments show that our approach is capable of providing a commercial-level service with a rather small number of nodes.

6. CONCLUSIONS

In this paper, we have shown that a massively parallel search engine capable of processing real-world scale data and query loads can be implemented using a DB-IR tightly integrated parallel DBMS. We have also presented the detailed implementation of such a system, ODYS. The DBMS used in the slaves of ODYS is Odysseus, which is a highly scalable object-relational DBMS that is tightly integrated with IR features [29]. Odysseus is capable of indexing 100 million Web pages, and thus, ODYS is able to handle a large volume of data even with a small number of machines. The tightly integrated DB-IR functionality enables ODYS to have a commercial-level performance for keyword queries. Furthermore, ODYS provides rich functionality such as SQL, schemas, and indexes for easy (and less error-prone) development and maintenance of applications [30].

We have also proposed a performance model that can estimate the performance of the proposed architecture. The model is a hybrid one that employs both an analytic approach based on the queuing model and an experimental approach of using a small-sized (five-node, in this paper) reference system to project the performance of a large target system. We have validated this model through comparison of the result projected by the model with the results measured using a ten-node system. Our estimation of the total response time is quite accurate since the bulk of the total response time is spent at the slave, and we derive the slave

[23]The average response time of a typical commercial search engine is known to be 200-250 ms [9, 13].

max time by measurement with accuracy. The result of the comparison indicates that the estimation error of the total query response time of the ten-node system is less than 2.13%. Such a modeling method is helpful in realistically estimating the performance of a system by using limited resources—without actually building a large-scale system.

Finally, we have estimated the performance of ODYS for real-world scale data and query loads. According to the performance model, with a small number of (i.e., 43,472) nodes, ODYS is capable of handling 1 billion queries/day for 30 billion Web pages at an average query response time of 194 ms. With twice as many nodes (i.e., half the query load per node), it can provide an average query response time of 148 ms. This clearly demonstrates the scalability and efficiency of our architecture. These results are even more marked since these are conservative results from a semi-cold start environment reflecting a lower-bound performance.

7. ACKNOWLEDGEMENTS

This work was supported by the National Research Foundation of Korea (NRF) grant funded by Korean Government (MEST) (No. 2012R1A2A1A05026326). We deeply appreciate incisive comments of anonymous reviewers, which made the paper far more complete. We also would like to acknowledge contributions of many people who worked on the Odysseus DBMS project over 23 years—in particular, Young-Koo Lee, Min-Jae Lee, Wook-Shin Han, Jae-Gil Lee, and Jae-Jun Yoo.

8. REFERENCES

[1] Abouzeid, A. et al., "HadoopDB: An Architectural Hybrid of MapReduce and DBMS Technologies for Analytical Workloads," In *Proc. Int'l Conf. on Very Large Data Bases (VLDB)*, pp. 922-933, Aug. 2009.

[2] Azure, http://www.microsoft.com/windowsazure.

[3] Barroso, L., Dean, J. and Holzle, U., "Web Search for a Planet: the Google Cluster Architecture," *IEEE Micro*, Vol. 23, No. 2, pp. 22-28, Mar. 2003.

[4] Budiu, M., 2009, available at http://budiu.info/work/dryad-talk-berkeley09.pptx.

[5] Cassandra, http://cassandra.apache.org.

[6] Chang, F. et al., "Bigtable: A Distributed Storage System for Structured Data," In *Proc. Symposium on Operating Systems Design and Implementation (OSDI)*, pp. 205-218, Nov. 2006.

[7] Cooper, R., *Introduction to Queuing Theory*, North Holland, 2nd ed., 1981.

[8] Dean, J., and Ghemawat, S., "MapReduce: Simplified Data Processing on Large Clusters," In *Proc. Symposium on Operating Systems Design and Implementation (OSDI)*, pp. 137-150 , Dec. 2004.

[9] Dean, J., "Challenges in Building Large-Scale Information Retrieval Systems," In *Proc. ACM Int'l Conf. on Web Search and Data Mining (WSDM)* (an invited talk), p. 1, Feb. 2009 (presentation slides available at http://research.google.com/people/jeff/WSDM09-keynote.pdf).

[10] Dean, J., "Designs, Lessons and Advice from Building Large Distributed Systems," a keynote at ACM SIGOPS Int'l Workshop on Large Scale Distributed Systems and Middleware (LADIS), Oct. 2009 (presentation slides available at http://www.odbms.org/download/dean-keynote-ladis2009.pdf).

[11] DeCandia, G. et al., "Dynamo: Amazon's Highly Available Key-Value Store," In *Proc. ACM Symposium on Operating Systems Principles (SOSP)*, Oct. 2007.

[12] Ghemawat, S., Gobioff, H., and Leung, S., "The Google File System," In *Proc. ACM Symposium on Operating Systems Principles (SOSP)*, Oct. 2003.

[13] Google, http://www.google.com/about/corporate/company/tech.html.

[14] Hadoop, http://hadoop.apache.org.

[15] HBase, http://hbase.apache.org.

[16] HDFS, http://hadoop.apache.org/hdfs.

[17] Javadi, B., Khorsandi, S., and Akbari, M., "Queuing Network Modeling of a Cluster-Based Parallel System," In *Proc. Int'l Conf. on High Performance Computing and Grid in Asia Pacific Region*, pp. 304-307, July 2004.

[18] Kemper, B. and Mandjes, M., Approximations for the Mean Sojourn Time in a Parallel Queue, Technical Report PNA-E0901, Centrum Wiskunde & Informatica, Mar. 2009.

[19] Kunder, M., http://www.worldwidewebsize.com.

[20] Lentz, A., "MySQL Storage Engine Architecture," In MySQL Developer Articles, MySQL AB, May 2004 (available at http://ftp.nchu.edu.tw/MySQL/tech-resources/articles/storage-engine).

[21] Lucene, http://lucene.apache.org.

[22] Moreira, J. et al., "Scalability of the Nutch search engine," In *Proc. Int'l Conf. on Supercomputing (ICS)*, pp. 3-12, June 2007.

[23] Nielsenwire, "Nielsen Reports February 2010 U.S. Search Rankings," Nielsen Report, Mar. 15, 2010 (available at http://blog.nielsen.com/nielsenwire/ online_mobile/nielsen-reports-february-2010-u-s-search-rankings).

[24] Özsu, M. and Valduriez, P., "Distributed Reliability Protocols," In Book *Principles of Distributed Database Systems,* Prentice Hall, 2nd ed., pp. 379-400, 1999.

[25] Richardson, M., Prakash, A., and Brill, E., "Beyond PageRank: machine learning for static ranking," In *Proc. Int'l Conf. on World Wide Web (WWW)*, pp. 707-715, May 2006.

[26] Shahhoseini, H. and Naderi, M., "Design Trade off on Shared Memory Clustered Massively Parallel Processing Systems," In *Proc. Int'l Conf. on Computing and Information*, Nov. 2000.

[27] Stonebraker, M. et al., "MapReduce and Parallel DBMSs: Friends or Foes?," *Communications of the ACM (CACM)*, pp. 64-71, Jan. 2010.

[28] Whang, K. et al., An Inverted Index Storage Structure Using Subindexes and Large Objects for Tight Coupling of Information Retrieval with Database Management Systems, U.S. Patent No. 6,349,308, Feb. 19, 2002, Application No. 09/250,487, Feb. 15, 1999.

[29] Whang, K. et al., "Odysseus: A High-Performance ORDBMS Tightly-Coupled with IR Features," In *Proc. Int'l Conf. on Data Engineering (ICDE)*, pp. 1104-1105, Apr. 2005. This paper recieved the Best Demonstration Award.

[30] Whang, K. et al., "DB-IR Integration Using Tight-Coupling in the Odysseus DBMS," submitted for publication, 2013.

[31] Yang, C. et al., "Osprey: Implementing MapReduce-Style Fault Tolerance in a Shared-Nothing Distributed Database," In *Proc. IEEE Int'l Conf. on Data Engineering (ICDE)*, pp. 657-668, Mar. 2010.

Massive Graph Triangulation*

Xiaocheng Hu[1] Yufei Tao[1,2] Chin-Wan Chung[2,3]
[1]Department of Computer Science and Engineering, CUHK, Hong Kong
[2]Division of Web Science and Technology, KAIST, Korea
[3]Department of Computer Science, KAIST, Korea

ABSTRACT

This paper studies I/O-efficient algorithms for settling the classic *triangle listing* problem, whose solution is a basic operator in dealing with many other graph problems. Specifically, given an undirected graph G, the objective of triangle listing is to find all the cliques involving 3 vertices in G. The problem has been well studied in internal memory, but remains an urgent difficult challenge when G does not fit in memory, rendering any algorithm to entail frequent I/O accesses. Although previous research has attempted to tackle the challenge, the state-of-the-art solutions rely on a set of crippling assumptions to guarantee good performance. Motivated by this, we develop a new algorithm that is provably I/O and CPU efficient at the same time, without making any assumption on the input G at all. The algorithm uses ideas drastically different from all the previous approaches, and outperformed the existing competitors by a factor over an order of magnitude in our extensive experimentation.

Categories and Subject Descriptors
H3.3 [**Information search and retrieval**]: Search process

Keywords
Graph, triangle, I/O-efficient algorithm

1. INTRODUCTION

In this paper, we revisit the classic *triangle listing problem*. The input is a graph[1] $G = (V, E)$, where V (E) is the set of vertices (edges). A *triangle* is a clique of 3 vertices u, v, w in G, and is denoted as Δ_{uvw}. The goal of triangle listing is to output all the triangles in G. For instance, if G is the graph in Figure 1, the set of triangles is $\{\Delta_{123}, \Delta_{234}, \Delta_{346}, \Delta_{368}, \Delta_{456}, \Delta_{568}\}$.

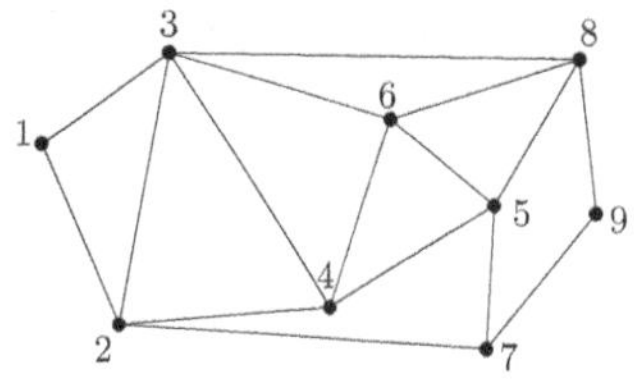

Figure 1: The input graph in our running example

The importance of triangle listing has long been recognized in the literatures of database, network analysis, knowledge discovery, and graph theory:

Dense Subgraph Mining. Given a graph G, a *dense neighborhood graph* (DN-graph) [23] is a subgraph of G, where each pair of connected vertices share at least a number of common neighbors. The most efficient known algorithm [23] for DN-graph discovery utilizes a triangle-listing algorithm as a black box. Hence, a faster solution to triangle listing automatically gives rise to an improved algorithm for mining DN-graphs.

Triangular Connectivity. Let u, v be vertices in a graph G. They are *triangularly connected* [4] if there is a sequence of triangles $(\Delta_1, \Delta_2, ..., \Delta_s)$ such that u (v) is a vertex in the first (last) triangle Δ_1 (Δ_s), and for every $1 \le i \le s-1$, Δ_i shares at least one vertex with Δ_{i+1}. In Figure 1, for instance, vertex 1 is triangularly connected to vertex 5 due to the sequence $(\Delta_{123}, \Delta_{346}, \Delta_{456})$. In *triangular clustering* [Section 5.1, [19]], the vertices in G are divided into equivalence classes such that, two vertices are in an equivalence class if and only if they are triangularly connected. The computation of equivalence classes is reduced to finding connected components after all the triangles have been obtained [19] (hence, fast triangle listing is again the key).

***k*-truss.** Given a graph G, its *k-truss* ($k \ge 3$) [10] is the maximum subgraph of G where every edge appears in at least $k-2$ triangles. This is a form of so-called *cohesive subgraphs* that reveal characteristics of social networks [10, 22]. Not surprisingly, the state-of-the-art algorithm [22] for k-truss computation deploys triangle listing as an initial step.

Network Measurement. A popular approach in studying networks is to interpret the measurements on certain key aspects. A well-known measurement is the (local) *clustering coefficient* [24]. Given a vertex v in a graph G, its clustering coefficient equals $t(v)/\binom{d(v)}{2}$, where $t(v)$ is the number of triangles containing v, and $d(v)$ is the degree of v. A large clustering coefficient indicates high density around v (i.e., many edges among the neighbors of v). The calcu-

*This work was supported in part by the WCU (World Class University) program under the National Research Foundation of Korea, and funded by the Ministry of Education, Science and Technology of Korea (Project No: R31-30007). Xiaocheng Hu and Yufei Tao were also supported in part by projects GRF 4166/10, 4165/11, and 4164/12 from HKRGC. Chin-Wan Chung was also supported in part by the National Research Foundation of Korea(NRF) grant funded by the Korea government(MEST) (No. 2012-0000182), and in part by Microsoft Research Asia through KAIST-Microsoft Research Collaboration Center.

[1]Unless otherwise stated, a graph in this paper is undirected and simple.

SIGMOD'13, June 22–27, 2013, New York, New York, USA.

lation of such coefficients requires computing $t(v)$ for all vertices v. Interestingly, as shown in [9], the most I/O-efficient algorithm for this purpose resorts to triangle listing, after which $t(v)$ can be obtained by simple counting.

1.1 Motivation

We consider that the input graph G does not fit in memory, and thus needs to be processed by an *external memory graph algorithm*. Recently, such algorithms have received considerable interests (see [6, 9, 13] and the references therein), in response to the practical need to analyze massive graphs whose scales exceed the memory capacity of a commodity machine. For example, as of 2011, the social network at Facebook contains more than 721 million active users (a.k.a. nodes), and over 69 billion friendship edges [3]. If each edge is represented by 2 integers, the entire graph occupies over 550 giga bytes of storage (4 bytes per integer).

I/O-efficient algorithms for triangle listing have been investigated previously. Next, we give an overview of the existing solutions (deferring a detailed coverage to Section 3). Henceforth, let M be the size of our memory, and B the size of a disk block, both measured in number of words. The values of M and B satisfy $M \geq 2B$, i.e., the memory contains at least two blocks. Finally, denote by K the number of triangles in G.

External Memory Compact Forward (EM-CF) [17]. Incurring $O(|E|+|E|^{1.5}/B)$ I/Os, this algorithm has two main defects. First, it performs at least $|E|$ I/Os, which is prohibitively expensive in most practical environments. Second, its I/O cost is insensitive to M, rendering the algorithm unable to benefit from the availability of extra memory. Note that the I/O complexity of EM-CF does not depend on K because it outputs all triangles in $O(K/B)$ I/Os whereas in general it holds that $K = O(|E|^{1.5})$ (as will be explained in the next section).

External Memory Node Iterator (EM-NI) [11]. This algorithm runs in $O(|E|^{1.5}/B \cdot \log_{M/B}(|E|/B))$ I/Os. As with EM-CF, its I/O complexity is (almost) insensitive to M, such that the dominating term $|E|^{1.5}/B$ receives no improvement even when memory is abundant.

Graph Partition [8, 9]. Neither of the above algorithms is *output sensitive*, namely, their I/O complexity is $\Omega(|E|^{1.5}/B)$, regardless of the output size K. Even though the term $O(|E|^{1.5}/B)$ is compulsory in the worst case where K reaches $\Omega(|E|^{1.5})$, the actual K in a realistic graph is far less than that extreme limit. This makes it interesting to design output sensitive algorithms that are more efficient when K is small.

Recently, Chu and Cheng [9] made some nice progress in this direction. The crucial idea is to target an I/O complexity of $O(|E|^2/(MB) + K/B)$. The rationale is that $|E|^2/(MB) < |E|^{1.5}/B$ whenever $|E|/M < \sqrt{|E|}$. To see why this is not a stringent inequality, note that even if the memory can hold only 1% of the edges, the inequality is still satisfied as long as $|E| > 10000$. In general, if the memory can accommodate a constant fraction of the input graph (a situation very likely in practice), $O(|E|^2/(MB) + K/B) = O(|E|/B + K/B)$, which is asymptotically optimal because any algorithm must read all edges at least once, and report all the triangles to the disk.

Utilizing several interesting ideas of graph partitioning, Chu and Cheng [9] presented two algorithms that achieve the desired $O(|E|^2/(MB)+K/B)$ bound under a set of assumptions. Unfortunately, as we analyze in Section 3, if any of those assumptions is violated, their algorithms fail to guarantee the target efficiency, and may even suffer from severe performance penalty.

1.2 Our Contributions

Our first contribution is a new algorithm that settles the triangle listing problem in $O(|E|^2/(MB) + K/B)$ I/Os in *all settings*, namely, with no assumption at all. The algorithm is based on ideas drastically different from those of [9]. Somewhat surprisingly, we show that the term $|E|^2/(MB)$ is inevitable, namely, it is impossible to achieve $o(|E|^2/(MB))$ I/Os for all inputs even if $M \ll |E|$.[2] This stands in sharp contrast to triangle listing in memory, where $o(|E|^2)$-time algorithms are well known (e.g., the algorithm of [7] runs in $O(|E|^{1.5})$ time). In external memory, the I/O complexity $O(|E|^2/(MB)+K/B)$ is thus already worst-case optimal within only a constant factor (even for $M \ll |E|$).

As the next step, we prove that the proposed algorithm is also CPU-efficient: it entails $O(|E|\log|E| + |E|^2/M + \alpha|E|)$ CPU time, where α is the *arboricity* of the input graph – a classic metric for measuring the density of a graph. Section 2 will present an extended introduction to α, while for now, it suffices to note that α never exceeds $O(\sqrt{|E|})$ even in the worst case [14], and is much smaller for graphs in reality [7, 16]. It can be shown that both the terms $|E|\log|E| + |E|^2/M$ and $\alpha|E|$ are inevitable, namely, no algorithm can perform only $o(|E|\log|E| + |E|^2/M)$ or $o(\alpha|E|)$ CPU time for all input graphs (even for $M \ll |E|$). This indicates that our algorithm is *both* I/O and CPU optimal by a constant factor in the worst case.

Besides designing new algorithms, this paper also enhances the understanding of existing algorithms. In this respect we present two new results. First, we prove that the I/O cost of EM-NI can actually be bounded by $O(\alpha \cdot SORT(|E|))$, where α as mentioned earlier is the arboricity, and $SORT(|E|)$ is the I/O cost of sorting $|E|$ elements. The finding reveals why EM-NI is very efficient when the input graph is sparse. In particular, $\alpha = O(1)$ for planar graphs, in which case the I/O complexity of EM-NI becomes $O(SORT(|E|))$. This phenomenon cannot be explained by the previous bound $O(|E|^{1.5}/B \cdot \log_{M/B}(|E|/B))$ on EM-NI.

Second, we revisit an elegant algorithm in [9] called *randomized graph partitioning* (RGP). We strengthen its analysis with a non-trivial argument to remove a restrictive assumption that was imposed on this algorithm. The removal reduces the remaining assumptions on RGP to some weak conditions that are almost always fulfilled, and thereby considerably improves its applicability.

1.3 Summary of Experiments

The paper also features an experimental study that is more extensive than those of all the previous work dealing with I/O-efficient triangle listing. We are the first to put all the known algorithms into a direct cross comparison (the papers [8, 9] that represent the state of the art unfortunately missed out EM-CF and EM-NI, which we will show are not always the slowest methods). Our experimentation involved both real and synthetic graphs. On the real side, we used *exactly* the same datasets deployed in [9] to establish the efficiency of DGP and RGP. On the synthetic side, we employed graphs of various distributions, including ones generated from the classic *small world* model [24] and the modern popular *recursive matrix* (R-MAT) model [5]. The results demonstrate that MGT outperformed all its competitors by a factor over an order of magnitude in both I/O and CPU efficiency. Furthermore, its performance is consistently good regardless of the graph distribution and size.

1.4 Paper Organization

Section 2 defines a set of frequent notations, and reviews some results from graph theory relevant to our discussion. Section 3 ana-

[2] The inevitability of $E^2/(MB)$ is trivial for $M = \Omega(|E|)$.

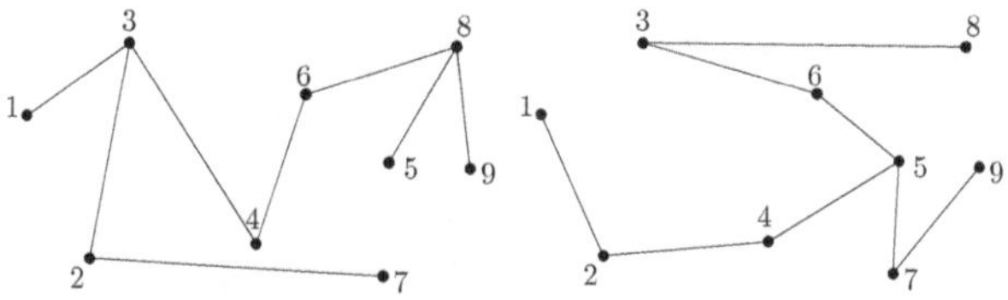

Figure 2: Two edge-disjoint trees covering all the edges of the graph in Figure 1

lyzes the previous I/O-efficient algorithms for triangle listing. Section 4 describes the proposed algorithm and proves its theoretical guarantees. Section 5 gives our new results on EM-NI and RGP, and elaborates on their significance. Section 6 presents an extensive experimental evaluation to demonstrate the superiority of the proposed technique over the existing solutions. Finally, Section 7 concludes the paper with a summary of our findings.

2. PRELIMINARIES

Basic Notations. As mentioned before, the input to the triangle listing problem is a simple undirected graph $G = (V, E)$, where V and E are the sets of vertices and edges, respectively. We represent an undirected edge between vertices u and v as (u, v) or equivalently as (v, u). For each $v \in V, \mathcal{N}(v)$ is the set of *neighbors* of v, where a neighbor is a vertex adjacent to v. Define the *degree* of v as $d(v) = |\mathcal{N}(v)|$.

We consider that G does not have any vertex v with $d(v) = 0$, i.e., an isolated vertex with no incident edge. In fact, if there are such vertices, they can be removed immediately because they obviously cannot appear in any triangle. Finally, we consider that G is given in *adjacency lists*, where the adjacency list of a vertex $v \in V$ stores $\mathcal{N}(v)$ in $O(1 + d(v)/B)$ consecutive blocks.

Arboricity. The *arboricity* is an important notion in graph theory for describing the density of a graph. Formally, the arboricity of a graph G, which is commonly denoted as α, is the minimum number of edge-disjoint forests needed to cover the edges of G. For example, the arboricity of the graph in Figure 1 is $\alpha = 2$, because its edges can be partitioned into 2 forests, as shown in Figure 2 (where each forest is actually a tree), whereas apparently no single forest can cover all the edges.

It is not immediately clear from the above definition why α is a metric for graph density. This is made explicit by a classic result due to Nash-Williams:

PROPOSITION 1 ([18]). *If G has at least 2 vertices, its arboricity α equals:*

$$\alpha = \max_{\forall G'} density(G')$$

where $G' = (V', E')$ is a subgraph of G with $|V'| \geq 2$, and

$$density(G') = \left\lceil \frac{|E'|}{|V'| - 1} \right\rceil.$$

Phrased differently, the arboricity is determined by the densest subgraph of G. In Figure 1, there is more than one densest subgraph: triangle Δ_{123}, for instance, is one, and has a density of $\lceil 3/(3-1) \rceil = 2$.

The proposition leads to the next well-known facts:

COROLLARY 1 ([7]). *The arboricity α of a graph $G = (V, E)$ satisfies:*

1. *$\alpha \leq \lceil \sqrt{|E|} \rceil$ in any case;*
2. *$\alpha = O(1)$ if G is planar.*

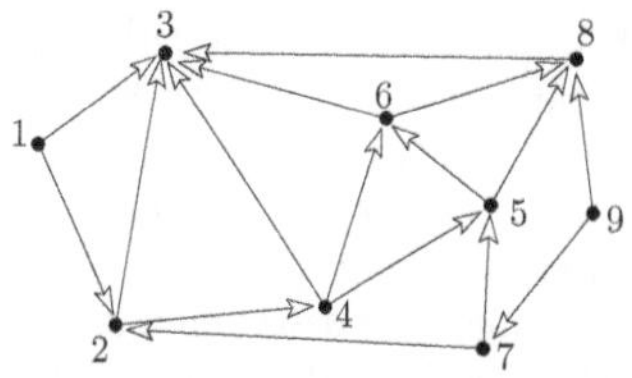

Figure 3: An oriented version of Figure 1

Note that α can reach $\Omega(\sqrt{E})$ when G is dense, e.g., when G is a complete graph so that $|E| = \frac{|V|}{2}(|V| - 1)$. In practice, a graph (e.g., a social network) is much sparser than a clique, and hence, its arboricity is much lower than $\sqrt{|E|}$ (see [7, 16]).

Number of Triangles. As mentioned before, we denote by K the number of triangles in the input graph G. Next, we will get some sense about how large K can possibly be. Consider an edge (u, v) in E. Clearly, any triangle Δ_{uvw} containing the edge must have the property that vertex w is a neighbor of both u and v. As u and v have $d(u)$ and $d(v)$ neighbors respectively, it thus follows that edge (u, v) can appear in at most $\min\{d(u), d(v)\}$ triangles. We therefore have:

$$3K \leq \sum_{(u,v) \in E} \min\{d(u), d(v)\}. \tag{1}$$

Chiba and Nishizeki [7] observed a delicate connection between the above and arboricity:

PROPOSITION 2 ([7]). *The right hand side of* (1) *is bounded by $O(\alpha|E|)$.*

It thus follows that $K = O(\alpha|E|)$. This, in turn, suggests $K = O(|E|^{1.5})$ by Corollary 1. These bounds are tight in the worst case: when the input G is a complete graph, $K = \binom{|V|}{3} = \Omega(|V|^3) = \Omega(|E|^{1.5})$, while $\alpha = \Omega(\sqrt{E})$ as analyzed before.

Oriented Input. As will be clear later, it is sometimes convenient to work with an *oriented* version $G^\star$ of G. To explain, let us define a total order $\prec$ on V: for any two vertices u, v in G, define $u \prec v$ if

- $d(u) < d(v)$, or
- $d(u) = d(v)$ but u has a smaller id than v.

$G^\star$ is obtained by giving a direction to each edge of G that respects $\prec$. That is, for each edge (u, v) of G, we direct it from u to v in $G^\star$ if $u \prec v$. Figure 3 shows the oriented version of the graph in Figure 1.

Henceforth, we will write $G^\star = (V, E^\star)$, where $E^\star$ is the set of directed edges decided as above. An edge $(u, v) \in E^\star$ points from u to v (namely, the vertex ordering in the pair is now important). For each vertex v, $\mathcal{N}^+(v)$ represents the set of its out-neighbors, that is, $\mathcal{N}^+(v) = \{u \mid (v, u) \in E^\star\}$. Define $d^+(v) = |\mathcal{N}^+(v)|$ as the *out-degree* of v.

$G^\star$ is stored in adjacency lists, where the adjacency list of a vertex v contains only $\mathcal{N}^+(v)$ in $O(1 + d^+(v)/B)$ consecutive blocks. For instance, in Figure 3, the adjacency list of vertex 4 is the set {(vertex) 3, 5, 6}. $G^\star$ can be easily computed from G in $O(SORT(|E|))$ I/Os by sorting.

3. PREVIOUS WORK ON TRIANGLE LISTING

The triangle listing problem has been extensively studied in internal memory, yielding a large number of algorithms [7, 12, 14,

15, 20]. All of them finish in time $O(|E|^{1.5})$, which is optimal in the worst case where $K = \Omega(|E|^{1.5})$, because $\Omega(K)$ time is needed just to report the triangles. However, these algorithms are not amenable to external memory, as they entail $\Omega(|E|^{1.5})$ I/Os in the worst case due to memory thrashing.

In this section, we extend the description in Section 1 about the existing I/O-efficient algorithms. Focus will be devoted to the solutions of [9] since they are the state of the art.

3.1 EM-CF

External memory compact forward (EM-CF) [17] accepts an oriented input $G^\star = (V, E^\star)$. For every edge $(u, v) \in E^\star$, it reports a triangle Δ_{uvw} for each $w \in \mathcal{N}^+(u) \cap \mathcal{N}^+(v)$. For example, given edge $(4, 6)$ in Figure 3, it outputs Δ_{463} because vertex 3 is the only common vertex in $\mathcal{N}^+(4) = \{3, 5, 6\}$ and $\mathcal{N}^+(6) = \{3, 8\}$.

Menegola [17] proved that $\mathcal{N}^+(u) \cap \mathcal{N}^+(v)$ can be obtained with $O(1 + \sqrt{|E|}/B)$ I/Os. Thus, the total I/O overhead is $O(|E| + |E|^{1.5}/B)$.

3.2 EM-NI

External memory node iterator (EM-NI) [11] also takes an oriented input $G^\star = (V, E^\star)$. It executes in two steps:

1. Obtain the set L of all pairs $(u, \{v, w\})$ such that $(u, v) \in E^\star$ and $(u, w) \in E^\star$.
2. For each $(u, \{v, w\}) \in L$, check whether $E^\star$ has an edge between v and w, and if so, report Δ_{uvw}.

For example, given the input of Figure 3, the first step returns $L = \{(1, \{2, 3\}), (2, \{3, 4\}), (4, \{3, 6\}), (4, \{5, 6\}), (4, \{3, 5\}), (5, \{6, 8\}), (6, \{3, 8\}), (7, \{2, 5\}), (9, \{7, 8\})\}$, where each number is a vertex id. The second step then verifies that every pair produces a triangle except $(4, \{3, 5\})$, $(7, \{2, 5\})$ and $(9, \{7, 8\})$.

Dementiev [11] showed how to perform the two steps in $O(|E|/B + |L|/B \cdot \log_{M/B}(|E|/B))$ I/Os. Menegola [17] further proved $|L| = O(|E|^{1.5})$. It thus follows that EM-NI terminates in $O(|E|^{1.5}/B \cdot \log_{M/B}(|E|/B))$ I/Os.

3.3 Graph Partition

Chu and Cheng [8, 9] proposed an algorithmic framework, which we call *graph partition* (GP), for triangle listing. As explained shortly, instantiation of the framework gives rise to different concrete algorithms.

The Framework. Given an input graph $G = (V, E)$ (*not* its oriented version), the framework divides V into disjoint *partitions* $V_1, ..., V_p$. The value of p and the partitioning strategy are precisely what are to be instantiated later. Every triangle Δ_{uvw} in G can now be classified into one of the following:

- **Type-I:** the three vertices u, v, w belong to the same partition.
- **Type-II:** two vertices are in the same partition, while the remaining vertex is in a different partition.
- **Type-III:** the three vertices are in distinct partitions.

For example, assume G to be the graph in Figure 1. Let $p = 3$ and $V_1 = \{1, 2, 3\}$, $V_2 = \{4, 5, 6\}$, and $\{7, 8, 9\}$. Then, Δ_{123}, Δ_{234} and Δ_{368} are of type-I, -II, and -III respectively.

Next, the GP framework reports all the type-I and -II triangles, by resorting to the concept of *extended subgraph*, each of which is a subgraph G_i $(1 \leq i \leq p)$ constructed from a partition V_i. Specifically, G_i is the subgraph induced by the edges adjacent to

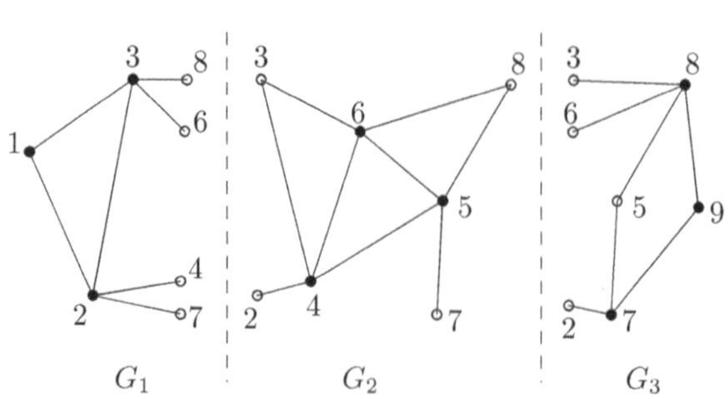

Figure 4: Extended subgraphs

the vertices of V_i. Figure 4 demonstrates G_1, G_2, G_3 in the aforementioned example on Figure 1. Note that an extended subgraph G_i may contain some vertices absent in V_i. For example, the white vertices 4, 6, 7, 8 are not in V_1, but appear in G_1 because each of them is a neighbor of a vertex in V_1.

Every triangle of type-I and -II exists in a unique extended subgraph. Making an assumption:

$\boldsymbol{A_1}$**:** Each extended subgraph fits in memory

the GP framework finds those triangles by loading each G_i into memory, and invoking an in-memory triangle listing algorithm.

It remains to report type-III triangles. The framework achieves this goal by converting type-III triangles to the previous types. Observe that a type-III triangle does not use any *intra edge*, i.e., an edge with *both* endpoints in the same partition (e.g., the edges between black vertices in Figure 4). Motivated by this, the GP framework removes all intra edges, and repeat the above on the remaining edges of G, i.e., launching another *iteration*. In a new iteration, the vertices are partitioned differently, so that a type-III triangle of a previous iteration may now become type-I or -II, and hence can be reported.

The partitioning strategy should guarantee $\Omega(M)$ intra edges in every iteration. Therefore, after $O(|E|/M)$ iterations, the left-over edges of G will fit in memory, at which point an in-memory algorithm is deployed to find all the missing triangles.

Deterministic Graph Partitioning (DGP). This algorithm, an instantiation of the above framework, adopts a deterministic strategy to partition V into $V_1, ..., V_p$. Assuming:

$$\boldsymbol{A_2}\textbf{:}\ |V| \leq M.$$

DGP first finds an *independent dominating set* D of V. Specifically, D is a maximal set of vertices such that (i) no two vertices in D are adjacent, and (ii) every vertex in V is either in D, or adjacent to a vertex in D. For example, in Figure 1, such a set can be $D = \{1, 4, 7, 8\}$. Then, DGP generates $p = \min\{|D|, \Theta(|E|/M)\}$ partitions based on D (see [9] for details).

Randomized Graph Partitioning (RGP). As another instantiation, RGP sets $p = \Theta(|E|/M)$ and generates $V_1, ..., V_p$ with a randomized approach: each vertex in V is independently assigned to V_i, where i is chosen uniformly at random from 1 to p.

Discussion on the Assumptions. The efficiency of the GP framework relies on Assumption $\boldsymbol{A_1}$. If $\boldsymbol{A_1}$ does not hold, the in-memory algorithm that the framework uses to find triangles in an extended subgraph G_i will incur memory thrashing, and thus suffer from heavy performance penalty.

Unfortunately, the assumption will *definitely* be violated on DGP in the worst case. To see this, consider that G is a complete graph such that $|V| < M \ll |E| = \binom{|V|}{2}$. It is easy to verify that D can contain only 1 vertex in this case. As a result, $p = 1$, and hence, the

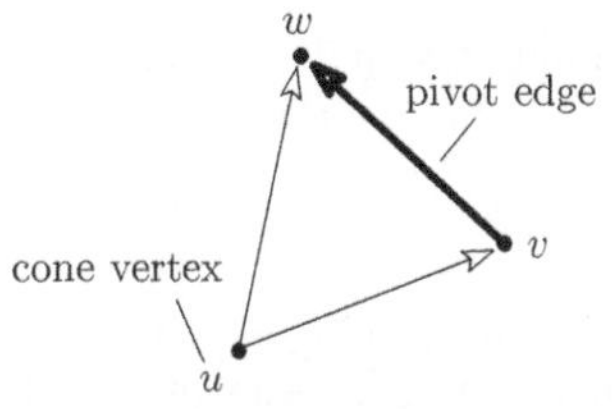

Figure 5: A triangle in $G^\star$ and its pivot edge ($u \prec v \prec w$)

extended subgraph G_1 obtained from V_1 is exactly G itself, which does not fit in memory.

On the other hand, the question whether $\boldsymbol{A_1}$ holds on RGP (with sufficiently high probability) was left open in [9], and still remains unanswered. In this paper, we will close the issue by proving a positive answer based on a non-trivial analysis in Section 5.2.

Chu and Cheng [9] showed that under the assumption:

$$\boldsymbol{A_3}\text{: } p = O(M/B), \text{ that is, } M = \Omega(\sqrt{|E| \cdot B})$$

DGP and RGP ensure I/O complexity[3] $O(|E|^2/(MB) + K/B)$, given the simultaneous satisfaction of Assumption $\boldsymbol{A_1}$ and (for DGP) $\boldsymbol{A_2}$.

It is worth mentioning that $\boldsymbol{A_3}$ is necessary to generate p extended subgraphs in $O(|E|/B)$ I/Os (because a block of memory needs to be reserved as the output buffer for each extended subgraph). This assumption can be removed by turning to sorting, but at the expense of increasing the I/O complexities of DGP and RGP to $O(|E|^2/(MB) \cdot \log_{M/B}(|E|/B) + K/B)$.

4. A NEW ALGORITHM

This section presents a new algorithm called *massive graph triangulation* (MGT), which settles triangle listing with $O(|E|^2/(MB) + K/B)$ I/Os in all circumstances, namely, needing no assumption at all. In the meantime, MGT entails only $O(|E| \log |E| + |E|^2/M + \alpha|E|)$ CPU time, where α is the arboricity of the input graph (see Section 2). Both the I/O and CPU complexities are worst-case optimal as we will prove later.

4.1 Guaranteeing I/O-Efficiency

We will first describe MGT by focusing *only* on I/O efficiency, i.e., pretending that all CPU operations were for free. The algorithm accepts an oriented input $G^\star = (V, E^\star)$ as defined in Section 2, which can be computed from the original input $G = (V, E)$ in $O(SORT(|E|))$ I/Os.

Pivot Edge. Let us make an observation about how a triangle Δ_{uvw} of G appears in the oriented graph $G^\star$. Recall that there is a total order $\prec$ on the vertices of V. Assume, without loss of generality, that $u \prec v \prec w$. Thus, the edges of Δ_{uvw} have directions as illustrated in Figure 5. In particular, u, v and w have 2, 1 and 0 outgoing edges in the triangle, respectively. We refer to the outgoing edge of v as the *pivot edge* of Δ_{uvw}, and u as the *cone vertex* of Δ_{uvw}.

Algorithm. MGT runs in *iterations*, each performing two steps:

1. Load into memory the next cM edges in $E^\star$, where $c < 1$ is a constant to be decided later. Let E_{mem} be the set of those edges.

2. Report all the triangles whose pivot edges are in E_{mem}.

MGT correctly finds all triangles because (i) Step 1 ensures every edge of $E^\star$ to appear in E_{mem} in a unique iteration, and (ii) for any triangle Δ, Step 2 guarantees its discovery in the iteration where E_{mem} contains the pivot edge of Δ.

[3]The complexity is expected for RGP.

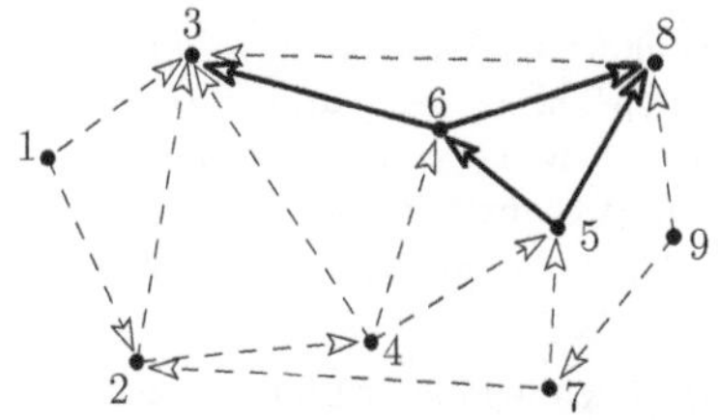

Figure 6: Illustration of Step 2 (solid edges are in E_{mem})

Details of Step 2. Next, we show how to implement Step 2 in $O(|E|/B)$ I/Os, plus the minimum cost of outputting the triangles found.

Algorithm 1: STEP 2 (VERSION 1)

Input: $G^\star = (V, E^\star)$ and a set E_{mem} of edges in memory
Output: All triangles whose pivot edges are in E_{mem}

```
obtain V_mem from E_mem
for each vertex u ∈ V do
    read N+(u) from disk to acquire N_mem(u) in memory
    S ← the set of edges from u to the vertices in N_mem(u)
    find in S ∪ E_mem all the triangles where u is the cone
    vertex
    release N_mem(u) and S from memory
return
```

Let V_{mem} be the set of vertices induced by the edges in the E_{mem} returned by Step 1. For example, suppose that E_{mem} consists of the solid edges in Figure 6; then $V_{mem} = \{3, 5, 6, 8\}$. In this case, Step 2 ought to output Δ_{436}, Δ_{456}, and Δ_{568} because their pivot edges $(3, 6)$, $(5, 6)$, and $(6, 8)$ are in E_{mem}.

Step 2 processes each vertex $u \in V$ in turn as follows. First, define:

$$\mathcal{N}_{mem}(u) \quad = \quad \mathcal{N}^+(u) \cap V_{mem} \tag{2}$$

namely, $\mathcal{N}_{mem}(u)$ is the set of out-neighbors of u that appear in V_{mem}. We obtain $\mathcal{N}_{mem}(u)$ by reading the adjacency list $\mathcal{N}^+(u)$ from the disk, while in the meantime adding a vertex $v \in \mathcal{N}^+(u)$ to $\mathcal{N}_{mem}(u)$ if $v \in V_{mem}$. Note that

$$|\mathcal{N}_{mem}(u)| \leq |V_{mem}| \leq 2|E_{mem}| \leq 2cM.$$

Hence, by setting c appropriately[4], E_{mem} and $\mathcal{N}_{mem}(u)$ together occupy at most M words of storage, and can co-exist in memory.

The knowledge of $\mathcal{N}_{mem}(u)$ essentially "augments" E_{mem} with up to $|\mathcal{N}_{mem}(u)|$ edges leaving u. For instance, the processing of vertex 4 in Figure 6 gives $\mathcal{N}_{mem}(4) = \{3, 5, 6\}$. Effectively, $\mathcal{N}_{mem}(4)$ permits us to "see" 3 more edges in memory: $(4, 3)$, $(4, 5)$ and $(4, 6)$.

As a crucial fact, *if a triangle Δ_{uvw} (where u is the cone vertex) should be reported by Step 2, it can now be discovered in memory.* To understand, recall that Step 2 needs to report Δ_{uvw} only if the pivot edge $(v, w) \in E_{mem}$. This implies that v and w both belong to V_{mem}, and hence, also to $\mathcal{N}_{mem}(u)$. It follows that edges (u, v) and (u, w) have been "augmented" into memory.

For illustration, consider again vertex 4 in Figure 6. As mentioned before, $\mathcal{N}_{mem}(4)$ reveals edges $(4, 3)$, $(4, 5)$ and $(4, 6)$ in

[4]For example, c can be $1/4$ in a naive implementation where an edge requires two words to store.

memory. At this moment, Δ_{463} and Δ_{456} (which are the triangles of vertex 4 that Step 2 needs to report) are memory resident.

After processing u, we clear $\mathcal{N}_{mem}(u)$ from memory, and move on to handle the next vertex of V. Note that E_{mem} is kept in memory throughout Step 2. Algorithm 1 summarizes the above in pseudocode.

I/O Complexity. Each iteration performs one scan over the adjacency lists of all vertices in $O(|E|/B)$ I/Os. The number of iterations is $\Theta(|E|/M)$ because each of them loads $\Theta(M)$ distinct edges of $E^\star$ into E_{mem}, except possibly the last iteration. This, as well as the fact that $\Theta(B)$ triangles can be reported in one I/O, proves that the I/O cost of MGT is bounded by $O(|E|^2/(MB) + K/B)$.

4.2 A CPU-Efficient Algorithm

The MGT algorithm described in the previous section does not achieve the desired bound $O(|E|\log|E| + |E|^2/M + \alpha|E|)$ on CPU time. Towards that purpose, we will modify the algorithm with extra ideas. This subsection will do so under the *small-degree assumption*:

$$d^+(v) \leq cM/2 \quad \text{for all } v \in V \tag{3}$$

where c is the same constant as in our earlier description. Recall that $d^+(v)$ is the out-degree of v in $G^\star$. Section 4.4 will remove this assumption, and obtain the final version of MGT that guarantees the claimed I/O and CPU bounds in all cases.

All-or-Nothing Requirement. Previously, the E_{mem} of an iteration is permitted to include cM arbitrary edges of $E^\star$. Now we require that E_{mem} should contain either *all* the outgoing edges of v or *none* of it, for every $v \in V$. For instance, the set E_{mem} in Figure 6 satisfies this *all-or-nothing requirement*.

We fulfill the requirement by processing one vertex at a time in Step 1 (of MGT). Specifically, let v be the next vertex whose outgoing edges have never appeared in E_{mem}. We add all its outgoing edges to E_{mem} if the size of the resulting E_{mem} does not exceed cM. Otherwise, v is left to the next iteration; and Step 1 terminates here by returning the current E_{mem}. This can also be described in pseudocode as:

Algorithm 2: STEP 1

```
Input: G* = (V, E*)
Output: A set E_mem of at least cM/2 edges in E*
E_mem ← ∅
for each vertex v ∈ V whose edges have never entered E_mem do
    if |N+(v)| + |E_mem| ≤ cM then
        add all the edges of v to E_mem
    else
        break
return E_mem
```

The above strategy may end up with an E_{mem} with less than cM edges. However, under the small-degree assumption, except the last iteration $|E_{mem}|$ must be at least $cM/2$, because if $|E_{mem}| < cM/2$, then E_{mem} should have been able to take in the (at most $cM/2$) outgoing edges of one more vertex.

Step 2 of MGT proceeds as described earlier. Since $|E_{mem}|$ is still $\Theta(M)$ except possibly in the final iteration, the I/O complexity of the algorithm remains bounded by $O(|E|^2/(MB) + K/B)$.

CPU-Implementation of Step 2. Our description so far has ignored all the in-memory operations, the details of which are to be filled in next. Define

$$V^+_{mem} = \{v \in V_{mem} \mid v \text{ has an outgoing edge in } E_{mem}\}$$

For example, in the example of Figure 6, $V^+_{mem} = \{5, 6\}$. Vertices 3 and 8, which belong to V_{mem}, are not in V^+_{mem} because they have no outgoing edge in E_{mem}.

We create hash structures on V_{mem}, V^+_{mem}, E_{mem} so that:

- Given any vertex v, whether $v \in V_{mem}$ and/or $v \in V^+_{mem}$ can be decided in $O(1)$ time.
- Given any vertices u, v, whether $(u, v) \in E_{mem}$ can be decided in $O(1)$ time.

Clearly, these hash structures occupy only $O(|E_{mem}|)$ space.

For each vertex $u \in V$, Step 2 needs to report all the triangles Δ_{uvw} where $u \prec v \prec w$ and the pivot edge (v, w) exists in E_{mem}. Expanding the procedure in Section 4.1, we first obtain $\mathcal{N}_{mem}(u)$ in $O(|\mathcal{N}^+(u)|)$ time, by using constant time to check whether $v \in V_{mem}$ for each $v \in \mathcal{N}^+(u)$. We then further acquire:

$$\mathcal{N}^+_{mem}(u) = \mathcal{N}_{mem}(u) \cap V^+_{mem}$$

in $O(|\mathcal{N}_{mem}(u)|) = O(|\mathcal{N}^+(u)|)$ time, by checking whether $v \in V^+_{mem}$ for each $v \in \mathcal{N}_{mem}(u)$. In Figure 6, for instance, when u is vertex 4, we have $\mathcal{N}_{mem}(4) = \{3, 5, 6\}$ and $\mathcal{N}^+_{mem}(4) = \{5, 6\}$.

Next, we use $O(|\mathcal{N}^+_{mem}(u)| \cdot |\mathcal{N}_{mem}(u)|)$ time to find the triangles of u that should be reported in the current iteration. For each vertex pair

$$(v, w) \in \mathcal{N}^+_{mem}(u) \times \mathcal{N}_{mem}(u) \text{ with } v \neq w$$

check in constant time whether $(v, w) \in E_{mem}$. If so, report Δ_{uvw}. For instance, to process vertex 4 in Figure 6, the algorithm probes edges $(5, 3)$, $(5, 6)$, $(6, 3)$ and $(6, 5)$ in E_{mem}. The second and third exist in E_{mem}, thus spawning Δ_{456} and Δ_{463}. Algorithm 3 restates the above details in pseudocode:

Algorithm 3: STEP 2 (DETAILS EXPANDED)

```
Input: G* = (V, E*) and a set E_mem of edges in memory
Output: All triangles whose pivot edges are in E_mem
obtain V_mem and V+_mem from E_mem
build hash structures on V_mem, V+_mem, and E_mem
for each vertex u ∈ V do
    read N+(u) from disk to acquire N_mem(u) in memory
    obtain N+_mem(u) from N_mem(u) in memory
    for each v ∈ N+_mem(u) do
        for each w ∈ N_mem(u) do
            if v ≠ w and edge (v, w) ∈ E_mem then
                output Δ_uvw
    release N_mem(u) and N+_mem(u) from memory
return
```

The complexity $O(|\mathcal{N}^+_{mem}(u)| \cdot |\mathcal{N}_{mem}(u)|)$ may appear expensive at first glance due to its quadratic nature. Somewhat surprisingly, when one adds up this complexity for all vertices throughout all iterations, the sum turns out to be $O(\alpha|E|)$, as we analyze next.

4.3 Bounding the CPU-Time

This subsection will analyze the CPU time of the modified MGT algorithm under the small-degree assumption. Let us start with a useful fact:

LEMMA 1. $\sum_{v \in V} (d^+(v))^2 = O(\alpha|E|)$.

PROOF. For any $v \in V$:

$$(d^+(v))^2 = d^+(v) \sum_{u \in \mathcal{N}^+(v)} 1 = \sum_{u \in \mathcal{N}^+(v)} d^+(v).$$

Hence:

$$\begin{aligned}
\sum_{v \in V} (d^+(v))^2 &= \sum_{v \in V} \sum_{u \in \mathcal{N}^+(v)} d^+(v) \\
&= \sum_{(v,u) \in E^\star} d^+(v) \\
&\le \sum_{(v,u) \in E^\star} d(v) \\
\text{(by how } (v,u) \text{ is directed)} &= \sum_{(v,u) \in E} \min\{d(v), d(u)\} \\
\text{(by Proposition 2)} &= O(\alpha|E|).
\end{aligned}$$

□

By the discussion of the previous subsection, in an iteration of MGT, Step 2 spends

$$\begin{aligned}
& O(|\mathcal{N}^+(u)| + |\mathcal{N}^+_{mem}(u)| \cdot |\mathcal{N}_{mem}(u)|) \\
= \; & O(|\mathcal{N}^+(u)| + |\mathcal{N}^+_{mem}(u)| \cdot |\mathcal{N}^+(u)|) \qquad (4)
\end{aligned}$$

time on each vertex $u \in V$. The terms $|N^+(u)|$ of all $u \in V$ add up to exactly $|E^\star| = |E|$. Hence, the total contribution by this term throughout all the $\Theta(|E|/M)$ iterations is $O(|E|^2/M)$. Henceforth, we will focus on the second term $|\mathcal{N}^+_{mem}(u)| \cdot |\mathcal{N}^+(u)|$.

Let $h = \Theta(|E|/M)$ be the number of iterations actually performed by MGT. Denote by $\mathcal{N}^+_{mem}(u, i)$ the content of $\mathcal{N}^+_{mem}(u)$ in the i-th iteration, for $1 \le i \le h$. In other words, the total contribution (to the CPU time) of the second term in (4) across all nodes u and all iterations i is at most

$$\sum_{i=1}^{h} \sum_{u \in V} O(|\mathcal{N}^+_{mem}(u, i)| \cdot |\mathcal{N}^+(u)|). \qquad (5)$$

Our all-or-nothing requirement (see Section 4.2) ensures:

LEMMA 2. *$\mathcal{N}^+_{mem}(u, 1)$, ..., $\mathcal{N}^+_{mem}(u, h)$ are mutually disjoint.*

PROOF. The all-or-nothing requirement guarantees that each vertex $v \in V$ belongs to V^+_{mem} in a unique iteration. In other words, the sets V^+_{mem} of all iterations are mutually disjoint. The lemma then follows from the fact $\mathcal{N}^+_{mem}(u, i)$ is a subset of the V^+_{mem} of iteration i, for $1 \le i \le h$. □

As $\mathcal{N}^+_{mem}(u, i) \subseteq \mathcal{N}^+(u)$ for each i, the lemma implies:

$$\sum_{i=1}^{h} |\mathcal{N}^+_{mem}(u, i)| \le |\mathcal{N}^+(u)| = d^+(u).$$

Hence:

$$\sum_{i=1}^{h} \left(|\mathcal{N}^+_{mem}(u, i)| \cdot |\mathcal{N}^+(u)|\right) \le (d^+(u))^2. \qquad (6)$$

Therefore:

$$\begin{aligned}
(5) &= \sum_{u \in V} \sum_{i=1}^{h} O\left(|\mathcal{N}^+_{mem}(u, i)| \cdot |\mathcal{N}^+(u)|\right) \\
\text{(by (6))} &= \sum_{u \in V} O(d^+(u))^2 \\
\text{(by Lemma 1)} &= O(\alpha|E|).
\end{aligned}$$

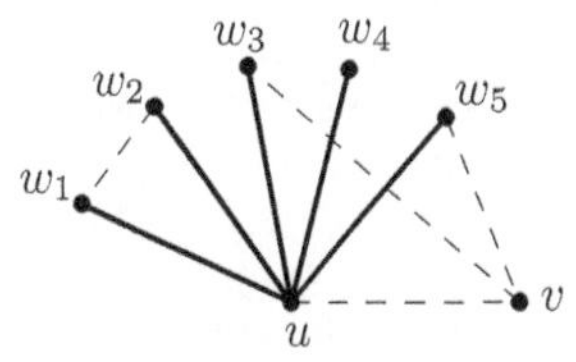

Figure 7: Illustration for the conversion algorithm (S consists of the solid edges)

Finally, recall that the input to the triangle listing problem is an undirected graph G, from which the oriented version $G^\star$ is computed by sorting, which (when implemented as the standard external sort [1]) takes $O(|E| \log |E|)$ CPU time. We thus have proved that MGT entails $O(|E| \log |E| + |E|^2/M + \alpha|E|)$ CPU time overall.

4.4 Removing the Small-Degree Assumption

This subsection presents the last component of our MGT algorithm, which deals with the case where the oriented input $G^\star$ does not satisfy the small-degree assumption (see (3)). In other words, there is at least one vertex v such that $d^+(v) > cM/2$.

MGT handles the case by working on the original (undirected) input G, instead of the oriented version $G^\star$. It removes certain edges of large-degree vertices, while ensuring that all the triangles involving those edges have been reported. The edge removal turns G into another graph G', whose oriented version $G'^\star$ satisfies the small-degree assumption. $G'^\star$ is then fed into the algorithm in Section 4.2 to report the remaining triangles.

Converting G to G'. Given $G = (V, E)$, we carry out the conversion as follows:

1. Identify a vertex $u \in V$ with $d(u) > cM/2$. If u does not exist, the conversion terminates with $G' = G$.
2. Load a set S of $cM/2$ edges[5] of u into memory.
3. Report all the triangles that involve at least one edge in S.
4. Remove the edges in S from E. Repeat from Step 1.

We refer to an execution from Step 1 to 4 as an *iteration*. The number of iterations is bounded by $\Theta(|E|/M)$ because $\Theta(M)$ edges are removed by an iteration. Next, we explain how to implement Step 3 efficiently.

The edges of S form a 2-level tree where u is the root, as shown in Figure 7 where the solid edges constitute S. Let T be the set of leaf vertices of this tree, e.g., $T = \{w_1, w_2, ..., w_5\}$ in Figure 7. Clearly, any triangle Δ involving at least an edge in S must have u as a vertex. Furthermore, Δ must be one of the types below:

- **Type-1:** 2 vertices of Δ are in T.
- **Type-2:** Only 1 vertex of Δ is in T.

In Figure 7, for instance, $\Delta_{uw_1w_2}$ and Δ_{uvw_5} are of type-1 and -2 respectively (note that $u \notin T$).

We create a hash structure on T to permit testing whether $v \in T$ in constant time for any $v \in V$. Both types of triangles can be found easily by a single scan on E. This is in fact obvious for type-1: for every edge $(v, w) \in E$, report Δ_{uvw} if and only if both v and w belong to T.

[5]The value $cM/2$ is chosen to facilitate understanding. In practice, one can load as many edges of u as the memory can accommodate. The algorithm still works the same way as described subsequently.

To find type-2 triangles, we process the adjacency list $\mathcal{N}(v)$ of each vertex $v \neq u$ as follows. First, check whether $u \in \mathcal{N}(v)$, and if not, we are done with v and move on to the next vertex. Otherwise, obtain $T(v) = \mathcal{N}(v) \cap T$ (e.g., $T(v) = \{w_3, w_5\}$ in Figure 7). So far we need to read $\mathcal{N}(v)$ from the disk once, and spend $O(|\mathcal{N}(v)|)$ CPU time. Finally, for every vertex $w \in T(v)$, output a triangle Δ_{uvw}; this requires $O(|T(v)|) = O(|\mathcal{N}(v)|)$ CPU time.

It is thus clear that each iteration of our conversion algorithm performs $O(|E|/B)$ I/Os, and entails $O(|E|)$ CPU time, plus the minimum output cost. Therefore, the overall algorithm has an I/O complexity $O(|E|^2/(MB) + K/B)$ and CPU complexity $O(|E|^2/M + K) = O(|E|^2/M + \alpha|E|)$ (recall from Section 2 that $K = O(\alpha|E|)$).

Putting Everything Together. The graph G' has the property that every vertex $v \in V$ has degree at most $cM/2$. Hence, its oriented version $G'^{\star}$ satisfies the small-degree assumption due to the obvious fact $d^+(v) \leq d(v)$. We can now apply the algorithm of Section 4.2 to find the remaining triangles. It is easy to verify that every triangle in G is reported exactly once. This completes the whole MGT algorithm, which brings us to this paper's first main result:

THEOREM 1. *The MGT algorithm solves the triangle listing problem in $O(|E|^2/(MB) + K/B)$ I/Os and $O(|E|\log|E| + |E|^2/M + \alpha|E|)$ CPU time.*

4.5 Worst-Case Optimality

We now explain why it is impossible to design an algorithm with I/O complexity $o(|E|^2/(MB))$ even when $M = o(|E|)$. Consider that the input G is a complete graph, and $M \geq |V| = \Theta(\sqrt{|E|})$. The number of triangles equals $\binom{|V|}{3} = \Omega(|V|^3)$. Therefore, any algorithm must incur

$$\begin{aligned}\Omega(|V|^3/B) &= \Omega(|E|^{1.5}/B)\\ &= \Omega(|E|^2/(|V|B)) = \Omega(|E|^2/(MB))\end{aligned}$$

I/Os just to report the triangles. This argument shows that the term $|E|^2/(MB)$ is compulsory in the worst case, implying that the I/O complexity in Theorem 1 is already optimal up to a constant factor. Note that *this optimality result holds for any M satisfying $M \geq |V|$*, that is, as long as all the vertices (but not edges) can be stored in memory.

The above finding also implies a lower bound of $\Omega(|E|^2/M)$ on CPU time because $\Omega(|V|^3) = \Omega(|E|^2/M)$ time is needed just to output triangles. This immediately rules out any algorithm with $o(|E|\log|E|)$ CPU time because $|E|\log|E| = o(|E|^2/M)$ when $M = \Theta(\sqrt{E})$. Given also the necessity of the term $\alpha|E|$ (see Section 2), it follows that any algorithm must incur $\Omega(|E|\log|E| + |E|^2/M + \alpha|E|)$ CPU time in the worst case, matching the upper bound in Theorem 1.

5. FINDINGS ON KNOWN ALGORITHMS

This section will strengthen the current understanding about two existing algorithms for triangle listing: EM-NI and RGP, as reviewed in Section 3. For EM-NI, we will reveal for the first time why the algorithm is especially efficient on sparse graphs. For RGP, we will remove a restrictive assumption imposed on its applicability.

5.1 EM-NI

We now prove:

THEOREM 2. *The EM-NI algorithm solves the triangle listing problem in $O(\alpha \cdot SORT(|E|))$ I/Os.*

PROOF. As mentioned in Section 3, the previous work has shown that EM-NI performs $O(\frac{|E|}{B} + \frac{|L|}{B}\log_{M/B}\frac{|E|}{B})$ I/Os. Below, we will show that $|L| = O(\alpha|E|)$ which therefore will establish the theorem because $SORT(|E|) = \Theta(|E|/B \cdot \log_{M/B}(|E|/B))$.

Let $G^{\star} = (V, E^{\star})$ be the oriented input to EM-NI. Recall that L is the set of all such pairs $(u, \{v, w\})$ that (u, v) and (u, w) are both in $E^{\star}$. For each $u \in V$, there are exactly $\binom{d^+(u)}{2}$ such pairs, where $d^+(u)$ is the out-degree of u. Therefore:

$$|L| = \sum_{u \in V}\binom{d^+(u)}{2} \leq \sum_{u \in V}(d^+(u))^2$$

which is $O(\alpha|E|)$ by Lemma 1. □

Previously, the I/O-complexity of EM-NI was understood as $O(|E|^{1.5}/B \cdot \log_{M/B}(|E|/B))$ (see Section 3). Hence, Theorem 2 is separated from the old result whenever $\alpha = o(\sqrt{|E|})$. Moreover, Theorem 2 clearly indicates that the I/O efficiency of EM-NI depends linearly on α, which as discussed in Section 2 measures the graph density. In particular, when G is planar, $\alpha = O(1)$ (see Corollary 1), in which case EM-NI finishes in $O(SORT(|E|))$ I/Os.

Theorem 2 makes it possible to compare EM-NI and our MGT algorithm in a more sensible manner. Interestingly, *EM-NI never has a better complexity as long as $M \geq |V|$*. To see this, first notice that:

$$\alpha \geq \frac{|E|}{|V| - 1}. \tag{7}$$

The above inequality results directly from the definition of α as the minimum number of edge-disjoint forests needed to cover all the edges of E: as each forest has at most $|V| - 1$ edges, at least $|E|/(|V| - 1)$ forests are needed to cover all the $|E|$ edges. Therefore, when $M \geq |V|$,

$$\alpha > |E|/|V| \geq |E|/M$$

which makes

$$|E|^2/(MB) < \alpha|E|/B < \alpha \cdot SORT(|E|)$$

namely, the I/O complexity in Theorem 2 is never better than that in Theorem 1.

5.2 RGP

Recall from Section 3 that the graph partition framework [9], which is the state of the art, relies on a key assumption $\boldsymbol{A_1}$ to attain its I/O efficiency. Chu and Cheng [9] instantiated the framework into the DGP and RGP algorithms. As explained in Section 3, unfortunately, Assumption $\boldsymbol{A_1}$ is inherent in DGP and thus impossible to remove. However, it remains open whether the assumption can be eliminated on RGP. The rest of the subsection will answer this question almost in all scenarios.

We will need the following Chernoff bound:

PROPOSITION 3 ([2]). *Let $X_1, ..., X_n$ be independent random variables between 0 and 1. Let $X = \sum_{i=1}^{n} X_i$ and $\mu = \sum_{i=1}^{n} \mathbf{E}[X_i]$. Then:*

$$\mathbf{Pr}[X \geq 2\mu] \leq \exp(-\mu/3).$$

The remainder of this subsection will follow the notations in Section 3.3. In addition, let d_{max} be the largest degree of the vertices in the input graph $G = (V, E)$. We now present the last main result of this paper:

THEOREM 3. *Under the condition:*

$$\boldsymbol{A_4}\text{: } M \geq 24 d_{max} \ln |E|,$$

Assumption $\boldsymbol{A_1}$ *holds with probability at least* $1 - 1/|E|$.

PROOF. Set $p = c|E|/M$ where c is a constant to be decided later. For each vertex $v \in V$ and each $i \in [1, p]$, define

$$X_i(v) = \begin{cases} d(v) & \text{if } v \in V_i \\ 0 & \text{otherwise} \end{cases}$$

As v is assigned to V_i with probability $1/p$, $\mathbf{E}[X_i(v)] = d(v)/p$.

Let $X_i = \sum_{v \in V} X_i(v)$, namely, X_i is the sum of the degrees of all vertices in G_i. Let Y_i be the number of edges in the extended subgraph G_i obtained from V_i. We observe:

$$Y_i \leq X_i. \tag{8}$$

The inequality holds because every edge in G_i is counted at least once by X_i. Clearly:

$$\mathbf{E}[X_i] = \sum_{v \in V} \mathbf{E}[X_i(v)] = \sum_{v \in V} \frac{d(v)}{p} = \frac{2|E|}{p} = \frac{2M}{c}.$$

The random variables $X_i(v)$ of different $v \in V$ are mutually independent. Furthermore, $X_i(v) \leq d_{max}$. Hence, applying Chernoff bound (Proposition 3) on the random variables $Z_i(v) = X_i(v)/d_{max}$ of all $v \in V$ gives:

$$\mathbf{Pr}\left[\sum_{v \in V} Z_i(v) \geq \frac{4M}{c \cdot d_{max}}\right] \leq \exp\left(-\frac{2M}{3c \cdot d_{max}}\right) \Rightarrow$$

$$\mathbf{Pr}\left[X_i \geq \frac{4M}{c}\right] \leq \exp\left(-\frac{2M}{3c \cdot d_{max}}\right) \tag{9}$$

When $M \geq 3c \cdot d_{max} \ln |E|$, it holds that

$$\exp\left(-\frac{2M}{3c \cdot d_{max}}\right) \leq \frac{1}{|E|^2} < \frac{1}{|E|} \cdot \frac{M}{c|E|} = \frac{1}{p|E|}$$

with which (9) gives:

$$\mathbf{Pr}\left[X_i \geq \frac{4M}{c}\right] \leq \frac{1}{p|E|} \tag{10}$$

G_i can be stored in at most $2Y_i$ words, which by (8) is at most $2X_i$ words. Setting $c = 8$, (10) shows that $2X_i \geq M$ occurs with probability at most $1/(p|E|)$ when $M \geq 24 d_{max} \ln |E|$, namely, the probability for G_i not to fit in memory is at most $1/(p|E|)$.

Therefore, when $\boldsymbol{A_4}$ holds, the probability that *any* of $G_1, ..., G_p$ does not fit in memory is at most $1/|E|$, thus completing the proof. □

For a massive input graph G with a massive E, Theorem 3 shows that $\boldsymbol{A_1}$ holds with extremely high probability as long as the memory is not too small. Note that condition $\boldsymbol{A_4}$ is tight up to only a logarithmic factor, because *when* $M < d_{max}$, $\boldsymbol{A_1}$ *can never be satisfied* such that not only RGP but also the graph partition framework itself will not be able to function. To see this, let v be the vertex in G with degree d_{max}, and suppose that $v \in V_i$, for some $i \in [1, p]$. Then, the extended subgraph G_i created from V_i must contain at least d_{max} edges, and therefore, does not fit in memory.

Theorem 3 has reduced the assumptions on RGP's applicability to only $\boldsymbol{A_3}$ and $\boldsymbol{A_4}$, both of which appear reasonable given the memory capacity of today's machines. Perhaps more important is the fact that $\boldsymbol{A_3}$ and $\boldsymbol{A_4}$ can be checked efficiently, by scanning the input graph at most once to glean $|E|$ and d_{max}. In contrast, there does not appear a way to check the original assumption $\boldsymbol{A_1}$, except for letting the algorithm run anyway.

6. EXPERIMENTS

In this section, we experimentally compare the proposed algorithm against the previous methods for triangle listing in external memory. The next subsection will explain the environments where our experiments were performed. Then, Section 6.2 (6.3) evaluates the efficiency of alternative solutions on real (synthetic) datasets.

6.1 Environmental Setup

All the experiments were performed under Linux (specifically Ubuntu 12.04) on a machine that was running an Intel 3GHz CPU (dual core) and was equipped with 8 giga bytes of memory. The block size B, which was fixed by the operating system, was equal to 4k bytes.

We compared our MGT algorithm against the existing I/O-efficient solutions to triangle listing, namely, EM-CF, EM-NI, DGP and RGP, all of which have been reviewed in Section 3. We implemented all the algorithms in C++, using the gcc compiler with the optimizer option O3. Our implementation is fully memory conscious. Namely, the binary executable of each algorithm accepts (among others) a parameter M that specifies in number of bytes how much memory can be used. It is guaranteed that the algorithm makes full use of the allocated memory, but its memory usage at any instant never exceeds M.

We measured the cost of an algorithm in two aspects: number of I/Os, and overall running time. The former was counted by strictly adhering to the standard external memory model [1], namely, an I/O reads a block from the disk into memory, or conversely, writes B words in memory to a disk block. The total running time, on the other hand, was measured as the amount of wall-clock time elapsed during the algorithm's execution.

In all cases, the input graph was given in adjacency lists *without* orientation. This is precisely the format assumed by DGP and RGP. If an algorithm (i.e., MGT, EM-CF, and EM-NI) requires an oriented version of the graph (as defined in Section 2), it carried out the orientation on the fly. For these algorithms, each cost we report later has always included the overhead incurred from performing the orientation. Finally, we exclude the output cost (i.e., the time to report the triangles found) because it is identical for all algorithms as they must return exactly the same set of triangles.

6.2 Performance on Real Data

Datasets and Methodology. We deployed exactly the same real datasets as were used in [9] where state-of-the-art DGP and RGP were developed. These datasets are named *LJ*, *USRD*, *WebUK* and *BTC* respectively, whose meta information is displayed as below[6]:

	LJ	*USRD*	*BTC*	*WebUK*
$\lvert V\rvert$	4,846,609	23,947,347	164,660,997	62,338,347
$\lvert E\rvert$	42,851,237	28,854,312	386,411,047	938,715,528
$\lvert E\rvert/\lvert V\rvert$	8.84	1.20	2.35	15.06
disk size	364 M	403 M	4.1 G	7.5 G

Table 1: Meta data of real graphs

More specifically, *LJ* represents a social network (see *http://www.livejournal.com*) where a vertex corresponds to an individual, and an edge indicates friendship between two persons. *USRD*, on the other hand, is a part of the US road network, where a vertex (edge) is a road junction (segment). *BTC* is an object relational graph where a vertex is a real-world object, and an edge

[6]The graph sizes listed here are different from those provided in [9], which, however, is due to the errors in [9], as has been verified by our communication with the authors of [9].

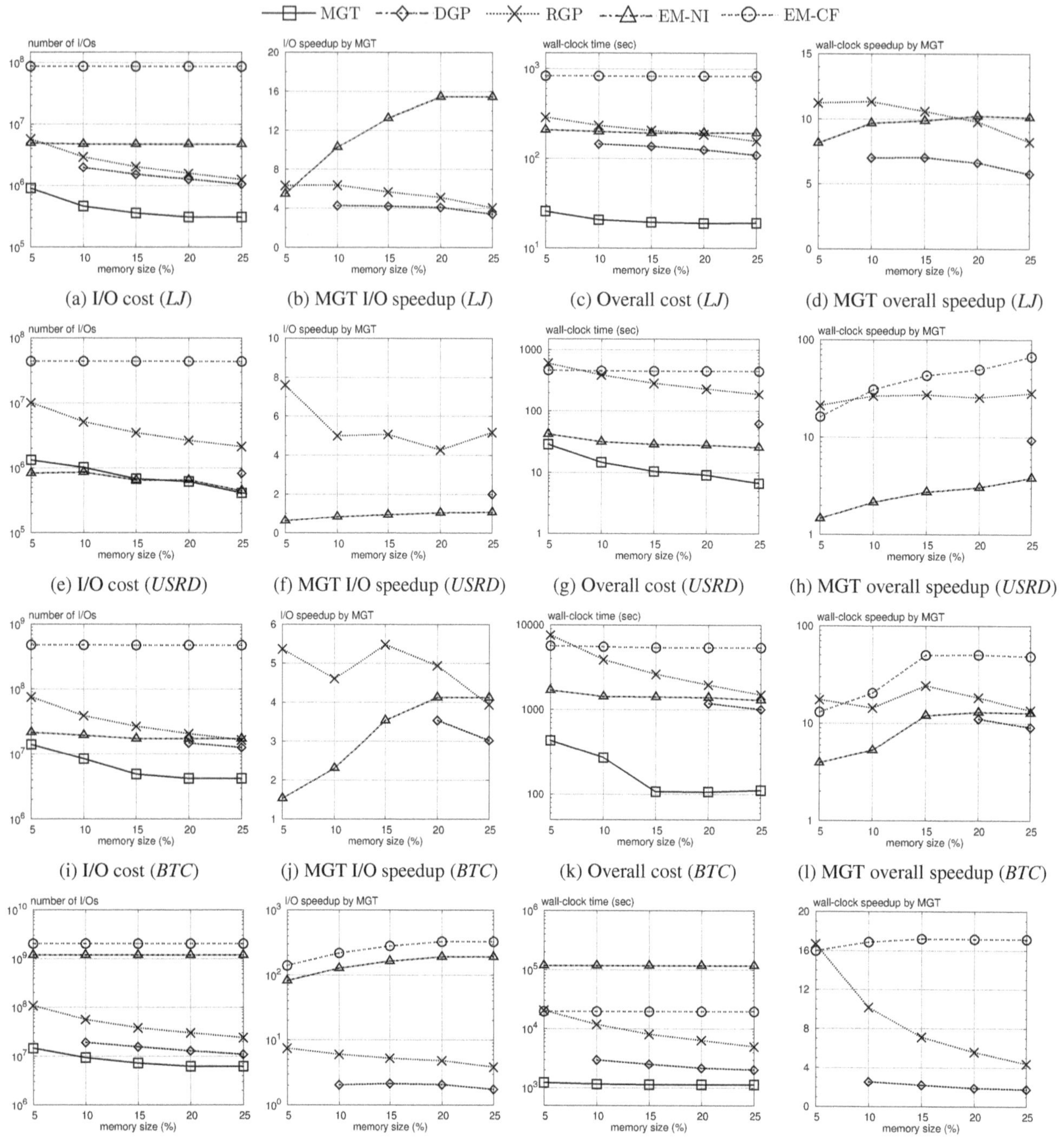

(a) I/O cost (*LJ*) (b) MGT I/O speedup (*LJ*) (c) Overall cost (*LJ*) (d) MGT overall speedup (*LJ*)

(e) I/O cost (*USRD*) (f) MGT I/O speedup (*USRD*) (g) Overall cost (*USRD*) (h) MGT overall speedup (*USRD*)

(i) I/O cost (*BTC*) (j) MGT I/O speedup (*BTC*) (k) Overall cost (*BTC*) (l) MGT overall speedup (*BTC*)

(m) I/O cost (*WebUK*) (n) MGT I/O speedup (*WebUK*) (o) Overall cost (*WebUK*) (p) MGT overall speedup (*WebUK*)

Figure 8: Efficiency comparison on real graphs

reflects a certain relationship between two objects (e.g., a person *owns* an item). This graph was obtained from the RDF dataset of the Billion Triple Challenge 2009 (*http://vmlion25.deri.ie*). Finally, *WebUK* captures the hyperlinks (i.e., edges) among a set of web pages (i.e., vertices) gathered for investigation of web spams (*http://barcelona.research.yahoo.net*).

Clearly, the amount M of memory allocated to an algorithm is the most crucial factor behind its efficiency. If M is so large that the entire input graph fits in memory, all algorithms will behave similarly because they essentially degenerate into in-memory triangle listing. The key of evaluating an external memory algorithm lies in examining how well it performs when only a fraction of the dataset fits in memory. Motivated by this, for each input graph, we varied M from 5% of the graph's disk size (see Table 1) to 25%, and in the meantime, compared the performance of different algorithms.

Results. Figure 8 presents all the results of the experiments on the real graphs. In the first row, Figure 8a plots the I/O cost of each algorithm on dataset *LJ* as a function of the memory size. Let the *I/O speedup* of MGT over another algorithm X be defined as the ratio between the numbers of I/Os entailed by X and MGT, respectively (e.g., an I/O speedup 2 means that MGT needs half as many I/Os as X). Figure 8b shows the I/O speedups of MGT over the other algorithms as the memory grows. Figures 8c and 8d demonstrate the corresponding results on the overall running time, noticing that *wall-clock speedup* of MGT is defined by extending I/O-speedup straightforwardly to wall-clock time. The second, third, and last rows of Figure 8 present the outcome of the same experiments on *USRD*, *BTC* and *WebUK*, respectively.

In Figure 8, EM-CF and EM-NI are sometimes omitted from a "speedup diagram" if MGT achieves an exceedingly high speedup over them. For example, EM-CF is absent from Figure 8b because it incurred over 100 times more I/Os than MGT (as a result, the inclusion of EM-CF would destroy the diagram's clarity). On the other hand, the disappearance of DGP from a diagram is *always due to its inapplicability*. Recall that this algorithm is subject to several assumptions as discussed in Section 3.3. If any of Assumptions $\boldsymbol{A_1}$, $\boldsymbol{A_2}$ and $\boldsymbol{A_3}$ is violated, DGP fails to execute. In fact, DGP failed in at least one setting on every dataset: specifically, $M = 5\%, \leq 20\%, \leq 15\%$ and $= 5\%$ for *LJ*, *USRD*, *BTC* and *WebUK*, respectively. All failures were due to violation of Assumption $\boldsymbol{A_2}$ with only one exception: the failure on *WebUK* ($M = 5\%$) was due to $\boldsymbol{A_1}$. RGP, on the other hand, never failed in any of our experiments. This is perfectly explainable: our analysis in Section 5.2 has reduced its assumptions to $\boldsymbol{A_3}$ and $\boldsymbol{A_4}$, both of which were easily satisfied in our settings.

It is evident from Figure 8 that MGT exhibited by far the best performance overall. In a majority of cases, it significantly outperformed all its competitors in both I/O and CPU efficiency. Further observe that, against every other method, MGT was faster in overall execution time by a factor over an order of magnitude in at least one experiment. These findings confirm the high effectiveness of the proposed techniques in practice, in addition to their rigorous theoretical guarantees which have already been established in earlier sections.

Regarding the other algorithms, EM-CF is clearly the worst-performing solution. This is not surprising because, as mentioned in Section 3.1, its I/O complexity is even greater than $\Omega(|E|)$, which is already prohibitively expensive in reality. EM-NI, on the other hand, is very sensitive to the graph density, as predicted by our analysis in Section 5.1. When the density is low, this algorithm can be fairly efficient, as can be seen from its performance on *USRD* (which is nearly planar). Unfortunately, with the increase of density, the cost of this algorithm grows dramatically, in fact to such an extent that it can be even more expensive than EM-CF (see Figure 8o). DGP is a capable method in the sense that, when it did not fail, it demonstrated acceptable performance (although still several times slower than MGT). Finally, RGP, which enjoys the same I/O complexity as MGT, apparently has a much larger hidden constant in its complexity.

6.3 Performance on Synthetic Data

Datasets and Methodology. Having established the superiority of our MGT algorithm on real data, we now proceed with a set of controlled experiments that aims at comparing the competing algorithms on different types of graphs, and evaluating their scalability with the graph size. Towards this purpose, we generated graphs of three distributions:

- **Random** (*RAND*): Given a pair of values n and m, we generated a random graph with n vertices by creating m edges, each of which connects a vertex pair chosen uniformly at random. This was followed by a clean-up process to eliminate duplicate edges between the same pair of vertices.

- **Recursive Matrix** (*R-MAT*): Proposed by Chakrabarti et al. [5], this model has gained considerable popularity due to its simplicity and ability to emulate a large variety of graphs in reality. It captures the fact that the vertex degree distribution of a real graph often *resembles but is not exactly* a power law. Given a pair of n and m, we created an *R-MAT* graph of n vertices and m edges using the generator published at *http://www.cse.psu.edu/~madduri/software/GTgraph* with its default parameters (the same *R-MAT* parameters were also used in the experiments of [21, 25]). Finally, duplicate edges were removed by a clean-up process.

- **Small World** (*S-WORLD*): This classic model was first described by Watts and Strogatz [24]. Given n and m where m is a multiple of $2n$, an *S-WORLD* graph was obtained as follows. First, imagine putting n vertices on a circle where each vertex v is connected to its $m/(2n)$ nearest neighbors on the left and right, respectively[7]. This creates m edges in total. Then, independently with probability p, each edge of v is replaced by an edge that connects v to another vertex chosen randomly. At the end, a clean-up process was invoked to remove duplicate edges. We set the model parameter p to 1%, as this was the median value in the experiments of the seminal work [24].

We set $m = 16n$ in all experiments. For each distribution, we generated 5 graphs by varying n from around 16 to 80 million. The following table gives the meta data of all the synthetic graphs after duplicate removal (these figures apply to all distributions):

$\|V\|$	16×2^{20}	32×2^{20}	48×2^{20}	64×2^{20}	80×2^{20}
$\|E\|$	2.7×10^8	5.4×10^8	8.1×10^8	10.7×10^8	13.4×10^8
disk size	2.1 G	4.2 G	6.4 G	8.5 G	10.6 G

Table 2: Meta data of synthetic graphs (all distributions)

For each graph, we inspected the efficiency of all algorithms by fixing the amount of allocated memory to 1 giga bytes. The only exception was EM-CF, which was omitted from further inspection due to its huge uncompetitive running time.

Results. Figure 9 demonstrates the comparison results of MGT, DGP, RGP and EM-NI on synthetic graphs, by focusing on the I/O and wall-clock time in the first and second rows, respectively. DGP has no results on *S-WORLD* graphs when $|V| \leq 32 \times 2^{20}$ because it failed due to the violation of $\boldsymbol{A_1}$.

The relative superiority of different algorithms generally follows the patterns observed earlier from real datasets. In every experiment, MGT outperformed all its competitors by a wide margin in both I/O and CPU efficiency. This phenomenon nicely complements the results of the preceding subsection in showing the robustness of MGT's performance, regardless of the graph distribution and the graph size.

7. CONCLUSIONS

Triangle listing is an important classic problem on graphs that has numerous applications in different domains. Although it has been well studied in internal memory, solving it I/O-efficiently on massive graphs exceeding the memory capacity still remains as a challenging task. Previously, there have been several attempts to tackle the challenge. However, even the state-of-the-art algorithms still entail lengthy execution time, and even so, are haunted by various assumptions that limit the applicability of those algorithms.

[7]The 1st left neighbor of v is the vertex immediately to the left of v on the ring, the 2nd neighbor is the vertex further to the left, and so on.

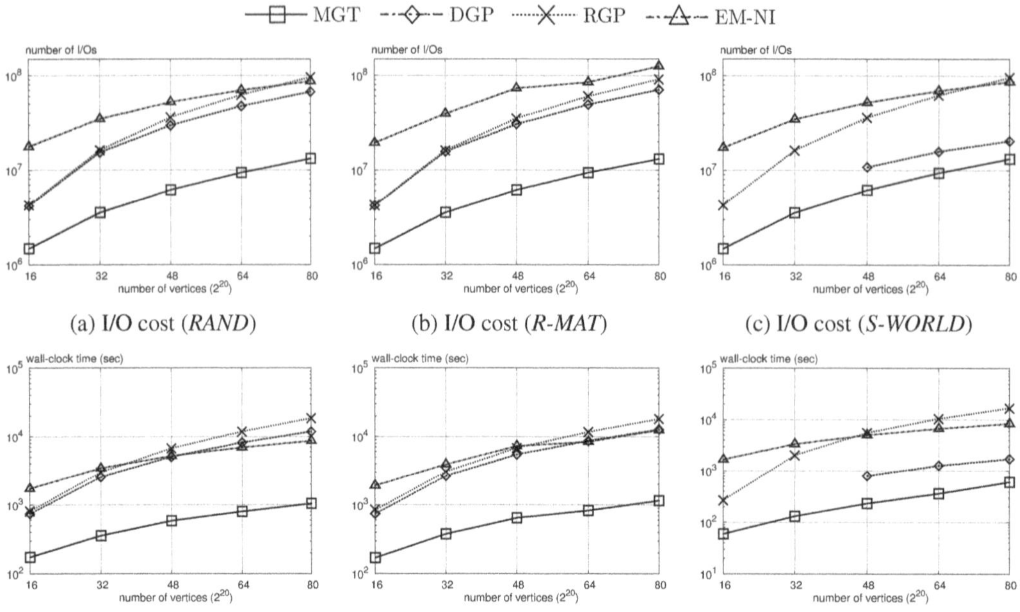

(a) I/O cost (*RAND*) (b) I/O cost (*R-MAT*) (c) I/O cost (*S-WORLD*)

(d) Overall cost (*RAND*) (e) Overall cost (*R-MAT*) (f) Overall cost (*S-WORLD*)

Figure 9: Efficiency comparison on synthetic graphs

In this paper, we have presented a new algorithm named MGT based on fresh ideas drastically different from the previous approaches. The proposed algorithm does not rely on any assumption, and outperformed every other alternative solution by a factor up to at least an order of magnitude in our extensive experimental evaluation. Furthermore, the MGT algorithm is based on a solid theoretical foundation, which proves its excellent efficiency in all settings, regardless of the graph distribution and size. In particular, we have shown that the I/O and CPU complexities of MGT are both optimal in the worst case.

8. REFERENCES

[1] A. Aggarwal and J. S. Vitter. The input/output complexity of sorting and related problems. *CACM*, 31(9):1116–1127, 1988.

[2] N. Alon and J. H. Spencer. *The Probabilistic Methods*. Wiley, New York, 2nd edition, 2000.

[3] E. Bakshy, I. Rosenn, C. Marlow, and L. A. Adamic. The role of social networks in information diffusion. *CoRR*, 2012.

[4] V. Batagelj and M. Zaversnik. Short cycle connectivity. *Discrete Mathematics*, 307:310–318, 2007.

[5] D. Chakrabarti, Y. Zhan, and C. Faloutsos. R-MAT: A recursive model for graph mining. In *SDM*, 2004.

[6] J. Cheng, Y. Ke, A. W.-C. Fu, J. X. Yu, and L. Zhu. Finding maximal cliques in massive networks. *TODS*, 36(4):21, 2011.

[7] N. Chiba and T. Nishizeki. Arboricity and subgraph listing algorithms. *SIAM J. of Comp.*, 14(1):210–223, 1985.

[8] S. Chu and J. Cheng. Triangle listing in massive networks and its applications. In *SIGKDD*, pages 672–680, 2011.

[9] S. Chu and J. Cheng. Triangle listing in massive networks. *TKDD*, 6(4):17, 2012.

[10] J. Cohen. Graph twiddling in a mapreduce world. *Computing in Science and Engineering*, 11(4):29–41, 2009.

[11] R. Dementiev. *Algorithm engineering for large data sets hardware, software, algorithms*. PhD thesis, Saarland University, 2006.

[12] D. Eppstein and E. S. Spiro. The h-index of a graph and its application to dynamic subgraph statistics. In *WADS*, pages 278–289, 2009.

[13] J. Hellings, G. H. L. Fletcher, and H. J. Haverkort. Efficient external-memory bisimulation on dags. In *SIGMOD*, pages 553–564, 2012.

[14] A. Itai and M. Rodeh. Finding a minimum circuit in a graph. *SIAM J. of Comp.*, 7(4):413–423, 1978.

[15] M. Latapy. Main-memory triangle computations for very large (sparse (power-law)) graphs. *TCC*, 407(1-3):458–473, 2008.

[16] M. C. Lin, F. J. Soulignac, and J. L. Szwarcfiter. Arboricity, h-index, and dynamic algorithms. *TCC*, 426:75–90, 2012.

[17] B. Menegola. An external memory algorithm for listing triangles. Technical report, Universidade Federal do Rio Grande do Sul, 2010.

[18] C. S. J. A. Nash-Williams. Decomposition of finite graphs into forests. *Journal of the London Mathematical Society*, 39(1):12, 1964.

[19] T. Schank. *Algorithmic Aspects of Triangle-Based Network Analysis*. PhD thesis, Universitat Karlsruhe, Fakultat fur Informatik, 2007.

[20] T. Schank and D. Wagner. Finding, counting and listing all triangles in large graphs, an experimental study. In *Workshop on Experimental Algorithms (WEA)*, pages 606–609, 2005.

[21] C.-H. Tai, P. S. Yu, D.-N. Yang, and M.-S. Chen. Privacy-preserving social network publication against friendship attacks. In *SIGKDD*, pages 1262–1270, 2011.

[22] J. Wang and J. Cheng. Truss decomposition in massive networks. *PVLDB*, 5(9):812–823, 2012.

[23] N. Wang, J. Zhang, K.-L. Tan, and A. K. H. Tung. On triangulation-based dense neighborhood graph discovery. *PVLDB*, 4(2):58–68, 2010.

[24] D. J. Watts and S. H. Strogatz. Collective dynamics of 'small-world' networks. *Nature*, 393:440–442, 1998.

[25] P. Zhao, C. C. Aggarwal, and M. Wang. gsketch: On query estimation in graph streams. *PVLDB*, 5(3):193–204, 2011.

Turbo$_{\text{ISO}}$: Towards UltraFast and Robust Subgraph Isomorphism Search in Large Graph Databases

Wook-Shin Han
School of Computer Science and Engineering
Kyungpook National University, Korea
wshan@knu.ac.kr

Jinsoo Lee
School of Computer Science and Engineering
Kyungpook National University, Korea
jslee@www-db.knu.ac.kr

Jeong-Hoon Lee
School of Computer Science and Engineering
Kyungpook National University, Korea
jhlee@www-db.knu.ac.kr

ABSTRACT

Given a query graph q and a data graph g, the subgraph isomorphism search finds all occurrences of q in g and is considered one of the most fundamental query types for many real applications. While this problem belongs to NP-hard, many algorithms have been proposed to solve it in a reasonable time for real datasets. However, a recent study has shown, through an extensive benchmark with various real datasets, that all existing algorithms have serious problems in their matching order selection. Furthermore, all algorithms blindly permutate all possible mappings for query vertices, often leading to useless computations. In this paper, we present an efficient and robust subgraph search solution, called Turbo$_{\text{ISO}}$, which is turbo-charged with two novel concepts, *candidate region exploration* and the *combine and permute* strategy (in short, COMB/PERM). The candidate region exploration identifies on-the-fly candidate subgraphs (i.e, candidate regions), which contain embeddings, and computes a robust matching order for each candidate region explored. The COMB/PERM strategy exploits the novel concept of the *neighborhood equivalence class* (NEC). Each query vertex in the same NEC has identically matching data vertices. During subgraph isomorphism search, COMB/PERM generates only combinations for each NEC instead of permutating all possible enumerations. Thus, if a chosen combination is determined to not contribute to a complete solution, all possible permutations for that combination will be safely pruned. Extensive experiments with many real datasets show that Turbo$_{\text{ISO}}$ consistently and significantly outperforms all competitors by up to several orders of magnitude.

Categories and Subject Descriptors

H.3.1 [**Information storage and retrieval**]: Content Analysis and Indexing—*Indexing methods*; H.3.3 [**Information storage and retrieval**]: Information Search and Retrieval—*Search process*

General Terms

Algorithm; Performance

Keywords

Subgraph Isomorphism; Candidate Region Exploration; Neighborhood Equivalence Class; Combine and Permute Strategy

1. INTRODUCTION

Graphs are prevalently used for modeling complex structures such as molecules, protein interaction networks, and program dependence. Along with the growing importance of graphs, considerable research efforts have focused on efficient graph data management.

One of the most fundamental graph queries in graph databases is the subgraph isomorphism search. That is, given a query graph q and a data graph g, the subgraph isomorphism problem is to find all distinct mappings (or embeddings) of q in g. Subgraph isomorphism search is actively used in many applications such as protein interaction analysis [21], graph classification [4], computer-aided design of electronic circuits [10], scene analysis [1], and chemical compound search [17]. Although, in theory, subgraph isomorphism search belongs to NP-hard, we can efficiently find embeddings in real graph databases in practice if we exploit a good matching order and powerful pruning techniques.

Although recent efforts [3, 12, 6, 21, 20] have seemed to enjoy some success, a recent study [8] has shown, through an extensive benchmark with many datasets, that all existing algorithms have serious performance problems for some query/data sets, which are summarized as follows: (P1) all methods have serious problems in their matching order selection, showing exponential behavior in some query/data sets, which means no methods show *robust* search performance. However, the good news is that, for each query/data set, there exists at least one method which processes such query set in a reasonable time; (P2) blind exploitation of neighborhood based filtering of GraphQL [6] and SPath [21] often negates their search performance in many query/datasets. In contrast, in those query/data sets, QuickSI [12] often outperforms more recent competitors, such as GraphQL and SPath, when it chooses a good matching order. This finding again reinforces the importance of choosing good matching orders; (P3) parameters of GraphQL and SPath significantly affect search performance. However, finding best parameter values in advance for each query is very difficult in practice.

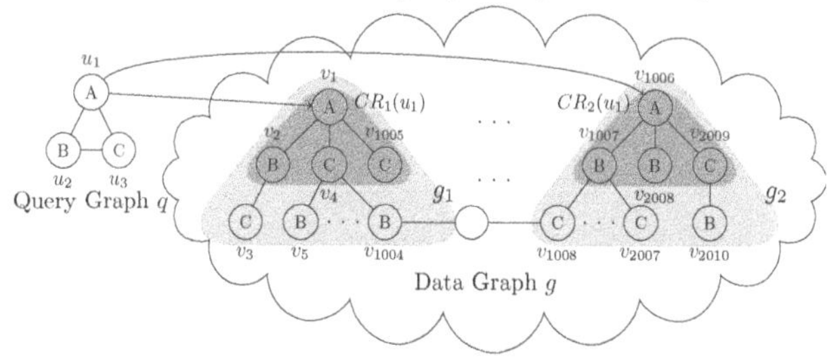

Figure 1: A query graph q and a data graph g.

Our new observation is that a good matching order for one data subgraph in g may be bad for other data subgraphs in g. Consider the two data subgraphs g_1 and g_2 in Figure 1. If we try to match a query vertex with a data vertex of g_1 using the matching order $O_1 = (u_1, u_2, u_3)$, after three matches (u_1, v_1), (u_2, v_2), (u_3, v_3), we know that there is no embedding in g_1. However, if we try to match using $O_2 = (u_1, u_3, u_2)$, for each child vertex v_c in v_4, we must match u_2 with every child vertex of v_4. Thus, the number of matching attempts using O_2 is 1003 (1 for u_1, 2 for u_3, and 1000 for u_2). Likewise, if we use O_1 for g_2, the number of matching attempts is 1003, while using O_2 requires only three.

In addition, we observe another new problem (P4) in the existing methods; exhaustive enumerations between query vertices and data vertices often lead to useless computations, resulting in significant performance degradation. Consider the query q and data graph g in Figure 2(a). Figure 2(b) shows a recursion tree T_r where each node in the tree corresponds to a match between a query vertex u and a data vertex v. For example, the first three recursive calls find the matches (u_1, v_1), (u_2, v_2), and (u_3, v_3) in this order. Given a matching order $(u_1, u_2, \cdots, u_7)$, all existing methods generate a similar recursion tree to T_r. However, when the seventh recursive call fails to match u_7 with v_7, we ensure that the subsequent recursive calls will not contribute to any valid embedding.

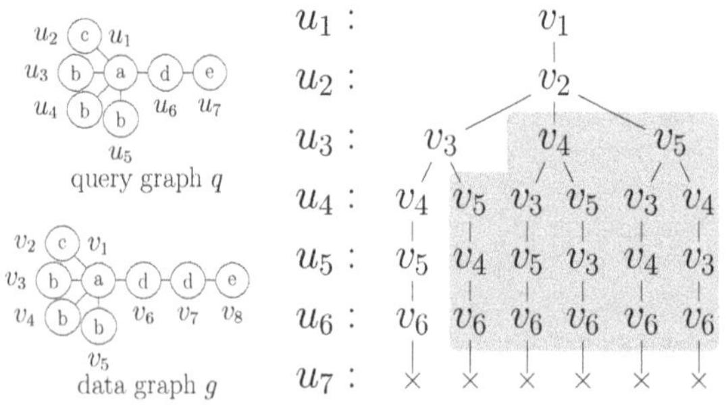

(a) a query and data graph. (b) a recursion tree T_r.

Figure 2: An example of useless enumerations.

These findings motivate us to develop a novel technique to efficiently and robustly process all such query/data sets. Our goal is to completely eliminate all these problems of existing methods. To this end, we propose 1) the novel concept of *candidate region exploration* and 2) a novel query processing strategy called *combine and permute* (in short, COMB/PERM). Candidate region exploration is a new approach for solving the matching order problem in subgraph isomorphism search, while COMB/PERM avoids the aforementioned useless enumerations between query/data vertices.

A candidate region for q is a data subgraph which may contain embeddings of the query graph. Additionally, if we perform subgraph isomorphism search on all candidate regions, we ensure that all embeddings can be obtained, avoiding all false negatives. For faster matching, minimizing the size of each data region is obviously important. Figure 1 illustrates two candidate regions, $CR_1(u_1)$ and $CR_2(u_1)$, for q, where both regions contain only four data vertices. The first matched vertex in each region is called the start vertex of each candidate region. v_1 and v_{1006} are the start vertices of $CR_1(u_1)$ and $CR_2(u_1)$, respectively.

In order to minimize the size of each candidate region, we first obtain a BFS search tree T_g from a selected root node u'_s of q so that each leaf is on the shortest path from u'_s. Then, for the start vertex v_s of each target candidate region, candidate region exploration identifies candidate data vertices for each query vertex by simply performing depth-first search using T_g starting from v_s. Next, we sort each path (accordingly, each leaf vertex) in T_g in ascending order of its number of candidate vertices and generate a matching order. Finally, given a candidate region, we find embeddings from candidate vertices for each query vertex (not from a data graph) according to the order obtained. For example, if we obtain a BFS search tree from q in Figure 1, the edge between u_2 and u_3 is removed. In $CR_1(u_1)$, a query vertex u_2 has a candidate vertex v_2, while u_3 has two candidate vertices v_4 and v_{1005}. Thus, a matching order (u_1, u_2, u_3) is obtained, and we next compute embeddings using these candidate vertices only. That is, we can easily determine that there are no embeddings in this region. Note that, for $CR_2(u_1)$, we obtain a different matching order (u_1, u_3, u_2) after candidate region exploration.

To avoid blindly permutating all possible mappings for query vertices u_3, u_4, and u_5 in Figure 2(a), the COMB/PERM strategy only generates combinations for such vertices. If a generated combination contributes to a valid mapping, the strategy permutes all possible mappings for the combination. Otherwise, it prunes out all other permutations for that combination. For example, we generate a combination (v_3, v_4, v_5) from data vertices $\{v_3, v_4, v_5\}$ for u_3, u_4, and u_5. If this combination fails to generate a valid mapping, then we do not permute the other combinations such as (v_3, v_5, v_4) and (v_4, v_3, v_5).

This presents a challenging question. "Which query vertices should be used for generating such combinations?" To answer this question, we propose the novel concept of *neighborhood equivalence class* (NEC). Each query vertex in the same NEC has identically matching data vertices. For example, u_3, u_4, and u_5 have the same matching data vertices $\{v_3, v_4, v_5\}$. Thus, u_3, u_4, and u_5 are in the same class. We need to identify all NECs before executing the subgraph isomorphism search. For this purpose, we propose an efficient polynomial-time algorithm called FINDNEC.

Our contributions are as follows: 1) We propose an efficient and robust subgraph search solution called $\text{Turbo}_{\text{ISO}}$ for completely solving the problems of existing methods. 2) We propose candidate region exploration to generate a robust matching order for each candidate region. 3) We propose a new concept of neighborhood equivalence class and the COMB/PERM strategy to generate only necessary enumerations. 4) Extensive experimental results show that $\text{Turbo}_{\text{ISO}}$ consistently and significantly outperforms the state-of-the-art methods by up to orders of magnitude.

The rest of this paper is organized as follows. Section 2 reviews subgraph isomorphism search and related work. Section 3 gives an overview of our solution for efficiently and robustly processing subgraph isomorphism queries. In Section 4, we propose the concept of neighborhood equivalence class and present an efficient algorithm to rewrite from an input query graph into an NEC tree. Section 5 presents an algorithm for performing candidate region exploration, and Section 6 presents a detailed matching algorithm based on COMB/PERM. Section 7 presents the results of performance evaluations. Section 8 summarizes and concludes the paper.

2. BACKGROUND

2.1 Problem Definition

A graph q is defined as (V, E, L) where V is the set of vertices, E ($\subseteq V \times V$) is the set of edges, and L is a label function that maps a vertex to a set of labels. Without loss of generality, all subgraph isomorphism algorithms can be easily extended to handle graphs whose edges have labels.

A graph $q = (V, E, L)$ is *isomorphic to a subgraph* of a data graph $g = (V', E', L')$ if there is an injection (or an embedding) $M : V \rightarrow V'$ such that, $\forall\, u \in V$, $L(u) \subseteq L'(M(u))$, and $\forall\, (u_i, u_j) \in E$, $(M(u_i), M(u_j)) \in E'$.

Now, the subgraph isomorphism problem is defined as follows: "Given a query graph q and a data graph g, find all distinct embeddings of q in g." In practice, however, we stop subgraph isomor-

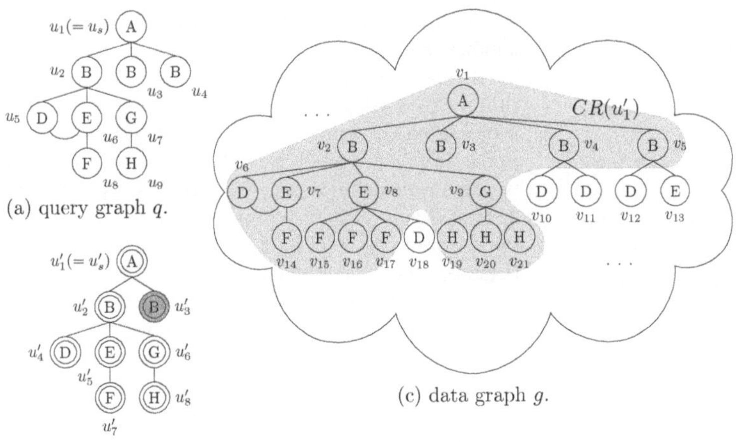

(a) query graph q.

(b) NEC tree q'.

(c) data graph g.

CR	candidate vertices
CR(u'_1, v^*_s)	$\{v_1\}$
CR(u'_2, v_1)	$\{v_2\}$
CR(u'_3, v_1)	$\{v_2, v_3, v_4, v_5\}$
CR(u'_4, v_2)	$\{v_6\}$
CR(u'_5, v_2)	$\{v_7, v_8\}$
CR(u'_6, v_2)	$\{v_9\}$
CR(u'_7, v_7)	$\{v_{14}\}$
CR(u'_7, v_8)	$\{v_{15}, v_{16}, v_{17}\}$
CR(u'_8, v_9)	$\{v_{19}, v_{20}, v_{21}\}$

(d) candidate subregions.

Figure 3: A running example

phism search after finding the first k embeddings. k is set to 1000 in [6, 21] and to 1024 in [14].

Consider a query graph q and a data graph g in Figure 1. Suppose that an edge between u_2 and u_3 is removed. Then, all embeddings of q in g are $\{(u_1, v_1), (u_2, v_2), (u_3, v_4)\}$, $\{(u_1, v_1), (u_2, v_2), (u_3, v_{1005})\}$, $\{(u_1, v_{1006}), (u_2, v_{1007}), (u_3, v_{2009})\}$, and $\{(u_1, v_{1006}), (u_2, v_{2008}), (u_3, v_{2009})\}$.

2.2 Related work

Most subgraph isomorphism algorithms [16, 3, 12, 6, 21, 20] are based on backtracking [8]. They first obtain a set of candidate vertices $C(u)$ for each query vertex u in a query graph q. For this purpose, each algorithm maintains a mapping table which maps a label to a list of vertices having that label. Given a matching order O, each algorithm invokes the main recursive subroutine SUBGRAPHSEARCH to match one query vertex with one data vertex at a time according to O. Note that the matching order plays a significant role in subgraph isomorphism performance.

In SUBGRAPHSEARCH, if the current query vertex u is selected, each algorithm refines $C(u)$ using its specific pruning rules. Then, for each candidate vertex refined v, each algorithm checks if the edges between u and already matched query vertices in q have corresponding edges between v and already matched data vertices of g. If v is qualified, we match u with v. Each algorithm then invokes SUBGRAPHSEARCH recursively by matching the remaining query vertices. We can finish the subgraph isomorphism search when all possible embeddings are obtained.

The Ullmann algorithm [16] is the first algorithm to tackle this problem. Since it uses the input order of query vertices and has almost no pruning rules to filter out candidate vertices, its performance is obviously the slowest among all existing algorithms. VF2 [3] optimizes Ullmann in the following aspect. In SUBGRAPHSEARCH, Ullmann chooses the current query vertex u arbitrarily, while VF2 chooses the u which is connected from the already matched query vertices. Note that, except for this constraint, VF2 does not define any matching order either. VF2 exploits this constraint to prune out candidate vertices from $C(u)$. The QuickSI algorithm proposes a matching order selection. Its matching order selection method chooses query vertices having infrequent vertex labels and infrequent, adjacent edge labels as early as possible. Although this greedy approach works for some datasets, it has a serious problem in its matching order for other datasets [8]. That is, choosing a more selective query edge can lead to a significantly less selective query path, which frequently occurs in the human protein interaction network. If we maintain statistics for all distinctive paths in the data graph, we can accurately calculate the selectivity of the path. However, this is infeasible in reality due to the huge amount of space and the expensive maintenance cost. GraphQL and SPath focus on minimizing the size of $C(u)$ by exploiting neighborhood-based filtering. GraphQL further minimizes it by performing the pseudo-isomorphism test, which generates BFS search trees for u and $v \in C(u)$, checks if the containment relationship exists between the two, and iterates this process by enlarging the BFS search trees. However, their matching order selection strategies using some simple formulae result in a serious problem in their matching orders. Furthermore, to store neighborhood information for each data vertex, some parameters must be provided by users.

Most recently, a new subgraph isomorphism algorithm was proposed in [14]. This algorithm is implemented in the memory cloud in Trinity [13]. It first decomposes a query into a set of basic query units called STwigs. Then, it obtains all possible intermediate results for each STwig. Here, a large amount of them must be transferred to other servers before join. Next, it performs block-based pipeline joins to merge all intermediate results. To define a join order, it uses a sampling based join optimization. However, it is unclear whether this algorithm is superior to the existing ones, since it has not been empirically compared with them. Its salient advantage is that it does not maintain any auxiliary index structure except the mapping table which maps a label to a list of vertices having that label. Thus, it can gracefully scale to support large graphs.

There are graph-index based subgraph isomorphism algorithms such as gIndex [17, 18], FG-Index [2], Tree+Δ [22], SwiftIndex [12], C-Tree [19], and gCode [23]. These utilize the filter-and-refinement strategy by using graph indexes. By using graph indexes as filters, we may prune out many unnecessary graphs at low cost during query processing. We store pairs of a graph feature and its posting list in the graph index. For a given query graph q, we enumerate all subgraphs of size up to $maxL$ for q and check whether such features are in the index. After finding features associated with their posting lists of graph IDs, we intersect all posting lists to obtain candidate graphs. Thus, the results of the filtering step are a set of graph IDs. If there is only a single, large graph in the database, using such graph indexes may not be useful, since the indexing-based algorithms must perform the subgraph isomorphism test if the query graph is contained in the single, large graph.

GraMi [11] is a frequent subgraph mining algorithm for a single graph g. It finds more generalized subgraph patterns where edges in a pattern correspond to distance-constrained paths in g. If at least σ embeddings of a pattern P exist in g (i.e., the support of $P \geq \sigma$), P is determined to be frequent in g. GraMi proposes a subgraph isomorphism algorithm based on a constraint satisfaction problem solver in order to find frequent patterns. However, the problem setting in [11] is completely different from the traditional subgraph isomorphism problem in that it uses the minimum image-based support (MNI) σ. That is, let M_j be the j-th embedding for P in g. Let ∇_i be $\bigcup_{j=1}^{|M|} M_j(u_i)$, where u_i is the i-th query vertex, and $|M|$ is the number of all possible embeddings. Then, $min_{u_i \in P}|\nabla_i|$ is used to calculate the support of a pattern. Thus, to check whether a given pattern P is frequent under the MNI frequency metric, the core idea is to check if there are at least σ data vertices that are valid assignments for each query vertex without enumerating all possible embeddings of P in g. If not, we can safely determine that P is infrequent. Note that this property can not be used for the traditional subgraph isomorphism problem. Regarding the matching order, GraMi selects the query vertex which has the largest number of query constraints without considering its selectivity. However, this heuristic again would result in similar performance problems as the existing subgraph isomorphism methods.GraMi also uses an optimization under the MNI frequency metric to handle a special case when a query graph itself is completely symmetric. It would be interesting to apply our techniques to this problem to speed up frequent subgraph mining.

Research efforts on approximate subgraph search algorithms [15, 9, 7] are also active. Here, to find approximate embeddings, each algorithm uses its own similarity measure. Note that both exact subgraph search and approximate subgraph search algorithms have their own applications [8].

3. OVERVIEW OF Turbo$_{\text{ISO}}$

In order to integrate the concept of neighborhood equivalence class in both candidate region exploration and the main recursive subroutine, Turbo$_{\text{ISO}}$ first rewrites a query graph q into an NEC tree q' by performing BFS search from a given start query vertex. Note that each vertex in q' corresponds to an NEC. This way, we only need to match one NEC vertex with the corresponding data vertices regardless of how many query vertices correspond to the NEC vertex. Consider a running example in Figure 3, where Turbo$_{\text{ISO}}$ first rewrites q in Figure 3 (a) into q' in Figure 3 (b). From a given start query vertex u_s, we obtain q'. Note that the NEC vertex u_3' corresponds to two query vertices u_3 and u_4, while the other vertices in q' correspond to a single vertex in q.

Next, the candidate region exploration process identifies candidate regions by performing a depth-first search for the start data vertex of each candidate region. After that, we obtain candidate data vertices for each NEC vertex. Here, candidate region exploration ensures that all candidate vertices for each NEC vertex u' have the same subtree as u'. Next, by ordering the leaf NEC vertices by the number of their candidate vertices, we can obtain a matching order for each candidate region. Here, we need to consider more sophisticated cases where 1) there exist non-tree edges in q, and 2) one NEC vertex corresponds to several query vertices, which will be elaborated in Section 5.3. In the running example, u_2' has one candidate vertex v_2, while u_3' contains four candidates $v_2 \sim v_5$. Since the leaf NEC vertices u_4', u_7', u_8', and u_3' have one, four, three, and four candidate vertices respectively, one possible generated order would be $O_3 = (u_1', u_2', u_4', u_6', u_8', u_5', u_7', u_3')$.

The main recursive subroutine, SUBGRAPHSEARCH, generates embeddings using candidate data vertices of the NEC vertices according to the matching order obtained. For example, given a matching order O_3, when we match u_5' with its candidate vertices v_7 and v_8, v_8 is pruned since it does not have an edge incident to v_6. When we match u_3' with its candidate vertices, v_2 is pruned since it has already been matched with u_2'. After matching all NEC vertices, we find an embedding $m = \{(u_1, v_1), (u_2, v_2), (u_3, v_3), (u_4, v_4), \cdots, (u_8, v_{14}), (u_9, v_{19})\}$. Then, with COMB/PERM, we generate another embedding, $m - \{(u_3, v_3), (u_4, v_4)\} \cup \{(u_3, v_4), (u_4, v_3)\}$.

Algorithm 1 outlines our subgraph isomorphism search algorithm, called Turbo$_{\text{ISO}}$. We first choose a start query vertex from q by calling CHOOSESTARTQVERTEX. Then, we obtain an NEC tree q' from q in Line 2. Next, for each start vertex of each region, we perform candidate region exploration from the root vertex u_s' of q' (Lines 3 $\sim$ 4). If we succeed in finding a region, we determine a matching order by calling DETERMINEMATCHINGORDER (Line 6). Now, we can map the start vertex u_s of q to the start vertex v_s of the region found by calling UPDATESTATE (Line 7). Like existing algorithms, we maintain two arrays M and F, where M is a mapping array, and F is an array storing information about which data vertices have been used in the current mapping. We next invoke the main recursive subroutine SUBGRAPHSEARCH to generate all possible embeddings for each region (Line 8). After we find all embeddings for each region, we restore the two arrays by RESTORESTATE (Line 9).

Algorithm 1 Turbo$_{\text{ISO}}(q, g)$

Input: query graph q, data graph g
Output: all embeddings of q in g

1: u_s := CHOOSESTARTQVERTEX(q, g);
2: q' := REWRITETONECTREE(q, u_s); // q' : NEC tree
3: **for each** v_s in $\{v | (v \in V(g))$ and $(L(u_s) \subseteq L(v))\}$ **do**
4:   **if** EXPLORECR($u_s', \{v_s\}, CR$) = FAIL **then**
5:     **continue**;
6:   order := DETERMINEMATCHINGORDER(q', CR);
7:   UPDATESTATE($M, F, \{u_s\}, \{v_s\}$);
8:   SUBGRAPHSEARCH($q, q', g, order$, 1);/* 1 means "the first query vertex to match."*/
9:   RESTORESTATE($M, F, \{u_s\}, \{v_s\}$);

4. QUERY REWRITE

In order to choose a start query vertex u_s which matches the start vertex of each region, we rank every query vertex by its value and select top-k query vertices by their ranking values. Here, we use a ranking function $Rank(u) = \frac{freq(g, L(u))}{deg(u)}$, where $freq(g, l)$ is the number of data vertices in g that have label l, and $deg(u)$ means the degree of u. In our experiment, we set k to 3. This ranking function favors lower frequencies and higher degrees. The rationale for this rule is that we want to minimize the number of candidate regions. This ranking function has been also used in [14]. Consider the running example in Figure 3. Since the rank value (= 1/3) of u_1 is the minimum, u_1 is selected as the start query vertex.

Among the top-three query vertices selected u_1, u_2, and u_3, we estimate the number of candidate regions more accurately by exploiting the following two filters whose costs are low. For each query vertex u selected, we obtain a set of candidate data vertices $C(u)$. Then, for each vertex v in $C(u)$, we first check if $deg(u) \leq deg(v)$. If qualified, we next exploit the *neighborhood label frequency filter* (NLF filter), which checks if $|adj(u, l)| \leq |adj(v, l)|$ for every distinct label l of the adjacent vertices of u. Here, $adj(u, l)$ represents a list of vertices having label l which are adjacent to u. Then, we can accurately estimate the number of candidate regions for each start query vertex selected. Lastly, we pick the one having the minimum number of candidate regions. Note that, we exclude any of u_2 or u_3 from applying these filters if its selectivity$(=\frac{|C(u)|}{|V(g)|}) > 5\%$. That is, we do not blindly apply these filters to such non-selective, start query vertices.

4.1 Neighborhood Equivalence Class

In this section, we formally define the concept of neighborhood equivalence class.

Definition 1. *Let $\simeq$ be an equivalence relation over all query vertices in q such that, $u_i(\in V(q)) \simeq u_j(\in V(q))$ if for every embedding m that contains (u_i, v_x) and (u_j, v_y) $(v_x, v_y \in V(g))$, there exists an embedding m' such that $m' = m - \{(u_i, v_x), (u_j, v_y)\} \cup \{(u_i, v_y), (u_j, v_x)\}$.*

The equivalence class of a query vertex u is a set of query vertices which are equivalent to (i.e., $\simeq$) u. This class is called *neighborhood equivalence class* (NEC). Consider a query q in Figure 3(a). Here, the query vertices u_3 and u_4 constitute one NEC, while each of the other vertices constitutes one NEC. Regarding the NEC of u_3 (= $\{u_3, u_4\}$), for every embedding m containing (u_3, v_3) and (u_4, v_4), there exists an embedding $m' = m - \{(u_3, v_3), (u_4, v_4)\} \cup \{(u_3, v_4), (u_4, v_3)\}$.

Let N_q be an NEC. Let $\mathcal{P}$ be a permutation of the vertices in N_q, and let M_{all} be a set of all embeddings. If $\{(\mathcal{P}[1], v_{i_1}), \cdots, (\mathcal{P}[|\mathcal{P}|], v_{i_{|\mathcal{P}|}})\} \subseteq m \in M_{all}$, then $\forall\ \mathcal{P}'$ in M_{all}, $m' = m - \{(\mathcal{P}[1], v_{i_1}), \cdots, (\mathcal{P}[|\mathcal{P}|], v_{i_{|\mathcal{P}|}})\} \cup \{(\mathcal{P}'[1], v_{i_1}), \cdots, (\mathcal{P}'[|\mathcal{P}|], v_{i_{|\mathcal{P}|}})\}$ for some $m' \in M_{all}$. Otherwise, $\forall\ \mathcal{P}'$, $\{(\mathcal{P}'[1], v_{i_1}), \cdots, (\mathcal{P}'[|\mathcal{P}|], v_{i_{|\mathcal{P}|}})\} \nsubseteq m'$ for all $m' \in M_{all}$.

We need to identify all neighborhood equivalence classes before executing subgraph isomorphism search. The following lemma states an important property of NEC which allows us to identify NECs by examining query vertices only.

Lemma 1. *Every query vertex u in an NEC N_q has the same label and the same set of adjacent query vertices. Otherwise, every query vertex u has the same label and is adjacent to every other vertex in N_q and has the same set $adj(u)$-N_q, where $adj(u)$ is the set of vertices adjacent to u. That is, all query vertices in N_q themselves form a clique.*

PROOF: We need to prove two conditions: 1) Suppose that every query vertex in N_q has the same label and same set of adjacent query vertices. Then, for any two query vertices u_i and u_j in N_q, it is clear that matching data vertices for u_i must be the same as those for u_j. Thus, for any embedding m, we can always find another embedding by exchanging u_i and u_j in m. 2) Suppose that every query vertex u has the same label and is adjacent to every other vertex in N_q and has the same set $adj(u)$-N_q. Then, $adj(u_i) - \{u_j\} = adj(u_j) - \{u_i\}$. Thus, for any two query vertices u_i and u_j, they match v_x and v_y respectively. Therefore, for any embedding m, we can always find another embedding by exchanging u_i and u_j in m. □

4.2 Rewrite to NEC tree

When we rewrite a query graph q into an NEC tree q', we need to achieve two goals: 1) candidate regions matching q' need to be minimized; and 2) all NECs must be efficiently obtained. It is obvious to exploit a BFS search tree from q to minimize the diameter of each candidate region on average. However, it is unclear whether we can efficiently identify all NECs using the BFS search tree. Lemma 2 states an important property of the NEC for this question. That is, we can achieve these two goals by performing a BFS search over the query graph.

Lemma 2. *Let $SP(u_s, u_i)$ be the set of all shortest paths from u_s to u_i. If the two query vertices u_i and u_j belong to the same NEC, for every shortest path $p_1 = p'(=(u_s, \cdots, u_x)) \bullet (u_x, u_i)$ in $SP(u_s, u_i)$, there exists a shortest path $p_2 = p' \bullet (u_x, u_j)$ in $SP(u_s, u_j)$, where $\bullet$ is the path concatenation operator. Thus, $|SP(u_s, u_i)| = |SP(u_s, u_j)|$.*

PROOF: According to Lemma 1, u_j must be adjacent to u_x as well, since u_i and u_j belong to the same NEC. Then, by substituting u_i with u_j in p_1, we can obtain p_2 whose length = $|p_1|$. Now, we need to show that p_2 is a shortest path from u_s to u_j. We prove this by contradiction. That is, suppose that p_1 is a shortest path from u_s to u_i, and that p_2 is not a shortest path. Then, there exists another shortest path $p_3 = (u_s, \cdots, u_y, u_j)$ whose length $< |p_2|$. According to Lemma 1, by substituting u_y and u_j with u_x and u_i in p_3, we can find a path $(u_s, \cdots, u_x, u_i)$ whose length = $|p_3| (< |p_1|)$. This contradicts the assumption that p_1 is a shortest path. □

Lemma 3 states the important relationship between the NEC of a vertex u' (denoted as $u'.NEC$) and the NEC of the child vertex u'_c of u' in the NEC tree. We exploit this relationship for both generating an NEC tree and performing subgraph isomorphism search.

Lemma 3. *Given any two NEC vertices u' and u'_c satisfying the parent-child relationship in the NEC tree, every query vertex u in $u'.NEC$ is adjacent to all vertices in $u'_c.NEC$.*

PROOF: We prove by contradiction. Suppose that there exists one query vertex u_j in $u'_c.NEC$ which is not adjacent to some vertex u_p in $u'.NEC$. Since u' and u'_c satisfy the parent-child relationship in the NEC tree, each query vertex in $u'_c.NEC$ must be adjacent to at least one query vertex in $u'.NEC$. Thus, there exists another query vertex u_i $(i \neq j)$ in $u'_c.NEC$ which is adjacent to u_p. According to Lemma 2, $|SP(u_s, u_i)| = |SP(u_s, u_j)|$. Consider a shortest path $p_1 = (u_s, \cdots, u_p, u_i)$ in $SP(u_s, u_i)$. According to Lemma 2, there also exists $p_2 = (u_s, \cdots, u_p, u_j)$ in $SP(u_s, u_j)$. This contradicts that u_j is not adjacent to u_p. □

According to Lemma 3, in order to create child NEC vertices of a given NEC vertex u', it is sufficient to examine the query vertices in $u'.NEC$. Algorithm 2 shows a rewrite algorithm, REWRITETONECTREE, which converts an input query graph into its NEC tree. REWRITETONECTREE first creates the root vertex of an NEC tree whose NEC is $\{u_s\}$ (Line 2). For enabling BFS search over q guided by the NEC tree being created so far, REWRITETONECTREE uses two lists $V_{current}$ and V_{next} to maintain NEC vertices at the current level and NEC vertices at the next level to visit, respectively. Initially, the NEC vertex that REWRITETONECTREE has to visit in the next level is set to the root node u'_s of the NEC tree (Line 4). By visiting all NEC vertices in the current level, REWRITETONECTREE creates all NECs in the next level (Lines 7 $\sim$ 16). For each NEC vertex u'_c in the current level, we first collect the adjacent and unvisited query vertices of all query vertices in $u'_c.NEC$ (Lines 7 $\sim$ 9). We then group those vertices by the vertex label (Line 12), and, for each group, we invoke FINDNEC to create the child NEC vertices of u'_c (Lines 13 $\sim$ 14). We repeat this process until V_{next} is empty (Line 17).

Algorithm 2 REWRITETONECTREE (q)

1: create a root NEC vertex u'_s;
2: $u'_s.NEC = [u_s]$;
3: mark u_s as visited;
4: $V_{current} = []$; $V_{next} = [u'_s]$;
5: **repeat**
6: $\quad V_{current} = V_{next}$; $V_{next} = \emptyset$;
7: $\quad$ **for each** NEC vertex u'_c in $V_{current}$ **do**
8: $\quad\quad C = adj(u'_c.NEC[1]) \cup \cdots \cup adj(u'_c.NEC[|u'_c.NEC|])$;
9: $\quad\quad$ remove all visited query vertices from C;
10: $\quad\quad$ mark all query vertices in C as visited;
11: $\quad\quad$ **if** C is non-empty **then**
12: $\quad\quad\quad$ group C by the vertex label into $G_1, \cdots, G_k$;
13: $\quad\quad\quad$ **for each** group G_i **do**
14: $\quad\quad\quad\quad$ $NECVertices$ =FINDNEC(G_i);
15: $\quad\quad\quad\quad$ append $NECVertices$ into V_{next};
16: $\quad\quad\quad\quad$ make u'_c be the parent of all $NECVertices$;
17: **until** (V_{next} is empty)

Consider the query graph in Figure 3 (a). REWRITETONECTREE first creates u'_1 whose NEC is $\{u_1\}$. Since the adjacent query vertices of u_1 are $\{u_2, u_3, u_4\}$, each of which has the same label B, we make one group containing all those query vertices. Then, by calling FINDNEC, we can create two NEC vertices u'_2 and u'_3 where u'_2.NEC $=\{u_2\}$, and u'_3.NEC $=\{u_3, u_4\}$. Now, V_{next} contains u'_2 and u'_3. We next examine all adjacent and unvisited vertices of the query vertices in u'_2.NEC, $\{u_5, u_6, u_7\}$. By grouping those query vertices by the vertex label, we obtain three groups, each of which is a singleton. By calling FINDNEC for each group, we can create three NEC vertices u'_4, u'_5, and u'_6 which are the child NEC vertices of u'_2. If we repeat this process, we can obtain the NEC tree finally as in Figure 3 (b). We explain another example using Figure 1. Here, u_1 is chosen as the start query vertex, and each query vertex corresponds to one NEC vertex. Thus, the resulting NEC tree q' is derived from q by removing the edge between u_2 and u_3. Thus, we have three NEC vertices u'_1, u'_2, and u'_3, which correspond to u_1, u_2, and u_3, respectively.

Now, we explain how to find NECs from a given set of candidate query vertices using FINDNEC. We first group those vertices by their adjacent vertices. According to Lemma 1, if the size of each group is larger than one, i.e., every query vertex in the group has the same label and the same set of adjacent query vertices, then we create an NEC vertex that contains all query vertices in the group. Otherwise, we examine all singleton groups to see if any groups can be merged into one NEC N_q such that every query vertex u_c in N_q has the same label and is adjacent to every other vertex in N_q and has the same set $adj(u_c)$-N_q Note that the worst time complexity of FINDNEC is $O(|G|^2)$.

5. CANDIDATE REGION EXPLORATION

As explained in the introduction, by performing subgraph isomorphism search for candidate regions only, we can obtain all embeddings for a given query graph q. In order to minimize the size of the candidate region, we rewrite q into an equivalent NEC tree q'. Here, by using q' instead of q, we can also accelerate the candidate region exploration process, since many query vertices in the same NEC are merged into one NEC vertex. The following section explains the concept of *candidate subregion* which stores candidate data vertices for each NEC vertex. Note that the union of all candidate subregions in a candidate region is equal to the candidate region.

5.1 Candidate Subregion

Given an NEC tree q' for a query graph q, we identify candidate regions by traversing g by using q'. For this purpose, the candidate region exploration process traverses the subgraph rooted at the start vertex of each candidate region.

During candidate region exploration, we can identify candidate data vertices for each NEC vertex, which will be used for subgraph isomorphism search. In order to store these data vertices, we propose the concept of the candidate subregion denoted as $CR(u', v)$, where u' is an NEC vertex, and v is a data vertex. $CR(u', v)$ contains data vertices such that they match u' and are child vertices of v in the DFS tree. We formally define $CR(u', v)$ in Definition 2.

Definition 2. *$CR(u', v)$ is a set of data vertices $\{v'\}$ such that 1) v' is a child vertex of v in the DFS search tree, 2) all NEC vertices on the path from u'_s to u' matches all data vertices on the path from v_s to v' in the DFS search tree, and 3) each subtree of u' matches the corresponding subtree of v' in the DFS search tree, where u'_s is the root vertex of q', and v_s is the start vertex of the candidate region.*

Figure 4 illustrates the semantics of $CR(u', v)$. To store a candidate vertex (i.e., v_s) for u'_s, we assume that there exists an artificial vertex v^*_s that is the parent of v_s.

Consider an NEC tree and a data graph in Figure 3. Here, $CR(u'_2, v_1) = \{v_2\}$, since v_2 can match u'_2, and the subtrees of u'_2 match those of v_2. Note that $CR(u'_2, v_1)$ does not contain v_3, v_4, or v_5, since their subtrees do not match those of u'_2. Similarly, $CR(u'_3, v_1) = \{v_2, v_3, v_4, v_5\}$. Figure 3(d) illustrates all candidate subregions for this example.

5.2 Algorithm and Data Structure

When we traverse a candidate region, we need to test if the data vertex v' which is adjacent to v can belong to $CR(u', v)$ for an NEC vertex u'. In order to speed up the test and prune out non-promising data vertices efficiently, we first check if $deg(u'.NEC[1]) \leq deg(v')$. Note that here we use the degree of the first query vertex $u'.NEC[1]$ rather than that of u'. For example, consider Figure 3(b), where $u'_1.NEC[1] = u_1$. When we try to match u'_1 with v_1 in Figure 3(c), the degree of u_1 is three while the degree of u'_1 is two. Thus, if the degree of v_1 is less than three, v_1 is safely pruned. Then, we exploit the NLF filter before traversing the subtree of v'. If not qualified, we prune such v' without traversing the subtrees of v'. Again, we invoke $NLF(u'.NEC[1], v')$ for this purpose.

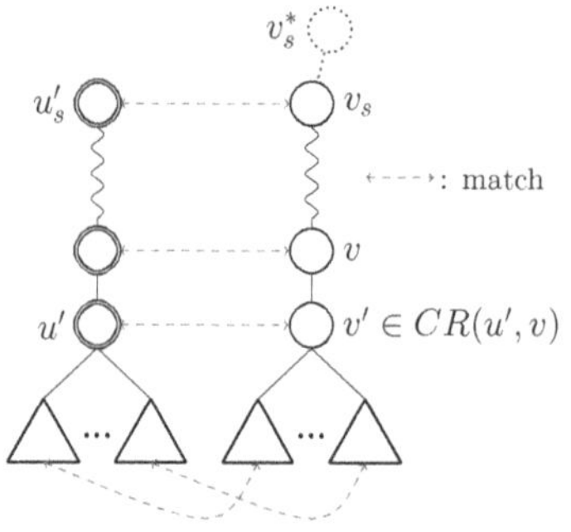

Figure 4: Semantics of $CR(u', v)$.

Algorithm 3 outlines the candidate region exploration process, EXPLORECR, which performs a depth-first search from the start vertex of a candidate region guided by an input NEC query tree. Inputs to EXPLORECR are an NEC vertex u', and a candidate data vertex set V_M for u'. For each unvisited data vertex v', EXPLORECR exploits the two tests to prune out unpromising data vertices (Line 2). If v' is qualified, we traverse the child vertices of v' by recursively calling EXPLORECR (Lines 6 $\sim$ 7). Here, we order child query vertices u'_cs of u' according to the size of $adj(v', \text{L}(u'_c))$ (Line 6). This would increase the probability that v' is to be pruned early if its subtrees do not match the subtrees of u'. If the subtrees of v' do not match the subtrees of u', we clear the candidate subregions for all visited vertices in the subtrees of v' (Lines 8 $\sim$ 9). Thus, we invoke CLEARCR for this purpose. If v' is qualified, we append it into $CR(u', v)$, where v is the parent vertex of v' in the DFS search tree (Line 15). If $|CR(u', v)| < |u'.NEC|$, we cannot map all query vertices in $u'.NEC$ to the vertices in $CR(u', v)$, and thus, we clear any subregions that we have found (Lines 16 $\sim$ 18).

Consider the running example in Figure 3. EXPLORECR performs depth-first search starting from v_1 using the NEC tree q' and identifies candidate vertices for each NEC vertex, which are stored in the corresponding candidate subregions. Note that v_{18} and $v_{10} \sim v_{13}$ are determined to be not in the candidate region by Line 6.

If v' is not qualified, CLEARCR should be invoked for *each subregion* for all visited vertices in the subtrees of v'. To speed up this process, we propose an efficient data structure for representing $CR(u', v)$s, where we maintain one array for each NEC vertex u' so that all $CR(u', v)$s are stored in the array $CR(u', -)$. Each element in $CR(u', -)$ consists of (v', a list L of ranges $[s,e]$) such that $|L|$ is equal to the number of child NEC vertices of u'. If the i-th child NEC vertex of u' is u'', then the candidate vertices for CR(u'', v') are stored from $CR(u'', -)[L_i.s]$ to $CR(u'', -)[L_i.e]$. By doing this, we only need to invoke CLEARCR for each descendent NEC vertex of u'.

Figure 5 shows an example of the data structure for $CR(u', -)$. Consider $CR(u'_1, -)$ which corresponds to $CR(u'_1, v^*_s)$. There is one element $(v_1, [1:1], [1:4])$ in $CR(u'_1, -)$. Since u'_1 has two child NEC vertices u'_2 and u'_3, the candidate vertex for $CR(u'_2, v_1)$ is stored in $CR(u'_2, -)[1]$, while the candidate vertices for $CR(u'_3, v_1)$ are stored from $CR(u'_3, -)[1]$ to $CR(u'_3, -)[4]$. Similarly, consider $CR(u'_5, -)$. The second element in $CR(u'_5, -)$ is $(v_8, [2:4])$. Thus, the candidate vertices for $CR(u'_7, v_8)$ are stored from $CR(u'_7, -)[2]$ to $CR(u'_7, -)[4]$.

Algorithm 3 EXPLORECR (u', V_M, CR)

```
for each unvisited data vertex v' in V_M do
  if deg(u'.NEC[1]) > deg(v') or NLF(u'.NEC[1], v') = FAIL
  then
    continue;
  mark v' as visited;
  matched := true;
  for each child query vertex u'_c of the u' ordered by the
  |adj(v', L(u'_c))| do
    if EXPLORECR(u'_c, adj(v', L(u'_c)), CR) = FAIL then
      for each visited child query vertex u''_c of u' except u'_c do
        CLEARCR(u''_c, v', CR);
      matched := false;
      break;
  mark v' as unvisited;
  if matched = false then
    continue;
  append {v'} into CR(u',v) such that v is the parent vertex of v' in
  the DFS search tree;
if |CR(u', v)| < |u'.NEC| then
  CLEARCR(u', v, CR);
  return FAIL;
return DONE;
```

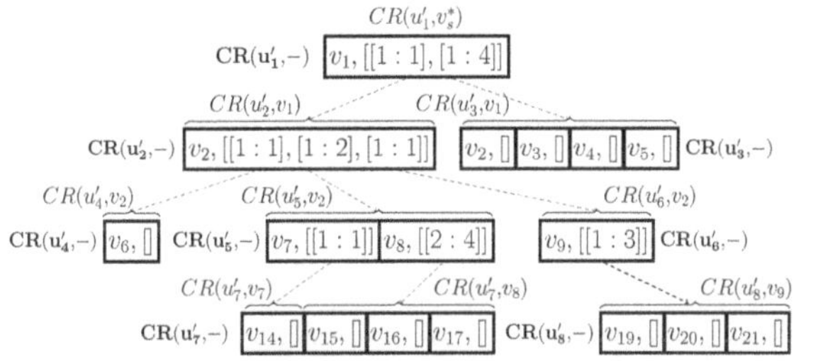

Figure 5: Representation of $CR(u', -)$.

Note that if a query is a path, and the start vertex of the query is at the end of the path, TurboISO can directly generate embeddings without calling the main recursive subroutine while we perform candidate region exploration. This simple optimization is typically effective if the query size is small as we will see in our experiments.

5.3 Matching Order Selection

If a query q has n vertices, $u_1, u_2, \cdots, u_n$, then the size of its search space becomes $|C(u_1)| \times |C(u_2)| \times \cdots \times |C(u_n)|$, where $C(u_i)$ is a set of candidate vertices that match u_i. Thus, we need to find a matching order so that the intermediate search space is minimized. However, this is a very difficult problem since we do not know the join selectivity of each pair of query vertices. Although every method tries to solve this problem using its own estimation formula, it fails to find a good matching order robustly due to serious problems in its estimation formula. For example, SPath finds the most selective path which starts from an already matched query vertex. Here, the selectivity function $sel(p)$ for a given path p is calculated as $\frac{2^{|V(p)|}}{\prod_{u \in V(p)} |C(u)|}$, where $V(p)$ denotes all vertices in a path p. Note that the denominator represents the join cardinality of the candidate sets for all query vertices in p. However, this overestimate leads to significant errors in estimating the join cardinality.

On the other hand, rather than relying on unrealistic estimation formulae, TurboISO performs candidate region exploration in order to count the number of candidate vertices for a given path in an NEC tree. This way, we can obtain almost *exact* selectivity for each query path from the start NEC vertex. Furthermore, we calculate the selectivity for each candidate region rather than for the whole graph. This is how TurboISO achieves more robust matching orders than the existing methods. Thus, we can exploit this precise information in selecting a matching order. Specifically, we sort each leaf vertex u' (each path, accordingly) by $|CR(u', -)|$. That is, we favor a path, such that the number of candidate vertices for the path is the smallest among the paths not selected yet. Consider Figure 6, where we have three query paths $p_1 \sim p_3$. For the first candidate region, through the candidate region exploration, we know that the cardinalities for those paths are 10, 10000, and 5, respectively. For the second candidate region, their cardinalities are 10000, 10, 5, respectively. If we perform the subgraph isomorphism search using p_1 and p_2 first, a lot of partial solutions will be enumerated. However, all of them will be eventually discarded by matching with p_3, since there are no edges between the data vertices having X and those having Z. On the other hand, if we perform the subgraph isomorphism search using p_1 and p_3, no results are generated, and thus, we can prune the entire search space. Accordingly, for the second candidate region, if we perform the subgraph isomorphism search using p_2 and p_3 first, we can prune the entire space. Otherwise, we are bound to enumerate a lot of partial solutions.

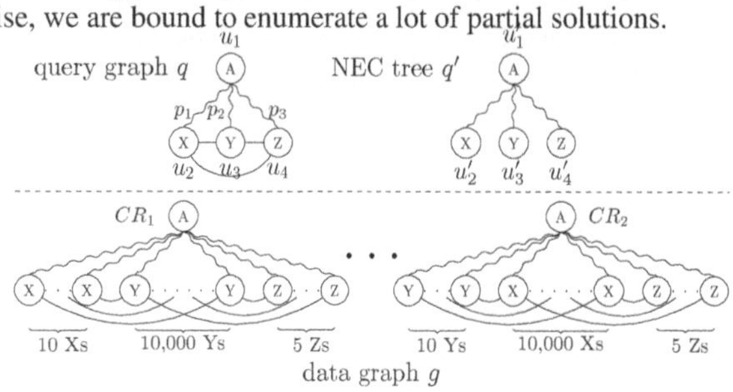

Figure 6: Importance of matching orders in different regions.

Here, we need to consider more sophisticated cases where 1) there exist non-tree edges in q, and 2) one NEC vertex corresponds to several query vertices. When we perform candidate region exploration, we do not consider non-tree edges in the query graph. Thus, we take this into account in estimating the number of candidate vertices for a given NEC vertex. Suppose that there are j non-tree edges incident to an NEC vertex u'. Then, we divide the number of candidate vertices for u' by $j+1$. This strategy is consistent with the computation of $Rank(u)$ in Section 4. We need to apply this reduction factor to subtrees of u'. For example, in Figure 3, the number of candidate vertices for u'_7 is four. However, since there is a non-tree edge between u_5 and u_6, we divide four by two, thereby our estimated value, two, becomes closer to the actual number, one (i.e., $|\{v_{14}\}|$). Thus, we obtain a matching order $O_4 = (u'_1, u'_2, u'_4, u'_5, u'_7, u'_6, u'_8, u'_3)$.

When a path p in the NEC tree consists of NEC vertices whose NEC sizes are greater than one, we have many corresponding query paths from p in the original query graph q. Since each query path in q has the same number of candidate vertices as that of p, we may still apply our strategy to this case as well. However, when we match the path p in the NEC tree with candidate vertices, we actually match many query paths from p at the same time. Thus, the actual number of candidate vertices for those paths are not the same as that for p. If there are many NEC vertices on p, we cannot know in advance the number of matches for the query paths without performing an expensive subgraph isomorphism search. The good news is that we can compute the exact number of candidate vertices when there exists only one NEC vertex whose NEC size > 1 at the end of the path, which frequently occurs in the query graph. Consider the NEC vertex u'_3 in Figure 3. For the NEC path $u'_1.u'_3$, we have two corresponding query paths $u_1.u_3$ and $u_1.u_4$. Thus, for the leaf query vertex pair of (u_3, u_4), we have six data vertex pairs, (v_2, v_3), (v_2, v_4), (v_2, v_5), (v_3, v_4), (v_3, v_5), and (v_4, v_5).

Thus, if the path p has an NEC node u' whose NEC size > 1 at the end of p, we compute the number of candidate vertices for the corresponding query vertices for u' by using Equation (1), where $P(u')$ is the parent NEC vertex of u'. For example, the number of candidate vertices for u'_3 ((u_3, u_4), accordingly) is $\binom{|CR(u'_3,v_1)|}{|u'_3.NEC|}$ ($= \binom{4}{2}$). Note that the formula $\binom{|CR(u',-)|}{|u'.NEC|}$ may not compute the correct value, since the selected data vertices such as v_3 and v_4 that match u_3 and u_4 respectively may not have the same parent data vertex in the DFS search tree that matches u_1.

$$\sum_{v \in CR(P(u'),-)} \binom{|CR(u',v)|}{|u'.NEC|} \quad (1)$$

6. MATCHING WITH COMB/PERM

Before explaining the subgraph isomorphism process, we explain the disk representation of a data graph. Turbo$_{\text{ISO}}$ represents a graph using two structures: 1) inverse vertex label list that allows access to the ordered vertex ID list by a given vertex label (see Figure 7(a)) and 2) adjacency list (see Figure 7(b)) of each vertex which stores adjacency information. Here, we group adjacent vertices by the label in the adjacency list. This way, we can efficiently compute $adj(v, l)$, which is used to prune unpromising vertices during candidate region exploration.

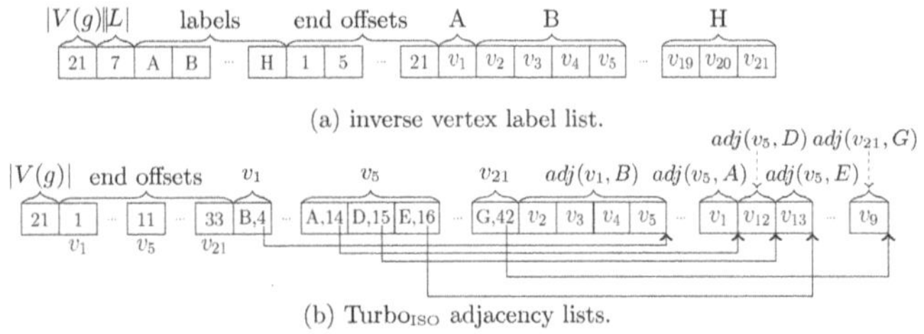

Figure 7: Disk representation of the data graph in Figure 3 (c).

6.1 Combine and Permute

In the subgraph isomorphism test, when we match the query vertices in $u'.NEC$ with a set of candidate data vertices C, we actually have to map all query vertices in $u'.NEC$ to some data vertices in C. For this purpose, we propose the combination operator, $NextComb(u', C)$. We elaborate how to find the set C in the next subsection. $NextComb(u', C)$ returns one $|u'.NEC|$-combination from C at a time whenever we invoke this function. Consider the running example in Figure 3. If we invoke $NextComb$ (u'_3, $\{v_3, v_4, v_5\}$), it first returns $[v_3, v_4]$. Thus, we can map u_3 and u_4 to v_3 and v_4, respectively. If we invoke $NextComb$ the next time, we can map u_3 and u_4 to v_3 and v_5, respectively.

Now, we explain the permutation operator $GenPerm(M, q', i)$, where M is the mapping table, q' is an NEC tree, and i is the index to a list of NEC vertices. In the main recursive subroutine of the subgraph isomorphism test, we invoke $GenPerm(M, q', 1)$ to process the first NEC vertex in q'. Repeatedly invoking $NextPerm$ (M, u') generates all possible permutations for the combinations generated by $NextComb$, where each combination is generated from one NEC vertex u'. We invoke $NextPerm(M, V(q')[i])$ to generate one permutation for $V(q')[i].NEC$ and to map the permutation to M accordingly (Line 6), where $V(q')[i]$ is the i-th NEC vertex in q'. Then, we recursively call $GenPerm(M, q', i+1)$ to generate permutations for the remaining $V(q')[i+1]$s (Line 7). Recall the running example in Figure 3 again. Suppose that an embedding M containing (u_3, v_3), (u_4, v_4) has been determined as a solution, we can generate all permutations for these query vertices, $[u_3, u_4]$ and $[u_4, u_3]$, and apply these permutations to the embedding, thereby generating two solutions.

Algorithm 4 GENPERM(M, q', i)

Input: M : a mapping table, q' : an NEC tree, i : index
1: **if** $i = |V(q')|+1$ **then**
2: report M and **return**; /*i.e., we have processed all NEC vertices */
3: **if** $|V(q')[i].NEC| = 1$ **then** /*$V(q')[i]$ denotes the i-th NEC vertex in q'*/
4: GENPERM($M, q', i+1$); /*Then, we don't need to generate permutations if the NEC size is one*/
5: **else**
6: **while** NEXTPERM($M, V(q')[i]$) $\neq$ DONE **do**
7: GENPERM($M, q', i+1$);

6.2 Main Recursive Subroutine

In candidate region exploration, we match an NEC vertex u' with data vertices. However, in subgraph isomorphism search, we have to match all query vertices in $u'.NEC$ with the corresponding data vertices. This presents the following challenging questions: (Q1) Given an NEC vertex u', which data vertices should be considered as candidates to match every query vertex in $u'.NEC$? (Q2) How should edges among the query vertices in $u'.NEC$ be handled? Note that these edges are not represented in the NEC tree.

Suppose that we try to match u' with the data vertices. Note that all query vertices in $P(u').NEC$ have already been matched with the corresponding data vertices, where $P(u')$ is the parent NEC vertex of u'. Then, in the mapping table M, query vertices $P(u').NEC[1]$, $\cdots$, $P(u').NEC[|P(u').NEC|]$ have already been mapped to $v_{M[P(u').NEC[1]]}, \cdots, v_{M[P(u').NEC[|P(u').NEC|]]}$, respectively. The following lemma answers the first question (Q1).

Lemma 4. *Given an NEC vertex u', a data graph g, and a mapping table M, any data vertex $v \in V(g)$ that u' matches must be in every $CR(u', v_{M[P(u').NEC[i]]})$ $(1 \leq i \leq |P(u').NEC|)$.*

PROOF: Proof by contradiction. Suppose that u' matches a data vertex v, but v is not in $CR(u', v_{M[P(u').NEC[i]]})$ for some i. That is, v is not connected to $v_{M[P(u').NEC[i]]}$. Then, some query vertex in $u'.NEC$ is not connected to $P(u').NEC[i]$. However, according to Lemma 2, every query vertex u in $P(u').NEC$ is connected to all vertices in $u'.NEC$. This contradicts the assumption that some query vertex in $u'.NEC$ is not connected to $P(u').NEC[i]$.

Consider an example in Figure 8. The data vertices v_5 and v_6 in $CR(u'_3, -)$ are considered as candidates since they are both in $CR(u'_3, v_2)$ and $CR(u'_3, v_3)$, while v_4 and v_7 are not considered as candidates for the query vertex u_4, since they are in either $CR(u'_3, v_2)$ or $CR(u'_3, v_3)$. That is, v_4 is not connected to v_3, and v_7 is not connected to v_2. However, their corresponding query vertices u_2 and u_3 are connected to u_4.

Now, we explain how to answer the second question. Here, the query vertices in $u'.NEC$ themselves must form a clique. If the query vertices in $u'.NEC$ form a clique, the corresponding candidate data vertices must form a clique as well. Otherwise, we can prune out those data vertices safely. Consider the example in Figure 8, where we match $u'_2.NEC$ with $\{v_2, v_3\}$. Since u_2 and u_3 in $u'_2.NEC$ themselves form a clique, the corresponding data vertices must form a clique. Otherwise, they are pruned.

SUBGRAPHSEARCH outlines the subgraph isomorphism search to generate embeddings. In Line 2, for an NEC vertex u', we obtain a set C of candidate vertices for $u'.NEC$ by intersecting all

$CR(u', v_{M[P(u').NEC[i]]})$s according to Lemma 4. Next, we obtain one $|u'.NEC|$-combination from C for the query vertices in $u'.NEC$ (Line 4). If any data vertex in the combination has already been mapped before, this combination is safely pruned (Lines 7 $\sim$ 8). Note that we push this constraint to generate the combination for speedup. Next, if all query vertices in $u'.NEC$ themselves form a clique, we check if the data vertices in the combination themselves form a clique as well (Lines 9 $\sim$ 11). Otherwise, we prune out these vertices. Next, by calling ISJOINABLE, we check if, for each query vertex u in $u'.NEC$, the edges between u and already matched query vertices of q have corresponding edges between $V[i]$ and already matched data vertices of g (Lines 13 $\sim$ 18). If every vertex in the combination is qualified, it is mapped to the corresponding query vertex u, and SUBGRAPHSEARCH updates status information by calling UPDATESTATE (Line 19). Once we examine all NEC vertices (all query vertices, accordingly), we generate embeddings by calling GENPERM (Line 21). Otherwise, SUBGRAPHSEARCH proceeds to match the remaining NEC vertices by recursively calling itself (Line 23). Finally, all changes done by UPDATESTATE are restored by calling RESTORESTATE.

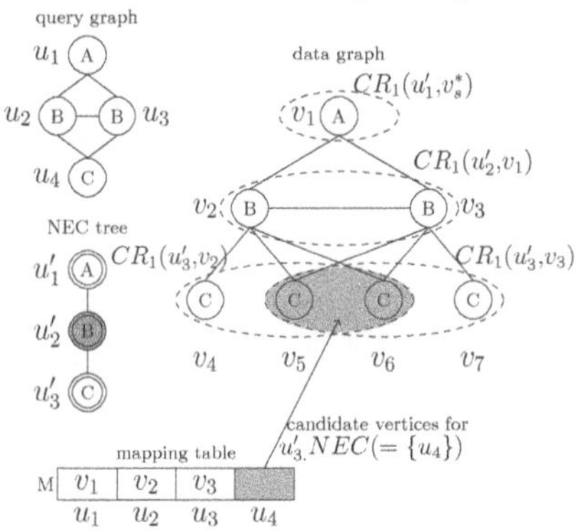

Figure 8: An example for Lemma 4.

Consider the running example in Figure 3. Given the matching order $O_4 = (u'_1, u'_2, u'_4, u'_5, u'_7, u'_6, u'_8, u'_3)$, when we match u'_5 with its candidate vertices, v_8 is pruned by Lines 14 $\sim$ 16. When we match u'_3 with its candidate vertices, v_2 is pruned by Lines 7 and 8. Since $u'_3.NEC$ contains two query vertices u_3 and u_4, we generate combinations from the candidate data vertices for u_3 and u_4 (Line 4) and then generate all possible permutations using those combinations (Line 21).

Unlike all existing algorithms, Turbo$_{\text{ISO}}$ has two phases to process subgraph isomorphism queries. One minor drawback of this approach is that, if we want to find k subgraph isomorphisms only, the existing approach may not access all data vertices in candidate regions for some queries, thus making early termination possible. To solve this problem, Turbo$_{\text{ISO}}$ *interleaves* the candidate region exploration process and the subgraph isomorphism process. That is, for each leaf in the NEC tree, if the number of vertices obtained by candidate region exploration exceeds k, we do not explore more vertices for the NEC vertex. Next, we estimate the number of candidate data vertices for each leaf NEC vertex using data vertices we have explored so far as a sample. Then, we execute the subgraph isomorphism test with the candidate vertices we have found so far. If we are unable to find k subgraph isomorphisms with these candidate vertices, we resume the candidate region exploration to find more candidate vertices. Thus, we can clearly avoid this drawback.

7. EXPERIMENTS

We evaluate the performance of the state-of-the-art algorithms against Turbo$_{\text{ISO}}$. The algorithms considered are as follows: (1) VF2 [3], (2) QuickSI [12] (in short, QSI), (3) GraphQL [6] (in short, GQL), (4) GADDI [20] (in short, GAD), and (5) SPath [21] (in short, SPA). Additionally, we compare Turbo$_{\text{ISO}}$ with the most recent state-of-the-art algorithm [14] in Section 7.5. Our main objective is to show that Turbo$_{\text{ISO}}$ 1) *consistently* outperforms all competing algorithms regardless of query/data sets and 2) *significantly* outperforms the competing algorithms by up to several orders of magnitude for datasets containing large graphs.

Algorithm 5 SUBGRAPHSEARCH $(q, q', g, order, d_c)$

1: $u' := order[d_c]$;
2: $C := CR(u', v_{M[P(u').NEC[1]]}) \cap \cdots \cap CR(u', v_{M[P(u').NEC[|P(u').NEC|]]})$;
3: **while true do**
4: $C' :=$ NEXTCOMB$(C, |u'.NEC|)$; // C' is a list
5: **if** $|C'| = 0$ **then**
6: **return**; /*That is, no more combination exists.*/
7: **if** $\exists v \in C'$ such that $F[v] =$ **true then**
8: **continue**;
9: **if** $u'.NEC$ form a clique **then**
10: **if** $\exists(v, v'), v, v' \in C'$ such that $v \neq v' \wedge (v, v') \notin E(g)$ **then**
11: **continue** ;
12: matched:=**true**;
13: **for** $i := 1$ to $|u'.NEC|$ **do**
14: **if not** ISJOINABLE$(q, g, M, u'.NEC[i], C'[i])$ **then**
15: matched:=**false**;
16: **break**;
17: **if** matched = **false then**
18: **continue**;
19: UPDATESTATE$(M, F, u'.NEC, C')$;
20: **if** $|V(q')| = d_c$ **then**
21: $GenPerm(M, q', 1)$;
22: **else**
23: SUBGRAPHSEARCH$(q, q', g, order, d_c + 1)$;
24: RESTORESTATE$(M, F, u'.NEC, C')$;

For comprehensive performance study, we use the same benchmark setting as [8]. For this purpose, we obtain the source code used in [8] and implement Turbo$_{\text{ISO}}$ on top of this framework for fair comparison. Regarding GraphQL and SPath, we use best parameter values for each dataset as in [8]. We use four datasets referred to here as AIDS, NASA, Yeast, and Human. These datasets have different characteristics. The AIDS dataset contains 10,000 small graphs whose average size is about 27 (in terms of the number of edges). The number of unique labels in AIDS is 51. The NASA dataset contains 36,790 trees where the average tree size is about 32, and the number of unique labels is much larger (=117,302) than AIDS. The Yeast dataset contains only one large graph having 3,112 vertices and 12,519 edges, where a vertex and an edge correspond to a protein and an interaction between two proteins, respectively. Since one protein can appear in several cellular components and biological processes, a vertex can have multiple labels. This graph is denser than those in AIDS and NASA. The Human dataset contains a large graph modeling a protein interaction network of 4,675 proteins (i.e., vertices) and 86,282 interactions (i.e., edges), which is larger and denser than Yeast. This graph has a fewer number of vertex labels (=90) and a larger average degree (=36.82) than Yeast (=8.05). The Human dataset also consists of vertices having multiple labels.

We use the same query sets as in [8]. Specifically, for the AIDS and NASA datasets, we use six query sets ($Q_4, Q_8, \cdots, Q_{24}$), each of which contains 1,000 query graphs of the same size. Note that in these query sets, a small size query graph q_s of size s is constructed from a large size query graph q_l of size $s + 4$ by removing edges until q_l is connected and contains s edges. Thus, the containment relationship between q_s and q_l is satisfied. For the Yeast and Human datasets, we use 10 query sets by varying the number of query sizes from 1 to 10. For those datasets, we use two more query sets (clique/path queries), generated by a tool used in [6]. These query sets do not satisfy the containment relationship. Since overall performance trends of the algorithms in the Yeast dataset are similar to those in the Human dataset, and thus, we omit them to save space.

We conducted all the experiments on a Windows Vista machine with Xeon Quad Core 2.27 GHz CPU and 8 GBytes RAM. We set the page size to 8 KBytes. We used the average number of SUBGRAPHSEARCH calls, and the average wall clock time as the performance metrics for query execution. We stopped subgraph isomorphism search after the first 1,000 subgraph isomorphisms were found, as it was done in [6, 21, 8]. For the database build time, since we do not maintain any auxiliary data structures, for AIDS and NASA, our building time is similar to VF2 which has the lowest database building time among all competitors. If there are multiple labels in data vertices as in Yeast and Human, since we group each adjacency list by label, our index building time is about 4-5 times slower than VF2 due to larger adjacency lists, but is still much faster than the other competitors. Since the subgraph isomorphism search is a CPU intensive task, $\text{Turbo}_{\text{ISO}}$ significantly outperforms all competitors for those datasets in spite of the increased reading time in Yeast and Human.

7.1 Experiment on the AIDS dataset

Figure 9 shows the experimental results for AIDS. All algorithms behave well since they choose relatively good matching orders for this dataset and prune unpromising candidates early. Here, as we increase the query size, the elapsed time of every algorithm decreases. Due to the containment relationship among the query sets in AIDS, as we increase the query size, the number of embeddings may decrease, and thus, we achieve better performance by pruning unpromising candidates early.

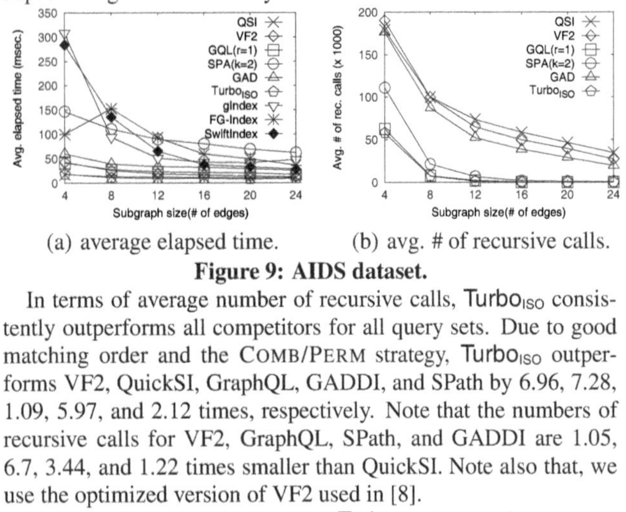

(a) average elapsed time. (b) avg. # of recursive calls.

Figure 9: AIDS dataset.

In terms of average number of recursive calls, $\text{Turbo}_{\text{ISO}}$ consistently outperforms all competitors for all query sets. Due to good matching order and the COMB/PERM strategy, $\text{Turbo}_{\text{ISO}}$ outperforms VF2, QuickSI, GraphQL, GADDI, and SPath by 6.96, 7.28, 1.09, 5.97, and 2.12 times, respectively. Note that the numbers of recursive calls for VF2, GraphQL, SPath, and GADDI are 1.05, 6.7, 3.44, and 1.22 times smaller than QuickSI. Note also that, we use the optimized version of VF2 used in [8].

In terms of average elapsed time, $\text{Turbo}_{\text{ISO}}$ also consistently outperforms all competitors for all query sets, although the ranking order ($\text{Turbo}_{\text{ISO}}$, QuickSI, VF2, GraphQL, GADDI, and SPath) is completely different. Since $\text{Turbo}_{\text{ISO}}$ has the candidate region exploration before executing the subgraph isomorphism test, this processing time is included in the elapsed time. Despite this overhead, $\text{Turbo}_{\text{ISO}}$ consistently outperforms all competitors. Although the average number of recursive calls for VF2 is slightly smaller than QuickSI, the average cost of recursive calls for VF2 is 2.82 times larger than that for QuickSI. This is because ISJOINABLE of $\text{Turbo}_{\text{ISO}}$ and QuickSI iterates through adjacent and already matched query vertices of u, while ISJOINABLE of VF2 iterates all adjacent query vertices of u. Regarding GraphQL, the filtering time spent for neighborhood based filtering and pseudo-isomorphism based pruning constitutes about 60 % of the total elapsed time, and the average cost of recursive calls for GraphQL is 1.94 times larger than VF2 due to 1) query optimization overhead and 2) absence of pruning rules in refining candidates. Regarding SPath, the additional times compared with $\text{Turbo}_{\text{ISO}}$ and QuickSI are due to 1) the filtering time spent for SPath neighborhood signature (about 62% of the total elapsed time), and 2) the reading times for accessing large SPath neighborhood signatures. In GADDI, due to the expensive NDS distance computation, the average cost of recursive calls for GADDI is about two times larger than VF2.

In addition, we perform experiments with the three best indexing methods in the iGraph package [5], gIndex, FG-Index, and SwiftIndex, for the AIDS dataset. Note that all indexing methods fail to create indexes for the NASA dataset due to the huge memory requirement (more than 50 GBytes) and exponential behavior in finding frequent subgraphs using their own subgraph isomorphism algorithms. Note that these methods report only the IDs of data graphs which contain a query graph along with only *one* embedding for each resulting data graph. Nevertheless, the experiments show surprising results that all these indexing methods perform poorer than $\text{Turbo}_{\text{ISO}}$. We analyze this phenomenon further. 1) For a given query graph q, they enumerate all subgraphs of size up to $maxL$ for q and check whether such subgraphs are in their indexes. However, this step constitutes a considerable performance bottleneck. Furthermore, this cost increases as we increase the query size. 2) After that, they intersect all relevant posting lists to obtain candidate graphs. Finally, they execute a subgraph isomorphism test for each candidate for refinement. However, the non-pruning ratios (or selectivities) using the indexes for $Q4 \sim Q24$ are considerably large, i.e., about 29.6% $\sim$ 0.18%. Considering that the index scan outperforms the sequential scan only when the selectivity is very small, these indexing-based methods cannot outperform the fast subgraph isomorphism algorithms using the sequential scan including $\text{Turbo}_{\text{ISO}}$. This indicates that we must reconsider the graph indexing problem itself.

7.2 Experiment on the NASA dataset

Figure 10 shows the experimental results for NASA. Although the NASA dataset contains only trees, VF2, QuickSI, and GADDI show exponential behaviors at the sizes of query sets 8, 12, and 8, respectively. GraphQL and SPath can finish their query processing in a reasonable time. However, if we use $r = 1$ and $k = 1$, both methods also fail at query sizes 16 and 12. Even if we use the best parameter values for GraphQL and SPath, $\text{Turbo}_{\text{ISO}}$ significantly outperforms them.

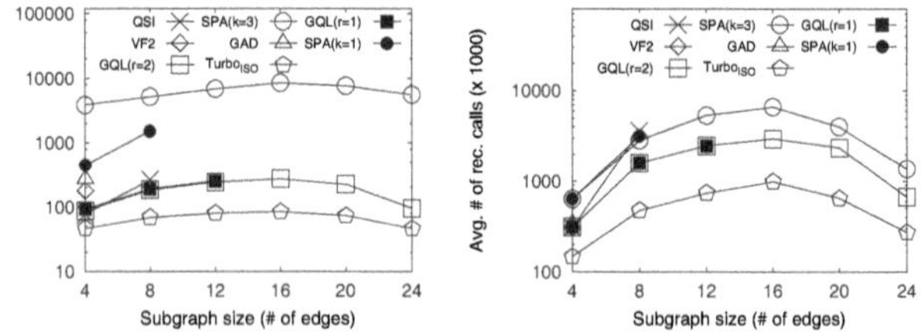

(a) average elapsed time. (b) avg. # of recursive calls.

Figure 10: NASA dataset.

The average numbers of recursive calls for $\text{Turbo}_{\text{ISO}}$ and GraphQL increase as we increase the query size up to 16. This is due to search space increments. However, when we increase the query size further, the average numbers of recursive calls decrease, since the matching orders of $\text{Turbo}_{\text{ISO}}$ and GraphQL significantly prune candidates, thereby significantly reducing the average number of recursive calls.

In the NASA dataset, there exist star-shaped queries having many of the same vertex labels. In GraphQL, by exploiting the pseudo-isomorphism test and signature-based filtering, it can gracefully handle such non-trivial queries. On the other hand, $\text{Turbo}_{\text{ISO}}$ processes such queries very efficiently by using the COMB/PERM strategy. In terms of the average elapsed time, $\mathsf{Turbo_{ISO}}$ significantly outperforms GraphQL and SPath by up to 3.22 and 119.49 times, respectively. We note that the overhead of executing the candidate region exploration for the NASA dataset is marginal to the overall query processing time.

7.3 Experiment on the Human dataset

Subgraph Queries: Figures 11(a) and 11(b) show the results of subgraph isomorphism search performance using subgraph queries for the Human dataset. Except GraphQL, all competitors fail to finish their query processing in a reasonable time. Specifically, VF2, GADDI, QuickSI, and SPath fail at query sizes 5, 7, 8, and 8. Note that GraphQL uses a large r value (=4) for this experiment. Otherwise, it also fails to complete its query processing.

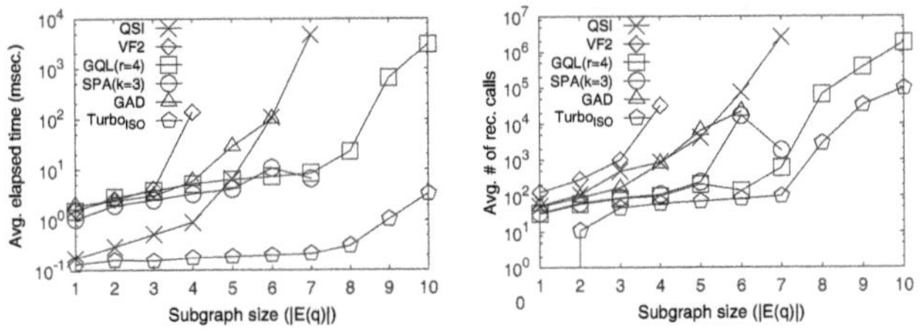

(a) average elapsed time. (b) avg. # of recursive calls.

Figure 11: Human dataset (Subgraph queries).

By using candidate region exploration and the COMB/PERM strategy, $\mathsf{Turbo_{ISO}}$ significantly outperforms GraphQL by up to 925.43 times! GraphQL prunes many candidates by using the pseudo-isomorphism test. However, since it uses the large r value, the performance overhead of the pseudo-isomorphism test becomes extremely expensive.

Clique Queries: Figures 12(a) and 12(b) show the performance results for the clique queries. Again, $\mathsf{Turbo_{ISO}}$ significantly outperforms all competitors. VF2 fails at query size 7. Since the Human dataset is denser than the Yeast dataset, matching orders generated by QuickSI are worse than those for Yeast. Thus, GraphQL outperforms QuickSI by 2.84 times on average.

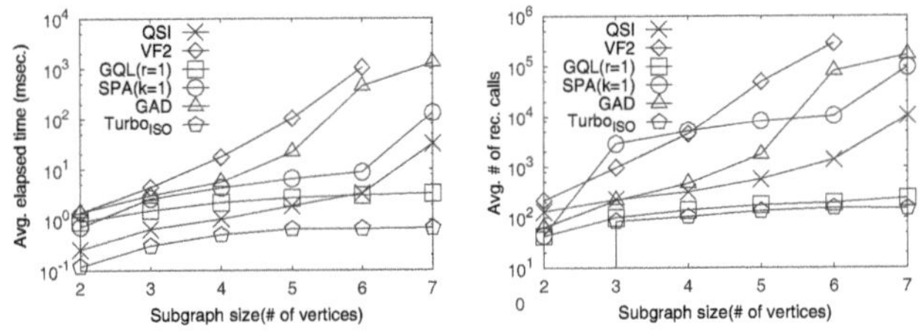

(a) average elapsed time. (b) avg. # of recursive calls.

Figure 12: Human dataset (Clique queries).

Path Queries: Figures 13(a) and 13(b) show the performance results for the path queries. Both VF2 and GADDI fail at query size 8. On average, $\mathsf{Turbo_{ISO}}$ is 3.79, 3.86, and 408.70 times faster than SPath, GraphQL, and QuickSI. Note that the performance of QuickSI for the Human dataset is much worse than that for the Yeast dataset due to the serious problem in its matching order selection. GraphQL shows more robust performance than QuickSI in the Human dataset, since it uses signature-based filtering and the pseudo-isomorphism test. Note that it uses a small r value (=0), and its elapsed time is reasonably good since the query type is path.

7.4 Scalability Test

We perform experiments by varying the number of vertices from 0.5 million to 4 million vertices (i.e., 8 datasets). The average degree is 8. That is, the largest graph contains 32 million edges. These

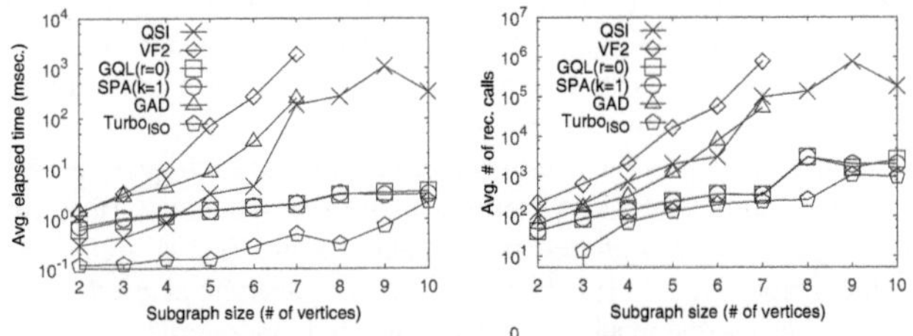

(a) average elapsed time. (b) avg. # of recursive calls.

Figure 13: Human dataset (Path queries).

datasets are generated by exploiting a graph generator provided by the GraphQL package where we make the generator produce multiple labels per vertex. The number of vertex labels is 500, and the average number of labels per vertex is about 8. We use one query set containing 1000 subgraph queries of size 15 for each dataset.

Figure 14 shows the average elapsed time for each query as we vary the number of data vertices. As we increase the number of vertices, the performance linearly increases mainly due to linearly increased graph loading time. If we exclude the loading time from the total elapsed time, the subgraph isomorphism performance of $\mathsf{Turbo_{ISO}}$ remains almost the same. This shows the excellent scalability of $\mathsf{Turbo_{ISO}}$ when varying the number of vertices.

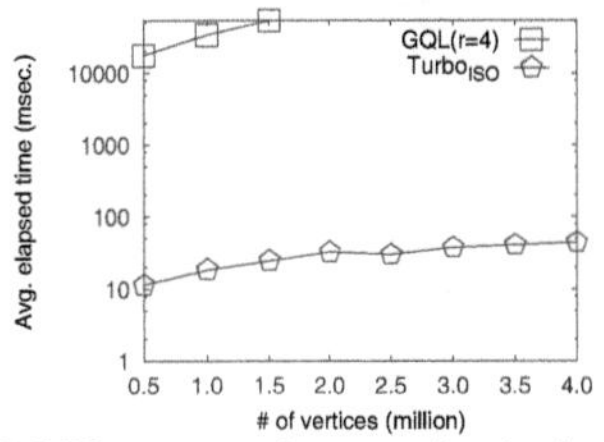

Figure 14: Scalability test using synthetic datasets (Subgraph queries).

Since GraphQL shows the best performance in the previous experiments, we perform the same scalability test using GraphQL. For the graph having one million vertices, $\mathsf{Turbo_{ISO}}$ outperforms GraphQL by 1836 times, finishing all 1000 queries in only 18 seconds, while GraphQL requires about 9.42 hours. The signature-based pruning and pseudo-isomorphism based pruning of GraphQL incur serious performance overhead when the number of vertices is very large. We see that the gap increases further as we increase the number of vertices.

7.5 Comparison with STW [14]

We compare $\mathsf{Turbo_{ISO}}$ with the most recent state-of-the-art in [14], referred to here as STW. Since we are unable to re-implement it due to unclarity in sampling-based join optimization of STW, we instead perform $\mathsf{Turbo_{ISO}}$ using the same real data sets as used in [14]. For fair comparison, we use a machine having the same CPU and OS as in [14] and also make the data graphs be resident in memory the same way as STW. Note that, like STW, there is no extra overhead in loading graphs into our database, since we do not maintain any auxiliary (index) structures. We stop subgraph isomorphism search after the first 1024 subgraph isomorphisms are found as done in [14]. We use the same two real data sets, US Patent and WordNet as in [14]. The US Patent graph consists of 3,774,768 vertices and 16,522,438 edges, having 418 labels. The WordNet graph contains 82,670 vertices, 133,445 edges and 5 labels. Due to unavailability of the query sets, according to the description in [14], we generate two query sets, referred to here as DFS and Random. While the query sets in [14] contain 100 queries, each of our query sets contains 10,000 queries for a more objective empirical comparison. We report the average elapsed time as in [14]. Since both datasets are directed graphs, the edge direction is considered in the adjacency list, the NEC tree rewrite, candidate region exploration, and the main recursive subroutine in $\text{Turbo}_{\text{ISO}}$.

Figure 15 shows the average elapsed time for each query as we vary the number of query vertices using *one* machine. Here, in this figure, we also plotted performance results (using *eight* machines) reported in [14] for comparison. The average elapsed times of STW using one machine for DFS and Random queries are about 21 seconds and 20 seconds, respectively [14]. $\text{Turbo}_{\text{ISO}}$ processes these query sets remarkably fast (1046 and 23024 times faster for DFS queries over US Patent and WordNet datasets, respectively!). This is again due to the good matching order selection and the COMB/PERM strategy. One author of STW kindly explains why it takes more than 20 seconds to process one query even if it terminates query processing as soon as it finds 1024 embeddings: From queries having 10 vertices and 20 edges, 6∼8 STwigs are generated. In STW, for each STwig, all partial solutions must be obtained first. Here, a large amount of them must be transferred to other servers. Then, STW performs 5∼7 block-based pipeline joins using the partial solutions for all STwigs. In [14], the block size, which means the number of partial solutions instead of the fixed memory bytes, is set to 8096. Thus, the number of the block-wise join result may grow up to about 64 million(=$(8096)^2$). In a clear contrast to STW which generates and transfers a large amount of intermediate STwig results, $\text{Turbo}_{\text{ISO}}$ directly accesses candidate regions without generating intermediate results, obtains good matching orders for them, and finds embeddings using those matching orders and the COMB/PERM strategy, leading to much earlier termination than STW. In addition, we generate 82,670 DFS queries for all vertices in WordNet, choose the top-100 slowest queries, and report the average time for those slowest queries. Nevertheless, $\text{Turbo}_{\text{ISO}}$ outperforms STW by up to 2851 times. This additional test *ensures* the superiority of $\text{Turbo}_{\text{ISO}}$ against STW.

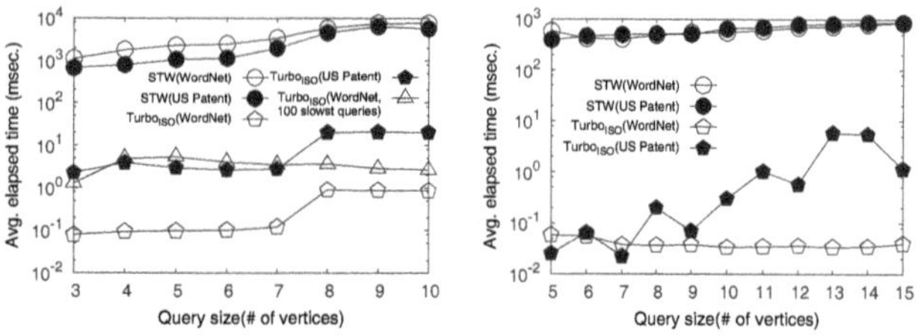

(a) DFS queries. (b) Random queries.

Figure 15: Comparison with STW.

8. CONCLUSION

In this paper, we presented an efficient and robust subgraph search solution called $\text{Turbo}_{\text{ISO}}$ in graph databases. We showed that our solution completely solved the problems of existing algorithms.

We first proposed the novel notion of neighborhood equivalence class (NEC), and then formally derived how to efficiently obtain NECs from a query graph. We then proposed the candidate region exploration process to efficiently identify candidate regions and find robust matching orders which are used for subgraph isomorphism search. We next proposed the COMB/PERM strategy to generate only necessary enumerations. That is, during subgraph isomorphism search, COMB/PERM generated only combinations for each NEC instead of permutating all possible enumerations. Thus, if a chosen combination is determined to not contribute to a complete solution, all possible permutations for the combination will be pruned without any enumeration, thereby significantly avoiding useless computations.

Through extensive experiments, we showed that our solution outperformed all competitors by up to orders of magnitude. Overall, we believe our subgraph isomorphism solution provides comprehensive insight and a substantial framework for future research.

9. ACKNOWLEDGEMENTS

This work was supported by the National Research Foundation of Korea(NRF) grant funded by the Korea government(MEST) (No. 2011-0016520) and Next-Generation Information Computing Development Program through the NRF funded by the Ministry of Education, Science and Technology (No. NRF-2012M3C4A7033342).

10. REFERENCES

[1] R. A. Baeza-Yates and G. Valiente. An image similarity measure based on graph matching. In *SPIRE*, pages 28–38, 2000.

[2] J. Cheng, Y. Ke, W. Ng, and A. Lu. Fg-index: towards verification-free query processing on graph databases. In *SIGMOD*, pages 857–872, 2007.

[3] L. P. Cordella, P. Foggia, C. Sansone, and M. Vento. A (sub)graph isomorphism algorithm for matching large graphs. *IEEE PAMI*, 26(10):1367–1372, 2004.

[4] M. Deshpande, M. Kuramochi, N. Wale, and G. Karypis. Frequent substructure-based approaches for classifying chemical compounds. *IEEE Trans. Knowl. Data Eng.*, 17(8):1036–1050, 2005.

[5] W.-S. Han, J. Lee, M.-D. Pham, and J. X. Yu. iGraph: A framework for comparisons of disk-based graph indexing techniques. *PVLDB*, 3(1):449–459, 2010.

[6] H. He and A. K. Singh. Graphs-at-a-time: query language and access methods for graph databases. In *SIGMOD*, pages 405–418, 2008.

[7] A. Khan, N. Li, X. Yan, Z. Guan, S. Chakraborty, and S. Tao. Neighborhood based fast graph search in large networks. In *SIGMOD*, pages 901–912, 2011.

[8] J. Lee, W.-S. Han, R. Kasperovics, and J.-H. Lee. An in-depth comparison of subgraph isomorphism algorithms in graph databases. *PVLDB*, 6(2), 2013, http://www-db.knu.ac.kr/vldb13.pdf.

[9] M. Mongiovi, R. D. Natale, R. Giugno, A. Pulvirenti, A. Ferro, and R. Sharan. Sigma: a set-cover-based inexact graph matching algorithm. *J. Bioinformatics and Computational Biology*, 8(2):199–218, 2010.

[10] M. Ohlrich, C. Ebeling, E. Ginting, and L. Sather. Subgemini: Identifying subcircuits using a fast subgraph isomorphism algorithm. In *DAC*, pages 31–37, 1993.

[11] M. E. Saeedy and P. Kalnis. Grami: Generalized frequent pattern mining in a single large graph.

[12] H. Shang, Y. Zhang, X. Lin, and J. X. Yu. Taming verification hardness: an efficient algorithm for testing subgraph isomorphism. *PVLDB*, 1(1):364–375, 2008.

[13] B. Shao, H. Wang, and Y. Li. The trinity graph engine. Technical Report 161291, Microsoft Research, 2012.

[14] Z. Sun, H. Wang, H. Wang, B. Shao, and J. Li. Efficient subgraph matching on billion node graphs. *PVLDB*, 5(9):788–799, 2012.

[15] Y. Tian and J. M. Patel. TALE: A tool for approximate large graph matching. In *ICDE*, pages 963–972, 2008.

[16] J. R. Ullmann. An algorithm for subgraph isomorphism. *J. ACM*, 23:31–42, January 1976.

[17] X. Yan, P. S. Yu, and J. Han. Graph indexing: A frequent structure-based approach. In *SIGMOD*, pages 335–346, 2004.

[18] X. Yan, P. S. Yu, and J. Han. Graph indexing based on discriminative frequent structure analysis. *ACM Trans. Database Syst.*, 30(4):960–993, 2005.

[19] S. Zhang, M. Hu, and J. Yang. Treepi: A novel graph indexing method. In *ICDE*, pages 966–975, 2007.

[20] S. Zhang, S. Li, and J. Yang. GADDI: distance index based subgraph matching in biological networks. In *EDBT*, pages 192–203, 2009.

[21] P. Zhao and J. Han. On graph query optimization in large networks. *PVLDB*, 3(1):340–351, 2010.

[22] P. Zhao, J. X. Yu, and P. S. Yu. Graph indexing: Tree + delta >= graph. In *VLDB*, pages 938–949, 2007.

[23] L. Zou, L. Chen, J. X. Yu, and Y. Lu. A novel spectral coding in a large graph database. In *EDBT*, pages 181–192, 2008.

Fast Exact Shortest-Path Distance Queries on Large Networks by Pruned Landmark Labeling

Takuya Akiba
The University of Tokyo
Tokyo, 113-0033, Japan
t.akiba@is.s.u-tokyo.ac.jp

Yoichi Iwata
The University of Tokyo
Tokyo, 113-0033, Japan
y.iwata@is.s.u-tokyo.ac.jp

Yuichi Yoshida
National Institute of Informatics,
Preferred Infrastructure, Inc.
Tokyo, 101-8430, Japan
yyoshida@nii.ac.jp

ABSTRACT

We propose a new exact method for shortest-path distance queries on large-scale networks. Our method precomputes distance labels for vertices by performing a breadth-first search from every vertex. Seemingly too obvious and too inefficient at first glance, the key ingredient introduced here is *pruning* during breadth-first searches. While we can still answer the correct distance for any pair of vertices from the labels, it surprisingly reduces the search space and sizes of labels. Moreover, we show that we can perform 32 or 64 breadth-first searches simultaneously exploiting bitwise operations. We experimentally demonstrate that the combination of these two techniques is efficient and robust on various kinds of large-scale real-world networks. In particular, our method can handle social networks and web graphs with hundreds of millions of edges, which are two orders of magnitude larger than the limits of previous exact methods, with comparable query time to those of previous methods.

Categories and Subject Descriptors

E.1 [**Data**]: Data Structures—*Graphs and networks*

General Terms

Algorithms, Experimentation, Performance

Keywords

Graphs, shortest paths, query processing

1. INTRODUCTION

A *distance query* asks the distance between two vertices in a graph. Without doubt, answering distance queries is one of the most fundamental operations on graphs, and it has wide range of applications. For example, on social networks, distance between two users is considered to indicate the closeness, and used in socially-sensitive search to help users to find more related users or contents [40, 42], or to analyze influential people and communities [19, 6]. On web graphs, distance between web pages is one of indicators of relevance, and used in context-aware search to give higher ranks to web pages more related to the currently visiting web page [39, 29]. Other applications of distance queries include top-k keyword queries on linked data [16, 37], discovery of optimal pathways between compounds in metabolic networks [31, 32], and management of resources in computer networks [28, 7].

Of course, we can compute the distance for each query by using a breadth first search (BFS) or Dijkstra's algorithm. However, they take more than a second for large graphs, which is too slow to use as a building block of these applications. In particular, applications such as socially-sensitive search or context-aware search should have low latency since they involve real-time interactions between users, while they need distances between a number of pairs of vertices to rank items for each search query. Therefore, distance queries should be answered much more quickly, say, microseconds.

The other extreme approach is to compute distances between all pairs of vertices beforehand and store them in an index. Though we can answer distance queries instantly, this approach is also unacceptable since preprocessing time and index size are quadratic and unrealistically large. Due to the emergence of huge graph data, design of more moderate and practical methods between these two extreme approaches has been attracting strong interest in the database community [12, 29, 41, 38, 4, 30, 17].

Generally, there are two major graph classes of real-world networks: one is road networks, and the other is complex networks such as social networks, web graphs, biological networks and computer networks. For road networks, since it is easier to grasp and exploit structures of them, research has been already very successful. Now distance queries on road networks can be processed in less than one microsecond for the complete road network of the USA [1].

In contrast, answering distance queries on complex networks is still a highly challenging problem. The methods for road networks do not perform well on these networks since structures of them are totally different. Several methods have been proposed for these networks, but they suffer from drawback of scalability. They take at least thousands of seconds or tens of thousands of seconds to index networks with millions of edges [41, 4, 2, 17].

To handle larger complex networks, apart from these exact methods, approximate methods are also studied. That is, we do not always have to answer correct distances. They are successful in terms of much better scalability and very small

SIGMOD'13, June 22–27, 2013, New York, New York, USA.

average relative error for random queries. However, some of these methods take milliseconds to answer queries [15, 38, 30], which is about three orders of magnitude slower than other methods. Some other methods answer queries in microseconds [29, 40], but it is reported that precision of these methods for close pairs of vertices is not high [30, 4]. This drawback might be critical for applications such as socially-sensitive search or context-aware search since, in these applications, distance queries are employed to distinguish close items.

1.1 Our Contributions

To address these issues, in this paper, we present a new method for answering distance queries in complex networks. The proposed method is an exact method. That is, it always answers exactly correct distance to queries. It has much better scalability than previous exact methods and can handle graphs with hundreds of millions of edges. Nevertheless, the query time is very small and around ten microseconds. Though our method can handle directed and/or weighted graphs as we mention later, in the following, we assume undirected, unweighted graphs for simplicity of exposition.

Our method is based on the notion of *distance labeling* or *distance-aware 2-hop cover.* The idea of 2-hop cover is as follows. For each vertex u, we pick up a set $C(u)$ of candidate vertices so that every pair of vertices (u, v) has at least one vertex $w \in C(u) \cap C(v)$ on a shortest path between the pair. For each vertex u and a vertex $w \in C(u)$, we precompute the distance $d_G(u, w)$ between them. We say that the set $L(u) = \{(w, d_G(u, w))\}_{w \in C(u)}$ is the *label* of u. Using labels, it is clear that the distance $d_G(u, v)$ between two vertices u and v can be computed as $\min\{\delta+\delta' \mid (w, \delta) \in L(u), (w, \delta') \in L(v)\}$. The family of labels $\{L(u)\}$ is called a *2-hop cover.* Distance labeling is also commonly used in previous exact methods [13,12,2,17], but we propose a totally new and different approach to compute the labels, referred to as the *pruned landmark labeling.*

The idea of our method is simple and rather radical: from every vertex, we conduct a breadth-first search and add the distance information to labels of visited vertices. Of course, if we naively implement this idea, we need $O(nm)$ preprocessing time and $O(n^2)$ space to store the index, which is unacceptable. Here, n is the number of vertices and m is the number of edges. Our key idea to make this method practical is *pruning* during the breadth-first searches. Let S be a set of vertices and suppose that we already have labels that can answer correct distance between two vertices if a shortest path between them passes through a vertex in S. Suppose we are conducting a BFS from v and visiting u. If there is a vertex $w \in S$ such that $d_G(v, u) = d_G(v, w) + d_G(w, u)$, then we *prune* u. That is, we do not traverse any edges from u. As we prove in Section 4.3, after this pruned BFS from v, the labels can answer the distance between two vertices if a shortest path between them passes through a vertex in $S \cup \{v\}$.

Interestingly, our method combines the advantages of three different previous successful approaches: landmark-based approximate methods [29, 38, 30], tree-decomposition-based exact methods [41, 4], and labeling-based exact methods [13, 12, 2]. Landmark-based approximate methods achieve remarkable precision by leveraging the existence of highly *central* vertices in complex networks [29]. This fact is also the main reason of the power of our pruning: by conducting breadth-first searches from these central vertices first, later we can drastically prune breadth-first searches. Tree-decomposition-based methods exploit the core–fringe structure of networks [10, 27] by decomposing tree-like fringes of low tree-width. Though our method does not explicitly use tree decompositions, we prove that our method can efficiently process graphs of small tree-width. This process indicates that our method also exploits the core–fringe structure. As with other labeling-based methods, the data structure of our index is simple and query processing is very quick because of the locality of memory access.

Table 1: Summary of experimental results of previous methods and the proposed method for exact distance queries.

Method	Network	$\|V\|$	$\|E\|$	Indexing	Query
TEDI	Computer	22 K	46 K	17 s	4.2 μs
[41]	Social	0.6 M	0.6 M	2,226 s	55.0 μs
HCL	Social	7.1 K	0.1 M	1,003 s	28.2 μs
[17]	Citation	0.7 M	0.3 M	253,104 s	0.2 μs
TD	Social	0.3 M	0.4 M	9 s	0.5 μs
[4]	Social	2.4 M	4.7 M	2,473 s	0.8 μs
HHL	Computer	0.2 M	1.2 M	7,399 s	3.1 μs
[2]	Social	0.3 M	1.9 M	19,488 s	6.9 μs
PLL	Web	0.3 M	1.5 M	**4 s**	0.5 μs
(this work)	Social	2.4 M	4.7 M	**61 s**	0.6 μs
	Social	1.1 M	**114 M**	15,164 s	15.6 μs
	Web	7.4 M	**194 M**	6,068 s	4.1 μs

Though this pruned landmark labeling scheme is already powerful by itself, we propose another labeling scheme with a different kind of strength and combine them to further improve the performance. That is, we show that labeling by breadth-first search can be implemented in a bit-parallel way, which exploits the property that the number of bits b in a register word is typically 32 or 64 and we can perform bit manipulations on these b bits simultaneously. By this technique, we can perform BFSs from $b + 1$ vertices simultaneously in $O(m)$ time. In the beginning, this bit-parallel labeling (without pruning) works better than the pruned landmark labeling since pruning does not happen much. Note that we are not talking about thread-level parallelism, and our bit-parallelism actually decreases the computational complexity by the factor of $b + 1$. We can also use thread-level parallelism in addition to these two labeling schemes.

As we confirm in our experimental results, our method outperforms other state-of-the-art methods for exact distance queries. In particular, it has significantly better scalability than previous methods. It took only tens of seconds for indexing networks with millions of edges. This indexing time is two orders of magnitude faster than previous methods, which took at least thousands of seconds or even more than one day. Moreover, our method successfully handled networks with hundreds of millions of edges, which is again two orders of magnitude larger than networks that have been previously used in experiments of exact methods. The query time is also better than previous methods for networks with the same size, and we confirmed that the query time does not increase rapidly against sizes of networks. We also confirm the size of an index of our method is comparable to other methods.

In Table 1, we summarize our experimental results and those of previous exact methods presented in these papers. We listed the results for the largest two real-world complex networks from each paper. In our experiments, we further compare our method with hierarchical hub labeling [2] and the tree-decomposition-based method [4].

In Section 2, we describe related works on exact and approximate distance queries. In Section 3, we give definitions and notions used in this paper. Section 4 is devoted to explain our first scheme, the pruned landmark labeling. We explain our second scheme, the bit-parallel labeling, in Section 5. In Section 6, we mention variants of distance queries we can handle by slightly modifying our method. We explain our experimental results in Section 7, and conclude in Section 8.

2. RELATED WORK

2.1 Exact Methods

For exact distance queries on complex networks such as social networks and web graphs, several methods are proposed recently.

Large portion of these methods can be considered as based on the idea of 2-hop cover [13]. Finding small 2-hop covers efficiently is a challenging and long-standing problem [13,12, 2]. One of the latest methods is *hierarchical hub labeling* [2], which is based on a method for road networks [1]. Another latest method related to 2-hop cover is *highway-centric labeling* [17]. In this method, we first compute a spanning tree T and use it as a "highway". That is, when computing distance $d_G(u, v)$ between two vertices u and v, we output the minimum over $d_G(u, w_1)+d_T(w_1, w_2)+d_G(w_2, v)$ where w_1 and w_2 are vertices in labels of u and v, respectively, and $d_T(\cdot, \cdot)$ is the distance metric on the spanning tree T.

An approach based on *tree decompositions* is also reported to be efficient [41,4]. A tree decomposition of a graph G is a tree T with each vertex associated with a set of vertices in G, called a *bag* [35]. Also, the set of bags containing a vertex in G forms a connected component in T. It heuristically computes a tree decompositions and stores shortest-distance matrices for each bag. It is not hard to compute distances from this information. The smaller the size of the largest bag is, the more efficient this method is. Because of the core–fringe structure of the networks [10, 27], these networks can be decomposed into one big bag and many small bags, and the size of the largest bag is moderate though not small.

2.2 Approximate Methods

To gain more scalability than these exact methods, approximate methods, which do not always answer correct distances, also have been studied.

The major approach is the *landmark-based approach* [36, 40]. The basic idea of these methods is to select a subset L of vertices as landmarks, and precompute the distance $d_G(\ell, u)$ between each landmark $\ell \in L$ and all the vertices $u \in V$. When the distance between two vertices u and v is queried, we answer the minimum $d_G(u, \ell) + d_G(\ell, v)$ over landmarks $\ell \in L$ as an estimate. Generally, the precision for each query depends on whether actual shortest paths pass nearby the landmarks. Therefore, by selecting central vertices as landmarks, the accuracy of estimates becomes much better than selecting landmarks randomly [29, 11]. However, for close pairs, the precision is still much worse than the average, since lengths of shortest paths between them are small and they are unlikely to pass nearby the landmarks [4].

To further improve the accuracy, several techniques were proposed [15,38,30]. They typically store shortest-path trees rooted at the landmarks instead of just storing distances from the landmarks. To answer queries, they extract paths from the shortest-path trees as candidates of shortest-paths, and improve them by finding loops or shortcuts. While they significantly improve the accuracy, the query time becomes up to three orders of magnitude slower.

Table 2: Frequently used notations.

Notation	Description
$G = (V, E)$	A graph
n	Number of vertices in graph G
m	Number of edges in graph G
$N_G(v)$	Neighbors of vertex v in graph G
$d_G(u, v)$	Distance between vertex u and v in graph G
$P_G(u, v)$	Set of all the vertices on the shortest paths between vertex u and v in graph G

3. PRELIMINARIES

3.1 Notations

Table 2 lists the notations that are frequently used in this paper. In this paper, we mainly focus on networks that are modeled as graphs. Let $G = (V, E)$ be a graph with vertex set V and edge set E. We use symbols n and m to denote the number of vertices $|V|$ and the number of edges $|E|$, respectively, when the graph is clear from the context. We also denote the vertex set of G by $V(G)$ and the edge set of G by $E(G)$. We denote the neighbors of a vertex $v \in V$ by $N_G(v)$. That is, $N_G(v) = \{u \in V \mid (u, v) \in E\}$.

Let $d_G(u, v)$ denote the distance between vertices u, v. If u and v are disconnected in G, we define $d_G(u, v) = \infty$. The distance in graphs is a metric, thus it satisfies the triangle inequalities. That is, for any three vertices s, t and v,

$$d_G(s, t) \leq d_G(s, v) + d_G(v, t), \quad (1)$$

$$d_G(s, t) \geq |d_G(s, v) - d_G(v, t)| \,. \quad (2)$$

We define $P_G(s, t) \subseteq V$ as the set of all vertices on the shortest paths between vertices s and t. In other words,

$$P_G(s, t) = \{v \in V \mid d_G(s, v) + d_G(v, t) = d_G(s, t)\} \,.$$

3.2 Problem Definition

This paper studies the following problem: given a graph G, construct an index to efficiently answer distance queries, which asks the distance between an arbitrary pair of vertices.

For simplicity of exposition, we mainly consider undirected, unweighted graphs. However, our algorithm can be easily extended for directed and/or weighted graphs, and we discuss about this extension in Section 6. Furthermore, our method can answer not only distances but also shortest-paths. This extension is also discussed in Section 6.

3.3 Labels and 2-Hop Cover

The general framework of *2-hop cover* [13, 12, 2], or sometimes called a *labeling method*, is as follows. Our method also follows this framework.

For each vertex v, we precompute a *label* denoted as $L(v)$, which is a set of pairs (u, δ_{uv}), where u is a vertex and $\delta_{uv} = d_G(u, v)$. We sometimes call the set of labels $\{L(v)\}_{v \in V}$ as an *index*. To answer a distance query between vertices s and

t, we compute and answer QUERY(s,t,L) defined as follows,

$$\text{QUERY}(s,t,L) = \\ \min\left\{\delta_{vs} + \delta_{vt} \mid (v,\delta_{vs}) \in L(s), (v,\delta_{vt}) \in L(t)\right\}.$$

We define QUERY$(s,t,L) = \infty$ if $L(s)$ and $L(t)$ do not share any vertex. We call L a *(distance-aware) 2-hop cover* of G if QUERY$(s,t,L) = d_G(s,t)$ for any pair of vertices s and t.

For each vertex v, we store the label $L(v)$ so that pairs in it are sorted by their vertices. Then, we can compute QUERY(s,t,L) in $O(|L(s)| + |L(t)|)$ time using a merge-join-like algorithm.

4. ALGORITHM DESCRIPTION

4.1 Naive Landmark Labeling

We start with the following naive method. As the index, we conduct a BFS from each vertex and store distances between all pairs. Though this method is too obvious and inefficient, for the exposition of the next method, we explain the details.

Let $V = \{v_1, v_2, \dots, v_n\}$. We start with an empty index L_0, where $L_0(u) = \emptyset$ for every $u \in V$. Suppose we conduct BFSs from vertices in the order of $v_1, v_2, \dots, v_n$. After the k-th BFS from a vertex v_k, we add distances from v_k to labels of reached vertices, that is, $L_k(u) = L_{k-1}(u) \cup \{(v_k, d_G(v_k,u))\}$ for each $u \in V$ with $d_G(v_k,u) \neq \infty$. We do not change labels for unreached vertices, that is, $L_k(u) = L_{k-1}(u)$ for every $u \in V$ with $d_G(v_k,u) = \infty$.

L_n is the final index. Obviously QUERY$(s,t,L_n) = d_G(s,t)$ for any pair of vertices s and t, and therefore, L_n is a correct 2-hop cover for exact distance queries. This is because, if s and t are reachable, then $(s,0) \in L_n(s)$ and $(s, d_G(s,t)) \in L_n(t)$ for example.

This method can be considered as a variant of landmark-based approximate methods, which we mentioned in Section 2.2. The standard landmark-based method can be regarded as a method that precomputes L_l instead of L_n and estimates distance between s and t by QUERY(s,t,L_l), where $l \ll n$ is a parameter expressing the number of landmarks.

4.2 Pruned Landmark Labeling

Then, we introduce *pruning* to the naive method. Similarly to the method above, we conduct *pruned* BFSs from vertices in the order of $v_1, v_2, \dots, v_n$. We start with an empty index L'_0 and create an index L'_k from L'_{k-1} using the information obtained by the k-th pruned BFS from vertex v_k.

We prune BFSs as follows. Suppose that we have an index L'_{k-1} and we are conducting a BFS from v_k to create a new index L'_k. Suppose that we are visiting a vertex u with distance δ. If QUERY$(v_k, u, L'_{k-1}) \leq \delta$, then we prune u, that is, we do not add (v_k, δ) to $L'_k(u)$ (i.e. $L'_k(u) = L'_{k-1}(u)$) and we do not traverse any edge from vertex u. Otherwise, we set $L'_k(u) = L'_{k-1}(u) \cup \{(v_k, \delta)\}$ and traverse all the edges from the vertex u as usual. As with the previous method, we also set $L'_k(u) = L'_{k-1}(u)$ for all vertices $u \in V$ that were not visited in the k-th pruned BFS. This algorithm, performing pruned BFSs, is described as Algorithm 1, and the whole preprocessing algorithm is described as Algorithm 2.

Figure 1 shows examples of pruned BFSs. The first pruned BFS from vertex 1 visits all the vertices (Figure 1a). During the next pruned BFS from vertex 2 (Figure 1b), when we visit vertex 6, since QUERY$(2,6,L'_1) = d_G(2,1) + d_G(1,6) = 3 = d_G(2,6)$, we prune vertex 6 and we do not traverse edges from it. We also prune vertices 1 and 12. As the number of performed BFSs increases, we can confirm that the search space gets smaller and smaller (Figure 1c,1d and 1e).

Algorithm 1 Pruned BFS from $v_k \in V$ to create index L'_k.

procedure PRUNEDBFS(G, v_k, L'_{k-1})
  $Q \leftarrow$ a queue with only one element v_k.
  $P[v_k] \leftarrow 0$ and $P[v] \leftarrow \infty$ for all $v \in V(G) \setminus \{v_k\}$.
  $L'_k[v] \leftarrow L'_{k-1}[v]$ for all $v \in V(G)$.
  while Q is not empty **do**
    Dequeue u from Q.
    if QUERY$(v_k, u, L'_{k-1}) \leq P[u]$ **then**
      continue
    $L'_k[u] \leftarrow L'_{k-1}[u] \cup \{(v_k, P[v_k])\}$
    for all $w \in N_G(v)$ s.t. $P[w] = \infty$ **do**
      $P[w] \leftarrow P[u] + 1$.
      Enqueue w onto Q.
  return L'_k

Algorithm 2 Compute a 2-hop cover index by pruned BFS.

procedure PREPROCESS(G)
  $L'_0[v] \leftarrow \emptyset$ for all $v \in V(G)$.
  for $k = 1, 2, \dots, n$ **do**
    $L'_k \leftarrow$ PRUNEDBFS(G, v_k, L'_{k-1})
  return L'_n

4.3 Proof of Correctness

In the following, we prove that this method computes a correct 2-hop cover index, that is, QUERY$(s,t,L'_n) = d_G(s,t)$ for any pair of vertices s and t.

THEOREM 4.1. *For any $0 \leq k \leq n$ and for any pair of vertices s and t,* QUERY$(s,t,L'_k) =$ QUERY(s,t,L_k).

PROOF. We prove the theorem by mathematical induction on k. Since $L'_0 = L_0$, it is true for $k = 0$. Now we assume it holds for $0, 1, \dots, k-1$ and prove it also holds for k.

Let s, t be a pair of vertices. We assume these vertices are reachable in G, since otherwise the answer ∞ can be obviously obtained. Let j be the smallest number such that $(v_j, \delta_{v_j s}) \in L_k(s), (v_j, \delta_{v_j t}) \in L_k(t)$ and $\delta_{v_j s} + \delta_{v_j t} =$ QUERY(s,t,L_k). We prove that $(v_j, \delta_{v_j s})$ and $(v_j, \delta_{v_j t})$ are also included in $L'_k(s)$ and $L'_k(t)$. This immediately leads to QUERY$(s,t,L'_k) =$ QUERY(s,t,L_k). Due to the symmetry between s and t, we prove $(v_j, \delta_{v_j s}) \in L'_k(s)$.

First, for any $i < j$, we prove by contradiction that $v_i \notin P_G(v_j, s)$. If we assume $v_i \in P_G(v_j, s)$, from Inequality 1

$$\begin{aligned}\text{QUERY}(s,t,L_k) &= d_G(s,v_j) + d_G(v_j,t) \\ &= d_G(s,v_i) + d_G(v_i,v_j) + d_G(v_j,t) \\ &\geq d_G(s,v_i) + d_G(v_i,t).\end{aligned}$$

Since $(v_i, d_G(s,v_i)) \in L_k(s)$ and $(v_i, d_G(t,v_i)) \in L_k(t)$, this contradicts to the assumption of the minimality of j. Therefore, $v_i \notin P_G(v_j, s)$ holds for any $i < j$.

Now we prove that $(v_j, d_G(v_j, s)) \in L'_k(s)$. Actually, we prove a more general fact: $(v_j, d_G(v_j, u)) \in L'_k(u)$ for all $u \in P_G(v_j, s)$. Note that $s \in P_G(v_j, s)$. Suppose that we

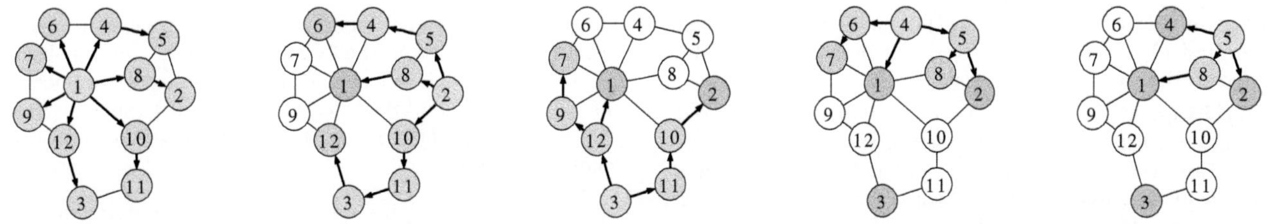

(a) First BFS from vertex 1. We visited all the vertices.

(b) Second BFS from vertex 2. We did not add labels to five vertices.

(c) Third BFS from vertex 3. We only visited the lower half of the vertices.

(d) Fourth BFS from vertex 4. This time we only visited the higher half.

(e) Fifth BFS from vertex 5. The search space was even smaller.

Figure 1: Examples of pruned BFSs. Yellow vertices denote the roots, blue vertices denote those which we visited and labeled, red vertices denote those which we visited but pruned, and gray vertices denote those which are already used as roots.

are conducting the j-th pruned BFS from v_j to create L_j. Let $u \in P_G(v_j, s)$. Since $P_G(v_j, u) \subseteq P_G(v_j, s)$ and $v_i \notin P_G(v_j, s)$ for any $i < j$, we have $v_i \notin P_G(v_j, u)$ for any $i < j$. Therefore, QUERY$(v_j, u, L'_{j-1}) > d_G(v_j, u)$ holds. Thus, we visit all vertices $u \in P_G(v_j, s)$ without pruning, and it follows that $(v_j, d_G(v_j, u)) \in L'_j(u) \subseteq L'_k(u)$. □

As a corollary, our method is proved to be an exact distance querying method by instantiating the theorem with $k = n$.

COROLLARY 4.1. *For any pair of vertices s and t,*

$$\text{QUERY}(s, t, L'_n) = d_G(s, t).$$

4.4 Vertex Ordering Strategies

4.4.1 Motivation

In the algorithm description above, we conducted pruned BFSs from vertices in the order of $v_1, v_2, \ldots, v_n$. We can freely choose the order, and moreover it turns out that the order is crucial for the performance of this method as we will see in the experimental results presented in Section 7.3.4.

To decide the order of vertices, we should select *central* vertices first in the sense that many shortest paths pass through these vertices. Since we would like to prune later BFSs as much as possible, we want to *cover* larger part of pairs of vertices by earlier BFSs. That is, the earlier labels should offer correct distances for as many pairs of vertices as possible, and therefore the earlier vertices should be those who many shortest paths passes through.

This problem is quite similar to the problem of selecting good landmarks for landmark-based approximate methods, which is discussed well in [29]. In that problem, we also want to select good landmarks so that many shortest path passes through these vertices or nearby vertices.

4.4.2 Strategies

Based on the results on landmark-based methods [29], we propose and examine the following three strategies. In experiments, we basically use the DEGREE strategy, and compare them empirically in Section 7.3.4.

RANDOM: We order vertices randomly. We use this method as a baseline to show the significance of other strategies.

DEGREE: We order vertices from those with higher degree. The idea behind this strategy is that vertices with higher degree have stronger connection to many other vertices and therefore many shortest paths would pass through them.

CLOSENESS: We order vertices from those with the highest closeness centrality. Since computing exact closeness centrality for all vertices costs $O(nm)$ time, which is too expensive for large-scale networks, we approximate closeness centrality by randomly sampling a small number of vertices and computing distances from those vertices to all vertices.

4.5 Efficient Implementation

4.5.1 Preprocessing (Algorithm 1)

Index: First, in the description above, we treated L'_{k-1} and L'_k separately and explained as if we copy L'_{k-1} to L'_k for simplicity of explanation. However, this copy can be easily avoided by keeping only one index and adding labels to it after each pruned BFS.

Initialization: Another important note is to avoid $O(n)$ time initialization for each pruned BFS. The reason why this method is efficient is that the search space of pruned BFSs gets much more smaller than the whole graph. However if we spend $O(n)$ time for initialization, it would be the bottleneck. What we want to do in the initialization is to set all values in the array storing tentative distances as ∞ (Line 3). We can avoid $O(n)$ time initialization as follows. Before we conduct the first pruned BFS, we set all values in the array P as ∞. (This takes $O(n)$ time but we do this only once.) Then, during each pruned BFS, we store all vertices we visited, and after each pruned BFS, we set $P[v]$ as ∞ for all each vertex v we have visited.

Arrays: For the array storing tentative distances, it is better to use 8-bit integers. Since networks of our interest are small-world networks, 8-bit integers are enough to represent distances. Using 8-bit integers, the array fits into low-level cache memories of recent computers, resulting in the speed up by reducing cache misses.

Querying: To evaluate queries for pruning (Line 7), it is faster to use an algorithm different from the normal one since we can exploit the fact here that we issue many queries whose one endpoint is always v_k. Before starting the k-th pruned BFS from v_k, we prepare an array T of length n initialized with ∞ and set $T[w] = \delta_{wv_k}$ for all $(w, \delta_{wv_k}) \in L'_{k-1}(v_k)$. To evaluate QUERY$(v_k, u, L'_{k-1})$, for all $(w, \delta_{wu}) \in L'_{k-1}(u)$, we compute $\delta_{wu} + T[w]$ and return the minimum. Though normal querying algorithm takes $O(|L'_{k-1}(v_k)| + |L'_{k-1}(u)|)$ time, this algorithm runs in $O(|L'_{k-1}(u)|)$ time. As Line 7 is the bottleneck of the algorithm, this technique speeds up preprocessing by about twice. Note that T should be represented by 8-bit integers as the same reason described above, and $O(n)$ time initialization for array T should be avoided in the same way for array P.

Prefetching: Unfortunately, we cannot fit the index and the adjacency lists into the cache memory for large-scale networks. However, we can manually prefetch them to reduce the cache misses, since vertices which we will access soon are in the queue. Manual prefetching speeds up preprocessing by about 20%.

Thread-Level Parallelism: As with parallel BFS algorithms [3], the pruned BFS algorithm can be also parallelized. However, for simple experimental analysis and fair comparison to previous methods, we did not parallelize our implementation in the experiments.

Sorting Labels: When applying merge-join-like algorithms to answer queries, pairs in labels need to be sorted by vertices. However, actually we do not need to sort explicitly by storing ranks of vertices instead of vertices. That is, when adding a pair (u, δ) in the i-th pruned BFS from vertex u, we add a pair (i, δ) instead. Then, since pairs are added from vertices with lower rank to those with higher rank, all the labels are automatically sorted.

4.5.2 Querying

Sentinel: We add a dummy entry, (n, ∞), to the label $L(v)$ for each $v \in V$. This dummy entry ensures that we find the same vertices, n, in the end when scanning two labels. Thus we can avoid to separately test whether we have scanned till the end.

Arrays: For each label $L(v)$, it is faster to store the array for vertices and the array for distances separately since distances are only used when vertices match [1]. We also align arrays to cache lines.

4.6 Theoretical Properties

4.6.1 Minimality

THEOREM 4.2. *Let L'_n be the index defined in Section 4.2. L'_n is minimal in the sense that, for any vertex v and for any pair $(u, \delta_{uv}) \in L'_n(v)$, there is a pair of vertices (s, t) such that, if we remove (u, δ_{uv}) from $L'_n(v)$, we cannot answer the correct distance between s and t.*

PROOF. Let $v_i \in V$ and $(v_j, \delta_{v_j v_i}) \in L'_n(v_i)$. This implies $j < i$. We show that if we remove $(v_j, \delta_{v_j v_i})$ from $L'_n(v_i)$ then we cannot answer the correct distance between v_i and v_j. We claim that, for any $k \neq j$, either (i) $(v_k, \delta_{v_k v_i}) \notin L'_n(v_i)$ or $(v_k, \delta_{v_k v_j}) \notin L'_n(v_j)$ holds, or (ii) $d_G(v_i, v_k) + d_G(v_k, v_j) > d_G(v_i, v_j)$ holds. Suppose $k < j$ and assume that (ii) does not hold. Then, (i) must hold since otherwise the j-th BFS should have pruned vertex v_i and $(v_j, \delta_{v_j v_i}) \notin L'_n(v_i)$. Suppose $k > j$ and assume that (ii) does not hold. Then, $v_k \in P_G(v_i, v_j)$ and therefore $(v_j, \delta_{v_j v_k}) \in L'_j(v_k)$, thus the k-th BFS prunes vertex v_j, leading to $(v_k, \delta_{v_k v_j}) \notin L'_n(v_j)$. □

4.6.2 Exploiting Existence of Highly Central Vertices

Then, we compare our method with landmark-based methods to show that our method also can exploit the existence of highly central vertices. We consider the standard landmark-based method [29,40], which do not use any path heuristics. As we stated in Section 2.2, by selecting central vertices as landmarks, it attains remarkable average precision for real-world networks. From the following theorem, we can observe that our method is efficient for networks whose distance can be answered by landmark-based methods with such high precision, and our method also can exploit the existence of these central vertices.

THEOREM 4.3. *If we assume that the standard landmark-based approximate method can answer correct distances to $(1-\epsilon)n^2$ pairs (out of n^2 pairs) using k landmarks, then the pruned landmark labeling method gives an index with average label size $O(k + \epsilon n)$.*

PROOF SKETCH. After conducting pruned BFSs from the k landmark vertices first, at most ϵn^2 pairs are added to the index in total, since we never add pairs whose distance can be answered from current labels. □

4.6.3 Exploiting Small Tree-width of Fringes

Finally, we show a theoretical evidence that our method can also exploit tree-like fringes efficiently. As we mentioned in Section 2.1, methods based on tree decompositions were proposed for distance queries [41, 4]. Both of them extend methods which work efficiently for graphs of small tree-width, and they exploit low tree-width of fringes in real-world networks by tree decompositions. Interestingly, though we do not use tree decompositions explicitly, we can prove that our method can efficiently process graphs of small tree-width. Thus, our method implicitly exploits this property of real-world networks too. For definitions of tree-width and tree decompositions, see [35].

THEOREM 4.4. *Let w be the tree-width of G. There is an order of vertices with which the pruned landmark labeling method takes $O(wm \log n + w^2 n \log^2 n)$ time for preprocessing, stores an index with $O(wn \log n)$ space, and answers each query in $O(w \log n)$ time.*

PROOF SKETCH. The key ingredient is the centroid decomposition [18] of the tree decomposition. First we conduct pruned BFSs from all the vertices in a centroid bag. Then, later pruned BFSs never go beyond the bag. Therefore, we can consider as we divided the tree decomposition into disjoint components, each having at most half of the bags. We recursively repeat this procedure. The number of recurrences is at most $O(\log n)$. Since we add at most w pairs to each vertex at each depth of recursion, the number of pairs in each label is $O(w \log n)$. At each depth of recursion, the total time consumed by pruned BFSs from the current components is $O(wm + w^2 n \log n)$, where $O(wm)$ is the time for traversing edges and $O(w^2 n \log n)$ is the time for pruning tests. □

5. BIT-PARALLEL LABELING

To further speed up both preprocessing and querying, we propose an optimizing method which exploits bit-level parallelism. Bit-parallel methods are those that perform different calculations on different bits in the same word to exploit the fact that computers can perform bitwise operations on a word at once. The word length is commonly 32 or 64 in computers of the day.

In the following, we denote the number of bits in a computer word as b and assume bitwise operations on bit vectors of length b can be done in $O(1)$ time. We propose an algorithm to conduct BFSs and compute labels from $b + 1$ roots

Algorithm 3 Bit-parallel BFS from $r \in V$ and $S_r \subseteq N_G(r)$.

```
procedure Bp-BFS(G, r, S_r)
    (P[v], S_r^{-1}[v], S_r^0[v]) ← (∞, ∅, ∅) for all v ∈ V
    (P[r], S_r^{-1}[r], S_r^0[r]) ← (0, ∅, ∅)
    (P[v], S_r^{-1}[v], S_r^0[v]) ← (1, {v}, ∅) for all v ∈ S_r
    Q_0, Q_1 ← an empty queue
    Enqueue r onto Q_0
    Enqueue v onto Q_1 for all v ∈ S_r
    while Q_0 is not empty do
        E_0 ← ∅ and E_1 ← ∅
        while Q_0 is not empty do
            Dequeue v from Q_0.
            for all u ∈ N_G(v) do
                if P[u] = ∞ ∨ P[u] = P[v] + 1 then
                    E_1 ← E_1 ∪ {(v, u)}
                    if P[u] = ∞ then
                        P[u] ← P[v] + 1
                        Enqueue u onto Q_1.
                else if P[u] = P[v] then
                    E_0 ← E_0 ∪ {(v, u)}
        for all (v, u) ∈ E_0 do
            S_r^0[u] ← S_r^0[u] ∪ S_r^{-1}[v]
        for all (v, u) ∈ E_1 do
            S_r^{-1}[u] ← S_r^{-1}[u] ∪ S_r^{-1}[v]
            S_r^0[u] ← S_r^0[u] ∪ S_r^0[v]
        Q_0 ← Q_1 and Q_1 ← ∅
    return (P, S_r^{-1}, S_r^0)
```

simultaneously in $O(m)$ time. Moreover, we also propose a method to answer distance queries for any pair of vertices via one of these $b+1$ vertices in $O(1)$ time.

5.1 Bit-parallel Labels

To describe the preprocessing algorithm and the querying algorithm, we first define what we store in the index.

As we explain in the next subsection, we conduct bit-parallel BFSs from a vertex r and a subset of its neighbors $S_r \subseteq N_G(r)$ with size at most b. We define

$$S_r^i(v) = \{u \in S_r \mid d_G(u,v) - d_G(r,v) = i\}.$$

Since vertices in S_r are neighbors of r, for any vertex $u \in S_r$ and any vertex $v \in V$, $|d_G(u,v) - d_G(r,v)| \leq 1$. Therefore, for each $v \in V$, S_r can be partitioned into $S_r^{-1}(v), S_r^0(v)$, and $S_r^{+1}(v)$. That is, $S_r^{-1}(v) \cup S_r^0(v) \cup S_r^{+1}(v) = S_r$.

We compute *bit-parallel labels* and store them in the index. For each vertex $v \in V$, we precompute a bit-parallel label denoted as $L_{\mathrm{BP}}(v)$. $L_{\mathrm{BP}}(v)$ is a set of quadruples $(u, \delta_{uv}, S_u^{-1}(v), S_u^0(v))$, where $u \in V$ is a vertex, $\delta_{uv} = d_G(u,v)$ and $S_u^i(v) \subseteq S_u$ is defined above. We store $S_u^{-1}(v)$ and $S_u^0(v)$ by bit vectors of b bits. Note that $S_u^{+1}(v)$ can be obtained as $S_u \setminus (S_u^{-1}(v) \cup S_u^0(v))$, but actually we do not use $S_u^{+1}(v)$ in the querying algorithm.

In order to describe subsets of S_r by bit vectors of b bits, we assign an unique number between one and $|S_r|$ to each vertex in S_r, and express presence of the i-th vertex by setting the i-th bit.

5.2 Bit-parallel BFS

We once put aside the pruning discussed in Section 4.2 and we make a bit-parallel version of the naive labeling method discussed in Section 4.1. We introduce pruning later in Section 5.4.

Let $r \in V$ be a vertex and $S_r \subseteq N_G(r)$ be a subset of neighbors of r with size at most b. We explain an algorithm to compute $d_G(r,v)$, $S_r^{-1}(v)$ and $S_r^0(v)$ for all $v \in V$ that are reachable from $\{r\} \cup S_r$. The algorithm is described as Algorithm 3. Basically we conduct a BFS from r computing sets S^{-1} and S^0.

Let v be a vertex. Suppose that we have already computed $S_r^{-1}(w)$ for all w such that $d_G(r,w) < d_G(r,v)$. We can compute $S_r^{-1}(v)$ as follows,

$$\{u \in S_r \mid u \in S_r^{-1}(w), w \in N_G(v), d_G(r,w) = d_G(r,v) - 1\},$$

since if u is in $S_r^{-1}(v)$, $d_G(u,v) = d_G(r,v) - 1$ and therefore u is on one of the shortest paths from r to v. Similarly, assuming that we have already computed $S_r^{-1}(w)$ for all w such that $d_G(r,w) \leq d_G(r,v)$ and $S_r^0(w)$ for all w such that $d_G(r,w) < d_G(r,v)$, we can compute $S_r^0(v)$ as follows,

$$\{u \in S_r \mid u \in S_r^0(w), w \in N_G(v), d_G(r,w) = d_G(r,v) - 1\}$$
$$\cup \{u \in S_r \mid u \in S_r^{-1}(w), w \in N_G(v), d_G(r,w) = d_G(r,v)\}.$$

Therefore, along with the breadth-first search, we can compute S_r^{-1} and S_r^0 alternately by dynamic programming in the increasing order of distance from r. That is, first we compute $S_r^{-1}(v)$ for all $v \in V$ such that $d_G(r,v) = 1$, next we compute $S_r^0(v)$ for all $v \in V$ such that $d_G(r,v) = 1$, then we compute $S_r^{-1}(v)$ for all $v \in V$ such that $d_G(r,v) = 2$, next we compute $S_r^0(v)$ for all $v \in V$ such that $d_G(r,v) = 2$, and so on. Note that operations on sets can be done in $O(1)$ time by representing sets by bit vectors and using bitwise operations.

5.3 Bit-parallel Distance Querying

To process a distance query between a pair of vertices s and t, as with normal labels, we scan bit-parallel labels $L_{\mathrm{BP}}(s)$ and $L_{\mathrm{BP}}(t)$. For each pair of quadruples that share the same root vertex, $(r, \delta_{rs}, S_r^{-1}(s), S_r^0(s)) \in L_{\mathrm{BP}}(s)$ and $(r, \delta_{rt}, S_r^{-1}(t), S_r^0(t)) \in L_{\mathrm{BP}}(t)$, from these quadruples we compute distance between s and t via one of vertices in $\{r\} \cup S_r$. That is, we compute $\delta = \min_{u \in \{r\} \cup S_r} \{d_G(s,u) + d_G(u,t)\}$. A naive way is to compute $d_G(s,u)$ and $d_G(u,t)$ for all u and take the minimum, which takes $O(|S_r|)$ time. However, we propose an algorithm to compute δ in $O(1)$ time by exploiting bitwise operations.

Let $\tilde{\delta} = d_G(s,r) + d_G(r,t)$. Since $\tilde{\delta}$ is an upper bound on δ and $d_G(s,u) \geq d_G(s,r) - 1, d_G(u,t) \geq d_G(r,t) - 1$ for all $u \in S_r$, $\tilde{\delta} - 2 \leq \delta \leq \tilde{\delta}$. Therefore, what we have to do is to judge whether the distance δ is $\tilde{\delta} - 2$, $\tilde{\delta} - 1$ or $\tilde{\delta}$.

This can be done as follows. If $S_r^{-1}(s) \cap S_r^{-1}(t) \neq \emptyset$, then $\delta = \tilde{\delta} - 2$. Otherwise, if $S_r^0(s) \cap S_r^{-1}(t) \neq \emptyset$ or $S_r^{-1}(s) \cap S_r^0(t) \neq \emptyset$, then $\delta = \tilde{\delta} - 1$, and otherwise $\delta = \tilde{\delta}$. Note that computing intersections of sets can be done by bitwise AND operations. Therefore, all these operations can be done in $O(1)$ time. Thus, the distance δ can be computed in $O(1)$ time, and, in total, we can answer each query in $O(|L_{\mathrm{BP}}(s)| + |L_{\mathrm{BP}}(t)|)$ time.

5.4 Introducing to Pruned Labeling

Now we discuss how to combine this bit-parallel labeling methods and the pruned labeling method discussed in Section 4.2. We propose a simple and efficient way as follows.

First we conduct bit-parallel BFSs without pruning for t times, where t is a parameter. Then, we conduct pruned BFSs using both the bit-parallel labels and normal labels for pruning.

This method exploits different strength of the pruned labeling method and the bit-parallel labeling method. In the beginning, pruning does not work much and pruned BFSs visits large portion of the vertices. Therefore, instead of pruned labeling, we use bit-parallel labeling without pruning to efficiently cover a larger part of pairs of vertices. Skipping the overhead of vain pruning tests also contributes the speed-up.

As roots and neighbor sets for bit-parallel BFSs, we propose to greedily use vertices with the highest priority: we select a vertex with the highest priority as the root r among remaining vertices, and we select up to b vertices with the highest priority as the set S_r among remaining neighbors.

As we see in the experimental results in Section 7, this method improves the preprocessing time, the index size and the query time. Moreover, as we also confirm in the experiments, if we do not set too large value as t, at least it does not spoil the performance. Therefore we do not have to be too serious about finding a proper value for t, and our method is still easy to use.

6. VARIANTS AND EXTENSIONS

Shortest-Path Queries: To answer not only distances but also shortest-paths, we store sets of tuples instead of pairs as labels. Label $L(v)$ is a set of triples (u, δ_{uv}, p_{uv}), where $p_{uv} \in V$ is the parent of u in the pruned breadth-first search tree rooted at u created by the pruned BFS from u. We can restore the shortest path between v and u by ascending the tree from v to the parents.

Weighted Graphs: To treat weighted graphs, the only necessary change is to perform pruned Dijkstra's algorithm instead of pruned BFSs. Bit-parallel labeling cannot be used for weighted graphs.

Directed Graphs: To treat directed graphs, we first redefine $d_G(u, v)$ as the distance from u to v. Then, we store two labels $L_{\mathrm{OUT}}(v)$ and $L_{\mathrm{IN}}(v)$ for each vertex. Label $L_{\mathrm{OUT}}(v)$ is a set of pairs (u, δ_{vu}), where $u \in V$ and $\delta_{vu} = d_G(v, u)$, and Label $L_{\mathrm{IN}}(v)$ is a set of pairs (u, δ_{uv}), where $u \in V$ and $\delta_{uv} = d_G(u, v)$. We can answer the distance from vertex s to vertex t by $L_{\mathrm{OUT}}(s)$ and $L_{\mathrm{IN}}(t)$. To compute these labels, from each vertex, we conduct pruned BFSs twice: once in the forward direction and once in the reverse direction.

Disk-based Query Answering: To answer a distance query, our querying algorithm only refers to two contiguous regions. Thus, if the index is disk resident, we can answer queries with two disk seek operations, which would be still much faster than an in-memory BFS.

7. EXPERIMENTS

We conducted experiments on a Linux server with Intel Xeon X5670 (2.93 GHz) and 48GB of main memory. The proposed method was implemented in C++. We used 8-bit integers to represent distances, 32-bit integers to represent vertices, and 64-bit integers to conduct bit-parallel BFSs. For vertex ordering, we mainly use the DEGREE strategy and we do not specify the vertex ordering strategy unless we use other strategies. For query time, we generally report the average time for 1,000,000 random queries.

Table 4: Datasets

Dataset	Network	$\|V\|$	$\|E\|$
Gnutella	Computer	63 K	148 K
Epinions	Social	76 K	509 K
Slashdot	Social	82 K	948 K
Notredame	Web	326 K	1.5 M
WikiTalk	Social	2.4 M	4.7 M
Skitter	Computer	1.7 M	11 M
Indo	Web	1.4 M	17 M
MetroSec	Computer	2.3 M	22 M
Flickr	Social	1.8 M	23 M
Hollywood	Social	1.1 M	114 M
Indochina	Web	7.4 M	194 M

7.1 Datasets

To show the efficiency and robustness of our method, we conducted experiments on various real-world networks: five social networks, three web graphs and three computer networks. We treated all the graphs as undirected, unweighted graphs. Basically we used five smaller datasets to compare the performance between the proposed method and previous methods and to analyze the behavior of these methods, and used larger six datasets to show the scalability of the proposed method. The types of networks, the numbers of vertices and edges are presented in Table 4.

7.1.1 Detailed Description

Gnutella: This is a graph created from a snapshot of the Gnutella P2P network in August 2002 [34].

Epinions: This graph is the on-line social network in Epinions (`www.epinions.com`), where each vertex represents a user and each edge represents a trust relationship [33].

Slashdot: This is the on-line social network in Slashdot (`slashdot.org`) obtained in February 2009. Vertices correspond to users and edges correspond to friend/foe links between the users [23].

NotreDame: This is a web graph between pages from University of Notre Dame (domain `nd.edu`) collected in 1999 [5].

WikiTalk: This is the on-line social network among editors of Wikipedia (`www.wikipedia.org`) created by communication on edits on talk pages by till January 2008 [21, 20].

Skitter: This is an Internet topology graph created from traceroutes run in 2005 by Skitter [22].

Indo: This is a web graph between pages in `.in` domain crawled in 2004 [9, 8].

MetroSec: This is a graph constructed from Internet traffic captured by MetroSec. Each vertex represents a computer and two vertices are linked if they appear in a packet as sender and destination [24].

Flickr: This is the on-line social network in a photo-sharing site, Flickr (`www.flickr.com`) [26].

Indochina: This is a web graph of web pages in the country domains of Indochina countries, crawled in 2004 [9, 8].

Hollywood: This is a social network of movie actors. Two actors are linked if they appeared in a movie together by 2009 [9, 8].

7.1.2 Statistics

First, we investigated the degree distribution of the networks, since degrees of vertices play important roles in our method when we use DEGREE strategy for vertex ordering.

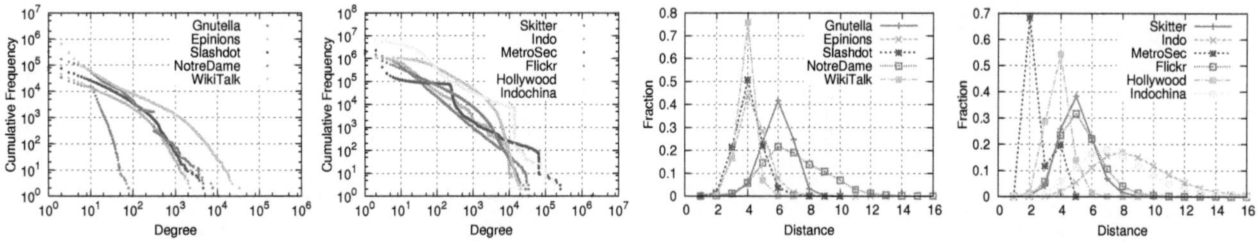

(a) Degree distribution of smaller five datasets.
(b) Degree distribution of larger six datasets.
(c) Distance distribution of smaller five datasets.
(d) Distance distribution of larger six datasets.

Figure 2: Properties of the datasets.

Table 3: Performance comparison between the proposed method and previous methods for the real-world datasets. IT denotes indexing time, IS denotes index size, QT denotes query time, and LN denotes average label size for each vertex. DNF means it did not finish in one day or ran out of memory.

Dataset	Pruned Landmark Labeling				Hierarchical Hub Labeling [2]				Tree Decomposition [4]			BFS
	IT	IS	QT	LN	IT	IS	QT	LN	IT	IS	QT	
Gnutella	54 s	209 MB	5.2 μs	644+16	245 s	380 MB	11 μs	1,275	209 s	68 MB	19 μs	3.2 ms
Epinions	1.7 s	32 MB	0.5 μs	33+16	495 s	93 MB	2.2 μs	256	128 s	42 MB	11 μs	7.4 ms
Slashdot	6.0 s	48 MB	0.8 μs	68+16	670 s	182 MB	3.9 μs	464	343 s	83 MB	12 μs	12 ms
NotreDame	4.5 s	138 MB	0.5 μs	34+16	10,256 s	64 MB	0.4 μs	41	243 s	120 MB	39 μs	17 ms
WikiTalk	61 s	1.0 GB	0.6 μs	34+16	DNF	-	-	-	2,459 s	416 MB	1.8 μs	197 ms
Skitter	359 s	2.7 GB	2.3 μs	123+64	DNF	-	-	-	DNF	-	-	190 ms
Indo	173 s	2.3 GB	1.6 μs	133+64	DNF	-	-	-	DNF	-	-	150 ms
MetroSec	108 s	2.5 GB	0.7 μs	19+64	DNF	-	-	-	DNF	-	-	150 ms
Flickr	866 s	4.0 GB	2.6 μs	247+64	DNF	-	-	-	DNF	-	-	361 ms
Hollywood	15,164 s	12 GB	15.6 μs	2,098+64	DNF	-	-	-	DNF	-	-	1.2 s
Indochina	6,068 s	22 GB	4.1 μs	415+64	DNF	-	-	-	DNF	-	-	1.5 s

Figures 2a and 2b are the log-log plot of degree complementary cumulative distribution. As expected, we can confirm that all these networks generally exhibit power-law degree distributions.

Then, we also examined the distribution of distances. Figures 2c and 2d show distribution of distances for 1,000,000 random pairs of vertices. As we can observe from these figures, these networks are also small-world networks, in the sense that the average distance is very small.

7.2 Performance

First we present the performance of our method on the real-world datasets to show the efficiency and robustness of our method. Table 3 shows the performance of our method for the datasets. IT denotes preprocessing time, IS denotes index size, QT denotes average query time for 1,000,000 random queries, and LN denotes the average label size for each vertex, in the format of the size of normal labels (left) plus the size of bit-parallel labels (right). We set the number of times we conduct bit-parallel BFSs as 16 for first five datasets and 64 for the rest.

In Table 3, we also listed the performance of two of the state-of-the-art existing methods. One is *hierarchical hub labeling* [2], which is also based on distance labeling. The other one is based on tree decompositions [4], which is an improved version of TEDI [41]. For these previous methods, we used the implementations by the authors of these methods, both in C++. Experiments for hierarchical hub labeling were conducted on a Windows server with two Intel Xeon X5680 (3.33GHz) and 96GB of main memory. Experiments for the tree-decomposition-based method were conducted on our environment described above. We also described the average time to compute distance by breadth-first search for 1,000 random pairs of vertices. Among these four methods including the proposed method, only the preprocessing of hierarchical hub labeling [2] was parallelized to use all the 12 cores. All the other timing results are sequential.

7.2.1 *Preprocessing Time and Scalability*

Our emphasis is particularly on the large improvement in the preprocessing time, leading to much better scalability. First, we successfully preprocessed the largest two datasets Hollywood and Indochina with millions of vertices and hundreds of millions of edges in moderate preprocessing time. This is improvement of two orders of magnitude on the graph size we can handle since, as we listed in Table 1, other existing exact distance querying methods take thousands or tens of thousands of seconds to preprocess graphs with millions of edges.

For next four datasets with tens of millions of edges, it took less than one thousand seconds, while the previous methods did not finish after one day or ran out of memory. For smaller six datasets, they took at most one minute, and about at least 50 times faster than the previous methods for the most of them.

7.2.2 *Query Time*

The average query time was generally microseconds and at most 16 microseconds. For almost all the smaller five datasets, the query time of the proposed method is faster than the query time of the previous methods. Indeed, from Table 1, we can also observe that the query time of our method is comparable to all the existing methods for graphs of these sizes. Moreover, we can confirm that the query time does not increase much for larger networks.

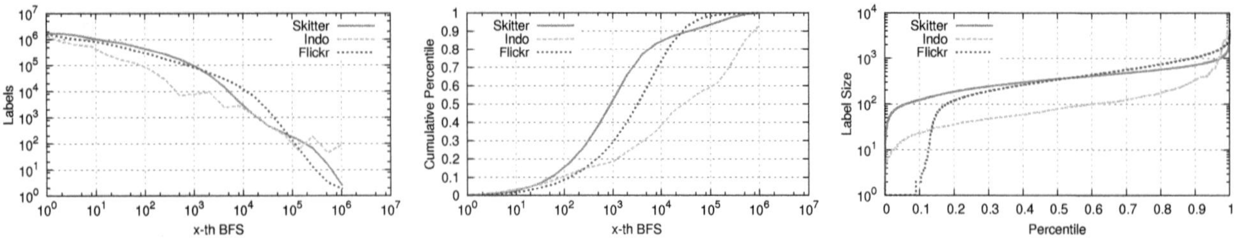

(a) Number of vertices labeled in each pruned BFS.

(b) Cumulative distribution of the number of vertices labeled in each pruned BFS.

(c) Distribution of the sizes of labels.

Figure 3: Effect of pruning and sizes of labels.

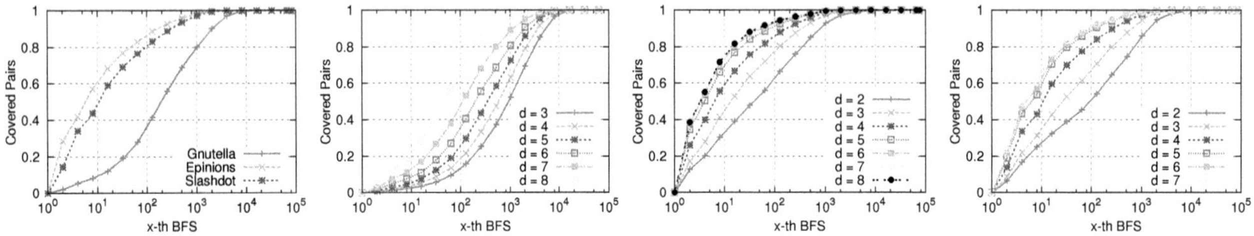

(a) Average

(b) Distance-wise, Gnutella

(c) Distance-wise, Epinions

(d) Distance-wise, Slashdot

Figure 4: Fraction of pairs of vertices whose distance can be answered by index, against number of performed pruned BFS.

7.2.3 *Index Size*

As for the smaller five networks, results demonstrate that our method is comparable to the previous methods with respect to index size. However, even though nowadays computers with tens of gigabytes of memory are neither rare nor expensive, reducing the index size can be an important next research issue.

7.3 Analysis

Next we analyze the behavior of our method to investigate why our method is efficient.

7.3.1 *Pruned BFS*

First we study how labels are computed and stored. Figure 3a shows the number of distances added to labels in each pruned BFS, and Figure 3b shows the cumulative distribution of it, that is, the ratio of the distances stored no later than each step to all the distances stored in the end. We did not use bit-parallel BFSs for these experiments.

From these figures, we can confirm the large impact of the pruning. Figure 3a shows that the number of distances added to labels in each BFS decreases so rapidly. For example, after 1,000 times of BFSs, for all the three datasets distances are added to the labels of only less than 10% of the vertices, and after conducting 10,000 times of BFSs, for all the three datasets distances are added to the labels of only less than 1% of the vertices. Figure 3b also shows that large portion of the labels are computed in the beginning.

7.3.2 *Sizes of Labels*

Figure 3c shows the distribution of the sizes of labels after the whole preprocessing, sorted in the ascending order of sizes. We can observe that the size of a label each vertex has do not differ much for different vertices, and few vertices have much larger labels than the average. This shows that the query time of our method is quite stable.

If you are anxious about vertices with unusually large labels, you can precompute the distance between these vertices and all the vertices and answer it directly, since the number of such vertices are few as shown in Figure 3c.

7.3.3 *Pair Coverage*

Figure 4a illustrates the ratio of the *covered* pairs of vertices, that is, the pairs of vertices whose distances can be answered correctly by current labels, at each step. We used 1,000,000 random pairs to estimate these ratios. We can observe that most pairs are covered in the beginning. This shows that such a large portion of pairs have the shortest paths that pass such a small portion of central vertices, which are selected by the DEGREE strategy. This is the reason why landmark-based approximate methods have good precision, and also the reason why our pruning works so effectively.

Figures 4b, 4c and 4d illustrate the ratio of the covered pairs of vertices at each step with pairs classified by distance. They show that generally distant pairs are covered earlier than close pairs. This is the reason why the precision of landmark-based approximate methods for close pairs are far worse than the precision for distant pairs. On the other hand, our method aggressively exploits this property: because distant pairs are covered in the beginning, we can prune distant vertices when processing other vertices, which results in fast preprocessing.

7.3.4 *Vertex Ordering Strategies*

Next we see the effect of vertex ordering strategies. Table 5 describes the average size of a label for each vertex using different vertex ordering strategies described in Section 4.4. We did not use bit-parallel BFSs for these experiments. As we can see, results are not so different between the DEGREE strategy and the CLOSENESS strategy. The DEGREE strategy might be slightly better. On the other hand,

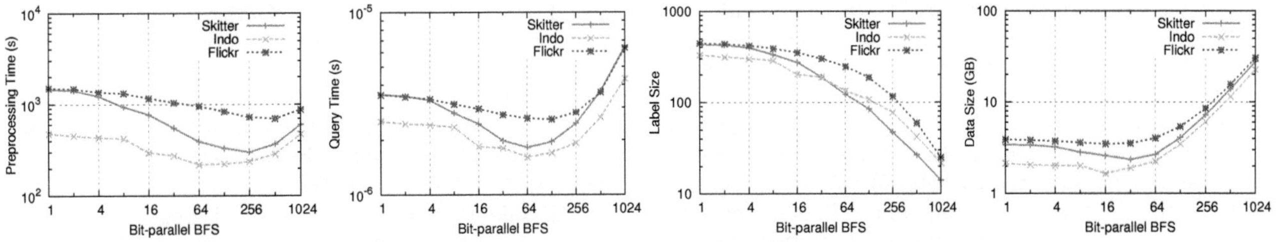

(a) Preprocessing time (b) Query time (c) Average size of a normal label (d) Index size

Figure 5: Performance against number of bit-parallel BFSs.

Table 5: Average size of a label for each vertex against different vertex ordering strategies.

Dataset	RANDOM	DEGREE	CLOSENESS
Gnutella	6,171	781	865
Epinions	7,038	124	132
Slashdot	8,665	216	234
NotreDame	DNF	60	82
WikiTalk	DNF	118	158

the result of the RANDOM strategy is much worse than other two strategies. This shows that by the DEGREE and CLOSENESS strategies we can successfully capture central vertices.

7.3.5 *Bit-parallel BFS*

Finally, we see the effect of bit-parallel BFSs discussed in Section 5. Figure 5 shows the performance of our method against different number of times we conduct bit-parallel BFSs.

Figure 5a illustrates preprocessing time. It shows that, with a proper number of bit-parallel BFSs, preprocessing time gets two to ten times faster, resulting in the further enhancement to the scalability of our method. Figure 5b illustrates query time. We can confirm that query time also gets faster. Figure 5c shows the average size of a normal label for each vertex. As we increase the number of bit-parallel BFSs, many pairs are covered by special labels computed by bit-parallel BFSs, and the size of normal labels decreases. Figure 5d shows the index size. With a proper number of bit-parallel BFSs, index size also decreases.

Another important finding from these figures is that the performance of our method is not too sensitive to the parameter of the number of bit-parallel BFSs. As they show, the performance of our method does not become worse much unless we choose a too big number. The proper parameters seem to common between different networks. Therefore, our method still is easy to use with this bit-parallel technique.

8. CONCLUSIONS

In this paper, we proposed a novel and efficient method for exact shortest-path distance queries on large graphs. Our method is based on distance labeling to vertices, which is common to the existing exact distance querying methods, but our labeling algorithm stands on a totally new idea. Our algorithm conducts breadth-first search (BFS) from all the vertices with pruning. Though the algorithm is simple, our pruning surprisingly reduce the search space and the labels, resulting in fast preprocessing time, small index size and fast query time. Moreover, we also proposed another labeling scheme exploiting bit-level parallelism, which can be easily combined with the pruned labeling method to further improve the performance. Extensive experimental results on large-scale real-world networks of various types demonstrated the efficiency and robustness of our methods. In particular, our method can handle networks with hundreds of millions of vertices, which are two orders of magnitude larger than the limits of the previous methods, with comparable index size and query time.

We plan to investigate ways to handle even larger graphs, where indices and/or graphs might not fit in main memory. The first way is to reduce the index size by reducing graphs exploiting obvious parts and symmetry [30, 14] and compressing labels by making dictionaries of common subtrees for shortest path trees [1]. Another way is disk-based or distributed implementation. As we stated in Section 6, disk-based query answering is obvious and ready, and the challenges are particularly on preprocessing. However, since our preprocessing algorithm is a simple algorithm based on BFS, we can leverage the large body of existing work on BFS. In particular, since pruning can be done locally, the preprocessing algorithm would perform well on BSP-model-based distributed graph processing platforms [25].

9. ACKNOWLEDGMENTS

We would like to thank Hiroshi Imai for critical reading of the manuscript, and Daniel Delling for providing us the experimental results of hierarchical hub labeling [2]. We would also like to thank the anonymous reviewers for their constructive suggestions on improving the paper. Yuichi Yoshida is supported by JSPS Grant-in-Aid for Research Activity Start-up (24800082), MEXT Grant-in-Aid for Scientific Research on Innovative Areas (24106001), and JST, ERATO, Kawarabayashi Large Graph Project.

10. REFERENCES

[1] I. Abraham, D. Delling, A. V. Goldberg, and R. F. Werneck. A hub-based labeling algorithm for shortest paths in road networks. In *SEA*, pages 230–241, 2011.

[2] I. Abraham, D. Delling, A. V. Goldberg, and R. F. Werneck. Hierarchical hub labelings for shortest paths. In *ESA*, pages 24–35. 2012.

[3] V. Agarwal, F. Petrini, D. Pasetto, and D. A. Bader. Scalable graph exploration on multicore processors. In *SC*, pages 1–11, 2010.

[4] T. Akiba, C. Sommer, and K. Kawarabayashi. Shortest-path queries for complex networks: exploiting low tree-width outside the core. In *EDBT*, pages 144–155, 2012.

[5] R. Albert, H. Jeong, and A. L. Barabasi. The diameter of the world wide web. *Nature*, 401:130–131, 1999.

[6] L. Backstrom, D. Huttenlocher, J. Kleinberg, and X. Lan. Group formation in large social networks: membership, growth, and evolution. In *KDD*, pages 44–54, 2006.

[7] S. Boccaletti, V. Latora, Y. Moreno, M. Chavez, and D. Hwang. Complex networks: Structure and dynamics. *Physics reports*, 424(4-5):175–308, 2006.

[8] P. Boldi, M. Rosa, M. Santini, and S. Vigna. Layered label propagation: a multiresolution coordinate-free ordering for compressing social networks. In *WWW*, pages 587–596, 2011.

[9] P. Boldi and S. Vigna. The webgraph framework I: compression techniques. In *WWW*, pages 595–602, 2004.

[10] D. S. Callaway, M. E. J. Newman, S. H. Strogatz, and D. J. Watts. Network robustness and fragility: Percolation on random graphs. *Physical Review Letters*, 85:5468–5471, 2000.

[11] W. Chen, C. Sommer, S.-H. Teng, and Y. Wang. A compact routing scheme and approximate distance oracle for power-law graphs. *TALG*, 9(1):4:1–26, 2012.

[12] J. Cheng and J. X. Yu. On-line exact shortest distance query processing. In *EDBT*, pages 481–492, 2009.

[13] E. Cohen, E. Halperin, H. Kaplan, and U. Zwick. Reachability and distance queries via 2-hop labels. In *SODA*, pages 937–946, 2002.

[14] W. Fan, J. Li, X. Wang, and Y. Wu. Query preserving graph compression. In *SIGMOD*, pages 157–168, 2012.

[15] A. Gubichev, S. Bedathur, S. Seufert, and G. Weikum. Fast and accurate estimation of shortest paths in large graphs. In *CIKM*, pages 499–508, 2010.

[16] H. He, H. Wang, J. Yang, and P. S. Yu. Blinks: ranked keyword searches on graphs. In *SIGMOD*, pages 305–316, 2007.

[17] R. Jin, N. Ruan, Y. Xiang, and V. Lee. A highway-centric labeling approach for answering distance queries on large sparse graphs. In *SIGMOD*, pages 445–456, 2012.

[18] C. Jordan. Sur les assemblages de lignes. *J. Reine Angew Math*, 70:185–190, 1869.

[19] D. Kempe, J. Kleinberg, and E. Tardos. Maximizing the spread of influence through a social network. In *KDD*, pages 137–146, 2003.

[20] J. Leskovec, D. Huttenlocher, and J. Kleinberg. Predicting positive and negative links in online social networks. In *WWW*, pages 641–650, 2010.

[21] J. Leskovec, D. Huttenlocher, and J. Kleinberg. Signed networks in social media. In *CHI*, pages 1361–1370, 2010.

[22] J. Leskovec, J. Kleinberg, and C. Faloutsos. Graphs over time: Densification laws, shrinking diameters and possible explanations. In *KDD*, pages 177–187, 2005.

[23] J. Leskovec, K. Lang, A. Dasgupta, and M. Mahoney. Community structure in large networks: Natural cluster sizes and the absence of large well-defined clusters. *Internet Mathematics*, 6(1):29–123, 2009.

[24] C. Magnien, M. Latapy, and M. Habib. Fast computation of empirically tight bounds for the diameter of massive graphs. *J. Exp. Algorithmics*, 13:10:1.10–10:1.9, Feb. 2009.

[25] G. Malewicz, M. H. Austern, A. J. Bik, J. C. Dehnert, I. Horn, N. Leiser, and G. Czajkowski. Pregel: a system for large-scale graph processing. In *SIGMOD*, pages 135–146, 2010.

[26] A. Mislove, M. Marcon, K. P. Gummadi, P. Druschel, and B. Bhattacharjee. Measurement and analysis of online social networks. In *IMC*, pages 29–42, 2007.

[27] M. E. J. Newman, S. H. Strogatz, and D. J. Watts. Random graphs with arbitrary degree distributions and their applications. *Physical Review E*, 64(2):026118 1–17, 2001.

[28] R. Pastor-Satorras and A. Vespignani. *Evolution and structure of the Internet: A statistical physics approach.* Cambridge University Press, 2004.

[29] M. Potamias, F. Bonchi, C. Castillo, and A. Gionis. Fast shortest path distance estimation in large networks. In *CIKM*, pages 867–876, 2009.

[30] M. Qiao, H. Cheng, L. Chang, and J. X. Yu. Approximate shortest distance computing: A query-dependent local landmark scheme. In *ICDE*, pages 462–473, 2012.

[31] S. A. Rahman, P. Advani, R. Schunk, R. Schrader, and D. Schomburg. Metabolic pathway analysis web service (pathway hunter tool at cubic). *Bioinformatics*, 21(7):1189–1193, 2005.

[32] S. A. Rahman and D. Schomburg. Observing local and global properties of metabolic pathways: 'load points' and 'choke points' in the metabolic networks. *Bioinformatics*, 22(14):1767–1774, 2006.

[33] M. Richardson, R. Agrawal, and P. Domingos. Trust management for the semantic web. In *ISWC*, volume 2870, pages 351–368. 2003.

[34] M. Ripeanu, A. Iamnitchi, and I. Foster. Mapping the gnutella network. *IEEE Internet Computing*, 6(1):50–57, Jan. 2002.

[35] N. Robertson and P. D. Seymour. Graph minors. III. Planar tree-width. *J. Comb. Theory, Ser. B*, 36(1):49–64, 1984.

[36] L. Tang and M. Crovella. Virtual landmarks for the internet. In *SIGCOMM*, pages 143–152, 2003.

[37] T. Tran, H. Wang, S. Rudolph, and P. Cimiano. Top-k exploration of query candidates for efficient keyword search on graph-shaped (RDF) data. In *ICDE*, pages 405–416, 2009.

[38] K. Tretyakov, A. Armas-Cervantes, L. García-Bañuelos, J. Vilo, and M. Dumas. Fast fully dynamic landmark-based estimation of shortest path distances in very large graphs. In *CIKM*, pages 1785–1794, 2011.

[39] A. Ukkonen, C. Castillo, D. Donato, and A. Gionis. Searching the wikipedia with contextual information. In *CIKM*, pages 1351–1352, 2008.

[40] M. V. Vieira, B. M. Fonseca, R. Damazio, P. B. Golgher, D. d. C. Reis, and B. Ribeiro-Neto. Efficient search ranking in social networks. In *CIKM*, pages 563–572, 2007.

[41] F. Wei. Tedi: efficient shortest path query answering on graphs. In *SIGMOD*, pages 99–110, 2010.

[42] S. A. Yahia, M. Benedikt, L. V. S. Lakshmanan, and J. Stoyanovich. Efficient network aware search in collaborative tagging sites. *PVLDB*, 1(1):710–721, 2008.

Improving Regular-Expression Matching on Strings Using Negative Factors

Xiaochun Yang
College of Information Science and Engineering
Northeastern University, China
yangxc@mail.neu.edu.cn

Bin Wang
College of Information Science and Engineering
Northeastern University, China
binwang@mail.neu.edu.cn

Tao Qiu
College of Information Science and Engineering
Northeastern University, China
qiutao@research.neu.edu.cn

Yaoshu Wang
College of Information Science and Engineering
Northeastern University, China
wangysneu@gmail.com

Chen Li
Dept. of Computer Science
UC Irvine, USA
chenli@ics.uci.edu

ABSTRACT

The problem of finding matches of a regular expression (RE) on a string exists in many applications such as text editing, biosequence search, and shell commands. Existing techniques first identify candidates using substrings in the RE, then verify each of them using an automaton. These techniques become inefficient when there are many candidate occurrences that need to be verified. In this paper we propose a novel technique that prunes false negatives by utilizing *negative factors*, which are substrings that *cannot* appear in an answer. A main advantage of the technique is that it can be integrated with many existing algorithms to improve their efficiency significantly. We give a full specification of this technique. We develop an efficient algorithm that utilizes negative factors to prune candidates, then improve it by using bit operations to process negative factors in parallel. We show that negative factors, when used together with necessary factors (substrings that must appear in each answer), can achieve much better pruning power. We analyze the large number of negative factors, and develop an algorithm for finding a small number of high-quality negative factors. We conducted a thorough experimental study of this technique on real data sets, including DNA sequences, proteins, and text documents, and show the significant performance improvement when applying the technique in existing algorithms. For instance, it improved the search speed of the popular Gnu Grep tool by 11 to 74 times for text documents.

Categories and Subject Descriptors

H.3 [**Information Storage and Retrieval**]: Content Analysis and Indexing;

D.2.8 [**Software Engineering**]: Metrics—*performance measures*

General Terms

Algorithms, Performance

Keywords

Regular expression, long sequence, performance

1. INTRODUCTION

This paper studies the problem of efficiently finding matchings of a regular expression (RE) in a long string. The problem exists in many application domains. In the domain of bioinformatics, users specify a string such as `TAC(T|G)AGA` and want to find its matchings in proteins or genomes [6, 13]. Modern text editors such as *vi*, *emacs*, and *eclipse* provide the functionality of searching a given pattern in a text document being edited. The shell command *grep* is widely used to search plain-text files for lines matching a regular expression. For instance, the command "`grep ^a.ple fruits.txt`" finds lines in the file called `fruits.txt` that begin with the letter `a`, followed by one character, followed by the letter sequence `ple`. The ability of processing regular expressions has been integrated into the syntax of languages (e.g., Perl, Ruby, AWK, and Tcl) and provided by other languages through standard libraries in .NET, Java, and Python.

A simple method to do RE search on a string is to construct an automaton for the RE. For each position in the string, we run the automaton to verify if a substring starting from that position can be accepted by the automaton. Notice that the verification step can be computationally expensive. The main limitation of this approach is that we need to do the expensive verification step many times. Various algorithms have been developed to speed up the matching process by first identifying candidate occurrences in the string, and then verifying them one by one [3, 4, 14]. These algorithms identify candidate places based on certain substrings derived from the RE that have to appear in matching answers, such as a prefix and/or a suffix. For instance, each substring matching the RE `xy(a|b)*zw*` should start with `xy` (a prefix condition) and end with `zw` or `z` (suffix conditions). Such substrings, called *positive factors* throughout the paper, can be used to locate candidate occurrences. Each of them will be further verified using one or multiple automata. Although these algorithms can eliminate many starting positions in the string, their efficiency can still be low when the positive factors generate too many candidate occurrences, especially when the text is long.

Contributions: In this paper we study how to improve the efficiency of existing algorithms for searching regular expressions in strings. We propose a novel technique that provides significant pruning power by utilizing the fact that we can derive substrings from the RE that *cannot* appear in an answer. Such substrings are called *negative factors.* We give an analysis to show that many candidates can be pruned by negative factors (Section 3).

In Section 4, we study how to use negative factors to speed up the matching process of existing algorithms. We show that negative factors can be easily integrated into these methods, and propose two bit-operation algorithms to do efficient search. In Section 4.3 we study the benefits of using negative factors. One interesting result is that considering necessary factors (substrings that have to appear in every answer) only does not provide much filtering power in prefix-based approaches. However, when combining both negative factors and necessary factors, we can gain much more pruning power. In Section 5 we study the problem of deciding a set of high-quality negative factors. There can be many negative factors, and the selected ones can greatly affect the performance of the matching process. To achieve a high efficiency, we propose an algorithm that only considers partial strings, and present an algorithm that can do early termination in the process of deciding negative factors. In Section 6 we present experimental results on real data sets including DNA sequences, protein sequences, and text documents, and demonstrate the space and time efficiency of the proposed technique. For instance, it improved the search speed of the popular Gnu Grep tool by 11 to 74 times for texts.

2. PRELIMINARIES

2.1 Regular Expression Matching

Let Σ be a finite alphabet. A *regular expression* (RE for short) is a string over $\Sigma \cup \{\epsilon, |, \cdot, *, (,)\}$, which can be defined recursively as follows:

- The symbol ϵ is a regular expression. It denotes an empty string (i.e., the string of length zero).
- Each string $w \in \Sigma^*$ is a regular expression, which denotes the string set $\{w\}$.
- If e_1 and e_2 are regular expressions that denote the set R_1 and R_2, respectively, then
  - (e_1) is a regular expression that represents the same set denoted by e_1.
  - $(e_1 \cdot e_2)$ is a regular expression that denotes a set of strings x that can be written as $x = yz$, where e_1 matches y and e_2 matches z.
  - $(e_1|e_2)$ is a regular expression that denotes a set of strings x such that x matches e_1 or e_2.
  - (e_1^+) is a regular expression that denotes a set of strings x such that, for a positive integer k, x can be written as $x = x_1 \ldots x_k$ and e_1 matches each string x_i $(1 \leq i \leq k)$. We use $\epsilon|e^+$ to express a Kleene closure e^*. In this paper, we consider the general case e^*.

Given an RE Q, we use $R(Q)$ to represent the set of strings that can be accepted by the automaton of Q. We use $|Q|$ to express the number of characters that Q contains. We use l_{min} to represent the length of the shortest string(s) in $R(Q)$. For example, for the RE $Q =$ (G|T)A*GA*T*, we have $|Q| = 6$ since it has six characters: G, T, A, G, A, and T. The set of strings $R(Q) =$ {GG, TG, GAG, TAG, GGA, TGA, GGT, TGT, GAGT, ...}. We have $l_{min} = 2$, since its shortest strings GG and TG have the length 2.

For a text (sequence) T of the characters in Σ, we use $|T|$ to denote its length, $T[i]$ to denote its i-th character (starting from 0), and $T[i, j]$ to denote the substring ranging from its i-th character to its j-th character.

For simplicity, in our examples we focus on the domain of genome sequences, where Σ={A, C, G, T}. We run experiments in Section 6 on other domains such as proteins and English texts, where the Σ has more characters.

Pattern Matching of an RE. Consider a text T of length n and an RE Q of length m. We say Q matches a substring $T[a, b]$ of T at position a if $T[a, b]$ belongs to $R(Q)$. The substring $T[a, b]$ is called an *occurrence* of Q in T. The problem of pattern matching for an RE is to find all occurrences of Q in T. Figure 1 shows an example text. Suppose $Q =$ (G|T)A*GA*T*. Then Q matches T at position 3, and the substring $T[3, 6]$ is an occurrence of Q in T.

0	1	2	3	4	5	6	7	8	9	10	11	12	13	14	15	16	17	18	19	20
T	A	C	T	A	G	A	C	G	T	T	A	A	T	T	T	A	C	G	T	A

Figure 1: An example text.

2.2 Prefix-Based Approaches

One naive approach for finding occurrences of an RE Q is to build an automaton for Q and run it from the beginning of the text T. An occurrence will be reported whenever a final state of the automaton is reached. The verification fails once a new feed character could not be accepted by the automaton. In this case, we move to the next position and repeat the verification process using the same automaton. We repeat the process for all starting positions in the text. Since the approach has to run the automaton for each position, it is very inefficient especially when T is very long (e.g., a chromosome of a human can contain 3 billion characters).

Recent techniques are developed for identifying sequences that contain at least one matching of an RE among multiple sequences. They utilize certain features of the RE Q to improve the performance of the automaton-based methods. Their main idea is to use *positive factors*, which are substrings of Q that can be used to identify candidate occurrences of Q in T. For instance, Watson in [14] used prefixes of strings in $R(Q)$ to find maximal safe shift distances to avoid checking every position in T. A prefix w.r.t. an RE Q is defined as a prefix with length l_{min} of a string in $R(Q)$. For example, for the RE $Q =$ (G|T)A*GA*T*, the prefixes w.r.t. Q are GA, TA, GG, and TG. There are other kinds of positive factors, which are discussed in Section 4.3.

Figure 2(a) shows the main idea of this approach using the running example. The substrings $T[0, 1]$, $T[3, 4]$, $T[5, 6]$, $T[10, 11]$, $T[15, 16]$, and $T[19, 20]$ are six matching prefixes for the RE Q. The approach only examines matching suffixes of the text T starting from these matching prefixes using the automaton of Q. The automaton keeps examining each matching suffix until it fails, and it reports an occurrence whenever a final state is reached. We call this kind of approach "algorithm PFILTER," where "P" stands for "Prefix."

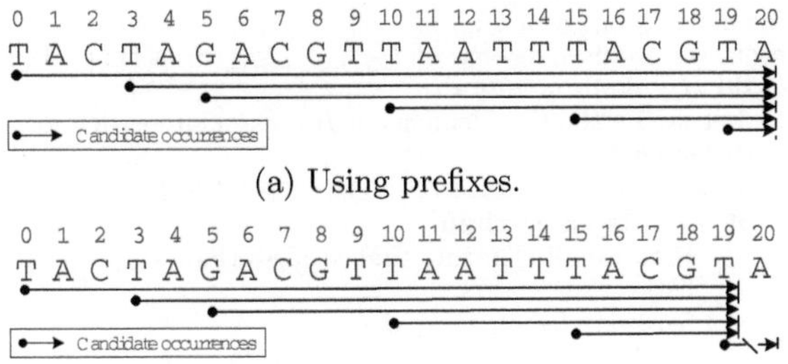

(a) Using prefixes.

(b) Combination of prefixes and last matching suffix.

Figure 2: Checking candidate occurrences of the RE Q = (G|T)A*GA*T*.

An alternative approach is adopted in NR-grep [9, 11], which uses a sliding window of size l_{min} on the text T and recognizes reversed matching prefixes in the sliding window using a reversed automaton. Similar to the definition of prefix, a suffix w.r.t. an RE Q is defined as a suffix with length l_{min} of a string in $R(Q)$. For example, for the RE Q = (G|T)A*GA*T*, the suffixes w.r.t. Q are TT, AT, AA, GA, GT, AG, GG, and TG, and the matching suffixes are $T[4,5]$, $T[5,6]$, $T[8,9]$, $T[9,10]$, $T[11,12]$, $T[12,13]$, $T[13,14]$, $T[14,15]$, and $T[18,19]$. We call the suffix-based approach "algorithm SFILTER," which is also similar to the algorithm PFILTER. It runs a reversed automaton from the end position of each suffix to the beginning of the text.

2.3 Improving Prefix-Based Approaches Using Last Matching Suffix

In Figure 2(a), the matching prefix $T[19,20]$ = TA could not be used to produce an answer string in $R(Q)$ since it is not among the suffixes identified above from the RE. Therefore, we could use the last matching suffix to do an early termination in each verification step. Figure 2(b) shows the example of improving the algorithm PFILTER. As we can see, by using the last matching suffix $T[18,19]$ = GT in the text T, a verification can terminate early at position 19. We call this approach the "algorithm PS." It only verifies those substrings starting from every matching prefix S_p to the last matching suffix S_s if the starting position of S_p is less than or equals to the starting position of S_s. We call S_s a *valid matching suffix* and each S_p a *valid matching prefix* w.r.t. its valid matching suffix S_s. For example, the substring $T[18,19]$ is a valid matching suffix and the substrings $T[0,1]$, $T[3,4]$, $T[5,6]$, $T[10,11]$, $T[15,16]$ are valid matching prefixes, whereas $T[19,20]$ is an invalid matching prefix. The algorithm PS requires $O(m{\cdot}n{\cdot}n'_p)$ time to do verifications for n'_p valid matching prefixes of T, assuming m is $|Q|$, and the verification for each valid matching prefix requires $O(m{\cdot}n)$ time.

3. NEGATIVE FACTORS

In this section, we develop the concept of negative factor, which can be used to improve the performance of matching algorithms. Contrary to positive factors, a negative factor is a substring that *must not* appear in an occurrence. We show that a negative factor can not only prune unnecessary verifications, but also terminate verifications early. We first present a formal definition of negative factors, then show a good pattern to prune candidates.

Definition 1. (Negative factor, or N-factor for short) Given a regular expression Q and a string w, a string w is called a *negative factor with respect to* Q, or simply a negative factor when Q is clear in the context, if there is no string $\Sigma^* w \Sigma^*$ does in $R(Q)$.

For a text T, an N-factor w.r.t. an RE Q must not appear in an answer to Q in T. For example, consider the RE Q = (G|T)A*GA*T*, the strings C, AGG, and TTA are N-factors, since they cannot appear in an answer as a substring.

LEMMA 1. *An N-factor w.r.t. an RE Q can not be a substring of a prefix or a suffix w.r.t. Q.*

THEOREM 1. *Given a text with length n, the number of N-factors w.r.t. an RE Q cannot be greater than $\sum_{i=1}^{n} |\Sigma|^i$.*

A PNS Pattern: Intuitively, we say a substring of T has a PNS pattern if it starts with a prefix of Q, has an N-factor in the middle, and ends with a suffix of Q. Formerly, let π_p, π_n, π_s be the set of starting positions of a matching prefix P, a matching N-factor N, and a matching suffix S in a text T, respectively. The substring $T[\pi_p, \pi_s + l_{min} - 1]$ conforms to a *PNS pattern* if N is a substring of $T[\pi_p, \pi_s + l_{min} - 1]$. Figure 3 shows that a substring conforms to a PNS pattern if and only if $\pi_p \leq \pi_n < \pi_s$ and $\pi_n + |N| \leq \pi_s + l_{min}$.

(a) A PNS pattern.

(b) Not a PNS pattern.

Figure 3: A substring conforming to a PNS pattern iff $\pi_p \leq \pi_n < \pi_s$ and $\pi_n + |N| \leq \pi_s + l_{min}$.

Obviously, a substring of T conforming to a PNS pattern cannot be an occurrence of Q. Based on this observation, we can prune unnecessary verifications using N-factors. Figure 4 shows an example of the benefit by using PNS patterns.

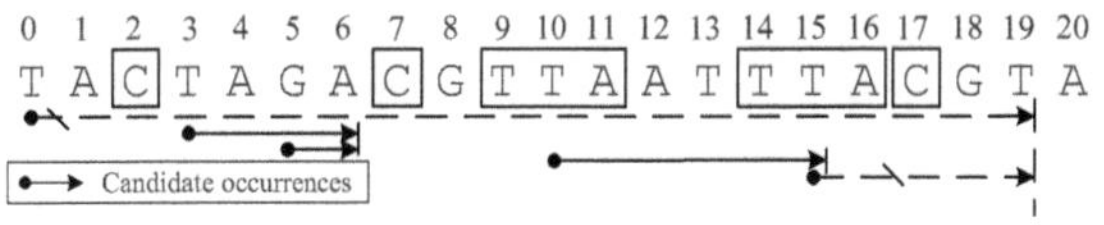

Figure 4: Using N-factors $T[2,2]$ and $T[17,17]$ to prune candidates of Q = (G|T)A*GA*T*. Compared with Figure 2(b), candidates $T[0,19]$ and $T[15,19]$ are pruned and the verifications starting from positions 3, 5, and 10 can be terminated early by using the N-factors $T[7,7]$ and $T[14,16]$, respectively.

Although the number of N-factors w.r.t. Q = (G|T)A*GA*T* is large, we can still generate a small number of high-quality N-factors, such as {C, AGG, ATA, ATG, GGG, GTA, GTG, TAT, TGG, TTA, TTG}. (We will provide details in Section 5.) For the example in Figure 2(b), all the five candidate substrings conform to a PNS pattern, in which two of them can be pruned using the N-factors $T[2,2]$ and $T[17,17]$. For instance, the substring $T[15,19]$ is such a substring that consists of a matching prefix $T[15,16]$ = TA, a matching suffix

$T[18,19]$ = GT, and an N-factor C at position 17. The N-factors can help us avoid the verifications of $T[0,19]$ and $T[15,19]$ (see Figure 2(b)). Furthermore, for the matching position of prefix $T[3,4]$ = TA, PNS can terminate the verification early when it meets the suffix $T[5,6]$ = GA, resulting in a better performance. Similarly, the verifications starting from the matching prefixes $T[5,6]$ = GA and $T[10,11]$ = TA can be terminated early at positions 6 and 15, respectively.

4. PRUNING UNNECESSARY CHECKS USING N-FACTORS

In this section we discuss how to combine N-factors with the algorithm PS to check candidate substrings that do not conform to a PNS pattern. In Section 4.1 we propose a merge algorithm to identify candidates and present two improved algorithms by using bit-parallel operations in Section 4.2. In Section 4.3 we show that negative factors, when used together with *necessary factors* (substrings that must appear in answers), can achieve better pruning power.

4.1 A Merging Algorithm

N-factors can be used to divide a text into a set of disjoint substrings, and we want to run the algorithm PS for each of them. Recall that the algorithm PS verifies substrings from every valid matching prefix to its corresponding valid matching suffix (see Section 2.3). For example, Figure 4 shows that the N-factors divide the text to disjoint substrings $T[0,1]$, $T[3,6]$, $T[8,10]$, $T[10,15]$, $T[15,16]$, and $T[18,20]$. Only $T[3,6]$ and $T[10,15]$ contain valid matching suffixes $T[5,6]$ and $T[14,15]$, respectively. The substrings $T[3,4]$ and $T[5,6]$ are valid matching prefixes w.r.t. the valid matching suffix $T[5,6]$, and $T[10,11]$ is a valid matching prefix w.r.t. the valid matching suffix $T[14,15]$, whereas $T[0,1]$, $T[15,16]$, and $T[19,20]$ are invalid matching prefixes.

In order to use N-factors in the PS approach, we sort starting positions of matches of prefixes, suffixes, and N-factors in the ascending order. A suffix trie of the text T can support this sorting operation with a large space overhead when T is long. To reduce the space cost, we can store the text T in a BWT format [7] and get an inverted list of starting positions for a substring α in a constant time ($O(|\alpha|)$) by simulating searches using BWT. For example, Figure 4 shows the inverted list of starting positions for the prefix TA is $\{0,3,10,15,19\}$ and the inverted list of starting positions for an N-factor C is $\{2,7,17\}$.

The basic idea of utilizing N-factors in the PS approach is to find a left valid matching suffix and valid matching prefixes in the text for each N-factor. The formal algorithm, called PNS-MERGE, is described in Algorithm 1 . It builds a min-heap H_N for all the N-factor lists, each of which is sorted in the ascending order. Let π_n be one element on the list of N. It pops π_n from the heap H_N and conduct a binary search for each suffix list specified by the largest element s_{max} ($< \pi_n + |N| - l_{min}$) to find a valid matching suffix starting at position s_{max} (lines 4 – 5). If such s_{max} exists, the algorithm PNS-MERGE verifies the candidate occurrence $T[\pi_p, s_{max}]$ for each unprocessed element π_p on prefix lists that is not greater than s_{max}. When s_{max} could not be found, it removes all the elements that are not greater than π_n on the prefix lists since they are all starting positions of invalid matching prefixes (lines 6 – 13). The algorithm then

Algorithm 1: PNS-MERGE

Input: An RE Q, Prefix lists $P_{set} = \{L_{P_1}, \ldots, L_{P_u}\}$, Suffix lists $S_{set} = \{L_{S_1}, \ldots, L_{S_v}\}$, Negative factor lists $L_{N_1}, \ldots, L_{N_w}$;

1 Calculate l_{min} given Q;
2 Insert the frontier records of $L_{N_1}, \ldots, L_{N_w}$ to a heap H_N;
3 **while** H_N *is not empty* **do**
4   Let π_n be the top element on H_N associated with an N-factor N;
5   $s_{max} \leftarrow$ FINDMAXSUFFIX($S_{set}, \pi_n + |N| - l_{min}$);
6   **if** s_{max} *is found* **then**
7   Remove all elements that are less than s_{max} in suffix lists;
8   **foreach** $L_{P_i} (\in P_{set})$ **do**
9   **for** *element* π_p ($\leq s_{max}$) *in the list* L_{P_i} **do**
10   VERIFY($T[\pi_p, s_{max}]$);
11   Remove π_p from L_{P_i};
12   **else**
13   Remove all elements that are not greater than π_n in prefix lists;
14   Pop π_n from H_N;
15   Push next record (if any) on each popped list to H_N;
16 **if** *there exists a non-empty list in* S_{set} **then**
17   $s_{max} \leftarrow$ FINDMAXSUFFIX($S_{set}, |T| - l_{min} + 1$);
18   VERIFY($T[\pi_p, s_{max}]$) for each π_p ($\leq s_{max}$) in prefix lists;

pops the top element π_n from the heap H_N and repeats the above steps until the heap H_N is empty.

If there exist non-empty suffix lists, the algorithm finds the largest element s_{max} among them and verifies the candidate occurrence $T[\pi_p, s_{max}]$ for each remaining element $\pi_p (\leq s_{max})$ on the prefix lists (lines 16 – 18).

The algorithm requires $O(n_p + m_n \cdot \log l_n + m_s \cdot \log l_s)$ time to generate candidates, where n_p is the number of prefixes in T, m_n and m_s are the number of N-factors and suffixes, respectively, l_n and l_s are the average length of the inverted list of each N-factor and suffix, respectively. The average length of each verification has been reduced to $\frac{n}{m_n \cdot l_n}$ since N-factors could divide the text into $m_n \cdot l_n$ disjoint substrings. Therefore, the algorithm PNS-MERGE only requires $O(\frac{m \cdot n}{m_n \cdot l_n} n_c)$ time to do verifications, where n_c is the number of candidates.[1]

4.2 Bit-Parallel Algorithms

In algorithm PNS-MERGE, we need to find valid matching suffixes and their corresponding valid matching prefixes to construct candidate occurrences for verification. We can accelerate the process by introducing the bit-parallel operations. We propose two algorithms in Sections 4.2.1 and 4.2.2.

4.2.1 *The* PNS-BITC *Algorithm under the Constraint* $|N| \leq l_{min}$

We use a bit vector $N_s = d_0 \ldots d_n$ to represent all the occurrences of N-factors in the text T. We set $N_s[d_i] = 1$ ($d_0 \leq d_i < d_n$) if an N-factor starts at the position d_i in T. We set the last bit $N_s[d_n] = 1$ to mark the end of T. Consider our running example shown in Section 2. Given the RE Q = (G|T)A*GA*T* and the text shown in Figure 1, the third row in Table 1 shows an example N_s, which represents the occurrences of N-factors w.r.t. Q in the text T. Similarly,

[1]According to the analysis in Section 5.4 and experimental results in Section 6, n_c is much smaller than n_p.

Algorithm 2: PNS-BitC

```
   Input: Bit vectors P_s, S_s, N_s, l_min;
1  Calculate vectors S_sm and P_c using Equation 1;
2  t ← the position of last suffix using S_sm;
3  Change S_sm[t] from 1 to 0;  π_s ← t;  π_p ← 0;
4  repeat
5  |  t ← the position of last suffix using S_sm;
6  |  repeat
7  |  |  π_p ← the position of last prefix using P_c;
8  |  |  Change P_c[π_p] from 1 to 0;
9  |  |  VERIFY(T[π_p, π_s + l_min − 1]);
10 |  until π_p < t;
11 |  Change S_sm[t] from 1 to 0;  π_s ← t;
12 until there is no 1 in S_sm or P_c;
```

we use vectors P_s and S_s for the occurrences of prefixes and suffixes in T respectively, in which $P_s[d_i] = 1$ (or $S_s[d_i] = 1$) indicates a prefix (or suffix) starting at position d_i in T.

We first consider a simple case where the length of each N-factor is no greater than the length l_{min}. Under this constraint, it is obvious that the case shown in Figure 3(b) cannot happen, i.e., if positions π_p, π_n, and π_s satisfy the condition $\pi_p < \pi_n < \pi_s$, there exists a PNS pattern. Under this constraint, a valid matching suffix means $\pi_s < \pi_n$ since a matching suffix and a matching N-factor cannot start at the same position, which suggest we can just use N_s, P_s, and S_s to calculate candidate occurrences.

Algorithm 2 shows the algorithm PNS-BitC that generates a candidate occurrence using a valid matching suffix and a corresponding valid matching prefix to do verifications. In line 1, the algorithm calculates two vectors S_{s_m} and P_c using Equation 1. In S_{s_m}, a bit $S_{s_m}[d_i] = 1$ if d_i is the starting position of a valid matching suffix, otherwise $S_{s_m}[d_i] = 0$. In P_c, a bit $P_c[d_i] = 1$ if d_i is the starting position of a valid matching prefix. Otherwise $P_c[d_i] = 0$.

$$
\begin{array}{lrcl}
\textit{Intermediate}: & A_0 & = & (N_s|S_s) - (N_s << 1), \\
 & S_{s_m} & = & (\sim A_0)\ \&\ S_s, \\
\textit{Intermediate}: & B_0 & = & N_s - S_{s_m}, \\
 & P_c & = & P_s\ \&\ B_0.
\end{array} \tag{1}
$$

For illustration purposes, we use an intermediate vector A_0 to show how to calculate S_{s_m}. The bit $A_0[d_i]$ is set to 0 if d_i is the starting position of a valid matching suffix. For example, the bits $A_0[5]$, $A_0[14]$, and $A_0[18]$ in Table 1 are all 0, and they mark the three valid matching suffixes. If there is no matching suffix between any two adjacent matching N-factors starting at d_i and d_j, the algorithm PNS-BitC sets $A_0[d_i] = 0$ and $A_0[d_l] = 1$ ($d_i < d_l < d_j$). Then we calculate S_{s_m} using $(\sim A_0)\&S_s$.

Table 1: Generate candidate regions using bit operations under the constraint $|N| \leq l_{min}$ ($l_{min} = 2$).

	Vector																					
	0					5					10					15					20	
P_s	1	0	0	1	0	1	0	0	0	0	1	0	0	0	0	1	0	0	0	1	0	0
S_s	0	0	0	0	1	1	0	0	1	1	0	1	1	1	1	0	0	0	1	0	0	0
N_s	0	0	1	0	0	0	0	1	0	0	0	0	0	0	0	0	0	1	0	0	0	1
A_0	1	1	1	0	1	0	1	1	1	1	0	1	1	1	0	1	1	1	0	1	1	1
S_{s_m}	0	0	0	0	0	1	0	0	0	0	0	0	0	0	1	0	0	0	1	0	0	0
B_0	0	0	0	1	1	1	0	0	1	1	1	1	1	1	1	0	0	0	1	0	0	1
P_c	0	0	0	1	0	1	0	0	0	0	1	0	0	0	0	0	0	0	0	0	0	0

Correspondingly we use another intermediate vector B_0 to represent the starting positions of all the possible valid matching prefixes. Figure 5 shows an example of partial bits in the vector B_0. The "1" bits correspond to the starting positions of valid matching prefixes.

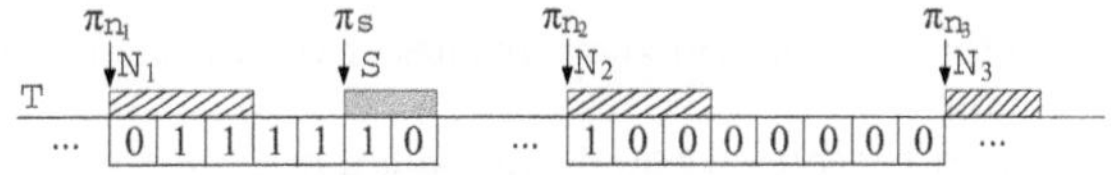

Figure 5: Explanation of the intermediate vector B_0.

The vector $P_c = P_s\ \&\ B_0$ denotes the starting positions of valid matching prefixes. Then the algorithm PNS-BitC gets each position pair π_p and π_s using bit operations (lines 2 and 7), which can be done in constant time.[2] It then verifies the corresponding candidate occurrence $T[\pi_p, \pi_s + l_{min} - 1]$ using P_c and S_{s_m} (line 9). For example, let $l_{min} = 2$. Table 1 shows the generated P_c and S_{s_m}. The candidate occurrences are $T[3, 6]$, $T[5, 6]$, and $T[10, 15]$, which are consistent with the candidate occurrences shown in Figure 4.

In general, the text string T can occupy the memory space of multiple words. The algorithm proceeds in the same fashion by computing S_{s_m} and P_c for all $\lceil \frac{n}{w} \rceil$ words, where w is the length of a word (e.g., 4 bytes). We only need to pay special attention to the case of processing (N_s<<1) and ($N_s - S_{S_m}$). For the current word N_s^{i-1}, when processing (N_s<<1), we need to maintain the first bit of its next word N_s^i and put it into the last bit of N_s^{i-1}. Similarly, the operation $N_s - S_{S_m}$ of the $(i-1)$st word is changed to $N_s^{i-1} - S_{S_m}^{i-1} - (N_s^i < S_{S_m}^i)$.

Let us analyze the space and time complexity of the algorithm. Let the word size be w. The algorithm requires $O(5\lceil \frac{n}{w} \rceil)$ to store the three input vectors and the two output vectors S_{S_m} and P_c. It takes $O(\lceil \frac{n}{w} \rceil)$ time to calculate S_{S_m} and P_c and $O(k_1 + k_2)$ time to generate candidate occurrences, where k_1 and k_2 are number of valid matching prefixes and valid matching suffixes, respectively. It requires the same verification time as the algorithm PNS-Merge.

4.2.2 *The* PNS-BitG *Algorithm without Constraints*

In Figure 3(b), the position relationship $\pi_p \leq \pi_n < \pi_s$ does not guarantee a PNS pattern. It means that the comparison between the end positions of the N-factor N_2 and the suffix S_2 is also needed, i.e., both conditions $\pi_p \leq \pi_n < \pi_s$ and $\pi_{n_e} \leq \pi_{s_e}$ need to be satisfied to make sure that a PNS can be found, where π_{n_e} and π_{s_e} are the end positions of the N-factor N_2 and the suffix B_2.

We can get an end position π_{s_e} by shifting its corresponding starting position π_s to the right for $l_{min} - 1$ bits since we know the length of each suffix is l_{min}, i.e., the vector for the end positions of the occurrences of N-factors $S_e = S_s >> (l_{min} - 1)$. However, the length of N-factors could be different, so we have to use another vector N_e to represent the end positions of the occurrences of N-factors. Equation 2 shows the bit operations to calculate candidate occurrences.

$$
\begin{array}{lrcl}
\textit{Intermediate}: & A_1 & = & (N_e|S_e) - (N_e<<1), \\
 & S_{e_m} & = & (\sim A_1)\ \&\ S_e\ \&\ (\sim N_e), \\
\textit{Intermediate}: & B_1 & = & (N_e - S_{e_m})\ \&\ (\sim N_e), \\
\textit{Intermediate}: & B_2 & = & \sim((S_{e_m}<<(l_{min}-1)) - S_{e_m}), \\
\textit{Intermediate}: & B_3 & = & (N_e\ \&\ A_1)\ |\ (N_e\ \&\ S_e), \\
\textit{Intermediate}: & B_4 & = & (N_s - B_3)\ \&\ (\sim N_s), \\
\textit{Intermediate}: & B_5 & = & (B_1\ \&\ B_2)\ |\ B_4, \\
 & P_c & = & P_s\ \&\ B_5.
\end{array} \tag{2}
$$

We consider the same example that matches the RE Q = `(G|T)A*GA*T*` on the text in Figure 1. Table 2 shows the

[2]http://graphics.stanford.edu/~seander/bithacks.html

input vectors and intermediate results of the bit operations in Equation 2.

Similar to the bit vector A_0 in Equation 1, in the intermediate bit vector A_1 in Equation 2, $A_1[d_i] = 0$ if d_i is the end position of a valid matching suffix. Then we can get the vector S_{e_m}, in which each bit 1 means an end position of a valid matching suffix. Notice that, different from S_{s_m} in Equation 1, the vector S_{e_m} needs to do an AND operation between $(\sim A_1)\&S_e$ and $(\sim N_e)$. Before we give the reason, let us consider the case where a matching suffix S has the same end position t with a matching N-factor N_1. According to the analysis in Section 4.1, this suffix S should not be used to generate candidate occurrences (see Figure 3(a)). In addition, if there is no suffix between the N-factor N_1 and its right neighbor N-factor N_2, then the bit $A_1[t]$ is 0. Therefore, the algorithm PNS-BitG may choose an invalid matching suffix setting $S_{e_m}[t] = 1$. In order to avoid choosing such invalid matching suffix S, we do the bit AND operation between $(\sim A_1)\&S_e$ and $(\sim N_e)$.

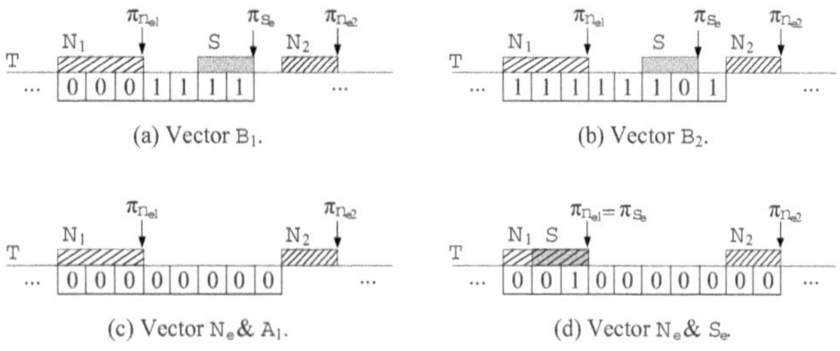

(a) Vector B_1. (b) Vector B_2. (c) Vector $N_e\& A_1$. (d) Vector $N_e\& S_e$.

Figure 6: Explanation of vectors.

For the purpose of calculating valid matching prefixes corresponding to each valid matching suffix, we use five intermediate vectors $B_1, \ldots, B_5$ to explain how the calculation works. Let S be the rightmost suffix between two N-factors N_1 and N_2. $B_1[d_i] = 1$ if $\pi_{n_{e1}} < d_i \leq \pi_{s_e}$. An example vector B_1 is shown in Figure 6(a). The vector B_2 sets all the bits to 1 except the bit $B_2[\pi_{s_e}]$, where π_{s_e} is the end position of a valid matching suffix. Figure 6(b) shows that $B_2[d_i] = 0$ ($\pi_{s_s} < d_i \leq \pi_{s_e}$), where π_{s_s} is the starting position of the valid matching suffix S.

Given two N-factors N_1 and N_2, if there is no suffix between them, we say N_1 is a *useless N-factor*. We use $B_3[\pi_{n_{e1}}] = 0$ to mark the useless N-factor N_1 and keep $B_3[\pi_{n_{e2}}] = 1$ at the same time. We use $N_e\&A_1$ to mark all the useless N-factors (see Figure 6(c)). However, a useless N-factor needs to be maintained if there is a suffix S happens ending at the same position with this N-factor. The reason is that a matching suffix $T[\pi_{s_s}, \pi_{s_e}]$ could be valid if there exists a prefix starting at position π_{p_s} and $\pi_{n_s} < \pi_{p_s} \leq \pi_{s_s}$, where π_{n_s} is the starting position of N_1 (see Figure 6(d)). We use $N_e\&S_e$ to specify all the same end positions of matching N-factors and valid matching suffixes. Furthermore we set each bit in $B_4[\pi_{n_s}+1, \pi_{s_e}]$ to 1. Then we use the vector B_5 to combine all cases of possible valid matching prefixes. Finally, the vector P_c marks all valid matching prefixes.

Table 2 shows the generated S_{e_m} and P_c, and the candidate occurrences are consistent with those shown in Figure 4.

We call the corresponding algorithm PNS-BitG. After using Equation 2 to get the two vectors S_{e_m} and P_c, the algorithm gets each position pair π_s and π_p from S_{e_m} and P_c, respectively. It then generates candidates $T[\pi_p, \pi_s]$ to do verification. The algorithm PNS-BitG requires the same time complexity as the algorithm PNS-BitC, but needs $O(6\lceil \frac{n}{w} \rceil)$ to store one more vector N_e than the algorithm PNS-BitC.

Table 2: Generate candidate regions using bit operations without any constraint ($l_{min} = 2$).

	Vector																					
	0					5					10					15					20	
P_s	1	0	0	1	0	1	0	0	0	0	1	0	0	0	0	1	0	0	0	1	0	0
S_e	0	0	0	0	0	1	1	0	0	1	1	0	1	1	1	1	0	0	0	1	0	0
N_s	0	0	1	0	0	0	0	1	0	1	0	0	0	0	1	0	0	1	1	0	0	1
N_e	0	0	1	0	0	0	0	1	0	0	0	1	0	0	0	0	1	1	0	0	1	1
A_1	1	1	1	0	0	1	0	1	0	1	0	1	1	1	1	0	0	1	0	0	0	1
S_{e_m}	0	0	0	0	0	0	1	0	0	0	1	0	0	0	0	1	0	0	0	1	0	0
B_1	0	0	0	1	1	1	1	0	1	1	1	0	1	1	1	1	0	0	1	1	0	0
B_2	1	1	1	1	1	1	0	1	1	1	0	1	1	1	1	0	1	1	1	0	1	1
B_3	0	0	1	0	0	0	0	1	0	0	0	1	0	0	0	0	0	1	0	0	0	1
B_4	0	0	0	0	0	0	0	0	0	0	1	1	0	0	0	0	0	0	0	0	0	0
B_5	0	0	0	1	1	1	0	0	1	1	1	1	1	1	1	0	0	0	1	0	0	0
P_c	0	0	0	1	0	1	0	0	0	0	1	0	0	0	0	0	0	0	0	0	0	0

4.3 Improving Pruning Power by Combining Negative Factors with Necessary Factors

Besides prefixes and suffixes, there is another type of positive factors, called *necessary factor*. A necessary factor w.r.t. an RE Q is a substring that must appear in every matching substring in the text T. For instance, `G` is a necessary factor w.r.t. the RE Q = `(G|T)A*GA*T*`. GNU grep 2.0 [4] employs a different heuristic approach for finding necessary factors w.r.t. an RE Q. The neighborhoods of these necessary factors are then verified using a lazy deterministic automaton.

Generally, a necessary factor (substring) divides Q into a left part and a right part. Two automata are constructed for verification in both directions. Figure 7(a) shows an example of this approach, call M algorithm. Since `G` is a necessary factor, the algorithm M builds an automaton A_r for the right part of the RE Q, i.e., `GA*T*`, and another automaton A_l for the left part of Q, i.e., `(G|T)A*G`. It then runs A_r on the suffixes of T starting at positions 5, 8, and 18, and runs A_l on the prefixes starting at these positions.

Now we analyze the effect of introducing necessary factors into the algorithms P, PS, and PNS. We call the corresponding algorithms PM, PMS, and PMNS, respectively. (In the case where there are no necessary factors, the approaches based on necessary factors can not be used.) Generally, an occurrence of Q in the text T must contain at least one necessary factor. Otherwise, the corresponding candidate can be pruned without verification. Now we show an interesting observation that using both negative factors and necessary factors together (i.e., algorithm PMNS) can enhance the filtering power significantly.

Figures 7(b) and 7(c) show the examples of introducing necessary factors into the algorithms P and PS, respectively. In Figures 7(b), the algorithm PM can prune the candidate $T[19, 20]$ since it does not contain a necessary factor. However, in Figure 7(c), the algorithm PMS cannot prune any more candidates because the necessary factor `G` at position 18 appears in the last matching suffix $T[18, 19]$ = `GT`. Generally, it has a high probability that a necessary factor appears in the late part of T, that is, each candidate occurrence might have a high probability to contain this necessary factor and could not be pruned.

However, the algorithm PNS generates candidates in a relatively short interval, in which at least one necessary factor is expected to be found, otherwise it must not be an occurrence. For example, the substring $T[10, 15]$ shown in

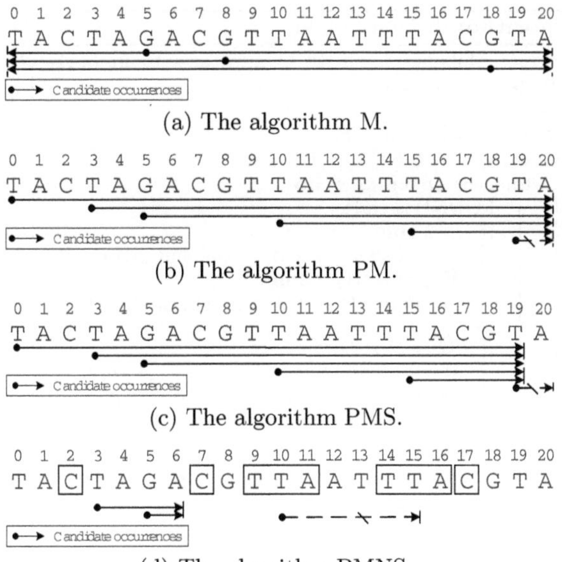

(a) The algorithm M.

(b) The algorithm PM.

(c) The algorithm PMS.

(d) The algorithm PMNS.

Figure 7: Checking candidate occurrences of the RE Q = (G|T)A*GA*T* using necessary factors, which are shown in bold font.

Figure 7(d) is unnecessary to be verified using the algorithm PMNS since it does not contain any necessary factor.

We can design algorithms using the ideas of PNS-MERGE and bit operations to combine necessary factors with PNS patterns. Due to space limitation we do not give the detail of these algorithms. In Section 6 we show our experimental results of the algorithm PMNS by using bit operations with constraints $|N| \leq l_{min}$, which is called PMNS-BITC.

5. CHOOSING GOOD N-FACTORS

The number of N-factors w.r.t. an RE could be large, and different N-factors could have different improvements on the matching performance of algorithms based on PNS patterns. For example, given an RE Q = C*AAA, both G and CGA are N-factors w.r.t. Q. It is obvious that any occurrence of CGA in a text T also contains an occurrence of G in T. Thus the N-factor CGA does not provide more filtering power than G. So a natural question is how to choose a small number of high-quality N-factors to maximize search performance. In this section we develop techniques to solve this problem. In Section 5.1 we show how to define a finite set of high-quality N-factors, called "core N-factors," and show an upper bound on the number of core N-factors w.r.t. an RE Q. Then in Section 5.2 we describe the challenge of efficiently constructing the core N-factors, and propose an efficient algorithm for constructing core N-factors. In Section 5.3 we develop a technique to speed up the generation of core N-factors by doing early termination.

5.1 Core N-Factors

Definition 2. (Core N-factor). An N-factor w.r.t. an RE Q is called a *core N-factor* if each of its proper subsequences is not an N-factor w.r.t. Q.[3]

For example, for the RE Q = C*AAA, the set of core N-factors w.r.t. Q is {G, T, AC, AAAA}. The substring GA is not a core N-factor since its subsequence G is an N-factor.

In order to compute an upper bound on the number of core N-factors w.r.t. an RE Q, we use a *factor automaton* [2] to check whether a string is an N-factor. A factor automaton is an automaton representing the set of all positive factors w.r.t. Q. For a given RE Q, we first construct a nondeterministic factor automaton A_f. Then A_f can be further transformed to a unique minimal deterministic factor automaton A_{f_m}, which accepts exactly the same set of strings [5]. Using A_{f_m} we can prove an upper bound on the number of core N-factors.

THEOREM 2. *Let Q be an RE and A_{f_m} be its minimized deterministic factor automaton. The length of a core N-factor w.r.t. Q cannot be greater than the number of states in the longest acyclic path of A_{f_m}.*

LEMMA 2. *The number of core N-factors w.r.t. an RE Q is upper bounded by $|Q|^2$.*

PROOF. An upper bound on the number of states in the longest acyclic path of the minimized deterministic factor automaton is the square of the number of characters that Q contains, i.e., $|Q|^2$. Therefore, the length of any core N-factor should be no greater than $|Q|^2$. □

5.2 Constructing Core N-Factors Online

One naive way to construct core N-factors is to enumerate strings with a length $\leq |Q|^2$ and check if they are core N-factors one by one (see Algorithm 3). The check process of a string s includes two phases: (i) the function CHECKSUBSEQUENCE checks if a subsequence of s is an N-factor (line 4), and (ii) otherwise, check if s itself is an N-factor, which can be determined by running the factor automaton $A_f(Q)$ (line 6).

Algorithm 3: NAIVECORE

```
  Input: Alphabet Σ, an RE Q, a factor automaton A_f(Q);
  Output: A set of core N-factors C_N;
1 C_N ← ∅;
2 for length l ← 1; l ≤ |Q|^2; l++ do
3     for each string s ∈ Σ^l do
4         FOUND ← CHECKSUBSEQUENCE(C_N, s);
5         if FOUND is false then
6             if s cannot be accepted by A_f(Q) then
7                 C_N ← C_N ∪ {s};
8 return C_N;
```

It can be time consuming to enumerate all the strings with a length $\leq |Q|^2$ and check each of them, especially when we have to do it for each search query. For instance, we need to enumerate 340 strings within 16 iterations for the RE Q = C*AAA. Next we present a more efficient method to construct core N-factors to reduce the computational cost.

Instead of enumerating all the strings (see line 3 in Algorithm 3), we can use two properties of core N-factors to generate them with a length l using a smaller set of strings with length $l-1$. Based on Definition 2, we show the properties and how to utilize them to improve the performance.

[3]We distinguish substring and subsequence in this paper. A substring of a string s has consecutive characters of s, while the characters in a subsequence may not be consecutive in s.

(1) *Generate core N-factors using substrings w.r.t. an RE Q.*

Property 1. If a string x is a core N-factor, then its prefix $x[0, |x|-2]$ and suffix $x[1, |x|-1]$ can be accepted by the factor automaton $A_f(Q)$.

This property helps us improve the performance of computing N-factors by "joining" a set of strings with length $l-1$ to generate strings with length l. The formal definition of *string-join* is given below.

Definition 3. (String-join) Given two strings s_1 and s_2, the *string-join* of s_1 and s_2, denoted by $\widehat{s_1 s_2}$, is computed as follows. If $|s_1| = |s_2| = l-1$ and $s_1[1, l-2] = s_2[0, l-3]$, then $\widehat{s_1 s_2}[0, l-2] = s_1$ and $\widehat{s_1 s_2}[l-1] = s_2[l-2]$; otherwise, $\widehat{s_1 s_2} = \emptyset$.

Definition 4. (String set self-join) Let $S = \{s_1, \ldots, s_k\}$ be a set of strings of length $l-1$. The *string set self-join* of S, denoted by $\widehat{S}$, is a set of non-empty strings $\widehat{s_i s_j}$ $(1 \leq i, j \leq k)$.

For example, let $S = \{s_1, s_2\}$, $s_1 =$ `ACG` and $s_2 =$ `CGT`, then $\widehat{S} = \{$`ACGT`$\}$.

Compared with Algorithm 3, we can get the same set of core N-factors with length l by self-joining the set of strings with length $l-1$, each of which can be accepted by the factor automaton $A_f(Q)$.

Let S' be the set of strings that can be accepted by $A_f(Q)$, where each string in S' has a length $l-1$, and $S = \widehat{S'}$. We use $S_Q(\Sigma^l) \subseteq \Sigma^l$ and $S_Q(S) \subseteq S$ to represent strings that can be accepted by $A_f(Q)$, and use $S_C(\Sigma^l) \subseteq \Sigma^l$ and $S_C(S) \subseteq S$ to represent the core N-factors.

THEOREM 3. *The two sets $S_Q(\Sigma^l)$ and $S_Q(S)$ are equivalent, and the two sets $S_C(\Sigma^l)$ and $S_C(S)$ are also equivalent.*

(2) *Avoid invoking* CHECKSUBSEQUENCE *for every generated string.*

Property 2. Given a core N-factor x with a length greater than 1, let s be a string whose prefix $s[0, |s|-2]$ and suffix $s[1, |s|-1]$ can be accepted by $A_f(Q)$. If x is subsequence of s, then $x[0] = s[0]$ and $x[|x|-1] = s[|s|-1]$.

Let $|x| = m$ $(1 < m \leq n)$. We construct string s as follows. Suppose S' is a set of strings with length $l-1$ that can be accepted by $A_f(Q)$. Let $S = (\widehat{S'})$ and $s \in S$. We know there must exist two strings $s_1, s_2 \in S'$, such that $s_1 = s[0, l-2]$ and $s_2 = s[1, l-1]$. Assuming $x[0] \neq s[0]$, since x is a subsequence of a string $s \in S$, we know x should be a subsequence of $s[1, l-1]$, i.e., x is a subsequence of s_2. It contradicts to the setting that any core N-factor is not a subsequence of a string in S. Therefore, $x[0]$ must be equivalent to $s[0]$. Similar, $x[m-1] = s[l-1]$.

Algorithm 4 is an improved algorithm by considering the above two properties in Algorithm 3. According to Property 1, the algorithm QUICKCORE in Algorithm 4 initially generates strings with length 1 and maintains those that can be accepted by the factor automaton $A_f(Q)$. Through self-joining the retained strings with length $l-1$, the algorithm generates the strings with one more character (lines 3 – 16).

Furthermore, when there exists a core N-factor x that does not satisfy $s[0] = x[0]$ and $s[l-1], x[|x|-1]$, then we do not need to invoke the function CHECKSUBSEQUENCE based on Property 2 (lines 7 – 9) . In the above example for Q = C^*AAA, among the 65 strings, only 8 strings need to be further checked using the function CHECKSUBSEQUENCE.

Algorithm 4: QUICKCORE

Input: Alphabet Σ, an RE Q, a factor automaton $A_f(Q)$;
Output: A set of core N-factors;
1 $C_N \leftarrow \emptyset$; $S \leftarrow \Sigma$;
2 Create a hash table H_T;
3 **for** *length* $l \leftarrow 1; l \leq |Q|^2; l{+}{+}$ **do**
4   **for** *each string* $s \in S$ **do**
5   FOUND $\leftarrow$ false;
6   **if** $l > 2$ **then**
7   New a string y, $y[0] \leftarrow s[0]$ and $y[1] \leftarrow s[l-1]$;
8   **if** *y is in H_T* **then**
9   FOUND $\leftarrow$ CHECKSUBSEQUENCE(C_N, s);
10   **if** *FOUND is false* **then**
11   **if** *s cannot be accepted by $A_f(Q)$* **then**
12         $C_N \leftarrow C_N \cup \{s\}$; $S \leftarrow S - \{s\}$;
13   Insert y into H_T, where $y[0] \leftarrow s[0]$ and $y[1] \leftarrow s[l-1]$;
14   **else**
15       $S \leftarrow S - \{s\}$;
16   $S \leftarrow \widehat{S}$;
17 return C_N;

5.3 Early Termination of Constructing Core N-Factors

We observe that the upper bound $|Q|^2$ on the length of an N-factor in Algorithm 4 is loose, which can result in many iterations in the algorithm (see line 2). As we can see in Table 3, all core N-factors have been generated before the fifth iteration. However, the absence of incremental core N-factors at an iteration cannot guarantee that there will not be any more core N-factors generated in the following iterations, i.e., a new core N-factor can still be generated even though nothing is produced in the previous iterations. So the question is whether there exists a tighter upper bound on the length using which we can terminate the iterations early. Next we show such a tighter bound.

Table 3: Early termination for Q = C^*AAA, where the underlined strings are core N-factors.

Iteration	Processing strings using Algorithm 4	Processing strings using Algorithm 5
1	A, C, T, G	A, C, T, G
2	AA, CA, CC, AC	AA, CA, AC
3	AAA, CAA, CCA, CCC	AAA, CAA
4	AAAA, CAAA, CCAA, CCCA, CCCC	AAAA, CAAA
5	CCAAA, CCCAA, CCCCA, CCCCC	$\emptyset$
6	CCCAAA, CCCCAA, CCCCCA, CCCCCC	
...	...	
16	...	

Observation 1. Let C be the set of characters in e^*, and k be the summation of frequencies of characters of C in Q. For any string s that matches the pattern e^* and $|s| > k$, we cannot find any string s' to make $\widehat{ss'}$ an N-factor.

As we can see in the second column in Table 3, Algorithm 4 keeps generating strings and checks if some of them are N-factors. In the second iteration, the string CC is used to generate strings CCA and CCC in the third iteration, and generate string CCAA, CCCA and CCCC in later iterations. As we know, CC is not an N-factor because C* exists in the RE Q. Any generated string based on CC cannot be an N-factor, since multiple Cs can always be accepted by the factor automaton $A_f(Q)$. Therefore, it is not needed to keep CC in the second iteration.

Based on this observation in Algorithm 5, we propose the algorithm EarlyCore to do early termination in the construction of core N-factors without any false dismissal. The algorithm first counts the frequency of each character in each Kleene closure e^* in Q (lines 2 – 7) and then uses it to check if a generated string needs to be reserved for self-joining in the next iteration (line 12).

Algorithm 5: EarlyCore

```
   Input: Alphabet Σ, an RE Q, a factor automaton A_f(Q);
   Output: A set of core N-factors;
1  C_N ← ∅; S ← Σ; C_S ← ∅;
2  for each expression e* in Q do
3      Let C ← the set of characters in e;
4      Let freq(C) ← 0;
5      for each character c in e do
6          freq(C) ← freq(C) + number of c in Q;
7      Insert C into C_S;
8  l ← 1;
9  while S is not empty do
10     for each string s ∈ S do
11         if ∃C ∈ C_S and s ∈ C^l then
12             if l = freq(C) + 1 then // bound of C
13                 S ← S − {s};
14         ... // see lines 5 - 15 in Algorithm 4
15     S ← Ŝ;    l ← l + 1;
16 return C_N;
```

Table 3 shows the number of iterations using Algorithm 4 and Algorithm 5, respectively. Algorithm 5 only needs 4 iterations compared with the 16 iterations in Algorithm 4.

Theorem 4. *The set S in Algorithm 5 always converges to an empty set.*

5.4 Pruning Power of N-factors

In this section, we analyze the pruning power of N-factors. We first present a theoretical analysis, then give an experimental result on a real data set.

Consider a substring $T[a, d]$ conforming to a PNS pattern, in which the substring $T[a, b]$ is a matching prefix and the substring $T[c, d]$ is a matching suffix ($a \leq b \leq c \leq d$). Let $p_1(n)$ denote the probability that the length of $T[b, c]$ is equal to n and $p_2(n)$ denote the probability that there exists at least one N-factor matching in $T[b, c]$. Then the probability of filtering any prefix matching in T using N-factors can be calculated as follows:

$$p_f = \sum_{n=0}^{|T|-2\cdot l_{min}} p_1(n) \times p_2(n). \quad (3)$$

We first calculate $p_1(n)$. Let $S = \{S_1, \ldots, S_h\}$ be the set of suffixes w.r.t. the RE Q. As defined in [14], each suffix in S has the same length l_{min}. Let $B_n(h, l_{min})$ denote the number of substrings $T[b, c]$ with a length n such that any suffix in S is not a substring of $T[b, c]$. Then we could get the following recurrence function for $n \geq 0$:

$$B_n(h, l_{min}) = \begin{cases} |\Sigma|^n & \text{if } n < l_{min}, \\ |\Sigma|\cdot B_{n-1}(h, l_{min}) - h\cdot B_{n-l_{min}}(h, l_{min}) & \text{otherwise.} \end{cases}$$

Then we have

$$p_1(n) = \frac{B_n(h, l_{min})}{|\Sigma|^n} \times \frac{h}{|\Sigma|^{l_{min}}}. \quad (4)$$

Similarly, let $N = \{N_1, \ldots, N_k\}$ be the set of N-factors w.r.t. the RE Q and each N-factor in N has a length l'. Then we have

$$p_2(n) = 1 - \frac{B_n(k, l')}{|\Sigma|^n}. \quad (5)$$

6. EXPERIMENTS

In this section, we present experimental results of the N-factor technique on multiple real data sets.

Experiment Setup. We conducted the experiments on three public data sets, including Human Genome, Protein sequences, and English texts.

- Human Genome: The genomic sequence (GRCh37) was assembled from a collection of DNA sequences, which consisted of 24 chromosomes with a length varying from 48 million to 249 million.[4]
- Protein sequences: We adopted the database Pfam 26.0 that contains a large amount of protein families and is composed of Pfam-A and Pfam-B.[5] The symbol set consists of all the capital English letters, excluding "O" and "J". We randomly picked text with a length varying from 101 to 9143 from Pfam-B.
- English texts: We used DBLP-Citation-network[6], which included 1,632,442 blocks, each of which corresponds to one paper. Each block contains several attributes of a paper, e.g., title, authors, abstract, etc. We extracted the abstract from every block. The symbol set consisted of 52 English letters, plus 10 digits.

We extracted several subsequences of length ranging from 10 million to 100 million from the Human Genome. For the other two data sets, the size of each data set varied from 10MB to 100MB. Since there is no "random" regular expression [12], we manually synthesized REs to cover different properties of the regular expression (see Table 4). The size of these REs was from 6 to 21 and l_{min} varied from 2 to 5. We ran each algorithm using the corresponding REs on different data sets. These REs were used as queries to compare the performance of different algorithms.

All the algorithms were implemented using GNU C++. The experiments were run on a PC with an Intel 3.10GHz Quad Core CPU i5 and 8GB memory with a 500GB disk, running a Ubuntu (Linux) 64-bit operating system. All index structures were in memory.

[4]http://hgdownload.cse.ucsc.edu/goldenPath/hg18
[5]ftp://ftp.sanger.ac.uk/pub/databases/Pfam/releases
[6]http://arnetminer.org/DBLP_Citation

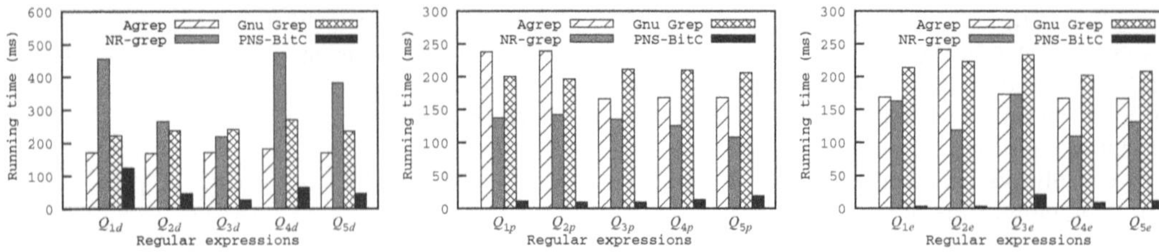

(a) DNA sequences. (b) Protein sequences. (c) English text.

Figure 8: Performance comparison of different algorithms.

Table 4: Synthesized regular expressions.

<table>
<tr><th>Data sets</th><th>Regular expressions Q</th></tr>
<tr><td>DNA</td><td>Q_{1_d} = C(TA)*(G)(TT)*(A|G)
Q_{2_d} = (CT|GT|AT)(CT)(A|T)*A
Q_{3_d} = ((TA)|(GG))*(GA)(AT|GC)
Q_{4_d} = (TG)*(C|A)(C)(GA)*(T)
Q_{5_d} = (TG)*(C|A)(C)GA*T</td></tr>
<tr><td>Protein</td><td>Q_{1_p} = (VYL|VAP|DD|LR)(PST)*(TT|FA|EMLA)
Q_{2_p} = (EV|NV|SS|PQ)(LSI)*(VR|SR|SV|VI)
Q_{3_p} = (EL)*(VR)(L|E)*G
Q_{4_p} = (LQ|LA)A*(V|L)
Q_{5_p} = (SL|LA)(A|L)*(EL)(S|L)*</td></tr>
<tr><td>English text</td><td>Q_{1_e} = (e|a|i)*(re|to)s
Q_{2_e} =(this|This|That|that)*(is)(c|d|e|f|g)
Q_{3_e} = (Auto|auto)*(ma|ta)
Q_{4_e} = S(e|a|i)*st
Q_{5_e} = (pa)t*(er|n)</td></tr>
</table>

Comparison of RE Matching Algorithms. Recall that the existing algorithms Agrep, Gnu Grep, and NR-grep are developed for matching REs on a set of short sequences. When a sequence contains more than one occurrences of a query, only the first occurrence of the query is returned. For the purpose of comparability, we modified the source code of them so that they can find all the occurrences as our algorithms do.

Figure 8 shows the performance comparison of Agrep, Gnu Grep, NR-grep, and our algorithms on the three data sets. Each data set contained sequences with length 50 million. The algorithm PNS-BitC achieved the best time performance. For instance, when querying Q_{3_d} on DNAs, PNS-BitC took 27ms only, compared to the 171ms, 241ms, and 219ms using Agrep, Gnu Grep, and NR-grep, respectively. The superiority was even more evident on English texts, where PNS-BitC was 74 times faster than the popular Gnu Grep tool, e.g., 3ms versus 242ms, 223ms, and 119ms for query Q_{2_e}. The difference was due to the fact that the pruning power of N-factors increased as the size of Σ increased.

Improving Existing Algorithms Using N-Factors. To evaluate the benefits of N-factors, we modified the three existing algorithms to utilize the N-factors. Figure 9 shows the benefits of N-factors. Each superscript N means that the algorithm was using N-factors. It can be seen that the modified algorithms achieved a better performance than the original algorithms. For instance, for the DNA data set, the N-factor improved the performance of the algorithms by about 3 times. Figure 9(a) shows that for the query Q_{1_d}, Agrep^N reduced the time of Agrep from 171ms to 42ms, Gnu Grep^N reduced the time of Gnu Grep from 222ms to 76ms, and NR-grep^N reduced the time of NR-grep from 456ms to 154ms. Figure 9(b) shows that Agrep and Gnu Grep were improved by more than 10 times when using N-factors for queries Q_{1_p} and Q_{2_p}.

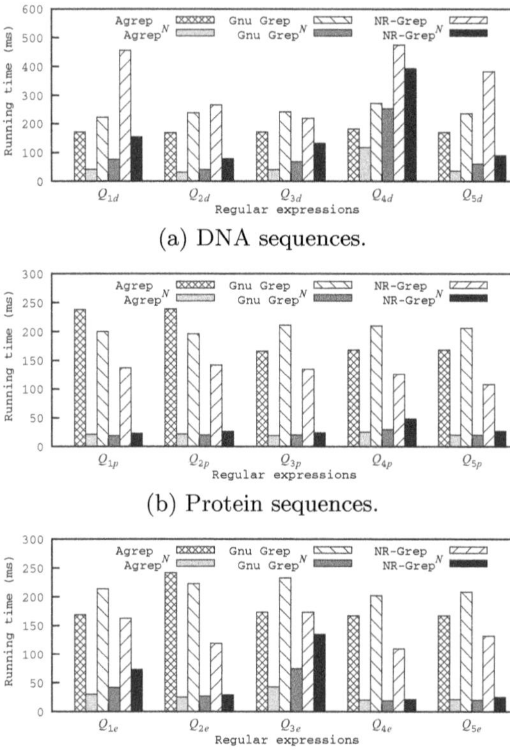

(a) DNA sequences.

(b) Protein sequences.

(c) English texts.

Figure 9: Improving existing approaches by using N-factors.

Scalability of Using N-Factors. Figure 10 shows the slowly increased running time when we increased the length of the sequence for different algorithms of using N-factors. We can see that the bit-parallel algorithms performed much better than the algorithm PNS-Merge. The algorithm PMNS-BitC was the most efficient one. For instance, when the length of the sequence was 100 million, the running time were 149ms, 168ms, and 215ms, respectively, for DNA sequences, the running time were 16ms, 17ms, and 25ms, respectively, for protein sequences, and the running time were 43ms, 44ms, and 62ms, respectively, for English texts.

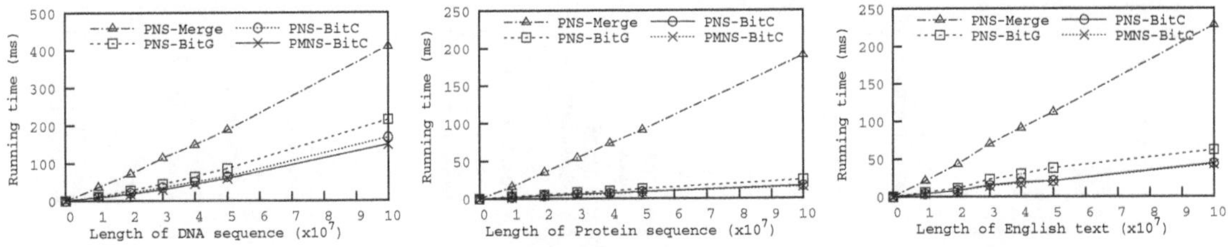

(a) DNA sequences. (b) Protein sequences. (c) English texts.

Figure 10: Scalability of approaches using N-factors.

Pruning Power of N-Factors. In Section 5.4 we analyzed the pruning power of N-factors. In order to calculate the probability value p_f in Equation 3 to see the pruning power of using N-factors for DNA sequences, we used three regular-expression workloads with query lengths 8, 12, and 15, respectively, each of which contained 100 REs, and $l_{min} = 5$. Each RE in a workload generated different numbers of suffixes and N-factors with different lengths. We ran the REs in each workload on DNA sequences with 50 million characters and calculated the average probability p_f. Figure 11 shows the pruning power of using N-factors. The dotted lines represent the computed values p_f, which ranged from 70.071% to 73.781% in the three workloads.

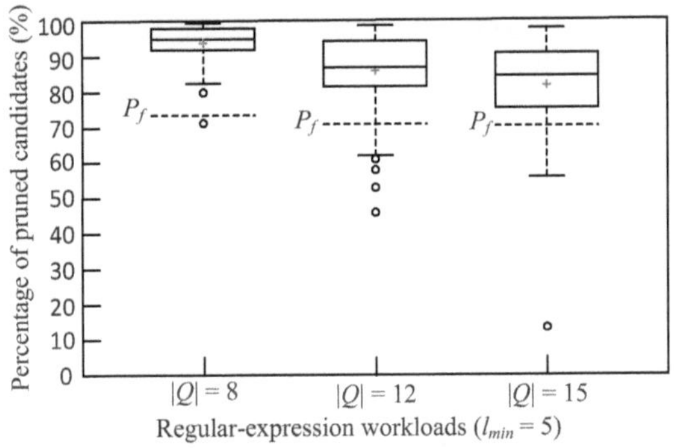

Figure 11: The ability of pruning false negatives using N-factors on DNA sequences.

Each box region in the figure represents the pruning power in the range between the first quartile (the top 25% REs) and the third quartile (the top 75% REs). The line in the box is the median value of the pruning power. The plus sign and the circles indicate the mean value of the pruning power and the outliers respectively. For the workload of $|Q| = 8$, the top 25% REs in the workload could prune 98.331% of the false negatives (i.e., substrings that do not need to be verified) and the top 75% REs could prune 92.008% of the false negatives. The other two workloads also provided significantly high pruning power. As we can see, the value p_f for each workload was lower than the experimental mean value. The reason is that our analysis is based on the assumption that data is evenly distributed, which may not be true in real data sets.

We got similar results for proteins and English texts (For space reason, we do not show the details.). The average probability value p_f for protein sequences was 72.115% when $|Q| = 19$ and $l_{min} = 4$, and the average probability value p_f for English texts was 61.870% when $|Q| = 23$ and $l_{min} = 4$.

We then tested the number of verifications when using different N-factor-based algorithms on the three data sets of size 100MB. As we can see from Figure 12, the algorithm PMNS-BitC, which considers the necessary factors, required fewer verifications in most cases. For example, in Figure 12(a), when the query was Q_{4_d}, the number of verifications using PMNS-BitC was 475,926, about the half of the number of the other algorithms. However, in most cases, the filtering advantage of PMNS-BitC was not evident. For example, in Figure 12(c), the number of verifications of algorithm PMNS-BitC was 63,861, which was similar to the number of algorithms PNS-BitC and PNS-BitG, and was even higher than that of PNS-Merge.

Construction of N-Factors. We compared the construction time of N-factors using different N-factor construction algorithms and give the experiment results in Table 5. We did not use the algorithm NaiveCore in the experiments due to its very poor performance. The time of the algorithm QuickCore was not stable, and it varied from 0.05ms to 648.08ms. The reason was that the number of sequences to be processed could grow exponentially if there exists a Kleene closure of size one. The algorithm EarlyCore was much more efficient than QuickCore. It was stable since it avoids generating N-factors due to Kleene closure. In the best situation, it only took 0.05ms to construct the N-factors, and the worst construction time was just 1.66ms.

7. RELATED WORK

Traditional techniques of finding occurrences of an RE Q of length m in a text T of length n is to convert Q to an automaton and run it from the beginning of T. An occurrence will be reported whenever a final state of the automaton is reached [1, 4, 8].

Recent techniques utilize positive factors of the RE Q to improve the traditional automata-based techniques. For instance, MutliStringRE [14] uses prefixes, Gnu Grep [4] uses necessary factors, and NR-grep [9, 11] uses reversed prefixes to identify initial matchings and then verify them using the automata (see Section 2.2 for details). All these approaches support finding initial matchings of positive factors. MutliStringRE and Gnu Grep use Shift-And algorithm [15], and NR-grep uses BNDM [10], where BNDM is a bit-parallel implementation of the reverse automaton. The above approaches cannot be directly used to find all occurrences of an RE in a long text (sequence), since they are mainly developed for identifying the sequences that contain at least one matching of the RE Q among a set of sequences. Agrep [15] is a different approach that supports approximate matching of regular expressions within a specified search region and

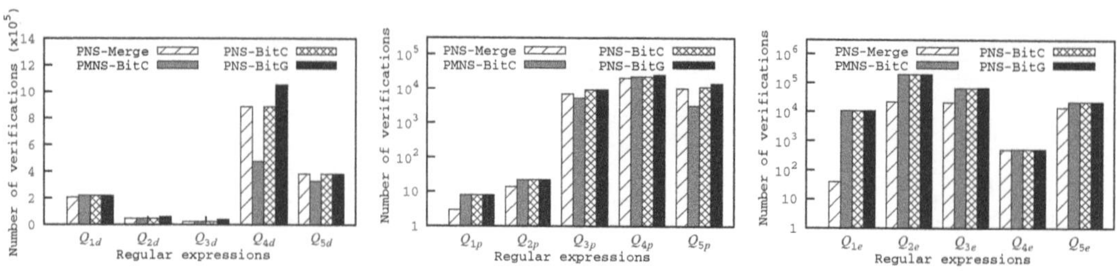

(a) DNA sequences. (b) Protein sequences. (c) English texts.

Figure 12: Comparison of verification numbers.

Table 5: Time for constructing Core N-factors.

Data set: DNA			Data set: Protein			Data set: English text		
REs	QuickCore	EarlyCore	REs	QuickCore	EarlyCore	REs	QuickCore	EarlyCore
Q_{1_d}	18.74ms	0.15ms	Q_{1_p}	2.02ms	1.99ms	Q_{1_e}	528.99ms	0.63ms
Q_{2_d}	648.08ms	0.09ms	Q_{2_p}	0.87ms	0.86ms	Q_{2_e}	1.71ms	1.66ms
Q_{3_d}	0.17ms	0.11ms	Q_{3_p}	13.37ms	0.16ms	Q_{3_e}	0.45ms	0.43ms
Q_{4_d}	0.05ms	0.05ms	Q_{4_p}	0.17ms	0.12ms	Q_{4_e}	215.80ms	0.37ms
Q_{5_d}	14.89ms	0.19ms	Q_{5_p}	429.48ms	1.01ms	Q_{5_e}	0.65ms	0.44ms

returns matching occurrences exactly. Compared to these existing approaches, our main contribution is to use negative factors to improve the matching performance.

8. CONCLUSION

In this paper, we proposed a novel technique called N-factor and developed algorithms to improve the performance of matching a regular expression to a sequence. We gave a full specification of this technique, and conducted experiments to compare the performance between our algorithms and existing algorithms,such as Agrep, Gnu grep, and NR-grep. The experimental results demonstrated the superiority of our algorithms. We also extended Agrep, Gnu grep, and NR-grep with the N-factor technique, and showed great performance improvement.

9. ACKNOWLEDGMENTS

The work is partially supported by the National Basic Research Program of China (973 Program) (No. 2012CB316201), the National NSF of China (Nos. 60973018, 61272178), the Joint Research Fund for Overseas Natural Science of China (No. 61129002), the Doctoral Fund of Ministry of Education of China (No. 20110042110028), the National Natural Science of China Key Program (No. 60933001), the National Natural Science Foundation for Distinguished Young Scholars (No. 61025007), and the Fundamental Research Funds for the Central Universities (No. N110804002).

10. REFERENCES

[1] R. A. Baeza-Yates and G. H. Gonnet. Fast text searching for regular expressions or automaton searching on tries. *J. ACM*, 43(6):915 – 936, 1996.

[2] M. Šimánek. The factor automaton. *Kybernetika*, 38(1):105 – 111, 2002.

[3] M. Crochemore, A. Czumaj, L. Gasieniec, S. Jarominek, T. Lecroq, W. Plandowski, and W. Rytter. Speeding up two strings matching algorithms. *Algorithmica*, 12(4/5):247 – 267, 1994.

[4] GNUgrep. ftp://reality.sgiweb.org/freeware/relnotes/fw-5.3/fw_gnugrep/gnugrep.html.

[5] J. E. Hopcroft and J. D. Ullman. *Introduction to Automata Theory, Languages, and Computation.* Addison-Wesley Publishing Company, Reading, Massachusetts, 1979.

[6] L. F. Kolakowski, J. Leunissen, and J. E. Smith. Prosearch: Fast searching of protein sequences with regular expression patterns related to protein structure and function. *Biotechniques*, 13:919 – 921, 1992.

[7] T. W. Lam, W. K. Sung, S. L. Tam, C. K. Wong, and S. M. Yiu. Compressed indexing and local alignment of DNA. *Bioinformatics*, 24(6):791–797, 2008.

[8] M. Mohri. String matching with automata. *Nordic Journal of Computing*, 4(2):217 – 231, 1997.

[9] C. Navarro. NR-grep: a fast and flexible pattern matching tool. *Software Practice and Experience (SPE)*, 31:1265 – 1312, 2001.

[10] C. Navarro and M. Raffinot. Fast and flexible string matching by combining bit-parallelism and suffix automata. *ACM Journal of Experimental Algorithmics (JEA)*, 5:4, 2000.

[11] C. Navarro and M. Raffinot. Compact DFA representation for fast regular expression search. In *Proceedings of WAE'01, Lecture Notes in Computer Science 2141*, pages 1 – 12, 2001.

[12] C. Navarro and M. Raffinot. New techniques for regular expression searching. *Algorithmica*, 41(2):89 – 116, 2004.

[13] R. Staden. Screening protein and nucleic acid sequences against libraries of patterns. *J. DNA Sequencing Mapping*, 1:369 – 374, 1991.

[14] B. W. Watson. A new regula grammar pattern matching algorithm. In *Proceedings of the 4th Annual European Sysmposium, Lecture Notes in Computer Science 1136*, pages 364 – 377. Springer-Verlag, 1996.

[15] S. Wu and U. Manber. Fast text searching allowing errors. *Comm. of the ACM*, 35(10):83 – 91, 1992.

String Similarity Measures and Joins with Synonyms

Jiaheng Lu †, Chunbin Lin †, Wei Wang ‡, Chen Li #, Haiyong Wang †
†School of Information and DEKE, MOE, Renmin University of China; Beijing, China
‡University of New South Wales,Australia, #University of California, Irvine, CA
†{jiahenglu,chunbinlin,why}@ruc.edu.cn, ‡weiw@cse.unsw.edu.au, #chenli@ics.uci.edu

ABSTRACT

A string similarity measure quantifies the similarity between two text strings for approximate string matching or comparison. For example, the strings "Sam" and "Samuel" can be considered similar. Most existing work that computes the similarity of two strings only considers syntactic similarities, e.g., number of common words or q-grams. While these are indeed indicators of similarity, there are many important cases where syntactically different strings can represent the same real-world object. For example, "Bill" is a short form of "William". Given a collection of predefined *synonyms*, the purpose of the paper is to explore such existing knowledge to evaluate string similarity measures more effectively and efficiently, thereby boosting the quality of string matching.

In particular, we first present an expansion-based framework to measure string similarities efficiently while considering synonyms. Because using synonyms in similarity measures is, while expressive, computationally expensive (NP-hard), we propose an efficient algorithm, called *selective-expansion*, which guarantees the optimality in many real scenarios. We then study a novel indexing structure called SI-tree, which combines both signature and length filtering strategies, for efficient string similarity joins with synonyms. We develop an estimator to approximate the size of candidates to enable an online selection of signature filters to further improve the efficiency. This estimator provides strong low-error, high-confidence guarantees while requiring only logarithmic space and time costs, thus making our method attractive both in theory and in practice. Finally, the results from an empirical study of the algorithms verify the effectiveness and efficiency of our approach.

Categories and Subject Descriptors

H.2.4 [**Database Management**]: Systems—*Textual Databases*; H.3.3 [**Information Storage and Retrieval**]: Information Search and Retrieval—*Search Process*

Keywords

Similarity Search, Similarity Join, Filter Estimation

1. INTRODUCTION

Approximate string matching is used heavily in areas such as data integration [2, 4], data deduplication [9], and data mining [10]. Most existing work that computes the similarity of two strings only considers syntactic similarities, e.g., number of common words or q-grams. Although syntactic similarities are indeed indicative, there are many important cases where syntactically different strings can represent the same real-world object. For example, "Bill" is a short form of "William", "Big Apple" is a synonym of "New York", and "Database Management Systems" can be abbreviated as "DBMS". Such equivalence information can help us identify semantically similar strings that may have been missed by syntactical similarity-based approaches.

In this paper, we study two problems related to approximate string matching with synonyms[1]. Firstly, how to define an effective similarity measure between two strings based on the synonyms? The traditional similarity functions cannot be easily extended to handle the synonyms in similarity matching. Secondly, how to efficiently perform similarity join based on newly defined similarity functions? That is, given two collections of strings, how to efficiently find similar string pairs from the collections? The two problems are closely related, because the similarity measures defined in the first problem will naturally provide a join predicate to the second.

We give several applications about approximate string measures and joins with synonyms to shed light on the importance of these two problems. In a gene/protein databases, one of the major obstacles that hinders the effective use is term variation [27], including Roman-Arabic (e.g. "Synapsin 3" and "Synapsin III"), acronym variation (e.g. "IL-2" and "interleukin-2"), and term abbreviation (e.g. "Ah receptor" and "Ah dioxin receptor"). A new similarity measure that can handle term variation may help users discover more genes/proteins of interest. New measures are also applicable in information extraction systems to aid mapping from text strings to canonical entries by similarity matching. More applications can be found in areas such as term classification and term clustering, which can be used for advanced information retrieval/extraction applications. String approximate join is typically useful in data integration and data cleaning. For example, in two representative data cleaning domains, namely addresses and academic publications, there often exist rich sources of synonyms, which can be leveraged to improve the effectiveness of systems significantly.

For the first problem of similarity measures, there is a wealth of research on string-similarity functions on the syntactical level, such as Levenshtein distance [29], Hamming distance [17], Episode

[1] For brevity, we use "*synonym*" to describe any kind of equivalent pairs which may include *synonym*, *acronym*, *abbreviation*, *variation* and other equivalent expressions.

ID	Name
q_1	Intl WH Conf 2012
q_2	VLDB
...	...

(a) Table Q

ID	Name
t_1	Very Large Scale Integeration
t_2	Intl Wireless Health Conference 2012 UK
...	...

(b) Table T

ID	Synonym pairs	ID	Synonym pairs
r_1	WH → Wireless Health	r_2	Conference → Conf
r_3	Intl → International	r_4	UK → United Kingdom
r_5	Wireless Health → WH	r_6	Conf → Conference
...	...	...	...

(c) Transformation synonym pairs

Figure 1: An example to illustrate similarity matching with synonyms

distance [11], Cosine metric [25], Jaccard Coefficient [9, 20], and Dice similarity [6]. Unfortunately, none of them can be easily extended to leverage synonyms to improve the quality of similarity measurement. One exception is the JaccT technique proposed by Arasu et al. [2], which generates all possible strings by applying synonym rewriting to both strings, and returns the maximum similarity among the transformed pairs of strings, as illustrated by the following example.

EXAMPLE 1. *Figure 1 shows an example of two tables Q and T and a set of synonyms. Consider two strings q_1 and t_2. Their token-based Jaccard similarity is only $\frac{2}{8}$. Now consider applying synonym pairs on them. Obviously, synonyms r_1, r_3 and r_6 can be applied to q_1, and r_2, r_3, r_4 and r_5 can be applied to t_2. We use $\mathcal{A}_{\mathcal{R}}(s)$ to denote the string generated by applying a set of synonym pairs $\mathcal{R}$ to the source string s. For example, $\mathcal{A}_{\{r_1,r_3\}}(q_1)$ is* "`International Wireless Health Conf 2012`".

[2] considers all the possible strings resulting from applying a subset of applicable synonyms on them, and then return the maximum Jaccard similarity. In the above example, it needs to consider $2^3 \cdot 2^4 = 128$ possible string pairs. The maximum Jaccard value is between $\mathcal{A}_{\{r_1,r_3,r_6\}}(q_1)$ and $\mathcal{A}_{\{r_3\}}(t_2)$, which is $\frac{5}{6}$.

The main limitation in the above approach is that its string similarity definition has to generate all possible strings and compare their similarity for each pair in the cross product. In general, given two strings s and t, assuming there are n_1 (resp. n_2) synonym pairs applied on s (resp. t), then the above approach needs to compute the similarities for $2^{n_1+n_2}$ pairs. Such a brute-force approach takes time exponential in the number of applicable synonym pairs. A special case of the problem for single-token synonyms is identified in [2] where the problem can be reduced to a maximum bipartite graph matching-based problem. Unfortunately, in practice, many synonyms contain multiple tokens, and even in the special case, it still has a worst-case complexity that is quadratic in both the number of string tokens and the number of applicable synonyms. Since such similarity measure has to be called for every candidate pairs when employed in similarity joins, it introduces substantial overhead.

In this paper we propose a novel *expansion-based* framework to measure the similarity of strings. Intuitively, given a string s, we first obtain its token set S, and then grow the token set by applying the applicable synonyms of s. When a synonym pair *lhs* → *rhs* is applied, we merge all the tokens in *rhs* to the token set, i.e., $S = S \cup rhs$. The similarity between two strings are the similarity between their expanded token sets. We have two key ideas here: (i) We can avoid the exponential computational complexity by expanding strings using *all* the applicable synonym pairs; (ii) it costs less to perform expanding operation than transforming operation, as illustrated below.

EXAMPLE 2. *(Continue the previous example.) We apply all the applicable synonym pairs to q_1 and t_2 to expand their token sets, and then evaluate the Jaccard similarity between the two expanded token sets. For instance, the fully expanded set of t_2 by applying synonym pairs r_2, r_3, r_4, and r_5 is* {`International, Intl, WH, Conf, 2012, Wireless, Health, Conference, United, Kingdom, UK`}. *The Jaccard similarity between two fully expanded token sets is $\frac{8}{11}$, which is also greater than the original similarity $\frac{2}{8}$ without synonyms.* ■

We note that the full expansion-based similarity illustrated in the above example is efficient to compute, and is also highly competitive in terms of effectiveness in modeling the semantic similarity between strings. Nonetheless, using all the synonym pairs to perform a full expansion may hurt the final similarities. Consider Example 2 again, where the use of rule r_4 on t_2 is detrimental to the similarity between q_1 and t_2, as none of the expanded tokens appears in q_1 or its expanded token set. Therefore, we propose a *selective expansion* measure, which selects only "good" synonym pairs to expand both strings (Section 3), and accordingly the similarity is defined as the maximum similarity between two appropriately expanded token sets of two strings. Unfortunately, *selective expansion* is proved to be *NP-hard* by a reduction from the 3SAT problem. To provide an efficient solution, we propose a greedy algorithm, called *SE* algorithm, which is *optimal* if the *rhs* tokens of the useful synonyms satisfy the *distinct* property (the precise definition will be described in Section 3.2). We empirically show that the condition is likely to be true in practice — the percentage of cases that such optimality hold in our experiments with three real-world data sets ranges between 70.0% and 89.8%. Figure 2 summarizes the results of the two new similarity algorithms, contrasted with results of existing methods [2].

Given the newly proposed similarity measures, it is imperative to study an efficient similarity join algorithm. In this paper, we first show a signature-based join algorithm, called *SN-Join*, by following the *filter-and-verification* framework (Section 4). It generates a set of tokens as signatures for each string using synonyms, finds candidate pairs that overlaps in the signatures, and finally verifies against the threshold using the above proposed similarity measure. In addition, we further propose the *SI-Join*, which speeds up the performance by using a native index, *SI-tree*, to reduce the candidate size with integrated signature and length filtering. Our join algorithms are also general enough to work with signatures generated by either prefix filtering or locality sensitive hashing (LSH).

The methods for selecting signatures of strings may significantly affect the performance of algorithms [20, 24]. Therefore, we propose, for the first time (to our best knowledge), an online algorithm to dynamically estimate the filtering power of a signature filter. In particular, we generate multiple signature filters using different strategies offline. Then given two tables to join online, we quickly estimate the performance of different filters and select the best one to perform the actual filtering. Our technical contribution here is to propose a novel, hash-based synopsis data structure, termed "*Two Dimensional Hash Sketch (2DHS)*", by extending the Flajolet-Martin sketch [13] on two join tables. We present novel estimation algorithms to provide high-confidence estimates to compare the filtering power of two filters. Our method carries both theoretical and practical significances. In theory, we can prove that, with any given high probability 1-δ, 2DHS returns correct estimates on upper and lower bounds, and its space and time complexities are logarithmic in the cardinality of input size. In practice, the experiments show that our estimation technique accurately predicts the quality of different filters in all three data sets and its running time

Similarity Algorithm	Computational Complexity	Effectiveness	Comment
Jacc	*O(L)*	*Low*	*Does not consider synonym pairs.*
JaccT [2]	$O(2^n(L+kn))$	*High*	*If only single token synonym pairs are allowed (implying k = 1), an optimal algorithm based on maximum bipartite matching can be used with a complexity of* $O(L^2 + Ln^2)$.
Full Expansion (ours)	*O(L+kn)*	*High*	*Most efficient and may have good quality.*
SE Algorithm (ours)	$O(L+kn^2)$	*High*	*SE is efficient and has good quality, it is optimal under the conditions of Theorem 2, and the complexity can be reduced to O(L+nlogn+kn).*

Figure 2: Comparison of String Similarity Algorithms with synonyms (Assume both strings have a length of L; The maximum number of applicable synonyms is n; k is the maximum size of the right hand side of a rule.)

is negligible compared to that of the actual filtering phase (accounting for only 1% of the total join time).

Finally, we perform a comprehensive set of experiments on three data sets to demonstrate the superior efficiency and effectiveness of our algorithms (Section 5). The results show that our algorithms are up to two orders of magnitude as efficient as the existing methods while offering comparable or better effectiveness.

2. RELATED WORK

String similarity measures: There is a rich set of string similarity measures including character n-gram similarity [17], Levenshtein Distance [15], Jaro-Winkler measure [31], Jaccard similarity [9], tf-idf based cosine similarity [25], and Hidden Markov Model-based measure [22]. A comparison of many string similarity functions is performed in [11]. These metrics can only measure syntactic similarity (or distance) between two strings, but cannot capture semantic similarities such as synonyms, acronyms, and abbreviations.

Machine learning-based methods [7, 27] have been proposed to improve the quality of traditional syntactic similarity-based approaches. In particular, learnable string similarity [7] presents trainable measures to improve the effectiveness of duplicate detection, and [27] uses logistic regression to learn a string similarity measure from an existing gene/protein name dictionary.

String similarity join: Majority of the state-of-the-art approaches [33, 24, 21, 29] for performing string similarity joins follow the *filtering-and-verification* framework. The basic idea is to first employ an efficient filter to prune string pairs that cannot be similar, and then verify the remaining string pairs by computing their real similarity. *Prefix filtering* [9] is a popular filtering scheme, which transforms each string to a set of tokens; then the tokens of each string are sorted based on a *global ordering*, and a prefix set for each string is selected based on a given similarity threshold to be signatures. Other efficient approaches are based on enumeration [4, 30, 21] or tries [28, 32].

LSH-based schemes are widely used to process the queries approximately, meaning that certain correct answers may be missed. For Jaccard similarity, one can generate l super-signatures, each of which is a concatenation of k minhashes [8] of the set s under a minwise independent permutation; only string pairs sharing one common super-signature are deemed as candidates. k and l are two parameters that can be tuned to achieve trade-off between efficiency and accuracy [33].

Estimation of set size: Our work is also related to the estimation of distinct pairs in set-union. There are many solutions proposed for the estimation of the cardinality of distinct elements. For example, in their influential paper, Flajolet and Martin [13] proposed a randomized estimator for distinct-element counting that relies on a hash-based synopsis; to this date, the Flajolet-Martin (FM) technique remains one of the most effective approaches for this estimation problem. FM sketch and its variation (e.g., [1, 14]) focus on one dimensional data, and we extend it to two-dimensional cases in this work.

Finally, the estimation of the result size of a string similarity join has been studied recently, e.g., in [18, 19], by using random sampling and LSH scheme. Note that these techniques cannot be directly applied here, since given a specific filter, our goal is to estimate the cardinality of candidates, which is often much greater than that of final results.

3. STRING SIMILARITY MEASURES

As described in Section 1, an expansion-based framework can efficiently measure the similarity of strings with synonyms to avoid the exponential computational complexity. In this section, we describe two expansion-based measures in detail. In particular, Section 3.1 describes an efficient full-expansion measure, and Section 3.2 shows a selective expansion to achieve better effectiveness. Finally, Section 3.3 analyzes the optimality of the methods.

3.1 Full Expansion

We first introduce notations. Given two strings s_1 and s_2, let S_1 and S_2 denote the sets generated from s_1 and s_2 respectively by tokenization (e.g., splitting strings based on delimiters such as white spaces). Let r denote a rule, which has the form: $lhs(r) \to rhs(r)$, where $lhs(r)$ and $rhs(r)$ are the left and right hand sides of r, respectively. Slightly abusing the notations, $lhs(r)$ and $rhs(r)$ can also refer to the *set* generated from the respective strings. Let $\mathbb{R}$ denote a collection of synonym rules, i.e., $\mathbb{R} = \{r\colon lhs(r) \to rhs(r)\}$. Given a string s, we say a rule $r \in \mathbb{R}$ is an *applicable rule* of s if $lhs(r)$ is a *substring* of s. We use $rhs(r)$ to expand the set S, that is, $S' = S \cup rhs(r)$. Let $sim(s_1, s_2, \mathbb{R})$ denote the similarity between s_1 and s_2 based on $\mathbb{R}$. Let $\mathcal{R}(s_1)$ and $\mathcal{R}(s_2)$ denote the *applicable rule set* of s_1 and s_2, respectively. Under the expansion-based framework, $sim(s_1, s_2, \mathbb{R}) = f(S_1', S_2')$, where S_1' and S_2' are expanded from S_1 and S_2 using some synonym rules in $\mathcal{R}(s_1)$ and $\mathcal{R}(s_2)$, and f is a set-similarity function such as Jaccard, Cosine, etc.

Based on how *applicable synonyms* are selected to expand S, there are different kinds of schemes. A simple one is the *full expansion*, which expands S using *all* their applicable synonyms. That is, the expanded set $S' = S \bigcup_{r \in \mathcal{R}(s)} rhs(r)$.

The full expansion scheme is efficient to compute. Let L be the maximum length of strings s_1 and s_2. The time cost of doing substring matching to identify the applicable synonym pairs is $O(L)$ using a suffix-trie-based method [12]. Then the complexity of the set expansion is $O(L + kn)$, where n is the maximum number of applicable synonym pairs for s_1 and s_2, and k is the maximum size of the right-hand side of a rule. As we will demonstrate in our experimental section, the full expansion provides a highly competitive performance with other optimized scheme to capture semantics of strings using synonyms.

3.2 Selective Expansion

We observe that, as mentioned in Section 1, the full expansion cannot guarantee that each applied rule is useful for similarity measure between two strings. Recall Example 2 and Figure 1. The use of rule r_4 on t_2 is detrimental to the similarity between q_1 and t_2, as "`United Kingdom`" does not appear in q_1. To address this issue, we propose an optimized scheme, called *selective expansion*, whose goal is to maximize the similarity value of two expanded sets by a judicious selection of applicable synonyms to apply. Given a collection of synonym rules $\mathbb{R}$ and two strings s_1 and s_2, the selective expansion scheme maximizes $f(S_1^{'}, S_2^{'})$. Suppose, without loss of generality, we use Jaccard Coefficient to measure the similarity between $S_1^{'}$ and $S_2^{'}$, which can be extended to other functions. The *Selective-Jaccard* similarity of s_1 and s_2 based on $\mathbb{R}$ (denoted by $SJ(s_1, s_2, \mathbb{R})$) is defined as follows:

$$SJ(s_1, s_2, \mathbb{R}) = \max_{\mathcal{R}(s_1)\subseteq\mathbb{R}, \mathcal{R}(s_2)\subseteq\mathbb{R}} \{Jaccard(S_1^{'}, S_2^{'})\}.$$

where $S_1^{'}$ and $S_2^{'}$ are the sets expanded from s_1 and s_2 using $\mathcal{R}(s_1)$ and $\mathcal{R}(s_2)$, respectively.

Unfortunately, we can prove that it is NP-hard to compute the *Selective-Jaccard* similarity with respect to the number of applicable synonym rules, by a reduction from the well-known 3SAT problem [16]. Due to space limitation, we leave the detailed proof in the full version. Since *Selective-Jaccard* is NP-hard, we design an efficient greedy algorithm that guarantees the optimality under certain conditions, which has been shown to be met in most cases in practice. Before presenting the algorithm, we will first define the notion *rule gain*, which can be used to estimate the fitness of a rule to strings.

Algorithm 1: Rule Gain

```
   Input  : r, s1, s2, R={ri: lhs(ri) → rhs(ri)}
   Output : the rule gain of r
1  U ← rhs(r) − S1; // r is applicable to s1, and S1 is the token set of s1
2  if (U = φ) then
3  └ return 0;
   //Let R' denote all applicable rules of S2
4  S2' ← S2 ∪_{ri∈R'} rhs(ri) //full-expanding S2
5  G ← (rhs(r) ∩ S2') − S1;
6  return |G|/|U|;
```

Given two strings s_1 and s_2, a collection of synonyms $\mathbb{R}$, and a rule $r\in\mathbb{R}$, we assume that r is an applicable rule for s_1. We denote the rule gain of r by $RG(r, s_1, s_2, \mathbb{R})$. When s_1, s_2, and $\mathbb{R}$ are clear from the context, we shall simply speak of $RG(r)$. Informally, the rule gain is defined by the number of useful elements introduced by r divided by the number of new elements in r. In particular, we say that a token $t \in rhs(r)$ in r is useful if t belongs to the full expansion set of s_2 and $t \notin s_1$. The reason we use the full expansion set of s_2 rather than the original set is that s_2 can be expanded using new rules, but all possible new tokens must be contained in the full expansion set. We now go through Algorithm 1. In line 1, we find the new elements U introduced by r. If $U = \varnothing$, then the rule gain is zero (lines 2 $\sim$ 3). line 4 fully expands s_2 and line 5 computes the useful elements G. Finally, the rule gain $RG(r) = \frac{|G|}{|U|}$ is returned (line 6).

We develop a "*selective expand*" algorithm based on rule gains, which is formally described in Algorithm 2. Before doing any expansion, we first compute a candidate set of rules (line 1), which only consists of applicable rules with relatively higher rule-gain values. In particular, in Procedure *findCandidateRuleSets*, we first let C_i contain all applicable rules whose rule gain is greater than zero (line 4), and then we iteratively remove the useless rules whose rule gain is too small from C_i (in lines 5$\sim$11). In lines 6$\sim$7, we use the elements in C_i to expand S_i to acquire S_i'. Then, in lines 9$\sim$11, any rule whose rule gain is less than $\frac{\theta}{1+\theta}$ is removed from C_i, where θ is defined as Jaccard similarity of the current expanded sets S_1' and S_2' (line 8), as its similarity is lower than the "average" similarity and its usage would be detrimental to the final similarity. Subsequently, in line 2, we iteratively expand s_1 and s_2 using the most gain-effective rule from the candidate sets. Note that after a new rule is used to expand the set, the rule gains of the remaining rules need to be recomputed in line 16, since the new elements U (in Algorithm 1) of the remaining rules will change.

Performance Analysis: The time complexity of *SE* algorithm is $O(L + kn^2)$, where L is the maximum length of s_1 and s_2, n is the total number of applicable synonyms for s_1 and s_2, and k is the maximum size of the right-hand side of a rule. More precisely, we use the suffix-trie to find applicable rule sets, and its complexity is $O(L)$. In Procedure *findCandidateRuleSet*, the complexity to perform full expansion (lines 6 $\sim$ 7) is $O(kn)$, and the iteration time is no more than n, thus the complexity is $O(L + kn^2)$.

Algorithm 2: SE Algorithm

```
    Input  : s1, s2, R={r: lhs(r) → rhs(r)}.
    Output : Sim(s1, s2, R).
1   C1, C2 ← findCandidateRuleSet(s1, s2, R);
2   θ ← expand(s1, s2, C1, C2);
3   return max(Jaccard(s1, s2), θ);

    Procedure findCandidateRuleSet(s1, s2, R)
4   Ci ← {r: r ∈ R ∧ lhs(r) is a substring of si(i=1 or 2) ∧ RG(r) > 0};
5   repeat
6   │ S1' ← S1 ∪_{r∈C1} rhs(r);
7   │ S2' ← S2 ∪_{r∈C2} rhs(r);
8   │ θ ← Jaccard(S1', S2')
9   │ for (r ∈ C1 ∪ C2 ) do
10  │   │ if (RG(r) < θ/(1+θ)) then
11  │   │ └ Ci ← Ci − r; //r ∈ Ci, i=1 or 2
    until (no rule can be removed in line 19);
12  return C1, C2

    Procedure expand(s1, s2, C1, C2,)
    //Let S1' and S2' denote the expanded sets of S1 and S2
13  S1' ← S1;
14  S2' ← S2;
15  while (C1 ∪ C2 ≠ φ) do
16  │ Find the current most gain-effective rule r ∈ Ci (i = 1 or 2);
17  │ if (RG(r) > 0) then
18  │ └ Si' ← Si' ∪ rhs(r);
19  └ Ci ← Ci - r;
20  return Jaccard(S1', S2');
```

3.3 Theoretical Analysis

In this subsection, we carve out one case and show that SE returns the optimal value, and analyze the reduced time complexity in this optimal case.

THEOREM 1. *Given two strings s_1 and s_2 and their applicable rule sets $\mathcal{R}(s_1)$ and $\mathcal{R}(s_2)$, we call a rule $r \in \mathcal{R}(s_i)$ (i = 1 or 2) useful if $RG(r) > 0$. We can guarantee that SE is optimal if the rhs tokens of all useful rules are distinct.*

PROOF. Let $\mathcal{R}^*$ denote the rule set used by the optimal algorithm. Let $\mathcal{R}$ denote the set $C_1 \cup C_2$ returned in line 1 of Algorithm 2. Then we will prove that $\mathcal{R}^* = \mathcal{R}$ as follows. Given an applicable rule r_i in $\mathcal{R}$, let G_i denote the useful elements, U_i denote the new elements, and let $Z_i = U_i - G_i$. Let θ^* and θ denote the full expansion similarity using $\mathcal{R}^*$ and $\mathcal{R}$ respectively. Note that all the rules in both $\mathcal{R}$ and $\mathcal{R}^*$ are useful. When all the rhs tokens are distinct, $\theta = \frac{|S_1 \cap S_2 + \sum G_i|}{|S_1 \cup S_2 + \sum Z_i|}$. For a rule $r^* \in \mathcal{R}^*$, we have $\frac{G^*}{Z^*} > \theta^* \geq \theta$, that is, $\frac{G^*}{U^*} > \frac{\theta}{1+\theta}$, i.e., $RG(r^*) > \frac{\theta}{1+\theta}$, which means that r^* will not be removed in Procedure *findCandidateRuleSet* (line 11) and $r^* \in \mathcal{R}$. Thus, $\mathcal{R}^* \subseteq \mathcal{R}$.

We then prove $\mathcal{R} \subseteq \mathcal{R}^*$ by contradiction. Assume that there exists a rule $r \in R$ but $r \notin R^*$, $\theta = \frac{|S_1 \cap S_2 + \sum G_i^* + G_i|}{|S_1 \cup S_2 + \sum Z_i^* + Z_i|}$. According to Algorithm 2, $\frac{G_i}{Z_i} > \theta$. Thus, $\theta > \frac{|S_1 \cap S_2 + \sum G_i^*|}{|S_1 \cup S_2 + \sum Z_i^*|} = \theta^*$, which contradicts to the optimal property and such r does not exist. Thus, $\mathcal{R} \subseteq \mathcal{R}^*$.

Finally, we show that all the candidate rules in $C_1 \cup C_2$ will be used in Procedure *expand* (line 2). If all the rhs tokens are distinct, the rule gain value will not change. The rule gain value of each rule is greater than zero (line 17), so all the rules will be used by SE in the expanding phase, which concludes the proof. □

Note that the condition in Theorem 1 does not require all the rhs tokens to be distinct. It only requires those from useful synonyms of s_1 and s_2 to be distinct, which are typically a very small subset. In addition, under the condition, the time complexity can be reduced to $O(L + n \log n + nk)$. The reason is that, the complexity to perform full expansion (lines 6∼7) is reduced to $O(1)$. Since the tokens are distinct, and that of expanding (lines 15∼19) is $O(n \log n)$, since the rule gain of each rule does not change, which can be implemented by a maximal heap. Finally, the Jaccard computation in line 20 needs $O(L + kn)$ time in the worst case. Therefore, the complexity of *SE* algorithm is $O(L+n \log n+nk)$.

4. STRING SIMILARITY JOINS

Given two collections of strings S and T, a collection of synonyms $\mathbb{R}$, and a similarity threshold θ, a *string similarity join* finds all string pairs $(s, t) \in S \times T$, such that $sim(s, t, \mathbb{R}) \geq \theta$, where *sim* is one of the similarity functions in Section 3.

One join algorithm is a signature-based nested-loop approach, called SN-Join, following the filtering-and-verification framework. That is, in the filtering step, SN-Join generates candidate string pairs by identifying all pairs (s, t) such that the signatures of s and t overlap. In the verification step, SN-Join checks if $sim(s, t, \mathbb{R}) \geq \theta$ for each candidate and outputs those that satisfy the similarity predicate.

To generate the signatures, one way is to extend the prefix-filter scheme. Given a string s, the signatures of s are a subset of tokens in s containing the $\lceil(1-\theta)|s|\rceil$ smallest elements of s according to a predefined global ordering. Therefore, we generate signatures for a string s as follows. Let $\mathcal{R} \subseteq \mathbb{R}$ be the set of n application synonym pairs for s. For each subset $\mathcal{R}_i$ of $\mathcal{R}$, we generate an expanded set S_i. For each S_i, we obtain one signature set (denoted by $sig(S_i)$). Note that the number of subset S_i is 2^n. The exponential number is due to the fact that we try to enumerate all possibilities of expanded sets for s with n synonym pairs. Finally, we generate a signature set for s by including all signatures of S_i: $Sig(s, \mathcal{R}) = \bigcup_{i=1}^{2^n} Sig(S_i)$. Note that this generation of signatures can be performed offline.

We observe that SN-join needs to check the signature overlap for each string pair $(s, t) \in S \times T$ to find the candidates, which can be time-consuming. In this section, we propose an optimized native indexes and the corresponding join algorithm (Section 4.1). We then study the impact of signature filters on the performance of algorithms in depth by proposing a novel hash-based synopsis data

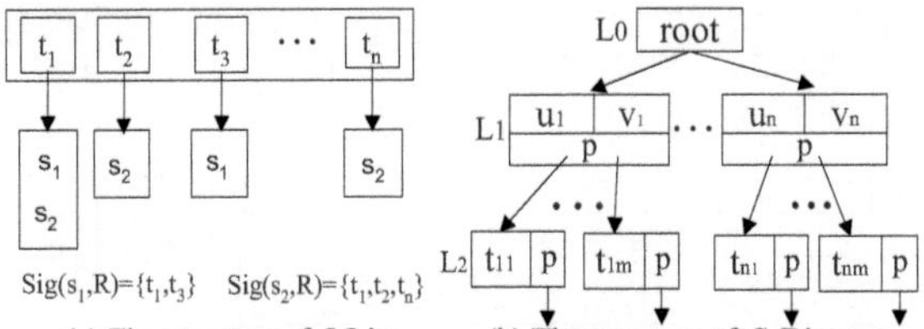

(a) The structure of I-List (b) The structure of S-Directory

Figure 3: The structure of I-List and S-Directory.

structure to effectively select signatures (Section 4.2). Finally we extend our discussion on LSH scheme (Section 4.3).

4.1 SI-Join Algorithm

To optimize the above SN-Join method, we show a native index by (i) avoiding signature-overlap checking; and (ii) reducing the number of candidates for the final verification, as follows.

Avoiding signature-overlapping check. We design a signature inverted list, called **I-List** (see Figure 3(a)). Each token t_i is associated with an inverted list including all string IDs whose signatures contain the token t_i. Thus, given a signature t_i, we can directly obtain all relevant string IDs without any signature-overlapping check.

Reducing the number of candidates. We extend the idea of *length filter* [6, 26] to reduce the number of candidates. Intuitively, given two strings s_1 and s_2 and a threshold value θ, if the size of the full expansion set of s_1 is much less than the size of $|s_2|$, then without checking the signatures of s_1 and s_2, one can claim that $sim(s_1, s_2, R)$ must be smaller than θ. Based on the observation, we propose a data structure, called **S-Directory**, to organize the strings by their lengths.

The S-Directory (see Figure 3(b)) is a tree structure with three levels, and nodes in different levels could be categorized into different kinds.

- *root-entry.* A node in level L_0 is a root entry, which has multiple pointers to the nodes in level L_1.
- *fence-entry.* A node in level L_1 is called *fence entry*, which contains three fields $\langle u, v, P\rangle$, where u and v are integers, and P is a set of of pointers to the nodes in L_2. In particular, u denotes the number of tokens of a string and v is the maximal number of tokens in the full expanded sets of strings whose length is u.
- *leaf-entry.* A node in level L_2 is called *leaf entry*, which contains two fields $\langle t, P\rangle$, where t is an integer to denote the number of the tokens in the full expanded set of a string whose length is u, and P is a pointer to an inverted list. As leaf entries are organized in the ascending order of t, $v_i = t_{im}$ (See Figure 3(b)).

We argue that S-Directory can easily fit in the main memory, as the size of S-Directory is only $O((v_{max} - u_{min})^2)$, which is quadratic to the difference between the maximal size of expanded sets and the shortest length of records. For example, in our implementation, to perform a self-join for a table with one million strings on USPS dataset, the size of S-Directory is only about 2.15KB.

To maximize the pruning power, we combine *I-List* and *S-Directory* together. That is, for each *leaf-entry*=$\langle t, P\rangle$, P points to a set of signatures (from the string whose size of the full expansion set is t) associated with multiple I-Lists. Thus, we have a combined index, called **SI-tree**, i.e., each leaf entry in S-Directory is associated with an I-List. Based on the SI-tree, we design a join algorithm (called **SI-Join**), which follows the filtering-and-verification framework and the verification phase is the same as that of SN-Join.

SI-Join (see Algorithm 3) has three steps in the filtering phase. In the first step (lines 2 ∼ 3), consider two fence-entries F_s and

ID	Strings	Signatures	L	F
q_1	2013 ACM Intl Conf on Management of Data USA	ACM, International, Conference, on	9	11
q_2	Very Large Data Bases Conf	Conf, Conference	5	7
q_3	VLDB Conf	Conf, Conference	2	7
q_4	ICDE 2013	ICDE	2	2

(a) Strings and signatures

ID	Synonym pairs	ID	Synonym pairs
r_1	Intl ⟶ International	r_3	VLDB ⟶ Very Large Data Bases
r_2	Conf ⟶ Conference	r_4	Very Large Data Bases ⟶ VLDB

(b) Synonym pairs

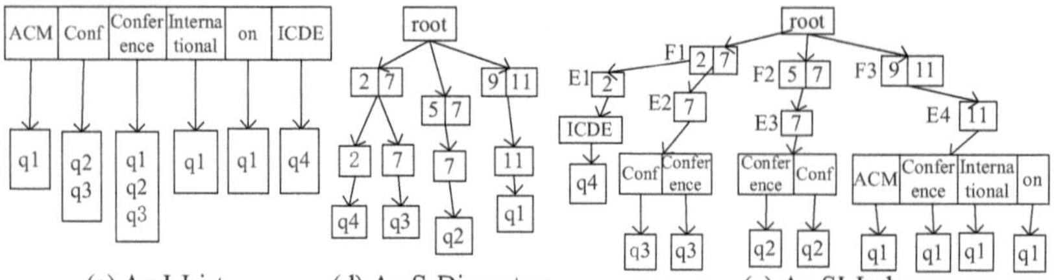

(c) An I-List (d) An S-Direcotry (e) An SI-Index

Figure 4: An example to illustrate the indexes. The column L and F denote the number of tokens in the string and in the full expanded set, respectively.

F_t. If the maximal size of expanded sets of strings below F_s (or F_t) is still smaller than θ times the length of original strings below F_t (or F_s) (i.e. u), then all pairs of strings below F_s and F_t can be pruned safely. Similarly, in the second step (lines $4 \sim 5$), given two leaf entries E_s and E_t, where all expanded sets have the same size, if the size of expanded sets below E_s (or E_t) is smaller than θ times the length of original strings below E_t (or E_s), then all string pairs below E_s and E_t can be pruned safely. In the third step (lines $6 \sim 10$), for each signature g that is an overlapping signature pointed by $E_s.P$ and $E_t.P$, Function getIList returns the I-List whose key is g. Then SI-Join generates string pair candidates for every two I-Lists.

Algorithm 3: SI-Join Algorithm

Input : SI-Trees SI_S for S and SI_T for T, threshold value θ, a collection of synonym pairs $\mathbb{R}$.
Output : $\mathbb{C}$: Candidate string pairs $(s, t) \in SI_S \times SI_T$

```
1  C ⟵ ∅;
2  for (∀ F_s in SI_S, ∀ F_t in SI_T) do
       //Fence-entry:F=<u, v, P>
3      if (min(F_s.v, F_t.v) ≥ θ × max(F_s.u, F_t.u)) then
4          for (∀ E_s∈F_s.P, ∀ E_t∈F_t.P) do
               //Leaf-entry:E=<t, P>
5              if (min(E_s.t, E_t.t) ≥ θ × max(F_s.u, F_t.u)) then
6                  for (∀ g is an overlapping signature pointed by E_s.P and E_t.P) do
7                      L_s=E_s.P→getIList(g);
8                      L_t=E_t.P→getIList(g);
9                      C={(s, t)|s ∈ L_s, t ∈ L_t};
10                     ℂ=ℂ∪ C;
11 return ℂ;
```

EXAMPLE 3. *We use this example to illustrate the SI-Join algorithm. Consider a self-join on the table in Fig. 4(a) with $\theta = 0.8$ and synonyms in Fig. 4(b). The corresponding I-Lists, S-Directory, and SI-index are shown in Figs. 4(c), (d) and (e). SI-Join prunes all the string pairs below F_1 and F_3, since $min(7, 11) < 0.8 \times max(2, 9)$ (lines 2~3). Similarly, all pairs below (E_1, E_3) can be pruned (lines 4~5). Then SI-Join uses the signatures "Conference" and "Conf" to get I-Lists below (E_2, E_3) (lines 7~8), since they are overlapping signatures pointed by E_2 and E_3 (line 6). Then a candidate (q_2, q_3) is generated and added to $\mathbb{C}$ (lines 9~10). The final results are (q_2, q_3) and $\{(q_i, q_i)|i \in [1, 4]\}$.*

4.2 Estimation-based signature selection

4.2.1 Motivation

The SI-join algorithm generates signatures for each string according to a global order of tokens. In theory, if N denotes the number of distinct tokens, there are $N!$ ways to permute the tokens to select signatures. Given two string tables for approximate join, it is impractical to design an efficient algorithm to select signatures for each string online. This is because even one scan of data is time consuming and it is meaningless to spend comparative time as the real join to find good signatures. In this section, we propose a novel strategy to solve this problem. Our main idea is to use multiple ways to generate signatures offline, and then given two tables to join, we quickly estimate the quality of each signature filter and select the best one to perform the actual filtering. The main challenge in this idea is two-fold. First, we need to select multiple promising signature filters offline. Second, the estimator should quickly determine the best filter online according to their filtering power.

To address the first challenge, we use the *itf*-based method ([2, 20]) to generate filters. In particular, let *tf(w)* denote the occurrences of token w appearing in the join tables, i.e., the frequency of w. Then the inverse term frequency of the token w, *itf(w)*, is defined as *1/tf(w)*. The global order is arranged in a descending order based on *itf* values. Intuitively, tokens with a high *itf* value are rare tokens in the collection and have a high probability not to be chosen as signatures. Since tokens come from two sources, tables and rules, there are multiple ways to compare the frequency of tokens as follows. (1) *ITF1*: sort the tokens from data tables and synonyms separately by decreasing *itf*, and then arrange tokens from tables first, followed by those from synonyms; (2) *ITF2*: sort separately again, but synonyms first, tables second; (3) *ITF3*: sort all the tokens together by a decreasing *itf* order; (4) *ITF4*: generate all possibilities of expanded sets for each string, then sort the tokens by the decreasing *itf* order in all the expanded sets.

In order to give an empirical study of the effect of different signatures on filtering power, we perform experiments using only signature filters with *ITF1*~*ITF4* against two datasets: CONF and USPS data. On the CONF dataset, we perform a join between two tables S and T using a synonym table R. Table S contains 1000 abbreviations of conference names, while table T has 1000 full expressions of conference names. On the USPS dataset, we perform a self-join on a table containing one million records, each of which contains a person name, a street name, a city name, etc., using 284 synonyms. The detailed description of the datasets can be found in Section 5.

Figure 5 reports the experimental results. We observe that (i) four signature filters achieve quite different filtering powers. The filtering power is measured by $\psi = \frac{|C|}{|N|}$, where $|C|$ denotes the number of pruned pairs and $|N|$ is the total string pairs. For instance, on the CONF dataset, when the join threshold is 0.7, the filtering power of ITF1 is 89.2%, while that of ITF2 is only 53.1%; and (ii) no signature filer can always perform the best in each dataset. For example, ITF1 performs the best in the USPS dataset, but it performs the worst in the CONF dataset. The main reason is that ITF1 gives a higher priority for the tokens in the data table to become signatures, but there are many overlaps in these signatures in the CONF dataset, resulting in a large number of candidates.

These results suggest that it is unrealistic to find a "one-size-fits-all" solution. Therefore, in the following, given two tables for join,

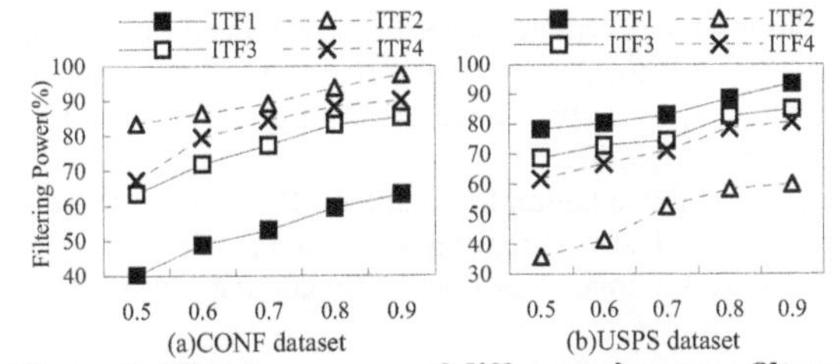

Figure 5: Filtering powers of different signature filters.

we propose an estimator to effectively estimate the filtering power of different filters to dynamically select the best filter.

4.2.2 Estimation-based selection algorithms

Let $\ell(S,g)=\{q_1^g, ..., q_n^g\}$ denote a list of string IDs (i.e., I-lists in Figs. 3 and 4) associated with the signature token g from the table S. Then an ID pair $(q_i^g, q_j^g) \in \ell(S,g) \times \ell(T,g)$ is an element of the cross-product of the two lists. Let G denote the set of all common signatures between S and T. Therefore, given a signature filter λ, the union of all ID pairs from all signatures in G constitutes the set of candidates after signature filtering, that is, $\bigcup_{g\in G} \ell(S,g) \times \ell(T,g)$.

We can use the following lemma to estimate the lower bound and the upper bound of the cardinality of candidates.

LEMMA 1. *Given a signature filter λ, the upper and lower bounds of the cardinality of the candidate pairs are:*

$$UB(\lambda) = \sum_{g\in G} (\|\ell(S,g)\| \times \|\ell(T,g)\|)$$

and

$$LB(\lambda) = max\{\|\ell(S,g)\| \times \|\ell(T,g)\|, g \in G\}$$

where $\|\ell(\cdot,g)\|$ denote the number of IDs in a list.

In the above lemma, the upper bound is defined as the total number of string pairs and the lower bound is the maximal number of string pairs associated with one signature. A signature λ guarantees to return fewer candidates than signature λ' if $UB(\lambda) < LB(\lambda')$. Obviously, the tighter the bound is, the better the results are, since a tighter bound implies more accurate estimates on the ability of a filter. Therefore, in the following, we introduce tighter upper and lower bounds by extending the Flajolet-Martin (FM) [13] technique.

The Flajolet-Martin estimator: The Flajolet-Martin (FM) technique [13] for estimating the number of distinct elements (i.e., set-union cardinality) relies on a family of hash functions $\mathcal{H}$ that map data values uniformly and independently over the collection of binary strings in the input data domain L. In particular, FM works as follows: (i) Use a hash function $h\in\mathcal{H}$ to map string ids to integers sufficiently uniformly in range $[0, 2^{L-1}]$; (ii) Initialize a bit-vector ν (also called synopses) of length L to all zeros and convert the integers into binary strings of length L; and (iii) Compute the position of the first 1-bit in the binary string (denoted as $p(h(i))$), and set the bit located at position $p(h(i))$ to be 1. Note that for any $i\in[0,2^{L-1}]$, $p(h(i)) \in \{0,\ldots,\log M\text{-}1\}$ and $Pr[p(h(i))=\ell]=\frac{1}{2^{\ell+1}}$, which means the bits in lower position have a higher probability to be set to 1. Figure 6 illustrates the FM method. Assume there are six strings. The length of the domain L=4. Finally, the synopsis ν is "1110".

Our two dimensional hash sketch (2DHS): In the following, we describe our ideas to extend FM sketch to provide better bounds to estimate the number of candidate pairs. The main challenge is that the existing FM-based methods [13, 14] are only applicable to one dimensional data, but we need to estimate the number of distinct

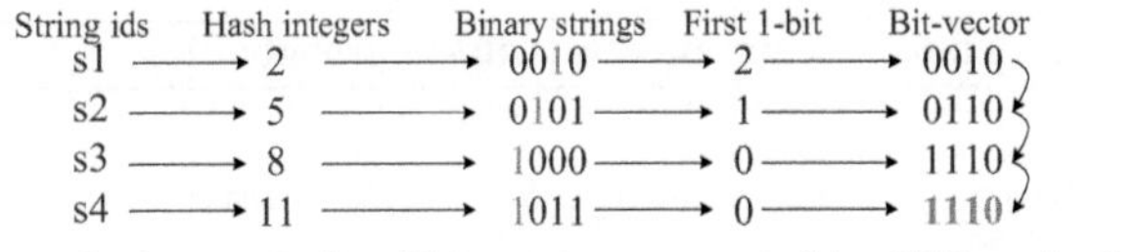

Figure 6: An example of bit-vector generated by FM method. (The first 1-bit is the left-most 1-bit.)

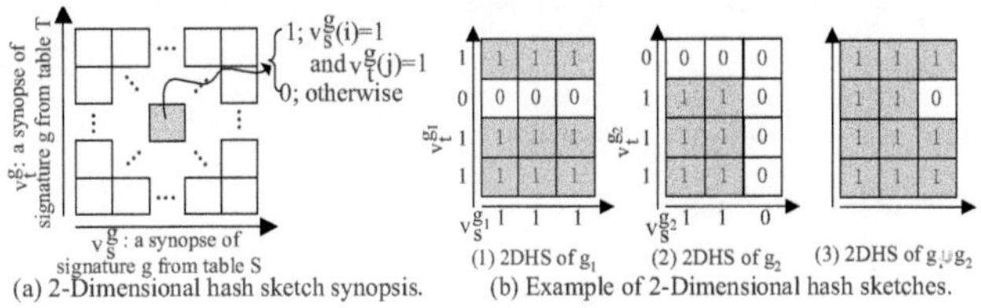

Figure 7: The structure of 2-dimensional hash sketch (2DHS)

pairs based on two independent FM sketches. In addition, the extra complication occurs, since we require the bounds to be correct with arbitrarily high probability. We now describe four steps to address the challenges.

Step 1 (Estimating the distinct number of one table): At first, we estimate the distinct number of string IDs for all signature tokens from one table, that is, μ_S and μ_T, where $\mu_S= \bigcup_{g\in G} \ell(S,g)$ and $\mu_T= \bigcup_{g\in G} \ell(T,g)$. Ganguly et al. [14] provide an (ϵ,δ)-*estimate* algorithm for μ_S (or μ_T) by using the extension of the FM technique, which estimates the quantity of μ_S (or μ_T) within a small relative error ϵ and a high confidence 1-δ. Space precludes detailed discussion about their method in this paper. However, readers may find it in Section 3.3 of [14]. Note that after the first step, we indeed obtain a new upper bound: $\mu_S \times \mu_T$. But it is still not tight enough. We proceed to the following steps to get a better value.

Step 2 (Constructing a two-dimensional hash sketch): Let ν_S^g and ν_T^g be an FM sketch of signature g in I-Lists of table S and table T respectively. We construct a 2-dimensional hash sketch synopsis $(2DHS)$ of signature g, which is a 2-dimensional bit-vector. The bucket (i,j) in a 2DHS is 1 if and only if $\nu_S^g(i)=1$ and $\nu_T^g(j)=1$. Further, let G be the set of common signatures of S and T. We construct a new $2DHS'$, which is the union of all 2DHS's of each signature, namely $\bigcup_{g\in G} 2DHS^g$, such that $2DHS'(i,j)$=1 if $\exists\, 2DHS^g(i,j)$=1.

EXAMPLE 4. *Figure 7 illustrates Step 2. Assume there are two common signatures g_1 and g_2 of S and T, $\nu_S^{g_1}=\{1,1,1\}$,$\nu_T^{g_1}=\{1,1,0,1\}$ and $\nu_S^{g_2}=\{1,1,0\}$,$\nu_T^{g_2}=\{1,1,1,0\}$. Figure 7(b1) is the 2DHS of g_1 and Figure 7(b2) is the 2DHS of g_2. Then the union $2DHS$ is shown in Figure 7(b3).*

Step 3 (Computing witness probabilities): Once the union *2DHS* is built, we select a bucket (i,j) to compute a witness probability as follows. We examine a collection of ω independent *2DHS* $(\nu_1^g,\nu_2^g,\ldots,\nu_\omega^g)$ (each copy using independently-chosen hash functions from $\mathcal{H}$). Algorithm 4 shows the steps to compute witness probabilities. In particular, let $R_s=\lfloor\log_2\mu_S\rfloor$ and $R_t=\lfloor\log_2\mu_T\rfloor$. We investigate a column of buckets (R_s, y) (line 2 $\sim$ 8), and a row of buckets (x, R_t) (line 9 $\sim$ 15), and select two smallest indexes y and x at which only a constant fraction 0.3ω of the sketch buckets turns out to be 1. As our analysis will show, the observed fraction $\hat{p}_s$ and $\hat{p}_t$ (line 16) and their positions can be used to provide a robust estimate for bounds in the next step.

Step 4 (Computing tighter upper and lower bounds): The final step is to compute the upper bound TUB and the lower bound TLB

Algorithm 4: Computing two witness probabilities

```
   Input  : ω independent 2-dimensional hash sketches
            (2DHS_1,2DHS_2,...,2DHS_ω), R_s and R_t.
   Output : p̂_s and p̂_t and two witness positions (R_s, y) and (x, R_t)
1  f=0.3ω;
2  for (y from 0 to R_t) do
3      count=0;
4      for (i from 1 to ω) do
5          if (2DHS_i[R_s][y]==1) then
6              count = count+1;
7      if (count≤f) then
8          p̂_s=count/ω and goto Line 9;
9  for (x from 0 to R_s) do
10     count=0;
11     for (i from 1 to ω) do
12         if (2DHS_i[x][R_t]==1) then
13             count = count+1;
14     if (count≤f) then
15         p̂_t=count/ω and goto Line 16;
16 return p̂_s, p̂_t and their witness positions (R_s, y), (x, R_t)
```

of a signature filter λ. Assume, without loss of generality, that $\mu_S \leq \mu_T$.

TUB(λ) $= \varphi_1 \cdot min(u_1, u_2)$, where

$$u_1 = \mu_S \cdot \frac{\ln(1-p_s)}{\ln(1-\frac{1}{2^y})}, \text{ and } p_s = \frac{\hat{p_s}}{1-(1-\frac{1}{2^{R_s}})^{\mu_S}};$$

$$u_2 = \mu_T \cdot \frac{\ln(1-p_t)}{\ln(1-\frac{1}{2^x})}, \text{ and } p_t = \frac{\hat{p_t}}{1-(1-\frac{1}{2^{R_t}})^{\mu_T}}$$

$$\text{TLB}(\lambda) = \varphi_2 \cdot \mu_S \cdot \frac{\ln(1-p_s')}{\ln(1-\frac{1}{2^y})}, \text{ where } p_s' = \frac{\hat{p_s}-\Delta p}{1-(1-\frac{1}{2^{R_s}})^{\mu_S}}$$

$$\Delta p = [1-(1-\frac{1}{2^{R_s+y}})^{\mu_S}] - \frac{1}{2^y} \times [1-(1-\frac{1}{2^{R_s}})^{\mu_S}]$$

where constants φ_1=1.43, φ_2=0.8, are derived in Theorem 2.

EXAMPLE 5. *This example illustrates the computation of TUB and TLB. Assume μ_S=100 and μ_T=200. Thus R_s=$\lfloor \log_2^{100} \rfloor$=6, R_t=$\lfloor \log_2^{200} \rfloor$=7. Assume, in Algorithm 4, that the returned values are $\hat{p_s}$=0.2, $\hat{p_t}$=0.19, x=5, and y=6. According to the formulas in Step 4, we have p_s=0.2522, p_t=0.24, u_1=1845, u_2=1729, Δp=0.0117, p_s'=0.2375, and the upper bound $TUB(\lambda)$ = 1.43*1729 = 2472 and $TLB(\lambda)$ = 1722×0.8=1278.*

Therefore, one filter is selected as the best one if its TUB is less than all the TLBs of other filters, which means that it returns the smallest number of candidates. In practice, if there are several filters whose bounds have overlaps, then it means that their abilities are similar with a high probability and we can arbitrarily choose one of them to break the tie.

Theoretical analysis: We first demonstrate that, with an arbitrarily high probability, the returned lower and upper bounds are correct, and then we analyze its space and time complexities. Due to space constraint, some proofs are omitted here.

It is important to note that given n distinct ID pairs and a position (x, y) in a 2DHS matrix, the probability that the bucket in (x, y) is 1 depends on the distribution of the input data. To understand it, consider the following two cases: One is (1,1), (2,1), ..., (n,1) and the other is (1,n+1), (2,n+2),...,(n,2n). Both cases have n distinct pairs, but their probabilities are different. The first case is $\frac{1}{2^y} \times [1-(1-\frac{1}{2^x})^n]$, but the second case is $[1-(1-\frac{1}{2^{x+y}})^n]$. Therefore, we need to differentiate the probabilities for these two extremes. Let $MIN(N, \mu_S, \mu_T, x, y)$ and $MAX(N, \mu_S, \mu_T, x, y)$ denote the minimum and maximum probabilities respectively that the bucket (x, y) is 1 with N distinct pairs, where μ_S and μ_T denote the number of distinct IDs in each dimension respectively. The computation of the accurate values of the MIN and MAX is highly complicated. But for the purpose of this paper to differentiate the ability of filters, we derive a lower (resp. upper) bound for the MIN (resp. MAX) probability.

The following lemma implies that the MIN and MAX probabilities are monotonically increasing on μ_S and μ_T. This monotonicity can ensure Lemmas 3 and 4 to compute the lower and upper bounds.

LEMMA 2. *If $\mu_S \geq \mu_S'$ and $\mu_T \geq \mu_T'$, then $MIN(N, \mu_S, \mu_T, x, y) \geq MIN(N, \mu_S', \mu_T', x, y)$ and $MAX(N, \mu_S, \mu_T, x, y) \geq MAX(N, \mu_S', \mu_T', x, y)$.*

LEMMA 3. *The lower bound of the MIN probability can be computed as:*

$$p_1 = [1-(1-\frac{1}{2^x})^{\mu_S}] \times [1-(1-\frac{1}{2^y})^{\frac{N}{\mu_S}}];$$

$$p_2 = [1-(1-\frac{1}{2^y})^{\mu_T}] \times [1-(1-\frac{1}{2^x})^{\frac{N}{\mu_T}}];$$

$$MIN(N, \mu_S, \mu_T, x, y) \geq max(p_1, p_2).$$

PROOF. *(Sketch) According to Lemma 2, the MIN probability is monotonically increasing with μ_S and μ_T. Therefore, the final MIN probability is greater than p_1 and p_2, since $\mu_S \geq \frac{N}{\mu_T}$ and $\mu_T \geq \frac{N}{\mu_S}$. That concludes the proof.* □

LEMMA 4. *Assume that $\mu_S \leq \mu_T$. Then the upper bound of the MAX probability can be computed as:*

$$p_1 = [1-(1-\frac{1}{2^x})^{\mu_S}] \times [1-(1-\frac{1}{2^y})^{\frac{N}{\mu_S}}];$$

$$p_2 = [1-(1-\frac{1}{2^{x+y}})^{\mu_S}] - \frac{1}{2^y} \times [1-(1-\frac{1}{2^x})^{\mu_S}];$$

$$MAX(N, \mu_S, \mu_T, x, y) \leq p_1 + p_2.$$

PROOF. *(Sketch) According to Lemma 2, with a fixed μ_S, the greater the value μ_T is, the greater the MAX probability is. In the worst case, μ_T = N. Therefore, the MAX probability p_{max} is no greater than:*

$$p_{max} \leq 1 - [(1-\frac{1}{2^x}) + \frac{1}{2^x} \cdot (1-\frac{1}{2^y})^{\frac{N}{\mu_S}}]^{\mu_S}$$

We then prove that $p_{max} - p_1 \leq p_2$. We can show that $p_{max} - p_1$ is a monotonically decreasing function when $N \geq \mu_S$. Therefore, when $N = \mu_S$ (in this case, $N = \mu_S = \mu_T$), we have the minimal value as follows.

$$p_{max} - p_1 \leq 1 - [(1-\frac{1}{2^x}) + \frac{1}{2^x} \cdot (1-\frac{1}{2^y})]^{\mu_S} - [1-(1-\frac{1}{2^x})^{\mu_S}] \times [1-(1-\frac{1}{2^y})] = p_2.$$ □

THEOREM 2. *Given a signature filter λ, with any high probability 1-δ, our algorithm guarantees to correctly return the upper bound and the lower bound to estimate the number of candidate pairs with λ.*

PROOF. *(Sketch) There are three steps in this proof. Firstly, we show that the estimated probabilities $\hat{p}_s$ and $\hat{p}_t$ returned by Algorithm 4 are low-error and high-confidence, and then we show our formulas TLB and TUB are correct. Finally, we show how to adjust formulas based on the estimated $\hat{p}_s$, $\hat{p}_t$ and μ_S, μ_T.*

First, in Algorithm 4, by Chernoff bound, the estimated $\hat{p}$=count/ω satisfies $|\hat{p} - p| \leq \epsilon p$ with a probability at least 1-δ as long as $\omega p \geq \frac{2\log(1/\delta)}{\epsilon^2}$. Let ϵ=0.15, Then $\omega p \geq 88\log(1/\delta)$. Since $\hat{p}_s$ and $\hat{p}_t$ returned in Algorithm 4 are the smallest indexes where only 0.3ω of sketches turn to be 1, their values are no less than 0.3/2=0.15. Therefore, $p \geq 0.15$, and we can generate enough number of sketches such that $\omega \geq 587\log(1/\delta) = \Theta(\log\frac{1}{\delta})$. Strictly speaking, the witness probabilities $\hat{p}_s$ and $\hat{p}_t$ are estimated values, and we need to use the Chernoff bound again to show that they are close to 0.15 with a high confidence. The details are omitted here.

Second, according to Lemmas 3 and 4, it is not hard to mathematically compute the lower bound and upper bound to estimate the number of distinct pairs number N.

Finally, the following two lemmas demonstrate that we only need to multiply a constant in the formulas to use the low-error estimated $\hat{p}_s$, $\hat{p}_t$, μ_S and μ_T for the accuracy guarantee. In particular, Lemma 5 is used to derive φ_1 in TUB and Lemma 6 for φ_2 in TLB, respectively. (A similar proof technique can be found in [5, 14], even though our estimation is quite different from theirs.)

LEMMA 5. *Let f(x) = $ln(1 - \frac{x}{1-(1-\frac{1}{2R_s})^{\mu_S(1+\varepsilon)}})$. If $y - x \leq 0.15x$ for some $x \leq 0.3$ and $\varepsilon \leq 0.1$, then $f(y) - f(x) \leq 0.43f(x)$.*

PROOF. *Since $1-(1-\frac{1}{2R_s})^{\mu_S(1+\varepsilon)} \approx 1-e^{-(1+\varepsilon)}$ and $\varepsilon \leq 0.1$, then $\frac{1}{1-e^{-(1+\varepsilon)}} \geq 1.5$. By Taylor series, there is a value $w \in (x, y)$ such that $ln(1-1.5y) = ln(1-1.5x)$-$1.5(y-x)/(1-1.5w)$. Thus, we have $f(y) - f(x) \leq \frac{1.5(y-x)}{1-1.5max(x,y)} \leq \frac{0.225x}{1-1.725x} \leq \frac{0.225x}{0.52} \approx 0.43x \leq -0.43ln(1-1.5x) \leq 0.43f(x)$.* □

LEMMA 6. *Let f(x) = $ln(1 - \frac{x-\Delta p}{1-(1-\frac{1}{2R_s})^{\mu_S(1+\varepsilon)}})$. If $x - y \leq 0.15x$ for some $x \leq 0.3$ and $\varepsilon \leq 0.1$, then $f(x) - f(y) \leq 0.2f(x)$.*

PROOF. *(Sketch) First, we can prove $\frac{\Delta p}{1-(1-\frac{1}{2R_s})^{\mu_S(1+\varepsilon)}} < 0.71$. The details are omitted here. Then by Taylor series again, there is a value $w \in (x, y)$ such that $\ln(1.71 - 1.5y) = \ln(1.71 - 1.5x) - (1.5(x-y))/(1.71 - 1.5w)$. Thus, we have $|f(y) - f(x)| \leq \frac{1.5(x-y)}{1.71-1.5\max(x,y)} \leq \frac{0.225x}{1.71-1.725x} \leq \frac{0.225x}{1.19} \approx 0.189x \leq 0.2\ln(1.71-1.5x)$, since by Maclaurin series, $\ln(1.71-1.5x) \approx \ln 1.71 - (1.5/1.71)x \approx 0.54 - 0.88x$.* □

THEOREM 3. *Given a high probability 1-δ, our estimator needs a total space of $\Theta(T \log M \log(1/\delta))$ bits, where T is the number of overlapping signatures and M is the maximal length of inverted list associated with a signature, and its computing complexity is $\Theta(T \log^2 M + \log M \log(1/\delta))$.*

PROOF. *The size of one FM sketch is $\log M$ and there are T signatures. So the space for storing all FM sketches is $2T \log M$. We need to generate a collection of ω=$\Theta(\log \frac{1}{\delta})$ sketches. Therefore, the total space requirement is $\Theta(T \log M \log(1/\delta))$. Further, to compute the time complexity, in step 1, the computing cost is $2\omega \log M$. The cost of Step 2 is $2T\log^2 M$ and that of Step 3 and 4 are $\omega \log M$ and O(1) respectively. Therefore the total cost is bounded by $\Theta(T \log^2 M + \log M \log(1/\delta))$.* □

4.3 Extension to LSH filters

Although we focus on prefix filters in the above discussion, our indexes and estimators can also be extended to other filters, such as LSH scheme. In particular, each signature s in LSH is a concatenation of a fixed number k of minhashes of the set and there are l such signatures (using different minhashes). Then, in the I-lists, each inverted list is associated with a pair (s, i), where i means that the signature s comes from the i-th minhash, $1 \leq i \leq l$. Therefore, by replacing the prefix signature g with (s, i), our SN-join (Algorithm 3) and 2DHS estimator can be directly applied on LSH scheme. As described in the next section, we implemented both LSH and prefix filters in our algorithms to make a comprehensive comparison.

Dataset	# of Strings	String Len (avg/max)	# of Synonym Pairs	# of Applicable Synonym Pairs Per String (avg/max)
USPS	1,000,000	6.75 / 15	300	2.19 / 5
CONF	10,000	5.84 / 14	1000	1.43 /4
SPROT	1,000,000	10.32 / 20	10,000	17.96 /68

Figure 8: Characteristics of Datasets.

5. EXPERIMENTAL RESULTS

In this section, we report an extensive experimental evaluation of algorithms on three real-world datasets. First, we show the effectiveness and efficiency of the expansion-based framework to measure the similarity of strings with synonyms. Second, we evaluate our SN-join, SI-Join and the state-of-the-art approaches to perform similarity join with prefixes and LSH signatures. Finally, we analyze the performance of 2DHS estimators.

All the algorithms were implemented in Java 1.6.0 and run on a Windows XP with dual-core Intel Xeon CPU 4.0GHz, 2GB RAM, and a 320GB hard disk.

5.1 Datasets and Synonyms

Data Sets. We use three datasets: US addresses (**USPS**), conference titles (**CONF**), and gene/protein data (**SPROT**). These datasets differ from each other in terms of rule-number, rule-complexity, data-size and string-length. Our goal in choosing these diverse sources is to understand the usefulness of algorithms in different real world environments.

USPS: We downloaded common person names, street names, city names, states, and zip codes from the United States Postal Service website (http://www.usps.com). We then generated one million records, each of which contains a person name, a street name, a city name, a state, and a zip code. USPS also publishes extensive information about the format of US addresses, from which we obtained 284 synonym pairs. The synonym pairs covers a wide range of alternate representations of common strings, e.g., *street* $\rightarrow$ *st.*

CONF: We collected 10,000 conference names from more than ten domains, including Medicine and Computer Science. We obtained 1000 synonym pairs between the full names of conferences and their abbreviations by manually examining conference websites or homepages of scientists.

SPROT: We obtained one million gene/protein records from the Expasy website (http://www.expasy.ch/sprot). Each record contains an identifier (ID) and its name. In this dataset, each ID has $5 \sim 22$ synonyms. We generated 10,000 synonym rules describing gene/protein equivalent expressions.

Figure 8 gives the characteristics of the three datasets.

5.2 Experimental results

5.2.1 *Quality and Efficiency of Similarity Measures*

The first experiment is to demonstrate the effectiveness and efficiency of the various similarity measures. We compared our two measures: full expansion (**Full**), and selective expansion (**SE**) with **Jaccard** without synonyms and **JaccT** using synonyms from [2].

For each of the three datasets, we performed the experiments by conducting a similarity join between a query table T_Q and a target table T_T as follows: (1) T_Q consists of 100 manually selected full names, and (2) T_T has 200 records where 100 of them are the correct abbreviations of the corresponding records in T_Q (i.e. the ground truth), and the other 100 "dirty" records are selected such that each of them is a similar record (in terms of Jaccard coefficient) to the corresponding records in T_Q. This is to ensure that there is only one correct matching record in T_T for each record in T_Q.

θ	CONF dataset												USPS dataset												SPROT dataset											
	Jacc			JaccT			Full			SE			Jacc			JaccT			Full			SE			Jacc			JaccT			Full			SE		
	P	R	F	P	R	F	P	R	F	P	R	F	P	R	F	P	R	F	P	R	F	P	R	F	P	R	F	P	R	F	P	R	F	P	R	F
0.50	0.04	0.44	0.07	0.45	0.83	0.60	0.43	0.91	0.58	0.67	0.94	0.78	0.01	0.74	0.02	0.08	0.95	0.15	0.06	0.95	0.11	0.05	1.00	0.10	0.01	0.54	0.01	0.07	0.81	0.12	0.05	0.72	0.09	0.05	0.94	0.10
0.60	0.14	0.44	0.21	0.47	0.83	0.60	0.50	0.85	0.63	0.69	0.90	0.78	0.01	0.42	0.02	0.08	0.82	0.15	0.12	0.93	0.21	0.10	0.95	0.19	0.01	0.32	0.02	0.07	0.72	0.13	0.08	0.68	0.15	0.10	0.90	0.18
0.70	0.44	0.40	0.42	0.52	0.80	0.63	0.51	0.82	0.63	0.72	0.85	0.78	0.06	0.42	0.11	0.22	0.82	0.35	0.26	0.93	0.41	0.36	0.93	0.52	0.05	0.32	0.08	0.19	0.71	0.30	0.18	0.65	0.28	0.33	0.87	0.48
0.80	0.63	0.35	0.45	0.76	0.74	0.75	0.55	0.70	0.62	0.87	0.84	**0.85**	0.21	0.42	0.28	0.39	0.73	0.51	0.61	0.80	0.70	0.79	0.91	0.85	0.16	0.32	0.21	0.33	0.62	0.43	0.52	0.64	0.58	0.69	0.83	0.75
0.90	0.82	0.21	0.33	0.80	0.71	0.75	0.68	0.60	0.64	0.89	0.80	0.84	0.71	0.42	0.53	0.61	0.73	0.66	0.84	0.75	0.79	0.96	0.89	**0.92**	0.54	0.32	0.40	0.48	0.57	0.52	0.69	0.61	0.65	0.83	0.82	**0.82**

Figure 9: Quality of similarity measures (P: precision, R: recall, F: F-measure).

CONF dataset			USPS dataset			SPROT dataset		
Jacc	0.14	s1= "Proceedings of the VLDB Endowment 2012: 38th International Conference on Very Large Databases, Turkey"	Jacc	0.00	s1= "University of Washington 1705 NE Pacific St Seattle, WA 98195"	Jacc	0.00	s1= "P93214"
JaccT	0.57	s2= "PVLDB 2012 Turkey"	JaccT	0.70	s2= "UW"	JaccT	0.75	s2= "14339_SOLL, 14-3-3 protein 9"
Full	0.93	r1:PVLDB->International Conference on Very Large Databases	Full	0.92	r1:UW->University of Washington r2:UW->1705 NE Pacific St Seattle, WA 98195	Full	0.83	r1:P93214->14339_SOLL r2:P93214->14-3-3 protein 9
SE	0. 93	r2:PVLDB->Proceedings of the VLDB Endowment	SE	1.00	r3:UW->University of Waterloo	SE	1.00	r3:14339_SOLL->UPI0000124DEC

Figure 10: Three examples to illustrate the quality of similarity measures.

Quality of Measures. In Figure 9, we report the quality of the measures by testing the *Precision* (short for "P"), *Recall* ("R"), and *F-measure*$=\frac{2\times P\times R}{P+R}$ ("F") on three datasets. We observe that:

- The similarity measures using synonyms (including *JaccT*, *Full* and *SE*) obtain higher scores than Jaccard which does not consider synonym pairs. The reason is that without using synonyms, Jaccard has no chance to improve the similarity.
- *SE* significantly outperforms *JaccT* in each dataset. For example, on SPROT dataset, the F-measures of *SE* and *JaccT* are 0.82 and 0.52 respectively. The main reason is that: an abbreviation may have various full expressions and the join records may contain the combination of multiple expressions. Therefore *SE* can apply multiple rules, while *JaccT* can apply only one. Note that such situation is not rare in the real world data, as one fragment of a string likely involves multiple synonym rules. We illustrate one example on each of three datasets in Figure 10 to compare the performance of four similarity measures.

Dataset	1000	3000	5000	7000	9000
USPS	70.0%	71.2%	72.8%	72.2%	70.8%
CONF	62.4%	67.6%	68.9%	71.2%	70.4%
SPROT	84.4%	86.7%	88.4%	89.8%	87.3%

Figure 11: Empirical Probabilities of Optimal Cases for SE

Optimality Scenarios of SE measure As described in Theorem 1, SE is optimal if the *rhs* tokens of useful rules are distinct. The purpose of this experiment is to verify how likely this optimal condition is satisfied in practice. We performed experiments on three datasets using different data sizes. The results are shown in Figure 11. The average percentages of optimal cases are 71.39%, 68.11%, and 87.32% in USPS, CONF and SPROT data, respectively. Therefore, the condition in Theorem 1 are likely to be met by the majority of candidate string pairs, which means that the values returned by the SE algorithm are optimal in most cases. Further, the percentage on SPROT data is larger than those on USPS and CONF. This is because many of the synonym pairs on SPROT are single-token-to-single-token synonyms, which are more likely to meet the distinct condition. In contrast, many of the synonyms of the USPS and CONF are multi-token synonyms.

Efficiency of Measures. Having verified the effectiveness of different measures, in the sequel we assess their efficiency. Figure 12(a) shows the time cost of the four measures on SPROT dataset (10K records) by running 10^8 times of string similarity measurement based on the nested-loop self-join. The x-axis denotes the number of synonym rules applied on one single string, and the y-axis is the total running time. We find that although the full-expansion needs to expand the string set using rules, its performance is comparable to that of Jaccard, which does not use any rules at all. This is because, the full-expansion adds all applied rules directly and its computing cost increases slowly with the number of rules. In contrast, JaccT needs to enumerate all the possible intermediate strings and its performance deteriorates rapidly with the increase of rules. Finally, SE is in the "middle" of the two extremes, which avoids enumerating all the possible strings to achieve better performance than JaccT, and which selects only appropriate rules to achieve better effectiveness than full-expansion in terms of F-measures (illustrated in Figure 9).

5.2.2 *Efficiency and Scalability of Join Algorithms*

The second experiment is to test the efficiency and scalability of various join algorithms. We compared our algorithms, **SN-Join**, and **SI-Join** with the algorithm in [2] (also termed **JaccT**). Our implementation of JaccT includes all the optimizations proposed in [2]. For our algorithms, since they can work with the two similarity measures (i.e., full expansion, selective expansion), we denote them as **SN(F)**, **SN(S)**, and **SI(F)** and **SI(S)** respectively. We implemented all algorithms using both prefix and LSH filters. Therefore, with respect to the algorithms using LSH scheme, we append "-L" to the name, e.g., JaccT-L denotes the JaccT algorithm using LSH scheme. Note that, we use the false negative ratio $\delta \leq 5\%$, i.e, the accuracy is $1-\delta \geq 95\%$. The parameters k and l should satisfy: $\delta \geq (1-\theta^k)^l$ [33]. For example, if threshold $\theta = 0.8$, $k = 3$, then l should be at least 5 to guarantee at least 95% accuracy.

Metrics. We took the following measures: (i) the size of signatures, (ii) the filtering ratio of the algorithms, which is typically defined as the number of pruned string pairs divided by the total number of string pairs; and (iii) the running time (including filtering time and verification time).

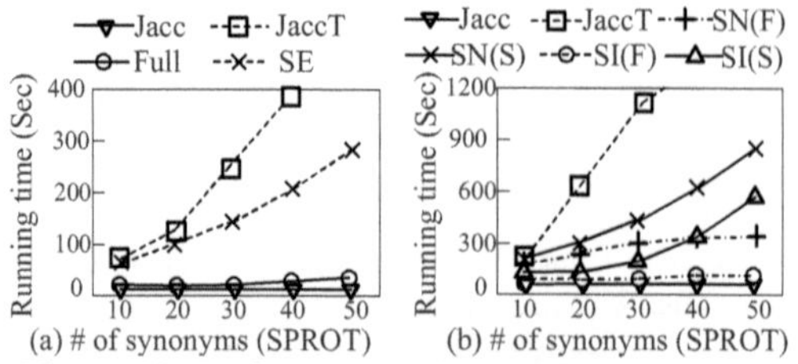

Figure 12: Performance with varying synonyms.

Number of Signatures. We first performed experiments to report the number of signatures of a query string. It has a major impact on the query time, as both JaccT and our join algorithms need to

θ	Prefix filtering scheme				Locality sensitive hashing (LSH) scheme					
	USPS		SPROT		USPS (k=4)			SPROT(k=6)		
	JaccT	Ours	JaccT	Ours	l	JaccT	Ours	l	JaccT	Ours
	Avg/max	Avg/max	Avg/max	Avg/max		Avg/max	Avg/max		Avg/max	Avg/max
0.95	1.415/5	1.137/3	8.363/17	7.432/16	**2**	3.384/8	3.254/8	**3**	14.87/46	12.16/44
0.90	1.527/6	1.447/6	8.654/18	8.322/16	**3**	4.576/19	4.499/18	**4**	19.84/58	19.44/57
0.85	2.078/8	2.201/7	9.532/18	8.953/17	**5**	8.952/21	8.911/20	**7**	34.72/72	34.58/71
0.80	3.780/9	2.349/7	10.79/19	9.512/19	**6**	11.14/29	11.09/27	**10**	49.62/103	48.19/100
0.75	3.913/9	2.806/8	11.55/19	10.10/21	**8**	15.52/36	14.15/35	**16**	69.36/192	68.73/185
0.70	4.456/10	3.568/10	13.07/20	12.97/23	**11**	20.09/51	19.21/51	**24**	75.04/297	74.92/294

Figure 13: Number of signatures (Prefix filtering scheme and LSH scheme).

θ	USPS (100K self-join)						SPROT(1000K self-join)					
	Filtering Ratio(%)			Candidate Size($x10^6$)			Filtering Ratio(%)			Candidate Size($x10^9$)		
	JaccT	SN-Join	SI-Join	JaccT	SN-Join	SI-Join	JaccT	SN-Join	SI-Join	JaccT	SN-Join	SI-Join
0.95	86.1	88.8	99.0	695.4	561.3	49.8	91.8	93.5	99.5	41.3	32.7	2.6
0.90	85.7	86.8	98.9	714.3	661.3	56.9	90.7	91.7	98.6	46.5	41.9	7.1
0.85	84.5	86.0	98.9	777.6	701.9	57.4	88.5	90.0	95.5	57.5	50.2	22.1
0.80	82.5	84.7	98.7	874.0	764.2	63.0	86.6	89.3	92.1	67.7	53.4	39.5
0.75	82.3	83.7	98.7	885.8	817.6	66.7	85.2	87.5	90.3	74.0	62.4	48.9
0.70	81.9	82.4	98.4	904.0	878.7	78.5	78.1	80.3	89.7	109.5	98.8	51.3

Figure 14: Filtering ratio with varying thresholds.

frequently check the overlaps of string signatures. The results are reported in Figure 13. For both prefix and LSH schemes, the number of signatures of our expansion-based algorithms is smaller than that of JaccT. The reason is that based on a transformation framework, JaccT is more likely to include new tokens into signatures than ours. In addition, we observe that the size of signatures in the LSH scheme is greater than that in prefix scheme, and the gap increases when the threshold decreases. As we will see shortly, this results in substantial overhead of filtering time for the LSH scheme.

Filtering Power. We then investigated the filtering power of different algorithms in Figures 14–15 using prefix and LSH schemes, respectively. The experiments were performed on USPS and SPROT datasets for self-join. For prefix-based algorithms, SN-Join is slightly better than JaccT, while SI-Join has a substantial lead over JaccT and SN-Join. These results are mainly because of the additional filtering power in SI-Join bought by length filtering and signature filtering. Next, for LSH-based algorithms, Figure 15 demonstrates the similar trend. That is, SI-Join is the winner in all settings by varying the parameters k and l. Compared to the prefix scheme, LSH has a slightly higher filtering ratio when parameters are set optimally (e.g. 99.2% v.s. 98.9% in USPS data, with threshold 0.9). On the other hand, note that LSH may filter away correct answers, resulting in false negatives, as can be seen from the false negative percentages shown in Figure 15.

Running Time and Scalability. Figure 16 and Figure 17 show the running time of five join algorithms based on prefix and LSH schemes respectively (the join threshold is 0.8). The x-axis represents the join data size. As shown, the running times of both JaccT and SN-Join (i.e., SN(F), SN(S)) have an exponential growth, whereas SI-Join (i.e., SI(F), SI(S)) scales better (i.e., linear) than SN-Join and JaccT. The reason is that SI-Join methods have more efficient filtering strategies and generate smaller size of candidates. In addition, in order to study the scalability of algorithms with the increase of the number of rules, we plot Figure 12(b), where SI(F) (i.e. SI-Join with the full-expansion) is a clear winner in algorithms using rules: it is insensitive to the number of rules and thus able to outperform other methods when one string involves more than 10 rules.

Prefix vs. LSH We then sought to analyze system performances with different signature schemes, namely, prefix vs. LSH. Figure 18 plots the running times of SI(S)-L (LSH) and SI(S) (Prefix) with varying join thresholds. Results on SI(F) and SN-join are similar. Note that, for SI(S)-L, the choice of k and l has substantial impact on the query time, hence we tuned and used the

k/L	USPS						SPROT					
	JaccT		SN-Join		SI-Join		JaccT		SN-Join		SI-Join	
	FR(%)	FN(%)	FR(%)	FN(%)	FR(%)	FN(%)	FR(%)	FN(%)	FR(%)	FN(%)	FR(%)	FN(%)
k=2,l=2	63.5	4.21	66.5	4.32	76.3	3.61	78.8	4.22	80.1	4.19	84.5	3.71
k=3,l=3	72.4	4.54	73.9	4.77	79.1	3.55	83.1	4.38	85.6	4.28	90.7	3.33
k=4,l=3	**87.9**	4.23	**89.4**	4.56	**99.2**	3.52	89.4	4.13	89.9	3.85	97.1	3.42
k=5,l=4	83.4	3.89	83.1	4.22	87.8	2.78	84.7	3.69	89.5	4.04	95.5	2.94
k=6,l=4	81.1	3.73	86.8	3.88	92.3	2.43	**92.3**	3.77	**93.7**	3.27	**99.8**	3.06
k=7,l=5	82.6	3.29	82.5	3.69	94.1	2.19	90.4	3.59	92.9	3.73	96.2	2.73

Figure 15: Filter ratio (FR) and false negative (FN) with varying parameters k and l. (accuracy=95%, threshold=0.9).

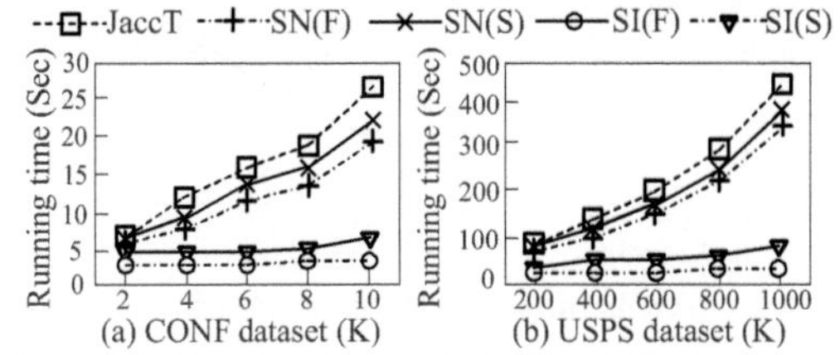

Figure 16: Running time in CONF and USPS datasets.

parameters of k and l for each threshold to achieve the best running time. Before we describe the results, it should be noted that the two schemes, LSH and prefix, have different goals and probably different application scenarios, as LSH is an *approximate* solution, but prefix must return *all* correct answers, making somewhat unfair for a direct comparison between them. We observe that LSH is faster than prefix when the threshold is approximately ≥ 0.8. This is mainly because more than one minhash signatures is combined (i.e, $k \geq 2$) in these settings, which makes LSH method quite selective. However, when the threshold is less than 0.8, we tried all reasonable combinations of k and l values and still cannot find a setting to beat prefix. This is because when the threshold is small, in order to improve the filtering power, we need to select a large k, which in turn requires a large l to maintain the same confidence level ($\geq 95\%$); this results in substantial overhead in filtering time. Therefore, LSH trades the filtering time for higher filtering power. Then the overall running time of LSH is greater than that of prefix in such case. This also the reason why the best running time achieved for threshold < 0.8 is with small k and l values to reduce the overall running time in Figure 18.

5.2.3 Estimation-based signature selection

The last set of experiments (Figure 19) studies the quality of *2DHS* synopsis on prefix and LSH schemes. For prefix filter, we use the four *frequency*-based signature filters, i.e., ITF1∼ITF4, which are described in Section 4.2. For LSH scheme, we vary the parameters k and l to generate six filters. The off-line processing time for the generation of all signatures of one filter is around 200s $\sim$ 300s, which is a one-time cost.

We first computed the upper bound (UB) and the lower bound (LB) of each filter by Lemma 1. One filter is returned as the best one if its UB is less than all the LBs of other filters, which means that it returns the smallest number of candidates. For example, in Figure 19(a), ITF2 is the best one in CONF dataset. If there is no filter which can beat all other filters using only UB and LB, then we further compute the tighter upper bound (TUB) and lower bound (TLB) using *2DHS* synopsis. Consequently, in Figure 19(b), ITF1 is the best filters in USPS dataset , as its TUB is less than all others' TLBs. Note that, our estimate correctly predicts the ability of four filters, which can be empirically verified in Figure 5 for prefix scheme. In addition, the estimate cost accounts for only 1% of the join time. For example, in USPS dataset, the time cost of

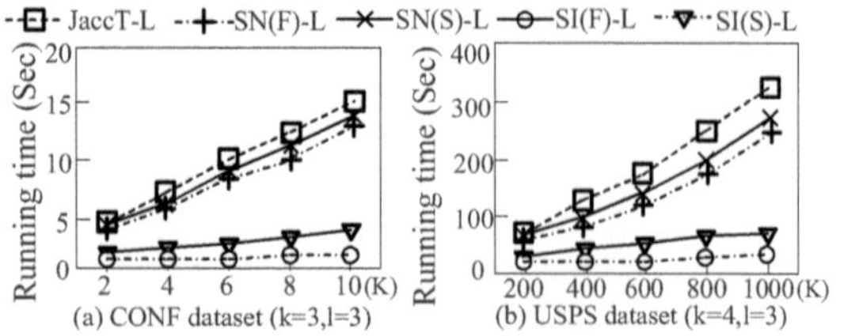

Figure 17: Performance on LSH signature scheme.

θ	k	l
0.95	4	2
0.90	4	3
0.85	2	3
0.80	2	3
0.75	1	3
0.70	1	3

(a) k,l settings

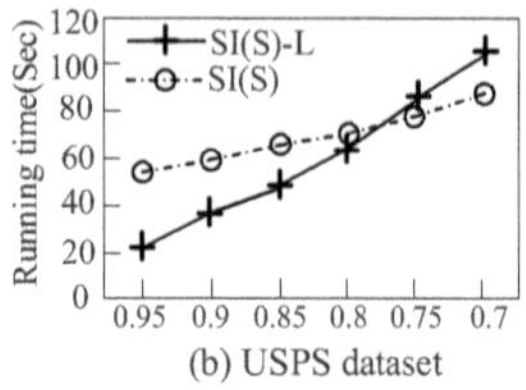

Figure 18: Prefix scheme vs. LSH scheme (with varying threshold values).

our estimator is only $0.81s$ while the filtering time is $83.7s$ and the total running time is $113.4s$.

Summary Finally, we summarize our findings.

(1) Considering four similarity measures. we observe that Jaccard is inadequate due to its complete neglect of synonym rules. JaccT is not efficient because it enumerates all transformed strings and entails large query overhead. Full-expansion is extremely efficiently, but its F-measure is not as good as Selective-expansion, which makes a good balance between effectiveness and efficiency.

(2) With respect to three similarity join algorithms, SI-join is the winner in all settings over JaccT and SN-join, by using SI-tree to efficiently perform length filtering and signature filtering. We achieve a speedup of up to 50∼300x on three data sets over the state-of-the-art approach.

(3) Finally, 2DHS synopsis offers very good results, and is extremely efficient to estimate the filtering power of different filters, (<1 second , accounting for only 1% of the total running time), which strongly motivates its application in practice.

6. CONCLUSIONS

In this paper, we studied the problem of strings similarity measures and joins with semantic rules (i.e. synonyms). We proposed two expansion-based methods to measure the similarity of strings and a novel index structure called SI-tree to perform the similarity join. We also proposed an estimator to select signatures online to optimize the efficiency of signature filters in join algorithms. The estimator provides provably high-confidence and low-error estimates to compare the filtering power of filters with the logarithmic space and time complexity. The extensive experiments demonstrated the advantages of our proposed approach over the state-of-the-art methods in three data sets.

7. ACKNOWLEDGEMENTS

This research is partially supported by 973 Program of China (Project No. 2012CB316205), NSF China (No. 60903056), 863 National High-tech Research Plan of China (No. 2012AA011001), Beijing Natural Science Foundation (No. 4112030), and New Century Excellent Talents in University. Wei Wang is supported by ARC Discovery Projects DP130103401 and DP130103405.

8. REFERENCES

[1] N. Alon, Y. Matias, and M. Szegedy. The space complexity of approximating the frequency moments. In *STOC*, pages 20–29, 1996.

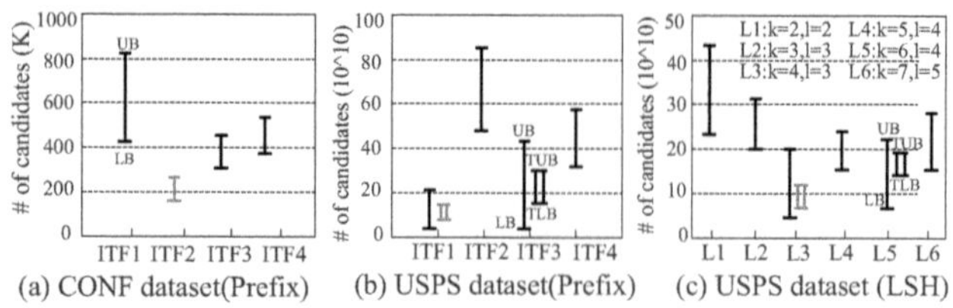

Figure 19: Estimation results of 2DHS synopsis for prefix and LSH schemes (threshold=0.90).

[2] A. Arasu, S. Chaudhuri, and R. Kaushik. Transformation-based framework for record matching. In *ICDE*, pages 40–49, 2008.

[3] A. Arasu, V. Ganti, and R. Kaushik. Efficient exact set-similarity joins. In *VLDB*, pages 918–929, 2006.

[4] Z. Bar-Yossef, T. S. Jayram, R. Kumar, D. Sivakumar, and L. Trevisan. Counting distinct elements in a data stream. In *RANDOM*, pages 1–10, 2002.

[5] R. J. Bayardo, Y. Ma, and R. Srikant. Scaling up all pairs similarity search. In *WWW*, pages 131–140, 2007.

[6] M. Bilenko and R. J. Mooney. Adaptive duplicate detection using learnable string similarity measures. In *KDD*, pages 39–48, 2003.

[7] A. Z. Broder, S. C. Glassman, M. S. Manasse, and G. Zweig. Syntactic clustering of the web. *Computer Networks*, 29(8-13):1157–1166, 1997.

[8] S. Chaudhuri, V. Ganti, and R. Kaushik. A primitive operator for similarity joins in data cleaning. In *ICDE*, page 5, 2006.

[9] S. Chaudhuri and R. Kaushik. Extending autocompletion to tolerate errors. In *SIGMOD Conference*, pages 707–718, 2009.

[10] W. W. Cohen, P. D. Ravikumar, and S. E. Fienberg. A comparison of string distance metrics for name-matching tasks. In *IIWeb*, pages 73–78, 2003.

[11] M. Farach. Optimal suffix tree construction with large alphabets. In *FOCS*, pages 137–143, 1997.

[12] P. Flajolet and G. N. Martin. Probabilistic counting algorithms for data base applications. *J. Comput. Syst. Sci.*, 31(2):182–209, 1985.

[13] S. Ganguly, M. N. Garofalakis, and R. Rastogi. Tracking set-expression cardinalities over continuous update streams. *VLDB J.*, 13(4):354–369, 2004.

[14] L. Gravano, P. G. Ipeirotis, H. V. Jagadish, N. Koudas, S. Muthukrishnan, and D. Srivastava. Approximate string joins in a database (almost) for free. In *VLDB*, pages 491–500, 2001.

[15] K. Iwama and S. Tamaki. Improved upper bounds for 3-sat. In *SODA*, 2004.

[16] G. Kondrak. *N*-gram similarity and distance. In *SPIRE*, pages 115–126, 2005.

[17] H. Lee, R. T. Ng, and K. Shim. Power-law based estimation of set similarity join size. *PVLDB*, 2(1):658–669, 2009.

[18] H. Lee, R. T. Ng, and K. Shim. Similarity join size estimation using locality sensitive hashing. *PVLDB*, 4(6):338–349, 2011.

[19] C. Li, J. Lu, and Y. Lu. Efficient merging and filtering algorithms for approximate string searches. In *ICDE*, pages 257–266, 2008.

[20] G. Li, D. Deng, J. Wang, and J. Feng. Pass-join: A partition-based method for similarity joins. In *VLDB*, 2012.

[21] D. R. H. Miller, T. Leek, and R. M. Schwartz. A hidden markov model information retrieval system. In *SIGIR*, pages 214–221, 1999.

[22] J. Qin, W. Wang, Y. Lu, C. Xiao, and X. Lin. Efficient exact edit similarity query processing with the asymmetric signature scheme. In *SIGMOD Conference*, pages 1033–1044, 2011.

[23] G. Salton and C. Buckley. Term-weighting approaches in automatic text retrieval. *Inf. Process. Manage.*, 24(5):513–523, 1988.

[24] S. Sarawagi and A. Kirpal. Efficient set joins on similarity predicates. In *SIGMOD Conference*, pages 743–754, 2004.

[25] Y. Tsuruoka, J. McNaught, J. Tsujii, and S. Ananiadou. Learning string similarity measures for gene/protein name dictionary look-up using logistic regression. *Bioinformatics*, 23(20):2768–2774, 2007.

[26] J. Wang, G. Li, and J. Feng. Trie-join: Efficient trie-based string similarity joins with edit-distance constraints. *PVLDB*, 3(1):1219–1230, 2010.

[27] J. Wang, G. Li, and J. Feng. Can we beat the prefix filtering?: an adaptive framework for similarity join and search. In *SIGMOD Conference*, pages 85–96, 2012.

[28] W. Wang, C. Xiao, X. Lin, and C. Zhang. Efficient approximate entity extraction with edit distance constraints. In *SIGMOD Conference*, pages 759–770, 2009.

[29] W. E. Winkler. The state of record linkage and current research problems. Technical report, Statistical Research Division, U.S. Census Bureau, 1999.

[30] C. Xiao, J. Qin, W. Wang, Y. Ishikawa, K. Tsuda, and K. Sadakane. Efficient error-tolerant query autocompletion. *PVLDB*, 2013.

[31] C. Xiao, W. Wang, X. Lin, J. X. Yu, and G. Wang. Efficient similarity joins for near-duplicate detection. *ACM Trans. Database Syst.*, 36(3):15, 2011.

Efficient Top-k Algorithms for Approximate Substring Matching

Younghoon Kim
Seoul National University
Seoul, Korea
yhkim@kdd.snu.ac.kr

Kyuseok Shim
Seoul National University
Seoul, Korea
shim@ee.snu.ac.kr

ABSTRACT

There is a wide range of applications that require to query a large database of texts to search for similar strings or substrings. Traditional approximate substring matching requests a user to specify a similarity threshold. Without top-k approximate substring matching, users have to try repeatedly different maximum distance threshold values when the proper threshold is unknown in advance.

In our paper, we first propose the efficient algorithms for finding the top-k approximate substring matches with a given query string in a set of data strings. To reduce the number of expensive distance computations, the proposed algorithms utilize our novel filtering techniques which take advantages of q-grams and inverted q-gram indexes available. We conduct extensive experiments with real-life data sets. Our experimental results confirm the effectiveness and scalability of our proposed algorithms.

Categories and Subject Descriptors

H.2 [**Database Management**]: Systems—*query processing, textual databases*

Keywords

Top-k approximate substring matching; edit distance; inverted q-gram index

1. INTRODUCTION

There is a wide range of applications that require to query a large database of texts to search for similar strings or substrings. A list of possible applications includes substring matching or short snippet suggestions for web search [23], named entity recognition [27], bio-informatics for finding DNA subsequences [20], music data retrieval [18] and spell checking [26]. These applications generally require high performance for real-time query processing to find similar substrings from text databases. While these applications are not all new, as there is an increasing trend of applications to deal with vast amounts of data, retrieving similar strings becomes a more challenging problem today.

To handle approximate substring matching, various string (dis)similarity measures, such as edit distance, hamming distance, Jaccard coefficient, cosine similarity and Jaro-Winkler distance have been considered [2, 10, 11, 19]. Among them, the edit distance is one of the most widely accepted distance measures for database applications where domain specific knowledge is not really available [10, 12, 20, 27].

Based on the edit distance, the approximate string matching problem is to find every string from a string database whose edit distance to the query string is not larger than a given maximum distance threshold. There are diverse applications requiring approximate string matching. For example, it is useful to check whether the names or addresses provided by users as input are correct by querying databases to search for the strings within a maximum distance threshold [29]. However, for databases with long strings, the containment search of a query string called *approximate substring matching* is more reasonable.

Id	String	Id	String
s_1	Jackson Pollock	s_4	Jacksomville
s_2	Jakob Pollack	s_5	Jakson Pollack
s_3	Jason Polock	s_6	Mackson Polock

Figure 1: An example of a string database D

Two different problem definitions have been introduced for approximate substring matching. In the first definition, the problem is to discover all substrings of each string in a database, whose edit distances to the query string are within the given maximum threshold [4, 17, 27]. Consider a query string 'Jackson' and a database shown in Figure 1. If the maximum edit distance threshold is 2, with 'Jackson Pollock' alone, the substrings of 'Jacks', 'Jackso', 'Jackson', 'ackson' and 'ckson' are all included in the query result.

Another popular definition of the approximate substring matching problem is to retrieve every string s whose *substring edit distance* to the query string σ is at most the given maximum threshold, where the substring edit distance between σ and s is the smallest edit distance among the ones between σ and all substrings in s [13, 25]. For example, let us reconsider the string database in Figure 1 and the query string 'Jackson'. If the maximum threshold is 2, the approximate substring matches are {'Jackson Pollock', 'Jason Polock', 'Jacksomville', 'Jakson Pollack', 'Mackson Polock'}.

All previous studies of approximate string or substring matching mentioned so far require each user to provide a maximum distance threshold. However, in many applications, it is very difficult for each user to know a proper

SIGMOD'13, June 22–27, 2013, New York, New York, USA.

threshold in advance since it depends on the application scenarios. An appealing alternative method is to compute the most similar k strings or substrings without the need to specify a maximum distance threshold. Without such top-k approximate matching, users have to try different distance threshold values, which may lead to empty results (if the threshold chosen is too low) or too many results with a long running time (if the threshold is too high). It also supports interactive applications, where users are presented with top-k most similar strings or substrings progressively.

In our paper, we propose the efficient algorithms for the top-k approximate substring matching problem which find the top-k strings whose substring edit distances to the query string are the smallest among all strings in a given database. Contrast to traditional approximate substring matching, top-k approximate substring matching (1) does not require each user to provide a maximum distance threshold, and (2) finds the top-k strings in data whose 'substring edit distances' to a given query string are the k smallest values. To the best of our knowledge, no existing work has addressed the top-k approximate substring matching problem and our algorithms presented in this paper are the first work for the problem.

EXAMPLE 1.1: *Consider the string data in Figure 1. Suppose that the query string σ is 'Jackson' and $k = 3$. Since s_1 has the substring which is exactly σ, its substring edit distance to σ is 0. For s_4 and s_5, the substring edit distances to σ are 1 since s_4 and s_5 have 'Jacksom' and 'Jakson' respectively. For other strings, the substring edit distances to σ are at least* 1. *Thus, the top-3 approximate substring matches are {'Jackson Pollock', 'Jacksomville', 'Jakson Pollack'}.* ∎

Given a set of strings D and a query string σ, a naive algorithm of top-k approximate substring matching examines every string s in D and compute the substring edit distance $d_{sub}(s, \sigma)$ one by one. We refer to the brute-force algorithm as *TopK-NAIVE*. Since computation of substring edit distance $d_{sub}(s, \sigma)$ is very expensive, we develop more efficient algorithms by utilizing q-grams in the query strings and available inverted q-gram indexes adopted widely to find approximate string matches [9]. This paper makes the following contributions:

- We first propose the algorithm *TopK-LB*, which reduces the number of substring edit distance computations in *TopK-NAIVE*, by checking each string s with a lower bound of $d_{sub}(s, \sigma)$ first based on dynamic programming.
- We next present the algorithm *TopK-SPLIT* which allows not to calculate the lower bounds of $d_{sub}(s, \sigma)$ for some strings by dividing data D into partitions based on q-grams and utilizing our proposed lower bound of $d_{sub}(s, \sigma)$ between σ and all strings in each partition.
- We also develop the algorithm *TopK-INDEX* that can speed up *TopK-SPLIT* by utilizing the posting lists of some q-grams in the query string, which can be obtained from the existing inverted positional q-gram index, whenever it is available by DBMSs.
- We conducted an extensive performance study of our proposed algorithms with real-life data sets. When there is no inverted q-gram index, we found that *TopK-SPLIT* is the best performer and faster than *TopK-NAIVE* by an order of magnitude. Whenever the inverted indexes are available, *TopK-INDEX* is the best and much faster than *TopK-SPLIT*. Experimental results also confirm that our algorithms outperform the extended traditional algorithms significantly and scale up well with large data sizes.

2. PRELIMINARIES

In this section, we provide definitions used in our paper and present a precise statement of the problem for the top-k approximate substring matching.

2.1 Notations and our Problem Definition

Let Σ be a finite alphabet of size $|\Sigma|$. For a string s of Σ^*, we denote the length of s with $|s|$. We use $s[i,j]$ with $1{\le}i{\le}j{\le}|s|$ to denote the substring of s which starts from position i and ends at position j. Similarly, $s[i]$ with $1{\le}i{\le}|s|$ denotes the character at the i-th position of s.

Edit distance: For two strings s_i and s_j, s_i can be transformed to s_j by applying repeatedly the three operations: insertion, deletion and substitution. The *edit distance* between s_i and s_j, which is denoted by $d(s_i, s_j)$, is defined as the minimum number of operations needed to transform s_i to s_j (or s_j to s_i). The dynamic programming algorithm to compute the edit distance between two strings s_i and s_j takes $O(|\sigma| \cdot |s|)$ time [14].

Substring edit distance: The substring edit distance from a string s to another string σ, which is represented by $d_{sub}(s, \sigma)$, is the minimum among the edit distance between σ and every substring of s. The $O(|\sigma|{\cdot}|s|)$-time algorithm based on dynamic programming to compute the substring edit distance is presented in [24]. (For more details, read [24, 25].)

We next present the definition of our *top-k approximate substring matching* problem.

DEFINITION 2.1: (Top-k Approximate Substring Matching) *Given a set of strings D and a query string σ, the top-k approximate substring matching problem is to find the k approximate strings $TOP_k(\sigma) = \langle s_1, s_2, ..., s_k \rangle$ in D which is an ordered sequence of k strings satisfying the following conditions:*

- $d_{sub}(s_1, \sigma) \le d_{sub}(s_2, \sigma) \le \cdots \le d_{sub}(s_k, \sigma)$ *holds.*
- *For every $s_j{\in}D$ such that $s_j {\notin} TOP_k(\sigma)$, we have* $d_{sub}(s_k, \sigma) \le d_{sub}(s_j, \sigma)$.

EXAMPLE 2.2.: *Consider the strings shown in Figure 1. Suppose that the query string σ is 'Jackson' and we are interested in the top-2 approximate substring matches $TOP_2(\sigma)$. Since s_1 includes σ as a substring, the substring edit distance $d_{sub}(s_1, \sigma)$ is 0. For the string s_4, $d_{sub}(s_4, \sigma)$ is 1 because s_4 has a substring 'Jacksom'. For other strings, the substring edit distances to σ are at least* 1. *Thus, we get* $TOP_2(\sigma)=\{s_1,s_4\}$. ∎

2.2 The q-grams and Inverted q-gram Indexes

We define q-grams and positional q-grams as follows.

DEFINITION 2.3.: *The* q-grams *of a string s are $s[i, i+q-1]s$ with all $1{\le}i{\le}(|s|{-}q{+}1)$. The* positional q-grams *of a string s are all pairs of each q-gram in s and its position (i.e., $(s[i, i+q-1], i)$ with $1{\le}i{\le}(|s|{-}q{+}1)$).*

EXAMPLE 2.4: *For the string s='Jackson' and q=3, ('Jac', 1), ('ack',2), ('cks',3), ('kso',4) and ('son',5) are the positional* 3*-grams of the string s.* ∎

Given a q-gram and a string containing the q-gram, a pair of its string id and the position where the q-gram occurs in the string is called a *posting*. With a set of strings D, the *posting list* of a q-gram is the list of postings for every occurrence of the q-gram in all strings in D. Note that every posting list is primarily sorted in increasing order of string

q-gram	posting list	q-gram	posting list	q-gram	posting list
Jac	$(s_1,1)$, $(s_4,1)$	llo	$(s_1,11)$	ack	$(s_2,11)$, $(s_5,12)$
ack	$(s_1,2)$, $(s_4,2)$, $(s_6,2)$	loc	$(s_1,12)$, $(s_3,10)$, $(s_6,11)$	Jas	$(s_3,1)$
cks	$(s_1,3)$, $(s_4,3)$, $(s_6,3)$	ock	$(s_1,13)$, $(s_3,11)$, $(s_6,12)$	aso	$(s_3,2)$
kso	$(s_1,4)$, $(s_4,4)$, $(s_5,3)$,$(s_6,4)$	Jak	$(s_2,1)$, $(s_5,1)$	omv	$(s_4,6)$
son	$(s_1,5)$, $(s_3,3)$, $(s_4,5)$, $(s_5,4)$, $(s_6,5)$	ako	$(s_2,2)$	mvi	$(s_4,7)$
on_	$(s_1,6)$, $(s_3,4)$, $(s_5,5)$, $(s_6,6)$	kob	$(s_2,3)$	vil	$(s_4,8)$
n_P	$(s_1,7)$, $(s_3,5)$, $(s_5,6)$, $(s_6,7)$	ob_	$(s_2,4)$	ill	$(s_4,9)$
_Po	$(s_1,8)$, $(s_2,6)$, $(s_3,6)$, $(s_5,7)$, $(s_6,8)$	b_P	$(s_2,5)$	lle	$(s_4,10)$
Pol	$(s_1,9)$, $(s_2,7)$, $(s_3,7)$, $(s_5,8)$, $(s_6,9)$	lla	$(s_2,9)$, $(s_5,10)$	aks	$(s_5,2)$
oll	$(s_1,10)$, $(s_2,8)$, $(s_5,9)$	lac	$(s_2,10)$, $(s_5,11)$	kso	$(s_5,3)$
olo	$(s_3,8)$, $(s_6,10)$	Mac	$(s_6,1)$	som	$(s_4,6)$

Figure 2: An inverted index for the database D

ids and secondarily sorted in ascending order of positions. With an *inverted q-gram index* of D, we can access the posting lists with q-grams as keys. In Figure 2, we show the inverted 3-gram index of the strings in Figure 1.

3. THE LOWER BOUNDS OF SUBSTRING EDIT DISTANCES

In this section, to identify the strings in D which do not need to compute actual substring edit distances, we present how to compute the lower bounds of substring edit distances by utilizing q-gram properties. For correctness and efficiency, we develop our techniques to guarantee *no false dismissals* and *few false positives*, respectively. To achieve these goals, we devise several filtering methods.

3.1 A Lower Bound of $d_{sub}(s, \sigma)$

We denote the lower bound of the edit distance $d(s,\sigma)$ between a string s and a query string σ by $\ell o(d(s,\sigma))$. The following lemma borrowed from [9] allows us to compute $\ell o(d(s,\sigma))$.

LEMMA 3.1: *[9] Given a query string σ and a string s, if s has at most c common q-grams with σ, the edit distance between $d(s,\sigma)$ satisfies the following inequality.*

$$d(s,\sigma) \geq \lceil(\max(|\sigma|,|s|) - q + 1 - c)/q\rceil$$

In other words, $\ell o(d(s,\sigma)) = \lceil(\max(|\sigma|,|s|) - q + 1 - c)/q\rceil$.

We now present the lemma below which allows us to compute a lower bound of the substring edit distance $d_{sub}(s,\sigma)$ between a string s and a query string σ. Remember that $s[i,j]$ denotes the substring of s which starts from position i and ends at position j.

LEMMA 3.2: *Consider a query string σ and a string s. Let c be the number of common q-grams between σ and s. Furthermore, let c_i be the number of common q-grams between σ and $s[i, i+|\sigma|\text{-}1]$. Then, the lower bound of $d_{sub}(s,\sigma)$, represented by $\ell o(d_{sub}(s,\sigma))$, is*

$$\ell o(d_{sub}(s,\sigma)) =$$
$$\begin{cases} \lceil(|\sigma| - q + 1 - c)/q\rceil, & \text{if } |s| < |\sigma|, \\ \min_{1\leq i\leq|s|-|\sigma|+1}\lceil(|\sigma| - q + 1 - c_i)/q\rceil, & \text{otherwise.} \end{cases} \quad (1)$$

Proof: If $|s| < |\sigma|$, σ cannot be a substring of s. Thus, the lower bound of $d_{sub}(s,\sigma)$ is the same as the lower bound of $d(s,\sigma)$ which is actually $\lceil(|\sigma|-q+1-c)/q\rceil$ by Lemma 3.1.

When $|s| \geq |\sigma|$, in order to compute the lower bound of $d_{sub}(s,\sigma)$, we can enumerate every substring s' of s and compute the lower bound of edit distance between σ and every substring s'.

Consider a substring $s[i,i+\ell-1]$ of length ℓ. If ℓ is larger than $|\sigma|$, the lower bound of $d(s[i,i+\ell-1],\sigma)$, denoted by $\ell o(d(s[i,i+\ell-1),\sigma))$, is at least $\ell o(d(s[i,i+|\sigma|-1],\sigma))$. It is because the lower bound derived by Lemma 3.1 monotonically grows with increasing the length of string s. Since computing a substring edit distance requires to find the substring with the minimum edit distance to σ, we can ignore the substrings of s whose lengths are larger than $|\sigma|$. Thus, $\ell o(d_{sub}(s,\sigma))$ is the minimum one among $\ell o(d(s[i,i+|\sigma|-1],\sigma))$s with $1\leq i\leq|s|-|\sigma|+1$. ∎

To compute $\ell o(d_{sub}(s,\sigma))$ based on the above Lemma, if we count the common q-grams between σ and every substring $s[i,i+|\sigma|-1]$ with $1\leq i\leq|s|-|\sigma|+1$, it takes $O(|\sigma|\cdot|s|)$ time. We now present the algorithm called *DYN-LB* which computes a tighter lower bound $\ell o(d_{sub}(s,\sigma))$ based on dynamic programming by utilizing the positions of matching q-grams with $O(\ell^2)$ time, where ℓ represents the number of matching q-gram pairs between s and σ. Note that we generally have $\ell \ll \min(|s|,|\sigma|)$.

Applying dynamic programming: We use the following notations for a query string σ and a string s in our dynamic programming formulation.

- Let $X_\sigma=\langle(x_1,p_1),\ldots,(x_{|X_\sigma|},p_{|X_\sigma|})\rangle$ be the sequence of positional q-grams from σ, each q-gram of which appears in the string s, satisfying $p_i < p_{i+1}$ for i=1,...,$|X_\sigma|-1$. Similarly, let $Y_s=\langle(y_1,r_1),\ldots,(y_{|Y_s|},r_{|Y_s|})\rangle$ be the sequence of positional q-grams from s, each q-gram of which occurs in σ, satisfying $r_i < r_{i+1}$ for i=1,...,$|Y_s|-1$.
- For a positional q-gram pair $\langle(x_i,p_i),(y_j,r_j)\rangle$ with $(x_i,p_i) \in X_\sigma$, $(y_j,r_j) \in Y_s$ and $x_i=y_j$, let $m[i,j]$ represent the lower bound of all edit distances $d(\sigma[1,p_i+q-1],s')$ where s' is every substring of s ending at position r_j+q-1.
- For two positional q-gram pairs $\{(x_u,p_u),(x_i,p_i)\} \subseteq X_\sigma$ and $\{(y_v,r_v),(y_j,r_j)\} \subseteq Y_s$ satisfying $x_u=y_v$, $x_i=y_j$, $p_u<p_i$ and $r_v<r_j$, let $\delta(p_u,p_i,r_v,r_j)$ denote the lower bound of the edit distance $d(\sigma[p_u,p_i+q-1],s[r_v,r_j+q-1])$.

Computing $m[i,j]$: For a positional q-gram pair $\langle(x_i,p_i),(y_j,r_j)\rangle$ such that $(x_i,p_i) \in X_\sigma$, $(y_j,r_j) \in Y_s$ and $x_i=y_j$, depending on whether x_i $(=y_j)$ is the only common q-gram between $\sigma[1,p_i+q-1]$ and every substring of s ending at position r_j+q-1 or not, we split into two cases.

(1) When x_i $(=y_j)$ is the only common q-gram between $\sigma[1,p_i+q-1]$ and every substring of s ending at position r_j+q-1, the edit distance between them is at least $\lceil(p_i-1)/q\rceil$ due to to Lemma 3.2.

(2) Otherwise, suppose that $\langle(x_u,p_u),(y_v,r_v)\rangle$ is the last positional q-gram pair satisfying $p_u<p_i$, $r_v<r_j$ and $x_u=y_v$, which minimizes $m[i,j]$. Then, for every such a matching q-gram pair $\langle(x_u,p_u),(y_v,r_v)\rangle$, $m[i,j]$ (i.e., the lower bound of the edit distance between $\sigma[1,p_i+q-1]$ and every substring of s ending at position r_j+q-1) is the sum of $m[u,v]$ and $\delta(p_u,p_i,r_v,r_j)$ (i.e., the lower bound of the edit distance $d(\sigma[p_u,p_i+q-1],s[r_v,r_j+q-1])$). Since showing the optimal substructure of this problem is easy, we omit the proof.

Since we do not know the positional q-gram pair $\langle(x_u,p_u),(y_v,r_v)\rangle$ satisfying $p_u<p_i$, $r_v<r_j$ and $x_u=y_v$ between $\sigma[1,p_i+q-1]$ and every substring of s ending at position r_j+q-1, we consider every $\langle(x_u,p_u),(y_v,r_v)\rangle \in X\times Y$ as the last matching pair followed by $\langle(x_i,p_i),(y_j,r_j)\rangle$ to compute $m[i,j]$. Thus, the recursive solution to compute $m[i,j]$ is

$$m[i,j] = \min\{\lceil(p_i-1)/q\rceil, \min_{\substack{\forall\langle(x_u,p_u),(y_v,r_v)\rangle\in X\times Y: \\ (x_u=y_v)\wedge(p_u<p_i)\wedge(r_v<r_j)}}\{m[u,v]+\delta(p_u,p_i,r_v,r_j)\}\}. \quad (2)$$

For every pair $\langle(x_1,p_1),(y_j,r_j)\rangle$ with $x_1=y_j$, there is only a single matching q-gram between $\sigma[1,p_1+q-1]$ and every substring of s ending at position r_j+q-1, and thus we set $m[1,j]$ to $\lceil(p_1-1)/q\rceil$ according to Lemma 3.2.

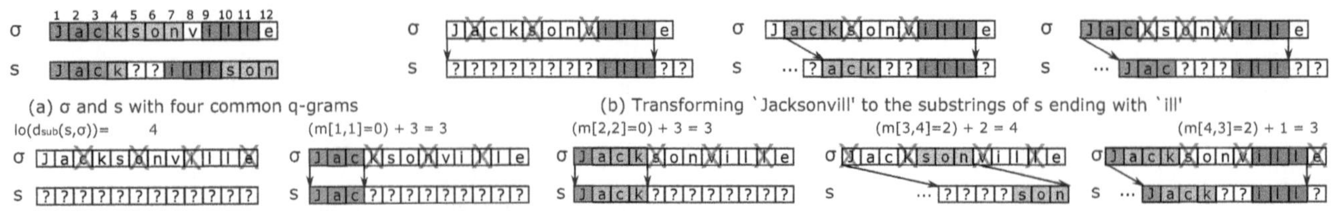

Figure 3: Computing the lower bound of $d_{sub}(s, \sigma)$ with DYN-LB

Computing $\ell o(d_{sub}(s, \sigma))$: Now we show how to compute $\ell o(d_{sub}(s, \sigma))$ using $m[i, j]$. When every q-gram in σ is modified, the lower bound of $d_{sub}(s, \sigma)$ is $\lceil (|\sigma| - q + 1)/q \rceil$ due to Lemma 3.2. Otherwise, suppose that the last matching q-gram pair is $\langle (x_i, p_i), (y_j, r_j) \rangle$ with $(x_i, p_i) \in X_\sigma$, $(y_j, r_j) \in Y_s$ and $x_i = y_j$. The lower bound of $d_{sub}(s, \sigma)$ is the sum of $m[i, j]$ and the minimum number of edit operations to modify every remaining q-gram in $\sigma[p_i+1, |\sigma|]$ so that there is no matching q-gram between $\sigma[p_i+1, |\sigma|]$ and $s[r_j+1, |s|]$, which is $\lceil (|\sigma| - p_i - q + 1)/q \rceil$ according to Lemma 3.2. Since we do not know the actual last matching positional q-gram pair, we consider every $\langle (x_i, p_i), (y_j, r_j) \rangle \in X \times Y$ such that $x_i = y_j$ as the last matching pair to compute $\ell o(d_{sub}(s, \sigma))$. Thus, the lower bound of $d_{sub}(s, \sigma)$ is

$$\min\{\lceil (|\sigma| - q + 1)/q \rceil, \min_{1 \le i \le |X_\sigma|, 1 \le j \le |Y_s|} \{m[i, j] + \lceil (|\sigma| - p_i - q + 1)/q \rceil\}. \quad (3)$$

Computing $\delta(\mathbf{p_u}, \mathbf{p_i}, \mathbf{r_v}, \mathbf{r_j})$: Given two positional q-gram pairs $\{(x_u, p_u), (x_i, p_i)\} \subseteq X_\sigma$ and $\{(y_v, r_v), (y_j, r_j)\} \subseteq Y_s$ satisfying $x_u = y_v$, $x_i = y_j$, $p_u < p_i$ and $r_v < r_j$, the transformation from $\sigma[p_u, p_i+q-1]$ to $s[r_v, r_j+q-1]$ by performing at least an edit operation on every q-gram in $\sigma[p_u, p_i+q-1]$ except the two q-grams (x_u, p_u) and (x_i, p_i) is the same as converting $\sigma[p_u+1, p_i+q-2]$ to $s[r_v+1, r_j+q-2]$ by modifying every q-gram in $\sigma[p_u+1, p_i+q-2]$ without exception.

The lower bound of the edit distance for the transformation performing at least an edit operation on every q-gram in $\sigma[p_u+1, p_i+q-2]$ is $\lceil (p_i - p_u - 1)/q \rceil$ $(= \lceil (((p_i+q-2) - (p_u+1) + 1) - q + 1 - 0)/q \rceil)$ due to Lemma 3.2. Furthermore, the difference between the lengths of two strings is a definite lower bound of the edit distance [9]. Thus, $\delta(p_u, p_i, r_v, r_j)$ becomes $\max\{\lceil (p_i - p_u - 1)/q \rceil, |(p_i - p_u) - (r_j - r_v)|\}$.

Time complexity: Let ℓ be the number of matching q-gram pairs $\langle (x_i, p_i), (y_j, r_j) \rangle \in X \times Y$ such that $x_i = y_j$. Since the number of entries $m[i, j]$ is ℓ and it takes $O(\ell)$ time to compute each $m[i, j]$ in Equation (2), the time complexity of *DYN-LB* is $O(\ell^2)$.

EXAMPLE 3.3: *Suppose we have σ='Jacksonville' of length 12 and s='Jack Willson'. The matching positional q-gram sets in σ and s are X_σ={(Jac,1), (ack,2), (son,5), (ill,9)} and Y_s={(Jac,1), (ack,2), (ill,7), (son,10)} respectively as illustrated in Figure 3(a). With the first matching q-gram 'Jac' in both X_σ and Y_s, $m[1,1]$ becomes 0. With the second matching positional q-gram pair (x_2, p_2)=(ack,2) in X_σ and (y_2, p_2)=(ack,2) in Y_s, $m[2,2]$ becomes 0. With the next matching q-grams (x_4, p_4)=(ill,9) in X_σ and (y_3, p_3)=(ill,7) in Y_s, we consider the following transformations, as shown in Figure 3(b):*

- *The transformation that modifies every q-gram except the last q-gram (ill,9) in σ, which takes at least 3 edit operations ($= \lceil (9-1)/3 \rceil$).*
- *Modifying $\sigma[1,4]$='Jack' to a substring of s ending with 'ack' followed by changing 'acksonvill' to 'ack Will', which requires at least 2 edit operations ($= m[2,2] + \max(\lceil (9-2-1)/3 \rceil, |10-8|)$).*
- *Transforming $\sigma[1,3]$='Jac' to $s[1,3]$='Jac' and converting 'Jacksonvill' to 'Jack Will', which needs at least 3 edit operations ($= m[1,1] + \max(\lceil (9-1-1)/3 \rceil, |11-9|)$).*

Now, $m[4,3]$ becomes 2. Similarly, we obtain $m[3,4]$=2. Finally, to compute the lower bound of $d_{sub}(s, \sigma)$ by Equation (3), we examine the lower bounds by the five transformations in Figure 3(c), such that every matching q-gram in X_σ is modified or each q-gram in X is the right most q-gram which is not changed. Then, we obtain 3 as the lower bound of $d_{sub}(s, \sigma)$. ∎

3.2 A Lower Bound of Substring Edit Distances between a Query and a Set of Strings

Previously, we could compute the lower bound of $d_{sub}(s, \sigma)$ using the common q-grams between a query string σ and the string s. However, we next show how to compute the lower bound of $d_{sub}(s, \sigma)$ using the mismatching q-grams from σ to s (i.e., the q-grams occurring in σ but not in s).

LEMMA 3.4: *Consider a query string σ and a string s. If the number of mismatching q-grams from σ to s is at least m, we have $d_{sub}(s, \sigma) \ge \lceil m/q \rceil$.*

Proof: When a string s_2 is obtained by applying a single edit operation on a string s_1, we have at most q mismatching q-grams from s_1 to s_2. Since at least m q-grams in σ do not appear in s, we need at least $\lceil m/q \rceil$ edit operations to convert σ to s (i.e., $\ell o(d(s, \sigma)) = \lceil m/q \rceil$). Furthermore, for every substring s' of the string s, since the number of mismatching q-grams from σ to s' is at least that of mismatching q-grams from σ to s, we can claim that the number of mismatching q-grams from σ to s' is at least m. Thus, we have $d(s', \sigma) \ge \lceil m/q \rceil$ for every substring s' of s and we can conclude $d_{sub}(s, \sigma) \ge \lceil m/q \rceil$. ∎

Consider a subset $G' \subseteq G$ where G is the set of all possible q-grams from σ. Assume that we partition D into $D^+_{G'}$ and $D^-_{G'}$ so that $D^+_{G'}$ is the set of strings in D which share at least a q-gram in G' and $D^-_{G'}$ is the rest of strings in D (i.e., $D^-_{G'} = D - D^+_{G'}$). Let $d_{sub}(D, \sigma)$ represent the smallest substring edit distance between σ and every string s in D. We denote the lower bound of $d_{sub}(D, \sigma)$ by $\ell o(d_{sub}(D, \sigma))$.

The lower bounds of $d_{sub}(D^-_{G'}, \sigma)$: We can compute a lower bound of the substring edit distances between σ and every string in $D^-_{G'}$ by the following lemma.

LEMMA 3.5: *Assume that we have a set of strings D and a query string σ. For each subset $G' \subseteq G$ where G is the q-gram set of σ, we have $d_{sub}(D^-_{G'}, \sigma) \ge \lceil |G'|/q \rceil$.*

Proof: Due to Lemma 3.4, for every string s in $D^-_{G'}$ which does not include any q-gram in G', $d_{sub}(s, \sigma) \geq \lceil |G'|/q \rceil$ holds. Thus, we have $d_{sub}(D^-_{G'}, \sigma) \geq \lceil |G'|/q \rceil$. ∎

While the lower bound of obtained by Lemma 3.5 is effective, it does not consider the positions of the q-grams in σ. In other words, we assumed that every q-gram in G' may overlap with another q-gram in G' in at least a position of σ. However, if we choose the q-grams for G' such that every q-gram in G' does not overlap with another q-gram in G', we can obtain a tighter lower bound of $\ell o(d_{sub}(D^-_{G'}, \sigma))$.

LEMMA 3.6.: *Let G be the set of all q-grams in a query string σ. If we select a subset $G' \subseteq G$ in which every q-gram does not overlap with another q-gram in G', we have $d_{sub}(D^-_{G'}, \sigma) \geq |G'|$.*

Proof: For each string s in $D^-_{G'}$, suppose that we perform edit operations on σ to convert it to a substring of s. Since every q-gram in G' does not appear in s, every q-gram in G' should be modified by at least an edit operation. However, every q-gram in G' does not overlap with another q-gram in G' and thus a single edit operation cannot affect multiple q-grams. Thus, for every string s in $D^-_{G'}$, we need at least $|G'|$ edit operations to transform σ to any substring of s. ∎

EXAMPLE 3.7: *Suppose we have a query string σ='Jackson' and G'={'Jac','kso'} in which every 3-gram does not overlap with another q-gram in G'. The strings in $D^-_{G'}$ are the strings which do not have even one of the 3-grams in G'. Since each 3-gram in G' does not overlap with another one, to transform σ to every substring of each string in $D^-_{G'}$, we need at least 2 edit operations (an edit operation on each of 'Jac' and 'kso') in σ. Note that we have $d_{sub}(D^-_{G'}, \sigma) \geq 2$ by Lemma 3.6.* ∎

If we fix the size of $G' \subseteq G$, we obtain the tightest lower bound $\ell o(d_{sub}(D^-_{G'}, \sigma))$ when G' is selected without any pair of overlapping q-grams.

COROLLARY 3.8: *Consider a query string σ and let G be the set of q-grams in σ. We obtain the tightest lower bound $\ell o(d_{sub}(D^-_{G'}, \sigma))$ among every possible $G' \subseteq G$ when the size of G' is $\lfloor |\sigma|/q \rfloor$.*

Proof: This is because we cannot select a set of q-grams with a larger size than $\lfloor |\sigma|/q \rfloor$ in which every q-gram does not overlap with another q-gram in the set. ∎

We now introduce the following lemma to use Lemma 3.6 effectively for top-k approximate substring matching.

LEMMA 3.9: *Consider a set of strings D, a query string σ, the q-gram set G of σ and a subset $G' \subseteq G$. Assume that we partitioned D into $D^+_{G'}$ and $D^-_{G'}$. While examining every string in $D^+_{G'}$, if there are at least k strings whose substring edit distances to σ are at most $\ell o(d_{sub}(D^-_{G'}, \sigma))$, we can find the top-$k$ approximate substring matches in D by examining the remaining strings in $D^+_{G'}$ only by ignoring the remaining strings in $D^-_{G'}$.*

Proof: While examining every string in $D^+_{G'}$ one by one, let s_k denote the string with the k-th smallest substring edit distance $d_{sub}(s_k, \sigma)$ so far. Since $d_{sub}(s_k, \sigma) \leq \ell o(d_{sub}(D^-_{G'}, \sigma))$, for every string $s' \in D^-_{G'}$, $d_{sub}(s', \sigma)$ cannot get smaller than $d_{sub}(s_k, \sigma)$ and we can not have any string of the top-k approximate substring matches in $D^-_{G'}$. ∎

```
Function TopK-LB (D, k, σ)
begin
   H_TopK = an empty max-heap storing ⟨dist, str⟩;
   G = {σ[i,i+q−1]|1≤i≤|σ|−q+1};
   for each string s in D do
      R = {(s[i,i+q−1], i) |∀i s.t.1≤i≤|s|−q+1, s[i,i+q−1]∈G};
      LB = DYN-LB(R, |σ|);
      if |H_TopK|<k or LB<H_TopK.getMax().dist then
         d = d_sub(s, σ);
         if |H_TopK| < k then H_TopK.insert(⟨d,s⟩);
         else if H_TopK.getMax().dist > d then
            H_TopK.insert(⟨d,s⟩);
            H_TopK.deleteMax();
   end for
   return H_TopK;
end
```

Figure 4: The TopK-LB algorithm

4. TOP-K ALGORITHMS FOR APPROXIMATE SUBSTRING MATCHING

We first introduce the brute-force algorithm *TopK-NAIVE* which blindly examines every string s in a set of strings D and computes substring edit distances $d_{sub}(s, \sigma)$ one by one. Since distance computations are very expensive, to reduce the number of substring edit distances to compute, we propose the algorithm *TopK-LB* which computes $d_{sub}(s, \sigma)$ only when the lower bound $\ell o(d_{sub}(s, \sigma))$ is smaller than the current k-th smallest substring edit distance. The lower bound $\ell o(d_{sub}(s, \sigma))$ is computed by our novel dynamic programming algorithm in *TopK-LB*.

Since *TopK-LB* utilizes the algorithm based on dynamic programming to compute the lower bound $\ell o(d_{sub}(s, \sigma))$ with *every* string s in D, we next propose the algorithm *TopK-SPLIT* which can even skip the expensive computation of $\ell o(d_{sub}(s, \sigma))$ for some strings s in D. *TopK-SPLIT* divides D into partitions for a given q-gram set G' and utilizes our new lower bound of $d_{sub}(s, \sigma)$. We also develop a novel dynamic programming algorithm to find the best q-gram set G' to be used at the beginning of *TopK-SPLIT*. Furthermore, whenever the k-th substring edit distance becomes smaller, *TopK-SPLIT* adaptively adjusts G' so that we can skip even more strings for computing the lower bounds of $d_{sub}(s, \sigma)$.

TopK-SPLIT still examines every string in D and thus its running time increases proportionally to the size of D. To speed up *TopK-SPLIT* further, we develop *TopK-INDEX* that does not need to check every string in D by utilizing the inverted q-gram indexes, whenever they are available.

We next present the above algorithms for finding the top-k approximate substring matches in more details.

TopK-NAIVE: The naive algorithm examines every string s in D and computes the substring edit distance $d_{sub}(s, \sigma)$. To find the top-k approximate substring matches in D, we maintain a max-heap H_{TopK} storing the k strings s' with the smallest $d_{sub}(s', \sigma)$s which are used as the keys in the max-heap H_{TopK}. If the size of H_{TopK} is less than k, we just insert the string s to H_{TopK}. Otherwise, we check whether $d_{sub}(s, \sigma)$ is smaller than $d_{sub}(s_R, \sigma)$ of the string s_R at the root of H_{TopK} (i.e., whether $d_{sub}(s, \sigma)$ is smaller than the k-th smallest substring edit distance so far). If it is satisfied, we delete the string at the root s_R of H_{TopK} and insert the string s to H_{TopK}. If not, we move to the next string and repeat the above step until we encounter the last string in D. We refer to the naive algorithm as *TopK-NAIVE*.

TopK-LB: Similar to *TopK-NAIVE*, we scan all strings in D. However, for each string s in D, we generate the list of common positional q-grams $R = \langle (g_1, p_1), \ldots (g_n, p_n) \rangle$ between σ and s in increasing order of positions where the position p_i of each (g_i, p_i) in R is the position in s at which the q-gram g_i appears. Then, we can compute the lower bound $\ell o(d_{sub}(s, \sigma))$ by invoking *DYN-LB* presented in Section 3.1. If $\ell o(d_{sub}(s, \sigma))$ is not smaller than the k-th smallest substring edit distance so far, we do not need to calculate the actual value of $d_{sub}(s, \sigma)$ since s cannot be a string of the top-k approximate substring matches. We call the algorithm *TopK-LB* and present its pseudocode in Figure 4.

EXAMPLE 4.1.: *Consider the set of strings D in Figure 1. Suppose the query string σ='Jacksen' of length 7 and we are interested in the top-2 approximate matches. The first two strings s_1 and s_2, whose substring edit distances to σ are 1 and 4 respectively, are inserted into the max-heap H_{TopK}. For the next string s_3='Jason Polock', the lower bound $\ell o(d_{sub}(s_3, \sigma))$ is 2 by* DYN-LB. *Since the second smallest substring edit distance in H_{TopK} is 4 and $\ell o(d_{sub}(s_3, \sigma))$ is smaller than 4, we have to compute $d_{sub}(s_3, \sigma)$, which turns out to be 3, and insert $(s_3, 3)$ into H_{TopK}. Now we have $\{(s_1, 1), (s_3, 3)\}$ in H_{TopK} and the second smallest substring edit distance so far becomes 3.*

With s_4='Jacksomville', $\ell o(d_{sub}(s_4, \sigma))$ becomes 1. Since $\ell o(d_{sub}(s_4, \sigma))$ is smaller than the second smallest substring edit distance in H_{TopK}, we have to compute $d_{sub}(s_4, \sigma)$ which is 2 and $(s_4, 2)$ is added to H_{TopK}. Then, the second smallest substring edit distance so far becomes 2. For s_5='Jakson Pollack', $\ell o(d_{sub}(s_5, \sigma))$ is 2 and thus we can skip computing expensive $d_{sub}(s_5, \sigma)$. Finally, with s_6='Mackson Polock', $\ell o(d_{sub}(s_5, \sigma))$ is 1 and we should compute $d_{sub}(s_5, \sigma)$. In summary, we calculated the substring edit distances with 5 strings out of 6 strings. ∎

TopK-SPLIT: Let G be the set of all q-grams in σ and let G' be a subset of G such that every q-gram in G' does not overlap with another q-gram in the set. We conceptually divide the strings in D into $D^+_{G'}$ and $D^-_{G'}$ where $D^+_{G'}$ is the set of strings in D each of which has at least a q-gram in G' and $D^-_{G'}$ is $(D - D^+_{G'})$. While scanning each string s, we can check easily whether the string s belongs to $D^+_{G'}$ or $D^-_{G'}$ by checking the q-grams in s.

Similar to *TopK-LB*, when examining every string s in D one by one, *TopK-SPLIT* generates the list of common positional q-grams R and skips computing $d_{sub}(s, \sigma)$ if $\ell o(d_{sub}(s, \sigma))$ is at least the k-th smallest substring edit distance so far. However, unlike *TopK-LB*, *TopK-SPLIT* can even skip computing $\ell o(d_{sub}(s, \sigma))$ by using Lemma 3.9 for each string as follows.

Let s_R denote the string whose substring edit distance to σ (i.e., $d_{sub}(s_R, \sigma)$) is the k-th smallest value among the strings examined so far. Among the unseen strings, we can skip distance computations for the strings whose substring edit distances to σ are at least $d_{sub}(s_R, \sigma)$. Since we split D into $D^+_{G'}$ and $D^-_{G'}$, after $d_{sub}(s_R, \sigma)$ becomes at most $\ell o(d_{sub}(D^-_{G'}, \sigma))$, we can skip every unseen string s belonging to $D^-_{G'}$. In this case, we have

$$d_{sub}(s_R, \sigma) \leq |G'| \leq d_{sub}(D^-_{G'}, \sigma) \qquad (4)$$

since the lower bound of $d_{sub}(D^-_{G'}, \sigma)$ is $|G'|$ due to Lemma 3.6 regardless of the q-grams in G'. However, for the unseen strings $s \in D^+_{G'}$, we still have to compute $d_{sub}(s, \sigma)$.

Intuitively, the larger $|G'|$ is, the earlier the condition of $d_{sub}(s_R, \sigma) \leq |G'|$ in Inequality (4) can be satisfied. Thus,

```
Function TopK-SPLIT (D, k, σ)
begin
  H_TopK = an empty max-heap storing ⟨dist, str⟩;
  G = {σ[i,i+q−1]|1≤i≤|σ|−q+1};
  τ = ⌊|σ|/q⌋;
  cond = false;
  for each string s in D do
    R = {(s[i,i+q−1], i) |∀i s.t.1≤i≤|s|−q+1, s[i,i+q−1]∈G};
    if cond=true and ∃(g_i, p_i) ∈ R, g_i ∈ G' then part = '+';
    else part = '−';
    if cond=false or part = '+' then
      LB = DYN-LB(R, |σ|);
      if |H_TopK|<k or LB<H_TopK.getMax().dist then
        d = d_sub(s, σ);
        if |H_TopK|<k then H_TopK.insert(⟨d,s⟩);
        else if H_TopK.getMax().dist>d then
          H_TopK.insert(⟨d,s⟩);
          H_TopK.deleteMax();
        if H_TopK.getMax().dist≤τ then
          cond = true;
          τ = H_TopK.getMax().dist;
          G' = BEST-G'(τ, G);
      if cond=true and H_TopK.getMax().dist<τ then
        τ = H_TopK.getMax().dist;
        G' = BEST-G'(τ, G);
  end for
  return H_TopK;
end
```

Figure 5: The TopK-SPLIT algorithm

when $|G'|$ is large, we have a smaller number of strings in D to examine before $d_{sub}(s_R, \sigma) \leq |G'|$ holds. However, once the inequality is satisfied, with a large $|G'|$, the number of the unseen strings belonging to $D^+_{G'}$ also becomes generally large.

To satisfy $d_{sub}(s_R, \sigma) \leq |G'|$ as soon as possible, we initially set $|G'|$ with $\lfloor |\sigma|/q \rfloor$. Note that the lower bound of $d_{sub}(D^-_{G'}, \sigma)$ is $|G'|$ and cannot be larger than $\lfloor |\sigma|/q \rfloor$ due to Corollary 3.8. Furthermore, note that we need G' to determine $D^+_{G'}$ to prune unseen strings only when $d_{sub}(s_R, \sigma) \leq |G'|$ is satisfied, since the inequality holds in the same location in D regardless of G' with the same size of G'. Thus, once $d_{sub}(s_R, \sigma) \leq \lfloor |\sigma|/q \rfloor$ holds, while scanning strings in D, we compute G' of size $d_{sub}(s_R, \sigma)$ and next examine the unseen strings in $D^+_{G'}$ only. For a given size ρ of G', we will discuss how to select such a subset G' minimizing the number of strings in $D^+_{G'}$ in Section 5. Thus, for the time being, we will assume that such a G' is provided by the function *BEST-G'(ρ)*.

Let τ be the k-th substring edit distance when $d_{sub}(s_R, \sigma) \leq \lfloor |\sigma|/q \rfloor$ is first satisfied. While we examine the strings in D, the k-the smallest substring edit distance monotonically decreases. When the k-the smallest substring edit distance is changed from τ to τ'', we can still test the unseen strings in $D^+_{G'}$ only. However, since any G'' satisfying $|G''| < |G'|$ and $d_{sub}(s_R, \sigma) = \tau'' \leq |G''|$ allows us not to examine $D^-_{G''}$ and we have $|D^-_{G''}| \leq |D^-_{G'}|$ generally, we can select such a G'' and check the unseen strings in $D^+_{G''}$ only. We can perform the above step whenever the k-th substring edit distance decreases.

The pseudocode of *TopK-SPLIT* is provided in Figure 5. The lower bound of $d_{sub}(D^-_{G'}, \sigma)$ (i.e., τ) is set to $\lfloor |\sigma|/q \rfloor$ initially which is the largest one according to Corollary 3.8. The variable *cond* has *false* initially representing that the k-th smallest substring edit distance so far exceeds τ. Until we set *cond* as *true*, while scanning each string s in D, if $LB = \ell o(d_{sub}(s, \sigma))$ computed by *DYN-LB* is smaller than the k-th smallest substring edit distance so far, we compute the actual value of $d_{sub}(s, \sigma)$ similar to *TopK-LB*. However, once the k-th smallest substring edit distance (i.e.,

```
Function TopK-INDEX (D, I, k, σ)
begin
1.  H_TopK = an empty max-heap storing ⟨dist, str⟩;
2.  G = {σ[i,i+q−1]|1≤i≤|σ|−q+1};
3.  τ = |G'|;
4.  cond = false;
5.  while D.end() = false do
6.    sid_D = D.getCurrentId();
7.    sid_I = I.getFrontierId(G);
8.    s = null;
9.    if cond = false and sid_I > sid_D then
10.     s = D.getString(sid_D);
11.     R = {(s[i,i+q−1], i) |∀i s.t.1≤i≤|s|−q+1, s[i,i+q−1]∈G};
12.     if ∃(g_i, p_i) ∈ R, g_i ∈ G' then part = '+';
13.     else part = '−';
14.   else
15.     (R, part) = I.getPosQgrams(sid_I);
16.   if cond = false or part = '+' then
17.     LB = DYN-LB(R, |σ|);
18.     if |H_TopK|<k or LB<H_TopK.getMax().dist then
19.       if s = null then s = D.getString(sid_I);
20.       d = d_sub(s, σ);
21.       if |H_TopK| < k then H_TopK.insert(⟨d,s⟩);
22.       else if H_TopK.getMax().dist > d then
23.         H_TopK.insert(⟨d,s⟩);
24.         H_TopK.deleteMax();
25.         if H_TopK.getMax().dist≤τ then
26.           cond = true;
27.           τ = H_TopK.getMax().dist;
28.           G' = BEST-G'(τ, G);
29.       if cond=true and H_TopK.getMax().dist<τ then
30.         τ = H_TopK.getMax().dist;
31.         G' = BEST-G'(τ, G);
32. end while
33. return H_TopK;
end
```

Figure 6: The TopK-INDEX algorithm

H_{TopK}.getMax().dist) becomes at most τ, we set *cond* to *true* and select G' by calling *BEST-G'* in lines 17–21 so that we can skip the computation of $d_{sub}(s,\sigma)$ for the unseen strings $s \in D^-_{G'}$ by Lemma 3.9. Furthermore, whenever the k-th smallest substring edit distance decreases, we select G' with size of H_{TopK}.getMax().dist again in lines 23–26.

EXAMPLE 4.2: *Consider the strings D in Figure 1. Suppose we want to find the top-2 approximate substring matches the query string* σ = *'Jacksen' using 3-grams. The lower bound of* $d_{sub}(D^-_{G'},\sigma)$ *(i.e.,* τ*)* τ *is initially set to* $2(=\lfloor 7/3 \rfloor)$.

First, the strings s_1 *and* s_2 *are inserted into* H_{TopK} *whose substring edit distances to* σ *are 1 and 4 respectively. With* s_3 *and* s_4*, we compute* $d_{sub}(s_3,\sigma)(=3)$ *and* $d_{sub}(s_4,\sigma)(=2)$*, and then the second smallest substring edit distance in* H_{TopK} *becomes 2.*

We now have 2 strings whose substring edit distances are at most τ*. After selecting the q-grams set* $G' \subseteq G$ *by* BEST-G'*, we can skip computing* $d_{sub}(s,\sigma)$ *with the strings* $s \in D^-_{G'}$ *due to Lemma 3.9. Suppose that the selected 3-gram set* G' *is {'Jac', 'kse'}. Then, for the strings* s_5 *and* s_6*, we can ignore them because they do not have any common 3-gram with* G'*. In summary, we could find the top-2 approximate substring matches by calculating the substring edit distances with 4 strings only.* ∎

TopK-INDEX: When the k-th smallest substring edit distance so far becomes at most $|G'|$ in *TopK-SPLIT*, we can even skip computing $\ell o(d_{sub}(s,\sigma))$ with the strings s $\in D^-_{G'}$. However, we still have to read unseen string s in D to determine whether s belongs to $D^-_{G'}$ by checking if s has at least a q-gram in G'. We will next improve the inefficiency by retrieving the unseen strings belonging to $D^+_{G'}$ only with utilizing inverted q-gram indexes when they are available.

While scanning each string in D, our new algorithm *TopK-INDEX* also scans the posting lists of the q-grams in G together. We assume that the strings in D are sorted with increasing order of string ids and we are also able to retrieve the strings in D with string ids as keys by random I/O access. We also assume that the posting list of every q-gram in G is stored with the increasing order of string id first and its position next in the inverted q-gram index. By reading the posting lists of the q-grams in G only, we can obtain the common q-gram list R for the strings which share at least a q-gram with σ. Whenever we need to compute the actual substring distance $d_{sub}(s,\sigma)$, we actually access the string s stored in D. Since the size of each string in D is generally much larger than that of the query string σ, using the posting lists of the q-grams in G only speeds up the generation of R and computation of $\ell o(d_{sub}(s,\sigma))$ significantly.

After the condition to apply Lemma 3.9 is satisfied (i.e., $d_{sub}(s_R,\sigma) \leq \ell o(d_{sub}(D^-_{G'},\sigma))$), instead of sequentially reading the unseen strings in D, we access the remaining strings $s \in D^+_{G'}$ only by random I/O access with utilizing the inverted q-gram index to skip the remaining strings $s \in D^-_{G'}$. Similar to *TopK-SPLIT*, whenever $d_{sub}(s_R,\sigma)$ decreases, we select a smaller G' with $|G'| = d_{sub}(s_R,\sigma)$ to reduce the size of $D^-_{G'}$.

The pseudocode of *TopK-INDEX* is presented in Figure 6. The difference from *TopK-SPLIT* is the lines 6–16 in which the common positional q-gram list R is produced by reading the posting lists of q-grams in G sequentially in increasing order of string ids.

Note that every posting list in the inverted index is sorted by string ids and positions. To obtain the list R in increasing order of string ids, we initially set the frontier of each posting list of a q-gram in G as the location of the first posting in the posting list. Then, we read the smallest id among the postings in all frontiers and move the frontier to the next posting in its posting list. Let I denote the given inverted index. The call of *I.getFrontierId(G)* returns the smallest string id sid_I among the ids in all frontiers, and *I.getPosQgrams(*sid_I*)* returns the common positional q-gram list R between the string of sid_I and the query string σ by reading all postings (g_i, p_i) from the posting lists of the q-grams in G such that $g_i = sid_I$. The invocation of *I.getPosQgrams* also informs whether the string belongs to $D^+_{G'}$ or $D^-_{G'}$.

If we just follow the posting lists of the q-grams in G only to generate the list R, there may exist a string s in D which may not have any common q-gram with the query string σ and we may miss all of such strings. Thus, while we move a cursor on D together in the increasing order of string ids, if the smallest frontier id sid_I is larger than the id sid_D of D which the current cursor indicates, we read the string of sid_D from D, generate R from the actual string in D, and then perform the computations of lower bound and actual distance if necessary.

After *cond* becomes *true*, we always go to line 15 to read the posting lists to obtain the common q-gram list R without reading strings from D. The reason is that, after we find at least k strings whose substring edit distances are at most $\ell o(d_{sub}(D^-_{G'},\sigma))$, if the query string σ and a string s in D do not share at least a q-gram, the string s belongs to $D^-_{G'}$ and thus we do not need to check such strings in D by Lemma 3.9. Furthermore, if the string s of sid_I shares at least a common q-gram with G' (i.e., *part* is '+'), we compute $\ell o(d_{sub}(s,\sigma))$ in line 17. If the lower bound

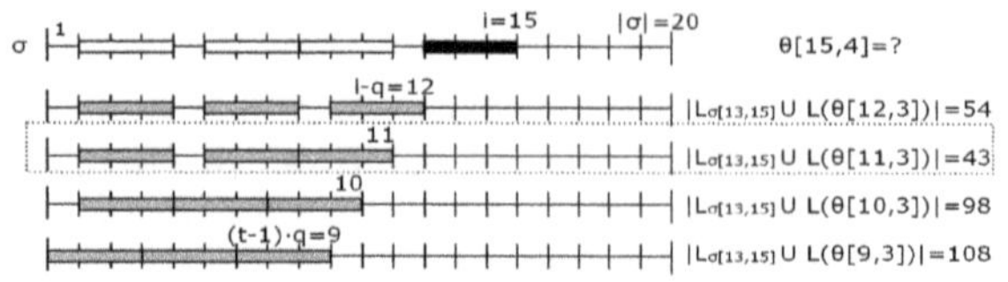

Figure 7: Computing $u[i,t]$ and $\theta[i,t]$

$\ell o(d_{sub}(s,\sigma))$ is smaller than the k-th smallest substring edit distance so far, we retrieve the string s from D by random I/O access to compute $d_{sub}(s,\sigma)$ as in line 20.

EXAMPLE 4.3: *Consider the strings D in Figure 1. Suppose that the query string σ is 'Jacksen' and we want to find the top-2 approximate substring matches from D using 3-grams. The 3-gram set G of σ is {'Jac', 'ack', 'cks', 'kse', 'sen'}. Initially, the lower bound τ of $d_{sub}(D^-_{G'},\sigma)$ is set to 2 (=$\lfloor 7/3 \rfloor$).*

At the beginning, the minimum string id among the frontiers of the posting lists of q-rams in G is s_1. The current cursor of D is also at s_1. Since we can obtain the common q-gram list R of s_1 from the posting lists, in each posting list, we read the frontier posting and move the frontier to the next. We also move the cursor of D to the next string without examining s_1. Since the current H_{TopK} is empty, we compute $d_{sub}(s_1,\sigma)$=1 and insert $(s_1, 1)$ into H_{TopK}.

Now, the minimum string id among the frontiers is s_4. However, since the current cursor of D indicates s_2, we read the s_2 and compute $d_{sub}(s_2,\sigma)$=4. Similarly, we read s_3 from D to calculate $d_{sub}(s_3,\sigma)$=3 and update H_{TopK}. Now the second smallest substring edit distance so far becomes 3.

We next read the frontier postings to obtain the common 3-gram list R between s_4 and σ which is {('Jac',1),('ack',2),('cks',3)}. The current cursor of D moves to the next string s_5. After we compute $d_{sub}(s_4,\sigma)$=2, the second smallest substring edit distance so far becomes 2. From now, since we already have 2 strings whose substring edit distances are at most τ=2, with G' of size 2 obtained by calling BEST-G', *we can find the top-2 approximate substring matches by considering the strings sharing at least a 3-gram in G' only due to Lemma 3.9. Let us assume that* BEST-G' *selects G'={'Jac', 'kse'}. Then, for the strings s_5 and s_6, we can ignore them because they do not appear in any posting list of 'Jac' or 'kse'. In summary, we can find the top-2 approximate substring matches by calculating the actual substring edit distances with 4 strings in D only.* ▮

5. SELECTING THE BEST G′ OF SIZE ρ

In the previous section, we assumed that $G' \subseteq G$ of size ρ is provided by the function *BEST-G'* for *TopK-SPLIT* and *TopK-INDEX*. Now, we present the algorithm *BEST-G'* which finds G' of size ρ such that the number of strings with at least a q-gram in G' in D (i.e., the size of $D^+_{G'}$) is the smallest. We use the following notations to describe our dynamic programming formulation to select such a G'.

- Let L_{g_i} be the set of the ids of strings containing the q-gram $g_i \in G$.
- For a q-gram set $Q \subseteq G$, let $L(Q) = \bigcup_{g_i \in Q} L_{g_i}$, which is the union of L_{g_i}s for all q-grams $g_i \in Q$, and we will use $|L(Q)|$ to represent the number of elements in $L(Q)$.
- Let $Q(i,t)$ be the set of all possible subsets Q of q-grams appearing in $\sigma[1,i]$ such that (1) $|Q|$=t, (2) the q-gram $\sigma[i-q+1,i]$ (i.e., the q-gram ending at the position i) always appears in Q and (3) all q-grams in Q does not overlap to each other.
- Let $\theta[i,t]$ denote the q-gram set Q in $Q(i,t)$ such that $|L(Q)|$ is the minimum among all q-gram sets in $Q(i,t)$.
- Let $u[i,t]$ represent $|L(\theta[i,t])|$.

Given the size ρ of G', we select Q with the minimum $|L(Q)|$ as G' among all subsets $Q \subseteq G$ consisting of ρ non-overlapping q-grams in σ. In every possible such Q, the ending position of the rightmost q-gram $\sigma[i-q+1,i]$ can be located in the positions i of σ with $\rho{\cdot}q \le i \le |\sigma|$. Thus, for every substring $\sigma[1,i]$ with $\rho{\cdot}q \le i \le |\sigma|$, we will enumerate the best ρ non-overlapping q-gram set Q which not only contains $\sigma[i-q+1,i]$ but also has the minimum $|L(Q)|$. The reason why we do not consider every i which is smaller than $(\rho{\cdot}q)$ is because the substring $\sigma[1,i]$ with $i < \rho{\cdot}q$ cannot have ρ non-overlapping q-grams. Since we use $\theta[i,\rho]$ to store the best Q with ρ non-overlapping q-grams which not only contains $\sigma[i-q+1,i]$ but also has the minimum $|L(Q)|$, we can find G' by selecting the $\theta[i,\rho]$ with the smallest $|L(\theta[i,\rho])|$ among $\theta[i,\rho]$s with $\rho{\cdot}q \le i \le |\sigma|$. In other words, if we compute $\theta[i,t]$s for every $1 \le t \le \lfloor |\sigma|/q \rfloor$ and $t \cdot q \le i \le |\sigma|$, we can select the q-gram set $\theta[i^*,\rho]$ as G' where i^* is chosen as follows:

$$i^* = \arg \min_{t \cdot q \le i \le |\sigma|} \{u[i,\rho]\} = \arg \min_{t \cdot q \le i \le |\sigma|} \{|L(\theta[i,\rho])|\}. \quad (5)$$

We next present a dynamic programming algorithm to compute $\theta[i,t]$ for $t = 1, \ldots, \lfloor |\sigma|/q \rfloor$ and $i = t \cdot q, \ldots, |\sigma|$.

Dynamic programming formulation: Since $\theta[i,t]$ contains t number of non-overlapping q-grams in the substring $\sigma[1,i]$ including $\sigma[i-q+1,i]$, we consider $\theta[j,t-1] \cup \{\sigma[i-q+1,i]\}$ with $1 \le j \le (i-q)$ to compute $\theta[i,t]$. However, $\theta[j,t-1]$ does not exist for j=1,...,$(t-1){\cdot}q-1$ because it is impossible to have $(t-1)$ non-overlapping q-grams in the substring $\sigma[1,j]$. Thus, we enumerate $\theta[j,t-1] \cup \{\sigma[i-q+1,i]\}$ for $(t-1) \cdot q \le j \le (i-q)$ only and select $\theta[j,t-1] \cup \{\sigma[i-q+1,i]\}$ with the smallest $|L(\theta[j,t-1]) \cup L_{\sigma[i-q+1,i]}|$ as $\theta[i,t]$. Our recursive definition for $\theta[i,t]$ is

$$\theta[i,t] = \theta[j^*,t-1] \cup \{\sigma[i-q+1,i]\} \quad (6)$$

where

$$j^* = \arg \min_{(t-1) \cdot q \le j \le i-q} \{|L_{\sigma[i-q+1,i]} \cup L(\theta[j,t-1])|\}. \quad (7)$$

In Figure 7, we show an example to illustrate how we compute $\theta[15,4]$. We enumerate $|L_{\sigma[13,15]} \cup \theta[j,3]|$ with $9 \le j \le 12$ and select $\{\sigma[13,15]\} \cup \theta[11,15]$ as $\theta[15,4]$ which minimizes $|L(\theta[15,4])|$.

If we compute $\theta[i,t]$ for every t from 1 to $\lfloor |\sigma|/q \rfloor$ and every i from $t{\cdot}q$ to $|\sigma|$ with the above dynamic programming algorithm, we can choose G' with a size ρ by Equation (5). We refer to this algorithm which finds G' with a given size ρ as *BEST-G′(ρ)*.

Note that *BEST-G′(ρ)* cannot find the optimal q-gram set G' because the optimal substructure property of our dynamic programming formulation is not satisfied. Suppose $\{\sigma[i-q+1,i]\} \cup Q$ is set to $\theta[i,t]$ in Equation (6) where Q is the optimal set with $(t-1)$ non-overlapping q-grams for $\sigma[1,j^*]$. Let Q' be a non-optimal q-gram set with $(t-1)$ non-overlapping q-grams in $\sigma[1,j^*]$ including the q-gram ending at the position j^*. Even though Q' is not an optimal q-gram set for $\sigma[1,j^*]$, if $L_{\sigma[i-q+1,i]}$ and $L(Q')$ share many common string ids so that $|L_{\sigma[i-q+1,i]} \cup L(Q')|$ becomes

g_1 \ g_2	-	Jac	ack	cks
Jac	100	-	-	-
ack	32	-	-	-
cks	16	-	-	-
kso	10	110	-	-
son	120	130	125	-
onv	40	120	43	50

(a) $|L_{g_1} \cup L_{g_2}|$ $(=|L(\{g_1, g_2\})|)$

	t=1		t=2	
i	θ[i,1]	u[i,1]	θ[i,2]	u[i,2]
3	{Jac}	100	-	-
4	{ack}	32	-	-
5	{cks}	16	-	-
6	{kso}	10	{Jac,kso}	110
7	{son}	120	{ack,son}	125
8	{onv}	40	{ack,onv}	43

(b) θ[i,t] and u[i,t]

Figure 8: Computations in *BEST-G′(ρ)*

smaller than $|L_{\sigma[i-q+1,i]} \cup L(Q)|$, we have $|L(Q')| > |L(Q)|$ and thus the computed $\theta[i,t]$ is not an optimal q-gram set for $\sigma[1,i]$. Thus, *BEST-G′(ρ)* finds an approximate q-gram set for G'. However, our performance study confirms that *BEST-G′(ρ)* obtains a good G' close to the optimal sets.

When *BEST-G′(ρ)* is invoked in *TopK-SPLIT* or *TopK-INDEX*, we need to know the actual size of $L(\theta[i,t])$ which is the union of the sets of string ids whose strings contain a q-gram in $\theta[i,t]$. We will use the MinHash technique [5, 7] to estimate the sizes of unions of sets in *BEST-G′(ρ)*.

Assume that for every q-gram g_i appearing in D, there is a MinHash signature of the set of string ids in which the q-gram g_i occurs. In *BEST-G′(ρ)*, we maintain the MinHash signature of $L(\theta[i,t])$ to compute $L_{\sigma[i-q+1,i]} \cup L(\theta[j,t-1])$ in Equation (7) with constant time.

Time complexity: In *BEST-G′(ρ)*, we have to compute $\theta[i,t]$ and $u[i,t]$ for every $1 \le t \le \lfloor|\sigma|/q\rfloor$ and every $t \cdot q \le i \le |\sigma|$. To compute each $\theta[i,t]$, it takes $O(|\sigma|)$ time. For each $u[i,t]$, it takes constant time since $u[i,t]$ is simply $|L(\theta[i,t])|$. Thus, the time complexity of *BEST-G′(ρ)* is $O(|\sigma|^3/q)$.

EXAMPLE 5.1.: *Consider the query string σ='Jacksonv' with $|\sigma| = 8$. Suppose that we should select the non-overlapping 3-gram set G' with size 2. For all possible non-overlapping 3-gram sets Q whose sizes are 1 or 2, $|L(Q)|$s are shown in Figure 8(a). We show all $\theta[i,t]$s and $u[i,t]$s computed by* BEST-$G'(\rho)$ *in Figure 8(b).*

Let us assume that we want to compute $\theta[8,2]$ that always includes the 3-gram $\sigma[6,8]$='onv'. We enumerate the following three cases of $|L_{onv} \cup L_{cks}|$(=50), $|L_{onv} \cup L_{ack}|$(=43) and $|L_{onv} \cup L_{Jac}|$(=120) by Equation (7), and select $\theta[8,2]$ = {'ack','onv'} with $u[8,2]$ = 43. Finally, to select the best G' with size 2 by Equation (5), we choose $\theta[8,2]$ = {'ack', 'onv'} for G' since $u[8,2]$ is the minimum among $u[6,2]$, $u[7,2]$ and $u[8,2]$. ∎

6. EXPERIMENTS

We empirically compared the performance of our proposed algorithms. All experiments reported in this section were performed on the machines with Intel Core[2] Duo 2.66GHz of processor and 2GB of main memory running Linux operating systems. All algorithms were implemented using C++ and compiled with GCC Compiler of version 4.1.3.

6.1 Implemented Algorithms

We implemented the following algorithms for our performance study.

- **TopK-NAIVE:** This represents the brute-force algorithm which computes the substring edit distance with every string in D to find the top-k approximate substring matches.
- **TopK-LB:** It is the implementation of *TopK-LB* which computes $d_{sub}(s,\sigma)$ only for the strings s in D whose lower bound $\ell o(d_{sub}(s,\sigma))$, obtained by calling *DYN-LB*, is smaller than the k-th smallest substring edit distance found so far.
- **TopK-SPLIT:** This is the algorithm which improves *TopK-LB* further by skipping even the computation of $\ell o(d_{sub}(s,\sigma))$ using the lower bound of substring edit distance between a query and a set of strings in Lemma 3.9.
- **TopK-INDEX:** This is the implementation of *TopK-INDEX* that utilizes the inverted q-gram indexes available to speed up *TopK-SPLIT*.
- **TopK-NGPP:** This is the modified version of *NGPP* in [27] to obtain the top-k approximate substring matches. The algorithm *NGPP* is the state-of-the-art algorithm to find all substrings of each string in D whose edit distances to a query string are at most a given maximum threshold τ. To adapt *NGPP* to top-k approximate substring matching, we first read the first k strings in D and set the k-th smallest one among their substring edit distances as the initial threshold τ. Then, as examining every string in D, if the k-th smallest substring edit distance becomes smaller than τ, we update the threshold τ to the k-th smallest substring edit distance.
- **TopK-FSS:** Similar to *TopK-NGPP*, we also extended *FSS* in [4] to compute the top-k approximate substring matches in the same manner.

Note that we used our own buffer management for reading the data strings in disk and accessing inverted indexes in all of our implementations without utilizing OS buffers to see the buffering effects for the tested algorithms more carefully. We report the native execution times (i.e., wall clock times) of the tested algorithms in this section.

6.2 Data Sets

To study the performance our proposed algorithms, we utilize the following two real-life data sets.

DBLP: For a short string data set, we used DBLP titles collected from `http://dblp.uni-trier.de/xml/`. However, since the original data is small, we increased its size by duplicating the original data 5 times. While we duplicate each string, we randomly performed an edit operation such as insert, delete and substitute on each position of the string with the probability of 0.1. The size of generated data is 635 MB with 13,966,030 strings whose average size is 48 bytes.

Wikipedia: This is the data set consisting of 106,185 web pages obtained from `http://en.wikipedia.org/wiki/Wikipedia:Database_download` for a long string data set. The data size is 1.1 GB and the average size is 11,027 bytes.

6.3 Queries Used

For DBLP, we randomly selected between 1 and 4 adjacent words appearing in DBLP titles to generate test queries. The range of query lengths is from 6 to 25 with average length 13.2. For Wikipedia, we sampled 50 entities from CoNLL data, which is a name entity data collected for Name Entity Recognition available for download at `http://www.cnts.ua.ac.be/conll2003/ner/`, as test queries. The lengths of selected queries are from 5 to 27 with average length 12.3.

Similarly, for our experiments with varying lengths of query strings, we also selected the query strings of lengths from 5 to 25 with DBLP titles and CoNLL data respectively. For each query length, 50 query strings were sampled.

6.4 Performance Results

We measured the performance of the algorithms for both DBLP and Wikipedia with varying k, the number of strings

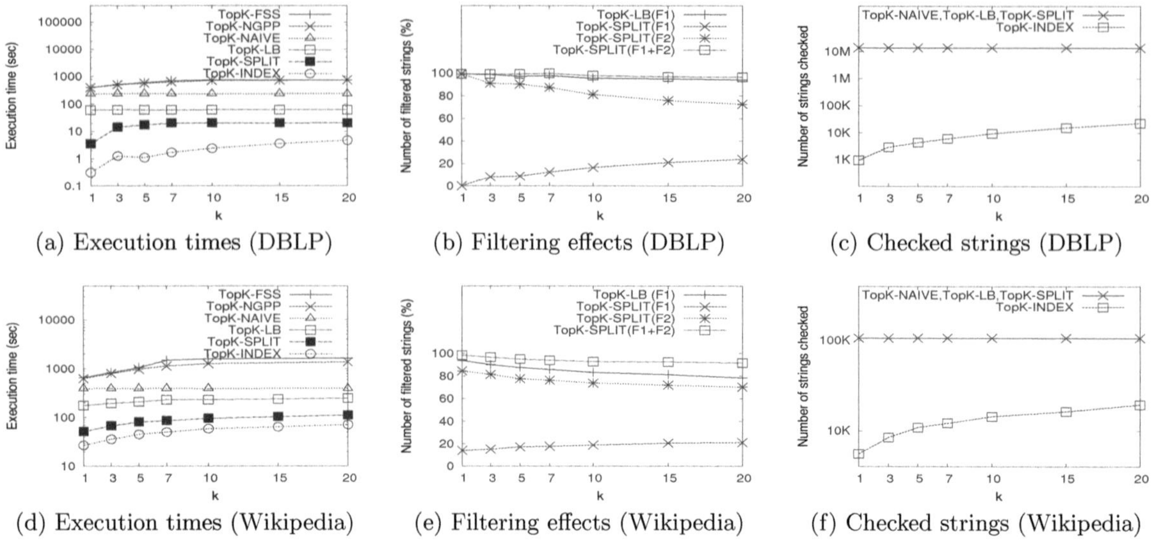

(a) Execution times (DBLP) (b) Filtering effects (DBLP) (c) Checked strings (DBLP)

(d) Execution times (Wikipedia) (e) Filtering effects (Wikipedia) (f) Checked strings (Wikipedia)

Figure 9: Varying k using DBLP and Wikipedia

n and the length of query strings L. Furthermore, we varied the length of q-grams q, MinHash signature size ℓ and buffer size B used. The default parameters are: k=5, q=3, ℓ=50 and B=512MB.

Varying k: We first report the execution times, the number of filtered strings and the percentage of strings read from D with varying k from 1 to 20 in Figure 9(a)–(f).

(1) Execution times: We show the execution times for DBLP and Wikipedia in Figure 9(a) and Figure 9(d) respectively. The log scale was used on the y-axises. In both data, *TopK-NGPP* and *TopK-FSS* show even worse performance than our naive algorithm *TopK-NAIVE*. The reason is that both of *TopK-NGPP* and *TopK-FSS* have to enumerate all substrings of every string in D to compute the substring edit distances. As expected from the experiments in [27], *TopK-NGPP* performs better than *TopK-FSS*.

As k is increased, the execution times for *TopK-LB*, *TopK-SPLIT* and *TopK-INDEX* grow gradually. Since the k-th smallest substring edit distance so far becomes larger with growing k, less number of strings are skipped for computing substring edit distances.

For every range of k, *TopK-INDEX* shows the best performance. *TopK-INDEX* is faster than *TopK-NAIVE* by at least 49.4 times and 5.5 times for DBLP and Wikipedia respectively. Furthermore, *TopK-SPLIT* is also faster than *TopK-NAIVE* by at least 11.6 and 3.5 times for DBLP and Wikipedia respectively.

(2) Filtering effects: To show the effectiveness of our filtering methods, we plotted the percentage of strings skipped for computing their substring edit distances in Figure 9(b) and Figure 9(e) with DBLP and Wikipedia respectively. Note that *TopK-LB(F1)* in the graphs represents the percentage of strings filtered with *TopK-LB* using the lower bounds $\ell o(d_{sub}(s, \sigma))$ obtained by *DYN-LB*. We also use *TopK-SPLIT(F1)* similarly in the graphs. *TopK-SPLIT(F2)* in the graphs represents the percentage of strings filtered by *TopK-SPLIT* using the lower bound of substring edit distances between a query string and a set of strings presented in Lemma 3.9. Furthermore, *TopK-SPLIT(F1+F2)* is the total ratio of strings filtered with *TopK-SPLIT*. Since the filtering effect of *TopK-INDEX* is exactly the same with that of *TopK-SPLIT*, we report the result of *TopK-SPLIT* only.

With every range of k, *TopK-SPLIT(F1+F2)* is always larger than *TopK-LB(F1)* in both data sets. For k=20 with Wikipedia, Figure 9(e) shows that *TopK-SPLIT* skips computing $d_{sub}(s, \sigma)$ with 17% more strings than *TopK-LB* does. Considering that *TopK-SPLIT* was 2.2 times faster than *TopK-LB* in Figure 9(d), we can conclude that using the lower bound by Lemma 3.9 improves the speed of query processing more than using the lower bound by *DYN-LB* does because the lower bound by Lemma 3.9 requires only to check whether each string contains at least a common q-gram with the query string in a constant time. With increasing k, both *TopK-LB(F1)* and *TopK-SPLIT(F1)* decrease slowly since the k-th smallest distance so far also becomes larger together with k. However, since the k-th substring edit distance found so far decreases slower as k grows, the chances that *TopK-SPLIT* skips the strings using the lower bound by *DYN-LB* increase on the contrary and thus *TopK-SPLIT(F2)* grows gradually.

(3) Number of strings read from D: We also plotted the number of data strings examined in disk with random I/O access by *TopK-INDEX* for DBLP and Wikipedia in Figure 9(c) and Figure 9(f) respectively. The y-axises are in a log scale. The graph confirms that *TopK-INDEX* effectively reduces the cost for reading the data strings in disk.

Varying n: With each of DBLP and Wikipedia, we selected the strings from the original data set to produce smaller data with varying the sampling rate from 6.25% to 100%. With varying the size of data, we plotted the execution times in Figure 10(a) for DBLP and in Figure 10(b) for Wikipedia. The graphs show that *TopK-INDEX* is the fastest in every range of data sizes. Both *TopK-NGPP* and *TopK-FSS* were even slower than *TopK-NAIVE* and their performance degrades linearly as data size grows because they have to examine every substring exhaustively. As the data size increases, the relative speedup of *TopK-INDEX* to *TopK-NAIVE* improves from 4.6 times to 8.6 times for Wikipedia. With DBLP, the speedup increases from 9.3 times to 24.5 times. Thus, we conclude that the performance of *TopK-INDEX*

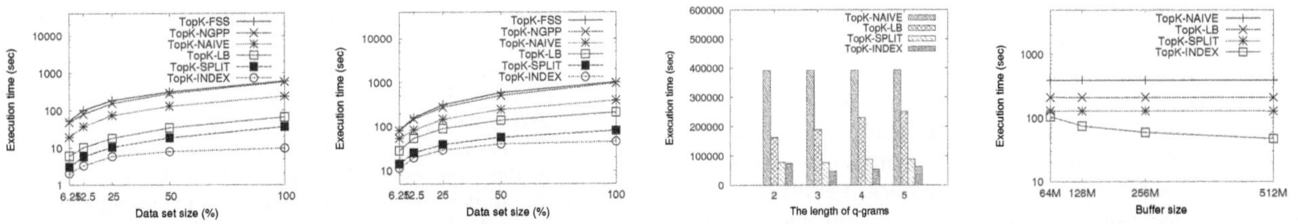

(a) Varying n (DBLP) (b) Varying n (Wikipedia) (c) Varying q (d) Varying B

Figure 10: Varying n, q and B

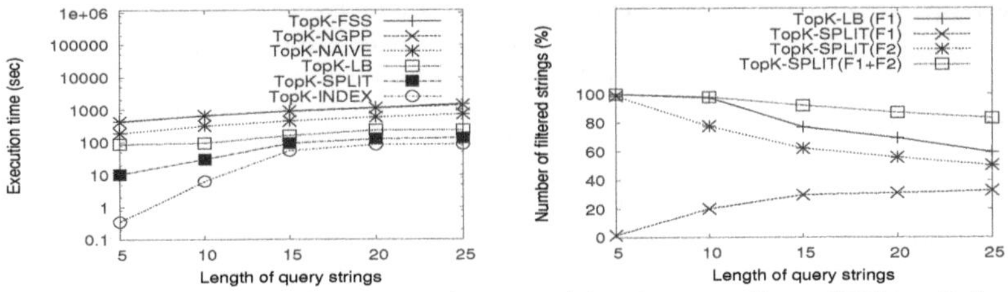

(a) Execution times (Wikipedia) (b) Filtering effects (Wikipedia)

Figure 11: Experiments with varying L

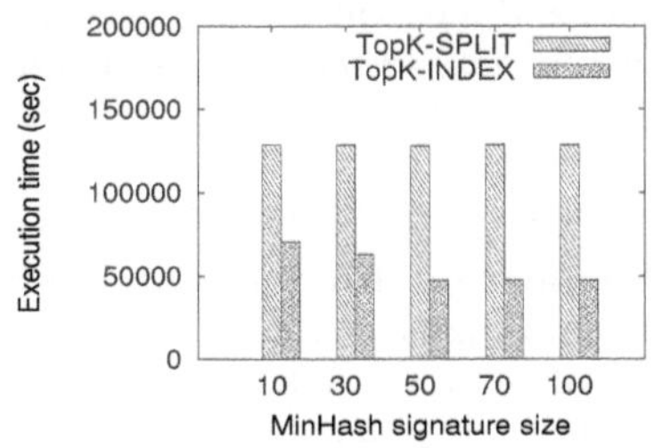

Figure 12: Varying ℓ (Wikipedia)

does not decline linearly with increasing data size and *TopK-INDEX* scales well to large data.

Varying L: With varying query lengths L from 5 to 25, we plotted the execution times for Wikipedia in Figure 11(a). The log scale was used on the y-axises. With every range of L, *TopK-INDEX* shows the best performance and *TopK-FSS* is the worst. When the lengths of query strings are 5 and 25, *TopK-INDEX* is 540 times and 8.44 times faster than *TopK-NAIVE* respectively. As L is increased, the execution times for all algorithms grow gradually. This is because there is a less chance that the strings in D have similar substrings to a longer query string and thus the k-th smallest substring edit distance so far becomes larger with growing L.

We also plotted the percentage of strings skipped for computing their substring edit distances $d_{sub}(s,\sigma)$ in Figure 11(b). With every range of L, *TopK-SPLIT* skips more strings for computing $d_{sub}(s,\sigma)$ than *TopK-LB* does. Furthermore, while *TopK-LB* computes $\ell o(d_{sub}(s,\sigma))$ based on dynamic programming algorithm *DYN-LB* for every string in D, *TopK-SPLIT* skips even computing $\ell o(d_{sub}(s,\sigma))$ for many strings. With increasing L, the gaps between the ratios of strings filtered by *TopK-SPLIT* and *TopK-LB* become larger because the query strings have more chance to have very selective q-grams resulting that more strings are filtered using the lower bound by Lemma 3.9.

Varying ℓ: We varied the MinHash signature size ℓ from 10 to 100 and plotted the running times of *TopK-SPLIT* and *TopK-INDEX* in Figure 12(a). Since the other algorithms do not estimate the computational cost to select G', they are not affected by the MinHash signature size. The graph shows that the performances of both algorithms are the worst when ℓ=10 and do not degrade that much with $\ell \le 50$. Thus, we used ℓ=50 as the default value in all our experiments.

Varying q: Figure 10(c) shows the graph of execution time as the length q of the q-grams used is varied from 3 to 5. Since *TopK-NAIVE* is not affected by the length of q-grams, its execution times are always constant. *TopK-LB* and *TopK-SPLIT* show the best performances when q=2. This is because, with a large q, the lower bound $\lceil(|\sigma|-q+1-n)/q\rceil$ in Lemma 3.2 decreases and thus, less strings are skipped for computing $d_{sub}(s,\sigma)$. Furthermore, since the maximum of $\ell o(d_{sub}(D^-_{G'},\sigma))$, which is $\lfloor|\sigma|/q\rfloor$, due to Corollary 3.8 also becomes smaller with a larger q, the critical point string where we meet the k-th string whose substring edit distance is at most $\ell o(d_{sub}(D^-_{G'},\sigma))$ appears later. However, *TopK-INDEX* shows the best performance when q=3 because the posting lists become very large with 2-grams.

Varying B: With varying the size of buffer B from 64 MB to 512 MB, we show the execution times in Figure 10(d). With increasing B, the speed of *TopK-INDEX* is improved gradually since we have more chance to hit the cached pages of inverted indexes with larger buffer sizes.

7. RELATED WORK

We present the previous work on approximate string matching first and then approximate substring matching.

Approximate string matching: For approximate *string* matching with a maximum distance threshold τ, the count filtering technique proposed in [9] utilizes the fact that if the *edit distance* between s and σ is at most τ, they must share at least $(\max(|s|,|\sigma|)-q+1-\tau\cdot q)$ q-grams. In [16], another algorithm is proposed to speed up approximate *string* matching by reducing the average size of inverted lists using variable length q-grams. However, this algorithm utilizes the length filtering or prefix filtering which cannot be used for approximate *substring* matching. In [1] and [22], the algorithms to find similar strings *probabilistically* were proposed, but we focused on the problem of finding the exact top-k approximate substring matches in this paper.

In [3] and [15], the algorithms using inverted q-gram indexes are presented. However, as mentioned in [27], to utilize the inverted q-gram indexes, the length of the q-grams to be used should be smaller than $(|\sigma|+1)/(\tau+1)$. Thus, depending on the value of τ and the q-grams used for accessing existing inverted indexes, it is not always possible to use existing inverted q-gram indexes for approximate string matching [27]. In [26] and [28], the top-k approximate *string* matching algorithms using inverted q-gram indexes are presented. However, as pointed out in [27], we cannot determine the q-gram size in advance to build indexes and thus these algorithms may not find the top-k approximate *string* matches correctly when using preexisting inverted q-gram indexes. One of our proposed algorithms also utilizes existing inverted indexes, but we still guarantee the correctness.

The algorithms in [6, 29] utilize the suffix tries which index a small portion of suffixes only in the data. However, to use suffix tries for approximate *substring* matching, we have to index every suffix appearing in the data, resulting large index sizes. Because of the high space requirements and poor locality of suffix tries, it is mentioned in [21] that the suffix trie based approaches are proper only when both of the data and index fit in main memory. Furthermore, since the approximate *string* matching algorithm with a maximum threshold τ using suffix tries in [8] has exponential space and time complexity to τ, it is hard to be extended for top-k approximate *substring* matching.

Approximate substring matching: Approximate substring matching has been studied in the context of approximate entity extraction in [4, 17, 27]. With a given threshold and a entity dictionary, these algorithms are actually join algorithms which find every substring in a database such that the edit distance between the substring and one of the strings in the entity dictionary is at most the threshold. The algorithms in [4, 27] can be extended for top-k approximate substring matching and thus we compared our proposed algorithms to our extended algorithms of [4, 27]. The algorithm in [17] utilizes inverted q-gram indexes but to use inverted indexes for top-k approximate substring matching, we have to ensure that the length of the q-grams used must be smaller than $(|\sigma|+1)/(\tau_k+1)$ where τ_k is the k-th smallest substring edit distance in D. Since we cannot know τ_k in advance to build indexes, we could not adapt the algorithm in [17] to our top-k approximate substring matching problem.

To the best of our knowledge, no previous work addresses the top-k approximate substring matching problem and our algorithms presented here are the first work for the problem.

8. CONCLUSION

In this paper, we studied the problem of top-k approximate substring matching. We first proposed efficient filtering methods using q-grams which may enable us to skip strings without computing the actual substring edit distances to the query string. We next presented two algorithms *TopK-LB* and *TopK-SPLIT* which efficiently find top-k approximate substring matches by utilizing the filtering techniques. Furthermore, we developed an improved algorithm *TopK-INDEX* which utilizes inverted q-gram indexes to speed up *TopK-SPLIT*. By experiment results, we show the effectiveness and scalability of our algorithms with real-life data sets.

Acknowledgment

This work was supported by the National Research Foundation of Korea(NRF) grant funded by the Korea government(MEST) (No. NRF-2009-0078828). It was also supported by Next-Generation Information Computing Development Program through the National Research Foundation of Korea(NRF) funded by the Ministry of Education, Science and Technology (No. NRF-2012M3C4A7033342).

9. REFERENCES

[1] A. Andoni and K. Onak. Approximating edit distance in near-linear time. In *STOC*, 2009.

[2] R. A. Baeza-Yates and B. A. Ribeiro-Neto. *Modern Information Retrieval - the concepts and technology behind search, Second edition*. Pearson Education Ltd., Harlow, England, 2011.

[3] A. Behm, S. Ji, C. Li, and J. Lu. Space-constrained gram-based indexing for efficient approximate string search. In *ICDE*, 2009.

[4] T. Bocek, E. Hunt, and B. Stiller. Fast similarity search in large dictionaries. In *Technical Report*, 2007.

[5] A. Z. Broder. On the resemblance and containment of documents. In *Proceedings of Compression and Complexity of SEQUENCES*, 1997.

[6] S. Chaudhuri and R. Kaushik. Extending autocompletion to tolerate errors. In *SIGMOD*, 2009.

[7] Z. Chen, F. Korn, N. Koudas, and S. Muithukrishnan. Selectivity estimation for boolean queries. In *PODS*, 2000.

[8] R. Cole, L.-A. Gottlieb, and M. Lewenstein. Dictionary matching and indexing with errors and don't cares. In *STOC*, 2004.

[9] L. Gravano, P. G. Ipeirotis, H. V. Jagadish, N. Koudas, S. Muthukrishnan, and D. Srivastava. Approximate string joins in a database (almost) for free. In *VLDB*, 2001.

[10] L. Jin and C. Li. Selectivity estimation for fuzzy string predicates in large data sets. In *VLDB*, 2005.

[11] N. Koudas, A. Marathe, and D. Srivastava. Flexible string matching against large databases in practice. In *VLDB*, 2004.

[12] H. Lee, R. T. Ng, and K. Shim. Extending q-grams to estimate selectivity of string matching with low edit distance. In *VLDB*, 2007.

[13] H. Lee, R. T. Ng, and K. Shim. Approximate substring selectivity estimation. In *EDBT*, 2009.

[14] V. I. Levenshtein. Binary codes capable of correcting deletions, insertions and reversals. *Soviet Phys. Dokl.*, 1985.

[15] C. Li, J. Lu, and Y. Lu. Efficient merging and filtering algorithms for approximate string searches. In *ICDE*, 2008.

[16] C. Li, B. Wang, and X. Yang. VGRAM: Improving performance of approximate queries on string collections using variable-length grams. In *VLDB*, 2007.

[17] G. Li, D. Deng, and J. Feng. Faerie: efficient filtering algorithms for approximate dictionary-based entity extraction. In *SIGMOD*, 2011.

[18] C.-C. Liu, J.-L. Hsu, and A. L. P. Chen. An approximate string matching algorithm for content-based music data retrieval. In *ICMCS*, 1999.

[19] A. Mazeika, M. H. Böhlen, N. Koudas, and D. Srivastava. Estimating the selectivity of approximate string queries. *ACM Trans. Database Syst.*, 32(2), 2007.

[20] G. Navarro. A guided tour to approximate string matching. *ACM Comput. Surv.*, 33(1):31–88, 2001.

[21] G. Navarro, E. Sutinen, and J. Tarhio. Indexing text with approximate q-grams. *J. Discrete Algorithms*, 2005.

[22] R. Ostrovsky and Y. Rabani. Low distortion embeddings for edit distance. *J. ACM*, 54(5), 2007.

[23] M. Sahami and T. D. Heilman. A web-based kernel function for measuring the similarity of short text snippets. In *WWW*, 2006.

[24] P. H. Sellers. The theory and computation of evolutionary distances: Pattern recognition. *J. Algorithms*, 1(4), 1980.

[25] E. Ukkonen. Finding approximate patterns in strings. *J. Algorithms*, 6(1):132–137, 1985.

[26] R. Vernica and C. Li. Efficient top-k algorithms for fuzzy search in string collections. In *KEYS*, 2009.

[27] W. Wang, C. Xiao, X. Lin, and C. Zhang. Efficient approximate entity extraction with edit distance constraints. In *SIGMOD*, 2009.

[28] Z. Yang, J. Yu, and M. Kitsuregawa. Fast algorithms for top-k approximate string matching. In *AAAI*, 2010.

[29] Z. Zhang, M. Hadjieleftheriou, B. C. Ooi, and D. Srivastava. Bed-tree: an all-purpose index structure for string similarity search based on edit distance. In *SIGMOD*, 2010.

Towards High-Throughput Gibbs Sampling at Scale: A Study across Storage Managers

Ce Zhang Christopher Ré
University of Wisconsin-Madison, USA
{czhang,chrisre}@cs.wisc.edu

ABSTRACT

Factor graphs and Gibbs sampling are a popular combination for Bayesian statistical methods that are used to solve diverse problems including insurance risk models, pricing models, and information extraction. Given a fixed sampling method and a fixed amount of time, an implementation of a sampler that achieves a higher throughput of samples will achieve a higher quality than a lower-throughput sampler. We study how (and whether) traditional data processing choices about materialization, page layout, and buffer-replacement policy need to be changed to achieve high-throughput Gibbs sampling for factor graphs that are larger than main memory. We find that both new theoretical and new algorithmic techniques are required to understand the tradeoff space for each choice. On both real and synthetic data, we demonstrate that traditional baseline approaches may achieve two orders of magnitude lower throughput than an optimal approach. For a handful of popular tasks across several storage backends, including HBase and traditional unix files, we show that our simple prototype achieves competitive (and sometimes better) throughput compared to specialized state-of-the-art approaches on factor graphs that are larger than main memory.

Categories and Subject Descriptors

H.2.4 [**Information Systems**]: Database Management; H.3.2 [**Information System**]: Information Storage and Retrieval—*Information Storage*

General Terms

Experimentation, Performance

Keywords

Gibbs sampling; storage manager; scalability

1. INTRODUCTION

Factor graphs capture and unify a range of data-driven statistical tasks in information extraction, text analytics, predictive analytics, and pricing and actuarial models that are used across many industries. For example, conditional random fields (CRF) are factor graphs that are used in industry for information extraction [22,42,43], e.g., Microsoft's EntityCube [46] and HP's IsWiki [9]. Moody's rating service uses Gibbs sampling and generalized linear models (GLMs) [39], as do leading insurance actuaries [4,13]. Increasingly, more sophisticated factor graph models are used. For example, Yahoo! and Google use latent Dirichlet allocation (LDA) for topic modeling [8, 23, 38], and Microsoft's EntityCube uses Markov logic [12,28,36,46]. Most inference or parameter estimation problems for factor graphs are intractable to solve exactly, e.g., segmenting a sentence using a skip-chain CRF, inverting the parameters of a GLM to estimate the risk of an actuarial model, or computing the parameters of an LDA model. To perform these tasks, one often resorts to sampling. Arguably the most popular of these approaches, and the one on which we focus, is Gibbs sampling [34].

Not surprisingly, frameworks that combine factor graphs and Gibbs sampling are popular and widely used. For example, the OpenBUGS framework has been used widely since the 1980s [25]. More recent examples include PGibbs [15] and Factorie [26]. For any factor graph, given a fixed time budget, an implementation of Gibbs sampling that produces samples at a higher throughput, achieves higher-quality results. Thus, a key technical challenge is to create an implementation of *high-throughput* Gibbs samplers.

Achieving high throughput for Gibbs sampling is well studied for factor graphs that fit in main memory, but there is a race to apply these approaches to larger amounts of data, e.g., in defense and intelligence [27], enterprise [17], and web applications [38].

A key pain point is that for each specific model, a scalable implementation is hand tuned, e.g., Greenplum's MADlib [17] and Yahoo! [38] implement hand-tuned versions of LDA. High-performance implementations of Gibbs sampling often require a tedious process of trial-and-error optimization. Further complicating an engineer's job is that the variety of storage backends has exploded in the last few years: traditional files, relational databases, and HDFS-based key-value stores, like HBase or Accumulo. The lack of scalable Gibbs samplers forces developers to revisit I/O tradeoffs for each new statistical model and each new data storage combination. We first show that a baseline approach that picks classically

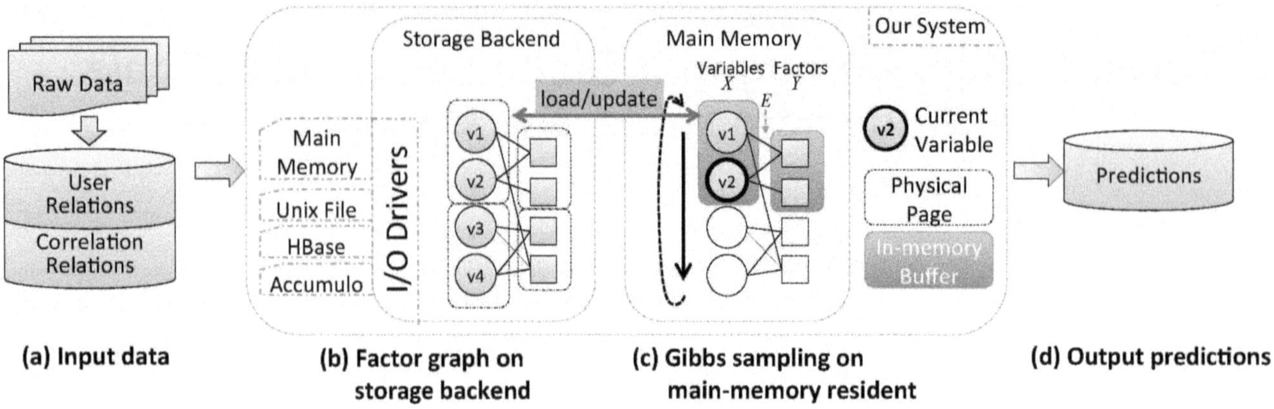

Figure 1: System overview. (a) The input to our system is a factor graph encoded in correlation relations (see Section 2). (b) Factor graphs are stored using several secondary storage backends, e.g., traditional unix file and HBase. (c) Gibbs sampling is performed. Our prototype loads only a portion of the factor graph into main memory, runs inference, and updates the state, which may be stored on secondary storage. (d) As is standard, these samples are summarized for use in the above applications.

optimal points in this tradeoff space may lose almost two orders of magnitude in throughput (see Figures 11 and 14).

We select three classical techniques that are used to improve query performance in database storage managers: materialization, page-oriented layout, and buffer-replacement policy. These techniques are simple to implement (so they may be implemented in practice), and they have stood the test of four decades of use.[1] Our study examines these techniques for a handful of popular storage backends: main-memory based, traditional unix files, and key-value stores.

Applying these classical techniques is not as straightforward as one may think. The tradeoff space for each technique has changed due to at least one of two new characteristics of sampling algorithms (versus join data processing): (1) data are mutable during processing (in contrast to a typical join algorithm), and (2) data are repeatedly accessed in an order that changes randomly across executions, which means that we cannot precompute an ideal order. However, within any given sampling session, the data is accessed in a fixed order. We consider the tradeoff space analytically, and use our analysis of the tradeoff space to design a simple proof-of-concept storage manager. We use this storage manager to validate our claimed tradeoff space in scaling Gibbs sampling.

As we show through experiments, our prototype system is competitive with even state-of-the-art, hand-tuned approaches for factor graphs that are larger than main memory. Thus, it is possible to achieve competitive performance using this handful of classical techniques.

Overview of Technical Contributions

In Section 2, we describe a representation of factor graphs that follows the work of Sen et al. [37] and Wick et al. [44].[2] We give a brief primer on factor graphs to provide context for our contributions, which we discuss at the end of this section.

A Primer of Gibbs Sampling on Factor Graphs. The input to Gibbs sampling is a factor graph, which is a labeled bipartite graph $G = (X, Y, E)$ where X and Y are sets of nodes and $E \subseteq X \times Y$ is a set of edges (illustrated in Figure 1). In a factor graph, X contains one node for each random variable, which is labeled with the current assignment to that variable, and Y contains a node for each factor. The factors define the correlation structure between the variables: two variables are connected to the same factor if they are correlated. A *factor function* is associated with each factor and numerically describes how sets of variables that are related by a factor are correlated. E describes which variables are associated with which factors.

The output of sampling is one or more samples for each variable in the factor graph. To obtain a sample for a single variable x, we perform three steps: (1) retrieve all neighboring factors and the assignments for all variables in those factors, (2) evaluate these neighboring factors with the retrieved assignments, and (3) aggregate the evaluation results to compute a conditional distribution from which we select a new value for x. This operation, which we call the *core operation*, is repeated for every variable in the factor graph (in a randomly selected order). We loop over the variables many times to obtain a high-quality sample.

Technical Contributions. Since the bulk (often over 99%) of the execution time is spent in the core operation, we focus on optimizing this operation. To this end, we identify three tradeoffs for the core operation of Gibbs sampling: (1) materialization, (2) page-oriented layout, and (3) buffer-replacement policy.

(1) Materialization tradeoffs. During Gibbs sampling, we access the bipartite graph structure many times. An obvious optimization is to materialize a portion of the graph to avoid repeated accesses. A twist is that the value of a random variable is updated during the core operation. Thus, materialization schemes that introduce redundancy may re-

[1] Although sampling approaches have been integrated with data processing systems, notably the MCDB project [20], the above techniques have not been applied to the area of high-throughput samplers.

[2] A minor difference is that we do not require, as Sen et al. [37] or PGibbs does, that one explicitly list the complete truth table for every factor (see Section 5).

Method	Comment
`void init(D[] vars)`	initialize this factor with a list of variable IDs
`float evaluate()`	evaluate the value of this factor

Figure 2: Interface for a factor function. Variable assignments are globally accessible.

quire many (random) writes. This introduces a new cost in materialization schemes, and so we re-explore lazy and eager materialization schemes, along with two co-clustering schemes [33, ch. 16]. The two co-clustering schemes together analytically and empirically dominate both eager and lazy schemes – but neither dominates the other. Thus, we design a simple optimizer based on statistics from the data to choose between these two approaches.

(2) Page-oriented layout. Once we have decided how to materialize or co-cluster, we are still free to assign variables and factors to pages to minimize the number of page fetches from the storage manager during the core operation. In cases in which the sampling is I/O bound, minimizing the number of page fetches helps reduce this bottleneck. Since Gibbs sampling proceeds through the variables in a random order, we want a layout that has good average-case performance. Toward this goal, we describe a simple heuristic that outperforms a naïve random layout by up to an order of magnitude. We then show that extending this heuristic is difficult: assuming $P \neq NP$, no polynomial time algorithm has a constant-factor approximation for the layout that minimizes page fetches during execution.

(3) Buffer-Replacement Policy. A key issue, when dealing with data that is larger than available main memory, is deciding which data to retain and which to discard from main memory, i.e., the buffer-replacement policy. Although the data is visited in random order, one will typically perform many passes over the data in the same random order. Thus, after the first pass over the data, we have a great deal of information about which pages will be selected during execution. It turns out that this enables us to use a classical result from Bélády in 1966 [7] to define a theoretically optimal eviction strategy: *evict the item that will be used latest in the future*. We implement this approach and show that it performs optimally, but that its improvement over more traditional strategies based on MRU/LRU is only 5–10%. It also requires some non-trivial implementation, and so it may be too complex for the performance gain. A technical serendipity is that we use Bélády's result to characterize an optimal buffer-replacement strategy, which is needed to establish our hardness result described in page-oriented layout.

We present background information on factor graphs and Gibbs sampling in Section 2, our technical contributions in Section 3, and an empirical validation in Section 4. We discuss related work in Section 5 and conclude in Section 6.

2. BACKGROUND

We describe factor graphs, the mechanics of Gibbs sampling, and how Gibbs sampling supports inference and query answering.

2.1 Factor Graphs

Factor graphs have been used to model complex correlations among random variables for decades [41], and have recently been adopted as one underlying representation for probabilistic databases [37,42,44]. A key principle of factor graphs is that random variables should be separated from the correlation structure. Following this principle, we define a probabilistic database to be $\mathcal{D} = (\mathcal{R}, \mathcal{F})$, where $\mathcal{R}$ is called the *user schema* and $\mathcal{F}$ is called the *correlation schema*. Relations in the user schema (resp. correlation schema) are called *user relations* (resp. *correlation relations*). A user's application interacts with the user schema, while the correlation schema captures correlations among tuples in the user schema. Figure 3 gives a schematic view of the concepts in this section.

User Schema. Each tuple in a user relation $R_i \in \mathcal{R}$ has a unique tuple ID, which takes values from a *variable ID domain* $\mathbb{D}$, and is associated with a random variable[3] taking values from a *variable value domain* $\mathbb{V}$. We assume that $\mathbb{V}$ is discrete (e.g., Boolean).[4] Each distinct *variable assignment* $\sigma : \mathbb{D} \mapsto \mathbb{V}$ defines a *possible world* I_σ that is equivalent to a standard database instantiation of the user schema.

Correlation Schema. The correlation schema defines a probability distribution over the possible worlds as follows. Intuitively, each correlation relation $F_j \in \mathcal{F}$ represents one type of correlation over the random variables in $\mathbb{D}$ by specifying *which* variables are correlated and *how* they are correlated. To specify *which*, the schema of F_j has the form $F_j(\underline{fid}, \bar{v})$ where fid is a unique factor ID taking values from a *factor ID domain* $\mathbb{F}$, and $\bar{v} \in \mathbb{D}^{a_j}$ where a_j is the number of random variables that are correlated by each factor.[5] In Figure 3, variables v_1 and v_4 are correlated. To specify *how*, F_j is associated with a function $f_j : \mathbb{V}^{a_j} \mapsto \mathbb{R}_+$. Given a possible world I_σ, for any $t = (fid, v_1, \ldots, v_{a_j}) \in F_j$, define $g_j(t, I_\sigma) = f_j(\sigma(v_1), \ldots, \sigma(v_{a_j}))$. Define $\text{vars}(fid) = \{v_1, \ldots, v_{a_j}\}$. To explain independence in the graph, we need the notion of the *Markov blanket* [30,41] of a variable v, denoted $\mathbf{mb}(v)$, and defined to be

$$\mathbf{mb}(v_i) = \{v \mid v \neq v_i,\ \exists fid \in \mathbb{F} \text{ s.t. } \{v, v_i\} \subseteq \text{vars}(fid)\}.$$

In Figure 3, $\mathbf{mb}(v_1) = \{v_2, v_4\}$. In general, a variable v is conditionally independent of a variable $v' \notin \mathbf{mb}(v)$ given $\mathbf{mb}(v)$. Here, v_1 is independent of v_3 given $\{v_2, v_4\}$.

To specify a factor function in our prototype, the user implements the C++ interface in Figure 2.[6]

Probability Distribution. Denote by $\mathcal{I}$ the set of all possible worlds. Define the *partition function* $Z : \mathcal{I} \mapsto \mathbb{R}_+$ over

[3] Either modeling the existence of a tuple (for Boolean variables) or in the form of a special attribute of R_i. The value of a random variable may be fixed as input.

[4] We describe factor graphs over continuous variables in the full version of this paper.

[5] Our representation supports factors with varying arity as well, but we focus on fixed-arity factors for simplicity.

[6] Our infrastructure also accepts higher level languages, e.g., OpenBUGS or Markov Logic, but this compilation is orthogonal to our contributions.

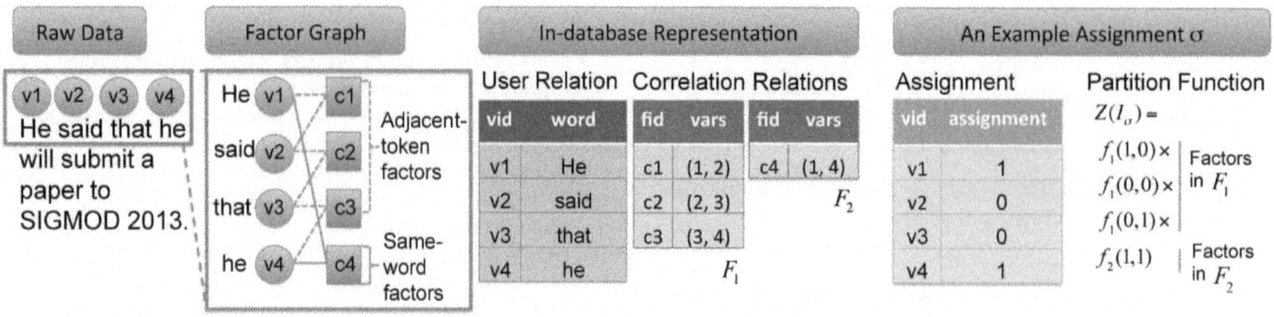

Figure 3: An example factor graph that represents a simplified skip-chain CRF; more sophisticated versions of this model are used in named-entity recognition and parsing. There is one user relation containing all tokens, and there are two correlation relations for adjacent-token correlation (F1) and same-word correlation (F2) respectively. The factor function associated to F1 (resp. F2), called f_1 (resp. f_2), is stored in a manner similar to a user-defined function.

any possible world $I \in \mathcal{I}$ as

$$Z(I) = \prod_{F_j \in \mathcal{F}} \prod_{t \in F_j} g_j(t, I) \tag{1}$$

The probability of a possible world $I \in \mathcal{I}$ is

$$\Pr[I] = Z(I) \left(\sum_{J \in \mathcal{I}} Z(J) \right)^{-1}. \tag{2}$$

We assume that $\sum_{J \in \mathcal{I}} Z(J) > 0$. It is well known that this representation can encode all discrete probability distributions over possible worlds [6].

2.2 Inference and Query Answering

In a factor graph, which defines a probability distribution, (marginal) *inference* refers to the process of computing the probability that a random variable will take a particular value. Marginal inference on factor graphs is a powerful framework. Following Sen et al. [37], we can use it to support sophisticated query answering via a two-stage process: (1) we first add a new user relation that describes the output of the query, and (2) we add in correlation relations as described by Sen et al.'s algorithm. This process creates a new factor graph, on which we perform marginal inference.

Gibbs Sampling. As exact inference for factor graphs is intractable, a commonly used inference approach is to sample, and then use the samples to compute the marginal probabilities of random variables (e.g., by averaging the outcomes). The main idea of Gibbs sampling is as follows. We start with a random possible world I_0. For each variable $v \in \mathbb{D}$, we sample a new value of v according to the conditional probability $\Pr[v|\mathbf{mb}(v)]$. A routine calculation shows that computing this probability requires that we retrieve the assignment to the variables in $\mathbf{mb}(v)$ and the factor functions associated with the factor nodes that neighbor v. Then we update v in I_0 to the new value. After scanning all variables, we obtain a first sample I_1. We repeat this process to generate I_{k+1} from I_k.

Example We continue our example (see Figure 3) of extracting information by labeling each token in a sentence using a skip-chain conditional random field [40], a type of

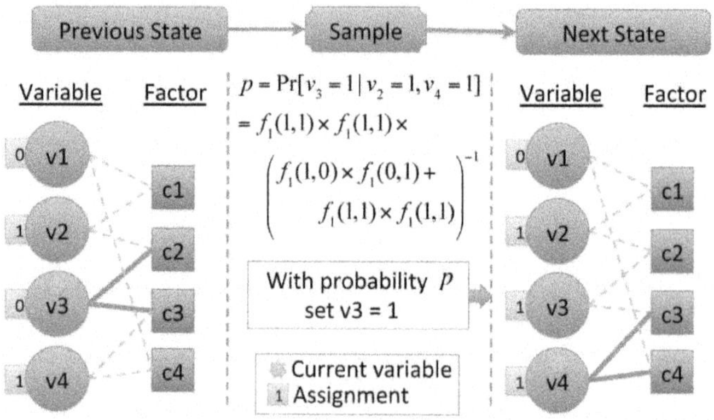

Figure 4: A step of Gibbs sampling. To sample a variable v_3, we read the current values of variables in $\mathbf{mb}(v_3) = \{v_2, v_4\}$ and calculate the conditional probability $\Pr[v_3|v_2, v_4]$. Here, the sample result is $v_3 = 1$. We update the value of v_3 and then proceed to sample v_4.

factor graphs used in named-entity recognition [14]. Figure 4 illustrates one step in Gibbs sampling to update a single variable, v_3: we compute the probability distribution over v_3 by retrieving factors c_2 and c_3, which determines $\mathbf{mb}(v_3)$. Then, we find the values of v_2 and v_4. Using Equation 2, one can check that the probability that $v_3 = 1$ is given by the equation in Figure 4 (conditioned on $\mathbf{mb}(v_3)$, the remaining factors cancel out).

There are several popular optimization techniques for Gibbs sampling that we implement in our prototype. One class of techniques improves the sample quality, e.g., *burn-in*, in which we discard the first few samples, and *thinning*, in which we retain every kth sample for some integer k [3]. A second class of techniques improves throughput using parallelism. The key observation is that variables that do not share factors may be sampled independently and so in parallel [45]. These techniques are essentially orthogonal to our contributions, and we do not discuss them further.

3. STORAGE-MANAGER TRADEOFFS TO SCALE GIBBS SAMPLING

We show that Gibbs sampling essentially performs joins and updates on a view over several base relations that represent the factor graph. Thus, we can apply classical data management techniques (such as view materialization, page-oriented layout, and buffer-replacement policy) to achieve scalability and high I/O efficiency.

3.1 Gibbs Sampling as a View

Given a database with a user schema and correlation schema as defined in the previous section, we define two simple relations that represent the edge relation of the factor graph and the sampled possible world:

$$E(v, f) = \{(v, f) | f \in \mathbb{F},\ v \in \text{vars}(f)\} \text{ and } A(\underline{v}, a) \subseteq \mathbb{D} \times \mathbb{V}$$

In Figure 3, E encodes the bipartite graph and each tuple in A corresponds to a possible assignment of a label of a variable. Note that each variable is assigned a single value (so v is a key of A) and A will be modified during Gibbs sampling.

The following view describes the input factor graph for Gibbs sampling:

$$Q(v, f, v', a') \leftarrow E(v, f), E(v', f), A(v', a'), v \neq v'.$$

When running Gibbs sampling, we group Q by the first field v. Notice that the corresponding group of tuples in Q contains all variables in the Markov blanket $\mathbf{mb}(v)$ along with all the factor IDs incident to v. This is all the information we need to generate a sample. For each group, corresponding to a variable v, we sample a new value (denoted by a) for v according to the conditional probability $\Pr[v|\mathbf{mb}(v)]$. The twist is that after we obtain a, we must update A before we proceed to the next variable to be sampled. In our implementation, we proceed through the groups in a random order.[7]

After one pass through Q, we obtain a new possible world (represented by A). We repeat this process to obtain multiple samples. By counting the number of occurrences of an event, e.g., a variable taking a particular value, we can use these samples to perform marginal inference.

We describe how we optimize the data access to Q using classical data management techniques such as view materialization and page-oriented layout. To study these tradeoffs, we implement a simple storage system. We store E and A using slotted pages [33, ch. 16] and a single-pool buffer manager.[8]

3.2 Materializing the Factor Graph

The view Q involves a three-way join. All join operators perform an index nested-loop join (see Figure 6) with a small twist: the join keys are also *record IDs*, hence we do not need to perform an actual index look-up to find the appropriate page. We examine materialization strategies to improve the performance of these joins.[9]

Materialization can reduce the number of random reads. However, a key twist is that the base relation A is updated after we examine each group. Thus, if we replicate A we could incur many random writes. We study this tradeoff by comparing four different materialization strategies in terms of random read/write costs and space requirements (see Figure 5).

- **Lazy:** we only materialize base tables. This strategy incurs the most random reads for on-the-fly joins, but the fewest random writes.
- **V-CoC:** we co-cluster on the variable side

$$QV(v, f, v') \leftarrow E(v, f), E(v', f), v \neq v'$$

  Compared to the lazy strategy, this strategy eliminates random reads on E and retains a single copy of A.
- **F-CoC:** we co-cluster on the factor side

$$QF(f, v', a) \leftarrow E(v', f), A(v', a)$$

  Compared to the lazy strategy, this strategy eliminates random reads on A at the cost of more random writes to update A within QF.
- **Eager:** we eagerly materialize Q. This strategy eliminates all random reads at the cost of high random writes during the core operation.

Figure 6 illustrates the two co-clustering strategies.

	Reads		Writes	Storage
	from A	from E	A	
Lazy	$\lvert\mathbf{mb}(v)\rvert$	d_v	1	$O(\lvert E\rvert + \lvert A\rvert)$
V-CoC	$\lvert\mathbf{mb}(v)\rvert$	0	1	$O(\sum_v \lvert\mathbf{mb}(v)\rvert + \lvert A\rvert)$
F-CoC	0	d_v	d_v	$O(\lvert E\rvert)$
Eager	0	0	$\lvert\mathbf{mb}(v)\rvert$	$O(\sum_v \lvert\mathbf{mb}(v)\rvert)$

Figure 5: I/O costs for sampling one variable under different materialization strategies. For a variable v, d_v is the number of factors in which v participates. Reads (resp. writes) are random reads (resp. random writes). The cost for each strategy is the total number of reads and writes.

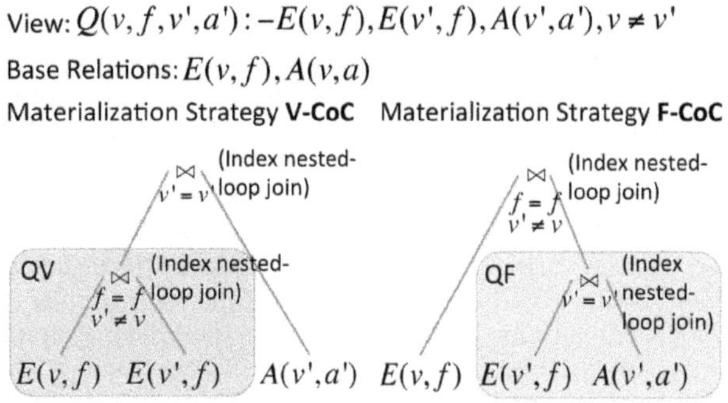

Figure 6: Strategies V-CoC and F-CoC.

[7]Our strategy is independent of the order. The order, however, empirically does change the convergence rate, and it is future work to understand the tradeoff of order and convergence.

[8]We use variable and factor IDs as record IDs, and so can look up the column v or f in both E and A using one random access (similar to RID lists [33, ch. 16]).

[9]Since we run many iterations of Gibbs sampling, the construction cost of materialized views is often smaller than the cost of running Gibbs sampling in all strategies. (In all of our experiments, the construction cost is less than 25% of the total run time.)

From Figure 5, we can see that V-CoC dominates Lazy and F-CoC dominates Eager in terms of random accesses (Assuming each factor contains at least two variables, $|\mathbf{mb}(v)| \geq 2d_v$). Our experiments confirm these analytic models (see Section 4.3). Therefore, our system selects between V-CoC and F-CoC. To determine which approach to use, our system selects the materialization strategy with the smallest random I/O cost according to our cost model.

3.3 Page-oriented Layout

With either V-CoC or F-CoC, Q is an index nested-loop join between one relation clustered on variables and another relation clustered on factors. How the data are organized into pages impacts I/O efficiency in any environment.

We formalize the problem of page-oriented layout for Gibbs sampling as follows, GLayout. The input to the problem is a tuple (V, F, E, μ, S, P) where (V, F, E) define a factor graph; that is, $V = \{v_1, \dots, v_N\}$ is a set of variables, $F = \{f_1, \dots, f_M\}$ is the set of factors, and $E = \{(v, f) \mid v \in \text{vars}(f)\}$ defines the edge relation. The order μ is a total order on the variables, V, which captures the fact that at each iteration of Gibbs sampling, one scans the variables in V in a random order, and S the page size (i.e., the maximum number of variables or factors a page can store), and P the set of pages.

Any solution for GLayout is a tuple (α, β, π) where $\alpha : V \mapsto P$ (resp. $\beta : F \mapsto P$) map variables (resp. factors) to pages. The order $\pi = (e_1, \dots, e_L)$ defines the order of edges that the algorithm visits. That is, given a fixed variable visit order $\mu = (v_1, \dots, v_N)$, we only consider tuple orders π that respect μ; we denote this set of orders as $\Pi(\mu)$.[10]

As we will see, it is possible in Gibbs sampling to construct an *optimal* page eviction strategy. For the moment, to simplify our presentation, we assume that there are only two buffer pages: one for variables and one for factors. We return to this point later. Then any ordering $\pi = (e_1, \dots, e_L)$ would incur an I/O cost (for fetching factors from disk):

$$\text{cost}(\pi, \beta) = 1 + \sum_{i=2}^{L} \mathbb{I}\left[\beta(e_i.f) \neq \beta(e_{i-1}.f)\right]$$

The goal is to find an ordering $\pi \in \Pi(\mu)$ and mapping β that minimizes the above I/O cost.

Algorithm. We use the following simple heuristic to construct (α, β, π) ordering F: we sort the factors in F in dictionary order by μ, that is, by the position of the earliest variable that occurs in a given factor. We then greedily pack F-tuples onto disk pages in this order. We show empirically that this layout has one order of magnitude improvement over randomly ordering and paging tuples.

Analysis. Extending this heuristic for better performance is theoretically challenging:

Proposition 3.1. *Assuming P≠NP, an algorithm does not exist that runs in polynomial time to find the optimal solution to* GLayout. *More strongly, assuming P≠NP, no polynomial time algorithm can even guarantee a constant approximation factor for* cost.

[10] $\Pi(\mu) = \{\pi = (e_1, \dots, e_L) \mid \forall i, j. 1 \leq i \leq j \leq L, e_i.v \preceq_\mu e_j.v\}$, where $x \preceq_\mu y$ indicates that x precedes y in μ.

We prove this proposition by encoding the multi-cut partition problem [2]. Under slightly more strict complexity assumptions (about randomized complexity classes), it also follows that getting a good layout *on average* is computationally difficult.

Multi-page Buffer. We return to the issue of more than two buffer pages. Since variables are accessed sequentially, MRU is optimal for the variable pages. One could worry that the additional number of buffer pages could be used intelligently to lower the cost. We show that we are able to reduce the multiple-page buffer case to the two-page case (and so an approximation result similar to Proposition 3.1); intuitively, given the instance generated for the two-buffer case, we include extra factors whose role in the reduction is to ensure that any optimal buffering strategy essentially incurs I/O only on the sequence of buffer pages that it would in the two-buffer case. Our proof examines the set of pages in Bélády's [7] optimal strategy, which we describe in the next section.

3.4 Buffer-Replacement Policy

When a data set does not fit in main memory, we must choose which page to evict from main memory. A key twist here is that we will be going over the same data set many times. After the first pass, we know the full reference sequence for the remainder of the execution. This enables us to use a classical result from Bélády in the 1960s [7] to define a theoretically optimal eviction strategy: *evict the item that will be used latest in the future.*

Recall that we scan variables in sequential order, so MRU is optimal for those pages. However, the factor pages require a bit more care. On the first pass of the data, we store the entire reference sequence of factors in a file, i.e., sequence $f_{i_1}, f_{i_2}, \dots$, lists each factor. For each reference, we then do a pass over this log to compute when each factor is used next in the sequence. At the end of the first scan, we have a log that consists of pairs of factor IDs and when each factor appears next. The resulting file may be several GB in size. However, during the subsequent passes, we only need the head of this log in main memory. We use this information to maintain, for each frame in the buffer manager, when that frame will be used next.

In our experiments, we evaluate under what situations this optimal strategy is worth the extra overhead. We find that the optimal strategy is close to the standard LRU in terms of run time–even if we allow the potentially unfair advantage of holding the entire reference sequence in main memory. In both cases, the number of page faults is roughly 5%–10% smaller using the optimal approach. However, we found that simple schemes based on MRU/LRU are essentially optimal in two tasks (called **LR** and **CRF** in the next section), and in the third task (called **LDA** in the next section) the variables share factors that are far apart, and so even the optimal strategy cannot mitigate all random I/O.

4. EXPERIMENTS

We validate that (1) our system is able to scale to factor graphs that are larger than main memory, and (2) for inference on factor graphs that are larger than main memory, we achieve throughput that is competitive with specialized approaches. We then validate the details of our technical claims about materialization, page-oriented layout, and

Systems	LR	CRF	LDA	Storage	Parallelism
Elementary	✓	✓	✓	Multiple	Multi-thread
Factorie	✓	✓	✓	RAM	Single-thread
PGibbs	✓	✓	✓	RAM	Multi-thread
OpenBUGS	✓		✓	RAM	Single-thread
MADlib			✓	Database	Multi-thread

Figure 7: Key features of each system that implements Gibbs sampling. OpenBUGS and MADlib do not support skip-chain CRFs. MADlib supports LR but not a full Bayesian (sampling) treatment; its support for LDA is via specialized UDFs.

buffer-replacement policy that we described in the previous section.

4.1 Experimental Setup

We run experiments on three popular statistical models: 1) logistic regression (**LR**), 2) skip-chain conditional random field [40] (**CRF**), and 3) latent Dirichlet allocation (**LDA**) [11]. We use **LR** and **CRF** for text chunking, and **LDA** for topic modeling. We select **LR** because it can be solved exactly and so can be used as a simple benchmark. We select **CRF** as it is widely used in text-related applications and inference is often performed with Gibbs sampling, and **LDA** as it is intuitively the most challenging model that is supported by all systems in our experiments.

Data Sets. To compare the quality and efficiency with other systems, we use public data sets that we call *Bench*. We run **LR** and **CRF** on CoNLL[12] and **LDA** on AP.[13] For scalability experiments and tradeoff efficiency experiments, we scale up *Bench* from 1x to 100,000x by adding more documents which are randomly selected from a one-day web crawl (5M documents, 400GB). We call the 1,000x data set *Perf* and the 100,000x data set *Scale*. Figure 8 shows the number of variables, factors, and size for each data set.

Metrics. We use two metrics to measure the quality: (1) the F1 score of the final result for data sets with ground truth (when ground truth is available) and (2) the *squared loss* [44] between the marginal probabilities that are the output of each sampling system and a gold standard on each data set (when there is no ground truth). For **LR**, we compute the gold standard using exact inference. For **CRF** and **LDA**, it is intractable to compute the exact distribution; and the standard approach is to use the results from Gibbs sampling after running many iterations beyond convergence [44]. In particular, we get an approximate gold standard for both **CRF** and **LDA** on *Bench* by running Gibbs sampling for 10M iterations. For efficiency, we measure the *throughput* as the number of samples produced by a system per second.

[11]As shown in the full version of this paper, following MADLib [17], we incrementally maintain the evaluation result of LDA factors with regard to changes of variable assignment. We implement this by attaching a fixed-size memory area to each factor. All tradeoffs, i.e., materialization, page-oriented layout, and buffer-replacement policy, still apply to this case.

[12]`http://www.cnts.ua.ac.be/conll2000/chunking/`

[13]`http://www.cs.princeton.edu/~blei/lda-c/`

Setting Name	Page Size	Buffer Size
Sp/Sb	4KB	40KB
Lp/Sb	4MB	40MB
Sp/Lb	4KB	4GB
Lp/Lb	4MB	4GB
Lp/MAXb	4MB	40GB

Figure 9: Different configuration settings of Elementary. Sp (resp. Lp) means *small (resp. large) page size*; Sb (resp. Lb) means *small (resp. large) buffer-size.*

Competitor Systems. We compare our system with four state-of-the-art Gibbs sampling systems: (1) PGibbs on GraphLab [15], (2) Factorie [26], and (3) OpenBUGS [25], which are main memory systems, and MADlib [17], a scalable in-database implementation of LDA. PGibbs and MADlib[14] are implemented using C++, OpenBUGS is implemented using Pascal and C, and Factorie is implemented using Java. We use Greenplum 4.2.1.0 for MADlib. The key features of each system are shown in Figure 7. For each model (i.e., **LR**, **CRF**, and **LDA**), all systems take the same factor graph as their input. We modify each system to output squared loss after each iteration, and we do not count this time as part of the execution time.

Details of our Prototype. We call our prototype system Elementary, and compare three variants of our system by plugging in different storage backends: **EleMM**, **EleFILE**, and **EleHBASE**. We use main memory, traditional unix files, and HBase, respectively, for these three variants. **EleMM** is used to compare with other main memory systems. **EleFILE** and **EleHBASE** use different secondary storage and are used to validate scalability and I/O tradeoffs.

Our system is implemented using C++ and bypasses the OS disk-page cache to support its own buffer manager. We compile all C++ code using GCC 4.7.2 and all Java code using Java 1.7u4. All experiments are run on a RHEL6.1 workstation with two 2.67GHz Intel Xeon CPUs (12 cores, 24 hyper-threaded), 128GB of RAM, and 12×2TB RAID0 drives. All data and temporary files are stored on a RAID, and all software is installed on a separate disk. We use the latest HBase-0.94.1 on a single machine[15] and follow best practices to tune HBase.[16]

We use various page-size/buffer-size combinations, as shown in Figure 9. These configuration settings correspond to small/large page sizes and small/large buffer sizes. We explore more settings in the full version, but the high-level conclusions are similar to these four settings so we omit those results. The **Lp/MAXb** setting is used for end-to-end experiments.

4.2 End-to-end Efficiency and Scalability

We validate that our system achieves state-of-the-art quality by demonstrating that it converges to the gold-standard probability distribution on each task. We then compare our

[14]`http://doc.madlib.net/v0.3/group__grp__plda.html`

[15]Our system can use HBase on multiple machines to get even higher scalability. We only discuss the one-machine case to be fair to other systems.

[16]http://hbase.apache.org/book/performance.html

Models	Bench (1x)			Perf (1,000x)			Scale (100,000x)		
	$\lvert V \rvert$	$\lvert F \rvert$	Size	$\lvert V \rvert$	$\lvert F \rvert$	Size	$\lvert V \rvert$	$\lvert F \rvert$	Size
LR	47K	47K	2MB	47M	47M	2GB	5B	5B	0.19TB
CRF	47K	94K	3MB	47M	94M	3GB	5B	9B	0.3TB
LDA	0.4M	12K	10M	0.4B	10M	9GB	39B	0.2B	0.9TB

Figure 8: Data sets sizes. We omit the 10x, 100x, and 10,000x cases from this table.

	# thread = 1			# threads = 20		
	LR	**CRF**	**LDA**	**LR**	**CRF**	**LDA**
EleMM	24	18	12	12x	9x	6x
EleFILE	34	24	33	9x	6x	4x
EleHBASE	101	70	92	9x	7x	4x
PGibbs	38	42	CRASH	9x	5x	CRASH
MADLib	N/A	N/A	17	N/A	N/A	8x
Factorie	95	120	6	N/A	N/A	N/A
OpenBUGS	150	N/A	CRASH	N/A	N/A	N/A

Figure 10: The time in seconds (speedup for 20-threads case) needed to achieve squared loss below 0.01 for *Bench* data set. N/A means that the task is not supported.

system's efficiency and scalability with that of our competitors.

Quality. We validate that our system converges to the gold-standard probability distribution on several tasks. We run all systems on *Bench* using the configuration **Lp/MAXb**. We take a snapshot after each system produces a sample; we output the squared loss and F1 score of that snapshot. Figure 10 shows the time that each system needs to converge to a solution with a squared loss less than 0.01. We chose 0.01 since a smaller loss does not improve the F1 score, i.e., when the loss is less than 0.01, **LR** converges to F1=0.79 and **CRF** to F1=0.81, which are the gold-standard values for these tasks. This validates that all systems achieve the same quality, and thus a more interesting question is to understand the rate at which they achieve the quality.

Efficiency. To understand the rate at which a system achieves the gold-standard quality, we run PGibbs, MADlib, Factorie, and OpenBUGS and measure when they are within 0.01 of the optimal loss. If a system can take advantage of multi-threading, we also run it with 20 threads and report the speedup factor compared with one thread. We chose our materialization strategy to be consistent with what is hard coded in state-of-the-art competitors, i.e., V-CoC for **LR** and **CRF**, and F-CoC for **LDA**. Figure 10 shows the results.

When there is 1-thread and all the data fit in main memory, we observe that all systems converge to gold-standard probability distribution within roughly comparable times. This is likely due to the fact that main memory Gibbs sampling uses a set of well-known techniques, which are widely implemented. There are, however, some minor differences in runtime. On **LR** and **CRF**, EleMM has comparable efficiency to PGibbs, but is slightly faster. After reviewing PGibbs' code, we believe the efficiency difference (<2x) is caused by the performance overhead of PGibbs explicitly representing factor functions as a table. For **LR** and **CRF**, EleMM is 4–10x faster than Factorie, and we believe that this is because Factorie is written in Java (not C++). OpenBUGS is more than one order of magnitude slower than EleMM. This difference in OpenBUGS is due to the inefficiency in how it records the samples of each variable. PGibbs requires explicit enumeration of all outcomes for each factor, and so the input size to PGibbs is exponential in the size of the largest factor. As **LDA** involves factors with hundreds or more variables, we could not run **LDA** on PGibbs. OpenBUGS crashed on **LDA** while compiling the model and data with the error message "illegal memory read." Elementary with secondary storage backends has similar performance trends, but is overall 2–5x slower than EleMM, due to the overhead of I/O.

For 20-thread cases, we observe speedups for all multi-threading systems. EleFILE and EleHBASE gets smaller speedups compared with EleMM because of the overhead of I/O requests. PGibbs also gets slightly smaller speedups than EleMM, and we believe that this marginal difference is caused by the overhead of MPI, which is used by PGibbs.

Scalability. We validate that our system can scale to larger data sets by using secondary storage backends. We run all systems on data sets scaling from 1x (*Bench*) to 100,000x (*Scale*) using one thread and **Lp/MAXb**. We let each system run for 24 hours and stop it afterwards. Figure 11 shows the results for **LR** and **LDA**.[17] We also run a baseline system, **Baseline**, that uses the file system as storage and disables all of our optimizations (lazy materialization, and no buffer management).

Not surprisingly, only systems that use secondary storage backends, i.e., EleFILE, EleHBASE, and MADlib (only for LDA), scale to the largest data sets; in contrast, main memory systems crash or thrash at scaling factors of 10x or more. As the core operation is scan based, it also not surprising that each system scales up almost linearly (if it is able to run).

However, the performance of the various approaches can be quite different. The Baseline system is three orders of magnitude slower than EleMM (it does not finish the first iteration within 24 hours on the 100x scale factor). This shows that buffer management is crucial to implementing an

[17] **CRF** is similar to **LR**, we include it in the full version.

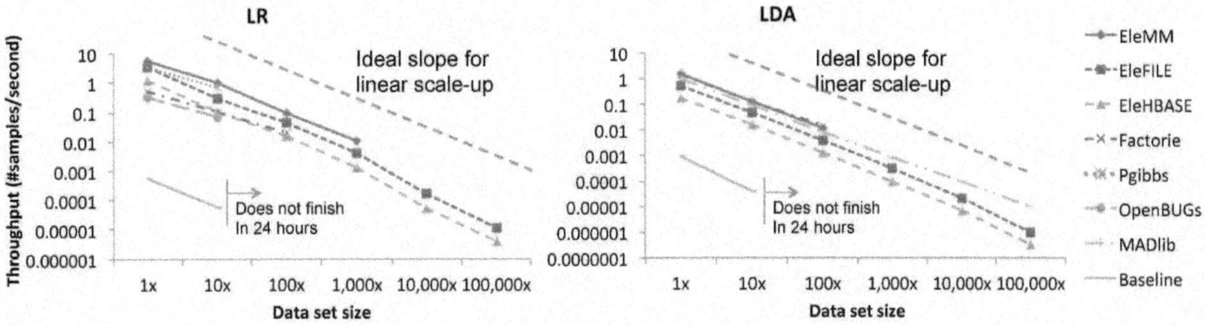

Figure 11: Scalability of Different Systems.

Model	A	E	QV	QF	Q
LR	0.18	1.4	1.4	1.4	1.4
CRF	0.18	2.0	3.2	2.0	3.2
LDA	1.66	9.0	100T+	9.0	100T+

Figure 12: Size of intermediate state in *Perf* dataset (see Sec. 3). All sizes in GB, except where noted.

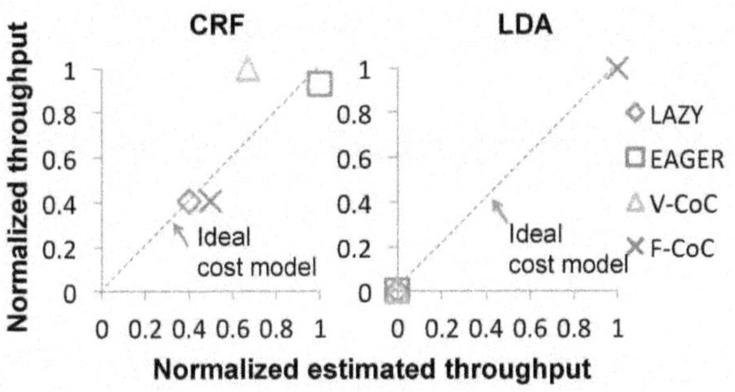

Figure 13: Accuracy of the cost model of different materialization strategies.

I/O-efficient Gibbs sampler. Due to higher I/O overheads, EleHBASE is 3x slower than EleFILE.

MADlib uses PostgreSQL as the storage backend, and is 2x faster than EleFILE. However, MADlib uses an approximate sampler for LDA, while our system implements an exact sampler. If we allow EleFILE to run this approximate sampler, EleFILE is between 10-20% faster.

4.3 I/O tradeoffs

We validate that both the materialization tradeoff and the page-oriented layout tradeoff in Section 3 affect the throughput of Gibbs sampling on factor graphs that are larger than main memory, while the buffer-replacement tradeoff only has a marginal impact. We also validate that we can automatically select near-optimal strategies based on our I/O cost model.

View Materialization. We validate that (1) the co-clustering strategies that we explored in Section 3 outperform both Lazy and Eager strategies, and (2) neither of the co-clustering strategies dominates the other. We compare the four materialization strategies; our GLAYOUT heuristic page-oriented layout is used in all settings. We report results for both EleFILE and EleHBASE on **CRF** and **LDA**.

As shown in Figure 14(a), for **CRF**, V-CoC dominates other strategies for all settings. We looked into the buffer manager; we found that (1) V-CoC outperforms Lazy (resp. F-CoC) by incurring 75% fewer read misses on **Sp/Sb** (resp. **Sp/Lb**); and (2) V-CoC incurs 20% fewer dirty page writes than Eager. The situation, however, is reversed in **LDA**. Here, F-CoC dominates, as both V-CoC and Eager fail to run **LDA** as they would require 100TB+ of disk space for materialization. Thus, neither co-clustering strategy dominates the other, but one always dominates both Eager and Lazy. The same observation holds for both EleFILE and EleHBASE.

A key difference between these tasks is that the number of variables in most factors in **LDA** is much larger (can be larger than 1,000) than **LR** and **CRF** (fewer than 3). Thus, some pre-materialization strategies are expensive in **LDA**. On the other hand, for **LR** and **CRF**, the time needed to look up factors is the bottleneck (which is optimized by V-CoC).

We then validate that one can automatically select between different materialization strategies by using the cost model shown in Figure 5. For each model and materialization strategy, we estimated the throughput as the inverse of the estimated total amount of I/O. For each materialization strategy, we plot its estimated and actual throughput. Figure 13 shows the results for EleFILE (**Sp/Lb**). We can see that the throughput decreases when the estimated throughput decreases. Based on this cost model, we can select the near-optimal materialization strategy.

Page-oriented Layout. We validate that our heuristic ordering strategy can improve sampling throughput over a random ordering. We focus on the F-CoC materialization strategy here, and report the V-CoC setting in the full version because the results are similar. We compare two page-oriented layout strategies: (1) **Shuffle**, in which we randomly shuffle the factor table, and (2) **Greedy**, which use our greedy heuristic to layout the factor table. As shown in Figure 14(b), **Greedy** dominates **Shuffle** on all data sets in both settings. For **CRF**, the heuristic can achieve two orders of magnitude of speedup. We found that for **Sp/Lb**, heuristic ordering incurs two orders of magnitude fewer page faults than random ordering. These results show that the tradeoff in page-oriented layout impacts the throughput of Gibbs sampling on factor graphs that do not fit in memory.

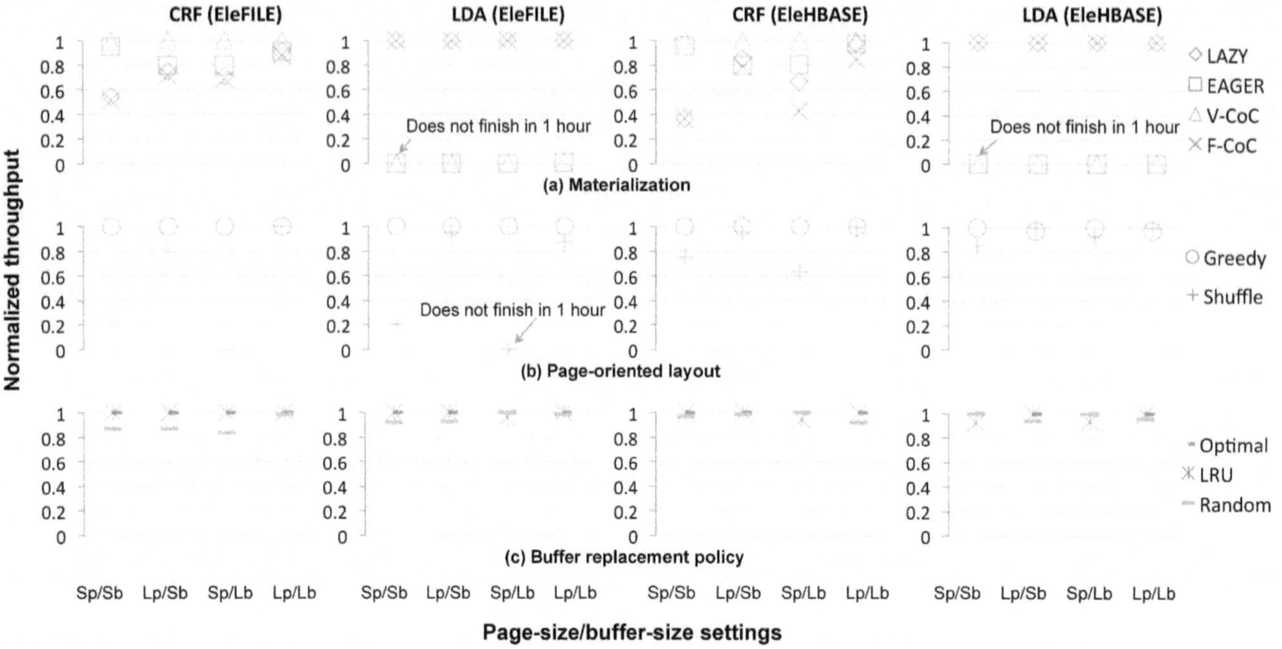

Figure 14: I/O tradeoffs on *Perf* dataset. Recall that Sp (resp. Lp) means *small (resp. large) page size*; Sb (resp. Lb) means *small (resp. large) buffer size*. See Figure 9 for the exact definitions of page and buffer size settings

Buffer-Replacement Policy. We validate that the optimal buffer-replacement strategy can only achieve a marginal improvement of sampling throughput over LRU. We compare three settings: (1) **Optimal**, which uses the optimal caching strategy on tables with random access, (2) **LRU**, which uses LRU on tables with random access; and (3) **Random**, which uses a random replacement policy. We use MRU on tables with sequential scan. We use V-CoC for **LR** and **CRF**, F-CoC for **LDA**, and **Greedy** for all page-oriented layouts because they are the optimal strategies for these tasks. As shown in Figure 14(c), **Optimal** achieves 10% higher throughput than **Random** for **CRF**, and 5% higher throughput than **LRU** for **LDA**. For **CRF**, the access pattern of factors is much like a sequence scan, and therefore **LRU** is near-optimal. As **Optimal** requires non-trivial implementation and is not implemented in existing data processing systems, an engineer may opt against implementing it in a production system.

Discussion. On this small set of popular tasks, our experiments demonstrate that our prototype can achieve competitive (and sometimes better) throughput and scalability than state-of-the-art systems for Gibbs sampling from factor graphs that are larger than main memory. What is interesting to us about this result is that we used a set of generic optimizations inspired by classical database techniques. Of course, in any given problem, there may be problem-specific optimizations that can dramatically improve throughput. For example, in higher-level languages like MCDB or Factorie, there may be additional optimization opportunities. Our goal, however, is not to exhaustively enumerate such optimizations; instead, we view the value of our work as articulating a handful of tradeoffs that may be used to improve the throughput of either specialized or generic systems for Gibbs sampling from factor graphs. These tradeoffs have not been systematically studied in previous work. Also, our techniques are orthogonal to optimizations that choose between various sampling methods to improve runtime performance, e.g., Wang et al. [42]. A second orthogonal direction is distributing the data to many machines; such an approach would allow us to achieve higher scalability and performance. We believe that the optimizations that we describe are still useful in the distributed setting. However, there are new tradeoffs that may need to be considered, e.g., communication and replication tradeoffs are obvious areas to explore.

5. RELATED WORK

We describe related work from the Gibbs sampling literature and the probabilistic databases literature.

Probabilistic graphical models [21] and factor graphs, in particular, are popular frameworks for statistical modeling. Gibbs sampling has been applied to a wide range of probabilistic models and applications [3], e.g., risk models in actuarial science [4], conditional random fields for information extraction [14], latent Dirichlet allocation for topic modeling [16, 17], and Markov logic for text applications [12, 28].

There are several recent general-purpose systems in which a user specifies a factor graph model and the system performs sampling-based inference. For example, Factorie [26] allows a user to specify arbitrary factor functions in Java; OpenBUGS [25] provides an interface for a user to specify arbitrary Bayes nets (which are also factor graphs) and performs Gibbs sampling on top of them; PGibbs [15] performs parallel Gibbs sampling over factor graphs on top of GraphLab [24]. We hope the tradeoffs we describe here add to this line of work for factor graphs that are larger than main memory.

To deploy sophisticated statistical analysis over increasingly data-intensive applications, there is a push to combine factor graphs and databases [37,44]. However, Sen et al. [37] did not consider Gibbs sampling. Most closely related to our work is Wick et al. [44], who do perform blocked Gibbs sampling and exploit a connection to materialized view maintenance. However, their approach performs the core operation in main memory. Hence, they did not consider the tradeoffs that we discuss in this paper.

Gibbs sampling is often optimized for specific applications. For example, a popular technique for implementing Gibbs sampling for latent Dirichlet allocation [16, 23, 32, 38] is to only maintain the sum of a set of Boolean random variables instead of individual variable assignments. A more aggressive parallelization strategy allows non-atomic updates to the variables to increase throughput (possibly at the expense of sample quality) [23,38]. Our prototype does allow this optimization, but it is orthogonal to our contributions (and we do not use it in our experiments).

One line of work tries to scale up these main-memory systems to support analytics on data sets that are larger than main memory. For example, the Ricardo system [11] integrates R and Hadoop to process terabytes of data stored on HDFS. However, Ricardo spawns R processes on Hadoop worker nodes, and still assumes that statistical analytics happen in main memory on a single node. Our system, however, studies how to scale up Gibbs sampling using both main memory and secondary storage. Systems like Ricardo could take advantage of our results to get higher scalability by improving single-node scalability. The MCDB system [20] is the seminal work of integrating sampling-based approaches into a database. MCDB scales up the sampling process using an RDBMS. However, it assumes that the classic I/O tradeoffs for an RDBMS work in the same way for sampling. Our work revisits these classical tradeoffs, and we hope that our study contributes to this line of work.

There is a rich literature on pushing probabilistic models and algorithms into database systems [1, 5, 10, 19, 29, 31, 35, 37, 42, 44]. Factor graphs [41] are one of the most popular and general formalisms [37, 42, 44]. There are alternative representation frameworks to factor graphs. For example, BayesStore [43] uses Bayes nets; Trio [1, 35], MayBMS [5], and MystiQ [10] use *c*-tables [18]; MCDB [19] uses VG functions; and Markov logic systems such as Tuffy [28] use grounded-clause tables. We focus on factor graphs but speculate that our techniques could apply to other probabilistic frameworks as well. PrDB [37] uses factor graphs and casts SQL queries as inference problems in factor graphs. While PrDB represents factor functions by enumerating all possible outcomes, we observe that such explicit enumeration is inefficient for factors involving hundreds of variables (e.g., in LDA), and so our system follows Factorie [26] and represents factor functions as C++ functions. PrDB could adopt this representation as well.

6. CONCLUSION

Motivated by problems in a variety of governmental and industrial applications, we studied how to make a highly scalable Gibbs sampler. All other things being equal, a Gibbs sampler that produces samples with higher throughput allows us to obtain high quality more quickly. Thus, the central technical challenge that we study is how to create a high-throughput sampler. In contrast to previous approaches that optimize sampling by proposing new algorithms, we examined whether or not traditional database optimization techniques could be used to improve the core operation of Gibbs sampling. In particular, we study the impact of a handful of classical data management tradeoffs on the throughput of Gibbs sampling on factor graphs that are larger than main memory. Our work articulates a handful of tradeoffs that may be used to improve the throughput of such systems, including materialization, page-oriented layout, and buffer-management tradeoffs. After analytically examining the tradeoff space for each technique, we described novel materialization strategies and a greedy page-oriented layout strategy for factor graphs.

Our experimental study found that our techniques allowed us to achieve up to two orders of magnitude improvement in throughput over classical techniques. Using a classical result due to Bélády, we implemented the optimal page-replacement strategy, but found empirically that it offered only modest improvement over traditional techniques. Overall, we saw that by optimizing for only these classical tradeoffs, we were able to construct a prototype system that achieves competitive (and sometimes much better) throughput than prior Gibbs sampling systems for factor graphs. As our optimization techniques are orthogonal to other techniques in the literature, we hope that our techniques will contribute to a wide array of sampling systems that have been developed in recent years.

7. ACKNOWLEDGMENT

We gratefully acknowledge the support of Defense Advanced Research Projects Agency (DARPA) DEFT Program under Air Force Research Laboratory (AFRL) prime contract No. FA8750-13-2-0039, the National Science Foundation EAGER Award under No. EAR-1242902 and CAREER Award under No. IIS-1054009, the Office of Naval Research under awards No. N000141210041 and No. N000141310129, Sloan Research Fellowship, American Family Insurance, and Google. Any opinions, findings, and conclusion or recommendations expressed in this material are those of the authors and do not necessarily reflect the view of DARPA, AFRL, ONR, NSF, or the US government.

8. REFERENCES

[1] P. Agrawal, O. Benjelloun, A. D. Sarma, C. Hayworth, S. Nabar, T. Sugihara, and J. Widom. Trio: A system for data, uncertainty, and lineage. In *VLDB*, 2006.

[2] K. Andreev and H. Räcke. Balanced graph partitioning. In *SPAA*, 2004.

[3] C. Andrieu, N. de Freitas, A. Doucet, and M. I. Jordan. An Introduction to MCMC for Machine Learning. *Machine Learning*, 2003.

[4] K. Antonio and J. Beirlant. Actuarial statistics with generalized linear mixed models. In *Insurance: Mathematics and Economics*, 2006.

[5] L. Antova, C. Koch, and D. Olteanu. Query language support for incomplete information in the MayBMS system. In *VLDB*, 2007.

[6] D. Barber. *Bayesian Reasoning and Machine Learning*. Cambridge University Press, 2012.

[7] L. A. Belady. A study of replacement algorithms for a virtual-storage computer. *IBM Syst. J.*, 1966.

[8] D. M. Blei, A. Y. Ng, and M. I. Jordan. Latent Dirichlet allocation. *J. Mach. Learn. Res.*, 2003.

[9] F. Chen, X. Feng, C. Re, and M. Wang. Optimizing statistical information extraction programs over evolving text. In *ICDE*, 2012.

[10] N. Dalvi, C. Re, and D. Suciu. Queries and materialized views on probabilistic databases. *JCSS*, 2011.

[11] S. Das, Y. Sismanis, K. S. Beyer, R. Gemulla, P. J. Haas, and J. McPherson. Ricardo: Integrating R and Hadoop. In *SIGMOD*, 2010.

[12] P. Domingos and D. Lowd. *Markov Logic: An Interface Layer for Artificial Intelligence.* Morgan and Claypool Publishers, 2009.

[13] N. Fenton and M. Neil. Combining evidence in risk analysis using Bayesian networks. *Agena*, 2004.

[14] J. Finkel, T. Grenager, and C. Manning. Incorporating non-local information into information extraction systems by Gibbs sampling. In *ACL*, 2005.

[15] J. Gonzalez, Y. Low, A. Gretton, and C. Guestrin. Parallel Gibbs sampling: From colored fields to thin junction trees. In *AISTATS*, 2011.

[16] T. L. Griffiths and M. Steyvers. Finding scientific topics. *PNAS*, 2004.

[17] J. M. e. a. Hellerstein. The MADlib analytics library: or MAD skills, the SQL. *PVLDB*, 2012.

[18] T. Imieliński and W. Lipski, Jr. Incomplete information in relational databases. *J. ACM*, 1984.

[19] R. Jampani, F. Xu, M. Wu, L. Perez, C. Jermaine, and P. J. Haas. The Monte Carlo database system: Stochastic analysis close to the data. *TODS*, 2011.

[20] R. Jampani, F. Xu, M. Wu, L. L. Perez, C. M. Jermaine, and P. J. Haas. MCDB: A Monte Carlo approach to managing uncertain data. In *SIGMOD*, 2008.

[21] D. Koller and N. Friedman. *Probabilistic Graphical Models: Principles and Techniques.* MIT Press, 2009.

[22] J. D. Lafferty, A. McCallum, and F. C. N. Pereira. Conditional random fields: Probabilistic models for segmenting and labeling sequence data. In *ICML*, 2001.

[23] Z. Liu, Y. Zhang, E. Y. Chang, and M. Sun. PLDA+: Parallel latent Dirichlet allocation with data placement and pipeline processing. *ACM TIST.*, 2011.

[24] Y. Low, J. Gonzalez, A. Kyrola, D. Bickson, C. Guestrin, and J. M. Hellerstein. Graphlab: A new parallel framework for machine learning. In *UAI*, 2010.

[25] D. Lunn, D. Spiegelhalter, A. Thomas, and N. Best. The BUGS project: Evolution, critique and future directions. *Statistics in Medicine*, 2009.

[26] A. McCallum, K. Schultz, and S. Singh. Factorie: Probabilistic programming via imperatively defined factor graphs. In *NIPS*, 2009.

[27] D. Newman, P. Smyth, and M. Steyvers. Scalable parallel topic models. *Journal of Intelligence Community Research and Development*, 2006.

[28] F. Niu, C. Ré, A. Doan, and J. W. Shavlik. Tuffy: Scaling up statistical inference in Markov logic networks using an RDBMS. *PVLDB*, 2011.

[29] D. Olteanu, J. Huang, and C. Koch. Sprout: Lazy vs. eager query plans for tuple-independent probabilistic databases. In *ICDE*, 2009.

[30] J. Pearl. *Probabilistic Reasoning in Intelligent Systems: Networks of Plausible Inference.* Morgan Kaufmann, 1st edition, Sept. 1988.

[31] L. Peng, Y. Diao, and A. Liu. Optimizing probabilistic query processing on continuous uncertain data. *PVLDB*, 2011.

[32] I. Porteous, D. Newman, A. Ihler, A. Asuncion, P. Smyth, and M. Welling. Fast collapsed Gibbs sampling for latent Dirichlet allocation. In *KDD*, 2008.

[33] R. Ramakrishnan and J. Gehrke. *Database Management Systems.* Osborne/McGraw-Hill, 2000.

[34] C. P. Robert and G. Casella. *Monte Carlo Statistical Methods (Springer Texts in Statistics).* Springer-Verlag New York, Inc., 2005.

[35] A. D. Sarma, O. Benjelloun, A. Halevy, S. Nabar, and J. Widom. Representing uncertain data: Models, properties, and algorithms. *The VLDB Journal*, 2009.

[36] S. Satpal, S. Bhadra, S. Sellamanickam, R. Rastogi, and P. Sen. Web information extraction using Markov logic networks. In *WWW*, 2011.

[37] P. Sen, A. Deshpande, and L. Getoor. PrDB: Managing and exploiting rich correlations in probabilistic databases. *The VLDB Journal*, 2009.

[38] A. Smola and S. Narayanamurthy. An architecture for parallel topic models. *PVLDB*, 2010.

[39] J. R. Sobehart, R. Stein, V. Mikityanskaya, and L. Li. Moody's public firm risk model: A hybrid approach to modeling short term default risk. *Moody's Investors Service, Global Credit Research, Rating Methodology*, 2000.

[40] C. Sutton and A. Mccallum. Collective segmentation and labeling of distant entities in information extraction. Technical Report #04-49, U. Mass, 2004.

[41] M. J. Wainwright and M. I. Jordan. Graphical models, exponential families, and variational inference. *Found. Trends Mach. Learn.*, 2008.

[42] D. Z. Wang, M. J. Franklin, M. Garofalakis, J. M. Hellerstein, and M. L. Wick. Hybrid in-database inference for declarative information extraction. In *SIGMOD*, 2011.

[43] D. Z. Wang, E. Michelakis, M. Garofalakis, and J. M. Hellerstein. BayesStore: Managing large, uncertain data repositories with probabilistic graphical models. *PVLDB*, 2008.

[44] M. Wick, A. McCallum, and G. Miklau. Scalable probabilistic databases with factor graphs and mcmc. *PVLDB*, 2010.

[45] T. Xu and A. T. Ihler. Multicore Gibbs sampling in dense, unstructured graphs. *AISTATS*, 2011.

[46] J. Zhu, Z. Nie, X. Liu, B. Zhang, and J.-R. Wen. StatSnowball: A statistical approach to extracting entity relationships. In *WWW*, 2009.

Latch-Free Data Structures for DBMS

Design, Implementation, and Evaluation

Takashi Horikawa
Knowledge Discovery Research Laboratories
NEC Corporation
Kawasaki, Japan
t-horikawa@aj.jp.nec.com

ABSTRACT

The fact that multi-core CPUs have become so common and that the number of CPU cores in one chip has continued to rise means that a server machine can easily contain an extremely high number of CPU cores. The CPU scalability of IT systems is thus attracting a considerable amount of research attention. Some systems, such as ACID-compliant DBMSs, are said to be difficult to scale, probably due to the mutual exclusion required to ensure data consistency. Possible countermeasures include latch-free (LF) data structures, an elemental technology to improve the CPU scalability by eliminating the need for mutual exclusion. This paper investigates these LF data structures with a particular focus on their applicability and effectiveness. Some existing LF data structures (such as LF hash tables) have been adapted to PostgreSQL, one of the most popular open-source DBMSs. The performance improvement was evaluated with a benchmark program simulating real-world transactions. Measurement results obtained from state-of-the-art 80-core machines demonstrated that the LF data structures were effective for performance improvement in a many-core situation in which DBT-1 throughput increased by about 2.5 times. Although the poor performance of the original DBMS was due to a severe latch-related bottleneck and can be improved by parameter tuning, it is of practical importance that LF data structures provided performance improvement without deep understanding of the target system behavior that is necessary for the parameter tuning.

Categories and Subject Descriptors

H.2.4 [**Database Management**]: Systems—*concurrency, relational databases, transaction processing*; D.1.3 [**Programming Techniques**]: Concurrent programming; C.4 [**Performance of Systems**]: Design studies, Measurement techniques, Performance attributes; D.2.4 [**Software/Program Verification**]: Formal methods

General Terms

Algorithms, Design, Performance, Measurement, Verification

SIGMOD'13, June 22–27, 2013, New York, New York, USA.

Keywords

Scalability, Database Management System, Bottleneck, Critical Section, Benchmark Program, Performance Tuning, Many-core System, Symmetric Multiprocessing, and Formal Verification

1. INTRODUCTION

When improving the performance of IT systems, we have no choice but to depend on the effective use of multi-core CPUs because the course of processor evolution has changed from boosting the clock rate to putting multiple cores on a single CPU chip [2]. Since a server machine can easily have plenty of CPU cores, CPU scalability has gradually acquired more importance and is now a major concern in IT systems. In this context, various methodologies and techniques have been developed to efficiently utilize many-CPU cores to improve the performance. Scale-out and many-core (a type of scale-up) architectures are typical examples.

Some systems, such as Web and application servers, are relatively easy to scale. Each process in the system shares only a little data, which means it can be executed independently from other processes. As for database systems, one possible approach to improving the CPU scalability is to relax the consistency model. The BASE[1] consistency model has been widely used, especially in systems related to big data. This approach can greatly improve the CPU scalability, and thus the scale-out architecture is suitable in this case.

In contrast, ACID[2]-compliant DBMSs are said to be difficult to scale despite their importance. Using the BASE consistency model requires a comprehensive change to the whole system architecture, and thus it can be difficult to apply it to existing systems, as usually performance improvement are required without modifying any application codes. There are also some mission critical systems for which the ACID consistency model is crucial. The reason systems using the ACID model have poor CPU scalability is that they use many dependent processes accessing many shared objects while enforcing isolation among them. A recent study pointed out that critical sections enforced by latches are reemerging as scalability concerns [10].

Latch-free data structures have been the focus of much research interest and many variations, latch-free hash tables [12] being one example, have been proposed as element technologies to improve CPU scalability. Because many studies have been performed on latch-free techniques and primitive mechanisms to implement the latch-free algorithm, usually atomic instructions of CPUs such as Compare-And-Swap (CAS), have been the same for a long time, the latch-free field seems fairly mature. The focus of the latch-free

[1] Basically Available, Soft state, Eventual consistency

[2] Atomicity, Consistency, Isolation, Durability

techniques has therefore gradually shifted to how effective and easy they are to use in real-world applications.

In this paper, I focus on latch-free data structures that I adapted to *PostgreSQL*, one of the most popular open-source DBMSs, and evaluate their applicability and effectiveness. Two latch-free data structures have been applied: 1) an existing latch-free hash table with a newly implemented built-in reference counter mechanism (crucial for using it in the DBMS) and an improved memory recycle mechanism, and 2) a newly developed latch-free lock algorithm that supports multiple-lock request modes. The accuracy of their operation is verified by a formal verification method using *SPIN*[9].

The majority of the performance evaluation was conducted with the *DBT-1* benchmark program [20], which simulates real-world transactions, and with a micro benchmark program (*pgbench*), which checks the behavior in an extreme situation. The results obtained from state-of-the-art 80-core machines showed that the latch-free data structures were effective for performance improvement in the many-core situation in that DBT-1 throughput increased by about 2.5 times. Although the poor performance of the original DBMS was due to a severe latch-related bottleneck and can be improved by parameter tuning, it is of practical importance that LF data structures improved the performance. Also significant is that because the improvement has been achieved on a conventional ACID-compliant DBMS, a great number of people will be able to take advantage of it. This is a promising approach for improving DBMS scalability that does not require introducing any radical change to the DBMS architecture (e.g., by using the BASE consistency model).

The are five primary contributions in this paper: 1) modifications to a latch-free hash table, including a built-in reference counter and an improved memory recycle mechanism; 2) a newly developed latch-free lock algorithm for the lock manager that supports multiple lock-request modes, which can be used even if the fast path lock mechanism, newly introduced in *PostgreSQL* 9.2, cannot be used; 3) verified operations by a formal verification method using *SPIN*, 4) implementation in one of the most popular open-source DBMSs, and 5) a demonstrated performance improvement through the DBMS measurements.

The rest of this paper is organized as follows. Section 2 describes the concept, design, and verification of the latch-free data structures, and in Section 3, they are applied in *PostgreSQL*. Section 4 presents the results of performance measurements along with a discussion. Section 5 discusses related work, followed by the conclusion of the paper in Section 6.

2. LATCH-FREE DATA STRUCTURES

2.1 Definitions

This paper will use a few technical terms, defined below.

Scalability in this paper is a property of systems to improve performance by adding CPU cores. A server machine is said to have good scalability if it can deliver a performance that is proportional to the number of CPU cores it contains.

Lock is a mechanism to protect "end-user visible resources" such as tables, rows in tables, transactions, sequences, materialized views, etc. from concurrent user access, i.e., serializing requests that cannot be done at the same time.

Latch is a mechanism to protect a program's internal data structures from being corrupted by multiple sessions/processes modifying them at the same time. "Mutex" often has a similar meaning to "latch", but in this paper I uses the word "mutex" to refer to the mutual exclusion mechanism that protects the status data of a latch. Examples include the LWLocks[3] used in *PostgreSQL*.

Latch-free means an algorithm or mechanism that enables multiple processes to access a data structure concurrently without race conditions or data corruption without mutual exclusion. The goal of latch-free in this paper is not to eliminate latches completely but to substantially reduce the influence of the latches. The latch is eliminated from a case in which the lock is available thus the process is possible to acquire the lock immediately. In the case of lock contention, on the other hand, the process may invoke a mutual exclusion enforced by latch, but its influence on the performance is small compared with the cost of sleep and wake-up operations carried out in the case of the lock contention.

Although "latch-free" seems to be used less commonly than "lock free" and sometimes used in a different way, as in a "latch-free wait event", this paper strictly follows the definition above. Since I focus on the internal aspects of DBMS, "lock-free" is not the subject of this paper; the lock requests are generated in application programs (i.e., outside the DBMS), and thus the DBMS plays no role in generating lock requests.

2.2 Latch-free hash tables

The latch-free hash table used in this paper is based on one proposed by Michael [12], a separate-chaining hash table that has a bucket array (hash head) in which each slot contains a pointer that points to a linked list containing the key-value pairs that are hashed to the same location. Some modifications–including a built-in reference counter, related API, and improved memory recycle mechanism–have been made; the first two are indispensable to use the hash table for the lock and buffer managers in DBMSs.

2.2.1 Latch-free list

The linked list structure is the core element in the separate-chaining hash table. The fundamental idea is that a latch-free hash table can be implemented by making the linked list used in the hash table latch-free [12]. CAS operations are used to insert (delete) a hash element into (from) the linked list. The delete operation of a hash element is performed in two steps (each using a CAS operation): 1) set the delete-mark bit, which is located at the lower side bit of the next-pointer, in the hash element (logical deletion), and 2) substitute the next-pointer in the previous hash element or the slot of the bucket array with the pointer value in the next-pointer of the hash element (physical deletion).

The latch-free hash table using the list is, however, still not sufficient for use in DBMSs, mainly due to their API consisting of FIND, INSERT[4], and DELETE. The next section describes the modification I applied to the latch-free hash table.

[3] *PostgreSQL* mainly uses three types of mutual exclusion mechanisms: spin locks intended for very short-term locks, light weight locks (LWLocks) typically used to interlock access to data structures in shared memory, and heavy weight locks usually used for all user-driven (meaning visible at the SQL level) lock requests.

[4] FIND and INSERT are sometimes combined into FIND_or_INSERT, in which the FIND operation is carried out first and the INSERT operation is executed if the FIND operation fails. If the FIND operation succeeds in finding the required hash element, the element will be returned as the return value of the API.

2.2.2 Built-in reference counter and API

The most significant drawback in previous latch-free hash tables is that there was the possibility of failure resulting from an inconsistent situation, i.e., a process could not access the correct data of the hash element that it obtained by the FIND API of the hash table, because the hash element could be deleted and recycled at any time between the instant when the process ordered the FIND API to obtain a particular hash element and the instant when the process accessed the hash element. The solution that this paper proposes is adding a reference-counter to each hash element and modifying the API in response to the addition of the mechanism.

Two versions of the API are used: one is designed for lock managers and the other is for buffer managers. The difference between the two is their different properties: while data relating to the lock status in a hash element is no longer necessary if its reference count becomes zero, valid data in the buffer page corresponding to a hash element has the possibility to be used in the near future even if the reference count of the hash element is zero.

As for the hash table for the lock manager, every hash element needs to be deleted as soon as its reference count becomes zero, so the reference count of zero has a special meaning in this hash table. In contrast, for the hash table for the buffer manager, every hash element should be kept in the hash table even if its reference count becomes zero. In order to delete a hash element, a special value of the reference count (minus one in this paper) is defined to mean that the hash element is being deleted.

Common API.

Both hash tables have the following APIs.

FIND The process tries to find the hash element specified by the given hash key. If the FIND operation does not find the required hash element, it returns a NULL pointer, meaning that this API has failed. In contrast, when the FIND operation finds the required hash element whose reference count is not the special value, the reference count is incremented and the API returns the hash element to the caller. If the reference count is the special value, the next operation depends on the type of hash table.

FIND_or_INSERT This is mostly the same as the rudimentary hash tables except 1) the reference count of the newly allocated hash element is set to one if the FIND operation fails, and 2) if the FIND operation succeeds in finding the required hash element, the reference count is incremented if the count is not the special value. If the count is the special value, the next operations depend on the type of hash table.

DECREMENT_REFERENCE_COUNT The reference count is decremented. This API is used for the hash element that was previously obtained by the FIND or FIND_or_INSERT API. As for the hash table for the lock manager, the hash element is deleted from the hash table when the decrement operation produces the reference count of zero.

API for lock manager.

The hash table for the lock manager has the same API as the common API described in the previous paragraph. What should be noted here is that when the FIND operation (in FIND or FIND_or_INSERT API) finds the specified hash element whose reference count is zero, the API deletes the hash element and restarts from the beginning. This control makes the hash table wait-free [1].

API for buffer manager.

The hash table for the buffer manager has the common API and the following additional API.

PREPARE_DELETE The reference count of the hash element is changed from zero to minus 1. If the count is not zero, this API fails.

DO_DELETE The specified hash element is deleted if the reference count is minus one. This API is supposed to be used for the hash element whose reference count is minus one.

As for the FIND operation, the process sleeps a little and then retries the operation from the beginning of the API when the FIND operation encounters the hash element whose reference count is minus one.

2.2.3 Memory recycle

The memory region allocated to a hash element is recycled if the hash element is deleted, which can cause the following two problems to arise: the ABA problem (Fig. 1), normally associated with CAS operations, and accessing a polluted pointer when traversing the list, a hash bucket of the hash table. The polluted pointer problem can occur when two concurrent operations conflict: one, a series of delete, reuse, and get operations (Fig. 2) carried out for a hash element, and the other, a traverse operation of a list that includes the hash element. When the conflict occurs, the process that traverses the list can read the value which is newly written by another process during its reuse operation for the element.

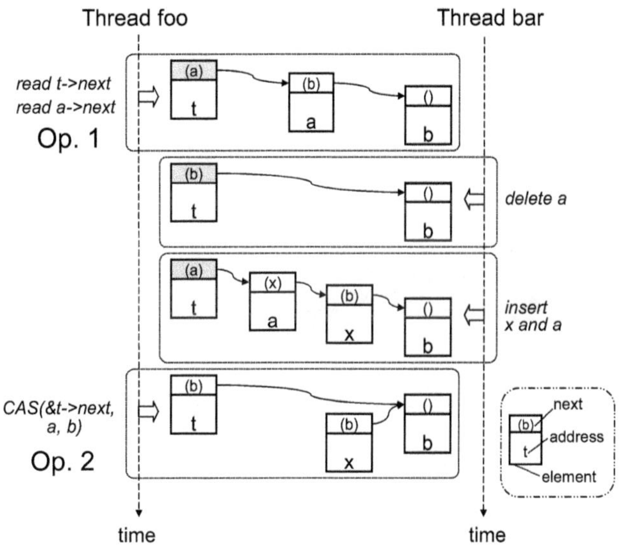

Figure 1: Example sequence resulting in ABA problem. Suppose the thread *foo* tries to delete the hash element *a*, performed by the non-atomic operations *OP. 1* and *OP. 2*. In their interval, if another thread *bar* deletes *a* and then inserts *x* and *a*, the next pointer of *t* has changed from *a* to *b* and then returns to *a*. Since *foo* is not aware of the *bar*'s operations, the CAS operation in *OP. 2* succeeds, resulting in an incorrect list structure.

The latch-free hash tables proposed in this paper adapt a hazard-pointer mechanism [13] as a possible countermeasure against these two problems. This mechanism prevents ABA problems from occurring by registering the address of the hash elements that are involved in the CAS operation. The registered hash elements are

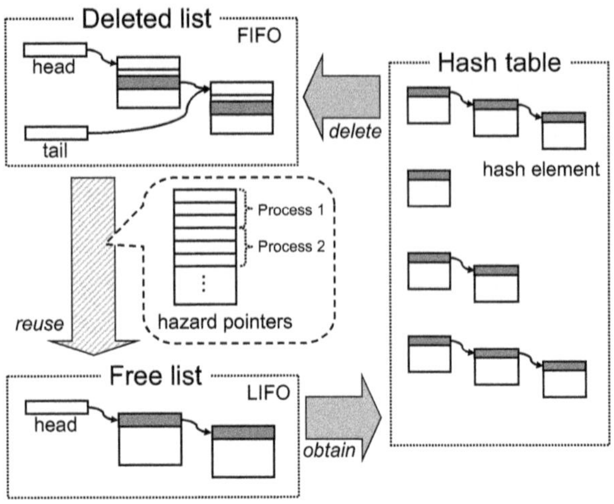

Figure 2: Memory recycle loop. As long as a hash element is in the deleted list, its next-pointer value is kept the same as at the time just before the move from the hash table to the deleted list. The link pointer used to form the deleted list is located at a separate area from that of the next pointer.

not moved from the deleted list to the free list, which results in the disconnection of the memory recycle loop (Fig. 2). Since an ABA problem can occur if a hash element goes around the loop in the intervening period between the instant when a pointer to the hash element is read and the instant when the CAS operation at the pointer is performed, this disconnection of the memory recycle loop produces the effect.

The hazard pointer mechanism has been adopted with the following modification to improve its performance: logically deleted hash elements are kept not in a pointer-array private to the process but in a particular linked list (deleted list) that is global among the processes concerning the hash table access. I verified this operation by a formal verification method (described in Section 2.4).

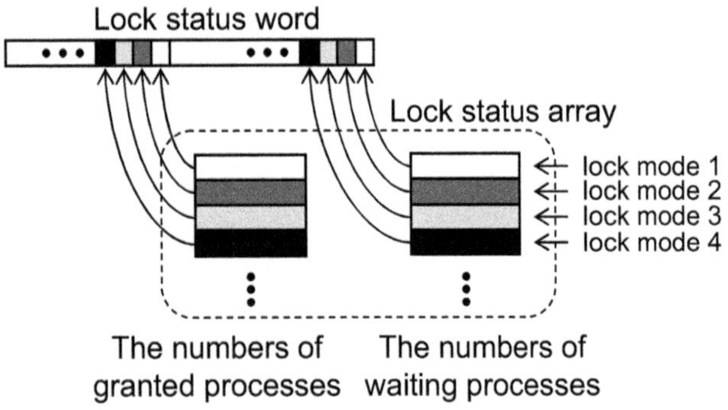

Figure 3: Data structure for latch-free lock. The lock status word can be handled by the CAS operation of the processor and each element of the lock status array can be handled by the atomic operations of the processor.

2.3 Mutual exclusion

2.3.1 Mutex-free latch

Latches usually require some mutual exclusion mechanism (i.e., a mutex) to protect the data structure by keeping the latch status consisting of the numbers of the granted processes and the waiting processes and the wait queue containing the waiting processes. A mutex can form a bottleneck, especially when the corresponding latch is frequently requested in a shared mode. LWLock, used in *PostgreSQL*, is an example of such a latch. It supports shared and exclusive lock requests and blocks processes, i.e., makes processes sleep, when the lock is not available.

The mutex can be eliminated if those status data can be updated atomically; as to a latch capable of supporting shared and exclusive mode requests, mutex-free atomic update of status data is possible with CAS operation. In for example, a 64-bit CPU, in which the length of CAS-accessible words is 64 bits, 21 bits can be assigned to express the number of the processes[5], which is enough for typical server machines.

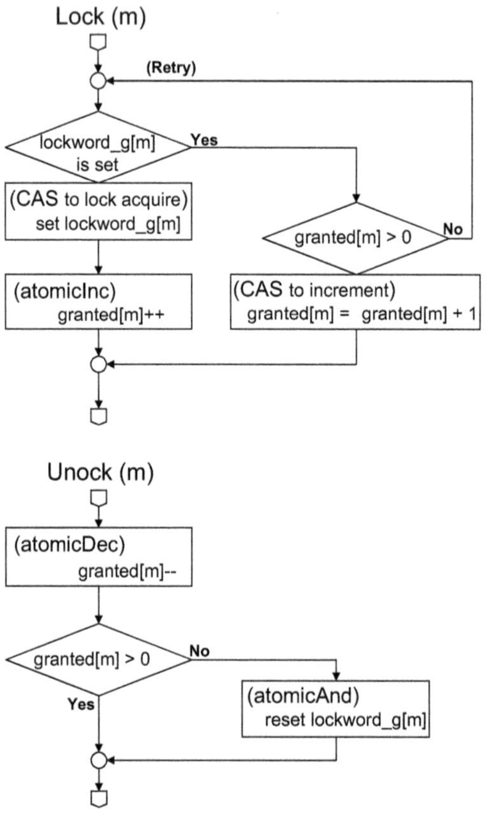

Figure 4: Basic algorithm of the lock and unlock procedures for lock mode m. For the sake of brevity, the operation flows of lock acquisition failure and CAS operation failure are not shown. If a CAS operation fails, the operation flow will restart from the condition-check step at just before the CAS operation. While CAS operations can fail, atomicInc(Dec) operations always succeed, i.e. they execute the atomic increment(decrement) unconditionally. The notations $lockword\_g[m]$ and $granted[m]$ indicate the left side of the lock status word and the lock status array, respectively, in Fig. 3.

For a latch implemented according to the above, a process can acquire the latch without using any mutex if it finds no contention

[5]In it, three sets of 21 bits are used to express the number of the shared latch holding processes, the number of shared latch waiting processes, and the number of exclusive latch waiting processes. The other one bit is for indicating whether an exclusive latch is held or not. Hence, $3x21bits + 1bit = 64bits$.

on the latch. In other words, the latch acquisition is carried out by one CAS operation to update the latch status. In contrast, in the case of latch conflict, the process that tries to acquire the latch updates the latch status to the number of the waiting process incremented and then puts itself into the wait queue, where a mutex to protect the wait queue is used.

2.3.2 *Latch-free lock*

In general, a lock supports multiple request modes. For example, *PostgreSQL* supports eight modes [16]. In such a situation, lock status data (more specifically, the sets of the numbers of lock granted and waiting processes) cannot be packed into a word that CAS operation can handle, and thus, some innovative mechanism is necessary to make a lock latch-free.

The key idea here is that the lock manager uses two types of variables (Fig. 3): lock status word and lock status array. Each variable in the lock status array keeps the number of the lock granted or the waiting processes corresponding to the variable and the lock status word keeps the aggregated status of the lock status array; each bit in the lock status word indicates whether the value of the corresponding element in the lock status array is zero or not. This design ensures that the lock status word provides enough information for the lock manager to determine whether the lock request made by a process should be granted or denied. The necessary information for the decision is not the exact number of processes but rather whether or not the number is zero.

The update of the lock status is carried out according to the algorithm shown in Fig. 4. The most important point in this algorithm is that there is a particular intermediate state: the relevant variable in the lock status array is zero and the corresponding bit in the lock status word is not zero. When the process that made the lock request detects such a state in the lock acquisition, it sleeps a little and then retries the lock acquisition from the beginning.

2.4 Verification

This section verifies the newly developed algorithms and the modifications made to the existing components. They are:

- Latch-free hash table operations in regard to the built-in reference counter
- Memory recycle mechanism
- Latch-free lock algorithm

As for the memory recycle mechanism and latch-free lock algorithm, *SPIN* was used to verify their operation when two or more processes were involved.

2.4.1 *Built-in reference counter*

Since the operation of the latch-free hash table has already been verified [12], the verification of the reference counter-related operations is relatively simple.

Hash table for lock manager.

This hash table faces the risk of producing an inconsistent state when two operations, FIND (including the FIND step in the FIND_or_INSERT) and DECREMENT_REFERENCE_COUNT, are being carried out concurrently for the same hash element whose reference count is one. In this case, the FIND operation has the potential to find the hash element in a intermediate state of DECREMENT_REFERENCE_COUNT. The reference count is zero and the element is still in the hash table, i.e., the element is not deleted.

Step I2 in Fig. 5 prevents the FIND and/or FIND_or_INSERT operation from incrementing the reference count from zero to one by using CAS operation for the increment. When the API execution finds the hash element whose reference count is zero, it will delete the element and retry from the beginning of the API. If this special care for the intermediate state was not taken, the API would return the hash element and it would soon be deleted from the hash table, resulting in an inconsistent state of the hash table.

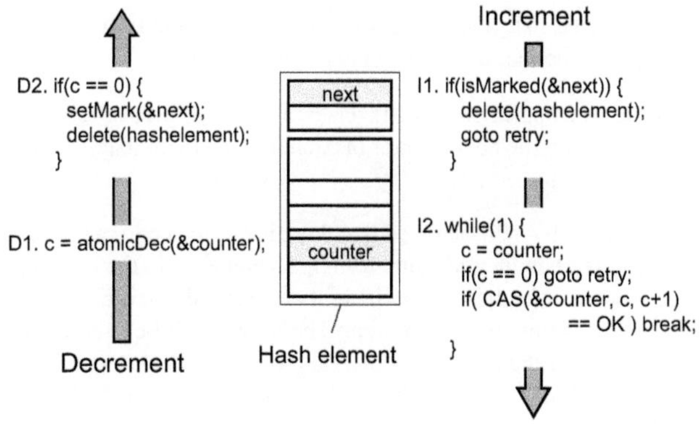

Figure 5: Contention between FIND (increment of the reference counter) and DECREMENT_REFERENCE_COUNT (decrement of the reference counter) operations. It is relatively easy to verify that every alternating occurrence of increment and decrement events produces an accurate state for the hash table.

Hash table for buffer manager.

The behavior of this hash table is quite simple: a hash element can be deleted by the execution of the DO_DELETE API only when its reference count is minus one, and thus no FIND_or_INSERT operation conflicts with the deletion of the element. When a FIND_or_INSERT operation finds the hash element whose reference counter is minus one, the process sleeps a little and then retries the operation from the beginning (as discussed in Section 2.2.2).

As for the state transition in regard to the reference counter, a hash element has three states–one or more than one, zero, and minus one–and every state transition is performed with one CAS operation. Consequently, there is no possibility of producing any inconsistent state in this hash table.

2.4.2 *Memory recycle mechanism*

The memory-recycle mechanism used in the latch-free hash tables differs from that of a conventional latch-free hash table in that logically deleted hash elements are kept in a particular global linked list. The behaviors within the list are verified in this section. The conventional latch-free hash table [12] keeps logically deleted hash elements in a pointer array located in the process local memory, which ensures that the deletion and recycle operations are not carried out concurrently.

Three types of operations should be taken into account in the verification:

Deletion An operation that links a hash element in the deleted list, i.e., the physical deletion of a hash element. Although a hash element is physically deleted, the next-pointer is still valid as long as the element is in the deleted list.

Recycle An operation consisting of the following steps: gather the non-null pointers from the hazard-pointer array into a local memory region, choose hash elements (none of which are found in the gathered hazard-pointers), and link the elements in a free list. Once a hash element is recycled, there is no guarantee that the next-pointer value is valid.

Traverse An operation that traverses a list in the hash table by following the next-pointer of each hash element that is linked in the list.

Verification by *SPIN* showed that there is no chance for a traverse process to read an invalid value form hash elements in the list if the recycle process fetches the variable that counts deleted list length and then performs the gather step. The length will be used as the limit number of the hash elements, each of which is checked to determine whether they can be linked in the free list or not. *SPIN* also showed that there is a chance for incorrect behavior if the counter fetch step and the gather step are conducted in reverse order.

2.4.3 *Latch-free lock algorithm*

SPIN was also used to verify the operation of the latch-free lock algorithm. A verification model of the lock algorithm, written in Promela [8], confirmed that there is no transition path leading to any invalid state. The lock intended for the verification supports the following three lock modes: exclusive, self-exclusive (conflicts with exclusive and itself, and shared.

Model checking was conducted for the situation in which five processes[6] try to acquire the lock for each request mode: two processes for the exclusive mode and three processes for shared followed by the lock promotion for the self-shared.

The key point in the transit to lock waiting is that the process has to re-check whether the lock is available or not after acquiring the mutex to protect the wait queue. If the process sleeps for the lock waiting without a re-check, the process is in danger of being left behind, i.e., it will not awaken, and thus sleeps forever.

3. APPLYING LATCH-FREE TO A DBMS

I applied latch-free data structures to one of the most widely used open-source DBMSs, *PostgreSQL*, to improve CPU scalability. This section describes the policy and method of the implementation.

3.1 Policy

I applied the latch-free data structures to the lock manager and buffer manager of a DBMS. Its heart is the hash table because it enables the high-speed searching of necessary data. Conventional hash tables use mutual exclusion, which causes a scalability bottleneck, so I have adopted this latch-free technique in order to improve the CPU scalability of the hash tables.

The policy in the implementation was based on a previous software performance engineering work[19] that suggested priority be determined by the magnitude of the influence on the system performance, with execution frequency being one such example.

Since fundamental hash operations (search, insert, and delete) are frequently executed, the latch-free hash table was implemented to support their concurrent execution by multiple processes. The following operations can also be performed in a mutex-free manner: obtaining a new hash element from the free list and appending the physically deleted element to the tail of the deleted list. In contrast, the recycle of hash elements in the deleted list is less frequently executed than the fundamental operations, and so a mutex is used to protect the head of the deleted list. Another mutex is used in the hash table so that the lock manager can protect the process wait queue, which is expected to have little influence on system performance (as described in Section 2.1).

3.2 Lock manager

3.2.1 *Overview*

A lock manager keeps the lock status for each object and is used to decide whether the lock request for the object made by a process should be granted or denied. As for hash table-based lock managers, each object is identified by a unique ID assigned to the object, which is used as the search key for the corresponding hash element that stores the lock status data on the object.

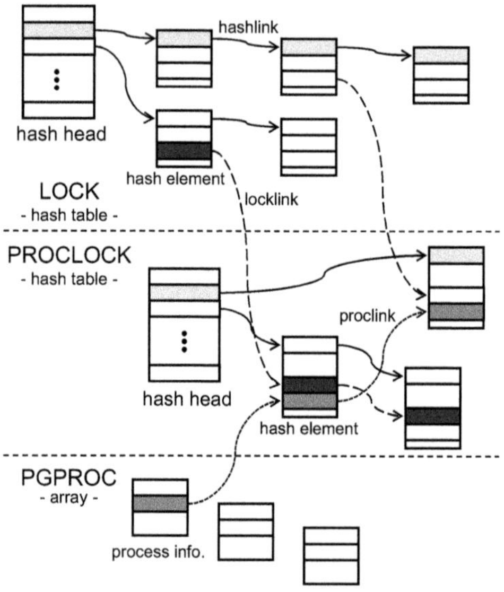

Figure 6: Data structures used in the PostgreSQL lock manager. Each hash element in the lock table has a locklink to connect the proclock elements corresponding to the lock object. Each proclock element is also connected with a proclink, starting from a particular PGPROC element corresponding to the process that owns the proclock element.

PostgreSQL uses two types of hash tables, as shown in Fig. 6: one for LOCK (lock table) and the other for PROCLOCK (proclock table). The lock table uses the object ID as the hash key and is intended to store the lock status of each object in the corresponding hash element. Meanwhile, the proclock table is intended to store each lock request made by a process. Although the hash element may be accessed by every process, it is to be inserted into and deleted from the proclock hash table only by the process that makes the lock request. The hash key of the proclock table is the combination of the object ID and the process ID[7].

A lock request is processed as follows. First, the lock manager obtains the existing or newly created hash element from the lock and proclock tables, and then it makes the decision about the lock request based on the lock status in the lock element. The procedure ends when the lock status is updated to reflect the decision and the proclock element is linked to the appropriate list in the lock element. An unlock request is processed as follows. The lock manager removes the proclock element from the list in the lock element and proclock hash table, and then it updates the lock status in the

[6]Five was the limitation due to the memory capacity and CPU power of the computer on which the model checking was performed.

[7]This is not a precise description of the PostgreSQL implementation but is correct in the semantic sense.

lock hash. If it finds that no process acquires the lock, it deletes the lock entry from the lock table.

Both procedures are carried out under mutual exclusion enforced by the corresponding latch (LWLock for *PostgreSQL*). *PostgreSQL* implementation does not use one latch per hash bucket but one latch for multiple hash buckets, called a 'partition'. The greater the number of lock partitions, the fewer the number of hash buckets that one latch covers.

3.2.2 Implementation

I modified the lock manager to use the latch-free hash table for the lock and proclock table, the latch-free lock for lock-checking, and the mutex-free latch for hierarchical locks. This modification was accomplished by making a few changes to the lock and unlock request handling procedures, as follows.

- The FIND_or_INSERT API is used to process the lock request and obtain the necessary hash elements from the lock and proclock tables.
- The lock-checking is carried out according to the latch-free lock algorithm.
- The DECREMENT_REFERENCE_COUNT API is used in the processing of the unlock request.

In this manner, the reference count has come to indicate the number of processes that are used in the lock acquisition, and thus the hash element can be deleted when the reference count becomes zero.

A mutual exclusion mechanism is still necessary in the lock manager to temporarily suspend the lock and unlock activities, which is necessary in specific situations such as deadlock checking. To implement this mutual exclusion, the mutex-free latch is used in the following manner. The lock and unlock procedures are carried out by acquiring the mutex-free latch in shared-mode, and deadlock checking, etc. are carried out by acquiring the mutex-free latch in exclusive-mode. In this way, deadlock checking, etc. can be executed by suspending the lock and unlock activities.

3.3 Buffer manager

3.3.1 Overview

In general, a buffer manager uses a hash table to find the page frame that contains the disk page specified by a given buffer tag, including the relation identifier and the block number relative to the beginning of the relation. Each hash element contains the index to specify the buffer descriptor, which keeps the page status including a dirty bit, the buffer, and the pin count for the page. It also implements a paging (or replacement) algorithm to choose what page has to be evacuated and replaced with the requested page in the case that the page is not found in the page frame.

As for *PostgreSQL*, the following characteristics are worthy to note here.

- It uses a hash table for which mutual exclusion is necessary, and thus a set of latches is used to protect the conflict of multiple processes accessing the same hash bucket.
- Its replacement algorithm is clock sweep, which uses the usage count in addition to the pin count to choose a victim buffer out of those buffers whose usage count and pin count are both zero.

3.3.2 Implementation

The buffer manager was modified to use the latch-free hash table. Since the reference count is used as the pin count, increment of the pin count is carried out in the FIND API execution.

It was somewhat complicated to determine a victim buffer in the case of buffer replacement. First, the process that tries to carry out a buffer replacement operation chooses a candidate buffer whose usage count is zero, and then the process invokes the PREPARE_DELETE API. If the execution of the API succeeds, the process determines the candidate buffer as the victim buffer to be replaced. Although there is the possibility that the chosen victim buffer will have a non-zero usage count, this unusual phenomenon, however, does not result in an incorrect DBMS status because the pin count of the buffer is zero[8], meaning no process uses the buffer. Since this unusual phenomenon is expected to be rare, this algorithm is correct in a practical sense.

4. EVALUATION

In this section, I examine the performance characteristics of latch-free data structures used in an ACID-compliant DBMS.

4.1 Target system

4.1.1 Workload

Performance measurement was conducted with two types of benchmark programs:

DBT-1 A fair usage implementation of the TPC-W [26] specification that simulates the activities of a business-oriented transactional Web e-Commerce system out of which the transaction pattern issued to the DB server was used in the performance measurement.

pgbench A simple program for running benchmark tests on *PostgreSQL* using a transaction scenario loosely based on TPC-B.

Both benchmark programs express measurement results in transactions per second (TPS) as primary performance metrics. CPU usage (%) and CPU activities measured with a built-in CPU performance counter were also examined for *DBT-1*.

DBT-1 was used to estimate the performance of DMBS in processing real-world business transactions. In the execution, the scale-factor of 'item' was 10,000 and the transaction type (profile) and that of 'customer' was 2,000, which results in an overall database size of about eight gigabytes. The transaction mix used in the measurement was a shopping mix [26], and the number of DBMS connections was the same as the number of cores. Both benchmark programs output benchmark results expressed in throughput (the number of transaction processed in a unit time) as the performance metrics of the measured system.

The *pgbench* was used to check the behavior under an extreme condition, i.e., when high-frequency shared-mode lock requests for relations were made. A select-only transactions mode, which generates a read-only workload consisting of numerous tiny queries to the DBMS, was used in the measurement. The database size was about eight gigabytes and created with a *pgbench* scale factor of 400.

[8]This can occur if another process pins or unpins the buffer accompanying the increment of the usage count within the period between the instant when the process reads the usage count and the instant when the process invokes the PREPARE_DELETE API. Even in this case, it is ensured that the pin count of the victim buffer is zero.

Just before the beginning of the performance measurement, the contents of the database were restored from their backup file (*DBT-1*) or initialized (*pgbench*), and thus all of the benchmark executions were started with exactly the same database contents.

4.1.2 DBMS

Variations.

The DBMSs used in the measurement were *PostgreSQL* version 9.2.2 and its variations. These were:

Original The first measured program was built from the original source code, obtained from the postgresql Web site, without any modification.

Baseline The original was modified in that the lock and buffer partitions were both enlarged from 16 to 128.

FPL_off The same as the 'baseline', except that the fast path lock (FPL) mechanism[5], a notable feature introduced in *PostgreSQL* version 9.2, for relations was turned off. [9]

Extended The number of lock and buffer partitions were both enlarged from 16 to 1024.

LF_lock The latch-free lock manager was used and the number of buffer partitions was enlarged from 16 to 128.

LF_lock_bufmgr The latch-free lock manager and buffer manager were used.

FPL_off was included in the measurement to investigate performance in the case that the FPL mechanism could not be used and thus a conventional hash-based lock manager is used (discussed in detail in Section 4.5).

Execution condition.

All variations of *PostgreSQL* were executed with default boot-up parameters except for the following modifications.

- 'shared_buffers' were enlarged to 12 gigabytes, enough space to store whole database files.
- 'synchronous_commit' was turned off to avoid log-related overhead.
- 'checkpoint_segments' were enlarged to 256 to mitigate checkpoint-related overhead.

4.1.3 Hardware and OS

The server machine used in this measurement was a state-of-the-art NUMA machine consisting of eight Intel E7-8870 CPUs driven by a 2.4-GHz clock, four Intel 7500 I/O hub chips, 128 of 4 gigabyte DDR3-1066 SDRAM DIMM (total: 512-gigabyte memory), and eight 146.5-gigabyte SAS hard drives (Fig. 7). CPUs were connected with Intel QuickPath Interconnect (QPI).

The hyper-threading mechanism was turned off to avoid hyper-threading-related resource conflicts and to exaggerate mutual exclusion effects. Since E7-8870 has ten CPU cores, this setting made the number of cores used 80.

The operating system was Linux [24] in 64-bit mode. Distribution was CentOS 6.3 [22] with a 2.6.32-279.el6.x86_64 kernel version.

[9]Two types of fast path lock have been introduced in *PostgreSQL* version 9.2: that for relations and that for virtual transaction IDs. The fast path lock for virtual transaction IDs was used in all test cases in this paper.

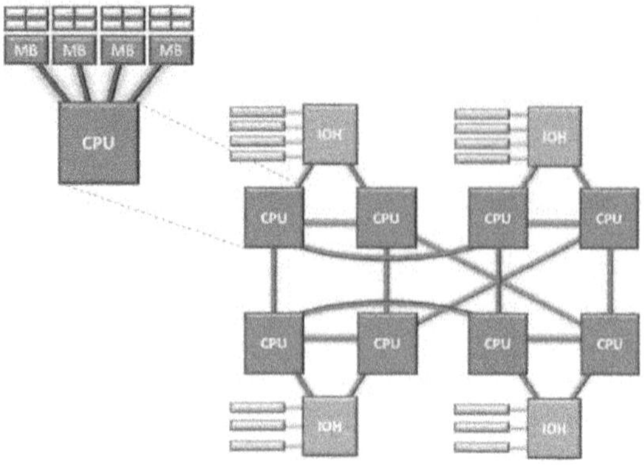

Figure 7: Architecture of the 80-core machine. As for the eight-socket configuration, each CPU can reach any memory chip located on another CPU within two hops through the QPI(s).

4.2 DBT-1 results

4.2.1 Primary results

Figure 8 shows the variation of throughput as a function of the number of emulated users (EU).

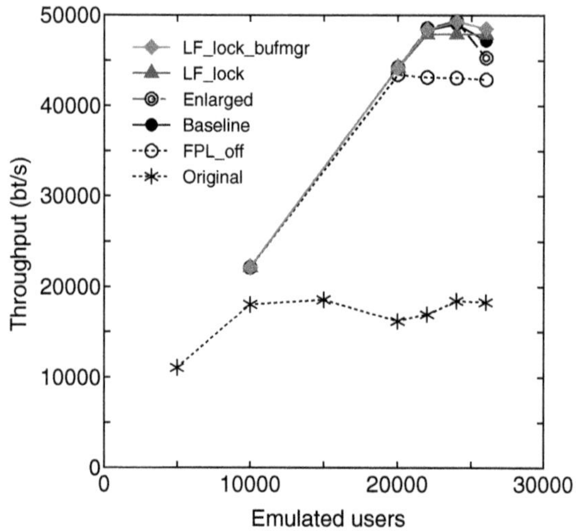

Figure 8: Variation of *DBT-1* throughput. Think time was set as 0.45 seconds.

The throughput of the *Original* case saturated at about 40% of the other cases. Fortunately, a relatively simple investigation of where the *PostgreSQL* processes slept revealed that this saturation was due to severe contention of the buffer partition; 16, the *PostgreSQL* default number of partitions, seemed too few for the 80-core server machine. This was because the baseline configuration of *PostgreSQL* for the measurements was determined in that the numbers of lock and buffer partitions were enlarged from 16 to 128.

It is significant to note that *LF_lock_bufmgr* improved the *DBT-1* throughput of *Original* by about 2.5 times and achieved almost the best performance without deep understanding of the target system behavior that is necessary for the parameter tuning. We also learned that the *PostgreSQL* default setting, used in most of the *PostgreSQL* binary packages, is not suitable for many-core machines.

4.2.2 *Heavy loaded situation*

Figure 9 shows the performance characteristics in the heavy loaded situation.

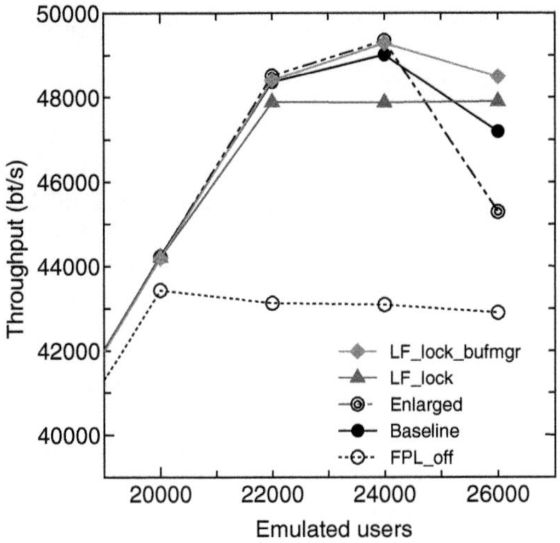

Figure 9: Enlarged view of heavy loaded region in Fig. 8.

Using the latch-free data structures (*LF_lock* and *LF_lock_bufmgr*) improved the *DBT-1* throughput of *FPL_off* by about 10%, which was almost the same as that of *Baseline* and *Extended.* While the fast path lock did not show negligible performance drop in the extra-heavy loaded situation (at 26000 EU), the performance drops of *LF_lock* and *LF_lock_bufmgr* were smaller.

4.2.3 *Variation with the number of cores*

Figure 10 shows the variation of saturation points of *DBT-1* throughput as a function of the number of cores[10].

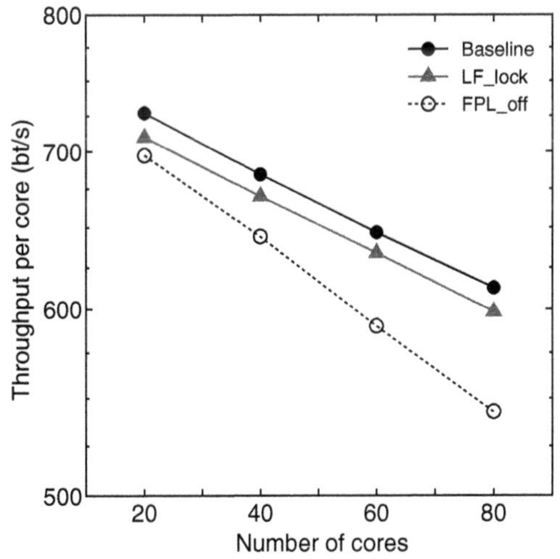

Figure 10: Variation of per core throughput.

While *LF_lock* and *Baseline* had a similar degree of decline in the throughput per core, *FPL_off* fell more rapidly, and thus the execution efficiency of *FPL_off*, i.e., a conventional hash table-based lock manager, become worse more quickly as the number of CPU cores increases compare with that of *LF_lock*, i.e., latch-free data structures, and of *Baseline*, which does not use a hash table-based lock manager.

In the near future, in server machines that use many-core CPUs– a 48-core CPU [4], for example–conventional hash table-based lock managers will become even more inefficient, and thus the importance of latch-free techniques as shown in this paper is expected to increase.

4.3 CPU activities

The CPU activities were measured with *oprofile*, a Linux tool using built-in CPU performance counters. As *oprofile* can count only one type of event per measurement, the benchmark executions were repeated with changing the type of event. Measured hardware events were `CPU_CLK_UNHALTED` and `INST_RETIRED`. The time interval between the start and the end of every *oprofile* measurement was 1000 seconds.

The remarkable thing with the CPU activities was the percentage of the CPU time consumed by the LWLock-related activity consisting of LWLockAcquire, LWLockRelease, and LWLockConditionalAcquire functions, shown in Fig. 11.

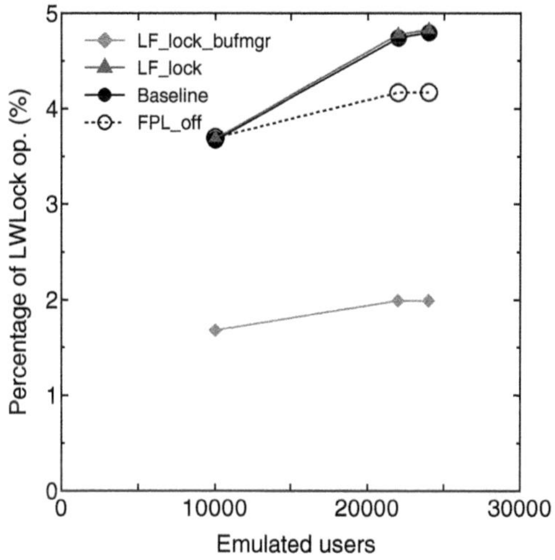

Figure 11: Percentage of CPU time consumed by the LWLock-related activity.

It is clear that

1. The percentages gradually increased with the load intensity, and

2. Using latch-free data structures for the buffer manager helped reduce the amount of LWLock-related activity.

In summary, half to one-third of LWLock-related activities in *PostgreSQL* executing *DBT-1* workload were attributed to the buffer manager and can be reduced by using latch-free data structures for the buffer manager. As for *FPL_off*, the percentage was smaller than that of *Baseline* and *LF_lock* in the heavy loaded situation, which likely relates to the measurement result (Fig. 9) showing that *FPL_off* delivered 10% less *DBT-1* throughput than *Baseline* and *LF_lock*.

[10]The number of cores was specified using a boot parameter of the Linux kernel: maxcpus = N. Although this method made the system behavior slightly differently from that of a real N-core machine, it was expected to produce a good estimate of the N-core machine's performance.

Figure 12 shows the measurement results of the number of instructions per transaction. Interestingly, in the heavy loaded situation, which is the area we should pay the most attention to, the number of instructions per transaction for all measurement cases converged at almost the same level.

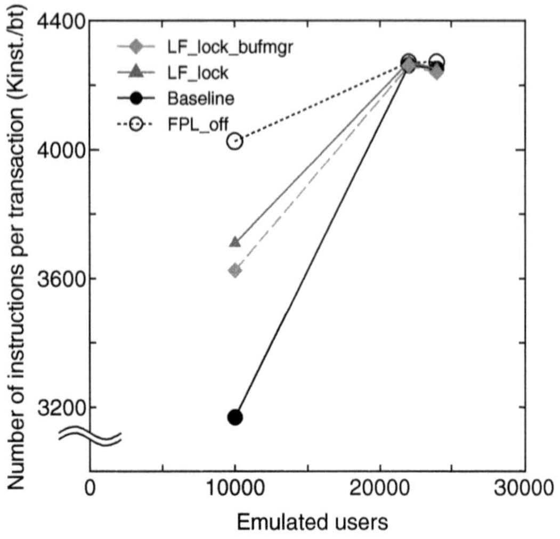

Figure 12: Number of instructions per transaction.

4.4 Pgbench result

The *pgbench* result is shown in Fig. 13. The most interesting finding here is that *Original* had a better performance than *FPL_off*, which is the reverse relationship to that found in the *DBT-1* result. Second is that the degree of performance improvement brought about by the latch-free data structure-based lock manager (*LF_lock_bufmgr* and *LF_lock*) over the traditional hash table-based lock manager (*FPL_off*) was less than that of the fast path lock manager, especially when the number of connections was high. This is in contrast with the *DBT-1* result, which showed significant improvement of *FPL_off* upon *Original*.

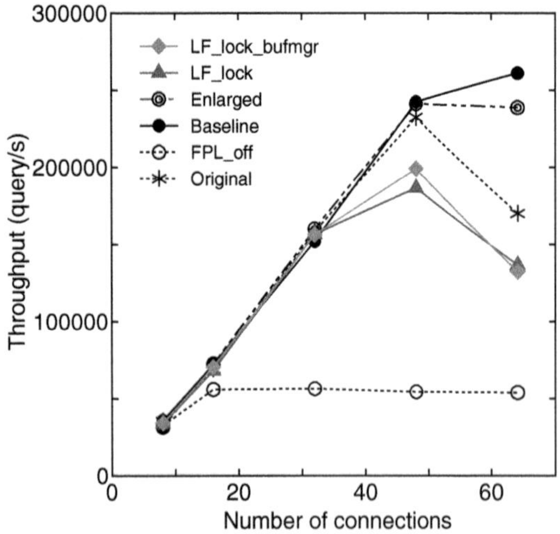

Figure 13: *pgbench* result.

4.5 Discussion

In this section, I discuss the effectiveness of the latch-free data structures mainly based on a performance comparison with the fast path lock. Since the main objective of both is to improve CPU scalability, it is worth comparing these different approaches.

4.5.1 Fast path lock

Features.

The fast path lock mechanism was introduced in *PostgreSQL* 9.2 to reduce the overhead of acquiring and releasing shared locks for relations. Its most unique point is that it does not use hash tables to store lock status data but rather uses only a PGPROC data structure (the bottom layer in Fig. 6). Although PGPROC elements are located in the shared memory region, each element is rarely accessed by processes other than its corresponding process; PGPROC elements are almost always local process data, and thus there is little contention among them.

In summary, the fast path lock mechanism exploits the fact that almost all of the lock requests to relations are made in shared-mode to avoid using the hash table-based lock manager. However, along with the performance advantage comes a couple of restrictions.

- It can only be applied for the shared-mode lock requests for relations.
- There is an upper limit to the number of relations for which the fast path lock can be applied.
- If an exclusive-mode lock is requested, the lock-status data will be transferred to the traditional hash table-based lock manager, producing a significant overhead.

Another partial disadvantage is that it brings an additional complexity to the program, which makes it more difficult to prevent false moves that violate the functional correctness of the program. It is difficult to verify the correctness of a program that controls a number of concurrent activities, i.e., operations carried out by simultaneous processes. A bug report [15] is a kind of proof of this wisdom.

In contrast, the latch-free lock is a mechanism that completely replaces the existing lock manager in *PostgreSQL*, and its operation has been verified using a formal verification method (Section 2.4). In addition, it is not incompatible but can be used with the fast path lock to handle lock requests that cannot be handled by the fast path lock.

Performance characteristics.

In the previous section, I showed that 1) the fast path lock improved performance to almost the same level as the latch-free data structures in the *DBT-1* workload, and 2) it outperformed the latch-free data structures in *pgbench* executed in the select-only mode, which generates a read-only workload consisting of numerous tiny queries to the DBMS. These results imply that *pgbench* tends to put more load on the lock manager–i.e., more shared lock requests for relations are made–than the *DBT-1* benchmark program, which made the fast path lock more effective in the *pgbench* workload.

This indicates that the characteristics of the workload have a considerable effect on the degree of efficacy brought by a countermeasure to improve the performance. While the fast path lock was more effective than the latch-free data structures for the *pgbench* workload, as discussed in this section, there was no apparent difference between them in the *DBT-1* workload.

4.5.2 *The numbers of latch and buffer partitions*

The numbers of the latch (LWLock in *PostgreSQL*) and buffer partitions are another important factor that affect the performance. Both are 16 in the *PostgreSQL* released on the official Web site, which seems too few for many-core server machines (as described in Section 4.2.1).

Of course, latch and buffer partitions are independent of each other, and thus it would be possible to further tune the number of partitions to bring more performance improvement than that shown in Section 4.2.1. Although this would be preferable from the system efficiency view point, such tuning would be time-consuming because choosing a suitable value requires trial-and-error adjustment while considering the disadvantages of increasing the number of partitions. Such a trade-off consideration is unnecessary if we use the latch-free lock mechanism in lock and buffer managers.

5. RELATED WORK

5.1 Overheads in DBMS

A previous study on overhead in a DBMS [6] showed that the major overheads in transaction processing are lock manager, buffer manager, latching, and logging. Although this result was obtained through experiments on a single-core machine and a different DBMS than the *PostgreSQL* that was used in the present study, it is consistent with the outcomes of the latch-free techniques described in this paper. The lock manager, buffer manager, and latching confined the CPU scalability and have been successfully improved by using the latch-free techniques.

The logging-related overhead is outside the scope of this paper. However, I feel it could be mitigated by improving I/O devices such as solid state drives (SSDs), including flash memory [3] and Fusion-io [23].

5.2 CPU scalability improvement in DBMS

Since critical sections are what constrict CPU scalability in ACID-compliant DBMS [10], there have been many studies conducted on this topic.

5.2.1 *Lock inheritance*

Lock inheritance was proposed to improve the CPU scalability of DBMS in executing OLTP workloads [11]. Its aim was to make hierarchical locking schemes more efficient by reducing the overhead due to processing shared lock and unlock requests, including the hash operations, i.e., creating and deleting the corresponding hash element. The key idea was that the process that acquires the lock in shared mode does not release but transfers the lock to another process that will soon request the lock in the same mode.

Although the lock inheritance was effective in terms of improving performance, its coverage is limited because it can only be applied to the shared-mode lock requests for relations. Furthermore, it may bring a risk of deadlock. On the other hand, the combination of the latch-free hash table and latch-free lock algorithm can be used as a comprehensive substitute of the existing lock manager, and thus there is no limitation in its coverage nor risk of deadlock.

5.2.2 *Latch-free buffer management*

A latch-free buffer manager was proposed in [27], in which a non-blocking replacement algorithm based on the CLOCK algorithm, called Nb-GCLOCK, was implemented. While the basics of the algorithm are almost the same as those described in Section 3.3, the implementation differs in that Nb-GCLOCK was implemented in Java, which embodies a garbage collection mechanism, while the latch-free buffer manager in *PostgreSQL* is written in the C language.

Since the reference count mechanism is a part of the garbage collection, it was unnecessary to take care of the reference count in the implementation of Nb-GCLOCK, and the hash element returned from the FIND API of the latch-free hash table is guaranteed not to be deleted as long as the program keeps the pointer to the element in a variable that the program uses. While the use of a programming language based on a garbage collection mechanism makes the implementation easy, it does suffer from the overheads associated with garbage collection.

On the other hand, special care is necessary to write a buffer manager using latch-free techniques in C-like languages. The latch-free hash table with built-in reference counter is one such example. It is suitable for the efficient execution of transactions on DBMSs written in C-like languages.

5.3 Distributed database systems

Using a distributed DBMS architecture modeled with sequencing, scheduling, and storage layers is one possible approach to improving performance by using many server nodes. Typical examples include the one proposed in [25], which advocated deterministic databases, and Postgres-XC [14].

Data stored in the DMBS is partitioned and distributed among the nodes, and two-phase commit is used to ensure data consistency. The scalability of this architecture can be bounded by the sequencing layer, which is the key component of a distributed database system, because it inputs all transaction requests and assigns a global serial order to each transaction.

However, the focus of this paper is the scheduling and the storage layers. Although the latch-free techniques described can be used for a distributed database system and improve the CPU scalability for each node, they might not do much to help improve the sequencing layer.

5.4 Latch-free techniques

5.4.1 *Latch-free hash tables*

The latch-free hash table used in this paper is based on one proposed in [12] but differs in the built-in reference counter and improved memory recycle mechanism (Section 2.2). Although the technical term 'latch-free hash table with reference counter' can be found in [21], the library downloadable from the site is not latch-free and no further concrete implementation ideas are described. Since such ideas cannot be found in other sites or previous papers, if the latch-free hash table described in this paper was not the first implementation, it would be at least one of the hardest-to-find implementations. The thing that improves the memory recycle mechanism is the use of the deleted list that stores all of the deleted hash elements. Although a similar mechanism, i.e., using data area other than the next pointer as the link pointer for the list, was mentioned [7], memory recycle was not considered in the paper. Thus, the latch-free hash table described in my present paper is the first implementation that uses a global deleted-list with a hazard-pointer mechanism to prevent ABA problems from occurring.

5.4.2 *Transactional memory*

Hardware transactional memories (HTMs), one example of which is described in [18], are innovative mechanisms that update multiple memory locations while maintaining a particular consistency constraint. Since HTMs have the excellent ability to update linked lists and/or lock status in one memory transaction, they can render the latch-free techniques obsolete. Currently, there are plans to implement an HTM using an Intel Haswell processor [17], but as HTMs are not commercially available, we cannot use or reap any benefit of an HTM at present.

In contrast, software transactional memories usually use atomic memory access (such as CAS) to implement their algorithms, and so the amount of necessary operations, and thus their performance, seems to be the same as that of the latch-free data structures in the bottom line. Since the latch-free data structures are streamlined for their intended functions, they are expected to outperform general purpose mechanisms such as software transaction memories in executing their functions.

6. CONCLUSION

In this paper, I proposed the application of latch-free data structures to ACID-compliant DBMS. A latch-free hash table has been adapted for and implemented in *PostgreSQL*, one of the most popular open-source DBMS, and a latch-free lock algorithm has been newly developed for and also implemented in *PostgreSQL*, with advance verification of their operations by a formal verification method.

The results of performance evaluations using state-of-the-art 80-core machines demonstrated that the latch-free data structures were effective for performance improvement in the many-core situation in which DBT-1 throughput increased by about 2.5 times without deep understanding of the target system behavior that is necessary for the parameter tuning.

Since multi-core CPUs have already fallen into common use and the number of CPU cores in one chip has continued to rise, scalability is becoming the most important property of IT systems. The latch-free data structures presented in this paper are a potential element technology to improve the scalability of server machines, as performance evaluation showed that a traditional hash table lock manager using latches worsened more quickly as the number of CPU cores increased than that using the latch-free hash table.

7. REFERENCES

[1] G. Barnes. A method for implementing lock-free shared-data structures. In *Proceedings of the fifth annual ACM symposium on Parallel algorithms and architectures*, pages 261–270. ACM, 1993.

[2] B. Cantrill and J. Bonwick. Real-world concurrency. *Communications of the ACM*, 51(11):34–39, 2008.

[3] S. Chen. Flashlogging: exploiting flash devices for synchronous logging performance. In *Proceedings of the 35th SIGMOD international conference on Management of data*, pages 73–86. ACM, 2009.

[4] COMPUTERWORLD. Intel working on 48-core chip for smartphones, tablets. http://www.computerworld.com/s/article/9233039/Intel_working_on_48_core_chip_for_smartphones_tablets.

[5] R. Haas. Performance improvements in postgresql 9.2, bigger servers, bigger problems. http://www.pgcon.org/2012/schedule/events/416.en.html.

[6] S. Harizopoulos, D. Abadi, S. Madden, and M. Stonebraker. Oltp through the looking glass, and what we found there. In *Proceedings of the 2008 ACM SIGMOD international conference on Management of data*, pages 981–992. ACM, 2008.

[7] T. Harris. A pragmatic implementation of non-blocking linked-lists. *Distributed Computing*, pages 300–314, 2001.

[8] G. Holzmann. Design and validation of computer protocols prentice hall. *New Jersey*, 1991.

[9] G. Holzmann. The model checker spin. *Software Engineering, IEEE Transactions on*, 23(5):279–295, 1997.

[10] R. Johnson, I. Pandis, and A. Ailamaki. Critical sections: re-emerging scalability concerns for database storage engines. In *Proceedings of the 4th international workshop on Data management on new hardware*, pages 35–40. ACM, 2008.

[11] R. Johnson, I. Pandis, and A. Ailamaki. Improving oltp scalability using speculative lock inheritance. *Proceedings of the VLDB Endowment*, 2(1):479–489, 2009.

[12] M. Michael. High performance dynamic lock-free hash tables and list-based sets. In *Proceedings of the fourteenth annual ACM symposium on Parallel algorithms and architectures*, pages 73–82. ACM, 2002.

[13] M. Michael. Hazard pointers: Safe memory reclamation for lock-free objects. *Parallel and Distributed Systems, IEEE Transactions on*, 15(6):491–504, 2004.

[14] Postgres-XC project Page. http://postgres-xc.sourceforge.net.

[15] PostgreSQL - hackers. bug in fast-path locking. http://postgresql.1045698.n5.nabble.com/bug-in-fast-path-locking-td5626629.html.

[16] PostgreSQL: Documentatoins: 9.2: Explicit locking. http://www.postgresql.org/docs/9.2/static/explicit-locking.html.

[17] J. Reinders. Transactional synchronization in haswell. http://software.intel.com/en-us/blogs/2012/02/07/transactional-synchronization-in-haswell.

[18] B. Saha, A. Adl-Tabatabai, and Q. Jacobson. Architectural support for software transactional memory. In *Microarchitecture, 2006. MICRO-39. 39th Annual IEEE/ACM International Symposium on*, pages 185–196. IEEE, 2006.

[19] C. U. Smith. *Performance Engineering of Software Systems*. Addison-Wesley Publishing Company, Reading, MA., 1990.

[20] SourceForge.net: osdldbt. http://sourceforge.net/apps/mediawiki/osdldbt/index.php?title=Main_Page.

[21] Sunrise Data Dictionary. A lock-free hash table library for c. http://www.sunrisetel.net/software/devtools/sunrise-data-dictionary.shtml.

[22] The Community ENTerprise Operating System. http://centos.org/.

[23] The Fusion-io Difference (SSD Differentiator). http://www.fusionio.com/white-papers/the-fusion-io-difference-ssd-differentiator/.

[24] The Linux Kernel Archives. http://www.kernel.org/.

[25] A. Thomson, T. Diamond, S. Weng, K. Ren, P. Shao, and D. Abadi. Calvin: Fast distributed transactions for partitioned database systems. In *Proceedings of the 2012 international conference on Management of Data*, pages 1–12. ACM, 2012.

[26] Transaction Processing Performance Council. Tpc-w. http://www.tpc.org/tpcw/.

[27] M. Yui, J. Miyazaki, S. Uemura, and H. Yamana. Nb-gclock: A non-blocking buffer management based on the generalized clock. In *Data Engineering (ICDE), 2010 IEEE 26th International Conference on*, pages 745–756. IEEE, 2010.

DBMS Metrology: Measuring Query Time

Sabah Currim
University of Arizona
scurrim@email.arizona.edu

Richard T. Snodgrass
University of Arizona
rts@cs.arizona.edu

Young-Kyoon Suh
University of Arizona
yksuh@cs.arizona.edu

Rui Zhang
Teradata
Rui.Zhang@teradata.com

Matthew Wong Johnson
Univ. of California, San Diego
mwj@email.arizona.edu

Cheng Yi
University of Arizona
yic@cs.arizona.edu

ABSTRACT

It is surprisingly hard to obtain accurate and precise measurements of the time spent executing a query. We review relevant process and overall measures obtainable from the Linux kernel and introduce a structural causal model relating these measures. A thorough correlational analysis provides strong support for this model. Using this model, we developed a timing protocol, which (1) performs sanity checks to ensure validity of the data, (2) drops some query executions via clearly motivated predicates, (3) drops some entire queries at a cardinality, again via clearly motivated predicates, (4) for those that remain, for each computes a single measured time by a carefully justified formula over the underlying measures of the remaining query executions, and (5) performs post-analysis sanity checks. The resulting query time measurement procedure, termed the *Tucson Protocol*, applies to proprietary and open-source DBMSes.

Categories and Subject Descriptors

H.2.4 [**Database Management**]: Systems—*Query Processing*

Keywords

accuracy; repeatability; Tucson Protocol

1. INTRODUCTION

A common approach for at least the last twenty-five years to measure database management system query time is as follows.

> "We used the UNIX *time* command to measure the elapsed time and CPU time. All queries were run 10 times. The resultant CPU usage was averaged." [8]

Consider the measured times in Table 1, for which considerable care (to be described in detail later) was taken to get repeatable results, and for which many sources of time variation (also to be discussed) were eliminated.

Even after taking these many proactive steps to improve the measurements, they still vary quite a lot, from 6290 msec to 8510 msec (with the lowest and highest numbers in **bold**), a range of 2220 msec, which is over 25% of the highest time. As we will see, this variability arises from necessary daemons and DBMS utility processes and their I/O and interactions with the DBMS.

The *accuracy* of any measurement system is the "closeness of agreement between a measured quantity value and a true quantity value of a measurand" while the *precision* of that system is the "closeness of agreement between ... measured quantity values obtained by replicate measurements on the same or similar objects under specified conditions" [9]. (Accuracy is termed *external validity* and precision, *repeatability*, in some contexts.)

In the following, we address the central question just raised: how to achieve precise and accurate measurements of query execution time? In considering the approach that is the norm, averaging ten runs, one asks, why average? In fact, why not minimum? Should all ten times be used? If some are dropped, how many should remain? Can additional information from the operating system help refine the determination of query processing time?

In this paper, we address both accuracy and precision in detail, along the way developing a comprehensive, carefully motivated query time measurement protocol. This protocol is much more precise, with a measurement resolution for many queries averaging ±1.2%. Due to the many external vagaries that have been eliminated, this protocol is also much more accurate.

While many (most?) database papers contain measurements, this is the first detailed time measurement protocol to be presented, providing a concrete and carefully specified sequence of steps to arrive at a defensible measurement of query evaluation time. Along the way, we present the first detailed causal model of the ways in which per-processor and overall measures are related and examine support for that model by a correlational analysis over hundreds of thousands of program runs.

2. BACKGROUND

There is a spectrum of granularities with regard to what is being measured and how it is measured, as summarized in the taxonomy shown in Figure 1. The first decision is whether to consider time as an *independent variable* (that is, specified when the experiment is run) or as a *dependent variable* (that is, measured). The TPC-C [12] benchmark is run for a user-specified length of time (minutes to hours),

	1	2	3	4	5	6	7	8	9	10	*Avg*	*Std Dev*
$Time_{meas}$ (msec)	**6530**	6571	**8764**	7961	8427	7829	8246	8506	8239	6991	7806	818

Table 1: Measured time of ten executions of a query on PostgreSQL

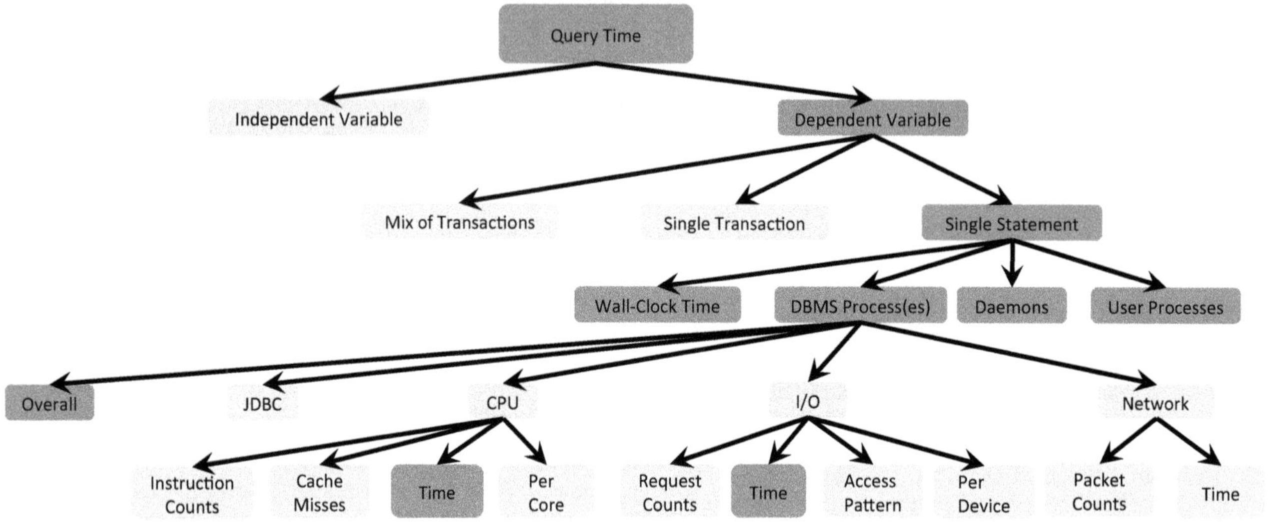

Figure 1: DBMS Time Taxonomy

long with the transaction mix (ratio of read and update transactions) and the number of completed transactions is measured, yielding a measured *transactions per minute.* We focus in this paper on measured query time. This could be of a mix of transactions, each with one or more queries and updates, of a single transaction, or of a single SQL statement (query or update). We focus here on measuring the total time of a single query. Some of these measurements can also be made of cloud databases, in which the queries are run over many distributed computers [4] or at a smaller scale, on a local distributed system [5].

When measuring how much time an individual query running on a single server requires, one can look again at wall clock time, which will include all the DBMS process(es), including those not actually evaluating the query, as well as operating system daemons and processes invoked by other users. The TPC-H [13] benchmark runs a host of queries over a prescribed database and measures total time for each, as do the XBench [16] and τBench [15] benchmarks. Or one can look more closely, restricting oneself to just those DBMS processes actually executing the query, or even to the time required for JDBC interaction, I/O, network, or CPU execution. One can measure I/O time, or obtain counts, such as the number of blocks read or written, perhaps differentiating between random and sequential disk I/O. One could also study the *pattern* of accesses, including differentiating synchronous from asynchronous I/O. For computation, one can also measure time or counts (such as number of CPU ticks). The same differentiation applies to measuring network activity. JDBC activity is generally composed of network activity (if the SQL statement initiator is running off-server) and computation. Finally, one can delve into the specifics of the CPU performance of a DBMS, examining for example processor cache effects [1] using profiling tools like Valgrind and Callgrind [14], which provide instruction and cache hit metrics. Counts are generally collected either through the operating system or instrumented DBMS or by running a disk or cache simulation on the instrumented DBMS [19].

The present paper will consider how to more accurately and precisely measure the time required to execute a single SQL statement, examining (a) overall wall clock time, (b) overall DBMS process time, (c) CPU time, and (d) I/O time. For understanding DBMS behavior, wall clock time is highly variable due to extraneous operating system daemons and user processes, which is why we focus in this paper on the harder problem: finer-grained measurements of DBMS process time and its CPU and I/O components. (Doing so can then provide insight into the additive effect of daemons and user processes.) We will extract counts from the operating system but as we are measuring proprietary DBMSes, we will not consider approaches that require that the DBMS itself be instrumented. Thus, we do not consider CPU or I/O simulation to obtain detailed counts and measures of cache performance nor of random versus sequential I/O (we *will* consider overall I/O time). We do not focus on measuring network time; instead, we reduce network time to the absolute minimum by mounting the disks on the server (not using a network file server). We minimize JDBC activity by returning a minimal result.

We show that it is possible to measure DBMS query process I/O and compute times, which when summed provides a much more stable measure of DBMS processing than wall clock time. This allows us to isolate the contribution of DBMS query processing in terms of compute and I/O time, within the context of realistic execution. By comparing these measures to those of non-DBMS processes, we can also characterize the contributions of those other processes, thereby achieving a more comprehensive picture.

Scenario (e.g., Exhaustive[1], OnePass[2])
  Experiment (query set (Q1-Q6), data spec, scenario parameter(s))
    DBMS (DB2, Oracle, PostgreSQL)
      Machine (sodb6–sodb12)
        Experiment Run (on a particular date)
          Query Instance (query number within query set)
            Query at Cardinality (10K–2M)
              Q@C Execution (1–10)

Figure 2: Hierarchy of Query-at-Cardinality (Q@C) executions

Indeed, our approach allows one to accurately measure all of the shaded variables in Figure 1.

Such measurements can be an initial step in broader studies, with these measures to be used as input to create more efficient query evaluation algorithms, to refine the query optimizer, such as its cost model (e.g., [7, 11]), to predict query performance (e.g. [2, 6, 8]), to characterize workloads (e.g., [17]), or to do provisioning and capacity planning (e.g., [18]).

3. TERMINOLOGY

Figure 2 presents a simple representation of the structure of our experiments, as a hierarchy of eight levels, ending at a particular query execution of a particular query at a particular cardinality for the underlying table(s), as part of a particular experiment run started on a stated date and time on a designated machine using a specified release of a specific DBMS, in the context of a specified experiment setup (stating the set of queries, the characteristics of the data, and various other parameters), of a selected experiment scenario.

As an example of this hierarchy, we previously presented in Table 1 measurements of 10 *Q@C Executions*. For the data in this table, we utilized the OnePass Scenario, an Experiment specifying a second set (Q2) of 20 queries (out of six such sets of queries), specifying data with a maximum cardinality of 2M rows, decreasing by 10K rows at a time, and specifying the scenario parameter of 10 executions per Q@C. We ran this query on the PostgreSQL DBMS, on the `sodb10` machine, from an experiment run started January 20, 2012 at 3:31pm, for query number 17, thus identifying a particular query instance running on a variable table with a cardinality of 1,770,000, and examining all ten Q@C executions. This paper concerns a total of 36 experiment runs, each taking a few days to a week on a single machine, involving a total of 353,630 query executions (35,363 Q@Cs) over the DB2, MySQL, Oracle, and PostgreSQL DBMSes running on the Linux operating system, totalling almost 3000 hours (4 months) of cumulative time.

4. MEASURING QUERY TIME

We now turn our attention to the central problem: measuring in a defensible manner the execution of a Q@C: a particular query at a specified cardinality on a particular machine for a specified DBMS within the context of a particular scenario and experiment.

[1]Executing a plan at each cardinality as cardinality changes.
[2]Executing a plan only when the current plan is different from the previous one as cardinality changes.

We execute in quick order, for a single query at a single cardinality, a certain number of Q@C executions. In our protocol, we execute each Q@C 10 times, which is sufficient for timing purposes. (As we'll see, Step 3-(iii) of the protocol drops Q@Cs with fewer than 6 query executions after many checks on these executions. This step retained 85% of the Q@Cs, indicating that 10 is about the right number of query executions to start with.) From various low-level measurements gathered during these multiple executions, we then compute a query execution time for that Q@C.

4.1 Wall-Clock Query Time

The Linux kernel provides several system calls that return the current time. (This method of measuring time is called *software monitoring*; it "is most suited for program-level measurements" [10].) The major difference among these functions is their measurement resolution. We use the Java method `currentTimeMillis()` which is based on the Linux `gettimeofday` system call. As we will see, milliseconds is actually a finer granularity than we will be able to achieve in the end, given all that is going on in a DBMS query.

Table 1 given on the second page of this paper is a pure cold cache measurement of query time using `currentTimeMillis` for 10 executions on PostgreSQL of the following query.

```
SELECT t0.id3, t1.id2
FROM ft_HT3 t3, ft_HT1 t1, ft_HT3 t2, ft_HT1 t0
WHERE t3.id3=t1.id2 AND t1.id2=t2.id1
      AND t2.id1=t0.id4
```

This query is on two tables. `ft_HT1` (the variable table) contains 177,000 tuples, each with four integers; `ft_HT2` (one of the constant tables) contains 2 million tuples, also each with four integers.

In these measurements we have taken the following steps: (a) stopped as many operating system daemons as possible, (b) eliminated network delays by running the executor on the same machine as the DBMS and by using a local disk, (c) eliminated user interactions by having the executor interact with an external lab DBMS to obtain the queries to be run and disallowing other user access, (d) ensured that the exact same query plan was being executed, on exactly the same database content, in exactly the same environment, to achieve data and within-run repeatability, and (e) ensured repeatability of I/O by clearing the many caches involved. Steps (a)–(c) improve accuracy while (d) and (e) address precision.

Most machines now have multiple cores, from 2 to 8 cores. As we will see, it is very difficult to get precise measurements for even a single core. Multiple cores are more complicated, as execution can continue as long as there are more unblocked processes as there are cores. Otherwise, one or more cores will be in an IOwait status for that tick. So we configure the Linux kernel to enable just one core, by adding `maxcpus=1` to the kernel arguments and verifying with `cat /proc/cpuinfo`. We applied this configuration to all the experimental machines. We note in passing that for all the DBMSes we measured, their default configuration limits query evaluation to just one process, so this is not a significant limitation, as for the great majority of the time the DBMS query process was the only one executing on the system.

As mentioned at the beginning of the paper, even when all of these other interactions have been eliminated to the extent possible, the measured times still vacillate a lot, by over 25% of the highest time. To reduce this variability, we need to use other information, specifically per-process and processor-wide measures provided by the O/S.

4.2 Per-Process Measures

By examining the measures in `/proc`, a pseudo-file system maintained by Linux which provides an interface to kernel data structures, the measurement protocol can obtain through file reads valuable *per-process* statistics for each active process identifier. Most are counts in units of *ticks*, which for our processors are exactly 10msec. The measures of interest to us are (a) *minflt* [3], the number of minor page faults, those which do not require loading a memory page from disk, and so do not incur I/O, (b) *majflt*, the number of major page faults, which cause the process to be blocked while that page is swapped in, thus incurring I/O, (c) *utime*, the number of ticks in which that process was running in user mode, (d) *stime*, the number of ticks in which a request from that process was being handled by the operating system, (e) *guest time*, the number of ticks in spent running a virtual CPU for a guest operating system (always 0 for our protocol). These values are cumulative for each process, counting from 0 when the process was instantiated/forked; hence, these values are also accessed both before and after the query. We retrieve these statistics with a `getProcs` method within the protocol that itself takes about 16 milliseconds. Note that thread synchronization costs are not recorded by the O/S, and thus cannot be measured in this way.

4.3 Overall Measures

There are a variety of other overall measures available. The per-processor cumulative counts include (a) *utime*, the number of ticks in which a user process was executing, (b) *user mode with low priority* in ticks (always 0, because lower-priority processes have already been eliminated), (c) *stime*, the number of ticks in which the operating system was servicing a system call or interrupt, (d) *idle time*, the number of ticks when the processor has nothing to do (almost always 0), (e) *IOwait time*, the number of ticks in which the system had no processes to run because all were waiting for I/O, (f) *irq* (interrupt requests) handled by the system, (g) *softirq*, the number of soft interrupt requests (these requests can be handled with further interrupts enabled, to allow high-priority interrupts to still get in in a timely manner), (h) *steal time*, the number of ticks spent in other operating systems when running in a virtualized environment (always 0 in our protocol) and (i) *processes*, the number of forks. Note that all of these values are cumulative, counting from 0 since the last system rebooted. In our protocol, these values are accessed before and after the query is evaluated (by a `getProcStat()` method within the protocol), with the first value subtracted from the second value to obtain the number performed during query execution. Each `getProcStat` takes about 0.13 milliseconds, because there is only one set of these measures.

We discovered that for some versions of the Linux operating system (e.g., Redhat Enterprise Linux 5.8), the *irq* overall measure is always zero. For the newest version, Redhat Enterprise Linux 6.3, the *irq* measure increases very slowly, just a few per hour, even when experiments are run continuously. This rate is sufficiently low that we don't consider such interrupts further.

5. A PROPOSED CAUSAL MODEL

We have seen that there are a variety of per-process measures: user time, system time, and guest time measured in ticks and minflt and majflt measured in counts, and a variety of overall measures: user time, user mode with low priority time, system time, idle time, IOwait ticks, and steal time measured in ticks and number of irq, softirq, and processes measured in counts. Per-process measures are measured at individual process level, extracted from the output of `getProcs()`. We define *per-type measures* as the aggregation of per-process measures for the DBMS query process(es) (this category is termed *query*), for the other DBMS processes (this category is termed *utility*), and for the remaining, operating system daemon processes (this category is termed *daemon*). (We also occasionally lump the second and third categories into what we call the *non-query processes*.) The goal is how to infer/calculate the total time used by the query process(es) to actually execute the query. The task before us is to allocate the appropriate portion of overall time to the query processes, using if possible the per-process and overall times and counts in this allocation.

As noted above, steal time and user model with low priority time are always 0. We already have counts for user and system time for those DBMS process(es). The challenge is to estimate the portion of overall IOwait ticks directly or indirectly caused by activities of the DBMS processes.

5.1 Structural Causal Model

Figure 3 provides an initial causal model of these measures. The model differentiates the DBMS query processes, which dominate the time and which is known to have significant I/O and CPU components, and is given in Figure 3a, from the non-query processes (utility and daemon processes), which contribute much shorter run times and for which it is not known whether they have significant I/O or CPU components, given in Figure 3b.

Within this composite model, nodes are variables to be measured and directed arcs hypothesize causal interactions. The variable denoted "# of IO Requests", a count of such requests, cannot be measured, and thus is considered a *latent variable*, depicted with an oval. (`/proc/`*pid*`/IO` provides bytes read, not I/O requests in counts of blocks read; `/proc/`*pid*`/mountstats` provides a count of `READ` and `WRITE` requests, but only to the network file server, not to the local disk [3]. Several of the DBMSes include page reads and writes in the statistics they maintain; we have not yet pursued that source of information.)

Some variables, specifically the number of Soft IRQ Requests and the number of IO Wait Ticks, are overall measures, and so represent the same values in both sub-models. For the other three measures, user time, number of major faults, and system time, we have both per-type and overall measures. For Figure 3a, "User Time" is a construct with four different operationalizations: user time of the DBMS query process(es), total user time of the utility DBMS process(es) (if any), user time of the daemon process(es) (if any), and total user time, aggregated over all processes. The other two variables, system time and major faults, have analogous operationalizations.

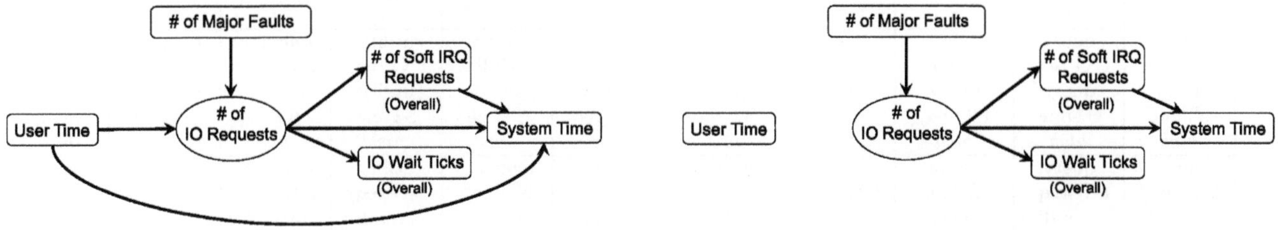

(a) Model for the DBMS Query Processes

(b) Model for Non-Query (Utility and Daemon) Processes

Figure 3: The Causal Model

The intuition behind this model is that the DBMS in its normal processing (measured by user time) reads data from the database, each read which induces an IO request to read in the block. That IO request incurs its own system time and interrupt requests, some of which are soft IRQs. If all processes are blocked on I/O, that request could add to IOwait ticks. All of these causal interactions are positive. For example, if user time increases for a different query, it is predicted that the number of IO requests might increase, which could itself increase the number of Soft IRQ requests, number of IO Wait ticks, and amount of system time. The DBMS presumably does other things that require system time. We don't expect to see a significant number of major faults caused by the DBMS query process, because after just a few query executions the entire query evaluator will have been faulted in, though if there were any major page faults, each would incur an IO Request to read the page in.

For all but the query process (that is, both utility and daemon processes), even though most of the obvious I/O-bound daemons are turned off, some I/O-bound daemons cannot be eliminated, such as `kjournald` and `pdflush`. On the other hand, some Linux kernel daemons are non-I/O bound. In either case, we don't know whether these non-query processes cause system time or major faults and therefore, in Figure 3b, there is no causal link predicted between user time and anything.

5.2 Predicted Correlations

This causal model relates 14 measures (four for each of user time, number of major faults, and system time plus single overall measures of number of soft IRQ requests and IOwait ticks), or a total of 182 interactions. For some pairs of measures, such as between daemon user time and daemon system time, there is no causal interaction predicted. For some other pairs of measures, such as daemon major faults and daemon system time, there is no direct causal link but there is an indirect causal link, in this case, along two paths, on involving number of soft IRQ requests. The overall model thus makes 45 specific predictions of correlations between pairs of measures, which we will now enumerate, motivating the strength of the correlation we expect to find for each. We identify expected an correlation of 0.7 or greater as a "high" level of correlation, from 0.3 to 0.7 as "medium" and those below that as a "low" level of correlation. Each correlation is positive: when one variable increases in value, we expect the other variable to increase in value.

We group these expected correlations that act in similar ways in Table 2. In each box is an interaction between two measures and a predicted level. We designate such pairs by group and letter within group. An example is correlation (*Ia*), the box at the top left, which concerns the interaction between query user time and query system time.

In general, we predict correlations between two different directly-linked measures for the same type of process (e.g., (*Ia*)) to be high. We predict overall correlations based on the strength of the associated per-type correlations. Similarly, indirectly-linked interactions are a sequence of directly-linked interactions: the correlation for the entire path generally won't be greater than that of any interaction along the way. An example is query major faults and query system time. For interactions involving a per-type and overall of different directly linked measures, as well as part-whole relationships (between a per-type and the overall operationalization of the same construct), we differentiate between query and non-query measures, because query processing dominates the computation. If the measure is only overall (that is, number of soft IRQ requests and number of IOwait ticks), or if there is a common ancestor, we do a case-by-case analysis.

The first group (Group I) involves correlations between two different measures, but for the same type of process (which can be either query, utility, or daemon). All such pairs are expected to be highly correlated, except for those involving major faults, because major faults are rare, and so their contribution to IO requests is minor. This group includes 11 predicted correlations.

The second group (II) involves correlation between the per-type measure and overall of a directly-linked different measure. The query process dominates the overall measure, but there are other things going on, so there will be some noise in overall, so we expect medium correlations. For utility and daemon processes, we expect only low correlation, for the same reason: the query process dominates the overall measure. Finally, concerning between IO requests and soft IRQ, we expect medium correlation, because prior investigation implied that IO requests generate soft IRQs.

The third group also involves correlations between two different measures, but for overall, expected to be correlated if all three per-type correlations in the first group are predicted. Also included in this group are such correlations involving measures that are only overall.

The fourth group involves correlation between a per-type measure and overall of an *indirectly-linked* different measure. Such correlations are expected to be of medium strength because they involve a sequence of other correlations.

The fifth group involves indirect correlations between two overall measures, because they don't differentiate the type of process. There are two cases. The first case is correlations involving user time. The interactions between user time and any other variable for non-IO bound processes are not in the model (Figure 3b).

	a	*b*	*c*	*d*	*e*	*f*	*g*	*h*	*i*	*j*	*k*
I	query UTime/ query STime *high*	query I/O req/ query STime *high*	query UTime/ query I/O req *high*	query MajFlts/ query I/O req *low*	query MajFlts/ query STime *low*	utility MajFlts/ utility I/O req *low*	utility MajFlts/ utility STime *low*	utility I/O req/ utility STime *high*	daemon I/O req/ daemon I/O req *low*	daemon MajFlts/ daemon STime *low*	daemon I/O req/ daemon STime *high*
II	query I/O req/ overall IO wait *med*	query I/O req/ overall Soft IRQ *med*	query Soft IRQ/ query STime *med*	utility I/O req/ overall I/O wait *low*	utility STime/ overall Soft IRQ *low*	daemon I/O req/ overall I/O wait *low*	daemon STime/ overall Soft IRQ *low*	utility I/O req/ overall Soft IRQ *med*	daemon I/O req/ overall Soft IRQ *med*		
III	overall MajFlts/ overall I/O req *low*	overall I/O req/ overall STime *high*	overal IO req/ overall I/O wait *low*	overall I/O req/ overall Soft IRQ *med*	overall Soft IRQ/ overall STime *med*						
IV	query UTime/ overall Soft IRQ *med*	query UTime/ overall IO wait *med*	query MajFlts/ overall Soft IRQ *med*	query MajFlts/ overall IO wait *med*	utility MajFlts/ overall Soft IRQ *low*	utility MajFlts/ overall IO wait *low*	daemon MajFlts/ overall Soft IRQ *low*	daemon MajFlts/ overall IO wait *low*			
V	overall UTime/ overall Soft IRQ *med*	overall UTime/ overall IO wait *med*	overall MajFlts/ overall Soft IRQ *med*	overall MajFlts/ overall IO wait *low*	overall MajFlts/ overall STime *low*						
VI	query UTime/ overall UTime *high*	query STime/ overall STime *high*	query IO req/ overall I/O req *high*	query MajFlts/ overall MajFlts *low*	utility MajFlts/ overall MajFlts *med*	daemon MajFlts/ overall MajFlts *med*					
VII	overall IO wait/ query STime *med*										

Table 2: Hypothesized Interactions and Hypothesized Levels

The sixth group involves part-whole relationships, that is, between the query component and the overall operationalization of the same construct. If the query process dominates the overall, the correlation will be high. If query process does not dominate, the correlation will be low. Query dominates for user, system and IO requests. Query does not dominate for major faults, which means that either or both utility and other contribute.

The seventh and final group involves implied relationships, that is, between variables that share a common ancestor, though there is no path between them. That said, we do so only for query measures, as less is known about non-query processes. Since there is no direct path, we expect the strength of the correlation to be smaller of the incoming arcs from the common ancestor.

6. TESTING THE CAUSAL MODEL

As mentioned, the seven group contribute 45 expected correlations. However, many involve the latent variable, number of IO requests, which by definition cannot be measured. We have a remaining 27 correlations not involving the latent variable. Our experiments provide a large amount of data that can be used to test this model, which we do now. Then, in Section 7, we will use this model to apportion I/O wait time to the DBMS processes and other processes.

We tested the model in two phases. In the first, *exploratory model analysis*, we ran a correlation analysis on a small portion of the query runs. We then examined our assumptions against the results of this analysis, and revised the model. The main changes suggested by this phase were to separate consideration of the query process, which we felt we understood much better, from the non-query processes, which we understand poorly. (Note that this paper is focused on measuring the query time, that is, the execution time of just the query process.) The result is that a single causal model was refined to the two-part model depicted in Figure 3.

Another aspect highlighted by the exploratory analysis was the role that major faults play in the model. The number of major faults generally is quite low, and almost non-existent for the query process (which made sense in retrospect, as the query code will have been swapped in at the beginning of the experiment and repeated executed).

The result to this point is a set of 27 correlations, each with an expected level: low, medium, or high. There are other interactions that are not predicted by our model. We then transitioned to the *confirmatory model analysis* stage of our testing, in which we did a correlational analysis of all 36 query runs, followed by a comparison of the actual level of correlation for each of the interactions in question with their level predicted by our model, for each DBMS.

In general, we found that the level predicted by our model either exactly matched that of the actual level (e.g., predicted high and actual high) or was close (e.g., predicted high and actual medium), for the majority of predicted interactions. For some interactions, the significance of the correlation was greater than 0.05, which means that there was insufficient data to determine if that interaction was present.

We now examine those few interactions where the prediction did not match the actual observed level of correlation, for each DBMS.

For DB2, there are five interactions of concern. Considering overall major faults, while we predicted the correlation with query major faults (interaction (*VId*)) would be low and with utility major faults (*VIe*) and with daemon major faults (*VIf*) would be medium, the actual correlations were query, high, and utility and daemon, not correlated with overall major faults. Looking into this further, we discovered that the *first* execution of a query in DB2 often experienced a few major faults and that these were often the only major faults in the execution, and so query dominated the total major faults.

The other discrepancy for DB2 was with the query user time and overall IO Wait ticks (*IVb*), which we predicted would have medium correlation but in fact were not correlated at all. We discovered that less than 2% of the DB2 query executions had *any* IO Wait ticks. That number of samples was too low to do a separate correlational analysis. This also explains the fifth interaction of concern, that of overall user time and overall IO Wait ticks (*Vb*).

For MySQL, there were three interactions of concern. The first is between overall soft IRQ and daemon system time (*IIg*), which was predicted to be low but whose actual correlation was high. Most queries in mySQL took a long time to complete. This resulted in both query and daemon processes causing a large number of major faults, so that both dominated the correlation between soft IRQ and system time and high correlations and observed correlations of high for both.

The second is *IVb*, discussed above. For MySQL, two things are going on. First, for many queries, there are no overall IOwait ticks. But there are also some long-running MySQL queries, in which the IOwait ticks accumulate, though still in low numbers: perhaps one or two dozen, representing less than 1% of the query user time. In both situations, the IOwait ticks is such a small component of the run time that no correlation was observed. Again, the exceptions, 0.97%, were so infrequent as to disallow a separate correlational analysis.

Finally, our model predicts a medium correlation for overall user time and overall IO Wait time (*Vb*), but no such correlation was observed. It seems that again, this is because of the very low amount of IO Wait ticks present in most of the query executions. For Oracle, we found that interaction (*IVf*), utility major faults and overall IO Wait ticks, was predicted to be low but was actually high. This is probably because the Oracle utility processes were being run intermittently, causing major faults which added to IO Wait ticks when contended with the Oracle query process. This also explains interaction (*Vd*), overall major faults and overall IOwait ticks, from expected low to actual high. For PostgreSQL, there was only one discrepancy (*IIg*), already discussed.

In summary, for the 108 testable interactions (27 interactions for each of four DBMSes), we encountered only eleven that were of concern, none of which presents a serious challenge to the model. Our conclusion is that the model is strongly supported by these experimental results. As we will see in Section 7.5, after cleaning up the query executions in Steps 2 and 3 of our protocol, the number of interactions of concern reduced dramatically.

We now delve into the details of the timing protocol.

7. TIMING PROTOCOL

In the following, we first discuss general data collection, then consider the intricacies of process interaction, and finally show how the data that was collected, in concert with the causal model shown in Figure 3, can be used to ascribe the portion of I/O time utilized by DBMS query evaluation.

7.1 Data Collection

Since the time to collect the per-type metrics is much longer than that taken to collect the overall metrics, we perform measurements in the following order: `getProcs()`→ `getProcStat()`→ `getTime()`→*execute query*→`getTime()`→ `getProcStat()`→`getProcs`, after which we compute the differences in the cumulative statistics.

This data needs to be carefully analyzed to understand how the processes interact when scheduled in an interleaved fashion, especially for allocating I/O among the processes. We found it to be useful to retain all of this data for *every* Q@C execution, but recording only those processes for which some activity was observed during the query execution.

7.2 Process Interactions

We now consider how individual processes interact with each other and with the measurement protocol. These interactions significantly complicate the timing of queries.

As illustrated in Figure 4, processes *P1*, *P2* and *P3* are recorded into a map, M_1, when the first `getProcs()` is invoked. Process *P4* might also appear in M_1, depending on exactly when it started (as `getProcs()` takes a while to execute, going through the processes one by one). Another map, M_2, built after the query has executed, records processes *P3*, *P6* and *P7*, and it might also have *P8*. We term process *P5* a *phantom process*, since it appears and completes its task before the query execution is finished, and thus will appear in neither M_1 or M_2. However, we can detect the presence of phantom process(es) by comparing the total number of executed processes (forks) extracted by `getProcStat()` before and after the query evaluation. Process *P4*, even if it is recorded in M_1, will not be considered to be a phantom process, because it did not start after the first `getProcStat()` was invoked.

The comparison between M_1 and M_2 reveals that processes *P1* and *P2* are present in M_1 but not in M_2. We term these processes *stopped processes*. It is evident that process *P2* overlaps the query execution, but it is not easy to differentiate process *P1* from *P2*. For example, both could have user ticks, even though only process *P2* actually overlapped with the query execution, contributing time measured by `gettime()`. If process *P4* was recorded in M_1, then it will also be considered a stopped process.

Processes *P6* and *P7* are located in M_2 but not in M_1. Process *P8* may also be in this situation as well, if it was caught by `getProcs()`. If caught, its ticks will be captured

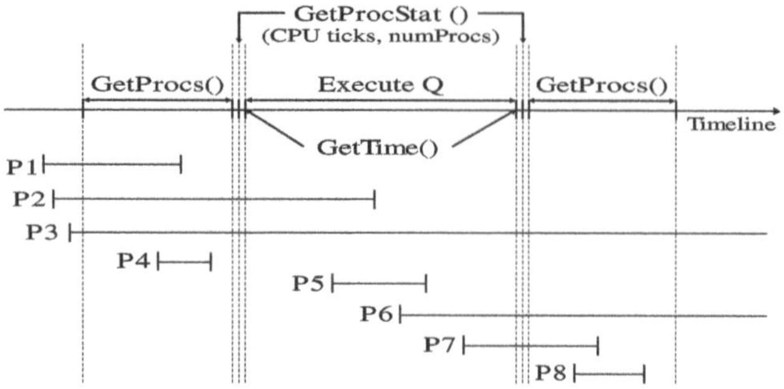

Figure 4: Processes considered when timing a query

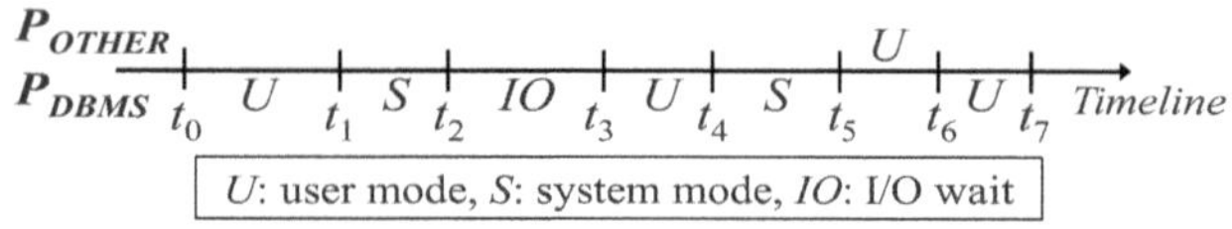

Figure 5: Two interleaved, running processes

in the per-type metrics, but not in the processor metrics.) We term these *started processes*. Note however that we know the amount of user and system time these processes incurred, because that information will be in M_2, unlike that for phantom processes.

7.3 Calculating the CPU Time

Generally, the CPU time is easy to calculate because we have per-type system and user time. However, we need to determine which DBMS process was actually running the query. For MySQL, there is only one DBMS process. For DB2, we can uniquely identify the query process (`db2sysc`). Oracle and PostgreSQL have multiple processes of the same name, one of which could be the one actually running the query. For such cases, we select the process that has the highest total user plus system time across all executions for a single Q@C as the one that is performing the query. Note that this could select the wrong process, if the query process ran very quickly and a DBMS utility process performed a lot of work during that same time frame. Hence, if the selected process does not appear in every query execution for a Q@C, we will drop that Q@C in Step 2-(i), below.

7.4 Calculating the I/O Time

Every tick can be in one of several modes [3]: running a user process (*user mode*), running a user process in low priority (*low priority mode*), running on behalf of user processes in the operating system (*system mode*), running on behalf of user processes in softirq (*softirq mode*), waiting for I/O, when all user processes are blocked (*IOwait mode*), or waiting for a user process, as there is no I/O or computation to be done (*idle mode*). The first three modes are illustrated in Figure 5, for two processes, the DBMS process and another process. Here the DBMS process starts in user mode for one tick, then switches to system mode, then to IOwait mode.

Our error model is that in the absence of non-query processes (utility and daemon), the measured time should be accurate, though it will vary somewhat with the vagaries of disk head position, so the number of user time plus system time and number of IOwait ticks will trade-off in slightly different ways for the Q@C executions. (We note in passing that this error model argues against taking the average mentioned at the start of this paper.) The utility processes when present will increase the total time through *their* user and system ticks, and will also probably increase the IOwait ticks, as there are generally only a few processes running at any one time. (On average, there are two or three additional processes running sometime during a Q@C execution, though there is a long tail to 18 processes, with one execution each with 20, 27, and 53 processes, out of the 350,000 executions examined.)

For our running example, the per-type metrics shown in Table 4 support this model. (In this table, the lowest and highest values for each row are in **bold**.) Note how stable the user times (U_{Qdbms}) and system times (S_{Qdbms}) are for the DBMS process performing the query ($SU_{query} = S+U$), with SU_{query} varying by only 7 ticks (less than 2%). For PostgreSQL, there is only one DBMS process, so we don't see any $SU_{utility}$ ticks (nor major faults, $MajFlt_{utility}$). For these executions, PostgreSQL has already faulted in all of the code to run the query, so $MajFlt_{query}$ is zero (though we do see non-zero values for this metric). The variance is contributed by the daemon processes that we cannot turn off, specifically SU_{daemon}, $SoftIrq$, and $MajFlt_{daemon}$ and by the interaction of those processes and the DBMS query process in $IOwait$ ticks.

So the challenge is in apportioning the $IOwait$ ticks to the query process. The model shown in Figure 3 and validated in Section 6 provides guidance on how to do so.

Algorithm measurementProtocol(*query*, *card*):
{turn off non-essential O/S daemons}
plan ← *GetQueryPlan*(*query*)
for *iterNum* ← 1 **to** 10 **do**
  timeSingleQuery(*iterNum*, *query*, *plan*, *card*)
end for
for *iterNum* ← 1 to 10 **do**
  dropQueryExecutions()
end for
if *dropQ@C*() **then**
  return null {Drop some Q@C's}
else
  calculateQueryTime() {Over remaining Q@C's}
end if

Figure 6: Measurement Protocol

7.5 Query Execution Time Computation

Recall that we start with a fixed number (10) of query executions for each Q@C. We desire an operationalization of the query execution time for that Q@C, which is a single time in milliseconds.

Our general protocol is to (1) perform sanity checks to ensure the validity of the data, (2) perhaps drop some query executions via clearly motivated predicates, (3) perhaps drop some entire Q@Cs, again via clearly motivated predicates, (4) for those Q@Cs that remain, for each compute a single measured time by a carefully-justified formula over the underlying measures of the remaining query executions, and (5) perform post-analysis sanity checks.

We now detail each step of this protocol, shown in Figure 6. We apply the protocol to our data, consisting of a total of 353,630 query executions (35,363 Q@Cs) over the four DBMSes.

	1	2	3	4	5	6	7	8	9	10	*Avg*	*Std Dev*
$Time_{meas}$ (msec)	**6530**	6571	**8764**	7961	8427	7829	8246	8506	8239	6991	7806	818
U_{total} (ticks)	303	315	**308**	300	—	303	301	**299**	309	—	305	5.1
L_{total} (ticks)	4	**0**	5	2	—	2	3	**26**	24	—	9	9.8
S_{total} (ticks)	171	**166**	171	183	—	176	176	**188**	185	—	177	7.7
Q_{total} (ticks)	**24**	27	44	42	-	39	43	**63**	48	-	41	11.4
$Idle_{total}$ (ticks)	0	0	0	0	—	0	0	0	0	—	0	0
IO_{total} (ticks)	150	**149**	**349**	269	—	262	301	275	258	—	253	65.1
$Time_{sum}$ (msec)	**6520**	6570	**8770**	7960	—	7820	8240	8510	8240	—	7829	845.4

Table 3: Measured time versus computed sum

	1	2	3	4	5	6	7	8	9	10	*Avg*	*Std Dev*
$Time_{meas}$ (msec)	**6530**	6571	**8764**	7961	8427	7829	8246	8506	8239	6991	7806	818
U_{query} (ticks)	289	293	**294**	286	—	287	288	**283**	290	—	289	3.6
S_{query} (ticks)	166	**161**	164	171	—	168	168	**177**	166	—	168	4.8
SU_{query} (ticks)	455	454	458	457	—	**453**	456	460	**460**	—	457	2.6
$SU_{utility}$ (msec)	0	0	0	0	—	0	0	0	0	—	0	0
SU_{daemon} (msec)	33	**37**	41	42	—	41	43	79	**84**	—	50	19.7
$MajFlt_{query}$	0	0	0	0	—	0	0	0	0	—	0	0
$MajFlt_{utility}$	0	0	0	0	—	0	0	0	0	—	0	0
$MajFlt_{daemon}$	17	**0**	7	**18**	—	0	0	0	0	—	5	7.9
$IOwait_{meas}$ (ticks)	150	**149**	**349**	269	—	264	301	275	258	—	252	69.5
$SoftIrq_{meas}$ (ticks)	**24**	27	44	42	—	39	42	**63**	48	—	40	14.2

Table 4: Breaking out the per-type metrics

Step 1: Perform Sanity Checks.

Before starting the query execution time computation, we assess the validity of our data by performing several *sanity checks*. These sanity checks serve only to indicate possible systematic errors across the entire experiment that need to be examined carefully before proceeding through the rest of the steps. (Sanity checks are always recommended within an experimental methodology to ensure data quality before analyzing the data.)

We have three different classes of such sanity checks, comprising twelve sanity checks in total.

Table 5 lists the first class: the overall cases for which not a single violation should occur in our data. The number of missing queries indicates how many queries were not executed, for whatever reason. The number of process info failures represents how many query executions do not have data stored about its processes, specifically, overall query execution information: overall ticks, number of started/stopped/ executed processes, phantom presence, total faults, and total daemon time. Finally, the unique plan violation checks how many Q@Cs have more than one query plan. All query executions of Q@C must have a single, identical query plan.

In prior testing, we encountered violations of several of these sanity checks, which suggested refinements to our protocol, thereby ensuring that there were no such violations for the runs examined in this paper.

The second class of sanity checks concerns query executions; see Table 6. Each of these six sanity checks could encounter a few isolated violations. However, we expect the violation percentage to be very low.

The DBMS time violation check identifies the percentage of query executions with the time taken by DBMS processes (query and utility) in total less than the time taken by daemon processes, since we expect query execution time to dominate. Fortunately, only about 0.01% DBMS time violations were observed across all query executions in our data. Second, the *zero* query time violation check indicates how many query executions have a query time of 0 ticks. We would not expect such query executions. Our data showed only 0.01% violations as well. Third, the query time violation check identifies the query executions in which the query time is greater than measured time. In our data, we uncovered 0.52%, which is a very low rate.

For the last three sanity checks in this class, one could be detected but should be very low and the other two should not be violated by any query execution. The no query process violation check indicates how many query executions do not have any query process. We got very low percentage (0.19%), with most of these query executions at the minimum cardinality (10K) or with a very short measured time, less than 10ms. Finally, we ensure that (query or utility) processes from another DBMS should not be running. We thus check how many query executions include other query or utility processes. There were no such query executions.

The final class involves three checks over each Q@C; see Table 7. The first detects excessive query process time variations, those in which the standard deviation of the query time (user mode ticks plus system mode ticks) is greater than 20% of the average query process time. We observed few violations. Monotonicity Violation identifies two Q@Cs for the same query plan having different cardinalities, for the query time of the Q@C's at a lower cardinality is greater than that of the Q@C at a higher cardinality. The query over the larger cardinality should take more time, so such instances indicate a problem; we term this *strict* monotonicity violation. We expect a small number of violations due to the small variance of query time at each query execution Due to the unavoidable variation of query times, we also

Number of Missing Queries	0
Number of Process Info Failures	0
Number of Unique Plan Violations	0

Table 5: Overall sanity checks

Percentage of DBMS Time Violations	0.01%
Percentage of Zero Query Time Violations	0.01%
Percentage of Query Time Violations	0.52%
Percentage of No Query Process Violations	0.19%
Percentage of Other Query Process Violations	0%
Percentage of Other Utility Process Violations	0%

Table 6: Query execution sanity checks

Percentage of Excessive Var. in Query Time	0.05%
Percentage of Strict Monotonicity Violation	0.29%
Percentage of Relaxed Monotonicity Violation	0.073%

Table 7: Q@C sanity checks

At Start of Step 2	353,630 QEs
At Start of Step 2	35,363 Q@Cs
After Step 2-(i)	350,830 QEs
After Step 2-(ii)	251,270 QEs
After Step 2-(iii)	249,110 QEs
After Step 2-(iv)	247,867 QEs
At Start of Step 3	31,658 Q@Cs
After Step 3-(i)	31,658 Q@Cs
After Step 3-(ii)	31,374 Q@Cs
After Step 3-(iii)	26,841 Q@Cs

Table 8: The number of Query Executions (QEs) and Q@Cs remaining after each sub-step

consider *relaxed* monotonicity violation in which half a standard deviation of query time is subtracted from the lower cardinality and half a standard deviation is added to the upper cardinality, to account for some of this variation.

Now that we see that the original data from our experiment passes all of these sanity checks, we can proceed onto the next step.

Step 2: Drop Query Executions.

In this step, we drop query executions that exhibit specific problems, in order to increase accuracy and precision.

First, we drop (i) the query executions identified as problematic in Table 6 as well as the first row of Table 7 to increase the precision of our measured query time. Table 8 shows how many query executions are valid at the beginning of Step 2 and after Step 2-(i): about 0.79% query executions were dropped.

Referring back to Figure 4 showing the interleaved processes, the total time (from the algorithm, $time_2 - time_1$) includes the time taken by the DBMS, the time taken by *P5*, and portions of processes *P2*, *P3*, *P5*, *P6*, and *P7*. For most of these processes, we have per-process information from `getProcs()`. Not so for the stopped process *P2* nor for the phantom process *P5*, because neither of those processes show up in map M_2. Due to this potentially large uncertainty, we (ii) drop any query execution that contains a stopped or phantom process.

Percentage of Excessive Var. in Query Time	0%
Percentage of Strict Monotonicity Violations	0.38%
Percentage of Relaxed Monotonicity Violations	0.076%

Table 9: Post (Q@C) sanity checks

If *P4* was included in M_1, then it will also be (conservatively) considered to be a stopped process (we know it started before the query and we only know it ended before we could get its per-process metrics). If that process was not included in M_1, then we don't need to worry about it.

Started processes (in this case, *P6* and *P7*) do not cause a problem, because we have per-process information for these processes in M_2. Even if process *P8* is included in M_2 that process will be ignored, as it is not a DBMS process.

We also (iii) drop query executions where the IOwait ticks is greater than two times the median IOwait ticks for the Q@C, when the median IOwait ticks is greater than zero. The rationale is that such a large number of IOwait ticks over the median could have only be caused by other processes. Because we allocate IOwait ticks in our computation of $Time_{calc}$, we need to be conservative.

When the median IOwait ticks is zero, a minority of query executions have a non-zero IOwait ticks. In such cases, we drop query executions for that Q@C whose number of IOwait ticks is greater than 2, because such query executions will be outliers (again, to be conservative).

The discussion in Section 6 identified two places where the overall IOwait ticks was problematic: when it was non-zero for DB2 (for a very small percentage of queries) and when it was significant for MySQL (also a very small percentage). Thus we (iv) drop DB2 query executions with non-zero IOwait ticks and drop MySQL query executions for non-zero IOwait ticks for which this time represents more than 1% of the query user time. The net take away is that for these two DBMSes, we need not concern ourselves with an adjustment to apportion IOwait time.

For our running example of query 17, execution 5 had one phantom and execution 10 had one phantom and one stopped process, so we drop those two query executions in Step 2-(ii). No other query executions from this query were dropped, as shown in Table 3.

Table 8 shows how many query executions remained after each sub-step in Step 2. As mentioned, 0.79% were dropped in Step 2-(i). 28.38% query executions were dropped due to stopped or phantom processes at Step 2-(ii). After Step 2-(iii), 0.86% query executions were dropped due to the high IOwait ticks. After Step 2-(iv), 0.50% query executions were dropped due to problematic IO Wait ticks from DB2 and MySQL. In summary, Step 2 in concert dropped 29.91% query executions, and based on the remaining query executions (247,867), a total of 31,658 Q@Cs were left, with each Q@C retaining an average of 7.83 query executions.

Step 3: Drop Selected Q@Cs.

In this step, we look at the query executions for each Q@C, and determine if these query executions *in concert* exhibit specific problems. If so, we drop the entire Q@C, to increase accuracy and precision.

All time metrics except for measured time via `getTime()` are in ticks. For very quick queries, which take only a few ticks, a single tick or two of additional IOwait ticks for a daemon process can throw off the total by a large percentage factor. Also, as noted in Section 7.3, very short execution times result in the wrong query process being chosen. Hence, we (i) drop any Q@C for which the identified query process does not appear in every query execution for that Q@C, (ii) drop Q@Cs with $Time_{meas}$ (average measured time across remaining executions) of 2 or less ticks, and (iii) drop those Q@Cs with less than six valid query executions. For our running example, none of these predicates dictated dropping this Q@C.

Table 8 shows how many Q@Cs are dropped after each sub-step in Step 3. As indicated by the last row for Step 2, we initially had 31,658 Q@Cs, and no Q@Cs were dropped at Step 3-(i) thanks to previously dropping query executions violating no query process sanity check. We dropped 0.90% Q@Cs at Step 3-(ii) and 14.5% at Step 3-(iii). Throughout Step 3, a total 15.2% of Q@Cs were discarded; each remaining Q@C had an average of 8.52 query executions.

We expect that cardinality of the result of each each successive step to monotonically decrease. As shown in Table 8, the cardinalities behave as expected.

Step 4: Calculate Query Time.

In this calculation, we include (a) DBMS user time, (b) DBMS system time, and (c) the portion of IOwait time due to DBMS I/O requests. Due to Step 2-(iii), the data from DB2 and MySQL will not have a meaningful number of IOWait ticks so component (c) does not pertain to these DBMSes.

According to the model shown in Figure 3 and validated in Section 6, there are four factors that cause IOwait ticks: query user time and query, utility, and daemon major faults. (All do so via the number of IO requests, which is a latent, and hence unmeasured, factor.) Of these three influences, only query user time and query major faults involve the query process.

We performed a regression, examining how much these three factors each contributed to IOwait ticks. We ran the following regression over the Q@C executions.

$$\begin{aligned} IOwait_{meas} &= a + b \times U_{query} \\ &\quad + c \times MajFlt_{query} \\ &\quad + d \times MajFlt_{utility} \\ &\quad + e \times MajFlt_{daemon} \qquad (1) \end{aligned}$$

This regression fits quite well with our error model. The variance explained is 67% for Oracle and 38% for PostgreSQL (due to the different characteristics of various DBMSes, we compute regression coefficients for each individual DBMS). None of the factors on the right dominate or appear to be collinear with *IOwait*. However, the $MajFlt_{query}$ factor is not a significant contributor; thus we do not use this factor.

The y-intercept for Oracle is 67 ticks and for PostgreSQL is 38 ticks. (Note that the model predicts that this intercept should be 0, though exogenous factors such as process startups and the latent variable contribute to this value).

We can then use the regression coefficient associated with the query process to determine the contribution of the IOwait time to the total query time. (As noted before, there is no reason to scale the IOwait time for DB2 nor for MySQL.)

$$\begin{aligned} IOwait_{calc} &= b \times U_{query} \qquad (2) \\ Time_{calc} &= (S_{query} + U_{query} + IOwait_{calc}) \\ &\quad \times 10msec \qquad (3) \end{aligned}$$

The regression (evaluated over the retained query executions) produced the needed regression coefficients of b (the multiplier for U_{query}) of 1.916 for Oracle and 0.259 for PostgreSQL. The resulting computed execution times ($Time_{calc}$) are shown in Table 10, with the median, 5308.3 msec, being the computed query time for this Q@C (in this case, there are an even number of remaining query executions, and so the median is the average of the two central times, with three times on each side). The last column indicates that this time is within one standard deviation of $\pm$1.7 ticks, or $\pm$0.3%. Across all runs, the computed time is within one average standard deviation of $\pm$2.9 ticks, or $\pm$1.2. Our conjecture is that unmeasurable factors such as thread synchronization are contained in this variance. In addition, we can report (see Figure 1) that the overall wall clock time ranged from 6.5 to 8.8 seconds, with an average of 7.38 sec $\pm$1.2 sec. The DBMS CPU time is 4570 $\pm$35 msec and the DBMS I/O time is 750 $\pm$1.4 msec. We could also report similar measures for the utility and daemon processes.

Step 5: Post Sanity Checks.

As post sanity checks, we re-examine excessively varying query time on the refined data, and check monotonicity violations based on the calculated query times.

Table 9 shows our post sanity check results. After our protocol was applied, no excessively varying query times were detected. Also, the rates of monotonicity violations increased just slightly. The total number of violations itself was reduced but relatively more Q@Cs were dropped by our protocol.

We reran the confirmatory correlation analysis discussed in Section 6 on the refined data. For DB2, four of the five interactions of concern in that prior analysis are now closer to the predicted, at most one level different, with three matching the predicted level exactly,. For MySQL, the number of interactions of concern went from three to one, for Oracle, two to one, and for PostgreSQL, the one concern was resolved. In sum, the refined data reduced the number of interactions of concern from 11 to 3, lending even stronger support for the causal model in Figure 3.

8. SUMMARY AND FUTURE WORK

Measuring query time is complex, as a DBMS interacts with other processes and with the operating system in quite involved ways.

This paper has considered these interactions in detail. We first articulated a structural causal model relating these measures. A thorough correlational analysis provided strong support for this model. Using this model, we developed a timing protocol that comprises *Isolation*: eliminating as many extraneous factors, including network delays, cache effects, and daemons; *Measurement*: specific metrics collected before and after the query execution, in a carefully prescribed order; and *Analysis*: a sequence that (i) performs initial sanity checks over the entire data, (ii) perhaps drops some Q@C executions, (iii) perhaps drops some entire Q@Cs, (iv) for those Q@Cs that remain, for each compute a single query time using the underlying measures of the remaining query executions, and finally, (v) does some final sanity checks. This protocol results in a more precise and more accurate timing of the query, reducing variance significantly.

	1	2	3	4	5	6	7	8	9	10	*Avg*	*Std Dev*
$Time_{meas}$ (msec)	**6530**	6571	**8764**	7961	8427	7829	8246	8506	8239	6991	7806	818
SU_{query} (ticks)	455	**454**	458	457	—	453	456	**460**	460	—	457	2.6
$MajFlt_{Qdbms}$ (msec)	0	0	0	0	—	0	0	0	0	—	0	0
$IOwait_{meas}$ (ticks)	150	**149**	**349**	269	—	264	301	275	258	—	252	69.5
$IOwait_{calc}$ (ticks)	74.9	75.9	**76.1**	74.1	—	74.3	74.6	**73.3**	75.1	—	74.8	0.9
$Time_{calc}$ (msec)	5298.5	5298.9	**5341.5**	5310.7	—	**5293.3**	5305.9	5333.0	5311.1	—	5311.6	17.1

Table 10: Final computed times

The *Tucson Protocol* is quite general, applicable to most versions of Unix that support `/proc`, and is also applicable to other operating domains in which measurements of multiple processes each doing computation and I/O is needed. While many of the specifics, such as clearing caches before executing a query, are well-known (though not well-documented), this is the first general query evaluation time measurement protocol to be articulated.

In subsequent work we plan to refine this query time measurement protocol to (a) incorporate network delays for a remote disk (which necessitates clearing the network file server cache for cold cache timings), (b) utilize block read and write statistics available from the DBMSes and bytes read and written from the O/S, (c) accommodate multiple disks, connected by a single or distinct channels, (d) accommodate multiple processor cores, (e) accommodate phantom processes while eliminating their impact on the computed time, (f) extend PostgreSQL to clear its cache, (g) ensure repeatability of file fragmentation, (h) support the Windows operating system, which has different per-process metrics, and thus might require an altered causal model and a different regression model and calculation of query time, and (i) accommodate multiple disks. We also want to extend the protocol to (a) measure single transactions that incorporate multiple statements and (b) measure a mix of transactions.

9. ACKNOWLEDGMENTS

This research was supported in part by NSF grants IIS-0639106, IIS-0415101, and EIA-0080123. We thank Benjamin Dicken, Preetha Chatterjee, Pallavi Chilappagari, David Gallup, Kevan Holdaway, Andrey Kvochko, and Lopamudra Sarangi for their contributions to the AZDBLAB and Phil Kaslo, Tom Lowry, and John Luiten for constructing and maintaining our experimental instrument, a laboratory of ten machines and associated software. Phil was particularly helpful in tracking down irq behavior. Finally, we thank Nikolaus Augsten for many helpful comments.

10. REFERENCES

[1] A. G. Ailamaki, D. J. DeWitt, M. D. Hill, and D. A. Wood, "DBMSes on modern processors: Where does time go?" University of Wisconsin Computer Sciences Technical Report 1394, February 25, 1999.

[2] M. Akswew, U. Cetintemel, M. Riondato, E. Upfal, and S. B. Zdonik, "Learning-based Query Performance Modeling and Prediction," in *ICDE'12*, pp. 390–411.

[3] D. Bovet, and M. Cesati, "Understanding the Linux Kernel, Third Edition," O'Reilly, 2003.

[4] B. F. Cooper, A. Silberstein, E. Tam, R. Ramakrishnan, and R. Sears, "Benchmarking Cloud Serving Systems with YCSB," in *Proceedings of the ACM Symposium on Cloud Computing*, New York, June 2010, pp. 143–154.

[5] R. F. Forman, J. M. Pechacek, and W. H. Schwane, "Apparatus and Method for Measure Transaction Time in a Computer System," IBM Patent, 2001.

[6] A. Ganapathi, H. A. Kuno, U. Dayal, J. L. Wiener, A. Fox, M. I. Jordan, and D. A. Patterson, "Predicting multiple performance metrics for queries: Better decisions enabled by machine learning," in *ICDE'09*.

[7] L. Gikoumakis and C. Galindo-Legaria, "Testing SQL Server's Query Optimizer: Challenges, Techniques and Experiences, *IEEE Data Eng. Bull.* 31(1): 36-43 (2008).

[8] H.-Y. Hwang and Y.-T. Yu, "An Analytical Method for Estimating and Interpreting Query Time," in *VLDB'78*.

[9] Working Group 2 of the Joint Committee for Guides in Metrology (JCGM/WG 2), **International Vocabulary of Metrology—Basic and General Concepts and Associated Terms**, 2008.

[10] K. Kant, **Introduction to Computer System Performance Evaluation**, McGraw-Hill, 1992.

[11] M. Stillger, G. M. Lohman, V. Markl, and M. Kaqndil, "LEO - DB2's Learning Optimizer," in *VLDB'01*.

[12] TPC, "Transaction Processing Performance Council—TPC-C," `http://www.tpc.org/tpcc/`. (accessed August 29, 2010)

[13] TPC, "TPC Transaction Processing Performance Council—TPC-H," `http://www.tpc.org/tpch/`. (accessed August 29, 2010)

[14] Valgrind Developers, "Callgrind: A Call-Graph Generating Cache and Branch Prediction Profiler," `http://valgrind.org/docs/manual/cl-manual.html`. (accessed October 27, 2010)

[15] S. W. Thomas, and R. T. Snodgrass and R. Zhang, "τBench: Extending XBench with Time," TIMECENTER TR-92, 2010.

[16] B. B. Yao, M. T. Özsu, and N. Khandelwal, N., "XBench benchmark and performance testing of XML DBMSs," in *ICDE'04*.

[17] P. Yu, M.-S. Chen, H.-U. Heiss, and S. Lee, "On workload characterization of relational database environments," *IEEE Transactions on Software Engineering*, 18:347–355, 1992.

[18] N. Zhang, J. Tatemura, J. M. Patel, and H. Hacǒgumus, "Towards Cost-Effective Storage Provisioning for DBMSs," *PVLDB*, Vol. 5, No. 4, pp. 274-285 (2011)

[19] R. Zhang, R. T. Snodgrass and S. Debray, "Micro-Specialization in DBMSes," in *ICDE*, pp. 690–701, April 2012.

Quality and Efficiency in Kernel Density Estimates for Large Data*

Yan Zheng, Jeffrey Jestes, Jeff M. Phillips, Feifei Li
School of Computing, University of Utah, Salt Lake City, USA
{yanzheng, jestes, jeffp, lifeifei}@cs.utah.edu

ABSTRACT

Kernel density estimates are important for a broad variety of applications. Their construction has been well-studied, but existing techniques are expensive on massive datasets and/or only provide heuristic approximations without theoretical guarantees. We propose randomized and deterministic algorithms with quality guarantees which are orders of magnitude more efficient than previous algorithms. Our algorithms do not require knowledge of the kernel or its bandwidth parameter and are easily parallelizable. We demonstrate how to implement our ideas in a centralized setting and in *MapReduce*, although our algorithms are applicable to any large-scale data processing framework. Extensive experiments on large real datasets demonstrate the quality, efficiency, and scalability of our techniques.

Categories and Subject Descriptors

H.2.4 [**Information Systems**]: Database Management – *Systems*

Keywords

Kernel density estimate (KDE), distributed and parallel KDE

1. INTRODUCTION

A kernel density estimate is a statistically-sound method to estimate a continuous distribution from a finite set of points. This is an increasingly common task in data analysis. In many scientific computing and data intensive applications, the input data set P is a finite number of observations or measurements made for some real-world phenomena, that can be best described by some random variable V with an unknown probability distribution function (pdf) f. For example, temperature readings from sensor nodes, collected over a period of time, represent a finite sample of a 1-dimensional random variable *temperature*.

Given a data set P consisting of values from a domain $\mathcal{M}$, a kernel density estimate is a function f_P that for any input in $\mathcal{M}$ (not necessarily in P) describes *the density* at that location. It is a fundamental data smoothing problem where inferences about the population are made, based on a finite data sample. That said, we view P as a finite, independent and identically distributed (iid) data sample drawn from a random variable V that is governed by an unknown distribution f. We are interested in estimating the shape of this function f. The kernel density estimate f_P approximates the density of f at any possible input point $x \in \mathcal{M}$ [31,37]. Figure 1 visualizes the kernel density estimate (KDE) in both 1 and 2 dimensions, using real data sets (a web trace in 1D and a spatial dataset from openstreetmap in 2D). Black dots represent a subset of points from P, and the blue curves or regions represent the KDE constructed from P.

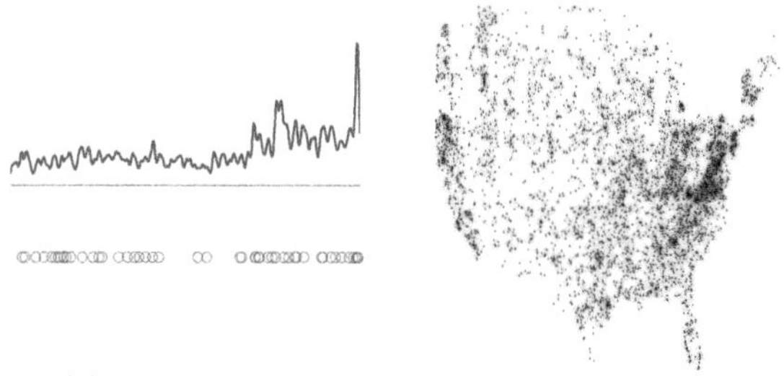

(a) KDE in 1D. (b) KDE in 2D.

Figure 1: Kernel density estimate (KDE).

A kernel density estimate has useful and important applications in databases. Suppose we have a set of customers labeled by their annual income P. Then we may ask do we have more customers with income about 100K or income about 50K (rather than specifying a rigid range). A kernel density estimate is a function f_P that for any input (such as $100K$ or $50K$) describes *the density* at that location. So we could return the values $f_P(100K)$ and $f_P(50K)$ to compare.

Alternatively, we may have a database storing the (two-dimensional) locations of crimes in a database, and we may want to compare the density of these crimes around two houses (that we may be considering buying). In this case, rigid notions of districts may not appropriately capture the density at houses near the borders of these districts.

Another family of applications originates from statistical physics where the KDE value is proportional to the force in a system of particles. In this setting, very high precision answers are needed to accurately carry out simulations.

Our contributions. A kernel density estimate serves two main purposes. First, it is a data structure that can process function evaluation queries. Second, it is a summarization, like a histogram, for quickly presenting the distribution of density over a domain. We will allow approximate kernel

*Thanks to support from NSF grants IIS-0916488, IIS-1053979, and CCF 1115677.

density estimate queries; most large data summarizations are by nature approximations, and density evaluations are models and thus should not be used to arbitrary precision. This approximation allows us to focus on a trade-off between the size of the data structure and the allowed approximation error; we focus on the strong ℓ_∞ error between the original kernel density estimate and its approximation.

Moreover, unlike histograms, kernel density estimates generalize naturally to more than one dimensional data. Since many spatial data sets lie naturally in $\mathbb{R}^2$, we focus primarily on one and two-dimensional data; however our techniques will scale naturally to higher dimensions; see Section 5.6.

With these goals in mind we investigate how to calculate such a data structure on an enormous scale (our experiments use 100 million points); our approximation (with theoretical bounds) is quite small in size (requires only megabytes in space) and is in fact independent of the original number of points, and offers very accurate queries. More importantly, our methods for computing these approximations are designed with parallel and distributed processing in mind, and we demonstrate how to adapt them in the popular MapReduce framework. But they can be easily adopted by any other parallel and distributed computation models.

The paper is organized as follows. Section 2 presents the problem formulation. Section 3 discusses background material and related work and Section 4 discusses the one dimension case. Section 5 presents the two dimension case. Section 6 reports experimental results and Section 7 concludes. Some technical proofs are relegated to the Appendix.

2. PROBLEM FORMULATION

Let P be an input point set of size n. We will either consider $P \in \mathbb{R}^1$ or $P \in \mathbb{R}^2$. We first describe the situation for $\mathbb{R}^d$, and then specify to one of these two common cases.

We restrict the *kernels* $K : \mathbb{R}^d \times \mathbb{R}^d \to \mathbb{R}^+$ we consider to satisfy the following three properties:

(K1) **mass preservation:** For any $p \in \mathbb{R}^d$, then
$$\int_{x \in \mathbb{R}^d} K(p,x)dx = 1.$$

(K2) **shift- and rotation-invariance:** There exists a function $\kappa : \mathbb{R}^+ \to \mathbb{R}^+$ such that for any $p, x \in \mathbb{R}^d$ we have $K(p,x) = \kappa(\|p - x\|)$, where $\|p - x\|$ denotes the ℓ_2 distance between p and x.

(K3) **monotonicity:** For $z < z'$ then $\kappa(z) > \kappa(z')$.

Examples of kernels include (described here for $\mathbb{R}^2$):

- Gaussian: $K(p,x) = \frac{1}{2\pi\sigma^2} \exp\left(\frac{-\|p-x\|^2}{2\sigma^2}\right)$
- Triangle: $K(p,x) = \frac{3}{\pi\sigma^2} \max\left\{0, 1 - \frac{\|p-x\|}{\sigma}\right\}$
- Epanechnikov: $K(p,x) = \frac{2}{\pi\sigma^2} \max\left\{0, 1 - \frac{\|p-x\|^2}{\sigma^2}\right\}$
- Ball: $K(p,x) = \begin{cases} 1/\pi\sigma^2 & \text{if } \|p - x\| < \sigma \\ 0 & \text{otherwise.} \end{cases}$

We use the Gaussian kernel by default (the most widely used kernel in the literature); although some scenarios favor the Epanechnikov kernel [39,42]. All kernel definitions have a σ term to controls the amount of data smoothing. In this paper we assume that σ is fixed; however, choosing the appropriate σ is an important problem and there is a large literature on doing so [23,35,44]. A notable property of our main techniques is that *they do not require knowledge of the kernel type or the value of* σ, it is only used in the evaluation step (although bounds are worse with the Ball kernel; details will appear in the extended version of this paper).

Given such a kernel K and a point set P in d-dimensions a *kernel density estimate* is formally defined as a function KDE_P which for *any query* $x \in \mathbb{R}^d$ evaluates as

$$\text{KDE}_P(x) = \frac{1}{|P|} \sum_{p \in P} K(p,x). \tag{1}$$

However, in many data-intensive applications, P could be large, e.g., sensor readings from numerous sensors over a long period of time. Thus, evaluating a kernel density estimate over P directly, which takes $O(n)$, can be prohibitively expensive in big data. Hence, our goal is to construct another point set Q (often $Q \subset P$, but not necessarily) so that KDE_Q approximates KDE_P well. More precisely,

Definition 1 (Approximate Kernel Density Esimate) Given the input P, σ, and some error parameter $\varepsilon > 0$, the goal is to produce a set Q to ensure

$$\max_{x \in \mathbb{R}^d} |\text{KDE}_P(x) - \text{KDE}_Q(x)| = \|\text{KDE}_P - \text{KDE}_Q\|_\infty \leq \varepsilon, \tag{2}$$

and we call this an ε*-approximation.*

We can also allow some failure probability, in which case an additional parameter $\delta \in (0,1)$ is introduced, and the goal is to produce Q to ensure

$$\Pr[\|\text{KDE}_P - \text{KDE}_Q\|_\infty \leq \varepsilon] \geq 1 - \delta, \tag{3}$$

and we call this an (ε, δ)*-approximation.*

Lastly, in some kernel density estimates, Q does not have to be a point set. Rather, it can be any succinct structure that approximates $\text{KDE}_P(x)$ well according to (2) or (3). □

Our objective is to find an approximate KDE_Q such that for any query x, evaluating $\text{KDE}_Q(x)$ is much cheaper than evaluating $\text{KDE}_P(x)$ which takes $O(n)$, and at the same time, $\text{KDE}_Q(x)$ approximates $\text{KDE}_P(x)$ well even in the worst case.

Often it will be useful to instead generate a weighted point set Q so there exists a weight $w : Q \to \mathbb{R}$ associated with every point in Q and in which case the kernel density estimate over Q is defined as:

$$\text{KDE}_Q(x) = \sum_{q \in Q} w(q) K(q,x). \tag{4}$$

3. BACKGROUND AND RELATED WORK

Around the 1980s kernel density estimates became the defacto way in statistics to represent a continuous distribution from a discrete point set [42] with the study initiated much earlier [37]. However, this work often implied brute force ($O(n)$ time) solutions to most queries.

The problem of evaluating kernel density estimates is a central problem in statistical physics and numerical analysis. These problems are often posed as n-body simulations where the force-interactions between all pairs of points need to be calculated [1], and the pairwise force is up to a constant described by the Gaussian kernel. This has resulted in many indexing type techniques that up to constant precisions can evaluate the kernel density estimate at all n points in roughly $O(n)$ time. These techniques are sometimes called *fast multi-pole methods* [4], and in practice these are typically implemented as quad trees which calculate the distance to roots of subtrees instead of all pairs when the distance becomes far enough. Numerical approximation techniques called the (Improved) Fast Gauss Transform (IFGT) [14, 36, 49, 50] can further improve these approaches. But the IFGT approach (in general fast multipole methods) is based on heuristics and does not offer formal theoretical guarantees on the approximation-time trade-off.

In order to have a formal theoretical guarantee to derive an (ε, δ)-approximation, random sampling is a baseline method, but it requires $O(\frac{1}{\varepsilon^2} \log \frac{1}{\delta})$ samples to be included in Q, which could lead to expensive query evaluations especially for small ε and/or δ values.

A recent technique using discrepancy theory [33] creates a small representation of a kernel density estimate (smaller than the random sampling approach) while still bounding the ℓ_∞ error. It works by creating a min-cost matching of points in P; that is P is decomposed into $|P|/2$ pairs so that the sum over all distances between paired points is minimized. Then it randomly removes one point from each pair reducing the size of P by half. This process is repeated until either the desired size subset or the tolerable error level is reached. However, computing the min-cost matching [11] is expensive, so this approach is only of theoretical interest and not directly feasible for large data. Yet, this will serve as the basis for a family of our proposed algorithms.

A powerful type of kernel is a *reproducing kernel* [2, 32] (an example is the Gaussian kernel) which has the property that $K(p, q) = \langle p, q\rangle_{\mathcal{H}_K}$; that is, the similarity between objects p and q defines an inner-product in a *reproducing kernel Hilbert space* (RKHS) $\mathcal{H}_K$. This inner-product structure (the so-called "kernel trick"), has led to many powerful techniques in machine learning, see [38, 40] and references therein. Most of these techniques are not specifically interested in the kernel density estimate; however, the RKHS offers the property that a single element of this space essentially represents the entire kernel density estimate. These RKHS approximations are typically constructed through some form of random sampling [41,48], but one technique known as "kernel herding" [7] uses a greedy approach and requires significantly smaller size in theory, however it bounds only ℓ_2 error as opposed to the sampling techniques which bound a stronger ℓ_∞ error [24].

Kernel density estimates have been used in the database and data mining community for density and selectivity estimations, e.g., [17,51]. But the focus in these works is how to use kernel density estimates for approximating range queries and performing selectivity estimation, rather than computing approximate kernel density estimates for fast evaluations. When the end-objective is to use a kernel density estimate to do density or selectivity estimation, one may also use histograms [16, 22, 26, 34] or range queries [12, 13, 19, 20, 47] to achieve similar goals, but these do not have the same smoothness and statistical properties of kernel density estimates [42]. Nevertheless, the focus of this work is on computing approximate kernel density estimates that enable fast query evaluations, rather than exploring how to use kernel density estimates in different application scenarios (which is a well-explored topic in the literature).

4. WARM-UP: ONE DIMENSION

Efficient construction of approximate kernel density estimates in one-dimension is fairly straightforward. But it is still worth investigating these procedures in more detail since to our knowledge, this has not been done at truly large scale before, and the techniques developed will be useful in understanding the higher dimensional version.

Baseline method: random sampling (RS). A baseline method for constructing an approximate kernel density estimate in one dimension is random sampling. It is well known that [7, 33] if we let Q be a random sample from P of size $O((1/\varepsilon^2)\log(1/\delta))$ then with probability at least $1 - \delta$ the random sample Q ensures that $\|\text{KDE}_P - \text{KDE}_Q\|_\infty \leq \varepsilon$.

That said, the first technique (RS) follows from this observation directly and just randomly samples $O((1/\varepsilon^2)\log(1/\delta))$ points from P to construct a set Q. In the centralized setting, we can employ the one pass reservoir sampling technique [46] to implement RS efficiently. For large data that is stored in distributed nodes, RS can still be implemented efficiently using the recent results on generating random samples from distributed streams [9].

The construction cost is $O(n)$. The approximate KDE has a size $O((1/\varepsilon^2)\log(1/\delta))$, and its query cost (to evaluate $\text{KDE}_Q(x)$ for any input x) is $O((1/\varepsilon^2)\log(1/\delta))$.

RS can be used as a preprocessing step for any other technique, *i.e.*, for any technique that constructs a KDE over P, we run that technique over a random sample from P instead. This may be especially efficient at extremely large scale (where $n \gg 1/\varepsilon^2$) and where sampling can be done in an efficient manner. This may require that we initially sample a larger set Q than the final output to meet the approximation quality required by other techniques.

Grouping selection (GS). A limitation in RS is that it requires a large sample size (sometimes the entire set) in order to guarantee a desired level of accuracy. As a result, its size and query cost becomes expensive for small ε and δ.

Hence, we introduce another method, called the *grouping selection* (GS) method. It leverages the following lemma, known as the γ-perturbation.

Lemma 1 *Consider n arbitrary values $\{\gamma_1, \gamma_2, \ldots, \gamma_n\}$ such that $\|\gamma_i\| \leq \gamma$ for each $i \in [n]$. Then let $Q = \{q_1, q_2, \ldots, q_n\}$ such that $q_i = p_i + \gamma_i$ for all $p_i \in P$. Then $\|\text{KDE}_P - \text{KDE}_Q\|_\infty \leq \gamma/\sigma$.*

PROOF. This follows directly from the $(1/\sigma)$-Lipschitz condition on kernel K (which states that the maximum gradient of K is $(1/\sigma)$), hence perturbing all points by at most γ affects the average by at most γ/σ. □

Using Lemma 1, we can select one point q in every segment ℓ of length $\varepsilon\sigma$ from P and assign a weight to q that is proportional to the number of points from P in ℓ, to construct an ε-approximate KDE of P. Specifically, GS is implemented as follows. After sorting P if it is not already sorted, we sweep points from smallest to largest. When we encounter p_i, we scan until we reach the first p_j such that $p_i + \varepsilon\sigma < p_j$. Then we put p_i (or the centroid of p_i through p_{j-1}) in Q with weight $w(p_i) = (j - i)/n$. Since Q constructed by GS is weighted, the evaluation of $\text{KDE}_Q(x)$ should follow the weighted query evaluation as specified in equation 4.

Theorem 1 *The method GS gives an ε-approximate kernel density estimate of P.*

PROOF. The weighted output of GS Q corresponds to a point set Q' that has $w(q)$ unweighted points at the same location of each $q \in Q$; then $\text{KDE}_Q = \text{KDE}_{Q'}$. We claim that Q' is an $\varepsilon\sigma$-perturbation of P, which implies the theorem.

To see this claim, we consider any set $\{p_i, p_{i+1}, \ldots, p_{j-1}\}$ of points that are grouped to a single point $q \in Q$. Since all of these points are within an interval of length at most $\varepsilon\sigma$, each $p_{i+\ell}$ is perturbed to a distinct point $q'_{i+\ell} \in Q$ (at location q) that is at distance $\gamma_{i+\ell} \leq \varepsilon\sigma$. $\square$

GS's construction cost is $O(n)$ if P is sorted, or $O(n \log n)$ otherwise. Its query cost is $O(|Q|)$, which in the worst case could be $|Q| = |P|$. And Q may be large depending on how densely points in P are co-located and the values of ε and σ. However, GS can be used as a post-processing step on top of any other method, such as using GS over the output of RS. This takes little overhead if the points are already sorted, such as in the output of SS (see below).

Sort-selection (SS). Our best method (SS) offers an ε-approximate kernel density estimate using only $O(\frac{1}{\varepsilon})$ samples in one-dimension, a significant improvement over random sampling. It leverages the following interesting result:

Lemma 2 *Consider a one dimensional sorted point set* $P = \{p_1, p_2, \ldots, p_n\}$ *where* $p_i \leq p_{i+1}$ *for all* i. *Let* $P_j = \{p_i \in P \mid (j-1)\varepsilon n < i \leq j\varepsilon n\}$ *for integer* $j \in [1, \lceil 1/\varepsilon \rceil]$ *such that* $P = \cup P_j$. *Then for any* $Q = \{q_1, q_2, \ldots, q_{\lceil 1/\varepsilon \rceil}\}$ *such that each* $q_j \in P_j$ *then* $\|\text{KDE}_P - \text{KDE}_Q\|_\infty \leq 2\varepsilon$.

If each $q_j = p_{\lceil (j-1/2)\varepsilon n \rceil}$, *then* $\|\text{KDE}_P - \text{KDE}_Q\|_\infty \leq \varepsilon$.

We now can construct the SS method based on Lemma 2. It simply selects $p_{\lceil (j-\frac{1}{2})\varepsilon n \rceil}$ from P into Q for each $j \in [1, \lceil 1/\varepsilon \rceil]$. This requires that P is sorted, and this can be done efficiently at very large scale using external merge sort. However, we can do better. Note that ε-approximate quantiles for $\lceil 1/\varepsilon \rceil$ quantile values are sufficient to construct Q, and we can use an efficient streaming or distributed algorithm for computing these ε-approximate quantiles [8,15,21, 27,28]. In particular, we only need to find the $\frac{\varepsilon n}{2}$th, $\frac{3\varepsilon n}{2}$th, $\frac{5\varepsilon n}{2}$th, ..., $(n - \frac{\varepsilon n}{2})$th quantile values from P. And it is easy to verify that ε-approximations of these quantiles are sufficient to establish the 2ε result in Lemma 2.

Using the ε-approximate quantiles, SS has a construction cost of $O(n \log \frac{1}{\varepsilon})$; otherwise its construction cost is $O(n \log n)$. In either case, its size is only $O(\frac{1}{\varepsilon})$ and its query cost is also just $O(\frac{1}{\varepsilon})$.

4.1 Efficient Evaluation

Once we have obtained a set Q above so KDE_Q approximates KDE_P, we need to efficiently answer queries of $\text{KDE}_Q(x)$ for any $x \in \mathbb{R}$. The first obvious choice is a brute force computation (BF) where we directly calculate $\frac{1}{|Q|}\sum_{q \in Q} K(q, x)$. This has little overhead and its cost is obviously $O(|Q|)$. It is most efficient if $|Q|$ is particular small.

A second approach (MP) is to use the one-dimensional variant of multi-pole methods. We build a B-tree (or binary tree if Q fits in memory) on Q. Each node v will store the weight (or count) w_v of all nodes in the subtree and the smallest v_s and largest v_l coordinates of the subtree. We traverse the tree as follows, starting at the root. If $x \in [w_s, w_l]$ visit each child and return their sum to the parent. If $|K(v_s, x) - K(v_l, x)| \leq \varepsilon$, then return $w_v K((v_l - v_s)/2, x)$ to the parent. Else, visit each child and return their sum to the parent. This approach may improve the query evaluation time in practice, especially when $|Q|$ is large.

5. TWO DIMENSIONS

In $\mathbb{R}^2$ we first describe baseline methods from the literature or based on simple extensions to existing methods. We then introduce our new methods. The first uses a randomized technique based on matchings, and the second is deterministic and based on space-filling curves.

5.1 Baseline Methods

Random sampling (RS). The first baseline (labeled RS) is to simply random sample a set Q from P. The same bound of $O((1/\varepsilon^2)\log(1/\delta))$ on the sample size from one dimension still holds in 2-dimensions, although the constant in the big-Oh is likely larger by a factor of about 2.

Improved fast Gauss transform (IFGT). A class of methods is based on *fast multi-pole methods* [4]. In practice in 2-dimensions these are implemented as quad trees which calculate the distance to roots of subtrees instead of all pairs when the distance becomes far enough. The Improved Fast Gauss Transform (IFGT) [14,36,49,50], is the state-of-the-art for fast construction and evaluation of approximate kernel density estimates (although only with Gaussian kernels). It improves multi-pole approaches by first building a k-center clustering over the data set P, and then just retaining a Hermite expansion of the kernel density estimates for the points associated with each k-centers. But the IFGT method is based on heuristics and does not offer any formal theoretical guarantees on the approximation-size trade-off. As a result, it involves a number of parameters that cannot be easily and intuitively set in order to derive a desired level of efficiency and accuracy tradeoffs.

Kernel herding (KH). Yet another possible approach is to explore the *reproducing kernel Hilbert space* (RKHS). As discussed in Section 3, these RKHS approximations are typically constructed through some form of random sampling [41,48], but one technique known as "kernel herding" [7] uses a greedy approach and requires significantly smaller size in theory, however it bounds only ℓ_2 error as opposed to the sampling techniques which bound a stronger ℓ_∞ error.

In particular, the state-of-the-art kernel herding technique from [7] is a greedy method. It adds at each step the single point $p \in P \backslash Q$ to Q which most decreases $\|\text{KDE}_Q - \text{KDE}_P\|_2$. This is possible to calculate efficiently through an approximate representation of KDE_Q and KDE_P in the RKHS. However, this still takes $O(|Q|n)$ time to construct $|Q|$ since at each step each point in $P \setminus Q$ needs to be evaluated to determine how much it will decrease the ℓ_2 error.

5.2 Randomized MergeReduce Algorithm

An interesting theoretical result built on discrepancy [5, 30] theory was recently proposed in [33] for constructing a small set Q so KDE_Q approximates KDE_P. It extends a classic method for creating ε-approximations of Chazelle and Matousek [6] (see also [5,30]), to ε-approximate kernel density estimates. These results are mostly of theoretical interest, the straightforward adaption is highly inefficient. Next we explain and overcome these inefficiencies.

5.2.1 The MergeReduce framework

Our algorithm leverages the framework of Chazelle and Matousek [6] and its generalizations. We first describe our overall framework, and then elaborate the most critical *reduce step* in further details. Roughly speaking, our algorithm repeatedly runs a merge-then-reduce step. Hence, we denote this framework as the *MergeReduce* algorithm.

Suppose the desired size of the compressed set Q is $|Q| = k$. The framework proceeds in three phases: an initialization phase, the combination phase, and the optional clean-up phase. The first phase is implicit, and the last phase is of theoretical interest only.

In the initialization phase we arbitrarily decompose P into disjoint sets of size k; call these $P_1, P_2, \ldots, P_{n/k}$. Since this is arbitrary, we can group data that is stored together into the same partition. This works well for distributed data or streaming data where consecutively encountered data are put in the same partition.

The combination phase proceeds in $\log(n/k)$ rounds. In each round, of the remaining sets of size k, it *arbitrarily* pairs them together, which we dub the *merge step*. For each pair say P_i and P_j, it runs *a reduce step* on the union of $2k$ points to create a single set of size k. At a high level, the *reduce step* has two parts. The first part is what we call a *matching operation*. It produces k pairs of points in a certain fashion over the $2k$ input points. The second part is trivial: it randomly selects one point from each pair to produce the final output of size k. The *merging operation* is the most critical part in a reduce step, and we will elaborate after presenting the overall MergeReduce framework.

That said, after i rounds of *merge and reduce*, there are $(n/k)/2^i$ sets of size k. This continues until there is one set remaining. Note that again the fact that we can pair sets (P_i and P_j) arbitrarily in a *merge step* is extremely convenient in a distributed or streaming setting.

The clean-up phase is not needed if the combination phase is run as above; see Section 5.2.4 for remaining details.

Importantly, we also note that this entire MergeReduce framework can be preceded by randomly sampling $O(1/\varepsilon^2)$ points from P which are then treated as the input. Then only $\log(1/\varepsilon)$ merge-reduce rounds will be needed.

The min-cost matching. The key part of this framework is to construct a *matching* in a set of points P. Suppose $|P| = n$, a *matching* consists of $\frac{n}{2}$ pairs of points, and every point in P belongs to exactly one pair in a *matching*.

The recent result from [33] implies that one can use the min-cost matching to derive an ε-approximate kernel density estimate. Note that a min-cost matching is a matching so that the sum of distances between matched points is minimized. Unfortunately, by using a min-cost matching, the algorithm in [33] is impractical. Here is why.

It is well known that a min-cost matching over n points can be done in $O(n^3)$ time using Edmonds' Blossom algorithm [11]. This quite complicated algorithm involves nonregular recursion, and it is clearly not scalable for large data sets. We use the state-of-the-art implementation [25] as a baseline for the matching operation and label it as Blossom-MR (MergeReduce with Blossom min-cost matching). This implementation of the Blossom algorithm requires first calculating $K(p,p')$ for all $O(n^2)$ pairs $p, p' \in P$ as input, which is part of the overall cost (which is $O(n^3)$).

There have been theoretical improvements [45] to Edmonds' algorithm for points in $\mathbb{R}^2$. These algorithms are considerably more complicated than that of Edmonds and no known efficient implementation exists; most likely the improvements are theoretical in nature only.

We have the following results concerning the Blossom-MR algorithm, and the Blossom-MR+RS algorithm that first randomly samples $O(1/\varepsilon^2)$ points.

Theorem 2 *For a point set $P \subset \mathbb{R}^2$ with n points, we can construct Q giving an ε-approximate KDE (with constant probability) in*

- $O(\frac{n}{\varepsilon^2}\log^2 n \log\frac{1}{\varepsilon})$ *time and* $|Q| = O(\frac{1}{\varepsilon}\log n\sqrt{\log\frac{1}{\varepsilon}})$ *using Blossom-MR, and*
- $O(n + \frac{1}{\varepsilon^4}\log^3\frac{1}{\varepsilon})$ *time and* $|Q| = O(\frac{1}{\varepsilon}\log^{1.5}\frac{1}{\varepsilon})$ *using Blossom-MR+RS.*

Lastly, the following greedy algorithm provides a two-approximation to the cost of the min-cost matching [10]. It finds the closest pair of points in P, matches them, removes them from P, and repeats. This algorithm can be implemented in $O(n^2 \log n)$ time as follows. Calculate all $O(n^2)$ pairwise distances and place them in a priority queue. Repeatedly remove the smallest pair from the queue (in $O(\log n)$ time). If both points are still in P, match them and mark them as no longer in P. We refer to the merge-reduce framework with this matching algorithm as the Greedy-MR method. Greedy-MR does improve the running time over Blossom-MR, however, it is still quite expensive and not scalable for large data. Furthermore, the result produced by Greedy-MR is not known to provide any approximation guarantees on the kernel density estimate.

5.2.2 More Efficient Reduce Step

The Blossom-MR algorithm and its heuristic variant Greedy-MR are too expensive to be useful for large data. Thus, we design a much more efficient *matching operation*, while still ensuring an ε-approximate kernel density estimate.

For any matching M, we produce an *edge map* E_M of that matching M as $E_M = \{e(p,q) \mid (p,q) \in M\}$ where $e(p,q)$ is an undirected edge connecting p and q. Given a disk B, for $e(p,q) \in E_M$ define $e(p,q) \cap B$ as follows.

- If both p and q are not covered by B, $e(p,q) \cap B = \emptyset$.
- If both p and q are covered by B, $e(p,q) \cap B = e(p,q)$.
- If either p or q is covered by B but not both. Suppose p is covered by B, and $e(p,q)$ intersects the boundary of B at a point s, $e(p,q) \cap B = e(p,s)$.

Then, we define $E_M \cap B$ as:

$$E_M \cap B = \{e(p,q) \cap B \mid e(p,q) \in E_m\}. \quad (5)$$

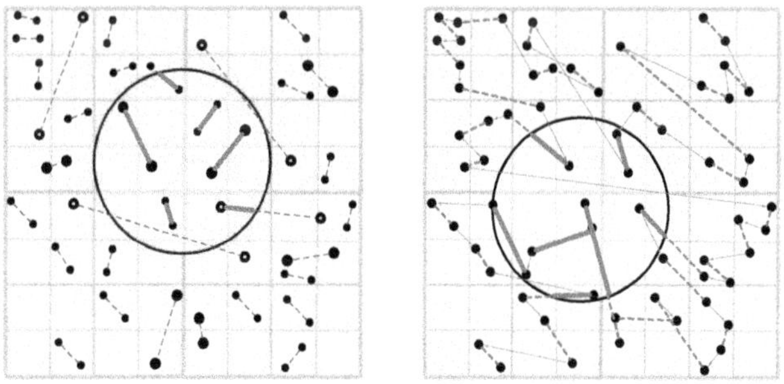

Figure 2: Intersection between a matching and a disk, solid red lines are included in $E_M \cap B$. Left shows Grid matching and right shows Z-order with every other edge in a matching.

An example of $E_M \cap B$ is shown in Figure 2. Essentially, we only want it to consider edges with at least one endpoint within B, and only the subset of the edge that is within B. We observe that in order to produce an ε-approximate kernel density estimate, the property the matching requires is in regards to any unit disk B. Specifically, we want

$$C_{M,B} = \sum_{e(p,q)\in E_M \cap B} \|p - q\|^2 \quad (6)$$

to be small. Let $C_M = \max_B C_{M,B}$.

The result in [33] says if M is the min-cost matching (minimizes $\sum_{(p,q)\in M} \|p-q\|$), then $C_M = O(1)$. But calculating the min-cost matching, both exactly and approximately, is expensive as we have shown in Section 5.2.1.

The grid matching. Here we present a novel solution which does have a bound on C_M and is efficient, including at very large scales. We progress in rounds until all points are matched. Starting with $i = 0$, in round i we consider a grid G_i on $\mathbb{R}^2$ where each grid cell has edge length $l_{\varepsilon,i} = \sqrt{2}\sigma\varepsilon 2^{i-2}$. Define cell $g_{r,c} \in G_i$ as $[rl_{\varepsilon,i}, (r+1)l_{\varepsilon,i}] \times [cl_{\varepsilon,i}, (c+1)l_{\varepsilon,i}]$ for integers r, c. Inside of each cell, match points arbitrarily. Only the unmatched points (one from any cell with an odd number of points) survive to the next round. Each cell in G_{i+1} is the union of 4 cells from G_i, thus in rounds $i > 0$ it can have at most 4 points. We refer to this matching algorithm as Grid; see example in Figure 2. For simpler analysis, we assume $\sigma > \varepsilon^c$ for some constant $c \geq 1$; typically $\sigma \gg \varepsilon$ and $\varepsilon < 1$, so this assumption is very mild. Alternatively, if we do not know σ ahead of time, we can recursively divide points that fall in the same grid cell into smaller and smaller levels until at most two are left in each cell (like a quad tree), and then move back up the recursion stack only with unmatched points; a careful implementation can be done in $O(n \log n)$ time [18]. Let P_0 be unmatched points after round 0, let $P' = P \setminus P_0$, and Q the final output.

Lemma 3 *Let $M'(P')$ be the matching on P' in Grid. For each edge $(p,q) \in M'(P')$ let $\hat{P}$ be where (w.l.o.g.) q is moved to location p. Then $\hat{P}$ is a $\varepsilon\sigma/2$-perturbation of P'.*

PROOF. Since all points matched in round 0 are in a grid cell of size at most $\varepsilon\sigma\sqrt{2}/4$, the point q in any edge is moved at most $\sqrt{2} \cdot \varepsilon\sigma\sqrt{2}/4 = \varepsilon\sigma/2$. □

Lemma 4 *Let $M_0(P_0)$ be the matching by Grid on P_0. Then $C_{M_0} = O(\log(1/\varepsilon))$ and Grid runs in $O(n \log \frac{1}{\varepsilon})$ time.*

PROOF. In each round, there are at most 2 matched pairs per grid cell. Each such pair has edge length at most $\sqrt{2}l_{\varepsilon,i} = \sigma\varepsilon 2^{i-1}$, and there are at most $(1/\sigma\varepsilon 2^{i-5/2})^2$ grid cells that intersect any unit ball. Thus the total squared-length of all matchings in round i is at most $((1/\sigma\varepsilon 2^{i-5/2})^2 \cdot (\sigma\varepsilon 2^{i-1})^2 = 2\sqrt{2}$. After $\log(1/\sigma\varepsilon) + 1$ rounds the total length of all matchings is at most $2\sqrt{2}(\log(1/\sigma\varepsilon) + 1)$, and in any ball, there are at most 4 remaining unmatched points. The last 4 points can each account for at most a squared-length of 4 within a unit ball B, so the total weight of edges in any unit ball B is at most $C_M \leq 2\sqrt{2}\log(1/\sigma\varepsilon) + 19 = O(\log(1/\varepsilon))$. Each round takes $O(n)$ time, and we can match points arbitrarily in $O(n)$ time after the $\log(1/\sigma\varepsilon) + 1$ rounds. □

We observe in most common scenarios C_M is close to 1.

With the Grid matching algorithm, we can instantiate the MergeReduce framework to get a Grid-MR algorithm, or if we first sample a Grid-MR+RS algorithm.

Theorem 3 *For a point set $P \subset \mathbb{R}^2$ with n points, we can construct Q giving an ε-approximate KDE (with constant probability) in*

- *$O(n \log \frac{1}{\varepsilon})$ time and $|Q| = O(\frac{1}{\varepsilon} \log n \log^{1.5} \frac{1}{\varepsilon})$ using Grid-MR, and*
- *$O(n + \frac{1}{\varepsilon^2} \log \frac{1}{\varepsilon})$ time and $|Q| = O(\frac{1}{\varepsilon} \log^{2.5} \frac{1}{\varepsilon})$ using Grid-MR+RS.*

Since Grid takes only $O(n \log \frac{1}{\varepsilon})$ time, the benefit of the initialization phase to split the data set into n/k pieces does not out-weigh its overhead in a centralized setting. In particular, we just run Grid once on all n_i points remaining in round i. This does not affect the runtime or error bounds.

Compared to the Blossom-MR and Greedy-MR algorithms, Grid-MR produces an ε-approximate kernel density estimate with about the same size, but with much cheaper construction cost. Grid-MR's running time only linearly depends on n, making it an ideal candidate to scale out to massive data.

5.2.3 Streaming and Distributed MergeReduce

Since the reduce step (the key computational component of the MergeReduce framework) is only run on select subsets, this allows the full framework to generalize to distributed and streaming settings.

Streaming variant. The streaming algorithm follows techniques for approximate range counting [3, 43]. Consecutive points are assigned to the same partitions P_i, and we pair and reduce partitions whenever there are two that represent the same number of points (one that has been merged i times represents $k2^i$ points). This means we only need to keep $\log \frac{n}{k}$ partitions, and thus only $O(k \log \frac{n}{k})$ points in memory at any given time. The dependence on n can be completely removed by first randomly sampling.

The final structure of the streaming algorithm has weighted points, where if a point is in a partition that has been reduced i times, its weight is 2^i. These weights can be removed to create just $5|Q|$ points instead of $|Q| \log \frac{|P|}{|Q|}$ by running the in memory matching algorithm on weighted points [29].

In particular, we can modify a matching algorithm to work with weighted points, specifically consider the Grid algorithm. In the 0th phase of Grid, a point with weight 2^i represents 2^i points that all fall in the same cell, and can be matched with themselves (this can be done by ignoring this point until the ith phase when its weight is 1).

Distributed variant. This framework is efficient on distributed data. Use the streaming algorithm on each distributed chunk of data, and then pass the entire output of the streaming algorithm to a central node, which can merge and reduce the union. The error caused by reducing on the central node is already accounted for in the analysis. Again, the dependence on $|P|$ can be removed by first sampling.

5.2.4 Other Extension

An alternative version of the combination phase is possible for the MergeReduce algorithm. Specifically, it considers some reduce step that takes time $O(n^\beta)$ on a set of size n, and instead sets $k = 4(\beta + 2)|Q|$ (where $|Q|$ is the desired size of the final output), and on every $(\beta+3)$th round, pairs sets but does not reduce them. Then the clean-up phase is used to reduce the single remaining set repeatedly until it is of size $|Q|$. When β is a constant, this saves a $O(\log n)$ from the size of the output Q (or $O(\log \frac{1}{\varepsilon})$ if we sampled first) [6].

More specifically, the output of this MergeReduce variant is then a set of size $|Q| = O(C_M \frac{1}{\varepsilon} \log^{0.5} \frac{1}{\varepsilon})$ for a reduce step that uses a matching algorithm which produces an output with cost C_M. If we use Grid, then Grid-MR produces an output of size $|Q| = O(\frac{1}{\varepsilon} \log^{1.5} \frac{1}{\varepsilon})$. And Blossom-MR outputs Q of size $|Q| = O(\frac{1}{\varepsilon} \log^{0.5} \frac{1}{\varepsilon})$ in $O(\frac{n}{\varepsilon^2} \log \frac{1}{\varepsilon})$ time.

But in practice, this variant is more complicated to implement and usually the overhead out-weighs its benefit. Hence we do not use this variant in this paper.

5.3 Deterministic Z-Order Selection

Inspired by one-dimensional sort-section (SS) and randomized two-dimensional Grid-MR algorithm, we propose a new deterministic two-dimensional technique based on space filling curves. A space filling curve puts a single order on two- (or higher-) dimensional points that preserves spatial locality. They have great uses in databases for approximate high-dimensional nearest-neighbor queries and range queries. The single order can be used for a (one-dimensional) B+ tree, which provides extremely efficient queries even on massive datasets that do not fit in memory.

In particular, the Z-order curve is a specific type of space filling curve that can be interpreted as implicitly ordering points based on the traversal order of a quad tree. That is if all of the points are in $[0,1]^2$, then the top level of the quad tree has 4 children over the domains $c_1 = [0, \frac{1}{2}] \times [0, \frac{1}{2}]$, $c_2 = [\frac{1}{2}, 1] \times [0, \frac{1}{2}]$, $c_3 = [0, \frac{1}{2}] \times [\frac{1}{2}, 1]$, and $c_4 = [\frac{1}{2}, 1] \times [\frac{1}{2}, 1]$. And each child's four children itself divide symmetrically as such. Then the Z-order curve visits all points in the child c_1, then all points in c_2, then all points in c_3, and all points in c_4 (in the shape of a backwards 'Z'); and all points within each child are also visited in such a Z-shaped order. See an example in Figure 2. Thus given a domain containing all points, this defines a complete order on them, and the order preserves spatial locality as well as a quad tree does.

The levels of the Z-order curve (and associated quad tree) are reminiscent of the grids used in the matching technique Grid. This insight leads to the following algorithm.

Compute the Z-order of all points, and of every two points of rank $2i$ and $2i+1$, discard one at random; repeat this discarding of half the points until the remaining set is sufficiently small. This approach tends to match points in the same grid cell, as with Grid, but is also algorithmically wasteful since the Z-order does not change between rounds.

Thus we can improve the algorithm by using insights from SS. In particular, we just run SS on the Z-order of points. So to collect $k = |Q|$ points, let the ith point retained $q_i \in Q$ be the point in rank order $\lceil (i - \frac{1}{2})\frac{|P|}{k} \rceil$. This selects one point from each set of $\frac{|P|}{k}$ points in the Z-order.

In fact, by setting $k = O(\frac{1}{\varepsilon} \log n \log^{1.5} \frac{1}{\varepsilon})$, if we randomly select one point from each Z-order rank range $[(i-1)\frac{|P|}{k}, i\frac{|P|}{k}]$ (call this algorithm Zrandom), then the resulting set Q has about the same guarantees as the Grid-MR algorithm, including Zrandom+RS which preprocesses by random sampling.

Theorem 4 *For a point set $P \subset \mathbb{R}^2$ with n points, we can construct Q giving an ε-approximate KDE (with constant probability) in*

- *$O(n \log n)$ time and $|Q| = O(\frac{1}{\varepsilon} \log n \log^{1.5} \frac{1}{\varepsilon})$ using Zrandom, and*
- *$O(n + \frac{1}{\varepsilon^2} \log \frac{1}{\varepsilon})$ time and $|Q| = O(\frac{1}{\varepsilon} \log^{2.5} \frac{1}{\varepsilon})$ using Zrandom+RS.*

PROOF. We prove this result by imagining that Zrandom does something more complicated than it actually does in order to relate it to Grid-MR. That is, we pretend that instead of just selecting a single points at random from each range $[(i-1)|P|/|Q|, i|P|/|Q|]$ in the Z-order rank, we proceed in a series of $\log(|P|/|Q|)$ rounds, and in each round the set P is reduced in size by half. Specifically, in each round, out of every two consecutive points in the Z-order (rank $2i$ and $2i+1$) we retain one at random. Since the Z-order is consistent across rounds, this results in a random point in the rank interval $[(i-1)|P|/|Q|, i|P|/|Q|]$ as desired.

Now if we consider the levels of the implicit quad tree defining the Z-order, this is equivalent to the grid used in Grid-MR. In each round, there are at most 3 edges within grid cell at level j, but that are not entirely in levels smaller than j. Since we still only care about $O(\log(1/\varepsilon))$ levels of the grid, the squared distance of these edges in that cell level account for at most $O(1)$ inside a unit square. Thus C_M is still at most $O(\log(1/\varepsilon))$. The remainder of the proof is the same as in Theorem 3. □

However, we find the implementation of the following deterministic algorithm to be more effective; but as the randomness is necessary for the proof, we do not provide bounds.

The construction of the Z-order can be done efficiently using its interpretation as bit-interleaving. Specifically, the *z-value* of a point is calculated by interleaving bits from the most significant bit to the least significant bit in the binary representation of a point's coordinates. For example, a two-dimensional point $(3, 5)$ expressed in its binary representation is $(011, 101)$. Its *z-value* is then $(011011)_2 = 27$.

Then we do not need to completely sort all points by z-value in order to select the proper k points, we can just approximately do this so that we have one point selected from each set of $\frac{|P|}{k}$ points in the sorted order. This can be done using an ε-approximate quantiles algorithm that is accurate up to $\varepsilon = 1/k$. This guarantees the existence in the quantile structure and its identification of at least one point within every consecutive set of $\frac{|P|}{k}$ points. We can just return this point for each range $[(i-1)\frac{|P|}{k}, i\frac{|P|}{k}]$ of ranks. We refer to this method as Zorder. Note that, following the discussion for SS in Section 4, we can use any of the existing efficient, large-scale ε-approximate quantiles algorithms in either the centralized or the distributed setting.

5.4 Efficient Query Evaluation

We can do efficient evaluations in $\mathbb{R}^2$ similar to BF and MP in $\mathbb{R}^1$, as discussed in Section 4.1. In fact, BF is exactly the same. MP uses a quad tree instead of a binary tree. It stores a bounding box at each node instead of an interval, but uses the same test to see if the difference between $K(x, \cdot)$ is within ε on the furthest and closest point in the bounding box to decide if it needs to recur.

5.5 Parallel and Distributed Implementation

As with one-dimensional methods, our two-dimensional methods can be efficiently implemented in distributed and streaming settings. Any algorithm using the MergeReduce framework can run in distributed and parallel fashion. As a result, Grid-MR, Zrandom, and Zorder are very efficient in any distributed and parallel environments, and they extend especially well for the popular MapReduce framework where data in each split is processed in a streaming fashion.

Among the baseline methods, RS can easily be implemented in any distributed and parallel environments. It takes some effort to make IFGT run in distributed and parallel fashion, but it is possible; we omit the details. Lastly, the KH can be approximated (without any bounds) by running its greedy step in each local piece of data independently, and then merging the results from local nodes.

5.6 Higher Dimensions

All two-dimensional algorithms described can be extended to higher dimensions. In particular, KH, RS, Blossom-MR,

Greedy-MR extend with no change, while Grid-MR and Zorder-MR extend in the obvious way of using a d-dimension grid or space-filling curve. In $\mathbb{R}^d$ the theoretical size bounds for RS increases to $O(\frac{1}{\varepsilon^2}(d+\log\frac{1}{\delta}))$ [24]; Grid-MR, and Zrandom-MR increases to $O(d^{d/2}/\varepsilon^{2-\frac{4}{d+2}}\log^{1+\frac{d}{d+2}}\frac{1}{\varepsilon}\log n)$ (and a $\log\frac{1}{\varepsilon}$ factor less for Blossom-MR). The increase in the second set is due to only being able to bound

$$C_M^d = \max_B \sum_{e(p,q)\in E_M \cap B} \|p-q\|^d$$

instead of equation (6) since the number of grid cells intersected by a unit ball now grows exponentially in d, and thus we need to balance that growth with the dth power of the edge lengths. The stated bounds, then results from [33] with an extra $\log n$ factor (which can be turned into a $\log\frac{1}{\varepsilon}$ by first random sampling) because we do not use the impractical process described in Section 5.2.4. In no case does the MergeReduce framework need to be altered, and so the construction times only increase by a factor d.

6. EXPERIMENTS

We test all methods in both the single-thread, centralized environment and the distributed and parallel setting. In the centralized case, we implemented all methods in C++ and obtained the latest implementation of the IFGT method from the authors in [36,49,50]. We then used MapReduce as the distributed and parallel programming framework. In particular, we implemented and tested all methods in a Hadoop cluster with 17 machines. The centralized experiments were executed over a Linux machine running a single Intel i7 cpu at 3.20GHz. It has 6GB main memory and an 1TB hard disk. The distributed and parallel experiments were executed over a cluster of 17 machines running Hadoop 1.0.3. One of the 17 machines has an Intel Xeon(R) E5649 cpu at 2.53 GHz, 100 GB of main memory, and a 2TB hard disk. It is configured as both the master node and the name node of the cluster. The other 16 machines in the Hadoop cluster (the slave nodes) share the same configuration as the machine we used for the centralized experiments. One TaskTracker and DataNode daemon run on each slave. A single NameNode and JobTracker run on the master. The default HDFS (Hadoop distributed file system) chunk size is 64MB.

Data sets. We executed our experiments over two large real datasets. In two dimensions, we used the OpenStreet data from the OpenStreetMap project. Each dataset represents the points of interest on the road network for a US state. The entire dataset has the road networks for 50 states, containing more than 160 million records in 6.6GB. For our experiments we focus on only the 48 contiguous states, excluding Hawaii and Alaska. Each record is a 2-dimensional coordinate, represented as 2 4-byte floating points. We denote this data as the *US* dataset.

In one dimension, we employed the second real dataset, *Meme*, which was obtained from the Memetracker project. It tracks popular quotes and phrases which appear from various sources on the internet. The goal is to analyze how different quotes and phrases compete for coverage every day and how some quickly fade out of use while others persist for long periods of time. A record has 4 attributes, the URL of the website containing the memes, the time Memetracker observed the memes, a list of the observed memes, and links accessible from the website. We preprocess the *Meme* dataset, and convert each record to have an 8-byte double to represent the *time* of a single observed meme and the URL of the website which published the meme, e.g. if an original record contained a list of 4 memes published at a given time at a website, 4 records would be produced in the new dataset. We view these records as a set of timestamps in 1d, reflecting the distribution of the Meme's publication time. After this preprocessing step, the *Meme* dataset contains more than 300 million records in 10.3GB.

In both 1d and 2d, whenever needed, we randomly sample records from the full *US* or the full *Meme* dataset to obtain a dataset of smaller size. Figure 1 in Section 1 visualizes the kernel density estimates built by our MergeReduce algorithms in 1d and 2d, over the full *Meme* and *US* datasets respectively (but only very few data points were plotted, to ensure that the figures are legible).

General setup. In all experiments, unless otherwise specified, we vary the values of one parameter of interest, while keeping the other important parameters at their default values. Also by default, we randomly generate 5,000 test points to evaluate the accuracy of an approximate kernel density estimate. Among these 5,000 points, 4,000 were randomly selected from the data set P, and the other 1,000 were randomly selected from the domain space $\mathcal{M}$ of P (but not from P itself). We use *err* to denote the *observed* ℓ_∞ *error* from an approximate kernel density estimate Q, which is computed from the evaluations of these 5,000 test points in KDE_Q and KDE_P respectively. We try to compare different methods by setting a proper ε value (the desired error in theory) for each of them so that they achieve the same observed error. All experiments report the *average of 10 random trials.*

6.1 Two Dimensions: Centralized

Default setup. Our default data set is a *US* data set with 10 million records. The default failure probability δ for the random sampling method (RS) is set to 0.001. To save space in the legend in all figures, we used G-MR and Z to denote the Grid-MR and Zorder methods respectively, and method+RS to denote the version of running method over a random sample of P (of size $O(\frac{1}{\varepsilon^2}\log\frac{1}{\delta})$), instead of running method over P directly. The default σ value in any kernel density estimate is 200, on a domain of roughly 50,000 × 50,000.

Our method+RS. We first study the effect of running our methods over a random sample of P, when compared against the results from running them directly over P. Figure 3 shows the results when we vary the value of the common input parameter for all of them, ε. Not surprisingly, as shown in Figure 3(a), the observed errors in all methods are smaller than the desired error ε. All methods produce smaller observed errors when smaller ε values were used. Furthermore, under the same ε value, G-MR+RS and Z+RS produce higher errors than their respective counterpart does, namely, G-MR and Z. However, the difference is fairly small. In fact, when *err* is about 10^{-2}, there are almost no difference between G-MR+RS (Z+RS) and G-MR (Z).

More importantly however, running a method over a random sample of P saves valuable construction time as shown in Figure 3(b). Figure 3(c) indicates the sizes of the final approximate kernel density estimates constructed by different methods are almost the same. This is because that whether running a method over P or a random sample of P, the final size of the kernel density estimate Q is largely determined by ε only. This also means that the query time of these

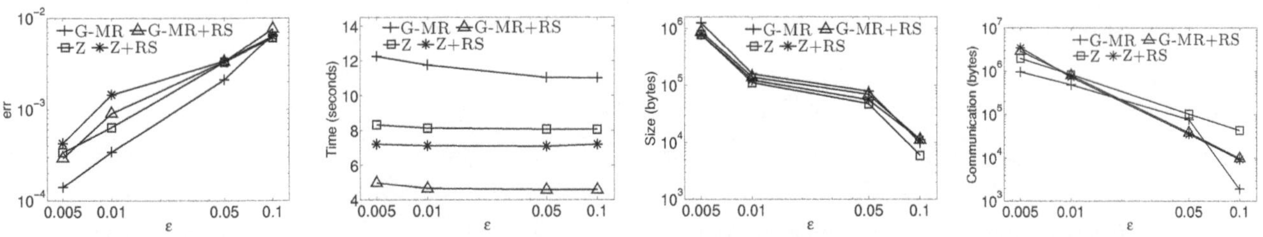

(a) *err* vs. ε. (b) Construction time. (c) Size. (d) Communication.

Figure 3: Effect of guaranteed error ε on the centralized G-MR, G-MR+RS, Z, Z+RS.

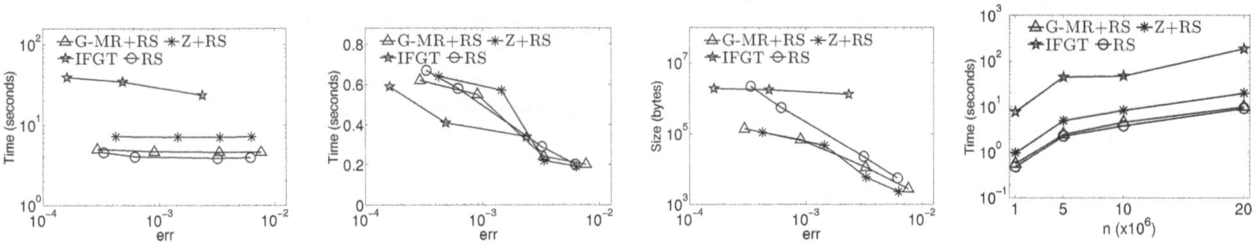

(a) Construction time vs *err*. (b) Query Time. (c) Size. (d) Construction time vs n.

Figure 5: Effect of measured ℓ_∞ error *err* and N on centralized IFGT, RS, G-MR+RS, Z+RS.

methods is almost the same, since the query time depends on only $|Q|$. Hence, we have omitted this figure.

Finally, we also investigate the impact to the communication cost if we run these methods in a cluster. Figure 3(d) shows that this impact is not obvious. Since G-MR and Z are very effective in saving communication cost already, collecting a random sample first does not lead to communication savings. In contrast, doing so might even hurt their communication cost (if the sample size is larger than what they have to communicate in our MergeReduce framework). Nevertheless, all methods are very efficient in terms of the total bytes sent: a few megabytes in the worst case when $\varepsilon = 0.005$ over a cluster for 10 million records in P.

In conclusion, these results show that in practice one can use our method+RS to achieve the best balance in construction time and accuracy for typically required observed errors.

Our method vs. baseline methods. We first investigate the construction cost of different alternatives in instantiating our MergeReduce framework, with different algorithm for the matching operation. We also include Kernel Herding (KH) as introduced in Section 5.1. In order to let these baseline methods complete in a reasonable amount of time, we used smaller data sets here. From the analysis in Section 5.2, Blossom-MR (denoted as B-MR, representing the theoretical algorithm [33]) with a $O(nk^2)$ cost for output size k and Greedy-MR with a $O(nk \log n)$ cost are much more expensive than G-MR. Similarly, KH with a $O(nk)$ cost is also much more expensive than G-MR which runs in roughly $O(n \log k)$ time. This is even more pronounced in Figures 4(a) and 4(b), showing the construction time of different methods when varying the observed error *err* and the size of the data sets respectively. G-MR is several orders of magnitude faster and more scalable than the other methods.

So the only competing baseline methods we need to consider further are the RS and IFGT methods. We compare these methods against our methods, G-MR+RS and Z+RS in Figure 5, using the default 10 million *US* data set. Figure 5(a) indicates that, to achieve the same observed error, RS is the most efficient method in terms of the construction time. However, our methods G-MR+RS and Z+RS are al-

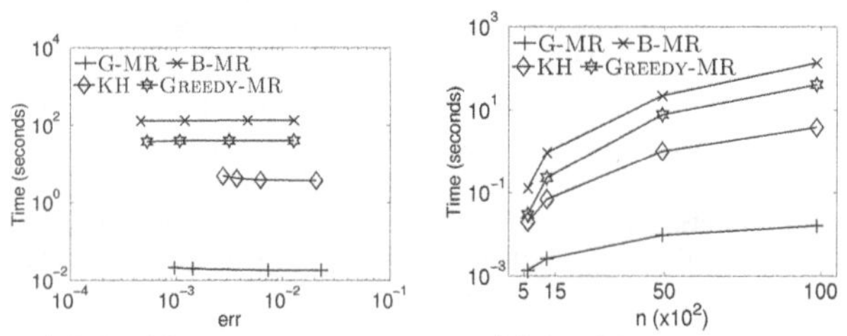

(a) Build time vs. *err*. (b) Build time vs. n.

Figure 4: Centralized G-MR, B-MR, Greedy-MR, KH.

most as efficient. In contrast, IFGT is almost one order of magnitude slower. In terms of the query time, Figure 5(b) shows that all methods achieve a similar query time given the same observed error, though IFGT does slightly better for very small *err* values. Note that we used the *multipole* (MP) query evaluation method for the kernel density estimates built from RS, G-MR+RS, and Z+RS. On the other hand, Figure 5(c) shows that the kernel density estimates built from both IFGT and RS have much larger size than that produced in our methods G-MR+RS and Z+RS, by 2 to 3, and 1 to 2 orders of magnitude respectively. Finally, Figure 5(d) indicates that all methods have very good scalability in their construction time when the data set size increases from 1 million to 20 million, but G-MR+RS, Z+RS, and RS are clearly much more efficient than IFGT.

In conclusion, our methods are almost as efficient as RS in terms of building a kernel density estimate, and they are much more efficient than IFGT. Our methods also share similar query time as IFGT and RS, while building much smaller kernel density estimates (in size) than both IFGT and RS.

6.2 Two Dimensions: Parallel and Distributed

Default setup. In this case, we change the default data set to a *US* data set with 50 million records, while keeping the other settings the same as those in Section 6.1. Furthermore, since IFGT is much slower in building a kernel density estimate (even more so for larger data sets), and it is also a heuristic without theoretical guarantees (in contrast to the other 3 methods), in the distributed and parallel setting, we focus on comparing our methods against the RS

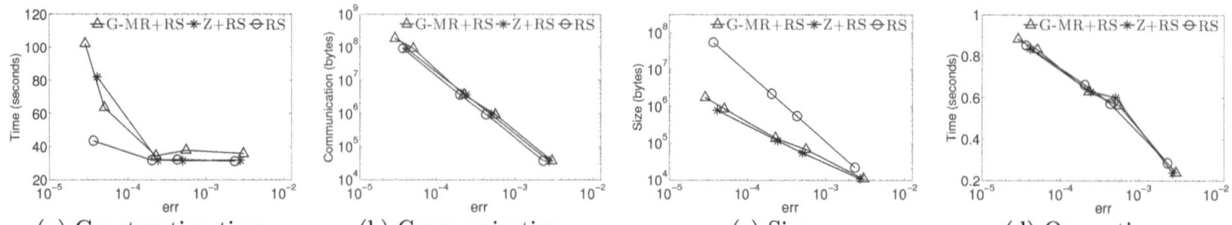

(a) Construction time. (b) Communication. (c) Size. (d) Query time.

Figure 6: Effect of measured ℓ_∞ error *err* on distributed and parallel G-MR+RS, Z+RS, RS.

method. Moreover, IFGT works only for the Gaussian kernel and needs to be provided the bandwidth σ ahead of time, whereas our methods and RS do not. For space, we omit experiments showing varying σ has mild effects on our algorithms and RS, but can lead to strange effects in IFGT.

Our methods vs. RS. We compare the performance of our methods, G-MR+RS and Z+RS, against RS on the aforementioned Hadoop cluster. Figure 6 reports the results when we vary the observed error *err* for different methods (by adjusting their ε values properly so they output roughly the same *err*). Figure 6(a) shows that RS is the most efficient method to construct an approximate kernel density estimate for small *err* values, but G-MR+RS and Z+RS become almost as efficient as RS once *err* is no smaller than 10^{-4} which is sufficient for many practical applications. In those cases, all three methods take less than 40 seconds to construct an approximate KDE for 50 million records. All methods are highly communication-efficient, as shown in Figure 6(b). There are almost no difference among the 3 methods: they communicate only a few MBs over the cluster to achieve an *err* of 10^{-4}, and tens or hundreds of KBs for *err* between 10^{-2} and 10^{-3}. In terms of the size of the approximate KDE_Q, not surprisingly, RS is always the largest. By our analysis in Sections 5.2 and Sections 5.3, $|Q|$ is $O(\frac{1}{\varepsilon^2}\log\frac{1}{\delta})$ for RS, and only $O(\frac{1}{\varepsilon}\log^{2.5}\frac{1}{\varepsilon})$ for both G-MR+RS and Z+RS. This is clearly reflected in Figure 6(c), where $|Q|$ is 1-2 orders of magnitude larger from RS than from G-MR+RS and Z+RS. Finally, we investigate the query time using Q in Figure 6(d). In general, the query time should be linear to $|Q|$. But in practice, since we have used the fast query evaluation technique, the *multipole* (MP) method as shown in Section 5.4, all three methods have similar query time.

We thus conclude that our methods, G-MR+RS and Z+RS perform better than RS. More importantly, they also have much better theoretical guarantees (in order to achieve to same desired error ε in theory), which is critical in practice since users typically use a method by setting an ε value, and for the same ε value, our methods will outperform RS by orders of magnitude ($O(\frac{1}{\varepsilon}\log^{2.5}\frac{1}{\varepsilon})$ vs. $O(\frac{1}{\varepsilon^2}\log\frac{1}{\delta})$). Nevertheless, to be as fair as possible, we experimentally compared methods by first running a few trials to set a proper ε value so each method has roughly the same observed error *err*.

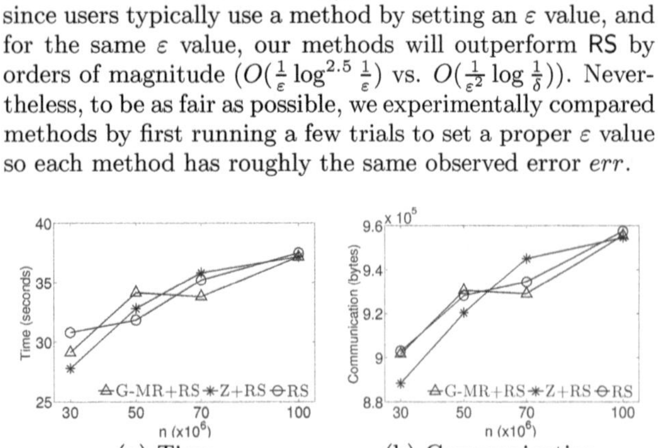

(a) Time. (b) Communication.

Figure 7: Effect of n on G-MR+RS, Z+RS, RS.

We also study the scalability of these methods in Figure 7 by varying the size of the data from 30 million to 100 million records. Not surprisingly, all three methods are extremely scalable in both their construction time (almost linear to n) and communication cost (almost constant to n). Communication only increases by 0.8×10^5 bytes when the total communication is about $9-10\times 10^5$ bytes; such increase is due to the overhead in Hadoop to handle more splits (as n increases), rather than the behavior of our algorithms which is independent from n in communication cost.

6.3 Two Dimensions: Is RS Good Enough?

To show our advantages over random sampling, we provide more centralized experiments here for higher precision. The trends in the parallel and distributed setting will be similar.

Getting higher precision results from a kernel density estimate can be very desirable. The error of kernel density estimates over samples is with respect to $\text{KDE}_P(x) = \frac{1}{|P|}\sum_{p\in P} K(p,x)$, but for large spatial data sets, often only a small fraction of points have non-negligible effect on a query x, so dividing by $|P|$ can make $\text{KDE}_P(x)$ quite small. Here it can be of critical importance to have very small error. Another use case of kernel density estimates is in n-body simulations in statistical physics [1], where high precision is required to determine the force vector at each step. Furthermore, note that a user typically uses these methods with a desirable error as the input, which is set as the input error parameter, the ε value; even though the observed error *err* on a data set may be smaller than ε. In that case, all of our methods have (roughly) a $O(\frac{1}{\varepsilon}/\log\frac{1}{\varepsilon})$ factor improvement in the KDE size, which is a critical improvement especially when ε needs to be small (for high precision applications).

We observe experiments in Figure 8 which compares G-MR+RS and Z+RS with RS in terms of construction time and size of the samples. (Note that figures for query time were omitted for the interest of space; but not surprisingly, they are roughly linear to the KDE size). We plot the figures based on input error parameter ε and observed error *err*. For the plot with respect to ε (Figure 8(a), 8(c)), when ε becomes smaller than $5*10^{-4}$, the construction time and size for RS remain constant as the sample size needed for RS becomes larger than the size of the original dataset. Since we then don't need to sample, the construction time and observed error for RS are 0. For small ε values, G-MR+RS and Z+RS are clever enough to test if random sampling is beneficial, and if not the random sampling step is bypassed.

For the higher precision observed error, the results (Figures 8(b), 8(d)) clearly demonstrate the superiority our proposed methods over RS, reducing both construction time and saving orders of magnitude in terms of both query time and size. We cannot achieve higher precision for RS when the observed error is smaller than 10^{-5}, since in those cases, ε is small enough that the random sample size is as big as the

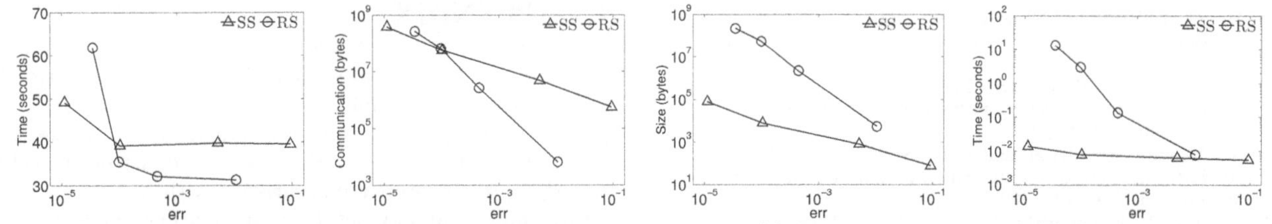

(a) Construction time. (b) Communication. (c) Size. (d) Query time.

Figure 9: Effect of varying measured *err* on RS, SS on one-dimensional data.

size of the original dataset (i.e., KDE from a random sample consists of the entire original dataset, leading to no error).

6.4 One Dimension: Parallel and Distributed

Default setup. We now shift our attention in 1d. The default data set is *Meme* with 50 million records, $\delta = 0.001$, and σ at 1 day, over 273 days of data. Since GS (grouping selection) is a complementary technique that works with any other method, we focus on RS and SS (sort selection). We only report the results from the parallel and distributed setting. The trends in the centralized setting are similar.

SS vs. RS. By varying the observed error *err*, Figure 9 compares the two methods across different metrics. To achieve smaller observed errors in constructing KDE_Q, SS is more efficient as shown in Figure 9(a), but RS becomes faster for larger observed errors. A similar trend is observed for the communication cost in Figure 9(b). In terms of reducing the size of Q, SS does a much better job than RS as shown in Figure 9(c), $|Q|$ in SS is 1-4 orders of magnitude smaller than $|Q|$ in RS, the gap is particularly large for smaller observed errors. This translates to the query time in Figure 9(d), where evaluating $\text{KDE}_Q(x)$ using Q produced by SS is much faster than doing so over Q from RS for most observed errors. When *err* becomes large, around 10^{-2}, the RS method catches up, corresponding to the sizes of Q becoming closer.

In conclusion, SS in general performs better than or comparable to RS on observed error. But it has much better theoretical guarantees in size and query time as shown in Section 4 ($\frac{1}{\varepsilon}$ vs. $O(\frac{1}{\varepsilon^2}\log\frac{1}{\delta})$), which is critical in practice since users generally use a method by setting an ε value.

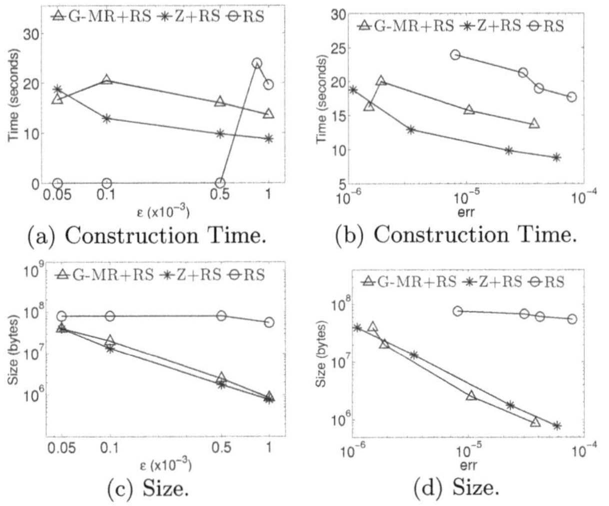

(a) Construction Time. (b) Construction Time.

(c) Size. (d) Size.

Figure 8: Effect of ε and ℓ_∞ error *err* on G-MR+RS, Z+RS, RS for high precision case.

7. CONCLUSION

This paper presents the new state-of-the-art for computing kernel density estimates over enormous real world data sets (up to 100 million points). These are essential statistical tools for large-scale data analysis and physical simulations. Our methods produce a coreset representation of the data which can be used as proxy for the true data while guaranteeing approximation error on size and runtime. Moreover, an extensive experimental study demonstrates that our methods provide clear improvements over existing techniques in terms of size, accuracy, and runtime. Interesting open problems include extending to kernel approximation on complex data types, such as graph and string kernels.

8. REFERENCES

[1] A. W. Appel. An efficient program for many-body simulation. *SIAM J.Scientific and Statistical Computing*, 6:85–103, 1985.

[2] N. Aronszajn. Theory of reproducing kernels. *Transactions AMS*, 68:337–404, 1950.

[3] A. Bagchi, A. Chaudhary, D. Eppstein, and M. T. Goodrich. Deterministic sampling and range counting in geometric data streams. *ACM Transactions on Algorithms*, 3:16, 2007.

[4] P. B. Callahan and S. R. Kosaraju. Algorithms for dynamic closest-pair and n-body potential fields. In *SODA*, 1995.

[5] B. Chazelle. *The Discrepancy Method*. Cambridge, 2000.

[6] B. Chazelle and J. Matousek. On linear-time deterministic algorithms for optimization problems in fixed dimensions. *Journal of Algorithms*, 21:579–597, 1996.

[7] Y. Chen, M. Welling, and A. Smola. Super-samples from kernel hearding. In *Conference on Uncertainty in Artificial Intellegence*, 2010.

[8] G. Cormode, F. Korn, S. Muthukrishnan, and D. Srivastava. Space- and time-efficient deterministic algorithms for biased quantiles over data streams. In *PODS*, 2006.

[9] G. Cormode, S. Muthukrishnan, K. Yi, and Q. Zhang. Optimal sampling from distributed streams. In *PODS*, 2010.

[10] R. Duan, S. Pettie, and H.-H. Su. Scaling algorithms for approximate and exact maximum weight matching. Technical report, arXiv:1112.0790, 2011.

[11] J. Edmonds. Paths, trees, and flowers. *Canadian Journal of Mathematics*, 17:449–467, 1965.

[12] S. Govindarajan, P. K. Agarwal, and L. Arge. CRB-tree: An efficient indexing scheme for range-aggregate queries. In *ICDT*, pages 143–157, 2003.

[13] J. Gray, A. Bosworth, A. Layman, and H. Pirahesh. Data cube: A relational aggregation operator generalizing group-by, cross-tab, and sub-total. In *ICDE*, 1996.

[14] L. Greengard and J. Strain. The fast Gauss transform. *Journal Scientific and Statistical Computing*, 12, 1991.

[15] M. Greenwald and S. Khanna. Space-efficient online computation of quantile summaries. In *SIGMOD*, 2001.

[16] S. Guha, N. Koudas, and K. Shim. Approximation and streaming algorithms for histogram construction problems. *ACM TODS*, 31:396–438, 2006.

[17] D. Gunopulos, G. Kollios, V. J. Tsotras, and C. Domeniconi. Approximating multi-dimensional aggregate range queries over real attributes. In *SIGMOD*, pages 463–474, 2000.

[18] S. Har-Peled. *Geometric Approximation Algorithms*. Chapter 2. American Mathematical Society, 2011.

[19] V. Harinarayan, A. Rajaraman, and J. D. Ullman. Implementing data cubes efficiently. In *ICDE*, 1997.

[20] C.-T. Ho, R. Agrawal, N. Megiddo, and R. Srikant. Range queries in OLAP data cubes. In *SIGMOD*, 1997.

[21] Z. Huang, L. Wang, K. Yi, and Y. Liu. Sampling based algorithms for quantile computation in sensor networks. In *SIGMOD*, pages 745–756, 2011.

[22] H. V. Jagadish, N. Koudas, S. Muthukrishnan, V. Poosala, K. Sevcik, and T. Suel. Optimal histograms with quality guarantees. In *VLDB*, 1998.

[23] M. C. Jones, J. S. Marron, and S. J. Sheather. A brief survey of bandwidth selection for density esimation. *American Statistical Association*, 91:401–407, 1996.

[24] S. Joshi, R. V. Kommaraju, J. M. Phillips, and S. Venkatasubramanian. Comparing distributions and shapes using the kernel distance. In *ACM SoCG*, 2011.

[25] V. Kolmogorov. BLOSSOM V: A new implementation of a minimum cost perfect matching algorithm. *Mathematical Programming*, 1(1), 2009.

[26] N. Koudas, S. Muthukrishnan, and D. Srivastava. Optimal histograms for hierarchical range queries. In *PODS*, 2000.

[27] X. Lin, J. Xu, Q. Zhang, H. Lu, J. X. Yu, X. Zhou, and Y. Yuan. Approximate processing of massive continuous quantile queries over high-speed data streams. *TKDE*, 18(5):683–698, 2006.

[28] G. S. Manku, S. Rajagopalan, and B. G. Lindsay. Approximate medians and other quantiles in one pass and with limited memory. In *SIGMOD*, pages 426–435, 1998.

[29] J. Matoušek. Approximations and optimal geometric divide-and-conquer. In *STOC*, 1991.

[30] J. Matoušek. *Geometric Discrepancy*. Springer, 1999.

[31] E. Parzen. On estimation of a probability density function and mode. *Annals of Mathematical Statistics*, 33:1065–1076, 1962.

[32] E. Parzen. Probability density functionals and reproducing kernel Hilbert spaces. In *Proceedings of the Symposium on Time Series Analysis*, pages 155–169, 1963.

[33] J. M. Phillips. ε-samples for kernels. In *SODA*, 2013.

[34] V. Poosala, Y. E. Ioannidis, P. J. Haas, and E. J. Shekita. Improved histograms for selectivity estimation of range predicates. In *SIGMOD*, pages 294–305, 1996.

[35] V. C. Raykar and R. Duraiswami. Fast optimal bandwidth selection for kernel density estimation. In *SDM*, 2006.

[36] V. C. Raykar, R. Duraiswami, and L. H. Zhao. Fast computation of kernel estimators. *J. of Computational and Graphical Statistics*, 19(1):205–220, 2010.

[37] M. Rosenblatt. Remarks on some nonparametric estimates of a density function. *A. Math. Stat.*, 27:832–837, 1956.

[38] B. Schölkopf and A. J. Smola. *Learning with Kernels: Support Vector Machines, Regularization, Optimization, and Beyond*. MIT Press, 2002.

[39] D. W. Scott. *Multivariate Density Estimation: Theory, Practice, and Visualization*. Wiley, 1992.

[40] J. Shawe-Taylor and N. Cristianini. *Kernel Methods for Pattern Analysis*. Cambridge University Press, 2004.

[41] Q. Shi, J. Petterson, G. Dror, J. Langford, A. Smola, and S. Vishwanathan. Hash kernels for structured data. *Journal of Machine Learning Research*, 10:2615–2637, 2009.

[42] B. W. Silverman. *Density Estimation for Statistics and Data Analysis*. Chapman & Hall/CRC, 1986.

[43] S. Suri, C. D. Tóth, and Y. Zhou. Range counting over multidimensional data streams. *Discrete and Computational Geometry*, 36:633–655, 2006.

[44] B. A. Turlach. Bandwidth selection in kernel density estimation: A review. Discussion paper 9317, Istitut de Statistique, UCL, Louvain-la-Neuve, Belgium.

[45] K. R. Varadarajan. A divide-and-conquer algorithm for min-cost perfect matching in the plane. In *FOCS*, 1998.

[46] J. S. Vitter. Random sampling with a reservoir. *ACM Transactions on Mathematical Software*, 11(1):37–57, 1985.

[47] J. S. Vitter, M. Wang, and B. Iyer. Data cube approximation and histograms via wavelets. In *CIKM*, 1998.

[48] K. Weinberger, A. Dasgupta, J. Attenberg, J. Langford, and A. Smola. Feature hashing for large scale multitask learning. In *ICML*, 2009.

[49] C. Yang, R. Duraiswami, and L. S. Davis. Efficient kernel machines using the improved fast gauss transform. In *NIPS*, 2004.

[50] C. Yang, R. Duraiswami, N. A. Gumerov, and L. Davis. Improved fast gauss transform and efficient kernel density estimation. In *ICCV*, 2003.

[51] T. Zhang, R. Ramakrishnan, and M. Livny. Fast density estimation using cf-kernel for very large databases. In *KDD*, pages 312–316, 1999.

9. APPENDIX

PROOF. OF LEMMA 2: We use a result from Joshi *et.al.* [24] (Theorem 5.1) that states that if $Q \subset P$ satisfies the following property (actually something more general), then $\|\text{KDE}_P - \text{KDE}_Q\|_\infty \leq \alpha$. For *any* interval $I = [a, b]$ we must have $||Q \cap I|/|Q| - |P \cap I|/|P|| \leq \alpha$. So we just need to show that the interval property is satisfied with $\alpha = 2\varepsilon$.

First note that any set P_j that is either entirely not in I (that is $|I \cap P_j| = 0$) or in I (that is $|P_j \cap I| = |P_j|$) contributes to $|Q \cap I|/|Q|$ the same as $|P \cap I|/|P|$ and this has no effect on the difference between the two. Since the sets are sorted, there are at most two sets $P_{j'}$ and $P_{j''}$ which contribute to the interval query error, depending on if $q_{j'}$ and $q_{j''}$ are in I or not. Since $|P_j|/|P|$ and $|\{q_j\}|/|Q|$ are at most ε, then the total error of leaving $q_{j'}$ and $q_{j''}$ in or out is at most $\alpha = \varepsilon + \varepsilon = 2\varepsilon$.

To see the tighter bound, note that if $q_{j'}$ (resp. $q_{j''}$) is in I, then at least half of $P_{j'}$ (resp. $P_{j''}$) is also in I. Thus each can contribute at most $\varepsilon/2$ to the error, leading to total error $\alpha = \varepsilon/2 + \varepsilon/2 = \varepsilon$. □

PROOF. OF THEOREM 2: MergeReduce takes $O(\log \frac{n}{k})$ rounds. In the ith round, we have $\frac{n}{2^{i-1}k}$ sets of points and each set has k points. We arbitrarily pair two sets, and run the Blossom matching algorithm over the union of $2k$ points. This step takes $O(\frac{n}{2^i k}(2k)^3)$ time. Note that the second part in a reduce step takes only linear time. Hence, the total running time is $\sum_{i=1}^{\log \frac{n}{k}} \frac{n}{2^i k}(2k)^3$ which is $O(nk^2)$.

The main result of [33] shows that each round on $n_i = n/2^{i-1}$ points produces a $O(\sqrt{\log n_i}/n_i)$-approximate KDE of the previous round, so after $\log \frac{n}{k}$ rounds the error is

$$\sum_{i=1}^{\log(n/k)} \frac{\sqrt{\log(n/2^i)}}{n/2^i} = O\left(\frac{1}{k} \log \frac{n}{k} \sqrt{\log k}\right)$$

with constant probability. Setting $k = O(\frac{1}{\varepsilon} \log n \sqrt{\log \frac{1}{\varepsilon}})$ achieves ε error total and a runtime of $O(\frac{n}{\varepsilon^2} \log^2 n \log \frac{1}{\varepsilon})$.

Sampling $O(\frac{1}{\varepsilon^2})$ points first takes $O(n)$ time and effectively sets $n = \frac{1}{\varepsilon^2}$ in the bound above. The with-sampling result follows. □

PROOF. OF THEOREM 3: MergeReduce has $O(\log \frac{n}{k})$ rounds. In the ith round, we have $\frac{n}{2^{i-1}k}$ sets of points and each set has k points. We arbitrarily pair all sets and for each pair run Grid over the union of $2k$ points, in total $O(\frac{n}{2^i k}(2k) \log \frac{1}{\varepsilon})$ time. Note that the second part in a reduce step takes only linear time. Hence, the total running time is $\sum_{i=1}^{\log \frac{n}{k}} \frac{n}{2^i k}(2k) \cdot \log(1/\varepsilon)$ which is $O(n \log(1/\varepsilon))$.

The main result of [33] (now adjusting for C_M) shows that each round on $n_i = n/2^{i-1}$ points produces a $O(C_M\sqrt{\log n_i}/n_i)$-approximate KDE of the previous round, so after $\log \frac{n}{k}$ rounds the approximation error is

$$\sum_{i=1}^{\log(n/k)} \frac{C_M\sqrt{\log(n/2^i)}}{n/2^i} = O\left(\frac{C_M}{k} \log \frac{n}{k} \sqrt{\log k}\right)$$

with constant probability. Since by Lemma 4 we have $C_M = O(\log(1/\varepsilon))$, setting $k = O(\frac{1}{\varepsilon} \log n \log^{1.5} \frac{1}{\varepsilon})$ achieves ε error total and a runtime of $O(n \log \frac{1}{\varepsilon})$ using Grid-MR.

Sampling $O(\frac{1}{\varepsilon^2})$ points first takes $O(n)$ time and effectively sets $n = \frac{1}{\varepsilon^2}$ in the bound above. The Grid-MR+RS result follows. □

Efficient Ad-hoc Search for Personalized PageRank

Yasuhiro Fujiwara†, Makoto Nakatsuji‡, Hiroaki Shiokawa†,
Takeshi Mishima†, Makoto Onizuka†
†NTT Software Innovation Center, 3-9-11 Midori-cho Musashino-shi, Tokyo, Japan
‡NTT Service Evolution Laboratories, 1-1 Hikarinooka Yokosuka-shi, Kanagawa, Japan
{fujiwara.yasuhiro, nakatsuji.makoto, shiokawa.hiroaki,
mishima.takeshi, onizuka.makoto}@lab.ntt.co.jp

ABSTRACT

Personalized PageRank (PPR) has been successfully applied to various applications. In real applications, it is important to set PPR parameters in an ad-hoc manner when finding similar nodes because of dynamically changing nature of graphs. Through interactive actions, interactive similarity search supports users to enhance the efficacy of applications. Unfortunately, if the graph is large, interactive similarity search is infeasible due to its high computation cost. Previous PPR approaches cannot effectively handle interactive similarity search since they need precomputation or approximate computation of similarities. The goal of this paper is to efficiently find the top-k nodes with exact node ranking so as to effectively support interactive similarity search based on PPR. Our solution is *Castanet*. The key Castanet operations are (1) estimate upper/lower bounding similarities iteratively, and (2) prune unnecessary nodes dynamically to obtain top-k nodes in each iteration. Experiments show that our approach is much faster than existing approaches.

Categories and Subject Descriptors

H.2.8 [**Database Applications**]: Data mining

General Terms

Algorithms, Theory

Keywords

Graph database, Personalized PageRank, Top-k search

1. INTRODUCTION

Large scale, highly interconnected networks, such as social networks and communication networks, have pervaded our society [26, 27]. There is a growing need for data management systems that can support the searching and mining of such network data. Since network data is naturally represented as a graph, graph databases have attracted significant attention in the database community. In recent years, various papers have been published on reachability queries [21], parallel algorithms [22], and graph clustering [32].

In the database community, link-based similarity measures have become popular since the publication of the PageRank paper [29]. The objective of link-based similarity measures is to extract similarities among nodes from the link structures of the graph; link-based similarity measures are used so as to find, classify, and analyze objects on graph databases [5]. Since then, there has been a surge of papers on link-based similarity measures such as ObjectRank [5] and SimRank [15]. From among them, *Personalized PageRank (PPR)* [4, 12], also known as Random Walk with Restart (RWR)[1] [14], has emerged as the most popular link-based similarity measure due to its effectiveness and solid theoretical foundation. Informally, PPR scores correspond to the stationary probabilities of random walks. At each step of PPR, an outgoing edge from the current node is randomly selected, and, with a certain probability, c, the walk is randomly restarted from a given query node. The probability c is called a scaling parameter [23]. The objective of this work is to enhance the efficacy of the following applications by finding top-k nodes with exact node ranking in an ad-hoc manner where PPR is used as the similarity measure:

Web prefetching. Web prefetching is a technique to download web pages before users demand them to reduce user-perceived latencies; this demands predicting which pages will be accessed by the users [10]. If most prefetched web pages are not visited by users in their subsequent accesses, the prefetching technique cannot effectively reduce access delays. Therefore, the success of the prefetching technique heavily relies on the accuracy of predictions. The approach proposed by Guo et al. offers effective predictions based on PPR [17]. Their approach sets user-specific query nodes in an ad-hoc manner according to the user's web logs, such as access frequency, which are updated by browsing actions. Their approach provides the user with top-5 prediction lists based on the PPR scores of the web pages and yields 23% higher accuracy than usage-based PageRank approach [11].

Word sense disambiguation. Queries for search engines are typically short, consisting of just 2.2 words on average [6]. Search engines need to derive what users want from this limited source of information. However, many words have multiple meanings and the correct meaning depends on the context in which they are used. Word sense disambiguation is the task of identifying the correct meaning of words [28]; it is a key technique in improving a search en-

[1] RWR is a special case of PPR as described in Section 3.

gine's performance. The PPR-based approach proposed by Agirre et al. performs word sense disambiguation by exploiting WordNet[2] as a graph [1]. This approach performs the disambiguation for arbitrarily given words to match the users' intentions; it applies PPR over the graph and assigns the meaning with the highest rank to the query word. Their approach outperforms the previous TextRank approach [25].

Automatic image annotation. The explosion in the number of images on the web necessitates an effective tool to search them. The traditional approach to finding images, practiced by librarians, is to annotate each image manually with keywords and then search on those keywords using a search engine; thus queries can be naturally specified by the user. However, the disadvantage with this approach is the cost and infeasibility of scaling it to large numbers of images. Automatic image annotation is the process by which metadata, in the form of keywords, is automatically assigned to a digital image [31]. It is achieved by finding high ranking keywords to the query image from a given collection of images and associated keywords on the fly. Pan et al. proposed a graph-based annotation method in which images and keywords are treated as nodes in a mixed media graph [30]. They utilized RWR to obtain top-5 ranking keywords for each query image from the large image collection. Their method can provide 10 percent higher annotation accuracy than a fine-tuned method.

Interactive similarity search is an important process to enhance the effectiveness of the above applications; interactive similarity search finds similar nodes in an ad-hoc manner for an arbitrary graph with the scaling parameter. The reasons are twofold. First, the graph can be fully known only after the query is submitted [8]. For example, in web prefetching, graphs are generated on the fly from the user's web logs, and mixed media graphs are created in an ad-hoc manner based on the arbitrarily given image for automatic image annotation. Second, the scaling parameter c has an impact on similarity scores and effectiveness of the applications. For example, Pan et al. reported that, for automatic image annotation, high quality results were achieved with $c = 0.1$ or 0.2 [30] while $c = 0.85$ is recommended for word sense disambiguation [1]. This indicates that the users dynamically change the scaling parameter c through their interactive actions based on search results [8]. However, this interactive approach has difficulty in achieving real-time response if the graph is large. This is because the computation cost of PPR is $O((N+M)T)$ where N, M, and T are the numbers of nodes, edges, and iterations until convergence, respectively.

Several approaches have been proposed to reduce the computation cost of PPR [2, 3, 4, 12, 14, 16, 33]. These approaches are distinguished as matrix-based approaches and Monte Carlo-based approaches. However, they are not appropriate for interactive similarity search. Matrix-based approaches utilize the property that the definition of PPR similarities permits their factorization into some canonical form. For example, Fujiwara et al. proposed efficient approaches for PPR and RWR that are based on QR and LU decompositions, respectively [14, 16]. However, these approaches cannot handle interactive similarity search. This is because these approaches need the precomputation step of QR/LU decomposition before the search process; QR/LU decomposition must be repeated once the graph structure changes.

[2] http://wordnet.princeton.edu/

In Monte Carlo-based approaches, random walks are performed to approximate similarity scores efficiently. The approximation approach proposed by Fogaras et al. [12] is one example of the Monte Carlo-based approach. They used random walks from the query nodes, which are stored in a disk; a fixed value of the scaling parameter c is used to compute approximate scores. However, approximate similarity scores are not desirable since it is difficult for any approximation to enhance the quality of real applications [14, 16]. Furthermore, the Monte Carlo-based approaches cannot effectively cope with on-the-fly changes of the given graph and the scaling parameter values since they precompute random walks before computing the similarity scores. Therefore, a fast approach that takes a different approach is demanded.

1.1 Problem statement

We address the following problem in this paper:

Problem (AD-HOC TOP-K SEARCH FOR PPR).

Given: *Graph G, the scaling parameter c, required number of answer nodes k, and set of query nodes $\mathbb{Q}$.*

Find: *Top-k nodes exactly where k nodes are arranged in descending order with respect to their PPR scores.*

This problem is designed not to compute exact similarities of top-k nodes but to rank top-k nodes exactly with respect to their similarity scores. This is because, in real applications, exact node ranking is more important than the exactness of the similarity scores as described in [23].

1.2 Contributions

In this paper, we propose an efficient approach called *Castanet* that identifies the top-k nodes with exact node ranking. In order to reduce search cost, the proposal utilizes the following two approaches: (1) Estimate upper/lower similarity bounds in iterative style and (2) Dynamically prune unnecessary nodes for top-k search in each iteration. Based on the two approaches, Castanet terminates the iterative computations if the exact ranking of top-k nodes is obtained. Castanet has the following attractive characteristics:

- **Fast**: Compared with the original iterative approach [20], Castanet achieves high speed search by using the above approaches to construct subgraphs for similarity computations; Castanet can avoid computing similarities from the whole graph (Section 4.5 and 5.1).
- **Exact**: While our approach achieves efficient similarity search, it theoretically guarantees not to sacrifice accuracy even though it exploits an estimation approach to prune unnecessary nodes (Section 4.5 and 5.2); it returns the top-k nodes with exact ranking.
- **No-precomputations**: Our approach does not require any precomputation step unlike the previous approaches (Section 4.4). Therefore, it can effectively handle ad-hoc search for any arbitrary graphs, the scaling parameter, and number of answer nodes.
- **Parameter-free**: The proposed approach dispenses with the need for the user to set inner-parameters (Section 4.4). Thus, it provides the user with a simple solution to PPR-based applications.

Even though interactive similarity search based on PPR is effective to enhance application quality, it has been difficult to utilize due to the limitations of the previous approaches. However, by providing a sophisticated approach that suits interactive similarity search, Castanet will help to improve the effectiveness of future PPR-based applications.

The remainder of this paper is organized as follows: Section 2 describes related work. Section 3 gives an overview of the background. Section 4 introduces the main ideas and details of the approaches. Section 5 reviews the results of our experiments. Section 6 details case-studies of Castanet. Section 7 provides our conclusions.

2. RELATED WORK

The previous approaches for PPR fall into two categories: matrix-based and Monte Carlo-based approaches. However, neither is really suitable for interactive similarity search since matrix-based approaches need precomputation and Monte Carlo-based approaches compute approximate similarities.

Tong et al. studied two types of matrix-based approaches; B_LIN and NB_LIN [33]. They used the idea that eigenvalue decomposition can yield approximate similarity scores for RWR. They showed the proof of an error bound for NB_LIN. However, their proof is based on the assumption the normalized graph Laplacian [34] can be exploited to represent a graph. Furthermore, their approaches require setting of the target rank of eigen-decomposition, which impacts the approximation quality. It is impractical to subject a large graph to eigen-decomposition since it is time-consuming as they themselves pointed out. Fujiwara el al. proposed efficient approaches for PPR and RWR [14, 16]. Their approaches utilize the property that similarity computations can be factorized by QR/LU decompositions, so their approaches first compute QR/LU decompositions before commencing the search process. Even though their approaches can find top-k nodes exactly, they cannot effectively handle interactive similarity search since they need precomputation with the specified scaling parameter c.

Fogaras et al. proposed a Monte Carlo-based approach for PPR [12]. To compute approximate scores, they used fingerprints from query nodes; a fingerprint of a node is a random walk starting from the node. They precompute fingerprints and store them on disk to approximate similarity scores from the ending nodes of these random walks. They exploited the linearity property of PPR to approximate similarity scores. Bahmani et al. described an efficient Monte Carlo algorithm that also utilizes precomputed random walks to find top-k nodes [4]. To approximate a node, they count total number of times the node is visited by random walks. Even though their approach can incrementally update similarity scores, and so supports dynamically changing graphs, their approach assumes that the scaling parameter has a fixed value; it cannot effectively support interactive similarity search. A subsequent study by Bahmani et al. investigated a fast MapReduce algorithm for Monte Carlo approximation [3]. However, this algorithm suffers high I/O cost since MapReduce is a disk-based approach; it cannot efficiently handle interactive similarity search. Avrachenkov et al. proposed two Monte Carlo-based approaches, MC End Point and MC Complete Path, to find top-k nodes for PPR where probability $1-c$ is used to restart from a query node [2]. To compute approximate similarities, MC End Point uses part of a random walk while MC Complete Path exploits the entire random walk. That is, MC End Point computes the similarity score of a node from the random walks that end at the node, and MC Complete Path evaluates the similarity score from the total number of visits to the node. Since MC Complete Path utilizes random walks more effectively than MC End Point, MC Complete Path theoretically requires approximately c times fewer random walks than MC End Point; MC Complete Path is faster than MC End Point. Since these approaches perform random walks with a given scaling parameter on the fly, they can compute top-k nodes in ad-hoc style even though they output approximate similarities. However, all Monte Carlo-based approaches require that the number of random walks be set to approximate similarity scores, which induces a trade-off between efficiency and approximation quality.

Table 1: Definition of main symbols.

Symbol	Definition
G	Given graph
N	Number of nodes in the graph
M	Number of edges in the graph
T	Number of iterations by the original iterative approach
c	Scaling parameter, $0 < c < 1$
k	Number of required answer nodes for top-k search
$\mathbb{V}$	Set of nodes in G
$\mathbb{E}$	Set of edges in G
$\mathbb{Q}$	Set of query nodes
$\mathbb{S}$	Set of selected nodes
$\mathbb{R}$	Set of reachable nodes to selected nodes
$\mathbb{L}$	Set of answer likely nodes
$\mathbb{D}$	Set of ranking determined nodes
$\mathbb{A}$	Set of answer nodes
$\mathbb{C}[u]$	Set of nodes adjacent to node u
$\mathbf{q}$	$N \times 1$ query node vector where $\sum q[i] = 1$
$\mathbf{s}$	$N \times 1$ similarity vector by PPR
$\mathbf{W}$	$N \times N$ column normalized adjacent matrix of G

Many other approaches have been proposed. For example, Cho et al. proposed the approach of computing lower bounding estimations for PPR-based web crawling [9]. To achieve this, they applied breadth-first search; they enumerate every possible path originating from the query nodes and compute the estimations through the enumeration. Even though their approach does not yield exact results, their lower bounding approach is acceptable for web crawling since their approach guarantees *not* to miss the high PPR pages (i.e. important pages). Jeh et al. suggested a framework that, for nodes that belong to a highly linked subset of hub nodes, provides a scalable solution for PPR [20]. Their approach precomputes similarity scores from hub nodes, and they approximately compute similarity scores from query nodes as a linear combination of the similarity scores from hub nodes. Basic Push Algorithm, studied by Gupta et al., exploits precomputed similarity scores of all nodes from hub nodes to find the top-k nodes [18]. The number of answer nodes yielded by this algorithm can be more than k since this algorithm uses upper similarity bounds. Unfortunately, the above approaches do not suit interactive similarity search since they compute approximate similarities or need precomputation with a fixed value scaling parameter.

3. PRELIMINARY

In this section, we formally define the notations and introduce the background of this paper. Table 1 lists the main symbols and their definitions. PPR is theoretically based on an intuitive "random surfer model", as same as for Google's PageRank [29]. Google's PageRank exploits the link structure of the graph to compute global importance, which can be used to rank nodes in the graph. PPR, introduced by Jeh and Widom [20], is based on the idea that this global notation of importance can be specialized to create personalized views of importance; importance scores of a node can be biased according to a user-specified set of nodes[3] (i.e., query nodes) and can be thought as the similarity to the nodes. RWR is a special case of PPR in that it has only a single node as a query node. Informally speaking, PPR is the steady-state probabilities of random walks; at each step in a random walk, it randomly selects an outgoing edge from the current node with probability c, and, with restart probability $1-c$, it jumps to a query node in accordance with its preference score. Let $\mathbb{V}$ and $\mathbb{E}$ be the set of nodes and edges in the given graph, respectively. That is, the given graph is represented as $G = \{\mathbb{V}, \mathbb{E}\}$. And let $\mathbf{s}$ be an $N \times 1$ PPR vector where the u-th element $s[u]$ denotes the PPR score of node u. $\mathbf{W}$ is a column-normalized adjacent matrix of the graph where its element $W[u, v]$ is the probability of node u being the next state given that the current state is node v. Computationally, the recursive PPR iteration propagates similarity scores until convergence as follows [20]:

$$\mathbf{s} = c\mathbf{W}\mathbf{s} + (1-c)\mathbf{q} \tag{1}$$

where $\mathbf{q}$ represents the query node vector in which the u-th element $q[u]$ corresponds to its preference score as a query node. If node u is not a query node, $q[u] = 0$. Elements in query nodes are normalized such that their sum is 1.

However, this iterative computation is not efficient if the top-k nodes are the target. This is because the similarity scores of all nodes are updated in the iterations. Furthermore, to find top-k nodes with exact node ranking, the exact similarity scores of all nodes must be obtained by applying the recursive procedures until convergence even though exact scores are not so important in top-k search [23]. This method takes $O((N+M)T)$ time to obtain exact similarities, which incurs excessive computational cost for large graphs and makes a fast solution essential as pointed out in [20].

4. PROPOSED METHOD

In this section, we present our proposal, Castanet, that efficiently finds top-k nodes with exact node ranking. First, Section 4.1 overviews the ideas underlying Castanet. That is followed by a full description including top-k search algorithm in Sections 4.2, 4.3, and 4.4. We also theoretically analyze its performance in Section 4.5.

4.1 Main ideas

The original iterative approach computes the similarities as the steady-state probabilities in the given graph as described in Section 3. This approach incurs high computational cost since it computes the similarities of all nodes by using the whole graph. To find top-k nodes efficiently, we update the similarity estimations of only selected nodes instead of all nodes in each iteration. Thus, we can avoid repeatedly processing the whole graph to find the top-k nodes.

In order to efficiently update the similarity estimations, each iteration dynamically extracts a subgraph by pruning unnecessary nodes and edges from the entire graph. Since the random walk probabilities that must be computed for the estimations are limited to existing edges in subgraphs, we can efficiently update similarity estimations. However, this raises a question; how can we dynamically identify the sets of necessary nodes and edges to find top-k nodes with exact node ranking? We dynamically estimate lower and upper similarity bounds in the iterations to identify unnecessary nodes and edges for top-k search [13]. The subgraphs are much smaller than the whole graph. As a result, we can obtain exact top-k nodes efficiently.

The subgraph approach requires fewer iterations than the original iterative approach. The original iterative approach applies recursive procedures until convergence to compute exact similarities. In contrast, our approach effectively utilizes lower and upper bounding estimations to obtain exact node ranking; if the ranking of a node is determined in an iteration, we do not reestimate the node in subsequent iterations. We terminate the search process once the node ranking is determined for all top-k nodes. This means that the search process is terminated without waiting for convergence; the number of iterations needed by our approach is smaller than that of the original iterative approach.

Our estimation approach provides a further advantage; this approach allows us to automatically determine the structures of subgraphs and the number of iterations. While previous approaches such as [2, 3, 4, 12, 33] require the setting of inner-parameters, which can impact search efficiency and approximation quality, our approach does not require any inner-parameter setting.

4.2 Similarity estimation

To realize efficient top-k search, we dynamically prune unnecessary nodes and edges by utilizing the lower and upper similarity estimations. We first introduce the notations used in the estimation in Section 4.2.1. We next formally define the lower and upper estimations in Section 4.2.2. We also show the theoretical aspects of the estimations.

4.2.1 Notation

To estimate lower and upper similarity bounds, we utilize $p_i[u]$, the random walk probability of length i which starts at a query node and ends at node u. In the random walk, we *do not* restart from a query node. Let $\mathbf{p}_i$ be the $N \times 1$ probability vector of i length random walk where u-th element corresponds to $p_i[u]$; $\mathbf{p}_i$ is computed as $\mathbf{p}_i = \mathbf{W}^i\mathbf{q}$ by exploiting i-th power of the adjacent matrix. Since it is clear that $\mathbf{p}_i = \mathbf{W}\mathbf{p}_{i-1}$, we can incrementally compute the random walk probability $\mathbf{p}_i$ from $\mathbf{p}_{i-1}$; the random walk probability of length i is computed as follows:

$$p_i[u] = \begin{cases} q[u] & (i = 0) \\ \sum_{v \in \mathbb{C}[u]} W[u, v] p_{i-1}[v] & (i \neq 0) \end{cases} \tag{2}$$

where $\mathbb{C}[u]$ is a node set whose edges are incident node u, i.e., $\mathbb{C}[u]$ is a set of directly adjacent nodes to node u in the original graph. In the i-th iteration ($i = 0, 1, 2, \ldots$), we select a set of nodes $\mathbb{S}_i$ for which we update lower and upper similarity bounds. The set of selected nodes initialized as the set of all nodes in the graph, i.e., $\mathbb{S}_0 = \mathbb{V}$, and nodes in $\mathbb{S}_i (i = 1, 2, \ldots)$ are selected as $\mathbb{S}_i$ is included in $\mathbb{S}_{i-1}$. Therefore $\mathbb{V} = \mathbb{S}_0 \supseteq \mathbb{S}_1 \supseteq \ldots \supseteq \mathbb{S}_i$. Details of the node selection are given in Section 4.3. To compute the upper similarity bound, we utilized $\mathbb{R}_i$, the set of nodes that is reachable [21] to any nodes in $\mathbb{S}_i$. Node u is reachable to node v if there is a path from node u to v in the original graph. Note that $\mathbb{S}_i \subseteq \mathbb{R}_i$, and, if $u \in \mathbb{S}_i$, it is obvious that $\mathbb{C}[u] \subseteq \mathbb{R}_i$. And $p_i[\mathbb{R}_i]$ indicates the probability of length i random walks that start at a query node and reaches a node in $\mathbb{R}_i$. That is, $p_i[\mathbb{R}_i] = \sum_{u \in \mathbb{R}_i} p_i[u]$. In addition, we use $W_{max}[u]$, the maximum probability incident to node u

[3] Called "preferred page" in [20].

in the matrix $\mathbf{W}$, i.e., $W_{max}[u] = \max\{W[u,v] : v \in \mathbb{V}\}$ so as to estimate the upper similarity bound.

4.2.2 Definition

We compute the lower similarity bound in each iteration by exploiting the random walk probabilities as follows:

Definition 1 (LOWER BOUND). *The lower estimation of node u in the i-th iteration, $\underline{s}_i[u]$, is defined as follows:*

$$\underline{s}_i[u] = \begin{cases} (1-c)p_i[u] & (i=0) \\ \underline{s}_{i-1}[u] + (1-c)c^i p_i[u] & (i \neq 0) \end{cases} \quad (3)$$

We show that Equation (3) has the lower bounding property in the next paragraph. This definition implies that (1) if $i = 0$, a lower estimate of node u is obtained by random walk probability $p_i[u]$ and the scaling parameter, and (2) otherwise, we can incrementally update the lower estimation $\underline{s}_i[u]$ by the random walk probability of the node and the scaling parameter. This definition also indicates that we can compute the lower estimate of a node in $O(1)$ time if the random walk probability $p_i[u]$ is already obtained.

We introduce the following lemma to show the property of the above estimation approach.

Lemma 1 (LOWER BOUND). *For any node in the graph, $\underline{s}_i[u] \leq s[u]$ holds in all iterations.*

Proof Prior to proving Lemma 1, we first prove that $\lim_{i\to\infty}(c\mathbf{W})^i = \mathbf{0}$ holds, i.e., the matrix $(c\mathbf{W})^i$ equal to a zero matrix after convergence. It is obvious $\lim_{i\to\infty} c^i = 0$ because $0 < c < 1$. Since matrix $\mathbf{W}$ is the column normalized adjacent matrix of the graph, the i-th power of adjacent matrix $\mathbf{W}^i$ corresponds to the probabilities of random walks of length i; none of the elements in $\mathbf{W}^i$ can be larger than 1 or smaller than 0. Therefore, we have

$$\lim_{i\to\infty}(c\mathbf{W})^i = \lim_{i\to\infty} c^i \lim_{i\to\infty} \mathbf{W}^i = \mathbf{0} \quad (4)$$

We next prove Lemma 1. From Equation (1), PPR scores can be obtained as follows:

$$\mathbf{s} = (1-c)(\mathbf{I} - c\mathbf{W})^{-1}\mathbf{q} \quad (5)$$

where $\mathbf{I}$ is the identity matrix and $(\mathbf{I} - c\mathbf{W})^{-1}$ is the inverse matrix of $\mathbf{I} - c\mathbf{W}$. As shown in [19], if $\lim_{i\to\infty}(c\mathbf{W})^i = \mathbf{0}$,

$$(\mathbf{I} - c\mathbf{W})^{-1} = \mathbf{I} + c\mathbf{W} + c^2\mathbf{W}^2 + \ldots = \textstyle\sum_{j=0}^{\infty}(c\mathbf{W})^j \quad (6)$$

by letting $(c\mathbf{W})^0 = \mathbf{I}$. From Equation (5) and (6), the following equation holds:

$$\mathbf{s} = (1-c)\left\{\textstyle\sum_{j=0}^{\infty}(c\mathbf{W})^j\right\}\mathbf{q} = (1-c)\textstyle\sum_{j=0}^{\infty} c^j \mathbf{p}_j \quad (7)$$

Equation (7) indicates that the u-th element of $\mathbf{s}$, $s[u]$, can be computed as follows:

$$s[u] = (1-c)\textstyle\sum_{j=0}^{\infty} c^j p_j[u] \quad (8)$$

From Equation (3), $\underline{s}_i[u]$ can be computed as follows:

$$\begin{aligned} \underline{s}_i[u] &= \underline{s}_{i-1}[u] + (1-c)c^i p_i[u] \\ &= \underline{s}_{i-2}[u] + (1-c)c^i p_i[u] + (1-c)c^{i-1}p_{i-1}[u] \\ &= (1-c)c^i p_i[u] + (1-c)c^{i-1}p_{i-1}[u] + \ldots + (1-c)p_0[u] \end{aligned} \quad (9)$$

Therefore, since $c > 0$ and $p_j[u] \geq 0$,

$$\underline{s}_i[u] = (1-c)\textstyle\sum_{j=0}^{i} c^j p_j[u] \leq (1-c)\textstyle\sum_{j=0}^{\infty} c^j p_j[u] = s[u] \quad (10)$$

which completes the proof. □

We exploit the lower similarity bound introduced in Definition 1 to estimate upper similarity bound. The definition of the upper similarity bound is given as follows by utilizing random walk probabilities:

Definition 2 (UPPER BOUND). *The upper estimation of node u in the i-th iteration, $\overline{s}_i[u]$, is defined as follows:*

$$\overline{s}_i[u] = \underline{s}_i[u] + c^{i+1}W_{max}[u]\, p_i[\mathbb{R}_i] \quad (11)$$

This definition represents that the upper bound estimate of node u can be updated in $O(1)$ time by c, $W_{max}[u]$, and $p_i[\mathbb{R}_i]$. We have the following lemma for the upper similarity bound in each iteration:

Lemma 2 (UPPER BOUND). *For any node in the graph, $\overline{s}_i[u] \geq s[u]$ holds in all iterations.*

Proof To prove the above lemma, we first show the property that $p_{i+j}[\mathbb{R}_{i+j}] \leq p_i[\mathbb{R}_i]$ $(j = 0, 1, \ldots)$ holds in all iterations by using mathematical induction.

Initial step: If $j=0$, it is obvious that $p_{i+j}[\mathbb{R}_{i+j}] = p_i[\mathbb{R}_i]$.

Inductive step: We assume that $p_{i+j-1}[\mathbb{R}_{i+j-1}] \leq p_i[\mathbb{R}_i]$. Since nodes are selected as $\mathbb{S}_{i+j} \subseteq \mathbb{S}_{i+j-1}$, it is obvious that $\mathbb{R}_{i+j} \subseteq \mathbb{R}_{i+j-1}$. Therefore, from Equation (2), we have

$$\begin{aligned} p_{i+j}[\mathbb{R}_{i+j}] &= \textstyle\sum_{v\in\mathbb{R}_{i+j}} p_{i+j}[v] \\ &= \textstyle\sum_{v\in\mathbb{R}_{i+j}} \sum_{w\in\mathbb{C}[v]} W[v,w]p_{i+j-1}[w] \\ &\leq \textstyle\sum_{w\in\mathbb{R}_{i+j-1}} \sum_{v\in\mathbb{R}_{i+j-1}} W[v,w]p_{i+j-1}[w] \\ &\leq \textstyle\sum_{w\in\mathbb{R}_{i+j-1}} p_{i+j-1}[w] = p_{i+j-1}[\mathbb{R}_{i+j-1}] \end{aligned} \quad (12)$$

This is because $\mathbb{C}[v] \subseteq \mathbb{R}_{i+j-1}$ and $\mathbf{W}$ is the column normalized adjacent matrix. As a result, $p_{i+j}[\mathbb{R}_{i+j}] \leq p_{i+j-1}[\mathbb{R}_{i+j-1}] \leq p_i[\mathbb{R}_i]$. This completes the inductive step.

By exploiting this property, we prove Lemma 2. From Equation (2), (8), and (10), PPR similarity of node u, $s[u]$, is computed as follows:

$$\begin{aligned} s[u] &= (1-c)\textstyle\sum_{j=0}^{i} c^j p_j[u] + (1-c)\sum_{j=i+1}^{\infty} c^j p_j[u] \\ &= \underline{s}_i[u] + (1-c)\textstyle\sum_{j=i+1}^{\infty}\sum_{v\in\mathbb{C}[u]} c^j W[u,v]p_{j-1}[v] \end{aligned} \quad (13)$$

Since $W[u,v] \leq W_{max}[u]$ and $\mathbb{C}[u] \subseteq \mathbb{R}_{j-1}$, we have

$$\begin{aligned} s[u] &\leq \underline{s}_i[u] + (1-c)W_{max}[u]\textstyle\sum_{j=i+1}^{\infty} c^j \sum_{v\in\mathbb{R}_{j-1}} p_{j-1}[v] \\ &= \underline{s}_i[u] + (1-c)W_{max}[u]\textstyle\sum_{j=i+1}^{\infty} c^j p_{j-1}[\mathbb{R}_{j-1}] \end{aligned} \quad (14)$$

Since $\sum_{j=i+1}^{\infty} c^j p_{j-1}[\mathbb{R}_{j-1}] = \sum_{j=0}^{\infty} c^{i+j+1} p_{i+j}[\mathbb{R}_{i+j}]$ and, as described above, $p_{i+j}[\mathbb{R}_{i+j}] \leq p_i[\mathbb{R}_i]$, we have

$$\begin{aligned} s[u] &\leq \underline{s}_i[u] + (1-c)W_{max}[u]\, p_i[\mathbb{R}_i] \textstyle\sum_{j=0}^{\infty} c^{i+j+1} \\ &= \underline{s}_i[u] + (1-c)W_{max}[u]\, p_i[\mathbb{R}_i] \frac{c^{i+1} - c^{\infty}}{1-c} \\ &\leq \underline{s}_i[u] + c^{i+1}W_{max}[u]\, p_i[\mathbb{R}_i] = \overline{s}_i[u] \end{aligned} \quad (15)$$

that completes the proof. □

We recursively compute lower and upper estimations in each iteration by using the random walk probability as shown in Definition 1 and 2. These estimations offer one significant advantage; their approximation performance improves with the number of iterations. We show this property by introducing the following lemma:

Lemma 3 (ENHANCING ACCURACY). *$\underline{s}_i[u] \geq \underline{s}_{i-1}[u]$ and $\overline{s}_i[u] \leq \overline{s}_{i-1}[u]$ hold in the i-th iteration.*

Proof We first prove that $\underline{s}_i[u] \geq \underline{s}_{i-1}[u]$. From Equation (3), we have $\underline{s}_i[u] - \underline{s}_{i-1}[u] = (1-c)c^i p_i[u] \geq 0$. We next prove that $\overline{s}_i[u] \leq \overline{s}_{i-1}[u]$. From Equation (3) and (11), $\overline{s}_i[u] - \overline{s}_{i-1}[u]$ is computed as follows:

$$\begin{aligned}&\overline{s}_i[u] - \overline{s}_{i-1}[u]\\ &= \underline{s}_i[u] - \underline{s}_{i-1}[u] + c^i W_{max}[u](cp_i[\mathbb{R}_i] - p_{i-1}[\mathbb{R}_{i-1}]) \quad (16)\\ &= c^i\{(1-c)p_i[u] + W_{max}[u](cp_i[\mathbb{R}_i] - p_{i-1}[\mathbb{R}_{i-1}])\}\end{aligned}$$

From Equation (2),

$$\begin{aligned}p_i[u] &= \textstyle\sum_{v\in\mathbb{C}[u]} W[u,v]\, p_{i-1}[v]\\ &\leq W_{max}[u] \textstyle\sum_{v\in\mathbb{R}_{i-1}} p_{i-1}[v] = W_{max}[u]\, p_{i-1}[\mathbb{R}_{i-1}]\end{aligned} \quad (17)$$

From Equation (12), $p_i[\mathbb{R}_i] \leq p_{i-1}[\mathbb{R}_{i-1}]$. Therefore,

$$\begin{aligned}&\overline{s}_i[u] - \overline{s}_{i-1}[u]\\ &\leq c^i W_{max}[u]\{(1-c)p_{i-1}[\mathbb{R}_{i-1}] + cp_{i-1}[\mathbb{R}_{i-1}] - p_{i-1}[\mathbb{R}_{i-1}]\} = 0\end{aligned} \quad (18)$$

This completes the proof. □

Lemma 3 ensures that our approach has the property of finding top-k nodes with exact node ranking without attempting to compute exact similarities until convergence as described in the next section. The lower/upper estimations have a property of converging to the exact values as follows:

Lemma 4 (CONVERGENCE OF ESTIMATIONS). *After convergence, lower and upper estimations are the same as the exact similarities for all nodes, i.e.,* $\underline{s}_\infty[u] = \overline{s}_\infty[u] = s[u]$.

Proof We first prove that $\underline{s}_\infty[u] = s[u]$. From Equation (10), it is clear that $\underline{s}_\infty[u] = (1-c)\sum_{j=0}^{\infty} c^j p_j[u] = s[u]$. We next prove that $\overline{s}_\infty[u] = s[u]$. From Equation (11), $\overline{s}_\infty[u] = \underline{s}_\infty[u] + c^\infty W_{max}[u]\, p_\infty[\mathbb{R}_\infty]$. Since $c^\infty = 0$, $0 \leq W_{max}[u] \leq 1$, and $0 \leq p_\infty[\mathbb{R}_\infty] \leq 1$, $c^\infty W_{max}[u]\, p_\infty[\mathbb{R}_\infty] = 0$. Therefore, $\overline{s}_\infty[u] = \underline{s}_\infty[u] = s[u]$ holds. □

Lemma 4 ensures that our approach has the property of ranking top-k nodes exactly as described in the next section.

4.3 Subgraph-based search

We dynamically construct subgraphs to efficiently compute random walk probabilities. We update the lower and upper estimations for selected nodes by using the random walk probabilities. In this section, we first detail our approach of selecting nodes in Section 4.3.1, and we formally define subgraphs in Section 4.3.2.

4.3.1 Node selection

In the proposed approach, we select a node to update the lower and upper similarity bounds of the node if (1) the node can be a top-k node (i.e., an answer-likely node) and (2) the ranking of the node in top-k nodes is *not* still determined by the estimations. Let θ_i be the k-th highest lower similarity bound among all nodes in the i-th iteration, a set of answer-likely nodes in the i-th iteration, $\mathbb{L}_i$, is defined as follows:

Definition 3 (ANSWER-LIKELY NODES). *The following equation gives the set of answer-likely nodes in the i-th iteration,* $\mathbb{L}_i$*, whose exact similarity can be higher than* θ_i*:*

$$\mathbb{L}_i = \{u \in \mathbb{V} : \overline{s}_i[u] \geq \theta_i\} \quad (19)$$

The above definition indicates that a node is an answer-likely node if its upper similarity bound is not lower than θ_i. This is because, if an upper estimation of a node is lower than θ_i, the exact similarity of the node cannot be more than θ_i. As shown in later, the sets of answer-likely nodes become smaller with each iteration. A set of ranking determined nodes in top-k nodes by the i-th iteration, $\mathbb{D}_i$, is defined as follows:

Definition 4 (RANKING DETERMINED NODES). *If* $|\mathbb{L}_i| = k$ *(i.e., the number of answer-likely nodes is k), the following equation gives the definition of the set of ranking-determined nodes,* $\mathbb{D}_i$*, whose exact ranks in top-k nodes are already fixed by the i-th iteration:*

$$\mathbb{D}_i = \{u \in \mathbb{L}_i : \underline{s}_i[u] > \overline{s}_i[v] \text{ or } \overline{s}_i[u] < \underline{s}_i[v], u \neq v, \forall v \in \mathbb{L}_i\} \quad (20)$$

Otherwise (i.e., $|\mathbb{L}_i| \neq k$*),* $\mathbb{D}_i$ *is defined as follows:*

$$\mathbb{D}_i = \emptyset \quad (21)$$

Definition 4 defines node u as a ranking-determined node if (1) the number of answer-likely nodes is k, and (2) there does not exist any node $v(\neq u)$ whose lower or upper similarity bound is between $\underline{s}_i[u]$ and $\overline{s}_i[u]$. That is, if there is a node whose lower or upper similarity bound is between $\underline{s}_i[u]$ and $\overline{s}_i[u]$, the rank of node u cannot be determined.

In Definition 4, if $|\mathbb{L}_i| = k$, it requires $O(k \log k)$ time to compute $\mathbb{D}_i$ since $\mathbb{D}_i$ can be obtained by sorting the nodes of $\mathbb{L}_i$ in the lower and upper estimations. If $|\mathbb{L}_i| \neq k$, it is unnecessary to compute $\mathbb{D}_i$ from Equation (21). By exploiting the definitions of $\mathbb{L}_i$ and $\mathbb{D}_i$, the set of selected nodes, $\mathbb{S}_i$ is defined as follows:

Definition 5 (SELECTED NODES). *The following equation gives the definition of the set of selected nodes,* $\mathbb{S}_i$*, whose lower/upper estimations are updated in the i-th iteration by random walk probabilities:*

$$\mathbb{S}_i = \begin{cases} \mathbb{V} & (i = 0) \\ \mathbb{L}_{i-1} \backslash \mathbb{D}_{i-1} & (i \neq 0) \end{cases} \quad (22)$$

In the above equation, $\mathbb{L}_{i-1} \backslash \mathbb{D}_{i-1}$ *represents the relative complement of* $\mathbb{L}_{i-1}$ *with respect to* $\mathbb{D}_{i-1}$ *which is given as* $\{u \in \mathbb{L}_{i-1} : u \notin \mathbb{D}_{i-1}\}$.

Definition 5 indicates that we first compute the lower/upper estimations for all nodes, and we do not update the estimations of a node if (1) the node is not an answer-likely node or (2) the ranking of the node has already been fixed by prior estimations. In other words, we update the estimation of a node if the node is an answer-likely node and its ranking has not been determined by prior estimations.

To show the property of the selected nodes, we introduce several lemmas on node sets $\mathbb{L}_i$ and $\mathbb{D}_i$. We first show the two properties of the set of answer-likely nodes $\mathbb{L}_i$ as follows by letting $\mathbb{A}$ be the set of answer nodes:

Lemma 5 (MONOTONIC DECREASE OF $\mathbb{L}_i$). *The elements in the node set of answer-likely nodes,* $\mathbb{L}_i$*, are monotonic decreasing in the iterations. That is,* $\mathbb{L}_i \subseteq \mathbb{L}_{i-1}$ *holds.*

Proof θ_i is the k-th highest lower estimation in the i-th iteration. Therefore, we have $\theta_i \geq \theta_{i-1}$ since lower bound estimations have monotonic increasing property as described in Lemma 3. As a result, (1) if node u is included in $\mathbb{L}_i$, the node must be included in $\mathbb{L}_{i-1}$ since $\overline{s}_{i-1}[u] \geq \overline{s}_i[u] \geq \theta_i \geq \theta_{i-1}$, and (2) otherwise, the node can be included in $\mathbb{L}_{i-1}$ since $\theta_i > \overline{s}_{i-1}[u] \geq \overline{s}_i[u] \geq \theta_{i-1}$ can be hold. □

Lemma 6 (CONVERGENCE OF $\mathbb{L}_i$). *The set of answer-likely nodes equals to the set of answer nodes after convergence, i.e.,* $\mathbb{L}_\infty = \mathbb{A}$.

Proof If θ is the k-th highest exact similarity among all nodes, we have $\theta_\infty = \theta$ after convergence from Lemma 4. Therefore, from Lemma 4, we have

$$\mathbb{L}_\infty = \{u \in \mathbb{V} : \overline{s}_\infty[u] \geq \theta_\infty\} = \{u \in \mathbb{V} : s[u] \geq \theta\} = \mathbb{A} \quad (23)$$

which completes the proof. □

Even though Definition 3 indicates that all the nodes in the original graph are needed to compute $\mathbb{L}_i$, we can efficiently compute $\mathbb{L}_i$ in the iterations. If $i \neq 0$ and $|\mathbb{L}_{i-1}| \neq k$, $\mathbb{L}_i$ is computed as follows:

$$\mathbb{L}_i = \{u \in \mathbb{L}_{i-1} : \overline{s}_i[u] \geq \theta_i\} \quad (24)$$

Equation (24) can be obtained by replacing $\mathbb{V}$ with $\mathbb{L}_{i-1}$ in Equation (19). That is, we can compute $\mathbb{L}_i$ from $\mathbb{L}_{i-1}$. This is because, if a node is not included in $\mathbb{L}_{i-1}$, the node cannot be included in $\mathbb{L}_i$ from Lemma 5. Moreover, if $i \neq 0$ and $|\mathbb{L}_{i-1}| = k$, $\mathbb{L}_i$ is computed as follows:

$$\mathbb{L}_i = \mathbb{L}_{i-1} \quad (25)$$

This is because $\mathbb{L}_i \subseteq \mathbb{L}_{i-1}$ and $\mathbb{L}_i$ converges to $\mathbb{A}$ from Lemma 5 and 6. We introduce the following properties of the set of ranking-determined nodes from Lemma 5 and 6:

Lemma 7 (MONOTONIC INCREASE OF $\mathbb{D}_i$). *The set of ranking-determined nodes, $\mathbb{D}_i$, has the property of monotonic increase; we have $\mathbb{D}_i \supseteq \mathbb{D}_{i-1}$ in the i-th iteration.*

Proof We first give proof of the case of $|\mathbb{L}_{i-1}| \neq k$. From Definition 4, in this case, we have $\mathbb{D}_{i-1} = \emptyset \subseteq \mathbb{D}_i$. We next show the proof of the case of $|\mathbb{L}_{i-1}| = k$. In this case, $\mathbb{L}_i = \mathbb{L}_{i-1} = \mathbb{A}$ holds due to Lemma 5 and 6. If node u is included in the node set $\mathbb{D}_{i-1}$, the node must be included in the node set $\mathbb{D}_i$ since (1) the estimations have the property of enhancing accuracy from Lemma 3, and (2) $\mathbb{L}_i = \mathbb{L}_{i-1}$. If node u is not included in node set $\mathbb{D}_{i-1}$, the node can be included in node set $\mathbb{D}_i$ due to the accuracy enhancement property of lower/upper estimations. □

Lemma 8 (CONVERGENCE OF $\mathbb{D}_i$). *After convergence, we have $\mathbb{D}_\infty = \mathbb{A}$; the set of ranking-determined nodes equals to the set of answer nodes.*

Proof We have $\underline{s}_\infty[u] = \overline{s}_\infty[u] = s[u]$ and $\mathbb{L}_\infty = \mathbb{A}$ after convergence from Lemma 4 and 6, respectively. Therefore, from Definition 4, we have,

$$\begin{aligned}\mathbb{D}_\infty &= \{u \in \mathbb{L}_\infty : \underline{s}_\infty[u] > \overline{s}_\infty[v] \text{ or } \overline{s}_\infty[u] < \underline{s}_\infty[v], u \neq v, \forall v \in \mathbb{L}_\infty\} \\ &= \{u \in \mathbb{A} : s[u] > s[v] \text{ or } s[u] < s[v], u \neq v, \forall v \in \mathbb{A}\} = \mathbb{A}\end{aligned} \quad (26)$$

Therefore, $\mathbb{D}_\infty = \mathbb{A}$ holds after convergence. □

Lemma 5 and 7 indicate that the set of nodes $\mathbb{L}_i$ and $\mathbb{D}_i$ have monotonic decrease and increase properties, respectively. Lemma 6 and 8 ensure that node sets $\mathbb{L}_i$ and $\mathbb{D}_i$ equal to the answer node set $\mathbb{A}$ after convergence. Therefore, we can introduce the following lemma for the selected nodes:

Lemma 9 (SET OF THE SELECTED NODES). *The set of selected nodes is monotonic decreasing and equals to an empty set after convergence. That is, $\mathbb{S}_i \subseteq \mathbb{S}_{i-1}$ and $\mathbb{S}_\infty = \emptyset$.*

Proof This is obvious from Lemma 5, 6, 7, and 8. □

Since, as described in Definition 5, the set of selected nodes is initialized to the set of nodes in the graph, the set of selected nodes has the property that $\mathbb{V} = \mathbb{S}_0 \supseteq \mathbb{S}_1 \supseteq \ldots \supseteq \mathbb{S}_i$. As shown in Section 4.2, this property enables our approach to compute the lower/upper estimations. Moreover, the property of $\mathbb{S}_\infty = \emptyset$ implies that our approach terminates in finite iteration number since $\mathbb{S}_\infty = \emptyset$ indicates that there is no node whose estimations are updated.

4.3.2 Subgraphs construction

In this section, we describe our approach that constructs subgraphs to efficiently update the estimations. A naive approach to updating the lower/upper estimations treats the whole graph in each iteration. However, this approach is too computationally expensive since it needs to obtain random walk probabilities of all nodes. Therefore, we construct subgraphs by pruning unnecessary nodes and edges from the original graph. In this section, we first define the subgraph and then show its properties. We also describe how to incrementally compute subgraphs in the iterations.

As shown in Definition 1 and 2, the lower and upper estimations are obtained by utilizing the random walk probabilities obtained by Equation (2). Therefore, the subgraphs are designed to efficiently compute random walk probabilities. To construct the subgraphs, we use the set of nodes, $\mathbb{H}_i$, whose number of hops from the query nodes is within i; $\mathbb{H}_i$ is composed of the nodes that are not more than i hops from the query nodes. We construct the subgraph in the i-th iteration, G_i, by exploiting $\mathbb{H}_i$ as follows:

Definition 6 (SUBGRAPH). *Let $G_i = \{\mathbb{V}_i, \mathbb{E}_i\}$ be the subgraph of G in the i-th iteration where $\mathbb{V}_i \subseteq \mathbb{V}$ and $\mathbb{E}_i \subseteq \mathbb{E}$, $\mathbb{V}_i$ and $\mathbb{E}_i$ are defined as follows:*

$$\mathbb{V}_i = \mathbb{H}_i \cap \mathbb{R}_i \quad (27)$$

$$\mathbb{E}_i = \{(u, v) \in \mathbb{E} : u \in \mathbb{V}_i, v \in \mathbb{V}_i\} \quad (28)$$

where (u, v) represents an edge from node u to v.

The above definition indicates that (1) subgraph G_i has a node in the original graph if the node is within i hops from the query nodes and is reachable to the selected nodes, and (2) an edge of the original graph exists in the subgraph if the nodes linked by the edge in the original graph exist in the subgraph. We introduce the following lemma to show the property of the subgraph.

Lemma 10 (LOWER/UPPER ESTIMATIONS BY SUBGRAPH). *The lower/upper estimations for the selected nodes in the i-th iteration are obtained from $\mathbb{V}_i$ and $\mathbb{E}_i$.*

Proof As described in Section 4.2.1, $p_i[u]$ is the random walk probability of length i that starts at a query node and ends at node u. So, if a node is more than i-hops away from the query nodes, the random walk probability of the node must be 0 in the i-th iteration. Therefore, we can obtain the lower/upper estimations with node set $\mathbb{H}_i$ and the set of edges that are incident to $\mathbb{H}_i$. From Equation (2), (3), and (11), it is clear that, if a node is *not* reachable to $\mathbb{S}_i$, the score of the random walk probability of the node does not affect the score of the lower/upper estimations of $\mathbb{S}_i$. This indicates that node set $\mathbb{R}_i$ and the set of edges that are incident from $\mathbb{R}_i$ need to be processed to compute the lower/upper estimations for selected nodes. As a result, we need only node set $\mathbb{V}_i = \mathbb{H}_i \cap \mathbb{R}_i$ and edge set $\mathbb{E}_i = \{(u, v) \in \mathbb{E} : u \in \mathbb{V}_i, v \in \mathbb{V}_i\}$ to obtain the lower/upper estimations of the selected nodes in the i-th iteration. □

This proof implies that we can compute random walk probabilities as well as the lower/upper estimations of the selected nodes by the subgraphs. We exploit the subgraphs to efficiently compute random walk probabilities as follows:

Definition 7 (PROBABILITY COMPUTATION BY SUBGRAPH). *Let $\mathbb{C}_i[u]$ be the set of nodes that are incident to node u in* *the subgraph G_i, we compute the random walk probability of node u in i-th iteration, $p_i[u]$, as follows:*

$$p_i[u] = \begin{cases} q[u] & (i=0) \\ \sum_{v \in \mathbb{C}_i[u]} W[u,v] p_{i-1}[v] & (i \neq 0) \end{cases} \quad (29)$$

The above equation can be obtained by replacing $\mathbb{C}[u]$ with $\mathbb{C}_i[u]$ in Equation (2). To find the top-k nodes, we compute the random walk probabilities of the nodes in the subgraphs by the above definition. We obtain the lower/upper estimations of selected nodes by exploiting Definition 1 and 2. Even though the naive approach processes the whole graph, we compute random walk probabilities from the subgraphs to reduce the computation cost.

However, it can require high computational cost to construct the subgraphs since this approach needs the whole graph to compute the subgraphs based on Definition 6. We, therefore, introduce an incremental approach to obtaining subgraphs that utilizes a set of nodes $\mathbb{h}_i$ and a set of edges $\mathbb{e}_i$. $\mathbb{h}_i$ is defined as the set of nodes that are i hops away from the query nodes. From this definition, it is clear that $\mathbb{h}_0 = \mathbb{H}_0 = \mathbb{Q}$ and $\mathbb{H}_i = \bigcup_{j=0}^{i} \mathbb{h}_j = \mathbb{H}_{i-1} + \mathbb{h}_i$. $\mathbb{e}_i$ is the set of edges that link node sets $\mathbb{h}_i$ and $\mathbb{H}_i$. That is, $\mathbb{e}_i = \{(u,v) \in \mathbb{E} : u \in \mathbb{h}_i, v \in \mathbb{H}_{i-1} \text{ or } u \in \mathbb{H}_{i-1}, v \in \mathbb{h}_i \text{ or } u \in \mathbb{h}_i, v \in \mathbb{h}_i\}$ since $\mathbb{H}_i = \mathbb{H}_{i-1} + \mathbb{h}_i$. Note that $\mathbb{h}_i$ and $\mathbb{e}_i$ can be obtained from a single breadth-first search rooted on the query nodes; $\mathbb{h}_i$ and $\mathbb{e}_i$ can be obtained within $O(N+M)$ time. We have the following lemma for these two sets:

Lemma 11 (Subgraph inclusion). *Let nodes and edges sets be $\mathbb{V}'_i = \mathbb{V}_{i-1} + \mathbb{h}_i$ and $\mathbb{E}'_i = \mathbb{E}_{i-1} + \mathbb{e}_i$, respectively, we have $\mathbb{V}_i \subseteq \mathbb{V}'_i$ and $\mathbb{E}_i \subseteq \mathbb{E}'_i$ if $i \neq 0$.*

Proof If $i \neq 0$, since $\mathbb{H}_i = \mathbb{H}_{i-1} + \mathbb{h}_i$ and $\mathbb{R}_i \subseteq \mathbb{R}_{i-1}$ hold, from Equation (27), we have

$$\mathbb{V}_i = (\mathbb{H}_{i-1} + \mathbb{h}_i) \cap \mathbb{R}_i \subseteq (\mathbb{H}_{i-1} + \mathbb{h}_i) \cap \mathbb{R}_{i-1} \quad (30)$$

Therefore,

$$\mathbb{V}_i \subseteq \mathbb{H}_{i-1} \cap \mathbb{R}_{i-1} + \mathbb{h}_i \cap \mathbb{R}_{i-1} \subseteq \mathbb{V}_{i-1} + \mathbb{h}_i = \mathbb{V}'_i \quad (31)$$

If $i \neq 0$, since $\mathbb{V}_i \subseteq \mathbb{V}_{i-1} + \mathbb{h}_i$, from Equation (28), we have

$$\mathbb{E}_i \subseteq \{(u,v) \in \mathbb{E} : u \in (\mathbb{V}_{i-1} + \mathbb{h}_i), v \in (\mathbb{V}_{i-1} + \mathbb{h}_i)\} \quad (32)$$

Therefore, since $\mathbb{V}_{i-1} = \mathbb{H}_{i-1} \cap \mathbb{R}_{i-1} \subseteq \mathbb{H}_{i-1}$, we have

$$\begin{aligned} \mathbb{E}_i \subseteq \{(u,v) \in \mathbb{E} : u \in \mathbb{V}_{i-1}, v \in \mathbb{V}_{i-1}\} + \\ \{(u,v) \in \mathbb{E} : u \in \mathbb{H}_{i-1}, v \in \mathbb{h}_i \\ \text{or } u \in \mathbb{h}_i, v \in \mathbb{H}_{i-1} \text{ or } u \in \mathbb{h}_i, v \in \mathbb{h}_i\} \end{aligned} \quad (33)$$

As a result, $\mathbb{E}_i \subseteq \mathbb{E}_{i-1} + \mathbb{e}_i = \mathbb{E}'_i$ holds. □

Based on Lemma 11, we incrementally construct the subgraphs in the iterations. Let a graph be $G'_i = \{\mathbb{V}'_i, \mathbb{E}'_i\}$, the graph G'_i can be incrementally obtained since $\mathbb{V}'_i = \mathbb{V}_{i-1} + \mathbb{h}_i$ and $\mathbb{E}'_i = \mathbb{E}_{i-1} + \mathbb{e}_i$. That is, graph G'_i can be obtained by adding i hop distant nodes and their corresponding edges to G_{i-1}. Since (1) $G_i \subseteq G'_i$ holds from the above lemma and (2) $\mathbb{h}_i$ and $\mathbb{e}_i$ can include nodes and edges that are not paths to $\mathbb{S}_i$, respectively, we compute subgraph G_i by determining the paths to $\mathbb{S}_i$ in graph G'_i by applying breadth-first search inversely from $\mathbb{S}_i$.

Algorithm 1 shows our incremental approach for subgraph construction. If $i = 0$, the algorithm initializes the node and edge sets to $\mathbb{V}_0 = \mathbb{Q}$ and $\mathbb{E}_0 = \{(u,v) \in \mathbb{E} : u \in \mathbb{Q}, v \in \mathbb{Q}\}$, respectively (lines 2-3). This is because $\mathbb{V}_0 = \mathbb{H}_0 \cap \mathbb{R}_0 = \mathbb{Q} \cap \mathbb{V} = \mathbb{Q}$ from Equation (22) and (27). Otherwise, it

Algorithm 1 Subgraph construction

Input: G_{i-1}, subgraph of previous iteration; $\mathbb{h}_i$, set of nodes; $\mathbb{e}_i$, set of edges; $\mathbb{S}_i$, set of selected nodes
Output: $\mathbb{G}_i$, subgraph in the i-th iteration

1: **if** $i = 0$ **then**
2: $\quad\mathbb{V}_0 := \mathbb{Q}$;
3: $\quad\mathbb{E}_0 := \{(u,v) \in \mathbb{E} : u \in \mathbb{Q}, v \in \mathbb{Q}\}$;
4: **else**
5: $\quad\mathbb{V}'_i := \mathbb{V}_{i-1} + \mathbb{h}_i$;
6: $\quad\mathbb{E}'_i := \mathbb{E}_{i-1} + \mathbb{e}_i$;
7: $\quad G'_i := \{\mathbb{V}'_i, \mathbb{E}'_i\}$;
8: $\quad$compute paths to $\mathbb{S}_i$ in G'_i;
9: $\quad$compute $\mathbb{V}_i$ and $\mathbb{E}_i$ from the paths;
10: **end if**
11: $G_i := \{\mathbb{V}_i, \mathbb{E}_i\}$;
12: **return** $\mathbb{G}_i$;

computes graph G'_i from the graph of the previous iteration, G_{i-1} (lines 5-7). It computes $\mathbb{V}_i$ and $\mathbb{E}_i$ from G'_i by utilizing breadth-first search (lines 8-9).

As shown in Algorithm 1, we can incrementally compute the subgraphs without using the whole graph; we can find answer nodes efficiently. The next section describes the top-k search algorithm based on the above subgraph approach.

4.4 Search algorithm

Algorithm 2 shows our algorithm Castanet. It first initializes the set of selected nodes (line 2), and computes the subgraph (lines 7-8). If a node is included in the subgraph, it computes the random walk probability of the node (lines 9-11) since such a node is necessary to obtain the estimations for the selected nodes (Lemma 10). And it computes the estimations of the selected node (lines 12-15). If $i = 0$, it computes $\mathbb{L}_i$ by Definition 3 (lines 16-17). Otherwise, it updates $\mathbb{L}_i$ from $\mathbb{L}_{i-1}$ (lines 18-24). Since $\mathbb{D}_i = \emptyset$ if $|\mathbb{L}_i| \neq k$ from Definition 4, it computes $\mathbb{D}_i$ when $|\mathbb{L}_i| = k$ (lines 25-26). It then updates the selected nodes (line 30). We terminate the iterations if there is no selected node (line 31). It obtains the node ranking by sorting the nodes of $\mathbb{D}_i$ in descending order of their lower estimations (line 32). Finally, it returns $\mathbb{D}_i$ as the set of answer nodes (lines 33-34).

As shown in Algorithm 2, our approach does not need any precomputation unlike the previous approaches. That is, we can effectively handle ad-hoc search. Our algorithm does not require any user-defined inner-parameter. Thus, it provides the user with a simple approach to finding the top-k nodes with enhanced search speed.

4.5 Theoretical analyses

We provide theoretical analyses on the search results and the computation cost of our algorithm. We introduce the following theorem that Castanet finds answer nodes exactly:

Theorem 1 (Exactness in top-k search). *Castanet finds the top-k nodes with exact node ranking.*

Proof Algorithm 2 computes the set of selected nodes until the set converges to an empty set, and it returns $\mathbb{D}_i$ as the answer nodes. If $\mathbb{S}_{i+1} = \emptyset$, we have $\mathbb{L}_i = \mathbb{D}_i$ from Definition 5. Since $\mathbb{L}_i \supseteq \mathbb{A}$ and $\mathbb{D}_i \subseteq \mathbb{A}$ from Lemma 5, 6, 7, and 8, we have $\mathbb{L}_i = \mathbb{D}_i = \mathbb{A}$ if $\mathbb{L}_i = \mathbb{D}_i$ holds. Therefore, we have $\mathbb{D}_i = \mathbb{A}$ if $\mathbb{S}_{i+1} = \emptyset$ holds. Since $\mathbb{D}_i = \mathbb{A}$, the ranking of all nodes in $\mathbb{D}_i$ are fixed after the iterations. Therefore, we can obtain the top-k nodes with exact node ranking. □

We discuss the time complexity of our approach. Let l and t be the average number of selected nodes and the number of iterations in our approach, respectively. And let n

Algorithm 2 Castanet

Input: G, original graph; c, the scaling parameter; k, number of answer nodes; $\mathbb{Q}$, set of query nodes
Output: $\mathbb{A}$, set of answer nodes

$i := 0$;
$\mathbb{S}_0 := \mathbb{V}$;
repeat
  if $i \neq 0$ **then**
    $i := i + 1$;
  end if
  compute $\mathbb{h}_i$ and $\mathbb{e}_i$ by breadth-first search;
  compute G_i by Algorithm 1;
  for each node $u \in \mathbb{V}_i$ **do**
    compute $p_i[u]$ from $\mathbb{G}_i$ by Equation (29);
  end for
  for each node $u \in \mathbb{S}_i$ **do**
    compute $\underline{s}_i[u]$ by Equation (3);
    compute $\overline{s}_i[u]$ by Equation (11);
  end for
  if $i = 0$ **then**
    compute $\mathbb{L}_i$ by Equation (19);
  else
    if $|\mathbb{L}_{i-1}| \neq k$ **then**
      compute $\mathbb{L}_i$ by Equation (24);
    else
      $\mathbb{L}_i := \mathbb{L}_{i-1}$;
    end if
  end if
  if $|\mathbb{L}_i| = k$ **then**
    compute $\mathbb{D}_i$ by Equation (20);
  else
    $\mathbb{D}_i := \emptyset$;
  end if
  $\mathbb{S}_{i+1} := \mathbb{L}_i \backslash \mathbb{D}_i$;
until $\mathbb{S}_{i+1} = \emptyset$
sort nodes of $\mathbb{D}_i$;
$\mathbb{A} := \mathbb{D}_i$;
return $\mathbb{A}$;

and m be the average numbers of nodes and edges of the subgraphs, respectively. Note that, the original iterative approach requires $O(N + M)T$ time.

Theorem 2 (COMPUTATIONAL COST). *Castanet requires $O((l + n + m + k \log k)t + N + M)$ time to find top-k nodes.*

Proof Our approach first constructs the subgraph which takes $O((n+m)t+N+M)$ time. This is because (1) nodes and edges in the subgraph of each iteration are computed by breadth-first search in $O((n + m)t)$ time, and (2) $\mathbb{h}_i$ and $\mathbb{e}_i$ are obtained in $O(N + M)$ time. It takes $O((n + m)t)$ and $O(l \cdot t)$ time to compute random walk probabilities and the lower/upper estimations from the subgraphs in the iterations, respectively. We can compute node sets $\mathbb{L}_i$ and $\mathbb{D}_i$ within $O(l \cdot t)$ and $O(k \log k \cdot t)$ time, respectively. After the iterations, we sort answer nodes to compute the node ranking which takes $O(k \log k)$ time. As a result, our approach requires $O((l + n + m + k \log k)t + N + M)$ time. □

As shown in the next section, $k \ll l \ll n \ll N$, $m \ll M$, and $t \ll T$ in practice. The original iterative approach needs $O((N+M)T)$ time; the proposed approach can find the top-k nodes much faster than the original iterative approach.

5. EXPERIMENTAL EVALUATION

We performed experiments to compare Castanet to the Monte Carlo-based approach proposed by Avrachenkov et al. [2], the matrix-based approach proposed by Fujiwara et al. [16], and the original iterative approach [29]. Avrachenkov et al. proposed two Monte Carlo-based approaches, MC Complete Path and MC End Point, both approximately find the top-k nodes in ad-hoc style unlike other approaches such as [4] and [12]. As described in their paper, MC Complete Path is faster than MC End Point. This is because MC Complete Path theoretically requires, approximately, c times fewer random walks than MC End Point as described in Section 2. Therefore, we selected MC Complete Path as a benchmark. The matrix-based approach by Fujiwara et al. is a state-of-the-art approach and can find top-k nodes exactly and efficiently by pruning unnecessary nodes. Their approach does not have the limitations of other matrix-based approaches such that (1) the exact top-k nodes are not guaranteed in the search results [33], or (2) only a single node is permitted as the query node [14]. Our experiments will demonstrate that:

- Efficiency: Castanet is much faster than the previous approaches for the real datasets tested (Section 5.1).
- Exactness: Unlike the previous approximate approach, the proposed approach can find the top-k nodes with exact ranking (Section 5.2).
- Applicability: Our approach can handle arbitrarily set the scaling parameters since it does not need precomputation (Section 5.3).

The experiments used the following four public datasets:

- Notredame[4]: This dataset was taken from the web pages of the University of Notre Dame[5]. In this graph, nodes represent pages from domain nd.edu and edges represent hyperlinks between them. There are 325, 729 nodes and 1, 497, 135 edges.
- CNR[6]: CNR (Italy's National Research Council)[7] is a public research organization. This graph is the result of a crawl of the Italian CNR domain where nodes and edges correspond to pages and hyperlinks, respectively. This graph has 325, 557 nodes and 3, 216, 152 edges.
- Email[8]: This is an email dataset from an European research institution. In this graph, each node corresponds to an email address. A directed edge between nodes u and v indicates that the owner of address u sent at least one message to address v. This dataset has 265, 214 nodes and 420, 045 edges.
- Social[9]: Slashdot[10] is a famous news website known for its specific user community. The graph is taken from Slashdot.org and contains interaction links among the users of Slashdot. The numbers of nodes and edges are 82, 144 and 549, 202, respectively.

In this section, "Castanet", "Monte", "Matrix", and "Original" represent the results of our approach, the Monte Carlo-based approach by Avrachenkov et al., the matrix-based approach by Fujiwara et al., and the original iterative approach, respectively. We randomly set three nodes as query nodes[11]. The preference scores were set to the same value. All experiments were conducted on a Linux quad 3.33 GHz Intel Xeon server with 32GB of main memory. We implemented all approaches using GCC.

[4] http://vlado.fmf.uni-lj.si/pub/networks/data/ND/NDnets.htm
[5] http://www.nd.edu/
[6] http://law.di.unimi.it/webdata/cnr-2000/
[7] http://www.cnr.it/sitocnr/home.html
[8] http://snap.stanford.edu/data/email-EuAll.html
[9] http://snap.stanford.edu/data/soc-sign-Slashdot090221.html
[10] http://slashdot.org/
[11] In word sense disambiguation, the number of query nodes is 2.2 on average as described in Section 1.

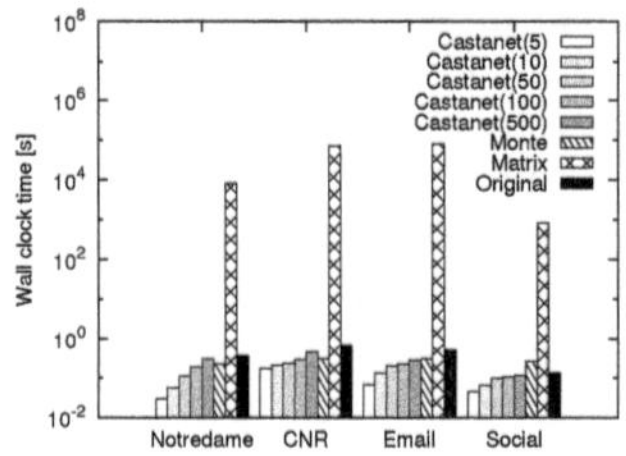

Figure 1: Search time of each approach.

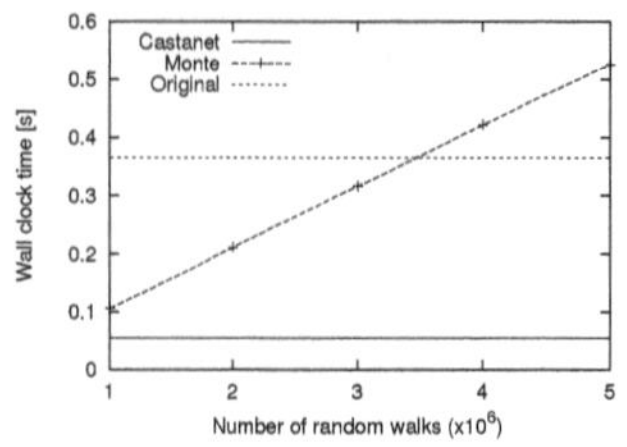

Figure 2: Efficiency versus number of random walks.

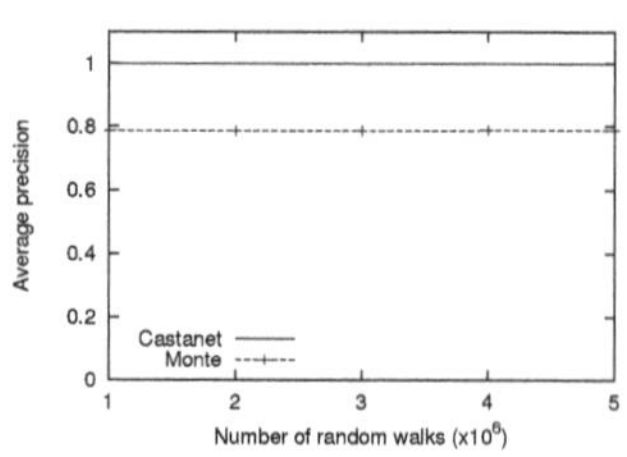

Figure 3: Accuracy versus number of random walks.

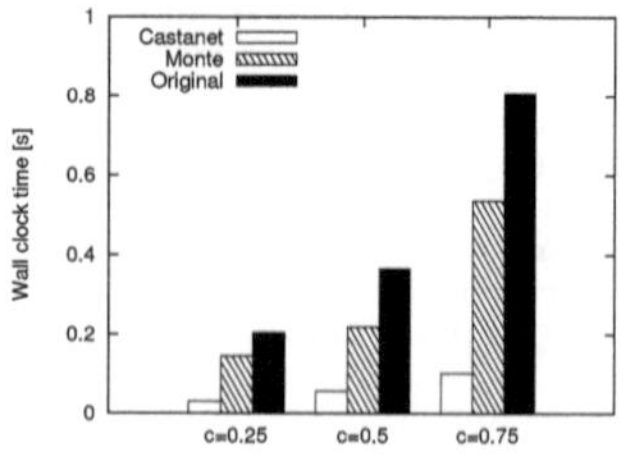

Figure 4: Efficiency versus the scaling parameters.

Table 2: Score of each parameter.

Parameter	Dataset			
	Notredame	CNR	Email	Social
N	3.25×10^5	3.25×10^5	2.65×10^5	8.21×10^4
l	2.29×10^4	2.13×10^4	2.27×10^4	7.92×10^3
n	5.12×10^4	7.01×10^4	5.98×10^4	2.88×10^4
M	1.49×10^6	3.21×10^6	4.20×10^5	5.49×10^5
m	7.30×10^4	5.70×10^5	9.76×10^4	2.17×10^5
T	30.8	32.8	56.0	28.0
t	15.5	24.3	15.7	13.1

Table 3: Breakdown of search time.

Approach	Search time [ms]		
	Precomputation	Top-k search	Overall
Castanet	–	5.52	5.52
Monte	–	21.8	21.8
Matrix	8.16×10^5	5.60×10^{-3}	8.16×10^5
Original	–	36.5	36.5

5.1 Efficiency of Castanet

We evaluated the search time of each approach. Figure 1 shows the results. In this figure, the results of the proposed approach are indicated by "Castanet(k)" where k is the number of answer nodes. We set the scaling parameter, c, to 0.5 and the number of random walks in the Monte Carlo-based approach to $2,500,000$. The impacts of the scaling parameter and the number of random walks are evaluated in later sections. Note that the number of answer nodes has, in the previous approaches, practically no impact on the search time. This is because (1) the similarities of all nodes must be computed to obtain similar nodes in the Monte Carlo-based and the original iterative approaches, and (2) precomputation time is dominant in the search time for the matrix-based approach. Table 2 details the parameters in Castanet and the original iterative approaches where $c = 0.5$ and $k = 10$. Table 3 shows the breakdown in the search time of each approach for Notredame where $c = 0.5$ and $k = 10$.

As shown in Figure 1, our approach is much faster than the original iterative approach. For example, our approach can cut the search time from the original iterative approach by up to 90% and 75% for Notredame and CNR, respectively. Note that Notredame and CNR have almost the same number of nodes. The result indicates that efficiency of our approach strengthens with the large effective diameter. The effective diameter is the 90-th percentile of shortest path length distribution [24]. Notredame and CNR have effective diameters of 9.3 and 5.6, respectively. If a graph has large effective diameter, the number of hops in the reachable node set is expected to be large. Therefore, the size of the node set $\mathbb{H}_i$ in the i-th iteration is likely to be small. As shown in Definition 6, the subgraph in the i-th iteration is obtained from the node set $\mathbb{H}_i$. Thus, the size of subgraphs is small for a large effective diameter graph as shown in Table 2, which yields the efficiency of our approach.

The result of Email and Social in Figure 1 indicates that our approach more efficiently find top-k nodes than the original iterative approach as graph size increases. These two graphs have effective diameter of 4.5 and 4.7, respectively; they are almost the same. As shown in Figure 1, our approach can cut the search time by up to 85% and 65% for Email and Social, respectively. This is because, if the given graph has large size, the sizes of subgraphs become relatively small compared to the whole graph.

Figure 1 also indicates that Castanet enhances the efficiency as the number of answer nodes k decreases. This is because the node sets $\mathbb{H}_i$ and $\mathbb{R}_i$ in Definition 6 have small size for small values of k. As shown in this figure, if $k = 500$, the Monte Carlo-based approach can be more efficient than our approach. However, this does not decrease the efficacy of our approach for the applications listed in Section 1. This is because k is typically much smaller than 500. For example, $k = 5$ in web prefetching and automatic image annotation [17, 30] as described in Section 1. Furthermore, the Monte Carlo-based approach does not find the top-k nodes exactly since it is an approximation approach. In addition, our approach is more efficient than the matrix-based approach under all conditions examined. This is because the precomputation time in the matrix-based approach is significantly high even though the top-k search time is small for other approaches as shown in Table 3. As a result, Castanet has superior search performance to the previous approaches.

5.2 Node ranking exactness

One major advantage of Castanet is that it guarantees the exactness of node ranking while the Monte Carlo-based approach does not. Since, as described in Section 2, the Monte Carlo-based approach approximates the similarity of a node by the total number of visits to the node via the random walks, the number of random walks is expected to impact the search time and approximation accuracy for the Monte Carlo-based approach. Therefore, we conducted comparative experiments using various numbers of random walks. Figure 2 and Figure 3 show the search time and the accuracy of each approach for Notredame, respectively, where $c = 0.5$ and $k = 10$. In Figure 3, we used average precision as the metric of accuracy; it is widely used to measure the accuracy of ranking models (see [7] for the definition of average precision.). Average precision outputs values between 0 and 1. Average precision is high as the ranking by Castanet or the Monte Carlo-based approach is similar to that by the original iterative approach; if average precision is 1, the ranking by Castanet or the Monte Carlo-based approach equals to that of the original iterative approach.

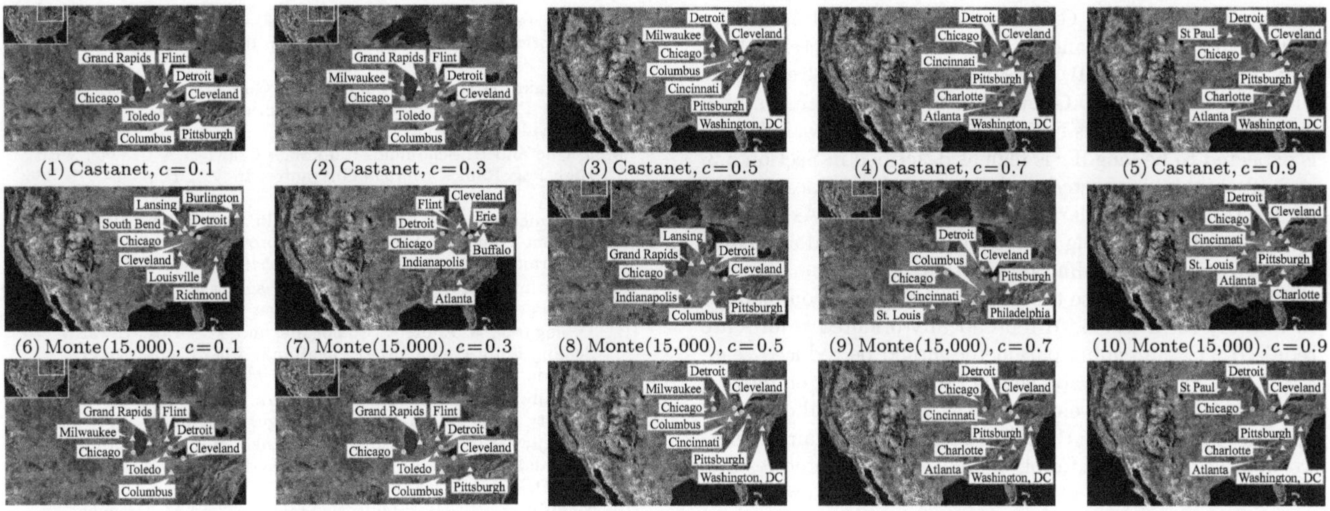

(1) Castanet, $c=0.1$ (2) Castanet, $c=0.3$ (3) Castanet, $c=0.5$ (4) Castanet, $c=0.7$ (5) Castanet, $c=0.9$

(6) Monte(15,000), $c=0.1$ (7) Monte(15,000), $c=0.3$ (8) Monte(15,000), $c=0.5$ (9) Monte(15,000), $c=0.7$ (10) Monte(15,000), $c=0.9$

(11) Monte(500,000), $c=0.1$ (12) Monte(500,000), $c=0.3$ (13) Monte(500,000), $c=0.5$ (14) Monte(500,000), $c=0.7$ (15) Monte(500,000), $c=0.9$

Figure 5: High similarity cities for Chicago, Detroit, and Cleveland as detected by each approach.

As shown in Figure 2, the Monte Carlo-based approach takes more computation time as the number of random walks increases. If the number of random walks is not properly set (e.g., 4,000,000 or 5,000,000), the Monte Carlo-based approach takes more computation time than the original iterative approach. Figure 3 shows that the average precision of Castanet is 1 since it finds top-k nodes with exact node ranking (Theorem 1). On the other hand, the Monte Carlo-based approach has lower average precision. Figure 2 and Figure 3 confirm that our approach is superior to the Monte Carlo-based approach in both speed and accuracy.

5.3 Flexibility to the scaling parameter

As mentioned in Section 1, interactive similarity search is important in real applications. Our approach can handle arbitrarily set the scaling parameters since it does not need precomputation as described in Section 4.4. To confirm this benefit, we evaluated the search time of each approach using the various scaling parameters. Figure 4 shows the results. In these experiments, we set $k = 10$ and used Notredame as the dataset. We omitted the results of the matrix-based approach since Figure 1 shows that the approach has significantly high search time than other approaches.

As shown in Figure 4, decreasing the score of the scaling parameter raises the efficiency of each approach in finding the answer nodes. This is explained below. Our approach updates the set of nodes subjected to lower/upper estimation in the each iteration. As shown in Equation (11), the upper estimation is obtained by adding $c^{i+1}W_{max}[u]\ p_i[\mathbb{R}_i]$ to the lower estimation. Therefore, if c is low, the upper estimation is expected to have a low score; this implies that we can more accurately compute the upper estimation if c is assigned a low score. As described in Section 2 , to obtain approximate similarities, the Monte Carlo-based approach computes random walks where probability c is used to select an outgoing edge from a current node at every step. This indicates that the random walk length is expected to be long if c is high. The computation time of the original iterative approach increases with the score of the scaling parameter, because the number of iterations required by the approach increases as c approaches to 1 as described in [23]. However, our approach can more efficiently find the answer nodes than the previous approaches; this implies that the proposed approach effectively supports interactive similarity search where the scaling parameter is set in ad-hoc style.

Table 4: Search time of each approach.

Approach	Search time [ms]				
	$c=0.1$	$c=0.3$	$c=0.5$	$c=0.7$	$c=0.9$
Castanet	1.18	2.02	3.27	5.76	8.78
Monte(15,000)	1.21	2.36	4.52	8.94	29.6
Monte(500,000)	33.8	79.0	149.5	296.6	986.5

6. CASE-STUDIES

To enhance the quality of applications, it is important to iteratively find the top-k nodes for an arbitrary graph in an ad-hoc manner. Our approach allows users to adjust the scaling parameter for a given graph on the fly. To validate our approach, we conducted case-studies on a real dataset using the various scaling parameters.

We used the city dataset[12] consisting of 71,959 direct flights between 456 cities in North America. Flights and cities correspond to edges and nodes, respectively. Edge weights are proportional to city proximities in terms of flight times. We detected five cities with high similarity, for Chicago, Detroit, and Cleveland, these three cities surround the Great Lakes. The preference scores were set to the same value. Figure 5 shows the results of our approach and the Monte Carlo-based approach. In these plots, circles and triangles represent query cities and high similarity cities, respectively. Note that our approach output the same results as the matrix-based approach and the original iterative approach, so we omit the results of these two approaches due to space limitations. Table 4 shows the search time of each approach. For the Monte Carlo-based approach, the number of random walks was set to 15,000 and 500,000. The results of these settings are referred as "Monte(15,000)" and "Monte(500,000)" in Figure 5 and Table 4.

If $c = 0.1$, our approach identified Pittsburgh, Columbus, Toledo, Flint, and Grand Rapids as high similarity cities. All these cities are also from around the Great Lakes. Since PPR computes random walks from the query nodes, major

[12] http://www.psi.toronto.edu/index.php?q=affinity propagation

cities surrounding the Great Lakes are detected as the results. On the other hand, if the scaling parameter is high (e.g., $c = 0.7$ or $c = 0.9$), cities distant from the Great Lakes such as Washington, D.C. or Atlanta were detected as high similarity cities. This is because (1) the random walk length is expected to be long if c is high as described in Section 5.3, and (2) highly connected nodes from other nodes are expected to be high similarity nodes in PPR [20]. As a result, large cities that have big airline hubs are detected as answer nodes for the large scaling parameters.

These results indicate that a user should be recommended to initially set c to 0.5. If more locally-oriented results are required, (1) the scaling parameter should be reduced (e.g., $c = 0.1$), and (2) the graph should be modified by employing locally-oriented edge weights such as geographical distances instead of flight times. Using road network, not airline network, is also preferable for obtaining locally-oriented results. If the user wants to extract large cities, the large scaling parameters are recommended where edge weighs are set in proportion to the number of passengers, which increases the edge weights to large cities. Since Castanet can efficiently find top-k nodes for an arbitrarily given graph with the flexible scaling parameter setting, it can support such interactive actions of the user to enhance application efficacy.

However, as shown in Figure 5, the results of the Monte Carlo-based approach are different from those of Castanet if the number of random walks is $15,000$; the results of the Monte approach contain many improper cities even though the Monte Carlo-based approach and Castanet have almost the same search time with this setting as shown in Table 4. If the number of random walks is increased to $500,000$, the Monte Carlo-based approach has the almost same results as Castanet as shown in Figure 5. However, this leads to high search times as shown in Table 4 since the search cost of the Monte Carlo-based approach is proportional to the number of random walks as described in Section 5.2.

7. CONCLUSIONS

We addressed the problems of efficiently finding the top-k nodes for PPR. Our solution, Castanet, is designed to support interactive similarity search and based on the idea to use lower/upper estimations and prune unnecessary nodes in the iterations. The experimental results show that our approach can achieve high efficiency while ensuring that the answer results offer exact node ranking. PPR is fundamental in many applications. Our approach allows many applications to be implemented more efficiently, and helps to improve the effectiveness of future applications.

8. REFERENCES

[1] E. Agirre and A. Soroa. Personalizing PageRank for Word Sense Disambiguation. In *EACL*, pages 33–41, 2009.

[2] K. Avrachenkov, N. Litvak, D. Nemirovsky, E. Smirnova, and M. Sokol. Quick Detection of Top-k Personalized PageRank Lists. In *WAW*, pages 50–61, 2011.

[3] B. Bahmani, K. Chakrabarti, and D. Xin. Fast Personalized PageRank on MapReduce. In *SIGMOD Conference*, pages 973–984, 2011.

[4] B. Bahmani, A. Chowdhury, and A. Goel. Fast Incremental and Personalized PageRank. *PVLDB*, 4(3):173–184, 2010.

[5] A. Balmin, V. Hristidis, and Y. Papakonstantinou. ObjectRank: Authority-based Deyword Search in Databases. In *VLDB*, pages 564–575, 2004.

[6] S. M. Beitzel, E. C. Jensen, A. Chowdhury, D. A. Grossman, and O. Frieder. Hourly Analysis of a Very Sarge Topically Categorized Web Query Log. In *SIGIR*, pages 321–328, 2004.

[7] B. Carterette, J. Allan, and R. K. Sitaraman. Minimal Test Collections for Retrieval Evaluation. In *SIGIR*, pages 268–275, 2006.

[8] S. Chakrabarti, A. Pathak, and M. Gupta. Index Design and Query Processing for Graph Conductance Search. *VLDB J.*, 20(3):445–470, 2011.

[9] J. Cho and U. Schonfeld. RankMass Crawler: A Crawler with High PageRank Coverage Guarantee. In *VLDB*, pages 375–386, 2007.

[10] J. Domènech, J. A. Gil, J. Sahuquillo, and A. Pont. Using Current Web Page Structure to Improve Prefetching Performance. *Computer Networks*, 54(9):1404–1417, 2010.

[11] M. Eirinaki and M. Vazirgiannis. Usage-based PageRank for Web Personalization. In *ICDM*, pages 130–137, 2005.

[12] D. Fogaras, B. Rácz, K. Csalogány, and T. Sarlós. Towards Scaling Fully Personalized PageRank: Algorithms, Lower Bounds, and Experiments. *Internet Mathematics*, 2(3), 2005.

[13] Y. Fujiwara, G. Irie, and T. Kitahara. Fast Algorithm for Affinity Propagation. In *IJCAI*, pages 2238–2243, 2011.

[14] Y. Fujiwara, M. Nakatsuji, M. Onizuka, and M. Kitsuregawa. Fast and Exact Top-k Search for Random Walk With Restart. *PVLDB*, 5(5):442–453, 2012.

[15] Y. Fujiwara, M. Nakatsuji, H. Shiokawa, and M. Onizuka. Efficient Search Algorithm for SimRank. In *ICDE*, 2013.

[16] Y. Fujiwara, M. Nakatsuji, T. Yamamuro, H. Shiokawa, and M. Onizuka. Efficient Personalized PageRank with Accuracy Assurance. In *KDD*, 2012.

[17] Y. Z. Guo, K. Ramamohanarao, and L. A. F. Park. Personalized PageRank for Web Page Prediction Based on Access Time-length and Frequency. In *Web Intelligence*, pages 687–690, 2007.

[18] M. S. Gupta, A. Pathak, and S. Chakrabarti. Fast Algorithms for Top-k Personalized PageRank Queries. In *WWW*, pages 1225–1226, 2008.

[19] D. A. Harville. *Matrix Algebra From a Statistician's Perspective*. Springer, 2008.

[20] G. Jeh and J. Widom. Scaling Ppersonalized Web Search. In *WWW*, pages 271–279, 2003.

[21] R. Jin, N. Ruan, S. Dey, and J. X. Yu. SCARAB: Scaling Reachability Computation on Large Graphs. In *SIGMOD Conference*, pages 169–180, 2012.

[22] U. Kang, D. H. Chau, and C. Faloutsos. Mining Large Graphs: Algorithms, Inference, and Discoveries. In *ICDE*, pages 243–254, 2011.

[23] A. N. Langville and C. D. Meyer. *Google's PageRank and Beyond: The Science of Search Engine Rankings*. Princeton University Press, 2006.

[24] J. Leskovec, J. M. Kleinberg, and C. Faloutsos. Graphs over Time: Densification Laws, Shrinking Diameters and Possible Explanations. In *KDD*, pages 177–187, 2005.

[25] R. Mihalcea. Unsupervised Large-vocabulary Word Sense Disambiguation with Graph-based Algorithms for Sequence Data Labeling. In *HLT/EMNLP*, 2005.

[26] M. Nakatsuji, Y. Fujiwara, T. Uchiyama, and K. Fujimura. User Similarity from Linked Taxonomies: Subjective Assessments of Items. In *IJCAI*, pages 2305–2311, 2011.

[27] M. Nakatsuji, Y. Fujiwara, T. Uchiyama, and H. Toda. Collaborative Filtering by Analyzing Dynamic User Interests Modeled by Taxonomy. In *ISWC*, pages 361–377, 2012.

[28] R. Navigli. Word Sense Disambiguation: A Survey. *ACM Comput. Surv.*, 41(2), 2009.

[29] L. Page, S. Brin, R. Motwani, and T. Winograd. The PageRank Citation Ranking: Bringing Order to the Web. Technical Report 1999-66, Stanford InfoLab, November 1999.

[30] J.-Y. Pan, H.-J. Yang, C. Faloutsos, and P. Duygulu. Automatic Multimedia Cross-modal Correlation Discovery. In *KDD*, pages 653–658, 2004.

[31] B. C. Russell, A. Torralba, K. P. Murphy, and W. T. Freeman. LabelMe: A Database and Web-based Tool for Image Annotation. *International Journal of Computer Vision*, 77(1-3):157–173, 2008.

[32] H. Shiokawa, Y. Fujiwara, and M. Onizuka. Fast Algorithm for Modularity-based Graph Clustering. In *AAAI*, 2013.

[33] H. Tong, C. Faloutsos, and J.-Y. Pan. Fast Random Walk with Restart and Its Applications. In *ICDM*, pages 613–622, 2006.

[34] D. Zhou, O. Bousquet, T. N. Lal, J. Weston, and B. Schölkopf. Learning with Local and Global Consistency. In *NIPS*, 2003.

Provenance-based Dictionary Refinement in Information Extraction

Sudeepa Roy*
University of Washington
sudeepa@cs.washington.edu

Laura Chiticariu
IBM Research-Almaden
chiti@us.ibm.com

Vitaly Feldman
IBM Research-Almaden
vitaly@post.harvard.edu

Frederick R. Reiss
IBM Research-Almaden
frreiss@us.ibm.com

Huaiyu Zhu
IBM Research-Almaden
huaiyu@us.ibm.com

ABSTRACT

Dictionaries of terms and phrases (e.g. common person or organization names) are integral to information extraction systems that extract structured information from unstructured text. Using noisy or unrefined dictionaries may lead to many incorrect results even when highly precise and sophisticated extraction rules are used. In general, the results of the system are dependent on dictionary entries in arbitrary complex ways, and removal of a set of entries can remove both correct and incorrect results. Further, any such refinement critically requires laborious *manual labeling* of the results.

In this paper, we study the *dictionary refinement problem* and address the above challenges. Using *provenance* of the outputs in terms of the dictionary entries, we formalize an optimization problem of maximizing the quality of the system with respect to the refined dictionaries, study complexity of this problem, and give efficient algorithms. We also propose solutions to address incomplete labeling of the results where we estimate the missing labels assuming a statistical model. We conclude with a detailed experimental evaluation using several real-world extractors and competition datasets to validate our solutions. Beyond information extraction, our provenance-based techniques and solutions may find applications in view-maintenance in general relational settings.

Categories and Subject Descriptors

H.0 [**Information Systems**]: General; I.7.m [**Document and Text Processing**]: Miscellaneous

Keywords

Information Extraction; Refinement; Provenance; Optimization

1. INTRODUCTION

Information Extraction, the problem of extracting structured information from unstructured text, is an essential component of many important applications including business intelligence, social media analytics, semantic search and regulatory compliance. The success of these applications is tightly connected with the quality of the extracted results, as incorrect or missing results may often render the application useless. Most information extraction systems use a set of *rules*, a number of *dictionaries* of terms and phrases (also known as *gazetteers* or *lists*) along with other basic features like *syntactic features* (*e.g.* regular expressions) and *morphological features* (*e.g.* part of speech) to identify common patterns in text; these are subsequently used to extract *entities* (*e.g.* Person, Organization, Location) and *relations* between entities (*e.g.* Person's birth date or phone number) from the text.

Developing and maintaining high-quality entity or relation extractors is an extremely laborious process. Typically, a developer starts by collecting an initial set of features and developing an initial set of rules. She then executes the extractor on a document collection, labels some of the results as *correct* (or, a *true positive*) and *incorrect* (or, a *false positive*), examines the causes of incorrect results, and refines the extractor in order to remove these incorrect results. This process is repeated until the developer is satisfied with the quality of the extractor. In this paper, we investigate in detail one of the most important parts of this process, that of *refining dictionaries* by suggesting to the human supervisor of the system a list of entries whose removal from the dictionaries will remove many false positives in the output without removing too many true positives. The supervisor may then decide to either: (1) delete these dictionary entries altogether, or (2) list them as ambiguous entries and move them to other dictionaries, or (3) update the rules in order to handle these entries appropriately.

Dictionaries are integral to information extraction systems [10, 9, 22]. For example, a Person extractor would make use of dictionaries of complete names (*e.g.* names of famous persons), as well as dictionaries of common first names and last names, and dictionaries of common titles (*e.g.* "Mr.", "Esq."). More sophisticated Person extractors may use a larger collection of more fine-grained dictionaries to improve accuracy (*e.g.* a dictionary of common first names that are also the names of major U.S. corporations). Dictionaries are even more relevant in the context of today's informal data sources (*e.g.* social media), which do not obey the constraints of formal language: syntactic features such as capitalization and punctuation are rarely present, and classic part of speech analyzers trained on formal text such as TreeBank have low accuracy [27].

Although many dictionaries are readily available from public or commercial sources, (*e.g.* the U.S. Census Bureau [1] provides extensive lists of first and last names, while [2] provides lists of locations containing millions of entries with detailed geographical information), inherent ambiguity in language prevents such exhaus-

*This work was done while the author was at the University of Pennsylvania and IBM Research-Almaden.

SIGMOD'13, June 22–27, 2013, New York, New York, USA.

tive dictionaries from being consumed directly, as they would lead to many false positives. Instead, these dictionaries require curation before they can be used effectively in an extractor, and the extent of the curation depends on the application, domain and language. For example, it has been observed that an extensive dictionary of location names is useful, whereas an extensive dictionary of person/organization names is not that effective [30, 21]. Dictionary entries are often collected from noisy sources [24, 31], or, generated automatically by a previous step of information extraction [33, 22]. One may frequently encounter in dictionaries of person names ambiguous entries such as "San", "Francisco", "Hong", "Kong", "April", "Costa" that mostly produce false positives. These entries must be either removed or treated differently in order to improve the quality of the system.

In addition to refining noisy dictionaries, it is important to derive dictionaries with high precision tailored to a particular domain of interest by refining more general dictionaries. For instance, there may be inherent overlap between dictionaries for different entities ("Chelsea" is a common first name, but also the name of a famous football club; "Victoria" or "Washington" can be a location or a person). While including "Chelsea" in a dictionary of names may work well in general, when the system is customized to process a corpus of sports news articles, we need to add a rule that can disambiguate "Chelsea". For example, the supervisor may decide to remove "Chelsea" from the dictionary of first names, and at the same time add "Chelsea" to a new dictionary of ambiguous names, along with a new rule that marks occurrences of ambiguous names as candidate persons only if another strong contextual (e.g., a title) clue is present in the nearby text. However, prior to adding the new rule, one must first determine the ambiguous entries in the dictionary. In practice, the decision whether to refine dictionaries or to add more sophisticated rules to directly handle all possible scenarios is usually carefully drawn on a case by case basis, by considering not only the overall improvement in accuracy, but also the ease of maintainability of the resulting extractor. Maintaining complex rules in general is a labor intensive process requiring expertise in the system's rule language. Building high precision dictionaries, especially for domain-specific applications, provides a low-overhead option requiring little or no knowledge of the system, and helps create, maintain and update extractor rules to further improve the quality of the system [26, 9, 17, 28].

To refine a dictionary, the system's supervisor would wish to examine a list of entries whose removal would lead to a significant improvement of the system by removing many false positives. This raises two technical challenges. *First*, a realistic extractor usually uses a number of dictionaries that are combined via complex rules. An output is determined by alternative or joint uses of multiple dictionary entries, and their arbitrary combinations. Therefore, when an entry is removed, some of the correct and incorrect results it has produced may get deleted and some may be retained depending on the other entries being removed. We need to consider the actual connection between dictionary entries and output results while refining the dictionaries. *Second, labeling* the outputs of extractors (as true and false positives) is a laborious task requiring substantial human effort. In addition, dictionaries frequently contain thousands of entries, therefore information about individual entries is sparse even when a large amount of labeled data is available. Nevertheless, one should ensure that the refined dictionaries perform well with respect to unlabeled data.

Our contribution. We systematically study the dictionary refinement problem in this paper. Note that in a Person extractor, if the entry "Chelsea" produces 15 true positives and 15 false positives, while "April" produces only 1 true positive and 5 false positives, it is not obvious which of these two entries should be removed first. Therefore, to balance the requirements of extraction *precision* (minimize false positives) and *recall* (avoid discarding correct answers), we maximize the standard objective of **F-score** (the harmonic mean of precision and recall) [38]. We study this maximization problem under two natural constraints that a human supervisor is likely to use: a limit on the number of dictionary entries to remove (*size constraints*), and the maximum allowable decrease in recall (*recall constraints*). The complex connection between dictionary entries and output results is captured using *provenance* of the results in terms of the entries as a boolean expression (which we call *provenance polynomials*) [19]. These polynomials are used to find the results that are deleted when a set of entries is removed.

To handle incomplete labeling of the results, we divide the dictionary refinement problem into two sub-problems: (a) *Label estimation* estimates the "fractional" labels of the unlabeled results assuming a statistical model for the labels. (b) *Refinement optimization* takes the (exact or estimated) labels of the results as input, and outputs a set of dictionary entries to remove in order to maximize the resulting F-score under size or recall constraint.

1. For **label estimation**, we give a method based on the well-known *Expectation - Maximization* (EM) algorithm [14]. Under our statistical model, we show that there is a closed-form expression for the update rules in EM for our application which can be efficiently evaluated.

2. To understand the complexity of the **refinement optimization** problem, we start with an important special case, called *single argument rules* (or, *simple rules*), where a *unique* dictionary entry is responsible for producing each output result. Then we move on to the case of general *multiple arguments rules* (or, *complex rules*). Besides serving as a stepping stone for complex rules, the case of simple rules has several practical applications including the initial refinement of a noisy dictionary generated from various sources, and the curation of specialized high-precision dictionaries (such as lists of organizations in healthcare and banking).

   The complex objective function of maximizing the F-score makes the refinement optimization step non-trivial even for simple rules, and even when the entire set of results is labeled. However, we give a poly-time optimal algorithm for simple rules under size constraints. The problem becomes NP-hard under recall constraints even for simple rules. Nevertheless, we show that an efficient near-optimal algorithm exists. In addition, we show that the estimated labels reduce to empirical estimates for simple rules, and therefore the label estimation step can be skipped in this case. For complex rules, the optimization problem is NP-hard even under size constraints and we propose efficient heuristics.

3. We conduct an extensive set of **experiments** on several real-world information extraction rulesets and competition datasets that validate the effectiveness of our techniques. The complexity of the extractor rules varies from one rule (for the simple rule case) to a highly refined extractor using over 400 rules (for the complex rule case). This demonstrates that our techniques are useful for both doing the initial refinement of a noisy dictionary and also to further improve the quality of an extractor that uses a sophisticated rule set.

Beyond information extraction, our approach has applicability in **view maintenance in general relational settings**. Our model and theoretical results can be used to refine erroneous source tuples in order to reduce the number of false positives in the output view without removing too many true positives (see Section 2).

Roadmap. We start with related work and preliminaries (Sections 2 and 3), and formalize the dictionary refinement problem in Section 4. Sections 5 and 6 present our technical contributions on estimation of labels for unlabeled results, and respectively, refinement optimization for simple and complex rules. We discuss our experimental results in Section 7 and conclude with directions for future work in Section 8.

2. RELATED WORK

Previous work on entity extraction from lists on the web (*e.g.* [15]), open information extraction (*e.g.* [4, 39]) and dictionary learning (*e.g.* [33]) addresses the problem of creating new dictionaries of terms from unstructured or semi-structured data sources by exploiting contextual patterns or the structure of web pages. Our work is complementary to these approaches, and can be used to further refine such automatically generated dictionaries. Our work is also orthogonal to *Named Entity Disambiguation* techniques (*e.g.* [20]), which, given an external catalog of entities, aim to associate an extracted named entity with an actual entity in the catalog. The goal of our techniques for complex rules is to find out entries that produce many false positives during the extraction process, so that the human supervisor can either remove them or update the rules. Our techniques are applicable not only to Named Entity Recognition tasks, but also other common tasks such as relationship or sentiment extraction; furthermore, they can be applied when the application cannot make use of an external catalog, for example due to license limitations or when speed of execution is critical.

Approaches for refining rule-based information extraction programs have been recently proposed in [34, 7, 26]. Shen et al. [34] propose an approach for refining rules by posing a series of template questions to the user, where each question asks for additional information about a specific (predefined) feature of the desired extracted data, whereas Chai et al. [7] allow users to update any (incorrect) intermediate result derived by the system and proposes techniques for incorporating these updates during program execution. In contrast, we develop techniques to automatically compute a (small) set of dictionary entries, therefore allowing the user to focus on a (small) set of base tuples whose removal results in highest quality improvements for the extractor. Liu et al. [26] proposed a provenance-based framework for refining information extraction rules. They showed how to use provenance to compute *high-level changes*, a specific intermediate result whose removal from the output of an operator causes the removal of a false positive from the result, and how multiple high-level changes can be realized via a *low-level change*: a concrete change to the operator that removes one or more intermediate results from the output of the operator. In this paper, we do rigorous theoretical analysis of one specific and important type of low-level change, that of refining dictionaries used in an extractor, especially in the presence of incomplete labeled data, which is an aspect not considered in [26].

Also related are recent studies on *causality* [29] and *deletion propagation* [6, 23] in general relational setting. In [29], the input consists of source tuples, an output boolean vector and a ground truth boolean vector, and the goal is to compute the *responsibility* of every source tuple using modifications such that the output is identical to the ground truth. In other words, the modifications should remove all incorrect results, while keeping all correct results. On the other hand, [6, 23] study the problem of deleting an incorrect answer tuple of an SPJU query while minimizing the *view-side-effect*, i.e. the number of other answer tuples deleted. We consider extractors consisting essentially of SPJU queries, where

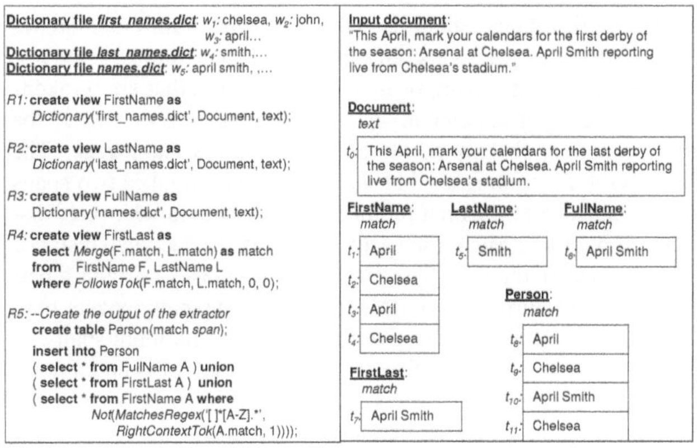

Figure 1: Example extraction program, input document D, and view instances created by the extraction program on D.

dictionary entries correspond to source tuples and extraction results correspond to outputs. As such, our work can be seen as an alternative objective for these related problems that tries to balance between the number of incorrect tuples retained and the number of correct tuples deleted. To the best of our knowledge, ours is the first formal study of dictionary refinement for information extraction with a well-defined objective of maximizing the F-score.

3. PRELIMINARIES

We illustrate the main components of a rule-based information extraction system in Figure 1 using a simplified Person extractor. An information extraction system typically consists of a set of *rules* (R_1 to R_5), and a set of *dictionaries* ("first_names.dict", "last_names.dict" and "names.dict"). Given one or a set of *input documents* (often called a *corpus*), such a system extracts the entities or relations specified in the *extractor* (view instance *Person* in Figure 1). In practice, the extractors are much more complex; one of the extractors used in our experiments uses more than 400 rules.

Rule Language. We use the *select-project-join-union* (SPJU) subset of SQL enriched with a number of basic extraction primitives to express information extraction rules[1]. This subset expresses a core set of functionality underlying most rule languages in common use today [5, 12, 25, 32, 35], and therefore our work can be easily applied to other rule languages. Specifically, we augment SQL with the following basic information extraction primitives. To model data values extracted from the input document we add a new atomic data type called *span*. A *span* is an ordered pair $\langle begin, end\rangle$ that identifies the region of an input document between the *begin* and *end* offsets. The input document is modeled as a table called Document with a single attribute of type *span* named *text*. We also add several predicates, scalar functions, and table functions to SQL's standard set of built-in functions as discussed below.

Example Rules. The program in Figure 1 consists of five rules labeled R_1 through R_5. Rules R_1 to R_4 define logical views, while R_5 materializes a table of extraction results. Rules R_1, R_2 and R_3 illustrate one of our text extraction additions to SQL: the *Dictionary* table function, which identifies all occurrences of a given set of terms specified as entries in a dictionary file. The dictionary files used in R_1 to R_3 contain a list of common first names, a list of common last names, and respectively a list of common full names. The three rules define three single-column views *FirstName*, *LastName* and *FullName* containing one intermediate tuple for each dictionary match in the document. We use w_i to denote dictionary entries

[1]The complex extractor used in our experiments also contains set difference operator (SQL minus) which we discuss in Section 7.1.

in order to distinguish them from their (possibly multiple) matches in a document (*e.g.* w_1 generates the intermediate tuples t_2 and t_4).

Rule R_4 identifies pairs of first and last names that are 0 tokens apart in the input document. The view definition uses two of the scalar functions that we add to SQL: *FollowsTok* and *Merge*. The *FollowsTok* function is used as a join predicate: it takes two spans as arguments, along with a minimum and maximum character distance, and returns *true* if the spans are within the specified distance of each other in the text. The *Merge* function takes as input a pair of spans and returns the shortest span that completely covers both input spans. (*Merge* is sensitive to the order of its input spans: if the second span appears before the first, the result of is undefined.) The *select* clause of R_4 uses *Merge* to define a span that extends from the beginning of each first name to the end of the last name.

Finally, rule R_5 materializes the table Person, which constitutes the output of our extractor. It uses a *union* clause to union together candidate name spans identified by rules R_3 and R_4, as well as candidates identified by R_1 that are not immediately followed by a capitalized word. Note the *where* clause of the last union operand of R_5 which uses two other additions to SQL: the *RightContextTok* function returns the span of a given length measured in tokens to the right of the input span, while the *MatchesRegex* predicate returns true if the text of the input span matches the given regular expression. In this case, the regular expression `'[ ]*[A-Z].*'` identifies a sequence of zero or more whitespaces, followed by an uppercase letter, followed by zero or more occurrences of any character.

Provenance of results in terms of dictionary entries. Following the existing work on data provenance, we assume a canonical algebraic representation of extraction rules as trees of operators. For the *select-from-where-union* subset of the language, the canonical representation is essentially the same as the representation of corresponding SQL statements in terms of relational operators σ, π, $\bowtie$ and $\cup$. When an extraction function such as *Dictionary* appears in the *from* clause of a *select* statement, we translate these table functions to operators by the same names.

The canonical rule representation enables us to express the *provenance* (or *lineage*) of extraction results. Provenance for database queries has been intensely studied in recent years (see, *e.g.* [8]). In this work, we use the notion of *how-provenance* to represent how an extraction result has been generated by the rules. Specifically, using the semiring framework of [19] we can encode the how-provenance of an output tuple t, denoted as $\texttt{Prv}(t)$, that describes how that output tuple has been derived from source or intermediate tuples using joins (multiplication $\cdot$) and union (addition $+$) operations; *e.g.* $\texttt{Prv}(t_{10}) = t_6 + t_7 = t_6 + t_3 \cdot t_5$, since $\texttt{Prv}(t_7) = t_3 \cdot t_5$. We call $\texttt{Prv}(t)$ the as *provenance polynomial* of t. We regard individual dictionary entries as the source of intermediate tuples generated by the *Dictionary* operator and express the provenance of an output tuple directly in terms of the entries that are responsible for generating that tuple. Since $\texttt{Prv}(t_3) = w_3$, $\texttt{Prv}(t_5) = w_4$ and $\texttt{Prv}(t_6) = w_5$, we have that $\texttt{Prv}(t_{10}) = w_5 + w_3 \cdot w_4$.

Simple and Complex Rules. To understand the complexity of the dictionary refinement problem, we classify the input extractors as (1) *single argument rules* (or, *simple rules*), and (2) *multiple arguments rules* (or, *complex rules*). Simple rules contain a single *Dictionary* table function (or *Dictionaries* for multiple dictionaries), whereas the extractor for complex rules can consist of a number of arbitrary rules involving one or more dictionaries (like the example in Figure 1). An example of a simple rule is

```
create view Person as
Dictionaries('name_USA.dict',
'name_German.dict', Document, text);
```

Here a *unique* dictionary entry is responsible for producing each output result and the provenance polynomial of a result tuple t is simply of the form $\texttt{Prv}(t) = w$. Besides being a fundamental special case for complex rules, the case of simple rules is of independent interest. Our solution for simple rules may be useful in initially refining manually or automatically generated dictionaries that can be used as basic features not only in rule-based, but also statistical (machine learning) information extraction systems. Other applications include the curation of specialized high-precision dictionaries (such as lists of organizations in healthcare and banking) and to create and refine complex extractor rules.

Precision, Recall and F-score. We now explain the standard measures for evaluating an extractor's quality, given a labeled dataset containing expected results for the extraction. With respect to the labeled dataset, an extracted result is either *a true positive* (correct) or a *false positive* (incorrect). The *precision*, or accuracy of the extractor is defined as the fraction of true positives among the total number of extracted results. An extractor with high precision outputs very few false positives. An expected mention that is not identified by the extractor is called a *missing result* (false negative). The *recall*, or coverage of the extractor is defined as the fraction of true positives among the total number of expected results. An extractor with high recall misses very few expected results. Finally, the standard *F-score*, also known as F_1*-score* or *F-measure* [38], combines precision and recall into a single measure computed as the harmonic mean of precision and recall $(2PR/(P+R))$.

4. DICTIONARY REFINEMENT PROBLEM

Let E be an extractor and let A be the set of all dictionary entries used by E (union of all dictionary). Given a set of documents $\mathbb{D}$, E produces a set of results, some of which are true positives (Good) and some are false positives (Bad). When a set of entries $S \subseteq A$ is removed from A, it results in another extractor E', which on the same set of documents $\mathbb{D}$ will produce a subset of the earlier results. Let $\bar{S} = A \setminus S$. Then the precision $P_{\bar{S}}$ and recall $R_{\bar{S}}$ of E' are:

$$P_{\bar{S}} = \frac{\text{No. of Good results with } \bar{S}}{\text{No. of Good results} + \text{No. of Bad results (with } \bar{S})} \quad (1)$$

$$R_{\bar{S}} = \frac{\text{No. of Good results with } \bar{S}}{\text{No. of Good results with } A} \quad (2)$$

It is not hard to see that the recall of E' will be at most that of E (i.e. 1), whereas the precision and therefore the F-score of E' can be more or less than that of E depending on the set S. For instance, in the output Person table of Figure 1, all results except "April Smith" are Bad, therefore the initial precision, recall and F-scores are $\frac{1}{4}, 1$ and $\frac{2}{5}$ respectively. If the entry w_1 = "Chelsea" is removed from the dictionary *first_names.dict*, the recall will remain the same, whereas the precision and F-score will improve to $\frac{1}{2}$ and $\frac{2}{3}$ respectively. The goal of the *dictionary refinement problem* is to compute a subset S whose removal results in an extractor E' having the maximum value of the F-score on $\mathbb{D}$.

4.1 Estimating Labels of Results for Incomplete Labeling

Even computing the F-score of an extractor requires knowing labels (Good/Bad) on the entire set of results, while often only a small fraction of the results is labeled. One possible approach is to ignore the unlabeled results altogether and try to maximize the F-score using the labeled results alone. But this may lead to overfitting and the solution may not work well for the entire result set. Estimating the labels empirically is a natural choice for simple rules (where each result is uniquely determined by an entry). However, the number of possible results may be very large for complex rules, and very few or zero labels are likely to be available for each result. This makes empirical estimates expensive as well as difficult. In Section 5, we propose a statistical model and give algorithms to estimate missing labels in the dataset.

4.2 Formal Problem Definition

We are given b dictionaries $A_1, \ldots, A_b$ and let n denote the total number of entries in $A = \cup_{\ell=1}^{b} A_\ell$. A result τ is produced by matches of one or more dictionary entries combined by the rules in the extractor; all such dictionary entries w are said to be in *provenance* of τ. How the entries produce τ is captured by the provenance polynomial $\texttt{Prv}(\tau)$ of τ (see Section 3); for all such entries w we say that $w \in \texttt{Prv}(\tau)$. Here every entry in A is treated as a unique boolean variable, and $\texttt{Prv}(\tau)$ is a boolean expression on these variables.

For simple rules, every result τ produced by an entry w has $\texttt{Prv}(\tau) = w$; when w is deleted exactly those results get deleted. However, for complex rules, some results τ such that $w \in \texttt{Prv}(\tau)$ can disappear when w is deleted, while some results may survive. In Figure 1, when w_3 = "april" is deleted, the result t_8 = "April" gets deleted, but t_{10} = "April Smith" survives (although $w_3 \in \texttt{Prv}(t_{10}) = w_5 + w_3 \cdot w_4$). This illustrates the following observation:

OBSERVATION 1. *When $S \subseteq A$ is removed, a result τ disappears from the result set if and only if its provenance polynomial* $\texttt{Prv}(\tau)$ *evaluates to* FALSE *by an assignment of* FALSE *(resp.* TRUE*) value to the variables corresponding to the entries in S (resp. $A \setminus S$).*

Let $\texttt{surv}(S)$ denote the set of results that survive when a set of entries S is deleted. For example, given three results τ_1, τ_2, τ_3 with provenance polynomials $uv, u+v, uw+uv$ respectively, when $S = \{u\}$ is deleted, the set $\texttt{surv}(S)$ will only contain τ_2. Let $\phi(\tau)$ denote the *label* for a result τ. When the entire result set is labeled, $\phi(\tau) = 1$ if τ is `Good`, and, = 0 if τ is `Bad`. Then rewriting (1) and (2), the "residual" precision ($P_{\bar{S}}$), recall ($R_{\bar{S}}$) and their harmonic mean F-score ($F_{\bar{S}}$) when S is deleted respectively are

$$P_{\bar{S}} = \frac{\sum_{\tau \in \texttt{surv}(S)} \phi(\tau)}{|\texttt{surv}(S)|}, \quad R_{\bar{S}} = \frac{\sum_{\tau \in \texttt{surv}(S)} \phi(\tau)}{\sum_{\tau} \phi(\tau)},$$

$$F_{\bar{S}} = \frac{2\sum_{\tau \in \texttt{surv}(S)} \phi(\tau)}{|\texttt{surv}(S)| + \sum_{\tau} \phi(\tau)} \quad (3)$$

For incomplete labeling, we extend the above definitions by allowing *fractional labels* $\phi(\tau)$, which intuitively denote the confidence that the label of the result is `Good`.

The refinement of an extractor is commonly done with human supervision. The supervisor may prefer to examine a small number of entries at a time, or may want to ensure that not too many original true positives are removed by the refinement. Therefore, we maximize the F-score under (1) **Size constraint:** Given an integer $k \leq n$, find a subset S, that maximizes $F_{\bar{S}}$, where $|S| \leq k$; and (2) **Recall constraint:** Given a fraction $\rho \leq 1$, find a subset S, that maximizes $F_{\bar{S}}$, where the residual recall $R_{\bar{S}} \geq \rho$. We study these optimization problems in Section 6. Note that both numerator and the denominator of $F_{\bar{S}}$ depend on the set S being removed, which makes the optimization and analysis non-trivial even for simple rules.

5. ESTIMATING LABELS

In this section we discuss our statistical data model and algorithms to estimate the missing labels.

5.1 The Statistical Model

A possible approach to estimate the missing labels is to group together the results with equal provenance (equivalent boolean expressions), and then estimate the labels empirically. The problem with this approach is that it is expensive, and it is likely that very few (if any) labels will be available for each result since the possible number of such expressions may be very large. At the same time it is quite likely that the correctness of individual entries will be similar across results with different provenance expressions. For example, the candidate last name ""Island"[2] can produce more than one `Bad` results like "Victoria Island" and "Baffin Island", and "Island" is a `Bad` *match*[3] as a last name in both results.

We represent this intuition by defining the model in the following way. We assume that each entry w has a fixed (and unknown) *entry-precision* p_w. For any given result τ such that $w \in \texttt{Prv}(\tau)$, the *match* of w for τ is correct with probability p_w and incorrect with probability $1 - p_w$ independent of the other results and other entries in $\texttt{Prv}(\tau)$. Further, we assume that the rules are correct, *i.e.* the label of τ is `Good` if and only if $\texttt{Prv}(\tau)$ evaluates to 1 given the correctness of the matches of individual entries (`Good` $\equiv 1$ and `Bad` $\equiv 0$). Next we discuss how we estimate the labels from the estimated entry-precisions, followed by our EM-based algorithm to estimate the entry-precisions from the available labeled data.

5.2 Estimating Labels from Entry-Precisions

Under our statistical model, the label $\phi(\tau)$ of a result τ can be estimated by evaluating the probability of its provenance $\texttt{Prv}(\tau)$, given p_w-s for all $w \in \texttt{Prv}(\tau)$. Computing the probability of a boolean expression ϕ given the probabilities of its constituent variables is in general *#P-hard* [37]; the classes of relational algebra queries for which the probability can be efficiently computed have been extensively studied (*e.g.*, see [13]). However, the provenance of the results involve a small number of variables (typically ≤ 10). So we compute $\phi(\tau)$ given p_w-s by an exhaustive enumeration.

5.3 Estimating Entry-Precisions by EM

Here we estimate the entry-precisions p_w given a set of results τ along with their provenance $\texttt{Prv}(\tau)$ and labels. We use the *EM (Expectation-Maximization)* algorithm to solve this problem. The EM algorithm [14] is a widely-used technique for the maximum likelihood estimation of parameters of a probabilistic model with hidden variables. It estimates the parameters iteratively either for a given number of steps or until some convergence criteria are met.

First, we introduce some notation to present the update rules of EM in terms of our problem. We index the entries arbitrarily as $w_1, \cdots, w_n$. Each entry w_i has an entry-precision $p_i = p_{w_i}$. There are N labeled results $\tau_1, \cdots, \tau_N$. We assume that $\tau_1, \cdots, \tau_N$ also denote the labels of the results $\phi(\tau_1), \cdots, \phi(\tau_N)$, so each τ_i is boolean, where $\tau_i = 1$ (resp. 0) if the label is `Good` (resp. `Bad`). If $w_i \in \texttt{Prv}(\tau_j)$, we say that $\tau_j \in \texttt{Succ}(w_i)$. For simplicity of notation, we assume that exactly b dictionary entries are involved in the expression $\phi_j = \texttt{Prv}(\tau_j)$ for each result τ_j; our implementation works for general cases. Hence each ϕ_j takes b inputs $y_{j1}, \cdots, y_{jb}$ and produces τ_j. Each $y_{j\ell}$ is boolean, where $y_{j\ell} = 1$ (resp. 0) if the match of dictionary entry corresponding to $y_{j\ell}$ is correct (resp. incorrect) while producing the label for τ_j. The entry corresponding to $y_{j\ell}$ will be denoted by $\texttt{Prv}_{j\ell} \in \{w_1, \cdots, w_n\}$.

To illustrate the notation, consider the *"firstname-lastname"* rule R_4 in Figure 1: the result is a person if it is a match from the dictionary *first_names.dict*, followed by a match from *last_name.dict*. In this example, $b = 2$ and for every result τ_j, $\tau_j = \phi_j(y_{j1}, y_{j2}) = y_{j1}y_{j2}$. For a `Good` result "April Smith", $\tau_j = 1, y_{j1} = 1$ (for "April"), and $y_{j2} = 1$ (for "Smith"), $\texttt{Prv}_{j1}$ = "April" and $\texttt{Prv}_{j2}$ = "Smith".

[2]"Island" is a last name (ref. *http://names.whitepages.com/last /island, http://www.surnamedb.com/Surname/Island*) in USA.

[3]A match is the tuple in the intermediate relation extracted by the Dictionary operator.

For a $\texttt{Bad}$ result "Victoria Island", $\tau_j = 0$, $y_{j1} = 1$ (for "Victoria"), and $y_{j2} = 0$ (for "Island").

Parameters and hidden variables for EM. For our problem, the vector of labels of the results $\vec{x} = \langle \tau_1, \cdots, \tau_N \rangle$ are the *observed variables*, the vector of vectors for the correctness of matches of individual entries for these results $\vec{\vec{y}} = \langle y_{j\ell} \rangle_{j \in [1,N], \ell \in [1,b]}$ are the *hidden variables*, and the vector of entry-precisions $\vec{\theta} = \{p_1, \cdots, p_n\}$ is the vector of unknown *parameters*.

Update rules for EM. Let $\vec{\theta}^t$ be the parameter vector at iteration t. The log-likelihood of the observed variables is $q(\vec{x}; \vec{\theta}) = \log P(\vec{x}|\vec{\theta}) = \sum_{j=1}^{N} \log P(\tau_i|\vec{\theta})$. The complete information for the problem includes the observed variables $\vec{x} = \langle \tau_1, \cdots, \tau_N \rangle$ as well as the hidden variables $\vec{\vec{y}} = \langle y_{j\ell} \rangle_{j \in [1,N], \ell \in [1,b]}$. The expected log-likelihood of the complete information given the observed variables $\vec{x}$ and current parameter vector $\vec{\theta}^t$ is $\mathbb{E}[q(\vec{x}, \vec{\vec{y}}; \vec{\theta})|\vec{x}, \vec{\theta}^t] = K$ (say). In the **E-step**, we compute the value of K in terms of p_i, $i \in [1,n]$, by using the current value of the parameters $\vec{\theta}^t$ In the **M-step**, we maximize K w.r.t. parameter vector $\vec{\theta}$, by differentiating K w.r.t. each p_i and equating $\delta K / \delta p_i$ to zero, to get the next guess of the parameters $\vec{\theta}^{t+1}$. We show that this gives a closed-form expression for each p_i which can be efficiently computed in each iteration of EM. The complete derivation is given in Appendix B.

Estimation for simple rules. Here we prove a simplifying observation which will be used in the next section:

OBSERVATION 2. *For simple rules, the entry-precision of an entry estimated by EM reduces to its empirical entry-precision. Further, EM converges in a single step.*

For simple rules, $\texttt{Prv}(\tau) = w$, where the result τ is a result of an entry w. (*i.e.* $b = 1$). Fix an arbitrary result τ_j, $j \in [1,N]$, and *the unique* entry w_i such that $\texttt{Prv}_{j,1} = w_i$. Then, at any time step t and for any values of the parameters $\vec{\theta}^t$, $c_{w_i,\tau_j,t} = \mathbb{E}[y_{j1}|\tau_j, \vec{\theta}^t] = \tau_j$. In other words, when the label of a result is given, whether or not the corresponding entry is a correct match for this result can be exactly inferred from the label of the result. Hence, the entry-precision p_i for any entry w_i is $p_i = \frac{C_1}{C_1 + C_2} = \frac{\sum c_{w_i,\tau_j,t}}{\sum c_{w_i,\tau_j,t} + \sum (1 - c_{w_i,\tau_j,t})}$ (the sums are over all τ_j such that $\tau_j \in \texttt{Succ}(w_i)) = \frac{\sum \tau_j}{\sum \tau_j + \sum (1 - \tau_j)}$ which equals the fraction of $\texttt{Good}$ results produces by w_i, *i.e.* the empirical entry-precision of w_i. Further, the EM algorithm will converge in a single step since this estimate is independent of the time-step t, and therefore label-estimation can be omitted altogether.

6. REFINEMENT OPTIMIZATION

Next we discuss the problem of maximizing the residual F-score for simple and complex rules (resp. Sections 6.1 and 6.2). This step takes the provenance polynomial and the (possibly fractional) label of all results as input, and outputs a set of entries to be deleted.

6.1 Simple Rules

The following observation simplifies the expressions of precision, recall, and F-score for simple rules.

OBSERVATION 3. *For simple rules, a result $\tau \in \texttt{surv}(S)$ if and only if the entry $w \notin S$ where $w = \texttt{Prv}(\tau)$.*

Let us denote the *frequency* of an entry w (*i.e.*, the number of results τ such that $\texttt{Prv}(\tau) = w$) by f_w. Then $|\texttt{surv}(S)| = \sum_{w \notin S} f_w$, and using Observation 2, $\sum_{\tau \in \texttt{surv}(S)} \phi(\tau) = \sum_{w \notin S} \sum_{\tau : w = \texttt{Prv}(\tau)} \phi(\tau) = \sum_{w \notin S} p_w f_w$. Here p_w is the (estimated) entry-precision of w.[4] Therefore, the expressions for $P_{\bar{S}}, R_{\bar{S}}, F_{\bar{S}}$ given in (3) reduce to:

$$P_{\bar{S}} = \frac{\sum_{w \notin S} p_w f_w}{\sum_{w \notin S} f_w},\; R_{\bar{S}} = \frac{\sum_{w \notin S} p_w f_w}{\sum_{w \in A} p_w f_w},\; F_{\bar{S}} = 2\frac{\sum_{w \notin S} p_w f_w}{\sum_{w \in A} p_w f_w + \sum_{w \notin S} f_w}$$

In Section 6.1.1, we give an optimal and efficient algorithm to maximize the F-score under size constraints. For recall constraints, in Section 6.1.2 we show that the exact optimization is NP-hard. However, we give a simple and efficient algorithm that is provably nearly optimal and works well in our tests.

Algorithm 1 Algorithm for size constraints (given k and Δ)

1: – Let $\theta_{low} = F_A$ and $\theta_{high} = 1$
2: **while** $\theta_{high} - \theta_{low} > \Delta$ **do**
3: Let $\theta = (\theta_{high} + \theta_{low})/2$ be the current guess.
4: Sort the entries w in descending order of $f_w(\theta - 2p_w)$.
5: Let S be the top $\ell \leq k$ entries in the sorted order such that $f_w(\theta - 2p_w) \geq 0$ for all $w \in S$.
6: **if** $\sum_{w \in S}[f_w(\theta - 2p_w)] \geq \sum_{w \in A} f_w(\theta - (2 - \theta)p_w)$ **then**
7: θ is feasible, set $\theta_{low} = F_{\bar{S}}$ and continue.
8: **else**
9: θ is not feasible, set $\theta_{high} = \theta$ and continue.
10: **end if**
11: **end while**
12: Output the set S used to define the most recent θ_{low}.

6.1.1 Size Constraints

Our goal is to maximize $F_{\bar{S}} = 2\frac{\sum_{w \notin S} p_w f_w}{\sum_{w \in A} p_w f_w + \sum_{w \notin S} f_w}$, where $|S| \leq k$. The main idea of our algorithm is that finding out whether there exists a dictionary with F-score of at least θ is a significantly simpler problem which overcomes the non-linearity of the objective function [16]. Accordingly, our algorithm *guesses* a value θ and then checks if θ is a feasible F-score for some S. The value of θ that maximizes $F_{\bar{S}}$ is then found via a binary search.

Checking if θ is a feasible F-score. We need to check whether there is a set S of entries such that $F_{\bar{S}} = 2\frac{\sum_{w \in A} p_w f_w - \sum_{w \in S} p_w f_w}{\sum_{w \in A} p_w f_w + \sum_{w \in A} f_w - \sum_{w \in S} f_w} \geq \theta$, *i.e.*, we need to find out whether there exists S such that

$$\sum_{w \in S} f_w(\theta - 2p_w) \geq \sum_{w \in A} f_w(\theta - (2 - \theta)p_w)$$

The right hand side of the inequality is independent of S, so it suffices to select the top-most (at most) k entries with non-negative value of $f_w(\theta - 2p_w)$ and check if the sum is at least $\sum_{w \in A} f_w(\theta - (2 - \theta)p_w)$. Clearly we want a subset S such that $F_{\bar{S}} \geq F_A$. Hence the guess θ is varied between F_A and 1. Algorithm 1 presents this idea in terms of an accuracy parameter Δ; the value of Δ for the optimal F-score will be discussed later.

Running time. There is an $O(n)$-time algorithm for the feasibility step 6: (i) Use the standard linear time selection algorithm to find the k-th highest entry, say u, according to $f_w(\theta - 2p_w)$, (ii) do a linear scan to choose the entries w such that $f_w(\theta - 2p_w) > f_u(\theta - 2p_u)$, and choose entries such that $f_w(\theta - 2p_w) = f_u(\theta - 2p_u)$ to get k entries in total, (iii) discard the selected entries with negative values of $f_w(\theta - 2p_w)$ and output the remaining $\leq k$ entries. However, we can have simpler implementations of the verification step - using a min-heap gives $O(n + k\log n)$ time, and a simple sorting gives $O(n \log n)$ time. Since values of the guesses are between 0 and 1, and the algorithm stops when the upper and lower bounds are less than Δ away, at most $\log(1/\Delta)$ steps will be required. Hence there is an implementation that runs in time $O(n\log(1/\Delta))$.

[4]For unlabeled results τ-s such that $\texttt{Prv}(\tau) = w$, estimated label $\phi(\tau) = p_w$. For the labeled results, the fraction having label 1 ($\texttt{Good}$) is p_w.

Value of Δ for optimal F-score. Let B be the number of bits to represent each p_w (fraction), f_w (integer) in the input. Consider any $F_{\overline{S}} = 2\frac{\sum_{w \notin S} p_w f_w}{\sum_{w \in A} p_w f_w + \sum_{w \notin S} f_w}$. B-bit numbers between 0 and 1 can represent values $t.2^{-B}$, for $0 \le t \le 2^B - 1$. Multiply both numerator and denominator of $F_{\overline{S}}$ by 2^B to get integer values in the numerator and denominator. Each of $p_w f_w$ and f_w in the denominator is $\le 2^{2B}$ after this multiplication, and there are at most $2n$ of them. The denominator of the fraction representing difference between two unequal F-score values is $\le n2^{2B+1}$, whereas the numerator of the fraction is ≥ 1. Hence the difference is $\ge \frac{1}{(n2^{2B+1})^2}$, and setting $\Delta = \frac{1}{(n2^{2B+1})^2}$ suffices. This leads to the following theorem:

THEOREM 1. *For simple rules, there is a poly-time optimal algorithm to maximize the F-score under size constraint. The algorithm runs in time $O(n \cdot (\log n + B))$, where B is the number of bits used to represent each p_w and f_w given to the algorithm.*

A natural question that may arise is whether selecting entries greedily (select the next entry that gives the maximum improvement in F-score and repeat for k steps) also gives an optimal solution. We give an example in Appendix A to show that greedy is not optimal.

6.1.2 Recall Constraints

First, we sketch the proof of NP-hardness. Then we give the near-optimal algorithm.

NP-hardness for exact optimization. We give a reduction from the *subset-sum problem* which is known to be NP-hard [18]. In the subset-sum problem the input is a set of positive integers $I = \{x_1, \cdots, x_n\}$[5], and an integer C, and the goal is to decide if there is a subset $S \subseteq I$ such that $\sum_{x_i \in S} x_i = C$.

Our reduction creates an instance of the refinement problem in which every number in the subset-sum instance corresponds to an entry with fixed and low entry-precision and frequency proportional to the number. In addition, we create a single word with high entry-precision. This word ensures that the highest F-score is achieved when the total frequency of the removed low precision words is the highest. Therefore, the maximum F-score can be achieved only when the recall budget is used exactly. The complete reduction is given in Appendix A.

Nearly Optimal Algorithm. We now describe a simple and efficient algorithm that gives a nearly optimal solution when used on a large corpus where frequencies of individual entries are small. Our algorithm sorts the entries in the increasing order of entry-precisions p_w, and selects entries according to this order until the recall budget is exhausted or there is no improvement of F-score by selecting the next entry (the pseudocode of the algorithm is straightforward and is omitted). Clearly the algorithm runs in time $O(n \log n)$. Formally, we prove the following theorem that gives a lower bound on the F-score of the solution.

THEOREM 2. *Let $w_1, \cdots, w_n$ be the entries sorted by the corresponding entry-precisions $p_1 \le \cdots \le p_n$ (here $p_i = p_{w_i}$). Let S^* be the set of entries whose removal gives the optimal F-score and $R_{\bar{S}^*} \ge \rho$. Let $r^* = \sum_{i \in \bar{S}^*} p_i f_i$ and let ℓ be the largest index for which $\sum_{i > \ell} p_i f_i \ge r^*$. Then the set S returned by our algorithm satisfies*

$$F_{\bar{S}} \ge \frac{2\sum_{i \in \bar{S}^*} p_i f_i}{\sum_{i \in \bar{S}^*} f_i + \sum_i p_i f_i + f_{max}/p_{\ell+1}}.$$

PROOF. Let $p_i = p_{w_i}$ and $f_i = f_{w_i}$, where $p_1 \le \cdots \le p_n$. Let $f_{max} = \max\{f_1, \ldots, f_n\}$, $S^i = \{w_j : 1 \le j \le i\}$ and $\overline{S} = A \setminus S$. Let $r^\ell = \sum_{i \in \overline{S^\ell}} p_i f_i = \sum_{i > \ell} p_i f_i$. By definition, $r^* + f_{max} \ge r^\ell \ge r^*$. Note that recall $R_{\overline{S^\ell}} = r^\ell / \sum_i p_i f_i \ge r^* / \sum_i p_i f_i = R_{\overline{S^*}} \ge \rho$. Due to the monotonicity check, the algorithm returns a solution with F-score $\ge F_{\overline{S^\ell}}$. Hence we give a lower bound on $P_{\overline{S^\ell}}$.

Observe that: (1) $\sum_{i \in \overline{S^\ell} \setminus \overline{S^*}} p_i f_i - \sum_{i \in \overline{S^*} \setminus \overline{S^\ell}} p_i f_i = \sum_{i \in \overline{S^\ell}} p_i f_i - \sum_{i \in \overline{S^*}} p_i f_i \le f_{max}$, and, (2) $\sum_{i \in \overline{S^\ell} \setminus \overline{S^*}} f_i \le \frac{\sum_{i \in \overline{S^\ell} \setminus \overline{S^*}} p_i f_i}{p_{\ell+1}} \le \frac{(\sum_{i \in \overline{S^*} \setminus \overline{S^\ell}} p_i f_i + f_{max})}{p_{\ell+1}} \le \sum_{i \in \overline{S^*} \setminus \overline{S^\ell}} f_i + \frac{f_{max}}{p_{\ell+1}}$. From (1), (2): $\sum_{i \in \overline{S^\ell}} f_i \le \sum_{i \in \overline{S^*}} f_i + \frac{f_{max}}{p_{\ell+1}}$. Hence $P_{\overline{S^\ell}} = \frac{r^\ell}{\sum_{i \in \overline{S^\ell}} f_i} \ge \frac{r^*}{\sum_{i \in \overline{S^*}} f_i + f_{max}/p_{\ell+1}}$, and, $F_{\overline{S^\ell}} = \frac{2}{1/R_{\overline{S^\ell}} + 1/P_{\overline{S^\ell}}} \ge \frac{2}{1/R_{\overline{S^*}} + 1/P_{\overline{S^\ell}}} \ge \frac{2\sum_{i \in \overline{S^*}} p_i f_i}{\sum_{i \in \overline{S^*}} f_i + \sum_i p_i f_i + \frac{f_{max}}{p_{\ell+1}}}$ □

Note that the lower bound guaranteed by the algorithm differs from the optimal F-score $F_{\bar{S}^*}$ only by the addition of the error term $\frac{f_{max}}{p_{\ell+1}}$ to the denominator. Individual frequencies are likely to be small when the given corpus and the dictionary are large. At the same time ℓ and hence $p_{\ell+1}$ are determined solely by the recall budget. Therefore the error term $\frac{f_{max}}{p_{\ell+1}}$ is likely to be much smaller than the denominator for a large dictionary. Our experiments support this argument. Another surprising property of this algorithm is that while it is not necessarily optimal in general, without the recall budget (*i.e.* $\rho = 0$), it finds the globally optimal solution; we defer the proof to the full version of the paper due to lack of space. Naturally, the slightly more involved Algorithm 1 with $k = n$ also gives the optimal solution for $\rho = 0$.

6.2 Complex Rules

The optimization problems become substantially harder for complex rules. In Section 6.2.1, we show that even for a complex rule as simple as "firstname-lastname" (rule R_4 in Figure 1) the optimization problem for size constraint is NP-hard. Further, the problem is NP-hard even when the independence and rule correctness assumptions we make in our statistical model hold. Note that this problem was shown to be poly-time solvable for simple rules. The case of recall constraint has already been shown to be NP-hard even for simple rules. Then in Section 6.2.2 we discuss efficient algorithms that we evaluate experimentally.

6.2.1 NP-hardness for Size Constraint

We give a reduction from the *k'-densest subgraph problem in bipartite graphs* [11]. Here the inputs are a bipartite graph $H(U,V,E)$ with n' vertices and m' edges, and an integer $k' < n'$. The goal is to select a subset of vertices $W \subseteq U \cup V$, $|W| = k'$, such that the subgraph induced on W has the maximum number of edges. We will denote the set of edges in the *induced subgraph* on W (every edge in the subgraph has both its endpoints in W) by $E(W)$.

For simplicity, first we prove a weaker claim: removing a subset S with *exactly* k (as opposed to *at most* k) vertices is NP-hard. Intuitively, the vertices correspond to entries and the edges correspond to results. We show that if the induced subgraph on a subset of vertices of size k' has a large number of edges, then removing entries in the *complement* of this subset gives high F-score.

Given an instance of the k'-densest subgraph problem, we create an instance of the dictionary refinement problem as follows. The vertices in U and V respectively correspond to the entries in the firstname and lastname dictionaries. Every edge $(u,v) \in E$ corresponds to a unique provenance expression $\phi_{u,v} = uv$, where the entries u and v are chosen from these two dictionaries respectively. For each $(u,v) \in E$, there is one result with label 1 (`Good`), and one with label 0 (`Bad`). The parameter k in the dictionary refinement problem is $k = n' - k'$. It is not hard to see that there is a subset $W \subseteq U \cup V$, such that $|W| = k'$ and $E(W) \ge q$ if and only if there is

[5]The subset-sum problem is NP-hard even for positive integers.

a subset S for the dictionary refinement problem such that $|S| = k$ and $F_{\bar{S}} \geq \frac{2}{\frac{m'}{q}+2}$ (proof is deferred to the full version).

The residual precision in the above reduction is a constant for all choices of S, and therefore, the F-score is a monotone function of the residual recall. Hence the above reduction does not work for the relaxed constraint $|S| \leq k$ (the residual recall is always maximized at $S = \emptyset$, i.e. when $k = 0$, independent of the k'-densest subgraph solution). Below we sketch the reduction for $|S| \leq k$, the complete reduction is deferred to the full version due to space constraint.

Outline of reduction for $|S| \leq k$. To strengthen the above reduction for $|S| \leq k$, we retain the graph with a good and a bad result for every edge as before. In addition, we add $s = mn$ `Good` results that are unrelated to anything; they will make the differences in the recall between solutions tiny (while preserving monotonicity in the size of $E(W)$). For every original entry $u \in U \cup V$, we add s `Bad` results (u, u^i) $1 \leq i \leq s$ connected to it. The entries $\bigcup_{u \in U \cup V}\{u_i : 1 \leq i \leq s\}$ are called auxiliary-bad entries. This way the precision will be roughly equal to $\frac{1}{n-k}$ (since these results dominate the total count) and hence solutions with smaller number of entries removed will have noticeably lower precision. Removing any of the auxiliary bad entries will have a tiny effect, so any optimal solution will always remove the entries corresponding to graph vertices $U \cup V$. Finally, it is easy to observe that labels for results that we create in this reduction can be obtained by assuming independent entry-precisions for all the dictionary entries created in the reduction. This proves the following theorem:

THEOREM 3. *For complex rules, maximizing the F-score under size constraint is NP-hard even for the firstname-lastname rule (i.e., the rule R_4 in Figure 1), and even when the entry-precisions satisfy independence.*

6.2.2 Refinement Algorithms

Since the dictionary refinement problem is NP-hard for complex rules under both size and recall constraints, we propose and evaluate efficient algorithms that work well in practice. These algorithms take the (actual or estimated) label and the provenance of each result as input, and produce a subset of entries to remove across all dictionaries.

Some natural and simple approaches that we examine for *size constraint* are (1) choosing (at most) top-k entries in decreasing order of *the fraction of* `Bad` *results* or *the number of* `Bad` *results* they produce, ignoring the actual provenance polynomials, and (2) greedily choosing (at most) k entries that give the maximum improvement in the F-score. Note that the implementation of these algorithms involves repeated computation of the `surv`(S) sets after each entry is included to S by evaluating the provenance polynomials of all results.

In addition, we improve the solution obtained by each of these algorithms by performing a *hill climbing* algorithm from the solution returned by the algorithm to find a local maximum. Here two solutions (set of entries to be deleted) S_1, S_2 are considered to be neighbors if S_2 can be obtained from S_1 by replacing an entry $w_1 \in S_1$ with a new entry $w_2 \notin S_1$. We iteratively choose the neighbor that gives the maximum improvement ΔF in the F-score. The algorithm stops if there is no more change in the set S of entries being removed, or a specified maximum number of iterations allowed is reached. The pseudocode for the generic hill-climbing algorithm is given in Algorithm 2.

For *recall constraint*, we use the same approach. However, while doing the local search using hill climbing, we maximize $\Delta F / \Delta R$ at each step (ΔR denotes the change in recall by deleting one additional entry), since we are trying to maximize F while still satisfying $R \geq \rho$ for a given recall budget ρ. These algorithms are empirically evaluated in Section 7.2.2.

Algorithm 2 Generic hill-climbing Algorithm for complex rules, size constraint (given maximum number of iterations *MAX*)

– Find an initial solution (an array) S.
while S changes and the no. of iterations is $\leq MAX$ **do**
  for each position i in S **do**
    Let $w = S[i]$, and let f be the current F-score
    for each entry $w' \notin S$ **do**
      Compute the new fscore $f_{w,w'}$ using $S \setminus \{w\} \cup \{w'\}$.
    end for
    Let $w_m = argmax_{w'} f_{w,w'}$.
    If $f_{w,w*} > f$, $S[i] = w_m$. Otherwise S is unchanged.
  end for
end while
Output the set S.

7. EXPERIMENTS

Now we present our experimental results. We discuss the datasets and extractors used in our experiments in Section 7.1. In Section 7.2, we evaluate the refinement algorithms on fully labeled datasets and compare their performance and efficiency; this supplements the theoretical results derived earlier. We evaluate our label estimation approach on partially labeled datasets in Section 7.3.

Experimental Settings. We used SystemT v1.0.0 [25, 32], enhanced with a framework to support provenance of the results [26]. The rules are specified in AQL (Annotation Query Language), which is the rule language of SystemT. All experiments were implemented in Java with JDK 6.0, and run on a 64-bit Windows 7 machine with Intel(R) Core^{TM} i7-2600 processor (4 GB RAM, 3.40 GHz).

7.1 Evaluation Datasets and Extractors

We used two labeled datasets in our experiments: CoNLL2003 (*CONLL* in short, with 945 documents) and ACE2005 (*ACE* in short, with 342 documents)[6]; both these datasets are frequently used in official Named Entity Recognition competitions [3, 36].

Each dataset contains *occurrences* identified by "(document id, begin offset, end offset)", and tagged with the corresponding entity name (Person, Location, Organization, etc.). Given an extractor, a result is `Good` (true positive) if it belongs to the set of occurrences for the corresponding entity, otherwise it is `Bad` (false positive).

We primarily considered two extractors to evaluate the cases of *simple rules* (provenance polynomials comprises a single variable) and *complex rules* (arbitrary provenance polynomials): (1) For simple rules a Person extractor is used, which comprises a single AQL rule (see Section 3) and a single dictionary "name.dict" containing contains both first and last names (12992 entries in total); (2) For complex rules, we use an Organization extractor which is part of a generic Named Entity Extractor for Person, Location and Organization ([9]). This extractor uses a variety of (over 400) rules and more than 120 dictionaries curated from public data sources such as the US Census Bureau (Census, 2007) and Wikipedia. There are dictionaries for common first and last names from different countries, salutation and suffixes for person names, different locations (cities, states, countries, etc.), industries and organizations (medical, gov-

[6]We do not consider larger labeled datasets because these are usually difficult to obtain in practice. However, we do show that the quality of the results output by the algorithm improves as more labeled data is available.

ernment, education, etc.), months and days and so on. In particular to extract Organization entities, it generates candidate mentions using dictionaries of full organization names, rules that combine syntactic features (capitalized tokens) with dictionaries of clues including industry suffixes (*e.g.*,"Technologies") or company suffixes ("Co.", "Ltd."), as well as complex filtering rules to disambiguate across different types of named entities.

Handling set-difference operation in the extractor. In practical extractors, including the complex extractor used in our experiments, *set-difference* operators (like SQL MINUS) are typically unavoidable. For instance, the extractor may output a person name if it appears in a dictionary of common names, and it does not appear in the dictionary of common organization names. In general, the extractor may output a tuple t if it appears in an intermediate view R_1 (as another tuple t_1) and does not appear in another view R_2. However, note that if t is output, there is no tuple t_2 in R_2, so it is not possible to write $\mathtt{Prv}(t)$ as $\mathtt{Prv}(t_1) \cdot \neg \mathtt{Prv}(t_2)$. In this case we store $\mathtt{Prv}(t) = \mathtt{Prv}(t_1)$ [26]. This approach is always sound (removing t_1 does remove t), and it is not hard to see that it is complete as well as long as there is no nested set-difference operations (in that case both $\mathtt{Prv}(t_1), \mathtt{Prv}(t_2)$ are monotone and the only way to remove a result t by deleting entries is by removing t_1). For nested difference operations, t_2 may appear (and as a result t disappears) if some entries are removed. However, to handle this we need to repeatedly run the complex extractor in our algorithms which is not a scalable approach. Therefore, we use $\mathtt{Prv}(t) = \mathtt{Prv}(t_1)$ (which are monotone boolean expressions) and our algorithms operate with these provenance polynomials as inputs.

Here we present results for the simple person extractor on the CONLL dataset (simple rule case), and the organization extractor from the sophisticated annotator mentioned above on ACE (complex rule case); results with other combinations of extractors and datasets are similar and are omitted for space limitations.

7.2 Dictionary Refinement with Full Labeling

Here we evaluate the algorithms proposed in Section 6 for simple and complex rules, both in terms of the resulting F-score after refinement and running time of the algorithms. In all experiments, we report F-score calculated by evaluating the new extractor (identical to the original extractor, but with suggested dictionary entries removed) against the labeled dataset.

7.2.1 Refinement Algorithms for Simple Rules

For both size and recall constraints, we compare our algorithms (Sections 6.1.1 and 6.1.2) with the greedy algorithms proposed for complex rules (Section 6.2.2) and two other natural approaches. The algorithms compared for **size constraint** are (see Figure 2 (i)): (1) *K-Optimal*: Algorithm 1 with $\Delta = 0.001$, (2) *K-Greedy*: the greedy algorithm for complex rules – the entry giving the maximum increment in F-score (*i.e.* ΔF) is selected next, (3) *K-BadFraction*: chooses the top-k entries in the decreasing order of the *fraction* of `Bad` results, (4) *K-BadCount*: chooses the top-k entries in the decreasing order of the *number* of `Bad` results.

The algorithms compared for **recall constraint** are (see Figure 2 (ii)): (1) *RecBudget-Near-Opt*: the near-optimal algorithm that selects entries in the decreasing order of the fraction of `Bad` results (see Section 6.1.2), (2) *RecBudget-Greedy-FR*: the greedy algorithm for complex rules that maximizes the incremental improvement in F-score relative to the decrease in recall (*i.e.* $\Delta F / \Delta R$) at each step, (3) *RecBudget-Greedy*: algorithm similar to K-Greedy that maximizes ΔF at each step, (4) *RecBudget-BadCount*: chooses the entries in the decreasing order of the *number* of `Bad` results. Each algorithm is run until the given recall budget ρ is exhausted.

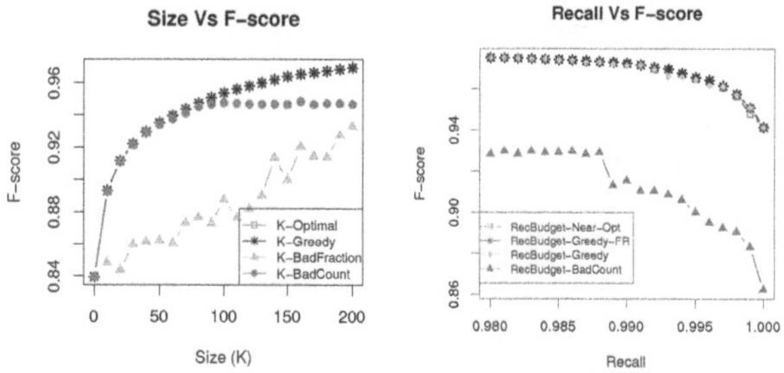

Figure 2: Refinement algorithms for simple rules: F-score.

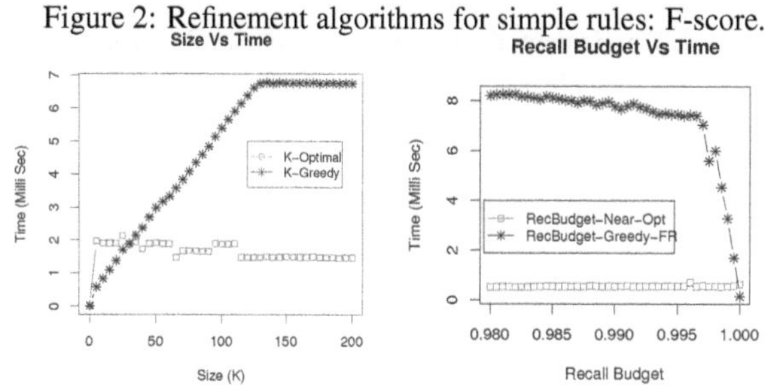

Figure 3: Refinement algorithms for simple rules: Running time.

Observations. First and foremost, Figure 2 shows that dictionary refinement improves the F-score for both size and recall constraints. For both constraints, the performance of our (near-) optimal algorithms and the greedy algorithms for complex rules are comparable on our datasets. They also perform as well or better than the other two algorithms. However, as we have shown in Example 1, the greedy algorithm may not give optimal solution for size constraint, and as discussed below, our algorithms run faster than the greedy algorithms.

Figure 3 gives the running time of the best two algorithms for both size and recall constraints, averaged over 100 runs. This figure shows that the algorithms are efficient and therefore can be embedded in interactive tools. After a certain value of size or recall budget, removing more dictionary entries does not improve the F-score; therefore the greedy algorithm stops and the curve becomes stable. For size (recall) constraint the greedy algorithms requires more time than the (near-) optimal algorithms at higher values of k (lower values of ρ, respectively). For size constraint, optimal and greedy algorithms run in $O(n \log n)$ and $O(kn)$ time respectively, n being the number of dictionary entries; the running times are similar for recall constraint. For $\Delta = 0.001$, K-Optimal converges in only 5 to 6 iterations. The advantage in running time of our algorithms is expected to be even more substantial for larger datasets.

7.2.2 Refinement Algorithms for Complex Rules

For complex rules, we compare the local search algorithms presented in Section 6.2 with other natural approaches. Similar to the case of simple rules, for **size constraint**, we test (1) *K-Greedy*: selects the next entry giving maximum ΔF, and (2) *K-BadCount* and (3) *K-BadFraction*: selects the next entry that has produced the maximum *number* and *fraction* of `Bad` results respectively. These algorithms are compared with (see Figure 4 (i)): (4) *K-LocalSearch*: our local search (hill-climbing) algorithm which finds the initial solution by K-BadFraction, and then finds the local maximum using Algorithm 2. Although we have also tried K-Greedy and K-BadFraction to give the initial solution, K-BadFraction outperforms these algorithms both as a standalone algorithm, and also when it is used as the initial solution for K-LocalSearch.

The corresponding algorithms for **recall constraint** are (1) *RecBudget-Greedy-FR* (selects the next entry that maximizes $\Delta F / \Delta R$ at each step), (2) *RecBudget-BadCount*, (3) *RecBudget-*

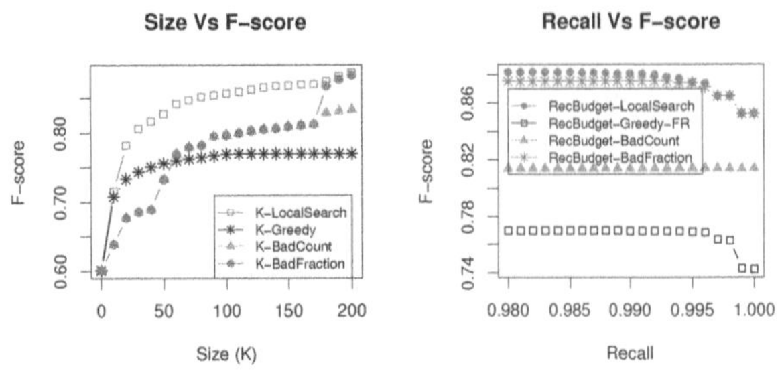

Figure 4: Refinement algorithms for complex rules: F-score.

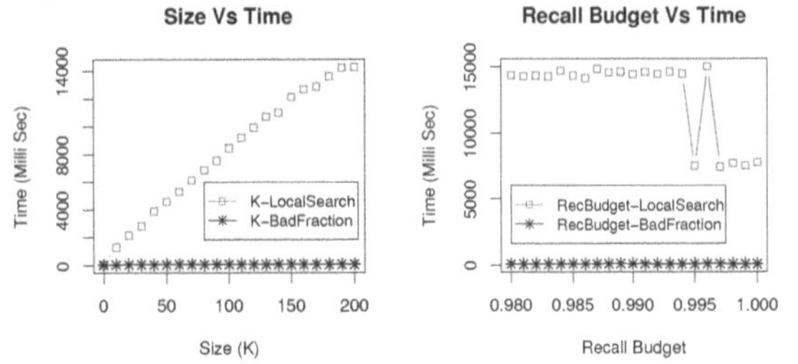

Figure 5: Refinement algorithms for complex rules: Running time.

BadFraction, and (4) *RecBudget-LocalSearch*: our proposed local search algorithm that finds the initial solution by RecBudget-BadFraction and then finds the local maximum by maximizing the value of $\Delta F/\Delta R$ at each step of the search (see Figure 4 (ii)).

Observations. Figure 4 shows that the proposed local search algorithms perform better than the other algorithms for both size and recall constraints. Figure 5 compares the running time of the best two algorithms for both size and recall constraints averaged over 10 runs (local search and sorting by the fraction of bad results). Naturally, K-BadFraction and RecBudget-BadFraction have much better running time than the local search algorithms as they involve a single round of sorting of the entries. The local search algorithms K-LocalSearch and RecBudget-LocalSearch first execute K-BadFraction and RecBudget-BadFraction respectively, and then continue searching for better solutions. Based on the application (*e.g.* for finding the obvious candidate entries to be removed), K-BadFraction may be used instead of K-LocalSearch for faster execution. The runtime for RecBudget-LocalSearch is high even at $\rho = 1.0$ (unlike K-LocalSearch at $k = 0$) since at $\rho = 1.0$ many entries may get deleted that produce *no* `Good` results. Further, running time of RecBudget-LocalSearch is not monotone with ρ unlike K-LocalSearch. For lower values of ρ the algorithm can choose entries that consume most of the recall budget and stop earlier which cannot be selected when ρ is high.

7.3 Refinement with Incomplete Labeling

Now we evaluate our label estimation approaches for *incomplete labeling* of the results. We estimate the label of each unlabeled result using the algorithms in Section 5; the actual labels are retained for labeled results. Then we run the refinement algorithms on the entire resultset. We call this the ESTIMATED approach, and compare it with the *NOT-ESTIMATED* approach, where the algorithms are run *only* on the labeled resultset.

In our tests we choose a random subset of the results in our dataset and define it to be the labeled resultset (that is, the rest of the labels are hidden from our label estimation and refinement algorithms). The set of deleted entries returned by each algorithm for both of these approaches are evaluated against the actual `Good`/`Bad` labels for the entire dataset to obtain the F-score after refinement. This is repeated 10 times, using different random subsets of labeled

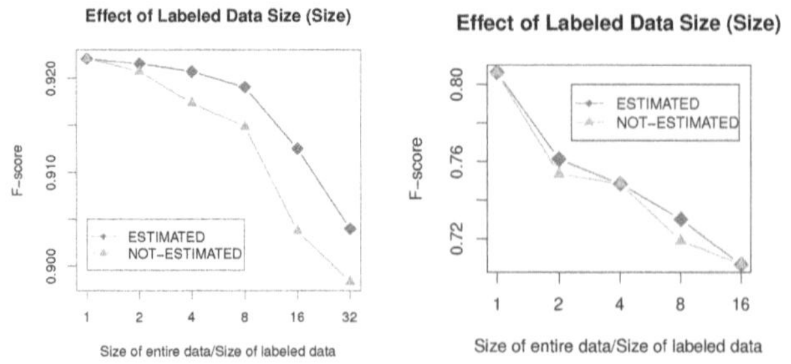

Figure 6: Effect of the labeled data size (simple and complex rules).

results and the mean F-scores are plotted in Figure 6 for different sizes of labeled result set and size constraint (measured as the fraction of all the results in the dataset). We omit the plots for recall constraints for due to lack of space, and discuss them in text.

7.3.1 *Incomplete Labeling for Simple Rules*

As mentioned in Section 5.3 (Observation 2), the label of a result produced by an entry is simply the fraction of `Good` results produced by that entry (entries with no labeled results are ignored), and therefore, the EM algorithm is not run for this case. Figure 6 (i) shows that, for size constraint, ESTIMATED approach gives better F-score over the NOT-ESTIMATED approach, and the benefit is higher when fewer results are labeled (indeed, both approaches are equivalent when fraction of labeled results equals 1). However, for recall constraint, these two approaches give essentially the same result. This is as expected, since our near-optimal algorithm chooses the entries according to the fraction of `Bad` results, which is the same for both labeled and the entire resultset.

7.3.2 *Incomplete Labeling for Complex Rules*

We first estimate the entry-precisions by EM that uses the provenance and labels of the labeled results (see Section 5.3). The EM algorithm is fast enough for practical purposes (it converges in about 15-20 steps and takes about 2 seconds to run). Then the missing labels are estimated by evaluating the provenance of the unlabeled results using the estimated entry-precisions (see Section 5.2). Figure 6 (ii) shows that the ESTIMATED approach is better or at least as good as the other approach. However, the improvement is not as significant as in the case of simple rules (also for recall constraint), possibly at least in part because of our simplifying independence assumption not holding in text data. Finding a more practical model toward estimating missing labels will be an interesting future work. Nevertheless, even a small improvement in F-score is of significance. Further, our label estimation technique may be useful in other applications, *e.g.* in view maintenance in relational setting, if the independence assumption in the source data holds.

7.4 Qualitative Evaluation

Figure 7 shows the first 10 entries returned by our (near-) optimal algorithms for simple rules when 10% of the results are labeled. We used the Person extractor described earlier, and indeed, these entries are incorrect or ambiguous as person names. We also see that the entries removed for recall constraint are the ones with all `Bad` results (they improve precision and F-score without reducing recall). However, for size constraint, entries with non-zero `Good` counts may also be chosen as the number of `Good` and `Bad` results also play an important role in this case.

For complex rules, we list the entries returned by K-LocalSearch for $k = 10$. The entries are *administration, coalition, force, government, guess, U.N., forces, lot*, some collected from more than one dictionaries (and therefore are treated as different entries). For

K-Optimal		
	$(good, bad)$ Count in Result Set	
Entry	Labeled	Labeled + Unlabeled
china	(0, 12)	(0, 100)
kong	(0, 11)	(0, 70)
june	(0, 9)	(0, 97)
hong	(1, 10)	(2, 71)
september	(0, 8)	(0, 101)
king	(0, 5)	(6, 20)
louis	(1, 6)	(4, 33)
long	(0, 4)	(0, 66)
cleveland	(0, 4)	(0, 30)
april	(0, 4)	(0, 30)

RecBudget-Near-Opt		
	$(good, bad)$ Count in Result Set	
Entry	Labeled	Labeled + Unlabeled
china	(0, 12)	(0, 100)
kong	(0, 11)	(0, 70)
june	(0, 9)	(0, 97)
september	(0, 8)	(0, 101)
king	(0, 5)	(6, 20)
long	(0, 4)	(0, 66)
cleveland	(0, 4)	(0, 30)
april	(0, 4)	(0, 42)
january	(0, 4)	(0, 28)
re	(0, 4)	(0, 54)

Figure 7: Top 10 entries output for size and recall constraints.

instance, the entry *U.N.* produces some `Good` results, *e.g. U.N. Security Council* and *U.N. Foundation*, and many `Bad` results when extracted by itself, because in these instances it overlaps with a person's job description, *e.g. Jeremy Greenstock, British Ambassador to U.N.*, and is labeled as part of Person mentions in [3]. Looking at these entries, the human supervisor may investigate the `Good` and `Bad` results they produce, and delete these entries or further refine the rules to remove the false positives in the output of the system. For instance, our system identifies *U.N.*, an example entry that could be handled by adding a special rule for filtering Organization mentions identified as part of a Person's position.

8. CONCLUSION AND FUTURE WORK

In this paper we studied one important aspect of building a high quality information extraction system, that of refining dictionaries used in the extractor. We provided rigorous theoretical analysis and experimental evaluation of the optimization problems that such refinement entails. We also proposed and evaluated a statistical approach for coping with small labeled data. First and foremost, our experimental results show that dictionary refinement can significantly increase the quality (F-score) of extraction using even a small amount of labeled data. Further, our experimental results validate the effectiveness of our algorithms, as well as show which of the several other natural algorithms perform better on real data sets.

There are several interesting future directions. Although the independence assumption in our statistical modeling is a good starting point, correlation among the results and their labels is highly likely to exist for text data. A more detailed modeling allowing correlation will be an interesting future work. Other interesting directions include adaptively labeling a corpus for dictionary refinement given a budget on the number of labels, and fully incorporating non-monotonic operators into our framework, including set difference and operators for removing span overlap.

9. REFERENCES

[1] In *www.census.gov*.

[2] In *www.geonames.org*.

[3] *Automatic Content Extraction 2005 Evaluation Dataset*. 2005.

[4] E. Agichtein and L. Gravano. *Snowball*: Extracting Relations from Large Plain-Text Collections. In *ACM DL*, pages 85–94, 2000.

[5] N. Ashish, S. Mehrotra, and P. Pirzadeh. XAR: An Integrated Framework for Information Extraction. In *WRI Wold Congress on Computer Science and Information Engineering*, 2009.

[6] P. Buneman, S. Khanna, and W.-C. Tan. On propagation of deletions and annotations through views. In *PODS*, pages 150–158, 2002.

[7] X. Chai, B.-Q. Vuong, A. Doan, and J. F. Naughton. Efficiently incorporating user feedback into information extraction and integration programs. In *SIGMOD*, 2009.

[8] J. Cheney, L. Chiticariu, and W. Tan. Provenance in databases: Why, how, and where. *Foundations and Trends in Databases*, 1(4):379–474, 2009.

[9] L. Chiticariu, R. Krishnamurthy, Y. Li, F. Reiss, and S. Vaithyanathan. Domain adaptation of rule-based annotators for named-entity recognition tasks. In *EMNLP*, pages 1002–1012, 2010.

[10] W. W. Cohen and S. Sarawagi. Exploiting dictionaries in named entity extraction: combining semi-markov extraction processes and data integration methods. In *KDD*, pages 89–98, 2004.

[11] D. G. Corneil and Y. Perl. Clustering and domination in perfect graphs. *Discrete Applied Mathematics*, 9(1):27 – 39, 1984.

[12] H. Cunningham. JAPE: a Java Annotation Patterns Engine. Research Memorandum CS – 99 – 06, University of Sheffield, May 1999.

[13] N. N. Dalvi, K. Schnaitter, and D. Suciu. Computing query probability with incidence algebras. In *PODS*, pages 203–214, 2010.

[14] A. P. Dempster, N. M. Laird, and D. B. Rubin. Maximum likelihood from incomplete data via the em algorithm. *JOURNAL OF THE ROYAL STATISTICAL SOCIETY, SERIES B*, 39(1):1–38, 1977.

[15] H. Elmeleegy, J. Madhavan, and A. Halevy. Harvesting relational tables from lists on the web. *PVLDB*, pages 1078–1089, 2009.

[16] D. Eppstein and D. S. Hirschberg. Choosing subsets with maximum weighted average. *J. Algorithms*, 24(1):177–193, 1997.

[17] O. Etzioni, M. Cafarella, D. Downey, A.-M. Popescu, T. Shaked, S. Soderland, D. S. Weld, and A. Yates. Methods for domain-independent information extraction from the web: an experimental comparison. In *AAAI*, 2004.

[18] M. R. Garey and D. S. Johnson. *Computers and Intractability: A Guide to the Theory of NP-Completeness*. 1979.

[19] T. J. Green, G. Karvounarakis, and V. Tannen. Provenance semirings. In *PODS*, pages 31–40, 2007.

[20] J. Hoffart, M. A. Yosef, I. Bordino, H. Fürstenau, M. Pinkal, M. Spaniol, B. Taneva, S. Thater, and G. Weikum. Robust disambiguation of named entities in text. In *Proceedings of the Conference on Empirical Methods in Natural Language Processing*, EMNLP '11, 2011.

[21] D. Jurafsky and J. Martin. *Speech and language processing: an introduction to natural language processing, computational linguistics, and speech recognition*. Pearson Prentice Hall, 2009.

[22] J. Kazama and K. Torisawa. Inducing gazetteers for named entity recognition by large-scale clustering of dependency relations. In *ACL*, pages 407–415, 2008.

[23] B. Kimelfeld, J. Vondrák, and R. Williams. Maximizing conjunctive views in deletion propagation. In *PODS*, pages 187–198, 2011.

[24] Z. Kozareva. Bootstrapping named entity recognition with automatically generated gazetteer lists. In *EACL: Student Research Workshop*, 2006.

[25] R. Krishnamurthy, Y. Li, S. Raghavan, F. Reiss, S. Vaithyanathan, and H. Zhu. SystemT: a system for declarative information extraction. *SIGMOD Record*, 37(4):7–13, 2008.

[26] B. Liu, L. Chiticariu, V. Chu, H. V. Jagadish, and F. R. Reiss. Automatic Rule Refinement for Information Extraction. *PVLDB*, 2010.

[27] M. P. Marcus, B. Santorini, and M. A. Marcinkiewicz. Building a large annotated corpus of english: The penn treebank. *COMPUTATIONAL LINGUISTICS*, 19(2):313–330, 1993.

[28] D. Maynard, K. Bontcheva, and H. Cunningham. Towards a semantic extraction of named entities. In *Recent Advances in Natural Language Processing*, 2003.

[29] A. Meliou, W. Gatterbauer, S. Nath, and D. Suciu. Tracing data errors with view-conditioned causality. In *SIGMOD*, 2011.

[30] A. Mikheev, M. Moens, and C. Grover. Named entity recognition without gazetteers. In *EACL*, pages 1–8, 1999.

[31] D. Nadeau, P. D. Turney, and S. Matwin. Unsupervised named-entity recognition: Generating gazetteers and resolving ambiguity. In *Canadian Conference on AI*, pages 266–277, 2006.

[32] F. Reiss, S. Raghavan, R. Krishnamurthy, H. Zhu, and S. Vaithyanathan. An algebraic approach to rule-based information extraction. In *ICDE*, pages 933–942, 2008.

[33] E. Riloff. Automatically constructing a dictionary for information extraction tasks. In *KDD*, 1993.

[34] W. Shen, P. DeRose, R. McCann, A. Doan, and R. Ramakrishnan. Toward best-effort information extraction. In *SIGMOD*, 2008.

[35] W. Shen, A. Doan, J. F. Naughton, and R. Ramakrishnan. Declarative information extraction using datalog with embedded extraction predicates. In *VLDB*, pages 1033–1044, 2007.

[36] E. F. Tjong Kim Sang and F. De Meulder. Introduction to the CoNLL-2003 shared task: language-independent named entity recognition. In *HLT-NAACL*, 2003.

[37] L. G. Valiant. The complexity of computing the permanent. *Theor. Comput. Sci.*, 8:189–201, 1979.

[38] C. J. van Rijsbergen. *Information Retrieval*. Butterworth, 1979.

[39] A. Yates, M. Banko, M.Broadhead, M. J. Cafarella, O. Etzioni, and S. Soderland. TextRunner: Open Information Extraction on the Web. In *HLT-NAACL (Demonstration)*, pages 25–26, 2007.

APPENDIX

A. PROOFS FROM SECTION 6.1

EXAMPLE 1. ***Greedy is not optimal.*** *Let* $n = 4$ *and* $k = 2$, $A = \{w_1, w_2, w_3, w_4\}$. *The pair of entry-precision and (relative) frequency* (p_{w_i}, f_{w_i}), $1 \leq i \leq 4$ *of these entries are* $(0.0284, 0.2374)$,

(0.0050, 0.2846), (0.0040, 0.2485), and (0.0033, 0.2295) respectively. Then the original F-score $F_A = 19.64 \times 10^{-3}$. Removing entries w_i, $1 \le i \le 4$ gives F-score 8.22×10^{-3}, 23.42×10^{-3}, 23.44×10^{-3}, and, 23.47×10^{-3} respectively. Hence greedy will choose entry w_4 in the first step. Given that w_4 is already chosen, removing w_1, w_2 and w_3 in addition gives resp. F-scores 8.90×10^{-3}, 31.21×10^{-3}, 30.70×10^{-3}. Hence the output of greedy is $\{w_4, w_2\}$. But the F-score after removing $\{w_2, w_3\}$ is 31.46×10^{-3}, which is better than the solution of greedy, and in this case also is the optimal solution. It can be verified that this example also shows non-optimality of other natural choices like choosing entries in the decreasing order of fraction *or* count *of* `Bad` *results.*

NP-hardness: Simple Rules, Recall Constraint. Given positive integers $I = \{x_1, \cdots, x_n\}$ and an integer C, the goal of the subset-sum problem is to decide if there is $S \subseteq I$ such that $\sum_{x_i \in S} x_i = C$.

Construction. There are n dictionary entries $A = \{w_1, \cdots, w_n\}$ corresponding to $x_1, \cdots, x_n$. Each w_i has $f_{w_i} = cx_i$, and $p_{w_i} = \frac{1}{c}$ (there are $p_{w_i} f_{w_i} = x_i$ `Good` results). We choose $c = 3 + K$. In addition, there is a special entry w^* such that $f_{w^*} = 1$ and $p_{w^*} = 1$. The recall budget $\rho = \frac{1+B}{1+K}$. The goal is to check if there is a subset S' such that the F-score $F_{\overline{S'}} \ge \frac{2(1+B)}{(1+K)+(1+cB)}$ and the recall $R_{\overline{S'}} \ge \rho$. The NP-hardness follows from the following lemma.

LEMMA 1. *There exists S' with $F_{\overline{S'}} \ge \frac{2(1+B)}{(1+K)+(1+cB)}$ and $R_{\overline{S'}} \ge \rho$, if and only if the subset-sum instance has a solution.*

PROOF. (if) Let the subset-sum instance have a solution S such that $\sum_{x_i \in S} x_i = C$, i.e. $\sum_{x_i \in I \setminus S} x_i = K - C = B$. Let $S' = \{w_i : x_i \in S\}$. First, $R_{\overline{S'}} = \frac{\sum_{w \notin S} p_w f_w}{\sum_{w \in A} p_w f_w} = \frac{1 + \sum_{x_i \in I \setminus S} x_i}{1 + \sum_{x_i \in I} x_i} = \frac{1+B}{1+K} = \rho$. Also $F_{\overline{S'}} = \frac{2 \sum_{w \notin S} p_w f_w}{\sum_{w \in A} p_w f_w + \sum_{w \notin S} f_w} = 2 \frac{1 + \sum_{x_i \in I \setminus S} x_i}{(1 + \sum_{x_i \in I} x_i) + (1 + \sum_{x_i \in I \setminus S} c x_i)} = \frac{2(1+B)}{(1+K)+(1+cB)}$.

(only if) Suppose S' is such that $F_{\overline{S'}} \ge \frac{2(1+B)}{(1+K)+(1+cB)}$ and $R_{\overline{S'}} \ge \rho = \frac{1+B}{1+K}$. Wlog., assume that $w^* \notin S'$, otherwise we can exclude w^* from S' without decreasing the values of precision or recall (hence also the F-score). Hence all entries in S' corresponds to integers in the subset-sum problem, and Let the corresponding set of integers in the subset-sum problem be S. Now $R_{\overline{S'}} = \frac{\sum_{w \notin S} p_w f_w}{\sum_{w \in A} p_w f_w}$ $= \frac{1 + \sum_{x_i \in I \setminus S} x_i}{1+K} \ge \frac{1+B}{1+K}$, or, $\sum_{x_i \in I \setminus S} x_i \ge B$ (I)

Also note that, $F_{\overline{S'}} = 2 \frac{\sum_{w \notin S'} p_w f_w}{\sum_{w \in A} p_w f_w + \sum_{w \notin S'} f_w} = \frac{2(1 + \sum_{x_i \in I \setminus S} x_i)}{(1+K) + (1 + c \sum_{x_i \in I \setminus S} x_i)}$ $\ge \frac{2(1+B)}{(1+K)+(1+cB)}$. Rearranging and simplifying both sides, $(c - 2 - K) \sum_{x_i \in I \setminus S} x_i \le (c - 2 - K)B$. Since $c = 3 + K$, $\sum_{x_i \in I \setminus S} x_i \le B$ (II)

From (I) and (II), $\sum_{x_i \in I \setminus S} x_i = B$, or, $\sum_{x_i \in S} x_i = K - B = C$. Therefore $S \subseteq I$ is a solution for the subset-sum problem. □

B. UPDATE RULES FOR EM

Here we derive the update rules for the EM-based algorithm described in Section 5.3. Let us denote the parameter vector at iteration t to be $\vec{\theta}^t$. Suppose $c_{w_i, \tau_j, t} = \mathbb{E}[y_j^\ell | \tau_j, \vec{\theta}^t]$, where $\tau_j \in \mathtt{Succ}(w_i)$ and $\mathtt{Prv}(y_j^\ell) = w_i$. We show that the update rules for parameters p_i has a nice closed form: $p_i = \frac{C_1}{C_1 + C_2}$, where $C_1 = \sum c_{w_i, \tau_j, t}$ and $C_2 = \sum (1 - c_{w_i, \tau_j, t})$, where the sum is over $1 \le j \le N$ such that $\tau_j \in \mathtt{Succ}(w_i)$. This gives $\vec{\theta}^{t+1}$, estimation of the parameters in the $t+1$-th round. The log-likelihood of the observed data

$$q(\vec{x}; \vec{\theta}) = \log P(\vec{x} | \vec{\theta}) = \sum_{j=1}^{N} \log P(\tau_i | \vec{\theta})$$

The complete data version of the problem will have the observed data $\vec{x} = \langle \tau_1, \cdots, \tau_N \rangle$ as well as the hidden data $\vec{y} = \langle y_j^\ell \rangle_{j \in [1,N], b \in [1,\ell]}$.

The expected log-likelihood of the complete data given the observed data $\vec{x}$ and current parameter vector $\vec{\theta}^t$ will be given by

$$\mathbb{E}[q(\vec{x}, \vec{y}; \vec{\theta}) | \vec{x}, \vec{\theta}^t] = \sum_{j=1}^{N} \sum_{\vec{y}_j} \Pr[\vec{y}_j | \tau_j, \vec{\theta}^t] \log \Pr[\tau_j, \vec{y}_j | \vec{\theta}]$$

$$= \sum_{j=1}^{N} \sum_{\vec{y}_j : \phi_j(\vec{y}_j) = \tau_j} \Pr[\vec{y}_j | \tau_j, \vec{\theta}^t] \log \Pr[\tau_j, \vec{y}_j | \vec{\theta}]$$

$$= \sum_{j=1}^{N} \sum_{\vec{y}_j : \phi_j(\vec{y}_j) = \tau_j} \Pr[\vec{y}_j | \tau_j, \vec{\theta}^t] \log [\Pr[\tau_j | \vec{y}_j, \vec{\theta}] \Pr[\vec{y}_j | \vec{\theta}]]$$

$$= \sum_{j=1}^{N} \sum_{\vec{y}_j : \phi_j(\vec{y}_j) = \tau_j} \Pr[\vec{y}_j | \tau_j, \vec{\theta}^t] \log \Pr[\vec{y}_j | \vec{\theta}] \quad = K(say)$$

In the third step of the above derivation, for $\vec{y}_j$ such that $\phi_j(\vec{y}_j) \neq \tau_j$, $\Pr[\vec{y}_j | \tau_j, \vec{\theta}^t] = 0$, and in the fifth step, for $\vec{y}_j$ such that $\phi_j(\vec{y}_j) = \tau_j$, $\Pr[\tau_j | \vec{y}_j, \vec{\theta}] = 1$. Note that, given the current guess of parameters $\vec{\theta}^t = \langle p_1^t, \cdots, p_n^t \rangle$, $\Pr[\vec{y}_j | \tau_j, \vec{\theta}^t]$ can be easily computed and is a constant. For $\vec{y}_j$ such that $\phi_j(\vec{y}_j) = \tau_j$, $\Pr[\vec{y}_j | \tau_j, \vec{\theta}^t] = \frac{\Pr[\vec{y}_j | \vec{\theta}^t]}{\Pr[\tau_j | \vec{\theta}^t]} = \frac{\prod_{y_j^\ell = 1} p^t_{\mathtt{Prv}(y_j^\ell)} \prod_{y_j^\ell = 0} (1 - p^t_{\mathtt{Prv}(z_j^\ell)})}{\sum_{\phi_j(\vec{z}_j) = \tau_j} \left[\prod_{z_j^\ell = 1} p^t_{\mathtt{Prv}(z_j^\ell)} \prod_{z_j^\ell = 0} (1 - p^t_{\mathtt{Prv}(z_j^\ell)}) \right]}$ (we slightly abuse the notation here: $p^t_{\mathtt{Prv}(y_j^\ell)} = p_i^t$, where $\mathtt{Prv}(y_j^\ell) = w_i$).

Next we rewrite K by expanding and collecting coefficients of $\log p_i$ and $\log(1 - p_i)$ for every word w_i, $i \in [1, n]$. Then, $K =$

$$\sum_{j=1}^{N} \sum_{\vec{y}_j : \phi_j(\vec{y}_j) = \tau_j} \Pr[\vec{y}_j | \tau_j, \vec{\theta}^t] \log \Pr[\vec{y}_j | \theta]$$

$$= \sum_{j=1}^{N} \sum_{\vec{y}_j : \phi_j(\vec{y}_j) = \tau_j} V_{jt} \log [\prod_{\ell=1}^{\ell} \Pr[y_j^\ell | \theta]] \quad \left(\text{let } V_{jt} = \Pr[\vec{y}_j | \tau_j, \vec{\theta}^t] \right)$$

$$= \sum_{j=1}^{N} \sum_{\vec{y}_j : \phi_j(\vec{y}_j) = \tau_j} V_{jt} \log [\prod_{y_j^\ell = 1} p_{\mathtt{Prv}(y_j^\ell)} \prod_{y_j^\ell = 0} (1 - p_{\mathtt{Prv}(y_j^\ell)})]$$

$$= \sum_{j=1}^{N} \sum_{\vec{y}_j : \phi_j(\vec{y}_j) = \tau_j} V_{jt} [\sum_{y_j^\ell = 1} \log [p_{\mathtt{Prv}(y_j^\ell)}] \sum_{y_j^\ell = 0} \log(1 - p_{\mathtt{Prv}(y_j^\ell)})]$$

$$= \sum_{i=1}^{n} \sum_{\substack{j=1, \tau_j \in \\ \mathtt{Succ}(w_i)}}^{N} \sum_{\substack{\vec{y}_j : \phi_j(\vec{y}_j) = \tau_j, \\ \mathtt{Prv}(y_j^\ell) = w_i}} V_{jt} \left[y_j^\ell \log p_i + (1 - y_j^\ell) \log(1 - p_i) \right]$$

$$= \sum_{i=1}^{n} \sum_{\substack{j=1, \tau_j \in \mathtt{Succ}(w_i) \\ \mathtt{Prv}(y_j^\ell) = w_i}}^{N} \mathbb{E}[y_j^\ell | \tau_j, \vec{\theta}^t] \log p_i + (1 - \mathbb{E}[y_j^\ell | \tau_j, \vec{\theta}^t]) \log(1 - p_i)$$

$$= \sum_{i=1}^{n} \sum_{\substack{j=1, \tau_j \in \mathtt{Succ}(w_i) \\ \mathtt{Prv}(y_j^\ell) = w_i}}^{N} c_{w_i, \tau_j, t} \log p_i + (1 - c_{w_i, \tau_j, t}) \log(1 - p_i)$$

In the above equations, $c_{w_i, \tau_j, t} = \mathbb{E}[y_j^\ell | \tau_j, \vec{\theta}^t]$. In the **E-step**, for every word w_i, and for every result $\tau_j \in \mathtt{Succ}(w_i)$, we compute the expectation of y_j^ℓ (the ℓ-th bit of $\vec{y}_j$) given the current parameter vector $\vec{\theta}^t$, where $\mathtt{Prv}(y_j^\ell) = w_i$. This can be computed from the probabilities $\Pr[\vec{y}_j | \tau_j, \vec{\theta}^t]$. So for every result τ_j, if ϕ_j takes b inputs, we have a vector of real numbers of size b after the E-step.

In the **M-step**, we maximize the expression K w.r.t. parameter vector $\vec{\theta}$ to get the next guess of the parameters $\vec{\theta}^{t+1}$.

For every $i \in [1, n]$, $\frac{\delta K}{\delta p_i} = 0 \Rightarrow \sum_{\substack{j=1, \tau_j \in \mathtt{Succ}(w_i), \\ \mathtt{Prv}(y_j^\ell) = w_i}}^{N} \left[\frac{c_{w_i, \tau_j, t}}{p_i} - \frac{1 - c_{w_i, \tau_j, t}}{1 - p_i} \right] = 0 \Rightarrow \frac{C_1}{p_i} - \frac{C_2}{1 - p_i} = 0$ (collecting the constants) $\Rightarrow p_i = \frac{C_1}{C_1 + C_2}$ □

CS2: A New Database Synopsis for Query Estimation

Feng Yu
Southern Illinois University
Carbondale, IL, 62901
fyu@cs.siu.edu

Wen-Chi Hou
Southern Illinois University
Carbondale, IL, 62901
hou@cs.siu.edu

Cheng Luo
Coppin State University
Baltimore, MD 21216
cluo@coppin.edu

Dunren Che
Southern Illinois University
Carbondale, IL, 62901
dche@cs.siu.edu

Mengxia Zhu
Southern Illinois University
Carbondale, IL, 62901
mzhu@cs.siu.edu

ABSTRACT

Fast and accurate estimations for complex queries are profoundly beneficial for large databases with heavy workloads. In this research, we propose a statistical summary for a database, called CS2 (Correlated Sample Synopsis), to provide rapid and accurate result size estimations for all queries with joins and arbitrary selections. Unlike the state-of-the-art techniques, CS2 does not completely rely on simple random samples, but mainly consists of correlated sample tuples that retain join relationships with less storage. We introduce a statistical technique, called reverse sample, and design a powerful estimator, called reverse estimator, to fully utilize correlated sample tuples for query estimation. We prove both theoretically and empirically that the reverse estimator is unbiased and accurate using CS2. Extensive experiments on multiple datasets show that CS2 is fast to construct and derives more accurate estimations than existing methods with the same space budget.

Categories and Subject Descriptors

H.2.4 [**Information Systems**]: Database Management, Systems, Query Processing

General Terms

Theory

Keywords

Query Optimization, Database Synopsis, Selectivity Estimation

1. INTRODUCTION

Query optimization has been a central research topic of Database Management Systems for many years [14, 25, 26, 30]. It aims to find the most efficient execution plans for queries. A query optimizer generally uses statistics about the database [22, 24], and assumptions about the attribute values [5, 25] to make cost estimations of alternative plans and selects the best one for execution. It is important to find the most efficient plans because studies [5, 19] have shown that executions with sub-optimal plans can be orders of magnitude slower than those with optimal plans. Unfortunately, due to the accuracy of the statistics stored in the database and the validity of assumptions made, query optimizers often cannot find the best plans in their search spaces for the queries. On the other hand, storing accurate statistics can require prohibitively large amounts of space. Thus, constructing a concise, accurate database synopsis has been a central issue of query optimization for decades. In this research, we are mainly concerned about queries with arbitrary select and equi-join operations.

There has been much effort to construct concise, accurate database synopses in the past. Among them, histograms [8, 15, 22, 24] have attracted the most attention. They are simple and effective for estimating low-dimensional queries, where the numbers of attributes of interest in a relation, including the selection and join attributes, are small. However, as the dimension increases, the storage space required by a multi-dimensional histogram can grow dramatically. In addition, the computations and maintenance of multi-dimensional histograms become very complex [21]. Some techniques, such as discrete cosine transform, wavelets, sketches [2, 16, 20], etc., have been proposed to compress the histograms. Unfortunately, these size reduction techniques become ineffective as the dimension increases.

There is also a long history of using sampling in databases [13, 12, 11, 18, 31]. With a small amount of sample tuples, accurate selectivity estimations can be obtained for select queries with arbitrary selection predicates. However, for joins, large estimation errors were observed when independent random samples of relations are used. To overcome this problem, Acharya et al [1] stored a join synopsis for each relation. The synopsis for a relation is a simple random sample of the result of the joins of the relation and all its descendant relations by the foreign-key relationships. Each join synopsis can then be used to generate simple random samples of the results of all subqueries that involve the source relation, and thus are very useful for estimations of a large set of queries.

Chaudhuri et al. in [3] proposed using the stratified sampling to improve estimations. However, workloads must be known beforehand for the stratified sampling to be effective.

SIGMOD'13, June 22–27, 2013, New York, New York, USA.

Moreover, the method is only applicable to "star queries" with foreign-key joins. Wu at el. in [31] used cumulative distributions to make estimations. But it mainly focuses on range queries over single relation.

Spiegel et al [27, 28] proposed an innovative approach to summarizing the correlations among the join and other attribute values in a data graph. Tuples in the graph are connected to nodes that represent their respective attribute values, and to tuples with which they join. To reduce the size of the data graph, tuples with similar join- and attribute-based characteristics are merged into clusters, and clusters with a similar value distribution for an attribute share the same (1-dimensional) histogram. This class of graph-based synopses, called TuG (Tuple Graph) synopses, can be applied to queries with joins of many-to-many and many-to-one relationships [29], and selections with table-level predicates.

Experimental results [27, 28] showed that histogram-based synopses are not as accurate as join synopses and TuG for complex join queries. Howerver, join synopses and TuG also have some limitations and shortcomings. For example, join synopses restrict their applications to foreign-key joins. In addition, a join synopsis is stored for each relation in the database, which raises concern about the total size of the synopses. As for TuG, its accuracy is heavily dependent on the quality of the clusterings performed. But as the number of attributes of interest increases and the relationships among attribute values becomes more complex, clusterings become less effective, and thus the accuracy of estimations deteriorates dramatically. The construction of a TuG synopsis is also very complex.

Motivated by the importance and continuing lack of an effective database synopsis, we set our goal to constructing a simple, concise, and accurate database synopsis. We have chosen to use sample tuples to construct the synopsis as intricate relationships among attribute values can be naturally embodied in the sample tuples. In addition, the space for storing a sample tuple only increases linearly with the number of attributes (of interest) in a relation. It makes sample tuples an effective tool for modeling multi-, and especially high-dimensional attribute value distributions. However, instead of storing independent random samples of relations, we propose to store correlated sample tuples to preserve the join relationships. That is, tuples of a relation are included in the sample of a relation if they join with already drawn sample tuples of other relations. Correlated sample tuples from relations form the correlated sample synopsis (CS2), which will be used for query size estimation, as well as approximate aggregate query answering.

While both the join synopses and the correlated sample synopsis attempt to capture relationships between tuples of different relations, there are many differences. The join synopses store samples of the results of joins, while the correlated sample synopsis stores a sample of correlated tuples from the relations. Besides this philosophical difference, the correlated sample synopsis is also more general than the join synopses. The join synopses are applicable only to the foreign-key join relationships, while the correlated sample synopsis can be applied to all types of join relationships, including many-to-one and many-to-many relationships. The join synopses assume no dangling tuples exist in the relations, but no such assumption is needed for the correlated sample synopsis. The join synopses rely on the simple random samples to make estimation and thus require constructing up to n synopses, where n is the number of relations in the join graph. The correlated sample synopsis can estimate with both random and correlated samples and needs just one synopsis for the entire database. This potential storage space advantage can translate into higher estimation accuracy for the correlated sample synopsis.

While TuG covers all types of joins, the selections are restricted to table-level selections. It cannot accommodate predicates like "R.age=30 OR S.salary > 50K" that cannot be pushed down to the individual tables. As for the correlated sample synopsis, there is no such restriction; it can be applied to any selection and join. In addition, selectivity estimates with statistical confidence levels and intervals can also be provided by using the correlated sample synopsis.

In this research, we propose to store a set of correlated sample tuples as the database synopsis. We have developed a powerful estimator, called the reverse estimator, that can fully utilize the correlated sample tuples to make accurate estimations, without relying on simple random sampling. The proposed reverse estimator represents a breakthrough in utilizing samples to make estimation. We have implemented the join synopses, TuG, and the correlated sample synopsis to compare their performance. The experimental results showed that both the join synopses (JS) and correlated sample synopsis (CS2) were much easier and several orders faster to construct than the TuG. In addition, they also generated more accurate estimates than TuG, with the correlated sample synopsis generating the most accurate estimates. The experimental results confirmed that the correlated sample synopsis is a simple, concise, and accurate summary of the database, not to mention that it is also the most general synopsis, applicable to queries with all types of join relationships and arbitrary selection conditions. It is the desired database synopsis that researchers have long been searching for.

The rest of paper is organized as follows. Section 2 introduces some background knowledge. Section 3 discusses the construction of a correlated sample synopsis. In Section 4, we describe selectivity estimation for queries with acyclic join graphs, and Section 5 cyclic graphs. Section 6 presents a method to improve estimation accuracy of commonly posted queries. Section 7 presents the experimental results and Section 8 is the conclusion.

2. PRELIMINARY

In this section, we define terminology that will be used to model the join relationships in a database. For simplicity, here we focus on equi-joins. The framework can be extended to other joins easily. Hereafter, a join refers to an equi-join.

2.1 Join Graphs

Definition 1. (**Join Graph of a Database**) The *join graph* $G(V, E)$ of a database consists of the set of all vertices $V = \{R_1, R_2, \ldots, R_n\}$ and a set of edges with each vertex denoting a relation in the database and each edge $\langle R_i, R_j \rangle \in E, R_i, R_j \in V$, the existence of a join relationship between R_i and R_j.

In this research, we make no assumption about the multiplicity of the join relationships, that is, they can be one-to-one, many-to-one, and many-to-many (often realized by many-to-one relationships in the relational model).

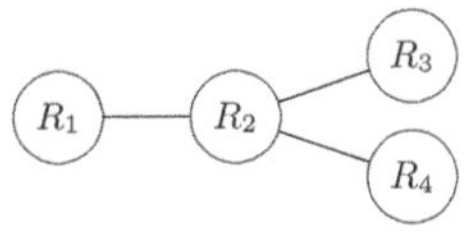

Figure 1: A Join Graph

Example 1. Figure 1 shows the join graph of a database where there are join attributes between R_1 and R_2, R_2 and R_3, and R_2 and R_4.

For simplicity and without loss of generality, we shall assume there is at most one join relationship between a pair of relations and each join relationship involves only one join attribute. The discussions here can be easily extended to general cases.

Definition 2. (**Join Graph of a Query**) Let Q be a query over a set of relations $V' \subseteq V$. The join graph of Q is a subgraph of G, denoted by $G'(V', E')$, where $V' \subseteq V$, $E' \subseteq E$, with each edge $\langle R_i, R_j \rangle \in E'$ corresponding to a join between R_i and R_j in Q.

If the join graph of a query or a database is disconnected, we can consider each connected component separately and then merge them by Cartesian products. Therefore, we shall assume hereafter all join graphs are connected.

Definition 3. (**Joinable Relations**) A pair of relations R_i and R_k, $i \neq k$, is said to be joinable, denoted by $J(R_i, R_k)$, if there is a path of length ≥ 1 between R_i and R_k in the join graph of the query. If there is an edge $\langle R_i, R_k \rangle \in E$, we say R_i and R_k are *directly joinable*; otherwise, they are *indirectly joinable*.

Definition 4. (**Joinable Tuples**) Assume R_i and R_k are a pair of joinable relations with a path $\langle R_i, R_{i+1}, ..., R_{k-1}, R_k \rangle$. A pair of tuples $t_i \in R_i$ and $t_k \in R_k$ are said to be joinable, denoted by $J(t_i, t_k)$, if t_i can find a match t_{i+1} in R_{i+1}, t_{i+1} can find a match t_{i+2} in $R_{i+2}, ...,$ and t_{k-1} can find a match t_k in R_k. Joinable tuples $t_i \in R_i$ and $t_k \in R_k$ are *directly joinable* if R_i and R_k are directly joinable, and they can match directly; otherwise, they are *indirectly joinable*.

3. CORRELATED SAMPLE SYNOPSIS CONSTRUCTION

Sample tuples naturally embody the intricate relationships of attribute values and thus can be good representatives of the underlying tuples of a relation. They are very effective in estimating the result sizes of select queries with arbitrary selection conditions [13]. Unfortunately, independent simple random samples, each of which consists of randomly drawn tuples from a participant relation of a query, generated a large error in join size estimation [13]. We observed that the large errors were caused by the independence of the sample tuples, disregarding the join relationships between tuples of participant relations. Preserving the join relationships may hold the key to the construction of an effective sample synopsis. With this principle in mind, we design a simple sampling scheme, called **correlated sampling**, that preserves the join relationships of tuples.

Table 1: Notation used in the paper

Symbol(s)	Meaning
R_i	Relation
$t \in R_i$	A tuple t in relation R_i
$G(V, E)$	Join graph of a database
$\langle R_i, R_k \rangle$	Edge in the join graph
$J(R_i, R_k)$	R_i and R_k are joinable relations
$J(t_i, t_k)$	t_i and t_k are joinable tuples
SRSWOR	Simple random sample without replacement
S_i^*	SRSWOR of R_i
S_i	Sample relation
$\mathbb{S}$	Correlated sample synopsis (CS2)
$\bowtie(...)$	Joins without order
Y	Query result size
Y_i	Number of result tuples generated by $t_i \in R_h$
y_i	Number of result tuples generated by $t_i \in S_h$
$\widehat{Y}, \widehat{Y}_p, \widehat{Y}_{RV}$	Estimations of Y
r_i	Joinable sampled tuple ratio (JR)
Z_i	Standard Total Number of Result Tuples (STNTR)
$\{z_i\}_{i=1}^{n_1}$	Reverse sample
R_h^J, $R_h^{J^c}$	Joinable and non-joinable partitions

3.1 Correlated Sampling

Correlated Sampling aims to gather a sample of joinable sample tuples from joinable relations in the database to form a synopsis, denoted by $\mathbb{S}$.

Definition 5. (**Correlated Sampling**) First, a relation, say R_1, is chosen as the **source relation**, from which a **simple random sample without replacement (SRSWOR)** [6] is collected into anther relation, denoted by S_1. We include S_1 into the synopsis, $\mathbb{S}$, and mark R_1 as visited. By induction, when R_i ($i > 1$) is visited, and S_i is the sample of R_i, we follow an unvisited edge $\langle R_i, R_j \rangle$ in the join graph of the database. Instead of SRSWOR, we collect the tuples in R_j that are directly joinable with the tuples in S_i. We include these correlated tuples into S_j, and repeat this procedure until all relations in the join graph are exhausted and all tuples directly or indirectly joinable with S_1 are collected. Finally, the synopsis $\mathbb{S} = \{S_1, ..., S_n\}$ is called a **Correlated Sample Synopsis** or **CS2**.

Note that, to emphasize S_1 is a SRSWOR of R_1, we use S_1^*, instead of S_1, in the future. All sampled relations S_1^* and other S_j's are called **sample relations**, and their tuples are called **sample tuples**. A sample relation S_j which is not a SRSWOR is called a **correlated sample relation**, the tuples of S_j are called **correlated sample tuples**, and R_j is called a **non-source relation**.

Algorithm 3.1 describes the general idea of the correlated sampling. We shall refine it later.

3.1.1 Sampling Path and Source Relation Selection

When choosing sampling order along the join graph, although one can follow any join relationship, e.g., a many-to-one, one-to-many, or many-to-many relationship, to gather correlated sample tuples, we suggest following a many-to-one relationship from a visited relation to another relation (visited or not). The rationale is that following one-to-many (and perhaps many-to-many) relationships can easily ex-

Algorithm 1 Correlated Sampling

Require: G — Join Graph of the Database; n_1 — Sample Size

1: R_a=Source_Selection(G) //source relation selection
2: $S_a^* = \emptyset$; $S_i = \emptyset$ ($\forall\, i \neq a$)
3: S_a^* = SRSWOR(R_a, n_1) //collect simple random sample
4: $W = \{R_a\}$ //mark R_a as visited
5: **while** $\exists$ unvisited edge $\langle R_i, R_j \rangle$ with $R_i \in W$ **do**
6: $\quad S_j = S_j \cup \{t | t \in R_j$, t is directly joinable with a tuple in $S_i\}$ //collect correlated sample tuples
7: $\quad W = W \cup \{R_j\}$ //mark R_j as visited
8: **end while**
9: $\mathbb{S} = \{S_a^*\} \cup (\cup_{j \neq a}\{S_j\})$
10: **return** $\mathbb{S}$ — Correlated Sample Synopsis

plode the size of the synopsis, and thus reduce the number of sample tuples that can be drawn from the source relation.

The same reasoning applies to the selection of the source relation. Thus, we prefer a relation that can reach the most relations, through only the many-to-one relationships directly or indirectly, to be the source relation. It is possible that the source relation may not reach all the relations in the graph through only the many-to-one relationships. Therefore, one may have to add additional source relations to cover unvisited relationships and relations.

3.1.2 Sample Size and Synopsis Maintenance

In Step (3) of Algorithm 3.1, we assume, for simplicity, the sample size n from the source relation is known beforehand. However, in reality, the sample size that meets the synopsis space requirement may not be known until the end of the sampling process. Given a synopsis space budget, the simplest way is to draw one tuple at a time from the source relation and collect related tuples along the sampling path. This process continues until the space budget is used up. If only the many-to-one relationships are followed in the sampling, one can also draw a number of sample tuples at a time until there is no budget left.

The correlated sample synopsis can be updated using existing algorithms [10]. Alternatively, since the construction of a synopsis takes just a few seconds (e.g., 10 seconds, as demonstrated in Section 7), one can simply reconstruct the synopsis periodically to keep it up to date.

3.2 A Primitive Correlated Sample Synopsis

For simplicity, we shall name the relations following the order in which they are sampled in the correlated sampling scheme described. That is, R_1 is the source relation, R_2 is sampled after the source relation, and then R_3, R_4, and etc. To explicitly specify the order, we modify the join graph into a directed **sampling order graph** (as shown in Figure 2(a)) in which a double-headed arrow from R_i to R_j indicates that R_j is sampled based on the sample tuples of R_i, or R_j is a child of R_i (equivalently, R_i is a parent of R_j). Ancestor and descendent relationships in a sampling order graph are defined in the same way as in an ordinary directed graph.

Example 2. (**A Primitive CS2**) Consider the order of sampling in Figure 2(a) and the join relationships among tuples in Figure 2(b). Each tuple is represented only by its ID for simplicity. $R_1 = \{1, 2, 3\}$, $R_2 = \{a, b, c\}$, $R_3 = \{A, B\}$ and $R_4 = \{\text{I}, \text{II}\}$. The lines, including both solid and dashed

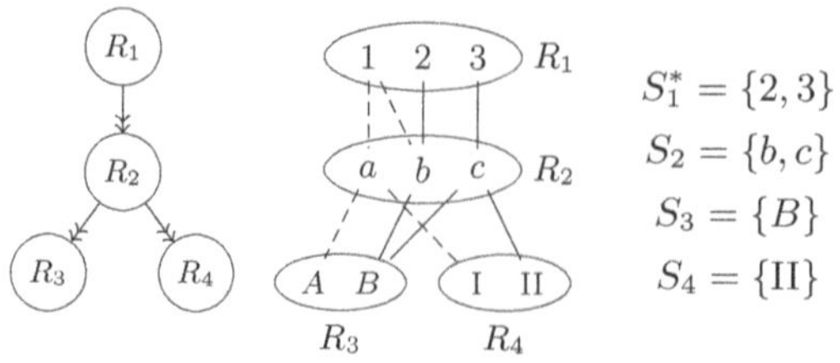

(a) Sampling Order Graph (b) Joinable Tuple IDs (c) CS2

Figure 2: A Primitive CS2

lines, between tuples represent the matching of join attribute values. R_1 and R_2 are in many-to-many relationship. The solid lines indicate that their end tuples are selected into the synopsis. That is, two tuples of R_1, 2 and 3, are first drawn into S_1^* (i.e., $S_1^* = \{2, 3\}$). Then b and c of R_2 are selected into S_2 because their join attribute values match those in S_1^*. After that, B is selected from R_3 into S_3 because of matching join attribute values with b, c in S_2. Finally, II of R_4 is selected into S_4 because it matches a of S_2. Therefore, the sample synopsis $\mathbb{S}$ consists of four sample relations as shown in Figure 2(c).

Note that the synopsis $\mathbb{S}$ described here is just in its primitive form.

Instead of storing all attributes of a tuple in the synopsis, one may choose to store only the join attributes and those attributes that are often referenced in the selection conditions. This would significantly reduce the size of a synopsis.

4. QUERY ESTIMATION

By evaluating queries against sample relations, we estimate query result sizes from the sample query results. We focus on queries that contain equi-joins and arbitrary selection predicates. Therefore, the query result size can be obtained by summing up the number of result tuples on each tuple of an arbitrary relation in the query. Due to space limitation, here we consider only a database with an acyclic join graph $G(V, E)$ and we assume no dangling tuples exist in the joins. Dangling tuples in the source relation will not generate result tuple. And dangling tuples in non-source relations are discussed in Section 4.2.3.

4.1 Source Query Estimation

A **source query** here refers to a query that has the source relation, R_1, as one of its operand relations.

Consider a source query over relations $R_1, R_2, ..., R_n$. Let $\{S_1^*, ..., S_n\}$ be the respective sample relations in the synopsis. Each result tuple of the query must be generated by a set of n tuples $\{t_1, ..., t_n\}$, $t_i \in R_i$, $1 \leq i \leq n$. We say that $t_i, 1 \leq i \leq n$, generates a result tuple. Let Y_i be the number of result tuples generated by the ith tuple $t_i \in R_1$, then the **Query Result Size**, $Y = \sum_{i=1}^{N_1} Y_i$, where $N_1 = |R_1|$. We propose the following unbiased estimator for Y.

THEOREM 1 (**Unbiasedness of CS2**). *Given S_1^*, a SRSWOR of the source relation R_1, the estimator*

$$\widehat{Y} = \frac{N_1}{n_1}\sum_{i=1}^{n_1} y_i \tag{1}$$

is an unbiased estimator of the query result size, Y, where $N_1 = |R_1|, n_1 = |S_1^*|$, and y_i is the number of result tuples generated by the ith tuple in S_1^*. Also, $v_1(\widehat{Y}) = \frac{N_1^2}{n_1}\varepsilon^2(1-f)$ is an unbiased estimator of $Var(\widehat{Y})$, where $f = \frac{n_1}{N_1}$ and $\varepsilon^2 = \frac{\sum_{i=1}^{n_1}(y_i - E(y_i))^2}{n_1 - 1}$.

PROOF. We only have to show that $\{y_j\}_{j=1}^{n_1}$ is a SRSWOR of $\{Y_i\}_{i=1}^{N_1}$. Then we can apply theorems in [6] to prove this theorem.

First of all, y_j is the total number of result tuples generated by tuple $u_j \in S_1^*$ when query Q is executed on the CS2, $\mathbb{S}$. According to Algorithm 3.1, the correlated sampling, for any correlated tuple $v_k \in R_j$ i.e. $J(v_k, u_i)$, we have $v_k \in S_j, j > 1$. That is, every result tuple generated by u_i on the original database, is also generated by u_i on $\mathbb{S}$.

On the other hand, $\mathbb{S}$ is a collection of sample relations, which are subsets of the original relations. Thus, for the same query Q, u_i can't generate more result tuples on $\mathbb{S}$ than the original database.

Hence, given $\forall u_j = t_i$, $u_j \in S_1^*, t_i \in R_1$, we have $y_j = Y_i$. Since S_1^* is a SRSWOR of R_1, $\{y_j\}_{j=1}^{n_1}$ is also a SRSWOR of $\{Y_i\}_{i=1}^{N_1}$.

By Theorem 2.1 and Theorem 2.4 of [6], this theorem is proved. □

Example 3. (**Source Query Estimation**) Consider the database and synopsis in Figure 2. We attempt to estimate the sizes of all queries that involve the source relation R_1, that is, $\bowtie(R_1, R_2)$, $\bowtie(R_1, R_2, R_3)$, $\bowtie(R_1, R_2, R_4)$, and $\bowtie(R_1, R_2, R_3, R_4)$. Here, $\bowtie(R_i,...,R_k)$ represents the joins of R_i,..., and R_k in no particular order.

First, we use S_1^*, S_2, S_3, and S_4 to compute the sample results of the queries.

$$|\bowtie(S_1^*, S_2)| = |S_1^* \bowtie S_2| = 2.$$
$$|\bowtie(S_1^*, S_2, S_3)| = |(S_1^* \bowtie S_2) \bowtie S_3)| = 2.$$
$$|\bowtie(S_1^*, S_2, S_4)| = |(S_1^* \bowtie S_2) \bowtie S_4)| = 1.$$
$$|\bowtie(S_1^*, S_2, S_3, S_4)| = |(S_1^* \bowtie S_2) \bowtie S_3) \bowtie S_4| = 1.$$

Then, the query sizes are estimated by Eq (1), where $N_1 = 3$ and $n_1 = 2$. So, the estimated query sizes of $\bowtie(R_1, R_2)$, $\bowtie(R_1, R_2, R_3)$, $\bowtie(R_1, R_2, R_4)$, $\bowtie(R_1, R_2, R_3, R_4)$ are 3, 3, $\frac{3}{2}$, and $\frac{3}{2}$, respectively, as compared to the exact sizes 4, 4, 2, and 2.

4.2 No-Source Query Estimation

A **no-source query** refers to a query that doesn't include the source relation.

Example 4. (**No-source Query**) In Figure 2, both $\bowtie(R_2, R_3)$ and $\bowtie(R_2, R_4)$ are no-source queries, since neither of their join graphs contain the source relation R_1.

The **highest relation** in a query refers to the relation with the least index according to the sampling order. For instance, in Example 4, R_2 is the highest relation in query $\bowtie(R_2, R_3)$.

For any no-source query Q with R_h as its highest relation in its join graph, let Y_j be the total number of result tuples generated by the jth tuple u_j in R_h. S_h is the sample relation of R_h. We want to estimate the query result size $Y_{R_h} = \sum_{j=1}^{N_h} Y_j$.

4.2.1 Estimation with Reverse Sampling

Since there is no SWRSOR of R_h, it is not straightforward how query result size Y_{R_h} can be derived from the sample of R_h directly. Therefore, we "back track" to the source relation and consider estimation of Y_{R_h} from R_1. We try to establish the relationship between Y_{R_h} and some derived values on tuples of R_1 based on Y_j. In order to establish the "reverse" connection from R_h to R_1, we introduce a definition called *Joinable Tuples Sampled Ratio* or *JR*.

Definition 6. (**Joinable Tuple Sampled Ratio** or **JR**) Considering R_1 as the source relation, $\forall u_i \in R_h$, $h > 1$, let C_i be the total number of tuples in R_1 that are joinable with u_i. Among these C_i joinable tuples, we assume D_i tuples are drawn into S_1^*, $0 \le D_i \le C_i$.

$$r_i = \frac{D_i}{C_i} \tag{2}$$

is called the *Joinable Tuples Sampled Ratio*, or *JR*, of u_i.

Now we show how to derive the result size Y_{R_h} from X_i in R_1. We assign a value X_i to the ith tuple, t_i, of R_1, as follows.

$$X_i = \sum_{j=1}^{N_h} A_j^i Y_j, \quad A_j^i = \begin{cases} 1, & \text{if } J(u_j, t_i), u_j \in R_h, t_i \in R_1 \\ 0, & \text{otherwise} \end{cases} \tag{3}$$

where $N_h = |R_h|$, and $J(u_j, t_i)$ is in definition 4. X_i is called the **Derived Total Number of Result Tuples** or **DTNRT**, generated by u_i in R_1. Using the C_i in JR, we adjust the weight of Y_j in X_i, denoted by Z_i, as follows.

$$Z_i = \sum_{j=1}^{N_h} \frac{A_j^i}{C_j} Y_j \tag{4}$$

where C_j is defined in Definition 6. We call Z_i the **Standard Total Number of Result Tuples** or **STNRT**.

Note that Z_i is associated with a tuple in R_1, but its value is from R_h. Therefore, the values in R_h are assigned to R_1 "reversely" along the sampling path. In order to estimate Y_{R_h}, we pick a SRSWOR of $\{Z_i\}$, and call it, a *reverse sample*.

Definition 7. (**Reverse Sample**) A *reverse sample*, denoted by $\{z_i\}_{i=1}^{n_1}$, is a SRSWOR of the STNRT set $\{Z_i\}_{i=1}^{N_1}$ s.t. Z_i is chosen into $\{z_i\}_{i=1}^{n_1}$ if and only if the tuple t_i of R_1 is sampled into S_1^*.

It is trivial that $y_j = Y_i$, if $t_i \in R_h$ is sampled into S_h as u_j, in which y_j is the total number of result tuples generated by u_j. Thus, according to (4), z_i can be expressed using values in S_h as follows.

$$z_i = \sum_{j=1}^{n_h} \frac{a_j^i}{C_j} y_j, \quad a_j^i = \begin{cases} 1, & \text{if } J(u_j', t_i'), u_j' \in S_h, t_i' \in S_1^* \\ 0, & \text{otherwise} \end{cases} \tag{5}$$

To estimate the no-source query result size Y_{R_h}, we propose the **Reverse (RV) Estimator** defined as

$$\widehat{Y}_{RV} = \frac{N_1}{n_1} \sum_{j=1}^{n_h} r_j y_j \tag{6}$$

where $N_1 = |R_1|$, $n_1 = |S_1^*|$, $n_h = |S_h|$, and y_j is the total number of result tuples generated by the jth tuple in S_h.

The significance of the RV Estimator is that, it can provide unbiased estimations for no-source queries using CS2. It is shown in the following theorem.

THEOREM 2 (**Unbiasedness of CS2**). *Given a no-source query with R_h as the highest relation in its join graph, $\widehat{Y}_{RV}$ in Eq(6) is an unbiased estimator of the query result size Y_{R_h}.*

PROOF. First of all, given R_1, S_1^*, R_h, S_h, we study the sum of Z_i as defined in Eq (4),

$$\sum_{i=1}^{N_1} Z_i = \sum_{i=1}^{N_1}\sum_{j=1}^{N_h} \frac{A_j^i}{C_j} Y_j = \sum_{j=1}^{N_h} \frac{(\sum_{i=1}^{N_1} A_j^i)}{C_j} Y_j \qquad (7)$$

By Definition 6, $\sum_{i=1}^{N_1} A_j^i = C_j$. Thus (7) can be written as $\sum_{i=1}^{N_1} Z_i = \sum_{j=1}^{N_h} Y_j = Y_{R_h}$, which means the sum of Z_i is actually equal to the query result size Y_{R_h}. Therefore, we can estimate the sum of Z_i for Y_{R_h}.

Second, we take a reverse sample $\{z_i\}_{i=1}^{n_1}$. By Definition 7, $\{z_i\}_{i=1}^{n_1}$ is a SRSWOR of $\{Z_i\}_{i=1}^{N_1}$. Therefore, we can use Eq (1), $\widehat{Y} = \frac{N_1}{n_1}\sum_{i=1}^{n_1} z_i$. By Theorem 1, $\widehat{Y}$ is an unbiased estimator of Y_{R_h}.

Finally, we prove $\widehat{Y} = \widehat{Y}_{RV}$. We express $\widehat{Y}$ in terms of y_i.

$$\widehat{Y} = \frac{N_1}{n_1}\sum_{i=1}^{n_1} z_i = \frac{N_1}{n_1}\sum_{i=1}^{n_1}\sum_{j=1}^{n_h} \frac{a_j^i}{C_j} y_j = \frac{N_1}{n_1}\sum_{j=1}^{n_h} (\frac{\sum_{i=1}^{n_1} a_j^i}{C_j}) y_j$$

By Definition 6, $\sum_{i=1}^{n_1} a_j^i = D_j$, we have

$$\widehat{Y} = \frac{N_1}{n_1}\sum_{j=1}^{n_h} \frac{D_j}{C_j} y_j = \frac{N_1}{n_1}\sum_{j=1}^{n_h} r_j y_j = \widehat{Y}_{RV}$$

The theorem is proved. □

THEOREM 3. *We provide an unbiased estimator of the variance of $\widehat{Y}_{RV}$.*

$$v_2(\widehat{Y}_{RV}) = \frac{N_1(N_1 - n_1)}{n_1^2}\sum_{i=1}^{n_1} z_i - \frac{2N_1(N_1 - n_1)}{n_1^2(n_1 - 1)}\sum_{i_1=1}^{n_1}\sum_{i_2>i_1}^{n_1} z_{i_1} z_{i_2}$$

where z_i is defined in the proof of Theorem 2.

This theorem can be proved by (9A.37) and (9A.44) of [6].

Example 5. (**No-Source Query Estimation with RV Estimator**) We attempt to use $\widehat{Y}_{RV}$ in Eq (6) to estimate the result size of a no-source query $\bowtie (R_2, R_3)$ executed on relations in Fig 3(a), denoted by Y_{R_2}. Note that $Y_a = Y_b = Y_c = 1$, because each tuple of R_2 produces exactly 1 result tuple. $|S_1^*| = 2$, and $N_1 = |R_1| = 3$. Thus $\frac{N_1}{n_1} = \frac{3}{2}$. Figure 3 shows the CS2 and JRs when $S_1^* = \{2, 3\}$ and $S_2 = \{b, c\}$. Tuples 1 and 2 of R_1 are joinable with b in S_2, but only tuple 1 is selected into S_1^*. Thus, $r_b = \frac{1}{2}$. Similarly, r_c=1. By Eq (6), for this given S_1^*, $\widehat{Y}_{RV} = \frac{3}{2}(\frac{Y_b}{2} + Y_c) = \frac{9}{4}$. In order to verify that $\widehat{Y}_{RV}$ is unbiased, we consider all possible SRSWOR of size 2 from R_1, i.e. S_1^*, and calculate the average of their estimates, $E(\widehat{Y}_{RV})$. Table 2 lists all calcualted $\widehat{Y}_{RV}$. As observed, $E(\widehat{Y}_{RV})$ is exactly the actual result size.

Table 2: Samples, RV Estimates($\widehat{Y}_{RV}$), and JR Values

S_1^*	S_2	JR	$\widehat{Y}_{RV}$
$\{1,2\}$	$\{a,b\}$	$r_a = r_b = 1$	$\frac{3}{2}(Y_a + Y_b) = 3$
$\{1,3\}$	$\{a,b,c\}$	$r_a = r_c = 1$, $r_b = \frac{1}{2}$	$\frac{3}{2}(Y_a + \frac{Y_b}{2} + Y_c) = \frac{15}{4}$
$\{2,3\}$	$\{b,c\}$	$r_a = \frac{1}{2}, r_c = 1$	$\frac{3}{2}(\frac{Y_b}{2} + Y_c) = \frac{9}{4}$
			$E(\widehat{Y}_{RV}) = 3$

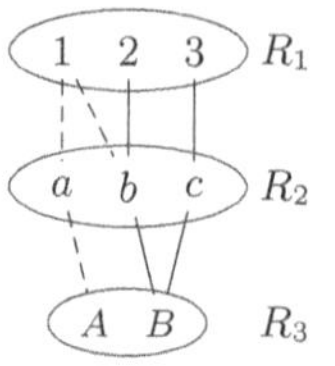

(a) Joinable Tuple IDs

$S_1^* = \{2, 3\}$

$S_2 = \{b, c\}$ $\quad J_2 = \{\frac{1}{2}, 1\}$

$S_3 = \{B\}$ $\quad J_3 = \{\frac{2}{3}\}$

(b) CS2 and JRs

Figure 3: CS2 and JRs when $S_1^* = \{2, 3\}$

4.2.2 JR Storage and Calculation

A CS2 is constructed for use by all possible queries. A JR value is stored with each correlated sample tuple in $S_i (i > 1)$ for use of all no-source query estimations.

As described in Algorithm 2, the JR values can be calculated in a top-down fashion following the sampling path. First, for each sample tuple u in the direct children of S_1^*, we calculate the $\mathbb{C}_u$ and $\mathbb{D}_u$, in which $\mathbb{C}_u$ comprises of IDs of u's joinable tuples in R_1, and $\mathbb{D}_u$ comprises of those in S_1^*. Then, each sample tuple in other sample relations will perform union (without duplicate) of $\mathbb{C}_u$ and $\mathbb{D}_u$ from joinable tuples in its parent sample relations. By definition 6, $C_u = \#(\mathbb{C}_u)$ and $D_u = \#(\mathbb{D}_u)$, in which $\#()$ is the cardinality of a set. Therefore, the JR value of tuple u is calculated as $r_u = \frac{\#(\mathbb{D}_u)}{\#(\mathbb{C}_u)}$. Finally, all the intermediate data, $\mathbb{C}_u$ and $\mathbb{D}_u$, will be removed after JR values are calculated.

In Algorithm 2, $\mathbb{C}_u$ and $\mathbb{D}_u$ are only calculated for correlated sample tuples, and they can be obtained in parallel with the procedure of correlated sampling (Algorithm 3.1). Therefore, the intermediate time and space overheads can be ignored when the sample size is small. In addition, in Section 7, we show that the estimation of CS2 is fairly satisfactory using only quite a small amount of sample.

4.2.3 Estimation Involving Non-joinable Tuples

Definition 8. (**Joinable and Non-joinable Partition**) Considering R_1 as the source relation, the *joinable partition* of R_h (with respect to R_1), denoted by R_h^J, refers to the subset of tuples in R_h, that are joinable with tuples in R_1. The complement of R_h^J in R_h is called *non-joinable partition* of R_h (with respect to R_1), denoted by $R_h^{J^c}$.

By Definition 8, there is no chance for tuples in $R_h^{J^c}$ to be selected into the correlated sample synopsis. In order to estimate the result size of no-source queries with R_h as the highest relation, we need to account for the number of result tuples generated by $R_h^{J^c}$.

Definition 9. (**Partition Difference**) For any given query Q, the total number of result tuples generated by R_h^J and

Algorithm 2 Calculate JR

```
Require: G(V, E): the acyclic join graph of the database;
    S = {S*_1} ∪ {S_i}_{i=2}^n: CS2 without JR
W = ∅ //the set of visited relations
//———Phase1: for direct children of R_1———
U = {S_i | S_i ∈ S s.t. R_i is a direct child of R_1 in G}
for all S_i ∈ U do
    for all u ∈ S_i do
        //IDs of tuples in R_1 and S*_1 joinable with u
        C_u = {t.ID | t ∈ R_1, J(t, u)}
        D_u = {t.ID | t ∈ S*_1, J(t, u)}
        u ← C_u //append to u
        u ← D_u
    end for
    W = W ∪ {S_i} //mark S_i as visited
end for
//———Phase2: for other correlated samples———
while W ≠ CS2 do
    pick S_i whose parent S_p is in W
    for all v ∈ S_i do
        //all the joinable tuples of v in S_i's parent relations
        J_v = {u | u ∈ S_p, J(u, v)}
        C_v = ∪_{u∈J_v} C_u //union without duplicate
        D_v = ∪_{u∈J_v} D_u
        v ← C_v //append to v
        v ← D_v
    end for
    W = W ∪ {S_i} //mark S_i as visited
end while
//———Phase3: calculate JR values———
for all S_i ∈ CS2 do
    for all u ∈ S_i do
        r_u = #(D_u)/#(C_u) //calculate JR
        u ← r_u //append JR to each sample tuple
        delete C_u, D_u //release extra space
    end for
end for
return S (CS2 with JRs calculated)
```

$R_h^{J^c}$ are Y^J and Y^{J^c}, respectively. The *partition difference* between R_h^J and R^{J^c} with respect to Q, denoted by μ, is defined as

$$\mu(R_h^J, R_h^{J^c}) = \left| \frac{n_{J^c} Y^J}{n_J Y^{J^c}} - 1 \right| \tag{8}$$

The partition difference μ is specified for a fixed query Q. To estimate their general difference for any query with R_h as the highest relation, one possible way is to select a set of sample queries from them, and calculate an averaged $\mu(R_h^J, R_h^{J^c})$. One can also check the distributions of tuples according to the join attributes of these queries.

Given a tolerance threshold, $\theta \in [0, 1]$, we claim that if $\mu(R_h^J, R_h^{J^c}) < \theta$, we can estimate Y^{J^c} as

$$\widehat{Y}^{J^c} = \frac{n_{J^c}}{n_J} \widehat{Y}^J_{RV} \tag{9}$$

where $\widehat{Y}^J_{RV}$ is the RV estimator for Y_h^J. The relative error of $E(\widehat{Y}^{J^c})$ is

$$\left| \frac{E(\widehat{Y}^{J^c}) - Y^{J^c}}{Y^{J^c}} \right| = \left| \frac{n_{J^c} Y^J}{n_J Y^{J^c}} - 1 \right| = \mu < \theta$$

That is, when $\mu < \theta$ the estimation relative error of $\widehat{Y}^{J^c}$ in Eq (9) is less than the tolerance threshold θ.

When $\mu(R_h^J, R_h^{J^c}) \geq \theta$, we have to estimate $R_h^{J^c}$ separately. An additional simple random sample S'_h, called a **supplement sampling**, is taken from from $R_h^{J^c}$, and correlated sample tuples are stored into respective sample relations of R_h in the join graph G.

To estimate Y^{J^c} using S'_h, we modify $\widehat{Y}$ in Eq(1) by treating $R_h^{J^c}$ as a source relation. That is

$$\widehat{Y}^{J^c} = \frac{N_h^{J^c}}{n_h^{J^c}} \sum_{i=1}^{n_h^{J^c}} y_i \tag{10}$$

where $N_h^{J^c} = |R_h^{J^c}|$, $n_h^{J^c} = |S'_h|$, and y_i is the number of result tuples generated by the ith tuple in S'_h.

Let $\widehat{Y}^J_{RV}$ be the RV estimator of Y^J. Since Y^J and Y^{J^c} are independent, we have the following theorem.

THEOREM 4. *$\widehat{Y}_h = \widehat{Y}^J_{RV} + \widehat{Y}^{J^c}$ is an unbiased estimator of the query result size Y_{R_h}. And $v_2(\widehat{Y}^J_{RV}) + v_1(\widehat{Y}^{J^c})$ is an unbiased estimator of $Var(\widehat{Y})$, in which v_1 and v_2 are defined as in Theorem 1 and Theorem 3.*

5. SELECTIVITY ESTIMATION FOR QUERIES WITH CYCLIC GRAPHS

If the join graph G' of a query is cyclic, and a query result tuple t^r involves in two different relation tuples, for example, t_1 and t_2 both in R_h. And there is a cycle in G' from t_1 to t_2. We say t^r is generated by t_1 instead of t_2. Hence, each result tuple still corresponds to one and only tuple in each relation when there is no dangling tuple.

Figure 4(a) shows a cyclic join graph and Figure 4(b) the join relationships. Let us use an example to illustrate the issues encountered in a cyclic join graph. Assume tuple 1 is first drawn from R_1. Then, following the correlated sampling (Figure 2), related tuples $A(\in R_2), b(\in R_3), \alpha, \beta(\in R_4), I(\in R_5), \Delta$ and $\Theta(\in R_6)$ are drawn into respective sample relations S_i, $2 \leq i \leq 6$, as shown in Figure 4(c). Note that S_4 contains tuples that are related to tuples in S_2 (i.e., A) and S_3 (i.e., b) because the two sampling branches from R_1 intersect at R_4.

While the synopsis (Figure 4(c)) is sufficient for estimating queries involving relations that are subsets of $\{R_1, R_2, R_4, R_6\}$ and $\{R_1, R_3, R_4, R_5, R_6\}$, it is not straightforward how queries involving relations from both sampling branches can be estimated. For example, consider the query $\bowtie (R_2, R_4, R_3)$, where R_2 and R_3 are on different branches. R_2 and R_3 both are candidates for the highest relation of the query. Assume we choose to use $S_2 = \{A\}$ to estimate the query size. From the synopsis, we know A is connected to α of R_4. Unfortunately, we do not know whether α is connected to any tuples in R_3 or not because we did not let α pierce through R_4 to reach related tuples in R_3 (i.e., a). A similar problem occurs if we use $S_3 = \{b\}$ to estimate the query size. That is, b is connected to $\beta(\in R_4)$, but we do not know whether β is connected to any tuples in R_2 because the sampling did not penetrate into R_2 to reach related tuples (i.e., B here).

Here, we propose two possible ways to handle this situation. The first is to estimate query sizes using the independence and uniformity assumptions. The second method is to enhance the synopsis by letting the sampling pierce through

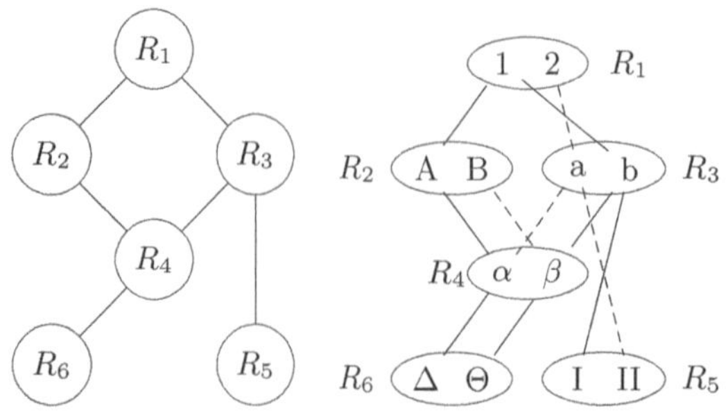

(a) A Cyclic Join Graph (b) Joinable Tuple IDs

$S'_1 = \{1\}$
$S_2 = \{A\}$
$S_3 = \{b\}$
$S_4 = \{\alpha, \beta\}$
$S_5 = \{I\}$
$S_6 = \{\Delta, \Theta\}$

(c) CS2

$S_3^+ = \{a\}$
$S_5^+ = \{II\}$

(d) Extended Samples

Figure 4: CS2 for a Cyclic Join Graph

the cycle-completing relation (e.g., R_4) and perhaps other relations.

5.1 Estimate using Independence and Uniformity Assumptions

Consider the query $\bowtie(R_2, R_4, R_3)$. Let T_{24} and T_{34} be the estimates for $|R_2 \bowtie R_4|$ and $|R_3 \bowtie R_4|$, respectively, derived using the method described in Section 4.2 using sample relations $\{S_2, S_4\}$ and $\{S_3, S_4\}$, respectively. Let N_4 be the number of tuples in R_4. Assume every tuple in R_4 is equally likely to participate in the result of $R_2 \bowtie R_4$ and $R_3 \bowtie R_4$. Then $|\bowtie(R_2, R_4, R_3)|$ can be estimated as

$$\frac{T_{24}T_{34}}{N_4}$$

This approach is simple. But, the accuracy of estimations may raise a concern because the use of the independence and uniformity assumptions.

5.2 Enhancing synopsis with extended samples

We allow the sampling to pier through the cycle-completing relation (e.g., R_4) and extend to any relation as desired. In general, we only extend to the relations that are often referenced in the queries together with the cycle-completing relation.

For example, we can let the sampling branch on the left (Figure 4) that goes from R_1, R_2 and R_4, extend to R_3 (or even to R_1 and R_5). An enhanced synopsis is shown in Figure 4(d), where the left sampling branch is extended to R_3 and R_5. In the figure, S_i^+ contains the extended sample tuples.

We do not need to differentiate S_i from S_i^+ in the sample evaluations unless R_i is the highest relation of the query. For example, consider the query $\bowtie(R_2, R_4, R_3, R_5)$ and the enhanced synopsis in Figure 4(c), 4(d). Assume R_2 is chosen to be the highest relation for evaluation. Consequently, S_2, without S_2^+, must be used. As for other relations, we can just use $S_i \cup S_i^+$. The sample query result can be obtained by $\bowtie(S_2, S_4, S_3 \cup S_3^+, S_5 \cup S_5^+)$, which is the same as $\bowtie(S_2, S_4, S_3^+, S_5^+)$. The latter may be more efficient, but the former is simpler, that is, always use $S_i \cup S_i^+$, except when S_i is the highest relation.

6. MULTI-SOURCE SYNOPSIS

Figure 5 shows a graph with two source relations R_A and R_B. Let A and B be the two groups of relations with R_A and R_B being their source relations respectively. The two

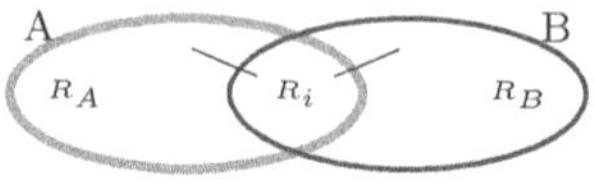

Figure 5: Multiple Source Relations

groups have a common relation R_i, but there can certainly be more. Note that the sampling processes that started from R_A and R_B would each draw their own related sample tuples from R_i and store them in S_i.

Given a query if there exists a sample penetrating all its operand relations, an estimate of the query size can be derived using the methods described in Section 4. If there does not exist a sample that penetrates all the operand relations, we resort to the estimation method based on the independence and uniformity assumptions in Section 5.

A multi-source synopsis arises from traversing only the many-to-one join relationships in the sampling. But there are other reasons for constructing a multi-source synopsis. In situations where there are multiple groups of relations that are often referenced together, we may select a source relation for each such group. Depending upon the importance of queries and desired accuracy, a multi-source synopsis allows a DBA to determine grouping of relations and sample sizes for individual groups. It can improve the accuracy of estimation for queries over relations in the same groups, however, decrease the accuracy for queries over relations across groups, due to the use of the independence and uniformity assumption in estimation. It can be a very flexible and effective way to build a synopsis.

7. EXPERIMENTS

In this section, we present the results of performance evaluations of TuG [27, 28], join synopses (JS) [1], and correlated sample synopsis (CS2).

The implementations of the join synopses and correlated sample synopsis are much simpler than TuG because TuG uses complex clustering and compression algorithms. We have implemented the TuG synopsis (whose code is not available to the public) following the descriptions in [27], including using the public Java source code [23] of CF-Tree and BIRCH [32] to conduct clustering, and implementing the Count-min Sketches [7] and histogram synopses [8] to reduce the size of histograms.

All programs are implemented in Java 1.6 and MySQL 5.1 on a Ubuntu 10.04 Linux system, equipped with an Intel

Table 3: Datasets

Name	Size	Comments
TPCH1G05	1GB	TPC-H skew factor z=0.5
TPCH1G1	1GB	TPC-H skew factor z=1.0
TPCH10G05	10GB	TPC-H skew factor z=0.5
TPCH10G1	10GB	TPC-H skew factor z=1.0
DBLP	692MB	DBLP online database

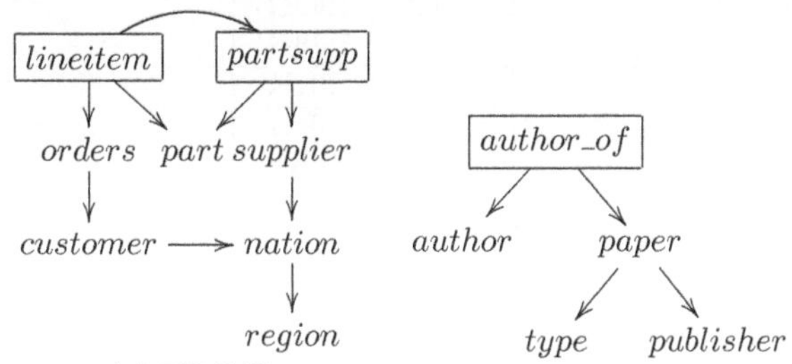

(a) TPC-H (b) DBLP

Figure 6: Join Graphs of Datasets (Boxed are Source Relations)

Core i7 3.4 GHz CPU, 4GB RAM and a 500GB hard disk (7200 RPM, Buffer size 16MB). All datasets and synopses are stored on the hard disk.

Using a large amount of memory only benefits TuG which utilizes clustering on large datasets. CS2 and JS only require small amounts of memory when constructing synopses.

7.1 Datasets

We conducted experiments on both synthetic data - TPC-H datasets with skewed data [4], and real-life data - DBLP dataset[17], which are listed in Table 3.

We generated 1GB and 10G TPC-H datasets with skew factors of z =0.5 and 1. Each TPC-H dataset has 8 relations, consisting of only the foreign-key join relationships. The arcs in Figure 6(a) indicate the many-to-one relationships, which also satisfy the foreign-key constraint for the TPC-H data, and the boxes indicate the source relations of CS2. Note that every relation is a source relation in JS.

The DBLP database listed more than 1.3 million articles in computer science by January 2010. Our DBLP dataset sources from a relational enhancement of the original DBLP data, named DBLP++[9]. We have replaced the many-to-many relationship between "author" and "paper" by two many-to-one relationships and a connecting relation "author_of", as JS does not apply to many-to-many relationships directly. However, CS2 is applicable to all types of relationships. In addition, we have also filtered out some data so that the foreign key constraint holds, as required by the JS. The join graph is shown in Fig 6(b).

7.2 Construction Time and Index

The average construction times of synopses in accuracy tests are presented in Table 4. As observed, the construction of TuG is significantly slower than JS and CS2 because it performs some time-consuming tasks, such as CV table building, all-but-one similar merges, BIRCH clustering, and etc. All of these tasks require tremendous amounts of disk I/O and CPU computation.

Building index will certiainly increase the construction speed of all the synopses. In our experiments, we built indexes on the join key attributes in both TPC-H and DBLP datasets.

Table 4: Average Construction Time of Synopses

Dataset	Space Budget	TuG	JS	CS2
TPCH1G05	29KB	639min	10sec	8sec
TPCH1G1	21KB	286min	10sec	8sec
TPCH10G05	100KB	∞	408sec	334sec
TPCH10G1	100KB	∞	340sec	300sec
DBLP	35KB	518min	8sec	3sec

7.3 Query Workload

We randomly generated queries involving different sets of relations with different numbers of selection predicates. For such queries, we randomly varied the ranges of attribute values in the selection criteria. Our experiments were designed to examine how joins and selections affect the accuracy of estimations.

Table 5 details the test queries and the space budgets used for each test. "DBLP Large/Small Range" refers to queries with large/small attribute value ranges specified in the selection predicates. "DBLP No-source" refers to queries that do not involve the source relation "author_of", which would require using the proposed RV estimator (Section 4). They are also among the queries used in the "DBLP Large / Small Range" experiments.

7.4 Synopsis Space Budget

According to Section 3.1.1 and Algorithm 3.1, in order to control the size of CS2, we chose "lineitem" of TPC-H and "author_of" of DBLP as the source relations. Our correlated sampling also followed many-to-one relationships in the join graphs. As Table 5 shows, the space of CS2 can be well controlled. Space budgets of CS2 are less than 20KB for 1GB TPC-H datasets, 100KB for 10GB TPC-H datasets, and less than 10KB for DBLP datasets.

Note that it is hard to control the final sizes of TuGs, even though we used the same clustering parameters to generate them on TPC-H datasets. We are not able to generate any TuG smaller than 20KB for TPC-H or 23KB for DBLP without generating large estimation errors, and thus their results are absent for the 3KB and 10KB tests in Figure 7.

7.5 Estimation Accuracy

Test queries were grouped based on the numbers of joins and selections placed on each relation. For example, in Figure 7(a), the query group 'j1s2' comprises queries with one join and at most 2 selections on each operand relation, with at most 4 selections per query.

Since JS and CS2 both need random sampling, they are not unique for a given DB. Therefore, for each dataset and given space budget, we generated 100 JSs and CS2s to observe their average performance. Each CS2/JS is used for estimations of all test queries. We use the absolute relative error to compare the accuracy of estimations, which is defined as

$$E = \left| \frac{\widehat{Y}^{Est} - Y^{Act}}{Y^{Act}} \right| \times 100\%$$

where Y^{Act} denotes the actual query result size and $\widehat{Y}^{Est}$ is

Table 5: Query Workloads and Space Budgets in Estimation Accuracy Tests

Figure	Tests	Data Size	Total Queries	Space Budget		
				TuG	JS	CS2
7(a)	TPCH1G05 Synopses 20KB	1GB	45	29KB	20KB	20KB
7(b)	TPCH1G05 Synopses 10KB	1GB	45	—	10KB	10KB
7(c)	TPCH1G1 Synopses 20KB	1GB	45	21KB	20KB	20KB
7(d)	TPCH1G1 Synopses 10KB	1GB	45	—	10KB	10KB
7(e)	TPCH10G05 Synopses 100KB	10GB	45	–	100KB	100KB
7(f)	TPCH10G1 Synopses 100KB	10GB	45	—	100KB	100KB
7(g)	DBLP Large Range 3KB	692MB	51	23KB	3KB	3KB
7(h)	DBLP Small Range 3KB	692MB	51	—	3KB	3KB
7(i)	DBLP Small Range 10KB	692MB	51	—	10KB	10KB
7(j)	DBLP No-source	692MB	36	—	3KB	3KB

the estimated result size. The results of accuracy tests are shown in Fig 7.

As shown in Figure 7(a) and Figure 7(c), TuG produced the worst relative errors generally. As mentioned earlier, TuG smaller than 20KB cannot generate meaningful estimations. JS and CS2 had similar accuracies for queries with small numbers of joins. However, JS's accuracy degraded quickly when the number of joins increased. CS2 produced the lowest relative errors in all cases of the TPC-H tests.

Figure 7(g) shows the results of DBLP large range query tests. Again, CS2 was superior to JS and TuG, with TuG performing the worst. As observed from Figures 7(g) and 7(h), small range queries gave higher errors than large range queries. Also, as the sizes of the synopses increased, the relative errors decreased (Figures 7(h) and 7(i)). The dominance of CS2 over JS became more obvious when the numbers of joins and selections increased, as shown in Fig 7(h).

Finally, we compare the accuracy of CS2 and JS for no-source queries. All queries were extracted from the previous tests. It is clear, as shown in Fig 7(j), that CS2 with the reverse estimator produced lower relative errors than JS.

In summary, TuG performed the worst among these three synopses. CS2 produced the smallest relative errors in all tests. In addition, CS2 increasingly outperformed JS as the numbers of joins and selections grew.

7.6 Unbiasedness of RV Estimator

In Section 4.2, we proposed the reverse estimator for all no-source queries, and proved theoretically that it is unbiased (Theorem 2). Here, we validate empirically the unbiasedness of this estimator using CS2. We also compare the results with JS.

For illustrative purposes, we select two queries for this bias test, one from group 'j2s1' and the other from 'j2s2' in the DBLP tests. A query is estimated each time using a different synopsis (or synopses) of the same size (3KB). We generated 100 synopses for this purpose. The absolute average relative error of the first i estimates is defined as

$$E_i = \left| \frac{\frac{\sum_{j=1}^{i} \widehat{Y}_j^{Est}}{i} - Y^{Act}}{Y^{Act}} \right| \times 100\%$$

where $i \geq 1$, Y^{Act} is the actual query size, $\widehat{Y}_j^{Est}$ is the estimated value derived from the jth synopsis (synopses), and $\frac{\sum_{j=1}^{i} \widehat{Y}_j^{Est}}{i}$ is the average of the first i estimates. For an unbiased estimator [6], the absolute average relative error should approach 0 as i (the number of tries) increases.

As observed in Figure 8(a), the errors of both CS2 (using the RV Estimator) and JS approached 0 as the number of tries increased. On the other hand, Figure 8(b) demostrates that the errors of CS2 converged to 0 earlier than JS within 100 rounds. i.e. CS2 yeilds a faster convergence speed than JS when more selections are added. Certainly, JS yields unbiased estimates as it uses simple random samples of join results. These experiments validate our earlier proofs of the unbiasedness of the RV estimator.

8. CONCLUSIONS AND FUTURE WORK

In this paper, we have presented an innovative approach to construct a database synopsis. The synopsis mainly consists of a set of correlated sample relations. We have designed a reverse estimator that can fully utilize the correlated sample tuples to make accurate estimations. Our experimental results show that the correlated sample synopsis is easy to construct and has better performance than existing synopses. It proves itself to be a simple, concise, and accurate synopsis.

There is still much work to do. We shall study the possibility of further reducing the size of the synopsis using other sampling techniques, such as subsampling. Finally, we shall explore the use of the correlated sample synopsis in approximate aggregate query answering.

9. ACKNOWLEDGMENTS

A special thanks to Dr. Sakthivel Jeyarathnam for his help in developing the reverse estimator. We are also grateful to Mr. Chase Abner for editing assistance.

10. REFERENCES

[1] S. Acharya, P. B. Gibbons, V. Poosala, and S. Ramaswamy. Join synopses for approximate query answering. *SIGMOD Rec.*, 28:275–286, June 1999.

[2] N. Alon, Y. Matias, and M. Szegedy. The space complexity of approximating the frequency moments. In *JOURNAL OF COMPUTER AND SYSTEM SCIENCES*, pages 20–29, 1996.

[3] S. Chaudhuri, G. Das, and V. Narasayya. Optimized stratified sampling for approximate query processing. *ACM Trans. Database Syst.*, 32(2), June 2007.

[4] S. Chaudhuri and V. Narasayya. Program for tpc-d data generation with skew. `ftp://ftp.research.microsoft.com/users/viveknar/tpcdskew`.

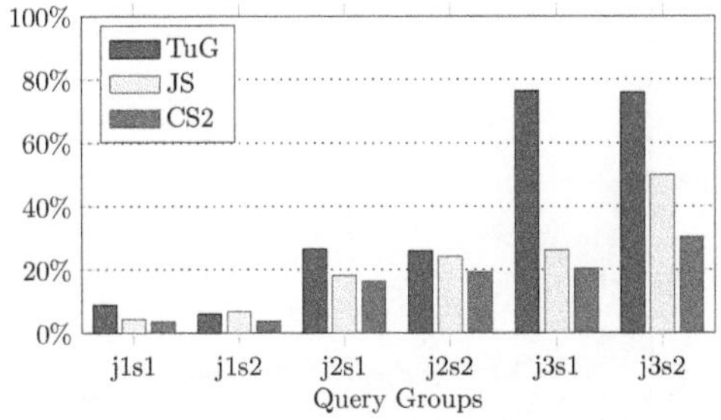

(a) TPCH1G05: TuG=29KB; JS,CS2=20KB

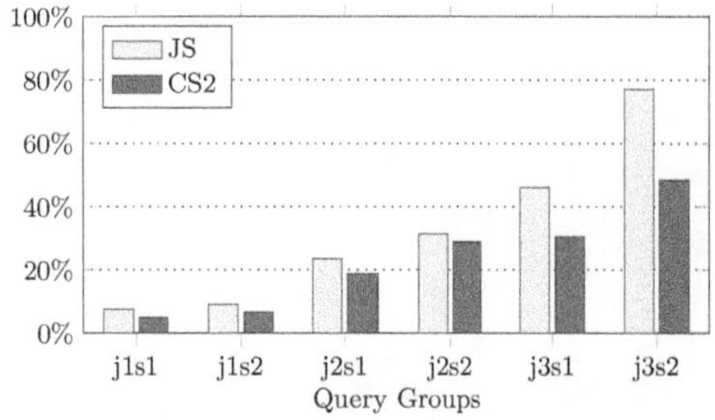

(b) TPCH1G05: JS,CS2=10KB

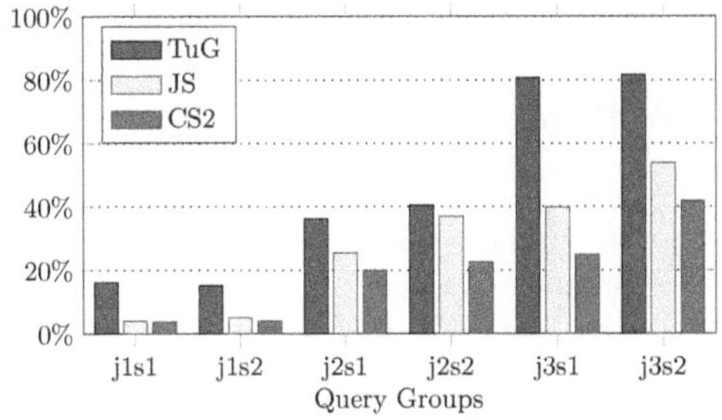

(c) TPCH1G1: TuG=21KB; JS,CS2=20KB

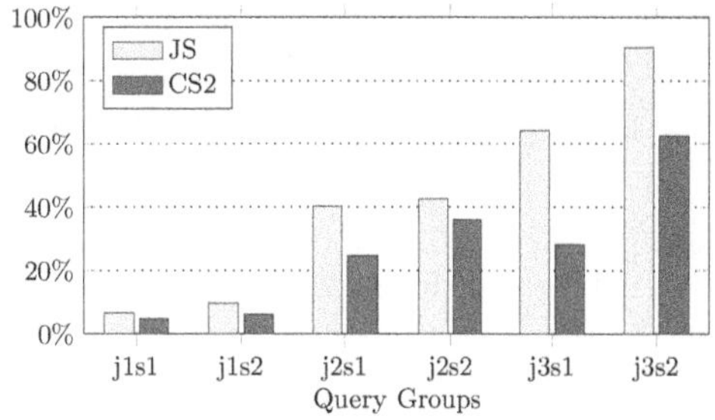

(d) TPCH1G1: JS,CS2=10KB

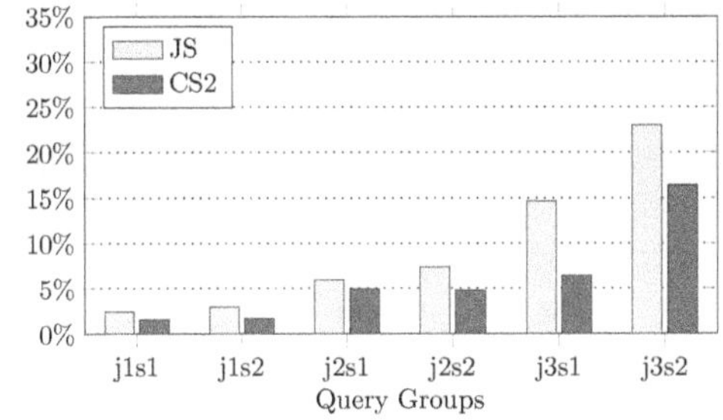

(e) TPCH10G05: JS,CS2=100KB

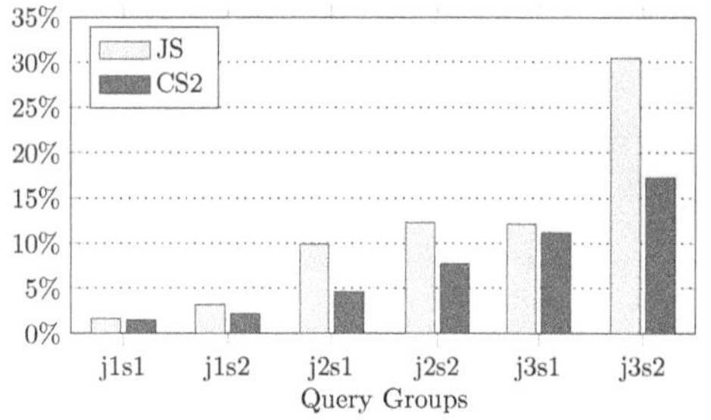

(f) TPCH10G1: JS,CS2=100KB

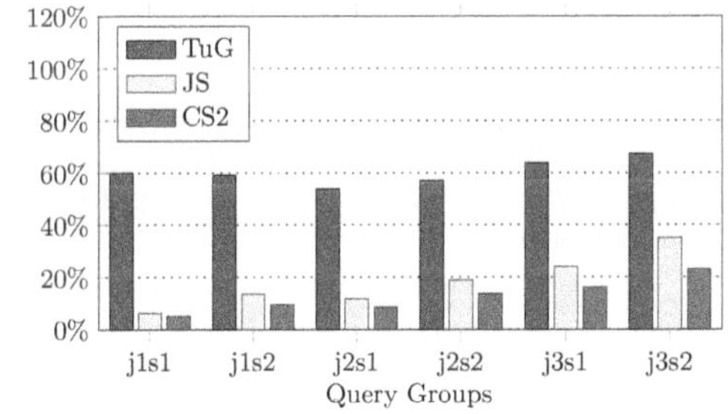

(g) DBLP Large Range: TuG=23K; JS,CS2=3KB

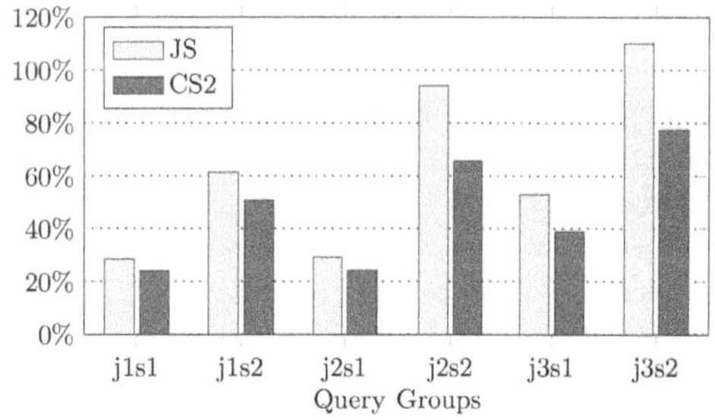

(h) DBLP Small Range: JS,CS2=3KB

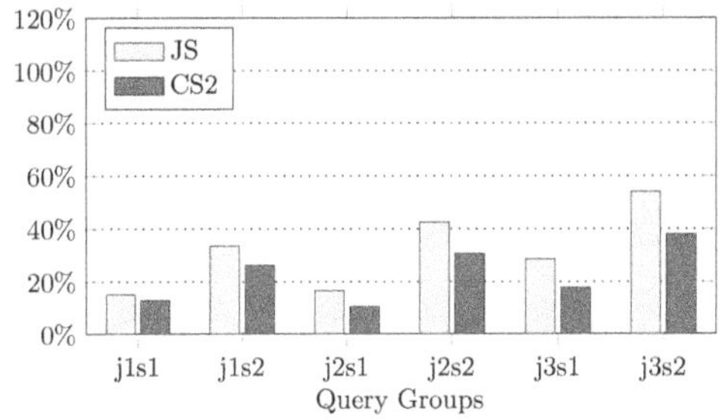

(i) DBLP Small Range: JS,CS2=10KB

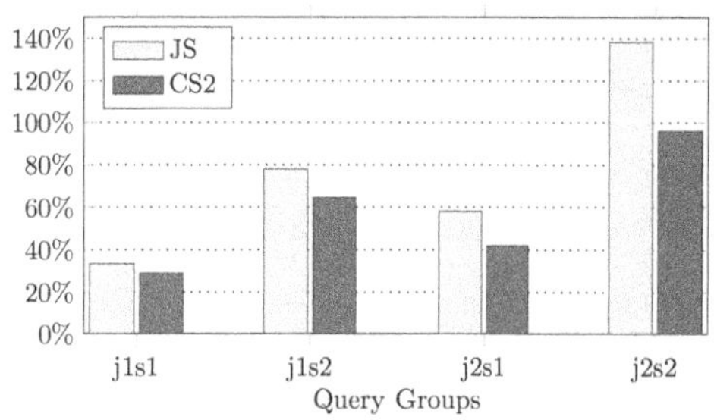

(j) DBLP No-source: JS,CS2=3KB

Figure 7: Absolute Relative Errors (%) in Accuracy Tests

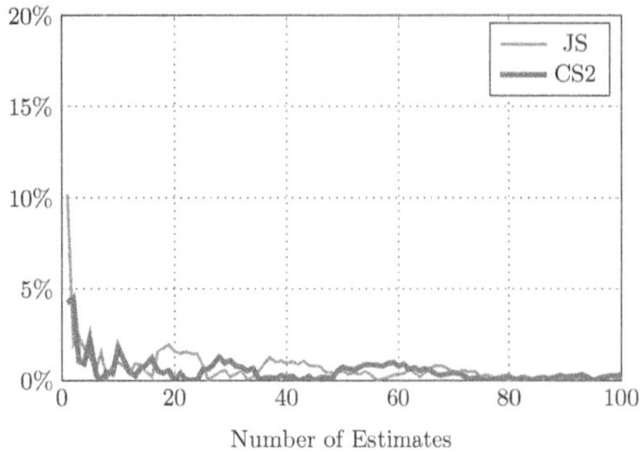

(a) Bias Test: DBLP No-source j2s1

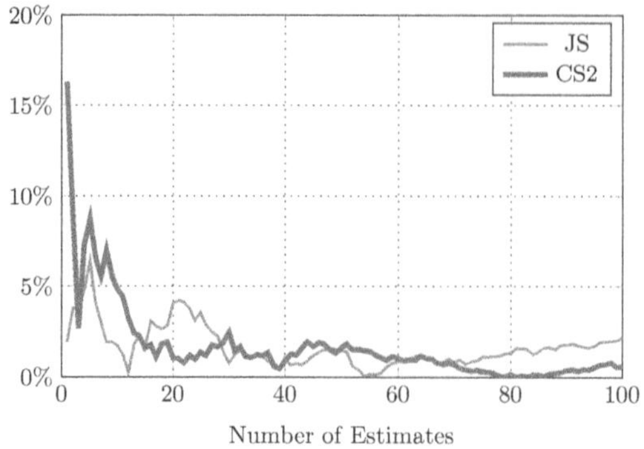

(b) Bias Test: DBLP No-source j2s2

Figure 8: Averaged Absolute Relative Errors (%) in Bias Tests

[5] S. Christodoulakis. Implications of certain assumptions in database performance evauation. *ACM Trans. Database Syst.*, 9:163–186, June 1984.

[6] W. G. Cochran. *Sampling Techniques, 3rd Edition.* John Wiley, 1977.

[7] G. Cormode and S. Muthukrishnan. An improved data stream summary: the count-min sketch and its applications. *J. Algorithms*, 55:58–75, April 2005.

[8] A. Deshpande, M. Garofalakis, and R. Rastogi. Independence is good: dependency-based histogram synopses for high-dimensional data. *SIGMOD Rec.*, 30:199–210, May 2001.

[9] J. Diederich. FacetedDBLP. `http://dblp.l3s.de/dblp++.php`.

[10] P. B. Gibbons, Y. Matias, and V. Poosala. Fast incremental maintenance of approximate histograms. VLDB '97, pages 466–475, 1997.

[11] P. J. Haas, J. F. Naughton, S. Seshadri, and A. N. Swami. Fixed-precision estimation of join selectivity. PODS '93, pages 190–201, 1993.

[12] P. J. Haas and A. N. Swami. Sequential sampling procedures for query size estimation. *SIGMOD Rec.*, 21:341–350, June 1992.

[13] W.-C. Hou, G. Ozsoyoglu, and B. K. Taneja. Statistical estimators for relational algebra expressions. PODS '88, pages 276–287, 1988.

[14] Y. E. Ioannidis and Y. C. Kang. Left-deep vs. bushy trees: an analysis of strategy spaces and its implications for query optimization. *SIGMOD Rec.*, 20:168–177, April 1991.

[15] R. P. Kooi. *The optimization of queries in relational databases.* PhD thesis, Cleveland, OH, USA, 1980. AAI8109596.

[16] J.-H. Lee, D.-H. Kim, and C.-W. Chung. Multi-dimensional selectivity estimation using compressed histogram information. *SIGMOD Rec.*, 28:205–214, June 1999.

[17] M. Ley. The DBLP computer science bibliography. `http://www.informatik.uni-trier.de/~ley/db/`.

[18] R. J. Lipton, J. F. Naughton, and D. A. Schneider. Practical selectivity estimation through adaptive sampling. *SIGMOD Rec.*, 19:1–11, May 1990.

[19] V. Markl, V. Raman, D. Simmen, G. Lohman, H. Pirahesh, and M. Cilimdzic. Robust query processing through progressive optimization. SIGMOD '04, pages 659–670, 2004.

[20] Y. Matias, J. S. Vitter, and M. Wang. Wavelet-based histograms for selectivity estimation. *SIGMOD Rec.*, 27:448–459, June 1998.

[21] Y. Matias, J. S. Vitter, and M. Wang. Dynamic maintenance of wavelet-based histograms. VLDB '00, pages 101–110, 2000.

[22] M. Muralikrishna and D. J. DeWitt. Equi-depth histograms for estimating selectivity factors for multi-dimensional queries. SIGMOD '88, pages 28–36, 1988.

[23] R. Perdisci. JBIRCH. `http://roberto.perdisci.com/projects/jbirch`.

[24] V. Poosala and Y. E. Ioannidis. Selectivity estimation without the attribute value independence assumption. VLDB '97, pages 486–495, 1997.

[25] P. G. Selinger, M. M. Astrahan, D. D. Chamberlin, R. A. Lorie, and T. G. Price. Access path selection in a relational database management system. SIGMOD '79, pages 23–34, 1979.

[26] J. M. Smith and P. Y.-T. Chang. Optimizing the performance of a relational algebra database interface. *Commun. ACM*, 18:568–579, October 1975.

[27] J. Spiegel and N. Polyzotis. Graph-based synopses for relational selectivity estimation. SIGMOD '06, pages 205–216, 2006.

[28] J. Spiegel and N. Polyzotis. Tug synopses for approximate query answering. *ACM Trans. Database Syst.*, 34(1):3:1–3:56, Apr. 2009.

[29] J. D. Ullman, H. Garcia-Molina, and J. Widom. *Database Systems: The Complete Book.* Prentice Hall PTR, Upper Saddle River, NJ, USA, 1st edition, 2001.

[30] E. Wong and K. Youssefi. Decomposition - a strategy for query processing. *ACM Transactions on Database Systems*, 1:223–241, 1976.

[31] Y.-L. Wu, D. Agrawal, and A. El Abbadi. Applying the golden rule of sampling for query estimation. *SIGMOD Rec.*, 30(2):449–460, May 2001.

[32] T. Zhang, R. Ramakrishnan, and M. Livny. Birch: an efficient data clustering method for very large databases. *SIGMOD Rec.*, 25:103–114, June 1996.

Branch-and-Bound Algorithm for Reverse Top-k Queries

Akrivi Vlachou[1,2], Christos Doulkeridis[1,3], Kjetil Nørvåg[1] and Yannis Kotidis[4]
[1]Norwegian University of Science and Technology (NTNU), Trondheim, Norway
[2]Institute for the Management of Information Systems, R.C. "Athena", Athens, Greece
[3]University of Piraeus, Piraeus, Greece
[4]Athens University of Economics and Business (AUEB), Athens, Greece
{vlachou,cdoulk,noervaag}@idi.ntnu.no, kotidis@aueb.gr

ABSTRACT

Top-k queries return to the user only the k best objects based on the individual user preferences and comprise an essential tool for rank-aware query processing. Assuming a stored data set of user preferences, reverse top-k queries have been introduced for retrieving the users that deem a given database object as one of their top-k results. Reverse top-k queries have already attracted significant interest in research, due to numerous real-life applications such as market analysis and product placement. Currently, the most efficient algorithm for computing the reverse top-k set is RTA. RTA has two main drawbacks when processing a reverse top-k query: (i) it needs to access all stored user preferences, and (ii) it cannot avoid executing a top-k query for each user preference that belongs to the result set. To address these limitations, in this paper, we identify useful properties for processing reverse top-k queries without accessing each user's individual preferences nor executing the top-k query. We propose an intuitive branch-and-bound algorithm for processing reverse top-k queries efficiently and discuss novel optimizations to boost its performance. Our experimental evaluation demonstrates the efficiency of the proposed algorithm that outperforms RTA by a large margin.

Categories and Subject Descriptors

H.2.4 [**Database Management**]: Systems—*Query processing*

General Terms

Algorithms, Experimentation, Performance

Keywords

Reverse top-k query, branch-and-bound algorithm

1. INTRODUCTION

Given a database of objects described by a set of numerical scoring attributes and a user with a preference function defined over these attributes, a top-k query retrieves the k objects with best score for the particular preference function. In the model that is widely used in related work [4, 10] and in practice, the users express their preferences through linear top-k queries, which are defined by assigning a weight to each of the scoring attributes, indicating the importance of each attribute to the user. Assuming a stored data set of user preferences, reverse top-k queries have been proposed [19,20] to retrieve the user preferences that make a given object belong to the respective top-k result set. From the perspective of a manufacturer, it is important to identify the customers who are potentially interested in her products and to estimate the visibility of a product based on the different user preferences for which it appears in the top-ranked positions. Hence, reverse top-k queries comprise an essential tool for business analysis, allowing manufacturers to assess the impact of their products in the market based on the competition.

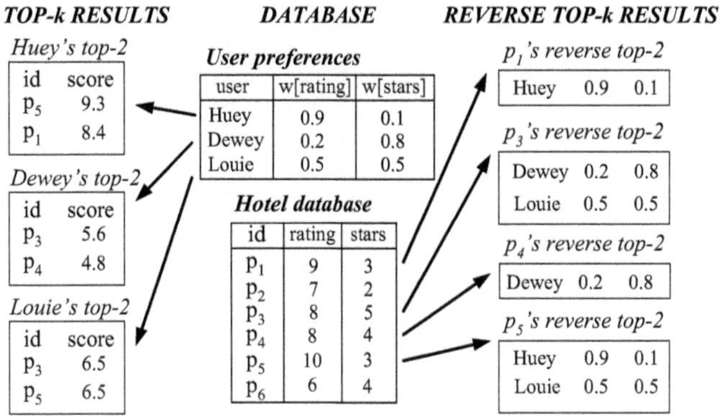

Figure 1: Example of reverse top-k queries.

More formally, a reverse top-k query returns for a point q and a positive integer k, the set of linear preference functions (in terms of weighting vectors) for which q is contained in their top-k result. Consider for example a database containing information about different hotels as well as user preferences, as depicted in Figure 1. For each of the six hotels, the rating and the number of stars are recorded, and maximum values on each attribute are preferable[1]. The database also stores the preferences of three users (Huey, Dewey and Louie) in terms of weights on each attribute. Different users may have different preferences about a potential hotel. For instance, Huey prefers hotels with high rating values, whereas Dewey is interested in hotels with many stars. Louie is indifferent or values equally rating and stars. On the left part of the figure, the top-2 hotels are depicted for each user along with their scores. On the right part, the reverse top-2 results are shown for the hotels. Notice

[1]In the remaining of this paper, minimum values will be preferable, without loss of generality.

that p_2 and p_6 have empty reverse top-2 result sets, i.e., they do not belong to the top-2 list of any user.

Currently, the most efficient algorithm for computing the reverse top-k set is the RTA algorithm [19]. RTA has two main drawbacks when processing a reverse top-k query: (i) it needs to access all stored user preferences, and (ii) it cannot avoid executing a top-k query for each user preference (determined by the corresponding user weights) that belongs to the result set. As a result, the performance of RTA is sensitive to the cardinality of the reverse top-k result; for queries with result sets of high cardinality RTA often becomes inefficient. Since we expect that reverse top-k queries will be posed for query points that are highly ranked, and therefore have a result set of high cardinality, this drawback severely limits the practicality of RTA.

To alleviate the shortcomings of RTA, in this paper, we study the conditions in which a set of weighting vectors (representing linear preference functions) can be immediately added to the result set. Therefore, we focus on whether a data point may be ranked higher than the query point for a set of weighting vectors. In addition, we address the question whether a set of weighting vectors can be excluded from the reverse top-k result. Based on these properties, we develop an efficient branch-and-bound algorithm assuming that both data sets are indexed by multidimensional access methods.

The contributions of this paper are summarized here:

- We introduce useful properties for processing reverse top-k queries without accessing each user's individual preferences nor executing the respective top-k query.
- We present a novel algorithm that processes sets of weighting vectors, without having to examine each vector individually, and use this algorithm as basic building block for our reverse top-k algorithms.
- We propose a framework for reverse top-k query processing that employs the branch-and-bound methodology and exploits the introduced properties.
- We present two optimizations of the basic branch-and-bound algorithm (BBR) that use result sharing ($BBR*$) and an aggregate R-tree ($BBRA$) to boost its performance.
- We conduct a thorough experimental evaluation that demonstrates the efficiency of our proposed algorithms.

The rest of this paper is structured as follows: Section 2 reviews related work. Section 3 presents some preliminaries, while Section 4 introduces the theoretical properties. Then, in Section 5, we present how sets of weighting vectors can be processed, without having to examine each one individually. Section 6 describes the branch-and-bound algorithm and its optimizations. In Section 7, we present the results of the experimental evaluation, and we conclude in Section 8.

2. RELATED WORK

Recently, the support of efficient top-k query processing has attracted much attention in the database research community. As reverse top-k queries are inherently related to top-k query processing, we summarize some representative work here. Onion [4] precomputes and stores the convex hulls of data points in layers. Then, the evaluation of a linear top-k query is accomplished by processing the layers inwards, starting from the outmost hull. Prefer [10] uses materialized views of top-k result sets, according to arbitrary scoring functions. During query processing, Prefer selects the materialized view corresponding to the function that is most similar to the query scoring function, and examines a subset of the data elements in this view. Efficient maintenance of materialized views for top-k queries is discussed in [26]. The robust index [24] is a sequential indexing approach that improves the performance of Onion [4] and Prefer [10]. The main idea is that a tuple should be placed at the deepest layer possible, in order to reduce the probability of accessing it at query processing time, without compromising the correctness of the result. Fagin et al. [7] introduce TA and NRA algorithms for computing the top-k queries over multiple sources, where each source provides a ranking of a subset of attributes only. Variations of them have been proposed that try to improve some of their limitations and have been studied in other application areas, leading to various threshold-based algorithms [1, 5, 9, 14]. Branch-and-bound processing of top-k queries has been studied in [17].

Reverse top-k queries [19, 20] have been proposed for assessing the impact of a potential product in the market, based on the number of users that deem this product as one of their top-k products according to their preferences. Recently, various applications of reverse top-k queries have appeared, including identifying the most influential products [22], and monitoring the popularity of locations based on user mobility [21].

Evaluation of multiple top-k queries has been studied in [8]. Given a data set of points and a set of ranking functions, the authors propose some methods to compute the top-k for all functions (all top-k query). The proposed methods exploit the fact that similar queries share common results to avoid evaluating the top-k queries one-by-one. The first algorithm (BINL) assumes that the data points are indexed by a multidimensional index and the functions are partitioned into groups based on their similarity. BINL processes each group of functions separately and uses bounds in order to avoid computing the exact score of the MBRs. Although BINL reduces the score computations that are required to retrieve the top-k sets of all functions, BINL does not support early termination, which means that the entire index of the data points has to be traversed once for each group of functions. The second algorithm (BLPTA) relies on materialized views. BLPTA answers multiple top-k queries by traversing each view once and can terminate early. In addition, the authors show that the proposed methods can be used also for processing reverse top-k queries. Obviously, if the result set for all top-k queries is known, it is trivial to find the reverse top-k set of a query point. Nevertheless, as shown in the experimental evaluation of [8], computing the all top-k query instead of a reverse top-k query is more expensive and it is useful only if the result of the all top-k query is maintained for answering multiple reverse top-k queries. A recent approach for evaluating multiple top-k queries has appeared in [27]. The proposed framework can be employed to process reverse top-k queries efficiently, however it requires to pre-process all top-k queries in W, and then build an index over the k-th ranked objects of each query. In contrast, our approach does not require such heavy pre-processing, and more importantly it avoids processing all top-k queries.

Different reverse query types, which take as input a data point and aim to find the queries that have this data point in their result set have been studied. Reverse nearest neighbor (RNN) queries were originally proposed in [11]. An RNN query finds the set of points that have the query point as their nearest neighbor. Recently, reverse furthest neighbor queries [25] are introduced, that are similar to RNN queries. The reverse skyline query [6, 13] identifies customers that would be interested in a product based on the dominance of the competitors products. In [3], the authors generalize the concept of reverse queries and propose the inverse queries that take as an input more than one data point. In particular, inverse

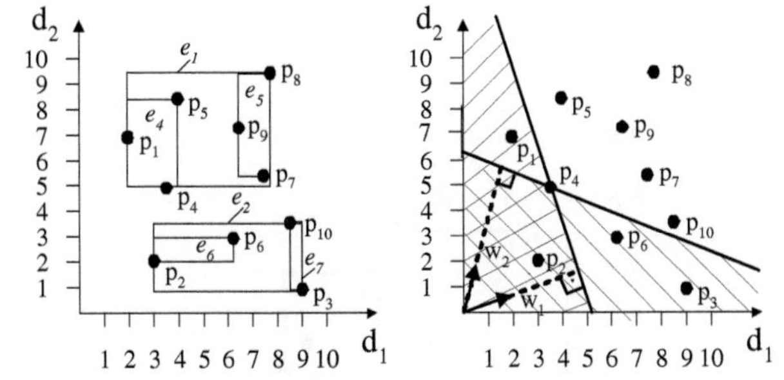

(a) Data set S (b) Reverse top-k query

Figure 2: Data set S and reverse top-k query.

range queries, inverse k-nearest neighbor queries, and inverse skyline queries are studied.

Several papers have proposed methods that aim to quantify the impact of products in the market. DADA [12] aims to help manufactures position their products in the market, based on three types of dominance relationship analysis queries. Creating competitive products has been recently studied in [23]. Nevertheless in these approaches, user preferences are expressed as data points that represent preferable products, whereas reverse top-k queries examine user preferences in terms of weighting vectors. Miah et al. [15] study a different problem, again from the perspective of manufacturers. The authors propose an algorithm that selects the subset of attributes that increases the visibility of a new product. Customer identification and product positioning has been recently studied in [2], where the attractiveness of a product is defined based on the concept of reverse skyline query.

3. PRELIMINARIES

Let D denote a data space defined by a set of n dimensions $\{d_1, \ldots, d_n\}$. Let S denote a set of database objects on D with cardinality $|S|$. Each dimension represents a numerical scoring attribute. A database object can be represented as a point $p \in S$, such that $p = \{p[1], \ldots, p[n]\}$, where $p[i]$ is a value on dimension d_i. Thus, the values $p[i]$ are numerical non-negative scores that evaluate the corresponding attributes of database objects. Without loss of generality, in this paper, we further assume that smaller score values are preferable.

In this paper, we assume that the data set S is indexed by a multidimensional index, such as an R-tree. The R-tree groups together nearby points in the data space and represents them by minimum bounding rectangles (MBRs) in the next higher level of the tree. An MBR is the smallest rectangle completely enclosing a set of points and each MBR contains at least one data point. Each MBR m is described by the coordinates of two of its opposite corners, namely the lower-left corner $(m.l)$ and the upper-right corner $(m.u)$. An intermediate entry e_i corresponds to the minimum bounding rectangle (MBR) $e_i.m$ that encloses the entries of the lower level, while a leaf entry corresponds to a data point. Figure 2(a) depicts an example of a data set S indexed by an R-tree.

3.1 Top-k Queries

Top-k queries are defined based on a scoring function f that aggregates the individual scores of an object into an overall score. The most important and commonly used case of scoring functions is the weighted sum function, also called linear. Each dimension d_i has an associated query-dependent weight $w[i]$ indicating d_i's relative importance for the query. The aggregated score $f_w(p)$ for

Symbols	Description
D	Data space
n	Data dimensionality
S	Data set of data points
W	Data set of weighting vectors
V	Subset of W
$p[i]$	Value of point p on dimension i
q	n-dimensional query point
w	Weighting vector
m	Minimum bounding rectangle (MBR)
$\ell_V(m)$	Lower bound of score of m based on V
$u_V(m)$	Upper bound of score of m based on V
$q \prec_V m$	q precedes m based on V
$RTOP_k(q)$	Reverse top-k result set

Table 1: Overview of symbols.

data point p is defined as a weighted sum of the individual scores: $f_w(p) = \sum_{i=1}^{n} w[i] \cdot p[i]$, where $w[i] \geq 0$ $(1 \leq i \leq n)$ and $\sum_{i=1}^{n} w[i] = 1$. Since the weights represent the *relative* importance between different dimensions the assumption $\sum_{i=1}^{n} w[i] = 1$ does not influence the definition of top-k queries.

DEFINITION 1. (Top-k query)*: Given a positive integer k and a user-defined weighting vector w, the result set $TOP_k(w)$ of the top-k query is a set of points such that $TOP_k(w) \subseteq S$, $|TOP_k(w)| = k$ and $\forall p_i, p_j : p_i \in TOP_k(w)$, $p_j \in S - TOP_k(w)$ it holds that $f_w(p_i) \leq f_w(p_j)$.*

A delicate situation arises when two (or more) objects share the same score for the k-th position. In this case, for simplicity reasons, we assume that it suffices to report any one of them as k-th result.

3.2 Reverse Top-k Queries

Given a query object q, the reverse top-k query identifies all weighting vectors for which q belongs to the top-k result set. The formal definition of the reverse top-k query follows. Notice that this definition corresponds to the bichromatic version of the reverse top-k query (cf. [19]), which assumes that a set of user preferences W exists.

DEFINITION 2. (Reverse top-k query [19])*: Given a point q and a positive number k, as well as two data sets S and W of data points and weighting vectors respectively, a weighting vector $w_i \in W$ belongs to the reverse top-k ($RTOP_k(q)$) result set of q, if and only if $\exists p \in TOP_k(w_i)$ such that $f_{w_i}(q) \leq f_{w_i}(p)$.*

In Figure 2(b), a data set S is depicted together with two different weighting vectors w_1 and w_2. Geometrically, in the Euclidean space a linear top-k query can be represented by a vector w. In this example, the dimension d_1 is preferable for w_1, whereas d_2 is more preferable for w_2. Assuming that p_4 is the query point, the shaded areas define its rank, which is equal to the number of the points enclosed in the corresponding shaded area of a weighting vector w_i. We notice that w_1 belongs to the reverse top-3 query result set, since only 2 objects are contained in the shaded area of w_1. However, w_2 belongs to the reverse top-4 query result set (but not to the reverse top-3), since there exist 3 objects in the shaded area of w_2.

4. THEORETICAL PROPERTIES

In this section we analyze the effect of a set $V \in W$ of weighting vectors on (a) the score of a single data point $p \in S$, and (b) on the score of a set of data points $\{p_i\} \in S$ (represented by an MBR m, i.e., each p_i is enclosed in m). In particular, we derive lower and upper bounds on the scores of p and m. The derived bounds establish score precedence relationships between a query point q and other data point(s). Eventually, this allows us to determine whether the rank of q based on V is affected by a set of data points. Table 1 summarizes the most important symbols used in this paper.

4.1 Score Bounds on Points and MBRs

First, we provide a formal definition of the *score* of a data point based on a weighting vector $w \in W$.

DEFINITION 3. (Score of point p): *Given a data point $p \in S$ and a weighting vector $w \in W$, the score of p is: $f_w(p) = \sum_{i=1}^{n} w[i] \cdot p[i]$.*

Given a set of weighting vectors $V \subseteq W$, we define the minimum and maximum score of a data point p based on V. We denote the score-lower-bound and score-upper-bound of p with $\ell_V(p)$ and $u_V(p)$ respectively.

DEFINITION 4. (Score-lower-bound of point p): *Given a set of weighting vectors V and a data point p, the score-lower-bound of p is: $\ell_V(p) = \sum_{i=1}^{n} min_{\forall w \in V}(w[i]) \cdot p[i]$.*

DEFINITION 5. (Score-upper-bound of point p): *Given a set of weighting vectors V and a data point p, the score-upper-bound of p is: $u_V(p) = \sum_{i=1}^{n} max_{\forall w \in V}(w[i]) \cdot p[i]$.*

Capitalizing on these scores of a point p with respect to a set of weighting vectors V, we are able to derive a *lower bound* and an *upper bound* of the score of p in a straightforward manner.

LEMMA 1. (Score bounds of p): *Given a set of weighting vectors V and a data point p, the score $f_w(p)$ of p is lower-bounded by $\ell_V(p)$ and upper-bounded by $u_V(p)$, i.e., it holds that $\forall w \in V$: $\ell_V(p) \leq f_w(p) \leq u_V(p)$.*

PROOF. It holds that: $f_w(p) = w[1] \cdot p[1] + \cdots + w[n] \cdot p[n] \leq max_{\forall w \in V}(w[1]) \cdot p[1] + \cdots + max_{\forall w \in V}(w[n]) \cdot p[n] = u_V(p)$. Similarly, it holds that: $f_w(p) = w[1] \cdot p[1] + \cdots + w[n] \cdot p[n] \geq min_{\forall w \in V}(w[1]) \cdot p[1] + \cdots + min_{\forall w \in V}(w[n]) \cdot p[n] = \ell_V(p)$. $\square$

In the following, we generalize the score bounds for the case of a set of data points that are represented by a minimum bounding rectangle (MBR) m and we denote as $m.l$ the lower-left corner and as $m.u$ the upper-right corner. Given a set of weighting vectors $V \subseteq W$ and an MBR m of data points, we can define a lower and upper bound of the scores of all data points that are enclosed in m based on any $w \in V$. The bounds are $\ell_V(m) = \ell_V(m.l)$ and $u_V(m) = u_V(m.u)$ respectively.

LEMMA 2. (Score bounds of MBR m): *Given a set of weighting vectors $w \in V \subseteq W$ and an MBR $m \in S$, the score $f_w(p)$ of every point $p \in m$ is lower-bounded by $\ell_V(m) = \ell_V(m.l)$ and upper-bounded by $u_V(m) = u_V(m.u)$, i.e., it holds that $\forall p \in m, \forall w \in V$: $\ell_V(m) \leq f_w(p) \leq u_V(m)$.*

PROOF. It holds that: $f_w(p) = w[1] \cdot p[1] + \cdots + w[n] \cdot p[n] \leq max_{\forall w \in V}(w[1]) \cdot p[1] + \cdots + max_{\forall w \in V}(w[n]) \cdot p[n] \leq max_{\forall w \in V}(w[1]) \cdot m.u[1] + \cdots + max_{\forall w \in V}(w[n]) \cdot m.u[n] = u_V(m)$. Similarly, it holds that: $f_w(p) = w[1] \cdot p[1] + \cdots + w[n] \cdot p[n] \geq min_{\forall w \in V}(w[1]) \cdot p[1] + \cdots + min_{\forall w \in V}(w[n]) \cdot p[n] \geq min_{\forall w \in V}(w[1]) \cdot m.l[1] + \cdots + min_{\forall w \in V}(w[n]) \cdot m.l[n] = \ell_V(m)$. $\square$

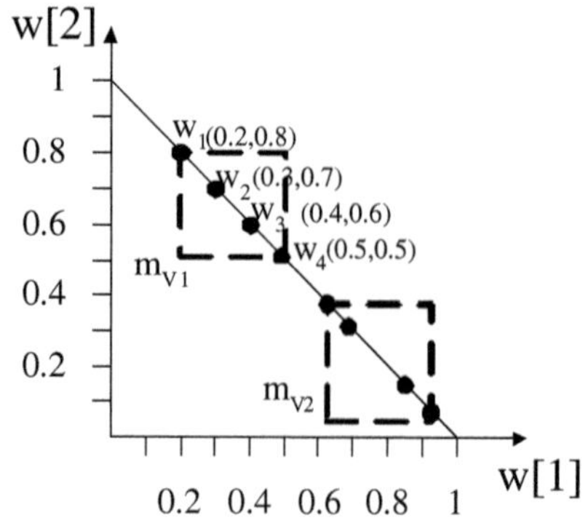

Figure 3: Example of data set W.

In the case in which an MBR m_V that encloses the set of weighting vectors V is given, the definition of the bounds $\ell_V(p)$ and $u_V(p)$ of the scores for a data point p can be derived by means of the lower-left corner and the upper-right corner of the MBR m_V respectively.

EXAMPLE 1. *In Figure 3, a set $V = \{w_1, w_2, w_3, w_4\}$ of four 2-dimensional weighting vectors is depicted, which are enclosed by an MBR defined by the lower-left corner $[0.2, 0.5]$ and the upper-right corner $[0.5, 0.8]$. Then, the values $\ell_V(p) = 0.2 \cdot p[1] + 0.5 \cdot p[2]$ and $u_V(p) = 0.5 \cdot p[1] + 0.8 \cdot p[2]$ define a lower and an upper bound respectively of the score $f_w(p)$ of any data point p based on V. For example, consider a data point p with $p[1] = 5$ and $p[2] = 3$, then $f_{w_1}(p) = 3.4$, $f_{w_2}(p) = 3.6$, $f_{w_3}(p) = 3.8$ and $f_{w_4}(p) = 4$, while $\ell_V(p) = 2.5$ and $u_V(p) = 4.9$.*

4.2 Score Precedence

Consider a reverse top-k query, defined by a query point q and a value k, and a multidimensional index (R-tree) over data set S. The goal is to find under which conditions a set of weighting vectors $V \subseteq W$ belongs to the reverse top-k result of q. In order to solve this problem, we first determine whether q has a better rank than a set of data points that are enclosed in an MBR m.

Given a set $V \subseteq W$ of weighting vectors, we can exploit the score bounds of data points and MBRs in order to map their potential scores to intervals. For instance, $\forall w \in V$ the score $f_w(q)$ of the query point belongs to the interval $[\ell_V(q), u_V(q)]$. Similarly, the score $f_w(p)$ of every point $p \in m$ belongs to the interval $[\ell_V(m), u_V(m)]$. We define a partial order between the query point and the MBRs of S based on the score bounds, which is used to compare the potential score of q to the score of the MBRs.

DEFINITION 6. (Score precedence): *Given a set $V \subseteq W$ of weighting vectors, a query point q, and an MBR m of data points, if $u_V(q) < \ell_V(m)$, then we say that q precedes m and we denote $q \prec_V m$. Similarly, if $u_V(m) < \ell_V(q)$, we say that m precedes q and we denote $m \prec_V q$. Otherwise, we say that q and m are incomparable and we denote $m \asymp_V q$.*

By studying the possible precedence relationships between the score interval of q and of an MBR m, we distinguish the following three cases (as depicted in Figure 4):

- **Case 1:** If $u_V(q) < \ell_V(m)$, i.e., q precedes m ($q \prec_V m$), then $\forall w \in V$ the score $f_w(q)$ of q is better than the score $f_w(p)$ of every point $p \in m$. Consequently, no point $p \in m$ can affect the rank of q for any weighting vector $w \in V$.

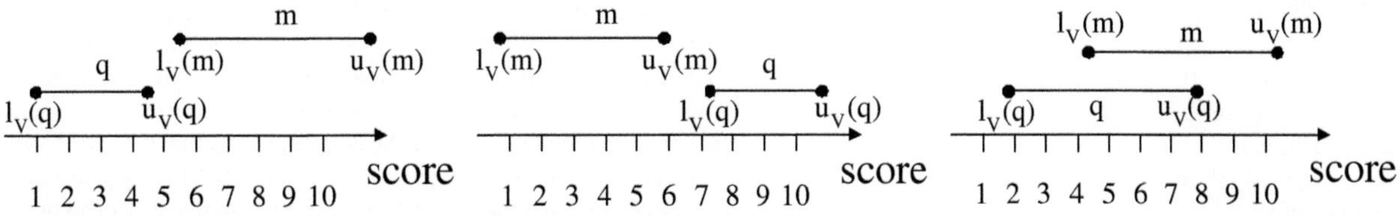

(a) Case 1: q precedes m ($q \prec_V m$) (b) Case 2: m precedes q ($m \prec_V q$) (c) Case 3: q, m incomparable ($m \asymp_V q$)

Figure 4: Intervals of scores and precedence relationships between query point q and MBR m.

- **Case 2:** If $u_V(m) < \ell_V(q)$, i.e., m precedes q ($m \prec_V q$), then every data point $p \in m$ has a better score than q for any weighting vector $w \in V$. This means that all points $p \in m$ have a better rank than q for any weighting vector $w \in V$.
- **Case 3:** If none of the above cases holds, then q and m are incomparable ($m \asymp_V q$) and there exists an overlap between the intervals. In this case, it cannot be determined whether q has a better or worse score than a data point $p \in m$ for a weighting vector $w \in V$. This means that q can have a better rank than some points of m for a weighting vector $w \in V$, while it can have a worse rank for other points of m or another $w' \in V$.

5. INTOPK ALGORITHM

To address limitations of existing approaches, the first step is to provide a method for determining if a given set of weighting vectors $V \subseteq W$ belongs to the reverse top-k results of q or not. To this end, we present the INTOPk algorithm that efficiently answers this question. Intuitively, INTOPk attempts to handle a set of weighting vectors without accessing each individual vector nor processing the top-k query, thus providing the missing functionality of RTA. This constitutes a key technical contribution of this paper. In the next section, we will describe how INTOPk can be exploited by a branch-and-bound algorithm that can directly compete with RTA.

In the following, a set $V \subseteq W$ of weighting vectors is represented by an MBR denoted as m_V. Given a data set S, the INTOPk algorithm takes as an input the MBR m_V, a query point q and a value k, and returns whether q belongs to the top-k result set for all or none of the weighting vectors enclosed in m_V. If none of these cases holds, the INTOPk algorithm returns that it cannot give a definite answer.

5.1 Pruning Property and Result Inclusion

By exploiting score precedence between the query point q and an MBR m_V of weighting vectors V, we can derive a useful pruning property for sets of weighting vectors $V \subseteq W$. The pruning property enables discarding MBRs of weighting vectors at once, without even accessing the individual vectors.

THEOREM 1. (Pruning property)*: Given a set of weighting vectors $V \subseteq W$ represented by an MBR m_V, and a reverse top-k query $RTOP_k(q)$, if k data items (MBRs or data points) precede q based on V, then m_V can be safely pruned, i.e., no weighting vector $w \in V$ belongs to the reverse top-k result of q.*

PROOF. By contradiction. Let us assume that $w \in V$ belongs to the reverse top-k result of q. Since k data items precede q based on V and any MBR encloses at least one data point, it holds that $\exists p_i$, $1 \leq i \leq k$ such that $u_V(p_i) < \ell_V(q)$, which leads to $f_w(p_i) \leq u_V(p_i) < \ell_V(q) \leq f_w(q)$. This means that there exist at least k data points with better score than q for any $w \in W$. This leads to a contradiction, since by definition if w belongs to the reverse top-k result of q, then at most $k-1$ data points p_i have a better score than q based on w. □

Additional pruning can be achieved in the case that V consists of a single vector w. Again, w can be discarded without evaluating the top-k query, based on the following lemma.

LEMMA 3. *Given a single weighting vector $w \in W$ and a reverse top-k query $RTOP_k(q)$, if for at least k data points p_i it holds that $u_{\{w\}}(q) > \ell_{\{w\}}(p_i)$, then the weighting vector $w \in W$ can be safely excluded from the reverse top-k result of q.*

PROOF. Let p_i, $1 \leq i \leq k'$ be the k' ($\geq k$) data points such that $u_{\{w\}}(q) > \ell_{\{w\}}(p_i)$. Moreover, for any data point by definition it holds that $\ell_{\{w\}}(p) = f_w(p) = u_{\{w\}}(p)$. Thus, $\forall p_i$ it holds that: $f_w(p_i) = \ell_{\{w\}}(p_i) < u_{\{w\}}(q) = f_w(q)$. Since for at least k data points it holds that $f_w(p) < f_w(q)$ (k data points have a better score than q for w), it means that w is not in the reverse top-k result of q. □

Notice that Lemma 3 does not hold for MBRs of weighting vectors, but only for a single weighting vector.

Furthermore, we derive a rule for immediate inclusion of an MBR of weighting vectors to the reverse top-k query result, without examining each weighting vector individually.

THEOREM 2. (Result inclusion)*: Given a set of weighting vectors $V \subseteq W$ represented by an MBR m_V, and a reverse top-k query $RTOP_k(q)$, if fewer than k data points p_i exist such that $u_V(q) > \ell_V(p_i)$, then all weighting vectors $w \in V$ can be safely added to the reverse top-k result of q.*

PROOF. Let p_i, $1 \leq i \leq k' < k$ be the k' data points such that $u_V(q) > \ell_V(p_i)$. Then, for all remaining points $p \in S - \{p_i\}$ it holds that $u_V(q) \leq \ell_V(p)$. We will prove the theorem by contradiction. Let us assume that $\exists w \in V$ that does not belong to the reverse top-k result of q. This means that there exist k data points p'_i such that $f_w(p'_i) < f_w(q)$ from which we derive that $\ell_V(p'_i) \leq f_w(p'_i) < f_w(q) \leq u_V(q)$, i.e., $\ell_V(p'_i) < u_V(q)$. Since $\forall p \in S - \{p_i\}$ it holds that $u_V(q) \leq \ell_V(p)$ and the size of set $\{p_i\}$ is k' ($< k$), this leads to a contradiction. □

The aforementioned theorems 1 and 2 and lemma 3 guide the design of an efficient algorithm for determining whether all weighting vectors in V or none of them belong to the reverse top-k results set of q.

5.2 Algorithmic Description

Algorithm 1 describes the pseudocode for the INTOPk algorithm. The algorithm contains an initialization phase, which is followed by a traversal of the R-tree of data set S. The algorithm uses two counters to determine whether m_V belongs to the result set or

Algorithm 1 INTOPk()

1: **Input:** MBR m_V of weighting vectors, query $RTOP_k(q)$
2: **Output:** -1: discard m_V, 0: inconclusive, 1: add m_V
3: $precincPoints \leftarrow 0$, $precEntries \leftarrow 0$
4: $e \leftarrow$ RtreeS.getRoot()
5: **if** $(u_V(q) > \ell_V(e.m))$ **then**
6:     *heapS*.enqueue(e)
7:     **if** $(e.m \prec_V q)$ **then**
8:         $precEntries$++
9: **while** (!*heapS*.isEmpty()) **do**
10:     $e \leftarrow$ *heapS*.dequeue()
11:     **if** $((precincPoints \geq k)$ **and** $(\ell_V(e.m) \geq \ell_V(q)))$ **then**
12:         **if** (m_V is a single w) **then**
13:             **return** -1
14:         **else**
15:             **return** 0
16:     **if** $(e.m \prec_V q)$ **then**
17:         $precEntries$– –
18:     $C \leftarrow expand(e)$
19:     **for all** $(e_i \in C)$ **do**
20:         **if** $(u_V(q) > \ell_V(e_i.m))$ **then**
21:             **if** $(e_i.m \prec_V q)$ **then**
22:                 $precEntries$++
23:                 **if** $(precEntries \geq k)$ **then**
24:                     **return** -1
25:             **if** (e_i is a data point) **then**
26:                 $precincPoints$++
27:             **else**
28:                 *heapS*.enqueue(e_i)
29: **if** $(precincPoints \geq k)$ **then**
30:     **return** 0
31: **else**
32:     **return** 1

not. The first counter denoted as $precEntries$ counts the entries e such that $e.m$ precede q based on V. If the number of these entries is greater than or equal to k, then we can exclude m_V from the result set based on Theorem 1. The second counter $precincPoints$ counts the data points that are either incomparable or precede q. Based on Theorem 2, if fewer than k such entries exist, m_V can be added to the result set[2].

In the initialization phase (lines 3–8), the root e of the R-tree is accessed. If $u_V(q) > \ell_V(e.m)$, then some of the data points enclosed in $e.m$ may have a better rank than q for some weighting vector enclosed in m_V. Therefore, the root entry is inserted into a heap (*heapS*) that contains entries of S that need to be further examined. This heap is sorted in ascending order of $\ell_V(m)$, because the entries with small (better) lower bound values have a higher probability to discard m_V. Then, the algorithm tests if $e.m$ precedes q. If that is the case, then all points enclosed in $e.m$ have a better rank than q for all weighting vectors in m_V. Since we assume that at least one data point is enclosed in each MBR $e.m$, $precEntries$ increases by one. Note that if q precedes the root entry $e.m$, then q has a better rank than any point of S, and the algorithm returns 1 (line 32) indicating that all weighting vectors of m_V can be added to the result set.

During the traversal of the R-tree (lines 9–28), in each iteration, the entry e of the heap with the best $\ell_V(m)$ value is examined. The INTOPk algorithm excludes m_V from the result set whenever it can safely decide that none of the weighting vectors in m_V can be included to the result set. Thus, if k data points have been retrieved that are either incomparable or precede q (line 11), it checks whether an MBR $e.m$ that has not been examined yet can exclude m_V from the result set. Since the MBRs are examined sorted based on $\ell_V(m)$, if the value $\ell_V(m)$ of the next MBR is larger or equal to $\ell_V(q)$, it means that there exists no other MBR that precedes q and m_V cannot be excluded from the result set. In addition, since k data points exist that are incomparable or precede q, m_V cannot be added to the result set. Therefore, INTOPk returns that it cannot give a definite answer, i.e., inconclusive. On the other hand, if m_V represents a single weighting vector (line 12), then based on Lemma 3 m_V can be discarded.

If $precincPoints$ is smaller than k, then the entry e will be expanded. If $e.m$ precedes q based on V, then we reduce $precEntries$ (line 17), since e will be expanded and the enclosed entries (MBRs or data points) will be counted. Since e is a non-leaf entry (only non-leaf entries are added to the heap), we expand the MBR and retrieve the list of children entries C. If q precedes a child entry, then this child entry is ignored, since it cannot influence the ranking of q. Note that also if $u_V(q) = \ell_V(e_i.m)$ the entry can be ignored, because based on the definition only points that have a better score influence the ranking of q. Otherwise, for each $e_i.m$ that precedes q, we increase $precEntries$ by one (line 22). In the case, where $e_i.m$ is a leaf entry, then we test if q precedes $e_i.m$ and if this is not the case we increase $precincPoints$ by one. Non-leaf entries are added to the heap and a new iteration of the algorithm starts. If all entries of S have been either discarded or examined and fewer than k data points that are incomparable or precede q have been found, then all weights of m_V can be added to the result set (line 32).

EXAMPLE 2. *In Figure 5, consider a reverse top-k query with $k = 2$ where the query point q has coordinates $q[1] = 5$ and $q[2] = 6.5$. Furthermore, let m_V be defined by the lower-left corner $m_V.l$=[0.2, 0.5] and the upper-right corner $m_V.u$=[0.5, 0.8]. Then, the lower and upper bound of q are $\ell_V(q)$=4.25 and $u_V(q)$=7.7, respectively. In the initialization phase, the root of the R-tree is accessed. Then, in the first iteration of INTOPk the root entry is expanded and entries e_1 and e_2 are inserted in heapS. Since e_2 has a smaller ℓ_V value, it is accessed first. During the expansion of e_2, entries e_6 and e_7 are inserted in the heap. Next, e_6 is accessed (based on the ℓ_V value) and the data points p_3 and p_5 are retrieved. The values of the counters become $precEntries = 1$ and $precincPoints = 2$. In the next iteration, e_7 is accessed and $precincPoints = 2 \geq k$, but the INTOPk algorithm continues with the next iteration. This is because $\ell_V(e_7.m) < \ell_V(q)$ and entries that may discard m_V can still be retrieved. Afterwards, e_7 is expanded and the data points p_8 and p_9 are retrieved. Point p_8 causes the increase of $precEntries = 2$ and therefore INTOPk terminates by returning -1 indicating that none of the weighting vectors of m_V belongs to the reverse top-2 result set of q.*

6. BRANCH-AND-BOUND ALGORITHM

In this section, we present the branch-and-bound algorithm for efficiently retrieving the reverse top-k result set of a query point q. First, we present the basic version of the algorithm in Section 6.1, and then we study two optimizations that boost its performance. In Section 6.2, we employ result sharing of consecutive INTOPk evaluations, in order to reduce the number of invocations that are required. Finally, in Section 6.3, we propose an algorithm that employs an aggregate R-tree, thus resulting in additional performance gains.

[2]For simplicity, we assume that q does not belong to S, but it is straightforward to adapt the algorithm for this case too.

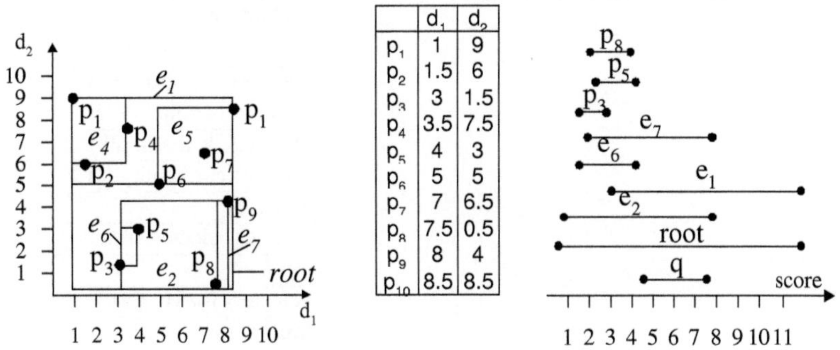

	d_1	d_2
p_1	1	9
p_2	1.5	6
p_3	3	1.5
p_4	3.5	7.5
p_5	4	3
p_6	5	5
p_7	7	6.5
p_8	7.5	0.5
p_9	8	4
p_{10}	8.5	8.5

Figure 5: Example of INTOPk algorithm.

6.1 Basic Branch-and-Bound Algorithm

Algorithm 2 describes our basic branch-and-bound algorithm (BBR). The algorithm uses an R-tree to index the data set of weighting vectors W. Intuitively, as our algorithm traverses this index, it bounds the search space of results for the reverse top-k query by discarding MBRs of weighting vectors that cannot contribute to the result set. Essentially, each time an entry of the R-tree is processed, our algorithm tests whether the weighting vectors that are enclosed by the MBR of the entry, forming a set V, may belong to the result set or whether it can be discarded. This test is accomplished in practice by using INTOPk algorithm, as described in Section 5. If INTOPk algorithm is inconclusive about V, the current entry of the R-tree needs to be expanded, and smaller subsets of V need to be examined for inclusion or pruning. The goal of BBR is to expand as few entries as possible by either discarding entries of the R-tree or by adding them to the result set immediately.

BBR traverses the R-tree that indexes the data set W and maintains a heap (*heapW*) of R-tree entries. Initially, the root of the R-tree is inserted in *heapW*. The entries in the heap are sorted based on their distance to a given weighting vector, for example their distance to the vector $w[i] = 1/n, \forall i$. Notice that the benefits of accessing weighting vectors based on their similarity to the given vector has been investigated and evaluated experimentally in [20]. Then, in each iteration an entry e (MBR) is accessed from the heap and the INTOPk algorithm is executed for its MBR $e.m$. Depending on the result of INTOPk algorithm, e is either added to the result set, or expanded or discarded. In the case that an entry is expanded, all its children entries are inserted in the heap (line 8). Otherwise, if the weighting vectors that correspond to an entry should be added, then all data points (i.e., weighting vectors) stored in the subtree rooted at e are retrieved and added to the result set (line 11). The $expandAll()$ method in the pseudocode retrieves all weighting vectors stored in the subtree rooted at e.

THEOREM 3. (Correctness of BBR): *The BBR algorithm always produces the correct reverse top-k result set.*

PROOF. *(Sketch)*: In BBR, every entry e of the R-tree indexing W is either added to the results or discarded (we note that expanding an entry also eventually results in adding or discarding the enclosed entries). Hence, it suffices to show that BBR never discards an entry that contains a weighting vector that is a reverse top-k result (false negatives), and never adds an entry that contains a weighting vector that is not a reverse top-k result (false positives).

- False negatives: Algorithm 1 decides to discard an entry e in two cases. In the first case, k discrete entries $e_i.m$ were found that precede q based on V and Theorem 1 verifies that no vector $w \in V$ can belong to the result. In the second case, only single weighting vectors are discarded, for which it holds that there exist at least k data points p_i such that $u_{\{w\}}(q) > \ell_{\{w\}}(p_i)$, and Lemma 3 proves that these weighting vectors can be safely discarded.

- False positives: Algorithm 1 adds an entry e to the result set, if fewer than k data points p_i exist such that $u_V(q) > \ell_V(p_i)$. Theorem 2 proves that in this case, any $w \in V$ belongs to the reverse top-k result.

□

Algorithm 2 BBR

```
1: Input: Point q, value k
2: Output: Reverse top-k result set RTOP_k(q)
3: heapW.enqueue(RtreeW.getRoot())
4: while (!heapW.isEmpty()) do
5:    e ← heapW.dequeue()
6:    i ← INTOPk(e.m, q, k)
7:    if i = 0 then
8:       heapW.enqueue(expand(e))
9:    else
10:      if i = 1 then
11:         RTOP_k(q) ← RTOP_k(q) ∪ expandAll(e)
12: return RTOP_k(q)
```

6.2 Branch-and-Bound with Result Sharing

As BBR traverses the R-tree indexing W, for each entry that needs to be processed, a traversal of the R-tree indexing S is initiated. Clearly, the performance of BBR depends on the number of invocations of the INTOPk algorithm, which is the cause of I/Os on the index of data set S. To improve the performance of BBR, it is beneficial to avoid INTOPk invocations (and the respective I/Os) when possible. Therefore, we employ a *result sharing* method that greatly reduces the accesses on this index. The new result sharing approach is termed $BBR*$ and is depicted in Algorithm 3.

$BBR*$ exploits previously computed results to avoid redundant processing. As explained in Section 5, Algorithm 1 achieves to discard an entry m_V due to the retrieval of k data items m_i (data points or MBRs) of the index on S that precede q on m_V. These data items can potentially lead to discarding subsequent weighting vectors, i.e., if m_i precede q based on the next entry m'_V. Therefore $BBR*$ maintains this set of MBRs in a list of bounded size k, denoted as *topk*, and uses this list for avoiding invocations of the INTOPk algorithm.

Algorithm 3 *BBR∗*

1: **Input:** Point q, value k
2: **Output:** Reverse top-k result set $RTOP_k(q)$
3: *heapW*.enqueue(RtreeW.getRoot())
4: **while** (!*heapW*.isEmpty()) **do**
5: $m_V \leftarrow$ *heapW*.dequeue()
6: $precEntries \leftarrow 0$
7: **for all** $(m_i \in topk)$ **do**
8: **if** $(u_V(m_i) \leq \ell_V(q))$ **then**
9: $precEntries$++
10: **if** $(precEntries < k)$ **then**
11: $i \leftarrow INTOPk(m_V, q, k)$
12: **if** $i = 0$ **then**
13: *heapW*.enqueue(expand(m_V))
14: **else**
15: **if** $i = 1$ **then**
16: $RTOP_k(q) \leftarrow RTOP_k(q) \bigcup$ expandAll(m_V)
17: **else**
18: update $topk$
19: **return** $RTOP_k(q)$

In the pseudocode of Algorithm 3, each time an entry m_V is accessed (line 5), a test is conducted between q and each of the MBRs maintained in the list $topk$ (lines 6– 9). If k MBRs precede q (line 8), then the INTOPk invocation based on m_V is avoided (line 10). The list $topk$ is updated each time the INTOPk algorithm results in discarding an entry m_V (line 18).

6.3 Branch-and-Bound with Aggregate R-tree

The aggregate R-tree (aR-tree) [16] is a variant of the R-tree that combines indexing with pre-aggregation. In the aggregate R-tree, each data object is associated with a score. In addition, each entry is annotated with a score value that aggregates the scores of all children entries. Even though different aggregation functions can be employed by an aggregate R-tree, we assume that each entry adds the scores of its children entries. Furthermore, the score of each data object is set equal to one. Thus, the score of each entry corresponds exactly to the number of all points contained in its subtree (i.e., all points enclosed by the entry's MBR).

By employing an aggregate R-tree for indexing the dataset S, the performance of the branch-and-bound reverse top-k algorithm can be improved even further. In Algorithm 1, the counter $precEntries$ estimates the number of points that precede q. Increasing the counter by one is a lower bound of the actual number of data points, since each MBR is assumed to enclose at least one data point. In the case of the aggregate R-tree, the exact number of points that are stored in the subtree rooted by an entry e_i is known. The only necessary modification in Algorithm 1 is to replace the increment (decrement) of $precEntries$ by one, with an increment (decrement) by the score of the respective entry (lines 8, 17 and 22). Then, $precEntries$ provides an exact value, rather than an estimate. By using the aggregate score, Algorithm 1 can determine faster whether m_V should be discarded, and thus fewer entries of the R-tree index on S are expanded. Similarly, the performance of $BBR*$ can be improved by the aggregate R-tree, if in Algorithm 3 the counter $precEntries$ is increased (line 9) based on the aggregate score of the respective entry.

7. EXPERIMENTAL EVALUATION

In this section, we present an extensive experimental evaluation of the proposed branch-and-bound algorithm for reverse top-k queries. All variants of the presented algorithms are implemented in Java and the experiments run on a server with 2x4 cores (AMD Opteron), 32GB RAM, and 2TB HDD. The block size is set to 4KB and the buffer of the R-tree has a size of 100 nodes.

Parameter	**Values**
Data dimensionality n	2,3,**4**,5,6,7,8,9
Data set S distribution	**UN**,CO,AC,CL,RE
Data set cardinality $\|S\|$	**100K**,1M,5M
Data set W distribution	**UN**,CL
Weights cardinality $\|W\|$	**100K**,1M
#queries	1000
Queries selected from	**k-skyband**,skyline
top-k	**10**,20,30,40,50
#clusters for W,S: C_W,C_S	5
Variance σ_W^2, σ_S^2	0.05^2

Table 2: Experimental parameters.

7.1 Experimental Setup

Data sets. In the experimental study, we employ both real (RE) and synthetic data sets, namely uniform (UN), correlated (CO), anti-correlated (AC), and clustered (CL). In the case of synthetic data sets, the generated values of each attribute belong to $[0, 10K]$. For the uniform data set, all attribute values are generated independently using a uniform distribution. The anti-correlated data set is generated by selecting a plane perpendicular to the diagonal of the data space using a normal distribution, and within the plane each attribute value follows a uniform distribution. Similarly, for the correlated data set, first a plane perpendicular to the diagonal of the data space is selected by using a normal distribution and within the plane, each attribute value is generated using a normal distribution.

We also use two real data sets. HOUSE (Household) consists of 127930 6-dimensional tuples, representing the percentage of an American family's annual income spent on 6 types of expenditure: gas, electricity, water, heating, insurance, and property tax. COLOR is a data set from UCI Machine Learning Repository that contains image features extracted from a Corel image collection. It consists of 68040 9-dimensional tuples describing features of images in HSV color space. Both data sets have been used before in research related to rank-aware query processing [18].

For the data set W of the weighting vectors, two different data distributions are examined, namely uniform (UN) and clustered (CL). For the clustered data set W, first C_W cluster centroids that belong to the (n-1)-dimensional hyperplane defined by $\sum w_i = 1$ are selected randomly. Then, each coordinate is generated on the (n-1)-dimensional hyperplane by following a normal distribution on each axis with variance σ_W^2, and a mean equal to the corresponding coordinate of the centroid.

Description of RTA. For comparative purposes, we evaluate the performance of the proposed branch-and-bound algorithm against the state-of-the-art algorithm for reverse top-k queries, named RTA [19, 20]. RTA works by examining each weighting vector and trying to avoid processing of the respective top-k, when RTA can safely decide that the vector cannot belong to the reverse top-k result. To achieve this, RTA uses a buffer of k entries to keep the results of the previously posed top-k query, and uses these results to prune the next weighting vectors. In RTA, the data set S is indexed by an R-tree and the underlying top-k processing is performed using a state-of-the-art branch-and-bound algorithm for top-k queries. The weighting vectors are examined in an order

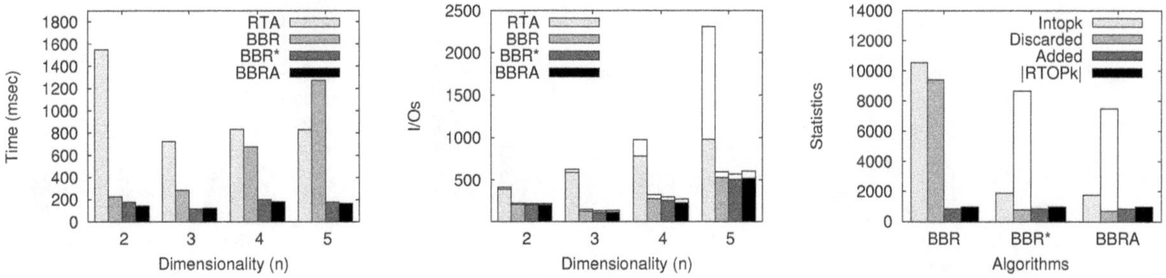

(a) Time. (b) I/Os. (c) Statistics.

Figure 6: Comparative performance of all algorithms for UN data set and varying dimensionality (n).

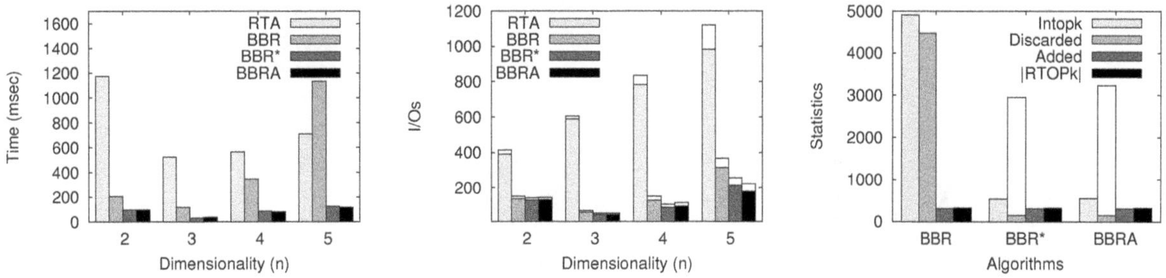

(a) Time. (b) I/Os. (c) Statistics.

Figure 7: Comparative performance of all algorithms for CL data set and varying dimensionality (n).

based on pairwise similarity, to increase the probability of pruning consecutive vectors. Hence, in the case of RTA, W is stored sorted on disk, while S is indexed by an R-tree.

Algorithms. We evaluate three variants of our branch-and-bound algorithm: basic (BBR), with result sharing ($BBR*$), and using aggregate R-tree ($BBRA$). The variants of the branch-and-bound algorithm use R-tree indexes on S and W, while $BBRA$ uses an aggregate R-tree on S.

Metrics. Our main metrics include: a) the query execution time required by each algorithm, and b) the I/Os used. The I/Os induced on S are buffered I/Os, while for the I/Os on W buffering is useless, since for a given query, W is not accessed multiple times. In the charts showing I/Os, each bar corresponds to the total number of I/Os induced by an algorithm, while the white part of the bar shows the I/Os induced on S and the colored part of the bar shows the I/Os induced on W. We also show the results of various statistics measured that clearly explain the behavior of each algorithm. We present average values over 1000 queries in all cases. The query points are randomly selected from a subset of the data points in S. To increase the probability of having non-empty result sets, this subset is either the k-skyband or the skyline set of S.

Parameters. We conduct experiments varying the dimensionality n (2-9), the cardinality $|S|$ (100K-5M), the cardinality $|W|$ (100K-1M), the value of k (10-50), and the data distributions for S and W. The default setup is: n=4, $|S|$=100K, $|W|$=100K, k=10, C_W=C_S=5, σ_W^2=σ_S^2=0.05^2, and we use UN distribution for both S and W. The experimental parameters together with default values (in bold) are shown in Table 2.

7.2 Experimental Results

Varying dimensionality n. Figure 6 presents the comparative performance of all algorithms for uniform data distributions of S and W, for varying n, and the default setup: $|S|$=100K, $|W|$=100K, k=10. In terms of execution time (Figure 6(a)), $BBR*$ and $BBRA$ improve the performance of RTA by a factor of 4 to 8, depending on the dimensionality. RTA is inefficient in the lower dimensions and improves its performance as the dimensionality increases. This is mainly because the performance of RTA depends on the cardinality of the reverse top-k result set, which gets smaller as the dimensionality increases (for $n = 2 : |RTOP_k(q)| = 13679.94$ while for $n = 4 : |RTOP_k(q)| = 32.31$). In contrast, the performance of BBR decreases as the dimensionality increases, because the processing of INTOPk becomes more expensive for higher dimensions. On the other hand, $BBR*$ and $BBRA$ scale with dimensionality.

In terms of I/Os (Figure 6(b)), again $BBR*$ and $BBRA$ are up to 4 times better than RTA. We stress that each bar corresponds to the total number of I/Os, while the white part of the bar shows the I/Os induced on S and the colored part of the bar shows the I/Os induced on W. This cost breakdown analysis shows that RTA uses more I/Os both for S and W. The branch-and-bound algorithms are very efficient in terms of I/Os on S due to the buffering employed. However, the important finding is that they all reduce the I/Os on W compared to RTA, which demonstrates the efficiency of the employed score bounds.

Figure 6(c) helps deriving some interesting insights about the branch-and-bound algorithms. The first bar shows the number of INTOPk evaluations for each algorithm. Both $BBR*$ and $BBRA$ consistently require fewer INTOPk evaluations that BBR. The second bar shows the number of discarded MBRs by each algorithm. For $BBR*$ and $BBRA$ the white part of the bar shows the number of MBRs discarded due to result sharing, i.e., without invoking INTOPk. This clearly demonstrates the value of result sharing. The third bar depicts the number of MBRs that were immediately added to the results by INTOPk. The significant finding is that all algorithms manage to add groups of weighting vectors to the result set,

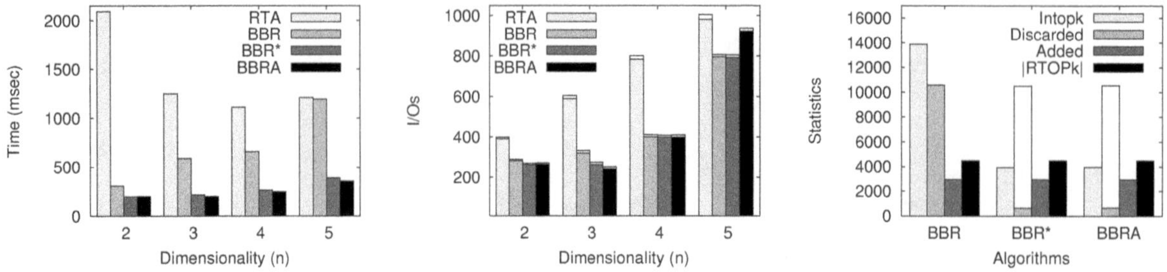

(a) Time. (b) I/Os. (c) Statistics.

Figure 8: Comparative performance of all algorithms for CO data set and varying dimensionality (n).

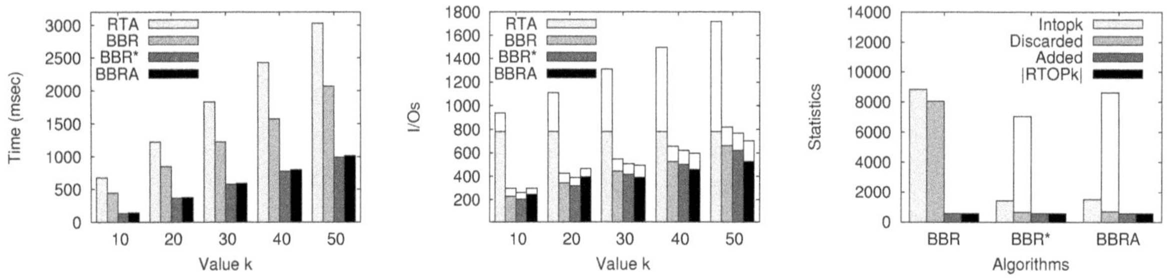

(a) Time. (b) I/Os. (c) Statistics.

Figure 9: Comparative performance of all algorithms for UN data set and varying value of k.

without examining each weighting vector individually. This becomes clear if we compare the cardinality of the result set (fourth bar), with the added elements (third bar). Since the added elements are fewer, this means all algorithms managed to add some groups of weighting vectors to the result.

Clustered data set W. In Figure 7, we use an identical setup with the previous experiment, only now the data set W is clustered. A clustered data set W simulates the case where user preferences are not independent, but there exist some groups of similar user preferences. The general observation is that both the execution time (Figure 7(a)) as well as the number of I/Os (Figure 7(b)) are smaller, when compared to the uniform data set W (see Figures 6(a) and 6(b)). Still, the relative performance between the different algorithms is similar as in the case of uniform data set W.

Correlated data set S. In Figure 8, we study the case of correlated data distribution for S. The results show that the branch-and-bound algorithms improve RTA in all setups both in terms of time and I/Os. This is quite important, because the CO data set is problematic for RTA even for small values of dimensionality. As shown in Figure 8(c), the reason for this behavior is the high cardinality $|RTOP_k|$ of the reverse top-k result in the case of CO data set. However, also in this case, the branch-and-bound algorithms significantly improve the performance of query processing. Notice that in the case of CO data set, the I/O cost is dominated by the I/Os induced on W, i.e., the bars in Figure 8(b) are completely colored, in contrast to the case of AC data set.

Varying k. Figure 9 shows the effect of increased values of k to time and I/Os for all algorithms. As shown in the chart, the branch-and-bound algorithms scale better than RTA as k increases.

Clustered data sets S and W. In Figure 10, we employ a clustered data set both for S and W. Again, the branch-and-bound algorithms are superior to RTA in all setups. An interesting observation is that when both data sets are clustered, $BBR*$ and $BBRA$ manage to discard a very high number of MBRs (shown in Figure 10(c)), thus causing only few INTOPk invocations.

Anti-correlated data set S. In Figure 11, the performance of our algorithms is studied for anti-correlated data distribution of data set S for varying dimensionality. This distribution is quite demanding for all algorithms, therefore the results are depicted in log scale at the y-axis. In all cases $BBR*$ and $BBRA$ outperform RTA, thus verifying their superiority. Notice that we use log-scale on the y-axis of Figure 11(b), hence the white part of the stacked bars is the dominant cost.

Varying cardinality of S. Figure 12 shows the performance of all algorithms for increasing the cardinality of data set S. Notice that the branch-and-bound algorithms maintain their advantage over RTA as the size of S increases. Moreover, the performance of our algorithms is influenced by the cardinality of S only slightly, showing the scalability of our algorithms with respect to S. This is clearly shown by the number of induced I/Os, depicted in Figure 12(b).

Varying cardinality of W. Figure 13 shows the performance of all algorithms for increasing the cardinality of data set W from 100K to 1M. When W increases in size, the performance of RTA drops significantly. In contrast, our algorithms $BBR*$ and $BBRA$ scale gracefully with $|W|$. This is a very strong result that demonstrates the efficiency of the branch-and-bound algorithms, in terms of pruning W.

Higher dimensions and skyline queries. In Figure 14, we conduct an experiment for high dimensions (6-9) to test the performance of all algorithms for stress conditions. Since in higher dimensionality the cardinality of the result set decreases, we generate the query workload by selecting queries out of the data set's skyline points. This means that on average each reverse top-k query will have more results, thus query processing becomes more expensive. As depicted in the charts, the performance of all algorithms dete-

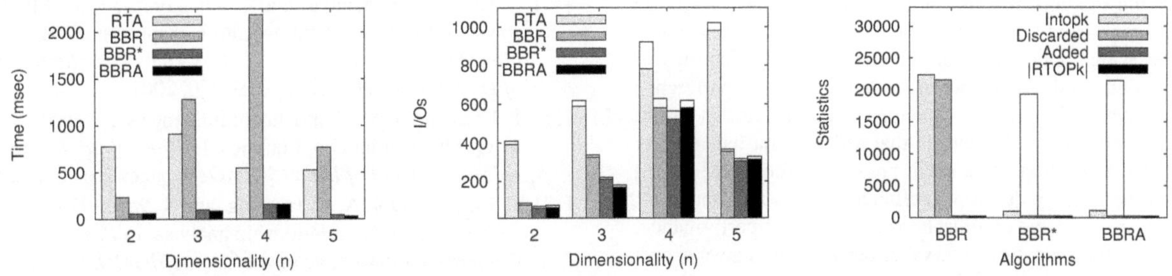

(a) Time. (b) I/Os. (c) Statistics.

Figure 10: Comparative performance of all algorithms for CL data sets S, W and varying dimensionality (n).

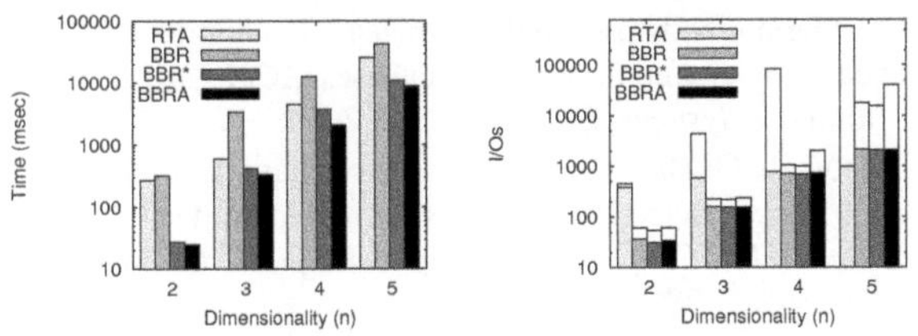

(a) Time. (b) I/Os.

Figure 11: AC data set and varying n.

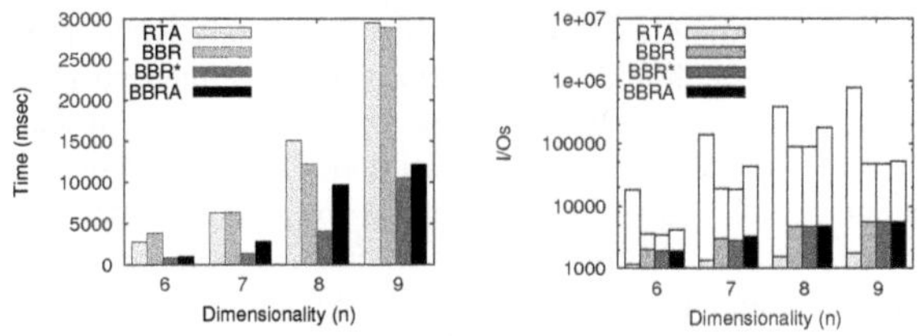

(a) Time. (b) I/Os.

Figure 14: Performance for high dimensions.

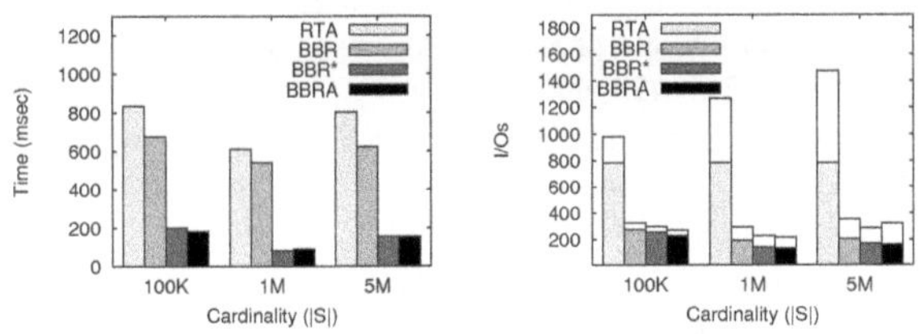

(a) Time. (b) I/Os.

Figure 12: Performance for varying $|S|$.

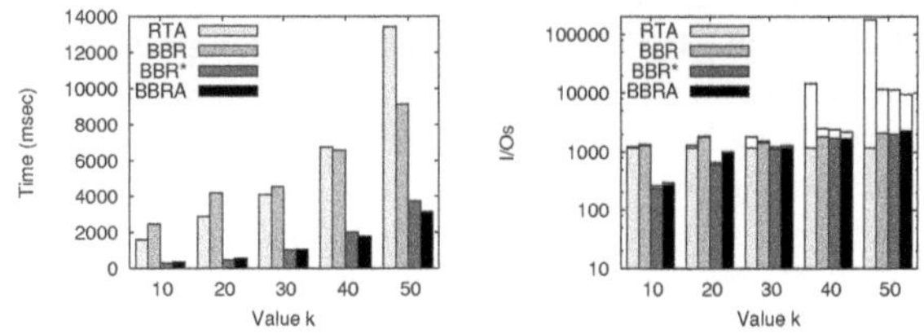

(a) Time. (b) I/Os.

Figure 15: Performance for HOUSE data set.

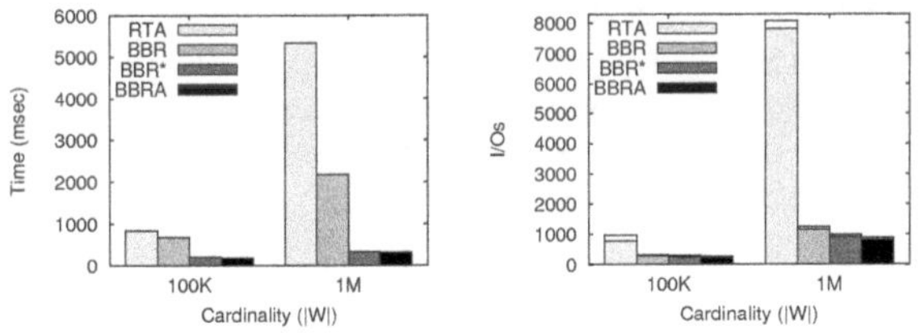

(a) Time. (b) I/Os.

Figure 13: Varying $|W|$.

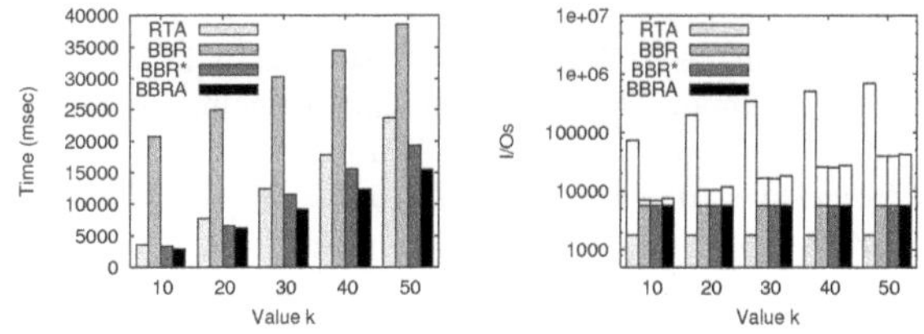

(a) Time. (b) I/Os.

Figure 16: Performance for COLOR data set.

riorates. However, $BBR*$ clearly outperforms all other algorithms in all setups consistently. Again, notice the use of log-scale in the y-axis of Figure 14(b).

Experiment with real data. Figure 15 shows the results from the first real data set (HOUSE) employed. Notice the log-scale in Figure 15(b). Also in these experiments, we use log-scale for the y-axis when reporting I/O. Clearly, $BBR*$ and $BBRA$ are more efficient than RTA, often by one order of magnitude. More importantly, the gain of our algorithms increases with the values of k. In Figure 16, we depict the results obtained in the case of the COLOR data set. Again, $BBR*$ and $BBRA$ outperform RTA, thus verifying their superiority also in the case of a demanding (9-dimensional) real data set. These results are in accordance with the study on the synthetic data. We conclude that our algorithms consistently improve the performance of RTA.

8. CONCLUSIONS

Reverse top-k queries constitute a useful tool for market analysis, since they help producers to identify those customers who are potentially interested in a particular product based on the customer preferences and the competitors' products. Currently, the state-of-the-art algorithm (RTA) needs to access each individual preference function and cannot add a preference function to the result set without evaluating the corresponding top-k query. In this paper, we propose a branch-and-bound algorithm for efficient reverse top-k query processing. Our algorithm alleviates the shortcomings of RTA by adding to the result set or discarding sets of preference functions instead of individual functions. To achieve this result, we study the conditions that ensure that a data point has a better rank than the query point for a set of preference functions. Based on these properties, we develop an efficient branch-and-bound algorithm and propose two optimizations that boost its performance. The experimental evaluation shows that our algorithm always outperforms RTA and performs efficiently in all cases.

9. ACKNOWLEDGMENTS

The work of Akrivi Vlachou was supported by the Action "Supporting Postdoctoral Researchers" of the Operational Program "Education and Lifelong Learning" (Action's Beneficiary: General Secretariat for Research and Technology), and is co-financed by the European Social Fund (ESF) and the Greek State. The research of Christos Doulkeridis was supported under the Marie-Curie IEF grant number 274063 with partial support from the Norwegian Research Council. The work of Yannis Kotidis has been co-financed by the European Union (European Social Fund - ESF) and Greek national funds through the Operational Program "Education and Lifelong Learning" of the National Strategic Reference Framework (NSRF) - Research Funding Program: RECOST.

10. REFERENCES

[1] R. Akbarinia, E. Pacitti, and P. Valduriez. Best position algorithms for top-k queries. In *Proc. of Int. Conf. on Very Large Data Bases (VLDB)*, pages 495–506, 2007.

[2] A. Arvanitis, A. Deligiannakis, and Y. Vassiliou. Efficient influence-based processing of market research queries. In *Proc. of Conf. on Information and Knowledge Management (CIKM)*, pages 1193–1202, 2012.

[3] T. Bernecker, T. Emrich, H.-P. Kriegel, N. Mamoulis, M. Renz, S. Zhang, and A. Züfle. Inverse queries for multidimensional spaces. In *Proc. of Int. Symposium on Spatial and Temporal Databases (SSTD)*, pages 330–347, 2011.

[4] Y.-C. Chang, L. D. Bergman, V. Castelli, C.-S. Li, M.-L. Lo, and J. R. Smith. The Onion technique: Indexing for linear optimization queries. In *Proc. of Int. Conference on Management of Data (SIGMOD)*, pages 391–402, 2000.

[5] S. Chaudhuri and L. Gravano. Evaluating top-k selection queries. In *Proc. of Int. Conf. on Very Large Data Bases (VLDB)*, pages 397–410, 1999.

[6] E. Dellis and B. Seeger. Efficient computation of reverse skyline queries. In *Proc. of Int. Conf. on Very Large Data Bases (VLDB)*, pages 291–302, 2007.

[7] R. Fagin, A. Lotem, and M. Naor. Optimal aggregation algorithms for middleware. In *Proc. of Symposium on Principles of Database Systems (PODS)*, pages 102–113, 2001.

[8] S. Ge, L. H. U, N. Mamoulis, and D. W. Cheung. Efficient all top-k computation: A unified solution for all top-k, reverse top-k and top-m influential queries. *IEEE Transactions on Knowledge and Data Engineering (TKDE)*, 25(5):1015–1027, 2013.

[9] U. Güntzer, W.-T. Balke, and W. Kießling. Optimizing multi-feature queries for image databases. In *Proc. of Int. Conf. on Very Large Data Bases (VLDB)*, pages 419–428, 2000.

[10] V. Hristidis, N. Koudas, and Y. Papakonstantinou. PREFER: a system for the efficient execution of multi-parametric ranked queries. In *Proc. of Int. Conference on Management of Data (SIGMOD)*, pages 259–270, 2001.

[11] F. Korn and S. Muthukrishnan. Influence sets based on reverse nearest neighbor queries. In *Proc. of Int. Conference on Management of Data (SIGMOD)*, pages 201–212, 2000.

[12] C. Li, B. C. Ooi, A. K. H. Tung, and S. Wang. DADA: a data cube for dominant relationship analysis. In *Proc. of Int. Conference on Management of Data (SIGMOD)*, pages 659–670, 2006.

[13] X. Lian and L. Chen. Monochromatic and bichromatic reverse skyline search over uncertain databases. In *Proc. of Int. Conference on Management of Data (SIGMOD)*, pages 213–226, 2008.

[14] A. Marian, N. Bruno, and L. Gravano. Evaluating top-k queries over web-accessible databases. *ACM Transactions on Database Systems*, 29(2):319–362, 2004.

[15] M. Miah, G. Das, V. Hristidis, and H. Mannila. Standing out in a crowd: Selecting attributes for maximum visibility. In *Proc. of Int. Conf. on Data Engineering (ICDE)*, pages 356–365, 2008.

[16] D. Papadias, P. Kalnis, J. Zhang, and Y. Tao. Efficient OLAP operations in spatial data warehouses. In *Proc. of Int. Symposium on Spatial and Temporal Databases (SSTD)*, pages 443–459, 2001.

[17] Y. Tao, V. Hristidis, D. Papadias, and Y. Papakonstantinou. Branch-and-bound processing of ranked queries. *Information Systems*, 32(3):424–445, 2007.

[18] Y. Tao, X. Xiao, and J. Pei. SUBSKY: efficient computation of skylines in subspaces. In *Proc. of Int. Conf. on Data Engineering (ICDE)*, page 65, 2006.

[19] A. Vlachou, C. Doulkeridis, Y. Kotidis, and K. Nørvåg. Reverse top-k queries. In *Proc. of Int. Conf. on Data Engineering (ICDE)*, 2010.

[20] A. Vlachou, C. Doulkeridis, Y. Kotidis, and K. Nørvåg. Monochromatic and bichromatic reverse top-k queries. *IEEE Transactions on Knowledge and Data Engineering*, 23(8):1215–1229, 2011.

[21] A. Vlachou, C. Doulkeridis, and K. Nørvåg. Monitoring reverse top-k queries over mobile devices. In *Proc. of Int. Workshop on Data Engineering for Wireless and Mobile Access (MobiDE)*, 2011.

[22] A. Vlachou, C. Doulkeridis, K. Nørvåg, and Y. Kotidis. Identifying the most influential data objects with reverse top-k queries. *PVLDB*, 3(1-2):364–372, 2010.

[23] Q. Wan, R. C.-W. Wong, I. F. Ilyas, M. T. Özsu, and Y. Peng. Creating competitive products. *PVLDB*, 2(1):898–909, 2009.

[24] D. Xin, C. Chen, and J. Han. Towards robust indexing for ranked queries. In *Proc. of Int. Conf. on Very Large Data Bases (VLDB)*, pages 235–246, 2006.

[25] B. Yao, F. Li, and P. Kumar. Reverse furthest neighbors in spatial databases. In *Proc. of Int. Conf. on Data Engineering (ICDE)*, 2009.

[26] K. Yi, H. Yu, J. Yang, G. Xia, and Y. Chen. Efficient maintenance of materialized top-k views. In *Proc. of Int. Conf. on Data Engineering (ICDE)*, pages 189–200, 2003.

[27] A. Yu, P. K. Agarwal, and J. Yang. Processing a large number of continuous preference top-k queries. In *Proc. of Int. Conference on Management of Data (SIGMOD)*, pages 397–408, 2012.

On the Correct and Complete Enumeration of the Core Search Space

Guido Moerkotte
University of Mannheim
Mannheim, Germany
moerkotte@informatik.uni-mannheim.de

Pit Fender
University of Mannheim
Mannheim, Germany
pfender@informatik.uni-mannheim.de

Marius Eich
University of Mannheim
Mannheim, Germany
meich@informatik.uni-mannheim.de

ABSTRACT

Reordering more than traditional joins (e.g. outerjoins, antijoins) requires some care, since not all reorderings are valid. To prevent invalid plans, two approaches have been described in the literature. We show that both approaches still produce invalid plans.

We present three conflict detectors. All of them are (1) correct, i.e., prevent invalid plans, (2) easier to understand and implement than the previous (buggy) approaches, (3) more flexible in the sense that the restriction that all predicates must reject nulls is no longer required, and (4) extensible in the sense that it is easy to add new operators. Further, the last of our three approaches is complete, i.e., it allows for the generation of all valid plans within the core search space.

Categories and Subject Descriptors

H.2.4 [**Database Management**]: query processing, relational databases

Keywords

query optimization, join ordering, non-inner joins

1. INTRODUCTION

For a DBMS that provides support for SQL, the query optimizer is a crucial piece of software. The declarative nature of a query allows its translation into many equivalent plans. The process of choosing a low cost plan from the alternatives is known as query optimization or, more specifically, plan generation. Essential for the costs of a plan is its ordering of join operations, since the runtime of plans with different join orders can vary by several orders of magnitude.

When designing a plan generator, there are two approaches suitable to find an optimal join order: bottom-up join enumeration via dynamic programming (DP) and top-down join enumeration through memoization. Both approaches face the same challenge: the considered plans must be *valid*, i.e., produce the correct result. This is simple if only joins are considered, since they are commutative and associative. Thus, every plan is a valid plan.

If more operators like left outerjoins, full outerjoins, antijoins, semijoins, and groupjoins are considered then no longer are all plans valid. In fact, in the literature we find only two ways of preventing invalid plans in a DP-based plan generator. The first approach (NEL/EEL) is by Rao, Lindsay, Lohman, Pirahesh, and Simmen [20, 21]. Their conflict detector allows for joins, left outerjoins and antijoins. The second approach (SES/TES) is by Moerkotte and Neumann [15]. As we will show in Sections 7 and 8, both approaches generate INVALID PLANS. This leaves the implementer of a plan generator with zero (correct) choices for a DP-based plan generator (cf. Sec. 8).

We found this situation unbearable and decided to do some research on it. Here, we present our results. The highlight will be the conflict detector CD-C, which is

1. correct,
2. complete,
3. easy to understand and implement,
4. flexible, and
5. extensible.

Correct means that only valid plans are generated. Complete means that all valid plans in the core search space (defined in Sec. 3) are generated. As we will see, this is not easily achieved. Obviously, easy to understand and implement is a nice feature. CD-C is flexible in two respects. First, NEL/EEL and SES/TES both require that all join predicates reject nulls. In our approach, we eliminate this restriction. Thus, within a query some predicates may reject nulls, while others do not. This is important, since SQL allows predicates which are not null rejecting (e.g., IS NOT DISTINCT FROM). Second, we allow (as did NEL/EEL and SES/TES) for *complex join predicates* to reference more than two relations. Extensibility allows to extend the set of binary operators considered by a conflict detector. We achieve extensibility by a table-driven approach: several tables encode the properties of the operators, and CD-C simply explores these tables to detect conflicts and prevent invalid plans.

The rest of the paper is organized as follows. Sec. 2 defines some preliminaries. Sec. 3 defines the core search space. In order to do so, the essential properties of binary operators are defined. Sec. 4 clearly states the goal of our paper and uses the well-known algorithm DPsub to illustrate how a conflict detector is integrated into DP-based plan generators.

SIGMOD'13, June 22–27, 2013, New York, New York, USA.

Sec. 5 presents three conflict detectors. Each of them is correct, and the last one is complete. Sec. 7 contains the experimental results. Sec. 8 discusses related work and presents invalid plans generated by NEL/EEL and SES/TES. Sec. 9 concludes the paper.

2. PRELIMINARIES

This section contains basic definitions.

LOP denotes the set of logical binary operators we allow for in our plans: join (⋈), full outerjoin (⟗), left outerjoin (⟕), left antijoin (▷), left semijoin (⋉), and groupjoin (⋈̄) [16]. In Sec. 6, we also consider cross products (×).

Null Rejecting for predicates is defined as follows [10]:

DEFINITION 1. *A predicate is null rejecting for a set of attributes A if it evaluates to* FALSE *or* UNKNOWN *on every tuple in which all attributes in A are* NULL.

For examples, we refer to the introduction and [10]. In the literature, some synonyms for null rejecting are used: null intolerant, strong, and strict.

Free Attributes and Tables $\mathcal{F}(\cdot), \mathcal{F}_{\mathbf{T}}(\cdot)$. As usual, we denote by $\mathcal{A}(e)$ the set of attributes/variables provided by some expression e and by $\mathcal{F}(e)$ the set of free attributes/variables in some expression e. For example, if $p \equiv R.a + S.b = S.c + T.d$, then $\mathcal{F}(p) = \{R.a, S.b, S.c, T.d\}$.

Set of tables ($\mathcal{T}$), and subtree operators (STO). For a set of attributes A, $\mathcal{T}(A)$ denotes the set of tables to which these attributes belong. We abbreviate $\mathcal{T}(\mathcal{F}(e))$ by $\mathcal{F}_{\mathrm{T}}(e)$. For p we have $\mathcal{T}(\mathcal{F}(e)) = \{R, S, T\}$. Let $\circ$ be an operator in the initial operator tree. We denote by left($\circ$) (right($\circ$)) its left (right) child. STO($\circ$) denotes the operators contained in the operator subtree rooted at $\circ$. $\mathcal{T}(\circ)$ denotes the set of tables contained in the subtree rooted at $\circ$.

NEL/SES model the producer/consumer constraints. [15] introduced the notion of the *syntactic eligibility sets* (SES for short). The SES are attached to operators and contain the set of tables that must be present before the operator can be applied. The producer/consumer constraints for a plan of the form plan(S_1) $\circ$ plan(S_2) are satisfied if SES($\circ$) $\subseteq S_1 \cup S_2$ holds. SES is also called NEL [21]. For non-dependent operators, their SES is equal to the set of attributes referenced in their predicate. For p as above, we have SES($\circ_p$) $= \{R, S, T\}$.

Degenerate Predicates contained in binary operators are those that do not reference tables from both of their inputs:

DEFINITION 2. *Let p be a predicate associated with a binary operator $\circ$ and $\mathcal{F}_T(p)$ the tables referenced by p. Then, p is called* degenerate *if $\mathcal{T}(left(\circ)) \cap \mathcal{F}_T(p) = \emptyset \vee \mathcal{T}(right(\circ)) \cap \mathcal{F}_T(p) = \emptyset$ holds.*

For example, in $\bowtie_{true}$ the predicate *true* is degenerate. Further, the expression is equivalent to a cross product. Since degenerate predicates are troublesome, we assume until Sec. 6 that no degenerate predicates (and, hence, no cross products) occur. In Sec. 6, we relax this assumption. Further, while presenting CALC_{SES} and CD-C, we will already take some care of degenerate predicates and cross products.

3. CORE SEARCH SPACE

This section defines the core search space. It is defined by a set of transformation rules exploring all valid alternatives to a given initial plan. Sec. 3.1 introduces these transformation rules and Sec. 3.2 defines the core search space.

3.1 Reorderability

Traditional join ordering approaches just reorder joins and no other binary operators. Since the join is commutative and associative, all plans are valid and there is no danger of generating invalid plans. Real plan generators must reorder more than just plain joins (e.g., ⋉, ▷, ⟕, ⟗, ⋈̄). In order to describe the reorderability properties of these operators, we need to carry over the notions of commutativity and associativity to pairs of operators. It is easy to see that some of these operators are commutative while others are not (see Table 1). If some binary operator $\circ$ is commutative, we denote this by comm($\circ$).

$\circ$	×	⋈	⋉	▷	⟕	⟗	⋈̄
comm($\circ$)	+	+	-	-	-	+	-

Table 1: The comm($\circ$)-property

Associativity is just a little more complex. We say that two not necessarily distinct operators $\circ^a$ and $\circ^b$ are *associative* if the following equivalence holds:

$$(e_1 \circ^a_{12} e_2) \circ^b_{23} e_3 \equiv e_1 \circ^a_{12} (e_2 \circ^b_{23} e_3). \qquad (1)$$

Here, we use the following convention. If operators do not carry a predicate or other expressions, their subscripts are immaterial and can be ignored. If an operator has a predicate, then ij indicates that it references attributes (and, thus, relations) from at most e_i and e_j. Thus, (for $1 \leq i,j \leq 3$, $i \neq j$) this also indicates that $\mathcal{F}(e) \cap e_k = \emptyset$ for $1 \leq k \leq 3$ and $k \notin \{i,j\}$. This ensures that the equivalence is correctly typed on both sides of the equivalence sign. For example, the predicate of $\circ^a_{12}$ accesses tables from e_1 and e_2, but not e_3. Note that $\circ^a_{12}$ may carry a complex predicate referencing more than two tables from e_1 and e_2. We will see an example in the next subsection. If some $\circ^a_{123}$ referenced tables in all three expression e_i, the expression on the left-hand side of Eqv. 1 would be invalid and the right-hand side would be valid, but could not be transformed into the left-hand side. For the purpose of conflict detection, complex predicates accessing more than two relations are no challenge, they just enlarge the set of tables that must be present before the complex predicate can be evaluated. The real challenge with complex predicates is to efficiently enumerate the now more restricted search space (cf. Sec. 6.1).

If for two operators $\circ^a$ and $\circ^b$ Eqv. 1 holds, we denote this by assoc($\circ^a, \circ^b$). It is important to note that assoc is not symmetric. Thus, the order of the operators (i.e., ($\circ^a, \circ^b$) vs. ($\circ^b, \circ^a$)) is important. Therefore, we tie the order in assoc to the syntactic pattern of Eqv. 1. It has to be the same order as on the left-hand side of the equivalence. This means that the left association has to be on the left-hand side and, consequently, the right association on the right-hand side of the equivalence.

If comm($\circ^a$) and comm($\circ^b$) holds, then assoc($\circ^a, \circ^b$) implies assoc($\circ^b, \circ^a$) and vice versa, as can be seen from

$$\begin{array}{rcll}
(e_1 \circ^a_{12} e_2) \circ^b_{23} e_3 & \equiv & e_1 \circ^a_{12} (e_2 \circ^b_{23} e_3) & \text{assoc}(\circ^a, \circ^b) \\
& \equiv & (e_2 \circ^b_{23} e_3) \circ^a_{12} e_1 & \text{comm}(\circ^a) \\
& \equiv & (e_3 \circ^b_{23} e_2) \circ^a_{12} e_1 & \text{comm}(\circ^b) \\
& \equiv & e_3 \circ^b_{23} (e_2 \circ^a_{12} e_1) & \text{assoc}(\circ^b, \circ^a) \\
& \equiv & (e_2 \circ^a_{12} e_1) \circ^b_{23} e_3 & \text{comm}(\circ^b) \\
& \equiv & (e_1 \circ^a_{12} e_2) \circ^b_{23} e_3 & \text{comm}(\circ^a).
\end{array}$$

Table 2 summarizes the associativity properties. Be careful, since assoc is not symmetric, $\circ^a$ must be looked up within a row and $\circ^b$ within a column, *not* vice versa. Entries with a footnote in Table 2 denote that assoc($\circ^a, \circ^b$) only holds if the predicates reject nulls (see Def. 1). For more details, see the corresponding footnotes at the bottom of Table 2.

$\circ^a$ \ $\circ^b$	×	⋈	⋉	▷	⟕	⟗	⋈̅
×	+	+	+	+	+	-	+
⋈	+	+	+	+	+	-	+
⋉	-	-	-	-	-	-	-
▷	-	-	-	-	-	-	-
⟕	-	-	-	-	+[1]	-	-
⟗	-	-	-	-	+[1]	+[2]	-
⋈̅	-	-	-	-	-	-	-

[1] if p_{23} rejects nulls on $\mathcal{A}(e_2)$ (Eqv. 1)
[2] if p_{12} and p_{23} reject nulls on $\mathcal{A}(e_2)$ (Eqv. 1)

Table 2: The assoc($\circ^a, \circ^b$)-property

Are we done? No! Consider the following well-known equivalence for the semijoin:

$$(e_1 \ltimes_{12} e_2) \ltimes_{13} e_3 \equiv (e_1 \ltimes_{13} e_3) \ltimes_{12} e_2.$$

It is easy to see that we cannot derive the plan on the right-hand side from the plan on the left-hand side using associativity and commutativity of $\ltimes$: neither holds. Thus, we need something new.

We define the *left asscom property* (l-asscom for short) as follows:

$$(e_1 \circ^a_{12} e_2) \circ^b_{13} e_3 \equiv (e_1 \circ^b_{13} e_3) \circ^a_{12} e_2. \quad (2)$$

We denote by l-asscom($\circ^a, \circ^b$) the fact that Eqv. 2 holds for $\circ^a$ and $\circ^b$.

Analogously, we can define a *right asscom property* (r-asscom):

$$e_1 \circ^a_{13} (e_2 \circ^b_{23} e_3) \equiv e_2 \circ^b_{23} (e_1 \circ^a_{13} e_3). \quad (3)$$

First, note that l-asscom and r-asscom are symmetric properties, i.e.,

$$\text{l-asscom}(\circ^a, \circ^b) \leftrightarrow \text{l-asscom}(\circ^b, \circ^a),$$
$$\text{r-asscom}(\circ^a, \circ^b) \leftrightarrow \text{r-asscom}(\circ^b, \circ^a).$$

The following reasoning

$$\begin{aligned}(e_1 \circ^a_{12} e_2) \circ^b_{23} e_3 &\equiv (e_2 \circ^a_{12} e_1) \circ^b_{23} e_3 && \text{if comm}(\circ^a_{12})\\ &\equiv (e_2 \circ^b_{23} e_3) \circ^a_{12} e_1 && \text{if l-asscom}(\circ^a_{12}, \circ^b_{23})\\ &\equiv e_1 \circ^a_{12} (e_2 \circ^b_{23} e_3) && \text{if comm}(\circ^a_{12})\\ &\equiv (e_1 \circ^a_{12} e_2) \circ^b_{23} e_3 && \text{if assoc}(\circ^a_{12}, \circ^b_{23})\end{aligned}$$

implies that

$$\text{comm}(\circ^a_{12}), \text{assoc}(\circ^a_{12}, \circ^b_{23}) \rightarrow \text{l-asscom}(\circ^a_{12}, \circ^b_{23}),$$
$$\text{comm}(\circ^a_{12}), \text{l-asscom}(\circ^a_{12}, \circ^b_{23}) \rightarrow \text{assoc}(\circ^a_{12}, \circ^b_{23}).$$

Thus, the l-asscom property is implied by associativity and commutativity, which explains its name. Quite similarly, the implications

$$\text{comm}(\circ^b_{23}), \text{assoc}(\circ^a_{12}, \circ^b_{23}) \rightarrow \text{r-asscom}(\circ^a_{12}, \circ^b_{23}),$$
$$\text{comm}(\circ^b_{23}), \text{r-asscom}(\circ^a_{12}, \circ^b_{23}) \rightarrow \text{assoc}(\circ^a_{12}, \circ^b_{23})$$

can be deduced.

Table 3 summarizes the l-/r-asscom properties. Again, entries with a footnote require that the predicates reject

∘	×	⋈	⋉	▷	⟕	⟗	⋈̅
×	+/+	+/+	+/-	+/-	+/-	-/-	+/-
⋈	+/+	+/+	+/-	+/-	+/-	-/-	+/-
⋉	+/-	+/-	+/-	+/-	+/-	-/-	+/-
▷	+/-	+/-	+/-	+/-	+/-	-/-	+/-
⟕	+/-	+/-	+/-	+/-	+/-	+[1]/-	+/-
⟗	-/-	-/-	-/-	-/-	+[2]/-	+[3]/+[4]	-/-
⋈̅	+/-	+/-	+/-	+/-	+/-	-/-	+/-

[1] if p_{12} rejects nulls on $\mathcal{A}(e_1)$ (Eqv. 2)
[2] if p_{13} rejects nulls on $\mathcal{A}(e_3)$ (Eqv. 2)
[3] if p_{12} and p_{13} rejects nulls on $\mathcal{A}(e_1)$ (Eqv. 2)
[4] if p_{13} and p_{23} reject nulls on $\mathcal{A}(e_3)$ (Eqv. 3)

Table 3: The l-/r-asscom($\circ^a, \circ^b$) property

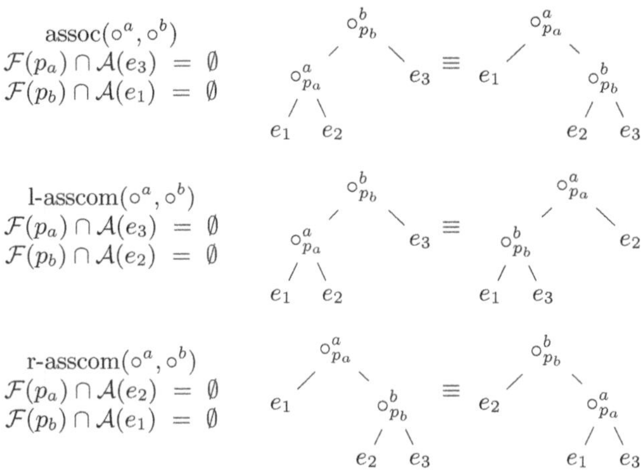

Figure 1: Transformation rules for assoc, l-asscom, and r-asscom

nulls. We assume that calls to assoc and l/r-asscom take care of this.

If an entry in one of the Tables 1 to 3 is marked with − or its condition in the footnote is violated, we say that there is a *conflict* regarding this property. A conflict means that the application of the corresponding transformation rule results in an invalid plan.

3.2 Definition of the Core Search Space

Typically, for a given input query, the query optimizer constructs an initial operator tree. In a transformation-based plan generator, all valid plans are then generated by exhaustively applying transformations to the initial plan.

If commutativity, associativity, l-asscom, and/or r-asscom hold, this gives rise to the according transformations. Except for commutativity, these are shown in Fig. 1. All equivalences can be applied from left to right and from right to left. We define the *core search space* for a given initial plan to be the set of plans generated by exhaustively applying these four transformations to the initial plan.

Fig. 2 shows a larger operator tree. Let us consider several possibilities for the predicates of the top-most operator $\circ^b$. If $p_b \equiv R_0.a + R_1.a + R_2.a + R_3.a = R_4.a * R_5.a$, then no reordering is possible, since all tables are referenced. If $p_b \equiv R_2.a + R_3.a = R_4.a * R_5.a$, then applying associativity is possible from a syntactic point of view, since $\mathcal{F}(p_b) \cap \mathcal{T}(e_1)$ becomes in our example $\{R_2, R_3, R_4, R_5\} \cap \{R_0, R_1\} = \emptyset$. In fact, although the predicate is complex, it references only tables below $\circ^2$ and $\circ^3$, whose subtrees correspond to e_2 and e_3 in Fig. 1. Accordingly, we would write $\circ^b_{12}$. Clearly,

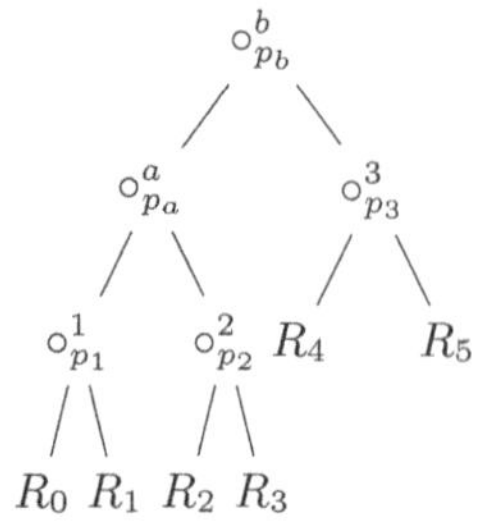

Figure 2: Example operator tree

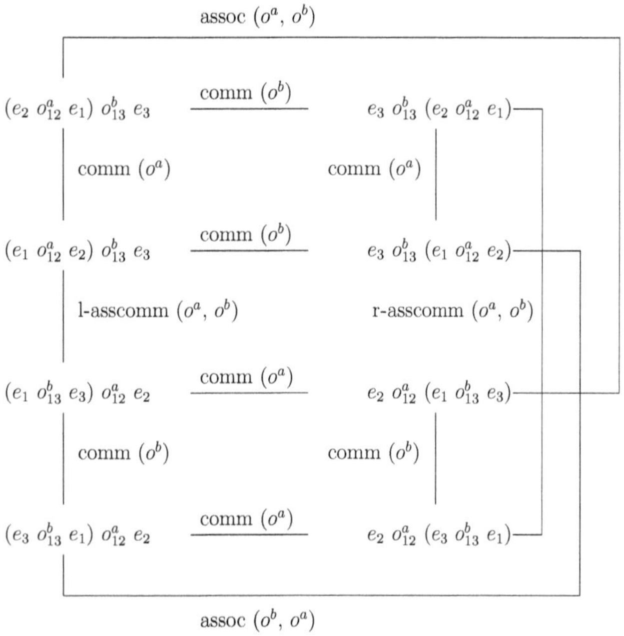

Figure 3: Core search space example

a binary predicate, e.g., $p_b \equiv R_0.a = R_5.a$, generates the largest search space and, thus, the highest opportunity for generating invalid plans and missing valid plans. This is the reason why we will restrict ourselves to binary predicates in Sec. 7.

Taking a look at the syntactic constraints shown in Fig. 1, we see that for non-degenerate predicates (see Def. 2) the following observation holds:

OBSERVATION 1. *The syntactic constraints for non-degenerate predicates imply that (1) either associativity or l-asscom can be applied for left nesting but not both, and (2) either associativity or r-asscom can be applied for right-nesting but not both.*

Thus, non-degenerate predicates simplify the handling of conflicts, since we have to take care of either associativity or l/r-asscom and never both at the same time.

Fig. 3 shows an example of the core seach space for the expression $(e_1 \circ^a_{12} e_2) \circ^b_{13} e_3$. We observe that any expression in the core search space can be reached by a sequence of at most two applications of commutativity, at most one application of associativity, l-asscom, or r-asscom, finally followed by at most two applications of commutativity. The total number of applications of commutativity can be restricted to 2. More specifically, one application of commutativity to each operator in the plan suffices.

```
DPSUBE
      ▷ Input: a set of relations R = {R_0, ..., R_{n-1}}
               a set of operators O with associated
               conflict descriptors
      ▷ Output: an optimal bushy operator tree
 1    for all R_i ∈ R
 2        BestPlan({R_i}) ← R_i
 3    for 1 ≤ i < 2^n − 1 ascending
 4        S ← {R_j ∈ R|(⌊i/2^j⌋ mod 2) = 1}
 5        if |S| = 1
 6            continue
 7        for all S_1 ⊂ S, S_1 ≠ ∅
 8            S_2 ← S \ S_1
 9            for all ∘ ∈ O
10                if APPLICABLE(∘, S_1, S_2)
11                    build and handle the plans
                          BestPlan(S_1) ∘ BestPlan(S_2)
12                    if comm(∘)
13                        build and handle the plans
                              BestPlan(S_2) ∘ BestPlan(S_1)
14    return BestPlan(R)
```

Figure 4: Pseudocode for DPSUBE

4. GOAL OF THE PAPER

This section discusses how the complete core search space can be explored by a plan generator.

Therefore, we extend the simple dynamic programming algorithm DPSUB [14] to one called DPSUBE. The resulting pseudo-code is shown in Fig. 4. As input, DPSUBE takes the set of n relations $R = \{R_0, \ldots, R_{n-1}\}$ and the set of operators O containing $n-1$ operators which DPSUBE has to apply in order to build a plan. First, it constructs a plan for single relations (Line 2). Then, it enumerates all subsets S of relations by decoding an integer, which is interpreted as a bitvector encoding a subset of the set of relations. For each set of relations S, DPSUBE then enumerates all subsets S_1 of S (Line 7) and their complements S_2 (Line 8). Both of them must be non-empty. For each pair (S_1, S_2), all operators $\circ$ in O are then tested for applicability via a call to APPLICABLE (Line 10). If the operator is applicable, the best plans P_1 for S_1 and P_2 for S_2 are recalled from the dynamic programming table (DP-table for short) via *BestPlan* and combined into the plan $P_1 \circ P_2$ for S (Line 11). The costs of this plan are then calculated, and if this plan is cheaper than the existing one, it is added to the DP-table. Since this piece of code is straightforward, we do not detail on it. Note that only if an operator is applicable, DPSUBE also considers commutativity. Thus, the plan $P_2 \circ P_1$ is built and handled if comm($\circ$) (Line 12) holds. The goal of the paper is to provide different implementations for APPLICABLE.

5. CONFLICT DETECTION

5.1 Outline

In order to open our approach for new algebraic operators, we use a table-driven approach. We use four tables which contain the properties of the algebraic operators. These contain the information of Tables 1, 2 and 3. (The latter includes two tables.) Extending our approach only requires to extend these tables!

We develop our final approach in three steps. In each step, we introduce one of our conflict detectors CD-A, CD-B, and

CD-C. For these conflict detectors, we present a complete bundle consisting of three components:

1. a representation for conflicts,
2. a conflict detection (CD) algorithm, which detects the conflicts in the initial operator tree and produces a conflict representation for each operator contained in it, and
3. the implementation of APPLICABLE, which uses the conflict representation for an operator and then determines whether the operator can be applied in a given context.

Each of the subsequently discussed bundles is correct, but only the last one is complete.

The main idea in the following (the same as in [15, 20, 21]) is to extend the producer/consumer constraints modeled through SES (NEL) by adding more tables to it in order to restrict the explored search space to valid plans only. This is possible, since SES is used to express the syntactic constraints: all referenced attributes/tables must be present before an expression can be evaluated. Therefore, if we add more tables, the explored search space becomes smaller.

Let us now define SES. First of all, SES contains the tables referenced by a predicate. If some operator like the groupjoin ⟗ [16] introduces new attributes, they are treated as if they belonged to a new table. This new table is present in the set of accessible tables after the groupjoin has been applied. Let R be a table and $\circ_p$ any of our binary operators except a groupjoin. We give the pseudo code for the SES calculation:

CALC$_{\text{SES}}(\circ_p)$

▷ **Input:** binary operator $\circ \in$ LOP carrying predicate p
if $\circ_p \in \{\bowtie, ⟗, ⟖, \triangleright, \ltimes\}$ ▷ and later: cross product $\times$
  return $\bigcup_{R \in \mathcal{F}_T(p)} \{R\} \cap \mathcal{T}(\circ_p)$
elseif $\circ_{p;a_1:e_1,\ldots,a_n:e_n} \in \{⟗\}$
  return $\bigcup_{R \in \mathcal{F}_T(p) \cup \mathcal{F}_T(e_i)} \{R\} \cap \mathcal{T}(\circ_p)$
else ▷ cross product $\times$
  return $\emptyset$

In case of non-degenerate predicates and in the absence of dependent operators (cf. Sec. 6.3) and table functions, CALC$_{\text{SES}}(\circ_p) = \mathcal{F}_T(p)$. Note that CALC$_{\text{SES}}$ handles cross products, which we will not need until Sec. 6.2.

All conflict representations have a component called *total eligibility set* (TES for short) which contains a set of tables. We always initialize TES with SES as calculated above. Further, we assume that our conflict representation has two accessors L-TES and R-TES returning

$$\begin{aligned} \text{L-TES}(\circ) &:= \text{TES}(\circ) \cap \mathcal{T}(\text{left}(\circ)) \text{ and} \\ \text{R-TES}(\circ) &:= \text{TES}(\circ) \cap \mathcal{T}(\text{right}(\circ)). \end{aligned}$$

This distinction is necessary since we want to consider commutativity explicitly, and in those cases where commutativity does not hold, we want to prevent operators which occurred on the left-hand side of an operator from moving to its right-hand side or vice versa.

All our implementations of APPLICABLE conjunctively include the test L-TES $\subseteq S_1 \wedge$ R-TES $\subseteq S_2$.

5.2 Approach CD-A

Let us first consider a simple operator tree with only two operators. Take a look at the upper half of Fig. 5. There,

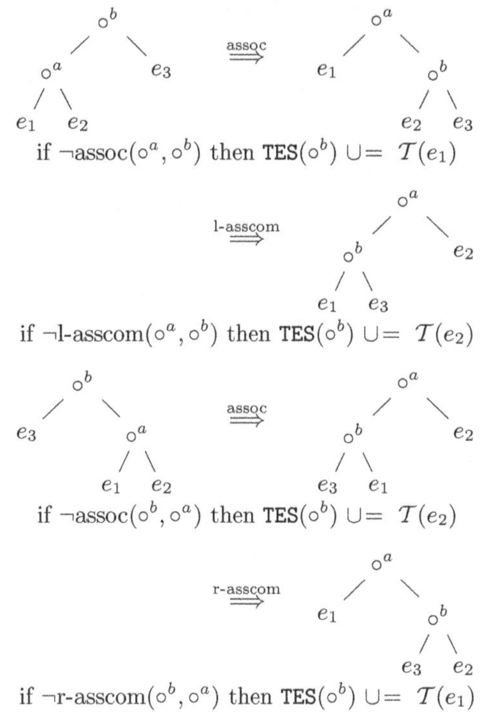

Figure 5: Calculating TES for simple operator trees

the application of associativity and l-asscom to some plan is illustrated. In case that associativity does not hold, we add $\mathcal{T}(e_1)$ to TES$(\circ^b)$. This prevents the plan on the right-hand side of the arrow marked with assoc. It does not, however, prevent the plan on the right-hand side of the arrow marked with l-asscom. Similarly, adding $\mathcal{T}(e_2)$ to TES$(\circ^b)$ does prevent the plan resulting from l-asscom but not the plan resulting from applying associativity. The lower part of Fig. 5 shows the actions needed if an operator is nested in the right argument. Again, we can precisely prevent the invalid plans.

There is only one more problem we have to solve. It occurs if a conflicting operator $\circ_a$ is not a direct child of $\circ_b$, but instead a descendant situated deeper in the operator tree. This is possible since in general, the e_i are trees themselves. Some reordering could possibly move a conflicting operator $\circ_a$ up to the top of an argument subtree.

Thus, we have to calculate the total eligibility sets bottom-up by applying CD-A to every operator $\circ^b$ in the operator tree. The pseudo code of CD-A is:

CD-A$(\circ^b)$

▷ **Input:** operator $\circ^b$
TES$(\circ^b) \leftarrow$ CALC$_{SES}(\circ^b)$
for $\forall\ \circ^a \in$ STO(left$(\circ^b)$)
  if $\neg$assoc$(\circ^a, \circ^b)$
    TES$(\circ^b) \leftarrow$ TES$(\circ^b) \cup \mathcal{T}(\text{left}(\circ^a))$
  if $\neg$l-asscom$(\circ^a, \circ^b)$
    TES$(\circ^b) \leftarrow$ TES$(\circ^b) \cup \mathcal{T}(\text{right}(\circ^a))$
for $\forall\ \circ^a \in$ STO(right$(\circ^b)$)
  if $\neg$assoc$(\circ^b, \circ^a)$
    TES$(\circ^b) \leftarrow$ TES$(\circ^b) \cup \mathcal{T}(\text{right}(\circ^a))$
  if $\neg$r-asscom$(\circ^b, \circ^a)$
    TES$(\circ^b) \leftarrow$ TES$(\circ^b) \cup \mathcal{T}(\text{left}(\circ^a))$

If we do not have degenerate predicates and cross products among the operators in the initial operator tree, we can safely use TES instead of $\mathcal{T}$.

The conflict representation comprises the TES for every operator. The pseudo code for APPLICABLE is:

APPLICABLE$_A(\circ, S_1, S_2)$

  ▷ **Input:** binary operator $\circ$, set of tables S_1, S_2

  return L-TES$(\circ) \subseteq S_1 \wedge$ R-TES$(\circ) \subseteq S_2$

Let us now see why APPLICABLE$_A$ is correct. We have to show that it prevents the generation of bad plans. Take the $\neg$assoc case with nesting on the left. Let the original operator tree contain $(e_1 \circ^a_{12} e_2) \circ^b_{23} e_3$. Define the set of tables $R_2 := \mathcal{F}_T(\circ^b_{23}) \cap \mathcal{T}(\text{left}(\circ^b_{23}))$ and $R_3 := \mathcal{F}_T(\circ^b_{23}) \cap \mathcal{T}(\text{right}(\circ^b_{23}))$. Then $\texttt{SES}(\circ^b_{23}) = R_2 \cup R_3$. Further, since $\neg\text{assoc}(\circ^a_{12}, \circ^b_{23})$, we have

$$\texttt{TES}(\circ^b_{23}) \supseteq \texttt{SES}(\circ^b_{23}) \cup \mathcal{T}(e_1).$$

Note that we used $\supseteq$ and not equality, since due to other conflicts, $\texttt{TES}(\circ^b)$ could be larger. Next, we observe that

$$\begin{aligned}\texttt{L-TES}(\circ^b_{23}) &\supseteq (\texttt{SES}(\circ^b_{23}) \cup \mathcal{T}(e_1)) \cap \mathcal{T}(\text{left}(\circ^b_{23}))\\ &\supseteq (\texttt{SES}(\circ^b_{23}) \cap \mathcal{T}(\text{left}(\circ^b_{23}))) \cup\\ &\quad\ (\mathcal{T}(e_1) \cap \mathcal{T}(\text{left}(\circ^b_{23})))\\ &\supseteq ((R_2 \cup R_3) \cap \mathcal{T}(\text{left}(\circ^b_{23}))) \cup (\mathcal{T}(e_1))\\ &\supseteq R_2 \cup \mathcal{T}(e_1)\end{aligned}$$

and

$$\begin{aligned}\texttt{R-TES}(\circ^b_{23}) &\supseteq (\texttt{SES}(\circ^b_{23}) \cup \mathcal{T}(e_1)) \cap \mathcal{T}(\text{right}(\circ^b_{23}))\\ &\supseteq \texttt{SES}(\circ^b_{23}) \cap \mathcal{T}(\text{right}(\circ^b_{23}))\\ &\supseteq R_3.\end{aligned}$$

Let S_1, S_2 be a pair of two arbitrary subsets of tables generated by DPSUBE. Then, the call APPLICABLE$(\circ^b, S_1, S_2)$ checks

$$\begin{aligned}\texttt{L-TES}(\circ^b_{23}) &\subseteq S_1 \text{ and}\\ \texttt{R-TES}(\circ^b_{23}) &\subseteq S_2,\end{aligned}$$

and fails if $S_1 \not\supseteq \mathcal{T}(e_1)$. Thus, neither $e_2 \circ^b_{23} e_3$ nor $e_3 \circ^b_{23} e_2$ will be generated and, hence, $e_1 \circ^a_{12} (e_2 \circ^b_{23} e_3)$ will not be generated either. Similarly, if $\neg$l-asscom$(\circ^a, \circ^b)$, $\texttt{L-TES}(\circ^b)$ will contain $\mathcal{T}(e_2)$, and the test prevents the generation of $e_1 \circ^b e_3$. The remaining two cases can be checked analogously.

From this discussion, it follows that DPSUBE generates only valid plans. However, it does not generate all valid plans. It is thus incomplete, as we can see from the example shown in Fig. 6. Since $\neg\text{assoc}(\ltimes_{0,1}, \rtimes_{2,3})$, $\texttt{TES}(\rtimes_{2,3})$ contains R_0 (line 4 of CD-A$(\rtimes_{2,3})$) . Thus, neither of the valid plans Plan 1 nor Plan 2 nor any of those derived from applying join commutativity to them will be generated.

5.3 Approach CD-B

In order to avoid this problem, we introduce the more flexible mechanism of *conflict rules*. A *conflict rule* (CR) is simply a pair of table sets denoted by $T_1 \to T_2$. With every operator node $\circ$ in the operator tree, we associate a set of conflict rules. Thus, our conflict representation now associates a TES and a set of conflict rules with every operator.

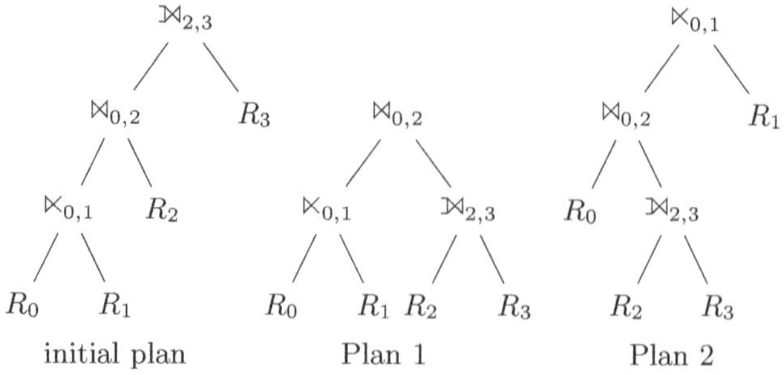

Figure 6: Example for incompleteness of CD-A

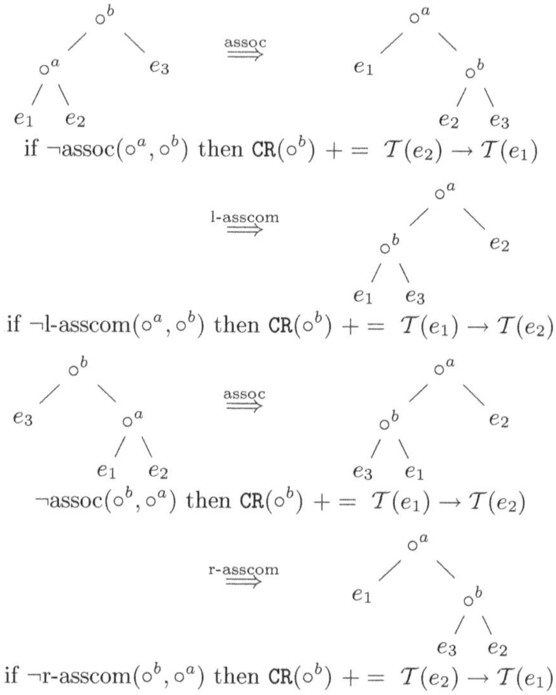

Figure 7: Calculating conflict rules for simple operator trees

Before we introduce their construction, let us illustrate their role in APPLICABLE$(\circ, S_1, S_2)$. A conflict rule $T_1 \to T_2$ is *obeyed* for S_1 and S_2 if with $S = S_1 \cup S_2$ the following condition holds:

$$T_1 \cap S \neq \emptyset \implies T_2 \subseteq S.$$

Thus, if T_1 contains a single table from S, S must contain all tables in T_2. Keeping this in mind, it is easy to see that the invalid plans are indeed prevented by the rules shown in Fig. 7 if they are obeyed. As we will see, the TES is restricted to SES in CD-B. Thus, the conflict rules allow for more flexibility: whereas the TES containment test is unconditioned, conflict rules represent a conditioned containment test.

The pseudo code for the new conflict detection is given in Fig. 8 with CD-B. As before, we apply CD-B bottom-up to every operator $\circ^b$ in the tree.

With the conflict rules, we need a new test for applicability. Now, the test given in Fig. 9 with APPLICABLE$_{B/C}(\circ, S_1, S_2)$ checks for two conditions:

1. L-TES $\subseteq S_1 \wedge$ R-TES $\subseteq S_2$ must hold (line 1), and
2. all rules in the rule set of $\circ$ must be obeyed (Lines 2-6).

CD-B($\circ^b$)

$\triangleright$ **Input:** operator $\circ^b$

TES($\circ^b$) $\leftarrow$ CALC$_{SES}$($\circ^b$)
for $\forall\ \circ^a \in$ STO(left($\circ^b$))
  if $\neg$assoc($\circ^a, \circ^b$)
    CR($\circ^b$) += $\mathcal{T}$(right($\circ^a$)) $\rightarrow$ $\mathcal{T}$(left($\circ^a$))
  if $\neg$l-asscom($\circ^a, \circ^b$)
    CR($\circ^b$) += $\mathcal{T}$(left($\circ^a$)) $\rightarrow$ $\mathcal{T}$(right($\circ^a$))
for $\forall\ \circ^a \in$ STO(right($\circ^b$))
  if $\neg$assoc($\circ^b, \circ^a$)
    CR($\circ^b$) += $\mathcal{T}$(left($\circ^a$)) $\rightarrow$ $\mathcal{T}$(right($\circ^a$))
  if $\neg$r-asscom($\circ^b, \circ^a$)
    CR($\circ^b$) += $\mathcal{T}$(right($\circ^a$)) $\rightarrow$ $\mathcal{T}$(left($\circ^a$))

Figure 8: Pseudocode for CD-B

Note that now all plans in Fig. 6 can be generated.

APPLICABLE$_{B/C}$($\circ, S_1, S_2$)

$\triangleright$ **Input:** binary operator $\circ$, set of tables S_1, S_2

1 **if** L-TES($\circ$) $\subseteq S_1 \wedge$ R-TES($\circ$) $\subseteq S_2$
2   **for all** $(T_1 \rightarrow T_2) \in$ CR($\circ$)
3   **if** $T_1 \cap (S_1 \cup S_2) \neq \emptyset$
4   **if** $T_2 \not\subseteq (S_1 \cup S_2)$
5   **return** FALSE
6   **return** TRUE
7 **else**
8   **return** FALSE

Figure 9: Pseudocode for APPLICABLE$_{B/C}$

Again, this implementation of APPLICABLE is correct but not complete, as the example in Fig. 10 shows. Since assoc($\bowtie_{0,1}, \ltimes_{1,3}$), assoc($\bowtie_{1,2}, \ltimes_{1,3}$) and l-asscom($\bowtie_{1,2}, \ltimes_{1,3}$), the only conflict occurs due to $\neg$r-asscom($\bowtie_{0,1}, \ltimes_{1,3}$). Thus,

$$\mathcal{T}(\{R_3\}) \rightarrow \mathcal{T}(\{R_1, R_2\}) \in \text{CR}(\bowtie_{0,1}).$$

The latter rule prevents the plan on the right-hand side of Fig. 10. Note that this is overly careful, since $R_2 \notin \mathcal{F}_T(\ltimes_{1,3})$. In fact, r-asscom would never be applied in this example, since $\bowtie_{0,1}$ accesses table R_1, and applying r-asscom would thus destroy the producer/consumer relationship ($\mathcal{F}_T(\bowtie_{0,1}) \cap \{R_1, R_2\} \neq \emptyset$) already checked by SES($\bowtie_{0,1}$).

5.4 Approach CD-C

The approach CD-C differs from CD-B only by the calculation of the conflict rules. The conflict representation and the procedure APPLICABLE remain the same. The idea is to learn from the above example and include only those tables under operator $\circ^a$ which occur in the predicate. However, we have to be careful to include special cases for degenerate predicates and cross products. The pseudo code is given with CD-C in Fig. 11. Let us revisit the example of Section 5.3. Since the only conflict occurs due to $\neg$r-asscom($\bowtie_{0,1}, \ltimes_{1,3}$), the rule set CR($\bowtie_{0,1}$) contains (Line 21 of CD-C) $\mathcal{T}(\{R_3\}) \rightarrow \mathcal{T}(\{R_1\}) \in$ CR($\bowtie_{0,1}$). As a consequence, the plan on the right of Fig. 10 will not be prevented anymore.

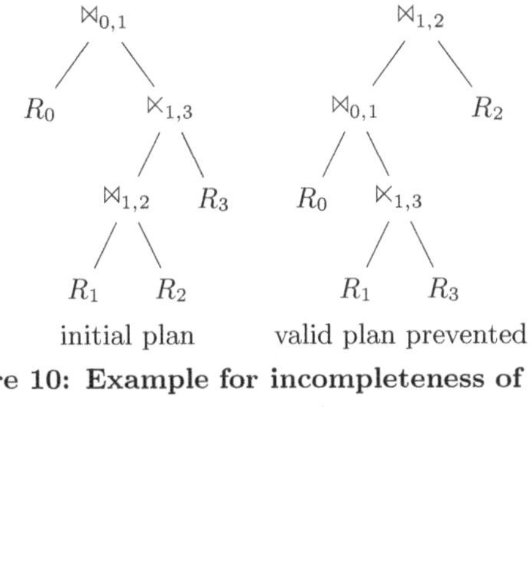

Figure 10: Example for incompleteness of CD-B

CD-C($\circ^b$)

$\triangleright$ **Input:** operator $\circ^b$

1 TES($\circ^b$) $\leftarrow$ CALC$_{SES}$($\circ^b$)
2 **for** $\forall\ \circ^a \in$ STO(left($\circ^b$))
3   **if** $\neg$assoc($\circ^a, \circ^b$)
4   **if** $\mathcal{T}$(left($\circ^a$)) $\cap\ \mathcal{F}_T(\circ^a) \neq \emptyset$
5   CR($\circ^b$) += $\mathcal{T}$(right($\circ^a$)) $\rightarrow$ $\mathcal{T}$(left($\circ^a$)) $\cap\ \mathcal{F}_T(\circ^a)$
6   **else**
7   CR($\circ^b$) += $\mathcal{T}$(right($\circ^a$)) $\rightarrow$ $\mathcal{T}$(left($\circ^a$))
8   **if** $\neg$l-asscom($\circ^a, \circ^b$)
9   **if** $\mathcal{T}$(right($\circ^a$)) $\cap\ \mathcal{F}_T(\circ^a) \neq \emptyset$
10   CR($\circ^b$) += $\mathcal{T}$(left($\circ^a$)) $\rightarrow$ $\mathcal{T}$(right($\circ^a$)) $\cap\ \mathcal{F}_T(\circ^a)$
11   **else**
12   CR($\circ^b$) += $\mathcal{T}$(left($\circ^a$)) $\rightarrow$ $\mathcal{T}$(right($\circ^a$))
13 **for** $\forall\ \circ^a \in$ STO(right($\circ^b$))
14   **if** $\neg$assoc($\circ^b, \circ^a$)
15   **if** $\mathcal{T}$(right($\circ^a$)) $\cap\ \mathcal{F}_T(\circ^a) \neq \emptyset$
16   CR($\circ^b$) += $\mathcal{T}$(left($\circ^a$)) $\rightarrow$ $\mathcal{T}$(right($\circ^a$)) $\cap\ \mathcal{F}_T(\circ^a)$
17   **else**
18   CR($\circ^b$) += $\mathcal{T}$(left($\circ^a$)) $\rightarrow$ $\mathcal{T}$(right($\circ^a$))
19   **if** $\neg$r-asscom($\circ^b, \circ^a$)
20   **if** $\mathcal{T}$(left($\circ^a$)) $\cap\ \mathcal{F}_T(\circ^a) \neq \emptyset$
21   CR($\circ^b$) += $\mathcal{T}$(right($\circ^a$)) $\rightarrow$ $\mathcal{T}$(left($\circ^a$)) $\cap\ \mathcal{F}_T(\circ^a)$
22   **else**
23   CR($\circ^b$) += $\mathcal{T}$(right($\circ^a$)) $\rightarrow$ $\mathcal{T}$(left($\circ^a$))

Figure 11: Pseudocode for CD-C

Correctness of CD-C. We show that APPLICABLE$_{B/C}$ for the $\neg$ assoc case with nesting on the left is correct. The remaining cases can be proven similarly. Let the original operator tree contain $(e_1 \circ^a_{12} e_2) \circ^b_{23} e_3$. Since $\neg$assoc($\circ^a, \circ^b$) (line 3 of CD-C($\circ^b$)), one of the following (line 5 or line 7) holds:

$$\begin{aligned} \text{CR}(\circ^b) \ &+= \ \mathcal{T}(e_2) \rightarrow \mathcal{T}(e_1) \text{ or} \\ &+= \ \mathcal{T}(e_2) \rightarrow \mathcal{T}(e_1') \text{ with } e_1' \subset e_1 \wedge e_1' \neq \emptyset. \end{aligned}$$

The second case subsumes the first case. Thus, it suffices to show the second case. To construct $e_1 \circ^a_{12} (e_2 \circ^b_{23} e_3)$ (right hand side of Eqv. 1), $(e_2 \circ^b_{23} e_3)$ must be constructed first. We show that APPLICABLE$_{B/C}$($\circ^b, S_1, S_2$) with either (A) $\mathcal{T}(e_2) \subseteq S_1 \wedge \mathcal{T}(e_3) \subseteq S_2$ or (B) $\mathcal{T}(e_3) \subseteq S_1 \wedge \mathcal{T}(e_2) \subseteq S_2$ returns FALSE. If the test in line 1 fails, FALSE is returned and we are done. Otherwise, L-TES($\circ$) $\subseteq S_1$ holds. Note that since we are trying to construct $(e_2 \circ^b_{23} e_3)$, $\mathcal{T}(e_1) \cap (S_1 \cup S_2) = \emptyset$ must hold. On the other hand, the conflict rule $T_1 \rightarrow T_2$ with $T_1 = \mathcal{T}(e_2)$ and $T_2 \supseteq \mathcal{T}(e_1')$ is contained in CR($\circ^b$). Thus, for this rule $T_1 \rightarrow T_2$: $T_1 \cap (S_1 \cup S_2) \neq \emptyset$ and $T_2 \not\subseteq (S_1 \cup S_2)$ hold in both cases (A) and (B). This cleary shows that FALSE is returned. Hence, CD-C and, consequently, CD-B are correct.

5.5 Rule Simplification

It is well-known that larger TES have a positive impact on the runtime of plan generators like DPHYP [15] or TDMC-CHYP [7] (see also Sec. 6). Further, reducing the number of rules slightly decreases plan generation time. Thus, applying laws like

$$\begin{aligned} R_1 \to R_2, R_1 \to R_3 &\equiv R_1 \to R_2 \cup R_3 \\ R_1 \to R_2, R_3 \to R_2 &\equiv R_1 \cup R_3 \to R_2 \end{aligned}$$

can be used to rearrange the rule set for efficient evaluation. However, we are much more interested in eliminating rules altogether by adding their right-hand side to the TES. For some operator $\circ$, consider a conflict rule $R_1 \to R_2$. If $R_1 \cap \text{TES}(\circ) \neq \emptyset$, we can add R_2 to TES due to the existential quantifier on the left-hand side of a rule in the definition of *obey*. Further, if $R_2 \subseteq \text{TES}(\circ)$, we can safely eliminate the rule. Applying these rearrangements is often possible, since both $\mathcal{T}(\text{left}(\circ^a)) \cap \mathcal{F}_T(\circ)$ and $\mathcal{T}(\text{right}(\circ^a)) \cap \mathcal{F}_T(\circ)$ will be non-empty.

6. MINOR ISSUES

6.1 Larger TES, Faster Plan Generation

Typically, a query graph is used to model the producer/consumer constraints defined in a given input query, and, thus, to represent the possible search space. For queries with complex predicates, i.e., predicates that reference more than two relations, the query graph is a hypergraph.

DEFINITION 3. *A* hypergraph *is a pair $H = (V, E)$ such that*

1. *V is a non-empty set of nodes, and*
2. *E is a set of hyperedges, where a* hyperedge *is an unordered pair (u, v) of non-empty subsets of V ($u \subset V$ and $v \subset V$) with the additional condition that $u \cap v = \emptyset$.*

We call any non-empty subset of V a hypernode.

Every plan generator based on dynamic programming or memoization constructs an optimal plan for a set of relations S by combining all suitable pairs of optimal subplans for sets of relations (S_1, S_2) where $S = S_1 \cup S_2 \wedge S_1 \neq \emptyset \wedge S_2 \neq \emptyset$ must hold (see Section 4). Furthermore, the producer/consumer constraints have to be met. Therefore, only certain sets S together with their combinations of S_1, S_2 are allowed. These combinations of S_1, S_2 are called csg-cmp pairs.

DEFINITION 4. *Let $H = (V, E)$ be a hypergraph and S_1, S_2 two non-empty subsets of V with $S_1 \cap S_2 = \emptyset$. Then, the pair (S_1, S_2) is called a* csg-cmp-pair *if the following conditions hold:*

1. *S_1 and S_2 induce a connected subgraph of H, and*
2. *there exists a hyperedge $(u, v) \in E$ such that $u \subseteq S_1$ and $v \subseteq S_2$.*

(See [15] for induced subgraphs and connectedness.)

Simple plan generators like DPSUB, DPSIZE [14], and MEMOIZATIONBASIC [6] generate various combinations for (S_1, S_2) and then possibly reject some (most) of them later on if they turn out to be invalid (APPLICABLE fails). This is not very efficient. In fact, the reason for DPHYP's [15] efficiency is that it only enumerates valid csg-cmp pairs. The above problem can be avoided if we use the TES (which are contained in all three conflict detectors and are (possibly) enlarged by rule simplification) to generate hyperedges instead of using them only within APPLICABLE. Hence, the hyperedges can directly cover most of the possible conflicts, if not all (see Sec. 7). The construction of the hyperedges proceeds as follows. For every operator $\circ$, we construct a hyperedge (l, r) such that $r = \text{TES}(\circ) \cap \mathcal{T}(\text{right}(\circ)) = \text{R-TES}(\circ)$ and $l = \text{TES}(\circ) \setminus r = \text{L-TES}(\circ)$. These hyperedges are then the input to DPHYP. Two things are important to observe. First, in case of non-empty rule sets, the applicable test must still be executed. Second, since $\text{SES} \subseteq \text{TES}$, no other hyperedges have to be constructed.

Let us now come to the question why larger TES result in higher efficiency. The efficiency of an advanced plan generator is directly correlated to the number of csg-cmp-pairs. Obviously, larger TES result in larger hypernodes in the hyperedges (l, r). Potentially, a hyperedge (l, r) gives rise to a csg-cmp-pair (l, r) if both l and r induce connected subgraphs. Further, every (S_1, S_2) with $S_1 \supseteq l$, $S_2 \supseteq r$, $S_1 \cap S_2 = \emptyset$ is a potential csg-cmp-pair. Thus, enlarging (l, r) decreases the number of csg-cmp-pairs.

6.2 Cross Products and Degenerate Predicates

Cross products and degenerate predicates are a little brittle. Consider the example $(R_1 \times R_2) \bowtie_{1,3} (R_3 \ltimes_{3,4} R_4)$. So far, nothing prevents DPSUBE to consider invalid plans like $R_1 \bowtie_{1,3} (R_3 \ltimes_{3,4} (R_2 \times R_4))$. Note that in order to prevent this plan, we would have to detect conflicts on the "other side" of the plan. Since cross products and degenerate predicates should be rare in real queries, it suffices to produce correct plans. We have no ambition to explore the complete search space. Thus, we just want to make sure that in these abnormal cases, the plan generator still produces a correct plan. This can be achieved by conjunctively adding the check

$$\mathcal{T}(\text{left}(\circ)) \cap S_1 \neq \emptyset \wedge \mathcal{T}(\text{right}(\circ)) \cap S_2 \neq \emptyset$$

to the test for APPLICABLE($\circ$, S_1, S_2). This results in a correct test, but about a third of the valid search space will not be explored if cross products are present in the initial operator tree. However, note that if the initial plan does not contain cross products and degenerate predicates, this test will always succeed such that in this case still the whole core search space is explored. Moreover, still a larger portion of the core search space is explored when comparing this approach to the one by Rao et al. [20, 21]. There, two separate runs of the plan generator for each of the arguments of a cross product are performed, which hinders any reordering of operators with cross products. Note that Moerkotte and Neumann's approach cannot handle cross products [14].

There is a second issue concerning cross products. In some rare cases, they might be beneficially introduced, even if the initial plan does not demand them. In this case, we can proceed as proposed by Rao et al. [20, 21]. For each relation R, a *companion set* is calculated which contains all relations that are connected to R only by inner join predicates. Within a companion set, all join orders and introductions of cross products are valid.

6.3 Unnesting

Dependent joins (d-joins, ⋈⃗) and the dependent variants of the other binary operators (⋉⃗, ▷⃗, ⟕⃗, ⟗⃗) play a central role in unnesting nested queries [2, 3, 8, 5]. Their incorporation into our approach is simple. In general, we just need to extend the matrices containing the assoc and l/r-asscom properties. In the special case of the dependent operators this is even simpler, since they have the same properties as their independent counterparts, except that they are not commutative. In any case, the conflict detectors can be used as is. However, the plan generator has to be adapted to dependent operators [14].

6.4 Pushing Grouping

Pushing group-by operators is a well-known technique to speed up data warehouse queries [24, 25]. To decide whether a group-by operator can be pushed and to do so is handled in Lines 11 and 13 of DPsube. Thus, these techniques are untouched by our conflict detector.

7. EVALUATION

In order to evaluate the different approaches, we implemented a transformation-based plan generator. It exhaustively applies the transformation rules defined in Sec. 3 until no new plan can be generated. Additionally, we implemented all known conflict detectors and used them within DPsube (see Sec. 4). Thereby, we modified DPsube such that it does not prune dominated plans but instead keeps all generated plans. This set of plans was then compared with the set of plans generated by the transformation-based plan generator. This way, we found (1) invalid plans and (2) valid plans not generated by DPsube equipped with some given conflict detector. Since NEL/EEL allows only for join, antijoin and left outerjoin but CD-X allow for more operators, we run experiments for two sets of operators ({⋈, ▷, ⟕} and {⋈, ⋉, ▷, ⟕, ⟗}).

For any given set of operators, we generated all possible initial plans for a given number of relations (varied between 3 and 7). For each initial plan, the different plan generators were called. The generation of all initial plans for n relations proceeds in three steps. In a first step, we unrank all integers from 1 to $\mathcal{C}(n-1)$, where $\mathcal{C}$ denotes the Catalan numbers ($\mathcal{C}(n)$ is the number of binary trees in n inner nodes), using the method proposed by Liebehenschel [13]. This gives us raw binary trees. In the second step, an operator from the operator set is attached to every inner node, making sure that every combination is generated exactly once. In the last step, we generate binary predicates by exploring all possibilities to reference one relation from the operator's left subtree and one from its right subtree. We did not generate complex predicates, since this simplifies the enumeration of the core search space (cf. Sec. 3.2).

Tables 4 and 5 show the results. The columns contain the number of relations (n), the number of distinct queries (initial operator trees), the number of plans the transformation-based plan generator generates for these queries, and for each conflict detector the number of invalid plans (I) and the number of plans not found (missing, M). The conflict detector EEL-F is a fixed version of the original NEL/EEL approach (see Sec. 8.1.1). Additionally, Table 5 contains for CD-C the number of rule sets which are empty after applying rule simplifications, and the number of non-empty rule sets.

From Table 4 we see that both the EEL/NEL approach and the SES/TES approach produce invalid plans. From Table 5 we see that CD-A and CD-B lose large fractions of the valid search space but CD-C does not. We also see that about 70% of all rule sets are empty if we apply rule simplification.

8. RELATED WORK

8.1 DP-based Plan Generation

If an input query involves binary operators other than ⋈ and ×, not all transformations as discussed in Section 3.2 are valid. Thus, any plan generator must be modified such that it restricts its search to valid transformations only. Otherwise, without these restrictions the generated plan may not be equivalent to the input query and, therefore, the result might be wrong.

There exist several proposals to restrict the search space. First, the problem of outerjoin simplification and reordering has been studied extensively by Galindo-Legaria and Rosenthal [23, 9, 10]. They identified a subclass of join/outerjoin queries where the query graph unambiguously determines the semantics of a query. For this type of queries, they proposed a procedure that analyzes paths in the query graph to detect conflicting reorderings. They enhanced a conventional dynamic programming algorithm to deal with these conflicts. Although very useful, their approach is restricted to joins and outerjoins and the query graph must exhibit special properties. In order to handle complex predicates, Bhargava, Goel and Iyer [1] extended this approach and present a conflict detection which analyzes paths in hypergraphs. Again, the approach is limited to joins and outerjoins. Rao et al. presented a method that is not restricted to joins/outerjoins. They additionally consider antijoins [21, 20]. They propose to use the initial operator tree instead of the query graph in order to maintain the semantics of the input query. Their idea is to calculate a set of relations associated with every predicate (operator). This set of relations (called EEL, for *extended eligibility list*) must be available before the predicate can be evaluated. EELs are a superset of `NEL`s. Moerkotte and Neumann [15] adopted the idea of `EEL` and called it `TES`. Their approach considers all join operators in `LOP` and their dependent counterparts. Additionally, they reformulated non-inner joins as complex predicates by modeling their reordering conflicts in the form of hyperedges in order to make plan generation more efficient.

Both the approach of Rao et al. as well as Moerkotte and Neumann's approach are not correct. Both generate invalid plans. We will present examples demonstrating why they fail. Further, we present a fix for the algorithm of Rao et al.

8.1.1 Outerjoin and Antijoin Reordering Using EELs

First, we explain the approach of Rao et al. in short [20, 21]. Then, we give a counter-example that shows the incorrectness of their method. After that, we make an attempt to repair the proposed EEL computation algorithm.

Conflict Detection with EELs The main idea of [20, 21] is to compute an *extended eligibility list* (`EEL`), which is a shorthand representation of possible reordering conflicts. In [20], Rao et al. proposed an algorithm called CALC_{EEL} to

n	#Queries	#Plans	EEL		EEL-F		TES		CD-A		CD-B		CD-C	
			I	M	I	M	I	M	I	M	I	M	I	M
3	26	88	0	0 %	0	1.14 %	0	0 %	0	0 %	0	0 %	0	0 %
4	344	4059	2	0 %	0	2.02 %	23	2.24 %	0	3.30 %	0	2.02 %	0	0 %
5	5834	301898	296	0 %	0	2.51 %	3964	6.47 %	0	8.54 %	0	5.38 %	0	0 %
6	117604	32175460	41108	0 %	0	2.70 %	605914	12.23 %	0	14.66 %	0	9.77 %	0	0 %
7	2708892	4598129499	6349126	0 %	0	2.71 %	99179293	19.05 %	0	21.06 %	0	15.04 %	0	0 %

Table 4: Small operator set: join, left outerjoin, antijoin

n	#Queries	#Plans	CD-A		CD-B		CD-C		Rule Sets	
			I	M	I	M	I	M	$\emptyset$	$\neg\emptyset$
3	62	203	0	0	0	0	0	0	107	17
4	1114	11148	0	473 (4.24 %)	0	246 (2.21 %)	0	0	2725	617
5	25056	934229	0	102019 (10.92 %)	0	55725 (5.96 %)	0	0	77484	22740
6	661811	108294798	0	20113801 (18.57 %)	0	11868102 (10.96 %)	0	0	2432717	876338
7	19846278	16448441514	0	4329578881 (26.32 %)	0	2793701760 (16.98 %)	0	0	83560096	35517572

Table 5: Large operator set: join, left/full outerjoin, semijoin, antijoin

compute the EEL for each predicate carried by a join operator $\circ \in \{⋈, ⟕, ▷\}$. The pseudo code of CALCEEL is shown in Fig. 12.

CALC$_{\text{EEL}}$ computes the EELs in a single bottom-up traversal (lines 4-20) of the initial operator tree. During the traversal, it maintains for each relation R an outerjoin set $outer_R$ and an antijoin set $anti_R$. Initially, both sets contain only the corresponding relation itself (lines 2, 3). Thereby, $outer_R$ stores all relations that are linked together through either inner or antijoin predicates (lines 13-16). And $anti_R$ keeps track of all relations $R \in \mathcal{T}(\text{left}(\circ)) \cap \texttt{NEL}(\circ)$ that are linked through $\circ \in \{⟕\}$ (lines 17-20). Essentially, this means that R has to be on the preserving side of a one-sided outerjoin predicate. As the name implies, $outer_R$ is used to compute the EEL for an outerjoin predicate (lines 6-8). Similarly, $anti_R$ is used to compute the EEL for an antijoin predicate (lines 9-12). The test of APPLICABLE is $\texttt{EEL} \subseteq S_1 \cup S_2$.

CALC$_{\text{EEL}}$

▷ **Input:** $\mathcal{T}(\circ)$, $\texttt{NEL}(\circ)$ where $\circ \in \{⋈, ⟕, ▷\}$
▷ **Output:** $\texttt{EEL}(\circ)$

1 **for each** $R \in \mathcal{T}(\text{topmost } \circ)$
2 $\quad outer_R \leftarrow \{R\}$
3 $\quad anti_R \leftarrow \{R\}$
4 **for each** operator $\circ$ during bottom-up traversal
5 $\quad \texttt{EEL}(\circ) \leftarrow \texttt{NEL}(\circ)$
6 $\quad$ **if** $\circ \in \{⟕\}$
7 $\quad\quad W \leftarrow \bigcup_{R \in \mathcal{T}(right(\circ)) \cap \texttt{NEL}(\circ)} outer_R$
8 $\quad\quad \texttt{EEL}(\circ) \leftarrow \texttt{EEL}(\circ) \cup W$
9 $\quad$ **elseif** $\circ \in \{▷\}$
10 $\quad\quad V \leftarrow \bigcup_{R \in \mathcal{T}(left(\circ)) \cap \texttt{NEL}(\circ)} anti_R$
11 $\quad\quad U \leftarrow \{R | R \in \mathcal{T}(right(\circ)) \cap \texttt{NEL}(\circ)\}$
12 $\quad\quad \texttt{EEL}(\circ) \leftarrow \texttt{EEL}(\circ) \cup V \cup U$
13 $\quad$ **if** $\circ \in \{⋈, ▷\}$
14 $\quad\quad W \leftarrow \bigcup_{R \in \texttt{NEL}(\circ)} outer_R$
15 $\quad\quad$ **for each** $R \in W$
16 $\quad\quad\quad outer_R \leftarrow W$
17 $\quad$ **elseif** $\circ \in \{⟕\}$
18 $\quad\quad V \leftarrow \bigcup_{R \in \mathcal{T}(left(\circ)) \cap \texttt{NEL}(\circ)} anti_R$
19 $\quad\quad$ **for each** $R \in \mathcal{T}(right(\circ)) \cap \texttt{NEL}(\circ)$
20 $\quad\quad\quad anti_R \leftarrow anti_R \cup V$

Figure 12: Pseudocode for CALC$_{\text{EEL}}$

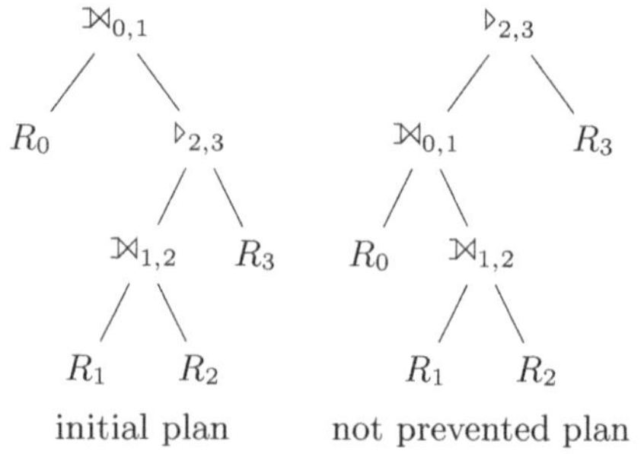

Figure 13: Example showing the incorrectness of CALC$_{\text{EEL}}$

The EEL computation is not correct. Fig. 13 shows an example where EELs as computed by CALC$_{\text{EEL}}$ do not prevent the generation of invalid plans. The initial plan is given on the left. The plan on the right of Fig. 13 can be derived by applying $\text{assoc}(⟕_{0,1}, ▷_{2,3})$. A look at Table 2 reveals that $\text{assoc}(⟕_{0,1}, ▷_{2,3})$ is not valid. Thus, the initial plan and the not prevented plan are not equivalent. We can verify this by using the relations in Table 6 as input for both plans. The result for the initial plan is given in Table 7. Clearly, this differs from the result of the invalid plan (Table 8).

Table 9 shows $anti_R$ and $outer_R$ during CALC$_{\text{EEL}}$ execution. Table 10 displays the results of CALC$_{\text{EEL}}$. According to $\texttt{EEL}(⟕_{0,1})$ and $\texttt{EEL}(▷_{2,3})$, the antijoin $▷_{2,3}$ can be applied on top of the outerjoin $⟕_{0,1}$, which is wrong. $\texttt{EEL}(⟕_{0,1})$ should contain $\{R_0, R_1, R_2, R_3\}$ in order to be correct because $\neg\text{assoc}(⟕_{0,1}, ▷_{2,3})$ holds.

R_0	R_1		R_2		R_3
A	A	B	B	C	C
1	1	1	1	1	1

Table 6: Example Relations.

$R_0 ⟕_{R_0.A=R_1.A} ((R_1 ⟕_{R_1.B=R_2.B} R_2) ▷_{R_2.C=R_3.C})$

$R_0.A$	$R_1.A$	$R_1.B$	$R_2.B$	$R_2.C$	$R_3.C$
1	NULL	NULL	NULL	NULL	NULL

Table 7: Result for executing initial plan Fig. 13 using relations of Table 6 as input.

$(R_0 ⟗_{R_0.A=R_1.A}(R_1 ⟗_{R_1.B=R_2.B} R_2)) \triangleright_{R_2.C=R_3.C}$

$R_0.A$	$R_1.A$	$R_1.B$	$R_2.B$	$R_2.C$	$R_3.C$
$\emptyset$					

Table 8: Result for executing initial plan Fig. 13 using relations of Table 6 as input.

R	$outer_R$	$anti_R$
R_0	$\{R_0\}$	$\{R_0\}$
R_1	$\{R_1\}$	$\{R_0, R_1\}$
R_2	$\{R_2, R_3\}$	$\{R_1, R_2\}$
R_3	$\{R_2, R_3\}$	$\{R_3\}$

Table 9: *$anti_R$* **and** *$outer_R$* **sets after executing** CALCEEL.

Fixing the EEL computation CALCEEL can be fixed: we only have to eliminate the intersection with NEL(∘) in Lines 7 and 18 as in

7 $\quad W \leftarrow \bigcup_{R \in \mathcal{T}(right(\circ))} outer_R$

With this fix, CALCEEL prevents reordering conflicts, but is not complete any more. Hence, we traded in correctness for incompleteness, which still is a better choice. This can be verified by using $R_0 ⟗_{0,1} (R_1 ⟗_{1,2} R_2)$ as input plan. The modified CALCEEL procedure now calculates $\texttt{EEL}(⟗_{0,1}) = \{R_0, R_1, R_2\}$, which prevents $(R_0 ⟗_{0,1} R_1) ⟗_{1,2} R_2$, although the latter is an equivalent and valid plan because assoc($⟗_{0,1}$, $⟗_{1,2}$) holds. Thus, $\texttt{EEL}(⟗_{0,1})$ should contain $\{R_0, R_1\}$ only.

8.1.2 Join Reordering using TESs

Before a join operator can be applied, the plan generator needs to ensure that the producer/consumer constraints are fulfilled. The conventional test is to check if the SES(∘) of some operator ∘ is a subset of $\mathcal{T}(\circ)$. Moerkotte and Neumann extend this test to prevent reordering conflicts [15]. Therefore, they introduce the notion of the *total eligibility set* (TES for short). The TES is defined to be a set of relations that is attached to any binary operator ∘. Before ∘ can be applied (line 11 of DPSUBE), APPLICABLE ensures that all elements of TES(∘) are present in $S_1 \cup S_2$. Since TES is an extension of SES, SES ⊆ TES holds.

Moerkotte and Neumann propose an algorithm called CALC$_{TES}$. It calculates the TES for every ∘ ∈ LOP. Its pseudo code can be found in [15]. As it turns out, Moerkotte's and Neumann's approach is neither correct nor complete: it generates wrong plans and misses good plans.

Fig. 14 contains an example showing the incorrectness of the SES/TES approach: the plan on the right is not equivalent to the initial plan on the left. Applying assoc($⟕_{1,2}, \triangleright_{2,3}$) as a first step and assoc($⟗_{0,1}, \triangleright_{2,3}$) thereafter transforms the initial plan into the plan on the right. To see that the plan on the right is invalid, consider the different results in Tables 11 and 12, which are based on the same input relations as before (Table 6).

∘	NEL	EEL
$⟗_{1,2}$	$\{R_1, R_2\}$	$\{R_1, R_2\}$
$\triangleright_{2,3}$	$\{R_2, R_3\}$	$\{R_1, R_2, R_3\}$
$⟗_{0,1}$	$\{R_0, R_1\}$	$\{R_0, R_1\}$

Table 10: Computed NEL and EEL after executing CALCEEL.

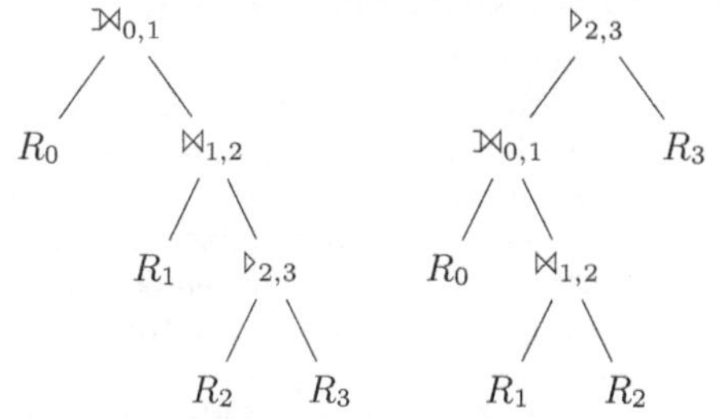

Figure 14: Example showing the incorrectness of CALC$_{TES}$

$R_0 ⟗_{R_0.A=R_1.A}(R_1 ⟕_{R_1.B=R_2.B}(R_2 \triangleright_{R_2.C=R_3.C} R_3))$

$R_0.A$	$R_1.A$	$R_1.B$	$R_2.B$	$R_2.C$
1	NULL	NULL	NULL	NULL

Table 11: Result for executing initial plan Fig. 14 using relations of Table 6 as input.

Table 13 shows the results of applying CALC$_{TES}$ to the initial plan. (For details, see [15].) Due to the actual values of TES($⟗_{0,1}$) and TES($\triangleright_{2,3}$), APPLICABLE allows that the antijoin $\triangleright_{2,3}$ moves on top of $⟗_{0,1}$, which is invalid since ¬assoc($⟗_{0,1}, \triangleright_{2,3}$) holds. In order to prevent the reordering, TES($⟗_{0,1}$) should contain $\{R_0, R_1, R_2, R_3\}$.

8.2 Transformation-Based Plan Generation

Besides DP-based and memoization-based algorithms for plan generation, there exists plenty of work on transformation-based plan generators [11, 17]. Unfortunately, transformation-based plan generators are less efficient. First, they are memory consuming, since they cannot prune plans because they need them to generate more plans via transformations. Second, they generate an exponential number of duplicates, as pointed out by Pellenkoft, Galindo-Legaria, and Kersten [17, 18, 19]. They also propose a solution to avoid the generation of duplicates, but this solution only works for acyclic query graphs. Thus, until better transformation-based algorithms are found, DP-based or memoization-based plan generators are the approaches of choice. Note that the latter also need a correct conflict detector.

$(R_0 ⟗_{R_0.A=R_1.A}(R_1 ⟕_{R_1.B=R_2.B} R_2)) \triangleright_{R_2.C=R_3.C} R_3$

$R_0.A$	$R_1.A$	$R_1.B$	$R_2.B$	$R_2.C$
$\emptyset$				

Table 12: Result for executing right plan Fig. 14 using relations of Table 6 as input.

∘	SES	TES
$\triangleright_{2,3}$	$\{R_2, R_3\}$	$\{R_2, R_3\}$
$⟕_{1,2}$	$\{R_1, R_2\}$	$\{R_1, R_2\}$
$⟗_{0,1}$	$\{R_0, R_1\}$	$\{R_0, R_1, R_2\}$

Table 13: Computed SES and TES after executing CALC$_{TES}$.

8.3 Beyond the Core Search Space

There exist several approaches to go beyond the core search space. The first one is based on generalized outerjoins [1, 4, 23]. To incorporate generalized outerjoins into our framework, we need to extend the property matrices. Another approach replaces all outerjoins by joins [12]. To make this work correctly, a complete semijoin reduction is performed upfront and virtual rows are introduced. Yet another interesting approach is proposed by Rao et al. [22]. They deliberately apply wrong reorderings and then compensate for it. For the compensation they rely on a new operator called best match that is relatively expensive. If no best-match operator is available in the runtime system, only compensation-free plans can be generated. However, whether a plan needs compensation or not is decided when the top-most operator is put in place. Hence, plans that need compensation are still built and have to be thrown away afterwards. Consequently, when compared to our approach far more (sub-) plans are generated but no cheaper plan is found. Moreover, our optimization techniques as described in Sec. 5.5 and Sec. 6.1 cannot be applied which renders modern plan generators like DPHYP [15] or TD-MCCHYP [7] almost useless. Furthermore, we conjecture that [22] does not cover the whole core search space. For example, for the initial plan $(R_1 ⟗_{p_{12}} R_2) ⟗_{p_{23}} R_3$, the alternative $R_1 ⟗_{p_{12}} (R_2 ⟗_{p_{23}} R_3)$ cannot be produced. It is future research to see how compensation can be incorporated into our approach.

9. CONCLUSION

We showed that existing approaches to reorder a not necessarily strict superset of $\{\bowtie, ⟕, \triangleright\}$ are incorrect: they produce invalid plans. We then presented the first valid conflict detectors. The third one of them, CD-C, is not only correct but also complete. It thus explores the full core search space. Further, our approach is extensible. If new algebraic operators pop up, we only need to extend four matrices containing their properties. The code itself remains unchanged.

Acknowledgements. We thank Simone Seeger for her help preparing the manuscript. We are also grateful to the anonymous referees for their comments, which helped us to significantly improve the paper.

10. REFERENCES

[1] G. Bhargava, P. Goel, and B. Iyer. Hypergraph based reorderings of outer join queries with complex predicates. In *SIGMOD*, pages 304–315, 1995.

[2] S. Cluet and G. Moerkotte. Nested queries in object bases. In *DBPL*, pages 226–242, 1993.

[3] S. Cluet and G. Moerkotte. Classification and optimization of nested queries in object bases. Technical Report 95-6, RWTH Aachen, 1995.

[4] U. Dayal. Of nests and trees: A unified approach to processing queries that contain nested subqueries, aggregates, and quantifiers. In *VLDB*, pages 197–208, 1987.

[5] M. Elhemali, C. Galindo-Legaria, T. Grabs, and M. Joshi. Execution strategies for SQL subqueries. In *SIGMOD*, pages 993–1003, 2007.

[6] P. Fender and G. Moerkotte. A new, highly efficient, and easy to implement top-down join enumeration algorithm. In *ICDE*, pages 864–875, 2011.

[7] P. Fender and G. Moerkotte. Top down plan generation: From theory to practice. In *ICDE*, pages 1105–1116, 2013.

[8] C. Galindo-Legaria and M. Joshi. Orthogonal optimization of subqueries and aggregation. In *SIGMOD*, pages 571–581, 2001.

[9] C. Galindo-Legaria and A. Rosenthal. How to extend a conventional optimizer to handle one- and two-sided outerjoin. In *ICDE*, pages 402–409, 1992.

[10] C. Galindo-Legaria and A. Rosenthal. Outerjoin simplification and reordering for query optimization. *TODS*, 22(1):43–73, Marc 1997.

[11] G. Graefe and W. McKenna. Extensibility and search efficiency in the volcano optimizer generator. In *ICDE*, pages 209–218, 1993.

[12] G. Hill and A. Ross. Reducing outer joins. *VLDB Journal*, 18:599–610, 2009.

[13] J. Liebehenschel. Ranking and unranking of lexicographically ordered words: An average-case analysis. *J. of Automata, Languages, and Combinatorics*, 2:227–268, 1997.

[14] G. Moerkotte and T. Neumann. Analysis of two existing and one new dynamic programming algorithm for the generation of optimal bushy trees without cross products. In *VLDB*, pages 930–941, 2006.

[15] G. Moerkotte and T. Neumann. Dynamic programming strikes back. In *SIGMOD*, pages 539–552, 2008.

[16] G. Moerkotte and T. Neumann. Accelerating queries with group-by and join by groupjoin. *PVLDB*, 4(11):843–851, 2011.

[17] A. Pellenkoft, C. Galindo-Legaria, and M. Kersten. Complexity of transformation-based optimizers and duplicate-free generation of alternatives. Technical Report CS-R9639, CWI, 1996.

[18] A. Pellenkoft, C. Galindo-Legaria, and M. Kersten. The complexity of transformation-based join enumeration. In *VLDB*, pages 306–315, 1997.

[19] A. Pellenkoft, C. Galindo-Legaria, and M. Kersten. Duplicate-free generation of alternatives in transformation-based optimizers. In *DASFAA*, pages 117–124, 1997.

[20] J. Rao, B. Lindsay, G. Lohman, H.Pirahesh, and D. Simmen. Using EELs: A practical approach to outerjoin and antijoin reordering. Technical Report RJ 10203, IBM, 2000.

[21] J. Rao, B. Lindsay, G. Lohman, H. Pirahesh, and D. Simmen. Using EELs: A practical approach to outerjoin and antijoin reordering. In *ICDE*, pages 595–606, 2001.

[22] J. Rao, H. Pirahesh, and C. Zuzarte. Canonical abstraction for outerjoin optimization. In *SIGMOD*, pages 671–682, 2004.

[23] A. Rosenthal and C. Galindo-Legaria. Query graphs, implementing trees, and freely-reorderable outerjoins. In *SIGMOD*, pages 291–299, 1990.

[24] W. Yan and P.-A. Larson. Performing group-by before join. In *ICDE*, pages 89–100, 1994.

[25] W. Yan and P.-A. Larson. Eager aggregation and lazy aggregation. In *VLDB*, pages 345–357, 1995.

Trinity: A Distributed Graph Engine on a Memory Cloud

Bin Shao
Microsoft Research Asia
Beijing, China
binshao@microsoft.com

Haixun Wang
Microsoft Research Asia
Beijing, China
haixunw@microsoft.com

Yatao Li*
HKUST
Kowloon, Hong Kong
ylibg@ust.hk

ABSTRACT

Computations performed by graph algorithms are data driven, and require a high degree of random data access. Despite the great progresses made in disk technology, it still cannot provide the level of efficient random access required by graph computation. On the other hand, memory-based approaches usually do not scale due to the capacity limit of single machines. In this paper, we introduce Trinity, a general purpose graph engine over a distributed memory cloud. Through optimized memory management and network communication, Trinity supports fast graph exploration as well as efficient parallel computing. In particular, Trinity leverages graph access patterns in both online and offline computation to optimize memory and communication for best performance. These enable Trinity to support efficient online query processing and offline analytics on large graphs with just a few commodity machines. Furthermore, Trinity provides a high level specification language called TSL for users to declare data schema and communication protocols, which brings great ease-of-use for general purpose graph management and computing. Our experiments show Trinity's performance in both low latency graph queries as well as high throughput graph analytics on web-scale, billion-node graphs.

Categories and Subject Descriptors

C.2.4 [**Computer-Communication Networks**]: Distributed Systems—*Distributed Databases*; D.4.2 [**Operating Systems**]: Storage Management—*Distributed memories*

Keywords

Distributed System; Memory Cloud; Graph Database

1. INTRODUCTION

Large graphs appear in a wide range of computational domains, and we are facing challenges at all levels ranging from the infrastructure to the programming model for managing and processing large graphs. Graph applications have varied needs. We may roughly classify such needs into two categories: online query processing, which requires low latency, and offline graph analytics, which requires high throughput. As an example, deciding instantly whether there is a path between two given persons in a social network belongs to the first category while computing PageRank for the WWW belongs to the second. Still, many sophisticated applications have both needs: Given two nodes in a graph, the "distance oracle" algorithm that estimates the shortest distance between the two nodes is an online algorithm. However, to estimate the distances, the algorithm relies on "landmark" nodes in the graph, and the optimal set of landmark nodes are discovered using offline analytics.

Despite the diversity of graph applications, graph computation has some unique characteristics [26]: It usually has a high data-access-to-computation ratio, in other words, it is I/O intensive. Furthermore, graph computation usually requires a high degree of random data access. This is particularly true for online queries as they usually require certain degree of graph exploration (e.g., BFS, sub-graph matching, etc.). Offline graph computations are usually performed in an iterative, batch manner. For iterative computations, keeping data in main memory can improve performance by an order of magnitude due to the reuse of intermediate results as illustrated by Spark [34]. Moreover, the scale of data makes distributed parallel computation the most promising solution for large graph processing. As we shall see, keeping the graph, at least the topology, in distributed memory not only improves the performance, but also enables a new set of graph computation paradigms.

In this paper, we introduce Trinity, a distributed graph engine on a memory cloud. Trinity supports both online graph query processing and offline graph analytics, and it has been used for real life applications, including knowledgebases [33], knowledge graphs [36], and social networks. Trinity is able to scale-out, which means it can host arbitrarily large graphs in the memory of a cluster of commodity machines[1]. Instead of optimizing for certain types of graph computation (e.g., BSP), Trinity directly addresses the random data access problem in large graph computation. Trinity implements a globally addressable distributed memory storage, and provides a random access abstraction for large

*The work was done at Microsoft Research Asia.

[1]Trinity usually makes the graph topology and frequently used information of the graph memory-resident. Trinity provides transparent access to other information associated with the graph in DBMSs.

SIGMOD'13, June 22–27, 2013, New York, New York, USA.

graph computation. The design of Trinity is based on the belief that, as high-speed network becomes more available and DRAM prices trends downward in the long run, all-in-memory solutions provide the lowest total cost of ownership for a large range of applications [8]. For instance, RAMCloud [30] envisioned that advances in hardware and OS technology will eventually enable all-in-memory applications, and low latency can be achieved by deploying faster NICs and network switches and by tuning the OS, the NIC, and the communication protocol. Trinity realizes this vision for large graph applications, and Trinity does not rely on hardware/platform upgrades and/or special OS tuning, although Trinity can leverage these techniques to achieve even better performance.

	Graph Database	Query Processing	Graph Analytics	Scale-out System
Neo4j [4]	Yes	Yes	Yes	No
HyperGraphDB [22]	Yes	Yes	No	No
GraphChi [25]	No	No	Yes	No
PEGASUS [23]	No	No	Yes	Yes
MapReduce [15]	No	No	Yes	Yes
Pregel [28]	No	No	Yes	Yes
GraphLab [1]	No	No	Yes	Yes

Table 1: Some Representative Graph Systems

Before we discuss the details of Trinity, we survey a few representative graph systems that have been proposed in the last few years. Table 1 summarizes our survey results. Among the existing graph systems, Neo4j [4] and HyperGraphDB [22] focus on supporting online transaction processing (OLTP) on graph data. However, they are not distributed: They do not handle graphs that are partitioned over multiple machines. This limits the size of the graphs they can *efficiently* handle. Furthermore, a single machine also does not have enough computation power compared with a distributed, parallel system. Thus, it is difficult for such systems to handle web-scale graphs.

On the other end of the spectrum are MapReduce [15], Pregel [28], GraphLab [1]. These are high latency, high throughput offline platforms. Unlike Neo4j and HyperGraphDB, they do not support online query processing, instead, they are optimized for analytics on large data partitioned over hundreds of machines. MapReduce computations on graphs depend heavily on interprocessor bandwidth, as graph structures are sent over the network iteration after iteration. Pregel and GraphLab mitigate this problem by passing computation results instead of graph structures between processors. In Pregel, GraphLab, and GraphChi, analytics on the graphs are expressed using a vertex centric computation paradigm. Although some well known graph algorithms, including PageRank, shortest path discovery, can be implemented through vertex centric computing with ease, there are a large range of sophisticated graph computations, for example, multi-level graph partitioning, that cannot be expressed in a succinct and elegant way.

Trinity itself is not a system that comes with comprehensive built-in graph computation modules. However, with its flexible data and computation modeling capability, Trinity enables the development of such modules and hence empowers a large variety of graph applications. In other words, it can easily morph into systems to support any specific graph applications.

The rest of the paper is organized as follows. In Section 2, we outline the design of the Trinity system. In Section 3, we introduce the Trinity's memory cloud. Section 4 describes the Trinity data model. Section 5 analyzes the computation paradigms of typical graph applications. Section 6 discusses some technical details in system implementation. Section 7 presents experimental results on Trinity. We discuss related work in Section 8 and conclude in Section 9.

2. AN OVERVIEW OF TRINITY

We show the architecture of Trinity in Figure 1. Trinity is a storage infrastructure and computation framework built on top of a cluster of well-connected machines. As a storage infrastructure, Trinity organizes the memory of multiple machines into a globally addressable, distributed memory address space (a memory cloud) to support large graphs. Trinity is designed for online query processing applications as well as offline analytics applications, and it supports user-friendly graph modeling, object-oriented data manipulation.

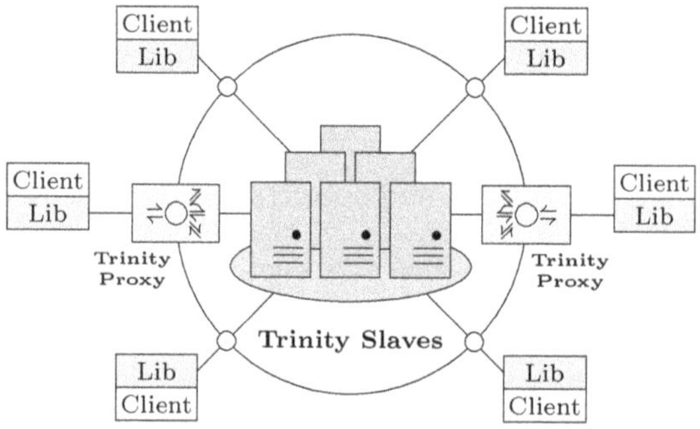

Figure 1: Trinity Cluster Structure

A Trinity system consists of multiple components that communicate through a network. According to the roles they play, we classify them into three types: slaves, proxies, and clients. A Trinity slave plays two roles: storing graph data and performing computation on the data. Computation usually involves sending messages to and receiving messages from other Trinity components. Specifically, each slave stores a portion of the data and processes messages received from other slaves, proxies, or clients. A Trinity proxy only handles messages but does not own any data. It usually serves as a middle tier between slaves and clients. For example, a proxy may serve as an information aggregator: It dispatches requests from clients to slaves and sends results back to the clients after aggregating partial results received from slaves. Proxies are optional, that is, a Trinity system does not always need a proxy. A Trinity client is responsible for enabling users to interacting with the Trinity cluster. It is a user interface tier between the Trinity system and end-users. Trinity clients are applications that are linked to Trinity library. They communicate with Trinity slaves and Trinity proxies through the APIs provided by the Trinity library.

Figure 2 shows the stack of Trinity system modules. The memory cloud is essentially a distributed key-value store, and it is supported by a memory storage module and a message passing framework. The memory storage module manages memory and provides mechanisms for concurrency control. The network communication module provides an efficient, one-sided, machine-to-machine message passing infrastructure.

Trinity Provides a specification language called TSL (Trinity specification language) that bridges the graph model and

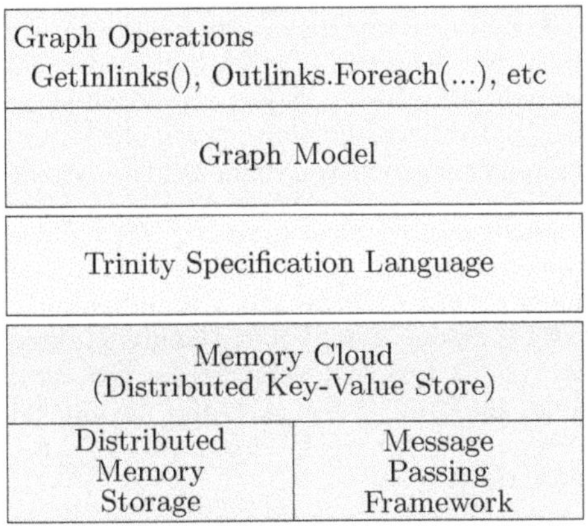

Figure 2: System Layers

the data storage. Due to the diversity of graphs and the diversity of graph applications, it is hard, if not entirely impossible, to support efficient general purpose graph computation using fixed graph schema. Instead of using fixed graph schema and fixed computation models, Trinity let users define graph schema, communication protocols, and computation paradigms through TSL.

3. THE MEMORY CLOUD

We create a distributed memory cloud as Trinity's storage infrastructure. The memory cloud consists of 2^p memory trunks, each of which is stored on a machine. Usually, we have $2^p > m$, where m is the number of machines. In other words, each machine hosts multiple memory trunks. The reason we partition a machine's local memory space into multiple memory trunks is twofold: 1) Trunk level parallelism can be achieved without any overhead of locking; 2) The performance of a single huge hash table is suboptimal due to a higher probability of hashing conflicts. Essentially, the entire memory cloud is partitioned into 2^p memory trunks. To support fault-tolerant data persistence, these memory trunks are also backed up in a shared distributed file system called TFS (Trinity File System), which is similar to HDFS [10].

On top of the memory cloud, we create a key-value store. A key-value pair forms the most basic data structure of the graph system or any system built on top of the memory cloud. Here, keys are 64-bit globally unique identifiers, and values are blobs of arbitrary length. As the memory cloud is distributed across multiple machines, we cannot address a key-value pair using its physical memory address. To address a key-value pair, Trinity uses a hashing mechanism. In order to locate the value of a given key, we first 1) identify the machine that stores the key-value pair, and then 2) locate the key-value pair in one of the memory trunks on that machine. Through this hashing mechanism (shown in Figure 3), we provide a globally addressable memory space.

Specifically, given a 64-bit key, to locate its corresponding value in the memory cloud, we hash the key to a p-bit value $i \in [0, 2^p - 1]$. This means the key-value pair is stored in memory trunk i within the memory cloud. To find out which machine memory trunk i is in, we maintain an "addressing table" that contains 2^p slots, where each slot stores a machine ID. Essentially, we implement a consistent hashing mechanism that allows machines to join and leave the memory cloud (described later). Furthermore, in order for global addressing to work, each machine keeps a replica of the addressing table, and we will describe how we ensure the consistency of the addressing tables in Section 6.2.

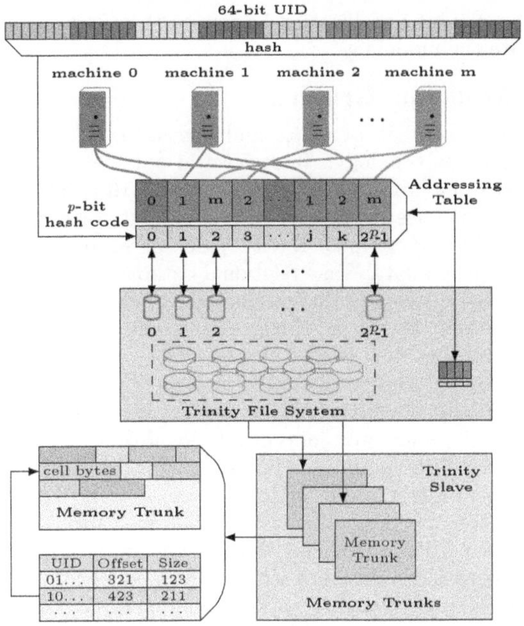

Figure 3: Data Partitioning and Addressing

We then locate the key-value pair in memory trunk i, which is stored on the machine whose ID is in slot i of the addressing table. Each memory trunk is associated with a hash table. We hash the 64-bit key again to find the offset and size of the key-value pair in the hash table. Given the memory offset and the size, we retrieve the key-value pair from the memory trunk.

The addressing table provides a mechanism that allows machines to dynamically join and leave the memory cloud. When a machine fails, we reload the memory trunks it owns from the TFS to other alive machines. All we need to do is to update the addressing table so that the corresponding slots point to the machines that host the data now. Similarly, when new machines join the memory cloud, we relocate some memory trunks to those new machines and update the addressing table accordingly.

Each key-value pair in the memory cloud may contain some meta data for various purposes. Most notably, we may associate each key-value pair with a spin lock. Spin locks are used for concurrency control and physical memory pinning. Multiple threads may try to access the same key-value pair concurrently. A physical key-value pair may also be moved by the memory defragmentation thread as elaborated in Section 6.1. Therefore, we must ensure a key-value pair is locked and pinned to a fixed memory position before allowing any thread to manipulate it. For applications that are not read-only, the spin lock mechanism allows a thread to access a pinned physical key-value pair exclusively by requiring all threads to acquire the lock before accessing or moving a cell.

4. DATA MODEL

Trinity is designed to handle graph data of diverse characteristics. In this section, we describe data modeling issues and the Trinity Specification Language that is designed to facilitate the modeling.

4.1 Modeling Graph

A graph consists of nodes and edges. But a graph is more than its topology: In real-world applications, nodes and edges in a graph are often associated with rich information. We may use relational databases, XML, or even plain text files to store graphs. But they do not support efficient access of graph data. Take relational databases as an example. We may use one table to store the nodes, and another table to store the edges. If edges represent more than one relationship, we may need multiple tables to store edges of difficult types. This seems to be simple and intuitive. However, graph operations usually involve graph traversal, which incurs costly, multi-way joins of relational tables. Thus, relational databases are not for processing graph data.

Trinity supports graphs on top of an in-memory key-value store. Here, the "key" is a system wide identifier, and the "value" is used for modeling application data. When the "value" is associated with a schema (defined in TSL, which is described in Section 4.2), we also call it a *cell*, and the (key, value) pair becomes a (cellId, cell) pair. To model graphs on top of a key-value store, we use a cell to implement a node in a graph. A cell may contain a lot of information. For undirected graphs, a cell (a graph node) contains a set of cellIds that represent its neighboring nodes. For directed graphs, a cell (a graph node) contains two set of cellIds, one for incoming links, and the other for outgoing links. A cell may contain additional data associated with a node, such as the name of the node, its description, etc.

Usually, there is no need to represent an edge as a cell. As mentioned above, we may represent a node's outgoing edges by the cellIds of the nodes they connect to. Additional data associated with an edge (e.g., its name, type, weight, etc.) can simply stay with the cellId as (cellId, associatedData) pairs. However, when edges are associated with rich information, we may represent edges using cells, and store the rich information associated with the edges in the edge cells. Correspondingly, a node will store a set of edge cellIds. We can also model hypergraphs in this way, as we can easily store a set of node cellIds in an edge cell.

4.2 Trinity Specification Language

We designed a high level language called TSL (Trinity Specification Language) for data and network communication modeling in Trinity. As we know, graphs have very diverse characteristics, and distributed algorithms on graphs have very diverse communication patterns. In face of these diversity, TSL brings great ease-of-use for general purpose graph management and computing. Its goals and benefits include the following:

- TSL provides object-oriented data manipulation for the underlying blob data in the memory cloud. This will be elaborated in Section 4.3.
- TSL facilitates data integration. It defines an interface between graphs and external data (e.g., data in an RDBMS). Through TSL, we can specify how nodes in a graph are associated with records in a relational table. This enables us to store graph topology and some critical data in Trinity's memory cloud, while leaving other rich information (such as images) on disk. This further enables transparent query processing over memory cloud and RDBMSs (but with dramatically improved performance as join relationships are materialized in Trinity), and automatic data conversion between memory cloud and external data sources.
- TSL facilitates system extension. With data schema and communication protocols defined in TSL, the TSL compiler generates highly efficient and powerful source code for data manipulation and communication, which greatly facilitates the development of advanced system modules in Trinity. For example, we implemented a sophisticated graph query language (TQL) within this framework.

Figure 4 gives an example of using TSL to model the data of a toy graph consisting of movies and actors.

```
[CellType: NodeCell]
cell struct Movie
{
    string Name;
    [EdgeType: SimpleEdge, ReferencedCell: Actor]
    List<long> Actors;
}
[CellType: NodeCell]
cell struct Actor
{
    string Name;
    [EdgeType: SimpleEdge, ReferencedCell: Movie]
    List<long> Movies;
}
```

Figure 4: Modeling a Movie and Actor Graph

The script above defines two types of graph nodes, namely Movie and Actor, using two `Cell structs`. A `Cell struct` is a basic element for modeling graph. It is a data container which may contain an arbitrary number of: 1) primitive data types, such as byte, int, and double; 2) data container types, such as Array, List, and BitArray; and 3) other user-defined structs. In our case, the Movie and Actor cells contain data elements `List<long> Actors` and `List<long> Movies`, which are outgoing edges from the cells. The "[...]" constructs (following C# convention) in the script describes the constructs that follow them. For example, it indicates Actors are `SimpleEdge` from Movie cells to Actor cells. Besides `SimpleEdge` (which is represented by a cellId), Trinity also supports `StructEdge` (which is an independent cell) and `HyperEdge` (hyperedges).

Besides modeling data, TSL also models network communication. This is important for the following reasons. First, graph algorithms have very diverse network communication patterns because they are data driven, and the data is distributed. It is extremely tedious for users to implement all kinds of message passing protocols (e.g., synchronous, asynchronous, etc.) Second, in vertex based computing and other algorithms, a large number of nodes send and receive messages simultaneously. The total number of messages in the system is huge although each message may be small. This incurs a huge cost if the system does not automatically pack small messages between two machines into a single transfer. Third, graph algorithms require a flexible message passing mechanism. The well known message passing framework MPI has drawbacks for distributed graph applications: It is optimized for two-sided bulk synchronous communication.

A lot of tuning is needed to write efficient, asynchronous, fine-grained message passing programs, and writing such code is tedious.

TSL provides an intuitive way of writing efficient message passing programs for graph computation. It provides one-sided communication based on the request-response communication paradigm, and it supports bulk synchronous message passing and transparent message packing for asynchronous messages to increase the network throughput.

```
struct MyMessage
{
    string Text;
}
protocol Echo
{
    Type: Syn;
    Request: MyMessage;
    Response: MyMessage;
}
```

Figure 5: Modeling Message Passing

Figure 5 shows an example. We implement a simple "Echo" protocol: A client sends a message to a server, and the server sends a message back. It is stated that "Echo" uses synchronous message passing, and the type of messages being sent and received is *MyMessage*. TSL compiles the script to generate an empty message handler *EchoHandler*, and the user only needs to implement the algorithm logic for the handler as if implementing a local method. Calling a protocol defined in the TSL is also like calling a local method. Trinity takes care of message dispatching, packing, etc., for the user.

4.3 Object-Oriented Cell Manipulation

The memory cloud provides a key-value pair store, where values are binary blobs. The TSL script in Figure 4 informs the Trinity system the schema of the data, so that Trinity knows how to manipulate the data, including, for example, integrating the data with data from external sources. Alternatively, we can implement graph nodes and edges as runtime objects. Unfortunately, we cannot reference objects across machine boundaries. Second, runtime objects incur significant storage overhead. For C# on the .Net framework, an empty runtime object (one that does not contain any data element) requires 24 bytes of memory on a 64-bit system and 12 bytes of memory on a 32-bit system. For billion-node graphs, this is a tremendous overhead. Third, although Trinity is an in-memory system, we do need to store memory trunks on disk or network for persistence. For runtime objects, we need serialization and deserialization operations, which is costly.

On the other hand, storing objects as blobs of bytes is compact, economical, with zero serialization and deserialization overhead. We can also make the objects globally addressable by giving them unique identifiers and using hash functions to map the objects to memory in a host machine as we have described. However, blobs are not user-friendly. We no long have an object-oriented interface, and we need to know the exact memory layout before we can manipulate the data in the blob (using pointers, address offsets, and casting to access data elements in the blob). This makes programming difficult and error-prone[2].

[2]Note that we cannot naively cast a blob to a structure defined in programming languages such as C or C# because the fields of a struct are not always flatly laid out in the memory. We cannot cast a flat memory region to a structured data pointer.

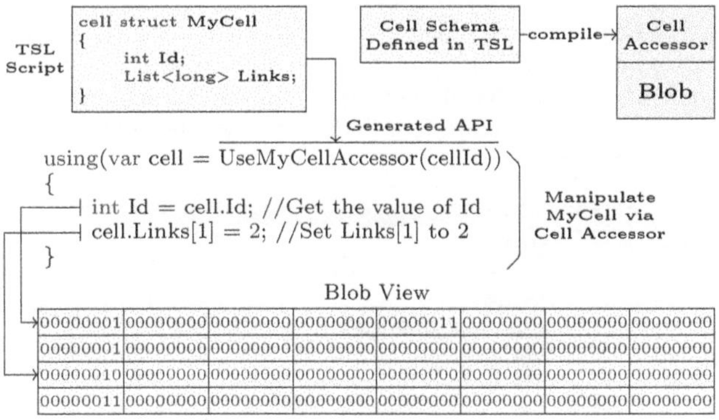

Figure 6: Cell Accessor

To address this problem, Trinity introduces a mechanism (the *cell accessor* mechanism) to support object-oriented data manipulation on blob data. Users first declare the schema of a cell in TSL, then Trinity automatically generates key-value store interfaces for manipulating cells stored as blob strings in the memory cloud. Specifically, Trinity compiles the TSL script to create a set of APIs for accessing, loading, and saving the data. One of the generated API is `UseMyCellAccessor`. Given a cellId, it returns an object of type `MyCellAccessor`, and users can manipulate its underlying blob data as a runtime object in an object-oriented manner. This is shown in Figure 6. As a matter of fact, a cell accessor is not a data container, but a data mapper. It maps the fields declared in the data structure to the correct memory locations in the blob. Any data accessing operation to a data field will be correctly mapped to the correct memory location with zero memory copy overhead.

4.4 Consistency

Using the spin lock associated with each key-value pair, Trinity guarantees the atomicity of the operation on a single cell (key-value pair). However, Trinity does not provide ACID transaction support. This means Trinity cannot guarantee serializability for concurrent threads. For applications that need transaction support, we can implement light-weight atomic operation primitives that span multiple cells, such as MultiOp primitives [13] and Mini-transaction primitives [7], on top of the atomic cell operation primitives.

5. GRAPH COMPUTATION PARADIGMS

Different graph computations have different data access and communication patterns. In this section, we discuss the graph computation paradigms supported by Trinity.

5.1 Traversal Based Online Queries

A lot of applications require graph exploration, the breadth-first search and the depth-first search being the most typical. Here, we use "people search" on a social network as an example to demonstrate the importance of efficient graph exploration to online query processing. The problem is the following: On a social network, for a given user, find anyone whose first name is "David" among his/her friends, his/her friends' friends, and his/her friends' friends' friends. This is a practical problem: While logged in on Facebook, a user performs a search in Bing. Bing explores the user's Facebook network to see if there is anything relevant. In the case as shown in Figure 7, it finds someone who is the user's friends' friend.

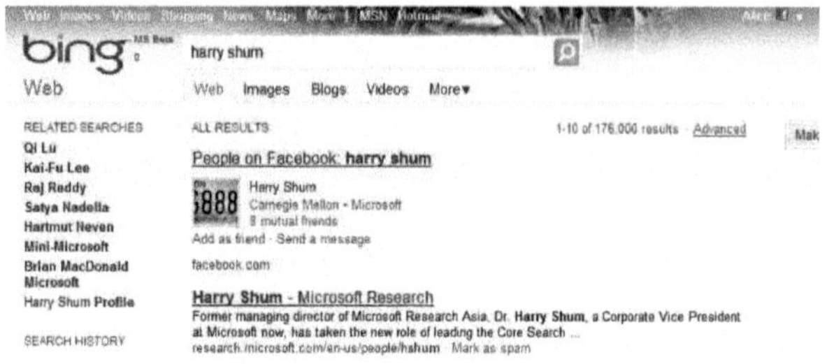

Figure 7: Facebook search in Bing

It is unlikely we can index the social network to solve the "David" problem. One option is to index the neighborhood for each user, so that given any user, we can use the index to check if there is any "David" within 3 hops of his/her neighborhood. However, the size and the update cost of such an index are prohibitive for a web-scale graph. The second option is to create an index to answer 3-hop reachability queries for any two nodes. This is infeasible because "David" is a popular first name, and we cannot check every David in the social network to see if he is within 3 hops to the current user.

Trinity solves the "David" problem by leveraging its very efficient memory-based graph exploration capabilities. We deployed a synthetic, power-law graph in an eight-machine cluster managed by Trinity. The graph has Facebook-like size and distribution (800 million nodes, 104 billion edges, with each node having on average 130 edges). We found that exploring the entire 3-hop neighborhood of any node in the graph takes less than 100 milliseconds on average. In other words, Trinity is able to explore $130 + 130^2 + 130^3 \approx 2.2$ million nodes distributed over eight machines in one tenth of a second. The algorithm simply sends asynchronous requests recursively to remote machines, and the performance is achieved by efficient memory access and optimization of network communication.

5.2 A New Paradigm for Online Queries

Trinity introduces a new paradigm for online graph processing by storing web-scale graphs in the memory of a distributed system, and relying on fast random access and parallel computing for query processing, as demonstrated by the above example.

In contrast, instead of storing graph in its native form, many existing graph systems store graph data in relational tables, or matrices, and use *join operations* to simulate graph exploration. The approach does not scale. In order to support more sophisticated online queries such as subgraph matching, existing systems rely on index. The reality is, none of the existing systems and methods support efficient subgraph matching on web-scale graphs. To understand the challenge, consider various kinds of indices developed to support query processing on graphs. Most of them require super-linear space and/or super-linear construction time. For example, the R-Join approach [14] for subgraph matching is based on the 2-hop index [11]. The complexity to build such an index is $O(n^4)$, where n is the number of vertices. It is obvious that in large graphs where the value of n is on the scale of 1 billion (10^9), any super-linear approach will become unrealistic, let alone an algorithm of complexity $O(n^4)$.

In Trinity, the combination of fast random access and parallel computing, offers a new paradigm which enables us to rethink efficient query processing on web-scale graphs. Figure 8(a) shows the performance of subgraph matching on web scale graphs. Here, the size of the graph ranges from 1 million to 128 million nodes, average node degree is 16, average query size is 10 (nodes), and queries are generated using two random methods, DFS and RANDOM [32]. It shows that without any index of graph structure, average query time is 1 second using just 8 machines for parallel query processing, and there is still a lot of room for improvement.

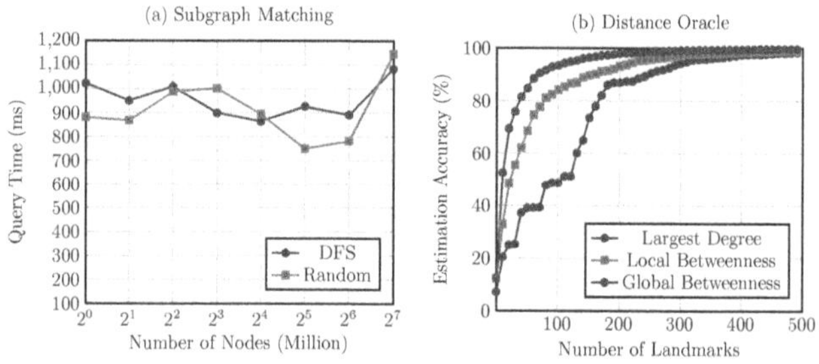

Figure 8: New paradigms of graph computation

5.3 Vertex Centric Offline Analytics

Trinity, as well as Pregel [28] and GraphChi [25], provide a vertex centric computation model for offline graph analytics. A computation task is expressed in multiple iterative super-steps and each vertex acts as an independent agent. During each super-step, each agent performs some computation and communication, independent of each other.

In the following, we first compare Pregel's vertex centric model with Trinity's vertex centric model. We will discuss GraphChi's computation model later at the end of this section.

- *A general model (Pregel).* In each super-step, a vertex may receive messages sent to it by *any* vertex in the previous super-step, send messages to *any* vertex, and modify its vertex values.
- *A restrictive model (Trinity).* In each super-step, a vertex may receive messages sent to it by *a fixed set* of vertices (usually its neighbors), send messages to *another fixed set* of vertices, and modify its vertex values.

As far as the above two computation models are concerned, Trinity is more restrictive than Pregel in the sense that in Trinity's computation model, a vertex only communicates with a subset of vertices (usually its neighbors). The reason Trinity focuses on the restrictive model is twofold. First, in a lot of well-known vertex centric computation, e.g. PageRank and shortest path, vertices only talk with their neighbors. In other words, the restrictive model can already support a large number of graph algorithms on its own. Second, the restrictive model introduces a lot of optimization opportunities. Since the communication is with a fixed set of vertices, the communication pattern is predictable iteration after iteration. This enables us to optimize messages delivery to maximize the performance. With the optimization techniques, Trinity achieves much better performance. With just 8 machines, one BSP iteration on a synthetic, power-law graph of 1 billion nodes and 13 billion edges takes less than 60 seconds. This enables Trinity to support algorithms such as PageRank and shortest distances very efficiently using vertex centric computation.

Before we describe the detail of how Trinity optimizes message passing for supporting the restrictive computation model in Section 5.4, we describe some related work. Recently, GraphChi [25] introduces a computation model which is even more restrictive. It supports asynchronous computation only, which means it cannot implement traversal based graph computation and synchronous graph computation efficiently. The benefit of doing so is that for analytics that can be implemented in an asynchronous manner, GraphChi can accomplish them using sequential disk access. It is clear that there is a compromise between the expressive power of a computation model and its efficiency.

However, unlike Pregel and GraphChi that are specialized systems focusing on one computation model, Trinity is not constrained by any computation model. For instance, Trinity can partition billion-node graphs within a few hours using a multi-level partitioning algorithm [6]. The quality of the partitioning is comparable to that of the best partitioning algorithm (e.g., METIS [24]). To the best of our knowledge, billion-node graph partitioning is an unsolved problem on general-purpose graph platforms. In summary, Trinity can adopt any computation model (BSP as in Pregel, restrictive vertex centric computation, or asynchronous model as in GraphChi), yet because Trinity deploys graphs on a memory cloud, it can express any algorithm using graph exploration, and is not constrained by any computation model.

5.4 Message Passing Optimization

In this section, we describe how Trinity optimizes message passing to support its vertex based computation model. Although a graph is distributed on multiple machines, from the point view of a local machine, vertices of the graph are in two categories: vertices on the local machine, and vertices on any of the remote machines. Figure 9(a) shows a local machine's bipartite view of the entire graph.

In vertex based computation, each vertex is scheduled to run a job. Before the job on a vertex can start running, the vertex must receive all the messages it needs. One naive approach is to wait until all messages to arrive before we start running the job on any of the local vertices. This means the local machine needs to buffer all the messages from remote vertices, and perform random access to retrieve the messages when running algorithms on the local vertices. Since the total amount of messages is too big to be memory resident, we need to buffer the messages on disk, and perform random accesses on the disk. This incurs significant cost.

Another naive approach is to run jobs on local vertices without preparing any messages in advance. When a local vertex is scheduled to run the job, we obtain remote messages for the vertex, and run the job immediately after they arrive. Since the system does not have space to hold all messages, we discard messages after they are used. For example, in Figure 9(a), in order to run the job on vertex x, we need messages from vertices u, v, and others. Later on, when y is scheduled to run, we need messages from u and v again. This means a single message needed to be delivered multiple times, which is unacceptable in an environment where network capacity is an extremely valuable resource.

In Trinity, we assume each vertex mainly communicates with a fixed set of vertices such as its neighbors (the restrictive vertex computation model). This provides opportunity of optimization, because at least we can prepare most of the messages a vertex needs before it is scheduled to run. To do this, we create a bipartite partition of the local graph as shown in Figure 9(b). In the ideal case, local vertices in a partition only needs messages from remote vertices in the same partition. Thus, as long as the local machine can buffer the messages required for each partition in memory, we can run the job on local vertices in the partition without waiting, and we also ensure that each message is delivered just once.

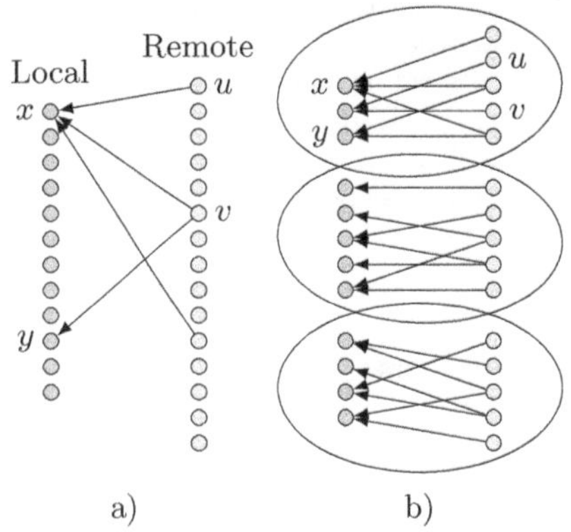

Figure 9: Bipartite View on a Local Machine

However, graph partitioning itself is a very costly task, and it is very difficult to create partitions of even size while minimizing the number of edge cuts. In Trinity, on each local machine, we differentiate remote vertices into 2 categories. The first category contains hub vertices, that is, vertices having a large degree and connecting to a great percentage of local vertices. The second category contains all of the remaining vertices. We buffer messages from vertices in the first category for the entire duration of one iteration. In other words, they will not participate in the partitioning process shown in Figure 9(b). For a scale-free graph, e.g., one generated by degree distribution $P(k) \sim ck^{-\gamma}$ with $c = 1.16$ and $\gamma = 2.16$, 20% hub vertices are sending messages to 80% of vertices. Even if we buffer messages from just 10% hub vertices, we have addressed 72.8% of message needs. Thus, after exclusing these frequently used messages, the partitioning becomes much easier.

In reality, vertices may need messages from vertices in other partitions, or from vertices other than a predefined fixed set of vertices such as their neighbors (the general vertex computaton model), these messages are obtained on demand. Let K_i be the remote vertices that do not belong to partition i but whose messages are needed by local vertices in partition i. We obtain messages from K_i while we are running algorithms on local vertices in partition $i - 1$. Usually, the size of K_i is small, and we can obtain messages from K_i before running the algorithms on local vertices in partition i.

The scheme described above requires remote messages to arrive in certain order (that is, partition by partition, including messages on cut edges K_i). To achieve this, after a local machine performs the partitioning, it sends out to each remote machine an "action script", which specifies the order of the messages it needs. Each machine merges the action scripts it receives from other machines. After the execution starts, each machine sends messages based on the merged script, iteration after iteration.

One observation we can make from Figure 9 is that unlike in online query processing, where it is impossible to predict which part of the graph the next query is going to access, the data access pattern in offline analytics jobs can be predicted. For example, for vertex centric computation, the execution is partition by partition. On each machine, the same sequence of execution will repeat over and over again.

Since we can predict the data access pattern, we no longer have to keep the entire graph memory resident. At any moment, we consider two types of vertices: A) vertices in a partition currently scheduled to run on a certain machine; and B) all of the other vertices in the graph. For a Type A vertex, we keep its cell structure in memory, the computation may need to access its neighbors, attributes, and local variables. For a Type B vertex, we only keep its message box in memory, since Type A vertices may need it. This is illustrated in Figure 10.

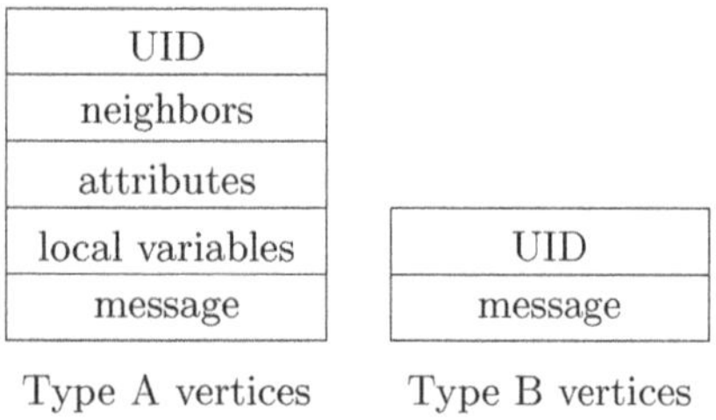

Figure 10: Memory Resident Cell Structures

This arrangement dramatically reduces the memory requirement. Originally, to keep the graph topology memory resident (also include some runtime information), the total memory we need is:

$$S = |V| \cdot (16 + k + l + m) + 8|E|$$

where 16 (bytes) is the space needed to store and access the UID, k, l, and m are the average sizes of attributes, local variables, and message, respectively. In the offline mode, the memory we need is

$$S' = p \cdot S + (1 - p) \cdot |V| \cdot (16 + m)$$

where p is the percentage of Type A vertices. Thus, the saved memory is:

$$S - S' = (1 - p)(k + l) \cdot |V| + (1 - p) \cdot 8|E|$$

Suppose $k = l = m = 8$ and $p = 0.1$, for the Facebook social graph, 708 GB memory space can be saved. This means the number of required machines can be reduced significantly without affecting the performance much.

5.5 A New Paradigm for Offline Analytics

Besides the capabilities mentioned above, Trinity also introduces a new paradigm for offline graph analytics. In Trinity, a web-scale graph is partitioned and stored on a number of machines. This leads to the following question: Can we perform graph computation locally on *each machine* and then aggregate their answers to derive the answer for the entire graph, or can we use probabilistic inference to derive the answer for the entire graph from the answer on *a single machine*? This paradigm has the potential to overcome the network communication bottleneck, as it minimizes or even abolishes network communication. The answer to the above question is positive. If a graph is partitioned over 10 machines, each machine has full information about 10% of the vertices and 10% of the edges. Besides, the edges link to a large amount of the remaining 90% of vertices. Thus, the sample actually contains a lot of information about the entire graph. Furthermore, when a graph is randomly partitioned, each machine holds a random sample of the graph, which enables us to perform probabilistic inference.

We experimented with this new paradigm in Trinity. In one example, we find landmark vertices, and use them to estimate shortest distances between any two nodes in a large graph [37]. In Figure 8(b), we show the effectiveness of using 3 methods to pick the landmark vertices. Here, the X axis shows the number of landmark vertices we use, and the Y axis shows estimation accuracy. The best approach is to use vertices that have the highest global betweenness, and the worst approach is to simply use vertices that have the largest degree. Our approach, which uses vertices that have the highest betweenness computed locally, actually has very close accuracy to the best approach. However, finding landmarks that have the highest global betweenness is significantly more costly than our approach.

6. IMPLEMENTATION DETAILS

We implemented Trinity on Microsoft .Net framework. In this section, we discuss some technical details in memory management and fault tolerance.

6.1 Circular Memory Management

Trinity memory cloud is a key-value store, and the value in a key-value pair is a blob of arbitrary size. Some (graph) applications need to manage billions of key-value pairs. Among these key-value pairs, some are very large (imagine a very popular celebrity on Facebook with a million fans), but most of them are small. It is a challenge to manage billions of key-value pairs of varied sizes in a very compact manner. Traditional memory management mechanisms that use memory buckets are extremely wasteful because they leave memory gaps between billions of key-value pairs. Furthermore, when we update a key-value pair, the size of the blob may increase or decrease, creating further challenges for memory management. For Trinity, the goal is to support fast memory allocation, efficient memory reallocation, and maintains a high memory utilization ratio.

Trinity implements a circular memory management mechanism, which tries to avoid memory gaps between large number of key-value pairs. When we initialize a memory trunk, we reserve a 2GB virtual memory address space from the operating system. As shown in Figure 11 (a), new key-value pairs are sequentially appended to the *committed memory* region. The pointer *append head* points to the next free memory byte. The memory space occupied by existing key-value pairs resides in the region between *committed tail* and *append head*.

When we expand a key-value pair or create a new key-value pair, we always allocate a new memory region from *append head* if there is enough *committed memory*. If no space is left, we allocate one or more new memory pages and advance *committed head*. Hence, memory allocation is efficient, because in most cases, we just advance the *append head*. Shrinking or expanding the size of a key-value pair may leave memory gaps in the *committed memory* region. Trinity activates a defragmentation daemon which scans the *committed memory* region, and moves key-value pairs toward *append head*. After a pass, the freed memory pages at the tail of *committed memory* is released and the *committed tail* is moved forward. In this process, the *committed head*, *append head*, and *committed tail* may move to the start of the memory trunk, performing an endless circular movement until all available memory is occupied.

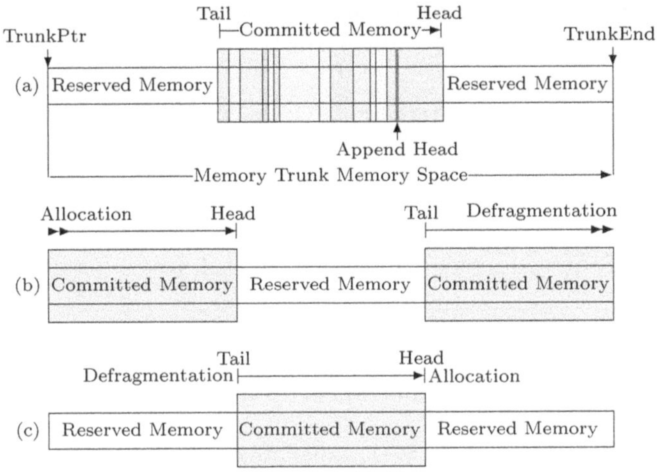

Figure 11: Circular Memory Management

For certain applications (e.g., graph generation, graph streams, etc.), the size of key-value pairs keep increasing (as new edges are added to the node cells). This creates tremendous overhead in committing and decommitting memory pages, and in moving key-value pairs around for defragmentation. To reduce the overhead, we devised a short-lived memory reservation mechanism to support frequent key-value pair reallocation. A naive idea is to reserve a few more bytes during a key-value pair expansion for future expansion. For example, if the current key-value pair needs to expand by 16 bytes, we allocate 32 bytes instead. The problem for this naive solution is that the memory utilization ratio will be lowered since a lot of reserved memory is actually not used. To address this issue, we make all memory reservation short-lived. One reservation is only valid in the interval between two defragmentation passes. The unused reserved memory will be released in next defragmentation. On the one hand, by memory reservation, we greatly decrease the chance of memory committing/decommitting and memory movement so that we can greatly improve the key-value pair expansion performance. On the other hand, through memory defragmentation, unused reserved memory is collected timely so that we can minimize the runtime memory overhead.

6.2 Fault Tolerance

As a distributed system, Trinity needs to deal with various fault-tolerance issues.

Shared Addressing Table Maintenance

Trinity uses a shared addressing table to locate a key-value pair, as elaborated in section 3. The addressing table is a shared global data structure. A centralized implementation is infeasible because of the performance bottleneck and the risk of single point of failure. A straightforward approach to these issues is to duplicate this table on each slave. However, this leads to potential problem of data inconsistency.

Trinity maintains a primary replica of the shared addressing table on a leader machine, and uses the fault-tolerant distributed file system TFS to keep a persistent copy of the primary addressing table. An update to the primary table must be applied to the persistent replica before committing.

Trinity uses heartbeat messages to proactively detect machine failures. Besides this, a machine A that attempts to access a data item on machine B which is down can detect the failure of machine B. In this case, machine A will inform the leader machine of the failure of machine B. After that, machine A will wait for the addressing table to be updated, and attempt to access the item again once the addressing table is updated.

On the confirmation of a machine failure, the leader machine will start the recovery process. During recovery, the leader reloads data owned by the failed machine to other alive machines, updates the primary addressing table and broadcasts it. Even if some slave machines cannot receive the broadcast message due to temporary network interruption, the protocol still works since a machine will always sync up with the primary addressing table replica when it fails to load a data item. If the leader machine fails, a new round of leader election will be triggered. The new leader marks a flag on the shared distributed fault-tolerant file system to avoid multiple leaders in the case that the cluster machines are partitioned into disjointed sets due to network failure.

Fault Recovery

For different computation models, we use different fault recovery mechanisms. For BSP based synchronous computation, we make check points every a few supersteps. These check points are written to the persistent file system for future failure recovery. For asynchronous computation, the fault recovery issue is subtler than that of its synchronous counterpart, as check points cannot be easily created when the computation is running in the asynchronous mode. Instead of adopting a complex checkpoint techniques, e.g. [21], we use a simple "periodical interruption" mechanisms to create snapshots. Specifically, Trinity issues an interruption signal periodically. On receiving this signal, all vertices will pause after finishing the job in hand. After issuing the interruption signal, Trinity calls Safra's termination detection algorithm [16] to check whether the system ceases. A snapshot is written to the persistent disk storage once the system ceases. For read-only queries, we just restart the failed node and reload the data from the persistent disk storage. For online update queries, we use the buffered logging mechanism proposed in RAMCloud to do failure recovery. The key idea is to log operations to remote memory buffers before committing them to the local memory. Detailed discussion about buffered logging can be found in [30, 29].

7. EXPERIMENTAL EVALUATION

We conduct a number of experiments to measure the performance of Trinity for online queries and offline analytics. All the following experiments are performed in a 16-machine cluster. Each machine has 96 GB DDR3 RAM and two 2.67 GHz Intel(R) Xeon(R) X5650 CPUs, each processor has 12 threads. The operating system is 64-bit Windows Server

2008 R2 Enterprise. There are dual network adapters on each machine, one is 40 Gbps Mellanox IPoIB Adapter and the other is 1 Gbps HP NC382i DP Multifunction Gigabit Server Adapter. Trinity is implemented using C# and complied with target platform x64. The Trinity runtime is .NET Framework 4.

People Search Query On Social Graph. We perform people search queries in a social network to measure the performance of data-intensive, traversal-based online graph queries. This experiment measures query response time of searching friends by name within 2 and 3 hops on synthetic social graphs. The out-degree of each node varies from 10 to 200. Eight machines are used in this experiment, the performance curves are shown in Figure 12(a). The response times of 2-hop queries are always under 10 ms. The response time of 3-hop search on the graph with 130 node degree is 96.2 ms in this experiment. Currently the average degree of Facebook is 130. This indicates people search queries on Facebook like social graphs can be answered within 100 ms.

Page Rank Calculation On Web Graph. Calculation of page rank is one of the commonest graph analytics tasks on web graphs. Here we use page rank calculation to measure the offline processing performance of Trinity. In this experiment, the page rank is calculated using synchronous vertex centric computation model on R-MAT graphs [12]. The number of vertices varies from 64 million to 1024 million. The average degree is 13. The computation time for one iteration (a super-step in BSP model) on 8, 10, 12 and 14 machines is shown in Figure 12(b). We can see that one page rank iteration on a graph with 1 billion node can be completed in merely one minute on 8 machines.

Breadth-first Search. Breadth-first search (BFS) is a fundamental graph computation operation. Many graph algorithms are built on BFS. Graph 500 Benchmark [5] adopts BFS as one of its two computation kernels. Figure 12(c) shows the performance curves of performing BFS on 8, 10, 12 and 14 machines. This experiment uses the same data as that in the page rank calculation experiment. For the 1 billion node graph, it takes 1028 seconds on 8 machines, while 644 seconds on 14 machines.

Trinity vs. PBGL. PBGL [19] is a generic C++ library for high-performance parallel and distributed graph Computation. We run BFS on RMAT graphs in a 16-machine cluster using PBGL and Trinity to compare their execution time and memory usage. The node count varies from 1 million to 256 million with average degree 4, 8, 16 and 32. The results in Figure 13 clearly show that Trinity runs 10x faster with 10x less memory footprint. When average degree is 32, PBGL runs out of memory on the 256 million graph. PBGL uses the "ghost cells" mechanism for message passing. This mechanism incurs great memory overhead, especially on not-well-partitioned graphs. It takes near 600 GB memory for the 256 million node graph when average degree is 16. In contrast, Trinity takes less than 65 GB memory for the same graph.

Trinity vs. Giraph. Giraph [3] is a publicly available pregel implementation. We run page rank on Giraph to compare its performance with Trinity. We deployed the latest Giraph on the 16-machine cluster. The required Hadoop version is 0.20.2-RC1. The JRE version is jre-6u31-windows-x64, and the maximum memory heap size is set to 81 GB. The experimental results are shown in Figure 12 (d). Each page rank iteration takes 2455 seconds on the graph with 256 million nodes and 2 billion edges. With half number of machines, each page rank iteration of Trinity on a graph with 1 billion nodes and 13 billion edges only takes 51 seconds. Trinity runs faster by two orders of magnitude. Note: when average degree is 16, Giraph run out of memory on the 256 million node graph. This indicates that the runtime memory footprint of Giraph is much larger Trinity.

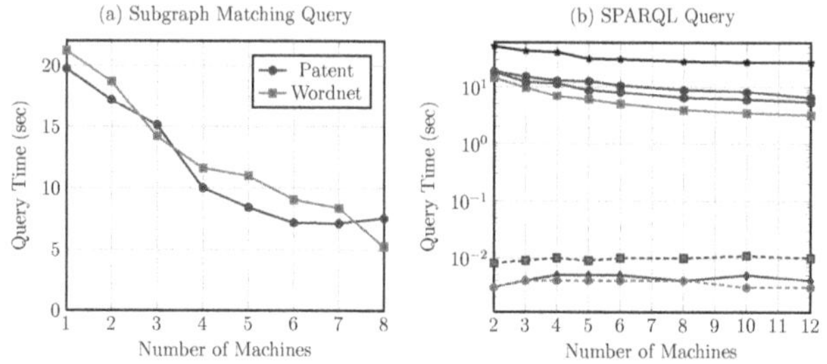

Figure 14: Parallel Speedup for Online Queries

Parallel Speedup. We have performed experiments to evaluate the distributed parallel speedup for both graph analytics jobs and online graph queries. The experimental results of page rank and BFS are shown in Figure 12 (b) and (c). The parallel speedup for online queries is shown in Figure 14. Figure 14 (a) shows the response time of subgraph match queries on two real-life graphs (Wordnet and US patent network), while (b) shows the response time of four SPARQL queries on a LUBM RDF data set [20] with 1,367,122,031 triples [36]. As the number of machines increases, the computation time is dramatically reduced for both offline graph analytics and online query processing. With more machines, the data partition on each machine is smaller, but the network message number will increase. Trinity is designed to scale out, with more machines, the performance would keep going up until the network communication limit is reached.

More Discussions on Scalability. An interesting observation is that Trinity has the least memory footprint when performing jobs on the same graph, compared with PBGBL and Giraph. PBGL and Giraph take more memory than trinity, while run much slower than Trinity. The reasons are twofold: i) Due to the random data access pattern, the graph data must be cached in memory during computation. However, in PBGL and Giraph, graph nodes exist as runtime objects in memory. They take much more memory than Trinity's plain blobs. 2) Trinity is an all-in-memory system, the graph data is loaded in memory before doing computation. So there is no cache-missing penalty. This mechanism is much more efficient than memory caching mechanism even a lot of memory is allocated as cache. Cache-misses hurt performance greatly even if there are only a few occurrences.

8. RELATED WORK

Many applications utilize large RAM storage to offer better performance. Large web applications, such as Facebook, Twitter, Youtube, and Wikipedia, heavily use memcached

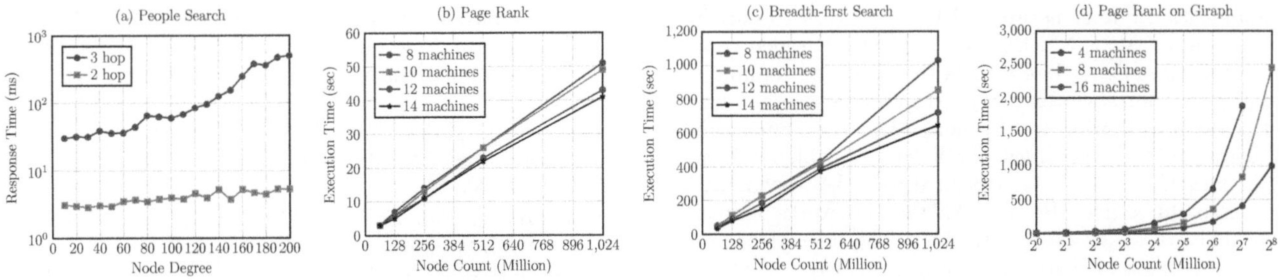

Figure 12: Trinity Performance Experiments

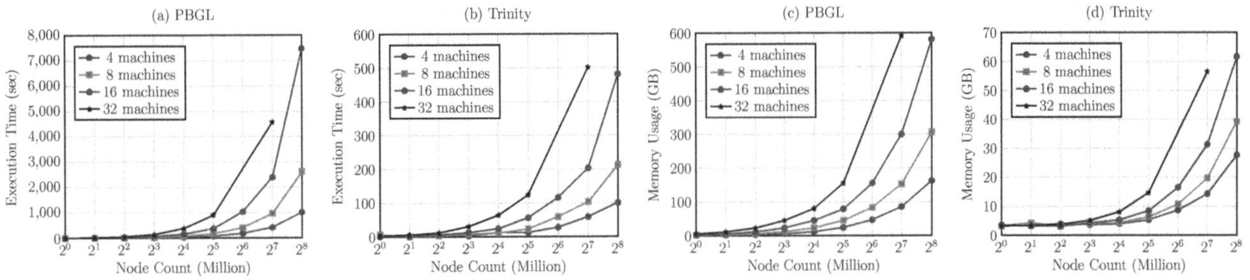

Figure 13: BFS in PBGL and Trinity

[17] to cache large volume of long-lived small objects. As the middle tier between data storage and application, caching systems offload the server side work by taking over some data serving tasks. Machines in a caching system are independent with each other. They do not communicate with each other to perform computation, hence they do not solve the computation latency problem.

Besides memcached, key-value stores such as Scalaris [31] and Redis [35] also use RAM as their main storage. Recently, RAMCloud [30] pushes the idea of RAM based applications to a new level. RAMCloud is a data storage system that hosts all its data permanently in memory. The memory cloud storage of Trinity resembles the concept proposed in RAMCloud. Although both RAMCloud and Trinity have a large distributed RAM storage, their design goals are quite different. RAMCloud tries to leverage the low latency and high throughput data access power of RAM to support large scale applications, especially large web applications. While Trinity focuses on utilizing the random data access trait of distributed RAM storage to support large graph processing applications, especially those need fast graph exploration. To the best of our knowledge, Trinity is the first mature system that turns the concept of ram cloud into a large graph processing platform.

Many systems have been devised to process large graphs. PEGASUS [23] is a graph mining system built on Hadoop [2], which is an open source implementation of the MapReduce framework [15]. Due to the challenges posed by parallel graph processing [26], MapReduce based approaches are often "ill-suited" for large graph processing as discussed in [28]. To overcome the challenges, Pregel [28], GraphLab [1], PowerGraph [18], and GraphChi [25] adopt vertex centric graph computation models. The idea of vertex centric computation can be traced back to the well studied synchronous and asynchronous network model [27]. The processors in a processor network becomes graph vertices, and communication channels becomes graph edges. To a large extent, these metaphors in the context of graph computation are the key innovations of vertex centric graph computation.

Due to the random data access problem, general purpose graph computations usually do not have efficient disk-based solutions. But under certain constraints, offline graph problems that can be solved by "divide-and-conquer" strategy sometimes have efficient disk based solutions. A typical example is GraphChi [25]. GraphChi can perform efficient disk based graph computation under an assumption that current computation has an asynchronous vertex centric solution. Asynchronous solution means a vertex can perform computation just based on partially updated information from its incoming links. This assumption, on the one hand, frees the need of passing messages of current vertex to all its outgoing links so that it can perform the graph computation block by block. On the other hand, it inherently cannot support traversal based graph computation and synchronous graph computation efficiently because it cannot access the neighborhood of a vertex efficiently. Disk based graph computation solutions are essentially cache mechanisms. If a problem can be well partitioned, then the sub-problems can be loaded in memory and efficiently handled one by one. However, as widely acknowledged [26], most graph problems are usually inherently irregular and hard to partition especially for online queries.

Besides various graph processing systems, a number of parallel graph processing libraries are also available for implementing parallel graph algorithms on large graph data, such as Parallel Boost Graph Library (PBGL) [19] and Multi-Threaded Graph Library (MTGL) [9]. PBGL provides graph data structures and message passing mechanisms to make graph algorithms run in parallel. It uses *ghost cells* (local replicas of remote cells) for message passing. As discussed in [26], the *ghost cell* mechanism only works well for well-partitioned graphs. Great memory overhead would be incurred for not-well-partitioned large graphs. This fact is clearly validated by our experimental results shown in Section 7. A big difference between PBGL and Trinity is their communication infrastructure. PBGL's network communication relies on MPI, which heavily utilizes two-sided communication paradigm. Trinity uses the one-sided communication paradigm, a vertex can send message to other vertices without any prior appointment. This communication paradigm makes fine-grained parallelism possible on large graph data [26]. MTGL is designed for massively multi-threaded architectures. However MTGL only works on massively multi-threaded machines. Thus, the dependence on architecture makes it hard to be adopted widely.

9. CONCLUSION

We introduce a graph engine called Trinity for building online query processing applications as well as offline graph analytics applications. The graph engine is built on top of a distributed memory storage infrastructure called memory cloud. Memory cloud is designed to address the random data access challenge of large graph processing. With this storage infrastructure, Trinity enables a large variety of efficient graph computing paradigms for web scale graphs.

10. REFERENCES

[1] `http://graphlab.org/`.

[2] `http://hadoop.apache.org/`.

[3] `http://incubator.apache.org/giraph/`.

[4] `http://neo4j.org/`.

[5] `http://www.graph500.org/`.

[6] How to partition a billion-scale graph. Technical report, Microsoft Research, 2012.

[7] M. K. Aguilera, A. Merchant, M. Shah, A. Veitch, and C. Karamanolis. Sinfonia: a new paradigm for building scalable distributed systems. SOSP '07, pages 159–174, 2007.

[8] D. G. Andersen, J. Franklin, M. Kaminsky, A. Phanishayee, L. Tan, and V. Vasudevan. Fawn: a fast array of wimpy nodes. SOSP '09, pages 1–14.

[9] J. Berry, B. Hendrickson, S. Kahan, and P. Konecny. Software and algorithms for graph queries on multithreaded architectures. In *IPDPS 2007*, pages 1–14, 2007.

[10] D. Borthakur. *The Hadoop Distributed File System: Architecture and Design*, 2007.

[11] R. Bramandia, B. Choi, and W. K. Ng. Incremental maintenance of 2-hop labeling of large graphs. *TKDE*, 22(5):682–698, 2010.

[12] D. Chakrabarti, Y. Zhan, and C. Faloutsos. R-mat: A recursive model for graph mining. SDM '04, 2004.

[13] T. D. Chandra, R. Griesemer, and J. Redstone. Paxos made live: an engineering perspective. PODC '07, pages 398–407, 2007.

[14] J. Cheng, J. X. Yu, B. Ding, P. S. Yu, and H. Wang. Fast graph pattern matching. In *ICDE*, pages 913–922, 2008.

[15] J. Dean and S. Ghemawat. Mapreduce: Simplified data processing on large clusters. OSDI '04, pages 137–150.

[16] E. W. Dijkstra. Shmuel Safra's version of termination detection. Jan. 1987.

[17] B. Fitzpatrick. Distributed caching with memcached. *Linux J.*, August 2004.

[18] J. E. Gonzalez, Y. Low, H. Gu, D. Bickson, and C. Guestrin. Powergraph: Distributed graph-parallel computation on natural graphs. In *OSDI*, pages 17–30, 2012.

[19] D. Gregor and A. Lumsdaine. The Parallel BGL: A generic library for distributed graph computations. POOSC '05.

[20] Y. Guo, Z. Pan, and J. Heflin. LUBM: A benchmark for OWL knowledge base systems. *Journal of Web Semantics*, 3(2-3):158–182, 2005.

[21] H. Higaki, K. Shima, T. Tachikawa, and M. Takizawa. Checkpoint and rollback in asynchronous distributed systems. INFOCOM '97, pages 998–, 1997.

[22] B. Iordanov. Hypergraphdb: a generalized graph database. WAIM '10, pages 25–36, 2010.

[23] U. Kang, C. E. Tsourakakis, and C. Faloutsos. Pegasus: A peta-scale graph mining system implementation and observations. ICDM '09, pages 229–238, 2009.

[24] G. Karypis and V. Kumar. Parallel multilevel k-way partitioning scheme for irregular graphs. Supercomputing '96.

[25] A. Kyrola, G. Blelloch, and C. Guestrin. Graphchi: Large-scale graph computation on just a pc. In *OSDI*, pages 31–46, 2012.

[26] A. Lumsdaine, D. Gregor, B. Hendrickson, and J. W. Berry. Challenges in parallel graph processing. *Parallel Processing Letters*, 17(1):5–20, 2007.

[27] N. A. Lynch. *Distributed Algorithms*. 1996.

[28] G. Malewicz, M. H. Austern, A. J. Bik, J. C. Dehnert, I. Horn, N. Leiser, and G. Czajkowski. Pregel: a system for large-scale graph processing. SIGMOD '10.

[29] D. Ongaro, S. M. Rumble, R. Stutsman, J. Ousterhout, and M. Rosenblum. Fast crash recovery in ramcloud. SOSP '11, pages 29–41, 2011.

[30] J. Ousterhout, P. Agrawal, D. Erickson, C. Kozyrakis, J. Leverich, D. Mazières, S. Mitra, A. Narayanan, G. Parulkar, M. Rosenblum, S. M. Rumble, E. Stratmann, and R. Stutsman. The case for ramclouds: scalable high-performance storage entirely in dram. *SIGOPS Oper. Syst. Rev.*, 43:92–105, 2010.

[31] T. Schütt, F. Schintke, and A. Reinefeld. Scalaris: reliable transactional p2p key/value store. ERLANG '08, pages 41–48, 2008.

[32] Z. Sun, H. Wang, H. Wang, B. Shao, and J. Li. Efficient subgraph matching on billion node graphs. *Proc. VLDB Endow.*, 5(9):788–799, May 2012.

[33] W. Wu, H. Li, H. Wang, and K. Zhu. Probase: A probabilistic taxonomy for text understanding. In *SIGMOD*, 2012.

[34] M. Zaharia, M. Chowdhury, M. J. Franklin, S. Shenker, and I. Stoica. Spark: cluster computing with working sets. HotCloud'10, pages 10–10, 2010.

[35] J. Zawodny. Redis: Lightweight key/value store that goes the extra mile. Linux Magazine, 2009.

[36] K. Zeng, J. Yang, H. Wang, B. Shao, and Z. Wang. A distributed graph engine for web scale RDF data. In *VLDB 2013*.

[37] X. Zhao, A. Sala, C. Wilson, H. Zheng, and B. Y. Zhao. Orion: shortest path estimation for large social graphs. WOSN'10, pages 9–9, 2010.

Characterizing Tenant Behavior for Placement and Crisis Mitigation in Multitenant DBMSs

Aaron J. Elmore[‡] Sudipto Das[$] * Alexander Pucher[‡]
Divyakant Agrawal[‡] Amr El Abbadi[‡] Xifeng Yan[‡]

[‡]University of California, Santa Barbara
Santa Barbara, CA, USA
{aelmore,pucher,agrawal,amr,xyan}@cs.ucsb.edu

[$]Microsoft Research
Redmond,WA USA
sudipto.das@microsoft.com

ABSTRACT

A multitenant database management system (DBMS) in the cloud must continuously monitor the trade-off between efficient resource sharing among multiple application databases (tenants) and their performance. Considering the scale of hundreds to thousands of tenants in such multitenant DBMSs, manual approaches for continuous monitoring are not tenable. A self-managing controller of a multitenant DBMS faces several challenges. For instance, how to characterize a tenant given its variety of workloads, how to reduce the impact of tenant colocation, and how to detect and mitigate a performance crisis where one or more tenants' desired service level objective (SLO) is not achieved.

We present **Delphi**, a self-managing system controller for a multitenant DBMS, and **Pythia**, a technique to learn behavior through observation and supervision using DBMS-agnostic database level performance measures. Pythia accurately learns tenant behavior even when multiple tenants share a database process, learns good and bad tenant consolidation plans (or packings), and maintains a per-tenant history to detect behavior changes. Delphi detects performance crises, and leverages Pythia to suggests remedial actions using a hill-climbing search algorithm to identify a new tenant placement strategy to mitigate violating SLOs. Our evaluation using a variety of tenant types and workloads shows that Pythia can learn a tenant's behavior with more than 92% accuracy and learn the quality of packings with more than 86% accuracy. During a performance crisis, Delphi is able to reduce 99th percentile latencies by 80%, and can consolidate 45% more tenants than a greedy baseline, which balances tenant load without modeling tenant behavior.

Categories and Subject Descriptors

H.2.4 [**Database Management**]: Systems—*Distributed databases*

Keywords

Multitenancy; elastic data management; database consolidation; tenant characterization; shared nothing architectures

*Work done while at UCSB

SIGMOD'13, June 22–27, 2013, New York, New York, USA.

1. INTRODUCTION

Cloud application platforms and large organizations face the challenge of managing, storing, and serving data for large numbers of applications with small data footprints. For instance, several cloud platforms such as Salesforce.com, Facebook, Google AppEngine, and Windows Azure host hundreds of thousands of small applications. Large organizations, such as enterprises or universities, also face a similar challenge of managing hundreds to thousands of database instances for different departments and projects. Allocating dedicated and isolated resources to each application's database is wasteful in terms of resources and is not cost-effective. **Multitenancy** in the database tier, i.e., sharing resources among the different applications' databases (or **tenants**), is therefore critical. We focus on such a multitenant database management system (**DBMS**) using the **shared process multitenancy** model where the DBMS comprises a cluster of database servers (or **nodes**) where each node runs a single database process which multiple tenants share.

1.1 Challenges in Multitenancy

A multitenant DBMS must minimize the impact of colocating multiple tenants. The challenge lies in determining *which* tenants to colocate and *how many* to colocate at a given server, i.e., learn good **tenant packings** that balance between over-provisioning and over-booking. Furthermore, the colocated tenants' resource requirements must be complementary to avoid heavy resource contention after colocation.

To ensure of service, a multitenant DBMS must also associate meaningful **service level objectives** (**SLOs**) in a consolidated setting. If a tenant's SLO is violated, the DBMS must adapt to this **performance crisis**. The challenge lies in mitigating the crisis which might be caused by a change in this tenant's behavior, a change in a colocated tenant's behavior, or a degradation in the node's performance. A tenant's behavioral change might be due to a change in the query pattern, data access distribution, working set size, access rates, or queries issued on non-indexed attributes while typical queries are on indexed attributes—complexity arises from the myriad of possibilities. Adapting to a crisis entails detecting changes, filtering erratic behavior, and devising mitigation strategies. Erratic behavior can arise from temporary shifts in application popularity, periodic analysis, or ad-hoc queries.

The problem of designing a self-managing controller is further complicated by the variety of tenant workload types. Many applications use their databases for multiple purposes, such as using the same database for serving, analysis, and logging. Therefore, in addition to workload variations across tenants, a single tenant might also exhibit different behaviors at different time instances. Behavioral changes might have patterns (e.g., diurnal trends of serving and reporting workloads) or might be erratic (e.g., flash crowds). Moreover, dynamics in the workload might or might not have correlation. For instance, hosted business applications observe a spike in multiple tenants' activity at the start of the business day. These behavioral dynamics, the interplay of shared resources among colocated tenants, and the complex interactions between the DBMS, OS, and the hardware make analytical models and theoretical abstractions impractical.

From the monitoring perspective, a system controller potentially receives hundreds of raw performance measures from the database process and the operating system (OS) at each node. Considering the scale of tens to hundreds of nodes, using all these raw signals to maintain an aggregate view of the entire system and the individual tenants results in an information deluge. One challenge in effective administration is to systematically filter, aggregate, and transform these raw signals to a manageable set of attributes and automate administration with minimal human guidance. An intelligent and self-managing system controller is a significant step towards achieving economies-of-scale and simplifying administration.

More than a decade of research has focused on effective multitenancy at different layers of the stack, including sharing the file system or the storage layer [15, 19], sharing hardware through virtualization [10], and in the application and web server layer [21]. Multitenancy in the database tier introduces novel challenges due to the richer functionality supported by the DBMS compared to the storage layer, and the complex interplay between CPU, memory, and disk I/O bandwidth observed in a DBMS compared to the stateless applications and web servers. Recent work has focused on various aspects of database multitenancy. Kairos [6] is a technique for tenant placement and consolidation for a set of tenants with known static workloads. Kairos uses direct measurements of the tenants' CPU, I/O, memory, and disk resource consumption to suggest consolidation plans. SmartSLA [24] is a technique for cost-aware resource management using direct resource utilization measurements to learn the average SLA penalty cost in a setting where each tenant has its independent database process and virtual machine. Ahmad and Bowman [1] use machine learning techniques to predict aggregate resource consumption for various workload combinations and proposes a technique that relies on static and known workloads. The authors argue that analytical models for performance and consolidation are hard due to complex component interactions and shifting bottlenecks. Lang et al. [14] propose a SLO-focused framework for static provisioning and placement where tenant workloads are known. In general, existing approaches do not target the problem of continuous tenant modeling, dynamic tenant placement, variable and unknown tenant workloads, and performance crisis mitigation in the shared process multitenancy model, which is critical for deploying shared database services.

1.2 Controller for a Multitenant DBMS

We present the design and implementation of **Delphi**, an intelligent self-managing controller for a multitenant DBMS that orchestrates resources among the tenants. Delphi uses **Pythia**, a technique to *learn* behavior through observation.[1] Pythia uses DBMS-agnostic database-level performance measures available in any standard DBMS and supervised learning techniques to learn a **tenant model** representing resource consumption. Pythia learns a **node model** to determine which combination of tenant types perform well after colocation (**good packings**) and which combinations do not perform well (**bad packings**). Pythia continuously models behavior and maintains historical behavior which allows it to detect a

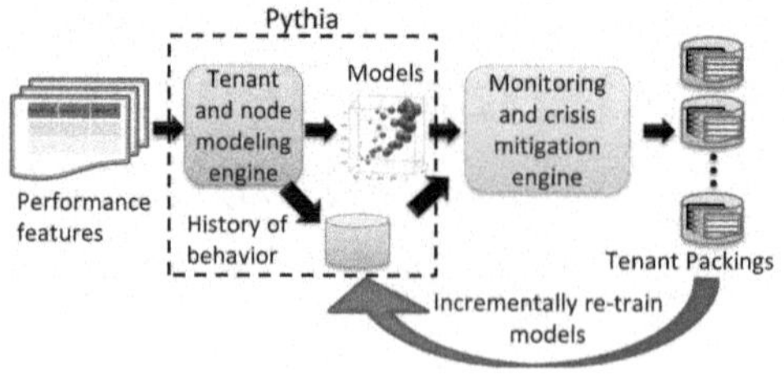

Figure 1: Pythia incrementally learns behavior.

change in a tenant's behavior. Once Delphi detects a performance crisis, it leverages Pythia to suggest remedial actions. Identifying a set of tenants to relocate, and finding destinations for these tenants to alleviate latency violations is the core challenge addressed by Pythia. Delphi employs a local search algorithm, hill-climbing, to prune the space of possible tenant packings and uses the node model to identify potential good packings. Pythia requires minimal human supervision, typically from a database administrator, only for training the supervised learning. Once the models are trained, Delphi can independently orchestrate the tenants, i.e., monitor the system to detect performance crises, load-balance and migrate tenants to mitigate a crisis and to ensure that tenant SLOs are being met. Figure 1 presents an overview of Delphi's design.

In contrast to existing techniques that directly use OS or VM level resource utilization, such as Kairos [6] and SmartSLA [24], Pythia uses database-level performance measures such as cache hit ratio, cache size, read/write ratio, and throughput. This allows Pythia to maintain a detailed per-tenant profile even when tenants share a database process. OS level measures either provide aggregate resource consumption metrics of all tenants, and the alternative of hosting one tenant per database process degrades performance [6]. In contrast, Pythia results in negligible performance impact by using performance measures available from any standard DBMS implementation. Additionally, Pythia learns tenant behavior without any assumptions or in-depth understanding of the underlying systems. In addition, unlike workload driven techniques [1,6,14], Pythia does not require advanced knowledge of the tenants' workload or limit the workload types. Moreover, Pythia does not require profiling tenants in a sandbox, a dedicated node for running tenants in isolation, thus making it applicable even in scenarios where production workloads cannot be replayed due to operational or privacy considerations [2]. Therefore, we expect Pythia to have applications in a variety of multitenant systems and environments, while requiring minimal changes to existing systems.

Delphi is the first end-to-end framework for the accurate and continuous modeling of tenant behavior in a shared process multitenancy environment. We built a prototype implementation of Delphi in a multitenant DBMS running a cluster of Postgres RDBMS servers. Our current implementation uses a set of **classifiers** to learn tenant and node models, although Pythia can be extended to use additional tenant resource models, or other machine learning techniques such as clustering or regression learning [23]. Pythia learns tenant models with a 92% accuracy, and node models with a 86% accuracy. Once a performance crisis is detected, Delphi can mitigate the crisis by reducing the 99th percentile latency violations by 80% on average.

This paper makes the following major contributions:

- Pythia, a technique to accurately learn tenant behavior using database-level attributes agnostic of a specific DBMS implementation. Pythia dynamically detects changes to a tenant's behavior even when tenants share a database process, and automatically learns good and bad tenant packings through observation.

[1]Delphi is an ancient Greek site, where the oracle Pythia resided.

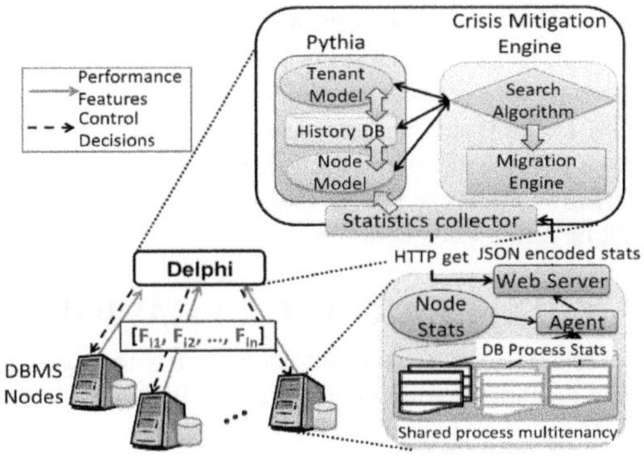

Figure 2: Overview of Delphi's architecture.

- An end-to-end design and implementation of Delphi, an intelligent self-managing controller for a multitenant DBMS. Delphi non-intrusively collects system wide statistics, load-balances to mitigate performance crises, and ensures tenant SLOs.
- A detailed evaluation and comparison against a greedy baseline, using a custom distributed multitenant benchmarking framework.

Organization: Section 2 provides background on database multitenancy and formulates the problem. Section 3 explains how Pythia learns the tenant and node models. Section 4 presents the detailed end-to-end implementation of Delphi. Section 5 presents a thorough evaluation using a variety of workloads and tenant types. Section 6 surveys the related work and Section 7 concludes the paper.

2. DATABASE MULTITENANCY

2.1 Multitenancy Models

Different multitenancy models arise from resource sharing at different levels of abstraction; the **shared hardware**, **shared process**, and **shared table** models are well known [13]. Salesforce.com [22] uses the shared table model where tenants share the database tables. SQL Azure [3] and Relational Cloud [7] use the shared process model where tenants share the database process. Xiong et al. [24] use the shared hardware model where tenants share the physical hardware but have independent VMs and database processes.

The choice of multitenancy model has implications on a system's performance, consolidation, and dynamics. For instance, the shared hardware model provides strong VM level isolation and elastic scaling. However, as shown in a recent study [6], such a model results in up to an order of magnitude lower performance and consolidation compared to the shared process model. On the other hand, the shared table model allows efficient resource sharing amongst tenants but restricts the tenant's schema and requires custom techniques for efficient query processing. The shared process model, therefore, provides a good balance of effective resource sharing, schema diversity, performance, and scale. The shared process model has also been widely adopted in commercial and research systems [3,7]. We therefore focus on the design of an autonomic controller for the shared process multitenancy model.

2.2 Delphi Architecture

Figure 2 provides an overview of the DBMS architecture we consider in this paper. The system consists of a cluster of shared-nothing DBMS nodes where each node runs an RDBMS engine which multiple tenants share. Delphi is the overall framework for a self-managing system controller and comprises Pythia, which models tenant and node behavior and maintains historical information, a **crisis detection and mitigation engine**, and a **statistics collector**, which gathers system-wide performance statistics.

Every DBMS node has a lightweight **agent** which collects usage statistics at that node. A lightweight embedded web server interfaces the agent to the statistics collector. Delphi periodically requests a snapshot of the performance measures from all nodes. On receipt of a snapshot request, the agent obtains per-tenant and aggregate performance statistics from the database process and the OS, collectively called the **performance features**. The agent then returns the snapshot to Delphi. We choose a pull based approach over a push based approach where the agents periodically push the snapshot to the Delphi. A pull based approach enables an agent to operate without any persistent state information and allows the snapshot frequency to be configured by Delphi. The agent collects and aggregates statistics only when requested by Delphi.

All snapshots collected by Delphi are stored in a **history database** that stores the per-tenant and per node history and serves as a persistent repository for historical information such as tenant behavior, packings, and actions taken by Delphi to mitigate a performance crisis. The history database can also be used for off-line analysis of Delphi's actions and performance by an administrator.

2.3 Service Level Objectives

In order for a shared multitenant DBMS to be attractive for the tenants, the DBMS must support some form of performance guarantees such as response times. Typically, the tenants and the DBMS provider agree on a set of service level agreements (**SLAs**). However, agreeing on SLAs is typically an arms race between the provider and the tenant often governed by business logic [2]. Automatically assigning performance SLAs based on workload characteristics is a hard problem and beyond the scope of this paper. Instead, we focus on service level objectives (SLOs) as a mechanism for quantifying the quality-of-service of a multitenant DBMS for a given tenant's workload. We rely on using a uniform percentile-based latency SLOs for all tenants.

2.4 Effects of Colocation

In the shared process multitenancy model, tenants share the DBMS, OS, and hardware. This includes sharing the DBMS's **buffer pool**, the OS's file system cache (or **page cache**), the available I/O bandwidth, and CPU cycles. DBMSs are typically optimized for scaling-up a single tenant and are not designed to fairly share resources among tenants. Therefore, it is critical to understand the impact of resource sharing and contention on performance. It is well understood that when colocating multiple tenants, no resource should be over-utilized. Approaches, such as Kairos [6], are known to determine which tenants can be colocated based on the tenant's resource consumption. Furthermore, it is also imperative that colocated tenants have complementary resource consumption. As an example, colocating a mix of disk-heavy and CPU-heavy tenants is probably better than colocating multiple disk-heavy tenants.

In addition to the above heuristics, when multiple tenants share the cache, it is important to consider how the tenants access the cache. Assume we have two tenant databases D_1, and D_2 colocated at a node with enough resources to serve both tenants. If D_1's throughput is higher than that of D_2, the least recently used (**LRU**) eviction policy, commonly used in buffer pool implementations, will result in D_1 stealing cache pages from D_2. This is because D_1 is accessing more pages, thus making D_2's pages candidates for likely eviction. This reduction in D_2's cache hit ratio will affect its performance. Figure 3 demonstrates this behavior in

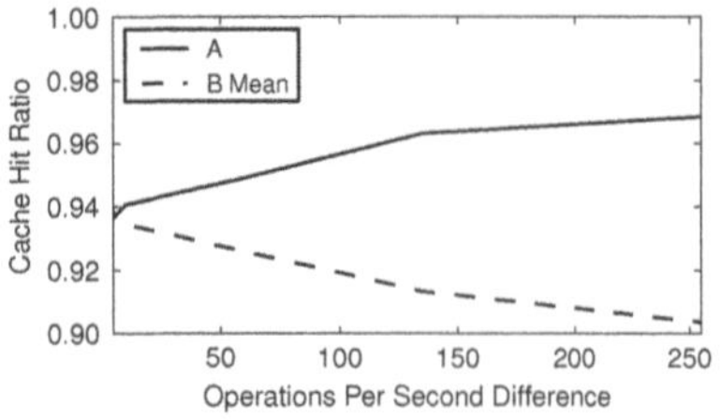

Figure 3: Effects of throughput on cache impedance.

an experiment on a node serving a set of identical tenants where a tenant A has its throughput gradually increasing while the other tenants (B) have a fixed throughput; B represents the average behavior of the remaining tenants. As the throughput difference increases, A steals more cache from the other tenants resulting in an increase in A's cache hit ratio and a decrease in the cache hit ratio of all the remaining tenants (B-Avg), thus affecting performance of the slower tenants.

We introduce the concept of **cache impedance** as a measure of compatibility between tenants to effectively share a cache. A scenario where one tenant dominates the cache over the other tenants is due to a cache impedance mismatch. Therefore, to ensure that tenants continue to perform well after colocation, it is important their cache impedance matches. Four major aspects affect cache access: key or tuple access distribution, database size, throughput, and the read/write distribution; though from our experiments, we have seen throughput to be the most dominant factor.

A similar impact of cache impedance is also observed for accesses to the OS page cache and how the tenants share the page cache. However, the interactions between the two levels of caches, the buffer pool and page cache, are complex due to the stateful interactions between the OS and DBMS [1]. We therefore take an empirical approach to infer a tenant's cache impedance through observed behavior, thus avoiding solutions tailored to a specific implementation. We incorporate the knowledge of cache impedance into the design of Pythia by using signals from both the buffer pool and the page cache to determine the class labels that represent tenant behavior. Pythia learns which combinations of tenant classes are amenable for colocation. While specialized solutions can be built with strong resource isolation between tenants or bypassing the page cache using direct I/O, we aim to present an approach requiring minimal changes to current DBMS architectures.

2.5 Problem Formulation

Let $\mathbb{D}$ be the set of tenant databases and $\mathbb{N}$ be the set of DBMS nodes. Each tenant $D_i \in \mathbb{D}$ is represented by a vector of performance features F_i and $\mathbb{F} = \{F_i | D_i \in \mathbb{D}\}$. Let $\mathcal{C}$ be a set of class labels corresponding to tenant behavior. Pythia learns the tenant model $\mathbb{T} : \mathbb{F} \rightarrow \mathcal{C}$, i.e., given a performance feature F_i of tenant D_i, the tenant model $\mathbb{T}$ assigns a label $c \in \mathcal{C}$ to D_i. Let P_j be the set of tenants at N_j, such that each tenant entry, D_i, has a corresponding class label $\mathcal{C}_i$ derived from $\mathbb{T}$ and performance measure (e.g.,latency), M_i, that constitutes the SLO. Pythia also learns the node model $\mathbb{P} : P_j \rightarrow \mathcal{G}$, i.e., given a set of tenants P_j, and thus corresponding labels, $\mathbb{P}$ assigns a label $g \in \mathcal{G}$ that indicates the packing's quality. We set $\mathcal{G} = \{\checkmark^+, \checkmark, \times\}$, where $\checkmark$ denotes a good packing, $\checkmark^+$ is a good packing with under-utilized resources, and $\times$ is a bad packing.

Delphi periodically collects snapshots from all the DBMS nodes. Each node reports the performance features of all the tenants hosted at that node and the overall node level usage statistics. Delphi monitors all the nodes and ensures that all the tenants' SLOs are being met and every node in the system is performing well, i.e., $\forall N_j \in \mathbb{N}, \mathbb{P}(P_j) \equiv \checkmark$. For every tenant, Pythia maintains a sliding window of the last $\mathbb{W}$ snapshots and their corresponding labels. Given a performance crisis at a node N_j, i.e., one or more tenants in the packing P_j are violating their SLOs, Delphi mitigates the crisis by finding a packing $P_j' \subset P_j$ such that $\mathbb{P}(P_j') \equiv \checkmark$. Delphi also finds destination node(s) (N_k) for the tenants $P_j - P_j'$ that must be moved out of N_j.

3. PYTHIA: LEARNING BEHAVIOR

Pythia seeks to learn tenant and node models through observation. Using machine learning classification, Pythia assigns a class label to a tenant that approximately describes the tenant's behavior and resource consumption. Pythia also learns which tenant packings are performing well and which ones are violating SLOs. Pythia's design goals are to learn behavior while: (i) requiring minimal changes to the underlying multitenant DBMS, (ii) having no foreknowledge or assumptions (such as static or predefined workloads or working set fitting in memory) on tenant workloads, and (iii) causing negligible performance impact.

Pythia uses supervised learning techniques, specifically classifiers, to learn tenant behavior. We use tenant classes that are representative of their resource consumption. Pythia also learns which combination of tenant types perform well together (good packings) and which tenant packings are likely to over consume resources or violate latency SLOs (bad packings). We now explain our feature selection process to identify a small set of performance features that can accurately model a tenant's behavior and then explain how Pythia uses these features to learn the tenant and node models.

3.1 Tenant Feature Selection

Pythia uses DBMS-agnostic database-level performance measures. Database-level performance measures allow per-tenant monitoring for detailed analysis even in shared process multitenancy. A plethora of performance measures can be extracted from any standard DBMS. Examples are number of cache accesses and cache misses, number of read/update/insert/delete requests, number of pages accessed by each transaction, average response time, and transactions per second. However, using all the measures to characterize a tenant is not desirable since the complex relationship between attributes can be difficult for classifiers to infer. We therefore use our domain knowledge to select a subset of measures.

The challenge lies in selecting the measures that correlate to tenants' behavior and resource requirements while ensuring high modeling accuracy. To allow Pythia to be used in a large variety of systems, we only select measures available from any standard DBMS implementation, be it SQL or NoSQL, with negligible or no impact on normal operation. We select the feature set guided by our knowledge of the attributes' semantics.

We now explain the different measures, some of which are derived from other raw measures, we choose as the tenant performance features and also explain the rationale behind their selection.

Write percent. The percentage of operations issued by a tenant that are writes, i.e., inserts, deletes, and updates. This measure gives an estimate of the rate at which the pages are updated and is also an indirect indicator of the expected disk traffic resulting from the writes due to cache pages being flushed, checkpointing, and appends to the transaction log.

Average operation complexity. Average number of (distinct) database pages accessed by a single transaction. When transactions are specified in a declarative language, such as SQL, operation complexity is a measure of the resources consumed (such as CPU cycles) to execute that operation. This measure differentiates a tenant issuing simple read/write transactions from one issuing complex

transactions performing joins or scans, even though both transaction types might issue the same number of SQL statements.
Percent cache hits. Number of database pages accessed that were served from the cache. This measure approximates the number of disk access requests issued by the database process for the tenant.
Buffer pool size. Number of pages allocated to the tenant in the DBMS buffer pool, approximates the tenant's memory footprint.
OS page cache size. Number of pages allocated in the OS page cache to the tenant's database files. Along with buffer pool size, provides an estimate of the tenant's total memory footprint.
Database size. Size of the tenant's persistent data and is representative of the disk storage consumption. Size has an indirect impact on the tenant's disk I/O.
Throughput (Transactions per second). Average number of transactions completed for a given tenant in a second. Transactions completed include both the transactions committed and rolled-back. Throughput is an indicator of behavior (such as cache impedance) and resource requirements (such as CPU and disk bandwidth).

Our experiments (Section 5) demonstrate that these attributes allow Pythia to train accurate models, representative of resource consumption, that can be used by Delphi for effective crisis mitigation.

3.2 Resource-based Tenant Model

We characterize a tenants' behavior in terms of its expected resource consumption. The rationale for selecting resource-based models is to allow Pythia to associate semantics to a tenant's behavior and reason about resources consumed. Furthermore, the number of critical resources are limited and known to a system administrator. Therefore, tenant behavior can be classified into a handful of resource-based classes without requiring knowledge of tenant workloads. Recent work has investigated classifying workload-based modeling by running queries in isolation [18]. However, using queries to build accurate models and understand tenant interaction, assumes new queries follow existing patterns and limits the opportunity for ad-hoc queries. Additionally, queries that rely on caching to minimize expensive operations, such as nested loop joins, can make modeling interactions difficult. In designing Pythia we sought to avoid these assumptions. We now explain how we select the resource-based class labels, how we determine the rules to assign labels to the tenants, and how we train the tenant model.

3.2.1 *Resource-based classes*

A tenant's resource consumption has four important components: CPU consumed to fulfill the tenant's requests, main memory (RAM) consumed to cache data, disk capacity consumed to store persistent data, and the disk I/O bandwidth (or disk **IOPS**) consumed. While networking is an important resource, for now we assume that database connections are ample due to connection pooling and workloads use minimal data transfer. In scenarios where this is critical, network attributes can be be added. In most cases, commodity servers have disks (order of terabytes) much larger than the tenants (order of few gigabytes). Therefore, disk capacity is almost always abundant. However, irrespective of how much RAM is provided, the DBMS and the OS in a running server will invariably use most of the available RAM to cache existing tenants. Therefore, RAM usage is almost always constrained and excess capacity for new tenants is not reserved. However, in practice, a large fraction of the cached pages are not actively used and a newly added tenant will carve out cache capacity, provided the tenant's cache impedance, as described in Section 2.4, matches that of the tenants already being served at the node. In addition to cache impedance, the disk IOPS and the available CPU capacity are two critical resources that determine how well the tenants perform after colocation. In a consolidated setting, we cannot directly determine the exact CPU and disk IOPS consumption or the cache impedance of each tenant, so we model them indirectly. We use the performance features to approximate resource consumption. We base our class labels based on three dimensions: expected disk IOPS (`D`), throughput (`T`), and operation complexity (`O`). We loosely associate `D`, `T`, and `O` to disk bandwidth consumption, cache impedance, and CPU consumption.

A human administrator is required to derive resource boundaries for the labels. These boundaries can be derived by observing resource distributions in a system where Pythia will be used. In our evaluation, we partition each continuous dimension into a few buckets whose boundaries are determined by analyzing the distribution of values obtained from an operational system. The `D` dimension is subdivided into four buckets: small (`DS`), medium (`DM`), large (`DL`), and extra-large (`DXL`). The `T` dimension is subdivided into three buckets: small (`TS`), medium (`TM`), and large (`TL`). The `O` dimension is subdivided into two buckets: small (`OS`) and large (`OL`). The rationale for such a subdivision is that the disk bandwidth is a critical resource for data intensive applications; a finer subdivision allows closer monitoring of a tenant's disk bandwidth consumption. Throughput impacts CPU consumption, disk IOPS, and cache impedance. We therefore consider throughput second after disk and use a coarser subdivision into three buckets. Operation complexity affects CPU consumption and is primarily targeted to differentiate tenants issuing complex queries such as scans, reports, or joins. Complexity comes last and is subdivided into two buckets.

We use class labels composed of `D`, `T`, and `O`. For instance, `DS-TS-OS` represents a tenant with low expected disk consumption, low throughput, and low complexity. Among the possible 24 classes, in practice, some classes fold into one encompassing class as some dimension override the others. As an example, a `DXL` tenant's resource consumption is high enough that the operation complexity does not matter; we only consider two throughput buckets for such tenants: `DXL-TL` and `DXL-TMS` (medium and small). Similarly, for a `DL-TL` tenant, complexity is irrelevant. Following is the set of class labels we used: $\mathcal{C}$ = `{DL-TL, DL-TM-OL, DL-TM-OS, DL-TS-OL, DL-TS-OS, DM-TL-OL, DM-TL-OS, DM-TM-OL, DM-TM-OS, DM-TS-OL, DM-TS-OS, DS-TL-OL, DS-TL-OS, DS-TM-OL, DS-TM-OS, DS-TS-OL, DS-TS-OS, DXL-TL, DXL-TMS}`.

3.2.2 *Training the model*

Throughput and operation complexity are directly measured from the database process. The number of disk requests issued per-tenant must be estimated since the OS only provides aggregate measures and the DBMS we use does not directly report resource metrics per-tenant. The database process provides a measure of the number of disk read requests issued to the OS. However, due to the OS page cache, an actual disk access happens only after a miss in the OS page cache. Our first approximation was that every access to the page cache has a uniform probability of a miss. This approach to modeling the OS page cache is inaccurate since it overlooks cache impedance in the page cache level. An artifact of using a DBMS that utilizes the page cache and does not use direct I/O. If a tenant D_1 misses the database cache more frequently compared to another tenant D_2, D_1 issues more requests to the page cache compared to D_2, thus dominating D_2 in the page cache. Therefore, a request by D_2 has a higher likelihood of a miss compared to that of D_1. The probability of a page cache miss is also dependent on other factors such as the tenant's database size, what fraction is cached, and the page cache eviction policy.

Let $P(A)$ be the probability that an access to a page missed the buffer pool. If h is the cache hit ratio, then $P(A) = 1 - h$. Let $P(B)$ be the probability of a miss in the page cache. If p is the total number of database pages for the tenant and m is the number of the tenant's pages in the page cache, then $P(B) = 1 - m/p$. The probability of a page being read from the disk is $P(A \cap B)$. For simplicity, if we assume that A and B are independent, then $P(A \cap B) = P(A)P(B) = (1-h)(1-m/p)$. The number of pages accessed per second is given as the product of the operation complexity (o) and throughput (t). Writes contribute to disk activity due to dirty buffer pages, and WAL writes. Update operations provide fixed disk-write activity due to logging, and have a probability of creating another disk-write, if a clean buffer page is dirtied. Outside of logging, updates to an already dirty buffer page may not force a new disk-write. This results in disk activity being difficult to accurately model. Let u be the update operations per second, d be the percentage of pages that are dirty in the buffer pool, and α be a slack variable for updates causing additional disk writes. Therefore, we have **Expected Disk IOPS** :

$$(o \times t)(1-h)(1-m/p) + u + \alpha(u \times d \times (1-h)) \quad (1)$$

This measure (1) is an approximation since it simplifies the effect of updates on disk-writes and assumes buffer pool misses and page cache misses are independent. However, our experiments in Section 5.2.1 reveal that (1) is close enough as a guideline for labeling the training set. We provide all the performance measures to the tenant classifier that *learns* the function using the attributes, but use the transformed expected disk IOPS in generating labels for our training set.

Training the tenant model requires minimal guidance from a human administrator. An administrator analyzes the distribution of the values along the dimensions `D`, `T`, and `O` to determine the boundaries for the buckets that form the class labels for training. For our evaluation, we derived boundaries by examining the distributions of attributes against server resource consumption when tenants were run in isolation. Once the bucket-boundaries are determined, the administrator assigns labels to the tenants based on their respective performance features. Pythia trains a classifier on the labeled training set to learn the tenant model $\mathbb{T}$.

Pythia is designed to work with various tenant models, as long as a model label exists that captures the multiple dimensions of resource utilization. Modeling database interaction in a multitenant environment is challenging due to shifting bottlenecks and unforeseen interactions. This work focuses on demonstrating the potential of a framework that relies on machine learning to model tenant behavior and predict interaction. The tenant model presented in this paper is a representative example. For future work, we plan to examine additional tenant models, such as online models based on query analysis [18], providing administrators feedback on models, and assisting tenant modeling through unsupervised learning.

3.3 Node Model for Tenant Packing

Pythia uses the tenant model to learn which tenant classes perform well together and which do not. The goodness of a packing depends on the class of tenants that comprise the packing. A node model is trained for a single hardware configuration.

A set of tenants at a node is represented as the **packing vector**. If $|\mathcal{C}|$ is the number of tenant classes, then a tenant packing is represented by a vector of length $|\mathcal{C}|$. A position in the vector represents a tenant class and the number of tenants of that class contained in the packing; if a type is absent in the packing, the corresponding count is set to 0. For example, if c_1, c_2, and c_3 are the known tenant classes and a packing had two tenants of type c_1 and three tenants of type c_3, the vector for the packing is $[2, 0, 3]$. The **node feature** representing a packing at a node is the packing vector.

We train the node model ($\mathbb{P}$) by providing a set of labels ($\mathcal{G}$) representing the goodness of a packing. In its simplest form, $\mathcal{G}$ can be $\{\checkmark^+, \checkmark, \times\}$ representing good or bad packings respectively. A packing is good ($\checkmark$) if all tenants meet their SLOs and under($\checkmark^+$) if SLOs are met and server resources are under-utilized. A latency SLOs is composed of an upper bound time for a given percentile. Let $\mathcal{S}$ be the set latencies, composed of s_i, the latency limit for the ith percentile in milliseconds. For our evaluation we set $\mathcal{S} = \{s_{95} : 500, s_{99} : 2000\}$ based on discussions with several cloud service providers. Relaxing or tightening SLOs depends entirely on the applications using the service.

The binary labeling technique captures the SLOs but does not consider utilization of the node. For instance, a packing might be good but the node's resources might be under-utilized or over-utilized. We therefore augment $\mathcal{G}$ to include information about utilization. As noted earlier, disk IOPS and CPU are two critical resources. We use idle CPU percent and the percentage CPU cycles spent on IO (IOWait) as indicators of node utilization both in terms of CPU and disk bandwidth; too many disk requests are reflected in high IOWait. A node's utilization is subdivided into three categories: if idle is above a certain upper bound ($\mathcal{U}_u$) then the node is under-utilized (`Under`), if idle is below a lower bound ($\mathcal{U}_l$) or IOWait is over a threshold $\mathcal{U}_w$ then the node is over-utilized (`Over`), idle percent in the range $(\mathcal{U}_l, \mathcal{U}_u]$ and IOWait less than $\mathcal{U}_w$ is considered good utilization (`Good`). If any tenant violates a latency SLO the node is labeled as Over, regardless of resource consumption. Composing the utilization based division with the SLO based division results in a set of labels that captures both utilization and SLOs: $\mathcal{G} = \{$`Under(`$\checkmark^+$`)`, `Good(`$\checkmark$`)`, `Over(`$\times$`)`$\}$.

To train the node models, a human administrator specifies the parameters $\mathcal{S}, \mathcal{U}_l, \mathcal{U}_u$, and $\mathcal{U}_w$. A simple rule-based logic assigns labels to the node based on the node feature. Once the training set is labeled, Pythia trains a classifier to learn the node model $\mathbb{P}$.. The node model is incrementally updated to reflect new observations in the running system.

3.4 Utilizing Machine Learning

We use Weka, an open-source machine learning library, to train Pythia's models. We experimented with multiple classifiers such as decision trees, random forests, support vector machines, and classifiers based on regression [23]. The training data is obtained by augmenting an operational system, for which Pythia will be trained, to collect the tenant and node features which are then labeled as described earlier. In our evaluation Pythia utilizes Random Forests, an ensemble decision tree classifier, due to its high accuracy and resistance to overfitting. Once the tenant and node models are trained, they are stored and served in-memory; Delphi uses these models for intelligent tenant placement.

In this section, we presented one way of training the models in Pythia as a representative example. However, Pythia can be adapted to work with a different set of performance features, tenant and node labels, and semantics associated with the label. The role of a domain expert or a system administrator is to determine representative features and assign labels so that the tenant and node models can be trained accordingly. For example, disk I/O is limited by the underlying hardware and experienced administrators can easily identify and categorize ranges of disk consumption. Moreover, Pythia can also be extended to use other forms of machine learning such as clustering or regression learning [23]. Exploring such directions are possible directions of future work; our initial focus was to leverage classification with domain knowledge to explore the end-to-end design space.

4. DELPHI IMPLEMENTATION

We implemented Delphi on a multitenant DBMS with each node running Postgres, an open-source RDBMS engine.[2] All the database level performance features ($\mathbb{F}$) are obtained using two Postgres extensions and without any modification to the Postgres code. Early in our project, we also explored MySQL and found the majority of performance measures comprising $\mathbb{F}$ are available through a third-party MySQL extension ExtSQL.[3] In this section, we explain Delphi's components other than Pythia, i.e., the statistics gathering component, and the crisis detection and mitigation component.

4.1 Statistics Collection

Each DBMS node has an agent which interfaces with Delphi. The agent collects the tenants' performance statistics by querying the database process. In our prototype, tenants share the same Postgres instance and have independent schemas (or databases, in Postgres terminology). To gather the performance statistics, we use two extensions to Postgres in addition to Postgres' internal statistics. The extension `pg_buffercache` provides detailed information about the state of the database buffer by table, and the extension `pgfincore` peeks into the OS's page cache to determine which parts of a tenant's database is cached by the OS. Both extensions expose the statistics as a table which the agent queries using SQL issued through a local JDBC connection. A number of queries are issued to Postgres, `pg_buffercache`, and `pgfincore` to obtain statistics such as per-tenant database and OS page cache allocation, cache-hit rations, number of dirty pages, and read/write ratios.

The agent also collects aggregate node-level usage statistics such as percentage idle CPU, CPU cycles blocked on I/O calls, CPU clock speed and number of cores, memory usage, number of disk blocks read or written, and disk I/O operations per second for all drives hosting database files or the transaction log. The agent can also be configured to follow database logs to record database events such as a checkpoint initialization or slow queries.

The statistics collector requests a snapshot via the agent's web server which obtains the performance measures from the local database; statistics are reset after collection. The response by the agent wraps all the statistics and the time since the last report in a flexible interchange format, JSON in our case, allowing easy extensibility. This entire process takes on the order of few milliseconds and allows lightweight statistics collection. The impact of monitoring on database latency was observed to be a few milliseconds.

4.2 Crisis Detection and Mitigation

4.2.1 Monitoring and Crisis Detection

The statistics collector periodically gathers statistics from all the DBMS nodes to create an aggregate view of the system. For every incoming snapshot, Delphi uses Pythia's tenant model to determine each tenant's class. Delphi maintains a per-tenant sliding window of the last $\mathbb{W}$ snapshots; all Delphi's actions are based on $\mathbb{W}$. The class labels in $\mathbb{W}$ are used to determine a representative label for each tenant. For instance, assume Delphi maintains 5 snapshots, and in this window a tenant D_i has 4 labels corresponding to class c_j and 1 label corresponding to c_k. Delphi represents D_i as $\{0.8c_j, 0.2c_k\}$, i.e., D_i is of type c_j with confidence 80% and type c_k with confidence 20%.

Delphi's use of a window $\mathbb{W}$, rather than using the last snapshot, provides a more confident view about shifts in behavior. It allows Delphi to filter spurious behavior, such as sudden spikes in activity or higher than average response times resulting from system maintenance activities such as checkpoints. Using percentile latency SLOs also limits the impact of a few queries with high latency. Crisis mitigation steps, such as migrating some tenants out of a node, are expensive and hence Delphi must filter out spurious behavior and react only when a shifting trend is observed.

For a given tenant packing P_j at node N_j, Delphi determines whether all tenants' SLOs, $\mathcal{S}$, are being met. If all SLOs are met and no resource is being over-utilized, then this packing is an instance of a good packing for the node model. The slack in resource consumption determines the aggressiveness of consolidation. If one or more SLOs are violated, then this packing is an instance of a bad packing. Once a performance crisis corresponding to a bad packing is detected, Delphi searches for a good packing and takes the remedial measures.

The node model $\mathbb{P}$ receives continuous feedback about good and bad tenant packings and is incrementally updated as Delphi observes new packings and their outcomes. We incrementally re-train $\mathbb{P}$ using the negative examples, i.e., cases where the model's prediction was inaccurate, and a sampling of positive examples that are not repetitive, as many packings and their outcomes are repetitive during steady state.

4.2.2 Crisis Mitigation

Mitigating a performance crisis for a bad packing P_j at node N_j entails identifying a packing $P'_j \subset P_j$ such that $\mathbb{P}(P'_j) \not\equiv \times$, where $\times$ corresponds to an over packing according to the node model $\mathbb{P}$. We formulate this problem of finding the packing P'_j as a search problem through the combinations of the tenant packings, a well-studied problem in artificial intelligence [17]. The search algorithm performs *what-if* analysis using the tenant model $\mathbb{P}$ to determine potential destinations node that can accommodate a subset of tenants in P_j^M without itself deteriorating to a bad packing as predicted by $\mathbb{P}$. Once a good packing P'_j is determined, the tenants $P_j^M = (P_j - P'_j)$ must be migrated out of N_j. Pythia must find one or more destination nodes that can accommodate P_j^M. Therefore any tenant in $p_j^M \in P_j^M$ requires a destination node N_k serving a packing P_k such that $\mathbb{P}(P_k) \not\equiv \times \wedge \mathbb{P}(P'_k) \not\equiv \times$ where $P'_k = P_k \cup p_j^M$. Destinations must be found for all tenants included in P_j^M.

We implemented a few different search algorithms in designing Pythia. *Breadth first search* (BFS) [17] first tries all combinations of migrating one tenant, then combinations of a pair of tenants, and so on until it finds a good packing according to $\mathbb{P}$. Using an exhaustive search algorithm would often not converge on a solution, either due to the search space complexity or not being able to satisfy a goal test of having no nodes in violation. Additionally, we do not expect BFS to scale with a large number of tenants and nodes. The local search algorithm, *hill-climbing* becomes the natural selection, due to the ability to provide a time-bounded best solution, and the ability to treat packing as an optimization problem [17]. With hill-climbing, all immediate neighbors (potential migrations) are examined, and the move providing the largest improvement is selected. Therefore only the local state is considered when making search decisions. This process is repeated, until no additional step can improve the state (a local maximum) or time has expired. Each step is evaluated with a heuristic cost estimate h to find a migration which provides the largest improvement to the tenant packing, by finding a local minimum for h. The naive cost function h attempts to minimize the number of nodes which are labeled as over($\times$).

$$h = \sum_{\{N_i \in N \mid \mathbb{P}(P_i) \equiv \times\}} 1 \qquad (2)$$

[2] http://www.postgresql.org/

[3] MySQL: http://www.mysql.com/, ExtSQL: http://www.extsql.com/.

However, in packings with minimal excess capacity, this cost function (2) to minimize the number of over nodes, would simply overload one node to the point of being unresponsive. The next step would be to minimize the number of tenants in violation. This requires we extend the node model to provide a confidence score λ for a given label. In place of a single label, most classifiers can produce a set of labels and confidences. We denote a function that provides a confidence rating given a packing and label, as $\lambda(\vec{\mathcal{C}}, \mathcal{G}) \to \mathbb{R} \in [0, 1]$. The new cost function follows as:

$$h = \sum_{N_i \in N} (\lambda(P_i, \times) \cdot |P_i|)^2 \quad (3)$$

This cost function has an artifact of migrating tenants between nodes that were not in violation, to reduce the overall score. Healthy nodes with a large number of nodes, can be labeled as having a small confidence of being over($\times$). This cost function would favor migrating from a large number of tenants with a low over-score, rather than a small number of tenants, in violation, with a higher over-score. We use a minimal threshold, σ for λ to register a score. After examining latencies and IO wait times for $\lambda(\vec{\mathcal{C}}, \times)$ we settled on $\sigma = 0.35$, due to reduced likelihood of high latencies or strained I/O. These results are included in Section 5.2.2. Our final cost function is set to:

$$h = \sum_{\{N_i \in N | \lambda(P_i, \times) > \sigma\}} (\lambda(P_i, \times) \cdot |P_i|)^2 \quad (4)$$

In case the search algorithm cannot find a suitable packing, or cannot converge after a few iterations, it concludes that new nodes need to be added to accommodate the changing tenant requirements and behaviors. In a cloud infrastructure, such as Amazon EC2, Delphi can automatically add new servers to elastically scale the cluster. In a statically-allocated infrastructure typical in classical enterprises, Delphi flags this event for capacity planning by a human administrator. Since the workloads are dynamic and we employ heuristics to find a solution, a stable state is not guaranteed. Additional heuristics, such as maximum allowed moves in a time period, are used to prevent excessive tenant movement.

Delphi must *migrate* the tenants p_j^M for which it found a potential destination node. This problem of migrating a tenant database in a live system is called **live database migration** [9]. Once a tenant is migrated, the outcome is recorded in the history database. Migrating a tenant incurs some cost, such as a few aborted transactions and an increase in response times. Our current search algorithm does not consider this cost in determining which tenants to migrate. Ideally, Delphi will factor migration cost into decision making, however this requires accurate models to predict migration cost, which is influenced by tenant attributes, colocated workloads, and network congestion. We evaluated regression models based on the attributes in Section 3.1 to predict migration cost, but interference from source and destination workloads resulted in inaccurate models. Accurate models to predict migration cost, augmenting the search algorithm to consider a predicted migration cost, and techniques to recognize patterns in workloads are worthwhile directions of future extensions.

It is possible to use replicas for crisis mitigation and load balancing in Pythia. Leveraging existing replicas to migrate workload instead of data migration reduces the migration cost. Synchronous replication protocols make this operation simple and quick, but at the cost of increased latency for update operations during normal operation. Asynchronous replication could also be used, but automating the process of migrating workload to a secondary replica, when the replicas can potentially be lagging, while preserving data consistency requires careful system design and additional approaches. Moreover, even in a system with multiple replicas, Pythia can help select a candidate replica to migrate the workload to. In scenarios where the existing replicas are not suitable destinations (since they might become overloaded as a result of this workload migration), Pythia can also help select a viable destination where a new replica can be regenerated. Our decision to focus on migration limits the problem's scope. In the future, we plan to explore how Pythia can be extended to support a hybrid of workload and data migration.

5. EXPERIMENTAL EVALUATION

We deployed and evaluated Delphi on a cluster of 16 servers dedicated to database processes, six servers dedicated to generating client workloads (workers), and one server dedicated to hosting Delphi and a benchmark coordinator. The database servers run PostgreSQL 9.1 on CentOS 6.3, with two quad-core Xeon processors, 32 GB RAM, 1 GB Ethernet, and 3.7 TB striped RAID HDD array. Adhering to PostgreSQL best practice, the buffer pool size is configured to 8 GB, with the remaining memory dedicated to use by the OS page cache. Default settings are used for other configuration options. The following section describes benchmarks used for workload generation, the methodology used to generate various tenant workloads, a validation of the tenant and node models, and a detailed evaluation of Pythia.

5.1 Benchmark and Tenant Description

Delphi targets multitenant environments that serve a wide variety of tenant types and workloads where the tenants often use their database for multiple purposes. Classical database benchmarks, such as the TPC suite, focus on testing the performance and limits of a single high performance DBMS dedicated either for transaction processing (TPC-C) or for data analysis (TPC-H). Existing benchmarks provide little support for evaluating the effects of colocating multiple tenants, systematically generating workloads for large numbers of small tenants, generating correlated and uncorrelated workload patterns, or generating workloads that change or evolve with time. We therefore designed and implemented a custom framework to evaluate and benchmark multitenant DBMSs.

Our multitenant benchmark is capable of generating a wide variety of workloads, such as lightweight tenants with minimal load and resource consumption, a mix of reporting and transactional workloads, and workloads that change behavior with time, thus emulating the variety of tenants a multitenant DBMS can host [2]. The benchmark is a distributed set of **load generator workers** orchestrated by a **master**. The core of the load generator comprises a set of configurable predefined workload types. Our current implementation supports the following workload classes: a light workload of short transactions, composed of 1-4 read and write operations; a lightweight market-based web application which tracks frequent clicks, reads products for browsing, places transactional orders, and reports on related items and popular ads; a time series database with a heavy insert workload and periodic reporting; a YCSB-like [5] workload on larger databases with 80% of operations, on 20% of the data; and a set of YCSB-like workloads with bounded random configurations. A tenant's workload is specified as one workload type, a database size varying between 100MB to 14 GB, and a vector of randomized configuration parameters, including throughput and number of client threads. Therefore a tenant's workload can potentially comprise multiple combinations of workload configurations in different time intervals. Using the randomized configuration, 350 tenants were generated and associated with a random id. Each tenant was run in isolation for a warm-up period of at least 30 minutes, and then latencies were measured over 10 minutes. To ensure tenants are amenable to consolidation with our latency SLOs, tenants with latency 95th percentile greater than 500 milliseconds (ms) or 99th percentile greater than 2000 ms are re-

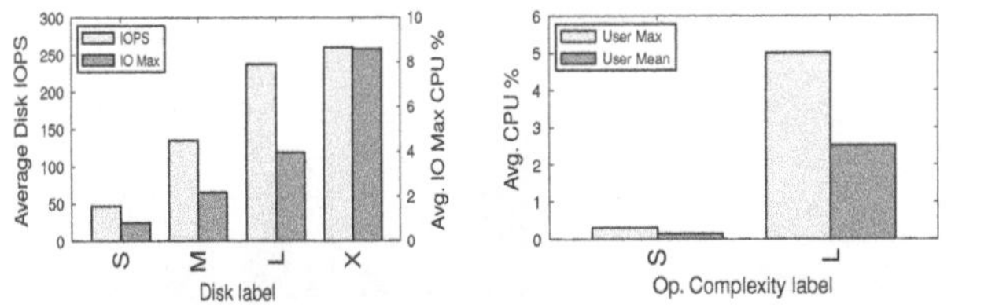

(a) Expected disk IOPS and CPU I/O Wait (b) Operation Complexity and CPU Utilization

Figure 4: Tenant model resource consumption when run in isolation.

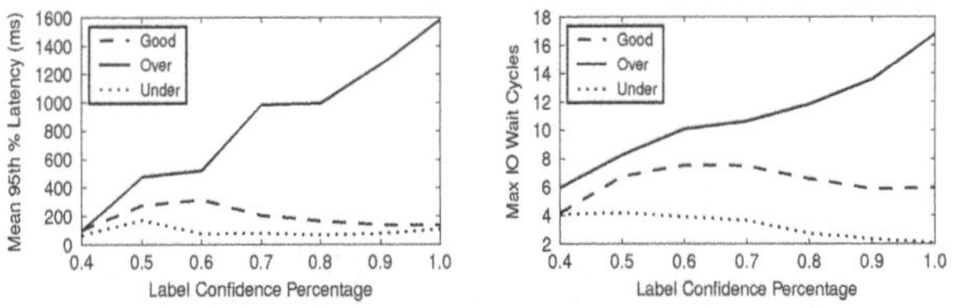

(a) Average tenant 95th percentile latency. (b) Average server max CPU cycles blocked on I/O.

Figure 5: Node model performance by label confidence

moved from the set of candidate tenants, which left 314 tenants. While this workload combination does not encapsulate the variety of workloads encountered in a real database platform, it is more robust than using a combination of heterogeneous workloads, such as only using YCSB or TPC-C for all tenants.

The benchmark master receives a mapping of tenants-to-servers from Delphi, and executes all workloads by distributing workloads at the thread granularity in round-robin to all worker nodes. Worker nodes connect directly to database servers via JDBC. Periodically the master collects rolling logs of all latencies, tagged by operation type, workload class, and tenant ID. Implementing such a distributed load testing environment is necessary to generate enough client load to stress 16 database servers concurrently, aggregate usage statistics, and emulate a distributed tenant query router.

5.2 Model Evaluation

Before describing the experimental evaluation of Pythia, we briefly revisit model generation and provide a basic validation that the proposed models capture behavior that Pythia utilizes for placement decisions. Pythia's models must be trained before Delphi can leverage Pythia for managing the tenants. Training data is collected from the operational system and a human administrator provides rules to label the training data, which is then fed into Pythia to learn tenant and node models. A model's accuracy is computed as the percentage of occurrences where Pythia's predicted tenant or node label matches that provided by the administrator. To measure accuracy, we used cross-validation, where the labeled data is partitioned into a *training set* and a *validation set*, the models are trained on the training set and tested on the validation set. Accuracy of the tenant model was about 92% while that of the node accuracy was about 86%. We also validated that when a node's resources are not thrashing, then a tenant's class label is static if the tenant's workload is static. When resource capacity becomes constrained, due to migration or thrashing, we did observe that tenant labels do fluctuate. Labeling based on a sliding window can reduce fluctuation, but fluctuations could result in a misclassification of a node, and requires additional iterations to resolve. Improving tenant interference modeling is left for future work.

Delphi is an initial step in building a multitenant controller, and to focus the problem on tenant placement we currently do not factor the cost of migration in placement decisions. Therefore in all evaluations, when any new combination of colocated tenants is evaluated (a **run**), the framework runs a staggered half-hour warm up period followed by a statistic reset. After warm up, evaluations run for a given time period with snapshots recorded every five minutes and node statistics captured every 30 seconds.

5.2.1 *Tenant Model Evaluation*

In determining which generated tenants are amenable to the defined latency SLOs, all tenants are run in isolation on a database server. Here the tenants' performance features are labeled using the rules described in Section 3.2. The labeled data set serves as our initial training set for tenant models. To validate that the resource-based tenant models do capture relative resource consumption, we examine the tenant models when run in isolation. The models are labeled using only the database features captured by an agent, and the servers resource utilization is only used for validation. Figure 4 shows that our models are representative of actual resource usage, without direct monitoring. Disk activity is examined in Figure 4(a) where we compare label buckets of **s**mall, **m**edium, **l**arge, and e**x**tra-large against average disk IOPS and the max CPU cycles blocked on I/O (**IO Max**). As predicted the disk component of a tenant's label corresponds to the average observed disk activity. Figure 4(b) shows that average operation complexity (number of pages accessed per transaction), which translates into CPU consumption. Our hypothesis is that high operation complexity includes CPU intensive queries, including, reporting queries that access many pages, complex join operations, or long running transactions that require concurrency validation. Here we show labels with **s**mall and **l**arge operation complexity against mean and max CPU cycles used on user processes, which is primarily composed of the database processes. The range for CPU cycles appear low, but these percentages are across 16 OS threads. Servers with fewer cores, would exhibit higher percentages.

To experiment with the robustness of the tenant model, we ran a TPC-C like tenant without having any TPC-C workloads in the training set. We ran the workload with five warehouses and a throttled single terminal. As expected the model labeled the tenant **DM-TS-OL**, as having medium disk access, low throughput and large operational complexity due to complex transactions.

5.2.2 *Node Model Evaluation*

In contrast to the tenant model, labeling the node training data can be substantially automated. The input to the node model is a vector of tenant model counts that are colocated on this node. The training requires observing many combinations of colocated tenant workloads. An administrator sets the parameters for determining a node's health, by determining acceptable ranges of resource consumption, such as disk IOPS or CPU consumption, and the percentile-based latency response time SLOs. With the model parameters defined and the ability to run synthetic workloads, Delphi is able to the automatically build the node model. Node models are valid for one type of hardware configuration.

Figure 5 presents average resource consumption by the node's label and Pythia's confidence of the provided label. Figure 5(a) shows the average tenant 95th percentile latency, and Figure 5(b), the average maximum percentage of CPU cycles blocked on I/O (**IO Wait**). The distribution for CPU utilization is similar to I/O, but with a sharp plateau for over labels. The corresponding graph is omitted for space. These results demonstrate that as Pythia becomes more confident about a predicted node label, the results trend

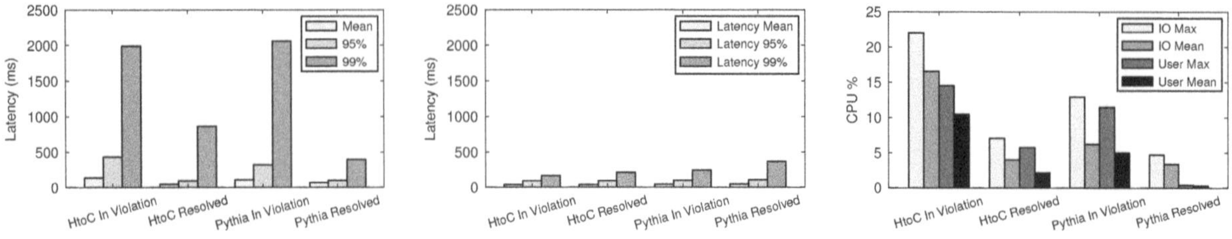

(a) Median latency for nodes experiencing SLO violations, before and after load-balancing.

(b) Median latency for nodes not initially experiencing SLO violations, before and after load-balancing.

(c) Change in CPU utilization for nodes in violation.

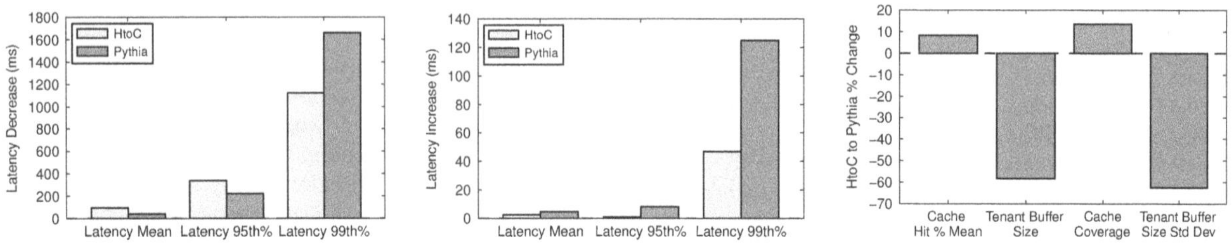

(d) Median latency decrease after crisis mitigation for nodes experiencing crisis.

(e) Median latency increase after crisis mitigation for nodes not initially in crisis.

(f) Relative differences from HtoC to Pythia's resolved state.

Figure 6: Comparing improvements to nodes in violation, and the impact on nodes not in violation

towards expected behavior. For example, as a node label increases in confidence of being over, we observe latencies, CPU utilization, and cycles blocked on I/O spike. As a node label becomes more confidently under, latencies, CPU utilization, and blocked I/O cycles decrease. These results imply that Pythia is able to predict the expected resource consumption for tenants. These figures include data collected from the experiments described in Section 5.3.

5.3 Crisis Mitigation

To evaluate Pythia's effectiveness in mitigating a performance crisis, we provide a random tenant packing with a set of nodes in violation, and initiate load-balancing to resolve the crisis. We then iteratively add new tenants to the system, which can result in new tenant violations. If any step does not contain a violation, we continue to add tenants to trigger a violation. The process is repeated until a violation cannot be resolved. We compare Pythia to a greedy baseline load-balancing algorithm **Hottest-to-Coldest (HtoC)**.

HtoC is modeled on the greedy load-balancing baseline used in the evaluation of the large scale storage system, Ursa [25]. This algorithm attempts to iteratively balance load, by moving tenants from over-loaded (hot) nodes to under-loaded (cold) nodes. Faced with a violation, non-violating nodes are inserted into a queue of possible destinations for violating tenants. The queue is sorted in descending order for excess CPU capacity (**Idle CPU**). Idle CPU capacity is a natural single metric to use for resource capacity, as non-idle cycles include cycles for the database process, kernel usage, and CPU cycles blocked on I/O. HtoC iterates through violating nodes by lowest idle cycles, and migrates one random tenant to a node removed from the head of the destination queue. This process repeats until a solution can be found, or until a maximum iteration count is reached and no solution is found. We compared moving a random tenant with moving all violating tenants, and found that a random tenant resulted in fewer violations, had lower average latencies, and resolved crisis with fewer iterations.

For this evaluation we initially assign a small uniform number (two or three) of tenants to all servers and iteratively run the following steps. Initially, all tenants are warmed up for thirty minutes, agent statistics are reset, and then collect a snapshot after running all tenants for five minutes. Delphi checks if any tenant is experiencing a performance crisis with any tenant violating performance SLOs. If no node is in violation, we distribute one new random tenant per server and repeat, starting with a new warm up. If any node is in violation, we attempt to mitigate the crisis by balancing the load through tenant migration. After the tenant repacking is executed, a snapshot is measured after warm up. This re-balancing is allowed to repeat for six iterations, if the re-packing cannot converge by then the experiment interval ends. We alternate complete incremental packing runs between Pythia and our greedy baseline load-balancing HtoC, giving both algorithms an identical list of tenants to use. We start with a low number of initial tenants, and allow each load-balancing algorithm to pack tenants incrementally to avoid using an arbitrary dense starting point that may favor one solution. This also allows both algorithms to be evaluated in light and dense tenant packings.

Because Pythia is more judicious with tenant packings, we can also use this experiment to evaluate the ability for tenant packing, or consolidation. Throughout all of these experiments, HtoC was never able to pack more tenants than Pythia. On average Pythia was able to successfully pack 71 tenants, a 45% improvement over HtoC's 49 tenants. The maximum number of tenants packed using Pythia was 80, and 64 for HtoC. We expect a larger number of tenants could have been packed for both algorithms if smaller tenants were used, durability settings were relaxed, or an array of SSDs were used. On successful load-balances, Pythia converged after 1.75 iterations, where HtoC resolved after 2.25 iterations on average. Pythia migrated an average 5.25 tenants per round, and HtoC migrated 2.25 tenants per round. One reason for increased tenants migrated is that Pythia would often shuffle tenants between non-violating nodes, in order to make capacity on ideal destinations for tenants from violating nodes.

Figure 6 demonstrates Pythia and HtoC's ability to mitigate a crisis by examining the impact of load balancing on tenant latency and resource consumption. The data here is captured from all incremental growth rounds that are successfully load-balanced. Fig-

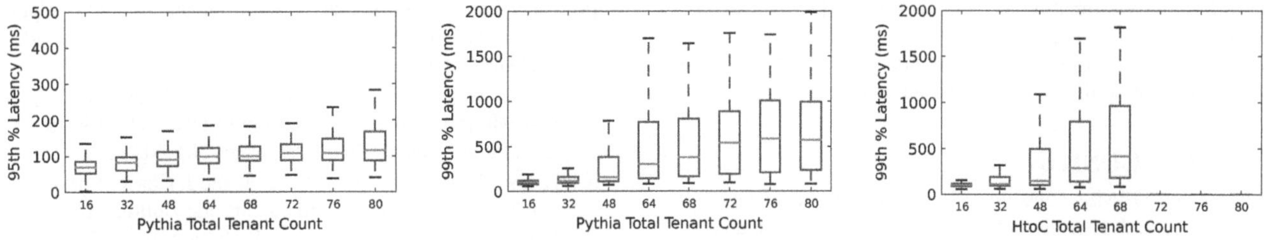

(a) Pythia 95th percentile

(b) Pythia 99th percentile

(c) HtoC 99th percentile

Figure 7: Tenant latencies by platform total tenant count.

ure 6(a) shows the before and after median tenant latencies hosted on nodes experiencing a performance crisis. Figure 6(d) shows the same data, but only the decrease in median latencies from load-balancing, instead of the before and after latencies. It is important to note, while HtoC and Pythia exhibit comparable performance gains for mean and 95th percentile latencies, Pythia decreases the 99th percentile latency by about 50% more, despite hosting 45% more tenants on average. Figures 6(b) and 6(e) show the impact of load-balancing on nodes not experiencing a SLO violation. As expected, Pythia has a larger impact on latency due to the increased number of tenants migrated from violating nodes. For both approaches, the increase in latency is small compared to the decrease in latency of violating nodes. Again, we assume that any database hosted in a multitenant environment can tolerate some variance in latency, provided latency SLOs are met. While violating latencies are similar for both approaches, Figure 6(c) shows HtoC's violating resource consumption is substantially worse than Pythia. Additionally, the resolved state for Pythia has lower CPU usage than non-violating nodes(not depicted) by 1% point on average.

A goal of load-balancing with Pythia is to implicitly consider cache impedance when matching tenants, in order to provide tenants with adequate cache access to meet latency SLOs. Figure 6(f) compares the relative differences in resource attributes between the resolved states of Pythia and HtoC. Pythia's resolved state results in a higher average tenant cache hit ratio and a higher percentage of the database that is in the page cache and buffer pool (**cache coverage**), which results in reduced disk activity for the tenants. An improvement of 13% on cache coverage and 8% on cache hit ratio alleviates a substantial amount of disk seeks, thus reducing disk contention between tenants. Interestingly, after Pythia mitigates a performance crisis, the tenants remaining on previously violating nodes have a higher cache hit ratio, a smaller average buffer size, and a lower variation in buffer size, when compared with the resolved HtoC nodes. The higher cache hit ratio combined with smaller buffer size suggests that tenants with smaller working sets remain together. The reduced variation, measured by standard deviation, means that the buffer size is more uniform, each tenant is getting a relatively equal share of the buffer pool, and that the cache is not cannibalized by dominate tenants. We therefore, conclude that Pythia is matching tenants' cache impedance when selecting the ideal packing to resolve a crisis.

To gather additional insight into the packing limits of both algorithms, we selected two successful packings of 64 tenants to grow at a smaller rate. We repeatedly grew these packings for both algorithms, by adding one tenant to four random nodes in each growth round. Pythia was able to successfully pack 72, 76, and 80 tenants; HtoC could not successfully pack beyond 68 tenants. Figure 7 shows latency distributions by total tenant count, for all successful growth rounds for both experiments described in this section. The boxplots show sampled minimum, lower quartile, median, upper quartile, and sampled maximum percentile latencies. The 95th percentile latencies for HtoC are very similar to Pythia's, so this graph is omitted. As we can see from Figure 7 the 99th percentile latencies are a primary driver for SLO violations, in both Pythia and HtoC. The sampled maximum and upper quartile latencies for HtoC rise much faster than Pythia, resulting in violations from fewer tenants. Our belief is that Pythia is optimizing packings for the 99th percentile, as most packing violations result in violations for the 99th percentile. This is a likely reason why this latency category has the biggest gains for Pythia. Experimenting with a 99th percentile latency of 10,000 ms and a 95th percentile of 500 ms, Pythia successfully packed 88 tenants, while HtoC could still not pack more than 68 tenants due to 95th percentile violations.

6. RELATED WORK

A vast corpus of research exists for problems related to Delphi's design. This includes database multitenancy, consolidation, resource orchestration, performance modeling, and crisis mitigation. Section 1.1 discusses the related work in managing multitenant DBMSs [1, 6, 14, 24]. Issues related to the design of multitenant systems are covered in Section 2.1 [3, 7, 13, 22].

Modeling resource consumption for application placement and load balancing has been successfully applied to many domains. Modeling performance of n-tiered web services has proven effective for predicting response time [20]. Regression based analytic modeling for n-tier applications has been used for capacity planning and placement, by approximating CPU demand [26]. These analytic models do not translate well for multitenant DBMS environments, due to dynamic and ad-hoc usage, and high latencies from shifting bottlenecks due to multivariate resource contention [1].

Storage systems are another domain which has utilized modeling for placement. Pesto, builds sampling-based models to understand workload performance, and load-balance I/O utilization [11]. The models are based on a linear relationship between outstanding I/O requests and latency, an assumption that does not hold for DBMSs. Similar to Pythia, Romano builds statistical models to predict workload performance, and to predict the impact of colocated workloads [16]. Load-balancing in Romano uses Simulated Annealing to avoid local maximums when finding new packing plans, and a greedy approach to minimize migrations when implementing the re-packing. Both Romano's interference models and search optimizations could extend Pythia in future work. Ursa, targets large scale storage systems by optimizing load balancing to only mitigate hot-spots and leverage topology-aware migrations to minimize re-packing costs [25]. This approach can be leveraged when migration costs are factored into Pythia.

Beyond provisioning and orchestration, Pythia's tenant model can be extended to better understand usage patterns. This can include characterizing service spikes [4], or predicting shifts in workloads [12]. Models for predicting storage consumption could extend disk-activity estimation of the tenant model [15]. In making placement decisions, additional tenant and workload combination models could improve interference prediction, when changing resource consumption limits resource-based models [8, 18].

7. CONCLUSION

Multitenant DBMSs consolidate large numbers of tenants with unpredictable and dynamic behavior. Designing a self-managing controller for such a system faces multiple challenges such as characterizing tenants, reducing the impact of colocation, adapting to changes in behavior, and detecting and mitigating a performance crisis. The complex interplay among tenants, DBMS, and the OS, as well as aggregated resource consumption measures make the task of monitoring and load balancing difficult. We designed and implemented Delphi, a self-managing controller for a multitenant DBMS that monitors and models tenant behavior, ensures latency SLOs, and mitigates performance crises without requiring major modifications to existing systems. Delphi leverages Pythia, a technique to classify tenant behavior, and learn good tenant packings. Pythia does not make assumptions about the tenant workloads or the underlying DBMS and OS implementations. Our analysis revealed unexpected interactions arising from tenant colocation and identified tenant behavior that are most sensitive to resource starvation. Our experiments, using a variety of tenant types and workloads, demonstrated that Pythia can learn a tenant's behavior with more than 92% accuracy and learn quality of packings with more than 86% accuracy. Using Pythia, Delphi can mitigate a performance crisis by selectively migrating tenants to improve 99th percentile response times by 80%.

Acknowledgments

The authors thank Neil Conway, Ken Salem, Jon Walker, Zhengkui Wang, Jerry Zheng, and the anonymous reviewers for providing useful feedback. This work is partly funded by NSF grants III 1018637, IIS 0905084, CNS 1053594, and NEC Labs America.

8. REFERENCES

[1] M. Ahmad and I. T. Bowman. Predicting system performance for multi-tenant database workloads. In *ACM DBTest*, pages 1–6, 2011.

[2] Personal communications with Jerry Zheng, VP Web Operations at AppFolio Inc., April 2011.

[3] P. A. Bernstein, I. Cseri, N. Dani, N. Ellis, A. Kalhan, G. Kakivaya, D. B. Lomet, R. Manner, L. Novik, and T. Talius. Adapting Microsoft SQL Server for Cloud Computing. In *ICDE*, pages 1255–1263, 2011.

[4] P. Bodík, A. Fox, M. J. Franklin, M. I. Jordan, and D. A. Patterson. Characterizing, modeling, and generating workload spikes for stateful services. In *SoCC*, pages 241–252, 2010.

[5] B. F. Cooper, A. Silberstein, E. Tam, R. Ramakrishnan, and R. Sears. Benchmarking Cloud Serving Systems with YCSB. In *SoCC*, pages 143–154, 2010.

[6] C. Curino, E. Jones, S. Madden, and H. Balakrishnan. Workload-Aware Database Monitoring and Consolidation. In *SIGMOD*, 2011.

[7] C. Curino, E. Jones, R. Popa, N. Malviya, E. Wu, S. Madden, H. Balakrishnan, and N. Zeldovich. Relational Cloud: A Database Service for the Cloud. In *CIDR*, pages 235–240, 2011.

[8] J. Duggan, U. Cetintemel, O. Papaemmanouil, and E. Upfal. Performance prediction for concurrent database workloads. In *SIGMOD*, pages 337–348, 2011.

[9] A. J. Elmore, S. Das, D. Agrawal, and A. El Abbadi. Zephyr: Live Migration in Shared Nothing Databases for Elastic Cloud Platforms. In *SIGMOD*, pages 301–312, 2011.

[10] L. Grit, D. Irwin, A. Yumerefendi, and J. Chase. Virtual machine hosting for networked clusters: Building the foundations for 'autonomic' orchestration. In *VTDC*, 2006.

[11] A. Gulati, G. Shanmuganathan, I. Ahmad, C. Waldspurger, and M. Uysal. Pesto: online storage performance management in virtualized datacenters. In *SOCC*, pages 19:1–19:14, 2011.

[12] M. Holze, A. Haschimi, and N. Ritter. Towards workload-aware self-management: Predicting significant workload shifts. In *ICDE Workshops*, pages 111 –116, 2010.

[13] D. Jacobs and S. Aulbach. Ruminations on multi-tenant databases. In *BTW*, pages 514–521, 2007.

[14] W. Lang, S. Shankar, J. Patel, and A. Kalhan. Towards multi-tenant performance slos. In *ICDE*, pages 702–713, 2012.

[15] O. Ozmen, K. Salem, M. Uysal, and M. H. S. Attar. Storage workload estimation for database management systems. In *SIGMOD*, pages 377–388, 2007.

[16] N. Park, I. Ahmad, and D. J. Lilja. Romano: autonomous storage management using performance prediction in multi-tenant datacenters. In *SoCC*, pages 21:1–21:14, 2012.

[17] S. J. Russell and P. Norvig. *Artificial Intelligence: A Modern Approach*. Prentice Hall, 3rd edition, 2009.

[18] M. B. Sheikh, U. F. Minhas, O. Z. Khan, A. Aboulnaga, P. Poupart, and D. J. Taylor. A bayesian approach to online performance modeling for database appliances using gaussian models. In *ICAC*, pages 121–130. ACM, 2011.

[19] G. Soundararajan, D. Lupei, S. Ghanbari, A. D. Popescu, J. Chen, and C. Amza. Dynamic resource allocation for database servers running on virtual storage. In *FAST*, pages 71–84, 2009.

[20] C. Stewart and K. Shen. Performance modeling and system management for multi-component online services. In *NSDI*, pages 71–84, 2005.

[21] B. Urgaonkar, P. Shenoy, and T. Roscoe. Resource overbooking and application profiling in shared hosting platforms. In *OSDI*, pages 239–254, 2002.

[22] C. D. Weissman and S. Bobrowski. The design of the force.com multitenant internet application development platform. In *SIGMOD*, pages 889–896, 2009.

[23] I. H. Witten and E. Frank. *Data Mining: Practical Machine Learning Tools and Techniques*. Data Management Systems. Morgan Kaufmann Publishers Inc., second edition, 2005.

[24] P. Xiong, Y. Chi, S. Zhu, H. J. Moon, C. Pu, and H. Hacigümüs. Intelligent management of virtualized resources for database systems in cloud environment. In *ICDE*, pages 87–98, 2011.

[25] G.-w. You, S.-w. Hwang, and N. Jain. Scalable load balancing in cluster storage systems. In *Middleware*, pages 101–122, 2011.

[26] Q. Zhang, L. Cherkasova, and E. Smirni. A regression-based analytic model for dynamic resource provisioning of multi-tier applications. In *ICAC*, pages 27–, 2007.

Minimal MapReduce Algorithms

Yufei Tao[1,2] Wenqing Lin[3] Xiaokui Xiao[3]

[1]Chinese University of Hong Kong, Hong Kong
[2]Korea Advanced Institute of Science and Technology, Korea
[3]Nanyang Technological University, Singapore

ABSTRACT

MapReduce has become a dominant parallel computing paradigm for *big data*, i.e., colossal datasets at the scale of tera-bytes or higher. Ideally, a MapReduce system should achieve a high degree of load balancing among the participating machines, and minimize the space usage, CPU and I/O time, and network transfer at each machine. Although these principles have guided the development of MapReduce algorithms, limited emphasis has been placed on enforcing serious constraints on the aforementioned metrics simultaneously. This paper presents the notion of *minimal algorithm*, that is, an algorithm that guarantees the best parallelization in multiple aspects at the same time, up to a small constant factor. We show the existence of elegant minimal algorithms for a set of fundamental database problems, and demonstrate their excellent performance with extensive experiments.

Categories and Subject Descriptors

F2.2 [**Analysis of algorithms and problem complexity**]: Nonnumerical algorithms and problems

Keywords

Minimal algorithm, MapReduce, big data

1. INTRODUCTION

We are in an era of information explosion, where industry, academia, and governments are accumulating data at an unprecedentedly high speed. This brings forward the urgent need of *big data processing*, namely, fast computation over colossal datasets whose sizes can reach the order of tera-bytes or higher. In recent years, the database community has responded to this grand challenge by building massive parallel computing platforms which use hundreds or even thousands of commodity machines. The most notable platform, which has attracted a significant amount of research attention, is *MapReduce*.

Since its invention [16], MapReduce has gone through years of improvement into a mature paradigm (see Section 2 for a review). At a high level, a MapReduce system involves a number of share-nothing machines which communicate only by sending messages over the network. A MapReduce algorithm instructs these machines to perform a computational task collaboratively. Initially, the input dataset is distributed across the machines, typically in a non-replicate manner, i.e., each object on one machine. The algorithm executes in *rounds* (sometimes also called *jobs* in the literature), each having three phases: *map*, *shuffle*, and *reduce*. The first two enable the machines to exchange data: in the map phase, each machine prepares the information to be delivered to other machines, while the shuffle phase takes care of the actual data transfer. No network communication occurs in the reduce phase, where each machine performs calculation from its local storage. The current round finishes after the reduce phase. If the computational task has not completed, another round starts.

Motivation. As with traditional parallel computing, a MapReduce system aims at a high degree of load balancing, and the minimization of space, CPU, I/O, and network costs at each individual machine. Although these principles have guided the design of MapReduce algorithms, the previous practices have mostly been on a best-effort basis, paying relatively less attention to enforcing serious constraints on different performance metrics. This work aims to remedy the situation by studying algorithms that promise outstanding efficiency in multiple aspects simultaneously.

Minimal MapReduce Algorithms. Denote by S the set of input objects for the underlying problem. Let n, the *problem cardinality*, be the number of objects in S, and t be the number of machines used in the system. Define $m = n/t$, namely, m is the number of objects per machine when S is evenly distributed across the machines. Consider an algorithm for solving a problem on S. We say that the algorithm is *minimal* if it has all of the following properties.

- *Minimum footprint:* at all times, each machine uses only $O(m)$ space of storage.
- *Bounded net-traffic:* in each round, every machine sends and receives at most $O(m)$ words of information over the network.
- *Constant round:* the algorithm must terminate after a constant number of rounds.
- *Optimal computation:* every machine performs only $O(T_{seq}/t)$ amount of computation *in total* (i.e., summing over all rounds), where T_{seq} is the time needed to solve the same problem on a single sequential machine. Namely, the algorithm should achieve a speedup of t by using t machines in parallel.

It is fairly intuitive why minimal algorithms are appealing. First, *minimum footprint* ensures that, each machine keeps $O(1/t)$ of the

SIGMOD'13, June 22–27, 2013, New York, New York, USA.

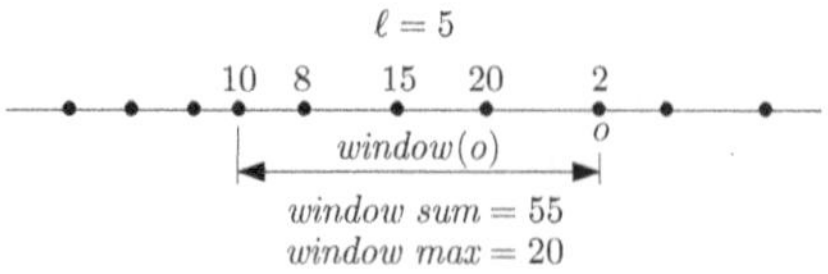

Figure 1: Sliding aggregates

dataset S at any moment. This effectively prevents *partition skew*, where some machines are forced to handle considerably more than m objects, as is a major cause of inefficiency in MapReduce [36].

Second, *bounded net-traffic* guarantees that, the shuffle phase of each round transfers at most $O(m \cdot t) = O(n)$ words of network traffic overall. The duration of the phase equals roughly the time for a machine to send and receive $O(m)$ words, because the data transfers to/from different machines are in parallel. Furthermore, this property is also useful when one wants to make an algorithm *stateless* for the purpose of fault tolerance, as discussed in Section 2.1.

The third property *constant round* is not new, as it has been the goal of many previous MapReduce algorithms. Importantly, this and the previous properties imply that there can be only $O(n)$ words of network traffic during the *entire* algorithm. Finally, *optimal computation* echoes the very original motivation of MapReduce to accomplish a computational task t times faster than leveraging only one machine.

Contributions. The core of this work comprises of neat minimal algorithms for two problems:

Sorting. The input is a set S of n objects drawn from an ordered domain. When the algorithm terminates, all the objects must have been distributed across the t machines in a sorted fashion. That is, we can order the machines from 1 to t such that all objects in machine i precede those in machine j for all $1 \leq i < j \leq t$.

Sliding Aggregation. The input includes

- a set S of n objects from an ordered domain, where every object $o \in S$ is associated with a numeric *weight*
- an integer $\ell \leq n$
- and a distributive aggregate function AGG (e.g., *sum*, *max*, *min*).

Denote by $window(o)$ the set of ℓ largest objects in S not exceeding o. The *window aggregate* of o is the result of applying AGG to the weights of the objects in $window(o)$. The *sliding aggregation problem* is to report the window aggregate of every object in S.

Figure 1 illustrates an example where $\ell = 5$. Each black dot represents an object in S. Some relevant weights are given on top of the corresponding objects. For the object o as shown, its window aggregate is 55 and 20 for AGG = *sum* and *max*, respectively.

The significance of sorting is obvious: a minimal algorithm for this problem leads to minimal algorithms for several fundamental database problems, including *ranking*, *group-by*, *semi-join* and *skyline*, as we will discuss in this paper.

The importance of the second problem probably deserves a bit more explanation. Sliding aggregates are crucial in studying time series. For example, consider a time series that records the Nasdaq index in history, with one value per minute. It makes good senses to examine *moving statistics*, that is, statistics aggregated from a sliding window. For example, a *6-month average/maximum* with respect to a day equals the average/maximum Nasdaq index in a 6-month period ending on that very day. The 6-month averages/maximums of *all* days can be obtained by solving a sliding aggregation problem (note that an average can be calculated by dividing a window sum by the period length ℓ).

Sorting and sliding aggregation can both be settled in $O(n \log n)$ time on a sequential computer. There has been progress in developing MapReduce algorithms for sorting. The state of the art is *TeraSort* [50], which won the Jim Gray's benchmark contest in 2009. *TeraSort* comes close to being minimal when a crucial parameter is set appropriately. As will be clear later, the algorithm requires manual tuning of the parameter, an improper choice of which can incur severe performance penalty. Sliding aggregation has also been studied in MapReduce by Beyer et al. [6]. However, as explained shortly, the algorithm is far from being minimal, and is efficient only when the window length ℓ is short – the authors of [6] commented that this problem is "notoriously difficult".

Technical Overview. This work was initialized by an attempt to justify theoretically why *TeraSort* often achieves excellent sorting time with only 2 rounds. In the first round, the algorithm extracts a random sample set S_{samp} of the input S, and then picks $t - 1$ sampled objects as the *boundary objects*. Conceptually, these boundary objects divide S into t segments. In the second round, each of the t machines acquires all the objects in a distinct segment, and sorts them. The size of S_{samp} is the key to efficiency. If S_{samp} is too small, the boundary objects may be insufficiently scattered, which can cause partition skew in the second round. Conversely, an over-sized S_{samp} entails expensive sampling overhead. In the standard implementation of *TeraSort*, the sample size is left as a parameter, although it always seems to admit a good choice that gives outstanding performance [50].

In this paper, we provide rigorous explanation for the above phenomenon. Our theoretical analysis clarifies how to set the size of S_{samp} to guarantee the minimality of *TeraSort*. In the meantime, we also remedy a conceptual drawback of *TeraSort*. As elaborated later, strictly speaking, this algorithm does not fit in the MapReduce framework, because it requires that (besides network messages) the machines should be able to communicate by reading/writing a common (distributed) file. Once this is disabled, the algorithm requires one more round. We present an elegant fix so that the algorithm still terminates in 2 rounds even by strictly adhering to MapReduce. Our findings of *TeraSort* have immediate practical significance, given the essential role of sorting in a large number of MapReduce programs.

Regarding sliding aggregation, the difficulty lies in that ℓ is not a constant, but can be any value up to n. Intuitively, when $\ell \gg m$, $window(o)$ is so large that the objects in $window(o)$ cannot be found on one machine under the *minimum footprint* constraint. Instead, $window(o)$ would potentially span many machines, making it essential to coordinate the searching of machines judiciously to avoid a disastrous cost blowup. In fact, this pitfall has captured the existing algorithm of [6], whose main idea is to ensure that *every* sliding window be sent to a machine for aggregation (various windows may go to different machines). This suffers from prohibitive communication and processing cost when the window length ℓ is long. Our algorithm, on the other hand, achieves minimality with a novel idea of *perfectly* balancing the input objects across the machines while still maintaining their sorted order.

Outline. Section 2 reviews the previous work related to ours. Section 3 analyzes *TeraSort* and modifies it into a minimal algorithm, which Section 4 deploys to solve a set of fundamental problems minimally. Section 5 gives our minimal algorithm for the sliding aggregation problem. Section 6 evaluates the practical efficiency of the proposed techniques with extensive experiments. Finally, Section 7 concludes the paper with a summary of findings.

2. PRELIMINARY AND RELATED WORK

In Section 2.1, we expand the MapReduce introduction in Section 1 with more details to pave the way for our discussion. Section 2.2 reviews the existing studies on MapReduce, while Section 2.3 points out the relevance of minimal algorithms to the previous work.

2.1 MapReduce

As explained earlier, a MapReduce algorithm proceeds in *rounds*, where each round has three phases: *map*, *shuffle*, and *reduce*. As all machines execute a program in the same way, next we focus on one specific machine $\mathcal{M}$.

Map. In this phase, $\mathcal{M}$ generates a list of key-value pairs (k, v) from its local storage. While the key k is usually numeric, the value v can contain arbitrary information. As clarified shortly, the pair (k, v) will be transmitted to another machine in the shuffle phase, such that the recipient machine is determined *solely* by k.

Shuffle. Let L be the list of key-value pairs that all the machines produced in the map phase. The shuffle phase distributes L across the machines adhering to the constraint that, pairs with the same key must be delivered to the same machine. That is, if $(k, v_1), (k, v_2), ..., (k, v_x)$ are the pairs in L having a common key k, all of them will arrive at an identical machine.

Reduce. $\mathcal{M}$ incorporates the key-value pairs received from the previous phase into its local storage. Then, it carries out whatever processing as needed on its local data. After all machines have completed the reduce phase, the current round terminates.

Discussion. It is clear from the above that, the machines communicate only in the shuffle phase, whereas in the other phases each machine executes the algorithm sequentially, focusing on its own storage. Overall, parallel computing happens mainly in reduce. The major role of map and shuffle is to swap data among the machines, so that computation can take place on different combinations of objects.

Simplified View for Our Algorithms. Let us number the t machines of the MapReduce system arbitrarily from 1 to t. In the map phase, all our algorithms will adopt the convention that $\mathcal{M}$ *generates a key-value pair* (k, v) *if and only if it wants to send* v *to machine* k. In other words, the key field is explicitly the id of the recipient machine.

This convention admits a conceptually simpler modeling. In describing our algorithms, we will combine the map and shuffle phases into one called *map-shuffle*. By saying succinctly that "*in the map-shuffle phase,* $\mathcal{M}$ *delivers* v *to machine* k", we mean that $\mathcal{M}$ creates (k, v) in the map phase, which is then transmitted to machine k in the shuffle phase. The equivalence also explains why the simplification is only at the logical level, while physically all our algorithms are still implemented in the standard MapReduce paradigm.

Statelessness for Fault Tolerance. Some MapReduce implementations (e.g., Hadoop) place the requirement that, at the end of a round, each machine should send all the data in its storage to a *distributed file system* (DFS), which in our context can be understood as a "disk in the cloud" that guarantees consistent storage (i.e., it never fails). The objective is to improve the system's robustness in the scenario where a machine collapses during the algorithm's execution. In such a case, the system can replace this machine with another one, ask the new machine to load the storage of the old machine at the end of the previous round, and re-do the current round (where the machine failure occurred). Such a system is called *stateless* because intuitively no machine is responsible for remembering any state of the algorithm [58].

The four minimality conditions defined in Section 1 ensure efficient enforcement of statelessness. In particular, *minimum footprint* guarantees that, at each round, every machine sends $O(m)$ words to the DFS, as is still consistent with *bounded traffic*.

2.2 Previous Research on MapReduce

The existing investigation on MapReduce can be coarsely classified into two categories, which focus on improving the internal working of the framework, and employing MapReduce to solve concrete problems, respectively. In the sequel, we survey each category separately.

Framework Implementation. *Hadoop* is perhaps the most popular open-source implementation of MapReduce nowadays. It was first described by Abouzeid et al. [1], and has been improved significantly by the collective findings of many studies. Specifically, Dittrich et al. [18] provided various user-defined functions that can substantially reduce the running time of MapReduce programs. Nykiel et al. [47], Elghandour and Agoulnaga [19] achieved further performance gains by allowing a subsequent round of an algorithm to re-use the outputs of the previous rounds. Eltabakh et al. [20] and He et al. [27] discussed the importance of keeping relevant data at the same machine in order to reduce network traffic. Floratou et al. [22] presented a column-based implementation and demonstrated superior performance in certain environments. Shinnar et al. [53] proposed to eliminate disk I/Os by fitting data in memory as much as possible. Gufler et al. [26], Kolb et al. [33], and Kwon et al. [36] designed methods to rectify *skewness*, i.e., imbalance in the workload of different machines.

Progress has been made towards building an *execution optimizer* that can automatically coordinate different components of the system for the best overall efficiency. The approach of Herodotou and Babu [28] is based on profiling the cost of a MapReduce program. Jahani et al. [29] proposed a strategy that works by analyzing the programming logic of MapReduce codes. Lim et al. [40] focused on optimizing as a whole multiple MapReduce programs that are interconnected by a variety of factors.

There has also been development of administration tools for MapReduce systems. Lang and Patel [37] suggested strategies for minimizing energy consumption. Morton et al. [46] devised techniques for estimating the progress (in completion percentage) of a MapReduce program. Khoussainova et al. [32] presented a mechanism to facilitate the debugging of MapReduce programs.

MapReduce, which after all is a computing framework, lacks many features of a database. One, in particular, is an expressive language that allows users to describe queries supportable by MapReduce. To fill this void, a number of languages have been designed, together with the corresponding *translators* that convert a query to a MapReduce program. Examples include SCOPE [9], Pig [49], Dremel [43], HIVE [55], Jaql [6], Tenzing [10], and SystemML [24].

Algorithms on MapReduce. Considerable work has been devoted to processing joins on relational data. Blanas et al. [7] compared the implementations of traditional join algorithms in MapReduce. Afrati and Ullman [3] provided specialized algorithms for multiway equi-joins. Lin et al. [41] tackled the same problem utilizing column-based storage. Okcan and Riedewald [48] devised algorithms for reporting the cartesian product of two tables. Zhang et al. [62] discussed efficient processing of multiway theta-joins.

Regarding joins on non-relational data, Vernica et al. [59], Metwally and Faloutsos [44] studied *set-similarity join*. Afrati et al. [2] re-visited this problem and its variants under the constraint that an algorithm must terminate in a single round. Lu et al. [42], on the other hand, investigated *k nearest neighbor join* in Euclidean space.

MapReduce has been proven useful for processing massive graphs. Suri, Vassilvitskii [54], and Tsourakakis et al. [56] considered *triangle counting*, Morales et al. [45] dealt with *b-matching*, Bahmani et al. [5] focused on the discovery of *densest subgraphs*, Karloff et al. [31] analyzed computing connected components and spanning trees, while Lattanzi et al. [39] studied *maximal matching*, *vertex/edge cover*, and *minimum cut*.

Data mining and statistical analysis are also popular topics on MapReduce. Clustering was investigated by Das et al. [15], Cordeiro et al. [13], and Ene et al. [21]. Classification and regression were studied by Panda et al. [51]. Ghoting et al. [23] developed an integrated toolkit to facilitate machine learning tasks. Pansare et al. [52] and Laptev et al. [38] explained how to compute aggregates over a gigantic file. Grover and Carey [25] focused on extracting a set of samples satisfying a given predicate. Chen [11] described techniques for supporting operations of data warehouses.

Among the other algorithmic studies on MapReduce, Chierichetti et al. [12] attacked approximation versions of the *set cover problem*. Wang et al. [60] described algorithms for the simulation of real-world events. Bahmani et al. [4] proposed methods for calculating personalized page ranks. Jestes et al. [30] investigated the construction of wavelet histograms.

2.3 Relevance to Minimal Algorithms

Our study of minimal algorithms is orthogonal to the *framework implementation* category as mentioned in Section 2.2. Even a minimal algorithm can benefit from clever optimization at the system level. On the other hand, a minimal algorithm may considerably simplify optimization. For instance, as the minimal requirements already guarantee excellent load balancing in storage, computation, and communication, there would be little skewness to deserve specialized optimization. As another example, the cost of a minimal algorithm is by definition highly predictable, which is a precious advantage appreciated by cost-based optimizers (e.g., [28, 40]).

This work belongs to the *algorithms on MapReduce* category. However, besides dealing with different problems, we also differ from the existing studies in that we emphasize on an algorithm's minimality. Remember that the difficulty of designing a minimal algorithm lies in excelling in *all* the four aspects (see Section 1) at the same time. Often times, it is easy to do well in only certain aspects (e.g., *constant rounds*), while losing out in the rest. Parallel algorithms on classic platforms are typically compared under multiple metrics. We believe that MapReduce should not be an exception.

From a theoretical perspective, minimal algorithms are reminiscent of algorithms under the *bulk synchronous parallel* (BSP) *model* [57] and *coarse-grained multicomputer* (CGM) *model* [17]. Both models are well-studied branches of theoretical parallel computing. Our algorithmic treatment, however, is system oriented, i.e., easy to implement, while offering excellent performance in practice. In contrast, theoretical solutions in BSP/CGM are often rather involved, and usually carry large hidden constants in their complexities, not to mention that they are yet to be migrated to MapReduce. It is worth mentioning that there has been work on extending the MapReduce framework to enhance its power so as to solve difficult problems efficiently. We refer the interested readers to the recent work of [34].

3. SORTING

In the *sorting problem*, the input is a set S of n objects from an ordered domain. For simplicity, we assume that objects are real values because our discussion easily generalizes to other ordered domains. Denote by $\mathcal{M}_1, ..., \mathcal{M}_t$ the machines in the MapReduce system. Initially, S is distributed across these machines, each storing $O(m)$ objects where $m = n/t$. At the end of sorting, all objects in $\mathcal{M}_i$ must precede those in $\mathcal{M}_j$ for any $1 \le i < j \le t$.

3.1 TeraSort

Parameterized by $\rho \in (0, 1]$, *TeraSort* [50] runs as follows:

Round 1. *Map-shuffle*(ρ)

Every $\mathcal{M}_i$ ($1 \le i \le t$) samples each object from its local storage with probability ρ independently. It sends all the sampled objects to $\mathcal{M}_1$.

Reduce (only on $\mathcal{M}_1$)

1. Let S_{samp} be the set of samples received by $\mathcal{M}_1$, and $s = |S_{samp}|$.
2. Sort S_{samp}, and pick $b_1, ..., b_{t-1}$ where b_i is the $i\lceil s/t \rceil$-th smallest object in S_{samp}, for $1 \le i \le t-1$. Each b_i is a *boundary object*.

Round 2. *Map-shuffle* (assumption: $b_1, ..., b_{t-1}$ have been sent to all machines)

Every $\mathcal{M}_i$ sends the objects in $(b_{j-1}, b_j]$ from its local storage to $\mathcal{M}_j$, for each $1 \le j \le t$, where $b_0 = -\infty$ and $b_t = \infty$ are dummy boundary objects.

Reduce:

Every $\mathcal{M}_i$ sorts the objects received in the previous phase.

For convenience, the above description sometimes asks a machine $\mathcal{M}$ to send data to itself. Needless to say, such data "transfer" occurs internally in $\mathcal{M}$, with no network transmission. Also note the assumption at the map-shuffle phase of Round 2, which we call the *broadcast assumption*, and will deal with later in Section 3.3.

In [50], ρ was left as an open parameter. Next, we analyze the setting of this value to make *TeraSort* a minimal algorithm.

3.2 Choice of ρ

Define $S_i = S \cap (b_{i-1}, b_i]$, for $1 \le i \le t$. In Round 2, all the objects in S_i are gathered by $\mathcal{M}_i$, which sorts them in the reduce phase. For *TeraSort* to be minimal, it must hold:

$\mathcal{P}_1$. $s = O(m)$.
$\mathcal{P}_2$. $|S_i| = O(m)$ for all $1 \le i \le t$.

Specifically, $\mathcal{P}_1$ is because $\mathcal{M}_1$ receives $O(s)$ objects over the network in the map-shuffle phase of Round 1, which has to be $O(m)$ to satisfy *bounded net-traffic* (see Section 1). $\mathcal{P}_2$ is because

$\mathcal{M}_i$ must receive and store $O(|S_i|)$ words in Round 2, which needs to be $O(m)$ to qualify *bounded net-traffic* and *minimum footprint*.

We now establish an important fact about *TeraSort*:

THEOREM 1. *When $m \geq t\ln(nt)$, $\mathcal{P}_1$ and $\mathcal{P}_2$ hold simultaneously with probability at least $1 - O(\frac{1}{n})$ by setting $\rho = \frac{1}{m}\ln(nt)$.*

PROOF. We will consider $t \geq 9$ because otherwise $m = \Omega(n)$, in which case $\mathcal{P}_1$ and $\mathcal{P}_2$ hold trivially. Our proof is based on the Chernoff bound[1] and an interesting bucketing argument.

First, it is easy to see that $\mathbf{E}[s] = m\rho t = t\ln(nt)$. A simple application of Chernoff bound results in:

$$\mathbf{Pr}[s \geq 1.6 \cdot t\ln(nt)] \leq \exp(-0.12 \cdot t\ln(nt)) \leq 1/n$$

where the last inequality used the fact that $t \geq 9$. The above implies that $\mathcal{P}_1$ can fail with probability at most $1/n$. Next, we analyze $\mathcal{P}_2$ under the event $s < 1.6t\ln(nt) = O(m)$.

Imagine that S has been sorted in ascending order. We divide the sorted list into $\lfloor t/8 \rfloor$ sub-lists as evenly as possible, and call each sub-list a *bucket*. Each bucket has between $8n/t = 8m$ and $16m$ objects. We observe that $\mathcal{P}_2$ *holds if every bucket covers at least one boundary object*. To understand why, notice that under this condition, no bucket can fall between two consecutive boundary objects (counting also the dummy ones)[2]. Hence, every S_i, $1 \leq i \leq t$, can contain objects in at most 2 buckets, i.e., $|S_i| \leq 32m = O(m)$.

A bucket β definitely includes a boundary object if β covers more than $1.6\ln(nt) > s/t$ samples (i.e., objects from S_{samp}), as a boundary object is taken every $\lceil s/t \rceil$ consecutive samples. Let $|\beta| \geq 8m$ be the number of objects in β. Define random variable x_j, $1 \leq j \leq |\beta|$, to be 1 if the j-th object in β is sampled, and 0 otherwise. Define:

$$X = \sum_{j=1}^{|\beta|} x_j = |\beta \cap S_{samp}|.$$

Clearly, $\mathbf{E}[X] \geq 8m\rho = 8\ln(nt)$. We have:

$$\begin{aligned}
\mathbf{Pr}[X \leq 1.6\ln(nt)] &= \mathbf{Pr}[X \leq (1-4/5)8\ln(nt)] \\
&\leq \mathbf{Pr}[X \leq (1-4/5)\mathbf{E}[X]] \\
\text{(by Chernoff)} &\leq \exp\left(-\frac{16}{25}\frac{\mathbf{E}[X]}{3}\right) \\
&\leq \exp\left(-\frac{16}{25} \cdot \frac{8\ln(nt)}{3}\right) \\
&\leq \exp(-\ln(nt)) \\
&\leq 1/(nt).
\end{aligned}$$

We say that β *fails* if it covers no boundary object. The above derivation shows that β fails with probability at most $1/(nt)$. As there are at most $t/8$ buckets, the probability that at least one bucket fails is at most $1/(8n)$. Hence, $\mathcal{P}_2$ can be violated with probability at most $1/(8n)$ under the event $s < 1.6t\ln(nt)$, i.e., at most $9/8n$ overall.

Therefore, $\mathcal{P}_1$ and $\mathcal{P}_2$ hold at the same time with probability at least $1 - 17/(8n)$. □

[1]Let $X_1, ..., X_n$ be independent Bernoulli variables with $\mathbf{Pr}[X_i = 1] = p_i$, for $1 \leq i \leq n$. Set $X = \sum_{i=1}^{n} X_i$ and $\mu = \mathbf{E}[X] = \sum_{i=1}^{n} p_i$. The Chernoff bound states (i) for any $0 < \alpha < 1$, $\mathbf{Pr}[X \geq (1+\alpha)\mu] \leq \exp(-\alpha^2\mu/3)$ while $\mathbf{Pr}[X \leq (1-\alpha)\mu] \leq \exp(-\alpha^2\mu/3)$, and (ii) $\mathbf{Pr}[X \geq 6\mu] \leq 2^{-6\mu}$.

[2]If there was one, the bucket would not be able to cover any boundary object.

Discussion. For large n, the success probability $1 - O(1/n)$ in Theorem 1 is so high that the failure probability $O(1/n)$ is negligible, i.e., $\mathcal{P}_1$ and $\mathcal{P}_2$ are almost never violated.

The condition about m in Theorem 1 is tight within a logarithmic factor because $m \geq t$ is an implicit condition for *TeraSort* to work, noticing that both the reduce phase of Round 1 and the map-shuffle phase of Round 2 require a machine to store $t-1$ boundary objects.

In reality, typically $m \gg t$, namely, the memory size of a machine is significantly greater than the number of machines. More specifically, m is at the order of at least 10^6 (this is using only a few *mega* bytes per machine), while t is at the order of 10^4 or lower. Therefore, $m \geq t\ln(nt)$ is a (very) reasonable assumption, which explains why *TeraSort* has excellent efficiency in practice.

Minimality. We now establish the minimality of *TeraSort*, temporarily ignoring how to fulfill the broadcast assumption. Properties $\mathcal{P}_1$ and $\mathcal{P}_2$ indicate that each machine needs to store only $O(m)$ objects at any time, consistent with *minimum footprint*. Regarding the network cost, a machine $\mathcal{M}$ in each round sends only objects that were already on $\mathcal{M}$ when the algorithm started. Hence, $\mathcal{M}$ sends $O(m)$ network data per round. Furthermore, $\mathcal{M}_1$ receives only $O(m)$ objects by $\mathcal{P}_1$. Therefore, *bounded-bandwidth* is fulfilled. *Constant round* is obviously satisfied. Finally, the computation time of each machine $\mathcal{M}_i$ ($1 \leq i \leq t$) is dominated by the cost of sorting S_i in Round 2, i.e., $O(m\log m) = O(\frac{n}{t}\log n)$ by $\mathcal{P}_2$. As this is $1/t$ of the $O(n\log n)$ time of a sequential algorithm, *optimal computation* is also achieved.

3.3 Removing the Broadcast Assumption

Before Round 2 of *TeraSort*, $\mathcal{M}_1$ needs to *broadcast* the boundary objects $b_1, ..., b_{t-1}$ to the other machines. We have to be careful because a naive solution would ask $\mathcal{M}_1$ to send $O(t)$ words to every other machine, and hence, incur $O(t^2)$ network traffic overall. This not only requires one more round, but also violates *bounded net-traffic* if t exceeds $\sqrt{m}$ by a non-constant factor.

In [50], this issue was circumvented by assuming that all the machines can access a distributed file system. In this scenario, $\mathcal{M}_1$ can simply write the boundary objects to a file on that system, after which each M_i, $2 \leq i \leq t$, gets them from the file. In other words, a brute-force *file accessing step* is inserted between the two rounds. This is allowed by the current Hadoop implementation (on which *TeraSort* was based [50]).

Technically, however, the above approach destroys the elegance of *TeraSort* because it requires that, besides sending key-value pairs to each other, the machines should also communicate via a distributed file. This implies that the machines are not share-*nothing* because they are essentially sharing the file. Furthermore, as far as this paper is concerned, the artifact is inconsistent with the definition of minimal algorithms. As sorting lingers in all the problems to be discussed later, we are motivated to remove the artifact to keep our analytical framework clean.

We now provide an elegant remedy, which allows *TeraSort* to still terminate in 2 rounds, and retain its minimality. The idea is to give *all* machines a copy of S_{samp}. Specifically, we modify Round 1 of *TeraSort* as:

Round 1. *Map-shuffle*(ρ)

After sampling as in *TeraSort*, each $\mathcal{M}_i$ sends its sampled objects to all machines (not just to $\mathcal{M}_1$).

Reduce

Same as *TeraSort* but performed on all machines (not just on $\mathcal{M}_1$).

Round 2 still proceeds as before. The correctness follows from the fact that, in the reduce phase, every machine picks boundary objects in exactly the same way from an identical S_{samp}. Therefore, all machines will obtain the same boundary objects, thus eliminating the need of broadcasting. Henceforth, we will call the modified algorithm *pure TeraSort*.

At first glance, the new map-shuffle phase of Round 1 may seem to require a machine $\mathcal{M}$ to send out considerable data, because every sample necessitates $O(t)$ words of network traffic (i.e., $O(1)$ to every other machine). However, as every object is sampled with probability $\rho = \frac{1}{m}\ln(nt)$, the number of words sent by $\mathcal{M}$ is only $O(m \cdot t \cdot \rho) = O(t\ln(nt))$ in expectation. The lemma below gives a much stronger fact:

LEMMA 1. *With probability at least* $1-\frac{1}{n}$, *every machine sends* $O(t\ln(nt))$ *words over the network in Round 1 of pure TeraSort.*

PROOF. Consider an arbitrary machine $\mathcal{M}$. Let random variable X be the number of objects sampled from $\mathcal{M}$. Hence, $\mathbf{E}[X] = m\rho = \ln(nt)$. A straightforward application of Chernoff bound gives:

$$\mathbf{Pr}[X \geq 6\ln(nt)] \leq 2^{-6\ln(nt)} \leq 1/(nt).$$

Hence, $\mathcal{M}$ sends more than $O(t\ln(nt))$ words in Round 1 with probability at most $1/(nt)$. By union bound, the probability that this is true for all t machines is at least $1 - 1/n$. □

Combining the above lemma with Theorem 1 and the minimality analysis in Section 3.2, we can see that *pure TeraSort* is a minimal algorithm with probability at least $1-O(1/n)$ when $m \geq t\ln(nt)$.

We close this section by pointing out that, the fix of *TeraSort* is of mainly theoretical concerns. Its purpose is to convince the reader that the broadcast assumption is not a technical "loose end" in achieving minimality. In practice, *TeraSort* has nearly the same performance as our *pure* version, at least on Hadoop where (as mentioned before) the brute-force approach of *TeraSort* is well supported.

4. BASIC MINIMAL ALGORITHMS IN DATABASES

A minimal sorting algorithm also gives rise to minimal algorithms for other database problems. We demonstrate so for *ranking*, *group-by*, *semi-join*, and 2D *skyline* in this section. For all these problems, our objective is to terminate in *one more round* after sorting, in which a machine entails only $O(t)$ words of network traffic where t is the number of machines.

As before, each of the machines $\mathcal{M}_1, ..., \mathcal{M}_t$ is permitted $O(m)$ space of storage where $m = n/t$, and n is the problem cardinality. In the rest of the paper, we will concentrate on $m \geq t\ln(nt)$, i.e., the condition under which *TeraSort* is minimal (see Theorem 1).

4.1 Ranking and Skyline

Prefix Sum. Let S be a set of n objects from an ordered domain, such that each object $o \in S$ carries a real-valued *weight* $w(o)$. Define *prefix*(o, S), the *prefix sum* of o, to be the total weight of the objects $o' \in S$ such that $o' < o$. The *prefix sum problem* is to report the prefix sums of all objects in S. The problem can be settled in $O(n \log n)$ time on a sequential machine. Next, we present an efficient MapReduce algorithm.

First, sort S with *TeraSort*. Let S_i be the set of objects on machine $\mathcal{M}_i$ after sorting, for $1 \leq i \leq t$. We solve the prefix sum problem in another round:

Map-shuffle (on each $\mathcal{M}_i$, $1 \leq i \leq t$)

$\mathcal{M}_i$ sends $W_i = \sum_{o \in S_i} w(o)$ to $\mathcal{M}_{i+1}, ..., \mathcal{M}_t$.

Reduce (on each $\mathcal{M}_i$):

1. $V_i = \sum_{j \leq i-1} W_j$.
2. Obtain *prefix*(o, S_i) for $o \in S_i$ by solving the prefix sum problem on S_i locally.
3. *prefix*$(o, S) = V_i +$ *prefix*(o, S_i) for each $o \in S_i$.

In the above map-shuffle phase, every machine sends and receives exactly $t - 1$ values in total: precisely, $\mathcal{M}_i$ $(1 \leq i \leq t)$ sends $t - i$ and receives $i - 1$ values. This satisfies *bounded net-traffic* because $t \leq m$. Furthermore, the reduce phase takes $O(m) = O(n/t)$ time, by leveraging the sorted order of S_i. Omitting the other trivial details, we conclude that our prefix sum algorithm is minimal.

Prefix Min. The *prefix min problem* is almost the same as prefix sum, except that *prefix*(o, S) is defined as the *prefix min* of o, which is the minimum weight of the objects $o' \in S$ such that $o' < o$. This problem can also be settled by the above algorithm minimally with three simple changes: redefine (i) $W_i = \min_{o \in S_i} w(o)$ in the map-shuffle phase, (ii-iii) $V_i = \min_{j \leq i-1} W_j$ at Line 1 of the reduce phase, and *prefix*$(o, S) = \min\{V_i, \textit{prefix}(o, S_i)\}$ at Line 3.

Ranking. Let S be a set of objects from an ordered domain. The *ranking problem* reports the *rank* of each object $o \in S$, which equals $|\{o' \in S \mid o' \leq o\}|$; in other words, the smallest object has rank 1, the second smallest rank 2, etc. This can be solved as a special prefix sum problem where all objects have weight 1 (i.e., prefix count).

Skyline. Let x_p (y_p) be the x- (y-) coordinate of a 2D point p. A point p *dominates* another p' if $x_p \leq x_{p'}$ and $y_p \leq y_{p'}$. For a set P of n 2D points, the *skyline* is the set of points $p \in P$ such that p is not dominated by any other point in P. The *skyline problem* [8] is to report the skyline of P, and admits a sequential algorithm of $O(n \log n)$ time [35].

The problem is essentially prefix min in disguise. Specifically, let $S = \{x_p \mid p \in P\}$ where x_p carries a "weight" y_p. Define the *prefix min* of x_p as the minimum "weight" of the values in S preceding[3] x_p. It is rudimentary to show that p is in the skyline of P, if and only if the prefix min of x_p is strictly greater than y_p. Therefore, our prefix min algorithm also settles the skyline problem minimally.

4.2 Group By

Let S be a set of n objects, where each object $o \in S$ carries a *key* $k(o)$ and a *weight* $w(o)$, both of which are real values. A *group* G is a maximal set of objects with the same key. The *aggregate* of G is the result of applying a distributive[4] aggregate function AGG to the weights of the objects in G. The *group-by* problem is to report the aggregates of all groups. It is easy to do so in $O(n \log n)$ time on a sequential machine. Next, we discuss MapReduce, assuming for simplicity AGG = *sum* because it is straightforward to generalize the discussion to other AGG.

[3]Precisely, given points p and p', x_p precedes $x_{p'}$ if (i) $x_p < x_{p'}$ or (ii) $x_p = x_{p'}$ but $y_p < y_{p'}$.

[4]An aggregate function AGG is *distributive* on a set S if AGG(S) can be obtained in constant time from AGG(S_1) and AGG(S_2), where S_1 and S_2 form a partition of S, i.e., $S_1 \cup S_2 = S$ and $S_1 \cap S_2 = \emptyset$.

The main issue is to handle large groups that do not fit in one machine. Our algorithm starts by sorting the objects by keys, breaking ties by ids. Consider an arbitrary machine $\mathcal{M}$ after sorting. If a group G is now completely in $\mathcal{M}$, its aggregate can be obtained locally in $\mathcal{M}$. Motivated by this, let $k_{min}(\mathcal{M})$ and $k_{max}(\mathcal{M})$ be the smallest and largest keys on $\mathcal{M}$ currently. Clearly, groups of keys k where $k_{min}(\mathcal{M}) < k < k_{max}(\mathcal{M})$ are entirely stored in $\mathcal{M}$, which can obtain their aggregates during sorting, and remove them from further consideration.

Each machine $\mathcal{M}$ has at most 2 groups remaining, i.e., with keys $k_{min}(\mathcal{M})$ and $k_{max}(\mathcal{M})$, respectively. Hence, there are at most $2t$ such groups on all machines. To handle them, we ask each machine to send at most 4 values to $\mathcal{M}_1$ (i.e., to just a single machine). The following elaborates how:

Map-shuffle (on each $\mathcal{M}_i, 1 \leq i \leq t$):

1. Obtain the total weight $W_{min}(\mathcal{M}_i)$ of group $k_{min}(\mathcal{M}_i)$, i.e., by considering only objects in $\mathcal{M}_i$.
2. Send pair $(k_{min}(\mathcal{M}_i), W_{min}(\mathcal{M}_i))$ to $\mathcal{M}_1$.
3. If $k_{min}(\mathcal{M}_i) \neq k_{max}(\mathcal{M}_i)$, send pair $(k_{max}(\mathcal{M}_i), W_{max}(\mathcal{M}_i))$ to $\mathcal{M}_1$, where the definition of $k_{max}(\mathcal{M}_i)$ is similar to $k_{min}(\mathcal{M}_i)$.

Reduce (only on $\mathcal{M}_1$):

Let $(k_1, w_1), ..., (k_x, w_x)$ be the pairs received in the previous phase where x is some value between t and $2t$. For each group whose key k is in one of the x pairs, output its final aggregate $\sum_{j|k_j=k} w_j$.

The minimality of our group-by algorithm is easy to verify. It suffices to point out that the reduce phase of the last round takes $O(t \log t) = O(\frac{n}{t} \log n)$ time (since $t \leq m = n/t$).

Categorical Keys. We have assumed that the key $k(o)$ of an object is numeric. This is in fact unnecessary because the key ordering does not affect the correctness of group by. Hence, even if $k(o)$ is categorical, we can simply sort the keys alphabetically by their binary representations.

Term Frequency. MapReduce is often introduced with the *term frequency problem*. The input is a document D, which can be regarded as a multi-set of strings. The goal is to report, for every distinct string $s \in D$, the number of occurrences of s in D. In their pioneering work, Dean and Ghemawat [16] gave an algorithm which works by sending all occurrences of a string to an identical machine. The algorithm is not minimal in the scenario where a string has an exceedingly high frequency. Note, on the other hand, that the term frequency problem is merely a group-by problem with every distinct string representing a group. Hence, our group-by algorithm provides a minimal alternative to counting term frequencies.

4.3 Semi-Join

Let R and T be two sets of objects from the same domain. Each object o in R or T carries a key $k(o)$. The *semi-join problem* is to report all the objects $o \in R$ that have a *match* $o' \in T$, i.e., $k(o) = k(o')$. The problem can be solved in $O(n \log n)$ time sequentially, where n is the total number of objects in $R \cup T$.

In MapReduce, we approach the problem in a way analogous to how group-by was tackled. The difference is that, now objects with the same key do not "collapse" into an aggregate; instead, we must output all of them if their (common) key has a match in T. For this reason, we will need to transfer more network data than group by, as will be clear shortly, but still $O(t)$ words per machine.

Define $S = R \cup T$. We sort the objects of the mixed set S by their keys across the t machines. Consider any machine $\mathcal{M}$ after sorting. Let $k_{min}(T, \mathcal{M})$ and $k_{max}(T, \mathcal{M})$ be the smallest and largest keys respectively, among the T-objects stored on $\mathcal{M}$ (a *T-object* is an object from T). The semi-join problem can be settled with an extra round:

Map-shuffle (on each $\mathcal{M}_i, 1 \leq i \leq t$):

Send $k_{min}(T, \mathcal{M}_i)$ and $k_{max}(T, \mathcal{M}_i)$ to *all* machines.

Reduce (on each $\mathcal{M}_i$):

1. K_{border} = the set of keys received from the last round.
2. $K(\mathcal{M}_i)$ = the set of keys of the T-objects stored in $\mathcal{M}_i$.
3. For every R-object o stored in $\mathcal{M}_i$, output it if $k(o) \in K(\mathcal{M}_i) \cup K_{border}$.

Every machine sends and receives $2t$ keys in the map-shuffle phase. The reduce phase can be implemented in $O(m + t \log t) = O(\frac{n}{t} \log n)$ time, using the fact that the R-objects on $\mathcal{M}_i$ are already sorted. The overall semi-join algorithm is minimal.

5. SLIDING AGGREGATION

This section is devoted to the *sliding aggregation problem*. Recall that the input is: (i) a set S of n objects from an ordered domain, (ii) an integer $\ell \leq n$, and (iii) a distributive aggregate function AGG. We will focus on AGG = *sum* because extension to other AGG is straightforward. Each object $o \in S$ is associated with a real-valued *weight* $w(o)$. The *window* of o, denoted as $window(o)$, is the set of ℓ largest objects not exceeding o (see Figure 1). The *window sum* of o equals

$$win\text{-}sum(o) = \sum_{o' \in window(o)} w(o')$$

The objective is to report $win\text{-}sum(o)$ for all $o \in S$.

5.1 Sorting with Perfect Balance

Let us first tackle a variant of sorting which we call the *perfect sorting problem*. The input is a set S of n objects from an ordered domain. We want to distribute them among the t MapReduce machines $\mathcal{M}_1, ..., \mathcal{M}_t$ such that $\mathcal{M}_i$, $1 \leq i \leq t-1$, stores *exactly* $\lceil m \rceil$ objects, and $\mathcal{M}_t$ stores all the remaining objects, where $m = n/t$. In the meantime, the sorted order must be maintained, i.e., all objects on $\mathcal{M}_i$ precede those on $\mathcal{M}_j$, for any $1 \leq i < j \leq t$. We will assume that m is an integer; if not, simply pad at most $t - 1$ dummy objects to make n a multiple of t.

The problem is in fact nothing but a small extension to ranking. Our algorithm first invokes the ranking algorithm in Section 4.1 to obtain the rank of each $o \in S$, denoted as $r(o)$. Then, we finish in one more round:

Map-shuffle (on each $\mathcal{M}_i, 1 \leq i \leq t$):

For each object o currently on $\mathcal{M}_i$, send it to $\mathcal{M}_j$ where $j = \lceil r(o)/m \rceil$.

Reduce: No action is needed.

The above algorithm is clearly minimal.

5.2 Sliding Aggregate Computation

We now return to the sliding aggregation problem, assuming that S has been perfectly sorted across $\mathcal{M}_1, ..., \mathcal{M}_t$ as described earlier. The objective is to settle the problem in just one more round. Once again, we assume that n is a multiple of t; if not, pad at most $t-1$ dummy objects with zero weights.

By virtue of the perfect balancing, the objects on machine i form a *rank range* $[(i-1)m+1, im]$, for $1 \le i \le t$. Consider an object o with $window(o) = [r(o)-\ell+1, r(o)]$, i.e., the range of ranks of the objects in $window(o)$. Clearly, $window(o)$ intersects the rank ranges of machines from α to β, where $\alpha = \lceil (r(o)-\ell+1)/m \rceil$ to $\beta = \lceil r(o)/m \rceil$. If $\alpha = \beta$, $win\text{-}sum(o)$ can be calculated locally by $\mathcal{M}_\beta$, so next we focus on $\alpha < \beta$. Note that when $\alpha < \beta - 1$, $window(o)$ *spans* the rank ranges of machines $\alpha+1, ..., \beta-1$.

Let W_i be the total weight of all the objects on $\mathcal{M}_i$, $1 \le i \le t$. We will ensure that every machine knows $W_1, ..., W_t$. Then, to calculate $win\text{-}sum(o)$ at $\mathcal{M}_\beta$, the only information $\mathcal{M}_\beta$ does *not* have locally is the objects on $\mathcal{M}_\alpha$ enclosed in $window(o)$. We say that those objects are *remotely relevant* to $\mathcal{M}_\beta$. Objects from machines $\alpha+1, ..., \beta-1$ are not needed because their contributions to $win\text{-}sum(o)$ have been summarized by $W_{\alpha+1}, ..., W_{\beta-1}$.

The lemma below points out a crucial fact.

LEMMA 2. *Every object is remotely relevant to at most 2 machines.*

PROOF. Consider a machine $\mathcal{M}_i$ for some $i \in [1, t]$. If a machine $\mathcal{M}_j$ stores at least an object remotely relevant to $\mathcal{M}_i$, we say that $\mathcal{M}_j$ is *pertinent* to $\mathcal{M}_i$.

Recall that the left endpoint of $window(o)$ lies in machine $\alpha = \lceil (r(o)-\ell+1)/m \rceil$. When $r(o) \in [(i-1)m+1, im]$, i.e., the rank range of $\mathcal{M}_i$, it holds that

$$\left\lceil \frac{(i-1)m+1-\ell+1}{m} \right\rceil \le \alpha \le \left\lceil \frac{im-\ell+1}{m} \right\rceil \Rightarrow$$
$$(i-1) - \left\lfloor \frac{\ell-1}{m} \right\rfloor \le \alpha \le i - \left\lfloor \frac{\ell-1}{m} \right\rfloor \quad (1)$$

where the last step used the fact that $\lceil x-y \rceil = x - \lfloor y \rfloor$ for any integer x and real value y.

There are two useful observations. First,integer α has only two choices satisfying (1), namely, at most 2 machines are pertinent to $\mathcal{M}_i$. Second, as i grows by 1, the two permissible values of α both increase by 1. This means that each machine can be pertinent to at most 2 machines, thus completing the proof. ☐

COROLLARY 1. *Objects in $\mathcal{M}_i$, $1 \le i \le t$, can be remotely relevant only to*

- *machine $i+1$, if $\ell \le m$*
- *machines $i+\lfloor(\ell-1)/m\rfloor$ and $i+1+\lfloor(\ell-1)/m\rfloor$, otherwise.*

In the above, if a machine id exceeds m, ignore it.

PROOF. Directly from (1). ☐

We are now ready to explain how to solve the sliding aggregation problem in one round:

Map-shuffle (on each $\mathcal{M}_i$, $1 \le i \le t$):

1. Send W_i to all machines.
2. Send all the objects in $\mathcal{M}_i$ to one or two machines as instructed by Corollary 1.

Reduce (on each $\mathcal{M}_i$):

For each object o already in $\mathcal{M}_i$ after perfect sorting:

1. $\alpha = \lceil (r(o)-\ell+1)/m \rceil$
2. w_1 = the total weight of the objects in $\mathcal{M}_\alpha$ that fall in $window(o)$ (if $\alpha < i$, such objects were received in the last phase).
3. $w_2 = \sum_{j=\alpha+1}^{i-1} W_j$.
4. If $\alpha = i$, set $w_3 = 0$; otherwise, w_3 is the total weight of the objects in $\mathcal{M}_i$ that fall in $window(o)$.
5. $win\text{-}sum(o) = w_1 + w_2 + w_3$.

We now analyze the algorithm's minimality. It is clear that every machine sends and receives $O(t+m) = O(m)$ words of data over the network in the map-shuffle phase. Hence, each machine requires only $O(m)$ storage. It remains to prove that the reduce phase terminates in $O(\frac{n}{t}\log n)$ time. We create a *range sum* structure[5] respectively on: (i) the local objects in $\mathcal{M}_i$, (ii) the objects received from (at most) two machines in the map-reduce phase, and (iii) the set $\{W_1, ..., W_t\}$. These structures can be built in $O(m \log m)$ time, and allow us to compute w_1, w_2, w_3 in Lines 2-4 using $O(\log m)$ time. It follows that the reduce phase takes $O(m \log m) = O(\frac{n}{t}\log m)$ time.

6. EXPERIMENTS

This section experimentally evaluates our algorithms on an in-house cluster with one master and 56 slave nodes, each of which has four Intel Xeon 2.4GHz CPUs and 24GB RAM. We implement all algorithms on Hadoop (version 1.0), and allocate 4GB of RAM to the Java Virtual Machine on each node (i.e., each node can use up to 4GB of memory for a Hadoop task). Table 1 lists the Hadoop parameters in our experiments.

Parameter Name	Value
fs.block.size	128MB
io.sort.mb	512MB
io.sort.record.percentage	0.1
io.sort.spill.percentage	0.9
io.sort.factor	300
dfs.replication	3

Table 1: Parameters of Hadoop

We deploy two real datasets named LIDAR[6] and PageView[7], respectively. 514GB in size, LIDAR contains 7.35 billion records, each of which is a 3D point representing a location in North Carolina. We use LIDAR for experiments on sorting, skyline, group by, and semi-join. PageView is 332GB in size and contains 11.8 billion tuples. Each tuple corresponds to a page on Wikipedia, and records the number of times the page was viewed in a certain hour during Jan-Sep 2012. We impose a total order on all the tuples by their timestamps, and use the data for experiments on sliding aggregation. In addition, we also generate synthetic datasets to

[5]Let S be a set of n real values, each associated with a numeric weight. Given an interval I, a *range sum* query returns the total weight of the values in $S \cap I$. A simple augmented binary tree [14] uses $O(n)$ space, answers a query in $O(\log n)$ time, and can be built in $O(n \log n)$ time.

[6]*Http://www.ncfloodmaps.com.*

[7]*Http://dumps.wikimedia.org/other/pagecounts-raw.*

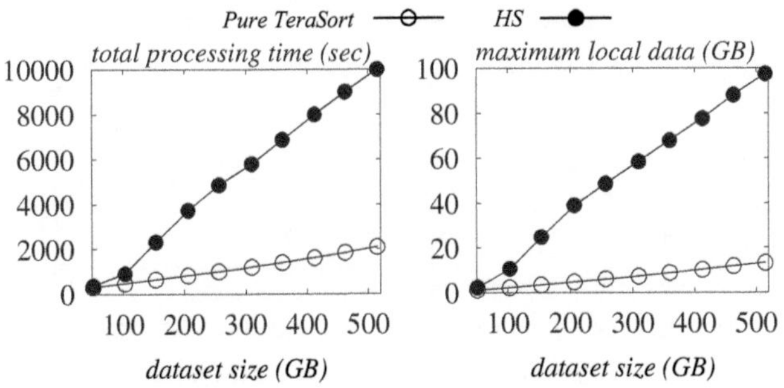

(a) Total time (b) Max. data volume on a slave

Figure 2: *Pure TeraSort* vs. *HS* on LIDAR.

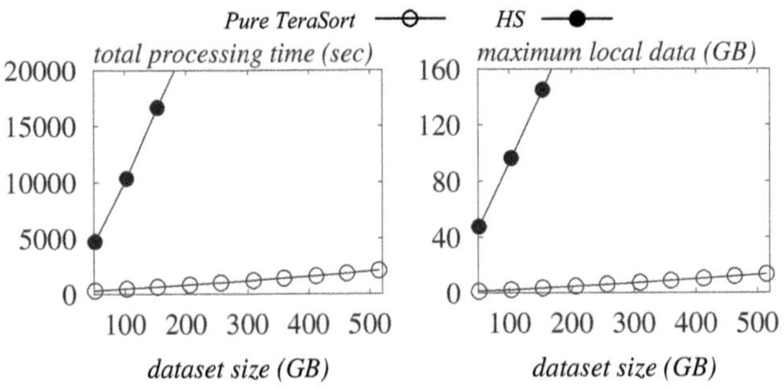

(a) Total time (b) Max. data volume on a slave

Figure 3: *Pure TeraSort* vs. *HS* on modified LIDAR

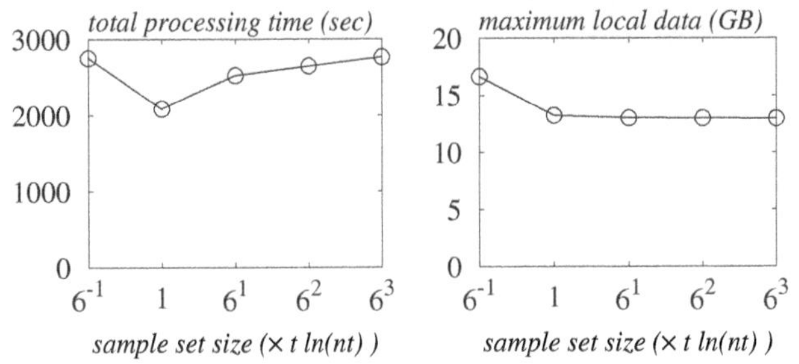

(a) Total time (b) Max. data volume on a slave

Figure 4: Effects of sample size on *pure TeraSort*

investigate the effect of data distribution on the performance of different algorithms. In each experiment, we run an algorithm 5 times and report the average reading.

6.1 Sorting

The first set of experiments compares *pure TeraSort* (proposed in Section 3.3) with Hadoop's default sorting algorithm, referred to as *HS* henceforth.

Given a dataset of k blocks long in the Hadoop Distributed File System (HDFS), *HS* first asks the master node to gather the first $\lceil 10^5/k \rceil$ records of each block into a set S – call them the *pilot records*. Next, the master identifies $t_{slave} - 1$ boundary points $b_1, b_2, \ldots, b_{t_{slave}-1}$, where b_i is the $i\lceil 10^5/t_{slave} \rceil$-th smallest record in S, and t_{slave} is the number of slave nodes. The mater then launches a one-round algorithm where all records in $(b_{i-1}, b_i]$ are sent to the i-th ($i \in [1, t_{slave}]$) slave for sorting, where $b_0 = 0$ and $b_t = \infty$ are dummies. Clearly, the efficiency of *HS* relies on the distribution of the pilot records. If their distribution is the same as the whole dataset, each slave sorts approximately an equal number of tuples. Otherwise, certain slaves may receive an excessive amount of data and thus become the bottleneck of sorting.

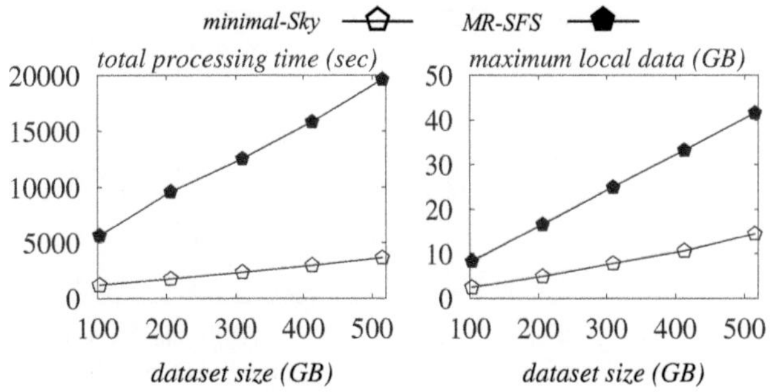

(a) Total time (b) Max. data volume on a slave

Figure 5: *Minimal-Sky* vs. *MR-SFS* on LIDAR

We implement *pure TeraSort* in a way similar to *HS* with the difference in how pilot records are picked. Specifically, the master now forms S by randomly sampling $t \ln t$ records from the dataset. Figure 2a illustrates the running time of *HS* and *pure TeraSort* in sorting LIDAR by its first dimension, when the dataset size varies from 51.4GB to 514GB (a dataset with size smaller than 514GB consists of random tuples from LIDAR, preserving their original ordering.) *Pure TeraSort* consistently outperforms *HS*, with the difference becoming more significant as the size grows. To reveal the reason behind, we plot in Figure 2b the maximum data amount on a slave node in the above experiments. Evidently, while *pure TeraSort* distributes the data evenly to the slaves, *HS* sends a large portion to a single slave, thus incurring enormous overhead.

To further demonstrate the deficiency of *HS*, Figure 3a shows the time taken by *pure TeraSort* and *HS* to sort a modified version of LIDAR, where tuples with small first coordinates are put to the beginning of each block. The efficiency of *HS* deteriorates dramatically, as shown in Figure 3b, confirming the intuition that its cost is highly sensitive to the distribution of pilot records. In contrast, the performance of *pure TeraSort* is not affected, owning to the fact that its sampling procedure is not sensitive to original data ordering at all.

To demonstrate the effect of sample size, Figure 4a shows the cost of *pure Terasort* on LIDAR as the number of pilot tuples changes. The result suggests that $t \ln(nt)$ is a nice choice. When the sample size decreases, *pure Terasort* is slower due to the increased unbalance in the distribution of data across the slaves, as can be observed from Figure 4b. On the opposite side, when the sample size grows, the running time also lengthens because sampling itself is more expensive.

6.2 Skyline

The second set of experiments evaluates our skyline algorithm, referred to as *minimal-Sky*, against *MR-SFS* [61], a recently developed method for skyline computation in MapReduce. We use exactly the implementation of *MR-SFS* from its authors. Figure 5a compares the cost of *minimal-Sky* and *MR-SFS* in finding the skyline on the first two dimensions of LIDAR, as the dataset size increases. *Minimal-Sky* significantly outperforms *MR-SFS* in all cases. The reason is that *MR-SFS*, which is not a minimal algorithm, may force a slave node to process an excessive amount of data, as shown in Figure 5b.

Figure 6 illustrates the performance of *minimal-Sky* and *MR-SFS* on three synthetic datasets that follow a correlated, anti-correlated, and independent distribution, respectively. 120GB in size, each dataset contains 2.5 billion 2D points generated by a publicly available toolkit[8]. Clearly, *MR-SFS* is rather sensitive to the dataset

[8] *Http://pgfoundry.org/projects/randdataset.*

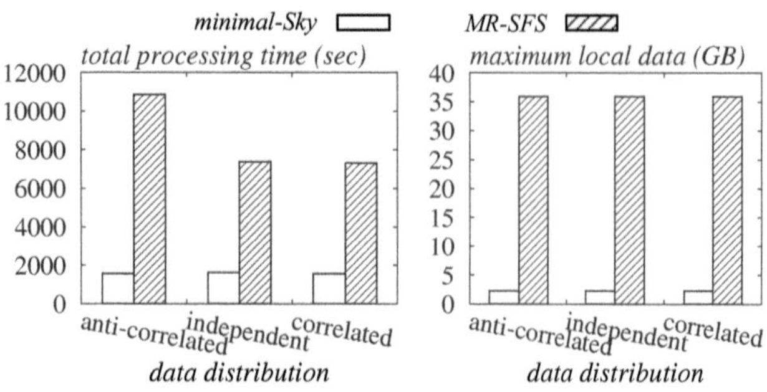

(a) Total time (b) Max. data volume on a slave

Figure 6: *Minimal-Sky* vs. *MR-SFS* on synthetic data

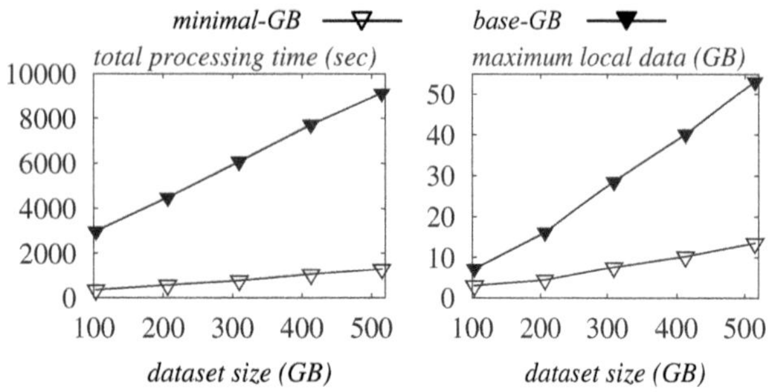

(a) Total time (b) Max. data volume on a slave

Figure 7: *Minimal-GB* vs. *base-GB* on LIDAR

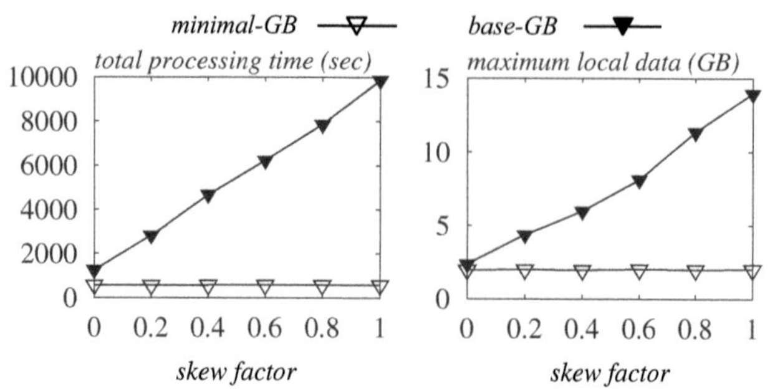

(a) Total time (b) Max. data volume on a slave

Figure 8: *Minimal-GB* vs. *base-GB* on synthetic data

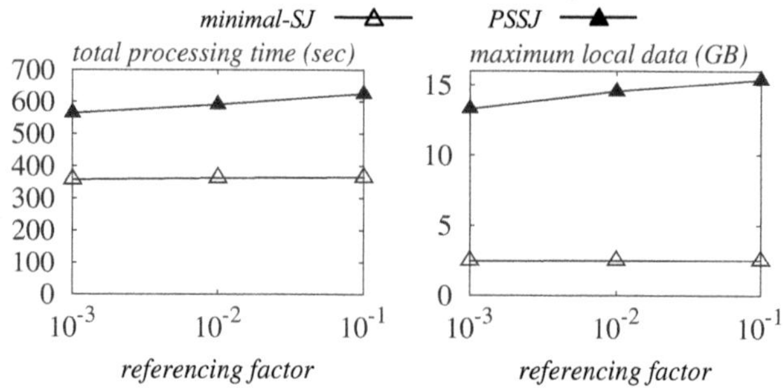

(a) Total time (b) Max. data volume on a slave

Figure 9: *Minimal-SJ* vs. *PSSJ* on various referencing factors

distribution, whereas the efficiency of *Minimal-Sky* is not affected at all.

6.3 Group By

Next, we compare our group by algorithm, referred to as *minimal-GB*, with a baseline approach called *base-GB*. Suppose that we are to group a dataset D by an attribute A. *Base-GB* first invokes a map phase where each tuple $t \in D$ spawns a key-value pair $(t[A], t)$, where $t[A]$ is the value of t on A. Then, all key-value pairs are distributed to the slave nodes using Hadoop's *Partitioner* program. Finally, every slave aggregates the key-value pairs it receives to compute the group by results.

Figure 7a presents the cost of *minimal-GB* and *base-GB* in grouping LIDAR by its first attribute. Regardless of the dataset size, *minimal-GB* is considerably faster than *base-GB* which, as shown in Figure 7b, is because Hadoop's *Partitioner* does not distribute data across the slaves as evenly as *minimal-GB*.

To evaluate the effect of dataset distribution, we generate 2D synthetic datasets where the first dimension (i) has an integer domain $[1, 2.5 \times 10^8]$, and (ii) follows a Zipf distribution with a skew factor between 0 and 1.[9] Each dataset contains 5 billion tuples and is 90GB in size. Figure 8 illustrates the performance of *minimal-GB* and *base-GB* on grouping the synthetic datasets by their first attributes. The efficiency of *base-GB* deteriorates as the skew factor increases. This is because *base-GB* always sends tuples with an identical group-by key to the same slave node. When the group-by keys are skewed, the data distribution is very uneven on the slaves, leading to severe performance penalty. In contrast, *minimal-GB* is completely insensitive to data skewness.

[9]Data are more skewed when the skew factor is higher. In particular, when the factor is 0, the distribution degenerates into uniformity.

6.4 Semi-Join

We now proceed to evaluate our semi-join algorithm, referred to as *minimal-SJ*, with *Per-Split Semi-Join* (*PSSJ*) [7], which is the best existing MapReduce semi-join algorithm. We adopt the implementation of *PSSJ* that has been made available online at *sites.google.com/site/hadoopcs561*. Following [7], we generate synthetic tables T and R as follows. The attributes of T are A_1 and A_2, both of which have an integer domain of $[1, 2.5 \times 10^8]$. T has 5 billion tuples whose A_1 values follow a Zipf distribution (some tuples may share an identical value). Their A_2 values are unimportant and arbitrarily decided. Similarly, R has 10 million tuples with integer attributes A_1 and A_3 of domain $[1, 2.5 \times 10^8]$. A fraction r of the tuples in R carry A_1 values present in T, while the other tuples have A_1 values absent from T. We refer to r as the *referencing factor*. Tuples' A_3 values are unimportant and arbitrarily determined.

Figure 9 compares *minimal-SJ* and *PSSJ* under different referencing factors, when the skew factor of $T.A_1$ equals 0.4. In all scenarios, *Minimal-SJ* beats *PSSJ* by a wide margin. Figure 10a presents the running time of *minimal-SJ* and *PSSJ* as a function of the skew factor of $T.A_1$, setting the reference factor r to 0.1. The efficiency of *PSSJ* degrades rapidly as the skew factor grows which, as shown Figure 10b, is because *PSSJ* fails to distribute the workload evenly among the slaves. *Minimal-SJ* is not affected by skewness.

6.5 Sliding Aggregation

In the last set of experiments, we evaluate our sliding aggregation algorithm, referred to as *minimal-SA*, against a baseline solution referred to as *Jaql*, which corresponds to the algorithm proposed in [6]. Suppose that we want to perform sliding aggregation over a set S of objects using a window size $l \leq n$. *Jaql* first sorts S with our ranking algorithm (Section 4.1). It then maps each record $t \in S$ to l key-value pair $(t_1, t), ..., (t_l, t)$, where $t_1, ..., t_l$ are the l largest objects not exceeding t. Then, *Jaql* distributes the key-value pairs to the slaves by applying Hadoop's *Partitioner*, and

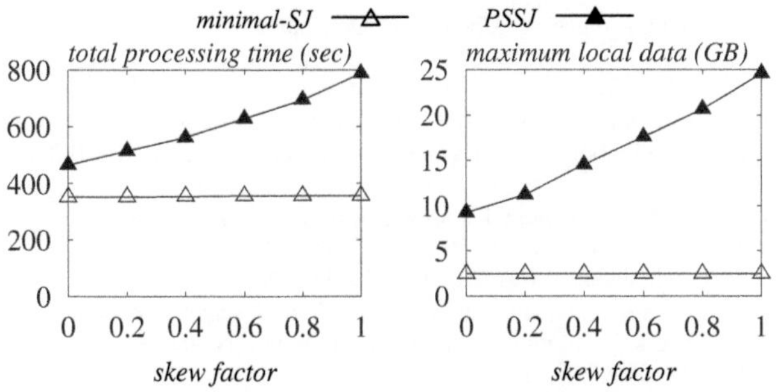

(a) Total time (b) Max. data volume on a slave

Figure 10: *Minimal-SJ* vs. *PSSJ* on various skew factors

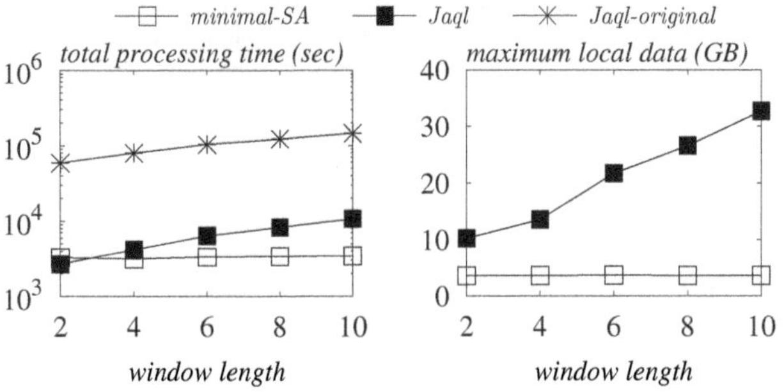

(a) Total time (b) Max. data volume on a slave

Figure 11: Sliding aggregation on small window sizes

instructs each slave to aggregate the key-value pairs with the same key. Besides our own implementation of *Jaql*, we also examine the original implementation released by the authors of [6], henceforth called *Jaql-original*.

Figure 11 demonstrates the performance of *minimal-SA*, *Jaql*, and *Jaql-original* on the PageView dataset, varying l from 2 to 10. *Minimal-SA* is superior to *Jaql* in all settings, except for a single case $l = 2$. In addition, *minimal-SA* is not affected by l, while *Jaql* deteriorates linearly. *Jaql-original* is slower than the other two methods by a factor of over an order of magnitude. It is not included in Figure 11b because it needs to keep almost the entire database on a single machine, which becomes the system's bottleneck.

Focusing on large l, Figure 12 plots the running time of *minimal-SA* when l increases from 10^5 to 10^9. We omit the Jaql implementations because they are prohibitively expensive, and worse than *minimal-SA* by more than a thousand times.

7. CONCLUSIONS

MapReduce has grown into an extremely popular architecture for large-scaled parallel computation. Even though there have been a great variety of algorithms developed for MapReduce, few are able to achieve the ideal goal of parallelization: balanced workload across the participating machines, and a speedup over a sequential algorithm linear to the number of machines. In particular, currently there is a void at the conceptual level as to what it means to be a "good" MapReduce algorithm.

We believe that a major contribution of this paper is to fill the aforementioned void with the new notion of "minimal MapReduce algorithm". This notion puts together for the first time four strong criteria towards (at least asymptotically) the highest parallel degree. At first glance, the conditions of minimality appear to be fairly stringent. Nonetheless, we prove the existence of simple yet elegant algorithms that minimally settle an array of important database problems. Our extensive experimentation demonstrates

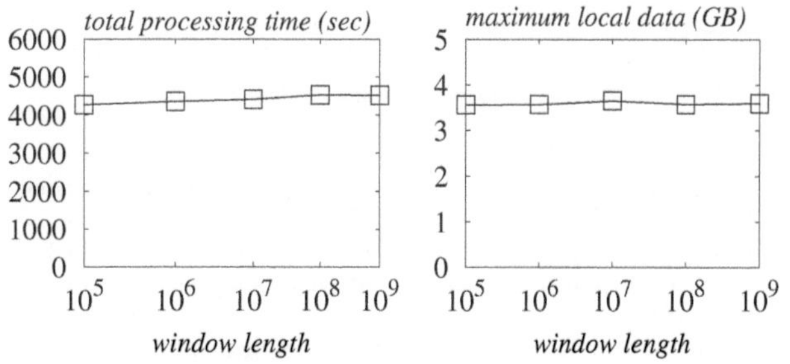

(a) Total time (b) Max. data volume on a slave

Figure 12: *Minimal-SA* on large window sizes

the immediate benefit brought forward by minimality that, the proposed algorithms significantly improve the existing state of the art for all the problems tackled.

ACKNOWLEDGEMENTS

Yufei Tao was supported in part by (i) projects GRF 4166/10, 4165/11, and 4164/12 from HKRGC, and (ii) the WCU (World Class University) program under the National Research Foundation of Korea, and funded by the Ministry of Education, Science and Technology of Korea (Project No: R31-30007). Wenqing Lin and Xiaokui Xiao were supported by the Nanyang Technological University under SUG Grant M58020016, and by the Agency for Science, Technology, and Research (Singapore) under SERC Grant 102-158-0074. The authors would like to thank the anonymous reviewers for their insightful comments.

8. REFERENCES

[1] A. Abouzeid, K. Bajda-Pawlikowski, D. J. Abadi, A. Rasin, and A. Silberschatz. Hadoopdb: An architectural hybrid of mapreduce and dbms technologies for analytical workloads. *PVLDB*, 2(1):922–933, 2009.

[2] F. N. Afrati, A. D. Sarma, D. Menestrina, A. G. Parameswaran, and J. D. Ullman. Fuzzy joins using mapreduce. In *ICDE*, pages 498–509, 2012.

[3] F. N. Afrati and J. D. Ullman. Optimizing multiway joins in a map-reduce environment. *TKDE*, 23(9):1282–1298, 2011.

[4] B. Bahmani, K. Chakrabarti, and D. Xin. Fast personalized pagerank on mapreduce. In *SIGMOD*, pages 973–984, 2011.

[5] B. Bahmani, R. Kumar, and S. Vassilvitskii. Densest subgraph in streaming and mapreduce. *PVLDB*, 5(5):454–465, 2012.

[6] K. S. Beyer, V. Ercegovac, R. Gemulla, A. Balmin, M. Y. Eltabakh, C.-C. Kanne, F. Özcan, and E. J. Shekita. Jaql: A scripting language for large scale semistructured data analysis. *PVLDB*, 4(12):1272–1283, 2011.

[7] S. Blanas, J. M. Patel, V. Ercegovac, J. Rao, E. J. Shekita, and Y. Tian. A comparison of join algorithms for log processing in mapreduce. In *SIGMOD*, pages 975–986, 2010.

[8] S. Borzsonyi, D. Kossmann, and K. Stocker. The skyline operator. In *ICDE*, pages 421–430, 2001.

[9] R. Chaiken, B. Jenkins, P. ake Larson, B. Ramsey, D. Shakib, S. Weaver, and J. Zhou. Scope: easy and efficient parallel processing of massive data sets. *PVLDB*, 1(2):1265–1276, 2008.

[10] B. Chattopadhyay, L. Lin, W. Liu, S. Mittal, P. Aragonda, V. Lychagina, Y. Kwon, and M. Wong. Tenzing a sql implementation on the mapreduce framework. *PVLDB*, 4(12):1318–1327, 2011.

[11] S. Chen. Cheetah: A high performance, custom data warehouse on top of mapreduce. *PVLDB*, 3(2):1459–1468, 2010.

[12] F. Chierichetti, R. Kumar, and A. Tomkins. Max-cover in map-reduce. In *WWW*, pages 231–240, 2010.

[13] R. L. F. Cordeiro, C. T. Jr., A. J. M. Traina, J. Lopez, U. Kang, and C. Faloutsos. Clustering very large multi-dimensional datasets with mapreduce. In *SIGKDD*, pages 690–698, 2011.

[14] T. H. Cormen, C. E. Leiserson, R. L. Rivest, and C. Stein. *Introduction to Algorithms, Second Edition*. The MIT Press, 2001.
[15] A. Das, M. Datar, A. Garg, and S. Rajaram. Google news personalization: scalable online collaborative filtering. In *WWW*, pages 271–280, 2007.
[16] J. Dean and S. Ghemawat. Mapreduce: Simplified data processing on large clusters. In *OSDI*, pages 137–150, 2004.
[17] F. K. H. A. Dehne, A. Fabri, and A. Rau-Chaplin. Scalable parallel geometric algorithms for coarse grained multicomputers. In *SoCG*, pages 298–307, 1993.
[18] J. Dittrich, J.-A. Quiane-Ruiz, A. Jindal, Y. Kargin, V. Setty, and J. Schad. Hadoop++: Making a yellow elephant run like a cheetah (without it even noticing). *PVLDB*, 3(1):518–529, 2010.
[19] I. Elghandour and A. Aboulnaga. Restore: Reusing results of mapreduce jobs. *PVLDB*, 5(6):586–597, 2012.
[20] M. Y. Eltabakh, Y. Tian, F. Ozcan, R. Gemulla, A. Krettek, and J. McPherson. Cohadoop: Flexible data placement and its exploitation in hadoop. *PVLDB*, 4(9):575–585, 2011.
[21] A. Ene, S. Im, and B. Moseley. Fast clustering using mapreduce. In *SIGKDD*, pages 681–689, 2011.
[22] A. Floratou, J. M. Patel, E. J. Shekita, and S. Tata. Column-oriented storage techniques for mapreduce. *PVLDB*, 4(7):419–429, 2011.
[23] A. Ghoting, P. Kambadur, E. P. D. Pednault, and R. Kannan. Nimble: a toolkit for the implementation of parallel data mining and machine learning algorithms on mapreduce. In *SIGKDD*, pages 334–342, 2011.
[24] A. Ghoting, R. Krishnamurthy, E. P. D. Pednault, B. Reinwald, V. Sindhwani, S. Tatikonda, Y. Tian, and S. Vaithyanathan. Systemml: Declarative machine learning on mapreduce. In *ICDE*, pages 231–242, 2011.
[25] R. Grover and M. J. Carey. Extending map-reduce for efficient predicate-based sampling. In *ICDE*, pages 486–497, 2012.
[26] B. Gufler, N. Augsten, A. Reiser, and A. Kemper. Load balancing in mapreduce based on scalable cardinality estimates. In *ICDE*, pages 522–533, 2012.
[27] Y. He, R. Lee, Y. Huai, Z. Shao, N. Jain, X. Zhang, and Z. Xu. Rcfile: A fast and space-efficient data placement structure in mapreduce-based warehouse systems. In *ICDE*, pages 1199–1208, 2011.
[28] H. Herodotou and S. Babu. Profiling, what-if analysis, and cost-based optimization of mapreduce programs. *PVLDB*, 4(11):1111–1122, 2011.
[29] E. Jahani, M. J. Cafarella, and C. Re. Automatic optimization for mapreduce programs. *PVLDB*, 4(6):385–396, 2011.
[30] J. Jestes, F. Li, and K. Yi. Building wavelet histograms on large data in mapreduce. In *PVLDB*, pages 617–620, 2012.
[31] H. J. Karloff, S. Suri, and S. Vassilvitskii. A model of computation for mapreduce. In *SODA*, pages 938–948, 2010.
[32] N. Khoussainova, M. Balazinska, and D. Suciu. Perfxplain: Debugging mapreduce job performance. *PVLDB*, 5(7):598–609, 2012.
[33] L. Kolb, A. Thor, and E. Rahm. Load balancing for mapreduce-based entity resolution. In *ICDE*, pages 618–629, 2012.
[34] P. Koutris and D. Suciu. Parallel evaluation of conjunctive queries. In *PODS*, pages 223–234, 2011.
[35] H. T. Kung, F. Luccio, and F. P. Preparata. On finding the maxima of a set of vectors. *JACM*, 22(4):469–476, 1975.
[36] Y. Kwon, M. Balazinska, B. Howe, and J. A. Rolia. Skewtune: mitigating skew in mapreduce applications. In *SIGMOD*, pages 25–36, 2012.
[37] W. Lang and J. M. Patel. Energy management for mapreduce clusters. *PVLDB*, 3(1):129–139, 2010.
[38] N. Laptev, K. Zeng, and C. Zaniolo. Early accurate results for advanced analytics on mapreduce. *PVLDB*, 5(10):1028–1039, 2012.
[39] S. Lattanzi, B. Moseley, S. Suri, and S. Vassilvitskii. Filtering: a method for solving graph problems in mapreduce. In *SPAA*, pages 85–94, 2011.
[40] H. Lim, H. Herodotou, and S. Babu. Stubby: A transformation-based optimizer for mapreduce workflows. *PVLDB*, 5(11):1196–1207, 2012.
[41] Y. Lin, D. Agrawal, C. Chen, B. C. Ooi, and S. Wu. Llama: leveraging columnar storage for scalable join processing in the mapreduce framework. In *SIGMOD*, pages 961–972, 2011.
[42] W. Lu, Y. Shen, S. Chen, and B. C. Ooi. Efficient processing of k nearest neighbor joins using mapreduce. *PVLDB*, 5(10):1016–1027, 2012.
[43] S. Melnik, A. Gubarev, J. J. Long, G. Romer, S. Shivakumar, M. Tolton, and T. Vassilakis. Dremel: Interactive analysis of web-scale datasets. *PVLDB*, 3(1):330–339, 2010.
[44] A. Metwally and C. Faloutsos. V-smart-join: A scalable mapreduce framework for all-pair similarity joins of multisets and vectors. *PVLDB*, 5(8):704–715, 2012.
[45] G. D. F. Morales, A. Gionis, and M. Sozio. Social content matching in mapreduce. *PVLDB*, 4(7):460–469, 2011.
[46] K. Morton, M. Balazinska, and D. Grossman. Paratimer: a progress indicator for mapreduce dags. In *SIGMOD*, pages 507–518, 2010.
[47] T. Nykiel, M. Potamias, C. Mishra, G. Kollios, and N. Koudas. Mrshare: Sharing across multiple queries in mapreduce. *PVLDB*, 3(1):494–505, 2010.
[48] A. Okcan and M. Riedewald. Processing theta-joins using mapreduce. In *SIGMOD*, pages 949–960, 2011.
[49] C. Olston, B. Reed, U. Srivastava, R. Kumar, and A. Tomkins. Pig latin: a not-so-foreign language for data processing. In *SIGMOD*, pages 1099–1110, 2008.
[50] O. O'Malley. Terabyte sort on apache hadoop. Technical report, Yahoo, 2008.
[51] B. Panda, J. Herbach, S. Basu, and R. J. Bayardo. Planet: Massively parallel learning of tree ensembles with mapreduce. *PVLDB*, 2(2):1426–1437, 2009.
[52] N. Pansare, V. R. Borkar, C. Jermaine, and T. Condie. Online aggregation for large mapreduce jobs. *PVLDB*, 4(11):1135–1145, 2011.
[53] A. Shinnar, D. Cunningham, B. Herta, and V. A. Saraswat. M3r: Increased performance for in-memory hadoop jobs. *PVLDB*, 5(12):1736–1747, 2012.
[54] S. Suri and S. Vassilvitskii. Counting triangles and the curse of the last reducer. In *WWW*, pages 607–614, 2011.
[55] A. Thusoo, J. S. Sarma, N. Jain, Z. Shao, P. Chakka, N. Zhang, S. Anthony, H. Liu, and R. Murthy. Hive - a petabyte scale data warehouse using hadoop. In *ICDE*, pages 996–1005, 2010.
[56] C. E. Tsourakakis, U. Kang, G. L. Miller, and C. Faloutsos. Doulion: counting triangles in massive graphs with a coin. In *SIGKDD*, pages 837–846, 2009.
[57] L. G. Valiant. A bridging model for parallel computation. *Commun. ACM*, 33(8):103–111, 1990.
[58] R. Vernica, A. Balmin, K. S. Beyer, and V. Ercegovac. Adaptive mapreduce using situation-aware mappers. In *EDBT*, pages 420–431, 2012.
[59] R. Vernica, M. J. Carey, and C. Li. Efficient parallel set-similarity joins using mapreduce. In *SIGMOD*, pages 495–506, 2010.
[60] G. Wang, M. A. V. Salles, B. Sowell, X. Wang, T. Cao, A. J. Demers, J. Gehrke, and W. M. White. Behavioral simulations in mapreduce. *PVLDB*, 3(1):952–963, 2010.
[61] B. Zhang, S. Zhou, and J. Guan. Adapting skyline computation to the mapreduce framework: Algorithms and experiments. In *DASFAA Workshops*, pages 403–414, 2011.
[62] X. Zhang, L. Chen, and M. Wang. Efficient multi-way theta-join processing using mapreduce. *PVLDB*, 5(11):1184–1195, 2012.

NADEEF: A Commodity Data Cleaning System

Michele Dallachiesa[†*] Amr Ebaid[‡*] Ahmed Eldawy[§*]
Ahmed Elmagarmid[♯] Ihab F. Ilyas[♯] Mourad Ouzzani[♯] Nan Tang[♯]

[♯]Qatar Computing Research Institute (QCRI)
[†]University of Trento [‡]Purdue University [§]University of Minnesota
dallachiesa@disi.unitn.it, aebaid@cs.purdue.edu, eldawy@cs.umn.edu
{aelmagarmid, ikaldas, mouzzani, ntang}@qf.org.qa

ABSTRACT

Despite the increasing importance of data quality and the rich theoretical and practical contributions in all aspects of data cleaning, there is no single end-to-end off-the-shelf solution to (semi-)automate the detection and the repairing of violations *w.r.t.* a set of heterogeneous and ad-hoc quality constraints. In short, there is no commodity platform similar to general purpose DBMSs that can be easily customized and deployed to solve application-specific data quality problems. In this paper, we present NADEEF, an extensible, generalized and easy-to-deploy data cleaning platform. NADEEF distinguishes between a *programming interface* and a *core* to achieve generality and extensibility. The programming interface allows the users to specify multiple types of data quality rules, which uniformly define *what* is wrong with the data and (possibly) *how* to repair it through writing code that implements predefined classes. We show that the programming interface can be used to express many types of data quality rules beyond the well known CFDs (FDs), MDs and ETL rules. Treating user implemented interfaces as black-boxes, the *core* provides algorithms to detect errors and to clean data. The *core* is designed in a way to allow cleaning algorithms to cope with multiple rules *holistically*, *i.e.,* detecting and repairing data errors without differentiating between various types of rules. We showcase two implementations for core repairing algorithms. These two implementations demonstrate the *extensibility* of our core, which can also be replaced by other user-provided algorithms. Using real-life data, we experimentally verify the generality, extensibility, and effectiveness of our system.

Categories and Subject Descriptors

H.2 [**Database Management**]: General—*integrity*

*Work done while interning at QCRI.

SIGMOD'13, June 22–27, 2013, New York, New York, USA.

Keywords

ETL, conditional functional dependency, matching dependency, data cleaning

1. INTRODUCTION

Data has become an important asset in today's economy. Extracting values from large amounts of data to provide services and to guide decision making processes has become a central task in all data management stacks. The quality of data becomes one of the differentiating factors among businesses and the first line of defense in producing value from raw input data. Ensuring the quality of the data with respect to business and integrity constraints has become more important than ever.

Despite the need of high quality data, there is no *end-to-end off-the-shelf* solution to (semi-)automate error detection and correction *w.r.t.* a set of *heterogeneous* and *ad-hoc* quality rules. In particular, there is no commodity platform similar to general purpose DBMSs that can be easily customized and deployed to solve application-specific data quality problems. Although there exist more expressive logical forms (*e.g.,* first-order logic) to cover a large group of quality rules, *e.g.,* CFDs, MDs or denial constraints, the main problem for designing an effective holistic algorithm for these rules is the lack of *dynamic semantics*, *i.e.,* alternative ways about *how* to repair data errors. Most of these existing rules only have *static semantics*, *i.e.,* *what* data is erroneous.

Emerging data quality applications place the following challenges in building a commodity data cleaning system.

Heterogeneity: Business and dependency theory based quality rules are expressed in a large variety of formats and languages from rigorous expressions (*e.g.,* functional dependencies), to plain natural language rules enforced by code embedded in the application logic itself (as in many practical scenarios). Such diversified semantics hinders the creation of one uniform system to accept heterogeneous quality rules and to enforce them on the data within the same framework.

Interdependency: Data cleaning algorithms are normally designed for one specific type of rules. [14] shows that interacting two types of quality rules (CFDs and MDs) may produce higher quality repairs than treating them independently. However, the problem related to the interaction of more diversified types of rules is far from being solved. One promising way to help solve this problem is to provide unified formats to represent not only the static semantics of various rules (*i.e.,* what is wrong), but also their dynamic semantics (*i.e.,* alternative ways to fix the wrong data).

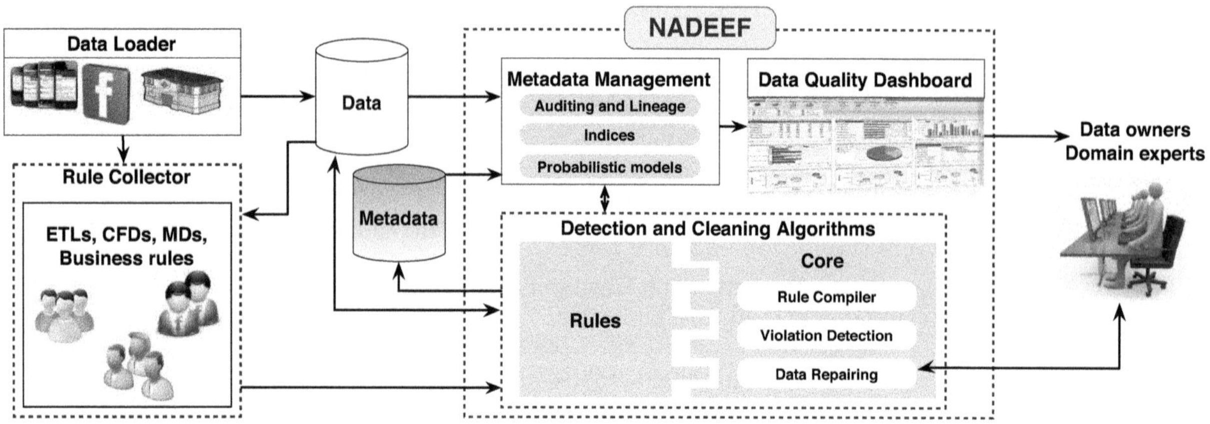

Figure 1: Architecture of NADEEF

Deployment and extensibility: Although many algorithms and techniques have been proposed for data cleaning [5, 14, 29], it is difficult to download one of them and run it on the data at hand without tedious customization. Adding to this difficulty is when users define new types of quality rules, or want to extend an existing system with their own implementation of cleaning solutions.

Metadata management and data custodians: Data is not born an orphan. Real customers have little trust in the machines to mess with the data without human consultation. Several attempts have tackled the problem of including humans in the loop (*e.g.,* [15, 26, 29]). However, they only provide users with information in restrictive formats. In practice, the users need to understand much more meta-information *e.g.,* summarization or samples of data errors, lineage of data changes, and possible data repairs, before they can effectively guide any data cleaning process.

We introduce NADEEF, a prototype for an extensible and easy-to-deploy cleaning system that leverages the separability of two main tasks: (1) isolating rule specification that uniformly defines *what* is wrong and (possibly) *how* to fix it; and (2) developing a core that holistically applies these routines to handle the detection and cleaning of data errors.

We show NADEEF's architecture in Fig. 1. In a nutshell, NADEEF first collects data and rules defined by the users. The rule compiler then compiles these *heterogeneous* rules into homogeneous constructs. Next, the violation detection module finds what data is erroneous and possible ways to repair them, based on user provided rules. After identifying errors, the data repairing module handles the *interdependency* of these rules by treating them holistically. Since data cleaning is usually an iterative process and new violations might be introduced when updating data values during repairing, NADEEF adopts a simple strategy to ensure that the process terminates. NADEEF also manages metadata related to its different modules. These metadata can be used to allow domain experts and users to actively interact with the system. We are working on augmenting NADEEF with a data quality dashboard that would exploit these metadata and provide information such as error summarization and error distribution; details on this component are left for future work.

Contributions. We make several notable contributions.

(1) We describe the first end-to-end commodity data cleaning system (Section 2).

(2) We propose a novel programming interface (Section 3) that supports the *generality* of NADEEF by providing users with ways to specify the semantics, both static and dynamic, of multiple types of data quality rules.

(3) We discuss basic error detection methods (Section 4). We also describe *partitioning* and *compression* as two techniques to improve violation detection. The former is to reduce the number of pairwise comparisons when computing violations, while the latter is to reduce the number of comparisons and the size of violations.

(4) To demonstrate the *extensibility* of our system, we present two core implementations for data cleaning algorithms (Section 5). The first one, which is designed to achieve higher accuracy, converts all violations and possible data changes to a variable-weighted conjunctive normal form (CNF). This CNF is then fed to a weighted MAX-SAT solver that computes repairs while minimizing their overall cost. The second one, which is designed to be more efficient, leverages the idea of equivalence classes [5]. It merges violating data into multiple equivalence classes and assigns a unique value to each equivalence class.

(5) We conduct extensive experiments to verify the generality, extensibility, and effectiveness of our system using real-life datasets (Section 6).

2. A MOTIVATING SCENARIO AND SYSTEM ARCHITECTURE

We present a detailed scenario to show the many features of NADEEF, followed by a discussion about its architecture.

2.1 A Motivating Scenario

Consider two databases D_1 and D_2 from a European bank: D_1 maintains customer information collected when credit cards are issued and D_2 records credit card transactions. The databases are specified by the following schemas:

bank (FN, LN, St, city, CC, country, tel, gd),
tran (FN, LN, str, city, CC, country, phn, when, where).

Here, a bank record specifies a credit card holder identified by first name (FN), last name (LN), street (St), city, country code (CC), country, phone number (tel) and gender (gd). A tran tuple is a record of a purchase paid by a credit card at time when and place where, by a customer identified by first name (FN), last name (LN), street (str), city, country code (CC), country and phone (phn). Example instances of bank and tran tables are shown in Figs. 2(a) and 2(b), respectively.

	FN	LN	St	city	CC	country	tel	gd
t_1:	David	Jordan	12 Holywell Street	Oxford	44	UK	66700543	Male
t_2:	Paul	Simon	5 Ratcliffe Terrace	Oxford	44	UK	44944631	Male

(a) D_1: An instance of schema bank

	FN	LN	str	city	CC	country	phn	when	where
r_1:	David	Jordan	12 Holywell Street	Oxford	44	UK	66700543	1pm 6/05/2012	Netherlands
r_2:	Paul	Simon	5 Ratcliffe Terrace	Oxford	44	UK	44944631	11am 2/12/2011	Netherlands
r_3:	David	Jordan	12 Holywell Street	Oxford	44	Netherlands	66700541	6am 6/05/2012	US
r_4:	Peter	Austin	7 Market Street	Amsterdam	31	UK	55384922	9am 6/02/2012	Netherlands

(b) Database D_2: An instance of schema tran

Figure 2: Example databases

Based on the application business logic, users may impose the following rules:

- φ_1: *(on table* tran*) if a customer's* CC *is 31, but his/her* country *is neither Netherlands nor Holland, update the* country *to Netherlands;*
- φ_2: *(on tables* bank *and* tran*) if the same person from different tables has different phones, the phone number from table* bank *is more reliable;*
- φ_3: *(on table* tran*) a country code* (CC) *uniquely determines a* country*;*
- φ_4: *(on table* tran*) if two purchases of the same person happened in the Netherlands and the US (East Coast) within 1 hour (assuming 6 hours' time difference between these two countries), these two purchases are either a fraud or were erroneously recorded.*

Figure 3 shows how these rules are represented in our system via a unified programming interface. In a nutshell, the users specify a rule's static semantics (*what* is wrong) over either one tuple or two tuples via a vio() function, where an error is represented by a set of attribute values. Moreover, the users can also, if possible, specify its dynamic semantics (*i.e.*, *how* to repair) by providing different alternatives to repair the data via a fix() function.

Rule1 (for φ_1) is a transformation rule on a single tuple on table tran. It states via a vio() function that if a tuple's CC is 31, but its country is neither Netherlands nor Holland, then it is problematic. It also states via a fix() function that the violating tuple's country should be updated to Netherlands.

Rule2 (for φ_2) is defined on two tables bank and tran. When it identifies that the same person from different tables has different phones (*i.e.*, the violation is not empty via a vio() function), it updates the phn value in tran to the tel value from bank (in fix()). Actually, the user indicates that the values from bank are more reliable. Here, the $\approx$ could be any (domain-specific) similarity function that a user defines.

Rule3 (for φ_3) specifies how to identify the violations via a vio() function on two tuples from table tran. It also defines via a fix() function two options to resolve a violation V: either update $V.s_2$[country] to $V.s_1$[country], or update $V.s_1$[country] to $V.s_2$[country].

Rule4 (for φ_4) only specifies how to detect a violation via a vio() function. No fix() function is given since the users do not know how to resolve this violation.

By allowing the expression of multiple types of rules (*e.g.*, eCFD [6] for the vio() of φ_1 and ETL for the fix() of φ_1, an MD φ_2, an FD φ_3 augmented with a fix() that changes values from the right hand side of the rule, and a custom rule φ_4) through our unified programming interface, NADEEF provides a simple way to determine what is wrong via vio() functions, and more importantly, it also captures how to repair it via a fix() function.

```
Class Rule1 {                                                /* for φ1 */
  set⟨cell⟩ vio(Tuple s1) {                          /*s1 in table tran */
    if (s1[CC]=31 ∧ (s1[country] ≠Netherlands ∨ s1[country] ≠Holland))
      return { s1[CC, country]; }
    return ∅;
  }
  set⟨Expression⟩ fix (set⟨cell⟩ V) {
    return { V.s[country] ← Netherlands; }
  } } /* end of class definition */
```

```
Class Rule2 {                                                /* for φ2 */
  set⟨cell⟩ vio (Tuple s1, Tuple s2) {         /*s1 in bank, s2 in tran */
    if (s1[LN, St, city]=s2[LN, str, city]∧s1[FN] ≈ s2[FN]∧s1[tel]≠s2[phn])
      return { s1[FN, LN, St, city, tel], s2[FN, LN, str, city, phn]; }
    return ∅;
  }
  set⟨Expression⟩ fix (set⟨cell⟩ V) {
    return { V.s2[phn] ← V.s1[tel]; }
  } } /* end of class definition */
```

```
Class Rule3 {                                                /* for φ3 */
  set⟨cell⟩ vio (Tuple s1, Tuple t2) {          /* s1, s2 in table tran */
    if (s1[CC] = s2[CC] ∧ s1[country] ≠ s2[country])
      return { s1[CC, country], s2[CC, country]; }
    return ∅;
  }
  set⟨Expression⟩ fix (set⟨cell⟩ V) {
    set⟨Expression⟩ fixes;
    fixes.insert(V.s1[country] ←V.s2[country]);
    fixes.insert(V.s2[country] ←V.s1[country]);
    return fixes;
  } } /* end of class definition */
```

```
Class Rule4 {                                                /* for φ4 */
  set⟨cell⟩ vio (Tuple s1, Tuple s2) {          /*s1, s2 in table tran */
    if (s1[LN, city, CC, tel] = s2[LN, city, CC, tel]
      ∧s1[where] = Netherlands ∧ s2[where] = US ∧ s1[FN] ≈ s2[FN]
      ∧(s1[when] − s2[when] ≥ 5) ∧ (s1[when] − s2[when] ≤ 7)
      return { s1[FN, LN, city, CC, tel, when, where],
        s2[FN, LN, city, CC, tel, when, where]; }
    return ∅;
  } } /* end of class definition */
```

Figure 3: Sample rules

Next, we show how the data in Fig. 2 can be repaired by the rules in Fig. 3 in a sequence of interdependent operations, as illustrated below:

(a) *Rule1* updates r_4[country] from UK to Netherlands.

(b) *Rule2* identifies that t_1 in D_1 and r_3 in D_2 are the same person, but with different phones. It updates r_3[phn] by taking 66700543 from t_1[tel], since bank is more reliable.

(c) *Rule3* detects that r_3 violates r_1 and r_2, *i.e.*, they have the same CC value but carry different country values. To resolve these two violations, one can either change r_3[country] from Netherlands to UK, or change both r_1[country] and r_2[country] from UK to Netherlands. A typical cleaning algorithm will choose the one with the minimum number of changes, *i.e.*, changing r_3[country] from Netherlands to UK.

(d) *Rule4* detects that the two purchases from the same person, r_1 and r_3, are problematic. Note that this rule only reports the violation, without repairing it.

Observe that only after changing r_3[phn] to 66700543 (the step (b) above), the violation in step (d) can be detected by a customized rule. We can see that (1) when taken together, different data quality rules help each other, and (2) to make practical use of their interaction, repairing operations for various types of data quality rules should be interleaved.

From this scenario, we can see that a commodity data cleaning system has to provide (a) a unified format for the users to specify *both* the static semantics *and* dynamic semantics of various types of rules, and (b) common data structures to represent data errors, which provide a natural way to design algorithms that holistically repair data.

2.2 Architecture Overview

Figure 1 depicts of the architecture of NADEEF. It contains three components: (1) the *Rule Collector* gathers user-specified quality rules; (2) the *Core* component uses a rule compiler to compile heterogeneous rules into homogeneous constructs that allow the development of default holistic data cleaning algorithms; and (3) the *Metadata management* and *Data quality dashboard* modules are concerned with maintaining and querying various metadata for data errors and their possible fixes. The dashboard allows domain experts and users to easily interact with the system.

Rule Collector. It collects user-specified data quality rules such as ETL rules, CFDs (FDs), MDs, deduplication rules, and other customized rules.

Core. The core contains three components: *rule compiler*, *violation detection* and *data repairing*.

(i) Rule Compiler. This module compiles all heterogeneous rules and manages them in a unified format.

(ii) Violation Detection. This module takes the data and the compiled rules as input, and computes a set of data errors.

(iii) Data Repairing. This module encapsulates holistic repairing algorithms that take violations as input, and computes a set of data repairs, while (by default) targeting the minimization of some pre-defined cost metric. This module may interact with domain experts through the *data quality dashboard* to achieve higher quality repairs.

Inside the core of NADEEF, we also implement an extensible Updater that decides which computed data changes will be finally committed. The Updater is needed since data cleaning is an expensive, (mostly) nondeterministic, and iterative process. When applied to the database, updates computed by repairing algorithms may trigger new violations and the cleaning process may not terminate. The Updater provides a termination test, ensuring that the entire data cleaning process terminates. We adopt a simple termination test in each iteration of the data repair process that is similar to data cleaning techniques proposed in [8,20]; the Updater applies the computed updates only if an attribute value is not changed more than x times (x is a parameter set to 2 by default). Otherwise, the Updater changes the attribute value to a special null value that eliminates any potential violations on this attribute value in the future.

Metadata management and data quality dashboard. Building a commodity data cleaning system requires collecting and handling several types of metadata to help in understanding and improving the cleaning process as well as supporting many features of NADEEF. The role of a metadata management module is to keep full lineage information about data changes, the order of changes, as well as maintaining indices to support efficient metadata operations. The data quality dashboard helps the users to understand the health of the database through progress indicators, data quality health information, as well as summarized, sampled or ranked data errors. It also facilitates the solicitation of users' feedback for data repairs. Details about this module are left for future work.

3. FUNDAMENTALS

In this section, we present the proposed programming interface for rule specification as well as some of the notations and concepts needed in NADEEF.

We consider a database $\mathcal{D} = \{D_1, \cdots, D_m\}$, where each D_j ($j \in [1, m]$) is an *instance* whose relation schema is R_j as $R_j = \{A_{j_1}, \cdots, A_{j_n}\}$. We use the term *cell* to denote a combination of a tuple and an attribute of a table, *i.e.*, $D.s[A]$. For simplicity, we write a cell as $s[A]$, when D is clear from the context.

For example, in Fig. 2, D_1 is an instance of relation bank, and t_1[FN] is a cell in instance D_1 whose value is David.

Data quality rules. The *programming interface* class *Rule* for defining the semantics of data errors and possible ways to fix them is as follows.

```
class Rule {
    set⟨cell⟩ vio (Tuple s1) { return ∅ };
    set⟨cell⟩ vio (Tuple s1, Tuple s2) { return ∅ };
    set⟨Expression⟩ fix (set⟨cell⟩) { return ∅ };
}   /* end of class definition */
```

In the above class we define three functions:

(1) vio(s) takes a single tuple s as input, and returns a set of problematic cells, *e.g.*, *Rule1* in Fig. 3. By default, it returns an empty set.

(2) vio(s_1, s_2) takes two tuples s_1, s_2 as input, and returns a set of problematic cells, *e.g.*, *Rule2*, *Rule3* and *Rule4* in Fig. 3. By default, it returns an empty set. Note that s_1, s_2 can come from the same relation or two different relations.

(3) fix (*set⟨cell⟩*) takes a nonempty set of problematic cells as input, and returns a set of suggested expressions to repair these data errors.

We refer to a class that inherits from *Rule* and implements at least one of the error detection functions vio() as a *data quality rule*, in order to express its static semantics (*what* is wrong). The function fix() is to reflect its dynamic semantics (*how* to repair errors). The presence of function fix() is optional, and its absence indicates that the users are not clear about its dynamic semantics, *e.g.*, *Rule4* in Fig. 3.

We can get φ_i ($i \in [1, 4]$) in Section 2 by instantiating *Rulei* in Fig. 3. In the rest of the paper, we shall use φ_i and *Rulei* interchangeably.

In contrast to traditional ways of defining data quality rules by strictly following some declarative logical formalism, the class *Rule* provides a *unified* and *generic* object-oriented programming interface. Such interface is expressive enough to allow users to easily capture both static and dynamic semantics of a large spectrum of data quality rules, as well as complex (*e.g.*, probabilistic or knowledge-based) processes.

Violations and candidate fixes. Violations specify what is wrong, while candidate fixes capture how to repair errors.

Violation. A *violation* is a nonempty set V of *cells* that are returned by the function vio(s) or vio(s_1, s_2) of a data quality rule φ, referred to as a violation of φ.

Intuitively, in a violation, at least one of the cells is erroneous and should be modified. For example, the two tuples r_1 and r_3 shown in Fig. 2 violate *Rule3*, since they have the same CC value but carry different country values. The corresponding violation consists of four cells $\{r_1[\mathsf{CC}], r_1[\mathsf{country}], r_3[\mathsf{CC}], r_3[\mathsf{country}]\}$.

For a database $\mathcal{D}$ and a data quality rule φ, we denote by $\mathsf{vio}(\mathcal{D}, \varphi)$ the set of all nonempty results returned by $\varphi.\mathsf{vio}(s)$ (*i.e.*, a single tuple) and $\varphi.\mathsf{vio}(s_1, s_2)$ (*i.e.*, a pair of tuples), where s is a single tuple in $\mathcal{D}$ and (s_1, s_2) is a pair of distinct tuples in $\mathcal{D}$, respectively. For a database $\mathcal{D}$ and a set Σ of rules, we denote by $\mathsf{vio}(\mathcal{D}, \Sigma) = \bigcup_{\varphi \in \Sigma} \mathsf{vio}(\mathcal{D}, \varphi)$ the set of all violations for data $\mathcal{D}$ and rules Σ.

In practice, many types of violations are usually defined on either a single tuple (*e.g.*, constant CFDs and many ETL rules), two tuples (*e.g.*, variable CFDs, MDs and deduplication rules), or a set of tuples (*e.g.*, aggregation constraints [21]). Supporting aggregation functions and other data quality rules defined on a subset of the data triggers a different class of challenges which are beyond the scope of this paper. This is *especially* true for the efficiency of the violation detection process. In this paper, we focus on the first two classes of violations, *i.e.*, violations defined on one tuple or two tuples. These two classes already cover a very large spectrum of data quality rules found in practice, thus not diminishing the expressiveness of NADEEF.

Candidate fix. A *candidate fix* F is a conjunction of expressions of the form "$c \leftarrow x$", where c is a cell, and x is either a constant value or another cell.

Intuitively, a candidate fix F is a set of expressions on a violation V, such that to resolve violation V, the modifications suggested by the expressions of F must be taken together. That is, to resolve a violation, more than one cell may have to be changed. In our example, each possible fix contains a single expression. For instance, consider *Rule3* in Fig. 3, each violation V has two candidate fixes, either assigning $V.s_2[\mathsf{country}]$ to $V.s_1[\mathsf{country}]$, or $V.s_1[\mathsf{country}]$ to $V.s_2[\mathsf{country}]$. Either way can resolve violation V.

Cost functions. As a database can be repaired in multiple ways, an immediate question is which repair to choose? Similarly to what most data cleaning methods use to make their decision, we adopt minimality, *i.e.*, compute an instance that repairs a database while incurring the least cost in terms of fixing operations. Let $\mathsf{cost}(c, v_1, v_2)$ be the cost of changing the cell c from value v_1 to v_2, and $\mathsf{cost}(\mathcal{D}, \mathcal{D}_r)$ is defined as the sum of $\mathsf{cost}(c, v_1, v_2)$ for each cell whose value is modified from $\mathcal{D}$ to a modified database $\mathcal{D}_r$. Since the users can plugin their own repairing algorithms, they can also replace the cost functions by their own.

Consistent database. Consider an instance $\mathcal{D}$ of $\mathcal{R}$, and a data quality rule φ, we say that $\mathcal{D}$ *satisfies* φ, denoted by $\mathcal{D} \models \varphi$, if (i) $\mathsf{vio}(s)$ returns an empty set for each tuple t in $\mathcal{D}$; and (ii) $\mathsf{vio}(s_1, s_2)$ returns an empty set for all pairs of distinct tuples s_1, s_2 in $\mathcal{D}$. We say that $\mathcal{D}$ *satisfies* a set Σ of data quality rules, denoted by $\mathcal{D} \models \Sigma$, if $\mathcal{D}$ *satisfies* each φ in Σ. We say that $\mathcal{D}$ is *consistent w.r.t.* Σ if $\mathcal{D} \models \Sigma$.

Fixed database. For an instance $\mathcal{D}$ of $\mathcal{R}$ and a data quality rule φ, we say that $\mathcal{D}$ is *fixed w.r.t.* φ, if for each violation V of $\mathcal{D}$ *w.r.t.* φ, $\mathsf{fix}(V)$ returns an empty set. We say that $\mathcal{D}$ is *fixed w.r.t.* a set Σ of data quality rules, if $\mathcal{D}$ is *fixed w.r.t.* each φ in Σ.

Consider our example in Section 2. After steps (a)-(d), we obtain a modified database $\mathcal{D}'$. While one violation still remains, *i.e.*, tuples (r_1, r_3) *w.r.t.* rule φ_4, it has no candidate fixes. Hence, the database $\mathcal{D}'$ is said to be *fixed*, although it is inconsistent, *e.g.*, it does not *satisfy* the rule φ_4 in Σ.

Unresolved violations. Note that, in our system, $\mathcal{D}_r$ must be *fixed* but may contain unresolved violations, *i.e.*, $\mathcal{D}_r$ may be inconsistent *w.r.t.* Σ. As opposed to traditional approaches that compute a fix $\mathcal{D}'_r$ that must be consistent, *i.e.*, $\mathsf{vio}(\mathcal{D}'_r, \varphi)$ is also empty for each φ in Σ, the problem we study only repairs dirty data for which candidate fixes are known. This is based on the fact that in practice and for some rules, there may not exist sufficient knowledge on how to resolve the corresponding violations; neither the users know *a priori* nor the data cleaning system could guess. Heuristically resolving such violations may introduce more errors, triggering a disastrous domino effect.

Further data quality aspects. There are several fundamental problems associated with quality rules. The *consistency problem* is to determine, given Σ and schemas $\mathcal{R}$, whether there exists a nonempty instance $\mathcal{D}$ (each table in $\mathcal{D}$ is nonempty) of $\mathcal{R}$ such that $\mathcal{D} \models \Sigma$. The *implication problem* is to decide, given Σ and another data quality rule ψ, whether Σ implies ψ. In simpler terms, the consistency problem is to decide whether the data quality rules are dirty themselves, and the implication problem is to decide whether a data quality rule is redundant. When treating the rules as black-boxes, it is difficult, if not impossible, to check whether they are internally consistent.

It has been verified in [14] that given CFDs only, or for CFDs and MDs taken together, the consistency (resp. implication) problem is NP-complete (resp. coNP-complete). However, when either the database schema is predefined or no attributes involved in the CFDs have a finite domain, the consistency check for CFDs is PTIME [14], which actually covers many practical applications. For the previous case or when the number of rules (*e.g.*, CFDs) is small, several algorithms have been proposed to check their consistency [12]. It is worth mentioning that we have implemented default classes for CFDs (FDs) and MDs; the consistency of such particular rules can be checked by these algorithms. In the following of this work, we assume collections of Σ and $\mathcal{D}$ that are consistent.

4. VIOLATION DETECTION

We describe a basic approach to compute violations as well as optimization techniques, namely partitioning and compression, that are possible under some restricted settings.

4.1 Finding Violations and Candidate Fixes

Given a database $\mathcal{D}$ and a set Σ of data quality rules, the method for violation detection, referred to as GetVio, returns a set $\mathcal{V}$ of violations and a set $\mathcal{F}$ of candidate fixes, where $\mathcal{V}$ (resp. $\mathcal{F}$) is the union of the violations (resp. candidate fixes) of $\mathcal{V}_\varphi$ (resp. $\mathcal{F}_\varphi$) for each φ in Σ. A straightforward way to compute $\mathcal{V}$ and $\mathcal{F}$ for each φ, is to invoke the functions $\mathsf{vio}(s)$ and $\mathsf{vio}(s_1, s_2)$ for each single tuple and each pair of tuples on which φ is defined, respectively. The $\mathsf{fix}()$ function will be invoked for each violation returned by $\mathsf{vio}(s)$ or $\mathsf{vio}(s_1, s_2)$. Since the quadratic time pairwise comparison for any two tuples is inherently expensive, we will discuss in Section 4.2 *partitioning* and *compression* as two techniques to improve its performance.

Rules	Violations	Candidate fixes
φ_1	V_1: $\{r_4[\mathsf{CC}, \mathsf{country}]\}$	F_1: $r_4[\mathsf{country}] \leftarrow$ Netherlands
φ_2	V_2:$\{t_1[\mathsf{FN}, \mathsf{LN}, \mathsf{St}, \mathsf{city}, \mathsf{tel}]$, $r_3[\mathsf{FN}, \mathsf{LN}, \mathsf{str}, \mathsf{city}, \mathsf{phn}]\}$	F_2: $r_3[\mathsf{phn}] \leftarrow t_1[\mathsf{tel}]$
φ_3	V_3: $\{r_1[\mathsf{CC}, \mathsf{country}]$, $r_3[\mathsf{CC}, \mathsf{country}]\}$	F_3: $r_1[\mathsf{country}] \leftarrow r_3[\mathsf{country}]$ F_4: $r_3[\mathsf{country}] \leftarrow r_1[\mathsf{country}]$
φ_3	V_4: $\{r_2[\mathsf{CC}, \mathsf{country}]$, $r_3[\mathsf{CC}, \mathsf{country}]\}$	F_5: $r_2[\mathsf{country}] \leftarrow r_3[\mathsf{country}]$ F_6: $r_3[\mathsf{country}] \leftarrow r_2[\mathsf{country}]$

Figure 4: Sample violations and candidate fixes

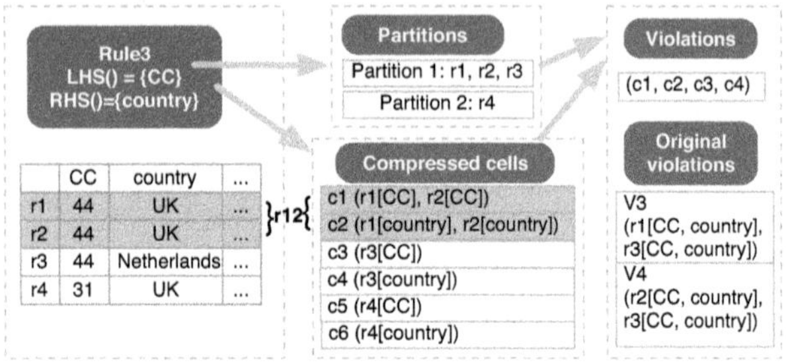

Figure 5: Partitioning and compression for a rule

Example 1: Consider steps (a-c) of the example in Section 2. There are 4 violations and 6 candidate fixes, as shown in Fig. 4. By applying φ_1 (resp. φ_2), we find a violation V_1 (resp. V_2) with two cells (resp. ten cells) involved from tuple r_4 (resp. tuples t_1 and r_3). The violation V_1 (resp. V_2) has a candidate fix F_1 (resp. F_2) that assigns Netherlands to $r_4[\mathsf{country}]$ (resp. $t_1[\mathsf{tel}]$ to $r_3[\mathsf{phn}]$). Moreover, attribute values from tuples r_1 and r_3 (resp. r_2 and r_3) violate φ_3, *i.e.*, violation V_3 (resp. V_4), leading to two candidate fixes F_3 and F_4 (resp. F_5 and F_6). Note that no violations of φ_4 exist before resolving the violations of φ_2. □

4.2 Optimizations for Violation Detection

In the general case, NADEEF has to trade in performance for generality and extensibility. For instance, violation detection upon all pairs of tuples using the vio() function is inherently expensive. However, it should be possible to do better in more restricted settings. One typical optimization is to divide large sets of input tuples into groups, referred to as *partitions*, such that violations are detected on each partition, provided that some information is known about the rules. For example, if we are resolving country code (CC) violations (*e.g.*, *Rule3* in Fig. 3), we may be able to divide them using the CC attribute. Thus, violations of tuples with the same CC but different country values need to be only detected inside each partition.

Another way to reduce the number of pairwise comparisons is to merge tuples. Specifically, two tuples t_1 and t_2 can be merged for a rule φ, if (1) (t_1, t_2) do not violate φ; and (2) for any t_3, $(t_1, t_3) \not\models \varphi$ iff $(t_2, t_3) \not\models \varphi$. Intuitively, the second condition requires that t_1 and t_2 can be merged if for any tuple t_3, they either both violate φ with t_3, or neither violates φ with t_3. This method is referred to as *compression* for violations.

In order to apply the above two techniques, we need users to provide some knowledge about their rules and how they use the attributes. Concretely, the system needs to know (a) the set of attributes that are used to indicate why two tuples should be compared; and (b) the set of attributes that need to be modified when there is a violation. We provide two functions LHS(φ) and RHS(φ) that the users need to

Algorithm ParComVio
Input: a database $\mathcal{D}$, a set Σ of data quality rules.
*Output:*the set $\mathcal{V}$ of all violations.

$\mathcal{V} = \emptyset$;
for each data quality rule φ in Σ **do**
  $\mathcal{P} = \mathsf{Partition}(\mathcal{D}, \varphi)$;
  $\mathcal{C} = \mathsf{Compress}(\mathcal{P}, \varphi)$;
  $\mathcal{V} = \mathcal{V} \cup \mathsf{DetectViolation}(\mathcal{P}, \mathcal{C}, \varphi)$;
while $\exists c_a, c_b \in \mathcal{V}$ such that $\mathsf{ext}(c_a) \cap \mathsf{ext}(c_b) \neq \emptyset$
  and $\mathsf{ext}(c_a) \neq \mathsf{ext}(c_b)$ **do**
    $\mathcal{V} = \mathsf{ExpandViolation}\ (c_a, \varphi_a, c_b, \varphi_b)$;
return $\mathcal{V}$;

Figure 6: Algorithm for partitioning and compression for multiple quality rules

implement to return the set of attributes for the above (a) and (b), respectively. For example, consider *Rule3* (φ_3) in Fig. 4, we have LHS(φ_3) = $\{\mathsf{CC}\}$ and RHS(φ_3) = $\{\mathsf{country}\}$.

Next, we first discuss the case for one data quality rule, and then extend to multiple quality rules. For simplicity, in the following, we focus our discussion on equality comparison. For various similarity comparisons, several blocking-based techniques are already in place and can be leveraged within NADEEF (see *e.g.*, [7,25]).

Single data quality rule. For a single data quality rule φ, *partitioning* groups all tuples whose LHS(φ) attribute values are the same. Using a hash table, the partitioning can be performed in linear time, assuming that a hash table requires a constant cost per operation.

For *compression*, two tuples t_1 and t_2 are merged into t_{12} *w.r.t.* φ if $t_1[\text{LHS}(\varphi) \cup \text{RHS}(\varphi)] = t_2[\text{LHS}(\varphi) \cup \text{RHS}(\varphi)]$. When they are merged, their cell values related to attributes LHS(φ) $\cup$ RHS(φ) are the same and will be compressed as $t_{12}[\text{LHS}(\varphi) \cup \text{RHS}(\varphi)] = t_1[\text{LHS}(\varphi) \cup \text{RHS}(\varphi)]$. We use the term *super cell* for a compressed cell. A super cell c is a cell with a set of identifers of original cells, referred to as the extension of cell c, denoted by $\mathsf{ext}(c)$. For the attributes that are irrelevant to φ, their cell values in t_{12} are set to null, and their extensions are empty.

It deserves to note that when similarity comparisons are considered, two cells whose values are similar cannot be compressed, if the similarity function is not transitive.

Example 2: Consider the database in Fig. 2 and the rule *Rule3* (φ_3) in Fig. 3. Figure 5 illustrates how the partitioning and compression techniques work. Here, LHS(φ_3) = $\{\mathsf{CC}\}$ and RHS(φ_3) = $\{\mathsf{country}\}$.

Partitioning table tran leads to two partitions: *Partition*1 with three tuples r_1–r_3 since their CC values are the same *i.e.*, 44, and *Partition*2 with one tuple r_4.

For compression, since $r_1[\mathsf{CC}, \mathsf{country}] = r_2[\mathsf{CC}, \mathsf{country}]$, the two tuples r_1 and r_2 (shaded tuples) will be merged into r_{12}. Their cells $r_1[\mathsf{CC}]$ and $r_2[\mathsf{CC}]$ (resp. $r_1[\mathsf{country}]$ and $r_2[\mathsf{country}]$) are merged into a super cell c_1 (resp. c_2) in r_{12} whose extension is $\mathsf{ext}(c_1) = \{r_1[\mathsf{CC}], r_2[\mathsf{CC}]\}$ (resp. $\mathsf{ext}(c_2) = \{r_1[\mathsf{country}], r_2[\mathsf{country}]\}$). The other cells of r_{12}, which are irrelevant to φ_3, have empty extensions and are omitted here. The other tuples (r_3 and r_4) are not compressed, and their cells c_3–c_6 are shown in Fig. 5.

From *Partition*1 and after compression (tuples r_{12} and r_3), one violation with four cells, *i.e.*, $\{c_1, c_2, c_3, c_4\}$, is detected. Note that this violation was originally represented by two violations as given in Fig. 5. There are no violations from *Partition*2. □

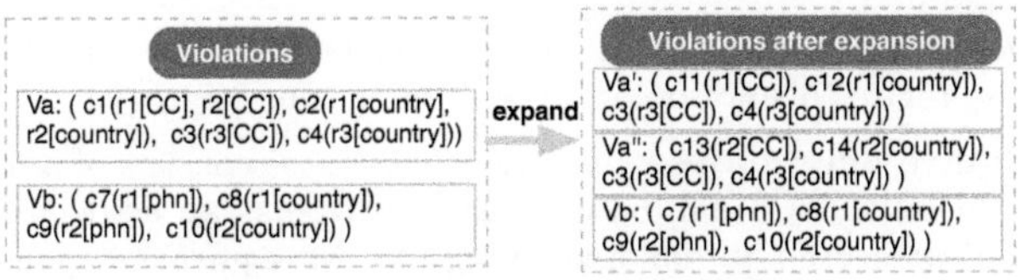

Figure 7: Expanding violations

Method	Comparisons	Violations
Brute force	1,199,880,000	130,038
Partitioning	6,797,429	130,038
Compression	52,512,009	4,434
Part. + Comp.	4,434	4,434

Figure 8: Benefits of partitioning and compression

Multiple data quality rules. The algorithm for detecting violations for multiple rules, referred to as ParComVio, is given in Fig. 6. Given a database $\mathcal{D}$ and a set Σ of data quality rules as input, the algorithm computes and returns a set $\mathcal{V}$ of all violations. It first creates partitions for each data quality rule (lines 2-3). It then compresses tuples for each partition (line 4). The violations for each rule will be computed within its partitions (line 5; see Example 2). After computing all violations, the algorithm needs to expand violations that have intersections across different rules (see Example 3 below) (lines 6-7). The violations are then returned (line 8).

Notably, a super cell is originally related to one rule (line 4), and all the cells in one super cell have the same value. Hence, extensions of any two super cells should be either the same, or disjoint, such that the value assignment to different super cells, for any cleaning algorithm, should be irrelevant. Otherwise, we need to expand these super cells (lines 6-7). We illustrate how the expansion works with the example below.

Example 3: For table tran (Fig. 2), assume that there is another rule φ_5 that states country uniquely determines phn. For simplicity, we only show one violation of φ_5, which is V_b as shown in Fig. 7. The violation V_a in Fig. 7 is the one derived in Fig. 5. Note that the two cells, c_2 in V_a and c_8 in V_b are not the same but overlap on r_1[country]. Hence, violation V_a needs to be expanded to V'_a and V''_a, as depicted in Fig. 7. □

One can derive original tuples from a compressed tuple, by uncompressing their super cells. Similarly, one can derive original violations from the violations given by super cells.

Complexity. The first loop (lines 2-5) runs in $O(|\mathcal{D}|^2|\Sigma|)$ time, by employing a hash table for partitioning, which is the worst case to detect violations pairwise without any compression. Similarly, the second loop runs in $O(|\mathcal{D}|^2|\Sigma|)$ time. In total, algorithm ParComVio runs in $O(|\mathcal{D}|^2|\Sigma|)$ time, where $|\Sigma|$ is typically small in practice.

Although the worst case complexity is the same as a brute force method, Fig. 8 shows the benefits of partitioning and compression using a 10K tuples HOSP data. Without any optimization, it requires 1 billion pairwise comparisons and produces 100K violations. With partitioning and compression, it requires only 4.4K pairwise comparisons and produces 4.4K violations.

5. DATA REPAIRING

In this section, we describe two algorithms for the data repairing module (implemented in NADEEF), referred to as GetFix. The first algorithm, which is designed to achieve higher accuracy, encodes a data cleaning problem to a variable-weighted conjunctive normal form (CNF) such that existing MAX-SAT solvers can be invoked to compute repairs with minimum cost. The second algorithm, which is designed to be more efficient, heuristically computes repairs by extending the idea of equivalence classes employed by many existing data cleaning algorithms. These two implementations illustrate the extensibility of our system using different repairing approaches. Better still, users can override these core classes with their own implementations.

5.1 A Variable-Weighted MAX-SAT Solver based Algorithm

Given a set $\mathcal{V}$ of violations and a set $\mathcal{F}$ of candidate fixes, the algorithm computes a set $\mathcal{F}'$ of fixes with the target that (1) when $\mathcal{F}'$ is applied to a database $\mathcal{D}$, the updated database $\mathcal{D}'$ is *fixed*, and (2) the overhead $\mathsf{cost}(\mathcal{D}, \mathcal{D}')$ of changing $\mathcal{D}$ to $\mathcal{D}'$ is minimum.

We propose to achieve the above target by converting our problem to a variable-weighted MAX-SAT problem, a well studied NP-hard problem. Given a CNF where each variable has an associated weight, this problem is to decide a set of Boolean assignments of variables such that (1) the maximum number of clauses can be satisfied (the whole CNF being satisfied translates to $\mathcal{D}'$ being fixed); and (2) the total weight of variable assignments to *true* is minimum, which translates to the cost of changing $\mathcal{D}$ to $\mathcal{D}'$ being minimum. Several high-performance tools for SAT (SAT-solvers) are in place [4] and have proved to be effective in areas such as software verification, AI, and operations research.

Weighted variables. Each assignment $t[A] \leftarrow a$ in a candidate fix F is represented by a Boolean variable $x^a_{t[A]}$. We denote by $\mathsf{wt}(x^a_{t[A]})$ the weight of $x^a_{t[A]}$. Intuitively, a variable $x^a_{t[A]}$ is *true* means that the attribute value of $t[A]$ should be changed to value a and if this update is applied to the database the cost is $\mathsf{wt}(x^a_{t[A]})$. Naturally, if $t[A] = a$, we have $\mathsf{wt}(x^a_{t[A]}) = 0$. Note that the compression technique discussed in Section 4 can be readily applied here. For each variable in a CNF corresponding to a super cell c, its weight is the cost of changing a normal cell multiplied by the cardinality of the super cell, *i.e.*, $|\mathsf{ext}(c)|$.

Clauses. The clauses are designed to represent three different semantics: (a) *inclusive* assignments: each cell that causes a violation should be assigned a (possibly) new value; (b) *exclusive* assignments: each cell can be assigned only one value; and (c) violation *avoidance*: cells that cause a violation cannot coexist with current values.

Given a set $\mathcal{F}$ of candidate fixes, let $\mathsf{val}(\mathcal{F}, t[A])$ denote $\{t[A]\} \cup \{a_i \mid (t[A] \leftarrow a_i) \in \mathcal{F}\}$, *i.e.*, the set of all values that $t[A]$ can be assigned to, including its current value. For example, for the candidate fix F_1 in Fig. 4, we have $\mathsf{val}(\{F_1\}, r_4[\mathsf{country}]) = \{\text{UK, Netherlands}\}$.

(a) Inclusive assignments. For each cell $t[A]$ such that $\mathsf{val}(\mathcal{F}, t[A])$ satisfies $n > 1$ where $n = |\mathsf{val}(\mathcal{F}, t[A])|$, we generate a clause with the form $(x^{a_1}_{t[A]} \vee \cdots \vee x^{a_n}_{t[A]})$. Intuitively, this clause is to ensure that at least one of the values should be assigned to $t[A]$.

(b) Exclusive assignments. For each cell $t[A]$ such that $\mathsf{val}(\mathcal{F}, t[A])$ satisfies $n > 1$ where $n = |\mathsf{val}(\mathcal{F}, t[A])|$, we generate $n(n-1)/2$ clauses, where each clause is in the form of $(\neg x^{a_i}_{t[A]} \vee \neg x^{a_j}_{t[A]})$, for each $a_i, a_j \in \mathsf{val}(\mathcal{F}, t[A])$, and $a_i \neq a_j$.

Intuitively, these clauses assure that at most one of the values can be assigned to $t[A]$.

(c) Violation avoidance. For each violation that consists of a set of n cells in the form of $t_i[A_i] = a_i$ for $i \in [1, n]$, A_i an attribute in t_i and a_i the current cell value of $t_i[A_i]$, we generate a clause $(\neg x^{a_1}_{t_1[A_1]} \vee \cdots \vee \neg x^{a_n}_{t_n[A_n]})$. Intuitively, this clause assures that these values cannot all be true simultaneously since they cause a violation when putting together.

Recall that the cost of each variable is determined by a function $\mathsf{cost}(c, v_1, v_2)$ that returns a value representing the cost of changing the value of cell c from v_1 to v_2. By default, it returns 1 (*i.e.*, unit update) when $v_1 \neq v_2$ and 0 otherwise.

Example 4: To better understand how the variable-weighted MAX-SAT solver works, we consider the six candidate fixes shown in Fig. 4. The variables with weight 1 are shown in the table below, *e.g.*, the variable $x^{Netherlands}_{r_4[\mathsf{country}]}$ indicates that $r_4[\mathsf{country}]$ can be changed to Netherlands. The variables with weight 0 are omitted.

$x^{Netherlands}_{r_4[\mathsf{country}]}$	$x^{66700543}_{r_3[\mathsf{phn}]}$	$x^{Netherlands}_{r_1[\mathsf{country}]}$	$x^{Netherlands}_{r_2[\mathsf{country}]}$	$x^{UK}_{r_3[\mathsf{country}]}$

We generate five *inclusive (resp. exclusive)* clauses, corresponding to the above five non-zero weight variables, as shown in the table below.

Inclusive assignments	Exclusive assignments
$(x^{UK}_{r_4[\mathsf{country}]} \vee x^{Netherlands}_{r_4[\mathsf{country}]})$	$(\neg x^{UK}_{r_4[\mathsf{country}]} \vee \neg x^{Netherlands}_{r_4[\mathsf{country}]})$
$(x^{66700541}_{r_3[\mathsf{phn}]} \vee x^{66700543}_{r_3[\mathsf{phn}]})$	$(\neg x^{66700541}_{r_3[\mathsf{phn}]} \vee \neg x^{66700543}_{r_3[\mathsf{phn}]})$
$(x^{UK}_{r_1[\mathsf{country}]} \vee x^{Netherlands}_{r_1[\mathsf{country}]})$	$(\neg x^{UK}_{r_1[\mathsf{country}]} \vee \neg x^{Netherlands}_{r_1[\mathsf{country}]})$
$(x^{UK}_{r_2[\mathsf{country}]} \vee x^{Netherlands}_{r_2[\mathsf{country}]})$	$(\neg x^{UK}_{r_2[\mathsf{country}]} \vee \neg x^{Netherlands}_{r_2[\mathsf{country}]})$
$(x^{UK}_{r_3[\mathsf{country}]} \vee x^{Netherlands}_{r_3[\mathsf{country}]})$	$(\neg x^{UK}_{r_3[\mathsf{country}]} \vee \neg x^{Netherlands}_{r_3[\mathsf{country}]})$

Moreover, four clauses are generated to avoid the four violations from Fig. 4, as shown in the table below, where "12…" is the abbreviation for "12 Holywell Street".

Avoid violations
$(\neg x^{31}_{r_4[\mathsf{CC}]} \vee \neg x^{UK}_{r_4[\mathsf{country}]})$
$(\neg x^{David}_{t_1[\mathsf{FN}]} \vee \neg x^{Jordan}_{t_1[\mathsf{LN}]} \vee \neg x^{12...}_{t_1[\mathsf{St}]} \vee \neg x^{Oxford}_{t_1[\mathsf{city}]} \vee \neg x^{66700543}_{t_1[\mathsf{tel}]}$ $\vee \neg x^{David}_{r_3[\mathsf{FN}]} \vee \neg x^{Jordan}_{r_3[\mathsf{LN}]} \vee \neg x^{12...}_{r_3[\mathsf{str}]} \vee \neg x^{Oxford}_{r_3[\mathsf{city}]} \vee \neg x^{66700541}_{r_3[\mathsf{phn}]})$
$(\neg x^{44}_{r_1[\mathsf{CC}]} \vee \neg x^{UK}_{r_1[\mathsf{country}]} \vee \neg x^{44}_{r_3[\mathsf{CC}]} \vee \neg x^{Netherlands}_{r_3[\mathsf{country}]})$
$(\neg x^{44}_{r_2[\mathsf{CC}]} \vee \neg x^{UK}_{r_2[\mathsf{country}]} \vee \neg x^{44}_{r_3[\mathsf{CC}]} \vee \neg x^{Netherlands}_{r_3[\mathsf{country}]})$

A variable-weighted MAX-SAT solver will take the conjunction of all the above clauses as input. There are two possible ways to fix the database, *i.e.*, the whole CNF is satisfiable, with a cost of 4 and 3 resp. as shown below.

Cost	Truth assignments of non-zero weight variables
4	$x^{UK}_{r_4[\mathsf{country}]}, x^{66700543}_{r_3[\mathsf{phn}]}, x^{Netherlands}_{r_1[\mathsf{country}]}, x^{Neterlands}_{r_2[\mathsf{country}]}$
3	$x^{UK}_{r_4[\mathsf{country}]}, x^{66700543}_{r_3[\mathsf{phn}]}, x^{UK}_{r_3[\mathsf{country}]}$

The variable-weighted SAT solver will choose the second option above, which will update three cells, *i.e.*, changing $r_4[\mathsf{country}]$ to UK, $r_3[\mathsf{phn}]$ to 66700543 and $r_3[\mathsf{country}]$ to UK, since it has the lowest total cost 3. □

5.2 An Equivalence Class based Algorithm

An alternative implementation of our core algorithm for data repairing is based on equivalence classes [8]. These were originally designed for FD and CFD violations. We first revise this notion and then present our strategy.

Equivalence classes. An *equivalence class* consists of a set E of cells. In a database $\mathcal{D}$, each cell c has an associated equivalence class, denoted by $\mathsf{eq}(c)$. An equivalence class E is associated with a set of candidate values, denoted by $\mathsf{cand}(E)$, and a unique *target* value, denoted by $\mathsf{targ}(E)$.

Given a set $\mathcal{V}$ of violations and a set $\mathcal{F}$ of candidate fixes as input, we build equivalence classes and find fixes as follows:

(i) Initialization. Each cell c involved in $\mathcal{V}$ is an equivalence class $\mathsf{eq}(c)$, and its candidate value is its current cell value.

(ii) Merge equivalence classes. (a) If there are two candidate fixes $c_1 \leftarrow c_2$ and $c_2 \leftarrow c_1$ in $\mathcal{F}$, the two equivalence classes for $\mathsf{eq}(c_1)$ and $\mathsf{eq}(c_2)$ will be merged into one, and the new set of candidate values is the union of the two sets of candidate values from $\mathsf{eq}(c_1)$ and $\mathsf{eq}(c_2)$, *i.e.*, $\mathsf{cand}(\mathsf{eq}(c_1)) \cup \mathsf{cand}(\mathsf{eq}(c_2))$. (b) If there is only one candidate fix $c_1 \leftarrow c_2$ (*i.e.*, $c_2 \leftarrow c_1$ is not a candidate fix), the candidate values of $\mathsf{eq}(c_1)$ will become $\mathsf{cand}(\mathsf{eq}(c_1)) \cup \mathsf{cand}(\mathsf{eq}(c_2))$.

(iii) Assign a target value. For each equivalence class E, select one target value $\mathsf{targ}(E)$ from its candidate values $\mathsf{cand}(E)$, such that the total cost of changing all cell values in E to $\mathsf{targ}(E)$ is minimum.

Using equivalence classes, we separate the decision of which cell values should be the same from the decision of what target value should be assigned to an equivalence class. We defer the assignment of $\mathsf{targ}(E)$ as late as possible to reduce poor local decisions. Note again that the compression technique discussed in Section 4 can be readily applied here. The cost of making a super cell value change in an equivalence class is multiplied by $|\mathsf{ext}(c)|$, the cardinality of the super cell (see Section 4.2).

6. EXPERIMENTAL STUDY

Using two real-life datasets, we evaluated our data cleaning system NADEEF along with four dimensions: (1) *Generality*: the programming interface of NADEEF can be used to specify multiple types of rules. (2) *Extensibility*: different core algorithms can be used to detect errors and clean data. (3) *Effectiveness*: while aiming to be generic, our method can find a *fixed* database with high accuracy compared with existing techniques. (4) *Efficiency*: our system can work on data in reasonable sizes.

Experimental Setting. We used two real-life datasets.

(1) HOSP *data* was taken from US Department of Health & Human Services (`http://www.hospitalcompare.hhs.gov`). It has 100K records with 9 attributes used in data quality rules: Provider Number (PN), zip, city, state, phone, Measure Code (MC), Measure Name (MN), condition, and stateAvg. We also downloaded another table of US ZIP codes from (`http://databases.about.com/od/access/a/zipcodedatabase.htm`). The table has 43K tuples with two attributes: zip and state.

(2) BUS *data* is a one table dataset obtained by joining 8 tables using primary-foreign key relationships. These tables were from the UK government public datasets (`http://data.gov.uk/data`). The table has 160K tuples with 16 attributes relevant to data quality rules: Locality Code (LC), Locality Name (LN), Locality Name Language (LL), Administrative Area Code (AC), Area District Code (AD), Cre-

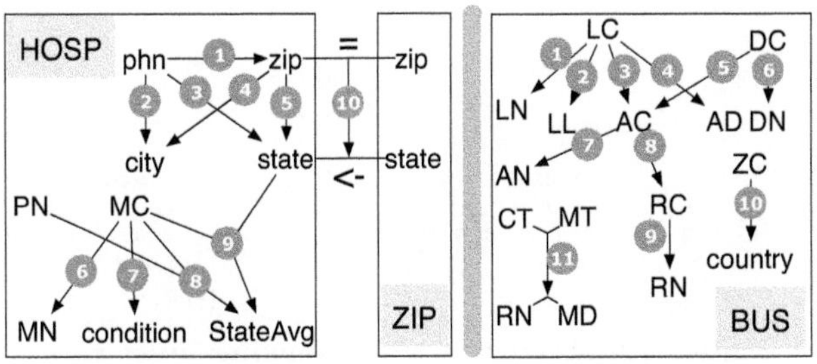

(a) HOSP dataset (b) BUS dataset

Figure 9: Data quality rules

ation DateTime (CT), Modification DateTime (MT), Revision Number (RN), Modification (MD), Area Name (AN), Region Code (RC), Region Name (RN), District Code (DC), District Name (DN), Bus Zone Code (ZC) and country.

Dirty datasets. Dirty data was generated as follows. For any dataset $\mathcal{D}$, we first cleaned $\mathcal{D}$ to get $\mathcal{D}'$ by using some cleaning algorithms followed by careful manual check, ensuring that $\mathcal{D}'$ is consistent *w.r.t.* the defined rules. We treated $\mathcal{D}'$ as the ground truth. We then added noise to $\mathcal{D}'$, which is controlled by noise rate noi%. Note that, we only added noise to the attributes that are used in data quality rules.

Data quality rules. All data quality rules have been designed manually (see Exp-1 below for details).

Algorithms. The system NADEEF was implemented in C++, including the following: (*i*) The algorithm for violation detection, using partitioning and compression techniques (Section 4.2) by default, referred to as GetVio. (*ii*) The algorithm for computing fixes using the variable-weighted SAT-solver (see Section 5.1), referred to as WSAT. We used a variable-weighted MAX-SAT solver from [22]. (*iii*) The algorithm for computing fixes using equivalence classes (Section 5.2), referred to as EQU. For comparison, we obtained the implementation of two algorithms for FD repairing, a cost-based heuristic method [5], referred to as HEU, and a vertex cover based approach [20], referred to as VER. Both approaches were implemented in Java.

We conducted all experiments on a Windows machine with an Intel 3.4GHz Intel CPU and 8GB of Memory.

Measuring Quality. To assess the accuracy of data cleaning algorithms, we used precision, recall and F-measure, which are commonly used in measuring the result of repairs, where

$$\text{F-measure} = 2 \cdot (\text{precision} \cdot \text{recall})/(\text{precision} + \text{recall}).$$

Here, precision is the ratio of attributes correctly updated to the number of all the attributes that have been updated, and recall is the ratio of correctly updated attributes to the number of all erroneous attributes.

Experimental Results. We now report our findings for the four dimensions mentioned earlier.

Exp-1: Generality. We show the *generality* of our framework by demonstrating that it can be used to specify multiple types of data quality rules. Fig. 9(a) depicts the rules defined for HOSP dataset and Fig. 9(b) depicts the rules for BUS dataset.

We defined 10 rules over the HOSP dataset, where rules 1-9 are all FDs and rule10 is an MD. For example, rule1 (resp. rule9) states that in table HOSP, phn (resp. MC and state) determines zip (resp. StateAvg). Rule10 states that if two

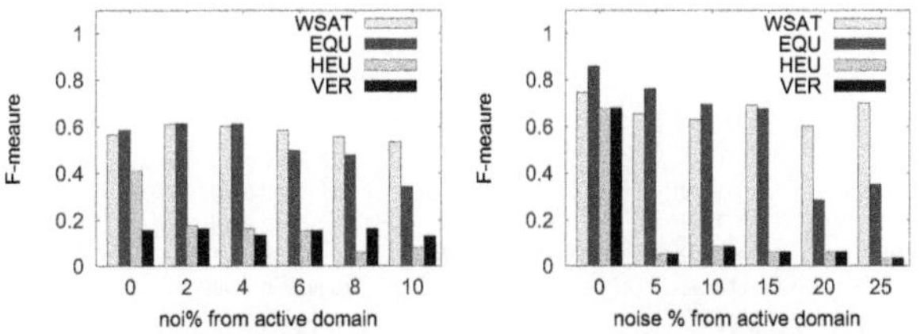

(a) HOSP (b) BUS

Active domain	WSAT	EQU	HEU	VER
0	132/186	137/187	73/73	39/220
2	141/195	141/195	72/553	40/237
4	137/199	139/199	70/606	42/374
6	127/178	126/250	67/612	39/265
8	132/204	136/301	59/1749	38/260
10	121/199	122/461	72/1543	26/189

Figure 10: Accuracy when the noise is from the active domain

zip code values from table HOSP and table ZIP are the same, but their state values are different, then the state value from ZIP table is more reliable. All of these data quality rules are defined over a pair of tuples.

There are 11 rules defined over the BUS dataset, where rules 1-10 are FDs, and rule11 is a customized rule. Rule11 states that, for each tuple, if its Creation DateTime (CT) and Modification DateTime (MT) are the same, then its Revision Number (RN) must be 0, and its status Modification (MD) must be new. We can use rule11 to fix erroneous cells as well as capturing missing values since the values for many RN and MD cells are missing. Remark that rules 1-10 are defined for a pair of tuples, and rule11 is defined on a single tuple.

For the rule classes that the users have to implement, FDs (resp. MDs) only require 65 and 34 (resp. 45 and 46) lines of code to define the functions for detecting violations and generating candidate fixes, respectively. For the customized rule (*i.e.*, rule11 for BUS data), the users need to write 50 lines of code in total. We see that using the concept of programming interface as defined in NADEEF, users will have to write only a few lines of code for data quality rules that are relevant to their dataset, without having to write an entire data cleaning system specially crafted for these rules. Note that for the FDs mentioned above, we assign them a default dynamic semantics of fixing errors by changing the values from the right hand side of the rules (see *e.g.*, *Rule2* in Fig. 3).

Remark. To ease the use of NADEEF, we have implemented some common classes that can be easily reused by users. Specifically, we have implemented *Rule* classes for CFDs (FDs) and MDs. For example, to specify various FDs, users only need to specify the left- and right-hand side attributes of each FD. We have also implemented some common similarity functions, with string edit distance by default.

Exp-2: Extensibility. We have already mentioned (Section 5) that we provide two different algorithms for fixing errors (*i.e.*, GetFix), namely WSAT and EQU. A user can specify in a configuration file which algorithm to use. Users can also specify a totally different core algorithm GetFix as long as that algorithm can take as input sets of violations and candidate fixes, and returns a set of fixes to be applied

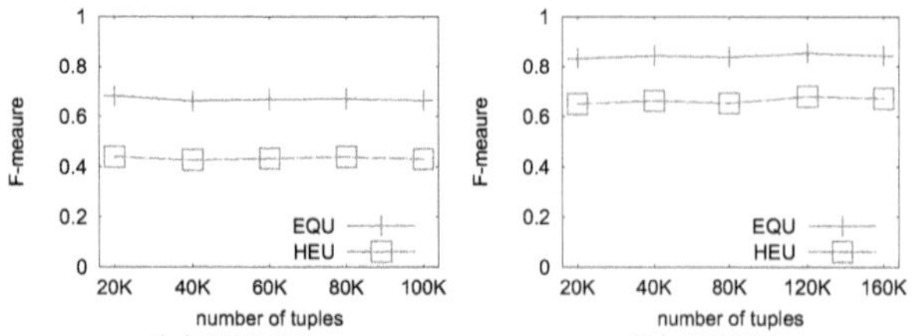

(a) HOSP (b) BUS

Figure 11: Accuracy when varying the size of data

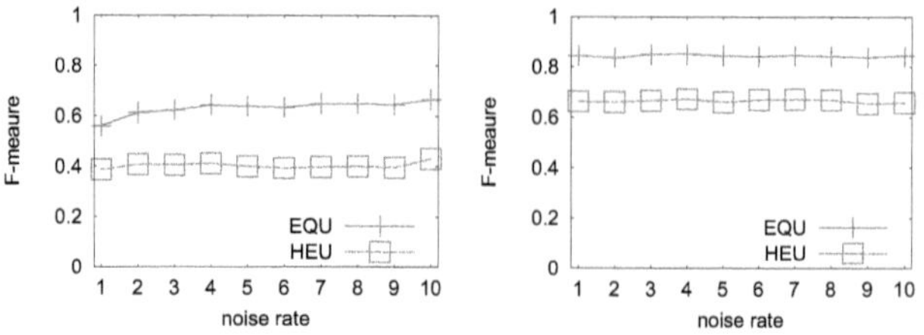

(a) HOSP (b) BUS

Figure 12: Accuracy when varying noise rate

to the database. Moreover, not only GetFix, but also the algorithm for GetVio, can be overridden.

Exp-3: Effectiveness. We evaluated the accuracy of different cleaning algorithms by varying noise rate (noi%) and the size of data. Noise is added by either introducing typos to an attribute value or changing an attribute value by another one from the active domain of that specific attribute.

Varying noise from the active domain. In this series of experiments, we fixed the overall noise rate to 1 percent and then varied the noise rate from the active domain (x-axis in both charts from Fig. 10). The results of comparing WSAT, EQU, HEU and VER are given in Fig. 10 (the y-axis represent F-measure values), where Fig. 10(a) is for HOSP data and Fig. 10(b) is for BUS data. We used 10K tuples for both datasets with FDs only.

Figure 10 shows that when there is no noise from active domain, *i.e.*, x-axis value is 0, both WSAT and EQU have comparable F-measure values with HEU as shown in Fig. 10(a) and 10(b). However, when there is noise from active domain, the F-measure values of both EQU and HEU drop quickly. This tells us that WSAT is not sensitive to noise from the active domain, while EQU and HEU are sensitive.

We explain the above results as follows: (1) WSAT is not sensitive to noise from active domain since it treats variables *independently* with the target of selecting variables with the least cost to satisfy the whole CNF or a maximum number of clauses. (2) EQU is sensitive since when there are erroneous values from the active domain, the algorithm merges (originally) irrelevant equivalence classes. Hence, when making decision to set an equivalence class a target value, many assignments are wrong. The case for HEU is similar. (3) VER is sensitive since when there are errors from the active domain, the algorithm will erroneously connect some tuples using hyper-edges (see [20]) as violations, which might connect two previously irrelevant violations and reduce the accuracy when repairing the data. (4) The reason that our approaches have higher accuracy is that users have to specify possible ways to fix errors, which avoids blindly making the database consistent by only targeting minimality.

We further explain the reason the recall of VER is low using the table in Fig. 10, the one for BUS data is similar and omitted for space constraints. The first column corresponds to the x-axis values in Fig. 10(a), *i.e.*, the percentage of noise from the active domain. Each cell in the table is for the number of correct changes over the number of changes. For example, the cell 132/186 represents that WSAT changed 186 values, and 132 of them are correct changes. We notice that when the noise from the active domain is large, *e.g.*, the last row, VER made only 189 changes to make the database consistent, while HEU made 1543 changes. Hence, VER uses less changes than HEU to compute a consistent database.

This group of experiments tells us that: (1) The new problem studied in this paper is meaningful, *i.e.*, instead of trying to compute a consistent database, we should try to resolve errors when candidate fixes are known. It highlights the need for users to provide useful information to guide the process of repairing data. (2) Equivalence class based solutions, which cover a large part of existing data cleaning algorithms, are sensitive to the noise from the active domain.

To favor the other approaches, in the following, we only consider noise from typos. Since WSAT and VER cannot scale well, we focus our comparisons mainly on EQU and HEU. Notice that for WSAT, we need a variable-weighted MAX-SAT solver. However, most popular SAT solvers are non-weighted or clause-weighted. While MiniSAT [18] is very efficient, its effectiveness was too low when we tried it and thus is not reported in this paper. Whenever a more robust variable-weighted MAX-SAT solver becomes available, we will evaluate it within our system.

Noise from typos only. We evaluated the effectiveness of different algorithms when there is only noise from typos. Figure 11(a) (resp. Fig. 11(b)) shows the case for HOSP (resp. BUS) when fixing noi% at 1% while varying the size of the data from 20K to 100K tuples (resp. 20K to 160K tuples). Moreover, Fig. 12(a) (resp. Fig. 12(b)) shows the result of HOSP (resp. BUS) data when varying the noise rate noi% from 1% to 10%, with 100K tuples (resp. 40K tuples). The results for the datasets of different sizes show similar trend, and hence are omitted here.

Figures 11(a) and 11(b) show that for different sizes of data, the F-measure values of different algorithms stay almost the same if the noise is only from typos, which verifies the previous group of experiments. The reason that EQU is better confirms that it is really helpful to have users specify the dynamic semantics of rules, *i.e.*, telling the system about the different alternatives to modify attributes when there is a violation.

Figures 12(a) and 12(b) show that when there is only noise from typos, existing algorithms are not sensitive to the noise rate. On the one hand, typos will only introduce independent violations. When treating these violations separately, the same algorithm will get a similar F-measure value. On the other hand, when there are errors from the active domain, most algorithms will associate (originally) irrelevant violations. This will negatively affect the results of most algorithms, which has been verified in Fig. 10.

Interleaving various types of data quality rules. We evaluated the effect of executing various types of data quality rules together versus executing them sequentially. Recall Fig. 9(a) for HOSP dataset, the MD rule10 overlaps with other FD rules. However, for BUS dataset, the customized rule11 has no overlap with other FD rules. Hence, we focus on evaluating the cleaning of HOSP in different rule order. For BUS,

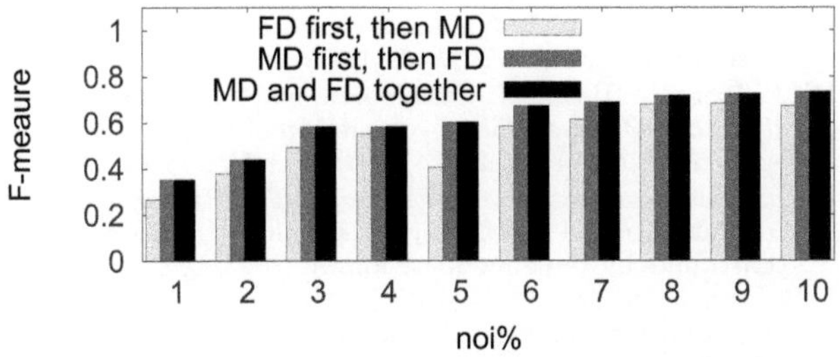

Figure 13: Interleaving various types of rules

since there is no overlap of rules, executing them in any order makes no difference.

We ran algorithm HEU on HOSP data with 100K tuples, varying the noise rate noi% from 1% to 10%. To clearly show the result, we added 5% extra noise to the attributes that are related to the intersected rules, *i.e.,* attributes zip and state. The result is shown in Fig. 13. When executing FDs first followed by MDs, the overall performance is worse than executing MDs first. Moreover, executing MDs and FDs together has the same performance as executing MDs first.

This experiment tells us that the order of executing multiple types of rules matters. That is, executing multiple types of rules in different orders will get different results. However, in practice, it is impossible to know the optimal order *a priori*. Hence, when having to deal with multiple types of rules, we should treat them *holistically*, as verified by Fig. 13.

Exp-4: Efficiency. In the last group of experiments, we studied the efficiency of various algorithms. We start by comparing EQU and HEU, followed by evaluating WSAT. Figure 14 shows running time of EQU and HEU: Fig. 14(a) relates to Fig. 11(a), and Fig. 14(b) relates to Fig. 11(b).

In these two figures, the x-axis represents the number of tuples and the y-axis the running time. We show two components of the running time of our method, where the lower part is for detecting violations (*i.e.,* GetVio) and the upper part is for repairing errors using EQU. The time for Updater is in milliseconds and thus not reported here.

The results show the following: (a) EQU and HEU deliver good results but for different applications, *e.g.,* HEU is faster for HOSP (Fig. 14(a)) while EQU is faster for BUS (Fig. 14(b)). (b) GetVio takes some time, but the time of EQU for computing fixes is quite efficient, which proves the benefit of our partitioning and compression techniques (see Fig. 8).

We also studied the efficiency of WSAT on HOSP and BUS data, where we fixed noi% at 1% while varying the size of data from 20K to 100K for HOSP and 20K to 160K for BUS. The running time is given in Fig. 15. The running times above 2 hours are not given since they did not run to completion. The high running times come from the inherent complexity of the problem of variable-weighted MAX-SAT problem, which is NP-hard. Thus, using WSAT for the whole dataset is not practical. However, it opens the opportunities to design an optimizer that first partitions the whole data cleaning problem into many smaller independent groups, then determines which algorithm, *e.g.,* HEU or WSAT, to invoke for each group.

Summary. From the above experimental study, we conclude that: (a) Providing a *generalized* programming interface, which requires minimum user efforts to specify data quality rules, is practically needed and is possible (Exp-1).

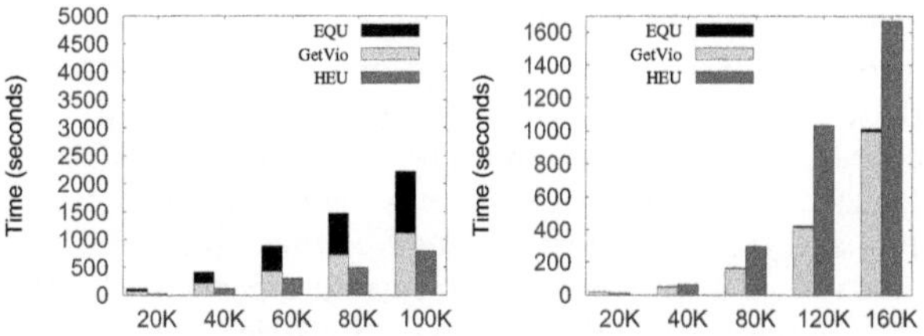

(a) HOSP (b) BUS

Figure 14: Efficiency study

HOSP	time (sec)	BUS	time (sec)
20K	617.4	20K	131.8
40K	4759.3	40K	482.1
60K	> 2 hours	80K	2473.2
80K	> 2 hours	120K	> 2 hours
100K	> 2 hours	160K	> 2 hours

Figure 15: Running time for WSAT

(b) By making our system *extensible*, we can benefit from algorithms that expert users implement for their own applications to replace the default core algorithms, especially for GetVio and GetFix (Exp-2). (c) Our systems can achieve better accuracy than existing methods since the users provide the system with the dynamic semantics to resolve violations (Exp-3). (d) Multiple types of data quality rules should be treated *holistically* (Exp-3), since in practice, it is difficult to know *a priori* the best order of sequential execution for algorithms designed for different rules. (e) Our system can work for data in reasonable sizes (Exp-4).

7. RELATED WORK

The first serious discussions and analyses of data repairing have emerged in [16]. After that, a large and growing body of literature has investigated ETL tools (see [2] for a survey), which support data transformations, and can be employed to merge and repair data [24]. Recently, there has been an increasing amount of literature on dependency theory (*a.k.a.* integrity constraints) to specify data consistency for data repairing, *e.g.,* FDs [28], its extension CFDs [8,12], MDs [13], FDs and INDs [5], and denial constraints [1]. However, they are in the class of universally quantified first-order sentences. Their limited expressiveness often does not allow to state problems commonly found in real life data as violations of these dependencies [11]. Through its programming interface, our framework is expressive enough to specify these problems as well as any of the existing constraints.

Data quality techniques often rely on domain-specific similarity and matching operators, beyond pure first-order logic. While these domain-specific operations may not be themselves expressible in any reasonable declarative formalism, it is still possible to integrate them into the framework of dependencies, especially for record matching (*a.k.a.* record linkage, entity resolution, and duplicate detection, see [10] for a survey). In contrast to matching rules (*e.g.,* [13,19,27]), our approach is more general since it also considers data repairing, among other things.

A general approach to tackle the problem of entity resolution is to define two functions, namely match and merge, over two tuples as proposed in [3], where match identifies duplicates and merge combines the two duplicated records into one. One can easily verify that the match can be naturally defined using function $\mathsf{vio}(s_1, s_2)$ to find duplicates, and fix() can be used to merge duplicates. However, merge cannot be used to represent updates of finer granularity (only some cell needs to be changed) as what fix() does in our system.

Several repairing algorithms have been proposed [5,8,15, 16,23,29]. Heuristic methods have been developed based on FDs and INDs [5], CFDs [12], and editing rules [16]. The methods of [5,8] employ confidence values provided by the users to guide a repairing process. Statistical inference is studied in [23] to derive missing values. To ensure the accuracy of the generate repairs, [23,29] require consulting the users. We do not assume the availability of confidence values in NADEEF. Moreover, while we do not support user interactions in the current implementation of NADEEF, the metadata we are handling can feed to a data quality dashboard that can then visualize the necessary information to understand the current health of the data and eventually allow the users to intervene to guide the cleaning process.

A number of studies have been proposed to tackle different data quality rules in one framework. The work [14] studies the interaction between record matching (MDs) and data repairing (CFDs). AJAX [17] and TAILOR [9] are toolboxes for record linkage. In contrast, the proposed system (a) covers a more general spectrum of data quality rules; (b) is extensible such that users can plug-in their own cores for error detection and data repairing, among other things.

8. CONCLUSION

We presented NADEEF, a commodity data cleaning system. The main design of NADEEF is to separate a *programming interface* that allows users to flexibly define multiple types of data quality rules about both their static semantics and dynamic semantics, and a *core* that implements algorithms to detect and repair dirty data by treating multiple types of quality rules holistically. We have demonstrated that our interface is general and expressive enough to define data quality rules beyond the well known ETL rules, CFDs and MDs. We have also shown the *extensibility* of NADEEF by showing that users can plug in other core algorithms, allowing experts to further customize our system.

Several extensions are underway. (1) To handle large volume of data, we plan to move our system from being memory-based to being disk-based, using an open source database *e.g.,* PostgresSQL. (2) We are designing more user friendly interface (*i.e.,* GUI) to help users define their rules easier. (3) We plan to incorporate various indices and blocking techniques in our framework to efficiently support similarity comparisons. (4) We plan to investigate techniques for partitioning a big cleaning problem into multiple small ones such that each one of them can be executed separately. This would provide opportunities for designing an optimizer to select the appropriate core implementation (*i.e.,* detection and repairing) for each partition as well running NADEEF in a parallel and distributed environment. (5) We will design and implement a live data quality dashboard on top of NADEEF and explore summarization techniques to more effectively involve users in the cleaning process.

9. REFERENCES

[1] M. Arenas, L. E. Bertossi, and J. Chomicki. Consistent query answers in inconsistent databases. *TPLP*, 3(4-5), 2003.

[2] C. Batini and M. Scannapieco. *Data Quality: Concepts, Methodologies and Techniques.* Springer, 2006.

[3] O. Benjelloun, H. Garcia-Molina, D. Menestrina, Q. Su, S. E. Whang, and J. Widom. Swoosh: a generic approach to entity resolution. *VLDB J.*, 18(1), 2009.

[4] A. Biere, M. Heule, H. van Maaren, and T. Walsh, editors. *Handbook of Satisfiability*, volume 185 of *Frontiers in Artificial Intelligence and Applications.* IOS Press, 2009.

[5] P. Bohannon, W. Fan, M. Flaster, and R. Rastogi. A cost-based model and effective heuristic for repairing constraints by value modification. In *SIGMOD*, 2005.

[6] L. Bravo, W. Fan, F. Geerts, and S. Ma. Increasing the expressivity of conditional functional dependencies without extra complexity. In *ICDE*, 2008.

[7] P. Christen. A survey of indexing techniques for scalable record linkage and deduplication. *TKDE*, 19(1), 2011.

[8] G. Cong, W. Fan, F. Geerts, X. Jia, and S. Ma. Improving data quality: Consistency and accuracy. In *VLDB*, 2007.

[9] M. G. Elfeky, A. K. Elmagarmid, and V. S. Verykios. Tailor: A record linkage tool box. In *ICDE*, 2002.

[10] A. K. Elmagarmid, P. G. Ipeirotis, and V. S. Verykios. Duplicate record detection: A survey. *TKDE*, 19(1), 2007.

[11] W. Fan. Dependencies revisited for improving data quality. In *PODS*, 2008.

[12] W. Fan, F. Geerts, X. Jia, and A. Kementsietsidis. Conditional functional dependencies for capturing data inconsistencies. *TODS*, 33(2), 2008.

[13] W. Fan, X. Jia, J. Li, and S. Ma. Reasoning about record matching rules. *PVLDB*, 2(1), 2009.

[14] W. Fan, J. Li, S. Ma, N. Tang, and W. Yu. Interaction between record matching and data repairing. In *SIGMOD Conference*, 2011.

[15] W. Fan, J. Li, S. Ma, N. Tang, and W. Yu. Towards certain fixes with editing rules and master data. *VLDB J.*, 21(2), 2012.

[16] I. Fellegi and D. Holt. A systematic approach to automatic edit and imputation. *J. American Statistical Association*, 71(353), 1976.

[17] H. Galhardas, D. Florescu, D. Shasha, E. Simon, and C.-A. Saita. Declarative data cleaning: Language, model, and algorithms. In *VLDB*, 2001.

[18] E. Giunchiglia and A. Tacchella, editors. *Theory and Applications of Satisfiability Testing*, SAT, 2004.

[19] M. A. Hernandez and S. Stolfo. Real-World Data is Dirty: Data Cleansing and the Merge/Purge Problem. *Data Mining and Knowledge Discovery*, 2(1), 1998.

[20] S. Kolahi and L. V. S. Lakshmanan. On approximating optimum repairs for functional dependency violations. In *ICDT*, 2009.

[21] G. M. Kuper. Aggregation in constraint databases. In *PPCP*, 1993.

[22] Y. S. Mahajan, Z. Fu, and S. Malik. Zchaff2004: An efficient sat solver. In *SAT (Selected Papers)*, 2004.

[23] C. Mayfield, J. Neville, and S. Prabhakar. ERACER: a database approach for statistical inference and data cleaning. In *SIGMOD*, 2010.

[24] F. Naumann, A. Bilke, J. Bleiholder, and M. Weis. Data fusion in three steps: Resolving schema, tuple, and value inconsistencies. *IEEE Data Eng. Bull.*, 29(2), 2006.

[25] G. Papadakis, E. Ioannou, C. Niederée, T. Palpanas, and W. Nejdl. Beyond 100 million entities: large-scale blocking-based resolution for heterogeneous data. In *WSDM*, 2012.

[26] V. Raman and J. M. Hellerstein. Potter's wheel: An interactive data cleaning system. In *VLDB*, 2001.

[27] S. E. Whang, O. Benjelloun, and H. Garcia-Molina. Generic entity resolution with negative rules. *VLDB J.*, 18(6), 2009.

[28] J. Wijsen. Database repairing using updates. *TODS*, 30(3), 2005.

[29] M. Yakout, A. K. Elmagarmid, J. Neville, M. Ouzzani, and I. F. Ilyas. Guided data repair. *PVLDB*, 4(5), 2011.

Don't be SCAREd: Use SCalable Automatic REpairing with Maximal Likelihood and Bounded Changes

Mohamed Yakout
Microsoft Corp.
myakout@microsoft.com

Laure Berti-Équille
Institut de Recherche pour le Développement
laure.berti@ird.fr

Ahmed K. Elmagarmid
Qatar Computing Research Institute
aelmagarmid@qf.org.qa

ABSTRACT

Various computational procedures or constraint-based methods for data repairing have been proposed over the last decades to identify errors and, when possible, correct them. However, these approaches have several limitations including the scalability and quality of the values to be used in replacement of the errors. In this paper, we propose a new data repairing approach that is based on maximizing the likelihood of replacement data given the data distribution, which can be modeled using statistical machine learning techniques. This is a novel approach combining machine learning and likelihood methods for cleaning dirty databases by value modification. We develop a quality measure of the repairing updates based on the likelihood benefit and the amount of changes applied to the database. We propose SCARE (SCalable Automatic REpairing), a systematic scalable framework that follows our approach. SCARE relies on a robust mechanism for horizontal data partitioning and a combination of machine learning techniques to predict the set of possible updates. Due to data partitioning, several updates can be predicted for a single record based on local views on each data partition. Therefore, we propose a mechanism to combine the local predictions and obtain accurate final predictions. Finally, we experimentally demonstrate the effectiveness, efficiency, and scalability of our approach on real-world datasets in comparison to recent data cleaning approaches.

Categories and Subject Descriptors

H.2.8 [**Database Applications**]: Data Mining; H.4 [**Information Systems Applications**]: Miscellaneous

Keywords

data cleaning, inconsistent data

1. INTRODUCTION

Data quality experts estimate that erroneous data can cost a business as much as 10 to 20% of its total system implementation budget [7]. They agree that as much as 40 to 50% of a project budget might be spent correcting data errors in time-consuming, labor-intensive and tedious processes. The proliferation of data also heightens the relevance of data cleaning and makes the problem more challenging: more sources and larger amounts of data imply larger variety and intrication of the data quality problems and higher complexity for maintaining the quality of the data in a cost-effective way. As a result, various computational procedures for data cleaning have been proposed by the database community to (semi-)automatically identify errors and, when possible, correct them.

Most existing solutions to repair dirty databases by value modification follow constraint-based repairing approaches [3, 19, 18], which search for minimal change of the database to satisfy a predefined set of constraints. While a variety of constraints (e.g., integrity constraints, conditional functional and inclusion dependencies) can detect the presence of errors, they are recognized to fall short of guiding to correct the errors; and worse, may introduce new errors when repairing the data [10]. Moreover, despite the research conducted on integrity constraints to ensure the quality of the data, in practice, databases often contain a significant amount of non-trivial errors. These errors, both syntactic and semantic, are generally subtle mistakes which are difficult or even impossible to detect and express using the general types of constraints available in modern DBMSs [20]. This highlights the need for different techniques to clean dirty databases.

In this paper, we address the issues on scalability and accuracy of replacement values by leveraging Machine Learning (ML) techniques for predicting better quality updates to repair dirty databases. Our proposed approach is complementary to existing efforts that leverage reference data [10] and user's interaction [22].

Statistical ML techniques (e.g., decision tree, Bayesian networks) can capture dependencies, correlations, and outliers from datasets based on various analytic, predictive or computational models [23]. Existing efforts in data cleaning using ML techniques mainly focused on data imputation (e.g., [20]) and deduplication (e.g., [6]). To the best of our knowledge, our work is the first approach to consider ML techniques for repairing databases by value modification.

Involving ML techniques for repairing erroneous data is not straightforward and it raises four major challenges: (1) Several attribute values (of the same record) may be dirty. Therefore, the process is not as simple as predicting values for a single erroneous attribute. This requires accurate modeling of correlations between the database attributes, which assumes that a subset is dirty and its complement is reliable. (2) A ML technique can predict an update for each tuple in the database; and the question is how to distinguish the predictions that should be applied. Therefore, a measure to quantify the quality of the predicted updates is required. (3) An over-fitting problem may occur when modeling a database with a large variety of dependencies that may hold locally for data subsets but do not hold globally. (4) Finally, the process of learning a model from a very large database is expensive, and the prediction model itself may not fit in the main memory. Despite the existence of scalable ML techniques for large datasets, they are either model dependent (*i.e.*, limited to specific models, for example SVM [21]) or data dependent (e.g., limited to specific types of datasets such as scientific data and documents repository). What is more, scalability is also an issue for constraint-based repairing approaches [8].

Such limitations motivate the need for effective and scalable methods to accurately predict cleaning updates with statistical guarantees. Precisely in this paper, our contributions can be summarized as follows:

- We formalize a novel data repairing approach that maximizes the likelihood of the data given the underline data distribution, which can be modeled using statistical ML techniques. The objective is to apply selected database updates that *(i)* will best preserve the relationships among the data values; and *(ii)* will introduce a small amount of changes. This approach enables a variety of ML techniques to be involved for the purpose of accurately repairing dirty databases by value modification. This way we eliminate the necessity to predefine database constraints, which requires the added expense of experts involvement. In contrast to the constraint-based data repair approaches, which find the minimum number of changes to satisfy a set of constraints, our likelihood-based repair approach finds the bounded amount of changes to maximize the data likelihood.

- One of the challenges is that *multiple* attributes values may be considered dirty. Therefore, we introduce a technique to provide predictions for multiple attributes at a time, while taking into account two types of dependencies: *(i)* the dependency between the identified clean attributes and dirty attributes; as well as, *(ii)* the dependency among the dirty attributes themselves. We present our technique by introducing the probabilistic principles which it relies upon.

- We propose SCARE (SCalable Automatic REpairing), a systematic scalable framework for repairing erroneous values that follows our approach and, more importantly, it is scalable for very large datasets. SCARE has a robust mechanism for horizontal data partitioning to ensure the scalability and enable parallel processing of data blocks; various ML methods are applied to each data block to model attributes values correlations and provide "local" predictions. We then provide a novel mechanism to combine the local predictions from several data partitions. The mechanism computes the validity of the predictions for the individual ML models and takes into account the models' reliability in terms of minimizing the risk of wrong predictions, as well as, the significance of partitions' sizes used in the learning stage. Finally, given several local predictions for repairing a tuple, we incorporate these predictions into a graph optimization problem, which captures the associations between the predicted values across the partitions and obtain more accurate, final tuple repair predictions.

- We present an extensive experimental evaluation to demonstrate the effectiveness, efficiency, and scalability of our approach on very large real-world datasets.

The rest of the paper is organized as follows: Section 2 defines the problem and introduces the notion of maximal likelihood repair. Section 3 presents our solutions for modeling dependencies and predicting accurate replacement values. Section 4 presents SCARE, our scalable solution to repair the data. We demonstrate the validity of our approach and experimental results in terms of efficiency and scalability in Section 5. We discuss related work in Section 6 and conclude the paper in Section 7.

2. PROBLEM DEFINITION AND SOLUTION APPROACH

In this section, we formalize our maximal likelihood repair problem and introduce our solution approach.

2.1 Problem Definition

We consider a database instance D over a relation schema $\mathcal{R}$ with $\mathcal{A}$ denoting its set of attributes. The domain of an attribute $A \in \mathcal{A}$ is denoted by $\mathtt{dom}(A)$.

In the relation $\mathcal{R}$, a set $F = \{E_1, \ldots, E_K\} \in \mathcal{A}$ represents the *flexible* attributes, which are allowed to be modified (in order to substitute the possibly erroneous values), and the other attributes $R = \mathcal{A} - F = \{C_1, \ldots C_L\}$ are called *reliable* with correct values. Hence, a database tuple t has two parts: the reliable part ($t[R] = t[C_1, \ldots C_L]$), and the flexible part ($t[F] = t[E_1, \ldots E_K]$). For short we refer to $t[R]$ and $t[F]$ as r and f, respectively (*i.e.*, $t = rf$). Note that the detection of the erroneous records is not the scope of our paper. We assume that it is possible to identify a subset $D_c \subset D$ of clean (or correct) tuples and $D_e = D - D_c$ represents the remaining *possibly* dirty tuples. This distinction does not have to be accurate in specifying the dirty records, but it should be accurate in specifying the clean records. Our objective is to learn from the correct tuples in D_c to predict accurate replacement values for the possibly dirty tuples in D_e.

There are various techniques to distinguish D_c as it is always possible to use reference data and existing statistical techniques (e.g., [17, 23]), as well as, database constraints (if available) to provide a score $P_e(t) \in [0..1]$ for each database tuple t for being erroneous. Applying a conservative threshold on the scores of each tuple $P_e(t)$, we can select high quality records to be used for training.

Example 1: Consider the example relation in Figure 1 with a sample of 8 tuples about some personal information: `Name`, `Institution`, area code `AC`, telephone number `Tel`, in addition to address information: `City`, `State` and `Zip`.

	Name	Institution	AC	Tel	City	State	Zip
t_1	H. Garcia-Molina	Stanford Univ.	650	723-0685	Santa Clara	CA	94305
t_2	S. Madden	MIT	617	258-6643	Cimradge	MA	02139
t_3	J. Han	UIUC	217	333-6903	Chicago	IL	61801
t_4	C. Clifton	Purdue Univ.	765	494-6005	Lafayette	IN	47906
t_5	W. Aref	Purdue Univ.	765	494-1997	WLafayette	IN	47907
t_6	E. Bertino	Purdue Univ.	765	496-2399	WLafayette	IN	47907
t_7	J. Widom	Stanford Univ.	650	723-7690	Stanford	CA	94305
t_8	M. Stonebraker	MIT	617	253-3538	Cambridge	MA	02139

Figure 1: Illustrative example

This data is a result of integrating professional contact information and lookup address database. Due to the integration process, we know that some of the address attributes (`City`, `State` and `Zip`) may contain errors. Therefore, we call the address attributes *flexible* attributes. After the integration process, we could separate high quality records by consulting other reference data or verifying some widely known relationships among the attributes. For this example, tuples $t_5, \ldots, t_8 \in D_c$ are identified as correct ones, while we are not sure about tuples $t_1, \ldots, t_4 \in D_e$. □

We introduce the data repair likelihood given the data distribution as a technique to guide the selection of the updates to repair the dirty tuples. Our approach is different from the maximum likelihood approach to learn a ML model parameter. In that case, the model's parameters and the captured distribution changes according to the observed data. In our case instead, we learn initially the data distribution from the set of clean tuples; and then, we change the dirty tuples *carefully* to maximize the data agreement with the learnt distribution. Our hypothesis is that the more the update will make the data follows the underline data distribution with least cost, the more likely the update to be correct.

Note that the tuples usually come to exist in the database independently (e.g., new customer records are inserted in the database independent from other customers information); errors in the tuples can be detected because of the existing values correlations among the database attributes that hold across the tuples. Such values correlations can be learnt using a ML model; and hence, the correctness probability of the tuples is conditionally independent given the learnt model. Consequently, the likelihood of the database D is the product of the tuples' probabilities given a probability distribution for the tuples in the database. Given the identified clean subset of the database D_c, we can model the probability distribution $P(R, F)$. Then, the likelihood of the possibly erroneous subset D_e can be written (as log likelihood):

$$L(D_e|D_c) = \sum_{t \in D_e} \log P(t \mid D_c) = \sum_{t=rf \in D_e} \log P(f \mid r) \quad (1)$$

where we use $P(t \mid D_c) = P(f \mid r)$, which we discuss in Section 3.

Assuming for a given tuple $t = rf$ a ML technique predicted f' instead of f. We say that the update u is predicted to replace f by f'. Applying u to the database will change the likelihood of the data; we call the amount of increase in the data likelihood given the data distribution as the likelihood benefit of u.

DEFINITION 1. ***Likelihood benefit of an update** u ($l(u)$):* *Given a database $D = D_c \cup D_e$, $t = rf \in D_e$ and an update u to replace f by f', the likelihood benefit of u is the increase in the database likelihood given the data distribution learnt from D_c, or $(L(D_e^u|D_c) - L(D_e|D_c))$, where D_e^u refers to D_e when the update u is applied. Using Eq. 1 we obtain:*

$$l(u) = \log P(f' \mid r) - \log P(f \mid r). \quad (2)$$

We also define the cost of an update as follows:

DEFINITION 2. ***Cost of an update** u ($c(u)$):* *For a given database tuple $t = rf$ and an update u to replace f by f', the cost of u is the distance between f and f',*

$$c(u) = \sum_{E \in F} d_E(f[E], f'[E]) \quad (3)$$

where $d_E(f[E], f'[E])$ is a distance function for the value domain of attribute E that returns a score between 0 and 1. Examples of distance functions for string attributes include the normalized Edit distance or Jaro coefficient; for numerical attributes, the normalized distance can be used, e.g., $d_E(a,b) = \frac{|a-b|}{max_E - min_E}$, where a and b are two numbers in $\mathrm{dom}(E)$, and max_E, min_E are the maximum and minimum values in $\mathrm{dom}(E)$ respectively.

Our objective is to modify the data to maximize its likelihood; however, and similar to existing repairing approaches, we need to be conservative in modifying the data. Therefore, we bound the amount of changes introduced to the database by a parameter δ. Hence, the problem becomes: given an allowed amount of changes δ, how do we best select the cleaning updates from all the predicted updates? This is a constrained maximization problem where the objective is to find the updates that maximizes the likelihood value under the constraint of a bounded amount of database changes, δ. We call this problem the "Maximal Likelihood Repair".

DEFINITION 3. ***Maximal Likelihood Repair:*** *Given a scalar δ and a database $D = D_e \cup D_c$. The Maximal Likelihood Repair problem is to find another database instance $D' = D'_e \cup D_c$, such that $L(D'_e \mid D_c)$ is maximum subject to the constraint $Dist(D, D') \leq \delta$.*

where $Dist$ is a distance function between the two database instances D and D' before and after the repairing and it can be defined as $Dist(D, D') = \sum_{\forall t \in D, A \in \mathcal{A}} d_A(t[A], t'[A])$, where $t' \in D'$ is the repaired tuple corresponding to tuple $t \in D$.

Note that δ can take values from 0 (*i.e.,* no changes to the data is allowed) to $|D_e| \times |F|$ (*i.e.,* change all flexible attributes of the dirty tuples). Regarding δ estimation, it is possible to use the score $P_e(t)$, which estimates the erroneousness of tuple t, to estimate $\delta = \epsilon \sum_{t \in D_e} P_e(t)$, where $\epsilon \in [0..1]$. The idea is that a possibly erroneous tuple is expected to be modified according to its score of being erroneous. ϵ can be chosen close to zero to be more conservative to the amount of introduced changes.

2.2 Solution Approach

For each tuple $t = rf$, we obtain the prediction f' that represents an update u to t. We compute the likelihood benefit and cost of u. Finally, we need to find the subset of updates that maximizes the overall likelihood subject to the constraint that the total cost is not more than δ, *i.e.*, $Dist(D, D') \leq \delta$.

Formally, given a set $\mathcal{U}$ of updates and, for each update u, we compute $l(u)$ and $c(u)$ using Eq. 2 and 3, respectively. Our goal is to find the set of updates $\mathcal{U}' \subseteq \mathcal{U}$, such that:

$$\sum_{\forall u \in \mathcal{U}'} l(u) \text{ is maximum} \quad \text{subject to: } \sum_{\forall u \in \mathcal{U}'} c(u) \leq \delta. \quad (4)$$

This is typically a 0/1 knapsack problem setting, which implies that the maximal likelihood repair problem is NP-complete.

Heuristic and quality measure: To solve the above problem, we use the famous heuristic to solve the 0/1 knapsack problem by processing the updates in decreasing order of the ratio $\frac{l(u)}{c(u)}$. This heuristic suggests that the "correctness measure" of an update u is *the ratio of the update's likelihood benefit to the cost of applying the update to the database* (*i.e.*, the higher the likelihood benefit with small cost, the more likely the update to be correct). Empirically, this gives good predictions for the updates as we will illustrate in our experiments.

Example 2: In Figure 1, assume that two updates were predicted to the database. u_1 updates t_3 such that f'_3={"Chicago", "IL", "60614"} and u_2 updates t_4 such that f'_4={"WLafayette", "IN", "47907"}. Assume also that both of $l(u_1), l(u_2)$ have the same likelihood benefit. In this case, u_2 will encounter lower cost in updating one character in both the `Zip` and the `City` attributes (update the `Zip` from"47906" to "47907" and the `City` from "Lafayette" to "WLafayette"), while u_1 will cost updating 4 characters in the `Zip` from "61801" to "60614". Hence, for $\delta \leq 2$ characters, only u_2 will be applied to the database. □

3. MODELING DEPENDENCIES AND PREDICTING UPDATES

The key challenge when considering data repair using the data distribution is that multiple attributes values may be dirty. In the case when a single attribute is erroneous, the problem is to model the conditional probability distribution of the erroneous attribute given the other attributes; and hence, a single classification model can be used to obtain the predicted values for the erroneous attribute. However, it is mostly the case that a set of attributes have low quality values and not a single attribute. Therefore, we need to model the probability distribution of the subset of dirty attributes given the other attributes that have reliable values (*i.e.*, most likely to be correct) to achieve a better prediction of the replacement values.

Example 3: In Figure 1 assuming we know that only the `City` attribute contains some errors. This is the simple case because a ML model can be trained by the database tuples considering the `City` as the label to be predicted. However in practice, more than one attribute can be dirty at the same time, for example, all the address attributes. In this case, we need a ML technique to model the distribution of the combination (`City`, `State`, `Zip`)—taking into account their possible inter-dependencies—given existing reliable values of attributes, e.g., (`Name`, `Institution`, `AC`, `Tel`). □

3.1 Modeling Dependencies

Let $\mathcal{S}_R = \texttt{dom}(C_1) \times \texttt{dom}(C_2) \cdots \times \texttt{dom}(C_L)$ denotes the space of possible reliable parts of tuples $t[C_1 \ldots C_L]$ (with clean attribute values), and $\mathcal{S}_F = \texttt{dom}(E_1) \times \texttt{dom}(E_2) \cdots \times \texttt{dom}(E_K)$ denotes the space of possible flexible parts of tuples $t[E_1 \ldots E_K]$ (with possibly erroneous values). Assuming that the tuples of D are generated randomly according to a probability distribution $P(R, F)$ on $\mathcal{S}_R \times \mathcal{S}_F$, $P(F|r)$ is the conditional distribution of F given $R = r$ and $P_{E_i}(E_i|r)$ is the corresponding marginal distribution of the values of attribute E_i,

$$P_{E_i}(e_i|r) = \sum_{f \in \mathcal{S}_F | f[E_i] = e_i} P(f \mid r)$$

Note that the posterior probability distribution $P(F \mid r)$ provides the means to analyze the dependencies among the flexible attributes. The distribution informs about the probability of each *combination* of values for the flexible attributes $\langle e_1, \ldots, e_K \rangle$, where $e_1 \in \texttt{dom}(E_1), \ldots, e_K \in \texttt{dom}(E_K)$.

Given a database tuple $t = rf$, the conditional probability of each combination of the flexible attribute values f can be computed using the product rule:

$$P(f \mid r) = P(f[E_1] \mid r) \prod_{i=2}^{K} P(f[E_i] \mid r, f[E_1 \ldots E_{i-1}]). \quad (5)$$

Note that we assume a particular order in the dependencies among the flexible attributes $\{E_1, \ldots, E_K\}$. To obtain this order, we leverage an existing technique [14] to construct a dependency network for the database attributes. The dependency network is a graph with the database attributes as the vertices; and there is a directed edge from A_i to A_j if the analysis determined that A_j depends on A_i. In our case, there will be two sets of vertices; the reliable set R and flexible set F. The first flexible attribute E_1 in the order is the one that has the maximum number of reliable attributes as its parents in the graph. Then subsequently, the next attribute in order i is the one with maximum number of parents that are either reliable attributes or flexible attributes with an assigned order. In our experiments, we followed this procedure by analyzing a sample of the database to determine the dependency order of the flexible attributes. Another alternative method to compute the conditional probability $P(f \mid r)$ without considering any particular order of the flexible attributes is to use Gibbs sampling [13]; however, it is very expensive to be applied to even moderate size databases. Please refer to [14] for further details.

In Section 3.2, we introduce an efficient way to obtain the predictions f' that is desirable for our cleaning approach and compute the conditional probabilities $P(f \mid r)$.

3.2 Predicting Updates

We use a ML model $\mathcal{M}$ (as predictor) to model the above joint distribution in Eq. 5. The model $\mathcal{M}$ is a mapping $\mathcal{S}_R \to \mathcal{S}_F$ that assigns (or predicts) the flexible attributes values f' for a database tuple $t = rf$ given the values r of the reliable attributes R. The prediction takes the form:

$$\mathcal{M}(r) = \langle M_1(r), \ldots, M_K(r) \rangle = f'.$$

To estimate the joint distribution of the flexible attribute values, $P(f \mid r)$ in Eq. 5, we learn K classification models $M_i(\cdot)$ on the input space $\mathcal{S}_R \times \texttt{dom}(E_1) \times \cdots \times \texttt{dom}(E_{i-1})$, (*i.e.*, using all the reliable attributes and the flexible attributes up to attribute E_i).

$$M_i : \mathcal{S}_R \times \texttt{dom}(E_1) \times \cdots \times \texttt{dom}(E_{i-1}) \to \texttt{dom}(E_i)$$

Algorithm 1 GetPredictions(Classification Model M_i, $\langle r, f[E_1], \ldots f[E_{i-1}] \rangle$ input tuple r_i, Probability P, Database Tuple $t = rf$)

1: **if** $(i > K)$ **then**
2: $f' = r_i - r$
3: AllPredictions = AllPredictions $\cup \{(f', P)\}$
4: **return**
5: **end if**
6: $f_{E_i} = M_i(r_i)$
7: $r_s = \langle r_i, f_{E_i} \rangle$
8: $P_s = P \times P(f_{E_i} \mid r_i)$
9: GetPredictions(M_{i+1}, r_s, P_s, t)
10: **if** $f_{E_i} \neq t[E_i]$ **then**
11: $r'_s = \langle r_i, t[E_i] \rangle$ {Adding the original E_i's value to the next input}
12: $P'_s = P \times P(t[E_i] \mid r_i)$
13: GetPredictions(M_{i+1}, r'_s, P'_s, t) {Predicting attribute E_i's value}
14: **end if**

We assume that M_i is a probabilistic classifier (e.g., Naïve Bayesian) that will be trained using D_c and produce a probability distribution over the values of the flexible attribute E_i given $\langle r, f[E_1], \ldots, f[E_{i-1}] \rangle$.

One efficient *greedy* way to approximate the optimal prediction f' is to proceed as follows: given a tuple $t = rf$, the classifier M_1 is used to predict the value of attribute E_1 (*i.e.*, $f'[E_1]$) given r. Then, M_2 predicts the value for attribute E_2 given r and $f'[E_1]$ as input. Proceeding in this way, M_i predicts the value of attribute E_i given r and $f'[E_1] \ldots f'[E_{i-1}]$. This approach can be considered as searching greedily for a path in a tree that has the possible values of $f' \in \mathcal{S}_F$ at the leaves. We call this tree as the *flexible attributes values search tree*. Needless to say this approach does not guarantee finding the prediction f' with the highest probability.

For a tuple t, to find a better prediction that is desired for our cleaning approach, we follow the conservative assumption in updating the database by considering and preferring the original attributes values in the tuple. Based on this assumption the best prediction will be among these explored tree paths, which involve the original values of the tuple t. Hence, we can compute, in addition to the greedy path, additional paths that assume that the original values in the tuple are the supposed predictions. The algorithm to compute a set of predictions for the flexible attributes F for a given tuple t is described in Algorithm 1, *GetPredictions*. Basically, *GetPredictions* proceeds recursively in the flexible attributes values search tree. At each node tree level i, two branches are considered when the prediction of attribute E_i is different from its original value in the tuple, otherwise, a single branch is considered. The initial call to Algorithm 1 to get predictions for tuple $t = rf$ is *GetPredictions(*M_0, r, *1.0*, $t = rf$*)*.

In Algorithm 1, Line 1 checks if we reached the prediction of the last flexible attribute E_K; and in this case, we add the flexible part f' of the obtained final tuple s to AllPredictions list. In Line 6, we predict the value f_{E_i} of attribute E_i. Lines 7 and 8 compose the new input r_s by adding f_{E_i} to r_i and compute the prediction probability so far, P_s. We then proceed recursively to get the prediction for the next flexible attribute $E_{(i+1)}$. The lines 11-13 are executed if the predicted value f_{E_i} is different from the original value $t[E_i]$. In this case, we compose another input r'_s using the original value $t[E_i]$ and compute the prediction probability so far using $P(t[E_i] \mid r_i)$ from the model M_i, then finally, proceed recursively to get a prediction for $E_{(i+1)}$.

Example 4: Consider the example relation in Figure 1. Assume that tuple t_4 was marked as erroneous and we want to obtain predictions for its flexible attributes. In *GetPredictions* initially r_i is the reliable attributes values {"C. Clifton", "Purdue Univ.", "765", "494-6005"}. In Line 6 the classifier M_0, which was trained using only the set of reliable attributes to predict the first flexible attribute `City`, provides the prediction to be "WLafayette". Then r_s is composed to be the input to the next classifier M_1, which was trained by the reliable attributes and the first flexible attribute `City` to predict the second flexible attribute `State`, r_s = {"C. Clifton", "Purdue Univ.", "765", "494-6005", "WLafayette"}. Since the predicted `City` is different from the one in the table, we compose another input to the classifier M_1 with the original `City` value, r'_s = {"C. Clifton", "Purdue Univ.", "765", "494-6005", "Lafayette"}. We obtain the prediction for the `State` given the two inputs r_s and r'_s and proceed recursively until we used M_3 to predict the `Zip`, and we finally extract f' from each r_i in Line 2 to end up with the list of AllPredictions. □

GetPredictions produces, for a given tuple t, at most 2^K predictions with their probabilities; however, in practice, the number of predictions are far less than 2^K. We select the prediction f' with the best benefit-cost ratio, *i.e.*, the update u that replaces f with f' and results in the highest $\frac{l(u)}{c(u)}$. Note that we need to compute $l(u)$ for only f' with $P(f' \mid r)$ being greater than $P(f \mid r)$, the probability of the original values, otherwise the likelihood benefit of the predicted update will be negative. Note also that $P(f \mid r)$ is included as well in the output of *GetPredictions*.

In Section 4, we present the method to scale up the maximal likelihood repair problem and get the predicted updates u along with their likelihood benefit $l(u)$. The cost $c(u)$ is straight forward to compute.

4. SCALING UP THE MAXIMAL LIKELIHOOD REPAIRING APPROACH

One of the key challenges in repairing dirty databases is the scalability [8]. In our case, the scalability issue is mainly due to learning a set of classification models to predict the flexible attributes values. The learning process in most ML techniques is known to be at least quadratic in the database size and the model itself may not fit in main memory. Indeed, there are efforts on learning from large scale datasets (e.g., scalable learning using SVM [21]). However, there is no much efforts in learning from large databases with most of attributes are string attributes and the number of correlations is large because of the large domain size of each database attribute.

In this section, we present a *model-independent* method to learn and predict updates to the database that is based on horizontally partitioning the database. Each database tuple will be a member of several partitions (or blocks). Each partition b is processed to provide predictions to the erroneous tuples $t \in b$ depending on the database distribution learnt from block b (*i.e., local* predictions). Finally, we present a novel mechanism to combine the local predictions from the different partitions and determine more accurate final predictions.

This method is in the flavor of learning *ensemble* models [5] or committee-based approaches, where the task is to predict a single class attribute by partitioning the dataset into several smaller partitions; then a model is trained by each data partition. For a given tuple, each model provide a prediction on the class attribute, and the final prediction is the one with the highest aggregated prediction probability. But, in our case, we want to predict the values of multiple flexible attributes together; and we are not limited to predict a single attribute value. Hence for a given tuple, we obtain a prediction (a combination f' of the flexible attribute values) from each data partition. We then propose a technique to combine the models' predictions into a graph optimization problem to find the final prediction for the flexible attributes. Our main insight is that

Algorithm 2 SCARE(D dirty database, $H = \{h_1, \ldots, h_J\}$ DB partitioning functions)

```
1:  Given H, partition D into blocks b_ij.
2:  for all block b_ij do
3:    Learn the models M_ij.
4:    for all tuple t = rf ∈ b_ij ∧ t ∈ D_e do
5:      Use M_ij to predict f'_j and get P_ij(f'_j | r) and P_ij(f | r)
6:      Store f'_j, P_ij(f'_j | r) and P_ij(f | r) in RS. {store in the
        Repair Storage.}
7:    end for
8:  end for
9:  for all tuple t = xy ∈ D do
10:   RS(t) = the candidate tuple repairs for t in RS.
11:   f' =SelectFinalPrediction(RS(t))
12:   For the update u to change f to f', compute the likelihood
      measure l(u) if f ≠ f'.
13: end for
```

the final (combinations of) predicted values are those which would maximize the associations among the predicted values across the partitions. Our mechanism to collect and incorporate the predicted updates takes into account the reliability of the learnt classification models themselves to minimize the risk of the predicted updates.

After obtaining the final predicted values with their likelihood benefit $l(u)$, we use them into the maximal likelihood repair problem (Eq. 4).

4.1 Process Overview

Algorithm 2 illustrates the main steps of the SCARE process to get the predicted updates along with their likelihood benefit. The primary input to the framework is a database instance D. The second input is a set of database partitioning functions (or criteria) $H = \{h_1, \ldots, h_J\}$.

There are two main phases for SCARE: (1) Updates generation phase (lines 1-8), and (2) Tuple repair selection phase (lines 9-13).

In Phase 1 (Line 1), each function $h_j \in H$ will partition D into blocks $\{b_{1j}, b_{2j}, \ldots\}$. Then, the loop in lines 2-8 processes each block b_{ij} as follows: *(i)* Learn the set of classifiers $\mathcal{M}_{ij}$ from the identified clean tuples in b_{ij} (lines 3); *(ii)* Use $\mathcal{M}_{ij}$ to predict the flexible attributes values for the possibly erroneous tuples in b_{ij} using Algorithm 1 (lines 4-7). For each tuple, the prediction is considered a *candidate tuple repair* and it is stored in a temporary repair storage, denoted as RS. Since each tuple will be a member of several data partitions, we will end up with a set of candidate tuple repairs for each possibly erroneous tuple. The details of the repair generation is provided in Section 4.2.

Phase 2 (lines 9-13) loops on each tuple $t \in D_e$ and retrieves all its candidate tuple repairs from the repair storage RS, then uses Algorithm 3 *SelectTupleRepair* to get the final tuple repair (update) with its estimated likelihood benefit. The details of the repair selection algorithm is provided in Section 4.3. Note that each iteration in Phase 1 does not depend on other iterations (similarly for the iterations of Phase 2). Hence, SCARE can be efficiently parallelized.

4.2 Repair Generation Phase

In this phase, the data is partitioned, as we will explain shortly, for two main benefits: *(i)* scale for large data by enabling independent processing for each partition; and *(ii)* more accurate and efficient learning of the classification models for the prediction task. The first benefit is obvious and the second benefit is obtained because of the following: When we train a classification model for prediction, ideally, we need the model to provide high prediction accuracy capturing all the possible dependencies from the data (we call it a model with *global view*). All the statistically significant dependencies are considered as the model's search space. However, if the space contains a lot of *weak* dependencies, most likely, the model will not be able to capture them. But if it does, the global view will not be accurate enough for prediction because of the model overfitting. Partitioning the database helps to capture local correlations that are significant within subsets of the database and that require a different degree of "zooming" to be recognized. Each of the partition functions $h \in H$ provides the search space partitioned according to the criteria shared by the tuples within the same block. If we train models on multiple blocks, we will have models with several *local views* (or specialized models, sometimes called *experts* [16]) for portions of the search space. Combining these local views, will result in a better prediction accuracy.

Partitioning the database: Each partition function or criterion $h(\cdot)$ maps each tuple to one of a set of partitions. Multiple criteria $H = \{h_1, \dots, h_J\}$ is used to partition the database in different ways. Each tuple t is mapped to a set of partitions, *i.e.*, $H(t) = \bigcup_{\forall j} h_j(t)$.

A simple way to choose the partition criteria is **Random** (*i.e.*, randomly partition the data many times). Another way to choose the criteria is **Blocking**, where partitions are constructed under the assumption that similar tuples will fit in the same block or inversely, tuples across different blocks are less likely to be similar. Many techniques for blocking have been introduced for the efficient detection of the duplicate records (refer to [6] for a survey).

It is worth mentioning that increasing the number of partition functions will result in a more accurate final prediction, because the variance in the predictions decreases as we increase the number of ways (partition functions) to partition the data. We found that partitioning the data using different blocking techniques provided more accurate predictions with less number of partition functions in comparison with the random partitioning.

Example 5: Consider again the relation in Figure 1. In this example, one may partition the database based on the `Institution` attribute (as a partition function) to get the tuples partitioned as follows: $\{t_1, t_7\}, \{t_2, t_8\}, \{t_3\}, \{t_4, t_5, t_6\}$. The result of the learning process from these data partitions will be expert models based on the person's institution. Another function may use the `AC` or a combination of attributes. Partition functions can be designed based on a signature based scheme or clustering as we elaborate in the experimental section. □

Reliability measure and risk minimization: In order to be conservative in considering the predictions from each block b_{ij} and its model $\mathcal{M}_{ij}$, we propose a mechanism to measure the reliability of a model and adapt the obtained prediction probability accordingly to support or detract the model's predictions.

Two major components help us judging the reliability of a model $\mathcal{M}_{ij}$: (*i*) the model quality, which is classically quantified by its *loss* $\mathcal{L}(\mathcal{M}_{ij}) = \frac{1}{|b_{ij}|} \sum_{t \in b_{ij}, t \in D_c, E \in F} d_E(f[E], f'_{ij}[E])$, where $|b_{ij}|$ is the number of tuples in partition b_{ij}, E is one of the flexible attributes F, d_E is a distance function for the domain of attribute E and f'_{ij} is the prediction of Model $\mathcal{M}_{ij}$ on the flexible attributes F for the tuple $t \in b_{ij}$ and $t \in D_c$; (*ii*) the second component is the size of the block: the smaller the block is, the less reliable the predictions will be. Hence, the reliability of model $\mathcal{M}_{ij}$ can be written as:

$$Re(\mathcal{M}_{ij}) = \frac{|b_{ij}|}{|D|} \left(1 - \mathcal{L}(\mathcal{M}_{ij})\right). \quad (6)$$

Finally, the prediction probabilities obtained from model $\mathcal{M}_{ij}$ are scaled to be: $\tilde{P}_{ij}(f' \mid r) = P_{ij}(f' \mid r) \times Re(\mathcal{M}_{ij})$.

Aggregating Suggestions: As mentioned earlier, a tuple $t = rf$ will be a member of $|H(t)|$ data partitions. From each partition, we get a candidate tuple repair for t, which are then stored in the storage RS with the following schema: $\{t\_id, partition, E_1, ..., E_K, \tilde{P}(f'|r), \tilde{P}(f|r)\}$, where *t_id* is the original tuple identifier, $partition$ is the partition name, $E_k \in F$,

RS(t_4)	City	State	Zip	P(f'|r)	P(f|r)
f'_1	WLafayette	IN	47907	0.7	0.6
f'_2	lafytte	IN	47906	0.6	0.5
f'_3	WLafayette	IN	47906	0.4	0.3
f'_4	Lafayette	IN	47907	0.8	0.6
f'_5	Lafayette	IL	47906	0.5	0.5

Figure 2: Generated predictions for tuple repairs with their corresponding prediction probabilities for tuple t_4 in Figure 1.

$\tilde{P}(f' \mid r)$ is the prediction probability of the repairing update f', and $\tilde{P}(f \mid r)$ is the probability of the original values in t. The space required for RS is of $O(|D| \times |H|)$.

Example 6: Consider tuple t_4 in Figure 1 and the flexible attributes are `City` and `State`, `Zip`. Assume that we used 5 partition functions and hence t_4 was a member of 5 partitions, consequently, we obtain 5 possible candidate tuple repairs. The table in Figure 2 illustrates the candidate tuple repairs of t_4, RS(t_4), with the corresponding prediction probabilities obtained from each partition. □

4.3 Tuple Repair Selection Phase

Once the candidate tuple repairs are generated, we need a repair selection strategy to pick the best one among the candidate set. One suggestion for a selection strategy can be the *majority voting*. For a tuple t, the majority voting can be done by selecting the most voted value from the partitions on each attribute E_i individually.

Majority Voting (MV): The majority voting strategy implies the assumption that each attribute was predicted independently from the others. For a tuple $t = rf$, we predict the combination of the flexible attributes f' together. Thus, the independence assumption of the attributes is not valid. Therefore, we propose a mechanism to vote for a final combination of the flexible attributes that takes into account the dependencies between the predicted values obtained from each partition.

Example 7: Consider the candidate tuple repairs of t_4 in Figure 2. Note that if we use the majority voting while using the prediction probability as the voter's certainty, the final prediction would be {"Lafayette", "IN", "47906"}. This solution does not take into account the dependencies between the predicted values within the same tuple repair. For example, there is a stronger association between "47907" and "IN" than between "47906" and "IN". This relationship is reflected on their corresponding prediction probabilities. The values "47907" and "IN" were predicted in f'_1, f'_4 with probabilities 0.7 and 0.8, while "47906" and "IN" were predicted in f'_2, f'_3 and their probabilities are smaller, 0.4 and 0.6. The same applies for the relationship between "WLafayette" and "IN", which have a stronger relationship than "Lafayette" and "IN". A more desired prediction will be {"WLafayette", "IN", "47907"}. □

For a given database tuple $t = rf$, our goal is to find the final combination $f'^* = \langle e_1^*, \dots, e_K^* \rangle$ such that $\sum_{b_{ij}, t \in b_{ij}} P(f'^* \mid r)$ is maximum. This requires the computation of the probability of each possible combination of the flexible attribute in each data block. Instead, we can search for the values that can maximize all the pairwise joint probabilities. In principle, if we maximize the pairwise association between the predicted values, then this implies maximizing the full association between the predicted values. Hence, the final update is the one that would maximize the prediction probabilities for each pair of attribute values. We formalize this problem as follows:

DEFINITION 4. *The Tuple Repair Selection Problem: Given a set of predicted combination for the flexible attributes RS(t)=* $\{f'_1, \dots, f'_{|H|}\}$ *for database tuple* $t = rf$ *along with the prediction probabilities of each combination, (i.e., for* $f'_j \in$*RS(t), we have the*

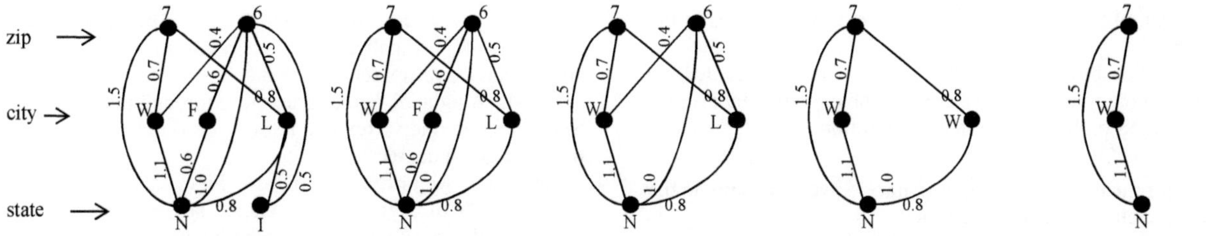

(a) Constructed Graph (b) After removing I (c) After removing F (d) After removing 6 (e) After removing W

Figure 3: Step by step demonstration for the SelectTupleRepair algorithm. At each iteration, the vertex with minimum weighted degree is removed as long as it is not the only vertex in its corresponding vertex set.

corresponding prediction probabilities $P(f'_j \mid r)$), the tuple repair selection problem for tuple t is to find $f'^* = \langle e^*_1, \ldots, e^*_K \rangle$ such that the following sum is maximum

$$\sum_{\forall\, e^*_i,\, e^*_k,\, i \neq k} \quad \sum_{\forall\, f' \in RS(t), e^*_i = f'[E_i],\, e^*_k = f'[E_k]} p(f' \mid r).$$

Solving the Tuple Repair Selection Problem: To find a solution, we map this problem to a graph optimization problem for finding the K-heaviest subgraph (KHS) [2] in a K-partite graph (KPG). The key idea is to process each database tuple t individually and use its set of candidate tuple repairs, RS(t), to construct a graph, where each vertex is an attribute value, and an edge is added between a pair of vertices *iff* the corresponding values co-occur in a prediction $f' \in$RS(t). The edges will have a weight derived from the obtained prediction probabilities. It is worth noting that this strategy is applied for each tuple on separate, therefore, this phase can be efficiently parallelized.

Finding KHS in KPG: The K-heaviest subgraph (KHS) problem is an NP optimization problem [2]. In an instance of the KHS problem, we are given a graph $G = (V_G, E_G)$, where V_G is the set of vertices of size n, E_G is the set of edges with non-negative weights (W_{wv} denotes the weight on the edge between vertices w, v), and a positive integer $K < n$.

The goal is to find $V' \subset V_G$, $|V'| = K$, where $\sum_{(w,v) \in E_G \cap (V' \times V')} W_{wv}$ is maximum. In other words, the goal is to find a K-vertex subgraph with the maximum weight.

A graph $G = (V_G, E_G)$ is said to be K-partite if we can divide V_G into K subsets $\{V_1, \ldots, V_K\}$, such that two vertices in the same subset can *not* be adjacent. We call *KHS in KPG problem*, the problem of finding KHS in a K-partite graph such that the subgraph contains a vertex from each partite.

DEFINITION 5. ***The KHS in KPG problem.*** *Given a K-partite graph $G = (V_1, \ldots, V_K, E_G)$, find $V' = \{v_1, \ldots, v_K\}$ such that $v_k \in V_k$ and $\sum_{(v_i,v_j) \in E_G \cap (V' \times V')} W_{v_i v_j}$ is maximum.*

LEMMA 1. *The KHS in KPG is NP-Complete.*

PROOF. This is a proof sketch. It is straight forward to see that we can reduce the problem of finding K-Clique (Clique of size K) in K-partite graph to the KHS in KPG problem. The problem of K-Clique in K-partite graph G is NP-complete by reduction from the problem of $(n - K)$-vertex cover in the complement K-partite graph G', which is NP-Complete (see [15] for details). ☐

Mapping the Tuple Repair Selection Problem to the KHS in KPG problem (KHSKPG): Given a set of predictions RS(t)= $\{f'_1, \ldots, f'_{|H|}\}$ for the flexible attributes of a tuple $t = rf$, where $f'_j = \langle e^{(j)}_1, \ldots, e^{(j)}_K \rangle$ and $K = |F|$ is the number of flexible attributes.

The repair selection problem can be mapped to the KHS in KPG problem using the following steps:

1. *Building vertex sets for each attribute E_k:* For each attribute E_k, create a vertex v for each distinct value in $\{e^{(1)}_k, \ldots, e^{(|H|)}_k\}$. Note that we have a set of vertices for each attribute E_k (*i.e.*, partite).
2. *Adding edges:* Add an edge between vertices v, w when their corresponding values co-occur in a candidate tuple repair. Note that v, w can not belong to the same vertex set.
3. *Assign edge weights:* For an edge between v, w, the weight is computed as follows: Let $f_{(v,w)} = \{f'_j | f'_j$ contains both $v, w\}$, *i.e.*, the set of predictions that contain both the values v, w.

$$W_{vw} = \sum_{f'_j \in f_{(v,w)}} P_{ij}(f'_j \mid r)$$

where $P_{ij}(f'_j \mid r)$ is the prediction probability of f'_j obtained from partition b_{ij}.

The graph construction requires a single scan over the predictions RS(t)= $\{f'_1, \ldots, f'_{|H(t)|}\}$, hence, it is of $O(K\,|H|)$. The number of vertices is the number of distinct values in the candidate tuple repairs.

Example 8: Figure 3(a) shows the constructed 3-partite graph from the predictions in Figure 2 for tuple t_4 in the original relation of Figure 1. For each attribute, there is a vertex set (or partite), e.g., the corresponding set of the `Zip` attribute contains {"47906", "47907"}. In the graph, we replaced the actual attributes values by a character abbreviation to have a more compact graph as follows: {"6" → "47906", "7" → "47907", "L" → "Lafayette", "W" → "Wlafayette", "F" → "lafytte", "N" → "IN", "I" → "IL"}.

Note that there is an edge between "W" and "N" with edge weight of 1.1 (= 0.4 + 0.7). This is because "WLafayette" and "IN" co-occur twice in f'_1 and f'_3 and their probabilities are 0.7 and 0.4 respectively. Also, there is an edge between "I" and "6" with weight of 0.5, because "IL" and "47906" co-occur once in f'_5 with probability 0.5. Similarly, the rest of the graph is constructed. ☐

Finally, finding the KHS in the constructed KPG is a solution to the tuple repair selection problem. The underlying idea is that the resulting K-subgraph $G'(V', E')$ will contain exactly a single vertex from each vertex set. This corresponds to selecting a value for each flexible attribute. Moreover, the weight of the selected subgraph corresponds to the result of maximizing the summation in Definition 4.

Computing the likelihood benefit: For a tuple $t = rf$, the solution of the KHS in KPG problem is the final prediction f' for the flexible attributes. The final prediction probability of f' is computed from the solution graph $G'(V', E')$ by

$$P(f' \mid r) = \frac{1}{|E'|} \sum_{e_{vw} \in E'} \frac{1}{|f_{(v,w)}|} \sum_{f'_j \in f_{(v,w)}} P_{ij}(f'_j \mid r).$$

The inner summation averages the probability of each pair of attribute values (*i.e.*, each edge in G') in the final prediction f'. The outer summation averages the probability over all the edges in the final graph G'.

The prediction probability of the original values in the flexible attribute f is computed following the ensemble method by averaging the obtained probability from each partition, *i.e.*, $P(f \mid r) = \frac{1}{|H|}\sum_{b_{ij}, t \in b_{ij}} P_{ij}(f \mid r)$.

Finally, for the update u changing f into f', we can compute the likelihood benefit $l(u)$ using Equation 2.

Example 9: Consider the constructed initial graph in Figure 3(a). Assuming that the solution for KHS in KPG is the subgraph {"W", "N", "7"} shown in Figure 3(e). Now, we have an update u to change the original values in tuple t_4 in Figure 1 from f ={"Lafayette", "IN", "47906"} to f' ={"WLafayette", "IN", "47907"}. From the RS(t_4) in Figure 2, we get $P(f \mid r) = avg\{0.6, 0.5, 0.3, 0.6, 0.5\} = 0.5$. For $P(f' \mid r) = \frac{1}{3}\left[\frac{1}{2}(0.7 + 0.4) + \frac{1}{2}(0.7 + 0.8) + 0.7\right] = 0.66$. Finally, we can use Eq. 2 to compute $l(u) = 0.12$. □

4.4 Approximate Solution for Tuple Repair Selection

For the general problem of finding the KHS, many approximate algorithms were introduced (e.g., [1, 2, 12]). For instance, in [1] the authors model the problem as a quadratic 0/1 program and apply random sampling and randomized rounding techniques resulting in a polynomial-time approximation scheme, and in [12], the algorithm is based on semi-definite programming relaxation.

If K is very small, then the optimal solution can be found by enumeration. For the case where K is not very small, we provide here an approximate solution that is inspired by the greedy heuristic discussed in [2]. For the general case graph problem, the heuristic repeatedly deletes a vertex with the least weighted degree from the current graph until K vertices are left. The vertex weighted degree is the sum of weights on the edges attached to it.

In the following, we follow the same heuristic for the case of K-partite graph. However, we iteratively remove the vertex with least weighted degree as long as it is *not* the only vertex left in the partite, otherwise, we find the next least weighted degree vertex. The algorithm is a greedy 2-approximation following the analysis discussed in [2].

Algorithm 3 SelectTupleRepair($G(V, E)$ graph, $\mathcal{S} = \{S_1, \ldots, S_K\}$)

1: **while** $\exists S \in \mathcal{S}$ s.t. $|S| > 1$ **do**
2: v =GetMinWeightedDegreeVertex($G, \mathcal{S}$)
3: **If** v = null **Then** break;
4: **for all** vertex $w \in V$ s.t. $e_{wv} \in E$ **do**
5: Remove e_{wv} from G.
6: Weighted_Degree(w) - = W_{wv}
7: **end for**
8: Remove v from its corresponding set S.
9: **end while**

Algorithm 3 shows the main steps to find the final tuple repair. There are two inputs to the algorithm: *(i)* the constructed graph $G(V_G, E_G)$ from the predictions; and *(ii)* the sets of vertices $\mathcal{S} = \{S_1, \ldots, S_K\}$, where each S_k represents the predicted values for attribute E_k. We store for each vertex v its current weighted degree in Weighted_Degree(v)=$\sum_{\forall e_{vw} \in E_G} W_{vw}$, which is the sum of the edges weights that are incident to v.

The algorithm proceeds iteratively in the loop illustrated in lines 1-9. The loop stops when a solution is found, where there is only one vertex in each vertex set, *i.e.*, $|S| = 1\ \forall S \in \mathcal{S}$. In each loop iteration, we start (Line 2) by finding the vertex v that has the minimum weighted degree using the Algorithm GetMinWeightedDegreeVertex($G, \mathcal{S}$). Then, we remove all the edges incident to v and update the WeightedDegree(w) by and subtracting W_{wv}, where w was connected to v by the removed edge e_{wv} (Lines 4-7). Finally, vertex v is removed from G and from its corresponding vertex set in Line 8.

GetMinWeightedDegreeVertex goes through the vertex sets that has more than one vertex and returns the vertex that has the minimum weighted degree.

Analysis: Algorithm 3 requires: First, visiting all n vertices to remove them except for K ones. For each vertex, each set $S \in \mathcal{S}$ of the K sets is visited to get its minimum vertex according to the weighted degree. This requires $O(nK \log |S|)$, where $n \approx O(K|H|)$ and $|S|$'s worst case is $O(|H|)$. Hence, visiting the vertices is of $O(K^2|H| \log |H|)$. Second, removing the vertices requires visiting their edges, $O(|E_G|)$, which has a worst case of $O(K^2|H|)$. Then, the overall complexity of Algorithm 3 is $O(K^2|H| \log |H|)$.

Example 10: The SelectTupleRepair algorithm is illustrated step-by-step in Figure 3. The algorithm looks for the vertex with the least weighted degree to be removed. The first vertex is "I", which has a weighted degree equal $1.0 = 0.5 + 0.5$, corresponding to the two incident edges in "I". This leaves the vertex set of the `State` attribute with only one vertex, "N". Therefore, we do not consider removing the vertex "N" in further iterations of the algorithm. The next vertex to remove is "F" to get Figure 3(c), and so on.

Finally, we got the final solution in Figure 3(e), which corresponds to a subgraph with 3 vertices —there is a vertex from each initial partite. This graph is the heaviest subgraph of size 3 (*i.e.*, the sum of the edges weight is the maximum), where each vertex belongs to a different partite. It is worth mentioning that the final graph does not have to be fully connected. Thus, the final prediction is {"WLafayette", "IN", "47907"}. □

5. EXPERIMENTS

In this section, we evaluate our data repair approach; specifically, the objectives of the experiments are as follows: (1) Quality evaluation of SCARE and the notion of maximal likelihood repair in comparison with the constraint-based repairing approaches of [3] and [11], the single model approach, and majority voting; (2) Comparison between SCARE and ERACER [20] for missing values prediction; (3) Study of SCARE parameters varying the number of changes, SCARE iterations and partition functions; (4) Assessment of the scalability of SCARE.

Datasets: In our evaluations, we use three datasets: *(i)* Dataset 1 is a real-world dataset obtained by integrating (anonymized) emergency room visits from 74 hospitals. This is the dataset we use for most of the quality experiments. Since such data is coming from several sources, a myriad of data quality issues arose due to the different health care information systems used by these hospitals and the different operators responsible for entering the data. We selected a subset of the available patient attributes, namely `Patient ID`, `Age`, `Sex`, `Classification`, `Complaint`, `HospitalName`, `StreetAddress`, `City`, `Zip`, `State` and `VisitDate`. This is in addition to the `Longitude` and `Latitude` of the address information. *(ii)* Dataset 2 is the US Census Data (1990) Dataset[1] containing about 2 M tuples. It has been used only in the scalability experiments. *(iii)* Dataset 3 is the Intel Lab Data (ILD[2]) used to evaluate SCARE for predicting missing values and compare it to ERACER [20], as a recent system that relies on relational learning for predicting missing data in relational databases.

Setup: To evaluate the quality of the repairing techniques in the first comparative study, we manually cleaned the dirty Dataset 1: we used addresses web sites and repositories, external reference

[1]http://archive.ics.uci.edu/ml/datasets/US+Census+Data+ (1990)
[2]http://db.csail.mit.edu/labdata/labdata.html.

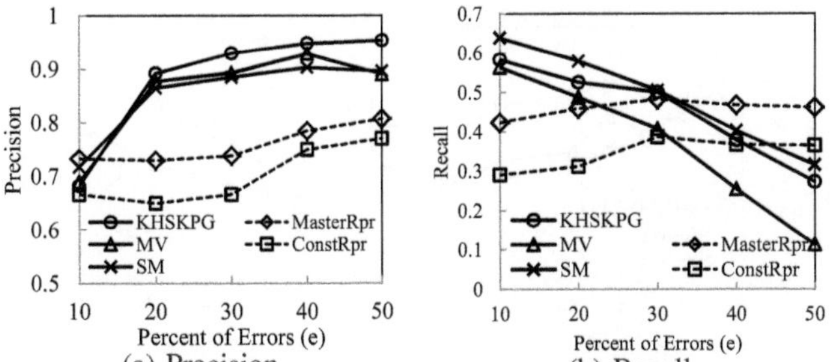

(a) Precision (b) Recall

Figure 4: Quality vs. the percentage of errors: SCARE maintains high precision by making the best use of δ, the allowed amount of changes in Dataset 1.

data sources, and visual inspection to obtain the clean dataset considered as the Golden Standard. We selected a set of attributes to be the flexible ones where we injected an increasing percentage of errors introduced in multiple attributes of the records. The flexible attributes of Dataset 1 that we considered for error injection and repairing were (`City`, `Zip`, `HospitalName`, `Longitude` and `Latitude`). Then, we compared the clean version of Dataset 1 (Golden Standard) with the repaired dataset outputs of each method (including ours).

Parameters: In our evaluations, we study several parameters that we list here with their assigned default values: (1) e: the percentage of the erroneous tuples in the dataset (default 30%), (2) d: the dataset size (default 10,000 tuples), (3) δ: the maximum amount of changes, as a fraction of d, the dataset size that SCARE is allowed to update (default 0.1 or 10% of d). (4) I: the number of iterations to run SCARE (default 1). (5) $|H|$: the number of partition functions (default 5).

Regarding the partition functions using blocking, we repeat the following process $|H|$ times: we randomly sample from the dataset a small number of tuples to be clustered in $\frac{|D|}{n_b}$ clusters, where n_b is the average number of tuples per partition. Then, each tuple is assigned to the closest cluster as its corresponding partition name. This process allows for having different blocking functions due to the random sample of tuples used in the clustering step of each iteration. The tuples that have been assigned to the same partition have common or similar features due to their assignment to the closest cluster. In all our quality experiments, we use blocking as the technique to partition the dataset. Another simple way to partition the dataset is to use random partitioning functions. In this case, given n_b, we assign each tuple to a partition name b_{ij}, where i is a random number from $\{1, \ldots, \frac{|D|}{n_b}\}$, and $j = 0$ initially. This process is repeated $|H|$ times while incrementing j each time.

All the experiments were conducted on a server running Linux with 32 GB RAM and 2 processors each with 3 GHz speed. We use MySQL to store and query the tuples. For the probabilistic classifiers, we use the Naïve Bayesian, specifically, we use the NBC WEKA implementation[3] with the default parameters settings. Java is used to implement our approach and we use Java Threads to benefit from a multiprocessor environment.

5.1 Quality Evaluation: Comparison with Constraint Based Approaches

In the following experiments, we use the standard precision and recall to measure the quality of the applied updates for string attributes.

The precision is defined as the ratio of the number of values that have been correctly updated to the total number of values that were updated, while the recall is defined as the ratio of the number of values that have been correctly updated to the number of incorrect values in the entire database. For numerical attributes, we use the mean absolute error (MAE): $\frac{1}{N}\sum_{i=1}^{d}|v_i - a_i|$ where v_i is the suggested value by SCARE, a_i is the actual value of the original data. We can compute these values since we know the ground truth for Dataset 1.

We report the quality results for four approaches:

- *KHSinKPG*: This is SCARE with the described tuple repair selection strategy as described in Section 4.3.
- *MV*: In this approach, SCARE uses directly the majority voting to select an attribute value from the candidate tuple repairs. We include this approach in the evaluation to compare our tuple repair selection strategy to the straight forward majority voting strategy.
- *SM*: The single model approach, where the whole dataset is considered as a single partition. Afterward, the likelihood benefit and cost are computed to select the best updates. This approach is included to show the advantages of combining several models with local views rather than using a single model with global view on the data.
- *ConstRepair*: One of the recent constraint-based repair approaches. We implemented (to the best of our understanding) the technique described in [3], which uses CFDs as constraints to find dirty tuples and derive repairs. We manually compiled a list of CFDs during the process of cleaning Dataset 1. Moreover, we implemented a CFD discovery algorithm [9] to be used as input to the repairing algorithm. To have a high quality rules and be fair to this approach, we discovered CFDs from the original "correct" data, which can not be the case in a realistic situation as we usually start with dirty data. We specified the rules support threshold to be 1%. Moreover, we assigned the attributes values correctness score following the technique described in [3]. The implementation to discover the CFDs is very time-consuming, therefore, this approach does not show up in all of our plots.
- *MasterRpr*: This is a recent data repair approach described in [11] that rely on a master clean data in addition to Matching Dependency (MD) rules as well as CFD rules. Since we split the database into D_c and D_e, we can use D_c as the master data. Also, we derived some MDs from the CFDs. More information on the MDs and how it can be used to clean the data is found in [11].

We use Dataset 1 and report in Figure 4 the precision and recall results for the applied updates while changing e, the percentage of tuples with erroneous values, from 10 to 50%. Generally, the approaches that maximize the data likelihood substantially outperform the constraint-based approach for the precision. Moreover, for the recall the likelihood approaches outperform the constraint-based approach when the errors is up to 30%, afterwards, the recall is comparable for all the approaches when errors is more than 30%.

SCARE with $KHSinKPG$ shows the highest precision. The precision increases using the three likelihood-based approaches with the increase in the amount of errors, but the recall is decreasing. For the `Longitude` and `Latitude` attributes, SCARE-based approaches ($KHSinKPG$ and MV) corrected these attributes with error rate between 1% and 5%.

For the SCARE-based approaches, the precision increases because we use a fixed δ. When the amount of errors in the data (noted e) is small (10 to 20%), SCARE-based approaches modify more data that allow for less accurate updates resulting in less precision and relatively high recall. As e increases, the data needs more updates to correct it, however, SCARE applies fewer, yet more accurate updates, and hence the precision increases, but the recall

[3]NBC WEKA available at http://www.cs.waikato.ac.nz/ml/weka

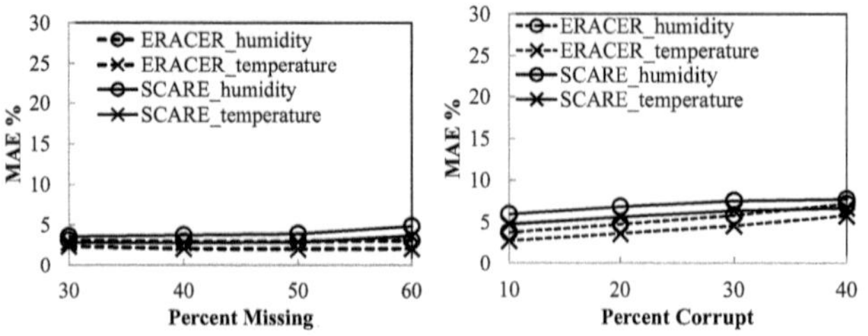

(a) (b)

Figure 5: Comparison between SCARE and ERACER to predict missing values. Generally, both SCARE and ERACER show high accuracy in predicting the missing values. SCARE uses in this experiment Naïve Bayesian model, while ERACER leverages domain knowledge interpreted in carefully designed Bayesian Network.

decreases (Figure 4(b)). The $KHSinKPG$ approach outperforms MV approach, because $KHSinKPG$ takes into account further associations between the predicted values across the data partitions. These associations are ignored in the MV approach. Both SCARE-based approaches that rely on data partitioning ($KHSinKPG$ and MV) show a comparable, and sometimes even better, accuracy than that of the SM approach.

The $ConstRepair$ and $MasterRpr$ have been outperformed by all the likelihood-based approaches. The $ConstRepair$ relies on the heuristics of finding values replacement that are close to the original data without considering any information on the data distributions and relationships. Moreover, the discovered CFDs that were used in $ConstRepair$ were not exhaustive enough to cover all the problems in the data and this explains the low recall in addition to the low precision. The $MasterRpr$ shows an improved performance over the $ConstRepair$ because, in addition to the CFDs, the $MasterRpr$ relies on a master clean data which helps in selecting the right replacement values through the MD rules. Therefore, both the precision and recall of $MasterRpr$ are better than those for the $ConstRepair$. But, the precision and recall are still low because, similarly with $ConstRepair$, the discovered CFDs and MDs are not exhaustive enough to cover the data problems. In contrast, SCARE relies on statistical ML techniques, which are able to cope with variable and multiple problems in the data and still rely on the data distributions to accurately predict the replacement values.

The recall of all the repairing approaches is in the range of 30 to 65%. However, for the likelihood-based approaches, the recall can be improved by running the approach again over the resulting database instance. We illustrate this improvement later in the experiment of Figure 7. But, the $ConstRepair$ approach achieves about 35% recall that can not be further improved given a fixed set of constraints.

To conclude, in comparison to the constraint-based repairing approaches, which demonstrated both low precision and recall, our likelihood based approach demonstrated accurate updates with high precision. Moreover, partitioning the data and combining the different predictions across the partitions provide more accurate predictions, because partitioning allows to learn data relationships at different granularity levels (local and global).

5.2 SCARE vs ERACER to predict missing values

In this experiment, we use Dataset 3, which includes a number of measurements taken from 54 sensors once every 31 seconds. It contains only numerical attributes. We include this dataset to evaluate SCARE for predicting missing values and compare it to ERACER. We used the same dataset with the same introduced errors as reported in ERACER evaluation of [20]. Thus, we were able to

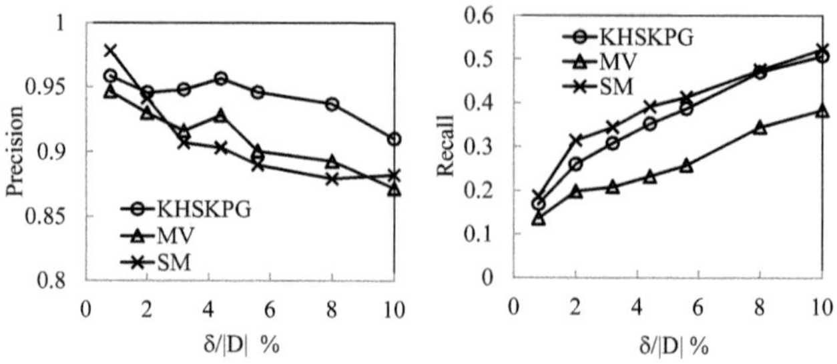

(a) (b)

Figure 6: δ controls the amount of changes to apply to the database: small δ guarantees high precision at the cost of the recall and vice versa.

compare the effectiveness results of ERACER based on the same dataset. The efficiency of ERACER was not demonstrated in [20] and it requires domain expertise unlike our approach.

ERACER is a recent machine learning technique for data cleaning; it is specifically dedicated to replace missing values but it can not be used for data repair by value modification. ERACER leverages domain expert knowledge about the dataset to design a Bayesian network. Then, ERACER uses an underlying relational database design to store all constructed model's parameters.

In Figure 5, we evaluate SCARE for predicting the missing values in comparison with ERACER. Here, we do not use δ as SCARE is not updating an existing database value. Instead, we consider all the predictions obtained from SCARE that fill a missing value.

Figure 5(a) reports the mean absolute error (MAE) while errors in the dataset are in the form of missing values. Figure 5(b) reports also the MAE, while errors are in the form of corrupting values, e.g., adding random values. More details on how this data was corrupted is provided in [20].

There are two major numerical attributes in the Dataset 3: humidity and temperature. In Figure 5(a), both SCARE and ERACER predict the missing values for the humidity and temperature with almost the same low error percentage (2 to 4 %); and also in Figure 5(a), they both behave similarly when increasing the percentage of corrupted data, and in this case, the error percentage in prediction is between 3 and 7 %.

These numbers show that both techniques provide high accuracy predictions. However, SCARE does not require the expensive domain expert to design a Bayesian network as for ERACER. For this experiment, SCARE used the Naïve Bayesian for the statistical models. The Naïve Bayesian did well when plugged into SCARE in comparison to the Bayesian network which has to be carefully designed for ERACER. This is thanks to the partitioning technique used in SCARE, which enables several local views of the data that are then combined at the end to obtain the most reliable global view for accurate predictions. Moreover, SCARE can benefit from carefully designed learning techniques, like ERACER, and plug it in the learning step to get more accurate predictions.

5.3 Parameters Study

Quality vs. the amount of changes δ: In this experiment, we study the effect of bounding δ, the number of changes fixed by the user on the repair quality. We report in Figure 6 the resulting precision and recall when $\frac{\delta}{|D|}$ changes from 1% to 10% (e.g., if $\frac{\delta}{|D|} = 5\%$, then SCARE can change up to 10% of the tuples by replacing a selected attribute value v by v' with distance $d(v, v') = 0.5$). Generally, low values of δ guarantee high precision and inversely. Increasing δ gives more chance to SCARE to modify the data. Hence, the recall increases as we increase δ, but updates with a lower confidence could be made. This justifies the decrease in the precision when we increase δ.

The conclusion from this experiment is that small δ guarantees high precision at the cost of the recall. However, the recall can be improved by further SCARE iterations over the data as we will see in the next experiment.

Quality vs. the number of SCARE iterations: This experiment shows the effect on the quality if we repeatedly execute SCARE over the dataset I times, $I = \{1, \ldots, 5\}$. After each iteration, the repaired tuples are considered members of the clean subset of the database, which is used in training the ML models. We report the obtained precision and recall in Figure 7. For all the SCARE-based approaches, the recall substantially improves from about 35% to close to 70% as we increase the number of iterations, while, the precision slightly decreases from the 90's to the 80's %. This indicates that the overall quality improves as we run more SCARE iterations. The $KHSinKPG$ outperforms the other approaches in terms of both precision and recall.

In each iteration, SCARE tries to repair the data to maximize the data likelihood given the learnt classification models subject to a constant amount of changes, δ. In the first few iterations, the discovered updates have higher correctness measure (*i.e.*, ratio of the likelihood benefit to the cost of the update, $\frac{l(u)}{c(u)}$) than those that are discovered later. Therefore, the applied updates in the first iterations have higher confidence, and hence, the precision starts high and decreases in later iterations. The recall increases faster than the decrease in precision, and therefore, the overall quality is improving. The main reason is that most of the applied updates are correct in the first few iterations, so the obtained database instances after each iteration are of higher quality to be learnt and modeled for predictions in the later iterations of SCARE. A stopping criteria for the iterations can be computed from the obtained overall likelihood benefit of the updates. If the benefit is not significant, then it is better to stop SCARE. In another setting, the user can be involved interactively (*e.g.*, [22]) to inspect very small number of the least beneficial updates after each iteration. If the least beneficial updates are correct, then most of the updates are correct according to the data distribution.

Quality vs. the partition functions: Here, we study the use of different partition functions (blocking techniques), as well as, the effect of the number of partition functions $|H|$ on the quality of SCARE on all the datasets. In Figure 8(a), we report the repair precision for Dataset 1 when we use four different blocking techniques as we increase the number of partition functions. One of the blocking techniques follows the clustering approach as described earlier in this section. The remaining three blocking techniques are signature based blocking, where we compute local sensitive hashing (LSH) for different attributes (`Zip`, `City`, `StreetAddress`) with different random seeds.

For each dataset, we note that as we increase the number of functions, the performances of all the blocking techniques improve. They all converge to obtain similar accuracy. Increasing $|H|$ will increase the chance that a tuple belongs to a larger number of partitions. SCARE learns a model from a local view (*i.e.*, from one partition) and predicts the values for the attributes of the considered tuple. Consequently, a larger number of candidate tuple repairs is proposed when increasing the number of partitions and the variance of the predictions decreases. The predictions become more independent from the blocking technique being used. The repair selection strategy combines the predictions of the local view models, and this increases the chance to obtain more accurate predictions.

5.4 SCARE Scalability

The scalability is one of the main advantages provided by SCARE, this is in addition to the quality of the updates demonstrated in the previous experiments. In the following, we assess the scalability of SCARE to large datasets.

In Figure 8(b), we report the scalability of SCARE on Dataset 2.

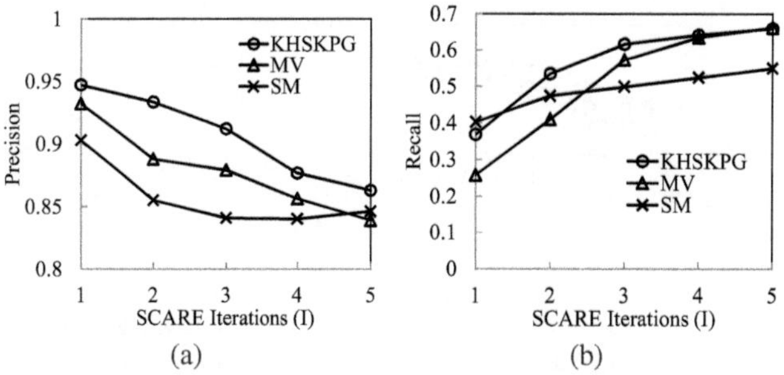

Figure 7: Using SCARE in an iterative way helps improving the recall and the overall quality of the updates. The decrease in the precision is small compared to the increase in the recall, achieving an overall high quality improvement demonstrated by the f-measure.

We report as well the fraction of time for each of the two phases of SCARE. The reported time includes the time for learning the classification models. SCARE scales linearly, because of its systematic process of handling each data partition. Note also that SCARE finished the processing of a 1 M tuples in less than 6 minutes. Phase 1, the updates generation, takes 80-85 % of the time because of the process of learning models and obtaining predictions.

In Figure 8(c), we report the overall time taken by SCARE to handle datasets from Dataset 1 with different size from 5,000 to 50,000 tuples. We use two different partition techniques: Random and Blocking. In general, SCARE still scales linearly with the dataset size. Moreover, it is noted that partitioning the data by blocking makes SCARE more efficient. The reason is that blocking makes a data partition containing less diversity of the domain values. This results in a faster processing to train the classification models for prediction.

Usually, the process of statistical modeling and prediction tasks is quadratic, but this is not the case with SCARE because of the robust mechanism of partitioning the data and the strategy used to combine multiple predictions.

Finally, we mentioned that SCARE can be efficiently parallelized. In our implementation we used Java Threads and in Figure 8(d), we demonstrate the speedup we obtain as we increase the number of processors. Note that SCARE achieves a linear speedup, which supports our claim.

6. RELATED WORK

Improving data quality has been the focus of a large body of research for decades. Our work is closely related to two research areas: *i)* constraint-based data repair; and *ii)* statistical machine learning techniques for data cleaning.

Constraint-based data repair: In this approach, usually we have a database instance that is inconsistent with a predefined set of constraints. The objective is to find another database instance that minimally differs from the original one and that is consistent with the constraints. For example in [3], conditional FDs (CFDs) are used as database constraints. The repairing technique is based on a cost-based greedy heuristic to decide upon a repair of errors. The authors use equivalent classes to group the attributes values that are equivalent in obtaining a final consistent database instance. The work in [18] uses FDs to map the repairing problem to hyper-graph optimization problem, where a heuristic vertex cover algorithm can help finding the minimal number of attributes values to modify in order to find a database consistent with the FDs. The main drawback of these approaches is that the data should be covered by a set of constraints that have been specified or validated by domain experts, which may be an expensive manual process and may not be affordable for all data domains. Moreover, the constraints usually fall short to correctly identify the right fixes [10].

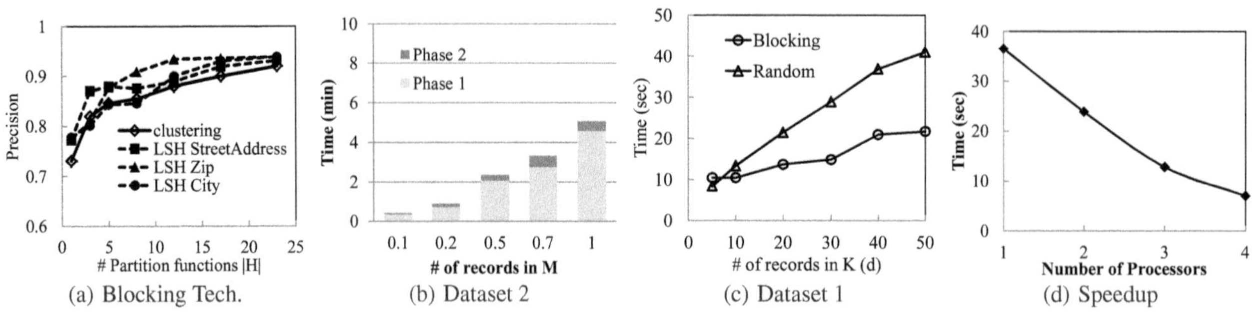

Figure 8: The effect of the blocking techniques and SCARE scalability experiments

The work in [11] presents an entropy based technique to provide a guarantee on the applied cleaning updates. For SCARE, since the data is partitioned and the predictions are aggregated, it is not clear how the entropy measures can be aggregated. Instead, we rely on the updates likelihood benefit-to-cost ratio as a measure for the updates quality. Our experiments demonstrate overall high precision in updating the database.

Statistical machine learning techniques for data cleaning: Data cleaning using ML techniques mainly focused on deduplication (refer to [6] for survey), data imputation (e.g., [20]) and errors detecting (e.g., [23, 17]). For instance, in [20], data imputation is based on relational learning to learn the characteristics of the attributes relationships in a relational database. Then, the learnt model is used to infer the missing values. This technique requires *a priori* knowledge about the relationships between the attributes to construct the appropriate Bayesian network. Most of similar techniques for data imputation are limited to numerical or categorical attributes. SCARE does not have such limitation. Our probabilistic setting is related to the efforts on predicting multiple class labels [4] (*i.e.*, multiple values for a single attribute). However, our task is to predict a single value from multiple attributes predictions.

The main challenges for ML techniques are mainly *(i)* the scalability for large databases to be modeled considering all existing significant data correlations; and *(ii)* the accuracy of the replacement values prediction due to the fact that existing methods usually capture either local or global data relationships and do not combine both views whereas SCARE approach does. Nevertheless, the usefulness of ML techniques can be leveraged inside the learning step of SCARE and help further improving the accuracy of the predicted updates to the data. Note that our approach is not limited to a specific (probabilistic) classifier. Moreover, it can also take advantage of DB constraints and FDs when they are available.

7. CONCLUSION

In this paper, we propose SCARE, a robust and scalable approach for accurately repairing erroneous data values. Our solution offers several advantages over previous methods for data repairing using database constraints: the accuracy of the replacement values and the scalability of the method are guaranteed; the cost of the repair is bounded by the amount of changes that the user is willing to tolerate; no constraint or editing rule is needed since SCARE analyzes the data, learns the correlations from the correct data and take advantages of them for predicting accurate replacement values. Finally, as shown in our experiments, SCARE outperforms existing methods on large databases with no limitation on the type of data (*i.e.*, string, numeric, ordinal, categorical) or on the type of errors (*i.e.*, missing, incomplete, outlying, or inconsistent values). Our current work is to extend SCARE to enable duplicate elimination while repairing errors both at the value and tuple levels.

Future work is to efficiently and interactively involve the user in a visual repairing scenario so that the selection of the candidate replacement values as well as the entire database repairing process can be user-approved in real-time.

8. ACKNOWLEDGMENT

This research is based in part upon work supported by QCRI and by NSF under Grant Number IIS 0916614.

9. REFERENCES

[1] S. Arora, D. Karger, and M. Karpinski. Polynomial time approximation schemes for dense instances of np-hard problems. In *STOC*, 1995.
[2] Y. Asahiro, K. Iwama, H. Tamaki, and T. Tokuyama. Greedily finding a dense subgraph. In *Journal of Algorithms*, 2000.
[3] G. Cong, W. Fan, F. Geerts, X. Jia, and S. Ma. Improving data quality: consistency and accuracy. In *VLDB*, 2007.
[4] K. Dembczynski, W. Cheng, and E. Hullermeier. Bayes optimal multilabel classification via probabilistic classifier chains. In *ICML*, 2010.
[5] T. G. Dietterich. Ensemble methods in machine learning. In *MCS workshop*, 2000.
[6] A. K. Elmagarmid, P. G. Ipeirotis, and V. S. Verykios. Duplicate record detection: A survey. *TKDE*, 2007.
[7] L. P. English. *Information quality applied: best practices for improving business information, processes and systems*. Wiley, 2009.
[8] W. Fan. Dependencies revisited for improving data quality. In *PODS*, 2008.
[9] W. Fan, F. Geerts, L. V. Lakshmanan, and M. Xiong. Discovering conditional functional dependencies. In *ICDE*, 2009.
[10] W. Fan, J. Li, S. Ma, N. Tang, and W. Yu. Towards certain fixes with editing rules and master data. *PVLDB*, 2010.
[11] W. Fan, J. Li, S. Ma, N. Tang, and W. Yu. Interaction between record matching and data repairing. In *SIGMOD*, 2011.
[12] U. Feige and M. Seltser. On the densest k-subgraph problem. *Algorithmica*, 1997.
[13] S. German and D. German. Neurocomputing: foundations of research. chapter Stochastic relaxation, Gibbs distributions, and the Bayesian restoration of images. 1988.
[14] D. Heckerman, D. M. Chickering, C. Meek, R. Rounthwaite, and C. Kadie. Dependency networks for inference, collaborative filtering, and data visualization. *J. Mach. Learn. Res.*, 2001.
[15] D. S. Hochbaum. Efficient bounds for the stable set, vertex cover and set packing problems. In *Discrete Applied Mathematics*, 1983.
[16] R. A. Jacobs, M. I. Jordan, S. J. Nowlan, and G. E. Hinton. Adaptive mixtures of local experts. *Neural Comput.*
[17] J. L. Y. Koh, M. L. Lee, W. Hsu, and K. T. Lam. Correlation-based detection of attribute outliers. In *DASFAA*, 2007.
[18] S. Kolahi and L. V. S. Lakshmanan. On approximating optimum repairs for functional dependency violations. In *ICDT*, 2009.
[19] A. Lopatenko and L. Bravo. Efficient approximation algorithms for repairing inconsistent databases. In *ICDE*, 2007.
[20] C. Mayfield, J. Neville, and S. Prabhakar. Eracer: a database approach for statistical inference and data cleaning. In *SIGMOD*, 2010.
[21] S. Sonnenburg, G. Rätsch, C. Schäfer, and B. Schölkopf. Large scale multiple kernel learning. *J. Mach. Learn. Res.*, 2006.
[22] M. Yakout, A. K. Elmagarmid, J. Neville, M. Ouzzani, and I. F. Ilyas. Guided data repair. *PVLDB*, 2011.
[23] X. Zhu and X. Wu. Class noise vs. attribute noise: a quantitative study of their impacts. *Artif. Intell. Rev.*, 22:177–210, November 2004.

Determining the Relative Accuracy of Attributes

Yang Cao[1,2] Wenfei Fan[1,2] Wenyuan Yu[1]
[1]School of Informatics, University of Edinburgh
[2]Big Data Research Center and SKLSDE Lab, Beihang University
{yang.cao@, wenfei@inf., wenyuan.yu@}ed.ac.uk

ABSTRACT

The *relative accuracy problem* is to determine, given tuples t_1 and t_2 that refer to the same entity e, whether $t_1[A]$ is more accurate than $t_2[A]$, *i.e.*, $t_1[A]$ is *closer to the true value* of the A attribute of e than $t_2[A]$. This has been a longstanding issue for data quality, and is challenging when the true values of e are unknown. This paper proposes a model for determining relative accuracy. (1) We introduce a class of accuracy rules and an inference system with a chase procedure, to deduce relative accuracy. (2) We identify and study several fundamental problems for relative accuracy. Given a set I_e of tuples pertaining to the same entity e and a set of accuracy rules, these problems are to decide whether the chase process terminates, is Church-Rosser, and leads to a unique *target tuple* t_e composed of the most accurate values from I_e for all the attributes of e. (3) We propose a framework for inferring accurate values with user interaction. (4) We provide algorithms underlying the framework, to find the unique target tuple t_e whenever possible; when there is no enough information to decide a complete t_e, we compute top-k candidate targets based on a preference model. (5) Using real-life and synthetic data, we experimentally verify the effectiveness and efficiency of our method.

Categories and Subject Descriptors

H.2 [**Database Management**]: General—*integrity*

Keywords

data accuracy, data cleaning

1. INTRODUCTION

One of the central issues of data quality is *data accuracy*. Given a set I_e of tuples pertaining to the same entity e, it aims to find the most accurate values for e. More specifically, it is to compute a tuple t_e, referred to the *target tuple for* e *from* I_e, such that for each attribute A of e, $t_e[A]$ is a value in I_e that is closest to the *true* A*-value* of e. The need for studying this is evident in *e.g.*, decision making [20], information systems [10] and data quality management [18].

Although important, data accuracy has not been well studied. Prior work on data quality has mostly focused on other issues such as data consistency [2, 12]. Consistency refers to the validity and integrity of the data. While there is an intimate connection between data accuracy and consistency, the two are *quite different*. Indeed, a database D may be consistent, but the values in D may still be inaccurate.

SIGMOD'13, June 22–27, 2013, New York, New York, USA.

Example 1: Consider relation stat given in Table 1, which collects performance statistics of Michael Jordan (Fig. 1) in the season of 1994-95, when Michael played for a baseball team Birmingham Barons in the Southern League (SL) in 1994, followed by his return to NBA, playing 27 games for Chicago Bulls in 1995. Each tuple in stat specifies the name (FN, MN, LN), performance (total points totalPts after rnds rounds played), jersey number J#, league, team and arena.

We want to find the target tuple for Michael from stat, consisting of the most accurate values for all the attributes at the end of 1994-95 NBA season. However, there are multiple values in stat for some attributes. For instance, we do not know whether 45 is more accurate than 23 for his J#.

The stat data is *consistent*. Indeed, constraints specifying its consistency include (a) functional dependency (FD [1]): [FN, MN, LN, league, rnds $\rightarrow$ totalPts], *i.e.*, player, rnds and league uniquely determine totalPts, and (b) conditional functional dependency (CFD [13]): [team = "Chicago Bulls" $\rightarrow$ arena = "United Center"], asserting that if team is Chicago Bulls, then arena must be United Center. While all tuples in stat satisfy these constraints and are hence *consistent*, most of the data values in stat are, however, *not accurate*. □

Not all is lost. An enterprise typically maintains *master data* [25], a single repository of high-quality data that provides various applications with a synchronized, consistent view of its core business entities. Leveraging master data, one is able to identify accurate values for *some* attributes. For example, a master relation nba is given in Table 2, in which a tuple specifies the FN, LN, league, season, and team of an NBA player. Then tuple s_1 in Table 2 tells us that in the 1994-95 season, Michael played for Chicago Bulls in NBA. Thus t_1 is *more accurate* than t_4 in *attribute* league (resp. team), denoted by $t_6 \prec_{\text{league}} t_1$ (resp. $t_4 \prec_{\text{team}} t_1$).

It is more challenging, however, to determine the *relative accuracy* of those attributes *in the absence of complete master data*. That is, given tuples t_1, t_2 and an attribute A, we want to know whether $t_1 \prec_A t_2$ when A is *not* covered by master data, such as J# in relation stat of Table 1. This is hard, but not hopeless. From the semantics of the data, one can derive accuracy rules (ARs), which tell us whether one tuple is more accurate than another in certain attributes.

Example 2: An analysis of the semantics of the stat data yields the ARs given in Table 1. Based on these rules, we can deduce relative accuracy as follows.

(1) We know that in a season, the number of rounds (rnds) monotonically increases (up to an bound). Hence for tuples t and t' referring to the same league, if $t[\text{rnds}] < t'[\text{rnds}]$, then $t \prec_{\text{rnds}} t'$, *i.e.*, $t'[\text{rnds}]$ is more current (and thus more accu-

	FN	MN	LN	rnds	totalPts	J#	league	team	arena
t_1:	MJ	null	null	16	424	45	NBA	Chicago	Chicago Stadium
t_2:	Michael	null	Jordan	27	772	23	NBA	Chicago Bulls	United Center
t_3:	Michael	null	Jordan	1	19	45	NBA	Chicago Bulls	United Center
t_4:	Michael	Jeffrey	Jordan	127	51	45	SL	Birmingham Barons	Regions Park

Table 1: Entity instance stat for Michael Jordon in the 1994-95 season

Figure 1: MJ's return

	FN	LN	league	season	team
s_1:	Michael	Jordan	NBA	1994-95	Chicago Bulls
s_2:	Michael	Jordan	NBA	2001-02	Washington Wizards

Table 2: Master data nba

φ_1: $\forall t_1, t_2 \in \textsf{stat}\ (t_1[\textsf{league}] = t_2[\textsf{league}] \wedge t_1[\textsf{rnds}] < t_2[\textsf{rnds}] \rightarrow t_1 \preceq_{\textsf{rnds}} t_2)$
φ_2 : $\forall t_1, t_2 \in \textsf{stat}\ (t_1 \prec_{\textsf{rnds}} t_2 \rightarrow t_1 \preceq_{\textsf{J\#}} t_2)$
φ_3: $\forall t_1, t_2 \in \textsf{stat}\ (t_1 \prec_{\textsf{rnds}} t_2 \rightarrow t_1 \preceq_{\textsf{totalPts}} t_2)$
φ_4 : $\forall t_1, t_2 \in \textsf{stat}\ (t_1 \prec_{\textsf{league}} t_2 \rightarrow t_1 \preceq_{\textsf{rnds}} t_2)$
φ_5 : $\forall t_1, t_2 \in \textsf{stat}\ (t_1 \prec_{\textsf{MN}} t_2 \rightarrow t_1 \preceq_{\textsf{FN}} t_2)$
φ_6 : $\forall t_m \in \textsf{nba}(t_m[\textsf{FN}, \textsf{LN}] = t_e[\textsf{FN}, \textsf{LN}] \wedge t_m[\textsf{season}] = \text{“1994-95”} \rightarrow t_e[\textsf{league}, \textsf{team}] = t_m[\textsf{league}, \textsf{team}])$

Table 3: Accuracy rules (ARs)

rate) than $t[\textsf{rnds}]$. This is expressed as rule φ_1 in Table 1. From φ_1 we can deduce that $t_i \prec_{\textsf{rnds}} t_2$ for $i \in [1, 3]$.

(2) For tuples t and t', if t' is more accurate than t in rnds, then $t \preceq_{\textsf{J\#}} t'$, denoting either $t[\textsf{J\#}] = t'[\textsf{J\#}]$ or $t \prec_{\textsf{J\#}} t'$; similarly for totalPts. That is, if t' is more accurate (current) than t in attribute rnds, then so are its *correlated attributes* $t'[\textsf{J\#}]$ and $t'[\textsf{totalPts}]$. These are expressed as rules φ_2 and φ_3 in Table 1, respectively. From these ARs and (1) we find that $t_2[\textsf{totalPts}] = 772$ and $t_2[\textsf{J\#}] = 23$ are more accurate than $t_i[\textsf{totalPts}]$ and $t_i[\textsf{J\#}]$, respectively, for $i \in [1, 3]$.

(3) We know that Michael ended up in NBA in the 1994-95 season. Moreover, if t' is more accurate than t in league, then so is t' in attributes rnds, totalPts, J# and arena. These can also be expressed as ARs, *e.g.*, φ_4. These tell us that t_i is more accurate than t_4 in these attributes, for $i \in [1, 3]$.

(4) For tuples t and t', if $t[A]$ is null but $t'[A]$ is not, then t' is more accurate than t in attribute A. This can also be expressed as an AR (not shown in Table 1). Moreover, if t' is more accurate than t in MN, then so is t' in the *correlated attribute* FN, as $t'[\textsf{MN}]$ and $t'[\textsf{FN}]$ typically *come together*. This is expressed as φ_5 in Table 1. These tell us that $t_4[\textsf{MN}]$=“Jeffrey” is most accurate in MN and $t_1 \prec_{\textsf{FN}} t_4$.

(5) As remarked earlier, we can use master data to find the most accurate values for certain attributes. This is shown as AR φ_6 in Table 1. It asserts that if there exists a master tuple $t_m \in \textsf{nba}$ such that $t_m[\textsf{FN}, \textsf{LN}] = t_e[\textsf{FN}, \textsf{LN}]$ and $t_m[\textsf{season}] =$ “1994-95”, then $t_e[\textsf{league}, \textsf{team}]$ should take the value of $t_m[\textsf{league}, \textsf{team}]$. Here t_e is the target tuple in which attributes $t_e[\textsf{FN}, \textsf{LN}]$ already find their most accurate values.

Putting these together, we can deduce the relative accuracy of attributes and better still, a large part of the target tuple t_e. Indeed, the values of t_e in FN, MN, LN, rnds, totalPts, league, team are found to be Michael, Jeffrey, Jordan, 27, 772, 23, NBA, and Chicago Bulls, respectively. □

This example tells us that *in the absence of true values* of an entity, one can still determine a large part of the target tuple, by taking together ARs and available master data. This, however, requires an inference system and efficient algorithms for deducing the relative accuracy of attributes.

Contributions. We make a first attempt to give a formal treatment of relative accuracy, from theory to practice.

(1) We propose a model for determining relative accuracy (Section 2). We introduce (a) *accuracy rules* (ARs) defined in terms of partial orders; and (b) a chase-like procedure [1] that, given a set I_e of tuples pertaining to the same entity e, a set Σ of ARs on I_e and (partial) master data I_m, infers relative accuracy and a target tuple by applying the ARs.

(2) We identify fundamental problems for relative accuracy (Section 3). Given I_e, Σ and I_m, these problems are to decide (a) whether the chase process on I_e terminates by applying Σ and I_m? (b) Whether do all the chase sequences lead to a unique target tuple t_e for e from I_e, *i.e.*, Church-Rosser [1], no matter in what orders the rules are applied? (c) If t_e is incomplete, *i.e.*, some of its attributes have the null value, can we make t_e complete while observing the ARs in Σ? We show that the chase process always terminates, the Church-Rosser property can be decided in $O((|I_e|^2 + |I_m|)|\Sigma|)$ time, whereas the last problem is NP-complete.

(3) We present a framework for deducing target tuples (Section 4). Given I_e, Σ and I_m, the framework checks whether the chase on I_e with Σ and I_m is Church-Rosser. If so, it *automatically deduces* as many accurate attribute values for t_e as possible. If t_e is incomplete, it computes top-k candidate targets based on a preference model. The users may check the candidate tuples, revise t_e, I_e and Σ, and invoke the process again until a satisfactory target tuple is found.

(4) We provide effective algorithms underlying the framework (Sections 5 and 6). We give an algorithm for deciding whether the chase is Church-Rosser given I_e, Σ and I_m, and deducing accurate attributes for target tuples. We also develop three algorithms for finding top-k candidate target tuples, with the *early termination* property without inspecting all possible tuples. In particular, one of the algorithms does not require ranked lists as input, and is *instance optimal w.r.t.* the number of visits to the data [11].

(5) We experimentally verify the effectiveness and efficiency of our method, using real-life and synthetic data (Section 7). We find that our approach is effective: for the real-life data, accurate values are automatically deduced for at least 73% of the attributes without user interaction, in 10 milliseconds (ms); moreover, at most 3-4 rounds of user interaction are needed to find complete target tuples. Our algorithms scale well with the sizes of entity instances, master data and ARs. We also evaluate our method for truth discovery, vs. prior approaches [8, 14]. We show that our model can accommodate trust in data sources [8] as well as data currency and consistency [14]. Even for truth discovery, our method performs as well as [8, 14] in their settings, or even better.

The analysis of relative accuracy helps us deduce the true value of an entity e. Even when we do not have enough information to decide the true values of all the attributes of e, partial true values deduced may still *enhance our trust* in values *critical to* decision making. In addition, relative accuracy helps us reduce search space and improve accuracy in data repairing, which is computationally costly [12]. Indeed, if $t_1 \prec_A t_2$ is deduced, we know that $t_1[A]$ is a better candidate than $t_2[A]$ for the A-attribute of these tuples. As will be seen shortly, relative accuracy is deduced via logical inference from data semantics. The inference can be *combined with* probabilistic analysis techniques (see below), to facilitate truth discovery, data repairing and decision making.

We contend that ARs, master data and inference algorithms yield a promising approach to determining relative accuracy. As shown in Example 2, while master data is helpful, it is *not* a must for the analysis of relative accuracy. In the absence of complete master data, we can still deduce true values for critical attributes based on accuracy rules and inference, as will be verified by our experimental study.

Related works. There has been a host of work on data quality issues such as data consistency, data currency, information completeness and entity resolution (see [2,12] for recent surveys). While data accuracy has long been advocated [2,16,23], the prior work has mostly focused on metrics for accuracy measurement; we are not aware of any formal treatment of relative accuracy in the absence of true values.

Rules and master data have been used in repairing data (data consistency) [3,15] and specifying relative information completeness [12]. This work differs from the prior work in the following. (1) ARs are quite different from the dependencies used for specifying consistency and completeness. As a result, the termination problem for rules of [15], for instance, is PSPACE-complete, while our inference (chase) process always terminates. (2) Data repairing and information completeness consider problems different from those studied here. (3) We give an operational semantics for ARs in terms of chase [1]. In contrast, chase was not considered in the prior work except [3]. While [3] adapted chase for data repairing [3] based on matching dependencies, it studied neither how to deduce relative accuracy, nor the complexity of determining whether a chase process is Church-Rosser.

Also related is prior work on truth discovery from data sources [4, 8, 14, 19, 27–30]. Those approaches include (i) dependencies on sources to detect copy relationships and identify reliable sources [8]; (ii) employing lineage and probabilistic [27]; (iii) vote counting and probabilistic analysis based on the trustworthiness of data sources [4, 19, 28–30]. In contrast, we deduce relative accuracy following a logical approach based on ARs and master data, without assuming knowledge about data sources. Our method is *complementary to* the prior approaches for truth discovery, and can be combined with them by deducing trust in attributes with ARs in truth discovery (see Sections 3 and 7 for details).

Closer to this work is [14], on conflict resolution by reasoning about data consistency and currency. It used partial orders, currency constraints and constant CFDs [13]. This work differs from [14] in the following. (1) We study relative data accuracy rather than conflict resolution. This said, currency orders and constant CFDs can be expressed as ARs and hence, our techniques can also be used in data fusion [5]. (2) We use ARs for actions in a chase process, as opposed to static dependencies of [14]. (3) Our approach is quite different from [14]. We infer accuracy via chase, use available master data to improve accuracy, and provide algorithms to compute top-k target tuples. These were not studied in [14].

Our algorithms for computing top-k target tuples are related to top-k query answering, which aims to retrieve top-k tuples from query result, ranked by a monotone scoring function [11,22]. One of our top-k algorithms extends algorithms for top-k rank join queries [21,26] by *embedding* score computation in top-k selection, rather than assuming that the scores are already given, and by additionally checking whether selected tuples observe ARs. We also provide a new algorithm that *does not* require the input to be ranked; it is instance optimal *w.r.t.* the number of visits to the data, and can be used to *compute rank joins on unranked lists.*

2. A MODEL FOR RELATIVE ACCURACY

We next present a model for determining relative accuracy. We first define ARs (Section 2.1), and then introduce a chase procedure for deducing relative accuracy (Section 2.2),

2.1 Rules for Specifying Relative Accuracy

Relative accuracy. Consider a relation schema $R = (A_1, \ldots, A_n)$, where the domain of attribute A_i is $\mathsf{dom}(A_i)$. We consider an *entity instance* I_e of R, which is a set of tuples pertaining to the *same* real-world entity e. Such an I_e is identified by entity resolution techniques [9,24], and is typically *much smaller* than a database instance in practice.

The problem of relative accuracy is to determine, given an attribute A_i of R and tuples $t_1, t_2 \in I_e$, whether t_2 is *more accurate than* t_1 *in attribute* A_i, denoted by $t_1 \prec_{A_i} t_2$.

More specifically, for each attribute A_i of I_e, $\prec_{A_i}$ is a *strict partial order* defined on the A_i attribute values in I_e. That is, $\prec_{A_i}$ is a binary relation that is irreflexive and transitive, and thus asymmetric. Initially, $\prec_{A_i}$ is *empty* for all $i \in [1, n]$, and we want to populate $\prec_{A_i}$ by deducing relative accuracy with accuracy rules. We also use $t_1 \preceq_{A_i} t_2$ to denote either $t_1[A_i] = t_2[A_i]$ or $t_1 \prec_{A_i} t_2$. Note that $\preceq_{A_i}$ is a partial order, referred to as the *accuracy order on attribute* A_i.

Ultimately we want to find a tuple t_e for I_e, referred to as the *target tuple for e from* I_e such that for each attribute A_i of R and all tuples $t \in I_e$, $t \preceq_{A_i} t_e$. Intuitively, t_e is a *new tuple* composed of the most accurate value of attribute A_i for all $i \in [1, n]$. It is easy to verify that if t_e exists, then it is *unique*. Note that I_e may not have enough information for us to deduce a complete t_e. If so, $t_e[A_i] = \mathsf{null}$ for some A_i, and we refer to t_e as an *incomplete target tuple* of I_e.

Accuracy rules (ARs). There are two forms of ARs. The first one is defined on tuples $t_1, t_2 \in I_e$ to deduce whether $t_1 \preceq_{A_i} t_2$, *i.e.*, their relative accuracy in an attribute A_i:

$$\varphi = \forall t_1, t_2 \ (R(t_1) \wedge R(t_2) \wedge \omega \rightarrow t_1 \ \preceq_{A_i} \ t_2) \qquad (1)$$

where ω is a conjunction of predicates of the form: (a) $t_1[A_l]$ op $t_2[A_l]$, where op is one of the comparison operators $=, \neq, >, <, \leq, \geq$; or (b) $t_i[A_l]$ op c for $i \in [1, 2]$, where c is a constant or $t_e[A_l]$; or (c) $t_1 \prec_{A_l} t_2$ or $t_1 \preceq_{A_l} t_2$. We refer to ω as $\mathsf{LHS}(\varphi)$ and $t_1 \preceq_{A_i} t_2$ as $\mathsf{RHS}(\varphi)$.

We denote by $(t_1, t_2) \models \omega$ if t_1 and t_2 satisfy the predicates in ω following the standard semantics of first-order logic. Intuitively, if $(t_1, t_2) \models \omega$, then $t_1 \prec_{A_i} t_2$ or $t_1 \preceq_{A_i} t_2$.

The second form of ARs is defined on (t_e, I_m), where t_e is the *target tuple template*, and I_m is an available master relation of schema R_m [25]. Note that R_m may not cover all the attributes of R. This form of ARs extends t_e by extracting accurate values from master relation I_m, as follows:

$$\varphi' = \forall t_m \ (R_m(t_m) \wedge \omega \rightarrow t_e[A_i] = t_m[B]) \qquad (2)$$

Here ω is a conjunction of predicates of the form $t_e[A_l] = c$ or $t_e[A_l] = t_m[B']$, where c is a constant and B' is an attribute of R_m. Intuitively, if t_e matches a master tuple t_m in I_m as specified by ω, then $t_e[A_i]$ is *instantiated* by taking the value of $t_m[B]$. We refer to ω as $\mathsf{LHS}(\varphi')$ and $t_e[A_i] = t_m[B]$ as $\mathsf{RHS}(\varphi)$. We write $(t_e, t_m) \models \omega$ if t_e and t_m satisfy ω.

Example 3: Recall the entity instance stat of Table 1, and master relation nba of Table 2. Then their ARs include φ_1–φ_6 given in Table 1. These ARs demonstrate how we can derive relative accuracy, in terms of (a) constants, built-in predicates and the semantics of the data such as φ_1, (b) data currency, *e.g.*, φ_2 and φ_3, (c) *co-existence* of attributes and known accuracy orders, such as φ_4 and φ_5, and (d) available master data such as φ_6. Additional ARs for stat include:

φ_7: $\forall t_1, t_2 \in \mathsf{stat}\ \big(t_1[A] = \mathsf{null} \wedge t_2[A] \neq \mathsf{null} \rightarrow t_1 \preceq_A t_2\big)$
φ_8: $\forall t_1, t_2 \in \mathsf{stat}\ \big(t_2[A] = t_e[A] \wedge t_e[A] \neq \mathsf{null} \rightarrow t_1 \preceq_A t_2\big)$
φ_9: $\forall t_1, t_2 \in \mathsf{stat}\ \big(t_1[A]{=}t_2[A] \rightarrow t_1 {\preceq_A} t_2\big)$
φ_{10}: $\forall t_1, t_2 \in \mathsf{stat}\ \big(t_1 \prec_{\mathsf{MN}} t_2 \rightarrow t_1 \preceq_{\mathsf{LN}} t_2\big)$
φ_{11}: $\forall t_1, t_2 \in \mathsf{stat}\ \big(t_1 \prec_{\mathsf{team}} t_2 \rightarrow t_1 \preceq_{\mathsf{arena}} t_2\big)$

Here φ_7–φ_9 are defined on all the attributes A of stat. Rule φ_7 says that the null value has the lowest accuracy; φ_8 asserts that if the target attribute $t_e[A]$ is defined, then it has the highest accuracy among all A-attribute values in I_e; and φ_9 says that for all t_1 and t_2, if $t_1[A] = t_2[A]$, then $t_1 \preceq_A t_2$. Rules φ_7–φ_9 are "axioms" that are included in any set of ARs. ARs φ_{10} and φ_{11} deduce accuracy from *correlated attributes* (*e.g.*, φ_{10}, if a tuple has a more accurate MN, then so does LN since the two attributes often come together).

Note that $t_1 \prec_A t_2$ iff $t_1 \preceq_A t_2$ and $t_1[A] \neq t_2[A]$. Hence when $\preceq_A$ is computed, we *can derive* $\prec_A$ *from* $\preceq_A$. □

Remark. Constant CFDs [13] developed for detecting data inconsistencies can be expressed as ARs. As an example, consider the CFD ψ given in Example 1: [team = "Chicago Bulls" → arena = "United Center"]. We can create a master relation of schema R_m with a tuple (team = "Chicago Bulls", arena = "United Center"), and express ψ as an AR

$$\forall t_m \in \mathsf{R_m}\ (t_m[\mathsf{team}] = t_e[\mathsf{team}] \rightarrow t_e[\mathsf{arena}] = t_m[\mathsf{arena}]),$$

which asserts that if the team of the target tuple t_e is Chicago Bulls, then its arena must be United Center. As we only need to assure the consistency of the target tuple t_e, general CFDs defined on two tuples are not needed here.

2.2 Inferring Relative Accuracy

We next present an inference system for relative accuracy, in terms of a chase-like procedure with ARs. The chase process gives an operational semantics for ARs.

We start with some notations. Consider an entity instance I_e, a master relation I_m, and a set Σ of ARs defined on I_e and I_m. (1) We use D to denote $(I_e, \preceq_{A_1}, \ldots, \preceq_{A_n})$, *i.e.*, I_e equipped with partial orders $\preceq_{A_i}$; we use $\preceq^D_{A_i}$ to denote the partial order $\preceq_{A_i}$ in D [3]. (2) We call $(D_0, t_e^{D_0})$ the *initial instance* of e, where $\preceq^{D_0}_{A_i}$ is empty, and $t_e^{D_0}$ is the target template with $t_e^{D_0}[A_i] = \mathsf{null}$ for all $i \in [1, n]$. (3) We refer to $S = (D_0, \Sigma, I_m, t_e^{D_0})$ as a *specification of entity* e. (4) We call (D, t_e^D) an *accuracy instance* of S, where t_e^D is *the target tuple template associated with* D, which is instantiated in the chase process, and may have null in some of its attributes.

In a nutshell, the chase starts with the initial instance $(D_0, t_e^{D_0})$. It deduces relative accuracy by *populating partial orders* and *instantiating the target tuple template*, yielding a sequence $(D_0, t_e^{D_0})$, $(D_1, t_e^{D_1})$, …, $(D_m, t_e^{D_m})$ of accuracy

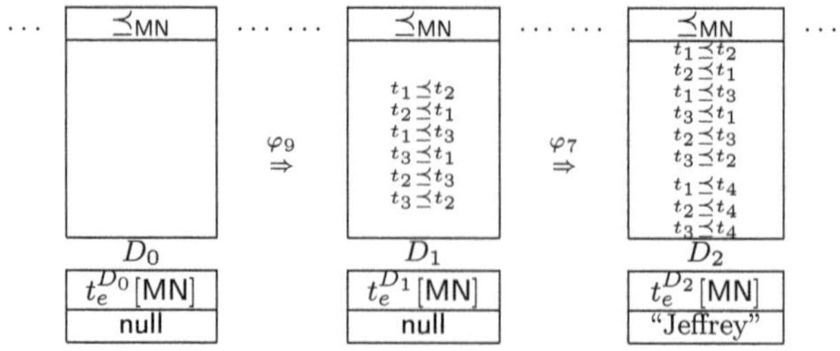

Figure 2: Single chase steps

instances. Each chase step applies an AR $\varphi \in \Sigma$ and I_m to an accuracy instance $(D_j, t_e^{D_j})$, and generates another instance $(D_{j+1}, t_e^{D_{j+1}})$. In other words, $(D_{j+1}, t_e^{D_{j+1}})$ is an updated version of $(D_j, t_e^{D_j})$, such that for some attribute A_i, either the partial order $\preceq^{D_{j+1}}_{A_i}$ extends $\preceq^{D_j}_{A_i}$ with a new pair, or $t_e^{D_j}[A_i] = \mathsf{null}$ is instantiated by letting $t_e^{D_{j+1}}[A_i]$ take a value from a master tuple in I_m or a value that is already determined most accurate for A_i. The process proceeds until no changes can be made to partial orders or the target tuple template. More specifically, these are stated as follows.

(1) A single chase step. We say that $(D_{j+1}, t_e^{D_{j+1}})$ is *an immediate result* of enforcing an AR $\varphi \in \Sigma$ on $(D_j, t_e^{D_j})$ with I_m, denoted by $(D_j, t_e^{D_j}) \mapsto_\varphi (D_{j+1}, t_e^{D_{j+1}})$, if $(D_j, t_e^{D_j}) \neq (D_{j+1}, t_e^{D_{j+1}})$ and one of the following conditions holds:

<u>*(a) When* $\varphi = \forall t_1, t_2 (R(t_1) \wedge R(t_2) \wedge \omega \rightarrow t_1 \preceq_{A_i} t_2)$.</u> Then there exist tuples $t_1, t_2 \in I_e$ such that

- $(t_1, t_2) \models \omega$;
- $D_{j+1} {=} (I_e, \preceq^{D_j}_{A_1}, \cdots, \preceq^{D_j}_{A_i} \cup \{(t_1, t_2)\}, \cdots, \preceq^{D_j}_{A_n})$; and
- $t_e^{D_{j+1}} {=} (t_e^{D_j}[A_1], \cdots, \lambda(t_e^{D_j}[A_i], \preceq^{D_{j+1}}_{A_i}) \cdots, t_e^{D_j}[A_n])$.

Here $\lambda(t_e^{D_j}[A_i], \preceq^{D_j}_{A_i}) {=} t[A_i]$ if there exists $t \in I_e$ such that for all $t' \in I_e$, $t' \preceq^{D_{j+1}}_{A_i} t$; and it is $t_e^{D_j}[A_i]$ otherwise.

Intuitively, $\preceq^{D_{j+1}}_{A_i}$ extends $\preceq^{D_j}_{A_i}$ by including $t_1 {\preceq_{A_i}} t_2$, and $t_e^{D_{j+1}}[A_i]$ takes the A_i value with the highest accuracy *w.r.t.* $\preceq^{D_{j+1}}_{A_i}$ if it exists. Note that D_{j+1} and D_j agree on every attribute and partial order other than $t_e^{D_j}[A_i]$ and $\preceq^{D_j}_{A_i}$.

<u>*(b) When* $\varphi = \forall t_m\ (R_m(t_m) \wedge \omega \rightarrow t_e[A_i] = t_m[A_i])$.</u> Then there exist tuples $t \in I_e$ and $t_m \in I_m$ such that

- $(t_e, t_m) \models \omega$, $D_{j+1} = D_j$, and
- $t_e^{D_{j+1}} = (t_e^{D_j}[A_1], \cdots, t_m[A_i], \cdots, t_e^{D_j}[A_n])$.

Here $t_e^{D_{j+1}}$ differs from $t_e^{D_j}[A_i]$ only in attribute A_i by taking master data $t_m[A_i]$, while D_{j+1} remains unchanged from D_j.

We say that $(D_j, t_e^{D_j}) \mapsto_\varphi (D_{j+1}, t_e^{D_{j+1}})$ is *valid* if (a) there exist no t_1 and t_2 such that both $t_1 \prec^{D_{j+1}}_{A_i} t_2$ and $t_2 \prec^{D_{j+1}}_{A_i} t_1$ (*i.e.*, $t_1 \preceq^{D_{j+1}}_{A_i} t_2$, $t_2 \preceq^{D_{j+1}}_{A_i} t_1$ but $t_1[A_i] \neq t_2[A_i]$), and (b) $t_e^{D_j}[A_i]$ is not changed if $t_e^{D_j}[A_i] \neq \mathsf{null}$. In the chase process we consider valid chase steps only.

Observe the following: (a) the entity instance I_e and the master data I_m remain unchanged when ARs are enforced; (b) $\preceq^{D_j}_{A_i}$ and $\preceq^{D_{i+1}}_{A_i}$ are partial orders for all attributes A_i, such that for all $t_1, t_2 \in I_e$, if $t_1 \preceq^{D_j}_{A_i} t_2$ and $t_2 \preceq^{D_j}_{A_i} t_1$ then $t_1[A_i] = t_2[A_i]$; and (c) if $t_e^{D_j}[A_i] \neq \mathsf{null}$, then $t_e^{D_{j+1}}[A_i] = t_e^{D_j}[A_i]$, *i.e.*, all non-null values of $t_e^{D_j}$ *remain unchanged.*

Example 4: Consider I_e = stat (Table 1), I_m = nba (Table 2), and Σ consisting of the ARs given in Example 3. Let D_0 be I_e with empty partial orders, and $t_e^{D_0}$ be the initial target template with $t_e^{D_0}[A]$ = null for all attributes A. After enforcing φ_9 on $(D_0, t_e^{D_0})$, it yields $(D_1, t_e^{D_1})$ as the first step in Fig. 2, in which $\preceq_{\mathsf{MN}}$ is extended on (t_1, t_2), (t_2, t_3) and (t_3, t_1). Similarly, after enforcing φ_7 on $(D_1, t_e^{D_1})$, it yields $(D_2, t_e^{D_2})$ as the second step in Fig. 2, which extends $\preceq_{\mathsf{MN}}$ on (t_1, t_4) and instantiates $t_e^{D_2}[\mathsf{MN}]$ = "Jeffrey". □

(2) Chase. A *chasing sequence* of D_0 by Σ and I_m is a sequence of accuracy instances $(D_0, t_e^{D_0})$, $(D_1, t_e^{D_1})$, ..., $(D_l, t_e^{D_l})$, ..., where for each $j \geq 1$, there exists some AR $\varphi \in \Sigma$ such that $(D_j, t_e^{D_j}) \mapsto_\varphi (D_{j+1}, t_e^{D_{j+1}})$ is valid.

A chasing sequence $(D_0, t_e^{D_0})$, ..., $(D_k, t_e^{D_k})$ is said to be *terminal* if it is finite and moreover, no more valid step can be enforced on $(D_k, t_e^{D_k})$. We refer to $t_e^{D_k}$ as a *deduced target tuple* of specification S, and $(D_k, t_e^{D_k})$ as the *terminal instance* of the chasing sequence.

Intuitively, the chase repeatedly applies ARs to deduce relative accuracy and instantiate the target tuple template, until it reaches an instance that cannot be further changed.

Example 5: Consider $D_0, t_e^{D_0}, \Sigma$ and I_m given in Example 4. By enforcing ARs φ_9, φ_7, φ_5, φ_{10}, φ_6, φ_1, φ_4, φ_2, φ_3 and φ_{11} on $(D_0, t_e^{D_0})$ in this order with I_m, one can get a deduced target tuple t_e[FN, MN, LN, rnds, totalPts, J#, league, team, arena] = (Michael, Jeffrey, Jordan, 27, 772, 23, NBA, Chicago Bulls, United Center). Note that t_e is a complete target tuple from stat, which draws values from *different tuples, e.g.,* t_2 and t_4 of stat and s_1 of nba. □

3. FUNDAMENTAL PROBLEMS

Given a specification $S = (D_0, \Sigma, I_m, t_e^{D_0})$ of an entity e, we want to know whether chasing on D_0 by Σ and I_m terminates? Whether will all chasing sequences of D_0 lead to the same deduced target tuple t_e? When the target tuple t_e is incomplete, can we make it complete while observing the ARs in Σ? Can we find top-k candidate targets for users to chose? This section studies these issues (due to the lack of space we defer all the proofs to the full version). As will be seen in Section 4, our framework for deducing relative accuracy and target tuples are based on these results.

(1) Termination of chase. Is every chasing sequence of D_0 by Σ and I_m an initial subsequence of a terminal chasing sequence? The answer to this question is affirmative.

Proposition 1: *Every chasing sequence of D_0 by Σ and I_m is finite and leads to a terminal instance in $O(|I_e|^2)$ steps, where $|I_e|$ is the size of the entity instance I_e in D_0.* □

(2) The Church-Rosser property. Another question asks whether different terminal chasing sequences of D_0 by Σ and I_m lead to *the same unique terminal instance*, no matter what rules in Σ are used and in what order they are applied. This is known as the *Church-Rosser property* (see, *e.g.,* [1]). If a specification S has the Church-Rosser property, we say that *S is Church-Rosser.* Obviously if S is Church-Rosser, then the uniquely deduced target tuple is *deterministic*, yielding a unique target that can be "trusted".

Unfortunately, not all specifications are Church-Rosser.

Example 6: Consider the specification S described in Example 5. One can verify that S is Church-Rosser. However, let us extend S to S' by adding an extra rule φ_{12}: $\forall t_1, t_2 \in$ stat $(t_1[\mathsf{league}] = \text{NBA} \wedge t_2[\mathsf{league}] = \text{SL} \rightarrow t_1 \preceq_{\mathsf{league}} t_2)$. Then S' is not Church-Rosser. Indeed, there are two chasing sequences that deduce different target tuples: one is the sequence given in Example 5 with $t_e[\mathsf{league}]$ = NBA, and the other is by enforcing ARs φ_7, φ_5, φ_{10} and φ_{12} in this order, yielding a target tuple t'_e with $t'_e[\mathsf{league}]$ = SL. □

This tells us that if S is not Church-Rosser, it may lead to multiple conflicting targets (*e.g.,* t_e and t'_e on league), which cannot be accurate at the same time. Thus specifications that are not Church-Rosser should be *identified and revised.*

To do this, we provide *a necessary and sufficient condition* for deciding whether a specification S is Church-Rosser. We say that a terminal chasing sequence $(D_0, t_e^{D_0})$, ..., $(D_k, t_e^{D_k})$ is *stable* if for all *invalid* chase steps that enforce an AR φ on $(D_k, t_e^{D_k})$, φ cannot be enforced on $(D_j, t_e^{D_j})$ as a valid step for all $j \in [0, k-1]$. That is, suppose that $(D_k, t_e^{D_k})$ can be further changed by φ by letting $t_e^{D_k}[A_i]$ change from a non-null value to another, or by allowing both $t_1 \preceq_{A_i}^{D_k} t_2$ and $t_2 \preceq_{A_i}^{D_k} t_1$ while $t_1[A_i] \neq t_2[A_i]$. Then the change cannot be inflicted to any $(D_j, t_e^{D_j})$ as a valid move. Intuitively, if φ could be enforced as a valid step, it would lead to a terminal sequence *different* from $(D_k, t_e^{D_k})$.

A stable chasing sequence prevents any conflicts in the chase such as those in Example 6, and allows us to efficiently determine whether S is Church-Rosser. In light of this, in the sequel we focus on Church-Rosser specifications only.

Theorem 2: *Given a specification $S = (D_0, \Sigma, I_m, t_e^{D_0})$, (a) S is Church-Rosser if and only if there exists a terminal chasing sequence of S that is stable; and (b) it is in $O((|I_e|^2 + |I_m|)|\Sigma|)$ time to decide whether S is Church-Rosser.* □

(3) Deducing candidate targets. When S is Church-Rosser, its deduced target tuple t_e may still be *incomplete, i.e.,* some attributes remain null. For example, if we drop AR φ_{11} of Example 3 from the specification of Example 5, the reduced specification is still Church-Rosser, but its deduced target is incomplete since the most accurate value of arena can no longer be determined, as indicated in Example 2.

This gives rise to the following question: can we find candidate targets and suggest them for the users to consider? More specifically, a complete tuple t'_e is called a *candidate target* of a specification $S = (D_0, \Sigma, I_m, t_e^{D_0})$ if

- for each attribute A_i, $t'_e[A_i] = t_e[A_i]$ if $t_e[A_i] \neq$ null, and $t'_e[A_i]$ is a value in $\mathsf{dom}(A_i)$ otherwise, where t_e is the unique deduced target tuple of S;
- $S' = (D_0, \Sigma, I_m, t'_e)$ is Church-Rosser and moreover, t'_e is the deduced target tuple of S'.

That is, a candidate target t'_e keeps the non-null values of t_e unchanged but instantiates those null attributes of t_e. Moreover, when we treat t'_e as the initial target template, the chase verifies that t'_e "satisfies" the constraints imposed by the ARs of Σ, and is deduced as the target tuple of S'.

The *candidate target problem* is to determine, given a specification S of an entity that is Church-Rosser, whether there exists a candidate target t'_e of S. It is, however, nontrivial.

Theorem 3: *The candidate target problem is* NP*-complete. It remains* NP*-hard for specifications $S = (D_0, \Sigma, I_m, t_e^{D_0})$ in which Σ consists of ARs of form (1) only, and when candidate targets t_e of S take values from I_e and I_m only.* □

The number of candidates t'_e for a Church-Rosser S could be quite large, exponential or even infinite.

Example 7: Consider $R = (A_1, \ldots, A_n)$, an entity instance I_e of R with tuples $t_1 = (0, \ldots, 0)$ and $t_2 = (1, \ldots, 1)$, and empty Σ and I_m. Then there are 2^n candidate targets with

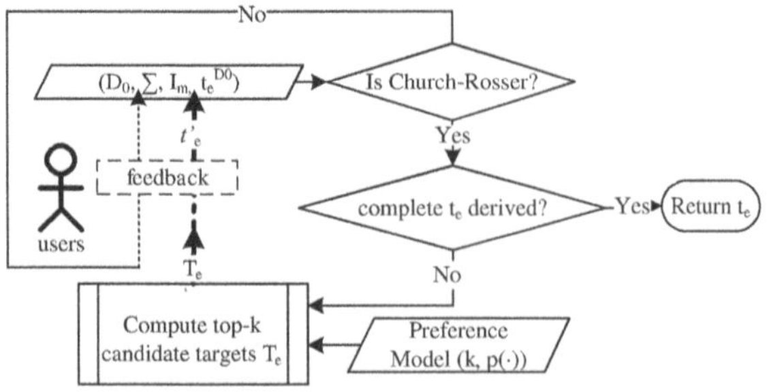

Figure 3: Framework overview

values from $\{0, 1\}$, *i.e.*, each tuple $t \in \{0, 1\}^n$ is a candidate target. Worse still, if some A_i of R has an infinite domain, there are possibly *infinitely many* candidate targets. □

(4) Finding top-k candidate targets. It is infeasible to enumerate all candidate targets. This suggests that we find top-k candidate targets for S based on a preference model.

We specify the preference model as a pair $(k, p(\cdot))$, where k is a natural number, and $p(\cdot)$ is a monotone scoring function such that given a set T_e of candidate targets, $p(T_e)$ is a real number. To simplify the discussion we assume that a real number $w_{A_i}(v)$ is associated with each value v in domain $\mathsf{dom}\ (A_i)$ (if $\mathsf{dom}\ (A_i)$ is infinite, $w_{A_i}(v)$ is the same for all v outside of I_e and I_m), referred to as the *score of* v. The score could be placed by the users as the confidence in v [12], found as probabilities by truth discovery algorithms [4, 19, 28–30] (see Section 7), or automatically derived by counting the occurrences of v in the A_i column and from co-existence of attributes and available scores. We define the *score*

$$p(T_e) = \sum_{t'_e \in T_e} \sum_{A_i \in \mathsf{attr}(R)} w_{A_i}(t'_e[A_i]).$$

Such preference is often too "soft" to be modeled as ARs or partial orders, and candidates derived from it may not be as "deterministic" ("certain") as deduced targets by the chase. Nonetheless, users often find such candidates helpful, as commonly practiced in data repairing heuristics [12].

For a Church-Rosser S, a preference model $(k, p(\cdot))$ and a number C, the *top-k candidate problem* is to decide whether there exists a set T_e of k candidate targets with $p(T_e) \geq C$.

Theorem 4: *The top-k candidate problem is* NP*-complete, and* NP*-hard under the same restriction of Theorem 3.* □

4. A FRAMEWORK

We now present a framework for deducing complete target tuples for entities. As depicted in Fig. 3, given a specification $S = (D_0, \Sigma, I_m, t_e^{D_0})$ of an entity e, it populates partial orders for relative accuracy and instantiates the target tuple template, based on the chase given in Section 2. It automatically deduces as many accurate values for e as possible, and interacts with the users to revise candidate targets, until a complete target tuple is found. It works as follows.

(1) *Church-Rosser checking.* It first inspects whether S is Church-Rosser via *automated reasoning*. The Church-Rosser property warrants a unique target tuple, in which the accurate values can be trusted (Section 3). If S is not Church-Rosser, the users are invited to revise S (see step (4) below), by following the "No" branch. The revised S is then checked.

(2) *Computing target tuple t_e.* When S is confirmed Church-Rosser, the framework computes the unique deduced target tuple t_e by means of the chase. It returns t_e if it is complete. Otherwise it computes a top-k set of candidate targets.

(3) *Computing top-k candidate targets.* As remarked in Section 3, t_e may be incomplete, and it is hard to identify (all) candidate targets (Theorem 3 and Example 7). To this end, the framework computes a top-k set T_e of candidate targets. It comes up with a preference model $(k, p(\cdot))$ following the practice of data repairing heuristics, which the users may opt to adjust. Based on $(k, p(\cdot))$, it computes T_e with k tuples such that (a) for each $t'_e \in T_e$, t_e is a candidate target of S, and (b) for all sets T'_e with k candidate targets, $p(T_e) \geq p(T'_e)$, *i.e.*, tuples in T_e have the highest scores. When there exist at least k candidate targets of S, T_e consists of k distinct tuples; otherwise T_e includes all candidate targets of S. The set T_e is then suggested to the users.

(4) *User feedback.* The users are invited to inspect T_e. They may opt to choose some $t'_e \in T_e$ as the target tuple (recall that for each candidate target t'_e, $t'_e[A] = t_e[A]$ if $t_e[A] \neq$ null); or revise S by instantiating $t_e[B]$ with either the value of some $t'_e[B]$ or a value $v \in \mathsf{dom}(B)$, for some $t_e[B] =$ null. The users are also allowed to revise S by editing ARs in Σ and tuples in I_e (D_0). The revised S with the designated initial values is then checked by step (1).

The process proceeds until a complete t_e is found.

In the rest of the paper we will provide algorithms underlying the framework: an algorithm for checking the Church-Rosser property of S and deducing t_e in Section 5, and algorithms for computing top-k candidate targets in Section 6.

Remark. (1) To find ARs as input of the framework, we need algorithms for discovering ARs from (*possibly dirty*) data. ARs of type (2) can be discovered along the same lines as matching dependencies (see, *e.g.*, [12] for a survey). ARs of type (1) could be found by mining first-order logic rules (*e.g.*, [17]). Given a relation r of schema R, one may also group pairs of its tuples (t_i, t_j) into classes based on their attribute values $(t_i[A], t_j[A])$ ($t_i, t_j \in r$, $A \in \mathsf{attr}(R)$) to denote accuracy orders, and discover ARs by analyzing the containment of those classes via a level-wise approach (*e.g.*, [7]). We defer a full treatment of AR discovery to future work.

(2) The framework can handle *possibly dirty* entity instances. Indeed, constant CFDs [13] for detecting data inconsistencies can be expressed as ARs (Section 2). Thus in the same framework the consistency of target tuples can be assured. The framework can also incorporate data repairing algorithms, which have been well studied (see, *e.g.*, [12]).

5. CHECK CHURCH-ROSSER PROPERTY

We next present an algorithm that, given a specification $S = (D_0, \Sigma, I_m, t_e^{D_0})$, checks whether S is Church-Rosser. If so, it computes the unique terminal instance (D, t_e), and returns *nil* otherwise. The algorithm is in $O((|I_e|^2 + |I_m|)|\Sigma|)$ time, and thus gives a constructive proof for Theorem 2(2).

The algorithm is denoted by IsCR and shown in Fig. 4. Following Theorem 2(1), IsCR checks whether S has a stable terminal chasing sequence, by simulating the chase. At each step of the chase, it collects all valid steps in a set $\mathcal{Q}$, and when the chase process proceeds, it checks whether any valid step in $\mathcal{Q}$ becomes invalid. If so, it concludes that S is not Church-Rosser. Indeed, an invalid step for an instance *remains invalid* in the rest of the chasing sequence. Hence if a valid step becomes invalid later, it will not lead to any stable terminal chasing sequence. If IsCR inspects all valid steps and if none of them becomes invalid, it actually identifies a stable terminal sequence, and thus concludes that S is Church-Rosser. In the process (D, t_e) is also constructed.

Algorithm IsCR makes use of (1) a procedure, denoted by Instantiation, as a preprocessing step to identify all single chase steps, and (2) an indexing structure $\mathcal{H}$ for efficiently locating applicable chase steps, described as follows.

Computing single chase steps. Procedure Instantiation pre-computes possible single chase steps, collected in a set Γ, by partially evaluating each AR $\varphi \in \Sigma$ on tuples in the entity instance I_e of D_0 and master relation I_m, as follows.

(1) When φ is of form (1) $\forall t_1, t_2(\omega \to t_1 \preceq_{A_k} t_2)$, for each pair (t_i, t_j) of tuples in I_e, it computes $\phi = (\omega' \to t_i \preceq_{A_k} t_j)$, where ω' is obtained by evaluating $\omega(t_i, t_j)$, which substitutes (t_i, t_j) for (t_1, t_2) in ω. More specifically, for each predicate in ω, (a) if it is of the form $t_1[A_l]$ op $t_2[A_l]$ or $t_s[A_s]$ op c ($s \in [1, 2]$), where op is one of $=, \neq, >, <, \leq, \geq$, then the predicate on (t_i, t_j) evaluates to true or false. If it is true, the predicate is not included in ω'. If it is false, ω' also becomes false. (b) If it is $t_1 \prec_{A_l} t_2$ (resp. $t_1 \preceq_{A_l} t_2$), the predicate is replaced by $t_i \prec_{A_l} t_j$ (resp. $t_i \preceq_{A_l} t_j$) in ω'. We include ϕ in Γ if ω' is not false. Intuitively, ϕ indicates a single chase step: if ω' is satisfied, then $t_i \preceq_{A_k} t_j$ could be deduced.

(2) When $\varphi = \forall t_m\ (R_m(t_m) \wedge \omega \to t_e[A_i] = t_m[B])$, *i.e.*, of form (2), for each $t' \in I_m$, it computes $\phi = (\omega' \to t_e[A_i] = c)$, where t_e is the target template, c is the constant $t'[B]$, and ω' is obtained from $\omega(t_m)$ by substituting constant $t'[B']$ for each $t_m[B']$ in ω. We include ϕ in Γ, which indicates that if ω' is satisfied, then $t_e[A_i]$ can be instantiated with c.

Note that no ϕ in Γ carries the $\forall$ quantifier. Moreover, each chase step can be carried out by enforcing some ϕ in Γ rather than ARs in Σ. We use LHS(ϕ) to denote ω'.

Example 8: The following single chase steps can be derived: (a) *true* $\to 16 \prec_{\text{rnds}} 27$ from t_1, t_2 of Table 1 and φ_1 (form (1)) of Table 3; (b) $16 \prec_{\text{rnds}} 27 \to 45 \prec_{\text{J\#}} 23$ from t_1, t_2 and φ_2 (form (1)); and (c) t_e[FN, LN] = (Michael, Jordan) $\to$ t_e[league, team] = (NBA, Chicago Bulls) from master tuple s_1 of Table 2 and φ_6 (form (2)) of Table 3. □

Building Indices. Algorithm IsCR uses an indexing structure $\mathcal{H}$ to speed up the process of finding next applicable chase steps. The structure $\mathcal{H}$ is defined as follows.

(1) For each $\phi \in \Gamma$, $\mathcal{H}$ contains a counter n_ϕ to keep track of the number of predicates in LHS(ϕ) that are not yet satisfied.

(2) For each predicate δ of the form of either $t_i \preceq_{A_k} t_j$ or $t_e[A_k] = c$, $\mathcal{H}$ maintains a set $\Phi_\delta = \{\phi \mid \phi \in \Gamma \wedge \delta \in \text{LHS}(\phi)\}$, *i.e.*, the set of ϕ's in Γ that contain δ in LHS(ϕ).

(3) A set $\mathcal{Q}$ is maintained by $\mathcal{H}$, which consists of all applicable single chase steps that were once valid. Initially, $\mathcal{Q} = \{\phi \mid \phi \in \Gamma \wedge n_\phi = 0 \wedge \phi$ was a valid step for $(D_0, t_e^{D_0})\}$.

Algorithm. We now present the main driver of IsCR. Given S, it first identifies all possible single steps and builds the index $\mathcal{H}$, by invoking procedures Instantiation and InitIndex (not shown), respectively (lines 1-2). It then initializes the accuracy instance template (D, t_e) with $(D_0, t_e^{D_0})$ (line 3).

After these, IsCR simulates the chasing of S (lines 3-13). When the set $\mathcal{Q}$ in $\mathcal{H}$ of valid steps is nonempty, it picks an applicable step ϕ from $\mathcal{Q}$ using a procedure NextStep (line 5, not shown), which removes ϕ from $\mathcal{Q}$. It then enforces ϕ as follows. If ϕ is derived from an AR of form (1) (lines 6-8), IsCR adds the derived partial order to D (line 7), and deduces $t_e[A_k]$ whenever possible (line 8). If ϕ is derived from

Input: A specification $S = (D_0, \Sigma, I_m, t_e^{D_0})$.
Output: The unique terminal instance (D, t_e) if S is Church-Rosser, and *nil* otherwise.

1. $\Gamma :=$ Instantiation(D_0, Σ, I_m);
2. $\mathcal{H} :=$ InitIndex$(\Gamma, D_0, t_e^{D_0})$; /*$\mathcal{Q}$ in $\mathcal{H}$ maintains single steps*/
3. $D := D_0$; $t_e := t_e^{D_0}$;
4. **repeat**
5. $\phi :=$ NextStep$(\mathcal{H})$;
6.   **if** $\phi = (\omega \to t_i \preceq_{A_k} t_j)$ (*i.e.*, form (1)) **then**
7. $D :=$ the transitive closure of $D \cup \{t_i \preceq_{A_k} t_j\}$;
8.   Update $t_e[A_k]$;
9.   **if** $\phi = (\omega \to t_e[A_i] = c)$ (*i.e.*, form (2)) **then**
10. $t_e[A_i] := c$;
11.   **if not** IsValid(ϕ, D, t_e) **then return** *nil*;
12.   Update $\mathcal{H}$;
13. **until** $\mathcal{Q}$ in $\mathcal{H}$ becomes empty $\emptyset$;
14. **return** (D, t_e)

Figure 4: Algorithm IsCR

an AR of form (2) (lines 9-10), IsCR sets $t_e[A_k] := c$ (line 10). If ϕ is invalid for (D, t_e), we can conclude that S is not Church-Rosser since there will be no stable terminal chasing sequences, as argued above, and IsCR returns *nil* (line 11). Otherwise IsCR updates $\mathcal{H}$ to reflect the changes to D and t_e (line 12): for each $t_i \preceq_{A_k} t_j$ derived, $n_{\phi'}$ is decreased by 1 for each $\phi' \in \Phi_{t_i \preceq_{A_k} t_j}$; and for each $t_e[A_k] = c$ derived, it decreases $n_{\phi'}$ by 1 for each $\phi' \in \Phi_{t_e[A_k]=c}$. For any ϕ' with $n_{\phi'} = 0$, ϕ' is added to $\mathcal{Q}$, *i.e.*, it now becomes a valid chase step, to be considered later. The process proceeds until no more steps in $\mathcal{Q}$ need to checked (line 13), and it returns (D, t_e) as the terminal instance (line 14).

Correctness & complexity. The correctness of IsCR follows from Theorem 2(1) and the argument above, since it checks all possible chase steps that are valid at some point of chasing. For the complexity, observe the following. (1) Instantiation is in $O(|\Sigma|(|I_e|^2 + |I_m|))$ time, which is also the bound on $|\Gamma|$. After Instantiation, IsCR no longer needs to visit I_e. (2) With the indices, NextStep takes O(1) time, and each ϕ is checked only once. (3) Each step derives new partial orders $\preceq_{A_k}$ and/or instantiates $t_e[A_k]$. Thus, the total number of steps processed (lines 5-12) is bounded by $O(|I_e|^2)$. Therefore, IsCR is in $O(|\Sigma|(|I_e|^2 + |I_m|))$ time. As remarked earlier, I_e is *much smaller* than a database instance. As will be seen in Section 7, IsCR takes about 10ms.

6. FIND TOP-k CANDIDATE TARGETS

We next provide algorithms that, given a Church-Rosser specification $S = (D_0, \Sigma, I_m, t_e^{D_0})$ and a preference model $(k, p(\cdot))$, compute a set T_e of top-k candidate targets. Here T_e consists of k distinct candidate targets of S with the maximum score $p(T_e)$ if there exist at least k such tuples of S; and otherwise T_e includes all candidate targets of S.

Theorem 4 tells us that the top-k candidate problem is NP-complete. Worse still, there exists no PTIME algorithm for it with a bounded approximation-ratio unless P = NP. Recall that NPO is the *class* of all NP optimization problems. An NPO-complete problem is NP-hard to optimize, and is among the hardest optimization problems.

Theorem 5: *The top-k candidate targets problem (optimization version) is* NPO*-complete.* □

Despite the hardness, we provide three algorithms to find top-k candidate targets, all with the *early termination* property, *i.e.*, they stop as soon as top-k candidate targets are found. The first two are exact algorithms. (1) The first one,

RankJoinCT, extends prior algorithms [21, 26] for computing top-k joins of ranked lists (Section 6.1). (2) The second one, TopKCT, is developed for a more general setting when the ranked lists are *not* given (Section 6.2). We show that TopKCT incurs *lower cost* than RankJoinCT, and is *instance optimal w.r.t.* the number of visits to the data needed. (3) The third one, TopKCT$_h$, is a PTIME heuristic version of TopKCT (Section 6.3). We also identify special cases when the top-k candidate targets problem is in PTIME.

6.1 RankJoinCT: An Algorithm based on Rank Join

Given a set of ranked lists and a monotone scoring function, *the top-k rank join problem* is to compute the top k join results of the lists with the highest scores. Our problem can be modeled as an extension of the top-k rank join problem as follows. Consider a Church-Rosser specification S, of which t_e is the unique deduced target tuple. Let Z be the set of attributes A such that $t_e[A_i]$ = null. Assume *w.l.o.g.* that Z consists of m attributes $A_1, \cdots, A_m$. Then a set T_e of top-k candidate targets is a set of top-k join results of values in each domain of Z such that it satisfies an *additional condition*: for each $t \in T_e$, the revised specification $S' = (D_0, \Sigma, I_m, t'_e)$ must also be Church-Rosser, where $t'_e[Z] = t[Z]$ and $t'_e[B] = t_e[B]$ for all $B \in R \setminus Z$.

In light of this, we develop algorithm RankJoinCT by extending top-k rank join algorithms [21, 26]. The algorithm assumes that the domain values of Z attributes are *ranked* based on their scores (see $w_{A_i}(\cdot)$ in Section 3). It takes as input S, $(k, p(\cdot))$, t_e and moreover, m lists $L_1, \cdots, L_m$, such that L_i is the ranked list of values in the *active domain* of A_i for all $i \in [1, m]$. It returns a top-k *list* T_e of candidate targets as required. Note that L_i is *finite*: the active domain of A_i is dom(A_i) if it is finite; otherwise it includes all A_i values from I_e or I_m and at most one more distinct value from dom(A_i), which suffices to denote values outside of I_e or I_m and is referred to as a *default value* (see Section 3). We omit the details of RankJoinCT for the lack of space, but give an example below to illustrate how it works.

Example 9: Consider the specification S of Example 5 and a preference model $(k = 2, p(\cdot))$, where $p(\cdot)$ counts value occurrences. Suppose that we drop team from φ_6 of Table 3. Then the deduced target t_e is incomplete since t_e[team] and t_e[arena] become null. To find top 2 candidate targets for S, RankJoinCT takes as input the modified S, $(2, p(\cdot))$ and two ranked list L_{team} and L_{arena} with $\perp_{\text{team}}$ and $\perp_{\text{arena}}$ as default values for team and arena, respectively. It maintains upper bounds u_{team} and u_{arena}, asserting that for all tuples with values in L_{team} (resp. L_{arena}), their scores are no higher than u_{team} (resp. u_{arena}). RankJoinCT iteratively retrieves candidate targets from the two lists. Initially, it picks top values for team and arena, and forms a candidate target t_1 with t_1[team, arena] = (Chicago Bulls, United Center) ($p(t_1) = 4$). It then updates both u_{team} and u_{area} to 3. After that, it picks the next top unseen value v from L_{arena} and chooses a candidate target from the join results of $\{v\}$ with other fixed values in t_1, which is t_2 with t_2[team, arena] = (Chicago Bulls, Chicago Stadium (or Regions Park)) ($p(t_2)$ = 3). Now $p(t_1)$ and $p(t_2)$ are no less than u_{FN} and u_{arena}.

Further, for each $t \in \{t_1, t_2\}$, RankJoinCT has to check the condition additional to [21,26], *i.e.*, whether t is a candidate target. This is done by procedure check, which is essentially IsCR of Fig. 4 by taking t as the initial target. As t_1 and t_2 pass check, they are returned as top-2 candidates. □

Input: S, $(k, p(\cdot))$ and t_e as for RankJoinCT, and heaps $H_1, \ldots, H_m$.
Output: A list T_e of top-k candidate targets of S.

1. $T_e := nil$;
2. **for each** $i \in [1, m]$ **do** $B_i := [H_i.\text{pop}()]$;
3. $o.t[Z] := (B_1[0], \cdots, B_m[0])$; $o.t[R \setminus Z] := t_e[R \setminus Z]$;
4. **for each** $i \in [1, m]$ **do** $o.p_i := 0$;
5. $o.w := p(\{o.t\})$;
6. $T := \{o.t\}$; $Q :=$ BrodalQueue($\{o\}$);
7. **while** $\|T_e\| < k$ **and** $\|Q\| > 0$ **do**
8. $o := Q.\text{pop}()$;
9.   **if** check($o.t$, S) **then** T_e.append($o.t$); /* add $o.t$ to T_e*/
10.   **for each** $i \in [1, m]$ **do**
11.   **if** len(B_i) $\leq o.p_i + 1$ **then** B_i.append(H_i.pop());
12. $o' := o$;
13. $o'.p_i := o'.p_i + 1$; $o'.t[A_i] := B_i[o'.p_i]$;
14. $o'.w := o.w - w_{A_i}(o.t[A_i]) + w_{A_i}(o'.t[A_i])$;
15.   **if** $o'.t \notin T$ **then** Q.push(o'); $T := T \cup \{o'.t\}$;
16. **return** T_e;

Figure 5: Algorithm TopKCT

Following [21], one can readily verify:

Proposition 6: RankJoinCT *finds top-k candidate targets with the early termination property,* i.e., *it does not need to check all tuples in the product of ranked lists.* □

However, RankJoinCT is not ideal. (1) In practice, domain values are often *not* given in ranked lists, and sorting the domains is costly. (2) RankJoinCT invokes procedure check for each tuple in the join result (Example 9); this yields *exponentially* many calls, each taking $O(|\Sigma|(|I_e|^2 + |I_m|))$ time.

6.2 TopKCT: A Brodal Queue Based Algorithm

To remedy the problems of RankJoinCT, we next present TopKCT. In contrast to RankJoinCT, TopKCT does not require ranked lists as input, and invokes check much less.

TopKCT maintains several structures: (1) a heap H_i for each $A_i \in Z$, to store the values in the active domain of A_i; it is able to pop up the top value in H_i in $O(\log |H_i|)$ time, and can be pre-constructed in linear time; (2) a Brodal queue Q, to keep track of tuples to be checked; Q is a worst-case efficient priority queue [6]; it takes $O(1)$ time to insert a tuple and $O(\log |Q|)$ time to pop up the top tuple; and (3) a hash set T to record tuples that were once pushed to Q.

TopKCT is shown in Fig. 5. Its input includes S, $(k, p(\cdot))$, t_e as for RankJoinCT; but instead of ranked lists, it takes m heaps $H_1, \cdots, H_m$ as input. It computes a top-k list T_e like RankJoinCT. The key idea behind TopKCT is that when T_e is nonempty, if t is the next best tuple, then there must exist a tuple $t' \in T_e$ such that t and t' differ in *only one* attribute. Hence it capitalizes on the heaps to pop up a tuple that is guaranteed to be the next best, one at time, rather than to compute costly ranked joins. The tuple is then validated by check, and is added to T_e if it is a candidate target. The process proceeds until either T_e is found or the search space is exhausted, with *the early termination property.*

More specifically, TopKCT first lets T_e be empty (line 1). It then pops the top values out of the m heaps $H_1, \cdots, H_m$ to m vectors $B_1, \cdots, B_m$, respectively (line 2), where B_i is a buffer of the values from H_i for $i \in [1, m]$. Note that $t_Z = (B_1[0], \cdots, B_m[0])$ is the tuple with the highest score. An object o is then formed (lines 3-5), with $2+m$ members: (1) $o.t$ is a tuple t_0, where $t_0[Z] = t_Z$ and $t_0[R \setminus Z] = t_e[R \setminus Z]$; (2) for $i \in [1, m]$, $o.p_i$ is an integer, initially 0; it is an index of B_i, indicating that $o.t[A_i]$ takes value from $B_i[o.p_i]$; and (3) $o.w$ is a real number, which is the score of $o.t$. The Brodal queue Q is initialized with $\{o\}$ only, and it lets the hash set $T := \{o.t\}$ (line 6). Note that when Q has multiple objects, it always pops up o' with the highest $o'.w$.

After these, TopKCT populates T_e by iterating the following until T_e has k tuples or Q becomes empty (lines 7-15, where $\|\cdot\|$ denotes cardinality). In each iteration, an object o is popped out from Q (line 8). If $o.t$ is verified a candidate target via check, $o.t$ is added to T_e (line 9). TopKCT then expands Q with tuples that differ from previous ones in *only one* attribute (lines 10-15). To do so, it first expands B_i by adding the top value from H_i to the end of B_i if $o.p_i$ already points to the last value of vector B_i, *i.e.,* all the values in B_i have been inspected (line 11). It then generates a new o' by letting $o.t[A_i] := B_i[o.p_i+1]$, *i.e.,* the value with the highest score next to o (lines 12-14; to simplify the discussion, we assume a weight w_{A_i} for each value when computing $o'.w$, as in Section 3; but this can be lifted). If o' has not been pushed to Q before, *i.e.,* $o' \notin T$, o' is added to Q and T (line 15).

Example 10: Consider the same S and $(2, p(\cdot))$ as in Example 9. Instead of ranked lists, TopKCT takes as input two heaps H_{team} and H_{arena} with the same values as the ranked lists for team and arena, respectively. It first pops the top values Chicago Bulls from H_{team} and United Center from H_{arena}, to form t_0 with $p(t_0) = 2+2 = 4$. It puts t_0 in a Brodal Queue Q. In the first iteration, TopKCT pops the top tuple out of Q (*i.e.,* t_0), and adds it to T_e since t_0 is a valid candidate target. It then pushes t_1 and t_2 to Q, where t_1[team, arena] = (Chicago, United Center) and t_2[team, arena] = (Chicago Bulls, Chicago Stadium). Then, t_1 (or t_2) is added to T_e as it is valid and is among the first popped from Q. Finally TopKCT returns $T_e = [t_0, t_1]$. □

Analysis. Algorithm TopKCT generates the next best candidate tuple by changing *one* attribute of some tuple already in T_e. As argued earlier, this strategy suffices to find top-k tuples. Better still, TopKCT has the following properties.

Proposition 7: TopKCT *has the early termination property,* i.e., *it stops as soon as T_e is found. In addition, it is instance optimal* w.r.t. *the number of visits of each heap* (pop*'s) among all exact algorithms that use heaps to find top-k candidate targets, with optimality ratio 1.* □

An algorithm A is said to be *instance optimal* if there exist constants c_1 and c_2 such that $cost(A, I) \le c_1 \cdot cost(A', I) + c_2$ for all instances I and all algorithms A' in the same setting as A, where $cost(A, I)$ is a *cost metric* of A on I [11]. The constant c_1 is called the *optimality ratio*. Here $cost(A, I)$ is the number of pop's performed on each heap by A on I.

Complexity. TopKCT incurs less cost than RankJoinCT. To see this, let n be the maximum size of H_i for $i \in [1, m]$, and the kth tuple in T_e correspond to the Kth tuple in the product of domain values. Then (1) pop of a heap takes at most $O(\log n)$ time, and there are at most $K + m$ such operations; (2) there are at most K pop operations on the queue Q, and each takes $O(\log Km)$ time; (3) there are at most Km push operations on Q, and each takes $O(1)$ time; and (4) check is invoked K times. Denote the cost of invoking check by c. Putting these together, TopKCT is in $O((K+m)\log n + K(m + \log K + \log m + \mathsf{c}))$ time, in contrast to exponential in K by RankJoinCT.

In light of the inherent intractability, however, K may be an exponential of n in the worst case, *e.g.,* when S does not have k candidate targets; in this case, TopKCT would inevitably exhaust the entire search space. Nevertheless, one can easily verify the following tractable special cases.

Proposition 8: TopKCT *is in* PTIME *when (1) ARs are of form (2) only, or (2) the schema R of I_e is fixed.* □

For instance, in case (1) one can easily see that $K = k$; hence from the analysis above it follows that RJCT is in PTIME, whereas TopKCT still takes exponential time.

As will be experimentally verified shortly, TopKCT actually scales well with real-life data. In addition, by modifying the check step for checking Church-Rosser, TopKCT can also be used to *compute top-k rank joins of unranked lists.*

6.3 TopKCT$_\mathsf{h}$: A Heuristic Algorithm

Finally we outline TopKCT$_\mathsf{h}$, a PTIME heuristic algorithm when all the attributes of R have an infinite domain.

TopKCT$_\mathsf{h}$ first finds a set of k tuples by simply invoking TopKCT without the check step (*i.e.,* line 9 in TopKCT). For each t returned by TopKCT, it greedily revises t with values from I_e and I_m until the revised t is verified a candidate target by check(t, S). It returns the revised tuples as T_e.

TopKCT$_\mathsf{h}$ is in $O((k+m)\log n + k(m+\log k+\log m) + km\mathsf{c})$ time, by the complexity of TopKCT ($k = K$ here), since revising k tuples takes $O(km\mathsf{c})$ time. It is heuristic in nature: while tuples in T_e are guaranteed to be candidate targets of S, they do not necessarily have the highest scores, a tradeoff between the cost and the quality of the solutions.

7. EXPERIMENTAL STUDY

Using both real-life data and synthetic data, we conducted five sets of experiments to evaluate: (1) the effectiveness of algorithm IsCR for deducing target tuples; (2) the effectiveness of RankJoinCT, TopKCT and TopKCT$_\mathsf{h}$ for computing top-k candidate targets; (3) rounds of user interactions; (4) the efficiency of RankJoinCT, TopKCT and TopKCT$_\mathsf{h}$; and (5) the effectiveness of TopKCT when being used for truth discovery, compared with the algorithms of [8, 14].

Experimental setting. Three real-life datasets (Med, CFP and Rest) and synthetic datasets (Syn) were used.

(1) Med was provided by a medicine distribution company (name withheld). It contained sale records of medicines from various stores, specified by a relation schema of 30 attributes such as name, regNo, manufacturer, whose values were not very accurate. Med consisted of 10K tuples for 2.7K entities, where each entity instance ranged from 1 to 83 tuples (4 in average). A set of reference data of 2.4K tuples with 5 attributes was also provided by the company, and we treated it as master data. We manually designed 105 ARs for Med, in which 90 were of form (1) and 15 of form (2).

(2) CFP was extracted from *call for papers/participation* found by Google (*e.g.,* WikiCFP[1], Dbworld[2]). Its attributes included venue, program, and deadline, with values varied in different versions of calls for the same conference. CFP consisted of 100 conferences (entities), with 503 tuples and 22 attributes. The entity instances ranged from 1 to 15 tuples (5 in average). We manually cleaned 55 entries from WikiCFP and treated them as master data, with 17 attributes. We found 43 ARs, with 28 of form (1) and 15 of form (2).

(3) Rest *data.* Rest was the restaurant data used by [8] from `http://lunadong.com/fusionDataSets.htm`. It consisted

[1] http://www.wikicfp.com/cfp/

[2] http://research.cs.wisc.edu/dbworld/browse.html

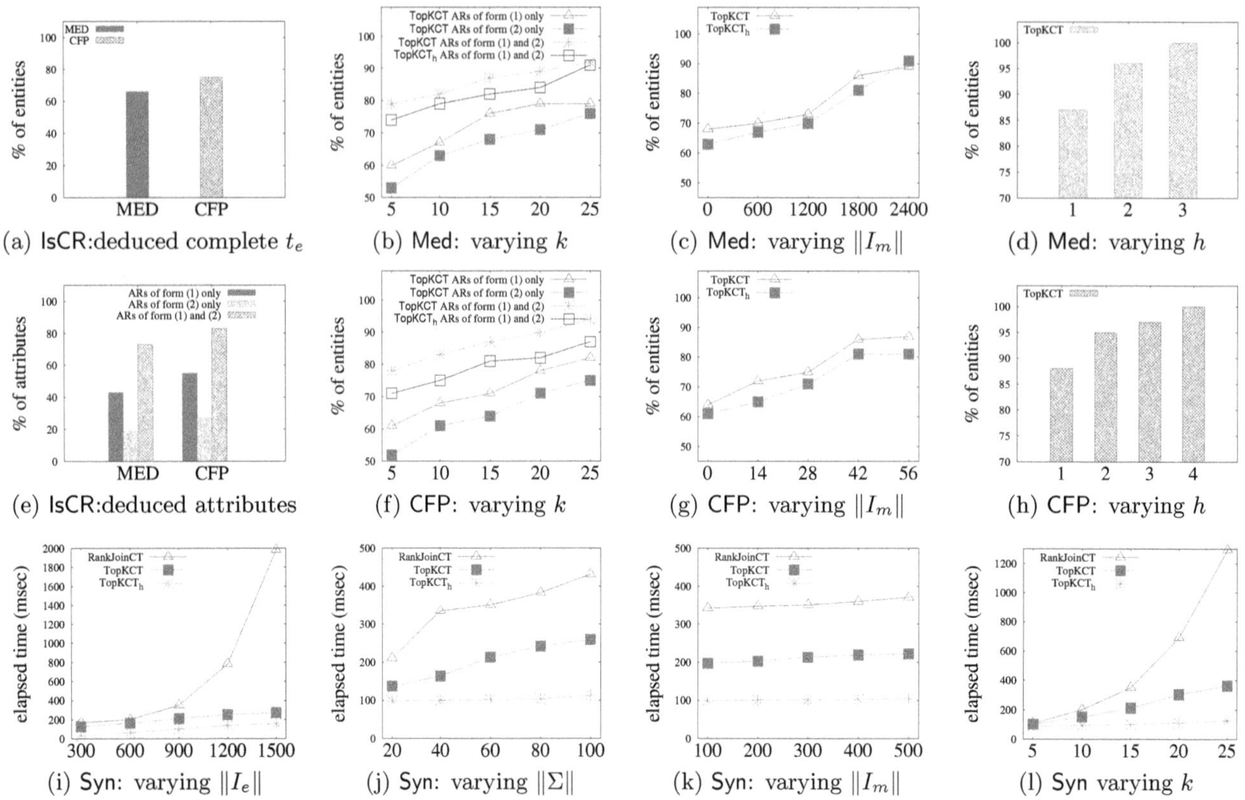

(a) IsCR:deduced complete t_e (b) Med: varying k (c) Med: varying $\|I_m\|$ (d) Med: varying h

(e) IsCR:deduced attributes (f) CFP: varying k (g) CFP: varying $\|I_m\|$ (h) CFP: varying h

(i) Syn: varying $\|I_e\|$ (j) Syn: varying $\|\Sigma\|$ (k) Syn: varying $\|I_m\|$ (l) Syn varying k

Figure 6: Experimental results

of 8 snapshots of 5149 restaurants in Manhattan, with 246K tuples, crawled from 12 Web sources in one-week intervals. Only the true value of a Boolean attribute closed? was to be determined. We found 131 ARs for Rest, all of form (1).

<u>*(4)*</u> *Syn data.* We generated a master relation I_m and entity instances I_e of 20 attributes by extending relations stat (Table 1) and nba (Table 2), respectively. The values in I_e and I_m were randomly drawn from the same domains. For its preference model, we assigned random scores to the values in the domains. We also randomly generated a set Σ of 100 ARs, in which 75% were of form (1) and 25% of form (2).

Remark. (1) The specifications for Med, CFP and Rest are Church-Rosser. (2) For preference we counted value occurrences (Section 3). (3) We used $k = 15$ by default in Experiments 1, 2 and 3, and $k = 1$ in Exp-5 (for truth discovery). (4) The ARs for each of the datasets have *similar* structures and often share the same LHS. For each attribute there are typically 3-4 ARs, and the large number of ARs comes from the number of attributes. One can also use profiling methods to *automatically discover* ARs [7,17] (see Section 4).

Implementation. We implemented the following, all in Python: (1) our algorithms IsCR, RankJoinCT, TopKCT and TopKCT$_h$; (2) a naive algorithm voting based on the preference model that only counts value occurrences, without using ARs; (3) the truth discovery algorithm DeduceOrder of [14] using currency constraints and constant CFDs (see Section 1); and (4) a probabilistic-based truth discovery algorithm copyCEF that utilizes a Bayesian model based on quality measures and copy relationships on data sources [8].

All experiments were conducted on a 64bit Linux Amazon EC2 High-CPU Extra Large Instance with 7 GB of memory, 20 EC2 Compute Units, and 1690 GB of storage. Each experiment was repeated 5 times, and the average is reported here.

Experimental results. We next present our findings.

Exp-1: Effectiveness of IsCR. Using real-life data Med and CFP, we evaluated the quality of target tuples deduced by IsCR: (a) the percentage of target tuples that were complete; and (b) the percentage of non-null attribute values.

<u>*Complete target tuples.*</u> Figure 6(a) shows that for 66% of the entities of Med and 72% of CFP, complete target tuples were automatically deduced by IsCR. That is, by leveraging ARs and master data, complete target tuples could be deduced for over 2/3 of the entities *without user interaction.*

<u>*Non-null values.*</u> Figure 6(e) reports the average percentage of the attributes in Med and CFP for which the most accurate values were deduced. It shows that IsCR found the most accurate values for 42%, 20%, and 73% (resp. 55%, 27%, and 83%) of the attributes in Med (resp. CFP), when ARs of form (1) only, (2) only, and both forms were used, respectively. This tells us the following: (a) IsCR is able to deduce accurate values for a large percentage of attributes, and (b) ARs of forms (1) and (2) interact with each other; indeed, when ARs of both forms were used, the number of accurate values deduced was larger than the *sum* of its counterparts when ARs of form (1) and (2) were used alone. Moreover, when ARs of form (1) or (2) were used only, no complete targets were deduced for Med and CFP (not shown).

Exp-2: Computing top-k candidates. We evaluated the effectiveness of TopKCT (RankJoinCT) and TopKCT$_h$ using Med and CFP. We manually identified the target tuple for each entity, and tested the percentage of entity instances for which the target tuple was among the top-k candidates found by our algorithms. We report the impact of the choice k, the forms of ARs and the size $|I_m|$ of master data on this. Since RankJoinCT and TopKCT are both exact algorithms, the two behaved the same in this set of experiments.

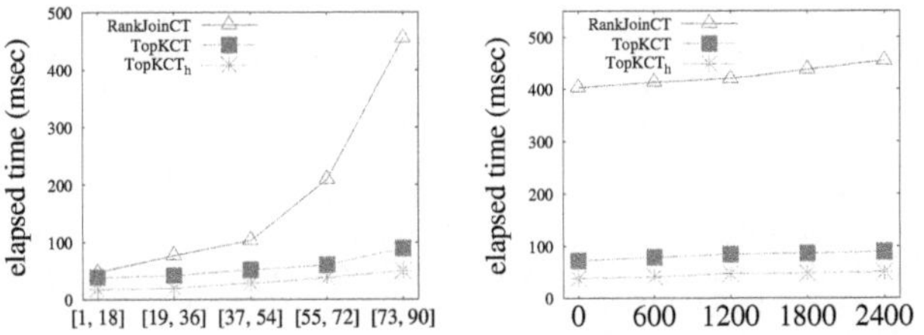

(a) Med: varying $\|I_e\|$ (b) Med: varying $\|I_m\|$

Figure 7: Experimental results

Impact of k. We report the results in Fig. 6(b) (resp. 6(f)) when k was varied from 5 to 25 for Med (resp. CFP). As shown there, (a) The larger k is, the more target tuples are covered by the top-k candidates. (b) To find the target tuples, k does not have to be large. Indeed, when $k = 25$, 92% (resp. 94%) were found by TopKCT and 91% (resp. 87%) by TopKCT$_h$ for Med (resp. CFP). (c) TopKCT did slightly better than TopKCT$_h$ in the quality of candidates found, while TopKCT$_h$ is more efficient than TopKCT (see Exp-4).

Impact of ARs. Figures 6(b) and 6(f) also report the results when Σ consisted of ARs of form (1) only, (2) only, or both. When both forms were used, TopKCT did better than when form (1) or (2) was used alone. In contrast to **Exp-1**, in the latter cases TopKCT could still find many target tuples: for both Med and CFP, it found the targets for 90% of entities when ARs of form (1) or (2) were used only, when $k = 25$.

Impact of $\|I_m\|$. We evaluated the impact of the size of I_m by varying the number of tuples in I_m from 0 to 2400 for Med (resp. 0 to 40 for CFP). As shown in Fig. 6(c) for Med (resp. Fig. 6(g) for CFP), (a) the larger $\|I_m\|$ is, the better TopKCT and TopKCT$_h$ perform, *i.e.,* master data helps improve the quality of top-k candidate targets found by our algorithms; and moreover, (b) even when master data is *unavailable* (*i.e.,* $|I_m| = 0$), TopKCT and TopKCT$_h$ *still work*. Indeed, they were still able to find the target tuples for 63% of Med entities and 64% for CFP, when $k = 15$.

We also tested voting in these settings, and found that voting performed much worse than TopKCT and TopKCT$_h$. It found no more than 50% of target tuples in all the cases.

Exp-3: User interactions. Using Med and CFP, we simulated user interactions as follows. When the deduced target t_e was incomplete, a single attribute B with $t_e[B] =$ null was randomly picked and assigned its accurate value; IsCR and TopKCT were then invoked on the revised t_e. The process repeated until the top-k candidates returned by TopKCT included the target tuple (manually identified, see **Exp-2**).

The results are reported in Figures 6(d) and 6(h) for Med and CFP, respectively, in which the x-axis indicates the number h of interaction rounds, and the y-axis shows the percentage of the target tuples found. The results show that few rounds of interactions are needed to deduce the targets for all the entities: at most 3 for Med, and 4 for CFP.

Exp-4: Efficiency. Using Syn and Med, we evaluated the efficiency of IsCR, RankJoinCT, TopKCT and TopKCT$_h$. To test the impact of I_e, Σ, I_m and k, we set ($\|I_e\|$, $\|I_m\|$, $\|\Sigma\|$, k) = (900, 300, 60, 15) for Syn, and varied one of the four: $\|I_e\|$ from 300 to 1500, $\|\Sigma\|$ from 20 to 100, $\|I_m\|$ from 100 to 500, and k from 5 to 25, while keeping the other three parameters unchanged. For Med we varied $\|I_e\|$ from [1, 18] to [73, 90] and $\|I_m\|$ from 0 to 2400, while keeping $k = 15$ and $\|\Sigma\| = 105$. We found that IsCR took *at most 10ms* in all these cases and hence, do not report it here.

As shown in Figures 6(i) and 7(a), on Med and Syn, (a) all three top-k algorithms are efficient (in less than 2s); (b) TopKCT and TopKCT$_h$ scale well with $\|I_e\|$; and (c) TopKCT outperforms RankJoinCT, and TopKCT$_h$ does better than TopKCT. They behaved consistently when one of $\|\Sigma\|$, $\|I_m\|$ and k was varied, as shown in Figures 6(j), 6(k) and 7(b), and 6(l), respectively. For Syn with $\|I_e\| = 1500$, $\|I_m\| = 300$ and $\|\Sigma\| = 50$, TopKCT$_h$, TopKCT and RankJoinCT took 159ms, 271ms and 1983ms, respectively.

Exp-5: Truth Discovery. Besides determining relative accuracy, we also evaluated the effectiveness of our algorithm TopKCT in truth discovery, against algorithms voting, DeduceOrder [14] and copyCEF [8] on Med, CFP and Rest. Here we used $k = 1$, to find a single target tuple as the true value, in favor of voting, DeduceOrder and copyCEF.

The algorithms were evaluated as follows. (1) We tested voting on Med, CFP and Rest. The results on Med are similar to those on CFP; thus only the results on CFP and Rest are reported here. (2) DeduceOrder was tested on CFP and Rest. For its rules, we extracted all ARs relevant to data currency as currency constraints, and all constant CFDs (which can be expressed as ARs, see Section 2), for each dataset. No such rules were found for Med, and hence only results on CFP and Rest are reported here. (3) We evaluated copyCEF on Rest only, because its required information on data sources is unavailable for Med and CFP. Indeed, Med was from a *single source*, and CFP was crawled from blog posts or Web pages for which the source accuracy could not be determined.

On CFP. On CFP, we tested how many true values (targets) were correctly derived for its entities by the algorithms. We found that voting, DeduceOrder and TopKCT deduced 37%, 0% and 70%, respectively. TopKCT performed almost twice better than voting. While DeduceOrder was not able to find the complete true values for any entity of CFP, it correctly derived 31% of attribute values, which are, however, still much lower than the 83% deduced by IsCR (Fig. 6(e)).

On Rest. On Rest, we evaluated the effectiveness of voting, DeduceOrder, copyCEF and TopKCT. Rest has only one attribute closed? to be determined. Hence we adopted the recall (r), precision (p) and F-measure (F_1) used in [8]: $r = \frac{|G \cap R|}{|G|}$, $p = \frac{|G \cap R|}{|R|}$ and $F_1 = \frac{2pr}{p+r}$, where R is the set of restaurants that were concluded to be closed by an algorithm, and G is the set of restaurants that were indeed closed.

As remarked earlier, our method is complementary to the probabilistic-based truth discovery approaches. Moreover, probabilities derived by these approaches can be incorporated into our model. Indeed, when the probabilities of attribute values returned by copyCEF are set as weights in our preference model, copyCEF can be treated as TopKCT with an empty set of ARs. When the weights in the preference model for TopKCT are set by value occurrences, voting is a special case of TopKCT with an empty set of ARs.

As reported in Table 4, DeduceOrder achieved 100% precision, but was bad on recall (0.15) and F-measure (0.26). While the F-measure of voting was reasonable (0.74), its precision was not very good (0.62). Algorithm copyCEF performed well with balanced precision (0.76) and recall (0.85), and did better in F-measure (0.8) than voting and DeduceOrder. Better still, ARs help here: with a small number of ARs, TopKCT that took value occurrences (like voting) as its preference outperformed copyCEF and voting on F-measure (0.83), and TopKCT that took the possibilities

Method	Prec	Rec	F-msr
DeduceOrder	1.0	0.15	0.26
voting	0.62	0.92	0.74
copyCEF	0.76	0.85	0.8
TopKCT (preference derived by voting)	0.73	0.95	0.82
TopKCT (preference derived by copyCEF)	0.81	0.88	0.85

Table 4: Truth Discovery on Rest

derived by copyCEF further improved copyCEF on precision (0.81) and recall (0.88), even without user interaction.

Observe the following. (1) DeduceOrder did not do well because there was not much currency and consistency information in CFP and Rest that could be utilized by DeduceOrder. Further, the assumption of [14] that the data has to be once correct was too strong for CFP and Rest. These further highlight the need for the study of relative accuracy with ARs. (2) Even without ARs, TopKCT can incorporate the source accuracy (copyCEF) and preference (voting), and performs well in truth discovery. (3) In contrast to Rest, many real-life datasets have a number of attributes that are logically correlated. TopKCT works better on such data than on Rest.

Summary. We find the following. (1) IsCR is effective: it is able to correctly and automatically deduce complete target tuples for at least 66% of the entities, and the most accurate values for 73% of the attributes in the real-life data. (2) ARs of form (1) and form (2) interact with each other and are effective in determining relative accuracy. (3) Our top-k algorithms RankJoinCT and TopKCT (resp. TopKCT_h) are capable of finding the target tuples for 93% (resp. 88%) of entities without user interaction, even when k is small. (4) Few rounds of user interactions are needed for our framework to deduce complete target tuples (3 for Med and 4 for CFP). (5) Our algorithms are efficient: IsCR takes less than 10ms, and TopKCT_h and TopKCT take 159ms and 271ms respectively, on entity instances consisting of 1500 tuples, I_m of 300 tuples and Σ of 50 ARs. (6) Our method is complementary to truth discovery algorithms, and can incorporate derived probabilities into our preference model. With a small number of ARs, TopKCT improves voting, DeduceOrder and copyCEF in truth discovery, with or without user interactions.

8. CONCLUSION

We have proposed a model for determining relative accuracy for entities in the absence of their true values. We have identified fundamental problems for accuracy, and established their complexity. Based on these, we have introduced a framework for deducing relative accuracy, and provided its underlying algorithms. Our experimental results have verified the effectiveness and efficiency of our techniques.

The study of data accuracy is still in its infancy. We are currently experimenting with large datasets from other domains to evaluate the techniques. We are also studying how to improve the accuracy of data in a database, which is often much larger than entity instances. Furthermore, discovery of ARs deserves a full treatment.

Acknowledgments. Fan and Yu are supported in part by EPSRC EP/J015377/1, the 973 Program 2012CB316200 and NSFC 61133002 of China. Cao is supported in part by the 973 Program 2011CB302602 and NSFC 91118008 of China.

9. REFERENCES

[1] S. Abiteboul, R. Hull, and V. Vianu. *Foundations of Databases.* Addison-Wesley, 1995.

[2] C. Batini and M. Scannapieco. *Data Quality: Concepts, Methodologies and Techniques.* Springer, 2006.

[3] L. Bertossi, S. Kolahi, and L. Lakshmanan. Data cleaning and query answering with matching dependencies and matching functions. In *ICDT*, 2011.

[4] L. Blanco, V. Crescenzi, P. Merialdo, and P. Papotti. Probabilistic models to reconcile complex data from inaccurate data sources. In *AISE*, 2010.

[5] J. Bleiholder and F. Naumann. Data fusion. *ACM Comput. Surv.*, 41(1), 2008.

[6] G. S. Brodal. Worst-case efficient priority queues. In É. Tardos, editor, *SODA*, pages 52–58. ACM/SIAM, 1996.

[7] F. Chiang and R. Miller. Discovering data quality rules. In *VLDB*, 2008.

[8] X. Dong, L. Berti-Equille, and D. Srivastava. Truth discovery and copying detection in a dynamic world. In *PVLDB*, 2009.

[9] A. K. Elmagarmid, P. G. Ipeirotis, and V. S. Verykios. Duplicate record detection: A survey. *TKDE*, 19(1):1–16, 2007.

[10] M. Eppler. *Managing information quality: Increasing the value of information in knowledge-intensive products and processes.* Springer, 2006.

[11] R. Fagin, A. Lotem, and M. Naor. Optimal aggregation algorithms for middleware. *JCSS*, 66(4):614–656, 2003.

[12] W. Fan and F. Geerts. *Foundations of Data Quality Management.* Morgan & Claypool Publishers, 2012.

[13] W. Fan, F. Geerts, X. Jia, and A. Kementsietsidis. Conditional functional dependencies for capturing data inconsistencies. *TODS*, 33(1), 2008.

[14] W. Fan, F. Geerts, N. Tang, and W. Yu. Inferring data currency and consistency for conflict resolution. In *ICDE*, 2013.

[15] W. Fan, J. Li, S. Ma, N. Tang, and W. Yu. Interaction between record matching and data repairing. In *SIGMOD*, 2011.

[16] C. Fisher, E. Lauria, and C. Matheus. An accuracy metric: Percentages, randomness, and probabilities. *JDIQ*, 1(3), 2009.

[17] P. A. Flach and N. Lachiche. Confirmation-guided discovery of first-order rules with Tertius. *Machine Learning*, 44(3):61–95, 2001.

[18] C. Fox, A. Levitin, and T. Redman. The notion of data and its quality dimensions. *IPM*, 30(1), 1994.

[19] A. Galland, S. Abiteboul, A. Marian, and P. Senellart. Corroborating information from disagreeing views. In *WSDM*, 2010.

[20] I. Gelman. Setting priorities for data accuracy improvements in satisficing decision-making scenarios: A guiding theory. *DSS*, 48(4), 2010.

[21] I. Ilyas, W. Aref, and A. Elmagarmid. Supporting top-k join queries in relational databases. *VLDB. J*, 13(3), 2004.

[22] I. Ilyas, G. Beskales, and M. Soliman. A survey of top-k query processing techniques in relational database systems. *CSUR*, 40(4), 2008.

[23] P. Narman, P. Johnson, M. Ekstedt, M. Chenine, and J. Konig. Enterprise architecture analysis for data accuracy assessments. In *EDOC*, 2009.

[24] F. Naumann and M. Herschel. *An Introduction to Duplicate Detection.* Morgan & Claypool Publishers, 2010.

[25] J. Radcliffe and A. White. Key issues for master data management. Technical report, Gartner, 2008.

[26] K. Schnaitter and N. Polyzotis. Evaluating rank joins with optimal cost. In *PODS*, 2008.

[27] J. Widom. Trio: A system for integrated management of data, accuracy, and lineage. In *CIDR*, 2005.

[28] M. Wu and A. Marian. A framework for corroborating answers from multiple web sources. *IS*, 36(2), 2011.

[29] X. Yin, J. Han, and P. Yu. Truth discovery with multiple conflicting information providers on the Web. *TKDE*, 20(6), 2008.

[30] B. Zhao, B. I. P. Rubinstein, J. Gemmell, and J. Han. A bayesian approach to discovering truth from conflicting sources for data integration. *PVLDB*, 5(6):550–561, 2012.

Photon: Fault-tolerant and Scalable Joining of Continuous Data Streams

Rajagopal Ananthanarayanan, Venkatesh Basker, Sumit Das,
Ashish Gupta, Haifeng Jiang, Tianhao Qiu, Alexey Reznichenko*,
Deomid Ryabkov, Manpreet Singh, Shivakumar Venkataraman
Google Inc.
{ananthr, vbasker, sumitdas}@google.com,
{agupta, jianghf, tianhao}@google.com, areznich@mpi-sws.org,
{rojer, manpreet, shivav}@google.com

ABSTRACT

Web-based enterprises process events generated by millions of users interacting with their websites. Rich statistical data distilled from combining such interactions in near real-time generates enormous business value. In this paper, we describe the architecture of Photon, a geographically distributed system for joining multiple continuously flowing streams of data in real-time with high scalability and low latency, where the streams may be unordered or delayed. The system fully tolerates infrastructure degradation and datacenter-level outages without any manual intervention. Photon guarantees that there will be no duplicates in the joined output (at-most-once semantics) at any point in time, that most joinable events will be present in the output in real-time (near-exact semantics), and exactly-once semantics eventually.

Photon is deployed within Google Advertising System to join data streams such as web search queries and user clicks on advertisements. It produces joined logs that are used to derive key business metrics, including billing for advertisers. Our production deployment processes millions of events per minute at peak with an average end-to-end latency of less than 10 seconds. We also present challenges and solutions in maintaining large persistent state across geographically distant locations, and highlight the design principles that emerged from our experience.

Categories and Subject Descriptors

H.2.4 [**Database Management**]: Systems — Distributed databases; H.3.5 [**Online Information Services**]: Web-based services

General Terms

Design, Performance, Reliability

Keywords

Continuous Streams, Fault-tolerance, Paxos, Stream joining

*Work done during internship with Google.

SIGMOD'13, June 22–27, 2013, New York, New York, USA.
Copyright 2013 ACM 978-1-4503-2037-5/13/06 ...$15.00.

1. INTRODUCTION

Joining data streams has received considerable attention in the past two decades [24, 25] due to its importance in numerous applications (e.g. IP network management, telephone fraud detection), where information arrives in the form of very high-speed streams that need to be processed online to enable real-time response [9].

With the explosive evolution of the Internet and the World Wide Web in the last several years, the need for similar technologies has grown multifold as web-based enterprises must process events generated by millions of users interacting with their websites. Users all over the world visit Google's web pages on a daily basis, issuing web-search queries, browsing search results, and clicking on ads (advertisements) shown on result pages.

Distilling rich statistical data from web user interactions in near real-time has a huge impact on business processes. The data enables advertisers to fine-tune their bids, budgets and campaigns, and vary the parameters in real-time to suit changing user behavior. It provides immediate feedback to advertisers on the effectiveness of their changes, and also allows Google to optimize the budget spent for each advertiser on a continuous basis.

To provide real-time statistical data, we built a system, called *Photon*, that can relate a primary user event (e.g. a search query) with subsequent events (e.g. a click on an ad) within seconds of the occurrence of such events. Photon joins multiple continuous streams of events using a shared identifier to combine the related events.

Let us illustrate the operational steps in Photon with an example of joining a click and a query event:

- When a user issues a search query (using terms such as "buy flowers") at google.com, Google serves ads to the user along with search results. The web server that serves the ad also sends information about this event to multiple *logs-datacenters*, where the data is stored persistently in the Google File System [14] (GFS). The logged data includes information such as advertiser identifier, ad text, and online ad auction parameters. This data is later used to generate reports for advertisers, perform quality analysis, etc. Each query event is assigned a unique identifier known as *query_id*. Figure 1 shows the query event happening at time t_1.

- After receiving the results of the search query, the user may click on one of the ads. The ad click request is sent to a backend server while the user is being forwarded/redirected to the advertiser's website. The

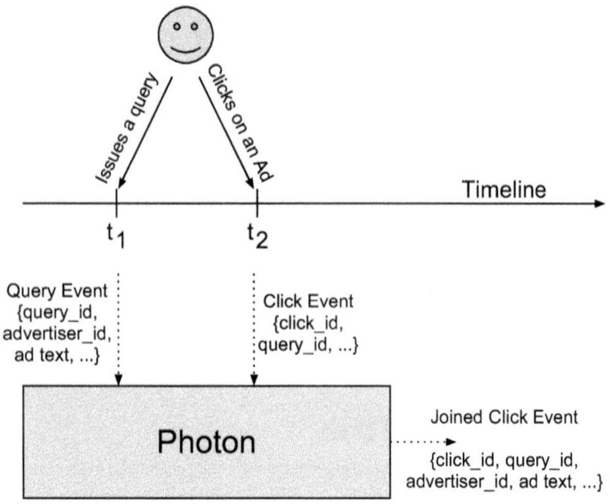

Figure 1: Joining query and click events in Photon

click event is also logged and copied to multiple logs datacenters. The logged data includes information of the ad that the user clicked, and is used to bill advertisers. The click event contains the query_id of the corresponding query. Each click event is assigned a unique identifier known as *click_id*. Figure 1 shows the click event happening at time t_2.

Continuing with the example, when a click event is shipped to logs datacenters, Photon joins the click event with its corresponding query event based on query_id. As part of the join, Photon copies all the details from the query event into a new joined click event (as shown in Figure 1). Photon reads input event streams from log files on GFS in different datacenters and writes joined events to new output log files on GFS in multiple datacenters. Joined logs are used to generate rich statistical data, combining the information from queries, ads and clicks.

Note that individual logs do not contain all the information necessary for generating rich statistical data. For example, when we compile statistics on a click event, we need access to the complete information recorded in the corresponding query event, such as other ads that were shown in the query result page, in addition to the ad recorded by this click event. It is possible to embed the query information in the Click URL sent to the user. However, sending extra data would increase latency of response and degrade user experience, as well as increase exposure to critical data. Moreover, URL length has an upper limit, thus restricting the amount of information we can propagate about a query. Hence, it is infeasible to include all the required information in the click event.

1.1 Problem Statement

Formally, given two continuously growing log streams such that each event in the *primary* log stream contains a unique identifier, and each event in the *foreign* log stream contains the identifier referring to an event in the primary log stream, we want to join each foreign log event with the corresponding primary log event and produce the joined event.

In relational database (RDBMS) terms, we can consider the two log streams as two tables with a foreign-key constraint [7]. The primary log stream is analogous to the primary table, and the foreign log stream corresponds to the foreign table. The stream joining problem is essentially an inner join between these two log streams. More specifically, the click logs mentioned above represent a foreign table that will be joined with the primary table (i.e., query logs). Hence, we refer to click events as foreign events, and query events as primary events, with the query_id as the key used in the joins. The resulting events are referred to as joined events. We use the generic terms in the rest of the paper, but we may use clicks and queries as illustrative examples.

The main goal of Photon is to perform continuous stream joining in real-time. We use this framework to join many different event streams at Google.

1.2 System Challenges

While building Photon to join continuous data streams, we face these challenges:

- ***Exactly-once semantics***: The output produced by Photon is used for billing advertisers, reporting revenue to investors in Wall Street, and so on. Photon must guarantee that a single click is never processed twice, since this leads to double-charging the advertisers. On the other hand, Google loses money for every click which is not processed by Photon. In practice, to meet the business needs, we require Photon to join 99.9999% events within a few seconds, and 100% events within a few hours. These requirements imply that Photon must provide: a) at-most-once semantics at any point of time, b) near-exact semantics in real-time, and c) exactly-once semantics eventually.

- ***Automatic datacenter-level fault-tolerance***: Datacenters regularly face different forms of outages. Some of these are planned (such as a software update or hardware replacement) and others are unplanned (like a power failure or network fiber cut). Service interruptions can last from a couple of minutes to a few days or even weeks. In this environment, a system designed to operate in a single datacenter suffers from serious drawbacks. After a failure, manual effort is required to setup the system in another datacenter, which can be tedious and error-prone. Reconstructing the state of the system can take hours, thus adversely affecting the overall availability of the system. In case of transient hiccups, it is difficult to decide whether to initiate the expensive effort of migrating the system to another datacenter, or try to ride out the outage, again impacting the system availability. Some distributed systems like GFS [14] and Bigtable [6] are excellent at handling a limited number of machine failures. But they are not designed to handle large-scale datacenter-level outages, and thus developers are responsible for designing their applications to handle outages gracefully. Given its direct impact on revenue, business needs mandate Photon to be a system with a very high degree of fault-tolerance that can automatically handle even a datacenter-level outage, with no manual operations and no impact on system availability.

- ***High scalability***: Not only does Photon need to handle millions of events per minute today, it must also be able to handle the ever-increasing number of events in the future.

- ***Low latency***: The output of Photon is used to compute statistics for advertisers and publishers on how their marketing campaigns are performing, detecting invalid clicks, optimizing budget, etc. Having Photon perform the join within a few seconds significantly improves the effectiveness of these business processes.

- ***Unordered streams***: Our primary stream (i.e. query) contains events approximately sorted by the timestamps of the events. However, the foreign stream (i.e. click) is typically not sorted by the query timestamp, since clicks can be arbitrarily delayed relative to the queries. This makes it very hard to apply window join algorithms [24, 25] proposed in literature.

- ***Delayed primary stream***: A click can only be joined if the corresponding query event is available in the logs datacenter. Logically, the query event always occurs before the corresponding click. However, the servers generating click events and query events are distributed throughout the world (to minimize end-user latency), and click and query logs are shipped independently to logs datacenters. The volume of query logs is orders of magnitude more than the volume of click logs, thus, it is not uncommon for a subset of query logs to be delayed relative to the corresponding click logs. Photon needs to be able to join whenever the query is available. This makes Photon different from standard RDBMS where a foreign key must always exist in the primary table.

1.3 Our Contributions

The key contributions from this paper are:

- To the best of our knowledge, this is the first paper to formulate and solve the problem of joining multiple streams continuously under these system constraints: exactly-once semantics, fault-tolerance at datacenter-level, high scalability, low latency, unordered streams, and delayed primary stream.

- We present challenges and solutions in maintaining persistent state across geographically distributed locations. While using commodity hardware resources, special attention is given to improving fault-tolerance and increasing throughput.

- The solutions detailed in this paper have been fully implemented and deployed in a live production environment for several months. Based on this real-world experience, we present detailed performance results, design trade-offs, and key design lessons from our deployment.

The rest of this paper is organized as follows. In section 2, we discuss how to store the critical state of our system in multiple datacenters while addressing all the systems challenges discussed above. Section 3 presents the detailed design and architecture of the Photon system. Section 4 describes our production deployment settings and measurements collected from the running system. Section 5 lists the lessons learnt from building Photon. Sections 6 and 7 describe related research, and summarize future work and conclusions.

2. PAXOS-BASED ID REGISTRY

The simplest way to achieve fault-tolerance on commodity hardware is through replication [22]. Extending this principle to a large collection of machines, we can withstand datacenter-level outage by running the same system in multiple datacenters in parallel. This approach has been applied to almost all web search servers and ad servers at Google to render the systems resilient to datacenter failures with no discontinuity in the level of service. Load balancers automatically redirect each user request to the closest running server, where it is processed without the need to consult any other server.

To provide datacenter-level fault-tolerance, Photon workers in multiple datacenters will attempt to join the same input event, but workers must coordinate their output to guarantee that each input event is joined at-most-once. The critical state shared between the workers consists of the set of event_ids (e.g. click_id) that have already been joined in the last N days. This state is stored in the *IdRegistry*. The constant N is determined by evaluating the trade-off between the cost of storage, and the cost of dropping events that are delayed by more than N days. Note that the system should always discard events delayed by N days as there is no way to detect duplicates among such events, and our goal is to avoid double-charging the advertisers.

Before writing a joined event to output, each worker verifies whether the event_id already exists in the IdRegistry. If the identifier exists, the worker skips processing the event. Otherwise, the worker attempts to write the event_id into the IdRegistry. The worker must successfully insert the event_id into the IdRegistry before it can write the joined event to output the logs. The IdRegistry must guarantee that once an event_id is written to it, subsequent requests to write the same identifier will fail.

The key requirements for the IdRegistry can be summarized as follows:

- *Fault-tolerance at datacenter-level*:
  The IdRegistry must be synchronously replicated to multiple datacenters so that its service is always available even when there is an outage in one or more datacenters. The maximum number of simultaneously tolerated datacenter outages should be configurable.

- *Read-modify-write transactions*:
  Workers must be able to perform conditional commits such as writing an event_id in the IdRegistry only if it does not exist in the IdRegistry yet.

Given the requirements of fault-tolerance and strong consistency, we implemented the IdRegistry using Paxos [18]. Paxos is a consensus algorithm executed by a set of replicas (e.g workers), to agree on a single value in the presence of failures. The algorithm guarantees synchronous replication of submitted values across the majority of replicas.

Figure 2 shows the high-level design of Photon to illustrate the use of the IdRegistry. We deploy the same Photon pipeline in multiple datacenters. Each pipeline processes all the events (e.g., clicks) present in the closest logs datacenter — at Google, logs are written to multiple geographically distributed datacenters. Each pipeline keeps retrying until the event is joined (i.e., written to the IdRegistry), which guarantees that each event is processed at least once by the system with minimal loss. To ensure that each event is processed at-most-once, the IdRegistry stores identifiers for the

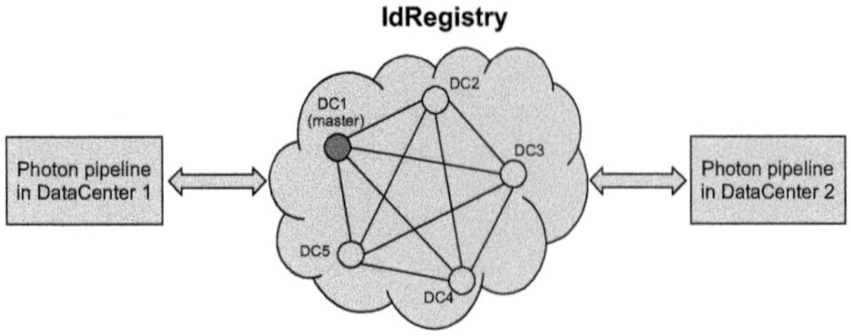

Figure 2: Photon pipeline running independently in two datacenters with the IdRegistry storing the global state synchronously in multiple datacenters.

events (e.g., click_id) that have been joined in the last N days. Since the global list of already joined events is stored in the IdRegistry, the Photon pipelines in multiple datacenters can work independently without directly communicating with each other.

2.1 IdRegistry Server Architecture

To implement an efficient IdRegistry, we use an in-memory key-value store that is consistently replicated across multiple datacenters using Paxos. By storing the id of an event as a key, the IdRegistry can quickly identify if an event is already joined or not. If the event_id already exists, it can fail the worker that tries to commit the same event_id. If the event_id does not exist, the IdRegistry does a Paxos commit to insert the new key with the condition that the key is still absent (i.e., using a read-modify-write transaction).

The IdRegistry is built on top of PaxosDB [4], a fault tolerant key-value in-memory store that uses the Paxos consensus algorithm. The PaxosDB implementation executes the consensus algorithm repeatedly for every incoming value to guarantee that each replica has access to the same sequence of submitted values. Each replica constructs its in-memory key-value store by processing the same sequence of submitted values. In other words, the in-memory key-value store at each caught-up replica is consistent. PaxosDB also guarantees that at most one of the group members will be the *master* at any given instant of time. Only the master can submit updates to Paxos. If the master dies, PaxosDB automatically elects a new master.

Figure 3 shows the architecture of a single IdRegistry server. The interaction between Photon workers and the IdRegistry follows a client-server model. Photon workers take the role of clients by sending two kinds of requests: (1) a lookup request to check if an event_id has already been committed; and (2) a conditional commit request to insert an event_id if and only if it is not present. The Remote Procedure Call (RPC) handler threads in the IdRegistry server accept incoming RPCs from clients. The handler is very lightweight in that it simply adds the input requests into an in-memory queue. A background thread dequeues requests, performs transactions on PaxosDB, and executes RPC callbacks which send responses to the client.

2.2 Scalable IdRegistry

To ensure that the outage of one relatively large geographical region does not affect the IdRegistry, we place IdRegistry replicas in different geographical regions such that replicas from more than one geographical region have to agree before a transaction can be committed into PaxosDB.

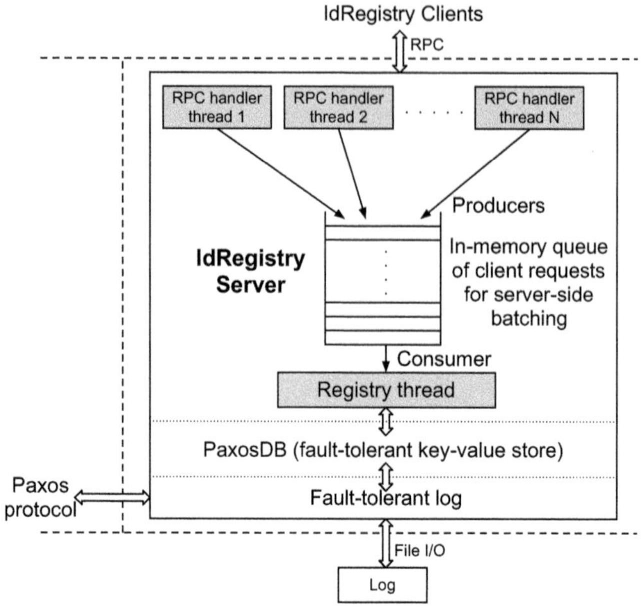

Figure 3: Architecture of a single IdRegistry server shard.

The downside of requiring such isolation zones is that the throughput of the IdRegistry will be limited by network latency. Based on typical network statistics, the round-trip-time between different geographical regions (such as east and west coasts of the United States) can be over 100 milliseconds. This would limit the throughput of Paxos to less than 10 transactions per second, which is orders of magnitude fewer than our requirements—we need to process (both read and write) tens of thousands of events (i.e., key commits) per second.

Although each client may be able to bundle multiple key commits into one RPC request, when there are a large number of clients, client-side batching is not always effective. We describe two mechanisms to achieve high scalability with the IdRegistry: server-side batching and sharding.

2.2.1 Server-side Batching

IdRegistry replicas are located in different geographical regions, hence a Paxos commit can take up to 100 milliseconds due to the round-trip latency. The latency mainly comes from the inherent network topology and not due to the amount of data we are sending around. In fact, each Paxos commit only needs to send a small amount of event-level data. Based on this observation, we implemented server-side batching to improve the throughput of each IdRegistry server. The key idea is to combine multiple event-level commits into one bigger commit. This is similar to the classic database technique of group commit [23].

As shown in Figure 3, the IdRegistry server has a single background thread (called registry thread) that dequeues client RPC requests, translates them to PaxosDB transactions, and sends the RPC response. The registry thread dequeues multiple requests and batches them into a single PaxosDB transaction.

Within a batch of requests, the registry thread performs application-level conflict resolution. Consider the case where multiple requests try to insert the same event_id into the Id-

Registry. If the event_id does not already exist, the registry thread will insert the event_id into PaxosDB, and respond with success to one client which marks the event as joined; other clients will receive a failure message which must drop the event. We take advantage of multi-row transactions in PaxosDB (updating multiple key/value pairs atomically with condition checks) to implement this behavior.

Assuming the size of an RPC for one event_id is less than 100 bytes, we can easily batch thousands of RPC requests into a single PaxosDB transaction. We do not enforce a minimum batch size, hence there is no tradeoff on latency.

2.2.2 *Sharding*

Although server-side batching improves the throughput of the IdRegistry significantly, it still fails to meet our requirements. The motivation for *sharding* comes from this observation: in the IdRegistry, events with different ids are processed independently of each other. To take advantage of the event_id independence, we partition the event_id space handled by the IdRegistry into disjoint *shards* such that event_ids from separate shards are managed by separate IdRegistry servers. The IdRegistry servers run in parallel and can accept requests for event_ids deterministically assigned to them. Figure 4 shows client requests being sent to different server shards, depending on their event_ids. The shard number is computed using a deterministic hash of the event_id, modulo the total number of shards. Note that each Photon worker can still process events from multiple shards; it can send RPCs to multiple IdRegistry server shards in parallel. This sharding approach ensures high scalability, and allows the IdRegistry to achieve the throughput we need.

Dynamically changing the number of shards

As the number of logged events increases, we need to add more shards to the IdRegistry. However, while adding more shards, simply changing the number of shards in the modulo can violate the deterministic property of the hash, and that can result in the same event_id to be mapped to a different shard number after increasing the shards. This is unacceptable because it will lead to duplicate events in the output logs. Thus, we need a deterministic mapping mechanism that allows dynamic changes of the number of shards while preserving mapping of existing event_ids across shards — the mapping mechanism must support backward compatibility.

To solve the above problem, we use a timestamp-based sharding configuration, which defines the number of shards to use at any given instance of time. We associate a timestamp with an event_id, and require that the clock skew of two timestamps is bounded by S seconds (using a global TrueTime [8] server, see section 3.1 for details). If the current time is t_1, we choose a future time $t_2 > t_1 + S$ and specify that events with timestamp less than t_2 should use hash(event_id) modulo the number of shards before increasing the shards, while the events with timestamp $>= t_2$ should use hash(event_id) modulo the number of shards after increasing the shards. This guarantees that we will deterministically compute the shard number for a given event_id.

As an example, if the IdRegistry has 100 shards, the sharding configuration will be:

$start\_time : 0, end\_time : \infty, number\_of\_shards : 100$

If we increase the number of shards from 100 to 120, current time is 5000, skew is 200, our sharding configuration will change to:

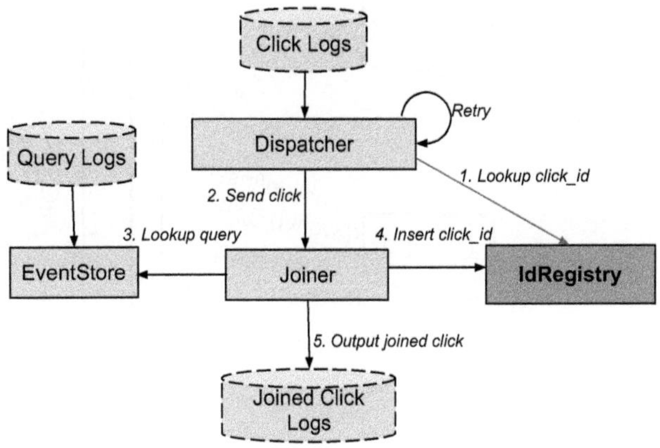

Figure 5: Components of pipeline in a single datacenter

$start\_time : 0, end\_time : 5200, number\_of\_shards : 100$
$start\_time : 5200, end\_time : \infty, number\_of\_shards : 120$

We store the sharding configuration inside PaxosDB to ensure that all the IdRegistry server shards and clients share the same configuration. Note that number of shards can be decreased in a similar way.

2.3 Deleting Old Keys

We can only keep a finite number of event_ids in the IdRegistry. Since each event_id is timestamped, the IdRegistry can delete ids older than N days. We refer to N as *garbage collection threshold.*

A background thread in each IdRegistry server periodically scans the old keys, and deletes them from the IdRegistry if the timestamp of these keys is older than the garbage collection threshold. The garbage collection thread runs only at the master IdRegistry replica. To guard against time differences between the different IdRegistry servers when the master changes, we store the garbage collection boundary timestamp in the IdRegistry servers, one timestamp for each IdRegistry server shard. This boundary timestamp is periodically updated by another thread using TrueTime [8] and we make sure it never goes back. The garbage collection thread only removes event_id entries whose timestamps are smaller than the recorded boundary timestamp.

If a client tries to insert or lookup an event older than the boundary timestamp, the IdRegistry sends failure response with a special error code, and the client skips processing the event.

3. SINGLE DATACENTER PIPELINE

As mentioned in Section 2, we deploy the same Photon pipeline in multiple datacenters. We now describe the architecture of a pipeline at a single datacenter, as shown in Figure 5. In the following examples, we use click and query logs as inputs, but the architecture applies to any similar event streams.

There are three major components in a single datacenter pipeline: *the dispatcher* to read clicks continuously and feed them to the joiner; the *EventStore* to provide efficient lookup for queries; and the *joiner* to find the corresponding query

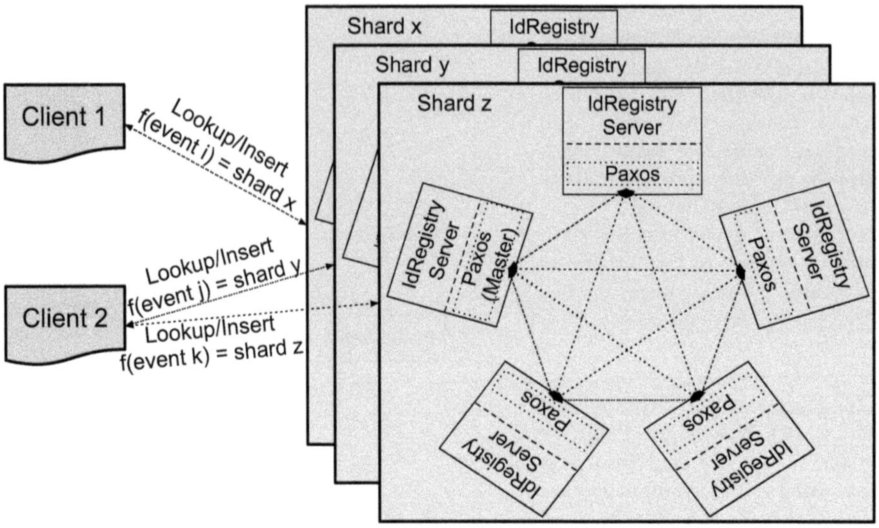

Figure 4: Sharding the IdRegistry to scale throughput

for a click using EventStore, deduplicate using the IdRegistry, and then generate joined output logs.

The sequence of steps to join a click with its corresponding query into a joined event are:

1. The dispatcher consumes the click events from the logs as they come in, and issues a lookup in the IdRegistry. If the click_id already exists in the IdRegistry, the dispatcher assumes that the click has already been joined and skips processing the click.
2. If the click_id does not exist in the IdRegistry, the dispatcher sends the click to the joiner asynchronously and waits for the response. If the joiner fails to join the click (say, due to a network problem, or because of a missing query event), the dispatcher will keep retrying by sending the click to another joiner instance after some backoff period. This guarantees at-least-once semantics with minimum losses.
3. The joiner extracts query_id from the click and does a lookup in the EventStore to find the corresponding query.
4. If the query is not found, the joiner sends a failure response to the dispatcher so that it can retry. If the query is found, the joiner tries to register the click_id into the IdRegistry.
5. If the click_id already exists in the IdRegistry, the joiner assumes that the click has already been joined. If the joiner is able to register click_id into the IdRegistry, the joiner stores information from the query in the click and writes the event to the joined click logs.

Note that the above algorithm is susceptible to losses if the joiner successfully registers the click_id to the IdRegistry but fails to write to output logs. Later, we present simple techniques to minimize the loss in Section 3.3.2, and also discuss procedures to recover missing output in Section 3.3.3.

Figure 6 depicts the same Photon pipeline running independently in multiple datacenters, with the global state maintained by the IdRegistry. The rest of this section describes in detail the basic architecture, the design of each component and the technical challenges involved.

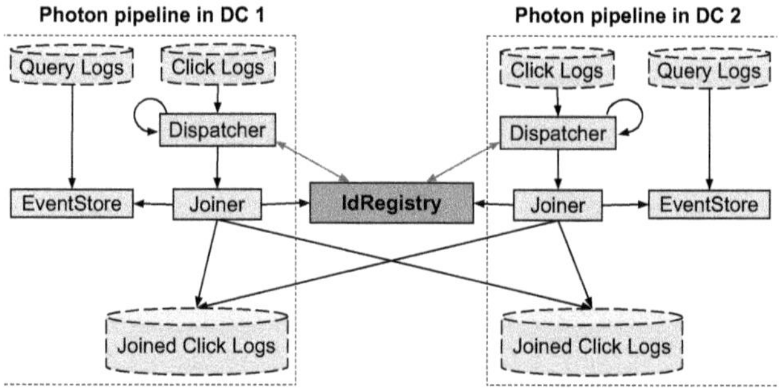

Figure 6: Components of pipelines running independently in two datacenters with the global state in the IdRegistry

3.1 Unique Event_Id Generation

Given the critical nature of the data they deal with, servers write all events (e.g. query and click) to a persistent storage like GFS [14] and also replicate them to multiple logs datacenters. When an event is recorded by a server, it is given a globally unique identifier (such as query_id or click_id as discussed before).

Production deployments consist of thousands of servers across the world that log all such events, a scale at which quick generation of event_ids is critical for a fast response to user actions. Independent generation of event_ids is a prerequisite to satisfy this requirement.

An event_id consists of three fields: *ServerIP*, *ProcessID* and *Timestamp*. These fields uniquely identify the server and the process on that server that generated an event, as well as the time the event was generated. Each server generates monotonically increasing timestamps for every event based on the current time. All the events in a log file are approximately sorted by their timestamp since multiple threads in the same process independently generate event_ids. This encoding of the location of an event, even if not entirely precise, plays a crucial role in finding the event in a large set of log files; this is discussed further in section 3.4.

Note that generating the timestamp for each event_id on each server locally may be adversely impacted by clock skew on the local machine. To limit the skew to S seconds, we use the TrueTime API [8] that provides clock synchronization primitives. By using GPS and atomic clocks, the primitives guarantee an upper bound on the clock uncertainty. Each server generating event_ids executes a background thread that sends an RPC to one of the TrueTime servers every S seconds to synchronize the local clock.

3.2 Dispatcher: Ensuring At-Least-Once Semantics

The input to Photon consists of events that are written to log files. Those files continuously grow in size. Events can overflow to new files when log files reach a maximum size. At any given time, a Photon instance has to track several thousands of growing log files. Thus, the main objectives of the dispatcher are: monitor the growth of log files continuously, read new events in a scalable and timely way, and dispatch them to the joiner with minimal latency.

The dispatcher periodically scans the directory where log files are located to identify new files and check the growth of existing files. The dispatcher stores a per-file state in the local GFS cell. This state includes the files encountered by the dispatcher, and the next byte offset to read from each file. To achieve a high degree of scalability, the dispatcher uses many worker processes to concurrently process the log files. With the persistent state, the processing information is preserved across restarts of workers. All the concurrent workers share the persistent file state locally so that they can work on different parts of log files without stepping onto each other.

Before sending events to the joiner, the dispatcher looks up each event_id in IdRegistry to make sure the event has not been joined. This optimization technique significantly improved performance as observed from the measured results (Section 4).

3.2.1 Retry Logic

Note that a click can only be joined if the corresponding query event is available in the logs datacenter. As mentioned in Section 1, it is not uncommon for a subset of query logs to be delayed relative to the corresponding click logs. In such cases, a joiner will not be able to process click events until corresponding query events have arrived in the logs datacenter.

After reading a click event from a log file, the dispatcher sends an RPC to the joiner, and asynchronously waits for the response. When the dispatcher fails to receive a successful response from the joiner for a click, it saves the click in local GFS and retries it later. This guarantees *at-least-once* semantics for every event with minimum losses. To limit the rate of retries in case of repeated failures (e.g. due to a network congestion), the dispatcher employs an exponential backoff algorithm. If the joiner still fails to join a click after a certain number of retries, and the click is older than a threshold, the joiner will mark the click as *unjoinable* and return success to the dispatcher. In practice, unjoinable events represent a very small fraction of all the events.

3.2.2 Handling Datacenter Outages

The file state maintained by the dispatcher is local to the datacenter where it runs. If the local GFS datacenter suffers an outage, the dispatcher will be stalled. This does not impact the end-to-end availability of the Photon system because we have at least two copies of the Photon pipeline in different datacenters each of which continues processing independent of the other. Once the datacenter that suffered the outage recovers to a healthy state, if the persistent state is intact, the dispatcher can resume where it left off and starts by processing the backlog. Since majority of backlog events would have been processed by the pipeline in the other datacenter, these events will already exist in the IdRegistry, and the dispatcher will catch-up quickly from the backlog to start processing recent events. We use appropriate throttling of outstanding requests to the IdRegistry to avoid overloading it, and ensure adequate performance during catch-up.

In rare cases where the dispatcher file state cannot be recovered after a datacenter outage, we could manually initialize it to ignore the backlog and immediately start processing latest events from the current time, assuming the pipeline in the other datacenter has been operating without interruptions.

3.3 Joiner

The joiner is implemented as a stateless RPC server that accepts requests from the dispatcher and coordinates with the EventStore and the IdRegistry to perform the join as well as any specific business logic.

3.3.1 Processing Logic

After accepting an incoming RPC from the dispatcher, the joiner extracts the click_id and query_id from the click event. Then the joiner sends an asynchronous RPC to EventStore to lookup the query for the corresponding query_id. If the EventStore cannot find the query, the joiner returns an error code to the dispatcher, so that the dispatcher can retry the request after some backoff time. When a joiner receives an event from the dispatcher, it first checks if there are already too many requests in flight. If so, the request will be rejected and the dispatcher will have to retry it later. Such throttling is essential to maintain the smooth flow of processing of events through the joiner.

A successful lookup to the EventStore returns the query corresponding to the click. As the next step in processing, the query and the click are passed to a library called the *adapter*. Usually, the adapter simply combines the two events into one joined event and passes the result back to the joiner. However, it may also apply application-specific business logic for filtering, or it can force the joiner to skip the click based on certain properties of the query. Isolating such business logic to the adapter adds flexibility to Photon, so that any two realtime data streams can be joined without modifying the core infrastructure.

After receiving the joined click event from the adapter library, the joiner will attempt to register the click_id into the IdRegistry using an asynchronous RPC. If successful, the joiner will then proceed to append the joined click to the output log, stored in the logs datacenters. Since the IdRegistry guarantees at-most-once semantics, for any given click_id at most one joiner will be able to successfully register it, preventing duplicate joined clicks to occur in the output logs.

If the joiner is unable to successfully register the click_id into the IdRegistry, it will drop the event. We consider this as a *wasted join*. In our production deployment, since we have dispatchers running in at least two datacenters, Photon reads each click at least twice. However, we minimize the wasted joins in the system by having the dispatcher do a lookup in the IdRegistry before sending the click to a joiner, and dropping the event if it is already present.

In contrast to the dispatcher, the joiner does not use a persistent storage to maintain any state. In addition, all joiners are functionally equivalent so we can use RPC-based load balancing to uniformly distribute the input requests from the dispatchers amongst all the joiners.

3.3.2 Minimizing Joiner Losses

The joiner writes an event to the output log only after successfully writing the event_id to the IdRegistry. Once an event_id is registered into the IdRegistry, another request to register the same event_id will fail. The IdRegistry guarantees this property. However, the lack of transactional atomicity between writing the output and registering the event_id can lead to problems as illustrated below while processing click events.

The problem arises when the IdRegistry successfully registers the click_id but the joiner times out or the RPC response to the register request gets lost in the network. Subsequent register requests from the same joiner will fail due to the existence of the click_id and the click will never be joined as a result. In our early test deployment, we observed a noticeable number of clicks missing from the joined output logs due to this reason.

To solve this problem, when a joiner commits a click_id to the IdRegistry, it also sends a globally unique *token* to the IdRegistry (consisting of the joiner server address, the joiner process identifier, and a timestamp) along with the click_id. The IdRegistry stores this information about the joiner as the value associated with the click_id. If the joiner does not receive response from IdRegistry within a certain timeout interval, it retries the request with the exact same token.

When the IdRegistry receives a request to register an existing click_id, it checks if the value for the click_id stored inside IdRegistry matches with the token in the request. If they match, it means the request is a retry from the same joiner that registered this click_id last time but did not receive the RPC response. In such a case, the IdRegistry returns *success* to the joiner, which will be able to output the joined click. This mechanism enables us to gracefully handle joiner retries and greatly reduce the number of missing clicks. In our production deployment of Photon, this technique reduced the number of missing clicks in joined output logs by two orders of magnitude.

Another potential source of event loss is due to unexpected crash of the joiner workers. Once a joiner sends an RPC to the IdRegistry, the latter may successfully register it into the IdRegistry but the joiner may crash and restart before receiving the acknowledgment and writing the joined click to output logs. Since Photon workers run on commodity hardware, such intermittent failures are inevitable, especially on large scale. After such a missed write, no other joiner can commit the event to output logs because the token kept in the IdRegistry does not belong to any joiner. We minimize the loss by enforcing an upper limit on the number of outstanding RPCs from any joiner to the IdRegistry. Once the joiner reaches the limit, it throttles the incoming requests from the dispatchers.

3.3.3 Verification and Recovery

As discussed above, Photon can miss events in the output joined logs due to absence of transactional atomicity between recording the event in the IdRegistry and recording in the output joined logs. Example scenarios that can surface this situation are: (a) the joiner crashes or restarts after writing to the IdRegistry, (b) logs storage loses data, (c) a bug in the code manifests itself after committing to the IdRegistry.

In normal conditions, observed losses represent a very small fraction – less than 0.0001 percent – of the total volume of joinable events. Consequently, the recovery scheme presented below is more useful to act as an insurance for rare cases such as bugs or catastrophic, uncontrollable failures.

Photon provides a verification system which takes each event in the input and checks its presence in the output. If an event in the IdRegistry is not present in the output log, we read the server address and process identifier from the token in the IdRegistry corresponding to the missing event, and identify the joiner. If the joiner had crashed or restarted, the event can be safely reprocessed without causing duplicates. To recover the event, we delete the missing event from the IdRegistry, and re-inject the event back into the dispatcher.

The recovery system only needs to read the tokens of events missing in the output logs. Hence, we can optimize storage cost of the IdRegistry by removing tokens of all joined events that have been successfully committed to the output logs. We scan the output joined logs continuously and clear the corresponding values from the IdRegistry. Thus the IdRegistry will only store tokens for lost events over a longer period of time, until they are recovered.

3.4 EventStore

EventStore is a service that takes a query_id as input and returns the corresponding query event. One simple approach to implement the lookup is to sequentially read the query logs and store the mapping from query_id to the log file name and byte offset where the query event is located. The mapping can be saved in a distributed hash table (e.g. BigTable [6]).

We built two implementations of EventStore based on the characteristics of our data: *CacheEventStore*, that exploits the temporal locality of events (for example, most of the ads are clicked shortly after the search query), and *LogsEventStore*, that exploits the fact that queries in a log file are approximately sorted by the timestamp of the events (see Section 3.1 for details).

3.4.1 CacheEventStore

CacheEventStore is an in-memory cache which provides high throughput and low-latency lookups for recent queries. It is a distributed key-value store similar to Memcached [12], where the key is the query_id and the value is the full query event. CacheEventStore is sharded by the hash of query_id and we use consistent hashing [17] to support smooth transitions during resharding. CacheEventStore is populated by a simple reader process that reads query logs sequentially and stores them in memory. CacheEventStore can keep several minutes worth of query events in memory. When it is full, the least recently used query events are evicted. Many of the events are never accessed because the number of foreign events is much smaller than the primary events stored in CacheEventStore. CacheEventStore is a best-effort system:

in case of a cache miss, the query lookup is forwarded to the LogsEventStore. It does not employ any kind of persistence mechanism and is there purely to optimize latency of primary event lookups, and save disk seeks by avoiding requests to the LogsEventStore: even though in order to populate it we end up reading all of primary logs, it is all in sequential reads and we avoid expensive random file access required by the LogsEventStore.

3.4.2 *LogsEventStore*

LogsEventStore serves requests that are not satisfied by the CacheEventStore. Normally such requests constitute only a small fraction (about 10%) of all lookups. But LogsEventStore may need to serve 100% of lookups during catch-up to process old logs, or when the CacheEventStore is having problems.

LogsEventStore serves requests by consulting a persistent *log file map* to determine the approximate position of an event in the primary log file. From that position, it reads a small amount of data sequentially to find the exact event. Log file map is a collection of entries that map an event_id to a particular offset within a log file where that event is located. These entries are emitted at regular intervals (every W seconds or M bytes) by the event reader as it reads primary log files to populate the CacheEventStore. Entries are stored in BigTable [6], which implements a distributed ordered map that allows efficient key range scans. To find the log file name and offset that is close to the event, the LogsEventStore scans a range of the file map BigTable key space beginning with *ServerIP:ProcessId:(Timestamp-W)* and ending just after *ServerIP:ProcessId:Timestamp*. It is not necessary for either of the keys to exist in the table, but as long as the primary event reader has been configured to emit map entries every W seconds, the result will contain at least one map entry which will put the reader within M bytes of the target event. By adjusting M and W we find the desired balance between the map table size and the amount of I/O required for each lookup.

4. PERFORMANCE RESULTS

Photon has been deployed in production for more than one year, and it has proven to be significantly more reliable than our previous singly-homed system. During this period, Photon has survived multiple planned and unplanned outages of datacenters without impacting the end-to-end latency. The physical placement of pipelines and the IdRegistry replicas is as follows:

- The IdRegistry replicas are deployed in five datacenters located in three geographical regions across the United States. These geographical regions are up to 100ms apart in round-trip latency. Each region has at most two IdRegistry replicas. Since we configured the IdRegistry to commit as long as three out of five replicas reach consensus, this setup ensures that we can cope with the complete outage of one region (as in case of a major natural disaster) without causing disturbance to production.
- All the other components in the pipelines (including dispatchers, joiners, etc.) are deployed in two geographically distant regions on the east and west coast of the United States. These two regions also have close physical proximity with logs datacenters.

The following statistics highlight the scale and efficiency of Photon:

- Photon produces billions of joined events per day. During the peak periods, Photon can scale up to millions of events per minute.
- Each day, Photon consumes terabytes of foreign logs (e.g. clicks), and tens of terabytes of primary logs (e.g. queries).
- More than a thousand IdRegistry shards run in each datacenter.
- Each datacenter employs thousands of dispatchers and joiners, and hundreds of CacheEventStore and LogsEventStore workers. These components are replicated in two or more datacenters globally.

To satisfy the mission-critical nature of the data, Photon pipelines monitor a wide variety of performance metrics. Below, we present some performance numbers from our real-world deployment. Note that the time range and granularity in some of the following graphs are not specified for business confidentiality reasons.

4.1 End-to-end Latency

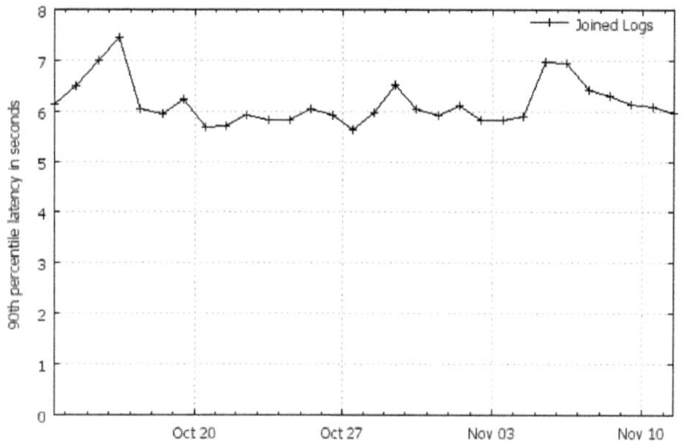

Figure 7: End-to-end latency of Photon

We define the end-to-end latency of each joined event as follows: when the joiner is ready to output a joined event, we export its latency as the current time minus the time when the event was logged — which is obtained from the event id's timestamp. The end-to-end 90th-percentile latency of Photon is computed based on the latency of each of the joined events.

Figure 7 plots the end-to-end 90th-percentile joining latency over a 30-day period. This graph shows that 90% of the events were joined in less than 7 seconds. This low latency is a direct result of the fact that the multiple stages in the pipeline communicate with each other through RPCs without the need to write intermediate data to disk storage (see Section 3).

One potential performance bottleneck arises from the time spent in disk seeks by LogsEventStore. With in-memory caching (i.e., CacheEventStore), Photon reduces the number of disk-based lookups significantly. Figure 8 shows the cache hit ratio for the CacheEventStore. The graph shows that most lookups are successfully handled by CacheEventStore

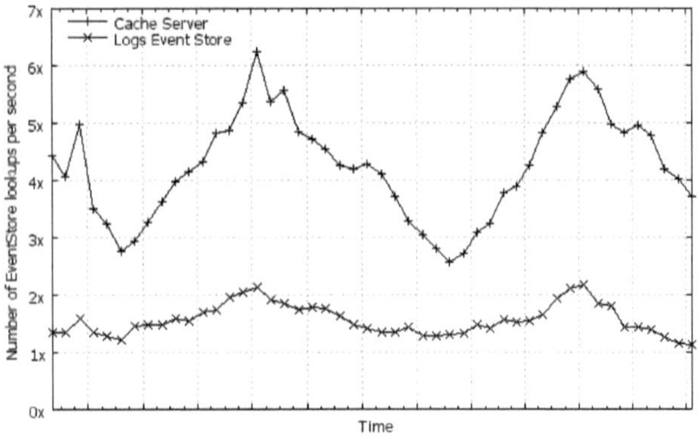

Figure 8: Photon EventStore lookups in a single datacenter

and only a small volume of traffic is processed by the slower LogsEventStore. Note that the volume of traffic to LogsEventStore stays relatively flat compared to the traffic growth - this means that we get even higher cache hit rate when the traffic increases.

4.2 Effect of Datacenter Outages

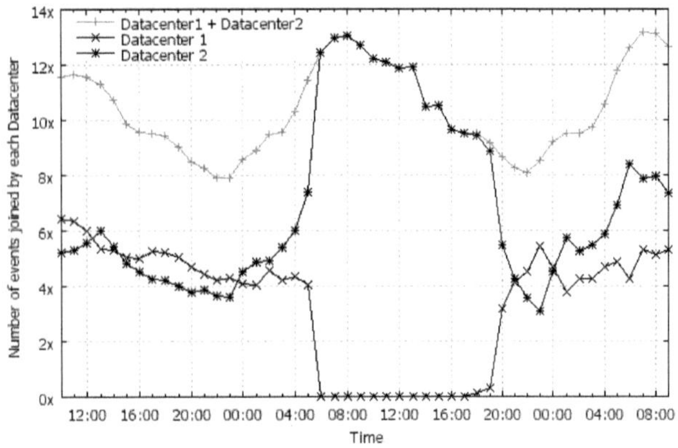

Figure 9: Photon withstanding a real datacenter disaster

Figure 9 shows the numbers of joined events produced by production pipelines in two separate datacenters over a period of time. When both datacenters are healthy, each processes half of the total events. However, when one of the datacenters suffers from a disaster, the other datacenter automatically starts handling the complete traffic without any manual intervention.

Similarly, when one of the IdRegistry datacenters goes down, the end-to-end performance of Photon is not impacted: since we are running five PaxosDB replicas in our setup, it lets us tolerate up to two datacenter-level outages.

4.3 IdRegistry Performance

In Section 2.2, we described how the IdRegistry batches multiple client requests into a single PaxosDB transaction to increase the throughput. Figure 10 shows the effectiveness of server-side batching at a single IdRegistry shard. This particular shard receives hundreds of client write requests per second. However, after batching, the number of PaxosDB transactions is only 6 to 12 per second.

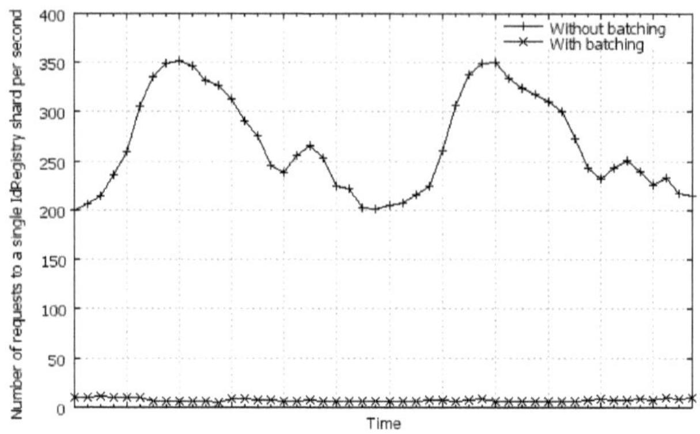

Figure 10: Effectiveness of server-side batching in the IdRegistry

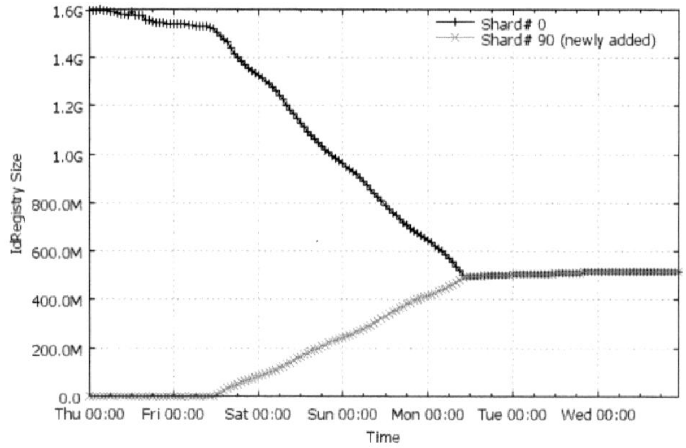

Figure 11: IdRegistry dynamic time-based upsharding

Figure 11 shows the effect of the IdRegistry dynamic resharding based on timestamp. Before upsharding, the size (= number of keys * bytes per key) of shard 0 was around 1.6GB. We tripled the number of shards and made it effective starting at Fri 12:00. This caused the size of shard 0 to drop and the size of newly added shard 90 to increase, until they both converged to 500MB. The IdRegistry garbage-collects event_ids that are older than 3 days, which explains why the old and new shards converge to the same size after 3 days.

4.4 Resource Efficiency

As mentioned in Section 2, we are able to tolerate datacenter-level failure by running independent pipelines in two datacenters, which clearly leads to some redundancy in the performed work. Recall from Section 3.2 that the dispatcher uses IdRegistry lookups to reduce the number of wasted joins.

Figure 12 shows that even though we read all events in both the datacenters, the optimization works very well in practice: less than 5% of the events are processed by both joiners.

This lookup technique also reduces the dispatcher catch-up time required after an extended downtime.

Figure 13 shows the dispatcher in one datacenter coming back after a 2-day downtime, and benefiting from the optimization. As soon as it was brought up, the dispatcher

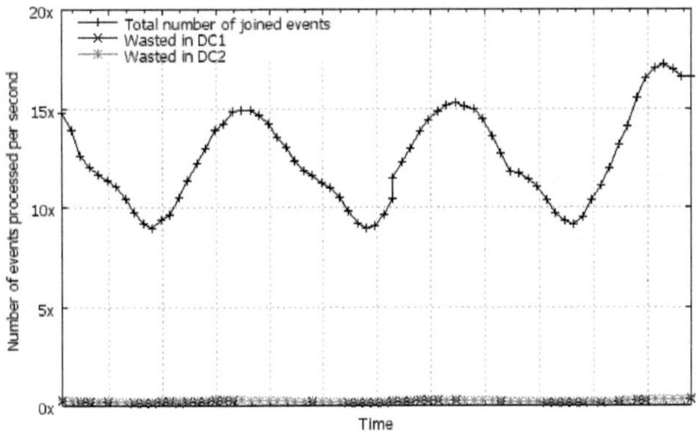

Figure 12: Wasted joins minimized by the dispatcher performing an IdRegistry lookup before sending events to the joiner

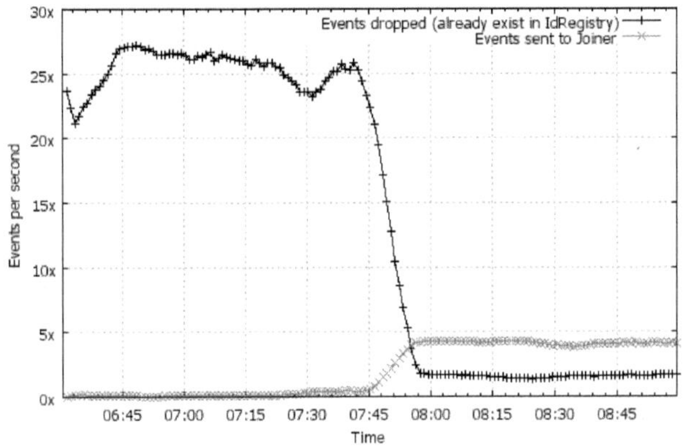

Figure 13: Dispatcher in one datacenter catching up after downtime

started to reprocess all the events of the last two days. Because a majority of these events had already been processed by the other healthy datacenter, the dispatcher caught up very quickly from the backlog.

5. DESIGN LESSONS

While designing and implementing many versions of the joining system, several design principles and lessons have emerged. Our experience is summarized below.

- To build a scalable distributed system based on Paxos, we need to minimize the critical state managed by the system, and ideally restrict it to meta-data only. Writing data through Paxos is very expensive because the data needs to be replicated to multiple datacenters across wide-area network in a synchronous fashion. Note that if the size of data is relatively small, it may be feasible to store the complete data (instead of meta-data) in Paxos as described in Spanner [8].
- In Photon, IdRegistry is the central point of communication among multiple pipelines maintaining consistent global state, and could turn into a bottleneck that limits scalability. We ensured that dynamic resharding of a running system is a first-class citizen in the design to avoid this limitation.
- RPC communication among workers helps in reducing the end-to-end latency, compared to using disk as the means of data communication. But using RPC requires application-level check for lost RPCs and retries to satisfy reliability guarantees. Special care should be exercised in throttling asynchronous RPCs to avoid overloading various servers such as the IdRegistry. Designating a single job (in this case, Dispatcher) to be responsible for retries facilitated the implementation of all other jobs to communicate via RPCs.
- It is better to isolate the specialized work to a separate pool of workers in order to make the system more scalable (in other words, divide and conquer). In our previous joining system, the work of the EventStore and the joiner was performed by the same component, and we did not have a CacheEventStore. Since LogsEventStore requires opening files and doing disk seeks, workers had affinity to only process the clicks where the corresponding query may be in the same physical file. This limited the scalability of the system. For a given category of work, designing each worker to be capable of operating on any particular piece of input makes the system more scalable.
- Some stream processing systems [26] recommend grouping individual events into a bigger batch. This works well only if all the events in a batch can be processed at the same time. For our case, it is very common to see a click event before its corresponding query event. If we group multiple clicks into a batch, then the whole batch cannot be committed until the corresponding queries are available. Hence, system designers need to make a careful decision on whether to batch or not.

6. RELATED WORK

There is a rich body of work on join algorithms in parallel and distributed RDBMS [19]. Over the last decade, researchers have also proposed techniques to join multiple streams continuously [1, 3, 5, 13, 15, 20, 24–26]. To the best of our knowledge, none of the existing literature addresses this problem under the following system constraints - eventually exactly-once semantics, fault-tolerance at datacenter-level, high scalability, low latency, unordered streams, delayed primary streams. Teubner et al. [24] used modern multi-core systems as opposed to commodity hardware. Blanan et al. [3] used MapReduce [10] to join streams, which is more suitable for a batch system rather than a continuously running one. Rao et al. [21] proposed using Paxos to maintain consistent database replication while being fault-tolerant. Unlike Photon, they store all Paxos replicas within a single datacenter, and hence are not impervious to datacenter disasters. Zaharia et al. [26] proposed breaking continuous streams into discrete units, which is not acceptable for Photon since we may see some clicks in a discrete stream before their corresponding query has arrived at the logs datacenter. Das et al. [9] proposed approximate joins as opposed to exact ones. Most of the existing join algorithms also assume that events in both input streams are sorted by the shared identifier, hence, they operate within a window to join [16]. In Photon, click can be arbitrarily delayed relative to its query.

Spanner [8], Megastore [2] and DynamoDB [11] provide consistent replication across datacenters as a storage service.

Both Spanner and Megastore do not currently allow applications to perform server-side batching of multiple client requests into a single Paxos commit.

7. CONCLUSIONS AND FUTURE WORK

In this paper, we described our experience in building and deploying a distributed stateful stream joining system that can withstand datacenter-level outages. The dispatcher keeps sending an event to the joiner until the IdRegistry server registers the event, ensuring at-least-once semantics. The IdRegistry is the heart of the system, as it ensures that no event is present in the output more than once. The dispatcher and the IdRegistry together guarantee that the only case where an event is lost is when the system commits the event to the IdRegistry, but fails to write the joined event to output. We presented an off-line mechanism to recover such unlikely losses. There is no single point of failure in the system, and all the components scale linearly with increased volume of traffic, including the scaling of critical state through resharding of IdRegistry. Asynchronous RPC-based communication among components reduces the latency, and helps achieve the goal of timely availability of rich statistical data.

We are working to extend Photon to join multiple continuous streams and scale sub-linearly. To reduce the end-to-end latency even further, we plan to have another fast, best-effort RPC path where the servers that generate query and click events directly send RPCs to the joiners (instead of the dispatcher waiting for these events to be copied to the logs datacenter). This will allow majority of events to be processed by the fast path, leaving the current logs-based system to process the missing events.

References

[1] D. J. Abadi et al. "The Design of the Borealis Stream Processing Engine". *Proc. of CIDR* 2005, pp.277-289.

[2] J. Baker et al. "Megastore: Providing scalable, highly available storage for interactive devices". *Proc. of CIDR* 2011, pp.223-234.

[3] S. Blanas et al. "A comparison of join algorithms for log processing in Mapreduce". *Proc. of SIGMOD* 2010, pp.975-986.

[4] T. D. Chandra, R. Griesemer, and J. Redstone. "Paxos made live: an engineering perspective". *Proc. of ACM PODC* 2007, pp.398-407.

[5] S. Chandrasekaran and M. J. Franklin. "Streaming queries over streaming data". *Proc. of VLDB* 2002, pp.203-214.

[6] F. Chang et al. "Bigtable: A Distributed Storage System for Structured Data". *ACM TOCS* 2008, 26.2, pp.4:1-4:26.

[7] E. F. Codd. "A Relational Model of Data for Large Shared Data Banks", *Communications of the ACM* 13 (6): p377-387, 1970.

[8] J. C. Corbett et al. "Spanner: Google's Globally-Distributed Database". *Proc. of OSDI* 2012.

[9] A. Das, J. Gehrke, and M. Riedewald. "Approximate join processing over data streams". *Proc. of SIGMOD* 2003, pp.40-51.

[10] J. Dean and S. Ghemawat. "MapReduce: Simplified data processing on large clusters". *Proc. of OSDI* 2004, pp.137-149.

[11] G. DeCandia et al. "Dynamo: Amazon's Highly Available Key-value Store". *Proc. of SOSP.* 2007, pp. 205-220.

[12] B. Fitzpatrick. "Distributed Caching with Memcached". Linux Journal, Issue 124, 2004, pp.5.

[13] B. Gedik, P. S. Yu, and R. R. Bordawekar. "Executing stream joins on the cell processor", *Proc. of VLDB* 2007, pp.363-374.

[14] S. Ghemawat, H. Gobioff, and S-T Leung. "The Google File System". *19th Symposium on Operating Systems Principles* 2003, pp.20-43.

[15] M. A. Hammad, W. G. Aref, and A. K. Elmagarmid. "Joining multiple data streams with window constraints". *Computer Science Technical Reports*, #02-115.

[16] J. Kang, J. F. Naughton, and S. D. Viglas. "Evaluating window joins over unbounded streams". *Proc. of VLDB* 2002, pp.341-352.

[17] D. Karger et al. "Consistent Hashing and Random Trees: Distributed Caching Protocols for Relieving Hot Spots on the World Wide Web". *Proc. of ACM SOTC* 1997, pp.654-663.

[18] L. Lamport. "The part-time parliament", *ACM TOCS* 16.2 1998, pp.133-169.

[19] P. Mishra and M. H. Eich. "Join processing in relational databases". *ACM Computing Surveys* 1992, 24(1), pp.63-113.

[20] L. Neumeyer et al. "S4: Distributed Stream Computing Platform". *Proc. of KDCloud* 2010.

[21] J. Rao, E. J. Shekita, and S. Tata. "Using Paxos to Build a Scalable, Consistent, and Highly Available Datastore". *Proc. of VLDB* 2011, pp.243-254.

[22] F. B. Schneider. "Implementing fault-tolerant services using the state machine approach: A tutorial", *ACM Computing Surveys* 22 1990, pp.299-319 (1990).

[23] D. Shasha and P. Bonnet. "Database Tuning: Principles, Experiments, and Troubleshooting Techniques". *Proc. of SIGMOD* 2004, pp.115-116.

[24] J. Teubner and R. Mueller. "How soccer players would do stream joins". *Proc. of SIGMOD* 2011, pp.625-636.

[25] J. Xie and J. Yang. "A survey of join processing in data streams". *Data Streams - Models and Algorithms* 2007, pp.209-236.

[26] M. Zaharia et al. "Discretized Streams: An Efficient and Fault-tolerant Model for Stream Processing on Large Clusters". *Proc. of HotCloud* 2012, pp.10-10.

Utility-Maximizing Event Stream Suppression *

Di Wang◇, Yeye He†, Elke Rundensteiner◇, Jeffrey F. Naughton‡
◇Department of Computer Science, Worcester Polytechnic Institute
†,‡ Department of Computer Sciences, University of Wisconsin-Madison
wangdi@cs.wpi.edu, heyeye@cs.wisc.edu, rundenst@cs.wpi.edu, naughton@cs.wisc.edu

ABSTRACT

Complex Event Processing (CEP) has emerged as a technology for monitoring event streams in search of user specified event patterns. When a CEP system is deployed in sensitive environments the user may wish to mitigate leaks of private information while ensuring that useful nonsensitive patterns are still reported. In this paper we consider how to suppress events in a stream to reduce the disclosure of sensitive patterns while maximizing the detection of nonsensitive patterns. We first formally define the problem of utility-maximizing event suppression with privacy preferences, and analyze its computational hardness. We then design a suite of real-time solutions to solve this problem. Our first solution optimally solves the problem at the event-type level. The second solution, at the event-instance level, further optimizes the event-type level solution by exploiting runtime event distributions using advanced pattern match cardinality estimation techniques. Our user study and experimental evaluation over both real-world and synthetic event streams show that our algorithms are effective in maximizing utility yet still efficient enough to offer near real-time system responsiveness.

Categories and Subject Descriptors

H.2 [**Information Systems**]: Database Management

Keywords

Complex Event Processing, Utility, Privacy

1. INTRODUCTION

Complex Event Processing (CEP) has gained increasing popularity for real-time pattern matching over event streams, and has received significant attention from both the research community [5, 22, 29] and industry [1, 3]. However, to date, the privacy implications of CEP applications have been overlooked. The privacy problems we study in this paper were motivated by real-world problems we encountered while developing and deploying CEP solutions for hospital environments. While our privacy problem is abstracted from this specific application domain, our problem formulation is sufficiently generic that it can be applied to general CEP applications. For concreteness, we begin with our motivating example.

Motivating Applications. Consider a CEP-powered health care system called HyReminder [27]. HyReminder, currently deployed at University of Massachusetts Memorial Hospital, is a hospital infection control system that aims to track, monitor and remind health-care workers with respect to hygiene compliance. In the hospital, each doctor wears an RFID badge that can be read by sensors installed throughout the hospital. As doctors move around in the hospital, sensor readings are triggered, which are then abstracted as events and transmitted to a CEP engine. Using CEP query processing techniques, event patterns that reveal hygiene compliance or violations can then be detected and reported in accordance with US hygiene regulations [7].

As an example of such a pattern, a doctor who exits a patient room (represented by an `Exit-patient-room` event) should perform hand sanitization (indicated by a `Sanitize` event) within a short period of time. We represent such a hygiene compliance pattern using Q1 below. Similarly, a doctor should wash hands (a `Wash` event) before entering an office (an `Enter-psychiatrist-office` event) to prevent spreading contagious diseases, as expressed by Q2 below. These regulations are commonly known as "wash-in, wash-out" in hospital jargon [7].

```
Q1: SEQ(Exit-patient-room, Sanitize)
WITHIN 2 min
Q2: SEQ(Wash, Enter-psychiatrist-office)
WITHIN 2 min
```

While the benefit of such CEP applications is apparent, some event patterns may be sensitive in that they reveal an individual's private information. For example, an observation that a doctor leaves a patient's room and then immediately enters a psychiatrist's office might serve as an indication that this patient is experiencing psychiatric problems. This event sequence, when expressed as a "private" pattern, can be written as:

```
P1: SEQ(Exit-patient-room, Enter-psychiatrist-office)
WITHIN 5 min
```

The issue is that when HyReminder monitors doctors' behaviors (the intended use of this application), the events being reported may disclose private information about individual patients as a side-effect. We observe that the simplistic approach of not directly reporting private patterns does not prevent their disclosure — the occurrence of several hygiene compliance patterns that HyReminder does report may be used by an adversary to infer the existence of private pattern matches.

As an example, in Figure 1, there is a stream of four events asso-

*This work is supported in part by NSF grant IIS-1018443, NIGMS grant R01LM011028-02, and UMMS-WPI CCTS Collaborative grant.
† Author's current affiliation: Microsoft Research.

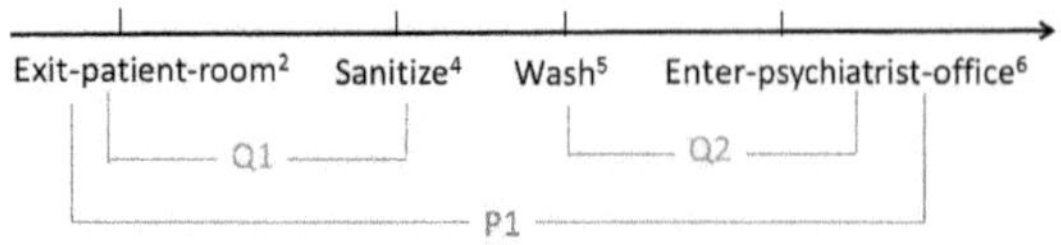

Figure 1: An adversarial attack using public pattern matches

ciated with the same doctor observed in HyReminder. Each event has a superscript indicating its timestamp in minutes. Over this particular event stream, there exists one match for Q1, (`Exit-patient-room`^{2}, `Sanitize`^{4}), and one match for Q2: (`Wash`^{5}, `Enter-psychiatrist-office`^{6}). Now by concatenating the matches of Q1 and Q2, an adversary can infer that a match for private pattern P1, namely (`Exit-patient-room`^{2}, `Enter-psychiatrist-office`^{6}) also exists. This example illustrates that the existence of private pattern matches can still be inadvertently revealed even when only legitimate queries are reported. It underlines the importance of taking private preferences into account when deploying CEP systems in sensitive environments like a hospital.

Of course, this hospital scenario is only one motivating example, that by no means cover the full spectrum of privacy threats with CEP systems – any time a CEP is deployed in a sensitive environment the possibility of a privacy breach exists. Furthermore, while one-off actions may be possible to mitigate privacy concerns within a particular application, our goal is broader — we wish to develop a general model for privacy and utility in CEP systems, and initial solutions to the problems that arise in that model.

At a high level, the problem we address can be described as follows. We consider two kinds of CEP patterns: those that should be detected and reported to data users (which we term *"public" patterns*), and those that users prefer not to reveal because of privacy concerns (which we term *"private" patterns*).

In this work we focus on the mechanism of *event suppression*, that is, deleting some events from the stream in order to "destroy" possible private pattern matches. For example, in Figure 1, dropping any event in the stream ensures that either a match of Q1 or Q2 would not be reported, thus preventing P1 from being inferred. In general, there exist numerous ways in which events could be suppressed. Note that dropping or keeping an event naturally represents a *trade-off* between reporting more useful public query matches and disclosing some undesirable private query matches. We thus provide a *utility-maximizing framework* that allows users to quantify their preferences by setting relative weights of public and private patterns, so that events can be suppressed in such a way that maximizes the utility of pattern matches that are preserved.

To the best of our knowledge, the work closest to ours is [15], which first identifies the privacy concern in CEP systems. However the work in [15] focuses on the theoretical hardness of a particular problem variant. Furthermore, no practical algorithm is designed nor empirical studies have been conducted. In this paper, we analyze possible variants of the more general version of the problem, develop practical algorithms that are useful in a real-time streaming environment, and experimentally evaluate our algorithms using both real-world and synthetic data.

Specifically, we make the following contributions in this work.

- We formally define the problem of utility-maximizing event suppression with privacy preferences. Our problem formulation enables users to quantify the relative importance of eliminating undesirable "private" matches versus producing useful "public" matches. Furthermore, we analyze problem variants (Section 3), and study their computational hardness (Section 4). We show that the problem in general is not only NP-hard, but also hard to approximate.
- Our second contribution is to develop a suite of real-time utility maximizing solutions. We first propose an approach based on linear programming that optimally solves the problem at the event-type level (which suppresses all events of the same type). For the computationally intractable instance-level problem (which suppresses individual events), we observe that our solution at the event-type level provides a useful basis for further optimization. Specifically, we introduce a *Hybrid solution* to tackle the instance-level problem by combining the solution at the event-type level with optimization heuristics based on run-time *pattern match cardinality estimation*. We further develop two techniques to address the sub-problem of pattern match cardinality estimation, one based on event arrival rates and the other based on periodicity using the state-of-the-art periodicity mining algorithms [11, 20]. To the best of our knowledge, the problem of event stream cardinality estimation has not been explored. Just like in relational databases, we think our cardinality estimation may be useful for resource allocation and query optimization in event stream systems. (Section 5).
- To better understand the effectiveness and performance of our proposed solutions, we conducted a user study and performed extensive experiments on both real-world and synthetic event streams. We show that our Hybrid solutions preserve significantly more utility than alternative approaches, while still efficient enough to ensure real time system responsiveness. In addition, we demonstrate in both our user study and experiments that in at least one real world scenario, periodicity information is needed to produce accurate cardinality estimation. The advantage of periodicity-based estimation is then reaffirmed using synthetic streams (Section 6).

2. PRELIMINARIES

2.1 Event Data Model

The input to a CEP system is a potentially infinite **event stream** composed of **event instances**. Each event instance, denoted by a lowercase e_i, corresponds to an instantaneous and atomic occurrence of interest [29]. Each event instance e_i is associated with a timestamp from a discrete time domain, denoted by $e_i.ts$. Event instances are conceptually grouped into **event types**. Let Σ be the set of all possible event types. Then each event type, denoted by an uppercase $E_i \in \Sigma$, is distinguished by its event type name (e.g., `Exit-patient-room`). Each event type has associated attributes as defined by the schema of the event type.

2.2 Event Query Model

In this work, we focus on the core CEP query functionality, the `SEQ` query operator [22, 29]. A SEQ query looks for a sequence of events in a specified temporal order within a given time window. A **SEQ pattern query** Q is of the form $Q = SEQ\ (E_1, E_2, ...\ E_n)$, where $E_k \in \Sigma$ are event types. For each query Q there is a specified time-window $Window(Q) \in \mathbb{R}^+$ over which Q will be evaluated. While multiple pattern match semantics exist (see [5] for a classification), in this work we use *skip till any match* semantic, defined as follows. A **pattern match** of Q over an event stream S is produced if there exists a temporally ordered subsequence $S' = (e_1, e_2, ...\ e_n)$, that is $e_i.ts < e_j.ts$ for all $1 \leq i < j \leq n$, such that for all $k \in [1, n]$, e_k is of type E_k, and $e_n.ts - e_1.ts \leq Window(Q)$. We say the sequence S' is a match of Q. As is common in current CEP engines [5, 22, 29], we assume the output of a pattern match is the concatenation of participating event instances. In this paper, we focus on queries with positive event types, while the problem of supporting CEP queries with negation is an interesting area for future work.

Individual Match vs. Aggregate Statistics. Many CEP applications are interested in individual query matches. For example, in our hospital setting, it is important to know which doctor enters which ICU after exiting a potentially-contagious patient's room without following sanitization procedures. There are also scenarios where aggregate statistics of CEP outputs are useful. For instance, the hospital leadership team is interested in knowing the aggregate hygiene-compliance-ratio in the hospital by month over the last 12 months, which is also a real output produced by our HyReminder.

While both of these scenarios are important, in this paper we focus on mitigating privacy risks when individual CEP matches are reported, which to our knowledge has not been systematically studied. Ensuring privacy for aggregate CEP statistics is also important, although for that problem existing techniques such as differential-privacy may be appropriate. The inapplicability of differential-privacy to reporting individual matches is discussed in Related Work (Section 7).

2.3 The Complication: Private Patterns

The notion of **private query patterns** sets our problem apart from the conventional CEP literature. In terms of syntax, private query patterns are just like SEQ queries, i.e., they consist of a sequence of events and an associated time window. The fundamental difference, however, is that while as many SEQ pattern matches as possible should be reported, private pattern matches would better be suppressed. In the remainder of this work we will refer to these two types of patterns as **private query patterns** and **public query patterns**, respectively. Q1 and Q2 in the motivating application, for example, are public query patterns, while P1 is a private query pattern. We denote the set of public query patterns by $\mathcal{Q}$ and the set of private query patterns by $\mathcal{P}$.

2.3.1 *Suppressing Private Pattern Matches*

A natural way to suppress a private pattern match is to suppress events that participate in the match. For example, in Figure 1, dropping any event in the stream ensures that one match of Q1 or Q2 would not be reported, thus preventing P1 from being inferred.

One important advantage of using event suppression is that the output is a subset of the original stream, so it remains an event stream with the same set of event-types as the original stream. Thus any stream-based application that can process the original stream can process the filtered stream without modification.

In addition, event suppression ensures the desirable *query-result subset property* when CEP queries with positive events are used. Namely we only report a *subset* of the original CEP query matches, which ensures that no spurious matches that do not exist in reality will ever be produced. This is desirable because the opposite is troubling — it would be disturbing if a hospital hygiene compliance system reported false hygiene compliance/violations because they were generated by the privacy protection system.

While we focus on event suppression in this work, other possible approaches also exist. In the classical database anonymization literature, a frequently used technique is *generalization* [25, 21], in which a specific value is "generalized" so that its presence reveals less information. Similarly one could adopt "event generalization" for our problem by generalizing detailed events into generic events. Although event generalization may mitigate some privacy concerns, it can cause trouble in producing meaningful query matches. For example, in Figure 1, if we only observe a generalized `Exit-room` event instead of the `Exit-patient-room`, we are not sure if matches of Q1 can be produced. Even if a probabilistic interpretation is acceptable, query results would violate the *subset property* that event suppression can offer.

Another possible data manipulation approach is to add noise to the timestamps of events. This approach is also problematic, because it risks introducing spurious query pattern matches, thus violating the *subset property* outlined above.

Since event suppression is a simple yet effective mechanism for addressing privacy preference in the context of CEP, in this paper we will focus on using event suppression. Alternative approaches are interesting directions for future work.

3. PROBLEM STATEMENT & TAXONOMY

In this section, we first formally define the problem of utility-maximizing stream suppression with privacy preferences. We further propose a problem taxonomy to better understand its variants.

3.1 Problem statement

Motivation of problem formulation. Since there are multiple ways in which events could be suppressed to preserve privacy, the question arises is which events should be dropped over others. An intuitive answer is to suppress events such that more "important" public pattern matches are kept. It practice, some pattern matches are naturally more important than others. For example, in the hospital where HyReminder is deployed, another public pattern, henceforth referred to as Q3, may be needed to produce a query match if a doctor exits a highly-contagious patient room, does not sanitize his hands, and immediately enters the ICU. A match for Q3 represents a grave violation of hygiene regulations, and is considered more "useful" than Q1 and Q2 by the user.

In order to capture this intuition, we define a positive **utility weight** $w(Q_i)$ for each public query Q_i, that quantifies the usefulness of reporting one match for Q_i. Q3 mentioned above, for example, should be assigned a higher utility weight than a match for query Q1 or Q2. Assigning appropriate weights to different queries in real-world applications requires domain expertise. In this work we assume that the utility weights for queries are provided by domain experts as part of the input to the system.

We then define *utility gain* as a weighted sum of all public pattern matches as below.

DEFINITION 1. *Let $w(Q_i) \in \mathbb{R}^+$ be the utility gain weight of public query $Q_i \in \mathcal{Q}$, let $\mathcal{C}(Q_i, S)$ be the number of matches for Q_i over stream S. The* ***utility gain*** *generated for query Q_i is:*

$$U(Q_i, S) = w(Q_i) \cdot \mathcal{C}(Q_i, S) \tag{1}$$

The utility gain generated over the entire query set $\mathcal{Q}$ on S is:

$$\mathcal{U}_{\mathcal{Q}} = \sum_{Q_i \in \mathcal{Q}} U(Q_i, S) \tag{2}$$

On the other hand, to model the fact that private pattern matches are undesirable, each such match is assigned a *negative* utility value, or a **utility penalty weight**. The resulting aggregate *utility loss* is the side-effect caused by private patterns. We then formally define utility loss as follows.

DEFINITION 2. *Let $w(P_j) \in \mathbb{R}^-$ be the utility penalty weight of private pattern $P_j \in \mathcal{P}$, and $\mathcal{C}(P_j, S)$ be the number of matches for P_j over event stream S. The* ***utility penalty*** *or* ***utility loss*** *associated with P_j is:*

$$U(P_j, S) = w(P_j) \cdot \mathcal{C}(P_j, S) \tag{3}$$

Since our goal is to balance the need to maximize utility gain and minimize utility loss, our objective function is simply defined as the sum of the two.

DEFINITION 3. *The overall utility generated by $\mathcal{Q} = \{Q_i\}$ and $\mathcal{P} = \{P_j\}$ on S is:*

$$\mathcal{U}_{\mathcal{Q}+\mathcal{P}} = \sum_{Q_i \in \mathcal{Q}} U(Q_i, S) + \sum_{P_j \in \mathcal{P}} U(P_j, S). \tag{4}$$

This objective function is an instance of *aggregate objective function* that is commonly used in the multi-objective optimization literature [24].

With these, we formally define the utility-maximizing stream suppression problem as follows.

PROBLEM 1. *Given an event stream S, a set of public queries $\mathcal{Q}$, a set of private queries $\mathcal{P}$, and a utility weight function $w(\cdot) \in \mathbb{R}$, find a subset S' of S such that the total utility $\mathcal{U}_{\mathcal{Q}+\mathcal{P}}$ is maximized for the chosen S' over all possible subsets of S.*

3.2 A Problem Taxonomy

3.2.1 Hard-constraint vs. Soft-constraint

In certain scenarios, users may demand that the adversary cannot infer even a single private pattern match. In other words, the constraints imposed by the private patterns are "hard", assuring no private pattern match is ever disclosed. We term such private pattern a **hard-constraint**. If every private pattern is a hard-constraint, the resulting problem is a hard-constraint utility maximization problem. In our formulation defined in Definition 2, utility penalty weights for private patterns can be set to *negative infinity* to enforce the hard-constraint.

Although the hard-constraint privacy is needed in some environments, there are cases in which reporting a public query match is of such paramount importance that it may override certain privacy concerns. As a concrete example, consider the public pattern Q3 in HyReminder discussed before, where a doctor enters an ICU without proper sanitization, which corresponds to a serious hygiene violation with dire consequences. On the other hand, there may also exist private patterns representing fairly innocuous privacy violations (e.g., a patient has his blood and urine tested). In such a scenario, it may be desirable to report the public pattern match Q3, even at the potential cost of leaking not-so-harmful private information.

Since such trade-offs are best decided using domain expertise, we want a problem formulation flexible enough to allow users to specify queries with overriding utilities that can trump privacy concerns if necessary. In the **soft-constraints** variant, not all private patterns are strictly prohibited. Instead, each such match is penalized by a utility loss, as defined in our utility framework in Definition 3. This allows *flexible trade-offs* between reporting useful public pattern matches and disclosing undesirable private pattern matches. Furthermore, it can degenerate into the Hard-Constraint model by using negative infinity query weights, and thus represents a more general problem formulation.

Choosing the Hard-constraint vs. the Soft-constraint model. Our hospital solution was developed in consultation with personnel in the hospital. Initially we favored the Hard-constraint problem formulation, for the simple reason that it offers precise privacy guarantees: anything that is labeled private will not appear in the result set.

While conceptually appealing, we later noticed that with this Hard-constraint approach, "utility" was significantly reduced. In particular, occasionally very important matches to public patterns, which must be reported in the hospital setting, were instead suppressed due to minor privacy concerns. For example, a query match that reports a grave hygiene violation (e.g., Q3 discussed earlier) must trigger alerts to the doctor as well as to the lead nurse on duty. However, in our initial experiments using the Hard-constraint approach, some such important matches were suppressed.

We were told this was unsatisfactory, because while it is important to mitigate privacy risks, ensuring hygiene compliance and controlling serious in-hospital infections are sometimes given higher priority. The system, after all, is used *internally* by medical workers; it is not an externally-facing system deployed on the Internet. We believe that this is a key distinction that makes our problem different from traditional privacy research.

Σ	set of all event types
$\mathcal{Q}$	set of all public patterns
$\mathcal{P}$	set of all private patterns
$w(Q_j)$	utility weight of pattern Q_j
λ_i	arrival rate of events of type E_i
$N_T(Q_j)$	expected number of matches of Q_j in a time span T

Table 1: Summary of symbols

This motivated us to study the more general Soft-constraint problem formulation, where private patterns are given negative weights, so that important public pattern matches may trump minor private matches, but at the same time serious private pattern matches can still be guaranteed to be hidden by setting their weights to negative infinity.

We realize that, intuitively, the Hard-constraint approach is more acceptable when talking about privacy. In this paper we chose to study the Soft-constraint problem not only because it is the one favored in our hospital scenario, but also because it is more generic: it subsumes the Hard-constraint variant because we can always simulate the Hard-constraint model by setting weights on private patters to negative infinity. The algorithms considered in this paper are applicable to both the Hard-constraint model and the Soft-Constraint model.

3.2.2 Type-level vs. Instance-level

Mirroring the classical taxonomy proposed for relational data privacy [17], our problem can be classified into "type-level" (corresponding to the "global recoding" in relational k-anonymity), or "instance-level" (corresponding to "local recoding").

More specifically, the **type-level** problem makes simplified suppression decisions at the *event type* level by either suppressing or preserving all events of the same type. That is, events of the same type are either all suppressed or all preserved, irrespective of when they occur in the stream.

On the other hand, the **instance-level** problem treats *each event differently* based on its run-time context, i.e., the previously arrived events in the active windows of queries, and the expectation of future events. An instance-level solution can suppress one event of a certain type while preserving another event of the same type. It thus allows flexible event suppression decisions that offer more opportunities for utility optimization, but as a consequence it presents a harder optimization problem.

3.2.3 Offline vs. Online

Orthogonal to the two dimensions above, our problem can be further classified into offline and online variants.

The **offline** variant produces decisions after the whole stream has arrived. Although this is not a practical assumption, studying the offline variant does allow us to eliminate the hardness arising from the randomness of the online problem and focus on optimal event suppression in a deterministic setting.

In the **online** variant, decisions have to be made in real-time for the currently arriving event without complete knowledge of future events. While this problem variant is more fitting for CEP applications, which typically demand real-time responsiveness, it is also intuitively more difficult. Challenges arise because (1) We must estimate future events and pattern matches that are probabilistic in nature, and (2) Even if future estimates are accurate, smart suppression decisions are still needed to maximize utility, which is in essence similar to the offline variant.

In the remainder of this paper we will focus on the online event suppression problem with soft-constraint, at both type-level and instance-level.

4. HARDNESS RESULTS

In this section, we study the hardness of the utility-maximizing event suppression problem. The proofs of our theorems are presented in Appendix. We first show in Theorem 1 that the instance-level offline variant is NP-hard.

THEOREM 1. *The problem of instance-level utility-maximizing event suppression with soft-constraint is NP-hard in the total number of events. It remains NP-hard even if each query contains exactly two event types.*

Moreover, we show that the instance-level problem is unlikely to be approximable in polynomial time.

THEOREM 2. *Let n be the total number of events in the stream. There is a fixed constant $\epsilon \geq 0$ such that if there is n^ϵ factor approximation algorithm for instance-level utility-maximizing event suppression with soft-constraint, then RP = NP.*

The hardness and inapproximability results illustrate the unfortunate fact that unless we are dealing with streams that have a small number of events, utility-maximizing event suppression at instance-level is unlikely to be even approximated efficiently. The problem is not much simpler even if we focus on very simple query constructs (e.g., two event types per query). Given that stream systems typically need to handle potentially a large number of event instances in real-time, efficient optimal solutions with a good quality guarantee are unlikely to exist.

Even for the less ambitious type-level variant, we show the surprising result that this variant exhibits a similar hardness as follows.

THEOREM 3. *The problem of type-level utility-maximizing event suppression with soft-constraint is NP-hard in the total number of event types.*

Despite the hardness result, we show in the following a *fixed-parameter-tractable* special case that under some natural assumptions, the type-level variant can be solved optimally.

PROPOSITION 1. *Suppose the expected number of matches for each query $Q \in \mathcal{Q}$ and $P \in \mathcal{P}$ over some standard time unit is known. Suppose the total number of public and private queries, $|\mathcal{P}| + |\mathcal{Q}|$, is some fixed constant. Then the problem of utility-maximizing online type-level event suppression can be solved in polynomial time to obtain the optimal solution in expectation.*

This proposition follows from a constructive algorithm to be described in Section 5.1. We would like to point out here that in comparison to the offline type-level variant, in the online version the solution is only optimal *in expectation*. The reason is because in the online version, only expectations of query matches are known and events can still arrive in an uncertain manner that deviates from the expectation. As such, one type-level solution may not be the optimal for all event stream instances. Rather it is optimal in the sense that in the long term, when the number of query matches converges to the expectation, the solution is optimal in expectation.

5. ONLINE SUPPRESSION ALGORITHMS

In this section, we devise two real-time event suppression strategies that maximize the overall utility. The first algorithm offers optimal suppression decisions at the event-type level (Sec. 5.1). Due to the fluctuations in the event stream, the optimal type-level decisions may not be the best decision for each event instance. This leads us to design the instance-level algorithm that tweaks type-level decisions based on run-time context, henceforth called *Hybrid* algorithm (Sec. 5.2). The key idea is that while the type-level approach provides a pretty good long-term decision, the instance-level decisions can fine-tune the type-level solution based on the events in the local windows.

Both of our algorithms need to estimate the cardinality of pattern matches as part of their decision making processes. Therefore, we propose two *cardinality estimation* approaches (Sec. 5.3). The first light-weight approach treats each type of event independent of each other, while the second sophisticated approach takes advantage of periodicities in the stream to produce more accurate estimations.

5.1 Optimal Type-Level Algorithm

Inspired by Proposition 1, we first explore the type-level variant. We propose to model the type-level suppression problem as an *integer linear program*. Specifically, let $\Sigma = \{E_i\}$ be the set of all event types. Let the integer $x_i \in \{0, 1\}$ be the decision variables to drop/keep all events of type E_i in order to ensure privacy, with $x_i = 1$ denoting to keep E_i, and $x_i = 0$ to drop E_i. Further let the integer $y_j \in \{0, 1\}$ denote whether or not public pattern $Q_j \in \mathcal{Q}$ will be output, and $z_k \in \{0, 1\}$ denote whether private pattern $P_k \in \mathcal{P}$ will be output.

Let $N_T(Q_j)$ and $N_T(P_k)$ be the expected number of pattern matches for Q_j and P_k produced over a standard time period T respectively. Using historical data, we can obtain statistics about the stream, like the average event arrival rate. These statistics then allow us to get a rough estimate of $N_T(Q_j)$ and $N_T(P_k)$ (we defer a detailed discussion on the orthogonal issue of cardinality estimation to Section 5.3). Now assume that $N_T(Q_j)$ and $N_T(P_k)$ are computed and treated as known constant values. The objective utility function then becomes:

$$\mathcal{U} = \sum_{Q_j \in \mathcal{Q}} w(Q_j) N_T(Q_j) y_j + \sum_{P_k \in \mathcal{P}} w(P_k) N_T(P_k) z_k \quad (5)$$

Recall that $w(\cdot)$ represents the utility weight function. We note that whether or not query Q_j can be reported (y_j is 0 or 1) depends on the values of the x_i's. Let $\sigma(Q_j)$ be the multi-set of all event types in Q_j. If one constituent event type E_i of a query pattern Q_j is dropped ($x_i = 0$, for $E_i \in \sigma(Q_j)$), then the query pattern can never be revealed ($y_j = 0$). We express the dependence using the following linear constraint. For all $Q_j \in \mathcal{Q}$, we have

$$0 \leq y_j \leq \frac{1}{|Q_j|} \sum_{E_i \in \sigma(Q_j)} x_i \quad (6)$$

Intuitively, this says that in a type-level solution, Q_j can be reported ($y_j = 1$) if and only if none of its participating event types are dropped.

Similarly, the variable $z_k \in \{0, 1\}$ is subject to the constraint:

$$1 \geq z_k \geq \frac{1}{|P_k|} - 1 + \frac{1}{|P_k|} \sum_{E_i \in \sigma(P_k)} x_i \quad (7)$$

This captures the fact that the private pattern will be reported ($z_k = 1$) when all its participating event types are preserved. When at least one constituent event type is absent, z_k gets a value of 0, which will avoid the utility penalty.

The problem of maximizing $\mathcal{U}$ is then an integer linear programming problem subject to the constraints in Equations (6) and (7). Putting the issue of estimating $N_T(Q_j)$ and $N_T(P_k)$ aside, this online type-level variant is really no different from the offline type-level variant. From Proposition 1, we know that it is solvable if the total number of event types or queries is limited.

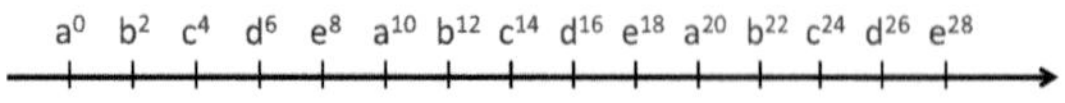

(a) Original event stream

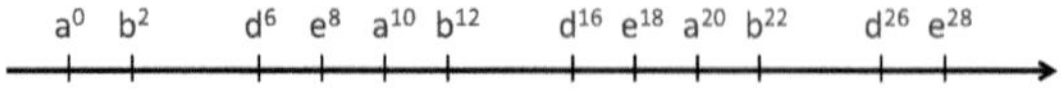

(b) With type-level suppression

Figure 2: Type-level LP-based algorithm

This is useful, for although the number of event instances may be unbounded in a stream system, the number of queries or event types tends to be limited (HyReminder, for example, has 16 event types and 14 queries and the corresponding LP can be solved in 20 ms). Furthermore, even when we are dealing with problems that have a large number of queries and events, since the type-level decisions would stay the same for every new arriving event, the LP only needs to be solved once, until new statistics arrive, at which point the decisions need to be re-computed. This approach thus provides a practical way to solve the type-level event suppression problem. We use Example 1 to illustrate this algorithm.

EXAMPLE 1. *Suppose we have five event types,* $\Sigma = \{A, B, C, D, E\}$. *A sample event stream is depicted in Figure 2a. The superscript of an event denotes its timestamp. As shown in the figure, events with different event types arrive with the same arrival rate, namely* 1 *event per* 10 *time units, in a simple and recurring pattern* (a, b, c, d, e). *Assume there are three public queries, namely*
$Q_1 = SEQ(B, C, D)$, $Window(Q_1) = 10$, $w(Q_1) = 5$;
$Q_2 = SEQ(A, B)$, $Window(Q_2) = 10$, $w(Q_2) = 20$;
$Q_3 = SEQ(D, E)$, $Window(Q_3) = 10$, $w(Q_3) = 20$;
and one private pattern,
$P_1 = SEQ(A, C, E)$, $Window(P_1) = 10$, $w(P_1) = -10$.

Let $[x_1, x_2, ..x_5]$ *be the decision variables of whether events of type* A, B, C, D, E *can be preserved,* $[y_1, y_2, y_3]$ *be the variables that indicate whether* Q_1, Q_2, Q_3 *can be reported, and* $[z_1]$ *be the variable indicating whether* P_1 *will be produced. Using Equations (5), (6) and (7), we obtain a linear program with the objective function:*

$$U = \frac{1}{10} \cdot 5 \cdot y_1 + \frac{1}{10} \cdot 20 \cdot y_2 + \frac{1}{10} \cdot 20 \cdot y_3 - \frac{1}{10} \cdot 10 \cdot z_1$$

where the four $\frac{1}{10}$*s are essentially* $N_T(Q_j)$ *and* $N_T(P_k)$*, i.e., the expected number of pattern matches over a time period* T*, subject to the constraints that can be instantiated from Equation (6) and (7).*

Solving the linear program gives us the optimal type-level solution, $[x_1, x_2, ...x_5] = [1, 1, 0, 1, 1]$. *Namely, events of type* C *will all be suppressed. This solution is intuitive. Dropping event type* C *ensures that no matches for* P_1 *and* Q_1 *will be produced. Since the arrival rate of* Q_1 *and* P_1 *are both* $\frac{1}{10}$, *and the weight* $w(Q_1) = 5$ *while* $w(P_1) = -10$, *it is profitable to drop event type* C.

Once the type-level decisions are computed, at execution time, all events of type C *will simply be suppressed, resulting in the event stream in Figure 2b.*

Discussion of LP-based algorithm. While this LP-based algorithm is practical for the type-level problem variant, it would be impractical for the instance-level variant. Recall that the instance-level variant makes suppression decisions at the granularity of event instances. Hence for an instance-level solution, a decision variable x_i is needed for *each event instance*, and each *pattern match* will be represented as a constraint. Note that both of these two can quickly become impractically large, resulting in too big a linear program to be solved efficiently. In particular, in our small-scale

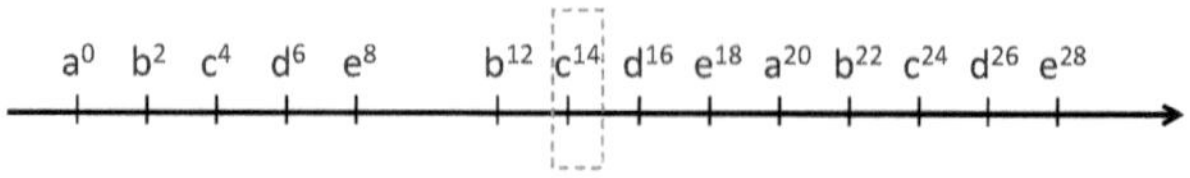

Figure 3: Motivation: suppressing c^{14} can be sub-optimal

experiment involving 50 event instances, the total time needed to solve the corresponding LP is around 16 minutes. In light of this prohibitive cost, in the next section we propose a hybrid approach that combines the type-level solution with instance-level heuristics.

5.2 Hybrid Instance-Level Algorithm

We now explore solutions to online instance-level event suppression, which can produce better utility than a type-level solution for the following reason. Recall that in the type-level solution, the expected number of pattern matches, $N_T(Q_j)$, is an average statistic produced over a long term. It is possible that over a short period of time event frequencies may deviate from their long term averages. Therefore, if the type-level solution is used as an instance-level solution, it may be sub-optimal in the short-term local windows. This observation is illustrated in the following example.

EXAMPLE 2. *We consider the same query patterns as in Example 1, now with a different event stream as shown in Figure 3. Recall that the type-level solution was to suppress event type* C.

Here, no a^{10} *arrives as expected, which is different from what the long-term statistics predict. Then when* c^{14} *arrives, there is no event of type* A *prior to* c^{14} *within* $Window(P_1) = 10$. *Hence, at time 14, no match for* $P_1 = SEQ(A, C, E)$ *can be produced even if* c^{14} *is kept. In that case, keeping* c^{14} *is essentially "free" (without any utility penalty). An optimal solution should keep* c^{14} *since it bears the potential of producing a match for* $Q_1 = SEQ(B, C, D)$. *The type-level solution in this example fails to make this optimal decision.*

The reasoning in the type-level solution, however, is not without merit. Over the long term, we expect one event of type A *prior to an event of type* C *within* $Window(P_1)$ *on average, which leads to one match of* P_1. *We also expect one match of* Q_1 *in which the same event of type* C *participates. So the type-level solution decides to suppress the event of type* C*, because the expected utility penalty of keeping it is* $w(P_1) = -10$*, which outweighs the expected utility gain* $w(Q_1) = 5$. *The particular case of* c^{14} *is different, because there is no previous event of type* A *in* c^{14}*'s active window. This deviation from the long term statistics renders the type-level solution sub-optimal.*

This example illustrates that due to fluctuations in event arrivals, the optimal type-level solution may *not* be the best decision. Instead it would be beneficial to deviate from the type-level decisions. This leads us to design an enhanced algorithm that extends type-level solution by instance-level heuristics that *"tweaks" type-level decisions based on run-time context.*

We describe our Hybrid algorithm in Algorithm 1. The overall flow of Algorithm 1 is summarized below. First it computes the expected utility gain of keeping the newly arrived event, e_i, by estimating the expected number of public query matches e_i could participate in. Then it computes the expected utility penalty if e_i is kept by estimating the expected number of private pattern matches e_i could be part of. It then decides to either suppress or keep e_i by comparing the expected utility gain and penalty.

We now describe Algorithm 1 in detail. First, the type-level decision for each event type is computed once in **Solve_LP**. Then, as each new event e_i arrives, we look up those events that have previously arrived for *partial matches* that e_i can participate in. Since

Algorithm 1 Hybrid Algorithm for Online Instance-level Suppression

```
Suppress_Hybrid_Instance_Level (history):
Suppress_T[] = Solve_LP(history)
while new_event arrives do
  utl_gain = 0
  for each partial_match of Q_j that new_event participates do
    exp_match ← Est_Match (partial_match, Suppress_T[])
    utl_gain += exp_match * w(Q_j)
  end for
  utl_penalty = 0
  for each partial_match of P_k that new_event participates do
    exp_match ← Est_Match (partial_match, Suppress_T[])
    utl_penalty += exp_match * w(P_k)
  end for
  if utl_gain + utl_penalty < 0 then
    suppress new_event
  else
    preserve new_event
  end if
end while
```

each such partial match is only a *"prefix"* of a full match, we then estimate in the subroutine **Est_Match** the number of matches for the *"suffix"* pattern from events that are expected to arrive in the future.

To produce an accurate estimate, two challenges arise: (1) to estimate the expected number of future matches of the "suffix" pattern, and (2) to estimate the event suppression decisions for the future events. We defer the first issue to Section 5.3. The second issue is also hard, because the suppression decision of a future event could affect the decisions about other future events thereafter. Our intuition, however, is that the type-level solution should provide guidance of what events tend to be suppressed in general. After all, instance-level decisions deviate from the type-level solution only when the local event distribution differs substantially from the long term average. It can be expected that suppression decisions should in general *converge to* the type-level solution. Thus we estimate the number of matches for the "suffix" of the partial match by making the assumption that events in the future will be suppressed in the same manner that the type-level solution dictates.

With that estimate in **Est_Match** we can calculate an expected utility gain for each partial match. Summing all the utility expectations gives us an estimation of the benefit of keeping the newly arrived event. We can perform a similar estimation of the total utility penalty that we expect to suffer if the new event is kept. In the end, by a simple comparison of total utility gain and utility penalty we can determine, based on the events that have arrived, whether to suppress the newly arrived event or to keep it. We use the running example in Example 3 to illustrate Algorithm 1.

EXAMPLE 3. *In Figure 4, we revisit the event stream in Example 2 while considering the same patterns. In Figure 4, event a^0 arrives first, which participates in $Q_2 = SEQ(A, B)$. According to the type-level decision, we expect events of type B will be kept in the future, with which a^0 is likely to contribute to matches of Q_2. Then the utility gain of keeping a^0 is expected to be $w(Q_2) = 20$. But a^0 also forms a partial match for $P_1 = (A, C, E)$. Suppose in the* ***Est_Match*** *procedure one match for the remaining suffix (C, E) is expected to arrive. However we reason that events of type C will most likely be suppressed, according to the type-level solution. As a result, the expected utility penalty of keeping a^0 is 0. Hence a^0 is preserved.*

Following the same logic, c^4 is suppressed and d^6, e^8 and b^{12} will be preserved. So far all the suppression decisions have been the same as the type-level solution.

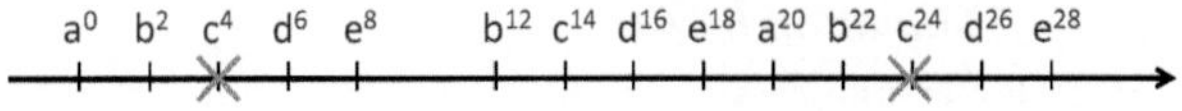

Figure 4: Running example of hybrid algorithm

Next we consider c^{14}. First, for the partial match (b^{12}, c^{14}) of Q_1 that it participates in, suppose ***Est_Match*** *again predicts that one event of type D will arrive in the remaining window, which amounts to a utility gain of 5. Then for P_1, in which c^{14} could participate, we find that from time 4 to 14, no event of type A exists, namely no partial match of P_1 that c^{14} could join with. Hence, keeping c^{14} will produce a net utility gain with no utility penalty. In this case we will keep it, which is a different decision from the type-level solution. This example manifests how the Hybrid algorithm can exploit local optimization opportunities to maximize utility.*

The upshot of this example is that the decisions converge to the type-level solution, which is an intuitive justification for our assumption that events which arrive in the future will most likely be suppressed as predicted by the type-level solution.

5.3 Pattern Match Cardinality Estimation

So far we have treated the computation of $N_T(Q_j)$, i.e., the number of matches of Q_j over a time span T in the type-level solution, and the cardinality estimation of **Est_Match** in the Hybrid solution as black boxes. Recall that the reason we need an estimate using $N_T(Q_j)$ in the type-level solution is to measure the expected utility that Q_j yields on average. The need of **Est_Match** is to weigh the utility gain and penalty of keeping the current event based on existing events in the active windows. The key issues behind both operations are essentially the same, which is to estimate the number of pattern matches over a time range T in the future.

In many applications the continuously arriving events tend to exhibit certain regular patterns [11, 20]. The problem then is to use historical data to estimate the cardinality of future pattern matches. Formally, given a pattern query $Q_j = SEQ(E_{j1}, E_{j2}, ..)$, and a time variable T, we want to estimate, using event arrival statistics, the number of matches for Q_j produced within T, henceforth referred to as $N_T(Q_j)$.

The time range T is a variable because it depends on how far apart in time the first event and the last event in the partial match are. For example, in Figure 4 of Example 3, when c^4 arrives, we need to estimate the number of events of type D that may arrive, which along with the existing partial match (b^2, c^4), can form full matches for query $Q_1 = SEQ(B, C, D)$. Because $Window(Q_1) = 10$, and the first event in the partial match is b^2, at current time 4, events of type D that arrive in the next $10-4+2 = 8$ time range can contribute to this particular match. This, then, is the value of T that we need to compute. However if the first event in the partial match is, say b^1 instead of b^2, then the window over which event of type D should be estimated is $10-4+1 = 7$, instead of 8. In other words the window of the partial suffix match is not fixed but rather varies. This makes the problem of cardinality estimation challenging (if the time range for cardinality estimation is always some fixed value then the problem can be solved by simply counting the historical data, with no computation involved).

In order for **Est_Match** to estimate the number of matches in the Hybrid solution, we can compute the corresponding value using the function $N_T(Q_j)$. Let $e_f.ts$ be the timestamp of the first event in the partial match, $e_c.ts$ be the timestamp of the current event under consideration, then the active window T can be computed as $Window(Q_j) - e_c.ts + e_f.ts$. Let Q_S be the suffix pattern that remains to be matched. Then **Est_Match** can be expressed as $N_{(Window(Q_j)-e_c.ts+e_f.ts)}(Q_S)$.

5.3.1 *Estimation by Arrival Rate*

Since Poisson process is a common approach to model arrivals in queuing theory and stream processing literature [6, 16], our first "baseline" estimation assumes that event arrivals follow the independent Poisson process. In the context of CEP, the Poisson process dictates that each type of event occurs continuously and independently of each other. Each type of event, E_i, arrives with an arrival rate λ_i, and the number of events that arrive in a fixed time period follows a Poisson distribution. In practice, when events arrive in a Poisson process, λ_i can be estimated by sampling the arriving events. Considering the fact that events may follow different distributions as time evolves, a moving sample of recently arrived events can be used to estimate the arrival rate [9].

Given the arrival rate λ_i for event type E_i, we describe how $N_T(Q_j)$ can be estimated. We first compute for each event type in Q_j the expected number of event occurrences in time range T, denoted by l_i. This can be computed as $l_i = \lambda_i T$. Further we denote by $\Gamma(Q_j)$ the multi-set of event types in Q_j, $\sigma(Q_j)$ the set of event types in Q_j, and $|Q_j|$ the pattern length of Q_j (for example, query $Q = SEQ(A, A, B)$ has $\Gamma(Q) = \{A, A, B\}$, $\sigma(Q) = \{A, B\}$, and $|Q| = 3$). Denote by $L_j = \sum_{E_i \in \sigma(Q_j)} l_i$ the expected number of occurrences of events relevant to Q_j in T. We can then estimate the expected number of query matches for Q_j in T as:

$$N_T(Q_j) = \binom{L_j}{|Q_j|} \prod_{E_i \in \Gamma(Q_j)} \frac{\lambda_i}{\sum_{E_k \in \sigma(Q_j)} \lambda_k} \qquad (8)$$

Equation (8) can be explained as follows. Given a total of L_j event occurrences in T, we need to pick $|Q_j|$ events to form one query match. Let us pick the first $|Q_j|$ events among the L_j events, and compute the probability that the first $|Q_j|$ events produce a match. Let the event at the first position of Q_j be of type E_{i_1}. The probability that the first event picked is actually of type E_{i_1} is $\frac{\lambda_{i_1}}{\sum_{E_k \in \sigma(Q_j)} \lambda_k}$, which is E_{i_1}'s arrival rate λ_{i_1} divided by the sum of arrival rates of all events in Q_j. For the second event in the sequence, the probability that it matches the event type at the second position of Q_j can be computed similarly. In the end the probability that the first $|Q_j|$ events all match the event types specified in Q_j and thus produces a query match is the cross product of individual terms, $\prod_{E_i \in \Gamma(Q_j)} \frac{\lambda_i}{\sum_{E_k \in \sigma(Q_j)} \lambda_k}$. Given that there are a total of $\binom{L_j}{|Q_j|}$ possible permutations out of L_j events and by symmetricity, the expected count of query matches can be expressed as the product of the two, thus Equation (8).

5.3.2 *Estimation by Periodicity*

Estimation using the event arrival rate is generally applicable in the sense that it does not assume dependencies between events of interest. However, in practice, event streams may exhibit certain *periodic patterns* that are highly regular. For example, in the hospital setting, a nurse may sanitize and enter patient rooms at a regular time interval, say every hour, for routine patient check-ups. Such patterns, being periodic and regular, can be leveraged to produce even more accurate pattern match cardinality estimation. We use Example 4 to illustrate this observation.

EXAMPLE 4. *Suppose we have two event types, A and B, as in Figure 5. From their arrival rates we know there will be two instances of A and B in a time period T. Knowing only this information, the best we can do is to use Equation* (8) *to produce an average estimate of the number of matches for pattern SEQ(A, B).*

If we can ascertain that events of type A and B follow certain periodic patterns, then we can do a significantly better job. Suppose A and B have the periodic pattern "A, B, A, B" as illustrated in Figure 5a. Then starting at 0 over a period of time T there are a total of three matches, namely $\{(a^1, b^2), (a^1, b^4), (a^3, b^4)\}$. *On the other hand, if the periodic pattern is of the form "B, B, A, A" as shown in Figure 5b, then even if the arrival rate of A and B stays the same over T, no match for SEQ(A, B) can be produced.*

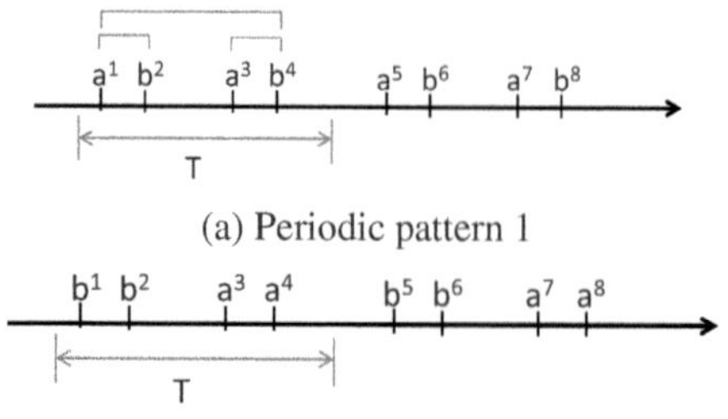

(a) Periodic pattern 1

(b) Periodic pattern 2

Figure 5: Estimating matches of SEQ(A,B) using periodic pattern

This illustrates the importance of discovering periodic patterns embedded in the event data, for if such patterns can be revealed and utilized, a much better pattern match estimate can be produced. This leads us to discover such periodic patterns in the input stream. The problem of periodicity mining has been extensively studied. In this work we adapt the techniques in [11, 20] to discover the periodic patterns.

Once such periodic patterns are discovered, we can compute the number of matches for pattern Q_j in each periodic cycle $\hat{T}$, denoted by $N_{\hat{T}}(Q_j)$. The problem that remains to be solved is to extrapolate the expected pattern match cardinality of an arbitrarily long time period T_X. More specifically, the problem can be stated as given a periodic cycle $\hat{T}$ and $N_{\hat{T}}(Q_j)$, what is the number of pattern matches of Q_j in time period T_X, or $N_{T_X}(Q_j)$? Care must be taken in calculating $N_{T_X}(Q_j)$. While it is tempting to think that if $T_X = 2\hat{T}$, then $N_{2\hat{T}}(Q_j)$ can be simply computed as $N_{2\hat{T}}(Q_j) = 2N_{\hat{T}}(Q_j)$, the analysis presented in Example 5 shows the error in this thinking.

EXAMPLE 5. *We revisit Example 4 in Figure 6. Given the periodic pattern "A, B, A, B" of stream in Figure 6a. Suppose we know that in the periodicity* $\hat{T}$, *there are two instances of A and B, respectively, denoted by* $N_{\hat{T}}(A) = N_{\hat{T}}(B) = 2$, *and three matches of pattern SEQ(A,B), or* $N_{\hat{T}}(AB) = 3$. *Then what is the number of pattern matches for SEQ(A, B) in* $2\hat{T}$? *Note that* $N_{2\hat{T}}(AB) = 2N_{\hat{T}}(AB) = 6$ *is problematic, because when the time period is extended from* $\hat{T}$ *to* $2\hat{T}$, *A-s in* T_1 *and B-s in* T_2 *also produce matches in a cross-product manner. In this particular case,* $N_{2\hat{T}}(AB) = N_{T_1}(AB) + N_{T_2}(AB) + N_{T_1}(A)N_{T_2}(B) = 3 + 3 + 2 * 2 = 10$. *Similarly, in the second periodic pattern in Figure 6b, the number of pattern matches* $N_{2\hat{T}}(AB)$ *follows the same formula:* $N_{2\hat{T}}(AB) = N_{T_1}(AB) + N_{T_2}(AB) + N_{T_1}(A)N_{T_2}(B) = 0 + 0 + 2*2 = 4$. *This corresponds to* $\{(a^3, b^5), (a^3, b^6), (a^4, b^5), (a^4, b^6)\}$.

In general, to compute $N_{n\hat{T}}(Q_j)$ given $N_{\hat{T}}(Q_j)$, where $n \in \mathbb{Z}^+$, Equation (9) can be used following the logic derived in Example 5. First, define a *continuous i-segmentation* of Q_j as a segmentation that breaks the event sequence of Q_j into i non-empty segments (for example, 2-segmentations of $Q = SEQ(A, B, C, D)$ include (A/BCD), (AB/CD), and (ABC/D)). Each segment in an i-segmentation is referred to as a *chunk* (for example, A and BCD are two chunks in the segmentation (A/BCD)). We denote all continuous i-segmentations of Q_j by $M_i(Q_j)$. Let $m = (c_1, c_2, ...c_i)$ be one such segmentation in $M_i(Q_j)$, where c_k is the k-th chunk in m. Let $D(m) = \prod_{c_k \in m} N_{\hat{T}}(c_k)$ be the cross-product of the count statistics of chunk c_k. Then the estimation of $N_{n\hat{T}}(Q_j)$ can be written as:

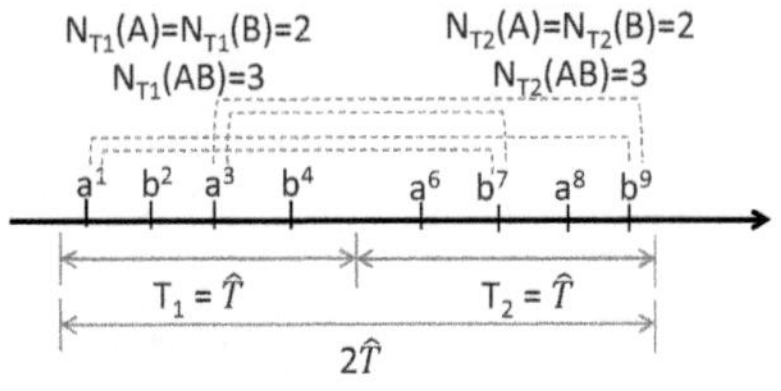

(a) Periodic pattern 1

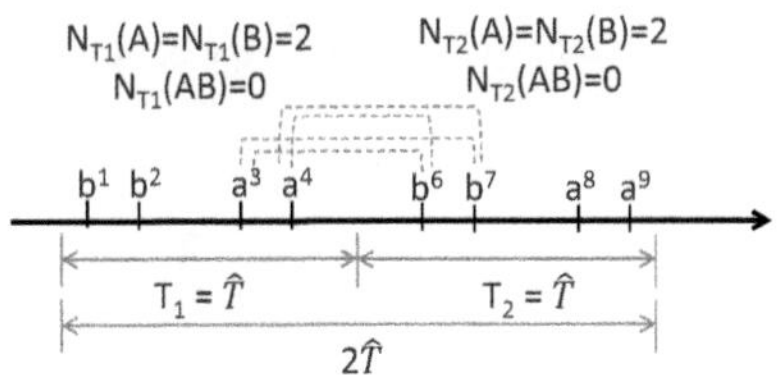

(b) Periodic pattern 2

Figure 6: Estimating via periodic pattern for time $2\hat{T}$

$$N_{n\hat{T}}(Q_j) = \sum_{i=1}^{n} \binom{n}{i} \sum_{m \in M_i(Q_j)} D(m) = \sum_{i=1}^{n} \binom{n}{i} \sum_{m \in M_i(Q)} \prod_{c_k \in m} N_{\hat{T}}(c_k) \tag{9}$$

So far we have only considered estimating pattern matches in a time period that is an exact multiple of a periodic cycle $\hat{T}$. Next we extend the logic to the general case. To estimate pattern match cardinality of a time period that is less than a full periodic cycle, we can detect the number of pattern matches within that time period from the known periodic pattern. To handle a time period that is longer than $\hat{T}$ but not an exact multiple of $\hat{T}$, we first estimate the utility within the time of a multiple of $\hat{T}$ using Equation (9), and then detect the number of matches within the remaining time period using the periodic pattern. Finally we combine the two parts of estimation to obtain a final estimate.

6. EXPERIMENTAL EVALUATION

We have implemented our proposed algorithms on the HP CHAOS stream engine [14], and used the OptimJ [2] module as the linear program solver. All experiments were conducted on a machine with an Intel Core 2 Duo 3.0GHz CPU and 3.2GB of RAM running Windows 7 and Java JRE 6.

Our experiments were conducted using both a real-world workload and a synthetic workload. The real-world workload was based on anonymized event streams collected from the University of Massachusetts Memorial Hospital where HyReminder is deployed.

In our real workload, public query patterns were created when HyReminder was developed from 2010 to 2012, following hygiene regulations established for US hospitals [7]. Examples of such queries include Q1, Q2, Q3 discussed earlier. As part of our new investigation, private patterns were constructed in consultation with domain experts familiar with the hospital application and privacy regulations. For example, P1 discussed earlier is a private query. A doctor checking-out some sensitive equipment (e.g. External Defibrillators) before entering a patient's room is another private query. We summarize the characteristics of these query patterns in Table 2.

In our experimental system, weights of query patterns were determined through a process in which we asked the domain experts the basic question "compared to a query match for Q_i, what is the relative importance of a match for Q_j (or P_k)." Suppose the weight of Q_i is initially set to w. For a private query P_k, if we determine that the benefit of reporting two matches of Q_i would negate the

Parameter	Value range
Pattern length	2 to 5
Time-based window size	1 min to 90 min
Weight of public patterns	1, 2, 3
Weight of private patterns	-1, -2, -3

Table 2: Pattern query characteristics

potential damage of revealing one match of P_k, we can then set weight of P_k to be $-2w$. Weights of public patterns can be determined similarly. This process is intuitive given the linearity of our objective function, and is easily comprehensible to non-technical users.

In our approach an important question arises as to how to identify all possible private queries a priori. In our hospital application, where we only have a small number of *event-types*, we can afford to exhaustively enumerate possible event-type combination to ensure that no bad queries are overlooked. Although this type of simplicity is not isolated (we know a few other CEP applications used in practice that can encode the domain of interest using a small number of event-types), we think it is an interesting area for future work to understand how to scale this process to problems with a large number of event types, possibly through some automatic process.

The synthetic event stream was produced with a parameterized *degree of periodicity*, where periodicity 1 corresponds to a perfectly periodic stream, while periodicity 0 means a perfectly random stream. We produced the synthetic stream by first generating a perfectly periodic stream. We then added "noise" to this stream by replacing events in the stream using different events with random timestamps and event-types drawn from Possion processes. In that way, an event stream with degree of periodicity $\gamma\%$ will have $\gamma\%$ of events generated through the addition of noise.

6.1 Algorithms Compared

We compare algorithms proposed in this work, namely the type-level LP-based solution (labeled as "Type-lvl"), the Hybrid solution with independent Poisson arrival estimation, ("Hybrid-I"), and the Hybrid solution with periodicity estimation ("Hybrid-P"). We also implemented two alternative event suppression solutions, namely the Hybrid-optimal algorithm ("Hybrid-opt") and the Greedy algorithm ("Greedy"), to compare against our proposed algorithms, in order to shed light on the performance of our algorithms.

Hybrid optimal. The first baseline approach is the so-called Hybrid-optimal. Recall that one key problem that we address in this work is to estimate the cardinality of pattern matches in the future. In this algorithm, we assume the Hybrid-optimal algorithm has perfect statistics, that is, it magically knows the actual number of pattern matches in the future. This can be implemented by looking at the events in the future and counting the number of matches. Comparing our approach with such an "oracle" algorithm that essentially "cheats" helps us to understand the utility loss due to inaccurate match cardinality estimations.

Global optimal. Note that there is still a gap between Hybrid-Optimal and global optimal. As such, we are interested in finding the size of this gap to establish a real utility upper-bound. For that, we randomly sampled a small number of events and used an LP-solver to solve the corresponding instance-level LP. This turns out to be very expensive; a stream of 50 events took about 16 minutes to finish. Over randomly sampled small-scale streams, we found a very small utility gap (2-4%) between the Hybrid-Optimal and the LP-solved global optimal. Given this result we regard Hybrid-Optimal as our approximate utility upper-bound.

Greedy solution. In addition, we experimented with a greedy algorithm that detects and eliminates breaches in a *detecting-then-removing* fashion [28]. Specifically, for each event e_i, it calculates

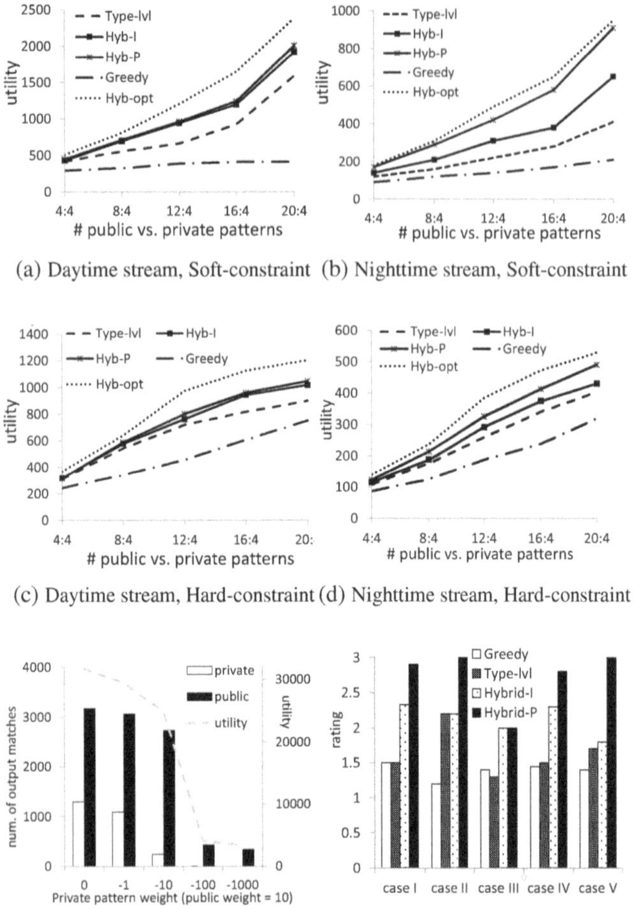

(a) Daytime stream, Soft-constraint (b) Nighttime stream, Soft-constraint

(c) Daytime stream, Hard-constraint (d) Nighttime stream, Hard-constraint

(e) Vary private query weights (f) User study results

Figure 7: Performance on hospital workload

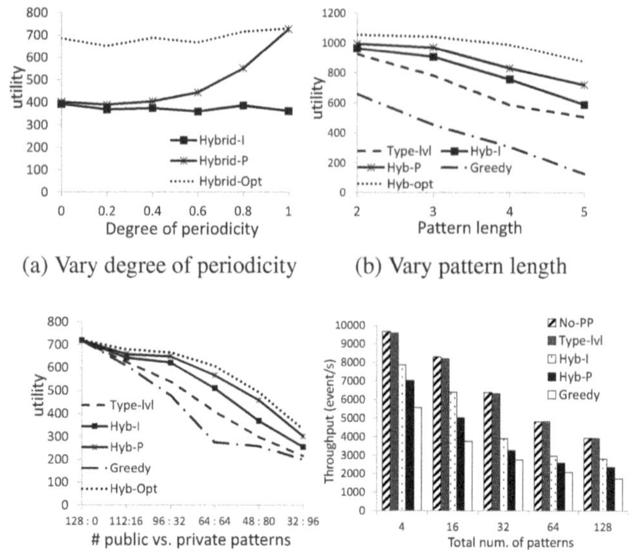

(a) Vary degree of periodicity (b) Vary pattern length

(c) Vary public/private patterns (d) Throughput

Figure 8: Performance on synthetic workload

the utility gain of public query matches that e_i triggers, as well as the utility loss of private query matches that e_i triggers over the stream of events output for public query matches. Both utility gain and loss are calculated using currently detected matches *without* estimating the effect of e_i on future matches. The greedy approach would suppress e_i if the utility loss outweighs the utility gain, and keeps e_i otherwise.

6.2 Experiments on Healthcare Workload

We observe that events of the health care workload during the day are dominated by random healthcare worker activities, which tend to be aperiodic. However, events during the night are more regular with a higher degree of periodicity, which may be due to the fact that at night nurses on duty typically only conduct routine check-ups in every room at regular intervals. We thus separate the stream into two sub-streams, one with day-time events and the other with night-time events.

Number of patterns vs. utility, using Soft-constraint. In this experiment, we have 4 private queries while varying the number of public queries from 4 to 20, over a stream of 20,000 events extracted from real stream trace collected during the daytime. Figure 7a shows the utility gain over the day-time stream. Clearly, Hybrid-opt has best utility gains. Our Hybrid-P approach comes second, slightly outperforming Hybrid-I. Both hybrid algorithms consistently outperform the Type-level algorithm by around 30%, and Hybrid-P outperforms the Greedy algorithm by up to 4x. This underlines the effectiveness of our Hybrid algorithms.

Figure 7b shows the utility of the same experiment using a stream of 10,000 events extracted from a night-time stream trace. In Figure 7b Hybrid-P produces 40% more utility than Hybrid-I. Note it has only 10% less utility than the Hybrid-opt. This is encouraging, because it shows that if the event stream exhibits periodic patterns, then our periodicity based cardinality estimation can capture these patterns and produce accurate estimations that ultimately lead to better utility-preserving decisions.

Number of patterns vs. utility, using Hard-constraint. We have mentioned that the algorithms considered in this paper are applicable to the Hard-constraint setting for strict privacy guarantees, by setting private weights to negative infinity and considering positive utility contribution of public queries in making suppression decisions. To explore this we conducted an additional set of experiments, where we used the same hospital data as in the previous experiment, but set all private pattern weights to minus infinity. This mimics a more strict environment where no private match is ever produced.

Figures 7c and 7d show similar trends for the Hard-constraint model — the Hybrid approaches also outperform alternative algorithms here. This suggests that Hybrid algorithms can be an attractive solution even when strict privacy guarantees are needed.

Pattern weight vs. number of output. In this experiment we vary weights of 4 private patterns from 0 to -1000, while fixing weights of 10 public pattern at 10. Results are reported using the same daytime stream used previously. Figure 7e shows the number of pattern matches produced by our Hybrid-P approach as well as the corresponding utility. As the weights become more negative, the number of private matches being output decreases. Observe that when the negative weight has significantly larger absolute value than the positive weight, no private match will be output at all. This also shows that our solutions can be configured with extremely low negative weights to solve the hard-constraint problem.

A user study on algorithm effectiveness. We invited 14 users, all familiar with HyReminder, to evaluate the output produced by the four algorithms considered in this work. We asked users to rate the effectiveness of algorithms by inspecting query matches produced by each algorithm, taking into account the perceived usefulness of public matches and potential damaging effects of private matches.

We created five test-cases for users to judge in the following manner. For each test-case, we randomly selected a subsequence of 100 events (all about a single healthcare worker) from the event trace. We also randomly picked 7 public patterns and 2 private patterns. We executed four algorithms using that workload, highlighted any remaining public and private query matches, and asked users to inspect the results. Users had their own intuitive ideas about the relative importance of the queries, but were not given the exact weights used by the system. The users were asked to rate the output of each algorithm as "bad" (score = 1), "fair" (2) or "good" (3), based on their subjective judgment of how well each algorithm makes the tradeoff between reporting useful public queries and hiding risky private queries.

Figure 7f summarizes the average score of each algorithm in five test-cases. Hybrid-P has an average score of 2.74 and ranks the highest across all test-cases. In test-case II and V, every user rated it as "good". Hybrid-I scores 2.12 on average, which is the second-best based on user ratings, while Greedy ranks the lowest with a score of 1.38. In summary, results of this user study are consistent with our utility-function based evaluation, confirming the effectiveness of our approach in capturing user's preferences, and affirming the usefulness of Hybrid algorithms.

6.3 Experiments on Synthetic Workload

Synthetic pattern queries were generated by randomly picking pattern lengths, event types, window sizes and weights using values listed in Table 2. For each experiment, numbers are reported using an averaged over 20 randomly generated workloads.

Periodicity degree vs. utility. Now we assess the relationship between the degree of periodicity of a stream and the resulting utility. Figure 8a compares algorithms with varying degrees of periodicity. We used 96 public patterns and 32 private patterns in this experiment, and executed algorithms over a stream of 10,000 events. With no periodicity Hybrid-P and Hybrid-I yield almost the same utility. As we move from a less periodic stream to a more periodic one, Hybrid-P achieves better utility preservation. The utility gain of Hybrid-P in the case of perfect periodicity (periodicity degree = 1) is almost 2x than that of Hybrid-I. It is also worth noting that even for streams with low degree of periodicity, say 0.2, there is a positive, albeit slight, utility advantage of using periodicity based cardinality estimation. For the remainder of experiments we fix the degree of periodicity at 0.4, a middle ground value.

Pattern length vs. utility. Next, we vary pattern complexity by changing pattern length from 2 to 5 and compare the utility of different algorithms. For each pattern length, we executed 96 public queries and 32 private queries over a stream of 10,000 events. As we can see in Figure 8b the utility drops as the pattern length increases. This is because the number of matches decreases when the pattern length increases. Our proposed Hybrid-P achieves only 12% less utility than the Hybrid-Opt, and outperforms all other approaches in this experiment.

Number of public/private patterns vs. utility. In Figure 8c we vary the ratio between the number of private patterns versus public patterns, while fixing the total number of patterns at 128, and report utility over a random stream with 10,000 events. As we can see, when there is no private pattern, each approach produces the same utility, as no event suppression is needed. As the number of private patterns increases, the proposed Hybrid-P and Hybrid-I outperform all other alternatives except for the oracle version Hybrid-Opt.

Number of patterns vs. throughput. Finally, we conduct a throughput test by increasing the total number of patterns. The ratio between the number of private patterns versus public patterns was fixed at 1:3. Figure 8d shows that the Hybrid-P algorithm attains at least 55% of the throughput of a baseline system where no privacy preservation is performed (labeled as "No-PP"). Its relatively efficiency and superior utility makes it an appealing approach. We also note that the Type-level approach achieves only slightly less throughput than No-PP. Considering the fact that Type-level significantly outperforms the Greedy approach in utility, it may also be an attractive alternative when system resources is a concern.

7. RELATED WORK

Complex Event Processing (CEP). CEP technologies exhibit sophisticated capabilities for pattern matching in high volume event streams [1, 5, 22, 29]. However, privacy-aware CEP is an emerging problem that has not been well studied. To the best of our knowledge the work closest to us is [15]. However the focus of [15] is on theoretical properties of the particular hard-constraint variant. It does not present solutions or empirical studies for the more general soft-constraint variant.

Privacy for data streams. Authors in [8, 31] consider k-anonymity in streaming data, where the aim is to generalize clusters of tuples into equivalence classes of size at least k. Differential privacy and its streaming variants (e.g., [10, 23]) have been proposed as a rigorous alternative. However, their applications are mostly limited to statistical aggregates (e.g., SUM query), and are not directly applicable to CEP pattern matching operation. Because many CEP applications are interested in individual pattern matches, and adding noise to individual matches (as opposed to aggregates) differentially privately can easily render the result useless.

In numerical streams, correlation attacks are studied in [18] and random noises are used to mitigate such attacks. Recently, authors in [13] consider the problem of filtering sensitive user location data in a stream to preserve privacy. These techniques, while useful for their respective purposes, are not applicable as they do not consider CEP pattern query semantics nor the utility optimization objective.

Hiding patterns in sequence databases. The problem of sequential pattern hiding was investigated in [4, 12] for static sequence databases. Their approaches operate on a set of sequences which are independent from each other. While in our CEP context, the single input stream contains potentially endless events that are temporally correlated. Therefore their approaches cannot be applied to solve our problem.

Combining global and local prediction. Lastly, the general idea of combining "global" (type-level) prediction and "local" (instance-level) prediction in our Hybrid algorithm has been applied to problems in completely different contexts, such as to predict the movement of mobile users [19], and to predict branches in the computer architecture literature [30].

8. CONCLUSIONS

In this paper we study the problem of utility-maximizing event stream suppression. We show that the Hybrid approach that combines LP-based solution and periodicity-based cardinality estimation is effective in maximizing utility while taking into account privacy penalties. in at least one real world scenario and many more synthetically generated datasets. Leveraging periodicity information for purposes beyond privacy (e.g., CEP query optimization) seems to be interesting areas for future research.

9. REFERENCES

[1] Microsoft StreamInsight: http://msdn.microsoft.com/en-us/sqlserver/ee476990.aspx.

[2] OptimJ: ateji.com/optimj.

[3] StreamBase: www.streambase.com.

[4] O. Abul, F. Bonchi, and F. Giannotti. Hiding sequential and spatiotemporal patterns. In *IEEE Trans. Knowl. Data Eng.*, volume 22, pages 1709–1723, 2010.
[5] J. Agrawal, Y. Diao, D. Gyllstrom, and N. Immerman. Efficient pattern matching over event streams. In *SIGMOD*, 2008.
[6] B. Babcock, S. Babu, R. Motwani, and M. Datar. Chain: Operator scheduling for memory minimization in data stream systems. In *SIGMOD*, 2003.
[7] J. M. Boyce and D. Pittet. Guideline for hand hygiene in healthcare settings. *MMWR Recomm Rep.*, 2002.
[8] C.-Y. Chow, M. F. Mokbel, and T. He. A privacy-preserving location monitoring system for wireless sensor networks. *IEEE Trans. Mob. Comput.*, 10(1):94–107, 2011.
[9] G. Cormode, S. Muthukrishnan, K. Yi, and Q. Zhang. Optimal sampling from distributed streams. In *PODS*, 2010.
[10] C. Dwork, M. Naor, T. Pitassi, G. N. Rothblum, and S. Yekhanin. Pan-private streaming algorithms. In *ICS*, 2010.
[11] M. G. Elfeky, W. G. Aref, and A. K. Elmagarmid. Stagger: Periodicity mining of data streams using expanding sliding windows. In *Proceedings of ICDM*, 2006.
[12] A. Gkoulalas-Divanis and G. Loukides. Revisiting sequential pattern hiding to enhance utility. In *ACM SIGKDD*, pages 1316–1324, 2011.
[13] M. Goetz, S. Nath, and J. Gehrke. Maskit: Privately releasing user context streams for personalized mobile applications. In *Proceedings of SIGMOD*, 2012.
[14] C. Gupta and S. W. et al. Chaos: A data stream analysis architecture for enterprise applications. In *CEC*, 2009.
[15] Y. He, S. Barman, D. Wang, and J. Naughton. On the complexity of privacy-preserving complex event processing. In *Proceedings of PODS*, 2011.
[16] Q. Jiang and S. Chakravarthy. Queueing analysis of relational operators for continuous data streams. In *Proceedings of CIKM*, 2003.
[17] K. LeFevre, D. J. DeWitt, and R. Ramakrishnan. Incognito: efficient full-domain k-anonymity. In *Proceedings of SIGMOD*, 2005.
[18] F. Li, J. Sun, S. Papadimitriou, G. A. Mihaila, and I. Stanoi. Hiding in the crowd: Privacy preservation on evolving streams through correlation tracking. In *ICDE*, 2007.
[19] T. Liu, P. Bahl, and I. Chlamtac. Mobility modeling, location tracking, and trajectory prediction in wireless atm networks. *IEEE Journal on Selected Areas in Communications*, 1998.
[20] H. J. Loether and D. G. McTavish. *Descriptive and inferential statistics, an introduction.* 1993.
[21] A. Machanavajjhala, D. Kifer, J. Gehrke, and M. Venkitasubramaniam. l-diversity: Privacy beyond k-anonymity. In *Proceedings of ICDE*, 2006.
[22] Y. Mei and S. Madden. Zstream: A cost-based query processor for adaptively detecting composite events. In *SIGMOD*, 2009.
[23] V. Rastogi and S. Nath. Differentially private aggregation of distributed time-series with transformation and encryption. *SIGMOD*, 2010.
[24] R. E. Steuer. *Multiple Criteria Optimization: Theory, Computations, and Application.* 1986.
[25] L. Sweeney. k-anonymity: a model for protecting privacy. *Int. J. Uncertain. Fuzziness Knowl.-Based Syst.*, 10, 2002.
[26] J. Tan. Inapproximability of maximum weighted edge biclique and its applications. In *Proceedings of TAMC*, 2008.
[27] D. Wang, E. Rundensteiner, and H. Wang. Active complex event processing: Applications in realtime health care. In *Proceedings of VLDB*, 2010.
[28] T. Wang and L. Liu. Butterfly: Protecting output privacy in stream mining. In *Proceedings of ICDE*, 2008.
[29] E. Wu, Y. Diao, and S. Rizvi. High-performance complex event processing over streams. In *SIGMOD*, 2006.
[30] T.-Y. Yeh and Y. N. Patt. Two-level adaptive training branch prediction. In *Proceedings of MICRO*, 1991.
[31] B. Zhou, Y. Han, J. Pei, B. Jiang, Y. Tao, and Y. Jia. Continuous privacy preserving publishing of data streams. In *Proceedings of EDBT*, 2009.

APPENDIX

A. PROOFS FOR HARDNESS RESULTS

Proof of Theorem 1.

PROOF. We reduce the problem of *Maximum Weighted Edge Biclique (MWEB)* [26] to offline instance-level event suppression problem with soft-constraint. In the decision version of MWEB, given a bipartite graph $G = (V_1, V_2, H)$ where edges take on both positive and negative weights $W(h) \in \mathbb{R}, h \in H$, the problem is to determine if there exists a bipartite subgraph whose sum of edge weights is no less than a given number U. For each vertex $v \in V_1 \cup V_2$, construct an event type E_v and one event e_v of type E_v. The input event sequence S is a randomly ordered sequence that consists of one e_v for all $v \in V_1 \cup V_2$. For each edge $h = (u, v) \in H$, if the edge weight is positive $W(h) > 0$, we build two public queries $Q_h = SEQ(E_u, E_v)$ and $Q'_h = SEQ(E_v, E_u)$, both with utility weight $W(h)$, and infinite window size. Similarly if the edge weight is negative, we build two private queries $P_h = SEQ(E_u, E_v)$ and $P'_h = SEQ(E_v, E_u)$ also with utility weight $W(h)$ and infinite window size. We first show that if there is a solution to MWEB with edge weight no less than U, then there exists a solution to the event suppression problem that has utility no less than U. Let $G' = \{V'_1, V'_2, H'\}$ be the subgraph of G that has weight C, where $C \geq U$. We can preserve every event e_v if $v \in V'_1 \cup V'_2$. The set of query matches would correspond directly to the set of edges H' in G', thus producing a total utility of C. Since we know $C \geq U$, this proves the forward direction. Now we need to show that if there is a solution to the event suppression problem with utility at least U, there is a bi-clique in the original graph that has an edge weight at least U. Let $T = e_v$ be the set of events preserved in event suppression solution. The subgraph G_T of G induced by $V = \{v : e_v \in T\}$ has a one-to-one correspondence between an edge in G_T and a query match in the solution T. The edge weight of G_T is thus the same as the utility of the solution T, which is no less than U. This completes our proof. □

Proof of Theorem 2.

PROOF. It was shown in [26] that there exists a constant $\epsilon > 0$, such that unless RP = NP, the MWEB problem cannot be approximated within a factor of n^ϵ in polynomial time, where n is the number of vertices in the graph. We note that the reduction from MWEB above is value preserving. That is, if a MWEB problem instance has a weight value of U, then the corresponding event suppression problem we construct also has a utility value of U. We show that the soft-constraint variant cannot be approximated within n^ϵ by contradiction. Suppose there exists an polynomial time algorithm that approximates the offline variant within a factor of n^ϵ. Then we would have found an algorithm that approximates MWEB within n^ϵ. This contradicts with the inapproximability result in [26] under standard complexity assumptions, thus proves the inapproximability of the offline soft-constraint variant of the event suppression problem. □

Proof of Theorem 3.

PROOF. We show this problem variant is NP-hard using a proof similar to the proof in Theorem 1, which is for the offline instance-level variant. In proving the hardness of offline instance-level variant, each problem instance we construct for each instance of MWEB problem has exactly one event instance per event type. In this particular case, an instance-level solution is also a type-level solution, and vice versa. Thus, using a similar proof, we can also show the hardness of the offline type-level variant. □

$\mathcal{E}$-Matching: Event Processing over Noisy Sequences in Real Time

Zheng Li
University of Massachusetts, Lowell
zli@cs.uml.edu

Tingjian Ge
University of Massachusetts, Lowell
ge@cs.uml.edu

Cindy X. Chen
University of Massachusetts, Lowell
cchen@cs.uml.edu

ABSTRACT

Regular expression matching over sequences in real time is a crucial task in complex event processing on data streams. Given that such data sequences are often noisy and errors have temporal and spatial correlations, performing regular expression matching effectively and efficiently is a challenging task. Instead of the traditional approach of learning a distribution of the stream first and then processing queries, we propose a new approach that efficiently does the matching based on an error model. In particular, our algorithms are based on the realistic Markov chain error model, and report all matching paths to trace relevant basic events that trigger the matching. This is much more informative than a single matching path. We also devise algorithms to efficiently return only top-*k* matching paths, and to handle negations in an extended regular expression. Finally, we conduct a comprehensive experimental study to evaluate our algorithms using real datasets.

Categories and Subject Descriptors

H.2.4 [**Database Management**]: Systems – *query processing.*

Keywords

Noisy stream; Complex event processing; Pattern matching.

1. INTRODUCTION

We live in an interesting world in the so-called "big data" era, where data is streaming to us at an unprecedented rate. Such data is generated by diverse sources such as smartphones (e.g., locations and health sensing), web logs, social networks, medical devices, highway sensors, and scientific experiments, to name a few. It is, then, really up to us to effectively use this data. Much of this data is produced at a high rate by unreliable devices, is often communicated through noisy channels (e.g., wireless networks), or is derived using incomplete knowledge based on raw data (e.g., trajectory mapping [24] and forecasting [4]). Consequently, noise and incompleteness in data are the norm rather than the exception.

Some queries are sensitive to the noise or uncertainty in data. Event pattern matching is such a type of query. Fundamentally, event queries map the observed data or events to characters in some alphabet, and then resort to regular expression matching [19, 1, 27] for finding patterns in a dynamically growing string that corresponds to the original stream. Clearly, if some crucial characters in the sequence are different from what they should be due to noise or incompleteness, an exact regular expression matching will fail to find the pattern. Let us look at some examples.

Example 1. Real-time ECG monitoring of heart disease patients has long been a critical method in cardiology [10, 11]. Devices such as Holter monitors are commonly used in practice. Recently, even iPhone has incorporated real-time ECG monitoring [3]. These real-time monitoring devices inevitably collect a noisy version of the original signal and the wireless communication to the central server can further introduce noise. Nonetheless, real-time ECG data is precious for doctors and nurses to catch emergent dangerous situations of patients and save their lives. Interestingly, we can use regular expressions (with some extensions as described below) to model common dangerous patterns.

Figure 1 (a) and (b) show two emergent conditions: Atrial Flutter (AF) and Premature Ventricular Contraction (PVC), respectively. As in a public dataset [31], the ECG time series can be digitized at 360 samples per second. Suppose that we discretize the signals into integer levels $[-6, 6]$, with 0 being the bottom level of the sawtooth waves in Figure 1(a) and the middle level in Figure 1(b), -6 being the lowest voltage level in Figure 1(b), and 6 being the highest level. Then the ECG signals become a sequence of characters with an alphabet $\{-6, -5, \ldots, -1, 0, 1, \ldots, 6\}$.

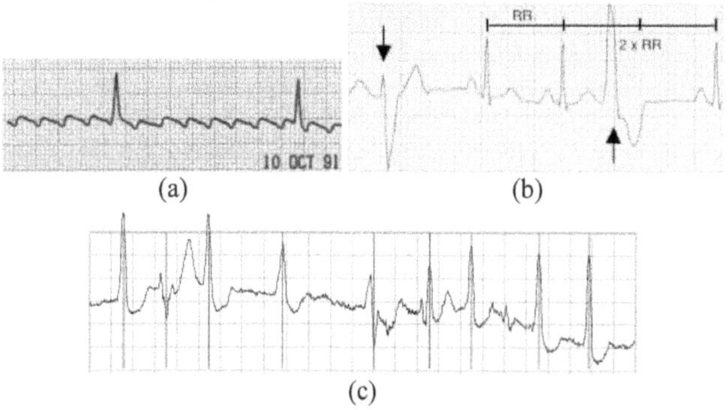

Figure 1. Two abnormal ECG patterns [30] and an actual ECG piece with noise. (a) Atrial Flutter (AF). It has a signature "sawtooth" pattern, showing many sawtooth-like waves between two peaks. (b) Premature Ventricular Contraction (PVC). The arrows indicate two different kinds of abnormal shapes. (c) A noisy ECG piece from a real dataset [31].

For AF (Fig. 1a), we can use the regular expression pattern:

$$r_1 = (5|6)0[(\bar{5}\bar{6})1(\bar{5}\bar{6})0]^{3+}(5|6) \quad (1)$$

where $5|6$ denotes either 5 or 6, $\bar{5}\bar{6}$ is a negation indicating that neither 5 nor 6 can occur in that position, and p^{3+} denotes that pattern p appears 3 or more times. Indeed, the first symbol $5|6$ indicates a peak signal (called R peak) in Figure 1(a), followed by a low value 0, and then three or more occurrences of the pattern $(\bar{5}\bar{6})1(\bar{5}\bar{6})0$, each of which is for one sawtooth wave. Finally another R peak is seen. The negations $\bar{5}\bar{6}$ are to ensure that we see enough sawtooth waves before the R peak.

For example, suppose a snippet of the observed ECG stream is $s = 5101010 \ldots 15$, where "..." refers to five repetitions of "10". Then there is an *exact* match of r_1 in s, where the first and last 5 in s matches the two $5|6$ sub-patterns in r_1 (two R peaks), respec-

SIGMOD'13, June 22–27, 2013, New York, New York, USA.

tively. Note that our semantics allows *interleaving irrelevant (i.e., non-matching) characters* in s, subject to a *window* constraint. For instance, the first and last 1's in s do not match any sub-patterns in r_1, and the window parameter w here can be 1 second, i.e., r_1 has to occur in the stream within a time window of 1 second (from the first to the last matching characters).

For PVC (Fig. 1b), we use the pattern:

$$r_2 = [-6\ (3|4|5)]\ |\ [6\ (-3|-4|-5)] \quad (2)$$

for a small window size (e.g., 0.3 seconds). r_2 matches two types of PVC patterns: a low valley (-6) followed by a small peak ($3|4|5$), or a high peak (6) followed by a valley ($-3|-4|-5$), illustrated in Fig. 1 (b) by the two arrows, respectively (r_2, for example, does not occur in the stream snippet s above). Several PVCs in a row become a form of ventricular tachycardia, which is much more dangerous. This can be detected by a pattern that consists of r_2 repeated multiple times within some time window.

For clarity of exposition, we show the clear-cut signals in Figure 1 (a, b). In reality, due to the noisy nature of both sensing devices and wireless communication, the received signals will be more like Figure 1 (c), which comes from a real dataset [31] (notice the baseline drift [29], etc.). We have to match r_1 and r_2 approximately or probabilistically, which is the focus of this work.

Example 2. Event pattern matching is fairly common in many data stream applications. As also discussed in [14], in a shopping mall, customers' locations (estimated from their smartphones' GPS or WiFi) combined with a map [25] give a noisy stream of each customer's visit sequence. This provides valuable information for business intelligence. For example, the shoe department manager at Macy's would like to find a pattern that "*a customer visited other shoe stores in the mall as well as Macy's and eventually decided to buy shoes at Macy's*". Suppose there are three shoe stores S_1, S_2, and S_3. Then we can use the pattern:

$$r_3 = [((S_1|S_2|S_3)^+M)|(M(S_1|S_2|S_3)^+)]\ B \quad (3)$$

where M is the event that the customer visited Macy's shoe department, and B is the event that she bought shoes at Macy's. Similarly, we can use:

$$r_4 = (\bar{S_1}\bar{S_2}\bar{S_3})N(\bar{S_1}\bar{S_2}\bar{S_3})B \quad (4)$$

to match the event that a customer did not go to any of the three shoe stores, but went to Nordstrom's shoe section (N), and eventually decided to buy shoes at Macy's. Such pattern queries also apply to RFID deployments in supermarkets to detect shoppers' shopping paths [13]. Approximate or probabilistic matching is required (otherwise we may miss true occurrences of a pattern).

There is previous work on approximate regular expression matching (ARM) based on the edit distance threshold (e.g., [18]). However, ARM does not consider the *correlation of errors* between neighboring characters of a string, which is common for data streams since those errors are likely caused by the same factor or the same source at some point in time. In Example 1, major noise sources of ECG include baseline drift and muscle tremor [29], both of which create local positive correlation of noise. Moreover, wireless communication also introduces temporal correlation of noise in the received streams [21]. Likewise, in Example 2, GPS and other positioning mechanisms are known to have temporal and spatial correlations of errors [23]. In our position tracking application, spatial correlations also translate to temporal correlations in data streams as a person/object moves around.

With such positive error correlations among neighboring characters, the matching probability can still be relatively high even though there are a large number of character mismatches. ARM, which is equivalent to assuming independent errors among characters, will either reject such matches, or accept them but cannot avoid many false positives due to the low threshold.

Furthermore, since there are often many matching paths (due to "or" and Kleene star operators), our probabilistic approach can return an aggregate probability (i.e., the probability that at least one of the matching paths is true), whereas the ARM approach is only concerned with one minimum edit distance path. Finally, unlike ARM, we extend regular expressions to handle negations in patterns, mixing in irrelevant events, and window constraints, which are essential for event pattern matching in data streams.

1.1 Our Contributions

We formulate the problem by first introducing the concepts of *extended* regular expressions (ERE) and *error models*, which are used to define the $\mathcal{E}$-Matching and top-k $\mathcal{E}$-Matching problems (**Sec. 2**). We modify and augment Thompson's automaton, and discuss a Markov chain error model (**Sec. 3**). We then present our main algorithm for $\mathcal{E}$-Matching (**Sec. 4**). Unlike most previous work, we do not attempt to first learn a probabilistic distribution of the sequence stream and then process queries over the distribution. Instead, we resort to an error model which is learned offline and is more stable than the dynamic data stream. In real time, our algorithm returns all matching paths with significant probabilities. These matching paths provide a lineage for users to trace back the basic events and tuples in the stream that cause the match.

However, when there is a large number of matching paths, it is desirable and much more efficient to return only the top-k paths with the highest probabilities. Thus, we devise a top-k matching algorithm, and quantify the average-case complexity regarding the number of matching paths to keep in the system (**Sec. 5**). Furthermore, we study *negations* in patterns, which are non-trivial and require our algorithm to maintain a "state vector" of error level probabilities (**Sec. 6**). Finally, we perform a comprehensive empirical study using real datasets to verify our approach (**Sec. 7**).

2. PROBLEM FORMULATION AND QUERY SEMANTICS

2.1 Preliminaries

We give some brief background on Markov chains. A Markov chain $\mathcal{M}$ is a discrete time stochastic process defined over a set of states S in terms of a matrix P of *transition probabilities* [17]. P has one row and one column for each state in S. The entry $\mathrm{P}[i,j]$ in the matrix (i-th row and j-th column) is the probability that the next state will be j, given that the current state is i. Thus, for all $i \in S$, $\sum_j \mathrm{P}[i,j] = 1$. An important property of a Markov chain is the *memorylessness property*: the future behavior of a Markov chain depends only on its current state, and not on how it arrived at the present state. If we denote by X_t the state of the Markov chain at time t, the above property can be stated formally as:

$$\mathbf{Pr}[X_{t+1} = j | X_0 = i_0, X_1 = i_1, \dots, X_t = i] = \mathbf{Pr}[X_{t+1} = j | X_t = i] = \mathrm{P}[i,j]$$

The *α-step transition probability* is defined as $\Pr[X_\alpha = j | X_0 = i]$, which can be easily shown to be $\mathrm{P}^\alpha[i,j]$, i.e., the i-th row and j-th column entry of matrix P^α (P to the α'th power).

Let $|S| = n$ (i.e., n states). Then a *stationary distribution* of the Markov chain is a probability distribution (over the states) $\vec{\lambda} = (\vec{\lambda}[1], \dots, \vec{\lambda}[n])$ such that $\vec{\lambda} = \vec{\lambda}\mathrm{P}$. Intuitively, if the Markov chain is in the stationary distribution at step t, it remains so at step $t+1$. Thus $\vec{\lambda}$ is the steady-state behavior of the chain. A finite, irreducible, and aperiodic Markov chain must have a unique stationary distribution. We refer the reader to [17] for details.

2.2 Problem Formulation

We are given an observed (noisy) sequence $o = o[1], o[2], \dots \dots$ where each character $o[i] \in \Sigma$, the *alphabet*. We use the terms *sequence*, *string*, and *stream* interchangeably, and use *character* and *letter* interchangeably in this work. Each $o[i]$ has a tag $t[i]$, also written as $t(o[i])$. If $t[i]$ is the timestamp when $o[i]$ is generated, we get *time-window* semantics. If $t[i]$ is a counter (i.e., $t[i] = i$), we get *count-window* semantics. The sequence o has increasing tags. For brevity, we sometimes write $o[i]$ as o_i.

We say that a *matching path* π of a regular expression r in stream s is a subsequence of s that causes a match of r, with each character in π matching a character in r. For example, if $s = 01151$ and $r = 1^*(2|5)$, then one matching path π consists of the 2nd and the 4th characters of s (i.e., 1, 5). Clearly there can be many matching paths for the same r (e.g., the 2nd, 3rd, and 4th characters of s form another matching path).

Definition 1 (ERE Matching). *An* extended regular expression (ERE) matching *is a regular expression matching extended by allowing mixing in irrelevant characters in the matching sequence, and augmented with window and negation constraints:*

The window constraint *with a parameter* w *requires that* $t(l) - t(f) \leq w$, *where* f *(*l*, resp.) is the first (last, resp.) character in a matching path.*

A negative character, *denoted as* $\bar{x}$ $(x \in \Sigma)$, *in an ERE requires that* x *must not appear in the context (in contrast to a positive character). More precisely,* $\bar{x}$ *requires the* absence *(instead of the presence) of* x *in a matching path between the two surrounding characters if they both exist. This is called a* surrounded negation.

If a negative character $\bar{x}$ *has no positive character before it in a matching path (i.e.,* $\bar{x}$ *is located at the front of the ERE), then* x *must not occur before the first positive character in a window. More precisely, there must not exist a character* x *in the stream with* $t(x) \in [t(l) - w, t(f)]$, *where* f *(*l*, resp.) is the first (last, resp.) positive character in a matching path. We call it a* front negation. *A* rear negation *is analogously defined (when* $\bar{x}$ *is located at the end of the ERE), requiring the absence of* x *in the stream with* $t(x) \in [t(l), t(f) + w]$.

Example 3. Consider $r_4 = (\bar{S_1}\bar{S_2}\bar{S_3})N(\bar{S_1}\bar{S_2}\bar{S_3})B$ in Eq. (4), with a window constraint $w = 3\ hours$. We have three surrounded negations between N and B (three negative characters $\bar{S_1}$, $\bar{S_2}$, and $\bar{S_3}$), and three front negations before the letter N. The three surrounded negations require that S_1 (S_2, S_3, resp.) must not occur in the stream between N and B of a matching path. The front negations require that S_1 (S_2, S_3, resp.) must not occur within a time window from $t(B) - 3\ hours$ to $t(N)$, where $t(B)$, $t(N)$ are the timestamps of B and N, respectively. Suppose we did not have the front negations in r_4; then the window constraint itself would only require the whole matching path, from $t(N)$ to $t(B)$, to be within 3 hours. Subject to these constraints, any other letters (events) may interleave in the time window of a matching path.

For ERE matching over a noisy sequence, we only need to know an error model, as defined below.

Definition 2 (Error Model). *For each character in a sequence, the* error is $e_i = e(o_i, x_i)$, *where* o_i *is the observed value of character* i *in the input sequence and* x_i *is its true value (without error). That is, the error is a function of* o_i *and* x_i. *An* error model *of the sequence is a joint distribution of the* e_i*'s.*

If o_i and x_i are numeric values (Example 1), it is often sufficient to define $e_i = o_i - x_i$. If o_i and x_i are categorical values (Example 2), it is not always obvious how to quantify the error. The easiest (and most faithful) way is to simply make e_i a 2-tuple (x_i, o_i), and leave the error model to specify the joint distribution.

For data streams, a realistic and computationally feasible error model is a Markov chain [17]. For instance, in Example 1, if an ECG signal has a positive error at time t, it is more likely to also have a positive error at time $t + 1$ rather than a negative error, due to the local correlation of error sources that create the errors. Likewise, in Example 2, (x_i, o_i) are the *actual* and the *estimated* locations of a customer, respectively. If the estimate at time t is off to the north, then, at time $t + 1$, it is also more likely to err on the same side than the other. In this work, we assume a Markov chain error model with $\Pr[e_i|e_{i-1}, \ldots, e_1] = \Pr[e_i|e_{i-1}]$. Note that a simpler (but less realistic) error model is independent errors for each character in the stream.

Example 4. Consider Example 2. It is easy to find the true (latitude, longitude) information of each interesting store/place in the ERE pattern (e.g., through the Google Maps API [8]). Then the alphabet of the string is all possible (latitude, longitude) pairs. Each character o_i in Definition 2 is such a pair as reported by a customer's smartphone, while x_i is her true location. The error of o_i is represented as a 2-tuple (x_i, o_i) and the error model is the joint distribution of all such 2-tuples for all i*'s* in the string.

Definition 3 ($\mathcal{E}$-Matching). *Given an observed sequence* $o = o_1, o_2, \ldots\ldots$ *where each character* $o_i \in \Sigma$, *an error model* $\mathcal{E}$, *an extended regular expression* r *with a window parameter* w, *and a probability threshold* τ, *the* $\mathcal{E}$-matching problem *is to report each index* i *of* o *together with the set of all matching paths* Π_i *at* i *if the following conditions are true: (1) Each* $\pi \in \Pi_i$ *has* o_i *as the last character; (2) Each* $\pi \in \Pi_i$ *has a match probability at least* τ *for the ERE* r *under the window size constraint; and (3)* $\Pi_i \neq \emptyset$. *Optionally, the user may also request the aggregate probability of* Π_i *(i.e.,* $\Pr[\exists\pi \in \Pi_i, s.t.\ \pi\ is\ a\ true\ match]$*).*

Example 5. To see a simple example, let the pattern $r = (a|b)c$ and a snippet of the sequence be $b'ea'fc'$, where a', b', and c' denote a noisy version of a, b, and c, respectively. For instance, with a certain probability, say, 0.6, the true value of a' is indeed a, while a' is not a with the remaining probability, 0.4. However, the errors of these characters are correlated, following an error model $\mathcal{E}$. When the last character of the sequence snippet, c', arrives, we report two matching paths $b'c'$ and $a'c'$ and their matching probabilities. Optionally, the user may request the probability that at least one of those two paths is an actual match.

Different from previous work [14, 20, 18], we report all significant matching paths (above a probability threshold, or top-k, as in the next definition). This is essentially the *lineage* of the matching query, which is important for event identification in data streams. The matching paths enable us to trace which events at the data sources trigger the pattern match, and what other information is associated with those events. For instance, for pattern r_3 in Example 2, the matching paths will help an analyst to identify which other shoe stores the customer has probably visited, how long she has stayed, and whether she bought anything there, etc.

One potential problem with $\mathcal{E}$-Matching is that there can be too many matching paths, which overwhelms the user and slows down the system. In fact, retrieving the top-*k* highest probability matching paths for each index i in the stream would be sufficient for most, if not all, applications, where k is a tunable parameter.

Definition 4 (Top-*k* $\mathcal{E}$-Matching). *The* top-*k* $\mathcal{E}$-matching *is the same as the* $\mathcal{E}$*-matching problem except that, when* $|\Pi_i| > k$, *we remove all but the* k *highest probability matching paths from* Π_i.

3. AUTOMATON AND ERROR MODEL

In this section, we present the building blocks of our matching algorithms, in particular, the augmented Thompson's automaton and error models in greater detail.

3.1 Augmented Thompson's Automaton

Starting from the classical construction of Thompson's automaton [2], which is a non-deterministic automaton accepting the language of a given regular expression, we describe a series of changes and decorations to the automaton, and call the resulting automaton an *augmented Thompson's automaton* (ATA).

Fig. 2 illustrates the basic construction operations of a Thompson's automaton. For instance, in r_3 of Eq. (3), α^+ is just $\alpha \cdot \alpha^*$. Any regular expression, however complex, can be recursively constructed from the four basic operations in Fig. 2, giving a Thompson's automaton. In particular, note that "back edges" – going from a state on the right to a state on the left – could only be introduced by Kleene stars in Fig. 2(d).

An ERE matching (Definition 1) may additionally have negative characters, interleaved irrelevant characters, and window constraints. Interleaved characters and window constraints will be taken care of by the $\mathcal{E}$-Matching algorithm in Sec. 4, while the changes in an ATA for negations are discussed in Sec. 6.

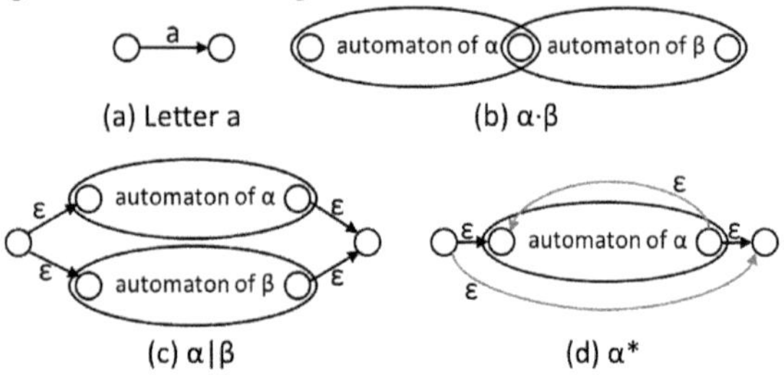

Figure 2. The construction of Thompson's automaton. (a) An elementary letter has a start and a final state. (b) Concatenation: α's final state merges with β's start state. (c) Or, α|β: create new start and final states. (d) Kleene star, α*: create new start and final states; note the new forward and back edges.

For our pattern matching algorithms, we have a simplification of the automaton constructed for an ERE:

Lemma 1. *We can remove all Kleene star (α^*) constructs from an ERE, which does not affect matching probability.*

Proof. Consider an ERE $r = \beta\alpha^*\gamma$, where β and γ denote the pieces of extended regular expression before and after α^*, respectively. Note that β or γ may also be an empty string if r begins or ends with α^*. Let $r' = \beta\gamma$. Firstly, any matching path of r' is also a matching path of r (by the definition of α^*). Secondly, in any possible world where a substring of the sequence o matches r, it must also match r' (since we allow interleaving irrelevant characters subject to a window constraint). Therefore, r and r' have the same matching probability for sequence o. □

Corollary 1. *The graph of an ATA, where vertices are states and directed edges are state transitions, is a DAG (directed acyclic graph).*

Corollary 1 is true because the only type of back edge in the original Thompson's automaton is created for Kleene star (Fig. 2d), but we remove all Kleene star operations in our ATA (Lemma 1). Since there are no back edges, the graph must be a DAG.

Lemma 2. *An ATA has $O(|r|)$ states in total, where $|r|$ is the number of characters and operators in the ERE r. Its states are in two categories:* (1) *an* L-state, *which has only one incoming edge with a letter on it, and* (2) *an* ε-state, *which has one or more incoming edges, all having a label ε. There is exactly one start and one final state, and we consider the start state as an L-state with an incoming edge labeled with an empty string.*

Lemma 2 is directly due to the construction of a Thompson's automaton [2], as evident from the recursive steps in Fig. 2 (it is true by induction as each of the four recursive steps preserves the properties in Lemma 2). From Lemma 2, we label each L-state with the letter on its (single) incoming edge. The next operation we perform on the automaton is that we *assign a unique ID to each state* in a *topological sort order* [12], since it is a DAG.

We then define $PL(s)$ as the set of previous L-states of an L-state s, i.e., for any $s' \in PL(s)$, we have that s' is an L-state, and exactly one letter is consumed from the stream to move from s' to s. We have the following simple and efficient algorithm to get $PL(s)$ for each L-state, and ensure the final states to be L-states.

The rationale of doing this is as follows. Intuitively, each L-state is a "trigger" that corresponds to one letter (on its incoming edge). When a new letter from the stream arrives, in our matching algorithm in Sec. 4, we will check each trigger to see if the L-state can "*consume*" the letter to bring the matching process forward.

Algorithm PREPAREPL&FINAL ($\mathcal{A}$)

1: **for each** state s of $\mathcal{A}$ in ID order **do**
2:   **for each** next state t of s **do**
3:     **if** s is an L-state **then**
4:       $PL(t) \leftarrow \{s\} \cup PL(t)$
5:     **else**
6:       $PL(t) \leftarrow PL(s) \cup PL(t)$
7:   **end for end if**
8:   **if** s is the final state but not an L-state **then**
9:     mark each state in $PL(s)$ as a final state
10: **end for end if**

The PREPAREPL&FINAL algorithm takes as input an automaton $\mathcal{A}$ and initialize a $PL(s)$ set to be $\emptyset$ for each state of $\mathcal{A}$ (omitted above for clarity). Here we generalize the PL set to ε-states as well for convenience, but we only use L-states and their PL sets in our matching algorithms. In line 2, each next state is found by traversing the outgoing edges of s. Then we either add s itself to $PL(t)$ (if s is an L-state) or pass $PL(s)$ to $PL(t)$ (if s is an ε-state). The algorithm is correct because any edge must go from a state with a smaller ID to one with a larger ID. In lines 8-9, changing the final state to be the previous L-states of the original ε-state is merely for algorithmic convenience (especially for negations in Sec. 6), as an ε-state does not consume any letter anyway.

3.2 Error Model

Our $\mathcal{E}$-Matching algorithms can work with any error model $\mathcal{E}$, which describes a *joint distribution* of the errors at each character of the sequence. The simplest error model is that each character's error is independently distributed. However, as discussed in Section 1.1, errors in data streams are often naturally correlated. As we have verified in our experiments using real world data (Section 7), using an independent error model can make the matching probability two or more orders of magnitude smaller than a Markov chain error model, which makes true occurrence of a pattern in the stream indiscernible from mismatching sequences.

In this work, we use *Markov chain* error models by default, which realistically capture the temporal and spatial correlation of streaming data. On the other hand, Markov chains are still reasonably simple and hence relatively efficient to perform probabilistic inference, which is crucial for our real time pattern matching goal. An error model $\mathcal{E}$ has n different error levels, corresponding to the n states of a Markov chain. The $P[i, j]$ in the transition matrix is the probability that the next position in the stream has error level j, given the current position has error level i. Thus, local correlations are encoded in the transition matrix.

The advantage of using an error model is that we do not need to learn the actual distribution of the streaming data itself, which is highly dynamic and needs to be constantly learned, a very challenging task for real time processing. An error model, or the distribution of noise, is relatively stable. For example, domain scientists perform extensive studies on error models of measuring devices and mechanisms, such as the temporal and spatial error correlations of GPS location and wireless networks [23, 21]. There are also a lot of studies that learn a Markov chain transition matrix from data (e.g., [22, 5]). This learning can be performed offline while our matching algorithms are run online in real time.

It is possible that the error source (ES) may change after some time, e.g., when the battery is replaced or the network link is repaired. But the key point is that such an "*ES change event*" is typically *infrequent* (while event matching queries are continuously run). The system can be *well-informed* about such an event; whatever "offline learning" algorithm used before can be run again to learn a new model. Moreover, an ES change event does not necessarily imply a model change – the same Markov chain transition matrix, reflecting the characteristics of *all errors of the device*, may be shared by multiple ES's which tend to cause errors in different directions. In this paper, we focus on the complex event matching, given an error model.

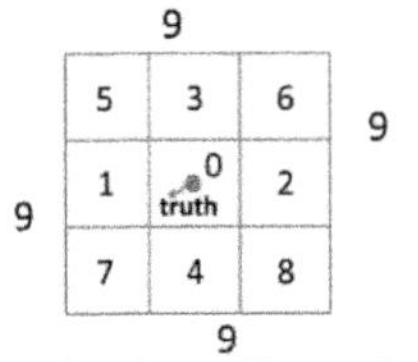

Figure 3. The error levels of two dimensional data such as (*latitude, longitude*). The point in the center is the true value.

For two dimensional data such as (latitude, longitude) as produced by GPS in Example 2 and our experiments, we use grid structure error levels as illustrated in Fig. 3. Since we know what we search for in the pattern (e.g., Macy's store in Example 2), the true value of a character, as shown at the center point of the figure, is easy to determine. Then the close region around the true value is error level 0; other levels, shown as 1 to 8 in Figure 3, are assigned accordingly. Finally, error level 9 is to accommodate all readings that do not fall in the previous levels (very large error or likely not for the intended true value).

Once we have the n error levels ($n = 10$ in Fig. 3), we have an $n \times n$ transition matrix P indicating the error correlation. For example, if the error level is 3 at index t in the sequence, then at index $t + 1$, the error level is more likely to be at levels 3, 5, or 6 than at levels 4, 7, or 8. As discussed earlier, this transition matrix can be obtained from the studies of domain scientists (e.g., [23, 21]) or by learning from historical or training data (e.g., [22, 5]). A simple way to learn an entry $\mathrm{P}[i, j]$ in a transition matrix through the training data is to calculate the frequency (a.k.a. empirical probability) of moving from error level i at time t to error level j at time $t + 1$.

Note that the choices of n and error levels here just exemplify a simple proof-of-concept error model (while the optimal error model requires domain knowledge and is beyond the scope of this paper). In this model, all surrounding areas of the central ground truth point (Fig. 3) are covered; the error level numbers are merely categorical and denote particular regions around the true point.

Interestingly, the data sequence that is input to our $\mathcal{E}$-Matching algorithms can simply be in its original format (latitude, longitude) in Example 2, while each letter in the ERE pattern is the true location of a known place (which can be easily looked up [8]). Error levels can be easily calculated from these readings during the matching algorithm dynamically (as the target "true" value varies at different letters of the pattern). The details will be presented in Sec. 4. Thus, our alphabet Σ of the string is a 2-tuple (latitude, longitude), whose size is infinite if we use real values.

Lemma 3. *If the following conditions are satisfied: (1) There are a finite number of error levels; (2) For each error level* i, $\mathrm{P}[i, i] > 0$, *i.e., it is possible for the error to stay at the same level at successive positions of the sequence; (3) At any position* t *in the sequence, there is a positive probability for any error level to occur in the future (i.e., at some position* $> t$*). Then the Markov chain error model has a unique stationary distribution.*

Proof. A state j in a Markov chain is periodic if $\exists$ an integer $\Delta > 1$ such that $\Pr[X_{t+s} = i | X_t = i] = 0$ unless s is divisible by Δ. Condition (2) ensure that the chain is aperiodic since $\Pr[X_{t+1} = i | X_t = i] > 0$ and 1 is not divisible by $\Delta > 1$. In addition, condition (3) ensures that the chain is irreducible for the following reason. First, any state of the chain can be reached (i.e., a positive probability). Consider any state i that occurs at some time t. With a positive probability the chain can reach any state j after t. Likewise, the chain can also go from state j to state i, giving the irreducibility. A finite, irreducible, and aperiodic Markov chain must have a unique stationary distribution [17]. □

All three conditions in Lemma 3 are realistic and reasonable. In particular, as we discussed, positive correlation between successive positions in the sequence is common, which entails that $\mathrm{P}[i, i]$ should actually be significant entries in the matrix (not only positive), explaining condition (2). Condition (3) states the fact that any error level may occur in the future, at least if we design the error levels in a reasonable way (recall Figure 3). Note that a positive probability could be tiny, even more ensuring that the conditions are practical. Lemma 3 indicates that a unique stationary distribution $\vec{\lambda} = (\vec{\lambda}[1], \dots, \vec{\lambda}[n])$ of the Markov chain error model exists. In fact, we can easily find it by solving a system of $n + 1$ linear equations: $\vec{\lambda}\mathrm{P} = \vec{\lambda}$ and $\sum_{i=1}^{n} \vec{\lambda}[i] = 1$. We use $\vec{\lambda}$ as the *marginal* distribution of the error levels in our algorithms.

4. $\mathcal{E}$-MATCHING

In this section, we present the $\mathcal{E}$-Matching algorithms without negations in patterns. Negations will be discussed in Sec. 6. To make the presentation clear, let us start with the notations that will be used in the rest of the paper for easy reference.

4.1 Notations and Some Intuition

We use $\mathcal{A}$ to denote an instance of ATA constructed based on the ERE in the query. Recall that each L-state of an ATA has a unique ID that is in topological sort order. $\mathcal{A}[i]$ denotes the *letter* at the L-state that has ID i in $\mathcal{A}$. We use $e(l_1, l_2)$ to denote the error level when the observed letter is l_1 while the true letter is l_2. A Markov chain error model $\mathcal{E}$ has a transition matrix P, and we use $\mathrm{P}[i, j]$ and $\mathrm{P}^{\alpha}[i, j]$ to denote the (i, j)-th entry of P and P^{α}, respectively. The stationary distribution of $\mathcal{E}$ is $\vec{\lambda} = (\vec{\lambda}[1], \dots, \vec{\lambda}[n])$, where n is the number of error levels.

During our algorithm, each L-state of $\mathcal{A}$ may contain a list of matching path *segments*. The basic idea is that, once we find a matching path at a final state, we can trace back to find all the *segments* of this path (instead of carrying the whole path along during the algorithm). Each matching path segment is $\pi = (j, i_p, j_p, id, j_0, p)$, where j is the value such that $o[j]$ matches this L-state. (i_p, j_p, id) points to the previous segment of this matching path in the previous state (with ID i_p), where $o[j_p]$ matched that state, and that segment is the id-th among all. j_0 is the value such that $o[j_0]$ is the first letter on this matching path, and p is the matching probability of this path so far (up to this L-state). We use $\pi.j$ or $\pi.p$ to denote the j or p value (resp.) of π, etc. Table 1 summarizes these notations for easy reference.

For instance, Fig. 4 shows an example where the pattern $r = -1(0|1)$ and the sequence contains $-1, 0, 1, -1$. The sequence and ATA are shown on the top-left of the figure, while the transition matrix P, P^2, and the stationary distribution $\vec{\lambda}$ are on the bottom (for now we ignore the table on the top-right of Fig. 4). The ATA $\mathcal{A}$ has states 0-3, with $\mathcal{A}[0] = \varepsilon$ (Lemma 2), $\mathcal{A}[1] = -1$, $\mathcal{A}[2] = 0$, and $\mathcal{A}[3] = 1$. When we observe a value 0 in the sequence, it may match state 1, with an error level $e(0, -1)$, as state 1's true value is $\mathcal{A}[1] = -1$. Example matrix entries include $P[3,2] = 0.1$ and $P^2[2,1] = 0.6$, assuming the 3 rows (or columns) correspond to error levels 1 to 3. An example matching path at state 3 is $\pi = (3, 1, 1, 0, 1, 0.68)$, indicating that $o[3] = 1$ matches this state, the previous matching state is 1 where $o[1]$ is used and the previous matching path segment is the 0'th at state 1. Moreover, π started at $o[1]$, and the matching probability is 0.68.

Table 1. Summary of Notations

Expression	Meaning
$\mathcal{A}[i]$	The letter of state i of an ATA $\mathcal{A}$
$e(l_1, l_2)$	Error level when observing l_1 for true value l_2
$P^\alpha[i,j]$	(i,j)-th entry of matrix P^α
$\vec{\lambda} = (\vec{\lambda}[1], \ldots, \vec{\lambda}[n])$	Stationary distribution of a Markov chain
$\pi = (j, i_p, j_p, id, j_0, p)$	Matching path segment at a state of $\mathcal{A}$ where $o[j]$ matches this state, (i_p, j_p, id) points to the previous segment, $o[j_0]$ started this path, and p is matching probability
$\pi.j$	j value of matching path segment π
$PL(s)$	Set of previous L-states of L-state s

4.2 $\mathcal{E}$-Matching Algorithm

Our algorithm incrementally discovers all qualified matching paths as characters stream in. When character $o[j]$ of sequence o arrives, we try to "trigger" each L-state of the ATA to see if it can bring a partial matching path forward. Clearly, if it is indeed a mismatch, the matching probability will soon decrease below the threshold. A path also has the option of not moving to a new state, which essentially allows "free" insertion of non-matching characters in stream, subject to the window constraint.

Another key idea of the algorithm is that for each (i, j) pair, where i is the ID of an L-state of the ATA and j is the index of a character in the sequence, we maintain a list of *partial* matching paths that end at state i. Since we record j, when we bring a path forward, we know how many characters (say, α) in stream we are skipping; then P^α is used to look up the transition probability.

The algorithm is shown below. In line 3, as each path segment records j_0, the index in stream that started the matching path, we remove it if it is too old (i.e., outside a window of size w). In lines 5-6, if a previous state is the start state, we are about to begin a matching path. Intuitively, the whole matching probability $p = p_0 p_{1|0} p_{2|1} \cdots p_{r|r-1}$, where p_0 is the (marginal) matching probability of the first letter in the matching path. For a Markov chain that has a unique stationary distribution (steady state), p_0 corresponds to one entry in the stationary distribution, based on the error level that enables the match of the first letter (line 6). Thereafter, we will use the conditional probability of matching letter i given the previous matching, $p_{i|i-1}$ $(1 \le i \le r)$, for the remaining r letters in the matching path. In lines 11-14, we try to trigger the current L-state and bring a matching path forward. The number of characters we skip in the sequence between matching this L-state and the previous is $j - j'$; hence, in line 12, for multi-step transition we use $P^{j-j'}$ to look up the transition probability (Sec. 2.1). Note that, for clarity, we omit the id setting when creating a new path segment; it can just be an increasing unique number per (i, j) pair.

Each state on the path only keeps a segment of the path; the complete path can be traced back and recovered only when necessary (i.e., sufficient probability remains at the final states).

Algorithm PATHFINDING $(o, e, P, \mathcal{A}, \tau)$

Input: o: an observed character sequence,
e, P: the error function and transition matrix,
$\mathcal{A}$: an augmented Thompson's automaton,
τ: probability threshold of matching paths
Output: matching paths

1: **for each** index $j = 1, 2, \ldots$ in sequence o **do**
2: **for each** L-state i of $\mathcal{A}$ in ID (topological sort) order **do**
3: remove paths at i that are too old (based on j_0, j, and w)
4: **for each** state $s \in PL(i)$ **do**
5: **if** s is the start state **then**
6: $p \leftarrow \vec{\lambda}[e(o[j], \mathcal{A}[i])]$ *// stationary distribution*
7: **if** $p < \tau$ **then continue end if**
8: add $(j, s, 0, id, j, p)$ to state i's path list
9: **continue**
10: **end if**
11: **for each** path $\pi' = (j', i_p, j_p, id', j_0, p')$ at s **do**
12: $p \leftarrow p' \cdot P^{j-j'}[e(o[j'], \mathcal{A}[s]), e(o[j], \mathcal{A}[i])]$
13: **if** $p < \tau$ **then continue end if**
14: add $\pi \leftarrow (j, s, j', id, j_0, p)$ to state i's path list
15: **end for end for**
16: **if** i is a final state **then**
17: report all paths at i
18: remove all paths at i
19: **end if**
20: **end for end for**

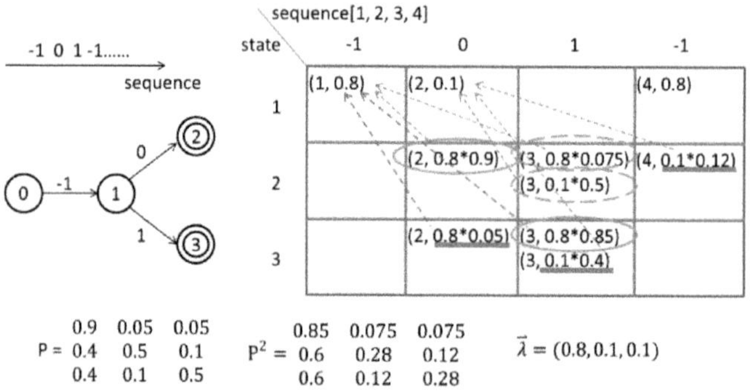

Figure 4. Illustrating PATHFINDING. The sequence and ATA are shown on the left, a table containing the matching path segments is shown on the right, and the transition matrix and stationary distribution are shown on the bottom. The red underlined paths are removed due to small probabilities. The circled paths will be output, with the solid-circled ones having higher probabilities than the dashed-circled ones.

Example 6. We illustrate how the algorithm works with a simple example, as shown in Figure 4. Let the pattern $r = -1(0|1)$ and the sequence be as shown on the top-left of Figure 4. We also show the ATA, the transition matrix P, P^2, and the stationary distribution in the figure. We have three error levels (1 to 3) corresponding to the difference between observed and true values being 0, 1, and -1, respectively (larger errors have probability 0). E.g., $e(0, -1) = 2$. Also, $\tau = 0.05$ and w is 3 time steps.

In the table in Figure 4, the rows are states and columns are characters in the sequence. Each pair in a table cell is a matching path segment. For clarity, we only show the first j and the last probability values in a path, but use dashed pointers to point to the previous path segment. The calculations of probabilities exactly follow the algorithm. The red underlined path segments have probabilities $< \tau$ and are removed. The green circled paths are complete and returned, with the solid-circled ones having much greater probabilities than the dashed-circled ones. Take the first path segment (denoted as π) in the cell at row 3 and column 3 of the table as an example. It is created when $o[3]$ in the stream arrives ($j = 3$), and we are considering state 3 of the ATA ($i = 3$). There is only one previous state in $PL(3)$, $s = 1$. s is not a start state, and there is one path segment there (top-left cell of the table), which has $j' = 1$ (line 11 of the algorithm), i.e., $o[1]$ matched there. Thus, in line 12, we multiply $p' = 0.8$ with $\mathrm{P}^{j-j'}[1,1] = \mathrm{P}^2[1,1] = 0.85$ to get the probability for π.

The correctness of the PATHFINDING algorithm is not hard to see. At the first matching character of a path, we use the marginal distribution for the error level in order to make first match happen. Thereafter, we use the Markov chain transition matrix raised to a certain power to look up the conditional probability.

A crucial point is that, although we do not really know the "true" value of an observed character, for ERE matching, it is sufficient to get only "what if" probabilities. That is, what if this observed character's true value matches that L-state letter? When we keep answering such questions, it turns out that we can efficiently and correctly calculate the matching probabilities.

In sharp contrast to the typical assumption of using machine learning techniques to learn a joint distribution of the stream first and then perform query processing, we only need to know the error model, which, as we have discussed, is much more stable than the dynamic stream. Different powers of the transition matrix P^{α} can be pre-computed ($\alpha \leq w$). Probabilistic inference is extremely fast at runtime – we just look up a matrix.

After retrieving a set of matching paths $\{\pi_1, \dots, \pi_r\}$ at some position of the stream, a user can optionally get the probability that at least one path is true by using the inclusion-exclusion principle [26]: $\Pr[\bigcup_{i=1}^{r} \pi_i] = \sum_{i=1}^{r} (-1)^{i-1} \sum_{I \subseteq \{1,\dots,r\}, |I|=i} \Pr[\bigcap_{j \in I} \pi_j]$. This requires, in the worst case, 2^r calculations of path probability, which is costly if the number of matching paths r is large. When there are too many matching paths, it would often suffice to retrieve top-k matching paths that have the highest probabilities, which is studied next. Indeed, even the cost of PATHFINDING itself is determined by how many matching paths are in the ATA, which heavily depends on the data in the sequence and the pattern.

Discussion. Thus far, we only consider a single error model. While this works well with our datasets and experiments (Sec. 7), it is conceivable that a complex event might consist of mixed *types* of events (characters) that originate from multiple devices with diverse error mechanisms. As such, each *type* (of events) may have a different transition matrix. We can easily generalize our matching algorithms for multiple types. Suppose there are t types of events. For each matching path segment π at an L-state s, we add t pairs of values $(\alpha_1, e_1), \dots, (\alpha_t, e_t)$, where (α_i, e_i) signifies that α_i events of type i have been skipped since the last time when a type i event was on this matching path, which has an error level e_i ($1 \leq i \leq t$). This information is carried along a matching path. When an event of type i triggers a match of the letter at the current L-state, we use $\mathrm{P}_i^{\alpha_i}$ matrix to look up the α_i-step transition probability (P_i is type i's transition matrix); e_i is used to determine an entry to use in the matrix (as before). The top-k matching algorithm (Sec. 5) can be extended similarly for each event type.

5. TOP-K $\mathcal{E}$-MATCHING

Since our goal is to obtain top-k paths with the highest probabilities across the final states, it seems natural to simply trim the low probability paths and only keep k highest probability paths at each state of the ATA. Unfortunately, this would not work. Consider a final state f and a state $i \in PL(f)$. Suppose $o[j]$ matches state f's letter and each path at state i becomes a candidate of top-k at state f. The problem is that each of those paths may get multiplied by a different probability, depending on j' where $o[j']$ matches the letter of state i (recall line 12 of PATHFINDING). Thus, a path that is top-k at f may not be in top-k at i before the extension.

To cope with this problem, it seems sufficient to keep top-k paths for each (i, j) pair, i.e., state i with $o[j]$ matching its letter. The reason is that an extension of a path from (i_1, j_1) to (i_2, j_2) will always get multiplied by the same probability since an error level is completely determined by (i, j), and the transition matrix is raised to the same power $j_2 - j_1$ (line 12 of PATHFINDING).

However, this still does not completely solve the problem. Matching paths get expired when the first matching symbol $o[j_0]$ is outside the current window. Thus, to ensure that we always have the current top-k at any time, we may have to keep top-k paths for each (i, j_0, j) triple, where j_0 is the stream index of the first letter in the path and j the last. The downside of this approach, of course, is that we have to keep $O(w^2 k)$ paths per state, where w is the number of characters in a stream window.

Our final solution is based on the observation that matching paths expire in the order of j_0 in the triple above. We illustrate this in Figure 5. Let j^* be the greatest j_0 for which there are top-k paths (between j^* and j). Then for $j_0 = j^* - 1$, we do not need to keep k paths, but only those that have a higher probability than at least one of the top-k paths at $j_0 = j^*$. This is because the paths with $j_0 = j^*$ expire *after* those with $j_0 = j^* - 1$. In general, for any j_0, we only need to keep paths that start at j_0 and are top-k among all paths that start at j_0 or after.

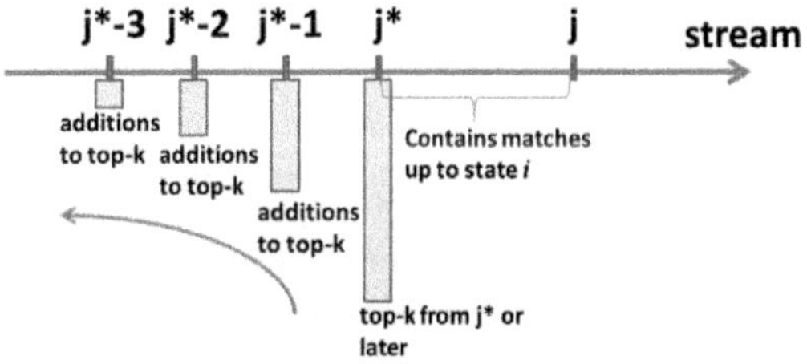

Figure 5. Adding matching path segments at state i of the automaton while stream is at index j. Find largest j_0 $(= j^*)$ that has k paths. This is the current top-k. Then for j_0 in descending order ($j^* - 1, \dots$), only add a path if it is ranked into the current top-k, which is constantly updated.

Our modification to the PATHFINDING algorithm is simple:

(1) In lines 8 and 14, we may add a set of "new" paths Π into state i (for the current j loop). Within Π, we first get k paths with the largest j_0 values (i.e., the j^* above). Then for each j_0 in descending order, we keep a path in Π only if it makes into the current top-k list.

(2) In line 17, we do not report the paths at a final state right away. Instead, after iterating through all final states, we select and return the top-k paths among all of them.

We first prove the correctness and then the average case complexity of our top-k algorithm.

Theorem 1. *The top-k $\mathcal{E}$-Matching algorithm returns the k highest probability matching paths at any stream index j.*

Proof. At *any time* t, at each L-state i of the ATA, for each stream index j, consider the set of matching paths (up to state i) in which $o[j]$ matches $\mathcal{A}[i]$. Let us denote this group of matching paths as $\Pi(i,j,t)$. We only need to prove the invariant that the top-k $\mathcal{E}$-Matching algorithm always keeps the top-k highest probability paths in $\Pi(i,j,t)$, if there are any. This can be proven by induction on i. First, it is trivially true at an initial state that matches the first letter, since there is at most one matching path in $\Pi(i,j,t)$ where $o[j]$ matches $\mathcal{A}[i]$.

For the induction step, consider an L-state i with previous L-states $PL(i)$. In order to get top-k of $\Pi(i,j,t)$, the algorithm goes through each $i' \in PL(i)$, and each $j' < j$. From the induction assumption, the algorithm has top-k in each $\Pi(i',j',t)$. From line 12 of PATHFINDING, each path in $\Pi(i',j',t)$ gets multiplied by the same probability $P^{j-j'}[e(o[j'],\mathcal{A}[i']), e(o[j],\mathcal{A}[i])]$. Thus, top-k in $\Pi(i',j',t)$ is sufficient to get top-k in $\Pi(i,j,t)$ (as a path ranked outside top-k in $\Pi(i',j',t)$ will never be top-k in $\Pi(i,j,t)$). The top-k in $\Pi(i,j,t)$ is selected by merging the results from different $\Pi(i',j',t)$, for $i' \in PL(i)$ and $j' < j$. The theorem is proven. □

We now quantify how many matching path segments we need to keep for each stream index j at state i. In the worst case, the top-k paths starting at $j^* - 1$ are all better (i.e., have higher probability) than top-k paths starting at j^* or after; the top-k paths starting at $j^* - 2$ are all better than $j^* - 1$, and so on, ending up with $O(kw)$ paths. However, this is clearly very unlikely. Therefore, we aim for an average case analysis based on a more realistic assumption of the starting position of a path versus its probability.

Theorem 2. *The expected number of paths we add at each state of an ATA for any stream index j is $O(k \log w)$, where w is the number of characters in a stream window. This is based on the distribution of starting position of a matching path being uniformly at random in its range.*

Proof. Consider Fig. 5 and step (1) of our modification to PATHFINDING. For starting position $j_0 \geq j^*$ our algorithm keeps exactly k paths. For $j_0 = j^* - 1$, the expected number of new paths that get added to the current top-k list is at most $k/2$. This is because all paths in the current top-k list have the same probability to be starting from $j^* - 1$ as to be starting from j^*. Note that it could be less than $k/2$ if there are not even $k/2$ paths starting from $j^* - 1$. Similarly, for $j_0 = j^* - 2$, the expected number of new paths that get added to the current top-k list is at most $k/3$. In general, we add in expectation $\frac{k}{\alpha+1}$ new paths for $j_0 = j^* - \alpha$ ($\alpha \leq w$). Thus, the expected total number of paths is at most $k\left(1 + \frac{1}{2} + \frac{1}{3} + \cdots + \frac{1}{w}\right) = O(k \log w)$ due to the Harmonic series [9]. □

6. NEGATION

We treat surrounded, front, and rear negations separately.

6.1 Surrounded Negation

We create *a single state* in the ATA for one or more neighboring negative letters (that have the same surrounding positive letters). This is also true for front and rear negations. For example, for r_4 in Eq. (4), we have one state for the first chunk of negative letters $\overline{S_1}\overline{S_2}\overline{S_3}$ right after the start state but before the state for N, and another state for the second chunk of $\overline{S_1}\overline{S_2}\overline{S_3}$ between the states for N and B. The reason is that a single state in the ATA is sufficient to simultaneously check the non-occurrence of a set of negative letters at the same location within a matching path. This state is treated as an L-state labeled with the negative letter(s). We only change the PATHFINDING regarding such a new state.

At this negation state, each path segment π also has an error level distribution vector $\vec{\sigma} = (\vec{\sigma}[1], \ldots, \vec{\sigma}[n])$, where $\vec{\sigma}[e]$ is the probability of error level e (for the current character). The rationale behind this vector is that we need to *continuously* ensure that a negative letter does not appear in the stream between the two surrounding positive letters in a matching path. Thus, as each letter in the stream arrives, we need to keep track of the probabilities of each *Markov chain state* (i.e., error level), since each may incur a different conditional probability for whether the next arriving letter matches the negative letter. Note that we do not need to do this before (without negations) because we do not have any constraints on the skipped letters between two matching letters.

Algorithm PATHFINDINGNEGATION $(o, e, \mathrm{P}, \mathcal{A}, \tau)$

Input: o: observed character sequence,
e, P: the error function and transition matrix,
$\mathcal{A}$, τ: an ATA and the probability threshold
Output: matching paths
1: **for each** index $j = 1, 2, \ldots$ in sequence o **do**
2: **for each** L-state i of $\mathcal{A}$ in ID (topological sort) order **do**
3: **if** state i is a negation **then**
4: **for each** path $(\pi, \vec{\sigma})$ at state i **do**
5: $\vec{\sigma} \leftarrow \vec{\sigma} \cdot \mathrm{P}$
6: $\vec{\sigma}[e(o[j], \mathcal{A}[i])] \leftarrow 0$
7: $\pi.p \leftarrow \sum_k \vec{\sigma}[k]$
8: **if** $\pi.p < \tau$ **then** remove $(\pi, \vec{\sigma})$ from state i **end if**
9: **end for**
10: **for each** state $s \in PL(i)$ **do**
11: **for each** new path π in s (added for this j) **do**
12: $\vec{\sigma} \leftarrow \vec{0}$
13: $\vec{\sigma}[e(o[j], \mathcal{A}[s])] \leftarrow \pi.p$
14: add path $(\pi, \vec{\sigma})$ to state i
15: **end if end for end for**
16: **for each** state $s \in PL(i)$ **do**
17: **if** s is a negation state **then**
18: **for each** path $(\pi', \vec{\sigma})$ at s **do**
19: $\vec{\sigma} \leftarrow \vec{\sigma} \cdot \mathrm{P}$
20: $p \leftarrow \vec{\sigma}[e(o[j], \mathcal{A}[i])]$
21: **if** $p < \tau$ **then continue end if**
22: $\pi \leftarrow (j, s, \pi'.j, id, \pi'.j_0, p)$
23: add π to state i
24: **end for end for end for end if end for**

The PATHFINDINGNEGATION algorithm is about moving paths into and out of the negation state. It is in addition to the previous PATHFINDING for regular states. Lines 4-9 are to keep track of the error level probability vector $\vec{\sigma}$ as discussed above, by multiplying the transition matrix P (line 5) and clearing the probability of error level corresponding to the negative letter (line 6). One of the error levels corresponds to the case where $o[j]$ matches the negative character $\mathcal{A}[i]$; we simply clear that entry in $\vec{\sigma}$ to be 0 (as it is disallowed) – essentially disregarding those possible worlds. As each character streams in, $\vec{\sigma}$ keeps evolving. Then the path probability is the sum of entries in $\vec{\sigma}$ (for allowed possible worlds). For clarity, we present it for the case when there is only one negative letter at this state. If there are multiple, then all error level entries for matching those letters need to be cleared. Lines 10-14 move a new path from the previous L-state to this negation state and construct the initial $\vec{\sigma}$ vector. The $\vec{0}$ in line 12 is an all-zero vector. Lines 16-23 are to move a matching path out of the negation state (s) to the next L-state (i). In line 20, we take the error level entry in $\vec{\sigma}$ that corresponds to matching the next positive letter $\mathcal{A}[i]$.

6.2 Front and Rear Negations

The front negation algorithm is based on PATHFINDINGNEGATION, with a few additions:

(1) At line 10, state $s \in PL(i)$ is the start state when i is a front negation state. Then we set $\vec{\sigma} \leftarrow \vec{\lambda}$ and $\vec{\sigma}[e(o[j], \mathcal{A}[i])] \leftarrow 0$. The new path probability is $\pi.p \leftarrow \sum_k \vec{\sigma}[k]$, and π has an extra field j_N, the index of the letter in stream that starts the mismatch of the negative letter. We add $(\pi, \vec{\sigma})$ to state i.

(2) At each "semifinal" state, i.e., a state in $PL(f)$ of a final state f, a path is withheld from extension to f until $j_N + w$.

In step (1), front negation takes $\vec{\sigma}$ from the marginal distribution $\vec{\lambda}$ for the front negation. In addition, the path needs to remember j_N, the start of the matching path window. Therefore, in step (2), we only need to change the semifinal states by making sure that each qualified path ends exactly at index $j_N + w$ of the sequence.

Rear Negation. The rear negation algorithm is also based on PATHFINDINGNEGATION, with a few exceptions:

(1) We do not create a state for a rear negative letter in ATA. But rather, we store the negative letter in the L-state for the positive letter immediately preceding the negative letter.

(2) When a path π reaches a final state i, we set $\vec{\sigma} \leftarrow \vec{0}$ and $\vec{\sigma}[e(o[j], \mathcal{A}[i])] \leftarrow \pi.p$. Thereafter, whenever a new stream letter at index j arrives, we do $\vec{\sigma} \leftarrow \vec{\sigma} \cdot \mathrm{P}$ and $\vec{\sigma}[e(o[j], c)] \leftarrow 0$, where c is the negative (disallowed) letter. Then set $\pi.p \leftarrow \sum_k \vec{\sigma}[k]$ (π gets removed if $\pi.p < \tau$). This continues until $j = \pi.j_0 + w$, when π is returned.

In step (2), we evolve the $\vec{\sigma}$ as before, since we have to delay a path at the final state until the end of the window $j = \pi.j_0 + w$ before it is reported (if it still has sufficient matching probability).

7. EXPERIMENTS

7.1 Datasets and Setup

We use the following real world datasets (which represent one-dimensional and two-dimensional noisy sequence data, respectively) to perform our experiments:

MIT-BIH Arrhythmia Database. This real dataset is part of the widely-used PhysioBank Archives and contains 48 half-hour excerpts of two-channel ambulatory ECG recordings, obtained from 47 subjects studied by the Boston's Beth Israel Hospital Arrhythmia Laboratory and MIT [31]. The recordings were digitized at 360 samples per second per channel with 11-bit resolution over a 10 mV range. The stream is discretized into integer levels from -6 to 6 by equally dividing the value range over all patients.

Microsoft Research GPS Dataset. This GPS trajectory dataset was collected in (Microsoft Research Asia) Geolife project by 182 users over five years [28]. A GPS trajectory is a sequence of time-stamped points, each of which contains the latitude, longitude and altitude (we only use latitude and longitude). This dataset contains 17,621 trajectories with a total distance of 1,292,951 kilometers and a total duration of 50,176 hours. These trajectories were recorded by different GPS loggers and GPS-phones, and have a variety of sampling rates. 91.5 percent of the trajectories are logged in a dense representation, e.g. every 1~5 seconds or every 5~10 meters per point. To avoid excessive granularity, we sample them so that we have 1 data point every 10 seconds.

We have implemented all the algorithms presented in the paper in Java. For comparison, we also implement an independent error model. All experiments are performed on a machine with an Intel Core i7 2.50 GHz processor and an 8GB memory.

7.2 $\mathcal{E}$-Matching

For the Arrhythmia dataset, we have 6 error levels based on the difference between the observed and the true values being 0, 1, -1, 2, -2, and all others, respectively. A 6×6 transition matrix is learned by inspecting training data pieces randomly chosen from the whole dataset. As discussed in Sec. 1, one of the most important error corrections of ECG signals is baseline correction. For ground truth, we assume that the level that occurs most frequent for a patient should be the baseline level 0. We then learn the errors and empirical transition probabilities from the training data. Likewise, for the GPS dataset, we have 10 error levels as depicted in Fig. 3, where a tile edge length $d = 0.006$ (in both latitude and longitude). We then learn a 10×10 transition matrix from training data which is random sequences from the whole dataset. For ground truth we map the traces to a map and assume that users should be at obvious places such as roads, buildings, shopping areas, and parks.

For comparison, we also implement an error model that assumes that the errors of characters in the sequence are completely independent. For fairness of comparison, the independent distribution of each character is the same as the marginal (i.e., stationary) distribution of the Markov chain error model that we use.

For the Arrhythmia dataset, in order to test performance, we issue a query with a higher selectivity (i.e., more matches) than r_1 and r_2 in Section 1: $r_5 = (-2|-1)012(3|4)54(3|2)0$, which would match an area around an R peak of a normal ECG. Such queries are practical because the R-peak detection is a crucial (yet challenging) problem in almost all kinds of electrocardiogram (ECG) applications (e.g., [15]). For the GPS dataset, we find that most locations are in Beijing. We issue a query with $r_6 = ((A|B|C)DE)|(ED(A|B|C))$, where A is Tiananmen Square, B is Palace Museum, C is Beihai Park, D is Wangfujing, and E is The Place. These places are in proximity to each other. A, B, and C are travel attractions while D and E are shopping areas. Imagine that for travel and shopping promotion, one will get a prize if she travels this pattern within a few hours. r_6 will find out such matches. As discussed in Example 2, such consumer location pattern queries are useful for business intelligence. The ECG queries above have much higher selectivities (i.e., more matching results) than the GPS queries, as R-peaks appear often. We will discuss this point shortly when we examine the throughputs.

Using the Arrhythmia dataset, we compare our Markov chain error model and the independent model. We use EREs of various *lengths* (defined as the number of letters in its longest serial path) from 3 to 15, as either sub-patterns from r_5 above or extensions to it (by padding 0's). The matching probabilities (of best paths) are shown in Fig. 6. All results displayed in this section are the averages of three runs (and the variances are insignificant).

The first fact we see here is that, as ERE pattern length ($|p|$) increases, the matching probability will always decrease. This is unavoidable because, even if an observed letter completely matched the required letter, the matching probability would still get multiplied by a transition probability that is less than 1 (there is always a positive probability for errors). This implies that the choice of τ (probability threshold) should be tuned based on $|p|$.

Secondly, we see that the independent error model results in matching probabilities as much as two or three orders of magnitude smaller than the Markov chain error model. In fact, such matching places in the data (as verified by visual inspection and the annotations in the dataset) are picked up by the Markov chain model. We find that the independent model cannot isolate many of the matches because they are disguised by too many false posi-

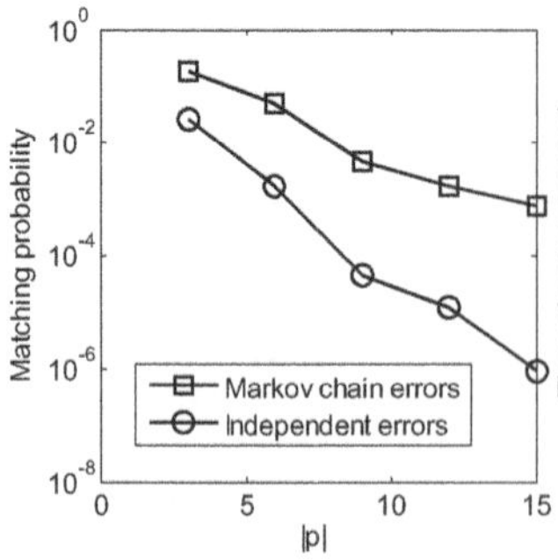

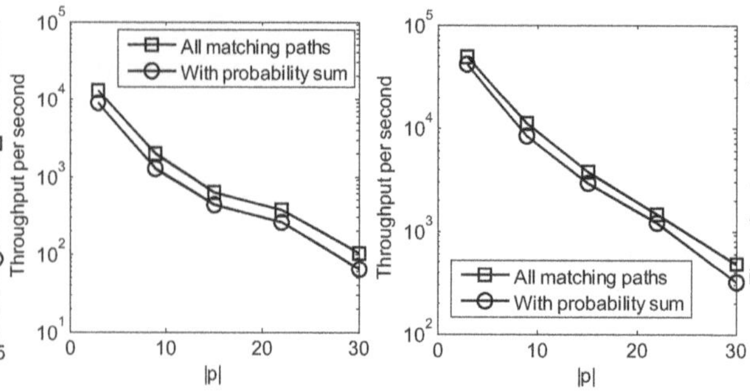

(a) (b)

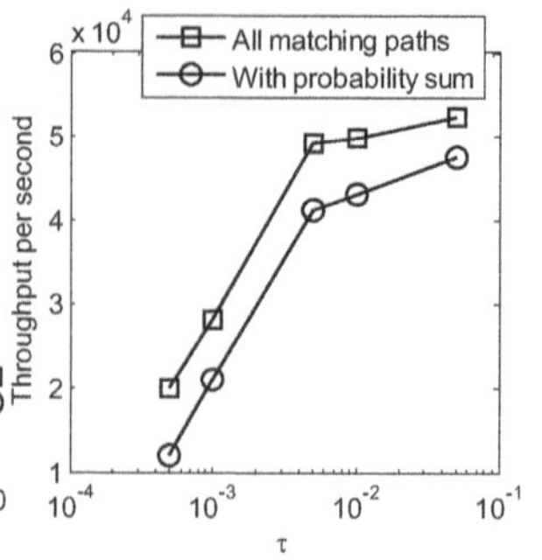

Fig. 6 Matching probability comparison **Fig. 7 Throughput vs. $|p|$ of (a) Arrhythmia, (b) GPS data** **Fig. 8 Throughput vs. τ**

tives (i.e., the false positives have similar or even higher matching probabilities). We get similar results with the GPS dataset.

Next, we examine the stream system throughput when running $\mathcal{E}$-Matching. The results for the Arrhythmia and the GPS datasets are shown in Fig. 7(a) and 7(b), respectively. The queries are variants of r_5 and r_6 with their lengths extended (to the needed $|p|$) based on the context of one occurrence of them in the datasets (e.g., for GPS data, we add more places into r_6 with *concatenation* and *or* constructs).

Firstly, for both datasets, the throughput decreases by about two orders of magnitude as $|p|$ increases from 3 to 20. This is because, as the automaton gets larger, many L-states will need to be examined and the number of incomplete matching paths will increase significantly. Nevertheless, for the Arrhythmia dataset, the data stream incoming rate is 360 samples per second, which allows $|p|$ to be as large as 25. For practical patterns, the serial path length is usually far less than 25 (e.g., r_1 and r_2 in Section 1). For GPS data, our stream incoming rate (per user) is 1 point every 10 seconds, which is far less than the throughput we can handle.

Secondly, we note the fact that the system throughput for the GPS dataset is about five times greater than that for the Arrhythmia dataset. This is because the ERE pattern we use for the Arrhythmia data has much more frequent occurrences in the sequence than the one for GPS data. Many real applications typically monitor rare patterns (e.g., security breach), which ensures a high system throughput.

Finally, recall that for $\mathcal{E}$-Matching a user can optionally obtain the probability sum of at least one matching path being true, by using the inclusion-exclusion principle. We discussed that this is costly if the number of matching paths is large. We verified that in the experiments. Indeed, Fig. 7 shows that the throughput can decrease by about 1/3 when calculating the probability sum.

We then look at the connection between probability threshold τ and system throughput, the result of which is shown in Fig. 8, based on the GPS dataset using query r_6. The throughput decreases as the probability threshold decreases. This is because, in the $\mathcal{E}$-Matching algorithm, a smaller τ implies that more partial matching paths will be considered and carried along within the states of the automaton, increasing the overhead. We note a sudden sharp drop of throughput at some point in the figure. This indicates that when the threshold τ drops below the matching probabilities of true matching paths, a large number of false positives (i.e., matches by chance) mix in, dramatically increasing the system load.

We now study the impact of window size constraints on system throughput, and show the result for Arrhythmia dataset in Fig. 9(a) and the GPS dataset in Fig. 9(b). The common trend between the results of the two datasets is that, as window size increases, throughput decreases. The reason is as follows: when window size increases, more matching paths will stay around in the system, which either eventually become true matches or get removed before they reach final states. These increase the overhead.

Another interesting fact is that the window sizes of the GPS data (minutes or hours) are significantly larger than those of the Arrhythmia data (< 1 *second*). This is due to the nature of the two datasets. The Arrhythmia stream is generated and changes at a much faster rate. For GPS data, people often stay in one location for some period of time. The data changes relatively slowly.

7.3 Top-*k* $\mathcal{E}$-Matching

Our next set of experiments is on the top-k $\mathcal{E}$-Matching algorithm. We first study the system performance under different k values, as shown in Fig. 10 for the Arrhythmia dataset. For $k = 0$, we display the result of $\mathcal{E}$-Matching, without top-k. For a small k, the throughput of top-k matching improves significantly over no top-k (almost 4 times). As k increases, the overhead increases. In addition, as k increases, the throughput difference with and without doing probability sum also increases. This is because, when the number of returned matching paths increases, the cost of computing their total probability increases significantly.

Now let us look at the impact of the window size parameter w on the performance of top-k $\mathcal{E}$-Matching using the Arrhythmia data. The result is shown in Fig. 11, where we use $k = 2$. When k is small, computing the probability sum has little overhead. When window size increases, the system throughput decreases.

However, if we compare Fig. 11 with Fig. 9(a), we find that the system throughput decrease in Fig. 11 is considerably less than $\mathcal{E}$-Matching without top-k. Specifically, for the same window size increase, the throughput reduces 18 times in $\mathcal{E}$-Matching, while only 7 times in top-k $\mathcal{E}$-Matching. This phenomenon can actually be explained by Theorem 2, which says that the expected number of matching paths we keep at state i for stream index j is $O(k \log w)$. By contrast, without top-k, this value is $O(w)$ since we have assumed there are a sufficient number of paths with starting position uniformly distributed. Thus, as w increases, the path number increase for top-k $\mathcal{E}$-Matching is much more moderate.

We then examine the probability threshold τ, using the GPS dataset. The result is shown in Fig. 12. We compare it with Fig. 8 which is without top-k. In Fig. 12, we also find that throughput decreases when τ decreases, as (low probability) matching paths will appear in states where previously do not have any paths. On the other hand, there is a remarkable difference between the two figures. For the same decrease in τ, the throughput of $\mathcal{E}$-Matching in Fig. 8 decreases by 2.6 times, while the throughput of top-k $\mathcal{E}$-Matching in Fig. 12 decreases only by 1.2 times. This is because top-k $\mathcal{E}$-Matching is relatively insensitive to probability threshold – it keeps fewer paths at each state and they often all exceed τ.

Finally, we vary the pattern length $|p|$. The result over the Arrhythmia dataset is shown in Fig. 13. As $|p|$ increases, the system throughput decreases since more ATA states will be processed and they carry more paths to be processed. Comparing with Fig. 7(a) where the throughput decreases 125 times, here it only decreases 43 times. This is because the number of paths at each state

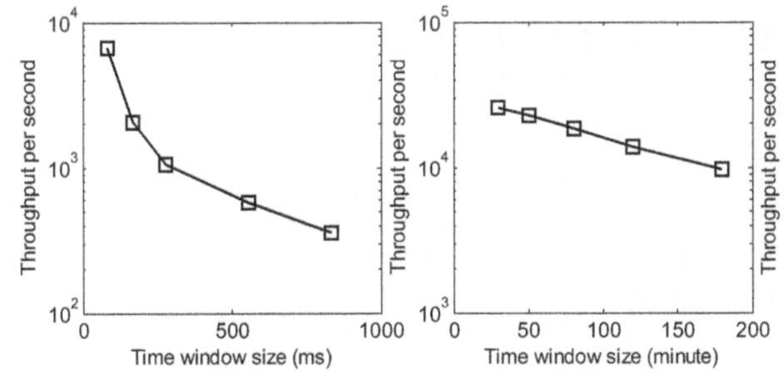

(a) **(b)**

Fig. 9 Throughput vs. *w* of (a) Arrhythmia, (b) GPS dataset

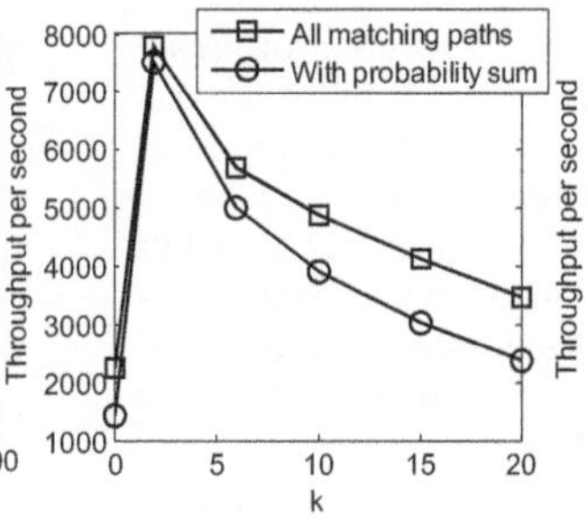

Fig. 10 Throughput vs. *k*

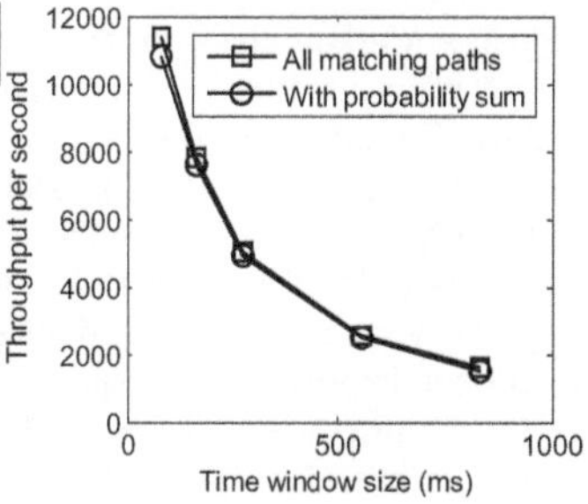

Fig. 11 Throughput vs. *w* for top-k

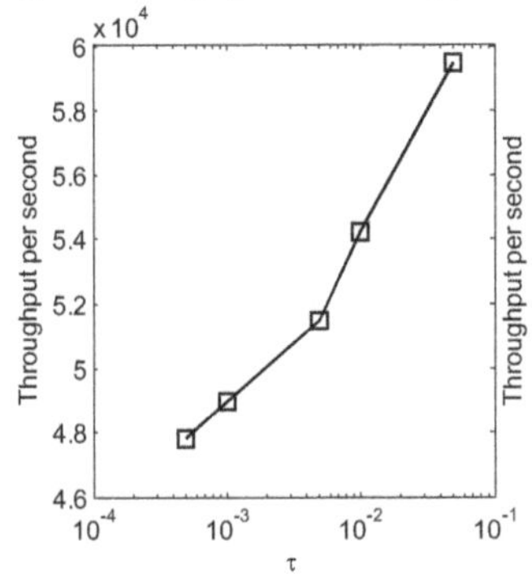

Fig. 12 Throughput vs. τ (top-k)

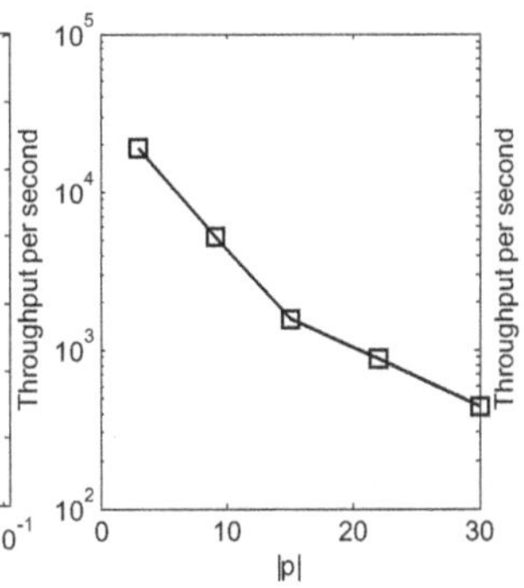

Fig. 13 Throughput vs. $|p|$

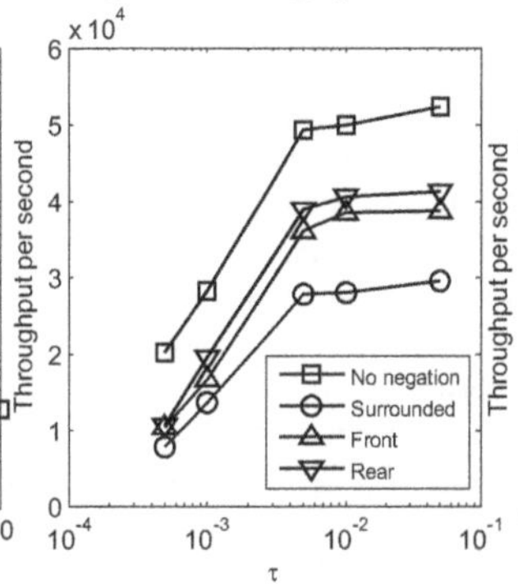

Fig. 14 Negation for various τ's

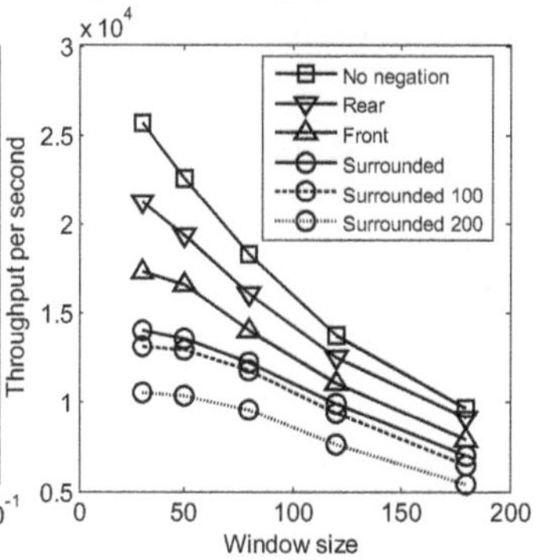

Fig. 15 Negation for various *w*'s

of the automaton is relatively stable for top-k matching, whereas it could grow and multiply fast without the top-k moderation.

7.4 Negations

We now study negations in an ERE pattern. Using the GPS dataset, we compare the cases of surrounded negations, front negations, and rear negations (by adding negative locations into r_6 in the middle, in the front, and in the rear, respectively). We also compare them with the original query without negation. Fig. 14 shows the system throughput when running these queries under different probability threshold τ, while Fig. 15 shows the system throughput under different window size parameters. In both figures, all types of queries have the same general trend, namely throughput increases when matching probability threshold τ increases and throughput decreases when window size w increases.

In both figures, no negation is the fastest. Surrounded negation is the slowest because in the PATHFINDINGNEGATION algorithm, in addition to what we do in PATHFINDING for positive states, we must: (1) Copy all paths from the previous states of the negation state to the negation state; (2) Do matrix multiplication to all paths at the negation state; and (3) Copy all paths to the next state(s). These together cause a significant overhead. Front negation is faster as we do not have step (1) above; as a result, the number of matching paths in subsequent steps is significantly fewer. Rear negation is the fastest because it only deals with matching paths at the final states (matrix multiplication on their error level vectors). However, the number of matching paths that can survive the whole matching and reach a final state is clearly fewer.

We also test the scalability of our algorithms as the number of error levels n increases. Recall that the transition matrix is $n \times n$. Originally $n = 10$; we increase n to various values including 100 and 200 (typically a few error levels would be sufficient for practical applications, but we test large n's just to see the scalability). It turns out that there is virtually no performance impact on the matching algorithm when there is no negation. This is because the PATHFINDING algorithm (line 12) merely looks up entries in a *pre-computed* (multi-step) transition matrix. The offline pre-computing of the multi-step transition matrices and the stationary distribution is also reasonably fast (within 1 second even for $n = 200$). There is some slow-down to the matching algorithm when there are negations. We add two lines in Fig. 15 for the results of surrounded negations when n is 100 (dashed line) and 200 (dotted line), respectively (the results for front/rear negations have a similar trend and are omitted). We see that the throughput is about 92% (78%, resp.) of the original when n is increased to 100 (200, resp.). This is because we have to do the multiplication between a vector and the transition matrix in the PATHFINDING-NEGATION (e.g., line 5), which is slower when n is larger.

Summary of experimental results. Our results in this section show that using a Markov chain error model is effective in discovering matches that are otherwise disguised by false positives under an independent model. The stream system throughput may vary considerably under different parameters such as pattern length, probability threshold, and window size; however, the $\mathcal{E}$-Matching algorithm is able to keep up with the stream input rates in the real datasets under practical parameter settings. Top-k $\mathcal{E}$-Matching improves the performance significantly over $\mathcal{E}$-Matching, especially for small k's (e.g., $k \leq 15$). Moreover, the performance of top-k matching is robust against adverse changes of parameters. Finally, surrounded negations have the most overhead among all negation types while rear negations have the least.

8. RELATED WORK

In the context of RFID data, there is previous work on event queries over probabilistic streams [20]. However, it has a very different focus and approach than our work. First, the query types are different. Unlike [20], we handle negations and window constraints, while [20] studies projection, join, and safe queries. In all our application examples, negations and window constraints are essential for specifying complex event patterns. In addition, we report multiple matching paths (useful for tracing relevant events at the sources) and their aggregate matching probability. Finally, for *real time* streams, [20] does not have access to correlation information and must assume each tuple is independent. By contrast, we use a Markov chain to model the correlation of *errors* and perform efficient inference of matching probability for real time streams. The efficiency stems from closely integrating Markov chain inference into matching algorithms based on an ATA.

Li et al. study windowed subsequence matching over probabilistic sequences [14]. Their exact algorithm uses dynamic programming. They also devise a randomized approximation algorithm to further improve performance, and a filtering technique adaptive to stream contents. Like us, they handle negations and window constraints. However, they only handle *subsequence* queries, while we match patterns in full-fledged *regular expressions*, which have proven to be much needed in complex event processing [19, 1, 27]. Secondly, [14] only handles a simple probability model where each character in the sequence is independently distributed, without the correlations that we deal with.

Dallachiesa et al. [6] also take into account the correlations among neighboring points when they study the uncertain time series similarity problem. They analyze and empirically compare a few techniques that assume independence among data points, together with a simple technique based on the moving average. However, they study similarity queries (between two time series) which are based on some distance function. Hence their techniques cannot be applied to our problem of *regular expression pattern* matching over a continuous *long sequence* extended with *negations* and *window constraints*, which is required for complex event detection. Moreover, as the authors point out [6], their technique does not provide any quality guarantees in terms of probabilistic measures, while we obtain the matching probabilities, which can be used in pruning, as well as in our top-k $\mathcal{E}$-Matching.

Using regular expressions for complex event processing has been well motivated and studied in both research and industry (e.g., [19, 1, 27]). This line of work assumes that the sequence is deterministic. However, as we argued earlier, in many applications where we need real time pattern matching and complex event processing, the sequence has noise and errors. Deterministic matching will not find the matches in these applications. Automata have also been used in complex event processing, e.g., [16, 7, 1, 27]. However, our design and usage of automata are radically different from theirs. For example, [16] uses automata to count the frequency of a *serial episode* φ. They initialize a new instance of the automaton every time the first event of φ comes into the window; thus they have many automata working at the same time for counting. In contrast, we only have one automaton for an ERE (which is more complex than a serial episode), working with an error model. [7] uses an nondeterministic automaton where edges are for predicates and nodes are for relations, while we use a deterministic automaton where each L-state is associated with only one incoming edge and one event. Unlike previous work, our automata handle uncertain/noisy sequences, achieved by working with an error model. We find *all* matching paths simultaneously, together with their matching probabilities (and the overall probability). Our top-k matching algorithm also adds to the novelty.

9. CONCLUSION

In this paper, we formalize the query semantics of using extended regular expression for complex event processing in real time. We then propose a novel approach that is based on an error model, rather than learning the distribution of data sequence first. Efficient algorithms are devised for the $\mathcal{E}$-Matching and top-k $\mathcal{E}$-Matching problems. We have also performed extensive experiments over real datasets to evaluate our approaches.

10. ACKNOWLEDGMENTS

This work was supported in part by the NSF, under the grants IIS-1149417 and IIS-1239176.

11. REFERENCES

[1] J. Agrawal, Y. Diao, D. Gyllstrom, N. Immerman. Efficient Pattern Matching over Event Streams. In *SIGMOD*, 2008.

[2] A. Aho. R. Sethi. J. Ullman. *Compilers: Principles, Techniques and Tools*. Addison-Wesley, 1985.

[3] T. Chan. The Incredible Success of a Heart Monitor Made for the iPhone. In *The Atlantic*, 2012.

[4] C. Chatfield. Model Uncertainty and Forecast Accuracy. In *Journal of Forecasting*, Vol. 15, 495-508, 1996.

[5] B. Craig, P. Sendi. Estimation of the transition matrix of a discrete-time Markov chain. In *Health Econ*., 2002.

[6] M. Dallachiesa, B. Nushi, K. Mirylenka, T. Palpanas. Uncertain time-series similarity: return to the basics. *VLDB*, 2012.

[7] A. Demers et al. Cayuga: A General Purpose Event Monitoring System. In *CIDR*, 2007.

[8] Google Maps API. https://developers.google.com/maps/.

[9] R. Graham et al. *Concrete Mathematics* (*2nd ed.*), 1989.

[10] T. Hilbel et al. Telemetry in the clinical setting. In *Herzschrittmachertherapie & Elektrophysiologie*, 2008.

[11] E. Jovanov et al. Real Time Holter Monitoring of Biomedical Signals. In *DSPS*, 1999.

[12] A Kahn. Topological sorting of large networks. *CACM* 1962.

[13] J. Larson et al. An Exploratory Look at Supermarket Shopping Paths. In *Inter. Journal of Research in Marketing*, 2005.

[14] Z. Li, T. Ge. Online Windowed Subsequence Matching over Probabilistic Sequences. In *SIGMOD*, 2012.

[15] M. Manikandan et al. A novel method for detecting R-peaks in electrocardiogram (ECG) signal. *Biomed. Sig. Proc.*, 2012.

[16] H. Mannila, H. Toivonen, A. Verkamo. Discovering frequent episodes in sequences. In *KDD*, 1995.

[17] R. Motwani, P. Raghavan. *Randomized Algorithms*. Cambridge University Press, 1995.

[18] E.W. Myers, W. Miller. Approximate matching of regular expressions. In *Bull. Math. Biol.*, 1989.

[19] Oracle Complex Event Processing: Lightweight Modular Application Event Stream Processing in the Real World. *An Oracle White Paper*, 2009.

[20] C. Re, J. Letchner, M. Balazinska, D. Suciu. Event queries on correlated probabilistic streams. In *SIGMOD*, 2008.

[21] U. Schilcher et al. Temporal correlation of interference in wireless networks with Rayleigh Block Fading. *TOMC* 2012.

[22] C. Sherlaw-Johnson et al. Estimating a Markov Transition Matrix from Observational Data. *J. Oper. Res. Society*, 1995.

[23] B. Stoew, G. Elgered. Spatial and temporal correlations of the GPS estimation errors. In *TOUGH Project Rep*., 2005.

[24] A. Thiagarajan et al. Accurate, Low-Energy Trajectory Mapping for Mobile Devices. In *NSDI*, 2011.

[25] A. Thiagarajan et al. VTrack: accurate, energy-aware road traffic delay estimation using mobile phones. *SenSys*, 2009.

[26] E. Weisstein. Inclusion-Exclusion Principle. From MathWorld-A Wolfram Web Resource.

[27] L. Woods, J. Teubner, G. Alonso. Complex Event Detection at Wire Speed with FPGAs. In *VLDB*, 2010.

[28] Y. Zheng et al. Mining interesting locations and travel sequences from GPS trajectories. In WWW, 2009. http://research.microsoft.com/en-us/downloads/b16d359d-d164-469e-9fd4-daa38f2b2e13/.

[29] http://www.cdc.gov/nchs/data/nhanes/nhanes3/cdrom/nchs/manuals/ecg.pdf.

[30] http://lifeinthefastlane.com/ecg-library/.

[31] http:// www.physionet.org/physiobank/database/mitdb/.

Toward Practical Query Pricing with QueryMarket

Paraschos Koutris, Prasang Upadhyaya,
Magdalena Balazinska, Bill Howe, and Dan Suciu
University of Washington, Seattle, WA
{pkoutris,prasang,magda,billhowe,suciu}@cs.washington.edu

ABSTRACT

We develop a new pricing system, QueryMarket, for flexible query pricing in a data market based on an earlier theoretical framework (Koutris et al., PODS 2012). To build such a system, we show how to use an Integer Linear Programming formulation of the pricing problem for a large class of queries, even when pricing is computationally hard. Further, we leverage query history to avoid double charging when queries purchased over time have overlapping information, or when the database is updated. We then present a technique that fairly shares revenue when multiple sellers are involved. Finally, we implement our approach in a prototype and evaluate its performance on several query workloads.

Categories and Subject Descriptors

H.2.4 [**Systems**]: Relational Databases

General Terms

Algorithms, Economics

Keywords

Data Pricing, Integer Linear Programming

1. INTRODUCTION

Data is increasingly sold and bought online. Apart from websites that sell data that they collect on their own [3, 5, 8], several web-based marketplace services have recently emerged: Azure Data Marketplace [1] and Infochimps [7] are primary examples. These marketplace services offer a public platform where data providers can upload and sell their data and data consumers can purchase it. However, the pricing schemes that are currently used to price data are either simplistic (a seller offers the whole dataset or parts of the dataset for fixed prices) or not flexible (only a limited class of queries is allowed). This limitation is problematic since recent work [17] demonstrated that buyers are interested in purchasing specific and complex information that requires combining subsets of data from multiple sources. In the absence of more flexible pricing schemes, buyers are forced to purchase supersets of the data they need.

In this work, we design and build a new system, called the *QueryMarket*, as a back-end engine to price and manage data in a marketplace service. QueryMarket enables practical and flexible pricing schemes: It enables sellers to upload their data and specify a set of price points in the form of *selection queries* over that data. Buyers can then purchase complex queries over all the data available for sale, thus having the flexibility to buy exactly the information needed. A buyer simply specifies her query and the system automatically computes the best set of selection queries to purchase in order to answer her query, given the current database instance and her past purchases. In prior work [13, 14] we studied the theory of flexible query pricing and showed that all but the simplest queries are hard to price. The main challenges for implementing a pricing system is thus to *(1) guarantee the efficient computation of prices for a large class of queries* and *(2) support the necessary functionality that a practical data marketplace requires*, which includes support for updates, queries over data from multiple vendors and avoiding double-charging for the same data. This paper takes an important first step toward addressing these two core challenges and outlines future work necessary to achieving a full-featured practical query pricing system.

In QueryMarket, the price the price depends only on the *information content* of the query, and not on the computational cost. Once the system computes a price, it fairly remunerates the various data providers involved in the transaction. Moreover, over time a data consumer is buying several queries, so the QueryMarket system must avoid double-charging the buyer for purchasing the same data. To achieve this, the system identifies redundant information between queries and adjusts the price accordingly. Hence, the price of a query also depends on the *query history* of a user. Since it is often the case that users ask closely related queries over a session, incorporating past purchases to avoid overcharging is a fundamental requirement. Finally, as users purchase data, sellers may add to it or may update it. QueryMarket supports various policies for selling updates, including providing updates for free and charging for updates in proportion to the amount of changed information.

The next example presents a practical case for pricing and discusses the challenges and requirements for QueryMarket.

EXAMPLE 1.1. *Our running example concerns selling data on word translation and word frequency. For any pair*

SIGMOD'13, June 22–27, 2013, New York, New York, USA.
Copyright 2013 ACM 978-1-4503-2037-5/13/06 ...$15.00.

of languages, e.g. *English, German, there exists a table* $T_{en,de}(w_1, w_2)$. *An entry* $T_{en,de}$*('thanks','danke') means that 'thanks' in English translates to 'danke' in German. Such data is currently sold through the Azure Marketplace [2], where the price depends on characters per month purchased. For example, 4 million characters per month cost $40.*

*Moreover, the dataset contains tables with frequency data about unigrams and bigrams for various genres (*e.g. *fiction, newspaper, music):* $UF(w, genre, freq, rank)$ *and* $BF(w_1, w_2, genre, freq, rank)$. *Such data is currently sold in [9] in a slightly different format. Both datasets can be purchased for $250 each (or subsets for a lower price).*

In current systems, our data consumer, Alice, can access this dataset in limited ways. The tables UF, BF *can only be bought in large chunks of words, even if Alice is interested in asking the frequency of a single word. The translation dataset enables translations of single words or text: for example, Alice can ask for the German translation of the word 'thanks':* $Q_1(x) = T_{en,de}('thanks', x)$. *However, Alice may be interested in more complex queries that combine multiple tables. Using the concise Datalog notation, the queries are:*

$$Q_2(x, y) = T_{de,en}(x, y), T_{de,fr}(x, y)$$
$$Q_3() = UF(\text{'rock'}, \text{'music'}, f_1, y), UF(\text{'pop'}, \text{'music'}, f_2, z), f_1 > f_2$$
$$Q_4(x, y) = UF(x, \text{'math'}, z, r), T_{en,de}(x, y), r \leq 100$$
$$Q_5(x) = T_{en,de}(x, x) \vee T_{en,fr}(x, x) \vee T_{en,sp}(x, x)$$

Query Q_2 *asks for all German words with identical English and French translations: 'Polizei' is such an example, since its English/French translation is 'police'.* Q_3 *asks if the word 'rock' appears in the genre 'music' more frequently than 'pop'.* Q_4 *asks for the German translation of the top 100 English math words. Finally,* Q_5 *asks for any English words such that its Spanish, German or French translation coincides with it. Obviously, in each case, Alice would like to pay only for the information content of that particular query. This is not possible in today's data markets, forcing Alice to buy entire datasets so as to answer complex queries.*

Additionally, multiple vendors may be necessary to answer each one of Alice's queries. For example, one seller S_T *may offer table* T *while another seller* $S_{UF,BF}$ *may sell the* UF *and* BF *tables. Today's data market services force users to purchase data separately from each vendor involved.*

Alice will also issue multiple queries over time. These queries may have overlapping information contents, for example, Alice may later decide that she needs the top 250 math words in English and issue query

$$Q_6(x, y) = UF(x, \text{'math'}, z, r), T_{en,de}(x, y), r \leq 250$$

similar to Q_4. *More subtle, if Alice issues* Q_5 *after* Q_4*, some of the same* $T_{en,de}(x, y)$ *tuples may need to be purchased for both queries. Ideally, Alice should not pay for information that she previously purchased. Today's data markets, however, commonly ignore any purchase history.*

Finally, the data may change over time. For example, the ranks and frequencies of various words may be updated and new words may be added. Today's marketplace services do not provide support for selling data updates.

QueryMarket is the first pricing system that supports the pricing of the above queries and also handles the other key technical challenges. Our main contributions in this paper can be summarized as follows.

An Implementation of the Static Pricing Framework. (Section 4) With our pricing scheme the seller specifies base prices for selection queries and the system then automatically computes the price of any user query. As argued in prior work [13], the pricing function must be *arbitrage-free*, meaning that no query can be answered from a set of cheaper queries. However, computing an arbitrage-free pricing function is NP-hard for a large class of practical queries, like those shown in Example 1.1. Thus, to design a system that prices an arbitrary query in reasonable time, we propose to formulate the pricing problem as an Integer Linear Program (ILP) and then call a state-of-the-art solver to compute the price. We show how to construct the ILP for a large class of queries, that includes unions of conjunctive queries (the class of SELECT-PROJECT-JOIN queries with disjunctions in SQL), query bundles and interpreted constraints (which add unary predicates for selections, theta joins, and even user-defined functions). We further describe how to incorporate additional knowledge about the data (in the form of key constraints) to the price computation.

This approach gives us a powerful tool to price a large subclass of SQL queries (with the exception of negation and aggregation). We further discuss several optimizations that minimize the size of the ILP to gain performance.

Pricing in a Dynamic Setting. (Section 5) Second, we study the case where a data consumer issues a series of queries over the database. In this case, there may be overlapping information between queries, a fact that reduces the information gain of a buyer. For example, if Alice issues first Q_4 and then Q_5, there may be a word that needs to be translated in both queries: in this case, it is fair to ask Alice to pay once. We propose and evaluate several methods to incorporate the query history of a user when computing the price. In particular, we show that one of our techniques is not only efficient to implement, but also captures well the information gain of the data consumer.

We further use query history to cope with pricing for *dynamic* databases, *i.e.* databases where the data is updated (*e.g.* the word frequency set may count the frequency of word in Twitter during a 24 hour window).

Revenue sharing. (Section 6) Finally, we discuss an extension of the basic single-vendor scenario, and consider the case when the data is contributed by multiple vendors. The buyer issues a query that integrates data from multiple vendors, and the challenge is to allocate the revenue fairly between the sellers. We present a solution to this problem, which only adds a modest amount of complexity over the basic pricing scheme for a single vendor, while ensuring that the revenue is shared fairly between sellers.

Prototype Implementation and Evaluation. (Section 7) We implement the above techniques in a prototype pricing system called *QueryMarket* and evaluate their performance on real data, as described in Example 1.1.

Organization. In Section 2, we review the pricing framework from our prior work [13]. In Section 4, we show how to implement pricing as an ILP and to optimize its construction. Section 5 discusses and compares our solutions for incorporating query history in pricing. Finally, in Section 7 we present and discuss our experimental findings.

2. BACKGROUND: PRICING FRAMEWORK

In prior work [13], we introduced a flexible data pricing framework, which requires that data sellers specify a small number of distinct price points for the data. It then uses these price points to automatically derive the price of any query submitted by buyers. The key objective is to limit the amount of work done by sellers, yet enable buyers to purchase and pay for personalized data products. A key concept of our framework and related frameworks [15] is that prices should be arbitrage-free. We adopt here the same principled approach to pricing; in this section we review briefly arbitrage-free pricing, following our prior work [13].

In the framework that we adopt, a data seller sells queries over a database D. Instead of specifying a price for every possible query, the seller instead specifies a set of explicit *price points* $\mathcal{S} = \{(V_1, p_1), \dots, (V_k, p_k)\}$, where a pair (V_i, p_i) denotes that the seller wishes to sell the view V_i over the database D for a price p_i. For example, a seller may decide to sell the set of words with any given rank for \$1: then there is a parameterized view, $V_k(w, g, f, r) = UF(w, g, f, r), r = k$, for each rank k. Thus, $\mathcal{S}$ contains a pair $(V_k, \$1)$ for every rank k. Even better, the prices can depend on the rank, *e.g.* the seller charges \$1 when the rank k is lower than 10, charges \$0.50 when the rank is between 10 and 99, and charges only \$0.10 for ranks 100 and up.

When the system receives a request by a data consumer to answer a query Q, it automatically computes a price $p_D^{\mathcal{S}}(Q)$. In fact, the framework defines the pricing function more generally, for an entire *query bundle* $\mathbf{Q} = \{Q_1, \dots, Q_k\}$, *i.e.* it allows the buyer to purchase simultaneously a set of queries, which will be priced together. This can be cheaper than pricing the queries separately, since it avoids double charging for overlapping information between queries. The pricing function must agree with the price points set by the seller, and, in addition, must satisfy the following properties:

Arbitrage-free: Whenever a query bundle $\mathbf{Q}$ can be answered entirely from the query bundles $\mathbf{V}_1, \dots, \mathbf{V}_k$, then it must hold that:

$$p_D^{\mathcal{S}}(\mathbf{Q}) \leq \sum_{i=1,\dots,k} p_D^{\mathcal{S}}(\mathbf{V}_i) \tag{1}$$

If this condition fails, then there exists an arbitrage situation: the buyer who wants to purchase $\mathbf{Q}$ has no incentive for paying the official price $p_D^{\mathcal{S}}(\mathbf{Q})$; instead she will purchase the view bundles $\mathbf{V}_1, \dots, \mathbf{V}_k$ and derive the answer to $\mathbf{Q}$ herself. Key in this definition is the concept of *answerability*, also called *determinacy* [18, 13]: a query bundle $\mathbf{Q}$ can be answered from the queries in the bundle $\mathbf{V} = \mathbf{V}_1 \cup \dots \cup \mathbf{V}_k$, in notation $D \vdash \mathbf{V} \twoheadrightarrow \mathbf{Q}$, if there exists a function that, given the answers to all queries in $\mathbf{V}$, computes the answers to all queries in $\mathbf{Q}$. Thus, there exists some way for the buyer to answer $\mathbf{Q}$ from $\mathbf{V}$, without access to the database D. The function needs to be correct only in the current state of the database D. In the rest of the paper, we will use the following alternative characterization of determinacy [13]: a set of views $\mathbf{V}$ determines a query $\mathbf{Q}$, $D \vdash \mathbf{V} \twoheadrightarrow \mathbf{Q}$, if for any database D' such that $\mathbf{V}(D') = \mathbf{V}(D)$, $\mathbf{Q}(D) = \mathbf{Q}(D')$.

For example, if $\mathbf{V}$ has two views, $R \bowtie S$ and $S \bowtie T$, and $\mathbf{Q}$ has one query, $R \bowtie S \bowtie T$, then for any database, $D \vdash \mathbf{V} \twoheadrightarrow \mathbf{Q}$: indeed, to answer $\mathbf{Q}$, simply perform a natural join of the two views. An arbitrage-free pricing function must be such that $p_D^{\mathcal{S}}(\mathbf{Q}) \leq p_D^{\mathcal{S}}(\mathbf{V})$. On the other hand, if we modify the two views to project out some attributes in S, then, in general, $\mathbf{V}$ no longer determines $\mathbf{Q}$, since the query can not be recovered from the views. In this case, the system may charge more for $\mathbf{Q}$ than for $\mathbf{V}$. However, assume that, in the current state of the database, one of the views is empty: then we have determinacy again, $D \vdash \mathbf{V} \twoheadrightarrow \mathbf{Q}$, because a savvy buyer can infer from $\Pi(R \bowtie S) = \emptyset$ that $R \bowtie S \bowtie T = \emptyset$, and the system must ensure $p_D^{\mathcal{S}}(\mathbf{Q}) \leq p_D^{\mathcal{S}}(\mathbf{V})$. Thus, even if the seller defines the price points independently of the database D (only dependent on the priced views), an arbitrage-free pricing function may depend indirectly on the database.

Discount-free: The prices offer no additional discounts than the ones specified by the data seller; equivalently, the pricing function is *maximum* among arbitrage-free prices.

A pricing function with such properties (if it exists) can be computed using the *arbitrage-price*. Recall that $\mathcal{S}$ are the price points explicitly defined by the seller. The *support* of a query bundle is:

$$supp_D^{\mathcal{S}}(\mathbf{Q}) = \{\mathcal{C} \subseteq \mathcal{S} \mid D \vdash \{V_i \mid (V_i, p_i) \in \mathcal{C}\} \twoheadrightarrow \mathbf{Q}\} \tag{2}$$

The support is the set of all subsets of price-points $\mathcal{C} \subseteq \mathcal{S}$ that are sufficient to answer $\mathbf{Q}$.

DEFINITION 2.1 (ARBITRAGE-PRICE). *The* arbitrage-price *of a query bundle* $\mathbf{Q}$ *is:*

$$p_D^{\mathcal{S}}(\mathbf{Q}) = \min_{\mathcal{C} \in supp_D^{\mathcal{S}}(\mathbf{Q})} \sum_{(\mathbf{V}_i, p_i) \in \mathcal{C}} p_i \tag{3}$$

The arbitrage-price represents the strategy of a savvy buyer: to purchase $\mathbf{Q}$, buy the cheapest support $\mathcal{C}$ for $\mathbf{Q}$, meaning the cheapest set of views that determine $\mathbf{Q}$. The arbitrage-price is always arbitrage free [13]; moreover, if it agrees with the seller's price points, then it is also the unique arbitrage-free, discount-free pricing function consistent with the seller's constraints. In other words, a pricing system must always compute the arbitrage price, Equation 3. Notice also that the arbitrage-price by definition is independent of the query plan that is used to compute the query.

EXAMPLE 2.2. *Continuing Example 1.1, we describe how a data seller, Bob, sets the price points for the data set. We will use selections as price points. Consider first $T_{en,de}$. Bob charges \$0.01 for every selection query of the form $V_a(x, y) = \sigma_{x=a}(T_{en,de}(x, y))$, for any word a. He charges \$0.02 for each selection of the form $\sigma_{y=a}(T_{en,de}(x, y))$. Essentially, a data consumer will pay \$0.01 to translate any English word to a German word, and \$0.02 for the inverse.*

As for the word frequency dataset, Bob prices two kinds of selections for the table UF: $\sigma_{w=a}(UF(w, g, f, r))$ for \$0.05, whereas the price of $\sigma_{r=n}(UF(w, g, f, r))$ depends on the rank. For the table BF, Bob chooses to price each selection on 2 attributes: $\sigma_{w_1=a,w_2=b}(BF(w_1, w_2, g, f, r))$ for \$0.1.

Under such price points, one can show (using results in [13]) that Q_2 can be priced efficiently in PTIME. However, Q_4 is NP-hard to price. Further, the pricing complexity of queries such as Q_3 or Q_5 is not formally known.

For the rest of the paper, we consider a database D, and allow the data seller to specify the price points only as *selection queries* over a single or multiple columns, as in Example 2.2. We assume that, for each column X of table R that the seller has specified prices, there exists a finite domain, denoted by $Col_{R.X}$: this *column*[1] is known to both

[1]The notion of a column should not be confused by the notion of the domain or the active domain of the database. To illustrate the distinction, consider a relation attribute representing English words. The domain is the set of strings of a given length, the active domain is the set of words in the database, the column is the set of all English words.

the seller and the buyer, and D is required to include values only from this column. The seller can specify explicit prices only for the values in the appropriate column. For a value $a \in Col(R.X)$, the explicit price of the selection $\sigma_{R.X=a}$ will be denoted by $p(\sigma_{R.X=a})$.

For each relation, we only require that at least one (and not necessarily all) attribute be priced. We also require that, for any priced attribute, prices are set for all values in the column. Otherwise, the price of the relation itself cannot be specified. For a relation R, let $att\_pr(R)$ denote the set of attributes that are priced by the seller; then, $att\_pr(R) \neq \emptyset$.

2.1 Alternative Pricing Models

We compare the framework presented above with two simple pricing schemes: (a) pay-per-tuple, and (b) sell only the pre-defined priced views. The comparison will be performed across three dimensions: system infrastructure, customer satisfaction and revenue for the seller.

In pay-per-tuple the buyer pays a uniform price for each output tuple. This is simple to implement and predictable: the more tuples returned, the higher the price. However, this scheme cannot put a price on negative information, which can be valuable. For example, a financial analyst sells stock recommendations, `StrongBuy(symb)`, and a user retrieves these stocks and their current price, $q(x, y) = \texttt{StrongBuy}(x), \texttt{List}(x, y)$. The query returns few answers, yet the user must pay dearly for them. The list of *all* stocks `List(symb,price)` is a superset of the query, but is freely available or cheap. Clearly, paying the same price per tuple makes no sense here from the seller's perspective. A more refined version of this scheme can differentiate the price paid for each tuple by charging each tuple depending on its provenance. While this fixes our toy example, it fails in more complex scenarios, e.g. when the user intersects the recommendations of two analysts, $q(x) = \texttt{StrongBuy1}(x), \texttt{StrongBuy2}(x)$. The absence of a stock from either recommendation is valuable important information, yet it is not captured by the provenance.

In fixed-views, the buyer can only purchase the views that are listed by the seller; if she needs to answer a query that is not on the list, she needs to determine herself which views to buy in order to answer her query. One advantage is that users obtain the entire views that determine their query and not just the final answer, at no additional cost and they may reuse these views for future queries. However, it is possible to achieve the same advantage in QueryMarket by recording the user's query history, Section 5. On the other hand, the fixed-views scheme, although simple to deploy, has three disadvantages. First, it moves the burden of computing the optimal set of views from the market maker to the buyer, who has to either do this manually (which is impractical), or could use a tool but that would be equivalent to our QueryMarket, simply running on the client rather than the server. Second, determining the optimal set of views to compute a query requires access to the current state of the database. For example, if the query is $q(x) = \texttt{StrongBuy1}(x), \texttt{StrongBuy2}(x)$ and stock A is not recommended by the second analyst, the buyer should buy only the information from the second analyst, and not have to pay the first analyst: QueryMarket can determine that, since it has access to the data, but the buyer does not. Finally, since the buyer cannot compute the optimal set of views to answer a query, she may later discover a cheaper way to buy the same query: this may become obvious by inspecting the views that she purchased, or she may learn this from another user. Such differential pricing is poorly received by customers and should be avoided at all costs [19].

To summarize, simpler pricing schemes either fail to capture the pricing needs of the seller or may defer the nontrivial problem of selecting the views to generate an answer to the buyer and hence making them impractical for buyers.

3. PROBLEM FORMULATION

We aim to develop a *practical* system for query-based data pricing. We build on the above theoretical framework and, to build a system, address the following three challenges.

Problem 1: Practical pricing of a large class of queries.

As discussed above, only a small class of queries (a subset of Conjunctive Queries) can be priced in PTIME. All other queries are NP-hard, even when price points are simple selection queries over single attributes. Our goal with building the QueryMarket system is to overcome this challenge and show that computing the price is a feasible task for a large class of queries common in practice. In particular, we demonstrate in Section 7 that our approach can price a large variety of queries over a real dataset in a few seconds.

We focus on the class of queries that can be expressed as Unions of Conjunctive Queries (UCQs) with interpreted predicates. This class of queries is of particular interest because it captures a large part of SQL (except for negations and aggregations): it captures SELECT-PROJECT-JOIN (SPJ) queries including theta joins, disjunctions, and conjunctions. Our approach also supports the pricing of user-defined functions. In our system, a user submits a query of the form $Q(x_1, \ldots, x_\ell) = R_1(\ldots), \ldots, R_n(\ldots)$, where the head Q of the query contains a (possibly empty) subset of variables from the query body. Each atom R_i in the query body is either a relation for sale available in the database D or the head of another rule in the query.

In order to compute prices, we take advantage of efficient state-of-the-art ILP solvers (*e.g.* GLPK, CPLEX, Mosek; we used GLPK [6] in Section 7) by casting the pricing problem as an integer linear program. Let us recall that to price the query, the system must compute the minimum-cost support for that query (Equation 3). The objective function of the ILP is then to minimize $\sum_{(V_i,p_i)\in\mathcal{S}} p_i x_i$, where (V_i, p_i) are all the price points in $\mathcal{S}$ and x_i is an indicator variable capturing whether the view V_i is being purchased to answer the query Q. The constraints of the ILP are expressed over the variables x_i and must be such that the set of purchased views forms a support for the query. The challenge is in determining how these constraints should be stated in order to achieve that goal.

Problem 2: Handle system dynamism.

The second problem that we address in the QueryMarket is that of system dynamism. First, we consider the problem of pricing a sequence of query bundles, $\mathbf{S} = \langle \mathbf{Q}_1, \mathbf{Q}_2, \ldots, \mathbf{Q}_k \rangle$, where the buyer purchases one query bundle $\mathbf{Q}_i \in \mathbf{S}$ at a time until all bundles in the sequence have been purchased. The ideal price that the buyer would like to pay is equal to purchasing all the bundles at once, namely $p_D^{\mathcal{S}}(\mathbf{Q}_{1:k})$, where $\mathbf{Q}_{1:k} = \bigcup_{i=1,\ldots,k} \mathbf{Q}_i$. But if she issues the queries one by one (over time), her total price is $\sum_i p^S_D(\mathbf{Q}_i)$. By arbitrage-freeness, the ideal price never exceeds the total price, and sometimes it can be strictly less, because it avoids double charging the buyer for the same data item; in an extreme case, if the buyer asks the same query repeatedly, $\mathbf{Q}_1 = \ldots = \mathbf{Q}_k = \mathbf{Q}$, then the ideal price is $p^S_D(\mathbf{Q}_{1:k}) = p^S_D(\mathbf{Q})$ (this follows from arbitrage-freeness), while the total price is k times larger. One would like the pricing system to account for past queries, and always charge the buyer the ideal prices, thus avoiding double charging. We demonstrate, however, that, in a dynamic setting, this is computationally too expensive, and propose a set of alternatives that closely approximate this ideal goal.

Second, we consider the problem of updates to the database D. We propose a flexible mechanism that enables sellers to determine their preferred pricing strategy for updated views that have previously been purchased by a buyer. To price updates, sellers define a function $p^u(V) \leq p(V)$ for each view. This function can be equal to zero or can be non-zero and can depend on a variety of parameters including time or the extent of the updates to V.

Problem 3: Ensure fairness of revenue sharing.

Finally, we consider an extension of the setting, where the data is contributed by multiple sellers. Thus, when a buyer issues a query, her answer integrates information from multiple vendors, and the issue is how to share the revenue fairly among the vendors. The arbitrage-free pricing function (Equation 3) is ignorant of multiple sellers: it finds a set of price points $\mathcal{C}$ of minimal total price, whose views are sufficient to answer the query. However, the set $\mathcal{C}$ is often not unique, and different choices correspond to wildly different ways of splitting the revenues between sellers. For a simple example, if the buyer purchases $\sigma_p(R) \bowtie \sigma_q(S)$, and the result is empty because both $\sigma_p(R)$ and $\sigma_q(S)$ are empty, then her payment can either be sent to the vendor of R (to pay for the information that R contains no records satisfying the predicate p), or to the vendor of S. A data market service must ensure *fairness* for the revenue sharing between sellers. In Section 6, we demonstrate that ignoring this problem by arbitrarily picking a solution can easily lead to unfairness, and develop a policy, FAIRSHARE, that ensures that each seller will be treated fairly in terms of revenue.

4. A PRACTICAL IMPLEMENTATION OF THE STATIC PRICING FRAMEWORK

In this section, we describe an efficient implementation of the pricing framework in the setting where a user issues a single query bundle for pricing.

4.1 ILP for Full Conjunctive Queries

The first step of the construction is to show how to construct the ILP for a full conjunctive query. In Datalog terminology, a full CQ is a query where every variable appears in the head. For example, Q_2 (Section 1) is a full CQ.

Given a full CQ $Q(x_1, \ldots, x_k)$, any tuple $t \in Col_{x_1} \times \cdots \times Col_{x_k}$ is a possible answer to Q (there are polynomially many such answers). Let t_R be the projection of a tuple $t \in Q(D)$ on the relation R in Q. Also, let $t[R.X]$ be the value of t at position $R.X$. Moreover, we say that a set of selection views $\mathbf{V}$ *covers* a tuple t_R if for some priced attribute $R.Y \in att\_pr(R)$, we have that $\sigma_{R.Y=a} \in \mathbf{V}$ and $t_R[R.Y] = a$. As an example, consider the set $\mathbf{V} = \{\sigma_{A=a_1}(R), \sigma_{A=a_1}(S)\}$ from Table 1. $\mathbf{V}$ covers both tuples $R(a_1), S(a_1, b)$, but not the tuples $S(a_2, b), S(a_3, b)$.

We now distinguish two cases depending on whether $t \in Q(D)$ or not. If $t \in Q(D)$, any set of views $\mathbf{V}$ that determines Q must make sure that any projection t_R of t to an atom R in Q belongs in R^D. To achieve this, $\mathbf{V}$ must cover t_R. In the case where $t \notin Q(D)$, $\mathbf{V}$ must discover a witness that t does not belong in the answer; in other words, $\mathbf{V}$ must discover an atom R such that $t_R \notin R^D$ and $\mathbf{V}$ must cover t_R. This intuition is formally captured by the following theorem.

THEOREM 4.1. *Let $Q(x_1, \ldots, x_k)$ be a full CQ, D be a database instance and $\mathbf{V}$ be a set of selection views s.t. $D \vdash \mathbf{V} \twoheadrightarrow Q$. Consider a tuple $t \in Col_{x_1} \times \cdots \times Col_{x_k}$.*

1. *If $t \in Q(D)$, then for each atom R in Q, there exists some priced attribute $R.X \in att\_pr(R)$ such that $\sigma_{R.X=t[R.X]} \in \mathbf{V}$.*
2. *If $t \notin Q(D)$, $\mathbf{V}$ includes at least one of the selections $\sigma_{R.X=t[R.X]}$, where $R.X \in att\_pr(R)$ and $t_R \notin D$.*

PROOF. For (1), assume that the claim does not hold. Then, for a tuple $t \in Q(D)$, there exists an atom R such that all selections of the form $\sigma_{R.X=t[R.X]}$, for any $R.X \in att\_pr(R)$, do not appear in $\mathbf{V}$. Notice that $t_R \in D$: consider a database D' where $D = D' - \{R(t_R)\}$. Clearly, $\mathbf{V}(D) = \mathbf{V}(D')$, since t_R does not belong in any of the views in $\mathbf{V}$. However, $t \notin Q(D')$, a contradiction.

For (2), assume again that the claim does not hold. Then, for any projection $t_R \notin D$, $\mathbf{V}$ does not include any of the views $\sigma_{R.X=t[R.X]}$, where $R.X \in att\_pr(R)$. Let D' be $D \cup \{R(t_R) \mid t_R \notin D\}$. Again, $\mathbf{V}(D) = \mathbf{V}(D')$, but now $t \in Q(D')$. $\square$

Exploiting Theorem 4.1, we can construct the linear program as follows. We introduce a variable $x_{R.X,a}$ for each selection of the form $\sigma_{R.X=a}$, where $R.X \in att\_pr(R)$ and $a \in Col_{R.X}$. The variable $x_{R.X,a}$ takes values from $\{0, 1\}$: it is 1 if the corresponding view is purchased, otherwise it is 0. Hence, the objective of the ILP is to minimize the total price captured by the following expression (where $att(Q)$ denotes the priced attributes of atoms in Q):

$$\textit{minimize} \quad \sum_{R.X \in att(Q)} \sum_{a \in Col_{R.X}} p(\sigma_{R.X=a}) x_{R.X,a}$$

We next discuss how to add the constraints for the ILP. There are two cases. (1) For each potential tuple $t \notin Q(D)$, we need to add one constraint as follows:

$$\forall t \notin Q(D): \quad \sum_{t.R \notin D, R.X \in att\_pr(R)} x_{R.X,t[R.X]} \geq 1$$

Notice that this forces, for any projection $t.R \notin D$, any solution to buy at least a selection view that will cover $t.R$. (2) For each tuple $t \in Q(D)$, and for each atom R in Q, we add the following constraint:

$$\forall t \in Q(D), \forall R \in \texttt{atoms}(Q): \quad \sum_{R.X \in att\_pr(R)} x_{R.X,t[R.X]} \geq 1$$

This construction produces an ILP that solves pricing for any full Conjunctive Query. Furthermore, notice that the construction does not prohibit the existence of constants in the CQ or self-joins (*i.e.* when a relation appears more than once in the query).

Schema: $R(A), S(A,B), T(A)$; **Domains:** $Col_A = \{a_1, a_2, a_3\}$, $Col_B = \{b\}$; **Database:** $R(a_1), S(a_1,b), S(a_2,b), T(a_1), T(a_2)$
Price points: $p(\sigma_{R.A=a_1}), p(\sigma_{R.A=a_2}), \dots, p(\sigma_{S.A=a_1}), \dots, p(\sigma_{S.B=b}), \dots, p(\sigma_{T.A=a_1}), \dots$
Objective Function: $\sum_{i=1}^{3} p(\sigma_{R.A=a_i}) x_{R.A,a_i} + \sum_{i=1}^{3} p(\sigma_{S.A=a_i}) x_{S.A,a_i} + p(\sigma_{S.B=b}) x_{R.B,b} + \sum_{i=1}^{3} p(\sigma_{T.A=a_i}) x_{T.A,a_i}$
Constraints: Query specific, as described below.

Type	Query	Generated ILP Constraints	Intuition
Full Queries	`Q(u,v) = R(u),S(u,v)`	$(a_1,b) \in Q$: $x_{R.A,a_1} \geq 1$, $x_{S.A,a_1} + x_{S.B,b} \geq 1$ $(a_2,b) \notin Q$: $x_{R.A,a_2} \geq 1$ $(a_3,b) \notin Q$: $x_{R.A,a_3} + x_{S.A,a_3} + x_{S.B,b} \geq 1$	(a_1,b) is in the answer, so we must purchase both $R(a_1)$ and $S(a_1,b)$ (by either buying $\sigma_{S.A=a_1}$ or $\sigma_{S.A=b}$); (a_2,b) is not in the answer, and the only way to find this out is to learn that $R(a_2)$ is not in the database; (a_3,b) is not in the answer, and we can learn this by learning that either $R(a_3)$ or $S(a_3,b)$ is not in the database.
Projections	`Q(v) = T(u),S(u,v)`	$(a_1,b) \in Q^f$: $x_{T.A,a_1} \geq z_1$, $x_{S.A,a_1} + x_{S.B,b} \geq z_1$ $(a_2,b) \in Q^f$: $x_{T.A,a_2} \geq z_2$, $x_{S.A,a_2} + x_{S.B,b} \geq z_2$ $b \in Q$: $z_1 + z_2 \geq 1$	To find out that b is in the answer, we need to learn either about (a_1,b) or (a_2,b): in each case, we cover the tuple as in the example on the previous line.

Table 1: An example on the ILP construction for queries on a database with three relations $R(A), S(A,B), T(A)$.

4.2 Extensions

In this subsection, we show how to extend the ILP construction for full conjunctive queries to include projections, UCQs, interpreted constraints, bundles, key constraints, as well as user-defined functions (UDFs).

Projections. Consider a query $Q(x_1,\dots,x_\ell)$, where the head variables are a strict subset of the body variables (or even an empty set if Q is boolean). Let Q^f be the corresponding full query of Q, *i.e.*, Q^f contains all the body variables as head variables. Take a tuple $t \in Col_{x_1} \times \dots Col_{x_\ell}$ and consider two cases.

If $t \in Q(D)$, for every tuple $t^f \in Q^f(D)$ that projects to t, introduce a constraint as in Q^f, with the only difference that the right side of the inequality is a new variable u_{t^f} (and not 1). Finally, introduce an additional constraint: $\sum_{t^f} u_{t^f} \geq 1$. Hence, every feasible solution has to satisfy the latter constraint, which means that one of the u_{t^f} will be set to 1: thus, the solution has to discover at least one t^f, which will imply that t will also be discovered as an answer. If $t \notin Q(D)$, for every tuple $t^f \notin Q^f(D)$ that projects to t, we construct the inequality constraint for Q^f as before; we need no additional constraints in this case. Indeed, if any of these inequalities fails to be satisfied, we do prove that t^f (and hence t) is indeed a non-answer.

Table 1 gives an illustrative example of the construction.

Interpreted Constraints. Here we address arbitrary selection conditions. The conditions may be unary (*e.g.* selections of the form $x = 1$) or of higher arity (*e.g.* $x = y$), and they may involve any conditional operator (*e.g.* inequalities $x < y$). Common queries that are used in practice are *theta joins* of the form $Q(x,y) = R(x), S(y), \theta(x,y)$, where θ is a predicate: *e.g.* $x > y$, $x \leq y$, $|x - y| < 2$ (band join).

For unary constraints, we assume a predicate $C(x)$. In this case, instead of using Col_x in the construction of the ILP, we use the *filtered* column $Col'_x = \{a \in Col_x \mid C(x)\}$. This transformation can be viewed as pushing the selection operator down the query plan, since it reduces the number of variables in the ILP. More generally, introducing a constraint of arbitrary arity $\theta(x_{i_1},\dots,x_{i_m})$, where $m \leq k$, modifies only how we define a potential tuple when constructing the ILP. Indeed, a potential tuple is now defined as $t \in \{\mathbf{a} \in Col_{x_1} \times \dots \times Col_{x_k} \mid \theta(a_{i_1},\dots,a_{i_m})\}$.

Query Bundles. Assume we want to formulate an ILP for a query bundle $\mathbf{Q} = \{Q_1,\dots,Q_k\}$. For each query Q_i, we construct independently the ILP constraints C_i. The constraints for the bundle $\mathbf{Q}$ will be the set of constraints $\{C_i \mid Q_i \in \mathbf{Q}\}$. As for the objective function of the ILP, this will be to minimize the sum of $p(\sigma_{R.X=a}) \cdot x_{R.X,a}$, where the sum is over any priced attribute for some relation that appears in some Q_i and $a \in Col_{R.X}$.

Selections on Multiple Attributes. We can formulate the ILP even in the case where price points are defined as selections over multiple attributes. For example, consider the bigram dataset in Example 1.1: it is reasonable for the data seller to price the selections on both words, *i.e.* $\sigma_{BF.w_1=a,BF.w_2=b}(BF)$. To incorporate this extension in the ILP, we can generalize Theorem 4.1 to take into account that a tuple t can now be *covered* not only by single-attribute, but also multiple-attribute selections. The generalization is straightforward and is omitted due to space constraints.

Unions of Conjunctive Queries. We will describe the ILP construction for a query $Q = Q_1 \cup Q_2$ that is the union of two CQs, Q_1, Q_2; the process can be easily generalized for the union of more than 2 queries.

For every potential tuple t, we distinguish several cases. If $t \notin Q(D)$, then it is neither in $Q_1(D)$ or $Q_2(D)$, so we construct the ILP constraints separately for Q_1, Q_2 as previously discussed. If $t \in Q(D)$, we distinguish two cases. If t belongs in $Q_1(D)$ and not in $Q_2(D)$, we introduce the constraint for $t \in Q_1(D)$ (symmetrically if $t \in Q_2(D)$ and not in $Q_1(D)$). Finally, if t belongs in both $Q_1(D), Q_2(D)$, we introduce the constraints for $Q_1(D), Q_2(D)$ as before, but now on the right side of the inequalities for Q_1 we replace 1 by a new binary variable $u_{t,1}$ and for Q_2 by a new binary variable $u_{t,2}$. Additionally, we require that $u_{t,1} + u_{t,2} \geq 1$.

Key Constraints. We discuss how to incorporate *key constraints* in our framework.

If the database schema defines a certain attribute as the key of a relation, we can take this information into account to lower the price offered to potential customers. Indeed, the key constraint is an additional piece of information about the database that the buyer knows, hence the buyer potentially needs less information to answer the same question without keys. Since the prices depend solely on information, less information implies a lower price.

EXAMPLE 4.2. *Assume that a data owner wants to sell the table $R(X,Y)$, where the instance is $R^D = \{(a_1,b_1)\}$, $Col_X = \{a_1\}$ is priced to \$10 and $Col_Y = \{b_1,b_2\}$ is priced to \$3 each. Assume we want to price the query $Q(x,y) = R(x,y)$. If no keys exist, then $\sigma_{Y=b_1}, \sigma_{Y=b_2}$ are the cheapest views that determine Q; hence, $p(Q) = 6$. Now, assume that the attribute X is a key for R. Then, purchasing the* *view $\sigma_{Y=b_1}$ suffices to determine Q, since the key constraint restricts a_1 to map to a single value of Y, which is b_1. In this case, $p(Q) = 3$.*

Assume that the attribute X is a key for $R(X, Y_1, \ldots, Y_k)$. Let us construct the constraints for the ILP as we have described before, but now we replace each variable $x_{R.X,a}$ with a new variable $y_{R.X,a}$. Furthermore, let $a \in Col_{R.X}$ map to the unique values $b_1, \ldots, b_k$. For each such value a, we introduce the following constraint:

$$y_{R.X,a} \leq x_{R.X,a} + \sum_{R.Y \in pr(R) \setminus X} x_{R.Y,b_i}$$

In other words, the answer to the selection view $\sigma_{R.X=a}$ is the single tuple $(a, b_1, \ldots, b_k)$, and, in order to buy it, it suffices to either buy it as is, or buy any of the other selection views on some b_i.

UDFs. We discuss how to model the pricing of user-defined functions in our pricing system. As a motivating example, suppose that a data seller wishes to sell a function *hashtag*(w), which determines whether the word w is a Twitter hashtag or not. The idea is to represent the function as a database relation *isHashtag*(X) that contains all the hashtags and then define a price point for each selection of the form $\sigma_{X=w} isHashtag(X)$, where w is a possible word. Thus, by representing any function $f(x_1, \ldots, x_k)$ for sale as a relation $is_f(X_1, \ldots, X_k)$, we can incorporate UDFs into our pricing system.

4.3 Optimizing the ILP

The resulting ILP can be typically large. Recall that we introduce a variable for every value of every attribute used for pricing. Moreover, the number of constraints varies according to the structure of the query and the attributes that are priced: for example, for a typical join $R(x, y) \bowtie S(y, z)$ where all columns are priced, the number of constraints will be $|Col_x| \cdot |Col_y| \cdot |Col_z|$. To overcome the problem of constructing a huge ILP, we develop several optimization techniques that reduce the size of the resulting ILP.

4.3.1 Independent Subproblems

This technique allows us to split the ILP into one or more smaller ILPs, solve each ILP independently and then efficiently combine their solutions. There are two cases where this technique can be applied.

First, when a CQ contains more than one connected component, it is possible to construct an ILP separately for each connected component and then combine their prices. For example, to compute the answer for $Q() = t_{gr}(x, x), t_{fr}(y, y)$, we independently price the components $Q_1() = t_{gr}(x, x)$ and $Q_2() = t_fr(y, y)$. If both are true, we add up their prices, if one is false we output its price and if both are false we output the minimum of the two prices.

This technique can also be applied in the case of bundles: if the queries in the bundle do not share any predicates, we can price each query separately and then add up their prices.

4.3.2 Problem Size Reduction

The second optimization technique we present reduces the number of variables or constraints of the ILP, which accelerates the price computation. We discuss below two cases where such a reduction of the ILP size is possible.

In the first case, the CQ contains a *hanging variable*, which is a variable that appears once in the body of the query. If the query Q is without self-joins any set of views that determines Q must either choose all the views from the hanging variable or none of them [13]. We can thus construct two separate ILPs: the first sets the prices of the views to zero (and automatically satisfies the relative constraints), whereas the second sets the prices to infinity (in practice we can remove the variables from the ILP).

In the second case, a CQ without self-joins contains a variable that appears multiple times in a single atom. Then, we can reduce the size of the ILP by keeping only one of the columns where this variable appears (see [13] for more details).

4.3.3 Coarse-Grained Pricing

To further reduce the size of the constructed ILP, we can use as price points selections not only on single values, but on groups of values or intervals. As we will discuss below, this also solves the problem of setting explicit price points on continuous or large domains.

EXAMPLE 4.3. *A data seller offers for purchase data on weather conditions. In particular, the table $Temp(x, y, t)$ denotes that a location with coordinates (x, y) has an average temperature t during 2011. Note that the column referring to the temperature is continuous and it makes no sense for the seller to set a price for specific values of the domain. The same problem appears when someone sells data on revenue for companies in the USA; even though the domain is not continuous, it is still impractical to price every value.*

To overcome these two problems, we propose a solution that is based on a more *coarse-grained* pricing. Instead of specifying price points as selections on single values, price points are specified as selections over disjoint groups of values that cover the column. This grouping can refer to a natural partition of a column into intervals, or, in the case of a finite column, an arbitrary partition of the values into groups.

EXAMPLE 4.4. *Continuing Example 4.3, a seller can partition the temperature column of the Temp table into ranges of 10 degrees Fahrenheit, $[-100, -90), \ldots, [90, 100)$, with two additional ranges $(-\infty, -100)$ and $[100, +\infty)$. A coarser pricing would partition into groups of 20 degrees. Moreover, the seller could also group price points on coordinates. For example, a reasonable partition would be to group coordinates based on zip code.*

As we show next, we can still transform the pricing problem into an ILP. However, the construction is not trivial, since joining attributes may be priced at a different granularity or using a different partitioning strategy.

Formally, the data seller can now define price points over some attribute X of relation R as $(\sigma_{R.X \in G_i}(R), p_i)$, where $\{G_i\}_{i=1,k}$ denotes a partition of $Col_{R.X}$ into k disjoint groups that cover $Col_{R.X}$.

Generalized Price Points. We next present an algorithm to compute the price in the case where the price points are groups of values and not single values. The algorithm transforms the problem to a single-value selection instance, which we have previously discussed how to price.

Let D be the database, $P_{R.X}$ be the partition into groups for an attribute $R.X$, and $\mathcal{S}$ be the price points in this case. Moreover, for a value $a \in Col_{R.X}$, let $G(a)$ be the (unique) group that a belongs to. We construct a database D' and price points $\mathcal{S}'$ as follows. The schema remains the same. For a relation R, we replace the column $Col_{R.X}$ for D with a column $Col'_{R.X}$, where each value in $Col'_{R.X}$ corresponds to a group in $P_{R.X}$. The price points are set such that the price of the selection is the same as the price of the group in $\mathcal{S}$. To construct the database D', for a tuple $t = (a_1, \ldots, a_k) \in R^D$, we introduce $G(t) = (G(a_1), \ldots, G(a_k)) \in R^{D'}$.

Finally, assume a given conjunctive query Q. We construct the corresponding query Q' for $\mathcal{S}'$ and D' as follows. If x is a join variable that appears in atoms $R_1, \ldots, R_m$, we replace its occurrence with $x^1, \ldots, x^m$ in $R_1, \ldots, R_m$ respectively and also introduce the predicate $\cap_{i=1} x^i \neq \emptyset$, *i.e.* that the conjunction of the corresponding groups must be non-empty. We prove next the validity of our construction.

THEOREM 4.5. *We have that* $p_D^{\mathcal{S}}(Q) = p_{D'}^{\mathcal{S}'}(Q')$.

PROOF. Notice that the price points are in one to one correspondence. Indeed, $\sigma_{R.X \in G}(R)$ is a price point in $\mathcal{S}$ iff $\sigma_{R.X = G}(R)$ is a price point in $\mathcal{S}'$. Hence, we need to show that $D \vdash \mathbf{V} \twoheadrightarrow Q$ iff $D' \vdash \mathbf{V} \twoheadrightarrow Q'$.

First, consider some $\mathbf{V}$ such that $D' \vdash \mathbf{V} \twoheadrightarrow Q'$. We will show that $D \vdash \mathbf{V} \twoheadrightarrow Q$. Indeed, consider a potential tuple $t = (a_1, \ldots, a_k) \in Q(D)$ and take its projection t_R for any atom R. By our construction, since $t_R \in R^D$, $G(t_R) \in R^{D'}$. Now, consider a join variable x which corresponds to the position i for t: let R_1, R_m the atoms that have x. Then, notice that the groups $G_1(a_i), \ldots, G_m(a_i)$ have a non-empty intersection, since a_i belongs in all of them. Thus, $G(t) \in Q'(D')$ and for each $G(t_R)$, at least one view covers it, which implies that at least one view will cover t_R as well. A similar proof holds when $t \notin Q(D)$. For the converse direction, assume that $D \vdash \mathbf{V} \twoheadrightarrow Q$. Then, take any tuple $t \in Q'(D')$ and suppose, for the sake of contradiction, that for any atom R, $\mathbf{V}$ does not cover t_R. Thus, we can find a tuple $a \in R^D$ such that $G(a) = t_R$ and this tuple is not covered by $\mathbf{V}$. Now, we also know that the intersection for the join variables is not-empty; hence, we can use any common value for the intersection and create a counterexample for determinacy. If $t \notin Q'(D')$, a similar construction holds. □

Notice that the transformation of the pricing problem to pricing single-valued selections does not increase the number of price points in the problem. Hence, the size of the resulting ILP depends directly on how coarse the partition of the column is.

Prices. Given a column $Col_{R.X}$, consider two partitions P_1, P_2 of the column such that P_1 is finer-grained than P_2, in the sense that, any group $G^2 \in P_2$ can be covered exactly by a disjoint set of groups from P_1. For example, the partition in Example 4.4 into 5-degree ranges is finer than the one into 20-degree ranges. Moreover, assume that the prices of P_1, P_2 are naturally set such that if a collection of groups $\{G^i\}_{i=1}^m$ from one partition covers a group G from the other partition, $\sum_{i=1}^m p(G^i) \geq p(G)$. In this case, it is easy to see that for any query Q, $p_D^{P_1}(Q) \leq p_D^{P_2}(Q)$ for the same database D[2]. Consequently, a more fine-grained partition will in general lead to lower prices for the buyers.

[2]Indeed, if $D \vdash \mathbf{V}^2 \twoheadrightarrow Q$ for P_2, we can cover each $V \in V^2$ by a collection of groups from P_1 of the same price. The resulting set of views may have redundant views, so the price may be even lower

5. PRICING IN A DYNAMIC SETTING

In the previous sections, we have only considered the case where a buyer purchases a single query bundle and the database is *static*, *i.e.* does not change over time. However, in order to build a practical pricing system, we need to consider the case where a data consumer is interested in several queries, which she issues at different times, and also study the case where the database is modified over time.

In both cases, queries may have overlapping content; hence, the information content that a data consumer has purchased in the past must be taken into account when we compute the price of a new query. In the extreme case that the content of a query is determined by previous queries asked, it must be offered for free, since the user has no information gain.

5.1 History

In this subsection, we discuss and explore various strategies for incorporating query history when computing the price. For the rest of the section, we consider the case of a buyer who wants to purchase a sequence of query bundles $\langle \mathbf{Q}_1, \mathbf{Q}_2, \ldots, \mathbf{Q}_k \rangle$. Notice that the queries are issued by the buyer in an *online* fashion; hence, we cannot assume that the buyer or the system knows the full query sequence from the start. Also, observe that the price for the information content of this sequence is $p(\mathbf{Q}_{1:k})$, *i.e.* the price of the bundle $\mathbf{Q}_{1:k} = \bigcup_{i=1,k} \mathbf{Q}_i$. For ease of exposition, let us denote by $p(\mathbf{Q}_i)$ the price of the bundle $\mathbf{Q}_i$ as a standalone query bundle.

Oblivious Pricing. This pricing strategy, which we denote by p^O, completely ignores the query history. Formally, when asking for the bundle $\mathbf{Q}_i$, we define $p^O(\mathbf{Q}_i) = p(\mathbf{Q}_i)$. The total cost for the sequence in the end will thus be $p^O(\langle \mathbf{Q}_1, \ldots, \mathbf{Q}_k \rangle) = \sum_i p(\mathbf{Q}_i)$. We will use this naive strategy as the baseline for comparison.

Bundle Pricing. The second strategy is to ensure that, after having asked queries $\mathbf{Q}_1, \ldots, \mathbf{Q}_k$, the user will have paid $p(\mathbf{Q}_{1:k})$, *i.e.* the price of the total bundle. In order to achieve this, the system charges for $\mathbf{Q}_i$, where $i > 1$, the price $p^B(\mathbf{Q}_i) = p(\mathbf{Q}_{1:i}) - p^B(\mathbf{Q}_{1:i-1})$. Moreover, $p^B(\mathbf{Q}_1) = p(\mathbf{Q}_1)$. It is easy to see that the definition implies that, for every $i = 1, \ldots, k$: $p^B(\langle \mathbf{Q}_1, \ldots, \mathbf{Q}_i \rangle) = p(\mathbf{Q}_{1:i})$. Hence, the total cost of the sequence is $p^B(\langle \mathbf{Q}_1, \ldots, \mathbf{Q}_k \rangle) = p(\mathbf{Q}_{1:k})$. Unfortunately, bundle pricing as a strategy is computationally inefficient, since now the price computation depends also on the size of the query history.

View Pricing. The third strategy leverages the query history by storing the information that the buyer has purchased. More precisely, when the system prices a query bundle $\mathbf{Q}_i$, it computes a set of views $\mathbf{V}$ of minimum cost that determines $\mathbf{Q}_i$. The pricing system will then consider that the user has purchased these views, and so will offer them for *free* when the same user issues another query. This strategy can be implemented efficiently, since the system will perform the same computation as pricing a standalone query, with the difference that the already purchased views will now be priced to zero. The only overhead of this strategy boils down to the system storing the views that have been purchased. Let us denote the price assigned by view pricing by p^V.

Conditional Pricing. The final pricing strategy we consider is *conditional pricing*, where we are looking for the minimum cost set of views that, together with $\mathbf{Q}_{1:i-1}$ determines $\mathbf{Q}_i$. For this, we use the following notation: $p^C(\mathbf{Q}_i) =$

$p(\mathbf{Q}_i|\mathbf{Q}_{1:i-1})$. Formally, the price will be equal to the minimum cost set of views $\mathbf{V}$ such that $D \vdash \mathbf{V}, \mathbf{Q}_{1:i-1} \twoheadrightarrow \mathbf{Q}_i$.

This notion is equivalent to the one presented in [15]. We do not explore this case in depth, since the problem becomes computationally very hard. In particular, deciding whether $p(Q|Q') = 0$ is equivalent to whether query Q' determines query Q, which is a problem in general harder than NP, even in the case where the price points are only selections.

When comparing the various pricing strategies, we are interested in two parameters. The first parameter is how efficient the computation of the price is (and whether it is independent from the size of the sequence or not). The second is how close the total price of the sequence will be to the price of the query bundle $\mathbf{Q}_{1:k}$. Regarding the second factor, we can formally show the following lemma.

LEMMA 5.1. *For any sequence* $\mathbf{S} = \langle \mathbf{Q}_1, \ldots, \mathbf{Q}_k \rangle$*:*

$$p(\mathbf{Q}_{1:k}) = p^B(\mathbf{S}) \leq p^V(\mathbf{S}) \leq p^C(\mathbf{S}) \leq p^O(\mathbf{S}) \quad (4)$$

$$p^O(\mathbf{S}) \leq k \cdot p(\mathbf{Q}_{1:k}) \quad (5)$$

PROOF. We first prove the first equation. It is easy to see that any strategy cannot do better than p^B. In order to show that $p^V(\mathbf{S}) \leq p^C(\mathbf{S})$, consider any bundle $\mathbf{Q}_i$ and let $\mathbf{V}$ be the set of views purchased so far by the view pricing strategy. By definition, $D \vdash \mathbf{V} \twoheadrightarrow \mathbf{Q}_{1:i-1}$. Hence, for any set of views $\mathbf{V}_i$ such that $D \vdash \mathbf{V}_i, \mathbf{Q}_{1:i-1} \twoheadrightarrow \mathbf{Q}_i$, it also holds that $D \vdash \mathbf{V}_i, \mathbf{V} \twoheadrightarrow \mathbf{Q}_i$, which implies that p^C will be at least as much as p^V. Finally, we show that $p^C(\mathbf{Q}_i) \leq p^O(\mathbf{Q}_i)$. Indeed, if $D \vdash \mathbf{V} \twoheadrightarrow \mathbf{Q}_i$, then trivially $D \vdash \mathbf{V}, \mathbf{Q}_{1:i-1} \twoheadrightarrow \mathbf{Q}_i$.

To show the second equation, notice that we have $p^O(\mathbf{S}) = \sum_i p(\mathbf{Q}_i) \leq k \cdot \max_i\{p(\mathbf{Q}_i)\}$. However, for any query bundle $\mathbf{Q}_i$, $p(\mathbf{Q}_i) \leq p(\mathbf{Q}_{1:k})$. It additionally holds that the bound is tight for p^V, *i.e.* there exists an instance such that $p^V(\mathbf{S}) = k \cdot p(\mathbf{Q}_{1:k})$. □

In Section 7, we experimentally compare the various strategies in terms of price and performance. We propose *view pricing* as the most suitable strategy for incorporating history, since the performance overhead over the oblivious strategy is small and the price is close to the total bundle price. Further, as we show in the next subsection, view pricing can be used to additionally model dynamic databases.

5.2 Updates

In this subsection, we discuss pricing in the presence of *updates*. Datasets that frequently change are often offered for sale: for example, the *hashtag*(X) table that contains all the words that are hashtags changes when new hashtags are added in the Twitter stream. Also, a dataset with stock prices may be updated daily.

Our framework does not enforce any constraints on how the prices are related when the database changes; however, if some part of the data has not been modified by the update, the pricing system should not charge the user again.

We use query history and the *view pricing* strategy to formalize this problem. The seller, apart from the base prices, can define an *update price* $p^u(V)$ for each view V, which defines how much a user must pay for updates to a view she has already purchased. Clearly, $p^u(V) \leq p(V)$. Moreover, the update price can be set to zero, *i.e.* after a view has been purchased, each modification is offered for free.

As we have discussed above, the data consumer keeps a log of the views that have been purchased: these views are now free for the user. When the database is updated, QueryMarket updates the prices of the purchased views accordingly: if a view has not been modified, its price remains zero. On the other hand, if a view V is modified, the price to purchase this view will be $p^u(V)$. This formulation allows to transform this problem into a regular pricing problem, thus not increasing the complexity of pricing.

6. REVENUE SHARING

Since the datasets may belong to several sellers, the revenue of a priced query must be shared between the sellers who contributed to answering the particular query Q. If a unique minimum-cost set of views $\mathbf{V}$ determines Q, distributing the profit among the sellers is trivial: the revenue of each seller is the sum of the prices of the views that she owns. However, it might be the case that the pricing problem admits *multiple* minimum-cost solutions.

EXAMPLE 6.1. *Consider* $Q(x,y) = R(x,y), S(y,z), y = 1$ *and assume that only the attributes* $R.y$ *and* $S.y$ *are priced uniformly at \$1. Moreover,* R *and* S *belong to different sellers. If both* $\sigma_{y=1}(R)$ *and* $\sigma_{y=1}(S)$ *are empty, we can determine* Q *by purchasing either* $\sigma_{y=1}(R)$ *from the one seller or* $\sigma_{y=1}(S)$ *from the other seller. In both cases, one seller will be rewarded with the total revenue (\$1) and the other will have zero profit.*

We next describe FAIRSHARE, a policy to ensure that the revenue will be fairly shared among the data sellers. Let a query bundle $\mathbf{Q}$ and $Sol(\mathbf{Q})$ the set of all the minimum-cost solutions. For a set of views $\mathbf{V}$ that determines $\mathbf{Q}$ and a seller s, let $\mathbf{V}_s$ be the set of views that belong to seller s. Moreover, for a seller s that may contribute to the price of $\mathbf{Q}$, define by $share(s, \mathbf{Q})$ the maximum revenue that seller s can get among all minimum-cost solutions for $\mathbf{Q}$:

$$share(s, \mathbf{Q}) = \max_{\mathbf{V} \in Sol(\mathbf{Q})} p(\mathbf{V}_s)$$

First, observe that one can compute the share for seller s using our standard ILP techniques, without needing to iterate over all possible solutions. For this, before we formulate the ILP, we give to all the views from seller s a tiny discount: a view that costs p will now cost $(1-\epsilon)p$ for an arbitrary small ϵ. The solution $\mathbf{V}$ with price $p'(\mathbf{V})$ of the ILP will now give us the share for seller s. Indeed, $p'(\mathbf{V}) = p'(\mathbf{V}_s) + p'(\mathbf{V} \setminus \mathbf{V}_s) = (1-\epsilon)p(\mathbf{V}_s) + p(\mathbf{V} \setminus \mathbf{V}_s) = (1-\epsilon)p(\mathbf{V}_s) + p(\mathbf{Q}) - p(\mathbf{V}_s) = p(\mathbf{Q}) - \epsilon p(\mathbf{V}_s)$. Thus, any solution with a larger share than $\mathbf{V}$ would give a smaller price than the optimal price of the ILP, a contradiction.

Intuitively, the share of a seller characterizes how much of the "burden" of answering $\mathbf{Q}$ she can afford. In the case of k sellers $s_1, \ldots, s_k$, it is easy to see that: $share(s_i, \mathbf{Q}) \leq p(\mathbf{Q}) \leq \sum_{i=1,k} share(s_i, \mathbf{Q})$.

Given that we know the shares for each of k sellers that may contribute to $\mathbf{Q}$, FAIRSHARE will distribute the revenue in proportion to the share of each seller, *i.e.* the revenue $rev(s_i, \mathbf{Q})$ of seller s_i will be:

$$rev(s_i, \mathbf{Q}) = \frac{share(s_i, \mathbf{Q})}{\sum_{j=1,k} share(s_j, \mathbf{Q})} \cdot p(\mathbf{Q})$$

Continuing Example 6.1, observe that the share of each seller is exactly \$1. Since the price of the query is also \$1, FAIRSHARE will distribute to each seller an equal part of the total price, *i.e.* \$0.5.

7. EVALUATION

In this section, we experimentally evaluate the QueryMarket pricing system. Our system (implemented in C++) runs as a middleware layer and can be used over any relational database management system (DBMS) supporting SQL: we evaluate our system on top of the lightweight SQLite DBMS. We use the open source GLPK ILP solver [6].

In QueryMarket, the explicit price points specified by the seller are stored as tables in the database itself. More precisely, for a priced attribute $R.X$, we create a table $Price[R.X](value, price)$, which stores the value of the selection attribute, along with the corresponding price. A similar construction holds when the price points refer to multiple attributes. In the case where the price is uniform for a specific attribute, we store only the attribute values.

In order to monitor the price tables introduced by the data sellers, QueryMarket keeps an index table, which we refer to as **price_info**, with the following structure:

$$price\_info(table\_name, column1, column2, column3,$$
$$uprice, price\_table, owner)$$

The column *uprice* refers to the case where the selection has a uniform price. As one can observe, the table also keeps track of the data owner in order to share the revenue.

In order to construct the ILP constraints, the system constructs and issues SQL queries over the price tables and the actual relations. Further, the system needs to store additional information so as to support the *view pricing* strategy discussed in Section 5. Hence, for each buyer u, QueryMarket keeps a table $Purchased\_Views[u]$ that stores the views that have been purchased by the user so far.

We evaluate the various queries and workloads over the database described in Example 1.1. More precisely, the database and price points are constructed as follows:

- $t_{en,de}(x, y)$: price points for both columns
- $t_{en,fr}(x, y)$: price points for column x
- $wf(w, g, f, r)$: price points for columns r and g
- $hashtag(x)$: price points for the unique column x

The prices are set uniformly for each attribute to some arbitrary price (the actual price value does not affect the runtime of pricing algorithms).

7.1 Evaluation of the ILP formulation

We first study the performance of our price computation algorithm that uses the ILP solver, for various sizes of the database and the columns (the original dataset has size in the order of 10^4, and for smaller sizes we consider subsets of it). In our setting, the size of each column is equal to the size of the projection of the relation on the priced attribute; the sizes of the relations are in general larger than the sizes of the columns, but of the same order of magnitude.

We issue various queries to the pricing system: selections on single attributes with or without projections (Q1 through Q5), selections with interpreted predicates (Q6), 2-way joins without projections (Q7-Q11), 2-way joins with projections (Q12-Q14) and 3-way joins (Q15). We conduct experiments to measure the time to price each query for columns with 10^2 and 10^3 rows[3]. The results are depicted in Figure 1,

[3]Our measurement study of Many Eyes shows that 90% of datasets contain fewer than 1000 rows [16].

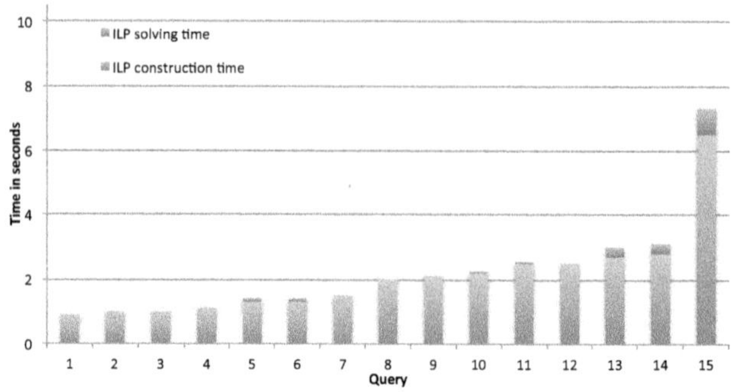

(a) Price columns with size 10^2. The construction time and total time lines almost overlap in this case.

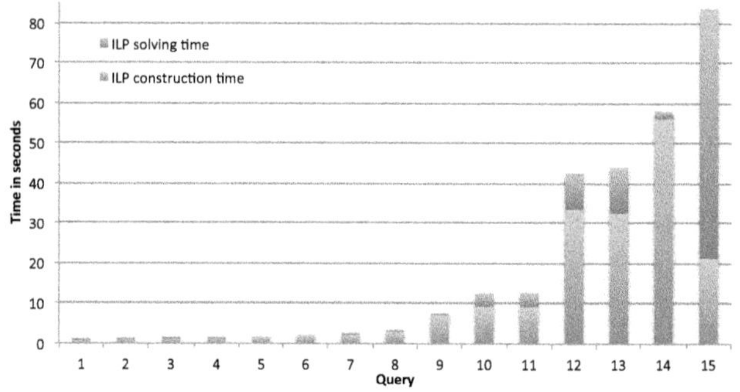

(b) Price columns with size 10^3.

Figure 1: Times for ILP construction and ILP solving for price columns of size 10^2(a) and 10^3(b), where the queries are in ascending order of total computation time.

where both the time to construct and the time to solve the ILP are measured.

As the figure shows, for the small-scale datasets, pricing is interactive: all but two queries are priced within 3 seconds. The slower two queries still take less than 10 seconds to price. In the larger configuration, 9 out of 15 queries are priced within 10 seconds, and all but one are priced within a minute. While these runtimes are no longer interactive, they are still drastically faster than the current approach, which requires human-to-human negotiations. The slower queries in both cases correspond to 2-way joins (for size 10^3), where the algorithm has to perform heavier computation in order to construct the ILP.

Discussion. The efficiency of our pricing algorithm depends heavily on the attributes that are priced. In general, it is a good practice to price as few attributes per relation as possible: pricing only one attribute (*i.e.* giving only one access point to the buyer) will make the ILP extremely efficient even for very large instances. If a buyer wishes to offer multiple access points to some relation, one strategy is to create copies of the same relation and for each copy offer a different access attribute: any buyer will not be aware that the data belongs in the same relation (that is exactly what the Azure Marketplace does when selling translations).

7.2 Query History

In this subsection, we evaluate the various strategies that we proposed to leverage query history discussed in Section 5 based on two parameters: performance and comparison of the prices to the optimal price, which is the price of the total bundle. The size of each column is in the order of 10^3 values.

In our experiment, we price three different query sequences of 30 queries $\langle Q_1, \ldots, Q_{30}\rangle$, which consist of a ran-

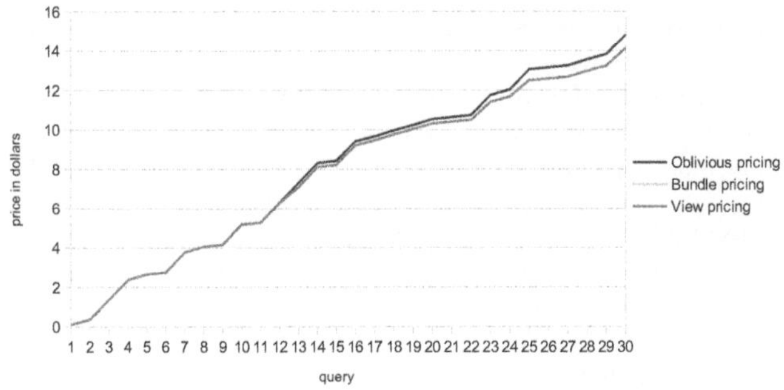

(a) Weakly overlapping query sequence

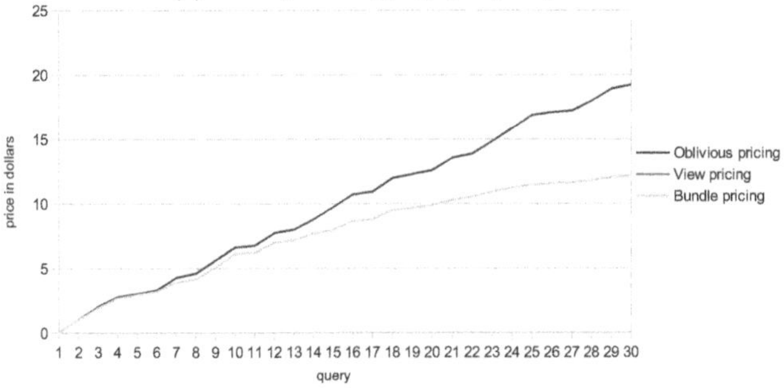

(b) Moderately overlapping query sequence

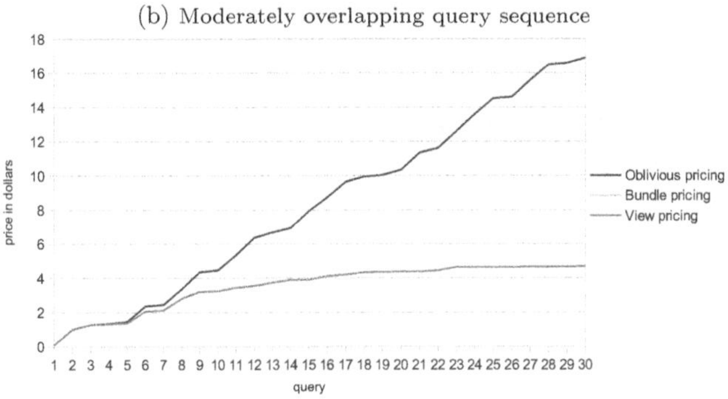

(c) Highly overlapping query sequence

Figure 2: Comparison of the pricing strategies. Oblivious pricing overcharges the users by 5% in (a) to 260% in (c). Bundle pricing computes the ideal price, but is too expensive to compute. View-pricing is easier to compute, and approximates bundle pricing almost perfectly (the graphs are overlapped in (a),(b) and (c)).

dom choice of selections on $t_{en,de}$ and $t_{en,fr}$ and joins between these two datasets and the *hashtag* table. Each query in the sequence is parametrized to access a small random set of English words. The three sequences differ in the amount of overlap between the sets of words: *weakly, moderately and highly overlapping.* We vary the overlap by varying the size of the set from which the set of English words is sampled: for the weakly overlapping set it is the whole column, for the moderately overlapping 20% of the column, and for the highly overlapping 0.05% of the column.

Figure 2a, Figure 2b and Figure 2c show the cumulative price at each point of the sequence for the following three pricing strategies: oblivious pricing (p^O), view pricing (p^V) and bundle pricing (p^B).

A first observation is that, in all three cases, the price for p^V is the same as p^B (although this will not always be the case). Moreover, in Figure 2a, since the information between the queries is essentially not overlapping, the price computed by all strategies is approximately the same, as expected. In contrast, in Figure 2c, where the information content is

Table 2: Performance comparison for the history pricing strategies.

Query Overlap	Oblivious	View	Bundle
Weak	142 sec	213 sec	> 20 min
Moderate	74 sec	129 sec	> 20 min
High	138 sec	165 sec	> 20 min

highly overlapping, the total price remains virtually constant after some point, which means that incoming queries can be answered almost for free, by using the views the user has already purchased. In this case, the user ends up paying 8X less than paying for each query independently.

Finally, we evaluate the time that it takes to price each of the three query sequences using each of the three pricing strategies. Table 2 shows the results. As the table shows, the overhead induced by storing and updating the purchased views is small: the time to price the whole sequence is only 20% to 75% longer than the time to price the same sequence using the oblivious pricing method. On the other hand, using bundle pricing makes price computation very costly, since the time to price the bundle $Q_{1:20}$, for example, takes as much as the cumulative time to price the queries $Q_1, \ldots, Q_{20}$ separately. And this cost is incurred repetitively, with each new query in the sequence.

8. DISCUSSION

We now discuss lessons learned and open research problems toward building a truly practical query pricing system.

Performance. As our experiments demonstrate, QueryMarket can price queries over small datasets interactively and over medium-size datasets within a minute or two. These query-pricing times are a first step toward a practical, automated query-pricing system, since they are much faster than the current approach of calling the data seller to negotiate a personalized data product. The ILP construction is the bottleneck step in query pricing, but QueryMarket can use *bucketization*, as described in Subsection 4.3, to reduce the number of price points and hence bring pricing back to interactive speeds, with the tradeoff of increasing the prices offered to the customers. Other optimizations may also be possible including pricing independent queries in parallel and combining ILP construction with ILP solving to reduce total processing times. Overall, however, scaling the pricing framework to datasets in the age of "Big Data" remains a challenging open problem.

We also learned that using history is critical in a dynamic setting. Bundle pricing offers the best functionality, but we discovered that it is too expensive. View pricing achieves a good trade-off between price reduction and efficiency.

Another interesting open problem is whether a system like QueryMarket could leverage approximations to give users an idea of a query's price without computing that price exactly such as to enable subsecond approximate query pricing.

Finally, in a practical system, it may be necessary to price queries based on both the value of the data and the cost of the resources necessary to process these queries.

Towards full SQL support. The current version of QueryMarket supports a large subset of SQL, but does not support aggregation or negation. Since queries with negation can be *non-monotone* and QueryMarket exploits the monotonicity property to compute a query price, using negation in queries would require new algorithms and theory for pricing non-monotone queries. As far as aggregation queries are concerned, the challenge is to fairly price such queries. For example, to determine a query Q that sums up the attribute X for the relation $R(X)$, one must purchase all the views of the form $\sigma_{X=a}(R)$. Thus, Q's cost under our framework is the same as purchasing the relation R, even though the sum operator offers significantly less information than the whole relation. There has been some work on pricing aggregates [15], but finding a way to integrate aggregation in a way that correctly captures the information content remains a challenging open problem.

Approximate Answers. A natural operation for a data marketplace is to allow the user to ask queries with a *budget limit*; if the query is above budget the system may return a good approximate answer (for example, a sample of the answer, or some summarization of the query) that falls within the given budget. This area opens several interesting research questions, such as to find what are relevant approximations of the queries, and further which one is the most informative under a given budget.

Data Integration. QueryMarket currently ignores all issues related to data integration. It can price queries across data providers assuming that the query produces a correct result. Interesting future work includes modeling and accounting for data overlap between multiple vendors, modeling differences in data quality and freshness across these vendors, and perhaps offering credits, free samples, or discounts whenever a buyer attempts to integrate datasets from different vendors but fails to achieve a desired result.

9. RELATED WORK

The notion of pricing in databases has been studied in various contexts, including resource management [20] and physical tuning [12, 21]. The concept of pricing *data*, however, has only recently emerged as a research topic [11, 17]. In this latter context, a series of recent papers [13, 14, 15] developed theoretical frameworks for flexible data pricing. Our paper builds on this theoretical foundation, but is the first towards a practical design and implementation of a pricing system. More specifically, Koutris *et al.* [13] present and study a formal framework for query-based pricing. Central to this framework are the notions of *arbitrage-free* and *discount-free* pricing. The authors explore in depth the case where the price points are selections on single attributes, and present a dichotomy on the complexity of pricing conjunctive queries without self-joins into NP-complete and PTIME. Further work [15] studies the same pricing framework in the case of *linear* aggregate queries. In contrast, our work focuses on developing and evaluating a practical system to price a large class of queries that can be expressed as Unions of Conjunctive Queries with interpreted predicates, while addressing practical concerns related to dynamic environments.

Digital market services for data have recently emerged in the cloud [1, 7]. Similar to our work, these services also implement data pricing systems, but with simplistic pricing schemes. In the case of Infochimps [7], the seller can either specify and price selection queries or entire datasets. On the Azure Marketplace [1], sellers specify parameterized selection queries over the base data or over pre-defined views. The prices are then set based on the number of output records returned (*subscriptions* give users access to a certain number of result pages in a month). Our pricing system is more powerful, since it can automatically price a much greater variety of queries.

There exist many independent vendors selling data online [4, 3, 8, 5, 10]. They either use simple and limited pricing options to sell data en masse or they negotiate custom products with individual buyers. Factual [4] offers their data through APIs and charges based on the number of API calls per day. Similarly, Xignite [10] sells data through annual subscriptions that come with a monthly limit on the number of returned records. Gnip [3] negotiates prices with individual customers. Finally, Aggdata [5] uses fixed prices for entire datasets or provides full access to their data library for a flat subscription cost.

10. CONCLUSIONS

We presented QueryMarket, a system that automatically prices a large class of SQL queries requested by buyers based on price-points specified by sellers. QueryMarket supports updates to the database and accounts for query history. The system also supports multiple sellers by sharing revenues fairly among them. Computing arbitrage-free prices is theoretically hard, and we described a novel approach for computing prices, by translating then into optimized Integer Linear Programs (ILPs).

11. ACKNOWLEDGMENTS

This work is partially supported by the National Science Foundation and Microsoft through NSF CiC grant CCF-1047815 and NSF grant IIS-0915054.

12. REFERENCES

[1] datamarket.azure.com/.

[2] datamarket.azure.com/dataset/bing/microsofttranslator.

[3] gnip.com.

[4] http://www.factual.com/.

[5] www.aggdata.com/.

[6] www.gnu.org/software/glpk/.

[7] www.infochimps.com/marketplace.

[8] www.patientslikeme.com.

[9] www.wordfrequency.info.

[10] www.xignite.com/.

[11] M. Balazinska, B. Howe, and D. Suciu. Data markets in the cloud: An opportunity for the database community. *PVLDB*, 4(12), 2011.

[12] D. Dash, V. Kantere, and A. Ailamaki. An economic model for self-tuned cloud caching. In *ICDE*, pages 1687–1693, 2009.

[13] P. Koutris, P. Upadhyaya, M. Balazinska, B. Howe, and D. Suciu. Query-based data pricing. In *PODS*, pages 167–178. ACM, 2012.

[14] P. Koutris, P. Upadhyaya, M. Balazinska, B. Howe, and D. Suciu. Querymarket demonstration: Pricing for online data markets. *PVLDB*, 5(12):1962–1965, 2012.

[15] C. Li and G. Miklau. Pricing aggregate queries in a data marketplace. In *WebDB*, 2012.

[16] K. Morton, R. Kosara, J. Mackinlay, M. Balazinska, and D. Grossman. Masses of visualizations: An analysis of usage patterns on many eyes and tableau public. Technical report, 2013.

[17] A. Muschalle, F. Stahl, A. Löser, and G. Vossen. Pricing approaches for data markets. In *BIRTE Workshop*, 2012.

[18] A. Nash, L. Segoufin, and V. Vianu. Determinacy and rewriting of conjunctive queries using views: A progress report. In *ICDT*, pages 59–73, 2007.

[19] C. Shapiro and H. R. Varian. Versioning: The smart way to sell information. *Harvard Business Review*, 76:106–114, 1998.

[20] Stonebraker et al. Mariposa: a wide-area distributed database system. *VLDB Journal*, 5(1):048–063, 1996.

[21] P. Upadhyaya, M. Balazinska, and D. Suciu. How to price shared optimizations in the cloud. *PVLDB*, 5(6):562–573, 2012.

Generalized Scale Independence Through Incremental Precomputation

Michael Armbrust[†‡]
marmbrus@google.com

Eric Liang[‡]
ericliang@berkeley.edu

Tim Kraska[*‡]
tim_kraska@brown.edu

Armando Fox[‡]
fox@cs.berkeley.edu

Michael J. Franklin[‡]
franklin@cs.berkeley.edu

David A. Patterson[‡]
pattrsn@cs.berkeley.edu

[*]Brown University [†]Google, Inc. [‡]University of California, Berkeley

ABSTRACT

Developers of rapidly growing applications must be able to anticipate potential scalability problems before they cause performance issues in production environments. A new type of data independence, called *scale independence*, seeks to address this challenge by guaranteeing a bounded amount of work is required to execute all queries in an application, independent of the size of the underlying data. While optimization strategies have been developed to provide these guarantees for the class of queries that are scale-independent when executed using simple indexes, there are important queries for which such techniques are insufficient.

Executing these more complex queries scale-independently requires precomputation using incrementally-maintained materialized views. However, since this precomputation effectively shifts some of the query processing burden from execution time to insertion time, a scale-independent system must be careful to ensure that storage and maintenance costs do not threaten scalability. In this paper, we describe a scale-independent view selection and maintenance system, which uses novel static analysis techniques that ensure that created views do not themselves become scaling bottlenecks. Finally, we present an empirical analysis that includes all the queries from the TPC-W benchmark and validates our implementation's ability to maintain nearly constant high-quantile query and update latency even as an application scales to hundreds of machines.

Categories and Subject Descriptors

H.2.4 [**Database Management**]: Systems

Keywords

Scalability; Scale Independence; Materialized view selection

1. INTRODUCTION

The ability to anticipate scalability problems is critical to fast-growing Internet services, such as Twitter and Facebook, both of whom have experienced long periods of exponential growth [15, 28]. When attempting to cope with this rapid influx of data, many scale-oriented developers have found that they prefer the straightforward pain of maintaining imperative implementations over the difficulty of identifying potentially expensive operations lurking beneath simple declarative expressions. Following this trend, NoSQL storage systems typically eschew declarative languages, sacrificing the productivity benefits these languages provide.

In our prior work, PIQL [4], we attempted to ensure that applications will perform predictably as they grow in popularity, while simultaneously preserving the many productivity benefits of the relational model. This syncretism was accomplished by introducing *scale independence* [5], a new type of data independence. As data sizes grow, even by orders of magnitude, a scale-independent system enforces strict invariants on the cost of query execution. Towards this end, PIQL incorporated an optimization algorithm that bounds the amount of work required to execute a given query. This technique was capable of handling SQL queries that could be answered scale-independently using only secondary indexes.

However, there are SQL queries, common in real world applications, where those previous techniques fall short. For these more complicated queries, on-demand execution could require reading unbounded amounts of data. For example, the popular online service Twitter needs to calculate the number of people following popular users. Executing this query on-demand could result in response time that grows with the size of the database. Fortunately, it is often possible to safely answer such queries at scale by leveraging *incremental precomputation*, effectively shifting some query processing work from execution time to insertion time.

We formally define two new classes of SQL queries where precomputation fundamentally changes the worst case execution cost at scale. Formalizing the characteristics of these classes allows us to construct a scale-independent view selection and maintenance system. PIQL's view selection system is unlike prior work on materialized views [2, 14, 17, 21], which attempted to minimize cost for a given workload. While these prior techniques select views that may speed up query execution on average, the overall performance of the application can unfortunately remain dependent on the size of the underlying database. Instead, PIQL focuses on ensuring scalability independent of data size and workload.

SIGMOD'13, June 22–27, 2013, New York, New York, USA.

PIQL's optimizer creates incrementally-maintained materialized views (IMVs) only when it is possible to verify the cost of storage and maintenance for these views will not itself introduce a scaling bottleneck. Potential scaling issues are avoided using novel static analysis algorithms that ensure a given view obeys invariants on both the size of the view and the work required by incremental maintenance. We also describe schema analysis and query rewriting techniques that allow PIQL to detect hotspots and mitigate the resulting performance degradation. In summary, we present the following contributions:

- We formalize the invariants and implicit assumptions from prior work on scale independence.
- Using these invariants, we define four levels of scale-independent query execution, two of which were not covered by existing execution techniques.
- We present a scale-independent view construction algorithm along with static analysis techniques to bound the cost of storage and maintenance.
- We describe a mechanism for automatically detecting and mitigating common temporal hotspots using a combination of load balancing and parallel execution.
- We present an empirical study, including all of the queries from the TPC-W benchmark, of the high quantile latency for query execution and maintenance operations as our system scales to hundreds of nodes.

2. SCALE-INDEPENDENT QUERY PROCESSING

As first described by our prior work [5], a scale-independent query processing system seeks to aid developers of rapidly growing applications by guaranteeing predictable query response time, independent of the size of the database. One technique for ensuring this predictability is to maintain invariants on the operations performed and resources required for all queries in an application.

In this section, we first describe the four levels of scale-independent query execution. We then briefly review the optimization techniques used by the initial version of PIQL [4] for queries that can be executed on-demand, formalizing the invariant used to ensure that a given query performs a bounded number of operations in the worst case. We also formalize implicit assumptions made by our prior work regarding the existence of a balanced partitioning for a given workload over a cluster of machines.

Building upon this foundation, we expand the discussion to include queries where previous techniques fall short, but where precomputation through the creation of an IMV can enable scale-independent execution. Since PIQL must ensure that these automatically created IMVs do not themselves threaten scalability, we place restrictions on the resources required for their storage and maintenance. Finally, we give an overview of the workflow used by PIQL to analyze all queries in an application and determine which scale-independent execution level should be used for each. This process results in a list of indexes and IMVs required.

2.1 Scale Independent Execution Levels

In order to help developers reason about the resource requirements of their application, we now define four levels of scale-independent query execution. Table 1 lists these levels and the invariants (Sections 2.2 and 2.3) on execution, update and storage costs that must be enforced for each.

The first level, Scale Independance Level 0 (SI-0), includes trivially scale-independent queries (e.g. `SELECT 1`) as well as queries that can be answered in a scale-independent manner using the clustered index on the primary key (e.g. a query that does a lookup by primary key). For queries in SI-1, it is similarly possible to bound the amount of work performed while executing the query, but only through the creation of a secondary index. Section 2.2 reviews existing optimization techniques that statically analyze queries to determine if they can be executed using one of these two levels.

In contrast to the queries in SI-0 and SI-1, some queries could require an unbounded amount of work to execute on-demand, even after the creation of secondary indexes. Often, precomputation by creating an IMV can fix this problem, enabling scale-independent execution by shifting work to insertion time. However, unlike with simple indexes, a scale-independent view selection system must also consider the scalability of storage and maintenance costs, and we reason about these costs using additional invariants. Section 2.3 introduces these new invariants, which ensure that IMVs themselves do not become a scaling bottleneck. Queries fall into SI-2 if they can be executed in a scale-independent manner using an IMV that satisfies both of the new invariants.

	SI-0	SI-1	SI-2	SI-3
Execution (Inv 1)	I	D	D	D
Execution w/ indexes (Inv 1)	-	I	D	D
IMV Update (Inv 2)	-	-	I	D
IMV Storage (Inv 3)	-	-	I	I
IMV Parallel Updates (Relaxed Invariant 2)	-	-	-	I

Table 1: The four levels of scale-independent execution. 'I' and 'D' denote respectively that the cost of executing a query for a given resource is independent or dependent on scale of the application. A '-' implies the cost is not applicable, and thus the query is trivially scale independent in this dimension.

For each of the aforementioned execution levels it is assumed that the workload can be evenly balanced over all of the machines in the system. Section 2.5 explains in detail why this balanced partitioning is required to avoid the increased query response time associated with hotspots. Prior definitions of scale independence [4] failed to deal with the fact that the naive use of secondary indexes can violate this assumption in cases where there is temporal locality of insertions relative to the value being indexed (e.g. an index over the attribute `created_on`). Fortunately, these hotspots can often be mitigated by spreading new insertions across the cluster and periodically computing aggregate results in parallel. However, since this execution pattern requires relaxing the invariant on the total work performed by an update, we place queries that utilize this strategy in the final query execution level, SI-3.

2.2 Scale-Independent Optimization

To review our prior work: PIQL takes as input the set of parameterized queries Q used by an application. The optimizer analyzes all queries in Q to ensure that the database can grow while maintaining consistent performance.

For the purposes of scale-independence, database growth occurs over the following three dimensions:

$\lvert R \rvert$	the size of all base relations
Δ_{rate}	the update rate for all base relations
q_{rate}	the rate of read queries in the system

PIQL achieved scale independence across these dimensions by designing the optimizer to select only physical plans that perform a bounded number of I/O operations, independent of $|R|$ (i.e., the size of all base relations). In contrast to standard average cost minimization, PIQL's optimization technique prevents the selection of query plans that may perform well for most users but that could violate an application's Service Level Objective (SLO) for statistical outliers. It also allows the database to warn the developer of queries that pose a potential scalability problem and provide suggestions for resolving the issue before the query can cause SLO violations in production. The invariant that is maintained by this optimization technique can be formalized as:

Invariant 1. Let $Exec(q_i)$ denote the number of operations[1] performed in the worst case by a query and $c_{ops}^{q_i}$ be a constant for a given query q_i. A scale-independent optimizer will only create physical query plans such that:

$$\forall q_i \in Q \exists c_{ops}^{q_i} : Exec(q_i) < c_{ops}^{q_i}$$

A system can verify that an application will satisfy this invariant by performing a static analysis of the application's schema and queries. For example, uniqueness constraints ensure that a query that performs a lookup by primary key will return at most one result, and thus require a bounded number of operations to execute.

To expand the space of queries that can be verified as scale independent, it is possible to employ language extensions to standard SQL. For example, Data Definition Language (DDL) cardinality constraints (introduced in [4]) allow developers to specify restrictions on the relationships present in their application, which are enforced at insertion time.

To understand this optimization technique more concretely, consider a simple application that stores documents along with associated tags with the following schema:

```
Tags(docId, tag, timestamp) WITH CARDINALITY(tag, K)
Documents(docId, timestamp, text, ...)
```

Italicized columns form the primary key of a relation and the `WITH CARDINALITY` clause denotes a cardinality constraint K on the number of unique values of `tag` that can exist for any given `docId`. An example of a scale-independent query on this schema is the following parametrized SQL, which returns the set of tags for a given document.

```
SELECT * FROM Tags WHERE docId = <doc>
```

For any value of the `<doc>` parameter, the query can be executed by scanning a bounded range of the clustered primary key index on `Tags` and will return at most K tuples. Thus, the optimizer can guarantee that this query will never violate Invariant 1.

2.3 Scale-Independent View Selection

Not all queries can be answered scale-independently using only indexes, and in this section we describe how the addition of IMV selection to PIQL enables the scale-independent execution of many of these previously unsafe queries. For example, the following shows the `twoTags` query, which returns the five newest documents assigned two user-specified tags.

```
SELECT t1.docId
FROM tags t1, tags t2, documents d
WHERE t1.docId = t2.docId AND
      t1.docId = d.docId AND
      t1.tag = <tag1> AND t2.tag = <tag2>
ORDER BY d.timestamp LIMIT 5
```

While a secondary index on `Tags.tag` would allow efficient lookup of the documents for a given tag, such an index is not sufficient to enable the scale-independent execution of the `twoTags` query. The performance of the query is potentially dependent on the size of the data due to the fact that during any given execution an unbounded number of rows matching `tag1` might need to be scanned before finding five documents that also match `tag2` or vice versa. In practice, developers faced with a query such as this one often utilize a technique known as intersection precomputation or caching [19], where all two tag combinations for a document are computed ahead of time (analogous to the creation of a join index [27]).

While there has been significant prior work on leveraging precomputation through automatic materialized view selection [2, 17, 21] and incremental maintenance [1, 6, 7, 13, 25], these approaches have focused on minimizing average cost for a given workload, rather than ensuring consistent resource requirements as the database grows. As such, these techniques could create a view that may speed up query execution on average, while the absolute performance of the query remains dependent on the size of the underlying data. Simply executing faster is not sufficient to guarantee SLO compliance as an application explodes in popularity.

In contrast, PIQL must only create an IMV when it will allow a query to be answered scale-independently. In addition to determining the scalability of the query when it is run over the materialized view, we must also ensure that the resources required to incrementally maintain and store the created materialized views do not themselves threaten the scalability of the application. To better explain the potential scalability threat posed by the inclusion of materialized views we now formalize the additional invariants that must be maintained by a scale-independent view selection system.

Bounding Update Cost

A scale-independent view selection system must avoid IMVs whose update cost increases with the scale of the application. To this end, the optimizer checks that there is an upper bound on the number of operations required to incrementally update all indexes and views given an update to a single tuple in a base relation. Said formally:

Invariant 2. Let $Update(r_i)$ denote the number of operations performed in the worst case by index and view maintenance when updating a single tuple in r_i, and let $c_{ops}^{r_i}$ be a constant for r_i. A scale-independent optimizer will create views such that the total maintenance costs will never violate the following condition:

$$\forall r_i \in R \exists c_{ops}^{r_i} : Update(r_i) < c_{ops}^{r_i}$$

For queries in SI-3, we relax Invariant 2 to permit queries where serial work performed by a single machine is bounded, instead of the total work for a single update.

[1]Operations are restricted to those with nearly constant latency. For example, a bounded lookup given an index.

Bounding Storage

It is possible for the size of an IMV to grow super-linearly with the size of the base relations, for example, due to an unconstrained join. Therefore, PIQL ensures that the size of each view is at most a constant factor larger than one of the base relations present in the view. Said formally:

Invariant 3. Let V be the set of all created views required to answer the queries in Q and let $c^{v_i}_{storage}$ be a constant for a view v_i. Let r_{v_i} be a relation in R and $|r_{v_i}|$ denote the number of tuples in r_{v_i}. A scale independent system creates IMVs with linear storage requirements by ensuring that:

$$\forall v_i \in V \exists c^{v_i}_{storage}, r_{v_i} \in R : |v_i| < c^{v_i}_{storage}|r_{v_i}|$$

2.4 Query Compilation

Figure 1 shows the five phases of PIQL, which are used to determine how to scale-independently execute a query. In addition to validating the scalability of all queries in an application and creating necessary indexes and IMVs, PIQL will also tell developers which level each query falls into so they can reason about its resource requirements and update latency characteristics.

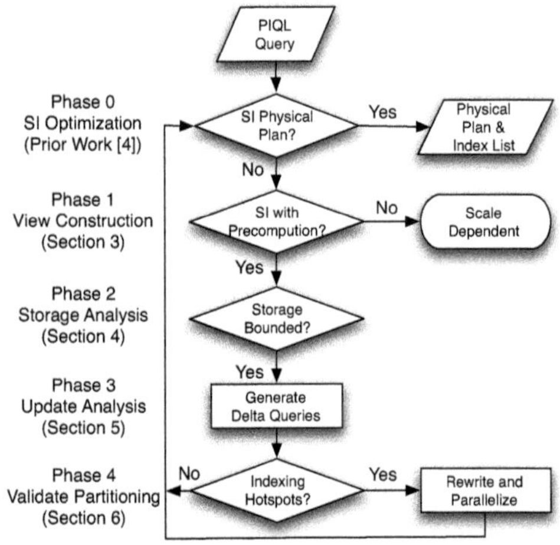

Figure 1: The phases of the scale-independent optimizer and view selection system.

Queries in level SI-0 or SI-1 are handled using prior techniques by generating a scale-independent physical execution plan (Phase 0), automatically creating indexes as needed. For cases where scale-independent physical plan for a query cannot be found by the optimizer, this paper describes how to expand a scale-independent relational system to answer the query instead by leveraging scale-independent precomputation (Phases 1-3). This view selection process occurs automatically through the creation of an IMV for queries that fall into SI-2. Additionally, PIQL ensures that common sources of hotspots are avoided (Phase 4), rewriting the query as a distributed staging step followed by a periodic parallel view refresh step. Since the resources required by the parallel view refresh step do not satisfy the strict form of Invariant 2, queries that require this transformation fall into SI-3.

2.5 Achieving Predictable Response Time

The bounds on execution cost enforced by Invariant 1 are useful not only for constraining resource requirements, but also for reasoning about performance. In [4], it was demonstrated empirically that bounding the number of operations performed by all queries in the worst case allows an application to achieve predictable response time as long as a scalable underlying storage system is used.

For example, many key/value stores can execute low-level operations such as `get(key)`, `getRange(prefix, limit)`, `put(key, value)` with consistent performance, even at high quantiles, by using a combination of autonomic techniques and over-provisioning [11, 26]. Since each query or update performs only a bounded number of these operations in the worst case, it is possible to reason about the probability distribution of the worst case execution time of each query [4]. This worst case reasoning is especially valuable for developers of interactive applications, who care about the response time for every user of their system.

While [4] demonstrated that it is possible to achieve nearly constant latency while scaling up, it is important to understand the implicit assumption that enables this predictability. Specifically, achieving consistent performance as the amount of data and number of machines grow is only possible when the growing workload can be spread evenly across machines in an ever growing cluster.

If no balanced partitioning of the workload exists, then eventually a single partition will become overloaded by the increased workload. As queues build on the overloaded machine, the latency for requests to this server will grow and eventually affect the overall response time of the application. For example, a hotspot will eventually occur when there is a query that requires a secondary index over the tuple creation timestamp field of a table. Maintaining this index naively would eventually result in a hotspot at the server holding the partition corresponding to the current time.

Section 6 describes how PIQL automatically avoids the creation of such indexes, instead utilizing workload balancing coupled with a periodic parallel collection step.

3. VIEW SELECTION

The first phase of PIQL's view selection system, view construction, is invoked when the optimizer is unable to find a scale independent physical plan for a query. Since this query does not fall into either SI-0 or SI-1, the optimizer will instead try to answer the query by creating an IMV. Note that this is only the first step in scale-independent view selection and merely constructs a view that *could* be used to answer the query while satisfying Invariant 1. The algorithms in this section do not yet ensure that this view will meet the other invariants regarding storage and maintenance costs. The general form of the IMVs created is as follows:

CREATE VIEW <viewName>
SELECT A_{view} [A_{agg}]
FROM $r_1, r_2, ...r_n$
WHERE P_{view} [GROUP BY A_{eq}]

A_{view} is an ordered list of the attributes projected by the IMV, while A_{agg} contains any aggregate expressions. The relations r_1 to r_n are the base relations present in the original query, and P_{view} is the set of predicates for the IMV. In the case of queries with aggregate expressions, a `GROUP BY` clause is also added to the IMV definition.

The construction algorithm ensures the created IMV will allow scale-independent execution of the original query by assuming that the underlying storage structure allows scale-independent access to tuples in the view given a prefix of the attributes present in A_{view}. Examples of acceptable storage systems include B-Trees and range-partitioned distributed key/value stores. We adopt the convention that the SQL expression used to define an IMV must specify not only which tuples are present in the view but also the ordering of attributes in the clustered index used to store the view. Thus, the definitions of created IMVs effectively define the spatial locality of the precomputed tuples.

3.1 View Construction Without Aggregates

The view construction algorithm presented in this section handles *select-project-join* queries with *conjunctive* predicates. Section 3.2 expands this algorithm to enable support for queries with aggregate expressions. At a high level, this algorithm is solving a variant of the view selection problem where the result of the target query must be computable by scanning a contiguous section of the view for any value of the runtime parameters. We start by describing how predicates that include runtime parameters are handled. Next, we describe the checks employed to ensure that the result of the original query can be obtained by scanning a contiguous section of the selected view. Finally, we describe the construction of the final view definition.

View construction starts by parsing predicates of the form *attr* `= <parameter>` or *attr* `{<, >, ≤, ≥} <parameter>`. Using these predicates, the algorithm constructs the sets A_{eq} and A_{ineq}, which contain attributes occurring in equality and inequality predicates respectively. These attribute sets are added to the prefix of the projection of the view, allowing the predicates of the original query to be evaluated efficiently using an index scan.

As a concrete example, for the **twoTags** query (Section 2) the set A_{eq} contains `{t1.tag, t2.tag}`, and A_{ineq} is empty.

Next, Algorithm 1 checks to ensure that the answer to the original query for any set of runtime parameters will be a contiguous set of tuples in the view. The requirements for this condition are as follows: Any number of attributes may be filtered by equality with a runtime parameter. In contrast, at most one attribute can be filtered by an inequality with a parameter, though this attribute may appear in more than one predicate (i.e., in the case of interval queries). This limitation is due to the fact that computing the intersection of two inequality predicates against different attributes may involve scanning over an arbitrary number of tuples in the view, and thus could violate Invariant 1. Similarly, any number of attributes may be specified in the `ORDER BY` clause, but this ordering must be prefixed by the inequality attribute, if one exists.

Algorithm 1 Confirming Adjacency of Result Tuples

if $|A_{ineq}| > 1 \lor (|A_{order}| > 0 \land A_{order}[0] \neq A_{ineq})$ **then**
    return *false*
end if
return *true*

If Algorithm 1 returns successfully, it then creates the set P_{view}. This step is accomplished by removing any predicates that involve a runtime parameter and then simplifying any redundant equality predicates.

To avoid changing the meaning of the query, it is important that this procedure does not inadvertently discard any transitive equality constraints present due to parameters that appear multiple times in the query. For example, given a query with the predicates a_1 `= <p1>` and a_2 `= <p1>`, P_{view} must contain the predicate $a_1 = a_2$. We account for these transitive equalities by generating predicates for the view from the equivalence classes defined by the equality predicates in the original query. Inequality predicates, in contrast, are copied directly from the original query. These predicates will eventually be turned into inequalities with parameters during delta query calculation (Section 5). Therefore, the rules regarding multiple attributes participating in inequalities still apply, and thus the creation of the view could be later be rejected due to a lack of a scale-independent maintenance strategy.

Algorithm 2 Generating View Predicates

1: $P :=$ set of all conjunctive predicates in the query of the form $v1\ op\ v2$
2: EquivalenceClasses(P) := set of equivalence classes under P
3: $P_{view} \leftarrow \{\}$
4: **for all** $X \in EquivalenceClasses(P)$ **do**
5:     $prevAttr := \varnothing$
6:     **for all** $v \in X$ **do**
7:         **if** $!isParam(v)$ **then**
8:             **if** $prevAttr \neq \varnothing$ **then**
9:                 $P_{view} := P_{view} + Equality(prevAttr, v)$
10:             **end if**
11:             $prevAttr := v$
12:         **end if**
13:     **end for**
14: **end for**
15: **for all** $p \in P$ **do**
16:     **if** $isInequality(p.op)$ **then**
17:         **if** $!isParam(p.v1) \land !isParam(p.v2)$ **then**
18:             $P_{view} := P_{view} + p$
19:         **end if**
20:     **end if**
21: **end for**

Algorithm 2 describes this process of creating P_{view}. Taking as input the set of conjunctive predicates (Line 1), the algorithm starts by partitioning values found in P into equivalence classes (Line 2). Next, for every equivalence class (Line 3), the algorithm adds an equality predicate to P_{view} for each attribute pair in the class (Line 4-11). Finally, the algorithm copies inequality predicates involving non-parameters into P_{view} (Line 15-21).

As an example, consider again the **twoTags** query. The predicates in this query define three equivalence classes:

```
{t1.docId, t2.docId, d.docId}, {t1.tag, <tag1>},
{t2.tag, <tag2>}
```

From these classes the following is produced for P_{view}:

```
{t1.docId = t2.docId, t1.docId = d.docId}
```

Once P_{view} has been constructed, the system next creates A_{view}. A_{view} contains the attributes in A_{eq} and A_{ineq} as well as any remaining key attributes from the top-level tables present in the original query. These key attributes are added to the projection in order to ensure the view can be efficiently maintained using production rules, as proposed by Ceri and Widom [7]. Specifically, the view selector ensures that there will be no duplicate tuples in the view and that all top-level table references are safe. Additionally, to avoid unnecessary redundancy, any key attributes that are unified by an equality predicate in the original query will only appear once in the projection of the view.

Algorithm 3 Choosing View Keys

1: $R :=$ the set of relations present in the original query
2: $A_{keys} := \{a : r \in R, a \in keyAttrs(r)\}$
3: $A_{view} \leftarrow []$
4: $A_{covered} \leftarrow \{\}$
5: **function** EQUIVALENCECLASS(P, a)
6:     return all values in P unified with a due to equality predicates, including a itself
7: **end function**
8: **for all** $a \in A_{eq} + A_{ineq} + A_{order} + A_{keys}$ **do**
9:     **if** $a \notin A_{covered}$ **then**
10:         $A_{view} := A_{view} + a$
11:         $A_{covered} := A_{covered} \cup EquivalenceClass(P, a)$
12:     **end if**
13: **end for**

Algorithm 3 describes the process used to populate A_{view} and starts by initializing A_{keys} to be the set of key attributes for all top-level tables from the original query (Line 2). Next, it initialises A_{view}, the ordered list of attributes that will appear in the view, and $A_{covered}$, the set of attributes already represented in the view definition considering unification, to be empty (Lines 3-4). Then, it iterates over the ordered concatenation of the attribute sets (Line 8) and adds to the view any attributes not yet present in the cover set $A_{covered}$ (Line 10). To prevent redundant values from appearing in the view, when an attribute is added, its entire equivalence class is added to $A_{covered}$ (Line 11).

Applying Algorithm 3 to the `twoTags` query, the attributes `t1.tag`, `t2.tag`, `d.timestamp`, and `d.docId` are selected. The first two attributes come from A_{eq}, `d.timestamp` comes from A_{order}, and `d.docId` from A_{keys}. By placing attributes from A_{eq} first, the view selector ensures that tuples satisfying the original query can be located by a prefix of the keys in the view. Including `d.timestamp` next ensures that the relevant tuples in the view will be sorted as specified by the `ORDER BY` clause. Finally, `d.docId` allows for safe view maintenance and the retrieval of the actual document.

Continuing the `twoTags` example, the following materialized view is created by the view constructor:

```
CREATE VIEW twoTagsView
SELECT t1.tag as t1tag, t2.tag as t2tag,
       d.timestamp, d.docId
FROM Tags t1, Tags t2, Documents d
WHERE t1.docId = t2.docId AND
      t1.docId = d.docId
```

Once the view has been constructed for a given query, the query is rewritten by replacing the top-level tables with the view and renaming any attributes to their equivalent attribute in the view. If there are any attributes that are present in the original query, but not in the view, they can be retrieved either by joining the view with the base relation on the keys that are present, or by adding the missing attributes to the view definition. The former will require more computation at query time while the latter will require more storage for the view. Since the method does not affect the scale independence of the query, the system decides which technique to use based on the predicted SLO compliance of the resulting query.

This final step rewrites the `twoTags` query to use the materialized view as follows:

```
SELECT t1.docId
FROM twoTagView
WHERE t1tag = <tag1> AND t2tag = <tag2>
ORDER BY timestamp LIMIT 5
```

3.2 View Construction With Aggregates

PIQL's view selection system is also capable of handling many queries that contain aggregates in the target list. In this subsection, we describe both the class of aggregates that are supported and the alternative view selection algorithm used when an aggregate is present in a query.

3.2.1 Scale-Independent Aggregates

The class of scale-independent aggregates is defined in part by the storage requirements for partial aggregate values. Using the categories of aggregates first defined by Gray et al. [12], PIQL can safely store partial aggregate values for both *distributive* aggregates (such as `COUNT` or `SUM`) and *algebraic* aggregates (such as `AVERAGE` and `VARIANCE`). Both of these categories have partial state records of fixed size. In contrast, *holistic* aggregates like `MEDIAN` can require an unbounded amount of partial state to be stored and thus conflict with our goal of scale independence.

Bounding the storage required for each partial aggregate value alone is not sufficient, as we must also ensure that efficient incremental maintenance of aggregated values is possible. Towards this end, we also require updates to the aggregate be both associative and commutative. While both `MIN` and `MAX` are distributive aggregates, updates to them do not always commute in the presence of deletions. For example, when the maximum value from a given group is deleted, the only way to update the aggregate is to scan over an unbounded set of tuples looking for the new maximum value.

3.2.2 View Selection with Aggregates

When PIQL's view selection system detects an aggregate in the projection of a scale-dependent query, it uses a slightly modified view construction algorithm. We explain these modifications in four parts.

Ordering Views containing aggregates cannot have any inequalities with parameters, as these could require unbounded computation to maintain. Additionally, since each query containing an aggregate will return only one tuple, there is no `ORDER BY` clause. These two changes eliminate the need for Algorithm 1.

Keys Views containing aggregates are maintained using techniques analogous to a counting solution [13]. Thus, it is not necessary to use Algorithm 3 to add keys for safe maintenance.

Aggregate Expressions The view selection algorithm must add partial aggregate values A_{agg} to the created view. In the case of distributive aggregates, only the aggregate expression itself must be added, while for algebraic aggregates more information may be required to ensure efficient incremental maintainability. For example, `AVERAGE` is computed by keeping both a `SUM` and a `COUNT`.

Group By Clause All of the attributes in A_{eq} are added to the group by clause of the created view.

The following is an example of how this modified algorithm would select a view for the countTags query, which calculates the number of documents assigned a given tag.

```
SELECT COUNT(*)           CREATE VIEW docsPerTag
FROM Tags                 SELECT tag, COUNT(*) as cnt
WHERE tag = <tag>         FROM Tags t
                          GROUP BY tag
```

3.3 Views for Window Queries

PIQL can handle many queries that operate over windows of data, and the techniques for handling these queries fall into two categories. For queries that operate over a fixed size tuple window, an index can be created on insertion timestamp. Since the tuple window bounds the number of tuples that will need to be retrieved from this index, scale independent optimization can then be performed on the rest of the query using standard techniques. Section 6 discusses the special consideration required when creating such indexes to avoid hotspots as the size of the database scales.

Aggregate queries that operate over a time window are handled by prepending an *epoch* identifier to the beginning of the view. The epoch identifier calculated using the following formula: $timestamp - (timestamp \mod windowSize)$. For example, consider modifying the countTags query from the previous section to count tags for a sliding window of length one minute. PIQL would create the following view (assuming timestamp is measured in milliseconds).

```
CREATE VIEW docsPerTagWindowed
SELECT (timestamp - (timestamp % (60*1000)),
       tag, COUNT(*) as count
FROM Tags t
GROUP BY (timestamp - (timestamp % (60*1000)), tag
```

Queries where the window size is larger than the slide amount can also be handled but will result in updates to all relevant epochs. Stale epochs can be garbage collected.

4. BOUNDING STORAGE COSTS

Once a candidate view has been produced by the selection algorithm described above, Phase 2 performs a static analysis of the maximum possible storage requirements. If the analysis determines that the view could grow super-linearly relative to the size of the base relations, the view is rejected, as its creation might violate Invariant 3.

PIQL's view size analysis utilizes dependency information from both the schema and the view definition. Note that the dependencies defined in this section subsume standard functional dependencies, where the latter can be represented as a cardinality dependency of weight one.

At a high level, the algorithm bounds the maximum size of a view by determining how many degrees of freedom remain after taking into account all of the tuples from a single relation in the view definition. In doing so, the algorithm determines whether the dependencies present are sufficient to ensure that the view is bounded in size by a constant factor relative to at least one base relation.

4.1 Enumerating Dependencies

The analysis starts by constructing the list of all dependencies for a given view definition. These dependencies are generated by analyzing the view as well as the schema of the application using the following four rules:

1. $(keyAttributes) \rightarrow (otherAttributes)$
   Add a dependency of weight one to represent the functional dependency due to the primary key's uniqueness constraint.
2. $(keyAttributes) \xrightarrow{cardinality} (constrainedFields)$
   Add a dependency for each relation that has a cardinality constraint declared in the schema, weighted by the cardinality of the constraint.
3. $attribute_1 \leftrightarrow attribute_2$
   Add a bidirectional dependency of weight one for each attribute pair present in an equality predicate in the WHERE clause of the view definition.
4. Fixed Value $\rightarrow$ *attr*
   Add a directional edge from a special fixed node to any attribute that is fixed by an equality predicate with a literal (e.g. $attr$ = true). This dependency is always implied, independent of what other dependencies are being considered.

Take, for example, the view definition of the twoTags query from the previous section. Given this view definition, the algorithm will produce the following list of dependencies. We omit trivial dependencies for the sake of brevity.

$$d.docId \rightarrow (d.timestamp, \ldots) \quad (1)$$

$$t1.docId \xrightarrow{K} t1.tag \quad (2)$$

$$t2.docId \xrightarrow{K} t2.tag \quad (3)$$

$$t1.docId \leftrightarrow t2.docId \quad (4)$$

$$t1.docId \leftrightarrow d.docId \quad (5)$$

First, dependency 1 is added to the set due to the primary key of the document relations. Next, dependencies 2 and 3 are added to the set due to the cardinality constraint that each document may have no more than K tags. Finally, dependencies 4 and 5 are added as a result of the equality predicates present in the view definition.

4.2 Bounding Size Relative to a Relation

The following algorithm determines if the maximum size of the view is linearly proportional to one of the relations present in the query, using the dependency list generated by the above rules. This analysis is performed by finding a relation present in the query such that all attributes present in the view are functionally dependent on the primary key of the selected relation. If independent attributes remain after the inclusion of all possible dependencies, then a bound on the size of the IMV does not exist relative to that relation. If no relation can be found such that all attributes are functionally dependent on its primary key, then the view is rejected due to a possible violation of Invariant 3.

Algorithm 4 describes this process formally, and takes as input the set of all relations present in the view and all dependencies for the IMV (Lines 1-2). It returns a boolean value indicating if there is an upper bound on the size of the view due to these dependencies. The algorithm iterates over all of the relations present in the view definition. For each relation, the set of attributes functionally dependent on this relation a_{dep} is initialized to the key attributes of the relation (Line 4). Then, the algorithm iteratively selects the set of attributes a that are functionally dependent on the attributes in a_{dep} given D but are not yet present in a_{dep} (Line 6). These new attributes are then added to a_{dep}

(Line 7). If a_{dep} now includes all attributes from the view, we know the view size is bounded relative to the relation r, thus, the algorithm returns *true* (Lines 8-10). The iteration stops if at any point there are no more attributes to add to the set (Line 11). If no bound can be found for any relation, the algorithm returns *false* (Line 13).

Algorithm 4 Bounding Maximum View Size

1: $R :=$ the set of all relations present in the view
2: $D :=$ the set of dependencies for the IMV
3: **for all** $r \in R$ **do**
4: $\quad A_{dep} := keyAttrs(r)$
5: $\quad$ **repeat**
6: $\quad\quad A := \{a \mid a \in attrs(R), a \notin a_{dep}, D \models A_{dep} \rightarrow a\}$
7: $\quad\quad A_{dep} := A_{dep} \cup A$
8: $\quad\quad$ **if** $A_{dep} \supseteq attrs(R)$ **then**
9: $\quad\quad\quad$ **return** *true*
10: $\quad\quad$ **end if**
11: $\quad$ **until** $|A| = 0$
12: **end for**
13: **return** *false*

To understand this process more concretely, consider again the definition of the IMV created by our system to answer the `twoTags` query. Algorithm 4 will start by selecting the Tags (t1) relation. This initializes a_{dep} to `{t1.id, t1.tag}`. On the first iteration, it will add `{t2.docId, d.docId}` to a_{dep} due to dependencies 4 and 5 respectively. Then, on the second iteration, it will add all remaining attributes due to dependencies 1 and 3. At this point, since all attributes in the query are in a_{dep}, the algorithm will return *true*.

Note that Algorithm 4 would return *false* were it not for the cardinality constraint on the number of tags per document (functional dependencies 2 and 3). To understand how this schema modification could cause the `twoTagView` definition to violate Invariant 3, consider the degenerate case of a database with only a single document. As the number of tags increases, the size of the view would grow quadratically.

4.3 Views with GROUP BY

When the view contains a `GROUP BY` clause, we must modify the procedure for determining if the storage required by the view is bounded. This modification is a result of the fact that the `GROUP BY` effectively collapses many tuples down to those with unique values for the attributes in the `GROUP BY`. Thus, instead of requiring attributes from all relations to be covered by the dependencies, it is sufficient to have dependencies that cover only the attributes being grouped on. This change can be implemented simply by substituting $attrs(R)$ with the set of attributes present in the `GROUP BY` on Line 8 of Algorithm 4.

5. BOUNDING MAINTENANCE COST

Once the view selection system has produced a candidate view and verified that a bound exists for the storage required by the view, Phase 3 ensures the existence of an upper bound on the number of operations required by incremental maintenance given a single update to any of the relations present in the view. In this section, we first review the standard techniques used to perform incremental maintenance. We then explain the analysis performed to ensure that the total number of operations required by this mechanism will be bounded.

5.1 Maintenance Using Production Rules

PIQL performs incremental maintenance using production rules [7] that execute each time a base relation is modified. At a high level, the production rules update the view by running a *delta query*. This delta query calculates all of the tuples that should be added or removed from the view due to a single tuple insertion or deletion. An updated tuple is processed as a delete followed by an insert.

Since PIQL's view construction algorithm ensures the safety of incremental maintenance, the delta query for an update can be derived by substituting the updated relation with the single tuple being inserted or deleted. In order to understand the delta query's derivation more concretely, consider the IMV `twoTagsView` when a new tag is inserted. PIQL's view selection system would calculate the first delta query by substituting the relation `t1` with the modified tuple in the view definition. Notationally, we represent the values of inserted or deleted tuple as `<parameters>` to the delta query. This substitution produces the following rule which will be run anytime a tuple is added to the `Tags` relation:

```
CREATE RULE newTag ON INSERT Tags
INSERT INTO twoTagsView
SELECT <tag>, t2.tag as t2tag, d.timestamp, d.docId
FROM Tags t2, Documents d
WHERE t2.docId = <docId> AND d.docId = <docId>
```

Update rules must be created for all of the relations present in the view definition, including another rule for the second instance of the `Tags` relation. Due to the presence of a self-join, the inserted tuple must also be joined with itself. We omit the other delta queries from the paper for brevity.

5.2 Maintenance Cost Analysis

Given all of the delta queries for a view, we must verify that none of them threaten the scalability of the application by requiring an unbounded number of operations during execution. Fortunately, since these delta queries are represented as SQL queries, we can reuse the optimization techniques from prior work [4] to perform this analysis. If the optimizer is able to find scale-independent plans for all of the delta queries, then we can certify that the addition of the view will not cause a violation of Invariant 2.

For example, consider the delta query `newTag` from the previous subsection. Due to the cardinality constraint on the number of tags per document, this query can always be executed by performing a single sequential scan.

Since verifying the scalability of the delta queries involves invoking the optimizer again, it is possible that the only scale-independent physical plan for a delta query will also require the creation of an index or materialized view. Thus, in some cases the creation of a materialized view could result in multiple *recursive* invocations of the view selection system. Fortunately, we can be assured that this recursion will always terminate since the degree of the query will decrease with each successive derivation [16].

5.3 Updating Aggregates

Materialized views that contain aggregates are also maintained using delta queries with one important distinction. Delta queries for aggregate functions return a list of updates to possibly existing rows instead of tuples that will be added or removed from the IMV. Notationally, we represent the update that will be applied to a given field in the view as an expression in the SELECT clause prefixed by a +.

The delta queries themselves are derived using rules similar to those used for other queries. Specifically, the inserted tuple is substituted for the relation being updated and simplified, leveraging the distributivity properties of joins and aggregates [16]. For example, considering the view for the countTags query, the following delta query is used for maintenance:

```
CREATE RULE ON INSERT INTO Tags
UPDATE twoTagsCount
SELECT <tag>, t2.tag, +1
FROM Tags t2
WHERE t2.docId = <docId>
```

When a new tag is inserted for a document, this query increments the count of all combinations of this tag and others already present for that document. The rules for deletions are symmetric and thus omitted for brevity.

6. AVOIDING COMMON HOTSPOTS

Preventing workload hotspots a critical when attempting to maintain consistent performance in a distributed query execution system. While clearly it is not possible to predict and avoid all possible hotspots, PIQL is able to detect some common cases using schema annotations provided by the developer. Based on these annotations, PIQL will avoid creating indexes that could result in a hotspot, and will instead suggest views that spread the insertions across the cluster. In this section we describe an addition to standard DDL and the technique used to rewrite potentially problematic queries.

6.1 DDL Annotations

PIQL allows developers to annotate columns whose values exhibit strong temporal locality with respect to insertions. Figure 2 shows the canonical example of such locality, an index over the creation timestamp for a given record. Since all records created within a short time period will have similar values for this attribute, all updates to an index ordered over this attribute will be routed to the same partition. While this concentration of updates will not result in performance issues at a small scale, it is in direct conflict of our goal of predictable performance as the system grows.

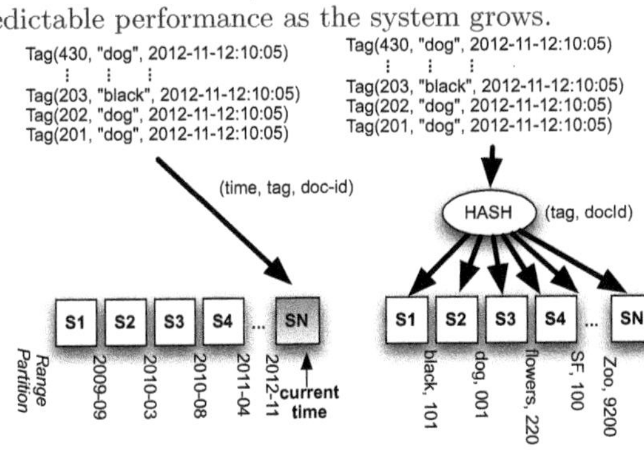

Figure 2: Indexes over timestamps can result in hotspots, denoted by the shaded server. In contrast, PIQL chooses to distribute insertions over all machines in the cluster.

Developers can warn the optimizer to avoid the creation of these hotspot prone indexes by using the TEMPORAL keyword. For example, consider the following modification to the Tags schema, first introduced in Section 2.

```
Tags(docId, tag, timestamp TEMPORAL) WITH ...
```

6.2 Query Rewriting

When PIQL detects a hot-spot prone index, it instead creates materialized views that can be used to answer the query using a two step process. As an example of a case where this process would occur, consider the following query, popularTags, which returns the most popular tags out of the most recent 5000 insertions.

```
SELECT tag, COUNT(*)
FROM (SELECT * FROM Tags
      ORDER BY timestamp
        LIMIT 5000)
GROUP BY tag
```

Using only prior techniques, the optimizer would classify this as SI-1 and attempt to execute it on-demand with an index over Tags.timestamp. This execution plan would be problematic at scale, however, as maintaining this index in a range partitioned system would eventually lead to an overloaded partition and subsequently high query latency.

Instead of creating this hot-spot prone index, PIQL will instead create a view that is hash partitioned by the primary key of the relation. In the example below, this partitioning can be seen though the HASH keyword at the beginning of the view definition. Within each partition the records are sorted by the TEMPORAL attribute (i.e., timestamp in this example). Any remaining required attributes are appended to the end of SELECT clause. This procedure results in the following materialized view for the popularTags query.

```
CREATE VIEW popularTagStaging
SELECT HASH(tag, docId), timestamp, tag
FROM Tags
```

Next, the original query is rewritten as a periodically updated materialized view by substituting the original relation with the hash-partitioned materialized view. For the popularTags query this transformation results in the following SQL.

```
CREATE VIEW popularTags PERIODIC 1 MIN
SELECT tag, COUNT(*)
FROM (SELECT * FROM popularTagStaging
      ORDER BY timestamp
        LIMIT 5000)
GROUP BY tag
```

The optimizer will choose a physical plan that executes the subquery in parallel on each partition. Since the tuples in each of the partitions are sorted by the desired ordering attribute, each partition will only need to scan over 5000 tuples in the worst case. Therefore, the total amount of work that needs to be performed serially has a constant upper bound. However, since the total amount of computation is now proportional to the number of machines in the cluster, this query now falls into SI-3, unlike the twoTags query from the previous sections, which falls into SI-2. Section 8.2.2 demonstrates that even though the total amount of work grows with the size of the cluster, the increased parallelism allows us to execute the query with only minor increases in the periodic update latency.

7. CONSISTENCY

PIQL's techniques are compatible with a variety of consistency guarantees, including online maintenance [20, 23] or deferred view maintenance [24, 9]. For applications with strong consistency requirements, a locking-based view maintenance mechanism can be used [23, 20]. However, depending on the data access patterns such locking-based techniques might create contention points and therefore potentially violate our goal of predictable performance at scale. As an alternative to locking-based techniques, many deferred view maintenance techniques, such as 2VNL [24], perform optimistic view maintenance. Finally, eventually consistent view maintenance techniques [23] provide the lowest overhead per update, but often at the price of a few concurrent updates never being reflected in the view (see also view maintenance anomalies [18]).

The current implementation uses the simplest technique, relaxed view maintenance. We, however, ensure that all updates are eventually reflected in the view using the following procedure: Delta queries execute under relaxed consistency, while background batch jobs check for and repair any inconsistencies that may arise by periodically reconstructing the entire materialized view. The frequency of the execution of these batch jobs can be tuned to meet the needs of a specific application. This approach provides a balance between low-latency updates, high availability, and consistency.

Clearly, the efficiency of PIQL could be improved by only checking for inconsistencies in those sections of the view that have changed recently as done in [24]. We believe this optimization as well as other mechanisms for eventually-consistent, distributed incremental view maintenance represent interesting future research problems.

8. EXPERIMENTS

In order to understand the effect the scale-independent invariants have on the latency of both query execution and view maintenance, we ran two sets of experiments. The first, a micro-benchmark based on the `twoTags` example query (Section 2), demonstrates the need for an IMV when answering a query in SI-2, as well as showing bounded latency for both query execution and the incremental maintenance of the view. The second experiment demonstrates the scalability of our system under a more holistic workload by running all queries from the TPC-W benchmark, using the modifications and IMVs suggested by PIQL's optimizer.

Experiments were run using Amazon EC2 m1.large instances, which have 7.5 GB of memory and CPU power roughly equivalent to a two-core, 2GHz processor. SCADS [5] was used for the underlying storage system and provisioned for each experiment such that all nodes were responsible for the same amount of data and workload.

8.1 TwoTags Benchmark

Without an IMV, the `twoTags` query can often be expected to return quickly, but common data access patterns can result in arbitrarily slow response times. For example, consider a case where a large number of documents are assigned `tag1` but few documents are also assigned `tag2`. With only an index, the system will need to read many of the documents with `tag1` during query execution, resulting in query latency that grows proportionally with the number of tuples touched. To validate whether this problematic scenario arises in practice, we construct datasets at varying scales in which document tags are sampled from a Zipf distribution (n=2000, s=0.1). We chose this distribution to approximate the frequency of tags in a social context [10, 22].

We measure the performance of the `twoTags` query at scale by partitioning the `Tags` relation as well as its materialized view across the cluster by key range, with two replicas per partition. Each experiment begins with 200,000 tags bulk loaded to each partition. A cardinality constraint of 10 tags per document is enforced, with an average of four tags per document initially. For each data point, we combine the results from multiple runs across different EC2 cluster instantiations, and discard the first run of any setup to mitigate JIT warm-up effects.

A 2:1 ratio of storage to client nodes is maintained across cluster sizes, with each client utilizing two reader and two writer threads to issue requests to storage concurrently. Since writes are significantly more expensive than reads, this results in a read-write ratio of approximately 25 to 1.

8.1.1 On-Demand vs. Materialization

Figure 3 shows that with on-demand execution, the 99th percentile latency grows linearly with the size of the data, and the query read latency quickly rises to over a second. The significant increase in response time clearly demonstrates the danger of allowing queries with scale-dependent plans to run in production. However, when the same query is answered using the IMV, the response time remains nearly constant, leveling off at a 99th percentile latency of 8ms.

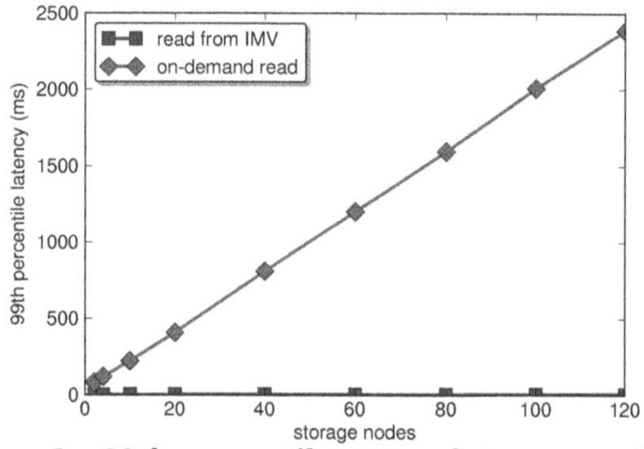

Figure 3: 99th-percentile query latency as cluster size grows with and without an IMV.

8.1.2 Cost of Incremental View Maintenance

Now that we have demonstrated bounded query latency by shifting some of the computational work to insertion time, we must now verify that we have not negatively impacted the scalability of writes to the application.

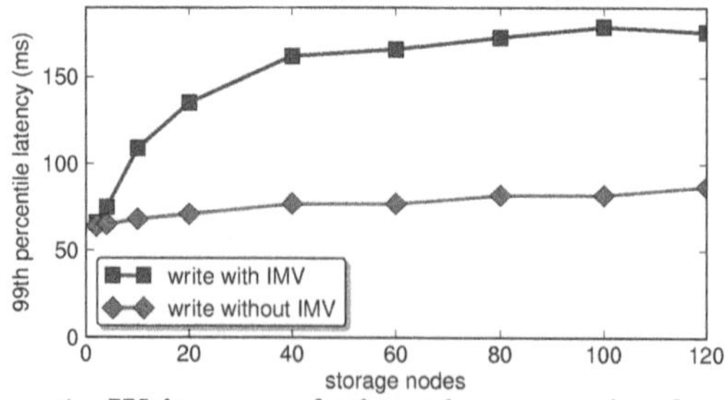

Figure 4: Write completion time remains bounded even with the overhead of incremental maintenance.

While the incremental view maintenance could be performed asynchronously, returning to the user immediately after the write is received, we modified the system to perform all maintenance synchronously for the purpose of this experiment. Figure 4 shows the effect that the maintenance of the materialized view has on write latency.

While latency of updates to the Tags relation is impacted by view maintenance, the effect is relatively small (~ 110ms in the worst case) and remains virtually constant for cluster sizes larger than 40 nodes. The initial increase in write latency as the cluster grows is due to the fact that the number of partitions in the system is small with respect to the cardinality constraint on tags. Specifically, for a smaller cluster, fewer partitions are often contacted per write, since some writes will go to the same machine. However, since Invariant 2 bounds the number of writes that will be performed in the worst case, eventually the maximum distribution is reached and the performance effect levels off.

8.2 TPC-W Benchmark

TPC-W[2] is a standard benchmark based on an online bookstore. Unlike prior work [4], where some TPC-W queries were excluded from scalability analysis, we include all web interactions in our evaluation. PIQL's automatic creation of IMVs allows for full execution of the benchmark, while still achieving consistent 99th percentile response time.

Two web interactions required slight modifications to avoid naive workload hotspots. The first, the BestSellerWI, returns the top 50 most popular items from the last 3333 orders. The second, AdminConfirmWI, returns the 5 most common items co-purchased with a specified item from the last 10,000 orders. Since executing either of these interactions on-demand would require an index over the creation time for a given order, PIQL suggested that we precompute the answer using periodically refreshed materialized views.

We went further and changed the tuple windows to instead calculate the result over hour-long time windows. TPC-W was initially designed to be run on a single machine and thus the queries were not written expecting arbitrarily high order rates. Since a time window both provides a more semantically consistent result as the system grows and requires strictly more work to maintain than simple tuple windows, we chose this implementation for our evaluation.

8.2.1 Query and Update Performance

After applying the scalability modifications, PIQL's optimizer was able to find query and update plans that satisfy all scale-independent invariants. Figure 5 shows the 99th percentile response time for the BuyConfirm web interaction. Since this interaction is the only one that actually places orders, all incremental view maintenance is performed during this action. Similar to the `twoTags` query, the strict upper bound on the number of operations performed in the worst case causes the increase in response time to eventually level off. Figure 6 shows that PIQL provides consistent 99th percentile response time for all web interactions.

Without view maintenance, the BuyConfirm interaction has a 99th percentile response time of 100ms. This means that, in the worst case, view maintenance adds nearly two seconds of latency to this web interaction. Fortunately, in a production system, this maintenance could be performed asynchronously and thus not affect end user experience.

A large majority of query processing time is due to network latency. For all TPC-W queries, we measured this

[2]http://www.tpc.org/tpcw/

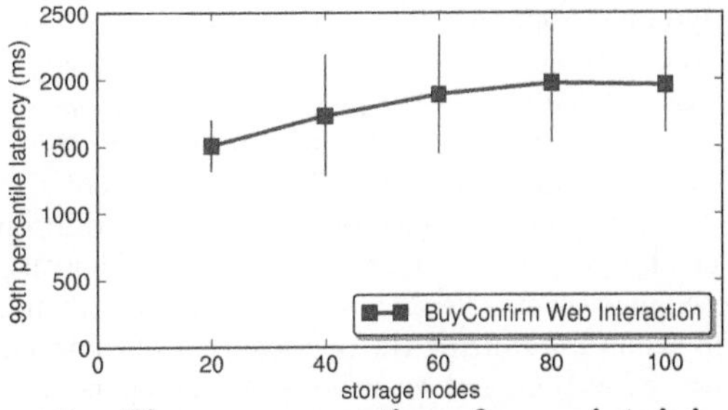

Figure 5: The response time for maintaining the IMVs for the TPC-W workload increases initially, but eventually levels off due to the limitations imposed by the scale-independent invariants.

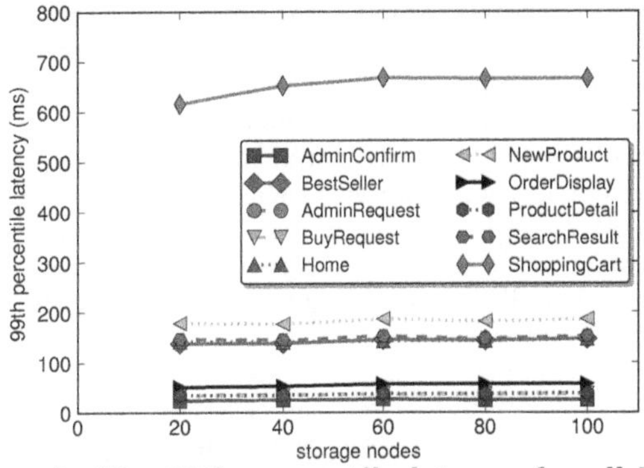

Figure 6: The 99th percentile latency for all TPC-W web interactions remains nearly constant as the number of machines increases

breakdown by comparing the time spent waiting for responses with the overall response time. The round trip latency to the storage nodes dominates query processing time, comprising on average 92% of total response time. In the worst case, local processing was responsible for 11% of latency, which is typical for short-running, distributed queries.

8.2.2 Latency of Parallel Refresh

The views used to answer queries such as BestSeller and AdminConfirm are updated periodically. Since we relax Invariant 2 to bound only the amount of work performed serially in each partition, instead of the total work required, these queries fall into SI-3. However, Figure 7 shows that since each partition can be processed in parallel, the overall time taken for the refresh step increases only slightly (less than a second) as we scale from 20 to 100 machines.

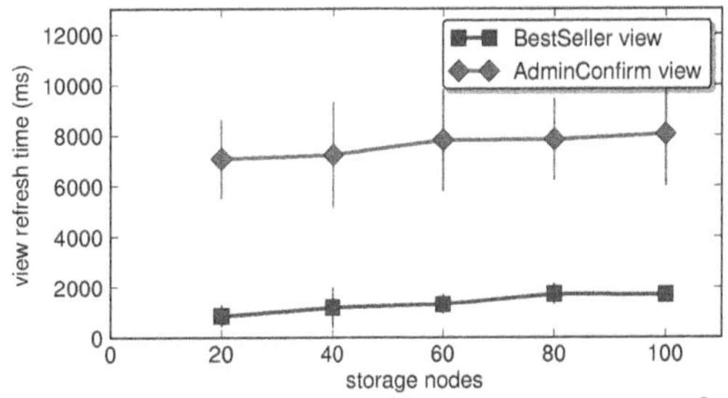

Figure 7: Periodic update latency stays nearly constant due to the requirement of bounded serial work.

9. RELATED WORK

Prior work on the automatic selection of materialized views, such as the static approach taken by Agrawal et al. [2]

or the dynamic approach taken by Kotidis and Rossopoulos [17], has focused on selecting views that will speed up a given workload. Generally the problem is framed as follows: Given a workload and a size bound, materialize the set of views that based on estimation will result in the greatest improvement in the performance of the system. Additionally, Gupta et al. [14] present algorithms that consider the cost of maintenance when selecting views. However, their techniques focus on minimizing the average cost of maintenance and query execution, not ensuring scale independence. In contrast, PIQL creates an IMV when it will fundamentally change the scalability of a query, not just when it could speed up execution. Thus, instead of just reducing response time, we ensure scale independence for an application before it is deployed to production. Additionally, our novel static analysis algorithms ensure that the size of the selected view can never grow faster than linearly relative to the base data.

DBToaster [3] also recursively creates materialized views to reduce the work of incremental maintenance. However, their system only works for views with aggregation and does not bound the total number of operations required.

Agrawal et al. [1] describe a large-scale declarative system that incrementally maintains materialized views. However, unlike PIQL, their query language does not support joins of more than two tables, unless they are all joined on the same attribute. Thus, PIQL's language extensions and recursive view creation allow the scale-independent maintenance of a wider range of views. Further expansion of scale independence may be possible. In particular better support for predicates with inequalities could be added through the inclusion of other data structures such as range trees [8].

10. CONCLUSION

The ability to anticipate and handle rapid growth is critical for modern large-scale interactive applications. Precomputation through the automatic creation of incrementally maintained materialized views is a powerful tool that can allow these sites to run more complex queries while still meeting their performance objectives. This technique shifts query processing work from execution time to insertion time, and can not only improve performance but also fundamentally change the scaling behavior of a wide range of queries.

In this paper, we presented a scale-independent view selection system, which not only recognizes such cases but also leverages novel static analysis techniques to ensure the automatically created views will not themselves become scaling bottlenecks. These algorithms ensure that created views will preserve invariants on both the storage required and the cost of maintenance as the scale of an application increases. Additionally, we described an annotation that allows PIQL to detect and mitigate common sources of workload hot spots. Together, these techniques allow PIQL to provide a relational engine that preserves the productivity benefits of SQL while maintaining the performance predictability of today's distributed storage systems.

Acknowledgments

We would like to thank Henry Cook, along with the reviewers, for feedback that significantly improved the content of this paper. This research is supported in part by NSF CISE Expeditions award CCF-1139158 and DARPA XData Award FA8750-12-2-0331, and gifts from Amazon Web Services, Google, SAP, Blue Goji, Cisco, Clearstory Data, Cloudera, Ericsson, Facebook, General Electric, Hortonworks, Huawei, Intel, Microsoft, NetApp, Oracle, Quanta, Samsung, Splunk, VMware and Yahoo!.

11. REFERENCES

[1] P. Agrawal et al. Asynchronous view maintenance for vlsd databases. In *SIGMOD*, 2009.

[2] S. Agrawal, S. Chaudhuri, and V. R. Narasayya. Automated selection of materialized views and indexes in sql databases. In *VLDB*, 2000.

[3] Y. Ahmad, O. Kennedy, et al. Dbtoaster: higher-order delta processing for dynamic, frequently fresh views. *Proc. VLDB Endow.*, 5(10), 2012.

[4] M. Armbrust, K. Curtis, T. Kraska, A. Fox, M. J. Franklin, and D. A. Patterson. PIQL: Success-tolerant query processing in the cloud. *PVLDB*, 5(3), 2011.

[5] M. Armbrust et al. Scads: Scale-independent storage for social computing applications. In *CIDR*, 2009.

[6] J. A. Blakeley, P.-Å. Larson, and F. W. Tompa. Efficiently updating materialized views. In *SIGMOD*, 1986.

[7] S. Ceri and J. Widom. Deriving production rules for incremental view maintenance. In *VLDB*, 1991.

[8] M. Chaabouni et al. The point-range tree: a data structure for indexing intervals. In *Proc. of ACM CSC*, 1993.

[9] L. S. Colby et al. Algorithms for deferred view maintenance. *SIGMOD Rec.*, 25(2), 1996.

[10] E. Cunha et al. Analyzing the dynamic evolution of hashtags on twitter: a language-based approach. In *Workshop on Languages in Social Media*, 2011.

[11] G. DeCandia et al. Dynamo: amazon's highly available key-value store. *SIGOPS*, 41, 2007.

[12] J. Gray, A. Bosworth, A. Layman, D. Reichart, and H. Pirahesh. Data cube: A relational aggregation operator generalizing group-by, cross-tab, and sub-totals. 1996.

[13] A. Gupta, D. Katiyar, and I. S. Mumick. Counting solutions to the view maintenance problem. In *Workshop on Deductive Databases, JICSLP*, 1992.

[14] H. Gupta and I. Mumick. Selection of views to materialize in a data warehouse. *Knowledge and Data Engineering, IEEE Transactions on*, 17(1), 2005.

[15] J. Kincaid. Zuckerberg: Online sharing is growing at an exponential rate. http://tinyurl.com/cskurl3.

[16] C. Koch. Incremental query evaluation in a ring of databases. In *PODS*, 2010.

[17] Y. Kotidis et al. Dynamat: a dynamic view management system for data warehouses. *SIGMOD Rec.*, 28(2), 1999.

[18] W. Labio et al. Performance issues in incremental warehouse maintenance. In *VLDB*, 2000.

[19] X. Long and T. Suel. Three-level caching for efficient query processing in large web search engines. In *WWW*, 2005.

[20] G. Luo et al. Locking protocols for materialized aggregate join views. In *VLDB*, 2003.

[21] H. Mistry, P. Roy, S. Sudarshan, and K. Ramamritham. Materialized view selection and maintenance using multi-query optimization. *SIGMOD Rec.*, 30(2), 2001.

[22] M. E. J. Newman. Power laws, pareto distributions and zipf's law. *Contemporary Physics*, 46, 2005.

[23] M. T. Özsu and P. Valduriez. *Principles of distributed database systems (2nd ed.)*. 1999.

[24] D. Quass and J. Widom. On-line warehouse view maintenance. In *SIGMOD*, 1997.

[25] K. Salem et al. How to roll a join: asynchronous incremental view maintenance. *SIGMOD Rec.*, 29(2), 2000.

[26] B. Trushkowsky et al. The scads director: scaling a distributed storage system under stringent performance requirements. In *FAST*, 2011.

[27] P. Valduriez. Join indices. *ACM Trans. Database Syst.*, 12(2), 1987.

[28] K. Weil. Measuring tweets. http://blog.twitter.com/2010/02/measuring-tweets.html.

Simulation of Database-Valued Markov Chains Using SimSQL

Zhuhua Cai
Rice University
Houston, TX, 77251
caizhua@gmail.com

Zografoula Vagena*
LogicBlox, Inc.
Atlanta, GA, 30309
foula@acm.org

Luis Perez
Rice University
Houston, TX, 77251
lp6@rice.edu

Subramanian Arumugam
Rice University
Houston, TX, 77251
propus@gmail.com

Peter J. Haas
IBM Almaden
San Jose, CA, 95120
phaas@us.ibm.com

Christopher Jermaine
Rice University
Houston, TX, 77251
cmj4@rice.edu

ABSTRACT

This paper describes the SimSQL system, which allows for SQL-based specification, simulation, and querying of database-valued Markov chains, i.e., chains whose value at any time step comprises the contents of an entire database. SimSQL extends the earlier Monte Carlo database system (MCDB), which permitted Monte Carlo simulation of static database-valued random variables. Like MCDB, SimSQL uses user-specified "VG functions" to generate the simulated data values that are the building blocks of a simulated database. The enhanced functionality of SimSQL is enabled by the ability to parametrize VG functions using stochastic tables, so that one stochastic database can be used to parametrize the generation of another stochastic database, which can parametrize another, and so on. Other key extensions include the ability to explicitly define recursive versions of a stochastic table and the ability to execute the simulation in a MapReduce environment. We focus on applying SimSQL to Bayesian machine learning.

Categories and Subject Descriptors

H.4 [**Information Systems Applications**]: Miscellaneous

Keywords

Markov chains; databases; machine learning

1. INTRODUCTION

SimSQL is a system that allows for SQL-based specification and large-scale, distributed simulation of database-valued Markov chains, i.e., chains whose value at any time step comprises the contents of an entire database. SimSQL employs many of the ideas first proposed in the context of the Monte Carlo database system (MCDB) [18], which is a prototype, SQL-based database system designed to support stochastic analytics. Both SimSQL and MCDB allow users to define—in addition to ordinary database tables—so-called *stochastic* database tables. In a stochastic table, some entries are random variables with associated probability distributions (not necessarily known in closed form) and others are ordinary, deterministic data values. Conceptually, when an SQL query is issued that includes stochastic tables, SimSQL and MCDB both use pseudo-random number generation techniques to instantiate each stochastic data value. Queries can be run over the resulting database instance (also called "possible world"); this process is repeated many times in a Monte Carlo fashion to obtain an empirical distribution of the query results. Both SimSQL and MCDB instantiate and process many possible worlds at the same time with high efficiency by sharing common costs using a "tuple bundle" approach.

SimSQL contains the basic functionality present in the original MCDB system, but also has some significant extensions. This paper focuses most closely on two key capabilities unique to SimSQL that are not present in MCDB and which significantly increase SimSQL's applicability vis-a-vis the earlier system.

1. SimSQL allows data in stochastic database tables to be used to parametrize the processes that stochastically generate the data in other stochastic database tables. This allows SimSQL to implement hierarchical stochastic models such as latent Dirichlet allocation (LDA) [5] for learning topics from text.

2. SimSQL allows both versioning and recursive definitions of stochastic database tables. For example, data in stochastic table A can be used to parametrize the stochastic generation of table B, which in turn can be used to parametrize the stochastic generation of a second version of table A, and so on.

Whereas MCDB merely allows generation of sample realizations of a given stochastic database D—in other words, a static database-valued random variable—the foregoing extensions enable SimSQL to generate realizations of a database-valued Markov chain $D[0]$, $D[1], D[2], \ldots$. That is, the stochastic mechanism that generates a realization of the ith database state $D[i]$ may explicitly depend on the prior state $D[i-1]$. Possible applications of this powerful functionality include Bayesian Machine Learning (ML) and massive stochastic agent-based simulations. In this paper we focus on ML applications.

*Work performed while Zografoula Vagena was affiliated with Rice University.

Material in this paper was supported by the National Science Foundation under grant number 0915315, and the Department of Energy under grant number DE-SC0001779.

SIGMOD'13, June 22–27, 2013, New York, New York, USA.

Scalable Bayesian Machine Learning in SimSQL. This paper gives several examples of how SimSQL can support Bayesian inference over large data sets. In Bayesian inference, it is assumed that a parametrized stochastic process generated the data. The parameters are uncertain, and the goal is to combine prior beliefs about the parameters with the observed data to infer distributional properties of the parameters. Depending upon the application, these parameters may describe clusters in the data, regression coefficients, or latent topics in text. Often, the "posterior distribution" on the parameters can be very difficult to describe analytically, so the most common analysis approach is to sample from the posterior distribution using Markov chain Monte Carlo (MCMC) simulation.

SimSQL's database-oriented approach gives a surprisingly appropriate set of abstractions for Bayesian ML. In most ML problems, there are a few classes of variables or parameters over which inference is to be performed. These might be latent variables (such as the identity of a cluster that produced a particular data point) or model parameters (such as the covariance matrices in a Gaussian mixture model). It is quite natural to group the members of such a class together and store them in a database table.

MCMC inference is natural in SimSQL because of the *VG function* abstraction that it borrows from MCDB. A VG function is a (nearly) arbitrary, (possibly) user-defined pseudo-random function that generates samples of uncertain data values; these samples are then used to construct sample realizations of stochastic tables. The sampling mechanism of a VG function depends on parameters that are provided as input tables. It is very easy to embed the sampling of the posterior distribution of a variable or parameter inside of a VG function, which is exactly what is needed for many MCMC algorithms. Furthermore, SQL is a very useful language for preparing complex parametrization of VG functions. This results in MCMC codes that are small and easy to understand "in the large"—that is, the specification for how variables fit together and parametrize each other is often remarkably simple.

Perhaps the most important advantage of running MCMC in SimSQL is that one can write SQL without worrying about how the code will be parallelized across many machines. SimSQL automatically takes care of the optimization and parallelization. SimSQL takes as input a specification written entirely in SimSQL's dialect of SQL, then optimizes it and executes the actual simulation in parallel on a Hadoop cluster, allowing for scalable processing.

Paper Highlights.

- This paper describes how SimSQL's dialect of SQL makes it very easy to declaratively specify Markov chain simulations.
- SQL codes for two Bayesian inference problems are given.
- Details are given on how SimSQL compiles Markovian simulations into computational plans that resemble classical database execution plans.
- Experiments show that SimSQL has reasonable performance for running large-scale, Markov chain simulations.

2. BAYESIAN LINEAR REGRESSION

To demonstrate, in a simple setting, the use of SimSQL for very large-scale Bayesian analysis, we describe how SimSQL can be used to implement MCMC inference for a very simple Bayesian linear regression model over a large database.

2.1 The Model

Suppose we have a large database table `myTable(x,y)` of n rows. Our goal is to learn two values a and b such that for an arbitrary observation $\mathtt{x}$, we can predict $\mathtt{y}$ via the formula $\mathtt{y} \approx a\mathtt{x} + b$. Although this is clearly a toy problem—in practice, with such a simple learning problem one is unlikely to resort to Bayesian methods—it makes a good first example.

To apply Bayesian methodology to such a problem, an analyst will first posit a stochastic generative process for the data:

1. $a \sim \text{Normal}(0, \sigma_0^2)$.
2. $b \sim \text{Normal}(0, \sigma_0^2)$.
3. $\sigma^2 \sim \text{InvGamma}(1, 1)$.
4. For each i in $\{1...n\}$, $\mathtt{y}_i \sim \text{Normal}(a\mathtt{x}_i + b, \sigma^2)$.

Here "$\sim$" should be read as "is sampled from" and InvGamma denotes the inverse gamma distribution.

We thus assume that the observed value $\mathtt{y}_i$ is normally distributed—with variance σ^2—around the predicted value $a\mathtt{x}_i + b$. The unknown parameters a and b are themselves treated as random variables and have normal "priors" with common variance σ_0^2 (which we take to be a known, constant "hyperparameter"). The term "prior" in Bayesian parlance refers to the probability distribution that we initially assume has produced the parameter values. The priors are based on previous knowledge or belief, or perhaps chosen for computational convenience. Our beliefs about the prior distribution are updated upon observation of the data in `myTable`, leading to a posterior distribution on the parameters; this posterior distribution is the ultimate object of our study. Choosing an appropriate generative process and priors is something of a "black art" and is beyond the scope of the paper. A reader who wants to learn more should look at an introductory text such as [4].

The specification of a stochastic generative process results in a probability density function (PDF) for the random data and parameters. In our example, we have:

$$\begin{aligned} &P(a, b, \sigma^2, \{\mathtt{y}_i\} | \{\mathtt{x}_i\}) \\ &= \text{Normal}(a|0, \sigma_0^2) \times \text{Normal}(b|0, \sigma_0^2) \\ &\quad \times \text{InvGamma}(\sigma^2|1, 1) \times \prod_i \text{Normal}(\mathtt{y}_i|a\mathtt{x}_i + b, \sigma^2) \end{aligned} \tag{1}$$

2.2 Inference

Our goal is to estimate the parameters a, b, and σ^2 after seeing the data in `myTable(x,y)`. That is, we wish to analyze the posterior distribution $P(a, b, \sigma^2 | \{\mathtt{x}_i, \mathtt{y}_i\})$. In practice, the posterior distribution is seldom amenable to closed-form analysis, and a common method for studying the posterior is to obtain samples from it that can be analyzed statistically. We accomplish this sampling using a particular MCMC algorithm called a "Gibbs sampler" [31]. Gibbs sampling is a technique for generating samples from a high-dimensional probability distribution function $P(X)$ that is known only up to a normalizing constant. A Gibbs sampler simulates a Markov chain whose stationary distribution is the desired target distribution. Briefly, the procedure works as follows: Assume that $X = (X_1, X_2, ..., X_d)$ is a $d-$dimensional vector of continuous and/or discrete random variables. A key requirement of the Gibbs sampler is that we can efficiently generate samples from the conditional distributions $P(X_j|X_{-j})$ for $j \in \{1..d\}$, where X_{-j} is the vector comprising all variables except X_j. To generate k samples the Gibbs sampler proceeds as follows:

1. Select an initial value $X^{(0)} = (X_1^{(0)}, X_2^{(0)}, \ldots, X_d^{(0)})$.
2. For each sample $i = \{1 \ldots k\}$, sample each variable $X_j^{(i)}$ from $P(X_j^{(i)}|X_1^{(i)}, \ldots, X_{j-1}^{(i)}, X_{j+1}^{(i-1)}, \ldots, X_d^{(i-1)})$.

```
CREATE TABLE tableA[0] (aValue) AS
  WITH   sampledVal AS Normal (SELECT * FROM VALUES (0, 10))
  SELECT *
  FROM   sampledVal;
CREATE TABLE tableB[0] (bValue) AS
  WITH   sampledVal AS Normal (SELECT * FROM VALUES (0, 10))
  SELECT *
  FROM   sampledVal;
```

Figure 1: Initializing a and b (σ_0^2 = 10).

```
CREATE TABLE variance[i] (s2Value) AS
  WITH sampledVal AS InvGamma (
    (SELECT 1 + dataNum/2
     FROM   metaData),
    (SELECT 1 + 0.5 *
            SUM ((y - aValue * x - bValue) *
                 (y - aValue * x - bValue))
     FROM   myData, tableA[i], tableB[i]))
  SELECT sampledVal.value
  FROM   sampledVal;
```

Figure 2: Updating the variance σ^2.

After running the simulation for k steps of a "burn in" period, the current state of the chain—which in our case would include $a^{(k)}$, $b^{(k)}$, and $\sigma^{2(k)}$—can be taken as a sample from the target distribution.

In in our example, we can use Bayes' rule together with the PDF in (1) to derive the following sampling distributions:

$$P(a|.) \propto \text{Normal}(a|0,\sigma_0^2) \times e^{(2\sigma^2)^{-1}\sum_i\{2(y_i-b)x_i a - x_i^2 a^2\}}$$

$$P(b|.) = \text{Normal}\Big(b \;\Big|\; \frac{\sum_i(y_i - ax_i)}{(\sigma^2/\sigma_0^2)+n}, \big(\frac{1}{\sigma_0^2}+\frac{n}{\sigma^2}\big)^{-1}\Big)$$

$$P(\sigma^2|.) = \text{InvGamma}\Big(\sigma^2 \;\Big|\; 1+\frac{n}{2}, 1+\frac{\sum_i(y_i - ax_i - b)^2}{2}\Big)$$

2.3 Learning the Model

A Gibbs sampler for this model must repeatedly update the values for a, b and σ^2 in a recursive fashion. The order in which to update these three parameters is arbitrary; we choose to first initialize a and b, and then update σ^2, a and b in sequence. We now describe how this recursion can easily be specified in SimSQL's SQL dialect.

Initialization. We begin by initializing the parameters a and b and storing each in its own one-row table: `tableA(aValue)` and `tableB(bValue)`. In SimSQL, a stochastic table can be annotated with a version number, which corresponds to a step of a Markov chain simulation or more generally to a level of recursion. In our case, `tableA[0]` denotes the initial version of `tableA`, and the SQL statement "`CREATE TABLE tableA[0] (aValue) AS`" in Figure 1 describes precisely how this table is to be created. Specifically, the VG function `Normal` is used to generate a temporary table `sampledVal`; the table-valued output of this VG function is then loaded into `tableA[0]` via the "`SELECT *`" subquery. The VG function `Normal` accepts a parameter table and outputs a result table of normally distributed samples.

Updating the parameters. The code to update σ^2, a and b—given in Figures 2 through 4—is similar to the code in Figure 1, with a few notable differences. First, the versioning variable `i` replaces the hard-coded `0`; this lets the SimSQL compiler know that this code is to be used to recursively define `variance`, `tableA` and `tableB`. Second, note the references to `variance[i-1]` in Figures 3 and 4, as well as the reference to `tableB[i-1]` in Figure 3. In this way, these stochastic table definitions reference

```
CREATE TABLE tableA[i] (aValue) AS
  WITH sampledVal AS SampleA (
    (SELECT * FROM VALUES (0, 10)),
    (SELECT 1 / (2 * var.s2Value)
     FROM   variance[i-1] as var),
    (SELECT SUM (2 * (y - bValue) * x), SUM (x * x)
     FROM   myTable, tableB[i-1]))
  SELECT sampledVal.value
  FROM   sampledVal;
```

Figure 3: Updating the value of a (σ_0^2 = 10).

```
CREATE TABLE tableB[i] (bValue) AS
  WITH sampledVal as Normal (
    (SELECT   SUM(y - aValue * x) /
              (var.s2Value / 10 + dataNum)
     FROM     variance[i-1] AS var, myData,
              tableA[i], metaData
     GROUP BY var.s2Value, dataNum),
    (SELECT   (1.0 / (1.0 / 10 + dataNum / var.s2Value))
     FROM     metaData, variance[i-1] AS var)
  )
  SELECT sampledVal.value
  FROM   sampledVal;
```

Figure 4: Updating the value of b (σ_0^2 = 10).

"older" versions of stochastic tables. Next, the code in Figure 3 uses the `SampleA` VG function. Since $P(a|.)$ has a non-standard distribution function, a library VG function cannot be used and the user-defined `SampleA` must be used instead; this VG function encapsulates a user-implemented "rejection" sampler [31] for $P(a|.)$. The three subqueries compute the statistics necessary to run the rejection sampler: the first (trivially) computes the parameter vector $(0, \sigma_0^2)$, the second computes $1/(2\sigma^2)$, and the third computes the quantities $\sum_i 2(y_i - bx_i)$ and $\sum_i x_i^2$ needed in the exponent that appears in the definition of $P(a|.)$. The situation is a bit simpler in Figures 2 and 4 in that the standard `InvGamma` and `Normal` VG functions are used to sample the updated values of σ^2 and b.

3. LATENT DIRICHLET ALLOCATION

We now turn to a more realistic example, and consider how SimSQL can be used to implement Bayesian inference for the popular LDA model [5]. LDA has many applications, from document classification to dimensionality reduction to document indexing. For reasons of exposition, we perform the inference using a "full" Gibbs sampler, as opposed to the "collapsed" sampler [29].

3.1 Model and Inference

LDA models a document as a bag of words where each word is generated by first selecting a latent (i.e., unobserved) topic from a document-specific topic distribution and then generating the word from a topic-specific word distribution. The topic distribution for each document is itself uncertain and has a Dirichlet prior. The Dirichlet family of "distributions over distributions" is the multivariate generalization of the beta distribution over $[0, 1]$; for $k \geq 2$ and parameter vector $\alpha = (\alpha_1, \alpha_2, \ldots, \alpha_k)$, the PDF is given by

$$\text{Dirichlet}(x_1, x_2, \ldots, x_k|\alpha) = \begin{cases} \frac{\Gamma(\sum_{i=1}^k \alpha_i)}{\prod_{i=1}^k \Gamma(\alpha_i)} \prod_{i=1}^k x_i^{\alpha_i - 1} & \text{if } x_i \geq 0 \text{ and } \sum_{i=1}^k x_i = 1; \\ 0 & \text{otherwise,} \end{cases}$$

where each α_i is positive and Γ is the standard gamma function. The word distribution for each topic is also uncertain, with a "symmetric" Dirichlet prior in which $\alpha_1 = \cdots = \alpha_k$. With a slight abuse of notation, we use a symbol such as α to denote both a

```
CREATE TABLE theta[0] (docID, topicID, prob) AS
    FOR EACH d IN documents
        WITH NewProbs AS Dirichlet
            (SELECT topicID, alpha
             FROM   topics, hyperparameters)
        SELECT d.docID, np.outID, np.probability
        FROM NewProbs AS np;
```

Figure 5: Initializing Θ

positive constant and the vector $(\alpha, \alpha, \ldots, \alpha)$, and simply write "Dirichlet(α)" to denote the corresponding symmetric prior.

Consider a large dataset of n documents with n_j words in the jth document and m distinct words overall. Assuming that t topics are present in the data and fixing hyperparameters α and β, the generative process underlying LDA is formally as follows:

1. For $i \in \{1...t\}$: $\Psi_i \sim$ Dirichlet(β)
2. For $j \in \{1...n\}$:
   (a) $\Theta_j \sim$ Dirichlet(α)
   (b) $z_j \sim$ Multinomial(n_j, Θ_j)
   (c) For $k \in \{1...t\}$: $w_{j,k} \sim$ Multinomial($z_{j,k}, \Psi_k$)

In step (1), we first produce a matrix Ψ with t rows and m columns; the row Ψ_i is a list of probabilities, where $\Psi_{i,d}$ is the probability that topic i will produce word d. Ψ_i is sampled from a Dirichlet(β) distribution. We subsequently use $\Psi_{*,d}$ to denote the column listing the probability that each topic will produce word d.

Next, we produce (for each document) a probability vector Θ_j, where $\Theta_{j,k}$ is the probability that a word in document j is generated from topic k. For document k, we sample z_j from a multinomial distribution with parameters n_j and Θ_j, so that $z_{j,k}$ records the number of words added to document j by topic k.

Finally, for document j, the quantity w_j is a matrix having t rows and m columns. $w_{j,k,d}$ tells us how many copies of word d were contributed to document j by topic k. Let $w_{j,k}$ denote the kth row in the w_j matrix, and let $w_{j,*,d}$ denote the dth column in this matrix. The kth row $w_{j,k}$ is sampled from a multinomial distribution with parameters $z_{j,k}$ and Ψ_k. After this process completes, the jth document in the corpus (represented as word frequencies) is $\delta_j = \sum_k w_{j,k}$. As discussed in Section 4, a typical goal of an LDA analysis is learning the posterior distribution of the Θ_j vectors, which describes the topic distribution within each document.

Our generative process is mathematically equivalent to the one described in the original LDA paper [5]; it differs slightly in that it is matrix- and vector-oriented, which leads to a simpler and more intuitive Gibbs sampler. It can be shown that the iterated sequence of updates required by the Gibbs sampler is as follows:

$$\Theta_j \sim \text{Dirichlet}(\alpha + z_j) \quad (2)$$

$$w_{j,*,d} \sim \text{Multinomial}(\delta_{j,d}, \Theta_j \times \Psi_{*,d}) \quad (3)$$

$$\Psi_i \sim \text{Dirichlet}(\beta + \sum_j w_{j,i}) \quad (4)$$

Here $\alpha + z_j$ denotes a vector addition and $\Theta_j \times \Psi_{*,d}$ denotes the item-by-item multiplication of the two vectors. We assume that the latter vector is normalized to a probability vector, if needed, prior to multinomial sampling. There is no need to explicitly sample z_j, because $z_{j,k}$ can always be computed as $\sum_d w_{j,k,d}$.

3.2 Specifying the Gibbs Sampler in SimSQL

To describe the above Gibbs sampler in SimSQL, we assume four database tables. The first two contain the topic and document

```
CREATE TABLE w[0] (docID, wordID, topicID, count) AS
    FOR EACH dw IN wordInDoc
        WITH TC AS Multinomial (
            (SELECT tm.topicID, tm.probability
             FROM theta[0] AS tm
             WHERE tm.docID = dw.docID),
            (SELECT dw.count))
        SELECT dw.docID, dw.wordID, tc.outID, tc.count
        FROM TC AS tc;
```

Figure 6: Initializing w

```
CREATE TABLE theta[i] (docID, topicID, prob) AS
    FOR EACH d IN documents
        WITH NewProbs AS Dirichlet
            (SELECT pw.topicID,
                    sum(pw.count) + hyperparameters.alpha
             FROM w[i-1] as pw, topics AS t, hyperparameters
             WHERE pw.docID = d.docID AND pw.topicID = t.topicID
             GROUP BY pw.topicID, hyperparameters.alpha)
        SELECT d.docID, np.outID, np.prob
        FROM NewProbs AS np;
```

Figure 7: Updating Θ

identifiers, and the third contains a single row with the positive, real-valued Dirichlet hyperparameters α and β (recall our assumption of symmetric Dirichlet priors). The fourth table stores the number of times that each unique word appears in each document.

```
topics(topicID)
documents(docID)
hyperparameters(alpha,beta)    % hyperparameters
wordInDoc(docID,wordID,count)  % words in documents
```

In addition, we have three stochastic tables; one (`psi`) to store the Ψ matrix, one (`theta`) to store the Θ matrix, and one (`w`) to store the various w matrices:

```
psi[i](topicID,wordID,prob)
theta[i](docID,topicID,prob)
w[i](docID,topicID,wordID,count)
```

Initialization. We begin by initializing the Θ and w matrices as shown in Figures 5 and 6. These codes are similar to the code in the previous section, with one big difference: the presence of the `FOR EACH` loop. Consider Figure 5. This code scans the `documents` table ("`FOR EACH d IN documents`") and, for each `d` encountered, invokes the `Dirichlet` VG Function via the `WITH` statement. The output schema for this VG function has two attributes: `outID`, the topic identifier, and `probability`, the word-production probability associated with that topic. The final `SELECT` query assembles the output from the VG function into a temporary table. All of the temporary tables created over all of the `d` values are then UNIONed to form `theta[0]`. Next, as shown in Figure 6, `w` is initialized by sampling, for each unique word in each document, the number of times that each topic produces the word, using the `Multinomial` VG function.

Updating the parameters. Figure 7 displays the SQL code for updating Θ. It is very similar to the initialization code in Figure 5; the key difference is in the parametrization of the `Dirichlet` VG function, which is based on the formula in (2). Similarly, the code to update `w`—shown in Figure 8—is very similar to the initialization code in Figure 6. Here the difference lies in the parametrization of the `Multinomial` VG function that allocates the number of appearances of a word in a document among the different topics. The parameter representing the probability that a given word in the document is associated with a given topic is computed as the product of the probability of the topic in the document and the probability that the topic produces the word, as required by (3).

```
CREATE TABLE w[i] (docID, wordID, topicID, count) AS
    FOR EACH dw IN wordInDoc
        WITH TC AS Multinomial(
            (SELECT tm.topicID, wpt.prob * tm.prob
             FROM psi[i-1] AS wpt, theta[i] AS tm
             WHERE wpt.wordID = dw.wordID AND
                   wpt.topicID = tm.topicID AND
                   tm.docID = dw.docID),
            (SELECT dw.count))
        SELECT dw.docID, dw.wordID, tc.outID, tc.count
        FROM TC AS tc;
```

Figure 8: Updating w

```
CREATE TABLE psi[i] (topicID, wordID, prob) AS
    FOR EACH t IN topics
        WITH NewProbs AS Dirichlet
            (SELECT pw.wordID,
                    sum(pw.count) + hyperparameters.beta
             FROM w[i] AS pw, hyperparameters
             WHERE pw.topicID = t.topicID
             GROUP BY pw.wordID, hyperparameters.beta)
        SELECT t.topicID, np.outID, np.probability
        FROM NewProbs AS np;
```

Figure 9: Updating Ψ

4. SPECIFYING AN ANALYSIS

We have shown how a database-valued Markov chain can be specified via a slight extension of standard SQL syntax. Denote by $D = (D[0], D[1], \ldots, D[M])$ the first $M + 1$ states of such a chain and recall that the overall goal of a SimSQL analysis is to study the (perhaps conditional) probability distribution of a query $Q = Q(D)$. (When using Gibbs sampling, the queries are usually of the specific form $Q(D[M])$, since interest centers on the state of the sampler after the burn-in period.) Here M is a maximum time-tick specified by the user—the current prototype requires that M be a fixed constant, but in future work we intend to relax this requirement. Conceptually, SimSQL first generates N samples from the distribution of D, i.e., N finite sample paths of the chain. SimSQL then applies Q to each of these sample paths to obtain a sample from the query-result distribution, and then uses these samples to estimate interesting features of the query-result distribution—such as moments, modes, and quantiles—or perhaps to visualize or perform statistical inference on the distribution.

In SimSQL, the user specifies an end-to-end simulation analysis using a novel SQL-like interface. Because of space constraints, we cannot describe the user interface in detail, and merely give a very brief example to show how a user might specify an analysis in the LDA scenario of Section 3. A typical goal of LDA is to study a quantity such as Θ_j, the (uncertain) topic probability vector for the jth document. Suppose that we wish to estimate $\tau_j = E[\Theta_j | w_j]$, the expected value of Θ_j, given the word data w_j. By the theory of Gibbs sampling, the sampled value $\Theta_j[M]$ after the Mth Gibbs iteration will be distributed approximately according to the distribution of $\Theta_j | w_j$ for M sufficiently large. Then we can estimate τ_j by $\hat{\tau}_j(N) = (1/N) \sum_{i=1}^{N} \Theta_j^{(i)}[M]$, where N is the number of Monte Carlo iterations (i.e., sample paths) and $\Theta_j^{(i)}[M]$ is the value of $\theta_j[M]$ in the ith iteration.

Suppose that $M = 50$ iterations is deemed large enough. Then, after defining the LDA model as in Section 3, the user can execute the program in Figure 10 to create a table of estimated topic-probability vectors, one per document. This table can then be further analyzed using standard SQL queries or other analysis tools. The `USING` clause specifies that $N = 100$ independent and identically distributed samples paths of the Gibbs-sampler Markov chain will be generated and used for subsequent averaging. The `WITH` clause specifies the query $Q(D)$ of interest. In this example, Q merely extracts the final (Mth) version of the `theta` table and returns this result as `lastTheta`. Note that the results from all N Monte Carlo iterations appear jointly in `lastTheta`. In particular, for any document j, the table contains the N sampled topic probability vectors $\Theta_j^{(1)}[M], \ldots, \Theta_j^{(N)}[M]$. The desired statistical summary of the Monte Carlo experiment is specified in the `COMPUTE` clause. For the LDA analysis, this summary is obtained simply by averaging the N Monte Carlo estimates of the topic probability, by document and topic.

```
USING IID(100)
WITH lastTheta(docID,topicID,prob,instanceID) AS
  (SELECT * FROM Theta[50])
COMPUTE
topicProbs(docID,topicID,prob) AS
  SELECT docID, topicID, AVERAGE(prob)
  FROM lastTheta
  GROUP BY docID, topicID
```

Figure 10: Syntax for an LDA analysis

5. IMPLEMENTATION OVERVIEW

The next few sections of the paper describe the SimSQL runtime. This section begins the description with an overview of the runtime.

Supporting huge plans. The defining characteristic of the MCMC simulations we would like to run in SimSQL is that the "query plans" are huge. A typical simulation may require tens to even hundreds of relational operations per iteration, so dozens of iterations may require thousands of operators.

One approach to running such a simulation would be to execute those thousands of operators as a single plan. However, there are problems with this approach. For example, cost-based optimization of such a huge plan is difficult because of the lack of reliable statistics over intermediate results. Estimating such statistics during optimization fails after the first few levels of the plan, due to the exponential propagation of the estimation errors [17].

A frame-based approach. We therefore perform incremental (re-)optimization and execution. Our approach is to partition the computation into sub-plans, called *frames*, which loosely correspond to the levels of recursive specification of the simulation. Each frame is optimized and executed in sequence: the output of one frame is provided as input to the next one. Dividing the computation into a sequence of frames provides an opportunity to collect precise statistics for each frame and use them when processing the next one. Most important, materializing the output of each frame makes it possible to checkpoint the computation. In addition to supporting recovery, checkpoints are crucial because they provide the ability to inspect intermediate states of a computation during a post-analysis phase. For example, imagine that after the completion of an 100 iteration MCMC process, a user wants to analyze the state of the Markov chain at the 20th iteration. Using a nearby checkpoint, the system can efficiently process that request.

Compiling and executing a simulation. The process, depicted in Figure 11, is as follows:

1. The SimSQL compiler parses the specification and creates a number of *template plans* that will be strung together to form the simulation. Template plans are so-named because they are the unoptimized building blocks from which a frame is constructed—they serve as templates for various parts of the frame. At a minimum, the system creates a template plan for each SQL code snippet that specifies the initial version

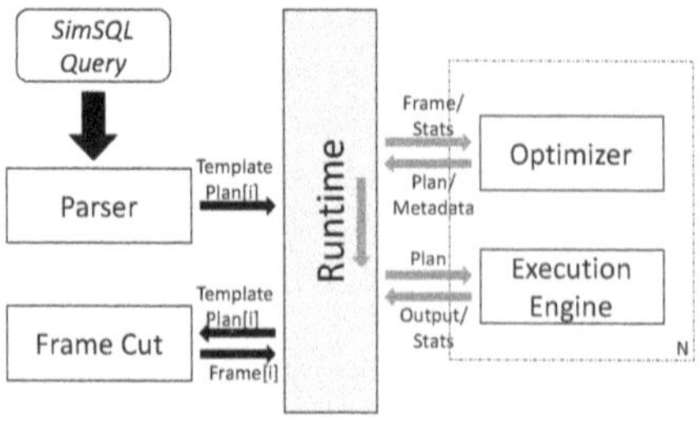

Figure 11: Overview of query processing in SimSQL.

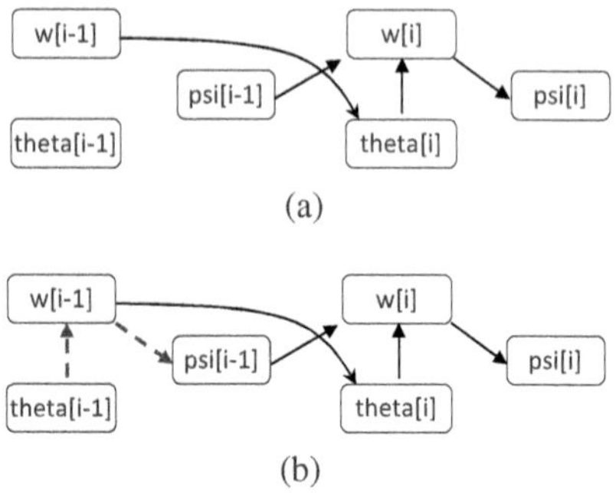

Figure 12: Determining whether a recursive query plan is valid.

of a stochastic table, and a template plan for each SQL code snippet that defines an intermediate stochastic table.

2. In a cost-based fashion, the set of template plans defining the intermediate tables are partitioned via a "frame cut" into two subsets. This partitioning determines where one frame ends and another begins, and is done so as to minimize the amount of data that needs to be materialized at the end of each frame.

3. The template plans for the initialization are appended with all of the template plans up to and including those that are part of the cut. This is the first frame, which is optimized.

4. After optimization, the deterministic parts of the first frame are identified, and the frame is run. As the frame is run, the deterministic parts are materialized.

5. While the result of running the frame is written out, statistics describing the resulting output tables are computed.

6. The next frame is created and optimized. The optimizer has the option of deciding (in cost-based fashion) to integrate the materialized, deterministic "views" from Step 4 into the plan for the frame.

7. The resulting plan for the frame is run by the SimSQL execution engine.

8. Steps (5) through (7) are repeated until completion.

6. QUERY PROCESSING IN DETAIL

This section describes various aspects of the aforementioned query processing steps in detail. A discussion of step (7) above—running a query plan—is deferred until the next full section of the paper.

6.1 Compilation

The SimSQL compiler performs multiple tasks: semantic checking of the SQL, flattening of nested queries, and generating template and actual plans.

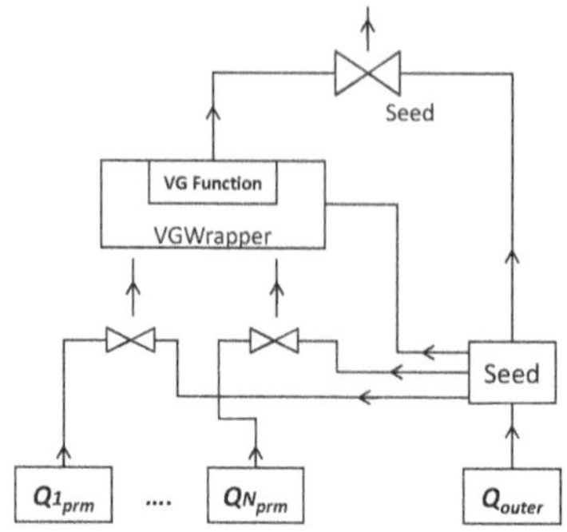

Figure 13: Template plan for creating a random table.

Checking for valid recursive definitions. The semantic checks that are performed by the query compiler are fairly standard, with an additional check for correctness of recursive table definitions. This latter check ensures that (1) the schema of a stochastic table `A[i]` is consistent, (2) each stochastic table has exactly one recursive definition, (3) a stochastic table with a constant index `A[const]` does not reference a stochastic table with a varying index `B[i]` and (4) at least one stochastic table with a constant index is defined. The current implementation assumes that a stochastic table `A` with index `i` can only reference another stochastic table `B` with index `i-1` or `i`.

The system also ensures that every stochastic table can be derived from stochastic tables with constant indices:

1. First a graph is generated whose nodes are the stochastic tables with indexes `i` and `i-1`, and the edges represent the dependence relationships among them. See, for example, Figure 12(a) for LDA.

2. As in Figure 12(b), edges among stochastic tables with index `i` are copied to the corresponding tables with index `i-1`.

3. If all the stochastic tables with index `i` can be accessed, then this check is passed.

Compilation into template plans. A template plan is simply an executable, unoptimized query plan. There are three types of template plans: *baseline*, *intermediate*, and *branch* template plans. Baseline plans correspond to stochastic table definitions with constant indices. In the LDA example, `theta[0]` and `w[0]` are compiled into baseline plans. Intermediate plans correspond to stochastic table definitions that recursively depend upon other stochastic tables, and are themselves used to parametrize other stochastic tables. In the LDA example, the `theta[i]`, `w[i]`, and `psi[i]` definitions are compiled into three intermediate template plans. Figure 14 shows the four template plans for the LDA example. Branch plans correspond to SQL queries that are run on top of stochastic tables to extract data or perform analysis.

Compiling a stochastic table definition into a template plan requires some explanation. The template plan for a generic stochastic table definition shown in Figure 13. Note that this template plan replaces the MCDB `Instantiate` operator, and is preferable in that it is an actual plan that is open to algebraic manipulation by the optimizer. In the figure, the plans $Q1_{prm}$ to QN_{prm} instantiate the tables that are used to parametrize the VG function, and Q_{outer} the "outer table" that corresponds to the tuples that are iterated over in the `FOR EACH` statement of a stochastic table definition. The `Seed` operator appends an integer (the "seed"), to every tuple from

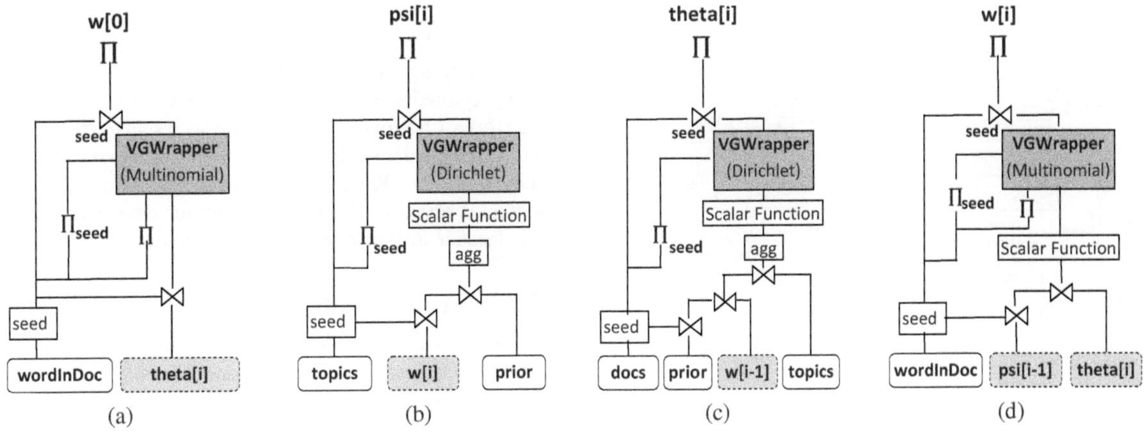

Figure 14: Template plans for LDA

Q_{outer}. The bottom level joins in the plan add seeds to each parameter stream based on the predicate in the `WHERE` clause of the SQL used to define the corresponding parameter tables. Seeds play three different roles in SimSQL. First, they seed the pseudorandom number generators (PRNGs) used within VG functions. Second, they are used as keys to match tuples from parameter streams with corresponding tuples in the outer table stream. Finally, seeds are used to link the output tuples of the VG function that correspond to a tuple in the outer table stream in the top level join operation. The actual VG function is run by the `VGWrapper` operator. It is described in detail in Section 7.3.

6.2 Frame Cut

As the execution of a frame is completed by SimSQL, the system checkpoints the state of the computation by writing out and saving the set of stochastic tables that will be used to parametrize the next frame. If this is done naively and very large tables parametrize the next frame, the size of the checkpoint may be huge. Thus, the SimSQL system chooses to end each frame at a "narrow" point in the computation, where the stochastic tables needed to parametrize the next frame take little space. The following algorithm computes the smallest checkpoint possible:

1. Given the template plans, a logical plan with two iterations is generated. This logical plan is optimized and executed to obtain statistics for each stochastic table.

2. An acyclic directed graph $G = (V, E)$ is defined, where V consists of stochastic tables with indices `i-1` and `i`, and E encodes the dependencies among them.

3. The *source* and *sink* are added. For each table `A` $\in V$, if `A` references tables with indices `i-2`, a direct edge from *source* to `A` is added; similarly, if `A` is referenced by tables with indices `i+1`, a directed edge from `A` to *sink* is added.

4. We assign the weight $+\infty$ to each edge $e \in E$ and the weight (cost) from Step 1 to each node $v \in V$. Our problem is then transformed to a max-flow/min-cut problem [11] with vertex capacities, and we apply the Edmonds-Karp algorithm.

Figure 15 shows the graph used to compute the LDA frame cut. The assigned weights (costs for materialization) are displayed for each stochastic table. After applying the Edmonds-Karp algorithm to compute the minimum cut, we find (as expected) the optimal frame cut is at {`psi[i-1]`,`theta[i]`}. Thus, these two tables will be checkpointed and will serve as input into every frame.

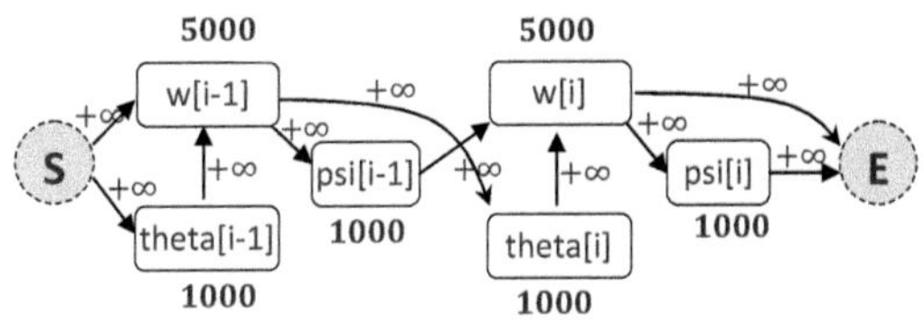

Figure 15: The graph used to determine the optimal frame cut.

6.3 Building/Optimizing Frames

The first frame is produced by starting with the template plans for the baseline tables, and then attaching (as specified by the SQL) all subsequent template plans up to and including those plans in the optimal cut, for `i` $= 0$. Subsequent frames are produced by assuming the results of the optimal cut as input, and then including all of the template plans in a full iteration. An example frame for LDA is shown in Figure 16.

This frame is then passed to the SimSQL query optimizer. Unfortunately, space precludes us from describing the extended SimSQL's query optimizer in detail. Briefly, the optimizer uses an A*-inspired search to optimize the plan. The cost of a plan is a weighted, linear combination of the total number of bytes input to and output from each intermediate plan operator. The weights on the various operator types capture the importance of each operator in the query cost estimation and are calculated using linear regression. SimSQL's optimizer has at its disposal all of the usual transformations (such as join re-orderings and push-down of selections) and also a list of SimSQL-specific transformations. An example of an SimSQL transformation is shown in Figure 17, where a random attribute called `count` is dropped and later re-created using the seed. Because random attributes are implemented as an array of random values, carrying them around can be quite expensive; thus dropping and re-creating a random attribute may result in a less expensive plan.

6.4 Materializing Deterministic Sub-Plans

The optimized frame may contain *deterministic sub-plans*, which are sub-plans of the query plan containing no `VGWrapper` operations, and where the initial input comes only from deterministic database tables. The output from such a plan can be re-used. To identify the deterministic sub-plans we employ a simple bottom-up algorithm. The algorithm visits each operator based on its topological ordering. An operator belongs to a deterministic plan if (1) it

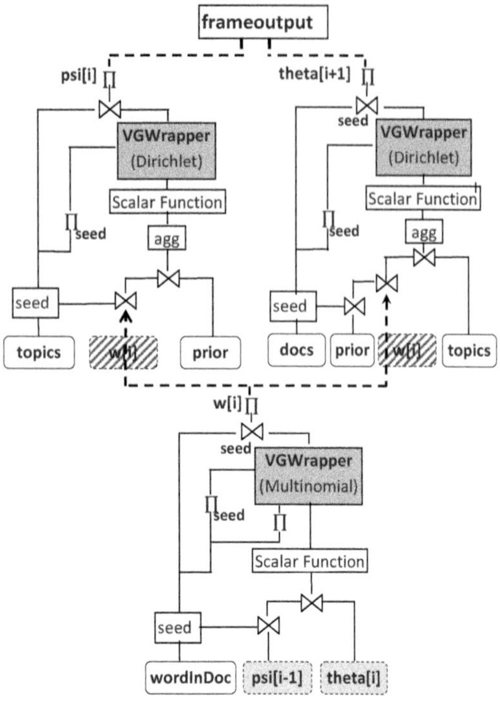

Figure 16: Frame to be optimized for execution.

is a deterministic database table scan or (2) all its descendants belong to a deterministic plan. Following standard methods used to incorporate materialized views into query plans [15], we give the optimizer the opportunity of re-using a deterministic sub-plan by introducing a plan transformation.

7. SIMSQL EXECUTION ENGINE

This section of the paper describes various aspects of the SimSQL execution engine.

7.1 Overview

The SimSQL execution engine is built on top of Hadoop, and written in both Java and C++. The ultimate output for the SimSQL compiler and optimizer (and the input into the SimSQL execution engine) is a specification for the query plan to be run, in a SimSQL-specific dataflow language that describes all of the relational operations in the plan, as well as how they fit together.

The SimSQL execution engine compiles this plan into a set of MapReduce jobs, and then, taking into account the dependencies among them, it runs them one at a time. To run a particular MapReduce job, SimSQL first "writes" (using a special macro-expansion facility) a Java code for the desired map task and a Java code for the the desired reduce task. These Java codes contain logic that is specifically tailored to the task at hand. For example, if the goal is to execute a relational join, the generated Java might contain (on the map side) specially generated code to run selection predicates over the two input relations, project away un-needed attributes, and compute hash keys over the input records. The generated Java code for the reduce side might contain code for the join predicate, as well as code for the final projection and any arithmetic or other functions that must be run to produce the final output.

Once the Java code for the task is generated, it is compiled and then executed. The reason that we employ this sort of dynamic code generation is to bypass the high CPU cost associated with interpreting, at runtime, data structures describing how to process the records dynamically; instead, we allow an optimizing compiler to generate byte code that does this far more efficiently. Others have explored this idea in the past few years (see, for example, the work of Neumann [26]). While such dynamic code generation has a cost—namely, the time required to generate and compile the code—in a MapReduce environment the additional fraction of a second is a small price to pay when one considers that the fastest MapReduce jobs take tens of seconds to run.

7.2 Tuple Bundles

Unlike in most applications of Hadoop, the data processed by SimSQL conform to a SimSQL-specific binary format instead of the usual text-based format. The important point to note is that the SimSQL format incorporates the MCDB "tuple bundle" trick [18]. Conceptually, SimSQL repeats the desired simulation N times to produce N mutually independent runs; in fact, the simulation is executed only once. This is made possible through SimSQL's use of *tuple bundles*, a concept borrowed from MCDB. Rather than running the simulation N times, a single set of tuple bundles that encodes each of the N independent possible worlds flows through a single query plan.

A tuple bundle t with schema S is, logically speaking, an array of N tuples, all having schema S. An attribute `att` is *constant* if $t[i]$.`att` $= c$ for some fixed value c and $i = 1, 2, \ldots, N$, otherwise it is *stochastic*. In our SimSQL implementation, the N tuples making up a single tuple bundle are stored in the obvious way: constant attributes are represented using a singleton value, and stochastic attributes are stored as arrays of values. A special stochastic attribute called `isPres` may also be present in the tuple bundle. The value of $t[i]$.`isPres` equals *true* if and only if the tuple bundle has a constituent tuple that appears in the ith possible world.

7.3 The VG Wrapper Operation

Most of SimSQL's MapReduce implementations of relational operations (the various joins such as the natural join, anti-join, and semi-join, de-duplication, selection, and so on) are straightforward. However, one operation that deserves a bit more explanation is SimSQL's `VGWrapper` operation. Each `VGWrapper` operation is run as part of a template plan, as shown in Figure 13 (this was discussed in the previous section), and the `VGWrapper` is tasked with parameterizing and executing a particular VG function.

Every VG function in SimSQL is a C++ class with (at least) four methods: `ClearParams`, `TakeParams`, `TakeSeed`, and `OutputVals`. `ClearParams` is called to let the VG function know that it is about to be parameterized. After `ClearParams`, `TakeParams` is called repeatedly to parameterize the VG function. When the `VGWrapper` is ready to use the function to produce random data, `TakeSeed` is called with the seed for the VG function's PRNG. The `VGWrapper` then repeatedly calls `OutputVals` to obtain random values from the VG function. When a `null` is eventually returned by the VG function (indicating that it is done producing values for the current possible world), the `VGWrapper` will then (optionally) call `ClearParams` to indicate that it wants to re-parameterize the function for the next trial (if the parameterization is constant across worlds, then no re-parameterization is needed). The `VGWrapper` then calls `TakeSeed`, followed by a sequence of calls to `OutputVals`, until a `null` is once again returned. This process is completed until all worlds have been computed.

To demonstrate this via an example, consider a `Multinomial` VG function and the `w[i]` stochastic table from the previous LDA example. Imagine that there are four tuple bundles, encoding three possible worlds, that are used to parameterize the function:

(tID: 0, prob: ⟨ 0.1, 0.2, 0.1 ⟩, isPres: ⟨ T, T, T ⟩)
(tID: 1, prob: ⟨ 0.4, 0.6, 0.5 ⟩, isPres: ⟨ F, T, F ⟩)
(tID: 2, prob: ⟨ 0.5, 0.2, 0.4 ⟩, isPres: ⟨ T, F, T ⟩)
(count: 14)

Here, a ⟨ ⟩ pair indicates an array of values, with each value being applicable to one of the three possible worlds. In our example, the VGWrapper will begin with the first possible world, calling ClearParams to indicate the start of a parameterization, followed by three calls to TakeParams, giving (0, 0.1), (2, 0.5), and (14) in sequence. The VGWrapper then calls TakeSeed, passing along the seed associated with the current dw value (see Figure 8) from the outer table stream (Q_{outer} in Figure 13). The VGWrapper then repeatedly calls OutputVals to obtain all output tuples for the first possible world. The VGWrapper then calls ClearParams and parameterizes the second possible world with (0, 0.2), (1, 0.6), and (14), and obtains the result with calls to OutputVals. Finally, it parameterizes the third possible world with (0, 0.1), (2, 0.4), and (14), obtains the result.

Note that we made the somewhat non-obvious decision to re-seed the VG function's PRNG for each and every possible world. This is in contrast to MCDB, where the VG function is seeded only once, and then the seed is used for all of the possible worlds. The reason that SimSQL re-seeds for each possible world is so that we can handle the presence of the isPres attribute in the outer input table with some efficiency. The stream of tuples from the outer input table supplies the seeded FOR EACH tuples to the VGWrapper. If one of these tuples has a false value in isPres, it means that the outer tuple has been removed from the database (perhaps via an earlier selection) and logically, it should not exist. A simple way to handle the non-existence would be to have the VGWrapper ignore it, knowing that it will be enforced by the top-level join in Figure 13. Although this solution is correct, it might be costly, since the VG function will be invoked needlessly.

Another solution would be to avoid running the VG function for possible worlds where isPres is false. This must be done with care. As discussed in the previous section, the optimizer is free to drop (project away) random attributes, and then generate them again later via a second execution of the VGWrapper operator. This transformation is depicted in Figure 17, and is useful if carrying around random data is more expensive than re-generating it. If the VGWrapper is invoked once, and then a subsequent operation removes an outer stream tuple from a possible world, the sequence of calls to the VG function will change the second time around, because that possible world will not be parameterized nor will OutputVals be called for that possible world. If the VG function was parameterized only once, at initialization, then the second use of the VGWrapper will produce different, inconsistent results because it will not be run for certain possible worlds.

Thus, in SimSQL the seed associated with a tuple from the outer table stream is not given directly to the VG function. Rather, it is used to seed an additional PRNG that is internal to the VGWrapper, and which is used to re-seed the VG function for each possible world via a call to TakeSeed. If isPres is false for any possible world, the new seed is discarded. That way, a possible world is always assigned the same seed, regardless of changes to the isPres attribute.

8. EVALUATION

In this section, we empirically evaluate the SimSQL system. Our goal is not to show that SimSQL can be used to implement the fastest distributed MCMC simulation possible—it would be unreasonable to think that a simulation coded using 47 lines of SQL (as with LDA) could possibly outperform a distributed simulation custom coded in Java or C. Rather, we wish to give some evidence that a simulation implemented and run on the SimSQL platform can have reasonable performance. "Reasonable" here might be a time that is within an order of magnitude (or two) of a special-purpose Java or C version. A $10X$ slowdown might be a big performance hit, but a distributed Java or C version might require several hundred times as much code, much more development time, and a much higher level of programming expertise.

8.1 Overview

Most of SimSQL as described in the paper has been implemented, with the exception of the analysis interface of Section 4. SimSQL consists of an SQL query compiler and query un-nester (approximately 40,000 lines of Java code), a cost-based query optimizer (approximately 11,000 lines of Prolog code), and a runtime (written in around 30,000 lines of Java and C/C++) that is built upon Hadoop. We use Amazon EC2 for all of our runs. The machines used are "High-Memory Quadruple Extra Large Instance" types, which have 8 relatively low-end virtual cores, two disks, and 68GB of RAM per machine.

Our high-level goal is examining SimSQL's feasibility. Along these lines, we wish to answer the questions: How well does SimSQL scale as the amount of data and computing resources increases? Can SimSQL run a distributed simulation quickly and (even more importantly) in a cost effective manner? To answer this question, we perform an experiment where the amount of data per compute node in a cluster is held constant, but an ever-increasing number of nodes are used to perform the simulation. If SimSQL scales perfectly, the time to run each simulation will stay constant as the number of nodes is increased.

We focus on two particular simulations: the MCMC simulation for the LDA model of Section 3 and a more complicated MCMC simulation for learning a Bayesian Gaussian mixture model (GMM) [4]. Unfortunately, space precludes us from providing the corresponding SQL code, but it totals 63 lines, and provides support for full (not just diagonal) covariance matrices. The LDA SQL code listed in the paper is compiled and run without modification. The LDA simulation compiles to a query plan with 45 operations in the baseline iteration, and 39 operations in the other iterations (that run in 22 and 20 MapReduce jobs, respectively). The GMM simulation has 40 operations in the baseline iteration, and 87 operations in the other iterations (running in 20 and 36 MapReduce jobs).

For the LDA model, we use the 20-newsgroups dataset [1] in our experiments. Since this dataset has only 16,330 documents, we create a database of (almost) arbitrary size by randomly picking two documents from the corpus and merging them—this gives us $\binom{2\times 16330}{2}$ distinct "documents". While this corpus of semi-simulated documents may not be the best testbed for evaluating the LDA model itself, we are interested in evaluating the SimSQL system, and this data should suffice. In our experiments, we use 100 topics and a dictionary of 10,000 words. For the GMM model, we use synthetically-generated ten dimensional data. The data are themselves generated by sampling from a Gaussian mixture model.

8.2 Benchmarks Run

Scalability. For the two models, we first choose a per-machine data size n, such that across experiments, when performing a simulation using m machines, the total amount of data processed is always $n \times m$, no matter the number of nodes. In the case of LDA, n is 250,000 documents. In the case of the GMM, n is 1,000,000 data

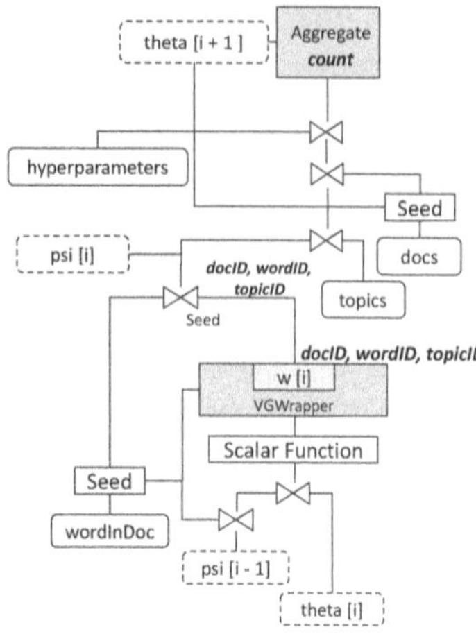

(a) Plan before transformation.

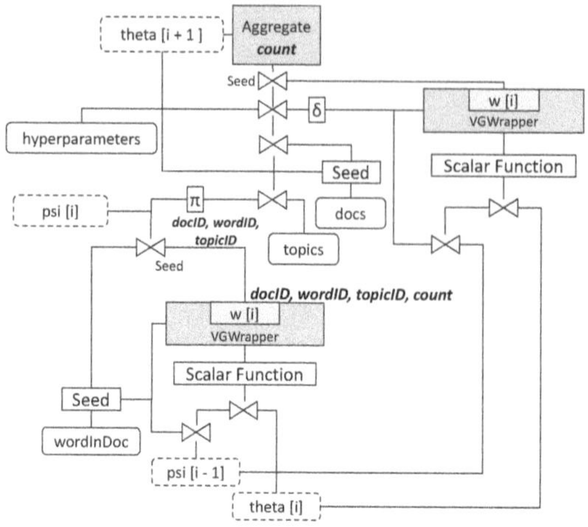

(b) Plan after transformation.

Figure 17: Transformation to drop and recreate a random attribute in SimSQL.

LDA Inference

Nodes	Iteration Number					
	0	1	2	3	4	5
5	2:22	2:33	2:28	2:25	2:29	2:22
10	2:33	2:35	2:30	2:28	2:32	2:30
20	2:34	2:27	2:30	2:28	2:30	2:34
50	2:44	2:39	2:37	2:41	2:52	2:44
100	3:24	3:16	3:17	3:18	3:13	3:04

Gaussian Mixture Model Inference

Nodes	Iteration Number					
	0	1	2	3	4	5
5	0:06	0:54	0:53	0:54	0:53	0:55
10	0:06	0:55	0:53	0:53	0:52	0:53
20	0:06	0:57	0:56	0:57	0:56	0:56
50	0:08	1:10	1:07	1:04	1:01	1:02
100	0:08	1:13	1:13	1:13	1:12	1:12

Figure 18: Running time (HH:MM) per iteration for GMM and LDA inference. Iteration zero is the initialization.

points. For each run, 10 different simulations are performed at the same time, so that 10 parallel Markov chains are simulated. We run the simulations for the two models using 5 nodes, 10 nodes, 20 nodes, 50 nodes, and 100 nodes. Figure 18 displays the results.

Work Sharing. To test the ability of the system to share work across possible worlds, we fix the number of nodes at 20. Then we vary n as follows. Let N be the number of Markov chains that are simulated in parallel. For LDA, we fix $n \times N$ to be $20 \times 10 \times 250,000$, and for the GMM, we fix $n \times N$ to be $20 \times 10 \times 1,000,000$, and then we perform five runs of the simulation, using $N = \{1, 5, 10, 20\}$. Thus, if $N = 10$, the run is identical to the scalability experiment with $m = 20$. But with $N = 20$, half the amount of data per machine is used, and if $N = 1$, ten times the amount of data per machine is used. Figure 19 gives the results.

8.3 Discussion

The system does appear to scale. The running time is more or less constant when the total data processed is held constant at $n \times m$. That said, not all of the rows in Figure 18 are identical for differing cluster sizes. Much of the increase in time is due to the fact that as the size of the problem increases, it becomes impossible for the system to pipeline expensive operations, such as joins. For example, in our Amazon cluster, we have approximately 6GB of RAM available for operation-specific, auxiliary data structures, for each Hadoop mapper and reducer. In the case of the GMM simulation, as we move from 10 to 20 machines (and 10 million to 20 million data points) it becomes impossible to buffer a copy of the entire data set in a 6GB hash table to run a join, and so certain joins switch from single-pass pipelined joins to full sort-merge joins, and the time increases slightly. As we move from 50 to 100 machines, we find that it is not always possible to store meta-data about all 100 million data points (such as the PRNG seed assigned to each) in RAM, and again we see an increase in running time. That said, for both GMM and LDA, at 100 machines, none of the varying-sized tables can be buffered in RAM, and so we would expect a more constant running time as the cluster size grows even larger.

Model	Number of parallel worlds			
	20	10	5	1
LDA	2:11	2:28	3:27	4:20
GMM	0:51	0:57	1:27	1:53

Figure 19: Avg running time per iteration (HH:MM), changing the number of parallel simulations while keeping the (number of data points) × (the number of simulations) constant.

Although the system appears to scale, it is reasonable to ask whether a running time of two or three hours per iteration is practical. To many practitioners of Bayesian machine learning, who have long been used to month-long simulation runs, the answer is affirmative. Additionally, we assert that the absolute time taken per iteration is perhaps not that important for a cloud-based platform. If the underlying architecture scales, the running time can be driven down dramatically at no additional cost by simply renting more machines. Specifically, our 100-node cluster costs around \$14 per hour (14 cents per machine per hour), and can run a GMM iteration in about 70 minutes—or a bit more than \$15 per iteration. We could instead rent 200 machines, at a cost of \$28 per hour, and as long as the running time per iteration is cut approximately in half, we will still spend \$15 per iteration, but would now have to wait only half as long for each iteration to finish. True, increasing cluster size past a certain point produces diminishing returns. In our Hadoop-based system it is impossible to push the per-iteration running time down below a few minutes (each GMM iteration requires 36 MapReduce jobs, which will always take at least seconds each, even in a small cluster). But in general, if the simulation takes too long, one can just rent a larger cluster.

Perhaps a more reasonable question is: Is the *cost* of learning a model reasonable? First, consider how many iterations are required for convergence. Burn-in periods of 1,000 or more iterations are common in the machine learning literature, but we question whether this is always a necessity. All of the standard Bayesian models with which we are familiar—including LDA, GMM, linear regression, conditional random fields, and matrix factorization—become quite stable after 100 iterations or so. For example, in Figure 20 we plot the θ vectors obtained in iterations 50-60 for three different documents from a run of LDA on the 20-newsgroups data set. There is little fluctuation, indicating stability in the model.

If we assume 100 iterations are desired, then at \$14 per iteration to handle 100 million data points (in the case of the GMM simulation), we have a cost of \$14 per million data points. Considering that we are running 10 simulations in parallel at that cost,[1] and that running a single simulation cuts the cost by a factor of five (see Table 19), we could run a single MCMC inference at the cost of around \$3 per million data points.

This is certainly not inexpensive, perhaps 10× to 100× more expensive than what one would obtain with a special-purpose, C or Java implementation, such as the LDA code written by Smola and Narayanamurthy [33]. That said, programmers who can write high-quality distributed or parallel C/Java code are very expensive themselves (and quite rare!), and so we argue that the fact that we obtain a cost of \$3 per million data points with only 63 lines of SQL makes our approach look very attractive—especially when the goal is fast prototyping of a particular inference algorithm.

9. RELATED WORK

Perhaps the work closest to our own in the database literature is the paper of Deutsch, Koch, and Milo on languages for specifying queries over Markov chains [13]. In contrast to our systems-oriented approach where the goal is to prototype a distributed platform suitable for performing large scale Bayesian MCMC, Deutch et al. are concerned with algorithmic aspects of the problem, showing how in certain cases it is possible to answer queries over a Markov chain without needing to actually simulate the chain many times. The setting that they consider is somewhat restrictive compared to our own (probabilistic databases with c-tables [16], or repair-keys [21]) and it is not immediately apparent how this work applies to common distributions such as the Dirichlet that accept real, vector-valued inputs and produce correlated, real, vector-valued outputs. However, there is a lot of merit to the development of algorithms to solve this problem efficiently, and the ultimate solution will include novel algorithmic as well as systems-oriented ideas.

MCMC for model inference over database data has been previously considered [36, 38]. In [36], the MCMC loop takes place within an external module. In [38] efficient SQL-based implementations of two MCMC algorithms were described. However, the work is not meant to provide general-purpose MCMC simulation.

[1]The advantage of running many simulations at the same time is that it generates many fully-independent models, without the need to continue to run a single chain, examining its state occasionally, to obtain more than one learned model.

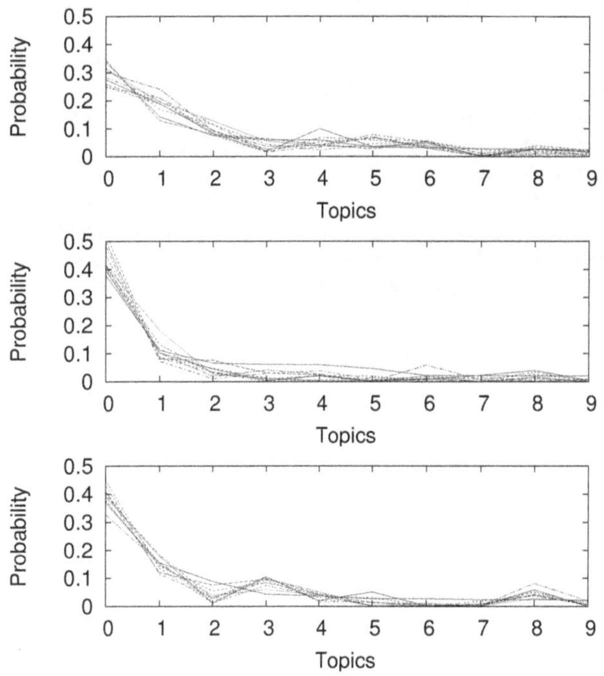

Figure 20: Parallel coordinates plot depicting sampled LDA θ vectors for three documents, iterations 50-60. The top ten topics for each document are shown, sorted in order of importance.

Jigsaw [20] is a system that uses VG functions to perform stochastic, what-if analysis. Jigsaw focuses not on systems issues (language, compilation, runtime), but instead on the problem of optimization over stochastic models; most of the technical innovation in the Jigsaw system is directed towards alleviating Monte Carlo overheads by decreasing the number of VG function invocations required when a stochastic simulation must be repeated for many different parameter configurations during the optimization.

Recent work in the machine learning and data mining communities has leveraged the MapReduce paradigm to either achieve high levels of parallelism [10, 24] or scale specific machine learning algorithms [3, 22, 23, 25, 27, 28, 32, 33]. These approaches require the detailed implementation of the model in a procedural language.

The SimSQL implementation described in this paper compiles simulations into MapReduce programs. The MapReduce framework has been employed to scale up other analytic tasks [12, 30].

The sequential execution of small frames in SimSQL is related to the repeated computation that is supported by the Pegasus [19], SystemML [14] and HaLoop [6] systems, though our emphasis on checkpointing and (re-)optimization is unique. SimSQL is closest in spirit to Haloop, which extends the MapReduce framework to efficiently support simple iterative or recursive computations.

A number of systems support SQL or SQL-inspired languages on top of MapReduce. These include DryadLINQ [37], SCOPE [7], HadoopDB [2], Hive [34], FlumeJava [8], and Tenzing [9].

Finally, there exists some recent work on scaling up specific classes of simulation using MapReduce, for example, agent-based simulations [35] and clustering for N-body simulations [22].

10. CONCLUSION

We have described the functionality, design and implementation of the SimSQL system, which allows for SQL-based specification, simulation, and querying of database-valued Markov chains. The key advantage of the SimSQL system is that allows a programmer to specify Markovian simulations of relatively high complexity in only a few dozen lines of SQL code; these simulations are then automatically distributed and run in parallel over a cluster of machines. As a proof-of-concept we described in detail the SQL specification of two real world Bayesian inference algorithms: MCMC inference for linear regression and for LDA. We also discussed possible SQL specifications of analysis tasks over the results of the performed simulation. Our experiments, using the LDA and GMM models, show that SimSQL has reasonable performance and scales well when running distributed Markov chain simulations.

11. REFERENCES

[1] 20Newsgroups Dataset. Available at: http://people.csail.mit.edu/jrennie/20newsgroups/.

[2] A. Abouzeid, K. Bajda-Pawlikowski, D. Abadi, A. Silberschatz, and A. Rasin. HadoopDB: An Architectural Hybrid of MapReduce and DBMS Technologies for Analytical Workloads. *PVLDB*, 2(1):922–933, 2009.

[3] B. Bahmani, K. Chakrabarti, and D. Xin. Fast Personalized Pagerank on MapReduce. In *SIGMOD*, 2011.

[4] C. M. Bishop. *Pattern Recognition and Machine Learning*. Springer, 2006.

[5] D. M. Blei, A. N. Ng, and M. I. Jordan. Latent Dirichlet Allocation. *JMLR*, 3:993–1022, 2003.

[6] Y. Bu, B. Howe, M. Balazinska, and M. D. Ernst. Haloop: efficient iterative data processing on large clusters. *PVLDB*, 3(1-2):285–296, 2010.

[7] R. Chaiken, B. Jenkins, P. Larson, B. Ramsey, D. Shakib, S. Weaver, and J. Zhou. SCOPE: easy and efficient parallel processing of massive data sets. *PVLDB*, 1(2):1265–1276, 2008.

[8] C. Chambers, A. Raniwala, F. Perry, S. Adams, R. R. Henry, R. Bradshaw, and N. Weizenbaum. Flumejava: easy, efficient data-parallel pipelines. In *PLDA*, 2010.

[9] B. Chattopadhyay, L. Lin, W. Liu, S. Mittal, P. Aragonda, V. Lychagina, Y. Kwon, and M. Wong. Tenzing a sql implementation on the mapreduce framework. *PVLDB*, 4(12):1318–1327, 2011.

[10] C.-T. Chu, S. K. Kim, Y.-A. Lin, Y. Yu, G. Bradski, A. Y. Ng, and K. Olukotun. Map-reduce for machine learning on multicore. In *NIPS*, 2006.

[11] T. Cormen, C. Leiserson, R. Rivest, and C. Stein. *Introduction to Algorithms*. McGraw-Hill, 2003.

[12] S. Das, Y. Sismanis, K. S. Beyer, R. Gemulla, P. J. Haas, and J. McPherson. Ricardo: Integrating r and hadoop. In *SIGMOD*, 2010.

[13] D. Deutch, C. Koch, and T. Milo. On probabilistic fixpoint and markov chain query languages. In *PODS*, pages 215–226, 2010.

[14] A. Ghoting, R. Krishnamurthy, E. Pednault, B. Reinwald, V. Sindhwani, S. Tatikonda, Y. Tian, and S. Vaithyanathan. SystemML: Declarative machine learning on mapreduce. In *ICDE*, 2011.

[15] J. Goldstein and P. Larson. Optimizing Queries Using Materialized Views: A practical, scalable solution. In *SIGMOD*, 2001.

[16] T. J. Green and V. Tannen. Models for incomplete and probabilistic information. *IEEE Data Eng. Bull.*, 29(1):17–24, 2006.

[17] Y. E. Ioannidis and S. Christodoulakis. Optimal histograms for limiting worst-case error propagation in the size of join results. *TODS*, 18(4):709–748, 1993.

[18] R. Jampani, F. Xu, M. Wu, L. L. Perez, C. Jermaine, and P. J. Haas. The Monte Carlo Database System: Stochastic analysis close to the data. *TODS*, 36(3):1–41, 2011.

[19] U. Kang, C. E. Tsourakakis, and C. Faloutsos. Pegasus: A peta-scale graph mining system - implementation and observations. In *ICDM*, 2009.

[20] O. Kennedy and S. Nath. Jigsaw: Efficient optimization over uncertain enterprise data. In *SIGMOD*, 2011.

[21] C. Koch. On query algebras for probabilistic databases. *SIGMOD Record*, 37(4):78–85, 2008.

[22] Y. Kwon, D. Nunley, J. D. Gardner, M. Balazinska, B. Howe, and S. Loebman. Scalable clustering for n-body simulations in a shared-nothing cluster. In *SSDBM*, 2010.

[23] Z. Liu, Y. Zhang, E. Y. Chang, and M. Sun. Plda+: Parallel Latent Dirichlet Allocation with Data Placement and Pipeline Processing. *ACM TIST*, 2(3):26:1–26:18, 2011.

[24] Y. Low, J. Gonzalez, A. Kyrola, D. Bickson, C. Guestrin, and J. M. Hellerstein. GraphLab: A New Parallel Framework for Machine Learning. In *UAI*, 2010.

[25] A. Mahout. Available at: http://mahout.apache.org/.

[26] T. Neumann. Efficiently compiling efficient query plans for modern hardware. *PVLDB*, 4(9):539–550, 2011.

[27] B. Panda, J. S. Herbach, S. Basu, and R. J. Bayardo. Planet: Massively parallel learning of tree ensembles with mapreduce. *PVLDB*, 2(2):1426–1437, 2009.

[28] S. Papadimitriou and J. Sun. DisCo: Distributed co-clustering with map-reduce: A case study towards petabyte-scale end-to-end mining. In *ICDM*, 2008.

[29] I. Porteous, D. Newman, A. T. Ihler, A. Asuncion, P. Smyth, and M. Welling. Fast collapsed Gibbs sampling for Latent Dirichlet Allocation. In *SIGKDD*, 2008.

[30] RHIPE: R and Hadoop Integrated Programming Environment. Available at: http://ml.stat.purdue.edu/rhipe/.

[31] C. P. Robert and G. Casella. *Monte Carlo Statistical Methods*. Springer, 2010.

[32] S. Singh, A. Subramanya, F. Pereira, and A. McCallum. Distributed MAP inference for undirected graphical models. In *NIPS Workshops*, 2010.

[33] A. J. Smola and S. Narayanamurthy. An Architecture for Parallel Topic models. *PVLDB*, 3(1):703–710, 2010.

[34] A. Thusoo, J. S. Sarma, N. Jain, Z. Shao, P. Chakka, S. Anthony, H. Liu, P. Wyckoff, and R. Murthy. Hive: a warehousing solution over a map-reduce framework. *PVLDB*, 2(2):1626–1629, 2009.

[35] G. Wang, M. V. Salles, B. Sowell, X. Wang, T. Cao, A. Demers, J. Gehrke, and W. White. Behavioral simulations in mapreduce. *PVLDB*, 3(1-2):952–963, 2010.

[36] M. Wick, A. McCallum, and G. Miklau. Scalable probabilistic databases with factor graphs and MCMC. In *VLDB*, 2010.

[37] Y. Yu, M. Isard, D. Fetterly, M. Budiu, U. Erlingsson, P. K. Gunda, and J. Currey. Dryadlinq: A system for general-purpose distributed data-parallel computing using a high-level language. In *OSDI*, 2008.

[38] D. Z. Zhang, M. J. Franklin, M. Garofalakis, J. M. Hellerstein, and M. L. Wick. Hybrid in-database inference for declarative information extraction. In *SIGMOD*, 2011.

Author Index

www.ingramcontent.com/pod-product-compliance
Ingram Content Group UK Ltd.
Pitfield, Milton Keynes, MK11 3LW, UK
UKHW051418290926
15471UKWH00009B/1673

9 781450 326131